The Enduring Vision

A History of the American People

Paul S. Boyer
University of Wisconsin, Madison

Clifford E. Clark, Jr.
Carleton College

Joseph F. Kett
University of Virginia

Thomas L. Purvis

Harvard Sitkoff
University of New Hampshire

Nancy Woloch
Barnard College

D. C. Heath and Company
Lexington, Massachusetts   Toronto

Acquisitions Editors: Linda Halvorson and James Miller
Developmental Editor: Sylvia Mallory
Production Editor: Rosemary R. Jaffe
Designer: Henry Rachlin
Production Coordinator: Michael O'Dea
Text Permissions Editor: Margaret Roll
Graphs: Boston Graphics, Inc.
Maps: Sanderson Associates
Photo Research: Martha Shethar with assistance from Sharon Donahue, Linda
              Finigan, Martha Friedman, Janet Goldman, Billie Ingram, and
              Sylvia Mallory

Cover: Appliqué Quilt (Detail), c. 1800. Sarah Furman Warner.
The Edison Institute, Henry Ford Museum & Greenfield Village.

ABOUT THE AUTHORS

Paul S. Boyer, Merle Curti professor of history at the University of Wisconsin, Madison, earned his Ph.D. from Harvard University. An editor of *Notable American Women, 1607–1950* (1971), he also coauthored *Salem Possessed: The Social Origins of Witchcraft* (1974), for which, with Stephen Nissenbaum, he received the John H. Dunning Prize of the American Historical Association. His other published works include *Purity in Print: Book Censorship in America* (1968), *Urban Masses and Moral Order in America, 1820–1920* (1978), and *By the Bomb's Early Light: American Thought and Culture at the Dawn of the Atomic Age* (1985). Also a frequent contributor to journals such as *American Quarterly* and *The New Republic,* he is currently researching another work on contemporary American culture. He is an elected member of the American Antiquarian Society.

Clifford E. Clark, Jr., professor of history at Carleton College, earned his Ph.D. from Harvard University. He has served as both chair of the history department and director of the American Studies program at Carleton. Clark is the author of *Henry Ward Beecher: Spokesman for a Middle-Class America* (1978), *The American Family Home, 1800–1960* (1986), and *American and Canadian Intellectual History, 1789 to 1960,* a volume in the forthcoming *General History of the Americas.* He has also edited and contributed to *Minnesota in a Century of Change: The State and Its People Since 1900* (1989) and serves on the editorial board of the *Winterthur Portfolio, A Journal of American Material Culture.* At present he is researching a study of a midwestern community that began as a planned railroad town.

Joseph F. Kett, professor of history and department chair at the University of Virginia, received his Ph.D. from Harvard University. His works include *The Formation of the American Medical Profession, 1780–1860: The Role of Institutions* (1968), *Rites of Passage: Adolescence in America, 1790–Present* (1977), *The American Family, 1978* (1978), and *The Dictionary of Cultural Literacy* (1988), of which he is a coauthor. His current

research project is on the diffusion of knowledge in the United States. He has participated on the Panel on Youth of the President's Science Advisory Committee, has served on the Board of Editors of the *History of Education Quarterly,* and is a past member of the Council of the American Studies Association.

Thomas L. Purvis, who has served as Editor of Publications at the Institute for Early American History and Culture and as adjunct associate professor of history at the College of William and Mary, received his Ph.D. from the Johns Hopkins University. He is the recipient of numerous academic honors and awards and a frequent contributor to journals such as the *William and Mary Quarterly* and *New Jersey History.* The author of *Proprietors, Patronage, and Paper Money: Legislative Politics in New Jersey, 1703–1776* (1986), for which he won the McCormick Prize, he is currently at work on a study of the Seven Years' War in America.

Harvard Sitkoff, professor of history at the University of New Hampshire and John Adams Professor of American Civilization in the Netherlands, earned his Ph.D. from Columbia University. He is the author of *A New Deal for Blacks* (1978) and *The Struggle for Black Equality* (1981); coeditor of *A History of Our Time* (1982, 1987); and editor of *Fifty Years Later: The New Deal Evaluated* (1985). A contributor to a number of edited collections, he has also published articles in many journals, among them *The Journal of American History, The Journal of Southern History,* and *The Wilson Quarterly.*

Nancy Woloch received her Ph.D. from Indiana University. She is the author of *Women and the American Experience* (1984), a coeditor of *Images of America: Selected Readings* (1978), and, with Walter LaFeber and Richard Polenberg, the coauthor of *The American Century: A History of the United States Since the 1890s* (1986). Currently working on a documentary history of early American women, she teaches American history at Barnard College.

PREFACE

The Enduring Vision

This is the story of America and of the visions that Americans have shared. The first vision was of the land itself. For the prehistoric adventurers who crossed the land bridge from Asia, for the Europeans who began to arrive in the sixteenth century, and for the later immigrants who poured in by the tens of millions, North America offered a haven for new beginnings. If life was hard in the Old World, it would be better in the New. And once here, the lure of the land continued—away from the crowded city, beyond the rim of settlement. If times were tough in the East, they would be better in the West. New Englanders migrated to Ohio; Ohioans migrated to Kansas; Kansans migrated to California. Southern blacks after the Civil War dreamed of new opportunities elsewhere:

> I got my ticket,
> Leaving the thicket,
> And I'm a-heading for the Golden Shore!

Even today, the land itself remains part of the vision. Indeed, it becomes more precious as we realize its vulnerability to pollution and exploitation. In this way, we share a link with those who went before us who also cherished this continent's forests, mountains, lakes, and rivers.

But the vision involves more than simply a love of the land. It also entails a commitment to an ongoing social and intellectual process: the process of creating a just social order. In pursuing this goal, we have experimented with new social forms and engaged in bitter debates. As the French immigrant Michel Crèvecoeur wrote in 1782: "The American is a new man, who acts upon new principles, . . . new ideas, and . . . new opinions."

Central to the American vision of the good society is the notion of individual freedom. To be sure, our commitment to freedom has frequently faltered in practice. The Puritans who sought freedom of worship for themselves often denied it to others. Southern whites who cheered the Declaration of Independence lived by the labor of black slaves. Many a capitalist tycoon conveniently forgot that economic exploitation can extinguish freedom as effectively as political tyranny or military force. And through much of our history, women—one-half the population—were relegated to second-class status. Yet the battered vision endured, prodding a sometimes reluctant nation to confront and explore its full meaning.

But freedom can be an empty and cheerless thing unless one is also part of a social group. The novelist O. E. Rolvaag, describing the emotions of a nineteenth-century Norwegian immigrant farm woman on the Great Plains, captured this feeling of social isolation:

> A sense of desolation so profound settled upon her that she seemed unable to think at all. . . . She threw herself back in the grass and looked up into the heavens. But darkness and infinitude lay there, also—the sense of utter desolation still remained. . . . Suddenly, for the first time, she realized the full extent of her loneliness. . . .

Thus the vision must also be one of community. John Winthrop, addressing a group of English immigrants aboard the *Arbella* on their way to America in 1630, eloquently summed up this dimension of the vision: "We must delight in each other, make others' conditions our own, rejoice together, mourn together, labor and suffer together: always having before our eyes our commission and community . . . as members of the same body."

The family, the town, the neighborhood, the church, and the nation itself have been ways by which Americans have woven into their lives a web of social meaning. And *community* is not just a high-sounding abstraction; it has political implications. If we are not just a fragmented collection of self-absorbed individuals but also a *people*, what obligations do we owe each other? What limitations on our freedom are we willing to accept in order to be part of a social group? In struggling with tough questions like these, we have further defined our vision of America.

Finally, this vision is one of renewal and new beginnings. The story of America is part of the human story, and thus it has its dark and shameful passages as well as its bright moments of achievement. Arrogance, injustice, callous blindness to suffering, and national self-delusion have all figured in our history. But balancing the times when we lost our way are the moments when we found our bearings and returned to the hard task of defining what America at its best might truly be.

This, then, is the essence of the vision: a vision not of a foreordained national destiny unfolding effortlessly but of a laborious, often frustrating struggle to define what our common life as a people shall be. For all the failures and the wrong turns, it remains a vision rooted in hope, not despair. In 1980 Jesse de la Cruz, a Mexican-American woman who had fought for years to improve conditions for California's migrant workers, summed up the philosophy that kept her going: "Is America progressing toward the better? . . . We're the ones that are gonna do it. We have to keep on struggling. . . . With us, there's a saying: *La esperanza muere al último.* Hope dies last. You can't lose hope. If you lose hope, that's losing everything."

No sentiment could better sum up the enduring vision of American history.

Introduction

In writing *The Enduring Vision,* our aim has been twofold: to do full justice to the history of public events, with maximum chronological clarity, and to bring into the story the rich findings of research into social and cultural history over the past few decades. In short, we set out to trace the interaction of public and private spheres in the American past. Times were ripe for such a venture. History is enjoying a long overdue resurgence in the undergraduate curriculum. Students come to American history eager for a compelling narrative, ready to encounter the grand sweep of the nation's past and to ponder America's identity as a nation. Their teachers reached intellectual maturity during and after the enormous expansion of history's domain that began in the 1960s with the absorption of social-science theory and a determination to study previously neglected social groups. The dual purpose of inquiring rigorously into a problem and of telling a story with grace and conviction has always guided the greatest practitioners of the craft of history. We have made it our purpose as well.

Our book maintains a reasonable level of rigor. We have not hesitated to take up challenging topics. But we have *explained* these matters clearly and shown how they are essential to understanding American history. Every step of the way, we and our editors have asked hard questions: what do college students beginning the study of American history need to know, and how does *this* particular piece of evidence fit into the picture?

Throughout, we have sought to describe the experiences and perspectives of ordinary people as well as to account for the motivations of history's great figures. Our view of history is neither rigidly "top-down" nor "bottom-up"; rather, we see a constant interplay between communities, regions, and nation. As frequently as possible, we introduce students to real people from the past and allow these participants to speak for themselves. The revealing anecdote or pungent quotation can be worth many words of abstract explanation, and we have ransacked our sources to find fresh material that piquantly captures the mentality of the era. Above all, we realize the importance of encouraging students to judge historical events with the values of the past in mind. There is no better way to foster respect for history.

Every working historian knows how difficult is the challenge of combining analysis and narrative. Our solution has been to break the narrative down into manageable, chapter-length chunks and to "stop the music" where appropriate in order to analyze the forces underlying events. We have tried to ensure that the reader always knows how private social interactions fit into larger patterns of public events yet never sees those events merely as a random progression of "facts" without social or cultural context.

We have tried to give our book character, to avoid impersonal blandness of style, to employ humor where appropriate, to communicate a sense of drama, and to evoke sympathy for those who have suffered. We hope that students will find the book's brisk, lively style readable and engrossing. But we also recognize that a textbook must "work" in hundreds of different courses, whose teachers may vary tremendously in pedagogical approach or interpretation. Here again, we felt an obligation to be as inclusive as possible. We have advanced our own views of controversial questions in such a way that instructors who think otherwise can engage our textbook in constructive debate. By thus seeing that the study of history is an ongoing inquiry rather than a handing-down of revealed truth, students can only be the gainers.

Plan of the Book

Our approach should be apparent from the opening pages. The Prologue offers a unique survey of the geographical foundations of American history—landforms, river systems, natural regions, climate, and vegetation. The theme of human interaction with the environment first appears here as well, as we describe precontact native American life. Chapter 1, analyzing the encounter and contrasting the cultures and societies of native Americans, West Africans, and Europeans, allows each people to speak for itself and offers a detailed, integrated portrait of native American history and culture. Against this comparative backdrop, we then take up the narrative of the planting of North America's first colonies. Chapters 2 and 3 discuss colonial society and culture in narratives that interlace chronological, regional, and topical presentations. Chapter 2, for example, contrasts New England, the English Caribbean, and the Chesapeake colonies throughout the seventeenth century; Chapter 3 introduces the Restoration colonies and the French and Spanish experiences, brings colonial society to maturity in the era of the Great Awakening and the Enlightenment, and discusses everyday life through the prism of family experiences over the life cycle.

The forging of the American nation is the theme of Chapters 4–6, from the onset of the imperial crisis to the Revolution and the Federalist decade. Here we rely primarily on narrative interspersed at key points with social analysis. Our story is essentially one of American unity in resistance to perceived British encroachments, and of civil war when the issue became independence and the disruption of traditional loyalties. The treatment of the Federalist era (Chapter 6) goes well beyond the usual dry survey of partisan bickering by studying the new nation region-by-region and stressing that the Republic's very survival was a matter of serious doubt.

The antebellum section—Chapters 7–12—begins with a chronological overview of political history from Jefferson to the Monroe Doctrine (Chapter 7), followed by a comprehensive social and economic introduction to the age of Jackson (Chapter 8). In Chapter 9 we take an innovative approach by treating Jacksonian political and reform movements as interlocking public and private attacks on social ills. We turn to the Old South in Chapter 10, offering a comprehensive portrait of this distinctive, self-sufficient, and viable region whose white citizens were deeply convinced that they had built a society worth defending. Chapter 11 provides a unique treatment of antebellum culture (using the word in its broadest sense) and of the rhythms of pre–Civil War daily life. Finally, Chapter 12 ties together a dual theme: the social change resulting from the great wave of immigration in the 1840s, and the expansionism of Manifest Destiny.

In Chapters 13–15 we consider the crisis of the Union, spanning the 1850s, the Civil War, and Reconstruction. The presentation strives to maintain a sense of drama and contingency—never, for example, assuming that northern victory and southern defeat were foreordained. In Chapter 14 we consider at length the war's powerful impact on the home front and on American culture, and in Chapter 15 we show how persistent racist assumptions and a preoccupation with other national issues eventually caused the North to lose interest in defending southern blacks' rights against the "redeemers."

We cover the post–Civil War decades in Chapters 16–20, whose unifying theme is the extraordinary social and cultural change triggered by industrial capitalism. Chapters on the West (16), industrialization (17), urbanization and immigration (18), and daily life (19) precede Chapter 20's narrative of Gilded Age politics and turn-of-the-century expansionism. However, Chapter 20 can also be read first without loss of continuity. Throughout, we have spotlighted the cultural ramifications of social change; explored the ways in which public and private issues intertwined; and stressed the autonomy of immigrants, workers, rural people, women, blacks, and native Americans.

In Chapters 21–25 our theme is the consequences of industrialization and urbanization, from progressivism to the New Deal. Chapter 21 presents progressivism as a multistranded movement, offering a variety of responses (not all of them benevolent) to the new industrial order. The treatment of World War I (Chapter 22) and of the 1920s (Chapter 23) comments at some length on the nation's cultural response to war and perseverant social tension. Finally, two chapters on the 1930s (24 and 25) assess the Great Depression as the most serious crisis yet faced by American industrial capitalism. In Chapter 24 we discuss the New Deal not as an array of alphabetical agencies but as the cradle of the modern welfare state; and Chapter 25's treatment of daily life and culture in the 1930s continues the text's approach of emphasizing the influence of individuals and communities on national social and political change.

The final cluster of chapters (26–31) extends from World War II to the present. Chapter 26 deals extensively with the home-front experience during World War II, integrating it into the narrative of military campaigns and global politics. We see in the immediate postwar years (Chapter 27) the end of American isolationism, a preoccupation with communism, and the nation's not always successful attempt to assimilate the New Deal; and in the 1950s (Chapter 28), an era of mature industrial society in which daily life assumed its essentially contemporary form through suburbanization and the expansion of leisure. The discussion of the tumultuous years from Kennedy's inauguration to Nixon's downfall (Chapters 29 and 30) focuses on modern industrial society's entrapment in Vietnam and ability to absorb the civil-rights revolution. We end the book not with the usual miscellaneous catalogue of unresolved contemporary problems but with an interpretation of recent history as the nation's gradual coming-to-terms with a sense of limits: the rise of ecological consciousness, the waning of global dominance, and the challenge of competing technological societies. By striving to put the recent past into a longer perspective, we are also in a position to round off the coverage of modern America with a unique Epilogue—a brief summing-up of our view of the lessons of history,

and an assessment of challenges that the nation's next generations will face.

Special Pedagogical Features

A range of useful and appealing study aids has been built into *The Enduring Vision*. Each chapter begins with a vivid vignette of a person or event that both swiftly draws the reader into the atmosphere and issues of the times and establishes the chapter's major themes. In every chapter there also appears an absorbing two-page illustrated essay, "A Place in Time," which explores in depth a single community's experiences in the era under consideration. Tables and chronological charts on special topics occur regularly throughout the text; and each chapter closes with a "Conclusion," an illustrated "Chronology" of pivotal events and developments, and a wealth of suggestions for further reading. The Appendix provides statistical tables; handy reference lists; and the text of the Declaration of Independence, the Articles of Confederation, and the Constitution (with its amendments).

The text's elegant full-color design features some 670 photographs and cartoons, over 100 maps, and 37 graphs. In the photographs we have taken care to avoid reproducing tired, overused images and have concentrated on historically accurate illustrations that, with rare exception, are contemporaneous with a chapter's time period. A special focus of the photographic selections has been material culture—the clothing, tools, housing, and other artifacts left by the peoples of the past. The strikingly beautiful quilts that grace *The Enduring Vision*'s covers reflect our fascination with this rich source of information about the daily lives of those gone before. The map and graph program encompasses exceptionally clear, accurate, and up-to-date illustrations, each accompanied by an explanatory caption.

Supplementary Program for *The Enduring Vision*

An extensive ancillary program accompanies *The Enduring Vision*. It has been designed not only to assist instructors, but to develop students' critical-thinking skills and to bolster readers' understanding of key topics and themes treated in the textbook.

The *Student Guide,* by Barbara Blumberg of Pace University, features (for each text chapter) review outlines, a statement of the central issues to understand, a vocabulary-building section, identifications, map exercises, sample test questions, and provocative exercises tracing the text authors' use of various historical sources. The *Instructor's Guide,* by Robert Grant of Framingham State College, offers innovative essays and handout masters centered on creative teaching techniques; summaries of each text chapter's main themes; and ideas for lecture, additional instruction, print and nonprint resources, and use of *Enduring Voices: Document Sets to Accompany The Enduring Vision.* In *Enduring Voices,* edited by James Lorence of the University of Wisconsin, Marathon Center, we provide a most unusual instructional resource. The package comprises sixty-two sets of primary-source documents for use with the text; the instructor may freely photocopy these materials for classroom discussions, course projects, or as parts of examinations. Each documentary set presents a variety of examples of primary documentary evidence—including excerpts from letters, diaries, contemporary fiction, speeches, and petitions, as well as song lyrics and advertisements—highlighting a topic or theme developed in the parallel text chapter. Rounding out the supplementary package are the *Heath Test Plus Computerized Testing Program,* which allows instructors to create customized problem sets for quizzes and examinations, and the accompanying *Test Item File,* in convenient printed format. Almost 3,000 questions, prepared by Kenneth Blume of Union College and the Albany College of Pharmacy, are available in the testing program. Finally, we have produced a large *Overhead-Transparency and Slide Package* comprising about 85 full-color illustrations based on text maps and graphs. In the supplements as in the textbook, our goal has been to make teaching and learning enjoyable and challenging.

Acknowledgments

Writing a textbook, especially one with multiple authors, is a team effort. *The Enduring Vision* has been five years in the making, and as we have planned the project, critiqued one anothers' chapters, responded to reviewers' suggestions, and watched our publisher produce the book, we have all felt a growing appreciation of the word *teamwork.* We want to take this opportunity to thank a number of individuals whose crucial role could never be appreciated by those who have not participated in such a project.

Sylvia Mallory, Senior Developmental Editor, has thrown heart and soul into the project since it was launched. She is a gifted stylist with a keen sense of how a chapter ought to flow and a realization (to quote Mark Twain) that the difference between the right word and an almost right word is like the difference between lightning and a lightning bug. She can put herself in the place of a student reader and spot where a passage will be obscure, while at the same time preserving the essence of a sophisticated idea. She worried about every detail, not only in the manuscript but also in the design, the illustration program, and the conceptualization of the supplementary materials. Through it all, she kept good humor, and we finish the job even better friends than when we began it. We also wish to thank Linda Halvorson and James Miller, successively Senior Acquisitions Editors. The first persuaded us to sign on (no mean feat), while the second cajoled us to get the job done on time. Rosemary Jaffe, Senior Production Editor, toiled with tremendous persistence—often long after closing hours—to shepherd the textbook through production, and meticulously kept track of innumerable details. In working with her during the year of actual production, we have greatly appreciated her enthusiasm and tact. Senior Designer Henry Rachlin contributed the book's clean, open, and arresting layout, whose excellence speaks for itself. Photo researcher Martha Shethar helped collect an array of fresh and intriguing illustrations—many of them real rarities—from which we had a hard time making final selections. Developmental Editor Patricia Wakeley worked with the supplements author team to produce what we believe is the fullest, most carefully executed set of ancillary materials available. Production Editor Cormac Morrissey contributed meticulous attention to the myriad details of producing the supplements. Permissions Editor

Margaret Roll spent many a long day securing rights to reproduce copyrighted material. At the end of the production process, Michael O'Dea, Manager of Manufacturing, worked his customary miracles to get the bound books delivered on time. Marketing Manager James Hamann shared with us the insights of his many years' experience in selling history textbooks.

Special words of thanks go to our many colleagues around the country who read and commented on the chapters, often at great length and with great insight. Ours was the final responsibility for sifting through their (occasionally contradictory) suggestions, but we want each of them to know that we have deeply appreciated their work. Many of them will see the stamp of their ideas in the book.

Our thanks go first to the members of the Editorial Review Board that D. C. Heath assembled to advise us and the editors in an ongoing way as our chapters were written and revised. They were:

Robert Abzug, University of Texas, Austin
Charles Alexander, Ohio University
Michael Bellesiles, Emory University
Jane De Hart, University of North Carolina, Chapel Hill
Ellen DuBois, University of California, Los Angeles
Karen Halttunen, Northwestern University
Richard Kirkendall, University of Washington
Richard L. McCormick, Rutgers University
Eric Monkkonen, University of California, Los Angeles
Walter Nugent, University of Notre Dame
James Ronda, Youngstown State University
Ronald Walters, Johns Hopkins University

The following scholars reviewed chapters in various stages of draft: **Richard Abbott,** Eastern Michigan University; **W. Andrew Achenbaum,** University of Michigan; **John L. Allen,** University of Connecticut; **Ted Alsop,** Brigham Young University; **Sharon Alter,** William Rainey Harper College; **David L. Ammerman,** Florida State University; **James Axtell,** College of William and Mary; **Edward Ayers,** University of Virginia; **William Barney,** University of North Carolina, Chapel Hill; **Susan Benson,** University of Missouri; **Dennis Berge,** San Diego State University; **Robert Berkhofer,** University of Michigan; **Chuck Bishop,** Johnson County Community College; **Julia Blackwelder,**
University of North Carolina, Charlotte; **Charmarie Blaisdell,** Northeastern University; **Sidney Bland,** James Madison University; **Barbara Blumberg,** Pace University; **Kenneth Blume,** Union College and Albany College of Pharmacy; **Nancy Bowen,** Del Mar College; **Paul Bowers,** Ohio State University; **James Broussard,** Lebanon Valley College; **Richard Buel,** Wesleyan University; **Frank Byrne,** Kent State University; **Betty Caroli,** Kingsborough Community College; **Patricia Cohen,** University of California, Santa Barbara; **Linda Cross,** Tyler Junior College; **John Cumbler,** University of Louisville; **David Danbom,** North Dakota State University; **George Daniels,** University of South Alabama; **Douglas Deal,** State University College of New York, Oswego; **Don Doyle,** Vanderbilt University; **Robert Dykstra,** State University of New York, Albany; **R. David Edmunds,** Indiana University; **Richard Ellis,** State University of New York, Buffalo; **Gary Fink,** Georgia State University; **Eric Foner,** Columbia University; **Sharon Fritz,** Moraine Valley Community College; **Richard Frucht,** Northwest Missouri State University; **David Glassberg,** University of Massachusetts, Amherst; **David Goldfield,** University of North Carolina, Charlotte; **Robert Grant,** Framingham State College; **Maurine Greenwald,** University of Pittsburgh; **Robert Griffith,** University of Maryland, College Park; **Ira Gruber,** Rice University; **Richard Haan,** Hartwick College; **Susan Hartmann,** Ohio State University; **Ellis Hawley,** University of Iowa; and **Jim Heath,** Portland State University.

Also, **Joan Hoff-Wilson,** Indiana University; **William Hogan,** Southeastern Massachusetts University; **William Holmes,** University of Georgia; **Michael Holt,** University of Virginia; **Robert Ireland,** University of Kentucky; **Jesse Jennings,** University of Utah; **Susan E. Kennedy,** Virginia Commonwealth University; **Peter Kolchin,** University of Delaware; **Michael Kurtz,** Southeastern Louisiana University; **Walter LaFeber,** Cornell University; **Walter Licht,** University of Pennsylvania; **Barbara Lindemann,** Santa Barbara City College; **John McCardell,** Middlebury College; **Jim McClellan,** Northern Virginia Community College; **J. Sears McGee,** University of California, Santa Barbara; **James McGovern,** University of West Florida; **Murdo McLeod,** University of Florida; **James McPherson,** Princeton University; **C. Roland Marchand,** University of California, Davis; **Jack**

Marietta, University of Arizona; Cathy Matson, University of Tennessee; Michael Mayer, University of Montana; James Merrell, Vassar College; Robert Messer, University of Illinois, Chicago; Douglas Miller, Michigan State University; James Mohr, University of Maryland, Baltimore County; H. Wayne Morgan, University of Oklahoma; Joseph Morice, Duquesne University; Jerome Mushkat, University of Akron; Gerald Nash, University of New Mexico; Michael Parrish, University of California, San Diego; J'Nell Pate, Tarrant County Community College; Michael Perman, University of Illinois, Chicago; Edward Pessen, Baruch College; Ronald Petrin, Oklahoma State University; Howard Rabinowitz, University of New Mexico; Elizabeth Raymond, University of Nevada, Reno; James Reed, Rutgers University; Daniel Richter, Dickinson College; Jere Roberson, Central State University; David Robson, John Carroll University; Roy Rosenzweig, George Mason University; David Rowe, Middle Tennessee State University; Jeffrey J. Safford, Montana State University; Neal Salisbury, Smith College; Martin Schiesl, California State University, Los Angeles; Judith Sealander, Wright State University; Richard Selcoe, Union Community College; Howard Shorr, Downtown Business Magnet High School; Joel Silbey, Cornell University; Neil Stout, University of Vermont; Alan Taylor, Boston University; Emory Thomas, University of Georgia; Robert Twombly, City College of New York; David Walker, University of Northern Iowa; Lynn Westerkamp, University of California, Santa Cruz; William Bruce Wheeler, University of Tennessee; Major Wilson, Memphis State University; Raymond Wolters, University of Delaware; Donald Worster, Brandeis University; Donald Wright, State University of New York, Cortland; Gavin Wright, Stanford University; Bertram Wyatt-Brown, University of Florida; and Kathleen Xidis, Johnson County Community College.

P. S. B.	T. L. P.
C. E. C.	H. S.
J. F. K.	N. W.

CONTENTS

1

The New and Old Worlds lii

8

The Transformation of American Society, 1815–1840 276

9

Politics, Religion, and Reform in Antebellum America 312

10   The Old South and Slavery, 1800–1860   350

13

From Compromise to Secession, 1850–1861   **452**

14

Reforging the Union: Civil War, 1861–1865   **486**

15   The Crises of Reconstruction, 1865–1877 **526**

16   The Frontier West **566**

17   The Rise of Industrial America   602

18

The Transformation of Urban America 640

19

Daily Life, Popular Culture, and the Arts, 1860–1900 674

22   World War I

23

The 1920s

24 Crash, Depression, and New Deal 866

25 American Life in a Decade of Crisis at Home and Abroad 900

28

America at Midcentury 1004

29

The Turbulent Sixties 1042

30 A Troubled Journey: From Port Huron to Watergate 1078

31 New Problems, Old Verities: From Watergate to the Present 1118

MAPS

CHARTS, GRAPHS, AND TABLES

American Land, Native Peoples

"The land was ours before we were the land's." So begins the poem "The Gift Outright," which the aged Robert Frost read at John F. Kennedy's inauguration in 1961. Frost's poem meditates on the interrelatedness of history, geography, and human consciousness. At first, wrote Frost, North American settlers merely possessed the land; but then, in a subtle spiritual process, they became possessed by it. Only by entering into this deep relationship with the land itself—"such as she was, such as she would become"—did their identity as a people fully take shape.

Frost's poem speaks of the encounter of English colonists with a strange new continent of mystery and promise; but of course, what the Europeans called the New World was in fact the homeland of the native American peoples whose ancestors had been "the land's" for at least fifteen thousand years. Native Americans had undergone an immensely long process of settling the continent, developing divergent cultures, discovering agriculture, and creating a rich spiritual life tightly interwoven with the physical environment that sustained them. Although the native Americans' story before the Europeans' incursion is recorded in archaeological relics rather than written documents, it is nonetheless fully a part of American history. Nor can we grasp the tragic conflict between Old and New World peoples that began soon after Columbus's arrival in 1492 without understanding the conti-nuities of native American history before and after contact with whites, or without appreciating the Indians' tenacious hold on their ancestral soil, forests, and waters.

This Prologue has a dual purpose. The first is to recount how the earliest Americans—the Indians—became "the land's." The second purpose is to tell the story of the land itself: its geological origins; its reshaping by eons of lifting, sinking, erosion, and glaciation; the opportunities and limitations that it presents to human endeavor. By weaving together the strands of geography and Indian experience, we shall consider as well the ultimate dependence of human beings on their environment.

To comprehend the American past we must first know the American land itself. The patterns of weather; the undulations of valley, plain, and mountain; the shifting mosaic of sand, soil, and rock; the intricate network of rivers, streams, and lakes—these have profoundly influenced United States history. North America's fundamental physical characteristics have shaped the course of human events from the earliest migrations from Asia to the later cycles of agricultural and industrial development, the rise of cities, the course of politics, and even the basic themes of American literature, art, and music. Geology, geography, and environment are among the fundamental building blocks of human history.

An Ancient Heritage

It is sobering to begin the study of American history by contrasting the recent rise of a rich, complex human society on this continent with the awesomely slow pace by which the North American environment took form. Geologists trace the oldest known rocks on the continent back some 3 billion years. The rocky "floor" known as the Canadian Shield first became visible on the surface of the northeastern United States and Canada during the earliest geologic era, the Precambrian, which ended 500 million years ago. Halfway between that remote age and the present, during the Paleozoic ("ancient life") era, forests covered much of what would eventually be the United States. From this organic matter, America's enormous coal reserves would be created, the largest yet discovered in the entire world. Only at the close of the Paleozoic, about 225 million years ago, did the continent become in a sense the "New World" by starting to split off from the single landmass that previously had encompassed all the earth's dry land surfaces. By a process known as plate tectonics—which continues today, at the rate of a few centimeters a year—the North American continent slowly began moving westward. At roughly the same time, the Appalachian Mountains arose in what is now the east-

200 million years ago

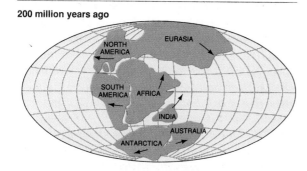

100 million years ago

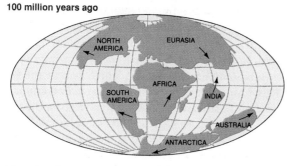

Present

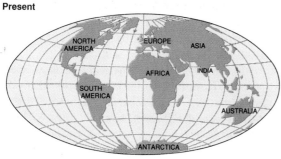

Movement of the Continents

(Top) The giant supercontinent of Pangaea; (center) continental positions 100 million years ago; (bottom) present position of the continents.

ern United States. Animal life had not as yet emerged from the sea. So enormous a gulf of time separates the origins of North America from the beginning of human history that, if those 225 million years were compressed into the space of a single twenty-four-hour day, everything that has happened since the Indians' ancestors first migrated here would flash by in the last half-second before midnight, and the New World's history since Columbus would occupy about five-thousandths of a second. In considering the sweep of geologic time, one inevitably wonders how ephemeral human history itself may yet prove to be.

Many millions of years after North America's initial separation, during the Mesozoic ("middle life") era—the age of the dinosaurs—violent movements of the earth's crust thrust up the Pacific Coastal, Sierra Nevada, and Cascade ranges on the continent's western edge. As the dinosaurs were dying out, toward the end of the Mesozoic some 65–70 million years ago, the vast, shallow sea that washed over much of west-central North America disappeared, having been replaced by the Rocky Mountains. By then, the decay and fossilization of plant and animal life were creating North America's once great petroleum deposits, which even a generation ago seemed almost limitless. Within the last 50 million years, volcanic eruptions raised the cones that now form the Hawaiian Islands, twenty-five hundred miles southwest of California. Active Pacific-rim volcanoes and powerful earthquakes all over the continent dramatically demonstrate that the molding of the American landscape still continues.

Volcanic Eruption, Hawaii

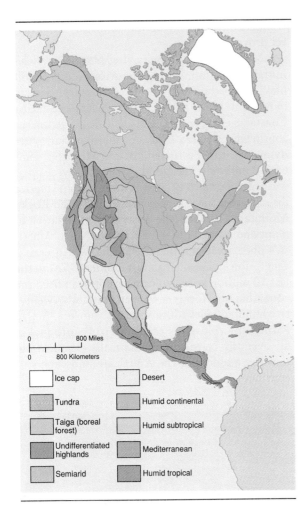

North American Climatic Regions

pockmarked the terrain over which the glaciers had spread, and areas adjacent to the ice sheets were covered with thick deposits of glacial outwash—sediment carried by streams from melting inland glaciers. Several thousand years passed before the Midwest and New England ceased to resemble present-day northern Alaska in climate and vegetation.

Like the slow but relentless shaping of landforms, the origins of the human species extend back to the mists of prehistoric time. Some 5 million years ago, direct human ancestors first evolved in the temperate grasslands of Africa. Between three hundred thousand and one hundred thousand years ago, *Homo sapiens* evolved and began migrating throughout the Old World. Then, late in the Ice Age, hunting bands pursuing large game animals reached northeastern Asia and the Alaska-Siberia land bridge. As the glaciers retreated, small hunting bands followed a corridor southward along the mountain slopes of northwestern Canada. Some of this movement occurred perhaps as early as forty thousand years ago, but most migration into the heart of the Americas can be dated very roughly to 20,000–10,000 B.C.

Almost all native American peoples were descended from these original migrants who ventured across the Alaska-Siberia land bridge. A few, however, were the offspring of more recent arrivals. Some four thousand years ago, for example, Eskimos and Aleuts from Siberia began paddling their kayaks to North America. These hardy peoples settled the coasts of the Bering Sea and the Arctic Ocean. Around the polar seas, they established a way of life based on small communities of remarkable resourcefulness and endurance. Most Eskimo peoples traded extensively with the Indians dwelling inland, but a few were so isolated that, as recently as the early twentieth century, some learned to their astonishment that they were not the only human beings on earth. Far more inviting to migrants, but even more isolated, were the Hawaiian Islands. About A.D. 400 and again about 1000, Polynesians from the South Pacific reached Hawaii in giant outrigger canoes. Part of the vast migrations then peopling the Pacific Islands, the Hawaiians created a vigorous warrior society that flourished undisturbed by outsiders until the English sea captain James Cook found his way there in 1778.

Between 2 million and ten thousand years ago, four great glaciations left a tremendous imprint on the land. The Ice Age staggers the imagination. A carpet of ice as thick as thirteen thousand feet extended over most of Canada and crept southward into what is now New England, New York State, and much of the Midwest. As the last ice caps retreated, water formerly locked in the ice sheets flooded shallow offshore regions like the land bridge that linked Alaska and Siberia. The climatic changes triggered by the melting ice drastically affected North American plant and animal life and helped turn the Southwest into a desert. Glacial runoff filled the Great Lakes and the Mississippi River basin. Ice and rocky debris

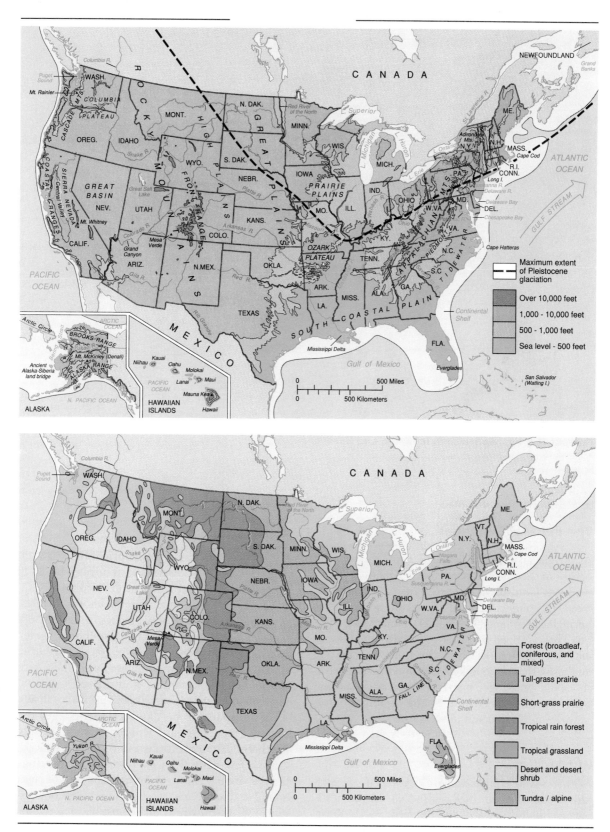

Above, **Physiographic Map of the United States**   *Below,* **Natural Vegetation of the United States**

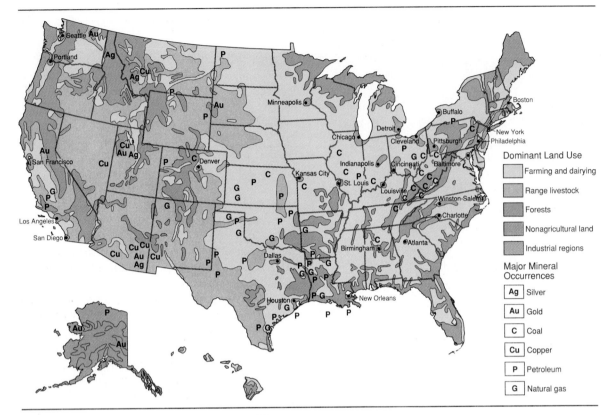

Present-Day U.S. Agriculture, Industry, and Resources

The Indians' Continent

As the glacial ice melted at last, raising the world's oceans to their present level, North America slowly warmed. Gradually the evergreens, the broadleaf trees, and temperate-zone animal life returned to once glaciated land. The hunters fanned out, too: small bands armed with flint-tipped weapons moved with the mammoths, mastodons, horses, camels, and bison that they stalked. Six thousand to twelve thousand years ago, many of these large species became extinct, destroyed by the combination of a warming climate and hunters' prowess.

The Northwest and the West

With its severe climate and profuse wildlife, Alaska still evokes the land that ancient North America's earliest migrants discovered. Indeed, Alaska's far north resembles a world from which ice caps have just retreated—a treeless tundra of grasses, lichens, and stunted shrubs. This region, the Arctic, is a stark wilderness in winter, reborn in fleeting summers of colorful flowers and returning birds. In contrast, the subarctic of central Alaska and Canada is a heavily forested country known as taiga. Here rises North America's highest peak, 20,300-foot Mt. McKinley, or Denali (the Indian name). Average temperatures in the subarctic range from the fifties above zero in summer to well below zero in the long, dark winters, and the soil is permanently frozen except during summer surface thaws.

The expanse from Alaska's glacier-gouged and ruggedly mountainous Pacific shore southward to northern California forms the Pacific Northwest. Only a few natural harbors break the shoreline, but they include the magnificent anchorages of Puget Sound and San Francisco Bay. Offshore, cool currents and warm winds make possible rich coastal fisheries.

The Pacific coastal region is in some ways a world apart. Vegetation and animal life, isolated

Mendenhall Glacier, Alaska

from the rest of the continent by deserts and mountains, include many species unfamiliar farther east. Warm, wet westerly winds blowing off the Pacific create a climate more uniformly temperate than anywhere else in North America. From Anchorage and the Alaska panhandle to a little south of San Francisco Bay, winters are cool, humid, and foggy, and the coast's dense forest cover includes the largest living organisms on earth, the giant sequoia (redwood) trees. Along the southern California coast, winds and currents generate a warmer, "Mediterranean" climate, and vegetation includes a heavy growth of shrubs and short trees, scattered stands of oak, and grasses able to endure prolonged seasonal drought.

The rugged Sierra Nevada, Cascade, and coastal ranges stretch the length of British Columbia, Washington, Oregon, and California. Their majestic peaks trap abundant Pacific Ocean moisture that gigantic clockwise air currents carry eastward. Between the ranges nestle flat, fertile valleys—California's Central Valley (formed by the San Joa-

Coastal Farming, Northern California

quin and Sacramento rivers), Oregon's Willamette Valley, and the Puget Sound region in Washington—that have become major agricultural centers in recent times.

Well east of the Pacific coastal band lies the Great Basin, encompassing Nevada, western Utah, southern Idaho, and eastern Oregon. The few streams here have no outlet to the sea. Much of the Great Basin was once covered by an inland sea holding glacial meltwater, a remnant of which survives in Utah's Great Salt Lake. Today, however, the Great Basin is dry and severely eroded, a cold desert rich in minerals, imposing in its austere grandeur and lonely emptiness. North of the basin, the Columbia and Snake rivers, which drain the plateau country of Idaho and eastern Washington and Oregon, provide plentiful water for farming.

Western North America's "backbone" is the Rocky Mountains. In turn, the Rockies form part of the immense mountain system that reaches from Alaska to the Andes of South America. Elevations in the Rockies rise from a mile above sea level at Denver at the foot of the mountains to permanently snowcapped peaks more than fourteen thousand feet above sea level. Beyond the front range of the Rockies lies the Continental Divide, the watershed separating the rivers flowing eastward into the Atlantic from those draining westward into the Pacific. The climate and vegetation of the Rocky Mountain high country resemble Arctic and subarctic types.

The Indians who settled the North and West between ten thousand and twenty thousand years ago adapted to their often severely challenging environments in diverse ways. For sustenance they depended on hunting, fishing, and gathering wild vegetation. Many of the plants they ate had to be leached of toxins. California Indians ground acorns into flour from which they made bread. Population densities varied enormously with locale. For example, in the forbidding subarctic North and the Great Basin, only scattered, wandering bands that occasionally converged in large winter encampments peopled the land, whereas mild and resource-rich California and the sheltered inlets of the northwestern coast supported many diverse cultures and the densest Indian populations in what would later be the United States. Abundant marine life, roots, and berries kept them well fed, and they excelled in intricate basket making. A Spanish friar who reached California overland from Mexico in 1770 wrote, "This land exceeds all the preceding territory in fertility and abundance of things necessary for sustenance."

Isolated from cultivators elsewhere, none of the Pacific coast Indians ever developed agriculture. Nevertheless, the same Spanish padre's 1770 account of the Chumash Indians gives a glimpse of a hardy, self-sufficient native California society. The Chumash, he found, were "well-appearing, of good disposition, affable, liberal [generous], and friendly towards the Spanish." Their villages were governed by civil chiefs who took multiple wives so that they could maintain kinship links with as many families as possible. Other males took but a single wife. Kin lived together in "neatly built" houses large enough for four or five families. The women carried their swaddled babies on their backs, strapped to boards, and thus were left "unencum-

Joshua Tree, Western Nevada

Maroon Bells of the Rocky Mountains, near Aspen, Colorado

bered for all their duties." Evidently, the Indians were exceedingly healthy before the sudden arrival of European peoples and their infectious diseases, which had a devastating effect.

The Southwest and the Origins of Agriculture

Arizona, southern Utah, western New Mexico, and southeastern California form America's southwestern desert. The climate is arid, searingly hot on summer days and cold on winter nights. Adapted to stringent environmental conditions, many plants and animals here could not survive elsewhere. Dust storms, cloudbursts, and flash floods have everywhere carved, abraded, and twisted the rocky landscape. Nature's fantastic sculpture appears on the most monumental scale in the Grand Canyon, where

for 20 million years the Colorado River has been cutting down to Precambrian bedrock.

In the face of such tremendous natural forces, human activity might well seem paltry and transitory. Yet here, sometime between 3000 and 2000 B.C., the first crop cultivation began on what is now United States soil. Agriculture probably originated when women noticed that wild seeds dropped to the ground could later sprout and bear new seeds, and when they realized that they might supplement their dwindling gatherings by reaping from what they had sown. For centuries crop cultivation remained a relatively minor source of food. But even as the Southwest slowly grew more arid, Indians preserved the precious water on which their corn, melons, and beans depended.

Agriculture supplied a major share of southwestern Indians' food after about 300 B.C., when new influxes of Indian peoples from Mexico brought more drought-resistant strains of corn to the Southwest. Within several centuries the possibility of more extensive crop cultivation nurtured several distinctive southwestern cultural traditions that live on today. One such tradition was the Hohokam culture of the peoples of Arizona's Gila River Valley, who diverted river water with networks of ditches. Another culture was the world of the pueblos—the massive "apartment-house" masonry villages that appeared in northern Arizona's and New Mexico's plateau country during the first millennium A.D.

Nothing in North America better embodies the human ability to thrive despite nature's inclemency than the enduring southwestern Indian cultures. By 1400 worsening desert conditions helped undermine the Hohokam culture. It yielded to the simpler but tenacious way of life of the Pima-Papago Indians who cultivated southern Arizona's river valleys using floodwater but not irrigation works. Meanwhile, the complex, tightly organized pueblo cultures also surmounted a prolonged crisis. By the late thirteenth century, increasing aridity forced the abandonment of many villages, particularly in the highlands (see "A Place in Time"). The center of pueblo life shifted to northeastern Arizona and to New Mexico's Rio Grande Valley. Pueblos grew even larger and more strongly fortified. Such precautions became necessary after the Southwest was invaded by marauding hunter-gatherer peoples from the Canadian subarctic, who formed the modern Navahos and Apaches. In the sixteenth century, an equally disruptive force would invade the region from the south: the Spanish.

The Heartland: Diffusion of Agriculture and Early Indian Civilization

North America's heartland comprises the area extending eastward from the Rockies to the Appalachians. This vast region forms one of the world's largest drainage systems. From it the Great Lakes empty into the North Atlantic through the St. Lawrence River, and the Mississippi-Missouri-Ohio river network flows southward into the Gulf of Mexico. Where the drainage system originates, at the northern and western reaches of the Great Lakes region, lie some of the world's richest deposits of

iron and copper ore. In our own time, the heartland's waterways have offered a splendid means of carrying this mineral wealth to nearby coal-producing areas for processing, unfortunately also spawning widespread environmental pollution.

The Mississippi—the "Father of Waters" to the Indians, and one of the world's longest rivers—carries a prodigious volume of water and silt. It has changed course many times in geological history. The lower Mississippi (below the junction with the Ohio River) meanders constantly. In the process, the river deposits rich sediments throughout its broad, ancient floodplain. Indeed, the Mississippi has carried so much silt over the millennia that in its lower stretches, the river flows *above* the surrounding valley, which it catastrophically floods when its high banks (levees) are breached. Over millions of years, such riverborne sediment covered what was once the westward extension of the Appalachians in northern Mississippi and eastern Arkansas. Only the Ozark Plateau and Ouachita Mountains remain exposed, forming the hill country of southern Missouri, north-central Arkansas, and eastern Oklahoma. These uplands have evolved into an economically and culturally distinctive region—beautiful but isolated and impoverished.

Below New Orleans the Mississippi empties into the Gulf of Mexico through an enormous delta with an intricate network of grassy swamps known as bayous. The Mississippi Delta offers good farm soil, capable of supporting a large population. Swarming with waterfowl, insects, alligators, and marine plants and animals, this environment has nurtured a distinctive way of life for the Indian, white, and black peoples who have inhabited it.

North of the Ohio and Missouri rivers, themselves products of glacial runoff, Ice Age glaciation molded the American heartland. Because the local terrain was generally flat prior to glaciation, the ice sheets distributed glacial debris quite evenly. Spread even farther by wind and rivers, this fine-ground glacial dust slowly created the fertile farm soil of the Midwest. Glaciers also dug out the five Great Lakes (Superior, Huron, Michigan, Ontario, and Erie), collectively the world's largest body of fresh water. Water flowing from Lake Erie to the lower elevation of Lake Ontario created Niagara Falls, comparable only to the Grand Canyon as testimony to nature's power.

Confluence of the Mississippi and Ohio Rivers near Cairo, Illinois

Cypress Pond in Bayou Country

Most of the heartland's eastern and northern sectors were once heavily forested. To the west thick, tall-grass prairie covered Illinois and parts of adjoining states, as well as much of the Missouri River basin and the middle Arkansas River basin (Oklahoma and central Texas). Beyond the Missouri the prairie gave way to short-grass steppe—the Great Plains, cold in winter, blazing hot in summer, and always dry. The great distances that separate the heartland's prairies and Great Plains from the moderating effects of the oceans have made this region's annual temperature range the most extreme in North America. As the traveler moves westward, elevations rise gradually, winds howl ceaselessly, trees grow only along streambeds, long droughts alternate with violent thunderstorms and tornadoes, and water and wood are ever scarcer.

From the Rockies to the wooded slopes of western Pennsylvania, the heartland was the habitat of the bison. Some twelve thousand years ago, Indian bands hunted a now extinct form of the

Mesa Verde in the Thirteenth Century

Mesa Verde Panorama, Showing the Cliff Palace

North of the desert lands of Arizona and New Mexico, the elevation gradually rises to a high plateau in the present-day Four Corners area, where Arizona, New Mexico, Colorado, and Utah meet. Modern-day scientists' analysis of ancient tree rings and pollen levels shows that a thousand years ago the plateau was somewhat wetter and more heavily forested than today, although rainfall was still sparse. But the environment was hospitable enough to support the emergence of new Indian cultures. Archaeologists call the early plateau peoples the Basketmakers, a name derived from the tightly woven basketry that the women fashioned from yucca fibers. About A.D. 700, Basketmaker mothers began to strap their infants to hard cradleboards, producing the flattened skull that for centuries would be the distinguishing physical characteristic of the plateau peoples. At the same time, the population first gathered in pueblos. Small in the beginning, the pueblos mushroomed in size over the centuries. They were generally located on the flat-topped elevations that the later Spanish invaders of the Southwest called mesas (after the Spanish word for *table*).

In about the year 1200, pueblo peoples of the Four Corners began to move from the mesas to cliffside caves that faced south for maximum sunlight. Protection against marauders must have been the reason, for living space was tighter in the new location. So it was that set-

tlers came to the Cliff Palace at Mesa Verde ("Green Table") in southwestern Colorado.

In this large settlement of some two hundred rooms, as many as a thousand people dwelled in cramped quarters. These conditions demanded effective public authority. Male societies organized to conduct religious rituals were one such form of social organization. For example, the Cliff Palace residents probably relied on a warrior society to mediate charges of antisocial behavior, whether theft, adultery, homicide, or witchcraft. Depending on circumstances, the people most likely recognized the leadership of

The Cliff Palace

two chiefs: a "civil chief" in peace-time and a "war chief" when they had to fight raiders or unfriendly pueblos. But no single person exercised leadership. Rather, it resided in the community as a whole, as expressed in the people's collective sense of what was proper behavior and what would please the gods who sent precious rain and made crops grow.

The supernatural penetrated all aspects of the people's everyday affairs. Omens and other signs of spiritual influence in daily life were interpreted by the community's shamans—individuals trusted for their ability to communicate with the spirit world. Ceremonies to honor the gods and ensure their favor went on continuously, performed without the slightest deviation from ancient ritual by the men of the pueblo's various religious societies who assembled in the kivas (ceremonial chambers). Cliff Palace had twenty-three kivas, each one closed to all but members of a single society. The most awful offense that anyone could commit was to reveal kiva secrets.

Thus accustomed to conform strictly to community standards, the Cliff Palace people went about their routines. Every day, men descended long ladders to the valley floor, where they worked the community's corn fields. By coiling and firing clay, women produced the highly distinctive Mesa Verde pottery—plain gray-white cookware for ordinary use and intricate black-on-white geometrically patterned vessels for ceremonial occasions. Women also looked after the community's turkeys and wove cotton fabric on looms. Everyone had to collect scarce rainwater; people even preserved early-morning dew on the rocks. No matter how generous the

Balcony House with Kiva, Mesa Verde

gods, farming was still intensely risky.

But at the end of the thirteenth century, the gods forsook Mesa Verde. A century-long climatic drying trend culminated in a terrible drought between 1276 and 1299, which possibly combined with epidemics or attacks by hostile neighbors to break the people's spirit. No telltale signs of violence survived. By 1300 the dwellers of the Cliff Palace and other Mesa Verde sites abandoned their pueblos and silently moved away. They probably regrouped to form the modern Hopi and Zuñi pueblos of Arizona and New Mexico. We do not even know what they had called themselves, although the Navahos who replaced them in the plateau region gave them the name by which the entire culture has become known: the Anasazis, or "Ancient Ones." Slowly the Mesa Verde cliff pueblos crumbled, bereft of inhabitants who could maintain the structures and the way

of life that they embodied. Whites first saw the ruins only in 1888. That year, some ranchers hunting for lost cattle happened into the valley and beheld the Cliff Palace, suspended ghostlike in a winter snowstorm.

Ancient Mesa Verde—type Pottery

A Folsom Point

This Folsom point is shown just as it was found, imbedded between two ribs of the extinct Bison taylori.

bison. The discovery in 1926 of the beautifully crafted "Folsom points" (stone spear points) in the bones of these ancient animals first proved how long ago the Indians' settlement of North America had occurred. Until the nineteenth century, bison herds supplied the greater part of the sustenance of many heartland Indian peoples. A Spanish trooper who saw the Great Plains in 1541–1542 wrote of the Indian inhabitants:

> *With the [bison's] skins they build their houses; with the skins they clothe and shoe themselves; from the skins they make rope and also obtain wool. With the sinews they make thread, with which they sew clothes and also their tents. With the bones they shape awls. The dung they use for firewood, since there is no other fuel in that land. The bladders they use as jugs and drinking containers. They sustain themselves on their meat, eating it slightly roasted and heated over the dung. Some they eat raw.*

Now much of this forested, grassy world is forever altered. The heartland has become open farming country. Gone are the flocks of migratory birds that once darkened the daytime skies of the plains; gone are the free-roaming bison. Forests now only fringe the heartland: in the lake country of northern Minnesota and Wisconsin, on Michigan's upper peninsula, and across the hilly uplands of the Appalachians, southern Indiana, and the Ozarks. The settlers who displaced the Indians have done most of the plowing up of prairie grass and felling of trees since the early nineteenth century, although Indians may have contributed to the deforestation, too, by burning large woodland areas centuries ago. Destruction of the forest and grassy cover has made the Midwest a "breadbasket" for the world market. But several times since the nineteenth century, inadequate irrigation and improper plowing have turned this matchless soil into a dustbowl.

Agriculture came to the heartland almost three millennia ago. Around 800 B.C. migrants from the Southwest or Mexico who were familiar with agriculture reached the Ohio Valley, where they created the Adena culture. Adena peoples buried their

Grain Harvesting in America's Heartland

Great Serpent Mound, Ohio

Embossed Copper Falcon, Hopewell Culture

This remarkable artifact was found in a mound at Mound City, Ohio. Predatory birds were a common motif among Hopewell peoples.

dead in earthen mounds. This custom, based on increasingly complex religious ideas, passed on to the Hopewell culture, which flourished between 100 B.C. and A.D. 550 in the same forested core of the Midwest. After about 550, the Hopewell culture faded away, but its place was taken about two centuries later by a similar religious cult whose surviving artifacts represent the Mississippian culture, which endured until about 1500. Mississippian settlements spread northward along the Mississippi-Missouri valleys and southward to Florida and Oklahoma, their denizens everywhere building extensive earthen mounds. Atop the mounds, Mississippians erected imposing temples and residences for their priest-kings, whose tombs they filled with a profusion of ceramic pottery and carved stone objects.

Encompassing more than fifteen hundred years before the coming of the Europeans, the Hopewell and Mississippian cultures marked the rise in North America of an early civilization. Possibly the people benefited from contact with the impressive empires in Mexico that had been developing since the first millennium B.C. and that culminated in the Maya and Aztec states. But archaeologists have not unearthed convincing evidence of direct Mexican influence. More likely, the Hopewell and Mississippian cultures were native North American developments, unfolding from an original religious impulse to provide for the afterlife and to appease the gods who ensured fertility. Archaeological findings suggest that in the Mississippian culture particularly, the priest-kings who organized religious ceremonials exercised strong, even despotic sway over their subjects. But their capacity for organizing society was formidable. The largest Mississippian community—Cahokia, which flourished near present-day St. Louis between about 1050 and 1250—was a city of up to thirty thousand inhabitants, a population as large as that of any medieval western European urban center. Moreover, the trade networks on which the Hopewell and Mississippian cultures depended were enormous, extending from the Gulf of Mexico to the upper Great Lakes and the Rockies.

Environmental change, primarily the long-term cyclic recurrence of a colder, drier climate, doubtless hastened the decline of the Hopewell world in the sixth century A.D. and the abandonment of Cahokia and other large Mississippian cities in the thirteenth century. Similar change adversely affected the pueblo peoples of the Southwest; in fact, the climatic shift had worldwide effects, contributing in the Old World to the decline of the Roman Empire and (a thousand years later) to a severe economic and demographic crisis in fourteenth-century Europe.

Civilizations and empires rise and fall, but life goes on. The decline of great religious centers such as Cahokia led to the diffusion of Mississippian cultural influence to tribal societies throughout the heartland and beyond. The way of life of the midwestern, southeastern, and eastern Indians who lived at some distance from the religious centers continued to take shape. Anthropologists call this way of life the Woodland culture. Woodland peoples formed tribal societies in small villages that shifted seasonally from corn fields and bean fields to hunting or fishing encampments. The Woodland culture eventually reached as far west as the Great Plains river valleys; and crossing the Appalachians, it also extended eastward to the Atlantic coast and New England.

The Atlantic Seaboard

The eastern edge of the heartland is marked by the ancient Appalachian Mountain chain, which over the course of 200 million years has been ground down to gentle ridges paralleling one another southwest to northeast. Between the ridges lie fertile valleys such as Virginia's Shenandoah. The Appalachian hill country's wealth is in thick timber and mineral beds—particularly the Paleozoic coal deposits—whose heavy exploitation since the nineteenth century has accelerated destructive soil erosion in this softly beautiful, mountainous land.

Descending gently from the Appalachians' eastern slope is the piedmont ("foot of the mountain"). In this broad, rolling upland extending from Alabama to Maryland, the rich red soil has been ravaged in modern times by excessive cotton and tobacco cultivation. The piedmont's modern pineywoods cover constitutes "secondary growth" replacing the sturdy hardwood trees that native Americans and pioneering whites and blacks once knew. The northward extension of the piedmont from Pennsylvania to New England has more broadleaf vegetation, a harsher winter climate, and (through the Hudson and Connecticut river valleys) somewhat better access to the piedmont itself. But unlike the piedmont, upstate New York and New England were shaped by glaciation: the terrain here comprises hills contoured by advancing and retreating ice, and numerous lakes scoured out by glaciers. Belts of debris remain, and in many

Cades Cove, Great Smoky Mountains; Tennessee Strip Mining

The impact of human hands is dramatically apparent in these two starkly contrasting Appalachian hill-country scenes.

places granite boulders shoulder their way up through the soil. Though picturesque, the land is the despair of anyone who has tried to plow it.

From southeastern Massachusetts and Rhode Island to south-central Alabama runs the fall line, the boundary between the relatively hard rock of the interior and the softer sediment of the coastal plain. Rivers crossing the fall line drop quickly to near sea level, thus making a series of rapids that block navigation upstream from the coast.

The character of the Atlantic coastal plain varies strikingly from south to north. In the extreme south, at the tip of the Florida peninsula, the climate and vegetation are subtropical. The southern coastal lands running north from Florida to Chesapeake Bay and the mouth of the Delaware River compose the tidewater region. This is a wide, rather flat lowland, heavily wooded with a mixture of

Boulders and Autumn Leaves, Washington, New Hampshire

Tidewater Wetlands, North Carolina

broadleaf and coniferous forests, ribboned with numerous small rivers, occasionally swampy, and often miserably hot and humid in summer. North of Delaware Bay, the coastal lowlands narrow and flatten to form the New Jersey Pine Barrens, Long Island, and Cape Cod—all of these created by the deposit of glacial debris. Here the climate is noticeably milder than in the interior. North of Massachusetts Bay, the land back of the immediate shoreline becomes increasingly mountainous.

Many large rivers drain into the Atlantic: the St. Lawrence, flowing out of the Great Lakes northeastward through eastern Canada; the Connecticut in New England; the Hudson, Delaware, Susquehanna, and Potomac in what are now the Middle Atlantic states; the Savannah in the South. Most of these originally carried glacial meltwater. The Susquehanna and the Potomac filled in the broad, shallow Chesapeake Bay, teeming with marine life and offering numerous anchorages for oceangoing ships.

North America's true eastern edge is not the coastline but the offshore continental shelf, whose relatively shallow waters extend as far as 250 miles into the Atlantic before plunging deeply. Along the rocky Canadian and Maine coasts, where at the end of the Ice Age the rising ocean half covered glaciated mountains and valleys, oceangoing craft may find numerous small anchorages. South of

Pemigewasset Wilderness, White Mountains, New Hampshire

The Tip of Cape Cod, Massachusetts

Massachusetts Bay, the Atlantic shore and the Gulf of Mexico coastline form a shoreline of sandy beaches and long barrier islands paralleling the mainland. Tropical storms boiling up from the open seas regularly lash North America's Atlantic shores, and at all times brisk winds make coastal navigation treacherous.

Crossing the Atlantic east to west can daunt even skilled mariners, particularly those battling against powerful winds by sail. Here, on one of the world's stormiest seas, the mighty Gulf Stream current sweeps from southwest to northeast. Winds off the North American mainland also trend steadily eastward, and dangerous icebergs floating south from Greenland's waters threaten every ship. Little wonder that in 1620 the *Mayflower* Pilgrims' first impulse on landing was to sink to their knees in thanks to God for having transported them safely across "the vast and furious ocean." Many a vessel went to the bottom.

But for millennia, the Atlantic coastal region of North America offered a welcoming haven to settlers. For example, ten thousand years ago, ancient Indian hunters followed a warming climate eastward across the Appalachians to the coast. Early in the first millennium A.D., eastern peoples began adopting the Woodland culture and agriculture from the heartland. Offshore, well within their reach, lay such productive fishing grounds as the Grand Banks and Cape Cod's coastal bays, where cool-water upwellings on the continental shelf have lured swarms of fish and crustaceans. "The abundance

of sea-fish are almost beyond believing," wrote a breathless English settler in 1630, "and sure I should scarce have believed it, except I had seen it with my own eyes."

Indian hands tended eastern North America's coastal lands with skill and care. From southern Maine to the Carolinas, great expanses of hardwood trees formed an open, parklike landscape, free of underbrush (which the Indians had systematically burned) but rich with grass and berry bushes that attracted a profusion of game. The Woodland peoples' "slash-and-burn" method of land management was environmentally sound and economically productive. Indians cleared the land by burning underbrush and destroying the larger trees' bark. Then, amid the leafless deadwood, they planted their corn, beans, and pumpkins in soil enriched by ash. After several years of abundant harvests, yields declined, and the Indians moved on to a new site to repeat the process. Soon groundcover reclaimed the abandoned clearing, restoring fertility naturally. Over time, rather than shifting their cultivation aimlessly through the wilderness, the Indians rotated their sowing around a series of fields.

The crop yields of Woodland Indians' agricultural lands, where corn, beans, and melons grew together in tangled plenty, astonished Europeans. "Small labor but great pleasure" was how New England's first white explorer described the Indians' supposedly carefree lives. His remark epitomized Europeans' misunderstanding of native American ways from the very outset. But Europeans also learned to benefit from the Indians' expertise in cultivating unfamiliar New World crops, and former Indian clearings were soon serving whites as farmsites as they advanced into the North American interior.

A Legacy and a Challenge

At least three thousand miles of open sea separates North America from Europe and Africa; and Asia, except for the subarctic region where Alaska and Siberia once joined, lies even more distant. Ever since the first human wanderers crossed over from Asia, geographical isolation and ecological variety

Rock-strewn Crystal River near Redstone, Colorado

have been the New World's most striking characteristics. Isolation made possible native Americans' social and cultural development untouched by alien influences and infectious diseases. Meanwhile, the great climatic and geographical variations among North American regions ensured that native cultures—all of them highly dependent on the natural environment—would be extremely diverse.

Yet despite North America's isolation, Indian history did not begin at Columbus's arrival, with everything before 1492 relegated to a dim, uneventful limbo of "prehistory." When Europeans "discovered" America in 1492, they did not enter an unchanging world of simple savages. To take but one example, during the fifteenth century, the five Iroquois tribes of western New York created their "Great League of Peace," a formidable confederacy with commercial and religious significance as well as growing military prowess. We can only guess what course native American cultural and social evolution might have taken had it remained untouched by alien influences. But there can be no doubt that native Americans in 1492 were caught up in long-range historical change rooted in thousands of years of prior development.

"A people come from under the world, to take their world from them"—thus an early-seventeenth-century Virginia Indian characterized the English invaders of his homeland. Indeed, the modern society that since the seventeenth century has arisen on the Indians' ancient continent bears little resemblance to the world that native Americans once knew. Only the land itself remains.

A lingering sense of isolation has stimulated European-descended Americans' hopes of keeping Old World problems away from the pristine New World, just as North America's fertile soil, virgin forests, and rich mineral resources have long conjured up visions of limitless wealth. But industrialization, urbanization, rapid mass transportation, and tremendous population growth stretched to the limits the American land's ability to maintain a modern society without irreversible ecological damage. And only in the twentieth century have Americans learned that global transportation networks and instantaneous communication make isolation impossible. At last, as ecologist Aldo Leopold put it, they have begun discovering that the earth's people "are only fellow voyagers in the odyssey of evolution." And that lesson has been hard learned. "It required 19 centuries to define decent man-to-man conduct and the process is only half-done," Leopold admonished; "it may take as long to evolve a code of decency for man-to-land conduct."

It is in evolving such a code, however, that the native American legacy may yet prove most enduring. Living in constant dependence on their environment, native Americans achieved a religious reverence for their land and all living beings that shared it. In recapturing a sense that the land—its life-sustaining bounty and its soul-sustaining beauty—is itself of inestimable value and not merely a means to the end of material growth, future American generations may reestablish a sense of historical and cultural continuity with their native American precursors. Thereby they can truly be possessed by their land instead of simply being its possessors.

CHRONOLOGY

c. 300,000– 100,000 B.C.	Migration of modern human beings throughout the Old World.
c. 40,000– 10,000 B.C.	Ancestors of New World's native population cross Alaska-Siberia land bridge.
c. 3000– 2000 B.C.	Crop cultivation begins on what is now U.S. soil.
c. 800 B.C.	Adena culture emerges in the Ohio Valley.
c. 300 B.C.	Agriculture supplies a major part of southwestern Indians' food.
c. 100 B.C.– A.D. 550	Hopewell culture flourishes in the Midwest.
c. A.D. 700	Mississippian culture takes shape near the junction of the Mississippi, Missouri, and Ohio rivers.
c. A.D. 1000	Pueblo culture emerges in the Southwest.
c. 1400– 1500	Iroquois "Great League of Peace" created.

CHAPTER 1

The New and Old Worlds

At ten o'clock on a moonlit night, the tense crew spotted a glimmering light. Then at two the next morning came the shout "Land! Land!" At daybreak they entered a shallow lagoon. The captain rowed ashore, the royal flag fluttering in the breeze. "And, all having rendered thanks to the Lord, kneeling on the ground, embracing it with tears of joy for the immeasurable mercy of having reached it, [he] rose and gave this island the name San Salvador." The date was October 12, 1492. The place was a tiny tropical island less than four hundred miles southeast of present-day Florida.

Besides his crew, the only witnesses to Christopher Columbus's landing were a band of Taino Indians peeking from the jungle as he claimed for his queen the island that they called Guanahaní. Soon curiosity overcame their fears. Gesturing and smiling, the Tainos walked down to the beach, where the newcomers quickly noticed the cigars they offered and the gold pendants in their noses.

The voyagers learned to savor the islanders' tobacco and to trade for golden ornaments as they sailed on among the West Indies, searching for the emperor of China's capital city. Although Columbus had found no Oriental potentates, he sensed that fabulous wealth lay within his grasp. He was sure that he had reached Asia—the Indies. Two months later, bringing with him some "Indians" and various souvenirs, he sailed home to tell of "a land to be desired and, once seen, never to be left."

Perhaps some Tainos would have agreed with the astonished Canadian Indian who saw his first shaggily bearded white man in 1632: "O, what an ugly man! Is it possible that any woman would look with favor on such a man?" Later Indians' accounts of their first sightings of Europeans also speak of wonder at seeing white-sailed "canoes" descending as from the sky and of fascination with the strangers' "magic"—their guns, gunpowder, durable metal pots and tools, woven cloth, glass beads, and alcohol. Because the white strangers were seldom prepared to survive unaided in the New World, the superbly adapted native people had ample opportunity to make themselves useful.

But the potential for deep misunderstanding was already present. From his first day in America, Columbus thought like a benevolent colonial master. "They should be good servants and of quick intelligence, . . . and I believe that they would easily be made Christians, for it appeared to me that they had no creed." The Europeans would soon realize that native Americans were neither gullible fools nor humble servants. Disillusioned, the newcomers would begin to see the Indians as lazy and deceitful "savages." Meanwhile, the native Americans found the Europeans' "magic"—which included their germs as well as their tools—very powerful. In much of what is now Latin America, the coming of the Europeans quickly turned into conquest. In the future United States and Canada, European mastery would come more slowly. But everywhere, the native Americans had to yield in the end.

Few stories in history are as familiar as Columbus's landing on San Salvador. And few dates are so truly epoch-making as October 12, 1492. From that moment, the American continents became the stage for the encounter of the Old and New Worlds.

New World Peoples

In 1492 the entire Western Hemisphere may have had a population of up to 80–100 million. Native Americans clustered most thickly in Mexico and Central America, the Caribbean islands, and Peru. Booty-seeking Spanish conquerors gravitated to these populous lands, especially to the highly organized Indian empires in Mexico and Peru.

North America—the future United States and Canada—seldom beckoned the first impatient European empire builders. Wealth was hard to find there, and no centralized states lay ready for European armies to conquer. For almost a century after 1492, Europeans therefore made few attempts to establish outposts in North America. Only between 1565 and 1630 did the first permanent European colonies appear in North America.

But North America was not an empty wasteland. In 1492 between 2 million and 10 million native Americans lived north of present-day Mexico, unevenly distributed. Sparse populations of nomads inhabited the Great Basin, the high plains, and the northern forests. Fairly dense concentrations, however, thrived along the Pacific coast, in the Southwest and Southeast, in the Mississippi Valley, and along the Atlantic coast. All these peoples grouped themselves in roughly 250 tribes, speaking many diverse languages and dialects. But the most important Indian social groups were the family, the village, and the clan. Within these spheres native Americans fed themselves well, reared their children, and tried to sort out the mysteries of life.

North American Indian Societies at the Moment of European Contact

Between the early sixteenth century and the 1630s, Europeans and Indians met in four regions of North America. These encounters took place along the East coast from the Arctic to the Carolinas; in the Southeast and the lower Mississippi Valley; fleetingly, on the edge of the Great Plains; and in the Southwest. Although Europeans' accounts were biased and confused, they help provide a vivid picture of native North American society on the eve of colonization, especially when they are combined with archaeological evidence and anthropologists' findings.

In the first zone of contact, eastern North America, early European explorers and settlers penned the most numerous reports of their impressions. Particularly with regard to social organization, these first white observers noted patterns of Indian life that were typical of native Americans throughout the continent. The European intruders' accounts also contained many telltale signs of their own Old World values.

For example, one of the early white visitors to travel far up the St. Lawrence Valley, about 1630, commented on a few features of Indian life that pleased him. This man, the French missionary Father Gabriel Sagard, happily reported an absence of "the vice" of kissing and otherwise publicly displaying affection, and he noted with satisfaction that marriage required the consent not only of parents but also of the bride. In other respects, however, Sagard was horrified. With parental connivance young Indians enjoyed premarital sex and entered into trial marriages. Divorce was casual, "it being sufficient for the husband to say to the wife's relatives and to herself that she is no good . . . [and] the wives also leave their husbands with ease when the latter do not please them. Hence it often happens that some . . . [women have] more than a dozen or fifteen husbands."

The French priest's initial observations in this Huron village in present-day Ontario, Canada, touched only the surface of the social system shared by native North Americans in many parts of the continent. Customs defining proper marriage partners varied greatly, but strict rules always prevailed. In most cultures young people married in their teens, after winning social acceptance as adults and generally following a period of sexual experimentation. Sometimes important men took multiple wives, but the nuclear families that married couples and their children formed never stood alone. Instead, strong ties of residence and deference bound each couple to one or both sets of parents, producing what scholars call extended families. The first European to sail very far along the coast of North America, Giovanni da Verrazano, in 1524 observed households of twenty-five to thirty persons in what is now Rhode Island.

Kinship cemented all Indian societies together. Ties to cousins, aunts, and uncles created complex

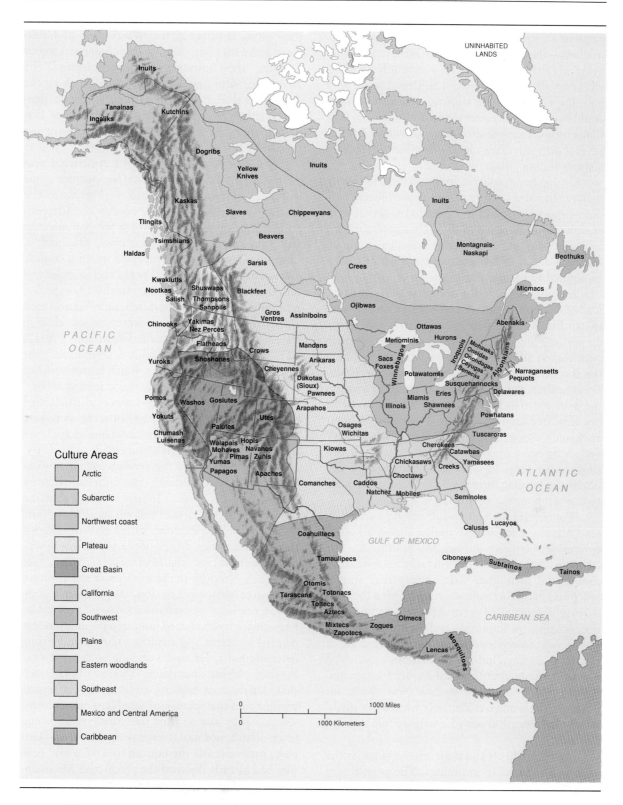

UNINHABITED LANDS

Inuits

Tanainas
Ingaliks
Kutchins

Dogribs

Yellow
Knives
Inuits

Kaskas

Tlingits
Slaves
Chippewyans

Tsimshians

Haidas

Beavers

Inuits

Sarsis

Montagnais-
Naskapi

Beothuks

Kwakiutls
Crees

Micmacs

Nootkas
Shuswaps
Blackfeet
Salish
Thompsons
Sanpoils

Ojibwas

Chinooks
Yakimas
Nez Percés

Gros
Ventres
Assiniboins

Ottawas

Abenakis

Flatheads

Crows

Mandans

Menominis
Hurons

Yuroks
Shoshones

Cheyennes

Arikaras

Sacs
Foxes

Mohawks
Oneidas
Onondagas
Cayugas
Senecas

Narragansetts
Pequots

Dakotas
(Sioux)
Pawnees

Potawatomis
Susquehannocks

Delawares

Pomos
Washos
Gosiutes

Arapahos

Miami
Illinois
Eries
Shawnees

Powhatans

Yokuts
Utes

Osages
Wichitas

Tuscaroras

Chumash
Luisenas
Paiutes

Cherokees
Catawbas

Kiowas

Yamasees

Walapais
Mohaves
Hopis
Navahos
Pimas Zunis
Yumas
Papagos

Chickasaws

Creeks

Apaches

Choctaws

Comanches
Caddos
Natchez
Mobiles

Seminoles

PACIFIC
OCEAN

ATLANTIC
OCEAN

Winnebagos

Algonkians

Iroquois

Calusas

Lucayos

Coahuiltecs

GULF OF MEXICO

Ciboneys

Subtainos

Tamaulipecs

Tainos

Otomis
Tarascans
Totonacs
Toltecs
Aztecs
Mixtecs
Zapotecs
Zoques
Olmecs

CARIBBEAN SEA

Lencas

Mosquitoes

Culture Areas

Arctic

Subarctic

Northwest coast

Plateau

Great Basin

California

Southwest

Plains

Eastern woodlands

Southeast

Mexico and Central America

Caribbean

| 0 | | 1000 Miles |
| 0 | | 1000 Kilometers |

**Cultural Divisions
Among the Native
Americans**

*By 1492 modern-day Canada and the United States may have had as many as 10
million Indian inhabitants, divided among more than fifty major linguistic groups
and at least ten major cultural groups that had adapted to the local environment.*

patterns of social obligation. So did membership in clans—the large networks of kin groups who believed in their descent from a common ancestor who embodied the admired qualities of some animal. Depending on the culture, clan membership could descend from either the mother or the father. Clans linked widely scattered groups within a tribe. Several different clans usually dwelled together in a single Indian village.

Kinship bonds counted for much more in Indian society than did nuclear-family units. Indians seldom expected spouses to be bound together forever, but kinship lasted for life. Thus native Americans could accept the divorce of individuals without feeling a threat to the social order. Such attitudes astounded European Christians.

Equally strange to Europeans was the Indians' way of work. "The men," recorded an English settler in Massachusetts in 1630, "for the most part do nothing but hunt and fish: their wives set their corn and do all their other work." In Europe hunting was an upper-class amusement, so Europeans never understood that it might constitute exhausting work for male Indians. Native Americans (who saw little of European women's housewifely labors) answered the newcomers' sneers about "lazy braves" and "exploited squaws" in kind: "they call the Englishmen fools in working themselves [in the fields] and keeping their wives idle," one white male visitor wrote of the northeastern Indians.

Women did the cultivating among northeastern Indians—and, indeed, among almost all other agricultural Indians outside the Southwest. For Indian women, field work easily meshed with child care, as did such other tasks as preparing animal hides and gathering wild vegetation. Men did jobs where children would get in the way: hunting, fishing, trading, negotiating, and fighting. Because Indian women often produced the greater share of the food supply, Indian communities accorded women more respect than did European societies. Among the Iroquois of upstate New York, for example, the women collectively owned the fields, distributed food, and played a weighty role in tribal councils.

In the Northeast and most other regions, tribes were generally loose groupings. The people of a tribe shared a common language and culture, and often they chose "civil chiefs" who mediated disputes between villages or clans, and "war chiefs" who led fights against outsiders. Chiefs had to prove their physical prowess, trustworthiness, and ability to persuade. But, noted a Frenchman in eastern Canada, "their authority is most precarious." The Europeans who first encountered chiefs along the Atlantic seaboard (as well as in the Southeast) generally either overestimated their powers or disdained them for not measuring up to European monarchs.

Nevertheless, in eastern North America, Europeans did find among the native peoples some instances of more centralized authority. In the eastern Great Lakes region between the fifteenth and the mid-sixteenth centuries, for example, the five Iroquois tribes (the Mohawks, Onondagas, Oneidas, Cayugas, and Senecas) formed a confederation to maintain mutual peace and to make war on outsiders. About this time in the Chesapeake, an even more centrally organized confederation took shape: the Powhatan Confederacy, whose chief in the early 1600s was also called Powhatan. "A tall, well proportioned man, with a sour look," the English leader Captain John Smith found him, "of a very able and hardy body to endure any labor." Powhatan's life-and-death powers evidently rested on the stores of corn that he collected as tribute and redistributed in lean times. "Their victuals are their only riches," Smith commented.

In the Southeast, the second region of early European-Indian contacts, the sixteenth-century Spanish invaders found Indian societies centered on larger, highly organized villages. Male (and occasionally female) chiefs called caciques headed these communities. Much of the southeastern way of life derived from the Mississippian culture (see Prologue). Although the Spanish never saw the most impressive Mississippian sites, they did come upon at least one southeastern town (in modern-day Alabama) with five hundred houses, a population segmented by status and wealth, a temple and strong defensive palisades, and a cacique borne on a litter by flute-playing attendants. This was thickly settled, fertile corn-farming country. But a female cacique told the Spanish of terrible recent epidemics, and they saw at least one formerly imposing town abandoned and overgrown with weeds. Diseases inadvertently introduced by Old World peoples had already doomed the productive Mississippian culture and threatened all southeastern native Americans.

The third zone of contact was the Great Plains, where Spanish soldiers briefly visited both agri-

Wichita Chief, Two Daughters, and a Warrior

On the plains sixteenth-century Spanish explorers encountered river-valley peoples such as these members of the Wichita tribe of eastern Kansas.

cultural and nomadic, nonagricultural Indians. Hoping to find dazzling cities to conquer, Francisco Vásquez de Coronado was disappointed by the plains and their buffalo-hunting peoples, although he conceded that they had "the best physiques of any I have seen in the Indies." The settled river-valley people whom Coronado also met on the plains, probably the Wichitas of eastern Kansas, seemed to him peaceful but poor. "The houses are of straw, and the people are savage. . . . They have no blankets, nor cotton with which to make them. All they have is the tanned skins of the cattle they kill. . . . They eat raw meat . . . [but] have the advantage over the others in their houses and in the growing of maize [corn]."

In the fourth region of European-Indian contact, the sunbaked Southwest, Coronado's quest for cities with gold-paved streets likewise ended in disillusionment. He reported little about the pueblo and river-valley peoples living there, and so modern scholars must rely on artifacts, ruins, and ecological evidence to piece together a picture of southwestern society at the moment of its first contact with Old World peoples.

Wresting a living from the severe southwestern environment demanded concentrated effort, but the native peoples succeeded remarkably well. The population was comparatively dense: a hundred thousand persons may have lived in the pueblos in the early sixteenth century, and intensive cultivation also supported large river-valley settlements. As in the rest of North America, extended families formed the foundation of southwestern village life in both the pueblos and the river valleys.

Stone Age Native American Culture

These laboriously made southwestern artifacts all date from before 1500. The photograph at the left includes a stone pick, mortar and pestle, drill, pipe, knife, and several axes and polishing stones, as well as a bone scraper and an awl. The painted figurine (right) was modeled from clay. Jewelry (center) made striking use of turquoise, a semiprecious stone traded as far as Mexico.

Southwestern patterns of property ownership and gender roles differed, not only from those of native Americans elsewhere but also among local cultures. Unlike Indians in other regions, here men and women shared agricultural labor. River-valley peoples of the Southwest owned land privately and passed it through the male line, and men dominated decision making. In pueblo society (which in this respect resembled societies in the Northeast and Southeast), land was communally owned, and women played an influential role in community affairs. A pueblo woman could end a marriage simply by tossing her husband's belongings out the door and sending him back to his kinfolk. Moreover, clan membership passed in the mother's line. Yet pueblo communities depended on secret male societies to perform the rituals that would secure the gods' blessing and ensure life-giving rain. In all respects, pueblo society strictly subordinated the individual to the group and demanded rigorous conformity. This cohesion would bolster the pueblo peoples when, after 1598, the Spanish conquered the Southwest and began imposing Christianity there.

Not only in the Southwest but throughout North America, almost every aspect of Indian life had some connection to the unseen world of spirits. Because many Indian peoples had no formal religious organizations, sixteenth-century Europeans such as Verrazano assumed "that they have no religion and that they live in absolute freedom, and that everything they do proceeds from Ignorance." Few more preposterous European misconceptions about the native Americans could be cited.

Indian Religion and Social Values

Most Indians explained the origin and destiny of the human race in deeply moving myths. In the beginning, said the Iroquois, was the sky world of unchanging perfection. From it fell a beautiful pregnant woman, whom the birds saved from plunging into the limitless ocean. On the back of a tortoise who rose from the sea, birds created the earth's soil, in which the woman planted seeds carried during her fall. From these seeds sprang all nature; from her womb, the human race.

Native American religion revolved around the conviction that all nature was alive, pulsating with a spiritual power—*manitou*, in the Algonkian lan-

guage of the northeastern Indians. A mysterious, awe-inspiring force that could affect human life for both good and evil, such power united all nature in an unbroken web. For most Indians, *manitou* was a far more vivid presence than the supreme, benevolent, but distant Good Spirit who they believed had created the universe. *Manitou* encompassed "every thing which they cannot comprehend," wrote the Puritan leader Roger Williams, one of the few European visitors who genuinely tried to understand the northeastern Indians' spiritual world. Their belief in *manitou* led most Indian peoples to seek constantly to conciliate all the spiritual forces in nature: living things, rocks and water, sun and moon, even ghosts and witches. For example, Indians were careful to pray to the spirits of the animals they hunted, justifying the killing of just enough game to sustain themselves. To the Indians, humanity was only one link in the great chain of living nature. The Judeo-Christian view that God had given humanity domination over nature was very strange to them.

Indians had many ways of gaining access to spiritual power. One was through dreaming: most native Americans took very seriously the visions that came to them in sleep. They also sought to link themselves to *manitou* by artificially altering their consciousness through difficult physical ordeals. Young men, for example, commonly endured a traumatic rite of passage before gaining recognition as adults. Such a rite often involved "questing"—going alone into a forest or up a mountain, fasting, sometimes taking a drug, and awaiting the mystical experience in which an animal spirit would reveal itself as a protective guide and offer a glimpse of the future. Girls went through comparable rituals at the onset of menstruation to initiate them into the spiritual world from which female reproductive power flowed. Moreover, entire communities often practiced collective power-seeking rituals such as the Plains Indians' Sun Dance, in which men tortured themselves not only to demonstrate indifference to pain but also to suffer on behalf of weaker members of their group (see Chapter 16).

Although on occasion all Indians tried to communicate directly with the spiritual world, they normally relied on shamans for help in understanding the unseen. The shamans ("medicine men" to whites) were healers who used both medicinal plants and magical chants, but their role in Indian society went further. They interpreted dreams, guided "questing" and other rituals, invoked war or peace spirits, and figured prominently in community councils. Chiefs had to maintain respectful relations with their people's shamans, and by the sixteenth century, shamans were forming organized priesthoods in the Southeast and Southwest.

Because most Indian cultures tried to maintain a sense of dependence among their people, native American communities demanded conformity and close cooperation. From early childhood Indians learned to be accommodating and reserved—slow to reveal their own feelings before they could sense others'. Although few native American peoples favored physical punishment in child rearing, Indian parents punished psychologically, by shaming. Throughout life the fear of becoming an isolated social outcast (a status that could mean death) forced individual Indians to maintain strict self-control. Communities took decisions by consensus, and leaders articulated slowly emerging agreements in memorable, persuasive, often passionate oratory. Shamans and chiefs therefore had to be dramatic orators. Noted John Smith, they spoke in public "with vehemency and so great passions that they sweat till they drop and are so out of breath they scarce can speak."

Because Indians highly valued consensus building in everyday life, their leaders' authority depended primarily on the respect that they invoked rather than what they could demand by compulsion. Distributing gifts was central to establishing and maintaining leadership with a native American community, as a Frenchman in early-seventeenth-century Canada clearly understood: "For the savages have that noble quality, that they give liberally, casting at the feet of him whom they will honor the present that they give him. But it is with hope to receive some reciprocal kindness, which is a kind of contract, which we call . . . 'I give thee, to the end thou shouldst give me.' "

Thus for Indians, trade was not merely an economic activity by which they acquired useful goods. It was also a means of ensuring goodwill with other peoples and of building their own prestige. European visitors almost always found native Americans eager to barter. For many centuries, trade among the Indians had spanned the continent. The Hurons of southern Ontario produced large agricultural surpluses for trade, and southwestern Indians' turquoise found its way to Mexico. Flint and other tool-making materials, salt, dyes, furs, and (in hard times) food and seeds were major objects of trade. So was tobacco, which Indians primarily regarded as a ceremonial drug, its fragrant smoke symbolizing the union of heaven and earth. Native Americans eagerly assimilated into their own way of life the new goods that European traders offered. Metal tools they valued for their practical, labor-saving benefits, while dyed cloth and glass objects quickly took on symbolic, prestige-enhancing qualities.

"They love not to be encumbered with too many utensils," remarked an early-seventeenth-century English visitor. Rather, prestige counted for everything in native American society. If Indians did accumulate possessions, it was primarily with the aim of giving them away, to win prestige. The most spectacular example of such gift-exchanging rituals was the Pacific Northwest potlatch ceremony. When a northwestern community's social hierarchy was shaken, an aspiring new leader would invite his neighbors to a potlatch, at which he would give away or destroy most of what he owned, all the while chanting about his own greatness and taunting his rivals. Those who received were expected later to give away even more. He who could give away the most gained the highest prestige and accumulated the greatest number of people obligated to him.

Scholars have used the word *reciprocity* to characterize native American religious and social values. Reciprocity involved mutual give-and-take, but its aim was not to confer equality. Instead, societies (like those of the Indians) based on reciprocity tried to maintain equilibrium and interdependence between individuals of unequal power and prestige. In their religious thinking, too, Indians applied the concept of reciprocity, in viewing nature as a web of interdependent power entities into which human beings had to fit. And in social organization, the Indians' principle of reciprocity required that communities be places of face-to-face, lifelong interaction. Trade and gift giving solidified such reciprocal bonds. The Indians' faith in social reciprocity also underlay their idea of property rights. They believed that the people of one area might agree to share with others the right to use the land for different but complementary pur-

Northwestern Totem Pole

The most famous symbol of northwestern Indian culture, totem poles served various purposes. Some advertised the genealogy and accomplishments of a clan, family, or individual. Others celebrated a successful potlatch. A few seem to have been intended to ridicule an enemy or simply to express the maker's whimsy and skill.

sessed a strong sense of order. Custom, the demands of social conformity, and the rigors of nature strictly regulated life, and the people's everyday affairs mingled with the spiritual world at every turn. Nature and the supernatural world could sometimes be frightening. For example, Indians feared ghosts and believed that nonconformists could invoke evil spirits by witchcraft—the most dreaded crime in Indian cultures. Much of Indian religion involved placating the evil spirits that caused sickness and death. The pueblo peoples, whose existence depended on carefully conserving a meager rainfall, relieved their constant anxiety by performing frequent rituals. And except in the Southwest, where stress on conformity minimized all competition, Indian life had an intensely competitive side. Individuals and communities eagerly strove to show physical prowess in ritualized games like football and lacrosse, and they bet enthusiastically on the outcome. "They are so bewitched with these . . . games, that they will lose sometimes all they have," said an Englishman of the Massachusett Indians about 1630. Such games served less as recreation than as a means of redistributing prestige.

The Mask of Death

In many Indian cultures, even individuals beloved in life could become malevolent ghosts after death. Rituals to placate the dead were common. This mask, representing the chief spirit of the dead, was made by the Kwakiutl people of the northwest coast.

poses: hunting, gathering, farming, trapping, or traveling. The notion (then emerging in Europe) that property ownership conferred perpetual and exclusive control of land was thus alien to Indians.

But native American society was hardly a simple, noncompetitive world. All Indian cultures pos-

The breakdown of order in Indian communities could bring fearful consequences: accusations of witchcraft, demands for revenge against wrongdoers, war against enemies. "They seldom make war for lands or goods," wrote Smith, "but for women and children [who would be adopted into the tribe], and principally for revenge." Going to war or exacting personal revenge was a ritualized way of restoring order that had broken down. A captured male could expect death after prolonged torture. Indian men learned from early childhood to inflict (and to bear) physical pain out of loyalty to kin and neighbors; they knew that they must withstand torture without flinching and death without fear. Endurance was central to Indian life.

"Many devilish gestures with a Hellish noise"—thus one Englishman dismissed native American religion. But at the same time, Europeans were apprehensive of shamans' power (they called them "priests of Satan") and feared Indian "savagery" as the evil influence of the devil, who was also a sinister figure in Christianity. As we shall see, the principle of social reciprocity also helped knit together Old World communities. But by 1492 reciprocity in Europe was starting to give way to a more impersonal social mentality, based on commercial exchange and an authoritarian chain of command. When Columbus encountered the Indians, Old and New World societies were moving apart, not converging.

Old World Peoples

The Old World gave birth to the human race. For several million years, early human beings went forth in waves from Africa's warm grasslands to people the globe. Then, over a span of at least five thousand years before 1492, a great range of societies arose, stretching from West Africa and Europe to Siberia and Polynesia. Complex networks of peaceful or aggressive interactions, cultural influences, and long-range trade linked many of these societies. Some Old World cultures were hunter-gatherer or simple agricultural communities. But throughout the Old World—as also in Mexico and Peru—there existed powerful states with armed forces, bureaucracies, religious institutions, proud aristocracies, and toiling common people.

West Africa

For almost five thousand years, the vast, barren Sahara Desert has lain between much of Africa and the rest of the world. In addition, West Africa was effectively isolated from the land to its north by the prevailing Atlantic winds, which could bring old-fashioned sailing ships south but hampered them from returning north. Moreover, the yellow fever rampant in the West African rain-forest coastline helped ward off outside intruders. If contracted in youth, yellow fever could be survived with lifelong immunity, but it generally killed adult newcomers lacking such defenses.

Nevertheless, between the formidable Sahara and the forbidding coast, a broad swath of grassland (savanna) offered a hospitable shelter. By about 3000 B.C., people here were growing grain and herding livestock. Late in the first millennium B.C., when knowledge of iron metallurgy reached the grasslands, the region's dark-skinned people began carrying their culture outward, eventually leaving their imprint on almost all of sub-Saharan Africa. By the sixteenth century, sub-Saharan Africa, twice the size of the United States, had a population of perhaps 20 million.

Despite its seeming isolation, West Africa looked northward. Camel caravans crossed the Sahara, and an important trade in gold and salt developed with North Africa's Mediterranean coast. From A.D. 600 to 1600, there arose in the grassland a series of West African empires—Ghana, Mali, and Songhai—that imposed tribute on their subject populations and taxed the merchant communities at the southern end of the caravan routes. Islam spread into West Africa from its Middle Eastern birthplace, and by the late eleventh century, the grassland empires became at least nominally Moslem. Their rulers kept records in Arabic and irregularly enforced Islamic law, but it was their wealth that made them famous throughout the Islamic world. By 1492 the last of the great West African empires, Songhai, stood at the height of its glory, with a bureaucracy and a vigorous army dominating much of the interior. Songhai's major city, Timbuktu, boasted flourishing markets and a famous Islamic university.

Compared with the grassland empires, coastal West Africa was relatively insignificant. In Senegambia at Africa's westernmost bulge, several small

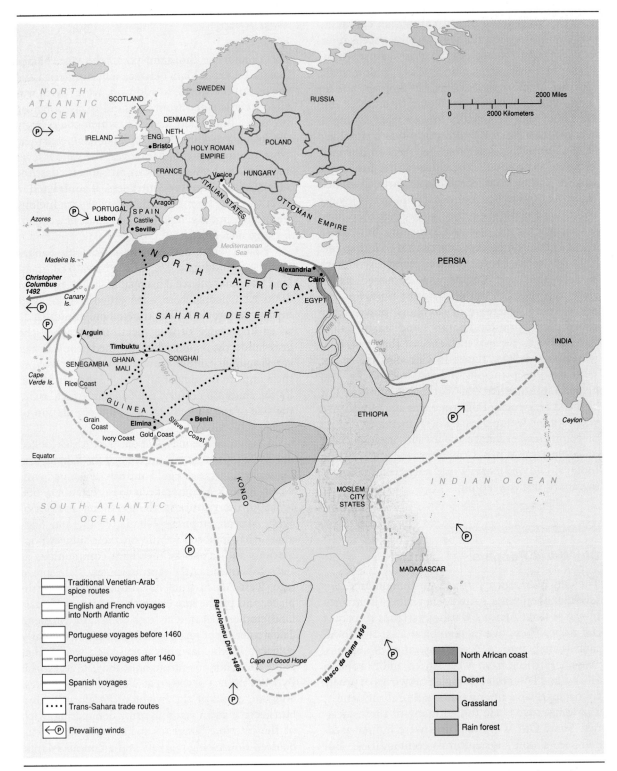

Europe, Africa, and the Near East in 1492

In 1492 Europeans had little knowledge of the outside world apart from the Mediterranean basin and Africa's west coast. Since the Azores and the Canary and Cape Verde Islands had been discovered recently in the eastern Atlantic, many Europeans were not surprised when Columbus found new islands farther west in 1492.

Bronze Head, Bini Tribe, Benin

Along with the Yoruba people of the city of Ife, the Bini tribe of Benin had by 1500 developed beautiful African art forms in their sculpture of human figures of ivory, terra cotta, and especially bronze.

Islamic states took root. Infestation by the tsetse fly, the carrier of sleeping sickness, kept livestock-herding peoples out of Guinea's coastal forests, but many small states arose here, too, during the first millennium A.D. Among these was Benin, where artisans had been fashioning magnificent iron-work for centuries.

Then in the fifteenth century, Guinea's population rose. Foreign demands for gold that Africans panned from streams or dug from the earth touched off the spurt. Grassland warriors and merchants poured into Guinea and Senegambia, seeking new opportunities and on occasion founding or expanding the region's tiny states. Similarly thirsting for fresh opportunities were the Portuguese, who in the mid-fifteenth century used new maritime techniques to sail up and down West Africa's coast in search of gold and slaves.

Parallels and contrasts between black African and native American societies before European contact are fascinating. Like the priest-kings who headed the complex Indian societies of the Mississippian culture, Mexico, and Peru, African grass-land emperors claimed semigodlike status, which they only thinly disguised when they adopted Islam. Small African kingdoms resembled the villages presided over by the caciques of southeastern North America. African kings' authority was primarily religious. Their power, like that of Indian chiefs, largely depended on their ability to persuade, to conform to custom, and sometimes to redistribute wealth justly among their people.

In Africa as in North America, the cohesiveness of kinship groups knitted society together. From childhood, Africans found themselves in a network of interlocking, mutual obligations to kinfolk. Not just parents but also aunts, uncles, distant cousins, and persons sharing clan ties formed an African's kin group and claimed his or her first loyalty. Africans held their grandparents in highest esteem and accorded village or clan elders great deference. In centuries to come, the tradition of strong extended families would help enslaved Africans in the New World to endure the breakup of nuclear families by sale.

Other aspects of family structure were also common to some native American and African societies. One was polygyny, the custom whereby a man married several wives and maintained numerous households. A second was bridewealth, a prospective husband's payment to his bride's kin before marriage. Christian Europeans wrongly interpreted both practices as demeaning to women and evidence of "barbarism." But an African man did not "buy" a wife; in effect, he posted bond for good behavior and acknowledged the relative prestige of his own and his bride's kin groups. Marrying several wives could cost a man heavily, so polygyny was largely confined to higher-status men who needed to establish marriage ties with more than one kin group. African and native American wives generally kept lifelong links with their own kin group, and in many societies children traced descent through the mother's, not the father's, bloodline. All this buttressed women's standing.

Still another parallel between the two cultures lay in their attitudes toward land and property. To Africans, kin groups not only enjoyed inalienable rights to the soil that their ancestors had always cultivated but also had a duty to honor ancestors and earth spirits by properly cultivating the land. Native Americans thought similarly, although their sense of proper land usage focused more on the village or tribe as a whole. Neither Africans nor native Americans treated land as a commodity to be bought and sold.

Cultivation was difficult in Africa and required the labor of both sexes. As in all tropical regions, scorching sunlight and frequent downpours prevented humus (slowly decaying vegetative matter) from accumulating in the African soil. Like Indians, Africans tried to maintain soil fertility by practicing slash-and-burn tillage (see Prologue). In the coastal rain forests, Africans grew root crops, primarily yams. On the grasslands the staff of life was grain, which in Senegambia meant rice. In the seventeenth and eighteenth centuries, both rice and the grain's enslaved Senegambian cultivators would be transplanted to the North American mainland.

Religion permeated African life. African, like native American, religion recognized spiritual presences pervading nature. The power of earth spirits and of agricultural ancestors reinforced the esteem that Africans accorded to cultivators. In the eighteenth century, Europeans got an authentic glimpse of African religion from Olaudah Equiano, a West African who eventually managed to purchase his freedom from slavery:

The natives believe that there is one Creator of all things, and that he lives in the sun, [and] . . . that he governs events. . . . Some . . . believe in the transmigration of souls [reincarnation] to some degree. Those spirits, who are not transmigrated, such as their dear friends or relations, they believe always attend them, and guard them from the bad spirits of their foes. For this reason, they always, before eating . . . put some small portion of the meat and pour some of their drink, on the ground for them; and they often make oblations [offerings] of the blood of beasts or fowls at their graves.

Magic and the placating of spiritual powers were as important in African as in Indian life, and the responsibility for maintaining contact with the spirit world fell to shamans. Africans explained misfortunes in terms of witchcraft, much as did Indians and Europeans. But African religion differed from native American religion in its focus on ancestor worship. Indians often regarded the dead with uneasiness, lest they become harmful ghosts, whereas Africans commonly venerated departed forebears as spiritual guardians.

Africa's magnificent artistic traditions were also steeped in religion. The ivory, cast-iron, and wood sculpture of West Africa, whose bold design would help mold the twentieth-century Western world's modern art, was used in ceremonies reenacting creation myths and honoring spirits. A strong moralistic streak ran through African folk tales. Oral reciters transmitted these stories in dramatic public presentations with ritual masks, dance, and music of a highly complex rhythmic structure now appreciated as one of the foundations of jazz.

Much in traditional African culture seemed to clash with the great monotheistic religions, Islam and Christianity. Among Africans, Islam appealed primarily to merchants trading with Moslem North Africa and the Middle East and to the grassland rulers eager to consolidate their power. Even these ambitious emperors were incompletely Islamicized—some learned with dismay that Islam limited them to four wives. By the sixteenth century, Islam had only begun to affect the daily lives of grassland cultivators and artisans. Christianity, arriving in West Africa with the Portuguese in the fifteenth and sixteenth centuries, demanded that Africans break even more radically with their traditional culture and until the nineteenth century had little impact.

European Culture and Society

When Columbus landed on San Salvador in 1492, Europe was approaching the height of a mighty cultural revival, the Renaissance. Contemporary intellectuals and poets believed that their age was witnessing a return to the standards of ancient Greek and Roman civilization. After a century-long economic recession, money had accumulated to pay for magnificent architecture, and wealthy patrons commissioned master painters and sculptors to create works glowing with idealized human beauty. Renaissance scholars strove to reconcile ancient philosophy with Christian faith, to explore the mysteries of nature, to map the world, and to explain the motions of the heavens.

But European society was quivering with tension. The era's artistic and intellectual creativity was partly inspired by intense social and spiritual stress, as Renaissance Europeans groped for stability by glorifying order, hierarchy, and beauty. A concern for power and rank ("degree") dominated European life between the fifteenth and seventeenth centuries. William Shakespeare (1564–1616), who expressed Renaissance values with incomparable eloquence, wrote:

> The heavens themselves, the planets and this
>   center [earth]
> Observe degree, priority, and place . . .
> Take but degree away, untune that string,
> And hark, what discord follows!

Gender, wealth, inherited position, and political power affected every European's status, and few lived outside the reach of some political authority's claim to tax and impose laws upon them. But this order was shaky. Conflicts between states, between religions, and between rich and poor constantly threatened the balance. All the more eagerly, then, did Europeans cling to their visions of order and hierarchy.

Atop the European hierarchy were enthroned the kings who governed most states. (Only a handful of republics existed, the most important of which were the two aristocratic city-states of Venice and Florence.) In 1492 the kingdoms of England, Scotland, France, Spain, and Portugal occupied roughly their present-day territories. Germany, Italy, and the Low Countries comprised a welter of smaller states. But the kings or the republican aristocrats

of all these lands only occasionally pursued national goals. Sometimes rulers did not even speak their subjects' language. These complications sprang from the intricate networks of marriages that ruling families arranged among themselves, often sowing the seeds of future conflicts over dynastic claims. Monarchs sought above all to consolidate their power and to that end waged wars with mercenary armies that cost mountains of money. The kings' forces spread disease and misery everywhere; they were "an unchristian, cursed tribe whose trade consists of gouging, pillaging, burning, murdering, gambling, drinking, whoring, blaspheming, willfully killing husbands and fathers, persecuting peasants . . . , stripping fields, and demanding tribute," a German chronicler wrote in 1531.

Kings' power depended on gaining the cooperation of the upper classes, usually by consulting such representative institutions as Parliament in England. The men who dominated these institutions generally saw officeholding as a form of property owning and a legitimate way to improve their fortunes. Society expected these aristocrats to spend freely even if they could not afford it. No king could ride roughshod over such men, and by defending their own liberties, they were also pre-

Marriage Feast at Bermondsey, *by Joris Hoefnagel, c. 1570 (Detail)*

Hoefnagel's canvas richly illustrates the festivities surrounding an important event in sixteenth-century European society—the alliance of two aristocratic families in marriage. In the background, various ordinary people lend a hand.

serving the principle of limited government against encroaching despotism.

At the bottom of the social heap toiled the ordinary people. In the overwhelmingly rural Europe of the times, peasants composed between 70 percent and 80 percent of the population. Peasants ranged from a few prosperous families with a large holding, such as the English yeomen, to landless laborers who barely scraped by on odd jobs. Taxes, rents, and other dues to landlords and the Church were heavy, and poor harvests or war drove even well-to-do peasants to starvation.

Europe's population increased between the late fifteenth and early seventeenth centuries from about 55 million in 1450 to almost 100 million by 1600. But without corresponding improvements in technology and agriculture, output did not rise to meet growing demand. Northern European and English peasant families cultivated wheat or rye, barley, and oats on long strips scattered through the village's three or more fields; one field lay fallow every third year to restore fertility. Yields were pitifully low. Families had to cooperate in plowing, sowing, and harvesting, as well as in grazing their livestock on the fallow field and the jointly owned "commons," or pastureland and forest. With new land at a premium, the commons could be a tempting prize for landlords to "enclose"—that is, to convert to private property. Peasants who had no *written* title to their land were especially vulnerable, but those with strong titles could either keep their land or profit from joining the landlord in enclosing.

The problems of peasant tenure were particularly acute in England, where some landlords and peasants united to divide the commons among themselves, raise sheep, and grow rich selling wool. "Your sheep . . . even eat up men," wrote Sir Thomas More (with some exaggeration) in his passionate protest against greed, *Utopia* (1516). "They devastate and destroy fields, houses, and towns. For in whatever parts of the kingdom . . . wool is produced, there the nobles and gentlemen . . . are not content with the rents and annual profits that their predecessors used to get from their farms. . . . They leave nothing for arable land, enclose everything for pasture. . . ."

European towns were numerous but small, typically with several thousand inhabitants each. A great metropolis like London, whose population ballooned from fifty-five thousand in 1550 to two

European Peasants

This small illustration from a fifteenth-century French manuscript accurately illustrates northern European peasant life. Plowing, carried out with a wheeled horse- or ox-drawn plow, often required cooperative effort, for not every household owned the necessary equipment. Once the field had been plowed, each household sowed and tended its own strips, but the entire community usually harvested together.

hundred thousand in 1600, was quite exceptional. But all towns were dirty and disease-ridden, and townspeople lived close-packed with their neighbors.

Unappealing as sixteenth-century towns might seem today, ambitious (or desperate) men and women of the time viewed them as growing, dynamic centers of opportunity. Immigration from the countryside—rather than an excess of urban births over deaths—accounted for towns' expansion. Most of the displaced country people who flocked into towns remained at the bottom of the social order, however, as servants or laborers who often failed to accumulate enough money to marry and live independently. Manufacturing took place in household workshops, where subordinate workers were dependent on an artisan master. Successful artisans and merchants formed guilds to control employment, prices, and the sale of goods. Dominated by the richest citizens, urban governments enforced social conformity by "sumptuary laws" that forbade dressing inappropriately to one's social rank. Thus the hopes and ambitions that drew thousands into towns usually ended in frustration. Commented the English writer Thomas Nashe on London's teeming populace in 1593:

> From the rich to the poor . . . there is ambition, or swelling above their states [proper place in society]; the rich citizen swells against the pride of the prodigal courtier; the prodigal courtier swells against the wealth of the citizen. One company swells against another. . . . The ancients [elderly], they oppose themselves against the younger, and suppress them and keep them down all that they may. The young men, they call [the elderly] dotards, and swell and rage. . . .

Conservative moralists like Nashe who thus condemned "overreaching" (individuals' attempts to rise in society) stoutly upheld the values of old-fashioned social reciprocity. As in the New World and Africa, in Europe traditional society rested on maintaining long-term, reciprocal relationships. Europeans' attempts to preserve reciprocity included their insistence on the joint use of common lands, their prohibitions against usury (charging interest on loans), and their bans on inappropriate dressing and "unjust" competition. Because its aim was the smooth functioning of social relationships between individuals of unequal status, reciprocity required the upper classes to act with self-restraint and dignity, while the lower classes had to show deference to their "betters." Finally, preserving reciprocity demanded strict economic regulation to ensure that sellers charged a "just price"—one that covered costs and allowed the seller a "reasonable" living standard but that barred him from taking advantage of buyers' and borrowers' misfortunes or of shortages to make "excessive" profits.

Yet for centuries Europeans had been compromising the ideals of traditional economic behavior. "In the Name of God and of Profit," thirteenth-century Italian merchants had written on their ledgers. By the sixteenth century, nothing could stop the charging of interest on borrowed money or sellers' price increases in response to demand. New forms of business organization slowly spread in the commercial world—especially the impersonal joint-stock company with many investors (see below), the ancestor of the modern corporation. Demand rose for capital investment, and so did the supply of accumulated wealth. Slowly a new economic outlook took form that justified both the unimpeded acquisition of wealth and unregulated economic competition, and insisted that individuals owed one another nothing but the money necessary to settle each market transaction. This new outlook, the central value system of capitalism or the "market economy," was the opposite of traditional demands for the strict regulation of economic activity to ensure social reciprocity and maintain "just prices."

In sixteenth- and seventeenth-century Europe, this new economic system was not yet dominant. Laws still sought to bolster the traditional goals of an unchanging, noncompetitive order of things, and peasants, artisans, and many small-scale merchants desperately supported these laws' enforcement. Even rich men tended to use their wealth to buy status rather than keep plowing profits back into production.

Sixteenth- and seventeenth-century Europeans therefore held conflicting attitudes toward economic enterprise and social change, and their ambivalence remained unresolved. In Europe itself and in transplanted Europeans' New World communities, a restless desire for fresh opportunity kept life simmering with competitive tension. But those who prospered still sought the security and pres-

The Banker and His Wife, by Quentin Metsys, 1514

Despite religious admonitions against excessive material gain, sixteenth-century Europeans were intensely money-conscious. In this portrait, a banker weighs gold coins to ensure their accurate value while his wife, watching him, holds a prayer book.

tige provided by traditional social distinctions, while the poor longed for the age-old values that they hoped would restrain irresponsible greed. Almost all intellectuals and clergymen defended traditional standards. When Europeans violated these standards, they did so with a bad conscience. Thus ideal and reality remained far apart.

Fundamental change in European society could also be seen in the growing importance of the nuclear family. The tradition of broad kinship networks did survive in the sense that nuclear families prudently tried to retain the goodwill of distant relatives, but these networks seldom overruled the male head of each nuclear family. In a common cliché of the age, the nuclear family was a "little commonwealth." The father's government within the family was supposed to mirror God's rule over Creation and kings' lordship over their subjects. Even grown sons and daughters regularly knelt for their father's blessing. The ideal, according to a German writer, was that "wives should obey their husbands and not seek to dominate them; they must manage the home efficiently. Husbands . . . should treat their wives with consideration and occasionally close an eye to their faults." In practice, the father's domination often had to make room for the wife's responsibility in managing family affairs and helping to run the farm or the workshop. And repeated male complaints (such as that of an English author in 1622) about wives "who think themselves every way as good as their husbands, and no way inferior to them," suggested that male domination had its limits.

Democracy had no place in Europe. A few late-medieval and sixteenth-century revolts had democratic overtones, but these uprisings were mercilessly suppressed. To Europeans of the era, democracy in practice meant mob rule and the destruction of social distinctions. Officials controlled crime, especially political and religious offenses by ordinary people, through brutal public punishments. Hierarchy implied subordination, strict rules, and the exercise of manly prowess.

Europeans and Their God

"In the beginning God created the heaven and the earth. . . . And God said, Let us make man in our image . . . and let them have dominion . . . over all the earth. . . . So God created man in his own image, . . . male and female he created them." Sixteenth-century Europeans firmly believed in this biblical explanation of the origins of the world and its peoples. Christianity, to which the vast majority of Europeans adhered, taught that Jesus Christ, God's Son, had redeemed sinners by suffering crucifixion and rising from the dead. Almost as vivid, perhaps, was Christians' belief in the devil, Satan, whom God had hurled from heaven soon after the Creation and who ceaselessly lured people to damnation by tempting them to do evil. The non-Christian European minority encompassed small Jewish communities, Moslem Turks, and descendants of medieval Spain's Arab conquerors. But all Europe's population—Christians, Jews, and Moslems—worshiped the same almighty Creator.

By the sixteenth century, Christianity (or Judaism or Islam) had sunk deep roots into the consciousness of most Europeans. But the people also retained beliefs in the supernatural that over the centuries had blended with their faith in Christ, the Christian saints, church ritual, and biblical teachings. Like native Americans and Africans, virtually all Europeans feared witches, and many thought that individuals could manipulate nature by invoking unseen spiritual powers—that is, by magic. (The most plausible alternative to magic was astrology, which insisted that a person's fate depended on the conjunction of various planets and stars.) Everyone envisioned nature as a "chain of being" infused by God with life and tingling with spiritual forces. Deeply embedded in European folklore, such supernaturalism also marked the "high culture" of educated medieval and Renaissance Europeans. Indeed, the sixteenth-century European "mentality" had more in common with Indian and African mind sets than any of these traditional belief systems have with the stereotypical "modern" world view.

Medieval churchmen asserted that Christ had founded the Church to save sinners from hell and lead them to heaven. All but a few heretics (religious dissenters) accepted the dictum "Outside the Church, no salvation." Christ's sacrifice was repeated every time a priest said Mass, and divine grace flowed to sinners through the sacraments that consecrated priests alone could administer—above all, baptism, confession, and the Eucharist (communion). In most of Europe in 1492, "the Church" was a huge network of clergymen, set apart from laypeople by the fact that they did not marry. At the top was the pope, God's "vicar" (representative), whose authority reached everywhere in Europe but Russia and the Balkan Peninsula.

The papacy wielded awesome spiritual power. Fifteenth- and early-sixteenth-century popes claimed the authority to dispense to repentant sinners extra blessings, or "indulgences," in return for such "good works" as donating money to the Church. Indulgences promised time off from future punishment in purgatory, where souls atoned for sins they had already confessed and been forgiven. (Hell, from which there was no escape, awaited those who died unforgiven.) The Church grew wealthy and corrupt by providing indulgences, which, given people's anxieties over "sinful" behavior, were enormously popular. The jingle of a successful indulgence seller in early-sixteenth-century Germany promised that

As soon as the coin in the cash box rings,
The soul from purgatory's fire springs.

The sale of indulgences, however, provoked a tremendous crisis for the Church. In 1517 the German monk Martin Luther (1483–1546) attacked the practice. When the papacy tried to silence him, Luther merely broadened his criticism to encompass the Mass, purgatory, priests, and the pope. Luther's revolt initiated the Protestant Reformation, which changed Christianity forever.

To Luther, indulgence-selling and similar examples of clerical corruption were evil not just because they bilked people. The Church, he charged, gave people false confidence that they could "earn" salvation by doing good works. His own agonizing search for salvation had convinced Luther that God alone chose whom to save from damnation and that believers could trust only God's love. Luther's spiritual struggle and experience of being "born again" constituted a classic conversion experience—the heart of Protestant religion as it would be preached and practiced for centuries in England and North America. "I did not love a just and angry God, but rather hated and murmured against him," recalled Luther. "Night and day I pondered until I saw the connection between the justice of God and the [New Testament] statement that 'the just shall live [be saved] by faith.' . . . Thereupon I felt myself to be reborn and to have gone through open doors into paradise."

A religious prophet of genius, Luther was socially conservative and politically naive. His assault on the Church's abuses won a fervent following among the German public, but Luther and his followers could carry out their program only with the aid of the German princes and city-states. Protestantism* thus had to allow civil governments broad control over reformed religion. Luther's dream of rallying all Christendom around God's Word soon crumbled.

Protestant reformers could not even agree on what God's Word really meant. Thus Luther and the great French reformer John Calvin (1509–1564) interpreted the spiritual meaning of the Eucharist—a vital issue in their day—quite differently. Calvin also focused more closely than Luther on the stark doctrine of predestination; that is, God's foreknowledge of who would be saved and who would be damned. But Calvinists and Lutherans, as the followers of the two Reformation leaders came to be called, were horrified when more radical Protestants questioned Christ's divinity. Moreover, Calvin and Luther soon had socially as well as religiously radical opponents. Among them were the Anabaptists, who appealed strongly to women and common people with their criticisms of the rich and powerful and sought to restrict baptism to "converted" adults. Most Anabaptists were pacifists, and some renounced private property and lived communally. Judging the Anabaptists a threat to the social order, governments and the mainstream churches persecuted them.

Still another disappointment for Protestants was the Catholic church's remarkable resilience. Catholic reform had begun in Spain even before Luther's revolt, and soon the papacy vigorously attacked corruption and combated Protestant viewpoints on major religious issues. The popes also sponsored a new religious order fervently committed to the papacy: the Jesuits, whose members would distinguish themselves for centuries as teachers, missionaries, and royal advisers. This Catholic revival, the Counter-Reformation, brought into existence the modern Roman Catholic church, which would endure little changed until the mid-twentieth century. But those in all camps who hoped that Christian concord would overcome religious quarrels were sadly disillusioned.

---

*The word *Protestant* comes from the *protest* of Luther's princely supporters against Holy Roman Emperor Charles V's anti-Lutheran policies.

John Calvin, *by Hans Holbein the Younger, Sixteenth Century*

Calvin was trained as a classical scholar before his religious conversion. He brought to Protestant theology a scholar's erudition, a lawyer's appreciation of the importance of God's sovereignty over Creation, and a religious zealot's intense faith.

The Reformation era left three great legacies. First, it created almost all the major Christian traditions that would eventually take root in American soil: Protestantism, modern Roman Catholicism, and many radical Protestant religious impulses that would later flower into dozens of denominations and visionary groups striving for human perfection. Second, Protestantism placed a high value on reading. Luther's own conversion had sprung from his long study of the Bible, and Protestants demanded that God's Word be read carefully by believers and preached by the minister. The new faith was spread best by the newly invented printing press; wherever Protestantism became estab-

lished, basic education and religious indoctrination followed. Third, Protestantism denied that God had endowed priests with special powers. Clergymen, Luther and Calvin insisted, could claim no more dignity than followers of any other honest profession. Work itself was dignified, and Christians should feel confident that God asked them only to fulfill the obligations of their station in life, however humble. Protestant leaders did not teach that work would earn salvation (no human effort could do that), and it did not necessarily follow that those predestined for salvation could be identified by their hard work or material success.

Overall, the Reformation was a conservative movement. It yearned to bring back the simplicity and purity of the ancient Christian church. Protestantism condemned the replacement of traditional reciprocity by marketplace values; even more than Catholicism, it questioned the pursuit of excessive wealth. In a world of troubling change, it could forge individuals of strong moral determination and equip them with the fortitude to survive and prosper. Protestantism's greatest appeal was to all those—ordinary people, merchants, and aristocrats alike—who brooded over their chances for salvation and valued the steady performance of duty.

Tudor England

The instability, tensions, and artistic creativity of sixteenth-century European life all converged in England. Deeply committed to the hierarchical view of society, English people faced major challenges: achieving political stability, settling the religious issues raised by the Reformation, and controlling social disorder. All three challenges were tightly intertwined and helped shape England's eventual involvement in North America.

Political instability weighed heavily upon the English. The ruling Tudor family had only recently (1485) come to the throne after bloody civil wars. The Tudor dynasty's fragility left Henry VIII (ruled 1509–1547) obsessed with producing a legitimate male heir. When his queen, Catharine of Aragon, failed to bear a son, Henry in 1527 asked the pope to annul his marriage. After the pope denied Henry's request, the king had Parliament dissolve his marriage and proclaim him "supreme head" of the Church of England (or Anglican church). The royal government executed a few opponents of the new church, and it closed monasteries and sold the extensive monastic lands to private buyers. At last one of Henry's later wives produced a male heir, the intelligent but sickly Edward VI (ruled 1547–1553), upon whose premature death the crown passed to Henry VIII's daughters—first Mary (ruled 1553–1558) and next Elizabeth I (ruled 1558–1603).

Rule by a woman frightened sixteenth-century people. Not only did they consider governance a male responsibility, but they also knew that a queen's marriage would ultimately transfer the crown to either a foreign dynasty or some domestic noble family. In this dangerous situation, Mary blundered repeatedly and saved the day only by dying soon. Elizabeth I, however, took her nation's interests to heart. Remaining the unmarried "virgin queen," she artfully managed Parliament, which represented the nation's landowning upper class and merchants. Parliament flooded her with advice, usually trying to push her further than she thought it prudent to go in dealing with political and religious issues. But by cleverly managing patronage—the distribution of royal favors and political offices—and by choosing shrewd advisers, Elizabeth remained in control of the kingdom's intricate political system and guided England through a perilous half-century.

Religion remained a source of trouble in England for well over a century after Henry VIII's break with Rome. The sale of monastic lands created a vested interest against returning to the old order. But Henry never quite decided whether he was a Protestant. Under Edward VI the church veered sharply toward Protestantism; then Mary tried to restore Catholicism by burning several hundred Protestants at the stake.

Elizabeth's reign, however, marked a crucial watershed. After "Bloody Mary," most English people were ready to become Protestant; *how* Protestant was the divisive question. A militant but minority religious viewpoint had arisen, called Puritanism. Puritans demanded a wholesale "purification" of the Church of England from "popish [Catholic] abuses." As Calvinists, Puritans affirmed predestination, denied Christ's presence in the Eucharist, denounced the ornate ritual of the Catholic Mass, and believed that hearing God's Word was the heart of true worship. The Puritan ranks

Elizabeth I, *by Nicholas Hilliard, 1572*
This miniature (created for a jeweled locket) portrays Queen Elizabeth at age thirty-nine. Unlike the more stylized portraits that date from her later years, the painting conveys Elizabeth's shrewd, sharp-witted character.

included aristocrats and other landowning gentlemen, university-educated clergymen and intellectuals, merchants, and hard-working, Bible-reading artisans and yeomen—but not Elizabeth, who distrusted Puritan militancy and preferred traditional, dignified ceremony in worship. The queen demanded, for example, that the Anglican church retain distinctive ceremonial attire for the clergy. Elizabeth even tried to avoid breaking with the papacy—until in 1570 the pope declared her a heretic and urged Catholics to overthrow her. Thereafter, the crown regarded English Catholics as potential traitors, and Elizabeth became more openly Protestant. But although Puritan sentiment gained ground in Parliament, Elizabeth never embraced it.

A troubled society lay beneath this political and religious turmoil. At the upper end of the social scale, only eldest sons inherited aristocratic titles; aristocrats' younger sons normally had to shift for themselves in a world of shrinking opportunities. The stagnant economy also pinched the gentry—the "respectable" landowners without aristocratic titles who traditionally lived without doing manual labor and played a prominent role in local government and Parliament. Everyone felt that the nation's population had grown too fast. With technology largely unchanged, per capita output and real household income fell. In effect, more workers competed for fewer jobs in the face of diminishing European markets for English cloth and rising prices for food. Enclosures aggravated the nation's unemployment problems, forcing great numbers of people to wander the countryside or pour into towns in search of work and so making England's population highly mobile. These "sturdy beggars" seemed to threaten law and order. To control them, Parliament passed "Poor Laws" that ordered vagrants whipped and sent home, where hard-pressed taxpayers had to maintain them on the dole. But Puritan and Anglican clergymen agreed that England's root problem was the irresponsible greed of the well-to-do, whom they charged with raising prices, goading the poor to revolt, and giving too little to charity. "You that eat till you blow, and feed till your eyes swell with fatness," preached moderate Puritan Henry Smith, ". . . impart some of your superfluity unto the poor. . . ."

By thus describing contemporary problems in moral terms, Smith displayed a traditional mentality. He—like Shakespeare, Luther, and Calvin—attributed social problems to people's improper behavior. In this respect, conservative European thinking paralleled the characteristic outlook of Africans and native Americans. But in the encounter of Old and New Worlds in the 150 years after 1492, the peoples on both sides of the Atlantic would find that they had little else in common with one another.

The Age of Discovery and the Beginnings of European Dominance

Europeans' outward thrust began centuries before Columbus's first voyage in 1492. In the tenth century, Scandinavian Vikings had reached Iceland and Greenland. From there, about A.D. 1000, Vikings made their way to North America. They established a settlement at "Vinland" (probably in Newfoundland) and may have explored the New England coast. But the Scandinavians soon abandoned and eventually almost forgot Vinland, and

the direction of European expansion changed. A series of crusading armies after 1096 struggled (ultimately in vain) to wrest Palestine from the Moslems. A brisk trade with the Middle East began in these years as the Europeans sold cloth and bought silks and the spices that they needed to preserve food and spark up a monotonous diet. Thirteenth-century merchants like Marco Polo even traveled overland to East Asia to buy directly from the Chinese. By the fourteenth and fifteenth centuries, the highly profitable spice and silk trade had enriched well-placed Italian merchants despite the era's generally depressed economic conditions, financed the cultural flowering of the early Renaissance, and excited the envy of all Europe.

Seaborne Expansion

Around 1460 a century of depression and population decline ended in Europe. An era of renewed economic and population growth opened. As Europeans competed for commercial advantage, they projected their power overseas.

Important changes in maritime technology occurred at this dawn of European expansion. In the early fifteenth century, shipbuilders and mariners along Europe's stormy Atlantic coast added the triangular Arab sail to the heavy cargo ship that they used for voyaging between England and the Mediterranean. They created a more maneuverable vessel, the caravel, that could sail against the wind. Sailors also mastered the compass and astrolabe, by which they got their bearings on the open sea. Without this "maritime revolution," European exploration would have been impossible.

Renaissance scholars' search for more accurate readings of ancient texts forced fifteenth-century Europeans to look at their world with new eyes. The great ancient Greek authority on geography was Ptolemy, but Renaissance scholars had to correct his data when they tried to draw accurate maps. Thus Renaissance "new learning" combined with older Arabic and European advances in mathematics to sharpen Europeans' geographic sense.

The adventuring spirit to explore new worlds first burned in impoverished little Portugal. Here zeal for continuing the struggle against the Moslems who had slowly been driven out of Spain and Portugal combined with an anxious search for new markets. Prince Henry "the Navigator" of Portu-

An Astrolabe

A device for calculating the position and altitude of the sun, stars, and planets, the astrolabe was one of the world's oldest scientific instruments. It was known to the ancient Greeks and perfected by the medieval Arabs. Ocean navigators found it indispensable. This brass English astrolabe, dating to 1326, may be the oldest such European instrument extant.

gal (1394–1460) embodied both urges. Henry encouraged Portuguese seamen to pilot the new caravels farther down the African coast searching for weak spots in the Moslem defenses and for opportunities to trade profitably. At the time of his death, the Portuguese had established a profitable slaving station at Arguin, and by the late fifteenth century, they had penetrated south of the equator. In 1488 Bartolomeu Días reached the Cape of Good Hope at Africa's southern tip. The Portuguese king John II seized the opportunity to open up direct contact with India, circumventing the Arabs and Venetians. In 1497 Vasco da Gama led a Portuguese fleet around the Cape of Good Hope and on to India.

Ultimately the Portuguese failed to destroy traditional Venetian-Arab commercial links, although for a century they remained an imperial presence in the Indian Ocean and present-day Indonesia. Already, however, they had brought Europeans face-to-face with black-skinned Africans.

The "New Slavery" and Racism

Slavery was well established in fifteenth-century West African life, as elsewhere. The grassland emperors, as well as individual families, depended heavily on slaves. Often, however, slaves or their children were absorbed into African families over time. The eighteenth-century West African Olaudah Equiano, who had suffered enslavement in the New World, thus explained the fate of war captives in his native society:

> *How different was their condition from that of the slaves in the West Indies! With us they do no more work than other members of the community, even their master. Their food, clothing, and lodging, were nearly the same as [free people's], except that they were not permitted to eat with those who were born free. . . . Some of these slaves even have slaves under them, as their own property, and for their own use.*

Outsiders—first Moslems, then Europeans—turned African slavery into an intercontinental business and tore slaves from their native society. A fifteenth-century Italian who witnessed Portuguese and Moslem slave trading reported that the Arabs "also have many Berber horses, which they trade, and take to the Land of the Blacks, exchanging them with the rulers for slaves. Ten or fifteen slaves are given for one of these horses, according to their quality. . . . These slaves are brought to the market town of Hoden; there they are divided. . . . [Some] are taken . . . and sold to the Portuguese leaseholders [of Arguin]. As a result every year the Portuguese carry away from [Arguin] a thousand slaves."

Equiano's eighteenth-century testimony paints a stark picture of slaves' experience in earlier centuries as well. Brought aboard a European slave ship, he wrote,

> *I was now persuaded that I had got into a world of bad spirits, and that they were going to kill me. Their complexions differing so much from ours, their long hair, and the languages they spoke . . . united to confirm me in this belief. . . . Quite overpowered with shock and horror,*

I . . . fainted. When I recovered a little, I found some black people around me, who I believed were some of those who brought me on board, and had been receiving their pay. . . . I asked them if we were not to be eaten by those white men with horrible looks, red faces, and long hair. They told me I was not. [But] soon after this the blacks who had brought me on board went off, and left me abandoned to despair. . . . I found some of my own nation [and] inquired . . . what was to be done with us? They gave me to understand that we were to be carried to these white people's country to work for them. I then was a little revived . . . but still I feared I should be put to death, the white people looked, as I thought, so savage. . . .

The Portuguese found slave trading lucrative and kept out competitors until about 1600. Although in 1482 they built an outpost, Elmina, on West Africa's Gold Coast, they exploited existing African commercial and social patterns. Often Portuguese merchants traded slaves and local products to other Africans for gold. The local African kingdoms were too strong for the Portuguese to attack, and black rulers traded—or chose not to trade—according to their own self-interest.

West African societies sometimes changed with the coming of Portuguese slavers. In Guinea and Senegambia, which supplied the bulk of sixteenth-century slaves, small kingdoms expanded to "service" the trade. Some of their rulers became comparatively rich. Farther south, in present-day Angola, the kings of Kongo used the slave trade to consolidate their power and voluntarily adopted Christianity. Kongo flourished until the late sixteenth century, when attackers from the interior destroyed it.

The slave-trading African kings and their communities used the trade as a way of disposing of "undesirables," including slaves whom they already owned, lawbreakers, and persons accused of witchcraft. But most slaves were simply victims of raids or wars. Moslem and European slave trading greatly stimulated conflicts among African communities.

Although European societies had used slaves since the time of ancient Greece and Rome, there were ominous differences in the European slavery that arose once the Portuguese began voyaging to West Africa. First, the new slave trade was a high-volume business that expanded steadily. Between

The Slave Trade: An African View

This iron casting from Benin shows a group of enslaved Africans, already dressed in western clothing.

1500 and 1600, perhaps 250,000 African slaves would land in the New World, and 50,000 would die en route. Another 200,000 would arrive between 1601 and 1621. Before the Atlantic slave trade finally ended in the nineteenth century, nearly 12 million Africans would be shipped in terrible conditions across the sea. Slavery on this scale had been unknown to Europeans since the collapse of the Roman Empire. Second, African slaves were treated exceptionally harshly. In medieval Europe slaves had primarily performed domestic service, but by 1450 the Portuguese and Spanish created large slave-labor plantations on their newly occupied islands along Africa's Atlantic coast, as well as in southern Portugal and on Spain's Mediterranean islands. These plantations produced sugar for European markets, using capital supplied by Italian investors to buy African slaves who toiled until death. In short, the African slaves owned by Europeans were destined for exhausting, mindless labor. By 1600 the "new slavery" had become a brutal link in an expanding commerce that ultimately would encompass all major Western nations.

Finally, race became the explicit basis of the "new slavery." Africans' blackness and their alien religion dehumanized them in European eyes. As their racial prejudice hardened, Europeans justified enslaving blacks with increasing ease. From the fifteenth century onward, European Christianity made few attempts to soften slavery's rigors, and race defined a slave. Because the victims of the "new slavery" were physically distinctive as well as culturally alien, slavery became a lifelong, hereditary, and despised status.

Columbus Reaches America

Europeans' varying motivations for expanding their horizons converged in the fascinating, contradictory figure of Christopher Columbus (1451–1509). The son of a ropemaker from the Italian port of Genoa, the young Columbus gained solid navigating experience as a sailor on voyages to West Africa and Iceland. His practical knowledge, self-taught geographical learning, and keen imagination drew him to speculations (circulating in late-fifteenth-century Europe) that Asia might be reached by sailing westward across the Atlantic. By the early 1480s this idea obsessed him. Religious fervor led Columbus to dream of carrying Christianity around the globe and liberating Jerusalem from Moslem rule, but he also burned with ambition to win wealth and glory. Although no portrait of Columbus painted from life exists, contemporaries agreed in describing him as a tall man of commanding presence, implacable in purpose.

Columbus would not be the first European to venture far out into the Atlantic. Besides the early Viking settlers at Vinland, fifteenth-century English fishermen may already have sailed as far west as the Grand Banks and even the North American coast. But Columbus was unique in the persistence with which he hawked his "enterprise of the Indies" around the royal courts of western Europe. John II of Portugal showed interest until Días's discovery of the Cape of Good Hope promised a surer way to India. Finally, in 1492, hoping to break a threatened Portuguese monopoly on direct trade with Asia, the rulers of newly united Spain—Queen Isabella of Castile and King Ferdinand of Aragon—accepted Columbus's offer. Picking up the westward-blowing trade winds at the Canary Islands, Columbus's three small ships reached San Salvador within a month.

Columbus's success derived from a gigantic miscalculation. North America lay about where he expected to find Japan, for he had combined Marco Polo's overestimate of Asia's eastward thrust with Ptolemy's underestimate of the earth's circumference. Another ancient Greek mathematician had calculated something close to the true circumference, and this figure was generally accepted by knowledgeable fifteenth-century Europeans; hence the skepticism that Columbus had aroused.

Word of Columbus's discovery caught Europeans' imaginations. It also induced Isabella and John II in 1494 to sign the Treaty of Tordesillas, which divided all future discoveries between Castile and Portugal. Meanwhile, Isabella had sent Columbus back to explore further, and he established a colony on Hispaniola, the Caribbean island today occupied by Haiti and the Dominican Republic. Columbus proved a poor administrator, and after his last voyages (1498–1502), he was shunted aside. He died an embittered man, convinced that he had reached the threshold of Asia, only to be cheated of his rightful rewards.

England's Henry VII (ruled 1485–1509) ignored Castile's and Portugal's claims of exclusive rights to new discoveries. In 1497 he sent the Italian navigator known in England as John Cabot westward into the Atlantic, tacking against the eastward winds of these latitudes. Cabot claimed for England either Nova Scotia or Newfoundland and the rich Grand Banks fisheries, but he disappeared at sea on a later voyage. Like Columbus, Cabot thought that he had reached Asia.

The more Columbus and others explored, the more apparent it became (to everyone except himself) that a vast landmass blocked the route to Asia. In 1500 the Portuguese claimed Brazil, and other voyages soon revealed a continuous coastline from the Caribbean to Brazil. In 1507 this landmass got its name when a publisher brought out a collection of voyagers' tales. One of the chroniclers was an Italian named Amerigo Vespucci. With a shrewd marketing touch, the publisher devised a catchy name for the new continent: America.

Getting past America and reaching Asia remained the early explorers' primary aim. In 1513 the Spaniard Vasco Núñez de Balboa chanced upon the Pacific Ocean when he crossed the narrow isthmus of Panama. Then in 1519 the Portuguese Ferdinand Magellan, sailing under the Castilian flag, began a voyage around the world by way of the stormy Magellan Straits at South America's southern tip. In an incredible feat of endurance, he crossed the Pacific to the Philippines, only to die fighting with local chiefs. One of his five ships and fifteen emaciated sailors finally returned to Spain in 1522, the first people to have sailed around the world.

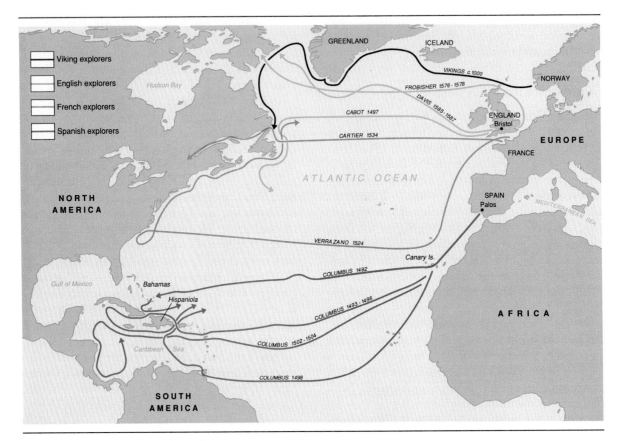

European Transatlantic Explorations, 1000–1587

Following Columbus's 1492 voyage, Spain's rivals soon began laying claim to parts of the New World based on the voyages of Cabot for England, Cabral for Portugal, and Verrazano for France. Later English and French exploration focused on finding a passage to Asia around or through Canada.

But Europeans hoped for easier access to East Asia's fabled wealth. The French king Francis I accepted the challenge of finding a "northwest passage" to Asia. In 1524 he dispatched the Italian navigator Verrazano to explore the North American coast from the Carolinas to Newfoundland. In two subsequent voyages, in 1534–1536, the French explorer Jacques Cartier carefully probed the coasts of Newfoundland, Quebec, and Nova Scotia and ascended the St. Lawrence as far as present-day Montreal. But Verrazano and Cartier found no gold and no northwest passage.

The Conquerors

Columbus was America's first slave trader and the first of the Spanish conquerors, or *conquistadores*. At his struggling colony on Hispaniola, he began exporting Indian slaves and created *encomiendas*—grants for the right to extract labor and other tribute from the Indians of a designated district. Other *conquistadores* would soon transplant this practice to the American mainland.

From the beginning *encomiendas* harshly exploited the native people, who died in droves from overwork, malnutrition, and disease. Portuguese slavers stepped in, supplying boatloads of Africans to replace the perishing Indians. But Spanish friars who came to Hispaniola to convert the Indians quickly sent back grim reports of Indian exploitation; and King Ferdinand (who had made money by selling *encomiendas*) felt sufficiently shocked to attempt to forbid the practice. No one, however, worried about the African slaves' fate.

Soon Spanish settlers were fanning out through the Caribbean in search of Indian slaves and gold.

In 1519 the restless nobleman Hernán Cortés (1485–1547) led a small band of followers to the Mexican coast. Destroying his boats and gathering Indian allies, he marched inland over towering mountain passes to conquer Mexico.

Spaniards had dreamed of a prize such as Mexico ever since they reached America. Mexico was rich: an impressive civilization had been evolving there for three thousand years, culminating in the mighty Aztec Empire. It was exotic: the priests and soldiers who dominated the empire raided neighboring peoples to seize victims for grisly human sacrifices. And Mexico was highly organized. The three hundred thousand inhabitants of the capital, Tenochtitlán, enjoyed fresh water supplied by means of elaborate engineering works; their urban society was highly stratified; and artisans produced a profusion of finely crafted pottery as well as stone, copper, silver, and gold implements. "We were amazed and said that it was like the enchantments they tell of [in stories], and some of our soldiers even asked whether the things that we saw were not a dream?" recalled one of Cortés's soldiers of his first glimpse of Tenochtitlán's pyramids, lakes, and causeways. Certainly the golden gifts that the Aztecs offered in the vain hope of buying off the invaders were no dream. "They picked up the gold and fingered it like monkeys," recalled an Indian. "Their bodies swelled with greed, and their hunger was ravenous. They hungered like pigs for that gold."

Cortés attacked and swiftly prevailed. He owed his astonishing victories partly to firearms and horses, which terrified the Aztecs, and partly to initial Aztec suppositions that the Spanish were the white, bearded gods whose return ancient legends had foretold. His success also resulted from his boldness and cunning, the Aztec emperor Moctezuma's fears, epidemics among the Indians, and the revolt of the Aztecs' subject peoples. By 1521 Cortés had overthrown the Aztecs and begun to build Mexico City on the ruins of Tenochtitlán. Soon the last Aztec emperor suffered defeat and execution, and within twenty years Central America lay at the Spaniards' feet. New Spain was born.

During the rest of the sixteenth century, other *conquistadores* and officials consolidated a great Hispanic empire stretching from New Spain (Mexico) to Argentina. Subduing America and enriching themselves never troubled the *conquistadores'* consciences. Before a battle a herald would reel off a proclamation in Spanish demanding the Indians'

Aztec Wealth

The Aztec emperors' power and wealth derived from tribute paid by subject peoples. Here, in a report prepared by Aztecs for their Spanish conquerors, is a list of the blankets, jewelry, and other finery that various Mexican cities formerly owed Emperor Moctezuma. Symbols denoting each city appear down the left margin.

conversion to Christianity and shifting onto them the guilt for bloodshed if they resisted. From the beginning, however, the Spanish church and government worried that the *conquistadores* were becoming too powerful and abusive. The monarchs sent over hundreds of bureaucrats to govern in the hierarchical European manner and to defend Indian rights. Another army of Spanish friars established missions among the Indians and tried to lessen the native people's suffering. But the whole system was too cumbersome. "I obey, but I do not fulfill" became a standard bureaucratic dodge.

The human cost of the conquest was enormous. Mourned a vanquished Aztec:

> Broken spears lie in the roads;
> We have torn our hair in our grief.
> The houses are roofless now . . .
> And the walls are splattered with gore . . .
> We have pounded our hands in despair
> Against the adobe walls.

When Cortés landed in 1519, central Mexico's population had been about 25 million. By 1600 it had shrunk to between 1 million and 2 million. Peru and other regions experienced similar devastation. America had witnessed the greatest demographic disaster in history.

Warfare, forced labor, starvation, and mass slaughter accounted for some of the catastrophe, but the greatest killers were microbes. Native Americans lacked antibodies to Old World infections—above all, the deadly, highly communicable smallpox. From the first years of contact, frightful epidemics decimated Indian communities. In the West Indian islands, the entire native population perished within a half-century. In return, a virulent form of venereal syphilis spread from the New World to Europe shortly after Columbus's first voyage.

Yet the "Columbian exchange"—the biological encounter of the Old and New Worlds—was not limited to deadly germs. In addition to diseases, sixteenth-century Europeans also brought horses, cattle, sheep, swine, chickens, wheat and other grains, sugar cane, and numerous fruits and garden vegetables to America, besides iron metallurgy, firearms, the wheel, and weeds. In the next century, African slaves carried rice and yams with them across the Atlantic. The list of New World gifts to the Old World was equally impressive: corn, many varieties of beans, white and sweet potatoes, the tropical root crop manioc, tomatoes, squash, pumpkins, peanuts, vanilla, cacao, coffee, avocados, pineapples, chilis, tobacco, turkeys, canoes and kayaks, hammocks, snowshoes, and moccasins. Often several centuries passed before new plants became widely accepted across the ocean; for example, many Europeans suspected that potatoes and tomatoes were either poisons or aphrodisiacs until the nineteenth century, and Indians at first had to be forced to grow wheat. However, the worldwide exchange of food products enriched human diets and later made possible enormous population growth.

Another dimension of the meeting of Old and New Worlds was the mixing of peoples. Throughout the sixteenth century, between one hundred thousand and three hundred thousand Spaniards immigrated, 90 percent of them male. Particularly in towns, a racially blended population arose. Blacks who were imported as slaves occasionally mated with Indians, and white men fathered numerous

The Exotic Weed

Among the notable New World plants involved in the Columbian exchange was tobacco. Central to Indian ritual, smoking tobacco quickly became popular among Europeans as well.

children with Indian and black women. Although these population transfers and mixtures were paltry compared to the wholesale extermination of native Americans through disease and violence, they helped save some offspring of the native American population by transmitting Old World antibodies.

The New World supplied seemingly limitless wealth for Spain. Not only did some Spaniards grow rich from West Indian sugar plantations and Mexican sheep and cattle ranches, but immense quantities of silver crossed the Atlantic after rich mines in Mexico and Peru began producing in the 1540s. A robust trade between America and Spain grew up, which Castilian officials tried to regulate. Spain took in far more American silver than its economy could absorb, setting off inflation that eventually engulfed all Europe. Bent on dominating Europe, the Spanish kings needed ever more American silver to pay their armies. Several times they went bankrupt, and their efforts to squeeze more taxes from their subjects provoked in the 1560s the revolt of Spain's rich Netherlands provinces—modern Belgium, Holland, and Luxembourg. In the end, gaining access to American wealth cost Spain dearly.

The bloody history of Spain's American conquests and efforts to dominate Europe helped spin the "Black Legend"—northern Europeans' vision of a tyrannical, fanatically Catholic Spain intent on conquering everything in sight. Ironically, much of the Black Legend's lurid picture of American horrors derived from the writings of a devout Spanish friar, Bartolomé de Las Casas (1474–1566), who had repented his own participation (as a layman) in the subjugation of Hispaniola. By the end of the sixteenth century, Las Casas's noble hopes of justice for the Indians lay in ruins. The Spanish church became increasingly bureaucratic, intolerant, and restrictive. All this fueled the Black Legend. As Spain's struggle to reconquer the Netherlands and to dominate France spilled ominously near their homeland, Protestant Britons shuddered. But they also looked for opportunities across the Atlantic with which to strike back at Spain—and to enrich themselves.

Footholds in North America

As early as 1510, the flow of wealth from the New World to Spain attracted swarms of northern European pirates. Over the next century, northern Europeans grew familiar with the North American coast through exploratory voyages, fishing expeditions, a small-scale fur trade, and piracy and smuggling.

But all non-Spanish sixteenth-century attempts to plant colonies in North America failed. Although England and France had laid claim to parts of North America on the basis of early voyages by the Cabots, Verrazano, and Cartier, these claims remained hollow pretensions as long as Spain could exclude other Europeans by force. Only in the early seventeenth century did Spain lose this power. In 1607–1608 the English and the French finally began to exploit knowledge gained during the previous century and established centers for permanent colonies. The Dutch, now free of Spain, followed their example

by 1614. Within less than twenty years of the initial successful settlements, each colony developed an economic orientation, pattern of Indian relations, and a natural direction of geographic expansion that would endure throughout the colonial era. The first quarter of the seventeenth century marked the formative period of North America's modern history.

New Spain's Northern Borderlands

The Spanish had built their New World empire by subduing the Aztec and other Indian states, whose riches had attracted the invaders like a magnet. But in the borderlands north of Mexico, the absence of visible wealth and organized states discouraged conquest. Good agricultural land did not suffice. "As it was his object to find another treasure like that . . . of Peru," a witness wrote of southeastern North America's would-be *conquistador*, Hernán de Soto, he "would not be content with good lands nor pearls."

However, a succession of hopeful emulators of Cortés did invade large parts of what would become the United States, although most perished in the attempt. The earliest was Juan Ponce de León, the conqueror of Puerto Rico, who in 1512–1513 and again in 1521 trudged through Florida in search of gold and slaves. His quest ended in death in an Indian skirmish. Legends notwithstanding, Ponce de León had not sought a "fountain of youth," although sometimes Indians managed to get rid of troublesome Spaniards by telling them tall tales of wonders elsewhere.

Dreams of conquest would not die, despite the failure of Ponce and several later adventurers. Lured by hopes of finding a new Peru, de Soto and his party in 1537–1543 blundered from Tampa Bay to the Appalachians and back to southern Texas. Scouring the land for gold, de Soto harried the Indians mercilessly. "Think, then," an Indian chief appealed to him vainly,

what must be the effect on me and mine, of the sight of you and your people, whom we have at no time seen, astride the fierce brutes, your horses, entering with such speed and fury into my country, that we had no tidings of your coming—things so absolutely new, as to strike awe and terror into our hearts.

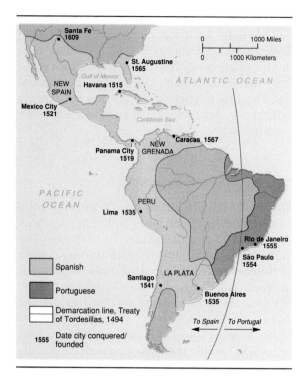

The Spanish and Portuguese Empires, 1610

By 1610 Spain dominated Latin America, including Portugal's possessions. Having devoted its energies to exploiting Mexico and the Caribbean, Spain had not yet expanded into what is now the United States, aside from establishing outposts in Florida and New Mexico.

De Soto also perished. Meanwhile, in 1540–1542 a second party under Coronado, drawn by rumors of a golden city called Cíbola, invaded the Southwest from Mexico. Coronado found the Grand Canyon, plundered the New Mexico pueblos, and roamed as far as Kansas before returning to Mexico, thinking himself a failure because he had found no gold. A third expedition, led by Juan Rodríguez Cabrillo, sailed along the California coast but likewise found nothing worth seizing.

For decades after these failed ventures, Spain's only interest in future U.S. lands lay in establishing a few strategic bases in Florida to keep out intruders. Later, in the 1580s, Spanish friars returned to the southwestern pueblo country, preaching Christianity and scouting the area's potential wealth. Encouraged by their reports, in 1598 Juan de Oñate led five hundred Spaniards into the upper Rio Grande Valley, where he proclaimed the royal colony of New Mexico, distributed *encomiendas,* and demanded tribute from the pueblo-dwelling Indians.

The new colony barely survived. The Spanish government had to replace Oñate in 1606 because of his excessive brutality. Finding no gold, many settlers went back. Those who stayed established Santa Fe in 1609, while others migrated to isolated ranches and fought off Navaho and Apache raiders. Eventually the missions' demands for labor service and their attempts to uproot pueblo religion produced an Indian backlash against Christianity (see Chapter 3). The Spanish would not be secure in New Mexico for a century.

Initial French Failures

In 1534 Jacques Cartier of France, searching for the northwest passage, identified the St. Lawrence River as one of North America's two primary avenues of entry. After 1600 this river would become the center of French colonization. (The other such avenue, also used by the French but in later years, was the Mississippi River.) Before finally planting permanent American colonies, however, France experienced more than a half-century of failure.

France made the first attempt at European colonization in North America in 1541, when ten ships carrying four hundred soldiers, three hundred sailors (including Cartier), and a few women sailed to the St. Lawrence Valley. Cartier returned to France in 1542 with what he thought were gold and diamonds but proved to be iron pyrite ("fool's gold") and quartz. The rest of the expedition ascended the St. Lawrence as far as the rapids, lost heart at the prospect of another Canadian winter, and went home.

The failed expedition of 1541–1542 seemed to verify the Spanish opinion, voiced by the cardinal of Seville, that "this whole coast as far [south] as Florida is utterly unproductive." The next French effort at colonization came in 1562, when French privateers (mariners licensed by their government to raid enemy shipping) briefly established a base in what is now South Carolina. In 1564 the French founded a settlement near modern-day Jacksonville, Florida, which the Spanish destroyed a year later, massacring all Frenchmen found to be Protestants. These failures, along with a civil war between French Catholics and Protestants, distracted the French from further colonization.

To lock France out of North America and to protect the Caribbean against seaborne northern European raiders, the Spanish in 1565 established the first permanent European settlement on future United States soil. This was the powerful fortress at St. Augustine, Florida. But because the Spanish considered Florida's interior worthless, St. Augustine never became more than a military stronghold and a base for religious missions.

Elizabethan England and the Wider World

In 1558, when Elizabeth I became queen, England was a minor power with a population of less than 5 million and stood on the sidelines as Spain and France grappled for supremacy in Europe. England's initial claims to North America had by now receded into the background, although hundreds of English fishing vessels voyaged annually to North American shores and to the Grand Banks. The English remained preoccupied with charting the direction of their religious Reformation and coping with domestic instability.

This instability, however, helped propel Elizabethan expansion. Shipping its unemployed poor overseas seemed a good solution to England's economic woes. "Surplus" English people transplanted to colonies across the ocean might not only provide raw markets for English cloth but also produce valuable export commodities. And the gentry of England's West Country (the southwestern peninsula jutting out into the Atlantic) itched for action. They were restless men, used to the sea, linked by family ties and Puritan sympathies, and frustrated by customs that limited the amount of family property inherited by younger sons. Sir Francis Drake, Sir John Hawkins, Sir Humphrey Gilbert, and Sir Walter Raleigh all fit this description and stood ready to lead England's overseas adventure.

But Spain blocked the way. When Elizabeth came to the throne, England and Spain were enjoying friendly relations. With the queen's support, Hawkins in the early 1560s made a tidy fortune raiding the Guinea coast for slaves and selling them legally to the Spanish; and Elizabeth stood by as the Spanish wiped out France's Florida colony in 1564. But the English worried about Spain's intervention in France's civil wars and its determined

Elizabethan Sea Dogs

Sir John Hawkins (1532–1595, right) and Sir Francis Drake (1540?–1596, center) led England's seaborne assault on Spain's New World empire. Thomas Cavendish (1555?–1592, left) followed Drake in sailing around the world in 1586–1588, capturing several Spanish galleons on the way. He later died at sea.

effort to crush the Netherlands revolt, as well as about the pope's call for Elizabeth's overthrow. Further, by now Englishmen had no incentive to trade legally with Spanish America: in 1568 the Spanish authorities in Mexico had chased Hawkins and Drake from the Caribbean. Secretly, Elizabeth stepped up her aid to French Protestants (the Huguenots), to the Calvinist rebels in the Netherlands, and to "sea dogs" like Hawkins and Drake—from whose voyages she took a share of the plunder. In the 1570s she encouraged merchants to invest in Atlantic-oriented ventures.

Meanwhile, the situation in Ireland, England's "back door," was deteriorating. As early as 1565, English troops fought to impose Tudor rule throughout the island. The conflict intensified when the pope and the Spanish began directly aiding Irish Catholics' resistance to the English. In the ensuing war that ground on through the 1580s, the English drove the Irish clans out of their strongholds (especially in northern Ireland, or Ulster) and established settlements ("plantations") of English and Scottish Protestant settlers—a profitable business for well-connected members of the gentry like Drake and Gilbert. Since Irish resistance did not depend on fortified cities or large armies, English commanders had to develop new tactics to subdue the mobile, armed Irish people, who could easily disappear into bogs and forests. The English practiced total war to break the rebellious population's spirit, inflicting starvation and mass slaughter by destroying villages in the winter. Commanders used terror to force local bands into submission. For example, Gilbert lined the path to his headquarters with Irish heads.

Elizabeth's generals justified these atrocities by claiming that the Irish were "savages." Ireland thus furnished precedents for strategies that the English later employed against North American Indians, whose customs, religion, and method of fighting likewise seemed to absolve Englishmen from guilt in waging exceptionally cruel warfare. Fighting in Ireland and settling fellow countrymen there, leading English colonizers such as Gilbert and Raleigh gained practical experience that they later applied in the New World.

England had two objectives in the Western Hemisphere in the 1570s. The first was to find the northwest passage to Asia and if possible to discover gold on the way; the second, in Drake's words, was to "singe the king of Spain's beard" by raiding Spanish fleets and ports from Spain to the West Indies. The search for the northwest passage only led to such embarrassments as explorer Martin Frobisher's return from the Canadian Arctic with a shipload of "fool's gold." However, privateering raids on the Spanish were both spectacularly successful and profitable for Drake's and Hawkins's financial backers, including merchants, gentry, government leaders, and Elizabeth herself. The most breathtaking enterprise was Drake's voyage around the world in 1577 in quest of sites for colonies. During this voyage he sailed up the California coast and entered San Francisco Bay.

Now deadly rivals, Spain and England sought to plant strategic bases against each other. In 1570–1571 the Spanish tried to establish a new outpost in Chesapeake Bay. They failed, largely because of Indian hostility. Then in 1578, Gilbert secured a royal patent (charter) to start an English colony in Newfoundland. Bad weather and unseaworthy ships at first prevented him from crossing the Atlantic, and after he at last took five ships to Newfoundland in 1583, he drowned on his return voyage.

But English colonial ventures did not cease. In 1584 Gilbert's half-brother Raleigh acquired the patent. Raleigh dispatched Arthur Barlowe to explore the coast farther south, closer to the Spanish—the region that the English had already named Virginia in honor of their virgin queen. Barlowe returned singing the praises of Roanoke Island (see "A Place in Time").

The Origins of Virginia

Claimed by the Spanish and English but occupied by neither, Virginia beckoned invaders. Although Barlowe and his fellow promoters exaggerated America's allure, here was a land of plenty.

The East Coast's native Americans spoke a variety of Algonkian languages and grouped themselves into numerous tribes. Early voyagers like Verrazano had commented on their large numbers, their health ("they live a long life and rarely fall sick"), their friendliness, and their eagerness to trade. Only the Maine Indians had been hostile—they had already learned to be wary of whites. Well they might be, for Europeans were unwittingly bringing them terrible tragedy. "The people began to die very fast, and many in a short space," an Englishman at Roanoke remarked, adding that the deaths invariably began after white men had visited an Indian village. From early in the sixteenth century, raging epidemics of smallpox and a dozen other Old World maladies scourged the defenseless Indians and exterminated entire tribes. Whole villages perished at once, with no one left to bury the dead. Ultimately up to 90 percent of the native population may have been lost. The Europeans came, one historian has written, not to a virgin land but to a widowed land.

But the English would find seizing Virginia no easy matter. Roanoke's sad fate illustrated several stubborn realities about early European experiences in North America. First, even a large-scale, well-financed colonizing effort could fail, given the settlers' unpreparedness for the American environment. Second, whites did not bring enough provisions for the first winter and consistently disdained growing their own food. Although some early English settlers were curious and open-minded about the Indians' way of life, all assumed that the Indians would feed them while they looked for gold—a sure recipe for trouble. Third, colonizing attempts would have to be self-financing: financially strapped monarchs like Elizabeth I would not throw good money after bad into America. Fourth, conflict with the Spanish hung menacingly over every European attempt to gain a foothold in North America.

In 1588 England won a spectacular naval victory over the Armada, a huge invasion fleet sent into the English Channel by Spain's Philip II. This famous victory preserved England's independence and demonstrated that the kingdom could repel attacks although it had little offensive military might. The war churned on as before. In 1595 Drake and Hawkins died fighting in the Caribbean. Raleigh wasted his political influence and physical health in fruitless quests for the legendary gilded king ("El Dorado") in South America. England, France, and the Netherlands formed an alliance to dismember the Spanish Empire, but the French backed out. Only the Netherlanders' naval assaults on Spanish and Portuguese* outposts around the world had devastating effects. England made no further moves to carve out American colonies until after 1600.

Yet overseas expansion still lured individual Englishmen. To sustain public interest in the New World, in 1589 and again in 1601 Richard Hakluyt published monumental collections of explorers' accounts, *The Principal Navigations, Voyages, and Discoveries of the English Nation*. But neither the English crown nor Parliament would agree to spend tax money on colonies, and Roanoke's failure had proved that private fortunes were inadequate to finance successful settlements. Only joint-stock companies—business corporations that would amass capital through sales of stock to the public—could raise funds for American settlement. Such stock offerings produced large sums, yet each investor could limit his risk to an amount that he could afford to lose. England's government henceforth would leave colonization to the private initiative of individuals or business groups and would spend no substantial sums on any colonies with the exception of (in the eighteenth century) Georgia and Nova Scotia.

Elizabeth died in 1603, and her cousin, the king of Scotland, ascended the English throne as James I. The cautious and peace-loving king signed a truce with Spain in 1604. Seriously alarmed by Dutch naval victories, the Spanish considered England the lesser danger. The new Spanish king, Philip III, therefore conceded what his predecessors had always refused: a free hand to another power in part of the Americas. Spain renounced its claims to Virginia; England could colonize unmolested.

On April 10, 1606, James I granted a charter authorizing overlapping grants of land in Virginia to two separate joint-stock companies, one based in London and the other in Plymouth. The Virginia Company of Plymouth received a grant extending south from modern Maine to the Potomac River, while the Virginia Company of London's lands ran north from Cape Fear to the Hudson River. Whichever group established the first successful colony would have its boundaries extended one hundred miles at the other's expense. The colonists would be business employees, not citizens of a separate political jurisdiction, and the stockholders of each company would regulate their behavior.

The Virginia Company of Plymouth sent 120 men to Sagadahoc, at the mouth of the Kennebec River. Half left in 1608 after a hard Maine winter, and the rest went back to England a year later with Raleigh Gilbert (Humphrey's son) when he returned home to collect an inheritance. Soon thereafter the company disbanded.

The wealthy merchant Sir Thomas Smythe provided the leadership necessary for the Virginia Company of London to avoid a similar failure. Smythe's first expedition to Virginia comprised 144 men, of whom 39 died at sea. The initial immigrants included many members of the gentry, most of whom expected riches to fall into their laps. They chose a site on the James River, which they named Jamestown, in May 1607. Discipline quickly fell apart after the discovery of iron pyrite sparked a fool's gold rush. By September only 59 colonists were still alive, and they had neglected to plant crops. When relief ships arrived in January 1608 with 120 reinforcements, only 38 survivors remained at Jamestown.

Although short of workers who could farm, fish, hunt, and do carpentry, Jamestown most

---

*Between 1580 and 1640, Portugal and its colonies were annexed to Spain.

Roanoke, 1584–1590

"We found the people most gentle, loving, and faithful, void of all guile and treason, and such as live after the manner of the golden age. The people only care how to defend themselves from the cold in their short winter, and to feed themselves with such meat as the soil affordeth. . . . The earth bringeth forth all things in abundance, as at the first creation, without toil or labor." Arthur Barlowe, who wrote these glowing words in 1584 after returning to England from Roanoke Island, on the coast of North Carolina, thought that he had found a paradise. To be sure, the native Americans seemed (to Barlowe) to fight cruel and bloody wars that had left them "marvelously wasted" and the country "desolate." But this was all the more reason why they should welcome English protection. To establish friendly reciprocity, the Indians' chief, Winginia, immediately offered to trade.

He beckoned us to come and sit by him, and being set he made all signs of joy and welcome, striking on his head and breast and afterwards on ours to show that we were all one, smiling and making show the best he could of all love and familiarity. After he had made a long speech unto us, we presented him with divers [various] things, which he received very joyfully and thankfully. . . . A day or two after this we fell to trading with them. . . . Of all things that he saw a bright tin dish most pleased him.

Sir Walter Raleigh (1552?–1618),
by an Unknown Artist

Raleigh was the foremost advocate of colonization at the English court.

Shortly thereafter Barlowe returned home, taking two kidnapped Indians so that Englishmen could see actual "savages" and teach them English.

The voyagers had been sent by Sir Walter Raleigh, who dreamed of founding an American colony where English, Indians, and even blacks liberated from Spanish slavery could live together productively. Barlowe reported just what Raleigh wanted to hear. Raleigh persuaded Queen Elizabeth to dispatch ships and a company of soldiers to launch a colony at Roanoke, accompanied by painter John White and scientist Thomas Harriot.

At first all went well. Harriot carefully studied Indian culture, and White captured the Indians' life in paintings of extraordinary delicacy. In awe of the English, the Indians eagerly traded and shared their corn—which they grew with amazing ease: "Their country corn," Barlowe had already reported, "groweth three times in five months. . . . Only they cast the corn into the ground, breaking a little of the soft turf with a wooden matlock, or pickax. . . . They have also beans very fair of divers colors and wonderful plenty. Some growing naturally and some in their gardens. . . ." Why should the English ever work?

So the English refused to try growing their own food—and by the first winter, they had outlived their welcome. Fearing that the Indians were about to attack them, the English killed Winginia in June 1586. When Raleigh's friend Drake arrived soon after with a shipload of blacks whom he had rescued from the Spanish and planned to settle at Roanoke, most of the English were ready to quit. Casually abandoning the blacks, the English sailed back across the Atlantic.

Raleigh did not give up yet. He sent another expedition in the summer of 1586 commanded by Richard Grenville, who left 15 men at Roanoke before hurrying off to fight the Spanish. In 1587 Raleigh dispatched White back to Roanoke with 110 settlers and their last Indian friend, Manteo, whom the English baptized and proclaimed "lord" of the local Indians. White found no trace of the little English

(Left) **A Carolina Indian Mother and Child,** *by John White, 1585*

(Right) **A Carolina Indian Warrior in Body Paint,** *by John White, 1585*

(Below) **Carolina Indians Fishing,** *by John White, 1585*

Using canoes, weirs, nets, and spears, coastal Indians depended on fishing as an important source of their food.

garrison. Leaving the settlers (including his newborn granddaughter), he went home to bring more supplies.

But Spain's attack in the English Channel intervened. Drake and every other English seaman were needed to help repel the Armada of 1588. Not until 1590 could White return to Roanoke—and found only rusty armor, moldy books, and the word *CROATOAN* cut into a post. What had happened to the "lost colony"? Were the settlers killed by Indians? Did they starve or die in a hurricane or drown attempting to move to the nearby island of Croatoan? Or did they join the Indians? (A persistent theory is that they were absorbed into a North Carolina tribe whose modern descendants have such English traits as blue eyes.) The most recent authority to tackle the question believes that Roanoke survivors moved closer to Chesapeake Bay, only to be wiped out by the Powhatan Confederacy when the next English settlement was planted

at Jamestown, in 1607. But historians will probably never know with certainty.

By the time England first attempted to found a colony in America, almost a century had passed since Christopher Columbus's discoveries. In that century Spain had already carved out an American empire vaster than the empire of ancient Rome at an

appalling cost in human lives. By the 1580s the English thought that they could do better: to provide the benevolent rule that would foster multiracial harmony and prosperity. But Roanoke was a miserable failure, and not for seventeen years would the English try again. English leaders' initial hopes of bringing freedom to America were a poignant casualty.

needed effective leadership on the council that directed Virginia's affairs. The council's first president hoarded supplies, and its second was lazy and indecisive. In September 1608 the councilors turned to a brash soldier of fortune whose eagerness to settle arguments with his fists had landed him in irons for most of the 1607 voyage: the magnificent braggart Captain John Smith.

Although only twenty-eight years old and of yeoman origin, Smith had experience fighting Spaniards and Turks that prepared him well to assume control in Virginia. Immediately organizing all but the sick in well-supervised work gangs, he ensured sufficient food and housing for winter. Applying lessons learned in his soldiering days, he laid down rules for maintaining sanitation and hygiene to limit disease. Above all, he brought order through military discipline. During the winter of 1608–1609, Smith lost just a dozen men out of two hundred.

Smith also became the colony's best Indian negotiator. After local native Americans captured him in late 1607, Smith displayed such impressive courage that Powhatan, the leader of the nearby Powhatan Confederacy, arranged an elaborate reconciliation ceremony in which his daughter, Pocahontas, "saved" Smith's life during a mock execution. Smith maintained satisfactory relations with the Powhatan Confederacy, in part through his personality, but he also employed calculated demonstrations of English military strength to mask the settlers' actual weakness.

John Smith prevented Virginia from disintegrating as Sagadahoc had. The company's shareholders reorganized the colonial government in 1609, however, and replaced the council's president with Thomas De La Warr. The new governor sailed for Virginia with six hundred settlers, but he and a third of the expedition were shipwrecked off Bermuda. De La Warr's loss left the colony without effective leadership, for Smith could no longer claim any authority. Discipline soon crumbled, and crops were neglected as settlers scattered to hunt for gold. Smith returned to England in September after suffering a serious wound from a gunpowder explosion.

The five hundred men and women who remained at Jamestown had not laid away sufficient food for the winter, and with Smith gone, the Indians turned hostile. A survivor of the winter left this account:

> So lamentable was our scarcity, that we were constrained to eat dogs, cats, rats, snakes, toadstools, horsehides, and what not; one man out of the misery endured, killing his wife powdered her up [with flour] to eat her, for which he was burned. Many besides fed on the corpses of dead men, . . . and indeed so miserable was our estate that the happiest day that some of them hoped to see was when the Indians had killed a mare, they wishing whilst she was boiling that Sir Thomas Smythe was upon her back in the kettle.

Of the five hundred residents at Jamestown in September 1609, about four hundred died by May 1610. The survivors stumbled down to a small ship and were sailing for home when they met Lord De La Warr and his shipwrecked contingent, just arriving in boats built on Bermuda. Their combined forces reoccupied Jamestown, but Virginia barely survived its "starving time."

De La Warr, a veteran of Irish campaigns, organized the settlers like a military garrison. The colony slowly grew, and by 1611 it had expanded forty miles beyond Jamestown, to modern-day Richmond. The English population remained small, just 380 in 1616, and it had yet to produce anything of value for the stockholders.

Tobacco emerged as Virginia's economic salvation. John Rolfe, an Englishman who married Pocahontas, spent several years perfecting a salable variety of tobacco and began planting it in Virginia. By 1618 the product commanded high prices, and that year Virginia exported large amounts of the crop. Thereafter Sir Thomas Smythe poured supplies and settlers into the colony.

To attract investment, the company started awarding large land grants to individuals who would pay the transportation of laborers to work their own property. Most of these laborers were indentured servants, who had to work for a fixed term of service (usually several years) in return for passage to America. The "plantations" that the new landowners established typically resembled the stockaded communities ("bawns") that English settlers built on confiscated lands in Ireland.

By 1622 Virginia still faced three serious problems. First, local officials systematically defrauded

Artifacts from Early Virginia

This double-edged sword (shown with fragments of its guard and pommel) and elaborate pipe tamper (featuring a man wearing armor and and smoking a pipe) were unearthed at Flowerdew Hundred, an early English settlement near present-day Hopewell, Virginia, and date from the first half of the seventeenth century.

the shareholders by embezzling treasury funds, overcharging for supplies, and using company laborers to work their own tobacco fields. They profited, but the company sank deeper into debt. Second, the colony's population suffered from an exceptionally high death rate. Most fatalities resulted from salt poisoning, typhus, or dysentery, contracted when the settlers drank water from the James River. For almost half the year, its downstream flow was insufficient to flush out the saltwater tide from the Atlantic. The river then became a stagnant, salty pool into which germs seeped from the settlers' outhouses. Most of the 3,500 immigrants entering Virginia from 1618 to 1622 died within three years. Finally, relations with the Indians steadily worsened after Pocahontas died in 1617, and Powhatan a year later. Leadership passed to the latter's brother, Opechancanough, who detested Powhatan's willingness to compromise and allow white settlement to expand. A powerful shaman also emerged among the Powhatans, who urged them to resist the English to the death. Opechancanough launched a surprise attack in 1622 that killed 347 of the 1,200 settlers. With much of their livestock destroyed, spring planting prevented, and disease spreading through cramped fortresses, hundreds more died in the ensuing months. At one point, the governor reported just 180 men fit for

military duty against an enemy numbering in the thousands.

Nevertheless, Opechancanough could not hold his forces together for a long siege. Reorganizing the settlers, Governor Francis Wyatt then took the offensive after the company sent more men. Wyatt used tactics developed during the Irish war. He inflicted widespread starvation by destroying food supplies, conducted winter campaigns to drive Indians from their homes when they would suffer most, and fought (according to John Smith) as if he had "just cause to destroy them by all means possible." By 1625 the English had won the war, and the Indians had lost their best chance of driving out the intruders.

The clash left the Virginia Company bankrupt and James I concerned over complaints against its officers. After receiving a report critical of the company's management, James revoked its charter in 1624, and the next year Virginia became a royal colony. Only about five hundred Old World settlers now lived in Virginia, including a handful of Africans of uncertain status who had been brought in since 1619.* So the roots from which would

---

*Whether or not these first Africans were—or remained—slaves is unknown. The emergence of Virginia's African-American population will be traced in Chapter 2.

grow the Anglo-American and African-American peoples of Virginia were fragile indeed.

French, Dutch, and Swedish Fur Colonies

French, like English, fishermen worked the plenteous Grand Banks fisheries throughout the sixteenth century. The French sailors bartered with coastal Indians for skins of the beaver, a species almost extinct in Europe. By the late sixteenth century, as European demand for beaver hats skyrocketed, France came to see North America primarily as a source for this valuable commodity.

Between 1598 and 1604, a series of government-sponsored French fur-trading outposts appeared in Acadia (modern-day Nova Scotia). But only in 1608 did the first enduring French settlement on Canadian soil begin, founded by Samuel de Champlain at Quebec, far up the St. Lawrence River. Champlain wintered there with twenty-eight men, of whom twenty died.

Shrewdly understanding how to keep his settlement going, Champlain arranged for the Hurons and other nearby tribes to collect furs from farther inland and deliver them to Quebec. He also dispatched French agents to live for long periods with the native Americans. These *coureurs de bois* (runners of the woods) integrated themselves into Indian communities and became a personal link uniting French and Indian interests. In 1615, when four Catholic priests arrived at Quebec, the French also began energetic missionary work among the Indians. Results came slowly, but eventually many Indians converted to Catholicism, and the missionaries (mostly Jesuits) learned to perform valuable services as diplomats, explorers, and even military strategists.

Preservation of good relations with Indian allies was critical to Champlain's success. Nevertheless, New France remained tiny. By 1650 just 675 French

European Settlements in North America, 1565–1625

Except for St. Augustine, all European settlements founded before 1607 were abandoned by 1625. Despite the migration of ten thousand Europeans to North America's Atlantic coast by 1625, the total number of Spanish, English, French, and Dutch on the continent was then about eighteen hundred, of whom two-thirds lived in Virginia.

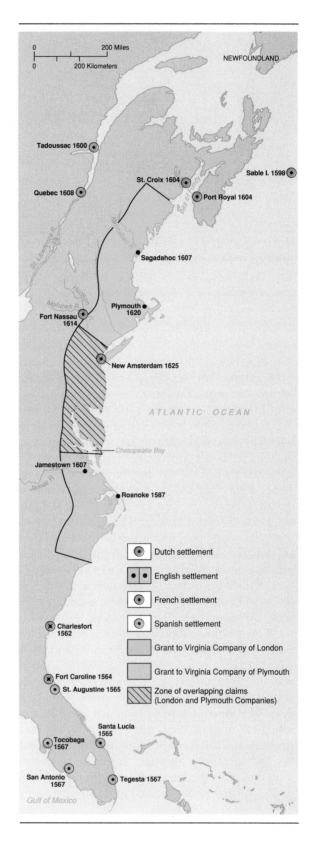

New Amsterdam

After the Dutch "purchase" of Manhattan Island, the fortified settlement of New Amsterdam grew only slowly, as this view from 1651 (the earliest known depiction) clearly shows. Except for the tip, the island remained farmland or forest. Corn brought by canoe-paddling Indians also helped feed the settlement. Note the windmill, where grain was ground.

lived there. Meanwhile, a formidable rival challenged New France's fur trade: the Dutch.

The Dutch Republic* was one of the seventeenth century's great powers. Mighty at sea, the Hollanders built an empire stretching from Brazil to West Africa and what is now Indonesia. North America was for them a relatively minor sphere of activity. Even so, the Dutch played a key role in opening North America to Europeans.

As early as 1609, the Dutch East India Company had become interested in North America when its merchants learned of the broad, deep Hudson River flowing from the interior of present-day New York. By 1611 Dutch oceangoing ships were sailing far up the Hudson, and in 1614 the company built Fort Nassau near what would become Albany. Then in 1625 a second Dutch joint-stock company, the new West India Company, erected another fort on an island at the mouth of the Hudson. A year later, the company's representative, Peter Minuit, bought the island from local Indians and began a second settlement there. The island was named Manhattan; the settlement, New Amsterdam; and the entire colony, New Netherland. As in New

France, immigrants trickled in slowly; by 1643 the Dutch colony had only sixteen hundred residents.

New Netherland became North America's first multiethnic society. Barely half the settlers were Dutch; most of the rest were Germans, French, and Scandinavians. In 1643 the population included Protestants, Catholics, Jews, and Moslems, and eighteen European and African languages were spoken. But religion counted for little (in 1642 the colony had seventeen taverns but not one place of worship), and the settlers' get-rich-quick attitude sapped company profits as private individuals persisted in trading illegally in furs. Eventually the company bowed to the inevitable and legalized private fur trading. Lacking self-restraint to avoid friction with the Indians, the colonists meanwhile failed to maintain enough military strength to deter attack.

New Netherlanders lived by the fur trade. The Dutch tried to use the Iroquois Confederacy as their Indian intermediary, much as the French depended on the Hurons. To stimulate a flow of furs to New Netherland, in the 1620s Dutch traders obtained from the Indians of Long Island Sound large quantities of wampum (tiny seashells traditionally denoting spiritual power, which native Americans had long traded throughout the continent's interior) and used it to buy beaver pelts inland. Backed respectively by the French and the Dutch, Hurons and Iroquois became embroiled in an ever-deep-

---

*By 1588 the independence of the northern, Dutch-speaking part of Spain's rebellious Netherlands provinces was secure, but the southern Netherlands (modern Belgium and Luxembourg) remained under Spanish rule until 1713.

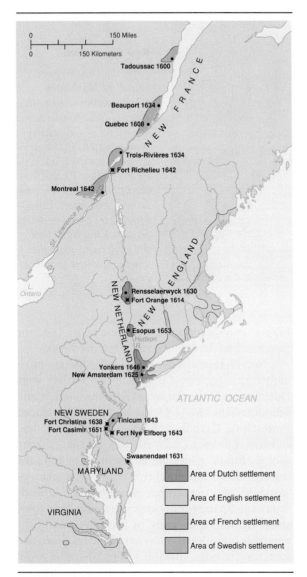

The Riverine Colonies of New France, New Netherland, and New Sweden, c. 1650

So that they could easily buy furs trapped by Indians farther inland, England's imperial rivals located their colonies along major river routes to the interior. The French settled along the St. Lawrence, the Dutch along the Hudson, and the Swedes along the Delaware.

ening contest to control the fur trade and maximize their profits in wampum, firearms, and alcohol. Overhunting soon drove up the price of beaver pelts, and intertribal wars grew correspondingly more violent. After 1642 the Dutch-armed Iroquois, in a series of bloody "beaver wars," destroyed

or scattered rival pro-French tribes like the Hurons. Then they attacked the French settlements along the St. Lawrence. "They come like foxes, they attack like lions, they disappear like birds," wrote a French Jesuit of the Iroquois.

Although the Dutch allied successfully with the Iroquois, their relations with their Indian neighbors, the Algonkians, were the worst of any Europeans. With its greedy settlers and military weakness, New Netherland had largely itself to blame. In 1643 all-out war erupted when Governor Willem Kiefft massacred previously friendly Algonkians, and by 1645 the Dutch could temporarily prevail only with English help and by inflicting terrible atrocities. But the fighting had cut New Netherland's population from sixteen hundred to seven hundred.

Another European challenger dangerously distracted the Dutch in their war with the Algonkians. In 1638 Sweden had planted a small fur-trading colony in the lower Delaware Valley. New Sweden diverted many furs from New Netherland. Annoyed, in 1655 the Dutch colony's stern, one-legged soldier-governor Peter Stuyvesant marched his militia against New Sweden. The four hundred residents of the rival colony peacefully accepted Dutch annexation. But New Netherland paid dearly for the victory. The Algonkians attacked during the militia's absence, this time destroying many scattered Dutch settlements and forcing Stuyvesant to ransom white captives.

Tiny though they were, the seventeenth-century French, Dutch, and Swedish colonies were not historically insignificant. New France became the nucleus of modern French Canada. New Netherland did not endure under Dutch rule (as we shall see in Chapter 3, in 1664 it fell to the English), yet the Dutch presence in what became New York lent a distinctive flavor to American life for centuries. Even short-lived New Sweden left a mark—the log cabin, that durable symbol of the American frontier, which Finnish settlers in the Swedish colony first introduced to the continent.

The Origins of New England: Plymouth Plantation

Still another rival entered the competition for the North American fur trade: the English who settled New England. In 1614 the ever-enterprising John

Smith, who explored its coast, gave New England its name. "Who," he asked, "can but approve this most excellent place, both for health and fertility?" An admirer of Cortés, Smith planned to conquer its "goodly, strong, and well-proportioned [Indian] people" and establish an English colony there. But his hope of settling an English colony in New England came to naught. As for the region's native peoples, microbes rather than soldiers did the grim business of destroying them as a terrible epidemic devastated the coastal tribes about 1616. In 1622 an Englishman found the ground littered with the "bones and skulls" of the unburied dead.

Against this tragic backdrop, in 1620 the Virginia Company of London gave a patent to some London merchants headed by Thomas Weston for a settlement near the Hudson River. Weston sent over 18 families (a total of 102 persons) in a small, leaky ship, the *Mayflower*. The colonists promised to send lumber, furs, and fish back to Weston in England for seven years, after which they would own the tract.

The expedition's leaders—but not all its members—belonged to a small religious community from the town of Scrooby in northern England. The group was made up of Puritans who had taken the radical step of withdrawing from the Church of England. Such "Separatists" risked the death penalty, and the Scrooby band had fled to the Netherlands to practice their religion freely. Unsatisfied there, they decided to immigrate to America under Weston's sponsorship.

The Pilgrims, as these people became known, missed their intended destination near the Hudson River. In November 1620 the *Mayflower* landed at Massachusetts Bay, outside the bounds of Virginia. Knowing that they had no legal right to be there, the Pilgrim leaders forced all the adult males in the group (including non-Separatists) to sign the Mayflower Compact before they landed. By this document they constituted themselves a "civil body politic"—that is, a civil government—under James I's sovereignty and established the colony of Plymouth Plantation.

Weakened by their journey and unprepared for winter, half the Pilgrims died within four months of landing. Those still alive in the spring of 1621 owed much to the aid of two Indians. One was Squanto, a local Indian who had been taken to Spain as a slave some years earlier, escaped to

Defending Plymouth Plantation

Nervous about their security despite the neighboring Indians' weakening through terrible epidemics, the Pilgrims at Plymouth used military force to overawe local tribes. This English helmet of steel and wrought iron was part of the equipment that a professional soldier like Miles Standish might have used to defend the settlement.

England, and made himself useful to potential New World colonists. Returning, he learned that he alone of his tribe of two thousand had survived an epidemic. The other friendly Indian, an Abenaki from Maine named Samoset, hoped to use the English as an ally against a rival tribe, the Narragansetts of modern-day Rhode Island. To stop the Pilgrims from stealing their food, the Indians taught the newcomers how to grow corn. The alliance that Squanto and Samoset arranged between Plymouth and local Wampanoag Indians headed by chief Massasoit united two weak parties, but with their firearms the Pilgrims became the dominant partner. By late 1621 Plymouth forced the local Indians to acknowledge English sovereignty. The Pilgrims' first Thanksgiving after the harvest of 1621 was a ceremony cementing the relationship, "at which time . . . we exercised our arms, many of the Indians coming amongst us, with some 90 men, whom for three days we entertained and feasted."

Plymouth's relations with the native Americans soon worsened, however. News of the Virginia massacre of 1622 hastened the Pilgrims' militarization of their colony (under the leadership of a professional soldier, Miles Standish) and threatening their Indian "allies" with their monopoly of firepower. By imposing stern discipline on themselves, the Pilgrims managed to become agriculturally self-sufficient. But they also offended the Indians by avoiding the close personal contact that the native peoples expected of an ally, and they made no attempt to convert the native Americans.

The Pilgrims were not so lucky—or shrewd—in dealing with their English patrons. Systematically cheated by their English sponsors, after seven years the Pilgrims had sunk so deeply into debt that they faced fifteen years' additional labor to free themselves. Fishing failed to be profitable, but they learned to trade their corn surpluses with the nonagricultural Indians of Maine for furs. By 1627 they had also agreed with the Dutch to divide the fur trade in the Connecticut River Valley. By the time Plymouth finally freed itself of obligations,

the settlement had grown to several hundred persons on Cape Cod and in the southeastern corner of present-day Massachusetts.

At first an almost insignificant group, the Pilgrims were only one of several small English bands that immigrated to New England in the 1620s. Their importance was twofold. First, they helped inspire the American vision of sturdy, self-reliant, God-fearing folk crossing the Atlantic to govern themselves freely. Second, they foreshadowed the methods that later generations of white Americans would use to gain mastery over the Indians. In both respects, the Pilgrims were the vanguard of a mighty, voluntary migration of Puritans to New England in the 1630s.

Conclusion

The founding of the first Old World colonies on the North American mainland came late in the Age of Discovery—the era spanning the mid-fifteenth to the mid-seventeenth centuries, during which Europeans enormously expanded their geographical horizons. Among the previously unknown peoples whom Europeans encountered were the native Americans of the Western Hemisphere and the dark-skinned Africans living south of the Sahara Desert. Indians and Africans alike had adapted well to their environments, but Europeans found them in many respects strange, even sinister.

The displacement of Indians and the enslavement of Africans tarnished the early history of European settlement in the New World. Despite devastation by disease, however, native Americans yielded only slowly to foreign incursions. As for Africans, even the horrors of the Atlantic slave trade did not strip them entirely of their heritage, which they later nurtured into a distinctive African-American culture.

During the first third of the seventeenth century, the general outlines of European land claims in North America emerged, as did the basic elements of the various colonies' economic life. Establishing ranches in New Mexico and fortresses in Florida, Spain advanced as far north as seemed worth going. Virginia's victory over the Indians left the English in control in the Chesapeake, where tobacco had become the principal commercial crop. Here and in the fragile Plymouth colony, English settlers depended primarily on farming. The Dutch, Swedish, and French colonies existed mainly to trade in fish and furs, which soon became important to New Englanders as well. Of the non-English colonies, New France was geographically the best positioned to expand deep into the continent. By 1630 North America stood poised for two surges in colonial development: the great English migration across the Atlantic, and the involuntary migration of Africans to New World servitude.

Given the thousands of lives lost and the fortunes wasted, the first tiny European outposts in North America may seem a minor achievement. By the 1630s they were just beginning to take on an air of permanence, leading discontented Europeans to imagine that new societies could be created across the Atlantic free from the Old World's inherited problems or without painful labor. These dreamers seldom dared to cross the ocean, and those who did generally lost their illusions—or their lives—when faced with the rigors of a strange environment. The transplantation of Europeans into North America was hardly a story of inevitable triumph.

CHRONOLOGY

c. 600–   Rise of the great West African empires.
1600

c. 1000   Vikings voyage to North America and establish a small settlement at Vinland.

c. 1400–   Renaissance era—first in Italy, then
1600   elsewhere in Europe.

1440   Portuguese slave trade in West Africa begins.

1488   Bartolomeu Días reaches the Cape of Good Hope.

1492   Christopher Columbus lands at San Salvador.

1497   John Cabot reaches Nova Scotia or Newfoundland.

1512–   Juan Ponce de León explores Florida.
1521

1513   Vasco Núñez de Balboa views the Pacific Ocean.

1517   Protestant Reformation begins in Germany.

1519   Ferdinand Magellan embarks on round-the-world voyage.
Hernán Cortés begins conquest of Aztec empire.

1524   Giovanni da Verrazano explores the North American coast.

1534   Jacques Cartier explores Canada for France.

1540–   Francisco Vásquez de Coronado explores the
1542   southwestern United States.

1558   Elizabeth I becomes queen of England.

1565   St. Augustine founded.

1565–   English attempt to subdue Ireland.
1580s

1577   Francis Drake circumnavigates the globe.

1578   Humphrey Gilbert secures a patent to establish an English colony in Newfoundland.

1585–   Roanoke colony explored and founded.
1587
1588   English defeat the Spanish Armada.

1598   New Mexico colony founded.

1603   James I becomes king of England.

1607   Jamestown colony founded.

1608   Samuel de Champlain founds Quebec.

1614   New Netherland colony founded.

1619   Large exports of tobacco from Virginia begin.
First Africans arrive in Virginia.

1620   Mayflower Compact signed; Plymouth Plantation founded.

1622 Powhatan Confederacy attacks Virginia colony.

1624 Revocation of Virginia Company's charter.

1625 Peter Minuit purchases Manhattan Island.

1638 New Sweden colony founded.

1643 War erupts between the Dutch and the Algonkian Indians.

1655 New Netherland colony peacefully takes over New Sweden.

For Further Reading

Paul Bohannan and Philip Curtin, *Africa and the Africans* (2d ed., 1971). A brief but comprehensive introduction to the African world—geography, society, culture, and history.

Fernand Braudel, *The Mediterranean and the Mediterranean World in the Age of Philip II* (2d ed., 1966; English trans., 1972). One of the greatest historical works of our time; examines the interactions of large "structures" of environment, economy, and events in sixteenth-century Europe and Africa.

Carl Bridenbaugh, *Vexed and Troubled Englishmen, 1590–1642* (1978). An excellent account of England during the age of expansion.

William Cronon, *Changes in the Land: Indians, Colonists, and the Ecology of New England* (1983). A pioneering study of the interactions of native Americans and European settlers with the New England ecosystem.

Francis Jennings, *The Invasion of America: Indians, Colonialism, and the Cant of Conquest* (1975). A brilliant, angry, and controversial corrective to traditional views of the settlement of North America.

Alvin Josephy, Jr., *The Indian Heritage of America* (1968). A comprehensive account of all Western Hemisphere native peoples, organized by cultural region and attentive to evolution over time.

D. W. Meinig, *The Shaping of America*, Vol. I: *Atlantic America, 1492–1800* (1986). A geographer's engrossing study of Europeans' encounter with North America and the rise of colonial society.

Roderick Nash, *Wilderness and the American Mind* (2d ed., 1973). An incisive essay on the changing ways in which untamed nature has captured the American imagination from colonial times to the rise of modern environmentalism.

J. H. Parry, *The Age of Reconnaissance* (1963). A comprehensive analysis of European exploration and the rise of European overseas empires from the fifteenth to the seventeenth centuries.

Additional Bibliography

Native Americans

James Axtell, *The European and the Indian: Essays on the Ethnohistory of Colonial North America* (1981) and *The Invasion Within: The Contest of Culture in Colonial North America* (1985); Harold Driver, *Indians of North America* (2d ed., 1969); Charles Hudson, *The Southeastern Indians* (1976); Jesse Jennings, ed., *Ancient North Americans* (1983); Karen Ordahl Kupperman, *Roanoke: The Abandoned Colony* (1984) and *Settling with the Indians: The Meeting of English and Indian Cultures in America, 1580–1640* (1980); Gary Nash, *Red, White, and Black: The Peoples of Colonial America* (2d ed., 1982); Neal Salisbury, *Manitou and Providence: Indians, Europeans, and the Making of New England, 1500–1643* (1982); Bernard Sheehan, *Savagism and Civility: Indians and Englishmen in Colonial Virginia* (1980); Anthony F. C. Wallace, *The Death and Rebirth of the Seneca* (1970); Wilcomb E. Washburn, *The Indian in America* (1975).

The Africans and Slavery

Philip Curtin, *The Atlantic Slave Trade: A Census* (1969) and *Economic Change in Precolonial Africa: Senegambia in the Era of the Slave Trade* (1975); Basil Davidson, *The African Genius* (1969); David Brion Davis, *The Problem of Slavery in Western Culture* (1966); J. S. Fage, *A History of Africa* (1978); Winthrop D. Jordan, *White Over Black: American Attitudes Toward the Negro 1550–1812* (1968); Robert July, *A History of the African People* (1970); Paul E. Lovejoy, *Transformations in Slavery: A History of Slavery in Africa* (1983); Richard Olaniyan, *African History and Culture* (1982); Jon Vogt, *Portuguese Rule on the Gold Coast, 1469–1682* (1979).

The Europeans

Fernand Braudel, *Civilization and Capitalism, 15th–18th Centuries* (3 vols., 1979; English trans., 1981); Peter Burke, *Popular Culture in Early Modern Europe* (1978); Carlo Cipolla, *Before the Industrial Revolution: Euro-*

pean Society and Economy, 1100–1700 (1976); L. A. Clarkson, *The Pre-Industrial Economy of England, 1500–1750* (1972); Patrick Collinson, *The Elizabethan Puritan Movement* (1967); Natalie Z. Davis, *Society and Culture in Early Modern France* (1975); A. G. Dickens, *The English Reformation* (1964); J. H. Elliott, *Imperial Spain, 1479–1716* (1963); G. R. Elton, *England Under the Tudors* (1974); J. R. Hale, *Renaissance Europe* (1971); Ralph Houlbrooke, *The English Family, 1450–1700* (1984); Peter Laslett, *The World We Have Lost: England Before the Industrial Age* (2d ed., 1971); Alan Macfarlane, *Witchcraft in Tudor and Stuart England* (1970); Stephen Ozment, *The Age of Reform, 1250–1550* (1980); Quentin Skinner, *The Origins of Modern Political Thought* (1978); Gerald Strauss, *Luther's House of Learning: Indoctrination of the Young in the German Reformation* (1978); Keith Thomas, *Religion and the Decline of Magic* (1971); Margo Todd, *Christian Humanism and the Puritan Social Order* (1988); Penry Williams, *The Tudor Regime* (1979); Keith Wrightson, *English Society, 1580–1680* (1982).

European Expansion and the Spanish Conquest

Fredi Chiappelli, ed., *First Images of America: The Impact of the New World on the Old* (2 vols., 1976); Alfred W. Crosby, Jr., *The Columbian Exchange: Biological and Cultural Consequences of 1492* (1972); Ralph Davis, *Rise of the Atlantic Economies* (1973); J. H. Elliott, *The Old World and the New, 1492–1650* (1970); Lewis Hanke, *The Spanish Struggle for Justice in the Conquest of America* (1965); Howard Mumford Jones, *O Strange New World* (1964); James Lockhart and Stuart B. Schwartz, *Early Latin America: A History of Colonial Spanish America and Brazil* (1983); S. E. Morison, *Admiral of the Ocean Sea: A Life of Christopher Columbus* (1942), *The European Discovery of America: The Northern Voyages*, A.D. *1500–1600* (1971), and *The Southern Voyages*, A.D. *1492–1616* (1974); J. H. Parry, *The Establishment of the European Hegemony: Trade and Expansion in the Age of the Renaissance* (1966); Carl O. Sauer, *Sixteenth Century North America* (1971).

Northern Europeans in North America

Nicholas P. Canny, *The Elizabethan Conquest of Ireland: A Pattern Established, 1565–1576* (1976); Thomas J. Condon, *New York Beginnings: Commercial Origins of the New Netherlands* (1968); Wesley Frank Craven, *Dissolution of the Virginia Company: The Failure of a Colonial Experiment* (1932); W. J. Eccles, *The Canadian Frontier, 1534–1760* (1969); George D. Langdon, Jr., *Pilgrim Colony: A History of New Plymouth, 1620–1691* (1966); Edmund S. Morgan, *American Slavery, American Freedom: The Ordeal of Colonial Virginia* (1975); David B. Quinn, *England and the Discovery of America, 1481–1620* (1974), *North America from Earliest Discovery to First Settlements: Norse Voyages–1612* (1977), and *Set Fair for Roanoke: Voyages and Colonies, 1584–1606* (1985); Oliver Rink, *Holland on the Hudson: An Economic and Social History of Dutch New York* (1986).

CHAPTER 2

Godly Order and Slavery: Seventeenth-Century New England, Caribbean, and Chesapeake Society

On the West Indian island of Barbados in 1692, a widowed Englishwoman named Sarah Horbin counted up her relatives to see who might deserve bequests of property in case her only son—a sailor whom Arab pirates were holding for ransom in an African prison—died. Through her kinsman John Seabury of Barbados, she had kept in contact with a dozen Seabury cousins in Massachusetts. She had also remained in touch with several Virginia relatives in the Empereur family and with a kinsman of her husband's, Andrew Rouse, who lived in the frontier zone between Virginia and Florida then simply called Carolina.

Sarah Horbin and her far-flung clan were part of a great migration of English women and men who built an empire almost absentmindedly for their mother country. From 1630 to 1660, at least 200,000 (and perhaps 250,000) English swarmed to foreign lands. By the mid-seventeenth century, England's population had reached 5.5 million, yet the kingdom was losing between 65,000 and 80,000 people every decade. Emigration from Spain, then a nation of 8 million, averaged about 20,000 per decade, while France, with a population of about 19 million, sent fewer than 10,000 persons overseas every ten years. About 1650 an English woman or man was five times more likely to emigrate than was a Spaniard, and twenty-five times more likely than an inhabitant of France.

About one-third of those leaving England went to Ireland or the Netherlands, but the migration chiefly scattered these refugees across the Atlantic. By 1700 there were almost 250,000 persons of English birth or parentage in the New World, including 200,000 within the modern-day United States. The vast exodus provided British North America with its first large wave of immigrant settlers. Perhaps every fourth American alive today could be descended from someone who crossed the Atlantic with this surge of desperate humanity.

Most of these refugees were the unwanted offspring of poverty and unemployment. Eighty percent of them were aged between fifteen and twenty-four. They generally had left their home communities looking for work, and, unsuccessful at finding it, signed on for America upon reaching a port city. The majority took ship only because they had no alternative.

The English government ignored this outpouring of youthful vigor. Its overseas possessions grew without any official plan for colonial expansion. The settlers who immigrated to—or found themselves stranded in—America received almost no financial help from the royal treasury and had to fend for themselves in a hostile world.

This freedom from centralized control allowed three very different societies to develop in seventeenth-century British North America: New England, the West Indies, and the Chesapeake. Each evolved distinctive systems of land use, labor, religious practice, and family and community experience. Barely one generation removed from England in 1690, Sarah Horbin on Barbados, her Seabury cousins in Massachusetts, and her Empereur kin in Virginia led lives that differed profoundly from one another.

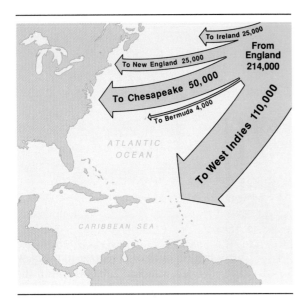

The Great English Migration, 1630–1660

During the great transatlantic English migration, the present-day United States received just one-third of English immigrants. The West Indies attracted twice as many colonists as went to the Chesapeake, and over four times as many as settled in New England.

The New England Way

Six years after returning to England from Jamestown, Captain John Smith led an expedition of whale hunters to that part of the North American coast then called Norumbega. He found no whales but came back with a profitable load of dried fish and a conviction that the land was destined for "men that have great spirits, but small means [or fortunes]." In 1616 Smith published *A Description of New England*, which gave the region its modern name.

Smith's pamphlet inspired persons discontented with the Church of England to view that area as a haven. The Pilgrims settled there by accident in 1620, and a few hundred others drifted in over the next decade, but not until 1630 did large-scale migration begin. Building communities based on religious ideals, these Puritans would found America's first utopian society.

The Puritan Impulse

Since the 1570s dissatisfied members of the Church of England had demanded that it be "purified" of traces of Roman Catholicism. These Puritans primarily wished to free the members of each congregation (laypersons) and their minister from outside interference by bishops. They also objected to ceremonies and practices inherited from Catholicism such as the Mass, elaborate church decoration, kneeling, and the use of priestly vestments or communion rails—the latter two implying that the clergy were separate from, and superior to, their congregations. Puritan ministers encouraged laypersons' participation in parish affairs and held simplified prayer meetings whose chief feature was a learned sermon.

Puritans differed among themselves about how to institute a reformed church. Non-Separatist Puritans upheld a state church, but one in which congregations were self-governing; they essentially attempted to reform the Church of England from within. Separatists, in contrast, rejected the concept of a state church and worshiped illegally outside the Church of England. Aside from the Separatists of Plymouth and Rhode Island, American Puritans were usually non-Separatists.

Insisting that it was not sufficient for a person to lead an outwardly moral life, Puritans argued that Christians must forge a commitment to serve God through a special act of spiritual rebirth (termed the *conversion experience, redemption,* or *sanctification*). At this moment of being "born again," a soul confronted the horrifying truth of its own unworthiness, sensed the majesty of God's righteousness, and felt the transcending power of divine love as God's saving grace made it worthy of entering heaven. Sanctification then cemented the individual to God as a "saint," or member of the "elect," who—though guaranteed eternal life in heaven—must still resist human sinfulness.

The conversion experience rarely came until an individual had deeply probed all personal weaknesses, learned to accept self-denial, and undergone repeated cycles of self-examination and repentance. For all but a few Puritans, this process, known as preparation for salvation, spanned several agonizing years spent in self-doubt and fear of losing one's soul, during which an individual struggled to gain self-mastery. Many saints who left accounts of their conversion experiences remembered a harrowing, exhausting sensation of relief and described themselves as having been "left smoking" or "bruised" by the powerful rush of God's grace.

For many Puritans, the conversion process was understandably a torturous process. Poverty, loneliness, and fear so pervaded England that even the middle classes could not avoid feeling anxious over the future. Chronic unemployment and low wages constantly tempted the hard-pressed to become petty cheats. Even honest individuals had difficulty showing charity, since they also found life insecure. In a nation of rampant unemployment, many persons unable to make a decent living had to fight with despair, the impulse to desert their families, and the urge to drink. Because the faltering economy forced half of all men and women to delay marriage until after age twenty-five, young adults had to battle sexual temptation through much of their lives. In such desperate times, it was natural for many to doubt that they could set the example expected of saints.

In preparing for spiritual rebirth, Puritans fought to gain mastery over their own wills, to internalize a highly idealistic code of ethics, and to forge the inner strength to live by an uncompromising moral standard. By the time of his or her redemption, a Puritan had undergone a radical personality transformation that replaced doubt with certainty. It was this reorientation of character that produced the Puritans' strong sense of purpose, willingness to sacrifice, and ironclad discipline. The conversion experience molded individuals like the Puritan military and political leader Oliver Cromwell, who felt confident that he could conquer any enemy because he had already conquered himself.

By bending their wills to a higher purpose while preparing for salvation, a generation of English men and women unknowingly steeled themselves to tame a hostile frontier. Temporarily blocked from reforming England, they attempted to build a righteous society in a distant land with rocky soil, a short growing season, and few natural resources.

Ultimately they had just two advantages in conquering this wilderness: a holy violence burning within and a stubborn refusal to accept defeat.

Errand into the Wilderness

By 1600 Puritans held considerable influence in the Church of England and enjoyed significant support from both commoners and gentry. Thereafter, as the political environment grew threatening and the economy worsened in England, many Puritans took interest in colonizing New England.

James I (ruled 1603–1625), the founder of England's Stuart dynasty, bitterly opposed Puritan efforts to eliminate the office of bishop. The monarchy's right to name bishops greatly strengthened its power because bishops composed about a quarter of the House of Lords, the upper chamber of Parliament, which at the time had a strong voice in enacting laws. Bishops also controlled the clergy and thus could silence ministers whose sermons or writings criticized government policies. James made it clear that he saw Puritan attacks on bishops as a direct threat to himself when he snapped, "No bishop, no king."

After Charles I became king in 1625, Anglican authorities undertook a systematic campaign to eliminate Puritan influence within the church. With the king's backing, bishops insisted that services be conducted according to the Book of Common Prayer, which prescribed rituals similar to Catholic practices, and they dismissed Puritan ministers who refused to perform these "High Church" rites. Church courts, which judged cases involving religious law, harassed the Puritan laity with fines or excommunication.

Besides persecution, economic distress also drove Puritans into exile. Between 1550 and 1650, wages fell by half. Bad harvests and depressions plagued England. A 30 percent rise in population from 1590 to 1640 spawned massive unemployment. When economic crisis and the outbreak of the Thirty Years' War on the European continent prevented Germany from importing large amounts of English cloth after 1618, a deep recession gripped England's weaving industry, taking a severe toll on the heavily Puritan southeastern counties. In 1629 the Puritan John Winthrop surveyed his home county of Suffolk, recently a busy center of cloth

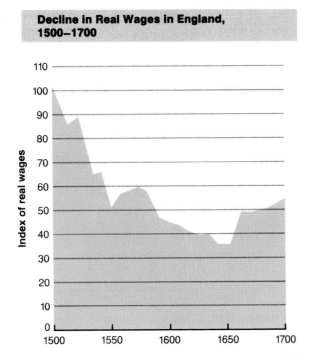

Decline in Real Wages in England, 1500–1700

This index of real wages, which measures the drop in purchasing power due to inflation and declining wages, indicates that as the Great Migration began around 1630, living standards for English workers had suffered a steady reduction of about 60 percent since the base year, 1500.

SOURCE: E. H. Phelps Brown and S. V. Hopkins, "Builders' Wage-Rates, Prices and Population: Some Further Evidence," *Economica*, XXVI (1959), 18–38; adapted from D. C. North and R. P. Thomas, *The Rise of the Western World: A New Economic History* (Cambridge, England: Cambridge University Press, 1973), 111.

of eleven ships and seven hundred passengers under John Winthrop, who would serve as a governor of Massachusetts Bay almost continuously until 1649. In midvoyage the governor delivered a lay sermon titled "A Model of Christian Charity," describing the colony as a utopian alternative to old England.

Winthrop boldly announced that "we shall be as a city upon a hill, the eyes of all people are upon us." The settlers would build a godly community whose compelling example would shame England into repenting. The English government would then truly reform the church, and a revival of piety would create a nation of saints.

Winthrop denounced the self-destructive economic jealousy that bred class hatred. God intended that "in all times some must be rich and some poor," the governor explained, in order that the saints could display virtue appropriate to their station in life. The rich had an obligation to show charity and mercy; those less wealthy should live out their faith in God's will by demonstrating patience and

production, and cried out in anguish, "Why meet we so many wandering ghosts in the shape of men, so many spectacles of misery in our streets?"

In 1628 several Puritan merchants bought the claims of the Virginia Company of Plymouth, England, to land north of Plymouth colony between the Charles and Merrimack rivers. This group obtained a royal charter in 1629 to settle and govern the area.

A City upon a Hill

Four hundred Puritans arrived at Salem, Massachusetts, later in 1629 to prepare the way for others. Then in 1630 the company sent out its "great fleet"

John Winthrop

During the passage to America, Winthrop urged his shipmates to build a society about which "men shall say of succeeding plantations: 'The Lord make it like that of New England.'"

fortitude. God expected the state's rulers to keep the greedy among the rich from exploiting the needy and to prevent the lazy among the poor from burdening their fellow citizens.

In outlining a divine plan in which all persons, rich and poor, depended on one another, Winthrop's sermon expressed a conservative European's understanding of traditional social reciprocity (see Chapter 1) and voiced the Puritans' deep dismay with the economic forces battering—and changing—English society. England had long since ceased to be a country of self-sufficient farm families living for generations in tight-knit communities. In most villages a handful of gentry landlords owned half the cultivated acreage; a small class of farmers known as yeomen—perhaps 20 percent of the rural population—held the rest; and about 30 percent of families achieved a decent standard of living by renting farms from the gentry or pursuing a craft. At the bottom of the social hierarchy, half or more of all English were landless laborers, servants, weavers, or spinners who had few possessions, raised little or none of their own food, and enjoyed no secure employment.

Winthrop's sermon implicitly criticized the breakdown of English society. Ever-growing numbers of desperate people tramped the road seeking work. Community ties frayed as villages experienced a turnover in population as high as 50 percent each decade. Family life deteriorated as household members scattered to find work. Perhaps a quarter of all children were hired out as servants to reside with strangers or were apprenticed to live with craftsmen willing to teach a trade that might save them from poverty.

The majority of England's people had no choice but to forsake their homes and compete fiercely for jobs. This floating population became increasingly individualistic, acquisitive, and materialistic. A new aggressiveness took root among vast numbers of brutalized people trapped in a market economy subject to frequent recessions.

Winthrop blamed this competitive spirit for fostering apathy toward human suffering. "What means then the bleating of so many oppressed with wrong," he had asked just before leaving England, "our shops full of rich wares, and under our stalls lye our own flesh in nakedness." Winthrop wanted charity to moderate the drive for profit, so that goods would be exchanged, wages set, and interest calculated in a manner that would allow a decent life for all. He expected the rich to serve God with their money, giving generously in time of need, and the less fortunate to sacrifice their time to serve in church, government, or the military.

Winthrop's shipboard sermon exemplified the main difference between New England's settlement and British colonization elsewhere. Other Englishmen in the New World would display the same acquisitive impulses transforming England, in particular by harshly exploiting labor. But the Puritans, while hoping for prosperity, believed that there were limits to legitimate commercial behavior. Puritans thought that moral self-restraint—or if need be, the government—should prevent merchants from taking advantage of shortages to squeeze out "excessive" profits. Above all, they hoped to turn religious idealism into a renewed sense of community. "It is a great thing," wrote an early New Englander, "to be a foundation stone in such a spiritual building." Massachusetts Bay would not be an extension of England but a reaction to it.

The Way of the Saints

Winthrop and the great fleet arrived in June 1630 at Boston harbor, and by fall six towns had sprung up in the city's modern limits. During the unusually severe first winter, 30 percent of Winthrop's party died, and an additional 10 percent went home in the spring. By mid-1631, however, thirteen hundred new settlers had landed, and more were on the way. The worst was over. The colony would never suffer another starving time. In contrast to early Virginia, Massachusetts Bay attracted disciplined, motivated men and women who established the colony on a firm basis within a year.

As non-Separatists, Massachusetts Puritans considered themselves spiritual members of the Church of England, but they created a system of church governance called congregationalism that completely ignored the authority of Anglican bishops. More than any other person, the Reverend John Cotton shaped American congregationalism. Called by some a walking library, this clergyman's prestige was so great that according to a fellow minister, Massachusetts settlers "could hardly believe that God would suffer Mr. Cotton to err."

Cotton's plan for governing the New England church placed control of each congregation squarely

Two Sketches of an Early Plymouth Meetinghouse *(left);* **Interior of the "Old Ship Church," Hingham, Massachusetts** *(right)*

One early New Englander boasted that his community's meetinghouse had been erected "by our own vote, framed by our own hammers and saws, and by our own hands set in the convenientest place for us all." Hingham's First Parish Meeting House (1681, right) was built by ship carpenters. They simply constructed a ship's keel in reverse for the interior roof.

in the hands of the male saints. By majority vote these men chose their minister, elected a board of "elders" to handle finances, decided who else deserved recognition as saints, and otherwise ran the church. In contrast, in a typical English parish, a powerful gentry family would select a new pastor (subject to a bishop's formal approval), and all other important decisions would be made by the parish council, or vestry, which was virtually always composed of wealthy landlords rather than ordinary church members. New England thus allowed for much more democratic control of the church than did Anglicanism.

Congregationalism fused separating and non-separating Puritanism. Congregational churches followed the Separatist tradition by allowing only

saints to take communion and baptize their children, but as in non-Separatist practice, they obliged all adults (except a few scandalously wicked individuals) to attend services and pay set rates (or tithes) for their support. New England thus had a state-sponsored, or "established," church, whose relationship to civil government was symbolized by the fact that a single building—called a meetinghouse rather than a church—was used for both religious services and town business.

This "New England Way" also diverged from English practices by setting higher standards for identifying the elect. English Puritans usually accepted as saints those who could correctly profess the faith, had repented their sins, and lived free of scandal. Massachusetts Puritans, however, insisted that candidates for membership undergo a soul-baring examination before the congregation and describe their spiritual life and conversion experience—a procedure called the conversion relation.

English Puritans strongly criticized the conversion relation as an unnecessary barrier to membership that would intimidate humble saints who felt awkward about having neighbors vote on their state of grace. Many early Puritans shared the reluctance of Jonathan Fairbanks, who refused to give a public profession of grace before the church in Dedham, Massachusetts, for several years, until the faithful persuaded him with many "loving conferences." One Dublin, New Hampshire, woman who was denied membership after being overcome by nervousness started sobbing uncontrollably and cried out, "*Christ* hath called me, and bid me *come* . . . and shall I now be put by?" Ashamed and somewhat misty-eyed themselves, the congregation relented, but the episode perfectly showed the conversion relation's potential for causing embarrassment and pain. The conversion relation would emerge as the New England Way's most vulnerable point and a major cause of its eventual demise.

New Englanders, like most European Protestants, could scarcely imagine conversion without literacy. Fathers drilled their children in the catechism, a simple question-and-answer summary of religious beliefs. Young people read the Bible to feel the quickening of God's grace, and saints often recorded their lapses and spiritual insights in diaries. In 1642 Massachusetts Bay colony, concerned about parental laxness, ordered households to conduct regular catechism sessions. Evidently this did not suffice, because in 1647 the colony passed its famous Old Deluder Act. The law ordered every town of fifty or more households to appoint one father to whom all children could come for instruction, and every town of at least one hundred households to maintain a grammar school and a teacher capable of preparing students for university-level instruction. The law's name derived from its declaration that "one chief project of that old deluder, Satan, [is] to keep men from knowledge of the Scriptures" by encouraging ignorance. By 1671 most other Puritan colonies enacted similar legislation, which represented New England's first step toward public education even though none of these laws

required school attendance, and though boys were more likely to be taught reading and writing than were girls. In any case, the family remained New England's chief bastion against ignorance, as Boston's First Church recognized in 1669 when it ordered the congregation's elders to visit all households "and see how they are instructed in the grounds [elements] of religion."

But however diligent laypeople might be in reading the Bible and indoctrinating their children, clergymen had responsibility for leading saints to repentance and stimulating piety. The minister's role was to stir his parishioners' faith with direct, logical, and moving sermons understandable by average listeners, not just by a well-educated elite. The Puritans' preference for this "plain style" of preaching did not blind them to the need for a highly educated clergy. To produce learned ministers, Massachusetts chartered Harvard College in 1636.

Harvard not only trained ministers but also offered instruction in the arts and sciences. Freshmen entered Harvard as young teen-agers after demonstrating an ability to write and speak Latin and a knowledge of Greek grammar. Harvard

Harvard College

An eighteenth-century woman depicted the college—an institution that excluded her gender—in needlework.

offered a single curriculum emphasizing classical languages, logic, philosophy, and divinity. All students left their tiny four-by-six-foot rooms at 4:30 A.M. for a breakfast of bread and beer. After prayers at 5:00 A.M., students went to study hall prior to lectures, all given in Latin, from 8:00 to 11:00 A.M. Then came the main meal, washed down with more beer and eaten indoors with everyone wearing hats. After a recreation hour, tutors quizzed underclassmen on the morning lecture as upperclassmen gave Latin speeches before the president. At 4:00 P.M. all students broke for additional beer and bread before attending prayers at 5:00 P.M., after which came a study hour, a light supper, another recreation hour, and finally bed at 9:00 P.M.

Harvard's insistence on high standards led Oxford University in England to recognize Harvard degrees as equivalent to its own by 1648. From 1642 to 1671, the college produced 201 graduates, including 111 ministers. Harvard's alumni made New England the only part of England's overseas empire to possess a college-educated elite during the seventeenth century, and they ensured that the New England Way would not falter for lack of properly trained clergy.

Dissent and Expansion

Some Puritans dissented from Winthrop's vision of the city upon a hill. The first to challenge the New England Way was Roger Williams, who arrived in America in 1631. Williams was one of those rare individuals who stir controversy without making personal enemies. Radiating the joy of serving God, he quickly became one of the most respected and popular figures in Massachusetts. But Williams questioned the legal basis of congregationalism. Once he began to insist that church and state be entirely separate, the Massachusetts Bay government moved to silence him.

Puritans agreed that the church must be free of state control, and they opposed theocracy (government run by clergy). However, they believed that a holy commonwealth required cooperation between church and state. Williams took a different stance, arguing that civil government should remain absolutely uninvolved with religious matters, whether blasphemy (cursing God), failure to pay tithes, refusal to attend worship, or swearing oaths on the Bible in court. He derived this posi-

tion from the sixteenth-century Anabaptist tradition (see Chapter 1), which held that the elect must limit their association with society's sinners to protect God's church from contamination. Williams opposed any kind of compulsory church service or interference with private religious beliefs, not because he felt that all religions deserved equal respect (for he did not) but because he feared that the state would eventually corrupt the saints.

Believing that the very purpose of founding Massachusetts Bay was to protect true religion and prevent heresy, the political authorities declared Williams's opinions subversive and banished him in 1635. At his friend Winthrop's suggestion, he went south with four companions to a place that he called Providence, which he purchased from the Indians. At Williams's invitation, a steady stream of malcontents drifted to the group of settlements near Providence on Narragansett Bay, which eventually joined to form Rhode Island colony. (Orthodox Puritans scorned the place as "Rogues Island.") In 1644 Williams obtained permission from England to establish a legal government. True to Williams's ideals, Rhode Island was the only New England colony to practice religious toleration. Growing slowly, the colony's four towns had eight hundred settlers by 1650.

A second challenge to the New England Way came from Anne Hutchinson, whom Winthrop described as "a woman of haughty and fierce carriage, of a nimble wit and active spirit." The controversy surrounding Hutchinson was especially ironic since her ideas derived from the much-respected John Cotton's theology. Cotton insisted that true congregationalism required the saints to be entirely free of religious or political control by anyone who had not undergone a conversion experience. His refusal to give any authority or power over religion to the nonelect applied even to persons who led upright, blameless lives—at least until they had been reborn spiritually.

Anne Hutchinson extended Cotton's main point—that the saints must be free from interference by the nonelect—into a broad attack on clerical authority. Dissatisfied with the dull minister of her church, she began implying that he was not among the elect, and then asserted that the saints in his congregation might ignore his views if they believed that he lacked saving grace. She eventually alleged that all the colony's ministers except John

Cotton and her brother-in-law John Wheelwright had not been born again and so lacked authority over those, like herself, who were already saved.

By casting doubt on the clergy's spiritual state and denying the right of unsaved ministers to judge the saints, Hutchinson undermined the clergy's moral authority to interpret and teach Scripture. Critics charged that her beliefs would delude individuals into imagining that they were accountable to no one but themselves. Her followers consequently were called Antinomians, meaning those opposed to the rule of law. Hutchinson bore the additional liability of being a woman challenging traditional male roles in the church and state. The authorities would have prosecuted Hutchinson had she been a man, of course, but her gender made her seem an especially dangerous foe.

By 1636 Massachusetts Bay split into two camps. Hutchinson's supporters included merchants (like her husband) who disliked the government's economic restrictions on their business; young men chafing against the rigid control of church elders; and most women, protesting their exclusion from voting in church affairs. In 1636 the Antinomians were strong enough to have their candidate elected governor, but they suffered defeat with Winthrop's return to office in 1637.

The victorious Winthrop brought Hutchinson to trial for heresy before the Massachusetts Bay legislature (the General Court). While John Cotton watched nervously, the legislators peppered her with questions. Hutchinson's knowledge of Scripture was so superior to that of her interrogators, however, that she would have been acquitted had she not claimed to have communicated directly with the Holy Spirit. Like virtually all Christians, orthodox Puritans believed that God had ceased to make known matters of faith by personal revelation since New Testament times. Thus Hutchinson's own words were sufficient to condemn her.

The General Court banished Hutchinson to Rhode Island. She later moved to New Netherland, where in 1643 she was killed by Indians. John Wheelwright led another exodus of Antinomians to Exeter, New Hampshire. Antinomianism's failure ended the last challenge capable of splitting congregationalism and ensured the New England Way's survival for two generations.

A less dramatic disagreement over the New England Way helped push yet a third wave of Puri-

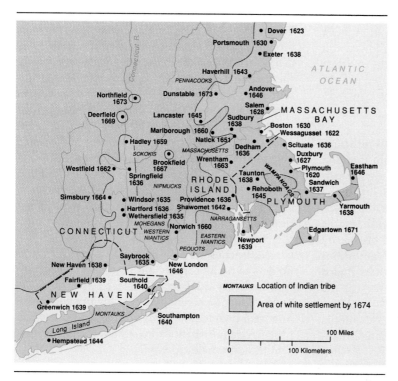

Colonizing New England, 1620–1674

Puritan expansion reached its maximum extent just before King Philip's War (see p. 59), which erupted largely as a result of the pressure of encroaching white settlement on the Wampanoags. New England's frontier did not expand beyond the area reached in 1674 until after 1715.

SOURCE: Frederick Merk, *History of the Westward Movement.* Copyright © 1979 by Lois Bannister Merk. Reprinted by permission of Alfred A. Knopf, Inc.

tans outside Massachusetts. Congregations at Dorchester and Newtown (present-day Cambridge) rejected the rigorous standards advocated by John Cotton for identifying the elect. Newtown's minister, Thomas Hooker, in particular took a more liberal attitude than Cotton toward admitting church members. Both groups asked the General Court's permission to relocate in the lower Connecticut River Valley, where unauthorized settlements had appeared at Windsor (1633) and Wethersfield (1634).

The General Court approved the settlers' plans, provided they would remain subject to Massachusetts authority for at least a year. In 1635 the Dorchester congregation went to Windsor. In 1636 Hooker and his congregation walked 120 miles to Hartford. Hooker's influence helped moderate Puritanism in Connecticut by establishing standards for church membership less strict than those in Massachusetts.

In 1639 Hartford, Windsor, and Wethersfield adopted a government, designed by Thomas Hooker, called the Fundamental Orders of Connecticut. Hooker modeled his government after that of Massachusetts Bay. Voting and officeholding were opened to all adult male landowners.

The southeastern third of modern-day Connecticut remained outside this agreement. Under John Davenport, a minister who felt that both Massachusetts Bay and Connecticut allowed too much moral laxness, this region set the strictest standards for verifying sainthood and based its laws most closely upon Old Testament examples. In 1643 the eight towns of this area united as the colony of New Haven.

The most fundamental threat to Winthrop's city upon a hill was that the people would abandon the ideal of a close-knit community to pursue self-interest. Although most Puritans welcomed the chance to found villages dedicated to stability, self-discipline, and a sense of mutual obligation, a large minority had come to America to find prosperity and social mobility. The most visibly ambitious colonists were merchants, whose activities fueled New England's economy but whose way of life challenged its ideals.

Merchants fit uneasily into a religious utopia that idealized social reciprocity and equated financial shrewdness with greed. They also clashed repeatedly with government leaders, who were trying to regulate prices so that consumers would

not suffer from the chronic shortage of manufactured goods that afflicted New England.

In 1635, when the Massachusetts General Court forbade the sale of any item above 5 percent of its cost, Robert Keayne of Boston and other merchants objected. These men argued that they had to sell some goods at higher rates in order to offset losses from other sales, shipwrecked cargoes, and inflation. In 1639, after selling nails at 25 percent to 33 percent above cost—hardly profiteering—Keayne was fined heavily in court and forced to make a humiliating apology before his congregation.

Though a pious Puritan whose annual profits averaged just 5 percent, Keayne symbolized the dangerous possibility that a headlong rush for profits would lead New Englanders to forget that they were their brothers' keepers. "Worldly gain was not the end design of the people of *New-England*," warned the Reverend John Higginson, "but *Religion*." Controversies like the one involving Keayne were part of a struggle for New England's soul. At stake was the Puritans' ability to insulate their city upon a hill from a market economy that would strangle the spirit of community within a harsh new world of frantic competition.

Power to the Saints

To preserve the New England Way, the Puritans evolved political and religious institutions far more democratic than those in the mother country. Unlike the Virginia Company of London, the Massachusetts Bay Company established its headquarters in America and gave the right of electing the governor and his executive council to all male saints. In 1634, after public protest that the governor and council held too much power, each town gained the option of sending two delegates to the General Court. In 1644 the General Court became a bicameral (two-chamber) lawmaking body when the towns' deputies separated from the Governor's Council to form the House of Representatives.

Massachusetts did not require voters or officeholders to own property but bestowed full citizenship on every adult male accepted as a saint. By 1641 about 55 percent of the colony's twenty-three hundred men could vote. By contrast, English property requirements allowed fewer than 30 percent of adult males to vote.

Old England's basic unit of local government was the county court. Its members, the justices of the peace, not only decided legal cases as judges but also performed such administrative tasks as supervising road repairs, maintaining public buildings, and assessing taxes for official expenses. Gaining office by royal appointment rather than election, the justices were always members of the gentry selected because of their wealth and political connections. But an ocean away, New England's county courts primarily functioned as courts of law, and the vital unit of local administration was the town meeting. Town meetings decentralized authority over political and economic decisions to a degree unknown in either Great Britain or its other overseas colonies.

New England legislatures established a town by awarding a grant of land to several dozen heads of families. These individuals enjoyed almost unlimited freedom to lay out the settlement, organize its church, distribute land among themselves, set local tax rates, and make local laws. Each town determined its own qualifications for voting and holding office in the town meeting, although custom dictated that all male taxpayers (including nonsaints) be allowed to participate. The meeting could exclude anyone from settling in town, or it could grant the right of sharing in any future land distributions to newcomers, whose children would inherit this privilege.

Community Life

The local economy and environment left their stamp on New England towns. Of these communities the seaports often seemed least tight-knit because of their transient population, while towns in Plymouth colony tended to be little more than a few stores, a mill, and a meetinghouse serving farmers dwelling over a wide distance. Nevertheless, towns in Massachusetts, Connecticut, and what would become New Hampshire (part of Massachusetts until 1679) were broadly uniform, since most were farm communities resembling traditional English villages.

The founders usually granted each family a one-acre house lot (just enough for a vegetable garden) within a half-mile of the meetinghouse. The town meeting also gave each household strips of land or small fields farther out for its crops and livestock. Often an individual owned several parcels of land in different locations and had the

The Whipple House

This Ipswich, Massachusetts, home, part of which dates to c. 1640, is thought to be one of the oldest Anglo-American dwellings extant.

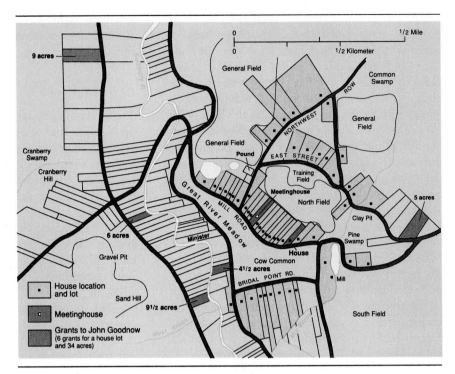

Land Divisions in Sudbury, Massachusetts, 1639–1656

Like other first-generation townsmen, John Goodnow lived on a small house lot near the meetinghouse. He pastured his livestock on "common" fields owned by the town and grew crops on thirty-four acres in five separate locations at a distance from his house.

SOURCE: Sumner Chilton Powell, *Puritan Village: The Formation of a New England Town* (Middletown, Conn.: Wesleyan University Press, 1963). Reprinted by permission.

right to graze a few extra animals on the town "commons."

Few aspects of early New England life are more revealing than the first generation's attempt in many, but not all, towns to keep settlement tightly clustered by granting families no more land than they needed to support themselves. Dedham's forty-six founders, for example, received 128,000 acres from Massachusetts Bay in 1636 yet gave themselves just 3,000 acres by 1656, or about 65 acres per family.

By separating a family's home from its farm acreage and forcing all residents to live within a mile of one another, town founders created a physical setting conducive to traditional reciprocity. In England, meanwhile, this mode of land division was coming to seem inefficient as farmers tried to produce a greater surplus for sale by consolidating their landholdings. By 1600 English agriculturalists preferred to live on scattered farms away from village centers, even though dispersion increased the difficulty of maintaining neighborly ties. New England's generally compact system of settlement forced people to interact with each other and also established an atmosphere of mutual watchfulness that promoted godly order.

Puritan Families

To the Puritans, society's foundation rested not upon the individual but upon the "little commonwealth"—the nuclear family. "*Well ordered families,*" declared minister Cotton Mather in 1699, "naturally produce a *Good Order* in other *Societies.*" In a proper Puritan family, the wife, children, and servants dutifully obeyed the husband. According to John Winthrop, a "true wife" thought of herself "in subjection to her husband's authority."

New Englanders defined matrimony as a contract subject to state regulation rather than a religious sacrament and so were married by justices of the peace instead of ministers. As a civil institution, a marriage could be dissolved by the courts in cases of desertion, bigamy, adultery, or physical cruelty. By permitting divorce, Puritans diverged radically from practices in England, where Anglican authorities rarely annulled marriages and civil divorces required a special act of Parliament. Still, New Englanders saw divorce as a remedy fit only for extremely wronged spouses, such as the Plymouth woman who discovered that her husband was simultaneously married to women in Boston, Barbados, and England. Massachusetts courts allowed just twenty-seven divorces from 1639 to 1692.

Because Puritans believed that healthy families were crucial to the community's welfare, they intervened whenever they discovered truly serious problems in a household. The courts disciplined unruly youngsters, disobedient servants, disrespectful wives, and violent or irresponsible husbands whose behavior seemed dangerous or unusually disruptive to a family. Churches also censured, and sometimes expelled, spouses who did not maintain domestic tranquillity. Negligent parents, one minister declared, "not only wrong each other, but they provoke God by breaking his law."

Although New England wives enjoyed significant legal protections against spousal violence and nonsupport and also had more freedom than their English counterparts to escape a failed marriage, they suffered the same legal disabilities borne by all Englishwomen. English common law allowed a wife no property rights independently of her husband unless he consented to a special prenuptial agreement giving her control over any property that she already owned. Only if a husband had no other heirs or wrote a will awarding his widow full control over their possessions could she claim rights over household property, although the law reserved lifetime use of a third of the estate for her support.

The structure and stability of New England families differed fundamentally from English households. In Great Britain infectious diseases combined with poor nutrition to produce steep levels of early death among adults, as well as high infant mortality. The typical male who reached age 18 could expect to die at about 53, while 18-year-old females on average faced an even shorter life span, to about 45, because so many pregnancies ended in death. English people married relatively late in the early seventeenth century, so that a typical family had just five children, of whom three would reach adulthood. Because perhaps one in six adults never married, this survival rate produced relatively modest population increases. So short was the span of life that, considering the late age of marriage, perhaps half of all English parents did not live long enough to see their first grandchild born. Most women who married in Manchester, England, in the 1650s, for example, were already orphans upon becoming brides.

In contrast, New England benefited from a remarkably benign disease environment. Although

Death in Seventeenth-Century New England

In the early years of settlement, the grave of the deceased was typically located on family land and marked by a plain stone. As the century unfolded, however, cemeteries increasingly sprang up near the meetinghouse, and intricately carved stones adorned the graves.

settlements were compact, minimal travel occurred between towns, especially in winter, when people were most susceptible to infection. Furthermore, easy access to land allowed families an adequate diet, which improved resistance to disease and lowered death rates associated with childbirth.

Consequently, New Englanders lived long and raised large families. Life expectancy for men reached 65, and women lived nearly that long. More than 80 percent of all infants survived long enough to get married. The 58 men and women who founded Andover, Massachusetts, for example, had 247 children; and by the fourth generation, the families of their descendants numbered 2,000 persons (including spouses who married in from other families). Despite the relatively small size and short duration of the Puritan exodus to New England (just 20,000 immigrants landed from 1630 to 1642, after which few newcomers arrived), the fact that about 70 percent of all settlers came as members of family groups soon resulted in a population evenly divided between males and females. This balance permitted rapid population growth without heavy immigration.

Its extraordinary rate of population growth enabled New England to become the only part of England's overseas empire that did not import large

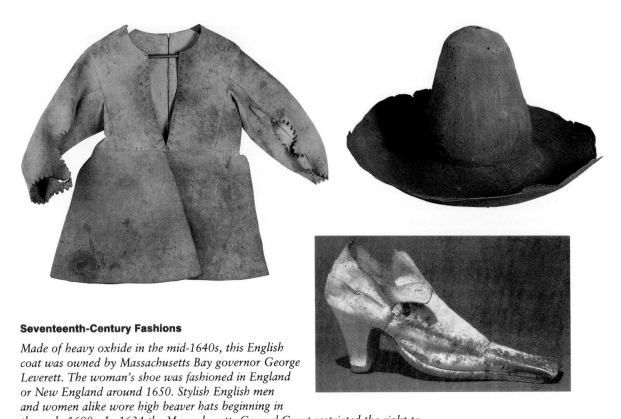

Seventeenth-Century Fashions

Made of heavy oxhide in the mid-1640s, this English coat was owned by Massachusetts Bay governor George Leverett. The woman's shoe was fashioned in England or New England around 1650. Stylish English men and women alike wore high beaver hats beginning in the early 1600s. In 1634 the Massachusetts General Court restricted the right to wear them to persons holding property valued at two hundred pounds or more.

numbers of indentured servants or slaves. Labor was in especially short supply in the first decades of settlement, when the colonists had to build towns and clear fields from dense forest. The first generation brought its labor with it, in the form of its own children.

Lacking any legal right to share in town land divisions until they became their fathers' heirs, the founding generation's children depended on their parents to provide them with acreage for a farm. Parents encouraged children, especially sons, to delay marriage and work for them in return for a bequest of land at a later date. Young males often stayed at home to till their fathers' fields until their late twenties, when they finally received their own land. Because the average family raised three or four boys to adulthood, parents could depend on thirty to forty years of work if their sons delayed marriage until about age twenty-six.

Families with more sons and daughters enjoyed a labor surplus that allowed them to send their children to work as apprentices or hired hands for others. However, this system of family labor was inefficient, for two reasons. First, the available supply of labor could not expand in times of great demand. Second, parents were reluctant to force their own children to work as hard as strangers. Nevertheless, family labor was the only system that New Englanders could afford.

Saddled with the triple burdens of a short growing season, rocky soil salted with gravel, and an inefficient system of land distribution that forced farmers to cultivate widely scattered strips, the colonists managed to feed large families and keep ahead of their debts, but few became wealthy from farming. Seeking greater fortunes than agriculture offered, seventeenth-century New Englanders soon turned lumbering, fishing, and rum distilling into major industries employing perhaps a fifth of all adults full-time and offering seasonal work to many farmers. As its economy became more diversified, New England prospered. But in the process, its inhabitants grew more worldly, only to discover that fewer and fewer of their children were emerging as saints.

The End of the Puritan Errand

As New Englanders struggled to make a living and curb dissent, old England fell into chaos. Charles I's efforts to impose taxes without Parliament's consent sparked a civil war in 1642. Alienated by years of religious harassment, Puritans gained control of the revolt, beheaded Charles in 1649, and eventually replaced the king with "Lord High Protector" Oliver Cromwell. Shortly after Cromwell's death, a provisional English government recalled the Stuarts and in 1660 crowned Charles II king.

The Stuart restoration doomed Puritanism in England. High Church Anglicans ruthlessly expelled Puritan ministers from their parishes and passed harsh laws forbidding Separatists from establishing churches and schools. One English saint summed up Puritan disillusionment: "God has spit in our face." The Restoration also left American Puritans without a mission. A generation of New England ministers had inspired their congregations to hope that their example would shame England into establishing a truly reformed church. However, having conquered a wilderness and built their city upon a hill, New Englanders discovered after 1660 that the eyes of the world were no longer fixed on them.

Simultaneously with the demise of English Puritanism, an internal crisis gripped the New England Way. The turmoil stemmed from the failure of the founding generation's children to declare themselves saints and accept full church membership. By 1650, for example, fewer than half the adults in John Winthrop's congregation were saints. The first generation believed that they had accepted a holy contract, or covenant, with God, which obliged them to establish a scripturally ordained church and charge their descendants with its preservation. In return for upholding this New England Way, God would make the city upon a hill prosper and shield it from corruption.

By 1650, however, relatively few second-generation Puritans had been willing to join the elect by making the required conversion relation before their congregation. One reason certainly was the second generation's understandable reluctance to subject themselves to a grilling before relatives and friends. All children who matured in Puritan towns must have witnessed at least one person suffer an ordeal like that of Sarah Fiske. For more than a year, Fiske answered petty charges of speaking uncharitably about her relatives—especially her husband, Phineas—and then was admitted to the Wenham, Massachusetts, church only after publicly denouncing herself as worse "than any toad."

Through its passivity, the second generation expressed its preference for a more inclusive religious community, organized on traditional English practices for admitting saints to Puritan congregations. In England non-Separatist ministers had routinely certified adults as members worthy of taking communion upon hearing a private conversion relation, and they baptized *all* children. The second generation in America also rejected the public conversion-relation ritual as an unnecessary source of division and bitterness that undermined Christian fellowship. In this they differed from their parents, who used the conversion relation to affirm godly order by setting the highest standards for moral conduct.

Because Puritan churches baptized only babies born to saints, the second generation's unwillingness to submit to the conversion relation confronted their parents with the prospect that their own grandchildren would remain unbaptized unless standards for church membership were loosened. In 1662 a convention of clergy and laity devised a compromise known as the Half-Way Covenant, which permitted the children of all baptized members, including nonsaints, to receive baptism. This covenant allowed the founders' descendants to transmit church membership to their children, but it left these offspring "halfway" members who could not take communion or vote in church affairs. When forced to choose between a church system founded on a pure membership of the elect and one that embraced the entire community, New Englanders eventually sacrificed purity for community.

The Half-Way Covenant signaled the end of the New England Way. The elect had been unable to bring up a new generation of saints whose religious fervor equaled their own. Most adults chose to remain in "halfway" status for life, and the saints became a shrinking minority as the third and fourth generations matured. Sainthood tended to flow in certain families, and by the 1700s there were more women among the elect than men in most congregations. But since women could not vote in church affairs, religious authority stayed in male hands.

The Eclipse of the Indians

One reason why the Puritans spread so rapidly across New England was the utter devastation of the region's native population well before the English arrived. Microbes introduced by fishermen and other casual visitors killed perhaps 90 percent of New England's coastal Indians between 1616 and 1618, and the earliest Puritan immigrants had faced little opposition from the demoralized native survivors. After declining from 20,000 in 1600 to a mere 750 in 1631, the Massachusett tribe came under attack by Micmacs from eastern Canada and soon emerged as the first native Americans to become a colonized people in their own land. The Massachusett people sought military protection from Winthrop's settlers so eagerly that they sold most of their land by 1636, surrendered their independence in 1644, and agreed to try Christianity and "civilization" by moving to "praying towns" like Natick, a place given them by the General Court. In the praying towns, leaders chosen by the Puritans would teach the native Americans Christianity and English ways.

The expansion of English settlement nevertheless aroused Indian resistance. As Puritans moved into the Connecticut River Valley, friction developed with the Pequots, a populous tribe less affected than others by earlier epidemics and whose name meant "Destroyer" in Algonkian. After an attack on two ships and the killing of several sailors near Pequot territory, an expedition from Puritan Massachusetts marched into Connecticut in 1636 to take revenge on that tribe, although the Indians' guilt in the incident had never been firmly established. An alarmed English farmer at Saybrook, Connecticut, angrily protested to the invaders, "You come hither to raise these wasps about my ears, and then you will take wing and flee away."

After clumsily plundering an Indian village, the Massachusetts troops did return home, leaving Connecticut's 800 settlers to face 3,500 enraged enemies. Pequot raids took about thirty lives through April 1637, by which time the settlers had won allies among the Mohegan and Narragansett Indians. Heeding Thomas Hooker's stern advice "not to do this work of the Lord's revenge slackly," Captain John Mason then waged a ruthless campaign, using tactics similar to those devised by the English to break Irish resistance during the 1570s (see Chapter 1). Mason's troops made no distinction between warriors and civilians—and they took few prisoners. By late 1637 perhaps 800 Pequots were killed, and the Puritans' native American allies were daily carrying heads to Hartford for rewards.

This so-called Pequot War tipped the balance of military power to the English by smashing the Pequots, the region's most feared Indian nation. Opening the way for central New England's swift settlement, the war sped up the tendency for small Indian tribes to become dependent on whites as they found themselves surrounded by white settlement. The English victory in 1637 proved so decisive that New England remained at peace until 1676.

As white settlers moved onto the Indians' traditional lands, Puritan missionaries, believing that Christianity was incompatible with native American culture, widened efforts to convert them. Unlike missionaries from France and Spain, who appealed to the Indians' appreciation of ceremony and related Catholic doctrines to native American beliefs, the Puritans insisted that the converts master a complex theology of salvation completely foreign to Indian thinking. Only after suffering the shock of disease and depopulation, cultural disintegration, economic dependence, and submission to white government did any New England Indians accept Protestantism. From the founding of Natick in 1651 to 1675, John Eliot, New England's foremost missionary, coaxed Indians into a total of fourteen praying towns, which in this way became Anglo-America's first Indian reservations.

The "praying Indians," as the converts were known, worshiped in their own language and listened to Scripture read from Eliot's Algonkian-language *Up-Biblum God,* the first Bible printed in Anglo-America (1663). Cut off from their own culture and bombarded with alien concepts of sinfulness, converted Indians often acquired a highly negative self-image, experiencing confusion, depression, and excessive preoccupation with shame and guilt. Few red Puritans were ever baptized as saints, and only two praying towns established congregations free of outside white control.

By 1675 European diseases had steadily reduced New England's Indian population from 140,000 in 1600 to 10,000, of whom 2,000 lived in praying

John Eliot

Eliot's Algonkian translation of the Bible, Up-Biblum God *(1663), was the first Bible printed in America.*

towns. Meanwhile, the number of English had swollen to 50,000. White-Indian conflict became acute during the 1670s because of pressure imposed on several major tribes, surrounded by white settlers, to accept the legal authority of colonial courts. Tension ran especially high in the Plymouth colony, where the English had engulfed the large Wampanoag tribe and forced a number of humiliating concessions on their leader Metacomet, or "King Philip," the son of Massasoit, the Pilgrims' onetime ally.

In 1675 Plymouth hanged three Wampanoags for killing a Christian Indian and threatened to arrest Philip. A minor incident in which several Wampanoags were shot while burglarizing a farmhouse produced a steady escalation of violence; and Philip soon organized about two-thirds of the native Americans, including perhaps a third of all praying Indians, into a military alliance. "But little remains of my ancestor's domain, I am resolved not to see the day when I have no country," Philip declared as he and his followers ignited the conflict known as King Philip's War.

Philip's forces—unlike the Indian combatants in the Pequot War, few of whom had fought with guns—were as well armed as the whites. The Indians attacked 52 of New England's 90 towns (of which 12 were entirely destroyed), burned 1,200 houses, slaughtered 8,000 head of cattle, and killed 600 colonists.

The tide turned against Philip in 1676. English militiamen and praying Indians destroyed their enemies' food supplies and sold hundreds of captives into slavery, including Philip's wife and child. "It must have been as bitter as death to him," wrote Puritan clergyman Cotton Mather, "to lose his wife and only son, for the Indians are marvellously fond and affectionate toward their children." Perhaps three thousand Indians starved or fell in battle, including Philip himself.

King Philip's War reduced New England's Indian population by almost 40 percent and eliminated native American resistance to white expansion everywhere in the region except Maine and along the Canadian border. It also generated in whites an abiding hatred of all native Americans, even the Christian Indians who fought Philip. In 1677 ten praying towns were disbanded and all Indians restricted to the remaining four; all Indian courts were dismantled; and "guardians" were appointed to supervise the native Americans. Missionary activity largely ceased. "There is a cloud, a dark cloud upon the work of the Gospel among the poor Indians," mourned John Eliot. The surviving Indians became a steadily dwindling underclass of servants and tenants widely afflicted by poverty, debt, and alcoholism.

Economics, Salem, and Satan

In the three decades after the Half-Way Covenant's adoption in 1662, New Englanders endured an endless stream of sermons called jeremiads (after ancient Israel's prophet Jeremiah), in which the clergy berated them for failing to preserve the idealism of the region's founding generation. The ministers complained not about rising sinfulness—for the people remained law-abiding, industrious, and sober—but about their parishioners' increasing tendency to forget, as one minister emphasized in 1663, "that New-England is originally a plantation of Religion, not a plantation of trade." The jeremiads indicted New Englanders for becoming more worldly, more individualistic, and less patient with restrictions on their economic behavior.

By the late seventeenth century, growing opportunities for personal success, born of an expanding economy, were changing New England's character. Although the earliest Puritan settlers had hardly lacked economic ambitions, their overriding need for cooperation and unity while building a society from scratch led them to emphasize collective welfare above individual interest. By 1690, however, the problems facing towns or congregations—far less serious than in the early years—no longer required the same degree of communal effort. New Englanders now turned their energies into producing more goods for export and otherwise profiting from overseas trade or the local market economy.

As New Englanders pursued economic gain more openly, the fabric of community loosened and populations began dispersing away from town centers. Eager to expand their agricultural output, townsmen voted themselves much larger amounts of land after 1660 and insisted that it be located in one place. For example, Dedham, which distributed only three thousand acres from 1636 to 1656, parceled out five times as much in the next dozen years. Rather than continue living close together, farmers built homes on their outlying tracts and thereby sacrificed the close, neighborly ties that previously had arisen from frequent association. This process of "hiving out" often generated friction between townspeople settled near the meetinghouse (who usually dominated politics) and the "outlivers," whose distance from the town center generally limited their influence over local affairs.

Although early New England was hardly a simple society of subsistence farmers, a rough equality had prevailed among its residents, most of whom were small landowners with few luxuries. By the late seventeenth century, however, the region's occupational structure had become very complex, especially in its several port cities, and the distribution of wealth was growing more uneven. These developments undermined the spirit of community by sowing jealousy and creating the anxiety that a small minority might be profiting at the majority's expense. At the same time, New England's rising involvement in international trade led individuals—in both cities and the countryside—to act more competitively, aggressively, and impersonally toward one another. John Winthrop's vision of a religiously oriented community

sustained by a sense of reciprocity and charity was giving way to a world increasingly like the materialistic, acquisitive society that the original immigrants had fled in old England.

Nowhere in New England did these trends have more disturbing effects than in Salem, Massachusetts, which grew rapidly after 1660 to become the region's second-largest port. Trade made Salem prosperous but also destroyed the relatively equal society of humble fishermen and small farmers that had once existed. A sharp distinction emerged between the port's residents—especially its rich merchants—and outlying farmers. Prior to 1661 the richest 10 percent of Salem residents owned 21 percent of the town's property, but by 1681 the richest tenth possessed 62 percent of all wealth.

Salem's farmers lost not only social standing to the merchants but also political power. Before 1665 twice as many farmers as merchants had held the town meeting's highest offices, but thereafter, merchant officeholders outnumbered those who were farmers by six to one. Salem became highly vulnerable to internal conflict between its prosperous merchants and its agricultural folk.

About six miles west of Salem's meetinghouse lay the precinct of Salem Village (now Danvers), an economically stagnant district whose residents resented Salem Town's political domination. The village was divided between supporters of the Porter and Putnam families. Well connected with the merchant elite, the Porters enjoyed political prestige in Salem Town and lived in the village's eastern section, whose residents farmed richer soils and benefited somewhat from Salem Town's prosperity. In contrast, most Putnams lived in Salem Village's less fertile western half, had little chance to share in Salem Town's commercial expansion, and had lost the political influence that they once held in town. The rivalry between Porters and Putnams mirrored the tensions between Salem's urban and rural dwellers.

In late 1691 several Salem Village girls encouraged a West Indian slave woman, Tituba, to tell fortunes and talk about sorcery. When the girls later began behaving strangely, villagers assumed that they were victims of witchcraft. Pressed to identify their tormenters, the girls named an ill-tempered beggar, a bedridden old woman, and Tituba.

So far the incident was not unusual. Until the late seventeenth century, belief in witchcraft was

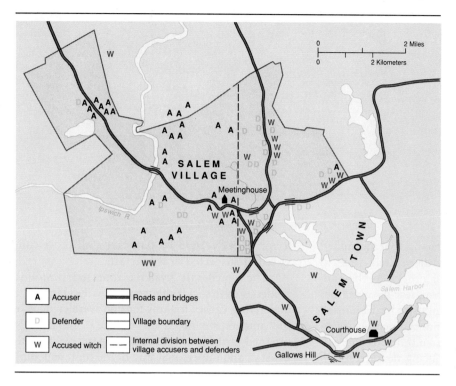

**The Geography
of Witchcraft:
Salem Village, 1692**

*Geographic patterns of
witchcraft testimony mir-
rored tensions within Salem
Village. Accused witches
and their defenders lived
mostly in the village's eastern division or in Salem
Town, while their accusers
overwhelmingly resided in
the village's western sector.*

SOURCE: Adapted from Paul
Boyer and Stephen Nissen-
baum, *Salem Possessed: The
Social Origins of Witchcraft*
(Cambridge, Mass.: Harvard
University Press, 1974).

very strong at all levels of European and American society. Between 1647 and 1691, New England courts tried eighty-one persons as witches, of whom sixteen were hanged. But unlike previous witch-craft episodes, in which officials questioned a few persons of low status in orderly hearings, events at Salem Village produced near panic and ensnared numerous prominent persons.

By April 1692 the girls had denounced two prosperous farm wives long considered saints in the local church, and they had identified the vil-lage's former minister as a wizard (male witch). In the judges' minds, fear of witchcraft overrode any doubts about the girls' credibility and led them to sweep aside normal procedural safeguards. Specif-ically the judges ignored the law's ban on "spectral evidence"—testimony that a spirit resembling the accused had been seen tormenting a victim. With the blessing of the village minister, himself a failed merchant, accusations multiplied until the jails overflowed with victims, including one suspect's four-year-old daughter, who would spend nine months in heavy chains.

The pattern of hysteria in Salem Village reflected that community's internal divisions. Most charges

came from the village's troubled western division, especially from Putnam family members, who lodged 46 of the 141 formal indictments. With two exceptions, those named as witches lived outside the village's western half; they primarily included persons connected economically or by marriage to the Porters—though no Porters were themselves named as witches—and several members of wealthy Salem Town families.

Anxieties concerning gender and age also influenced who became victims. Two-thirds of all accusers were girls aged between eleven and twenty, products of a society that had little sympathy for the emotional complexity of adolescence and that expected children to act like adults well before they possessed the self-control to do so. Those most fre-quently named as witches were middle-aged wives or widows, the very persons who most closely resembled an adolescent girl's mother. To a large extent, a group of immature girls were displacing resentment felt toward their mothers (who had the primary responsibility for bringing up daughters) onto other women whose families were viewed by the girls' parents or neighbors with jealousy or hostility.

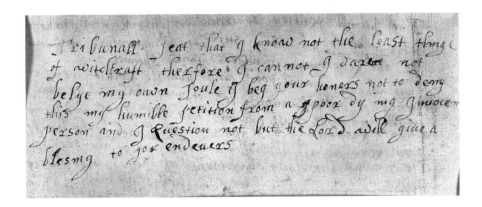

Petition of Mary Easty, 1690

In her petition Easty swore that "I know not the least thing of witchcraft."

The number of persons facing trial multiplied quickly. Those found guilty desperately tried to stave off death by implicating others. As the pandemonium spread beyond Salem, fear dissolved ties of friendship and family. A minister heard himself condemned by his own granddaughter. A seven-year-old girl helped send her mother to the gallows. A wife and daughter facing death testified against their own husband and father. Fifty persons saved themselves by confessing. Twenty others who would neither disgrace their name nor betray the guiltless went to their graves. Shortly before she was hanged, a victim of the witch hunters named Mary Easty begged the court to come to its senses: "I petition your honors not for my own life, for I know I must die . . . [but] if it be possible, that no more innocent blood be shed."

By late 1692 most Massachusetts ministers had expressed doubt that justice was being done. The clergy primarily objected that most convictions depended heavily upon spectral evidence. Increase Mather (Cotton's father, and a leading Puritan minister) in particular insisted that spectral evidence lacked legal credibility because the devil could manipulate it. Mather concluded that by accepting such evidence in court, New Englanders had fallen victim to a deadly game of "blind man's buffet" set up by Satan and were "hotly and madly, mauling one another in the dark." Backed by the clergy (and alarmed by an accusation against his wife), Governor William Phips forbade any further imprisonments for witchcraft in October—by which time more than a hundred individuals were in jail and twice that many stood accused—and shortly thereafter he suspended all trials. Phips ended the terror in early 1693 by pardoning all those convicted or suspected of witchcraft.

The witchcraft hysteria reflected profound anxieties over social change in New England. The underlying causes for this tension were evident in the antagonism of Salem Village's communally oriented farmers toward the competitive, individualistic, and impersonal way of life represented by Salem Town. In this clash of values, the rural villagers assumed the symbolic role of purging their city upon a hill of its commercial witches, only to leave the landscape desecrated by their gallows.

By the last years of the seventeenth century, the New England Way of John Winthrop had lost its relevance for the generation reaching maturity. Eighteenth-century New Englanders would be far less willing to accept society's right to restrict their personal behavior and economic freedom. The anxieties arising from this shift in values, which lay at the core of the witchcraft hysteria, faded after 1700 because of a general awareness that New England's stingy soil, harsh climate, and meager natural resources forced its inhabitants to become economically enterprising if they wished to avoid poverty.

By 1700 New Englanders had begun a transition from Puritans to "Yankees." True to their Puritan roots, the people would retain strong religious convictions and an extraordinary capacity for perseverance. Out of the striving to wring a living from an unsparing environment evolved the Yankee traits of ingenuity, shrewdness, and a sharp eye for opportunity, on which New Englanders would build a thriving international commerce—and later an industrial revolution.

The English Caribbean

Simultaneously with the appearance of New England's earliest settlements in the 1620s, a second wave of English colonization swept the West Indies. Between 1630 and 1642, more than twice as many British immigrants landed in the Caribbean as went to New England; indeed, almost 60 percent of the seventy thousand British who drifted overseas during these years embarked for either the Caribbean or the Western Atlantic provisioning base at Bermuda.

The English West Indies strongly influenced British North America. The Caribbean islands became the major market for New England's surplus foodstuffs, dried fish, and lumber. In the 1640s the British West Indians began adapting their economy to large-scale slave labor and devising a code of social conduct for nonwhites. In this way, the West Indies pioneered techniques of racial control that would later appear in the mainland colonies' plantation societies. After 1660 a large outmigration of English islanders added significantly to British North America's population.

No Peace Beyond the Line

In the sixteenth century, Spain claimed all the Caribbean, but the Spanish eventually concentrated on holding the four largest islands: Santo Domingo (or Hispaniola), Puerto Rico, Cuba, and Jamaica. By 1600 the West Indies had become a diplomatic no man's land, a region outside the legal limits of European treaties. Anyone sailing past the mid-Atlantic and south of the Tropic of Cancer's line forfeited the protection of international law. English, French, and Dutch felt free to settle uninhabited islands, and the Spanish felt equally free to exterminate trespassers on sight. Undeclared war was the normal state of affairs, and life was cheap, for no peace existed "beyond the line."

Successful English colonies appeared in the Caribbean only after Spain and the Dutch Republic went to war in 1621. Gambling that the Dutch would distract Spain from launching attacks against isolated outposts, English freebooters began seizing islands vacated by the Spanish. St. Kitts (St.

Christopher) was first in 1624, and by 1640 the English had established nearly twenty communities from the Bahamas to the waters off Nicaragua. Spanish troops soon destroyed most of these fledgling settlements but left the English entrenched on St. Kitts, Barbados, Montserrat, Nevis, and Antigua. Later, in 1655, Jamaica also fell to an English force.

Born of war, England's West Indian colonies matured in turmoil. Between 1640 and 1713, every major island but Barbados suffered at least one invasion by Carib Indians, Spaniards, French, or Dutch. After 1680 pirates from the Bahamas menaced British shipping until the Royal Navy exterminated them during the 1720s. Seven slave revolts rocked the English islands prior to 1713, and they left a bitter legacy of racial hatred on the crowded West Indies.

Sugar and Slaves

The English West Indies initially developed along lines similar to Virginia. Strong demand for tobacco led the first settlers to cultivate that plant almost exclusively. Even after the boom collapsed in 1629, the Caribbean colonists kept growing tobacco in hopes that prices would recover.

Since a single worker could tend only three acres per year, tobacco farming supported a large population on Barbados, St. Kitts, Antigua, Nevis, and Montserrat. By 1640 more colonists lived on these five islands (collectively half the size of Rhode Island) than in Virginia.

Tobacco was inexpensive to raise; it needed no equipment more costly than a curing shed. Thus tobacco growing gave individuals with small savings a chance to improve themselves. Although low prices inhibited upward mobility, and there emerged a distinct group of planters profitably working their estates with servant labor, through the 1630s the English West Indies remained a society with a large percentage of independent landowners, an overwhelmingly white population, and no extreme inequality of wealth.

An alternative to tobacco soon appeared, however, that rapidly revolutionized the islands' economy and society. During the early 1640s, Dutch merchants familiar with Brazilian methods of sugar production began encouraging the English to grow sugar cane. In return for selling their harvest to the

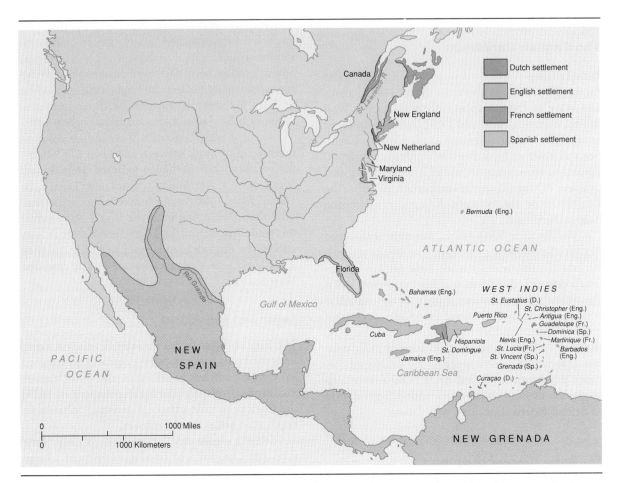

The Caribbean Colonies, 1660 *Aside from Jamaica, England's sugar colonies were clustered in the eastern Caribbean's Leeward Islands. Lying within easy reach of seaborne attack, every English island but Barbados was the scene of major fighting.*

Dutch, wealthy English planters learned how to raise and process this highly profitable crop.

Sugar could make a settler fabulously wealthy because it sold at unusually high prices, which escalated steadily for a century after its introduction on the islands. But sugar manufacture was also a complex process that required grinding, boiling, refining, and (for rum) distilling the cane immediately after cutting—before it lost its sweetness—and therefore was a very costly venture. Besides a large labor force, a sugar producer needed a mill, several caldrons, a still, and a number of outbuildings. Growing sugar required more capital than ordinary tobacco farmers possessed or could borrow as long as tobacco prices stayed low. Aggressively buying land, a few sugar planters on Bar-

bados closed off opportunity to small farmers by bidding up real-estate prices about 1,000 percent from 1643 to 1650. By 1680 a mere 7 percent of property owners held over half the agricultural acreage on Barbados, which grew 60 percent of the sugar exported to Britain. A typical sugar planter owned an estate of two hundred acres, while most Barbadians scratched a pitiful living from farms of ten acres or less.

Because the profit from sugar vastly exceeded that from any other crop, West Indian planters soon turned all available acreage into cane fields. They deforested every English island except mountainous Jamaica and greatly reduced the amount of land available for grain and livestock. The West Indies then quickly became dependent on outside sources for lumber and foodstuffs, and a flourishing market thus opened up for New England farmers, fishermen, and loggers.

Because planters needed three times as many workers per acre to raise cane as tobacco, rising sugar production greatly multiplied the demand for labor. Before 1640 West Indians had imported white servants who signed an indenture, or contract, to work without pay for four to six years in return for free passage to America. After 1640, however, sugar planters increasingly purchased slaves from the Dutch to do common field work and instead employed the indentured servants who came from Britain as overseers or skilled artisans.

Although slavery had died out in England after the eleventh century, English immigrants to the Caribbean quickly copied the example set there by Spanish slaveowners. On Barbados, for example, British newcomers imposed slavery on both blacks and Indians immediately after settling on that island in 1627. The Barbadian government in 1636 condemned every black brought there to lifelong bondage. All other English islanders likewise plunged into slaveowning with gusto.

Sugar planters preferred slaves to white servants because slaves could be driven harder and maintained less expensively. Unlike European servants, who wilted in the tropics, Africans could endure Caribbean conditions, because they had grown up in a hot, humid climate. White servants could use their contracts to demand decent food, clothes, and housing; but slaves, as mere property, had no rights, and masters could spend the bare minimum necessary to keep them alive. Most servants ended their indentures after four years, just as they were becoming efficient workers, but slaves toiled on until death. Although slaves initially cost two to four times more than servants, they proved a more economical long-term investment.

By 1670 the sugar revolution had transformed the British West Indies into a predominantly black and unfree society. In 1713 slaves outnumbered whites by a margin of four to one. Although the number of slaves shot up from approximately 40,000 in 1670 to 130,000 in 1713, the white population remained stable at about 33,000 because the planters' preference for slave labor greatly reduced the importation of indentured servants after 1670.

Declining demand for white labor in the West Indies diverted the flow of English immigration from the islands to mainland North America and so contributed to population growth there. Further, because the expansion of West Indian sugar plantations priced land beyond the reach of most whites, perhaps thirty thousand people left the islands from 1655 to 1700. Most whites who quit the West Indies also migrated to the mainland colonies—especially the Chesapeake, where they could continue growing tobacco.

West Indian Society

Within a generation of 1640, sugar transformed the West Indies into a starkly unequal world of haves and have-nots. At the pinnacle of society were a few fabulously rich families; composing just 7 percent of all whites, they owned more than half the land and held more than a hundred slaves apiece. The great majority of whites, however, survived on plots of ten acres or less and led a hardscrabble existence growing tobacco, cotton, or food crops.

At the bottom of Caribbean society were the slaves, who lived under a ruthless system of racial control imposed by the islands' European minority through laws known as slave codes. In 1661 Barbados passed the first comprehensive slave code, which served as a model for all colonies in the Caribbean and several on the North American mainland. The Barbados code professed to guarantee decent treatment for slaves (as did certain laws protecting indentured servants), but it failed to define an adequate diet or shelter, aside from requiring masters to furnish each woman with a dress and every man with a pair of pants and a hat. In effect, the code allowed owners to let their slaves run almost naked, house them in rickety shacks, and work them to exhaustion. Moreover, the Barbados code stripped slaves of all legal rights protected under English law. Unlike white servants, slaves could not be tried by juries. The law gave slaves no guarantee of a fair legal hearing and did not even forbid testimony obtained by torture.

In this way, West Indian governments allowed masters almost complete control over their human property. Their laws purposefully placed no limits on how or why a master could punish a slave. Consequently, slaves suffered vicious beatings and whippings. If a master killed a slave, he could not be punished unless a jury determined that he acted

View of Bridge Town, Barbados, in 1695 *One historian has called this rare sketch, which was drawn on the deck of a ship, "the finest and most accurate seventeenth-century view of an English seaport in the New World."*

intentionally, and even then he could only be fined, not jailed or executed. The slave codes effectively legalized assault, battery, and involuntary manslaughter.

Slave codes, moreover, left those in bondage defenseless against *all* whites, not just their masters. Slaves could not testify in court against free persons. Barbados allowed any ordinary white who caught a slave at large without a pass to give him a "moderate whipping," which could include beatings of up to fifty lashes.

Finally, slave codes attempted to terrorize those in bondage into obedience through cruel and extreme punishments. Judges could order ears sliced off for theft of food, have slaves torn limb from limb for allegedly poisoning masters, and sentence rebels to be burned alive. Heads or other body parts of executed slaves often dangled gruesomely in public places to generate an atmosphere of dread.

Life in the Caribbean endured amid the constant violence inflicted on Catholic by Protestant, slave by master, and man by nature. Of the seventy-four settlers who founded Barbados in 1627, only six remained alive just eleven years later. A bubonic-plague epidemic killed an estimated one-third of the islanders from 1647 to 1649. Up to five thousand militiamen (every sixth Englishman in the Caribbean) perished while fighting to capture Jamaica from Spain in the 1650s. Hundreds regularly lost their lives in hurricanes. In 1692 an

BARBADOS. 1695 By Samuel Copen

earthquake killed almost seven thousand Jamaicans out of a population of forty thousand. Malaria and yellow fever never ceased their slaughter. Immigrants usually died less than twenty years after arriving, at about thirty-eight years of age.

Mortality among blacks was especially frightful. Sugar production required arduous labor, but it was so profitable that planters had little incentive to keep their slaves healthy; they could well afford to replace those killed by overwork. Slaves usually arrived on the islands as men and women in their early twenties, and within ten years most were dead of exhaustion and abuse. So rapidly did the planters wear out field hands that, although they imported 264,000 Africans to the English West Indies between 1640 and 1699, the slave population stood at just 100,000 in 1700.

Despite these appalling conditions, enslaved Africans did what they could to maintain a semblance of normal existence. They were more likely than island whites to start families, since the ratio of male to female slaves neared equality by 1670. (Still, a staggering mortality rate among slave spouses cut most marriages short, and half or more of all slave children died before age five.) In their daily lives, slaves retained much of their native heritage. African music survived in work songs and ceremonial dances and chants, including the mournful laments in which newly arrived Africans grieved over their fate. Very few converted to

Christianity; most clung to faith in ancestral spirits, and some committed suicide in the belief that their ghosts would return home. They also re-created African family structures, as well as marriage and funeral customs. In short, the islands' black culture displayed a far stronger African imprint than did the African-American way of life that would eventually emerge on the North American mainland.

Among white islanders, family cohesion was weak. Because about 80 percent of servants were male, most British settlers led wild lives as bachelors. Not until after 1700 did a sufficient number of white women inhabit the islands to give all white men the option of marriage. Even then high death rates robbed most children of at least one parent well before they reached maturity.

Organized religion withered in the English Caribbean. The number of clergymen never met the colonists' needs, so the majority of churches had no minister. Aside from the small Jewish minority, most whites rarely attended religious services. English islanders spent far more time in taverns drinking rum (popularly known as Old Kill-Devil) than in church. According to an old Caribbean joke, upon founding a new settlement, the Spanish first constructed a church, the Dutch first built a fort, and the English immediately set up a barroom. If drinking habits on Bermuda in the 1620s were typical, the average English islander consumed well over a gallon of distilled liquor each month.

Few white residents demonstrated any sense of community. The rich generally hired overseers to manage their estates and retired in luxury to England. The poor left in droves for other colonies. In sum, the English Caribbean was a society of materialistic fortune seekers trying to get rich quickly before death overtook them, and of slaves being worked to death.

The West Indian colonies were the first of England's overseas possessions to evolve into plantation societies. The most extreme examples of labor exploitation, racial subordination, and social stratification could indeed be found in these Caribbean colonies, but a similar pattern of development also characterized English settlements in Chesapeake Bay. By 1700 the Chesapeake resembled the Caribbean far more than it resembled New England, but only after enduring a tortured history of economic depression and violent unrest.

Chesapeake Society

Virginia's survival was no longer at stake when James I took control of the colony in 1624 from the bankrupt Virginia Company. The company had built a colony but destroyed itself in the process. Charles I ignored his new province. He and his successors refused to spend any significant amount of money on Virginia, even for the governors whom they appointed—whose salaries instead came from local taxes.

Royal indifference worked to the colonial elite's advantage by minimizing outside interference. Virginia's leaders experimented with various systems of local administration and succeeded in forcing reluctant governors to cooperate with their legislature. As in the West Indies, the environment and the dominant regional crop—tobacco in Virginia's case—determined the colonists' destiny. These same forces shaped life in Maryland and northeastern North Carolina, which, with Virginia, evolved a common Chesapeake culture.

State and Church

Virginia's first elected assembly did not meet until 1619 but thereafter convened regularly until the Virginia Company's charter was revoked. King James I, who then took over direct control of the colony, disliked representative government and planned to rule Virginia through a governor of his own choosing, who would appoint (and could dismiss) advisers to the newly created Royal Council. But Virginians petitioned repeatedly that their legislature be revived. In 1628 the new king, Charles I, grudgingly relented, but only to induce the assembly to lay a tax on tobacco exports that would transfer the cost of the colony's government from the crown to Virginia's taxpayers.

After 1630 the need for additional taxes led royal governors to call regular assemblies. The small number of elected representatives, or burgesses, initially met as a single body with the council to pass laws. During the 1650s the legislature split into two chambers—the House of Burgesses and the Governor's Council, whose members held lifetime appointments. Later royal colonies all established bicameral legislatures like Virginia's.

Local government varied widely during Virginia's first quarter-century. All individuals who commanded the militia, enforced the law, or held courts were appointed to office rather than elected. After experimenting with various institutions of local administration, in 1634 Virginia's settlers adopted England's county-court system. The courts' members, or justices of the peace, acted as judges; they also set local tax rates, paid county officials, and saw to the construction and maintenance of roads, bridges, and public buildings. As in England, this system was undemocratic, for the justices and the sheriffs, who administered the counties during the courts' recesses, gained office by the royal governor's appointment instead of by citizens' votes. Everywhere south of New England, unelected county courts would become the basic unit of local government by 1710.

First instituted in 1618, Anglican vestries governed each parish. The six vestrymen handled all church finances, determined who was deserving of poor relief, and investigated complaints against the minister. The taxpayers, who were legally obliged to pay fixed rates to the Anglican church, elected vestries until 1662, when the assembly made them self-recruiting and independent of the voters.

Because few counties supported more than one parish, many residents could not conveniently attend services. A chronic shortage of clergymen left many communities without functioning congregations. In 1662 just ten ministers served Virginia's forty-five parishes. Compared to New Englanders, Chesapeake dwellers felt religion's influence lightly, though not as lightly as English West Indians.

First Families

Virginia encountered great difficulty in developing a social elite able and willing to provide disinterested public service. The gentry sent by the Virginia Company to supervise its affairs were rarely suited for a frontier society. By 1630 all but a few of these gentlemen had either died or returned to England.

The next cycle of leaders were primarily middle class in origins, but over time they acquired great wealth. Most worked their way up into the company's highest positions and then built large estates by defrauding the stockholders. Others were rough-hewn gamblers who risked all on tobacco and won big. From 1630 to 1660, these individuals dominated Virginia's Royal Council and became even richer through land grants, tax exemptions, and public salaries. Because they had few or no children to assume their place in society, however, their influence died with them.

From 1660 to 1675, a third cycle of immigrants, who generally arrived after 1645, assumed political power. Principally members of English merchant families engaged in trade with Virginia, they had become planters. They usually emigrated with wealth, education, and burning ambition. By 1670 they controlled the Royal Council. Most of them profited from "public" service by obtaining huge land grants.

Unlike their predecessors, this group bequeathed their wealth and power to future generations, later known as the First Families of Virginia. Among them were the Burwell, Byrd, Carter, Harrison, Lee, Ludwell, Randolph, and Taylor families. Not only would the First Families dominate Virginia politics for two centuries, but a fifth of all American presidents would be descended from them.

Maryland

Until 1632 English colonization had resulted from the ventures of joint-stock companies, but afterward the crown repeatedly made presents of the Virginia Company's forfeited territory to reward English politicians. Overseas settlement thereafter resulted from grants of crown land to proprietors, who assumed the responsibility for peopling, governing, and defending their colonies.

In 1632 the first such grant went to Lord Baltimore (Cecilius Calvert) for a large tract of land north of the Potomac River and east of Chesapeake Bay, which he named Maryland in honor of England's Queen Henrietta Maria. Lord Baltimore also secured freedom from royal taxation, the power to appoint all sheriffs and judges, and the privilege of creating a local nobility. The only checks on the proprietor's power were the crown's control of war and trade and the requirement that an elected assembly approve all laws.

With Charles I's agreement, Lord Baltimore intended to create an overseas refuge for English Catholics, who constituted about 2 percent of England's population. Although English Catholics were rarely molested and many (like the Calverts) were very wealthy, they could not worship in public, had to pay tithes to the Anglican church, and could not hold political office.

In making Maryland a Catholic haven, Baltimore had to avoid antagonizing English Protestants. He sought to accomplish this by transplanting to the Chesapeake the old English institution of the manor—an estate on which a lord could maintain private law courts and employ as his chaplain a Catholic priest. Local Catholics could then come to the manor to hear Mass and receive the sacraments privately. Baltimore adapted Virginia's headright system by offering wealthy English Catholic aristocrats large land grants on condition that they bring settlers at their own cost. Anyone transporting five adults (a requirement raised to twenty by 1640) received a two-thousand-acre manor. Baltimore hoped that this arrangement would allow Catholics to survive and prosper in Maryland while making it unnecessary to pass any special laws alarming to Protestants.

Maryland's initial colonization proceeded quite smoothly. In 1634 the first two hundred settlers landed. Maryland was the first colony spared a starving time, thanks to the Calvert family's careful study of Virginia's early history. The new colony's success showed that English overseas expansion had come of age. Baltimore, however, stayed in England, governing as an absentee proprietor, and few Catholic settlers went to Maryland. From the outset, Protestants formed the majority of the population. Maryland became a society of independent landowners because land prices were low and few settlers consequently were willing to become tenants on the manors. These conditions doomed the Calverts' dream of creating on the Chesapeake a manorial system of mostly Catholic lords collecting rents. By 1675 all of Maryland's sixty nonproprietary manors had evolved into plantations.

There was little religious tension in Maryland in the colony's first years, although gradually the situation worsened. The Protestant majority dominated the colonial assembly's elective lower house, but many Catholics (including several Calvert relatives) became large landowners, held high public office in the colony, and dominated the appointive upper house. Serious religious problems first emerged in 1642, when Catholics and Protestants in the capital at St. Mary's argued over use of the city's chapel, which both groups had shared until that time. As antagonisms intensified, Baltimore

drafted the Act for Religious Toleration, which the assembly passed in 1649. Baltimore hoped that the statute would reinforce the Catholic minority's legal rights, but the law also reflected his consistent support for freedom of conscience. The toleration act was America's first law affirming liberty of worship. However, it did not protect non-Christians, nor did it separate church and state, since it empowered the government to punish religious offenses such as blasphemy.

The toleration act did not secure religious peace. In 1654 the Protestant majority barred Catholics from voting, ousted Governor William Stone (himself a Protestant), and repealed the toleration act. In 1655 Stone raised an army of both faiths to regain the government but was defeated at the Battle of the Severn River. The victors imprisoned Stone and hanged three Catholic leaders. Catholics in Maryland actually experienced more trouble than did their counterparts during the English Civil War, in which Catholics were seldom molested by the victorious Puritans.

Maryland remained in Protestant hands until 1658. Ironically, Lord Baltimore resumed control by order of the Puritan authorities then ruling England. Even so, the Calverts encountered enormous obstacles in governing Maryland during the next four decades because of Protestant resistance to any political influence by Catholics.

Life in the Chesapeake

Compared to colonists on England's tiny Caribbean sugar islands or in New England's compact towns (where five hundred people often lived within a square mile of the meetinghouse), Chesapeake residents had few neighbors. A typical community comprised about two dozen families in an area of twenty-five square miles, or about six persons per square mile. Friendship networks seldom extended beyond a three-mile walk from one's farm and rarely included more than twenty adults. Many, if not most, Chesapeake inhabitants lived in a constricted world much like that of Robert Boone, a Maryland farmer described by an Annapolis paper as having died at age seventy-nine "on the same Plantation where he was born in 1680, from which he never went 30 Miles in his Life."

The isolated folk in Virginia and Maryland and in the unorganized settlements of what would

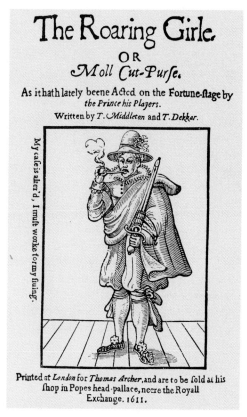

"The Roaring Girl"

A picture of a smoker adorns the title page of this 1611 English play. Smoking tobacco had become a popular pastime in England, which by 1620 was a major market for American leaf.

become North Carolina shared a way of life shaped by one overriding fact: their future depended on the price of tobacco. Tobacco had dominated Chesapeake agriculture since 1618, when demand for the crop exploded and prices spiraled to dizzying levels. The boom ended in 1629 after prices sank a stunning 97 percent, from a high of 36 pence per pound to a penny. After stabilizing near 2.4 pence, tobacco rarely again fetched more than 10 percent of its former high.

Despite its plunge, tobacco stayed profitable as long as it sold for over two pence per pound *and* was cultivated on fertile soil near navigable water. The plant grew best on level ground with good internal drainage, so-called light soil, which was usually found beside rivers. Locating a farm along Chesapeake Bay or the region's web of rivers also

minimized transportation costs by permitting tobacco to be loaded on ships at wharves near one's home. Perhaps 80 percent of all Chesapeake homes lay within a half-mile of a riverbank, and most within six hundred feet of the shoreline.

From such waterfront bases, wealthy planters built wharves that served not only as depots for tobacco exports but also as distribution centers for imported goods. The planters' control of both export and import commerce stunted the growth of towns and the emergence of a powerful merchant class. Urbanization therefore proceeded slowly in the Chesapeake, even in a capital like Maryland's St.

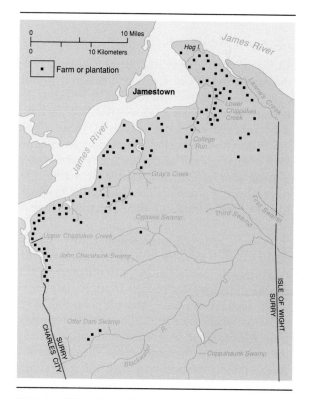

Pattern of Settlement in Surry County, Virginia, 1620–1660

Unlike the New England colonists, whose settlements were tightly nucleated around a town center (see the map of Sudbury, Massachusetts, on page 54), the Chesapeake population distributed itself thinly along the banks of rivers and creeks.

SOURCE: Thad W. Tate and David Ammerman, eds., *The Chesapeake in the Seventeenth Century* (Chapel Hill: University of North Carolina Press, 1979). Published for the Institute of Early American History and Culture. Reprinted by permission.

Mary's, which as late as 1678 was still a mere hamlet of thirty scattered houses.

Although the tobacco crash left small producers struggling to support themselves, cultivating the "weed" could generate a large income for anyone with a sizable work force. Tobacco thus sustained a sharp demand for labor that lured about 110,000 Britons to the Chesapeake from 1630 to 1700. Ninety percent of these immigrants were indentured servants. Virginia and Maryland encouraged masters to import workers by offering headrights (usually of fifty acres) for each person transported. Men were more valued as field hands than women, so 80 percent of servants were males aged about twenty.

Domestic Relations

So few women immigrated to the Chesapeake in the early years of colonization that barely a third of all male servants could find brides before 1650. Further, marriage occurred relatively late, because most inhabitants immigrated as servants whose indentures forbade them to wed before completing their term of labor. Their own scarcity gave women a great advantage in negotiating favorable marriages. Female indentured servants often managed to have their suitors buy their remaining time of service.

Death ravaged seventeenth-century Chesapeake society mercilessly and left domestic life exceptionally fragile. Before 1650 the greatest killers were diseases contracted from contaminated water: typhoid, dysentery, and salt poisoning. After 1650 malaria became epidemic as sailors returning from Africa, along with a few Africans, carried it into the marshy lowlands, where the disease was spread rapidly by mosquito bites. Life expectancy in the 1600s was about forty-eight for men and forty-four for women—slightly less than in England but nearly twenty years less than in New England. Servants died at horrifying rates, with perhaps 40 percent going to their graves within six years of arrival, and 70 percent by age forty-nine. Such high death rates severely crippled family life. Half of all persons married in Charles County, Maryland, during the late 1600s became widows or widowers within seven years. The typical Maryland family saw half of its four children die in childhood.

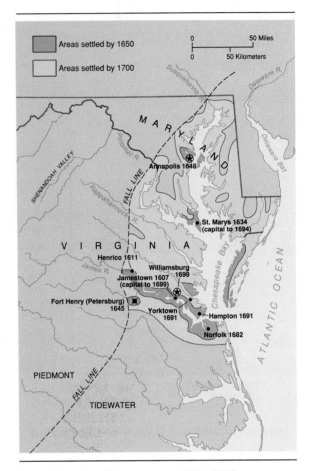

Colonizing the Chesapeake, 1607–1660

The Chesapeake frontier expanded slowly until after Indian defeat in the Second Powhatan War of 1644–1646. By 1700, when the European and African population had reached 110,000, newcomers had spread virtually throughout the tidewater.

Chesapeake women who lost their husbands tended to enjoy greater property rights than widows elsewhere. To ensure that their own children would inherit the family estate in the event that their widows remarried, Chesapeake men often wrote wills giving their wives perpetual and complete control of their estates. A widow in such circumstances gained economic independence yet still faced enormous pressure to marry a man who could produce income by farming her fields.

The combination of predominantly male immigration and devastating death rates notably retarded population growth. Although the Chesapeake had received perhaps 110,000 British immigrants between 1630 and 1700, its white population stood at just 69,000 in 1700. By contrast, a benign disease environment and a more balanced sex ratio among the 25,000 Puritans who immigrated to New England during the 1600s allowed that region's white population to climb to 91,000 by 1700.

The Chesapeake's dismal demographic history began improving in the late seventeenth century. By then resistance acquired from childhood immunities allowed native-born residents to survive into their fifties, or ten years longer than immigrants. As the number of families slowly rose, the ratio of men to women became more equal, since half of all children were girls. By 1690 an almost even division existed between the sexes. Thereafter, the white population grew primarily through an excess of births over deaths rather than through immigration, so that by 1720 the Chesapeake was primarily a native-born society.

Tobacco's Troubles

The massive importation of servants into the seventeenth-century Chesapeake made society increasingly unequal. Taking advantage of the headright system, a few planters built up large landholdings and then earned substantial incomes from their servants' labor. The servants' lot was harsh. Most were poorly fed, clothed, and housed. The exploitation of Chesapeake labor was hardly equaled anywhere in the English-speaking world outside the West Indies.

Servants faced a bleak future when their indentures ended. Having received no pay, they entered into freedom without savings. Virginia obliged masters to provide a new suit of clothes and a year's supply of corn to a freed servant. Maryland required these items plus a hoe and an ax and gave the right to claim fifty acres whenever an individual could pay to have the land surveyed and deeded.

Maryland's policy of reserving fifty acres for ex-servants permitted many of its so-called freedmen to become landowners. Two-thirds of all Chesapeake servants went to Virginia, however, where no such entitlement existed. After 1650 Virginia speculators monopolized most of the light

soil along riverbanks so essential for a profitable farm, and freedmen found land ever more unaffordable. Upward mobility was possible, but few achieved it.

After 1660 upward mobility almost vanished from the Chesapeake as the price of tobacco fell far below profitable levels, to a penny a pound. So began a depression lasting over fifty years. Despite their own tobacco losses, large planters earned other income from rents, interest on loans, some shopkeeping, and government fees.

Most landowners held on by offsetting tobacco losses with small sales of corn and cattle to the West Indies. A typical family nevertheless inhabited a shack barely twenty feet by sixteen feet and

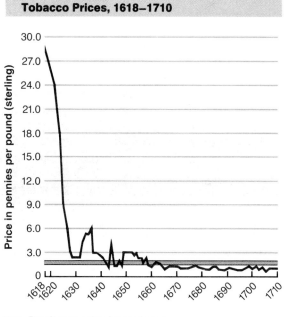

Tobacco Prices, 1618–1710

Break-even price for producers

Even after its great plunge in the 1620s, tobacco remained profitable until about 1660, when its price fell below the "break-even" point—the income needed to support a family or pay off a farm mortgage.

SOURCE: Russell R. Menard, "The Chesapeake Economy, 1618–1720: An Interpretation" (unpublished paper presented at the Johns Hopkins University Seminar on the Atlantic Community, November 20, 1973), and "Farm Prices of Maryland Tobacco, 1659–1710," *Maryland Historical Magazine*, LVIII (Spring 1973), 85.

owned no more property than Adam Head of Maryland possessed when he died in 1698: three mattresses without bedsteads, a chest and barrel that served as table and chair, two pots, a kettle, "a parcell of old pewter," a gun, and some books. Most tobacco farmers lacked furniture, lived on mush or stew because they had just one pot, and slept on the ground—often on a pile of rags. Having fled poverty in England or the Caribbean for the promise of a better life, they found utter destitution in the Chesapeake.

Servants who completed their indentures after 1660 fared even worse, for the depression slashed wages well below the level needed to build savings and in this way placed landownership beyond their means. Lacking capital, those living as tenants could not afford to breed cattle for the West Indies, and they had little corn to sell after meeting their own needs. Ex-servants formed a frustrated and embittered underclass that seemed destined to remain landless and poor.

Bacon's Rebellion

By the 1670s these bleak conditions trapped most Virginia landowners in a losing battle against poverty and left the colony's freedmen verging on despair. Both groups were capable of striking out in blind rage if an opportunity presented itself to stave off economic disaster. In 1676 this human powder keg exploded in violence that left hundreds of Indians dead, dozens of plantations looted, and Virginia's capital, Jamestown, burned. The person who lit the match was Nathaniel Bacon, a wealthy, well-educated young Englishman who had immigrated to Virginia in 1674 and established a plantation. He was a bold man and an inspiring speaker, and Governor William Berkeley, a distant relative, had immediately appointed him to the Royal Council.

Virginia had been free of serious conflict with native Americans since the Second Powhatan War of 1644–1646. During that struggle, forces under Opechancanough, then nearly a century old but able to direct battles from a litter, killed five hundred of the colony's eight thousand whites before meeting defeat. By 1653 tribes encircled by English settlement began agreeing to remain within boundaries set by the government—in effect, on reservations. White settlement then expanded north

Virginia Indian, c. 1645

At the time that this contemporary sketch was made, Virginia's white settlers and Indians were embroiled in the Second Powhatan War.

to the Potomac River, and by 1675 Virginia's four thousand Indians were greatly outnumbered by forty thousand whites.

Provoked by white settlers, Indians in the Potomac Valley in 1676 made several attacks, in which thirty-six Virginians, including Bacon's overseer, died. Governor Berkeley proposed defending the panic-stricken frontier with an expensive chain of forts linked by patrols. Stung by low tobacco prices and taxes that took almost a quarter of their yearly incomes, small farmers preferred the less costly solution of waging a war of near extermination. Despite orders from Berkeley not to retaliate, three hundred settlers elected Bacon to lead them against nearby Indians in April 1676. Bacon's expedition found only peaceful Indians but massacred them anyway.

When he returned in June 1676, Bacon sought authority to wage war "against all Indians in generall." Bacon's new-found popularity forced the governor to grant his demand. The legislature voted a program designed to appeal to both hard-pressed taxpayers and ex-servants desperate for land. The assembly defined as enemies any Indians who left their villages without English permission (even if they did so out of fear of attack by Bacon), and declared their lands forfeited. Bacon's troops were free to plunder all "enemies" of their furs, guns, wampum, and corn harvests and also to keep Indian prisoners as slaves. The assembly's incentives for enlisting were directed at land-bound buccaneers eager to get rich quickly by seizing land and enslaving any Indians who fell into their clutches.

But Berkeley soon had second thoughts about letting Bacon's thirteen hundred men continue their frontier slaughter and called them back. The governor's order spared more Indians from attack, leading Bacon's men to rebel and march on Jamestown. Forcing Berkeley to flee across Chesapeake Bay, the rebels burned Jamestown, offered freedom to any servants or slaves owned by Berkeley's supporters who joined them, and then looted their enemies' plantations. At the very moment of triumph, however, Bacon died of dysentery in late 1676, and his followers dispersed.

The tortured course of Bacon's Rebellion revealed a society under deep internal stress. The revolt began as an effort to displace escalating tensions within white society onto local Indians. Because social success in Virginia depended on accumulating land and labor, small farmers and landless ex-servants alike responded enthusiastically to the prospect of taking Indian lands, stealing their furs, wampum, and harvests, and enslaving prisoners. So easily did the insurrection disintegrate into an excuse to plunder other whites, however, that it appears that the rebels were driven as much by economic opportunism as by racism. Bacon's Rebellion was an outburst of long-pent-up frustrations by marginal taxpayers and ex-servants, driven to desperation by the tobacco depression.

Slavery

Bacon's Rebellion exposed the crackling tensions underlying class relations among Chesapeake whites. This social instability derived in large part from the massive importation of indentured servants, who later became free agents in an economy

that offered them little but poverty while their former masters seemingly prospered. But even before Bacon's Rebellion, the acute potential for class conflict was diminishing as Chesapeake planters gradually substituted black slaves for white servants (see "A Place in Time").

Early Virginians were still inching toward a system of racial bondage long after English West Indian planters had taken the plunge. A Dutch privateer sold the first Africans to Virginia in 1619, but it is unknown whether these individuals were treated as indentured servants or slaves. Very few blacks entered the Chesapeake before 1649 (the date of the earliest known contract for importing African slaves); of these, most became free, some bought farms and raised families, and a few later purchased other Africans.

Racial slavery developed in three stages in the Chesapeake. Blacks first began appearing from 1619 to 1640. Although Anglo-Virginians carefully dis-

Tobacco Label

Dating from about 1700, this English label for smoking tobacco features slaves on a Virginia tobacco plantation.

Middlesex County, Virginia, in the Seventeenth Century

On a sandy peninsula between tidewater Virginia's Rappahannock and Piankatank rivers lies Middlesex County, carved in 1668 out of sprawling Lancaster County. In the late 1640s, families had begun appropriating land here. Settlement was well under way by February 1651, when little Richard Perrott became "the first Man Child that was gott and borne in Rappahannock River of English parents." Richard's parents, like all the 83 families residing in Middlesex by 1668, lived on isolated "plantations" that raised corn and livestock for food and tobacco for sale.

These 83 families comprised 513 free people. They accounted for roughly half the county's residents and owned the other half of the population: 334 English indentured servants (mostly males aged 15–25) and 65 blacks brought from the West Indies. Servants and slaves were as much the head of household's responsibility as children. Blacks' conditions of servitude were still fluid, although a trend toward lifetime bondage had begun. Servants typically owed between four and twelve years' service, and half of those with four or more years to go would not live to enjoy freedom. Their lot was hard, but their labor essential. Each hoe-wielding laborer could cultivate two to three acres of tobacco plants, and owners could increase input only by adding to their labor force. Because planters such as Peter Montague faced "the whole loss of the . . . Cropp" when a servant ran away at the height of

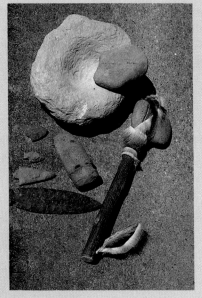

Indian Artifacts from Middlesex County

These early Indian relics include a grinding stone (top), several spear points (left), and a stone ax head (right). Native Americans continued to live in Middlesex County after the arrival of the first permanent English settlers around 1650 but gradually moved westward.

the season, unfree workers had some bargaining leverage.

Death lurked everywhere. On average, adult men and women died at ages 48 and 39 respectively—a life expectancy of fifteen years less than that of New Englanders. Thirty percent of all children under 18 lost both parents. The appearance of a highly lethal strain of malaria (which coincided with increasing imports of African-born slaves after 1680)

kept death rates high.

The prevalence of early death produced complex households in which stepparents might raise children with two or three different surnames. Mary, George Keeble's wife, bore seven children before being widowed at age 29, whereupon she immediately became Robert Beverley's wife. Mary died in 1678 at age 41 after having five children by Beverley, who then married Katherine Hone, a widow with one child. Upon Beverley's death in 1687, Katherine quickly wed Christopher Robinson, who had just lost his wife and needed a mother for his four children. Christopher and Katherine's household included children named Keeble, Beverley, Hone, and Robinson. This tangled chain of six marriages among seven people eventually produced twenty-five children who lived at least part of their lives with one or more stepparents.

For a sense of belonging, residents relied primarily on kin networks. Twice monthly, however, they could gather in the parish church for a short sermon, communion, and a chance to gossip, trade news, and sell livestock—always using tobacco as the medium of exchange. Monthly court sessions likewise brought people together to resolve disputes and see the county's prominent men installed in the petty local offices that helped define their status.

Property also counted in determining status. Toward the end of the century, a landowner's ability to work a holding depended pri-

Hewick Manor

Christopher Robinson arrived in Virginia from England about 1666 and built this stately brick home in 1678. Robinson, who served two terms in the Virginia House of Burgesses, was named England's secretary of foreign plantations in 1692, but he died the following year.

Christ Episcopal Church

This handsome brick structure was erected in 1714 on the site of an earlier wooden church. The churchyard contains the elaborately carved table-top tombs of many seventeenth-century Middlesex County residents, among them members of the Beverley, Churchill, and Corbin families.

marily on owning slaves, for since the 1670s the supply of indentured English servants had been drying up. In 1698 the county's population stood at 1,771—30 percent unfree. But by a four-to-one margin, these unfree laborers were now black. Although slaves cost two or three times the going rate for servants, black teen-agers who survived could give twenty years' service before becoming "old"; further, immunities acquired from African ancestors gave slaves a greater likelihood of warding off malaria. In addition, many black women produced large new generations of slaves. Sharlott, for example, who came from Africa at age 12, bore thirteen children. By age 56 her master, Henry Thacker, owned twenty-two of her descendants, representing a 2,500 percent profit over her purchase price.

Facing narrowing opportuni-

ties in the 1690s, poorer whites began leaving Middlesex County at a rate of about two hundred per decade. In Virginia's interior they found abundant land and a more healthful climate. As whites who remained grew steadily more nervous about the rising number of enslaved blacks, local slave codes became more stringent. Masters, seldom gentle with white servants (who nevertheless lived with the family), used often brutal punish-

ments to keep slaves in line and generally housed their bondspeople in separate huts. In 1700 the county demanded "that Negroes not be kept att Quarters without overseers."

Between 1668 and 1740, Middlesex County's population was transformed from 93 percent white to 54 percent black. Half the population still owned the other half. But the race of the unfree laborers had changed, and they were now chattel slaves.

tinguished blacks from whites in official documents—in a manner that seems to show a tendency to discriminate according to race—they did not assume that every African was sold as a slave rather than as a servant who would eventually become free. During the second phase, spanning the years 1640–1660, unmistakable evidence survives that many blacks were treated as slaves and that their children inherited that status. Customary behavior apparently required that all blacks be treated as inferior to whites—even whites like indentured servants, who owed labor service to others. In the final phase, after 1660, whites officially recognized slavery and regulated it by law. Maryland first defined slavery as a lifelong, inheritable, racial status in 1661. Virginia followed suit in 1670. By 1705 strict legal codes defined the place of slaves in society and set standards of racial etiquette. Although this period saw slavery mature into a legal system, most of the specific practices enacted into law had evolved into custom before 1660.

Slavery was never considered a status appropriate for any white. Although the English could have enslaved enemies such as the Irish, Scots, and Spanish, they always reserved this complete denial of human rights for nonwhites. The English embarked on slavery as an "unthinking decision," one in which they unconsciously acted on the basis of a profoundly negative, emotional response to blackness and assumed that Africans were inferior to whites—and so uniquely suited for slavery.

As late as 1660, fewer than a thousand slaves lived in Virginia and Maryland. The number in bondage first became truly significant in the 1680s, when the Chesapeake's slave population almost tripled, rising from forty-five hundred to about twelve thousand. By 1700 nearly twenty thousand slaves resided in the region, and they made up 22 percent of the inhabitants. Even so, indentured servants still composed half of all unfree laborers in 1700.

Slavery replaced indentured servitude for economic reasons. First, it became more difficult to import indentured servants as the seventeenth century advanced, because a gradual decline in England's population between 1650 and 1700 reduced the number of persons willing to emigrate overseas. As England's population decreased, labor became more valuable at home, and wages rose by about 50 percent. Second, before 1690 the Royal African Company, which held a monopoly on selling slaves to the English colonies, shipped nearly all its cargoes to the West Indies, a situation that left few blacks available for sale to the Chesapeake. During the 1690s this monopoly was broken, and rival companies soon expanded the supply of slaves. Large shipments of Africans then began reaching the Chesapeake, though not in sufficient numbers to change the region's racial composition radically. Unlike the West Indies, the Chesapeake (including its backcountry) would remain predominantly white.

The emergence of slavery was critical in relaxing the economic strains within white society that had helped precipitate Bacon's Rebellion. Gradually after 1690, nonslaveowners came to see themselves as sharing a common interest with the upper class in maintaining social control over a race regarded as alien and threatening.

Conclusion

By 1690 England had planted three distinctive societies in the New World. At the northern and southern extremes were New England and the West Indies, which were appropriately polar opposites in regard to their racial composition, their organization of labor, their inhabitants' sense of community, the influence of religion, and the degree to which materialism governed social relations. Nevertheless, these two societies—like the rich and poor in John Winthrop's "A Model of Christian Charity"—had critical need of each other. The sugar islands could not feed themselves or supply their own lumber requirements, and New England relied on the Caribbean to purchase its surpluses of these goods.

The third English sphere in the New World, the Chesapeake, represented a middle ground, a place closely akin to the exploitative, uncertain, market-economy world of old England that most of its residents had left. As in the Old World, in the Chesapeake prosperity proved elusive during the seven decades after 1630, and economic hardship ultimately produced the chaos of Bacon's Rebellion. By 1700, however, a new mix of races and labor organization was emerging in the Chesapeake that would lay the basis for a remarkably vibrant society. At the core of this future dynamism would be a small, enterprising elite of "First Families" that would dominate the region's politics, economy, and culture very much in the manner of England's landed gentry.

In the course of the seventeenth century, New England evolved from a highly religious, community-oriented society to a region characterized by rising worldliness, individualism, and competitiveness. New Englanders ceased to be Puritans and became Yankees sometime in the early eighteenth century. Their collective character nevertheless continued to exhibit many traits rooted in the Puritan experience. In the Chesapeake, social development evolved in the opposite direction. As the number of blacks in their midst swelled and caused them to replace their former class antagonisms with a heightened sense of racial solidarity, the region's whites moved away from a fiercely competitive, openly materialistic, and frankly exploitative ethos toward a growing sense of community among themselves.

CHRONOLOGY

1603 James I becomes king of England.

1619 Virginia's first elected assembly meets.
Dutch privateer sells first African slaves to Virginia.

1625 Charles I becomes king of England.

1630 John Winthrop, "A Model of Christian Charity."
Massachusetts Bay colony founded.

1630– 1660 The great English migration to North America.

1633 First English settlements in Connecticut.

1634 Cecilius Calvert (Lord Baltimore) founds proprietary colony of Maryland.

1635 Roger Williams is banished from Massachusetts Bay; founds Providence, Rhode Island, in 1636.

1636 Harvard College established.

1637 Anne Hutchinson is tried by Massachusetts Bay colony and banished to Rhode Island.
Pequot War.

1639 Fundamental Orders of Connecticut.

1640s Large-scale slave-labor system takes hold in the West Indies.

1642 English Civil War begins.

1643 New Haven colony founded.

1644 Williams obtains permission to establish a legal government in Rhode Island.

1649 Earliest known contract for importing slaves to the Chesapeake.

1649 Lord Baltimore drafts Maryland's Act for
(cont.) Religious Toleration.

King Charles I beheaded.

1651– Natick, Massachusetts, and other New
1675 England "praying towns" established.

1653 First Indian reservation established in Virginia.

1660 Charles II becomes king of England in the
Stuart restoration.

1661 Barbados government creates first
comprehensive slave code.

Maryland defines slavery as a lifelong,
inheritable racial status.

1662 Half-Way Covenant drafted.

1670 Virginia defines slavery as a lifelong, inheritable
racial status.

1675– King Philip's (Metacomet's) War in New
1676 England.

1676 Bacon's Rebellion in Virginia.

1690s Collapse of the Royal African Company's
monopoly on selling slaves to the English
colonies; large shipments of Africans begin
reaching the Chesapeake.

1692– Salem witchcraft trials.
1693

For Further Reading

Bernard Bailyn, *The New England Merchants in the Seventeenth Century* (1955). A masterful examination of the challenge posed to Puritan ideals by New England's merchants.

Jack P. Greene, *Pursuits of Happiness: The Social Development of Early Modern British Colonies and the Formation of American Culture* (1988). A brilliant synthesis of Chesapeake, Caribbean, and New England history.

Winthrop D. Jordan, *The White Man's Burden: Historical Origins of Racism in the United States* (1974). A brief yet definitive analysis of racism's origins.

Edmund S. Morgan, *American Slavery, American Freedom: The Ordeal of Colonial Virginia* (1975). The most penetrating analysis yet written on the origins of southern slavery.

Darrett B. Rutman, *Winthrop's Boston: A Portrait of a Puritan Town, 1630–1649* (1965). An illuminating description of the disintegration of Winthrop's "city upon a hill."

Darrett B. Rutman and Anita H. Rutman, *A Place in Time: Middlesex County, Virginia, 1650–1750* (1984). The best examination of community life in the early Chesapeake.

Alan Simpson, *Puritanism in Old and New England* (1955). The best short introduction to Puritanism ever written.

Additional Bibliography

Early New England

David Grayson Allen, *In English Ways: The Movement of Societies and the Transferral of English Local Law and Custom* (1981); James Axtell, *The School upon a Hill: Education and Society in Colonial New England* (1974); Emery Battis, *Saints and Sectaries: Anne Hutchinson and the Antinomian Controversy in the Massachusetts Bay Colony* (1962); Theodore Dwight Bozeman, *To Live Ancient Lives: The Primitivist Dimension in Puritanism* (1988); Charles L. Cohen, *God's Caress: The Psychology of Puritan Religious Experience* (1986); David Cressy, *Coming Over: Migration and Communication Between England and New England in the Seventeenth Century* (1987); Richard S. Dunn, *Puritans and Yankees: The Winthrop Dynasty of New England, 1630–1717* (1962); Stephen Foster, *Their Solitary Way: The Puritan Social Ethic in the First Century of Settlement in New England* (1971); Philip F. Gura, *A Glimpse of Sion's Glory: Puritan Radicalism in New England, 1620–1660* (1984); David D. Hall, *The Faithful Shepherd: A History of the New England Ministry in the Seventeenth Century* (1972); Charles E. Hambrick-Stowe, *The Practice of Piety: Puritan Devotional Disciplines in Seventeenth Century New England* (1982); Christine Leigh Heyrman, *Commerce and Culture: The Maritime Communities of Colonial Massachusetts* (1984); Kenneth A. Lockridge, *A New England Town: The First*

Hundred Years: Dedham, Massachusetts, 1636–1736 (1970); Robert Middlekauff, *The Mathers: Three Generations of Puritan Intellectuals, 1596–1728* (1971); Perry Miller, *The New England Mind*, 2 vols. (1939–1953); Edmund S. Morgan, *The Puritan Dilemma: The Story of John Winthrop* (1958) and *Visible Saints: The History of a Puritan Idea* (1963); Sumner Chilton Powell, *Puritan Village: The Formation of a New England Town* (1964); Darrett B. Rutman, *Husbandmen of Plymouth: Farms and Villages in the Old Colony, 1620–1649* (1967).

Witchcraft

Paul Boyer and Stephen Nissenbaum, *Salem Possessed: The Social Origins of Witchcraft* (1974); John P. Demos, *Entertaining Satan: Witchcraft and the Culture of Early New England* (1982); Carol F. Karlsen, *The Devil in the Shape of a Woman: Witchcraft in Colonial New England* (1987); Keith Thomas, *Religion and the Decline of Magic* (1971); Richard Weisman, *Magic, Science, and Religion in Seventeenth-Century Massachusetts* (1982).

The English West Indies

Carl Bridenbaugh and Roberta Bridenbaugh, *No Peace Beyond the Line: The English in the Caribbean, 1624–1690* (1972); Michael Craton and James Walvin, *A Jamaican Plantation: The History of Worthy Park, 1670–1970* (1970); Richard S. Dunn, *Sugar and Slaves: The Rise of the Planter Class in the English West Indies, 1624–1713* (1972); Richard B. Sheridan, *Sugar and Slavery: An Economic History of the British West Indies, 1623–1775* (1973).

Indian-White Relations

James Axtell, *The Invasion Within: The Contest of Cultures in Colonial North America* (1985); William Cronon, *Changes in the Land: Indians, Colonists, and the Ecology of New England* (1983); Francis Jennings, *The Invasion of America: Indians, Colonialism, and the Cant of Conquest* (1975); Yasuhide Kawashima, *Puritan Justice and the Indian: White Man's Law in Massachusetts, 1630–1763* (1986); Howard S. Russell, *Indian New England Before the Mayflower* (1980); Neal Salisbury,

Manitou and Providence: Indians, Europeans, and the Making of New England, 1500–1643 (1982); Alden T. Vaughan, *The New England Frontier: Puritans and Indians, 1620–1675* (1965).

Gender and Family

John P. Demos, *A Little Commonwealth: Family Life in Plymouth Colony* (1970); Philip Greven, *Four Generations: Population, Land, and Family in Colonial Andover, Massachusetts* (1970); Lyle Koehler, *A Search for Power: The "Weaker Sex" in Seventeenth-Century New England* (1980); Edmund S. Morgan, *The Puritan Family: Religion and Domestic Relations in Seventeenth-Century New England* (1966); Marylynn Salmon, *Women and the Law of Property in Early America* (1986); Roger Thompson, *Women in Stuart England and America: A Comparative Study* (1974); Laurel Thatcher Ulrich, *Good Wives: Image and Reality in the Lives of Women in Northern New England, 1650–1750* (1982); Nancy Woloch, *Women and the American Experience* (1984).

The Chesapeake

Warren M. Billings, ed., *The Old Dominion in the Seventeenth Century: A Documentary History of Virginia, 1606–1689* (1975); Timothy H. Breen and Stephen Innes, *"Myne Own Ground": Race and Freedom on Virginia's Eastern Shore, 1640–1676* (1980); Lois Green Carr et al., *Colonial Chesapeake Society* (1988); Wesley Frank Craven, *The Southern Colonies in the Seventeenth Century* (1949) and *White, Red, and Black: The Seventeenth-Century Virginian* (1971); Carville Earle, *The Evolution of a Tidewater Settlement Pattern: All Hallow's Parish, Maryland, 1650–1783* (1975); Ivor Noel Hume, *Martin's Hundred* (1982); Aubrey C. Land et al., eds., *Law, Society, and Politics in Early Maryland* (1977); Gloria L. Main, *Tobacco Colony: Life in Early Maryland, 1650–1720* (1982); William L. Shea, *The Virginia Militia in the Seventeenth Century* (1983); Thad Tate and David Ammerman, eds., *The Chesapeake in the Seventeenth Century: Essays on Anglo-American Society* (1979); Wilcomb E. Washburn, *The Governor and the Rebel: A History of Bacon's Rebellion in Virginia* (1957).

CHAPTER 3

Colonial Society Comes of Age, 1660–1750

Alexander Garden was furious with the young Anglican minister George Whitefield. Just over from England, Whitefield was stating publicly that the rest of Garden's ministers were unsaved and endangering their parishioners' souls. Garden, as the bishop of London's commissary (representative) in Charles Town, South Carolina, was responsible for the Church of England's well-being in the southern British colonies. He thought that he had plenty to contend with already—most pressingly, the numbing indifference of most of his flock—and did not appreciate one of his ministers' making waves. With Whitefield's descent on the colonies like a hurricane, Garden sensed that 1740 would not be a good year for established religion.

Calling Whitefield in for an interview, Garden demanded that the preacher explain his repeated attacks on South Carolina's Anglican ministry. He got more than he bargained for. Whitefield, it seemed, thought that Garden "was as ignorant as the rest" of the local clergy because he failed to teach the central Protestant doctrine of justification by faith alone (see Chapter 1). And Whitefield threatened to speak out against the commissary if Garden refused to condemn dancing and other public entertainments. Thunderstruck, Garden shot back that Whitefield would be suspended if he preached in any church in the province—to which Whitefield retorted that he would treat such an action as he would an order from the pope.

Garden got Whitefield out of his house but not out of his hair. The two men carried their dispute to the public. Garden accused Whitefield of jeopardizing the stability of colonial society. Whitefield accused the Anglican clergy of abandoning Calvinist doctrine in favor of the cold heresy of reason. An extraordinary orator, Whitehead stirred his listeners' passions, calling forth an "enthusiasm" for religion that undermined traditional order and deference. He inspired members of congregations to think themselves as good as, if not superior to, their ministers; wives, to question their husbands' piety; children, to claim divine grace that their parents did not feel; slaves, to believe that they too had souls; and common people, to insist that they were the equal of anyone else.

That was Whitefield's greatest crime—to be heard throughout America. He became the first national figure in North America, traveling thousands of miles to spread his doubts about the established religious order. Everywhere he went, the people poured out by the thousands to listen and feel, to sense individually the overwhelming power of a direct connection with God.

Sweeping through British North America in the 1740s, Whitefield encountered a vibrant society, a rapidly growing economy, and the beginnings of a richly diverse culture. By 1750 the colonies could claim the world's largest concentration of overseas Europeans; besides those of English stock, significant numbers descended from German, Irish, Scottish, Dutch, and French settlers. North America was also the enforced home of a burgeoning African population, by now slowly becoming English-speaking and Christian. Geographically, however, the people remained isolated from one another. Whitefield found it quicker to make the hazardous, disease-ravaged transatlantic voyage than to go overland from New England to Georgia.

A generation of imperial crisis and war with the French from 1685 to 1713 had forged among Anglo-America's whites a strong sense of shared allegiance to the English crown and of deeply felt Protestant heritage. Then, during the era of peace between 1713 and 1744, British Americans' provincialism faced the dual challenge of two vital yet conflicting European cultural currents. The first of these was the Enlightenment—the dissemination among the educated public of faith in reason rooted in an appreciation of natural science—which found its foremost American exponent in Benjamin Franklin. The second current was the religious revival pulsing across Protestant Europe in the 1730s

and 1740s, one of whose greatest prophets was George Whitefield. That Franklin and Whitefield became the first two Anglo-American public figures to win fame not only throughout the colonies but also in the entire Western world testifies to America's active participation in the culture of the age.

The peace and prosperity that characterized mid-eighteenth-century British North America would have astonished seventeenth-century colonists, clinging to their uncertain footholds on the edge of the transatlantic wilderness. But even though by 1740 life was becoming reasonably stable and secure, especially for upper-class Anglo-Americans, the Great Awakening let loose spiritual and social tremors that jolted colonial self-confidence. Alexander Garden's nervousness was hardly unreasonable.

The Restoration Colonies

In 1660 mainland Anglo-America remained a loose cluster of Chesapeake settlements with about thirty thousand struggling tobacco producers, and a New England enclave where some thirty-three thousand stubborn Puritans had built their city upon a hill. In between lay thinly populated New Netherland, an outpost of England's great commercial rival, the Dutch Republic.

With the end of the English Revolution and the Stuart restoration in 1660, English authorities almost immediately busied themselves with their North American colonies. Their least effective initiative was the revived Church of England's attempt to clean up organized religion in the Chesapeake— a "Sodom of uncleaness [sic] & a Pest house of iniquity," as one overwrought Anglican minister in Maryland described that colony about 1660. But because educated English clergymen resisted taking American parishes, reform of American Anglicanism never got very far.

Second, Parliament began passing laws collectively known as the Navigation Acts, designed to benefit England's commercial interests. Expanding upon a 1651 law, the Navigation Acts of 1660 and 1663 barred colonial merchants from exporting such commodities as sugar and tobacco anywhere except to England, and from importing goods in

non-English ships. The act of 1672 provided administrative machinery to enforce these rules.

Third, the Restoration set in motion a new wave of colony building that gave England control of the North American coast from Maine to South Carolina. A series of "Restoration colonies" appeared—Carolina, New York, New Jersey, and Pennsylvania. Before 1720 most settlers in the new colonies came from existing British North American provinces; but thereafter, these provinces attracted masses of Irish and German immigrants, in the process altering the colonies' purely English character.

English domestic politics figured prominently in the Restoration government's plans for America. Charles II (ruled 1660–1685) had clamoring supporters to reward. The Navigation Acts favored powerful commercial interests in England. The king entrusted the creation of the new colonies to important English politicians—the proprietors who organized settlement, oversaw governance (subject to loose control from London), and expected to profit handsomely.

In every Restoration colony, the proprietors created a system of land distribution that would bring them high income and ensure a stable social hierarchy. But, as earlier in Maryland, their plans

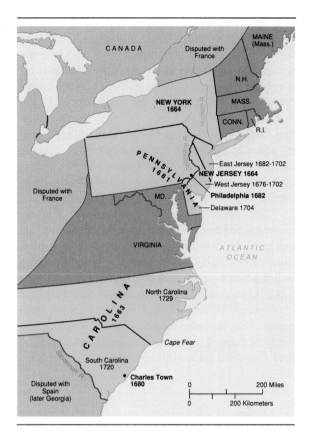

The Restoration Colonies

England's Restoration colonies were carved out of the claims or earlier colonial territory of rival European powers. Spain claimed the territory chartered as Carolina in 1663. Out of England's takeover of Dutch New Netherland in 1664 came the colonies of New York, East Jersey, West Jersey, Pennsylvania, and Delaware.

collided with the colonists' determination to better themselves. Dreams of stability soon waned, and by 1689 English attempts to impose a uniform system of rule across the Atlantic provoked a series of colonial rebellions, linked to an anti-Stuart revolution in England itself.

Carolina

During the 1650s several struggling, unauthorized little outposts were formed along the swampy coast from just south of Virginia to Spanish Florida by a few English settlers—"the dregs and gleanings of all other English Colonies," an early-eighteenth-century clergyman recalled. Some of these "dregs and gleanings" were New Englanders; others were

people who had failed to profit from the West Indian sugar boom. In 1663 Charles II bestowed this unpromising coast on several English supporters. The grateful proprietors named their colony Carolina in honor of Charles (*Carolus* in Latin).

Carolina grew haltingly at first. The proprietors organized the existing little settlements in the northern part of their domain as a separate district and established a bicameral legislative body for it. Then in 1669 one of the proprietors, Anthony Ashley Cooper, speeded up settlement by offering immigrants fifty-acre land grants for every family member, indentured servant, or slave they brought in. Cooper's action marked a turning point. In 1670 settlement of southern Carolina began when two hundred Barbadian and English settlers landed near modern-day Charleston, "in the very chops of the Spanish." Narrowly escaping destruction when a hurricane scattered Spanish warships sent to attack them, they wintered without enduring a "starving time." Soon they formed the colony's nucleus, with their own bicameral legislature distinct from that of the northern district.

Cooper and his secretary—John Locke, later acclaimed as one of the great philosophers of the age—devised an intricate plan for Carolina's settlement and government. Their Fundamental Constitutions of Carolina attempted to ensure the colony's stability by decreeing that political power and social rank should accurately reflect settlers' landed wealth. Thus they invented three orders of nobility, with "proprietors" on top, "landgraves" in the middle, and "caciques" at the bottom. Together this elite would hold two-fifths of all land, make laws through a Council of Nobles, and dispense justice through manorial law courts. Ordinary Carolinians with smaller landholdings were expected to defer to nobility, although they would enjoy religious toleration and the benefits of English common law.

The reality of Carolina's early settlement bore small resemblance to Locke's scheme. New arrivals who could get all the land they needed saw little reason to obey pseudofeudal lords and all but ignored most of the plans drawn up for them across the Atlantic.

Until 1680 about half the settlers of southern Carolina came directly from overcrowded Barbados, bringing with them a few slaves. Other settlers drifted in from mainland colonies to the north, as did a trickle of French Protestant refugees. The first colonists raised "Hoggs, & Cattle which they sell to the New-Comers, and with which they purchase Cloathes, and tools from them," and also sold beef to the West Indies. Cattle raising discouraged the widespread use of slaves, for herding required only a small labor force and afforded bondsmen too many tempting opportunities to run away. Because ranching yielded only modest profits, few striking disparities of wealth arose, and the slaves who accompanied the first Carolinians seem to have been spared the brutality widely meted out to blacks in the British Caribbean.

In northern Carolina life was much the same. Settled by Virginians and Marylanders, the region exported tobacco, lumber, and pitch, giving local people the name tarheels. As in southern Carolina, these activities did not at first produce enough profit to warrant maintaining many slaves, and so self-sufficient white families predominated. As late as 1720, the region was nine-tenths white.

But Carolina had not been created so that settlers could merely eke out a marginal existence.

Like the first Virginians, southern Carolinians sought a staple crop that could make them rich. By the early 1690s, they found it—rice. The grain was probably first brought by West Africans, for it constituted the basic foodstuff in Senegambia. Because rice, like sugar, enormously enriched a few men with capital to invest in costly dams, dikes, and slaves, it remade southern Carolina into a society resembling that of the West Indies. By earning annual profits of 25 percent, rice planters within a generation became the only colonial elite whose wealth rivaled that of the Caribbean sugar planters.

The Carolina rice planters' huge profits had to be reaped at someone's expense, however. No matter how inhumanly they might be driven, indentured English servants simply could not work in humid rice paddies swarming with mosquitoes. The planters' solution was to import an ever-growing force of African slaves. Unfortunately for these people, they had two major advantages to masters. First, perhaps 15 percent of the slaves imported into Carolina had cultivated rice in their home-

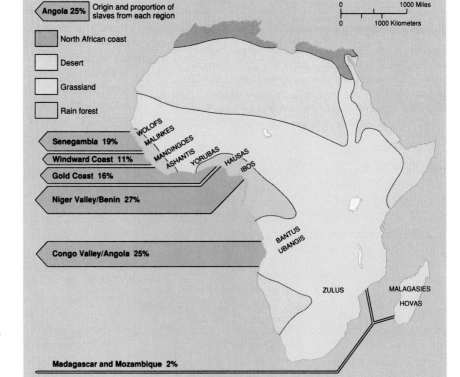

Old World Origins of North American Slaves, 1690–1807

Three-quarters of all Africans brought to British North America were sold to Europeans by African merchants operating between the Niger and Senegal rivers. Most slaves were captured or bought several hundred miles inland and marched to the coast for export.

land, and their expertise was vital in teaching whites how to raise the unfamiliar crop. Second, many Africans had partial immunity to malaria, the highly infectious and deadly disease transmitted by mosquito bites, which was endemic to coastal regions of West Africa and which African-born slaves (and infected slave ships' crews) carried to the New World. (Tragically, the antibody that helps ward off malaria also tends to produce the sickle-cell trait, a hereditary genetic condition often fatal to those children who inherit it.) The Africans' relatively low death rate from malaria made possible commercial rice production in Carolina. A tremendous demand for black slave labor resulted, for a typical rice planter farming 130 acres needed sixty-five slaves. The proportion of slaves in southern Carolina's population spurted from 17 percent in 1680 to 67 percent in 1720, when the region officially became the colony of South Carolina. South Carolina was Britain's sole eighteenth-century mainland colony with a black majority.

Rice thrived only within a forty-mile-wide coastal strip extending from Cape Fear (now in North Carolina) to present-day Georgia. The hot, humid, marshy lowlands quickly became infested with malaria. Carolinians grimly joked that the rice belt was a paradise in spring, an inferno in summer, and a hospital in the wet, chilly fall. In the worst months, planters' families usually escaped to the relatively cool and more healthful climate of Charles Town and let overseers supervise their harvests.

As long as Europeans outnumbered Africans, race relations could be somewhat relaxed. But as a black majority emerged and swelled, whites increasingly relied on force and fear to control their slaves. In 1696 Carolina adopted the galling restrictions and gruesome punishments of the Barbados slave code (see Chapter 2). Bondage in the mainland colony was becoming as cruel and harsh as in the West Indies.

In contrast to South Carolina, northern Carolina was long spared large-scale slavery; but tragedy also marred its early history as whites and native Americans there became locked in a bloody struggle. In 1711, provoked by white encroachments on their land and by several instances of whites' kidnapping Indians as slaves, the Tuscarora tribe destroyed New Bern, a frontier settlement of seven hundred Swiss immigrants. In retaliation, colonial

militia and the Tuscaroras' Indian enemies rampaged through the offending tribe's villages. By 1713, with a thousand of their people killed or enslaved (about one-fifth of the total population), the Tuscaroras surrendered. Nearly half the survivors migrated to New York, where they became the Sixth Nation of the Iroquois Confederacy.

Disunity was costly for Carolina Indians. After helping whites crush the Tuscaroras, the Yamasees of the southern Carolina lowlands found themselves beset by colonial fur traders who cheated, abused, and enslaved them. Finally, in 1715, the Yamasees led most nearby tribes in attacks that drove the settlements back to the coast. But the next year, the Carolina militia, which barely equaled the thousand warriors then harassing Charles Town, enrolled six hundred slaves and drove the Indians from the area suitable for rice production.

The Tuscarora and Yamasee wars cracked Indian opposition to Old World peoples' expansion in the Carolinas. The Tuscaroras largely abandoned the region. The Yamasees practically disappeared as a people, for those who were not killed in fighting, enslaved, or doomed by disease blended into the Creek nation farther inland.

The first two generations of Carolina settlers had cleared the unhealthy coastal regions, developed profitable exports, enslaved thousands of blacks, and crushed Indian resistance—all with little aid from the faraway proprietors, whose main activities had been vetoing many laws passed by the Carolina assemblies and appointing unpopular governors. Carolinians came to regard the proprietors as indifferent even to their defense. Exasperated, the southern Carolina assembly asked the British monarchy to take control, and in 1720 the king complied by making South Carolina a royal province. Proprietary rule finally ended in 1729, when North Carolina also became a royal colony.

Ten years later, in 1739, South Carolina was rocked by a powerful slave uprising, the Stono Rebellion. It began when twenty slaves robbed guns and ammunition from a store twenty miles from Charles Town, at the Stono River Bridge. Marching under a makeshift flag and crying "Liberty!" they collected eighty men and headed for Spanish Florida, a well-known refuge for runaways. Along the way they burned seven plantations and killed twenty whites, but they spared a Scottish innkeeper who "was a good Man and kind to his slaves."

Within a day mounted militia surrounded the slaves by a riverbank, cut them down mercilessly, and spiked a rebel head on every milepost between that spot and Charles Town. Disturbances elsewhere in the colony required more than a month to suppress, with insurgents generally "put to the most cruel Death." But white apprehension ran high, expressed in a new slave code that would remain essentially in force until the Civil War. The code kept South Carolina slaves under constant surveillance. Further, it threatened masters with fines for not disciplining slaves and required legislative approval for manumission (freeing of individual slaves). The Stono Rebellion thus speeded South Carolina's emergence as a rigid, racist, and fear-ridden society—and its failure showed slaves that armed uprisings were suicidal. Slaves still resisted after the revolt, but typically by feigning stupidity, running away, committing arson or sabotage, or poisoning masters. Not until 1831 would significant slave violence again break out on the mainland.

The Carolinas' rise had cost innumerable lives and untold suffering for enslaved blacks and displaced native Americans. Whites lived in an atmosphere of anxiety. Grim reality had triumphed over hazy English dreams of a stable society.

New York and the Jerseys

Like Carolina, the English colonies of New York and New Jersey had their origins in the speculative enterprise of Restoration courtiers close to Charles II. As in Carolina, here too upper-class proprietors hoped to create a hierarchical society in which they could profit from settlers' rents. These plans for the most part failed in New Jersey, as in Carolina. Only in New York did they come close to success.

In 1664, waging war against the Dutch Republic, Charles II dispatched a naval force to conquer New Netherland. Weakened by an earlier clash with local Indians, Dutch governor Peter Stuyvesant and four hundred poorly armed civilians surrendered peacefully. Nearly all the Dutch (including Stuyvesant himself) remained in the colony on generous terms.

Charles II made his brother James, Duke of York, proprietor of the new province and renamed it New York. When the duke became King James II in 1685, he proclaimed New York a royal colony. Immigration from New England, Britain, and France

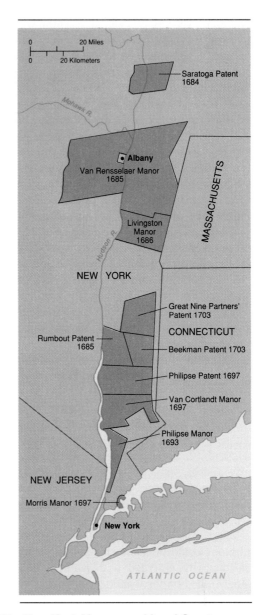

The New York Manors and Land Grants

Between 1684 and 1703, English governors awarded most of the best land east of the Hudson River as manors to prominent politicians—the majority of them Dutch—whose heirs became the wealthiest elite in the rural northern colonies.

boosted the population from five thousand in 1664 to twenty thousand in 1700, of whom just 44 percent were descended from the original New Netherlanders.

Abraham Wendell, *by an Unknown Artist, c. 1737*

Prosperous eighteenth-century Dutch residents of the Hudson River Valley commonly sat for their portraits. Among them was the well-to-do Albany patroon Abraham Wendell, shown here standing before his own land, stream, and mill.

New York's governors rewarded their most influential political supporters with large land grants. By 1703 five families held approximately 1.75 million acres (about half the area east of the Hudson River and south of Albany), which they withheld from sale in hope of creating manors with numerous rent-paying tenants. But the *patroons*—the Dutch name for manor lords—never became European-style lords oppressing peasant tenants, for unlike Europe, America had plenty of good land and too few farmers. The easy availability of other land along the Hudson kept the manors under-populated and unprofitable until after 1700. *Patroons* could only attract tenants by offering favorable terms—building mills, lowering rents, and giving young families farm tools—and by dispensing evenhanded justice in their manor courts. Individual tenants thus did well, but their landlords did even better. Earning an enormous income from their rents, the New York *patroons* by 1750 formed

a landed elite second only in wealth to the Carolina rice planters.

Ambitious plans likewise collided with American realities in New Jersey, which also was carved out of New Netherland. Immediately after the Dutch province's conquest in 1664, the Duke of York named two court favorites, Lord Berkeley and Sir Philip Carteret, as joint proprietors of New Jersey, an area then inhabited by less than six thousand native Americans and a few hundred Dutch and Swedes. From the beginning the New Jersey proprietors had difficulty controlling their province. By 1672 several thousand New Englanders had settled along the Atlantic shore. Quarreling with the absentee proprietors, they renounced allegiance to them at an extralegal meeting that the proprietary governor sneered at as the "disorderly assembled." Soon Berkeley and Carteret tired of wrangling with the unruly Puritans and sold the region to a group of even more contentious religious dissenters, called Quakers, who split the territory into the two colonies of West Jersey (1676) and East Jersey (1682).

East Jersey's new proprietors, a group of mostly Scottish Quakers, could no more successfully work with the local Puritans than had Berkeley and Carteret, while West Jersey's English Quakers squabbled constantly among themselves. The Jerseys' mix of Quakers, Anglicans, Puritans, Scottish Presbyterians, Dutch Calvinists, and Swedish Lutherans got along poorly with each other and even worse with the proprietors. The governments collapsed between 1698 and 1701 as mobs disrupted the courts. In 1702 the disillusioned proprietors finally surrendered their political powers to the crown, which proclaimed New Jersey a royal province.

Quaker Pennsylvania

The noblest attempt to carry out European-born concepts of justice and stability in founding a Restoration colony began in 1681. That year, Charles II paid off a huge debt to a supporter's heir by making this man, William Penn, the proprietor of the last unallocated tract of American territory at the king's disposal. Penn (1644–1718) had two aims in developing his colony. First, he was a Quaker and wanted to launch a "holy experiment" based on the teachings of the extremely radical English preacher George Fox. Second, "though I desire to extend religious freedom," he explained, "yet I want some recompense for my trouble." But Penn did not intend "Penn's Woods" to become merely a hunting ground for get-rich-quick speculators.

Quakers in late-seventeenth-century England stood well beyond the fringe of respectability. They appealed strongly to men and women at the bottom of the economic ladder, and they challenged the conventional foundation of the social order. George Fox, the movement's originator, had received his inspiration while wandering civil war–torn England's byways and searching for spiritual meaning among distressed common people. Tried on one occasion for blasphemy, he warned the judge to "tremble at the word of the Lord" and was ridiculed as a "quaker." Fox's followers called themselves the Society of Friends, but the name Quaker stuck. They were among the most radical of the many religious sects born in England during the 1640s and 1650s.

The core of Fox's theology was his belief that the Holy Spirit or "Inner Light" could inspire every soul. Mainstream Christians, by contrast, found any such claim of special communication with God highly suspicious, as Anne Hutchinson's banishment from Massachusetts Bay colony in 1636 had revealed. While trusting direct inspiration, Quakers also took great pains to ensure that individual opinions would not be mistaken for God's will. They felt confident that they understood Inner Light only after having reached near-unanimous agreement through intensive and searching discussion led by "Public Friends"—ordinary laypeople. In their simple religious services ("meetings"), Quakers sat silently until the Inner Light prompted one of them to speak.

Some of their beliefs led English Quakers to behave in ways that seemed disrespectful to government and the social elite and so aroused fierce hostility. For example, insisting that individuals deserved recognition for their spiritual state rather than their wealth or family status, Quakers refused to tip their hats to their social betters. For the same reason, they would not use the pronoun *you* (customarily employed when commoners spoke to members of the gentry), instead addressing everyone *thee* and *thou* as a token of equality. By wearing their hats in court, moreover, Quakers appeared to mock the state's authority; and by taking literally Scripture's ban on swearing oaths, they seemed to place themselves above the law. The Friends'

refusal to bear arms appeared unpatriotic and cowardly to many. Finally, Quakers accorded women unprecedented equality. The Inner Light, Fox insisted, could "speak in the female as well as the male." A number of fiery Quaker proselytizers were women, including Mary Dyer, a Rhode Island merchant's wife whom Fox converted when the couple returned to England. She went back to Rhode Island in 1658, helped organize Quaker groups there, and eventually was condemned for sedition and hanged in Massachusetts in 1660.

Not all Quakers came from the bottom of society. The movement's emphasis on quiet introspection and its refusal to adopt a formal creed also attracted well-educated and well-to-do individuals disillusioned by the quarreling of rival faiths. The possessor of a great fortune, William Penn was hardly a typical Friend, but there were significant numbers of merchants among the estimated sixty thousand Quakers in the British Isles in the early 1680s. Moreover, the industriousness that the Society of Friends encouraged in its members ensured that many humble Quakers were already accumulating money and property.

Quakers in England faced intense pressure to conform to the established church, but they throve on persecution. The courts severely fined those absent from Anglican services. Constables commonly collected fines by seizing Quakers' farm tools, equipment, or livestock and by destroying their looms or workbenches. Between 1660 and 1685, fifteen thousand Quakers were jailed, and many others suffered public whippings or facial disfigurements. Through all this adversity, they won a reputation for industriousness, even in prison. Jailed in 1669, William Penn found his fellow Quaker inmates busily engaged at crafts like weaving and spinning and absorbed in prayer during their work breaks. "The jail by that means became a meeting-house and a work-house," Penn proudly wrote, "for *they would not be idle anywhere.*"

Much care lay behind the Quaker migration to Pennsylvania that began in 1681, and it resulted in the most successful initial transplantation of Europeans in any North American colony. Penn sent an advance party to the Delaware Valley, where a thousand Swedes and Dutch already lived. After an agonizing voyage in which one-third of the passengers died, Penn arrived in 1682. Choosing a site for the capital, he named it Philadelphia—the "City

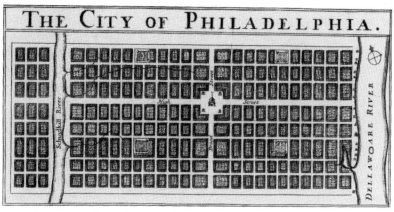

THE CITY OF PHILADELPHIA.

William Penn's Map of Philadelphia, c. 1681; Portrait of Penn,
by Francis Place

*Central to William Penn's master plan for Philadelphia was the idea that
each residence should stand in the middle of its plot, encircled by gardens
and orchards. This pastel portrait is thought to be the most accurate likeness
of Penn extant.*

of Brotherly Love." By 1687 some eight thousand
English Quaker refugees had joined Penn across
the Atlantic. (Pennsylvania was the only Restoration colony besides West Jersey whose colonists
before 1720 came primarily from Europe rather
than other colonies.) Because most Quakers immigrated in family groups rather than as single males,
a high birthrate resulted, and the population grew
rapidly. In 1698 a Quaker reported that in Pennsylvania one seldom met "any young Married
Woman but hath a Child in her belly, or one upon
her lap."

As planned by its founder, Pennsylvania offered
Friends the freedom not only to live diligently but
also to make laws according to their ideals. Having
experienced persecution, Penn hated intolerance and
arbitrary government. Thus in drafting the colony's constitution, he proposed "to leave myself and
my successors [as proprietor] no power of doing
mischief, that the will of One man may not hinder
the good of the whole company." But the Frame
of Government (constitution) that Penn devised went
through at least seven drafts before he was satisfied. After wavering between authoritarian and more
democratic plans, Penn finally opted for a system
with a strong executive branch (a governor and
governor's council) and granted the lower legislative chamber (the assembly) only limited powers.
Friends, forming the majority of the colony's pop-

ulation, dominated this elected assembly. Penn
named Quakers (or persons sympathetic to them)
as governor, judges, and sheriffs. Hardly a democrat, he feared "the ambitions of the populace which
shakes the Constitution," and he intended to check
"the rabble" as much as possible. Because he also
insisted on the orderly disposition of property and
hoped to avoid unseemly wrangling, he carefully
oversaw land sales in the colony. To prevent haphazard growth and social turmoil in his "greene
country towne," Philadelphia, Penn designed the
city with a grid plan, laying out the streets at right
angles and reserving small areas for parks.

Good planning ensured that Pennsylvania suffered no initial "starving time." The colony was
also fortunate in experiencing no large-scale wars
with native Americans for seventy years. Partly this
resulted from the sparse Indian population in the
Delaware Valley—probably no more than twenty
thousand in the 1680s. To the Indians, Penn
expressed a wish "to live together as Neighbours
and Friends," and he tried to buy land fairly from
them. However, Pennsylvania was not immune from
localized Indian violence.

Pennsylvania seemed an ideal colony—intel-
ligently organized, well financed, tolerant, open to
all industrious settlers, and largely at peace with
the Indians. Rich, level lands and a lengthy growing season produced bumper crops. Sharp West

Indian demand for its grain quickly generated widespread prosperity and by 1700 made Philadelphia a major port.

But like other attempts to base new American societies on preconceived plans or lofty ideals, Penn's "peaceable kingdom" soon bogged down in human bickering. In 1684 the founder returned to England to resolve boundary disputes with adjacent Maryland, and in his absence (until 1699) the settlers quarreled incessantly. Although Penn spent much money on his colony, an opposition party attacked his efforts to monopolize foreign trade and to make each landowner pay him a small annual fee. Bitter struggles between Penn's supporters in the governor's council and opponents in the assembly deadlocked the government. From 1686 to 1688, the legislature passed no laws and the council once ordered the lower house's speaker arrested. Penn's brief return to Pennsylvania from 1699 to 1701 helped little, but just before he sailed home, he made the legislature a unicameral (one-chamber) assembly and allowed it to initiate measures.

In addition, religious conflict shook Pennsylvania during the 1690s, when George Keith, a college-educated Public Friend, urged Quakers to adopt a formal creed. This would have changed the democratically functioning Quaker sect—in which the humblest member had equal authority in interpreting the Inner Light—into a more traditional church dominated by an educated clergy. The majority of Quakers rejected Keith's views in 1692, whereupon he joined the Church of England, taking some Quakers with him. Keith's heresy began a major decline in the Quaker share of Pennsylvania's population. The proportion fell further once Quakers ceased immigrating in large numbers after 1710. Finally, in 1748 Penn's heirs became Anglican. Pennsylvania's highest political offices thereafter went to Anglicans, although Friends remained predominant in the assembly.

William Penn met his strongest opposition in the counties on the lower Delaware River, where the best lands had been taken up by Swedes and Dutch. In 1704 these counties gained the right to elect their own legislature, but Penn continued to name their governor. Although the new colony of Delaware's separation temporarily strengthened the proprietor's party in what remained of Pennsylvania, by then the founder's dream of a harmonious society was dashed.

Sadness darkened Penn's last years. Having sunk a fortune into Pennsylvania, he later spent some months in a debtor's prison and died in debt. Long before, he had despaired at having to battle with the legislature's politicians, bent on economic and political advantage. As early as 1685, he begged them, "For the love of God, me, and the poor country, be not so governmentish; so noisy and open in your disaffection."

Penn's anguish summed up the dilemmas of the late-seventeenth-century Englishmen who had planned the Restoration colonies so carefully. Very little went according to expectation. Yet the Restoration colonies were a solid success. Before they were a quarter-century old, the middle colonies demonstrated that British America could benefit by encouraging pluralism. New York and New Jersey successfully integrated New Netherland's Swedish and Dutch population; and Pennsylvania, New Jersey, and Delaware refused to require residents to pay support for any official church. But meanwhile, the virtual completion of English claim staking along the Atlantic coast had set England on a collision course with France and Spain, the other European powers vying for North American territory.

Rivals for North America

France and Spain had established far-flung inland networks of fortified trading posts and missions that stood in marked contrast to England's compact settlements. To offset the English colonists' superiority in numbers, France and Spain enlisted native Americans as trading partners and military allies, and the two Catholic nations had far more success than English Protestants in converting Indians to Christianity. By 1720 a handful of missionaries, fur traders, and merchants—who rarely benefited from any military protection—had spread French and Spanish influence through two-thirds of the present-day United States.

England's rivals exercised varying degrees of control in developing their American colonies. Louis XIV's France, the supreme power in late-seventeenth-century Europe, poured in state resources, whereas Spain, then in deep decay, made little attempt to influence North American affairs from afar. In both cases, local officials and settlers assumed the primary burden for extending imperial control.

France Claims a Continent

By 1663 more than half a century's efforts had yielded little success for the struggling colony of New France. The Iroquois were choking its livelihood by intercepting convoys of beaver pelts from the interior. French settlement had advanced no farther up the St. Lawrence River than Jacques Cartier had penetrated 129 years before. The colony's white population of twenty-five hundred was less than half that of tiny New Netherland.

But 1663 marked the turning point for New France. That year, the trading company that had founded the colony relinquished control to Louis XIV. From 1663 to 1672, the French crown energetically built up the new royal colony's population by dispatching about six hundred settlers each year. About half were indentured servants who received land after three years' work and could marry among the hundreds of "kings' girls," female orphans shipped over with dowries. The royal government also sent fifteen hundred soldiers (most of whom eventually became settlers) to stop Iroquois interference with the French fur trade. In 1666 these troops marched into present-day New York, pan-

icking the local Mohawks into fleeing without a fight. Sobered by the burning of four villages, well stocked with winter food, the Iroquois Confederacy made a peace that lasted until 1680. Subsequently, New France enormously expanded its North American fur exports. The colony also began attracting hardy and ambitious upper-class adventurers such as the Sieur de La Salle, a former candidate for the priesthood who arrived in 1663 to seek his fortune but later had to evade creditors eager to clap him in a debtor's prison.

French activity quickly penetrated deep into the continent. Frenchmen swarmed westward seeking furs, and by 1670 one-fifth of them were *coureurs de bois*—independent traders unconstrained by government authority or dubious pasts. Living and intermarrying with the Indians, the *coureurs* built for France an empire resting solely on trade and goodwill among native peoples all over central North America. As early as 1672, fur trader Louis Joliet and Jesuit missionary Jacques Marquette became the first white men known to have reached the upper Mississippi River (near modern Prairie du Chien, Wisconsin); they later paddled twelve hundred miles downstream, to the Mississippi's junction with the Arkansas River. Ten years later, the Sieur de La Salle descended the entire Mississippi to the Gulf of Mexico. When he reached the delta, La Salle formally claimed all the Mississippi basin—half the territory of the present-day

The Old World Encounters the New

Alexandre de Batz, a French visitor to New Orleans in 1735, drew these members of various native American tribes that French missionaries described. The six Indians at the center were Illinois people, a tribe among whom Father Marquette worked. Trade goods, including cured skins and kegs of fat, are lined up in the foreground.

continental United States—for Louis XIV, in whose honor he named the territory Louisiana. A small band of curious Indians watched the ceremony and then drifted away, serenely unaware that anything had changed for them.

Having asserted title to this vast empire, the French began settling the southern gateway into it. In 1698 the first French colonizers arrived near the mouth of the Mississippi. A year later, the French erected a fort near present-day Biloxi, Mississippi. In 1702 they occupied what is now Mobile, Alabama, as a fur-trading station. Founded in 1718, New Orleans became Louisiana's capital and port.

In no time Louisiana acquired a foul reputation, and few French immigrated there willingly. To boost its population, the government deported paupers and criminals, recruited German refugees, and encouraged large-scale slave imports. By 1732

two-thirds of lower Louisiana's fifty-eight hundred people were slaves. Life was dismal, even for whites. A thoroughly corrupt government ran the colony. The settlers could barely feed themselves, often escaping famine only by trading gunpowder for the Indians' corn. Even the priests reportedly could not get along with each other.

France's vast North American empire existed primarily to support trade with the Indians for furs. By 1744 *coureurs de bois* had explored as far west as North Dakota and Colorado and were buying beaver pelts and Indian slaves on the Great Plains. Only at widely scattered places did the French attempt other kinds of enterprise: for example, mining iron in modern-day Missouri and farming in what is now Illinois. Fewer than a thousand fur traders and soldiers held an immense domain for France. The all-important factor was maintaining

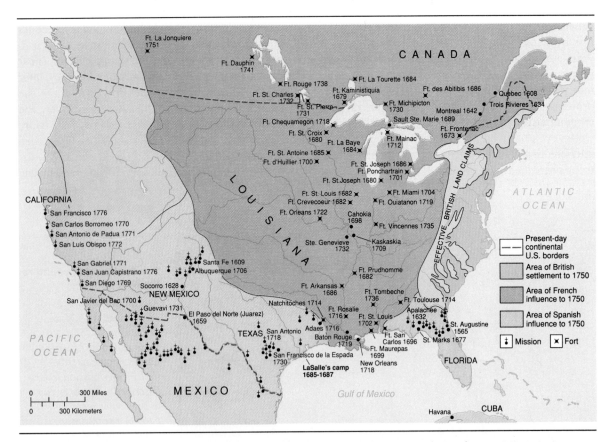

French and Spanish Occupation of North America, to 1776   *French fur traders became entrenched along the Great Lakes and upper Mississippi River between 1666 and 1700, after which they built many settlements in territory claimed by Spain along the Gulf of Mexico. Spanish colonization was concentrated in Florida, central Texas, the Rio Grande Valley, and southern California.*

good relations with the Indians, who after 1720 were the real bar to Spanish and English expansion.

Spain's Borderlands

In the 1680s the Spanish had meanwhile grown alarmed. La Salle had temporarily occupied an outpost near modern-day Houston from 1685 to 1687. To defend their borderland holdings, Spanish authorities in Mexico proclaimed the province of Texas (or Tejas) in 1691. But no permanent Spanish settlements appeared there until 1716, when Spaniards established four missions and a small garrison. The most flourishing of these was San Antonio de Valero, where friars constructed a fortified mission building later famous as the Alamo. The Spanish presence in Texas remained weak, however. By 1742 only eighteen hundred Spaniards and thirteen hundred Catholic Indians blocked the French intruders, and Spain displayed little urgency in building up the province.

Spanish preoccupation with unrest in New Mexico was a primary reason for this neglect of Texas. By 1680 about 2,800 Europeans—many of them scattered on isolated *ranchos* (ranches)—and 30,000 pueblo-dwelling Indians lived in New Mexico's Rio Grande Valley. That year, an Indian named Popé led a revolt, sparked by Spanish priests' efforts to outlaw the religious rituals central to the pueblo peoples' way of life. Popé's forces killed 400 whites (including most priests), captured Santa Fe, and drove the survivors south to El Paso (modern Juarez, Mexico). The pueblo peoples held Santa Fe until Popé died, in 1692, and their resistance seriously threatened Spanish rule down to the 1720s.

To repopulate New Mexico, Spain gave land grants of approximately twenty-six square miles wherever ten or more families founded a town. Strong fortifications arose to protect against future Indian attacks. As in the early New England towns, the settlers built homes on small lots around the church plaza, farmed separate fields nearby, grazed livestock at a distance, and shared a community woodlot and pasture.

By 1750 the Spanish in New Mexico numbered just 5,200, half of them in four towns. Meanwhile, the reduction of the pueblo population by an astonishing 55 percent since 1680, to a mere 13,500, finally eased the danger to Spanish settlements from this quarter, although nomadic Apaches and Navahos remained a menace to outlying *ranchos*. These livestock-raising centers, radiating out for many miles from little clusters of houses, monopolized vast tracts along the Rio Grande and blocked further town settlement. On the *ranchos* mounted cattle and sheep herders (*vaqueros*) created the way of life later associated with the American cowboy—featuring lariat and roping skills, cattle drives, roundups, and brandings. In this way, the horse reached the native Americans.

Recognizing the advantage that mounted men held over foot warriors, the Spanish tried to keep their horses away from the Indians, but horses escaped, were stolen, and were surreptitiously sold. Trade and natural increase spread the animals over the Southwest and the Great Plains. The introduc-

The Alamo

The eighteenth-century Franciscan mission stands today as a powerful symbol of the spirit of resistance felt by a small group fighting in 1836 for Texan Independence from Mexico (see Chapter 12).

Mission Life

*At top left, two priests greet an Indian chief and his three wives; below them, diso-
bedient Indians are punished; right, demons dance as priests offer Mass and perform
sacraments.*

tion of the horse, which took place between the
late sixteenth and the eighteenth centuries, was a
pivotal event for the Plains Indians. Peaceful peoples who once had migrated slowly on foot, they
became flamboyant mounted warriors.

It was missionaries, however, not farmers and
herders, who shouldered the main burden of colonizing Spain's borderlands. Most often the first
Spaniards to explore and map an area, the padres
persuaded native American tribes to accept Spanish allegiance by gathering at a mission. Because
soldiers seldom accompanied them, the missionaries organized their converts as defense forces
against raiders. Thus new missions created a military shield for older Spanish settlements.

In this process, the native Americans often suffered unintentionally. Mission life slowly cut them
off from their religion, traditional work habits, and
language. Most devastating of all, the dense concentration of native peoples at places where they
were exposed to Old World diseases spawned ter-

rible epidemics among them. The graveyards around
the adobe mission churches were soon filled with
hundreds of little crosses commemorating deceased
Indian converts.

Spain's final burst of North American expansion began in 1700. That year, Austrian-born friar
Eusebio Kino came north from Mexico to found
Arizona's first mission (near present-day Tucson),
and his explorations from this base disproved the
longstanding myth that California was an island
incapable of being settled. But not until 1769 did
Franciscan friars led by Father Junípero Serra
establish California's first mission, at San Diego.
Over time, a string of missions inched up the coast,
a day's march apart, to San Francisco. Government
officials encouraged this mission-building effort
mainly to plant a firm Spanish presence in California and thus forestall a coastal expansion of
Russian outposts, which in the 1720s had sprung
up in Alaska to tap the fur trade.

California's potential wealth in minerals and

agricultural land remained largely unexploited during the years of Spanish—and later Mexican—occupation. The Spanish crown awarded immense grants of California land to ex-soldiers and other pioneers for cattle ranches. With the best lands belonging to large estate owners or the church, all but a few California Indians lived rather humbly as farmers or artisans at the missions. Between 1785 and 1803, 40 percent of California's Indians became Catholic. But the white and mestizo (mixed Indian and European) population never rose above 4,000 during the eighteenth century, and exposure to European diseases reduced the mission Indians from an initial total of some 54,000 converts to 17,000 by 1832.

Spain also attempted an ambitious missionizing effort in Florida. By 1665, when scarcely 2,000 whites inhabited Florida, some 13,000 Indians were gathered in a chain of thirty-two missions near the border with southern Carolina. However, Spain's grip was uncertain, for after 1690 southeastern native peoples, among them the Creeks, fiercely retaliated against the English and their Indian allies, who had been plundering native villages for slaves. In light of the Spaniards' reluctance to give their Indian converts enough guns to protect themselves, mission building was less successful in Florida than elsewhere in Spanish North America.

By the mid-eighteenth century, the French and Spanish empires had reached their limits in North America. Spain controlled much of the southern Atlantic and Pacific coastlines. France exercised a subtle influence over the Mississippi, Ohio, and Missouri River valleys. Both empires, spread thin, depended heavily on Indian goodwill or acquiescence. In contrast, British North America was compact, aggressively expansionist, and usually antagonistic toward the native Americans.

Rebellion and War

As France and Spain widened their influence throughout North America, England's colonies seethed with unrest, triggered by the Stuart monarchs' attempt to tighten political control over the colonists. By the late 1680s, the monarchy had kindled sullen resistance as it assumed direct rule over

New England and squelched representative government in eight provinces.

But royal centralization collapsed in 1689, after a revolution in England forced King James II into exile. In North America this rebellion sparked several uprisings and ushered in a long period of war with France. Most important, James's successors, William and Mary, reversed several objectionable royal policies and largely returned control of local affairs to the colonial elites.

Stuart Policies

As the sons of a king executed by Parliament, the last two Stuart monarchs disliked representative government. Charles II called Parliament into session rarely from 1674 to 1679, and not at all from 1681 until his death in 1685. James II (ruled 1685–1688) hoped to reign as an "absolute" monarch like France's Louis XIV, who never had to face a national parliament. Not surprisingly, neither English king had much sympathy for the American colonial assemblies.

Royal intentions of extending direct political control to North America first became evident in New York. The proprietor, Charles II's brother James, the Duke of York, considered elected assemblies "of dangerous consequence" and forbade legislatures to meet from 1664 to 1682. He relented from 1682 to 1686 but thereafter called none. Meanwhile, Charles showed a clear preference for naming high-ranking army men as colonial governors. Despite their new civilian status, these governors were the militia's commanders in chief, and their background made them well suited to crushing civilian dissent with armed force. From 1660 to 1685, Charles appointed former army officers to about 90 percent of all gubernatorial positions, thereby compromising the time-honored English tradition of holding the military strictly accountable to civilian authority. By 1680 such "governors general" ruled 60 percent of all American colonists. James II later continued this policy.

Ever resentful of outside meddling, New Englanders proved most stubborn in defending self-government and resisting Stuart policies. As early as 1661, the Massachusetts assembly politely but firmly declared its citizens exempt from all laws and royal decrees from England except for a declaration of war. The colony ignored the Navigation

Acts (see below) and continued welcoming Dutch traders. "The New England men break through and . . . trade to any place that their interest lead them," claimed Virginia's governor William Berkeley.

Soon Charles II targeted Massachusetts for special punishment. In 1679 he carved out of its territory a new royal colony, New Hampshire. Then in 1684 he declared Massachusetts itself a royal colony and revoked its charter, the very foundation of the Puritan city upon a hill. Puritan minister Increase Mather responded by openly calling on colonists to resist to the point of martyrdom.

Royal centralization in America culminated after James II ascended to the throne. In 1686 the new king consolidated Massachusetts, New Hampshire, Connecticut, Rhode Island, and Plymouth into a single administrative unit, the Dominion of New England. He added New York and the Jerseys in 1688. With this bold stroke, all legislatures in these colonies ceased to exist, and still another former army officer, Sir Edmund Andros, became the governor of the Dominion of New England, at Boston.

Massachusetts soon burned with hatred for the new governor. By "Exercise of an arbitrary Government," preached Salem's minister, "ye wicked walked on Every Side & ye Vilest of men ware [sic] exalted." Andros was indeed brutally arbitrary. He suppressed the legislature, limited towns to a single annual meeting, and jailed prominent citizens to crush protests. Further, Andros hit a raw nerve by forcing a Boston Puritan congregation to share its meetinghouse with an Anglican minister, and he even looked into the finances of Harvard College. Naturally, he also strictly enforced the Navigation Acts. "You have no more privileges left you," Andros reportedly told a group of outraged colonists, "than not to be sold for slaves." Other than his soldiers and a handful of recently arrived Anglican immigrants, however, Andros had no base of support in Massachusetts.

Tensions also ran high in New York, where Catholics held high political and military posts under the Duke of York's rule. By 1688 citizens feared that these Catholic officials would betray the colony to France. Many colonists had reason to believe that Andros's local deputy, Captain Francis Nicholson, was pro-Catholic. When Nicholson allowed the harbor's forts to deteriorate and reacted skeptically to rumors of Indian hostility, New Yorkers suspected the worst.

The Glorious Revolution in England and America

New England Puritans' fury at Andros's forcing them to tolerate Anglicanism was matched by English Protestants' growing worries about the Stuarts' obvious predilection for Catholicism. The Duke of York became a Catholic in 1676, and Charles II converted on his deathbed. Both rulers violated Parliament's laws by issuing decrees that allowed Catholics to hold high office and worship openly. When seven Anglican bishops denounced one such edict in 1688, James II tried them as state enemies. English Protestants' fears that they would have to accept Catholicism intensified after both kings expressed their preference for allying with France just as Louis XIV was launching new persecutions of that country's Protestants in 1685.

The English tolerated James II's Catholicism only because his heirs, his daughters Mary and Anne, had remained Anglican. Then in 1688 James's wife bore a son, who would be raised—and might someday reign—as a Catholic. Aghast at the thought of a Catholic monarchy, some English politicians asked Mary and her husband, William of Orange (the Dutch Republic's leader) to intervene. When William and Mary led a small army to England in November 1688, most royal troops defected to them, and James II fled to France.

This bloodless revolution of 1688, also called the Glorious Revolution, created a "limited monarchy" as defined by England's Bill of Rights of 1689. The crown promised to summon Parliament annually, sign all its bills, and respect traditional civil liberties. The Glorious Revolution's vindication of limited representative government burned deeply into English political consciousness, and Anglo-Americans never forgot it. Anglo-Americans not only came to share English Protestants' pride in the Glorious Revolution but also struck their own blows for liberty. Soon Massachusetts, New York, and Maryland all rose up against local representatives of the Stuart regime.

By 1688–1689 New Yorkers and New Englanders felt increasingly threatened by French aggression. Rumors flew that a French fleet was planning to take New York and that Indians would

**King William and
Queen Mary**

raid Albany. By early 1689 pro-French Indians assaulted English settlements in Maine. Andros promptly led a force of English troops and Massachusetts militia to defend Maine. But when he refused to attack neutral Indians, the colonists suspected him of protecting treacherous French allies. Ordering his soldiers to guard the Maine frontier, Andros returned to Boston defenseless in the event of trouble there.

Meanwhile, news that England's Protestant leaders had risen up against James II had electrified New Englanders. On April 18, well before confirmation of the English revolt's success, Boston's militia arrested Andros and his councilors. (The governor tried to flee in women's clothing but was caught after an alert guard spotted a "lady" in army boots.) The "sensible Gentlemen" of Massachusetts—the old political leadership—acted in the name of William and Mary, risking their necks should James return to power in England. Massachusetts and every other New England colony swiftly resumed self-government.

William and Mary would have preferred continuing the Dominion, but in the face of single-minded colonial determination to break it up, they wisely desisted. They gave official consent to dismantling the Dominion and restored to the citizens of Connecticut and Rhode Island the right of electing their own governors. However, they kept Massachusetts a royal colony, and, though allow-

ing the province to absorb Plymouth, refused to let it regain New Hampshire.

In other respects, too, Massachusetts won only a partial victory. Despite Increase Mather's lobbying in London, the new royal charter of 1691 reserved to the crown the right of appointing the governor. Moreover, property ownership, not church membership, became the criterion for voting. Worst of all, the Puritan colony had to tolerate Anglicans, who were proliferating in the port towns. In a society trembling at divine displeasure over its ungodliness (see Chapter 2), this was indeed bitter medicine to swallow.

New York's counterpart of the anti-Stuart uprising was Leisler's Rebellion. Emboldened by news of Boston's April 18 coup and startled by rumors that Andros's deputy Nicholson had threatened to burn New York, the city's militia seized the harbor's main fort on May 31, 1689. With his authority strangled, Nicholson sailed for England. Captain Jacob Leisler of the militia took over command of the colony, repaired its run-down defenses, and called elections for an assembly. When English troops arrived at New York in 1691 and Leisler denied them entry to key forts for fear that their commander was loyal to James II, a skirmish resulted, and Leisler was arrested.

"Hott brain'd" Leisler unwittingly had set his own downfall in motion. He had jailed many New Yorkers for questioning his authority, only to find that his former enemies had gained the new governor's ear and persuaded him to charge Leisler with treason for firing on royal troops. A packed jury found Leisler and his son-in-law, Jacob Milborne, guilty. Both men went to the gallows insisting that they were dying "for the king and queen and the Protestant religion."

Quickly wresting control of the council and legal system, Leisler's enemies used the courts to plunder their opponents' estates. Their rampage ceased in 1695, when Parliament reversed Leisler's and Milborne's convictions and ordered them reburied with full honors. Following a triumphant, emotional procession in which half of New York's adults marched in a pouring rain to reinter the two martyrs, the Leislerians inflicted stinging reprisals on their enemies and would have executed Leisler's bitterest antagonist if a sympathetic governor had not pardoned him. Both parties fought ruthlessly to destroy the other; but not until most of their leaders had died, by about 1720, did Jacob Leisler's vengeful ghost cease stalking New York.

By 1689 Maryland too had suffered political turmoil revolving around the issues of arbitrary government and Catholic plots. The Protestant-dominated lower house and the Catholic officials in the upper chamber feuded endlessly. Lurking behind it all was the uncertainty of having a pro-Stuart Catholic as the colony's absentee proprietor. News of England's Glorious Revolution naturally heartened Maryland's Protestant majority, which had long chafed under Catholic rule. Hoping to prevent a repetition of minor religion-tinged uprisings that had flared in 1676 and 1681, Lord Baltimore sent a messenger from England in early 1689 to command Maryland's obedience to William and Mary. But the courier died en route. The colony's Protestants widely began to fear that their proprietor was a traitor who supported James II.

Soon John Coode, a leader of the 1681 revolt, and three others organized the Protestant Association to secure Maryland for William and Mary. These conspirators seem to have been motivated far more by their exclusion from high public office than by religion, for three of the four had Catholic wives. Coode's group seized the capital in July 1689, removed all Catholics from office, and requested that the crown take over the colony. They got their wish. Maryland became a royal province in 1691, and in 1692 it made the Church of England the established religion. Catholics, who composed less

than one-fourth of the population, lost the right to vote and thereafter could worship only in private.

Maryland stayed in royal hands until 1715. At that point, the fourth Lord Baltimore joined the Church of England and regained his proprietorship. (Ironically, the children of John Coode and of another Protestant Association mastermind then turned Catholic.) Maryland continued as a proprietary colony until 1776.

The revolutionary events of 1688–1689 decisively changed the colonies' political climate by reestablishing legislative government and ensuring religious freedom for Protestants. Dismantling the Dominion of New England and directing governors to call annual assemblies, William and Mary allowed the colonial elite to reassert control over local affairs and encouraged American political leaders to identify their interests with England. A foundation was thus laid for an empire based on voluntary allegiance rather than submission to raw power imposed from faraway London. The crowning of William and Mary opened a new era in which Americans drew rising confidence from their relationship to the English throne. "As long as they reign," wrote a Bostonian who helped topple Andros, "New England is secure."

A Generation of War

The Revolution of 1688 ushered in a quarter-century of warfare that convulsed Europe and the colonies alike. In 1689 England joined a general European coalition against France's Louis XIV, who supported James II's claim to the English crown. The resulting War of the League of Augsburg (which Anglo-Americans called King William's War) was the first struggle to embroil the colonies in European rivalries. For the next seventy-five years, North American soil would be an extension of Europe's battlefields.

In the American theater of King William's War, New Yorkers and Yankees launched a two-pronged invasion of Canada in 1690, with one prong aimed at Montreal and the second at Quebec. Lack of supplies caused the Anglo-American expedition marching on Montreal to disintegrate in the New York wilderness. Meanwhile, their strength sapped by smallpox, half-rations, and insufficient ammunition, two thousand Massachusetts militiamen eventually abandoned a lengthy siege of Quebec.

The war then degenerated into a series of cruel but inconclusive border raids against civilians on both sides.

Already weary from a new wave of Beaver Wars fought against Indians in the Ohio Valley since 1680 (see Chapter 1), the Iroquois of New York bore the bloodiest fighting in King William's War. Standing almost alone against their foes, the Five Nations faced overwhelming odds. Not only did their own English and Dutch allies meet with little success intercepting enemy war parties, but *coureurs de bois* had enlisted virtually all other Indians of the region as French combatants. In 1691 every Mohawk and Oneida war chief died in battle; by 1696 French armies had destroyed the villages of every Iroquois nation but the Cayugas and Oneidas. Hundreds of tribe members defected to the French and moved to Canada.

Although the war ended in 1697, the Iroquois staggered under Algonkian invasions until 1700. By then one-quarter of the Five Nations' 2,000 warriors had been killed or taken prisoner, or had deserted to Canada. The total Iroquois population declined 20 percent over twelve years, from 8,600 to 7,000. (By comparison, fewer than 900 English and Dutch, and perhaps no more than 400 French, died during the same period.)

In 1701, under French pressure, the Iroquois agreed not only to let Canada's governor settle their disputes with other Indians but also to stay neutral in future wars. Thereafter, the Iroquois perfected a delicate diplomacy that played off the English and French. Skillful negotiations brought the Iroquois far more success than had war by allowing them to keep control of their lands, rebuild their decimated population, and gain recognition as holding the balance of power along the Great Lakes.

In 1702 European war again erupted when England fought France and Spain in the War of the Spanish Succession, called Queen Anne's War by England's American colonists. This conflict taught Anglo-Americans painful lessons about their military weakness. Raiders from Canada destroyed several towns in Massachusetts and Maine. The Spanish invaded southern Carolina and nearly took Charles Town in 1706. Enemy warships captured many colonial vessels and landed looting parties along the Atlantic coast. Colonial sieges of Quebec and St. Augustine ended as expensive failures.

English forces had more success than their colonial counterparts and occupied the Hudson's

French Fort Builders

The French mania for establishing forts in America is the subject of this German engraving of c. 1700.

Bay region, as well as previously French Newfoundland and Acadia (later called Nova Scotia). When peace came in 1713 after nineteen years of vicious combat, however, the French and Indian hold on the continent's interior remained unbroken.

The most important consequence of the colonial wars was political in nature, not military. The wars instilled in Anglo-Americans a profound sense of dependence on Great Britain. The clashes with France vividly reminded Americans of the loyalty they owed William and Mary for ousting James II, who the colonists believed would have persecuted Protestants and ruled despotically. Anglo-Americans also came to recognize their own military weakness and the extent to which their shipping needed the Royal Navy's protection. Even as a new generation of English colonists matured, war was thus reinforcing their sense of British identity by buttressing their loyalty to the crown.

Peace and Expansion

The end of Queen Anne's War in 1713 introduced a generation of peace lasting until 1744. Britain's mainland colonies enjoyed exceptional growth in these years, with their population tripling from about 330,000 to 1 million. Settlement spread to the foothills of the Appalachians, and the new colony of Georgia was born. Rising prosperity dramatically improved living standards for most Americans and allowed the upper ranks of society to become graciously cultured and "enlightened."

A Burgeoning, Diversifying Population

In 1751 Pennsylvania businessman, publicist, and scientist Benjamin Franklin (1706–1790) wrote in an essay, *Observations Concerning the Increase of Mankind and the Peopling of the Colonies*, that "people increase in proportion to the number of marriages, and that is greater in proportion to the ease and convenience of supporting a family. When families can be easily supported, more persons marry, and earlier in life." Cities, he noted, retarded such growth: they were unhealthy and contained many people too poor to marry and rear families. But British America, with its small cities and great expanses of rural space, clearly seemed destined to grow and flourish. Estimating the colonies' population at 1 million, Franklin calculated that this number would double every twenty-five years. He exulted: "What an accession of power to the British empire!" Franklin knew whereof he spoke: he was the tenth child among seventeen siblings. He estimated colonial growth trends with amazing precision, and modern research has confirmed his reasoning about the factors driving population change in his era.

Every North American colony followed a similar demographic pattern. In the first years of settlement, numbers increased only through a continuous influx of immigrants, for settlers always died more quickly than children could be born to replace them. But at some point, males ceased to outnumber females, so that most adults could find mates. Moreover, because colonists married young and had large families, the population finally started inching up by natural increase (the excess of births over deaths). Rapid growth, however, began only when settlers also enjoyed good nutrition and a healthy environment—conditions that lowered infant mortality and extended adult life expectancy.

By 1645 the male-female ratio almost equalized in New England (see Chapter 2). Thereafter, favorable environmental conditions caused the population to shoot up. By 1690 the same spurt began in the Middle Atlantic colonies.

Demographic "takeoff" reached the South last. Only with the heavy importation of indentured servants did the southern population continue to expand in the seventeenth century. Even after 1690, when the southern colonies finally had roughly equal numbers of men and women, growth was slow because epidemic disease haunted the marshy tidewater. After Queen Anne's War, however, southern whites left the tidewater in droves, and by 1750 a majority of them resided in the piedmont, where the life expectancy equaled that in New England. Slaves came to form the greater part of the eighteenth-century tidewater population, but their death rate was lower than whites' because of their partial immunity to malaria.

After 1700, when life expectancy and family size in the South rose to levels typical of the North, British North America's growth rate far outpaced Great Britain's. Colonial women had an average of eight children and forty-two grandchildren; British women at the time typically bore five infants and had fifteen grandchildren. The ratio of Britain's population to that of the mainland colonies plummeted from 20 to 1 (1700) to 3 to 1 (1775).

Fully half of all colonial women bore more than eight children. This exceptionally high birthrate produced families like that of New Jersey resident Daniel Robbins, described in the *New England Weekly Journal* in 1733. By the time Robbins was 66, his wife had 13 children, of whom 11 had married and borne 62 offspring of their own. None of the Robbins's descendants had yet died, and more grandchildren were on the way. "Thus it appears," the *Weekly Journal* declared, "that said Daniel Robbins has successfully kept and fulfilled that great and necessary Commandment of *Multiply, be Fruitful*, and *Replenish the Earth*." Such remarkable fertility was responsible for two-thirds of colonial population growth after 1700.

In the eighteenth century, immigration continued to contribute significantly to colonial population growth, though it became less important than natural increase. In the forty years after Queen Anne's War, the colonies absorbed 350,000 newcomers, 40 percent of them (140,000) slaves who had survived a sea crossing of sickening brutality. The approximately 210,000 whites who immi-

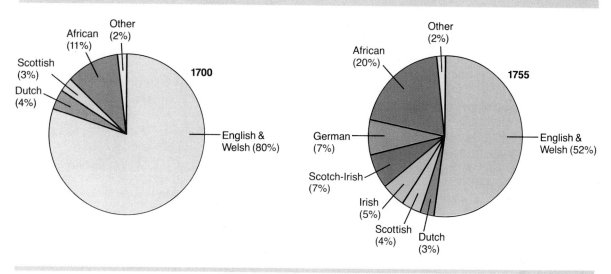

Distribution of Ethnic and Racial Groups Within the British Mainland Colonies, 1700–1755

Other (2%)
African (11%)
Scottish (3%)
Dutch (4%)
1700
English & Welsh (80%)

Other (2%)
African (20%)
German (7%)
Scotch-Irish (7%)
Irish (5%)
Scottish (4%)
Dutch (3%)
1755
English & Welsh (52%)

The impact of heavy immigration from 1720 to 1755 can be seen in the reduction of the English-Welsh stock from four-fifths of all colonists to a slight majority; in the doubling of the African-American population; and in the sudden influx of Germans and Irish, who together composed a fifth of all Anglo-Americans by 1755.

SOURCE: Thomas L. Purvis, "The European Ancestry of the United States Population," *William & Mary Quarterly,* LXI (1984), 85–101.

grated during these years included a sharply reduced share from England compared to the seventeenth century. Whereas between 1630 and 1700 an average of 2,000 English settlers landed annually (constituting 90 percent of all European immigrants), after 1713 the English contribution dropped to about 500 a year. Rising employment and higher wages in eighteenth-century England simply made voluntary immigration to America far less attractive than before. But economic hardship elsewhere in the British Isles and northern Europe supplied a steady stream of immigrants, and their coming ensured that white North Americans were growing more ethnically diverse.

Immigrants usually found the passage to America harrowing. A German in 1750 remembered "the ship . . . full of pitiful signs of distress . . . , all of them caused by the age and the highly salted state of the food . . . , as well as by the very bad and filthy water, which brings about the miserable destruction and death of many. . . . All this misery reaches its climax when . . . one

must suffer through two or three days and nights of storm, with everyone convinced that the ship with all aboard is bound to sink." This man's voyage lasted fifteen weeks.

The largest eighteenth-century white immigrant contingent comprised 100,000 newcomers from Ireland, two-thirds of them "Scots-Irish" descendants of sixteenth-century Scottish Presbyterians who had settled in northern Ireland. After 1718 Scots-Irish fled to America to escape rack renting (frequent increases in farm rents), and they commonly came as complete families. In contrast, 90 percent of all Catholic Irish immigrants arrived as unmarried male indentured servants. Rarely able to find Catholic wives, they generally abandoned their faith to marry Protestant women.

Meanwhile, from Germany came a wave of 65,000 settlers, most of them refugees from terrible economic conditions in the Rhine Valley. Wartime devastation had compounded the misery of Rhenish peasants, many of whom were squeezed onto plots of land too small to feed a family. One-third of these people financed their voyage as "redemptioners"—that is, they had sold themselves or their children as indentured servants. Most Germans were either Lutherans or Calvinists. But a significant minority belonged to small, pacifist religious sects that desired above all to be left alone.

Overwhelmingly, the eighteenth-century immigrants were poor. Those who became indentured servants had to give one to four years of work to an urban or rural master, who might well exploit them cruelly. Servants could be sold or rented out, beaten, granted minimal legal protection, kept from marrying, and sexually harassed; and attempted escape usually meant an extension of their service. But at the end of their term, most managed to collect "freedom dues," which could help them to marry and acquire land.

Whether or not they had been servants, few immigrants settled permanently in those parts of North America where land was relatively scarce and expensive—New England, New Jersey, lower New York, and the southern tidewater. (New Englanders in particular did not welcome people who might become public charges: "these confounded Irish will eat us all up," snorted one Bostonian.) Philadelphia became the immigrants' primary port of entry. So many foreigners passed through the "City of Brotherly Love" into underpopulated Pennsylvania that by 1755 the original English stock accounted for only one-third of the colony's population; the rest were mostly Germans, Irish, and Scots.

Rising numbers of immigrants traveled to the piedmont region, stretching along the eastern slope of the Appalachians. A significant German community developed in upper New York, and thousands of other Germans as well as Irish fanned southward from Pennsylvania into western Maryland. Many other Irish, Germans, and Scots arrived in the second-most popular gateway to eighteenth-century America, Charles Town, whence they would move on to settle the South Carolina piedmont. There they raised grain, livestock, and tobacco, generally without slaves. After 1750 both streams of immigration merged with an outpouring of Anglo-Americans from the Chesapeake in the rolling, fertile hills of western North Carolina. In 1713 few Anglo-Americans had lived more than fifty miles from the sea, but by 1750 one-third of all colonists resided in the piedmont.

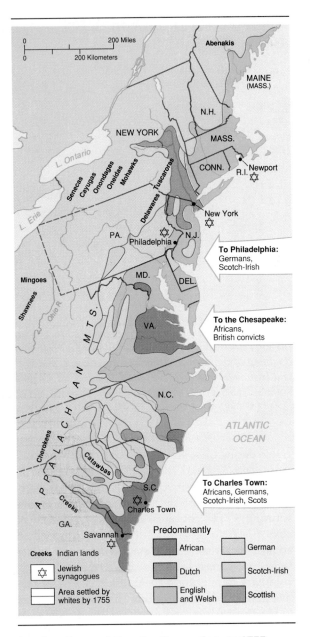

Immigration and Frontier Expansion, to 1755

A sharp rise in the importation of African slaves made much of the southern tidewater a predominantly black region. Immigrants from Germany, Ireland, and Scotland tended to settle in the piedmont. A significant Jewish population emerged in the seaports.

Immigrants found the piedmont rather easy to settle. Disease and war had already destroyed or scattered most of the native American population.

Only in upper New York did a continuing Indian presence block further white expansion (see "A Place in Time"). Elsewhere after 1713, few Indians remained within the triangular region bounded by Philadelphia, Albany, and southern Maine. The Chesapeake tribes had moved beyond Virginia's Shenandoah Valley, and in the Carolina piedmont, the remnants of the Tuscaroras and Yamasees drifted away. Then in the 1730s, smallpox killed perhaps half the fifty thousand Cherokees and Catawbas remaining in the Carolina piedmont. Native Americans explained their own depopulation in supernatural rather than scientific terms, but their conclusion was not far from the mark. "They have a superstition," wrote a Pennsylvania German in 1700, "that as many Indians die each year, as the number of Europeans that newly arrive."

English-stock colonists did not relish the influx of so many foreigners. Franklin spoke for many when he asked in his 1751 essay on population,

> *why should the Palatine boors [Germans] be suffered to swarm into our settlements, and, by herding together, establish their language and manners, to the exclusion of ours? Why should Pennsylvania, founded by the English, become a colony of aliens, who will shortly be so numerous as to Germanize us instead of us Anglicizing them, and will never adopt our language or customs any more than they can acquire our complexion?*

In the same ungenerous spirit, Franklin objected to the slave trade largely because it would increase America's black population at the expense of industrious whites.

On another occasion, Franklin suggested that the colonists send rattlesnakes to Britain in return for the convict laborers dumped on American shores. Deportation of lawbreakers to America had been common enough in the seventeenth century, and between 1718 and 1783, some thirty thousand convicts arrived. A few were murderers; most were thieves; some were guilty of the most trivial offenses, like a young Londoner who "got intoxicated with liquor, and in that condition attempted to snatch a handkerchief from the body of a person in the street to him unknown. . . ." Convicts were sold as servants on arrival. Relatively few continued to commit crimes in America, and some managed eventually to establish themselves as back-country farmers. But like many contemporary Americans, colonial citizens seldom wished to absorb the victims of other nations' social problems.

Georgia

Yet for Parliament, solving England's social problems was a chief motive in chartering the new colony of Georgia in 1732. Parliament intended Georgia as a refuge where bankrupt debtors (who normally rotted in jail until their debt was repaid) could settle, their presence protecting South Carolina against attacks from Spanish Florida to the south. Meanwhile, the new colony's sponsors hoped that Georgia would flourish by exporting expensive commodities like wine and silk. Parliament even spent money to ensure the success of the colony, which became the only North American province (except Nova Scotia) in which the British government actually invested funds.

The moving spirit behind Georgia's foundation was tough-minded James Oglethorpe (1696–1785). He guided the colony's charter through Parliament (of which he was a member) and for the first ten years of Georgia's existence dominated the board of trustees that administered the province. A puritanical bachelor, he yearned to do good for the downtrodden. Although a soldier of fortune, he admired the pacifist Quaker William Penn, whom in several respects he resembled. Like Penn, he was doomed to disappointment.

Georgia took shape slowly during its first decade. Oglethorpe founded the port of entry, Savannah, in 1733, and by 1740 a small contingent—2,800 colonists—had settled in the province. Almost half the immigrants came from Germany, Switzerland, and Scotland, and most had their overseas passage paid by the government. A small number of Jews were among the early settlers. Georgia thus began as the least English of all colonies. In 1742 Oglethorpe led 650 men in repelling 3,000 Spanish troops and refugee South Carolina slaves who had invaded Georgia aiming to destroy all English settlements as far as Charles Town. When peace returned in 1744, Georgia's survival was assured.

Idealistic concerns about human welfare, along with practical considerations of security, prompted Oglethorpe to try banning slavery and rum from Georgia, as well as to deal fairly with the Indians.

Geneseo, New York, in 1750

In 1750, about forty miles south of Lake Ontario lay the Seneca Indian village of Geneseo. Comprising about a hundred houses set amidst vast fruit orchards and beautiful vegetable fields, Geneseo was the largest community of the Senecas, the westernmost Iroquois people. The high seventeenth-century stockade had slowly crumbled during the long peace since 1713. As the village outgrew its former fortifications, the Senecas abandoned their decrepit homes and built replacements wherever they pleased, so that Geneseo sprawled without plan across a lovely meadow.

Decades of peace had brought the Senecas prosperity. In exchange for the furs that they sold at Albany, Seneca hunters kept Geneseo well supplied with British manufactures. Every Seneca household owned a gun, several metal pots, woven blankets, steel knives and hatchets, animal traps, iron needles, scissors, ready-made shirts, bells, mirrors, tweezers for extracting body hair, a mouth harp, copper armbands, rings, metallic earrings, and assorted charms. Dutch and English merchants did a lucrative business providing the Iroquois with these wares, as well as with enormous quantities of gunpowder, bullets, and whiskey. The Senecas dressed, slept, cooked, hunted, and entertained themselves using European goods, which they incorporated into their way of life without changing their underlying culture and values.

Iroquois life revolved around the longhouse. Measuring as much as seventy-five feet long and fifteen

Iroquois Silver Craft

Though lacking knowledge of silver and other metals until whites introduced them, the Iroquois thereafter became highly skilled metal crafters.

feet wide, the longhouse was a barracks that could hold up to sixty persons. Each family occupied a compartment twelve or fifteen feet long containing two sets of double-decker bunk beds about six feet wide. There was little privacy, for one hallway connected every compartment and people tramped through at all hours. An open fire smoldering all day in every family's quarters kept the atmosphere smoke-filled and stuffy.

Each longhouse sheltered the members of a particular clan, its symbol carved above the main entrance. Because ancestry was traced through the mother's line, women dominated the longhouse's social and economic activities. Elder women resolved problems between clan members and oversaw the distribution of property.

By raising the community's crops, women also bore the chief responsibility for preventing famine. An individual woman could claim exclusive rights to a field or an orchard, but few did so. The women cleared, planted, weeded, and harvested the fields of their clan in a leisurely but highly efficient fashion by organizing "working bees," during which they joked, sang, or gossiped their way through each day's labor. Aside from meat and fish that the men brought in, a mother furnished her family's entire diet: fruit, squash, pumpkins, herbs, bark teas, and especially succotash, a bean-corn mixture that provided all a healthy adult's protein needs. Iroquois women were such productive farmers that the Seneca nation, which numbered just thirty-five hundred people in 1750, raised perhaps a million bushels of corn each year.

The Iroquois also gave women considerable opportunity to influence the choice of leaders and other political decisions. The forty-nine Seneca clans sent representatives to the council of the League of the Iroquois, and whenever a delegate died, the senior women of the clan named his successor. Although men had formal responsibility for war and diplomacy, women's views carried substantial weight at village meetings. Women rarely spoke there, but they persuaded important individuals from their clans to voice females' views, and they lobbied undecided leaders to support their spokesmen. Because native Americans made decisions by persuasion

Hendrick, a Mohawk Chief, c. 1710

Hendrick, who posed for this formal portrait during a visit to London, sported European-style dress but personalized it with Iroquois touches such as the woven sash and wampum belt that he is holding. The Iroquois readily adopted European attire.

and consensus rather than by a simple majority vote, women were guaranteed a hearing—and they often prevailed.

As head of their clans, women could, moreover, insist that their kinsmen attack enemies for revenge or to seize a captive to replace a dead relative. Although such demands could not be legally enforced, they imposed a moral burden that men could not escape without seriously damaging their reputation. Consequently, Iroquois women instigated many small-scale military actions by demanding vengeance or prisoners. Even during the relatively peaceful decades after Queen Anne's War ended in 1713, Seneca matrons sent several dozens of war parties against the Catawba Indians of South Carolina. The fate of Catawbas dragged back by these raiders depended on the women, who adopted most captives into their families but shared fully in slowly torturing to death those who seemed unfit to replace fallen relatives.

So the Senecas, like all Iroquois, depended heavily on women's contributions. The men roamed over a million square miles from South Carolina north to Hudson's Bay and west to the Mississippi River; frequently gone for several months at a stretch while trapping furs, they went off for shorter periods while hunting game, conducting diplomacy, or seeking captives. But during these absences, economically self-sufficient women could be counted on to feed the village. Additionally, in times of a conflict such as King William's War, when the Iroquois lost perhaps half their senior leaders in battle, elder women's political skills and wisdom guided untested younger men who were suddenly thrust into positions of high responsibility. And in more peaceful times, women preserved the memory of the past, passed traditions on to children, and kept peace within the cramped, smoke-filled longhouses. In short, women provided the economic self-sufficiency, political wisdom, and cultural memory that were essential to the Iroquois' continuation as a great people.

Family Life in a Seneca Longhouse

The baby hangs in a cradle-board; the man carves a wooden bowl.

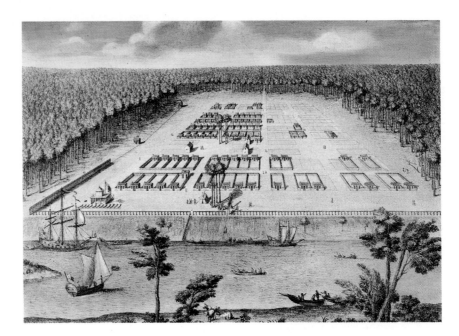

Earliest-Known View of Savannah, c. 1734

Oglethorpe hated slavery. "They live like cattle," he wrote to the trustees after viewing Charles Town's slave market. "If we allow slaves, we act against the very principles by which we associated together, which was to relieve the distressed." Slavery, he thought, degraded blacks, made whites lazy, and presented a terrible risk. South Carolina's Stono Rebellion of 1739 particularly alarmed him. Oglethorpe worried that wherever whites relied on a slave labor force, they courted slave revolts, which the Spanish could then exploit. As an abstainer from hard liquor (a trait that made him unusual in eighteenth-century America), he disapproved of the importation and distilling of spirits, and as the man responsible for the colony's security, he feared the effects of encouraging nearby Indians to drink. Oglethorpe was also atypical of his era in admiring the native Americans' seemingly simple, dignified way of life, and they responded by trusting him. As long as he remained the colony's leader, Georgia enjoyed good relations with the southeastern tribes.

At Oglethorpe's insistence, Parliament made Georgia the only colony where slavery was forbidden. He also pushed through a requirement that landholdings remain relatively small and that a male always occupy each farm. Thus fathers could pass on property only if they had male heirs. These measures were aimed at keeping rural Georgia populated by white farmer-soldiers, ready to leap to the colony's defense and uncorrupted by the urge to speculate in real estate or build up slave-labor plantations.

But Oglethorpe's well-intentioned plans failed completely. Few debtors arrived because Parliament set impossibly stringent conditions for their release from prison. Limitations on settlers' rights to sell or enlarge their holdings, as well as the ban on slavery, also kept settlement low. Raising exotic export crops proved impractical; as in South Carolina, only rice yielded a profit. Oglethorpe struggled against economic reality for a decade and then gave up. After the early 1740s, he took little part in Georgia's affairs. Then in 1750 the trustees finally legalized slavery, and other restrictions on the market for land also fell by the wayside. As a result, Georgia boomed. The population rose from four thousand residents in 1750 (including up to a thousand hitherto illegal slaves) to twenty-three thousand inhabitants in 1770, 45 percent of them blacks.

Georgia's settlement completed British colonization of the Atlantic seaboard. Having held Georgia against Spain and pushed the frontier west 150 miles, British expansion virtually halted after 1750. Anglo-Americans would not settle beyond the Appalachians until the 1770s. Nevertheless, the colonial population continued to grow rapidly,

James Oglethorpe and the Indians

In 1734 Oglethorpe visited London with Indians who had sold him land. Here the native Americans meet with Englishmen who have invested in the Georgia colony.

doubling every twenty-six years—almost exactly what Franklin had predicted in 1751. Had this rate continued, the U.S. population today would number around 850 million, second only to China's.

A Maturing Colonial Economy and Society

Britons who visited mid-eighteenth-century America were generally impressed at the sight of a sophisticated society and widespread economic prosperity. "The nobleness of the town," wrote an English naval officer after first viewing New York in 1756, "surprized me more than the fertile appearance of the country. I had no idea of finding a place in America, consisting of near 2,000 houses, elegantly built of brick, raised on an eminence and the streets paved and spacious, . . . but such is this city that very few in England can rival it in its show." Seven years later, when issuing orders for demobilizing royal troops stationed in the colonies, General Jeffery Amherst advised his regimen-

tal commanders to discourage their men from returning to the British Isles to be mustered out because "I would much rather they would take their Discharges in this country, where they can get their Livelyhood by working Easier than at Home."

The prosperity and social development that European visitors recorded, as well as the underlying rapid population growth and wide expansion of frontier settlement, were relatively new. By 1750 the colonies' brisk economic growth had been under way for only fifty to seventy-five years, depending on the region. Throughout the first half of the eighteenth century, colonial exports climbed steadily and allowed Anglo-Americans to enjoy a relatively high standard of living despite external controls imposed by Parliament.

British Economic Policy Toward America

Between 1651 and 1733, Parliament enacted a series of laws governing commerce between the British Isles and the overseas colonies. Historians label the rules of trade set forth in these laws the "navigation system," and they use the word *mercantilism* to describe the assumptions on which these laws rested. Both the navigation system and mercantilist thinking remained vigorously alive from the late seventeenth to the late eighteenth century, and they deeply affected North America's relationship with Great Britain.

Mercantilism was not a carefully elaborated economic theory. Rather, the word refers to European policymakers' aim of guaranteeing prosperity by making their own country as self-sufficient as possible—by eliminating dependence on foreign suppliers, damaging foreign competitors' commercial interests, and increasing their nation's net stock of gold and silver by selling more abroad than they bought. Mercantilist policies generally had the additional effect of favoring special interests such as chartered companies and merchants' guilds. Mercantilism was the antithesis of a competitive free-market system, which received its first great theoretical defense in Scottish economist Adam Smith's *The Wealth of Nations,* published in 1776. Until that revolutionary year, mercantilist thinking would dominate British policy almost unchallenged.

Parliament enacted England's first Navigation Act in 1651 to undercut the Dutch Republic's economic preponderance. Dutch shippers and merchants then controlled oceanic trade and probably owned three-quarters of northern Europe's commercial vessels; few Englishmen could compete with the well-financed and experienced Dutch traders. By the Navigation Acts, Parliament sought to exclude the Dutch from English trade and thereby to force England to build up its own merchant marine. Immediately after the Stuart restoration in 1660, Parliament reiterated these rules and also began protecting English manufactures from foreign competition. By 1750 a long series of Navigation Acts were in force, affecting the colonial economy in four major ways.

First, the laws limited all imperial trade to *British* ships, defined as those with British ownership and whose crews were three-quarters British. (Because Parliament wanted only to exclude the Dutch, not to discriminate against Americans, it classified all colonists, even blacks, as British.) When Parliament began strictly to enforce this requirement in the late seventeenth century, American colonists and some elements of the English business community alike objected, because the Dutch

offered better prices, credit, and merchandise. After 1700, however, when Britain's merchant marine became equal to its Dutch competitors, this cause for complaint evaporated.

This new shipping restriction not only contributed to Great Britain's rise as Europe's foremost shipping nation but also laid the foundations for an American merchant marine. By the 1750s one-third of all imperial vessels were American-owned. The swift growth of this merchant marine diversified the colonial economy and made it more self-sufficient. The expansion of colonial shipping in turn hastened urbanization by creating a need for centralized docks, warehouses, and repair shops in America. By 1770 Philadelphia was the British Empire's second-largest port, after London, and New York City was not far behind. Shipbuilding emerged as a major colonial industry in these years, and by 1770 one-third of the "British" merchant marine was actually American-built.

The second major way in which the Navigation Acts affected the colonies lay in their barring the export of certain "enumerated goods" to foreign nations unless these items first passed through England or Scotland. The mainland's chief "controlled" items were tobacco, rice, furs, indigo (a Carolina plant that produced a blue dye), and naval stores (masts, hemp, tar, and turpentine). Parliament never restricted grain, livestock, fish, lumber, or rum, which altogether made up 60 percent of colonial exports. Further, American exporters of tobacco and rice—the chief commodities affected by enumeration—had their burdens reduced by two significant concessions. First, Parliament gave Americans a monopoly over the British market by excluding foreign tobacco, even though this hurt British consumers. (Rice planters enjoyed a natural monopoly because they had no competitors.) Second, Parliament tried to minimize the added cost of landing tobacco and rice in Britain (where customs officials collected duties on both) by refunding these duties on all tobacco and rice that the colonists later shipped to other countries. About 85 percent of all American tobacco and rice was eventually reexported and sold outside the British Empire.

The navigation system's third impact on the colonies was to encourage economic diversification in America. Parliament used British tax money to pay modest bounties to Americans producing

New York Harbor, c. 1760 *New York was a bustling colonial port in the mid-eighteenth century. In this colorful panorama, a group of militiamen drill, center; a French ship, possibly the catch of a privateer, is anchored to the left.*

such items as silk, iron, dyes, hemp, and lumber, which Britain would otherwise have had to import from other countries, and it raised the price of commercial rivals' imports by imposing protective tariffs on them.

On the surface, the trade laws' fourth consequence for the colonies was negative: they forbade Americans from competing with British manufacturers of clothing and steel. In practice, however, this prohibition had little effect, for it banned only *large-scale* manufacturing; colonial tailors, hatters, and housewives could continue to make any item of dress in their households or small shops. Manufactured by low-paid labor, British clothing imports to America generally undersold whatever the colonists could have produced at their higher labor costs. For this reason, Americans failed to establish a profitable clothing industry until after 1820. Steel manufacturing also depended on cheap labor, and not until the 1840s did either Great Britain or America develop a successful steel industry. The colonists were free to produce iron, however, and by 1770 they had built 250 ironworks employing thirty thousand men, a work force larger than the entire population of Georgia or of any provincial city. At the American Iron Company's

complex of eleven forges and furnaces near Ringwood, New Jersey, five hundred workers manned eleven furnaces that annually consumed eight square miles of timber as fuel. By 1770 British North America produced more iron than England and Wales, and only Sweden and Russia exceeded the colonies' output.

Colonial complaints against the navigation system raged in the late seventeenth century but rarely were heard after 1700. The trade regulation primarily burdened tobacco and rice exporters, whose income nevertheless was reduced by less than 3 percent. The commercial laws did raise the cost of non-British merchandise imported into the colonies, but seldom by enough to encourage smuggling (except in the case of tea from India and molasses from the French Caribbean). The great volume of colonial trade proceeded lawfully, and Americans probably smuggled much less than did Britons themselves. Anglo-American commerce provided mutual advantages for Britain and its colonies, and when Americans lost their trading rights in 1783, their commerce declined greatly. Although Parliament intended the laws only to benefit Britain, the navigation system had far from crippled the provincial economy. Rather, British North

Colonial Exports and Their Average Annual Value, 1768–1772

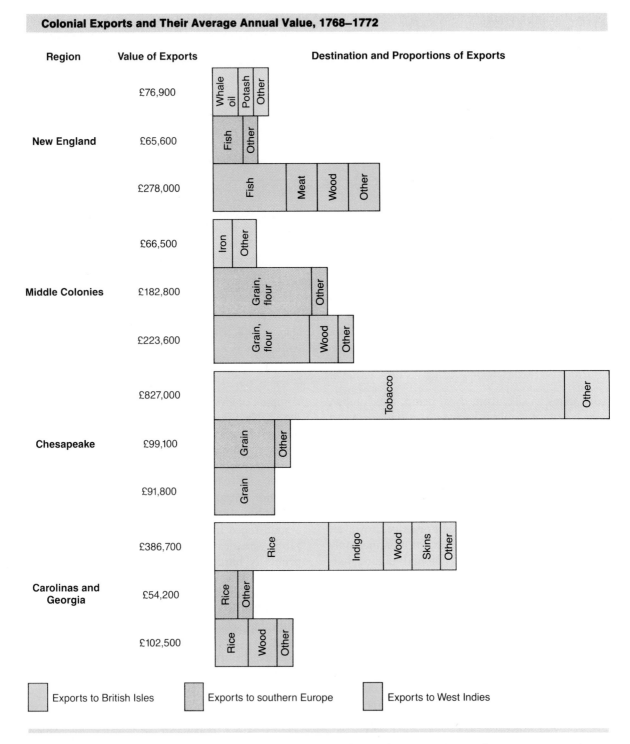

Export patterns varied greatly among colonial regions. The South sent almost 80 percent of its exports to Great Britain, while more than half of northern exports went to the West Indies and another quarter was sold in southern Europe. The value of Chesapeake tobacco equaled that of almost all northern exports combined.

NOTE: Unlabeled segments represent miscellaneous exports.

SOURCE: James F. Shepherd and Gary M. Walton, *Shipping, Maritime Trade and the Economic Development of Colonial North America* (Cambridge, England: Cambridge University Press, 1972), 211–227.

America's economy grew at a per capita rate of 0.6 percent annually from 1650 to 1770, a pace twice that of Britain.

Eighteenth-Century Living Standards

Propelled by a tenfold increase in the volume of exports, colonial living standards rose dramatically from 1700 to 1770. Nowhere was Americans' newfound prosperity more evident than in the Chesapeake, which in the late seventeenth century had been a region of impoverished tenants battered by depressed tobacco prices. Not only did tobacco exports triple from 1713 to 1774, but prices slowly crept upward, in large part owing to a 75 percent reduction in marketing costs. The Chesapeake economy further benefited from sharply higher exports of wheat and corn, which by 1770 equaled 25 percent of tobacco sales. Thus within three generations of Bacon's Rebellion, the Chesapeake had ceased to be a region locked in pervasive poverty; instead, poverty was confined to a small underclass of whites attempting to farm marginal-quality soil. At the same time, a landholding small-planter element arose, so large that perhaps 30 percent of all white families owned slaves. Atop Chesapeake society, moreover, an elite of wealthy large landowners and slavemasters flourished after about 1700.

Living standards were highest in the mid-Atlantic, spanning the area from New York south to Delaware. In 1770 per capita wealth here exceeded the colonial average by 40 percent. These colonies' striking prosperity owed much to rich soils, a long-term climatic warming that lengthened the growing season after 1700, and brisk demand for livestock, wheat, and corn in the West Indies and (to a lesser extent) southern Europe.

Of all Anglo-Americans, New Englanders prospered least. Though hardly poor, Yankees were on average only half as wealthy as colonists elsewhere. Plagued by mediocre soil and a short growing season, New Englanders had to import grain to feed themselves. Yankees sent two-thirds of their livestock, lumber, and fish exports to the West Indies, and while their cattle raising remained profitable, a long-term decline in lumber prices stung the local economy. By the 1750s most New England towns had become overpopulated, bursting with more young men than could acquire enough land to support a family. In subsequent decades only migration to the frontier—to Vermont, Maine, Nova Scotia, and upper New York—would ease the pressure.

Many New Englanders survived economically by turning to the sea. By 1700 the Yankee merchant marine and fishing industry were the largest in the colonies, providing employment for every seventh man. This prosperity came at a heavy cost, however, for the sea was cruel and took perhaps every fifth sailor to a watery grave. (For this reason, the balcony on a ship captain's home from which his wife could watch for her husband's return to harbor became known as the widow's walk.)

Taken as a whole, the American colonies by the mid-eighteenth century enjoyed a standard of living that greatly exceeded that of Scotland or Ireland and approximated that of England and Wales. Steady overseas demand for colonial products spawned a prosperity that enabled Americans to consume a huge volume of British products. Consequently, the share of British exports sold to the colonies spurted from just 5 percent in 1700 to almost 40 percent by 1760. "You may depend upon it," remarked Pennsylvania judge William Allen in commenting on prospects for self-improvement, "this is one of the best poor man's countries in the world."

Rural Family Life

Although economic opportunity abounded for eighteenth-century immigrants and American-born colonists alike, personal success was hard won. A case in point is that of Aaron Leaming, the penniless orphan of a crippled English immigrant. By 1740 Leaming had risen through hard work to become one of New Jersey's richest residents. His rags-to-riches climb was certainly atypical, but his blunt advice to would-be emulators captured the essence of colonial opportunity: "Those who [do] not intend to die as poor as they were born must bestir themselves with great industry."

Because the vast majority of landowners had just enough acreage for a working farm, they could not provide their children with land of their own when they married. Moreover, since couples typically started having children in their mid-20s, had their last babies sometime after 40, and lived past 60, all but their youngest children would be approaching middle age before receiving any inheritance. Even children who obtained inheritances before turning 30 rarely got more than a sixth or seventh of their parents' estate, because most families wrote wills that divided property evenly—or almost so—among all daughters and sons. A young male had to build savings to buy farm equipment by working (from about age 16 to 23) as a field hand for his father or neighbors. Because mortgages usually required down payments of 33 percent, a young husband normally supported his growing family by renting a farm from the local gentry until his early or mid-30s.

Landownership came quickest to those farmers who could find seasonal or part-time work. Some learned a craft like carpentry that earned money year-round. Many more trapped furs, gathered honey and beeswax, or made cider, shingles, turpentine, or wampum. Whenever possible, farmers found wintertime jobs draining meadows, clearing fields, or fencing land for wealthier landowners who did not own slaves or indentured servants. Such nonagricultural work might gain an industrious farmer half again of his total income from selling crops and livestock.

Families worked off mortgages slowly because the long-term cash income from a farm (6 percent) about equaled the interest on borrowed money (5–8 percent). After making a down payment of one-third, a husband and wife generally satisfied the next third upon inheriting shares of their deceased parents' estates. They paid off the final third when their children reached their teens and the family could thus expand farm output with two or three full-time workers. Only by their late 50s, just as their youngest offspring got ready to leave home, could most colonial parents hope to free themselves of debt.

In general, the more isolated a community or the less productive its farmland, the more self-sufficiency and bartering its people practiced, although only the remotest settlements were completely self-sufficient. Almost all rural families depended heavily on wives' and daughters' production. Women contributed to their household's financial success by manufacturing items that the family would otherwise have to purchase. Besides cooking, cleaning, and washing, wives preserved food, boiled soap, made clothing, and tended the garden, dairy, orchard, poultry house, and pigsty. Women often sold dairy products to neighbors or export merchants, spun yarn into cloth for tailors, knitted

"The Queen of Sheba"

Mary Williams, a young girl of Massachusetts or New Hampshire, completed this brightly colored needle-point work in 1744. Though reflecting contemporary European design, the picture is distinctively American in composition and in the architectural and clothing styles that it depicts.

various garments for sale, and even vended their own hair for wigs. A farm family's ability to feed itself and its animals was worth about half of its cash income (a luxury that few European tenants had), and women did no less than men in meeting this end.

Legally, however, colonial American women found themselves constrained (see Chapter 2). A woman's single most autonomous decision was her choice of a husband. Once married, she lost control of her dowry (unless she was a New Yorker subject to old Dutch custom, which allowed her somewhat more authority). Still, widows controlled between 8 and 10 percent of all property in eighteenth-century Anglo-America, and some—among them Eliza Pinckney of South Carolina, the mother of several Revolutionary-era leaders—held large estates.

City women shared their country cousins' legal disability, and they worked equally hard to help support their households. Yet in one respect most city women differed. They and their families had to contend with narrowing, not expanding, economic prospects.

The Urban Paradox

The cities were colonial America's economic paradox. They shipped the livestock, grain, and lumber that enriched the countryside but were caught in a downward spiral of declining opportunity.

After 1740 economic success proved ever more elusive for the 4 percent of colonists who lived in cities. Poverty escalated rapidly in the three major seaports of Philadelphia, New York, and Boston. Debilitating ocean voyages left many immigrants too weak to work, and every incoming ship from Europe carried numerous widows and orphans. Moreover, the cities' poor rolls always bulged with the survivors of mariners lost at sea. High population density and poor sanitation in urban locales allowed contagious diseases to run rampant, so that half of all city children died before age twenty-one and urban adults lived ten years less on average than country folk.

Even the able-bodied found cities economically treacherous. Early-eighteenth-century urban artisans typically trained apprentices and employed them as journeymen for many years until the latter opened their own shops. After 1750, however, more and more employers kept their labor force only as long as business was brisk, and released workers when sales slowed; in 1751 a shrewd Benjamin Franklin recommended this practice as an intelligent way to use expensive labor. Recessions hit more frequently after 1720 and created longer spells of unemployment. As urban populations ballooned, wages correspondingly tended to shrink, while the cost of rents, food, and firewood shot up.

Urban poverty grew from insignificance before 1700 into a major problem in the mid-eighteenth century. By 1730 Boston could no longer shelter its destitute in the almshouse built in 1685, and by 1741 the town had declared every sixth citizen too poor to pay taxes. Not until 1736 did New York need a poorhouse (for just forty persons), but by 1772, 4 percent of its residents (over eight hundred people) required public assistance to survive. The number of Philadelphia families listed as poor on tax rolls jumped from 3 percent in 1720 to 11 percent by 1760.

Economic frustration disposed townspeople to turn to violence to defend their interests. Before 1710, for example, few serious disorders disrupted Boston, but between that year and 1750, the city experienced five major riots, aimed at suppressing prostitution, stopping the navy from drafting sailors, or protesting wartime profiteering. However, citizens used force only as a last resort to curb public nuisances. They usually achieved their goals through intimidation or property damage, after which they disbanded and let the law resume its course.

Most southern cities were tiny. Charles Town, however, became North America's fourth-largest

Lamplighter on Broad Street, *by William Chappel*

A lamplighter makes his rounds on New York City's Broad Street. Eighteenth-century American cities were crowded, disease-infested places where poverty was rampant.

city. South Carolina's capital offered gracious living to the wealthy planters who flocked to their townhouses during the months of worst heat and insect infestation on their plantations. But shanties on the city's outskirts sheltered a growing crowd of destitute whites. The colony encouraged whites to immigrate in hopes of reducing blacks' numerical preponderance, but some European newcomers could not reach frontier farms or find any work except as ill-paid roustabouts. Like their counterparts in northern port cities, Charles Town's poor whites competed for work with urban slaves whose masters rented out their labor, and racial tensions simmered.

Slavery's Wages

From 1713 to 1754, five times as many slaves poured onto mainland North America than in all the preceding years. The proportion of blacks in the colonies doubled, rising from 11 percent at the beginning of the century to 20 percent by midcentury. Slavery was primarily a southern institution, but 15 percent of its victims lived north of Maryland, mostly in New York and New Jersey. By 1750 every seventh New Yorker was a slave.

Because West Indian and Brazilian slave buyers outbid the mainland colonists, a mere 5 percent of transported Africans were ever sold within the present-day United States. Unable to buy as many male field hands as they needed, mainland masters had no choice but to accept numerous female workers, and they protected their investments by maintaining the slaves' health. These factors promoted family formation and increased life expectancy far beyond the levels in the Caribbean, where family life was unstable and high death rates resulted from overwork and disease (see Chapter 2). On the mainland by 1750, the rate of natural increase for African-Americans almost equaled that for whites.

For slaves, the economic progress achieved in colonial America by about 1750 meant primarily that masters could usually afford to keep them healthy. Rarely, however, did masters choose to make their human chattels comfortable. A visitor to a Virginia plantation from Poland (where most peasants lived in dire poverty) gave this impression of slaves' quality of life:

> We entered some Negroes huts—for their habitations cannot be called houses. They are far

Blacks as a Percentage of the Total Population in Anglo-America 1650–1770

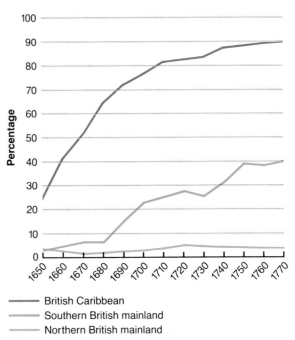

— British Caribbean
— Southern British mainland
— Northern British mainland

Wide differences developed in the racial composition of Britain's American colonies. By the mid-eighteenth century, the Caribbean sugar islands were almost 90 percent black, whereas the mainland colonies north of Maryland had become about 95 percent white. By 1750 slaves composed almost 40 percent of all mainland colonists south of Pennsylvania.

SOURCE: Robert W. Fogel and Stanley L. Engerman, *Time on the Cross* (Boston: Little, Brown, 1974), 21.

more miserable than the poorest of the cottages of our peasants. The husband and wife sleep on a miserable bed, the children on the floor . . . a little kitchen furniture amid this misery . . . a teakettle and cups . . . five or six hens, each with ten or fifteen chickens, walked there. That is the only pleasure allowed to the negroes.

To maintain slaves, masters normally spent just 40 percent of the amount paid for the upkeep of indentured servants. While white servants ate two hundred pounds of beef or pork yearly, most slaves consumed only fifty pounds of meat. The value of the beer and hard cider given to a typical servant alone equaled the expense of feeding and clothing the average slave. Masters usually provided adult slaves with eight quarts of corn and a pound of pork each week but expected them to grow their own vegetables, forage for wild fruits, and perhaps raise poultry.

Slaves worked for a far longer portion of their lives than whites. Slave children went to the fields as part-time helpers soon after reaching seven years and began working full-time between eleven and fourteen. Unlike white women, who did only light work in their dairies and gardens, female blacks routinely tended tobacco or rice crops, even when pregnant, and often worked outdoors in winter. Most slaves toiled until they died, although those in their sixties rarely performed hard labor.

The rigors of bondage did not, however, crush its victims' spirits. Slaves experienced love and formed families, and they constantly strove to win concessions from their owners. Despite the odds against them, slaves accumulated small amounts of property by establishing exclusive rights over their gardens and poultry, and they sometimes sold food to their masters. In 1769, for example, Thomas Jefferson made several purchases like the following:

gave negro for watermelon	7 pence
paid Fanny for 6 chickens	2 shillings
paid Cato for 1 doz eggs	3 pence

House slaves widely insisted on being tipped by guests for shining shoes and stabling horses. They sometimes sought presents aggressively on holidays, as a startled New Jersey tutor on a Virginia plantation discovered in 1774 when slaves demanding gifts of cash roused him from bed early Christmas morning.

In the South Carolina and Georgia rice country, slaves working under the highly favorable task system had control of about half their waking hours. Under tasking, each slave spent some hours caring for a quarter-acre—usually a half-day—after which his or her duties ended. By 1750 this system permitted certain slaves to keep hogs and sell surplus vegetables in Charles Town. A remarkable but atypical slave named Sampson earned enough money in his off-hours to hire another to work his own task, and became free in 1728.

By midcentury slaves made up 20 percent of New York City's population and formed a majority in Charles Town and Savannah. City life offered slaves advantages, most notably the chance for those with skills to hire themselves out and keep part of their wages. Many urban slaves could afford to dress well and to patronize taverns catering to black customers. By 1770 one-tenth of Savannah's slaves lived in rented rooms away from their owners. Though still in bondage, these blacks forced urban whites to allow them a substantial measure of personal freedom. But urban racial tensions could also

John Potter and His Family   *The Potters of Matunuck, Rhode Island, relax at tea. Note the presence of the black servant.*

run high, as in New York City in 1741, when nine slaves were burned at the stake for allegedly plotting arson.

Although slaves improved themselves and generally experienced robust health, most led lives of drudgery, lightened by few physical comforts. Prosperity also proved elusive for numerous white residents of the seaports, increasingly buffeted by poverty. These exceptions aside, middle-class eighteenth-century Anglo-Americans achieved a remarkably high standard of living, exceeded only by the Dutch and perhaps the English. The relatively few Americans at the top of the social pyramid lived more comfortably than the colonial middle class, but even the richest provincials enjoyed nothing like the opulence of Europe's titled aristocrats and the West Indian sugar kings.

The Consolidation of the Colonial Elites

"A man who has money here, no matter how he came by it, he is everything, and wanting [lacking] that he's a mere nothing, let his conduct be ever so irreproachable." Thus a Rhode Islander in 1748 described how colonial Americans defined high status. But once having achieved wealth, a man was expected by his contemporaries to behave with an appropriate degree of responsibility, to display dignity and generosity, and to be a community leader. In short, he was expected to act like a gentleman.*

Before 1700 the colonies' class structure was not readily apparent, because the rural elite's preference for buying land, servants, or slaves instead of luxuries perpetuated a homespun quality among the wealthy. In 1715 a traveler visiting one of Virginia's richest planters, Robert Beverley, noticed that his host owned "nothing in or about his house but just what is necessary, . . . [such as] good beds but no curtains and instead of cane chairs he hath stools made of wood." Unlike the British gentry, who did no manual labor, the colonial upper class included many individuals like West Jersey's Lieutenant Governor Thomas Olive, who commonly set aside his plowing to hold spontaneous court

sessions amid tree stumps as a favor to neighbors seeking his folksy "Jersey justice."

After 1720 well-to-do colonists began displaying their wealth more openly, particularly in their housing. The greater gentry—the richest 2 percent, who held about 15 percent of all property—constructed residences such as the Low House, New Jersey's most splendid home in 1741, and the Shirley mansion in Virginia. The lesser gentry, or second-wealthiest 2 to 10 percent, who held about 25 percent of all property, typically lived in a more modest fieldstone dwelling such as Pennsylvania's Lincoln homestead or a wood-frame house such as Whitehall in Rhode Island. In contrast, middle-class farmers commonly inhabited one-story wooden buildings with four small rooms and a loft.

The gentry also exhibited their wealth after 1720 by living in imitation of the European "grand style." They wore costly English fashions, drove carriages instead of wagons, and bought expensive chinaware, books, furniture, and musical instruments. They pursued a gracious life by studying foreign languages, learning formal dances, and cultivating polite manners. In sports their preference shifted to horse racing (on which they bet avidly) and away from cockfighting, a less elegant diversion. Their diets gained variety (as did those of most other eighteenth-century Americans), and gentry families indulged in rich, often unwholesome delicacies. A few young colonial males even got an English education.

For some rich colonials, affluence meant simply an opportunity to behave irresponsibly, but if they did so they generally incurred censure. For example, one young heir of the wealthy Livingstone family of New York was, his relatives complained, such a spendthrift that he was "scarce ever worth a groat in cash," the result of having "murdered his days with gamesters and Debauchers, and as he lived without a Fame, died without a memory."

For Chesapeake gentlemen, debt was a problem even if they lived virtuously. Tobacco planters were perpetually short of cash and in hock to British merchants who bought their crops and sold them imported goods on credit at high prices. Noted the Maryland assembly in 1697: "The trade of this province ebbs and flows according to the rise or fall of tobacco in the market of England." Planters could respond only in two ways. First, they could strive for as much self-sufficiency as possible on

---

*In the eighteenth century, the word *gentleman* meant an individual who not only conformed to socially accepted standards of behavior but also belonged to the upper class, or *gentry*.

The Shirley Plantation

The Shirley plantation on Virginia's James River was the nucleus of a self-contained world containing its own blacksmith, cooper, cobbler, and, of course, field slaves. Rare, gleaming silver graces the interior.

their estates—for example, by training their slaves to manufacture glass, bricks, tools, nails, and carriages. Second, they could diversify away from the region's tobacco monoculture (dependence on a single staple crop) by growing wheat or cutting timber. Self-sufficiency and diversification became more widely accepted objectives as the eighteenth century wore on, and after 1750 landowners like George Washington and Thomas Jefferson strongly advocated them.

In the eighteenth-century colonial cities, wealth remained highly concentrated. For example, New York's wealthiest 10 percent owned about 45 percent of the property throughout the eighteenth century. Similar patterns existed in Boston and Philadelphia. Set alongside the growth of a poor underclass in these cities, such statistics underscored the polarization of status and wealth in urban America on the eve of the Revolution. But as serious as this problem was becoming, no American cities experienced the vast gulf between elite wealth and mass poverty that was commonplace in eighteenth-century European towns.

The American colonial gentry and urban elite not only set the tone for society at large but also

dominated politics. Governors invariably appointed members of the greater gentry to sit on their councils or as judges on the highest courts. Most representatives elected to the legislatures' lower houses (assemblies) also ranked among the wealthiest 2 percent, as did majors and colonels in the militia. In contrast, members of the lesser gentry sat less often in the legislature, but they commonly served as justices of the peace on the county courts and as militia officers up to captain.

Colonial America's only high-ranking elected officeholders were the members of the legislature's lower house. But outside New England (where any voter could hold office), legal requirements barred 80 percent of white men from running for the assembly, most often by specifying that a candidate must own a minimum of a thousand acres. (Farms then averaged 180 acres in the South and 120 acres in the mid-Atlantic colonies.) Even had there been no such property qualifications, however, few ordinary citizens could have afforded the high costs of elective office. Assemblymen received only living expenses, which might not fully cover the cost of staying at their province's capital, much less compensate a farmer or an artisan for his absence from farm or shop for six to ten weeks a year. Even members of the gentry grumbled about legislative duty, many of them viewing high office as "a sort of tax on them to serve the public at their own Expense besides the neglect of their business," according to Governor Lewis Morris of New Jersey.

For these reasons, political leadership fell to certain wealthy families with a tradition of public service. Nine families, for example, provided one-third of Virginia's royal councilors during the century after 1680. John Adams, a rising young Massachusetts politician, estimated that most towns in his colony chose their legislators from among just three or four families.

The colonies set liberal qualifications for male voters, but all provinces excluded women, blacks, and Indians from elections. In seven colonies voters had to own land (usually forty to fifty acres), and the rest demanded that an elector have enough property to furnish a house and work a farm with his own tools. About 40 percent of free men could not meet these requirements, but nearly all of these were indentured servants, single sons still living with parents, or young men just beginning family life. Nevertheless, most white males in America would vote by age forty, whereas two-thirds of all men in England and nine-tenths in Ireland could not and would never vote.

In rural areas voter participation was low unless a vital issue was at stake. The difficulties of voting limited the average rural turnout to about 45 percent. (This rate of participation was, however, better than in typical American elections today, apart from those for president.) Outside New England and Pennsylvania, which held regularly scheduled elections, governors changed legislatures according to no set pattern, so that elections might lapse for years and suddenly be held on very short notice. Colonists in isolated areas thus often had no knowledge of an upcoming contest. The fact that all polling took place at the county seat discouraged many electors from traveling long distances over poor roads to vote. Moreover, in New York, New Jersey, the Chesapeake colonies, and North Carolina, voters had to state their choice publicly, often face-to-face with the candidates. This procedure naturally inhibited participation on the part of those who might dissent. Finally, the absence of political parties also played a role in the turnout:

no institutional means existed to stimulate popular interest in politics and to mobilize voters in support of candidates. Office seekers nominated themselves and usually ran on their reputation rather than issues that might spur public interest.

In view of these various factors, indifference toward politics was not uncommon by the mid-eighteenth century. For example, to avoid paying legislators' expenses at the capital, numerous Massachusetts towns refused to choose assemblymen; in 1763, 64 of 168 towns held no elections. Thirty percent of men elected to South Carolina's assembly neglected to take their seats from 1731 to 1760, including a majority of those chosen in 1747 and 1749. Apathy would have been even greater had candidates not freely plied voters with alcohol. This "swilling the planters with bumbo" was most popular among Virginians: George Washington dispensed almost two quarts of liquor for each voter at the courthouse when first elected to the assembly in 1758. Such practices helped the elite in most eighteenth-century colonies build up a tradition of community leadership that would serve them well in the years of revolutionary crisis after 1763.

Only in the major seaports did a truly competitive political life flourish. Voter turnout was relatively high in the cities because of greater population density, better communications, and the use of secret ballots (except in New York). Further, the cities' acute economic difficulties stimulated political participation among urban voters, ever hopeful that the government might ease their problems. In politics as in economics, cities were an exception to the general pattern for Anglo-America.

The most significant political development after 1700 was the rise of the assembly as the preponderant force in American government. Except in Connecticut and Rhode Island (where voters elected their governor), the crown or the proprietors in England chose each colony's governor, who in turn named a council, or upper house of the legislature. Thus only through the assembly could members of the gentry defend their own interests. Until 1689 governors and councils took the initiative in drafting laws, and the assemblies rather passively followed their lead; but thereafter, the assemblies assumed a more central role in politics.

Colonial leaders argued that their legislatures should exercise the same rights as those won by Parliament in its seventeenth-century struggle with royal authority. Indeed, Americans saw their assemblies as miniature Houses of Commons, and they assumed that governors possessed only those powers exercised by the British crown. Since Parliament had won supremacy over the monarchy through the Bill of Rights in 1689, colonials felt that their governors had strictly limited powers and should defer to the assemblies in cases of disagreement.

The lower houses steadily asserted their prestige and authority by refusing to permit outside meddling in their proceedings, taking firm control over taxes and the budget, and especially by keeping a tight rein on executive salaries. Although governors had considerable powers (including the right to veto acts, call or dismiss assembly sessions at will, and schedule elections anytime), they were quite vulnerable to legislatures' financial pressure because they received no salary from British sources and relied on the assemblies for their income. Only through this "power of the purse" could assemblies force governors to sign laws opposed by the crown.

Moreover, because the British government had little interest in eighteenth-century colonial politics, the assemblies could seize considerable power at the governors' expense. The Board of Trade, which Parliament established in 1696, was charged with monitoring American developments and advising the crown on colonial affairs. But aside from its first decade and a vigorous period from 1748 to 1753, the board's small, inefficient staff lacked the vision and energy to provide the strong support needed by embattled governors wrestling to maintain royal authority. The board could have easily frustrated the assemblies' rise to power by persuading the crown to disallow objectionable colonial laws signed by the governors; but of 8,563 acts sent from the mainland between 1696 and 1776, the board had just 469 disapproved. The Board of Trade's ineffectiveness left a vacuum in royal policy that allowed the colonies to become self-governing in most respects except for trade regulation, restrictions on printing money, and declaring war.

Thus during the first half of the eighteenth century, most Americans prospered and some grew wealthy. Gradually, class distinctions became more sharply etched. But British North America had no centuries-old institutions to bolster aristocratic privilege: no hereditary nobility, powerful

bureaucracy, standing army, or royal court. Even the Anglican church was weak, lacking American bishops. Without these traditions of rigid hierarchy, social expectations largely sufficed to ensure that the American upper class would receive appropriate deference and act with a sense of public responsibility.

Enlightenment and Awakening

Anglo-America was probably the world's most literate society in the eighteenth century. Perhaps 90 percent of New England's adult white male population and 40 percent of the women could write well enough to sign documents, thanks to the region's traditional support for primary education. Among white males elsewhere in the colonies, the literacy rate varied from about 35 percent to more than 50 percent. (In England, by contrast, no more than one-third of all males could read and write.) But how readily most of these people could (or would) read a book or write a letter was another matter. Ordinary Americans' reading fare at best encompassed only a few well-thumbed books: an almanac, a psalter, and the Bible. Colonial farmers and artisans inhabited the world of oral culture, in which ideas and information passed through the spoken word—a conversation with neighbors, an exchange of pleasantries with the local gentleman, a hot debate at the town meeting, a sermon by the minister. When uttered with feeling and sincerity, spoken words could move them with tremendous force.

But members of the gentry, well-to-do merchants, educated ministers, and a few self-improving artisans also lived in the world of print culture. Though costly, books and writing paper could open up eighteenth-century European civilization to men and women who could read. And a rich, exciting world it was. Great advances in natural science seemed to explain the laws of nature; human intelligence appeared poised to triumph over ignorance and prejudice; life itself looked as if it would at last become pleasant. Eminent men of letters such as France's Voltaire (1694–1778) corresponded with kings, awed the literate public, and dared to attack religious bigotry. For those who had the time to read and think, an age of optimism and progress had dawned: the Enlightenment. Upper-class Americans could not resist its charms and could be powerfully moved by the promise of its written words.

Enlightened Americans

American intellectuals like the self-taught scientist Benjamin Franklin drew their inspiration from Enlightenment ideals, which combined confidence in human reason with skepticism toward beliefs not founded on science or strict logic. One source of Enlightenment thought lay in the writings of English physicist Sir Isaac Newton (1642–1727), who in 1687 explained how universal gravitation ruled the universe. Newton's work captured Europe's imagination by demonstrating the harmony of natural laws and stimulated others to search for rational principles in medicine, law, psychology, and government.

> *Nature and Nature's laws lay hid in night:*
> *God said: Let Newton be! and all was light*

wrote English poet Alexander Pope, expressing the wonder that educated Europeans felt at Newton's revelations.

In the second quarter of the eighteenth century, no American more fully embodied the Enlightenment spirit than Franklin. Born in Boston in 1706, Franklin migrated to Philadelphia at age seventeen. He brought along skill as a printer, considerable ambition, and insatiable intellectual curiosity. In 1727 he gathered a small group of young men, mostly aspiring artisans like himself, into a club called the Junto, whose members pledged themselves to debate highbrow questions and collect useful information for their "mutual improvement."

In moving to Philadelphia, Franklin put himself in the right place at the right time, for the city was growing much more rapidly than Boston and was attracting English and Scottish merchants who shared Franklin's zest for learning. These men nudged Franklin's career along by lending him books and securing him printing contracts. In 1732 Franklin began to publish *Poor Richard's Almanack,* a collection of maxims and proverbs that made him famous. By age forty-two Franklin had

earned enough money to retire from printing and devote himself to science and community service.

These dual goals—science and community benefit—were intimately related in Franklin's mind, for he believed that all true science would be useful in the sense of making everyone's life more comfortable. For example, experimenting with a kite, Franklin demonstrated in 1752 that lightning was electricity, a discovery that led to the useful lightning rod. Building on his Junto activities, Franklin organized the American Philosophical Society in 1743 to encourage "all philosophical experiments that let light into the nature of things, tend to increase the power of man over matter, and multiply the conveniences and pleasures of life." By 1769 this society had blossomed into an intercolonial network of amateur scientists.

Franklin left his mark on Philadelphia in other ways. He established its first volunteer fire company—complete with engine—in 1736, inspired the creation of a circulating library that held America's finest collection of scientific books, and in 1740 founded an academy that became the College of Philadelphia (now the University of Pennsylvania). From this institution sprang the colonies' first medical school in 1765.

Although several southern plantation owners, including Thomas Jefferson, ardently championed progress through science, the Enlightenment's primary centers in America were the seaboard cities, where the latest books and ideas from Europe circulated and gentlemen and self-improving artisans met in small societies to investigate nature. In the eyes of many of these individuals, the ideal was the Royal Society in London, the foremost learned society in the English-speaking world. Franklin and Cotton Mather became members of the Royal Society. In this respect, the Enlightenment, at least initially, strengthened the ties between colonial and British elites. While confident that science would benefit everyone, Enlightened Americans envisioned progress as gradual and proceeding from the top down. They trusted reason far more than they trusted the common people, whose judgment, especially on religious matters, seemed too easily deranged.

Just as Newton inspired the scientific bent of Enlightenment intellectuals, English philosopher John Locke's *Essay Concerning Human Understanding* (1690) led many to embrace "reasonable" or "rational" religion. Locke contended that ideas, including religion, are not inborn but are acquired by toilsome investigation of and reflection upon experience. To most Enlightened intellectuals, the best argument for the existence of God seemingly could be derived through study of the harmony and order of nature, which pointed to a rational Creator. Some individuals carried this argument a step further by insisting that where the Bible conflicted with reason, one should follow the dictates of reason rather than the Bible. Those who took the argument furthest were called Deists. Deists concluded that God, having created a perfect universe, did not miraculously intervene in its workings but rather left it alone to operate according to natural laws.

Americans influenced by the Enlightenment usually described themselves as Christians and attended church. But they feared Christianity's excesses, particularly as indulged in by fanatics who persecuted others in religion's name, and by "enthusiasts" who claimed miraculous visions and direct mandates from God. Mindful of Locke's caution that a human can never be *absolutely* certain of anything but his or her own existence, they distrusted zealots. Typically, Franklin contributed money to most of the churches in Philadelphia but thought that the religion's value lay mainly in its encouragement of virtue rather than in theological hair splitting.

Prior to 1740 Enlightened Americans usually associated fanaticism and bigotry with the bygone days of the early Puritans, and they looked on their own time as an era of progressive reasonableness. But a series of religious revivals known as the Great Awakening would soon shatter their complacency.

The Great Awakening

Viewing the world as orderly and predictable, rationalists were inclined to a sense of smug self-satisfaction. Franklin took the occasion of writing his will in 1750 to thank God for giving him "such a mind, with moderate passions" and "such a competency of this world's goods as might make a reasonable mind easy." But many Americans lacked a comfortable competency of worldly goods and lived neither orderly nor predictable lives. For example, in 1737 and 1738 an epidemic of diphtheria, a contagious throat disease, killed every tenth child under sixteen from New Hampshire to Pennsylvania. Such an event starkly reminded the colonists of the fragility of earthly life and turned their thoughts to religion.

A quickening of religious fervor began at scattered places in the colonies in the mid-1730s. Then in the 1740s, an outpouring of passionate Christian revivalism swept all of British North America. This "Great Awakening" cut across lines of class, status, and education. Even elites found themselves

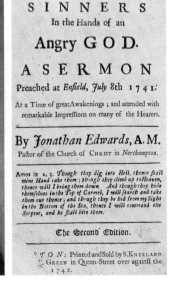

Jonathan Edwards; Title Page from "Sinners in the Hands of an Angry God"

Edwards's famous sermon warned the wicked of the terrible punishments awaiting them in the afterlife.

caught up in it, realizing the inadequacy of reason alone to move their hearts. Above all, the Great Awakening represented an unleashing of anxiety and longing among ordinary people living in a world of oral culture—anxiety about sin, and longing for salvation. And the answers that they received were conveyed through the spoken word. Some preachers of the Great Awakening were themselves intellectuals, comfortable amid the books and ideas of the print culture. But for all, religion was primarily a matter of emotional commitment.

In contrast to rationalists, who stressed the human potential for betterment, the ministers who roused their congregations into outbursts of religious fervor during the Great Awakening's revivals depicted the emptiness of material comfort, the utter corruption of human nature, the fury of divine wrath, and the need for immediate repentance. Although he was a brilliant intellect, well aware of contemporary science, the Congregationalist Jonathan Edwards, who led a revival at Northampton, Massachusetts, in 1735, drove home this message with breathtaking clarity. "The God that holds you over the pit of Hell, much as one holds a spider or other loathsome insect over the fire, abhors you," Edwards intoned in one of his famous sermons, "Sinners in the Hands of an Angry God." "His wrath toward you burns like fire; He looks upon you as worthy of nothing else but to be cast into the fire."

Even before Edwards's Northampton revival, two ministers in central New Jersey—the Presbyterian William Tennent and the Dutch Reformed Theodore Frelinghuysen—had stimulated conversions in prayer meetings called the Refreshings. But the event that brought these isolated threads of revival together was the arrival in 1739 of the charismatic George Whitefield, an English clergyman who had been stoking the fires of revival in the Anglican church. So overpowering was Whitefield's presence that some joked that he could make crowds swoon simply by saying "Mesopotamia," and English author Samuel Johnson thought Whitefield's magnetic appeal so potent that the priest would have been adored even if he preached from a tree wearing only a nightcap. Crowds exceeding twenty thousand could hear his booming voice clearly, and many wept at his eloquence.

Whitefield's American tour inspired thousands to seek salvation. Most converts were young

adults in their late twenties. In Connecticut alone, the number joining churches jumped from 630 in 1740 to 3,217 in 1741, and within four years of Whitefield's arrival, every fifth man and woman under forty-five had been "born again."

Whitefield's allure was so mighty that he even awed potential critics. Hearing him preach in Philadelphia, Benjamin Franklin first vowed to contribute nothing to the collection but gradually melted. So admirably did Whitefield conclude his sermon, Franklin recalled, "that I empty'd my Pocket wholly into the Collector's Dish, Gold and all." But divisions over the revivals quickly developed in Whitefield's wake and were widened by the tactics of some of his more extreme followers. For example, after leaving Boston in October 1740, Whitefield invited Gilbert Tennent (William's son) to follow "in order to blow up the divine flame lately kindled there." Denouncing Boston's established clergymen as "dead Drones" and lashing out at aristocratic fashion, Tennent built a following among the city's poor and downtrodden. So did another firebrand, the Congregationalist James Davenport, who once bellowed at his Southold, New York, congregation for twenty-four hours.

Exposing colonial society's social divisions, Tennent and Davenport corroded support for the revivals among established ministers and officials. Increasingly, the lines hardened between the revivalists, known as New Lights, and the rationalist clergy, or Old Lights, who dominated the Anglican, Presbyterian, and Congregational churches. In 1740 Gilbert Tennent published *The Danger of an Unconverted Ministry*, which hinted that most Presbyterian ministers lacked saving grace and hence were bound for hell, and urged their parishioners to abandon them for the New Lights. By thus sowing the seeds of doubt about individual ministers, Tennent was undermining one of the foundations of social order, for if the people could not trust their own ministers, whom could they trust?

Old Light rationalists fired back. In 1742 Charles Chauncy, a well-known Boston Congregationalist, condemned the revival as an epidemic of the "enthusiasm" that Enlightened intellectuals so loathed. Chauncy particularly blasted those enthusiasts who mistook the ravings of their overheated imaginations for direct communications from God. He even provided a kind of checklist for spotting enthusiasts: look for "a certain wildness" in their eyes, the "quakings and tremblings" of their limbs, and foaming at the mouth, Chauncy suggested. Put simply, the revival had unleashed "a sort of madness."

The Great Awakening opened unprecedented splits in American Protestantism. In 1741 New and Old Light Presbyterians formed rival branches that did not reunite until 1758, when the revivalists emerged victorious. The Anglicans lost many members to New Light preachers, especially to Presbyterians and Baptists. Congregationalists splintered so badly that within twenty years of 1740, New Lights had seceded from one-third of all churches and formed separate parishes.

In Massachusetts and Connecticut, where the Congregational church was established by law, the secession of New Light parishes provoked bitter conflict. To force New Lights into paying tithes to their former church, Old Lights repeatedly denied new parishes legal status. Connecticut passed repressive laws forbidding revivalists to preach or perform marriages, and the colony expelled many New Lights from the legislature. In Connecticut's Windham County, an extra story had to be added to the jail to hold all the New Lights arrested for not paying tithes. Elisha Paine, a revivalist imprisoned at Windham for illegal preaching, continued giving sermons from his cell and drew such crowds that his followers built bleachers nearby to hear him. Paine and his fellow victims generated widespread sympathy for the New Lights, who finally won control of Connecticut's assembly in 1759.

Although New Lights made steady gains until the 1770s, the Great Awakening peaked in 1742. The revival then crested everywhere but in Virginia, where its high point came after 1755 with an upsurge of conversions by Baptists, who also suffered considerable legal harassment.

For all the commotion it raised at the time, the Great Awakening's long-term effects exceeded its immediate impact. First, the revival started the decline in the influence of Quakers (who were not significantly affected by the Great Awakening), Anglicans, and Congregationalists. As these churches' importance waned, the number of Presbyterians and Baptists increased after 1740, and that of Methodists (pro-revival offshoots of Anglicanism) rose after 1770. Ever since the late 1700s, these three churches have dominated American Protestantism. Second, the Great Awakening stimulated the founding of new colleges, for existing colleges were scarred in their opponents' eyes by their affiliations with either Old or New Lights. In 1746 New Light Presbyterians established the College of New Jersey (Princeton). Then followed King's College (Columbia) for Anglicans in 1754, the College of Rhode Island (Brown) for Baptists in 1764, Queen's College (Rutgers) for Dutch Reformed in 1766, and Dartmouth College for Congregationalists in 1769. Third, the revival

Nassau Hall *Officially chartered as the College of New Jersey, Princeton was popularly known in its early years as Nassau Hall, after the name of its principal building (center).*

marked the real emergence of black Protestantism, which was almost nonexistent before 1740. New Lights reached out to slaves, some of whom joined white churches and even preached at the revivals. Conversions came slowly, but by 1790 many blacks were Christians.

The Great Awakening also had the unintended effect of fostering religious toleration by blurring theological differences among New Lights. Though an Anglican who helped found Methodism, George Whitefield preached with Presbyterians such as Gilbert Tennent and Congregationalists like Jonathan Edwards. Revivalism emphasized inner experience over doctrine and implied that the true church was a fellowship of saints who shared saving grace. Revivalism thus prepared Americans to accept denominationalism, which today assumes that all Judeo-Christian churches are legitimate expressions of belief in God and deserve equal freedom and respect. Denominationalism would slowly emerge after the Revolution as the best means of accommodating religious diversity.

Historians have disagreed over whether the Great Awakening had political as well as religious effects. Although Tennent and Davenport called the poor "God's people" and flayed the wealthy, they never advocated a social revolution, and the Awakening did not produce any distinct political ideology. Yet by sensitizing the public to the corruption of those in authority, New Light ministers laid some of the groundwork for political revolutionaries a generation later, who would contend that royal government in America had grown corrupt and unworthy of obedience.

Conclusion

The aura of sanctified purpose lingered over Whitefield and his religious revival even after his death in Boston in 1770. In September 1775 a ragtag army of American rebels, marching through Massachusetts, paused on their way to attack the British stronghold at Quebec. Hoping to win a blessing for their risky venture, they broke open a tomb and prayed over a holy man's remains. The corpse was George Whitefield's.

By the 1750s the British mainland colonies had taken on the look of mature societies. For fifty years their population and wealth had been rising impressively. The mainland provinces were more populous than Scotland and almost one-third the size of England. White colonists' standard of living far exceeded those of Scotland and Ireland and equaled that of England. Literacy had spread widely in the northern colonies, and by 1766 Anglo-America had more institutions of higher learning than England, Scotland, and Ireland together. A self-confident Anglo-American upper class had garnered expertise in law, trade, finance, and politics.

While the mainland colonies had developed mature political systems that could even challenge royal authority, the Glorious Revolution of 1688–1689 and the imperial wars of 1689–1713 had bolstered the colonists' dependence on—and loyalty to—the British monarchy. Nonetheless, the colonists' British patriotism, which would be proven under enemy fire between 1744 and 1760, hinged on the assumption that they shared Britons' political rights. In particular, a crucial principle for them was the rough equality of power between the colonial legislatures and Great Britain's Parliament.

In 1763 Britain began challenging Americans' longstanding conceptions of their political rights and attempted to subordinate the colonies to Parliament's authority. In ignoring the colonies' tradition of self-government, however, Parliament would underestimate the vigor with which the colonial elite stood ready to defend local autonomy, even to the point of revolution. Nor did the British upper class have any inkling of the depth of righteous conviction that many ordinary Americans would feel in linking their defense of liberty with their obedience to God. Out of that potent mixture of self-reliant confidence and God-given mission, Americans would begin to forge a national consciousness.

CHRONOLOGY

1651– Parliament creates the navigation system to
1733   regulate British imperial commerce.

1660 Restoration of the Stuart dynasty to English throne.

1663 Sir John Colleton and others obtain title to Carolina.

1664 English conquer the Dutch colony of New Netherland, which becomes the English colony of New York.

Sir Philip Carteret and John, Lord Berkeley, become joint proprietors of the Jersey colony.

1670 Settlement of southern Carolina begins.

1672 Louis Jolliet and Jacques Marquette explore the Mississippi River.

1676 Quakers organize the colony of West Jersey.

1680– Pueblo revolt in New Mexico.
1692

1681 William Penn founds the colony of Pennsylvania.

1682 Quakers organize the colony of East Jersey.

The Sieur de la Salle descends the Mississippi River to the Gulf of Mexico and claims the Mississippi basin for France.

1685 James II becomes king of England.

1686– Dominion of New England.
1689

1688 Glorious Revolution in England; James II is deposed.

1689 William and Mary ascend to English throne. Protestant Association organized in Maryland. Leisler's Rebellion in New York.

1689– King William's War.
1697

1690 John Locke, *Essay upon Human Understanding.*

1698 French begin settlements near the mouth of the Mississippi River.

1700 Father Eusebio Kino founds first Arizona mission.

1701 Iroquois adopt neutrality policy in future colonial wars.

1702– Queen Anne's War.
1713

1711– Tuscarora War in North Carolina.
1713

1715– Yamasee War in South Carolina.
1716

1718 New Orleans founded.

1732 Georgia colony chartered.

1739 Great Awakening begins. Stono Rebellion in South Carolina.

1743 Benjamin Franklin founds American Philosophical Society.

1769 Franciscan priests establish first California mission, at San Diego.

For Further Reading

Bernard Bailyn, *Voyagers to the West: A Passage in the Peopling of America on the Eve of the Revolution* (1986). Pulitzer Prize–winning study that, though dealing primarily with British immigration in the 1770s, throws important light on the motives of immigrants throughout the eighteenth century.

Richard L. Bushman, *From Puritan to Yankee: Character and the Social Order in Connecticut, 1690–1765* (1967). The best examination of social and cultural maturation in any colony.

Jack P. Greene and J. R. Pole, eds., *Colonial British America: Essays in the New History of the Early Modern Era* (1984). Essays by sixteen leading authorities summarizing the current status of scholarship on early America.

Rhys Isaac, *The Transformation of Virginia, 1740–1790* (1982). Pulitzer Prize–winning study of class relationships, race relations, and folkways at the time of the Great Awakening.

James H. Merrell, *The Indians' New World: Catawbas and Their Neighbors from European Contact Through the Era of Removal* (1989). A pathbreaking examination, with broad implications for understanding the native American past, of the interaction between South Carolina colonists and Catawba Indians.

Edwin J. Perkins, *The Economy of Colonial America* (2d ed., 1988). An authoritative, commonsensical, and highly readable overview of economic life in early America.

Phinizy Spalding, *Oglethorpe in America* (1977). An excellent introduction to Georgia's early struggle for survival.

Peter H. Wood, *Black Majority: Negroes in Colonial South Carolina from 1670 Through the Stono Rebellion* (1974). An engrossing study of slavery and racism as they evolved in the Lower South.

Additional Bibliography

The Restoration Colonies

Melvin B. Endy, Jr., *William Penn and Early Quakerism* (1973); Sung Bok Kim, *Landlord and Tenant in Colonial New York: Manorial Society, 1664–1775* (1978); Daniel C. Littlefield, *Rice and Slaves: Ethnicity and the Slave Trade in Colonial South Carolina* (1981); John A. Munroe, *Colonial Delaware: A History* (1973); Gary B. Nash, *Quakers and Politics: Pennsylvania, 1681–1726* (1968); John E. Pomfret, *The Province of East New Jersey, 1609–1702: The Rebellious Province* (1962), and *The Province of West New Jersey, 1609–1702: A History of the Origins of an American Colony* (1956); Robert C. Ritchie, *The Duke's Province: A Study of New York Politics and Society, 1664–1691* (1977); W. Stitt Robinson, *The Southern Colonial Frontier, 1607–1763* (1979); Robert M. Weir, *Colonial South Carolina: A History* (1983).

French and Spanish Expansion

John Francis Bannon, *The Spanish Borderlands Frontier, 1513–1821* (1970); W. J. Eccles, *The Canadian Frontier, 1534–1760* (1969), and *France in America* (1972); Charles Edwards O'Neill, *Church and State in French Colonial Louisiana: Policy and Politics to 1732* (1966); Edward H. Spicer, *Cycles of Conquest: The Impact of Spain, Mexico, and the United States on the Indians of the Southwest, 1533–1960* (1962); David J. Weber, ed., *New Spain's Far Western Frontier: Essays on Spain in the American West* (1979).

Rebellion and Imperial Warfare

Lois Green Carr and David W. Jordan, *Maryland's Revolution of Government, 1689–1692* (1974); Michael G. Hall, *Edward Randolph and the American Colonies, 1676–1703* (1960); Richard R. Johnson, *Adjustment to Empire: The New England Colonies, 1675–1715* (1981); David S. Lovejoy, *The Glorious Revolution in America, 1660–1692* (1972); Howard H. Peckham, *The Colonial Wars, 1689–1762* (1964); William Saunders Webb, *The Governors General: The English Army and the Definition of the Empire, 1569–1681* (1979).

Society, Economics, and Population Growth

Philip D. Curtin, *The Atlantic Slave Trade: A Census* (1969); Oliver M. Dickerson, *The Navigation Acts and the American Revolution* (1951); Thomas M. Doerflinger, *A Vigorous Spirit of Enterprise: Merchants and Economic Development in Revolutionary Philadelphia* (1986); A. Roger Ekirch, *Bound for America: The Transportation of British Convicts to the Colonies, 1718–1775* (1987); Richard Hofstader, *America at 1750: A Social Portrait* (1971); N. E. H. Hull, *Female Felons: Women and Serious Crime in Colonial Massachusetts* (1987); Allan Kulikoff, *Tobacco and Slaves: The Development of Southern Cultures in the Chesapeake, 1680–1800* (1986); Audrey Lockhart, *Some Aspects of Emigration from Ireland to the North American Colonies Between 1660 and 1775* (1976); John J. McCusker and Russell R. Menard, *The Economy of British America, 1607–1789* (1985); Edgar J. McManus, *Black Bondage in the North* 1973); Donald W. Meinig, *The Shaping of America: A Geographical Perspective on Five Hundred Years of History: Volume I, Atlantic America, 1492–1800* (1986); Gerald W. Mullin, *Flight and Rebellion: Slave Resistance in Eighteenth-Century Virginia* (1972); Gary B. Nash, *The Urban Crucible: The Northern Seaports and the Origins of the American Revolution* (abridged ed., 1986); Sharon V. Salinger, *"To Serve Well and Faithfully": Labor and Indentured Servants in Pennsylvania, 1682–1800* (1987); Daniel Blake Smith, *Inside the Great House: Family Life in Eighteenth-Century Chesapeake Society* (1980); Mechal Sobel, *The World They Made Together: Black and White Values in Eighteenth-Century Virginia* (1987); Gary M. Walton and James F. Shepherd, *The Economic Rise of Early America* (1979); Robert V. Wells, *The Population of the British Colonies in America Before 1776: A Survey of Census Data* (1975); Betty Wood, *Slavery in Colonial Georgia, 1730–1775* (1984).

The Enlightenment, Religion, and Politics

Patricia U. Bonomi, *Under the Cope of Heaven: Religion, Society, and Politics in Colonial America* (1986); Henry S. Commager, *The Empire of Reason: How Europe Imagined and America Realized the Enlightenment* (1977); Bruce C. Daniels, ed., *Power and Status: Essays on Officeholding in Colonial America* (1986); Robert J. Dinkin, *Voting in Provincial America: A Study of Elections in the Thirteen Colonies, 1680–1776* (1977); Edwin S. Gaustad, *The Great Awakening in New England* (1957); Jack P. Greene, *The Quest for Power: The Lower Houses of Assembly in the Southern Royal Colonies, 1689–1776* (1963); Thomas L. Purvis, *Proprietors, Patronage, and Paper Money: Legislative Politics in New Jersey; 1703–1776* (1986); Sally Schwartz, *A Mixed Multitude: The Struggle for Toleration in Colonial Pennsylvania* (1987); Charles S. Sydnor, *American Revolutionaries in the Making: Political Practices in Washington's Virginia* (1965); Patricia J. Tracy, *Jonathan Edwards, Pastor: Religion and Society in Eighteenth-Century Northampton* (1980); Carl J. Vipperman, *The Rise of Rawlins Lowndes, 1721–1800* (1978); Marilyn J. Westerkamp, *Triumph of the Laity: Scots-Irish Piety and the Great Awakening, 1625–1760* (1988); Esmond Wright, *Franklin of Philadelphia* (1986).

CHAPTER 4

The Road to Revolution, 1748–1776

In 1769 Benjamin Franklin was an agent for several American colonial assemblies and living in London, where he obtained an anonymous English pamphlet entitled *Good Humour*. Franklin bristled at the unknown author's charges that the colonists' recent opposition to parliamentary taxes represented "*a posture of hostility* against Great Britain." "There was no Posture of Hostility in America," Franklin angrily scribbled in the margin, "but Britain put herself in a Posture of Hostility against America."

As Franklin wrote those words, a constitutional crisis gripped the British Empire and was markedly affecting Britain's relationship with its overseas colonies. The conflict between the mother country and the American colonies arose suddenly after 1763, when Parliament attempted to tighten control over economic and political affairs in the colonies. Long accustomed to legislating for themselves, Americans resisted this unexpected effort to centralize decision making in London. American leaders like Franklin interpreted Britain's clampdown as calculated antagonism and were certain that Parliament's efforts to tax them would make a mockery of self-government in America.

Despite their apprehension over parliamentary taxes, colonial politicians usually expressed their opposition peacefully from 1763 to 1775, through such tactics as legislative resolutions and commercial boycotts. Few lost their lives during the twelve years prior to the battles at Lexington and Concord, the first military clashes of the Revolution, and all of those killed were American civilians rather than royal officials or soldiers. Even after fighting broke out, some colonists agonized for more than a year over whether to sever their political relationship with England—which even native-born Americans sometimes referred to affectionately as "home." Of all the world's colonial peoples, none became rebels more reluctantly than did Anglo-Americans in 1776.

Imperial Warfare

Between 1713, when Queen Anne's War ended, and the early 1740s, the American colonies enjoyed a generation of peace, punctuated only by a brief war with Spain fought in Georgia from 1739 to 1742. But then two major European wars spilled over into the New World. The first was known in Europe as the War of the Austrian Succession (1740–1748) and in America as King George's War (1744–1748). A second, far more decisive European struggle, the Seven Years' War (1756–1763), had as its American counterpart the French and Indian War, which engulfed the colonies from 1754 to 1760. These conflicts originated in rivalries among the great powers of Europe—Britain, France, Austria, Prussia, and Russia—but few colonists doubted that King George's War was also *their*

127

war, or that their prosperity depended on a British victory in the Seven Years' War.

Yet these wars produced an ironically mixed effect. On one hand, they fused the bonds between the British and the Anglo-Americans. Fighting side by side, shedding their blood in the same cause, the British and the American colonists came to rely on each other as rarely before. At the same time, the conclusion of each war planted the seeds first of misunderstanding, then of suspicion, and finally of hostility between the former compatriots.

King George's War

King George's War largely followed the pattern of earlier conflicts under William and Mary and Queen Anne (see Chapter 3). Few battles involved more than six hundred men, most of the skirmishes consisted of raids and counterattacks along the Canadian border, and the French and their Indian allies attacked no English settlements south of New York.

King George's War produced just one major engagement, which would later embitter Anglo-American relations. In 1745 almost four thousand New Englanders under William Pepperell of Maine assaulted the French bastion of Louisbourg on the northern tip of Nova Scotia, which guarded the entrance to the St. Lawrence River. Upon learning that the expedition of raw recruits planned to take a fortress defended by 250 cannons mounted on stone walls thirty feet high, Benjamin Franklin (then a member of the Pennsylvania assembly) feared the worst. "Fortified towns are hard nuts to crack," he warned his brother in Boston, "and your teeth are not accustomed to it."

Unable to bring artillery with them, Franklin's Yankee countrymen obtained siege guns by storming the enemy's outer batteries and then captured ammunition from several unsuspecting French supply ships that sailed into their clutches. For almost seven weeks they shelled Louisbourg, lobbing in nine thousand cannonballs and six hundred bombs until every building was either crumbling or on fire. On June 17, 1745, Pepperell took the fortress and almost 1,500 prisoners, at a loss of only 167 of his troops.

The colonists did not enjoy the fruits of victory for long. After three more years of inconclusive warfare, Britain and France signed a treaty in 1748 that exchanged Louisbourg for a British outpost in India that the French had taken during the war.

The memory of how their stunning achievement at Louisbourg went for naught would rankle the colonists for a decade.

A Fragile Peace

King George's War had failed to establish either Britain or France as the dominant power in North America, and each side soon began preparations for another war. The French governor of Canada continued to maintain two forts on New York soil, at Niagara and Crown Point, as well as a pair of garrisons in territory claimed by Britain's King George II as part of Nova Scotia. It was the Ohio Valley, however, that became the tinderbox for Anglo-French conflict. Pennsylvania traders took advantage of the peace to surge into the valley, where they briefly established a flourishing fur trade with the local Indians. French soldiers responded by harassing and arresting the Pennsylvanians, and even killing some, until all were driven out by 1752. In 1753 the Canadians began building a chain of forts that would link the Ohio River with Louisiana and block British expansion westward. In the interwar years, the French also strengthened their military alliances with the western Indians and even gained some prestige among the Iroquois, who had taken no part in King George's War.

In response to French aggression, in mid-1754 delegates from seven colonies north of Virginia

"Join or Die," 1754

Benjamin Franklin published this well-known cartoon just before the Albany Congress convened. The snake symbolized the colonies' considerable divisions—a disunity that political leaders would have to struggle against in years to come.

gathered at Albany, New York, to lay plans for their mutual defense. By showering the wavering Iroquois with thirty wagonloads of presents, the colonists kept most of these Indians neutral. The delegates then endorsed a proposal for a colonial confederation, the so-called Albany Plan of Union, largely based on the ideas of Pennsylvania's Franklin and Massachusetts's Thomas Hutchinson. The plan called for a "Grand Council" representing all the colonial assemblies, with a crown-appointed "president general" as its executive officer. The Grand Council would devise policies regarding military defense and Indian affairs, and if necessary, it could demand funds from the colonies according to an agreed-upon formula. Although it provided a precedent for later American unity, the Albany Plan came to nothing, primarily because no colonial legislature would surrender the least control over its powers of taxation, even to fellow Americans and in the face of grave mutual danger.

Virginians meanwhile were on the verge of provoking an international incident in the Ohio Valley, which Virginia claimed. In 1753 the colony sent a twenty-one-year-old surveyor, George Washington, to demand that the French abandon their forts on the Allegheny River. The French refused, but Washington reported that Virginia might still block further Canadian expansion by occupying the strategic point where the Allegheny and Monongahela rivers joined to form the Ohio—the site of present-day Pittsburgh.

Returning in 1754 with three hundred colonial volunteers and one hundred British regulars, Washington found the French already occupying the juncture of the rivers and constructing Fort Duquesne there. He then built a crude defensive position about sixty miles southeast called Fort Necessity, near which his men killed several French soldiers in an ambush that brought swift retaliation. On July 4, 1754, after losing one-fourth of his men in a daylong battle, Washington surrendered Fort Necessity to an enemy force four times larger than his own and led the survivors home.

The Seven Years' War in America

Although France and Britain remained at peace in Europe until 1756, the action at Fort Necessity created a virtual state of war in North America. In response, nearly eight thousand Americans enlisted during 1755 to attack the Canadian strongholds menacing New York and Nova Scotia. That same year, British general Edward Braddock and a thousand Irish regulars arrived in North America to take Fort Duquesne.

Stiff-necked and scornful of colonial soldiers, Braddock expected his disciplined British regulars to make short work of the enemy and only dimly perceived the strength and resourcefulness of the forces gathering against him. Washington's failure in the Ohio Valley had driven the western Indians into an alliance with the French. On July 9, 1755, about nine hundred Canadians and Indians ambushed Braddock's force of British regulars and the Virginia volunteers under Washington nine miles east of Fort Duquesne. Riddled by three hours of steady fire from an unseen foe, Braddock's regulars finally broke and left Washington's Virginians to hold off the enemy while they retreated. Nine hundred regular and provincial soldiers died in Braddock's defeat, including Braddock himself, who succumbed on the retreat.

Following this engagement, Indian raids convulsed Pennsylvania, Maryland, Virginia, and even parts of New Jersey—all colonies that had escaped attack in previous wars. Meanwhile, neither of two Anglo-American armies that marched against the French fortresses at Niagara and Crown Point in New York reached its objective in 1755. The only successful British expedition that year was undertaken by two thousand New Englanders who seized two French forts that were putting Nova Scotia at risk. This campaign was memorable less for its military significance than for its tragic aftermath. Following the takeover of the French forts, the governor of Nova Scotia ordered the troops to drive thousands of local French-Canadian civilians, the Acadians, from their homes—often with nothing more than they could carry in their arms—and to burn their villages. This cruel expulsion stemmed from the Acadians' refusal to promise not to bear arms for France. Almost 5 percent of Canada's population was eventually deported in this way to the British colonies, from which many migrated to French Louisiana. There they became known as Cajuns.

Although Anglo-Americans outnumbered Canadians twenty to one, the French commander in chief, Louis Joseph Montcalm, maintained the offensive in 1756 and 1757. A daring and resourceful general, Montcalm benefited from large numbers of French regulars in Canada, over-

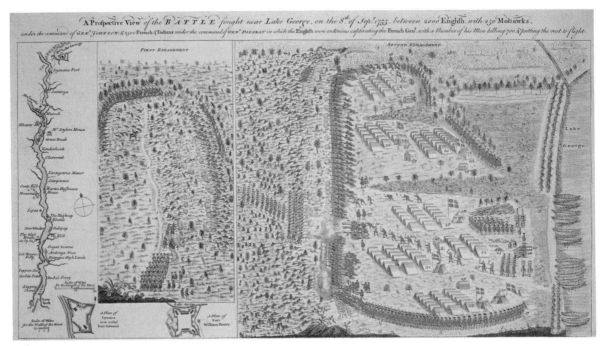

The Battle of Lake George   *This contemporary drawing records the battle of September 8, 1755, in intricate detail. A force of 3,500 American provincials and 300 Indians under William Johnson defeated a mixed force of 2,000 French regulars, Canadians, and Indians, led by Baron Ludwig Dieskau, who were defending Crown Point.*

whelming Indian support, and the mobilization of nearly every able-bodied Canadian into a formidable militia that fought with the courage of desperate men. In contrast, the American colonies balked at providing many troops and frequently sent poorly trained men who had been enlisted for only a few months. "I would rather have no Troops," wrote a despairing British colonel in 1757, "than to be at the Trouble & expence to form them, & when they could begin to be able to perform their Duty, be oblig'd to disband them."

Confronted by the numerically superior but disorganized Anglo-Americans, the French seized Fort Oswego on Lake Ontario in 1756 and took Fort William Henry on Lake George in 1757. By now the French threatened central New York and western New England. In Europe, too, the war was going badly for Britain, which by 1757 seemed to be facing defeat on all fronts.

In this dark hour, one of the British ministers, William Pitt, took control of military affairs in the royal cabinet and reversed the downward course. Imaginative and single-minded in his conception of Britain's imperial destiny, Pitt saw himself as the man of the hour. "I know," he declared, "that I can save this country and that no one else can." True to his word, Pitt reinvigorated British patriotism throughout the empire. By the war's end, he was the colonists' most popular hero, the symbol of what Americans and Englishmen could accomplish when united.

Hard pressed in Europe by France and its allies (which included Spain after 1761), Pitt preferred not to send large numbers of British regulars to America. Fewer than four thousand British troops arrived on the mainland from mid-1757 until Canada's conquest. Rather, Pitt believed that the key to crushing Canada lay in the mobilization of colonial soldiers. To encourage the Americans to assume the military burden, he promised that if the colonies raised the necessary men, Parliament would bear most of the cost of maintaining them.

Pitt's offer to free Americans from the war's financial burdens generated unprecedented support. The colonies organized twenty-one thousand troops in 1758, more soldiers than the crown sent

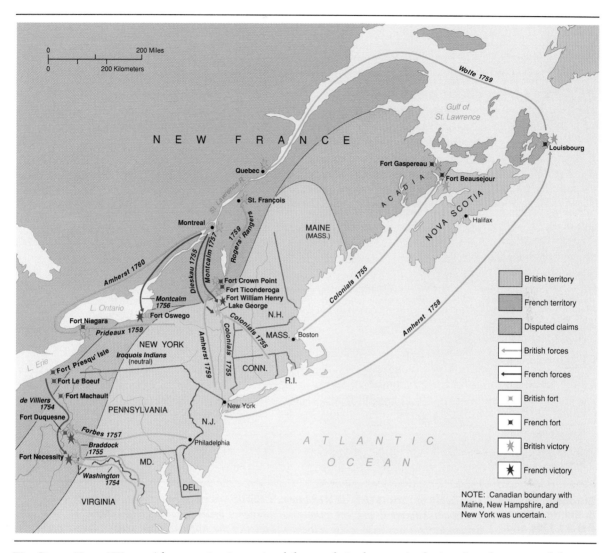

The Seven Years' War in America

After experiencing major defeats early in the war, Anglo-American forces turned the tide against the French by taking Fort Duquesne in late 1757 and Louisbourg in 1758. After Canada fell in 1760, the fighting shifted to Spain's Caribbean colonies.

NOTE: The Canadian boundary with Maine, New Hampshire, and New York was uncertain.

to the mainland during the entire war, and raised an equal number in 1759. The resulting offensive under General Jeffery Amherst captured Fort Duquesne and Louisbourg by late 1758 and drove the French from northern New York the next year. In September 1759 Quebec fell after General James Wolfe defeated Montcalm on the Plains of Abraham outside that city, where both commanders died in battle. Canadian resistance ended in 1760, when Montreal surrendered.

France ceded all its territories on the North American mainland by the Treaty of Paris of 1763, which officially ended the Seven Years' War in both America and Europe. France gave Britain all of its lands east of the Mississippi and transferred title to its claims west of that river to Spain, which also gained New Orleans. In return for Cuba, which a British expedition had taken over in 1762, Spain ceded Florida to Britain. Spain's vast New World empire thus remained intact, but France's formerly

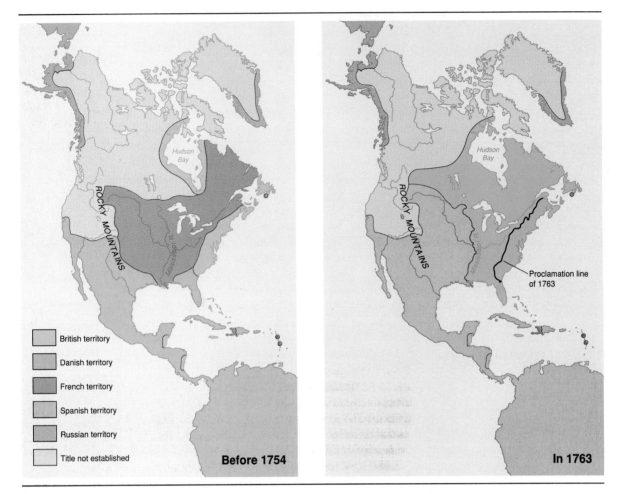

European Powers in the New World Before 1754 and in 1763

The Treaty of Paris (1763) divided France's North American empire between Britain and Spain. Hoping to prevent unnecessary violence between whites and Indians, Britain forbade any new white settlements west of the Appalachians' crest in the Proclamation of 1763.

extensive holdings were reduced to a few tiny fishing islands off Newfoundland and several thriving sugar islands in the West Indies. Britain seemed supreme in eastern North America.

Friction Between Allies

In England, public opinion assumed that credit for the North American victory belonged to the professional soldiers sent over from Britain. In fact, however, two of every five regulars who served had enlisted in America. Benjamin Franklin once complained that, although the force that captured two French forts on Nova Scotia's border in 1755 comprised two thousand Massachusetts troops and fewer than three hundred British regulars, "yet it could not be discovered by the Account . . . published in the London Gazette, that there was a single New England man concern'd in the Affair."

The failure of the British people to understand Pitt's strategy had led them to underestimate the colonial soldiers' contribution to the war. Though realizing that the newly formed colonial units would not perform as well as veteran regiments, Pitt had nevertheless placed the American enlistees in charge of vital support roles: forming the reserve force in battle, performing essential supply functions, and holding frontier forts. This plan had the advantage of freeing the greatest number of British regulars for combat against the highly trained French, but it led the British public mistakenly to infer that the Americans had dodged their share of the fighting.

Pitt's promise to reimburse the colonial assemblies for their military expenses, moreover, angered Britons, who concluded that the colonists were escaping scot-free from the war's financial burden. Resentment amounting to rage against the colonists flared in Britain, especially among England's heavily taxed landlords. These members of the gentry had seen Britain's national debt nearly double during the war, from £72 million to over £123 million. At a time when the total debt of all the colonies collectively amounted to less than £1 million, the interest charges alone on the British debt came to more than £4 million a year. Staggering under the twin burdens of debt and taxes, the British thought it outrageous to repay Americans for defending themselves against an enemy on their own borders.

Worse, victory over the French did not end the British taxpayers' woes, for the settlement of the war indirectly spurred new Indian-white conflicts that drove the British debt even higher. With the French vanquished, the Indians feared that Anglo-American settlers would flock to areas of the Appalachian Mountains where the British military seemed determined permanently to occupy the western forts captured from France. To check British ambitions, an Ottawa chieftain named Pontiac forged an alliance among several western tribes and in May 1763 launched an offensive that sacked eight British forts near the Great Lakes and besieged two others at Pittsburgh and Detroit. After a relief column of Royal Americans and Scottish Highlanders routed a large Indian force at Bushy Run, Pennsylvania, an uneasy truce prevailed until a peace was negotiated in 1764.

Yet despite the native American defeat at Bushy Run, Pontiac's Alliance had not been decisively beaten. Hoping to conciliate the Indians and end the frontier fighting, the British government issued the Proclamation of 1763, which banned white settlement beyond the crest of the Appalachians. The proclamation angered colonies with western land claims, but it was intended only as a temporary measure to calm Indian fears about white expansion. The British, in fact, moved the line west just five years later to accommodate colonial land spec-

ulators. (One of those speculators was George Washington, who astutely kept buying western land because "any person who . . . neglects the present opportunity [*sic*] of hunting out good Lands . . . will never regain it.") The real barrier to Anglo-American expansion into the Ohio Valley was not the Proclamation of 1763 but continuing Indian strength, which prevented whites from occupying lands west of Pittsburgh until 1775.

Pontiac's War also led the British government to conclude that ten thousand British soldiers should remain in North America to occupy the western territories that France had ceded and to intimidate the Indians. The British expected to spend £220,000 annually to maintain these troops, but the actual expense soared to nearly twice that figure. With the £20,000 needed to establish civil governments in Canada and Florida factored in, the burden of maintaining control over Britain's newly acquired territories would reach almost half a million pounds a year, fully 6 percent of Britain's peacetime budget. Britons considered it perfectly reasonable for the colonists to help offset this expense, which the colonists, however, saw as none of their responsibility. Added to British misunderstanding of the American role in the Seven Years' War, the question of who would pay this new debt further clouded relations between the peoples of Britain and the mainland colonies.

Imperial Reorganization

The Seven Years' War ended the era of "salutary neglect" that had characterized imperial oversight during most of the preceding half-century. Before 1763 Parliament had made few laws affecting the colonies, aside from the various Navigation Acts controlling trade (see Chapter 3). These laws, moreover, had not provoked dissatisfaction, for Americans widely accepted Britain's right to regulate their commerce but customs officers enforced the law loosely.

During the early 1760s, Parliament changed course, stirring up controversy in the process. The discontent centered first on new regulations that denied to Americans suspected of smuggling traditional rights essential for a fair trial. But the most striking departure from prior imperial practices came in Parliament's attempts to tax the colonies. Because Britain tightened its imperial grip gradually, however, Americans were slow to appreciate the extent of the changes under way. Following a minor dispute in 1761 over the use of legally dubious search warrants and growing friction raised by the Sugar Act of 1764, a major confrontation over parliamentary taxation flared in 1765 over the passage of the Stamp Act.

These measures coincided with the beginning of the reign of George III (ruled 1760–1820), who ascended to the throne at age twenty-two. In contrast to his immediate predecessors, George I and George II, who had been largely content to let veteran politicians in Parliament run the country, the new king distrusted the British political establishment. He was determined to have a strong influence on government policy, but he wished to reign as a constitutional monarch who cooperated with

George III, *Studio of A. Ramsay, c. 1767*

Although unsure of himself and emotionally little more than a boy upon his accession to the English throne, George III possessed a deep moral sense and a fierce determination to rule as well as to reign.

Parliament and worked through prime ministers. However, neither his experience, his temperament, nor his philosophy suited George III to the formidable task of selecting satisfactory prime ministers to oversee the passage of imperial laws. Frequent clashes of personality and policy prompted the king to make abrupt changes in leadership at the very time when British government was trying to implement a massive reorganization of the empire. George's first prime minister, his friend and former tutor Lord Bute, lasted only from 1760 to 1763. Then in quick succession came the ministry of George Grenville from 1763 to 1765, that of the Marquis of Rockingham in 1766, the ministry of the ailing William Pitt in 1766, and a period of uncertain leadership that ended only in 1770, with the appointment of the ministry led by Frederick, Lord North.

The Writs of Assistance

British attempts to halt American merchants from trading with the enemy in the French West Indies during the Seven Years' War produced a crackdown on smuggling. In 1760 the royal governor of Massachusetts authorized revenue officers to employ a document called a writ of assistance to seize illegally imported goods. The writ was a general search warrant that permitted customs officials to enter any ships or buildings where smuggled goods might be hidden. Because the document required no evidence of probable cause for suspicion, most English legal authorities considered it unconstitutional. The writ of assistance also threatened the traditional respect accorded the privacy of a family's place of residence, since most merchants conducted business from their homes, where they might store inventory anywhere. The writ allowed a customs agent to ransack a merchant's house in search of illegal goods, even if there was no evidence of lawbreaking. (Today such warrants are illegal in Great Britain and the United States.)

Writs of assistance proved a powerful weapon against smuggling. In quick reaction to the writs, merchants in Boston, virtually the smuggling capital of the colonies, hired lawyer James Otis to challenge the constitutionality of these warrants. (Otis, a former prosecuting attorney for Boston's vice-admiralty court, had resigned his post in protest against the writs.) Arguing his case before the Massachusetts supreme court in 1761, Otis proclaimed that "an act against the Constitution is void"—even one passed by Parliament. But the court, heavily influenced by the opinion of Chief Justice Thomas Hutchinson, who noted the continuing use of identical writs in England, ruled against the merchants.

Despite having lost the case, Otis had expressed with absolute clarity the colonists' fundamental conception of Parliament's role under the British constitution. The British constitution was not a written document but a collection of customs and accepted principles that guaranteed certain rights to all citizens. Most British politicians assumed that Parliament's laws were themselves part of the constitution and hence that Parliament could alter the constitution at will. Like other Americans, Otis contended that Parliament possessed no authority to violate any of the traditional "rights of Englishmen," and he asserted that there were limits "beyond which if Parliaments go, their Acts bind not."

The Sugar Act

In 1764, just three years after Otis's court challenge, Parliament passed the Sugar Act with the goal of raising £100,000, a sum that would offset one-fifth of the military expenses in North America. Its enactment triggered a new round of tension between Britain and the colonies, for the Sugar Act ended Britain's longstanding policy of exempting colonial trade from revenue-raising measures. The Navigation Acts had not been designed to bring money into the British treasury but rather to benefit the imperial economy indirectly, by stimulating trade and protecting English manufacturers from foreign competition. The taxes that Parliament levied on colonial products entering Britain were paid by English importers who passed them on to consumers; they were not taxes paid by American producers. So little revenue did the Navigation Acts bring in (just £1,800 in 1763) that they did not even pay for the cost of their own enforcement, which came to about £8,000.

The Sugar Act amended the old Molasses Act of 1733, which had taxed all foreign molasses entering British America at 6 pence per gallon. Parliament had never intended this law to raise revenue but rather to serve as a protective tariff excluding French West Indian molasses from entering British North America, where the colonists distilled it into rum. The Molasses Act increased the cost of rum by about half for all distillers using French molasses but allowed distillers to import molasses from the British West Indies duty-free. However, the British West Indies produced such large amounts of rum for local use that little surplus molasses remained for export. Mainland distillers needed about 3.5 million gallons of molasses annually, and they had no choice but to buy it from the French West Indies, which had huge surpluses to export. Because the Molasses Act's 6 pence duty was too high to pass on to consumers, American importers had commonly bribed customs officials into taking 1½ pence per gallon to look the other way when French molasses was unloaded. Aware of the widespread bribery, Parliament assumed, erroneously, that rum drinkers could stomach a 3 pence duty per gallon.

New taxes were not the only feature of the Sugar Act objectionable to Americans. The act's principal architect, British prime minister George Grenville, viewed it as a weapon against what he saw as an epidemic of colonial smuggling. Grenville exaggerated the extent of colonial smuggling, which was largely confined to tea and to French molasses, and he ignored the fact that illegal trade was rampant in Great Britain. In any event, the Sugar Act targeted a broad range of colonial commercial activities for control by establishing a host of new regulations. The law stipulated that colonists could export lumber, iron, skins, hides, whalebone, logwood, and many other commodities to foreign countries only if the shipments landed first in Britain. Previously, American ships had taken these products directly to the Netherlands or the German states, where captains purchased local goods and then sailed straight back to the colonies. By channeling this trade through Britain, Parliament hoped that colonial shippers would purchase more *imperial* wares for the American market and buy fewer goods from foreign competitors. Moreover, by slapping a heavy tax on the formerly thriving American business of carrying duty-free Portuguese wine from Madeira and the Azores to the colonists, the law also aimed to increase English merchants' sales of European wine.

These restrictions financially burdened several important sectors of American commerce that previously had been legal. The Sugar Act hit New

England especially hard, since its economy had depended heavily on exporting these items to continental Europe and also on quenching the colonists' thirst with Portuguese wine. By interfering with a profitable trade developed through American enterprise, the Sugar Act had the perverse effect of creating a new category of smuggling where none had existed before, because many colonial merchants ultimately ignored the law, which in their view senselessly sacrificed their interests.

The Sugar Act also vastly complicated the requirements for shipping colonial goods. A captain now had to fill out a confusing series of documents to certify his trade as legal, and the absence of any of them left his entire cargo liable to seizure. Moreover, the Sugar Act defined oceanic commerce so broadly that much of the trade between colonies, never before regulated, became subject to complex rules for compliance. The law's petty regulations made it virtually impossible for a great many colonial shippers to avoid committing technical violations of the Sugar Act, even if they traded in the only manner possible under local circumstances.

Finally, the Sugar Act disregarded many traditional English protections for a fair trial. First, the law allowed customs officials to transfer smuggling cases from the colonial courts (in which juries decided the outcome) to vice-admiralty courts, where a judge alone gave the verdict. Because the Sugar Act (until 1768) awarded vice-admiralty judges 5 percent of any confiscated cargo, judges had a financial incentive to find every defendant guilty. Second, until 1767 the law did not permit defendants to be tried where their offense allegedly had taken place (usually their home province) but required all cases to be heard in the vice-admiralty court at Halifax, Nova Scotia. Third, the law reversed normal courtroom procedures, which presumed innocence until guilt was proved, by requiring the defendant to disprove the prosecution's charge.

The Sugar Act was no idle threat. George Grenville ordered the navy to enforce the measure, and it did so vigorously. A Boston resident complained in 1764 that "no vessel hardly comes in or goes out but they find some pretense to seize and detain her." That same year, Pennsylvania's chief justice reported that customs officers were extorting fees from small boats carrying lumber across

the Delaware River to Philadelphia from New Jersey and seemed likely "to destroy this little River-trade." "Men of war, cutters, marines with their bayonets fixed, judges of admiralty, collectors, comptrollers, searchers, . . . and a whole catalogue of pimps are sent hither," scowled a Massachusetts merchant in 1765, "not to protect our trade, but to distress it."

The Sugar Act alarmed colonists by sacrificing their economic interests and legal rights for the benefit of British merchants. Rather than pay the 3 pence tax, Americans continued smuggling molasses until 1766. Then, to discourage smuggling, Britain lowered the duty to 1 penny—less than the customary bribe American shippers paid to get their cargoes past inspectors. The law thereafter raised about £30,000 annually in revenue until 1775.

The Sugar Act confused Americans. They understood (correctly) that the Molasses Act of 1733 had never been meant as a revenue measure; in their eyes, it was a legitimate law intended to regulate trade. They therefore hesitated to denounce the Sugar Act as unconstitutional, for it seemingly only amended the Molasses Act. Notwithstanding, nine provincial legislatures protested that in passing the Sugar Act, Parliament had abused its authority to regulate trade. But seven of these objected on narrow grounds—either to its economic consequences for distillers or to its denial of traditional guarantees of a fair trial. Thus opposition to the Sugar Act failed to crystallize into a general defense of the no-taxation-without-representation principle. The law's burden fell overwhelmingly on Massachusetts, New York, and Pennsylvania, and other provinces had little interest in resisting a measure that did not affect them directly. In the end, the Sugar Act's immediate impact was minor. Soon a far more controversial issue would overshadow it—the Stamp Act.

The Stamp Act

The revenue raised by the Sugar Act did little to ease Britain's financial crisis. The national debt continued to rise, and the British public groaned under the weight of the second-highest tax rates in Europe. Particularly irritating to Britons was the fact that by 1765 their rates averaged 26 shillings per person, while the colonial tax burden varied

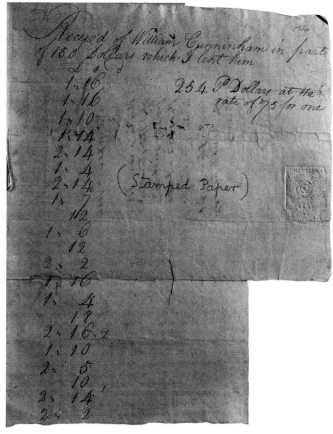

Tax Stamps

Under the Stamp Act, all legal and commercial documents had to bear tax stamps such as those shown here in closeup and on a business document.

from ½ to 1½ shillings per inhabitant, or barely 2 percent to 6 percent of the British rate. Well aware of how lightly the colonists were taxed, Grenville thought that fairness demanded a larger contribution to the empire's need.

To force the colonists to pay their share of imperial expenses, Parliament passed the Stamp Act in March 1765. The law obliged Americans to purchase and use special stamped (watermarked) paper for newspapers, customs documents, various licenses, college diplomas, and numerous legal forms necessary for recovering debts, buying land, and making wills. As with the Sugar Act, violators would face prosecution in vice-admiralty courts, without juries. The prime minister projected yearly revenues of £60,000 to £100,000, which would offset 12 percent to 20 percent of North American military expenses. Unlike the Sugar Act, which was an *external* tax on trade that fell mainly on merchants and ship captains, the Stamp Act levied an *internal* tax that few colonists could escape. Any-

one who made a will, transferred property, borrowed money, or bought playing cards or newspapers would pay the tax.

To Grenville and most of his supporters in Britain, the new tax seemed a small price for the benefits of the empire. Nevertheless, some Britons objected in principle to the tax, most notably William Pitt, who was Grenville's brother-in-law. In challenging the Stamp Act, Pitt emphasized that the colonists had never been subject to British revenue bills and taxed themselves through their own local assemblies.

Grenville agreed with Pitt that Parliament could not tax any British subjects unless they enjoyed representation in that body. But, Grenville and his followers contended, Americans *were* represented in Parliament, even if not one American actually elected any members. Americans, the prime minister claimed, shared the same status as the majority of British adult males, who either lacked sufficient property to vote or lived in large cities like

Sheffield, Manchester, and Birmingham—some more populous than the entire colony of Georgia in the mid-1760s—which had no seats in Parliament. Such persons were considered to be "virtually" represented in Parliament. The theory of virtual representation held that every member of Parliament stood above the narrow interests of his constituents and considered the welfare of *all* subjects when deciding issues. By definition, then, no Briton was represented by any particular individual in the House of Commons, but rather all imperial subjects, including Americans, could depend on each member of Parliament to protect their well-being.

Grenville and his supporters also denied that Americans were entitled to any exemption from British taxation because they elected their own assemblies. These legislative bodies were allegedly no different from English or Scottish town councils, whose local powers to pass laws and taxes did not nullify Parliament's authority over them. Accordingly, colonial assemblies were an adaptation to unique American circumstances and possessed no more power than Parliament allowed them to exercise.

The Colonial Perspective

The Stamp Act forced a choice on Americans. They would either have to confront the issue of parliamentary taxation head-on or surrender any claim to meaningful rights of self-government. However much they might admire and respect Parliament, few colonists imagined that it represented them. American spokesmen accepted the theory of virtual representation as valid for England and Scotland, but they denied that it could be extended to inhabitants of the colonies. In the American view, unless a lawmaker shared the interests of his constituents, he would have no personal stake in opposing bills contrary to their welfare. Americans recognized that members of Parliament would not impose oppressive taxes on their fellow residents of Great Britain, because the same taxes would also fall on their own estates and fortunes. The same members of Parliament, if left free to collect revenue in America, would have a clear incentive to shift the government's financial burden from themselves and their constituents onto the American colonists.

To Americans, Parliament's passage of the Stamp Act demonstrated both its indifference to their interests and the shallowness of the theory of virtual representation. Colonial agents in London had lobbied against passage of the law, and provincial legislatures had sent petitions—carefully worded statements of principle—warning against passage, but all to no avail. Parliament had dismissed the petitions without even a hearing. Parliament "must have thought us Americans all a parcel of Apes and very tame Apes too," concluded Christopher Gadsden of South Carolina, "or they would have never ventured on such a hateful, baneful experiment."

Although Americans rejected Parliament's claim to tax them, they did concede that it possessed *limited* powers of legislation. For example, the colonists believed that Parliament could standardize legal procedures throughout the realm to permit every British subject equal access to royal justice. The colonists also accepted the practical necessity for Parliament to regulate the empire's trade, even if their commerce was inconvenienced in the process.

Anglo-Americans considered the essential obligation of British allegiance to be loyalty to the crown, and their one unequivocal duty to be helping to defend the empire in wartime. The colonists insisted that they enjoyed a substantial measure of self-governance similar to that of Ireland, whose Parliament alone could tax its people but could not interfere with laws, like the Navigation Acts, passed by the British Parliament. In a speech before the Boston town meeting opposing the Sugar Act, James Otis expressed Americans' basic argument: "that by [the British] Constitution, every man in the dominions is a free man: that no parts of His Majesty's dominions can be taxed without consent: that every part has a right to be represented in the supreme or some subordinate legislature." In essence, Americans assumed that the empire was a loose federation in which their legislatures possessed considerable autonomy, rather than an extended nation governed directly from London.

Resisting the Stamp Act

Unlike the Sugar Act, the Stamp Act generated a political storm that rumbled through all the colonies in 1765. Every rank in society was caught up in the tempest—artisans, small farmers, planters, and merchants; women as well as men. Before the protest was over, upper-class community leaders had assumed direction of the colonial resistance movement.

In late May Patrick Henry, a twenty-nine-year-old Virginia lawyer with a talent for fiery oratory, dramatically conveyed the rising spirit of resistance. Henry persuaded the Virginia House of Burgesses to adopt several strongly worded resolutions denying Parliament's power to tax the colonies, and in the debate over the resolutions, the Speaker of the House cut him off just short of his uttering a treasonous wish that "some good American would stand up for his country"—presumably by assassinating the British tyrant responsible. Rather garbled accounts of Henry's resolutions electrified other Americans, and by the year's end, eight other colonial legislatures took a firm stand against British taxation.

Meanwhile, active resistance to the law was taking shape. In Boston by late summer, a group of mostly middle-class artisans, shopkeepers, and businessmen joined together as the Loyal Nine to fight the Stamp Act. They recognized that the stamp distributors, who alone could accept money for watermarked paper, were the law's weak link. If the public could pressure them into resigning before taxes became due on November 1, the Stamp Act would become inoperable. The Loyal Nine would propel Boston to the forefront of resistance.

It was no accident that Boston set the pace in opposing Parliament. Bostonians lived primarily by trade and distilling, and in 1765 they were not living well. No other port suffered so much from the Sugar Act's trade restrictions. The law burdened rum producers with a heavy tax on molasses, dried up a flourishing business of importing Portuguese wines, and prohibited the direct export of many New England products to profitable overseas markets. The city, moreover, was still struggling to recover from a great fire in 1760 that had burned 176 warehouses and left every tenth family homeless.

Widespread economic distress produced an explosive situation in Boston. A large segment of its population had good reason to blame British policies for the town's hard times. The situation was unusually dangerous because Bostonians were not only used to violence but seemed to enjoy mayhem for its own sake. The high point of each year was November 5, Guy Fawkes Day, when thousands gathered to commemorate the failure of a Catholic plot in England in 1606 to blow up Parliament and kill King James I. On that day each year, mobs from the North End and the South End customarily burned gigantic figures of the pope. High spirits usually overflowed into violent confrontations in which unruly crowds battled each other with fists, stones, and barrel staves. After the brawlers in 1764 killed a small child who got in the way, the rival mobs made a truce that united them under a South End shoemaker named Ebenezer MacIntosh. MacIntosh commanded two thousand young toughs who could not imagine getting through 1765 without a major riot. The Loyal Nine soon enlisted these frustrated street fighters against Boston's stamp distributor, Andrew Oliver.

The morning of August 14 found a likeness of Oliver swinging from a tree guarded by a menacing crowd. Oliver apparently did not realize that the Loyal Nine were warning him to resign immediately, so at dusk MacIntosh and several hundred shouting followers demolished a new building of Oliver's at the dock. The mob then surged toward Oliver's house, where they ceremoniously beheaded his effigy and "stamped" it to pieces, an exercise designed in part to give him time to flee to safety. The crowd then shattered the windows of his home, smashed his furniture, and even tore out the paneling. When Lieutenant Governor Thomas Hutchinson and the sheriff tried to disperse the crowd, they were driven off under a barrage of rocks. Surveying his devastated home the next morning, Oliver announced his resignation.

Groups similar to the Loyal Nine but calling themselves the Sons of Liberty began forming throughout the colonies to follow Boston's example. A second house wrecking occurred at Newport, Rhode Island, on August 27, after the local stamp distributor ignored a fair warning to resign; he ruefully did so the next day. Upon seeing his store pulled down, Maryland's stamp master rode off in panic until his horse dropped dead of exhaustion in New Jersey. Most other distributors followed the example of James McIvers of New York, who fled the office as soon as he learned of Oliver's fate: "a storm was riseing," McIvers explained, "and I should soon feel it." Virginia's distributor abandoned his duties after learning that his own father was attacking him in the press. By November 1 every stamp man but two had resigned, and the holdouts did so shortly. Within a mere three months, a movement with no central direction had made Grenville's tax a dead letter.

Bitterness against the Stamp Act unleashed spontaneous, contagious violence. Twelve days after the first Boston riot, MacIntosh's mob demolished the elegant home of Thomas Hutchinson. The crowd indulged in a ten-hour orgy of drunken vandalism. This attack occurred in part because smugglers held grudges against Hutchinson for certain decisions he had given as chief justice and also because many financially pinched citizens saw him as a symbol of the royal policies crippling Boston's already troubled economy. Others lashed out in reaction to Hutchinson's efforts to stop the destruction of his brother-in-law Andrew Oliver's house. Ironically, Hutchinson privately opposed the Stamp Act.

Violence also got out of hand in Newport, Rhode Island. Unwilling to do their own dirty work, local merchants had arranged for John Webber, an English sailor just four days in town, to lead a gang of seamen against the provincial stamp distributor. Having accomplished that task, Webber turned on the merchants, publicly humiliated the sheriff, and seemed on the verge of plundering the town. The deposed stamp master—who was also the colony's attorney general—ended Newport's descent into anarchy by clapping Webber in jail.

The ten weeks from August 14 to November 1, 1765, were the most disorderly period of American opposition to British authority. The Sons of Liberty directed their violence against property, however, and invariably left avenues of escape for their victims. No one was killed or tarred and feathered, although some stamp distributors had their pride deeply wounded. Nevertheless, Webber's rampage and the frenzied assault on Hutchinson's mansion were instances of simple lawlessness. By September 1765 the leaders of the Sons of Liberty recognized that unless they prevented similar sprees in the future, they would discredit their cause. Thereafter, they directed public demonstrations with firm discipline and sometimes used military formations to maneuver hundreds of protesters like a small army. Especially fearful that a royal soldier or revenue officer might be shot or killed, the Sons of Liberty forbade their followers to carry weapons, even when facing armed adver-

saries. Realizing the value of martyrs, they resolved that the only lives lost over the issue of British taxation would come from their own ranks.

In October 1765 representatives of nine colonies met in New York City in the so-called Stamp Act Congress. The session was remarkable for the colonies' agreement on and bold articulation of the general principle that Parliament lacked authority to levy taxes outside Great Britain and to deny any person a jury trial. Only once before had a truly intercolonial meeting taken place—the Albany Congress, in 1754—and, as we have seen, its plea for unity had fallen on deaf ears. In 1765 the colonial response was entirely different. "The Ministry never imagined we could or would so generally unite in opposition to their measures," wrote a Connecticut delegate to the congress, "nor I confess till I saw the Experiment made did I."

Declarations of principle like these resolutions of the Stamp Act Congress helped to embolden and unify Americans, but words seemed futile in view of Parliament's earlier refusal to consider colonial objections to the stamp duties. "The most effectual way to procure a repeal," an anonymous writer in the *New York Gazette* suggested, "is to shew them [the British] that nothing will execute it but down right force. This will make them despair of ever executing it at all."

Indeed, the British were finding the Stamp Act unenforceable, and governmental business began grinding to a halt. By late 1765 most stamp distributors had resigned or fled under popular compulsion, and without the watermarked paper required by law, most royal customs officials and court officers were refusing to perform their duties. In response, legislators compelled the reluctant officials to resume operation by threatening to withhold their pay. At the same time, merchants obtained sailing clearances by insisting that they would sue if cargoes spoiled while delayed in port. By late December the courts and harbors of almost every colony were again functioning.

Thus the American upper class assumed control of the public outcry against the Stamp Act. Respectable gentlemen moved to keep an explosive situation from getting out of hand by taking over leadership of local Sons of Liberty groups, by coordinating protest through the Stamp Act Congress, and by having colonial legislatures restore normal business. Colonial leaders feared that chaos was

"The Fatal To-Morrow"

In his October 31, 1765, edition, the Pennsylvania Journal's *publisher explained to subscribers how the Stamp Act, which would take effect the following day, was forcing him to stop publishing awhile in order to "deliberate whether any methods can be found to elude the chains forged for us."*

about to break out, particularly if British troops landed to enforce the Stamp Act. A letter from an influential Pennsylvanian, John Dickinson, to William Pitt summed up how responsible colonials envisioned the dire consequences of revolutionary turmoil: "a multitude of Commonwealths, Crimes, and Calamities, Centuries of mutual jealousies, Hatreds, Wars of Devastation, till at last the exhausted provinces shall sink into savagery under the yoke of some fortunate Conqueror."

Such extreme consequences did not come to pass, though the Stamp Act still remained in effect. To force its repeal, New York's merchants agreed on October 31, 1765, to boycott all British goods, and businessmen in other cities soon followed their example. Because Americans purchased about 40 percent of England's manufactures, this nonimportation strategy put the English economy in danger of recession. The colonial boycotts consequently triggered panic within England's business community, whose members descended on Parliament to warn that the Stamp Act's continuation would stimulate a wave of bankruptcies, massive unemployment, and political unrest.

For reasons unconnected with the Stamp Act, George Grenville had fallen from George III's favor in mid-1765 and had been succeeded by the Marquis of Rockingham. The new prime minister hesitated to advocate repeal because the overwhelming majority within the House of Commons was outraged at colonial defiance of the law. Then in January 1766 William Pitt, a steadfast opponent of the Stamp Act, boldly denounced all efforts to tax the colonies, declaring, "I rejoice that America has resisted." Parliamentary support for repeal thereafter grew, though only as a matter of practicality, not as a surrender of principle. In March 1766 Parliament revoked the Stamp Act, but only in conjunction with passage of the Declaratory Act, which affirmed parliamentary power to legislate for the colonies "in all cases whatsoever."

Because the Declaratory Act was written in general language, Americans interpreted its meaning to their advantage. Most colonial political leaders recognized that the law was modeled after an earlier statute of 1719 regarding Ireland, which was considered exempt from British taxation. The measure therefore seemed no more than a parliamentary exercise in saving face to compensate for the Stamp Act's repeal, and Americans ignored it. The House of Commons, however, intended that the colonists take the Declaratory Act literally to mean that they could not claim exemption from *any* parliamentary statute, including a tax law. The Stamp Act crisis thus ended in a fundamental disagreement between Britain and America over the colonists' political rights.

Although the Stamp Act crisis had not resolved the underlying philosophical differences between Britain and America, most Americans were eager to put the events of 1765 behind them, and they showered both king and Parliament with loyal statements of gratitude for the Stamp Act's repeal. The Sons of Liberty disbanded. Americans manifestly still possessed a deep emotional loyalty to "Old England" and concluded with relief that their active resistance to the law had slapped Britain's leaders back to their senses. Despite the unpleasant memories retained by each side after the Stamp Act's repeal, the empire remained in a position to mend its wounds with time.

Era of Crisis

From 1767 to 1773, Parliament pursued a confrontational policy that gradually corroded Americans' trust of Britain. British actions in these years created a climate of fear and alienation on the mainland that left most Americans convinced that the Stamp Act had not been an isolated mistake but part of a deliberate design to undermine colonial self-governance. Burdened by historically high levels of taxation, the British public strongly supported politicians who would compel Americans to contribute toward the cost of royal government in the colonies. Two untested leaders in the House of Commons responded to this public pressure: Charles Townshend and Lord North, neither of whom had much sympathy for the American position.

The Rise of Charles Townshend

In August 1766, in a move arising out of British politics, George III dismissed the Rockingham government and summoned William Pitt to form a cabinet. An opponent of taxing the colonies, Pitt had the potential to repair the Stamp Act's damage, for no man was more respected in America. However, Pitt's health collapsed in March 1767, and effective leadership passed to his chancellor of the exchequer (or treasurer) Charles Townshend. Townshend, who had earned a resolution of gratitude from the Massachusetts assembly for voting against the Stamp Act, seemed well suited to reassure the nervous colonists. What Americans did not know was that he was fickle, hungry for power, and believed that Parliament could tax them. As responsibility for the empire shifted to "Champagne Charley" (a name bestowed on Townshend after he delivered an extraordinarily rousing dinner speech while drunk), policy lurched in the same direction as George Grenville had taken.

Just as Townshend took office, a conflict arose with the New York legislature over the Quartering Act of 1765 (also known as the Mutiny Act). This law ordered colonial legislatures to pay for certain goods needed by soldiers stationed within their respective borders. The necessary items were relatively inexpensive barracks supplies such as candles, windowpanes, mattress straw, polish, and a small liquor ration. The Quartering Act applied only to troops in settled areas, not on the frontier. It did not force citizens to accept soldiers in private homes or require legislatures to build new barracks. Just five colonies fell under its provisions, and four of these generally complied.

Despite its seemingly petty stipulations, the law aroused resentment, for it constituted an *indirect* tax; that is, while it did not (like the Stamp Act) empower royal officials to collect money directly from the colonists, it obligated particular assemblies to raise a stated amount of revenue by whatever means they considered appropriate. The act fell lightly or not at all on most colonies; but New York, where more soldiers were stationed than any other province, found compliance very burdensome and refused to grant any supplies.

New York's resistance to indirect taxation produced a torrent of anti-American feeling in the House of Commons, whose members remained bitter at having had to withdraw the Stamp Act. Townshend responded by drafting the New York Suspending Act, which threatened to nullify all laws passed by the colony after October 1, 1767, if the assembly still refused to vote the supplies. By the time that George III signed the measure in June, however, New York had already appropriated the necessary funds.

Although New York's retreat averted further confrontation, the conflict over the Quartering Act revealed the full extent of anticolonial sentiment in the House of Commons. The incident demonstrated that British leaders would not hesitate to defend Parliament's sovereignty through the most drastic of all steps: by interfering with American claims to self-governance. What Townshend and others did not realize was that such a course of action would soon undermine a loyal people's political allegiance.

Townshend's Financial Policies

The new wave of British resentment toward the colonies coincided with an outpouring of British frustration over the government's failure to cut taxes from wartime levels. Discontent raged among the landed gentry, whose members took advantage of their domination of the House of Commons to slash their own taxes by 25 percent in 1767. This move cost the government £500,000 and prompted Townshend to propose laws that would increase colonial customs revenue and tax imports entering America.

Townshend reasoned that a closer surveillance of colonial trade would intercept more smuggled goods, pressure colonial merchants to rely more on legal imports, and thus enlarge customs duties. In 1767 he introduced legislation creating the American Board of Customs Commissioners, whose members would strictly enforce the Navigation Acts. This law raised the number of port officials, funded the construction of a colonial coast guard, and provided money for secret informers.

At the same time, Townshend sought to tax the colonists by exploiting an oversight in their arguments against the Stamp Act. In confronting the Stamp Act, Americans had emphasized their opposition to *internal* taxes—that is, to taxes levied directly on property, goods, or government services in the colonies—but had said little about Parliament's right to tax imports as they entered the colonies. Townshend and other British leaders chose to interpret this silence as evidence that the colonists accepted Britain's right to tax their trade—to impose "external" taxes. Yet not all British politicians were so mistaken. "They will laugh at you,"

predicted a now much wiser George Grenville, "for your distinctions about regulations of trade." Brushing aside Grenville's warnings, Parliament passed Townshend's Revenue Act of 1767 (popularly called the Townshend duties) in June and July 1767. The new law taxed glass, paint, lead, paper, and tea imported into the colonies.

On the surface, Townshend's contention that the Americans would submit to this external tax on imports was convincing, for the colonists had long accepted Parliament's right to regulate their overseas trade and had in principle acknowledged taxation as a legitimate form of regulation. Even the Sugar Act had not primarily aroused opposition in the colonies because it imposed taxes; rather, Americans had protested the law because it instituted impractical regulations for conducting trade and violated traditional guarantees of a fair trial.

Townshend's Revenue Act differed significantly from what Americans had long seen as a legitimate way of regulating trade through taxation. To the colonists, charging a duty was a lawful way for British authorities to control trade only if that duty excluded foreign goods by making them prohibitively expensive to consumers. The Revenue Act of 1767, however, set moderate rates that did not price goods out of the colonial market; clearly, its purpose was to collect money for the treasury. Thus from the colonial standpoint, Townshend's duties were taxes just like the Stamp Act duties.

Although Townshend had introduced the Revenue Act in response to the government's budgetary problems, he had an ulterior motive for establishing an American source of revenue. Traditionally, royal governors had depended on colonial legislatures to vote their salaries; for their part, the legislatures had often refused to allocate these salaries until governors had signed certain bills to which they were opposed. Through the Revenue Act, Townshend hoped to establish a fund that would pay the salaries of governors and other royal officials in America, thus freeing them from the assemblies' control. In effect, by stripping the assemblies of their most potent weapon, the power of the purse, the Revenue Act threatened to tip the balance of constitutional power away from elected colonial representatives and toward unelected royal officials.

In reality the Revenue Act would never yield anything like the income that Townshend anticipated. Of the various items taxed, only tea produced any significant revenue—£20,000 of the £37,000 that the law was expected to yield. And because the measure would serve its purpose only if British tea was affordable to colonial consumers (who could easily smuggle Dutch tea), Townshend eliminated £60,000 worth of import fees paid on East Indian tea entering Britain before transhipment to America. On balance, the Revenue Act *worsened* the British treasury's deficit by £23,000. By 1767 Britain's financial difficulties were more an excuse for, than the driving force behind, political demands to tax the colonies. From Parliament's standpoint, the conflict with America was becoming a test of national will over the *principle* of taxation.

The Colonists' Reaction

Parliament gave the colonists little time to plan resistance against the Townshend duties. Americans only learned of the Revenue Act shortly before it went into operation, and they hesitated over the appropriate response. The strong-arm tactics that sent stamp tax collectors into panicky flight would not work against the Townshend duties, which the navy could easily collect offshore, safe from any Sons of Liberty.

Resistance to the Revenue Act remained weak until December 1767, when John Dickinson published twelve essays entitled *Letters from a Farmer*. (Dickinson was in fact a lawyer, but he preferred to portray himself as a son of the soil because the legal profession was unpopular among the general population.) The essays, which appeared in nearly every colonial newspaper, emphasized that, although Parliament could regulate trade by voting duties capable of providing small amounts of "incidental revenue," it had no right to tax commerce for the single purpose of raising revenue. In other words, the legality of any external tax depended on its intent. No tax designed to produce revenue could be considered constitutional unless a people's elected representatives voted for it. Dickinson said nothing that the colonists had not stated or implied during the Stamp Act crisis. Rather, his contribution lay in persuading Americans that the many arguments that they had marshaled against the Stamp Act also applied to the Revenue Act.

For all their clarity and eloquence, the *Letters from a Farmer* did not suggest tactics for resisting the Townshend duties, which had already taken effect. Dickinson was a conservative, deeply opposed to turmoil: he averred that "the cause of liberty is a cause of too much dignity to be sullied by turbulence and tumult." Yet resistance quickly took shape, aided immeasurably by the leadership of Massachusetts and by the blundering of the British government.

Dickinson himself had grasped the critical importance of mobilizing the citizens of Massachusetts. In a letter to James Otis, the Boston lawyer famed for his arguments in the writs-of-assistance case, Dickinson acknowledged that "whenever the Cause of American Freedom is to be vindicated, I look towards the Province of Massachusetts Bay. She must, as she has hitherto done, first kindle the Sacred Flame that on such occasions must warm and illuminate the Continent." Soon after receiving the letter, Otis chaired a Boston town meeting that asked the Massachusetts legislature to oppose the Townshend duties. In response, the assembly in early 1768 called on one of its members, Samuel Adams, to draft a "circular letter" to every other legislature. Harvard-educated yet possessing a flair for the push-and-shove of local politics, Adams had helped bring the Sons of Liberty under respectable leadership in 1765. In time he would acquire a reputation in Britain as a fanatic for colonial rights, but he deliberately phrased the circular letter in moderate language in order to give it a wide appeal. Adams's circular letter forthrightly condemned both taxation without representation and the threat to self-governance posed by Parliament's making governors and other royal officials financially independent of the legislatures. Nonetheless, the document acknowledged Parliament as the "supreme legislative Power over the whole Empire," and it advocated no illegal activities.

Virginia's assembly warmly approved Adams's eloquent message and sent out a more strongly worded circular letter of its own, urging all colonies to oppose imperial policies that would "have an immediate tendency to enslave them." But most colonial legislatures reacted indifferently to these letters. In fact, resistance to the Revenue Act might have disintegrated had the British government not overreacted to the circular letters.

Indeed, parliamentary leaders regarded even the mild Massachusetts letter as "little better than an incentive to Rebellion." Disorganized by Townshend's sudden death in 1768, the king's Privy

Samuel Adams

A central player in the drive for American liberty, Adams wrote in 1774 that "I wish for a permanent union with the mother country, but only in terms of liberty and truth. No advantage that can accrue to America from such a union, can compensate for the loss of liberty."

Council directed Lord Hillsborough, first appointee to the new post of secretary of state for the colonies, to express the government's displeasure. Hillsborough flatly told the Massachusetts assembly to disown its letter, forbade all overseas assemblies to endorse it, and commanded royal governors to dissolve any colonial legislature that violated his instructions. George III later commented that he never met "a man of less judgment than Lord Hillsborough." A wiser man might have tried to divide the colonists by appealing to their sense of British patriotism, but Hillsborough had chosen a course guaranteed to unite them in anger.

To protest Hillsborough's crude bullying, many legislatures previously indifferent to the Massachusetts circular letter now adopted it enthusiastically. The Massachusetts House of Representatives voted 92–17 not to recall its letter. The number 92 immediately acquired symbolic significance for Americans; colonial politicians on more than one occasion drank 92 toasts in tipsy salutes to Mas-

sachusetts's action. In obedience to Hillsborough, royal governors responded by dismissing legislatures in Massachusetts and elsewhere. These moves played directly into the hands of Samuel Adams, James Otis, and John Dickinson, who wished to ignite widespread opposition to the Townshend duties.

While increasingly outraged over the Revenue Act, the colonists still needed some effective means of bringing pressure on Parliament for its repeal. One approach, non-importation, seemed especially promising because it offered an alternative to violence and would distress Britain's economy. In August 1768 Boston's merchants therefore adopted a non-importation agreement, and the tactic slowly spread southward. "Save your money, and you save your country!" became the watchword of the Sons of Liberty, who began reorganizing after two years of inactivity. Not all colonists supported non-importation, however. Its effectiveness ultimately depended on the compliance of merchants, whose livelihood relied, in turn, on buying and selling imports. In several major communities, including Philadelphia and Baltimore, merchants continued buying British goods until early 1769, and Charles Town (Charleston), South Carolina, did not cut off its purchases until July 1769. Far from complete, the boycott probably kept out no more than 40 percent of all imports from Britain.

Nevertheless, the exclusion of 40 percent of imports inflicted serious losses on British merchants and thereby heightened pressure within Britain for repeal of the Townshend duties. Yet the tactical value of non-importation was not restricted to damaging Britain's economy. It also hinged on convincing the British—and the colonists themselves—that all Americans were determined to sustain resistance, and on demonstrating that the American cause rested on the foundations of impeccable morality and sensible moderation. Colonial rhetoric therefore frequently included traditional religious appeals and harped on familiar lessons from ancient history. And it provided a unique opportunity for women to join in the protest against unconstitutional laws.

The Mobilization of Opinion

Samuel Adams once expressed hope that America would become a "Christian Sparta." By linking religion and ancient history, Adams was combining two of colonial leaders' most potent rhetorical appeals in rallying public protest. Almost every eighteenth-century American had been steeped in Protestantism since earliest childhood; and all whose education had gone beyond the basics had imbibed Greek and Latin learning, as well as seventeenth-century English literature. All these hallowed traditions, Americans believed, confirmed the legitimacy of their cause. "Having been initiated in youth, in the doctrines of civil liberty, as they were taught by such men as Plato . . . [and] Cicero . . . among the ancients; and such as . . . Milton [and] Locke . . . among the moderns," wrote the minister Jonathan Mayhew, "[and] having earlier still learnt from the holy scriptures, that wise, brave, and virtuous men were always friends of liberty . . . I would not, I cannot now, relinquish the fair object of my youthful affections, LIBERTY. . . ."

Recalling in later years the inspiring debate over the Stamp Act that he had witnessed in Virginia's House of Burgesses in 1765, Thomas Jefferson said of Patrick Henry that "he appeared to me to speak as Homer wrote." Jefferson was a typical educated man of his day in revering the ancient republics of Greece and Rome for their supposedly stern, virtuous devotion to liberty. The pamphlets, speeches, and public declarations that gentlemen like Jefferson and Dickinson wrote resounded with quotations from the ancient classics. These allusions served as constant reminders to upper-class Americans of the righteous dignity of their cause. But appeals to ordinary Americans had to draw upon deeper wellsprings of belief. Significantly, the power of Henry's oratory also reflected his ability (unique among Virginia political leaders) to evoke the colonists' religious fervor, which the Great Awakening had stirred.

Beginning with the Stamp Act protest, New England's clergymen mounted their pulpits and summoned their flocks to stand up for God and liberty. "A just regard to our liberties . . . is so far from being displeasing to God that it would be ingratitude to him who has given them to us to . . . tamely give them up," exhorted one minister. "We are bound in conscience to stand fast in the liberty with which Christ has made us free." Not quite so quickly, but in the end with equally heartfelt intensity, Baptist and other dissenting preachers took up the cause. Only Anglican ministers, who were accustomed to insist on the religious duty of obe-

dience to the crown, tried to stay neutral or opposed the protest; and many pacifist Quakers kept out of the fray. But to most American Protestant clergymen, memories of battling for the Lord in the old Calvinist tradition proved too powerful to resist.

Voicing such a message, "the black regiment" of clergymen in their dignified gowns exerted an enormous influence on public opinion. Far more Americans heard sermons (or read them in printed form) than had access to newspapers or pamphlets, and ministers always got a respectful hearing at town meetings. Community leaders' proclamations of days of "fasting and public humiliation"— in colonial America, a familiar means of focusing public attention on an issue and invoking divine aid—inspired sermons on the theme of God's sending the people woes only to strengthen and sustain them until victory. Even Virginia gentlemen not notable for their piety felt moved by such proclamations and ordered their families to comply. Moreover, protest leaders' calls for boycotting British luxuries meshed neatly with traditional pulpit warnings against frivolity and wastefulness. Few ordinary Americans escaped the unceasing public reminders that community solidarity against British tyranny and "corruption" meant rejecting sin and obeying God.

By associating their cause with Christian faith and ancient virtue, Americans were not using a particularly original strategy, for such allusions were commonplace eighteenth-century ways of appealing to public opinion. But another American means of mobilizing support was novel: the involvement of women in the protest movement. Women's enlistment in the cause unfolded slowly. Calling themselves the Daughters of Liberty, upper-class female patriots had played only a minor part in defeating the Stamp Act. Some had attended political rallies during the Stamp Act crisis, while others had reinforced colonial resolve by turning a cold shoulder to men unwilling to resist Grenville's tax.

In contrast, women assumed a highly visible role during the Townshend crisis. Clearly believing that colonial women could exert a persuasive moral influence on public opinion, American leaders encouraged them to protest the Revenue Act's tax on tea. Accordingly, in early 1770 more than three hundred "mistresses of families" in Boston denounced the consumption of the beverage. In some ways, such nonconsumption was a more

Mr. and Mrs. Thomas Mifflin, *by John Singleton Copley, 1773*

The Mifflins were prominent Philadelphians. Thomas, a merchant in his early years, sat in the Pennsylvania assembly, served as one of the youngest members of the First Continental Congress, and later joined the Continental Army, where he quickly rose to officer's rank. An ardent supporter of the American cause, Sarah Morris Mifflin here demonstrates her patriotism by spinning her own thread.

effective tactic than non-importation, for while a minority of merchants might ignore non-importation on the basis of principle or financial interest, a refusal by colonists to consume imports would chill merchants' economic incentive to continue bringing in English products.

Nonconsumption agreements therefore quickly became popular and were extended to include English manufactures (mostly clothing) as well as tea. Again women played a vital role, because the boycott would fail unless the colonists replaced British imports with apparel of their own making. Responding to leaders' pleas that they expand domestic cloth production, women of all social ranks, even those who customarily did not weave their own fabric or sew their own clothing, orga-

nized spinning bees. These events attracted intense publicity as evidence of American determination to fight parliamentary taxation. The colonial cause, noted a New York woman, had enlisted "a fighting army of amazons . . . armed with spinning wheels."

Spinning bees not only helped undermine the masculine prejudice that women had no place in public life but also endowed spinning and weaving, previously considered routine household tasks, with special political virtue. "[W]omen might recover to this country the full and free enjoyment of all our rights, properties and privileges," exclaimed the Reverend John Cleaveland of Ipswich, Massachusetts, in 1769; he then added with more than usual honesty that this "is more than the men have been able to do."

Spinning bees, combined with female support for boycotting tea, were dramatic demonstrations of American determination. Colonial leaders were waging a battle to convince public opinion in Britain that their society would stand firm in opposing unconstitutional taxes. Only if the British people believed that Americans—male and female—were truly united would they accept repeal of the Townshend duties. Female participation in symbolic protests forced the British public to appreciate the depth of colonial commitment to maintaining the non-importation agreements and so contributed significantly to Parliament's reluctant decision to rescind most of the Townshend duties.

Repeal of the Townshend Duties

In January 1770 Lord North became prime minister. Although described as a "great, heavy, booby-looking man" and noted for occasionally sleeping through debates in the House of Commons, North had ability and would retain his office until 1782. North favored eliminating most of the Townshend duties to prevent the American commercial boycott from widening, but to underscore British authority, he insisted on retaining the tax on tea. Parliament agreed, and in April 1770, giving in for the second time in three years to colonial pressure, it repealed most of the Townshend duties.

Parliament's partial repeal produced a dilemma for American politicians. They considered it intolerable that taxes remained on tea, the most profitable item for the royal treasury. Colonial leaders were unsure whether they should press on with the non-importation agreement until they achieved total victory, or whether it would suffice to maintain a selective boycott of tea. When the non-importation movement collapsed in July 1770, the Sons of Liberty resisted external taxation by voluntary agreements not to drink British tea. Through nonconsumption they succeeded in limiting revenue from tea to about one-sixth the level originally expected. This amount was far too little to pay the salaries of royal governors as Townshend had intended.

Yet American leaders took little satisfaction in having forced Parliament to compromise. The tea duty remained as a galling reminder that Parliament refused to retreat from the broadest possible interpretation of the Declaratory Act. Thus although the crisis passed in 1770, its legacy lingered long afterward. The tax on tea acted like a festering sore that slowly poisoned relations between Britain and its colonies. The Townshend crisis had begun the gradual process by which a loyal people lost all sense of allegiance to their mother country.

Customs Racketeering and Escalating Violence

Although few Americans had objected to the establishment in 1767 of the American Board of Customs Commissioners, that institution soon became a major source of controversy in the colonies. Townshend had wanted the board to bring honesty, efficiency, and more revenue to overseas customs operations, but it accomplished none of his goals. Instead, the new commissioners grew notorious for abusing the law rather than enforcing it, in order to enrich themselves through confiscated ships or cargoes.

The rapid expansion of the American customs service in 1767 coincided with new legal provisions that awarded a revenue officer one-third of the value of all goods and ships appropriated through a conviction of smuggling. The fact that fines could be tripled under certain circumstances provided an even greater incentive to seize illegal cargoes. Smuggling cases were heard in vice-admiralty courts, moreover, where the probability of conviction was extremely high. Had the new customs commissioners done their duty honestly and pursued smugglers vigorously, little dissension would have developed. But the prospect of accumulating a small fortune through seizures proved too tempting. Soon revenue agents commonly perverted the law by filing charges for technical violations of the Sugar Act, even when no evidence existed of intent to conduct illegal trade.

Indeed, the Sugar Act afforded unscrupulous excise officials a virtual gold mine of opportunities to accuse honest shipowners and merchants of smuggling. Revenue agents most often exploited the provision that declared any cargo illegal unless it had been loaded or unloaded with a customs officer's written authorization. Many vessels transporting lumber or tobacco found it impossible to comply, because they typically picked up these items piecemeal at a succession of small wharves far from a customhouse. Previously, a ship captain received certification of such cargoes for overseas passage at the nearest harbor, but after 1764 such a procedure violated the Sugar Act, even if the captain had no intention of smuggling.

Under the new rules, even a captain who threw rotting provisions overboard while at sea could be found guilty of illegally unloading. One common device by which customs officials created opportunities for seizures was to accommodate local circumstances by bending the rules for a time (particularly by relaxing the strict loading requirements) and then suddenly to enforce the letter of the law. The American Board of Customs Commissioners thus embarked on a program of "customs racketeering" that constituted little more than a system of legalized piracy operating through the vice-admiralty courts to achieve its objectives.

Directly or indirectly, the Board of Customs Commissioners fed an upsurge in popular violence. Above all, customs commissioners' use of paid spies provoked retaliation. The *Pennsylvania Journal* in 1769 scorned these agents as "dogs of prey, thirsting after the fortunes of worthy and wealthy men." By the very fact that they betrayed the trust of employers, and sometimes of friends, informers aroused wild hatred in their victims and were roughly handled whenever found. Nearly all instances of tarring and feathering in these years were acts of private revenge against informers rather than acts of political reprisal.

Customs commissioners also fanned angry passions by invading the traditional rights of sailors. Longstanding maritime custom allowed a ship's crew to supplement their incomes by making small sales between ports. Anything stored in a sailor's chest was considered private property that did not have to be listed as cargo on the captain's manifest and so was exempt from the regulations of the Navigation Acts. After 1767, however, revenue agents began treating such belongings as cargo, thus establishing an excuse to seize the entire ship.

Under this new policy, crewmen saw their trunks ruthlessly broken open by arrogant inspectors and then lost trading stock worth several months' wages because it was not listed on the captain's loading papers. Sailors developed deep hatred for customs officers and eagerly awaited chances to get even. Not surprisingly, after 1767 inspectors fell increasingly victim to riots dominated by vengeful seafaring men. By enforcing the letter of the law while violating its spirit, the American Board of Customs Commissioners created a superheated climate that made such riots and assaults inevitable.

In British eyes, the violence perpetrated against customs officials not only tarnished the colonists' efforts to defend their rights but also seemed part of an American campaign to destroy royal authority. However, this perception was wrong. Although colonial leaders could not channel all resistance into peaceful petitions and boycotts (as they had done in protesting the Townshend duties) and could not always prevent periodic eruptions of outrage against royal officials' excesses, they vehemently opposed such tactics as counterproductive. "Let this be the language of all," wrote a Son of Liberty in the *Boston Gazette*: "no mobs, no confusion, no tumults."

Nowhere were customs agents and informers more detested than in Boston, where in June 1768 citizens finally retaliated against their tormentors. The occasion was the seizure of the colonial merchant John Hancock's sloop *Liberty*. A group of nearby sailors mercilessly beat the customs agents on the wharf and then decided to give every excise man in town the same lesson. The crowd swelled to several hundred as it surged through the streets hunting down its prey, and by day's end, the rioters had driven all revenue inspectors from Boston.

Hancock, reportedly North America's richest merchant and a leading opponent of British taxation, had become a chief target of the customs commissioners. Although a significant minority of Boston's merchants did smuggle, no firm evidence exists that Hancock was among them. Nevertheless, in

John and Dorothy Hancock, *by Edward Savage*

As president of the Second Continental Congress, Hancock, shown here with his wife, Dorothy, was the first to sign the Declaration of Independence.

1768 the customs commissioners used a perjured statement from a customs inspector to seize the *Liberty* for allegedly avoiding £700 in duties on Madeira wine worth £3,000. By then requesting the payment of triple charges on the wine, they made Hancock liable for a total fine of £9,000, an amount almost thirteen times greater than the taxes supposedly evaded.

Several flagrant violations of Hancock's right to a fair trial tainted his prosecution. For example, a customs inspector who refused to sign false statements against Hancock was fired but then promised the return of his job and a secret payment if he would cooperate. The Boston grand jury charged another customs inspector with lying under oath. The most damaging evidence against Hancock came from a customs informer, whose testimony would not have been allowed in any other English court because he stood to gain a third of the £9,000 fine that Hancock would pay if convicted. Furthermore, the presiding judge did not allow Hancock's lawyer to cross-examine prosecution witnesses; and because the judge questioned Hancock's witnesses privately, in his own chambers, Hancock's lawyer could not be sure whether their evidence had hurt or helped his case. Since the hearing took place in a vice-admiralty court, moreover, Hancock's fate depended not on a jury but on the same judge whose actions had prejudiced his defense.

Hancock's case forced Americans to reevaluate their former acceptance of the principle that Parliament had limited authority to pass laws for them. Prior to 1768 colonial leaders had single-mindedly denied Britain's power to tax them, without considering that freedoms of equal importance might also be jeopardized by other kinds of legislation. But by 1770 it was becoming clear that measures like the Sugar Act and the act creating the American Board of Customs Commissioners seriously endangered property rights and civil liberties. This realization led many Americans to expand their opposition from a rejection of taxation without representation to a more broadly based rejection of legislation without representation. By 1774 there would emerge a new consensus that Parliament possessed no lawmaking authority over the colonies except the right to regulate imperial commerce through statutes like the old Navigation Acts.

By 1770 the British government, aware of its customs officers' excesses, began reforming the service. The smuggling charges against Hancock were finally dropped because the prosecution feared that Hancock would appeal a conviction to England, where honest officials would take action against the persons responsible for violating his rights. But although the abuses largely ended by the early 1770s, the damage had been done. Townshend's American Board of Customs Commissioners contributed enormously to the colonists' growing suspicion of British motives and their progressive alienation from the mother country.

The Boston Massacre

As another consequence of the violence stirred up by the customs commissioners, a force of seventeen hundred British troops landed in Boston during the six weeks after October 1, 1768. By 1770 this military occupation, which directly resulted from the *Liberty* riots, provoked a fresh round of violence.

Boston rapidly took on the atmosphere of an occupied city and crackled with tension as armed sentries and resentful civilians traded insults. The mainly Protestant townspeople found it especially galling that many soldiers were Irish Catholics and a few, mostly drummers, were blacks. The majority of enlisted men, moreover, were free to seek employment following the morning muster. Often agreeing to work for less than local laborers, they generated fierce hostility in a community still plagued by unemployment.

The situation in Boston was tailor-made for a man like Samuel Adams, whose genius lay in shaping public opinion. Adams once said that his task

The Landing of British Troops in Boston, 1768

The patriot silversmith and engraver Paul Revere recorded the controversial event for posterity in this engraving. Revere also described the redcoats' "insolent Parade, [with] Drums beating, Fifes playing, and Colours flying up King Street."

was not to make events but to improve on them. By imposing nearly two thousand redcoats on a crowded, economically distressed, and violence-prone city of twenty thousand bullheaded Yankees, the British government gave Adams all the grist that he needed for his propaganda mill.

In October 1768 Adams began publishing the *Journal of the Times,* a magazine claiming to offer a factual account of abuses committed by the army and the customs service in Boston. Adams intended to make a bad situation worse by kindling outrage that would harden popular resistance against British authority. Although the troops behaved well by the period's standards (often better than the townspeople), the *Journal* rarely lacked for stories of civilians who were assaulted, insulted, or simply annoyed at hearing regimental musicians play mocking versions of "Yankee Doodle" on fifes and drums. Adams exaggerated every incident, published all rumors as if they were true, and invented stories whenever the times grew dull. Bostonians came to hate the redcoats more with every issue of Adams's *Journal,* and Americans elsewhere worried that their communities might be the next site of a military occupation.

Still, Bostonians endured their first winter as a garrison town without undue trouble and saw half the British troops sail home in mid-1769. Relations between the remaining soldiers and civilians then abruptly worsened. The deep-seated resentment against all who upheld British authority suddenly boiled over on February 22, 1770, when an unpopular customs informer fired bird shot at several children bombarding his house with rocks and killed an eleven-year-old German boy. The ever crafty Samuel Adams made sure that the tragedy served his cause well. He organized a burial procession to maximize the sense of horror at a child's death, relying on grief to unite the community in opposition to British policies. "My Eyes never beheld such a funeral," wrote his cousin John Adams. "A vast Number of Boys walked before the Coffin, a vast Number of Women and Men after it. . . . This Shews there are many more Lives to spend if wanted in the Service of their country."

Although the army had played no part in the shooting, it became a natural target for the townspeople's frustration and rage. A week after the boy's funeral, a disorderly crowd went looking for trouble and found it at the guardpost protecting the

The Boston Massacre, 1770, *Engraving by Paul Revere*

Shortly after the "massacre," one Bostonian observed that "unless there is some great alteration in the state of things, the era of the independence of the colonies is much nearer than I once thought it, or now wish it."

customs office. They pelted the sentry with insults, ice, rocks, and lumber until a captain and seven soldiers arrived. While the officer tried to disperse the mob, his men endured a steady barrage of flying objects and dares to shoot. One soldier finally did fire, after having been knocked down by a block of ice, and the others pulled their triggers without orders. Their uneven volley hit eleven persons, five of whom eventually died.

Burning hatreds produced by an intolerable situation underlay this so-called Boston Massacre. Once again Samuel Adams orchestrated a funeral fit for martyrs and used the occasion to solidify American opposition to British authority. Most colonists accepted the distorted account of the event published in Adams's *Journal* and reinforced by Paul Revere's famous engraving (see illustration above): that it was a ruthless attack on unarmed civilians who dared to stand up to military bullies. The "massacre" profoundly affected Americans, forcing many to confront the stark possibility that the British government might be bent on coercing them into paying unconstitutional taxes through naked force.

Drift and Division

The shock that followed the March 5 bloodshed marked the emotional high point of the Townshend crisis. Royal authorities in Massachusetts tried to defuse the situation in Boston by isolating all British soldiers on a fortified island in the harbor, and Governor Thomas Hutchinson promised that the soldiers who had fired would be tried. Patriot leader John Adams served as their attorney, with the intention not only to demonstrate Americans' commitment to impartial justice but also "to lay before [the people of Boston], the Law as it stood, that they might be apprized of the Dangers ... which must arise from intemperate heats and irregular commotions." All but two of the soldiers were acquitted, and the ones found guilty suffered only a branding on their thumbs. Meanwhile, Parliament soon repealed all external taxes except the tea duty, leaving most colonists uncertain about whether their rights were still endangered. To the extent that Americans resisted at all, they did so passively by drinking smuggled tea.

From mid-1770 to 1772, Lord North's government virtually ignored the colonies. North's inaction undercut the influence of firebrands like Samuel Adams, who were left without an issue that could be used to stir discontent. The minister of John Hancock's congregation expressed the mood of the times well when he wrote in January 1771 that "there seems ... to be a Pause in Politics."

During the lull Americans increasingly quarreled among themselves. New Hampshire and New York argued over title to modern-day Vermont, where settlers from both colonies fought a minor guerrilla war. Pennsylvania waged a frustrating legal battle with Virginia to defend its territory near Pittsburgh and had similar problems with Connecticut, which issued land grants around Wilkes-Barre and settled several hundred squatters there. But the most dramatic example of colonial divisiveness occurred in North Carolina, where widespread discontent over corrupt, inefficient government sparked a brief civil war between provincial officials and the so-called Regulators. The Regulators aimed to redress the grievances of North Carolinians living in the colony's western regions, who were underrepresented in the colonial assembly and who found themselves exploited by dishonest, self-serving officeholders appointed to their posts by eastern politicians. The Regulator movement climaxed on May 16, 1771, at the Battle of Alamance Creek. Leading an army of perhaps 1,300 eastern militia, North Carolina's royal governor defeated about 2,500 Regulators in a clash that left almost three hundred casualties. Although the Regulator uprising then disintegrated, it crippled the colony's subsequent ability to resist British authority.

The Committees of Correspondence

The truce in Anglo-American antagonisms lasted until 1772. In the fall of that year, Lord North's ministry began preparing to implement Townshend's goal of paying the royal governors' salaries out of customs revenue. The colonists had always viewed this intention to free the governors from legislative domination as a fundamental threat to representative government. In response, Samuel Adams persuaded Boston's town meeting to request that every Massachusetts community appoint persons responsible for exchanging information and coordinating measures to defend colonial rights. Of approximately 260 towns, about half immediately established "committees of correspondence," and most others did so within a year. From Massachusetts the idea spread throughout New England.

The committees of correspondence were the colonists' first attempt to maintain close and continuing political cooperation over a wide area. By linking almost every interior community to Boston through a network of dedicated activists, the system allowed Adams to conduct a campaign of political education for all of Massachusetts, and increasingly for all of New England. Adams sent out messages for each town's local committee to read at its town meeting, which would then debate the issues and adopt a formal resolution. Forcing tens of thousands of citizens to consider evidence that their rights were in danger, the system committed them to take a personal stand by voting.

Adams's most successful venture in whipping up public alarm came in June 1773, when he publicized certain letters of Massachusetts governor Thomas Hutchinson that Benjamin Franklin had obtained. Massachusetts town meetings discovered through the letters that their own chief executive had advocated "an abridgment of what are called English liberties" and "a great restraint of natural liberty." The publication of the Hutchinson correspondence confirmed American suspicions that a plot was afoot to destroy basic freedoms.

The shock produced by Hutchinson's letters led many colonists to take seriously the warnings of well-known English political writers like Lord Bolingbroke, John Trenchard, and Thomas Gordon. Beginning in the early eighteenth century, these and other "oppositionist" authors had argued that since 1720 prime ministers had exploited the treasury's vast resources to provide pensions, contracts, and profitable offices to politicians or had bought elections by bribing voters in small boroughs. According to these men, most members of Parliament no longer represented the true interests of their constituents but rather had sold their political souls for financial gain.

Often referring to themselves as the "country interest" (or "country party"), these writers expressed the frustrations of landowning taxpayers who were forced to support an expensive government dominated by a "court party" of nonelected officials close to the king. Eventually, this "country ideology" predicted, a power-hungry prime minister or a group of anonymous conspirators would use a corrupted Parliament to gain absolute power for themselves. By 1773 many Americans believed that this scenario was indeed unfolding and that the assault on their rights was part of a plot to establish a despotism.

Even before the committees of correspondence sprang up, an incident had occurred that reinvigorated American discontent. On June 9, 1772, the customs schooner *Gaspee* ran aground near Providence, Rhode Island. One of the last revenue cutters to engage in customs racketeering by plundering cargoes for technical violations of the Sugar Act, the *Gaspee* had acquired an odious reputation among Rhode Islanders. Its crew had frequently landed to steal fruit, unfenced livestock, and firewood, and the captain was said to be "more imperious and haughty than the Grand Turk himself." Now helplessly stuck in the mud, the *Gaspee* presented too tempting a target for local inhabitants to resist. That night, more than one hundred disguised men burned it to the waterline, not for political reasons but for the simple pleasure of revenge.

The British government dispatched a commission to look into the attack, with instructions to send all suspects to England for trial. The investigators failed to identify any raiders and came back empty-handed. Nevertheless, Americans were alarmed that the ministry intended to dispense with another essential civil liberty, an accused citizen's right to be tried by a local jury.

In reaction to the *Gaspee* commission's instructions, Patrick Henry, Thomas Jefferson, and fellow Virginian Richard Henry Lee proposed in March 1773 that Virginia establish a permanent committee for corresponding with other colonies. Within a year every province but Pennsylvania had followed its example. By early 1774 colonial leaders were linked by a communications web for the first time since 1766.

In contrast to the brief, intense Stamp Act crisis, the dissatisfaction spawned by the Townshend duties and the American Board of Customs Commissioners persisted and gradually poisoned relations between Britain and America. In 1765 feelings of loyalty and affection toward Britain had remained strong in America and thus had helped disguise the depth of the division over the constitutional issue of taxation. By 1773, however, colonial allegiance was becoming conditional and could no longer be assumed.

Toward Independence

Although the British Empire remained superficially tranquil in early 1773, it had resolved none of its underlying constitutional problems. To a large degree, Americans ignored the continued taxation of tea because of a widespread expectation that Lord North would eventually have the duty repealed. Parliament suddenly blasted this unrealistic hope when it passed the Tea Act in 1773. This measure set off a chain reaction that started with the Boston

Tea Party in late 1773 and was followed by Parliament's attempt to retaliate through the Intolerable Acts in 1774, the First Continental Congress in September 1774, the outbreak of fighting in April 1775, and the colonists' declaration of their independence in July 1776.

The Tea Act

Colonial smuggling and nonconsumption had taken a heavy toll on Britain's East India Company, which enjoyed a legal monopoly on importing tea into the British Empire. By 1773, with tons of tea rotting in its warehouses, the East India Company was teetering on the brink of bankruptcy. But Lord North could not let the company fail. Not only did it pay substantial duties on the tea it imported into Britain, but it also provided huge indirect savings for the government by maintaining British authority in India at its own expense.

If the company could only control the colonial market, North reasoned, its chances for returning to profitability would greatly increase. Americans supposedly consumed more than a million pounds of tea each year, but by 1773 they were purchasing just one-quarter of it from the company. In May 1773, to save the beleaguered East India Company from financial ruin, Parliament passed the Tea Act, which eliminated all remaining import duties on tea entering England and thus lowered the selling price to consumers. (Ironically, the same saving could have been accomplished by repealing the Townshend tax, which would have ended colonial objections to the company's tea and produced enormous goodwill toward the British government.) To lower the price further, the Tea Act also permitted the company to sell its tea directly to consumers rather than through wholesalers.

These two concessions reduced the cost of East India Company tea in the colonies well below the price of all smuggled competition. Parliament expected simple economic self-interest to overcome American scruples about buying taxed tea. With the resulting revenue, the British government would finally be able to achieve Townshend's goal of making the royal governors independent of colonial assemblies by paying their salaries.

But the Tea Act alarmed many Americans, above all because they saw in it a menace to colonial representative government. By making taxed tea competitive in price with smuggled tea, the law in all likelihood would raise revenue, which the British government would use to pay royal governors. The law thus threatened to corrupt Americans into accepting the principle of parliamentary taxation by taking advantage of their weakness for a frivolous luxury. Quickly, therefore, the committees of correspondence decided to resist the importation of tea, though without violence and without the destruction of private property. Either by pressuring the company's agents to refuse acceptance or by intercepting the ships at sea and ordering them home, the committees would keep East India Company cargoes from being landed. In Philadelphia an anonymous "Committee for Tarring and Feathering" warned harbor pilots not to guide any ships carrying tea into port.

In Boston, however, this strategy failed. On November 28, 1773, the first ship came under the jurisdiction of the customhouse, to which duties would have to be paid on its cargo within twenty days. Otherwise, the cargo would be seized from the captain and the tea claimed by the company's agents (who included two of Governor Hutchinson's sons) and placed on sale. When Samuel Adams, John Hancock, and other leading citizens repeatedly asked the customs officers to issue a special clearance for the ship's departure, they found themselves blocked by the governor's refusal to compromise.

On the evening of December 16, Samuel Adams convened a meeting in Old South Church. He informed the five thousand citizens of Hutchinson's insistence upon landing the tea, told them that the grace period would expire in a few hours, and announced that "this meeting can do no more to save the country." About fifty young men disguised as Indians thereupon yelled a few war whoops and headed for the wharf, followed by most of the crowd.

Adams's disciplined band of youths assaulted no one and damaged nothing but the hated cargo. Thousands lined the waterfront to see them heave forty-five tons of tea overboard. For almost an hour, the onlookers stood silently transfixed, as if at a religious service, while they peered through the crisp, cold air of a moonlit night. The only sounds were the steady chop of hatchets breaking open wooden

The Boston Tea Party, 1773

This 1793 engraving is the earliest-known American depiction of the event.

chests and the soft splash of tea on the water. When their work was finished, the participants left quietly, and the town lapsed into a profound hush—"never more still and calm," according to one observer.

The Intolerable Acts

Boston's "Tea Party" inflamed the British. Lord North fumed that only "New England fanatics" could imagine themselves oppressed by inexpensive tea. A Welsh member of Parliament drew wild applause by declaring that "the town of Boston ought to be knocked about by the ears, and destroy'd." In vain did the great parliamentary orator Edmund Burke plead for the one action that could end the crisis. "Leave America . . . to tax herself. . . . Leave the Americans as they anciently stood. . . ." The British government, however, swiftly asserted its authority by enacting four Coercive Acts that, together with the unrelated Quebec Act, became known to Americans as the Intolerable Acts.

The first of the Coercive Acts, the Boston Port Bill, became law on April 1, 1774. It ordered the navy to close Boston harbor unless the Privy Council certified by June 1 that the town had arranged to pay for the ruined tea. Lord North's cabinet deliberately imposed this impossibly short deadline in order to ensure the harbor's closing, which would lead to serious economic distress. The government therefore refused to let a group of London merchants post bond for the necessary £9,000.

The second Coercive Act, the Massachusetts Government Act, had actually been under consideration before the Boston Tea Party. This law revoked the Massachusetts charter and restructured the government to make it less democratic. The colony's upper house would no longer be elected annually by the assembly but appointed for life by the crown. The governor gained absolute control over the naming of all judges and sheriffs. Jurymen, previously elected, were now appointed by sheriffs. Finally, the new charter forbade communities to hold more than one town meeting a year without the governor's permission. These changes brought Massachusetts's government into line with that of other royal colonies, but the colonists interpreted them as evidence of hostility toward representative government.

The final two Coercive Acts—the Administration of Justice Act and the Quartering Act—rubbed salt into the wounds. The first of these permitted any person charged with murder while enforcing royal authority in Massachusetts (such as the British soldiers indicted for the Boston Massacre) to be tried in England or in other colonies. The second allowed the governor to requisition *empty* private buildings for housing troops. These measures, along with the appointment of General Thomas Gage, Britain's military commander in North America, as the new governor of Massachusetts,

Thomas Gage

The commander in chief of Britain's forces in America from 1763 to 1775, Gage in April 1775 would issue the fateful order for British troops to march to Concord and seize the rebel arms stored there (p. 158).

struck New Englanders as proof of a plan to place them under a military despotism.

Americans learned of the Quebec Act along with the previous four statutes and associated it with them. Intended to cement loyalty to Britain among conquered French-Canadian Catholics, the law established Roman Catholicism as Quebec's official religion. This provision alarmed Protestant Anglo-Americans, who widely associated Catholicism with arbitrary government. Furthermore, the Quebec Act gave Canada's governors sweeping powers but established no legislature. It also permitted property disputes (but not criminal cases) to be decided by French law, which did not use juries. Additionally, the law extended Quebec's territorial claims south to the Ohio River and west to the Mississippi, a vast area in which several colonies had land claims.

The Intolerable Acts convinced New Englanders that the crown was plotting to corrode traditional English liberties throughout North America. Many believed that after starving Boston into submission, the governor of Massachusetts would appoint corrupt sheriffs and judges to crush political dissent through rigged trials. The Quartering Act would repress any resistance by forcing troops on an unwilling population. The Administration of Justice Act, which the colonists cynically called the Murder Act, would encourage massacres by preventing local juries from convicting soldiers who killed civilians. Once resistance in Massachusetts had been smashed, the Quebec Act would serve as a blueprint for extinguishing representative government throughout the colonies. Parliament would revoke every colony's charter and introduce a government like Quebec's. Elected assemblies, freedom of religion for Protestants, and jury trials would all disappear.

Intended by Parliament simply to punish Massachusetts—and particularly that rotten apple in the barrel, Boston—the Intolerable Acts instead pushed most colonies to the brink of revolution. Repeal of these laws became, in effect, the colonists' nonnegotiable demand. Of the twenty-seven reasons justifying the break with Britain that the Americans cited in their 1776 Declaration of Independence, six concerned these statutes.

Virginia's response to the Intolerable Acts was particularly important because that colony could provide more military manpower than any other. Sentiment for active resistance first solidified in the Virginia assembly, whose members returned to their counties and enlisted the local gentry in the cause of firmly opposing the offensive laws. As the upper class quickly pulled together, the leading planters undertook a program of political education for the colony's ordinary citizens, who up to that point had been apathetic about the Anglo-American confrontation. On public occasions such as court days and militia musters, the gentry spoke repeatedly of the need to support Massachusetts, persuading voters to commit themselves to resistance by signing petitions against the Intolerable Acts. Within two years the gentry had mobilized Virginia's free population overwhelmingly against Parliament, and it was clear that if war broke out, the British Army would face united resistance not only in New England but also in Virginia.

The First Continental Congress

In response to the Intolerable Acts, the extralegal committees of correspondence of every colony but Georgia sent delegates to a Continental Congress in Philadelphia. Among those in attendance when the Congress assembled on September 5, 1774, were the colonies' most prominent politicians: Samuel and John Adams of Massachusetts; John Jay of New York; Joseph Galloway and John Dickinson of Pennsylvania; and Patrick Henry, Richard Henry Lee, and George Washington of Virginia. The fifty-six delegates had come together to find a way of defending American rights short of war, and in interminable dinner parties and cloakroom chatter, they took one another's measure.

The First Continental Congress opened by endorsing a set of extreme statements of principle called the Suffolk Resolves that recently had placed Massachusetts in a state of passive rebellion. Adopted by delegates at a convention of Massachusetts towns just as the Continental Congress was getting under way, the resolves declared that the colonies owed no obedience to any of the Intolerable Acts, that a provisional government should collect all taxes until the former Massachusetts charter was restored, and that defensive measures should be taken in the event of an attack by royal troops. The Continental Congress also voted to boycott all British goods after December 1 and to cease exporting almost all goods to Britain and its West Indian possessions after September 1775 unless a reconciliation had been accomplished. This agreement, the Continental Association, would be enforced by locally elected committees of "observation" or "safety," whose members in effect were usurping control of American trade from the royal customs service.

Such bold defiances were not to the liking of all delegates. Jay, Dickinson, Galloway, and other moderates who dominated the middle-colony contingent most feared the internal turmoil that would surely accompany a head-on confrontation with Britain. These "trimmers" (John Adams's scornful phrase) vainly opposed non-importation and tried unsuccessfully to win endorsement of Galloway's plan for a "Grand Council," an American legislature that would share with Parliament the authority to tax and govern the colonies.

Finally, however, the delegates summarized their principles and demands in their Declaration of Rights. This document conceded to Parliament the power to regulate colonial commerce, but it argued that all previous parliamentary efforts to impose taxes, enforce laws through admiralty courts,

suspend assemblies, and unilaterally revoke charters were unconstitutional. By addressing the Declaration of Rights to the king rather than Parliament, Congress was imploring George III to end the crisis by dismissing those ministers responsible for passing the Intolerable Acts.

The Fighting Begins

Most Americans hoped that their resistance would jolt Parliament into renouncing all authority over the colonies except trade regulation. But a minority of the colonial elite took alarm, and bonds between men formerly united in outlook sometimes snapped. John Adams's onetime friend Jonathan Sewall, for example, charged that the Congress had made the "breach with the parent state a thousand times more irreparable than it was before." Fearing that Congress was enthroning "their *High Mightinesses,* the MOB," he and like-minded Americans fell back on their loyalty to the king. In England meanwhile, George III sniffed rebellion in the Congress's actions. His instincts, and those of American loyalists, were correct. A revolution was indeed brewing.

To solidify their defiance, the American resistance leaders coerced waverers and loyalists (or "Tories," as they were often called). Thus the elected committees that Congress had created to enforce the Continental Association often turned themselves into vigilantes, compelling merchants who still traded with Britain to burn their imports and make public apologies, browbeating clergymen who preached pro-British sermons, and pressuring Americans to adopt simpler diets and dress in order to relieve their dependence on British imports. Additionally, in colony after colony, the committees took on governmental functions by organizing volunteer military companies and extralegal legislatures. By the spring of 1775, colonial patriots had established provincial "congresses" that paralleled and rivaled the existing colonial assemblies headed by royal governors.

The uneasy calm was first broken in April 1775, in Massachusetts. There as elsewhere, citizens had prepared for the worst by collecting arms and organizing extralegal militia units (locally known as minutemen) whose members could respond instantly to an emergency. The British government ordered Massachusetts governor Gage to quell the "rude rabble" by arresting the principal patriot leaders. Aware that most of these had already fled Boston, Gage instead sent 700 British soldiers on April 19, 1775, to seize military supplies that the colonists had stored at Concord. Two couriers, William Dawes and Paul Revere, quickly alerted nearby towns of the British troops' movements and target. At Lexington about 70 minutemen hastily drawn up on the town green attempted to oppose the soldiers. After a confused skirmish in which 8 minutemen died and a single redcoat was wounded, the British pushed on to Concord. There they found few munitions but encountered a growing swarm of armed Yankees (see "A Place in Time"). When some minutemen mistakenly became convinced that the town was being burned, they exchanged fire with the British regulars and touched off a running battle that continued most of the sixteen miles back to Boston. By day's end the redcoats had lost 273 men, but they had gained some respect for Yankee courage.

These engagements awakened the countryside, and by the evening of April 20, some twenty thousand New Englanders were besieging the British garrison in Boston. Acting on their own authority, on May 10 Vermonter Ethan Allen and a motley collection of New Englanders overran Fort Ticonderoga on Lake Champlain, partly with the intent of using its captured cannon in the siege of Boston. That same day, the Second Continental Congress convened in Philadelphia. Most delegates still opposed independence and at Dickinson's urging agreed to send a "loyal message" to George III. Dickinson composed what became known as the Olive Branch Petition; excessively polite, it nonetheless presented three demands: a cease-fire at Boston, repeal of the Intolerable Acts, and negotiations to establish guarantees of American rights. Events quickly overtook this effort at reconciliation. The Olive Branch Petition reached London at the same time as news of a battle fought just outside Boston on June 17. In this engagement British troops attacked colonists entrenched on Breed's Hill and Bunker Hill. Although successfully dislodging the Americans, the British suffered 1,154 casualties out of 2,200 men, compared to a loss of 311 Yankees. After Bunker Hill the British public wanted retaliation, not reconciliation, and on August 23 the king proclaimed New England in a state of rebellion. In December Parliament declared all the colonists rebellious and made their ships subject to seizure.

The Failure of Reconciliation

Despite the turn of events, most Americans clung to hopes of reconciliation. Even John Adams, who believed in the inevitability of separation, described himself as "fond of reconciliation, if we could reasonably entertain Hopes of it on a constitutional basis." Yet the same Americans who pleaded for peace passed measures that Britain could only construe as rebellious. Before the delegates to the Continental Congress even heard about the Battle of Bunker Hill, they voted to establish an "American continental army" and appointed George Washington its commander.

Still, most Americans resisted independence, partly because they clung to the notion that evil ministers rather than the king were forcing unconstitutional measures on them and partly because they expected that saner heads would rise to power in Britain. On both counts they were wrong. The Americans exaggerated the influence of Pitt, Burke, and their other friends in Britain. For example, when Burke proposed in March 1775 that Parliament acknowledge the colonists' right to raise and dispose of taxes, he was voted down by a thumping majority in Parliament. Lord North's sole counterproposal was to allow the colonists to tax themselves, but on condition that they collect whatever sum of money Parliament ordered. This concession amounted to no more than involuntary self-taxation, and it had the full endorsement of George III, who consistently supported the North ministry.

The Americans' sentimental attachment to the king, the last emotional barrier to their accepting independence, finally crumbled in January 1776 with the publication of Thomas Paine's *Common Sense*. A former corsetmaker and schoolmaster, Paine immigrated to the colonies from England late in 1774 with a letter of introduction from Benjamin Franklin, a penchant for radical politics, and a gift for writing plain and pungent prose that anyone could understand. Paine told Americans what they had been unable to bring themselves to say: kingship was an institution dangerous to liberty, undemocratic, and inappropriate to Americans. The king was "the royal brute" and a "hardened, sullen-tempered Pharaoh." By repudiating monarchy and creating a republic, "we have it in our power to begin the world over again."

By Paine's estimate *Common Sense,* printed in both English and German, sold more than one hundred thousand copies within three months, equal to one for every fourth or fifth adult male. The *Connecticut Gazette* described it as "a landflood that sweeps all before it." By the spring of 1776, Paine's pamphlet had dissolved lingering allegiance to George III and removed the last psychological barrier to independence.

Independence at Last

John Adams described the movement toward independence as a coach drawn by thirteen horses, which could not reach its destination any faster than the slowest ones were willing to run. New England was already in rebellion, and Rhode Island declared itself independent in May 1776. The middle colonies hesitated to support revolution because they feared, correctly, that the war would largely be fought over control of Philadelphia and New York. Following the news in April that North Carolina's congressional delegates were authorized to vote for

independence, the South began pressing for separation. Virginia's extralegal legislature soon instructed its delegates at the Second Continental Congress to propose independence, which Richard Henry Lee did on June 7. Formally adopting Lee's resolution on July 2, Congress created the United States of America.

The task of drafting a statement to justify the colonies' separation from England fell to Virginia delegate Thomas Jefferson. Congress reviewed his manuscript on July 3 and approved it the next day. The Declaration of Independence never mentioned Parliament by name—even though the central point of dispute since 1765 had been Parliament's legislative powers—because Congress was unwilling to imply, even indirectly, that it held any authority over America. Jefferson instead indicted the king for "repeated injuries and usurpations, all having in direct object the establishment of an absolute tyranny over these states." The declaration recited these "injuries" but above all emphasized the crown's apparent intention to establish a "despotism."

Jefferson elevated the colonists' grievances from a dispute over English freedoms to a struggle for

History Preserved

The Pennsylvania State House was the site of the Declaration of Independence's signing (at which this inkstand was used) and of the constitutional convention. During the latter, Washington sat in this handsome mahogany half-sun chair.

Concord, Massachusetts, in 1775

About 2 A.M. on April 19, 1775, the alarm bell in Concord, Massachusetts, started to ring furiously. Normally, it summoned men to turn out with fire buckets, but on this night drowsy citizens (including the town's minister, Reverend William Emerson) ambled toward the town square clutching muskets. Concord's minutemen were gathering to oppose 750 British troops marching to seize arms and ammunition stored in their town. Concord's mobilization on that chilly spring night was sure evidence that the colonies were teetering on the brink of revolution.

Until recently, the citizens had been loyal British subjects. Like other rural New Englanders, they had been indifferent to the British Empire's political crisis until they had debated Boston's circular letter of November 20, 1772. Thereafter, Concord's town meeting endorsed a steady flow of correspondence from Boston denouncing unconstitutional parliamentary laws. In June 1774, 80 percent of Concord men signed a strongly worded pledge to boycott British goods until the Intolerable Acts were repealed. By March 6, 1775, all but three men in town had sworn to uphold the Continental Congress against Massachusetts's royal governor, General Thomas Gage. Within the brief span of thirty months, Concord had shed its apathy and become united in resisting the Intolerable Acts.

As dawn approached, the townspeople hid bullets and gunflints throughout their houses, concealed gunpowder in the woods, and buried cannon and muskets. Fifteen-year-old Milicent Barrett, the granddaughter of the minutemen's colonel, supervised teen-age girls in the manufacture of cartridges. Reinforcements for Concord's 150 minutemen arrived from nearby towns. Word came that the British had opened fire on Lexington's minutemen, but no one knew if blood had been shed.

At daybreak Captain David Brown marched his company toward Lexington and promptly ran into the British. Sizing up the situation, Brown swung back to Concord with drums beating and fifes squealing. "We had grand music," Corporal Amos Barrett later recalled. Badly outnumbered, Colonel James Barrett evacuated the town center and took up position on high ground overlooking the Concord River bridge to await reinforcements.

After posting a guard at the bridge, just out of the minutemen's range, the British scoured the town for military equipment. Much of what little remained behind was saved by the town's women, who outwitted redcoats sent to search their homes. Mrs. Amos Wood tricked an officer who correctly suspected the presence of hidden ammunition into believing that a locked room sheltered panic-stricken women. "I forbid anyone entering this room," commanded the chivalrous Englishman. Hannah Barnes bluffed a search party out of entering a room that contained a chest filled with money needed to buy additional military supplies.

The British regulars dumped five hundred pounds of bullets into a pond, destroyed sixty barrels of flour, and found two cannon. They also accidentally set fire to the courthouse and a blacksmith shop,

"The White Cockade" *Fifer Luther Blanchard and drummer Francis Barker played this martial tune shortly before the skirmish near the bridge.*

Concord, April 19, 1775 *In a contemporary illustration, engraver Amos Doolittle recorded the British troops' arrival in town.*

which they saved before serious damage resulted. But the minutemen on the ridge became enraged by the rising smoke.

"Will you let them burn the town down?" screamed hotheaded Lieutenant Joseph Hosmer at Colonel Barrett. Now commanding four hundred men, Barrett decided to reenter the town and led his men toward the hundred redcoats guarding the bridge. The British withdrew across the river and fired several warning shots. One round wounded Luther Blanchard, a fifer who had been merrily playing a marching tune. Suddenly, smoke billowed from the British ranks and musketballs whistled across the water. Captain Isaac Davis and Private Abner Hosmer, volunteers from nearby Acton, fell dead. "For God's sake, fire," shouted Captain Jonathan Buttrick to his Concord company, which shot a volley at the British that killed three soldiers and wounded nine others.

The skirmish lasted only two or three minutes. The British withdrew to the town center. The min-

British Looters

A colonial cartoonist caught the redcoats in a looting spree during their retreat from Concord.

utemen crossed the river but then broke ranks and milled about in confusion. Both sides kept their distance until noon, when the British started to march back to Boston.

The British delay in leaving Concord allowed hundreds of minutemen to arrive from neighboring towns. At Meriam's Corner, these reinforcements began harassing the redcoats in a running battle that continued for sixteen miles. "Every man," recalled Private Thaddeus Blood, "was his own commander." By day's end almost three hundred royal troops were killed, wounded, or missing, and eighty colonists lay dead or injured.

Concord citizens escaped the day with slight losses: four men wounded, none dead. The war, however, had barely begun, and before it was over, Concord sent off every able-bodied man between the ages of eighteen and forty to serve in the army. After the war the fight at the bridge assumed mythic dimensions for Americans, who celebrated the patriots who dared death at "the rude bridge that arched the flood" and "fired the shot heard 'round the world." But Concord citizens were too familiar with the events to romanticize them. In 1792 they unemotionally tore up the historic bridge and built a more convenient crossing several hundred yards down river.

universal human rights. His eloquent emphasis on the equality of all individuals and their natural entitlement to justice, liberty, and self-fulfillment expressed the Enlightenment's deepest longing for a government that would rest on neither legal privilege nor the exploitation of the majority by the few.

Jefferson addressed the Declaration of Independence as much to Americans uncertain about the wisdom of independence as to world opinion, for he wanted to convince his fellow citizens that social and political progress could no longer be accomplished within the British Empire. The declaration never claimed that perfect justice and equal opportunity existed in the United States; rather, it challenged the Revolutionary generation and all who later inherited the nation to bring this ideal closer to reality.

Conclusion

The most moving section of the Declaration of Independence's original draft was directed to the people of England, whom Jefferson regretfully reminded that "we might have been a free and great people together." Congress eliminated these words, which expressed the feelings of most Americans all too well, for in a civil war it is never wise to dwell on the matter of shedding common blood. Throughout the long imperial crisis, Americans had repeatedly pursued the goal of reestablishing the empire as it had functioned before 1763, when colonial trade was protected and encouraged—not taxed and plundered—by the Navigation Acts, and when colonial assemblies had exercised exclusive power over taxation and internal legislation. These reluctant revolutionaries now had to face the might of Europe's greatest imperial power and win their independence on the battlefield. They also had to decide to what degree they would implement the idealistic vision evoked in Jefferson's declaration. Neither task would prove simple or easy.

CHRONOLOGY

1733 Molasses Act.

1744–1748 King George's War.

1754–1760 French and Indian War (in Europe, the Seven Years' War, 1756–1763).

1760 George III becomes king of Great Britain.

1763 Pontiac's War.

1764 Sugar Act.

1765 Stamp Act.
Quartering Act.
Loyal Nine formed in Boston to oppose the Stamp Act.
Sons of Liberty band together thoughout the colonies.
Stamp Act Congress.
Colonists begin boycott of British goods.

1766 Stamp Act repealed.
Declaratory Act.

1767 New York Suspending Act.

American Board of Customs Commissioners created.

Revenue Act (Townshend duties).

John Dickinson, *Letters from a Farmer.*

1768 Massachusetts "circular letter."

Boston merchants adopt the colonies' first non-importation agreement.

John Hancock's ship *Liberty* seized by Boston customs commissioner.

British troops arrive in Boston.

1770 Townshend duties, except tea tax, repealed.

Boston Massacre.

1771 Battle of Alamance Creek in North Carolina.

1772 Gaspee incident in Rhode Island.

Committees of correspondence begin in Masschusetts and rapidly spread.

1773 Tea Act.

Boston Tea Party.

1774 Coercive (Intolerable) Acts.

Quebec Act.

First Continental Congress meets and adopts Suffolk Resolves.

Continental Association.

Colonists' Declaration of Rights and Grievances.

1775 Battles of Lexington and Concord.

Second Continental Congress meets.

Olive Branch Petition.

Battles at Breed's Hill and Bunker Hill.

1776 Thomas Paine, *Common Sense.*

Declaration of Independence.

For Further Reading

Bernard Bailyn, *The Ideological Origins of the American Revolution* (1967). Pulitzer Prize–winning examination of the political heritage that shaped colonial resistance to British authority.

Jack P. Greene, *Peripheries and Center: Constitutional Development in the Extended Politics of the British Empire and the United States 1607–1788* (1987). A thorough study of how inherited English legal traditions and colonial political experience not only influenced Americans from 1763 to 1776 but also shaped the later course of American constitutional thought.

Robert A. Gross, *The Minutemen and Their World* (1976). An eloquent and evocative examination of Concord, Massachusetts, in the Revolutionary era.

Pauline Maier, *From Resistance to Revolution: Colonial Radicals and the Development of American Opposition to Britain, 1765–1776* (1972). An insightful, definitive examination of how colonial leaders strove to force the repeal of unconstitutional laws with a minimum use of violence.

Robert Middlekauff, *The Glorious Cause: The American Revolution, 1763–1789* (1982). A judicious, learned, and highly readable narrative of the events leading to Independence.

Edmund S. Morgan and Helen M. Morgan, *The Stamp Act Crisis: Prologue to Revolution* (rev. ed., 1963). The most penetrating, and now classic, analysis of colonial constitutional principles regarding the limits on Parliament's taxing power.

Robert R. Palmer, *The Age of the Democratic Revolution: Vol. I, The Challenge* (1959). Bancroft Prize–winning examination of the American Revolution in comparison to events in England, Ireland, and France.

Additional Bibliography

The Military Background

Fred Anderson, *A People's Army: Massachusetts Soldiers and Society in the Seven Years' War* (1984); Sylvia R. Frey, *The British Soldier in America: A Social History of Military Life in the Colonial Period* (1981); Douglas E. Leach, *Arms for Empire: A Military History of the British Colonies in North America, 1607–1763* (1973); Richard Middleton, *The Bells of Victory: The Pitt-Newcastle Ministry and the Conduct of the Seven Years' War, 1757–1762* (1985); John Shy, *Toward Lexington: The Role of the British Army in the Coming of the American Revolution* (1965).

Taxing and Regulating Trade

Thomas C. Barrow, *Trade and Empire: The British Customs Service in Colonial America* (1967); Oliver M. Dickerson, *The Navigation Acts and the American Revolution* (1951); Michael Kammen, *Empire and Interest: The American Colonies and the Politics of Mercantilism* (1970); John P. Reid, *In a Rebellious Spirit: The Argument of Facts, the Liberty Riot, and the Coming of the American Revolution* (1979); John W. Tyler, *Smugglers and Patriots: Boston Merchants and the Advent of the American Revolution* (1986); Carl Ubbelohde, *The Vice-Admiralty Courts and the American Revolution* (1960).

Constitutional Issues

Richard L. Bushman, *King and People in Provincial Massachusetts* (1985); David L. Jacobson, ed., *The English Libertarian Heritage: From the Writings of John Trenchard and Thomas Gordon in "The Independent Whig" and "Cato's Letters"* (1965); Richard Koebner, *Empire* (1961); John G. A. Pocock, *Three British Revolutions: 1641, 1688, 1776* (1980); Jack R. Pole, *Political Representation in England and the Origins of the American Republic* (1966); John P. Reid, *Constitutional History of the American Revolution: The Authority of Rights* (1986), *Constitutional History of the American Revolution: The Power to Tax* (1987), and *In a Defiant Stance: The Conditions of Law in Massachusetts Bay, the Irish Comparison, and the Coming of the American Revolution* (1977).

Religious Influences

Ruth H. Bloch, *Visionary Republic: Millennial Themes in American Thought, 1756–1800* (1985); Patricia U. Bonomi, *Under the Cope of Heaven: Religion, Society, and Politics in Colonial America* (1986); Carl R. Bridenbaugh, *Mitre and Sceptre: Transatlantic Faiths, Ideas, Personalities, and Politics, 1689–1775* (1962); Jack P. Greene and William G. McLaughlin, *Preachers and Politicians: Two Essays on the Origin of the American Revolution* (1977); Nathan O. Hatch, *The Sacred Cause of Liberty: Republican Thought and the Millennium in Revolutionary New England* (1977).

Resistance

David Ammerman, *In the Common Cause: American Response to the Coercive Acts of 1774* (1974); Richard D. Brown, *Revolutionary Politics in Massachusetts: The Boston Committees of Correspondence and the Towns, 1772–1774* (1970); Ian R. Christie and Benjamin W. Labaree, *Empire or Independence, 1760–1776: A British-American Dialogue on the Coming of the American Revolution* (1976); Peter C. Hoffer, *Revolution and Regeneration: Life Cycle and the Historical Vision of the Generation of 1776* (1983); Michael G. Kammen, *A Rope of Sand: The Colonial Agents, British Politics, and the American Revolution* (1968); Benjamin W. Labaree, *The Boston Tea Party* (1964); Mary Beth Norton, *Liberty's Daughters: The Revolutionary Experience of American Women, 1750–1800* (1980); Richard A. Ryerson, *The Revolution Is Now Begun: The Radical Committees of Philadelphia, 1765–1776* (1978); John Sainsbury, *Disaffected Patriots: London Supporters of Revolutionary America, 1769–1782* (1987); Peter Shaw, *American Patriots and the Rituals of Revolution* (1981); Neil R. Stout, *The Perfect Crisis: The Beginnings of the Revolutionary War* (1976); Peter D. G. Thomas, *The Townshend Duties Crisis: The Second Phase of the American Revolution, 1767–1773* (1987); Robert W. Tucker and David C. Hendrickson, *The Fall of the First British Empire: Origins of the War of American Independence* (1982); Hiller B. Zobel, *The Boston Massacre* (1970).

Biographies

Bernard Bailyn, *The Ordeal of Thomas Hutchinson* (1974); Richard R. Beeman, *Patrick Henry: A Biography* (1974); John Brooke, *King George III* (1972); Milton E. Flower, *John Dickinson: Conservative Revolutionary* (1983); Eric Foner, *Tom Paine and Revolutionary America* (1976); William M. Fowler, Jr., *The Baron of Beacon Hill: A Biography of John Hancock* (1979); Pauline Maier, *The Old Revolutionaries: Political Lives in the Age of Samuel Adams* (1980); Dumas Malone, *Jefferson the Virginian* (1948); John C. Miller, *Sam Adams: Pioneer in Propaganda* (1936); Peter D. G. Thomas, *Lord North* (1974).

CHAPTER 5

The Forge of Nationhood, 1776–1788

In November 1775 General George Washington ordered Colonel Henry Knox to bring the British artillery recently captured at Fort Ticonderoga to the siege of Boston. Washington knew firsthand of the difficulties of wilderness travel, especially in the winter, and he must have wondered if this city-bred officer was up to the task. Only twenty-five years old and a Boston bookseller with little experience in the woods, Knox was nevertheless the army's senior artillerist, largely because he had read several books on the subject while business in his store was dull.

Knox and his men built crude sleds to haul their fifty-nine cannons through dense forest covered by two feet of snow. On good days they moved these sixty tons of artillery about seven miles. On two very bad ones, they shivered for hours in freezing water while retrieving guns that had fallen through the ice at river crossings. As their oxen grew weak from overexertion and poor feed, the men had to throw their own backs into pulling the cannons across New York's frozen landscape. On reaching the Berkshire Mountains in western Massachusetts, their pace slowed to a crawl as they trudged uphill through snow-clogged passes. Forty days and three hundred miles after leaving Ticonderoga, Knox and his exhausted New Yorkers reported to Washington in late January 1776. The Boston bookseller had more than proved himself: he had accomplished one of the Revolution's great feats of endurance.

The guns from Ticonderoga placed the outnumbered British in a hopeless position and forced them to evacuate Boston on March 17, 1776. A lifelong friendship formed between Washington and Knox. Knox served on the Virginian's staff throughout the war and accepted his request to be the nation's first secretary of war in 1789.

Friendships like the one between Washington and Knox were almost as revolutionary as the war that produced them. Because inhabitants of different colonies had little opportunity to become acquainted before 1775, their outlooks had remained narrowly confined within the borders of their provinces. This localism was well entrenched at the start of the war. George Washington at first described New Englanders as "an exceeding dirty and nasty people." Yankee soldiers irritated troops from distant colonies such as Virginia with smug assumption of superiority expressed in their popular marching song "Chester," whose rousing lyrics rang out:

> Let tyrants shake their iron rod,
> and slavery clank her galling chains.
> We fear them not, we trust in God.
> New England's God forever reigns.

The Revolution gave northerners and southerners their first real chance to learn what they had in common, and they soon developed mutual admiration. George Washington, who in the war's early days dismissed New England officers as "the most indifferent kind of people I ever saw," changed his mind after meeting men like Henry Knox.

In July 1776 the thirteen colonies had out of desperation declared independence and established a new nation. But it took the War for Independence to create American citizens. Only as a result of the collective hardships experienced during eight years of terrible fighting did the inhabitants of the thirteen states cease to see themselves simply as military allies and come to accept each other as fellow citizens.

The return of peace in 1783 left Americans with a false sense of security. Major problems remained unsolved and ignored. The national government's authority withered as the states increasingly failed to provide the financial support nec-

essary to finance federal operations. During the 1780s far-sighted leaders perceived two great challenges. Could they preserve the national spirit born during the war before it evaporated? If so, could they find a means of providing the central government with the ability to uphold its financial obligations and command respect from foreign countries, and yet not threaten interference with each state's right to legislate for itself or endanger individual liberties? They would not even begin to overcome these challenges until 1789.

America's First Civil War

The Revolution was both a collective struggle that marched a sizable portion of the American people against Britain and a civil war between inhabitants of North America. Eventually, it would degenerate into a brothers' war of the worst kind, conducted without the restraint, mutual respect, and compassion that would characterize the next prolonged encounter between Americans, the bloody Civil War of the 1860s. From a military standpoint, the Revolution's outcome depended not only on the ability of the supporters of independence, called the Whigs, to wear down the British army but also on the Whigs' success in suppressing fellow North Americans' opposition to independence. The magnitude of these tasks frequently disheartened the Whigs, but it also united them. Without the disappointments and sacrifices suffered from 1775 to 1783, Americans might never have developed the commitment to nationhood essential to prevent their new country from splintering into several smaller republics.

The Loyalists

As late as January 1776, most colonists still hoped that declaring independence from Britain would not be necessary. Not surprisingly, when separation came six months later, many Americans remained unconvinced that it was justified. About 20 percent of all whites either opposed the rebellion actively or refused to support the Continental Congress unless threatened with fines or imprisonment. While these internal enemies of the Rev-

olution called themselves loyalists, they were "Tories" to their Whig foes. Whigs remarked, but only half in jest, that "a tory was a thing with a head in England, a body in America, and a neck that needed stretching."

Loyalists avowed many of the same political values as did the Whigs. Like the Whigs, they usually opposed Parliament's claim to tax the colonies. Many loyalists thus found themselves fighting for a cause with which they did not entirely agree, and as a result large numbers of them would find it relatively easy to change sides during the war. Most doubtless shared the apprehension expressed in 1775 by the Reverend Jonathan Boucher, a well-known Maryland loyalist, who preached with two loaded pistols lying on his pulpit cushion: "For my part I equally dread a Victory by either side."

Loyalists disagreed, however, with the Whigs' insistence that only independence could preserve the colonists' constitutional rights. The loyalists denounced separation as an illegal act certain to ignite an unnecessary war. Above all, they retained a profound reverence for the crown and deeply believed that if they failed to defend their king, they would sacrifice their personal honor.

The most important factor in determining loyalist strength in any area was the degree to which prominent local Whigs had successfully convinced the mass of voters that representative government was endangered by the king and Parliament. Town leaders in New England, the Virginia gentry, and the rice planters of South Carolina's seacoast all

vigorously pursued a program of political education and popular mobilization from 1772 to 1776.
Repeatedly explaining the issues at public meetings, these elites shook the mass of citizens from
their apathy and persuaded the overwhelming
majority in favor of resistance. As a result, probably no more than 5 percent of whites in these
areas were committed loyalists in 1776. Where the
leading families acted indecisively, however, their
communities remained divided when the fighting
began. Because the gentry of New York and New
Jersey were especially reluctant to declare their
allegiance to either side, the proportion of loyalists
was highest there. Those two states eventually furnished about half of the twenty-one thousand
Americans who fought in loyalist military units.

The next most significant factor influencing
loyalist military strength was the geographical distribution of recent British immigrants, who closely
identified with their homeland, not America, and
overwhelmingly opposed independence. Among
these newcomers were thousands of British soldiers who had served in the French and Indian War
and then remained in the colonies, usually in New
York, where they could obtain two-hundred-acre
land grants. Further, more than 125,000 English,
Scots, and Irish landed from 1763 to 1775—the
greatest number of Britons to arrive during any
dozen years of the colonial era. Major centers of
loyalist sympathy existed wherever large concentrations of such British-born people lived. In New
York, Georgia, and the backcountry of North and
South Carolina, where the native-born Britons were
heavily concentrated, the proportion of loyalists
among whites probably ranged from 25 percent to
40 percent in 1776. In wartime the British army
organized many Tory units comprising immigrants
from the British Isles, including the Loyal High-
land Emigrants, the North Carolina Highlanders, and the Volunteers of Ireland. After the war
foreign-born loyalists composed a majority of
those persons compensated by the British for property losses during the Revolution—including
three-quarters of all such claimants from the Carolinas and Georgia.

Loyalism also fed on the presence of ethnic
and religious minorities outside of the main currents of colonial society. For example, a small
number of German, Dutch, and French religious
congregations that resisted use of the English lan-

guage felt indebted to the British government for
their religious freedom and doubted that their rights
would be as safe in an independent nation dominated by Anglo-Americans. Yet on balance, these
ethnic and religious minorities provided few loyalists. The great majority of Germans in Pennsylvania, Maryland, and Virginia, for example, had
started to assimilate into the English-speaking
mainstream by 1776 and would overwhelmingly
support the Whig cause.

One group with distinctive ethnic and religious characteristics—Canada's French Catholics—composed the most significant North American minority to hold loyalist sympathies. Although
they had fought against the British in the French
and Indian War, French-Canadian Catholics feared
domination by the Anglo-Americans. The Quebec
Act of 1774 had guaranteed their religious freedom and their continued use of French civil law.
Remembering that the American colonists had
denounced this measure and demanded its repeal,
French Catholics worried that their privileges would
disappear if they were absorbed into an independent Protestant America.

Canadian anxieties intensified in mid-1775,
when the Continental Congress ordered Continental forces to "free" Canada from British tyranny
unless this action was "disagreeable" to the French
population. In reality, Congress cared little what
the French-Canadians thought, for Congress
believed that a conquest of Canada was essential
to block a British invasion from the north. In 1775
Continental armies (one of them led by Benedict
Arnold, a fervent patriot who later turned traitor)
marched into Canada and attacked Quebec but
suffered defeat on December 31, 1775. French
Catholics emerged from the shock of invasion more
loyal to the crown than ever before. The Whigs
never even attempted to win over the other recently
founded mainland colonies—Nova Scotia and East
and West Florida—whose small populations of
mainly recent immigrants were firmly dominated
by British military authorities.

American loyalists would also draw wartime
support from both slaves and native Americans.
As a deeply alienated group within society, slaves
quickly realized that the Revolution was not
intended to benefit them. In 1766, when a group
of slaves, inspired by the protests against the Stamp
Act, had marched through Charleston, South Car-

olina, shouting "Liberty!" they had faced arrest for inciting a rebellion. By 1775 it was the British who most often offered liberty to enslaved Americans. For example, in 1775 Lord Dunmore, governor of Virginia, promised freedom to any slave who enlisted in the cause of restoring royal authority. About eight hundred blacks joined him before he fled the colony. During the war at least twenty thousand American slaves ran away to sign on as laborers or soldiers in the Royal Army. Among the Whig slaveholders who saw many of his slaves escape to British protection was Thomas Jefferson.

Native Americans had long resented the presence of white colonists on their lands, and during the war only the Oneidas and Tuscaroras (two member tribes of the Iroquois Confederacy) in New York and the Catawbas in South Carolina supported the Whig cause. Elsewhere in the original thirteen colonies and throughout the region west of the Appalachian Mountains, the British could count on Indian support or neutrality.

Toward loyalists collectively, Whigs reserved an intense hatred, far greater than their antipathy toward the British army, and loyalists responded with equal venom. Each side saw its cause as so sacred that opposition by a fellow American was an unforgivable act of betrayal. The worst atrocities committed during the war were inflicted by Americans upon each other.

The Opposing Sides

Britain entered the war with two major advantages. First, in 1776 the 11 million inhabitants of the British Isles greatly outnumbered the 2.5 million Americans, one-third of whom were either slaves or loyalists. Second, Britain possessed the world's largest navy and one of its best professional armies. Nevertheless, the royal military establishment grew during the war years to a degree that strained Britain's resources. The army more than doubled from 48,000 to 111,000 men, not only in North America but also in the British Isles and the West Indies. To meet its manpower needs, the British government had to raise the recruiting bonuses paid to get men to enlist, lower physical requirements, widen age limits, and sometimes enroll soldiers forcibly. But even these measures failed to provide the required numbers. Without hiring 30,000 German mercenaries known as Hessians

Woodcut from "A New Touch on the Times . . . . By a Daughter of Liberty, Living in Marblehead," 1779

Americans on the home front as well as in the front lines experienced stunning wartime hardships. This illustration of a female partisan holding a musket accompanied a poem by Molly Gutridge, whose theme was women's sacrifice and suffering in a seaport economy upset by war.

and later enlisting 21,000 loyalists, Britain could not have met its manpower needs.

Despite its smaller population, the United States mobilized its people more effectively than did Britain. By the end of the war, the Americans had enlisted or drafted into the Continental Army or the state militias perhaps half of all free males from age sixteen to forty-five—about 220,000 troops—compared to the 162,000 Britons, loyalists, and Hessians who served in the British army.

Britain's ability to crush the rebellion was further weakened by the decline in its seapower that had resulted from peacetime budget cuts after 1763. Midway through the war, half of the Royal Navy's ships sat in dry dock awaiting major repairs.

Although the navy expanded rapidly from 18,000 to 111,000 sailors, it lost 42,000 men to desertion and 20,000 to disease or wounds. In addition, Britain's merchant marine suffered mightily from raids by the numerous American privateers newly outfitted from the colonies' thriving merchant marine. During the war rebel privateers and the fledgling U.S. Navy would capture over 2,000 British merchant vessels and 16,000 crewmen.

Britain could ill afford these losses, for it faced a colossal task in trying to supply its troops in America. While at one time or another the British army controlled all the major American cities, British soldiers ventured into the agricultural hinterland only at their peril and hence could not easily round up supplies. In fact, almost all the food consumed by the army, a third of a ton per soldier per year, had to be imported from Britain. Seriously overextended, the navy barely kept the army supplied and never effectively blockaded American ports.

Mindful of the enormous strain that the war imposed, British leaders faced serious problems maintaining their people's support for the conflict. The war more than doubled the national debt. Bur-

An American Soldier of 1778,
by Friedrich von Germann

dened by record taxes, the politically influential landed gentry could not be expected to vote against their pocketbooks forever.

The United States faced different but no less severe wartime problems. First, one-fifth of its free population was openly disloyal. Second, although the state militias sometimes performed well in hit-and-run guerrilla skirmishes and were also effective in intimidating loyalists and wavering Whigs and in requisitioning war supplies, they lacked the training to fight pitched battles. Congress recognized that independence would never be secured if the United States relied on guerrilla tactics, avoided major battles, and allowed the British to occupy all major population centers. Moreover, because European powers would interpret U.S dependence on guerrilla warfare as evidence that Americans could not drive out the British army, that strategy would doom efforts by the Continental Congress to gain foreign loans and diplomatic recognition.

The Continental Army thus had to fight in the standard European fashion of the times. Professional eighteenth-century armies relied on expert movements of mass formations. Victory often depended on rapid maneuvers to crush an enemy's undefended flank or rear. Attackers needed exceptional skill in close-order drill in order to fall on an enemy before he could reform and return fire. Because muskets had a range of under one hundred yards, armies in battle were never far apart. Battles usually occurred in open country with space for maneuver. The troops advanced within musket range of each other, stood upright without cover, and fired volleys at one another until one line weakened from its casualties. Discipline, training, and nerve were essential if soldiers were to stay in ranks while comrades fell beside them. The stronger side then attacked at a quick walk with bayonets drawn and drove off its opponents.

In 1775 Britain possessed a well-trained army with a strong tradition of bravery under fire. In contrast, the Continental Army had neither an inspirational heritage nor many experienced officers or sergeants who might turn raw recruits into crack units. Consequently, the Americans experienced a succession of heartbreaking defeats in the war's early years. Yet to win the war, the Continentals did not have to destroy the British army but only prolong the rebellion until Britain's taxpayers lost patience with the struggle. Until then,

American victory would hinge heavily on the ability of one man to keep his army fighting despite defeat. He was George Washington.

George Washington

Few generals ever looked and acted the role as much as Washington. He spoke with authority and comported himself with dignity. At six feet two inches, he stood a half-foot taller than the average man of his day. Powerfully built, athletic, and hardened by a rugged outdoor life, he was one of the war's few generals whose presence on the battlefield could inspire troops to heroism.

Washington's military experience began at age twenty-two, when he had taken command of a Virginia regiment raised to resist French claims in the Ohio Valley (see Chapter 4). He had lost his first battle to a force vastly outnumbering his own. A year later, at Braddock's defeat, he had placed himself at the point of greatest danger and had two horses killed under him, besides having his hat shot off and his coat ripped by five bullets. His reputation for courage reached England, where he had briefly become a minor hero. Above all, Washington's early military experience—his mistakes and lost battles—taught him lessons that he might not have learned from easy, glorious victories. He discovered the dangers of overconfidence and the need for determination in the face of defeat. He also learned much about American soldiers, especially that they performed best when led by example and treated with respect.

With Virginia's borders safe from attack in 1758, Washington had resigned his commission and become a tobacco planter. He had sat in the Virginia House of Burgesses, where his influence had grown, not because he thrust himself into every issue but because others respected him and sought his opinion. Having emerged as an early, though not outspoken, opponent of parliamentary taxation, he had also sat in the Continental Congress. In the eyes of the many who valued his advice and remembered his military experience, Washington was the logical choice to head the Continental Army.

War in Earnest

Henry Knox's successful transport of artillery from Ticonderoga to Boston prompted the British to evacuate Boston in March 1776 and to move on to New York, which they wished to seize and use as a base for conquering New England. Under two brothers—General William Howe and Admiral Richard, Lord Howe—130 warships carrying 32,000 royal troops landed near New York harbor in the summer of 1776. Defending New York, America's second-largest city, were 18,000 poorly trained soldiers under George Washington.

On August 27, 15,000 of William Howe's men nearly overwhelmed the 10,500 troops whom Washington had stationed on Long Island, just across a river from New York City. Inflicting over 1,000 casualties while losing fewer than 400 men, the British were on the verge of annihilating the Americans. But Washington executed a masterful night evacuation to New York City, saving 9,500 soldiers and most of his artillery from certain capture. He himself was the last American to board a boat.

By the third week of September 1776, the Continental Army around New York included more than 16,000 men fit to bear arms. Over the next three months, the British killed or took prisoner one-quarter of these troops and drove the survivors into headlong retreat across New Jersey. By early December, when Washington crossed the Delaware River from New Jersey into Pennsylvania, he had fewer than 7,000 troops fit for duty. Thomas Paine accurately described these demoralizing days as "the times that try men's souls."

With the British in striking distance of Philadelphia, Washington decided to seize the offensive before the morale of his army and country collapsed completely. On Christmas night, 1776, he led his troops back into New Jersey and attacked a Hessian garrison at Trenton, where he captured 918 Germans and lost only 4 Continentals. Washington then attacked 1,200 British at Princeton on January 3, 1777, and killed or took captive one-third of them while sustaining only 40 casualties.

These American victories at Trenton and Princeton had several important consequences. At a moment when defeat seemed inevitable, they boosted civilian and military morale. In addition, by checking the British offensive, they frustrated Howe's plans to pacify New Jersey by persuading inhabitants opposed to or skeptical of independence to rally to the British cause. Although nearly 5,000 New Jerseyans with loyalist sympathies swore allegiance to the crown late in 1776, Washington's victories forced the British early in 1777 to remove

The Battle of Princeton (1777), *by William Mercer, c. 1790*

In the battle's first phase, fought south of the town, the American advance guard clashed with redcoats who were en route to Trenton, where they planned to link up with Lord Cornwallis. The British had the upper hand until George Washington and the main Continental force arrived, attacked, and drove them off.

virtually all their New Jersey garrisons to New York, while Washington established winter quarters at Morristown, New Jersey, only twenty-five miles from New York City.

As long as they had enjoyed the support of the redcoats, New Jersey's loyalists had plundered local Whigs. Now stripped of British protection, the loyalists fell prey to the rebel militia, who drove thousands of loyalists into British-held New York, where many joined the Royal Army. Other loyalists formed guerrilla bands to raid their former neighbors; still others fled into South Jersey's forbidding Pine Barrens, from which they pillaged their ex-tormentors. Until 1782, when the state militia destroyed the last band of Pine Barren Tories, New Jersey's Whigs fell victim to a barrage of ambushes and assassinations. The state suffered civil war at its worst.

While lingering until 1782, New Jersey loyalism never recovered from the blow it received when the British evacuated the state early in 1777. The state militia became a relentless police force dedicated to rooting out political dissent. The mili-

tia disarmed known loyalists, jailed their leaders, and kept a constant watch on suspected Tories. Ironically, the British themselves contributed to the undermining of New Jersey loyalism, for prior to the Battle of Trenton, British commanders had failed to prevent an orgy of looting by their troops that damaged loyalists and Whigs equally. Surrounded by armed enemies and facing constant danger of arrest, most loyalists who remained in the state bowed to the inevitable and swore allegiance to the Continental Congress; more than a few ex-loyalists themselves joined the rebel militia. The same process was eventually repeated following British invasions of New York in 1777, Georgia in 1778, and the Carolinas in 1779. Upon regaining the upper hand, Whig militias ruthlessly pursued loyalists aiding the redcoats, forced many to flee, and coerced most into renouncing the crown.

Not all loyalists shifted sides, however. The war drove perhaps one of every six loyalists into exile in Canada, Britain, or the West Indies. Twenty percent of all New Yorkers may have left the United States by 1784. When the British evacuated Savannah in 1782, 15 percent of all whites in Georgia accompanied them. Most of those who departed were evidently British immigrants, whose mobility and lack of local roots made exile easier. Whether loyalists changed sides or became political refugees, loyalism declined as a force during the war. By 1782 few active loyalists remained outside British lines.

The Turning Point

Shortly after the battles of Trenton and Princeton, the Marquis de Lafayette, a young French aristocrat, joined Washington's staff. Lafayette was twenty years old, highly idealistic, very brave, and infectiously optimistic. Given Lafayette's close connections with the French court, his presence in America indicated that the French king, Louis XVI, might recognize U.S. independence and perhaps declare war on Britain. Before recognizing the United States, however, Louis wanted proof that the Americans could win a major battle, a feat they had not yet accomplished.

Louis did not have to wait long. In the summer of 1777, the British launched a two-pronged assault intended to crush American resistance in New York State and thereby isolate New England. Pushing off from Montreal, a force of regulars and their Iroquois allies, marching under Lieutenant Colonel Barry St. Leger, would proceed south along Lake Ontario and invade central New York from Fort Oswego in the west, while General John Burgoyne would lead the main British force south from Quebec through eastern New York and link up with St. Leger near Albany.

The British would have faced a formidable task under any circumstances; but to complicate matters, General William Howe, the British commander in chief in North America, chose to launch a *second* major campaign in the summer of 1777, which was aimed at the American capital, Philadelphia. Howe intended to draw the Continentals south to the defense of their capital, defeat them in battle, and then use Philadelphia as a base for building loyalist support in the mid-Atlantic region. Howe's fateful decision to move against Philadelphia meant that neither he nor the modest force that he had left behind in New York City under General Henry Clinton could decisively aid St. Leger or Burgoyne if their invasion of New York misfired.

Unfortunately for Howe, nothing went according to plan in New York. St. Leger's force of 1,900 advanced a hundred miles and halted to besiege 750 New York Continentals at Fort Stanwix. Unable to take the post after three weeks, and finding himself deserted by the Iroquois, who suffered heavy losses in a battle with the local militia near Oriskany, St. Leger retreated in late August 1777.

Meanwhile, on July 6 Burgoyne's 8,300 British and Hessians had taken Fort Ticonderoga, about a hundred miles north of Albany. But by now Burgoyne's supply lines were overstretched, and a force that he dispatched to seize supplies at Bennington, Vermont, was repulsed with heavy losses. Along with the 900 troops that Burgoyne had detached to garrison Fort Ticonderoga, his losses in Vermont depleted his army and gave General Horatio Gates time to collect nearly 17,000 American troops for an attack. Gates fought two indecisive battles near Saratoga in the fall, inflicting another 1,200 casualties on Burgoyne. Surrounded and hopelessly outnumbered, Burgoyne's 5,800 troops honorably laid down their arms on October 17, 1777.

The diplomatic impact of the Battle of Saratoga rivaled its military significance and made it the war's turning point. Early in December 1777, news of the battle reached France, where Benjamin Franklin had recently arrived as the U.S. ambassador. Although one of America's wealthiest, wisest, and most sophisticated men, Franklin shrewdly captured the French imagination by appearing in a fur cap and playing the part of an innocent backwoods philosopher. Turning himself into the court's latest fad, Franklin won widespread French sympathy for the United States. Then with the victory at Saratoga, France became convinced that the Americans could win the war and thus deserved diplomatic recognition.

In February 1778 France therefore formally recognized the United States. Four months later, it went to war with Britain. Spain declared war on Britain in 1779, but as an ally of France, not the United States, and the Dutch Republic joined them in the last days of 1780. Now facing a coalition of enemies, Britain had no allies of its own.

Of all the American allies, only France sent troops to the United States, and they did nothing of significance until 1781. Nonetheless, the coalition forced Britain to send thousands of soldiers to Ireland and the West Indies to guard against

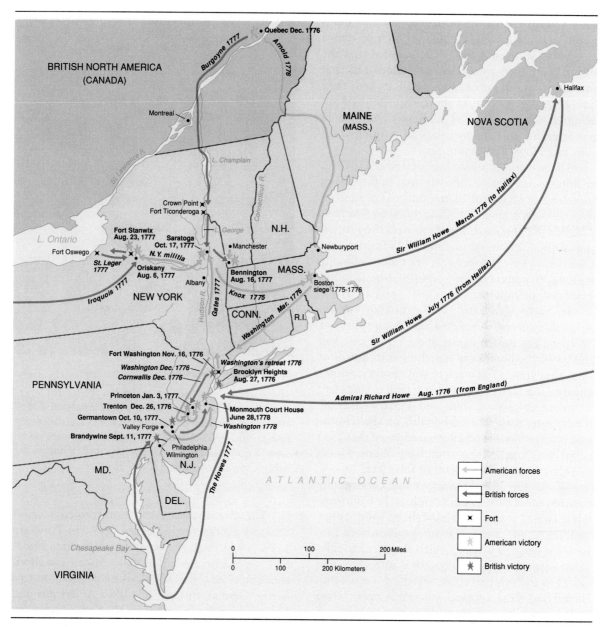

The War in the North, 1776–1779

Following the British evacuation of Boston, the war shifted to New York City, which the British held from 1776 to 1783. In 1777 Britain's success in taking the U.S. capital, Philadelphia, was offset by defeat in upstate New York. The hard-fought battle of Monmouth Court House, New Jersey, ended the northern campaigns in 1778.

French invasion, thus reducing the manpower available to fight in the United States. The French and Spanish navies, which together approximately equaled the British fleet, won several large battles, denied Britain control of the sea, and punctured the Royal Navy's blockade.

The Continentals Mature

While Gates and Burgoyne maneuvered in upstate New York, Howe landed 18,000 troops near Philadelphia in late August. With Washington at their head and Lafayette at his side, 16,000 Continentals paraded through the imperiled city on August 24,

1777. "They marched twelve deep," John Adams wrote to his wife Abigail, "and yet took up above two hours in passing by." Adams noted that the troops were well armed and uniformed but that they did not keep their heads straight or wear their hats cocked properly—in short, they still had not acquired "quite the air of soldiers." They would pay a fearful price for their lack of training when they met Howe's professionals.

The two armies collided on September 11, 1777, at Brandywine Creek, Pennsylvania. In the face of superior British discipline, not only did most Continental units crumble but Congress soon fled Philadelphia in panic, enabling Howe to occupy America's capital. Howe again defeated Washington at Germantown on October 4. In one month's bloody fighting, 20 percent of the Continentals were killed, wounded, or captured.

In early December 1777, 11,000 tentless American survivors huddled round campfires at Whitemarsh, Pennsylvania. Short on rations and chilled to the bone from marching into a wall of sleet, they took a full week to walk to their winter quarters fourteen miles away. A fourth of them had worn out at least one shoe, and on days when the roads froze, they suffered horribly on the ice-covered ridges. Washington later remembered that "you might have tracked the army from White Marsh to Valley Forge by the blood of their feet."

While the British army rested comfortably eighteen miles away in Philadelphia, the Continentals stumbled around the bleak hills of Valley Forge, building crude huts. The troops somehow preserved a sense of humor, which they occasionally demonstrated by joining together in a thousand voices to squawk like crows watching a cornfield. Underlying these squawks was real hunger: James Varnum reported on December 20 that his Connecticut and Rhode Island troops had gone the two previous days without meat and three days without bread.

The army slowly regained its strength but still lacked training. The Continentals had forced Burgoyne to surrender more by their overwhelming numbers than by their skill. Indeed, when Washington's men had met Howe's forces on equal terms, they lost badly. The Americans mainly lacked the ability to march as compact units and maneuver quickly. Regiments often straggled single-file into battle and then wasted precious time forming to attack, and few troops were expert in bayonet drill.

Friedrich von Steuben

The Prussian-born Steuben arrived in the United States in December 1777. Although the government and the army alike felt deep disillusionment over the value of foreign officers at that time, the talented Steuben overcame this disability and was appointed the Continental Army's major-general in 1778.

The Continental Army's ill-trained recruits received a desperately needed boost in February 1778, when the German soldier of fortune Friedrich von Steuben arrived at Valley Forge. The short, squat Steuben did not look like a soldier, but this earthy German instinctively liked Americans and became immensely popular. He had a talent for motivating men (sometimes by staging humorous tantrums featuring a barrage of German, English, and French swearing); but more important, he possessed administrative genius. In a mere four months, General Steuben almost single-handedly turned the army into a formidable fighting force.

General Henry Clinton, now British commander in chief, evacuated Philadelphia in mid-1778 and marched to New York. The Continental Army got its first opportunity to demonstrate Steuben's training when it caught up with Clinton's rear guard at Monmouth Court House, New Jersey, on June 28, 1778. Although the Americans initially faltered, Washington re-formed them along a strong defensive position. Clinton ordered his best units against Washington's line, only to see them thrown back at bayonet point. The battle raged for six hours in one-hundred-degree heat until Clinton broke off contact. Expecting to renew the fight at daybreak, the Americans slept on their arms, but Clinton's army slipped away before then. The British would never again win easy victories, except when they faced more militiamen than Continentals.

The Battle of Monmouth ended the contest for the North. Clinton occupied New York, which the Royal Navy made safe from attack. Washington kept his army nearby to watch Clinton. Meanwhile, the Whig militia hunted down the last few Tory guerrillas and extinguished loyalism.

Frontier Campaigns

A different kind of war developed west of the Appalachians and along the western borders of New York and Pennsylvania. The numbers engaged in these frontier skirmishes were relatively small, but the fighting was fierce and the stakes were high. In 1776 few Anglo-Americans had a clear notion of the western boundaries of the new nation; by 1783, when the Peace of Paris concluded the war, whites had established enough settlements west of the Appalachians to justify their claim to the Mississippi River as their western border. So while the frontier campaigns did not determine the outcome of the war, they had a significant impact on the future shape of the United States.

In the 1760s Daniel Boone and other "long knives" had begun exploring west of the Cumberland Gap, the main pass through the southern Appalachians. They were astonished to find no permanent Indian settlements within the sixty thousand square miles of what are now Kentucky and central Tennessee. This vast area could be opened to settlement if the native Americans would sell their claims to it. The Iroquois sold their title in 1768, as did the Cherokees in 1775. The Shawnees, who dwelled in what is now Ohio, also accepted whites' occupation of Kentucky, but only after their defeat in 1774 by the Virginia militia in Lord Dunmore's War. Having surrendered their claims at gunpoint, the Shawnees felt no obligation to honor Dunmore's treaty, and for the next forty years, this embittered Indian nation would stand at the forefront of resistance to white expansion in the Ohio Valley.

The permanent settlement of Kentucky began in 1775, and of central Tennessee the year after. White expansion into the Ohio Valley made the western Indians firm British allies. Native Americans elsewhere overwhelmingly supported the British.

As Daniel Boone's career in Kentucky illustrates, Anglo-Americans paid a heavy price holding the West for the Continental Congress. Boone survived numerous ambushes, at least seven skirmishes, and three pitched battles. In 1778 he and thirty men, assisted by their wives and children, stood off more than four hundred Indians at Boonesborough. Boone himself was twice shot and twice captured. Indians also killed two of his sons, a brother, and two brothers-in-law, besides wounding another brother four times and capturing a daughter, who was herself later wounded as well.

However, the Indian attacks failed to drive white settlers from Kentucky (see "A Place in Time"). In June 1778, 175 militiamen left what is now Louisville to put an end to British authority north of the Ohio River. Their leader was George Rogers Clark, a twenty-six-year-old colonel who had spent the previous four years fighting native Americans in Kentucky. Clark used news of the recent French-American alliance to persuade the militia at the distant French settlements in present-day Illinois and at Vincennes, Indiana, to become U.S. citizens. He then established his headquarters at Kaskaskia, Illinois.

But Britain's commander at Detroit, Colonel Henry Hamilton, leading five hundred regulars and Indians who outnumbered Clark's riflemen more than four to one, retook Vincennes in December. A realistic officer might have retreated, and a brave officer might have prepared to defend Kaskaskia, but Clark decided to attack Vincennes. In the dead of winter, he led his Kentuckians through 180 miles of barren plains flooded by heavy rains. They waded across three icy rivers, all shoulder-deep. The men survived on half-rations because the downpours had driven most wildlife to higher ground.

Clark had gambled that Hamilton's Indians would have gone home, but he learned with dismay that two hundred remained at Vincennes. Undaunted, the resourceful Clark now resorted to espionage. He employed a French spy to deceive

Bryan's Station, Kentucky, in 1782

The War for American Independence was more than a military clash between British redcoats and American continentals disciplined to fight in rigid formations. The conflict also pitted American against American, as loyalist and patriot bands met in hundreds of small, bloody backcountry encounters. And for thousands of native Americans, the war meant a chance to defend their homeland against the settlers spilling westward across the Appalachians.

In 1782 the war came to Bryan's Station, five miles east of Lexington, Kentucky. Founded three years earlier by five of Daniel Boone's brothers-in-law, the fort was surrounded by a twelve-foot-high stockade and sheltered thirty-nine houses. The settlers risked attack by Indians every time they ventured out—even the women, who left the fort regularly, under armed escort, to milk cows, weed gardens, and draw water from a nearby spring. In August Bryan's Station got word to send its men to join a local militia rally, for a pro-British force of three hundred Wyandot Indians and sixty white Canadians, led by the Pennsylvania loyalist Captain William Caldwell, was raiding Kentucky. At neighboring Hoy's Station, the attackers had abducted two children and ambushed a rescue party.

Caldwell's men headed straight for Bryan's Station, silently surrounding it on the night of August 15 as the settlement's men and women were casting bullets and readying their muskets. At daybreak, as the fort's captain, John Craig, prepared to lead forty-three men to Hoy's Station, an African-born slave noticed that the usual chorus of singing birds had given way to an eerie silence. In broken English he warned of an unseen enemy. Soon the defenders shot a poorly concealed Indian, whose companions, however, did not betray their presence by firing back—not even to stop two Bryan's Station men who trotted off to summon help. Craig realized that the attackers were waiting to ambush the main body of men just outside the fort.

The defenders of Bryan's Station practiced their own deception. They desperately needed water in order to avoid dehydration while fighting under the broiling sun; but men trying to reach the spring would be cut down in a crossfire. If the Indians' intent, however, was to lull the settlers' suspicions, the native Americans might let women through. So, pretending total ignorance of danger, the women went to fetch the water. They walked barefoot as usual (although shoes would have helped them run faster if pursued), and they took a dozen girls, one of them shielding her mother by walking in front. Even when one woman saw a hand

Bryan's Station

A Kentucky Rifle *It is believed that a resident of Bryan's Station used this rifle in the defense of the fort in 1782.*

clutching a hatchet under a bush, they maintained their composure at the spring and resisted the urge to rush to safety. After fifteen agonizing minutes, they returned with the water.

Caldwell's men attacked at midmorning. A few Indian decoys had tried to lure the defenders away from one side of the fort, but Craig's men kept their discipline and drove back the main force when it swarmed toward them. A steady pounding of musket fire and a rain of flaming arrows followed. While their men held the enemy at bay, the women reloaded guns and molded bullets while their children pulled flaming arrows out of roofs and doused fires. Little Betsy Johnson calmly plucked a blazing arrow from her infant brother Richard's cradle.

Help arrived by late afternoon, when the defenders' ammunition was running so low that their wives had begun melting pewter plates into bullets. Fourteen mounted militiamen galloped through a hail of enemy fire to reach the fort safely. Meanwhile, thirty other unmounted men in the relief party engaged the foe in a confused hand-to-hand fight. Outnumbered ten to one, the reinforcements lost six men before breaking off the battle.

Certain that more militiamen were on the way, Caldwell ended the siege. But that night, the settlers listened helplessly as the jeering loyalists trampled their crops and killed their livestock. The next morning's light unveiled a scene of desolation. A hundred acres of corn lay wasted, most of the potatoes and vegetables had been uprooted, and the carcasses of five hundred cattle, hogs, and sheep littered the ground.

The defenders had lost two men but had killed or wounded thirty attackers. Bryan's Station never again came under siege, and within two years its residents abandoned it for isolated farms; but war with the Indians went on for a decade. Richard Mentor Johnson, whose cradle had been hit by a fiery arrow, later received a gold sword from Congress for bravery in the War of 1812, and in 1837 he became vice president of the United States.

Fetching Water *In a twentieth-century reenactment, Bryan's Station women leave the safety of the fort to draw water from the nearby spring.*

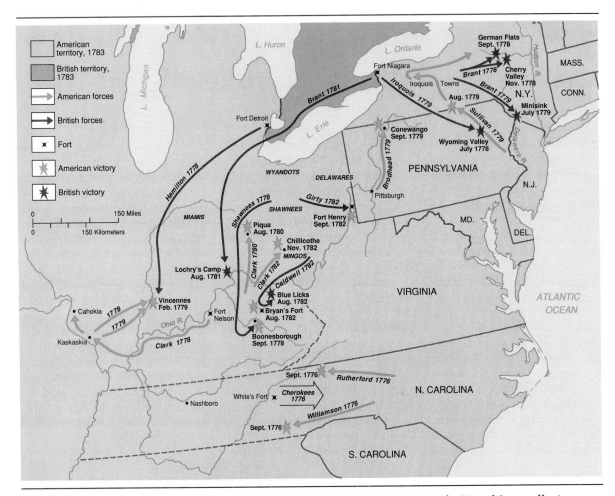

The War in the West, 1776–1779

George Rogers Clark's victory at Vincennes in 1779 gave the United States effective control of the Ohio Valley. Carolina militiamen drove attacking Cherokees far back into the Appalachians in 1776. In retaliation for their raids on New York and Pennsylvania, John Sullivan inflicted widespread starvation on the Iroquois by burning their villages and winter food supplies in 1779.

the native Americans into believing that he commanded a thousand men, prompting the Indians to flee. Carefully hiding his true strength, he then besieged the fort. The British commander surrendered Vincennes and twelve cannons on February 24, 1779, because he too concluded that he was badly outnumbered. Clark's victory not only eliminated British forts south of Detroit but also gave the United States a strong claim to retain the region north of the Ohio River.

In the East meanwhile, the Iroquois in New York remained neutral until 1777. Then the Six Nations of the Iroquois Confederacy split, with all

but the Tuscaroras and most Oneidas providing warriors for St. Leger's invasion of New York. Led by the exceptionally gifted Mohawk Joseph Brant, the Iroquois devastated the Pennsylvania and New York frontiers in 1778; they killed 340 Pennsylvania militia at Wyoming, Pennsylvania, alone and probably slew an equal number in their other raids. In 1779 the U.S. general John Sullivan retaliated by invading the Iroquois country with 3,700 Continentals and several hundred Tuscaroras and Oneidas. Sullivan fought just one battle, near present-day Elmira, New York, in which his artillery routed Brant's warriors. After he subsequently

Detroit in 1794

Detroit was a French outpost from 1701 to 1760. The British occupied it for the next thirty-six years, using it after 1775 as a staging area for their frontier forays on white settlers.

burned two dozen Indian villages and destroyed a million bushels of corn, most Iroquois fled without food into Canada. Untold hundreds starved during the next winter, when more than sixty inches of snow fell.

In 1780 Brant's thousand warriors fell upon the Tuscaroras and Oneidas and then laid waste to Pennsylvania and New York for two years. But this final whirlwind of Iroquois fury masked reality: Sullivan's campaign had destroyed the Iroquois peoples' heartland, and by 1783 their population had declined by perhaps one-third in eight years. The Six Nations would never truly recover.

Victory in the South

After 1778, as Britain formulated a new strategy that reflected changed circumstances, the war's focus shifted to the South. With the entry of France and Spain into the war, the conflict had acquired international dimensions; Britain was suddenly locked in a struggle that raged from India to Gibraltar to the West Indies and the American mainland. By

securing ports in the South, the British would acquire the flexibility to move their forces back and forth between the West Indies and the United States as necessity dictated. In addition, the South looked like a relatively easy target. General Henry Clinton recalled that in 1778 a British force of 3,500 troops had taken Savannah, Georgia, without great difficulty, and he expected that a renewed invasion of the South would tap a huge reservoir of loyalist support. In sum, the British plan was to seize key southern ports and, with the aid of loyalist militiamen, move back toward the North, pacifying one region after another.

The plan unfolded smoothly at first. Sailing from New York with 9,000 troops, Clinton forced the surrender of Charleston, South Carolina, and its 3,400-man garrison on May 12, 1780. Clinton then returned to New York with a third of his army, leaving mopping-up operations in the South to Lord Charles Cornwallis, now in command of British forces in that region. However, the British quickly found that there were fewer loyalists than they had expected. The Carolinas and Georgia did contain a sizable loyalist population, whose members enlisted by the thousands in royal militia units. Most were British immigrants, and Scots were especially prominent. But southern loyalism had suffered a serious blow in 1776, when Britain's Cherokee allies, settling scores of their own, had attacked the Carolina frontier and killed residents indiscriminately. Numerous Tories had switched sides, joining the Whig militia to defend their homes.

After the British capture of Charleston, the loyalist militia, embittered by countless instances of harsh treatment under Whig rule, lost little time in taking revenge. Whigs struck back whenever possible. So began an escalating cycle of revenge, retribution, and retaliation that engulfed the Lower South through 1782.

This southern war became intensely personal. Individuals often chose sides not for political rea-

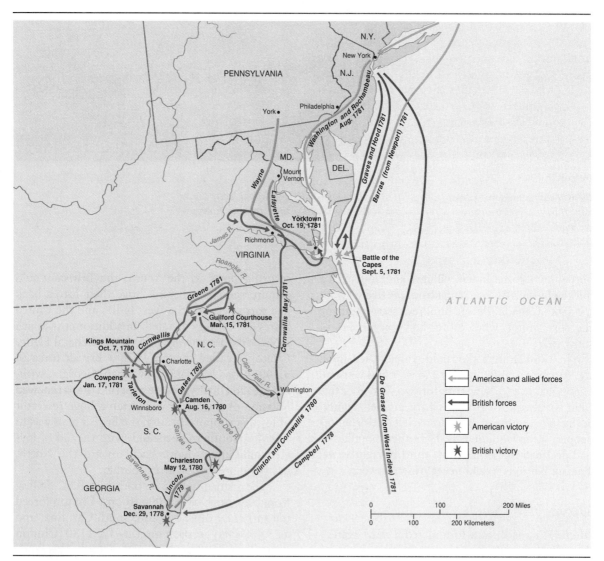

The War in the South, 1778–1781   *By 1780 Britain held the South's major cities, Charleston and Savannah, but could not establish control over the backcountry because of resistance from Nathaniel Greene's Continentals. By invading Virginia, Lord Cornwallis placed himself within striking distance of Washington's U.S. and French forces, a decision that rapidly led to the British surrender at Yorktown in October 1781.*

sons but to avenge an outrage perpetrated by the other. For example, Thomas Sumter and Andrew Pickens, South Carolina's two foremost Whig guerrillas, both took up arms after Tories plundered their plantations in 1780. And when another South Carolinian, the Tory William Cunningham, learned that his brother had been whipped to death by Whig militiamen from Ninety-Six, South Carolina, he grimly walked sixty miles to Ninety-Six to find and kill the officer responsible. Afterward, while leading loyalist guerrillas, Cunningham earned the nickname Bloody Bill.

An obscure rebel whose involvement in these confused vendettas seems typical was the Whig sympathizer Andrew Meaden of North Carolina. For Meaden, the Revolution was a true civil war: he never once saw a British regular during his two years' service but did all his fighting against loyalists or Cherokees. Meaden later recalled how in July 1780, he "volunteered under Captain George Wailes from Rowan Co. . . . to march in his company against some Tories, who had shot Capt. Yorke while a prisoner. . . . We made great exertions to take Capt. Fannan, a Tory, who had shot Capt. Yorke. . . . But he eluded our pursuit. . . . We took some Tories prisoner, whipped some, and compelled them to take the oath of allegiance." Like many of his generation, Meaden, fighting more for vengeance than politics, slowly became brutalized.

But the southern conflict was not all guerrilla warfare. Washington, forced by Clinton's continued occupation of New York City to stay in the North with most of the Continental Army, sent General Horatio Gates to take command in the South. With only a small force of Continentals at his disposal, however, Gates had to rely on poorly trained militiamen. In August 1780 Cornwallis inflicted a crushing defeat on Gates at Camden, South Carolina. Fleeing after firing a single volley, Gates's militia left his badly outnumbered Continentals to be overrun. Camden was the worst American defeat of the war.

Washington responded by relieving Gates of command and sending General Nathaniel Greene to confront Cornwallis. Greene subsequently fought three major battles between March and September 1781, and he lost all of them. "We fight, get beat, rise, and fight again," he wrote back to Washington. Still, Greene won the campaign, for he gave the Whig militia the protection they needed to hunt down loyalists, stretched British supply lines until they began to snap, and sapped Cornwallis's strength by inflicting much heavier casualties than the British general could afford. Greene's dogged resistance forced Cornwallis to leave the Carolina backcountry in American hands and to lead his battered troops into Virginia.

Secure in New York City, Clinton wanted Cornwallis to return to Charleston and renew his Carolina campaign, but Cornwallis had a mind of his own and established a new base at Yorktown, Virginia, near the coast. From Yorktown Cornwallis hoped to fan out into Virginia and Pennsylvania, but he never got the chance. Cornwallis's undoing began on August 30, 1781, when a French fleet from the West Indies, commanded by Admiral De Grasse, dropped anchor off the Virginia coast and landed troops near Yorktown. Soon Lafayette joined them, leading a small force of Continentals. Meanwhile, Washington made enough feints at New York City to prevent Clinton from coming to Cornwallis's aid and then moved his army south to tighten the noose around the British. Trapped in Yorktown, Cornwallis's 6,000 British stood off 8,800 Americans and 7,800 French for three weeks. They finally surrendered with military honors on October 19, 1781.

The Peace of Paris

"Oh God!" Lord North exclaimed upon hearing of Yorktown, "It's all over." Indeed, Cornwallis's surrender drained the will of England's overtaxed gentry to fight and forced the government to commence peace negotiations. John Adams, Benjamin Franklin, and John Jay were America's principal diplomats at the peace talks in Paris, which began in June 1782.

Military realities largely influenced the terms of the peace. Britain recognized American independence and stipulated the evacuation of all royal troops from U.S. soil. Although the vast majority of Americans lived in the thirteen states clustered near the eastern seaboard, the British had little choice but to award the United States all lands east of the Mississippi, for by 1783 twenty thousand Anglo-Americans lived west of the Appalachians, and Clark's victories had given Americans control of the Northwest. The treaty also gave the United

States important fishing rights off the Grand Banks of Canada.

On the whole, the settlement was highly favorable to the United States, but it did not resolve all disputes. In a separate treaty, Britain transferred East and West Florida back to Spain, but the boundaries designated by this treaty were ambiguous. Spain interpreted the treaty to mean that it regained the same Florida territory that it had ceded to Britain in 1763. But Britain's treaty with the United States named the thirty-first parallel as the Floridas' northern border, well south of the area claimed by Spain. Spain and the United States would dispute the northern boundary of Florida until 1795.

The Peace of Paris also planted the seeds of several future disputes between Britain and the United States. Although the United States promised to urge the state legislatures to compensate loyalists for their property losses and agreed that no legal bars would prevent British creditors from collecting prewar debts, several state governments later refused to pay back loyalists and erected barriers against British creditors. In response, the British failed to honor their treaty pledge to return slaves confiscated by their troops.

The Peace of Paris ratified American independence, but winning independence had exacted a heavy price. At least 5 percent of all free white males aged sixteen to forty-five died in the war. If the present-day U.S. population fought a war with comparable casualties, 2.5 million people would be killed. Only the Civil War produced a higher ratio of casualties to the nation's population. Further, while the war secured American independence, it did not settle two important issues: what kind of society America was to become and what sort of government the new nation would possess. Yet the war had a profound impact on both questions.

Revolutionary Society

Two forces shaped the social effects of the Revolution: first, the principles articulated in the Declaration of Independence; and second, the dislocations caused by the war itself. These factors combined to change relationships between members of different classes, races, and sexes momentously.

Egalitarianism

Between 1700 and 1760, social relations between elites and the common people had grown more formal, distant, and restrained. Members of the gentry had attempted to emphasize their social position by living far beyond the means of ordinary families. As the 1760s unfolded, however, the need to mobilize widespread support for the rising Whig movement had led the upper class to minimize their displays of wealth. Members of the gentry instinctively realized that by dressing in a fashion closer to the average citizen, they could build a sense of common cause. Thus the upper classes began wearing homespun rather than imported English clothes as early as 1768 and subsequently watched their popularity soar. When the First Families of Virginia organized minutemen companies in 1775, they threw away their expensive militia uniforms and dressed in homespun hunting shirts; then even the poorest farmer would not be too embarrassed to enlist because of his humble appearance. By 1776 the visible distinctions of wealth had been noticeably reduced.

Then came war, which accelerated the erosion of class differences by forcing the gentry, who held officers' rank, to show respect to the ordinary folk serving as privates. Indeed, the soldiers demanded to be treated with consideration, especially in light of the ringing words of the Declaration of Independence, "All men are created equal." The soldiers would follow commands, but not if they were addressed as inferiors. General Steuben reported to a European army officer: "You say to your soldier, 'Do this,' and he doeth it, but I am obliged to say 'This is the reason why you ought to do that,' and he does it."

The best officers realized this fact immediately. Some, among them General Israel Putnam of Connecticut, went out of their way to show that they felt no superiority to their troops. While inspecting a regiment digging fortifications around Boston in 1776, Putnam saw a large stone nearby and told a noncommissioned officer to throw it onto the outer wall. The individual protested, "Sir, I am a corporal." "Oh," replied Putnam, "I ask your pardon, sir." The general then dismounted his horse and hurled the rock himself, to the immense delight of the troops working there.

A majority of men of military age were exposed to treatment of this sort in the course of the war. Soldiers came to expect that their worth as individuals would be recognized by their officers, at least within the limits allowed by the army. After these common soldiers returned to civilian life, they retained a sense of self-esteem and insisted on respectful treatment. As these feelings of personal pride gradually translated into political behavior and beliefs, it became highly unlikely that the majority of voters would again accept candidates who scorned the common people. The war thus subtly but fundamentally democratized Americans' political assumptions.

The gentry's sense of social rank also diminished as they met men who rose through ability rather than through advantages of wealth or family. The war produced numerous examples like James Purvis, the illiterate son of a nonslaveowning Virginia farmer, who joined the First Virginia Regiment as a private in 1775, soon rose to sergeant, and then taught himself to read and write so that he could perform an officer's duties. Captain Purvis fought through the entire war and impressed his well-born officers as "an uneducated man, but of sterling worth." As elites saw more and more middle-class farmers and even artisans performing responsibilities previously thought to be above their station in life, they developed a new appreciation that a person's merit was unrelated to his wealth.

This new emphasis on equality did not extend to blacks, women, or native Americans, but it undermined the tendency to believe that wealth or distinguished family background conferred a special claim to public office. "[O]ne should consider himself as good a man as another," declared the *New Jersey Gazette* in 1780, "and not be brow beaten or intimidated by riches or supposed superiority." After the war even a fraternal organization of veteran Continental Army officers, the Society of the Cincinnati, evoked widespread alarm because its charter gave membership to sons and their descendants who, it was feared, might evolve into a hereditary aristocracy.

In short, Revolutionary-generation Americans came to insist that virtue and sacrifice defined a citizen's worth independently of his wealth. Citizens widely began to view members of the "natural aristocracy"—those who had demonstrated fitness for government service by personal accomplishments—as the ideal candidates for political office. This natural aristocracy had room for a few self-made men such as Benjamin Franklin, as well as for those, like Jefferson and John Hancock, born into wealth. Voters still elected the wealthy to office, but not if they flaunted their money. And members of the gentry increasingly acted like the "harmless aristocrats" of Virginia described by Judge St. George Tucker, who "never failed to pull off their hats to a poor man whom they met, and generally appeared to me to shake hands with every man in a Court-yard or a Church-yard."

A Revolution for Blacks

The wartime situation of African-Americans contradicted the ideals of equality and justice for which Americans were fighting. About five hundred thousand blacks—20 percent of the total population—inhabited the United States in 1776, of whom all but about twenty-five thousand lived in bondage. Even those who were free could not vote, lived under curfews and other galling restrictions, and lacked the guarantees of equal justice held by the poorest white criminal. Free blacks could expect no more than grudging toleration, and few slaves ever gained their freedom.

Although the United States was a "white man's country" in 1776, the war opened some opportunities to blacks. Amid the confusion of war, some slaves, among them Jehu Grant of Rhode Island, ran off and posed as freemen. Grant later recalled his excitement "when I saw liberty poles and the people all engaged for the support of freedom, and I could not but like and be pleased with such a thing." Blacks also made their way into the Continental Army. Even though the army late in 1775 forbade the enlistment of any African-Americans, some blacks were already fighting in units during the siege of Boston, and the ban on black enlistments started to collapse in 1777. All states but Georgia and South Carolina eventually recruited blacks.

Approximately five thousand blacks served in the Continental forces, most from the North. The majority of blacks who enlisted were slaves serving with their masters' consent, usually in integrated units. In 1781 a German mercenary described Rhode Island's black regiment as "the most neatly dressed, the best under arms, and the most precise in its maneuvers."

For the most part, these wartime opportunities for blacks grew out of the army's need for manpower rather than a white commitment to equal justice for African-Americans. In fact, until the mid-eighteenth century, few in the Western world had criticized slavery at all. Like disease and sin, slavery was considered part of the natural order. But in the decade before the Revolution, American opposition to slavery had swelled. The first American prohibition against slaveowning came from the annual leadership conference (known as the yearly meeting) of the New England Quakers in 1770. The yearly meetings of New York and Philadelphia Quakers followed suit in 1776, and by 1779 the Quakers had compelled their members to free 80 percent of their slaves.

While the Quakers aimed mainly to abolish slaveholding within their own ranks, the Declaration of Independence's broad assertion of natural rights and human equality spurred a more general attack on the institution of slavery. Between 1777 and 1784, Vermont, Pennsylvania, Massachusetts, Rhode Island, and Connecticut ended slavery. New York did so in 1799, and New Jersey in 1804. New Hampshire, unmoved by petitions like that written in 1779 by Portsmouth slaves demanding liberty "to dispose of our lives, freedom, and property," never freed its slaves; but by 1810 there were none in the state.

The movement against slavery reflected the Enlightenment's emphasis on gradual change, initiated by leaders who carefully primed public opinion. The Revolutionary generation, rather than advocating slavery's immediate abolition, favored steps that would weaken the institution and in this way bring about its eventual demise. Most state abolition laws provided for gradual emancipation, typically declaring all children born of a slave woman after a certain date—often July 4—free. (Such individuals still had to work, without pay, for their mother's master for up to twenty-eight years.) Furthermore, the Revolution's leaders did not press for decisive action against slavery in the South, out of fear that widespread southern emancipation would either bankrupt or end the Union. Instead, a southern slave's claim to freedom had to be balanced by an owner's demand for compen-

Alexander Spotswood Payne with His Brother, John Robert Dandridge Payne, and Their Nurse, c. 1790–1800

The Payne children, members of a wealthy eighteenth-century family, posed with their black nurse. The Revolution vastly modified the social and intellectual climate in which slavery had flourished in America for more than a century without substantial challenge.

sation for lost labor. But the United States, already deeply in debt as a result of the war, could not have financed immediate abolition in the South, and any attempt to have done so without compensation would have driven that region into secession. "Great as the evil is," observed Virginia's James Madison in 1787, "a dismemberment of the union would be worse."

Yet even in the South, slavery worried the consciences of prominent Whigs. When one of his slaves ran off to join the British and later was recaptured, Madison concluded that it would be hypocritical to punish the runaway "merely for coveting that liberty for which we have paid the price of so much blood." Still, Madison did not free the slave, and no state south of Pennsylvania abolished slavery. Nevertheless, every state but North Carolina passed laws making it possible for masters to manumit (set free) slaves without posting large sums of money as bond for their good behavior. By 1790 the number of free blacks in Virginia and Maryland had risen from about four thousand in 1775 to nearly twenty-one thousand, or about 5 percent of all African-Americans there.

These "free persons of color" faced the future destitute of money. Most had purchased their freedom by spending their small cash savings earned in off-hours and were past their physical prime. Once free, they found whites reluctant to hire them or to pay equal wages. Black ship carpenters in Charleston, South Carolina, for example, earned one-third less than their white coworkers in 1783. Under such circumstances, most free blacks remained poor laborers or tenant farmers. However, even under such extreme disadvantages, some free blacks became landowners or skilled craftsmen. One who achieved considerable fame was Benjamin Banneker of Maryland, a self-taught mathematician and astronomer. Later, in 1789, he served on the commission that designed Washington, D.C., and after 1791 he published a series of almanacs.

Free blacks relied on one another for help. Self-help among African-Americans largely flowed through religious channels. Because racially separate churches provided mutual support, self-pride, and a sense of accomplishment, free blacks began founding their own Baptist and Methodist congregations after the Revolution. In 1787 black Methodists in Philadelphia started the congregation that by 1816 would become the African Methodist Episcopal church. Black churches, the greatest source of inner strength for most African-Americans ever since, had their origins in the Revolutionary period.

Most states granted important civil rights to free blacks during and after the Revolution. Free blacks had not participated in colonial elections in the North, but they gained this privilege everywhere there by 1780. Most northern states repealed or stopped enforcing curfews or other colonial laws restricting their freedom of movement. Free blacks in the South could cast ballots in North Carolina, Maryland, and Delaware by 1783 and soon gained this right in Kentucky and Tennessee. These same states generally changed their laws to guarantee free blacks equal treatment in court hearings.

The Revolution neither ended slavery nor brought equality to free blacks, who continued to be treated as second-class citizens. But it did begin a process by which slavery could be extinguished. In half the nation, public opinion no longer condoned human bondage, and southerners increasingly viewed slavery as a necessary evil—an attitude that implicitly recognized its immorality. Slavery had begun to crack, and even the hold of racism seemed to be weakening.

Women in the New Republic

"To be adept in the art of Government is a prerogative to which your sex lay almost exclusive claim," wrote Abigail Adams to her husband John in 1776. She was one of the era's shrewdest and tartest political commentators and her husband's political confidante and best friend, but she had no public role. Indeed, for most women and almost all men in the 1780s, a woman's duty was to maintain her household and raise her children.

Apart from the fact that some states eased women's difficulties in obtaining divorces, the Revolution did not significantly affect the legal position of women. Women did not gain any new political rights, although New Jersey's 1776 constitution did not exclude them from voting and a law in force in that state from 1790 to 1807 referred to voters as "he and she." On the whole, the Revolution did far more for African-Americans than for white women. The assumption that women were naturally dependent—either as children subordinate to their parents or as wives to their husbands—continued to dominate discussions of the female role.

Nonetheless, the Revolutionary era witnessed the beginnings of a challenge to this attitude. Throughout the 1760s Whig orators had pointed to women's sacrifices to keep their families clothed during the colonial boycotts as evidence of Americans' patriotic solidarity. While these effusive declarations of women's importance to the patriot cause were meant mainly for British ears, American women heard them and took them seriously. For example, Massachusetts's Mercy Otis Warren, known before the imperial crisis for her polished, nonpolitical poetry, turned her pen to political satire in the early 1770s. In her play *The Group* (1775), she lampooned leading Massachusetts Tories under such names as Judge Meagre, Sir Spendall, and Hum Humbug.

Gradually, the subordination of women, which once was taken for granted, became the subject of debate. The Massachusetts essayist and poet Judith Sargent Murray contended in 1779 that the sexes had equal intellectual ability and deserved equal education. Murray hoped that "sensible and informed" women would improve their minds, not

Women in Revolutionary Society

As republican ideals and the female wartime experience joined forces to alter both women's self-images and prevailing social attitudes, postwar America witnessed notable changes in the lives of white women. (Left) Mrs. William Moseley, a republican mother idealized in portraiture with her son; (center) Judith Sargent Murray, a proponent of equal education for women; and (right) the Westtown Boarding School, established by the Society of Friends in 1794 to expand women's educational opportunities in the mid-Atlantic states.

rush into marriage (as she had at eighteen), and instill republican ideals in their children. After 1780 the urban upper class founded numerous private schools, or academies, for girls, and these provided to American women their first widespread opportunity for advanced education. Massachusetts also established an important precedent in 1789, when it forbade any town to exclude girls from its elementary schools. Further, American women who chafed at the restrictions of their domestic role took heart from the publication in 1792 of the English radical Mary Wollstonecraft's *Vindication of the Rights of Women*. While feeling obliged to condemn Wollstonecraft's intemperate language and sexually liberated lifestyle, many American women approved her passionate defense of female moral equality.

Although the great struggle for female political equality would not begin until the nineteenth century, the frequent Revolutionary-era assertions that women were intellectually and morally men's peers provoked scattered calls late in the eighteenth century for political equality. In 1793 Priscilla Mason, a spunky schoolgirl graduating from one of the

female academies, blamed "*Man*, despotic man" for shutting women out of the church, the courts, and government. In her salutatory oration, she urged that a women's senate be established by Congress to evoke "all that is human—all that is *divine* in the soul of woman."

Priscilla Mason had pointed out a fundamental problem in republican egalitarianism: what, besides being a virtuous wife and mother, should a woman *do* with her education? Men and women would grapple to resolve this question for generations to come.

The Revolution and Social Change

The American Revolution left the overall distribution of wealth in the nation unchanged. Because the 3 percent of Americans who fled abroad as loyalists represented a cross-section of society, their departure left the new nation's class structure unaltered. Loyalists' confiscated estates tended to be bought up by equally well-to-do Whig gentlemen. Overall, the American upper class seems to have owned about as much of the national wealth in 1783 as it did in 1776.

In short, the Revolution did not obliterate social distinctions nor even challenge all of them. Class distinctions, racial injustice, and the subordination of women persisted into the nineteenth century. In particular, the institution of slavery survived intact in the South, where the vast majority of slaves lived. Yet the Revolutionary era set in motion significant social changes. Increasingly, the members of the gentry had to earn respect by demonstrating their competence and by treating the common people with dignity. The Revolution dealt slavery a decisive blow in the North, greatly enlarged the free-black population, and awarded free people of color important political rights. While the momentous era did not bring women political equality, it placed new issues pertaining to the relations between the sexes on the agenda of national debate. And inevitably, the social changes wrought by the Revolution also deeply affected American political values.

Forging a Government

Americans had drawn many political conclusions from the imperial crisis of the 1760s, including the conviction that without vigilance by the people, governments would become despotic. But before the Declaration of Independence, few Americans had given much thought to forming governments of their own. While guiding and inspiring the Whigs, the Continental Congress lacked the sovereign powers usually associated with governments, including the authority to impose taxes.

During the war years, Whigs quickly recognized the need to establish governmental institutions to sustain the war effort and to buttress the United States' claim to independent nationhood. But the task of forging a government would prove arduous, in part because of the inevitable upheavals of war. In addition, the state governments that Americans formed after the Declaration of Independence reflected two different and often conflicting impulses: on one hand, the traditional ideas and practices that had guided Anglo-Americans for much of the eighteenth century; on the other, the

republican ideals that found a receptive audience in America in the 1760s and early 1770s.

"Can America be happy under a government of her own?" asked Thomas Paine in 1776. He answered his own question: "as happy as she pleases: she hath a blank sheet to write upon."

Tradition and Change

In establishing the Revolutionary state governments, Whigs relied heavily on ideas about government inherited from the colonial experience. For example, most Whigs took for granted the value of bicameral legislatures. As we have seen, the colonial legislatures in the royal provinces had consisted of two houses: an elected lower chamber (or assembly) and an upper chamber (or council) appointed by the governor or chosen by the assembly. These two-part legislatures resembled Parliament's division into the House of Commons and House of Lords and symbolized the assumption that a government should give separate representation to aristocrats and common people.

Revolutionary Americans also accepted the longstanding practice of setting property requirements for voters and elected officials. In the prevailing view, only the ownership of property, especially land, made it possible for voters to think and act independently. Whereas tenant farmers and hired laborers might sell their votes or vote against their best judgment to avoid displeasing their landlords or employers, property holders could express their opinions freely. This association between property and citizenship was so deeply ingrained that even radical firebrands such as Samuel Adams opposed allowing all males—much less women—to vote and hold office.

The notion that elected representatives should exercise independent judgment in leading the people rather than simply carry out the popular will also survived from the colonial period and restricted the democratization of politics. Although Americans today take political parties for granted, the idea of parties as necessary instruments for identifying and mobilizing public opinion was alien to the eighteenth-century political temper, which equated parties with "factions"—selfish groups that advanced their own interests at the expense of the public good. In general, candidates for office did not present voters with a clear choice between pol-

Revolutionary Americans

The Revolutionary generation witnessed the emergence of a new brand of politics as ideals of liberty and equality accelerated longstanding tendencies among the people.

icies calculated to benefit rival interest groups; instead, they campaigned on the basis of their personal reputations and fitness for office. As a result, voters did not know where office seekers stood on specific issues and hence found it hard to influence governmental actions.

Another colonial practice that persisted into the 1770s and 1780s was the equal (or nearly equal) division of legislative seats among all counties or towns, regardless of differences in population. Inasmuch as representation had never before been apportioned according to population, a minority of voters normally elected a majority of assemblymen. Additionally, many offices that later would become elective—such as sheriffs and justices of county courts—were appointive in the eighteenth century.

In sum, the colonial experience provided no precedent for a democratization of the United States during the Revolutionary era. Whigs showed little inclination to extend the vote to all free males. Nor did they favor the election of county officials, representation in assemblies based on population, or the development of a party system that would encourage candidates to state their political beliefs forthrightly.

Yet without intending to extend political participation, Whigs found themselves pulled in a democratic direction by the logic of the imperial crisis of the 1760s and 1770s. The colonial assemblies, the most democratic parts of colonial government, had led the fight against British policy during Americans' ideological clash with the mother country, while the executive branch of colonial governments, filled by royal governors and their appointees, had repeatedly locked horns with the assemblies. Whigs entered the Revolution dreading executive officeholders and convinced that even elected governors could no more be trusted with power than could monarchs. Recent history seemed to confirm the message hammered home by British country ideology (see Chapter 4) that those in power tended to become either corrupt or dictatorial. Consequently, Revolutionary statesmen proclaimed the need to strengthen legislatures at the governors' expense.

Despite their preference for vesting power in popularly elected legislatures, Whigs described themselves as republicans rather than democrats. Although used interchangeably today, these words had different connotations in the eighteenth century. At worst, democracy suggested mob rule; at best, it implied the concentration of power in the hands of an uneducated multitude. In contrast, republicanism presumed that government would be entrusted to capable leaders, elected for their superior talents and wisdom. For most republicans, the ideal government would delicately balance the interests of different classes to prevent any one group from gaining absolute power. Some Whigs, including John Adams, thought that a republic could include a hereditary aristocracy or even a monarchy as part of this balance, but most thought otherwise. Having blasted one king in the Declaration of Independence, Whigs had no desire to enthrone another. Still, their rejection of hereditary aristocracy and monarchy posed a problem for Whigs as they set about drafting state constitutions: how to maintain balance in government amid pervasive distrust of executive power.

Reconstituting the States

The state governments that Americans constructed during the Revolution reflected both the traditional and radical features of their thought. In keeping with colonial traditions, eleven of the thirteen states established bicameral legislatures. In all but a few states, the great majority of officeholders, at both the state and the county level, were still appointed rather than elected. Only one state, Pennsylvania, attempted to ensure that election districts would be roughly equal in population, so that a minority of voters could not elect a majority of legislators. Nine of the thirteen states reduced property requirements for voting, but none abolished such qualifications entirely, and most of the reductions were quite modest.

Yet the persistence of these conservative features should not obscure the pathbreaking components of the state constitutions. Above all, they were *written* documents whose adoption usually required popular ratification and which could be changed only if the people voted to amend them. In short, having rejected Parliament's right to tax them, Americans also jettisoned the British conception of a constitution as a body of customary arrangements and practices, insisting instead that constitutions were written compacts that defined and limited the powers of rulers. Moreover, as a final check on governmental power, the revolutionary constitutions spelled out citizens' fundamental rights. By 1784 all state constitutions included explicit bills of rights that outlined certain freedoms beyond governmental control. In sum, governments were no longer to serve as the final judge of the constitutionality of their activities.

The state constitutions reflected Whig thought in other ways, too. In most states the governor became an elected official, and elections themselves occurred far more frequently. Prior to 1776 colonial elections, typically called at the governor's pleasure, most often took place every three or four years. In contrast, after 1776 each state scheduled annual elections except South Carolina, which held them every two years. While most state and county offices remained appointive, the power

of appointments was transferred from the governor to the legislature. Legislatures usually appointed judges and could reduce their salaries or impeach them (try them for wrongdoing). But the new constitutions took their largest bite out of the governors' powers. Pennsylvania actually eliminated the office of governor, while other states stripped the executive branch of nearly all authority. By relieving governors of most appointive powers, denying them the right to veto laws, and making them subject to impeachment, the constitutions turned governors into figureheads who simply chaired an executive council that made militia appointments and supervised financial business.

As the new state constitutions weakened the executive branch and vested more power in the legislatures, they also made the legislatures, especially the upper chambers, more responsive to the will of the people. Nowhere could the governor appoint the upper chamber. Eight constitutions written before 1780 allowed voters to select both houses of the legislature, one (Maryland) used a popularly chosen "electoral college" for its upper house, and the remaining "senates" were filled by vote of their assemblies. Pennsylvania and Georgia abolished the upper house and substituted a single-chamber unicameral legislature. The Whigs' assault on the executive branch and their enhancement of legislative authority reflected their bitter memories of royal governors who had acted arbitrarily to prorogue (dismiss) assemblies and control government through their power of appointment, and it underscored the influence of "country-party" ideologues, who had warned that republics' undoing began with executive usurpation of authority.

In their first flush of revolutionary enthusiasm, few Whigs imagined that the legislatures themselves could become tyrannical. Yet most were familiar with the argument of the French Baron de Montesquieu (1689–1755) in *The Spirit of the Laws* that a proper division of political power would balance the executive, legislative, and judicial branches. By concentrating power in legislatures, the state constitutions provided no such balance. Gradually, however, Whigs paid more attention to the principle of balanced government. For example, Massachusetts revised its constitution in 1780 to strengthen the office of governor, while Georgia and Pennsylvania substituted bicameral for unicameral legislatures by 1790. Other states raised property qualifications for members of the upper chamber in a bid to encourage the "senatorial element" and to make room for men of "Wisdom, remarkable integrity, or that Weight which arises from property."

In general, the state constitutions written in the 1780s balanced power more evenly among branches of the government than had those composed in 1776–1777. Nonetheless, in comparison to the colonial-era royal governors, state executives continued to be relatively weak. Further, despite Whigs' efforts to bolster the upper chamber, or senate, as a balance against excesses of the lower house, the individuals elected to state senates did not seem notably wealthier or wiser than the members of the lower house. Even after Whigs raised the property requirements for senators, voters sent virtually indistinguishable groups to both houses. This failure of the "senatorial element" to emerge led republicans to reevaluate the purpose of bicameral legislatures. While social distinctions existed in the United States, none were so extreme as to merit institutionalization in a separate branch of the legislature. Whigs gradually altered their defense of bicameral legislatures by emphasizing that these bodies could act as useful checks on each other rather than as institutional embodiments of different social classes. If either house passed unwise measures, the other could block their enactment. Thus bicameralism itself became a functional safeguard against legislative abuses.

The Whigs' deference to the principle of balanced government revealed a central feature of their thought. Gradations among social classes and restrictions on the expression of popular will troubled them far less than the prospect of tyranny by those in power. But Whigs also believed that social divisions, if deep-seated and permanent, could jeopardize republican liberty. While more committed to liberty than to equality, some Whig leaders attempted to implement major social changes through legislation by the new state governments. In Virginia, for example, between 1776 and 1780 (when he became governor), Thomas Jefferson drafted a series of bills to promote greater equality. In October 1776 he persuaded the Virginia legislature to abolish entails, legal requirements that prevented an heir and all his descendants from selling or dividing an estate. Although entails were easy to break through special laws—Jefferson himself had escaped from the restrictions of one—he hoped that their elimination would strip wealthy families of the opportunity to amass land continuously and become an overbearing aristocracy. Through Jefferson's efforts, Virginia also ended primogeniture, the legal requirement that the eldest son inherit all a family's property in the absence of a will. Thereby, Jefferson hoped to ensure a continuous division of wealth. By 1791 no state provided for primogeniture, and just two allowed entails.

These years also witnessed the end of state-established churches in most of the country. New England, whose political climate was the nation's most conservative, resisted this reform, and the Congregational church continued to collect tithes (church taxes) until 1817 in New Hampshire, 1818 in Connecticut, and 1833 in Massachusetts. But in every state where colonial taxpayers had supported the Anglican church, such support was abolished by 1786. Thomas Jefferson best expressed the ideal behind disestablishment in his Statute for Religious Freedom (1786), whose preamble resounded with a defense of religious freedom at all times and places. "Truth is great," proclaimed Jefferson, "and will prevail if left to itself."

The American Revolution, wrote Thomas Paine in 1782, was intended to ring in "a new era and give a new turn to human affairs." This was an ambitious declaration and seemed to conflict with the Whigs' tendency to borrow from the past institutions such as state senates and property requirements for voting. Paine's point was not that the unique features of some constitutions, such as the termination of primogeniture and the disestablishment of the Anglican church, outweighed the traditional elements of the constitutions. Instead, he was expressing the Whigs' view—which lay at the heart of their republican ideal—that *all* political institutions now were being judged by the standard of whether they served the public good rather than the interests of the powerful few. More than any single innovation of the era, it was this new way of thinking that made the Whigs revolutionary.

The Articles of Confederation

While Whigs poured most of their political energies into the state governments, in 1776 John Dickinson, who had stayed in Congress despite having refused to sign the Declaration of Independence, drafted a proposal for a national government, which he called the Articles of Confederation. Congress adopted a weakened version of the Articles and sent it to the states for ratification in 1777. The Articles established a single-chamber national Congress, elected by the state legislatures, in which each state had only one vote. Congress could request funds from the states but could enact no tax of its own without every state's approval, nor could it regulate interstate or overseas commerce.

The proposed government's omissions were notable. The Articles did not provide for an executive branch. Rather, congressional committees oversaw financial, diplomatic, and military affairs. Nor was there a judicial system by which the national government could compel allegiance to its

laws. Finally, the Articles would not become operational until approved by all thirteen state legislatures. Twelve states agreed to the new government by 1779, but Maryland delayed, refusing to sign until all states claiming lands north of the Ohio River turned these territories over to the United States. Maryland lawmakers wanted to keep Virginia and New York from expanding to such a degree that they would dominate the new nation. Beginning in 1781, northwestern claims by individual states were abandoned, and the Articles finally became law in March.

The Articles explicitly reserved to each state "its sovereignty, freedom and independence" and established a form of government in which Americans were citizens of their own states first and of

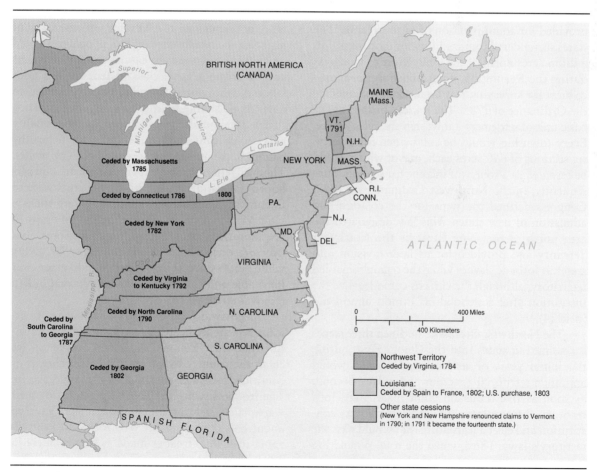

State Claims to Western Lands, and State Cessions to the Federal Government, 1782–1802

Eastern states' surrender of land claims paved the way for new state governments in the West. Georgia was the last state to cede its western lands, in 1802.

the United States second. As John Adams later explained, the Whigs of 1776 never thought of "consolidating this vast Continent under one national Government" but instead erected "a Confederacy of States, each of which must have a separate government." Much as they distrusted the concentration of power in the hands of executives on the state level, Whigs had deep misgivings about a strong national government.

The Articles worked satisfactorily during the war, as the fear of military defeat ensured cooperation from the states. The advent of peace, however, made most politicians complacent and exposed the Confederation's impracticalities. The United States ended the Revolution burdened with difficult problems that could not be solved by a government with so little power.

Yet in its brief history, the Confederation not only achieved American independence but also provided for administration of western lands. The states surrendered responsibility for more than 160 million acres north of the Ohio River to Congress during the Revolution. To establish uniform procedures for surveying this land, Congress enacted the Ordinance of 1785. The law established as the basic unit of settlement a township six miles square. Every township would be subdivided into thirty-six sections of 640 acres each, one of which would be reserved as a source of income for schools. Subsequently, in the Northwest Ordinance of 1787, Congress defined the steps for the creation and admission of new states. This law designated the area north of the Ohio River as the Northwest Territory and provided for its later division into states. It forbade slavery while the region remained a territory, although the citizens could legalize the institution after statehood (as Illinois almost did in 1824).

The Northwest Ordinance outlined three stages for admitting states into the Union. First, during the initial years of settlement, Congress would appoint a territorial governor and judges. Second, as soon as five thousand adult males lived in a territory, the people would write a temporary constitution and elect a legislature that would pass the territory's laws. Third, when the total population reached sixty thousand, the settlers would write a state constitution, which Congress would have to approve before granting statehood.

The Ordinance of 1785 and the Northwest Ordinance became the Confederation's major contributions to American life. These laws set the basic principles for surveying the frontier, allowed territorial government at an early stage of settlement, and provided reasonable standards for statehood. Both measures served as models for organizing territories later acquired west of the Mississippi River. The Northwest Ordinance also established a significant precedent for banning slavery from certain territories. But because Indians, determined to keep out white settlers, controlled virtually the entire region north of the Ohio River, the Confederation's ordinances respecting the Northwest had no immediate effect.

The Northwest Territory seemed to offer enough rich land to guarantee future citizens landownership for centuries. This fact satisfied American republican sentiment, which placed great importance upon opening the West for settlement out of fears that the rapidly growing U.S. population would quickly exhaust the land east of the Appalachians and so create a large class of tenants and poor laborers who would lack the property needed to vote. By poisoning politics through class conflict, such a development would undermine the equality that republicans thought essential for a healthy nation. In the anticipated westward push by whites, Thomas Jefferson and other republican thinkers hoped to avoid conflict with the northwestern Indians by assimilating them into white society. However, since native Americans had no desire to abandon their own culture, republican anxieties over preserving economic opportunity by giving white settlers access to western lands made war inevitable and sowed the seeds of eventual Indian removal farther west.

At postwar treaty negotiations, native Americans repeatedly heard U.S. commissioners scornfully declare: "You are a subdued people . . . we claim the country by conquest." Under threats of continued warfare, the Indians initially gave in. The Iroquois, who lost about 10 percent of their warriors by fighting on the British side, gave up about half their land in New York and Pennsylvania in several treaties made at Fort Stanwix in 1784. Then at the Treaty of Fort McIntosh in 1785, the major northwestern tribes signed away most of present-day Ohio. These settlements outraged most

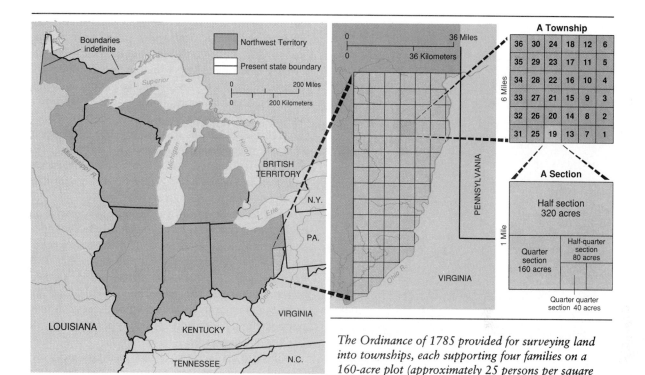

The Northwest, 1785–1787

The Ordinance of 1785 provided for surveying land into townships, each supporting four families on a 160-acre plot (approximately 25 persons per square mile). In 1787 the Northwest Ordinance stipulated that states would ultimately be created in the region.

native Americans, who denied that their negotiators had authority to give up tribal lands. By 1786 the Indians had repudiated both treaties.

The Indians' resistance stemmed in large part from their confidence that the British—still a presence in the West—would provide the arms and ammunition they needed to defy the United States. Britain had refused to abandon seven forts on the nation's northwestern frontier, officially because several state legislatures had blocked the collection of prewar debts owed British merchants and had also refused to compensate loyalists for wartime property losses. In April 1784, however, well before Britain knew about the violation of these provisions of the peace treaty, its colonial office had secretly ordered the governor of Canada to hold those forts. With Indian support, Britain hoped eventually to reestablish its claim to the Northwest Territory.

The Mohawk Joseph Brant emerged as the inspiration behind Indian resistance to white encroachments. Courageous in battle, skillful in diplomacy, and highly educated (he had translated the Bible into Iroquois), Brant became a minor celebrity when he visited King George at London in 1785. At British-held Fort Detroit in 1786, he helped organize the northwestern Indians into a military alliance to exclude white settlers north of the Ohio River. But Brant and his Mohawks, who had relocated beyond American reach in Canada, could not win support from the Iroquois still living in New York. John Sullivan's campaign of 1779 (see above) had left the Six Nations unwilling to risk another such invasion.

The Confederation confronted similar problems in the Southeast, where Spanish officials were goading Indians to harass Anglo-American settlers in Tennessee and Georgia. The Spanish found a brilliant ally in the Creek Alexander McGillivray, a sickly but shrewd diplomat who was three-quarters white. In the Treaty of Augusta (1783), the Creeks had surrendered extensive territory in Georgia that McGillivray intended to regain. Patiently holding back his warriors for three years, McGillivray negotiated a secret treaty with Spain that promised the Creeks weapons so that they

Joseph Brant, *by Wilhelm von Moll Berczy, c. 1800*

In the 1780s several Indian leaders—among them Brant (a Mohawk), Blue Jacket (a Shawnee), and Little Turtle (a Miami)—worked to create a northwestern Indian confederation that would strengthen native American resolve not to bargain with land-hungry whites.

could protect themselves "from the Bears and other fierce Animals." When McGillivray finally unleashed his forces in 1786, he assaulted only occupants on the disputed lands and wisely offered a cease-fire after winning his objective. Eager to avoid voting taxes for a costly war, state politicians let him keep the land.

Besides intriguing with the southeastern Indians, Spain attempted to deny western settlers permission to ship their crops down the Mississippi River to New Orleans, the only port from which they could profitably export their goods. Having negotiated a separate treaty with Britain (see above), Spain had not signed the Peace of Paris, by which Britain promised the United States export rights down the Mississippi, and in 1784 the Spanish closed New Orleans to Anglo-American commerce. To negotiate trading privileges at New Orleans, the United States sent John Jay to Spain. Jay failed to win concessions, but he returned with a treaty that opened up valuable Spanish markets to eastern merchants and renounced Spanish claims to disputed southwestern lands—at the cost, however, of relinquishing American export rights through New Orleans for twenty years. Although Congress rejected this Jay-Gardoqui Treaty in 1786, the treaty infuriated westerners and southerners, whose interests seemed to have been sacrificed to benefit northern commerce.

The Confederation was no more successful at prying trade concessions from Britain. Before Independence almost 60 percent of northern exports had gone to the British West Indies, but after 1783 Britain closed West Indian ports to the Yankee merchant marine. The loss of these island markets contributed mightily to an economic depression that gripped the nation, and especially its seaports, in 1784 (see Chapter 6).

Next to its lack of success in diplomacy, the Confederation's greatest failure lay in its inability to prevent national bankruptcy. Winning the war had cost the nation's six hundred thousand taxpayers a staggering $160 million, a sum that exceeded by 2,400 percent the taxes raised to pay for the Seven Years' War. To finance the War for Independence, which cost far more than the nation could immediately collect through taxation, the government had borrowed funds from abroad and printed its own paper money, called Continentals. Lack of public faith in the government destroyed 98 percent of the value of the Continentals from 1776 to 1781, an inflationary disaster that gave rise to the expression "not worth a Continental."

Faced with a desperate financial situation, Congress turned to a wealthy, self-made Philadelphia merchant, Robert Morris, who in 1781 became the nation's superintendent of finance. Morris proposed that the states authorize the collection of a national import duty of 5 percent to finance the congressional budget and to guarantee interest payments on the war debt. Because the Articles stipulated that every state had to approve the levying of national taxes, the import duty failed to pass in 1782 when Rhode Island alone rejected it.

Hoping to panic the country into creating a regular source of national revenue, Morris and New York congressman Alexander Hamilton then engi-

Robert Morris

Morris assumed almost dictatorial powers over the nation's finances in his role as superintendent of finance. As a delegate to the Philadelphia Convention in 1787, he would support a strong federal government.

neered a dangerous gamble known later as the Newburgh Conspiracy. In 1783 the two men secretly persuaded the army's officers (then encamped at Newburgh, New York) into bluffing that they would mutiny unless the treasury obtained the taxation authority needed to raise their pay, which was months in arrears. But George Washington, learning of the conspiracy before it was carried out, ended the plot by delivering a speech that appealed to his officers' honor and left them unwilling to proceed. Although Morris never intended that a mutiny actually occur, his willingness to take such a risk demonstrated the country's perilous financial straits.

When peace came in 1783, Morris found it impossible to secure adequate funding for the United States. That year, Congress sent another tax measure to the states, but once again a single legislature, this time New York's, blocked it. From then on, the states steadily decreased their contributions to Congress. By the late 1780s, the states had fallen behind nearly 80 percent in providing the

funds that Congress requested to operate the government and honor the national debt.

In sum, the Articles of Confederation had achieved nothing significant except the ordinances of 1785 and 1787. The government's disunity and financial embarrassments invited both foreign aggression and attacks by western Indians on frontier settlers. "I see one head gradually turning into thirteen," George Washington soberly commented in 1780; "I see the powers of Congress declining too fast." By 1787 his apprehensions had become a reality.

Shays's Rebellion

But for an outbreak of violence in Massachusetts late in 1786, the Confederation might have tottered on indefinitely. Since 1784 a recession had gripped Massachusetts after the state had lost its best market, the British West Indies. To worsen matters, the state legislature voted early in 1786 to pay off its Revolutionary debt in three years. This ill-considered policy necessitated a huge tax hike that exceeded the ability of many marginal farmers to pay. The plight of Massachusetts farmers was especially severe in the western counties, where agriculture was least profitable. Late in 1786 farmer and former Revolutionary War officer Daniel Shays led some two thousand angry men in an attempt to shut down the courts in three of these western counties, and thereby stop sheriffs' auctions for unpaid taxes and prevent foreclosures on farm mortgages. Although routed by the state militia after several skirmishes, Shays's followers won control of the Massachusetts legislature in 1787, cut taxes, and secured a pardon for their leader.

Shays's supporters had limited objectives, were dispersed with relatively little bloodshed, and never seriously posed the danger of anarchy. But his uprising symbolized for critics of the weak national government the Republic's fragility under the Confederation. By threatening to seize weapons from a federal arsenal at Springfield, Massachusetts, the Shaysites had unintentionally reminded nationalists how pitifully defenseless the United States had become. At the same time, rumors were flying that the Spanish had offered export rights at New Orleans to westerners if they would secede from the Union. Nationalists wondered whether Shays's Rebellion might trigger secessionist movements elsewhere. Washington had earlier worried that one head was turning into thirteen, but now it seemed possible that one might turn into thirty or forty separate heads.

Not everyone shared these apprehensions. In contrast to New England, the mid-Atlantic and southern states were emerging from a depression, thanks to rising tobacco and food exports to Europe. Taxpayers in these sections, moreover, were paying off war debts easily. Further, the regions' numerous small farming families, living in relatively isolated communities and trading largely with neighbors, were in quiet times widely indifferent to national politics. But the minority of people intensely dissatisfied with the Confederation was growing. Urban artisans, for example, hoped for a stronger national government that would impose a uniformly high tariff and thereby protect them from foreign competition. Merchants and shippers wanted a government powerful enough to secure trading privileges for them, while land speculators and western settlers preferred a government capable of pursuing a more activist policy against the Indians. To these groups were now added those political leaders who saw in Shays's Rebellion a sign of worse things to come.

Shortly before the outbreak of the rebellion, delegates from five states had assembled at Annapolis, Maryland. They had intended to discuss means of promoting interstate commerce but instead called for a general convention to propose amendments to the Articles of Confederation. Accepting their suggestion, Congress asked the states to appoint delegations to meet in Philadelphia.

The Philadelphia Convention

In May 1787 fifty-five delegates from every state but Rhode Island began gathering at the Pennsylvania State House in Philadelphia, later known as Independence Hall. Among them were figures of established reputation like George Washington, Benjamin Franklin, John Dickinson, and Robert Morris, as well as talented newcomers such as Alexander Hamilton and James Madison. Most were wealthy and in their thirties or forties, and nineteen owned slaves. More than half had legal training.

The convention immediately closed its sessions to the press and the public, kept no *official* journal, and even appointed chaperones to accompany the

aged and talkative Franklin to dinner parties lest he disclose details of what was happening. Although these measures opened the members of the convention to the charge of acting undemocratically and conspiratorially, the delegates thought secrecy essential to ensure themselves freedom of debate without fear of criticism from home.

The delegates shared a "continental" or "nationalist" perspective, instilled through their extended involvement with the national government. Thirty-nine had sat in Congress, where they had seen the Articles' defects firsthand. These delegates had outgrown the localism that was typical of state politicians and had come to appreciate how much Americans were alike. In the postwar years, they had become convinced that unless the national government were freed from the state legislatures' control, the country would fall victim to foreign aggression or simply disintegrate.

The convention faced two basic issues. The first was whether to tinker with the Articles (as the state legislatures had formally instructed the delegates to do) or to scrap the Articles and draw up an entirely new frame of government. The second fundamental question was how to balance the conflicting interests of large and small states. James Madison of Virginia, who had entered Congress in 1780 at twenty-nine, proposed an answer to each issue. Despite his youth and almost frail build, Madison commanded enormous respect for his profound knowledge of history and the passionate intensity that he brought to debates.

Madison's Virginia Plan, introduced by his fellow Virginian Edmund Randolph in late May, boldly called for the establishment of a national government rather than a federation of states. Madison's blueprint gave Congress virtually unrestricted rights of legislation and taxation, the power to veto any state law, and authority to use military force against the states. As delegate Charles Pinckney of South Carolina immediately saw, the Virginia Plan was designed "to abolish the State Govern[men]ts altogether." The Virginia Plan specified a bicameral legislature and fixed representation in both houses of Congress proportionally to each state's population. The voters would elect the lower house, which would then choose delegates to the upper chamber from nominations submitted by the legislatures. Both houses would jointly name the country's president and judges.

The Assembly Room In Independence Hall

Much history was made in this room. The Declaration of Independence was signed here in 1776, and the constitutional-convention delegates met in this chamber in 1787.

Madison's scheme aroused immediate opposition, however, especially his call for the states to be represented according to their population—a provision highly favorable to his own Virginia. On June 15 William Paterson of New Jersey offered a counterproposal, the so-called New Jersey Plan, which recommended a single-chamber congress in which each state had an equal vote, just as under the Articles.

Despite their differences over representation, Paterson's and Madison's proposals alike would have strengthened the national government at the states' expense. No less than Madison, Paterson wished to empower Congress to raise taxes, regulate interstate commerce, and use military force against the states. The New Jersey Plan, in fact, was the first to define congressional laws and treaties as the "supreme law of the land"; it would also have established courts to force reluctant states and their citizens to accept these measures.

The New Jersey Plan was highly significant because it exposed the convention's great stumbling block: the question of representation. The Virginia Plan would have given the four largest states a majority in both houses. The New Jersey Plan would have allowed the seven smallest states, which included just 25 percent of all Americans, to control Congress. By July 2 the convention had arrived "at a full stop," as Roger Sherman of Connecticut noted. To end the impasse, the delegates

assigned a member from each state to a "grand committee" dedicated to compromise. The panel adopted a proposal offered earlier by the Connecticut delegation: an equal vote for each state in the upper house and proportional voting in the lower house. Madison and the Virginians doggedly fought this so-called Connecticut Compromise, but they were voted down on July 17. The convention overcame the remaining hurdles rather easily in the next two months.

As finally approved on September 17, 1787, the Constitution of the United States was an extraordinary document, and not merely because it successfully reconciled the conflicting interests of the large and small states. Out of hard bargaining among different states' representatives emerged the Constitution's delicate balance between the desire of nearly all delegates for a stronger national government and their fear that governments tended to grow despotic. The Constitution augmented national authority in several ways. Although it did not incorporate Madison's proposal to give Congress a veto over state laws, it vested in Congress the authority to lay and collect taxes, to regulate commerce among the states (interstate commerce), and to conduct diplomacy. States could no longer coin money, interfere with contracts and debts, or tax interstate commerce. All acts and treaties of the United States became "the supreme law of the land." All state officials had to swear to uphold the

James Madison

Although one of the Philadelphia Convention's youngest delegates, Madison of Virginia was among its most politically astute. He played a central role in the Constitution's adoption.

Constitution, even against acts of their own states. The national government could use military force against any state.

These provisions added up to a complete abandonment of the principle on which the Articles of Confederation had rested: that the United States was a federation of independent republics known as states, with all authority concentrated in their legislatures. Yet still concerned about too strong a federal system, the Constitution's framers devised two ways to restrain the power of the new national government. First, they established three distinct branches—executive, legislative, and judicial—within the national government; and second, they designed a system of checks and balances to prevent any one branch from dominating the other two. The framers systematically applied to the national government the principle of a *functional* separation of powers, an idea that had been evolving in the states since about 1780. In the bicameral Congress, states' equal representation in the Senate was offset by the proportional representation, by population, in the House; and each chamber could

block hasty measures demanded by the other. Further, where the state constitutions had deliberately weakened the executive, the Constitution gave the president the power to veto acts of Congress; but to prevent capricious use of the veto, Congress could override the president by a two-thirds majority in each house. The president could conduct diplomacy, but only the Senate could ratify treaties. The president named his cabinet, but only with Senate approval. The president and all his appointees could be removed from office by a joint vote of Congress, but only for "high crimes," not for political disagreements.

To further ensure the independence of each branch, the Constitution provided that the members of one branch would not choose those of another, except for judges, whose independence was protected by lifetime appointment. For example, the president was to be selected by an electoral college, whose members the states would select as their legislatures saw fit. The state legislatures also elected the members of the Senate, while the election of delegates to the House of Representatives was achieved by popular vote.

In addition to checks and balances, the founders improvised a novel form of federalism—a system of shared power and dual lawmaking by the national and state governments—in order to place limits on central authority. Not only did the state legislatures have a key role in electing the president and senators, but the Constitution could be amended by the votes of three-fourths of the state legislatures. Thus the convention devised a form of government that differed significantly from Madison's plan to establish a "consolidated" national government entirely independent of, and superior to, the states.

A key assumption behind federalism was that the national government would limit its activities to foreign affairs, national defense, regulating commerce, and coining money. The states otherwise had full freedom to act autonomously on purely internal matters. Regarding slavery in particular, each state retained full authority.

The Philadelphia Convention treated slavery as a political, not a moral issue; it allowed three-fifths of all slaves to be counted for congressional representation (a formula used since 1783 to assess state contributions to Congress). The Constitution forbade any state's people to prevent the return of runaway slaves to another state. The only cases in which the Constitution interfered with slavery were such national matters as overseas commerce and (presumably) administration of the territories (since the Constitution did not repudiate the Northwest Ordinance's law on slavery). The Constitution explicitly permitted Congress to ban the importation of slaves after 1808.

While leaving much authority to the states, the Constitution established a national government clearly superior to the states in several spheres, and it utterly abandoned the notion of a federation of virtually independent states. Having thus strengthened national authority, the convention had to face the issue of ratification. For two reasons, it seemed unwise to submit the Constitution to state legislatures for ratification. First, the framers realized that the state legislatures would reject the Constitution, which shrank their power relative to the national government. Second, most of the framers repudiated the idea—implicit in ratification by existing state legislatures—that the states composed the foundation of the new government. The opening words of the Constitution—"We the People of the United States"—underlined the delegates' growing conviction that the government had to be based on the consent of the American people themselves, "the fountain of all power" in Madison's words.

In the end, the Philadelphia Convention provided for the Constitution's ratification by special state conventions composed of delegates elected by the people. Approval by only nine such conventions would put the new government in operation. Because any state refusing to ratify would remain under the Articles, the possibility existed that the country might divide into two nations.

Under the Constitution the framers expected the nation's "natural aristocracy" to continue exercising political leadership; but did they also intend to rein in the democratic currents set in motion by the Revolution? In one respect they did, by curtailing what most nationalists considered the excessive power of popularly elected legislatures. But the Constitution made no attempt to control faction and disorder by suppressing liberty—a "remedy," wrote Madison, that would be "worse than the disease." The framers did provide for one crucial democratic element in the new government, the House of Representatives. Equally important,

the Constitution recognized the American people as the ultimate source of political legitimacy. Moreover, by making the Constitution flexible and amendable (though not easily amendable) and by dividing political power among competing branches of government, the framers made it possible for the national government to be slowly democratized in ways unforeseen in 1787, without turning into a tyranny of ideologues or temporary majorities. Madison eloquently expressed the founders' intention of controlling the dangers inherent in any society:

> *If men were angels, no government would be necessary. If angels were to govern men, neither external nor internal controls on government would be necessary. In framing a government which is to be administered by men over men, the great difficulty lies in this: You must first enable the government to control the governed; and in the next place, oblige it to control itself. A dependence on the people is no doubt the primary control on the government; but experience has taught mankind the necessity of external precautions.*

Ratification

The Constitution's supporters began the campaign for ratification without significant national support. Most Americans had expected that the Philadelphia Convention would offer only limited amendments to the Articles. A majority therefore hesitated to adopt the radical restructuring of government that had been proposed. Undaunted, the Constitution's friends moved decisively to marshal political support. In a clever stroke, they called themselves Federalists, a term that implied that the Constitution balanced the relationship between the national and state governments and thereby lessened the opposition of those hostile to a centralization of national authority.

The Constitution's opponents commonly became known as Antifederalists. This negative-sounding title probably hurt them, for it did not convey the crux of their argument against the Constitution—that it was not "federalist" at all since it failed to balance the power of the national and state governments. Indeed, many Antifederalists doubted whether any such balance was possible. In their view, either the national or the state gov-

George Mason

Mason fought the Constitution's ratification, insisting on the inclusion of a bill of rights. He deeply opposed the delegates' compromise on the slave trade, a practice that he deemed "disgraceful to mankind."

ernments would dominate the Republic; no even division of power could be achieved. By augmenting national authority, Antifederalists maintained, the Constitution would ultimately doom the states.

The Antifederalist arguments expressed a deep-seated Anglo-American suspicion of concentrated power. Unquestionably, the Constitution gave the national government unprecedented authority in an age when almost all writers on politics taught that the sole means of preventing despotism was to restrain the power of government officials. Compared to a national government, which inevitably would be distant from the people in an era when news traveled slowly, the state governments struck Antifederalists as far more responsive to the popular will. "The vast Continent of America cannot be long subjected to a Democracy if consolidated into one Government. You might as well attempt to rule Hell by Prayer," wrote a New England Antifederalist. True, the framers had

devised a system of checks and balances to guard against tyranny, but no one could be certain that the untried scheme would work. For all its checks and balances, in addition, the Constitution nowhere contained ironclad guarantees that the new government would protect the liberties of individuals or the states. The absence of a bill of rights made an Antifederalist of Madison's nationalist ally and fellow Virginian, George Mason, the author of the first such state bill in 1776.

Although the Antifederalists advanced some formidable arguments, they rarely matched their opponents in vigor. The intellectual horizons of the Antifederalists usually were bounded by the state politics with which they were familiar; few of them had acquired the national outlook that service in the Continental Army or Congress had imparted to their opponents. The Antifederalists could count among their number the Virginia firebrand Patrick Henry but no one with Madison's learning, Hamilton's genius, or the national prestige of Washington and Franklin. While their antagonists carefully planned how to elect sympathetic delegates to the ratifying conventions, the Antifederalists failed to create a sense of urgency among their supporters, assuming incorrectly that a large majority would rally to them. Only one-quarter of the voters turned out to elect delegates to the state ratifying conventions, however, and most had been mobilized by Federalists.

Federalist delegates prevailed in eight conventions between December 1787 and May 1788, in all cases except one by margins of at least two-thirds. Such lopsided votes usually reflected the Federalists' greater organizational skills compared to their opponents, rather than the degree of popular support for the Constitution. Advocates of the new plan of government did indeed ram through approval in some states "before it can be digested or deliberately considered" (in the words of a Pennsylvania Antifederalist). Only Rhode Island and North Carolina rejected the Constitution and thus refused to join the new United States.

But unless Virginia and New York ratified, the new government would not be workable. Antifederalist sentiment in both states (and elsewhere) ran high among small farmers, who saw the Constitution as a scheme favoring city dwellers and monied interests. Prominent political leaders in these two states called for refusing ratification, includ-

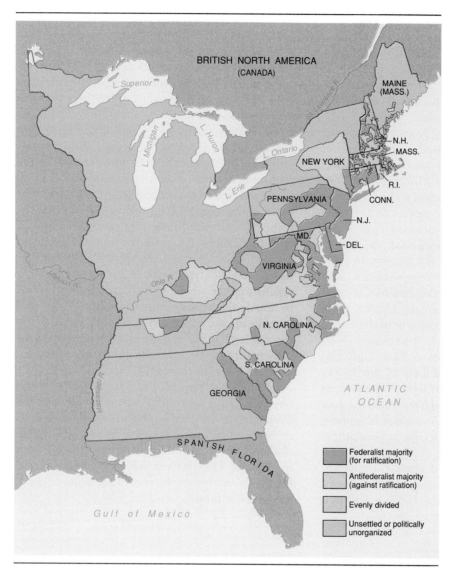

Federalists and Anti-federalist Strongholds, 1787–1790

Antifederalist support came from interior regions where geographic isolation bred a narrow, localistic perspective. Federalists drew their primary backing from densely populated areas along major transportation routes, where trade, mobility, and frequent contact with persons in other states encouraged a nationalistic identity. Some frontier regions, too, among them Georgia and western Virginia, voted for a stronger central government that would push back the Indians or the Spanish.

Map legend:
- Federalist majority (for ratification)
- Antifederalist majority (against ratification)
- Evenly divided
- Unsettled or politically unorganized

ing New York governor George Clinton and Virginia's Richard Henry Lee, George Mason, Patrick Henry, and future president James Monroe.

The Constitution became the law of the land on June 21, 1788, when the ninth state, New Hampshire, ratified by the close vote of 57–47. At that moment debate was still under way in the Virginia convention. The Federalists won crucial support from the representatives of the Alleghany counties—modern West Virginia—who wanted a strong national government capable of ending Indian raids across the Ohio River. Western Vir-

ginians' votes, combined with James Madison's logic and the growing support for the Constitution among tidewater planters, proved too much for Henry's spellbinding oratory. On June 25 the Virginia delegates ratified by a narrow 53 percent majority.

The struggle was even closer and more hotly contested in New York. Antifederalists had solid control of the state convention and would probably have voted down the Constitution, but then news arrived of New Hampshire's and Virginia's ratification. The Federalist forces, led by Alexander Hamilton and John Jay, began hinting strongly that if the convention voted to reject, pro-Federalist New York City would secede from the state and join the Union alone, leaving upstate New York a landlocked enclave. When a number of Antifederalist delegates took alarm at this threat and switched sides, New York ratified on July 26, by a 30–27 vote.

So the Antifederalists went down in defeat, and they did not survive as a political movement. Yet they left an important legacy. At their insistence, the Virginia, New York, and Massachusetts conventions ratified the Constitution with the accompanying request that the new charter be amended to include a bill of rights protecting Americans' basic freedoms. So widespread was the public demand for a bill of rights that it became an inevitable item on the new government's agenda, even as the states were choosing members of Congress and as presidential electors were unanimously designating George Washington president of the United States, with John Adams as vice president.

Antifederalists' objections in New York also stimulated a response in the form of one of the greatest works of political analysis ever written: *The Federalist,* a series of eighty-five newspaper essays penned by John Jay, Alexander Hamilton, and James Madison. *The Federalist* papers probably had little or no influence on the voting in the New York State convention. Rather, their importance lay in providing a glimpse of the framers' intentions in designing the Constitution, and thus powerfully shaping the American philosophy of government. The Constitution, insisted *The Federalist*'s authors, had a twofold purpose: first, to defend the minority's rights against majority tyranny; and second, to prevent a stubborn minority from blocking well-considered measures that the majority believed necessary for the national interest. Critics, argued *The Federalist,* had no reason to fear that the Constitution would allow a single economic or regional interest to dominate. In the profoundest essay in the series, *Federalist* No. 10, Madison rejected the Antifederalist argument that establishing a republic for a nation as large as the United States would unleash a chaotic contest for power and ultimately leave the majority exploited by a minority. "Extend the sphere," Madison insisted, "and . . . you make it less probable that a majority of the whole will have a common motive to invade the rights of other citizens, . . . [or will be able to] act in unison with each other." The country's very size and diversity would theoretically neutralize the attempts of factions to manipulate unwise laws through Congress.

Madison's analysis was far too optimistic, however. As the Antifederalists predicted, the Constitution afforded enormous scope for special interests to influence the government. The great challenge for Madison's generation would be how to maintain a government that would provide equal benefits to all but at the same time accord special privileges to none.

Conclusion

The entry of North Carolina into the Union in late 1789 and of Rhode Island in May 1790 marked the final triumph of the nationalism born of the War for Independence. The devastating eight-year conflict swept up half of all men of military age and made casualties of one-fifth of these. Never before had such a large part of the population been called on to make sacrifices in a common cause of this magnitude.

The collective experience of fighting together as countrymen made many veterans self-consciously American. After several years in the army, General Nathaniel Greene of Rhode Island condemned the "prejudices" of those with "local attachments." "I feel the cause and not the place," Greene said; "I would as soon go to Virginia [to fight] as stay here [New England]." The distractions of peace almost allowed this sentiment to evaporate, but the Constitution offered the firmest proof that a growing number of Americans now felt comfortable viewing themselves as a common people rather than citizens of allied states.

CHRONOLOGY

1770 Yearly Meeting of New England Quakers prohibits slaveowning—first American ban on slaveholding.

1775 Virginia governor Lord Dunmore promises freedom to any slave assisting in the restoration of royal authority.

First white settlement in Kentucky.

Mercy Otis Warren, *The Group.*

1776 British troops evacuate Boston.

British defeat American forces under George Washington in fighting around New York City.

American victory in Battle of Trenton.

1777 American victory in Battle of Princeton.

British general John Burgoyne surrenders at Saratoga.

Battle of Brandywine Creek; British occupy Philadelphia.

British general William Howe defeats Washington at Battle of Germantown.

1778 France formally recognizes the United States.

France declares war on Britain.

Philadelphia evacuated by British general Henry Clinton; Battle of Monmouth Court House (New Jersey).

George Rogers Clark captures Kaskakia (Ill.), Cahokia (Ill.), and Vincennes (Ind.).

British occupy Savannah.

1779 Spain declares war on Britain.

George Rogers Clark's recapture of Fort Vincennes.

1780 British seize Charleston.

Dutch Republic declares war on Britain.

1781 Articles of Confederation become law.

Battle of Yorktown; British general Charles Cornwallis surrenders.

1782 British evacuate Savannah.

Paris peace negotiations begin.

1783 Peace of Paris.

1784 Spain closes New Orleans to American trade.

1785 Ordinance of 1785.

Treaty of Fort McIntosh.

1786 Congress rejects Jay-Gardoqui Treaty.

Fort Detroit Indian conference leads to resumption of Indian warfare.

Virginia adopts Thomas Jefferson's Statute of Religious Freedom.

1786– Shays's Rebellion in Massachusetts.
1787

1787 Northwest Ordinance.

Philadelphia Convention; federal Constitution signed.

1788 James Madison, Alexander Hamilton, and John Jay, *The Federalist.*

Federal Constitution becomes law.

1792 Mary Wollstonecraft, *Vindication of the Rights of Women.*

For Further Reading

Jack P. Greene, ed., *The American Revolution: Its Character and Limits* (1987). Leading scholars' analysis of how Americans dealt with the problem of applying their political ideals to an imperfect society without endangering the nation's survival.

Don Higginbotham, *The War of American Independence: Military Attitudes, Policies, and Practice, 1763–1789* (1971). An excellent examination of how military policies and events affected society and reflected contemporary attitudes toward war.

Linda K. Kerber, *Women of the Republic: Intellect and Ideology in Revolutionary America* (1980). A pathbreaking study of how the Revolution affected women's legal and social status.

Robert Middlekauff, *The Glorious Cause: The American Revolution, 1763–1789* (1982). The best comprehensive account of military and political developments through the Philadelphia Convention.

Benjamin Quarles, *The Negro in the American Revolution* (1961). An authoritative study of blacks' role in the War for Independence and the struggle's consequences for them.

Charles Royster, *A Revolutionary People at War: The Continental Army and American Character* (1980). An illuminating analysis of how Revolutionary Americans created and fought in an army and what this reveals about their emotions, attitudes, and ideals.

Gordon Wood, *The Creation of the American Republic, 1776–1787* (1969). The most comprehensive treatment of the evolution of American political thought from the creation of the first state governments to the Philadelphia Convention.

Additional Bibliography

The Military Struggle

Wallace Brown, *The King's Friends: The Composition and Motives of the American Loyalist Claimants* (1965); Richard Buel, Jr., *Dear Liberty: Connecticut's Mobilization for the Revolutionary War* (1980); Robert M. Calhoon, *The Loyalists in Revolutionary America, 1760–1781* (1973); E. Wayne Carp, *To Starve the Army at Pleasure: Continental Army Administration and American Political Culture, 1775–1783* (1984); Lawrence D. Cress, *Citizens in Arms: The Army and the Militia in American Society to the War of 1812* (1982); Jonathan R. Dull, *A Diplomatic History of the American Revolution* (1985); William M. Fowler, *Rebels Under Sail: The American Navy During the Revolution* (1976); Barbara Graymont, *The Iroquois in the American Revolution* (1972); Ira D. Gruber, *The Howe Brothers and the American Revolution* (1972); Ronald Hoffman and Peter J. Albert, eds., *Arms and Independence: The Military Character of the American Revolution* (1984); Ronald Hoffman and Thad W. Tate, eds., *An Uncivil War: The Southern Backcountry During the American Revolution* (1985); James K. Martin and Mark E. Lender, *A Respectable Army: The Military Origins of the Republic, 1763–1789* (1982); William H. Nelson, *The American Tory* (1961); James O'Donnell, *Southern Indians in the American Revolution* (1973); Howard H. Peckham, *The Toll of Independence: Engagements and Battle Casualties of the American Revolution* (1974); John Shy, *A People Numerous and Armed: Reflections on the Military Struggle for American Independence* (1976); Paul H. Smith, *Loyalists and Redcoats: A Study in British Revolutionary Policy* (1964); Jack M. Sosin, *The Revolutionary Frontier, 1763–1783* (1967).

Revolutionary Society

Robert A. Becker, *Revolution, Reform, and the Politics of American Taxation, 1763–1783* (1980); Ira Berlin and Ronald Hoffman, eds., *Slavery and Freedom in the Age of the American Revolution* (1983); Joy Day Buel and Richard Buel, Jr., *The Way of Duty: A Woman and Her Family in Revolutionary America* (1984); Jeffrey J. Crow and Larry E. Tise, *The Southern Experience in the American Revolution* (1978); Linda Grant DePauw, *Founding Mothers: Women in America in the Revolutionary Era* (1975); Peter C. Hoffer, *Revolution and Regeneration: Life Cycle and the Historical Vision of the Generation of 1776* (1983); Rhys Isaac, *The Transformation of Virginia, 1740–1790* (1982); Michael Kammen, *A Season of Youth: The American Revolution and the Historical Imagination* (1978); Duncan J. MacLeod, *Slavery, Race, and the American Revolution* (1974); Jackson Turner Main, *The Social Structure of Revolutionary America* (1965); John E. Selby, *The Revolution in Virginia, 1775–1783* (1988); Kenneth Silverman, *A Cultural History of the American Revolution: Painting, Music, Literature, and the Theatre in the Colonies and the United States from the Treaty of Paris to the Inauguration of George Washington, 1763–1789* (1976).

Politics and Constitutionalism

Willi Paul Adams, *The First American Constitutions: Republican Ideology and the Making of the State Constitutions in the Revolutionary Era* (1980); Richard Beeman et al., eds., *Beyond Confederation: Origins of the Constitution and American National Identity* (1987); Van Beck Hall, *Politics Without Parties: Massachusetts,*

1780–1791 (1972); Donald S. Lutz, *Popular Consent and Popular Control: Whig Political Theory in the Early State Constitutions* (1980); Forrest McDonald, *E Pluribus Unum: The Formation of the American Republic, 1776–1790* (1965), and *Novus Ordo Seclorum: The Intellectual Origins of the Constitution* (1985); Jackson Turner Main, *The Antifederalists: Critics of the Constitution, 1781–1788* (1961), and *Political Parties Before the Constitution* (1973); Anne M. Ousterhout, *A State Divided: Opposition in Pennsylvania to the American Revolution* (1987); John G. A. Pocock, *The Machiavellian Moment: Florentine Political Thought and the Atlantic Republican Tradition* (1975); Norman K. Risjord, *Chesapeake Politics, 1781–1800* (1978); David P. Szatmary, *Shays' Rebellion: The Making of an Agrarian Insurrection* (1980).

Biographies

James T. Flexner, *Washington: The Indispensable Man* (1974); Don Higginbotham, *Daniel Morgan: Revolutionary Rifleman* (1961); Isabel Thompson Kelsay, *Joseph Brant, 1743–1807: Man of Two Worlds* (1984); Ralph Ketcham, *Benjamin Franklin* (1966), and *James Madison: A Biography* (1971); Dumas Malone, *Jefferson and the Rights of Man* (1951); David Nelson, *Anthony Wayne, Soldier of the Early Republic* (1985), and *William Alexander, Lord Stirling* (1987); Charles Royster, *Light-Horse Harry Lee and the Legacy of the American Revolution* (1981); George T. Thayer, *Nathaniel Greene: Strategist of the American Revolution* (1960); Carl J. Vipperman, *The Rise of Rawlins Lowndes, 1721–1800* (1978); William B. Willcox, *Portrait of a General: Sir Henry Clinton in the War of Independence* (1964).

CHAPTER 6

Launching the New Republic,
1789–1800

Early in 1789 a mysterious stranger from New Orleans named André Fagot appeared in Nashville, Tennessee. Fagot was officially there to talk business with local merchants, but in reality he was a Spanish agent sent to stir up discontent. For years, westerners had agonized over the American government's failure to win Spanish permission for them to export crops through New Orleans, without which their settlements would never flourish. Fagot made westerners a tempting offer—unrestricted export privileges at New Orleans, which promised to ensure them prosperity. But in return, they would have to request that Spain annex Tennessee to its Louisiana colony.

Fagot found many local residents willing to discuss becoming Spanish subjects. One of his more enthusiastic contacts was a young lawyer recently arrived from the Carolinas. Aware that poor communities could support only poor lawyers, the Carolinian was drawn irresistibly to the plot. Learning that Spain would give valuable land grants in the lower Mississippi Valley to anyone who renounced United States citizenship, the lawyer began visiting Spanish Louisiana regularly to investigate settling there. Fagot probably placed little reliance on this brash conspirator, who had a wild temper and a reputation for gambling and drinking. In 1789 he seemed just another frontier opportunist. But in little more than a quarter-century, the Nashville lawyer would become the country's most popular hero and the symbol of American nationalism. He was Andrew Jackson.

The fact that even Jackson could talk secession to Spanish agents underscores the fragility of the United States in 1789, one year after the Constitution's ratification. North Carolina (which controlled Tennessee territory) and Rhode Island had not yet joined the Union. Westerners appeared to be abandoning the new government. The United States faced the prospect that foreign powers would slice off western territory. The nation could conceivably have disintegrated into several smaller republics, much as Latin America would splinter into numerous nations after rebelling against Spain in the early nineteenth century.

Few incoming American presidents have confronted as many grave problems as did George Washington in 1789. The West might well have separated from the Union. Indians and frontier whites fought endlessly. Foreign restrictions on U.S. exports threatened the nation's economy. The treasury was bankrupt, and the government's credit a shambles.

The most serious obstacles facing the United States in 1789 were overcome by the time Washington's second administration ended in 1797, but only at the price of unleashing fiercely emotional party divisions among citizens. By 1798 a sense of crisis gripped the nation. The party in power resorted to political repression. Fearing that a fair election might be impossible and that the national government was slipping into despotism, the opposing party desperately tried to justify the right of state legislatures to veto federal laws. In the election of 1800, each side damned the other in increasingly irresponsible rhetoric. Only when the election had been settled—by the narrowest of margins—could it be said that the United States had managed to avoid dissolution and preserve civil liberties for its citizens.

The Fragile New Nation

By 1789 six years had elapsed since Britain had recognized U.S. independence, but for many Americans peace had brought problems rather than prosperity. Restrictions on export markets endangered the livelihoods of innumerable farmers, sailors, and merchants. Foreign efforts to prevent Americans from settling the frontier frustrated influential land speculators and toiling pioneers. The Confederation's default on the national debt had injured tens of thousands of Revolutionary creditors from all levels of society by delaying their compensation, and even after 1788 there was no guarantee that the new government would honor their claims fully. All these conditions had helped convince prominent Americans that a new constitution and a new government were desperately needed. But Antifederalists had not disappeared from public life, and supporters of the new government faced enormous pressure to succeed.

In the first two decades under the Constitution, it proved impossible for the government to devise policies that would provide equal benefits throughout the land. The different regions' interests varied greatly and often conflicted. Other fissures also became apparent in American society: among blacks, Indians, and whites; between emerging capitalists and wage-earning workers; above all, among citizens who interpreted the republican ideology of the Revolutionary years in different ways.

Regional and ideological conflicts would split the new nation's Congress, first into factions and then into hostile parties—just what the Constitution's framers had hoped to avoid. And political polarization would also bring into focus something else that few members of the Philadelphia Convention had favored: a rising demand for a *democratic* republic.

The West

Most U.S. territory from the Appalachians to the Mississippi River belonged to those peoples whom the Declaration of Independence had condemned as "merciless Indian savages." Divided into more than eighty tribes and numbering perhaps 150,000

persons in 1789, these native Americans were struggling to preserve their way of life. During the Revolutionary War, Anglo-Americans had dealt the Iroquois and Cherokees a punishing series of blows. But most Indians, although bloodied, continued to resist threats to their land. Tribes in the Ohio Valley formed a defensive confederacy in 1786 (see Chapter 5). The powerful southeastern tribes refused to acknowledge American rule. Great Britain openly backed Indian resistance in the Northwest, and Spain armed the southeastern native Americans. As the Constitution took effect, the federal government faced the prospect of having to force Britain and Spain to abandon the Indians and then of negotiating land purchases from them.

Confronting the inland Indians were approximately two hundred thousand whites and blacks who had hacked homesteads out of the raw wilderness. Although their ranks included some well-to-do planters and merchants, most families found life exceedingly harsh. Above all, frontier settlers were isolated and vulnerable. By 1786 a succession of Indian war parties spread death, destruction, and anxiety from Pennsylvania to Georgia. In Kentucky alone, where just 74,000 settlers lived in 1790, more than 1,500 pioneers were killed or captured in Indian raids from 1784 to 1790—a casualty rate twice as high as that of the Revolutionary War. Frontier people retaliated ruthlessly. "The people of Kentucky," wrote an army officer trying to end the fighting, "will carry on private expeditions against the Indians and kill them whenever they meet them, and I do not believe there is a jury in all Kentucky will punish a man for it."

Whites could conquer the Indians only by mustering overwhelming military force and threatening entire tribes with starvation by ravaging their villages and stocks of winter food. Such large-scale operations lay beyond the capability of poorly equipped, ill-trained frontier militia. This fact became obvious in 1786, when a lack of supplies forced 1,200 Kentuckians marching under George Rogers Clark against the Indians of the Great Lakes region to abandon their campaign. If Clark, who had prevailed against enormous odds during the

Revolution, found himself thus overwhelmed, clearly only federal forces could defeat the Indians. But in 1789 the U.S. Army's total strength was 672 soldiers, less than half the number of warriors that the northwestern Indian confederation could raise. Little wonder that the weakness of the U.S. government caused many frontier folk to despair—and to decide that the United States had forfeited their loyalty. Clark spoke for untold Kentuckians in 1788 when he declared that "no property or person is safe under a government so weak as that of the United States."

Nevertheless, militia raids across the Ohio River did force the Miamis, Shawnees, and Delawares gradually to evacuate southern Indiana and Ohio. These Indians' withdrawal northward, toward the Great Lakes, tempted whites to make their first settlements in what is now Ohio. In the spring of 1788, about fifty New Englanders sailed down the Ohio River in a bullet-proof barge named the *Mayflower* and founded the town of Marietta. That same year, some Pennsylvanians and New Jerseyites established a second community north of the Ohio, on the site of modern-day Cincinnati. By then the contest for the Ohio Valley was nearing a decisive stage.

Westerners felt a special bitterness toward the British. The recent enemy's continued occupation of seven forts on American soil seemed the mainspring of the unceasing border fighting. Royal diplomats justified this violation of the Peace of Paris by citing certain states' failure to compensate loyalists for confiscated property and to honor prewar debts owed by U.S. citizens. But these complaints served only as pretexts for retarding American expansion westward until Britain could sponsor an Indian buffer state south of the Great Lakes and possibly annex the region to Canada. Meanwhile, the lingering British presence in the Northwest allowed Canadian fur traders to maintain a brisk business there.

Spaniards' intentions of acquiring U.S. territory were equally transparent, particularly when they hinted that Indian raids on the frontier would stop if the settlers asked for Spanish citizenship. Spain exerted even more formidable leverage on westerners by closing New Orleans to American commerce in 1784. This action lured some leading westerners into a web of secret negotiations known

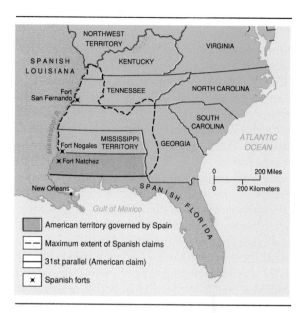

Spanish Claims to American Territory, 1783–1796

Spain refused to recognize Britain's 1783 cession to the United States of all territory north of the 31st parallel. The Spanish occupied Florida as it had been ceded to Britain in the Treaty of Paris (1763) and claimed all or part of five future states south of the Tennessee River and west of the Flint River.

as the Spanish Conspiracy. Noting that Congress under the Articles of Confederation seemed ready to accept the permanent closing of New Orleans in return for Spanish concessions elsewhere (see Chapter 5), many westerners began talking openly of secession. "I am decidedly of the opinion," anxiously wrote Kentucky's attorney general in 1787, "that this western country will in a few years Revolt from the Union and endeavor to erect an Independent Government." In 1788 Tennessee conspirators boldly advertised their flirtation with Spain by naming a large district along the Cumberland River after Spain's governor in New Orleans. Most westerners who accepted Spanish favors and gold meant only to pocket badly needed cash in return for vague promises of goodwill. The episode showed, however, that leading citizens were susceptible to foreign manipulation and subversion. As young Andrew Jackson concluded in 1789, making some arrangements with the Spanish seemed "the only immediate way to obtain peace with the Savage [Indians]."

The South

Meanwhile, southerners watched the deterioration of Anglo-American fortunes in the West with particular concern. Many southern citizens had acquired a personal stake in trans-Appalachian affairs because Virginia and North Carolina had rewarded Revolutionary soldiers with western land. Whether these veterans intended to move west themselves or to profit by selling their rights to others, all wanted to see the western territories prosper. Hoping to make a quick fortune in land speculation, southern planters (including George Washington) had borrowed heavily to buy frontier real estate; but uncertainty about the West's future made them worry that land prices would crash. By 1789 a potent combination of small farmers and landed gentry in the South had become enraged at foreign barriers to frontier expansion and eagerly supported politicians, among them Thomas Jefferson and James Madison, who advocated strong measures against the British and Spanish.

Aside from the frustrated ambitions of southern land speculators, however, the region's economy had largely recovered from the Revolution. The South was exporting as much tobacco by 1786 as before the Revolution and was earning prices that equaled or exceeded prewar levels. Furthermore, the southern economy had become increasingly diversified as grain harvests rose sharply in the Chesapeake, hemp production expanded noticeably in Virginia, and indigo culture temporarily revived in South Carolina and Georgia. Agricultural income seemingly was growing less dependent on the fate of one or two staple crops than during the colonial era. The South's recovery lagged only in the coastal districts of South Carolina, where the war had taken an especially destructive course. By 1789 agriculture and commerce had recuperated to such an extent that every southern state except South Carolina had made substantial progress in retiring its war debt.

The North

In the North, in such states as Pennsylvania and New York, agricultural production benefited from a steady demand for foodstuffs and by 1788 had largely recovered from the Revolution's ravages. As famine stalked Europe, American farmers in the Delaware and Hudson River valleys prospered from climbing export prices.

New Englanders were not so fortunate. A short growing season and poor soil kept yields so low, even in the best of times, that farmers barely produced enough grain for local consumption. New Englanders also faced both high taxes to repay the money borrowed to finance the Revolution and a tightening of credit that spawned countless lawsuits against debtors. These problems had sparked Shays's Rebellion in 1786 and still defied solution. Whereas most southern states had largely eliminated their war debts and the Middle Atlantic states had made great progress in managing theirs, New England taxpayers remained under a crushing obligation. Economic depression only aggravated the region's chronic overpopulation. Young New England men continued migrating to the frontier

Regional Diversity, c. 1790–1800

(Right) Rockett's Landing on the James River, in the heart of fertile land near the head of the tidewater; (center) the New England countryside near Worcester, Massachusetts; (far right) a Pennsylvania barn. The interests and commercial activities of the sections varied markedly in the Republic's early years.

or to the cities, and their discontent and restless mobility loosened the bonds of parental authority and left many women without marriage prospects.

New England's fishing fleet and merchant marine also discovered the high price of independence. Prior to 1775, when every colonial vessel enjoyed the protection of the Navigation Acts, the region's maritime community had employed approximately 15 percent of all adult males. After Independence, however, Britain quickly slapped strict limitations on U.S. commerce. The new republic's ships lost all rights to carry cargoes to the West Indies and faced high customs fees for landing products in Great Britain. For the most part, American foodstuffs, lumber, and tobacco were welcome in Britain only if they arrived in British ships. Because half of all U.S. exports went to Great Britain or its West Indian colonies, these restrictions allowed British shippers to increase their share of the Atlantic trade at American expense.

Only with difficulty did the U.S. merchant marine survive in these years. Resourceful captains took cargoes to the French West Indies, Scandinavia, and even China. Wily Yankee skippers were also surprisingly successful in smuggling foodstuffs to the British West Indies under the very nose of the Royal Navy. Nevertheless, British policies imposed real hardship on New England, whose economy depended heavily on fishing and ocean commerce. By 1791 discriminatory British treatment had reduced the number of seamen in the Massachusetts cod and whale fisheries by 42 percent compared to the 1770s. Recognizing that Great Britain could not be forced to grant trade concessions, New England's leaders preferred to solve the problem through peaceful accommodation, an approach entirely opposite to western and southern preferences for direct confrontation with Britain—even at the risk of war.

Entrepreneurs, Artisans, and Wage Earners

After 1783, through the enterprise of an ambitious, aggressive class of businessmen, the northern economy became less dependent on farming. Most of these individuals had begun as merchants, and they now used their profits to invest in factories, ships, government bonds, and banks (see "A Place in Time"). These men believed that the United States would gain strength if Americans balanced agriculture with banking, manufacturing, and commerce, and they wanted to limit American dependence on imported British manufactures. They also insisted that the nation needed a healthy merchant marine standing ready to augment U.S. naval forces in wartime.

Philadelphia in the 1790s

From 1790 to 1800, Philadelphia was the United States' capital, largest city, main financial market, and intellectual and scientific center. Home to forty-four thousand people in 1790, by 1800 Philadelphia almost doubled its population. This growth occurred despite a frightful yellow-fever epidemic in 1793, which cost several thousand lives and sent everyone (including President Washington and the entire federal government) fleeing until cooler weather killed the infection-bearing mosquitoes. A constant stream of country people and foreign immigrants poured in, and large numbers of Germans, French, Irish, and Scots kept Philadelphia's population diverse.

Most Philadelphians belonged to artisan families practicing such trades as carpentry, bricklaying, tailoring, and leatherworking. These crafts supplied the city's elite with elegant imitations of the latest European fashions in dress, furniture, and housing. Modestly endowed artisans, small merchants, and professional men lived comfortably, if not opulently. Such was not the case for many of the newcomers, who generally found themselves trapped amid the expanding ranks of propertyless, ill-paid wage workers.

Among poor Philadelphians were 1,640 blacks counted by the 1790 census, all but 210 of them free. (Pennsylvania had enacted gradual emancipation in 1780.) Whereas some slaves had been trained in skilled trades like blacksmithing, young free men of color

Delaware River Front, Philadelphia, *by Thomas Birch*

The port of Philadelphia hummed with activity in the 1790s. Its wharves welcomed goods from all over the world, and Pennsylvania manufactures and farm products lined the riverfront, waiting for export.

found themselves excluded from such crafts and relegated to menial work. Still, free blacks strove to improve their lot: they maintained seven schools and a Methodist congregation led by a former slave. All these were segregated.

The richest 10 percent of Philadelphians owned about half the city's wealth. This upper crust included old Quaker merchant families, recent wartime profiteers, and hustling new entrepreneurs. Philadelphia was still a preindus-

trial city entirely dependent on foreign trade for its existence, and most of its wealthiest men made their fortunes in commerce.

Philadelphia's economic environment was treacherous, however. Given rapidly changing market conditions, merchants had to be ever ready to act decisively. They repeatedly gambled everything in hopes of developing new overseas markets for Delaware Valley foodstuffs or of expanding the sphere within which they could retail European-made

The Bank of Pennsylvania, *by Benjamin Latrobe, 1798*

Philadelphia, William Penn's "greene country towne," was a major financial center from 1790 to 1800. The city's banks and merchant exchange were among the United States' finest buildings in these years. The writer James Fenimore Cooper remarked that Philadelphia's splendid architecture was "a tribute to [the] gold . . . to be expected here."

imports. Overseas trade was the most nerve-wracking of all Philadelphia businesses. From 1785 to 1791, bankruptcies reduced the number of trading firms from 514 to 440. Of the sixty-five wealthiest traders operating in 1779, only nine were still in business seventeen years later. The survivors were calculating, daring, and grasping.

In 1776, into this competitive commercial world came the half-blind French immigrant Stephen Girard. Relying on a quick mind and a scrappy, abrasive personality, Girard struggled for years just to avoid bankruptcy. But he exemplified the traits necessary for commercial success in Philadelphia—a determination to conduct his business personally (even when laid up with a painful head wound) and a willingness to take chances. "Since I have not as much as I desire, it seems necessary for me to take some risks or remain always poor." By

1795 he ranked high among the city's wealthiest individuals.

Girard's phenomenal success stemmed from his refusal to imitate conservative businessmen, who demonstrated a "prudence that will risk nothing." He and his fellow entrepreneurs helped propel Philadelphia into the industrial age. They provided two essential elements that would transform the city's economy—capital amassed from foreign trade, and a readiness to take chances by investing in business ventures unrelated to commerce. Merchants had founded the city's banking system in 1781; later merchants would pool funds to establish competing banks. Among these was one started by Girard in 1812 that remained in operation until the 1970s. These banks were critical in providing venture capital for the building of factories. Many merchants also lent directly to entrepreneurs who were unable to obtain

loans from commercial banks, thus expanding opportunity for new areas of economic activity. Some merchants even invested in factories directly and lent important managerial skills that contributed to the success of these infant industries.

Amid the shifting sands of precarious commerce and embryonic industrial capitalism, Girard and his competitors in the 1790s helped a flourishing, cultured city continue to prosper. The well-to-do could even afford to send their daughters to the Young Ladies' Academy, founded in 1787 by Dr. Benjamin Rush. "The patriot—the hero—the legislator," Dr. Rush grandly proclaimed, "would find the sweetest reward for their toils, in the approbation of their wives"—and how better could young women bestow this approval than by being educated themselves? Among the subjects that they studied was bookkeeping.

Philadelphia's bustling commerce and entrepreneurial enterprise produced social strain. Journeymen printers and leatherworkers, for example, organized and struck in a vain attempt to avoid becoming permanent wage earners. Yet the city's most notable political pressure group of the 1790s did not promote class conflict. In this organization, Philadelphia's Democratic Society, artisan masters rubbed shoulders with members of the professional elite like Dr. Rush and famed scientist David Rittenhouse—and with entrepreneur Stephen Girard. What united these republican enthusiasts were a conviction that individuals of talent and ambition ought not be held back by special interests, an admiration for revolutionary France, and a determination to preserve the liberty so hard won in the American Revolution.

Such entrepreneurs stimulated a flurry of innovative business ventures that pointed toward the future. The country's first private banks were founded in the 1780s in Philadelphia, Boston, and New York. Philadelphia merchants created the Pennsylvania Society for the Encouragement of Manufactures and the Useful Arts in 1787. This organization promoted the immigration of English artisans familiar with the latest industrial technology, including Samuel Slater (see Chapter 8), who established the nation's first modern water-powered textile factory at Pawtucket, Rhode Island, in 1793. In 1791 investors from New York and Philadelphia started the Society for the Encouragement of Useful Manufactures, which attempted to demonstrate the potential of large-scale industrial enterprises by building a factory town at Paterson, New Jersey. That same year, New York merchants and insurance underwriters organized America's first formal association for trading government bonds, out of which the New York Stock Exchange evolved.

Many of these early enterprises ended in financial ruin, however, because they proved premature or unrealistic. Not a few of their promoters shared the fate of Philadelphia businessman Robert Morris, who had signed both the Declaration of Independence and Constitution yet would spend three years in a debtor's prison after 1798. But the vision of these men was ultimately vindicated, for as often happens, failure preceded success: in the nineteenth century, the United States gradually became an industrial society.

Yet in 1789 the northeastern cities remained overwhelmingly preindustrial, without large factories. Half the urban work force consisted of "mechanics," whose ranks included both master artisans and journeymen. Mechanics manufactured goods by hand, typically in workshops where the master and his family employed a few journeymen or apprentices. Journeymen changed jobs frequently; those hired in Samuel Ashton's Philadelphia cabinet shop, for example, stayed an average of just six months between 1795 and 1803. Moreover, well-to-do artisan households, as well as professional and upper-class families, employed numerous servants. And masters and other employers could draw upon the growing ranks of low-paid day workers, who included most free blacks and many orphans, widows, and drifters.

Certificate of the "New York Mechanick Society," c. 1785

In the face of changing times and narrowing opportunity, many urban artisans organized societies to set wages and working hours.

Mechanics tended to follow in their fathers' occupational footsteps. They lived in close-knit neighborhoods with others who practiced their trade and with whom they enjoyed such traditional pastimes as drinking, marching, and "mobbing." Their wives and daughters often helped in the shop but rarely sought outside employment unless widowed or orphaned. Despite their industriousness and thrift, mechanics faced stiff competition from British manufacturers, who increasingly used labor-saving machinery and unskilled, low-paid labor. Consequently, American mechanics were disposed to support political leaders willing to raise the price of imported British goods through a national tariff. Most mechanics had supported the Constitution, hoping that it would create a strong and assertive national government.

A few artisans succeeded in adapting techniques of large-scale production to their crafts. The textile-finishing, printing, furniture-making, and construction trades most successfully exploited new technology or unskilled wage labor; they offered many opportunities for master artisans to establish flourishing family businesses. But most mechanics were either reluctant to abandon traditional household-oriented shops for an impersonal factory system or else could not modernize for lack of credit, which was scarce and expensive. Many artisans thus found opportunity shrinking, and they responded by organizing societies to set wages and working hours. Over the long run, the artisan community would contract as mechanics themselves became wage earners working for entrepreneurial industrialists; but in the 1790s these trends were only beginning to emerge.

In 1789 virtually all politically conscious Americans—entrepreneurs and merchants, urban mechanics and frontier settlers, nationalists and Antifederalists, northerners and southerners—expressed their hopes for the nation's future in terms of republican ideals. These lofty goals of selfless service to the general good had helped community leaders rally the public behind them in resisting British encroachments since the 1760s. Republican ideology had guided the men who hammered out state constitutions and the new federal Constitution, and it had also helped Antifederalists state their case against the Constitution. Now in the 1790s, how to interpret republican ideals, with their abiding distrust of government power, became a nagging question in the cut-and-thrust of everyday politics. Most Americans thought that they knew what republican virtue meant, and most tended to condemn rivals' views as the road to corruption. Noting in *The Federalist* the numerous divergent meanings of the word *republican,* James Madison had concluded that "no satisfactory one would ever be found."

Constitutional Government Takes Shape

Traveling slowly over the nation's miserable roads, the men entrusted with launching the federal experiment began assembling in New York, the new national capital, in March 1789. Because so few members were on hand, Congress opened its session a month late. George Washington did not arrive until April 23 and only took his oath of office a week later.

The slowness of these first halting steps, however, disguised the seriousness of the tasks at hand. The country's elected leaders had to make far-reaching decisions on several critical questions left

unresolved by the Constitution's framers. For example, the Constitution gave the president no formal responsibility for preparing a legislative agenda, although it allowed him wide discretion by directing him to make periodic reports on the state of the Union and by permitting him to recommend matters for Congress's consideration. The Philadelphia Convention likewise had not specified whether cabinet officers would be accountable to Congress or to the president. Nor did the Constitution say how the federal court system should be structured. Finally, widespread distrust of any government unrestrained by a bill of rights required that Congress prepare amendments for the states' consideration, but the exact scope and character of these amendments remained to be determined. "We are in a wilderness," wrote James Madison, "without a footstep to guide us."

Consequently, even though the Constitution had been ratified as the supreme law of the land, its framers' intentions might still have been reversed. The First Congress could easily have weakened presidential authority, limited access to federal courts, or passed amendments resurrecting features of the Articles of Confederation. Antifederalists conceivably could have convoked another constitutional convention, ostensibly to prepare a bill of rights but actually to rewrite the entire Constitution. In 1789 the nation's future remained unsettled in these, as in many other, regards.

Defining the Presidency

No office in the new government aroused more suspicion than the presidency. Many feared that the president's powers could make him a virtual king. Public apprehension remained in check only because of George Washington's reputation for honesty. Washington tried to calm fears of unlimited executive power. His careful behavior established important precedents that until the 1820s generally restrained his successors from becoming actively involved in preparing legislation.

The Constitution mentioned the executive departments only in passing, required the president to obtain the Senate's approval for his nominees to head these bureaus, and made all executive personnel liable to impeachment. Otherwise, Congress was free to determine the organization and accountability of what became known as the cabinet. The first cabinet, established by Congress, consisted of four departments, headed by the secretaries of state, treasury, and war and by the attorney general. Vice President John Adams's tie-breaking vote defeated a proposal that would have forbidden the president from dismissing cabinet officers without Senate approval. This outcome reinforced the president's authority to make and carry out policy; it also separated the powers of the executive and legislative branches beyond what the Constitution required, and so made the president a more equal partner with Congress.

President Washington suggested few laws to Congress. Rarely did he speak out against opponents of government policy, and generally he limited his public statements to matters of foreign relations and military affairs. He deferred to congressional decisions concerning domestic policy whenever possible and cast only two vetoes during his eight-year tenure (1789–1797).

Washington tried to reassure the public that he was above favoritism and conflicts of interest. Believing himself duty-bound to seek advice from a wide range of opinions, he balanced his cabinet with southerners and northeasterners. When Secretary of State Thomas Jefferson opposed certain policies of Secretary of the Treasury Alexander Hamilton, Washington implored Jefferson not to leave his post, even though the president supported Hamilton.

"He is polite with dignity, affable without familiarity, distant without haughtiness, grave without austerity, modest, wise, and good." So Abigail Adams, the wife of the vice president, described Washington. Once the government had settled into Philadelphia (the nation's capital from 1790 to 1800), the president enjoyed the private company of wealthy citizens, but he felt truly comfortable only at his Virginia estate, Mount Vernon, or on the Pennsylvania farm he rented. More than any other national leader, Washington sincerely strove to understand the aspirations of the two groups that dominated American society—northeastern merchants and entrepreneurs, and southern planters. Like most republican leaders, he believed that the proper role for ordinary citizens was not to set policy through elections but rather to choose well-educated, politically sophisticated men who would make laws in the people's best interest, though independently of direct popular influence.

The president endured rather than enjoyed the pomp of office. Suffering from a variety of ailments that grew as the years passed, Washington longed to escape the presidency. Only with difficulty was he persuaded to accept reelection in 1792. He feared dying while in office and thus setting the precedent for a lifetime presidency. With great anxiety he realized that "the preservation of the sacred fire of liberty and the destiny of the republican model of government are . . . *deeply*, perhaps *finally*, staked on the experiment entrusted to the hands of the American people." Should he contribute to that experiment's failure, he feared, his name would live only as an "awful monument."

National Justice and the Bill of Rights

The Constitution merely authorized Congress to establish federal courts below the level of the Supreme Court; it had offered no guidance as to how the judicial system should be structured. And although the Constitution specifically barred the federal government from committing such abuses as passing ex post facto laws* and bills of attainder,† the absence of a comprehensive bill of rights had led several delegates at Philadelphia to refuse to sign the Constitution and had been a major point of attack by Antifederalists. The task of filling in these gaps fell to the First Congress.

In 1789 many citizens feared that the new federal courts would ride roughshod over local customs. Every state had gradually devised a unique, time-honored blend of judicial procedures appropriate to local circumstances. Any attempt to force states to abandon their legal heritage would have produced strong counterdemands that federal justice be narrowly restricted. Bowing to such sentiments, Congress might have drastically curtailed the scope and power of the federal judiciary or

---

*Ex post facto law: a law criminalizing previously legal actions and punishing those who have been engaging in such actions.

†Bill of attainder: a legislative act proclaiming a person's guilt and stipulating punishment without a judicial trial.

limited the federal judicial system to the Supreme Court. Congress might also have forbidden federal judges to accept cases from the states on a range of subjects (as permitted by Article III, Section 2). Such actions by Congress would have tipped the balance of power in the new nation to the states.

But when it passed the Judiciary Act of 1789, which created the federal-court system, Congress did not seek to hobble the national judiciary. Yet the act managed to quiet popular apprehensions by establishing in each state a federal district court that operated according to local procedures. A district-court ruling could be appealed to a federal circuit court. Each circuit court consisted of one district-court judge and two Supreme Court justices (who would travel among certain states between Supreme Court sessions), and the three would decide cases according to state laws. But as the Constitution stipulated, the Supreme Court exercised final jurisdiction. Congress had struck a reasonable compromise that respected state traditions while offering wide access to federal justice.

In fulfilling its mandate to guarantee personal liberties, the First Congress sifted through 210 proposals for constitutional amendments. There was no consensus, however, as to what a bill of rights should provide, and a strong possibility existed that Antifederalists would manipulate the widespread public desire for protection of individual rights into a campaign to return power to the states. James Madison, who had been elected to the House of Representatives, battled fiercely to keep the Constitution's opponents from undermining the powers essential for a firm national government. It was Madison who played the leading role in drafting the ten amendments that became known as the Bill of Rights when ratified by the states in December 1791.

Madison insisted that the first eight amendments guarantee personal liberties, not strip the national government of any necessary authority. All but one of these eight affirmed the rights of individuals rather than of state governments. Their most important provisions protected public debate, religious beliefs, and procedures for fair trials. The Ninth and Tenth amendments reserved to the people or to the states powers not allocated to the federal government under the Constitution, but Madison headed off proposals to limit federal power

more explicitly. In general, the Bill of Rights imposed no serious check on the framers' nationalist objectives.

The Bill of Rights made only one concession toward what would soon be termed states' rights. That sole exception was the Second Amendment, ensuring the *collective* right of each state's populace to maintain a militia free of federal interference. The implications of this "right to keep and bear arms" were profoundly disturbing. Its prominence as the second of the ten amendments, moreover, emphasized lingering fears that a powerful central government might degenerate into tyranny. In adopting the Second Amendment, the nation's politicians were playing with fire, for it represented nothing less than an invitation to civil war.

Once the Bill of Rights was in place, the federal judiciary moved decisively to establish its authority. In 1793, in *Chisholm v. Georgia*, the Supreme Court ruled that a state could be sued in federal courts by nonresidents. In 1796 the Court declared its right to determine the constitutionality of congressional statutes in *Hylton v. United States* and to strike down state laws in *Ware v. Hylton*. But Congress had already decided that the Court had encroached too far on states' authority in *Chisolm*, and in 1794 it had voted to overturn this decision through a constitutional amendment. Ratified in 1798, the Eleventh Amendment revised Article III, Section 2, so that private citizens could no longer undermine states' financial autonomy by using federal courts to sue another state's government in civil cases and claim money from that state's treasury. The defeat of *Chisholm* stands as one of the handful of instances in American history whereby the Supreme Court was subsequently overruled by a constitutional amendment.

By endorsing the Eleventh Amendment, Congress expressed its recognition that federal power could threaten vital local interests. Such awareness had been growing since the early 1790s, rupturing the nationalist coalition that had written the Constitution, secured its ratification, and dominated the First Congress. A dramatic sign of this split was James Madison's shift from nationalist to critic of excessive federal power in 1790–1791. Up to this time, Madison and most of his fellow nationalists had not thought very deeply about how federal power should be used. The chief exception was

Alexander Hamilton, whose bold program alienated many like-minded nationalists by demonstrating that federal policies could be shaped to reward special interests.

National Economic Policy and Its Consequences

Realizing that war would jeopardize national survival, Washington concentrated his attention on diplomacy and military affairs. His reluctance to become involved with pending legislation enabled his energetic secretary of the treasury, Alexander Hamilton, to set the administration's domestic priorities. Hamilton quickly emerged as the country's most imaginative and dynamic statesman by formulating a sweeping program for national economic development. But Hamilton's agenda proved deeply divisive.

Hamilton and His Objectives

Born in the West Indies in 1755, Hamilton had sailed to New York in 1772 to enroll at King's College (now Columbia University), where he had emerged as a passionate defender of American rights. He had entered the Continental Army in 1775, distinguished himself in battle several times, and won the nickname the Little Lion.

During his four years on Washington's staff, Hamilton developed an exceptionally close relationship with his commander in chief. Hamilton's mother had been the mistress of a Scottish merchant who had abandoned her and their children when Alexander was about ten. For Hamilton, Washington helped fill the emotional void created by his own father's desertion. At the same time, for the childless Washington, Hamilton became almost a son. Hamilton thus gained extraordinary influence over Washington, who despite misgivings frequently supported the younger man's policies.

Hamilton formulated his financial proposals to strengthen the nation against foreign enemies and also to lessen the threat of disunion. The most immediate danger concerned national security: the possibility of war with Great Britain, Spain, or both.

The Republic could finance a full-scale war only by borrowing heavily, but because Congress under the Articles of Confederation had failed to redeem or pay interest on the Revolutionary debt, the nation's credit had been largely ruined abroad and at home. The country's economy also seemed unequal to fighting a major European power. War with Britain would mean a blockade, which would strangle commerce and stop the importation of necessary manufactured goods. French assistance had overcome this danger during the Revolution; but France's navy had declined greatly since 1783 (while the British had vastly improved theirs). Moreover, growing political instability in France was transforming America's wartime ally into an uncertain friend. Unless the United States achieved self-sufficiency in the manufacture of vital industrial products and maintained a strong merchant marine ready for combat, its chances of surviving a second war with Britain appeared slim.

Hamilton also feared that the Union might disintegrate because of Americans' tendency to think first of their local loyalties and interests. He himself felt little personal identification with his adopted state, New York. His six years in the Continental Army produced a burning nationalistic faith. For him, the Constitution's adoption had been a close victory of national over state authority. Now he worried that the states might reassert power over the new government. If this happened, he doubted whether the nation could prevent ruinous trade discrimination between states, deter foreign aggression, and avoid civil war.

Both his wartime experiences and his view of human nature forged Hamilton's political beliefs. An enthusiastic young patriot who had fought bravely during the Revolution's darkest hours, Hamilton had grown profoundly disillusioned by civilian profiteering. Like many disappointed idealists, he became a cynic who believed that few could live up to his own standards. Thus he came to share the conviction of many other nationalists that the Republic's population (like the rest of humanity) would never show limitless self-sacrifice and virtue. Hamilton concluded that the federal government's survival depended on building support among politically influential citizens through a straightforward appeal to their financial interests. Private ambitions would then serve the national welfare.

Charming and brilliant, vain and handsome, a notorious womanizer, and thirsting for fame and power, Hamilton himself exemplified the worldly citizen whose fortunes he hoped to link to the republic's future. But to the growing ranks of his opponents, Hamilton would embody the dark forces luring the Republic to its doom—a man who, Jefferson wrote, believed in "the necessity of either force or corruption to govern men."

Report on the Public Credit

Seeking guidance on how to restore the nation's credit worthiness, in 1789 Congress directed the Treasury Department to evaluate the status of the Revolutionary debt. Hamilton seized the opportunity to devise policies that would not only rebuild the country's credit but also entice a key sector of the upper class to place their prestige and capital at its service. Congress received his Report on the Public Credit in January 1790. The report listed $54 million in United States debt: $42 million owed to Americans, and the rest to foreigners. Hamilton estimated that on top of the national debt, the states had debts of $25 million, an amount that included several million dollars that the United States had promised to reimburse, such as Virginia's expenses in defending settlements in the Ohio Valley.

Hamilton's first major recommendation was that the federal government compensate anyone possessing debt certificates issued by the Continental Congress at their full value. The government would obtain the necessary money by "funding" the debt—that is, raising the $54 million needed to honor the national debt by selling an equal sum in new bonds. Holders of the original debt could then be repaid in full unless they preferred to receive the reissued bonds. Retainers of the new bonds would earn 4 percent interest, and to pay that interest, Congress would levy duties on imports.

Second, the report proposed that the federal government pay off the state debts remaining from the Revolution. Such obligations would be funded along with the national debt in the manner described above. Once again, current holders would receive full value with interest.

Hamilton argued that the continued failure of certain states to honor their obligations would undermine U.S. credit in overseas markets. While this reasoning contained a kernel of truth, it masked his most important motive. He saw the federal assumption of state debts as a chance for the national government to win the gratitude and loyalty of state creditors by honoring their claims before the remaining states could manage to pay them. Since legislatures awash in debt wanted to avoid piling more taxes on the voters, they would accept any relief, regardless of Hamilton's actual intentions.

Hamilton exhorted the government to use the money earned by selling federal lands in the West to pay off the $12 million owed to Europeans as quickly as possible. The Treasury could easily accumulate the interest owed on the remaining $42 million by collecting customs duties on imports and excise taxes on whiskey distillers. An essential feature of Hamilton's plan was the creation of a "sinking fund"—a sum of money reserved solely for guaranteeing future interest payments, into which revenues would be "sunk." This precaution would establish public confidence by assuring bond holders that their investments would be safe because the government would always have funds to pay them their interest promptly. Furthermore, Hamilton proposed that money owed to American citizens should be made a permanent debt. That is, he urged that the government *not* attempt to repay the $42 million principal but instead keep paying interest to persons wishing to hold bonds as an investment. If Hamilton's recommendation were adopted, the only burden on the taxpayers would be the small annual cost of 4 percent interest. It

Continental Currency

Alexander Hamilton, *by John Trumbull, 1792*

Hamilton's self-confident pride clearly shows through in this portrait, painted at the height of his influence in the Washington administration.

would then be possible to uphold the national credit at minimal expense, without ever having to pay off the debt itself.

Hamilton advocated a perpetual debt above all as a lasting means of uniting the economic fortunes of the nation's creditors to the United States. In an age when financial investments were notoriously risky, the federal government would protect the savings of wealthy bond holders through conservative policies but still offer an interest rate competitive with the Bank of England's. The guarantee of future interest payments would act as the explicit link uniting the interests of the moneyed class with those of the government. Few other investments would entail so little risk.

The Report on the Public Credit provoked immediate controversy. While no one in Congress doubted that its provisions would fully restore the country's fiscal reputation, many objected that those

least deserving of reward would gain the most. The original owners of more than three-fifths of the debt certificates issued by the Continental Congress (ranging from George Washington to Revolutionary patriots of modest means) had long before sold theirs at a loss, many out of dire financial necessity. Foreseeing Hamilton's intentions, wealthy speculators, on the other hand, had by then accumulated large holdings at the expense of unsuspecting original owners. Now these astute speculators stood to reap huge gains, even collecting interest that had fallen due before they had purchased the certificates. "That the case of those who parted with their securities from necessity is a hard one, cannot be denied," Hamilton admitted. But making exceptions would be even worse.

To Hamilton's surprise, Madison—once an advocate of national assumption of state debts—emerged as one of the chief opponents of reimbursing current holders at face value. Madison tried but failed to obtain compensation for original owners who had sold their certificates. Congress rejected his suggestions partly because some congressmen were themselves speculators but primarily because preventing fraudulent claims would have been impossible.

Had Congress allowed popular pressure to influence how it repaid public creditors, however, the nation would have found it very hard to borrow money during future emergencies. Hamilton's policy was defensible and virtually inevitable; but it generated widespread resentment because it rewarded rich profiteers while ignoring the wartime sacrifices of ordinary citizens.

Opposition to assuming the state debts also ran high. Only the New England states, New Jersey, and South Carolina had failed to make effective provisions for paying their creditors. Understandably, the issue stirred the fiercest indignation in the South, which except for South Carolina had extinguished 83 percent of its debt. To allow residents of the laggard states to escape heavy taxes while others had liquidated theirs at great expense seemed to reward irresponsibility. Many Virginians, among them Madison, opposed Hamilton not only for reasons of high principle but also because of their state's self-interest. South Carolina became the sole southern state that supported Hamilton's policies.

Southern hostility almost defeated assumption. In the end, however, Hamilton managed to save his proposal by exploiting the strong desire among Virginians to relocate the national capital in their region. Virginians expected that moving the capital would make their state the crossroads of the country and thus help preserve its position as the nation's largest, most influential state. In return for the northern votes necessary to transfer the capital to the Potomac River, Hamilton secured enough Virginians' support to win the battle for assumption. Yet the debate over state debts alienated most southerners by confirming their suspicions that other regions monopolized the benefits of a stronger union.

Congressional enactment of the Report on the Public Credit dramatically reversed the nation's fiscal standing. Formerly scorned as a beggar country, the United States saw its financial reputation soar in 1790. Europeans grew so enthusiastic for U.S. bonds that by 1792 some securities were selling at 10 percent above face value.

Reports on the Bank and Manufactures

In December 1790 the secretary of the treasury presented Congress with a second message, the Report on a National Bank. Having managed to restore full faith in greatly undervalued certificates, Hamilton in effect had significantly expanded the stock of capital available for investment. He intended to direct that money toward projects that would diversify the national economy through a federally chartered bank.

The proposed bank would raise $10 million through a public stock offering. The Treasury would hold one-fifth of the stock and name one-fifth of the directors, but four-fifths of the control would fall to private hands. Private investors could purchase shares by paying for three-quarters of their value in government bonds. In this way, the bank would capture a significant portion of the recently funded debt and make it available for loans; it would also receive a substantial and steady flow of interest payments from the Treasury. Anyone buying shares under these circumstances had little chance of losing money and was positioned to profit handsomely.

Hamilton argued that the Bank of the United States would cost the taxpayers nothing and greatly benefit the nation. It would provide a safe place for the federal government to deposit tax revenues,

make inexpensive loans to the government when taxes fell short, and help relieve the scarcity of hard cash by issuing paper notes that would circulate as money. Furthermore, it would possess authority to regulate the business practices of state banks. Above all, the bank would provide much needed credit to expand the economy.

Finally, Hamilton called for American economic self-sufficiency. He admired the "prodigious effect" on Great Britain's national wealth that the recent expansion of factories had stimulated in that nation, and he wanted to encourage similar industrialization in the United States. His Report on Manufactures of December 1791 advocated protective tariffs on foreign imports to foster domestic manufacturing, which in turn would both attract immigrants and create national wealth. Elsewhere the secretary called for assisting the merchant marine against British trade restrictions by reducing duties on goods imported into the United States on American ships and by offering subsidies (called bounties) for fishermen and whalers. These measures would also indirectly protect the national bank's loans to industrialists and shippers.

Hamilton's Challenge to Limited Government

In the eyes of many of the new government's supporters, Hamilton's plan to establish a permanent national debt violated the principle of equality among citizens; it seemed to favor the interests of public creditors over those of other Americans. Hamilton's critics also denounced his proposal for a national bank, interpreting it as a dangerous scheme that would give a small, elite group special power to influence the government.

The bank issue drew Thomas Jefferson into the ranks of Hamilton's opponents. It was almost an article of faith among Revolutionary-generation Americans like Madison and Jefferson that the Bank of England had undermined the integrity of government in Britain. Shareholders of the new Bank of the United States could just as easily become the tools of unscrupulous politicians. If significant numbers in Congress also owned bank stock, they would likely vote in support of the bank even at the cost of the national good. To Jefferson, the bank was "a machine for the corruption of the legislature [Congress]." Senator John Taylor of Virginia predicted that its vast wealth would enable the bank to take over the country, which would thereafter, he quipped, be known as the United States of the Bank.

Opponents' strongest argument against the bank was their claim of its unconstitutionality. The Constitution had given Congress no specific authorization to issue charters of incorporation. Unless Congress adhered to a "strict interpretation" of the Constitution, critics argued, the central government might oppress the states and trample individual liberties, just as Parliament had done to the colonies. Strictly limiting the powers of the government seemed the surest way of preventing the United States from degenerating into a corrupt despotism, as Britain had.

Congress approved the bank by only a thin margin. Doubtful of the bank's constitutionality, Washington turned for advice to both Jefferson and Hamilton. Jefferson scarcely understood banking, but he deeply feared political corruption and did not want to extend government power beyond the letter of the Constitution. "To take a single step beyond the boundaries thus specifically drawn around the powers of Congress is to take possession of a boundless field of power no longer susceptible of any definition," warned Jefferson. Hamilton fought back, urging Washington to sign the bill. Because Congress could enact all measures "necessary and proper" (Article I, Section 8), Hamilton contended that the only unconstitutional activities were those actually *forbidden* to the national government. In the end, the president accepted Hamilton's cogent argument for a "loose interpretation" of the Constitution. In February 1791 the Bank of the United States obtained a charter guaranteeing its existence for twenty years. Washington's acceptance of the principle of loose interpretation was the first victory for those advocating an active, assertive national government.

Madison and Jefferson also strongly opposed Hamilton's proposal to encourage industry through protective tariffs on foreign manufactures. They viewed such protectionism as an unfair subsidy promoting uncompetitive industries that would founder without government support. Moreover, tariffs doubly injured the majority of citizens, first by imposing heavy import taxes that were passed on to consumers and then by reducing the incentive for American manufacturers to produce goods

at a lower cost than imports. Together these results unjustifiably raised prices. The only beneficiaries would be individuals shielded from overseas competition and institutions, like the bank, that lent them money. Fearing that American cities might develop a dangerous class of dependent and politically volatile poor people, Jefferson and Madison saw industrialization as a potential menace to the Republic's stability.

Congress ultimately refused to approve a high protective tariff. Nevertheless, Hamilton succeeded in setting higher duties on goods imported into the United States by British vessels than on items carried by American ships. As a result, the tonnage of such goods carried by the American merchant marine more than tripled from 1789 to 1793. Congress also approved subsidies for New England's beleaguered whale and cod fisheries in 1792.

Hamilton's Legacy

Hamilton's attempt to erect a base of political support by appealing to economic self-interest proved highly successful. His arrangements for rescuing the nation's credit provided enormous gains for the speculators, merchants, and other "monied men" of the port cities who by 1790 held most of the Revolutionary debt. As holders of bank stock, these same groups had yet another reason to use their prestige on behalf of national authority. Assumption of the state debts liberated taxpayers from a crushing burden in New England, New Jersey, and South Carolina. Hamilton's efforts to promote industry, commerce, and shipping struck a responsive chord among the Northeast's budding entrepreneurs and hard-pressed artisans,

Those attracted to Hamilton's policies called themselves Federalists, in large part to imply (incorrectly) that their opponents had formerly been Antifederalists. Despite the Federalists' effort to associate themselves with the Constitution, they actually favored a "consolidated" (centralized) national government instead of a truly federal system with substantial powers left to the states. Federalists dominated public opinion in New England, New Jersey, and South Carolina besides enjoying considerable support in Pennsylvania and New York.

However, Hamilton's program sowed dissension in sections of the country where Federalist economic policies provided few benefits. Resentment ran high among those who felt that the government appeared to be rewarding special interests. This situation appeared a perversion of the common understanding that the Constitution had been ratified to bring equal advantages to all Americans. Southern reaction to Hamilton's program, for example, was overwhelmingly negative. Few southerners (aside from some wealthy Charleston merchants) had retained Revolutionary certificates until 1789. By that date only South Carolina of all the southern states had any significant remaining Revolutionary debt. The Bank of the United States had few southern stockholders, and it allocated very little capital for loans there.

Hamilton's plans for commercial expansion and industrial development likewise seemed irrelevant to the interests of the West, where agriculture promised to be exceptionally profitable if only the right to export through New Orleans would be guaranteed. In Pennsylvania and New York, too, the uneven impact of Hamiltonian policies generated dissatisfaction. Resentment against a national economic program whose main beneficiaries seemed to be eastern "monied men" and Yankees who refused to pay their debts gradually united westerners, southerners, and many individuals in the mid-Atlantic region into a political coalition that challenged the Federalists for control of the government and called for a return to the "true principles" of republicanism.

The Whiskey Rebellion

Hamilton's financial program not only sparked an angry political debate in Congress but also helped ignite a civil insurrection called the Whiskey Rebellion. Severely testing the federal government's authority, this insurrection was the young republic's first serious crisis.

Because the national government's assumption of state debts required more revenue than import duties alone could provide, Hamilton had recommended an excise tax on domestically produced whiskey. He insisted that his proposal would distribute the expense of financing the national debt evenly across the United States. He even alleged that the country's morals would improve if higher prices induced Americans to drink less liquor, a contention enthusiastically endorsed by Philadel-phia's College of Physicians. Though Congress complied with Hamilton's request in March 1791, many members doubted that Americans (who on average annually imbibed six gallons of hard liquor per adult) would submit tamely to sobriety. James Jackson of Georgia, for example, warned the administration that his constituents "have long been in the habit of getting drunk and that they will get drunk in defiance of a dozen colleges or all the excise duties which Congress might be weak or wicked enough to pass."

The accuracy of Jackson's prophecy became apparent in September 1791, when a crowd tarred and feathered an excise agent near Pittsburgh. Western Pennsylvanians found the new tax especially burdensome. Unable to ship their crops to world markets through Spanish New Orleans, most farmers had grown accustomed to distilling their rye or corn into alcohol, which could be carried across the Appalachians at a fraction of the price charged for bulky grain. Hamilton's excise equaled 25 percent of whiskey's retail value, enough to wipe out a frontier farmer's profit.

The law furthermore specified that all trials concerning tax evasion be conducted in federal courts. Any western Pennsylvanian indicted for noncompliance thus had to travel three hundred miles to Philadelphia. Not only would the accused then face a jury of unsympathetic easterners, but he would have to bear the cost of a long journey and lost earnings while at court, in addition to fines and other court penalties if found guilty. Consequently, western Pennsylvanians had justifiable reasons for complaining that local circumstances made the whiskey tax excessively burdensome.

Moreover, Treasury officials rarely enforced the law rigorously outside western Pennsylvania. An especially diligent excise inspector lived near Pittsburgh, whose efforts to collect the tax increasingly enraged local residents and in time touched off massive resistance.

Initially, most residents preferred to protest the tax peacefully, through mass meetings and petitions to Congress. Only a frustrated, reckless minority resorted to violence. However, these hotheads not only attacked federal revenue officers without giving Congress a chance to respond to their grievances but even turned on their own neighbors, destroying property and occasionally pinning down farmers with rifle fire for hours. In several instances the rebels terrorized or tarred and feathered others simply for criticizing their actions. Opposition to the whiskey tax degenerated into random violence that overshadowed the legitimate complaints of western Pennsylvanians.

Large-scale resistance erupted in July 1794. One hundred men attacked a U.S. marshal serving sixty delinquent taxpayers with summonses to appear in court at Philadelphia. A crowd of five hundred burned the chief revenue officer's house after a shootout with federal soldiers assigned to protect him. Roving bands torched buildings, assaulted tax collectors, chased government supporters from the region, and flew a flag symbolizing an independent country that they hoped to create from six western counties.

The frontier turmoil played directly into the Washington administration's hands. Hamilton blasted the rebellion as simple lawlessness, in particular because Congress had reduced the tax rate per gallon in 1792 and just recently had voted to allow state judges in western Pennsylvania to hear trials. Washington concluded that failure to respond strongly to the uprising would encourage similar outbreaks in other frontier areas where lax enforcement had allowed distillers to escape paying taxes.

Washington accordingly summoned 12,900 militiamen from Pennsylvania, Maryland, Virginia, and New Jersey to march west under his command. Opposition evaporated once the troops reached the Appalachians, and the president left Hamilton in charge of making arrests. Of about 150 suspects seized, Hamilton sent twenty in irons to Philadelphia. Two men received death sentences, but Washington eventually pardoned them both, noting that one was a "simpleton" and the other "insane."

The Whiskey Rebellion was a milestone in determining limits on public opposition to federal policies. In the early 1790s, many Americans still assumed that it was legitimate to protest unpopular laws using the same tactics with which they had blocked parliamentary measures like the Stamp Act. Indeed, western Pennsylvanians had justified their resistance with exactly such reasoning. Before 1794 the question of how far the people might go in resisting federal laws remained unresolved because, as Washington declared, "We had given no testimony to the world of being able or willing to support our government and laws." But by firmly suppressing the first major challenge to national authority, Washington served notice that if citizens wished to change the law, they could do so only through constitutional procedures—by making their dissatisfaction known to their elected representatives and if necessary electing new representatives.

The United States in a Hostile World

By 1793 disagreements over foreign affairs had emerged as the primary source of friction in American public life. The political divisions created by Hamilton's financial program hardened into ideologically oriented factions that argued vehemently over whether the country's foreign policy should be pro-French or pro-British.

The United States faced a particularly hostile international environment in the 1790s. European powers restricted American trade, stirred up Indian raids on the frontier, claimed large areas of western territory, and maintained military garrisons on U.S. soil. Because the United States was a weak nation whose economic well-being depended heavily on exports, foreign-policy issues loomed large in national politics. Disputes over foreign relations would poison public life from 1793 to 1815.

Defending the West

The most serious perils to the nation's future rose from British and Spanish attempts to detach the West from the United States. In the early years of Washington's administration, Spanish officials commonly bribed numerous well-known political figures in Tennessee and Kentucky, among them a former general on Washington's staff, James Wilkinson, whose unscrupulous intrigues would continue well past 1800. Thomas Scott, a congressman from western Pennsylvania, meanwhile schemed with the British. Between 1791 and 1796, the federal government anxiously admitted Vermont, Kentucky, and Tennessee to the Union, partly in the hope of strengthening their sometimes flickering loyalty to the United States.

Like all subsequent strong presidents, Washington jealously guarded his prerogative to conduct foreign affairs. Consulting with the Senate as the Constitution required, he nevertheless tried to keep tight control of foreign policy. Realizing that he could not quickly resolve the complex western problem, Washington pursued a course of patient diplomacy that was intended "to preserve the country in peace if I can, and to be prepared for war if I cannot." The prospect of peace improved in 1789 when Spain unexpectedly opened New Orleans to American commerce, although exports remained subject to a 15 percent duty that westerners bitterly resented. Still, secessionist sentiment gradually subsided.

Washington now moved to weaken Spanish influence in the West by neutralizing Spain's most important ally, the Creek Indians. The Creeks numbered more than twenty thousand, including perhaps five thousand warriors, and they bore a fierce hostility toward Georgian settlers, whom they called *Ecunnaunuxulgee,* or "the greedy people who want our lands." In 1790 the Creek leader Alexander McGillivray signed a peace treaty with the United States (a secret provision of which promised him a large annual bribe) that permitted whites to occupy lands in the Georgia piedmont fought over since 1786, but which in other respects preserved Creek territory against white expansion. Washington insisted that Georgia restore to the Creeks' allies, the Chickasaws and Choctaws, the vast area along the Mississippi River known as the Yazoo Tract, which Georgia claimed and had begun selling off to white land speculators.

Hoping to conclude a similar agreement with Great Britain's Indian allies, the United States sent an envoy to the Great Lakes tribes in 1790. The Miamis responded by burning a captured American to death. Late that same year, the president's first effort to force peace through military action failed when General Josiah Harmar abandoned his march against the Miamis after the loss of nearly two hundred of his soldiers. A second campaign ended in disaster on November 4, 1791, when Indians killed nine hundred men out of a force of fourteen hundred led by General Arthur St. Clair.

Washington's efforts to pacify the frontier lay in a shambles. Not only had two military expeditions suffered defeat in the Northwest Territory, but in 1792 the Spanish had persuaded the Creeks to renounce their treaty with the federal government and to resume hostilities. Ultimately, the damage done to U.S. prestige by these setbacks convinced many Americans that the combined strength of Britain and Spain could be counterbalanced only by an alliance with France.

France and Factional Politics

One of the most momentous events in history, the French Revolution began in 1789 with the meeting (for the first time in almost two centuries) of France's legislative assembly, the Estates General. Americans remained fundamentally sympathetic to the revolutionary cause as the French abolished nobles' privileges, wrote a constitution, and bravely repelled invading armies from Austria and Prussia. France became a republic in September 1792; it then pro-

"The Contrast"

In a contemporary cartoonist's view, the winning of American liberty seemed an orderly and peaceful process as compared to the bloody struggle for French liberty.

claimed a war of all peoples against all kings, in which it assumed that the United States would eagerly enlist.

Enthusiasm for a pro-French foreign policy raged in the South and on the frontier, in particular after France went to war against Spain and Great Britain in 1793. Increasingly, western settlers and southern speculators in frontier lands hoped for a decisive French victory in Europe that, they reasoned, would leave Britain and Spain militarily too exhausted to continue meddling in the West. The United States could then insist on free navigation of the Mississippi, force the evacuation of British garrisons, and end both nations' support of Indian resistance.

Moreover, a slave uprising in France's Caribbean colony of Saint Domingue (modern-day Haiti), in which the British became involved, soon generated passionate anti-British sentiment in the South. White southerners grew alarmed for the future of slavery and their own lives as thousands of terrified French planters fled to the United States from Saint Domingue with accounts of how British invaders in 1793 had supported the rebellious slaves. The blacks had fought with determination and inflicted heavy casualties on the French. Southern whites concluded that the British had intentionally sparked a bloodbath on the island and worried that a British-inspired race war would engulf the South as well. Anti-British hysteria even began to undermine South Carolina's loyalty to Federalist policies.

After 1790 American reactions to the French Revolution diverged sharply in the North and the South, in large measure for economic reasons. In the North merchants' growing antagonism toward France reflected not only their conservatism but also their strong awareness that good relations with Britain were essential for their region's prosperity. Virtually all the nation's merchant marine operated from northern ports, and by far the largest share of U.S. foreign trade was with Great Britain. Merchants, shippers, and ordinary sailors in New England, Philadelphia, and New York feared that an alliance with France would provoke British retaliation against this valuable commerce, and they argued that the United States could win valuable concessions by demonstrating friendly intentions toward Great Britain. Indeed, important members of Parliament, including Prime Minister William Pitt the Younger, seemed to favor liberalizing trade with the United States.

Southerners had no such reasons to favor Britain. Southern spokesmen like Jefferson and Madison viewed Americans' reliance on British commerce as a menace to national self-determination and wished to divert most U.S. trade to France. Jefferson and Madison repeatedly demanded that British imports be reduced through the imposition of discriminatory duties on cargoes shipped from England and Scotland in British vessels. Their recommendations gravely threatened the economic well-being of Britain, which sold more manufactured goods to the United States than to any other country. In the heat of the debate, Federalist opponents of a discriminatory tariff warned that the English would not stand by while a weak French ally pushed them into depression. If Congress adopted this program of trade retaliation, Hamilton predicted in 1792, "there would be, in less than six months, an open war between the United States and Great Britain."

After declaring war on Britain and Spain in 1793, France actively tried to embroil the United States in the conflict. (The treaty of alliance of 1778 still bound the United States to come to France's aid.) The French dispatched Edmond Genêt as minister to the United States with orders to enlist American mercenaries to conquer Spanish territories and attack British shipping. Much to the French government's disgust, however, President Washington issued a proclamation of American neutrality on April 22.

Meanwhile, Citizen Genêt (as he was known in French Revolutionary style) had arrived on April 8. He found no shortage of southern volunteers for his American Foreign Legion despite America's official neutrality. Making generals of George Rogers Clark of Kentucky and Elisha Clarke of Georgia, Genêt directed them to seize the Spanish garrisons at New Orleans and St. Augustine. Clark openly defied Washington's Neutrality Proclamation by advertising for recruits for his mission in Kentucky newspapers; Clarke began drilling three hundred troops on the Florida border. But the French failed to provide adequate funds for either campaign. And as for the American recruits, while all were willing to fight for France, few were

The Frigate L'Embuscade ("Ambush")

During Washington's presidency, French-outfitted raiders such as L'Embuscade snatched merchant vessels from American coasts. The seizures defied U.S. authority and hindered the Republic's quest for neutrality in the war between France and Britain.

willing to fight without pay, and so both expeditions eventually disintegrated in 1794 for lack of French money to supply them.

However, Genêt did not need funds to outfit privateers, whose crews were paid from captured plunder. By the summer of 1793, almost a thousand Americans were at sea in a dozen ships flying the French flag. These privateers seized more than eighty British vessels and towed them to United States ports, where French consuls sold the ships and cargoes at auction.

The British Crisis

Even though the Washington administration swiftly closed the nation's harbors to Genêt's buccaneers and requested the French ambassador's recall, his exploits provoked an Anglo-American crisis. George III's ministers decided that only a massive show of force would deter further American aggression. Accordingly, on November 6, 1793, the Privy Council issued secret orders confiscating any foreign ships trading with French islands in the Caribbean. The council purposely delayed publishing these instructions until after most American ships

carrying winter provisions to the Caribbean left port, so that their captains would not know that they were sailing into a war zone. The Royal Navy then seized more than 250 American vessels, a high price for Genêt's troublemaking.

Meanwhile, the U.S. merchant marine was suffering a second galling indignity—the drafting of its crewmen into the understrength Royal Navy. Thousands of British sailors, including numerous naval deserters, had previously fled to U.S. ships, where they hoped to find an easier life than under the tough, poorly paying British system. In late 1793 British naval officers began routinely inspecting American crews for British subjects, whom they then impressed (forcibly enlisted) as the king's sailors. Overzealous commanders sometimes broke royal orders by taking U.S. citizens, and in any case the British did not recognize former subjects' right to adopt American citizenship. Impressment scratched a raw nerve in most Americans, who recognized that the federal government's willingness to defend its citizens from such contemptuous abuse was a critical test of national character.

Next the British boldly challenged the United States for control of the West. In February 1794

Canada's royal governor delivered an inflammatory speech at an Indian council, denying U.S. claims north of the Ohio River and urging his listeners to destroy every white settlement in the Northwest. Soon British troops were building an eighth garrison on U.S. soil, Fort Miami, near present-day Toledo, Ohio. Meanwhile, the Spanish encroached further upon territory owned by the United States by building Fort San Fernando in 1794 at what is now Memphis, Tennessee.

Hoping to halt the drift toward war, Washington launched a desperate diplomatic initiative in 1794. He sent Chief Justice John Jay to Great Britain, dispatched Thomas Pinckney to Spain, and authorized General Anthony Wayne to negotiate a treaty with the Indians of the Ohio Valley.

Having twice defeated federal armies, the Indians scoffed at Washington's peace offer. But the tide turned as Wayne led three thousand regulars and Kentucky militiamen deep into the Indian homeland and ruthlessly razed every village within his reach. On August 20, 1794, his troops routed a thousand Indians at the Battle of Fallen Timbers just two miles from British Fort Miami. Wayne's

army marched past the post in a provocative victory parade and then built an imposing stronghold to challenge British authority in the Northwest, appropriately named Fort Defiance. Indian morale plummeted. In August 1795 Wayne compelled twelve northeastern tribes to sign the Treaty of Greenville, which opened most of modern-day Ohio to white settlement and ended Indian hostilities for sixteen years.

Wayne's success allowed John Jay to win a major diplomatic victory in London: a British promise to withdraw troops from American soil. He also managed to gain access to West Indian markets for small American ships, but only by bargaining away U.S. rights to load cargoes of sugar, molasses, and coffee from the Caribbean. On other points, Jay found the British unyielding. Aside from fellow Federalists, few Americans could interpret Jay's Treaty as preserving peace with honor.

Jay's Treaty left Britain free not only to violate American neutrality but also to ruin a profitable commerce by restricting U.S. trade with French ports during wartime. Many opponents, moreover, passionately decried Jay's failure to end

Negotiating the Treaty of Greenville

In this detail of a contemporary painting believed to have been done by a member of General Wayne's staff, Chief Little Turtle speaks to Wayne, who stands with one hand behind his back.

impressment and predicted that Great Britain would thereafter force even more Americans into the Royal Navy. And southerners resented that Jay had not achieved their long-sought goal of compensation for slaves taken away by the British army during the Revolution. As the Federalist-dominated Senate ratified the treaty by a one-vote margin in 1795, Jay nervously joked that he could find his way across the country by the fires of rallies burning him in effigy.

Despite its unpopularity, Jay's Treaty probably represented the utmost that a weak, politically divided United States could have extracted from mighty Britain. Although enormously unpopular, the treaty was one of the Washington administration's major accomplishments. First, it defused an explosive crisis with Great Britain before war became inevitable. Second, it ended a twelve-year British occupation of U.S. territory. Third, the treaty provided for the settlement, by arbitration, of the claims of British merchants who were owed American debts from before 1776, and it also arranged for U.S. citizens' compensation for property seized by the Royal Navy in 1793 and 1794. Americans benefited disproportionately when these accounts were finally settled by 1804: they received $10,345,000, compared to just $2,750,000 awarded to the British creditors.

Although the Senate rejected the provision granting limited trading rights with the West Indies in return for a British monopoly over certain commodities, Jay's Treaty played a critical role in stimulating an enormous expansion of American trade. British governors in the West Indies used the treaty's ratification as an excuse to proclaim their harbors open to U.S. ships. Other British officials permitted Americans to develop a thriving commerce with India, even though this trade infringed on the East India Company's monopoly. Within a few years after 1795, American exports to the British Empire shot up 300 percent because the United States had unofficially gained "most-favored-nation" status as a means of restoring good relations.

On the heels of Jay's Treaty came an unqualified diplomatic triumph engineered by Thomas Pinckney. Ratified in 1796, the Treaty of San Lorenzo with Spain (also called Pinckney's Treaty) won westerners the right of unrestricted, duty-free access to world markets via the Mississippi River. Spain also promised to recognize the 31st parallel as the United States' southern boundary, to dismantle all fortifications on American soil, and to discourage Indian attacks against western settlers.

By 1796 the Washington administration thus had successfully defended the country's territorial integrity, restored peace to the frontier, opened the Mississippi for western exports, made it possible for northeastern shippers to regain British markets, and kept the nation out of a dangerous European war. As the popular outcry over Jay's Treaty demonstrated, however, the nation's foreign policy had left Americans much more deeply divided in 1796 than they had been in 1789.

Battling for the Nation's Soul

Neither the Constitution nor *The Federalist* had envisioned organized political parties, and none existed in 1789 when Washington became president. By the end of his second term, however, politically conscious Americans had split into two hostile parties, Federalists and Republicans.

The unfolding struggle transcended the economic and sectional differences so evident in earlier disputes about Hamiltonian finance and the possibility of war with Britain. After 1796 a battle raged over the very future of representative government, culminating in the election of 1800, whose outcome would determine whether the nation's political elite could accommodate demands from ordinary citizens for a more active and influential role in determining government policy. No issue was more important or hotly argued than the matter of officeholders' accountability to their constituents.

Ideological Confrontation

By the mid-1790s the French Revolution had forced Americans to reassess their political values. American attitudes toward events in France divided sharply after that nation's revolutionary regime turned radical in 1793–1794, sending thousands of "counterrevolutionaries" to the guillotine. The polarization of American opinion assumed a strongly, though not completely, regional dimension.

The Republican Court, *by Daniel Huntington*

Federalists emphasized the dignity of the national government by staging sumptuous balls and formal receptions. Administration critics saw these affairs as an effort to emulate European court life. Washington, although mindful of upholding presidential dignity, found public functions tedious, and his stiff formality often masked his personal discomfort.

For northern Federalists, revolutionary France became an abomination—"an open hell," thundered Massachusetts Federalist Fisher Ames, "still ringing with agonies and blasphemies, still smoking with sufferings and crimes." New England was the nation's most conservative, religiously oriented region, and most of its people came to detest the French government's disregard for civil rights and its attempt to substitute the adoration of Reason for the worship of God. Middle Atlantic businessmen, who were perhaps less religious than New Englanders but hardly less conservative, condemned French leaders as evil radicals who incited the poor against the rich. A minority of well-off northern merchants and professional men, however, continued to look favorably upon the French Revolution, primarily out of loyalty to deeply felt republican principles.

Federalists trembled at the thought of guillotines and "mob rule" looming in the United States' future. Memories of Shays's Rebellion and the Whiskey Rebellion made their fears reasonable. So did the tendency of artisans in Philadelphia and New York to bandy the French revolutionary slogan "Liberty, Equality, Fraternity" and to admire pro-French political leaders such as Jefferson. Moreover, Citizen Genêt had openly encouraged

vocal opposition to the Washington administration until the faction in the French government that he represented fell from power—and even more troubling, he had found hundreds of Americans willing to fight for France. Federalists worried that all of this was just the tip of an iceberg.

By the mid-1790s Federalist leaders had concluded that it was unwise and perhaps dangerous to involve the public too deeply in politics. The people, they believed, were not evil-minded but simply undependable and could easily fall prey to such a rabble rouser as Genêt. As Senator George Cabot of Massachusetts put it, "The many do not think at all." For Federalists, democracy meant "government by the passions of the multitude," though they also felt that the people, if properly led, could stand as a powerful (but passive) bulwark against anarchy. Indeed, they *did* trust ordinary property owners to judge a candidate's personal fitness for high office. Federalists consequently argued that citizens need not be presented with choices over policy during elections; instead, voters ought to choose candidates according to their personal merits. Thus they favored a representative government, in which elected officials would rule in the people's name but would be independent of direct popular influence.

"Where Liberty Dwells, There Is My Country"

Motifs of republican virtue and liberty were widely reproduced in the nation's early years. In this coverlet of toile manufactured in England for American sale, the shield-bearing Columbia, symbolizing the United States, leads a fur-capped Benjamin Franklin in his elevation to divine status.

Preserving order, the Federalists maintained, required demonstrating the dignity of the government and forging a close, visible relationship between the government and the upper class. Such a spectacle would not only reassure citizens that their future was in competent hands but also set high standards that few radicals could meet. As early as 1789, Vice President John Adams had tried to give the president and other high officials royal-sounding titles like "His High Mightiness." (Adams had failed amid much ridicule, including being lampooned as "His Rotundity.") During the 1790s government officials continued to dramatize their social distance from average citizens. Members of Congress and the cabinet dressed in high fashion, traveled in expensive coaches, appeared with retinues of servants, and attended endless formal dinners and balls, which served as grand opportunities for the upper class to flaunt its wealth. Federalists insisted that they ruled *of* and *for* the people, but they took pains to symbolize that their government was not *by* the people.

The Federalists aimed to limit public office to wise and virtuous men who would vigilantly protect liberty. This objective was consistent with eighteenth-century fears that corruption and unchecked passion would undermine society, for in republican theory a "virtuous" government need not be directly responsible to public opinion. If (as many assumed) democracy meant "mob rule," then political virtue and direct democracy were incompatible. The Federalists' profound suspicion of the common people therefore was deeply rooted not only in old-fashioned social reciprocity (see Chapter 1) and in conservative colonial political traditions but also in republican ideology itself.

A very different understanding of republican ideology influenced Jefferson, Madison, and others alienated by Federalist measures. Although some critics of the administration surfaced in New England and the Middle Atlantic states, anti-Federalist sentiment ran particularly high in the South. Indeed, the southern interpretation of republicanism stressed the corruption inherent in a powerful government dominated by a highly visible few, and southerners widely insisted that liberty would be safe only if power was diffused among virtuous, independent citizens. Thus anti-Federalist southerners feared popular participation in politics far less than northern Federalists. Further, few southern planters were strongly religious, and many had absorbed the Enlightenment's faith that the free flow of ideas would inevitably ensure progress. They also felt confident of their ability to lead (and be elected by) the smaller farmers. Consequently, southerners felt exhilarated by the events unfolding in France; they saw the French as fellow republicans, carrying on a work of universal revolution that would replace hereditary privilege with liberty, equality, and brotherhood. Unlike northern Federalists, nervous about urban mobs, southern planters faced the future with optimism and viewed attempts to inhibit widespread political participation as unworthy of educated gentlemen.

Self-interest, too, drove men like Jefferson and Madison to rouse ordinary citizens' concerns about civic affairs. Political apathy was widespread in the early 1790s, a situation that favored the Federalists by making it unlikely that they would be criticized for passing unwise laws. If, however, the Federalists could be held accountable to the public, they would think twice before enacting measures opposed by the majority; or if they persisted in advocating misguided policies, they would ultimately be removed from office. Such reasoning led Jefferson, a wealthy landowner and large slaveholder, to say, "I am not among those who fear the people; they and not the rich, are our dependence for continued freedom."

Efforts to turn public opinion against the Federalists had begun in October 1791 with the publication of the nation's first opposition newspaper, the *National Gazette.* Then in 1793–1794, popular dissatisfaction with the government's policies led to the formation of several dozen Democratic (or Republican) societies, primarily in seaboard cities but also in the rural South and in frontier towns. Their memberships ranged from planters and merchants to artisans and sailors. Conspicuously absent were clergymen, the poor, and blacks.

Sharply critical of the Federalists, the societies spread dissatisfaction with the Washington administration's policies. Because many of the clubs arose during Genêt's ministry, and because all of them also acclaimed revolutionary France, Federalists assumed (wrongly) that their members were acting as foreign agents. Federalists interpreted their emotional appeals to ordinary people as demagoguery and denounced the societies' followers as "democrats, mobocrats, & all other kinds of rats."

The Federalists feared that the societies would grow into revolutionary organizations. Washington privately warned that "if [the clubs] were not counteracted (not by prosecutions, the ready way to make them grow stronger) or did not fall into disesteem . . . they would shake the government to its foundation." During the Whiskey Rebellion, the president publicly denounced "certain self-created societies." So great was his prestige that the societies temporarily broke up. But by attacking them, Washington had at last ended his nonpartisan stance and identified himself unmistakably with the Federalists. The censure would cost him dearly.

The Republican Party and the Election of 1796

Neither Jefferson nor Madison belonged to a Democratic society. However, these private clubs helped publicize administration critics' views, and they initiated into political activity numerous voters who would later support Jefferson's and Madison's Republican party. Ironically, Madison had earlier been one of the most outspoken opponents of political parties.

In the early 1790s, politically active Americans believed that deliberately organizing a political faction or party was a corrupt, subversive action. The Constitution's framers had neither wanted nor planned for political parties, and in *The Federalist No. 10*, Madison had claimed that the Constitution would prevent the rise of national political factions. Republican ideology commonly assumed that factions or parties would fill Congress with politicians of little ability and less integrity, pursuing selfish goals at the expense of national welfare. Good citizens, it was assumed, would shun partisan scheming. These ideals, however, began to waver as controversy mounted over Hamilton's program and foreign policy. President Washington still tried to set an example of impartial leadership by seeking advice from both camps. (He did not know that in their partisan zeal both Hamilton and Jefferson maintained indiscreet contacts with British and French diplomats, respectively.) But Jefferson finally resigned from the cabinet in 1793, and thereafter even the president could not halt the widening political split. Each side saw itself as the guardian of republican virtue and attacked the other as an illegitimate "cabal" (faction).

In 1794 party development reached a decisive stage. Shortly after Washington had openly identified himself with Federalist policies, followers of Jefferson who called themselves Republicans* successfully attacked the Federalists' "pro-British" leanings in many local elections and won a slight majority in the House of Representatives. The election signaled the Republicans' transformation from a faction of officeholders to a broad-based party capable of coordinating local political campaigns throughout the nation.

Federalists and Republicans alike used the press to mold public opinion in the 1790s. In this decade American journalism came of age as the number of newspapers multiplied from 92 to 242, mostly in New England and the Middle Atlantic states. By 1800 newspapers had perhaps 140,000 paid subscribers (about one-fifth of the eligible voters), and their secondhand readership probably exceeded 300,000. Newspapers of both camps were libelous and irresponsible. They cheapened the quality of public discussion through incessant fear mongering and character assassination. Republicans stood accused of plotting a reign of terror and of wishing to turn the nation over to France. Federalists faced repeated charges of favoring a hereditary aristocracy and even of planning to establish an American dynasty by marrying off John Adams's daughter to George III. Such tactics whipped up mutual distrust and made political debate emotional and subjective. Nevertheless, the newspaper warfare stimulated many citizens to become politically active, even if for the wrong reasons.

Behind the inflammatory rhetoric, the Republicans' central charge was that the Federalists had evolved into a faction bent on enriching wealthy citizens at the taxpayers' expense. In 1794 a Republican writer claimed that Federalist policies would create "a privileged order of men . . . who shall enjoy the honors, the emoluments, and the patronage of government, without contributing a farthing to its support." Although almost every Republican leader, too, was well born, Republicans asserted that the Federalists planned to re-create the atmosphere of a European court through highly publicized state dinners, formal balls, and other dazzling entertainments. The Republicans

*Jefferson and Madison preferred the party name *Republican* rather than the radical-sounding *Democratic.*

George Washington, *by Jean Antoine Houdon, 1788–1792*

The French sculptor Houdon created this magnificent life-size statue of Washington from a life mask and exact measurements. It depicts Washington in a role with which he was comfortable: that of an ordinary citizen-farmer.

erred in claiming that their opponents were scheming to introduce legal privilege, aristocracy, and monarchy. But they correctly identified the Federalists' fundamental assumption: that citizens' worth could be measured in terms of their money.

Republican charges that the president secretly supported alleged Federalist plots to establish a monarchy enraged Washington. "By God," Jefferson reported him swearing, "he [the president] would rather be in his grave than in his present situation . . . he had rather be on his farm than to be made *emperor of the world.*" Further, the president took alarm at the stormy debate over Jay's Treaty, and he dreaded the nation's polarization into hostile factions. Republicans' abuse sharply stung him. "As for you, sir," sneered Thomas Paine in a pamphlet, "treacherous in private friendship . . . and a hypocrite in public life, the world will be puzzled to decide whether you are an apostate or an impostor, whether you have abandoned good principles or ever had any." Lonely and surrounded by mediocre advisers after Hamilton's return to private life, Washington decided in the spring of 1796 to retire after two terms. Four years earlier, Madison had drafted the president's parting message to the nation; but now Washington called on Hamilton to give a sharp political twist to his Farewell Address.

The heart of Washington's message was a vigorous condemnation of political parties. Partisan alignments, he insisted, endangered the republic's survival, especially if they became entangled in disputes over foreign policy. Washington warned that the country's safety depended on citizens' avoiding "excessive partiality for one nation and excessive dislike of another." Otherwise, independent-minded "real patriots" would be overwhelmed by demagogues championing foreign causes and paid by foreign governments. Aside from scrupulously fulfilling its existing treaty obligations and maintaining its foreign commerce, the United States must avoid "political connection" with Europe and its wars. If the United States gathered its strength under "an efficient government," it could defy any foreign challenge; but if it became sucked into Europe's quarrels, violence, and corruption, then the republican experiment was doomed. Washington and Hamilton had skillfully turned the central argument of republicanism against their Republican critics. They had also evoked a vision of America virtuously isolated from foreign intrigue and power politics, which would remain a potent inspiration until the twentieth century.

Washington left public office in 1797 and died in 1799. Like many later presidents, he went out amid a barrage of criticism. During his brief retirement, the nation's political division into Republicans and Federalists hardened. Each party consolidated its hold over particular states and groups of voters, leaving the electorate almost equally divided.

As the election of 1796 approached, the Republicans cultivated a large, loyal body of voters. Their efforts to marshal support marked the first time since the Revolution that the political elite had effectively mobilized ordinary Ameri-

cans to take an interest in public affairs. The Republicans' constituency included the Democratic societies, workingmen's clubs, and immigrant-aid associations.

Immigrants became a prime target for Republican recruiters. During the 1790s the United States absorbed perhaps twenty thousand French refugees from Saint Domingue and more than sixty thousand Irish, including some conspirators exiled for plotting against British rule. Although potential immigrant voters were few—composing less than 2 percent of the electorate—the Irish in particular could exert crucial influence in Pennsylvania and New York, where public opinion was closely divided and a few hundred immigrant voters could tip the balance away from the Federalists. In short, Irish immigrants could provide the Republicans with a winning margin in the two states, and the Republicans' pro-French and anti-British rhetoric ensured enthusiastic Irish support.

In 1796 the presidential candidates were Vice President John Adams, supported by the Federalists, and the Republicans' Jefferson. Republicans expected to win as many southern electoral votes and congressional seats as the Federalists counted on in New England, New Jersey, and South Carolina. The crucial "swing" states were Pennsylvania and New York, where the Republicans tried mightily to tip the balance by wooing the large immigrant (particularly Irish) vote. In the end, however, the Republicans took Pennsylvania but not New York, and so Jefferson lost the presidency by just three electoral votes. The Federalists narrowly regained control of the House and maintained their firm grip on the Senate. But by a political fluke possible under the Constitution at the time, Jefferson became vice president.*

The new president exemplified both the strengths and the weaknesses of an intellectual. His brilliance, insight, and idealism have rarely been equaled among American presidents. Like most intellectuals, however, Adams was more comfortable with ideas than with people, more theoretical than practical, and rather inflexible. He inspired trust and often admiration but could not command

---

*The Constitution then stipulated that the presidential candidate with the second-highest electoral vote would become vice president. This was one example of the Constitution's failure to provide for political partisanship.

Adams Family Farm
John Adams, *by Gilbert Stuart, 1826 (Detail)*

The Adamses hailed from Quincy, Massachusetts. John Adams was born in the house at the right; his son, John Quincy Adams, in the saltbox at the left. Soon after the elder Adams's death, John Quincy Adams, himself now president, commissioned a final portrait; this gentle and distinguished canvas was the result.

personal loyalty. His wisdom and historical vision were drowned out in highly emotional political debate. Adams's rational, reserved personality was likewise ill suited to inspiring the electorate, and he ultimately proved unable to unify the country.

The French Crisis

Adams was initially fortunate, however, that French provocations produced a sharp backlash against the Republicans. The French interpreted Jay's Treaty as an American attempt to assist the British in their war against France. On learning of Jefferson's defeat, the French ordered the seizure of American ships carrying goods to British ports; and within a year the French had plundered more than three hundred vessels. The French government rubbed in its contempt for the United States by directing that every American captured on a British naval ship (even those involuntarily impressed) should be hanged.

Hoping to avoid war, Adams sent a peace commission to Paris. But the French foreign minister, Charles de Talleyrand, refused to meet the delegation, instead promising through three unnamed agents ("X, Y, and Z") that talks could begin after he received $250,000 and France obtained a loan of $12 million. This barefaced demand for a bribe became known as the XYZ Affair. Americans reacted to it with outrage. "Millions for defense, not one cent for tribute" became the nation's battle cry as the 1798 congressional elections began.

The XYZ Affair discredited the Republicans' foreign policy views, but the party's leaders compounded the damage by refusing to condemn French aggression and opposing Adams's call for defensive measures. The Republicans tried to excuse French behavior, while the Federalists rode a wave of militant patriotism. In the 1798 elections, Jefferson's supporters were routed almost everywhere, even in the South.

Congress responded to the XYZ Affair by arming fifty-four ships to protect American commerce. The new warships were at once put to use in what has become known as the Quasi-War—an undeclared Franco-American naval conflict in the Caribbean from 1798 to 1800, during which U.S.

forces seized ninety-three French privateers at the loss of just one vessel. The British navy meanwhile extended the protection of its convoys to America's merchant marine. By early 1799 the French were a nuisance but no longer a serious threat at sea.

Despite the president's misgivings, the Federalists in Congress tripled the regular army to ten thousand men in 1798, with an automatic expansion of land forces to fifty thousand in case of war. But the risk of a land war with the French was minimal. In reality, the Federalists primarily wanted a military force ready in the event of a civil war, for the crisis had produced near-hysteria about conspiracies that were being hatched by French and Irish malcontents flooding into the United States.

Federalists were well aware that the French legation was not only engaged in espionage but also making treasonous suggestions to prominent persons. The government knew, for example, that in 1796 General Victor Collot had traveled from Pittsburgh to New Orleans under orders to investigate the prospects for establishing a pro-French, independent nation west of the mountains, and also that he had examined strategic locations to which rebellious frontier dwellers might rally. The State Department heard in 1798 that France had created in the West "a party of mad Americans ready to join with them at a given Signal."

The Alien and Sedition Acts

The Federalists, moreover, insisted that the likelihood of open war with France required stringent legislation to protect national security. In 1798 the Federalist-dominated Congress accordingly passed four measures known collectively as the Alien and Sedition Acts. Adams neither requested nor particularly wanted these laws, but he deferred to congressional judgment and signed them.

Both parties cooperated in writing the first of the four laws, the Alien Enemies Act, which was designed to prevent wartime spying or sabotage. This measure outlined procedures for determining whether the citizens of a hostile country posed a threat to the United States; if so, they were to be deported or jailed. The law established fundamental principles for protecting national security and respecting the rights of enemy citizens. It was to

operate only if Congress declared war and so was not used until the War of 1812 (see Chapter 7).

Second, the Alien Friends Act was a peacetime statute enforceable until June 25, 1800. It authorized the president to expel any foreign residents whose activities he considered dangerous. The law did not require proof of guilt, on the assumption that spies would hide or destroy evidence of their crime. Republicans maintained that the law's real purpose was to deport prominent immigrants critical of Federalist policies.

Republicans also denounced the third law, the Naturalization Act. This measure increased the residency requirement for U.S. citizenship from five to fourteen years (the last five continuously in one state), with the purpose of reducing Irish voting.

Finally came the Sedition Act, the only one of these measures enforceable against U.S. citizens. Although its alleged purpose was to distinguish between free speech and attempts at encouraging others to violate federal laws or to overthrow the government, the act nevertheless defined criminal activity so broadly that it blurred any real distinction between sedition and legitimate political discussion. Thus it forbade an individual or group "to oppose any measure or measures of the United States"—wording that could be interpreted to ban any criticism of the party in power. Another clause made it illegal to speak, write, or print any statement about the president that would bring him "into contempt or disrepute." Under such restrictions, for example, a newspaper editor might face imprisonment for disapproving of an action by Adams or his cabinet members. The Federalist *Gazette of the United States* expressed the twisted logic of the Sedition Act perfectly: "It is patriotism to write in favor of our government—it is sedition to write against it."

Sedition cases were heard by juries, which could decide if the defendant had really intended to stir up rebellion or was merely expressing political dissent. But whatever way one looked at it, the Sedition Act interfered with free speech. Ingeniously, the Federalists wrote the law to expire in 1801 (so that it could not be turned against them if they lost the next election) and to leave them free meanwhile to heap abuse on the *vice* president, Jefferson.

Federalist enforcement of the first of the repressive new laws, the Alien Friends Act, produced mixed results. The president signed a deportation order for French agent Collot, who escaped capture. No expulsions were actually carried out under the law, although two of Collot's assistants and several dozen other French sailed home before they could be forcibly removed.

The real target of Federalist repression was the U.S. opposition press. Four of the five largest Republican newspapers were charged with sedition just as the election of 1800 was getting under way. The attorney general used the Alien Friends Act to threaten an Irish journalist, John Daly Burk, with expulsion (Burk went underground instead). Scottish editor James T. Callender was on the verge of being deported when he suddenly qualified for citizenship. Now unable to expel Callender, the government tried him for sedition before an all-Federalist jury, which sent him to prison for criticizing the president.

Federalist leaders never intended to fill the jails with Republican martyrs. Rather, they wanted to use a small number of highly visible prosecutions to intimidate most journalists and candidates into keeping quiet during the election of 1800. The attorney general charged seventeen persons with sedition and won ten convictions. Among the victims was the Republican congressman Matthew Lyon of Vermont ("Ragged Matt, the democrat," to the Federalists), who spent four months in prison for publishing a blast against Adams.

Vocal criticism of Federalist repression erupted only in Virginia and Kentucky. During the summer of 1798, militia commanders in these states mustered their regiments, not to drill but to hear speeches demanding that the federal government respect the Bill of Rights. Entire units then signed petitions denouncing the Alien and Sedition Acts. The symbolic implications of these protests were sobering. Young men stepped forward to sign petitions on drumheads with a pen in one hand and a gun in the other, as older officers who had fought in the Continental Army looked on approvingly. It was not hard to imagine Kentucky rifles being substituted for quill pens as the men who had led one revolution took up arms again.

Ten years earlier, opponents of the Constitution had warned that giving the national government extensive powers would eventually endanger freedom. By 1798 their prediction had come true.

Shocked Republicans realized that because the Federalists controlled all three branches of the government, neither the Bill of Rights nor the system of checks and balances protected individual liberties. In this context, the doctrine of states' rights was first advanced as a means of preventing the national government from violating basic freedoms.

Madison and Jefferson anonymously wrote two manifestoes on states' rights that the assemblies of Virginia and Kentucky officially endorsed in 1798. Madison's Virginia Resolutions and Jefferson's Kentucky Resolutions declared that the state legislatures had never surrendered their right to judge the constitutionality of federal actions and that they retained an authority called interposition, which enabled them to protect the liberties of their citizens. A set of Kentucky Resolutions adopted in November 1799 added that objectionable federal laws might be "nullified" by the states. The terms *interposition* and *nullification* were not defined, but their intention was obviously to prevent residents from being tried for breaking an unconstitutional law. The Virginia and Kentucky legislatures must have understood that interposition would ultimately challenge the jurisdiction of federal courts and perhaps require that state militia march into a federal courtroom to halt proceedings at bayonet point.

Although no other states endorsed these resolutions (most in fact expressed disapproval), their passage demonstrated the great potential for violence in the late 1790s. So did a minor insurrection called the Fries Rebellion, which broke out in 1799 when crowds of Pennsylvania German farmers released prisoners jailed for refusing to pay taxes needed to fund the national army's expansion. Fortunately, the disturbance collapsed just as federal cavalry arrived, and the only casualties were several head of rebellious cattle shot by trigger-happy soldiers.

The nation's leaders increasingly acted as if a crisis were imminent. Vice President Jefferson hinted that events might push the southern states into secession from the Union. The normally sensible President Adams hid guns in his home. After passing through Richmond and learning that state officials were purchasing thousands of muskets for the militia, an alarmed Supreme Court justice wrote in January 1799 that "the General Assembly of

Virginia are pursuing steps which will lead directly to civil war." A tense atmosphere hung over the Republic as the election of 1800 neared.

The Election of 1800

In the election the Republicans rallied around Jefferson for president and the wily New York politician Aaron Burr for vice president. The Federalists meanwhile became mired in wrangling between Adams and the extreme "High Federalists" who looked to Alexander Hamilton for guidance. That the nation survived the election of 1800 without a civil war or the disregard of voters' wishes owed chiefly to the good sense of the more moderate leaders of both parties. Thus Jefferson and Madison discouraged radicalism that might provoke intervention by the national army. Even more credit belonged to Adams for rejecting High Federalist demands that he ensure victory by deliberately sparking an insurrection or asking Congress to declare war on France.

"Nothing but an open war can save us" argued Adams's High Federalist secretary of the treasury. But when the president suddenly discovered the French willing to seek peace in 1799, he proposed a special diplomatic mission. "Surprise, indignation, grief & disgust followed each other in quick succession," said a Federalist senator on hearing the news. Adams obtained Senate approval for his envoys only by threatening to resign and so make Jefferson president, an action that he later described with justifiable pride as "the most disinterested . . . in my whole life." The High Federalists were so outraged that they tried unsuccessfully to dump Adams. Hamilton denounced him as a fool, but this ill-considered maneuver rallied most New Englanders around their stubborn, upright president.

Adams's negotiations with France did not achieve a settlement until 1801, but the expectation that normal—and perhaps friendly—relations with the French would resume prevented the Federalists from exploiting charges of Republican sympathy for the enemy. Without the immediate threat of war, moreover, voters grew resentful that in merely two years, taxes had soared 33 percent to support an army that had done nothing except chase terrified Pennsylvania farmers. As the danger of war receded, voters gave the Federalists less credit

for standing up to France and more blame for ballooning the national debt by $10 million.

Two years after their triumph in the 1798 elections, support for the Federalists had eroded sharply. High Federalists who had hoped for war spitefully withheld the backing that Adams needed to win. The Republicans meanwhile redoubled their efforts to elect Jefferson. They were especially successful in mobilizing voters in Philadelphia and New York, where artisans, farmers, and some entrepreneurs were ready to forsake the Federalists, whom they saw as defenders of entrenched privilege and upstart wealth. Amid the excitement, political apathy waned. Voter turnouts in 1800 leaped to more than double those of 1788, rising from about 15 percent to almost 40 percent, and in hotly contested Pennsylvania and New York more than half the eligible voters participated.

Playing on their opponent's reputation as a religious free thinker, the Federalists forged a case against Jefferson that came down to urging citizens to vote for "GOD—AND A RELIGIOUS PRESIDENT; or impiously declare for JEFFERSON—AND NO GOD!!!" But this ploy did not prevent thousands of deeply religious Baptists, Methodists, and other dissenters from voting Republican. Nor did voters know that Adams was scarcely more conventional in his religious views than Jefferson.

Adams lost the presidency by just 8 electoral votes out of 138. He would have won if his party had not lost control of New York's state senate, which chose the electors, after a narrow defeat in New York City. Unexpectedly, Jefferson and his running mate Burr also carried South Carolina because his backers made lavish promises of political favors to that state's legislators.

Although Adams lost, Jefferson's election was not assured. The Republicans had failed to select in advance one elector who would not vote for Burr, so the electoral college deadlocked in a Jefferson-Burr tie.* The choice of president devolved upon the House of Representatives, where thirty-five ballots over six days produced no result. Finally, Delaware's only representative, a Federalist, aban-

---

*The Twelfth Amendment (ratified in 1804) eliminated the possibility of such problems. It stipulated that electors vote separately for presidential and vice-presidential candidates; no longer would the runner-up in the presidential contest become vice president.

doned Burr and gave Jefferson the presidency by history's narrowest margin.

Deferring Equality

The election of 1800 did not make the United States more democratic. Rather, it prevented rigidly anti-democratic prejudices from blocking future political liberalization. The Republican victory also repudiated the Federalist willingness, so evident in Hamilton's plans, to create a base of support for the government through special-interest legislation. Such self-serving goals led critics like Madison to condemn the Federalists for "substituting the motive of private interest for public duty." After 1800 government policies would be judged by Jefferson's standard of "equal rights for all, special privileges for none."

But not all Americans won equal rights. Women took no part in politics, and few people felt that they should. As for the native Americans, the nation's diplomatic gains came largely at their expense; and foreign-policy issues rarely concerned the aspirations of African-Americans. Moreover, in the Republic's early years, white Americans lost much of the idealism that Revolutionary ideology had inspired, and they began to assume that racial minorities could never be more than second-class citizens at best.

Indian Decline

By 1795 most eastern Indian tribes had suffered severe reductions in population and territory. Innumerable deaths had resulted from battle, famine, exposure to the elements during flight from enemies, and disease. From 1775 to 1795, the Cherokees declined from 16,000 to 10,000 and the Iroquois fell from about 9,000 to 4,000. Meanwhile, in the quarter-century before 1800, Indians may have forfeited more land than the area inhabited by whites in 1775.

Frontier warfare had sapped the strength of many Indian cultures. Young adults grew indifferent toward traditional ways. Unable to strike back at whites, Indians inflicted violence on one another and often consumed enormous quantities of whis-

Osage Warrior, *by Charles de Saint-Mémin, c. 1804*

As the nineteenth century opened, many native Americans found themselves torn between their traditional lifestyles and pressure to adopt white ways.

key. The situation among the Iroquois was all too typical. "The Indians of the Six Nations," wrote a federal official in 1796, "have become given to indolence, drunkenness, and thefts, and have taken to killing each other."

The Indians' predicament spawned a profound social and moral crisis within the tribes, most notably among the Iroquois. Handsome Lake, an Iroquois tribal leader, tried to halt his people's decline by borrowing from the white man's world. Despite his own problems with liquor, he sought to end alcoholism among Indians by appealing to their religious traditions. Even more radically, he welcomed Quaker missionaries and federal aid earmarked for teaching whites' agricultural methods to Iroquois men, who had to look for a new livelihood after the loss of their hunting grounds. Some, to be sure, sneered at advice that they should work like white farmers; said one, only "squaws and hedgehogs are made to scratch the ground." But

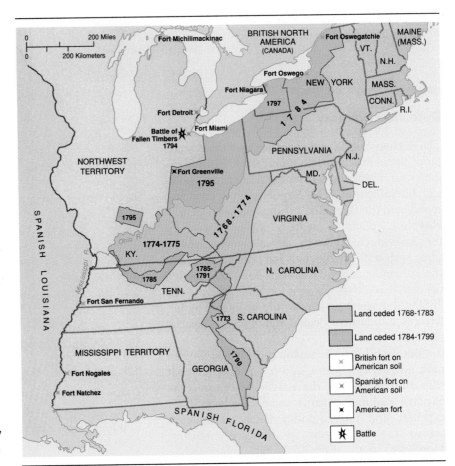

Indian Land Cessions, 1768–1799

Between 1768 and 1775, western Indians sold off vast territories, though only in undesirable mountainous regions or unoccupied Kentucky hunting grounds. Pressure by U.S. military forces from 1784 to 1799 led to the native Americans' first involuntary cessions since the early eighteenth century of large, inhabited Indian lands.

many Iroquois men welcomed the change. It was the women who resisted most, because they stood to lose their collective ownership of farmland, their control of the food supply, and their place in tribal councils. Women who did not accept Handsome Lake's and the Quakers' urging to exchange farming for housewifery found themselves accused of witchcraft, and some were killed. Even so, cultural conversion proceeded very slowly.

White attitudes toward native Americans would change significantly after the 1790s. Eighteenth-century Anglo-Americans attributed the Indians' distinctive way of life to their upbringing and expected that the native peoples would eventually match whites' cultural achievements. Indians—unlike blacks—did not seem to eighteenth-century whites a separate race. But the Iroquois' partial willingness to adopt white ways proved quite exceptional: in contrast, most native Americans

clung tightly to traditional values, much to whites' frustration and annoyance. By 1800 whites were growingly perceiving native Americans as incapable of change—as "redskins," a distinct and inferior race that white American society could never absorb. Native Americans, in short, were becoming aliens in their own land, regarded by more and more whites as a deadweight on the nation's progress.

Redefining the Color Line

The Republic's first years marked the high tide of black Americans' Revolutionary era success in bettering their lot. Although racism had not disappeared, Jefferson's eloquent words "all men are created equal" had awakened many whites' consciences. By 1790, 8 percent of all African-Americans enjoyed freedom—many having purchased

Number and Percentage of Free Blacks, by State, 1800

State	Total Number of Free Blacks	Free Blacks as a Percentage of Total Black Population
Massachusetts	7,378	100%
Vermont	557	100%
New Hampshire	855	99%
Rhode Island	3,304	90%
Pennsylvania	14,564	89%
Connecticut	5,300	85%
Delaware	8,268	57%
New York	10,374	33%
New Jersey	4,402	26%
Maryland	19,587	16%
Virginia	20,124	6%
North Carolina	7,043	5%
South Carolina	3,185	2%
Georgia	1,019	2%
Kentucky	741	2%
Tennessee	309	2%
UNITED STATES	108,395*	11%

*Total includes figures from the District of Columbia, Mississippi Territory, and Northwest Territory. These areas are not shown on the chart.

Within a generation of the Declaration of Independence, a large free black population emerged that included every ninth African-American. In the North, only in New Jersey and New York did most blacks remain slaves. Almost half of all free blacks lived in the South. Every sixth black in Maryland was free by 1800.

SOURCE: U.S. Bureau of the Census.

liberty or earned it through wartime service. Ten years later, 11 percent controlled their own fate. Various state reforms meanwhile attempted to improve slaves' conditions. In 1791, for example, the North Carolina legislature declared that the former "distinction of criminality between the murder of a white person and one who is equally an human creature, but merely of a different complexion, is disgraceful to humanity" and authorized the execution of whites who murdered slaves. By 1794 most states had outlawed the Atlantic slave trade.

Hesitant measures to ensure free blacks' legal equality also appeared in the 1780s and early 1790s. Most states dropped restrictions on their freedom of movement, protected their property, and allowed them to enroll in the militia. Of the sixteen states in the Union by 1796, all but three either permitted free blacks to vote or made no specific attempt to exclude them. Further, the federal Constitution required no racial test for citizenship and counted everyone except slaves equally for congressional representation. But before the 1790s ended, the trend toward lessening social and legal distances between the races ended. Abolitionist sentiment ebbed, slavery became more entrenched, and whites demonstrated unmistakable reluctance to accept even free blacks as fellow citizens.

Federal law led the way in restricting blacks' rights. When Congress established procedures for naturalizing aliens in 1790, it limited eligibility to foreign whites. The federal militia law of 1792 required whites to enroll in local units but allowed states to exclude free blacks, an option that state governments increasingly chose. The navy and the marine corps forbade nonwhite enlistments in 1798. Delaware stripped free blacks of the vote in 1792, and by 1807 Maryland, Kentucky, and New Jersey had followed suit. Free blacks continued to vote and serve in integrated militia organizations in many localities after 1800 (including the slave states of North Carolina and Tennessee), but the number of places that treated them as the political equals of whites dropped sharply in the early 1800s.

An especially revealing indication of changing racial attitudes occurred in 1793, when Congress enacted the Fugitive Slave Law. This law required judges to award possession of a runaway slave upon any formal request by a master or his representative. Accused runaways not only were denied a jury trial but also were sometimes refused permission to present evidence of their freedom. Slaves' legal status as property disqualified them from claiming these constitutional privileges, of course, but the Fugitive Slave Law denied *free* blacks the legal protections that the Bill of Rights guaranteed them as citizens. Congress nevertheless passed this measure without serious opposition. The law marked a striking departure from the atmosphere of the 1780s, when state governments had invariably given whites and free blacks the same legal privileges. By 1793 white Americans clearly found it easy to forget that the Constitution had not limited citizenship to their race, and fewer of them felt honorbound to protect black rights.

The bloody slave revolt on Saint Domingue notably undermined the trend toward abolition and reinforced the kind of fears that spawned racism. Reports of the slaughter of French slaveowners made Americans hesitate to criticize slavery in the United States and helped transform the image of blacks from that of victims of injustice to one of a potential menace. In August 1800 smoldering southern white fears were kindled when a slave insurrection broke out near Virginia's capital, Richmond. Having secretly assembled weapons, more than a thousand slaves planned to march on Richmond. State militiamen, called out by Governor James Monroe, swiftly put down the conspiracy and executed some thirty-five slaves, including the leader, Gabriel Prosser. "I have nothing more to offer than what General Washington would have had to offer, had he been taken by the British officers and put to trial by them," said one rebel before his execution. "I have ventured my life in endeavoring to obtain the liberty of my countrymen, and I am a willing sacrifice to their cause."

Gabriel's Rebellion confirmed whites' anxieties that Saint Domingue's terrifying experience could be replayed on American soil. For years thereafter, isolated uprisings occurred, and rumors persisted that a massive revolt was brewing. Antislavery sentiment diminished quickly. By 1810 abolitionists ceased to exert political influence, and not until the 1830s would the antislavery movement recover from the damage inflicted by the Saint Domingue revolt.

By the time Thomas Jefferson assumed the presidency in 1801, free blacks had suffered a subtle erosion of their substantial political gains since 1776, and slaves were no closer to freedom. Two vignettes poignantly communicate blacks' plight. In 1799, near death, George Washington freed all of his relatively few slaves and gave them small sums of money to start a new life. But Martha Washington refused to emancipate the much larger group of Mount Vernon slaves who were her personal property. Meanwhile, across the Potomac, work was proceeding on the new national capital that would bear the first president's name. Enslaved blacks performed most of the labor. African-Americans were manifestly losing ground.

Conclusion   The United States had survived the perils of birth. By 1801 the dangers of civil war and national disintegration had abated, though they had not vanished. A peaceful transition of power, unprecedented in history, occurred when the Federalists allowed Thomas Jefferson to become president. But ideological hatreds remained strong, and the West's allegiance to the Union was by no means assured. Racial tensions were growing, not diminishing. It remained to be seen whether Jefferson's liberal version of republicanism could serve as a better philosophy of government than the Federalists' conservative republicanism.

CHRONOLOGY

1787 Pennsylvania Society for the Encouragement of Manufactures and the Useful Arts established.

1789 George Washington sworn in as first president.
Judiciary Act of 1789.
French Revolution begins.

1790 Alexander Hamilton submits his Report on the Public Credit and Report on a National Bank to Congress.

1791 Bank of the United States is granted a twenty-year charter.
Vermont admitted to the Union.
Bill of Rights ratified.
Slave uprising begins in French colony of Saint Domingue.
Society for the Encouragement of Useful Manufactures founded.
Hamilton submits his Report on Manufactures to Congress.

1792 Kentucky admitted to the Union.

1793 Fugitive Slave Law.
Chisholm v. *Georgia.*
Large-scale exodus of French planters from Saint Domingue to the United States.
France declares war on Britain, Spain, and Holland.

1793 Washington's Neutrality Proclamation.
(cont.) Democratic societies established.

1794 Whiskey Rebellion in western Pennsylvania.
General Anthony Wayne's forces rout Indians in the Battle of Fallen Timbers.

1795 Jay's Treaty with Britain ratified.
Treaty of Greenville.

1796 *Hylton* v. *United States.*
Ware v. *Hylton.*
Tennessee admitted to the Union.
Treaty of San Lorenzo (Pinckney's Treaty) ratified.
Washington's Farewell Address.
John Adams elected president.

1798 XYZ Affair.
Alien and Sedition Acts.
Eleventh Amendment to the Constitution ratified.

1798– Virginia and Kentucky Resolutions.
1799

1798– United States fights Quasi-War with France.
1800

1799 Fries Rebellion in Pennsylvania.

1800 Gabriel's Rebellion in Virginia.
Thomas Jefferson elected president.

For Further Reading

Lance Banning, *The Jeffersonian Persuasion: Evolution of a Party Ideology* (1978). A fresh interpretation of the intellectual assumptions that underlay Jeffersonian political principles.

Richard Buel, Jr., *Securing the Revolution: Ideology in American Politics, 1789–1815* (1972). A detailed examination of the party battles of the 1790s and the factors that contributed to the Jeffersonians' eventual victory.

Ralph Ketcham, *Presidents Above Party: The First American Presidency, 1789–1829* (1984). A comprehensive study of the ideals of nonpartisan leadership that guided the behavior of the first six presidents.

Drew R. McCoy, *The Elusive Republic: Political Economy in Jeffersonian America* (1980). An insightful portrayal of the influence of economic considerations on early national political thought.

Charles R. Ritcheson, *Aftermath of Revolution: British Policy Toward the United States, 1783–1795* (1969). A judicious, thoroughly researched account of Anglo-American diplomacy to Jay's Treaty.

James M. Smith, *Freedom's Fetters: The Alien and Sedition Laws and American Civil Liberties* (rev. ed., 1966). The most comprehensive study of the country's first great crisis in civil rights.

Gerald Stourzh, *Alexander Hamilton and the Idea of Republican Government* (1970). A bold, sweeping description of Hamilton's personal values, understanding of republicanism, and political policies.

Additional Bibliography

Early National Society

Ira Berlin, *Slaves Without Masters: The Free Negro in the Antebellum South* (1974); James Essig, *Bonds of Wickedness: American Evangelicals Against Slavery, 1770–1808* (1982); Alfred N. Hunt, *Haiti's Influence on Antebellum America* (1989); Robert McColley, *Slavery and Jeffersonian Virginia* (1964); Curtis P. Nettles, *The Emergence of a National Economy, 1775–1815* (1962); Douglass C. North, *The Economic Growth of the United States, 1790–1860* (1961); Howard B. Rock, *Artisans of the New Republic: The Tradesmen of New York City in the Age of Jefferson* (1979); George C. Rogers, Jr., *Charleston in the Age of the Pinckneys* (1969); Bernard W. Sheehan, *Seeds of Extinction: Jeffersonian Philanthropy and the American Indian* (1973); Charles G. Steffen, *The Mechanics of Baltimore: Workers and Politics in the Age of Revolution, 1763–1812* (1984); Barbara M. Tucker, *Samuel Slater and the Origins of the American Textile Industry, 1790–1860* (1984); Anthony F. C. Wallace, *The Death and Rebirth of the Seneca* (1970).

Diplomatic, Military, and Western Affairs

Harry Ammon, *The Genêt Mission* (1973); Steven R. Boyd, ed., *The Whiskey Rebellion: Past and Present Perspectives* (1985); Colin G. Calloway, *Crown and Calumet: British-Indian Relations, 1783–1815* (1987); Jerald A. Combs, *The Jay Treaty: Political Battleground of the Founding Fathers* (1970); Alexander DeConde, *Entangling Alliance: Politics and Diplomacy under George Washington* (1958), and *The Quasi-War: The Politics and Diplomacy of the Undeclared War with France, 1797–1801* (1966); Felix Gilbert, *To the Farewell Address: Ideas of Early American Foreign Policy* (1961); Reginald Horsman, *The Frontier in the Formative Years, 1783–1815* (1970); Richard H. Kohn, *Eagle and Sword: The Federalists and the Creation of the Military Establishment in America, 1783–1802* (1975); Daniel G. Lang, *Foreign Policy in the Early Republic: The Law of Nations and the Balance of Power* (1985); Bradford Perkins, *The First Rapprochement: England and the United States, 1795–1805* (1955); Thomas P. Slaughter, *The Whiskey Rebellion: Frontier Epilogue to the American Revolution* (1986); William Stinchcombe, *The XYZ Affair* (1980); Wiley Sword, *President Washington's Indian War: The Struggle for the Old Northwest, 1790–1795* (1985); Mary K. B. Tachau, *Federal Courts in the Early Republic: Kentucky, 1789–1816* (1978); J. Leitch Wright, *Britain and the American Frontier, 1783–1815* (1975).

Politics

Joyce Appleby, *Capitalism and a New Social Order: The Republican Vision of the 1790s* (1984); Richard Beeman, *The Old Dominion and the New Nation, 1788–1801* (1972); Rudolph M. Bell, *Party and Faction in American Politics: The House of Representatives, 1789–1801* (1974); William N. Chambers, *Political Parties in a New Nation: The American Experience, 1776–1809* (1963); Noble E. Cunningham, Jr., *The Jeffersonian Republicans: The Formation of Party Organization, 1789–1801* (1957); Paul Goodman, *The Democratic Republicans of Massachusetts* (1964); John F. Hoadley, *Origins of American Political Parties, 1789–1803* (1986); Stephen G. Kurtz, *The Presidency of John Adams: The Collapse of Federalism, 1795–1800* (1957); John C. Miller, *The Federalist Era, 1789–1801* (1960); Carl E. Prince, *New*

Jersey's Jeffersonian Republicans: The Genesis of an Early Party Machine, 1789–1817 (1967); Lisle A. Rose, *Prologue to Democracy: The Federalists in the South, 1789–1800* (1968); Robert A. Rutland, *The Birth of the Bill of Rights, 1776–1791* (1955); Bernard Schwartz, *The Great Rights of Mankind* (1977); Donald H. Stewart, *The Opposition Press of the Federalist Period* (1969); Alfred F. Young, *The Democratic Republicans of New York: The Origins, 1763–1797* (1967); John Zvesper, *Political Philosophy and Rhetoric: A Study of the Origins of American Party Politics* (1977).

Biographies

John R. Alden, *George Washington: A Biography* (1984); Ralph A. Brown, *The Presidency of John Adams* (1975); Gerard H. Clarfield, *Timothy Pickering and American Diplomacy, 1795–1800* (1969); Jacob E. Cooke, *Alexander Hamilton* (1982); Marcus Cunliffe, *George Washington: Man and Monument* (1958); Ralph Ketcham, *James Madison: A Biography* (1971); Adrienne Koch, *Jefferson and Madison: The Great Collaboration* (1950); Milton Lomask, *Aaron Burr: The Years from Princeton to Vice President, 1756–1805* (1979); Forrest McDonald, *Alexander Hamilton: A Biography* (1979); Dumas Malone, *Jefferson and the Ordeal of Liberty* (1962); Richard B. Morris, *John Jay: The Nation and the Court* (1967); Paul D. Nelson, *Anthony Wayne: Soldier of the Early Republic* (1985); Merrill Peterson, *Thomas Jefferson and the New Nation: A Biography* (1970); Peter Shaw, *The Character of John Adams* (1976); Page Smith, *John Adams* (1962).

CHAPTER 7

Jeffersonianism and the Era of Good Feelings

Arriving at a diplomatic reception in 1803, the British minister to the United States, Anthony Merry, was aghast to find the American president, Thomas Jefferson, "ACTUALLY STANDING IN SLIPPERS DOWN AT THE HEELS." Such "utter slovenliness and indifference to appearances," Merry concluded, could only be "intended as an insult, not to me personally, but to the sovereign I represented." In fact, Jefferson intended no insult. He never paid much attention to his dress and believed that pomp and fanfare had gotten out of hand in the administrations of George Washington and John Adams. Jefferson's casual dress, including his penchant for wearing slippers on public occasions, reflected both his personal preference and his desire to restore "republican simplicity" to the American government. That same desire led Jefferson to walk to his inaugural and then back to his boarding house, and later to substitute written messages for personal appearances before Congress.

The appearance of the new capital, Washington, reinforced Merry's impression of Americans' shabbiness. Designed for the traffic of London and the elegance of Versailles, Washington possessed neither in 1800. It could boast of two public buildings of note, the president's mansion and the Capitol, both unfinished and separated by a mile and a half of swampy terrain. The best that could be said for the place, a British visitor observed, was that the partridges nesting around the Capitol's wall provided excellent shooting.

Washington's spare arrangements mirrored conditions in the young nation. In 1800 the two most populous states, Virginia and Pennsylvania, contained fewer than fourteen inhabitants per square mile. At a time when London reported more than a million inhabitants and Paris more than half a million, no American city held even seventy thousand people. The poor quality or utter lack of roads forced Americans to live very isolated from each other. Stagecoaches running between Baltimore and Washington, for example, had to pass through a virtually trackless forest. To get to Washington from Monticello, his home in Virginia, President Jefferson had to cross five rivers that lacked bridges.

This isolation ensured that the political horizons of most Americans were limited by the physical boundaries of their own towns or villages. Republicans and Federalists clashed venomously in Washington, but in many rural areas, neither party aroused intense support. The outgoing president, John Adams, had not seen himself as the leader of a political party. The incoming president, Thomas Jefferson, did play the role of party leader and in this respect was a more modern figure than Adams. But neither Jefferson's Republicans nor the rival Federalists had any effective grassroots organization. However sharp the clashes between Republicans and Federalists in Washington, national issues only occasionally concerned ordinary Americans. Women, slaves, and the propertyless were legally barred from voting, and even those citizens who were eligible to vote often found national issues remote and uninteresting. Few voters ever laid eyes on a president. Jefferson, for example, had not been in New England since 1784, and he never did venture west of the Appalachian Mountains or south of Virginia.

Despite its deeply ingrained localism, America was to experience the most extraordinary national events between 1800 and 1820. In swift succession, the United States would double its land area; survive a bizarre scheme by a former vice president to divide the Union; stop all its trade with Europe in an effort to avoid war, and then go to war anyway and nearly lose; conclude a peace more favorable than it had a right to expect; and almost disintegrate in a battle over statehood for Missouri while simultaneously profiting from European power concessions that would extend its territorial claims from the Atlantic to the Pacific.

The intrusion of so dizzying a sequence of events upon a society known for its sleepy provinciality was not altogether accidental. Because communications were poor, the age proved congenial to adventurers like Jefferson's vice president, Aaron Burr, who hatched wild conspiracies with the hope of succeeding before his plans became common knowledge. Furthermore, the strength of local attachments among the common people somewhat insulated leaders like Jefferson and his successor, James Madison, from their constituents. This insulation, in turn, enabled Jefferson and Madison to view politics on a grand scale. In their eyes, politics was more a process for transforming philosophical ideas into realities than for accommodating the special needs of diverse groups.

America's newness also contributed to the philosophical or ideological cast of its politics. Because there had never before been a transfer of political power from a defeated party to a victorious party, no one was sure how the Republicans would behave in office or what would become of the Federalists. The absence of precedents that might have quietly settled certain issues meant that seemingly minor questions such as replacement of Federalist officeholders became occasions for major philosophical clashes between the Republicans and the Federalists. In sum, one of the tasks that faced Jefferson and Madison was to devise and gain popular acceptance of ground rules to guide the operations of republican government.

The Age of Jefferson

Although basically a dispassionate man, Thomas Jefferson aroused deep emotions in others. His admirers saw him as a vigilant defender of popular liberty, an aristocrat who trusted the people. His detractors, pointing to his doubts about some Christian doctrines and to his early defense of the French Revolution, portrayed him as an infidel and a frenzied radical. Jefferson had so many facets that it was hard not to misunderstand him. Trained in law, he spent much of his prepresidential life in public office—as governor of Virginia, secretary of state under Washington, and vice president under John Adams. His interests included the violin, architecture, languages, and science. He designed his own mansion, Monticello, in Virginia; studied Latin, Greek, French, Italian, Anglo-Saxon, and several Indian languages; and served for nearly twenty years as president of the American Philosophical Society, the nation's first and foremost scientific

organization. He viewed himself as a stronger friend of equality than either Washington or Adams; yet he owned more than two hundred slaves.

History convinced Jefferson that republics collapsed from within, not from without. Hostile neighbors notwithstanding, the real threat to freedom was posed by governments that progressively undermined popular liberty. Taxes, standing armies, and corrupt officials had made governments the masters, rather than the servants, of the people. Anyone who doubted this lesson of history needed only to look at the French Revolution; Jefferson had greeted it with hope and then watched in dismay as Napoleon Bonaparte assumed despotic power in 1799.

To prevent the United States from sinking into tyranny, Jefferson advocated that state governments retain considerable authority. He reasoned that in a vast republic marked by strong local

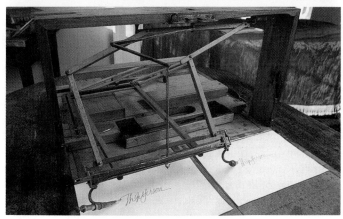

Jefferson's Monticello

Located in Virginia's piedmont region, Jefferson's mansion Monticello revealed his taste, scientific curiosity, and penchant for gadgetry. The device on his desk, known as a polygraph, enabled him to duplicate his letters in a pre-photocopier age.

attachments, state governments were more immediately responsive to the popular will than was the government in Washington. He also believed that popular liberty required popular virtue. For republican theorists like Jefferson, virtue consisted of a disposition to place the public good ahead of one's private interests and to exercise vigilance to keep governments from growing out of control. To Jefferson, the most vigilant and virtuous people were educated farmers, who were accustomed to act and think with sturdy independence. The least vigilant were the inhabitants of cities. Jefferson regarded cities as breeding grounds for mobs and as menaces to liberty. When the people "get piled upon one another in large cities, as in Europe," he wrote, "they will become corrupt as in Europe."

Despite his deep philosophical beliefs, Jefferson was not impractical. Of all the charges leveled at him by contemporaries, the most inaccurate was that he was a dreamy philosopher incapable of governing. "What is practicable," he wrote, "must often control pure theory." He studied science not because he liked to ponder abstract puzzles but because he believed that every scientific advance would increase human happiness. All true knowledge was useful knowledge. This practical cast of mind revealed itself both in his inventions—he designed an improved plow and a gadget for duplicating letters—and in his presidential agenda.

Jefferson's "Revolution"

Jefferson described his election as a revolution, but the revolution he sought was to restore the country to the liberty and tranquillity it had known before Alexander Hamilton's economic program and John Adams's Alien and Sedition Acts: to reverse the drift into despotism that he had detected during the 1790s. One alarming sign of this drift was the growth of the national debt by $10 million under

Explosion of the Intrepid

In September 1804 the American fireship Intrepid, *loaded with powder and intending to penetrate Tripoli harbor and explode enemy ships, blew up before reaching its target, killing Captain Richard Somers and his crew. Seven months earlier, commanded by Lieutenant Stephen Decatur, the* Intrepid *had destroyed the American frigate* Philadelphia, *which had fallen into Tripolitan hands. Britain's Lord Nelson reportedly described Decatur's exploit as "the most bold and daring act of the age."*

the Federalists. Jefferson and his secretary of the treasury, the Swiss-born Albert Gallatin, objected to the debt on both political and economic grounds. Hamilton had argued that by giving creditors a financial stake in the health of the federal government, a national debt would strengthen that government. Jefferson and Gallatin disagreed. Merely to pay the interest on the debt, there would have to be taxes, which Jefferson and Gallatin opposed for many of the same reasons that they opposed the debt. Taxes would suck money from industrious farmers, the backbone of the Republic, and put it in the hands of wealthy creditors, parasites who lived off interest payments. Further, Jefferson and Gallatin feared that revenue from taxes would tempt the government to build such a menace to liberty as a standing army.

Jefferson and Gallatin succeeded in getting Congress to repeal most internal taxes, but this repeal left the government dependent on revenue from the tariff, which was inadequate to pay off the debt. The only alternative was to slash expenditures. Jefferson closed American embassies in Madrid, Lisbon, and The Hague to save money and to signal his intention of pulling the United States out of European entanglements, and he cut the army from 4,000 to 2,500 men. The navy, however, was a different matter. In 1801 he ordered a naval squadron into action in the Mediterranean against the so-called Tripolitan (or Barbary) pir-

ates of North Africa. For centuries, the Moslem rulers of Tripoli, Morocco, Tunis, and Algiers had solved their own budgetary problems by engaging in piracy and extorting tribute in exchange for protection; seamen whom they captured were held for ransom or sold into slavery. Most European powers handed over the fees demanded, but Jefferson calculated that going to war would be cheaper than paying high tribute to maintain peace. While suffering its share of reverses during the ensuing fighting, the United States did not come away empty-handed. In 1805 it was able to conclude a peace treaty with Tripoli for roughly half the price that it had been paying annually for protection.

Jefferson was not a pacifist and would continue to use the navy to gain respect for the American flag, but he and Gallatin placed economy ahead of military preparedness. Gallatin calculated that the nation could be freed of debt in sixteen years if administrations held the line on expenditures. In Europe, the Peace of Amiens (1802) brought a temporary halt to the hostilities between Britain and France that had threatened American shipping in the 1790s, and buoyed Jefferson's confidence that minimal military preparedness was a sound policy. The Peace of Amiens, he wrote, "removes the only danger we have to fear. We can now proceed without risks in demolishing useless structures of expense, lightening the burdens of our constituents, and fortifying the principles of free government." This may have been wishful thinking, but it rested on a sound economic calculation, for the vast territory of the United States could never be secured from attack without astronomical expense.

Jefferson and the Judiciary

In his inaugural address, Jefferson reminded Americans that their agreements were more basic than their disagreements. "We have called by different name brothers of the same principle," he proclaimed. "We are all republicans; we are all federalists." He was enough of a realist to know that the political conflict would not evaporate, but he sincerely hoped to allay fear of the Republican party and to draw moderate Federalists over to his side. There was a chance of success. He and John Adams had once been friends. The two shared many views, and each was suspicious of Hamilton. But the eventual reconciliation between Adams and Jefferson (they renewed their friendship after Jefferson's presidency), and more generally between Federalists and Republicans, would not occur during Jefferson's administration, largely because of bitter feelings over the composition and control of the judiciary.

In theory, Jefferson believed that talent and virtue rather than political affiliation were the primary qualifications for judgeships. In theory, the Federalists believed the same, but they had rarely detected either talent or virtue among the Republicans, and in 1800 not a single Republican sat on the federal judiciary. For Republicans, the crowning blow was the Federalist-sponsored Judiciary Act, passed on February 27, 1801. On the surface, this law had a nonpartisan purpose. By creating sixteen new federal judgeships, the act promised to relieve Supreme Court justices of the burden of riding far from Washington to hear cases. But the act contained several features that struck Jefferson as objectionable, including a provision to reduce the number of justices on the Supreme Court from six to five. This provision threatened both to strip Jefferson of his first opportunity to appoint a justice and to perpetuate Federalist domination of the judiciary.

Recalling the federal courts' zealousness in enforcing the Alien and Sedition Acts, and dismayed by the absence of Republicans on the fed-

eral judiciary, Jefferson saw in the Judiciary Act of 1801 a confirmation of his fears that the Federalists were retreating into the judiciary as a stronghold, "and from that battery all the works of Republicanism are to be beaten down and erased." Any lingering doubts Jefferson might have had about Federalist intentions were swept away by the actions of outgoing president John Adams during his last days in office. Between December 12, 1800, the day on which Adams's defeat in the election became clear, and March 4, 1801, the date of Jefferson's inauguration, Adams appointed several last-minute, or "midnight," judges. All federal judges appointed by Adams under provisions of the Judiciary Act were prominent Federalists. Some had been defeated for office during the election of 1800. One had captained a loyalist regiment during the Revolution, and three were brothers or brothers-in-law of John Marshall, the Federalist chief justice who was also the reputed author of the Judiciary Act of 1801.

Some radical Jeffersonians believed that judges should be elected, but Jefferson himself had no quarrel with the practice of appointing judges to serve during "good behavior" (normally for life); indeed, he thought that an independent judiciary was vital to the success of republican government. But the Federalists seemed to be turning the judiciary into an arm of their party, and in defiance of the popular will. Ironically, it was not the midnight appointments that Adams actually made but one that he left unfinished that stiffened Jefferson's resolve to seek repeal of the Judiciary Act. On his last day in office, Adams appointed an obscure Federalist, William Marbury, as justice of the peace in the District of Columbia but then failed to deliver Marbury's commission before midnight. With Jefferson in office, the new secretary of state, James Madison, refused to release the commission. Marbury petitioned the Supreme Court for a writ of mandamus,* ordering Madison to make the delivery. Chief Justice Marshall then called on Madison to show cause why he should not be compelled to hand over the commission. Although the Supreme Court did not decide the case of *Marbury* v. *Madison* until 1803, Jefferson detected in Marshall's

---

*Mandamus: an order from a higher court commanding that a specified action be taken.

John Marshall, *by Chester Harding*

Marshall served as U.S. chief justice under six presidents, several of whom were infuriated by his opinions. During Marshall's tenure, the Supreme Court asserted its authority to declare laws passed by Congress unconstitutional and affirmed the supremacy of the national government over state governments.

maneuvers the early signs of still another Federalist scheme to use the judiciary to advance partisan interests, and in 1802 he won congressional repeal of the Judiciary Act. The Federalists were in despair. The Constitution, moaned Federalist senator Gouverneur Morris, "is dead. It is dead."

As John Marshall would soon demonstrate, however, the Federalist judiciary was alive and brimming with energy. Like Jefferson, Marshall was a Virginian, but he was the son of an ordinary farmer, not an aristocrat. Marshall's service in the Continental Army during the Revolution had instilled in him (as in Alexander Hamilton) a burning attachment to the Union rather than to any state, and in the 1790s he had embraced the Federalist party. In 1803 Marshall's long-awaited

decision in *Marbury* v. *Madison* came down. Marshall tossed the Republicans a few crumbs by ruling that the Supreme Court could not compel Madison to deliver William Marbury's commission. With twisting logic, Marshall then argued that the Court could not issue a writ of mandamus (the writ Marbury sought) in its original jurisdiction because its power to do so, although explicitly granted by Congress in the Judiciary Act of 1789, was not explicitly granted by the Constitution. Hence that part of the Judiciary Act of 1789 that gave the Court power to issue writs of mandamus was unconstitutional. Next Marshall proceeded to trample on the crumbs by lecturing Madison about his moral duty (as opposed to his legal obligation) to have delivered the commission.

From the perspective of constitutional history, the key part of Marshall's decision is not that he left a minor official like Marbury without legal recourse nor that he delivered an uncalled-for lecture to Madison, but that he declared part of the Judiciary Act of 1789 unconstitutional. This was the first time that the Court had declared an act of Congress unconstitutional. It would not do so again until 1857, but an important precedent had been set.

Marshall's decision, however, had a different significance for Jefferson. Along with most mainstream Republicans, Jefferson thought that the courts did have a right to engage in judicial review (that is, to declare legislative acts unconstitutional). As far as judicial review went, Jefferson merely held that courts had no *exclusive* right of review; other branches of the government should also have the right to review the constitutionality of measures before them. Since Marshall's decision in *Marbury* did not assert that courts alone could declare laws unconstitutional, Jefferson had no quarrel with the principle of judicial review as Marshall advanced it. What infuriated Jefferson was Marshall's gratuitous lecture to Madison, which was really a lecture to Jefferson as Madison's superior. The lecture struck Jefferson as another example of Federalist partisanship with respect to the judiciary.

While the *Marbury* decision was brewing, the Republicans had already taken the offensive against the judiciary by moving to impeach (charge with wrongdoing) two Federalist judges, John Pickering of the New Hampshire District Court and Samuel

Chase of the United States Supreme Court. The particulars of the two cases differed. Pickering was an insane alcoholic who behaved in a bizarre manner in court. In one case, he decided against the prosecution before hearing any of its witnesses and then taunted the district attorney that even if he could present forty thousand witnesses, "they will not alter the decree." Chase, a notoriously partisan Federalist, had rigorously enforced the Sedition Act of 1798 and had jailed several Republican editors, including one whom Jefferson had befriended. To Republicans, Chase was the devil incarnate; all of them knew that Chase's name formed the correct ending of a popular ditty:

> *Cursed of thy father, scum of all that's base,*
> *Thy sight is odious, and thy name is . . .*

Despite these differing details, the two cases raised the same issue. The Constitution provided that federal judges could be removed solely by impeachment, which could be considered only in cases of "Treason, Bribery and other high Crimes and Misdemeanors." Was impeachment an appropriate way to get rid of judges who were insane or excessively partisan? Despite misgivings among Federalists and some Republicans about charging an obviously insane man with crimes and misdemeanors, the Senate voted to convict Pickering on March 12, 1804. That same day, the House of Representatives voted to indict Chase. John Randolph, one of Jefferson's supporters in Congress, so completely botched the prosecution of Chase that he failed to obtain the necessary two-thirds majority for conviction on any of the charges. But even if Randolph had done a competent job, Chase might still have gained acquittal, because moderate Republicans were coming to doubt whether impeachment was a solution to the issue of judicial partisanship.

Chase's acquittal ended Jefferson's skirmishes with the judiciary. Although his radical followers continued to attack the principles of judicial review and an appointed judiciary as undemocratic, Jefferson objected to neither. He merely challenged Federalist use of judicial power for political goals. Yet there was always a gray area between law and politics. Federalists did not necessarily see a conflict between protecting the Constitution and advancing their party's cause. Nor did they use their control of the federal judiciary to undo Jefferson's "revolution" of 1800. The Marshall court, for example, upheld the constitutionality of the repeal of the Judiciary Act of 1801. For his part, Jefferson never proposed to impeach Marshall. In supporting the impeachments of Pickering and Chase, Jefferson was trying to make the judiciary more responsive to the popular will by challenging a pair of judges whose behavior had been outrageous. No other federal judge would be impeached for more than fifty years.

The Louisiana Purchase

Jefferson's goal of avoiding foreign entanglements would remain beyond reach as long as European powers had large landholdings in North America. In 1800 Spain, a weak and declining power, controlled East and West Florida as well as the vast Louisiana Territory. The latter alone was equal in size to the United States at that time. In the Treaty of San Ildefonso (October 1, 1800), Spain ceded the Louisiana Territory to France, which was fast emerging under Napoleon Bonaparte as the world's foremost military power. It took six months for news of the treaty to reach Jefferson and Madison but only a few minutes for them to grasp its significance.

Jefferson had long dreamed of an "empire of liberty" extending across North America and even into South America, an empire to be gained not by military conquest but by the inevitable expansion of the free and virtuous American people. An enfeebled Spain constituted no real obstacle to this expansion. As long as Louisiana had belonged to Spain, time was on the side of the United States. But Bonaparte's capacity for mischief was boundless. What if Bonaparte and the British reached an agreement that gave England a free hand in the Mediterranean and France a license to expand into North America? Then the United States would be sandwiched between the British in Canada and the French in Louisiana. What if Britain refused to cooperate with France? In that case, Britain might use its naval power to seize Louisiana before the French took control, thereby trapping the United States between British forces in the South and West as well as in the North and West.

Although Americans feared these two possibilities, Bonaparte actually had a different goal. During the 1790s he had dreamed of a French empire in the Middle East, but his defeat by the British fleet at the Battle of the Nile in 1798 had blasted this dream. Now Bonaparte devised a plan for a new French empire, this one bordering the Caribbean and the Gulf of Mexico. The fulcrum of the empire was to be the Caribbean island of Santo Domingo (today comprising Haiti and the Dominican Republic). He wanted to use Louisiana not as a base from which to threaten the United States but as a breadbasket for an essentially Caribbean empire. His immediate task was to subdue Santo Domingo, where a bloody slave revolution in the 1790s had resulted by 1800 in the takeover of the government by the black statesman Toussaint L'Ouverture (see Chapter 6). Bonaparte dispatched an army to reassert French control and to reestablish slavery, but yellow fever and fierce resistance on the part of former slaves combined to destroy the army.

As a slaveholder himself, Jefferson tacitly approved Bonaparte's attempted reconquest of Santo Domingo; as a nationalist, he continued to fear a French presence in Louisiana. This fear intensified in October 1802, when the Spanish colonial administrator in New Orleans issued an order prohibiting the deposit of American produce in New Orleans for transshipment to foreign lands. Because American farmers west of the Appalachians depended on New Orleans as a port for the cash crops that they shipped down the Mississippi River, the order was a major provocation to Americans. The order had in fact originated in Spain, but most Americans assumed that it had come from Bonaparte, who, while he now owned Louisiana, had not yet taken possession of it. An alarmed Jefferson wrote to a friend that "the day that France takes possession of N. Orleans . . . we must marry ourselves to the British fleet and nation."

The combination of France's failure to subdue Santo Domingo and the termination of American rights to deposit produce in New Orleans stimulated two crucial decisions, one by Jefferson and the other by Bonaparte, that ultimately resulted in the United States' purchase of Louisiana. First, Jefferson nominated James Monroe and Robert R. Livingston to negotiate with France for the purchase of New Orleans and as much of the Floridas as possible. (Because West Florida had repeatedly changed hands between France, Britain, and Spain,

no one was sure who owned it.) Meanwhile, Bonaparte, mindful of his military failure in Santo Domingo and of American opposition to French control of Louisiana, had concluded that his projected Caribbean empire was not worth the cost. In addition, he planned to recommence the war in Europe and needed cash. Accordingly, he decided to sell *all* of Louisiana. After some haggling between the American commissioners and Bonaparte's minister, Talleyrand, a price of $15 million was settled upon. (One-fourth of the total represented an agreement by the United States to pay French debts owed to American citizens.) For this sum the United States gained an immense, uncharted territory west of the Mississippi River. No one knew its exact size; Talleyrand merely observed that the bargain was noble. But the purchase virtually doubled the area of the United States at a cost, omitting interest, of 13½¢ an acre. It is small wonder that at the signing of the treaty, Livingston claimed that "this is the noblest work of our whole lives. . . . From this day the United States take their place among the powers of the first rank."

Because Jefferson's commissioners had exceeded their instructions, however, the president had doubts about the constitutionality of the purchase. No provision of the Constitution explicitly gave the government authority to acquire new territory or to incorporate it into the Union. Jefferson therefore drafted a constitutional amendment that authorized the acquisition of territory and prohibited the American settlement of Louisiana for an indefinite period. Fearing that an immediate and headlong rush to settle the area would lead to the destruction of the Indians and to an orgy of land speculation, Jefferson wanted to control development so that Americans could advance "compactly as we multiply." Few Republicans, however, shared Jefferson's constitutional reservations, and the president himself soon began to worry that ratification of an amendment would take too long and that Bonaparte might in the meantime change his mind about selling Louisiana. Consequently, he quietly dropped the amendment and submitted the treaty to the Senate, where it was quickly ratified.

It is easy to make too much of Jefferson's dilemma over Louisiana. He was wedded to strict construction of the Constitution, believing that the Constitution should be interpreted according to its letter. But he was also committed to the principle of establishing an "empire of liberty." Doubling the size of the Republic would guarantee land for American farmers, the backbone of the Republic and the true guardians of liberty. Like the principle of states' rights to which Jefferson also subscribed, strict construction was not an end in itself but a means to promote republican liberty. If that end could be achieved by some way other than strict construction, so be it. In addition, Jefferson was alert to practical considerations. Most Federalists opposed the Louisiana Purchase on the grounds that it would decrease the relative importance of their strongholds on the eastern seaboard. As the leader of the Republican party, Jefferson saw no reason to hand the Federalists an issue by dallying over ratification of the treaty.

The Lewis and Clark Expedition

Louisiana dazzled Jefferson's imagination. Here was an immense territory about which Americans knew virtually nothing. No one was sure of its western boundary. A case could be made for the Pacific Ocean, but Jefferson was content to claim that Louisiana extended at least to the mountains west of the Mississippi. No one, however, was certain of the exact location of these mountains, because

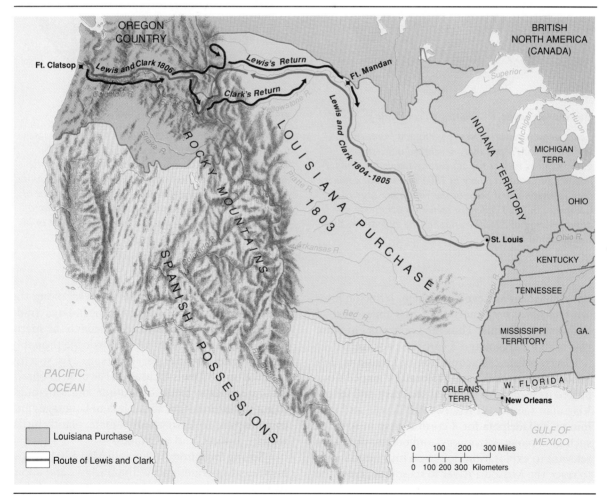

The Louisiana Purchase and the Exploration of the West   *The explorations of Lewis and Clark demonstrated the vast extent of the area purchased from France.*

Meriwether Lewis, *by Charles Wilson Peale*

Lewis grew up near Jefferson's Virginia home and, under Jefferson's guidance, developed a thirst for knowledge as well as for adventure. Lewis became Jefferson's personal secretary in 1801 and in that capacity read Jefferson's first State of the Union message to Congress. In 1803 Jefferson secured a congressional appropriation of $2500 to finance the expedition that Lewis would lead.

William Clark, *by Charles Wilson Peale*

Brother of the famed Indian fighter George Rogers Clark, William Clark served at the Battle of Fallen Timbers. William Clark's daring and resourcefulness aided the Louisiana expedition in times of crisis, as did his skill at map making. He later became governor of the Missouri Territory and an outspoken advocate of the interests of the Indians whom he had fought in his youth.

few Americans had ever seen them. Jefferson himself had never been more than fifty miles west of his home in Virginia. Thus the Louisiana Purchase was both a bargain and a surprise package.

Even before the acquisition of Louisiana, Jefferson had planned an exploratory expedition; picked its leader, his personal secretary and fellow Virginian Lieutenant Meriwether Lewis; and sent him to Philadelphia for a crash course in sciences such as zoology, astronomy, and botany that were relevant to exploration. Jefferson instructed Lewis to trace the Missouri River to its source, cross the western highlands, and follow the best water route to the Pacific. In requesting congressional funding for the expedition, Jefferson stressed the commer-

cial possibilities that it might uncover; along the line of the Missouri and beyond, the Indians' trade in pelts might be diverted from Canada to the south. But the advance of scientific knowledge probably had a higher priority for Jefferson. His specific instructions to Lewis focused on the need to obtain accurate measurements of latitude and longitude; to gather information about Indian languages and customs; and to learn about climate, plants, birds, reptiles, insects, and volcanoes.

Setting forth from St. Louis in May 1804, Lewis, his second-in-command William Clark, and about fifty others followed the Missouri River and then the Snake and Columbia rivers. In the Dakota country, Lewis and Clark hired a French-Canadian

Calumet

This calumet, a pipe used by the North American Indians for such ceremonies as the ratification of treaties (and hence called a peace pipe), was typical of the items that Lewis and Clark brought back from their exploration of the Louisiana Territory.

fur trader, Toussaint Charbonneau, as a guide and interpreter. Slow-witted and inclined to panic in crises, Charbonneau proved a mixed blessing, but his wife, Sacajawea, who accompanied him on the trip, made up for his failings. A Shoshone and probably no more than sixteen years old in 1804, Sacajawea had been stolen by a rival tribe and then claimed by Charbonneau, perhaps in settlement for a gambling debt. When first encountered by Lewis and Clark, she had just given birth to a son; indeed, her infant's presence helped to reassure Indian tribes of the expedition's peaceful intent. Additionally, Sacajawea showed Lewis and Clark how to forage for wild artichokes and other plants, often their only food, by digging into the dens where rodents stored them. Clutching her baby, she rescued most of the expedition's scientific instruments after a storm capsized one of its boats on the Missouri River.

The group finally reached the Pacific in November 1805 and then returned to St. Louis, but not before collecting a mass of scientific information, including the disturbing fact that more than three hundred miles of mountains separated the Missouri from the Columbia. It also produced a sprinkling of tall tales, many of which Jefferson believed, about gigantic Indians, soil too rich to grow trees, and a mountain composed of salt. Jefferson's political opponents railed that he would soon be reporting the discovery of a molasses-filled lake. For all the ridicule, the expedition stimulated rather than dampened interest in the West.

The Election of 1804

Jefferson's acquisition of Louisiana left the Federalists dispirited and without a popular national issue. As the election of 1804 approached, the main threat to Jefferson was not the Federalist party but his own vice president, Aaron Burr. In 1800 Burr had tried to take advantage of a tie in the electoral college to gain the presidency, a betrayal in the eyes of most Republicans, who assumed that he had been nominated for the vice presidency. While the adoption in 1804 of the Twelfth Amendment, which required separate and distinct ballots in the electoral college for the presidency and vice presidency, put an end to the possibility of an electoral tie for the presidency, it did not put an end to Burr. Between 1801 and 1804, Burr entered into enough intrigues with the Federalists to convince the Republicans that it would be unsafe to renominate him for the vice presidency. The Republicans in Congress rudely dumped Burr in favor of George Clinton. Without a hope of success, the Federalists nominated Charles C. Pinckney and Rufus King and then watched their candidates go down to crushing defeat in the election. The Federalists carried only two states, failing to hold even Massachusetts. Jefferson's overwhelming victory brought his first term to a fitting close; between 1801 and 1804, the United States had doubled its territory, taken steps to pay off its debt, and remained at peace. In short, Jefferson basked in the sun of success.

The Election of 1804		
Candidates	*Parties*	*Electoral Vote*
THOMAS JEFFERSON	Democratic-Republican	162
Charles C. Pinckney	Federalist	14

The Gathering Storm

The sky was not cloudless for long. In gaining control of Louisiana, the United States had benefited from the preoccupation of European powers with their own struggles. The nation would again benefit from this preoccupation between 1814 and 1823. But between 1803 and 1814, the renewal of the Napoleonic wars in Europe turned the United States into a pawn in a chess game played by others and helped to make Jefferson's second term far less successful than his first. In fact, the very success of his first administration contained the germs of problems that would plague his second term. As long as the two parties could compete on a more or less even basis, as in the election of 1800, leaders within each party could demand unity as a prerequisite for victory. But as the Federalist opposition weakened, unity among Republicans became less important, and they increasingly fell victim to internal squabbles.

Jefferson's Coalition Fragments

For the moment, the election of 1804 eliminated the Federalists as a force in national politics. More troubling to Republicans than Federalist opposition was factionalism within their own party, much of it the product of the inventive and perverse mind of Aaron Burr. Burr suffered a string of reverses in 1804. After being denied renomination as vice president, he entered into a series of intrigues with a faction of despairing and extreme (or "High") Federalists in New England. Led by Senator Timothy Pickering of Massachusetts, these High Federalists plotted to sever the Union by forming a pro-British "Northern Confederacy," composed of Nova Scotia (part of British-owned Canada), New England, New York, and even Pennsylvania. Although most Federalists disdained the plot, Pickering and others settled on Burr as their leader and helped him gain the Federalist nomination for the governorship of New York. Alexander Hamilton, who had thwarted Burr's plans for the presidency in 1800 by throwing his weight behind Jefferson, now foiled Burr a second time by allowing the publication of his "despicable opinion" of Burr. Defeated by a Republican in the election for New York's governor, Burr challenged Hamilton to a duel and mortally wounded him at Weehawken, New Jersey, on July 11, 1804.

Under indictment in two states for his murder of Hamilton, Burr, still vice president, now hatched a scheme so bold that it gained momentum initially because his political opponents seriously doubted that even Burr was capable of such machinations. He allied himself with the unsavory general James Wilkinson, formerly the highest military officer in the U.S. Army and now military governor of the Louisiana Territory. Wilkinson had been on Spain's payroll intermittently as a secret agent since the 1780s. Together Burr and Wilkinson conspired to separate the western states into an independent confederacy south of the Ohio River. In addition, Wilkinson had long entertained the idea of an American conquest of Mexico, and Burr now added West Florida as a possible target. They presented these ideas to westerners as having the covert support of the administration, to the British as a way to attack Spanish-owned Mexico and West Florida, and to the Spanish (removing Mexico and West Florida as targets) as a way to divide up the United States.

Jefferson, who described Burr as a crooked gun that never shot straight, let the plot germinate for more than a year before taking action. In October 1806 he finally denounced the conspiracy publicly. By that time Burr and about sixty followers had left their staging ground, an island in the upper Ohio River, and were making their way down the Ohio and Mississippi rivers to join Wilkinson at Natchez. But Wilkinson was not there to greet Burr and his several boatloads of conspirators with their many conspiracies. Recognizing that Jefferson was now moving against Burr and that the British were uninterested in supporting the plot, Wilkinson wrote to Jefferson to report the conspiracy and then took refuge in New Orleans, where he proclaimed himself the most loyal of the president's followers.

A few weeks later, Jefferson officially denounced the conspiracy. Now Burr panicked. He tried to escape to West Florida but was intercepted; brought back to Richmond, he was put on trial for treason. Chief Justice Marshall presided at the trial and charged the jury that the prosecution had to prove not merely that Burr had treasonable intentions but also that he had committed treasonable acts, a virtually impossible task inasmuch as the conspiracy had fallen apart before Burr accomplished what he had planned. Jefferson was furious, but Marshall was merely following the clear wording of the Constitution, which deliberately made treason difficult to prove. The jury returned a verdict of "not proved," which Marshall entered as "not guilty." Still under indictment for his murder of Hamilton, Burr fled to Europe, where he tried to interest Napoleon in making peace with Britain as a prelude to a proposed Anglo-French invasion of the United States and Mexico. He returned to the United States in 1812 and, in keeping with his reputation as a womanizer, fathered two illegitimate children in his seventies and was divorced for adultery at eighty. Perhaps the most puzzling man in American history, he died in 1836.

Jefferson and the Quids

In addition to the Burr conspiracy, Jefferson faced a challenge from a group of Republicans known as the Quids*, who were led by fellow Virginian John Randolph. Randolph was a man of abounding eccentricities. An early illness had left him beardless, with a soprano voice, and probably sexually impotent. Like a dart, his wit was sharp and piercing. For all his peculiarities and biting witticisms, however, Randolph was a man of principle. Although much younger than Jefferson, he stood squarely in the tradition of the "country" ideology of the 1770s, that set of beliefs that had celebrated the honest wisdom of the plain farmer against the corruption of rulers and "court" hangers-on and that had warned incessantly against the natural tendency of all governments to encroach upon liberty. Jefferson had started out with the same beliefs but had gradually recognized their limitations. By definition, country ideology was a stance for those out of power, an ideology of opposition rather than of governance. In gaining political power, Jefferson had learned the need for compromise. Randolph, in contrast, remained frozen in an earlier time and denounced every change as a decline from the purity of 1776. He once said that he would throw all politicians to the dogs if he had less respect for dogs.

After serving in the House of Representatives between 1801 and 1805, Randolph began to turn on Jefferson. First, he blasted Jefferson for backing a compromise in the Yazoo land scandal. In 1795 the Georgia legislature had sold the huge "Yazoo" tract (35 million acres of land comprising most of present-day Alabama and Mississippi) for a fraction of its value to four land companies that had bribed virtually the entire legislature. Following public outrage, the next legislature canceled the sale, but not before many investors had purchased land in the expectation of reselling it at a higher price. The cancellation of the sale threatened to bankrupt these investors, who had bought land to which they now no longer held legal title. For Jefferson, the scandal posed a moral challenge, since some of the purchasers, knowing nothing of the bribery, had bought the land in good faith. It also confronted him with a political challenge, since some of the buyers were northerners whom Jefferson hoped to woo into the Republican party. In 1803 a commission that included Secretary of State Madison and Treasury Secretary Gallatin awarded 5 million acres to Yazoo purchasers as a compromise. For Randolph, the compromise was itself a scandal, further evidence of the decay of republican virtue.

Randolph next collided with Jefferson over the president's request for a congressional appropriation of $2 million to purchase East and West Florida from Spain. Characteristically, Randolph raged less at the idea of obtaining the Floridas than at Jefferson's apparent act of deception in requesting money for extraordinary diplomatic expenses without officially informing Congress of the real object of the expenditures. Jefferson had sound reasons for preferring to keep negotiations over the Floridas out of the limelight, and he privately informed members of Congress, including Randolph, of his plans for the purchase; but to Randolph, it all seemed like another betrayal of virtue. He proclaimed, "I don't understand this double set of opinions and principles—the one ostensible, the other real; I hold true wisdom and cunning to be utterly incompatible."

The Suppression of American Trade

Burr's acquittal and Randolph's taunts shattered the aura of invincibility that had surrounded Jefferson after the Louisiana Purchase and the election of 1804. Now foreign affairs began to pose an even sharper challenge to his administration. In 1803 the Peace of Amiens collapsed. Britain and

---

*Quid: a name taken from the Latin *tertium quid* or "third thing." Roughly, a dissenter.

France resumed their war. While the United States remained neutral, many European nations joined the fray. Britain reacted to American neutrality with contempt. Much of Britain's information about the United States came from Federalists, who viewed the American republic as feeble and Jefferson as a pro-French romantic, and from British visitors to the United States, usually aristocrats, who sent back unflattering portraits of a rudderless democracy without effective leadership.

Britain concluded that there was little to fear from America, but the British attitude contained a dose of envy as well as contempt for the United States. While Britain was locked in a struggle against Napoleon, whom the British viewed as the enemy of all humanity, the United States was prospering at Britain's expense. Between 1790 and 1810, American ship tonnage nearly tripled. American vessels carried sugar and coffee from French and Spanish colonies in the Caribbean to Europe. This trade not only provided Napoleon with supplies but also drove down the price of sugar and coffee from the British West Indies by adding to the glut of these commodities on world markets. It was easy for the British to conclude that American prosperity was the cause of Britain's economic difficulties.

The basis of the American prosperity was the reexport trade—an American adaptation to the British Rule of 1756, which stated that trade closed in time of peace could not be opened in time of war. For example, in peacetime, France usually restricted to French ships the transportation of products such as sugar from the French West Indies. According to the Rule of 1756, the ships of a neutral country such as the United States could not replace French ships as carriers now that the war between France and Britain made French vessels fair game for the British navy. The American response to the Rule of 1756 was the "broken voyage." American vessels would carry produce from the Spanish and French West Indies to an American port, unload it and pass it through customs, then reload it and reexport it to Europe as *American* produce. Between 1795 and 1805, the British tolerated broken voyages but thereafter charted a new course. Seeking now to strangle French commerce as well as to defeat Napolean's armies, Britain pursued total war against France. A sign of the new policy was a British court's decision in the 1805 *Essex* case declaring broken voyages illegal.

The British followed the *Essex* decision in May 1806 with the first of several trade regulations known as Orders in Council, which established a blockade of part of the continent of Europe. In theory, this Order in Council softened the *Essex* decision by allowing American vessels to trade with French possessions as long as they carried their cargoes to Britain rather than to a continental port controlled by France. But Napoleon responded in November 1806 with his Berlin Decree, which proclaimed a blockade of the British Isles; any ship attempting to enter or leave a British port was now subject to seizure by France. The British answered the Berlin Decree with another Order in Council, this one requiring all neutral ships trading in the blockaded zones of Europe to stop at British ports to secure licenses. Napoleon replied in December 1807 by tightening his so-called Continental System with the Milan Decree, which proclaimed that any vessel that submitted to British regulations or allowed itself to be searched by the Royal Navy was subject to seizure by France.

This dizzying sequence of proclamations and counterproclamations effectively outlawed virtually all American trade. If an American ship submitted to search by a British ship or secured a British license to trade, it became a French target; if it avoided the British and reached a French-controlled port, it became a British target. Both Britain and France seized American ships, but British seizures were far more humiliating to Americans. France was a weaker naval power than Britain; much of the French fleet had been destroyed by the British at the Battle of Trafalgar in October 1805. Accordingly, most of France's seizures of American ships occurred in European ports where American ships had been lured by Napoleon's often inconsistent enforcement of his Continental System. In contrast, British warships hovered just beyond the American coast. Off New York, for example, the Royal Navy stopped and searched virtually every American vessel. At times, U.S. ships had to line up a few miles from the American coast to be searched by the Royal Navy.

Impressment

On top of these provocations, the British added that of impressment. At issue was the seizure from American merchant ships, and the subsequent pressing into service, of purported British sailors who had deserted from the Royal Navy.

British sailors had good reason to be discontented with the navy. Aside from the fact that discipline on the Royal Navy's "floating hells" was often brutal, wages were much lower than on American ships. The pay of an able-bodied seaman on a British ship was only around seven dollars a month, compared to twenty-five to thirty-five dollars a month on American ships. As a result, at a time when war intensified Britain's need for sailors, the Royal Navy suffered a high rate of desertion to U.S. ships; for example, in 1807 the American frigate *Constitution* carried a crew of 419 men, of whom 149 were British subjects.

Impressed sailors led harrowing lives that included frequent escapes and recaptures. One seaman suffered impressment on eleven separate occasions; another, on the verge of his third recapture, drowned himself rather than spend another day in the Royal Navy. The British practice of impressment was not only cruel to individuals but galling to American pride, because many deserters from the Royal Navy had acquired American naturalization papers and become American citizens. The British impressed these men anyway on the principle that once a Briton, always a Briton. At times, the British also impressed American-born citizens, even when the latter produced documentation proving their American birth. Americans with Irish-sounding names were especially suspect. One New Englander related how a British captain barked at him that "I was a damned Irish Yankee and I have as good a right [duty] to serve his majesty as he had." Between 1803 and 1812, the British impressed over six thousand American citizens. Although impressment did less damage to the American economy than the seizure of ships, it was even more humiliating.

Any doubts that Americans had about British arrogance evaporated in June 1807 when a British warship, HMS *Leopard,* patrolling off Hampton Roads, Virginia, attacked an unsuspecting American frigate, USS *Chesapeake,* and forced it to surrender. The British then boarded the vessel and seized four supposed deserters. One, a genuine deserter, was later hanged; the other three were former Britons, now American citizens, who had "deserted" only from impressment. Even the British had never before asserted their right to seize

deserters off government ships. The so-called *Chesapeake* Affair enraged the country. Jefferson remarked that he had not seen so belligerent a spirit in America since 1775. Yet while making some preparations for war, the president sought peace —first by conducting fruitless negotiations with Britain to gain redress for the *Chesapeake* outrage, and second by steering the Embargo Act through Congress in December 1807.

The Embargo

By far the most controversial legislation of either of Jefferson's administrations, the Embargo Act prohibited vessels from leaving American ports for foreign ports. Technically, it prohibited only exports, but its practical effect was to stop imports as well, for few foreign ships would venture into American ports if they had to leave without cargo. Amazed by the boldness of the act, a British newspaper described the embargo as "little short of an absolute secession from the rest of the civilized world."

Jefferson advocated the embargo as a means of "peaceable coercion." By restricting French and British (especially British) trade with the United States, he hoped to pressure both nations into respecting American neutrality. But the embargo did not have the effect that Jefferson intended. Although British sales to the United States dropped 50 percent between 1807 and 1808, the British quickly found new markets in South America, where rebellions against Spanish rule had flared up, and in Spain itself, where a revolt against Napoleon had opened trade to British shipping. Further, the Embargo Act itself contained some loopholes. For example, it allowed American ships blown off course to put in at European ports if necessary; suddenly many captains were reporting that adverse winds had forced them across the Atlantic. Treating the embargo as a joke, Napoleon seized whatever American ships he could lay hands on and then informed the United States that he was only helping to enforce the embargo. The British were less amused, but the embargo confirmed their view that Jefferson was an ineffectual philosopher, an impotent challenger compared with Napoleon.

The harshest effects of the embargo were felt not in Europe but in the United States. Some thirty thousand American seamen found themselves out of work. Merchants stumbled into bankruptcy by

Joseph Peabody, *by Charles Osgood*

The Revolutionary soldier Joseph Peabody (1757–1844) built a large fleet of seafaring vessels after the war and became the leading merchant in Salem, Massachusetts. The embargo severely disrupted Peabody's thriving importation of pepper, tea, indigo, and other products from China, the Mediterranean, and the West Indies.

twice the ship tonnage per capita of any other state and more than a third of the entire nation's ship tonnage in foreign trade. (The earnings of the Massachusetts merchant fleet that year were equal to the entire revenue of the U.S. government in 1806.) For a state so dependent on foreign trade, the embargo was a calamity. Wits reversed the letters of *embargo* to form the phrase "O grab me."

The picture was not entirely bleak. The embargo forced a diversion of merchants' capital into manufacturing. In short, unable to export produce, Americans began to make products. Before 1808 the United States had only fifteen mills for fashioning cotton into textiles; by the end of 1809, an additional eighty-seven mills had been constructed. But none of this comforted merchants already ruined or mariners driven to soup kitchens. Nor could New Englanders forget that the source of their misery was a policy initiated by one of the "Virginia lordlings," "Mad Tom" Jefferson, who knew little about New England and who had a dogmatic loathing of cities, the very foundations of New England's prosperity. A Massachusetts poet wrote:

*Our ships all in motion once whitened the
　ocean,
They sailed and returned with a cargo;
Now doomed to decay they have fallen a prey
To Jefferson, worms, and embargo.*

The Election of 1808

Even before the Embargo Act, Jefferson had announced that he would not be a candidate for reelection. With his blessing, the Republican congressional caucus nominated James Madison and George Clinton for the presidency and vice presidency, while the Federalists countered with Charles C. Pinckney and Rufus King, the same ticket that had made a negligible showing in 1804. In 1808 the Federalists staged a modest comeback, gaining twenty-four congressional seats. Still, Madison won 122 of 175 electoral votes for president, and the Republicans retained comfortable majorities in both houses of Congress.

Several factors contributed to the Federalists' revival in 1808. First, the embargo gave them the national issue that they had long lacked. Also, younger Federalists, represented by men like Har-

the hundreds, and jails swelled with debtors. A New York City newspaper ruefully noted that the only activity still flourishing in the city was prosecution for debt. Farmers, too, were devastated. Unable to export their produce or sell it at a decent price to hard-pressed urban dwellers, many farmers could not earn enough cash to pay their debts. In desperation, one farmer in Schoharie County, New York, sold his cattle, horses, and farm implements, worth eight hundred dollars before the embargo, for fifty-five dollars. Speculators who had purchased land expecting to sell it later at a higher price also took a beating, because cash-starved farmers stopped buying land. "I live and that is all," wrote one New York speculator. "I am doing no business, cannot sell anybody property, nor collect any money."

The embargo fell hardest on New England and particularly on Massachusetts, which in 1807 had

The Election of 1808

Candidates	Parties	Electoral Vote
JAMES MADISON	Democratic-Republican	122
Charles C. Pinckney	Federalist	47
George Clinton	Democratic-Republican	6

rison Gray Otis of Massachusetts and Robert G. Harper of South Carolina, were making their influence felt. Old-time Federalists, expecting the voters to defer naturally to gentlemen, had refused to campaign actively for votes, and they judged it disgraceful that their Republican opponents treated voters to barbecues and staged mass meetings. The younger Federalists, on the other hand, deliberately imitated the vote-winning techniques that had proved successful for the Republicans.

The Failure of Peaceable Coercion

To some contemporaries, the diminutive "Little Jemmy" Madison (he was only five feet, four inches tall) seemed a weak and shadowy figure alongside the commanding presence of Jefferson. But in fact, Madison, who faced a situation that would have confused anyone, brought to the presidency an intelligence and a capacity for systematic thought that matched Jefferson's. Like Jefferson, Madison believed that American liberty had to rest on the virtue of the people and that that virtue was critically tied to the growth and prosperity of agriculture. More clearly than Jefferson, Madison also recognized that agricultural prosperity depended on the vitality of American trade, for Americans would continue to enter farming only if they could get their crops to market. In particular, the British West Indies, dependent on the United States for much of their lumber and grain, struck Madison as a natural trading partner for the United States. Britain alone could not fully supply the West Indies. Therefore, if the United States embargoed its own trade with the West Indies, Madison reasoned, the British would be forced to their knees before Americans could suffer severe losses from the embargo. Britain, he wrote, was "more vulnerable in her commerce than in her armies."

The problem was that the American embargo was coercing no one. Increased trade between Canada and the West Indies after 1808 made a shambles of Madison's plan to pressure Britain by blocking American trade to the West Indies. On March 1, 1809, Congress repealed the Embargo Act and substituted the weaker, although face-saving, Non-Intercourse Act. This act opened American trade to all nations except Britain and France and authorized the president to restore trade with either nation if it ceased to violate neutral rights. But the act failed to persuade the British or the French to respect American shipping. Grasping at straws, Madison then negotiated an agreement with David Erskine, the British minister in Washington, to reopen American trade in return for a British promise to revoke its Orders in Council. That same day, June 10, 1809, some six hundred American ships sailed for Britain. But Erskine had acted without orders. British Foreign Secretary George Canning disavowed the Erskine agreement as soon as he got wind of it, and Madison was forced to reembargo trade with Britain.

Madison called Canning's policy a "mixture of fraud and folly," but Canning thought that he was pursuing a level-headed course of action and had trouble understanding American belligerence. Canning and most British statesmen saw the world as containing a few great powers like Britain and France and innumerable small and weak powers. When great powers waged war against each other, there were no neutrals. Weak nations such as the United States should logically seek the protection of a great power. Since Britain was a natural trading partner for the United States, Americans should recognize, the reasoning went, that their best interests would be served by peacefully submitting to dependency on Britain. The problem was that Jefferson and Madison refused to accept this British conception of power relationships. In their view, the United States, however weak its military, was a nation founded on majestic principles that made it morally superior to Europe. The stepchildren of vanity and ambition, Europe's wars were of no concern to Americans. Jefferson wrote of France and England: "The one is a den of robbers and the other of pirates."

As an economic boom swept across Britain in 1809, the failure of the American policy of peaceable coercion was becoming obvious. Nor was that policy having a noticeable impact on France. Holding the same view of international power relations as the British, Napoleon tried to manipulate the United States into a collision course with Britain. Confronted by implacable hostility from Britain and France, Congress continued to drift. In May 1810 it substituted Macon's Bill No. 2 for the Non-Intercourse Act. The Macon legislation reopened trade with Britain and France and then offered a clumsy bribe to each: if either Britain or France repealed its restrictions on neutral shipping, the United States would halt all commerce with the other. Jumping at the opportunity presented by Macon's Bill No. 2, Napoleon promised to repeal his edicts against American trade. Madison snapped at the bait and proclaimed non-intercourse against Britain. But Napoleon had no intention of respecting American neutrality. His plan all along had been to trick the Americans into a posture of hostility toward Britain, and he continued to seize American ships spotted in French-controlled ports. Peaceable coercion had become a fiasco.

The Push into War

Madison soon found himself faced not only by a hostile Britain and France but by militants within his own party who demanded more aggressive policies. Most of these men were southerners and westerners. Coming from regions where honor was a sacred word, they were infuriated by insults to the American flag. In addition, when an economic recession struck the South and West between 1808 and 1810, South Carolina's John C. Calhoun and others realized that British policies were wrecking the economies of their regions. Consequently, a war spirit began to pulsate in the veins of several young congressmen elected in 1810. Drawn mainly from the South and West, these hotbloods formed a cohesive group, dubbed the "war hawks," in the House of Representatives. Their leader was a thirty-four-year-old Kentuckian, Henry Clay, who preferred war to the "putrescent pool of ignominious peace." With the support of the other war hawks, such as Calhoun, Richard M. Johnson of Kentucky, and William R. King of North Carolina—all of them future vice presidents—Clay was elected to the speakership of the House over the aging Nathaniel Macon, the author of Macon's Bill No. 2.

Tecumseh and the Prophet

Voicing a more emotional and pugnacious nationalism than Jefferson and Madison, the war hawks called for the expulsion of the British from Canada and the Spanish from the Floridas. Their demands merged with western settlers' fears that the British in Canada were actively recruiting the Indians to halt the march of American settlement. These fears, groundless but plausible, became intense when the Shawnee chief Tecumseh and his half-brother the Prophet sought to unite several tribes in Ohio and the Indiana territory against American settlers. Demoralized by the continuing loss of Indian lands to the whites and by the ravages of Indian society

Tenskwatawa, the Prophet

In periods of crisis, the native American cultures often gave rise to prophets—religious revivalists of sorts—such as Tecumseh's brother Tenskwatawa. Known to non-Indians as the Prophet, Tenskwatawa tried to revive traditional Indian values and customs such as the common ownership of land and the wearing of animal skins and furs. His religious program blended with Tecumseh's political program to unite the western tribes.

by alcoholism, Tecumseh and the Prophet (himself a reformed alcoholic) tried to unify their people and revive traditional Indian virtues. Both men believed that the Indians had to purge themselves of liquor and other corrupting messengers of white civilization as part of this revival. For example, to express his rejection of the whites' ways, Tecumseh long refused to learn English.

The aspirations of these Shawnee leaders set them on a collision course with Governor William Henry Harrison of the Indiana Territory. A wily bargainer, Harrison had purchased much of central and western Indiana from the Miami and the Delaware Indians in the Treaty of Fort Wayne (1809) for the paltry sum of ten thousand dollars. When Tecumseh's Shawnee people had refused to sign the treaty, however, Harrison began to regard the brilliant and charismatic Indian leader as an enemy.

With white settlers in Indiana convinced that Tecumseh's effort to unite the Indians was a British-inspired scheme, Harrison gathered an army in September 1811 and marched against a Shawnee encampment, the Prophet's Town, at the junction of the Wabash and Tippecanoe rivers. Then in November the Shawnees, led by the Prophet (Tecumseh was off recruiting Creek Indians), attacked Harrison. In the ensuing Battle of Tippecanoe, the Shawnees were beaten, the Prophet's Town was destroyed, and the Prophet was discredited in Tecumseh's eyes for his premature attack. Ironically, the Battle of Tippecanoe, which made Harrison a national hero, accomplished precisely what it had been designed to prevent. Never before a British agent, Tecumseh now joined with the British.

Congress Votes War

By the spring of 1812, President Madison had reached the decision that war with Britain was inevitable. On June 1 he sent his war message to Congress. Meanwhile, an economic depression struck Britain, partly because the American policy of restricting trade with that country had finally started to work. Under pressure from its merchants, Britain repealed the Orders in Council on June 23, but by then Congress, unaware that the British were contemplating repeal of the orders, had passed the declaration of war. It was still possible, of course, for Madison to revoke the declaration now that the maritime issue had been partly

settled. The British cabinet believed that he would do so. What the British failed to comprehend, however, was how much more belligerent American political leaders, particularly Republicans, had become between 1810 and 1812.

While both war hawks and westerners had contributed to this hostile mood, neither held the key to the vote in favor of war. The war hawks composed a minority within the Republican party; the West was still too sparsely settled to have many representatives in Congress. Rather, the votes of Republicans in populous states like Pennsylvania, Maryland, and Virginia were the main force propelling the war declaration through Congress. Most opposition to war came from Federalist strongholds in Massachusetts, Connecticut, and New York. Because Federalists were so much stronger in the Northeast than elsewhere, congressional opposition to war revealed a sectional as well as a party split. In general, however, southern Federalists opposed the war declaration, while northern Republicans supported it. In other words, the vote for war followed party lines more closely than sectional lines. Much like James Madison himself, the typical Republican advocate of war had not wanted war in 1810 nor even in 1811 but had been led by the accumulation of grievances to demand it in 1812.

The Causes of the War

In his war message, Madison listed impressment, the continued presence of British ships in American waters, and British violations of neutral rights as grievances that justified war. But none of these complaints was new. Taken together, they do not fully explain why Americans went to war in 1812 rather than earlier—for example, in 1807 after the *Chesapeake* affair. Madison also listed British incitement of the Indians as a stimulus for war. This grievance of recent origin contributed to war feeling in the West. "The War on the Wabash," a Kentucky newspaper proclaimed, "is purely British. The British scalping knife has filled many habitations both in this state as well as in the Indiana Territory with widows and orphans." But the West had too few American inhabitants to account for the nation's being propelled into war. A more important underlying cause was the economic recession that affected the South and West after

1808—and the conviction, held by John C. Calhoun and others, that British policy was damaging America's economy. Finally, the fact that Madison rather than Jefferson was president in 1812 was of major importance. Jefferson had believed that the only motive behind British seizures of American ships was Britain's desire to block American trade with Napoleon. Hence Jefferson had concluded that time was on America's side; the seizures would stop as soon as the war in Europe ceased. In contrast, Madison had become persuaded that Britain's real motive was to strangle American trade once and for all and thereby eliminate the United States as a trading rival. War or no war in Europe, Madison saw Britain as a menace to America. In his war message, he stated flatly that Britain was meddling with American trade not because that trade interfered with Britain's "belligerent rights" but because it "frustrated the monopoly which she covets for her own commerce and navigation."

The War of 1812

The popular American war slogan in June 1812 was "Free Trade and Sailors' Rights," and maritime issues had indeed been the centerpiece of Madison's war message. Yet Americans marched rather than sailed to war; they aimed at Canada, not at the British fleet. There were several reasons for this strategy. First, the growth of Canadian exports to the West Indies after 1808 had convinced Madison that Canada was not a snowbound wasteland but a key prop of the British Empire, an indispensable component of Britain's designs to strangle American trade. Moreover, an attack on Canada seemed a practical tactic. Between 1800 and 1812, the Republicans had consistently preferred economy to preparedness. They had shrunk the national debt from $83 million to $27.5 million, and as a result the American navy contained only six frigates, three sloops of war, and a number of smaller vessels, including gunboats. A brainchild of Jefferson, the gunboats were little more than floating gun docks designed for harbor defense. They often sank when they ventured forth to sea and at times could not even hold anchor in harbors. When a hurricane blew one gunboat eight

miles inland onto a cornfield, the Federalists mordantly toasted it as the finest ship "upon earth."

Thus unable to challenge Britain at sea, Americans looked north to Canada as a practical objective. Few Americans expected a prolonged or difficult struggle. The United States outstripped Canada in everything: 25 to 1 in population, 9 to 1 in militia, 7 to 5 in regular army soldiers. Further, not only were the best British troops in Europe fighting Napoleon but three out of every five settlers in Canada were Americans from New York, Pennsylvania, and Connecticut. These settlers, now technically Canadians, had been lured north by cheap land but feared the British more than they feared their kin on the American side. To Jefferson, the conquest of Canada seemed "a mere matter of marching."

Expectations of an easy victory, however, rested on a much shakier foundation than many Americans realized. First, the British had an invaluable ally in the native Americans, who proved to be terrifying as well as tough warriors. Although not the only ones to commit atrocities, the Indians struck fear in beholders by dangling scalps from their belts. The British quickly learned to play on this fear, in some cases forcing Americans to surrender by hinting that the Indians might be uncontrollable in battle. Second, most American generals were aged and incompetent, and one of the only good ones, Andrew Jackson, was long denied a federal commission, on political grounds. And the American state militias, the darlings of republican theorists because they seemed a safe alternative to a standing army, were filled with Sunday soldiers who "hollered for water half the time, and whiskey the other. . . ." Their lack of training aside, few militiamen really understood the goals of the war. In fact, outside Congress, there simply was not much blood lust in 1812. In New England, where opposition to the war was widespread, the people had little stomach for an invasion of Canada. (The loyal minority in New England, however, did provide the army with more regiments than either the middle states or the South.) President Madison was able to raise only 10,000 one-year volunteers out of the 50,000 authorized by Congress. In Kentucky, the home of the prominent war hawk Henry Clay (who boasted that his constituents were spoiling for a fight), only 400 answered the first call for volunteers. This lukewarm response in all sections indicates not only that most people viewed Canada as remote but also that national political issues did not necessarily penetrate deeply into American society in 1812. Local attachments remained stronger than national ones.

The military campaigns of the war developed in two broad phases. From the summer of 1812 to the spring of 1814, the Americans assumed the offensive position, launching a succession of poorly coordinated and generally unsuccessful attacks on Canada. From the spring of 1814 into early 1815, the British took the offensive and achieved some spectacular victories while losing key battles.

On to Canada

Whereas some Americans wanted to commence the war with an attack on Montreal, the ardor of western politicians dictated that the opening offensive occur in the West. In July 1812 sixty-year-old General William Hull led an American army from Detroit into Canada, but the ingenious Tecumseh cut his supply line. Hull then retreated to Detroit. Unnerved by the sight of Tecumseh and by the hint of the British commander, General Isaac Brock, that "the numerous body of Indians who have attached themselves to my troops will be beyond my control the moment the contest commences," Hull surrendered two thousand men to thirteen hundred British and native American troops.

Now the British concentrated their strength against a mixed force of regulars and New York militia menacing Canada north of Niagara Falls. While the American regulars marched into Canada, the New York militiamen, contending that they had volunteered only to protect their homes, not to invade Canada, refused to cross their state line. As the militia looked on from the American side, a detachment of American regulars was crushed by the British at the Battle of Queenston (October 12, 1813). Again the daunting Indian presence proved decisive. Winfield Scott, later to become a candidate for the presidency of the United States, negotiated the American surrender as Mohawk Indians were attacking his men. The third American offensive of 1812 never got off the ground. The sixty-two-year-old general Henry Dearborn was to have moved on Montreal via Lake Champlain. He had advanced twenty miles north of Plattsburgh by November 19, when the militia refused to go any further. Thus Dearborn returned to Plattsburgh.

Under General William Henry Harrison, the Americans renewed their offensive in 1813 and tried to retake Detroit. A succession of reverses convinced Harrison that offensive operations were futile as long as the British controlled Lake Erie. During the winter of 1812–1813, Captain Oliver H. Perry constructed a little fleet of vessels out of green wood, cannon captured in a raid on York (Toronto), and supplies dragged across the snow from Pittsburgh to his headquarters at Presqu'ile (Erie). Perry encountered and destroyed a British squadron at Put-in-Bay on the western end of Lake Erie on September 10, 1813, reporting "We have met the enemy, and they are ours." Losing control of Lake Erie, the British pulled back from Detroit, but Harrison overtook and defeated a combined British and Indian force at the Battle of the Thames on October 5. Tecumseh, now a legend among the whites, died in the battle; Colonel Richard Johnson's claim, never proved, to have killed Tecumseh later contributed to Johnson's election as vice president of the United States.

The Naval War

Even before their victory at Put-in-Bay, Americans had achieved sensational successes on the high seas. Republican tightfistedness had not altogether succeeded in starving the United States Navy. However small, the navy had entered the war with three of the largest and fastest frigates afloat — the *Constitution,* the *United States,* and the *President.* On August 19, 1812, the *Constitution* destroyed HMS *Guerrière* in the mid-Atlantic and on December 29 wrecked HMS *Java* off Brazil. In October the *United States,* under Captain Stephen Decatur, captured HMS *Macedonian* off the African coast and brought the ship back to New London, Connecticut, as a prize. But these victories had more psychological than strategic value. While they gave Americans something to cheer, the British clamped a blockade on the American coast, starting with Delaware Bay and Chesapeake Bay in the fall of 1812 and extending to New York in the spring of 1813 and to New England in the spring of 1814. The *United States* was now corked in the bottle of New York harbor, the *President* in New Haven, and the *Constitution* in Boston. Nor did Perry's victory on Lake

The Constitution Ranging Alongside the Guerrière, *by Michael Felice Corne, 1812 (Detail)*

The Constitution *won more battles than any other early American frigate. Its most famous victory was over H.M.S.* Guerrière *in August 1812. Known affectionately as Old Ironsides, it was saved from demolition in 1830 by the poet Oliver Wendell Holmes, became a schoolship for the U.S. Naval Academy, was nearly confiscated by the fledgling Confederate navy in 1861, and today survives as a naval relic in Boston harbor.*

Erie and Harrison's at the Battle of the Thames hasten the conquest of Canada. Efforts to invade Canada in the Niagara area, and to gain control of Lake Ontario, failed.

The British Offensive

Britain's military fortunes crested in the spring of 1814. After his disastrous invasion of Russia in 1812 and a series of defeats in 1813, France's Napoleon abdicated as emperor in April 1814, and Britain began to move regulars from Europe to North America. The British quickly found, however, that earlier defeats had toughened the Americans, who were now fighting to defend their homes rather than to invade Canada. The first sign of trouble for the British came on the Niagara front in July 1814, when attacking redcoats were stopped by fierce American resistance at the battles of Chippewa (July 5) and Lundy's Lane (July 25).

The main British thrust came not on the Niagara front but down Lake Champlain. At the head of ten thousand British veterans, the largest and best-equipped British army ever sent to North America, General Sir George Prevost advanced south via the lake at the end of August and reached Plattsburgh on September 6. Prevost's plan was to

split the New England states from the rest of the country. At Plattsburgh, however, he encountered a well-entrenched American army. Resolving that he had to control the lake before attacking Plattsburgh, Prevost called up his fleet, but an American naval squadron under Captain Thomas Macdonough defeated the British squadron on September 11. Dispirited, Prevost abandoned the campaign.

Ironically, the British achieved a far more spectacular success in an operation originally designed merely as a diversion from their main thrust down Lake Champlain. In 1814 a British army sailed from Bermuda for Chesapeake Bay, landed near Washington, and on August 24 met a larger American force, composed mainly of militia, at Bladensburg, Maryland. The Battle of Bladensburg quickly became the "Bladensburg races" as the American militia fled, almost without firing a shot. The British then descended on Washington. Madison, who had witnessed the Bladensburg fiasco, escaped into the Virginia hills. His wife, Dolley, pausing only long enough to load her silver, a bed, and a portrait of George Washington onto her carriage, hastened to join her husband, while British troops ate the supper prepared for the Madisons at the presidential mansion. Then they burned the mansion along with other public buildings in Washington. A few weeks later, the British attacked

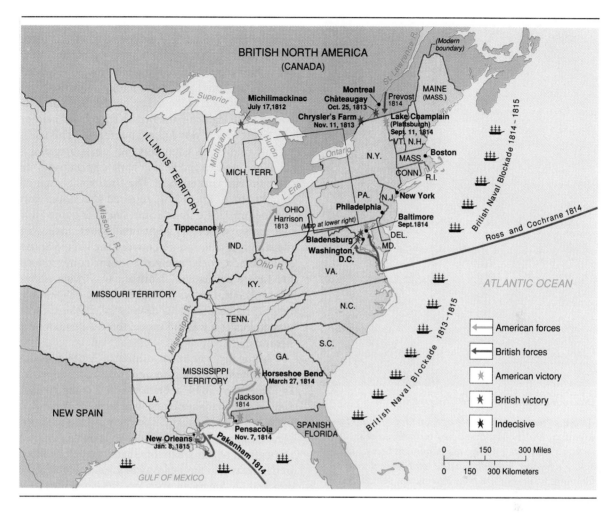

Major Battles of the War of 1812

*Most of the war's major engagements
occurred on or near the United States' northern frontier; but the Royal Navy blockaded
the entire Atlantic coast, and the British army
penetrated as far south as Washington and
New Orleans.*

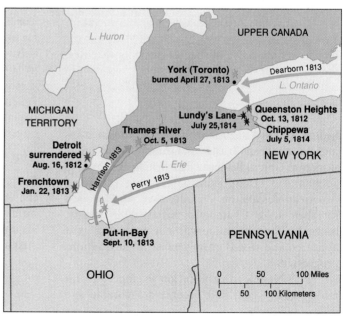

Dolley Madison, *by Gilbert Stuart, 1804*

As the attractive young wife of Secretary of State James Madison, Dolley Madison acted virtually as the nation's First Lady during the administration of Jefferson, a widower. Friendly, tactful, and blessed with an unfailing memory for names and events, she added to her reputation as an elegant hostess after her husband became president.

Baltimore, but after failing to crack its defenses, they broke off the operation.

The Treaty of Ghent

In August 1814 negotiations to end the war commenced between British and American commissioners at Ghent, Belgium. The British appeared to command a strong position. Having frustrated American designs on Canada, they stood poised for their Lake Champlain initiative. In reality, however, their position was not as strong as it appeared and would grow weaker as negotiations progressed.

With Napoleon's abdication as emperor, Britain's primary goal had become a favorable and lasting peace in Europe; the British had little to gain from prolonging a minor war in America. Mindful of their superior military position, they demanded territorial concessions from the United States. The American naval victory at Plattsburgh, however, brought home to Britain the fact that after two years of fighting, the British controlled neither the Great Lakes nor Lake Champlain. The spectacular raid on Washington had no strategic significance, and so the British gave way on the issue of territorial concessions. The final treaty, signed on Christmas Eve 1814, restored the status quo ante bellum*: the United States neither gained nor lost territory. Several additional issues, including the fixing of a boundary between the United States and Canada, were referred to joint commissions for future settlement. Nothing was done about impressment, but with Napoleon out of the way, neutral rights became a dead issue. Because there was no longer a war in Europe, there were no longer neutrals.

Ironically, the most dramatic American victory of the war came after the conclusion of peace. In December 1814 a British army, composed of veterans of the Napoleonic wars and commanded by General Sir Edward Pakenham, descended on New Orleans. On January 8, 1815, two weeks after the signing of the Treaty of Ghent but before word of the treaty had reached America, Pakenham's force attacked an American army under General Andrew ("Old Hickory") Jackson. Already a legend for his ferocity as an Indian fighter, Jackson inspired little fear among the British, who advanced into battle far too confidently, but he did strike enough terror in his own men to prevent another American rout. In an hour of gruesome carnage, Jackson's troops shredded the line of advancing redcoats, killing Pakenham and inflicting more than two thousand casualties while losing only thirteen Americans.

The Hartford Convention

Because the Treaty of Ghent had already concluded the war, the Battle of New Orleans had little significance for diplomats. Indirectly, however, it had an impact on domestic politics by eroding Federalist strength.

---

*Status quo ante bellum: Latin for the state of affairs before the war.

The comeback that the Federalists had made in the election of 1808 had continued into the 1812 campaign. Buoyed by hostility to the war in the Northeast, the Federalists had thrown their support behind DeWitt Clinton, an antiwar Republican. Although Madison won the electoral vote 128–89, Clinton carried all of New England except Vermont, as well as New York and New Jersey. American military setbacks in the war intensified Federalist disdain for the new Madison administration. Indeed, from their bastions in New England (see "A Place in Time"), Federalists saw a nation misruled for over a decade by Republican bunglers. Jefferson's attack on the judiciary had seemed to threaten the rule of law. His purchase of Louisiana, a measure of doubtful constitutionality, had enhanced Republican strength and reduced the relative importance of Federalist New England in the Union. The Embargo Act had severely damaged New England's commerce. Now "Mr. Madison's War" was bringing fresh misery to New England in the form of the British blockade. A few Federalists began to talk of New England's secession from the Union. Most, however, rejected the idea, believing that they would soon benefit from popular disfavor with the war and spring back into power.

In late 1814 a Federalist convention met in Hartford, Connecticut. While some advocates of secession were present, moderates took control and passed a series of resolutions summarizing New England's grievances. At the root of these grievances lay the belief that New England was becoming a permanent minority in a nation dominated by southern Republicans who failed to understand New England's commercial interests. Accordingly, the convention proposed to amend the Constitution to abolish the three-fifths clause (which gave the South a disproportionate share of votes in Congress by allowing it to count slaves as a basis of

representation), to require a two-thirds vote of Congress to declare war and to admit new states into the Union, to limit the president to a single term, to prohibit the election of two successive presidents from the same state, and to bar embargoes lasting more than sixty days. As bold as these proposals were, their timing was disastrous for the Federalists. News of the Treaty of Ghent and of Jackson's victory at New Orleans dashed the Federalists' hopes of gaining broad popular support. The goal of the Hartford Convention had been to assert states' rights rather than disunion, but to many the proceedings smelled of a traitorous plot. The restoration of peace, moreover, stripped the Federalists of the primary grievance that had fueled the convention. In the election of 1816, Republican James Monroe, Madison's hand-picked successor, swept the nation over negligible Federalist opposition. He would win reelection in 1820 with only a single dissenting electoral vote. As a force in national politics, the Federalists were finished.

The Election of 1816

Candidates	Parties	Electoral Vote
JAMES MONROE	Democratic-Republican	183
Rufus King	Federalist	34

The Election of 1820

Candidates	Parties	Electoral Vote
JAMES MONROE	Democratic-Republican	231
John Quincy Adams	Independent Republican	1

The Election of 1812

Candidates	Parties	Electoral Vote
JAMES MADISON	Democratic-Republican	128
DeWitt Clinton	Federalist	89

The Awakening of American Nationalism

The United States emerged from the War of 1812 bruised but intact. In its first major war since the Revolution, the American republic had demonstrated not only that it could fight on even terms

Bulfinch's Boston

During the first quarter of the nineteenth century, Boston shed its quaint colonial-era character and was transformed into a bustling commercial hub and one of the most important towns in the independent nation. Formerly a community dotted with frame houses and boxy brick residences—most with small farms, gardens, and orchards—Boston became a prosperous seaport in the early years of the republic, a charming place dominated by tree-fringed streets and stately brick homes inhabited by the town's elites.

Bostonians' success in maritime industry underlay this metamorphosis. Shipping, cod fishing, and whaling thrived in the port town. Boston's waterfront was ever alive with graceful, gently bobbing sailing ships—a riot of masts. Bostonians going about their business on the harborfront clomped along in their wagons, their horses' progress sometimes impeded by the ships' bowsprits jutting out into the streets. Along the way they passed wharf after wharf lined with the brick warehouses and countinghouses that had sprung up to manage Bostonians' widening sea trade. In 1794 eighty humming quays gave a distinctive commercial flavor to the waterfront.

A highly profitable commerce with Europe, the East Indies, and China fueled the furious seaside activity, along with shipping to ports in the East Indies and elsewhere in the United States. Boston merchants and sea captains built fortunes from their shipping and fish-

ing ventures; some voyages realized profits of more than $100,000, a huge take for the times. New England cotton manufacturers benefited handsomely too as savvy Yankees began to turn a former home industry into a large-scale business operation that supplied the duck and canvas for the harbor's panorama of sails. The fledgling American navy also needed sails; those for the *Constitution* had to be made in an old grain storehouse because no other town structure was long enough.

Even before the imposition of the embargo that stifled this lucrative trade, Boston, the home of many of President Thomas Jefferson's most bitter Federalist critics, among them George Cabot and Harrison Gray Otis, was a thorn in Jefferson's side. A Federalist elite ran the city, dominating its politics and culture as well as its maritime economy. Composing the elite were not only the merchants upon whom the town's commercial prosperity rested but also the lawyers who controlled its judicial offices, as well as men who had made a fortune in real estate. These upper-crust Bostonians supported the town's cultural institutions, such as the Boston Athenaeum, the nation's largest private library; the American Academy of Arts and Sciences; and Harvard College in nearby Cambridge. Austere and even frigid in their manners, Boston's Federalist leaders were a study in contrast to friendly, backslapping Virginia squires.

Following a grand tour of Europe, the architect Charles Bul-

Charles Bulfinch, *by Mather Brown, 1786*

Bulfinch learned about architecture as a boy by browsing in the well-stocked architectural library of his maternal grandfather, the wealthy Charles Apthorp. In the 1780s Bulfinch's interest was further stimulated by his visits to Rome, Florence, and London and by the encouragement of Thomas Jefferson.

finch, in love with the classical style that he had seen in ancient Roman ruins, designed the majestic Massachusetts State House (completed in 1798) and the gracious mansions on Beacon Hill from which Boston's Federalists looked down upon "their" prosperous city. Bulfinch did more than cater to the elite; the scion of colonial aristocrats, he was part of the elite and served as Boston's police chief. The vast majority of Bostonians, of course, shared none of the privileges and splendor enjoyed by Bulfinch and others of the elite; artisans, mariners, and laborers looked up to Beacon Hill, not down from it. Yet even when Jefferson's Republicans began to score victories in Massachusetts, Boston stayed solidly Federalist.

How could the Federalists retain their political control for so long? Part of the answer is that Boston artisans and laborers remembered how the elite families had supported the Revolution and the Constitution. In addition, the Federalist elite profited from the attitude still prevailing among the common people that social superiors deserved respect and even obedience. Historians call this attitude deference, and there was a lot of it in Boston. To secure deference, the elite paid careful attention to dress. Powdered wigs, lace ruffles, silk stockings, and gold canes were all part of a carefully fashioned image that members of the elite projected when they walked the streets. This attention to image was important, especially among elite families like

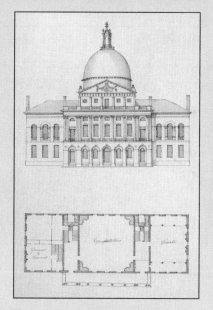

Massachusetts State House

Like Jefferson, Bulfinch admired the classical style of ancient Greece and Rome. But Bulfinch was less inclined than Jefferson to copy ancient buildings literally. Bulfinch's design for the Massachusetts State House reflects the symmetry of neoclassicism; unlike Jefferson's plan for the Virginia Capitol, it is not based on any particular Roman structure.

the Cabots and the Lowells, recent arrivals to Boston who had made their fortunes during and after the Revolution. If deference showed any sign of weakening, the Boston elite could and did fall back on its control of elections. Until 1822, for example, Boston Brahmins beat back efforts to establish decentralized polling places. All Bostonians voted in Faneuil Hall under the eyes of the elite, and only after presenting evidence of property owning.

Bulfinch advised young men against becoming architects, for he believed that few new buildings would be constructed in Boston. His attitude reflected the fact that Boston's population had grown by only 10 percent between 1743 and 1790. Immigrants avoided stuffy Federalist Boston. Adventurers and radicals found New York and Philadelphia more congenial. Yet even as Bulfinch designed his stately mansions, the city was changing. Its population rose from 18,000 in 1790 to nearly 34,000 in 1810, and to 58,000 in 1826. By the 1820s the city had become too large and diverse to follow the leadership of a single elite. By the late 1820s, new political alignments had shattered Federalist domination of Boston's politics.

The Tea Party, *by Henry Sargent, c. 1821 (Detail)*

Bulfinch's Federalist patrons craved elegant interiors and could afford wall-to-wall carpeting. Tea parties like this unified as well as entertained Boston's elite.

Manuscript for "The Star-Spangled Banner" *(Detail)*

against a major power but also that republics could fight wars without turning themselves into despotisms. The war produced more than its share of symbols of American nationalism. Whitewash cleared the smoke damage to the presidential mansion; thereafter, it became known as the White House. The British attack on Fort McHenry, guarding Baltimore, prompted a young observer, Francis Scott Key, to compose "The Star-Spangled Banner." The Battle of New Orleans boosted Andrew Jackson onto the stage of national politics and became a source of legends about why the Americans had won the battle. It appears to most scholars today that the British lost because Pakenham's men, advancing within range of Jackson's riflemen and cannon, unaccountably paused and became sitting ducks. But in the wake of the battle, Americans spun a different tale. The legend arose that Jackson owed his victory not to Pakenham's blundering tactics but to hawk-eyed Kentucky frontiersmen whose rifles picked off the British with unerring accuracy. In fact, many frontiersmen in Jackson's army had not carried rifles; even if they had, gunpowder smoke would have obscured the enemy. But none of this mattered at the time. Just as Americans preferred militia to professional soldiers, they chose to believe that their greatest victory of the war was the handiwork of amateurs.

Madison's Nationalism and the Era of Good Feelings

The War of 1812 had three major political consequences. First, it eliminated the Federalists as a national political force. Second, it went a long way toward convincing the Republicans that the nation was strong and resilient, capable of fighting a war while maintaining the liberty of its people. The third consequence was an outgrowth of the first two. With the Federalists tainted by disloyalty and with fears about the fragility of republics fading, Republicans increasingly embraced some doctrines long associated with the Federalists. In a message to Congress in December 1815, Madison called for federal support for internal improvements, tariff protection for the new industries that had sprung up during the embargo, and the creation of a new national bank. (The charter of the first Bank of the United States had expired in 1811.) In Congress another Republican, Henry Clay of Kentucky, proposed similar measures, which he called the American System, with the aim of making the nation economically self-sufficient and free from dependency on Europe. In 1816 Congress chartered the Second Bank of the United States and enacted a moderate tariff. Federal support for internal improvements proved to be a thornier problem. Madison favored federal aid in principle but believed that a constitutional amendment was necessary to authorize it. Accordingly, he vetoed an internal-improvements bill passed in 1817.

As Republicans adopted positions that they had once disdained, an "Era of Good Feelings" dawned on American politics. A Boston newspaper, impressed by the warm reception accorded President Monroe while touring New England, coined the phrase in 1817. It has stuck as a description of Monroe's two administrations, from 1816 to 1824.

Compared with Jefferson and Madison, Monroe was neither brilliant, polished, nor wealthy, but he keenly desired to heal the political divisions that a stronger intellect and personality might have inflamed. The phrase "Era of Good Feelings" reflects not only the war's elimination of some divisive issues but also Monroe's conscious effort to avoid political controversies. But the good feelings were paper-thin. Madison's 1817 veto of the internal-improvements bill revealed the persistence of disagreements about the role of the federal government under the Constitution. Furthermore, the embargo, the War of 1812, and the continuation of slavery had aroused sectional animosities that a journalist's phrase about good feelings could not dispel. Not surprisingly, the postwar consensus began to unravel almost as soon as Americans recognized its existence.

John Marshall and the Supreme Court

Jefferson's old antagonist John Marshall continued to preside over the Supreme Court during the Monroe administrations and in 1819 issued two opinions that stunned Republicans. The first case, *Dartmouth College* v. *Woodward,* centered on the question of whether New Hampshire could transform a private corporation, Dartmouth College, into a state university. Marshall concluded that the college's original charter, granted to its trustees by George III in 1769, was a contract. Since the Constitution specifically forbade states to interfere with contracts, New Hampshire's effort to turn Dartmouth into a state university was unconstitutional. The implications of Marshall's ruling were far-reaching. Charters or acts of incorporation provided their beneficiaries with various legal privileges and were sought by businesses as well as by colleges. In effect, Marshall said that once a state had chartered a college or business, it surrendered both its power to alter the charter and, in large measure, its authority to regulate the beneficiary.

A few weeks later, the chief justice handed down an even more momentous decision in the case of *McCulloch* v. *Maryland.* The issue here was whether the state of Maryland had the power to tax a national corporation, specifically the Baltimore branch of the Second Bank of the United States. The bank was a national corporation, chartered by Congress, but most of the stockholders were private citizens who reaped whatever profits the

bank made. Speaking for a unanimous Court, Marshall ignored these private features of the bank and concentrated instead on two issues. First, did Congress have the power to charter a national bank? Nothing in the Constitution, Marshall conceded, explicitly granted this power. But the Constitution did authorize Congress to lay and collect taxes, to regulate interstate commerce, and to declare war. Surely these enumerated powers, he reasoned, implied a power to charter a bank. Marshall was clearly engaging in a broad, or "loose," rather than strict, construction (interpretation) of the Constitution. The second issue was whether a state could tax an agency of the federal government that lay within its borders. Marshall argued that any power of the national government, express or implied, was supreme within its sphere. States could not interfere with the exercise of federal powers. A tax by Maryland on the Baltimore branch was such an interference and hence was plainly unconstitutional.

Marshall's decision in the *McCulloch* case dismayed many Republicans. Although Madison and Monroe had supported the establishment of the Second Bank of the United States, the bank had made itself unpopular by tightening its loan policies during the summer of 1818. This contraction of credit triggered a severe depression, the Panic of 1819, that gave rise to considerable distress throughout the country, especially among western farmers. At a time when the bank was widely blamed for the panic, Marshall's ruling stirred controversy by placing the bank beyond the regulatory power of any state government. His decision, indeed, was as much an attack on state sovereignty as it was a defense of the bank. The Constitution, Marshall argued, was the creation not of state governments but of the people of *all* the states and thus was more fundamental than state laws. His reasoning assailed the Republican theory, best expressed in the Virginia and Kentucky resolutions of 1798–1799, that the Union was essentially a compact among states. Republicans had continued to view state governments as more immediately responsive to the people's will than was the federal government and to regard the compact theory of the Union as a guarantor of popular liberty. As Republicans saw it, Marshall's *McCulloch* decision, along with his decision in the *Dartmouth College* case, stripped state governments of the power to impose the will of their people upon corporations.

The Missouri Compromise

The fragility of the Era of Good Feelings again became apparent in the prolonged controversy between 1819 and 1821 over the territory of Missouri. In February 1819 the House of Representatives was considering a bill to admit Missouri as a slave state. James Tallmadge, Jr., a New York Republican, offered an amendment that prohibited the further introduction of slaves into Missouri and provided for the emancipation, at age twenty-five, of all slave offspring born after Missouri's admission as a state. Following bitter debate, the House approved the bill with Tallmadge's amendment. The Senate, after an equally rancorous debate, struck the amendment from the Missouri bill. In each chamber the vote on the Tallmadge amendment followed sectional lines, with the South virtually unanimously opposed to the provisions regarding slavery and the North predominantly in support. "This momentous question," Jefferson worried, "like a fire bell in the night, awakened and filled me with terror."

American politics had long been torn by sectional conflict, and slavery had at times figured in this discord, notably in the debate at the Constitutional Convention over the three-fifths clause. Yet prior to 1819 slavery had not been the primary factor in sectional division. Issues like Alexander Hamilton's economic program and the Jay Treaty had done more than slavery to polarize the country along sectional lines. During the 1790s Jefferson's main fear had been that Federalist economic policies were favoring northern commercial development at the expense of southern agriculture. After 1800 Federalist opposition to the Louisiana Purchase and to the War of 1812 grew mainly out of concern that the now dominant Republicans were

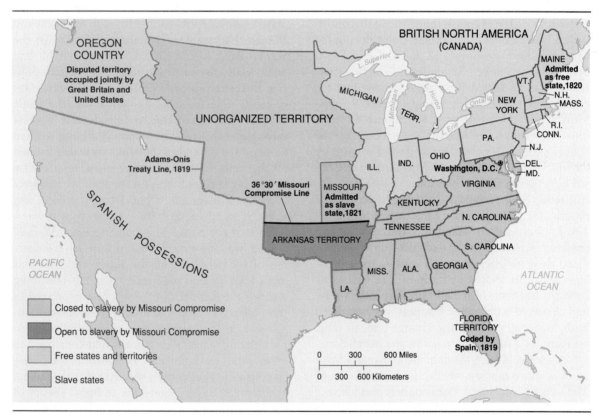

The Missouri Compromise, 1820–1821   *The Missouri Compromise temporarily quelled controversy over slavery by admitting Maine as a free state and Missouri as a slave state, and by prohibiting slavery in the remainder of the Louisiana Purchase north of 36° 30'.*

sacrificing New England's political and commercial interests to those of the South and West. The Hartford Convention of 1814 had been a reaction not so much to the spread of slavery as to the decline of New England's political influence.

For various reasons, the Missouri question thrust slavery into the center of this long-standing sectional conflict. In 1819 the Union had eleven free and eleven slave states. The admission of Missouri as a slave state would upset this balance to the advantage of the South. Noting that every president since John Adams had been a Virginian, Federalists portrayed the admission of Missouri as part of a conspiracy to perpetuate the rule of Virginia slaveholders. Republicans countered by pointing to the relatively sudden emergence in the House of Representatives of a vocal antislavery block, which included many northern Federalists, and to the growing number of Federalist-dominated societies in the North that promoted the manumission (freeing) of slaves. In response to these developments, some Republicans began to view all efforts to restrict slavery as part of a plot by the Federalists to divide northern and southern Republicans and thus regain political power. In sum, by 1819 the slavery issue had become intertwined with the prevailing distrust between the parties and between the sections.

Virtually every issue that was to wrack the Union during the next forty years was present in the controversy over Missouri: southern charges that the North was conspiring to destroy the Union and to end slavery; accusations by northerners that southerners were conspiring to extend the institution. For a while, leaders doubted that the Union would survive the crisis. House Speaker Henry Clay wrote that the words *civil war* and *disunion* were commonly uttered, almost without emotion. But a series of congressional agreements in 1820 and 1821, known collectively as the Missouri Compromise, resolved the crisis.

The first of these agreements involved the balance between slave states and free states. At the same time that Congress was considering statehood for Missouri, Maine was seeking admission as a free state. In 1820 Congress agreed to admit Maine as a free state, to pave the way for Missouri's admission as a slave state, and to prohibit slavery in the remainder of the Louisiana Purchase territory north of 36°30' (the southern boundary of Missouri). But compromise did not come easily. The components of the eventual compromise passed by close and ominously sectional votes. Additionally, no sooner had the compromise been forged than it nearly fell apart. As a prelude to statehood, Missourians drafted a constitution that prohibited free blacks from entering their territory. This provision raised a thorny question, for some eastern states recognized free people of color as citizens, who, as such, were protected from discrimination by the federal Constitution, which clearly stated that "Citizens of each State shall be entitled to all Privileges and Immunities of Citizens in the several States." Balking at Missourians' exclusion of free blacks, antislavery northerners barred Missouri's admission into the Union until 1821, when Henry Clay engineered a new agreement. This second Missouri Compromise prohibited Missouri from discriminating against citizens of other states but left open the issue of whether free blacks were citizens.

The Missouri Compromise was widely viewed as a southern victory. The South had gained admission of Missouri, whose acceptance of slavery was controversial, while conceding to the North the admission of Maine, whose rejection of slavery inspired no controversy at all. Yet the South had conceded to freedom a vast block of territory north of 36°30'. While much of this territory was unorganized Indian country that some viewed as unfit for white habitation, it would not remain a wilderness for long. Also, the Missouri Compromise reinforced the principle, originally set down by the Northwest Ordinance of 1787, that Congress had the right to prohibit slavery in some territories. Southerners had implicitly accepted the argument that slaves were not like other forms of property that could be moved from place to place at will.

Foreign Policy Under Monroe

American foreign policy between 1816 and 1824 reflected more consensus than conflict. The end of the Napoleonic Wars and the signing of the Treaty of Ghent had removed most of the foreign-policy disagreements between Federalists and Republicans. Moreover, Monroe was fortunate to have as his secretary of state an extraordinary diplomat,

John Quincy Adams. An austere and scholarly man whose library equaled his house in monetary value, Adams was a tough negotiator and a fervent nationalist. Although he was the son of the last Federalist president, he had been the only Federalist in the Senate to support the Louisiana Purchase. He later backed the embargo, joined the Republican party, served as minister to Russia, and was one of the negotiators of the Treaty of Ghent.

As secretary of state, Adams moved quickly to strengthen the peace with Great Britain. During his term the United States and Britain signed the Rush-Bagot Treaty of 1817, which effectively demilitarized the Great Lakes by severely restricting the number of ships that the two powers could maintain there. Next the British-American Convention of 1818 fixed the boundary between the United States and Canada from the Lake of the Woods west to the Rockies and restored to Americans the same fishing rights off Newfoundland that they had enjoyed before the War of 1812. As a result of these two agreements, for the first time since Independence, the United States had a secure border with British-controlled Canada and could turn its attention southward and westward.

Adams's dealings with the Spanish, who still owned East Florida and claimed West Florida, were also successful. It had never been clear whether the Louisiana Purchase included West Florida. Acting as if it did, the United States in 1812 had simply added a slice of West Florida to the state of Louisiana and another slice to the Mississippi Territory. In 1818 Andrew Jackson, the American military commander in the South, seizing upon the pretext that Florida was both a base for Seminole Indian raids into American soil and a refuge for fugitive slaves, invaded East Florida, hanged two British subjects, and captured Spanish forts. Jackson had acted without explicit orders, but Adams supported the raid, guessing correctly that it would panic the Spanish into further concessions. In 1819 Spain agreed to the Adams-Onís (or Transcontinental) Treaty. By its terms, Spain ceded East Florida to the United States, renounced its claims to all of West Florida, and agreed to a southern border of the United States that ran from the Mississippi River along the Sabine River (separating Texas from Louisiana) and then westward along the Red and Arkansas rivers to the Rocky Mountains, finally following the forty-second parallel to the Pacific. For the first time, the United States had a legitimate claim to the Pacific coast.

The Monroe Doctrine

John Quincy Adams had long believed that God and nature had ordained that the United States would eventually span the entire continent of North America. Throughout his negotiations leading up to the Adams-Onís Treaty, he made it clear to Spain that should the Spanish not concede some of their territory in North America, the United States might seize all of it, including Texas and even Mexico. Americans were fast acquiring a reputation as an aggressive people. Yet Spain was concerned with larger issues than the encroachment of Americans. Its primary objective was to suppress the revolutions against Spanish rule that had broken out in South America. To accomplish this, Spain sought support from the European monarchs who had organized the Holy Alliance in 1815. The brainchild of the czar of Russia, the Holy Alliance proclaimed lofty Christian principles as a justification for quashing revolutions everywhere. Although most of the crowned heads of Europe joined the alliance, the British, distracted by trouble at home, stayed aloof. Britain's main goal was to prevent a new eruption of revolutionary France. To this end, Britain had joined the Quadruple Alliance (Austria, Britain, Prussia, and Russia) and, since there was some overlap in the members of the two leagues, hoped to control the Holy Alliance without actually joining it. But the Holy Alliance had a mind of its own, and by 1822 its members were talking of helping Spain suppress the South American revolutions. In response, British foreign minister George Canning proposed that the United States and Britain issue a joint statement opposing any European interference in South America while pledging that neither would annex any part of Spain's old empire in the New World.

This was the background of the Monroe Doctrine, as President Monroe's message to Congress on December 2, 1823, later came to be called. The message announced three key principles: that unless American interests were involved, the United States' policy was to abstain from European wars; that the "American continents" were not "subjects for future colonization by any European power"; and that any attempt at European colonization in the New World would be construed by the United States as an unfriendly act. Monroe's message was in harmony with some aspects of Canning's proposals. But Monroe accepted the position of Secretary of State Adams that it was better for the United States to make a declaration of policy on its own than to "come in as cock-boat in the wake of the British man-of-war." Specifically, Monroe and Adams rejected Canning's insistence that both Britain and the United States pledge never to annex any part of Spain's former territories. Adams had long believed that Texas and Cuba would one day fall under American control as a consequence of the law of "political gravitation." "We have no intention of seizing either Texas or Cuba," Adams wrote. "But the inhabitants of either or both of them may exercise their primitive rights, and solicit a union with us. . . . Without entering now into the enquiry of the expediency of our annexing Texas or Cuba to our Union, we should at least keep ourselves free to act as emergencies arise and not tie ourselves down to any principle which might immediately afterward be brought to bear against ourselves."

As Adams wished, the Monroe Doctrine kept open the American option to extend control over Texas and Cuba while simultaneously sanctioning American recognition of the new Latin American governments. It is easy to ridicule the doctrine as merely a unilateral pronouncement by the United States. It was in fact widely derided in Europe. Fear of the British navy, not the Monroe Doctrine, prevented the Holy Alliance from intervening in South America. Yet by keeping open its options to annex territory, the United States was using the Monroe Doctrine to claim a preeminent position in the New World.

Conclusion

Although the diplomatic achievements of John Quincy Adams and James Monroe were formidable, the greatest accomplishment of the early Republic's leaders was to fashion a workable body of political institutions and customs to govern the young nation. The framers of the Constitution had not anticipated the rise of political parties, and when Jefferson took office in 1801, it was unclear how a victorious party would behave. The range of possibilities was great. Some feared that the Republicans would amend the Constitution to ensure their political ascendancy. One reason why Jefferson's early actions against the judiciary had terrified Federalists was that they viewed his maneuverings as part of a larger plan to destroy them.

As it turned out, Jefferson did not destroy the Federalists; they destroyed themselves. Until the embargo, they failed to come up with a popular national issue, and then they rode opposition to the embargo and to the War of 1812 for too long. When the war ended, a surge of national pride swept the Federalists aside. The election of 1800 had generated anxiety bordering on hysteria; that of 1820 produced yawns. Indeed, the nation was almost too peaceful. Federalist collapse and the embrace by the Republicans of former Federalist policies like the tariff and national banking blurred divisions once sharp.

James Monroe's reelection in 1820 marked the high point of the Republican surge. Even as Republicans congratulated themselves on the emergence of an era of apparent good feelings, the signs of future divisions were growing. The furor over the Missouri Compromise shattered sectional harmony. Subtle changes were starting to occur in American society—changes that would create new political issues and divisions by 1830.

CHRONOLOGY

1800– John Adams's midnight
1801 appointments.

1801 Thomas Jefferson's inauguration.

1802 Repeal of the Judiciary Act of 1801.
Yazoo land compromise.
American right of deposit at New Orleans revoked.

1803 *Marbury* v. *Madison*.
Conclusion of the Louisiana Purchase.

1804 Judge John Pickering convicted by the Senate.
Impeachment of Justice Samuel Chase.
Aaron Burr kills Alexander Hamilton in a duel.
Jefferson elected to a second term.

1804– Lewis and Clark expedition.
1806

1805 Start of the Burr conspiracy.
Chase acquitted by the Senate.
Essex case.

1806 British government issues the first Order in Council.
Napoleon's Berlin Decree.

1807 Burr acquitted of treason.
Chesapeake Affair.
Napoleon's Milan Decree.
Embargo Act passed.

1808 James Madison elected president.

1809 Non-Intercourse Act passed; Embargo Act repealed.

1810 Macon's Bill No. 2.

1811 Battle of Tippecanoe.

1812 Orders in Council revoked.
United States declares war on Britain.
Madison reelected to a second term.
General William Hull surrenders at Detroit.
USS *Constitution* defeats HMS *Guerrière*.
Battle of Queenston.

1813 Battle of Lake Erie (Put-in-Bay).
Battle of the Thames.

1814 Battles of Chippewa and Lundy's Lane.
Battle of Bladensburg.

British burn Washington, D.C.
Captain Thomas Macdonough's naval victory at the Battle of Plattsburgh.
Hartford Convention.
Treaty of Ghent signed.

1815 Battle of New Orleans.

1816 James Monroe elected president.
Second Bank of the United States chartered.

1817 Rush-Bagot Treaty.

1818 British-American Convention of 1818.
Andrew Jackson invades East Florida.

1819 Adams-Onís (Transcontinental) Treaty.
Dartmouth College v. *Woodward*.
McCulloch v. *Maryland*.

1820 Monroe reelected to a second term.

1820– Missouri Compromise.
1821

1823 Monroe Doctrine.

For Further Reading

Henry Adams, *History of the United States During the Administrations of Jefferson and Madison*, 9 vols. (1889–1891). A classic study by the great-grandson of John Adams.

Irving Brant, *James Madison*, vols. 4–6 (1953–1961). The standard biography of Madison.

Forrest McDonald, *The Presidency of Thomas Jefferson* (1976). A lively overview.

Dumas Malone, *Jefferson and His Time*, vols. 4 and 5 (1970, 1974). An extremely comprehensive biography.

Merrill Peterson, *Thomas Jefferson and the New Nation: A Biography* (1970). The best one-volume biography of Jefferson.

Marshall Smelser, *The Democratic Republic, 1801–1815* (1968). A thorough general work.

J. C. A. Stagg, *Mr. Madison's War: Politics, Diplomacy and Warfare in the Early Republic* (1983). An important reinterpretation of the causes of the War of 1812.

Additional Bibliography

Political Ideologies

Joyce Appleby, *Capitalism and a New Social Order: The Republican Vision of the 1790s* (1984); Lance Banning, *The Jeffersonian Persuasion: Evolution of a Party Ideology* (1978); Drew McCoy, *The Elusive Republic: Political Economy in Jeffersonian America* (1980).

Political Parties

James Banner, *To the Hartford Convention: The Federalists and the Origins of Party Politics in the Early Republic, 1789–1815* (1967); Noble E. Cunningham, *The Jeffersonian Republicans and Power: Party Operations, 1801–1809* (1963); David Hackett Fischer, *The Revolution of American Conservatism: The Federalist Party in the Era of Jeffersonian Democracy* (1965); Ronald P. Formisano, *The Transformation of Political Culture: Massachusetts Parties, 1790s–1840s* (1983); Robert M. Johnstone, Jr., *Jefferson and the Presidency: Leadership in the Young Republic* (1978); David P. Jordan, *Political Leadership in Jefferson's Virginia* (1983); Linda K. Kerber, *Federalists in Dissent: Imagery and Ideology in Jeffersonian America* (1970); Shaw Livermore, *The Twilight of Federalism: The Disintegration of the Federalist Party, 1815–1830* (1962); James S. Young, *The Washington Community: 1800–1828* (1966).

Political Leaders

Thomas P. Abernethy, *The Burr Conspiracy* (1954); Robert Dawidoff, *The Education of John Randolph* (1979); Milton Lomask, *Aaron Burr*, 2 vols. (1979, 1982); Samuel Eliot Morison, *Harrison Gray Otis, 1765–1848: The Urbane Federalist* (1962); Robert Shalhope, *John Taylor of Caroline: Pastoral Republican* (1978).

Law and the Judiciary

Leonard Baker, *John Marshall: A Life in Law* (1974); Albert J. Beveridge, *John Marshall*, 4 vols. (1916–1919); Richard E. Ellis, *The Jeffersonian Crisis: Courts and Politics in the Young Republic* (1971); Charles G. Haines, *The Role of the Supreme Court in American Government and Politics, 1789–1835* (1944); Peter C. Hoffer and N. E. H. Hull, *Impeachment in America, 1635–1805* (1984); Morton J. Horwitz, *The Transformation of American Law, 1780–1860* (1977).

The War of 1812 and Its Prologue

Pierre Berton, *The Invasion of Canada* (1980); Roger H. Brown, *The Republic in Peril* (1964); A. L. Burtt, *The United States, Great Britain, and British North America* (1940); Harry L. Coles, *The War of 1812* (1965); Reginald Horsman, *The Causes of the War of 1812* (1962); Bradford Perkins, *Prologue to War: England and the United States, 1805–1812* (1961); Julius W. Pratt, *Expansionists of 1812* (1925); Louis M. Sears, *Jefferson and the Embargo* (1927); Burton Spivak, *Jefferson's English Crisis: Commerce, Embargo, and the Republican Revolution* (1979).

Nationalism and Sectionalism

Harry Ammon, Jr., *James Monroe: The Quest for National Identity* (1971); George Dangerfield, *The Awakening of American Nationalism, 1815–1828* (1965) and *The Era of Good Feelings* (1952); Don E. Fehrenbacher, *The South and Three Sectional Crises* (1980); Glover Moore, *The Missouri Compromise, 1819–1821* (1953); Donald L. Robinson, *Slavery in the Structure of American Politics, 1765–1820* (1971).

John Quincy Adams and the Monroe Doctrine

Samuel F. Bemis, *John Quincy Adams and the Foundations of American Foreign Policy* (1949); Walter LaFeber, ed., *John Quincy Adams and the American Continental Empire* (1965); Ernest R. May, *The Making of the Monroe Doctrine* (1975); Dexter Perkins, *Hands Off: A History of the Monroe Doctrine* (1951) and *The Monroe Doctrine, 1823–1826* (1927).

CHAPTER 8

The Transformation of American Society, 1815–1840

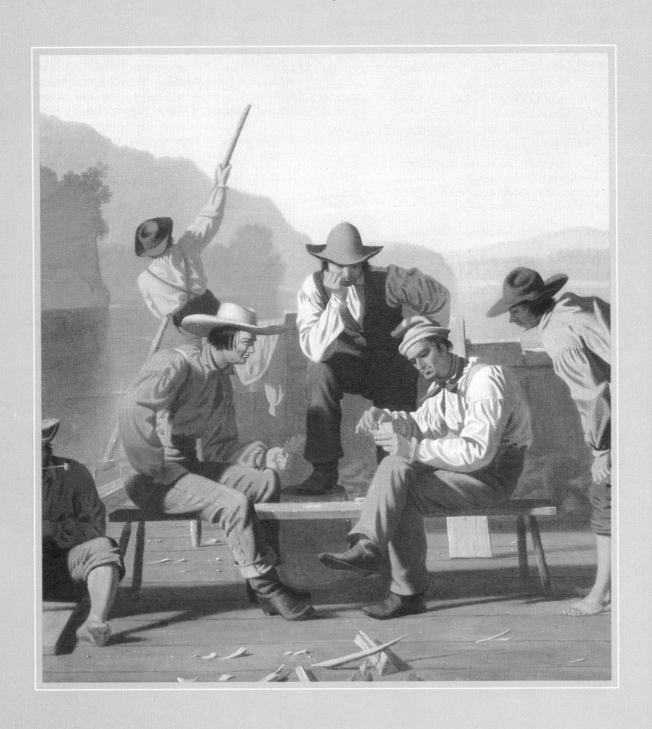

In 1835 William Kirkland and his wife, Caroline, left the private school that they had run in Geneva, New York, and moved to Detroit, in the Michigan Territory. William's plan was simple. He and Caroline would teach in Detroit long enough to earn money to invest in land. Detroit was being flooded by immigrants from the East who, as Caroline wrote, "came to buy land,—not to clear and plough, but as men buy a lottery ticket or dig for gold—in the hope of unreasonable and unearned profits." Although William intended to found a settlement in the wilderness rather than merely to buy and sell land, he, too, hoped to get rich in the West.

Reared in cultivated refinement in New York City and educated at excellent Quaker schools, Caroline had her own notions about the West. The novels and travelers' accounts that she had read projected conflicting but invariably rosy images of the frontier: the West was a land of boundless treasure, a vast garden eager to yield the fruits of its soil, and a romantic wilderness through which one could easily drive a carriage on a moonlit night.

After serving for a year as the principal of a school for young ladies in Detroit, William acquired thirteen hundred acres of land in Livingston County, sixty miles northwest of Detroit, and laid out his settlement around the village of Pinckney. But life in Pinckney failed to live up to the Kirklands' expectations. Instead of a quaintly romantic cottage, Caroline found herself forced to live in a tiny log cabin, far too small for her fancy eastern furniture. Equally disconcerting to the Kirklands was westerners' attitude toward others' possessions.

Frontier people thought that they had a right to borrow anything that Caroline owned, with no more than a blunt declaration that "you've got plenty." "For my own part," Caroline related, "I have lent my broom, my thread, my tape, my spoons, my cat, my thimble, my scissors, my shawl, my shoes; and have been asked for my combs and brushes: and my husband, for his shaving apparatus and his pantaloons."

Other surprises were in store for the Kirklands. Accustomed to servants, Caroline found that even poor western girls refused to hire themselves out permanently as household help. As William noted, occasionally a poor girl would enter service long enough to earn money for a new dress, "but never as a regular calling, or with an acknowledgement of inferior station." Yet the Kirklands gradually realized that the peculiarities of westerners sprang not from selfishness or laziness but from an underlying belief in equality. For example, westerners' penchant for borrowing arose from their attitude that frontier men and women had to share and share alike, or go under.

Caroline turned her experiences in Michigan to good advantage by writing a fictionalized account of them, A New Home—Who'll Follow? (1839). Justly hailed as the first realistic account of western life, A New Home established Caroline's literary reputation, which she continued to build after she and William returned to New York in 1843.

Between 1815 and 1840, many Americans like the Kirklands ventured into the West and had their visions of easy living punctured by the harsh realities of the frontier. Even those who remained in the East had to adjust—to the successive waves of economic and social change that swept the nation after the conclusion of the War of 1812. For westerners and easterners alike, improvements in transportation (the so-called transportation revolution) were spearheaded by the completion in 1825 of the Erie Canal. This "revolution" both stimulated interregional trade and migration and encouraged an unprecedented development of towns and cities. The new urban dwellers, in turn, formed a market not only for agricultural produce but also for the products of the industries springing up in New England and the major northeastern cities.

Viewed superficially, these changes did not greatly affect the way most Americans lived. Whether in 1815 or 1840, the majority of Americans dwelled outside of cities, practiced agriculture for a living, and traveled on foot or by horse. Yet this surface impression of continuity is misleading, because by 1840 many farmers had moved to the West. The nature of farming had also changed, as farmers increasingly raised crops for sale in distant markets rather than merely for their families' consumption. While most Americans still depended on agriculture, by 1840 alternatives to farming abounded. The rise of such alternatives, in turn, had an impact on some of the most basic social relationships: between parents and children, and between wives and husbands.

Westward Expansion and the Growth of the Market Economy

The spark that ignited these changes was the spread of Americans across the Appalachian Mountains. In 1790 the vast majority of the people resided east of the mountains and within a few hundred miles of the Atlantic Ocean. But by 1840 one-third lived between the Appalachians and the Mississippi River. In this area, known at the time as the West, settlers were buffeted by a succession of unexpected social and economic forces.

The Sweep West

This outward thrust of the population occurred in a series of bursts. The first began even before the 1790s and was reflected in the admission of four new states into the Union between 1791 and 1803: Vermont, Kentucky, Tennessee, and Ohio. Then, after an interlude of over ten years that saw the admission of only one new state, Louisiana, six states entered the Union between 1816 and 1821: Indiana, Mississippi, Illinois, Alabama, Maine, and Missouri. Even as Indiana and Illinois were gaining statehood, settlers were pouring farther west into Michigan. Ohio's population jumped from 45,000 in 1800 to 581,000 by 1820 and 1,519,000 by 1840; Michigan's, from 5,000 in 1810 to 212,000 by 1840.

An adventuring spirit carried some Americans far beyond the Mississippi. The Lewis and Clark expedition whetted interest in the Far West, and in 1811 a New York merchant, John Jacob Astor, founded the fur-trading post of Astoria at the mouth of the Columbia River in the Oregon Country. In the 1820s and 1830s, fur traders also operated along the Missouri River from St. Louis to the Rocky Mountains and beyond. At first, whites relied on the native Americans to bring them furs, but during the 1820s white trappers or "mountain men"—among them, Kit Carson, Jedidiah Smith, and the mulatto Jim Beckwourth—gathered furs on their own while performing astounding feats of survival in harsh surroundings.

Jedidiah Smith was representative of these men. Born in the Susquehanna Valley of New York in 1799, Smith moved west with his family to Pennsylvania and Illinois and in 1822 signed on with an expedition bound for the upper Missouri River. In the course of this and subsequent explorations, he was almost killed by a grizzly bear in the Black Hills of South Dakota, learned from the Indians to trap beaver and shoot buffalo, crossed the Mojave Desert into California, explored California's San Joaquin Valley, and hiked back across the Sierras and the primeval Great Basin to the Great Salt Lake, a trip so forbidding that even the Indians avoided it.

Their exploits popularized in biographies, the mountain men became legends in their own day.

The Mountain Men

Rocky Mountain trappers or "mountain men" were among the most colorful and individualistic of nineteenth-century Americans. Entrepreneurs who trapped beavers for their pelts (which were used until the 1830s to make hats), the mountain men were also hunters, explorers, and adventurers who lived "a wild Robin Hood kind of life" with "little fear of God and none at all of the Devil."

They were, however, atypical migrants. For most pioneer settlers, the West meant the area between the Appalachians and the Mississippi River, the region today known as the Midwest, and before 1840 very few ventured into the Far West. In contrast to Jedidiah Smith, whose unquenchable thirst for adventure led to his death at the hands of Comanches in 1831, most pioneers sought stability and security. The newspaper reports, pamphlets, and letters home that told easterners what to expect in the West usually stressed that western living was bountiful rather than harsh or even risky. A legislator in the Missouri Territory wrote in 1816 that in the states west of the Appalachians, "there neither is, nor, in the nature of things, can there ever be, any thing like poverty there. All is ease, tranquility and comfort."

Western Society and Customs

In their desire for stability, pioneers usually migrated as families rather than as individuals. Because they needed to get their crops to market, most settlers between 1790 and 1820 clustered near the navigable rivers of the West, especially the magnificent water system created by the Ohio and Mississippi rivers. Only with the spread of canals in the 1820s and 1830s, and later of railroads, did westerners feel free to venture far from rivers. In addition, westerners often clustered with people who hailed from the same region back east. For instance, in 1836 a group of farmers from nearby towns met at Castleton, Vermont, listened to a minister intone from the Bible, "And Moses sent them to spy out the land of Canaan," and soon established the town of Vermontville in Michigan. Other migrants to the West were less organized than these latter-day descendants of the Puritans, but most hoped to settle among familiar faces in the West. Finding southerners already well entrenched in Indiana, for example, New Englanders tended to prefer Michigan.

Far from seeking isolation, most westerners craved sociability. Even before there were towns and cities in the West, farm families joined with their neighbors in group sports and festivities. Men met for games that, with a few exceptions like marbles (popular among all ages), were tests of strength or agility. These included wrestling, lifting weights, pole jumping (for distance rather than height), and a variant of the modern hammer toss. Some of these games were brutal. In gander pulling, horseback riders competed to pull the head off a gander whose neck had been stripped of feathers and greased. Women usually combined work and play in quilting and sewing parties, carpet tackings, and even chicken and goose pluckings. Social activities brought the sexes together. Group corn huskings usually ended with dances; and in a variety of "hoedowns" and "frolics," even westerners who in theory might disapprove of dancing promenaded to singing and a fiddler's tune.

Within western families, there was usually a clear division of labor between men and women. Men performed most of the heaviest labor such as cutting down trees and plowing fields, but women had many chores. Women usually rose first in the morning, because their work included milking the cows as well as preparing breakfast. Women also fashioned the coverlets that warmed beds in unheated rooms, and prior to the spread of factory-made clothing in the 1830s, they made shirts, coats, pants, and dresses on home spinning wheels for family use. They often helped butcher hogs. They knew that the best way to bleed a hog was to slit its throat while it was still alive, and after the bleeding, they were adept at scooping out the innards, washing the heart and liver, and hanging

them to dry. There was nothing dainty about the work of pioneer women.

Most western sports and customs had been transplanted from the East. Gander pulling, for example, had been a popular pastime in Virginia before it made its way to the frontier. Yet the West had a character of its own. Before 1830 few westerners could afford elegant living. Cowpaths did double duty as sidewalks in country towns. The West contained no more than a sprinkling of elegant mansions. Even in the wealthy cotton-growing regions of Alabama and Mississippi, most planters lived in rough conditions prior to 1830. Their relative lack of refinement made westerners easy targets for easterners' contemptuous jibes. Criticisms of the West as a land of half-savage yokels tended, in turn, to give rise to counterassertions by westerners that they lived in a land of honest democracy and that the East was soft and decadent. The exchange of insults fostered a regional identity among westerners that further shaped their behavior. Priding themselves on their simple manners, westerners were often not only hostile to the East but also intolerant of those westerners who had pretensions to gentility. On one occasion, a traveler who hung up a blanket in a tavern to cover

Merrymaking at a Wayside Inn, *by Pavel Svinin*

Country inns served as social centers for rural neighborhoods as well as stopping places for travelers.

his bed from public gaze had it promptly ripped down. On another, a woman who improvised a screen behind which to retire in a crowded room was dismissed as "stuck up." And a politician who rode to a public meeting in a buggy instead of on horseback lost votes.

The Federal Government and the West

Of the various causes of expansion to the Mississippi from 1790 to 1840, the one that operated most generally and uniformly throughout the period was the growing strength of the federal government. Even before the Constitution's ratification, several states had ceded their western land claims to the national government, thereby creating the bountiful public domain. The Land Ordinance of 1785 had set forth plans for surveying and selling parcels of this public treasure to settlers. The Northwest Ordinance of 1787 provided for the orderly transformation of western territories into states. The Louisiana Purchase of 1803 brought the entire Mississippi River under American control, and the Transcontinental Treaty of 1819 wiped out the last vestiges of Spanish power east of the Mississippi. The federal government directly stimulated settlement of its expanding landholdings by inducing soldiers to enlist during the War of 1812 in return for promises of land after the war. With 6 million acres allotted to these so-called military bounties, many former soldiers pulled up roots and tried farming in the West. To facilitate westward migration, Congress authorized funds in 1816 for continued construction of the National Road, a highway begun in 1811 that reached Wheeling, Virginia, on the Ohio River, in 1818 and Vandalia, Illinois, by 1838. Soon the road was thronged with settlers. "Old America seems to be breaking up," a traveler on the National Road wrote in 1817. "We are seldom out of sight, as we travel on this grand track towards the Ohio, of family groups before and behind us."

While whites gained innumerable advantages from having a more powerful national government behind them, the rising strength of that government brought misery to the Indians. Virtually all the foreign-policy successes during the Jefferson, Madison, and Monroe administrations worked to the native Americans' disadvantage. Both the Louisiana Purchase and the Transcontinental Treaty

stripped them of Spanish protection. In the wake of the Louisiana Purchase, Lewis and Clark bluntly told the Indians that they must "shut their ears to the counsels of bad birds" and listen henceforth only to the Great Father in Washington. The outcome of the War of 1812 also worked against the native Americans; indeed, the Indians were the only real losers of the war. Early in the negotiations leading to the Treaty of Ghent, the British had insisted on the creation of an Indian buffer state in the Old Northwest, between the United States and Canada. But after the American victory at the Battle of Plattsburgh, the British dropped the demand and essentially abandoned the Indians to the Americans.

The Removal of the Indians

As white settlers poured into the West, they found in their path sizable pockets of Indians, particularly in the South. The Cherokees, Creeks, Choctaws, Chickasaws, and Seminoles—whom non-Indians collectively called the Five Civilized Tribes—occupied large parts of Tennessee, Georgia, Alabama, Mississippi, and Florida. Years of commercial dealings and intermarriage with non-Indians had created in all these tribes an influential minority of mixed-bloods, who had heeded the call of white missionaries to embrace Christianity and agriculture. Among the Cherokees, for example, not only was agriculture practiced, but some Indians built looms and gristmills and even owned slaves. One of their chiefs, Sequoyah, devised a written form of the Cherokee language, while other Cherokees published their own newspaper, the *Cherokee Phoenix*.

In whites' eyes, these were extraordinary accomplishments, and the federal government welcomed them as signs of advancing "civilization" among the Indians. But "civilizing" the native Americans did not always work to the government's advantage. While some assimilated mixed-bloods willingly sold tribal lands to the government and moved west, others, recognizing that their prosperity depended on commercial dealings with whites, resisted removal. In addition, within the "civilized" tribes, the majority of Indians were full-bloods. Although some full-bloods willingly moved west, most were keen to retain their ancestral lands in the East and were contemptuous both of whites

Tahlequah, Indian Territory

The sufferings of the southeastern Indian tribes along the Trail of Tears did not end when the Cherokees, Choctaws, Chickasaws, Creeks, and other nations arrived in the Indian Territory that is now Oklahoma. Most of the tribes found that the federal government failed to deliver fully on promises of supplies and that white merchants, who had contracted to feed the native Americans until they could raise their own crops, often cheated them. At times, white contractors bought up Indian claims for corn rations for cash, which the Indians then spent on whiskey. One white agent reported seeing two thousand drunken Creeks, more than 10 percent of the entire tribe, on a single day in 1837.

Yet left to their own devices, the southeastern Indians were thriving in their new western home by the 1840s. In addition to establishing farms and small factories, the native Americans developed a passion for education. With the aid of white missionaries, they built elementary schools and academies. They operated printing presses that turned out schoolbooks, hymnals, and catechisms in the Creek, Choctaw, and Cherokee languages as well as in English. Some historians have concluded that the native Americans' school system was the best west of the Mississippi in the 1840s. As white Americans trekked to Texas and California during that decade, moreover, they came to depend on the food and other supplies that they purchased from the transplanted southeastern Indians.

With prosperity, the tribes gradually overcame their internal political divisions. Rival Cherokee factions, for example, united in 1839 and established a seat of government at Tahlequah, a village in present-day eastern Oklahoma, near the Illinois River. But the "civilized" tribes continued to suffer from raids by the nomadic prairie Indians such as the Osages and Comanches. In June 1843 Tahlequah became the scene of a most extraordinary council of tribes. Some four thousand delegates from seventeen Indian nations, including the seven-foot-tall Osage leader Black Dog and the son of Tecumseh, crowded into Tahlequah to hear the presiding Cherokee chief, John Ross, proclaim: "By peace our condition has been improved in the pursuits of civilized life. We should, therefore, extend the hand of peace from tribe to tribe, till peace is established between every nation of red men within the reach of our voice." In addition to destroying a thousand gallons of whiskey, the council agreed on a compact that provided for punishment of offenders from one tribe who raided another tribe.

No Indian council, however, could remove the source of intertribal raiding: the steady shrinkage of the nomadic Indians' hunting grounds caused by the relentless advance of white settlement and by the very prosperity of the civilized Indians. Reduced to near starvation, the Osages and Comanches continued to raid the civilized tribes' livestock until these nomads themselves were forced onto reservations.

Cherokee Hunter,
*by Baroness Hyde de Neuville, 1820
On the eve of their removal to the West, the Cherokees and the other southeastern tribes had increasingly abandoned their traditional hunting, fishing, and gathering for agriculture and trade.*

Chief John Ross, *by John Rubens Smith, 1841*

After becoming the principal chief of the eastern Cherokees in 1828, Ross, who was only one-eighth Cherokee himself, emerged as a leading opponent of Jackson's Indian-removal policy.

Choctaw Girls

These young Choctaws, members of one of the Five Civilized Tribes, were photographed in the Oklahoma Indian Territory.

Tahlequah Council, 1843, *by John Mix Stanley*

The seventeen-tribe council of the summer of 1843 was intended to establish friendly ties between the Cherokee exiles and the Indian Territory's Plains peoples.

and of mixed-bloods who bartered away tribal land to whites. When the Creek mixed-blood chief William McIntosh sold to the government all Creek lands in Georgia and two-thirds of Creek lands in Alabama in the Treaty of Indian Springs (1825), other Creeks executed him.

As whites' demands for Indian lands reached the boiling point during the 1820s, the traditional policy of negotiating treaties piecemeal with the Indians came under fire. Andrew Jackson embodied the whites' new militancy. Jackson was one of the first prominent government officials to recognize that the balance of power between native Americans and whites had shifted drastically since the American Revolution. His victory over the Creeks at the Battle of Horseshoe Bend in 1814 had convinced him that the Indians were much weaker than whites often realized. And because they were weakening, Jackson could see no justification for continuing "the farce of treating with the Indian tribes." The Indians were not independent nations, Jackson argued, but were subject to the laws of whatever state they resided in.

When Jackson became president in 1829, he promptly instituted a more coercive removal policy. His policy reflected not only his disdain for the Indians but also his conviction that, as long as the Indians stayed in the East, the "real" Indians who still retained their "savage" ways would be exploited by mercenary whites and self-serving mixed-bloods. In 1830 he secured from a divided Congress passage of the Indian Removal Act, which granted the president funds and authority to remove native Americans by force if necessary. By then, Georgia and other states were putting overwhelming pressure on the Indians. Resolutions pushed through the Georgia legislature provided that after 1830 Indians could not be parties to or witnesses in legal cases involving whites. By the late 1820s, the Creeks in Georgia and Alabama started to move west. In 1836 the Georgia militia attacked Creeks still in the state, and when starving Creeks raided white settlements for food, federal troops finished the job begun by the militia. In 1836 fifteen thousand Creek Indians, most of the Creek nation, were removed, many in chains and handcuffs, and resettled west of the Mississippi.

A similar fate befell the other "civilized" tribes of the South. Treaties signed in 1830 and 1832 achieved the removal of the Choctaws from Mississippi and the Chickasaws from northern Mississippi and northwestern Alabama. The visiting Frenchman Alexis de Tocqueville witnessed the arrival of the Choctaws, including "the wounded, the sick, newborn babies, and the old men on the point of death," at Memphis on the Mississippi. "I saw them embark to cross the great river, and the sight will never fade from my memory. Neither sob nor complaint rose from that silent assembly. Their afflictions were of long standing, and they felt them to be irremediable." Most Seminoles were removed from Florida, but only after a bitter war between 1835 and 1842 that cost the federal government $20 million.

The Cherokees, the most assimilated of all southern tribes, staged the most ingenious defense by petitioning the U.S. Supreme Court for an injunction against enforcement of the Indian Removal Act of 1830. Although the Cherokees had drafted a constitution in 1827 for a Cherokee republic within Georgia, Chief Justice John Marshall, in the case of *Cherokee Nation* v. *Georgia* (1831), ruled that the Cherokees were neither a state nor a foreign nation and hence lacked standing to bring suit. But Marshall acknowledged that prolonged occupancy gave the Cherokees a right to their land, and a year later, he clarified the Cherokees' legal position in *Worcester* v. *Georgia,* by holding that they were a "domestic dependent nation" entitled to federal protection from molestation by Georgia.

But Marshall's decision had little impact. Jackson ignored it, reportedly sneering, "John Marshall has made his decision; now let him enforce it." The Cherokees themselves were divided into a majority anti-removal faction and a minority pro-removal faction. Federal agents persuaded a pro-removal chief to sign the Treaty of New Echota (1835), which ceded all Cherokee land to the United States for $5.6 million and free transportation west. Most Cherokees denounced the treaty, and on June 22, 1839, a party of Cherokees took revenge by murdering its three principal signers, including a former *Cherokee Phoenix* editor. But the Cherokees' fate had already been sealed. Between 1835 and 1838, bands of Cherokees straggled west to the Mississippi along the so-called Trail of Tears. Unlike the Creeks, the Cherokees policed their own removal, but this fact did not lessen their physical and spiritual sufferings. Between 2,000 and 4,000 of the 16,000 migrating Cherokees died.

Indians in the Northwest Territory fared no

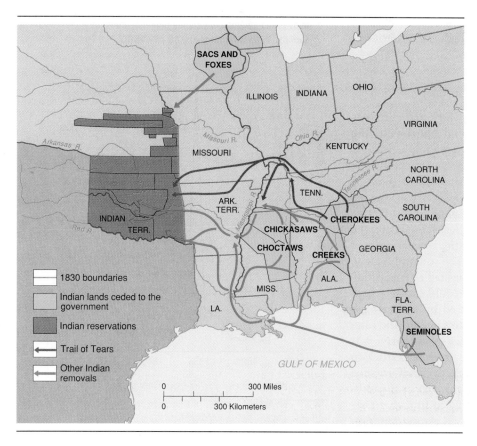

The Removal of the Native Americans to the West, 1820–1840

The so-called Trail of Tears, followed by the Cherokees, was one of several routes along which various tribes migrated on their forced removal to reservations west of the Mississippi.

better. A series of treaties extinguished their land titles, and most moved west of the Mississippi. The removal of the northwestern Indians was notable for two uprisings. The first, led by Red Bird, a Winnebago chief, began in 1827 but was quickly crushed. The second was led by a Sac and Fox chief, Black Hawk, who resisted removal until 1831 and then moved his people west of the Mississippi, only to return the following year. In June 1832 federal troops and Illinois militia furiously attacked his band and virtually annihilated Black Hawk's followers as they tried to recross the Mississippi into Iowa. Black Hawk's downfall induced the other Old Northwest tribes to cede their lands. Between 1832 and 1837, the United States acquired nearly 190 million acres of Indian land in the Northwest for $70 million in gifts and annuities.

The Agricultural Boom

In pushing Indians from the path of white settlers, the federal government was responding to whites' demands for land and more land. Depleted soil and

overcrowding had long driven eastern farmers west, but after the War of 1812, a new incentive—the bounding prices of agricultural commodities such as wheat, corn, and cotton—pulled settlers westward in search of better farmland. Several factors accounted for the skyrocketing farm prices. First, Britain and France, exhausted by the Napoleonic Wars, were importing wheat and corn from America, and the United States had swiftly captured former British markets in the West Indies and former Spanish markets in South America. In addition, the beginnings of industrialization in New England even before the war combined with the westward migration of New England farmers to create a demand in the eastern United States for western foodstuffs. So as domestic and foreign demand intensified, commodity prices rose between 1815 and 1819. The West's splendid river systems made it possible for farmers in Ohio to ship wheat and corn down the Ohio River to the Mississippi and then down the Mississippi to New Orleans. There wheat and corn were either sold or transshipped to the East, the West Indies, South America, or

Europe. Just as government policies were making farming in the West possible, high prices for food-stuffs were making it attractive.

Eli Whitney and the Cotton Gin

While the prospect of raising wheat and corn was pulling farmers toward the Old Northwest, the irresistible lure of cotton was creating a frenzied rush to settle the Old Southwest, particularly the states of Alabama and Mississippi on the Gulf of Mexico.

As early as the 1790s, demand in the British textile industry for raw cotton was stimulating the cultivation of the crop along the coastal strip of South Carolina and Georgia. The soil and climate there were ideal for growing long-staple "sea-island" cotton, a variety whose fibers could easily be separated from its shiny black seed by squeezing it through rollers. But in the South's upland and interior regions, the only cotton that would thrive was the short-staple variety, whose green seed stuck so tenaciously to the fibers that rollers merely crushed the seeds and ruined the fibers. It was as if southerners had discovered gold only to find that they could not mine it. But in 1793 a Connecticut Yankee, Eli Whitney, rescued the South by inventing the cotton gin during a brief stopover at the Georgia plantation of a Yale classmate. Whitney's gin was simplicity itself. He impaled short-staple cotton fibers onto iron pins that he inserted into a cylinder, then rotated the cylinder to push the fibers through iron guards. As the seeds dropped conveniently into a box below, the fibers were gathered by rotating brushes positioned on the far side of the guards.

Whitney and his classmate quickly patented the gin, but neither made much money off it. The device was so simple that it was easy to copy, and within a few years, other inventors marked improved gins that used saw-toothed cylinders rather than iron pins. But Whitney's invention removed at a stroke one of the main obstacles to the spread of cotton planting. Short-staple cotton quickly proved itself a wonderful crop. The British could not get enough of it. The explosive thrust of small farmers and planters from the seaboard South into the Old Southwest resembled a gold rush. By 1817 "Alabama fever" gripped the South. At the United States land office in Huntsville, sales of public land in 1818 reached $7 million; good land sold for $30

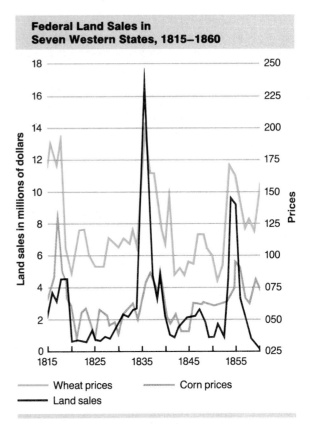

Federal Land Sales in Seven Western States, 1815–1860

Land sales from the public domain tended to rise and fall with the prices of wheat and corn. The higher the price that farmers could obtain for these commodities, the more land they purchased.

SOURCE: Douglass North, *The Economic Growth of the United States 1790–1860* (New York: Norton, 1966), 137.

to $50 an acre. By 1820 half of the nation's cotton was being produced west of the Appalachians in the gulf states of Alabama and Mississippi. Cotton production tripled between 1816 and 1826, and the story was only beginning. Between 1831 and 1836, the value of cotton exports rose 300 percent. Accounting for less than a quarter of all American exports between 1802 and 1807, cotton composed just over half by 1830 and nearly two-thirds by 1836.

The Rise of the Market Economy

To farmers, the high prices of agricultural commodities between 1815 and 1819 appeared an unmixed blessing. Most planned to grow enough food to feed their families (called subsistence agriculture) *and* a cash crop like wheat or cotton to sell in local or distant markets (called commercial agriculture, or the "market economy"). Farming for markets was not new; many farmers had done so during the colonial era. What was new after the War of 1812 was the extent to which farmers entered the market economy. High crop prices tempted many former subsistence farmers into the commercial economy. Often these individuals had little experience with commercial dealings and little idea of what they were getting into. Commercial agriculture exposed farmers to innumerable new risks. First, cash crops like wheat and cotton were sold to persons whom the farmers themselves frequently never met, in places that they never saw. Second, farmers had no control over the fluctuations of distant markets. Further, there was inevitably an interval, often a long one, between harvesting a cash crop and selling it. To sustain themselves during the interval, farmers had to borrow money. Thus commercial agriculture forced farmers into short-term debt in the hope of long-term profit.

The debt was frequently worse than most had expected. In the first place, many western farmers had to borrow money to buy their land. The roots of this indebtedness for land lay, in turn, in the federal government's inability to devise an effective policy for transferring the public domain directly into the hands of small farmers.

Federal Land Policy

Partisan and sectional pressures buffeted federal land policy like a kite in a March wind. The result was a succession of land laws between 1796 and 1820, each of which sought to undo the damage caused by its predecessor.

Because their political bases lay in the East, the Federalists had been reluctant during the 1790s to encourage headlong settlement of the West. Nevertheless, they were eager to raise revenue for the federal government from land sales. They reconciled these goals—retarding actual settlement while gaining revenue—by encouraging the sale of huge tracts of land to wealthy speculators, individuals who did not intend to farm the land but planned instead to hold it until its value rose and then sell off parcels to farmers. Even during the 1790s, land speculators were swarming through the area east of the Appalachians. The Holland Land Company, for example, composed mainly of Dutch investors,

bought up much of western New York and western Pennsylvania. A federal land law passed in 1796 reflected Federalist aims by establishing a minimum purchase of 640 acres at a minimum price of two dollars an acre and by allowing only a year for full payment. Few small-scale farmers could afford land from the public domain on these terms.

Believing that the small farmer was the backbone of the Republic, and fully aware of Republican political strength in the West, Thomas Jefferson and the Republicans took a different tack. Starting in 1800, federal land laws increasingly reflected the Republicans' desire to ease the transfer of the public domain to farmers. Even so, few proposed giving land to farmers outright. The Republicans needed revenue from land sales if they were to extinguish the national debt. Accordingly, the land law of 1800 dropped the minimum purchase to 320 acres and allowed up to four years for full payment but kept the minimum price at $2.00 an acre. In 1804 the minimum purchase came down to 160 acres; and in 1820, to 80 acres. The minimum price also declined from $2.00 an acre in 1800 to $1.64 in 1804 and to $1.25 in 1820.

Although land policy was steadily liberalized, small farmers did not necessarily benefit immediately. Federal land laws between 1800 and 1820 were nervous responses to the fact that much of the public domain was still being bought up by speculators, no matter what Congress did. All land in the public domain was first sold at auction, usually for much more than the two-dollar minimum. With agricultural prices soaring, speculators assumed that land would continue to rise in value and accordingly were willing to bid high on new land. In ignorance of their real value, veterans of the War of 1812 often sold their land warrants to speculators. Josiah Meigs, the commissioner of the government's General Land Office, reported cases of veterans who had sold warrants for 160 acres for as little as two hundred dollars.

The growing availability of credit after the War of 1812 fed speculation. The chartering of the Second Bank of the United States in 1816 had the dual effect of increasing the amount of money in circulation and stimulating the chartering of private banks within states (state banks). The circulation of all banks grew from $45 million in bank notes in 1812 to $100 million in 1817. The stockholders and directors of these banks viewed them less as a sound investment for their capital (many directors

Independence, Squire Jack Porter, *by Francis Blackwell Mayer, 1858*

This painting of Captain John Porter, a War of 1812 veteran who later owned a farm in western Maryland, captures the independence and self-sufficiency that antebellum Americans associated with agriculture. With no boss to command him, Squire Porter relaxed and smoked his pipe whenever he chose.

actually had very little capital when they started state banks) than as agencies that could lend them money for land speculation. Secretary of the Treasury William H. Crawford observed in 1820 that banks had been incorporated "not because there was capital seeking investment, not because the places where they were established had commerce and manufacturers which required their fostering aid; but because men without active capital wanted the means of obtaining loans, which their standing in the community would not command from banks or individuals having real capital and established credit." In short, banks were founded so that they could lend their directors money for personal investment in land speculation. The result was an orgy of land speculation between 1815 and 1819. In 1819 sales of public land were over 1,000 percent greater than the average of the 1800–1814 period.

The Speculator and the Squatter

Nevertheless, most of the public domain eventually found its way into the hands of small farmers. Because speculators gained nothing by holding land for prolonged periods, they were only too happy to sell it when the price was right. In addition, a familiar frontier type, the squatter, exerted a restraining influence on the speculator.

Even before the creation of the public domain, squatters had helped themselves to western land; George Washington himself had been unable to drive squatters off lands that he owned in the West. Squatters were an independent and proud lot, scornful of their fellow citizens, who were "softened by Ease, enervated by Affluence and Luxurious Plenty, & unaccustomed to Fatigues, Hardships, Difficulties or dangers." Disdaining land speculators above all, squatters formed claims associations to police land auctions and prevented speculators from bidding up the price of land. Squatters also pressured Congress to allow them "preemption" rights—that is, the right to purchase at the minimum price land that they had already settled on and improved. Seeking to undo the pernicious effects of its own laws, Congress responded by passing special preemption laws for squatters in specific areas and finally, in 1841, acknowledged a general right of preemption.

But preemption laws were of no use to farmers

who arrived after speculators had already bought up land. Having spent their small savings on livestock, seed, and tools, these settlers then had to buy land from speculators on credit at vicious interest rates that ranged as high as 40 percent. Saddled by steep indebtedness, many western farmers had no choice but to skimp on subsistence crops while expanding cash crops in the hope of paying off their creditors. Farmers in these years were not merely entering the market economy; they were lunging into it.

Countless farmers who had carried basically conservative expectations to the West and who had hoped to establish self-sufficient farms in a land of abundance quickly became economic adventurers. Wanting land that they could call their own, but forced to raise cash crops in a hurry, many farmers worked their acreage to exhaustion and thus had to keep moving in search of new land. The phrase "the moving frontier" refers not only to the obvious fact that with each passing decade, the line of settlement shifted farther west but also to the fact that the same people kept moving. The experience of Abraham Lincoln's parents, who migrated from the East through several farms in Kentucky and then to Indiana, was representative of the westward trek.

The Panic of 1819

In 1819 the land boom collapsed like a house of cards, the victim of a financial panic. The Panic of 1819 had several long-term causes, all of which illustrated how deeply the American economy—and "independent" American farmers—had become dependent on foreign trade and loose credit. The textile factories that had sprung up during the embargo had not shared in the postwar economic boom. With the conclusion of the Napoleonic Wars in 1815, British exporters unloaded their overflowing textile inventories on the American market at bargain prices that undercut American-made textiles. Because bank credit was readily available, Americans had enough cash to purchase these British manufactures. In the case of agriculture, despite the postwar boom in agricultural exports to Europe, the United States actually *imported* more than it exported between 1815 and 1819. In addition, after 1817 the combination of a bumper crop in Europe and a business recession in Britain trimmed the foreign demand for American wheat, flour, and cotton at the very time when American farmers were becoming more dependent on agricultural exports to pay their debts.

Closer to home, the loose practices of state banks contributed mightily to the panic. Like the Bank of the United States, the state banks issued their own bank notes. In the absence of any national system of paper money, these notes served as a circulating medium. A bank note was just a piece of paper with a printed promise from the bank's directors to pay the bearer on demand a certain amount of specie (gold or silver coinage). State banks had long emitted far more bank notes than they could redeem. Further, because the Bank of the United States had more branches than any state bank, notes of state banks were often presented by their holders to branches of the Bank of the United States for redemption. Whenever the Bank of the United States redeemed a state bank note in specie, it became a creditor of the state bank.

In reaction to the overemission of state bank notes, the Bank of the United States began in the summer of 1818 to insist that state banks redeem in specie their notes that were held by the Bank of the United States. To pay their debts to the Bank of the United States, state banks had to demand that borrowers repay loans. The result was a general curtailment of credit throughout the nation, but particularly in the West.

The biggest losers were the land speculators, who had bought huge tracts with the expectation that prices would rise but now found prices tumbling. Land that had once sold for as much as $69 an acre dropped to $2 an acre. Land prices fell, in turn, because the credit squeeze drove down the market prices of staples like wheat, corn, cotton, and tobacco. Cotton, which sold for 32¢ a pound in 1818, sank as low as 17¢ a pound in 1820. Since farmers could not get much cash for their crops, they could not pay the debts that they had incurred to buy land. Since speculators could not collect money owed them by farmers, the value of land that they still held for sale collapsed.

The significance of the panic lay not only in the economic damage it did but also in the conclusions that many Americans drew from it. First, the panic left a bitter taste about banks, particularly the Bank of the United States, which was widely blamed for the hard times. In addition, the panic dramatized the vulnerability of American factories to cheap foreign competition (a vulnerability evident even before the economic downturn) and thereby stimulated demands for the protection of domestic industries. These demands would lead to the passage of higher tariffs in 1824 and 1828. Finally, plummeting prices for cash crops demonstrated how much farmers were coming to depend on distant markets. In effect, it took a severe business reverse to show farmers the extent to which they had become businessmen. The fall in the prices of cash crops intensified the search for better forms of transportation to reach those faraway markets. If the cost of transporting crops could be cut, farmers could keep a larger share of the value of their crops and thereby adjust to falling prices.

The Transportation Revolution: Steamboats, Canals, and Railroads

Most forms of transportation available to Americans in 1820 had severe drawbacks. The great rivers west of the Appalachians ran primarily from north to south and hence could not by themselves connect western farmers with eastern markets. The National Road, with its crushed-stone surface, was a well-built highway that advanced farther west each year. In addition, between 1815 and 1825, several northern states chartered private companies to build toll roads (turnpikes). But roads could not solve the nation's transportation problems. Aside from the fact that horse-drawn wagons could carry limited produce, roads were expensive to maintain. Turnpike companies generally found the income from tolls inadequate to cover the outlays for repairs. After 1825 the pace of investment in turnpikes slackened, and the interest of both public and private investors shifted toward the development of waterways.

In 1807 Robert R. Livingston and Robert Fulton successfully introduced a steamboat popularly known as the *Clermont* on the Hudson River. Livingston and Fulton soon gained a monopoly from the New York legislature to run a ferry service on the Hudson between New York and New Jersey. So spectacular were their profits that rival entrepreneurs secured a license from Congress to operate a competing ferry service and thereby challenged the Livingston-Fulton monopoly. A long court battle followed. Finally, in 1824 the U.S.

Supreme Court decided against the monopoly in the famous case of *Gibbons* v. *Ogden*. Speaking for a unanimous Court, Chief Justice John Marshall ruled that commerce included not merely the exchange of products but navigation as well. This was an important finding, because the Constitution clearly empowered Congress to regulate commerce "among the several States." In the event of a conflict between state and congressional regulation of commerce, Marshall continued, the congressional power must prevail. Thus Marshall upheld the competitors (who had a license from Congress) and effectively broke the Livingston-Fulton monopoly. In the wake of Marshall's decision, state efforts to establish monopolies over river trade quickly collapsed. The number of steamboats operating on western rivers jumped from 17 in 1817 to 69 in 1820 and to 727 by 1855.

Prior to the introduction of steamboats on the Mississippi, flatboats (simply floating rafts) carried produce downriver. Since they were unable to navigate upstream, the flatboats were broken up and sold for firewood in New Orleans. The return voyage was made either by foot or horse through Indian country, or by sailing vessels from New Orleans to Philadelphia or New York and then by foot or horse across the Appalachians to the West.

Interior of a Flatboat, *by Charles-Alexandre Lesueur, 1826*

Not all flatboats that carried produce and pioneers on American rivers were floating rafts. Many had roomy interiors that accommodated whole families, provisions, and even barn animals.

Keelboats—similar to flatboats but moved by a rudder—could make the upstream voyage, though at a snail's pace. It took a keelboat three or four months to complete the 1,350-mile journey from New Orleans to Louisville. In contrast, steamboats could travel upstream at a relatively fast speed. As early as 1817, a steamboat made the trip in twenty-five days. Moreover, although the English had developed steam-propulsion technology in the eighteenth century, between 1820 and 1840, Americans discovered many practical techniques for increasing the effectiveness of steamboats. The gradual introduction of long, shallow hulls made steamboats suitable for use in shallow water (particularly the stretch of the Mississippi-Ohio river system from Louisville to Pittsburgh). The result was an extension of the navigation season; hot, dry summer weather that lowered water levels no longer forced steamboats out of service.

Steamboats became more ornate as well as more practical. To compete for passengers, they began to offer luxurious cabins and lounges (called saloons). The saloon of the *Eclipse,* a Mississippi steamboat, was the length of a football field and featured skylights, chandeliers, a ceiling criss-crossed by Gothic arches, and mahogany furniture covered with velvet. Such "elegance bordering on magnificence" helped to reassure westerners that whatever easterners might say, they were not savage backwoods people but polished and urbane citizens. Yet most steamboat passengers only glimpsed this elegance. Saloons were reserved for the small minority who booked "cabin" passage. The majority of travelers purchased "deck" passage, which entitled them to sleep on a cotton bale if they were lucky enough to find one, on the floor if they were not.

Whether cabin or deck passengers, all steamboat travelers confronted the hazards of this mode of navigation. Fires were common—not surprisingly, in view of the fact that steamboats needed huge furnaces and often carried combustible cargoes like oil and hay. Collisions claimed many lives. The worst, occurring in 1837 on the Mississippi, killed several hundred Creek Indians who were being transported by steamer to reservations in the West. Submerged snags often cracked the fragile hulls of fast-moving steamers: British novelist Charles Dickens described the Mississippi above Cairo, Illinois, as "an enormous ditch . . . choked and obstructed everywhere by huge logs and whole forest trees." Moreover, because little was known about the reaction of metals under stress, boiler explosions destroyed many steamboats, not to mention their passengers. So common were such explosions that one company introduced a line of steamboats on the Hudson River that, for safety's sake, carried the passengers in tow on a barge. Yet nothing could stifle Americans' love of steamboats; for all their perils, they could navigate swiftly upriver.

Once steamboats had demonstrated the feasibility of upriver navigation, popular enthusiasm for internal improvements shifted away from turnpikes and toward canals. As late as 1816, the United States had only a hundred miles of canals. Not only did Americans know little about building canals in these early years, but the capital required to construct them was mind-boggling. Even Thomas Jefferson dismissed the idea of canals as "little short of madness." However, the invention of the steamboat, the abundance of western settlers desperate for access to markets, and the natural endowment of the Great Lakes combined to make the lure of canals irresistible. Canals offered the prospect of connecting the superb Mississippi-Ohio river system with the Great Lakes, and the Great Lakes with eastern markets.

The construction of the Erie Canal was the first major canal project. Started by New York State in 1817, the canal at its completion stretched for 363 miles between Albany and Buffalo. The Erie Canal was ten times longer than any previous American canal and by far the longest in the Western world. More than a waterway, it was a capstone of the sometimes fragile Era of Good Feelings, a symbol of American ingenuity and peaceful progress. As part of the celebration of its completion in 1825, a procession of American steamboats formed a perfect circle of salute around two British warships anchored in New York Harbor. The British responded by striking up "Yankee Doodle," to which the Americans replied with "God Save the King." Through the Erie Canal, New York City was linked by inland waterways (the Hudson River, the canal itself, and Lake Erie) all the way to Ohio.

In New England the Blackstone Canal (1824–1828) created a water highway between Worcester, Massachusetts, and the Narragansett Bay in Rhode Island. By 1834 the Main Line (or Pennsylvania) Canal connected eastern Pennsylvania with Pitts-

Erie Canal, *by John William Hill, 1831*

Construction of the Erie Canal was a remarkable feat—all the more so because the United States did not possess a single school of engineering at the time. The project's heroes were lawyers and merchants who taught themselves engineering, and brawny workmen, often Irish immigrants, who hacked a waterway through the forests and valleys of New York.

burgh. The Main Line Canal was an even more remarkable feat of engineering than the Erie because it crossed the Allegheny Mountains with the aid of a railroad. Canal boats on this system had to be built in collapsible sections; they were disassembled upon reaching the mountains and then carried up one side and down the other on cable cars. As these canals spread like fingers from east to west, a similar system of canals was under construction from west to east. By 1836 the Ohio and Erie Canal stretched from Portsmouth on the Ohio River to Cleveland on Lake Erie. The Miami and Erie Canal ran from Cincinnati to Dayton, where plans called for it to join a railroad line to Sandusky on Lake Erie. From Lake Erie, packets and steamboats could carry produce to the Erie Canal and on to Albany and New York City. In 1836, 365,000 bushels of western wheat entered the milling city of Rochester on the Erie Canal and left as 369,000 barrels of flour bound for eastern New York.

The canal boom drastically cut shipping costs. In 1817, just before construction began on the Erie Canal, the cost of transporting wheat from Buffalo to New York City was three times the market value of wheat in New York City, while the transportation costs for corn and oats over the same route were, respectively, six and twelve times their market value in New York City. Average freight charges between Buffalo and New York City dropped from 19¢ a ton per mile in 1817 to less than 2¢ a ton per mile in 1830. Throughout the nation, canals reduced shipping costs from 20¢ to 30¢ a ton per mile before 1815 to 2¢ to 3¢ a ton per mile by the 1830s.

When another economic depression hit in the late 1830s, various states found themselves overcommitted to costly canal projects and ultimately scrapped many. Yet even as the canal boom was ending, railroads were spreading. In 1825 the world's first railroad devoted to general transportation began operation in England, and by 1840 some three thousand miles of track had been laid in America, about the same as the total canal mileage in 1840. During the 1830s investment in American railroads actually exceeded that in canals. Cities like Baltimore and Boston, which lacked major inland waterway connections, turned to railroads to enlarge their share of the western market. The Baltimore and Ohio Railroad, chartered in 1828, took business away from the Chesapeake and Ohio Canal farther south. Blocked by its Berkshire Mountains from building a canal to the Erie, Massachusetts chartered the Boston and Worcester Railroad in 1831 and the Western Railroad (from Worcester to Albany) in 1833.

Faster, cheaper to build, and able to reach more places, railroads had obvious advantages over canals and contributed to the growth of communities that were remote from waterways. But railroads' potential was only slowly realized. Most early railroads ran between cities in the East rather than from east to west and carried more passengers than freight. Not until 1849 did freight revenues exceed passenger revenues, and not until 1850 was the East Coast connected by rail to the Great Lakes.

Several factors explain the relatively slow spread of interregional railroads. Unlike canals, which were built directly by state governments, most railroads

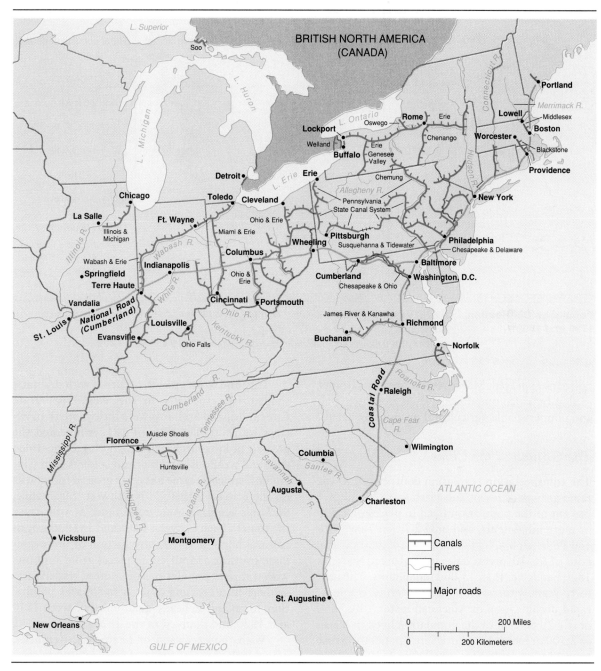

Major Rivers, Roads, and Canals, 1825–1860

Railroads and canals increasingly tied the economy of the Midwest to that of the Northeast.

were constructed by private corporations seeking quick profits. To minimize their original investment, railroad companies commonly resorted to cost-cutting measures such as covering wooden rails with iron bars. As a result, while relatively cheap to build, American railroads needed constant repairs and were even more vulnerable than canals to economic fluctuations. In contrast, while expensive to construct, canals needed relatively little maintenance and were kept in operation for decades after

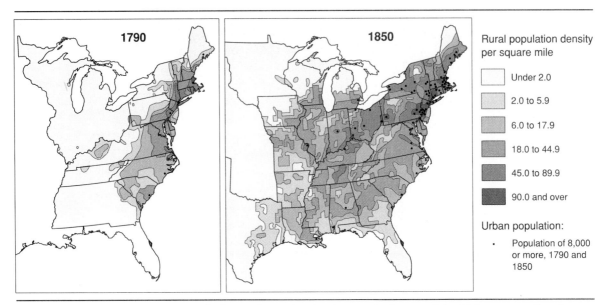

Population Distribution, 1790 and 1850 *By 1850 high population density characterized parts of the Midwest as well as the Northeast.*
SOURCE: *1900 Census of Population, Statistical Atlas,* plates 2 and 8.

railroads appeared. Moreover, it remained cheaper to ship bulky commodities such as iron ore, coal, and nonperishable agricultural produce by canal.

The Growth of the Cities

The transportation revolution contributed to the rapid growth of towns and cities. In 1820 only 6.1 percent of the population lived in places of 2,500 or more inhabitants, and only 2 cities, New York and Philadelphia, had more than 100,000 people. Four of the 10 largest cities in the United States in 1820 had fewer than 15,000 inhabitants. The next forty years witnessed, in relative terms, the most rapid urbanization in American history. By 1860 nearly 20 percent of the population lived in places of 2,500 or more. New York City's population rose from 124,000 in 1820 to 800,000 in 1860. By 1860 there were 8 American cities larger than the largest city in 1820. An even more revealing change was the transformation of sleepy villages of a few hundred into thriving towns of several thousand. In 1820 only 56 incorporated towns could boast between 2,500 and 10,000 inhabitants; by 1850 there were over 350 such towns. The Erie Canal transformed Rochester, New York, for example, from a village of a few hundred people in 1817 to a thriving town of 9,000 by 1830.

City and town growth occurred with dramatic suddenness, especially in the West. Pittsburgh, Cincinnati, and St. Louis were little more than villages in 1800. The War of 1812 stimulated the growth of Pittsburgh, whose iron forges provided shot and weapons for American soldiers, and Cincinnati, which became a staging ground for attacks on the British in the Old Northwest. Meanwhile, St. Louis acquired some importance as a fur-trading center. Then between 1815 and 1819, the agricultural boom and the introduction of the steamboat transformed all three places from outposts with transient populations of hunters, traders, and soldiers into bustling cities. Cincinnati's population, for example, nearly quadrupled between 1810 and 1820 and doubled in the 1820s.

With the exception of Lexington, Kentucky, whose lack of access to water forced it into relative stagnation after 1820, all the prominent western cities were river ports: Pittsburgh, Cincinnati, and Louisville on the Ohio; St. Louis and New Orleans on the Mississippi. Except for Pittsburgh, all were essentially commercial hubs rather than manufacturing centers and were flooded by individuals extremely eager to make money. In 1819 land speculators in St. Louis were bidding as much as a thousand dollars an acre for lots that had sold for thirty dollars an acre in 1815. Waterfronts endowed

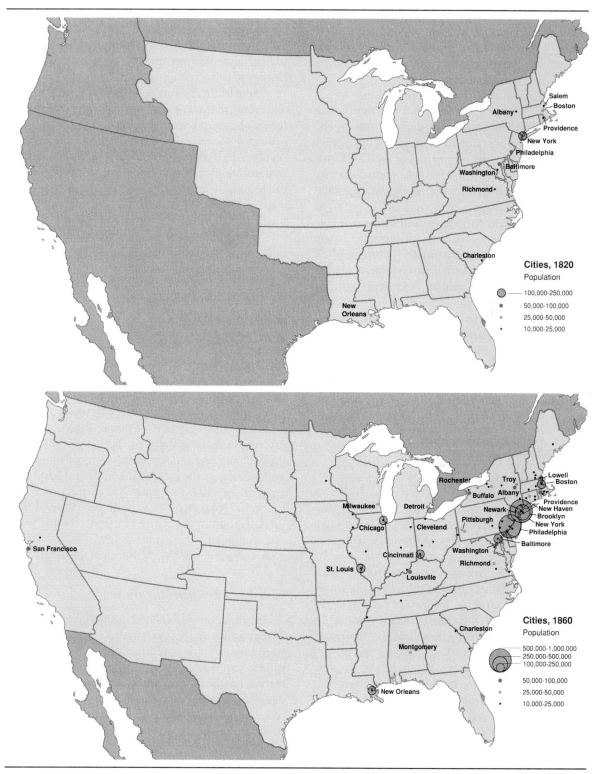

American Cities, 1820 and 1860

In 1820 most cities were seaports. By 1860, however, cities dotted the nation's interior, in large measure because of the transportation revolution.

SOURCE: *Statistical Abstract of the United States.*

with natural beauty were swiftly overrun by stores and docks. "Louis Ville, by nature is beautiful," a visitor wrote, "but the handy Work of *Man* has instead of improving destroy'd the works of Nature and made it a detestable place."

The transportation revolution acted like a fickle god, selecting some cities for growth while sentencing others to relative decline. Just as the steamboat had elevated the river cities over land-locked Lexington, the completion of the Erie Canal shifted the center of western economic activity toward the Great Lakes. The result was a gradual decline in the importance of river cities and a rise between 1830 and 1860 in the importance of lake cities such as Buffalo, Cleveland, Detroit, Chicago, and Milwaukee. In 1830 nearly 75 percent of all western city dwellers lived in the river ports of New Orleans, Louisville, Cincinnati, and Pittsburgh, but by 1840 the proportion had dropped to 20 percent.

The growth of cities and towns was spurred initially by the transportation revolution and the development of interregional trade. Urban expansion received an added boost from the rise of manufacturing between 1815 and 1840.

The Rise of Manufacturing

Today we customarily equate the word *manufacturing* with industrialization—that is, with large factories, machinery, and mass production. But the literal meaning of *manufacturing* is "making by hand." During the colonial era, most products were made by hand, either in households or in the workshops of skilled artisans. The period between 1815 and 1860 marked a transition from colonial to modern manufacturing. Household, or "cottage," industries declined, while large factories and power-driven machinery came to dominate the production of cotton textiles. But small shops were still responsible for a great deal of manufacturing. As late as 1860, the average manufacturing establishment contained only eight workers.

Few Americans believed in 1860 that they lived in an industrial society; most continued to think of the United States as a nation of farmers and small producers. This self-image, however, was misleading. By 1850 the 20 percent of the labor force engaged in manufacturing produced about 30 percent of the national output. Furthermore, industrialization was starting to affect many crafts besides textile making.

Industrialization was not a single occurrence, a kind of tidal wave that washed away traditional forms of manufacturing. Rather, it was a gradual process with several distinct stages. First, the tasks involved in making a product were subdivided, so that instead of making a whole product, each worker made only a part. Next, workers were gathered into factories with rooms devoted to specialized operations performed by hand or by simple machines. Finally, power-driven machinery replaced fabrication by hand. These three stages arrived quickly and almost simultaneously in New England's cotton textile industry, but many crafts—including the making of shoes, hats, guns, trunks, and saddles—experienced at least the first two stages before 1860. Many variations of this pattern appeared between 1815 and 1860. In some crafts, task subdivision and simple machinery were introduced without the creation of large factories. In others, like shoe manufacturing, the subdivision of tasks and the emergence of large factories occurred before the introduction of power-driven machinery. Because the growth of industrialization was gradual and uneven, it was not always clear to men and women at the time that traditional hand fabrication by skilled artisans was in the process of becoming obsolete. They still imagined skilled artisans to be at the center of manufacturing without recognizing the extent to which industrialization was tumbling them from their pedestals.

Causes of Industrialization

A host of factors stimulated industrialization. The Embargo Act of 1807 persuaded merchants barred from foreign trade to redirect their capital into factories. The War of 1812 sparked support for protective tariffs to end American economic dependence on Europe; particularly in the 1820s, tariffs reduced imports of English cloth and contributed to the 15.4 percent average annual rise in American cloth products between 1815 and 1833. Improvements in transportation made it possible for manufacturers to sell finished products in distant markets and provided an incentive to increase production. In addition, a popular preference for factory-made rather than homemade products developed wherever the transportation revolution reached. Household production declined not only in cities but in rural areas along canals and railroads and never gained a secure footing in the West. The more farmers went into the business of selling as well as raising crops, the more they were inclined to buy articles like shoes and clothes rather than make them.

Industrialization also depended on immigration. Five million people migrated from Europe to the United States between 1790 and 1860. Some came to escape political oppression (the United States was the only nation in which a large segment of the working class could vote), but more immigrated in search of economic opportunity. The bulk of these newcomers were either German or Irish, and over 80 percent arrived after 1840 (see Chapter 12). All contributed to industrialization as laborers and as consumers. But the immigrants who played the greatest role in launching industrialization were not the Germans or the Irish but the much smaller numbers of British immigrants. Industrialization had started in Britain during the mid-eighteenth century, and by 1790 Britain had a class of artisans who understood the workings of machines. Men like Samuel Slater learned the "mystery" of textile production as apprentices to factory masters in England and then evaded British laws against emigration (Slater did so by leaving in disguise), carrying their knowledge of machines to America in their heads.

Although Britain had a head start in developing the technology relevant to industrialization, Americans made contributions of their own. Unlike Britain, America had no craft organizations (called guilds) that tied artisans to a single trade. As a result, American artisans freely experimented with machines outside their craft. In the 1790s wagon maker Oliver Evans of Delaware, for example, built an automated flour mill that required only a single supervisor to look on as the grain poured in from one side and was discharged from the other as flour. In addition, the relatively high wages paid to American workers gave manufacturers an incentive to find substitutes for expensive hand labor in order to make products as quickly and cheaply as possible. After inventing the cotton gin, Eli Whitney in 1798 filled a government contract for ten

thousand muskets by using unskilled workers to make identical parts that could be interchanged from musket to musket. The idea of interchangeable parts actually originated in Europe, but the United States led all nations in applying the idea in factories—so much so that it came to be called the American system of manufacturing.

New England Industrializes

New England became America's first industrial region. The gradual strangulation of American trade by Britain's Orders in Council, Napoleon's Continental System, and Jefferson's embargo hit New England more severely than regions less dependent on European trade. Incentives were thus provided for New England's merchants to invest in manufacturing. In addition, New England's rivers were numerous, swift-flowing, and ideally suited to provide water power for mills. At the same time, the region's soil, thin and rocky in many places, forced young men off the land and into the westward flow of migration, while leaving villages and towns with a surplus of young women. The textile mills that multiplied in New England after 1815 depended on the labor of the sisters who had stayed at home while their brothers headed west or moved to the cities.

Within New England the main innovation came in the manufacture of cotton textiles. In 1790 Samuel Slater arrived in Pawtucket, Rhode Island, and established there the first permanent American mill for spinning cotton into yarn through the use of the spinning frame invented by the Englishman Richard Arkwright. Starting with nine workers, Slater had a hundred by 1800 and constructed other mills around Rhode Island and Massachusetts. Slater's mills performed only two of the many operations needed to turn raw cotton into clothing: carding, or fashioning broad laps of cotton into fine strands or slivers, and spinning these strands into yarn. The actual weaving of yarn Slater contracted out to women working in their homes. This "putting-out" system reinforced rather than challenged the traditional position of household, or "cottage," industry.

The incorporation in 1813 of the Boston Manufacturing Company by a group of merchant capitalists called the Boston Associates began a new chapter in the relationship between factories and

Samuel Slater's Mill

Slater's mill in Pawtucket, Rhode Island, was the birthplace of the U.S. textile industry.

cottage industries. Starting with a capital stock of $400,000 (more than ten times the stock of a typical Rhode Island mill), the Boston Manufacturing Company in quick succession established cotton textile factories in the Massachusetts towns of Waltham on the Charles River and Lowell on the Merrimack. By 1836 the Boston Associates had a total investment of $6.2 million in eight companies employing more than six thousand workers.

Size was not the only factor that distinguished these new mills from Slater's. In contrast to Slater's mills, the Waltham and Lowell factories produced finished products and thus challenged the cottage industries that Slater's system had sustained. Additionally, the Waltham and Lowell mills upset the traditional ordering of New England society to a degree that Slater never contemplated. Slater had sought to preserve tradition by hiring entire families to work in his mill complexes, just as entire families had traditionally worked on farms. He hired men to raise crops on nearby land owned by the factory while their wives and children tended the machines inside. Under this arrangement, children were never out of parental sight for long. In contrast, 80 percent of the workers in the mills operated by the Boston Manufacturing Company were unmarried women between the ages of fifteen and thirty, who had been lured from New England's farms by the promise of factory work. Mary Paul,

a Vermont teen-ager, settled her doubts about leaving home for work in Lowell by concluding that "I . . . must work where I can get more pay." While these young women often wrote home, they rarely saw their parents. In place of traditional family discipline, the Waltham and Lowell operatives, as the mill workers were called, experienced new kinds of restraints. The Boston capitalists who financed the mills did not personally oversee them; rather, they delegated oversight to managers, who imposed their own forms of discipline on the work force. Operatives had to live either in boarding houses built by the factory owners or in licensed private dwellings. Company regulations required operatives to attend church on the Sabbath, to observe a 10:00 P.M. curfew, and to accept what one minister called the "moral police of the corporations." At least initially, most young female operatives submitted without complaint to the "moral police."

A major reason why the corporations enforced high moral standards was to give the mills a good reputation so that New England farm girls would continue to be attracted into factory work. Yet mill conditions were far from attractive. To prevent the threads from snapping, the factories had to be kept humid. To create this condition, overseers nailed the windows shut and sprayed the air with water. Operatives also had to contend with flying dust and the deafening roar of the machines. Then keener

Mill Girls

New England's humming textile mills were a magnet for untold numbers of independence-seeking young women in antebellum America.

Manufacturing in New York City and Philadelphia

With their large size, reliance on female labor, and dependence on machinery, the Lowell and Waltham textile mills were the most conspicuous examples of industrialization before 1840. In contrast to such planned factory towns, cities like New York and Philadelphia during the 1820s and 1830s witnessed an industrialization that lacked even the appearance of orderliness, depended far less on machinery and on female workers, occurred in small firms as well as in large ones, and encompassed a greater range of products, including shoes, saddles, tools, rope, hats, and gloves.

While diverging from the Lowell-Waltham model, the factories of New York and Philadelphia exposed workers to some of the same forces encountered by New England mill girls. By expanding the market for manufactures, the transportation revolution had turned some urban craftsmen, auctioneers, and merchants into aggressive merchandisers who scoured the country for orders. As a result, by 1835 New York City's ready-made clothing industry, for example, was supplying cheap dungarees and shirts to western farmers and even southern slaves; in the 1840s it was providing expensive suits for well-to-do customers. In turn, the possibility of reaching distant markets intensified competition and spurred businessmen to slash the cost of their products by increasing output, cutting wages, or both. In New England the Boston Associates had responded by introducing machines, but New York City lacked an easily harnessable source of water power, and before 1840 few machines existed that could speed up the fabrication of products like shoes. Thus factory owners in cities like New York and Philadelphia had to use different tactics to increase their share of the marketplace: they hired large numbers of unskilled or semiskilled workers, many of them women, and paid them low wages to perform simple, specialized hand operations like stitching cloth and soling shoes. In place of the colonial artisan who had fabricated the whole shoe on demand for a customer, such unskilled or semiskilled laborers no longer made whole shoes and rarely even saw a customer.

This subdivision of tasks (without the use of machines) characterized a great deal of industrialization before 1840 and occurred in a variety of

competition and a worsening economy in the late 1830s led the mill owners to reduce wages and speed up work schedules. Such conditions were common in nineteenth-century factories, but in Lowell and Waltham, they were intensified by the basic impersonality of the system. Each of the major groups that contributed to the system lived in a self-contained world. The Boston Associates raised capital but rarely visited the factories. Their agents, all men, gave orders to the operatives, mainly women. Some 800 Lowell mill women quit work in 1834 to protest a reduction in wages. Two years later, there was another "turnout," this time involving 1,500 to 2,000 women. These were the largest strikes in American history to that date. They are noteworthy as strikes not only of employees against employers but also of women against men.

work settings. In the boot and shoe industry that developed after 1820 in eastern Massachusetts, especially at Lynn, workers were gradually gathered into large factories to perform specialized operations in different rooms. In metropolises like New York and Philadelphia, the pattern was a little different. Here, while some large factories appeared in nearly all crafts, much of the subdivision of tasks took place in small shops, garrets, or homes. Because of the population density in these cities, it was unnecessary to gather workers into large factories. Middlemen could simply subcontract tasks out to widows, immigrants, and others who would fashion parts of shoes or saddles or dresses anywhere that light would enter. "We have been in some fifty cellars in different parts of the city," a New York *Tribune* reporter wrote in 1845, "each inhabited by a shoe-maker and his family. The floor is made of rough plank laid loosely down, and the ceiling is not quite so high as a tall man. The walls are dark and damp and . . . the miserable room is lighted only by a shallow sash partly projecting above the surface of the grounds and by the little light that struggles from the steep and rotting stairs. In this apartment often lives the man and his work bench, the wife, and five or six children of all ages; and perhaps a palsied grandfather and grandmother and often both. . . . Here they work, here they cook, they eat, they sleep, they pray. . . ."

In further contrast to places like Lowell and Waltham, which had not even existed in the eighteenth century, New York and Philadelphia were home to artisans with proud craft traditions and independence. Those with a skill like cutting leather or clothing, which was still in demand and took years to master, continued to earn good wages. Others grew rich by turning themselves into businessmen who spent less time making products than taking trips to obtain orders and who then hired workers to fill the orders. Thus industrialization did not reduce all artisans to misery. But many artisans, even though skilled, found themselves on the downslope. Increasingly faced with factory competition, they could either eke out a living as independent artisans by working longer hours and by skimping on food or other necessaries, or enter factories at low wages as semiskilled or unskilled workers. In 1835 Philadelphia shoemakers complained that factory owners had reaped "large fortunes, by reducing wages, making huge quantities of work, and selling at reduced prices, while those

of us who have served time to the trade and have been anxious to foster its interests, have had to abandon the business and enter the system of manufacturing."

In the late 1820s, skilled artisans in New York, Philadelphia, and other cities began to form trade unions and "workingmen's" political parties to protect their interests. Disdaining association with unskilled workers, most of these groups initially sought to restore privileges and working conditions that artisans had once enjoyed rather than to act as leaders of unskilled workers. But the steady deterioration of working conditions in the early 1830s tended to throw skilled and unskilled workers into the same boat. When coal heavers in Philadelphia struck for a ten-hour day in 1835, they were quickly joined by carpenters, cigar makers, shoemakers, leather workers, and other craftsmen in the United States' first general strike.

The emergence of organized worker protest underscored the mixed blessings of economic development. While some benefited from the new commercial and industrial economy, others found their economic position deteriorating. By the 1830s many Americans wondered whether their nation was truly a land of equality.

Equality and Inequality

Observers of antebellum (pre–Civil War) America sensed that changes were sweeping the country but had trouble describing them or agreeing on their direction. Alexis de Tocqueville, a French nobleman who spent nine months in America in 1831–1832, and whose two-volume *Democracy in America* (1835, 1840) contained both extraordinary insights and oversights, pinpointed the "general equality of condition among the people" as the fundamental fact from which all other characteristics of American society flowed. Yet Tocqueville's oft-cited observation about equality represented only part of his thinking about the extent of social democracy in America. He filled his private journal with references to inequalities. Tocqueville believed that these inequalities were less visible, but not necessarily less authentic, than those in France. He was struck by how American servants insisted on being called the "help" and on being viewed as neighbors invited to assist in running a household rather than as a class of permanent menials. But he certainly recognized that there were rich and poor in America.

While Tocqueville argued with himself, Americans disagreed with each other. Some insisted that wealth was "universally diffused." Others, like New York merchant Philip Hone, described an unhappy society in which "the two extremes of costly luxury in living, expensive establishments, and improvident waste are presented in daily and hourly contrast with squalid misery and hopeless destitution."

What assumptions and considerations explain these conflicting evaluations? Tocqueville viewed everything in comparative terms. America had more social equality than France. It was not just that American *servants* took on airs; in America, *merchants,* who in France were disdained by the titled nobility, were among other groups who considered themselves equal to anyone. Other observers generalized about the whole society after examining only part of it. Almost all contemporaries struggled to find the right words to describe the changes. They applied traditional terms like *artisan* and *farmer* to people whose activities no longer conformed to the conventional image of what artisans and farmers did. Similarly, they tossed around words like *democracy* and *equality* without always recognizing that equality before the law was one thing, equality of opportunity another, and social equality a third.

For all these reasons, it is difficult to get what mariners call a fix on American society before the Civil War. Using refined techniques of measurement, however, historians have drawn a more detailed and complete portrait of antebellum society than the profile sketched by contemporaries. The following discussion applies mainly to northern society. The South, whose "peculiar institution" of slavery created a distinctive social structure and set of social relationships, is examined separately in Chapter 10.

Growing Inequality:
The Rich and the Poor

The gap between the rich and the poor, which had increased during the late eighteenth century, widened further during the first half of the nineteenth

century. Although Americans portrayed them as oases of equality, farm areas contained a good deal of inequality. In 1850 the poorest 40 percent of native-born farmers owned less than one hundred dollars worth of property, while the richest 30 percent to 40 percent of farmers owned three-fourths or more of the total farm property. But the truly striking inequalities developed in the cities, where a small fraction of the people owned a huge share of urban wealth. In Boston, for example, the richest 10 percent of the population owned a little over half of the city's real estate and personal property in 1771. By 1833 the richest 4 percent owned 59 percent of the wealth, and by 1848 nearly two-thirds of the wealth. By 1848, 81 percent of Boston's population owned only 4 percent of its wealth. In New York City, the richest 4 percent owned nearly half the wealth in 1828 and more than two-thirds by 1845. These statistics are representative of trends that affected all major cities. By 1860 the wealthiest 10 percent in Baltimore, St. Louis, and New Orleans held more than 80 percent of the wealth. A similar if less extreme trend toward the concentration of wealth affected towns like Jacksonville, Illinois, and Poughkeepsie, New York.

Although commentators celebrated the self-made American who rose "from rags to riches," few individuals actually accumulated their wealth in this way. The vast majority of those who became extremely rich started out with considerable wealth. Fewer than five of every hundred wealthy men started poor, and close to ninety of every hundred started rich. The old-fashioned way to make money was to inherit it, marry into more, and then invest wisely. There were just enough instances of fabulously successful poor boys like John Jacob Astor, who built a fur-trading empire, to sustain popular belief in the rags-to-riches myth, but not enough to turn that myth into a reality.

Their splendid residences as well as their wealth set the rich apart. The urban rich built imposing mansions clustered in neighborhoods. In 1828 over half of the 500 wealthiest families in New York City lived on only 8 of the city's more than 250 streets, while during the early 1830s, half of Boston's wealthy families lived on but 8 of its 325 streets. Social clubs also separated the rich from others. The Philadelphia Club, founded in 1834, was a stronghold for proper Philadelphians. By the late 1820s, New York City had a club so exclusive that it was called just The Club. Tocqueville noted

View of St. Louis, *by Leon Pomarede, 1832*

When the trans-Mississippi fur trade declined in the 1830s, the steamboats that plied the Mississippi and Missouri rivers became the key to St. Louis's expansion. The economic gap between the city's rich and poor widened as St. Louis grew.

that in America "the wealthiest and most enlightened live among themselves." Yet Tocqueville was also struck by how the rich feigned respect for equality when they moved about in public. They rode in ordinary rather than sumptuous carriages, brushed elbows easily with the less privileged, and avoided the conspicuous display of wealth that marked their private lives.

At the opposite end of the social ladder were the poor. By today's standards, most antebellum Americans were poor: they lived "close to the margin" of poverty, depended heavily on their children's labor to meet expenses, had little money to spend on medical care or recreation, and were subject to unemployment, not just during general economic downturns but from month to month, even in times of prosperity. Freezing weather, for instance, could temporarily throw day laborers, factory workers, and boatmen out of work. In 1850 an estimated three out of eight males over the age of twenty owned little more than their clothing and the cash in their pockets.

In evaluating economic status, it is important to recognize that statistics on the distribution of wealth to some extent mask the fact that the accumulation of property takes place over an entire lifetime and increases with age. With its extraordinary high birthrate, antebellum America was overwhelmingly a nation of young people with little property; not all of them would remain propertyless as they grew older.

We must also keep in mind that when antebellum Americans themselves spoke of poverty, they were not thinking of the condition of hardship that affected most people. Instead, they were referring to a state of dependency, a total inability to fend for oneself, that affected *some* people. They often called this dependency pauperism. The absence of health insurance and old-age pensions condemned many infirm and aged people to pauperism. Widows whose children had left home might also have a hard time avoiding pauperism. Contemporaries usually classified all such people as the "deserving" poor and contrasted them with the "undeserving" poor—such as indolent loafers and drunkards whose poverty was self-willed. Most moralists claimed that America was happily free of a permanent class of paupers. They assumed that since pauperism resulted either from circumstances beyond anyone's control, such as old age and disease, or from voluntary decisions to squander money on liquor, it could not afflict entire groups generation after generation.

This assumption was comforting but also misleading, because a class of people who could not escape poverty was emerging in the major cities during the first half of the nineteenth century. One source of this class was immigration. As early as 1801, a New York newspaper called attention to boatloads of immigrants with large families, without money or health, and *"expiring from the want of sustenance."* The arrival of huge numbers of Irish immigrants during the 1840s and 1850s made a bad situation worse. The Irish were among the poorest immigrants ever to arrive in America. Fleeing famine in Ireland, they found even worse conditions in noxious slums like New York's infamous Five Points district. Starting with the conversion of a brewery into housing for hundreds of people in 1837, the Five Points became probably the worst slum in America.

The Irish were not only poor but, as Catholics, also belonged to a church despised by the Protestant majority. In short, they were different and had little claim on the kindly impulses of most Protestants. But even the Protestant poor came in for rough treatment in the years between 1815 and 1840. The more Americans convinced themselves that success was within everyone's grasp, the less they accepted the traditional doctrine that poverty was ordained by God, and the more they were inclined to hold the poor responsible for their own poverty. Ironically, even as many Americans blamed the poor for being poor, they practiced discrimination that kept some groups mired in enduring poverty. Nowhere was this more true than in the case of northern free blacks.

Free Blacks in the North

Prejudice against blacks was deeply ingrained in white society throughout the nation. Although slavery had largely disappeared in the North by 1820, laws penalized blacks in many ways. One form of discrimination was to restrict the blacks' right to vote. In New York State, for example, a constitutional revision of 1821 eliminated property requirements for white voters but kept them for blacks. Rhode Island banned blacks from voting in 1822; Pennsylvania did so in 1837. Throughout the half-century after 1800, blacks could vote on equal terms with whites in only one of the nation's major cities, Boston. Efforts were also made to bar free blacks from migrating to other states and cities. Missouri's original constitution authorized the state legislature to prevent blacks from entering the state "under any pretext whatsoever." Free blacks were often barred from public conveyances and facilities and were either excluded from public schools in major cities or forced into segregated schools. Segregation was the rule in northern jails, almshouses, and hospitals. But of all restrictions on free blacks, the most damaging was the social pressure that forced them into the least skilled and lowest-paying occupations throughout the northern cities. Recollecting his youthful days in Providence, Rhode Island, in the early 1830s, the free black William J. Brown wrote: "To drive carriages, carry a market basket after the boss, and brush his boots, or saw wood and run errands was as high as a colored man could rise." Although a few free blacks became successful entrepreneurs and grew moderately wealthy, urban free blacks were only half as likely as city dwellers in general to own real estate.

The "Middling Classes"

The majority of antebellum Americans lived neither in splendid wealth nor in grinding poverty. Most belonged to what men and women of the time called the middling classes. Even though the wealthy owned an increasing proportion of all wealth, most people's standard of living rose between 1800 and 1860, particularly between 1840 and 1860, when per capita income grew at an annual rate of around 1.5 percent.

Americans applied the term *middling classes* to farmers and artisans, whose ideal was self-employment. These were the nation's sturdy "producers." Commentators criticized the rich for luxury and the poor for depravity, but they rarely had anything bad to say about the middling classes, whom they regarded as steady and dependable, the

The Blacksmith's Shop, *by Eastman Johnson, 1863*

Blacksmiths were indispensable artisans in antebellum America. At their forges, which served as both social and industrial centers, they made or repaired horseshoes, nails, rifles, saws, wagon axles, chains, bear traps, and farm implements of every sort.

real America. Yet life in the middle was unpredictable, filled with jagged ups and downs. Words like *farmer* and *artisan* were often misleading, for they gave a greater impression of steadiness and stability than was really the case. For example, Asa G. Sheldon, born in Massachusetts in 1788, described himself in his autobiography as a farmer, offered advice on growing corn and cranberries, and gave speeches about the glories of farming. While Sheldon undoubtedly knew a great deal about farming, he actually spent very little time tilling the soil. In 1812 he began to transport hops from New England to brewers in New York City, and he soon extended this business to Philadelphia and Baltimore. He invested his profits in land, but rather than farm the land, he made money selling its timber. When a business setback forced him to sell his property, he was soon back in operation "through the disinterested kindness of friends" who lent him money, with which he purchased carts and oxen. These he used to get contracts for filling in swamps in Boston and for clearing and grading land for railroads. From all this and from the backbreaking labor of the Irish immigrants he hired to do the

shoveling, Sheldon the "farmer" grew prosperous. But his prosperity in fact owed little to farming.

The increasingly commercial and industrial economy of antebellum America created opportunities for success and forced individuals like Sheldon to make adaptations. Not everyone, though, had an opportunity for success. Had it not been for the intervention of wealthy friends, Sheldon would have ended up in a poorhouse. Many lacked kindly friends with money to lend. Some, like Sheldon, rose. Others, like Allan Melville, father of novelist Herman Melville, slipped down the slope. An enterprising import merchant, Allan Melville had an abounding faith in his nation, in "our national Eagle, 'with an eye that never winks and a wing that never tires,'" and in the inevitable triumph of honesty and prudence. The Melvilles lived comfortably in Albany and New York City, but in the late 1820s, Allan's business, never robust, sagged. By 1830 he was begging his father for a loan of $500, proclaiming that "I am destitute of resources and without a shilling—without immediate assistance I know not what will become of me." He got the $500 plus an additional $3,000, but the downward spiral continued. In 1832 he died, broken in spirit and nearly insane.

The case of artisans also illustrates the perils of life in the middling classes. During the colonial period, artisans had formed a proud and cohesive group whose members often attained the goal of self-employment. They owned their own tools, made their own products on order from customers, boarded their apprentices and journeymen in their homes, and passed their skills on to their sons. By 1850, in contrast, artisans had entered a new world of economic relationships. This was true even of a craft like carpentry that did not experience any industrial or technological change. Town and city growth in the wake of the transportation revolution created a demand for housing. Some carpenters, usually those with access to capital, became contractors who took orders for more houses than they could build themselves and who then hired large numbers of journeymen to do the construction work. Likewise, as we have seen, in the early industrialization of shoe manufacturing during the 1820s, some shoemakers spent less time crafting shoes than making trips to obtain orders for their products, then hired workers to fashion parts of shoes. In effect, the old class of artisans was breaking apart into two new groupings. On one side were artisans who had become businessmen or entrepreneurs; on the other, journeymen with little prospect of self-employment.

An additional characteristic of the middling classes (one that they shared with the poor) was a high degree of transiency, or "spatial mobility." Farmers who cultivated land intensively in order to raise a cash crop and so get out of debt exhausted their land quickly and had to move on. Artisans displaced from skilled jobs by machines found that much unskilled work was seasonal and that they had to move from job to job to survive. Canal workers and boatmen had to secure new work when waterways froze. Even for city dwellers, to shift jobs often meant changing residences, for the cities were spreading out at a much faster rate than was public transportation. Some idea of the degree of transiency can be gained from a survey made by the Boston police on Saturday, September 6, 1851. At a time when Boston's population was 145,000, the survey showed that from 6:30 A.M. to 7:30 P.M., 41,729 people entered the city and 42,313 left.

Alcohol in the Early Republic

Antebellum economic change improved many lives but also imposed new pressures. In a society in which some individuals outstripped others in the race for riches, most felt compelled to succeed. But when they failed, more and more Americans came to believe that their failure was not the product of fate or divine will, as had traditionally been thought, but of individual lack of enterprise. By stripping away the older idea that personal failure reflected God's will, the commercialization and industrialization of American society made the individual bear the whole burden of failure. In this context, Americans increasingly turned to alcoholic binges in these years, as a way not to explain their inadequacies but to soften them, by retreating into the mellow stupor of intoxication.

A tradition of drinking had been inherited from the eighteenth century, and the spread of the population across the Appalachians further stimulated the production and consumption of liquor. Before 1830 western farmers commonly distilled grain into spirits. Annual per capita consumption of rum, whiskey, gin, and brandy rose until it exceeded seven gallons by 1830, nearly triple today's rate.

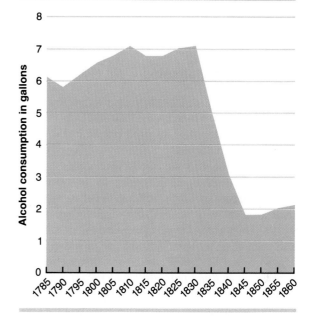

Absolute Alcohol Consumption, per Capita, of Drinking-Age (15+) Population

The temperance movement, which arose in the late 1820s and was dedicated to encouraging abstinence from alcoholic beverages, had a decisive impact on American drinking patterns.

SOURCE: From *The Alcoholic Republic: An American Tradition* by W. J. Rorabaugh. Copyright 1979 by Oxford University Press, Inc. Reprinted by permission.

By the late 1820s, the average adult male was drinking a half-pint of liquor a day. So much a part of the cultural scene did drinking become that one enterprising Irish immigrant, Sam Patch, even charged spectators to watch him jump, inebriated, into rivers. In 1829 he finally miscalculated and drunkenly plunged to his death in Genesee Falls near Rochester, New York. Far more typical than Patch's spectacular leaps were brawls among drunken lumbermen and canal workers. But it was not just manual workers who fell victim to the "demon" of liquor, for many physicians, lawyers, and bankers sought in intoxication a temporary feeling of achievement, power, and success.

The multiplying risks and opportunities that confronted Americans both widened the gap between social classes and increased the psychological burdens on individuals. Commercial and industrial growth also placed pressure on such basic social relationships as those between lawyers and their clients, ministers and their parishioners, and children and their parents.

The Revolution in Social Relationships

Following the War of 1812, the growth of interregional trade, commercial agriculture, and manufacturing disrupted many traditional social relationships and forged new ones. Two broad generalizations encompass these changes. First, Americans questioned authority to an unprecedented degree. In 1775 they had rebelled against their king. Now, it seemed, they were rebelling as well against their lawyers, physicians, ministers, and even their parents. An attitude of individualism sprouted and took firm root in antebellum America. Once *individualism* had meant nothing more than selfishness, but now Americans used the word to signify positive qualities: self-reliance and the conviction that each person was the best judge of his or her own true interests. Ordinary Americans might still agree with the opinions of their leaders, but only after they had thought matters through on their own. Those with superior wealth, education, or social position could no longer expect the automatic deference of the common people.

Second, even as Americans widely proclaimed themselves a nation of self-reliant individualists and questioned the traditional basis of authority, they sought to construct new foundations for authority. For example, among middle-class women, the idea developed that they possessed a "separate sphere" of authority in the home. In addition, individuals increasingly joined with others in these years to form voluntary associations through which they might influence the direction that their society would take.

The Attack on the Professions

The first phase in this alteration of social relationships was the erosion of traditional forms of authority. In the swiftly changing antebellum society, claims to social superiority were questioned as never before. The statesman Harrison Gray Otis put it in a nutshell in 1836: "Everywhere the disposition is found among those who live in the val-

leys to ask those who live on the hills, 'How came we here and you there?' "

Intense criticism of lawyers, physicians, and ministers exemplified this assault on authority. As far back as the 1780s, Benjamin Austin, a radical Boston artisan, had complained that lawyers needlessly prolonged and confused court cases so that they could charge high fees. Between 1800 and 1840, a wave of religious revivals known as the Second Great Awakening (see Chapter 9) sparked new attacks on the professions. Some revivalists blasted the clergy for creating complicated theologies that ordinary men and women could not comprehend, for drinking expensive wines, and for fleecing the people. One religious revivalist, Elias Smith, extended the criticism to physicians, whom he accused of inventing Latin and Greek names for diseases in order to disguise their own ignorance of how to cure them.

Attacks on the learned professions peaked between 1820 and 1850. In medicine a movement arose under the leadership of Samuel Thomson, a farmer's son with little formal education, to eliminate all barriers to entry into the medical profession. Thomson believed that anyone could understand the principles of medicine and become a physician. His crusade was remarkably successful. By 1845 every state had repealed laws that required licenses and education to practice medicine. Meanwhile, attacks on lawyers sharpened, and relations between ministers and their parishioners grew tense and acrimonious. In colonial New England, ministers had usually served a single parish for life, but by the 1830s a rapid turnover of ministers was becoming the norm as finicky parishioners commonly dismissed clergymen whose theology displeased them. Ministers themselves were becoming more ambitious—more inclined to leave small, poor congregations for large, wealthy ones.

The increasing commercialization of the economy contributed both to the growing number of professionals and to the attacks on them. The rise of the market economy intensified the demand for lawyers and physicians; the number of medical schools, for example, grew from one in 1765 to twenty in 1830 and sixty-five in 1860. Like so many other antebellum Americans, these freshly minted lawyers and doctors often were transients without deep roots in the towns that they served and without convincing claims to social superiority.

Describing lawyers and physicians, a contemporary observer wrote: "Men dropped down into their places as from clouds. Nobody knew who or what they were, except as they claimed, or as a surface view of their character indicated." A horse doctor one day would the next day hang up his sign as "Physician and Surgeon" and "fire at random a box of his pills into your bowels, with a vague chance of hitting some disease unknown to him, but with a better prospect of killing the patient, whom or whose administrator he charged some ten dollars a trial for his marksmanship."

The questioning of authority was particularly sharp on the frontier. Here, to eastern and foreign visitors, it seemed that every man they met was a "judge," "general," "colonel," or "squire." In a society in which everyone was new, such titles were easily adopted but just as easily challenged. Where neither law nor custom sanctioned claims of superiority, would-be gentlemen substituted an exaggerated sense of personal honor. Obsessed with their fragile status, many of these "gentlemen" reacted testily to the slightest insult. Dueling became a widespread frontier practice. At a Kentucky militia parade in 1819, a colonel's dog jogged onto the field and sat at his master's knee. Enraged by this breach of military decorum, the regiment's general ran the dog through with his dress sword. A week later, general and colonel met with pistols at ten paces. The colonel was killed; the general, crippled for life.

The Challenge to Family Authority

In contrast to the public, philosophical attacks on the learned professions, children engaged in a quiet questioning of parental authority. Economic change created new opportunities that forced young people to choose between staying at home to help their parents and venturing out on their own. Writing to her parents in Vermont shortly before taking a job in a Lowell textile mill, eighteen-year-old Sally Rice quickly got to the point: "I must of course have something of my own before many more years have passed over my head and where is that something coming from if I go home and earn nothing. You may think me unkind but how can you blame me if I want to stay here. I have but one life to live and I want to enjoy myself as I can while I live."

A similar desire for independence propelled young men to leave home at earlier ages than in the past and to strike out on their own. Although the great migration to the West was primarily a movement of entire families, movement from farms to towns and cities within regions was frequently spearheaded by restless and single young people. Two young men in Virginia put it succinctly: "All the promise of life seemed to us to be at the other end of the rainbow—somewhere else—anywhere else but on the farm. . . . And so all our youthful plans had as their chief object the getting away from the farm."

Antebellum Americans also widely wished to be free of close parental supervision, and their changing attitudes influenced courtship and marriage. Many young people who no longer depended on their parents for land insisted on privacy in courting and wanted to decide for themselves when to marry. Increasingly, too, romantic love between the partners rather than parental preferences determined decisions to marry. Where seventeenth-century Puritans had advised young people to choose marriage partners whom they *could* love, by the early 1800s, young men and women viewed romantic love as the indispensable basis for a successful marriage. "In affairs of love," a young lawyer in Maine wrote, "young peoples hearts are generally much wiser than old peoples heads."

One sign of young people's growing control over courtship and marriage was the declining likelihood that the young women of a family would marry in their exact birth order. Traditionally, fathers had wanted their daughters to marry in the order of their birth, to avoid planting the suspicion that there was something wrong with one or more of them. Toward the end of the eighteenth century, however, the practice ceased to be customary, as daughters were making their own marital decisions. Another mark of the times was the growing number of long engagements. Having made the decision to marry, some young women were reluctant to tie the knot, fearing that marriage would snuff out their independence. For example, Caroline and William Kirkland were engaged for seven years before their marriage in 1828. Equally striking was the increasing number of young women who chose not to marry. Catharine Beecher, the daughter of the prominent minister Lyman Beecher, broke off her engagement to a young man during the 1820s, despite her father's pressure to marry him. She later renewed the engagement, but after her fiancé's death in a shipwreck, she remained single for the rest of her life.

Thus young people lived more and more in a world of their own. Not surprisingly, moralists reacted with alarm and flooded the country with books of advice to youth such as William Alcott's *The Young Man's Guide,* which went through thirty-one editions between 1833 and 1858. The number of such advice books sold in antebellum America was truly vast, but to an amazing extent, they all said the same thing. They did not advise young men and women to return to farms, and they assumed that parents had little control over them. Rather, their authors exhorted youths to develop habitual rectitude, self-control, and "character." It was an age not just of the self-made man but also of the self-made youth.

Wives, Husbands

Another class of advice books pouring from the antebellum presses counseled wives and husbands on their rights and duties. These were a sign that relations between spouses, too, were changing. Young men and women who, as teen-agers, had grown accustomed to making decisions on their own were more likely than their ancestors to approach wedlock as a compact between equals. Of course, wives remained unequal to their husbands in many tangible ways, the most obvious being the continuation into the 1830s of the traditional legal rule that married women could not own property. But relations between wives and husbands were changing during the 1820s and 1830s toward a form of equality.

One source of the change was the rise of a potent ideology known as the doctrine of separate spheres. Traditionally, women had been viewed as subordinate to men in all spheres of life. Now middle-class men and women developed a kind of separate-but-equal doctrine that portrayed men as superior in making money and governing the world and women as superior for their moral influence on family members. One of the most important duties assigned to the sphere of women was the raising of children. During the eighteenth century, ministers had addressed sermons to fathers to remind them of their duty to govern the family, but by the 1830s child-rearing manuals increasingly appealed to mothers rather than fathers. "How entire and

perfect in this dominion over the unformed character of your infant," the popular writer Lydia Sigourney proclaimed in her *Letters to Mothers* (1838). Advice books instructed mothers to discipline their children by loving them and withdrawing affection when they misbehaved rather than by using corporal punishment. A whipped child might become more obedient but would remain sullen and bitter. In contrast, the gentler methods advised in manuals promised to penetrate to the child's heart, to make the child want to do the right thing.

The idea of a separate women's sphere blended with a related image of the family and the home as secluded refuges from a society marked by commotion and disorder. The popular culture of the 1830s and 1840s painted an alluring portrait of the pleasures of home life through songs like "Home, Sweet Home" and poems such as Henry Wadsworth Longfellow's "The Children's Hour" and Clement Moore's "A Visit from St. Nicholas." The publication of Moore's poem coincided with the growing popularity of Christmas as a holiday season in which family members gathered to exchange warm affection. Even the physical appearance of houses changed as architects offered new designs for the ideal home. The prominent architect Andrew Jackson Downing published plans for peaceful single-family homes that he hoped would offset the "spirit of unrest" and the feverish pace of American life. In Downing's view, houses should contain welcoming porches, comfortable piazzas, overhanging roofs with high gables, and deep eaves to evoke sentiment. He wrote of the ideal home: "There should be something to love. There must be nooks about it, where one would love to linger; windows, where one can enjoy the quiet landscape at his leisure; cozy rooms, where all fireside joys are invited to dwell."

As a prophet, Downing deserves high marks, because one of the motives that has impelled many Americans to flee cities for suburbs in the twentieth century has been the desire to achieve ownership of a single-family residence. However, in the 1820s and 1830s, this ideal was beyond the reach of most people—not just blacks, immigrants, and sweatshop workers, but much of the middle class as well. In the countryside, while middle-class farmers still managed productive households, these were anything but tranquil: wives milked cows and bled hogs, and children fetched wood, drove cows to pasture, and chased blackbirds from cornfields.

The Ephraim Hubbard Foster Family, *by Ralph E. W. Earl, c. 1824*

This painting literally captures the child-centeredness of middle-class families in antebellum America by placing a child in the middle of the family group.

In the cities, middle-class families often had to sacrifice their privacy by taking in boarders to supplement family income.

Still, the doctrine of separate spheres for men and women, and the image of the home as a calming refuge from a harsh world, were powerful ideals, and virtually the only ones projected in antebellum magazines. Although they were ideals rather than descriptions of reality, they did intersect with the real world at *some* points. For example, the decline of cottage industries and the rising number of urban families headed by merchants, lawyers, or brokers (all of whom worked away from their homes) gave married women more time to spend on child rearing. Above all, even if they could not afford to live in a Downing-designed house, married women found that they could use the doctrine of separate spheres and the image of the home as a refuge to gain new power within their families. A subtle implication of the doctrine of separate spheres was that women should have control not only over the discipline of children but also over the more fundamental issue of the number of children that they would bear.

In 1800 the United States had had one of the highest birthrates ever recorded for a civilized nation. The average woman bore 7.04 children. It is safe to say that married women had become pregnant as often as possible. In the prevailing farm economy, children were valuable for carrying out essential tasks and, as time passed, for relieving aging parents of the burden of heavy farm labor. Most parents had assumed that the more children, the better. However, the spread of a commercial economy raised troublesome questions about children's economic value. Unlike a farmer, a merchant or lawyer could not send his children to work at the age of seven or eight. The average woman, who had borne 7.04 children in 1800, was bearing only 5.02 by 1850, and 3.98 by 1900. The birthrate remained high among blacks and among many immigrant groups, but it slumped drastically among native-born whites, particularly in towns and cities. The birthrate also declined in rural areas, but more sharply in rural villages than on farms, and more sharply in the East, where land was scarce, than in the West, where abundant land created continued incentives for parents to have many children.

For the most part, the decline in the birthrate was accomplished by abstinence from sexual intercourse or by *coitus interruptus* (withdrawal of the male organ before ejaculation) or by abortion. By the 1840s such abortionists as New York City's notorious Madame Restell advertised remedies for "female irregularities," a common euphemism for unwanted pregnancies. There were no foolproof birth-control devices, and as much misinformation as information circulated about the techniques of birth control. Nonetheless, interest in birth-control devices was intensifying. In 1832 Charles Knowlton, a Massachusetts physician, described the procedure for vaginal douching in his book *Fruits of Philosophy*. Although Knowlton was frequently prosecuted and once jailed for obscenity, efforts to suppress his ideas only resulted in their being publicized even more. By 1865 popular tracts had familiarized Americans with a wide range of birth-control methods, including the rubber condom and the vaginal diaphragm. Whatever the method, the decision to limit family size was usually reached jointly by wives and husbands. Economic and ideological considerations blended together. Husbands could note that the economic value of children was declining; wives, that having fewer children would give them more time to nurture each one and thereby carry out the duties of the woman's sphere.

Supporters of the ideal of separate spheres did not advocate full legal equality for women. Indeed, the idea of separate spheres was an explicit *alternative* to legal equality. But the concept did enhance women's power within marriage by justifying their demands for influence over such vital issues as child rearing and the frequency of pregnancies. In addition, it allowed some women a measure of independence from the home. For example, it sanctioned Catharine Beecher's travels to lecture women on better ways to raise children and manage their households.

Horizontal Allegiances and the Rise of Voluntary Associations

As some forms of authority, such as that of parents over their children and of husbands over their wives, were weakening, Americans devised new ways through which individuals could extend their influence over others. The pre–Civil War period witnessed the widespread substitution of *horizontal* allegiances for *vertical* allegiances. An example of vertical allegiance is found in the traditional patriarchal family, wherein a wife and children looked up to the father for leadership. Another example occurs in the small eighteenth-century workshop, where apprentices and journeymen took direction from the master craftsman and even lived in the craftsman's house, subject to his authority. Common to these examples is the idea of authority

flowing from the top down. In a vertical allegiance, people in a subordinate position identify their best interests with the interests of their superiors rather than with those of other individuals in the same subordinate position.

When social relationships began to assume a horizontal form, several new patterns emerged. While the older kind of vertical relationships did not disappear, they became less important in people's lives. Relationships now arose that linked those in a similar position. For example, in large textile mills during the 1830s, many operatives discovered that they had more in common with each other than with their managers and overseers. Similarly, wives were increasingly inclined to form associations that bound them with other married women. Young men formed associations with other young men. None of these associations was intended to overthrow traditional authority. Many of them in fact professed to strengthen the family or community. But all represented the substitution of new allegiances for old ones.

A sign of the change can be seen in the large number of voluntary associations formed in the 1820s and 1830s. These were associations that arose apart from government and sought to accomplish some goal of value to their members. Tocqueville observed that in France the government stood at the head of every enterprise but that in America "you will be sure to find an association."

At the most basic level, the voluntary associations encouraged sociability. As transients and newcomers flocked into towns and cities, they tended to join with others who shared similar characteristics, experiences, or interests. Gender was the basis of many voluntary societies. Of twenty-six religious and charitable associations in Utica, New York, in 1832, for instance, one-third were exclusively for women. Race was still another basis for voluntary associations. Although their names did not indicate it, Boston's Thompson Literary and Debating Society, its Philomathean Adelphic Union for the Promotion of Literature and Science, and New York City's Phoenix Society were all organizations for free blacks.

Promoting sociability, however, was not the only benefit of voluntary associations. These associations also allowed their members to assert their influence at a time when traditional forms of authority were weakening. For example, voluntary associations proved compatible with the idea that women had a separate sphere. As long as a woman could argue that her activities were in the best interests of the home, she could escape the kitchen long enough to join maternal associations (where mothers exchanged ideas about child rearing), temperance associations (where they promoted abstinence from alcoholic beverages), and moral-reform societies. These latter societies, which multiplied in the 1830s and 1840s, combated prostitution.

Temperance and moral-reform societies had a dual purpose. They sought to suppress well-known vices *and* to enhance women's power over men. Temperance advocates assumed that intemperance was a male vice. Moral reformers attributed the prevalence of prostitution to the lustfulness of men who, unable to control their passions, exploited poor and vulnerable girls. While exhorting prostitutes to give up their line of work, moral reformers also tried to shame brothel patrons into chastity by publishing their names in newspapers. Just as strikes in Lowell in the 1830s were a form of collective action by working women, temperance and moral-reform societies represented collective action by middle-class women to increase their influence in society. Here as elsewhere, the tendency of the times was to forge new forms of horizontal allegiance between like-minded Americans.

Conclusion

Alexis de Tocqueville described the United States of the 1830s as remarkable not for "the marvellous grandeur of some undertakings" but for the "innumerable multitude of small ones." In fact, a number of grand enterprises *were* undertaken between 1815 and 1840, among them the construction of the Erie Canal and the establishment of the Lowell mills. But Tocqueville was basically correct. The distinguishing feature of the period was the amount of small to medium-size enterprises that Americans embarked upon: commercial farms of modest proportions, railroads that ran for a few hundred miles, manufacturing companies that employed five to ten workers.

The changes of the period were modest in comparison to those that would come in the late nineteenth century, when industrial firms routinely employed hundreds of workers and railroads spanned the continent. Nevertheless, to antebellum Americans, it seemed as if the world of their ancestors was breaking apart. In 1800 no human or machine had been able to sustain motion at more than ten miles an hour. The railroads changed that. In 1800 it had been natural to assume that the limits of trade were set by the limits of rivers. Canals changed that. Everywhere traditional assumptions about what was "natural" were challenged.

As traditional assumptions eroded, new ones took their place. Ties to village leaders and even to parents weakened, but new bonds with the like-minded and with age peers emerged. Individualism became a major force in the sense that a widening circle of Americans insisted on the right to shape their own economic destinies. "No man in America is contented to be poor," a magazine proclaimed, "or expects to continue so." Yet Americans did not desire isolation from each other. Voluntary associations based on the personal preferences of their members, rather than on custom, proliferated. A host of advice books aimed at young people, wives, and husbands tried to teach Americans how to play the new roles thrust upon them by economic and social change. The marriage manual was as much a part of antebellum America as the Erie Canal or the Boston Manufacturing Company.

The social transformations of 1815 to 1840 not only changed the private lives of Americans but also brought a host of new political issues to the fore, as we shall see in Chapter 9.

CHRONOLOGY

1790 Samuel Slater opens his first Rhode Island mill for the production of cotton yarn.

1793 Eli Whitney invents the cotton gin.

1807 Robert R. Livingston and Robert Fulton introduce the steamboat *Clermont* on the Hudson River.

1811 Construction of the National Road begins at Cumberland, Maryland.

1813 Incorporation of the Boston Manufacturing Company.

1816 Second Bank of the United States chartered.

1817 Erie Canal started.

1819 Economic panic, ushering in four-year depression.

1820– Growth of female moral-reform societies.
1850

1820s Expansion of New England textile mills.

1824 *Gibbons* v. *Ogden.*

1825 Completion of the Erie Canal.

1828 Baltimore and Ohio Railroad chartered.

1830 Indian Removal Act passed by Congress.

1831 *Cherokee Nation* v. *Georgia.*
Alexis de Tocqueville begins visit to the United States to study American penitentiaries.

1832 *Worcester* v. *Georgia.*

1834 First strike at the Lowell mills.

1837 Economic panic begins a depression that lasts until 1843.

1840 System of production by interchangeable parts perfected.

For Further Reading

Rowland Berthoff, *An Unsettled People: Social Order and Disorder in American History* (1971). A stimulating interpretation of American social history.

Ray A. Billington, *Westward Expansion: A History of the American Frontier* (1949). The standard study of westward movement and settlement.

Daniel Boorstin, *The Americans: The National Experience* (1965). A provocative interpretation of American society in the first half of the nineteenth century.

Carl Degler, *At Odds: Women and the Family in America from the Revolution to the Present* (1980). A fine overview of the economic and social experiences of American women.

George R. Taylor, *The Transportation Revolution, 1815–1860* (1951). The standard general study of the development of canals, steamboats, highways, and railroads.

Sean Wilentz, *Chants Democratic: New York City and the Rise of the American Working Class, 1788–1850*

(1983). A stimulating synthesis of economic, social, and political history.

Additional Bibliography

Agriculture and the Westward Movement

Thomas D. Clark, *The Rampaging Frontier* (1939); Charles Danhof, *Change in Agriculture: The Northern United States, 1820–1870* (1969); Paul W. Gates, *The Farmer's Age: Agriculture, 1815–1860* (1960); William H. Goetzmann, *Explorations and Empire: The Explorer and the Scientist in the Winning of the American West* (1966); Malcolm Rohrbough, *The Land Office Business: The Settlement and Administration of American Public Lands, 1789–1837* (1968).

Indians

Robert F. Berkhofer, Jr., *The White Man's Indian: Images of the American Indian from Columbus to the Present*

(1979); John R. Finger, *The Eastern Band of Cherokees, 1819–1900* (1984); Michael D. Green, *The Politics of Indian Removal: Creek Government and Society in Crisis* (1982); William G. McLoughlin, *Cherokees and Missionaries, 1789–1839* (1984); Roy H. Pearce, *The Savages of America* (1965); Richard Slotkin, *Regeneration Through Violence: The Mythology of the American Frontier, 1600–1860* (1973); Wilcomb E. Washburn, *The Indian in America* (1975).

The Transportation Revolution

Albert Fishlow, *American Railroads and the Transformation of the Ante-Bellum Economy* (1965); Robert W. Fogel, *Railroads and American Economic Growth: Essays in Econometric History* (1964); Carter Goodrich, *Government Promotion of American Canals and Railroads, 1800–1890* (1960); Erik F. Haites, James Mak, and Gary M. Walton, *Western River Transportation: The Era of Early Internal Development, 1800–1860* (1975); Harry N. Scheiber, *The Ohio Canal Era: A Case Study of Government and the Economy, 1820–1861* (1969); R. E. Shaw, *Erie Water West* (1966).

Communities

Stuart Blumin, *The Urban Threshold: Growth and Change in a Nineteenth-Century American Community* (1976); Don H. Doyle, *The Social Order of a Frontier Community: Jacksonville, Illinois, 1825–1870* (1978); Clyde Griffen and Sally Griffen, *Natives and Newcomers: The Ordering of Opportunity in Mid-Nineteenth-Century Poughkeepsie* (1978); Paul Johnson, *A Shopkeeper's Millennium: Society and Revivals in Rochester, New York, 1815–1837* (1978); Richard C. Wade, *The Urban Frontier* (1964); Anthony F. C. Wallace, *Rockdale: The Growth of an American Village in the Early Industrial Revolution* (1977).

Immigrants

Rowland Berthoff, *British Immigrants in Industrial America* (1953); Kathleen N. Conzen, *Immigrant Milwaukee, 1836–1860* (1976); Jay P. Dolan, *The Immigrant Church: New York's Irish and German Catholics, 1815–1860* (1975); Oscar Handlin, *Boston's Immigrants: A Study in Acculturation* (rev. ed., 1959); Marcus L. Hansen, *The Atlantic Migration, 1607–1860* (1940); Philip Taylor, *The Distant Magnet: European Emigration to the United States of America* (1971); Carl Wittke, *The Irish in America* (1956).

Technology

Siegfried Giedion, *Mechanization Takes Command* (1948); H. J. Habakkuk, *American and British Technology in the Nineteenth Century* (1962); Otto Mayr

and Robert C. Post, eds., *Yankee Enterprise: The Rise of the American System of Manufactures* (1981); Merritt R. Smith, *Harpers Ferry Armory and the New Technology* (1977).

Manufacturing and Economic Growth

W. Elliot Brownlee, *Dynamics of Ascent* (1974); Stuart Bruchey, *The Roots of American Economic Growth, 1607–1861* (1965); Thomas C. Cochran, *Frontiers of Change: Early Industrialism in America* (1981); Alan Dawley, *Class and Community: The Industrial Revolution in Lynn* (1976); Thomas Dublin, *Women at Work: The Transformation of Work and Community in Lowell, Massachusetts, 1826–1860* (1979); Bruce Laurie, *Working People of Philadelphia, 1800–1850* (1980); Douglass North, *The Economic Growth of the United States, 1790–1860* (1961); Peter Temin, *The Jacksonian Economy* (1969); Barbara Tucker, *Samuel Slater and the Origins of the American Textile Industry, 1790–1860* (1984).

Rich and Poor

Leonard P. Curry, *The Free Black in Urban America, 1800–1850* (1981); Peter Knights, *The Plain People of Boston, 1830–1860* (1971); Raymond A. Mohl, *Poverty in New York, 1785–1825* (1971); Edward Pessen, *Riches, Class, and Power Before the Civil War* (1973); William J. Rorabaugh, *The Alcoholic Republic: An American Tradition* (1979); Stephan Thernstrom, *Poverty and Progress* (1964).

Professions

Daniel H. Calhoun, *Professional Lives in America: Structure and Aspiration, 1750–1850* (1965); Donald M. Scott, *From Office to Profession: The New England Ministry, 1750–1850* (1978); Richard Shryock, *Medical Licensing in America, 1650–1965* (1967).

Women and the Family

Nancy F. Cott, *The Bonds of Womanhood: 'Woman's Sphere' in New England, 1780–1835* (1977); Suzanne Lebsock, *The Free Women of Petersburg: Status and Culture in a Southern Town, 1784–1860* (1984); James C. Mohr, *Abortion in America: The Origins and Evolution of National Policy, 1800–1900* (1978); Glenda Riley, *Women and Indians on the Frontier, 1825–1915* (1984); Ellen K. Rothman, *Hands and Hearts: A History of Courtship in America* (1987); Mary Ryan, *Cradle of the Middle Class: The Family in Oneida County, New York, 1790–1865* (1981); Kathryn K. Sklar, *Catharine Beecher: A Study in American Domesticity* (1973); Gwendolyn Wright, *Building the Dream: A Social History of Housing in America* (1981).

CHAPTER 9

Politics, Religion, and Reform
in Antebellum America

In 1824 the Marquis de Lafayette, former major general in the Continental Army and a Revolutionary War hero, accepted the invitation of President James Monroe and Congress and revisited the United States. For thirteen months as "the Nation's Guest," Lafayette traveled to every state and received a welcome that fluctuated between warm and tumultuous. There seemed no limits to what Americans would do to show their admiration for this "greatest man in the world." "There were," a contemporary wrote, "*La Fayette* boots—*La Fayette* hats —*La Fayette* wine—and *La Fayette* everything." In New York City, some fervid patriots tried to unhitch the horses from Lafayette's carriage and pull it up Broadway themselves.

Lafayette had contributed mightily to the Revolution's success. Americans venerated him as a living embodiment of the entire Revolutionary generation fast passing from the scene. The majority of Americans alive in 1824 had been born since George Washington's death in 1799. John Adams and Thomas Jefferson survived, but they were along in years. Both would die on July 4, 1826, fifty years to the day since the signing of the Declaration of Independence. Seizing on Washington's remark that he loved Lafayette "as my own son," Americans toasted the Frenchman as a cherished member of the family of Revolutionary heroes. In Charleston the toast ran: "WASHINGTON, our Common Father—*you* his favorite *son*"; in New Jersey, "LA FAYETTE, a living monument of greatness, virtue, and faithfulness still exists—a second Washington is now among us."

The festive rituals surrounding Lafayette's visit symbolized Americans' conviction that they had remained true to their heritage of republican liberty. The embers of conflict between Federalists and Republicans that once had seemed to threaten the Republic's stability had cooled; the Era of Good Feelings still reigned over American politics in 1824. Yet even as Americans were turning Lafayette's visit into an affirmation of their ties to the Founders, those ties were fraying in the face of new challenges. Westward migration and growing economic individualism, the forces underlying these challenges, shaped politics mightily between 1824 and 1840. The impact of economic and social change shattered old assumptions and contributed to a vigorous new brand of politics.

This transformation led to the birth of a second American party system, in which two new parties, the Democrats and the Whigs, replaced the Republicans and the Federalists. More was at work here than a change of names. The new parties took advantage of the transportation revolution to spread their messages to the farthest corners of the nation and to arouse voters in all sections. The new parties' leaders were more effective than their predecessors at organizing grassroots support, more eager to make government responsive to the popular will, and more likely to enjoy politics and welcome conflict as a way to sustain interest in political issues.

Not all Americans looked to politics as the pathway to their goals. Some, in fact, viewed politics as suited only to scoundrels and could identify with the sentiments of the Detroit workingman who wrote in 1832 that he "did not vote. I'll [have] none of sin." Despairing of politics, many men and women became active in reform movements pursuing various goals, among them the abolition of slavery, the suppression of the liquor trade, improved public education, and equality for women. Strongly held religious beliefs impelled reformers into these causes, while simultaneously increasing their distrust of politics. Yet even reformers hostile to politics gradually found that the success of their reforms depended on their ability to influence the political process.

During the 1820s and 1830s, the political and reform agendas of Americans diverged increas-ingly from those of the Founders. The Founders had feared popular participation in politics, enjoyed their wine and rum, left an ambiguous legacy on slavery, and displayed only occasional interest in women's rights. Yet even as Americans shifted their political and social priorities, they continued to venerate the Founders, who in death meant even more than in life. Histories of the United States, biographies of Revolutionary patriots, and torch-light parades that bore portraits of Washington and Jefferson alongside those of Andrew Jackson all helped to reassure the men and women of the young nation that they were remaining loyal to their republican heritage.

The Transformation of American Politics, 1824–1832

In 1824 Andrew Jackson and Martin Van Buren, who would lead the Democratic party in the 1830s, and John Quincy Adams and Henry Clay, who would help to guide the rival National Republican (or Whig) party in the 1830s, all belonged to the same political party—the Republican party of Thomas Jefferson. Yet by 1824 the Republican party was coming apart at the seams under pressures generated by industrialization in New England, the spread of cotton cultivation in the South, and westward expansion. These forces sparked issues that would become the basis for the new political division between Democrats and Whigs. In general, those Republicans (augmented by a few former Federalists) who retained Jefferson's suspicion of a strong federal government and preference for states' rights became Democrats; those Republicans (along with many former Federalists) who believed that the national government should actively encourage economic development became Whigs.

Regardless of which path a politician chose, all leaders in the 1820s and 1830s had to adapt to the rising democratic idea of politics as a forum for the expression of the will of the common people rather than as an activity that gentlemen conducted for the people. Gentlemen could still gain election to office, but their success now depended less on their education or wealth than on their ability to identify and follow the will of the majority. Americans still looked up to their political leaders, but the leaders could no longer look down on the people.

Democratic Ferment

The process by which politics gradually became more democratic took several forms. In one state after another, the requirement, common in the eighteenth century, that voters own property was scaled down to a stipulation that voters merely pay poll taxes. Maryland, South Carolina, Massachusetts, Connecticut, and New York all liberalized their suffrage laws for white voters between the 1790s and 1821, and none of the eight new states admitted between 1796 and 1821 required voters to own property. Moreover, written ballots replaced the old custom of voting aloud (called *viva voce* or "stand up" voting), which had enabled social superiors to influence their inferiors at the polls. Many appointive offices became elective. In 1821, for example, New York abolished its five-member Council on Appointments, which had controlled the appointment of some fifteen thousand public officials, including every mayor in the state. While the electoral college remained in place, the practice of allowing state legislatures to choose presidential electors gave way to the selection of electors by popular vote. In 1800, rather than voting for Thomas Jefferson or John Adams, most Americans could do no more than vote for the men who would vote for the men who would vote for Jefferson or Adams. By 1824, however, legislatures chose electors in only six states, and by 1832 in only one (South Carolina).

Nothing did more to undermine the old barriers to the people's expression of their will than a fierce tug of war between the Republicans and the Federalists in the 1790s and early 1800s. Since party survival depended on the ability to win elections, political parties had to court voters. First the Republicans and then the Federalists learned to woo voters by staging grand barbecues at which men from Massachusetts to Maryland washed down free clams and oysters with free beer and whiskey. Wherever one party was in the minority, it sought to increase the number of eligible voters in order to turn itself into the majority party. In the South, where the Republicans were strong, they showed little interest in increasing the size of the electorate, but in the North they built a following by advocating expanded suffrage. Federalists played the same game when it suited their needs; the initiator of suffrage reform in Maryland, for example, was an aristocratic Federalist.

The democratization of politics developed at an uneven pace, however. As late as 1820, the Republican and Federalist parties continued to be organized from the top down. To nominate candidates, for example, both parties relied on the caucus, a meeting of party members in the legislature, rather than on popularly elected nominating conventions. Moreover, few party leaders rushed to embrace the *principle* of universal white manhood suffrage. Even the newly admitted western states tried at first to imitate the suffrage restrictions of the East and abandoned them only when

it became clear that in a region where nearly everyone's land title was in dispute, to require property ownership for voting merely invited fraud. Nor did the democratization of politics necessarily draw more voters to the polls. Waning competition between the Republicans and the Federalists between 1816 and 1824—the years spanning the Era of Good Feelings—deprived voters of clear choices and turned national politics into a boring spectacle.

Yet no one could mistake the tendency of the times: to oppose the people or democracy had become a formula for political suicide. The people, a Federalist moaned, "have become too saucy and are really beginning to fancy themselves equal to their betters." Whatever their convictions, politicians learned to adjust.

The Election of 1824

Partially submerged political tensions surfaced in the election of 1824 and inflicted sudden death on the Era of Good Feelings. Even before the election, President Monroe's Republican coalition was cracking under pressure from its rival sectional components. In 1824 five candidates, all Republicans, ended up vying for the presidency. John Quincy Adams emerged as New England's favorite. South Carolina's brilliant John C. Calhoun contended with Georgia's William Crawford, an old-school Jeffersonian, for southern support. Out of the West marched Henry Clay of Kentucky, ambitious, crafty, and confident that his American System of protective tariffs and federally supported internal improvements would endear him to the manufacturing regions of the East as well as to the New West.

Clay's belief that he was holding a solid block of western states was punctured by the rise of a fifth candidate, Andrew Jackson of Tennessee. At

The Election of 1824				
Candidates	Parties	Electoral Vote	Popular Vote	Percentage of Popular Vote
JOHN QUINCY ADAMS	Democratic-Republican	84	108,740	30.5
Andrew Jackson	Democratic-Republican	99	153,544	43.1
William H. Crawford	Democratic-Republican	41	46,618	13.1
Henry Clay	Democratic-Republican	37	47,136	13.2

first, none of the other candidates took Jackson seriously. But he was popular on the frontier and in the South and stunned his rivals by gaining the support of opponents of the American System from Pennsylvania and other northern states.

Although the Republican congressional caucus chose Crawford as the party's official candidate early in 1824, the caucus could no longer unify the party. Three-fourths of the Republicans in Congress had refused to attend the caucus. Crawford's already diminished prospects evaporated when he suffered a paralyzing stroke. Impressed by Jackson's support, Calhoun withdrew from the race and ran unopposed for the vice presidency. In the election, Jackson won more popular and electoral votes than any other candidate (Adams, Crawford, Clay) but failed to gain a majority, as required by the Constitution. Thus the election was thrown into the House of Representatives, whose members had to choose from the three top candidates—Jackson, Adams, and Crawford. Hoping to forge an alliance between the West and Northeast in a future bid for the presidency, Clay gave his support to Adams. Clay's action secured the presidency for Adams, but when Adams promptly appointed Clay his secretary of state, Jackson's supporters raged that a "corrupt bargain" had cheated Jackson of the presidency. Although there is no evidence that Adams had traded Clay's support for an explicit agreement to appoint Clay his secretary of state (an office from which Jefferson, Madison, Monroe, and Adams himself had risen to the presidency), the allegation of a corrupt bargain was widely believed. It formed a cloud that hung over Adams's presidency.

John Quincy Adams as President

Adams's appointment of Clay as his secretary of state was the first of several clumsy miscalculations that cloaked his presidency in controversy. Basically, Adams failed to understand the changing political climate. In his first annual message to Congress in December 1825, the president made a series of proposals that might have won acclaim in 1815 but that only antagonized interests that had grown more powerful and alert in the ensuing decade. He proposed, for example, a program of federal support for internal improvements, an idea that

John Quincy Adams

John Quincy Adams was the first president to pose for the camera. His expression here reveals his austere and determined personality.

had gained support from Republicans like Henry Clay, the architect of the American System, after the War of 1812. Between 1819 and 1825, however, opponents of the American System had multiplied. Strict Jeffersonians (often called Old Republicans), among them the Virginian John Randolph, had consistently attacked federal aid for internal improvements as unconstitutional, but they were no longer the mainstays of the opposition. Adams's call for federal support for improvements came within a few months of New York's completion of the Erie Canal. Because New York had built the canal with its own money, its senator, Martin Van Buren, opposed federal aid for internal improvements; such support would only enable other states to construct rival canals.

In addition, Adams infuriated southerners by proposing to send American delegates to a conference of newly independent Latin American nations in Panama. Southerners feared that U.S. attendance would imply recognition of Haiti, a black republic that had gained its independence from France through a slave revolution. Both the sharp debate over the Missouri Compromise in 1819–1820 and the discovery of a planned slave revolt in South Carolina in 1822 (organized by a free black, Denmark Vesey) had shaken southern slaveholders and generated hostility to Adams's proposal. If Adams had simply recognized that he was antagonizing important groups and responded by seeking new bases of support, he might have saved himself. But he clung to an increasingly obsolete notion of the president as a custodian of the public good who stayed aloof from factions and parties. Far from purging his political opponents, he appointed several to high office and thereby alienated even his friends. As late as 1829, he wrote blithely: "I have no wish to fortify myself by the support of any party whatever."

The Rise of Andrew Jackson

As Adams's popularity ebbed, Andrew Jackson's star rose. Jackson's victory over the British in the Battle of New Orleans in 1815 had given him a national reputation. The fact that he was a Tennessee slaveholder, a renowned Indian fighter, and a militant advocate of Indian removal endeared Jackson to the South. Where Adams tried to uphold treaties between the federal government and the Indians that gave the native Americans the option of staying in the East, Jackson urged that southerners be allowed a free hand in pushing the Indians westward. Southerners praised Jackson's stance as a noble application of the Jeffersonian principle of states' rights and recognized that it would satisfy their hunger for land. Furthermore, as the only presidential candidate in the election of 1824 with no connection to the Monroe administration, Jackson was in an ideal position to capitalize on what John C. Calhoun called "a vague but widespread discontent" in the wake of the Panic of 1819 that left people with "a general mass of disaffection to the Government" and "looking out anywhere for a leader."

While Adams moved sluggishly, Jackson's supporters swiftly established committees throughout the country. Two years before the election of 1828, towns and villages across the United States buzzed with furious but unfocused political activity. With the exception of the few remaining Federalists, almost everyone called himself a Republican. There were Republicans who were "Adams men," others who were "Jackson men," and still others who styled themselves "friends of Clay." Amid all the political confusion, few realized that a new political system was being born. The man most alert to the signs of the times was Martin Van Buren, who was to become vice president during Jackson's second term and president upon Jackson's retirement.

Van Buren exemplified a new breed of politician debuting on the national scene in the 1820s. A tavernkeeper's son, he had started his political career at the bottom, in county politics, and worked his way up to New York's governorship. In Albany he built a powerful political machine, the Albany Regency, composed mainly of men like himself from the lower and middling ranks. His archrival in New York politics, DeWitt Clinton, was all that Van Buren was not—tall, handsome, aristocratic, and brilliant. But Van Buren had a geniality that made ordinary people feel comfortable and an uncanny ability to sense in which direction the political winds were about to blow. Van Buren loved politics, which he viewed as a wonderful game; he was one of the first prominent American politicians to make personal friends from among his political enemies.

The election of 1824 convinced Van Buren of the need for renewed two-party competition. Without the discipline imposed by a strong opposition party, the Republicans in 1824 had splintered into sectional pieces. No candidate had secured an electoral majority, and the House of Representatives had decided the outcome amid charges of intrigue and corruption. It would be better, Van Buren concluded, to let all the shades of opinion in the nation be reduced to two. Then the parties would clash, and a clear popular winner would emerge. Jackson's strong showing in the election persuaded Van Buren that "Old Hickory" could lead a new political party. In the election of 1828, this party, which gradually became known as the Democratic party, put up Jackson for president and Calhoun for vice president. Its opponents, increasingly calling themselves the National Republicans, rallied behind Adams and his running mate, treasury secretary Richard Rush. Slowly but surely, the second American party system was taking shape.

The Election of 1828

The 1828 campaign was a vicious, mudslinging affair. The National Republicans attacked Jackson as a murderer (between duels and military executions, he was directly responsible for the deaths of several men), a drunken gambler, and an adulterer. The adultery charge caused Jackson the greatest pain. His wife, the beloved, ailing, and soon-to-die Rachel, had sought a divorce from her first husband, Lewis Robards. She had married Jackson believing that her divorce was complete, only to find that it was not. "Ought a convicted adulteress and her paramour husband," the Adams men taunted, "be placed in the highest office of this free and Christian land?" Jackson's supporters replied in kind. They accused Adams of wearing silk underwear, being rich, being in debt, and having gained favor with the czar of Russia by trying to provide him with a beautiful American prostitute.

Although both sides engaged in mudslinging, Jackson's men had better aim. Charges by Adams's supporters that Jackson was an illiterate backwoodsman only added to Jackson's popular appeal by making him seem just like an ordinary citizen. Jackson's supporters portrayed the clash as one between "the *democracy* of the *country*, on the one hand, and a *lordly purse-proud aristocracy* on the other." Jackson, they said, was the common man incarnate—his mind unclouded by learning, his morals simple and true, his will fierce and resolute. In contrast, Jackson's men represented Adams as an aristocrat, a dry scholar whose learning obscured the truth, a man who could write but not fight. Much of this, of course, was wild exaggeration. Jackson was a wealthy planter, not a simple backwoodsman. But it was the kind of exaggeration that people wanted to hear. Uncorrupt, natural, plain, Jackson was presented as the common man's image of his better self.

The election swept Jackson into office with more than twice the electoral vote of Adams. Yet the popular vote, much closer, made it clear that the people were not simply responding to the personalities or images of the candidates (though these dominated the campaign). The vote also reflected

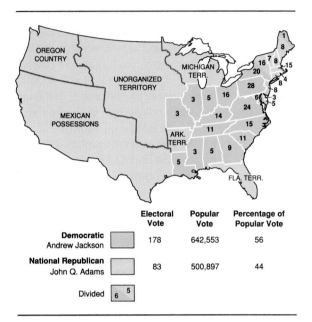

	Electoral Vote	Popular Vote	Percentage of Popular Vote
Democratic Andrew Jackson	178	642,553	56
National Republican John Q. Adams	83	500,897	44
Divided	6 5		

The Election of 1828

the strongly sectional bases of the new parties. The popular vote was close only in the middle states and the Northwest. Adams gained double Jackson's vote in New England; Jackson received double Adams's vote in the South, and nearly triple Adams's vote in the Southwest.

Jackson in Office

For all its fanfare, the campaign had revealed little about Jackson's stands on major issues. On such key questions as federal aid for internal improvements and the tariff, Jackson had sent out conflicting signals. In Tennessee he had aggressively pursued wealth and opposed legislation for the relief of debtors. Yet he understood the popular feelings that had carried him to the presidency and, once in office, played the role of defender of the people against the forces of privilege.

His first policy on coming to office was to openly support the principle of "rotation in office"—the removal of officeholders of the rival party—which critics called the spoils system. Jackson did not invent this policy: many of his predecessors had employed it. Nor did he pursue it with unusual thoroughness, for he removed only about one-fifth of the federal officeholders whom he inherited from Adams. But Jackson defended removal on new and democratic grounds. The duties of officeholders were so plain and simple, he argued, that any intelligent man could perform them. By moving civil servants into and out of office at will, Jackson hoped not only to give as many individuals as possible a chance to work for the government but also to prevent the emergence of an elite bureaucracy that operated beyond the will of the people.

Although Jackson's policy toward the civil service ruffled feathers, it did not produce deep sectional or ideological division. But the issues of federal support for internal improvements and protective tariffs ignited sectional controversy. The South had fewer canals and roads than other sections and, in 1830, fewer plans to build them. Its main cash crop, cotton, was nonperishable and could be transported by rivers and the ocean. Accordingly, southerners were cool toward spending federal money for internal improvements. Jackson, whose firmest political base was in the South, became convinced that federal support for internal improvements was a lavish giveaway program prone to corruption. He also believed that such funding violated the principle that Congress could appropriate money only for objectives shared by *all* Americans, such as national defense, not for the objectives of particular sections or interests. Accordingly, in 1830 Jackson vetoed a bill to provide federal support for a road in Kentucky between Maysville and Lexington.

Coupled with the almost simultaneous passage of the Indian Removal Act (see Chapter 8), the Maysville Road veto enhanced Jackson's popularity in the South. The tariff issue, however, sternly tested the South's allegiance to Jackson. In 1828, while John Quincy Adams was still in office, Jackson's supporters in Congress had contributed to the final passage of a bill that favored western agricultural interests by raising tariffs (import taxes) on imported hemp, wool, fur, flax, and liquor as well as New England manufacturing interests by raising the tariff on imported textiles. The South, which had few industries to protect from foreign competition, was left high and dry, for tariffs effectively raised the cost of manufactured goods for southerners. Jackson's followers had assumed that the support of the South could be taken for granted in the upcoming election and that embittered southerners would blame the Adams administration for this "Tariff of Abominations." In reality,

Jackson rather than Adams would bear the brunt of the South's ire over the tariff.

Nullification

The tariff of 1828 laid the basis for a rift between Jackson and his vice president, John C. Calhoun, that was to shake the foundations of the Republic. Early in his career, Calhoun had been an ardent nationalist. He had entered Congress in 1811 as a "war hawk," supported the protectionist tariff of 1816, and dismissed strict construction of the Constitution as refined philosophical nonsense. During the late 1820s, however, Calhoun changed course. Calhoun the nationalist gradually became Calhoun the states' rights sectionalist. The reasons for his shift were complex. He had supported the tariff of 1816 essentially as a measure conducive to national defense in the wake of the War of 1812. By encouraging infant industries, he had reasoned, the tariff would free the United States from dependence upon Britain and provide revenue for military preparedness. By 1826, however, few Americans perceived national defense as a priority. Further, the infant industries of 1816 had grown into troublesome adolescents that demanded higher and higher tariffs.

There was also the matter of Calhoun's fierce ambition. He longed to be president. Jackson had stated that he would serve only one term, and as vice president, Calhoun assumed that he would succeed Jackson. To do so, however, he had to maintain the support of his native South Carolina and of the South in general. As the center of cotton production shifted to the Southwest—Alabama and Mississippi—South Carolina's economy declined during the 1820s, and South Carolinians largely blamed protective tariffs. Tariffs not only drove up the price of manufactured goods but also threatened to reduce the sale of British textile products in the United States. Such a reduction might eventually lower the British demand for southern cotton and cut cotton prices. The more New England industrialized, the clearer it became that tariff laws were pieces of sectional legislation. New Englanders like Massachusetts's eloquent Daniel Webster swung toward protectionism; southerners responded with militant hostility.

Calhoun followed the Virginia and Kentucky resolutions of 1798–1799 in viewing the Union as a compact by which the states had conferred lim-

Andrew Jackson, *by Thomas Sully, 1845*

John C. Calhoun, *by Charles Bird King, c. 1825*

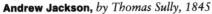

*Jackson, defeated in the presidential election of 1824, won handily four years later.
The magnetic Calhoun, Jackson's vice president, broke with Jackson over nullification and the Peggy Eaton affair and resigned the vice presidency in 1832.*

ited and specified powers on the federal government. While the Constitution did empower Congress to levy tariffs, Calhoun insisted that only tariffs
that raised revenue for such common purposes as
defense were constitutional. Set so high that it
deterred foreign exporters from shipping their
products to the United States, the tariff of 1828
could raise little revenue, and hence it failed to
meet Calhoun's criterion of constitutionality: that
federal laws benefit everyone *equally*. In 1828 Calhoun anonymously wrote the widely circulated
South Carolina Exposition and Protest, in which
he spelled out his argument that the tariff of 1828
was unconstitutional and that aggrieved states
therefore had the right to nullify, or override, the
law within their borders.

Vehement opposition to tariffs in the South,
and especially in South Carolina, rested on more
than economic considerations, however. Southerners feared that a federal government that passed
tariff laws favoring one section over another might
also pass laws meddling with slavery. Because Jackson himself was a slaveholder, the fear of federal
interference with slavery was perhaps farfetched.
But South Carolinians, long apprehensive of assaults

on their crucial institution of slavery, had many
reasons for concern. South Carolina was one of
only two states in which blacks composed a majority of the population in 1830. Moreover, in 1831
a bloody slave revolt led by Nat Turner boiled up
in Virginia. That same year, William Lloyd Garrison established *The Liberator,* an abolitionist
newspaper. These developments did not add up to
a real challenge to slavery. However, they were
enough to convince many troubled South Carolinians that a line had to be drawn against tariffs and
the possibility of future interference with slavery.

Jackson Versus Calhoun

Like Calhoun, Jackson was strong-willed and proud.
Unlike Calhoun, he was already president and the
leader of a national party that included supporters
in pro-tariff states like Pennsylvania (which had
gone for Jackson in the election of 1828). Thus to
retain key northern support while soothing the
South, Jackson devised two policies.

The first was the distribution of surplus federal revenue to the states. Tariff schedules kept some
goods out of the United States but let many others

in for a price. The price, in the form of duties on imports, became federal revenue. In these years before federal income taxes, tariffs were a major source of federal revenue. Jackson hoped that this revenue, fairly distributed among the states, would remove the taint of sectional injustice from the tariff and force the federal government to restrict its own expenditures. All of this was good Jeffersonianism. Second, Jackson hoped to ease tariffs down from the sky-high tariff of 1828.

Calhoun disliked the idea of distributing federal revenue to the states because he believed that such a policy could become an excuse to maintain tariffs forever. But he was loath to break openly with Jackson. Between 1828 and 1831, Calhoun muffled his protest, hoping that Jackson would lower the tariff and that he, Calhoun, would retain both Jackson's favor and his chances for the presidency. Congress did pass new, slightly reduced tariff rates in 1832, but these did not come close to satisfying South Carolinians.

Even before passage of the tariff of 1832, two issues that had nothing to do with tariffs ruptured personal relations between Calhoun and Jackson. In 1829 Jackson's secretary of war, John H. Eaton, married the daughter of a Washington tavern-keeper. By her own account, Peggy O'Neale Eaton was "frivolous, wayward, [and] passionate." Before the marriage Peggy had acquired the reputation of being too forward with the boarders in her father's tavern, one of whom had been Eaton. After the marriage she and Eaton were snubbed socially by Calhoun's wife and by his friends in the cabinet. Peggy's only supporters were Martin Van Buren, the secretary of state, and President Jackson himself, who never forgot how his own wife had been wounded by slander during the campaign of 1828. Jackson concluded that the entire Eaton affair was a plot inspired by Calhoun to discredit him and advance Calhoun's own presidential aspirations.

To make matters worse, in 1830 Jackson received convincing documentation of his suspicion that back in 1818, Calhoun, as secretary of war under President Monroe, had urged that Jackson be punished for his unauthorized raid into Spanish Florida. The revelation that Calhoun had tried to stab him in the back in 1818, combined with the snubbing of Peggy Eaton, convinced Jackson that he had to "destroy [Calhoun] regardless of what injury it might do me or my administration." A symbolic confrontation occurred between

Jackson and Calhoun at a Jefferson Day dinner in April 1830. Jackson proposed the toast: "Our Union: It must be preserved." Calhoun responded: "The Union next to Liberty the most dear. May we always remember that it can only be preserved by distributing equally the benefits and burdens of the Union."

The stage was now set for a direct clash between the president and his vice president over nullification. In 1831 Calhoun acknowledged his authorship of the *South Carolina Exposition and Protest*. In November 1832 a South Carolina convention nullified the tariffs of 1828 and 1832 and forbade the collection of customs duties within the state. Jackson reacted quickly. He despised nullification, calling it an "abominable doctrine" that would reduce the government to anarchy, and he loathed the South Carolina nullifiers as "unprincipled men who would rather rule in hell, than be subordinate in heaven." Jackson even began to send arms to loyal Unionists in South Carolina, and in December 1832 he issued a proclamation that while promising South Carolinians further tariff reductions, lambasted nullification as itself unconstitutional. The Constitution, he emphasized, had established "a single nation," not a league of states.

The crisis eased in March 1833 when Jackson signed into law two measures—"the olive branch and the sword," in the words of one historian. The olive branch was the tariff of 1833 (also called the Compromise Tariff), which provided for a gradual but significant lowering of duties between 1833 and 1842. The sword was the Force Bill, authorizing the president to use arms to collect customs duties in South Carolina.

Like most of the accommodations by which the Union lurched from one sectional crisis to the next before the Civil War, the Compromise of 1833 grew out of a mixture of partisanship and statesmanship. The moving spirit behind the Compromise Tariff was Kentucky's senator Henry Clay, who had long favored high tariffs. A combination of motives brought Clay and the nullifiers together in favor of tariff reduction. Clay feared that without concessions to South Carolina on tariffs, the Force Bill would produce civil war. Further, he was apprehensive that without compromise, the principle of protective tariffs would disappear under the wave of Jackson's immense popularity. In short, Clay would rather take responsibility for lowering tariffs than allow the initiative on tariff questions to pass to the Jacksonians. For their part, the nullifiers hated Jackson and defiantly toasted "Andrew Jackson: On the soil of South Carolina he received an humble birthplace. May he not find it in a traitor's grave!" While recognizing that South Carolina had failed to gain support for nullification from other southern states and that they would have to bow to pressure, the nullifiers preferred that Clay, not Jackson, be the hero of the hour. Accordingly, they supported Clay's Compromise Tariff and formally rescinded the nullification proclamation. Everywhere Americans now hailed Clay, once known as hotheaded and impetuous, as the Great Compromiser. Even Martin Van Buren frankly stated that Clay had "saved the country."

The Bank Veto

One reason why Jackson signed Clay's compromise tariff into law was that he did not have strong convictions about an alternative. Inclined to react passionately to most issues, Jackson was relatively flexible and open-minded on the subject of tariffs. In sharp contrast, as a result of some disastrous financial speculations early in his career, Jackson had come to office with a deep suspicion of all banks, all paper money, and all exclusive monopolies. On each count, the Bank of the United States was a likely target.

In 1816 the Second Bank of the United States had received a twenty-year charter from Congress. As a creditor of state banks, the Bank of the United States could contract the lending capacity of the state banks whenever it chose by demanding that they redeem in specie (gold or silver coinage) their bank notes that were held by the Bank of the United States. Because most banks emitted more notes than they could redeem in specie, the Bank of the United States exerted an often healthy restraint on excessive lending by state banks.

Many aspects of the Bank of the United States, however, made it controversial. As we have seen, its decision to contract credit had precipitated the Panic of 1819, for which it was widely blamed. Furthermore, at a time when privilege was coming under fire, the bank was undeniably a privileged institution. First, it was the official depository for federal revenue, a fact that greatly increased its capacity to lend money and that gave it a commanding position over all state banks. Second, while the federal government accorded it privileges not

available to any other bank, the Bank of the United States was only remotely under the federal government's control. The bank's stockholders were private citizens—a "few Monied Capitalists," in Jackson's words. Although chartered by Congress, the bank was located not in Washington but in Philadelphia. The federal government appointed a majority of the bank's directors but allowed them considerable independence.

No one better typified the bank's distance from the push and shove of politics than its president, Nicholas Biddle. A polished aristocrat, Biddle had once edited a literary magazine (after his marriage to an heiress freed him of the need to make money), and he continued to write poetry in his spare time. As bank president, he viewed himself as a public servant whose duty was to keep the bank above politics. Knowing nothing of Jackson's loathing of banks, Biddle had voted for Jackson in 1824 and 1828. Jackson would give Biddle many opportunities to repent these votes.

In his first annual message to Congress in 1829, Jackson questioned "both the constitutionality and expediency" of the Bank of the United States. Strongly influenced by Henry Clay, Biddle resolved to seek recharter of the bank in 1832, four years before its existing charter expired. With his eyes on the presidential election of 1832, Clay sensed that a pro-bank stand would boost his own chances in the election. Although Biddle and Clay secured congressional approval to recharter, Jackson promptly vetoed the recharter bill. He denounced the bank as a private and privileged monopoly that drained the West of specie, was immune to taxation by states (as Chief Justice Marshall had established in his 1819 *McCulloch* v. *Maryland* decision), gathered inordinate power into the hands of a few men, and made "the rich richer and the potent more powerful." Failing to persuade Congress to override Jackson's veto, Clay now pinned his hopes on gaining the presidency himself.

The Election of 1832

By 1832 Jackson's views on major issues were considerably clearer than in 1828. The Indian Removal Act, his vetoes of the Maysville Road Bill and the recharter of the Bank of the United States, his policy of distributing federal revenues, and his lowering of tariffs all marked him as a strong defender of states' rights. But at the same time, his vigorous

The Election of 1832

Candidates	Parties	Electoral Vote	Popular Vote	Percentage of Popular Vote
ANDREW JACKSON	Democratic	219	687,502	55.0
Henry Clay	National Republican	49	530,189	42.4
William Wirt	Anti-Masonic	7 }	33,108	2.6
John Floyd	National Republican	11 }		

response to nullification had established him as a staunch Unionist. States' rights and Unionism were compatible doctrines. While cherishing the Union, Jackson believed that the states were far too diverse to accept strong, purposeful direction from the federal government. The safest course was to allow the states considerable freedom, so that they would remain contentedly within the Union and reject dangerous doctrines like nullification.

Despite earlier statements to the contrary, Jackson ran again, selecting Martin Van Buren, now clearly the heir apparent, as his running mate to replace Calhoun, who had resigned. Against Jackson the National Republicans put up Henry Clay. Clay's platform was his American System of protective tariffs, national banking, and federal support for internal improvements. The election of 1832, the first in which national nominating conventions chose the candidates, was more issue-oriented than the vicious campaign of 1828. But Jackson continued to benefit from his great personal popularity. He carried 219 electoral votes to Clay's 49 and even took pro-bank and pro-tariff Pennsylvania. Clay's economic nationalism made him popular in pro-tariff New England. But Clay could not topple Jackson's stronghold in the South, while Jackson chalked up support in the North and West as well as the South. Secure in office for another four years, Jackson was ready to finish the job of dismantling the Bank of the United States.

The Bank Controversy and the Second Party System

Coming late in Andrew Jackson's first term, the veto of the bank's recharter had relatively little impact on the election of 1832. However, between 1833 and 1840, banking became an issue that ignited extraordinary popular passion. In no period of American history have issues relating to banking generated keener public interest than during these seven years. Jackson's veto of recharter unleashed a tiger that threatened to devour all banks.

Why did banking so raise people's temperature? Part of the answer lay in the fact that the U.S. government did not issue paper currency of its own; there were no "official" dollar bills as we know them today. Paper money took the form of notes (promises to redeem in specie) emitted by private banks. As a consequence, private bankers had enormous influence over economic transactions and could easily be viewed by ordinary people as sinister. In addition, a basic issue lurked behind most of the banking debates of the 1830s. What sort of society would the United States become? If paper money circulated in abundance, businessmen and farmers could readily obtain loans to open factories or buy more land. Such an economy would be speculative in the sense that it would raise expectations for profit while posing risks. A sudden slump in the prices of industrial or agricultural products would leave businessmen and farmers mired in debt. Furthermore, a speculative economy would not benefit everyone equally. Factory owners would reap profits, but their employees would have to perform poorly paid and often unhealthy work. Would the United States be a nation that embraced swift economic development, even at the price of allowing some to get rich quickly off investments while others languished? Or would it be a nation characterized by more modest growth in traditional molds, but one anchored by "honest" manual work and frugality?

Before the answer to any of these questions was clear, the banking issue dramatically transformed American politics. It contributed mightily to the emergence of opposition to the Democrats and to the steady expansion of popular interest in politics.

The War on the Bank

Once reelected, Jackson could have allowed the bank to die a natural death when its charter ran out in 1836. But viewing the bank not only as a monopoly but as a symbol of all the exclusive privileges that were robbing the nation of its republican ideals, Jackson and several of his rabid followers feared the bank as a kind of dragon that would grow new limbs even as old ones were cut off. As Frederick Robinson, a radical New York Jacksonian, put it: "Kill the great monster and the whole brood which are hatched and nourished over the land will fall an easy prey. But if we suffer it to escape with life, however wounded, maimed, and mutilated, it will soon recover its wonted strength, its whole power to injure us, and all hope of its destruction must be forever renounced." When Biddle, in anticipation of further moves against the bank by Jackson, began to call in the bank's loans and contract credit during the winter of 1832–1833, Jacksonians saw their darkest fears confirmed. The bank, Jackson assured Van Buren, "is trying to kill me, but I will kill it."

Rather than allow the bank to die naturally, Jackson embarked on a policy of removing federal deposits from the Bank of the United States and placing them in state banks. The policy was controversial even within the administration; Jackson dismissed two secretaries of the treasury before he finally found one, Maryland's Roger B. Taney, who would implement the policy.

Once in place, the policy of removing deposits only raised a new and even thornier issue. Those state banks that became the depositories for federal revenue could use that revenue as the basis for issuing more paper money and for extending more loans. In short, the removal policy enabled state banks to increase their lending capacity. But Jackson hated both paper money and a speculative economy in which capitalists routinely took out large loans. The policy of removal seemed a formula for producing exactly the kind of economy that Jackson wanted to abolish. Jackson recognized the danger and hoped to sharply limit the number of state banks that would become depos-

itories for federal revenue. But as state banks increasingly clamored for the revenue, the number of state-bank depositories soon multiplied beyond Jackson's expectations. There were twenty-three by the end of 1833. Critics dubbed them "pet banks" because they were usually selected for their loyalty to the Democratic party. During the next few years, fueled by paper money from the pet banks and by an influx of foreign specie to purchase cotton and for investment in canal projects, the economy entered a heady expansion. Jackson could not stem the tide. In 1836, pressured by Congress, he reluctantly signed into law the Deposit Act, which both increased the number of deposit banks and loosened federal control over them.

Jackson's policy of removing deposits deepened a split within his own Democratic party between advocates of soft money (paper) and those of hard money (gold or silver coinage, or specie). Both sides agreed that the Bank of the United States was evil, but for different reasons. Soft-money Democrats resented the bank's role in periodically contracting credit and restricting the lending activities of state banks; their hard-money counterparts disliked the bank because it sanctioned an economy based on paper money. Prior to the Panic of 1837, the soft-money position was more popular among Democrats outside of Jackson's inner circle of advisers than within that circle. For example, western Democrats had long viewed the Bank of the United States' branch in Cincinnati as inadequate to supply their need for credit and favored an expansion of banking activity.

Aside from Jackson and a few other figures within the administration, the most articulate support for hard money came from a faction of the Democratic party in New York called the Locofocos. The Locofocos grew out of various "workingmen's" parties that had sprouted during the late 1820s in northern cities and that called for free public education, the abolition of imprisonment for debt, and a ten-hour workday. Most of these parties had collapsed within a few years, but in New York the "workies" had gradually been absorbed by the Democratic party. Once in the party, the workingmen were hard to keep in line. Composed of a mixture of intellectuals and small artisans and journeymen threatened by economic change, they worried about inflation, preferred to be paid in specie, and distrusted banks and paper

Jackson Versus the Bank

Andrew Jackson, aided by Martin Van Buren (center), attacks the Bank of the United States, which, like the many-headed serpent Hydra of Greek mythology, keeps sprouting new heads. The largest head belongs to Nicholas Biddle, the Bank's president.

money. In 1835 a faction of workingmen had broken away from Tammany Hall, the main Democratic party organization in New York City, and held a dissident meeting in a hall whose candles were illuminated by a newfangled invention, the "loco foco," or match. Thereafter, these radical workingmen were known as Locofocos.

The Rise of Whig Opposition

During Jackson's second term, the opposition National Republican party changed its name to the Whig party. More important, the opposition began to broaden its base in both the South and the North. Jackson's magnetic personality had swept him to victory in 1828 and 1832. But as the profile of Jackson's administration became more sharply delineated—as Jackson's vague Jeffersonianism of 1829 gave way to hard-and-fast positions against the Bank of the United States, federal aid for internal improvements, protective tariffs, and nullification—the opposition drew into its fold increasing numbers alienated by Jackson's policies.

Jackson's crushing of nullification, for example, led some of its southern supporters into the Whig party, not because the Whigs favored nullification but because they opposed Jackson. Jackson's war on the Bank of the United States produced the same result. His policy of removing deposits from the bank pleased some southerners but dismayed others who had been satisfied with the bank and who did not share westerners' mania for even cheaper and easier credit. Jackson's opposition to federal aid for internal improvements also alienated some southerners who feared that the South would languish behind the North unless it began to push ahead with improvements. Because so much southern capital was tied up in slavery, pro-improvement southerners looked to the federal government for aid, and when they met with a cold shoulder, they drifted into the Whig party. None of this added up to an overturning of the Democratic party in the South; the South was still the Democrats' firmest base. But the Whigs were making significant inroads, particularly in southern market towns and among planters who had close ties to southern bankers and merchants.

Meanwhile, in the North, social reformers were infusing new vitality into the opposition to Jackson. These reformers wanted to improve American society by attacking the sale of liquor, opposing slavery, bettering public education, and elevating public morality. Most opponents of liquor (temperance reformers) and most public-school reformers gravitated to the Whigs. Whig philosophy was more compatible with the reformers' goals than Democratic ideals. Where Democrats maintained that the government should not impose a uniform standard of conduct on a diverse society, the Whigs' commitment to Clay's American System implied an acceptance of active intervention by the government to change society. Reformers wanted the government to play a positive role specifically by suppressing the liquor trade and by establishing centralized systems of public education. Thus a shared sympathy for active government programs tended to unite Whigs and reformers.

Reformers also indirectly stimulated new support for the Whigs from native-born Protestant workers. The reformers, themselves almost all Protestants, widely distrusted immigrants, especially the Irish, who viewed drinking as a normal recreation and who, as Catholics, suspected (correctly) that the public schools favored by reformers would teach Protestant doctrines. The rise of reform agitation and its frequent association with the Whigs drove the Irish into the arms of the Democrats but, by the same token, gained support for the Whigs from many native-born Protestant workers who were contemptuous of the Irish.

Of all the sources of Whig strength, none, however, was more remarkable than Anti-Masonry, a protest movement against the secrecy and exclusiveness of the Masonic lodges, which had long provided prominent men with fraternal fellowship and exotic ritual. The spark that set off the Anti-Masonic crusade was the abduction and disappearance in 1826 of William Morgan, a stonemason in Genesee County, New York, who had threatened to expose the secrets of the Masonic order. Every effort to solve the mystery of Morgan's disappearance ran into a stone wall because local sheriffs, judges, and jurors were themselves Masons seemingly bent on obstructing the investigation. Throughout the Northeast the public became increasingly aroused against the Masonic order, and rumors spread that Masonry was a powerful conspiracy of the rich to suppress popular liberty, a secret order of men who loathed Christianity, and an exclusive retreat for drunkards.

Beginning as a movement of moral protest in New York, Anti-Masons soon organized the Anti-Masonic party and scored remarkable successes, gaining temporary control of Vermont and Penn-

sylvania and holding the balance of power in New York and Massachusetts. As the political power of Anti-Masonry became evident, both parties courted it, the Whigs more successfully than the Democrats. The Whigs' ability to capitalize on Anti-Masonry partly reflected the fact that Anti-Masons displayed the same hatred for vice as the Whig reformers. Anti-Masons usually advocated temperance, and some attacked slavery. They insisted that membership in Masonic lodges, like the consumption of liquor, was sinful. A number of leading Whigs, among them Henry Clay, were themselves Masons, but they knew a good thing when they saw it; by 1834 the Whigs were rapidly absorbing Anti-Masonry. Anti-Masonry brought into the Whig party in the North a broadly based constituency that protested "aristocracy" with the same zeal as the Jacksonians did. In this way, Anti-Masonry helped to free the Whig party of the charge that it was merely a tool of the rich.

By 1836 the Whigs had become a national party with widespread appeal. In both the North and South, they attracted those with close ties to the market economy—commercial farmers, planters, merchants, and bankers. In the North they also gained support from reformers, evangelical clergymen (especially Presbyterians and Congregationalists), Anti-Masons, and manufacturers. In the South they appealed to some former nullificationists; Calhoun himself briefly became a Whig. Everywhere the Whigs assailed Jackson as an imperious dictator, "King Andrew I"; indeed, they had taken the name "Whigs" to associate their cause with that of the American patriots who had opposed King George III in 1776.

The Election of 1836

As the election of 1836 approached, the Whigs lacked only a national leader. Henry Clay came close, but he was scarred by many political battles and additionally could not shake his reputation as a man who spent his days at the gaming table and his nights in brothels. Unable to agree on a single candidate, the Whigs ran four sectional candidates: William Henry Harrison of Ohio in the Old Northwest, Hugh Lawson White of Tennessee and W. P. Mangum of North Carolina in the South, and Daniel Webster of Massachusetts in the East. The Whig strategy was to prevent Vice President

The Election of 1836				
Candidates	Parties	Electoral Vote	Popular Vote	Percentage of Popular Vote
MARTIN VAN BUREN	Democratic	170	765,483	50.9
William H. Harrison	Whig	73 ⎫		
Hugh L. White	Whig	26 ⎪		
Daniel Webster	Whig	14 ⎬	739,795	49.1
W. P. Mangum	Whig	11 ⎭		

Martin Van Buren, the Democratic candidate, from gaining the required majority of electoral votes. That would force the election into the House of Representatives, where the Whigs thought that they had a chance to win.

Van Buren, whose star in the Democratic party had risen as Calhoun's had fallen, captured 170 electoral votes to 124 for the four Whigs combined. The Whig strategy obviously had backfired, but there were signs of trouble ahead for the Democrats. In the South the Whigs ran virtually even in the popular vote and captured Georgia and Tennessee. Even in the southern states held by Van Buren, the Democratic proportion of the popular vote was much smaller than in 1832; in North Carolina, for example, it dropped from 70 percent to 53 percent.

The Panic of 1837

Jackson left office in March 1837 in a sunburst of glory. Hailed as "the greatest man of his age" and presented with innumerable children named after him, his return to his Nashville home became a triumphant procession. But the public's mood quickly became less festive, for no sooner was Van Buren in office than a severe depression began.

The years 1835 and 1836 had witnessed a speculative boom fed by Jackson's policy of removing federal deposits from the Bank of the United States and placing them in state banks. In 1830 there were 329 banks in the nation with a total capital of $110 million. By 1835 the number of banks had increased to 704, with a total capital of $231 million. The value of bank notes in circulation grew from $61 million in 1830 to $149 million in 1837. Commodity prices rose an average of 13 percent a year in 1835 and 1836. Land sales

skyrocketed. States made new commitments to build canals. In 1836, for example, Illinois began construction of the Illinois and Michigan Canal in order to link Lake Michigan with the Illinois and Mississippi rivers. Then in May 1837 prices began to tumble, and bank after bank suspended specie payments. After a short rally, the economy crashed again in 1839. The Bank of the United States, which had continued to operate as a state bank with a Pennsylvania charter, failed. Nicholas Biddle himself was charged with fraud and theft. Banks throughout the nation again suspended specie payments.

The ensuing depression was far more severe and prolonged than the economic downturn of 1819. Those lucky enough to find work saw their wage rates drop by roughly one-third between 1836 and 1842. In despair, many workers turned to the teachings of William Miller, a New England religious enthusiast whose reading of the Bible convinced him that the end of the world was imminent. Dressed in black coats and stovepipe hats, Miller's followers roamed urban sidewalks and rural villages in search of converts. Many Millerites sold their possessions and purchased white robes to ascend into heaven on October 22, 1843, the date on which Millerite leaders calculated the world would end. Ironically, by then the worst of the depression was over, but at its depths in the late 1830s and early 1840s, the economic slump fed the gloom that made poor people receptive to Miller's predictions. A New Yorker rich enough to afford a private joke confided to his diary that people everywhere were "out of kash, out of kredit, out of karacter and out of klothes."

The origins of the depression were both national and international. In July 1836 Jackson had issued a proclamation called the Specie Circular, which

Note of the "Humbug Glory Bank"

In the Panic of 1837, many notes from real banks were not worth much more than this funny money, adorned by an ass and a shady character.

provided that after August 15 only specie was to be accepted in payment for public lands. The Specie Circular was one of Jackson's final affirmations of his belief that paper money encouraged people to embark on speculative, get-rich-quick schemes, sapped "public virtue," and robbed "honest labour of its earnings to make knaves rich, powerful and dangerous." He hoped that the Specie Circular would reverse the damaging effects of the Deposit Act of 1836, which he had signed reluctantly. The Specie Circular took the wind out of the speculative boom by making banks hesitant to issue more of the paper money that was fueling the boom, because western farmers eager to buy public lands would now demand that banks immediately redeem their paper in specie. Although the Specie Circular chilled bankers' confidence, it was not the sole or even the major reason for the depression. There were international causes as well, most notably the fact that in 1836, Britain, in an effort to restrain the outflow of British investment, checked the flow of specie from its shores to the United States.

The Search for Solutions

Van Buren came to office with a well-deserved reputation as a crafty politician; contemporaries called him the "sly fox" and the "little magician." Now he had to act decisively, for the depression was causing misery not only for ordinary citizens but for the Democratic party as well. Railing against "Martin Van Ruin," the Whigs in 1838 swept the governorship and most of the legislative seats in Van Buren's own New York.

To regain the political initiative, the president called for the creation of an Independent Treasury. Instead of depositing its revenue in state banks, the federal government would keep the revenue itself and thereby withhold public money from the grasp of business corporations. Introduced in Congress in 1837, the Independent Treasury Bill finally passed in 1840. With a flourish, Van Buren signed it into law on July 4, 1840; his supporters hailed it as America's second Declaration of Independence.

The establishment of the Independent Treasury reflected the basic Jacksonian suspicion of an alliance between the federal government and banking. From the moment that it was introduced, the Independent Treasury Bill promised not only to give the Democrats a clear national issue around which to rally but to get the federal government out of the banking business. But the Independent Treasury proposal failed to address the banking issue on the state level. Jackson's dismemberment of the Bank of the United States had not slowed the establishment of state banks, whose number by 1840 had grown to over nine hundred. While holding charters from state governments, these banks were privately controlled institutions whose loans to businessmen and farmers fueled the kind of speculative economy that Jacksonians feared.

Whigs and Democrats differed sharply in their approach to the multiplication of state banks. Eager to encourage economic development, Whigs in New York and elsewhere introduced the idea of "free banking." Free banking allowed any group to start a bank as long as its members met general state requirements. In the eyes of Whigs, Jackson's Specie Circular, not banks themselves, had caused the depression. In contrast, Democrats took a different view of both the causes of the depression and the value of state banks. Disillusioned by the collapse of the speculative boom of 1835–1836, a growing number of Democrats blamed the depression on banks and paper money and adopted the hard-money stance long favored by Jackson and his advisers. In Louisiana and Arkansas, Democrats successfully prohibited banks altogether. Elsewhere, Democrats imposed severe legislative restrictions on banks—for example, by banning the emission of paper money in small denominations. In sum, after 1837 the Democrats became an anti-bank, hard-money party.

The Election of 1840

Despite the depression, Van Buren gained his party's renomination. Avoiding their mistake of 1836, the Whigs settled on a single candidate, Ohio's William Henry Harrison, and ran former Virginia senator John Tyler as vice president. A relatively minor force in the Whig party, Harrison was sixty-seven years old and barely eking out a living on a farm. The Whigs picked him because he had few enemies. Early in the campaign, the Democrats made a fatal mistake by ridiculing Harrison as "Old Granny," a man who desired only to spend his declining years in a log cabin sipping cider. Without knowing it, the Democrats had handed the

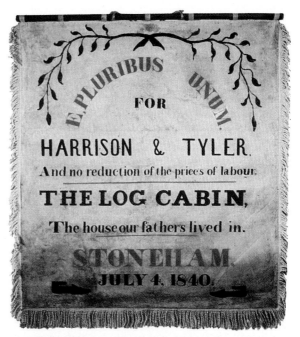

Harrison and Tyler Log Cabin Banner

By July 1840 few Americans needed to be reminded that "the house our fathers lived in" was a log cabin, the Whig campaign symbol.

Whigs the most famous campaign symbol in American history. The Whigs immediately reminded the public that Harrison had been a rugged frontiersman, the hero of the Battle of Tippecanoe, and a defender of all frontier people who lived in log cabins.

Refusing to publish a platform, the Whigs ran a "hurrah" campaign. They used log cabins for headquarters, sang log-cabin songs, gave out log-cabin cider, and called their newspaper the *Log Cabin.* For a slogan, they trumpeted "Tippecanoe and Tyler too." When not celebrating log cabins, they attacked Van Buren as a soft aristocrat who lived in "regal splendor." While Harrison was content to drink hard cider from a plain mug, the Whigs observed, Van Buren had turned the White House into a palace fit for an oriental despot and drank fine wines from silver goblets while he watched people go hungry in the streets.

The election results gave Harrison a clear victory. Van Buren carried only seven states and failed even to hold his own New York. The depression would have made it difficult, if not impossible, for any Democrat to have triumphed in 1840, but Van

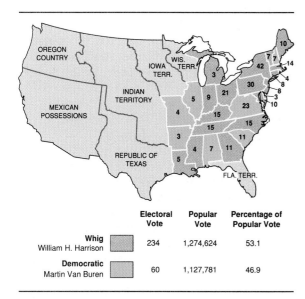

	Electoral Vote	Popular Vote	Percentage of Popular Vote
Whig William H. Harrison	234	1,274,624	53.1
Democratic Martin Van Buren	60	1,127,781	46.9

The Election of 1840

Buren had other disabilities besides the economic collapse. Unlike Harrison and Jackson, he had no halo of military glory. Moreover, Van Buren ran a surprisingly sluggish campaign. Prior to 1840 the Whigs had been slower than the Democrats to mobilize voters by new techniques. But in 1840 it was Van Buren who directed his campaign the old-fashioned way by writing encouraging letters to key supporters, while Harrison broke with tradition and went about the country (often on railroads) campaigning. Ironically, Van Buren, the master politician, was beaten at his own game.

The Second Party System Matures

In losing the presidency in 1840, Van Buren actually received 400,000 more popular votes than any previous presidential candidate. The total number of votes cast in presidential elections had risen from 1.2 million in 1828 to 1.5 million in 1836 to 2.4 million in 1840. The leap in the size of the popular vote between 1836 and 1840, 60 percent, is the greatest proportionate jump between consecutive elections in American history. Neither lower suffrage requirements nor population growth was the main cause of this change. Rather, the spurt in the popular vote resulted from a jump in the percentage of eligible voters who *chose* to vote. In the three elections before 1840, the proportion of white males who voted had fluctuated between 55 percent and 58 percent; in 1840 it rose to 80 percent.

Both the depression and the frenzy of the log-cabin campaign had jolted previously indifferent voters to go to the polls. Yet voter turnouts stayed up even after prosperity returned in the 1840s. The second party system, which had been developing slowly since 1828, reached a high plateau in 1840 and remained there for more than a decade. What gave politicians their appeal in the eyes of ordinary people were not only their rousing campaign techniques but also the strong contrasts and simple choices that they could present. The gradual hardening of the line between the two parties stimulated enduring popular interest in politics.

No less than the tariff and banking, reform also aroused partisan passions by 1840. Yet many of the seeds of the reform movements that burst upon the national scene in the 1830s were initially sown in the field of religion rather than politics.

The Rise of Popular Religion

In *Democracy in America,* Alexis de Tocqueville pointed out an important difference between France and the United States. "In France I had almost always seen the spirit of religion and the spirit of freedom pursuing courses diametrically opposed to each other; but in America I found that they were intimately united, and that they reigned in common over the same country." From this assertion Tocqueville drew a startling conclusion: religion was "the foremost of the political institutions" of the United States.

In calling religion a political institution, Tocqueville did not mean that Americans gave special political privileges to any particular denomination. Rather, he was referring to the way in which religious impulses reinforced American democracy and liberty. Just as Americans demanded that politics be made accessible to the average person, they insisted that ministers preach doctrines that appealed to ordinary people. The most successful ministers were those who used plain words to move the heart, not those who tried to dazzle their listeners with theological complexities. Increasingly, too, Americans demanded theological doctrines that put individuals in charge of their own religious destiny. They thrust aside the Calvinist doctrine that God had arbitrarily selected some people for salvation and others for damnation and substituted the belief that anyone could attain heaven.

Thus heaven as well as politics became democratized in these years. This harmony between religious and democratic impulses owed much to a series of religious revivals known as the Second Great Awakening.

The Second Great Awakening

The Second Great Awakening had begun in Connecticut during the 1790s and set ablaze one section of the nation after another during the following half-century. At first, educated Congregationalists and Presbyterians such as Yale University's president Timothy Dwight had dominated the revivals. But as they moved from Connecticut to frontier states like Tennessee and Kentucky, the

Methodist Camp Meeting *Frontier revivals occurred outdoors, lasted for days, and attracted an abundance of women and children as well as men.*

revivals had undergone striking changes that were typified by the rise of camp meetings. Camp meetings were gigantic revivals in which members of several denominations gathered together in sprawling open-air camps for up to a week to hear revivalists proclaim that the Second Coming of Jesus was near and that the time for repentance was now. The most famous camp meeting had occurred at Cane Ridge, Kentucky, in August 1801, when a huge crowd had come together on a hillside to listen to thunderous sermons and to sing hymns and experience the influx of divine grace. One eyewitness vividly described the meeting:

At night, the whole scene was awfully sublime. The ranges of tents, the fires, reflecting light amidst the branches of the towering trees; the candles and lamps illuminating the encampment; hundreds moving to and fro, with lights or torches, like Gideon's army; the preaching, praying, singing, and shouting, all heard at once, rushing from different parts of the ground, like the sound of many waters, was enough to swallow up all the powers of contemplation.

The Cane Ridge revival had been an episode of the larger Great Kentucky Revival of 1800–1801.

Among the distinguishing features of these frontier revivals was the appearance of "exercises" in which men and women rolled around like logs, jerked their heads furiously (a phenomenon known simply as the jerks), and grunted like animals (the "barking exercise"). Observing the apparent pandemonium that had broken loose, critics had blasted the frontier frenzy for encouraging fleshly lust more than spirituality and complained that in revivals, "more souls were begot than saved." In fact, the early frontier revivals had challenged traditional religious customs. The most successful frontier revivalist preachers were not educated men but ordinary farmers and artisans who had experienced powerful religious conversions and who had contempt for learned ministers with their dry expositions of doctrine.

No religious denomination had been more successful on the frontier than the Methodists. With fewer than seventy thousand members in 1800, the Methodists had by 1844 become America's largest Protestant denomination, claiming a little over a million members. In contrast to New England Congregationalists and Presbyterians, Methodists emphasized that religion was primarily a matter of the heart rather than the head. Too, the frontier

Methodists disdained a "settled" ministry—that is, ministers tied to fixed parishes. Instead, they preferred itinerant circuit riders—young, unmarried men—who moved on horseback from place to place and preached in houses, open fields, or wherever else listeners gathered.

Although the frontier revivals disrupted religious custom, they also worked to promote law, order, and a sense of morality on the frontier. For all the jerks, rolls, and barks that they produced, they ultimately advanced values such as sobriety, hostility to dueling, and an abhorrence of the violence so common in frontier living. Drunken rowdies who tried to invade camp meetings met their match in brawny itinerants like the Methodist Peter Cartwright. It was not only in camp meetings that Cartwright and his peers sought to raise the moral standard of the frontier. The basic unit of Methodist discipline on the frontier was the "class." When revivals broke up, the converted formed these tiny groups of twelve or so members who met weekly to provide mutual encouragement of both religion and morality. In these class meetings, Methodists chastised each other for drunkenness, fighting, fornication, gossiping, and even sharp business practices.

Eastern Revivals

By the 1820s the center of the Second Great Awakening was shifting from the frontier back to the East. The revival fires glowed with peculiar intensity in an area of western New York that became known as the Burned-Over District. Although not a frontier area in the 1820s, western New York was filled with transplanted New Englanders whose ancestors had experienced the Great Awakening in the eighteenth century and who hungered for their own religious experiences. After the completion of the Erie Canal, the region was also a magnet for winners and losers in the restless pursuit of wealth. In sum, it was a fertile field of high expectations and bitter discontent.

The man who harnessed these anxieties to religion was Charles G. Finney. Finney began his career as a lawyer, but after a religious conversion in 1821, which he described as a "retainer from the Lord Jesus Christ to plead his cause," he became a Presbyterian minister and conducted revivals in towns along the canal like Rome and Utica. While he also found time for trips to New York and Boston, his greatest "harvest" came in the thriving canal city of Rochester in 1830–1831.

The Rochester revival had several features that justify Finney's reputation as the "father of modern revivalism." First, it was a citywide revival in which all denominations participated. Finney was a pioneer of cooperation among Protestant denominations. In addition, in Rochester and elsewhere, Finney introduced devices for speeding conversions. Among these were the "anxious seat," a bench to which those ready for conversion were led so that they could be made objects of special prayer, and the "protracted meeting," which went on nightly for up to a week. Finney's emphasis on revival techniques sharply distinguished him from eighteenth-century revivalists, including Jonathan Edwards. Where Edwards had portrayed revivals as the miraculous work of God, Finney made them out to be human creations. The divine spirit flowed in revivals, but humans made them happen. Finally, although a Presbyterian, Finney flatly rejected the Calvinist belief that humans had a natural and nearly irresistible inclination to sin (the doctrine of "human depravity"). Rather, he affirmed, sin was purely a voluntary act; no one *had* to sin. Men and women could will themselves out of sin just as readily as they had willed themselves into it. Indeed, he declared, it was theoretically possible for men and women to will themselves free of all sin — to live perfectly. Those who heard Finney and similar revivalists came away convinced that they had experienced the washing away of all past guilt and the beginning of a new life. "I have been born again," a young convert wrote. "I am three days old when I write this letter."

The assertions that people could live without sin ("perfectionism") and that revivals were human contrivances made Finney a controversial figure. Yet his ideas came to dominate "evangelical" Protestantism, forms of Protestantism that focused on the need for an emotional religious conversion. He was successful because he told people what they wanted to hear: that their destinies were in their own hands. A society that celebrated the "self-made" individual found plausible Finney's assertion that even in religion, people could make of themselves what they chose. Moreover, compared to most frontier revivalists, Finney had an unusually dignified style. Taken together, these factors gave him a potent appeal to merchants, lawyers, and small manufacturers in the towns and cities of the North. Finally, more than most revivalists, Finney recognized that without the mass participation of women, few revivals would have gotten off the ground. During the Second Great Awakening, female converts outnumbered male converts by about two to one. Finney encouraged women to give public testimonials of their religious experiences in church, and he often converted husbands by first converting their wives and daughters. After a visit by Finney, Melania Smith, the wife of a Rochester physician who had little time for religion, greeted her husband with a reminder of "the woe which is denounced against the families which call not on the Name of the Lord." Soon Dr. Smith heeded his wife's pleading and joined one of Rochester's Presbyterian churches.

Critics of Revivals: The Unitarians

Whereas some praised revivals for saving souls, others doubted that they produced permanent changes in behavior and condemned them for encouraging "such extravagant and incoherent expressions, and such enthusiastic fervor, as puts common sense and modesty to the blush."

One small but influential group of revival critics was the Unitarians. The basic doctrine of Unitarianism—that Jesus was not divine but merely an exemplary human being—had gained quiet acceptance among religious liberals during the eighteenth century. However, it was not until the early nineteenth century that Unitarianism emerged as a formal denomination with its own churches, ministry, and national organization. In New England in these years, hundreds of Congregational churches were torn apart by the withdrawal of socially prominent families who had embraced Unitarianism and by legal battles over which group—Congregationalists or Unitarians—could occupy church property. Although Unitarians won relatively few converts outside New England, their tendency to attract the wealthy and educated gave them influence beyond their numbers.

Unitarians criticized revivals as uncouth emotional exhibitions and argued that moral goodness should be cultivated by a gradual process of "character building," in which the individual learned to model his or her behavior on that of Jesus rather

than by a sudden emotional conversion as in a revival. Yet Unitarians and revivalists shared the belief that human behavior could be changed for the better. Both rejected the Calvinist emphasis on innate human wickedness. William Ellery Channing, a Unitarian leader, claimed that Christianity had but one purpose: "the perfection of human nature, the elevation of men into nobler beings."

The Rise of Mormonism

The Unitarians' assertion that Jesus Christ was human rather than divine challenged a basic doctrine of orthodox Christianity. Yet Unitarianism proved far less controversial than another of the new denominations of the 1820s and 1830s, the Church of Jesus Christ of Latter-day Saints, or Mormons. Its founder, Joseph Smith, grew to manhood in one of those families that seemed in constant motion to and fro but never up. After moving his family nearly twenty times in ten years, Smith's ne'er-do-well father settled in Palmyra, New York, in the heart of the Burned-Over District. As a boy, Smith's imagination teemed with plans to find buried treasure, while his religious views were convulsed by the conflicting claims of the denominations that thrived in the region. "Some were contending for the Methodist faith, some for the Presbyterian, and some for the Baptists," Smith later wrote. He wondered who was right and who wrong, or whether they were "all wrong together."

The sort of perplexity that Smith experienced was widespread in the Burned-Over District, but his resolution of the confusion was unique. Smith claimed that an angel led him to a buried book of revelation and to magic stones for use in translating it. He completed his translation of this Book of Mormon in 1827. The Book of Mormon tells the story of an ancient Hebrew prophet, Lehi, whose descendants came to America and created a prosperous civilization that looked forward to the appearance of Jesus as its savior. Jesus had actually appeared and performed miracles in the New World, the book claimed, but the American descendants of Lehi had departed from the Lord's ways and quarreled among themselves. God had cursed some with dark skin; these were the American Indians, who, when later discovered by Columbus, had forgotten their history.

Despite his astonishing claims, Smith quickly

gathered followers. The appeal of Mormonism lay partly in its positioning of America at the center of Christian history and partly in Smith's assertion that he had discovered a new revelation. The idea of an additional revelation beyond the Bible appeared to some to resolve the turmoil created by the Protestant denominations' inability to agree on what the Bible said or meant.

Smith and his followers steadily moved west from New York to Ohio and Missouri and then to Illinois, where they built a model city, Nauvoo, and a magnificent temple supported by thirty huge pillars. By moving west, the Mormons hoped to draw closer to the Indians, whose conversion was one of their goals, and to escape persecution. Smith's claim to have received a new revelation virtually guaranteed a hostile reception for the Mormons wherever they went, because Smith had undermined the authority of the Bible, one of the two documents (the other being the Constitution) upon which the ideals of the American republic rested.

Smith added fuel to the fire when he reported in 1843 that he had received still another revelation, this one sanctioning the Mormon practice of having multiple wives, or polygyny. Although Smith did not publicly proclaim polygyny as a doctrine, its practice among Mormons was a poorly kept secret. Smith's self-image also intensified the controversy that boiled around Mormonism. Refusing to view himself as merely the founder of another denomination, he saw himself as a prophet, the "Second Mohammed," and believed that Mormonism would be to Christianity what Christianity had been to Judaism: a grand, all-encompassing, and higher form of religion. He himself was the "King of the Kingdom of God." In 1844 he announced his candidacy for the presidency of the United States. But the state of Illinois was already moving against him. Charged with treason, he was jailed in Carthage, Illinois, and along with his brother, murdered there by a mob in June 1844.

Despite persecution, the Mormons won converts, not only in the United States but in the teeming slums of English factory cities from which Mormon agents brought thousands to America. In the thirty years after 1840, the number of Mormons grew from six thousand to two hundred thousand. After Smith's death a new leader, Brigham Young, led the main body of Mormons from Nauvoo to the Great Salt Lake Valley in Utah, which

Handcart Pioneers

The painter of these pioneer Mormons trekking to Utah, Carl Christian Anton Christensen, was attracted to Mormonism by missionaries in his native Denmark. Christensen immigrated to America in 1857 and with his bride walked thirteen hundred miles from Iowa City to Utah, pulling his possessions in a crude, two-wheeled handcart.

then was still under the control of Mexico. There Mormons established an independent republic, the state of Deseret. A thousand miles from Illinois, they prospered. Their isolation, combined with the firm control of Young, the "Old Boss," kept the rank and file in line. Polygyny, which Young officially proclaimed as a church doctrine, did not produce the hoped-for increase in Mormon numbers, but it did guarantee that Mormons would remain a people apart from the mainstream of American society. Above all, the Mormons were industrious and deeply committed to the welfare of other Mormons. Cooperation among Mormons took several forms, not the least of which was the practice of devoting each Mormon's "surplus" production to public projects like irrigation. Mormons transformed the valley into a rich oasis. When Utah came under American control after the Mexican War, they dominated its government.

Although Mormonism is one of the few religions to have originated in the United States, the antebellum Mormons pushed against the currents of American religion and society. They rejected the Bible as the sole source of revelation, substituted polygyny for monogamy, and elevated economic cooperation above competitiveness. Mormonism appealed to the downtrodden and insecure rather than to the prosperous and secure. It offered the downcast an explicit alternative to dominant religious and social practices. In this respect, Mormonism mirrored the efforts of several religious communal societies whose members resolutely set themselves apart from society. In general, these religious communitarians were less numerous, controversial, and long-lasting than the Mormons, but one group among them, the Shakers, has continued to fascinate Americans.

The Shakers

The leader of the Shakers (who derived their name from a convulsive religious dance that was part of their ceremony) was Mother Ann Lee, the illiterate daughter of an English blacksmith. Lee had set sail for America in 1774, and her followers soon organized a tightly knit community in New Lebanon, New York. In this and in other communities, the Shakers proved themselves able craftsmen. Shaker furniture became a byword for its beauty and strength. But for all their achievements as craftsmen, the Shakers were fundamentally otherworldly and hostile to materialism. Lee insisted that her followers abstain from sexual intercourse, believed that the end of the world was imminent, and derived many of her doctrines from trances and heavenly visions that she claimed to have. Among these doctrines was her conviction that at the Second Coming, Jesus would take the form of a woman, herself.

Her teachings about the evils of sexual relations would quickly have doomed the Shakers to extinction had it not been for the spread of religious revivalism in 1790. Turning up at Cane Ridge and other revival sites, Shaker missionaries made off with converts whom the revivals had loosened

**Shakers,
New Lebanon, New York**   *Opposed to marriage, Shakers could increase their numbers only by gaining converts. After the Civil War, they failed in this mission. When this photograph was taken, about 1872, there were just over two thousand Shakers in the United States.*

from their traditional religious moorings. At their peak during the second quarter of the nineteenth century, the Shakers numbered about six thousand in eight states.

Shakers and Mormons chose to live apart from society. But the message of most evangelical Protestants, including Charles G. Finney, was that religion and economic individualism—a person's pursuit of wealth—were compatible. Most revivalists told people that getting ahead in the world was acceptable as long as they were honest, temperate, and bound by the dictates of their consciences. By encouraging assimilation into rather than retreat from society, evangelicalism provided a powerful stimulus to the manifold reform movements of the 1820s and 1830s.

The Age of Reform

Despite rising popular interest in politics between 1824 and 1840, large numbers of people were excluded from politics. Women were not allowed to vote, and blacks generally suffered rather than benefited from the gradual liberalization of voting requirements. By 1860 most northern states denied free people of color the right to vote. Too, the political parties did not welcome the intrusion of controversial issues like slavery, nor did they show much interest in women's rights.

During the 1820s and 1830s, unprecedented numbers of men and women overcame the limits of political parties by joining organizations that aimed to improve society. Some sought to abolish slavery; others, to elevate the position of women, to suppress liquor, or to improve the treatment of criminals and the insane. Many worked for the betterment of public education, and a resourceful minority attempted to establish utopian communities in which individuals could live harmoniously apart from society in idyllic settings. At times, the reformers cooperated with politicians, and when they did, it was usually with Whigs rather than Democrats. But the reformers' primary allegiance was to their own causes rather than to political parties. Indeed, politics struck most reformers as a sorry spectacle that allowed a man like Andrew Jackson, a duelist who married a divorcée, to become

president and that routinely rewarded persons who would sacrifice any principle for victory at the polls.

Reformers were energized by the moral exhilaration that came from believing that they were on God's side of any issue. Religious revivalism contributed to their intense moralism. Virtually all prominent temperance reformers of the 1820s and 1830s, for example, had been inspired initially by revivals. Religious conversions also propelled some men and women into abolition. However, revivalism and reform were not always so intimately linked. Prominent school reformers were frequently religious liberals either hostile or indifferent to revivals, and similarly a disproportionate number of early women's rights advocates were either Unitarians or Quakers. And while some abolitionists owed their first flush of idealism to revivals, others did not, and almost all came to criticize the Protestant churches for condoning slavery. Yet even those reformers opposed to revivalism borrowed the evangelical preachers' language and psychology by looking upon drunkenness, ignorance, and inequality as sins that called for immediate repentance and change.

Historians have advanced conflicting interpretations of antebellum reformers. Some see reformers as noble and tireless crusaders for a better society; others portray them as unbalanced fanatics who would hammer all people into a single, arbitrary standard of righteousness. Both sides have a point. Reformers were usually high-minded men and women who gained neither wealth nor security from their commitment to causes. Yet reform did have a dark side. Reformers did not hesitate to coerce people into righteousness. They pushed for legal prohibition of liquor and for compulsory education. For criminals they designed penitentiaries on highly repressive principles. In retrospect, their priorities were often misplaced. Assailing intemperance with fury, they paid less attention to the slums and working conditions that stimulated drinking. Reform enlisted far more advocates of temperance than of women's rights, and more supporters of public-school reform than of the abolition of slavery.

Although the reform movements appealed to those excluded from or repelled by politics, most lacked the political parties' national organizations. The primary center of reform was New England and those areas of New York and the

Midwest settled by New Englanders. Southerners actively suppressed abolition, displayed only mild interest in temperance and education reform, ignored women's rights, and looked upon utopian communities as signs of the mental instability of northern reformers.

The War on Liquor

Agitation for temperance (either total abstinence from alcoholic beverages or moderation in their use) intensified during the second quarter of the nineteenth century. Temperance reformers addressed a growing problem: per capita consumption of alcohol had risen steadily between 1800 and 1830. With some justification, reformers saw alcoholic excess as a male indulgence whose bitter consequences (spending wages on liquor instead of food) were suffered by women and children. Not surprisingly, temperance was a banner behind which millions of women were to march during the nineteenth century.

There had been agitation against intemperance before 1825, but that year the Connecticut revivalist Lyman Beecher ushered in a new phase when, in six widely acclaimed lectures, he thundered against all use of alcohol. A year later, evan-

gelical Protestants created the American Temperance Society, the first national temperance organization. By 1834 some five thousand state and local temperance societies were loosely affiliated with the American Temperance Society. Where previous temperance supporters had advised moderation in the use of spirits, the American Temperance Society followed Beecher in demanding total abstinence. The society flooded the country with tracts denouncing the "amazing evil" of strong drink and urged churches to expel any members who condoned alcohol.

Among the main targets of the evangelical temperance reformers were moderate drinkers among the laboring classes. In the small shops where a handful of journeymen and apprentices worked informally, passing the jug every few hours was a time-honored way to relieve fatigue and monotony. But with the rise of large factories, new demands arose for a disciplined work force. Factory owners with precise production schedules to meet needed orderly and steady workers. Thus evangelical temperance reformers quickly gained manufacturers' support. In East Dudley, Massachusetts, for example, three factory owners refused to sell liquor in factory stores, calculating that any profits from the sale would be more than offset by

Politicians in a Country Bar, *by James Clooney, 1844*

The temperance movement did not deter politicians from soliciting voters in a likely place.

Rochester, New York, in the 1820s and 1830s

When Captain Oliver H. Perry defeated the British at the Battle of Lake Erie (1813), he did an unsought favor for a tiny settlement started by Colonel Nathaniel Rochester in western New York. Perry's victory, while giving the Americans control of Lake Erie, reminded them of their inability to control Lake Ontario. The original plans for a waterway across New York had projected a route from Albany on the Hudson River to Oswego on Lake Ontario. But since the Lake Ontario border with Canada remained insecure, canal planners shifted to a southerly and much longer route, from Albany to Lake Erie, that passed through Rochester. Situated at the falls of the Genesee River, with abundant water power for flour mills, Rochester was already producing 26,000 barrels of flour a year in 1818. The completion of the Erie Canal in 1825 transformed Rochester from a small milling center into America's first inland boom town (see Chapter 8). In 1828 Rochester exported 200,000 barrels of flour. Its population leaped from 1,500 in 1820 to more than 12,000 by 1834.

During the 1820s Rochester experienced growing social fragmentation. Increasingly, a spirit of acquisitiveness took root in the town. In past days master artisans had boarded and supervised a few journeymen in their own homes and exclusively served local customers. Now the master craftsmen traveled through the countryside in search of more business. To fill the additional orders from distant buyers, they subdivided the tasks of making shoes and other commodities and gradually replaced the semiskilled journeymen whom they had once boarded with unskilled laborers who lived apart, in working-class neighborhoods. Increasing rowdiness accompanied this growing division of the social classes. Taverns multiplied; in 1827 alone almost a hundred persons procured licenses to sell liquor. Town fathers blamed liquor for a horrifying spectacle in 1829, when hundreds paid to see the none-too-sober Sam Patch plunge to his death in a widely publicized leap over the main falls of the Genesee.

With social upheavals came political divisions. By the mid-1820s

Genesee Scenery, *by Thomas Cole*

Cole captured the beautiful countryside around Rochester in this colorful view featuring the falls of the Genesee.

Early View of Rochester

This 1835 view looks eastward across the Erie Canal. Buffalo Street (now Main Street) is at the center.

the handful of elite families like that of Nathaniel Rochester could no longer govern the town's diverse interests. The Anti-Masonic movement, which began near Rochester, acted as a magnet for those discontented with the leading families, virtually all of whose male members were Masons. "Reason seems to have lost her empire," a member of the Rochester clan complained, "and Charity to have resigned her seat."

For merchant Josiah Bissell, Sam Patch's fatal leap was the last straw. Long dismayed by rampant drunkenness and Sabbath breaking

Nathaniel Rochester,
by John James Audubon, 1824

in Rochester, Bissell and like-minded citizens had tried in 1828 to suppress stagecoach and boat travel on Sunday, to force observance of the Sabbath on *"that large mass of the community who neither fear God nor obey man."* On the Sunday after Sam Patch's death, Bissell invited the leading evangelist, Charles G. Finney, to conduct a revival in Rochester.

Finney's revivals in Rochester during 1830 and 1831 drew hundreds into the churches. Now demure women were shouting "Blessed be the Name of Jesus" in church. "We are either marching toward heaven or towards hell," a convert wrote to his sister. "How is it with you?"

Nevertheless, the revivals failed to unify the town. The rise of Anti-Masonry in the 1820s had fragmented Rochester's politics to the point where no leader, religious or political, could mend the pieces. Rather than restoring unity, Finney contributed a new and ideological basis to the town's divisions by tying religious conversion to temperance. During the 1830s most town supporters of the revivals became Whigs: evangelical Presbyterians, including numerous manufacturers and merchants converted by Finney, soon formed the core of Roch-

ester's Whig party. A respectable number of anti-liquor workers followed their lead. In contrast, the Jacksonian Democrats drew their support from Catholics, unchurched Protestant workers, and grocers and retailers who served working-class neighborhoods. Opposing restrictions on the sale of liquor, Rochester's Jacksonians took the view that the individual's conscience rather than legislation should guide morality, and they opposed efforts to force the substitution of cold water for liquor. Asked how her husband would vote, a woman in a working-class neighborhood replied: "Why he has always been [for] Jackson, and I don't think he has joined the Cold Water."

The temperance issue acted as a filter through which national issues like the Bank of the United States made their way into Rochester during the 1830s. The same people who opposed Jackson's removal of deposits from the bank supported temperance. Yet temperance was more than just another issue at election time. It served as the *premier* issue in Rochester. Their response to temperance shaped the basic political orientation of Rochester's voters and guided their allegiances when a controversial issue like banking appeared on the horizon.

lost working time and "the scenes of riot and wickedness thus produced."

Workers showed little interest in temperance before the late 1830s. But after the Panic of 1837, a new stage of temperance agitation sprang up in the form of the Washington Temperance Societies. Starting in Baltimore in 1840, the Washingtonians were more likely to be mechanics (workingmen) and laborers than ministers and manufacturers. Many were reformed drunkards, and most had concluded that their survival in the harsh climate of depression depended on their commitment to sobriety and frugality. For example, Charles T. Woodman, a baker, had been forced by the collapse of his business to flee Boston for Philadelphia to escape his creditors. Like most Washingtonians, Woodman blamed his ruin on the revival of his "old habit" of drink. The forces dislocating workers in the late 1830s were often far beyond their control. Part of the appeal of temperance was that it lay *within* their control. Take care of temperance, a Washingtonian assured a Baltimore audience, and the Lord would take care of the economy.

For all their differences from earlier temperance associations, the Washingtonians reflected the impact of revivals even more than did the American Temperance Society. Viewing drinking as sinful, they held "experience meetings," in which members described their "salvation" from liquor and their "regeneration" through abstinence (or "teetotalism"*). Their wives joined "Martha Washington" societies, in which they pledged to smell their husbands' breath each night and paraded with banners that read "Teetotal or No Husband." The Washingtonians spread farther and faster than any other antebellum temperance organization.

As temperance won new supporters, anti-alcohol crusaders gradually shifted their tactics from calls that individuals abstain to demands that cities and towns, and even states, ban all traffic in liquor (see "A Place in Time"). This shift from moral suasion to legal prohibition was controversial even within the movement. But by the late 1830s, prohibition was scoring victories. In 1838 Massachusetts prohibited the sale of distilled spirits in amounts less than fifteen gallons; in 1851 Maine banned the manufacture and sale of all intoxicating beverages. Controversial though these laws were, the temperance movement earned a measure of success. After rising steadily between 1800 and 1830, per capita consumption of distilled spirits began to fall during the 1830s. The rate of consumption during the 1840s was less than half that in the 1820s.

Public-School Reform

No less than temperance reformers, school reformers worked to encourage orderliness and thrift in the common people. Rural America's so-called district schools provided reformers with one of their main targets. One-room log or clapboard cabins containing pupils aged anywhere from three to twenty or more, the district schools taught farmers' children to read and count but little more. Those who attended the district schools never forgot their primitive conditions or harsh discipline: "the woodpile in the yard, the open fire-place, the backless benches," and the floggings until "the youngster vomited or wet his breeches."

For all their drawbacks, the district schools enjoyed support from rural parents, who financed them by a mixture of tuition payments, property taxes, and fuel contributions and by boarding the teachers in their homes. But reformers saw these schools in a different light. Centered in industrializing states like Massachusetts and Connecticut, the reformers insisted that schools had to equip children for the emerging competitive and industrial economy. The most articulate and influential of the reformers, former Massachusetts lawyer and state senator Horace Mann, in 1837 became the first secretary of the newly created Massachusetts Board of Education, and for the next decade, he promoted a sweeping transformation of public education. Mann's goals included shifting the burden of financial support for schools from parents to the state, grading the schools (that is, classifying pupils by age and attainment), extending the school term from two or three months to as many as ten months, introducing standardized textbooks, and compelling attendance. In place of loosely structured schools that were mere appendages of the family, Mann and other reformers advocated highly structured institutions that would occupy most of the child's time and energy.

School reformers hoped not only to combat ignorance but to spread uniform cultural values by

---

*Teetotal: coined by an English laborer at a temperance meeting in 1834, *teetotal* was merely an emphatic form of *total*.

exposing all children to identical experiences. Children would arrive at school at the same time and thereby learn punctuality. Graded schools that matched children against their age peers would stimulate the competitiveness needed in a rapidly industrializing society. Children would all read the same books and absorb such common sayings as "Idleness is the nest in which mischief lays its eggs." The McGuffey readers, which sold 50 million copies between 1836 and 1870, created a common curriculum and preached industry, honesty, sobriety, and patriotism.

But antebellum educational reformers faced challenges at every turn. Mindful that the short terms and informal arrangements of district schools harmonized with the farming seasons, rural people resisted standardization and centralization. In Massachusetts, representatives of farm areas nearly succeeded in abolishing Mann's board of education in 1840. From a different direction, urban Catholics sniped at the reformers' rigid Protestantism. In New York City, Bishop John Hughes led demands during the early 1840s for public support of parochial schools. Hughes pointed out that the textbooks used in public schools contained anti-Catholic and anti-Irish barbs; one textbook warned, for example, that Catholic immigrants threatened to turn America into the "common sewer of Ireland." And in both rural and urban areas, the laboring poor opposed compulsory education as a menace to parents dependent on their children's wages.

Yet the reformers enjoyed remarkable success in overcoming opposition. Although reform did not make significant gains in the South (see Chapter 10), much of the North remodeled its schools along the lines advocated by Mann. Most northern states continued to finance schools by a mixture of public tax support and tuition payments, but the balance gradually shifted toward tax support. School terms lengthened, and schools increasingly were graded. In 1852 Massachusetts passed the nation's first compulsory-attendance law.

The school reformers prevailed, in part, because their opposition was fragmented. Neither Protestant farmers nor urban Catholics thought much of school reform, but these groups thought even less of each other. In part, too, reformers succeeded because they gained influential allies. The so-called workingmen's parties that arose in the late 1820s shared the school reformers' enthusiasm for free public education. Manufacturers, who needed a disciplined work force, could not help but notice how much emphasis reformers placed on punctuality. Many merchants, lawyers, and progressive farmers sensed that the district schools were unsuited to an age of rapid economic change and accordingly supported reform. And reform-minded women not only preferred the gentle methods of discipline that Mann advocated but recognized, too, that the grading of schools would facilitate women's entry into teaching. It was widely believed that a woman could never control the assortment of three- to twenty-year-olds found in a one-room schoolhouse, but managing a class of eight- or nine-year-olds was a different matter. Catharine Beecher stated bluntly: "A profession is to be created for women. . . . This is the way in which thousands of intellectual and respectable women, who toil for a pittance scarcely sufficient to sustain life, are to be relieved and educated." Whereas in 1800 most teachers had been male, women gradually took the place of men in the classroom wherever school reform left its mark. By 1900 about 70 percent of the nation's schoolteachers were women.

School reform also appealed to native-born Americans alarmed by the swelling tide of immigration. The public school emerged as the favorite device by which reformers forged a common American culture out of an increasingly diverse society. "We must decompose and cleanse the impurities which rush into our midst" through the "one infallible filter—the SCHOOL."

School reformers were assimilationists in the sense that they hoped to use public education to give children common values through shared experiences. In one respect, however, these reformers wore blinders on the issue of assimilation, for few stressed the integration of black and white children. When black children were fortunate enough to get any schooling, it was usually in segregated schools. Black children who entered integrated public schools met with such virulent prejudice that black leaders in northern cities frequently preferred segregated schools.

Abolition

Antislavery sentiment among whites flourished in the Revolutionary era but declined in the early nineteenth century. The main antislavery organization founded between 1800 and 1830 was the

**Game of Chance:
Auctioneers and Slaves**

Games and toys were meant to educate as well as to amuse children. This game, manufactured in Maine in the mid-nineteenth century, encouraged children to abhor slavery.

American Colonization Society (1817), which displayed little moral outrage against slavery. The society proposed a plan for gradual emancipation, with compensation to the slaveowner, and the shipment of freed blacks to Africa. This proposal attracted support from some slaveholders in the Upper South who would never have dreamed of a general emancipation.

At its core, colonization was hard-hearted and softheaded. Colonizationists assumed that blacks were a degraded race that did not belong in American society, and they underestimated the growing dependence of the South's economy on slavery. Confronted by a soaring demand for cotton and other commodities, few southerners were willing to free their slaves, even if compensated. In any event, the American Colonization Society never had enough funds to buy freedom for more than a fraction of slaves. Between 1820 and 1830, only 1,400 blacks migrated to Liberia, and most were already free. In striking contrast, the American slave population, fed by natural increase (the excess of births over deaths), rose from 1,191,000 in 1810 to more than 2,000,000 in 1830.

During the 1820s the main source of radical opposition to slavery was blacks themselves. Blacks had little enthusiasm for colonization. Most American blacks were native- rather than African-born. How, they asked, could they be sent back to a continent that they had never left? "We are *natives* of this country," a black pastor in New York proclaimed. "We only ask that we be treated as well as *foreigners*." In opposition to colonization, blacks formed scores of abolition societies. In 1829 the Boston free black David Walker published an *Appeal* for a black rebellion to crush slavery.

Not all whites acquiesced to the continuance of slavery. In 1821 the Quaker Benjamin Lundy began a newspaper, the *Genius of Universal Emancipation,* and put forth proposals that no new slave states be admitted, that the internal slave trade be outlawed, that the three-fifths clause of the Constitution be repealed, and that Congress abolish slavery wherever it had the authority to do so. In 1828 Lundy hired a young New Englander, William Lloyd Garrison, as an assistant editor. Prematurely bald and with steel-rimmed glasses, and typically donning a black suit and black cravat, Garrison looked more like a schoolmaster than a rebel. But in 1831, when he launched his own newspaper, *The Liberator,* he quickly established himself as the most famous and controversial white abolitionist. "I am in earnest," Garrison wrote. "I will not equivocate—I will not excuse—I will not retreat a single inch—AND I WILL BE HEARD."

Garrison's battle cry was "immediate emancipation." In place of exiling blacks to Africa, he substituted the truly radical notion that blacks should enjoy civil (or legal) equality with whites. He greeted slaves as "a Man and a Brother," "a Woman and a Sister." Even Garrison, however, did not think that all slaves could be freed overnight. "Immediate emancipation" meant that all people had to realize that slavery was sinful and its continued existence intolerable.

Garrison quickly gained support from the growing number of black abolitionists. A black barber in Pittsburgh sent Garrison sixty dollars to help with *The Liberator.* Black agents sold subscriptions. Three-fourths of *The Liberator's* subscribers in the early years were black. The escaped slave Frederick Douglass and a remarkable freed slave who named herself Sojourner Truth proved eloquent lecturers against slavery. Douglass could rivet an audience with an opening line. "I appear before the immense assembly this evening as a thief and a robber," he gibed. "I stole this head, these limbs, this body from my master, and ran off with them."

Relations between black and white abolitionists were not always harmonious. White abolitionists called for legal equality for blacks but not necessarily for social equality. Not without racial prejudice, they preferred light- to dark-skinned Negroes and, Garrison excepted, were hesitant to admit blacks to antislavery societies. Yet the prejudices of white abolitionists were mild compared to those of most whites. A white man or woman could do few things less popular in the 1830s than become an abolitionist. Mobs, often including colonizationists, repeatedly attacked abolitionists. For example, a Boston mob, searching for a British abolitionist in 1835, found Garrison instead and dragged him through town on the end of a rope. An abolitionist editor, Elijah Lovejoy, was murdered by a mob in Alton, Illinois, in 1837.

Abolitionists drew on the language of revivals and described slavery as sin, but the Protestant churches did not rally behind abolition as strongly as behind temperance. Lyman Beecher roared against the evils of strong drink but whimpered about those of slavery and in 1834 tried to suppress abolitionists at Cincinnati's Lane Theological Seminary. In response, Theodore Dwight Weld, an idealistic follower of Charles G. Finney, led a mass withdrawal of students. These "Lane rebels" formed the nucleus of abolitionist activity at the antislavery Oberlin College.

As if external hostility were not enough, abolitionists argued continually with each other. The American Anti-Slavery Society, founded in 1833, was the scene of several battles between Garrison and prominent New York and midwestern abolitionists such as the brothers Lewis and Arthur Tappan, Theodore Dwight Weld, and James G. Birney. One of the issues between the two sides was whether abolitionists should enter politics as a distinct party. In 1840 Garrison's opponents ran Birney for president on the ticket of the newly formed Liberty party. As for Garrison himself, he was increasingly rejecting *all* laws and governments, as well as political parties, as part of his doctrine of "nonresistance." In 1838 he and his followers had founded the New England Non-Resistance Society. The

starting point of the doctrine was the fact that slavery depended on force. Garrison then added that all governments ultimately rested on force; even laws passed by elected legislatures needed police enforcement. Because Garrison viewed force as the opposite of Christian love, he concluded that Christians should refuse to vote, hold office, or have anything to do with government. It is a small wonder that many abolitionists thought of Garrison as extreme, or "ultra."

The second issue that divided the American Anti-Slavery Society concerned the role of women in the abolitionist movement. In 1837 Angelina and Sarah Grimké, daughters of a South Carolina slaveholder, embarked on an antislavery lecture tour of New England. Women had become deeply involved in antislavery societies during the 1830s, but always in female auxiliaries affiliated with those run by men. What made the Grimké sisters so controversial was that they drew mixed audiences of men and women to their lectures at a time when it was thought indelicate for women to speak before male audiences. Clergymen chastised the Grimké sisters for lecturing men rather than obeying them.

Such criticism backfired, however, because the Grimkés increasingly took up the cause of women's rights. In 1838 each wrote a classic of American feminism. Sarah produced her *Letters on the Condition of Women and the Equality of the Sexes,* while Angelina contributed her *Letters to Catharine E. Beecher* (Lyman Beecher's daughter and a militant opponent of female equality). Some abolitionists tried to dampen the feminist flames. The abolitionist poet John Greenleaf Whittier dismissed women's grievances as "paltry" compared to the "great and dreadful wrongs of the slave." Even Theodore Dwight Weld, who had married Angelina Grimké, wanted to subordinate women's rights to antislavery. But the fiery passions would not be extinguished. Garrison, welcoming the controversy, promptly espoused women's rights and urged that women be given positions equal to men in the American Anti-Slavery Society. In 1840 the election of a woman, Abby Kelley, to a previously all-male committee split the American Anti-Slavery Society wide open. A substantial minority of pro-feminist delegates left—some to join the Liberty party, others to follow Lewis Tappan into the new American and Foreign Anti-Slavery Society.

The disruption of the American Anti-Slavery

Society did not greatly damage abolitionism. The national society had never had much control over the local societies that had grown swiftly during the mid-1830s. By 1840 there were more than fifteen hundred local societies, principally in Massachusetts, New York, and Ohio. By circulating abolitionist tracts, newspapers, and even chocolates with antislavery messages on their wrappers, these local societies kept the country ablaze with agitation.

One of the most disruptive abolitionist techniques was to flood Congress with petitions calling for an end to slavery in the District of Columbia. Congress had no time to consider all the petitions, but to refuse to address them meant depriving citizens of their right to have petitions heard. In 1836 southerners secured congressional adoption of the "gag rule," which automatically tabled abolitionist petitions and thus prevented discussion of them in Congress. Ex-president John Quincy Adams, then a representative from Massachusetts, led the struggle against the gag rule and finally secured its repeal in 1845. The debate over the gag rule subtly shifted the issue from the abolition of slavery to the constitutional rights of free expression and petitioning Congress. Members of Congress with little sympathy for abolitionists found themselves attacking the South for suppressing the right of petition. In a way, the gag-rule episode vindicated Garrison's tactic of stirring up emotions on the slavery issue. By holding passions over slavery at the boiling point, Garrison kept the South on the defensive. The less secure southerners felt, the more they were tempted into clumsy overreactions like the gag rule.

Women's Rights

The position of American women in the 1830s contained many contradictions. Women could not vote. If married, they had no right to own property (even inherited property) or to retain their own earnings. Yet the spread of reform movements provided women with unprecedented opportunities for public activity without challenging the prevailing belief that their proper sphere was the home. By suppressing liquor, for example, women could claim that they were transforming wretched homes into nurseries of happiness.

The argument that women were natural guardians of the family was double-edged. It jus-

tified reform activities on behalf of the family, but it undercut women's demands for legal equality. Let women attend to their sphere, the counterargument ran, and leave politics and finance to men. So deeply ingrained was sexual inequality, indeed, that most feminists did not start out intending to attack it. Instead, their experiences in other reform movements, notably abolition, led them to the issue of women's rights.

Among the early women's rights advocates who started their reform careers as abolitionists were the Grimké sisters, the Philadelphia Quaker Lucretia Mott, Lucy Stone, and Abby Kelley. Like abolition, the cause of women's rights revolved around the conviction that differences of race and gender were unimportant and incidental. "Men and women," Sarah Grimké wrote, "are CREATED EQUAL! They are both moral and accountable beings, and whatever is *right* for man to do, is *right* for woman." The most articulate and aggressive advocates of woman's rights, moreover, tended to gravitate to William Lloyd Garrison rather than to more moderate abolitionists. Garrison, himself a vigorous feminist, repeatedly stressed the peculiar degradation of women under slavery. The early issues of *The Liberator* contained a "Ladies' Department" headed by a picture of a kneeling slave woman imploring, "Am I Not a Woman and a Sister?" It was common knowledge that slave women were vulnerable to the sexual demands of white masters. Garrison denounced the South as a vast brothel and described slave women as "treated with more indelicacy and cruelty than cattle."

While their involvement in abolition aroused advocates of women's rights, the discrimination that they encountered within the abolition movement infuriated them and impelled them to make women's rights a separate cause. In the 1840s Lucy Stone became the first abolitionist to lecture solely on women's rights. When Lucretia Mott and other American women tried to be seated at the World's Anti-Slavery Convention in London in 1840, they were relegated to a screened-off section. The incident made a sharp impression not only on Mott but on Elizabeth Cady Stanton, who had elected to accompany her abolitionist husband to the meeting as a honeymoon trip. In 1848 Mott and Stanton organized a women's rights convention at Seneca Falls, New York, that proclaimed a Declaration of Sentiments. Modeled on the Declaration of Independence, the Seneca Falls Declaration began

Elizabeth Cady Stanton *(far left)* **and Lucretia Mott**

Most newspapers ridiculed the Seneca Falls convention that Stanton and Mott organized to advance women's rights. Over three hundred people attended.

with the assertion that "all men and women are created equal." The convention passed twelve resolutions, and only one, a call for the right of women to vote, failed to pass unanimously; but it did pass. Ironically, after the Civil War, the call for woman suffrage became the main demand of women's rights advocates for the rest of the century.

Although its crusaders were resourceful and energetic, women's rights had less impact than most other reforms. Temperance and school reform were far more popular, and abolitionism created more commotion. Women would not secure the right to vote throughout the nation until 1920, fifty-five years after the Thirteenth Amendment would abolish slavery. One reason for the relatively slow advance of women's rights was that piecemeal gains —such as married women's securing the right to own property in several southern states by the late 1830s—satisfied many women. The cause of women's rights also suffered from a close association with abolitionism, which was unpopular. In addition, the advance of feminism was slowed by the competition that it faced from the alternative ideal of domesticity. By sanctioning activities in reforms such as temperance and education, the cult of domesticity provided many women with worthwhile pursuits beyond the family. In this way, it blunted the edge of female demands for full equality.

Penitentiaries and Asylums

Reform efforts took shape during the 1820s to combat poverty, crime, and insanity by establish-

ing highly regimented institutions, themselves products of striking new assumptions about the causes of deviancy.

In the colonial era, Americans had viewed poverty as neither the fault of its victims nor a sign of a defective social order. Rather, poverty was seen as a permanent condition of society, ordained by God to test Christians' humility and charity. Men and women thought of crime, too, as an enduring feature of society. Faced with punishment, individual criminals might mend their ways, but new lawbreakers would take their place. So ingrained were the defects of human nature that some would always choose the way of crime.

Several developments undermined these assumptions during the first half of the nineteenth century. Not only were poverty and crime rising, but in the swiftly growing cities, each was more visible than in the past. Alarmed legislators launched investigations into the causes of both indigence and crime, from which they concluded that deviant behavior often resulted from exposure to drunken fathers and broken homes. The failure of parental discipline, not the will of God or the wickedness of human nature, lay at the root of evil.

Few Americans would have reached these conclusions (or even undertaken the investigations that led to them) had it not been for their growing belief that the moral qualities of the individual were changeable rather than fixed. Both religious revivalists and reformers increasingly came to think that human nature could be altered by the right combination of moral influences. Most grasped the optimistic implications. "The study of the *causes of crime*," William Ellery Channing concluded, "may lead us to its *cure*."

To cure crime, reformers created substitutes for parental discipline, most notably the penitentiary. Penitentiaries were prisons marked by an unprecedented degree of order and discipline. Of course, colonial Americans had incarcerated criminal offenders, but jails had been used mainly to hold prisoners awaiting trial or to lock up debtors. For much of the eighteenth century, the threat of the gallows rather than of imprisonment had deterred wrongdoers. In contrast, nineteenth-century reformers believed that rightly managed, penitentiaries would bring about the sincere reformation of offenders.

To purge offenders' violent habits, reformers usually insisted on solitary confinement. Between 1819 and 1825, New York built penitentiaries at Auburn and Ossining (Sing Sing), in which prisoners were confined by night in small, windowless cells. By day they could work together but never speak and rarely even look at each other. Some reformers criticized this "Auburn system" for allowing too much contact and preferred the rival "Pennsylvania system," in which each prisoner spent all of his or her time in a single cell (each with a walled courtyard for exercise) and received no news or visits from the outside.

Antebellum America also witnessed a remarkable transformation in the treatment of poor people. The prevailing colonial practice of offering relief to the poor by supporting them in a household ("outdoor relief") gradually gave way to the construction of almshouses for the infirm poor and workhouses for the able-bodied poor ("indoor relief"). The argument for indoor relief was much the same as the argument for penitentiaries: plucking the poor from their demoralizing surroundings and exposing them to a highly regimented institution could change them into virtuous, productive citizens. However lofty the motives behind workhouses and almshouses, the results were often abysmal. In 1833 a legislative committee found that the inmates of the Boston House of Industry were packed seven to a room and included unwed mothers, the sick, and the insane as well as the poor.

As for insane people, those living in a work-

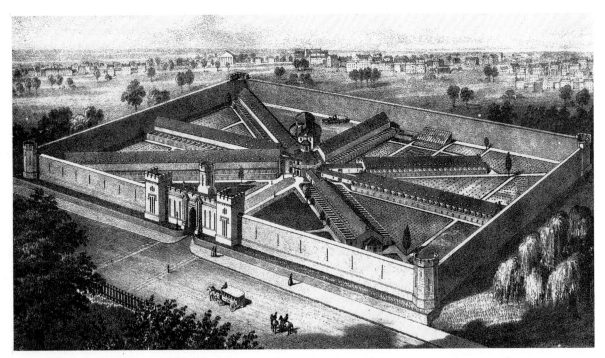

The Eastern Penitentiary   *Built in Pennsylvania in 1820, this prison, in its geometrically precise layout, reflected prison reformers' concern with total control.*

house such as the Boston House of Industry were relatively well off, for many experienced even worse treatment by confinement in prisons. In 1841 an idealistic Unitarian schoolteacher, Dorothea Dix, was teaching a Sunday school class in a jail in East Cambridge, Massachusetts, and discovered there insane people kept in an unheated room. Dix pursued her investigation and visited jails and almshouses throughout the state. In 1843 she presented a memorial to the state legislature, which described the insane confined "in *cages, closets, cellars, stalls, pens*! *Chained, naked, beaten with rods, and lashed into obedience.*" With the support of Horace Mann and the Boston reformer Samuel G. Howe, she encouraged legislatures to build insane asylums, and by the time of the Civil War, twenty-eight states, four cities, and the federal government had constructed public mental institutions.

Penitentiaries, workhouses, and insane asylums all reflected the same optimistic belief that deviancy could be erased by resettling deviants in the right environment. But what was the "right" environment? In some aspects, the answer was clear-cut. Heated rooms were better than frigid ones, and sober parents preferable to drunkards. But reformers demanded much more than warm rooms and responsible parents. Reformers were convinced that the unfettered freedom and individualism of American society were themselves defects in the environment and that the poor, criminal, and insane needed extraordinary regimentation if they were to change. Prison inmates were to march around in lock step; in workhouses the poor, treated much like prisoners, were often forbidden to leave or receive visitors without permission. The idealism behind such institutions was genuine, but later generations would question reformers' underlying assumptions.

Utopian Communities

The belief that individuals could live perfectly, which tinged most antebellum reform movements, took its most extreme form in the experimental societies or "utopian" communities that flourished in these years. Although varying widely in their philosophies and arrangements, utopian communities had some common features. Their founders were intellectuals who designed their communities as alter-natives to the prevailing competitive economy and as models whose success would inspire imitation. Unlike the Shakers and the Mormons, the utopians did not claim to have visions of God or visits from angels. Nor did they burn their bridges to society.

American interest in utopian communities first spurted during the 1820s. In 1825 British industrialist and philanthropist Robert Owen founded the New Harmony community in Indiana. Owen had already acquired a formidable reputation (and a fortune) from his management of cotton mills at New Lanark, Scotland. His innovations at New Lanark had substantially improved his workers' educational opportunities and living conditions and left him convinced that similar changes could transform the lives of working people everywhere. He saw the problem of the early industrial age as social rather than political. The form of government (whether republican, aristocratic, or monarchical) mattered less than the arrangement of work and living conditions. If social arrangements could be perfected, all vice and misery would disappear; human character was formed, "without exception," by people's surroundings or environment. The key to perfecting social arrangements lay, in turn, in the creation of small, planned communities—"Villages of Unity and Mutual Cooperation," each to contain a perfect balance of occupational, religious, and political groups.

Lured to the United States by cheap land and by Americans' receptivity to experiments, Owen confidently predicted that by 1827 the northern states would embrace the principles embodied in New Harmony. Unfortunately, by 1827 there was little left to embrace, for the community had quickly fallen apart. New Harmony had attracted more than its share of idlers and fanatics, and Owen had not always helped matters. He had spent too much time on the road publicizing the community and not enough time managing it. He had clashed with clergymen, who still believed that Original Sin, not environment, shaped human character. Yet Owenism survived the wreckage of New Harmony. The ideas that the human character was formed by environment and that cooperation was superior to competition had a potent impact on urban workers for the next half-century. Owen's ideas, for example, impelled workingmen's leaders to support educational reform during the late 1820s.

In the early 1830s, the utopian impulse weakened, only to revive amid the economic chaos of the late 1830s and 1840s. Appalled by the misery that came with economic depression, small bands of idealists gathered anew in experimental communities whose names—Hopedale, Fruitlands, Brook Farm—suggested idyllic retreats. Their founders' visions were fired by intense but unconventional forms of Christianity. Adin Ballou, a Universalist minister who founded Hopedale, near Milford, Massachusetts, described it as a "miniature Christian republic." Brook Farm, near Boston, was mainly the creation of a group of religious philosophers called transcendentalists. Most transcendentalists, including Ralph Waldo Emerson and George Ripley, had started as Unitarians but sought to revitalize Unitarianism—and indeed, all denominations—by proclaiming the infinite spiritual capacities of ordinary men and women.

Like other utopias, Brook Farm was both a retreat and a model. Convinced that the competitive commercial life of the cities was unnatural, philosophers welcomed the opportunity to engage in elevated discussions after a day perspiring in the cabbage patch. Although Brook Farm never had more than a hundred residents, it attracted several renowned writers. Emerson visited it, and novelist Nathaniel Hawthorne lived there for a period; Brook Farm's literary magazine, *The Dial,* became a forum for transcendentalist ideas about philosophy, art, and literature (also see Chapter 11). The utopians at Brook Farm also tried out the scheme of social organization devised by the French utopian Charles Fourier. Fourier's ideas, which resembled Owen's, called for dividing society into small cooperative units called phalanxes. In the words of one historian, Fourierism "offered a rigid, almost regimented plan designed to free people to be what nature meant them to be." Fourierism caught on as far west as Wisconsin and Iowa; at least twenty-eight Fourierist communities sprang up between 1841 and 1858.

Few utopias enjoyed success to match their ambition. Brook Farm disbanded in 1849; Hopedale, in 1853. In general, utopian communities were less durable and attracted fewer people than religious communities such as those of the Shakers and Mormons. In contrast to the religious communitarians, the utopians kept open their avenues to society and moved back and forth between their communities and antislavery or women's rights conventions. Utopians neither sought nor attained the kind of grip on the allegiance of their members held by a Mother Ann Lee or a Joseph Smith.

Oneida

A notable exception to this generalization—a reform community that was both durable and exclusive—was the Oneida community in New York State. Started by Yale graduate John Humphrey Noyes in 1847, Oneida lasted until 1881. A friend of many reformers, Noyes in 1834 took Charles G. Finney's idea of perfectionism to a logical extreme by announcing that he had achieved perfection and was henceforth incapable of sinning. By 1837 Noyes had decided that those who could not sin had no need for exclusive institutions like marriage. Within a few years, he put "communism in love" to practical effect by exchanging wives with one of his followers.

To ordinary minds, Noyes was simply an adulterer; indeed, one reason why he fled to Oneida was to avoid prosecution for adultery. But Noyes preferred to call his doctrine "complex marriage"; a man or woman who had achieved perfection could have sexual intercourse with any number of perfected partners. Despite appearances, Noyes did not view complex marriage as a way to loosen sexual standards. Rather, he created elaborate rules to restrict the occasions of intercourse. The general idea was for the most spiritually advanced members of the community to father the most children. Appropriately, "Father" Noyes fathered more than anyone else.

Noyes's ideas about sex reflected his belief that any exclusive attachment between husband and wife worked against the interests of women by burdening them with excessive numbers of children and with "kitchen slavery." By establishing rules to govern intercourse, he hoped to reduce the number of children. Other arrangements at Oneida also evidenced Noyes's commitment to greater equality for women. Not only were women given a voice in decisions that affected the community, but they were relieved of much household drudgery by Noyes's decree that Oneidans eat only one formal meal a day (breakfast). Even child rearing became a communal, rather than exclusively maternal, responsibility at Oneida. As soon as children were able to walk, they were placed in a communal nursery.

Oneida's significance went beyond complex marriage. Noyes was an abolitionist. By the 1850s, when southerners thought about abolitionists, they thought of Noyes as well as Garrison. To defenders of slavery, the North seemed in the grip of licentious crackpots whose calls for the abolition of slavery were only the first step in a barbaric restructuring of all social relationships.

Conclusion

During the 1820s and 1830s, American society burst beyond its traditional physical and intellectual boundaries. Everywhere the old leadership provided by the Revolutionary generation gave way to new leaders born after 1775. Surrounded by weak foreign neighbors and at peace with the great powers of Europe, Americans, without much restraint from traditional or external threats, grappled with the implications of a changing society.

Political parties, religious revivals, and reform movements responded to social change in ways that were novel and inventive but never uniform. By reducing the innumerable interests and opinions that composed American society to two alternatives—the Democrats and the Whigs—the second party system gave direction to the conflicts that were created by economic and social change. Those excluded from politics or dismayed by the compromises into which politicians routinely entered turned to the churches and to reform movements as vehicles for change. Yet religion and reform were not simply alternatives to politics, for each intersected politics at scores of points. The closer one drew to 1840, the greater were the number of intersections. Temperance advocates began to demand legal prohibition of liquor; some abolitionists turned to the Liberty party; some feminists demanded the vote; utopians became political targets. Politics became a medium that even those antagonistic to politics had to understand.

CHRONOLOGY

1800–
1801   Great Kentucky Revival.

1817   American Colonization Society founded.

1824   John Quincy Adams elected president by the House of Representatives.

1826   American Temperance Society organized.

1828   Andrew Jackson elected president.
Congress passes the "Tariff of Abominations."
John Calhoun anonymously writes *South Carolina Exposition and Protest*.

1830   Jackson's Maysville Road Bill veto.
Indian Removal Act.

1830– 1831   Charles G. Finney's Rochester revival.

1831   William Lloyd Garrison starts *The Liberator*.

1832 Jackson vetoes recharter of the Bank of the United States.

Jackson reelected president.

South Carolina Nullification Proclamation.

1833 Force Bill.

Compromise Tariff.

American Anti-Slavery Society founded.

South Carolina nullifies the Force Bill.

1834 Whig party organized.

1836 Congress imposes the gag rule.

Deposition Act.

Specie Circular.

Martin Van Buren elected president.

1837 Horace Mann becomes secretary of the Massachusetts Board of Education.

Economic depression sets in.

Murder of Elijah Lovejoy by proslavery mob.

Grimké sisters set out on lecture tour of New England.

1838 Garrison's New England Non-Resistance Society founded.

Publication of Sarah Grimké's *Letters on the Condition of Women* and Angelina Grimké's *Letters to Catharine E. Beecher.*

1839 Depression deepens as the Bank of the United States fails.

1840 Independent Treasury Act passed.

William Henry Harrison elected president.

First Washington Temperance Society started.

1841 Dorothea Dix begins exposé of prison conditions.

Brook Farm Community founded.

1848 Seneca Falls Convention.

For Further Reading

Lee Benson, *The Concept of Jacksonian Democracy: New York as a Test Case* (1961). A major revisionist interpretation of the period.

William W. Freehling, *Prelude to Civil War* (1966). A major study of the nullification crisis.

Richard P. McCormick, *The Second American Party System: Party Formation in the Jacksonian Era* (1966). An influential work stressing the role of political leaders in shaping the second party system.

Edward Pessen, *Jacksonian America: Society, Personality, and Politics* (rev. ed., 1979). A comprehensive interpretation of the period that emphasizes the lack of real democracy in American society and politics.

Arthur M. Schlesinger, Jr., *The Age of Jackson* (1945). A classic study, now dated in some of its interpretations but still highly readable.

Fred Somkin, *Unquiet Eagle: Memory and Desire in the Idea of American Freedom, 1815–1860* (1967). A penetrating study of American political values.

Alice F. Tyler, *Freedom's Ferment* (1944). A comprehensive survey of reform movements.

Ronald G. Walters, *American Reformers, 1815–1860* (1978). An insightful study of nineteenth-century reform, incorporating recent scholarship.

Chilton Williamson, *American Suffrage: From Property to Democracy, 1760–1860* (1960). The standard study of changing requirements for voting.

Additional Bibliography

Political Leaders

Donald B. Cole, *Martin Van Buren and the American Political System* (1984); James C. Curtis, *The Fox at Bay: Martin Van Buren and the Presidency, 1837–1841* (1970); Richard B. Latner, *The Presidency of Andrew Jackson: White House Politics, 1829–1837* (1979); John Niven, *Martin Van Buren and the Romantic Age* (1983); Major L. Wilson, *The Presidency of Martin Van Buren* (1984); C. M. Wiltse, *John C. Calhoun: Nullifier, 1829–1839* (1949).

Political Parties

Jean H. Baker, *Affairs of Party: The Political Culture of Northern Democrats in the Mid-Nineteenth Century* (1983); Ronald P. Formisano, *The Birth of Mass Political Parties, 1827–1861* (1971) and *The Transformation of American Political Culture: Massachusetts Parties, 1790s–1840s* (1983); Daniel W. Howe, *The Political Culture of the American Whigs* (1980); Robert V. Remini,

The Election of Andrew Jackson (1963) and *Andrew Jackson and the Course of American Empire* (1977); Harry L. Watson, *Jacksonian Politics and Community Conflict: The Emergence of the Second American Party System in Cumberland County, North Carolina* (1981); Sean Wilentz, *Chants Democratic: New York City and the Rise of the American Working Class, 1788–1850* (1983).

Banking and the Economy

Bray Hammond, *Banks and Politics in America from the Revolution to the Civil War* (1957); John M. McFaul, *The Politics of Jacksonian Finance* (1972); William G. Shade, *Banks or No Banks: The Money Question in Western Politics* (1972); James Roger Sharp, *The Jacksonians Versus the Banks: Politics in the United States After the Panic of 1837* (1970); Peter Temin, *The Jacksonian Economy* (1965).

Religious Revivals

Sydney E. Ahlstrom, *A Religious History of the American People,* 2 vols. (1975); Leonard J. Arrington, *The Mormon Experience* (1979) and *Brigham Young: American Moses* (1985); John Boles, *The Great Revival, 1787–1805* (1972); Whitney Cross, *The Burned-Over District* (1950); Klaus J. Hansen, *Mormonism and the American Experience* (1981); William G. McLoughlin, *Modern Revivalism* (1959); Donald G. Mathews, *Religion in the Old South* (1977).

Relationships Between Religion and Reform

Gilbert Barnes, *The Anti-Slavery Impulse* (1933); Clifford S. Griffin, *Their Brothers' Keepers: Moral Stewardship in the United States* (1960); Mary Ryan, *Cradle of the Middle Class: The Family in Oneida County, New York, 1790–1865* (1981); Timothy L. Smith, *Revivalism and Social Reform* (1957).

Temperance

Jed Dannenbaum, *Drink and Disorder: Temperance Reform in Cincinnati from the Washingtonian Revival to the WCTU* (1984); Ian Tyrrell, *Sobering Up: From Temperance to Prohibition in Antebellum America* (1979).

Educational Reform

Carl F. Kaestle, *Pillars of the Republic: Common Schools and American Society, 1780–1860* (1983); Carl F. Kaestle and Maris A. Vinovskis, *Education and Social Change in Nineteenth-Century Massachusetts* (1980); Michael B. Katz, *The Irony of Early School Reform* (1968); Stanley K. Schultz, *The Culture Factory: Boston Public Schools 1789–1860* (1973).

Abolitionists

Robert H. Abzug, *Passionate Liberator: Theodore Dwight Weld and the Dilemma of Reform* (1980); David B. Davis, *The Problem of Slavery in the Age of Revolution, 1770–1823* (1975); Lawrence J. Friedman, *Gregarious Saints: Self and Community in American Abolitionism, 1830–1870* (1982); Blanche Glassman Hersh, *The Slavery of Sex: Feminist Abolitionists in America* (1978); Jane A. Pease and William H. Pease, *They Who Would Be Free: Blacks' Search for Freedom, 1830–1861* (1974); Lewis Perry, *Radical Abolitionism: Anarchy and the Government of God in Antislavery Thought* (1973); Benjamin Quarles, *Black Abolitionists* (1969); Leonard L. Richards, *"Gentlemen of Property and Standing": Anti-Abolition Mobs in Jacksonian America* (1970); Ronald G. Walters, *The Antislavery Appeal: American Abolitionists After 1830* (1976); Bertram Wyatt-Brown, *Lewis Tappan and the Evangelical War Against Slavery* (1969).

Women's Rights

Lois Banner, *Elizabeth Cady Stanton* (1980); Barbara J. Berg, *The Remembered Gate — The Woman and the City, 1800–1860* (1978); Carl N. Degler, *At Odds: Women and the Family in America from the Revolution to the Present* (1980); Ellen C. DuBois, *Feminism and Suffrage: The Emergence of an Independent Women's Movement in America, 1848–1869* (1978); Elisabeth Griffith, *In Her Own Right: The Life of Elizabeth Cady Stanton* (1984); Gerda Lerner, *The Grimké Sisters from South Carolina: Rebels Against Slavery* (1967); Keith Melder, *Beginnings of Sisterhood: The American Woman's Rights Movement, 1800–1850* (1977).

Institutional Reformers

Gerald W. Grob, *Mental Institutions in America: Social Policy to 1875* (1973); W. David Lewis, *From Newgate to Dannemora: The Rise of the Penitentiary* (1965); Robert Mennel, *Thorns and Thistles* (1973); David Rothman, *The Discovery of the Asylum* (1971).

Utopian Communities

Arthur E. Bestor, *Backwoods Utopias: The Sectarian and Owenite Phases of Communitarian Utopianism in America, 1663–1829* (1950); Maren Lockwood Carden, *Oneida: Utopian Community to Modern Corporation* (1969); Michael Fellman, *The Unbounded Frame: Freedom and Community in Nineteenth-Century America Utopianism* (1973); J. F. C. Harrison, *Quest for the New Moral World: Robert Owen and the Owenites in Britain and America* (1969).

CHAPTER 10

The Old South and Slavery, 1800–1860

During the winter of 1831–1832, an intense debate over the future of slavery galvanized Virginians. A slave insurrection led by Nat Turner in August 1831 aroused new anxieties, particularly among the nonslaveholding whites in the western part of the state. "What is to be done?" an editorial writer in the *Richmond Enquirer* queried. "Oh my God, I don't know, but something must be done." Plans for a gradual emancipation of slaves, one of them advanced by Thomas Jefferson's grandson, leaped onto the state's political agenda. For a period, opponents of slavery held the initiative and protested against the institution with a fury that would have cheered antislavery northerners. Slavery, according to one Virginian, was "a mildew which has blighted in its course every region it has touched from the creation of the world." In the words of another, slavery "is ruinous to whites; retards improvements; roots out our industrious population; banishes the yeomanry from the country; and deprives the spinner, the weaver, the smith, the shoemaker, and the carpenter of employment and support." In the end, the advocates of emancipation went down to defeat, but only narrowly, and mainly because the state legislature was grossly malapportioned in favor of eastern slaveholders and against western nonslaveholders.

However narrow, the defeat of Virginia's emancipationists at the start of the 1830s marked a point of no return for the region known to history as the Old South. The Old South gradually took shape between the 1790s and 1860. As late as the American Revolution, *south* referred more to a direction than to a place. But by the 1850s, southerners were publishing books with titles like *Sociology for the South* and *Social Relations in Our Southern States* that took for granted the South's separate regional identity. The distinctive feature of the Old South was that it condoned slavery at a time when the institution had come under attack everywhere else in the civilized world. In 1775 slavery had known no sectional boundaries in America. However, by 1800 nearly every northern state had either abolished slavery or adopted a plan for the gradual emancipation of slaves within its borders, and Congress banned the importation of slaves in 1808. Thereafter, opposition to slavery intensified, not only in the United States, but in Europe and South America. Without too much exaggeration, Senator James Buchanan of Pennsylvania proclaimed in 1842: "All Christendom is leagued against the South upon the question of domestic slavery."

Virginians' debate over slavery in 1831–1832 underscored the internal divisions within Virginia and the South as a whole. In every southern state, nonslaveholding farmers, or yeomen, composed a majority of the white population throughout the antebellum period. Further, among the states that would secede and in 1861 form the Confederate States of America, there was a basic distinction between the Upper South (Virginia, North Carolina, Tennessee, and Arkansas) and the Lower, or Deep, South (South Carolina, Georgia, Florida, Alabama, Mississippi, Louisiana, and Texas). Socially and economically, the Upper South relied far less than the Lower South on slavery and on cotton. With varied agricultural economies based on the raising of wheat, tobacco, hemp, vegetables, and livestock, the states of the Upper South bore many resemblances to the free states of the North. Politically, the Upper South approached secession far more reluctantly than the Lower South.

For all of its internal variety, however, the Old South possessed strong bonds of unity that derived from slavery. The defense of slavery gradually united white opinion in the South. After reaching a climax in Virginia in 1831–1832, southern white opposition to slavery steadily weakened, and most whites came to dread the thought of a general emancipation of slaves. Although the Upper South

hesitated about secession in 1861, it withdrew from the Union not because of doubts about slavery but because of doubts as to whether secession would defend slavery. In the final analysis, the Upper and Lower Souths were merely parts of a single Old South, because slavery gave southern society such a distinctive cast. Although reminded by daily contact with whites of the contempt in which their race was held, blacks could do little to escape bondage. Slavery scarred all social relationships in the Old South: between blacks and whites, among whites, and even among blacks. Without slavery there never would have been an Old South.

King Cotton

The traditional cash crops of the South declined in the late eighteenth century. That old standby tobacco, a crop notorious for depleting soil nutrients, depended on foreign markets that were essentially undependable, especially after Independence stripped American trade of British protection. Tidewater Virginia, once the center of tobacco production, had dwindled economically to a shadow of its former self. North Carolina, whose soil had been depleted by tobacco, so languished that contemporaries called it the Rip Van Winkle of the Union. Rice provided the coastal region of South Carolina with a major cash crop, but rice could not be grown inland. Cotton growing was also

confined to seaboard areas. Indeed, in 1790 the South's population was concentrated in states bordering on the Atlantic. Three out of every four southerners lived in Maryland, Virginia, North Carolina, and South Carolina, and one out of every three in Virginia alone.

The contrast between the South of 1790 and that of 1850 was stunning. By 1850 only one out of every seven white southerners lived in Virginia. One out of every three white southerners lived in seven flourishing states (Alabama, Arkansas, Florida, Louisiana, Mississippi, Missouri, and Texas) admitted to the Union after 1800. What had transformed the stagnant South of 1800 into the dynamic

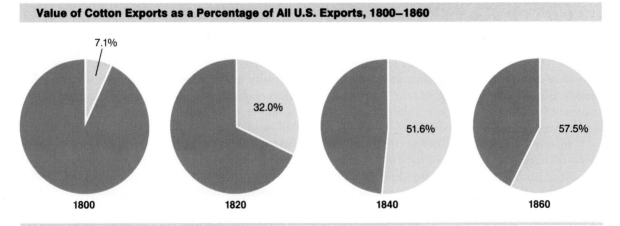

Value of Cotton Exports as a Percentage of All U.S. Exports, 1800–1860

7.1%   1800

32.0%   1820

51.6%   1840

57.5%   1860

By 1840 cotton accounted for more than half of all U.S. exports.

and bustling South of 1850? The answer, in a word, is cotton. The growth of the British textile industry in the late eighteenth century had created a huge demand for cotton and provided a stimulus to the development of the cotton gin. The removal of the Indians (see Chapter 8) opened the way to the expansion of cotton production in new territories. Armed with cotton gins, settlers swept into Alabama and Mississippi after 1815. By 1860 Mississippi had become the leading cotton producer in the nation, and settlers had already pushed farther west, into east Texas. At its peak the cotton belt (or "Cotton Kingdom") stretched from South Carolina, Georgia, and northern Florida in the east through Alabama, Mississippi, central and western Tennessee, and Louisiana, and from there on to Arkansas and Texas.

The Lure of Cotton

To British traveler Basil Hall, it seemed that all southerners could talk about was cotton. "Every flow of wind from the shore wafted off the smell of that useful plant; at every dock or wharf we encountered it in huge piles or pyramids of bales,

and our decks were soon choked with it. All day, and almost all night long, the captain, pilot, crew, and passengers were talking of nothing else." With its warm climate, wet springs and summers, and relatively dry autumns, the Lower South was especially suited to the cultivation of cotton. In contrast to the sugar industry, which thrived in southeastern Louisiana, cotton required neither expensive irrigation canals nor costly machinery. Sugar was a rich man's crop that demanded a considerable capital investment to grow and process. But cotton could be grown profitably on any scale. A cotton farmer did not even need to own a gin; commercial gins would serve him. Nor did a cotton farmer have to own slaves; in 1860, 35 percent to 50 percent of all farmers in the cotton belt owned no slaves. Cotton was profitable for anyone, even nonslaveholders, to grow; it promised to make poor men prosperous and rich men kings.

Although modest cotton cultivation did not require slaves, large-scale cotton growing and slavery grew together. As the southern slave population nearly doubled between 1810 and 1830, cotton employed three-fourths of all southern slaves. Owning slaves made it possible to harvest vast tracts

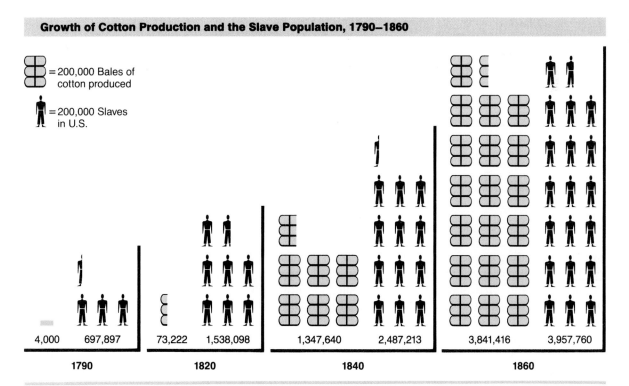

Growth of Cotton Production and the Slave Population, 1790–1860

= 200,000 Bales of cotton produced

= 200,000 Slaves in U.S.

| 4,000 | 697,897 | 73,222 | 1,538,098 | 1,347,640 | 2,487,213 | 3,841,416 | 3,957,760 |

| **1790** | **1820** | **1840** | **1860** |

Cotton and slavery rose together in the Old South.

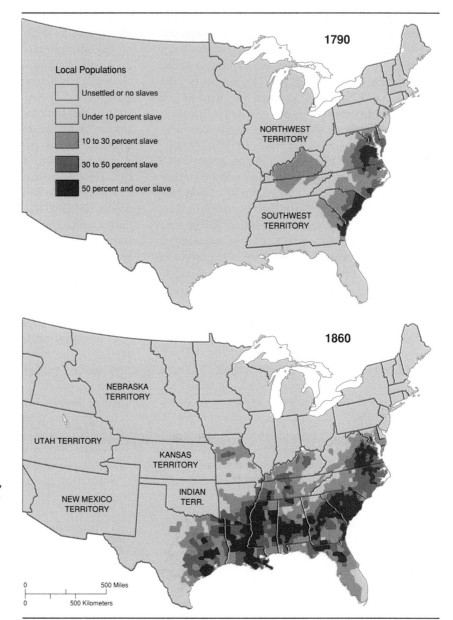

Distribution of Slaves, 1790 and 1860

In 1790 the majority of slaves resided along the southeastern seaboard. By 1860, however, slavery had spread throughout the South, and slaves were most heavily concentrated in the Deep South states.

SOURCE: Reprinted with permission of Alfred A. Knopf, Inc. from *Ordeal by Fire: The Civil War and Reconstruction* by James M. McPherson. Copyright 1982 by Alfred A. Knopf, Inc.

of cotton speedily, a crucial advantage because a sudden rainstorm at harvest time could pelt cotton to the ground and soil it. Slaveholding also enabled planters to increase their cotton acreage and hence their profits.

An added advantage of cotton lay in its compatibility with the production of corn. Corn could be planted earlier or later than cotton and harvested before or after. Since the cost of owning a slave was the same whether or not he or she was working, corn production enabled slaveholders to utilize slave labor when slaves were not employed on cotton. Nonslaveholding cotton growers also found it convenient to raise corn, and by 1860 the acreage devoted to corn in the Old South actually *exceeded* that devoted to cotton. Corn fed both families and the livestock that flourished in the South (in 1860 the region had two-thirds of the nation's hogs). From an economic standpoint, corn and cotton gave the South the best of both worlds. Fed by intense demands in Britain and New England, the price of cotton remained high, with the result that money flowed into the South. Because of southern self-sufficiency in growing corn and in raising hogs that thrived on the corn, money was not drained out of the region to pay for food produced in the North. In 1860 the twelve wealthiest counties in the United States were all in the South.

Ties Between the Lower and Upper South

Sugar and cotton were the main cash crops in the Lower South. The agriculture of the Upper South, founded on tobacco, hemp, wheat, and vegetables, depended far less than that of the Lower South on a few great cash crops. Yet the Upper South identified with the Lower South rather than with the agricultural regions of the free states. The reasons were social, political, and even psychological. Many settlers in states like Alabama and Mississippi had

come from Upper South states like Virginia and North Carolina. All white southerners benefited from the three-fifths clause of the Constitution, which enabled them to count slaves as a basis for congressional representation. All southerners were stung by abolitionists' criticisms of slavery, drawing no distinction between the Upper and Lower South. Importantly, too, economic ties linked the Upper and Lower South. The profitability of cotton and sugar in the Lower South increased the value of slaves throughout the South. Between 1790 and 1860, perhaps a million or more slaves were herded across state lines in the Old South. Roughly three-fourths of these slaves moved with their masters, while the remainder were sold as individuals. The sale of slaves from states with declining or stagnant plantation economies (Maryland, Virginia, and South Carolina) to those with booming economies (Alabama, Mississippi, Louisiana, Arkansas, and Texas) became a huge business. Arguing against a proposal for the gradual emancipation of slaves, Professor Thomas R. Dew of Virginia's College of William and Mary stated in

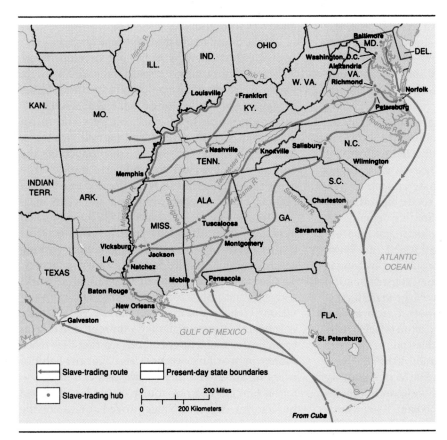

The Internal Slave Trade, 1810–1860

An internal slave trade developed after the slave trade with Africa ended in 1808. With the growth of cotton production, farmers in the Upper South found it profitable to sell their slaves to planters in the Lower South.

1832, "Virginia is, in fact, a *negro* raising State for other States; she produces enough for her own supply, and six thousand a year for sale." Without the sale of its slaves, Dew concluded, "Virginia will be a desert."

The North and South Diverge: Economic Patterns

The South had emerged from a slump in the last quarter of the eighteenth century to become a region of dynamic change between 1800 and 1860. But it had changed in ways that only widened the distance between it and the North. At a time when the North was experiencing rapid urbanization, the South remained predominantly rural. In 1820 the proportion of the southern population living in urban areas was about half that of New England and the mid-Atlantic states; by 1860 the proportion had dropped to a third.

One reason for the rural character of the South was that it contained very little industry. Although a third of the population of the United States in 1850 lived there, the South accounted for only 10 percent of the nation's manufacturing. The industrial output of the entire South in 1850 was less than that of New Hampshire and only one-third that of Massachusetts. Between 1840 and 1860, the South's share of the capital invested in American manufacturing actually *declined,* from 20 percent to 16 percent.

Yet the South had advocates of both industrialization and factories. A minority of southerners, among them editor J. D. B. De Bow of New Orleans, applauded industrialization as a way to revive the economies of older states such as Virginia and South Carolina, to retard migration to the Southwest, to reduce the South's dependency on northern manufactured products, and by proving that slavery had not transformed the South into a backwater, to quiet "the slanderous tongue of northern fanatics." Pleas for industrialization met with some success as a few large manufacturing companies took root. In South Carolina William Gregg, a prosperous Charleston jewelry merchant, zealously advocated industrialization after touring New England's textile mills in 1844. A year later, he started the Graniteville Manufacturing Company, which owned nine thousand spindles and three hundred looms by the late 1840s. Graniteville became a company town, with lumber mills,

gristmills, and a machine shop as well as textile mills. In Richmond Joseph Reid Anderson guided the Tredegar Iron Works to success. By 1860 the Tredegar Works ranked fourth among the nation's largest producers of iron products, and during the Civil War, it contributed greatly to the Confederate cause. Farther southwest, Daniel Pratt constructed an industrial village near Montgomery, Alabama, in which he produced cotton textiles and ginned raw cotton.

These striking examples of industrial success in the Old South, however, do not change the general picture. Industrial output in the South ran somewhat behind that of the West and far behind that of New England and the Middle Atlantic states. Compared to factories in New England, New York, and Pennsylvania, those of the South were small; they produced mainly for nearby markets; and they were much more closely tied to agriculture. The leading northern industries turned hides into tanned leather and leather into shoes, or cotton into threads and threads into suits. In contrast, while the South had some textile and shoe factories, its leading industries were only a step removed from agriculture. They turned grain into flour, corn into meal, and trees into lumber.

If the South could develop some large and successful industries, why did it not develop more? Slavery did not in itself impede industrial growth, for slaves were widely employed in factories. In the Tredegar Iron Works, for example, Anderson overcame opposition from white workers and introduced slaves into skilled rolling-mill positions. Indirectly, however, slavery did undercut the enthusiasm of whites for industrialization. The prospect of industrial slavery troubled most slaveholders. Slaves who were hired out to factory masters in cities like New Orleans and Richmond could pass themselves off as free, and often they acted as if they were free by negotiating better working conditions and by shifting from factory to factory. The same objection applied to small rural workshops. Even rural factories drew slaves off the plantations, where discipline could be more easily enforced. A Virginia planter who rented his slaves to an iron manufacturer complained that they made money by working overtime and "got the habit of roaming about and *taking care of themselves.*"

White laborers, of course, could be employed in factories. William Gregg proved at Graniteville that supposedly unruly southern whites could be

Port and City of New Orleans,
by Marie Adrien Persac, 1858

The South's largest city, New Orleans was also the main port of exit for cotton and Mississippi Valley produce.

forged into a disciplined labor force. But any effort to introduce extensive industrialization faced a major problem: to raise capital for industrialization, planters would have had to sell their slaves. They had little incentive to do so. Cash crops like cotton and sugar were proven winners, while the benefits of industrialization remained remote and doubtful. Moreover, industrialization threatened to disrupt social relations, a southerner contended, by introducing "filthy, overcrowded, licentious factories" and by attracting antislavery white immigrants to the South. As long as southerners believed that an economy founded on cash crops would remain profitable, they had little reason to leap into the uncertainties of industrialization.

The North and South Diverge: Education in a Cotton Economy

Compared to the antebellum North, the Old South made only meager provisions for public elementary schools. Flurries of enthusiasm for public education periodically swept the South, but without much effect. Southerners flatly rejected the idea of com-

pulsory education, which was gaining ground in the North by the 1850s, and they were reluctant to tax property to support education. The idea of educating slaves in any kind of school became increasingly abhorrent to southern legislatures; indeed, lawmakers made it a crime even to teach slaves to read. Some public aid flowed to state universities and to schools for white paupers, but for most whites, the only available schools were private. As a result, white illiteracy, which had been more extensive in the South than in the North during the eighteenth century, remained high in the South even as it declined in the North during the antebellum period. For example, nearly 60 percent of the North Carolinians who enlisted in the United States Army before the Civil War were illiterate. The comparable proportion for northern enlistees was less than 30 percent.

Various factors help to explain why the South lagged behind the North in the field of public education. Because the Lower South's economy relied so heavily on cotton, state revenues rose and fell with the price of cotton, and so did legislative enthusiasm for education. In addition, the South's

357

low population density made it difficult to provide public schools for all children. The idea of having a public school within walking distance of each child was appealing until one realized just how far each child would have to walk. But a low population density did not stop midwestern states from energetically promoting public education. The most probable reason for the South's failure to develop effective public schools was widespread indifference to the idea.

As was true of southern arguments in favor of industrialization, pro-education proclamations abounded, but these issued from a small segment of the leadership and often fell on deaf ears. Agricultural, self-sufficient, and independent, the middling and poor whites of the South remained unconvinced of the need for public education. They had little dependency on the printed word, few complex commercial transactions, and infrequent dealings with urban people. Even the large planters, some of whom did support public education, had a less intense commitment to it than did northern manufacturers. Where many northern businessmen accepted Horace Mann's argument that public schools would create a more orderly and alert work force, planters had no need for an educated white work force, for they already had a black one that they were determined to keep illiterate lest it acquire through books ideas about freedom.

Cotton and Southern Progress

Because the South diverged so sharply from the North, it is tempting to view the South as backward and lethargic, doomed to be bypassed by its more energetic northern sisters. Increasingly, northerners associated the spread of cities and factories with progress. Finding few cities and factories in the South, they concluded that the region was a stranger to progress as well. A northern journalist wrote of white southerners in the 1850s: "They work little, and that little, badly; they earn little, they sell little; they buy little, and they have little—very little—of the common comforts and consolations of civilized life."

Yet the white South did not lack progressive features. In 1840 per capita income in the white South was only slightly below the national average, and by 1860 it exceeded the national average. While it is true that southerners made few contri-butions to technology to rival those of northerners, many southerners had a progressive zeal for agricultural improvement. The Virginian Edmund Ruffin, who allegedly touched off the Civil War by firing the first cannon on Fort Sumter in 1861 and committed suicide in despair at the South's defeat in 1865, was an enthusiastic supporter of crop rotation and of the use of fertilizer and an important figure in the history of scientific agriculture.

Rather than viewing the Old South as economically backward, it is better to see it merely as different. Cotton was a wonderful crop, and southerners could hardly be blamed for making it their ruler. "No! You dare not make war upon cotton; no power on earth dares to make war upon it," a senator from South Carolina proclaimed in 1858. "Cotton is king."

Social Relations in the White South

Antislavery northerners often charged that slavery twisted the entire social structure of the South out of shape. By creating a permanent black underclass of bondsmen, they alleged, slavery robbed lower-class whites of the incentive to work, reduced them to shiftless misery, and rendered the South a premodern throwback in an otherwise progressive age.

Stung by northern allegations that slavery turned the white South into a region of rich planters and wretchedly poor common folk, Alabama lawyer Daniel R. Hundley retorted that "the middle classes of the South constitute the greater proportion of her citizens, and are likewise the most useful members of her society" and that even the planters "wear homespun every day and work side by side with their slaves." Turning the tables on his northern antagonists, Hundley contended that the real center of white inequality was the North, where merchants and financiers paraded in fine silks and never soiled their hands with manual labor.

In reality, what makes the white South both difficult and interesting to study is that it was a curious amalgam of aristocratic and democratic, premodern and modern features. Although it contained considerable class inequality, property ownership was widespread. Rich planters occupied seats in state legislatures out of proportion to their numbers in the population, but they did not necessarily get their way, nor did their political agenda always differ from that of other whites. Practices like slaveholding and dueling not only survived but intensified in the Old South at a time when they were dying out elsewhere in the civilized world. Visitors to the South sometimes thought that they were traveling backward in time. "It seems as if everything had stopped growing, and was growing backwards," novelist Harriet Beecher Stowe wrote of the South. Yet like northerners, white southerners were restless, acquisitive, eager to make money, skillful at managing complex commercial enterprises, and when they chose, even capable of becoming successful industrialists.

The Social Groups of the White South

While all agricultural regions of the South contained slaveholders and nonslaveholders, there was considerable diversity within each group. There were slaveholders in every southern state who owned vast estates, magnificent homes, and hundreds of slaves, but most lived more modestly. In 1860 one-quarter of all white families in the South owned slaves. Of these, nearly half owned fewer than five slaves, and nearly three-quarters had fewer than ten slaves. Only 12 percent owned twenty or more slaves, and only 1 percent had a hundred or more. Large slaveholders clearly were a minority within a minority. Nonslaveholders also formed a diverse group. Most were landowners whose farms drew on the labor of family members, but the South also contained nonslaveholding whites who squatted on land in the so-called pine barrens or piney woods and who scratched out a livelihood by raising livestock, hunting and fishing, and planting a few acres of corn, oats, or sweet potatoes.

Despite all the diversity, one might reasonably divide the South's social structure into four main groups—the planters, the small slaveholders, the yeomen (or family farmers), and the people of the pine barrens—although even this classification is a little arbitrary. Historians usually classify as planters those who owned twenty or more slaves, the minimum number considered necessary for specialized plantation agriculture. Yet in any group of twenty slaves, some were likely to be too old and others too young to work. Arguably, a planter needed more than twenty slaves to run a plantation. Similarly, those with fewer than twenty slaves

are usually described as small slaveholders, but an obvious difference separated an individual who owned ten to nineteen slaves and one who owned fewer than five. The former was close to becoming a planter; the latter was only a step removed from the yeomen. A great deal depended on where one lived. In the low country and delta regions of the South, the planters dominated; most small slaveholders in these areas had dealings with the planters and looked to them for leadership. In the hilly upland regions, the yeoman were dominant, and small slaveholders tended to acquire their outlook.

Of course, many lawyers, physicians, merchants, and artisans, who did not fall into any of these four main groups, also made the Old South their home. But because the South was fundamentally rural and agricultural, those outside of agriculture usually identified their interests with one or another of the four agricultural groups. Rural artisans and merchants had innumerable dealings with the yeoman. Urban merchants and lawyers depended on the planters and absorbed their outlook on most issues. (Some of the most articulate defenders of plantation slavery, including Daniel R. Hundley, were trained as lawyers.) Similarly, slave traders relied on the plantation economy for their livelihood. Nathan Bedford Forrest, the uneducated son of a humble Tennessee blacksmith, made a fortune as a slave trader in Natchez, Mississippi. When the Civil War broke out, Forrest enlisted in the Confederate army as a private and rose swiftly to become the South's greatest cavalry general. "That devil Forrest," the Yankees called him. Plantation slavery directed Forrest's allegiances as surely as it did those of planters like Jefferson Davis, the Confederacy's president.

Planters and Plantation Mistresses

With porticoed mansion and fields teeming with slaves, the plantation still stands at the center of the popular image of the Old South. This romanticized view, reinforced by novels and motion pictures like *Gone with the Wind,* is not entirely misleading, for the South contained plantations that travelers found "superb beyond description." Whether devoted to cotton, tobacco, rice, or sugar, the plantations were characterized by a high degree of division of labor. In the 1850s Bellmead, a tobacco plantation on Virginia's James River, was virtually an agricultural equivalent of a factory village. Its more than one hundred slaves were classified into the domestic staff (butlers, waiters, seamstresses, laundresses, maids, and gardeners), the pasture staff (shepherds, cowherds, and hog drivers), outdoor craftsmen (stonemasons and carpenters), indoor craftsmen (blacksmiths, carpenters, shoemakers, spinners, and weavers), and the field hands. Such a division of labor was inconceivable without an abundance of slaves and land. Wade Hampton's cotton plantation near Columbia, South Carolina, encompassed twenty-four hundred acres of land. With such resources, it is not surprising that large plantations could generate incomes that contemporaries viewed as immense ($20,000—$30,000 a year). Immense is an even better description of the worth (rather than income) of some planters. At his death in 1851, South Carolina's Nathaniel Heyward owned fourteen rice plantations; a cotton plantation; a sawmill and pine land; horses, mules, and cattle worth $20,000; nine residences in Charleston; and furniture valued at $180,000, silver plate at $15,000, old wine at $3,000, and securities and cash amounting to $200,000. This represented the *small* part of his estate. The large portion was his more than two thousand slaves valued at over a million dollars.

During the first flush of settlement in the piedmont and trans-Appalachian South, in the eighteenth century, most well-off planters had been content to live in simple log cabins. In contrast, between 1810 and 1860, elite planters often vied with each other to build stately mansions. Some, like Lyman Hardy of Mississippi, hired architects. Hardy's "Auburn," built in 1812 near Natchez, featured Ionic columns and a portico thirty-one feet long and twelve feet deep. Others copied designs from books like Andrew Jackson Downing's *The Architecture of Country Houses* (1850), which sold sixteen thousand copies between 1850 and 1865. Nor did the popular Greek Revival and Georgian styles exhaust planters' options. In 1859 Joseph A. S. Acklen, who owned several plantations near the junction of the Red and Mississippi rivers, began a country house in the style of a Gothic castle, with a great hall and more than fifty rooms.

However impressive, these were not typical planters. The wealth of most planters, especially in states like Alabama and Mississippi, consisted primarily in the value of their slaves rather than

Lyman Hardy's Auburn, Natchez, Mississippi

Designed by one transplanted Yankee and owned by another, Auburn, with its tall columns topped by lavish Ionic capitals, showed the influence of neoclassical architecture in the Old South.

in such finery as expensive furniture or silver plate. In monetary terms, slaves were worth a great deal, as much as seventeen hundred dollars for a field hand in the 1850s. Planters could convert their wealth into cash for purchasing luxuries only by selling slaves. A planter who sold his slaves ceased to be a planter and relinquished the South's most prestigious social status. Not surprisingly, most planters clung to large-scale slaveholding, even if it meant scrimping on their lifestyles. A northern journalist observed that in the Southwest, men worth millions lived as if they were not worth hundreds.

Planters had to worry constantly about profitability, for the fixed costs of operating plantations—including hiring overseers, housing and feeding slaves, and maintaining cotton gins and other equipment—were considerable. Their drive for profits led planters to search constantly for more and better land, to organize their slaves into specialized work gangs for maximum efficiency, and to make their plantations self-sufficient in food. Their quest for profits also impelled planters to cultivate far-flung commercial connections. Like any commodity, cotton went up and down in price. Sometimes the fluctuations were long-term; more often, the price fluctuated seasonally. In response to these rises and falls, planters assigned their cotton to commercial agents in cities. These agents held the cotton until the price was right and extended credit to enable the planters to pay their bills before the cotton was sold. Thus indebtedness became part of the plantation economy. Persistent debt intensified the planters' quest for more profits to escape from the burden of debt. Planters enjoyed neither repose nor security.

Plantation agriculture placed psychological strains as well as economic burdens on planters and their wives. Frequent moves disrupted circles of friends and relatives, all the more so because migration to the Southwest carried families into progressively less settled, more desolate areas. In 1850 those regions of the South with thriving plantation economies—notably Alabama, Mississippi, and southeastern Louisiana—had only recently emerged from the frontier stage; as late as 1860, the Mississippi Delta contained vast tracts of unsettled land. In the 1850s New York journalist Frederick Law Olmsted was surprised to find planters in the Southwest living in fairly crude homes whose only distinguishing features were whitewashed exteriors and, at times, expensive rugs over roughly planked floors. "Their early frontier life," Olmsted wrote, "seems to have destroyed their capacity to enjoy many of the usual luxuries of civilized life."

For plantation women, migration to the Southwest often amounted to a fall from grace, for many of them had grown up in seaboard elegance, only to find themselves in isolated regions, surrounded by slaves, and bereft of the companion-

Sugar Mill on Bayou Teche, Olivier Plantation, *by Marie Adrien Persac, 1861*
Elite southerners, chickens, and a peacock enjoy a sunny day in this placid scene of a gracious Louisiana sugar plantation.

ship of white social peers. "I am sad tonight, sickness preys on my frame," wrote a bride who moved to Mississippi in 1833. "I am alone and more than 150 miles from any near relative in the wild woods of an Indian nation." At times wives lacked even their husbands' companionship. Plantation agriculture kept men on the road, scouting new land for purchase, supervising outlying plantations, and transacting business in New Orleans or Memphis. "Almost four weeks, and am I to be depriv'd of the pleasure of seeing you for weeks to come, it makes the tears fall fast from my poor Eyes," a lonely wife wrote her distant husband.

Planters and their wives found various ways to cope with their isolation from civilized society. Many spent long periods of time in cities and left the management of plantations to overseers. In 1850 fully one-half the planters in the Mississippi Delta were absentees living in or near Natchez or New Orleans rather than on their plantations. Yet in 1850 only 30 percent of planters with a hundred or more slaves employed white overseers; the majority did not escape from the task of managing their estates. In response, many made plantation life more sociable by engaging in lavish hospitality. But hospitality imposed enormous burdens on plantation wives, who might have to entertain as many as fifteen people for breakfast and attend to the needs of visitors who stayed for days. Indeed, in the plantation economy, wives had even less leisure than their husbands. Aside from raising their own children and caring for guests, plantation mistresses supervised house slaves, made carpets and clothes, looked after outlying buildings like smokehouses and dairies, and planted garden fruits and vegetables. Plantation women were anything but the delicate idlers of legend. In the absence of their husbands or fathers, they frequently kept the plantation accounts. An Alabama politician expected his daughter to report the exact amounts of corn and cotton planted at each of his plantations.

Among the greatest sorrows of some plantation mistresses was the presence of the mulatto children, who stood as daily reminders of their husbands' infidelity. Mary Boykin Chesnut, an astute Charleston woman and famous diarist, commented: "Any lady is ready to tell you who is the father of all the mulatto children in everybody's household but her own. These, she seems

to think, drop from clouds." Insisting on sexual purity for white women, southern gentlemen followed a looser standard for themselves. After the death of his wife, the brother of the famous abolitionist sisters Sarah and Angelina Grimké fathered three mulatto children. The gentlemanly code usually tolerated such transgressions as long as they were not paraded in public—but at times, even if they were. Richard M. Johnson of Kentucky, the man who allegedly killed Tecumseh during the War of 1812, was elected vice president of the United States in 1836 despite having lived openly for years with his black mistress.

The isolation, drudgery, and humiliation that planters' wives experienced turned very few against the system. When the Civil War came, they supported the Confederacy as enthusiastically as any group. However much they might hate living as white islands in a sea of slaves, they recognized no less than their husbands that their wealth and position depended on slavery.

The Small Slaveholders

In 1860, 88 percent of all slaveholders owned fewer than twenty slaves, and most of these possessed fewer than ten slaves. Some slaveowners were not even farmers: one out of every five was employed outside of agriculture, usually as a lawyer, physician, merchant, or artisan.

As a large and extremely diverse group, small slaveholders experienced conflicting loyalties and ambitions. In the upland regions, they absorbed the outlook of yeomen (nonslaveowning farmers), the numerically dominant group. Typically, small upland slaveholders owned only a few slaves and rarely aspired to become large planters. In contrast, in the low country and delta regions, where planters formed the dominant group, small slaveholders often aspired to planter status. In these planter-dominated areas, someone with ten slaves could realistically look forward to the day when he would own thirty. The deltas were thus filled with ambitious and acquisitive individuals who linked success to owning more slaves. Whether one owned ten slaves or fifty, the logic of slaveholding was much the same. The investment in slaves could be justified only by setting them to work on profitable crops. Profitable crops demanded, in turn, more and better land. Much like the planters, the small slaveholder of the low country and delta areas were restless and footloose.

The social structure of the deltas was fluid but not infinitely so. Small slaveholders were usually younger than large slaveholders, and many hoped to become planters in their own right. But as the antebellum period wore on, a clear tendency developed toward the geographical segregation of the small slaveholders from the planters in the cotton belt. Small slaveholders led the initial push into the cotton belt in the 1810s and 1820s, while the large planters, reluctant to risk transporting their hundreds of slaves into the still turbulent new territory, remained in the seaboard South. Gradually, however, the large planters ventured into Alabama and Mississippi. Colonel Thomas Dabney, a planter originally from tidewater Virginia, made several scouting tours of the Southwest before moving his family and slaves to the region of Vicksburg, Mississippi, where he started a four-thousand-acre plantation. The small slaveholders already on the scene at first resented Dabney's genteel manners and misguided efforts to win friends. He showed up at house raisings to lend a hand, but the hands he lent were not his own, which remained gloved, but those of his slaves. The small slaveholders muttered about transplanted Virginia snobs. Dabney responded to complaints simply by buying up much of the best land in the region. In itself, this was no loss to the small slaveholders. They had been first on the scene, and it was their land that the Dabneys of the South purchased. Dabney and men like him quickly turned the whole region from Vicksburg to Natchez into one of large plantations. The small farmers took the proceeds from the sale of their land, bought more slaves, and moved elsewhere to grow cotton. Small slaveholders gradually transformed the region from Vicksburg to Tuscaloosa, Alabama, into a belt of medium-size farms with a dozen or so slaves on each.

The Yeomen

Nonslaveholding family farmers, or yeomen, composed the largest single group of southern whites. Most were landowners. Landholding yeomen, because they owned no slaves of their own, frequently hired slaves at harvest time to help in the fields. In an area where the land was poor, like eastern Tennessee, the landowning yeomen were typically subsistence farmers, but most grew some crops for the market. Whether they engaged in subsistence or commercial agriculture, they controlled landholdings far more modest than those of the planters—more likely in the range of fifty to two hundred acres than five hundred or more acres. Yeomen could be found anywhere in the South, but they tended to congregate in the upland regions. In the seaboard South, they populated the piedmont region of Georgia, South Carolina, North Carolina, and Virginia; in the Southwest they usually lived in the hilly upcountry, far from the rich alluvial soil of the deltas. A minority of yeomen did not own land. Typically young, these men resided with and worked for landowners to whom they were related.

The leading characteristic of the yeomen was the value that they attached to self-sufficiency. As nonslaveholders, they were not carried along by the same logic that impelled slaveholders to acquire more land and plant more cash crops. Although most yeomen raised cash crops, relative to planters, they devoted a higher proportion of their acreage to subsistence crops like corn, sweet potatoes, and oats than to cash crops. The ideal of the planters was profit with modest self-sufficiency; that of the yeomen, self-sufficiency with modest profit.

Yeomen dwelling in the low country and delta regions dominated by planters were often dismissed as "poor white trash." But in the upland areas, where they constituted the dominant group, the yeomen were highly respectable. There they coexisted peacefully with the slaveholders, who typically owned only a few slaves (large planters were rare in the upland areas). Both the small slaveholders and the yeomen were essentially family farmers. With or without the aid of a few slaves, fathers and sons cleared the land and plowed, planted, and hoed the fields. Wives and daughters planted and tended vegetable gardens, helped at harvest, occasionally cared for livestock, cooked, and made clothes for the family.

In contrast to the far-flung commercial transactions of the planters, who depended on distant commercial agents to market their crops, the economic transactions of yeomen usually occurred within the neighborhood of their farms. Yeomen

Corn Husking, *by Eastman Johnson, 1860*

Grown by the South's nonslaveholding yeomen, corn rather than cotton was the region's principal crop. Yeomen ate corn in various forms, including bread and grits, and fed corn to their livestock, which provided them with meat and milk.

often exchanged their cotton, wheat, or tobacco for goods and services from local artisans and merchants. In some areas they sold their surplus corn to the herdsmen and drovers who made a living in the South's upland regions by specializing in the raising of hogs. Along the French Broad River in eastern Tennessee, some twenty thousand to thirty thousand hogs were fattened for market each year; at peak season, a traveler would see a thousand hogs a mile. When driven to market, the hogs were quartered at night in huge stock stands, veritable hog "hotels," and fed with corn supplied by the local yeomen.

The People of the Pine Barrens

One of the most controversial groups in the Old South comprised independent whites of the wooded "pine barrens." In a region marked by slaveholding, widespread landownership, and agriculture, these people stood out as deviants. Composing about 10 percent of southern whites, they were neither slaveholders nor (as a rule) landowners nor primarily farmers. Rather, they typically put up crude cabins, cleared a few acres of surrounding land (on which they usually squatted), planted some corn

between tree stumps, and grazed hogs and cattle in the woods. Their simple diet—cornmeal and pork supplemented by fish and game—did not differ much from that of the yeomen or slaves. But their way of life was different. They did not raise cash crops, nor did they engage in the daily routine of orderly work that marked family farmers. With their ramshackle houses and handful of stump-strewn acres, they appeared to be lazy and shiftless.

Antislavery northerners cited the people of the pine barrens as proof that slavery degraded nonslaveholding whites. A southern defender of slavery, Daniel R. Hundley, summarized the antislavery argument: "Look at the Poor Whites of the South, . . . and behold the fruits of slavery." Then he attacked the argument. The pine barrens folk were poor, he conceded, but unlike the paupers of the northern cities, they could fend for themselves. Hundley's contention was well founded. The people of the pine barrens acquired a degree of self-sufficiency to which the South's climate and customs contributed. Mild winters made it possible to graze livestock in the woods for much of the year. Furthermore, the South retained the legal tradition (rapidly being dismantled in the antebellum North) of treating unfenced and unimproved land as available for public use. Despite complaints, the people of the pine barrens (along with many yeomen) hunted on land belonging to others as long as it was neither enclosed nor improved.

The economic independence of the pine barrens dwellers shaped their attitudes toward work. The men were reluctant to hire themselves out as farm laborers, and even when they did, they refused to perform "slave" tasks like caring for cattle and fetching wood and water. The women had similar attitudes. They might sew or quilt on hire, but they refused to become servants.

It is misleading to think of these people as victimized or oppressed. Many lived in the pine barrens out of choice. The grandson of a farmer who had migrated from Emanuel County, Georgia, to the Mississippi pine barrens explained his grandfather's motives in these words: "The truth is it looks like Emanuel County. The turpentine smell, the moan of the winds through the pine trees, and nobody within fifty miles of him, [were] too captivating . . . to be resisted, and he rested there."

Conflict and Consensus
in the White South

Planters tangled with yeomen on several issues in the Old South. With their extensive economic dealings and need for credit, planters and their urban commercial allies inclined toward the Whig party, which was generally more sympathetic to banking and economic development. Cherishing their self-sufficiency, and economically independent, the yeomen tended to be Democrats.

The occasions for conflict between these groups were minimal, however, and an underlying political unity reigned in the South. Especially in the Lower South, each of the four main social groups—planters, small slaveholders, yeomen, and pine barrens people—tended to cluster in different regions. The delta areas that planters dominated contained relatively small numbers of yeomen. In other regions small slaveowners, families with ten to fifteen slaves, predominated. In the upland areas far from the deltas, the yeomen congregated. And the people of the pine barrens lived in a world of their own. There was more geographical intermingling of groups in the Upper South than in the Lower, but throughout the South each group attained a degree of independence from the others. With widespread

landownership and relatively few factories, the Old South basically was not a place where whites worked for other whites, and this tended to minimize friction among whites.

In addition, the white South's political structure was sufficiently democratic to prevent any one social group from gaining exclusive control over politics. It is true that in both the Upper and the Lower South, the majority of state legislators were planters. Large planters, those with fifty or more slaves, were represented in legislatures far out of proportion to their numbers in the population. Yet these same planters owed their election to the popular vote. The white South was affected by the same democratic currents that swept northern politics between 1815 and 1860, and the newer states of the South had usually entered the Union with democratic constitutions that included universal white manhood suffrage—the right of all adult white males to vote.

While yeomen often voted for planters, the nonslaveowners did not issue their elected representatives a blank check to govern as they pleased. During the 1830s and 1840s, Whig planters who favored banks faced intense and often successful opposition from Democratic yeomen. These yeomen blamed banks for the Panic of 1837 and pressured southern legislatures to restrict bank operations. On banking issues, nonslaveholders got their way often enough to nurture their belief that they ultimately controlled politics and that slaveholders could not block their goals.

Conflict over Slavery

Nevertheless, there was considerable potential for conflict between the slaveholders and nonslaveholders. The white carpenter who complained in 1849 that "unjust, oppressive, and degrading" competition from slave labor depressed his wages surely had a point. Between 1830 and 1860, slaveholders gained an increasing proportion of the South's wealth while declining as a proportion of its white population. The size of the slaveholding class shrank from 36 percent of the white population in 1831 to 31 percent in 1850 to 25 percent in 1860. A Louisiana editor warned in 1858 that "the present tendency of supply and demand is to concentrate all the slaves in the hands of the few, and thus excite the envy rather than cultivate the sympathy of the people." That same year, the governor of Florida proposed a law guaranteeing to each white person the ownership of at least one slave. Some southerners began to support the idea of Congress's reopening the African slave trade to increase the supply of slaves, bring down their price, and give more whites a stake in the institution.

As the debate over slavery in Virginia during 1831–1832 (see this chapter's introduction) attests, slaveholders had good reasons for uncertainty over the allegiance of nonslaveholders to the "peculiar institution" of slavery. The publication in 1857 of Hinton R. Helper's *The Impending Crisis of the South,* which called upon nonslaveholders to abolish slavery in their own interest, revealed the persistence of white opposition to slavery. On balance, however, slavery did not create profound and lasting divisions between the South's slaveholders and nonslaveholders. Although antagonism to slavery flourished in parts of Virginia up to 1860, proposals for emancipation dropped from the state's political agenda after 1832. In Kentucky, a state with a history of antislavery activity that dated back to the 1790s, calls for emancipation were revived in 1849 in a popular referendum. But the pro-emancipation forces went down to crushing defeat. Thereafter, the continuation of slavery ceased to be a political issue in Kentucky and elsewhere in the South.

The rise and fall of pro-emancipation sentiment in the South raises a key question. Since the majority of white southerners were nonslaveholders, why did they not attack the institution more consistently? To look ahead, why were so many of them to fight ferociously and die bravely during the Civil War in defense of an institution in which they appeared not to have had any real stake? There are various answers to these questions. First, some nonslaveholders hoped to become slaveholders. Second, most simply accepted the racist assumptions upon which slavery rested. Whether slaveholders or nonslaveholders, white southerners dreaded the likelihood that emancipation might encourage "impudent" blacks to entertain ideas of social equality with whites. Blacks might demand the right to sit next to whites in railroad cars and even make advances to white women. "Now suppose they [the slaves] was free," a white southerner told a northern journalist in the 1850s, "you see they'd all think themselves just as good as we; of

course they would if they was free. Now just suppose you had a family of children, how would you like to hev a niggar steppin' up to your darter?" Slavery, in short, appealed to whites as a legal, time-honored, and foolproof way to enforce the social subordination of blacks. Finally, no one knew where the slaves, if freed, would go or what they would do. After 1830 a dwindling minority of northerners and southerners still dallied with the idea of colonizing freed blacks in Africa, but that alternative increasingly seemed unrealistic in a society where slaves numbered in the millions. Without colonization, southerners concluded, emancipation would produce a race war. In 1860 Georgia's governor sent a blunt message to his constituents, many of them nonslaveholders: "So soon as the slaves were at liberty thousands of them would leave the cotton and rice fields . . . and make their way to the healthier climate of the mountain region [where] we should have them plundering and stealing, robbing and killing." There was no mistaking the conclusion. Emancipation would not merely deprive slaveholders of their property, it would jeopardize the lives of nonslaveholders.

The Proslavery Argument

As slaveholders and nonslaveholders closed ranks behind slavery, southerners increasingly defended the institution as a positive good rather than as a necessary evil. Between 1830 and 1860, southern intellectuals such as James Henry Hammond, Edmund Ruffin, and William Gilmore Simms of South Carolina and Nathaniel Beverley Tucker, George F. Holmes, and George Fitzhugh of Virginia constructed a theoretical defense of slavery. They contended that slavery was a venerable institution that had flourished in the most refined civilizations. A slave society in ancient Athens, Holmes noted, had produced Plato and Aristotle, and Roman slaveholders had "conquered the world, legislated for all succeeding ages, and laid the broad foundations of modern civilization and modern institutions." In the eyes of these apologists for slavery, the antiquity and universality of the institution proved that inequality was a natural human condition.

Furthermore, they noted, inequality existed in the North as well as the South, with the difference that northern inequality resulted in the exploita-

Old Kentucky Home, *by Eastman Johnson, 1859*

This portrait of banjo-plucking, carefree slaves projected the white South's view of slavery as a benign institution.

on slavery. During the 1790s and early 1800s, some Protestant ministers had assailed slavery as immoral. By the 1830s, however, most members of the clergy had convinced themselves that slavery was not only compatible with Christianity but also necessary for the proper exercise of the Christian religion. Like the proslavery intellectuals, clergymen contended that slavery provided the opportunity to display Christian responsibility toward one's inferiors, while it helped blacks develop Christian virtues like humility and self-control. With this conclusion solidified, southerners increasingly attacked antislavery evangelicals in the North for disrupting the allegedly superior social arrangement of the South. In 1844 the Methodist Episcopal church split into northern and southern wings. In 1845 Baptists formed a separate Southern Convention. Even earlier, southerners and conservative northerners had combined in 1837 to drive the antislavery New School Presbyterians out of that denomination's main body. All this added up to a profound irony. In 1800 southern evangelicals had been more critical of slavery than southerners as a whole. Yet the evangelicals effectively seceded from national church organizations long before the South seceded from the Union.

Honor and Violence in the Old South

Almost everything about the Old South struck northern visitors as extreme. Although inequality certainly flourished in the North, no group in northern society was as deprived as the slaves. The Irish immigrants who arrived in the North in great waves in the 1840s often owned no property, but unlike the slaves, they were not in themselves a form of property. Not only did northerners find the gap between the races in the South extreme, but individual southerners seemed to run to extremes. One minute they were hospitable and gracious; the next, savagely violent. Abolitionists were not the only ones to view the Old South as a land of extremes. "The Americans of the South," Alexis de Tocqueville asserted, "are brave, comparatively ignorant, hospitable, generous, easy to irritate, violent in their resentments, without industry or the spirit of enterprise."

tion of the weak, while southern inequality led to the protection of the weak by the strong. Northern mill owners used their "wage slaves" and then discarded them; in contrast, southern masters and slaves were bound together by a "*community* of interests." Southerners portrayed slavery as a costly and inefficient labor system, but one that allowed and even compelled masters to treat slaves well by attending to their health, clothing, and discipline. "You have been chosen," Tucker told students at the College of William and Mary, "as the instrument, in the hand of God for accomplishing the great purpose of his benevolence."

The rise of the proslavery argument coincided with a shift in the position of the southern churches

Violence in the White South

No one who lived in a southern community, a northern journalist noted in the 1850s, could fail to be impressed with "the frequency of fighting with deadly weapons." Throughout the colonial and antebellum periods, violence deeply colored the daily lives of white southerners. In the 1760s a minister described backcountry Virginians "biting one anothers Lips and Noses off, and gowging one another—that is, thrusting out anothers Eyes, and kicking one another on the Cods [genitals], to the Great damage of many a Poor Woman." In the 1840s a New York newspaper described a fight between two raftsmen on the Mississippi that started when one accidentally bumped the other into shallow water. When it was over, one raftsmen was dead; the other boasted, "I can lick a steamboat. My fingernails is related to a sawmill on my mother's side, . . . and the brass buttons on my coat have all been boiled in poison." Gouging out eyes became a specialty of sorts among poor whites. On one occasion, a South Carolina judge entered his court to find a plaintiff, a juror, and two witnesses all missing one eye. Stories of eye gougings and ear bitings lost nothing in the telling and became part of the folklore of the Old South. Mike Fink, a legendary southern fighter and hunter, boasted that he was so mean that in infancy, he refused his mother's milk and cried out for a bottle of whiskey. Yet beneath the folklore lay the reality of violence that gave the Old South a murder rate as much as ten times higher than that of the North.

The Code of Honor and Dueling

At the root of most violence in the white South lay intensified feelings of personal pride that themselves reflected the inescapable presence of slaves. Every day of their lives, white southerners saw slaves who were degraded, insulted, and powerless to resist. This experience had a searing impact on whites, for it encouraged them to react violently to even trivial insults in order to demonstrate that they had nothing in common with slaves. Among gentlemen this exaggerated pride took the form of a code of honor. In this context, honor can best be defined as an extraordinary sensitivity to one's reputation, a belief that one's self-esteem depends on the judgment of others. In the antebellum North, moralists celebrated a rival ideal, character—the quality that enabled an individual to behave in a steady fashion regardless of how others acted toward him or her. A person possessed of character acted out of the promptings of conscience. In contrast, in the honor culture of the Old South, the slightest insult, as long as it was perceived as intentional, could become the basis for a duel (see "A Place in Time").

Formalized by British and French officers during the Revolutionary War, dueling gained a secure niche in the Old South as a means by which gentlemen dealt with affronts to their honor. To outsiders, the incidents that sparked duels seemed so trivial as to be scarcely credible: a casual remark accidentally overheard, a harmless brushing against the side of someone at a public event, even a hostile glance. Yet dueling did not necessarily terminate in violence. Dueling constituted part of a complex code of etiquette that governed relations among gentlemen in the Old South and, like all forms of etiquette, called for a curious sort of self-restraint. Gentlemen viewed dueling as a refined alternative to the random violence of lower-class life. The code of dueling did not dictate that the insulted party leap at his antagonist's throat or draw his pistol at the perceived moment of insult. Rather, he was to remain cool, bide his time, settle on a choice of weapons, and agree to a meeting place. In the interval, negotiations between friends of the parties sought to clear up the "misunderstanding" that had evoked the challenge. In this way, most confrontations ended peaceably rather than on the field of honor at dawn.

Although dueling was as much a way of settling disputes peaceably as of ending them violently, the ritual could easily terminate in a death or maiming. Dueling did not allow the resolution of grievances by the courts, a form of redress that would have guaranteed a peaceful outcome. As a way of settling personal disputes that involved honor, recourse to the law struck many southerners as cowardly and shameless. Andrew Jackson's mother told the future president: "The law affords no remedy that can satisfy the feelings of a true man."

In addition, dueling rested on the assumption that a gentlemen could recognize another gentleman and hence would know when to respond to a challenge. Nothing in the code of dueling compelled a gentleman to duel someone beneath his status, because such a person's opinion of a gentleman hardly mattered. An insolent porter who insulted a gentleman might get a whipping but did not merit a challenge to a duel. Yet it was often difficult to determine who was a gentleman. The Old South teemed with pretentious, would-be gentlemen. A clerk in a country store in Arkansas in the 1850s found it remarkable that ordinary farmers who hung around the store talked of their honor and that the store's proprietor, a German Jew, carried a dueling pistol.

The Southern Evangelicals and White Values

With its emphasis on the personal redress of grievances and its inclination toward violence, the ideal of honor had a potential for conflict with the values preached by the southern evangelical churches, notably the Baptists, Methodists, and Presbyterians. These evangelical denominations were on the rise even before the Great Kentucky Revival of 1800–1801 and continued to grow in the wake of the revival. With forty-eight thousand southern members in 1801, for example, the Methodists reported eighty thousand by 1807. All of the evangelical denominations stressed humility and self-restraint, virtues that stood in contrast to the entire culture of show and display that buttressed the extravagance and violence of the Old South.

Prior to 1830 most southern gentlemen looked down on the evangelicals as uncouth fanatics, and even after 1830 evangelical values scarcely dominated the South's white leadership. But evangelicals gradually shed their image as illiterate backwoods people by founding colleges like Randolph Macon (Methodist, 1830) and Wake Forest (Baptist, 1838) and by exhorting pious women, who composed two-thirds of the membership of evangelical churches, to make every home "a sanctuary, a resting place, a shadow from the heats, turmoils, and conflicts of life, and an effectual barrier against ambition, envy, jealousy, and selfishness." During the 1830s evangelical values and practices like revivalism began to penetrate even the Episcopal church, the denomination long preferred by the gentry.

Southern evangelicals rarely attacked honor as such, but they railed against dueling, brawling, intemperance, and gambling and, in the words of

a Georgia woman, the "*Revenge, Ambition, Pride*" that undergirded these practices. By the 1860s the South contained many Christian gentlemen like the bible-quoting Presbyterian general Thomas J. "Stonewall" Jackson, fierce in a righteous war but a sworn opponent of strong drink, the gaming table, and the duel.

Life Under Slavery

Slavery, the institution that lay at the root of the code of honor and other distinctive features of the Old South, has long inspired controversy among historians. Some have portrayed slavery as a benevolent institution in which blacks lived contentedly under kind masters; others, as a cruel and inhuman system that drove slaves into constant rebellion. Neither view is accurate, but both contain a germ of truth. There were kind masters who accepted the view expressed by a Baptist minister in 1854: "Give your servants that which is just and equal, knowing that you also have a Master in heaven." Moreover, some slaves developed genuine affection for their masters. Yet slavery was an inherently oppressive institution that forcefully appropriated the life and labor of one race for the material benefit of another. Despite professions to the contrary by apologists for slavery, the vast majority of slaveholders exploited the labor of blacks to earn a profit. Kind masters might complain about cruel overseers, but the masters hired and paid the overseers to get as much work as possible out of blacks. When the master of one plantation chastised his overseer for "barbarity," the latter replied: "Do you not remember what you told me the time you employed me that [if] I failed to make you good crops I would have to leave?" Indeed, kindness was a double-edged sword, for the benevolent master came to expect grateful affection from his slaves and then interpreted that affection as loyalty to the institution of slavery. In fact, blacks felt little, if any, loyalty to slavery. When northern troops descended upon plantations during the Civil War, masters were dismayed to find many of their most trusted slaves deserting to Union lines.

While the kindness or cruelty of masters made some difference to slaves, the most important

Edgefield District, South Carolina, in the Antebellum Era

Pierce Mason Butler

A leading Edgefield politician, Butler was befriended early in his career by John Calhoun, who secured an army commission for him. Joining Calhoun in the early 1830s in support of nullification, Butler was elected governor of South Carolina in 1836. He led the Palmetto regiment in the Mexican War and was killed in action in 1847.

Francis Wilkinson Pickens

Pickens came to Edgefield to study and practice law. A relative of Calhoun, he favored nullification. Elected governor of South Carolina just before its secession from the Union in 1860, Pickens once said that "before a free people can be dragged into a war, it must be in defense of great national right as well as national honor."

Located on the western edge of South Carolina near the Georgia border, Edgefield District combined features of the aristocratic lowcountry, to which it was linked by the Savannah River, and the yeoman-dominated upland regions of the Old South. Most Edgefield whites were small farmers or agricultural workers. In 1860 a majority did not own any slaves, and a sizable minority had no land. Yet the invention of the cotton gin had attracted wealthy lowcountry planters to Edgefield, and by 1860 the district had become the state's leading cotton producer. These planters formed the nucleus of the district's elite. By 1860 the wealthiest 10 percent of white heads of household in Edgefield controlled 57 percent of the district's real and personal property. Intermarriage strengthened ties within the elite. By the time of the Civil War, the leading families, among them the Butlers, Bonhams, Brookses, Simkinses, and Pickenses, had intermarried.

Black slaves were the basis of upper-crust Edgefield's wealth. By 1860 slaves outnumbered whites by 50 percent in the district. The vast majority of Edgefield's black bondsmen were field slaves. Almost all of those dwelling on the great plantations worked under the "gang" system, by which they were divided into a number of groups, each performing a specified amount of work. (The gang system stood in contrast to the "task" system, in which individual slaves carried out designated chores.) The plantations' "plow gangs" comprised

strong young men and occasionally some women, whereas "hoe gangs" generally included elderly slaves and women. A small number of Edgefield's slaves were skilled artisans who did blacksmithing and carpentry on the district's omnipresent farms. Whether field hands or skilled craftsmen, most slaves lived with their families in simple, rude one-room cabins in close proximity to the dwellings of other slaves. An Edgefield black born into slavery in

1852 recalled that the slaves "had houses of weatherboards, big enough for [a] chicken coop—man, wife, and chillun [live] dere."

Only one-quarter of Edgefield's whites owned twenty or more of such slaves in 1860. This elite minority accounted for possession of nearly two-thirds of the district's slaves. Using their slaves not only as agrarian workers but as collateral for loans, the great planters agreed with John C. Calhoun's northern-bred son-in-law Thomas Green Clemson—the owner of the Edgefield plantation called Cane-break—that "slaves are the most valuable property in the South, being the basis of the whole southern fabric." Yet despite the yawning gap between the wealth of the planters and the income of most other whites, class conflict did not convulse antebellum Edgefield's white society, which as a whole was tightly unified. Verbal assaults on "aristocrats" did sweep through the district from time to time, but lawyers (whom the people treated with suspicion because they did not work with their hands) rather than planters bore the brunt of these attacks.

Religion contributed mightily to this harmony reigning within Edgefield's white society. Indeed, religion was at the core of both family life and community life in the district and significantly molded the world view of the people. Although many churches dotted the countryside, so dispersed was Edgefield's population—the district contained only two incorporated towns—that ministers were limited. Thus devout Episcopalian planters and zealous Baptist yeomen farmers often found themselves sitting side by side listening to whatever traveling preacher had happened through their neighborhood. As a further boon to white solidarity, Edgefield's small farmers depended on the plantation lords to gin and market their cotton, and during the harvest they often rented slaves from the great planters. Nonslaveholding yeomen were likelier than small slaveowners to be dissatisfied with their lot in life, and many moved west into the states of Georgia, Alabama, Mississippi, and Louisiana rather than stay and complain about the rich. Nearly 60 percent of Edgefield's white heads of household in 1850 no longer

Trinity Episcopal Church

Well-known local families, among them the Butlers, Brookses, Pickenses, and Wigfalls, were members of this elite Edgefield church.

resided in the district in 1860.

The code of honor further unified the whites. Like southern gentlemen elsewhere, Edgefield's male elite saw affronts to honor behind every bush. Two military officers once fought a duel because one questioned the other's chess moves. Louis Wigfall, an Edgefield planter who later served as a Confederate senator from Texas and who was rumored to be "half drunk all the time," posted signs denouncing as cowards those who refused to accept his innumerable challenges to duels. Yet however much the code of honor set individual against individual, it could unify a region. For example, in 1856 Preston Brooks, a United States congressman from Edgefield, brutally caned Massachusetts senator Charles Sumner on the Senate floor after Sumner had delivered an antislavery oration that

dealt roughly with one of Brooks's relatives. As Representative Brooks later wrote to his constituents, it was not just the honor of a relative that he sought to defend. Rather, he had set himself up as a "sentinel" guarding the honor of every white South Carolinian against the slanderous tongues of northerners. By the mid-1850s growing attitudes like this were demonstrating that the battle lines clearly had been drawn between southerners and northerners. The time seemed to be fast approaching when, as Edgefield newspaper editor Arthur Simkins observed, southern planters' "rich blessings . . . inherited from a virtuous ancestry" would lead them to band together to strongly oppose "mobocratic tendencies in American society" flourishing in the Northeast's "larger cities and more populous manufacturing towns."

determinants of their experiences under slavery depended on such impersonal factors as the kind of agriculture in which they were engaged, whether they resided in rural or urban areas, and whether they lived in the eighteenth or nineteenth century. The experiences of slaves working on cotton plantations in the 1830s differed drastically from those of slaves in 1700, for reasons unrelated to the kindness or brutality of masters.

The Maturing of the Plantation System

Slavery changed significantly between 1700 and 1830. In 1700 the typical slave was a young man in his twenties who had recently arrived aboard a slave ship from Africa or the Caribbean and worked in company with other recent arrivals on isolated small farms. Drawn from different African regions and cultures, few such slaves spoke the same language. Because commercial slave ships contained twice as many men as women, and because slaves were widely scattered, blacks had difficulty finding sexual partners and creating a semblance of family life. Further, as a result of severe malnutrition, black women who had been brought to North America on slave ships bore relatively few children. Thus the slave trade had a devastating effect on natural increase among blacks. Without importations, the number of slaves in North America would have declined between 1710 and 1730.

In contrast, by 1830 the typical North American slave was as likely to be female as male, had been born in America, spoke a form of English that made possible communication with other slaves, and worked in the company of numerous other slaves on a plantation. The key to the change lay in the rise of plantation agriculture in the Chesapeake and South Carolina during the eighteenth century. Plantation slaves had an easier time finding mates than those on the remote farms of the early 1700s. As the ratio between slave men and women fell into balance, marriages occurred with increasing frequency between slaves on the same or nearby plantations. The native-born slave population began to rise after 1730 and soared after 1750. Importations of African slaves gradually declined after 1760, and Congress banned them in 1808.

Work and Discipline of Plantation Slaves

In 1850 the typical slave experience was to work on a large farm or plantation with at least ten fellow bondsmen. That year, almost three-quarters of all slaves were owned by masters with ten or more slaves, and just over one-half lived on units of twenty or more slaves. To understand the daily existence of the typical antebellum slave, then, requires an examination of the work and discipline routines common on large-scale farming operations.

The day of antebellum plantation slaves usually began an hour before sunrise with the sounding of a horn or bell. After a sparse breakfast, slaves marched to the fields. A traveler in Mississippi described a procession of slaves on their way to work. "First came, led by an old driver carrying a whip, forty of the largest and strongest women I ever saw together; they were all in a simple uniform dress of bluish check stuff, the skirts reaching little below the knee; their legs and feet were bare; they carried themselves loftily, each having a hoe over the shoulder, and walking with a free, powerful swing, like *chasseurs* on the march." Then came the plow hands, "thirty strong, mostly men, but few of them women. . . . A lean and vigilant white overseer, on a brisk pony, brought up the rear."

As this account indicates, slave men and women worked side by side in the fields. Female slaves who did not labor in the fields scarcely idled their hours away. A former slave, John Curry, described how his mother milked cows, cared for the children whose mothers worked in the fields, cooked for field hands, did the ironing and washing for her master's household, and took care of her own seven children. Plantations never lacked tasks for slaves of either sex. As former slave Solomon Northup noted, "ploughing, planting, picking cotton, gathering the corn, and pulling and burning stalks, occupies the whole of the four seasons of the year. Drawing and cutting wood, pressing cotton, fattening and killing hogs, are but incidental labors." Regardless of the season, the slave's day stretched from dawn to dusk. Touring the South in the 1850s, Frederick Law Olmsted prided himself on rising early and riding late but added: "I always found the negroes in the field when I first looked out, and generally had to wait for the negroes to come from the field to have my horse fed when I stopped

Black Women and Men on a Trek Home, South Carolina

Much like northern factories, large plantations made it possible to impose discipline and order on their work force. Here black women loaded down with cotton join their men on the march home after a day in the fields.

for the night." When darkness made field work impossible, slaves toted cotton bales to the gin-house, gathered wood for supper fires, and fed the mules. Weary from their labors, they slept in log cabins on wooden planks. "The softest couches in the world," a former bondsmen wryly observed, "are not to be found in the log mansions of a slave."

Although virtually all antebellum Americans worked long hours, no laboring group experienced the same combination of long hours and harsh discipline as slave field hands. Northern factory workers did not have to put up with drivers who, like one described by Olmsted, walked among the slaves with a whip, "which he often cracked at them, sometimes allowing the lash to fall lightly upon their shoulders." The lash did not always fall lightly. The annals of American slavery contain stories of repulsive brutality. Pregnant slave women were sometimes forced to lie in depressions in the ground and endure whipping on their backs, a practice that supposedly protected the fetus while abusing the mother. The disciplining and punishment of slaves was often left to white overseers and

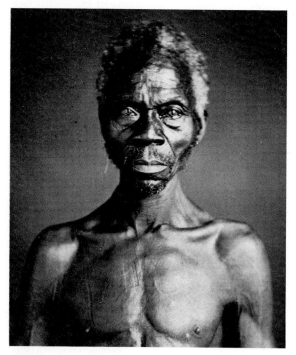

Renty

Renty, a native of the Congo, served on a South Carolina plantation in 1850, the year this daguerreotype was taken.

black drivers rather than to masters. "Dat was de meanest devil dat ever lived on the Lord's green earth," a former Mississippi slave said of his driver. The barbaric discipline meted out by others twinged the conscience of many a master. But even masters who professed Christianity viewed the disciplining of slaves as a priority—indeed, as a Christian duty to ensure the slaves' proper "submissiveness." The black abolitionist Frederick Douglass, once a slave, recalled that his worst master had been converted at a Methodist camp meeting. "If religion had any effect on his character at all," Douglass related, "it made him more cruel and hateful in all his ways."

Despite its relentless, often brutal discipline, plantation agriculture gave a minority of slaves opportunities for advancement, not from slavery to freedom but from unskilled and exhausting field work to semiskilled or skilled indoor work. Some slaves developed skills like blacksmithing and carpentry and learned to operate cotton gins. Others were trained as cooks, butlers, and dining-room attendants. These house slaves became legendary for their arrogant disdain of field hands of poor whites. The legend often distorted the reality, for house slaves were as subject to discipline as field slaves. "I liked the field work better than I did the house work," a female slave recalled. "We could talk and do anything we wanted to, just so we picked the cotton." Yet slave craftsmen and indoor servants occupied higher rungs than field hands on the social ladder of slavery.

The Slave Family

Masters thought of slaves as naturally promiscuous and flattered themselves into thinking that they alone held slave marriages together. Masters did have an incentive to encourage slave marriages in order to bring new slaves into the world and to discourage slaves from running away. Some masters baked wedding cakes for slaves and later arbitrated marital disputes. James Henry Hammond, the governor of South Carolina and a large slaveholder, noted in his diary how he "flogged Joe Goodwyn and ordered him to go back to his wife. Ditto Gabriel and Molly and ordered them to come together. Separated Moses and Anny finally."

Yet this picture of benevolent masters holding together naturally promiscuous slaves is misleading. The keenest challenge to the slave family came not from the slaves themselves but from slavery. The law provided neither recognition of nor protection for the slave family. While some slaveholders were reluctant to break slave marriages by sale, such masters could neither bequeath this reluctance to their heirs nor avoid economic hardships that might force them to sell off slaves. The reality, one historian has calculated, was that on average,

Slave Market in Richmond, Virginia, *by Eyre Crowe, 1852*

The sale of enslaved blacks in antebellum markets such as this made stable family life an impossibility for innumerable southern slaves.

The Hermitage *These slave quarters were part of the Hermitage plantation in Savannah, Georgia.*

a slave would witness in a lifetime the sale of eleven family members.

Naturally, the commonplace buying and selling of slaves severely disrupted the slaves' attempts to create a stable family life. Poignant testimony to the effects of sale on slave families, and to the desire of slaves to remain near their families, was provided by an advertisement for a runaway slave in North Carolina in 1851. The advertisement described the fugitive as presumed to be "lurking in the neighborhood of E. D. Walker's, at Moore's Creek, who owns most of his relatives, or Nathan Bonham's who owns his mother; or, perhaps, near Fletcher Bell's, at Long Creek, who owns his father." Small wonder that a slave preacher pronounced a slave couple married "until death or *distance* do you part."

Aside from their disruption by sale, slave families experienced separations and degradations from other sources. The marriage of a slave woman gave her no protection against the sexual demands of a master nor, indeed, of any white. The slave children of white masters at times became targets of the wrath of white mistresses. Sarah Wilson, the daughter of a slave and her white master, remembered that as a child, she was "picked on" by her

mistress until the master ordered his wife to let Sarah alone because she "got big, big blood in her." Slave women who worked in the fields usually were separated from their children by day; young sons and daughters often were cared for by the aged or by the mothers of other children. When slave women took husbands from nearby (rather than their own) plantations, the children usually stayed with the mother. Hannah Chapman remembered that her father tried to visit his family under cover of darkness "because he missed us and us longed for him." But if his master found him, "us would track him the nex' day by de blood stains."

Despite enormous obstacles, the relationships within slave families were often intimate and, where possible, long-lasting. In the absence of legal protection, slaves developed their own standards of family morality. A southern white woman observed that slaves "did not consider it wrong for a girl to have a child before she married, but afterwards were extremely severe upon anything like infidelity on her part." When given the opportunity, slaves sought to solemnize their marriages before clergymen. White clergymen who accompanied the Union army into Mississippi and Louisiana in the closing years of the Civil War conducted thousands of marriage rites for slaves who had long viewed themselves as married and who now desired a formal ceremony and registration.

Although slaves tried to solemnize their marriage vows in the same fashion as whites, the slave family did not merely copy the customs of white families. In white families, for example, the parent-child bond overrode all others; slaves, in contrast, emphasized ties between children and their grandparents, uncles, and aunts as well as parents. Such broad kinship ties marked the West African cultures from which many slaves had originally been brought to America, and they were reinforced by the separations between children and one or both parents that routinely occurred under slavery. Frederick Douglass never knew his father and saw his mother infrequently, but he vividly remembered his grandmother, "a good nurse, and a capital hand at making nets for catching shad and herring." In addition, slaves often created "fictive" kin networks; in the absence of uncles and aunts, they simply named friends their uncles, aunts, brothers, or sisters. In effect, slaves invested non-kin relations with symbolic kin functions. In this way, they helped protect themselves against the involuntary disruption of family ties by forced sale and established a broader community of obligation. When plantation slaves greeted each other as "brudder," they were not making a statement about actual kinship but about obligations that they felt for each other. Apologists for slavery liked to argue that a "community of interests" bound masters and slaves together. In truth, the real community of interests was the one that slaves developed among themselves in order to survive.

The Longevity, Diet, and Health of Slaves

In general, slaves in the United States reproduced faster and lived longer than slaves elsewhere in the Western Hemisphere. The evidence comes from a compelling statistic. In 1825, 36 percent of all slaves in the Western Hemisphere lived in the United States, while Brazil accounted for 31 percent. Yet of the 10 million to 12 million African slaves who had been imported to the New World between the fifteenth and nineteenth centuries, only some 550,000 (about 5 percent) had come to North America, while 3.5 million (nearly 33 percent) had been brought to Brazil. Mortality had depleted the slave populations of Brazil and the Caribbean to a far greater extent than in North America.

Several factors account for the different rates between the United States on one hand and Brazil and the Caribbean on the other. First, the sex ratio among slaves equalized more rapidly in North America, encouraging earlier and longer marriages and more children. Second, because growing corn and raising livestock were compatible with cotton cultivation, the Old South produced plenty of food. The normal ration for a slave was a peck of corn-meal and three to four pounds of fatty pork a week. Slaves often supplemented this nutritionally unbalanced diet with vegetables grown in small plots that masters allowed them to farm and with catfish and game. In the barren winter months, slaves ate less than in the summer; in this respect, however, they did not differ much from most whites.

As for disease, slaves had greater immunities to both malaria and yellow fever than did whites, but they suffered more from cholera, dysentery, and diarrhea. In the absence of privies, slaves usually relieved themselves behind bushes; urine and feces washed into the sources of drinking water and caused many diseases. Yet slaves developed some remedies that while commonly ridiculed by whites, were effective against stomach ailments. For example, the slaves' belief that eating white clay would cure dysentery and diarrhea rested on a firm basis, for we know now that kaolin, an ingredient of white clay, is a remedy for these ailments.

Although slave remedies were often more effective than those of white physicians, slaves experienced higher mortality rates than whites. At any age, a slave looked forward to a shorter life than a white, but most strikingly in infancy. Rates of infant mortality for slaves were at least twice those of whites. Between 1850 and 1860, fewer than two out of three black children survived to the age of ten. Whereas the worst mortality occurred on plantations in disease-ridden, low-lying areas, pregnant, overworked field hands often miscarried or gave birth to weakened infants even in healthier regions. Masters allowed pregnant women to rest, but rarely enough. "Labor is conducive to health," a Mississippi planter told a northern journalist; "a healthy woman will rear most children."

Slaves off Plantations

Although plantation agriculture gave some slaves, especially males, opportunities to acquire specialized skills, it imposed a good deal of supervision on them. The greatest opportunities for slaves were reserved for those who worked off plantations and farms, either as laborers in extractive industries like mining and lumbering or as artisans in towns and cities. Because the lucrative cotton growing attracted so many whites onto small farms, a perennial shortage of white labor plagued almost all the nonagricultural sectors of the southern economy. As a consequence, there was a steady demand for slaves to drive wagons, to work as stevedores (ship-cargo handlers) in port cities, to man river barges, and to perform various tasks in mining and lumbering. In 1860 lumbering employed sixteen thousand workers, most of them slaves who cut trees, hauled them to sawmills, and fashioned them into useful lumber. In sawmills black engineers fired and fixed the steam engines that provided power. In iron-ore ranges and ironworks, slaves not only served as laborers but occasionally supervised less skilled white workers. In Richmond and Petersburg in Virginia, some six thousand slaves processed chewing tobacco. In addition, just as mill girls composed the labor force of the booming textile industry in New England, slave women and children worked in the South's infant textile mills.

Behind all of this were some basic, long-standing features of southern society. Even before the rise of cotton, the profitability of southern cash crops like rice and indigo had pulled white labor out of towns and cities and indirectly provided considerable scope for slaves to work as skilled artisans. In the eighteenth century, cities like Charleston and Savannah had a large class of highly skilled slave blacksmiths and carpenters. This tradition continued into the next century and affected both enslaved and free blacks. Whether slave or free, blacks generally found it easier to work in skilled occupations in southern cities than in northern cities during the antebellum period. Not only did tradition open up skilled crafts to blacks, but the South did not attract the same flow of immigrant labor to compete with blacks as did the North.

As a result, despite slavery's stranglehold on black society, some southern blacks enjoyed opportunities in cities that were denied to blacks in northern cities. For the most part, enslaved blacks who worked in factories or in extractive industries like lumbering and mining were not owned by their employers. Rather, they were hired out by their rural masters to urban employers. If conditions in factories or mines deteriorated to the point where slaves grew ill or died, rural masters would refuse

to provide urban employers with more slaves. So it was in the interest of white supervisors to keep conditions of work for slaves off the plantations at a tolerable level. Watching the loading of a steamboat with cotton bales, Frederick Law Olmsted was amazed to see slaves sent to the top of the bank to roll the bales down to Irishmen who stowed them on the ship. Asking the reason for this arrangement, Olmsted was told: "The niggers are worth too much to be risked here; if the Paddies [Irish] are knocked overboard, or get their backs broke, nobody loses anything."

Life on the Margin: Free Blacks in the Old South

When the British were marching on New Orleans late in 1814, Andrew Jackson called upon the free blacks of the city to rally to the American flag. Many did, and they played a significant role in Jackson's victory early in 1815 at the Battle of New Orleans. Indeed, free blacks were more likely than

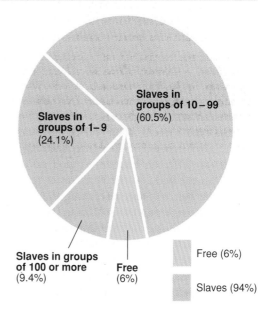

Black Society in the Old South, c. 1860

Slaves in groups of 10–99 (60.5%)

Slaves in groups of 1–9 (24.1%)

Slaves in groups of 100 or more (9.4%)

Free (6%)

Free (6%)

Slaves (94%)

(For all states in which slavery was legal in 1860)

Slaves greatly outnumbered free blacks in the Old South. Most slaves were owned by masters with ten or more slaves.

SOURCES: *Eighth Census of the United States, 1860: Population by Age, Sex, Race,* and Lewis C. Gray, *History of Agriculture in the Southern United States* (New York: Kelley, 1933).

southern blacks in general to live in cities. In 1860 one-third of the free blacks in the Upper South and more than half in the Lower South were urban.

The relatively specialized economies of the cities provided free people of color with opportunities to become carpenters, coopers (barrel makers), barbers, and even small traders. A visitor to an antebellum southern market would find that most of the meat, fish, vegetables, and fruit had been prepared for sale by free blacks. Urban free blacks formed their own fraternal orders and churches; a church run by free blacks was often the largest house of worship in a southern city. In New Orleans free blacks had their own literary journals and opera. In Natchez a free black barber, William Tiler Johnson, invested the profits of his shop in real estate, acquired stores that he rented out, purchased slaves and a plantation, and even hired a white overseer.

As Johnson's career suggests, some free blacks were highly successful. But free blacks were always vulnerable in southern society and became more so as the antebellum period wore on. While free blacks continued to increase in absolute numbers (a little more than a quarter-million free people of color dwelled in the South in 1860), the rate of growth of the free black population slowed after 1810. Between 1790 and 1810, this population had more than tripled, to 108,265. The reason for the slowdown after 1810 was that fewer southern whites were setting slaves free. Until 1820 masters with doubts about the rightness of slavery frequently manumitted (freed) their black mistresses and mulatto children, and some set free their entire work forces (as Jefferson had done upon his death in 1826). In the wake of the Nat Turner rebellion in 1831 (see below), laws restricting the liberties of free blacks were tightened. During the mid-1830s, for example, most southern states made it a felony to teach blacks to read and write. Every southern state forbade free blacks to enter that state, and in 1859 Arkansas ordered all free blacks to leave.

So while a free black culture flowered in cities like New Orleans and Natchez, that culture did not reflect the conditions under which most free blacks lived. Free blacks were tolerated in New Orleans, in part because there were not too many of them. A much higher percentage of blacks were free in the Upper South than in the Lower South. Further, although a disproportionate number of

free blacks lived in cities, the majority lived in rural areas, where whites lumped them together with slaves. Even a successful free black like William Tiler Johnson could never dine or drink with whites. When Johnson attended the theater, he sat in the colored gallery.

The position of free blacks in the Old South contained many contradictions. So did their minds. As the offspring, or the descendants of offspring, of mixed liaisons, a disproportionate number of free blacks had light brown skin. Some of them were as color-conscious as whites and looked down on "darky" field hands and coal-black laborers. Yet as whites' discrimination against free people of color intensified during the late antebellum period, many free blacks realized that such a future as they had was as blacks, not as whites. Feelings of racial solidarity grew stronger among free blacks in the 1850s, and after the Civil War, the leaders of the freedmen were usually blacks who had been free before the war.

Slave Resistance

The Old South contained the seeds of organized slave insurrections. In the delta areas of the Lower South, where blacks outnumbered whites, enslaved blacks experienced continuous forced labor on plantations and communicated their bitterness to each other in the slave quarters. Free blacks in the cities could have provided leadership for rebellions. Rumors of slave conspiracies flew around the southern white community, and all whites knew of the massive black insurrection that had destroyed French rule in Santo Domingo.

Yet only three organized rebellions occurred in the Old South, and taken together, they illustrate more the futility than the possibility of a slave insurrection. In 1800 Virginia slave Gabriel Prosser's planned slave uprising was betrayed by other slaves, and Prosser and his followers were executed. That same year, a South Carolina slave, Denmark Vesey, won fifteen hundred dollars in a lottery and bought his freedom. Purchasing a carpentry shop in Charleston and becoming a preacher at that city's African Methodist Episcopal church, Vesey built a cadre of dedicated black followers, including a slave of the governor of South Carolina and a black conjurer named Gullah Jack. In 1822 they devised a plan to attack Charleston and seize all the city's arms and ammunition, but they were betrayed by other slaves and executed.

The Nat Turner rebellion, which occurred in 1831 in Southampton County, Virginia, was the only one of the three slave insurrections to result in the death of whites. Gloomy and introspective by nature, Nat Turner taught himself to read and write in childhood and became a prodigious reader of the Bible. He gained recognition from slaves as a preacher of electrifying sermons delivered in woodland clearings or in the shacks where slaves gathered to hear "real preachin'." Soon he added a reputation for visions and prophecy; he told, for example, of seeing white and black angels warring in the sky. Yet for all his gifts—a white later said that Turner had "a mind capable of attaining anything"—Turner's life was one of onerous field work, punctuated by a sale that separated him from his wife and that reminded him that whites measured his value only in cash.

In 1831 Turner's conviction of the injustice of slavery, intensified by his reading of the Bible and by his own experiences, boiled over. Slaves who had long venerated him as a prophet now took him as their "general." In August he set out with a handful of slaves armed with axes and clubs. Gathering recruits as they moved from plantation to plantation, Turner and his followers killed all white men, women, and children they encountered. Before the rebellion was suppressed and Turner hanged, fifty-five whites had been slain, a number roughly equal to Turner's force at its peak strength.

Turner's rebellion stunned the South. In the widely circulated *Confessions of Nat Turner,* which Turner dictated to a white lawyer while awaiting execution, Turner's steadfast belief in the justice of his cause flashed again. When asked, "Do you not find yourself mistaken now?," Turner replied, "Was not Christ crucified?" In company with the earlier slave uprising in Santo Domingo, Turner's rebellion convinced white southerners of the ever-present threat of a slave insurrection. Yet neither the Turner rebellion nor the Prosser and Vesey plots ever had a chance of success. The latter two were conspiracies that never got off the ground. During the Turner rebellion, several slaves alerted their masters to the threat, less out of loyalty to slavery than from a correct assessment of Turner's chances. Despite constant fears of slave rebellion, the Old South experienced far less in the way of organized

Slave with Bells

Like cats, some slaves were belled to make escape difficult.

rebellion than did the Caribbean region and South America.

Why is this so? First, although slaves formed a majority in South Carolina and a few other states, they did not constitute a *large* majority in any state. Second, in contrast to the Caribbean, an area of absentee landlords and sparse white population, the white presence in the Old South was formidable, and the whites had all the guns and soldiers. Reviewing Gabriel's Rebellion, Governor James Monroe of Virginia commented: "The superiority in point of numbers, in the knowledge and use of arms, and indeed every other species of knowledge which the whites have over the blacks in this Commonwealth, is so decisive that the latter could only sustain themselves for a moment in a rebellion against the former." The rumors of slave conspiracies that periodically swept the white South demonstrated to blacks the promptness with which whites could muster forces and mount slave patrols. Third, the development of family ties among slaves made them reluctant to risk death and leave their children parentless. Finally, blacks who ran away or plotted rebellions had no allies. Southern Indians routinely captured runaway slaves and exchanged them for rewards; some Indians even owned slaves.

Short of rebellion, slaves could try to escape to freedom in the North. Perhaps the most ingenious, Henry Brown, induced a friend to ship him from Richmond to Philadelphia in a box and won immediate fame as "Box" Brown. Some light mulattoes passed as whites. More often, fugitive slaves borrowed, stole, or forged passes from plantations or obtained papers describing them as free. Frederick Douglass borrowed a sailor's papers in making his escape from Baltimore to New York City in 1838. Some former slaves, among them Harriet Tubman and Josiah Henson, made repeated trips back to the South to help other slaves escape. These sundry methods of escape fed the legend of the "Underground Railroad," supposedly an organized network of safe houses owned by white abolitionists who spirited blacks to freedom. In reality, fugitive slaves owed very little to abolitionists. Some white sympathizers in border states did provide safe houses for blacks, but these houses were better known to watchful slave catchers than to most blacks.

Escape to freedom was a dream rather than an alternative for most blacks; out of millions of slaves, probably fewer than a thousand escaped to the North. Yet slaves often ran away from masters, not to escape to freedom but to visit spouses or avoid punishment. Most runaways remained in the South; indeed, some returned to former, kinder masters. During the eighteenth century, African slaves had often run away in groups to the interior and sought to create self-sufficient colonies or villages of the sort that they had known in Africa. But once the United States had acquired Florida, long a haven for runaways, few uninhabited places remained in the South to which slaves could escape.

Despite poor prospects for permanent escape, slaves could disappear for prolonged periods into the free black communities of southern cities. Because whites in the Old South depended so heavily on black labor, slaves enjoyed a fair degree of practical freedom to drive wagons to market and to come and go when they were off plantations. Slaves hired out or sent to a city might overstay their leave and even pass themselves off as free.

The experience of slavery has sometimes been compared to the experience of prisoners in penitentiaries or on chain gangs, but the analogy is misleading. The supervision that slaves experienced was sometimes intense (for example, when working at harvest time under a driver), but often lax; it was irregular rather than consistent.

The fact that antebellum slaves frequently enjoyed some degree of practical freedom did not change the underlying oppressiveness of slavery. But it did give slaves a sense that they had certain rights on a day-to-day basis, and it helped to deflect slave resistance into forms that were essentially furtive rather than open and violent. Theft was so common that planters learned to keep their tools, smokehouses, closets, and trunks under lock and key. Overworked field hands might leave valuable tools out to rust, or feign illness, or simply refuse to work. As an institution, slavery was vulnerable to such tactics; unlike free laborers, slaves could not be fired for negligence or malingering. Frederick Law Olmsted found slaveholders in the 1850s afraid to inflict punishment on slaves "lest the slave should abscond, or take a sulky fit and not work, or poison some of the family, or set fire to the dwelling, or have recourse to any other mode of avenging himself."

Olmsted's reference to arson and poisoning reminds us that not all furtive resistance was peaceful. Arson and poisoning, both common in African culture as forms of vengeance, were widespread in the Old South, and the fear of each even more so. Dysentery and similar ailments afflicted whites as well as blacks. Masters could never be sure about why they were sick; to put it differently, they could never be sure that they had not been poisoned.

Arson, poisoning, work stoppages, and negligence were alternatives to violent rebellion. Yet these furtive forms of resistance differed from rebellion. The goal of rebellion was freedom from slavery. The goal of furtive resistance was to make slavery bearable. The kind of resistance that slaves usually practiced sought to establish customs and rules that would govern the conduct of masters as well as that of slaves without challenging the institution of slavery as such. Most slaves would have preferred freedom but settled for less. "White folks do as they please," an ex-slave said, "and the darkies do as they can."

The Emergence of African-American Culture

A distinctive culture emerged among blacks in the slave quarters of antebellum plantations. This culture drew on both African and American sources, but it was more than a mixture of the two. Enslaved blacks gave a distinctive twist to the American as well as African components of their culture.

The Language of Slaves

Before slaves could develop a common culture, they had to be able to communicate with each other. During the colonial period, verbal communication among slaves had often been difficult, for most slaves had been born in Africa, which contained an abundance of cultures and languages. The captain of a slave ship noted in 1744:

> As for the languages of Gambia [in West Africa], they are so many and so different that the Natives on either Side of the River cannot understand each other; which, if rightly consider'd, is no small happiness to the Europeans who go thither to trade for slaves.

In the pens into which they were herded before shipment and on the slave ships themselves, however, Africans developed a "pidgin"—that is, a language that has no native speakers but in which people with different native languages can communicate. Pidgin is not unique to black people. When Tarzan announced, "Me Tarzan, you Jane," he was speaking English pidgin. Nor is English pidgin the only form of pidgin; slaves sent to South America developed Spanish and Portuguese pidgins.

Many of the early African-born slaves learned English pidgin poorly or not at all, but as American-born slaves came to compose an increasingly large proportion of all slaves, English pidgin took root. Indeed, it became the only language most slaves knew. Like all pidgins, this was a simplified language. Slaves usually dropped the verb *to be* (which had no equivalent in African tongues) and either ignored or confused genders. Instead of saying "Mary is in the cabin," they said, "Mary, he in cabin." To negate, they substituted *no* for *not*, saying, "He no wicked." English pidgin contained several African words. Some, like *banjo*, became part of standard English; others, like *goober* (peanut), became part of southern white slang. Although they picked up pidgin terms, whites ridiculed field hands' speech. Some slaves, particularly house servants and skilled artisans, learned to speak standard English but had no trouble understanding the pidgin of field hands. However strange pidgin sounded to some, it was indispensable for communication among slaves.

African-American Religion

The development of a common language marked the first step in the forging of African-American culture. No less important was the religion of the slaves.

Africa contained rich and diverse religious customs and beliefs. Some of the early slaves were Moslems; a few had acquired Christian beliefs either in Africa or in the New World. But the majority of the slaves transported from Africa were neither Moslems nor Christians but rather worshipers in one of many native African religions. Most of these religions, which whites lumped together as heathen, drew little distinction between the spiritual and material worlds. Any event or development, from a storm to an earthquake or an illness, was assumed to stem from supernatural forces. These forces were represented by God, by spirits that inhabited the woods and waters, and by the spirits of ancestors. In addition, the religions of West Africa, the region from which most American slaves originally came, attached special significance to water, which suggested life and hope.

The majority of the slaves brought to America in the seventeenth and eighteenth centuries were young men who may not have absorbed much of this religious heritage before their enslavement. In any case, Africans differed from each other in their specific beliefs and practices. For these reasons, African religions could never have unified blacks in America. Yet some Africans probably clung to their beliefs during the seventeenth and eighteenth centuries, a tendency made easier by the fact that whites undertook few efforts before the 1790s to convert slaves to Christianity. Further, dimly remembered African beliefs such as the reverence for water may have predisposed slaves to accept Christianity when they were finally urged to do so, because water had a symbolic significance for Christians, too, in the sacrament of baptism. The Christianity preached to slaves by Methodist and Baptist revivalists during the late eighteenth and nineteenth centuries, moreover, resembled African religions in that Christianity also drew few distinctions between the sacred and the secular. Just as Africans believed that a crop-destroying drought or a plague resulted from supernatural forces, the early revivalists knew in their hearts that every drunkard who fell off his horse and every Sabbath-breaker struck by lightning had experienced a deliberate and direct punishment from God.

By the 1790s blacks formed about a quarter of the membership of the Methodist and Baptist denominations. Yet masters continued to fear that a Christianized slave would be a rebellious slave. Converted slaves in fact played a significant role in each of the three major slave rebellions in the Old South. The leaders of Gabriel Prosser's rebellion in 1800 used the Bible to prove that slaves, like the ancient Israelites, could prevail against overwhelming numbers. Denmark Vesey read the Bible, and most of the slaves executed for joining his conspiracy belonged to Charleston's African Methodist church. Nat Turner was both a preacher and a prophet.

Despite the subversive impact of Christianity on some slaves, however, these uprisings, particularly the Nat Turner rebellion, actually stimulated Protestant missionaries to intensify their efforts to convert slaves. Missionaries pointed to the self-taught Turner to prove that slaves would hear about Christianity in any event and that organized efforts to convert blacks were the only way to ensure that slaves learned correct versions of Christianity, which emphasized obedience rather than rebellion. Georgia missionary and slaveholder Charles Colcock Jones reassuringly told white planters of the venerable black preacher who, upon receiving some abolitionist tracts in the mails, promptly turned them over to the white authorities for destruction. A Christian slave, the argument ran, would be a better slave rather than a bitter slave. For whites, the clincher was the split of the Methodists, Baptists, and Presbyterians into northern and southern wings by the mid-1840s. Now, they argued, it had finally become safe to convert slaves, for the churches had rid themselves of their antislavery wings. Between 1845 and 1860, the number of black Baptists doubled.

Bibby Mosby

Bibby Mosby was a "mammy" enslaved to the family of a Charlottesville, Virginia, judge from about 1830 to 1863.

The experiences of Christianized blacks in the Old South illustrate many of the contradictions of life under slavery. Urban blacks often had their own churches, but in the rural South, where the great majority of blacks lived, slaves worshiped in the same churches as whites. Although the slaves sat in segregated sections, they heard the same sermons and sang the same hymns as whites. Some black preachers actually developed followings among whites, and Christian masters were sometimes disciplined by biracial churches for abusing Christian slaves in the same congregation. The churches were, in fact, the most interracial institutions in the Old South. Yet none of this meant that Christianity was an acceptable route to black liberation. Ministers went out of their way to remind slaves that spiritual equality was not the same as civil equality. The effort to convert slaves gained momentum only to the extent that it was becoming certain that Christianity would not change the basic inequality of southern society.

Although they listened to the same sermons as whites, slaves did not necessarily draw the same conclusions. It was impossible to Christianize the slaves without telling them about the Chosen People, the ancient Jews whom Moses led from captivity in Pharaoh's Egypt into the Promised Land of Israel. Inevitably, slaves drew parallels between their own condition and the Jews' captivity. Like the Jews, blacks concluded, they themselves were "de people of de Lord." If they kept the faith, then, like the Jews, they too would reach the Promised Land. The themes of the Chosen People and the Promised Land ran through the sacred songs, or "spirituals," that blacks sang, to the point where Moses and Jesus almost merged:

> *Gwine to write to Massa Jesus,*
> *To send some Valiant Soldier*
> *To turn back Pharaoh's army, Hallelu!*

A listener could interpret a phrase like "the Promised Land" in several ways; it could refer to Israel, to heaven, or to freedom. From the perspective of whites, the only permissible interpretations were Israel and heaven, but some blacks, like Denmark Vesey, thought of freedom as well. The ease with which slaves constructed alternative interpretations of the Bible also reflected the fact that many plantations contained black preachers, slaves trained by white ministers to spread Christianity among blacks. When in the presence of masters or white ministers, these black preachers usually just repeated the familiar biblical command: "Obey your master." Often, however, slaves met for services apart from whites, usually on Sunday evenings but at times during the week as well. Then the message changed. A black preacher in Texas related how his master would say "tell them niggers iffen they obeys the master they goes to Heaven." The minister quickly added, "I knowed there's something better for them, but I daren't tell them 'cept on the sly. That I done lots. I tells 'em iffen they keep praying, the Lord will set 'em free."

Some slaves privately interpreted Christianity as a religion of liberation from the oppression of slavery, but most recognized that their prospects for freedom were slight. On the whole, Christianity did not turn them into revolutionaries. Neither did it necessarily turn them into model slaves. What it did accomplish was to provide slaves with a view of slavery different from their masters' outlook. Where the masters argued that slavery was a benign and divinely ordained institution in blacks'

best interests, Christianity told them that slavery was really an affliction, a terrible and unjust institution, but one that God had allowed in order to test their faith. For having endured slavery, he would reward blacks. For having created it, he would punish masters.

Black Music and Dance

Compared to the prevailing cultural patterns among elite whites, the culture of blacks in the Old South was extremely expressive. In religious services, blacks shouted "Amen" and let their bodily movements reflect their feelings long after white religious observances, some of which had once been similarly expressive, had grown sober and sedate. Northern journalist Frederick Law Olmsted recorded how, during a slave service in New Orleans during the 1850s, parishioners "in indescribable expression of ecstasy" exclaimed every few moments: "Glory! oh yes! yes!—sweet Lord! sweet Lord!"

Slaves also expressed their feelings in music and dance. Drawing on their African musical heritage, which used hand clapping to mark rhythm, American slaves made rhythmical hand clapping—called patting juba—an indispensable accompaniment to dancing, because southern law forbade them to own "drums, horns, or other loud instruments, which may call together or give sign or notice to one another of their wicked designs and intentions." Slaves also played an African instrument, the banjo, and beat tin buckets as a substitute for drums. Whatever instrument they played, their music was tied to bodily movement. Sometimes slaves imitated white dances like the minuet, but in a way that ridiculed the high manners of their masters. More often, they expressed themselves in a dance African in origin, emphasizing shuffling steps and bodily contortions rather than the erect precision of whites' dances.

Whether at work or at prayer, slaves liked to sing. Work songs describing slave experiences usually consisted of a leader's chant and a choral response:

> *I love old Virginny*
>   *So ho! boys! so ho!*
> *I love to shuck corn*
>   *So ho! boys! so ho!*
> *Now's picking cotton time*
>   *So ho! boys! so ho!*

The Banjo Lesson, *by Henry O. Tanner, c. 1893*

Tanner, a black artist, captured African-Americans' rich musical traditions and close family bonds in this evocative painting.

Masters encouraged such songs, believing that singing induced the slaves to work harder and that the innocent content of most work songs proved that the slaves were happy. Recalling his own past, Frederick Douglass came closer to the truth when he observed that "slaves sing most when they are most unhappy. The songs of the slave represent the sorrows of his heart; and he is relieved by them, only as an aching heart is relieved by its tears."

Blacks also sang religious songs, later known as spirituals. The origin of spirituals is shrouded in obscurity, but it is clear that by 1820 blacks at camp meetings had improvised what one white described as "short scraps of disjointed affirmations, pledges, or prayers lengthened out with long repetition choruses." As this description suggests, whites usually took a dim view of spirituals and tried to make slaves sing "good psalms and hymns" instead of "the extravagant and nonsensical chants, and catches, and hallelujah songs of their own composing." Indeed, when around whites, blacks often sang hymns like those of Isaac Watts and other great white evangelicals, but nothing could dampen slaves' enthusiasm for songs of their own making.

Spirituals reflected the potent emphasis that the slaves' religion put on deliverance from earthly travails. To a degree, the same was true of white hymns, but spirituals were more direct and concrete. Slaves sang, for example,

> *In that morning, true believers,*
> *In that morning,*
> *We will sit aside of Jesus*
> *In that morning,*
> *If you should go fore I go,*
> *In that morning,*
> *You will sit aside of Jesus*
> *In that morning,*
> *True believers, where your tickets*
> *In that morning,*
> *Master Jesus got your tickets*
> *In that morning.*

Another spiritual proclaimed: "We will soon be free, when the Lord will call us home."

Conclusion

The emergence of an African-American culture was one among many features that made the Old South distinctive. With its huge black population, lack of industries, and dispersed white population, the South seemed a world apart. Even while finding individual southerners agreeable, northerners increasingly recognized the differences between their region and the South in the antebellum years. Whether or not they believed that the federal government should tamper with slavery, northerners grew convinced that slavery had cut the South off from progress and had turned it into a region of "sterile land, and bankrupt estates."

Conversely, to most white southerners, the North, and especially the industrial Northeast, appeared to be the region that deviated from the march of progress. Southerners noted that most Americans—indeed, most people throughout the world—practiced agriculture and that agriculture made the South a more comfortable place for millions than factories rendered the North. In reaction to northern assaults on slavery, southerners portrayed the institution as a time-honored and benevolent response to the natural inequality of the black and white races. Southerners pointed to the slaves' adequate nutrition, their embrace of evangelical Protestantism, the affection of some slaves for their masters, and even their work songs as evidence of the slaves' contentment.

In reality, few if any slaves accepted slavery. Although slaves rebelled infrequently and had little chance for permanent escape, they often engaged in covert resistance to their bondage. The slaves embraced Christianity, but they understood it differently than whites. Where Christianity taught whites the need to make slaves submissive, it taught slaves the gross injustice of human bondage.

CHRONOLOGY

1790s Methodists and Baptists start to make major strides in converting slaves to Christianity.

1793 Eli Whitney invents the cotton gin.

1800 Gabriel Prosser leads a slave rebellion in Virginia.

1808 Congress prohibits external slave trade.

1812 Louisiana, the first state formed out of the Louisiana Purchase, is admitted to the Union.

1816–
1819 Boom in cotton prices stimulates settlement of the Southwest.

1817 Mississippi enters the Union.

1819 Alabama enters the Union.

1819–
1820 Missouri Compromise.

1822 Denmark Vesey's conspiracy is uncovered in South Carolina.

1831 William Lloyd Garrison starts *The Liberator*. Nat Turner leads a slave rebellion in Virginia.

1832 Virginia legislature narrowly defeats a proposal for gradual emancipation.

Virginia's Thomas R. Dew writes an influential defense of slavery.

1835 Arkansas admitted to the Union.

1837 Economic panic begins, lowering cotton prices.

1844– Methodist Episcopal and Baptist churches
1845   split into northern and southern wings over slavery.

1845 Florida and Texas admitted to the Union.

1849 Sugar production in Louisiana reaches its peak.

1849– Period of high cotton prices.
1860

1857 Hinton R. Helper, *The Impending Crisis of the South*.

1859 John Brown's raid on Harpers Ferry.

1860 South Carolina secedes from the Union.

For Further Reading

John B. Boles, *Black Southerners, 1619–1869* (1983). An excellent synthesis of recent scholarship on slavery.

Orville Vernon Burton, *In My Father's House Are Many Mansions: Family and Community in Edgefield, South Carolina* (1985). An extremely valuable study of the South Carolina upcountry.

Wilbur J. Cash, *The Mind of the South* (1941). A brilliant interpretation of southern history.

Bruce Collins, *White Society in the Antebellum South* (1985). A very good, brief synthesis of southern white society and culture.

William J. Cooper, *Liberty and Slavery: Southern Politics to 1860* (1983). A valuable synthesis and interpretation of recent scholarship on the antebellum South in national politics.

Clement Eaton, *The Growth of Southern Civilization, 1790–1860* (1961). A fine survey of social, economic, and political change.

Robert W. Fogel and Stanley L. Engerman, *Time on the Cross: The Economics of American Negro Slavery* (1974). A controversial book that uses mathematical models to analyze the profitability of slavery.

Eugene D. Genovese, *Roll, Jordan, Roll: The World the Slaves Made* (1974). The most influential work on slavery in the Old South written during the last twenty years; a penetrating analysis of the paternalistic relationship between masters and slaves.

James Oakes, *The Ruling Race: A History of American Slaveholders* (1982). An important attack on the ideas of Eugene D. Genovese.

U. B. Phillips, *American Negro Slavery* (1918). A work marred by racial prejudice but containing a wealth of information about the workings of slavery and the plantation system. The same description fits another major book by Phillips, *Life and Labor in the Old South* (1929).

Kenneth M. Stampp, *The Peculiar Institution: Slavery in the Ante-Bellum South* (1956). A standard account of the black experience under slavery.

Charles S. Sydnor, *The Development of Southern Sectionalism, 1819–1848* (1948). A description of the growing split between North and South over slavery and related issues.

William R. Taylor, *Cavalier and Yankee: The Old South and American National Character* (1961). An imaginative study of the northern and southern mind through the eye of literature.

Additional Bibliography

The Economic and Social Structure of the White South

William L. Barney, *The Road to Secession* (1972); Fred Bateman and Thomas Weiss, *A Deplorable Scarcity: The Failure of Industrialism in the Slave Economy* (1981); Orville V. Burton and Robert McMath, eds., *Class, Conflict, and Consensus* (1982); Mary B. Chesnut, *A Diary from Dixie* (edited by Ben Ames Williams, 1949); Blanche Henry Clark, *The Tennessee Yeoman, 1840–1860* (1942); Catherine G. Clinton, *The Plantation Mistress: Women's World in the Old South* (1982); Barbara J. Fields, *Slavery and Freedom on the Middle Ground: Maryland During the Nineteenth Century* (1985); Elizabeth Fox-Genovese, *Within the Plantation Household: Black and White Women of the Old South* (1988); Eugene Genovese, *The Political Economy of Slavery* (1965); Steven Hahn, *The Roots of Southern Populism: Yeomen Farmers and the Transformation of the Georgia Upcountry, 1850–1890* (1983); Daniel R. Hundley, *Social Relations in Our Southern States* (1860); Suzanne Lebsock, *The Free Women of Petersburg: Status Culture in a Southern Town, 1784–1860* (1984); Forrest McDonald and Grady McWhiney, "The Antebellum Southern Herdsman: A Reinterpretation," *Journal of Southern History* 41 (May 1975): 147–66; Frank L. Owsley, *Plain Folk of the Old South* (1949); Whitman H. Ridgway, *Community Leadership in Maryland, 1790–1840* (1979); Anne F. Scott, *The Southern Lady: From Pedestal to Politics, 1830–1930* (1970); Julia F. Smith, *Slavery and Plantation Growth in Antebellum Florida* (1973); Herbert Weaver, *Mississippi Farmers, 1850–1860* (1945); Ralph A. Wooster, *Politicians, Planters, and Plain Folk* (1975); Gavin Wright, *The Political Economy of the Cotton South* (1978).

The Values of the White South

Edward L. Ayers, *Vengeance and Justice: Crime and Punishment in the Nineteenth-Century American South* (1984); David T. Bailey, *Shadow on the Church: Southwestern Evangelical Religion and the Issue of Slavery, 1783–1860* (1985); Dickson D. Bruce, *Violence and Culture in the Antebellum South* (1979); William J. Cooper, *The South and the Politics of Slavery, 1829–1856* (1978); Clement Eaton, *The Mind of the Old South* (1964); James D. Essig, *The Bonds of Wickedness: American Evangelicals Against Slavery, 1770–1808* (1982); Drew G. Faust, *A Sacred Circle: The Dilemma of the Intellectual in the Old South, 1840–1860* (1977) and *James Henry Hammond and the Old South: A Design for Mastery* (1982); John Hope Franklin, *The Militant South* (1966); George M. Fredrickson, *The Black Image in the White Mind: The Debate on Afro-American Character and Destiny, 1817–1914* (1971) and *White Supremacy: A Comparative Study in American and South African History* (1981); Alison G. Freehling, *Drift Toward Dissolution: The Virginia Slavery Debate of 1831–1832* (1982); Elliott J. Gorn, " 'Gouge and Bite, Pull Hair and Scratch': The Social Significance of Fighting in the Southern Backcountry," *American Historical Review* XC (February 1985): 18–43; Michael Hindus, *Prison and Plantation: Crime, Justice, and Authority in Massachusetts and South Carolina, 1767–1878* (1980); John McCardell, *The Idea of a Southern Nation: Southern Nationalists and Southern Nationalism* (1979); Donald G. Mathews, *Religion in the Old South* (1977); Ronald Takaki, *A Pro-Slavery Crusade: The Agitation to Reopen the African Slave Trade* (1980); J. Mills Thornton, *Politics and Power in a Slave Society: Alabama, 1800–1860* (1978); Bertram Wyatt-Brown, *Southern Honor: Ethics and Behavior in the Old South* (1982).

Black Experience and Culture in the Old South

Ira Berlin, *Slaves Without Masters: The Free Negro in the Antebellum South* (1974); John Blassingame, *The Slave Community* (1972); Judith Wragg Chase, *Afro-American Art and Craft* (1971); Leonard P. Curry, *The Free Black in Urban America, 1800–1850: The Shadow of the Dream* (1981); Carl N. Degler, *Neither Black Nor White: Slavery and Race Relations in Brazil and the United States* (1971); Dena J. Epstein, *Sinful Tunes and Spirituals: Black Folk Music to the Civil War* (1977); Claudia D. Goldin, *Urban Slavery in the American South, 1820–1860* (1976); Herbert G. Gutman, *The Black Family in Slavery and Freedom, 1759–1925* (1976); Vincent Harding, *There Is a River: The Black Struggle for Freedom in America* (1981); Jacqueline Jones, *Labor of Love, Labor of Sorrow: Black Women, Work, and the Family from Slavery to the Present* (1985); Lawrence W. Levine, *Black Culture and Black Consciousness: Afro-American Folk Thought from Slavery to Freedom* (1977); Stephen B. Oates, *The Fires of Jubilee* (1975); Leslie H. Owens, *This Species of Property: Slave Life and Slave Culture in the Old South* (1976); Albert J. Raboteau, *Slave Religion* (1978); George P. Rawick, *From Sundown to Sunup: The Making of a Black Community* (1972); Robert S. Starobin, *Industrial Slavery in the Old South* (1970); Thomas L. Webber, *Deep Like Rivers: Education in the Slave Quarters, 1831–1865* (1978).

Yet progress had its darker side. Spread unevenly throughout the society, technological advances neither prevented nor ameliorated the depression of the late 1830s and early 1840s and had little positive impact on the poor. Periodic cholera epidemics reminded Americans that technology, in the shape of railroads and steamboats, could transport disease as well as food. Leading writers of the period, among them the philosopher and essayist Henry David Thoreau, questioned the easy assumption that material progress would stimulate moral progress. For the first time, widespread anxieties arose about the despoliation of the American landscape, and conscious efforts were launched to preserve enclaves of nature as parks and retreats safe from the advance of civilization.

Technology and Economic Growth

As evidence that they were a progressive people, Americans increasingly pointed to the march of "technology." The word *technology* was popularized after 1829 to describe how an understanding of scientific principles could be used to transform the practical conveniences of life. "We have invented more useful machines within twenty years," a Bostonian wrote in the 1830s, "than have been invented in all Europe." To those familiar with the progress of invention, *DeBow's Review* observed in 1846, "scarcely anything now will appear impossible."

Belief in the progressive effects of technology sprang from widely varying quarters. In 1836 the conservative Whig Daniel Webster contended that machines would advance civilization because they could perform the work of ten people without consuming food or clothing. At the other end of the political spectrum, a Lowell mill girl and labor organizer, Sarah Bagley, wrote in 1847: "It is emphatically the age of improvement. The arts and sciences have been more fully developed and the great mass of society are feeling its improvement." Practical science promised to make everyone's life more comfortable. The benefits of technology seemed to be democratic.

The technical innovations that transformed the quality of life in antebellum America included the steam engine, the cotton gin, the reaper, the use of interchangeable parts in manufacturing, the sewing machine, and most dazzling of all, the telegraph. Several of these innovations, including the steam engine and the principle of interchangeable parts, had originated in Europe. But Americans had a flair for investing in others' inventions and for perfecting their own, to the point where the inventions became profitable. Improvements in Eli Whitney's cotton gin between 1793 and 1860, for example, led to an eightfold increase in the amount of cotton that could be ginned in a day. Of course, technology did not benefit everyone. Improve-

Woman at Singer Sewing Machine

Asked to repair a sewing machine that did not do continuous stitching, Isaac M. Singer invented one that did. Patented in 1851, the Singer machine quickly dominated the market. Although most early sewing machines were used in factories, some had made their way into households by 1860.

ments in the cotton gin served to rivet slavery firmly in place by making the South more dependent on cotton. Technology also rendered many traditional skills obsolete and thereby undercut the position of artisans. But technology contributed to improvements in transportation and increases in productivity, which in turn lowered commodity prices and raised the living standards of a sizable body of free Americans between 1840 and 1860.

Agricultural Advancement

Confronted by the superior fertility of western soil, many easterners abandoned wheat production and migrated to the West or took jobs in America's expanding factories. Others developed new agricultural techniques and specialties. In Orange County, New York, for example, farmers fed their cows on the best clover and bluegrass and emphasized cleanliness in the processing of dairy products. Through these practices, they produced a superior butter that commanded more than double the price of ordinary butter and even gained a reputation in Europe. Still other eastern farmers continued to produce wheat, but to stay competitive with westerners, they turned to the use of fertilizers. By fertilizing their fields with plaster left over from the construction of the James River Canal, Virginia wheat growers raised their average yield per acre to fifteen bushels by the 1850s, up from an average of only six bushels in 1800. Similarly, during the 1840s American cotton planters began to import guano, left by the droppings of sea birds on islands off Peru, for use as a fertilizer. Fertilizers helped eastern cotton farmers close the gap created by the greater fertility of southwestern soil for cotton.

Like cotton, wheat presented a harvesting problem. Use of the traditional hand sickle consumed prodigious amounts of time and labor, all the more so because cut wheat had to be picked up and bound. Ever since the eighteenth century, inventors in Europe had experimented with horse-drawn machines to replace sickles. But until Cyrus McCormick came on the scene, the absence of the right combination of technical skill and business enterprise had relegated mechanical reapers to the realm of tinkerers' dreams. In 1834 McCormick, a Virginian, patented a mechanical reaper that both drew on and improved previous designs. Opening

a factory in Chicago in 1847, McCormick began to manufacture reapers by mass production and introduced aggressive marketing techniques such as deferred payments and money-back guarantees.

The North rather than the South provided the main market for McCormick's reaper and for those of his many competitors. With its reliance on slave labor, the South had far less incentive to mechanize agriculture. Even without the reaper, wheat was fast becoming to the midwestern farmer what cotton was to his southern counterpart. "The wheat crop is the great crop of the North-west, for exchange purposes," an agricultural journal noted in 1850. "It pays debts, buys groceries, clothing and lands, and answers more emphatically the purposes of trade among the farmers than any other crop." By harvesting grain seven times more rapidly than traditional methods, and with half the labor force, the reaper guaranteed the preeminence of wheat on the midwestern prairies of Illinois, Indiana, Iowa, and Missouri. McCormick sold 80,000 reapers by 1860, and this was only the beginning. During the Civil War, he made immense profits by selling more than 250,000 reapers. Ironically, just as a Connecticut Yankee, Eli Whitney, had stimulated the foundation of the Old South's economy by his invention of the cotton gin, Cyrus McCormick, a proslavery southern Democrat, would help the North win the Civil War. The reaper would keep northern agricultural production high at a time when labor shortages caused by the mobilization of troops might otherwise have slashed production.

Technology and Industrial Progress

Although Americans had made several important technical innovations before 1820, the early growth of American manufacturing depended mainly on *imported* technology. Gradually, however, American industries gained a reputation abroad for their own innovations. As early as 1835, a British observer reported that a woolen mill in Lowell, Massachusetts, contained a remarkable number of labor-saving contrivances. In 1853 a small-arms factory in England reequipped itself with machine tools (machines that shaped metal products) manufactured by two firms in the backwoods of Vermont. Americans had relatively few reservations about investing in technology. After finishing a tour of American factories in 1854, a noted British engineer concluded that "wherever [machinery] can be introduced as a substitute for manual labor, it is universally and willingly resorted to."

During the 1840s and 1850s, American industries advanced toward perfecting manufacturing by the use of interchangeable parts. Eli Whitney had introduced this idea (often called the American system of manufacturing) to the United States in 1798, but in Whitney's day the manufacture of guns or other items by the use of interchangeable parts required a great deal of time-consuming hand filing before the parts could be fitted together. In the 1840s American factories immeasurably improved the quality of their machine tools and thereby eliminated much of the need for hand filing. As a result, it became possible to substitute parts that were made in one year for those fabricated in another. In 1853 a British commission investigating American technology looked on in amazement as the superintendent of the Springfield, Massachusetts, armory ordered rifles produced in ten consecutive years to be stripped and their parts reassembled at random.

The American system of manufacturing contained several distinctive advantages. Traditionally, damage to any part of a mechanical contrivance had rendered the whole useless, for no new part would fit. With the perfection of manufacturing by interchangeable parts, however, replacements could be ordered for damaged parts. In addition, the improved machine tools upon which the American system depended enabled entrepreneurs to push inventions swiftly into mass production. The likelihood that inventions would quickly enter production in turn attracted investors. By the 1850s Connecticut firms like Smith and Wesson were mass-producing the revolving pistol, which Samuel Colt had invented in 1836. Sophisticated machine tools made it possible, a manufacturer wrote, to increase production "by confining a worker to one particular limb of a pistol until he had made two thousand." The sewing machine, invented in 1846 by Elias Howe, entered mass production only two years later.

Americans also displayed an eagerness to eliminate the constraints of time and space. An impatient people inhabiting a huge area, they seized enthusiastically on Samuel F. B. Morse's invention of the telegraph in 1844. "The advantages to be

Samuel F. B. Morse

Morse had various interests besides the telegraph. In the 1820s he became a well-known portrait painter and in the 1830s a leading anti-Catholic. He later grew interested in women's higher education and co-founded Vassar College in 1865.

derived from the adoption of the Electric Telegraph," a British engineer noted in 1854, "have in no country been more promptly appreciated than in the United States. A system of communication that annihilates distance was felt to be of vital importance, both politically and commercially, in a country so vast, and having a population so widely scattered." The speed with which Americans formed telegraph companies and erected lines stunned the British. "No private interests can oppose the passage of a line through any property," the same British engineer wrote. "There are no committees, no counsel, no long array of witnesses and expensive hearings; compensation is made simply for damage done, the amount being assessed by a jury, and generally on a most moderate estimate. With a celerity that is surprising a company is formed, a line is built, and operations are commenced." Although telegraph lines usually transmitted political and commercial messages, some cities adapted them for reporting fires. By the early 1850s, Boston had an elaborate system of telegraph stations from which news of a blaze could be swiftly transmitted to fire companies throughout the city. Whatever their use, telegraph lines spread rapidly. By 1852 more than fifteen thousand miles of lines connected cities as distant as Quebec, New Orleans, and St. Louis.

The Railroad Boom

The same penchant for overcoming the natural limits imposed by time and space drove antebellum Americans to make an extraordinary investment in railroads. To an even greater degree than the telegraph, the railroad embodied progress through technology.

In 1790 even European royalty could travel no faster than fourteen miles an hour, and that only with frequent changes of horses. Yet by 1850 an ordinary American could travel on a train at three times that speed. The swift, comfortable transport that American railroads provided for the common man and woman dramatized the democratic promise of technology more vividly than any other technological innovation of the time.

In Europe railroads usually had several classes of travel. The common people were traditionally herded into crowded cars and seated on wooden benches or chairs. Only those who paid to travel first-class enjoyed a modicum of luxury. In contrast, in America there was only *one* class of railroad travel (except for blacks, who were often forced to sit separately). Furthermore, American inventors introduced a level of comfort that astonished Europeans. They experimented with adjustable upholstered seats that could be turned in whatever direction the train was traveling and that could be converted into couches at night. In effect, everyone could travel first-class. Americans, a Frenchman observed, had "a perfect passion for railroads" and loved them "as a lover loves his mistress."

Yet in the 1830s little about the railroads appeared lovable. The first trains were drawn by horses rather than by locomotives; a few actually used sails for power. Those with locomotives showered their passengers' clothing with sparks, for the riding cars were often open to the air. In the absence of brakes, passengers at times had to get out and pull trains to stops. Without means of

illumination, trains rarely ran at night. Scheduling posed problems because the United States did not adopt standard time until 1883 (see Chapter 17); at noon in Boston, it was twelve minutes before noon in New York. Moreover, trains en route faced innumerable delays. Because most railroads owned only a single track, trains had to wait on sidings for other trains to pass. Since a train's whereabouts remained a mystery once it had left a station, such waits could seem interminable.

Between 1840 and 1860, a stunning transformation occurred in the size of the rail network and in the power and convenience of trains. Railroad track increased from three thousand to thirty thousand miles. Passengers now traveled in flat-roofed coaches. Illumination by kerosene lamps made night travel possible. Locomotives gained in power to the point where they no longer had to be pulled uphill by horses or by stationary engines. Fifty thousand miles of telegraph wires enabled dispatchers to communicate with trains on route and to reduce delays.

Passengers nevertheless still confronted inconveniences. Sleeping accommodations remained crude and schedules erratic. Since individual railroads continued to use track of different gauges, frequent changes of train (eight between Charleston and Philadelphia in the 1850s) remained a necessity. Yet nothing could slow the advance of railroads or cure Americans' mania for them. By 1860 the United States had more track than the rest of the nations of the world combined.

Just as canals had spearheaded the first phase of the transportation revolution, railroads led the second phase during the 1840s and 1850s. Canals were not abandoned; the Erie Canal, for example, did not reach its peak volume until 1880. But railroads, providing much faster transport and being less vulnerable to winter frosts, gradually overtook canals, first in passenger and then in freight traffic. By 1860 the value of goods transported by railroad greatly exceeded that carried by canals.

As late as 1860, few rail lines extended west of the Mississippi, but railroads had spread like spiderwebs east of the great river. The 1840s saw vigorous railroad construction in New England; by 1850 Massachusetts had half of the track that it would possess in 1950. Elsewhere to the east of the Mississippi, the railroad boom developed mainly in the 1850s, when twenty-two thousand miles of

The Express Train

Snaking through the wilderness, trains promised to conquer distance without upsetting nature's harmony.

Railroad Growth, 1850–1860

Rail ties between East and Midwest greatly increased during the railroad "boom" of the 1850s.

track were added to the nation's rail network. In the South railroads transformed places like Chattanooga and Atlanta into thriving commercial hubs. The most important development of the 1850s, however, lay in the forging of rail lines between the East and the Midwest (or "Old Northwest"). The New York Central and the Erie railroads joined eastern New York to Buffalo; the Pennsylvania Railroad connected Philadelphia and Pittsburgh; and the Baltimore and Ohio linked Baltimore to Wheeling, Virginia (now West Virginia). Simultaneously, intense construction in Ohio, Indiana, and Illinois created trunk lines that joined each of these routes. By 1860 rail lines ran from Buffalo to Cleveland, Toledo, and Chicago; from Pittsburgh to Fort Wayne; and from Wheeling to Cincinnati and on to St. Louis.

The completion of rail links between the East and Midwest rerouted much of the commerce of the nation's interior. Before the 1850s most of the agricultural surplus of the Upper Mississippi Val-ley had made its way down the river to New Orleans for transshipment to the East. Although a railroad between New Orleans and Cincinnati was finally completed in 1859, the earlier completion of the east-west trunk lines had already deflected the flow of grain, livestock, and dairy products directly to the East, bypassing the Mississippi Valley. Gradually, Chicago supplanted New Orleans as the nation's main interior commercial hub. In 1849 Chicago had virtually no rail service, but by 1860 eleven railroads radiated from it.

Too, the forging of east-west rail trunks dramatically stimulated the settlement and agricultural development of the Midwest. By 1860 Illinois, Indiana, and Wisconsin had replaced Pennsylvania, Ohio, and New York as the leading wheat-growing states. Although settlers usually arrived in advance of the railroads, the trains gave hot pursuit. Further, by enabling midwestern farmers to speed their produce to the East, railroads greatly increased the value of their farms and thereby promoted additional settlement. By encouraging settlement, moreover, railroads indirectly stimulated the industrial development of the Midwest, because new settlers needed lumber for fences and houses, and mills to grind wheat into flour. Cities like Chicago, Davenport, Iowa, and Minneapolis grew not only as railroad hubs but as centers of lumber and flour trade.

Railroads also propelled the growth of small towns along their routes. The Illinois Central Railroad, which had more track than any other road in 1855, made money not only from its traffic but also from real-estate speculation. Purchasing land for stations along its route, the Illinois Central then laid out towns around the stations. The selection of Manteno, Illinois, as a stop of the Illinois Central, for example, transformed the site from a crossroads without a single house in 1854 into a bustling town of nearly a thousand in 1860, replete with hotels, lumberyards, grain elevators, and gristmills. (The Illinois Central even dictated the naming of streets. In the towns along its route, streets running east and west were always named after trees, and those running north and south were numbered. Soon one town looked much like the next.) By the Civil War, few thought of the railroad-linked Midwest as a frontier region or viewed its inhabitants as pioneers.

As the nation's first big business, the railroads transformed the conduct of business. During the early 1830s, railroads, like canals, depended on financial aid from state governments. With the onset of depression in the late 1830s, however, state governments scrapped overly ambitious railroad projects. Convinced that railroads burdened them with high taxes and blasted hopes, voters turned against state aid, and in the early 1840s, several states amended their constitutions to bar state funding for railroads and canals. The federal government took up some of the slack, but federal aid did not provide a major stimulus to railroads before 1860. Rather, part of the burden of finance passed to city and county governments in agricultural areas that wanted to attract railroads. Municipal governments, for example, often gave railroads rights-of-way, grants of land for stations, and public funds.

The dramatic expansion of the railroad network in the 1850s, however, strained the financing capacity of local governments and required a turn toward private investment, which had never been absent from the picture. Well aware of the economic benefits of railroads, individuals living near the roads had long purchased railroad securities issued by governments and had directly bought stock in railroads, often paying by contributing their labor to building the roads. But the large roads of the 1850s needed more capital than such small investors could generate. Gradually, the center of railroad financing shifted to New York City, and in fact, it was the railroad boom of the 1850s that helped to make Wall Street the nation's greatest capital market. The securities of all the leading railroads were traded on the floor of the New York Stock Exchange during the 1850s. In addition, the growth of railroads turned New York City into the center of modern investment firms. The investment firms evaluated the securities of railroads in Toledo or Davenport or Chattanooga and then found purchasers for these securities in New York, Philadelphia, Paris, London, Amsterdam, and Hamburg. Controlling the flow of funds to railroads, the investment bankers began to exert influence over the railroads' internal affairs by supervising administrative reorganizations in time of trouble. A Wall Street analyst noted in 1851 that railroad men seeking financing "must remember that money is power, and that the [financier] can dictate to a great extent his own terms."

Rising Prosperity

Technological advances also improved the lives of consumers by bringing down the price of many commodities. For example, clocks that cost $50 to fabricate by hand in 1800 could be produced by machine for 50¢ by 1850. In addition, the widening use of steam power contributed to a 25 percent rise in the average worker's real income (actual purchasing power) between 1840 and 1860. Early-nineteenth-century factories, which had depended on water wheels to propel their machines, of necessity had to shut down when the rivers or streams that powered the wheels froze. With the spread of steam engines, however, factories could stay open longer and workers could increase their annual wages by working more hours. Cotton textile workers were among those who benefited: although their hourly wages showed little gain, their average annual wages rose from $163 in 1830 to $176 in 1849 to $201 by 1859.

Standard Workingman's Budget, New York City, 1853	
Item of Expenditure	*Amount*
Groceries	$273.00
Rent	100.00
Clothing, bedding, etc.	132.00
Furnishings	20.00
Fuel	18.00
Lights	10.00
Taxes, water, commutation	5.00
Physicians' and druggists' charges	10.00
Traveling	12.00
Newspapers, postage, library fees	10.00
	$590.00
Church, charity, etc.	10.00
Total annual expenditures	$600.00

SOURCE: *New York Times,* November 8, 1853. The expenditures are supposed to be those of a family of four, "living moderately."

Workingman's Budget, Philadelphia, 1851	
Item of Expenditure	*Amount*
Butcher's meat (2 lb. a day)	$ 72.80
Flour (6½ barrels a year)	32.50
Butter (2 lb. a week)	32.50
Potatoes (2 pecks a week)	26.00
Sugar (4 lb. a week)	16.64
Coffee and tea	13.00
Milk	7.28
Salt, pepper, vinegar, starch, soap, soda, yeast, cheese, eggs	20.80
Total expenditures for food	$221.52
Rent	$156.00
Coal (3 tons a year)	15.00
Charcoal, chips, matches	5.00
Candles and oil	7.28
Household articles (wear, tear, and breakage)	13.00
Bedclothes and bedding	10.40
Wearing apparel	104.00
Newspapers	6.24
Total annual expenditures	$538.44

SOURCE: *New York Daily Tribune,* May 27, 1851. These amounts are supposed to be the minimum upon which a family of five could live. Items have been rearranged and converted to an annual basis for this table.

The growth of towns and cities also contributed to an increase in average annual wages. Farmers experienced the same seasonal fluctuations as laborers in the early factories. In sparsely settled rural areas, the onset of winter traditionally brought hard times; as demand for agricultural labor slumped, few alternatives existed to take up the slack. "A year in some farming states such as Pennsylvania," a traveler commented in 1823, "is only of eight months duration, four months being lost to the laborer, who is turned away as a useless animal." In contrast, densely populated towns and cities offered more opportunities for annual work. The urban dockworker thrown out of his job as a result of frozen waterways might find work as a hotel porter or an unskilled indoor laborer.

Towns and cities also provided women and children with new opportunities for paid work. (Women and children had long performed many vital tasks on farms, but rarely for pay.) The wages of children between the ages of ten and eighteen came to play an integral role in the nineteenth-century family economy. Family heads who earned more than $600 a year might have been able to afford the luxury of keeping their children in school, but most breadwinners were fortunate if they made $300 a year. Although the cost of many basic commodities fell between 1815 and 1860 (another consequence of the transportation revolution), most

families lived close to the margin. Budgets of workingmen's families in New York City and Philadelphia during the early 1850s reveal annual expenditures of $500–$600, with more than 40 percent spent on food, 25–30 percent on rent, and most of the remainder on clothing and fuel. Such a family obviously could not survive on the annual wages of the average male head of household. It needed the wages of its children and, at times, those of the wife as well.

Life in urban wage-earning families was not necessarily superior to life in farming communities. A farmer who owned land, livestock, and a house did not have to worry about paying rent or buying fuel for cooking and heating, and rarely ran short of food. Many Americans continued to aspire to farming as the best of all occupations. But to purchase, clear, and stock a farm involved a considerable capital outlay that could easily amount to five hundred dollars, and the effort promised no rewards for a few years. The majority of workers in agricultural areas did not own farms and were exposed to the seasonal fluctuations in demand for agricultural labor. In many respects, they were worse off than urban wage earners.

The economic advantages that attended living in cities help to explain why so many Americans moved to urban areas during the first half of the nineteenth century. As a further attraction, during the 1840s and 1850s, cities also provided their residents with an unprecedented range of comforts and conveniences.

The Quality of Life

In addition to large-scale transformations in production, transportation, and income, the two decades before the Civil War witnessed subtle alterations in the quality of everyday life in the United States. Less visible and dramatic than those wrought by the railroad, these changes in everyday experiences occurred for the most part within the privacy of homes and affected such routine activities as eating, drinking, and washing. Technological improvements in these years made the daily home-life experiences of Americans far more comfortable. "Think of the numberless contrivances and inventions for our comfort and luxury which the last half dozen years have brought forth," the poet Walt Whitman exclaimed to his readers, and you will "bless your star that fate has cast your lot in the year of Our Lord 1857." Indeed, the patent office in Washington was flooded with sketches of reclining seats, sliding tables, beds convertible into chairs, lounges convertible into cradles, street-sweeping machines, and fly traps. Machine-made furniture began to transform the interiors of houses. Stoves revolutionized heating and cooking. By bringing fresh vegetables to city dwellers, railroads stimulated important changes in diet.

Despite all of the talk of comfort and progress, many Americans, however, experienced little improvement in the quality of their lives. Technological advances made it possible for the middle class to enjoy luxuries formerly reserved for the rich but often widened the distance between the middle class and the poor. At a time when the interiors of urban, middle-class homes were becoming increasingly lavish, the urban poor congregated in cramped and unsightly tenements. In addition, some aspects of life remained relatively unaffected by scientific and technical advances. Medical science, for example, made a few advances before 1860, but none that rivaled the astonishing changes wrought by the railroad and the telegraph.

The benefits rather than the limitations of progress, however, gripped the popular imagination. Few Americans accepted the possibility that progress could neglect such an important aspect of everyday life as health. Confronted by the failure of the medical profession to rival the achievements of Cyrus McCormick and Samuel F. B. Morse, Americans embraced popular health movements that sprang up outside of the medical profession and promised to conquer disease by the precepts of diet and regimen.

Housing

During the early 1800s, urban dwellings had grown far more standardized than previously. Builders had responded to the swift growth of cities by erecting quickly constructed row houses—uniform attached dwellings increasingly made of brick. Where city dwellers in the eighteenth century usually had lived in unattached frame houses of one or two stories, all of which looked different and faced in different directions, their nineteenth-century counterparts were more likely to inhabit row houses. Some praised the uniformity of row houses as democratic, but others condemned the structures as monotonous. "The great defect in the houses," an English visitor observed, "is their extreme uniformity—when you have seen one, you have seen all."

The average row house was narrow and long, fifteen to twenty feet across, thirty to forty feet from front to back. Most had open spaces in the rear for gardens, pigs, privies, and cisterns. Row houses were not all alike. In the nineteenth century, middle-class row houses were larger (3 to 3½ stories) than working-class row houses (2 to 2½ stories). Between 1830 and 1860, moreover, the interiors of middle-class row houses became more elaborate than those of common laborers. Such features as cast-iron balconies (especially popular in the South), elegant doors, curved staircases, carved columns between rooms, and rooms with fanciful, asymmetrical shapes distinguished the row houses of the middle class from those of the less fortunate.

As land values rose in the early nineteenth century (as much as 750 percent in Manhattan between 1785 and 1815), renting rather than owning homes became more common. By 1815 more than half of the homes in the large cities were rented, usually by artisans, journeymen, and day laborers. Soaring land values also led to the subdividing of many row houses for occupancy by several families or boarders. The worst of these subdivided houses were called tenements and became the usual habitats of Irish immigrants and free blacks.

In rural areas, the quality of housing depended on the date of settlement as much as on social class. In recently settled areas, the standard dwelling was a rude, one-room log cabin with floors made of split logs that allowed drafts to seep in, roofs that let in snow, crude chimneys made of sticks and clay, and windows covered by oiled paper or cloth. As rural communities matured, however, log cabins gave way to frame houses of two or more rooms with glass windows and better insulation. Most of these houses were built on a principle known as the balloon frame. Originally, *balloon frame* was a term used by traditional artisans to express their contempt for houses that appeared so flimsily constructed as to risk blowing away. In place of foot-thick heavy timbers that were laboriously fitted together, the balloon-frame house had a skeleton of thin sawed timbers nailed together in such a way that every strain ran against the grain of the wood. The strength of balloon-frame houses soon confounded their critics, while their simplicity and cheapness endeared them to western builders with neither the time nor the skill to cut heavy beams and fit them into each other.

Home Furniture

Furniture trends between 1840 and 1860 revealed the widening gap between the lifestyles of the prosperous and those of the poor. Families in the middle and upper classes increasingly decorated their parlors with a style of furniture known as French antique or rococo. Rococo furniture reflected both the affluence and the formality of middle- and upper-class families. In such households, the ideal

Family Group

In this daguerreotype taken about 1852, a family relaxes in their parlor, which is furnished in the ornate style popular during this period.

parlor required a seven-piece matched set: an armchair for the husband, a smaller and less expensive lady's chair for his wife, a sofa, and four parlor chairs for guests and children. Rococo furniture was by definition ornate. Upholstered chairs, for example, displayed intricate scrolls depicting vines, leaves, or flowers and had curved legs with ornamental feet (called cabriole legs). The heavily upholstered backs of sofas often contained designs of rose blossoms topped by carved medallions. Artisans framed hanging mirrors with intricately fashioned and gilded moldings that depicted birds, flowers, and even young women. The finished products frequently weighed so much that they threatened to tumble from the wall.

The highly ornamented rococo furniture marked its possessors as people of substantial wealth. At the same time, the rise of mass production in such furniture centers as Grand Rapids, Michigan, and Cincinnati brought the rococo style within the financial reach of the middle class and thereby helped to close the gap between the truly wealthy (who often imported their furniture from France) and those who were merely well off. Unable to afford even mass-produced rococo pieces, however, the great majority of Americans had to be content with simpler furniture. Technological advances in the fabrication of furniture tended to level taste between the middle and upper classes while simultaneously marking those classes off from everyone else.

Heating, Cooking, and Diet

In the 1840s the transportation and industrial revolutions affected such basic household features as heating, cooking, and diet. As soon as the transportation revolution had opened distant markets, some iron foundries began to specialize in the production of cast-iron stoves. By the late 1840s, stoves were rapidly displacing open hearths for both heating and cooking.

The blaze of the open hearth had a romantic attraction for poets, but the hearth was an inefficient source of warmth: most of the heat was lost up the chimney. Because of their superior ability to retain heat, stoves allowed families to reduce expenditures on wood and coal. Stoves were also superior to hearths for cooking. Housewives could leave meals unattended on stoves, and they no longer

ran the danger of scorching their dresses while bending to reach into open flames. In addition, several dishes could be cooked at once on a stove. In this way, stoves contributed to the growing variety of the American diet.

By the 1840s most stoves burned coal rather than wood. Before 1830 English and Welsh immigrants had taught Americans how to hew coal (that is, mine it with heavy instruments), and the discovery in eastern Pennsylvania of a superior variety of coal called anthracite guaranteed a steady supply. Coal was not without drawbacks, however. A faulty coal-burning stove could fill a room with poisonous carbon monoxide. But coal burned far longer than wood and reduced the time and expense that families had traditionally devoted to acquiring fuel.

As more and more people congregated in towns and cities, and as transportation improved, urban markets for the sale of country produce multiplied. Railroads brought fresh vegetables, which in the eighteenth century had been absent even from lavish banquet tables, into towns and cities. Railcars also carried in fresh fish, poultry, and fruit. By 1860 Boston and St. Louis each had ten large public markets. Even small towns in the Midwest were likely to have public markets by the 1840s.

Despite the improvements wrought by the transportation revolution, personal diets were still subject to seasonal fluctuations. Only the rich could afford fruits out of season, for they alone could afford to buy sugar in sufficient quantities to preserve fruit. (The Florida and California citrus fruit industries still lay in the future.) Indeed, preserving almost any kind of food presented problems. Although Americans pioneered technical advances in the harvesting and storing of ice before 1840, home iceboxes were rare before 1860. One contemporary writer recommended that housewives bury meat in the snow to keep it from spoiling, but salt remained the most widely used preservative. One reason why antebellum Americans ate more pork than beef was that salt affected the taste of pork less objectionably than the flavor of beef.

Water and Sanitation

Rural homes rarely had running water. Water was brought in from wells, springs, or cisterns; used; carried outside again; and dumped. During the early

1800s, the same had been true in cities, but with increasing population density, alarm rose about the threat to well water posed by leakage from outdoor privies. In response, some cities had constructed public waterworks. In 1823 Philadelphia had completed a system that brought water along aqueducts and through pipes from the Schuylkill and Delaware rivers to street hydrants. Visiting Philadelphia in 1842, Charles Dickens marveled that the city "is most bountifully provided with fresh water, which is showered and jerked about, and turned on, and poured off every where." During the 1840s and 1850s, several other major cities constructed similar waterworks. New York City completed the Croton aqueduct (which brought water into the city from reservoirs to the north) in the 1840s, and Cleveland, Detroit, Hartford, Louisville, and Cincinnati built waterworks during the 1850s. By 1860 sixty-eight public water systems operated in the United States.

Although these municipal water systems stood among the most impressive engineering triumphs of the age, their impact is easily exaggerated. Many small cities like Rochester and Poughkeepsie, New York, had no waterworks in 1860. As late as 1862, Louisville had only 239 houses connected to its system. The 53,000 customers of New York City's system in 1856 composed less than a tenth of the city's population. Even with the establishment of waterworks, few houses had running water; the incoming water usually ended its journey at a street hydrant. As in rural areas, families had to carry water into and out of houses. Moreover, houses blessed with running water rarely possessed hot water. Before one could take a bath, water had to be heated on the stove or over the fireplace. Not surprisingly, people rarely bathed. A New England physician claimed in 1832 that not one in five of his patients took one bath a year. Fewer than fourteen hundred baths served New York City in 1855.

Because Americans bathed infrequently, their bodily odors undoubtedly were pungent, but so were smells of every sort. Even fashionable residential streets often contained stables backed by mounds of manure. Municipal sanitation departments were virtually nonexistent. Street cleaning was mainly the responsibility of private contractors, who gained a reputation for slackness in discharging their duties. To supplement the work of such undependable contractors, Americans relied on hogs, which they let roam freely and scavenge.

Thomas Dusenberry, Plumber

Advertisements pointed out the marvelous possibilities of fresh water from New York City's Croton reservoir.

(Scavenging hogs that turned down the wrong street often made tasty dinners for the poor.) The abundance of outdoor privies added to the stench. Flush toilets were rare outside of cities, and within cities provisions for sewerage lagged behind those for waterworks. With a population of 178,000 in 1860, Boston had only about five thousand flush toilets, a far higher ratio of toilets to people than most cities could report. Americans normally answered calls of nature by trips to outdoor privies, whose unpleasant smells they suppressed mainly by the application of shovelsful of dirt.

Comforts and conveniences later taken for granted were still rare in 1860. Conveniences like stoves and folding beds that made their way into the home, far from liberating women from housework, merely elevated the standards of housekeeping. In her widely popular *Treatise on Domestic*

Economy (1841), Catharine Beecher used technological advances to justify her contention that women had a duty to make every house a "glorious temple" by utilizing space and other resources more efficiently. None of this, however, changes the fact that middle-class antebellum Americans increasingly boasted of how comfortable their lives were becoming and pointed to the steady improvement in wages, diet, and water supplies as tangible marks of betterment.

Disease and Health

Despite a slowly rising standard of living, Americans remained vulnerable to disease. Between 1793, when an outbreak of yellow fever had devastated Philadelphia, and 1918–1919, when an influenza epidemic killed more than half a million Americans (and at least 20 million people worldwide), epidemics posed a constant but unpredictable threat. In 1832–1833 the combined effects of cholera and yellow fever had killed perhaps a fifth of New Orleans's population. Cholera returned to the United States in 1849 and carried off 10 percent of St. Louis's population while dealing staggering blows to most other cities.

Although not the only threats to health, epidemic diseases were the most visible and feared dangers. With grim irony, the transportation revolution increased the peril from epidemics. The cholera epidemic of 1832 had the dubious distinction of being America's first national epidemic. Its course followed that of the transportation revolution. One route of the epidemic ran from New York City up the Hudson River, across the Erie Canal to Ohio, and down the Ohio River to the Mississippi and New Orleans; the other route followed shipping up and down the East Coast from New York City.

Each major antebellum epidemic of cholera or yellow fever intensified public calls for the establishment of municipal health boards, and by the 1850s most major cities had formed such agencies. However, so few powers did city governments give them that the boards could not even enforce the reporting of diseases. In fact, public health generally remained a low-priority issue, because many doubted that any project supported by the widely distrusted medical profession could be of much value. Distrust of physicians in part grew out of the long-standing popular belief that an elite med-

Cholera

So full did some cemeteries become during the 1832 cholera epidemic that the residents of certain communities were directed to bury their dead elsewhere.

ical profession had no place in a democracy (see Chapter 8). But the inability of physicians to find a satisfactory explanation for epidemic diseases also contributed to hostility toward the profession.

Prior to 1860 no one understood that tiny organisms called bacteria caused both cholera and yellow fever. Rather, rival camps of physicians battled furiously and publicly over the merits of the "contagion" theory versus those of the "miasm" theory. Insisting that cholera and yellow fever were transmitted by touch, contagionists called for vigorous measures to quarantine affected areas. In contrast, supporters of the miasm theory argued that poisonous gases (miasms) emitted by rotting vegetation or dead animals carried disease through the air. The miasm theory led logically to the conclusion that swamps should be drained and streets cleaned. Neither theory, however, was consistent with the evidence. Quarantines failed to check cholera and yellow fever (an argument against the contagionist theory), while many residents of filthy slums and stinking, low-lying areas contracted neither of the two diseases (a refutation of the miasm theory). Confronted by this inconclusive debate between medical experts, municipal leaders refused to delegate more than advisory powers to health boards dominated by physicians. After the worst epidemic in the city's history, a New Orleans editor stated in 1853 that it was "much safer to follow the common sense and unbiased opinion of the intelligent mass of the people than the opinions of medical men . . . based upon hypothetical theories."

Although most epidemic diseases baffled antebellum physicians, a basis for forward strides in surgery was laid during the 1840s by the discovery of anesthetics. Prior to 1840 young people often entertained themselves at parties by inhaling nitrous oxide, or "laughing gas," which produced sensations of giddiness and painlessness; and semicomical demonstrations of laughing gas became a form of popular entertainment. (Samuel Colt, the inventor of the revolver, had begun his career as a traveling exhibitor of laughing gas.) But nitrous oxide had to be carried around in bladders, which were difficult to handle, and in any case, few recognized its surgical possibilities. Then in 1842 Crawford Long, a Georgia physician who had attended laughing-gas frolics in his youth, employed sulfuric ether (an easily transportable liquid with the same properties as nitrous oxide) during a surgical operation. Long failed to follow up on his discovery, but four years later William T. G. Morton, a dentist, successfully employed sulfuric ether during an operation at Massachusetts General Hospital in Boston. Within a few years, ether came into wide use in American surgery.

The discovery of anesthesia improved the public image of surgeons, long viewed as brutes who hacked away at agonized patients. Furthermore, by making longer operations possible, anesthesia encouraged surgeons to take greater care than previously during surgery. Nevertheless, the failure of most surgeons to recognize the importance of clean hands and sterilized instruments partially offset the benefits of anesthesia before 1860. In 1843 Boston physician and poet Oliver Wendell Holmes, Sr., published an influential paper on how the failure of obstetricians to disinfect their hands often spread a disease called puerperal fever among mothers giving birth in hospitals. Still, the medical profession only gradually accepted the importance of disinfection. Operations remained as dangerous as the diseases or wounds that they tried to heal. The mortality rate for amputations hovered around 40 percent, and during the Civil War, 87 percent of soldiers who suffered abdominal wounds died from them.

Popular Health Movements

Doubtful of medicine and skeptical of the benefits of public health, antebellum Americans turned to a variety of therapies and regimens that promised to give them healthier and longer lives. One popular response to disease was hydropathy, or the "water cure," which filtered into the United States from Europe during the 1840s. By the mid-1850s the United States had twenty-seven hydropathic sanatoriums, which claimed to offer by cold baths and wet packs "an abundance of water of dewy softness and crystal transparency, to cleanse, renovate, and rejuvenate the disease-worn and dilapidated system." The water cure held a special attraction for well-off women, partly because hydropathics professed to relieve the pain associated with childbirth and menstruation and partly because hydropathic sanatoriums were congenial gathering places in which middle-class women could relax and exercise in private.

In contrast to the water cure, which necessitated the time and expense of a trip to a sanatorium, a health system that anyone could adopt was propounded by Sylvester Graham, a temperance reformer turned popular health advocate. Alarmed by the 1832 cholera epidemic, Graham counseled changes in diet and regimen as well as total abstinence from alcohol. Contending that Americans ate too much, he urged them to substitute vegetables, fruits, and coarse, whole-grain bread (called Graham bread) for meat and to abstain from spices, coffee, and tea as well as from alcohol. Soon Graham added sexual "excess" (by which he meant most sex) to his list of forbidden indulgences. Vegetables were preferable to meat, according to Graham, because they provoked less hunger. The food cravings of the "flesh-eater" were "greater and more imperious" than those of the vegetarian.

Many of Graham's most enthusiastic disciples were reformers. Grahamites had a special table at the Brook Farm community. Until forced out by outraged parents and hungry students, one of Graham's followers ran the student dining room at reformist Oberlin College. Much like Graham, reformers traced the evils of American society to the unnatural cravings of its people. Abolitionists, for example, contended that slavery intensified white men's lust and contributed to the violent behavior of white southerners. Similarly, Graham believed that eating meat stimulated lust and other aggressive impulses.

Yet Graham's doctrines attracted a broad audience that extended beyond the perimeters of the reform movements. Many towns and cities had boarding houses whose tables were set according to his principles. His books sold well, and his public lectures were thronged. Like hydropathy, Grahamism addressed the popular desire for better health at a time when orthodox medicine seemed to do more damage than good. Graham used religious phrases that were familiar to churchgoers and then channeled those concepts toward nonreligious goals. Luxury was "sinful," disease resembled hell, and health was a kind of heaven on earth. In this way, he provided simple and familiar assurances to an audience as ignorant as he was of the true causes of disease.

Phrenology

The belief that each person was ultimately the master of his or her own destiny marked the popular antebellum health movements. A similar impulse underlay phrenology, the most popular of the scientific fads that swept antebellum America.

Originating with the Viennese physician Franz J. Gall, phrenology centered on the idea that the human mind was composed of thirty-seven distinct faculties, or "organs," each localized in a different part of the brain. Phrenologists thought that the degree of each organ's development determined the shape of the skull, so that they could accurately analyze an individual's character by examining the bumps and depressions of the skull. During the 1830s Johann Spurzheim, a student of Gall, and George Combe, a Scot, transported phrenology to the United States, where it commanded serious attention from educated dabblers in science, including Horace Mann and Henry Ward Beecher, Lyman Beecher's son and, after midcentury, the most prominent American clergyman.

In the 1840s phrenology entered a new phase in the hands of the brothers Orson and Lorenzo Fowler. A graduate of Amherst College, where he had been a classmate of Henry Ward Beecher, Orson Fowler originally intended to become a Protestant missionary. Instead, he became a missionary for phrenology and opened a publishing house in New York City (Fowlers and Wells) that marketed books on phrenology everywhere. When some critics argued that phrenology was godless because it eliminated the idea of the human soul, the Fowlers pointed to a huge organ called Veneration to establish that people were naturally religious. When others said that phrenology was pessimistic because a person presumably could not change the shape of his or her skull, the Fowlers retorted that every desirable organ could be improved by exercise. Lorenzo Fowler reported that several of his skull bumps had actually grown. Orson Fowler wrapped it all into a tidy slogan: "Self-Made, or Never-Made."

Drawing phrenological charts of oneself or one's friends became a parlor game of sorts during the 1840s and 1850s, but phrenology appealed to Americans less as a pastime than as a "practical" science. In a mobile and individualistic society where people routinely transacted business with strangers, phrenology promised to provide at a glance a quick assessment of others. Merchants used phrenological charts to pick suitable clerks, and young maidens induced their fiancés to undergo phrenological analyses before tying the knot. Before phrenology, a supporter declared, "the wisest of men had no means of deciding, with anything like certainty, the talents or character of a stranger."

Phrenology did not cure disease, but phrenologists had close ties to the popular health movement. Fowlers and Wells issued the *Water-Cure Journal* after 1848 and brought out Sylvester Graham's *Lectures on the Science of Human Life*. Orson Fowler filled his popular phrenological books with tips on the evils of coffee, tea, meat, spices, and sex that could have been plucked from Graham's writings. As a "science," phrenology sprang from the same impulse as the health movements—the belief that anyone could understand and obey the "laws" of life.

Unlike hydropathy, phrenology did not require any investment of money. Unlike Grahamism, it did not call for painful abstinence. Easily understood and practiced by the average person, and filled with the promise of universal betterment, phrenology was the ideal science for antebellum America. Just as Americans invented machines to better their lives, they were not above inventing "sciences" that promised human betterment.

Democratic Pastimes

Between 1830 and 1860, technology increasingly transformed leisure as well as work. At times, the impact of technology on leisure was indirect. For example, as factory-made clothing displaced homespun, many middle-class women had more free time and occupied it by reading. By 1860 women composed the bulk of the novel-reading public, and fiction by and about women so flooded the country that Nathaniel Hawthorne complained of competition from a "damned pack of female scribblers." But technology's main effect on leisure was direct. In the years before the Civil War, Americans became dependent on types of recreation that were manufactured and sold. Recreation became a commodity that people purchased in the form of cheap newspapers and novels as well as affordable tickets to plays, museums, and lectures.

Just as the Boston Associates had daringly capitalized on new technology to produce textiles at Lowell and Waltham, imaginative entrepreneurs utilized technology to make and sell entertainment. Men like James Gordon Bennett, one of the founders of the penny press in America, and P. T. Barnum, the greatest showman of the nineteenth century, amassed fortunes by sensing what people wanted and then employing available technology to satisfy their desire. To a degree, indeed, these men induced the public to want what they had to sell. Barnum, for example, had a genius for using newspaper publicity to pique popular interest in curiosities that he was about to exhibit.

Bennett and Barnum thought of themselves as purveyors of democratic entertainment. They would sell their wares cheaply to anyone. Barnum's famous American museum in New York City catered to a wide variety of social classes that paid to view paintings, dwarfs, mammoth bones, and other attractions. By marketing the American Museum as family entertainment, Barnum helped to break down barriers that had long divided the pastimes of husbands from those of their wives. Similarly, the racy news stories in Bennett's *New York Herald* provided its vast audience with a common stock of information and topics for conversation. In these ways, the impact of technology on amusement was democratic.

Technology also ignited the process by which individuals became spectators rather than the creators of their own amusements. Americans had long found ways to enjoy themselves. Even the gloomiest Puritans had indulged in games and sports. After 1830, however, the burden of providing entertainment began to shift from individuals to entrepreneurs who supplied ways to amuse the public.

Newspapers

In 1830 the typical American newspaper was a mere four pages long, with the front and back pages devoted almost wholly to advertisements. The second and third pages contained editorials, details of ship arrivals and of their cargoes, reprints of political speeches, and notices of political events. Few papers depended on their circulation for profit; even the most prominent papers had a daily circulation of only one thousand to two thousand. Rather, papers often relied on subsidies from political parties or factions. When a party gained power, it inserted paid political notices only in papers loyal to it. "Journalists," a contemporary wrote, "were usually little more than secretaries dependent upon cliques of politicians, merchants, brokers, and office seekers for their prosperity and bread."

Newspaper Boy, *by Edward Bannister, 1869*

Newsboys such as this one poignantly painted by the black artist Edward Bannister were a familiar sight on nineteenth-century street corners.

As a result, newspapers could be profitable without being particularly popular. Because of their potential for profit, new papers were constantly being established. But most had limited appeal. The typical paper sold for six cents an issue at a time when the average daily wage was less than a dollar. Papers often seemed little more than published bulletin boards. Merely records of events, they typically lacked the exciting news stories and eye-catching illustrations that later generations would take for granted.

The 1830s witnessed the beginnings of a stunning transformation. Technological changes, most of which originated in Europe, vastly increased both the supply of paper (still made from rags) and the speed of printing presses. The substitution of steam-driven cylindrical presses for flatbed hand presses led to a tenfold increase in the number of printed pages that could be produced in an hour. Enterprising journalists, among them the Scottish-born James Gordon Bennett, grasped the implications of the new technology. Newspapers could now rely on vast circulation rather than on political subsidies to turn a profit. To gain circulation, journalists like Bennett slashed the price of newspapers. In 1833 the *New York Sun* became America's first penny newspaper, and Bennett's *New York Herald* followed in 1835. By June 1835 the combined daily circulation of New York's three penny papers reached 44,000; in contrast, before the dawn of the penny press in 1833, the city's eleven dailies had a combined daily circulation of only 26,500. Spearheaded by the penny papers, the combined daily circulation of newspapers throughout the nation rose from roughly 78,000 in 1830 to 300,000 by 1840. The number of weekly newspapers spurted from 65 in 1830 to 138 in 1840.

Cheapness was not the only feature of the penny papers. Dependent on circulation and advertising rather than on subsidies, the penny press revolutionized the marketing and format of papers. Where single copies of the six-cent papers were usually available only at the printer's office, newsboys hawked the penny papers on busy street corners. Moreover, the penny papers subordinated the recording of political and commercial events to human-interest stories of robberies, murders, rapes, and abandoned children. They dispatched reporters to police courts and printed transcripts of trials. As

sociologist Michael Schudson observes, "The penny press invented the modern concept of 'news.'" Rather than merely recording events, the penny papers wove events into gripping stories. They invented not only news but also news reporting. Relying on party stalwarts to dispatch copies of speeches and platforms, and reprinting news items from other papers, the older six-cent papers did little, if any, reporting. In contrast, the penny papers employed their own correspondents and were the first papers to use the telegraph to speed news to readers.

Some penny papers were little more than scandal sheets, but the best, like Bennett's *New York Herald* and Horace Greeley's *New York Tribune* (1841), pioneered modern financial and political reporting. From its inception, the *Herald* contained a daily "money article" that substituted the analysis and interpretation of financial events for the dull recording of commercial facts. "The spirit, pith, and philosophy of commercial affairs is what men of business want," Bennett wrote. The relentless snooping of the *Tribune*'s Washington reporters outraged politicians. In 1848 *Tribune* correspondents were temporarily barred from the House floor for reporting that Representative Sawyer of Ohio ate his lunch (sausage and bread) each day in the House chamber, picked his teeth with a jackknife, and wiped his greasy hands on his pants and coat.

The Popular Novel

Like newspapers, novels became enormously popular between 1830 and 1860. Of course, novels had been read long before 1830, and some authors, among them the Scot Sir Walter Scott, had gained a wide following. But the cost of novels before 1830 had restricted their sales. Each of Scott's novels, for example, was issued in a three-volume set that retailed for as much as thirty dollars. During the 1830s and 1840s, the impact of the transportation revolution and technical advances in printing brought down the price of novels. As canals and railroads opened crossroads stores to the latest fiction, publishers in New York and Philadelphia vied to deliver inexpensive novels to the shelves. By the 1840s cheap paperbacks that sold for as little as seven cents began to flood the market.

Those who did not purchase such fictional books could read serializations in newspapers that were devoted mainly to printing novels. The most successful of these story papers was the *New York Ledger*, which a young Scotch-Irish immigrant, Robert Bonner, started in the mid-1840s. Like James Gordon Bennett, the lord of the penny press, Bonner had a genius for identifying what the public wanted and for launching publicity extravaganzas. To herald the serialization of one novel, Bonner spent twenty thousand dollars and arranged the firing of a one-hundred-gun salute in City Hall Park. By 1860 the *Ledger* had an astonishing weekly circulation of four hundred thousand.

The most popular fiction on the market in the 1840s and 1850s was the sentimental novel, which sought to evoke feelings or emotions. The tribulations of orphans and the deaths of children filled the pages of these tearjerkers. In Susan Warner's *The Wide, Wide World* (first serialized in 1850), the heroine burst into tears on an average of every other page for two volumes. Sentimentalism was not confined to novels. The popular writer Lydia Sigourney wrote a poem on the death of a canary that had accidentally been starved to death.

Women contributed the main audience for sentimental novels. This genre was a kind of women's fiction, written by women about women and mainly for women. The most lucrative occupation open to women before the Civil War, writing often attracted those in desperate need of cash. Hard times had lured many renowned female novelists into the field. Susan Warner, for example, had been brought up in luxury and then tossed into poverty by the financial ruin of her father in the Panic of 1837. Mrs. E. D. E. N. Southworth, who gained fame and fortune from *The Hidden Hand* (first serialized in 1859) and other novels, turned to writing after a broken marriage left her supporting two children on a teacher's salary of $250 a year.

Women's fiction dealt with more than the flow of tears. A major theme in the novels of Susan Warner and Mrs. Southworth was that women could conquer any obstacle. Women's novels challenged the stereotype of the male as the trusty provider and of the female as the delicate dependent by portraying men as liars, drunken lechers, or vicious misers and depicting women as resourceful and strong-willed. In the typical plot, a female orphan or a spoiled rich girl thrown on hard times, or a dutiful daughter plagued by a drunken father, learned grittily to master every situation. The moral was clear. Women could overcome trials and make the world a better place. Few of the novelists were active feminists, but their writings provided a glimpse into the private feelings of their female readers.

The Theater

During the 1850s novelists like the Englishman Charles Dickens and the American Harriet Beecher Stowe, the author of *Uncle Tom's Cabin*, were as well known through dramatizations of their work as by sales of their books. Antebellum theaters were large (twenty-five hundred to four thousand seats in some cities) and crowded by all classes. With seats as cheap as twelve cents and rarely more than fifty cents, the typical theater audience included lawyers and merchants and their wives, artisans and clerks, sailors and noisy boys, and a sizable body of prostitutes. Prostitutes usually sat in the top gallery, called the third tier, "that dark, horrible, guilty" place. The presence of prostitutes in theaters was taken for granted; the only annoyance came when they left the third tier to solicit customers in the more expensive seats.

The prostitutes in attendance were not the only factor that made the antebellum theater vaguely disreputable. Theatrical audiences were notoriously rowdy. They showed their feelings by stamping their feet, whistling, hooting at villains, and throwing potatoes or garbage at the stage when they did not like the characters or the acting. Individual actors developed huge followings, and the public displayed at least as much interest in the actors as in the plays. In 1849 a long-running feud between the leading American actor, Edwin Forrest, and the popular British actor William Macready ended with a riot at New York City's Astor Place that left twenty people dead.

The Astor Place riot demonstrated the broad popularity of the theater. Forrest's supporters included a following of Irish workers who loathed the British and appealed to the "working men" to rally against the "aristocrat" Macready. Macready, who projected a more polished and intellectual image than Forrest, attracted the better-educated classes. Had not all classes patronized the theater, the riot probably would never have occurred.

The plays themselves were as diverse as the audiences. Most often performed were melodramas, whose plots resembled those of sentimental novels. Vice was punished, virtue rewarded, and the heroine finally married the hero. Yet the single most popular dramatist was William Shakespeare. In 1835 audiences in Philadelphia witnessed sixty-five performances of Shakespeare's plays. Americans who may never have read a line of Shakespeare grew familiar with Othello, King Lear, Desdemona, and Shylock. Theatrical managers adapted Shakespeare to a popular audience. They highlighted the swordfights and assassinations, cut some speeches, omitted minor characters, and pruned words or references that might have offended the audience's sense of propriety. For example, they substituted *pottels* for *urinals* and quietly advanced Juliet's age at the time that she falls in love with Romeo from fourteen to eighteen. They occasionally changed sad endings to happy ones. The producers even arranged for short performances or demonstrations between acts of Shakespeare—and indeed, of every play. During such an interlude, the audience might have observed a brief impersonation of Tecumseh or Aaron Burr, jugglers and acrobats, a drummer beating twelve drums at once, or a three-year-old who weighed a hundred pounds.

Minstrel Shows

The Yankee or "Brother Jonathan" figure who served as a stock character in many antebellum plays helped audiences to form an image of the ideal American as rustic, clever, patriotic, and more than a match for city slickers and decadent European aristocrats. In a different way, the minstrel shows that Americans thronged to see in the 1840s and 1850s forged enduring stereotypes that buttressed white Americans' sense of superiority by diminishing black people.

Minstrel shows arose in northern cities in the 1840s, as blackfaced white men took to the stage to present an evening of songs, dances, and humorous sketches. Minstrelsy borrowed some authentic elements of African-American culture, especially dances characterized by the sliding, shuffling step of southern blacks, but most of the songs had origins in white culture. Such familiar American songs as Stephen Foster's "Camptown Races" and "Massa's in the Cold Ground," which first aired in min-

Dan Bryant, the Minstrel

Bryant was one of many antebellum popularizers of black minstrelsy. One of the earliest known minstrelsy performances occurred in Boston in 1799, when the white man Gottlieb Graupner, reportedly made up as a black, sang and accompanied himself on the banjo.

strel shows, reflected white Americans' notions of how blacks sang more than it represented authentic black music. In addition, the images of blacks projected by minstrelsy both catered to and reinforced the prejudices of the working-class whites who dominated the audience of minstrel shows. Minstrel troupes usually depicted blacks as stupid, clumsy, and obsessively musical and emphasized the Africanness of blacks by giving their characters names like the Ethiopian Serenaders and their acts titles like the Nubian Jungle Dance and the African Fling. At a time of intensifying political conflict over race, minstrel shows planted images and expectations about blacks' behavior through stock characters. These included Uncle Ned, the tattered, humble, and docile slave, and Zip Coon, the arrogant urban free black who paraded around in a high hat, long-tailed coat, and green vest and who lived off his girlfriends' money. Minstrels lampooned blacks who assumed public roles by portraying them as incompetent stump speakers who called Patrick Henry "Henry Patrick," referred to John Hancock as "Boobcock," and confused the word *statute* with *statue*.

By the 1850s major cities from New York to San Francisco had several minstrel theaters. Touring professional troupes and local amateur talent even brought minstrelsy to small towns and villages. Mark Twain later recalled how minstrelsy had burst upon Hannibal, Missouri, in the early 1840s as "a glad and stunning surprise." So popular was the craze that minstrels even visited the White House and entertained Presidents John Tyler, James K. Polk, Millard Fillmore, and Franklin Pierce.

P. T. Barnum

The remarkable career of P. T. Barnum exemplified the intersection of virtually all of the forces that made entertainment a profitable business in antebellum America. As a young man in his native Bethel, Connecticut, Barnum savored popular journalism by starting a newspaper, the *Herald of Freedom*, that assailed wrongdoing in high places. Throughout his life, he thought of himself as a public benefactor and pointed to his profits as proof that he gave people what they wanted. Yet honesty was never his strong suit. As a small-town grocer in Connecticut, he regularly cheated his customers on the principle that they were trying to cheat him. Barnum, in short, was a hustler raised in the land of the Puritans, a cynic and an idealist rolled into one.

After moving to New York City in 1834, Barnum started a new career as an entrepreneur of popular entertainment. His first venture exhibited a black woman, Joice Heth, whom Barnum billed as the 169-year-old former slave nurse of George Washington. Barnum neither knew nor cared how old Joice was (in fact, she was probably around 80); it was enough that people would pay to see her. Strictly speaking, he cheated the public, but he knew that many of his customers shared his doubts about Joice's age. Determined to expose Barnum's gimmick, some poked her to see whether she was really a machine rather than a person. He was playing a game with the public, and the public with him.

In 1841 Barnum purchased a run-down museum in New York City, rechristened it the American

P. T. Barnum and Tom Thumb

Charles Stratton, whom Barnum renamed General Tom Thumb, was a midget. When discovered by Barnum in Bridgeport, Connecticut, in 1842, Tom was nearly five years old, stood only two feet tall, and had gained a mere six pounds since birth. Characteristically, Barnum immediately advertised Tom as an eleven-year-old and took him on tour.

Museum, and opened a new chapter in the history of popular entertainment. The founders of most earlier museums had intended an educational purpose. They exhibited stuffed birds and animals, specimens of rock, and portraits. Most of these museums, however, had languished for want of public interest. Barnum, in contrast, made piquing public curiosity the main goal. To attract people, he added collections of curiosities and faked exhibits. Visitors to the American Museum could see ventriloquists, magicians, albinos, a five-year-old midget whom Barnum named General Tom Thumb and later took on a tour of Europe, and the "Feejee Mermaid," a shrunken oddity that Barnum billed as "positively asserted by its owner to have been taken alive in the Feejee Islands." By 1850 the American Museum had become the best-known museum in the nation and a model for popular museums in other cities.

Blessed with a genius for publicity, Barnum recognized that newspapers could invent as well as report news. One of his favorite tactics was to puff his exhibits by writing letters (under various names) to newspapers, in which he would hint that the scientific world was agog over some astonishing curiosity of nature that the public could soon see for itself at the American Museum. But Barnum's success rested on more than publicity. A staunch temperance advocate, he provided regular lectures at the American Museum on the evils of alcohol and soon gave the place a reputation as a center for safe family amusement. Finally, Barnum tapped the public's insatiable curiosity about natural wonders. In 1835 the editor of the *New York Sun* had boosted his circulation by claiming that a famous astronomer had discovered pelicans and winged men on the moon. At a time when each passing year brought new technological wonders, the public was ready to believe in anything, even the Feejee Mermaid.

The Quest for Nationality in Literature and Art

Sentimental novels, melodramas, minstrel shows, and the American Museum belonged to the world of popular culture. All these genres lacked the dignity and originality that would endear them to those seeking cultural expressions that would reflect the American national spirit and command respect abroad. The limits of the popular genres—with their frequent crudity and their interchangeable plots, characters, and themes—did not escape the notice of reflective observers. During the 1830s Ralph Waldo Emerson emerged as the most influential spokesman for those who sought a national literature and art.

"Our day of dependence, our long apprenticeship to the learning of other lands, draws to a close," Emerson announced in his address "The American Scholar" (1837). For too long, Emerson affirmed, Americans had deferred to European precedents in literature and learning. Now the time had come for the American people to trust themselves. Let "the single man plant himself indomitably on his instincts and there abide," and "the huge world will come round to him."

Contemporaries proclaimed "The American Scholar" an intellectual Declaration of Independence and praised Emerson for having "cut the cable" that still moored the United States to European thought. Yet Emerson's plea for cultural autonomy was hardly new; ever since the Revolution, Americans had been calling for cultural as well as political independence from Britain. In the 1780s Noah Webster, the famous compiler of textbooks and dictionaries that substituted phonetic American spellings for British spellings, had warned that basing American literature on European taste and manners was as foolish as constructing "a durable and stately edifice . . . upon the mouldering pillars of antiquity."

"The American Scholar" had an electrifying effect for several reasons. First, as Emerson recognized, the democratic spirit of the age had made Americans more self-reliant. Successful in their political and material lives, they no longer felt the need to defer to European standards. In addition, the dramatic impact of Emerson's address reflected his ability to adapt an international literary movement known as romanticism to American conditions. Originating in Europe in the second half of the eighteenth century, romanticism challenged the rival impulse known as classicism (or neoclassicism). Classicists described standards of beauty and taste as universal and decreed that the most desirable literary productions display elegance and polish. In contrast, romantics argued that each nation had to discover its own unique literary genius. They further insisted that great literature reflect not only national character but also the most profound emotions of the writer. Where classicists expected that all fine literature and art would conform to an identical standard of elegance, romantics sought individuality in literary and artistic expression.

As we have seen, during the 1830s the transcendentalist movement emerged as a challenge to Unitarianism, and in their literary work, Emerson and other transcendentalists evolved a uniquely American form of romanticism. Dismissing the prevailing idea that all knowledge came through the senses, transcendentalists argued instead that such basic conceptions as those of God and freedom were inborn. Knowledge resembled sight—

an instantaneous, direct perception of truth. Emerson concluded that learned people enjoyed no special advantages in the pursuit of truth. All persons could see the truth if only they would trust the promptings of their hearts. Applied to the United States, transcendentalist doctrine led to the exhilarating conclusion that a young, democratic society could produce as noble a literature and art as the more traditional societies of Europe. While such a fledgling, democratic society might lack elegance and polish, it could draw upon the inexhaustible resources of the common people.

Literary Geography

Emerson's "The American Scholar" coincided with a flowering of distinctively American literature and art, often called the American Renaissance, that had been gaining momentum since the 1820s. By 1837 the American public had grown as familiar with native-born authors such as Washington Irving and James Fenimore Cooper as with such lions of the British literary world as Sir Walter Scott and Charles Dickens. Emerson did not initiate this outpouring of native talent, but he expressed its ideals and helped to shape its direction.

Of all the regions of the United States, New England had the most fertile soil for literature. Its poets ranged from the urbane Henry Wadsworth Longfellow and polished Boston aristocrats like Oliver Wendell Holmes, Sr., and James Russell Lowell to the farm-born, self-taught Quaker John Greenleaf Whittier. Boston also became the home of George Bancroft, William Hickling Prescott, Francis Parkman, and John Lothrop Motley, the four most distinguished historians of the antebellum period. Twenty miles from Boston lay Concord, the home of Emerson, Nathaniel Hawthorne, the eccentric Henry David Thoreau, and the brilliant philosopher and critic Margaret Fuller. Not far from Concord lay Fruitlands, a utopian community where Louisa May Alcott, the author of *Little Women* (1868), passed part of her childhood under the sometimes dizzying influence of her unworldly father, Bronson Alcott. Farther to the west was Amherst, the residence of Emily Dickinson. Shy and reclusive, she lived out her entire fifty-six years on the same street ("I do not go from home," she stated with characteristic pithiness), where she wrote exquisite poems that examined, in her own words, every splinter in the groove of the brain. Dreading the corruption of her art by commercialism, she staunchly refused to publish her verse.

Most New Englanders did not share Emily Dickinson's horror of publicity. Nineteenth-century New England writers and publishers widely exported their region's culture. By the end of the century, schoolchildren throughout the nation were turning pages of Longfellow's *Evangeline* (1847) and *The Song of Hiawatha* (1855), Whittier's *Snow-Bound* (1866), and Lowell's antislavery *The Biglow Papers* (1848). What had begun as a regional culture became enshrined as a national culture, and for this reason alone, New England's literary renaissance deserves special recognition.

New England, however, always faced a challenge from New York, the home of Irving, Cooper, and later of Walt Whitman and Herman Melville. Even before the flowering of American literature, New York had abounded with literary clubs, composed for the most part of wealthy young lawyers and merchants. It was in New York that the wealthy and gifted Irving had made his reputation with the publication of the comedic *Diedrich Knickerbocker's A History of New York* (1809). After serving in the War of 1812, Irving had left the United States for Europe and had not returned until 1832. Yet his *Sketch Book* (1820), which contained "Rip Van Winkle" and "The Legend of Sleepy Hollow," continued to endear him to Americans, who displayed a boastful pride in the literary accomplishments of their best-known writer.

The literary flowering affected all regions. Southerners such as William Gilmore Simms, the author of *The Yemassee* (1835), acquired reputations that spread beyond their native section. Although he did most of his writing in New York and Philadelphia, Edgar Allan Poe was a Virginian by upbringing and emotional identification. In the lower and westerly regions of the Old South, Augustus B. Longstreet and Johnson J. Hooper crafted humorous sketches that captured a kind of backcountry roguishness and rowdiness so extravagant that it became hilarious. Longstreet's *Georgia Scenes* (1835) described gander pulling, eye gouging, and other frontier pastimes. Hooper's *Some Adventures of Captain Simon Suggs* (1846) related how Suggs cheated his own father at cards to obtain a horse and how he went to a camp meeting to get religion and came away with the contents of the collection box instead.

Washington Irving; Rip Van Winkle

Visiting Britain in 1817, Irving met Sir Walter Scott, who urged him to study German legends for fictional material. Irving took this advice and borrowed heavily from the German legend of "Peter Klaus" for "Rip Van Winkle," his most famous tale.

Not all antebellum writers, however, have passed the test of time. Irving's writings now strike critics as examples of a comfortable second-rateedness. Although polished poets, neither Longfellow nor Whittier was notably innovative. Dickinson was a genius, but born in 1830, she did most of her writing after 1860. In retrospect, regional humorists like Longstreet and Hooper are significant mainly because they foreshadowed a far greater humorist, Mark Twain.

Yet within the large circle of antebellum writers, the genius of seven individuals continues to shine: Cooper, Emerson, Thoreau, Whitman, Hawthorne, Melville, and Poe. Cooper and Emerson basked in public esteem in their day, but neither Hawthorne nor Poe gained the popular audience that each believed he deserved. The antebellum public largely ignored the remaining three—Thoreau, Whitman, and Melville. Creativity rather than popularity became the unifying characteristic of these seven writers. Each challenged existing literary conventions and created new ones. Cooper demonstrated the possibility of writing a novel using distinctively American literary themes. Emerson gave a new direction to an old literary form, the essay. Thoreau wrote about nature in a way that captured not only its beauty but its constant activity. By breaking with the conventions of rhyme and

meter, Whitman breathed new vitality into poetry. As a writer of both short fiction and poetry, Poe went far to free literature from the insistence that it preach a moral and to establish the principle that fiction and poetry be judged by the pleasure that they imparted. Hawthorne and Melville turned the novel into a vehicle for exploring the depths of human psychology.

James Fenimore Cooper and the Quest for Literary Independence

Until well after 1800, British literature had dominated American literary taste. With the publication of *Waverley* (1814), a historical novel set in Britain in the 1740s, the star of Sir Walter Scott had begun its spectacular ascent on the American horizon. Americans had named more than a dozen towns Waverley; advertisements for subsequent novels by Scott had borne the simple caption, "By the author of *Waverley*."

Because he wrote historical novels under Scott's influence, James Fenimore Cooper, born in 1789, has often been called the American Scott. But this designation is misleading, for the enormously popular Cooper achieved a remarkable creativity in his own right. His most important innovation was to introduce to fiction such an American type as the frontiersman Natty Bumppo ("Leatherstocking") and such a distinctly American theme as the conflict between the customs of primitive life on the frontier and the irresistible advance of civilization. Starting with the publication of *The Pioneers* (1823), both the career of Leatherstocking and the conflict between nature and civilization unfolded in Cooper's novels, notably *The Last of the Mohicans* (1826), *The Pathfinder* (1840), and *The Deerslayer* (1841). Cooper's popularity was enhanced by his remarkable productivity. He averaged a novel a year for thirty-one years and once said that he found it harder to read his novels than to write them. The reading public knew what to expect of Cooper and rewarded him with its patronage.

Cooper's success marked the first step in a process that saw Americans develop an imaginative literature of their own. They still read British novels, but they increasingly enjoyed American writers. In 1800 American authors accounted for a negligible proportion of the output of American publishers. By 1830, 40 percent of the books published in the United States were written by Americans; and by 1850, 75 percent.

Emerson, Thoreau, and Whitman

Emerson's advocacy of a national literature extended beyond his urgings in "The American Scholar." In writings of his own, he tried (not always successfully) to capture the brisk language of the common people of the United States. Furthermore, he encouraged younger American writers like Thoreau and Whitman. Whitman, extravagantly patriotic, contrasted sharply with Emerson and Thoreau, who often criticized the materialism and aggressiveness of their countrymen. The ideal of nationality in literature clearly did not always mean the uncritical celebration of Americans and American policies. But the uniquely American prose or poetry that flowed from the pens of these three writers did share a strong common feature: it emphasized the spontaneous and vivid expression of personal feelings over learned analysis, which the writers associated with European traditions.

Born in 1803, Emerson served briefly as a Unitarian minister. During the 1830s he carved out a new career for himself as a public lecturer. The topics of his addresses, most of which he published as essays, appeared to be broad and general: "Beauty," "Nature," "Power," "Representative

Men," and "New England Reformers." But a unique pungency and vividness characterized his language. For example, in "The American Scholar," in which Emerson emphasized the importance of independent thought on the part of the true scholar, his language was striking: "Let him [the scholar] not quit his belief that a popgun is a popgun, though the ancient and honorable of the earth affirm it to be the crack of doom." Equally remarkable was Emerson's way of developing his subjects. A contemporary compared listening to Emerson to trying to see the sun in a fog; one could see light but never the sun itself. As a transcendentalist who believed that knowledge reflected the voice of God within every person and that truth was inborn and universal, Emerson never amassed evidence or presented systematic arguments to prove his contentions. Rather, he relied on a sequence of vivid and arresting though often unconnected assertions. The argument was hard to follow (one listener thought she might have better understood Emerson if she had stood on her head), but the overall effect dazzled the audience.

Emerson had a magnetic attraction for intellectually inclined young men and women who did not fit easily into American society. Henry David Thoreau, born in 1809 in Concord, Massachusetts, where Emerson took up residence during the 1830s, was representative of the younger Emersonians. Yet a crucial difference separated the two men. Adventurous in thought, Emerson was basically unadventurous in action. As contemplative as Emerson, Thoreau was more of a doer. At one point, Thoreau went to jail rather than pay his poll tax. This revenue, he knew, would support the war against Mexico, which he viewed as part of a southern conspiracy to extend slavery. The experience led Thoreau to write *Civil Disobedience* (1849), in which he defended the right to disobey unjust laws.

In the spring of 1845, Thoreau moved a few miles from Concord into the woods near Walden Pond. There he constructed a simple cabin on land owned by Emerson and spent the next two years providing for his wants away from civilization. Thoreau's stated purpose in retreating to Walden was to write a description (later published) of a canoe trip that he and his brother had taken down the Concord and Merrimack rivers in 1839. During his stay in the woods, however, he conceived and wrote a much more important book, *Walden*

(1854). A contemporary described *Walden* as "the log-book of his woodland cruise," and indeed, Thoreau filled its pages with descriptions of hawks and wild pigeons, his invention of raisin bread, his trapping of the woodchucks that despoiled his vegetable garden, and his construction of a cabin for exactly $28.50. Few writers have matched Thoreau's ability to capture both the details and the cycles of nature and to give the reader the sensation of being present at the scene. But true to transcendentalism, Thoreau had a larger message. His woodland retreat taught him that he (and by implication, others) could satisfy material wants with only a few weeks' work each year and thereby leave more time for reexamining life's purpose. The problem with Americans, he said, was that they turned themselves into "mere machines" to acquire wealth without asking why. Thoreau bore the uncomfortable truth that material and moral progress were not as intimately related as Americans liked to think.

One of Ralph Waldo Emerson's qualities was an ability to sympathize with such dissimilar personalities as Thoreau and Walt Whitman—the former eccentric, reclusive, and critical; the latter self-taught, outgoing, exuberant, and in love with virtually everything about America except slavery. Born in 1819, Whitman left school at eleven and became a printer's apprentice and later a journalist and editor for various newspapers in Brooklyn, Manhattan, and New Orleans. A familiar figure at Democratic party functions, he marched in the vanguard of party parades and put his pen to the service of the party's free-soil wing.

Journalism gave Whitman an intimate knowledge of ordinary Americans; the more he knew them, the more he liked them. His reading of Emerson nurtured his belief that America was to be the cradle of a new citizen in whom natural virtue would flourish unimpeded by European corruption, a man like Andrew Jackson, that "massive, yet most sweet and plain character." The threads of Whitman's early career came together in his major work, *Leaves of Grass*, a book of poems first published in 1855 and reissued with additions in subsequent years.

Leaves of Grass shattered most existing poetic conventions. Not only did Whitman write in free verse (that is, most of his poems had neither rhyme nor meter), but the poems were also lusty and blunt at a time when delicacy reigned in the literary world.

Walt Whitman

Whitman is today considered one of the major nineteenth-century poets, but in his day many derided his verse as indecent. In 1865 Whitman lost his job with the U.S. government when his superiors found out that he was the author of Leaves of Grass.

Whitman wrote of "the scent of these arm-pits finer than prayer" and "winds whose soft-tickling genitals rub against me." No less remarkably, Whitman intruded himself into his poems, one of which he titled "Song of Walt Whitman" (and later retitled "Song of Myself"). Although Whitman thought well of himself, it was not egotism that propelled him to sing of himself. Rather, he viewed himself—crude, plain, self-taught, and passionately democratic—as the personification of the American people. He was

> Comrade of raftsmen and coalmen, comrade
>   of all who shake hands and welcome to
>   drink and meat,
> A learner with the simplest, a teacher of the
>   thoughtfullest.

By 1860 Whitman had acquired a considerable reputation as a poet. Nevertheless, the original edition of *Leaves* (a run of only about eight hundred copies) was ignored or derided as a "heterogeneous mass of bombast, egotism, vulgarity, and nonsense." One reviewer suggested that it was the work of an escaped lunatic. Only Emerson and a few others reacted enthusiastically. Within two weeks of publication, Emerson, never having met Whitman, wrote: "I find it the most extraordinary piece of wit and wisdom that America has yet contributed." Emerson had long called for the appearance of "the poet of America" and knew in a flash that in Whitman, that poet had arrived.

Hawthorne, Melville, and Poe

In "The American Scholar," Emerson called upon American writers to create a democratic literature by comprehending "the near, the low, the common"—the everyday experiences of ordinary Americans. However exhilarating a message, Emerson's plea had a negligible impact on the major writers of fiction during the 1840s and 1850s—Nathaniel Hawthorne, Herman Melville, and Edgar Allan Poe. Hawthorne, for example, set *The Scarlet Letter* (1850) in New England's Puritan past, *The House of the Seven Gables* (1851) in a mansion haunted not by ghosts but by memories of the past, and *The Marble Faun* (1859) in Rome. Poe set several of his short stories such as "The Murders in the Rue Morgue" (1841), "The Masque of the Red Death" (1842), and "The Cask of Amontillado" (1846) in Europe; as one critic has noted, "His art could have been produced as easily had he been born in Europe." Melville did draw materials and themes from his own experiences as a sailor and from the lore of the New England whaling industry, but for his novels *Typee* (1846), *Omoo* (1847), and *Mardi* (1849), he picked the exotic setting of islands in the South Seas; and for his masterpiece *Moby-Dick* (1851), the ill-fated whaler *Pequod*. If the only surviving documents from the 1840s and 1850s were its major novels, historians would face an impossible task in describing the appearance of antebellum American society.

The unusual settings favored by these three writers partly reflected their view that American life lacked the materials for great fiction. Hawthorne, for example, bemoaned the difficulty of writing about a country "where there is no shadow, no antiquity, no mystery, no picturesque and gloomy wrong, nor anything but a commonplace prosperity in broad and simple daylight, as is happily the case with my dear native land." In addition, psychology rather than society riveted the attention of these three writers; each probed the depths of the human mind rather than the intricacies of social

relationships. Their preoccupation with analyzing the mental states of their characters grew out of their underlying pessimism about the human condition. Emerson, Whitman, and (to a degree) Thoreau optimistically believed that human conflicts could be resolved if only individuals followed the promptings of their better selves. In contrast, Hawthorne, Melville, and Poe viewed individuals as bundles of conflicting forces that, even with the best intentions, might never be reconciled.

Their pessimism led them to create characters obsessed by pride, guilt, a desire for revenge, or a quest for perfection and then to set their stories along the byways of society, where they would be free to explore the complexities of human motivation without the jarring intrusion of everyday life. For example, in *The Scarlet Letter* Hawthorne turned to the Puritan past in order to examine the psychological and moral consequences of the adultery committed by Hester Prynne and the minister Arthur Dimmesdale. So completely did Hawthorne focus on the moral dilemmas of his central characters that he conveyed little sense of the social life of the Puritan village in which the novel is set. Melville, who dedicated *Moby-Dick* to Hawthorne, shared the latter's pessimism. In the novel's Captain Ahab, Melville created a frightening character whose relentless and futile pursuit of the white whale fails to fill the chasm in his soul and brings death to all of his mates save the narrator, Ishmael. Poe also channeled his pessimism into creative achievements of the first rank. In perhaps his finest short story, "The Fall of the House of Usher" (1839), he demonstrated an uncanny ability to weave the symbol of a crumbling mansion with the mental agony of a crumbling family.

Hawthorne, Melville, and Poe did not heed Emerson's call to write about the everyday experiences of their fellow countrymen. Nor did they follow Cooper's lead by creating distinctively American heroes. Yet each contributed to an indisputably American literature. Ironically, their conviction that the lives of ordinary Americans provided inadequate materials for fiction led them to create a uniquely American fiction, one marked less by the description of the complex social relationships of ordinary life than by the analysis of moral dilemmas and psychological states. In this way, they unintentionally fulfilled a prediction made by Alexis de Tocqueville that writers in democratic nations, while rejecting many of the traditional sources of fiction, would explore the abstract and universal questions of human nature.

American Landscape Painting

American painters also sought to develop nationality in art between 1820 and 1860. Lacking a mythic past of the sort represented by the gods and goddesses of the ancient world, Americans subordinated history and figure painting to landscape painting. Yet just as Hawthorne had complained about the flat, commonplace character of American society, the painters of the Hudson River school recognized that the American landscape lacked the European landscape's "poetry of decay" in the form of ruined castles and crumbling temples. Like everything else in the United States, the landscape was fresh, relatively unencumbered by the human imprint. This fact posed a challenge to the Hudson River school painters.

The Hudson River school flourished from the 1820s to the 1870s. Numbering more than fifty painters, it is best represented by Thomas Cole, Asher Durand, and Frederic Church. All three men painted scenes of the region around the Hudson River, a waterway that Americans compared in majesty to the Rhine. But none was exclusively a landscapist. Some of Cole's most popular paintings were allegories, including *The Course of Empire*, a sequence of five canvases depicting the rise and fall of an ancient city and clearly implying that luxury doomed republican virtue. Nor did these artists paint only the Hudson. Church, a student of Cole and internationally the best known of the three, painted the Andes Mountains during an extended trip to South America in 1853. After the Civil War, the German-born Albert Bierstedt applied many Hudson River school techniques in his monumental canvases of the Rocky Mountains.

The writings of Washington Irving and the

Twilight in the Wilderness,
by Frederick E. Church, 1860

Like many Hudson River school paintings, Church's Twilight in the Wilderness, *often considered his masterpiece, creates a mood of almost religious majesty.*

Central Park, New York City, in 1858

In 1858 Frederick Law Olmsted and Calvert Vaux entered the competition for the design of New York City's proposed Central Park. Already famous for his newspaper accounts of his tours through the slave states, Olmsted was keenly interested in landscapes. The British-born Vaux had been a partner of Andrew Jackson Downing, who, before his untimely death in 1852, had gained renown as America's foremost landscape architect. Both Olmsted and Vaux shared the widening fear that urban and industrial growth was destroying the American landscape and robbing the nation of its natural treasures. By the 1830s factory villages like Lowell and Waltham had turned into bustling cities, and by 1850 New York City had become a metropolis of more than half a million people. Pavement and houses threatened eventually to obliterate every parcel of open land. The "march of improvement," an observer warned in 1835, "is as destructive in its course, of everything verdant in nature, as the passage of an army of locusts over a field of grain."

So Olmsted and Vaux called for the creation of parks—enclaves of unspoiled nature in or near cities. They drew inspiration from a movement that developed in the 1830s to construct artistically landscaped "rural" cemeteries on the outskirts of cities. This movement for rural cemeteries addressed the practical problems spawned as urban developers churned up graves and as entrepreneurs plastered tombstones with handbills announcing

Frederick Law Olmsted

Olmsted's design for Central Park brought him fame and many commissions. Over his long career, he designed almost eighty parks, including Brooklyn's Prospect Park, Chicago's Jackson Park, and Boston's Back Bay Park. He also designed thirteen college campuses, among them those of Stanford University and the University of California at Berkeley.

new business ventures. But the rural-cemetery movement also reflected the ideal expressed by Emerson and Thoreau that nature was a source of spiritual refreshment. The opening of the Mount Auburn Cemetery just outside Boston in 1831 prompted an orator to proclaim that cemeteries "are not for the dead. They are for the living." Cemeteries modeled on Mount Auburn bore names that evoked images of pastoral beauty—"Laurel Hill," "Harmony Grove," "Wood Lands,"

"Green Mount," and "Greenwood." Like Mount Auburn, which some thirty thousand people a year were visiting by midcentury, they became tourist attractions.

From the cemetery movement and other sources, Olmsted and Vaux derived the principle that nature could always be improved upon by moving earth to form little hills and valleys. The result would be "picturesque"; that is, it would remind viewers of the landscapes that they had seen in pictures. Some advocates of the picturesque, among them the painter Frederic Church, preferred a wild and sublime naturalism, signified by jutting mountains and raging rivers, but Olmsted and Vaux favored gentle, pastoral scenery marked by rolling hills and placid lakes. With the blessing of the venerable Washington Irving, whose early writings had popularized the scenery along the Hudson River, Olmsted and Vaux wove their ideas into a plan called "Greensward." Not only did Greensward win the competition, but Olmsted secured the coveted appointment as the park's architect in chief.

Greensward prevailed over competing plans based on profoundly different visions of the ideal public park. Its main opposition came from advocates of bisecting the park with a grand boulevard, like the Champs Elysées in Paris, that would run from Fifty-ninth Street to the south wall of an existing reservoir with the aid of a suspension bridge across water and "a flight of marble steps" up to the reservoir. Olmsted and Vaux, in contrast, wanted the park to look as rural as possible, showing nothing of the city. A bordering line of trees screened out buildings. Within the park, brooks were filled in ("mere rivulets are uninteresting," Olmsted and Vaux proclaimed), and ninety-five miles of drainage pipes were dug to create lakes from the reservoir's water. Made as unobtrusive as possible, four sunken thoroughfares were cut through the park to carry coaches from east to west. The effect was to make Central Park an idealized version of nature. As Olmsted recognized, "The Park throughout is a single work of art."

Viewing Central Park as a secluded retreat in the heart of the city, Olmsted hoped that the park would encourage harmony between the rich and the poor by providing all classes with a meeting place free of the tensions generated by acquisitiveness. In cities, he wrote, our minds are "brought into close dealings with other minds without any friendly flowing toward them, but

Underpass and Traffic on Transverse Road

Olmsted used depressed roadways so that those who came to Central Park for enjoyment would not be upset by urban traffic.

rather a drawing from them." Most of the city's laboring poor, however, equated the value of the park with the employment opportunities, rather than the recreational prospects, that it offered. The city's Democratic administration used the construction jobs created by the park to reward its largely immigrant following. Olmsted complained that "the pretense of work was merely a form of distributing public money to the poor, and my office was for several days regularly surrounded by an organized mob carrying a banner inscribed 'Bread and Blood.' This

mob sent in to me a list of 10,000 names of men alleged to have starving families, demanding that they should immediately be put to work."

Olmsted kept his workers in line by "rigidly discharging any man who failed to work industriously and behave in a quiet and orderly manner." "Quiet and orderly" is a fair description of Olmsted's expectations of the appropriate behavior not only of his laborers but of all city dwellers. Noise so jangled his nerves that he worked late into the night, and he assumed that others shared his longing for quiet. But in fact, the laboring poor usually preferred more boisterous amusements than Central Park could provide. Frequenting the saloon, cheering at the prizefight, and running with the city's fire companies were more typical working-class entertainments than strolling in the park. And those laborers who did prefer the park often lived too far away and worked too long a day for a visit. An observer noted in 1873 that "the greater part of the laboring population" did not have the free time to enjoy the park. Even before it became clear that the park's clientele would be drawn mainly from the middle and upper classes, the bloody draft riots of 1863 (see Chapter 14), in which Irish mobs took over much of the city and lynched blacks, underscored the fact that Central Park had only limited potential to blunt social strife.

Skating in Central Park

Olmsted designed Central Park for all forms of outdoor amusements, including the highly popular ice skating.

413b

opening of the Erie Canal had sparked artistic interest in the Hudson during the 1820s. Interest was kept alive in subsequent decades by popular fears that, as one contemporary expressed it in 1847, "the axe of civilization is busy with our old forests." As the "wild and picturesque haunts of the Red Man" became "the abodes of commerce and the seats of civilization," he concluded, "it behooves our artists to rescue from its grasp the little that is left before it is too late."

The Hudson River painters wanted to do more than preserve a passing wilderness. Their special contribution to American art was to emphasize emotional effect over accuracy. Cole's use of rich coloring, billowing clouds, massive gnarled trees, towering peaks, and deep chasms so heightened the dramatic impact of his paintings that the poet and editor William Cullen Bryant compared them to "acts of religion." Similar motifs marked Church's paintings of the Andes Mountains, which used erupting volcanoes and thunderstorms to evoke dread and a sense of majesty (see "A Place in Time"). Lacking the ruined castles and crumbling temples that dotted European landscapes, the Americans strove to capture the natural grandeur of their own landscape.

The "Diffusion" of Literature and Art

Just as Emerson contended that the democratizing spirit of his age would encourage Americans to discover their cultural identity, many of his contemporaries argued that in a democratic society, the educated had a duty to "diffuse" or spread enlightenment among the common people. Some hoped that inexpensive books and magazines would automatically bring fine literature to the masses. Reflecting on the declining cost of printed material, a clergyman concluded in 1841 that "genius sends its light into cottages." Many others, however, feared that the public would prefer the sensational penny-press fiction and the predictable sentimental novels to more elevating intellectual fare, and they pointed to the need for organized efforts to instruct and uplift American minds.

Advocates of systematic popular instruction turned not only to the public schools but also to lyceum lectures to popularize knowledge. The brainchild during the 1820s of Josiah Holbrook, an eccentric Connecticut inventor and educator, lyceums were essentially local organizations that

sponsored public lectures. The topics and audiences of these lectures were diverse. In the winter of 1851–1852, for example, the lyceum in Belfast, Maine, sponsored lectures on astronomy, biology, physiology, geology, conversation, reading, the cultivation of memory, popular illusions concerning the Middle Ages, Iceland, the equality of the human condition, the true mission of women, and the domestic life of the Turks. Audiences usually included professional men, merchants, farmers, artisans, and a large number of middle-class women.

The lecturers were also a diverse lot. Prior to 1840 most were well-known locals who wished to show off their learning before admiring neighbors. But between 1840 and 1860, the spread of railroads contributed to the creation of a group of nationally known lecturers, a virtual road show of the American Renaissance. Emerson, for example, delivered some sixty lectures in Ohio alone between 1850 and 1867. Known in the 1830s as a radical and eccentric Yankee philosopher, he acquired a reputation throughout the North as a venerable sage by 1860. Another popular lecturer, the poet and world traveler Bayard Taylor, enthralled audiences everywhere with his descriptions of Arabia, Greece, Russia, and Japan. Taylor's frequent appearances in the garb of a cossack or an Arab (complete with scimitar) only heightened the effect. Tickets to lectures sold for as little as twelve cents, but so large were the crowds (up to two thousand) that some literary figures could command the then astounding fee of $125 per lecture. Most lecturers were content with more modest rewards; one stalwart of the lyceum circuit claimed that he did it for "F.A.M.E.—Fifty and My Expenses." Herman Melville, no more popular as a lecturer than as a novelist, pledged, "If they will pay expenses and give a reasonable fee, I am ready to lecture in Labrador or on the Isle of Desolation off Patagonia."

Railroads, the spread of public education, and lower costs for newspapers and books helped bring audiences and lecturers together. Newspapers, for example, announced the comings and goings of lecturers. Bayard Taylor began to receive invitations to lecture only after the public had read his published accounts of his travels. Originating in New England, lyceums expanded quickly across the northern states and made inroads into the South.

The spread of lyceums revealed a broad popular hunger for knowledge and refinement. By 1840 thirty-five hundred towns had lyceums. Yet 1840 was also the year of the log-cabin campaign, which blasted Martin Van Buren for displays of refinement as fully as Andrew Jackson's supporters had earlier gouged John Quincy Adams for being a man of learning. Americans clearly were of two minds on the subject of learning.

This ambivalence toward refined knowledge was nowhere sharper than in the West. Westerners often prided themselves on their rough ways. Western almanacs sprinkled stories of Davy Crockett and other unlettered western heroes among their weather predictions and planting advice, and some western writers fiercely resisted cultural penetration from the East. Yet the West was filled with eastern missionaries who were eager to dispel the notion that westerners were crude backwoods folk and who cultivated learning as well as Protestantism by building scores of colleges, academies, and lyceum halls. In 1800 there was only one college in what is now the Midwest; by 1850 there were nearly seventy, more than in any other region. "They drive schools along with them, as shepherds drive their flocks," clergyman Henry Ward Beecher observed of westerners. "They have herds of churches, academies, lyceums, and their religious and educational institutions go lowing along the western plains, as Jacob's herd lowed along the Syrian hills." Western newspapers sometimes railed at transplanted easterners for "namby-pamby, uptownish" lyceum lectures, but audiences flocked to listen to emissaries of eastern refinement.

Antebellum America contained missionaries for art as well as for knowledge. During the 1840s the American Art Union tried to cultivate popular interest in art by catering to the people's penchant for gambling. For five dollars a year, subscribers to the union received both an engraving of an American painting and a lottery ticket for an original American painting. With agents in towns from Maine to Missouri, the American Art Union had sixteen thousand subscribers by 1849 and half a million visitors to its gallery in New York City. At a time when few American homes had wallpaper, which was imported and expensive, picture collecting became a fad.

The movements to popularize knowledge and art bridged the cultural gap between classes but never closed it. Further, the popularization of culture carried a hidden price tag. In bringing learning and art to the masses, creative thinkers had to soften their ideas. Lyceum lecturers, for example, usually avoided controversy. Even Emerson, whose early pronouncements on religion were extremely controversial, learned to pull his punches on the lyceum circuit. While his epigrammatic style of presenting his ideas made him eminently quotable, his vagueness made it possible to quote him on both sides of most issues. Similarly, while the American Art Union distributed some paintings by Thomas Cole, it also disseminated a lot of mediocre paintings that the public liked. Charged with encouraging mediocrity, the Art Union responded bluntly that, since "no one affects to fear mediocrity in religion or learning, why should we fear it in art?"

Conclusion

Hailed as progressive and democratic, technological advances transformed the lives of millions of Americans between 1840 and 1860. The introduction of the mechanical reaper increased wheat production and substantiated a federal official's contention in 1860 that "the ratio of increase of the principal agricultural products of the United States had more than kept pace with the increase of population." The gradual introduction of steam power reduced the vulnerability of factories to the vagaries of the weather, stretched out the employment season, and increased both productivity and annual income. The widespread introduction of coal-burning stoves not only warmed houses but, in conjunction with the spread of railroads, brought greater variety to the American diet. Technology also left an enduring mark on leisure pursuits. By bringing down the cost of printing, technical advances stimulated the rise of the penny press and the inexpensive novel, vastly increased the size of the reading public, and encouraged efforts to popularize knowledge.

Even dissenters usually directed their fire at technology's effects rather than at technology itself. Sylvester Graham wanted Americans to return to simpler lives, but he understood that vegetarianism depended on railroads to bring fresh produce into cities. The bright possibilities rather than the dark potential of technology impressed most antebellum Americans. Yet technology scarcely obliterated class and ethnic differences, nor did it quiet sectional strife. Even as the penny press and the telegraph spread throughout the nation, Americans were finding that speedier communication could not bridge their differences over slavery.

CHRONOLOGY

1820 Washington Irving, *The Sketch Book.*

1823 Philadelphia completes the first urban water-supply system.
James Fenimore Cooper, *The Pioneers.*

1826 Josiah Holbrook introduces the idea for lyceums.
Cooper, *The Last of the Mohicans.*

1831 Mount Auburn Cemetery opens.

1832 A cholera epidemic strikes the United States.

1833 The *New York Sun*, the first penny newspaper, is established.

1834 Cyrus McCormick patents the mechanical reaper.

1835 James Gordon Bennett establishes the *New York Herald.*

1837 Ralph Waldo Emerson, "The American Scholar."

1841 P. T. Barnum opens the American Museum.

1842 Edgar Allan Poe, "The Murders in the Rue Morgue."

1844 Samuel F. B. Morse patents the telegraph.
The American Art Union is established.
Poe, "The Raven."

1846 W. T. G. Morton successfully uses anesthesia.

1849 Second major cholera epidemic.
Astor Place theater riot leaves twenty dead.

1850 Nathaniel Hawthorne, *The Scarlet Letter.*

1851 Hawthorne, *The House of the Seven Gables.*
Herman Melville, *Moby-Dick.*
Erie Railroad completes its line to the West.

1852 Pennsylvania Railroad completes its line between Philadelphia and Pittsburgh.

1853 Ten small railroads are consolidated into the New York Central Railroad.

1854 Henry David Thoreau, *Walden.*

1855 Walt Whitman, *Leaves of Grass.*

1856 Pennsylvania Railroad completes Chicago link.
Illinois Central completed between Chicago and Cairo, Illinois.

1857 Baltimore–St. Louis rail service completed.

1858 Frederick Law Olmsted is appointed architect in chief for Central Park.

For Further Reading

Carl Bode, *The Anatomy of American Popular Culture, 1840–1861* (1959). A useful general survey.

E. Douglas Branch, *The Sentimental Years, 1836–1860* (1934). A gracefully written, breezy, and informative narrative.

Ann Douglas, *The Feminization of American Culture* (1977). An analysis of the role of the middle-class women and liberal ministers in the cultural sphere during the nineteenth century.

Siegfried Giedion, *Mechanization Takes Command*

(1948). An interpretive overview of the impact of technology on Europe and America.

Barbara Novak, *Nature and Culture: American Landscape Painting, 1825–1875* (1982). An insightful study of the relationships between landscape painting and contemporary religious and philosophical currents.

Gwendolyn Wright, *Building the Dream: A Social History of Housing in America* (1981). An exploration of the ideologies and policies that have shaped American housing since Puritan times.

Additional Bibliography

Technology, Progress, and the Standard of Living

Ruth Schwartz Cowan, *More Work for Mother: The Ironies of Household Technology from the Open Hearth to the Microwave* (1983); Durand Echeverria, *Mirage in the West: A History of the French Image of American Society to 1815* (1957); H. J. Habakkuk, *American and British Technology in the Nineteenth Century* (1962); Dolores Hayden, *The Grand Domestic Revolution: A History of Feminist Designs for American Homes, Neighborhoods, and Cities* (1981); David A. Hounshell, *From the American System to Mass Production, 1800–1932* (1984); John F. Kasson, *Civilizing the Machine: Technology and Republican Values in America, 1776–1900* (1976); Stanley Lebergott, *The Americans: An Economic Record* (1984); Edgar W. Martin, *The Standard of Living in 1860* (1942); Susan Strasser, *Never Done: A History of American Housework* (1983).

Railroads

Eugene Alvarez, *Travel on Southern Antebellum Railroads, 1828–1860* (1974); Alfred D. Chandler, *The Visible Hand: The Managerial Revolution in American Business* (1977); Thomas C. Cochran, *Railroad Leaders, 1845–1890* (1953); Stewart H. Holbrook, *The Story of American Railroads* (1947); Edward C. Kirkland, *Men, Cities and Transportation: A Study in New England History, 1820–1900* (1948); Robert J. Parks, *Democracy's Railroads: Public Enterprise in Michigan* (1972); John F. Stover, *American Railroads* (1961).

Disease and Health

John D. Davies, *Phrenology: Fad and Science* (1955); John S. Haller, Jr., *American Medicine in Transition, 1840–1910* (1981); Stephen Nissenbaum, *Sex, Diet, and Debility in Jacksonian America: Sylvester Graham and Health Reform* (1980); Martin S. Pernick, *A Calculus of Suffering: Pain, Professionalism, and Anesthesia in Nineteenth-Century America* (1985); Charles Rosen-

berg, *The Cholera Years: The United States in 1832, 1849, and 1866* (1962); Paul Starr, *The Social Transformation of American Medicine* (1982).

Popular Culture

Jean H. Baker, *Affairs of Party: The Political Culture of Northern Democrats in the Mid-Nineteenth Century* (1983); Carl Bode, *The American Lyceum: Town Meeting of the Mind* (1968); David Grimsted, *Melodrama Unveiled: American Theater and Culture, 1800–1850* (1968); Karen Halttunen, *Confidence Men and Painted Women: A Study in Middle-Class Culture in America, 1830–1870* (1982); Neil Harris, *Humbug: The Art of P. T. Barnum* (1973); Russell Lynes, *The Tastemakers* (1949); Dan Schiller, *Objectivity and the News: The Public and the Rise of Commercial Journalism* (1981); Michael Schudson, *Discovering the News: A Social History of American Newspapers* (1978); Donald Scott, "The Popular Lecture," *Journal of American History* 66 (March 1980):791–809; Robert C. Toll, *Blacking Up: The Minstrel Show in Nineteenth-Century America* (1974).

Literature

Nina Baym, *Woman's Fiction: A Guide to Novels by and About Women in America, 1820–1870* (1978); Vincent Buranelli, *Edgar Allan Poe* (1977); William Charvat, *The Profession of Authorship in America, 1800–1870* (edited by Matthew J. Bruccoli, 1968); David Levin, *History as Romantic Art: Bancroft, Prescott, Motley, and Parkman* (1963); Kenneth S. Lynn, *Mark Twain and Southwestern Humor* (1972); James Mellow, *Nathaniel Hawthorne in His Time* (1980); Henry Nash Smith, *Democracy and the Novel: Popular Resistance to Classic American Writers* (1978); Benjamin T. Spencer, *The Quest for Nationality: An American Literary Campaign* (1957); Tony Tanner, *The Reign of Wonder: Naiveté and Reality in American Literature* (1965); Larzer Ziff, *Literary Democracy: The Declaration of Cultural Independence in America* (1981).

Visual Arts

Elizabeth Barlow, *Frederick Law Olmsted's New York* (1972); Thomas Bender, *Toward an Urban Vision: Ideas and Institutions in Nineteenth-Century America* (1975); Albert Fein, *Frederick Law Olmsted and the Environmental Tradition* (1972); Neil Harris, *The Artist in American Society: The Formative Years, 1790–1860* (1966); Louis L. Noble, *The Life and Times of Thomas Cole* (1964); Raymond J. O'Brien, *Landscape and Scenery of the Lower Hudson Valley* (1981); Laura Wood Roper, *FLO: A Biography of Frederick Law Olmsted* (1973); Bryan J. Wolf, *Romantic Re-Vision: Culture and Consciousness in Nineteenth-Century American Painting and Literature* (1982).

CHAPTER 12

Immigration, Expansion, and Sectional Conflict, 1840–1848

Considering themselves uniquely civilized and progressive, many antebellum Americans found the idea that God had ordained the spread of their civilization over all of North America irresistible. "Americans regard this continent as their birthright," proclaimed Sam Houston, the first president of the independent republic of Texas, in 1847. Those whom Americans saw as less civilized, notably the Indians and the Mexicans, could rightfully be dispossessed of their land in order to make way for "our mighty march."

This was not idle talk. In less than a thousand days of feverish activity during the administration of President James K. Polk, the United States increased its land area by 50 percent. The nation not only annexed Texas and successfully negotiated with Britain to acquire that part of Oregon south of the forty-ninth parallel but also fought a war with Mexico that led to the acquisition of California and New Mexico. Americans justified these takeovers on some of the same grounds that they had used earlier to dispossess the Indians of their lands. South Carolina's John C. Calhoun boasted that nothing could prevent Americans, "an industrious and civilized race," from "passing into an uninhabited country where the power of the owners is not sufficient to keep them out." Some commentators even contended that expansion was a blessing in disguise for peoples whom Americans deemed less progressive than themselves. Calling in 1848 for the annexation of all of Mexico, a New York journalist argued that the acquisition of that territory would give "an entirely new character and new development to her population."

Beyond expanding its physical boundaries, the United States swelled dramatically in population during the 1840s and 1850s, in part because of a spectacular rise in European immigration. The number of immigrants who entered the United States in these two decades alone exceeded the nation's entire population in 1790. European immigration soared during the mid-1840s, at the same time that the nation plunged into expansion.

Although antebellum immigration and territorial expansion had different sources, the two developments became closely linked. For example, as the penny press whipped up fervor for expansion among the urban immigrant masses, they increasingly championed efforts to push the national boundary to the Pacific. Most immigrants, moreover, supported the Democratic party, which embraced expansion far more enthusiastically than the rival Whig party. The immigrant vote helped to tip the election of 1844 to the Democrats and brought an ardent expansionist, James K. Polk, to the White House.

Beyond these direct connections between immigration and expansion, immigration indirectly stimulated expansion. New immigrants, particularly the Irish, crowded into cities and factory towns in search of work at a time when the post-1837 depression kept the wages of native-born workers low. Ugly outbursts of anti-immigrant feeling reflected the mounting tensions between the immigrant and native-born populations. A number of influential Democrats concluded that the best solution to the intensifying class and ethnic conflict lay in expanding the national boundaries, bringing more land under cultivation, and attracting immigrants to that land, in the process recapturing the ideal of America as a nation of self-sufficient farmers.

Moreover, Democrats advocated expansion as a means of reducing strife between the sections. Expansion into Oregon would gratify the North; expansion into Texas would please the South. Some influential Democrats even argued that Texas would become a kind of highway along which slaves and free blacks alike would wend their way over the horizon and into Mexico. In this way, the argument ran, expansion would gradually drive the sectionally divisive issue of race out of politics.

In reality, expansion brought sectional antagonism to the boiling point, split the Democratic party in the late 1840s, and set the nation on the path to the Civil War.

Newcomers and Natives

Between 1815 and 1860, 5 million European immigrants landed in the United States. Of these, 4.2 million arrived between 1840 and 1860; 3 million of them came in the single decade from 1845 to 1854. This ten-year period witnessed the largest immigration proportionate to the total population (then around 20 million) in American history. The Irish led the way as a source of immigration between 1840 and 1860, with the Germans running a close second. Smaller contingents continued to immigrate to the United States from England, Scotland, and Wales, and a growing number came from Norway, Sweden, Switzerland, and Holland. But by 1860 fully three-fourths of the 4.1 million foreign-born Americans were either Irish or German.

Expectations and Realities

A desire for religious freedom drew some immigrants to the United States. For example, when Mormon missionaries actively recruited converts in the slums of English factory towns, a number of English migrated to America. Many emigrants from Norway were Quakers fleeing persecution by the official Lutheran clergy. But a far larger number of Europeans sailed for America to better their economic condition. Their hope was fed by a continuous stream of travelers' accounts and letters from relatives describing America as a utopia for poor people. German peasants learned that they could purchase a large farm in America for the price of renting a small one in Germany. English men and women were told that enough good peaches and apples were left rotting in the orchards of Ohio to sink the British fleet.

Hoping for the best, emigrants often encountered the worst. Their problems began at ports of embarkation, where hucksters frequently sold them worthless tickets and where ships scheduled to leave in June might not sail until August. Countless emigrants spent precious savings in waterfront slums while awaiting departure. The ocean voyage itself proved terrifying; many emigrants had never set foot on a ship. Most sailed on cargo ships as steerage passengers, where, for six weeks or more, they endured quarters almost as crowded as on slave ships.

For many emigrants, the greatest shock came when they landed. "The folks aboard ship formed great plans for their future, all of which vanished quickly after landing," wrote a young German from Frankfurt in 1840. Immigrants quickly discovered that farming in America was a perilous prospect at best. Aside from lacking the capital to start a farm, most immigrants had to confront the fact that farming in the United States bore little resemblance to farming in Europe. European farmers valued the associations of their communities. Their social and cultural lives revolved around villages that were fringed by the fields that they worked. In contrast, as many immigrants quickly learned, American farmers lived in relative isolation. They might belong to rural neighborhoods in which farmers on widely scattered plots of land met occasionally at revivals or militia musters. But they lacked the compact village life of European farmers, and

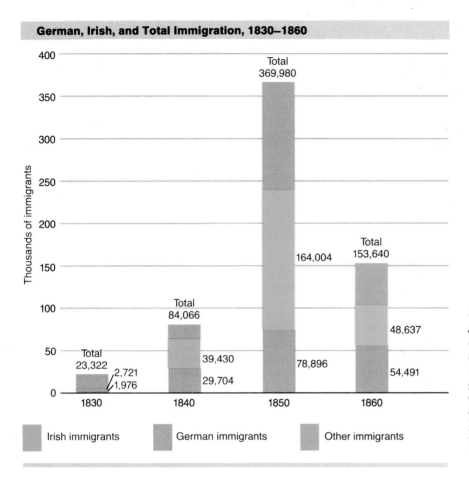

German, Irish, and Total Immigration, 1830–1860

Thousands of immigrants

Total
369,980

Total
164,004

Total
153,640

Total
84,066

Total
23,322

2,721
1,976

2,704

39,430
29,704

78,896

54,491

48,637

1830   1840   1850   1860

Irish immigrants   German immigrants   Other immigrants

Irish and German immigrants led the more than tenfold growth of immigration between 1830 and 1860.

SOURCE: U.S. Bureau of the Census, *Historical Statistics of the United States, Colonial Times to 1970*, Bicentennial Edition (Washington, D.C., 1975).

they possessed an individualistic psychology that led them to speculate in land and to move frequently. One Irish immigrant farmer, writing home to complain of the distance between farms, noted bitterly, "I can hardly yet forgive the persons that advised me to come here."

Despite the shocks and dislocations caused by migration, certain patterns emerged in the distribution of immigrants within the United States. Initially shaped by trade routes, these patterns were then perpetuated by custom. Most of the Irish settlers before 1840 departed from Liverpool on sailing ships that carried English manufactures to eastern Canada and New England in return for timber. On arrival in America, few of these Irish had the capital to become farmers, and hence they crowded into the urban areas of New England, New York, Pennsylvania, and New Jersey, where they could more easily find jobs. In contrast, German emigrants usually left from continental ports on ships

engaged in the cotton trade with New Orleans. However, deterred from settling in the South by the presence of slavery, the oppressive climate, and the lack of economic opportunity, the Germans congregated in the upper Mississippi and Ohio valleys, especially in Illinois, Ohio, Wisconsin, and Missouri. Geographical concentration also characterized most of the smaller groups of immigrants. More than half of the Norwegian immigrants, for example, settled in Wisconsin, where they typically became farmers.

On balance, immigrants were less likely to pursue agriculture in the New World than in Europe. Both the Germans and, to an even greater degree, the Irish tended to concentrate in cities. By 1860 these two groups formed more than 60 percent of the population of St. Louis; nearly half the population of New York City, Chicago, Cincinnati, Milwaukee, Detroit, and San Francisco; and well over a third that of New Orleans, Baltimore, and Boston. These fast-growing cities created an intense demand for the labor of people with strong backs and a willingness to work for low wages. Irish construction gangs built the houses, new streets, and aqueducts that were changing the face of urban America and dug the canals and railroads that threaded together the rapidly developing cities. A popular song recounted the fate of the thousands of Irishmen who died of cholera contracted during the building of a canal in New Orleans:

> *Ten thousand Micks, they swung their picks,*
> *To build the New Canal*
> *But the choleray was stronger 'n they.*
> *An' twice it killed them awl.*

The cities provided immigrants with the sort of community life that seemed lacking in farming settlements. Immigrant societies like the Friendly Sons of St. Patrick took root in cities and combined with associations like the Hibernian Society for the Relief of Emigrants from Ireland to welcome the throngs of newcomers.

The Germans

In the mid-nineteenth century, the Germans were an extremely diverse group. In 1860 Germany was not a nation-state like France or Britain, but a collection of principalities and small kingdoms. German immigrants thought of themselves as Bavarians, Westphalians, or Saxons rather than as Germans. Moreover, the German immigrants included Catholics, Protestants (usually Lutherans), and Jews as well as a sprinkling of freethinkers who denounced the ritual, clergy, and doctrines of all religions. Although few in number, these critics were vehement in their attacks on the established churches. A pious Milwaukee Lutheran complained in 1860 that he could not drink a glass of beer in a saloon "without being angered by anti-Christian remarks or raillery against preachers."

German immigrants came from a wide range of social classes and occupations. The majority had engaged in farming, but a sizable minority were professionals, artisans, and tradespeople. Heinrich Steinweg, an obscure piano maker from Lower Saxony, arrived in New York City in 1851, anglicized his name to Henry Steinway, and in 1853 opened the firm of Steinway and Sons, which quickly

Levi Strauss's Jeans

A far cry from today's designer jeans, Levi Strauss's sturdy work pants quickly caught on with laborers.

achieved international acclaim for the quality of its pianos. Levi Strauss, a Jewish tailor from Bavaria, migrated to the United States in 1847. Upon hearing of the discovery of gold in California in 1848, Strauss gathered rolls of cloth and sailed for San Francisco. When a miner told him of the need for durable work trousers, Strauss fashioned a pair of overalls from canvas. To meet a quickly skyrocketing demand, he opened a factory in San Francisco; his cheap overalls, later known as blue jeans or Levi's, made him famous as well as rich.

For all their differences, the Germans were bound together by their common language, which strongly induced recent immigrants to the United States to congregate in German neighborhoods. Even prosperous Germans bent on climbing the social ladder usually did so within German neighborhoods. Germans formed their own militia and fire companies, sponsored parochial schools in which German was the language of instruction, started German-language newspapers, and organized their own balls and singing groups. The range of voluntary associations among Germans was almost as broad as among native-born Americans.

Other factors beyond their common language brought unity to the German immigrants. Ironically, the Germans' diversity also promoted their solidarity. For example, because they were able to supply their own doctors, lawyers, teachers, journalists, merchants, artisans, and clergy, the Germans had little need to go outside their own neighborhoods. Moreover, economic self-sufficiency conspired with the strong bonds of their language to encourage a clannish psychology among the German immigrants. While admiring the Germans' industriousness, native-born Americans resented their economic success and disdained their clannishness. German refugee Moritz Busch complained that "the great mass of Anglo-Americans" held his countrymen in contempt. The Germans responded by becoming even more clannish. In turn, their psychological separateness made it difficult for the Germans to be as politically influential as the Irish immigrants.

The Irish

Between 1815 and 1860, Irish immigration to the United States passed through several stages. Irish soldiers who fought against the United States in the War of 1812 had returned to their homeland with reports that America was a paradise filled with fertile land and abundant game, a place where "all a man wanted was a gun and sufficient ammunition to be able to live like a prince." Among the Irish who subsequently emigrated between 1815 and the mid-1820s, Protestant small landowners and tradespeople in search of better economic opportunity predominated.

From the mid-1820s to the mid-1840s, the character of Irish immigration to the United States gradually changed. Increasingly, the immigrants were Catholics drawn from the poorer classes, many of them tenant farmers whom Protestant landowners had evicted as "superfluous." Protestant or Catholic, rich or poor, 800,000 to a million Irish immigrants entered the United States between 1815 and 1844. Then, between 1845 and the early 1850s, a blight destroyed every harvest of Ireland's potatoes, virtually the only food of the peasantry, and spawned one of the most gruesome famines in history. The Great Famine inflicted indescribable suffering on the Irish peasantry and killed perhaps a million people. One landlord characterized the surviving tenants on his estate as no more than "famished and ghastly skeletons." To escape the ravages of famine, 1.8 million Irish migrated to the United States in the decade after 1845. Whereas earlier Irish immigrants had been predominantly

poor and Catholic, the famine Irish were overwhelmingly so. Indeed, a quarter to a third of the Irish who arrived during the years 1845–1855 could speak only Irish.

Irish Catholics usually entered the work force at or near the bottom. The popular image of Paddy with his pickax and Bridget the maid contained a good deal of truth. Irish men in the cities dug cellars and often lived in them; outside the cities, they dug canals and railroad beds. Irish women often became domestic servants. Compared to other immigrant women, a high proportion of Irish women entered the work force, if not as maids then often as textile workers. By the 1840s Irish women were displacing native-born women in the textile mills of Lowell and Waltham. Poverty drove Irish women to work at early ages, and the outdoor, all-season work performed by their husbands turned many of them into working widows. Winifred Rooney became a nursemaid at the age of seven and an errand girl at eleven. She then learned needlework, a skill that helped her support her family after her husband's early death. The high proportion of employed Irish women reflected more than their poverty. Compared to the predominantly male German immigrants, more than half of the Irish immigrants were women, most of whom were single adults. In both Ireland and America, the Irish usually married late, and many never married. For Irish women to become self-supporting was only natural.

The lot of most Irish people was harsh. One immigrant described the life of the average Irish laborer in America as "despicable, humiliating, [and] slavish"; there was "no love for him—no protection of life—[he] can be shot down, run through, kicked, cuffed, spat upon—and no redress, but a response of 'served the damn son of an Irish b____ right, damn him.'" Yet some Irish struggled up the social ladder. In Philadelphia, which had a more varied industrial base than Boston, Irish men made their way into iron foundries, where some became foremen and supervisors. Other Irish rose into the middle class by opening grocery and liquor stores.

The varied occupations pursued by Irish immigrants brought them into conflict with two quite different groups. The poorer Irish who dug canals and cellars, hauled cargo on the docks, washed

Irish Emigrants

Eager Irish emigrants crowd to board a County Kerry mail coach that will carry them to a port town and eventually to a new life in America.

laundry for others, and served white families competed directly with equally poor free blacks. This competition stirred up Irish animosity toward blacks and a hatred of abolitionists. At the same time, enough Irish men eventually secured skilled or semiskilled jobs that clashes with native-born white workingmen became unavoidable.

Anti-Catholicism, Nativism, and Labor Protest

The hostility of native-born whites toward the Irish often took the form of anti-Catholicism. Anti-Catholicism had been a strong, if latent, impulse among American Protestants since the early Puritan days. The surge of Irish immigration during the second quarter of the nineteenth century revived anti-Catholic fever. For example, in 1834 rumors circulated among Boston Protestants that a Catholic convent in nearby Charlestown contained dungeons and torture chambers. The mother superior turned away a delegation of officials demanding to inspect the convent. Soon the building lay in ashes, the victim of a Protestant mob. In 1835 Samuel F. B. Morse, the future inventor of the telegraph, warned that the despotic governments of Europe were systematically flooding the United States with Catholic immigrants as part of a conspiracy to destroy republican institutions. "We must first stop this leak in the ship," he wrote, "through which the muddy waters from without threaten to

sink us." That same year, the combative evangelical Protestant Lyman Beecher issued *A Plea for the West*, a tract in which he warned faithful Protestants of an alleged Catholic conspiracy to send immigrants to the West in sufficient numbers to dominate the region. A year later, the publication of Maria Monk's best-selling *Awful Disclosures of the Hotel Dieu Nunnery in Montreal* rekindled anti-Catholic hysteria. Although Maria Monk was actually a prostitute who had never lived in a convent, she professed to be a former nun. In *Awful Disclosures,* she described how the mother superior forced nuns to submit to the lustful advances of priests who entered the convent by a subterranean passage.

At the root of a great deal of the anti-Catholicism of the 1830s and 1840s lay native-born Americans' escalating fears of cheap competition from Irish workers. Increasingly tense rivalry for jobs was a strong impulse, for example, behind the burning of the Charlestown convent in 1834. Compared to fantastic notions of Catholic conspiracies to take over the country, anxieties over cheap Irish competition for jobs were fairly realistic. The Irish were crowding into the United States at a time when the wages of Protestant, native-born artisans and journeymen were already being depressed by the subdivision of tasks that accompanied early industrialization and by the aftermath of the Panic of 1837 (see Chapter 9). In response, young Protestant workingmen in their twenties, threatened by Irish competition, formed the backbone of the many nativist (anti-immigrant) societies that multiplied during the 1840s. Most of these societies eventually developed political offshoots. The Order of the Star-Spangled Banner, for example, by 1854 evolved into the Know-Nothing or American party, which became a major political force in the 1850s.

Nativist outbursts were not labor's only response to the wage cuts that accompanied the depression. Some agitators began to advocate land reform as a solution to workingmen's economic woes. Americans had long cherished the notion that a nation so blessed by abundant land as the United States need never give rise to a permanent class of factory "wage slaves." In 1844 the English-born radical George Henry Evans organized the National Reform Association and rallied supporters with the slogan "Vote Yourself a Farm." Evans advanced neo-Jeffersonian plans for the establishment of "rural republican townships," composed of 160-acre plots for workers. He quickly gained the backing of artisans who preferred such "agrarian" notions to a further advance of the industrial order that was undermining their position. Evans was also supported by a number of middle-class intellectuals, among them Horace Greeley, the editor of the *New York Tribune.*

Land reformers argued that workers' true interests could never be reconciled with an industrial order in which factory operatives sold their labor for wages. By engaging in wage labor, they said, workers abandoned any hope of achieving economic independence. These reformers most appealed to articulate and self-consciously radical workers, particularly artisans and small masters whose independence was being threatened by factories and who feared that American labor was "fast verging on the servile dependence" common in Europe. But land reform offered little to factory operatives and wage-earning journeymen who completely lacked economic independence. In an age when a horse cost the average worker three months' pay and most factory workers dreaded "the horrors of wilderness life," the idea of solving industrial problems by resettling workers on farms seemed a pipe dream.

The land reformers believed that only a fundamental restructuring of economic relations would improve the condition of workers. They therefore opposed strikes for short-term wage increases. In contrast, labor unions, less idealistic in their goals, were more sympathetic to strikes. Unions had flourished in a number of cities during the mid-1830s and then experienced a resurgence in the mid-1840s as the effects of the depression wore off. They appealed to several groups indifferent to land reform. For example, as refugees from an agricultural society, desperately poor Irish immigrants could more realistically hope to improve their status through unions and strikes rather than through farming. The most celebrated strike in the New York City area in the 1840s was organized by Irish dockworkers in Brooklyn. Women workers also formed unions in the 1840s. In 1845 tailoresses and seamstresses organized the Ladies Industrial Association in New York City; their leader, Elizabeth Gray, proclaimed, "Too long have we been bound down by tyrant employers."

Agitation by labor unionists generated considerable commotion in the 1840s and resulted in a few victories for workers. In the landmark case of *Commonwealth* v. *Hunt* (1842), the Massachusetts Supreme Court ruled that labor unions, or "combinations," were not illegal monopolies that restrained trade. But because less than 1 percent of the work force belonged to a labor union during the 1840s, there were sharp limits to the impact of unions.

Although immigrant and native-born workers at times united to support land reform or unions, profound divisions along ethnic and religious lines split the antebellum working class. Even after labor had gained a modest victory in the *Commonwealth* v. *Hunt* decision, employers freely fired union agitators and replaced them with cheap immigrant labor. "Hundreds of honest laborers," a labor paper reported in 1848, "have been dismissed from employment in the manufactories of New England because they have been suspected of knowing their rights and daring to assert them." This kind of repression effectively blunted agitation for the ten-hour day (at a time when workers typically toiled for twelve to fourteen hours). The drive for a shorter workday had gained support in the 1840s from a number of organizations, among them the Lowell Female Reform Association.

During the 1830s and 1840s, tensions between

native-born and immigrant workers inevitably became intertwined with the political divisions of the second party system.

Labor Protest and Immigrant Politics

Very few immigrants had ever cast a vote in an election prior to their arrival in America, and only a small fraction were refugees from political persecution. Political upheavals had erupted in Austria and several of the German states in the turbulent year of 1848 (the so-called Revolutions of 1848), but among the million German immigrants to the United States, only about ten thousand were political refugees, or "Forty-Eighters."

Once they had settled in the United States, however, many immigrants became politically active. They quickly found that urban political organizations, some of them dominated by earlier immigrants, would help them to find lodging and employment—in return for votes. Both the Irish and the Germans identified overwhelmingly with the Democratic party. An obituary of 1837 that described a New Yorker as a "warm-hearted Irishman and an unflinching Democrat" could have been written of millions of other Irish. By 1820 the Irish had taken over Tammany Hall, the New York City Democratic organization. Similarly, the Germans became stalwart supporters of the Democrats in cities like Milwaukee and St. Louis.

The immigrants' worries about staying financially afloat partly explain their widespread Democratic support. Andrew Jackson had given the Democratic party an antiprivilege and anti-aristocratic coloration, and most immigrants, especially the Irish, saw the Democrats as more sympathetic than the Whigs to the common people. Moreover, many Irish immigrants turned to the Democrats because antislavery was more closely identified in the North with the Whig party than with the Democratic party. The Irish loathed abolitionism out of fear that emancipated slaves would migrate north and compete with them for unskilled jobs.

Beyond these economic considerations, most Irish and German immigrants saw the Whigs as more of a threat than the Democrats to their moral and religious values. The identification of the Whigs with temperance reform, for example, pushed the Irish and Germans toward the Democrats, for both immigrant groups had hearty traditions of drinking. The fact that some prominent temperance reformers, including Lyman Beecher, were also leading anti-Catholics further strengthened the allegiance of Catholic immigrants to the anti-temperance Democrats. Public-school reform, a major Whig goal, also drew fire from immigrants. The Irish looked upon school reform as a menace to the Catholicism of their children; the Germans saw it as a threat to the integrity of their language and culture.

These economic, moral, and religious views composed a volatile mixture in the immigrants' minds and turned them against the Whig party. The emotional cleavage between the two parties at times provoked violence. For example, in Philadelphia, contention between Irish Democrats and native-born Whigs over temperance became intertwined in the early 1840s with a conflict over the use of the Protestant King James rather than the Catholic Douay version of the Bible for the scriptural readings that began each school day in the public schools. Fiery Protestant politicians hostile to Catholics and Democrats mounted soapboxes to denounce "popery" and the alleged efforts of Catholics to "kick " the Bible out of the schools. Soon Protestant mobs descended on Catholic neighborhoods, and before the militia quelled these "Bible Riots," thirty buildings lay in charred ruins and at least sixteen people had been killed.

The Bible Riots spotlighted not only the interplay of nativism, religion, and politics but also the way in which local issues shaped the immigrants' political allegiances. Liquor regulations and school laws, for example, were city or state concerns rather than federal responsibilities. Yet the Democratic party that the immigrants so widely supported in their battles over local matters served them as a kind of school of broad, national principles. It taught them to venerate George Washington, to revere Thomas Jefferson and Andrew Jackson, and to view "monied capitalists" as parasites who would tremble when the people spoke. It introduced immigrants to Democratic newspapers, Democratic picnics, and Democratic parades. The Democrats, by identifying their party with all that they thought best about the United States, helped give immigrants a sense of themselves as Americans. By the same token, the Democratic party introduced immigrants to national issues. It redirected politi-

The Bible Riots *Religious differences and job competition between native-born Americans and immigrants triggered Philadelphia's bloody Bible Riots in June 1844.*

cal loyalties that often had been forged on local issues into the arena of national politics. During the 1830s the party had persuaded immigrants that national measures like the Bank of the United States and the tariff, seemingly remote from their daily lives, were vitally important to them. Now during the 1840s, the Democrats would try to convince immigrants that national expansion advanced their interests.

The West and Beyond

As late as 1840, Americans who referred to the West still meant the area between the Appalachian Mountains and the Mississippi River or just beyond, a region that included much of the present-day Midwest. Beyond the states bordering the Mississippi lay an inhospitable region unlike any that the earlier settlers had ever known. Those who ventured west of Missouri encountered the Great Plains, a semiarid plateau with few trees. Winds blowing east from the Rocky Mountains sucked the moisture from the soil. Bands of nomadic Indians— including the Pawnees, Kiowas, and Sioux—roamed

this territory and gained sustenance mainly from the buffalo. They ate its meat, wore its fur, and covered their dwellings with its hide. Aside from some well-watered sections of northern Missouri and eastern Kansas and Nebraska, the Great Plains presented would-be farmers with massive obstacles.

The formidable barrier of the Great Plains did not stop settlement of the West in the long run. Temporarily, however, it shifted public interest toward the verdant region lying beyond the Rockies, the Far West.

The Far West

With the Transcontinental (or Adams-Onís) Treaty of 1819, the United States had given up to Spain its claims to Texas west of the Sabine River. This had left Spain in undisputed possession not only of Texas but also of California and the vast territory of New Mexico. Combined, California and New Mexico included all of present-day California and New Mexico as well as modern Nevada, Utah, and Arizona, and parts of Wyoming and Colorado. Two years later, a series of revolts against Spanish rule had culminated in the independence of Mexico and in Mexico's takeover of all North

American territory previously claimed by Spain. The Transcontinental Treaty also had provided for Spain's cessation to the United States of its claims to the country of Oregon north of the forty-second parallel (the northern boundary of California). Then in 1824 and 1825, Russia abandoned its claims to Oregon south of 54°40′ (the southern boundary of Alaska). In 1827 the United States and Britain, each of which had claims to Oregon based on discovery and exploration, revived an agreement (originally signed in 1818) for joint occupation of the territory between 42° and 54°40′, a colossal area that contemporaries could describe no more precisely than the "North West Coast of America, Westward of the Stony [Rocky] Mountains" and that included all of modern Oregon, Washington, and Idaho as well as parts of present-day Wyoming, Montana, and Canada.

Collectively, Texas, New Mexico, California, and Oregon composed an area larger than Britain, France, and Germany combined. Such a vast region should have tempted any nation, but during the 1820s Mexico, Britain, and the United States viewed the Far West as a remote and shadowy frontier. By 1820 the American line of settlement had only reached Missouri, well over 2,000 miles (counting detours for mountains) from the West Coast. El Paso on the Rio Grande and Taos in New Mexico lay, respectively, 1,200 and 1,500 miles north of Mexico City. Britain, of course, was many thousands of miles from Oregon.

Far Western Trade

The earliest American and British outposts on the West Coast were trading centers established by merchants who had reached California and Oregon by sailing around South America and up the Pacific. Between the late 1790s and the 1820s, for example, Boston merchants had built a thriving exchange of coffee, tea, spices, cutlery, clothes, and hardware—indeed, anything that could be bought or manufactured in the eastern United States—for furs (especially those of sea otters), cattle, hides, and tallow (rendered from cattle fat and used for making soap and candles). Between 1826 and 1828 alone, Boston traders took more than 6 million cattle hides out of California; in the otherwise undeveloped California economy, these hides, called "California banknotes," served as the main medium

of exchange. During the 1820s the British Hudson's Bay Company developed a similar trade in Oregon and northern California.

The California trade occasioned little friction with Mexico. Producing virtually no manufactured goods, Hispanic people born in California (called *californios*) were as eager to buy as the traders were to sell—so eager that they sometimes rowed out to the vessels laden with goods, thus sparing the traders the trip ashore. Those traders who did settle in California, like the American Thomas O. Larkin and the Swiss-born John Sutter, quickly learned to speak Spanish and became assimilated into Mexican culture.

Farther south, trading links developed during the 1820s between St. Louis and Santa Fe along the famed Santa Fe Trail. The Panic of 1819 left the American Midwest short of cash and its merchants burdened by unsold goods. Pulling themselves up from adversity, however, plucky midwesterners loaded wagon trains with tools, utensils, clothing, windowpanes, and household sundries each spring and rumbled westward to Santa Fe, where they traded their merchandise for mules and New Mexican silver. To a far greater extent than had Spain, Mexico welcomed this trade. Indeed, by the 1830s more than half the goods entering New Mexico by the Santa Fe Trail trickled into the mineral-rich interior provinces of Mexico such as Chihuahua and Sonora, with the result that the Mexican silver peso, which midwestern traders brought back with them, quickly became the principal medium of exchange in Missouri.

Some Americans ventured north from Santa Fe to trap beaver in what is today western Colorado and eastern Utah. The profitability of the beaver trade also encouraged merchants and trappers like the "mountain man" Jedidiah Smith (see Chapter 8) to venture directly from St. Louis into the Rockies in competition with both the Santa Fe traders and agents of the Hudson's Bay Company. On the Green River in Mexican territory, the St. Louis–based trader William Ashley in 1825 inaugurated an annual rendezvous or encampment where traders exchanged beaver pelts for supplies, thereby saving themselves the trip to St. Louis. With the aid of Ashley's encampments, the St. Louis traders gradually wrested the beaver trade from their Santa Fe competitors.

For the most part, American traders and trap-

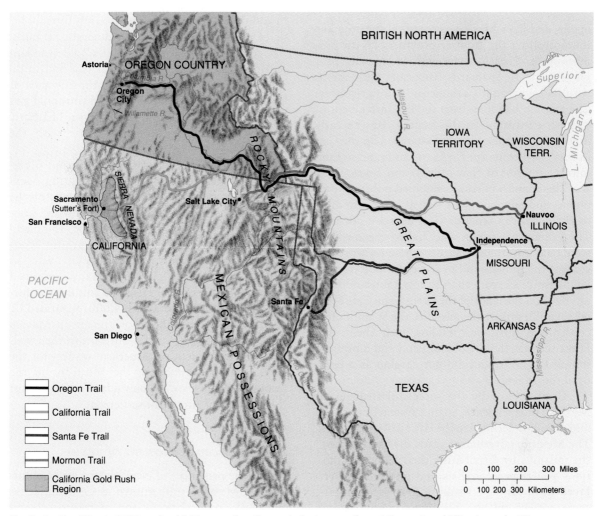

Trails to the West, 1840   *By 1840 several trails carried pioneers from Missouri and Illinois to the West.*

pers operating on the northern Mexican frontier in the 1820s and 1830s posed more of a threat to the beaver than to Mexico's provinces. (If silk hats had not become fashionable in Europe in the mid-1830s, the beaver might have been hunted to extinction.) Not only did the Mexican people of California and New Mexico depend on the American trade for manufactured goods, but Mexican officials in both provinces relied on customs duties to support their governments. In New Mexico the government often had to await the arrival of the annual caravan of traders from St. Louis before it could pay its officials and soldiers.

Although the relations between Mexicans and Americans were mutually beneficial during the 1820s, the potential for conflict was never absent. Spanish-speaking, Roman Catholic, and accustomed to a more hierarchical society, the Mexicans formed a striking contrast to the largely Protestant, individualistic Americans. And while few American traders themselves became permanent residents of Mexico, many returned with glowing reports of the climate and fertility of Mexico's northern provinces. By the 1820s American settlers were already moving into eastern Texas. At the same time, the ties that bound the central government of Mexico to its northern frontier provinces were starting to fray.

Mexican Government in the Far West

Spain, and later Mexico, recognized that the key to controlling the frontier provinces lay in promoting their settlement by civilized Hispanic people—that is, by Spaniards, Mexicans, and Indians who had embraced Catholicism and agriculture. The mission had long been the key instrument of Spanish expansion on the frontier. By the early nineteenth century, missions stretched up the California coast from San Diego to San Francisco and into the interior of New Mexico and Texas.

The Spanish mission combined political, economic, and religious goals—an arrangement alien to the American separation of church and state. The Franciscan priests who staffed the missions were paid government agents who endeavored to convert the Indians and to settle them on mission lands. By 1823 more than twenty thousand Indians lived on the lands of the twenty-one California missions. To protect the missions, the Spanish often constructed forts, or presidios, near them. San Francisco was the site of a mission and a presidio founded in 1776 and did not develop as a town until the 1830s.

Dealt a blow by the successful struggle for Mexican independence, Spain's system of missions and presidios declined in the late 1820s and 1830s. The Mexican government gradually "secularized" the missions by distributing their lands to ambitious government officials and private ranchers. Freed from the supervision of Franciscan priests, some former mission-dwelling Indians became forced laborers in white communities, but many returned to their nomadic ways and joined with Indians who had always resisted the missions. During the 1820s and 1830s, these "barbaric Indians"—notably, the Comanches, Apaches, Navahos, and Utes—terrorized the Mexican frontier by stealing livestock and carrying off Hispanic women and children. Apaches and Comanches attacked New Mexico and Texas, and the Comanches swept into northern Mexico, striking within 150 miles of Mexico City. The legislature of the Mexican state of Chihuahua complained in 1846 that "we travel the roads at their [the Indians'] whim; we cultivate the land where they wish and in the amount that they wish."

Mexican policy was partly responsible for this upsurge in terrorism. With the secularization of the missions, Hispanic ranchers had turned some native Americans into virtual slaves on ranches now bloated by the addition of former mission lands. In addition, Mexican frontier dwellers thought little of raiding Indian tribes for domestic servants. "To get Indian girls to work for you," a descendant of Hispanic settlers recalled, "all you had to do was organize a company against the Navahos or Utes or Apaches and kill all the men you could and bring captive the children." In short, the "barbaric Indians" had many scores to settle with the Mexicans.

Because the overofficered and corrupt Mexican army had little taste for frontier fighting, Mexican settlers on the frontier could not rely on the military for protection against the Indians. Consequently, few Mexicans ventured into the undeveloped, lawless territories. Few areas in the Western Hemisphere potentially so rich were so underpopulated. In 1836 New Mexico contained about 30,000 people of Hispanic culture; California, about 3,200; and Texas, 4,000. Separated by vast distances from their government in Mexico City, which often seemed indifferent to their welfare, and dependent on American traders for the necessities of civilization, the Mexicans of the frontier provinces formed only a frail barrier against the advance of American settlement.

The American Settlement of Texas

Unlike the provinces of New Mexico and California, the Mexican state known as Coahuila-Texas lacked the natural protection of mountains and deserts. During the post-1815 cotton boom, small bands of southern farmers began to push across the Sabine River into eastern Texas in search of more land for cotton cultivation. In addition, after the Panic of 1819, many debt-ridden Americans in the Midwest and South found flight into Texas a convenient escape from creditors. By 1823 some three thousand Americans lived in eastern Texas. In 1824 the Mexican government began actively to encourage American colonization of Texas as a way to bring in manufactured goods (of which the Mexicans produced virtually none) and to gain protection against the Indians. Expecting that American settlers would live peacefully under Mexican rule, the Mexican government bestowed generous land grants on agents (known as *empresarios*) who contracted to bring Americans into Texas. The most successful of these *empresarios*, Stephen F. Austin, had attracted some three hundred

Stephen F. Austin

By founding Anglo-American settlements in Texas in the 1820s, Austin and other empresarios *helped the Mexican government fill the sparsely populated region.*

American families to Texas by 1825. Other *empresarios* followed suit, and by 1830 some seven thousand Americans lived in Texas, more than double the Mexican population dwelling there.

Although Mexico gained some advantages from the American immigration into Texas, the Americans proved a mixed blessing to the Mexican people. Some unscrupulous American traders, like the notorious Harlan Coffee, provoked the Indians to raid Mexican settlements and seize livestock to trade for American liquor and guns. Other American immigrants were roustabouts who moved to Texas to escape debts and sheriffs. But even law-abiding Americans posed a problem. Unlike the relatively assimilated American traders in California, the settlers of Texas were farming families who dwelled in eastern Texas, apart from the Mexicans who had congregated in the western part of the state. Although naturalized as Mexican citizens, the American settlers distrusted the Mexicans and complained constantly about the creaking, erratic Mexican judicial system. Above all, Mexico had not bargained for the size and speed of the American immigration. The first news of the Americans, Mexican general Manuel Mier y Terán wrote in 1828, "comes from discovering them on land already under cultivation." Four years later, Mier y Terán committed suicide in despair over Mexico's inability to stem and control the American advance.

As early as 1826, an American *empresario*, Haden Edwards, led a revolt against Mexican rule, but Mexican forces, aided by Stephen F. Austin, quickly crushed the uprising. Although, like Austin, most Americans were still willing to live in Texas as naturalized Mexican citizens, during the early 1830s, the allegiance of the Americans to the Mexican government was severely eroded. In 1830 Mexico closed Texas to further immigration from the United States and, having emancipated its own slaves in 1829, forbade the introduction of more slaves to Texas. The latter measure struck directly at the Americans, many of whom were slaveholders. However, Mexico lacked the military might to enforce its decrees. Between 1830 and 1834, the number of Americans in Texas doubled. In 1834 Austin secured repeal of the 1830 prohibition on American immigration, and by 1835 an estimated one thousand Americans a month were crossing into Texas. In 1836 Texas contained some 30,000 white Americans, 5,000 black slaves, and 4,000 Mexicans.

As American immigration swelled, Mexican politics grew increasingly unstable. "The political character of this country," Austin wrote, "seems to partake of its geological features—all is volcanic." From its inception, the government of the Mexican republic had rested on a precarious balance between liberals (or federalists), who favored popular liberty and decentralized government, and conservative centralists, who sought to concentrate power in the hands of military and church officials in Mexico City. In 1834 Mexican president Antonio López de Santa Anna ousted leading liberals from his government and began to restrict the powers of the regimes in Coahuila-Texas and other Mexican states. His actions ignited a series of rebellions in the Mexican states, the most important of which became known as the Texas Revolution.

The Texas Revolution

Santa Anna's brutality in crushing most of the rebellions alarmed Austin and others. Austin initially had taken a moderate position. He hoped to cooperate with Mexican liberals to restore the Mexican Constitution of 1824 and to secure greater autonomy for Texas within Mexico. At the outset, he did not favor Texas's independence from Mexico. When Santa Anna invaded Texas in the fall of 1835, however, Austin cast his lot with the more radical Americans who wanted outright independence.

At first, Santa Anna's army met with success. In late February 1836, his force of 4,000 men laid seige to San Antonio, whose 200 Texan defenders retreated into an abandoned mission, the Alamo. After repelling repeated attacks and inflicting more than 1,500 casualties on Santa Anna's army, the remaining 187 Texans, including such famed frontiersmen as Davy Crockett and Jim Bowie, were wiped out to the last man on March 6. A few weeks later, Mexican troops massacred some 350 Texas prisoners at Goliad.

Even before these events, Texas delegates had met in a windswept shed in the village of Washington, Texas, and declared Texas independent of Mexico. The rebels by then had settled on a military leader, Sam Houston, for their president. A

Sam Houston

This photo, taken in his sixties, shows Houston as a prosperous and successful statesman. But in his youth Houston had a reputation for wildness. In 1829 he resigned Tennessee's governorship and lived dissolutely for three years among the Cherokees.

giant man who wore leopard-skin vests, Houston retreated east to pick up recruits (mostly Americans who crossed the border to fight Santa Anna). Houston turned and surprised Santa Anna on a prairie near the San Jacinto River in April. Shouting "Remember the Alamo," Houston's army of eight hundred tore through the Mexican lines, killing nearly half of Santa Anna's men in fifteen minutes and taking Santa Anna himself prisoner. Houston then forced Santa Anna to sign a treaty (which the Mexican government never ratified) recognizing the independence of Texas.

American Settlements in California, New Mexico, and Oregon

California and New Mexico, both less accessible than Texas, exerted no more than a mild attraction for American settlers during the 1820s and 1830s. Only a few hundred Americans resided in New Mexico in 1840; that same year, California con-

Major Battles in the Texas Revolution, 1835–1836

Sam Houston's victory at San Jacinto was the decisive action of the war and avenged the massacres at the Alamo and Goliad.

tained perhaps four hundred Americans. A contemporary observed that the Americans living in California and New Mexico during these years "are scattered throughout the whole Mexican population, and most of them have Spanish wives. . . . They live in every respect like the Spanish."

Yet the beginnings of change were already evident. California's Hispanic population generally welcomed American immigration as a way to encourage economic development. In addition, some Americans who settled in California before 1840 sent back highly favorable reports of the region to induce immigration. California was said to be a land of "perpetual spring," inhabited only by lazy Mexicans. One story, tongue-in-cheek, told of a 250-year-old man who had to leave the region when he finally wanted to die. Such reports produced their intended effect. During the 1840s an ever-widening stream of Americans migrated to the interior Sacramento Valley, where they lived geographically and culturally apart from the Mexicans. For these land-hungry settlers, no sacrifice seemed too great if it led to California. In 1848 John and Cornelia Sharp abandoned their hardscrabble farm in Ohio and built a flatboat that carried them and their seven children on the Ohio and Missouri rivers to Independence, Missouri. Arriving nearly destitute, they worked for almost four years to earn enough to continue their journey to California.

Oregon, with its abundant farmland, beckoned settlers from the Mississippi Valley. During the 1830s missionaries like the Methodist Jason Lee moved into Oregon's Willamette Valley, and by 1840 the area contained some five hundred Americans. Enthusiastic reports sent back by Lee piqued interest in Oregon. An orator in Missouri described Oregon as a "pioneer's paradise" where "the pigs are running around under the great acorn trees, round and fat and already cooked, with knives and forks sticking in them so that you can cut off a slice whenever you are hungry." Indeed, to some Oregon seemed even more attractive than California. Oregon was already jointly occupied by Britain and the United States, and its prospects for eventual U.S. annexation appeared better than California's.

The Overland Trail

Whatever their destination, Americans who journeyed west in the 1840s faced extraordinary obstacles. Little was known about the terrain between Missouri and the West Coast. In fact, little was known about the coast itself; as late as 1846, no detailed map of California existed. The few available guidebooks contained as much myth as truth. Lansford Hastings's *Emigrant's Guide to Oregon and California* (1845) deliberately tried to steer settlers away from Oregon and toward California.

Westport Landing, *by W. H. Jackson*

Now part of Kansas City, Westport Landing was typical of the Missouri River towns from which wagon trains began the long journey to the West.

LAND HO!

"WESTWARD THE STAR OF EMPIRE TAKES ITS WAY."

WANTED,

Ten good, substantial, intelligent, and independent-minded FARMERS, who either own farms in this region worth $3000 each, or who can command $1500 each on or before the first day of June next, and $1500 more in one year from that date, to form a Company and go to Illinois for the purpose of settling *together* on 3500 acres of land, (being 350 acres a-piece) each having 250 acres of first rate prairie, and 100 acres of excellent timber contiguous. Also, to become interested in 640 acres more adjoining, commanding a water power as great as that of Rochester, and a beautiful Town site, late the residence of a celebrated Indian Chief, who owned the whole tract; hence these lands have remained unsettled, whilst the surrounding country is settled with industrious and prosperous farmers. The title of the purchaser from the Indian has lately been confirmed by an act of Congress and sanctioned by the President, and is therefore perfect. These lands are situated on the banks of a beautiful river, near the Illinois & Michigan Canal,—now nearly completed,—and in the bosom of a country, which, for scenic beauty and fertility, is not surpassed on this side of the Rocky Mountains.

The subscriber has the above tract of land at his disposal, and no better lands or pleasanter location can be found in the whole range of the vast regions of the West. Come on, then, gentlemen, to the number of seven more (*three* are already waiting for you) and make out the number, and then depute some two, three, or four, of the wisest ones amongst you, to go and examine for you all. There is no romance about this, of which you can be convinced by calling on the subscriber, at B. Newton's Tavern, Palmyra, where maps of the lands may be seen, and where he will explain to you more fully the objects in view, and the advantages of obtaining a portion of these lands, water power and village property. Those who wish to make inquiry will please call soon, as the subscriber is about to depart for the west in a few weeks.

N. B.—The undersigned has two or three farms for sale in this county, which will be sold cheap for prompt pay. Also a house and lot in this village.

Palmyra, Oct. 29, 1841.

A. H. HOWLAND.

Land Ho!

Dwelling on the quality of farmland and the availability of timber and water power, advertisements lured pioneers westward with promises of prosperity and comfort rather than romance and adventure.

Unfortunately, Hastings devised shortcuts to California that drastically understated the distance across such formidable barriers as the Great Salt Desert. One victim of Hastings's misguidance, the Donner party, which set out from Illinois in 1846, lost so much time following his advice that its members became snowbound in the High Sierra and reached California only after the survivors had turned to cannibalism.

Emigrants responded to the extraordinary challenges of the overland trail by cooperating closely with each other. Most set out in huge wagon trains rather than as individuals; so large did the trains become that the voyagers found it necessary to draw up codes of law and elect officers for the trip. But even the most dedicated officers were hard pressed to coordinate the schedules of hundreds of wagons, and in practice the caravans often splintered into smaller parties composed of friends and relatives.

The family represented the most important single form of cooperation on the overland trail. Even before their departure from midwestern farms, women often spent months preserving food and making clothes for the trip. Once under way, women packed and unpacked the wagon each day, milked the cows brought along to stock the new farm in the West, cooked meals on open fires (even if it meant standing for hours with an umbrella to protect the flame from rain), and assisted with the childbirths that occurred on the trail at about the same frequency as in the nation as a whole. Men yoked and unyoked the oxen, drove the wagons and stock, and went off with other men on hunting parties. Men occasionally tried their hand at cooking, but as one noted briskly, "It is more slavish work than I had anticipated." On balance, the division of men's and women's work on the trail reflected firmly entrenched traditions.

One additional task of men was to stand guard against Indian raids, but most emigrants found the Indians whom they encountered cooperative. Indeed, emigrants came to depend on the native Americans as guides for crossing dangerous rivers like the Columbia and as couriers to carry messages back to eastern settlements. Soon the emigrants complained less about the violence of the Indians than about their shrewdness at driving bargains. "The Indian is a financier of no mean ability," a female emigrant wrote, "and invariably comes out A–1 in a bargain." The Indians profited not only by selling fish and vegetables to emigrants but also by exacting tribute for the right to pass through their territory and by collecting tolls for passage over crude bridges. Emigrants who refused to pay usually found that their livestock disappeared. The Indians' pilfering from the wagon trains was far more common than violent assaults on emigrants. The popular image of the isolated wagons surrounded by war-whooping Indians is misleading, because the wagons rarely traveled alone and the native Americans rarely attacked.

Yet tales of Indian massacres increasingly blazed in the eastern press during the 1840s and 1850s. In 1855 several newspapers reported the annihilation of 300 travelers in a wagon train by 2,000 bloodthirsty Sioux and Cheyenne Indians and then described how the sole survivor walked all the way to Oregon. This story and others like it were as fictional as they were juicy. But fraudulent reports of Indian attacks predisposed emigrants to distrust all native Americans. Nervous, trigger-happy emigrants at times provoked Indian assaults. Yet the number of emigrants killed by native Americans on the overland trail remained modest. Between 1840 and 1860, fewer than 400 emigrants lost their lives in Indian attacks, whereas slightly more than 400 Indians were killed by emigrants.

Between 1840 and 1848, an estimated 11,500 emigrants followed an overland trail to Oregon, while some 2,700 reached California. These numbers were modest and concentrated in the years from 1844 to 1848. Yet even small numbers could make a huge difference in the Far West, for the British could not effectively settle Oregon at all, and the Mexican population in California was small and scattered. By 1845 California clung to Mexico by the thinnest of threads. The territory's Hispanic population, the *californios*, felt little allegiance to Mexico, which they contemptuously referred to as the "other shore." Nor did they feel any allegiance to the United States. Some *californios* wanted independence from Mexico; others looked to the day when California might become a protectorate of Britain or perhaps even France. But these *californios*, with their shaky allegiances, now faced a growing number of American settlers whose political sympathies were not at all divided.

The Politics of Expansion

The major issue that arose as a by-product of westward expansion was whether the United States should annex the independent Texas republic. In the mid-1840s the Texas-annexation issue generated the kind of political passions that banking questions had ignited in the 1830s, and became

entangled with equally unsettling issues relating to California, New Mexico, and Oregon. Between 1846 and 1848, a war with Mexico and a dramatic confrontation with Britain settled all these questions on terms favorable to the United States.

Yet at the start of the 1840s, western issues occupied no more than a tenuous position on the national political agenda. From 1840 to 1842, questions relating to economic recovery—notably, banking, the tariff, and internal improvements—dominated the attention of political leaders. Only after politicians failed to address the economic issues coherently did opportunistic leaders thrust issues relating to expansion to the top of the political agenda.

The Whig Ascendancy

The election of 1840 brought the Whig candidate William Henry Harrison to the presidency and installed Whig majorities in both houses of Congress. The Whigs had raced to power with a program, based on Henry Clay's American System, to stimulate economic recovery, and they had excellent prospects of success. They quickly repealed Van Buren's darling, the Independent Treasury. They then planned to substitute some kind of national "fiscal agent," which, like the defunct Bank of the United States, would be a private corporation chartered by Congress and charged with regulating the currency. The Whigs also favored a tariff, but with a twist. In the past, Whigs had supported a "protective" tariff, one set so high as to discourage the importation of goods that would compete with the products of American industries. Now the Whigs proposed a modification in the form of a "revenue" tariff, one high enough to provide "incidental" protection for American industries but low enough to allow most foreign products to enter the United States. The duties collected on these imports would accrue to the federal government as revenue. The Whigs then planned to distribute this revenue to the states for internal improvements, a measure as popular among southern and western Whigs as the tariff was among northeastern Whigs.

The Whig agenda might have breezed into law had it not been for the untimely death of Harrison after only one month in office. With Harrison's demise, Vice President John Tyler, an upper-crust Virginian who had been put on the ticket in 1840 to strengthen the Whigs' appeal in the South, assumed the presidency. From virtually every angle, the new president proved a disaster for the Whigs.

Tyler, a former Democrat who had become a Whig mainly out of dismay at Andrew Jackson's tendency to veto acts of Congress, favored the Democratic policy of states' rights. Ironically, as president, Tyler himself used the veto to shred his new party's program. In August 1841 a Whig bill to create a new national bank became the first casualty of Tyler's veto. Stunned, the Whig majority in Congress quickly passed a modified banking bill, only to see Tyler veto it as well.

Congressional Whigs fared little better on the issues of the tariff and the distribution of tariff revenues to the states. The Compromise Tariff of 1833 had provided for a gradual scaling down of tariff duties, until none was to exceed 20 percent by 1842. Amid the depression of the early 1840s, however, the provision for a 20 percent maximum tariff appeared too low to generate revenue. Without revenue, the Whigs would have no money to distribute among the states for internal improvements and no program with national appeal. In response, the Whig congressional majority passed two bills in the summer of 1842 that simultaneously postponed the final reduction of tariffs to 20 percent and ordered distribution to the states to proceed. Tyler promptly vetoed both bills. Tyler's mounting vetoes infuriated the Whig leadership. "Again has the imbecile, into whose hands accident has placed the power, vetoed a bill passed by a majority of those legally authorized to pass it," screamed the *Daily Richmond Whig*. Some Whigs talked of impeaching Tyler. Finally, in August, Tyler, needing revenue to run the government, signed a new bill that maintained some tariffs above 20 percent but abandoned distribution to the states.

Tyler's erratic course confounded and disrupted his party. By maintaining some tariffs above 20 percent, the tariff of 1842 satisfied northern manufacturers, but by abandoning distribution, it infuriated many southerners and westerners. Northern Whigs succeeded in passing the bill with the aid of many northern Democrats, particularly pro-tariff Pennsylvanians, while large numbers of Whigs in the Upper South and West opposed the tariff of 1842.

In the congressional elections of 1842, the Whigs paid a heavy price for failing to enact their program. While retaining a slim majority in the Senate, they lost control of the House to the Democrats. Now the nation witnessed one party in control of the Senate, its rival in control of the House, and a president who appeared to belong to neither party.

Tyler and the Annexation of Texas

Although a political maverick disowned by his party, Tyler ardently desired a second term as president. Domestic issues offered him little hope of building a popular following, but foreign policy was another matter. In 1842 Tyler's secretary of state, Daniel Webster, concluded a treaty with Great Britain, represented by Lord Ashburton, that settled a long-festering dispute over the boundary between Maine and the Canadian province of New Brunswick. Awarding more than half the disputed territory to the United States, the Webster-Ashburton Treaty was popular in the North. Tyler reasoned that if he could now arrange for the annexation of Texas, he would build a national following.

The issue of slavery, however, had long clouded every discussion of Texas. By the late 1830s, antislavery northerners, among them John Quincy Adams, had concluded that both the Texas Revolution and subsequent proposals to annex Texas formed the core of an elaborate southern conspiracy to extend slavery into the Southwest. Several pieces of evidence seemed to point to this conclusion. Settled by slaveholders, Texas would certainly become a slave state. In fact, some southerners had talked openly of creating as many as four or five slave states out of the vast region encompassed by Texas. Further, as Adams pointed out in 1838, the slaveholding president Andrew Jackson had raised no objection when southerners had violated American neutrality by crossing into Texas in time to fight in the Battle of San Jacinto. All of this occurred, Adams added, at a time when southerners had started to defend slavery as a positive good rather than as a necessary evil.

Nevertheless, Tyler was not deterred from throwing the full weight of his administration behind the annexation of Texas. In the summer of 1843, the president launched a propaganda campaign for annexation. He justified his crusade by reporting that he had learned of certain British designs on Texas, which Americans, he argued, would be prudent to forestall. Tyler's campaign was fed by reports from his unofficial agent in London, Duff Green, a protégé of John C. Calhoun and a man whom John Quincy Adams contemptuously dismissed as an "ambassador of slavery." Green assured Tyler that as a prelude to undermining slavery in the United States, the British would pressure Mexico to recognize the independence of Texas in return for the abolition of slavery there. Calhoun, who became Tyler's secretary of state early in 1844, embroidered these reports with fanciful theories of British plans to use abolition as a way to destroy rice, sugar, and cotton production in the United States and gain for itself a monopoly on all three staples.

In the spring of 1844, Calhoun and Tyler submitted to the Senate for ratification a treaty, secretly drawn up, annexing Texas to the United States. Among the supporting documents accompanying the treaty was a letter from Calhoun to Richard Pakenham, the British foreign minister in Washington, that defended slavery as beneficial to blacks, the only way to protect them from "vice and pauperism." Antislavery northerners no longer had to look under the carpet for evidence that the impulse behind annexation lay in a desire to protect and extend slavery; now they needed only to read Calhoun's words. Both Martin Van Buren, the leading northern Democrat, and Henry Clay, the most powerful Whig, came out against immediate annexation, on grounds that annexation would provoke the kind of sectional conflict that each had sought to bury. By a vote of 35–16, the treaty went down to crushing defeat in the Senate. Decisive as it appeared, however, this vote only postponed the final decision on annexation to the upcoming election of 1844.

The Election of 1844

Tyler's ineptitude turned the presidential campaign into a free-for-all. The president hoped to succeed himself in the White House, but he lacked a base in either party. Testing the waters as an independent, he could not garner adequate support and was forced to drop out of the race.

Henry Clay had a secure grip on the Whig nomination. Martin Van Buren appeared to have an equally firm grasp on the Democratic nomination, but the issue of annexation split his party.

1844 Campaign Banner

Clay hoped to convince the public that the Whig programs of high tariffs and the distribution of tariff revenues would restore prosperity, here represented by a well-dressed farmer and his well-fed horse.

Trying to appease all shades of opinion within his party, Van Buren stated that he would abide by whatever Congress might decide on the annexation issue. Van Buren's attempt to evade the issue succeeded only in alienating the modest number of northern annexationists, led by Michigan's former governor Lewis Cass, and the much larger group of southern annexationists. At the Democratic convention, Van Buren and Cass effectively blocked each other's nomination. The resulting deadlock was broken by the nomination of James K. Polk of Tennessee, the first "dark-horse" nominee in American history.

Although little known outside the South, the slaveholding Polk was the favorite of southern Democrats, who accurately described him as the "bosom friend of [Andrew] Jackson, and a pure whole-hogged Democrat, the known enemy of banks and distribution." On the Texas issue, Polk supported immediate "reannexation," a curious turn of phrase that reflected Andrew Jackson's belief that Texas had been part of the Louisiana Purchase until unwisely ceded to Spain by the Transcontinental Treaty of 1819. Indeed, Polk followed Old Hickory's lead so often that he became known as Young Hickory.

Gibing "Who is James K. Polk?" the Whigs derided Polk's nomination. Polk himself marveled at his turn of fortune, for he had lost successive elections for the governorship of Tennessee. Yet he proved a wily campaign strategist. To satisfy pro-tariff Pennsylvania Democrats, Polk adjusted his position on the tariff to hold out some hope for protection. In addition, Polk and supporters like Senator Robert J. Walker of Mississippi managed to convince many northerners that the annexation of Texas would advance their interests. By foiling alleged British plans to abolitionize Texas, Walker contended, annexation would make Texas a safe haven for slavery and draw both slaves and free blacks away from states bordering the North. Failure to annex, on the other hand, would prevent the westward dispersal of the South's slave population, intensify racial tensions in the existing slave states, and increase the chances of a race war that would spill over into the North. However farfetched, Walker's arguments played effectively on the racial phobias of many northerners and helped Polk detach annexation from Calhoun's narrow, pro-southern defense of it.

In contrast to the Democrats, who established a clear direction in their arguments, Clay kept muddying the waters. In the spring of 1844, he had opposed the annexation treaty. Then he sent conflicting messages to his followers throughout the summer of 1844, saying that he had nothing against annexation as long as it would not disrupt sectional harmony. Finally, in September 1844 he again came out against annexation. Clay's shifts on annexation alienated his southern supporters and prompted a small but influential body of northern antislavery Whigs to desert to the Liberty party, which had been organized in 1840. Devoted to the abolition of slavery by political action, the Liberty party nominated Ohio's James G. Birney for the presidency.

Annexation was not the sole issue of the campaign. The Whigs' failure to enact their tariff and banking policies under Tyler alienated some traditional Whig support. In addition, as the Philadelphia Bible Riots demonstrated, long-simmering tensions between native-born Americans and immigrants were boiling over in key northern states in 1844. The Whigs infuriated immigrant voters by nominating Theodore Frelinghuysen as Clay's running mate. A leading Presbyterian layman, Frelinghuysen gave "his head, his hand, and his heart" to temperance and an assortment of other Protestant causes. His presence on their ticket fixed the image of the Whigs as the orthodox Protestant party and roused the largely Catholic foreign-born voters to turn out in large numbers for the Democrats.

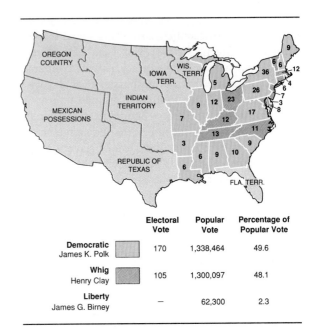

	Electoral Vote	Popular Vote	Percentage of Popular Vote
Democratic James K. Polk	170	1,338,464	49.6
Whig Henry Clay	105	1,300,097	48.1
Liberty James G. Birney	—	62,300	2.3

The Election of 1844

On the eve of the election in New York City, so many Irish marched to the courthouse to be qualified for voting that the windows had to be left open for people to get in and out. "Ireland has re-conquered the country which England lost," an embittered Whig moaned. Polk won the electoral vote 170–105, but his margin in the popular vote was only 38,000 out of 2.6 million votes cast, and he lost his own state of Tennessee by 113 votes. In most states the two main parties contended with each other on close terms, a sign of the maturity of the second party system. A shift of 6,000 votes in New York, where the immigrant vote and Whig defections to the Liberty party hurt Clay, would have given Clay both the state and the presidency.

Manifest Destiny

The election of 1844 demonstrated one incontestable fact: the annexation of Texas had more national support than Clay had realized. The surging popular sentiment for expansion that made the underdog Polk rather than Clay the man of the hour reflected a growing conviction among the people that America's natural destiny was to expand into Texas and all the way to the Pacific.

Expansionists emphasized extending the "area of freedom" and talked of "repelling the contaminating proximity of monarchies upon the soil that we have consecrated to the rights of man." For contemporary young Americans like Walt Whitman, such restless expansionism knew few limits. "The more we reflect upon annexation as involving a part of Mexico, the more do doubts and obstacles resolve themselves away," Whitman wrote. "Then there is California, on the way to which lovely tract lies Santa Fe; how long a time will elapse before they shine as two new stars in our mighty firmament?"

Americans awaited only a phrase to capture this ebullient spirit of continentalism. In 1845 John L. O'Sullivan, a New York Democratic journalist, wrote of "our manifest destiny to overspread and to possess the whole of the continent which Providence has given us for the development of the great experiment of liberty and federated self-government entrusted to us."

Advocates of Manifest Destiny used lofty language and routinely invoked God and Nature to sanction expansion. Inasmuch as most spokesmen for Manifest Destiny were Democrats, many of whom supported the annexation of Texas, northern Whigs frequently dismissed Manifest Destiny as a smoke screen aimed at concealing the evil intent of expanding slavery. In reality, many advocates of Manifest Destiny were neither supporters of slavery nor zealous annexationists. Oregon and California loomed more prominently in their minds than Texas. For despite their flowery phrases, these expansionists rested their case on hard material calculations. Most blamed the post-1837 depression on the failure of the United States to acquire markets for its agricultural surplus and saw the acquisition of Oregon and California as solutions. A Missouri Democrat observed that "the ports of Asia are as convenient to Oregon as the ports of Europe are to the eastern slope of our confederacy, with an infinitely better ocean for navigation." An Alabama Democrat praised California's "safe and capacious harbors," which, he assured, "invite to their bosoms the rich commerce of the East."

Expansionists desired more than profitable trade routes, however. At the heart of their thinking lay an impulse to preserve the predominantly agricultural character of the American people and thereby to safeguard democracy. Most expansionists associated the industrialization that was transforming America with social stratification and class strife, and many saw the concentration of impov-

erished Irish immigrants in cities and factory towns as evidence of the common people's shrinking opportunities for economic advancement. After a tour of New England mill towns in 1842, John L. O'Sullivan warned Americans that should they fail to encourage alternatives to factories, the United States would sink to the level of Britain, a nation that the ardent Democratic expansionist James Gordon Bennett described as a land of "bloated wealth" and "terrible misery."

Most Democratic expansionists came to see the acquisition of new territory as a logical complement to their party's policies of low tariffs and opposition to centralized banking. Where tariffs and banks tended to "favor and foster the factory system," expansion would provide farmers with land and with access to foreign markets for their produce. As a consequence, Americans would continue to become farmers, and the foundations of the Republic would remain secure. The acquisition of California and Oregon would provide enough land and harbors to sustain not only the 20 million Americans of 1845 but the 100 million that some expansionists projected for 1900 and the 250 million that O'Sullivan predicted for 1945.

The expansionists' message, especially as delivered by the penny press in such newspapers as Bennett's *New York Herald*, made sense to the laboring poor of America's antebellum cities. The *Herald*, the nation's largest-selling newspaper in the 1840s, played upon the anxieties of its working-class readers by arguing relentlessly for the expulsion of the British from Oregon and for thwarting alleged British plans to abolitionize the United States. These readers, many of them fiercely antiblack, anti-British Irish immigrants, welcomed any efforts to open up economic opportunities for the common people. Most also favored the perpetuation of slavery, for the freeing of slaves would throw masses of blacks into the already intense competition for jobs.

The expansionists with whom these laboring-class readers sided drew ideas from Thomas Jefferson, John Quincy Adams, and other leaders of the early Republic who had proclaimed the American people's right to displace uncivilized or European people from the path of their westward movement. Early expansionists, however, had feared that overexpansion might create an ungovernable empire. Jefferson, for example, had proposed an indefinite restriction on the settlement of Louisiana. In contrast, the expansionists of the 1840s, citing the virtues of the telegraph and the railroad, believed that the problem of distance had been "literally annihilated." James Gordon Bennett claimed that the telegraph would render the whole nation as compact and homogeneous as New York City. Ironically, while many expansionists pointed with alarm to the negative effects of industrialization on American society, their confidence in technology convinced them that the nation could expand with minimal risk to the people.

Polk and Oregon

The most immediate impact of the growing spirit of Manifest Destiny was to escalate the issue of Oregon. To soften northern criticism of the still-pending annexation of Texas, the Democrats had included in their platform for the election of 1844 the assertion that American title "to the whole of the Territory of Oregon is clear and unquestionable." Taken literally, the platform committed the party to acquire the entire area between California and 54°40', the southern boundary of Alaska. Since Polk had not yet been elected, the British could safely ignore this extraordinary claim for the moment, and in fact, the Oregon issue had aroused far less interest during the campaign than had the annexation of Texas. But in his inaugural address, Polk reasserted the "clear and unquestionable" claim to the "country of Oregon." If by this Polk meant all of Oregon, then the United States, which had never before claimed any part of Oregon north of the forty-ninth parallel, had executed an astounding and belligerent reversal of policy.

Polk's objectives in Oregon, however, were more subtle than his language. He knew that the United States could never obtain all of Oregon without a war with Britain, and he wanted to avoid that. He proposed to use the threat of hostilities to persuade the British to accept what they had repeatedly rejected in the past: a division of Oregon at the forty-ninth parallel. Such a division would give the United States both the excellent deep-water harbors of Puget Sound and the southern tip of British-controlled Vancouver Island. For their part, the British had long held out for a division along the Columbia River, which entered the Pacific far south of the forty-ninth parallel.

Polk's comments in his inaugural speech roused among westerners a furious interest in acquiring

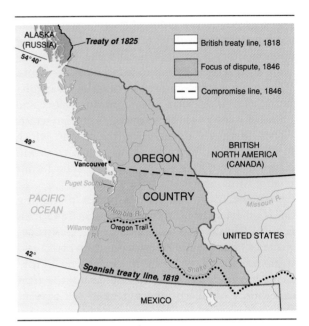

Oregon Boundary Dispute

Although demanding that Britain cede the entire Oregon Territory south of 54°40', the United States settled for a compromise at the forty-ninth parallel.

the whole territory. Mass meetings adopted such resolutions as "We are all for Oregon, and *all* Oregon in the West" and "The Whole or None!" Further, each passing year brought new American settlers into Oregon. Even John Quincy Adams, who advocated neither the annexation of Texas nor the 54°40' boundary for Oregon, believed that the American settlements in Oregon gave the United States a far more reasonable claim to the territory than mere exploration and discovery gave the British. The United States, not Britain, Adams contended, was the nation bound "to make the wilderness blossom as the rose, to establish laws, to increase, multiply, and subdue the earth," all "at the first behest of God Almighty."

In April 1846 Polk secured from Congress the termination of joint British-American occupation of Oregon and promptly gave Britain the required one year's notice. With joint occupation abrogated, the British could either go to war over American claims to 54°40' or negotiate. They chose to negotiate. Although the British raged against "that ill-regulated, overbearing, and aggressive spirit of American democracy," they had too many domestic and foreign problems to welcome a war over what Lord Aberdeen, the British foreign secretary, dismissed as "a few miles of pine swamp." The ensuing treaty provided for a division at the forty-ninth parallel, with some modifications. Britain retained all of Vancouver Island as well as navigation rights on the Columbia River. The Senate ratified the treaty (with the proviso that Britain's navigation rights on the Columbia were merely temporary) on June 15, 1846.

The Origins of the Mexican War

Even as Polk was challenging Britain over Oregon, the United States and Mexico moved steadily toward war. The impending conflict had both remote and immediate causes. One long-standing grievance lay in the failure of the Mexican government to pay some $2 million in debts owed to American citizens. In addition, bitter memories of the Alamo and of the Goliad massacre continued to arouse in Americans a loathing of Mexicans. Above all, the issue of Texas embroiled relations between the two nations. Mexico still hoped to regain Texas or at least to keep it independent of the United States, a nation whose policies toward blacks seemed to most Mexicans evidence of an inherent national cruelty. Once in control of Texas, the Mexicans feared, the United States might seize other Mexican provinces, perhaps even Mexico itself, and treat the citizens of Mexico much as it had treated its slaves.

Unfortunately for Mexico, Polk's election boosted the strength of pro-annexation forces in the United States. The arguments that Polk and Senator Robert J. Walker had put forth during the election campaign of 1844 had persuaded many northerners of the national, rather than purely sectional, benefits of annexing Texas. Recognizing the growing popularity of annexation, both houses of Congress passed a resolution in February 1845 to annex Texas. Soon after taking office, Polk dispatched agents to the Texas republic to gain acceptance of annexation. Some Texans feared that annexation would provoke an invasion of Texas by Mexico, which had never formally recognized Texas's independence and which now served notice that it "would consider equivalent to a declaration of war against the Mexican Republic the passage of an act for an incorporation of Texas with the territory of the United States."

Confronted by Texan timidity and Mexican belligerence, Polk moved on two fronts. To sweeten the pot for the Texans, he supported their claim to the Rio Grande as the southern boundary of Texas. This claim ran counter to Mexico's view that the Nueces River, a hundred miles northeast of the Rio Grande, bounded Texas. The area between the Nueces and the Rio Grande was largely uninhabited, but the stakes were high. Although only a hundred miles southwest of the Nueces at its mouth on the Gulf of Mexico, the Rio Grande meandered west and then north for nearly two thousand miles and encircled a huge slice of territory, including part of New Mexico. The Texas that Polk proposed to annex thus encompassed far more land than the Texas that had gained independence from Mexico in 1836. Reassured by Polk's support, a Texas convention voted overwhelmingly on July 4, 1845, to accept annexation. In response to Mexican war preparations, Polk then made a second move, ordering American troops under General Zachary Taylor to the edge of the disputed territory. Taylor took up a position at Corpus Christi, a tiny Texas outpost situated just south of the Nueces and hence in territory still claimed by Mexico.

Never far from Polk's thoughts in his insistence on the Rio Grande boundary lay his desire for California and for its fine harbors of San Diego and San Francisco. In fact, Polk had entered the White House with the firm intention of extending American control over California. By the summer of 1845, his followers were openly proclaiming that if Mexico went to war with the United States over Texas, "the road to California will be open to us." Then in October 1845, Polk received a dispatch from Thomas O. Larkin, the American consul at Monterey, California, that warned darkly of British designs on California but ended with the optimistic assurance that the Mexicans in California would prefer American to British rule. Larkin's message gave Polk the idea that California might be acquired by the same methods as Texas: revolution followed by annexation.

Visions of new territorial acquisitions were dancing merrily in Polk's mind when Texas accepted annexation in July 1845. With Taylor's troops at Corpus Christi, the next move belonged to Mexico. Unfortunately, Mexico had difficulty making any firm moves, for its politics had slipped again into turmoil with the ouster of Santa Anna by General José Herrera in December 1844. Herrera's own position in Mexican politics was shaky, and prodded by the British, he agreed to receive a delegation from the United States to reach an amicable settlement. Simultaneously, Polk, locked in a war of words with the British over Oregon, decided to give negotiations with Mexico a try. In November 1845 he sent an emissary, the Spanish-speaking John Slidell, to Mexico City. Slidell's final instructions were to gain Mexican recognition of the annexation of Texas, including the Rio Grande boundary, in return for the United States' assumption of all financial claims on the part of American citizens against the Mexican government. Polk also authorized Slidell to offer up to $25 million for New Mexico and California or, failing this, to offer $5 million for New Mexico alone.

By the time Slidell reached Mexico City on December 6, 1845, the threat of a military revolt led by General Mariano Paredes had pushed the Herrera government to the brink of collapse. Too weak to negotiate any concessions to the United States, Herrera refused to receive Slidell. In response to Mexico's refusal to negotiate, Polk now ordered Taylor to march from Corpus Christi southward to the north bank of the Rio Grande. Still viewing the Rio Grande as the key to the Far West, Polk hoped that Taylor's presence on the river would spur the Mexicans to attack. Mexican aggression, the president anticipated, would unify Americans and would quiet northerners who were suspiciously contrasting Polk's willingness to compromise on Oregon with his continuing belligerence toward Mexico. "Why," a Chicago newspaper asked, "should we not compromise our difficulties with Mexico as well as with Great Britain?" Polk had no intention of compromising on the Texas boundary, but if it came to war, he wanted a united country behind him.

On May 9, 1846, Polk notified his cabinet that he could no longer await a Mexican attack and that he must send a war message to Congress. A few hours after the cabinet adjourned, news arrived that a Mexican force had crossed the Rio Grande and ambushed two companies of Taylor's troops. Now the prowar press had its martyrs. "*American blood has been shed on American soil!*" one of Polk's followers proclaimed. On May 11 Polk informed Congress that war "exists by the act of Mexico herself" and called for a $10 million appropriation to fight the war.

Polk's disarming assertion that the United States was already at war provoked furious opposition in Congress, where John C. Calhoun briefly united with antislavery Whigs to protest the president's high-handedness. Polk's opponents pointed out that the Mexican attack on Taylor's troops had occurred in territory that no previous administration had claimed as part of the United States. By announcing that war already existed, moreover, Polk seemed to be undercutting Congress's power to declare war and using a mere border incident as a pretext for plunging the nation into a general war to acquire more slave territory. The pro-Whig *New York Tribune* warned its readers that Polk was "precipitating you into a fathomless abyss of crime and calamity." Antislavery poet James Russell Lowell of Massachusetts wrote of the Polk Democrats:

> *They just want this Californy*
> *So's to lug new slave-states in*
> *To abuse ye, an' to scorn ye,*
> *An' to plunder ye like sin.*

But Polk had maneuvered the Whigs into a corner. Few Whigs could forget that the opposition of the Federalists to the War of 1812 had wrecked the Federalist party, and few wanted to appear unpatriotic by refusing to support Taylor's beleaguered troops. Swallowing their outrage, most Whigs backed appropriations for war against Mexico.

Throughout the negotiations with Britain over Oregon and with Mexico over Texas, Polk had demonstrated his ability to pursue his goals unflinchingly. A humorless, austere man who banned dancing and liquor at White House receptions, Polk inspired little personal warmth, even among his supporters. But he possessed clear objectives and a single-mindedness in their pursuit. At every point, he had encountered opposition on the home front: from Whigs who saw him as a reckless adventurer; from northerners of both parties opposed to any expansion of slavery; and from John C. Calhoun, who loathed Polk for his high-handedness and feared that a war with Britain would strip the South of its market for cotton. Yet Polk triumphed over all opposition, in part because of his opponents' fragmentation, in part because of expansion's popular appeal, and in part because of the weakness of his foreign antagonists. Reluctant to fight over Oregon, Britain chose to negotiate. Too weak to negotiate, Mexico chose to fight over territory that it had already lost (Texas) and for territories over which its hold was feeble (California and New Mexico).

The Mexican War

Most European observers expected Mexico to win the war. With a regular army four times the size of the American forces, Mexico had the added advantage of fighting on home ground. The United States, which had botched its one previous attempt to invade a foreign nation, Canada in 1812, now had to sustain offensive operations in an area remote from American settlements.

In contrast to the Europeans, expansionists in the United States hardly expected the Mexicans to fight at all. A leading Democrat confidently predicted that Mexico would offer only "a slight resistance to the North American race" because its mixed Spanish and Indian population had been degraded by "amalgamation." Newspaper publisher James Gordon Bennett proclaimed that the "imbecile" Mexicans were "as sure to melt away at the approach of [American] energy and enterprise as snow before a southern sun."

In fact, the Mexicans did not prove to be superior in battle, but neither were they cowardly. They fought bravely and stubbornly, though with little success. In May 1846 Taylor, a sixty-two-year-old veteran of the War of 1812, defeated the Mexicans in two battles north of the Rio Grande and then crossed the river to defeat them again at Matamoros and to capture the major northern Mexican city of Monterrey in September. Taylor's victories touched off a wave of enthusiasm in the United States. Recruiting posters blared: "Here's to Old Zach! Glorious Times! Roast Beef, Ice Cream, and Three Months' Advance!" Already the Whigs were touting Taylor, "Old Rough and Ready," for the presidency in 1848.

After taking the supposedly impregnable Monterrey, however, Taylor, starved for supplies, granted the Mexicans an armistice by which he pledged not to pursue them for eight weeks. Eager to undercut Taylor's popularity, and judging him "wholly unqualified for the command he holds," Polk now stripped Taylor of half his men and assigned them to General Winfield Scott. Polk ordered Scott to prepare an amphibious assault on Vera Cruz, a city on the Gulf of Mexico far to the south, and to proceed overland to Mexico City. Before Scott could attack Vera Cruz, however, Taylor gained even greater fame. Seeking to win an easy victory over Taylor's depleted army, Santa Anna, who had made another of his many comebacks in Mexican politics, led an army of twenty thousand men north to dislodge Taylor. The two armies met at the Battle of Buena Vista, February 22–23, 1847. After a series of futile charges, Santa Anna's men, demoralized by the superior American artillery, retreated.

The Siege of Vera Cruz (above)

War News from Mexico (left), *by Richard Caton Woodville, 1848; The Mexican conflict was the first war that sent newspaper reporters to the front. Americans hungrily read their accounts of such engagements as the siege of Vera Cruz.*

Battle of Buena Vista, *by Carl Nebel, 1847*

Zachary Taylor's victory over the Mexicans at Buena Vista made him a national hero.

While Taylor was winning fame in northern Mexico, and before Scott had launched his attack on Vera Cruz, American forces farther north were dealing decisive blows to the remnants of Mexican rule in New Mexico and California. In the spring of 1846, Colonel Stephen Kearny marched an army from Fort Leavenworth, Kansas, toward Santa Fe. Like the pioneers on the Oregon Trail, Kearny's men faced immense natural obstacles as they marched over barren ground. "No grass for 4 days," one of Kearny's officers wrote his wife. "The regulars have spirit, and volunteers would not make it without them." Finally reaching New Mexico, Kearny took the territory by a combination of bluff, bluster, and perhaps bribery, without firing a shot. The Mexican governor, following his own advice that "it is better to be thought brave than to be so," fled at Kearny's approach. After suppressing a brief rebellion by Mexicans and Indians, Kearny sent a detachment of his army south into Mexico. There, having marched six thousand miles from Fort Leavenworth, these troops joined Taylor in time for the Battle of Buena Vista.

Like New Mexico, California fell easily into American hands. In 1845 Polk had ordered Commodore John D. Sloat and his Pacific Squadron to occupy California's ports in the event of war with Mexico. To ensure victory, Polk also dispatched a courier overland with secret orders for one of the most colorful and important actors in the conquest of California, John C. Frémont. A Georgia-born adventurer, Frémont had married Jessie Benton, the daughter of the powerful senator Thomas Hart Benton of Missouri. Benton used his influence to have accounts of Frémont's explorations in the Northwest (mainly written by Jessie Benton Frémont) published as government documents. All of this earned glory for Frémont as "the Great Pathfinder." Finally overtaken by Polk's courier in Oregon, Frémont was instructed to proceed to California and to "watch over the interests of the United States." Interpreting his orders liberally, Frémont rounded up some American insurgents, seized the town of Sonoma, and proclaimed the independent "Bear Flag Republic" in June 1846. The combined efforts of Frémont, Sloat, his successor David Stockton, and Stephen Kearny (who arrived in California after capturing New Mexico) quickly established American control over California.

The final and most important campaign of the war saw the conquest of Mexico City itself. In March 1847 Winfield Scott landed near Vera Cruz at the head of twelve thousand men and quickly pounded the city into submission. Moving inland, Scott encountered Santa Anna at the seemingly impregnable pass of Cerro Gordo, but a young captain in Scott's command, Robert E. Lee, helped to find a trail that led around the Mexican flank to a small peak overlooking the pass. There Scott planted howitzers and, on April 18, stormed the pass and routed the Mexicans. Scott now moved directly on Mexico City. Taking the key fortresses of Churubusco and Chapultepec (where another young captain, Ulysses S. Grant, was cited for bravery), Scott took the city on September 13, 1847.

In virtually all these encounters on Mexican

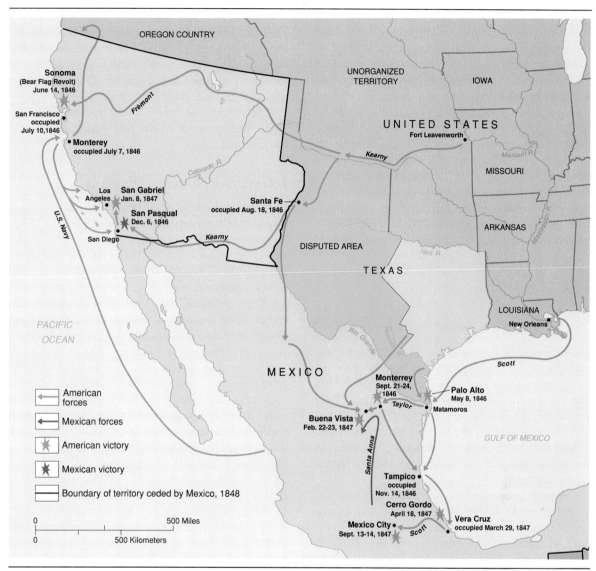

Major Battles of the Mexican War *The Mexican War's decisive campaign began with General Winfield Scott's capture of Vera Cruz and ended with his conquest of Mexico City.*

soil, the Mexicans enjoyed numerical superiority. In the final assault on Mexico City, Scott commanded eleven thousand troops against Santa Anna's twenty-five thousand. But doom stalked the Mexican army. Hampered by Santa Anna's nearly unbroken string of military miscalculations, the Mexicans fell victim to the vastly superior American artillery and to the ability of the Americans to organize massive military movements. The "barbarians of the North" (as the Mexicans called the American soldiers) died like flies from yellow fever, and they carried into battle the agonies of

venereal disease, which they picked up (and left) in every Mexican town that they took. But the Americans benefited from the unprecedented quality of their weapons, supplies, and organization.

By the Treaty of Guadalupe Hidalgo (February 2, 1848), Mexico ceded Texas with the Rio Grande boundary, New Mexico, and California to the United States. In return, the United States assumed the claims of American citizens against the Mexican government and paid Mexico $15 million. Although the United States gained the present states of California, Nevada, New Mexico, Utah, most of Arizona, and parts of Colorado and Wyoming, some rabid expansionists in the Senate denounced the treaty because it failed to include all of Mexico. But the acquisition of California, with its excellent Pacific ports of San Diego and San Francisco, satisfied Polk. Few senators, moreover, wanted to annex the mixed Spanish and Indian population of Mexico. A writer in the *Democratic Review* expressed the prevailing view that "the annexation of the country [Mexico] to the United States would be a calamity," for it would incorporate into the United States "ignorant and indolent half-civilized Indians," not to mention "free negroes and mulattoes" left over from the British slave trade. In this way, the virulent racism of American leaders allowed the Mexicans to retain part of their nation. On March 10, 1848, the Senate ratified the treaty by a vote of 38 to 10.

The Mexican War in the Popular Mind

Occurring amid the rise of the penny press and the popular novel, the Mexican War became the most fully reported war that America had yet fought and the first conflict in which war correspondents were employed. The extensive coverage given to battlefield victories fueled the soaring nationalism and helped to submerge political divisions. "We are now all Whigs and all Democrats," an Indiana newspaper declared.

Romance as well as patriotism gripped the popular mind. Writers portrayed the war as evidence that the noble, chivalric streak in the American character could prevail over the grasping materialism of American society. To a generation fed on the historical novels of Sir Walter Scott, it seemed that the age of chivalry had returned. Innumerable popular war novels, with titles like *The Texan Ranger; or, The Maid of Matamoros*, mingled patriotism and romance by relating how American soldiers routed Mexican men only to fall in love with Mexican women.

The main beneficiary of the publicity swirling out of the war was Zachary Taylor. Taylor had the right combination of qualities to enchant a people in search of heroes. To those who danced to the hastily composed "Rough and Ready Polka" and the "General Taylor Quick Step," Taylor's military genius seemed equaled only by his democratic bearing and conspicuously ordinary manner. In

contrast to the more soldierly Winfield Scott ("Old Fuss and Feathers"), Taylor went into battle wearing a straw hat and plain brown coat. To an idolizing public, even Taylor's short stature and inclination to corpulence became an advantage; some said that he resembled Napoleon.

The war made Taylor a military hero. The conflicts that spun out of the war would now boost his political career.

Intensifying Sectional Divisions

Despite the wartime patriotic enthusiasm, sectional conflict sharpened between 1846 and 1848. To a degree, this conflict intensified over issues unrelated to expansion. Many of the problems stemmed from Polk's uncompromising and literal-minded Jacksonianism.

Once in office, Polk not only had restored the Independent Treasury, a measure that dismayed the Whigs, but also had eroded the unity of his own party by pursuing Jacksonian policies on tariffs and internal improvements. The numerous northern Democrats who supported a modestly protective tariff had taken heart during the 1844 campaign from Polk's promise to combine a revenue tariff with a measure of protection. But Polk's administration, glutted with southerners, quickly abandoned any talk of protection. The tariff of 1846, fashioned by Robert J. Walker, who became Polk's secretary of the treasury, slashed all duties to the minimum necessary for revenue. Polk then disappointed western Democrats, thirsting for federal aid for internal improvements, by vetoing a law that they supported, the Rivers and Harbors Bill of 1846. To these western Democrats, this veto appeared to be another sign of the pro-southern tilt of Polk's presidency and did more to weaken western support for Polk than his abandonment of the fight for the 54°40′ boundary of Oregon.

Ultimately, however, sectional conflict over tariffs and internal improvements proved of far less importance than the battles generated by territorial expansion. Polk held true to his belief that expansion had provided an "additional guaranty for the preservation of the Union itself." Like most Jacksonian Democrats, he saw the bursting of the nation's boundaries as a way to disperse the population, weaken dangerous tendencies toward centralized government, and retain the agricultural and democratic character of the United States. In Polk's judgment, expansion would accomplish these objectives whether the new territory acquired were slave or free. Focusing attention on slavery in the territories struck him as "not only unwise but wicked." The Missouri Compromise, prohibiting slavery north of 36°30′, impressed him as a simple and permanent solution to the problem of territorial slavery.

Yet many northerners were coming to see slavery in the territories as a profoundly disruptive issue that could not be resolved merely by extending the 36°30′ line to the Pacific. Some antislavery Whigs, especially those from abolitionist strongholds in New England and Ohio, opposed *any* extension of slavery, on moral grounds. But these Whigs, still a minority in their party, posed no immediate threat to Polk. A more damaging challenge emerged within Polk's own party: from a group of northern Democrats who, while not viewing slavery as morally evil, feared that an extension of slavery into California and New Mexico (parts of each lay north of 36°30′) would deter free laborers from settling those territories. These Democrats argued that competition with slave labor clearly degraded free labor, that the westward extension of slavery would create a barrier to the westward migration of free labor, and that such a barrier would intensify the social problems already evident in the East: excessive concentration of population, labor protest, class strife, and social stratification.

The Wilmot Proviso

A young Democratic congressman from Pennsylvania, David Wilmot, became the spokesman for these disaffected northern Democrats. On a sizzling night in August 1846, he introduced an amendment to an appropriations bill for the upcoming negotiations with Mexico over Texas, New Mexico, and California. This amendment, known as the Wilmot Proviso, stipulated that slavery be prohibited in any territory acquired by the negotiations. Neither an abolitionist nor a critic of Polk on tariff policy, Wilmot spoke for those loyal Democrats who had supported the annexation of Texas on the assumption that Texas would be the last slave state. Wilmot's intention was not to split his party along sectional lines but to hold Polk to

what Wilmot and other northern Democrats took as an implicit understanding: Texas for the slaveholders, California and New Mexico for free labor. With strong northern support, the proviso passed in the House but stalled in the Senate. Polk refused to endorse it, and most southern Democrats opposed any barrier to the expansion of slavery south of the Missouri Compromise line. Accepting the view that the westward extension of slavery would reduce the concentration of slaves in the older regions of the South and thus lessen the chances of a slave revolt, southern Democrats tried to put as much distance as possible between themselves and Wilmot.

The proviso raised unsettling constitutional issues. Calhoun and fellow southerners contended that since slaves were property, slaveholders enjoyed the Constitution's protection of property and could carry their slaves wherever they chose. This position led to the conclusion (drawn explicitly by Calhoun) that the Missouri Compromise of 1820, prohibiting slavery in the territories north of 36°30′, was unconstitutional. On the other side were many northerners who cited the Northwest Ordinance of 1787, the Missouri Compromise, and the Constitution itself, which gave Congress the power to "make all needful rules and regulations respecting the territory or other property belonging to the United States," as justification for congressional legislation over slavery in the territories. With the election of 1848 approaching, politicians of both sides, eager to hold their parties together and avert civil war, searched frantically for a middle ground.

The Election of 1848

The Whigs now confronted a major problem and a splendid opportunity. The problem derived from the fact that the nation had returned to prosperity after 1843 without any apparent help from the Whig economic program of national banking, high tariffs, and federal aid for internal improvements. After having asserted that their policies alone could pull the nation out of the depression, the Whigs had watched in dismay as the nation returned to prosperity under the Democrat Polk's program of an independent treasury, low tariffs, and no federal aid for internal improvements. Never before had Clay's American System seemed so irrelevant. The Whigs' opportunity grew out of the fact that the Wilmot Proviso had gravely embarrassed southern

San Francisco in the Gold Rush

San Francisco became a favorite destination for newcomers in the gold rush. Its population spurted from 1,000 in 1849 to 50,000 in 1856. Few American towns had presented less likely prospects for growth. The Spanish had constructed a presidio and a mission on the site in 1776, and a small town Yerba Buena, had sprung up around the mission. But when the United States took possession of Yerba Buena in July 1846, the town stretched for only a few streets in each direction and contained a mere 150 people who huddled amid its low mountains and fog-enshrouded sand hills. Arriving in the summer of 1846, a boatload of 200 Mormons more than doubled the population of Yerba Buena, which became San Francisco in 1847.

The gold rush transformed the town into "a pandemonium of city" in the words of John Woodhouse Audubon, who became stranded there by Christmas 1849, on his way to the gold fields. San Francisco quickly emerged as the main supply depot for miners and prospectors in the interior. At first, virtually all commodities that passed through the city originated outside of California. Lumber came from Maine and Oregon, flour from Chile and Virginia, sugar from Hawaii, and manufactured goods from the eastern states and Britain. This reliance on imports shaped the town's occupational structure between 1849 and 1853. San Francisco's economy was so top-heavy with merchants and storekeepers that those willing to drive carts (draymen) or unload ships or build houses could command wages that elsewhere would have seemed unbelievable. A New

Montgomery Street, San Francisco, 1850, *Daguerreotype by Frederick Coombs*

In the view of historian William H. Goetzmann and art historian William N. Goetzmann, San Francisco was "the final living embodiment of Manifest Destiny, a golden dream city of great instant wealth."

England–born lawyer seriously considered giving up his practice to become a drayman, for "they pay a man to drive a cart fifteen to twenty dollars a day," a generous wage at the time. By the mid-1850s the establishment of iron foundries and flour mills relieved the growing city's dependence on imports, but the supply of commodities remained uncertain, and commodity prices continued to gyrate crazily. Flour that cost $10 a barrel one month might jump to $19 the next. Real-estate prices also soared during the early rush, particularly near the waterfront. The city's economy was vulnerable to crashes as precipitous as its booms. A commercial panic in 1855 produced nearly two

hundred bankruptcies and left close to $7 million in uncollectable debts.

The variety of San Francisco's population rivaled the volatility of its economy. Emigrants came from the four corners of the globe. By the 1850s the Irish outnumbered every other group of foreign-born immigrants. Many Irish were convicts who arrived by way of Australia, to which they had been exiled as punishment for their crimes. China, France, and Italy, nations that did not contribute many immigrants to other parts of the United States before 1860, all sent sizable contingents to San Francisco. Part of the city's tiny black population was also foreign-born. Richard Dalton, for example, came from the West Indies as a steward on a steamer and then labored on the ships that plied the Sacramento and San Joaquin rivers to Sacramento and Stockton. Indeed, no other U.S. city contained people from more parts of the world, and only two, St. Louis and Milwaukee, had a higher proportion of foreign-born residents in 1860. In addition, by the early 1850s, San Francisco contained six to ten times as many men as women.

In a city bursting with rival ethnic and racial groups and lacking the constraints imposed by family responsibilities, violence became a principal noncommercial activity. Audubon reported how the place teemed with men "more blasphemous, and with less regard for God and his commands than all I have ever seen on the Mississippi." A young clergyman wrote in 1851 that "most of our citizens if not all go armed" and confessed that he carried a harmless-looking cane, which "will be found to contain a sword two-and-a-half feet long." The city's small fledgling police force posed little challenge to criminals. For protection, some businessmen organized disbanded soldiers into an extralegal force called the Hounds. Unfortunately, the Hounds soon terrorized the people whom they were supposed to protect. In response, in 1851 San Francisco's merchants organized the first of

several Committees of Vigilance, which patrolled the streets, deported undesirables, and tried and hanged thieves and murderers.

The vigilantes turned out during subsequent outbursts of lawlessness. In 1855 a gambler named Charles Cora insulted the wife of William Richardson, a U.S. marshal. Richardson then insulted Cora's mistress, a prostitute. A crusading editor, William King, joined the fight on Richardson's side, and a political hack and longtime antagonist of King, James Casey, added his barbs to the fray. The outcome revealed much about law and order in early San Francisco. Richardson armed himself and sought out Cora in a saloon, only to be shot to death by Cora; Casey shot and killed King on a street. Vigilantes then seized Cora and Casey, tried them in secret, and hanged them.

These incidents underscore the city's religious and ethnic tensions as well as its atmosphere of easy violence. Richardson was a southerner and a Protestant, and his supporter King crusaded against the Catholic church. While less than models of virtue, their opponents Cora and Casey had been raised Catholics and resented attacks on the religion of their parents. Americans thought of the Far West as a land of opportunity where past antagonisms and traditions would

be eradicated, but all the divisions of the larger society were reproduced in San Francisco. The major racial, regional, religious, and ethnic groups kept their distance from each other. Blacks were forced to sit in segregated parts of theaters and to attend segregated schools. Southern and New England Protestants worshiped at different churches. Immigrants from Europe also divided on the basis of language and nationality. German, Polish, Russian, and Anglo-American Jews each maintained separate religious congregations.

Regional and ethnic antagonisms even threatened at times to disrupt the harmony within the city's political parties. Transplanted southerners and Irish immigrants, for example, vied with each other for control of the Democratic party. But at election time, these groups laid aside their antagonisms and united against the rival parties. The Germans usually joined the Irish to ally with the Democrats, whereas the Whigs (and later the Know-Nothings and the Republicans) drew support from former New Englanders, from temperance advocates, and from some immigrants who resented the brash and brawling Irish. In this way, party politics gave coherence to the city's divisions and provided a generally peaceful outlet for the populace's overheated tempers.

San Francisco Saloon, *by Frank Marryat*

Mexicans, Chinese, Yankees, and southerners drink together in an ornate San Francisco saloon in the booming gold-rush days.

The Election of 1848				
Candidates	Parties	Electoral Vote	Popular Vote	Percentage of Popular Vote
ZACHARY TAYLOR	Whig	163	1,360,967	47.4
Lewis Cass	Democratic	127	1,222,342	42.5
Martin Van Buren	Free-Soil		291,263	10.1

Democrats. Although many antislavery northern Whigs had supported Wilmot's amendment, the proviso's origin in the Democratic party provided southern Whigs with a windfall, for they could now portray themselves as the only dependable guardians of the South's interests.

These considerations inclined the majority of Whigs toward Zachary Taylor. As a Louisianian and large slaveholder, Taylor had an obvious appeal to the South. As a political newcomer who had never voted in a presidential election, he had no loyalty to Clay's American System. As a war hero, he might have a broad national appeal. Nominating Taylor, the Whigs presented him as an ideal man "without regard to creeds or principles" and ran him without any platform.

Because Wilmot was one of their own, the Democrats faced a greater challenge. They could not ignore the issue of slavery in the territories, but if they embraced the positions of either Wilmot or Calhoun, they would suffer an unmendable sectional fracture. With Polk declining to stand for reelection, the Democrats nominated Lewis Cass of Michigan, who solved their problem by evolving a doctrine of "squatter sovereignty," or popular sovereignty as it was later called. Cass argued that the issue of slavery in the territories should be kept out of Congress "and left to the people of the confederacy in their respective local governments." In other words, let the actual settlers in each territory decide the issue for themselves. Cass's position benefited from both its arresting simplicity and its vagueness. Was he saying that Congress had the power to prohibit slavery in the territories but, in the interests of sectional harmony, should leave the issue to each territory? Or did he mean that Congress lacked any power to legislate on slavery in the territories? As a further complication, the doctrine of squatter sovereignty did not establish a clear time frame for territorial action. Did the doctrine mean that the first territorial legislature could

abolish slavery, or did it intend that the final decision on slavery had to await the moment of admission to the Union? In actuality, few Democrats wanted definitive answers to these questions. The very vagueness of squatter sovereignty added to its appeal, for Democrats north and south were free to interpret it to their own advantage to their constituents.

Although both parties tried to steer around the issue of slavery in the territories, neither one fully succeeded. A pro–Wilmot Proviso faction of the Democratic party in New York, called the Barnburners, broke away from the party. Proclaiming their dedication to "Free Trade, Free Labor, Free Speech, and Free Men," the Barnburners courted Liberty party abolitionists and antislavery "Conscience" Whigs, who were dismayed by their party's nomination of the slaveholding Taylor. In August 1844 Barnburners, Conscience Whigs, and former Liberty party adherents met in Buffalo, created the Free-Soil party, and nominated Martin Van Buren on a platform opposing any extension of slavery. Van Buren's motives in accepting this third-party nomination reflected both lingering bitterness at his rejection by the Democrats in 1844 (a defeat engineered largely by Lewis Cass) and alarm at the increasingly southern domination of the party under Polk.

The Whig candidate, Taylor, benefited from the opposition's alienation of key northern states over the tariff issue, from Democratic disunity over the Wilmot Proviso, and from his glowing military record. He captured a majority of the electoral votes in both the North and the South. While failing to carry any state, the Free-Soil party ran well enough in the North to demonstrate the grassroots popularity of opposition to the extension of slavery. Defections to the Free-Soilers, for example, probably cost the Whigs the state of Ohio. Van Buren wrote that the new party had gained "more than we had any right to expect." Indeed, by showing that opposition to the spread of slavery had far greater popular appeal than the abolitionism of the old Liberty party, the Free-Soilers sent the Whig and Democratic parties a message that these parties would be unable to ignore in future elections.

The California Gold Rush

When Wilmot had first made public his proviso, the issue of slavery in the Far West was more abstract than practical, because Mexico had not yet ceded any territory and relatively few Americans resided in either California or New Mexico. Nine days before the signing of the Treaty of Guadalupe Hidalgo, however, an American carpenter discovered gold while constructing a sawmill in the foothills of California's Sierra Nevada range. A frantic gold rush was on within a few months. A San Francisco paper complained that "the whole country from San Francisco to Los Angeles, and from the shore to the base of the Sierra Nevada, resounds with the sordid cry to gold, GOLD, GOLD! while the field is left half-planted, the house half-built, and everything neglected but the manufacture of shovels and pickaxes." (Deprived of its staff, advertisers, and subscribers, the newspaper then suspended publication.) By December 1848 pamphlets with titles like *The Emigrant's Guide to the Gold Mines* had hit the streets of New York City.

To speed the gold-rushers to their destination, builders constructed sleek clipper ships like Donald McKay's *Flying Cloud*, which made the eighteen-thousand-mile trip from New York to San Francisco around Cape Horn in a record eighty-nine days on its maiden voyage in 1851. But most gold-rushers traveled overland. Overland emigrants to California rose from 400 in 1848 to 25,000 in 1849 and to 44,000 in 1850 (see "A Place in Time").

With the gold rush, the issue of slavery in the Far West became practical as well as abstract, and immediate rather than remote. In 1849 gold attracted a hundred thousand newcomers to California, including Mexicans, free blacks, and slaves brought by planters from the South. White prospectors loathed the thought of competing with any of these groups and wanted to drive all of them out of the gold fields. Spawned by disputed claims and prejudice, violence mounted, and demands grew for a strong civilian government in California to replace the ineffective military government left over from the war. Polk began to fear that without a satisfactory congressional solution to the slavery issue, Californians might organize a government independent of the United States. The gold rush thus guaranteed that the question of slavery in the Mexican cession would be the first item on the agenda for Polk's successor and, indeed, for the nation.

Conclusion

By calling their destiny manifest, Americans of the 1840s implied that they had no other course than to annex Texas, seize California and New Mexico, and secure the lion's share of Oregon. Obstacles might arise, but most believed that barriers to expansion would melt away in the face of a dynamic and resolute people.

This image of expansion as inevitable had deep roots in the experiences and values of the American people. Fed by immigration, the population continued to leap forward; by 1850 the United States had nearly five times its population in 1800. The fate of Mexican rule in Texas was sealed as much by the overwhelming numerical superiority of the American settlers as by Sam Houston's brilliant victory at the Battle of San Jacinto. In addition, expansion rested on a sequence of propositions that seemed self-evident to many antebellum Americans: that a nation of farmers would never experience sustained misery; that given the chance, most Americans would rather work on farms than in factories; and that expansion would provide more land for farming, reduce the dangerous concentration of people in cities, and restore opportunity for all.

Beyond all the talk of inevitable expansion, however, Americans saw their society's divisions deepen in the 1840s, not only between native-born and immigrant people but also between northerners and southerners. Expansion proved so controversial that it split the Democratic party over the Wilmot Proviso, widened the gap between northern and southern Whigs, and spurred the emergence of the Free-Soil party. Victorious over Mexico and enriched by the discovery of gold in California, Americans counted the blessings of expansion in these years but began to fear its costs.

CHRONOLOGY

1818 The United States and Britain agree on joint occupation of Oregon for a ten-year period.

1819 Transcontinental (Adams-Onís) Treaty.

1821 Mexico gains independence from Spain.

1822 Stephen F. Austin founds the first American community in Texas.

1824–1825 Russia abandons its claims to Oregon south of 54°40′.

1826 Haden Edwards leads an abortive rebellion against Mexican rule in Texas.

1827 The United States and Britain renew their agreement on joint occupation of Oregon for an indefinite period.

1830 Mexico closes Texas to further American immigration.

1834 Antonio López de Santa Anna comes to power in Mexico.
Austin secures repeal of the ban on American immigration into Texas.

1835 Santa Anna invades Texas.

1836 Texas declares its independence from Mexico.
Fall of the Alamo.
Goliad massacre.
Battle of San Jacinto.

1840 William Henry Harrison elected president.

1841 Harrison dies; John Tyler becomes president.
Tyler vetoes Whig National Banking Bill.

1842 Whigs abandon distribution.
Webster-Ashburton Treaty.

1843 Tyler launches campaign for Texas annexation.

1844 Philadelphia Bible Riots.
Senate rejects treaty annexing Texas.
James K. Polk elected president.

1845 Congress votes joint resolution to annex Texas.
Texas accepts annexation by the United States.
Mexico rejects Slidell mission.

1846 Congress ends the joint occupation of Oregon.
Zachary Taylor defeats the Mexicans in two battles north of the Rio Grande.
The United States declares war on Mexico.
John C. Frémont proclaims the Bear Flag Republic in California.
Congress votes to accept a settlement of the Oregon boundary issue with Britain.
Walker Tariff (tariff of 1846).
Colonel Stephen Kearny occupies Santa Fe.
Wilmot Proviso introduced.
Taylor takes Monterrey.

1847 Taylor defeats Santa Anna at the Battle of Buena Vista.
Vera Cruz falls to Winfield Scott.
Mormons establish the state of Deseret.
Mexico City falls to Scott.
Lewis Cass's principle of "squatter sovereignty."

1848 Gold discovered in California.
Treaty of Guadalupe Hidalgo signed.
Taylor elected president.

For Further Reading

Ray A. Billington, *The Far Western Frontier, 1830–1860* (1956). A comprehensive narrative of the settlement of the Far West.

William R. Brock, *Parties and Political Conscience: American Dilemmas, 1840–1850* (1979). An excellent interpretive study of the politics of the 1840s.

William H. Goetzmann, *When the Eagle Screamed: The Romantic Horizon in American Diplomacy, 1800–1860* (1966). A lively overview of antebellum expansionism.

Thomas R. Hietala, *Manifest Design: Anxious Aggrandizement in Late Jacksonian America* (1985). A fine revisionist study that stresses the economic impulse behind expansion.

Maldwyn A. Jones, *American Immigration* (1960). An excellent brief introduction to immigration.

Charles G. Sellers, *James K. Polk: Continentalist, 1843–1846* (1966). An outstanding political biography.

Henry Nash Smith, *Virgin Land: The American West as Symbol and Myth* (1950). A classic study of westward expansion in the American mind.

Additional Bibliography

Immigration, Nativism, and Labor Protest

Lee Benson, *The Concept of Jacksonian Democracy: New York as a Test Case* (1961); Ray A. Billington, *The Protestant Crusade, 1800–1860: A Study of the Origins of Nativism* (1938); R. A. Burchell, *The San Francisco Irish, 1848–1880* (1980); Kathleen Conzen, *Immigrant Milwaukee, 1836–1860* (1976); Alan Dawley, *Class and Community: The Industrial Revolution in Lynn* (1976); Hasia R. Diner, *Erin's Daughter in America* (1983); Oscar Handlin, *Boston's Immigrants* (rev. ed., 1969); Bruce Laurie, *Working People of Philadelphia, 1800–1850* (1980); Lawrence J. McCaffrey, *The Irish Diaspora in America* (1984); Kerby A. Miller, *Emigrants and Exiles: Ireland and the Irish Exodus to North America* (1985); Earle F. Niehaus, *The Irish in New Orleans, 1800–1860* (1965); LaVern J. Rippley, *The German-Americans* (1976); Dennis P. Ryan, *Beyond the Ballot Box: A Sound History of the Boston Irish, 1845–1917* (1983); Norman Ware, *The Industrial Worker, 1840–1860* (1964); Sean Wilentz, *Chants Democratic: New York City and the Rise of the American Working Class, 1788–1850* (1984); Carl Wittke, *The Irish in America* (1956).

The Far West

John W. Caughey, *The California Gold Rush* (1975); Malcolm Clark, Jr., *Eden Seekers: The Settlement of Oregon, 1818–1862* (1981); Douglas H. Daniels, *Pioneer Urbanites: A Social and Cultural History of Black San Francisco* (1980); Arnoldo De Leon, *They Called Them Greasers: Anglo Attitudes Toward Mexicans in Texas, 1821–1900* (1983); John Mack Faragher, *Women and Men on the Overland Trail* (1979); William H. Goetzmann, *Exploration and Empire: The Explorer and the Scientist in the Winning of the American West* (1966); Neal Harlow, *California Conquered: War and Peace on the Pacific, 1846–1850* (1982); Theodore J. Karaminski, *Fur Trade and Exploration: Opening of the Far Northwest, 1821–1852* (1983); Robert J. Loewenberg, *Equality on the Oregon Frontier* (1976); Roger W. Lotchin, *San Francisco, 1846–1856: From Hamlet to City* (1974); Frederick Merk, *History of the Westward Movement* (1978); R. W. Paul, *California Gold* (1947); Leonard Pitt, *The Decline of the Californios: A Social History of the Spanish-Speaking Californians, 1846–1890* (1966); Alfred Robinson, *Life in California* (1891); John I. Unruh, Jr., *The Plains Across: Overland Emigrants and the Trans-Mississippi West, 1840–1860* (1979); David J. Weber, *The Mexican Frontier, 1821–1846: The American Southwest Under Mexico* (1982).

The Politics and Diplomacy of Expansion

K. Jack Bauer, *The Mexican War, 1846–1848* (1974); William C. Binkley, *The Texas Revolution* (1952); Gene M. Brack, *Mexico Views Manifest Destiny* (1976); Seymour Connor and Odie Faulk, *North America Divided: The Mexican War, 1846–1848* (1971); William J. Cooper, *Liberty and Slavery: Southern Politics to 1860* (1983); Bernard DeVoto, *The Year of Decision, 1846* (1943); Norman A. Graebner, *Empire on the Pacific: A Study in American Continental Expansion* (1955); Reginald Horsman, *Race and Manifest Destiny: The Origins of American Racial Anglo-Saxonism* (1981); Marquis James, *The Raven: The Story of Sam Houston* (1929); Robert W. Johannsen, *To the Halls of the Montezumas: The Mexican War in the American Imagination* (1985); Ernest McPherson Lander, Jr., *Reluctant Imperialist: Calhoun, the South Carolinian, and the Mexican War* (1980); Frederick Merk, *Slavery and the Annexation of Texas* (1972); David M. Pletcher, *The Diplomacy of Annexation: Texas, Oregon, and the Mexican War* (1973); Joseph G. Raybeck, *Free Soil: The Election of 1848* (1970); John H. Schroeder, *Mr. Polk's War: American Opposition and Dissent, 1846–1848* (1971); Charles G. Sellers, *James K. Polk: Jacksonian, 1795–1843* (1957); Joel H. Silbey, *The Shrine of Party: Congressional Voting Behavior, 1841–1852* (1967); Otis A. Singletary, *The Mexican War* (1960).

CHAPTER 13

From Compromise to Secession, 1850–1861

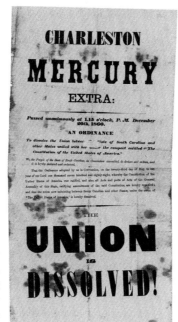

Between December 1859 and February 1860, Washington's political community witnessed one of the most remarkable deadlocks in the history of the House of Representatives. After forty-four ballots the House had still failed to elect a Speaker, the individual responsible for appointing the committees that the House needed to function. Too weak to elect one of their own, southerners repeatedly blocked the election of the early front-runner, Ohio Republican John Sherman.

Elections for the speakership had produced prolonged deadlocks in the past, but never before had tempers so flared. Now many congressmen armed themselves before entering the House chamber. During one debate a pistol fell from the pocket of a New York representative; other congressmen, thinking that he had drawn his pistol, leaped at him. A South Carolinian observed that "the only persons who do not have a revolver and a knife are those who have two revolvers." Although the election of the obscure and inoffensive William Pennington of New Jersey finally broke the deadlock, the tense atmosphere in Congress mirrored the division between the North and the South that would soon lead to the secession of the slave states from the Union.

Secession, a southern newspaper editor conceded in 1861, was a desperate measure. But, he quickly added, "We must recollect that we live in desperate times." A series of confrontations with the North over the status of slavery in the territories fed this growing sense of desperation in the South. Viewing the West as a boundless field of

economic opportunity for themselves, northerners abhorred the idea of competing with slaves there for jobs and thus zealously resisted the westward advance of slavery. During the 1850s a growing number of northerners embraced the doctrine known as free soil, the belief that Congress had to prohibit slavery in all the territories. Free-soilers like New York's Republican senator William H. Seward and Illinois's senatorial candidate Abraham Lincoln did not call for the abolition of slavery in the southern states, but they did define the conflict between slavery and freedom as national in scope. In 1858 Seward spoke of an "irrepressible conflict" between slavery and freedom and predicted that either the wheat fields of the North would become slave or the cotton fields of the South free. Invoking the biblical warning that "a house divided against itself cannot stand," Lincoln made the same point in 1858: "I believe that this nation cannot exist permanently half slave and half free." In the eyes of these men, the only solution lay in a congressional prohibition of slavery in the territories.

The doctrine of free soil ultimately rested on an image of the good society as one in which free individuals worked to achieve economic self-sufficiency as landowning farmers, self-employed artisans, and small shopkeepers. Like free-soil northerners, white southerners valued economic independence, but they insisted that without slaves to do society's menial jobs, common white people could never attain economic self-sufficiency. By 1850 most southern whites had persuaded themselves that slavery was an institution that treated blacks humanely while enabling whites to enjoy comfortable lives.

These differing images of the good society made conflict over slavery in the territories virtually unavoidable. White southerners interpreted free-soil attacks on territorial slavery as slaps in their faces. Nothing infuriated them more than the idea that they could not take their property, slaves, anywhere that they chose. Increasingly, too, southerners viewed free-soilers' hostility as a thinly disguised attempt to corrode the foundations of slavery in both the territories and the South itself. When the abolitionist John Brown recklessly attempted to spark a southern slave insurrection in 1859, innumerable southerners concluded that only the extreme step of secession could safeguard the South against northern onslaughts. "Not only our property," a southern newspaper editor proclaimed in 1861, "but our honor, our lives and our all are involved."

The Compromise of 1850

Ralph Waldo Emerson had predicted that an American victory in the Mexican War would be akin to swallowing arsenic, and his forecast proved disturbingly accurate. When the Treaty of Guadalupe Hidalgo was signed in 1848 to end the war, the United States contained an equal number (fifteen) of free and slave states. The vast territory ceded by Mexico (the Mexican cession) threatened to upset this balance in ways that few could have foreseen. Further, all of the proposed solutions to the problem of slavery in the Mexican cession—a free-soil policy, extension of the Missouri Compromise line, and popular sovereignty—ensured controversy. The prospect of "Free Soilism, Wilmot Provisoism, and all such tomfoolery" horrified southerners. The idea of extending the Missouri Compromise line, 36°30′, to the Pacific, which would allow slavery in New Mexico and southern California, antagonized northerners committed to free soil. (This second proposal simultaneously angered southern extremists, notably John C. Calhoun and his followers, by conceding to Congress the right to bar slavery in any of the territories.) The third solution, popular (or "squatter") sovereignty, which promised to ease the issue of slavery extension out of national politics by allowing each territory to decide the question for itself, offered the greatest hope for compromise. Yet popular sovereignty would appease neither those opposed in principle to the expansion of slavery nor those opposed to prohibitions on its expansion.

As statesmen fashioned their positions on slavery extension, the flow of events plunged the nation into a crisis. In the spring of 1849, the nonslaveholding Mormons in Deseret drew up a constitution and sought admission to the Union. (The state of Deseret had been established by Brigham Young's followers on soil that had become part of the United States with the Treaty of Guadalupe Hidalgo.) Then in the fall of 1849, Californians, their numbers swollen by thousands of gold-rushers, framed a constitution that banned slavery, and in 1850 they petitioned for statehood. (From the standpoint of popular sovereignty, California had jumped the gun, for Congress had not yet recognized it as a territory.) To complicate matters, Texas, admitted as a slave state in 1845, laid claim to the eastern half of New Mexico, a region where the future of slaves remained in doubt.

By 1850 these territorial issues had become intertwined with two other concerns. Northern orators had long denounced slavery and the sale of slaves in the District of Columbia, within the shadow of the federal government. For their part, southerners had often complained that northerners were flouting the Fugitive Slave Act, which Congress had passed in 1793, and were actively frustrating slaveholders' efforts to catch runaways on northern soil and return them to the South. Any broad compromise between the sections would have to take into account northern demands for a restriction on slavery in the District of Columbia and southern insistence on a more effective fugitive-slave law.

Zachary Taylor at the Helm

Although elected president in 1848 without a platform, Zachary Taylor came to office with a clear position on the issue of slavery in the Mexican cession. A slaveholder himself, he took for granted the South's need to defend slavery. Taylor insisted that southerners would best protect slavery if they refrained from rekindling the issue of slavery in the territories. He rejected Calhoun's idea that the protection of slavery in the southern states ultimately depended on the expansion of slavery into the western territories. In Taylor's eyes, neither California nor New Mexico was suited to slavery; in 1849 he told a Pennsylvania audience that "the people of the North need have no apprehension of the further extension of slavery."

Although Taylor looked to the exclusion of slavery from California and New Mexico, his position differed from that embodied in the Wilmot Proviso, the free-soil measure proposed in 1846 by a northern Democrat. The proviso had insisted that *Congress* bar slavery in the territories ceded by Mexico. Taylor's plan, in contrast, left the decision to the states. Recognizing the preponderance of free-staters in California, Taylor had prompted Californians to bypass the territorial stage that normally preceded statehood, to draw up their constitution in 1849, and to apply directly for admission as a free state. The president strongly hinted that he expected New Mexico, where slavery had been abolished under Mexican rule, to do the same.

Taylor's strategy appeared to promise a quick, practical solution to the problem of slavery extension. It would give the North two new free states. At the same time, it would acknowledge a position upon which all southerners agreed: a *state* could bar or permit slavery as it chose. This conviction in fact served as the very foundation of the South's defense of slavery, its armor against all the onslaughts of the abolitionists. Nothing in the Constitution forbade a state to act one way or the other on slavery.

Despite its practical features, Taylor's plan dismayed southerners of both parties. Having gored the Democrats in 1848 as the party of the Wilmot Proviso, southern Whigs expected more from the president than a proposal that in effect yielded the proviso's goal—the banning of slavery in the Mexican cession. Many southerners, in addition, questioned Taylor's assumption that slavery could never take root in California or New Mexico. To one observer, who declared that the whole controversy over slavery in the Mexican cession "related to an imaginary negro in an impossible place," south-

erners pointed out that both areas already contained slaves and that slaves could be employed profitably in the mining of gold and silver. "California is by nature," a southerner proclaimed, "peculiarly a slaveholding State." Calhoun trembled at the thought of adding more free states. "If this scheme excluding slavery from California and New Mexico should be carried out—if we are to be reduced to a mere handful . . . wo, wo, I say to this Union." Disillusioned with Taylor, nine southern states agreed to send delegations to a southern convention that was scheduled to meet in Nashville in June 1850.

Henry Clay Proposes a Compromise

Taylor might have been able to contain mounting southern opposition if he had held a secure position in the Whig party. But the leading Whigs, among them Daniel Webster of Massachusetts and Kentucky's Henry Clay, each of whom had presi-

Henry Clay

Although unsuccessful in five presidential bids, Clay was a towering figure in the Senate, to which he was first elected during Jefferson's presidency. Ultimately, his long congressional service worked against his presidential aspirations, for he made many enemies over the years. But his knowledge of the Senate gave him the tools to forge compromises.

dential aspirations, never reconciled themselves to Taylor, a political novice. Early in 1850 Clay boldly challenged Taylor's leadership by forging a set of compromise proposals to resolve the range of contentious issues. Clay proposed (1) the admission of California as a free state; (2) the division of the remainder of the Mexican cession into two territories, New Mexico and Utah (formerly Deseret), without federal restrictions on slavery; (3) the settlement of the Texas–New Mexico boundary dispute on terms favorable to New Mexico; (4) as a pot-sweetener for Texas, an agreement that the federal government would assume the considerable public debt of Texas; (5) in the District of Columbia, the continuance of slavery but the abolition of the slave trade; and (6) a more effective fugitive-slave law.

Clay rolled all of these proposals into a single "omnibus" bill, which he hoped to steer through Congress. The debates over the omnibus during the late winter and early spring of 1850 witnessed the last major appearances on the public stage of Clay, Webster, and Calhoun, the trio of distinguished senators whose lives had mirrored every public event of note since the War of 1812. Clay played the role of the conciliator, as he had during the controversy over Missouri in 1820 and again during the nullification crisis in the early 1830s. He warned the South against the evils of secession and assured the North that nature would check the spread of slavery more effectively than a thousand Wilmot Provisos. Gaunt and gloomy, a dying Calhoun listened as another senator read his address, in which Calhoun summarized what he had been saying for years: the North's growing power, enhanced by protective tariffs and by the Missouri Compromise's exclusion of slaveholders from the northern part of the Louisiana Purchase, had created an imbalance between the sections. Only a decision by the North to treat the South as an equal could now save the Union. Three days later, Daniel Webster, who believed that slavery, "like the cotton-plant, is confined to certain parallels of climate," delivered his memorable "Seventh of March" speech. Speaking not "as a Massachusetts man, nor as a Northern man, but as an American," Webster chided the North for trying to "reenact the will of God" by legally excluding slavery from the Mexican cession and declared himself a forthright proponent of compromise.

However eloquent, the conciliatory voices of Clay and Webster made few converts. With every call for compromise, some northern or southern speaker would rise and inflame passions. The antislavery New York Whig William Seward, for example, enraged southerners by talking of a "higher law than the Constitution"—namely, the will of God against the extension of slavery. Clay's compromise became tied up in a congressional committee. To worsen matters, Clay, who at first had pretended that his proposals were in the spirit of Taylor's plan, broke openly with the president in May, while Taylor attacked Clay as a glory-hunter.

As the Union faced its worst crisis since 1789, a series of events in the summer of 1850 eased the way toward a resolution. When the Nashville convention assembled in June, extreme advocates of "southern rights," called the fire-eaters because of their recklessness, boldly made their presence felt. But talk of southern rights smelled suspiciously like a plot to disrupt the Union. "I would rather sit in council with the six thousand dead who have died of cholera in St. Louis," Senator Thomas Hart Benton of Missouri declared, "than go into convention with such a gang of scamps." Only nine of the fifteen slave states, most in the Lower South, sent delegates to the convention, and moderates took control and isolated the extremists. Then Zachary Taylor, after eating and drinking too much at an Independence Day celebration, fell ill with gastroenteritis and died on July 9. His successor, Vice President Millard Fillmore of New York, quickly proved himself more favorable than Taylor to the Senate's compromise measure by appointing Daniel Webster as his secretary of state. Next, after the compromise suffered a devastating series of amendments in late July, Stephen A. Douglas of Illinois took over the floor leadership from the exhausted Clay. Recognizing that the compromise lacked majority support in Congress, Douglas jettisoned Clay's strategy by chopping the omnibus into a series of separate measures and seeking to secure passage of each bill individually. This ingenious tactic worked beautifully. By summer's end, in the Compromise of 1850, Congress had passed each component of Clay's plan: statehood for California; territorial status for Utah and New Mexico, allowing popular sovereignty; resolution of the Texas–New Mexico boundary disagreement; federal assumption of the Texas debt; abolition of the

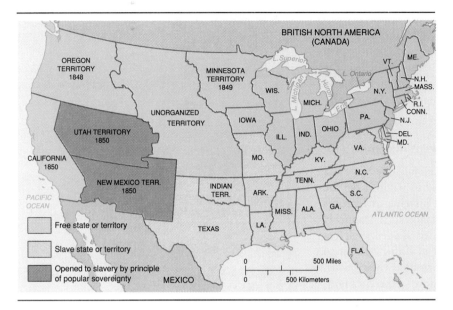

The Compromise of 1850

The Compromise of 1850 admitted California as a free state. Utah and New Mexico were left open to slavery or freedom on the principle of popular sovereignty.

slave trade in the District of Columbia; and a new fugitive-slave law.

Assessing the Compromise

President Fillmore hailed the compromise as a "final settlement" of sectional divisions, and Clay's reputation for conciliation reached new heights. Yet the compromise did not bridge the underlying differences between the two sections. Far from leaping forward to save the Union, Congress had backed into the Compromise of 1850; the majority of congressmen in one or another section opposed virtually all of the specific bills that made up the compromise. Most southerners, for example, voted against the admission of California and the abolition of the slave trade in the District of Columbia; the majority of northerners opposed the Fugitive Slave Act and the organization of New Mexico and Utah without a forthright congressional prohibition of slavery. These measures passed only because the minority of congressmen who genuinely desired compromise combined with the majority in either the North or the South who favored each specific bill.

Each section both gained and lost from the Compromise of 1850. The North won California as a free state, New Mexico and Utah as likely future free states, a favorable settlement of the Texas–New Mexico boundary (most of the disputed area was awarded to New Mexico, a probable free state), and the abolition of the slave trade in the District of Columbia. The South's benefits were cloudier. By stipulating popular sovereignty for New Mexico and Utah, the compromise, to most southerners' relief, had buried the Wilmot Proviso's insistence that Congress formally prohibit slavery in these territories. But to southerners' dismay, the position of the free-soilers remained viable, for the compromise left open the question of whether Congress could prohibit slavery in territories outside of the Mexican cession.

Not surprisingly, southerners reacted ambivalently to the Compromise of 1850. In southern state elections during the fall of 1850 and in 1851, pro-compromise, or Unionist, candidates thrashed anti-compromise candidates who talked of southern rights and secession. But even southern Unionists did not dismiss the possibility of secession. Unionists in Georgia, for example, forged the celebrated Georgia platform, which threatened secession if Congress either prohibited slavery in New Mexico or Utah or repealed the fugitive-slave law.

The one clear advantage gained by the South, a more stringent fugitive-slave law, quickly proved a mixed blessing. Because few slaves had been taken into the Mexican cession, the question of slavery there had a hypothetical quality. However, the issues raised by the new fugitive-slave law were far from hypothetical, because the law authorized real southerners to pursue real fugitives on northern soil. Here was a concrete issue to which the average northerner, who may never have seen a slave and who cared little about slavery a thousand miles away, would respond with fury.

Enforcement of the Fugitive Slave Act

Northern moderates accepted the Fugitive Slave Act as the price that the North had to pay to save the Union. But the law contained a string of features distasteful to moderates and outrageous to staunchly antislavery northerners. It denied alleged fugitives the right of trial by jury, did not allow them to testify in their own behalf, permitted their return to slavery merely on the testimony of the claimant, and enabled court-appointed commissioners to collect ten dollars if they ruled for the slaveholder but only five dollars if they ruled for the fugitive. In authorizing federal marshals to raise posses to pursue fugitives on northern soil, the law threatened to turn the North into "one vast hunting ground." In addition, the law targeted not only recent runaways but also those who had fled the South *decades* earlier. For example, it allowed slave-catchers in 1851 to wrench a former slave from his family in Indiana and return him to the master from whom he had fled in 1832. Above all, the law brought home to northerners the uncomfortable truth that the continuation of slavery depended on their complicity. By legalizing the activities of slave-catchers on northern soil, the law reminded northerners that slavery was a national problem, not merely a peculiar southern institution.

Antislavery northerners assailed the law as the "vilest monument of infamy of the nineteenth century." "Let the President . . . drench our land of freedom in blood," proclaimed Ohio's Whig congressman Joshua Giddings, "but he will never make us obey that law." His support for the law turned Senator Daniel Webster of Massachusetts into a villain in the eyes of the very people who for years had revered him as the "godlike Daniel." The abolitionist poet John Greenleaf Whittier wrote of his fallen idol:

> *All else is gone; from those giant eyes*
> *The soul has fled:*
> *When faith is lost, when honor dies,*
> *The man is dead.*

Advertisement for an Antislavery Play

This banner, promoting a spectacle of realistic scenes of slavery, illustrates the zeal and indignation of the antislavery movement.

Efforts to catch and return fugitive slaves inflamed feelings in both the North and the South. In 1854 a Boston mob, aroused by antislavery speeches, broke into a courthouse and killed a guard in an abortive effort to rescue the fugitive slave Anthony Burns. Determined to prove that the law could be enforced "even in Boston," President Franklin Pierce sent a detachment of federal troops to escort Burns to the harbor, where a ship carried him back to slavery. No witness would ever forget the scene. As five platoons of troops marched with Burns to the ship, some fifty thousand people lined the streets. As the procession passed, one Bostonian hung from his window a black coffin bearing the words "THE FUNERAL OF LIBERTY." Another draped an American flag upside down as a symbol that "my country is eternally disgraced by this day's proceedings." The Burns incident shattered the complacency of conservative supporters of the Compromise of 1850. "We went to bed one night old fashioned conservative Compromise Union Whigs," the textile manufacturer Amos A. Lawrence wrote, "and waked up stark mad Abolitionists." A Boston committee later successfully purchased Burns's freedom, but the fate of many fugitives was far less happy. One such unfortunate was Margaret Gaines, who, about to be captured and sent back to Kentucky as a slave, slit her daughter's throat and tried to kill her other children rather than witness their return to slavery.

In response to the Fugitive Slave Act, vigilance committees sprang up in many northern communities to spirit endangered blacks to safety in Canada. As another ploy, lawyers used obstructive tactics to drag out legal proceedings and thus raise the slave-catchers' expenses. Then during the 1850s, nine northern states passed "personal-liberty laws." By such techniques as forbidding the use of state jails to incarcerate alleged fugitives, these laws aimed to bar state officials from enforcing the law.

Northern resistance to the Fugitive Slave Act affected not only slaves who ran away from the South but also those who fled from masters visiting the North. In 1852 Juliet Lemmon of Virginia took eight of her slaves to New York City, where a judge set free all eight, on grounds that New York law prohibited slavery. In conjunction with the frequent cold stares, obstructive legal tactics, and occasional violence encountered by slaveholders who ventured north to capture runaways, incidents like this one helped demonstrate to southerners that opposition to slavery boiled only shallowly beneath the surface of northern opinion. In the eyes of most southerners, the South had gained little more from the Compromise of 1850 than the Fugitive Slave Act, and now doubts surrounded even that northern concession. After witnessing riots against the Fugitive Slave Act in Boston in 1854, a young Georgian studying law at Harvard wrote to his mother: "Do not be surprised if when I return home you find me a *confirmed disunionist.*"

Uncle Tom's Cabin

The publication in 1852 of Harriet Beecher Stowe's novel *Uncle Tom's Cabin* aroused wide northern sympathy for fugitive slaves. Stowe, the daughter of the famed evangelical Lyman Beecher and the younger sister of Catharine Beecher, the stalwart advocate of domesticity for women, greeted the Fugitive Slave Act with horror and outrage. In a memorable scene from the novel, she depicted the slave Eliza escaping to freedom, clutching her infant son while bounding across ice floes on the Ohio River. Yet Stowe targeted slavery itself more than

merely the slave-catchers who served the institution. Much of her novel's power derives from its intimation that even good intentions cannot prevail against so evil an institution. Torn from his wife and children by sale and shipped on a steamer for the Lower South, the black slave Uncle Tom rescues little Eva, the daughter of kindly Augustine St. Clare, from drowning. In gratitude, St. Clare purchases Tom from a slave-trader and takes him into his home in New Orleans. But after St. Clare's death, his cruel widow sells Tom to the vicious (and northern-born) Simon Legree, who whips Tom to death. Stowe played effectively on the emotions of her audience by demonstrating to an age that revered family life how slavery tore the family apart.

Three hundred thousand copies of *Uncle Tom's Cabin* were sold in 1852, and 1.2 million by the summer of 1853. Dramatized versions, which added dogs to chase Eliza across the ice, eventually reached perhaps fifty times the number of people as the novel itself. As a play, *Uncle Tom's Cabin* enthralled working-class audiences normally indifferent, if not hostile, to abolitionism. During one stage performance, a reviewer for a New York newspaper

Uncle Tom and Little Eva *(detail)*

The American public became familiar with Uncle Tom and Little Eva not only through Harriet Beecher Stowe's novel but also through paintings like this 1853 scene by the black artist Robert Stuart Duncanson.

observed that the gallery was filled with men "in red woollen shirts, with countenances as hardy and rugged as the implements of industry employed by them in the pursuit of their vocations." Astonished by the silence that fell over these men at the point when Eliza escapes across the river, the reviewer turned to discover that many of them were in tears.

The impact of *Uncle Tom's Cabin* cannot be precisely measured. Although the novel stirred deep feelings, it reflected the prevailing stereotypes of blacks far more than it overturned commonly held views. Stowe portrayed only light-skinned blacks as aggressive and intelligent; she depicted dark-skinned blacks such as Uncle Tom as docile and submissive. In addition, some of the stage dramatizations softened the novel's antislavery message. In one version, which P. T. Barnum produced, Tom was rescued from Legree and returned happily as a slave to his original plantation.

Surgery on the plot, however, could not fully excise the antislavery message of *Uncle Tom's Cabin.* Although the novel hardly lived up to the prediction of proslavery lawyer Rufus Choate that it would convert 2 million people to abolitionism, it did push many waverers toward a more aggressively anti-southern and antislavery stance. Indeed, fear of its impact inspired a host of southerners to pen anti–Uncle Tom novels. As historian David Potter has concluded, the northern attitude toward slavery "was never quite the same after *Uncle Tom's Cabin.*"

The Election of 1852

The issue of the enforcement of the Fugitive Slave Act fragmented the Whig party. The majority of northern Whigs, strongly supportive of free soil, had opposed the passage of the Fugitive Slave Act and now were leading defiance of the law. This increasingly vocal and potent northern free-soil wing put southern Whigs on the spot, for these southerners had long come before the southern electorate as the party best able to defend slavery within the Union.

The Whigs' nomination in 1852 of General Winfield Scott, the Mexican War hero, in place of the pro-compromise Millard Fillmore, widened the sectional split in their party. Although a Virginian, Scott had fallen under the influence of Senator William H. Seward of New York, a leader of the party's free-soil wing, and owed his nomination to northern votes. During the campaign Scott issued only a single, feeble endorsement of the Compromise of 1850, far less than southern Whigs needed if they were to brand the Democrats as the party of disunion and portray themselves as the party of both slavery and the Union.

The Democrats suffered from divisions of their own. In 1848 defectors from the Democratic party, led by Martin Van Buren, had formed the core of the Free-Soil party, which had gained over 10 percent of the popular vote. By 1852, however, most of the Free-Soilers of 1848, hungry for the spoils of office, returned to the Democratic party. As an idea rather than as a third party, free soil continued to win adherents between 1848 and 1852, but most converts to the idea of free soil gravitated to the Whig rather than the Democratic party.

The Democratic convention began as a three-sided struggle among Lewis Cass of Michigan, James Buchanan of Pennsylvania, and Stephen A. Douglas of Illinois but ended with the nomination of a dark horse, Franklin Pierce of New Hampshire. Handsome, charming, and friendly, Pierce had served in Congress and in the Mexican War. But his appeal to the Democrats rested less on his political experience or his undistinguished war record (during a battle near Mexico City, he had passed out after having been thrown from his horse) than on his acceptability to all factions of the party. The

The Election of 1852				
Candidates	Parties	Electoral Vote	Popular Vote	Percentage of Popular Vote
FRANKLIN PIERCE	Democratic	254	1,601,117	50.9
Winfield Scott	Whig	42	1,385,453	44.1
John P. Hale	Free-Soil		155,825	5.0

"ultra men of the South," a friend of Pierce noted, "say they can cheerfully go for him and none, none say they cannot." In both the North and the South, the Democrats rallied not only behind the Compromise of 1850 but behind the idea of applying popular sovereignty to *all* the territories. In the most one-sided election since 1820, Pierce swept twenty-seven of the thirty-one states and won the electoral vote 254–42. The outcome was particularly galling for southern Whigs, who had soared to new heights four years previously. Compared to the 49.8 percent of the popular vote in the South won by Zachary Taylor in 1848, in 1852, Scott could claim only 35 percent of the southern vote. In state elections during 1852 and 1853, moreover, the Whigs were devastated in the South; one Whig stalwart lamented "the decisive breaking-up of our party."

The Collapse of the Second Party System

Franklin Pierce had the dubious distinction of being the last presidential candidate for eighty years to win the popular and electoral vote in both the North and the South. Not until 1932 did another president, Franklin D. Roosevelt, repeat this accomplishment. Pierce was also the last president to hold office under the second party system—Whigs against Democrats. For two decades the Whigs and the Democrats had battled, often on even terms, in both national sections. Then, within the four years of Pierce's administration, the Whig party disintegrated. In its place two new parties, first the American ("Know-Nothing") party, and then the Republican party, arose.

Unlike the Whig party, the Republican party was a purely sectional, northern party. Its support came from former northern Whigs and from discontented northern Democrats. The Democrats survived as a national party, but with a base so shrunken in the North that in 1856, the Republican party, although scarcely a year old, swept two-thirds of the free states.

For decades the second party system had kept the conflict over slavery in check by giving Americans other issues—banking, internal improvements, tariffs, nativism, and temperance—to argue over. Support for banks, paper money, tariffs, and temperance had helped to unify northern and southern Whigs, while opposition to the Whigs on these issues bound northern and southern Democrats together. By the early 1850s, however, some of the issues that Whigs had long used to court voters in both sections had lost their clarity and urgency. This development exposed the Whigs' internal division over free soil as a raw wound. When Stephen A. Douglas in 1854 put forth a proposal to organize the vast Nebraska territory without restrictions on slavery, he ignited a firestorm that consumed the Whig party.

The Waning of the Whigs

Even before the conflagration created by Douglas's Nebraska bill, the Whig party's grip on its constituents was weakening. An economic boom from the late 1840s to the mid-1850s made the Whigs' policy of a high protective tariff seem unnecessary, because the boom occurred at a time when the *low* Walker Tariff of 1846 was in force. The Whigs also suffered from a severe miscalculation on immigration. The spectacular rise in immigration between 1845 and 1854 impaled the Whigs on the horns of a dilemma. Most immigrants settled in the North and voted Democratic. The Whigs could have responded to this fact either by continuing to align themselves with prohibition and nativism or by bidding for the immigrant (largely Catholic) vote. In 1844 and again in 1848, they had chosen the former strategy, but every year brought more immigrants and greater risks to Whigs who ignored the power of the immigrant vote. In the presidential campaign of 1852, New York Whig senator William H. Seward had tried to reverse his party's direction by touting the Whig Winfield Scott as sympathetic to Catholicism. Scott had allowed his daughters to attend a Catholic convent school, and during the Mexican War, he had been careful to respect property belonging to the Catholic church in Mexico. Seward's strategy backfired, however: Catholic immigrants continued to vote Democratic, and native-born Protestant Whigs were outraged by this softening of their party's anti-immigrant stand.

As the Whigs' traditional stands on the tariff and nativism lost their potency, the party was increasingly unable to disguise its internal split over slavery. Of the two parties—Whig and Democratic—the Whigs had the larger, more aggressive free-soil wing. By the early 1850s, the Fugitive Slave Act had widened the chasm between antislavery "Conscience" Whigs, such as senators Charles Sumner of Massachusetts and Benjamin Wade of Ohio, and the so-called Cotton Whigs, northern manufacturers and southern planters with a shared financial stake in cotton. Sumner's contemptuous description of the Cotton Whigs as an alliance of "the lords of the loom" and "the lords of the lash" underscored the Whig party split. Only the thinnest of threads held the Whig party together by 1852, and these would soon snap under the pressure of mounting conflict over the future of slavery in the Nebraska Territory.

The Kansas-Nebraska Act

Signed by President Pierce at the end of May 1854, the Kansas-Nebraska Act dealt a shattering blow to the already weakened second party system. Moreover, the law triggered a renewal of the sectional strife that many Americans believed that the Compromise of 1850 had buried. The origins of the act lay in the seemingly uncontroversial advance of midwestern settlement. Farm families in Iowa and Missouri had long dreamed of establishing homesteads in the vast prairies to their west, and their congressional representatives had repeatedly introduced bills to organize the territory west of these states, so that Indian land titles could be extinguished and a basis for government provided. Too, since the mid-1840s, advocates of national expansion had looked to the day when a railroad would link the Midwest to the Pacific; and St. Louis, Milwaukee, and Chicago had vied to become the eastern end of the projected Pacific railroad.

In January 1854 Senator Stephen A. Douglas of Illinois proposed a bill to organize Nebraska as a territory. An ardent expansionist, Douglas had formed his political ideology in the heady atmosphere of Manifest Destiny during the 1840s. As early as the mid-1840s, he had embraced the ideas of a Pacific railroad and the organization of Nebraska as ways in which to guarantee a continuous line of settlement between the Midwest and the Pacific. While he preferred a railroad from his home town of Chicago to San Francisco, Douglas dwelled on the national benefits that would attend

construction of a railroad from *anywhere* in the Midwest to the Pacific. Such a railroad would enhance the importance of the Midwest, which could then hold the balance of power between the older sections of the North and South and guide the nation toward unity rather than disruption. In addition, westward expansion through Nebraska with the aid of a railroad struck Douglas as an issue, comparable to Manifest Destiny, around which the contending factions of the Democratic party would unite.

Douglas recognized two sources of potential conflict over his Nebraska bill. First, some southerners advocated a rival route for the Pacific railroad that would start at either New Orleans or Memphis. Second, Nebraska lay within the Louisiana Purchase and north of the Missouri Compromise line of 36°30′, a region closed to slavery. Unless Douglas made some concessions, southerners would have little incentive to vote for his bill, because the organization of Nebraska would simultaneously create a potential free state and increase the chances for a northern, rather than a southern, railroad to the Pacific. As the floor manager of the Compromise of 1850 in the Senate, Douglas thought that he had an ideal concession to offer to the South. The Compromise of 1850 had applied the principle of popular sovereignty to New Mexico and Utah, territories outside of the Louisiana Purchase and hence unaffected by the Missouri Compromise. Why not assume, Douglas reasoned, that the Compromise of 1850 had taken the place of the Missouri Compromise *everywhere*? Believing that expansion rather than slavery was uppermost in the public's mind, Douglas hoped to avoid controversy over slavery by ignoring the Missouri Compromise. But he quickly came under pressure from southern congressmen, who wanted an explicit repudiation of the Missouri Compromise. Soon southerners forced Douglas to state publicly that the Nebraska bill "superseded" the Missouri Compromise and rendered it "void." Still under pressure, Douglas next agreed to a division of Nebraska into two territories: Nebraska to the west of Iowa, and Kansas to the west of Missouri. Because Missouri was a slave state, most congressmen assumed that the division aimed to secure Kansas for slavery and Nebraska for free soil.

The modifications of Douglas's original bill set off a storm of protest. Congressmen quickly

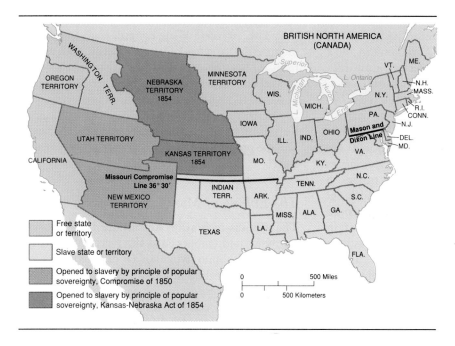

The Kansas-Nebraska Act, 1854

Kansas and Nebraska lay within the Louisiana Purchase, north of 36°30', and hence were closed to slavery until Stephen A. Douglas introduced his bills in 1854.

tabled the Pacific railroad (which, in the turn of events, would not be built until after the Civil War) and focused on the issue of slavery extension. A group of "Independent Democratic" northern congressmen, composed of Conscience Whigs and free-soil Democrats, assailed the bill as "part and parcel of an atrocious plot" to violate the "sacred pledge" of the Missouri Compromise and to turn Kansas into a "dreary region of despotism, inhabited by masters and slaves." Their rage electrified southerners, many of whom initially had reacted indifferently to the Nebraska bill. Some southerners had opposed an explicit repeal of the Missouri Compromise from fear of stimulating sectional discord; others doubted that Kansas would attract many slaveholders. But the furious assault of antislavery northerners united the South behind the Kansas-Nebraska bill by turning the issue into one of sectional pride as much as slavery extension.

Despite the uproar, Douglas successfully guided the Kansas-Nebraska bill through the Senate, where it passed by a vote of 37 to 14. In the House of Representatives, where the bill passed by little more than a whisker, 113 to 100, the true dimensions of the conflict became apparent. Not a single northern Whig representative in the House voted for the bill, while the northern Democrats divided evenly, 44 to 44.

The Surge of Free Soil

Douglas obviously had miscalculated the reaction to his Kansas-Nebraska bill. Amid the clamor over the bill, he conceded that he could now travel to Chicago by the light of his own burning effigies. Yet Douglas was neither a fool nor a political novice. Rather, he was the victim of a political force, the surge of feeling for free soil, that exploded under his feet.

Support for free soil united northerners who could agree on little else. Many northern free-soilers were racists who opposed letting any blacks, free or slave, into the West. In 1851 and 1853, racist free-soil advocates in Iowa and Illinois secured the passage of laws prohibiting settlement by black people; and in Iowa, Michigan, and Wisconsin, free-soilers refused by overwhelming majorities to allow blacks to vote. In Oregon, after rejecting slavery by a three-to-one majority in 1857, voters excluded all blacks from the state by an eight-to-one majority. But laws excluding blacks from western settlement were not always enforced, and not all free-soilers were racist. Some rejected slavery on moral grounds and opposed blatantly racist legislation. However, as the abolitionist George W. Julian accurately observed, the antislavery convictions of many westerners were grounded on a "perfect, if not supreme" hatred of blacks.

Although split over the morality of slavery, free-soilers agreed that slavery impeded whites' progress. Most free-soilers accepted Abraham Lincoln's portrayal of the North as a society of upwardly mobile farmers, artisans, and small businessmen and subscribed to the doctrine of "free labor"—the idea that in America, any enterprising individual could escape the class of wage labor and attain self-employment. "The man who labored for another last year," Lincoln insisted, "this year labors for himself, and next year he will hire others to labor for him." Because a slave worked for nothing, the free-soil argument ran, no free laborer could compete with a slave. A territory might contain only a handful of slaves or none at all, but as long as Congress refused to prohibit slavery in the territories, the institution could gain a foothold. Then slavery would grow, and free labor would wither; competition with slave labor would either drive out free labor or deter free labor from entering. Wherever slavery appeared, a free-soiler proclaimed, "labor loses its dignity; industry sickens; education finds no schools; religion finds no churches, and the whole land of slavery is impoverished."

Furthermore, free-soilers flatly rejected the idea that slavery had natural limits. As long as slaves could enter a territory, they believed, slaveholders would find tasks for them. In 1851 a free-soiler warned that "slavery is as certain to invade New Mexico and Utah, as the sun is to rise." By 1854 free-soilers were predicting that once secure in Kansas, slavery would invade the Minnesota Territory.

One free-soiler articulated the growing suspicions of many when he branded the Kansas-Nebraska Act "a part of a continuous movement of slaveholders to advance slavery over the entire North." At every turn, the free-soilers contended, the spread of slavery depended on the complicity of politicians. At the heart of the free-soil argument lay the belief that southern planters, southern politicians, and their northern dupes like Stephen A. Douglas were conspiring to spread slavery. And rather than any single event, there emerged a *pattern* of events—the Fugitive Slave Act, the repeal of the Missouri Compromise, and the Kansas-Nebraska division—that convinced free-soilers that a diabolical Slave Power was spreading its tentacles like an octopus. "I voted for the compromise measures of 1850, with the exception of the fugitive slave law," wrote a Whig congressman from Massachusetts, "and had little sympathy with abolitionists, but the repeal of the Missouri Compromise, that most wanton and wicked act, so obviously designed to promote the extension of slavery, was too much to bear. I now advocate the freedom of Kansas under all circumstances and at all hazards, and the prohibition of slavery in all territories now free."

The Ebbing of Manifest Destiny

The Kansas-Nebraska Act strained Democratic harmony and embarrassed the Pierce administration. The hubbub over the law doomed Manifest Destiny, the issue that had unified the Democrats in the 1840s.

Pierce had come to office as a champion of Manifest Destiny. In 1853 his emissary James Gadsden concluded a treaty with Mexico for the purchase of a strip of land south of the Gila River (now southern Arizona and part of southern New Mexico), an acquisition favored by advocates of a southern railroad route to the Pacific. The fiercely negative reaction to the so-called Gadsden Purchase, however, pointed up the mounting suspicions of expansionist aims. Encountering stiff northern opposition, Gadsden's treaty gained Senate approval in 1854 only after an amendment slashed nine thousand square miles from the purchase. Clearly, the same sectional rivalries that were brewing conflict over the existing territory of Nebraska were threatening to engulf proposals to gain *new* territory.

Pierce encountered even more severe buffeting when he tried to acquire the island of Cuba. Even as Congress was wrestling with the Kansas-Nebraska bill, Mississippi's former senator John A. Quitman was planning a massive filibustering (unofficial) military expedition—to seize Cuba from Spain. Pierce himself wanted to purchase Cuba and may have encouraged Quitman as a way to scare Spain into selling the island. However, northerners, aroused by the Kansas-Nebraska bill, increasingly viewed filibustering as another manifestation of the Slave Power's conspiracy to grab more territory for the "peculiar institution." Pierce, alarmed by northern reaction to the Kansas-Nebraska bill and by signs that Spain planned to defend the island militarily, forced Quitman to scuttle the planned expedition.

Pierce still hoped to purchase Cuba, but events quickly slipped out of his control. In October 1854 the American ambassadors to Great Britain, France, and Spain, two of them from the South, met in Belgium and issued the unofficial Ostend Manifesto, which called upon the United States to acquire Cuba by any necessary means, including force, and then to welcome the island "into that great family of states of which the Union is the Providential Nursery." Already beset by the storm over the Kansas-Nebraska Act, and faced by northern outrage at the threat of aggression against Spain, Pierce quickly repudiated the manifesto.

Despite the Pierce administration's opposition to the Ostend Manifesto, the idea of expansion into the Caribbean continued to attract southerners, including the Tennessee-born adventurer William Walker. Slightly built and so shy and unassuming that he usually spoke with his hands in his pockets, Walker seemed an unlikely soldier of fortune. Yet between 1854 and 1860, the year when he was executed by a firing squad in Honduras, Walker led a succession of filibustering expeditions into Central America. Taking advantage of civil chaos in Nicaragua, he made himself the chief political force in that nation, reinstituted slavery there, and talked openly of making Nicaragua a United States colony. Southern expansionists also kept the acquisition of both Cuba and parts of Mexico at the top of their agenda and received some support from northern Democrats. As late as 1859, President James Buchanan, Pierce's successor, tried to persuade Congress to appropriate funds for the purchase of Cuba.

For all of the proclamations and intrigues that surrounded the movement for southern expansion in the 1850s, the expansionists' actual strength and goals remained open to question. Many planned filibustering expeditions never got off the ground. With few exceptions the adventurers were shady characters whom southern politicians might admire but upon whom they could never depend. Moreover, a sizable body of southerners did not support the idea of southward expansion. The largely Whig sugar planters in Louisiana, for example, opposed acquiring Cuba, on grounds that once Cuba was annexed, its sugar would enter the United States duty-free and compete with American sugar.

Still, southern expansionists created enough commotion to worry antislavery northerners that the South aspired to establish a Caribbean slave empire. Like a card in a poker game, the threat of expansion southward was all the more menacing for not being played. As long as the debate over the extension of slavery focused on territories in the continental United States, slavery's prospects for expansion were limited and, Kansas aside, seemed fairly dim. If parts of the Caribbean were added to the United States, however, all these calculations would have to change.

The Rise and Fall of the Know-Nothings

While fracturing the harmony of the Democrats, the Kansas-Nebraska Act also wrecked the Whig party. In the immediate aftermath of the law, most northern Whigs hoped to blame the Democrats for the act, revive their fortunes in the North, and entice defectors from the free-soil Democrats to their side. In the state and congressional elections of 1854, the Democrats were drubbed, losing sixty-six congressional seats in the north. But the Whig party failed to benefit from the backlash against the Democrats. However disillusioned they were by the Kansas-Nebraska Act, few northern Democrats would align with their traditional Whig opponents, while many northern Whigs, mindful of southern Whig support for the Kansas-Nebraska Act, decided to quit the party. In the Midwest defecting Whigs and free-soil Democrats turned to a bewildering variety of new parties that bore such names as the Peoples', Independent, and Republican parties. "The Whig party, *as a party*, are completely disbanded," an Indiana Democrat wrote. "They have not *as a party*, brought out a single candidate."

In the traditional Whig strongholds of the Northeast, the new American, or Know-Nothing, party emerged as the principal alternative to the Whigs and Democrats. The Know-Nothings evolved out of a secret nativist organization, the Order of the Star-Spangled Banner, founded in 1849. (The party's popular name, Know-Nothing, derived from the standard response that members gave to inquiries about its activities: "I know nothing.") One of many such societies that mushroomed in response to the unprecedented immigration of the 1840s, the Order of the Star Spangled Banner had sought to rid the

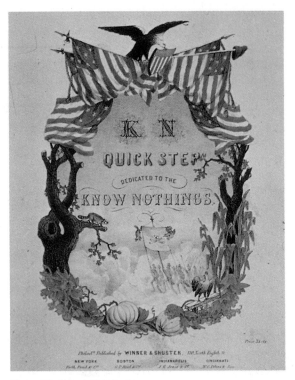

Know-Nothing Quickstep

By 1856, when the American (or Know-Nothing) party ran Millard Fillmore for president, the Know-Nothings had shed their secrecy to the point of commissioning party songs.

United States of immigrant and Catholic political influence by pressuring the existing parties to nominate only native-born Protestants to office and by advocating an extension of the naturalization period before immigrants could vote. Late in 1853 the order made inroads in politics as the American party. The Know-Nothings often astonished political observers by electing candidates whom the regular parties did not even know were running. The party received an additional boost when northern voters, disillusioned with the traditional parties over passage of the Kansas-Nebraska Act, turned to the Know-Nothings. In 1854 Know-Nothings captured the governorship, all the congressional seats, and almost all the seats in the state legislature in Massachusetts. By 1855 they controlled all of the New England states except Vermont and Maine and even made gains in Kentucky, Maryland, Missouri, and Texas.

Explaining the success of the Know-Nothings, one politician observed that the people "want a Paddy [Irish] hunt and on a Paddy hunt they will go." Indeed, hostility to immigrants and Catholics lay at the core of Know-Nothingism. Yet the Know-Nothings added some new dimensions to the long-standing nativist antagonism against Catholics and immigrants. Remembering the abortive attempt of some Whigs to court the Catholic vote in the election of 1852, the Know-Nothings trusted neither of the traditional parties. As Senator Charles Sumner of Massachusetts put it, "The people are tired of the old parties and they have made a new channel." Most Know-Nothing leaders were young, few were wealthy, and all dismissed the old parties as run by cliques of corrupt politicians. In addition, Know-Nothings stressed their opposition to the Slave Power and to slavery extension and presented themselves not only as anti-Catholic but also as antislavery. Indeed, an obsessive fear of conspiracies unified the Know-Nothings' stands on both Catholicism and slavery. Just as they declaimed against the pope for allegedly conspiring to subvert the American republic, they saw everywhere the evil influence of the Slave Power.

After rising spectacularly between 1853 and 1855, the star of Know-Nothingism nevertheless plummeted and gradually disappeared from the horizon after 1856. Various factors account for the Know-Nothings' failure to sustain their early success. First, the Know-Nothings proved as vulnerable as the Whigs and the Democrats to sectional splits over slavery. Although stronger in the North than in the South, the Know-Nothings developed a southern wing composed mainly of former Whigs, and in 1856 the northern and southern wings of the American party nominated different presidential candidates. Second, the former northern Whigs in search of an antislavery alternative to the Democrats found it impossible to reconcile the antislavery position of northern Know-Nothings with the latter's anti-Catholicism and nativism. One such Whig refugee, Illinois congressman Abraham Lincoln, asked pointedly: "How can anyone who abhors the oppression of negroes be in favor of degrading classes of white people?" We began by declaring, Lincoln continued, "that 'all men are created equal.' We now practically read it 'all men are created equal except negroes.' When the Know-

Nothings get control, it will read 'All men are created equal, except Negroes and foreigners and Catholics.'" Third, the secrecy of the Know-Nothings, which seemed as darkly conspiratorial as the very evils that Know-Nothings claimed to attack, also contributed to the party's demise. Finally, even success worked against the Know-Nothings, for once in office they proved unable to stop immigration or to suppress Catholicism, and soon they began to look like just another bunch of bumbling politicians.

The Republican Party

Even before the luster started to wear off Know-Nothingism, the Republican party, which sprang up in several states in 1854 and 1855, emerged as a refuge for antislavery voters. The new party was basically a coalition of "formers": former northern Whigs enraged at the southern Whigs' support for the Kansas-Nebraska Act; former northern Democrats dismayed by southerners' domination of their party; and in time, former Know-Nothings.

The need to harmonize these diverse constituencies forced Republican leaders into a juggling act. Because the Republican party contained a sizable group of former Democrats and former Whigs, issues like the tariff, banking, and internal improvements, which traditionally had divided Whigs and Democrats, had the potential to sever Republican unity. To maintain internal harmony during their early years, the Republicans thus usually ignored national economic issues. Similarly, anti-immigrant feeling and anti-Catholicism were potentially divisive issues for the new party. Many ex-Whig converts to the Republican party persisted in their anti-immigrant, anti-Catholic stance. But because the new party included former Democrats, the Republicans usually avoided public blasts at immigrants, who had traditionally voted Democratic. Even on the slavery issue, the Republican party held various shades of opinion in uneasy balance: at one extreme, conservatives who merely wanted to restore the Missouri Compromise; at the other, a small faction of former Liberty party abolitionists; and in the middle, a sizable body of free-soilers.

No single issue did more to unify the Republicans around their free-soil center and to build the new party's fortunes than the outbreak of violence in Kansas, which quickly gained for the territory the name Bleeding Kansas.

Bleeding Kansas

In the wake of the Kansas-Nebraska Act, Boston-based abolitionists had organized the New England Emigrant Aid Company to send antislavery settlers into Kansas. The abolitionists' aim was to stifle escalating efforts to turn Kansas into a slave state. But antislavery New Englanders arrived slowly in Kansas; the bulk of the territory's early settlers came from Missouri or elsewhere in the Midwest. Very few of these early settlers opposed slavery on moral grounds. Some, in fact, favored slavery; others wanted to keep all blacks, whether slave or free, out of Kansas. "I kem to Kansas to live in a free state," exclaimed a clergyman, "and I don't want niggers a-trampin' over my grave."

Despite most settlers' racist leanings and utter hatred of abolitionists, Kansas became a battleground between proslavery and antislavery forces. In March 1855 thousands of proslavery Missourian "border ruffians," led by Senator David R. Atchison, crossed into Kansas to vote illegally in the first election for a territorial legislature. Drawing and cocking their revolvers, they quickly silenced any judges who questioned their right to vote in Kansas. These proslavery advocates probably would have won an honest election, because they would have been supported by the votes both of slaveholders and of nonslaveholders horrified at rumors that abolitionists planned to use Kansas as a colony for fugitive slaves. But by stealing the election, the proslavery forces committed a grave tactical blunder. A cloud of fraudulence thereafter hung over the proslavery legislature subsequently established at Lecompton, Kansas. "There is not a proslavery man of my acquaintance in Kansas," wrote the wife of an antislavery farmer, "who does not acknowledge that the Bogus Legislature was the result of a gigantic and well planned fraud, that the elections were carried by an invading mob from Missouri." This legislature then further darkened its image by expelling several antislavery legislators and passing a succession of outrageous acts. These laws limited officeholding to individuals who would swear allegiance to slavery, punished the

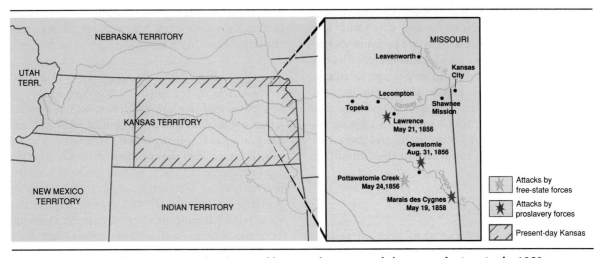

Bleeding Kansas *Kansas became a battleground between free-state and slave-state factions in the 1850s.*

harboring of fugitive slaves by ten years' imprisonment, and made the circulation of abolitionist literature a capital offense.

The legislature's actions set off a chain reaction. Free-staters, including a small number of abolitionists and a much larger number of settlers enraged by the proceedings at Lecompton, organized a rival government at Topeka, Kansas, in the summer and fall of 1855. In response, the Lecompton government in May 1856 dispatched a posse to Lawrence, where free-staters, heeding the advice of antislavery minister Henry Ward Beecher that rifles would do more than Bibles to enforce morality in Kansas, had taken up arms and dubbed their guns "Beecher's Bibles." Riding under flags emblazoned "SOUTHERN RIGHTS" and "LET YANKEES TREMBLE AND ABOLITIONISTS FALL," the proslavery posse tore through the town like a hell-bent mob. Although the intruders did not kill anyone, they burned several buildings and destroyed two free-state printing presses—enough to earn their actions in the Republican press as "THE SACK OF LAWRENCE."

The next move belonged to John Brown. The son of a Connecticut abolitionist, Brown had drifted through business failures, bankruptcy, and even a charge of embezzlement, sustained only by his belief that God had ordained his misfortunes to test him. The sack of Lawrence convinced Brown that God now beckoned him, in the words of a neighbor, "to break the jaws of the wicked." In late May Brown led seven men, including his four sons and his son-in-law, toward the Pottawatomie Creek near

Lawrence. Setting upon five men associated with the Lecompton government, they shot one to death and hacked the others to pieces with broadswords. Brown's "Pottawatomie massacre" struck terror into the hearts of southerners and completed the transformation of "bleeding Kansas" into a battleground between the South and the North. A month after the massacre, a South Carolinian living in Kansas wrote to his sister:

> *I never lie down without taking the precaution to fasten my door and fix it in such a way that if it is forced open, it can be opened only wide enough for one person to come in at a time. I have my rifle, revolver, and old home-stocked pistol where I can lay my hand on them in an instant, besides a hatchet and an axe. I take this precaution to guard against the midnight attacks of the Abolitionists, who never make an attack in open daylight, and no Proslavery man knows when he is safe in this Ter[ritory.]*

In Kansas popular sovereignty flunked its major test. Instead of quickly resolving the issue of slavery extension, popular sovereignty merely institutionalized the division over slavery by creating two rival governments, in Lecompton and Topeka. The Pierce administration then shot itself in the foot by denouncing the Topeka government and recognizing only its Lecompton rival. Pierce had forced northern Democrats into the awkward position of appearing to ally with the South in support of the fraudulently elected legislature at Lecompton. Nor did popular sovereignty keep the slavery issue out of national politics. On the day before the sack of Lawrence, Republican senator Charles Sumner of Massachusetts delivered a bombastic and wrathful speech, "The Crime Against Kansas," in which he verbally whipped most of the United States Senate for complicity in slavery and singled out Senator Andrew Butler of South Carolina for his choice of "the harlot, slavery" as his mistress and for the "loose expectoration" of his speech (a nasty reference to the aging Butler's tendency to drool). Sumner's oration stunned most senators. Douglas wondered aloud whether Sumner's real aim was "to provoke some of us to kick him as we would a dog in the street." Two days later a relative of Butler, Democratic representative Preston Brooks of South Carolina, strode into the Senate chamber, found Sumner at his desk, and struck him repeatedly with a cane. The hollow cane broke after five or six blows, but Sumner required stitches, experienced shock, and did not return to the Senate for three years. Brooks became an instant hero in the South, and the fragments of his cane were "begged as sacred relics." A new cane, presented to Brooks by the city of Charleston, bore the inscription "Hit him again."

Now "Bleeding Kansas" and "Bleeding Sumner" united the North. The sack of Lawrence, Pierce's recognition of the proslavery Lecompton government, and Brooks's actions seemed to clinch the Republican argument that an aggressive slaveocracy held white northerners in contempt. Abolitionists remained unpopular in northern opinion, but southerners were becoming even less popular than abolitionists. Northern migrants to Kansas coined a name reflecting their feelings toward southerners: "the pukes." Other northerners attacked the slaveholding migrants to Kansas as the "Missouri savages." By denouncing the Slave Power more than slavery itself, Republican propagandists sidestepped the issue of slavery's morality, which divided their followers, and focused on portraying southern planters as arrogant aristocrats and the natural enemies of the laboring people of the North.

The Election of 1856

The election of 1856 revealed the scope of the political realignments of the preceding few years. In this, its first presidential contest, the Republican party nominated John C. Frémont, the famed

"pathfinder" who had played a key role in the conquest of California during the Mexican War. The Republicans then maneuvered the northern Know-Nothings into endorsing Frémont. The southern Know-Nothings picked the last Whig president, Millard Fillmore, as their candidate, while the Democrats dumped Pierce for the seasoned James Buchanan of Pennsylvania. A four-term congressman and long an aspirant to the presidency, Buchanan finally secured his party's nomination because he had the good luck to be out of the country (as minister to Great Britain) during the furor over the Kansas-Nebraska Act. As a signer of the Ostend Manifesto, he was popular in the South: virtually all of his close friends in Washington were southerners.

The campaign quickly turned into two separate races—Frémont versus Buchanan in the free states and Fillmore versus Buchanan in the slave states. In the North the candidates divided clearly over slavery extension; Frémont's platform called for a congressional prohibition of slavery in the territories, while Buchanan pledged congressional "non-interference." In the South Fillmore appealed to traditionally Whig voters and called for moderation in the face of secessionist threats. But by nominating a well-known moderate in Buchanan, the Democrats undercut some of Fillmore's appeal. Although Fillmore garnered more than 40 percent of the popular vote in ten of the slave states, he carried only Maryland. In the North Frémont outpolled Buchanan in the popular vote and won eleven of the sixteen free states; if Frémont had carried Pennsylvania and either Illinois or Indiana, he would have won the election. As it turned out, Buchanan, the only truly national candidate in the race, secured the presidency.

The election yielded three clear conclusions. First, the American party was finished as a major national force. The Know-Nothings had made fools out of themselves by endorsing Frémont, widely (although incorrectly) rumored to be a Roman Catholic, and by nominating Fillmore, who had never even attended a meeting of a Know-Nothing lodge. In the wake of the election, most northern Know-Nothings went over to the Republicans, while the southerners who had voted for Fillmore were left without any real party home. Second, although in existence scarcely more than a year, lacking any base in the South, and running a political novice, the Republican party did very well. A purely sec-

The Election of 1856				
Candidates	Parties	Electoral Vote	Popular Vote	Percentage of Popular Vote
JAMES BUCHANAN	Democratic	174	1,832,955	45.3
John C. Frémont	Republican	114	1,339,932	33.1
Millard Fillmore	American	8	871,731	21.6

tional party had come within reach of capturing the presidency. Finally, as long as the Democrats could unite behind a single national candidate, they would be hard to defeat. To achieve such unity, however, the Democrats would have to find more James Buchanans—"doughface" moderates who would be acceptable to southerners and who would not drive even more northerners into Republican arms.

The Crisis of the Union

No one ever accused James Buchanan of impulsiveness or fanaticism. Although he disapproved of slavery, he believed that his administration could neither restrict nor end the institution. In 1860 he would pronounce secession a grave wrong, but he would again affirm that his administration could not stop it. Understandably, contemporaries hailed his election as a victory for moderation. Yet his administration encountered a succession of controversies, first over the famed *Dred Scott* decision of the Supreme Court, then over the proslavery Lecompton constitution in Kansas, next following a raid by John Brown on Harpers Ferry, Virginia, and finally concerning secession itself. Ironically, a man who sought to avoid controversy presided over one of the most controversy-ridden administrations in American history. Buchanan's problems arose less from his own actions than from the fact that the forces driving the nation apart were already spinning out of control by 1856. By the time of Buchanan's inauguration, southerners who looked north saw creeping abolitionism in the guise of free soil, while northerners who looked south saw an insatiable Slave Power. Once these images had taken hold in the minds of the American people, politicians like Buchanan had little room for maneuver.

The Dred Scott *Case*

Pledged to congressional "non-interference" with slavery in the territories, Buchanan had long looked to the courts for a judicious and nonpartisan resolution of the vexatious issue of slavery extension. A case that appeared to promise such a solution had been winding its way through the courts for years; on March 6, 1857, two days after Buchanan's inauguration, the Supreme Court handed down its decision in *Dred Scott* v. *Sandford*.

Dred Scott, a slave, had been taken by his master during the 1830s from the slave state Missouri into Illinois and the Wisconsin Territory, areas respectively closed to slavery by the Northwest Ordinance of 1787 and by the Missouri Compromise. After his master's death, Scott sued for his freedom on the grounds of his residence in free territory. A jury sided with Scott and set him free. On appeal, however, the Missouri supreme court overturned the jury's decision in 1852 and returned Scott to slavery. Subsequently, Scott's new owner moved to New York while leaving Scott in Missouri, a turn of events that encouraged Scott to sue in the federal courts (which had jurisdiction over suits brought by citizens of one state against those of another). In 1856 the case finally reached the Supreme Court.

The Court faced two key issues. Did Scott's residence in free territory during the 1830s make him free? Next, regardless of the answer to this question, did Scott, again enslaved in Missouri, have a right to sue in the federal courts? The Court could have resolved the case on narrow grounds by answering the second question in the negative, but Buchanan wanted a far-reaching decision that would deal with the broad issue of slavery in the territories.

In the end, Buchanan got the broad ruling that he sought, but one so controversial that it settled little. In the most important of six separate majority opinions, Chief Justice Roger B. Taney, a

James Buchanan

Polished, affable, and cosmopolitan, Buchanan loathed extremists and instinctively searched for the middle ground on every issue. It was his misfortune to be president at a time when the middle ground was disappearing.

seventy-nine-year-old Marylander whom Andrew Jackson had appointed to succeed John Marshall in 1835, began with the narrow conclusion that Scott, a slave, could not sue for his freedom. Then the thunder started. No black, whether a slave or a free person decended from a slave, could become a citizen of the United States, Taney continued. Next Taney whipped the thunderheads into a tornado. Even if Scott had been a legal plaintiff, Taney ruled, his residence in free territory years earlier did not make him free, because the Missouri Compromise, whose provisions prohibited slavery in the Wisconsin Territory, was *itself* unconstitutional. The compromise, declared Taney, violated the Fifth Amendment's protection of property (including slaves) from deprivation without due process of law.

Contrary to Buchanan's hopes, the decision touched off a new blast of controversy over slavery in the territories. The antislavery press flayed it as a "willful perversion" filled with "gross historical falsehoods." Taney's ruling gave Republicans more evidence that a fiendish Slave Power conspiracy gripped the nation. Although the Kansas-Nebraska Act had effectively repealed the Missouri Compromise, the Court's majority now rejected even the *principle* behind the compromise, the idea that Congress could prohibit slavery in the territories. Five of the six justices who rejected this principle were from slave states. The Slave Power, a northern paper bellowed, "has marched over and annihilated the boundaries of the states. We are now one great homogenous slaveholding community."

Like Stephen Douglas after the Kansas-Nebraska Act, President Buchanan now appeared as another northern dupe of the slaveocracy. Republicans restrained themselves from open defiance of the decision only by insisting that it did not bind the nation; Taney's comments on the constitutionality of the Missouri Compromise, they contended, amounted merely to *obiter dicta*, opinions unnecessary to settling the case.

Reactions to the decision underscored the fact that by 1857 no "judicious" or nonpartisan solution to slavery extension was possible. Anyone who still doubted this needed only to read the fast-breaking news from Kansas.

The Lecompton Constitution

While the Supreme Court wrestled with the abstract issues raised by the expansion of slavery, Buchanan sought a concrete solution to the gnawing problem of Kansas, where the free-state government at Topeka and the officially recognized proslavery government at Lecompton viewed each other with profound distrust. Buchanan's plan for Kansas looked simple: an elected territorial convention would draw up a constitution that would either permit or prohibit slavery; Buchanan would submit the constitution to Congress; Congress would then admit Kansas as a state.

Unfortunately, no sooner had Buchanan devised his plan than it began to explode in his face. Popular sovereignty, the essence of Buchanan's plan, demanded fair play, a scarce quality in Kansas. The territory's history of fraudulent elections left both sides reluctant to commit their fortunes to the polls. An election for a constitutional convention took place in June 1857, but free-staters, by now a majority in Kansas, boycotted the election on grounds that the proslavery side would rig it. Dominated by proslavery delegates, a constitutional convention then met and drew up a frame of government, the Lecompton constitution, that protected the rights of those slaveholders already living in Kansas to their slave property and provided for a referendum in which voters could decide whether to allow in more slaves.

The Lecompton constitution created a dilemma for Buchanan. A supporter of popular sovereignty, he had gone on record in favor of letting the voters in Kansas decide the slavery issue. Now he was confronted by a constitution drawn up by a convention that had been elected by less than 10 percent of the eligible voters, by plans for a referendum that would not allow voters to remove slaves already in Kansas, and by the prospect that the proslavery side would conduct the referendum no more honestly than it had others. Yet Buchanan had compelling reasons to accept the Lecompton constitution as the basis for Kansas's admission as a state. The South, which had provided him with 112 of his 174 electoral votes in 1856, supported the constitution. Buchanan knew, moreover, that only about two hundred slaves resided in Kansas, and he believed that the prospects for slavery in the remaining territories were slight. The contention over slavery in Kansas struck him as another example of how extremists could turn minor issues into major ones. To accept the constitution and speed the admission of Kansas as either a free state or a slave state seemed the best way to pull the rug from beneath the extremists and quiet the commotion in Kansas. Accordingly, in December 1857 Buchanan formally endorsed the Lecompton constitution.

Buchanan's decision provoked a bitter attack from Senator Stephen A. Douglas. What rankled Douglas and many others was that the Lecompton convention, having drawn up a constitution, then allowed voters to decide only whether more slaves could be brought into the territory. "I care not whether [slavery] is voted down or voted up," Douglas declared. But to refuse to allow a vote on the constitution itself, with its protection of existing slave property, smacked of a "system of trickery and jugglery to defeat the fair expression of the will of the people."

Even as Douglas broke with Buchanan, events in Kansas took a new turn. A few months after electing delegates to the convention that drew up the Lecompton constitution, Kansans had gone to the polls to elect a territorial legislature. So flagrant was the fraud in this election—one village with thirty eligible voters returned more than sixteen hundred proslavery votes—that the governor disallowed enough proslavery returns to give free-staters a majority in the legislature. After the drafting of the Lecompton constitution, this territorial legislature called for a referendum on the entire document. Where the Kansas constitutional convention's goal had been to restrict the choice of voters to the narrow issue of the future introduction of slaves, the territorial legislature sought a referendum that would allow Kansans to vote against the protection of existing slave property as well as the introduction of more slaves.

In December 1857 the referendum called earlier by the constitutional convention was held. Boycotted by free-staters, the constitution with slavery passed overwhelmingly. Two weeks later, in the election called by the territorial legislature, the proslavery side abstained, and the constitution went down to crushing defeat. Having already cast his lot with the Lecompton convention's election, Buchanan simply ignored this second election. But he could not ignore the obstacles that the division in Kansas created for his plan to bring Kansas into the Union under the Lecompton constitution. When he submitted the plan to Congress, a deadlock in the House forced him to accept a proposal for still another referendum. This time, Kansans were given the choice between accepting or rejecting the entire constitution, with the proviso that rejection would delay statehood. Despite the proviso, Kansans overwhelmingly voted down the constitution.

Not only had Buchanan failed to tranquilize Kansas, but he had alienated northerners in his own party. His support for the Lecompton constitution confirmed the suspicion of northern Democrats that the southern Slave Power pulled all the important strings in their party. Douglas became the hero of the hour for northern Democrats and even for some Republicans. "The bone and sinew of the Northern Democracy are with you," a New Yorker wrote to Douglas. Yet Douglas himself could take little comfort from the Lecompton fiasco, as his cherished formula of popular sovereignty increasingly looked like a prescription for civil strife rather than harmony.

The Lincoln-Douglas Debates

Despite the acclaim that he gained in the North for his stand against the Lecompton constitution, Douglas faced a stiff challenge in Illinois for re-election to the United States Senate. Of his Republican opponent, Abraham Lincoln, Douglas said: "I shall have my hands full. He is the strong man of his party—full of wit, facts, dates—and the best stump speaker with his droll ways and dry jokes, in the West."

Physically as well as ideologically, the two men formed a striking contrast. Tall (6′4″) and gangling, Lincoln once described himself as "a piece of floating driftwood." Energy, ambition, and a passion for self-education had carried him from the Kentucky log cabin where he was born in 1809 through a youth filled with odd occupations (farm laborer, surveyor, rail-splitter, flatboatman, and storekeeper) into law and politics in his adopted Illinois. There he had capitalized on westerners' support for internal improvements to gain election to Congress in 1846 as a Whig. Having opposed the Mexican War and the Kansas-Nebraska Act, he joined the Republican party in 1856.

Douglas was fully a foot shorter than the towering Lincoln. But his compact frame contained astonishing energy. Born in New England, Douglas appealed primarily to the small farmers of southern origin who populated the Illinois flatlands. To these and others, he was the "little giant," the personification of the Democratic party in the West. The campaign quickly became more than just another Senate race, for it pitted the Republican party's rising star against the Senate's leading Democrat and, thanks to the railroad and the telegraph, received unprecedented national attention.

Although some Republicans extolled Douglas's stand against the Lecompton constitution, to Lincoln nothing had changed. Douglas was still Douglas, the author of the infamous Kansas-Nebraska Act and a man who cared not whether slavery was voted up or down as long as the vote was honest. Opening his campaign with the "House Divided" speech ("this nation cannot exist permanently half slave and half free"), Lincoln reminded his Republican followers of the gulf that

still separated his doctrine of free soil from Douglas's popular sovereignty. Douglas dismissed the house-divided doctrine as an invitation to secession. What mattered to him was not slavery, which he viewed as merely an extreme way to subordinate an allegedly inferior race, but the continued expansion of white settlement. Like Lincoln, he wanted to keep slavery out of the path of white settlement. But unlike his rival, Douglas believed that popular sovereignty was the surest way to attain this goal without disrupting the Union.

The high point of the campaign came in a series of seven debates held from August 21 to October 15, 1858. The idea for the debates was floated by Lincoln, who hoped to gain by them public recognition, and accepted by Douglas, who viewed the encounters as a way of putting an end to Lincoln's practice of speaking in each Illinois town as soon as Douglas had left. The Lincoln-Douglas debates mixed political drama with the atmosphere of a festival. For the debate at Galesburg, for example, dozens of horse-drawn floats descended on the town from nearby farming communities. One bore thirty-two pretty girls dressed in white, one for each state, and a thirty-third, who dressed in black with the label "Kansas" and carried a banner proclaiming "THEY WON'T LET ME IN."

Douglas used the debates to portray Lincoln as a virtual abolitionist and advocate of racial equality. Both charges were calculated to doom Lincoln in the eyes of the intensely racist Illinois voters. In response, Lincoln affirmed that Congress had no constitutional authority to abolish slavery in the South, and in one debate he asserted bluntly that "I am not, nor ever have been in favor of bringing about the social and political equality of the white, and black man." However, fending off charges of extremism was getting Lincoln nowhere; so in order to seize the initiative, he tried to maneuver Douglas into a corner.

In view of the *Dred Scott* decision, Lincoln asked in the debate at Freeport, could the people of a territory lawfully exclude slavery? In essence, Lincoln was asking Douglas to reconcile popular sovereignty with the *Dred Scott* decision. Lincoln had long contended that the Court's decision rendered popular sovereignty as thin as soup boiled from the shadow of a pigeon that had starved to death. If, as the Supreme Court's ruling affirmed, Congress had no authority to exclude slavery from

Abraham Lincoln

Clean-shaven at the time of his famous debates with Douglas, Lincoln would soon grow a beard to give himself a more distinguished appearance.

Stephen A. Douglas

Douglas's politics were founded on his unflinching conviction that most Americans favored national expansion and would support popular sovereignty as the fastest and least controversial way to achieve it. Douglas's self-assurance blinded him to rising northern sentiment for free soil.

a territory, it seemingly followed that a territorial legislature created by Congress also lacked power to do so. To no one's surprise, Douglas replied that notwithstanding the *Dred Scott* decision, the voters of a territory *could* effectively exclude slavery simply by refusing to enact laws that gave legal protection to slave property.

Douglas's "Freeport doctrine" salvaged popular sovereignty but did nothing for his reputation among southerners, who preferred the guarantees of the *Dred Scott* decision to the uncertainties of popular sovereignty. While Douglas's stand against the Lecompton constitution had already tattered his reputation in the South ("he is already dead there," Lincoln affirmed), his Freeport doctrine stiffened southern opposition to his presidential ambitions.

Lincoln faced the problem throughout the debates that free soil and popular sovereignty, although distinguishable in theory, had much the same practical impact. Neither Lincoln nor Douglas doubted that popular sovereignty, if fairly applied, would keep slavery out of the territories. In order to keep the initiative and sharpen their differences, Lincoln shifted in the closing debates toward attacks on slavery as "a moral, social, and political evil." He argued that Douglas's view of slavery as merely an eccentric and rather unsavory southern custom would dull the nation's conscience and facilitate the legalization of slavery everywhere. But Lincoln compromised his own position by rejecting both abolition and equality for blacks.

Neither man scored a clear victory in argument, and the senatorial election itself settled no major issues. Douglas's supporters captured a majority of the seats in the state legislature, which at the time was responsible for electing United States senators. But despite the racist leanings of most Illinois voters, Republican candidates for the state legislature won a slightly larger share of the popular vote than did their Democratic rivals. Moreover, in its larger significance, the contest solidified the sectional split in the national Democratic party and made Lincoln famous in the North and infamous in the South.

John Brown's Raid

Although Lincoln explicitly rejected abolitionism, he often spoke of free soil as a step toward the "ultimate extinction" of slavery in the South. Predictably, many southerners ignored the distinction between free soil and abolition and concluded that Republicans and abolitionists were inseparable components of an unholy alliance against slavery. Indeed, to many southerners, the entire North seemed locked in the grip of demented leaders bent on civil war. One of the South's more articulate defenders of slavery, for example, equated the doctrine of the abolitionists with those of "Socialists, of Free Love and Free Lands, Free Churches, Free Women and Free Negroes—of No-Marriage, No-Religion, No-Private Property, No-Law and No-Government."

No single event did more to rivet this image of the North in southerners' minds than the raid in 1859 on the federal arsenal at Harpers Ferry, Virginia, by John Brown, the brooding religious zealot responsible for the Pottawatomie massacre in Kansas three years earlier. At the head of twenty-one

men, Brown seized the arsenal on October 16, 1859, in the hope of igniting a massive slave uprising, first in Virginia and then throughout the South. But Brown neglected to inform the slaves of his plans and even failed to provision his men with enough food to last a day. A detachment of federal troops, commanded by Lieutenant Colonel Robert E. Lee, quickly overpowered the raiders. Convicted of treason, Brown was hanged on December 2, 1859.

If this had been the whole story, southerners might have dismissed the raid as the act of an isolated lunatic. Captured correspondence, however, revealed that Brown, far from acting alone, had extensive ties to prominent northern abolitionists. These northerners had provided both moral and financial support for Brown's plan to invade Virginia, free the slaves, and "purge this land with blood." Any lingering southern doubts about the scope of the conspiracy vanished when parts of the North responded to Brown's execution with memorial services and tolling bells. Ralph Waldo Emerson exulted that Brown would "make the gallows as glorious as the cross," and William Lloyd Garrison proclaimed his support for "every slave insurrection at the South and in any slave country." Republicans, including Lincoln and Senator William Seward of New York, denounced Brown's raid, but southerners suspected that Brown's failure, rather than the deed itself, provoked the repudiation.

Although Brown had failed to start a slave insurrection, his abortive raid rekindled southern fears of slave uprisings. Every village church bell in the North that tolled in honor of Brown, a South Carolinian declared, "proclaims to the South the approbation of that village of insurrection and servile war." In the wake of Brown's raid and throughout 1860, rumors flew around the South of assorted slave plots to devastate the region. Vigilantes turned out to battle conspiracies that existed only in their own minds. For example, a horde of southern defenders mobilized to rout the thousands of abolitionists who were rumored to be conspiring to pillage northeastern Texas. In North Carolina white mobs raided an encampment of Irish canal workers said to be in league with the slaves. In various other incidents, vigilantes rounded up thousands of slaves, whipped some into confessing to nonexistent plots, and then lynched them. The hysteria played into the hands of the southern-rights extremists known as the fire-eaters. Indeed, this faction actively encouraged the witch hunt by

The Last Moments of John Brown
by Thomas Hovenden

By the day of his hanging, Brown had become a martyr in northern eyes. Although the artist showed Brown kissing a black child, in fact no blacks were present. On his way to the gallows, Brown handed a note to a guard predicting that "the crimes of this guilty land will never be purged away but with Blood."

spreading tales of slave conspiracies in the press so that southern voters would turn to them as alone able to "stem the current of Abolition."

Although southern fears of slave insurrections proved unfounded, nothing calmed those apprehensions. Nor did it make any difference to southerners that Seward and Lincoln denounced Brown's raid. Most southerners interpreted the evidence linking Brown to abolitionists as just the tip of an iceberg and concluded that the abolitionists themselves were mere agents of the Republican party. Had not the Republicans repeatedly assailed slavery and sought unconstitutionally to bar its expansion? Had not Seward spoken of an "irrepressible conflict" between freedom and slavery? The incident at Harpers Ferry, declared resolutions passed by the Tennessee legislature, was "the natural fruit of this treasonable 'irrepressible conflict' doctrine put forth by the great head of the Black Republi-

can party and echoed by his subordinates." In the final analysis, southerners contended, John Brown, abolitionists, and Republicans all rested their case on the same premise: that slaves were somehow an illegitimate form of property and that the South deserved only scorn for its "peculiar institution."

The South Contemplates Secession

Convinced that they were menaced not only by the eccentric William Lloyd Garrisons of the North but also by the Republican party that had swept two-thirds of the northern states in the election of 1856, southerners increasingly spoke of secession from the United States as their only recourse. "The South must dissever itself," a South Carolinian insisted, "from the rotten Northern element."

Southerners reached this conclusion gradually,

and often reluctantly. In 1850 few southerners could have conceived of transferring their political and emotional allegiances from the United States to some new nation. Relatively insulated from the main tide of immigration, southerners thought of themselves as the most American of Americans. The fire-eaters, many of whom ardently desired secession, by no means represented southern thought. But the events of the 1850s brought a growing number of southerners to the conclusion that the North had deserted the true principles of the Union. Southerners interpreted northern resistance to the Fugitive Slave Act and to slavery in Kansas as either illegal or unconstitutional, and they viewed headline-grabbing phrases like "irrepressible conflict" and "a higher law" as virtual declarations of war on the South. In southerners' eyes, it was the North, not the South, that had grown peculiar.

This sense of the North's deviance tinged reports sent home by southern visitors to the North during the 1850s. Southerners complained bitterly of the "impudence and want of politeness" of northern free blacks. A Mississippi planter could scarcely believe his eyes, for example, when he witnessed a group of northern free blacks refusing to surrender their seats to a party of white women. Abolitionist hecklers rankled southern lecturers in the North. When assured by their northern friends that such hostility to the South's institutions did not reflect the whole of northern opinion, southerners could only wonder why northerners kept electing Republicans to office. Southerners even began to question whether it was wise to allow southern youth to attend northern colleges, where their minds might be poisoned by descriptions of their slaveholding parents as "graceless barbarians." Southern visitors increasingly described their northern trips as ventures into "enemy territory" and "a totally different country."

In this context of fraying sectional ties, John Brown's raid had an electrifying effect on southern opinion. Thousands of southerners, a Richmond newspaper editor observed after the raid, "who, a month ago, scoffed at the idea of a dissolution of the Union as a madman's dream . . . now hold the opinion that its days are numbered, its glory perished." Another southerner proclaimed that the Brown incident had revealed "the width and depth of the abyss which renders asunder two nations, apparently one." A pamphlet published in 1860

embodied in its title the growing conviction of southerners that *The South Alone Should Govern the South*.

Viewed as a practical tactic to secure concrete goals, secession did not make a great deal of sense. Some southerners contended that secession would make it easier for the South to acquire more territory for slavery in the Caribbean; yet the South was scarcely united in desiring additional slave territory in Mexico, Cuba, or Central America. States like Alabama, Mississippi, and Texas contained vast tracts of unsettled land that could be converted to cotton cultivation far more easily than the Caribbean. Other southerners continued to complain that the North blocked the access of slaveholders to territories in the continental United States. But it is unclear how secession would solve this problem. If the South were to secede, the remaining continental territories would belong exclusively to the North, which could then legislate for them as it chose. Nor would secession stop future John Browns from infiltrating the South to provoke slave insurrections.

Yet to dwell on the impracticality of secession as a choice for the South is to miss the point. Talk of secession was less a tactic with clear goals than an expression of the South's outrage at the irresponsible and unconstitutional course that southerners viewed the Republicans as taking in the North. It was not merely that Republican attacks on slavery sowed the seeds of slave uprisings. More fundamentally, southerners believed that the North was treating the South as its inferior—indeed, as no more than a slave. "Talk of Negro slavery," exclaimed southern proslavery philosopher George Fitzhugh, "is not half so humiliating and disgraceful as the slavery of the South to the North." Having persuaded themselves that slavery made it possible for them to enjoy unprecedented freedom and equality, white southerners took great pride in their homeland. They bitterly dismissed Republican portrayals of the South as a region of arrogant planters and degraded white common folk. Submission to the Republicans, declared the Democratic senator Jefferson Davis of Mississippi, "would be intolerable to a proud people."

Nevertheless, as long as the pliant James Buchanan occupied the White House, southerners did no more than *talk* about secession. Once aware that Buchanan had declined to seek reelection, however, they anxiously awaited the election of 1860.

The Election of 1860

As a single-issue, free-soil party, the Republicans had done well in the election of 1856. To win in 1860, however, they would have to broaden their appeal in the North, particularly in states like Pennsylvania and Illinois that they had lost in 1856. To do so, Republican leaders had concluded, they needed to forge an economic program to complement their advocacy of free soil.

A severe economic slump following the so-called Panic of 1857 furnished the Republicans a fitting opening. The depression shattered more than a decade of American prosperity and thrust economic concerns to the fore. In response, in the late 1850s, the Republicans developed an economic program based on support for a protective tariff (popular in Pennsylvania) and on two issues favored in the Midwest, federal aid for internal improvements and the granting of free 160-acre homesteads to settlers out of publicly owned land. By proposing to make these homesteads available to immigrants who were not yet citizens, the Republicans went far to shed their nativist image that lingered from their early association with the Know-Nothings. Carl Schurz, an 1848 German political refugee who had campaigned for Lincoln against Douglas in 1858, now labored mightily to bring his antislavery countrymen over to the Republican party.

The Republicans' desire to broaden their appeal also influenced their choice of a candidate. At their convention in Chicago, they nominated Abraham Lincoln over the early front-runner, William H. Seward of New York. Although better known than Lincoln, Seward failed to convince his party that he could carry the key states of Pennsylvania, Illinois, Indiana, and New Jersey. (Rueful Republicans remembered that their presidential candidate John C. Frémont would have won in 1856 if he had carried Pennsylvania and one of the remaining three states.) Lincoln held the advantage not only of hailing from Illinois but also of projecting a more moderate image than Seward on the slavery issue. Seward's penchant for controversial phrases like "irrepressible conflict" and "higher law" had given him a radical image. Lincoln, in contrast, had repeatedly affirmed that Congress had no constitutional right to interfere with slavery in the South and had explicitly rejected the "higher law" doctrine. The Republicans now needed only to widen their northern appeal.

The Democrats, however, who still claimed to be a national party, had to bridge their sectional divisions. The *Dred Scott* decision and the conflict over the Lecompton constitution had weakened the northern Democrats and emboldened the southern Democrats. While Douglas desperately defended popular sovereignty against the free-soil doctrine, southern Democrats increasingly abandoned popular sovereignty for the crisp assurances of the *Dred Scott* decision. Heartened by Chief Justice Taney's ruling that Congress lacked the power to exclude slavery from the territories, many southerners now concluded that Congress had an obligation to safeguard slavery in any territory. In February 1860 Senator Jefferson Davis of Mississippi introduced a set of resolutions calling for the federal government to enforce the *Dred Scott* decision by actively protecting territorial slavery.

The Davis resolutions never stood a chance of adoption by Congress. Nevertheless, they embarrassed the Douglas Democrats. No northern Democrat could win an election on a platform calling for the congressional protection of slavery in the territories. As a Georgia Democrat opposed to the Davis resolutions commented: "Hostility to Douglas is the sole motive of the movers of this mischief. I wish Douglas defeated . . . , but I do not want him and his friends crippled or driven off. Where are we to get as many or as good men in the North to supply their places?"

The Democratic party's internal turmoil boiled over at its Charleston convention in the spring of 1860. Failing to force acceptance of a platform guaranteeing federal protection of slavery in the territories, the delegates from the Lower South stalked out. The convention adjourned to Baltimore, where a new fight broke out over the question of seating hastily elected, pro-Douglas slates of delegates from the Lower South states that had seceded from the Charleston convention. The decision to seat these pro-Douglas slates led to another walkout, this time by delegates from Virginia and other states in the Upper South. The remaining delegates nominated Douglas, while the seceders marched off to another hall in Baltimore and nominated Buchanan's vice president, John C. Breckenridge of Kentucky, on a platform calling for the

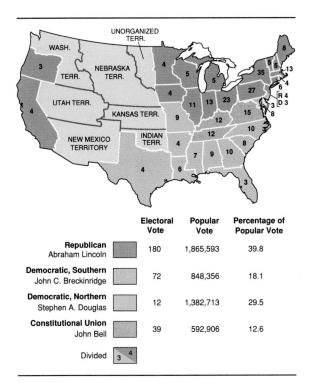

	Electoral Vote	Popular Vote	Percentage of Popular Vote
Republican Abraham Lincoln	180	1,865,593	39.8
Democratic, Southern John C. Breckinridge	72	848,356	18.1
Democratic, Northern Stephen A. Douglas	12	1,382,713	29.5
Constitutional Union John Bell	39	592,906	12.6
Divided	3 4		

The Election of 1860

congressional protection of slavery in the territories. Unable to rally behind a single nominee, the divided Democrats thus ran two candidates, Douglas and Breckenridge. The disruption of the Democratic party was now complete.

The South still contained an appreciable number of moderates, often former Whigs who had joined with the Know-Nothings behind Fillmore in 1856. In 1860 these moderates, aided by former northern Whigs who opposed both Lincoln and Douglas, forged the new Constitutional Union party and nominated John Bell, a Kentucky slaveholder who had opposed both the Kansas-Nebraska Act and the Lecompton constitution. Calling for the preservation of the Union, the new party took no stand on the divisive issue of slavery extension.

With four candidates in the field, voters faced a relatively clear choice. Lincoln conceded that the South had a constitutional right to preserve slavery but demanded that Congress prohibit its extension. At the other extreme, Breckenridge insisted that Congress had to protect slavery in any territory that contained slaves. This left the middle ground to Bell and Douglas, the latter still committed to popular sovereignty but in search of a verbal for-

mula that might reconcile it with the *Dred Scott* decision. Despite this four-way race, Lincoln won a clear majority of the electoral vote, 180 to 123 for his three opponents combined. Although Lincoln gained only 39 percent of the popular vote, his popular votes were concentrated in the North, the majority section, and were sufficient to carry every free state. Douglas ran a respectable second to Lincoln in the popular vote but a dismal last in the electoral vote. As the only candidate to campaign in both sections, Douglas suffered from the scattered quality of his votes and carried only Missouri. Bell won Virginia, Kentucky, and Tennessee, while Breckenridge captured Maryland and the Lower South.

The Movement for Secession

As the dust from the election settled, southerners faced a disconcerting fact: a man so unpopular among southerners that his name had not even appeared on the ballot in much of their section was now president. Lincoln's election struck most of the white South as a calculated northern insult. The North, a South Carolina planter told a visitor from England, "has got so far toward being abolitionized as to elect a man avowedly hostile to our institutions." Few southerners believed that Lincoln would fulfill his promise to protect slavery in the South, and most feared that he would act as a mere front man for more John Browns. "Now that the black radical Republicans have the power I suppose they will Brown us all," a South Carolinian lamented. An uneducated Mississippian residing in Illinois expressed his reaction to the election more bluntly:

> It seems the north wants the south to raise cotton and sugar rice tobacco for the northern states, also to pay taxes and fight her battles and get territory for the purpose of the north to send her greasy Dutch and free niggers into the territory to get rid of them. At any rate that was what elected old Abe President. Some professed conservative Republicans Think and say that Lincoln will be conservative also but sir my opinion is that Lincoln will deceive them. [He] will undoubtedly please the abolitionists for at his election they nearly all went into fits with Joy.

Some southerners had threatened secession at the prospect of Lincoln's election; now the moment

Charleston in the Secession Crisis, 1860–1861

After securing the nomination of Pennsylvania's James Buchanan for the presidency in 1856, northern Democrats made a conciliatory gesture to the South. They agreed to hold their party's 1860 convention in Charleston, South Carolina. Time would give northerners many opportunities to regret that gesture. Long in decline, with only a few overpriced hotels, Charleston offered little as a convention city. The supporters of Stephen A. Douglas had to convert the second floor of a meeting hall into a giant dormitory, where they slept in rows of beds and baked in one-hundred-degree heat. Far more troubling to the delegates who descended on the city in April 1860 was the hysteria that consumed Charleston in reaction to John Brown's raid on Harpers Ferry six months earlier. Mounted police, armed with swords and muskets, patrolled the streets, and vigilantes combed the byways in search of abolitionists. Panicked Charlestonians viewed every northerner in the city—whether a politician, a traveling salesman, or a schoolteacher—as "necessarily imbued with doctrines hostile to our institutions."

Suspicion and harassment greeted northern sojourners, but Charleston's blacks endured a virtual reign of terror after "the late outrage at Harpers Ferry." A little under half the city's population in 1860 was black, and 81 percent of the blacks were slaves. White southerners distrusted urban slaves, most of whom lived apart from their rural

Slave Badges

The badges that they were forced to wear constantly reminded Charleston's slaves of their bondage.

masters and were hired out to city employers. Indeed, some slaves took advantage of their distance from their masters to hire themselves out for wages, a practice that whites feared would infect slaves with the notion that they were free. In addition, white workingmen resented competition from urban slaves in the skilled trades, and they used the furor over John Brown's raid to pressure the city's mayor into enforcing an old and long-neglected ordinance that slaves working away from their masters wear badges. Those without badges were rounded up and jailed, and their masters fined.

Charleston's enslaved blacks were not the sole targets of the city's increasingly repressive mood. Few southern cities had more visible or well-organized communities of free blacks than Charleston. Composed mainly of mulattos who

took pride in their light skin and assembled in the Brown Fellowship Society, Charleston's free people of color formed a brown aristocracy of skilled tailors, carpenters, and small tradesmen. Free blacks like John Marsh Johnson worshiped in the same Episcopal church as such elite whites as Christopher G. Memminger, a prominent lawyer and politician who would soon become the Confederacy's secretary of the treasury. The financial prosperity of these free blacks depended on the white aristocrats who frequented their stores, admired their thrift and sobriety, and took comfort in their apparent loyalty. When a bill calling for the enslavement or expulsion of South Carolina's free blacks came before the state legislature in 1859, Memminger reminded the legislators that a free black had helped to expose Denmark Vesey's planned uprising of slaves back in 1822. Heartened by the support of Memminger and others, John Marsh Johnson congratulated himself for predicting "from the onset that nothing would be done affecting our position."

Johnson little realized the extent to which the world of Charleston's free blacks was in danger of falling apart. The city had been a center of southern-rights radicalism since the days of the nullification crisis. Charleston was the home of the fire-eater, Robert Barnwell Rhett; and it always rolled out the welcome carpet for Edmund Ruffin, a Virginia drumbeater for slavery. Further, after John Brown's raid, even moderate citizens, including former

Unionists, were embracing secession. The cause of secession demanded, in turn, that elite whites unite with working-class whites in a common front against the North. During the 1850s Charleston's working-class whites had grown increasingly powerful and aggressive; the increase in their numbers gave the city a white majority in 1860, for the first time in its history. Working-class whites feared competition from any blacks but had a special loathing for free blacks, who on Sundays dared "to draw up in fine clothes" and "wear a silk hat and gloves" and who celebrated weddings by drinking champagne and riding to the church in elegant carriages.

Soon free blacks became the victims of the growing cooperation between elite and working-class whites. Indeed, by August 1860 Charleston was in the grip of an "enslavement crisis." The same police dragnets that had snared urban slaves without badges now trapped innumerable free blacks as well. Unenslaved blacks suddenly had to prove that they were free, a tall order inasmuch as South Carolina had long prohibited the freeing of slaves. For decades white masters who wanted to free favored slaves had resorted to complicated legal

First Shots of the Civil War

Stunned Charleston residents crowded the city's rooftops to view the firing on Fort Sumter—a siege that lasted thirty-four hours.

ruses, with the result that many blacks who had lived for years as free people could not prove that they were free and were forced back into slavery. Abandoning his initial optimism, John Marsh Johnson wrote nervously to his brother-in-law to report "cases of persons who for 30 yrs. have been paying capitation Tax [as free persons of color] & one of 35 yrs. that have to go back to bondage & take out their Badges." Many other free African-Americans fled to the North.

A religious man, Johnson believed that God helped those who helped themselves. Rather than "supinely wait for the working of a miracle by having a Chariot let down to convey us away," he resolved in late August 1860 to stay and endure the "present calamity." By then, however, the Democratic party had snapped apart under the pressure of southern demands for the congressional recognition of slavery in all the territories. "The last party pretending to be a national party, is broken up," the secessionist Charleston *Mercury* exulted, "and the antagonism of the sections of the Union has nothing to arrest its fierce collision." In December 1860 another convention meeting in Charleston would proclaim South Carolina's secession from the United States. In April 1861, only a year after the Democratic delegates had assembled in Charleston for their party's convention, shore batteries along Charleston's harbor would open fire on Fort Sumter. This action set in motion a train of events leading to the extinction of slavery itself. Ironically, after the Civil War, the free blacks who had weathered the enslavement crisis of 1860 would emerge as the leaders of the city's black people, all of them now free.

View of Charleston, 1846, *by Henry Jackson*

Picturesque Charleston was home to many of South Carolina's most rabid secessionists.

of choice had arrived. On December 20, 1860, a South Carolina convention voted unanimously for secession; and by February 1, 1861, Alabama, Mississippi, Florida, Georgia, Louisiana, and Texas had followed South Carolina's lead (see "A Place in Time"). On February 4 delegates from these seven states met in Montgomery, Alabama, and established the Confederate States of America.

Despite the abruptness of southern withdrawal from the Union, the movement for secession had been, and continued to be, laced with uncertainty. Many southerners had resisted calls for immediate secession. Even after Lincoln's election, fire-eating secessionists had met fierce opposition in the Lower South from so-called cooperationists, who called upon the South to act in unison or not at all. Many cooperationists had hoped to delay secession in order to wring concessions from the North that might remove the need for secession. Jefferson Davis, who was inaugurated in February 1861 as the first president of the Confederacy, was a most reluctant secessionist, and he remained in the United States Senate for two weeks after his own state of Mississippi had seceded. Even zealous advocates of secession had a hard time reconciling themselves to secession and believing that they were no longer citizens of the United States. "How do you feel now, dear Mother," a Georgian wrote, "that *we* are in a foreign land?"

In the month after the establishment of the Confederate States of America, moreover, secessionists suffered stinging disappointments in the Upper South. Virginia, North Carolina, Tennessee, Arkansas, and the border slave states of Maryland, Kentucky, Delaware, and Missouri all rejected calls for secession. Various factors account for the Upper South's reluctance to embrace the movement. In contrast to the Lower South, which had a guaranteed export market for its cotton, the Upper South depended heavily on economic ties to the North, bonds that would be severed by secession. Further, with proportionately far fewer slaves than the Lower South, the states of the Upper South and the border states doubted the loyalty of their sizable nonslaveholding populations to the idea of secession. Virginia, for example, had every reason to question the allegiance to secession of its nonslaveholding western counties, which would soon break away to form Unionist West Virginia. Few in the Upper South could forget the raw nerve touched by the

Jefferson Davis

Davis brought an abundance of public experience to the Confederate presidency. Wounded in the Mexican War, he had served in the U.S. Senate, became secretary of war under President Franklin Pierce, and negotiated the Gadsden Purchase.

publication in 1857 of Hinton R. Helper's *The Impending Crisis of the South*. A nonslaveholding North Carolinian, Helper had described slavery as a curse upon poor white southerners and thereby questioned one of the most sacred southern doctrines, the idea that slavery rendered all whites equal. If secession were to spark a war between the states, moreover, the Upper South appeared to be the likeliest battleground. Whatever the exact weight assignable to each of these factors, one point is clear: the secession movement that South Carolina so boldly started in December 1860 seemed to be falling apart by March 1861.

The Search for Compromise

The lack of southern unity confirmed the long-standing belief of Lincoln and most Republicans that the secessionists' talk, and even their actions, contained more bluster than substance. Seward

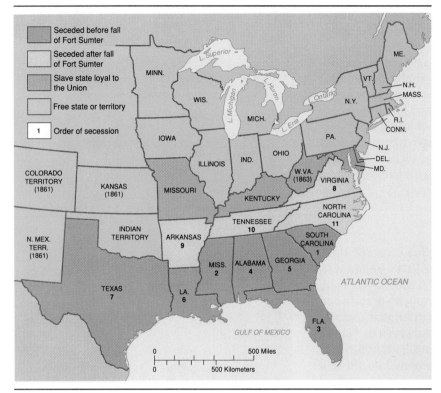

Seceded before fall of Fort Sumter

Seceded after fall of Fort Sumter

Slave state loyal to the Union

Free state or territory

1   Order of secession

Secession

Four key states—Virginia, Arkansas, Tennessee, and North Carolina—did not secede until after the fall of Fort Sumter. The border slave states of Maryland, Delaware, Kentucky, and Missouri stayed in the Union.

described secession as the work of "a relatively few hotheads," and Lincoln expected that the loyal majority of southerners would soon wrest the initiative from the fire-eating minority.

This perception among the Republicans stiffened their resolve to resist the compromises that some moderates were trying to forge. In the immediate wake of South Carolina's secession, Senator John J. Crittenden of Kentucky brought forth the most important of the compromises. Crittenden's plan included calls for the compensation of owners of runaway slaves, the repeal of the North's personal-liberty laws, a constitutional amendment to prohibit the federal government from ever interfering with slavery in the southern states, and another constitutional amendment that would restore the Missouri Compromise line for the remaining territories and guarantee federal protection of slavery below the line. This last amendment proved to be the sticking point. Lincoln stood firm against any abandonment of free soil. "On the territorial issue," he wrote to a southerner, "I am inflexible." In the face of steadfast Republican opposition, the Crittenden plan collapsed.

Lincoln's opposition to compromise rested partly on his belief that a loyal majority of southerners would soon overturn secession. The president-elect, however, almost certainly exaggerated the strength and dedication of southern Unionists. In reality, many of the southern opponents of the fire-eating secessionists were sitting on the fence and hoping for major concessions from the North; their allegiance to the Union was conditional, not unconditional. Lincoln can be faulted for his misreading of southern opinion. But even if his assessment had been accurate, it is unlikely that he would have accepted the Crittenden plan. Republicans viewed the plan as a surrender rather than a compromise, because it hinged on the abandonment of free soil, the principle on which the Republican party had been founded. In addition, as Lincoln well knew, some southerners still talked of seizing more territory for slavery in the Caribbean. In proposing to extend the 36°30′ line, the Crittenden plan specifically referred to territories "hereafter acquired," a veiled reference to future Caribbean expansion. If he were to accept the Crittenden compromise, Lincoln feared that it would be only a matter of time "till we shall have to take Cuba as a condition upon which they [the seceding states] will stay in the Union."

Beyond these considerations, the precipitous secession of the Lower South subtly changed the question that Lincoln faced. The issue was no longer slavery extension but secession. The Lower South had left the Union in the face of losing a fair election. For Lincoln to have caved in to such pressure would have violated majority rule, the principle upon which the nation, not just his party, had been founded.

The Coming of War

By the time that Lincoln took office in March 1861, little more than a spark was needed to ignite a war. Lincoln pledged in his inaugural address to "hold, occupy, and possess" federal property in the seven states that had seceded, an assertion that committed him to the defense of Fort Pickens in Florida and Fort Sumter in the harbor of Charleston, South Carolina. William Seward, whom Lincoln had appointed secretary of state, now became obsessed with the idea of conciliating the Lower South in order to hold the Upper South in the Union. In addition to advising the evacuation of federal forces from Fort Sumter, Seward proposed a scheme to reunify the nation by threatening a war with France and Spain. But Lincoln brushed aside Seward's advice. Instead, the president informed the governor of South Carolina of his intention to supply Fort Sumter with much-needed provisions, but not with men and ammunition. To gain the dubious military advantage of attacking Fort Sumter before the arrival of relief ships, Confederate batteries began to bombard the fort shortly before dawn on April 12. The next day, the fort's garrison surrendered.

Proclaiming an insurrection in the Lower South, Lincoln now appealed for seventy-five thousand militiamen from the loyal states to suppress the rebellion. His proclamation pushed citizens of the Upper South off the fence upon which they had perched for three months. "I am a Union man," one southerner wrote, "but when they [the Lincoln administration] send men south it will change my notions. I can do nothing against my own people." In quick succession, Virginia, North Carolina, Arkansas, and Tennessee leagued with the Confed-

Lincoln's First Inauguration

In his inaugural, Lincoln, in the shadow of the still unfinished Capitol dome, assured the South that he would not interfere with slavery in states where it existed, but he warned that "the central idea of secession is the essence of anarchy."

eracy. After acknowledging that "I am one of those dull creatures that cannot see the good of secession," Robert E. Lee resigned from the United States Army rather than lead federal troops against his native Virginia.

The North, too, was ready for a fight, less to abolish slavery than to punish secession. Worn out from his efforts to find a peaceable solution to the issue of slavery extension, and with only a short time to live, Stephen Douglas assaulted "the new system of resistance by the sword and bayonet to the results of the ballot-box" and affirmed: "I deprecate war, but if it must come I am with my country, under all circumstances, and in every contingency."

Conclusion   Thus during the 1850s the gap widened between northerners and southerners on the vexing issue of slavery extension. Popular sovereignty, which in 1850 struck many Americans as a practical solution to slavery in the territories, foundered in Kansas amid civil strife and turmoil over the Lecompton constitution. As support for popular sovereignty withered, sentiment for free soil gained ground in the North. In the South the *Dred Scott* decision provided judicial support for the position that Congress had to protect slavery in whatever territories it appeared.

Although the differences between northern and southern opinion on the slavery-extension issue sharpened and widened during the tempestuous decade, the two sections stood far apart by 1850. The Compromise of 1850 merely papered over an already considerable gulf. Decades of industrial expansion had convinced northerners of the value of free labor, a view that excluded competition with slaves. Yet decades of agricultural prosperity had persuaded southerners of the economic and moral value of slavery. The success of their system made southerners antagonistic to any suggestion that slave property was inferior to other property.

Despite this clear division by 1850, secession germinated for ten years before flowering. More than a broad disagreement over slavery in the territories was needed to push the South into secession. Before the South took that drastic step, it had to convince itself that the North aimed not merely to bar the spread of slavery but also to corrode the moral and political foundations of southern society. Several events persuaded the South that such was indeed the North's intention: northern fury over the Kansas-Nebraska bill, the emergence of the purely sectional Republican party, northern opposition to the *Dred Scott* decision, and John Brown's raid on Harpers Ferry. Once southerners came to believe that northern attacks on slavery's expansion were tactics in a wider campaign to reduce the South to subjection and "slavery," secession became a natural recourse.

As an expression of principled outrage, secession fittingly capped a decade in which each side had clothed itself in principles. The conflicts over principle that marked the 1850s were deeply embedded in the nation's political heritage. Both sides, North and South, laid claim to the ideals of the Constitution, but each understood those ideals differently. For northerners wedded to free soil, liberty meant an individual's freedom to pursue self-interest without competition from slaves. For white southerners, liberty meant their freedom to dispose of their legally acquired property as they saw fit. Similarly, both sides subscribed to the rule of law, which each accused the other of deserting. Northerners found evidence of southern treachery in the voting fraud that culminated in the Lecompton constitution. Southerners pointed to northern defiance of the Fugitive Slave Act and, later, of the *Dred Scott* decision, and to northern complicity in John Brown's raid. In the end, war broke out between siblings who, although they claimed the same inheritance, had become virtual strangers to each other.

CHRONOLOGY

1846 Wilmot Proviso.

1848 Treaty of Guadalupe Hidalgo ends Mexican War.
Free-Soil party formed.
Zachary Taylor elected president.

1849 California seeks admission to the Union as a free state.

1850 Nashville convention assembles to discuss the South's grievances.
Compromise of 1850.

1852   Harriet Beecher Stowe, *Uncle Tom's Cabin*.
Franklin Pierce elected president.

1853   Gadsden Purchase.

1854   Ostend Manifesto.
Kansas-Nebraska Act.
William Walker leads a filibustering expedition into Nicaragua.

1854–   Know-Nothing and Republican parties
1855   emerge.

1855   Proslavery forces steal the election for a territorial legislature in Kansas.
Proslavery Kansans establish a government in Lecompton.
Free-soil government established in Topeka, Kansas.

1856   The "Sack of Lawrence."
John Brown's Pottawatomie massacre.
James Buchanan elected president.

1857   *Dred Scott* decision.
President Buchanan endorses the Lecompton constitution in Kansas.
Panic of 1857.

1858   Congress refuses to admit Kansas to the Union under the Lecompton constitution.
Lincoln-Douglas debates.

1859   John Brown's raid on Harpers Ferry.

1860   Abraham Lincoln elected president.
South Carolina secedes from the Union.

1861   The remaining Lower South states secede.
Confederate States of America established.
Crittenden compromise plan collapses.
Lincoln takes office.
Firing on Fort Sumter; Civil War begins.
Upper South secedes.

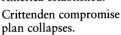

For Further Reading

Eric Foner, *Free Soil, Free Labor, Free Men: The Ideology of the Republican Party Before the Civil War* (1970). An outstanding analysis of the thought, values, and components of the Republican party.

Michael F. Holt, *The Political Crisis of the 1850s* (1978). A lively reinterpretation of the politics of the 1850s.

Allan Nevins, *The Ordeal of the Union* (vols. 1–2, 1947). A very detailed, highly regarded account of the coming of the Civil War.

David Potter, *The Impending Crisis, 1848–1861* (1976). The best one-volume overview of the events leading to the Civil War.

Additional Bibliography

The Compromise of 1850 and Its Aftermath

Stephen W. Campbell, *The Slave Catchers* (1968); Thomas F. Gossett, *Uncle Tom's Cabin and American Culture* (1985); Holman Hamilton, *Prologue to Conflict: The Crisis and Compromise of 1850* (1964); Thelma Jennings, *The Nashville Convention* (1980); Thomas D. Morris, *Free Men All: The Personal Liberty Laws of the North, 1780–1861* (1974); Chaplain W. Morrison, *Democratic Politics and Sectionalism: The Wilmot Proviso Controversy* (1967).

Political Realignment, 1852–1856

Carleton Beales, *Brass Knuckles Crusade: The Great Know-Nothing Conspiracy* (1961); Eugene Berwanger, *The Frontier Against Slavery: Western Anti-Negro Prejudice in the Slavery Extension Controversy* (1967); Ronald P. Formisano, *The Birth of Mass Political Parties: Michigan, 1827–1861* (1971); Michael F. Holt, *Forging a Majority: The Formation of the Republican Party in Pittsburgh* (1969); James A. Rawley, *Race and Politics: "Bleeding Kansas" and the Coming of the Civil War*

(1969); Geoffrey W. Wolff, *The Kansas-Nebraska Bill* (1977).

The South and the Sectional Crisis

Charles H. Brown, *Agents of Manifest Destiny: The Lives and Times of the Filibusterers* (1978); Avery Craven, *The Growth of Southern Nationalism, 1848–1861* (1953); Clement Eaton, *The Mind of the Old South* (1967); John Hope Franklin, *The Militant South, 1800–1861* (1970) and *A Southern Odyssey: Travelers in the Antebellum North* (1976); Michael P. Johnson and James L. Roark, eds., *No Chariot Let Down: Charleston's Free People of Color on the Eve of the Civil War* (1984); John McCardell, *The Idea of a Southern Nation: Southern Nationalists and Southern Nationalism, 1830–1861* (1979); Robert E. May, *The Southern Dream of a Caribbean Empire, 1854–1861* (1973); Rollin G. Osterweiss, *Romanticism and Nationalism in the Old South* (1949); Ronald L. Takaki, *A Proslavery Crusade: The Agitation to Reopen the African Slave Trade* (1971); J. Mills Thornton, *Politics and Power in a Slave Society* (1978).

The Disruption of the Union

William L. Barney, *The Road to Secession* (1972) and *The Secessionist Impulse* (1974); Steven A. Channing, *Crisis of Fear: Secession in South Carolina* (1970); Ollin-

ger Crenshaw, *The Slave States in the Presidential Election of 1860* (1969); David Donald, *Charles Sumner and the Coming of the Civil War* (1960); Don E. Fehrenbacher, *The Dred Scott Case* (1978) and *Prelude to Greatness: Lincoln in the 1850s* (1962); George B. Forgie, *Patricide in the House Divided: A Psychological Interpretation of Lincoln and His Age* (1979); Henry V. Jaffa, *Crisis of the House Divided: An Interpretation of the Lincoln-Douglas Debates* (1959); Robert W. Johannsen, *Stephen A. Douglas* (1973); Michael Johnson, *Secession and Conservatism in the Lower South: The Social and Ideological Bases of Secession in Georgia, 1860–1861* (1983); Albert J. Kirwan, *John J. Crittenden: The Struggle for the Union* (1962); Milton Klein, *President James Buchanan: A Biography* (1962); Paul C. Nagel, *One Nation Indivisible: The Union in American Thought* (1964); Allan Nevins, *The Emergence of Lincoln* (2 vols., 1950); Roy F. Nichols, *The Disruption of American Democracy* (1948); Stephen B. Oates, *To Purge This Land with Blood: A Biography of John Brown* (1970); David Potter, *Lincoln and His Party in the Secession Crisis* (1942); Elbert B. Smith, *The Presidency of James Buchanan* (1975); Kenneth Stampp, *And the War Came: The North and the Secession Crisis, 1860–1861* (1970); R. A. Wooster, *The Secession Conventions of the South* (1962).

CHAPTER 14

Reforging the Union:
Civil War, 1861–1865

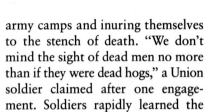

With the fall of Fort Sumter in April 1861, northerners and southerners rushed to arms. "They sing and whoop, they laugh: they holler to de people on de ground and sing out 'Good-bye,'" remarked a slave watching rebel troops depart. "All going down to die." Longing for the excitement of battle, the first volunteers enlisted with hopes of adventure and glory. Garish uniforms reflected their expectation of martial romance. Gaudiest of all were the northern Zouave regiments, whose members patterned their dress on that of French troops in North Africa, who, in turn, modeled their uniforms on a notion of what the Turks wore into battle: baggy red pantaloons, spotless white gaiters, and fezzes. Marching to war in dashing attire provided more than an outlet for romantic yearnings: it also gave boys a chance to act like men. A contemplative New Yorker, who sent two teen-aged sons to enlist, marveled how the war provided "so much manhood suddenly achieved." In their early letters home, victorious soldiers exulted over their transformation in battle. "With your first shot you become a new man," an Alabama volunteer wrote to his father. Neither volunteers nor politicians expected a long or bloody war. Most northern estimates ranged from one month to a year. Southerners also looked forward to a speedy war. One rebel could lick ten Yankees, southerners liked to think, because "the Yankee army is filled with the scum of creation."

These expectations of military glory and quick fame proved the first of many miscalculations. Actual battlefield experiences scarcely conformed to the early volunteers' rosy visions. For most soldiers, achieving manhood meant surviving in fetid army camps and inuring themselves to the stench of death. "We don't mind the sight of dead men no more than if they were dead hogs," a Union soldier claimed after one engagement. Soldiers rapidly learned the value of caution in battle. When "solid shot is cracking skulls like eggshells," a northern volunteer wrote, "the consuming passion is to get out of the way." You learn, a southerner wrote, to become "cool and deliberate."

These were the reactions of the lucky ones. One out of every five soldiers who fought in the Civil War died in it. The 620,000 American soldiers who lost their lives between 1861 and 1865 nearly equaled the number of American soldiers killed in all the nation's earlier and later wars combined. The war's gruesome destructiveness shattered politicians' expectations as well as soldiers' romantic visions. Once it became clear that the war could not be ended by a few battles, leaders on both sides contemplated strategies once unpalatable and even unthinkable. The South, where the hand of government had always fallen lightly on the citizenry, found that it had to draft men into its army and virtually extort supplies from its civilian population. By the end of the war, the Confederacy was even prepared to arm its slaves in an ironically desperate effort to save a society founded on slavery. The North, which began the war with the restricted objective of overcoming secession, and which explicitly disclaimed any intention of interfering with slavery, found that in order to win, it had to shred the fabric of southern society by destroying slavery. For politicians as well as soldiers, the war turned into a series of surprises.

Mobilizing for War

North and South alike were unprepared for war. In April 1861 the Union had only a small army of sixteen thousand men, scattered all over the country, mostly in the West. One-third of the officers of the Union army had resigned to join the Confederacy. The Union seemed to hang by a thread politically. The nation had not had a strong president since James K. Polk in the 1840s. Its new president, Abraham Lincoln, struck many observers as a yokel. That such a government could marshal its people for war seemed at best a doubtful proposition. The federal government had levied no direct taxes on its citizens for decades, and it had never drafted anyone into its army. Fortunately for the Union, the Confederacy was even less prepared, for it had no tax structure, no navy, only two tiny gunpowder factories, and poorly equipped, unconnected railroad lines.

During the first two years of the war, both sides would have to overcome these deficiencies, raise and supply large armies, and finance the heavy costs of war. In each region mobilization for war expanded the powers of the central government to an extent that few had anticipated.

Recruitment and Conscription

The Civil War armies were the largest organizations ever created in America; by the end of the war, over 2 million men would have served in the Union army and 800,000 in the Confederate army. In the first flush of enthusiasm for war, volunteers rushed to the colors. "I go for wiping them out," a Virginian wrote to his governor. A similar zest for enlistment engulfed the North. "Without seriously repressing the ardor of the people, I can hardly stop short of twenty regiments," the governor of Ohio informed Lincoln. "War! and volunteers are the only topics of conversation or thought," an Oberlin College student wrote to his brother in April 1861. "I cannot study. I cannot sleep. I cannot work, and I don't know as I can write."

At first, the raising of armies depended on local efforts rather than on national or even state direction. Citizens opened recruiting offices in their hometowns, held rallies, and signed up volunteers. "The walls are covered with placards from military companies offering inducements to recruits," a war

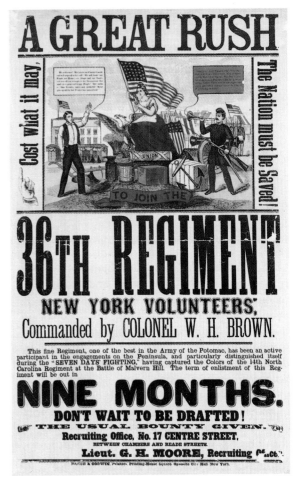

"A Great Rush"

This recruiting poster lured volunteers by promises of bounties and threats of the draft.

correspondent wrote from New York, where shops were "devoted to . . . rifles, pistols, swords, plumes, long boots, saddles, bridles, camp beds, canteens." As a consequence of this recruitment system, regiments were usually composed of soldiers from the same locale. Localism and voluntarism did not stop with the recruitment of troops. In the South cavalrymen were expected to provide their own horses, and uniforms everywhere were left mainly to local option. In both armies officers up to the rank of colonel were elected by other officers and enlisted men.

This informal and democratic way of raising and organizing soldiers conformed to the nation's political traditions. Americans had argued for generations that the freely given consent of the people, not the dictates of the government, could alone create an army in a republic. Because of its length and gruesome destructiveness, the Civil War would place insupportable stress on this tradition, however. As early as July 1861, the Union instituted examinations for officers, and its practice of electing officers gradually died out. In addition, as casualties mounted, military demand soon exceeded the supply of volunteers. Because nearly half of its 1861 volunteers had enlisted for only a year, the Confederacy felt the pinch first and in April 1862 enacted the first conscription law in American history. All able-bodied white males aged eighteen to thirty-five would be required to serve in the military for three years. Subsequent amendments raised the age limit to forty-five and then to fifty, and lowered it to seventeen.

The Confederacy's Conscription Act aroused little enthusiasm among southerners. Opponents charged that the draft was an assault on state sovereignty by a despotic regime and that the law would "do away with all the patriotism we have." Exemptions applied to many occupations, from religious ministry to shoemaking, and these angered the nonexempt. So did a loophole, closed in 1863, that allowed the well-off to purchase substitutes. Hostility also mounted over an amendment, the so-called 20-Negro law, that exempted an owner or overseer of twenty or more slaves from service. Although southerners widely feared that the slave population could not be controlled if all able-bodied white males were away in the army, the 20-Negro law evoked complaints about "a rich man's war but a poor man's fight."

Despite opposition, the Confederate draft became increasingly hard to evade, and this fact stimulated volunteering. Only one soldier in five was a draftee, but four out of every five eligible white southerners served in the Confederate army. In addition, a new conscription law, passed in 1864, required all soldiers then in the army to stay in for the duration of the war. This requirement ensured that a high proportion of Confederate soldiers would be battle-hardened veterans.

Once the army was raised, the Confederacy faced the challenge of supplying it. At first, the South lacked facilities to produce arms and ammunition and relied on imports from Europe, weapons confiscated from federal arsenals situated in the South, and guns captured on the battlefield. These stopgap measures bought time until an industrial base was established. By 1862 the Confederacy had a competent head of ordnance (weaponry), Josiah Gorgas. Working through Gorgas and other officials, the Confederacy assigned ordnance contracts to privately owned factories like the Tredegar Iron Works in Richmond, provided loans to establish new factories, and created government-owned industries like the giant Augusta Powder Works in Georgia, the largest in North America at the time. The South lost few, if any, battles for want of munitions.

The Confederacy was less successful in supplying its troops with clothing and food. Southern soldiers frequently went without shoes; during the South's invasion of Maryland in 1862, thousands of Confederate soldiers had to be left behind because they could not march barefoot on Maryland's macadamized roads. Late in the war, Robert E. Lee's Army of Northern Virginia ran out of food but never out of ammunition. The South's supply problems had several sources: railroads that fell into disrepair or were captured, an economy that relied more heavily on producing tobacco and cotton than growing food, and Union invasions early in the war that overran the livestock and grain-raising districts of central Tennessee and Virginia. Close to desperation, the Confederate Congress passed the Impressment Act in 1863, which authorized army officers to take food from reluctant farmers at prescribed rates. This law was even more unpopular than the Conscription Act, and farmers regarded impressment agents as legalized thieves. The same law empowered agents to impress slaves into labor for the army, a provision that provoked even more resentment. Slaveowners were willing to give up their relatives to military service, a Georgia congressman noted, "but let one of their negroes be taken and what a howl you will hear."

The industrial North could more easily supply its troops with arms, clothes, and food than could the South. However, keeping a full army was another matter. When the initial tide of enthusiasm for enlistment passed and the terms of the early recruits ended, Congress followed the Confederacy's example and turned to conscription. The Enrollment Act of March 1863 made every able-bodied white male citizen aged twenty to forty-five eligible for draft into the Union army.

Like the Confederate conscription law of 1862, the Enrollment Act granted exemptions, although only to high government officials, ministers, and

Union Forces

Total size ▮ 2,100,000

Total Draftees and Substitutes   164,000

Draftees ▮ 46,000

Substitutes ▮ 118,000

Total Desertions   200,000

Caught and returned ▮ 80,000

Total Deaths   360,000

Battle wounds ▮ 110,070

Disease ▮ 249,930

Confederate Forces

Total size ▮ 800,000

Total Draftees and Substitutes   190,000

Draftees ▮ 120,000

Substitutes ▮ 70,000

Total Desertions   104,000

Caught and returned ▮ 21,000

Total Deaths   258,000

Battle wounds ▮ 94,000

Disease ▮ 164,000

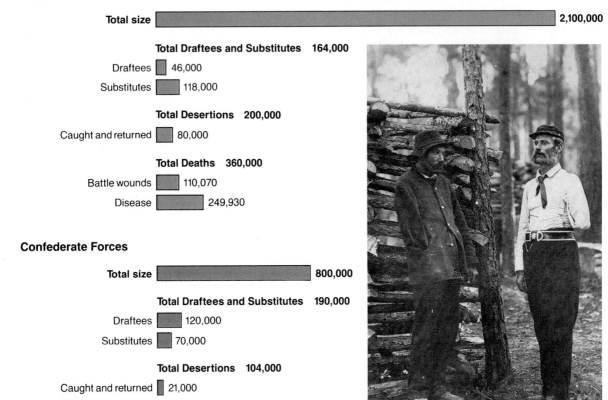

Total Civil War Deaths Compared to U.S. Deaths in Other Wars

Civil War ▮ 618,000

World War II ▮ 318,000

World War I ▮ 115,000

Vietnam War ▮ 56,227

Korean War ▮ 33,000

Mexican War ▮ 13,270

Spanish-American War and Philippine Insurrection ▮ 9,700

Revolutionary War ▮ 4,044

War of 1812 ▮ 2,200

The Civil War had profound human costs. North and South, there was hardly a family that did not grieve for a loved one or friend killed during the war. Armless or legless veterans were a common sight in American cities, towns, and rural districts well into our present century.

men who were the sole support of widows, orphans, or indigent parents. It also offered two means of escaping the draft: substitution, or paying another man who would serve instead; and commutation, paying a $300 fee to the government. To provide draft machinery, the law divided each state into enrollment districts and gave them quotas to meet, first through volunteers and then through the draft. The new system was difficult to administer and chaotic in practice. Enrollment districts often competed for volunteers by offering cash payments (bounties); dishonest "bounty jumpers" repeatedly registered and deserted after collecting their payment. And as in the South, conscription aroused opposition. Democrats denounced it as a violation of individual liberties and states' rights, while ordinary citizens of little means resented the commutation and substitution provision and leveled their own "poor man's fight" charges. Still, as the Confederates had learned, the law stimulated volunteering. Only 8 percent of Union soldiers were draftees or substitutes.

Financing the War

The recruitment and supply of huge armies lay far beyond the capacity of American public finance at the start of the war. During the 1840s and 1850s, annual federal spending had averaged only 2 percent of the gross national product.* With such meager expenditures, the federal government could meet its revenue needs from tariff duties and from income brought in by the sale of public lands. In fact, the government had not imposed any direct taxes on its citizens for thirty years. During the war, however, annual federal expenditures gradually rose to 15 percent of the gross national product, and the need for new sources of revenue became urgent. Yet even in the face of massive wartime expenditures, neither the Union nor the Confederacy initially showed much enthusiasm for imposing taxes. Aside from the fact that Americans were unaccustomed to paying taxes to their national government, both sides expected the war to be short, and neither wanted the knock of the tax collector

to dampen patriotic spirit. In August 1861 the Confederacy enacted a small property tax and the Union an income tax, but both measures were halfhearted, and neither raised much revenue. The Union's first income-tax law actually postponed collection until 1863.

Still needing revenue, both sides turned to war bonds; that is, to loans from citizens, to be repaid by future generations. The patriotic fervor of the early war years helped to sell these bonds. Southerners quickly bought up the Confederacy's first bond issue ($15 million) in 1861. That same year, a financial wizard, Philadelphia banker Jay Cooke, led a successful campaign to induce the northern public to subscribe to a much larger bond issue ($150 million). But in themselves bonds did not answer the requirements of wartime finance, because they had to be paid for in gold or silver coin (specie), which was in short supply. Soaking up most of its available specie, the South's first bond issue threatened to be its last, while in the North many hoarded their gold rather than spend it on bonds.

Recognizing the limitations of taxation and of bond issues, the Union and the Confederacy began to print paper money. Early in 1862 Lincoln signed into law the Legal Tender Act, which authorized the issue of $150 million of the so-called greenbacks. Christopher Memminger, the Confederacy's treasury secretary, and Salmon P. Chase, his Union counterpart, shared a distrust of paper money, but each came around to the idea because, as Chase bluntly put it, *"The Treasury is nearly empty."* The availability of paper money would make it easier to pay soldiers, to levy and raise taxes, and to sell war bonds. The Legal Tender Act not only authorized the issuance of the greenbacks but also provided for the emission of $500 million of war bonds purchasable with greenbacks.

Yet doubts about paper money lingered. Unlike gold and silver, which had established market values, the value of paper money depended mainly on the public's confidence in the government that issued it. To bolster that confidence, Union officials made the greenbacks legal tender (that is, acceptable in payment of most public and private debts) and then overcame their early reservations about taxes by imposing increasingly stiff taxes on everything from income to liquor, yachts, and billiard tables. The steady flow of tax revenue into the federal treasury strengthened public confidence in the government's ability to meet its obligations and helped

---

*Gross national product (GNP): the sum, measured in dollars, of all goods and services produced in a given year. By contrast, in the 1980s the federal budgets averaged about 25 percent of GNP.

to check the inflationary tendency inherent in paper money.

In contrast, the Confederacy never made its paper money legal tender, an omission that inevitably raised the suspicion that the southern government had little confidence in its own paper issues. To compound the problem, the Confederacy raised less than 5 percent of its wartime revenue from taxes. (The comparable figure for the North was 21 percent.) The Confederacy did enact a comprehensive tax measure in 1863, but Union invasions disrupted its ability to collect taxes. In addition, the South's relatively undeveloped system of internal transportation made tax collection a hit-or-miss proposition. For example, the Confederacy's tax measures of 1863 included a tax-in-kind, a sort of tithe. After feeding their families, farmers had to pledge one-tenth of their crops to the government. Because thousands of agents were sent to collect it, the tax-in-kind brought results, but it fell disproportionately on farmers who lived near the railroads traveled by tax collectors. Some of the food collected, moreover, rotted in government warehouses for want of transportation. To many farmers, it seemed that the Confederacy's tax policies were both unfair and incompetently administered.

In the face of the Confederacy's sorry performance in collecting taxes, confidence in the South's paper money quickly evaporated, and the value of Confederate paper in relation to gold plunged disastrously. The Confederacy responded by printing more paper money, a billion dollars of it by 1865, but this action merely accelerated southern inflation. While prices in the North rose about 80 percent during the war, the Confederacy suffered an inflation rate in excess of 9,000 percent. What cost a southerner one dollar in 1861 cost forty-six dollars by 1864.

By raising taxes, floating bonds, and printing paper money, both the Union and the Confederacy broke with the hard-money, minimal-government traditions of American public finance. For the most part, these changes occurred as unanticipated and often reluctant adaptations to wartime conditions. But in the North the Republicans took advantage of the departure of the southern Democrats from Congress to push through one measure that they and their Whig predecessors had long advocated, a system of national banking. In February 1863 Congress passed the National Bank Act over the concerted opposition of the northern Democrats. This law established criteria by which a bank could obtain a federal charter and issue national bank notes (notes backed by the federal government). One intended effect of the law was to give private bankers an incentive to purchase war bonds, because once a private bank had obtained a federal charter, it could issue national bank notes up to 90 percent of the value of the war bonds that it held.

The North's ability to revolutionize its system of public finance during the war reflected not only its longer experience with the complex financial transactions required by its industrial and commercial economy but also its greater political cohesion during the war.

Political Leadership in Wartime

The Civil War pitted rival political systems as well as armies and economies against each other. The South entered the war with several apparent political advantages. Lincoln's call for militiamen to suppress the rebellion had transformed hesitators in the South into tenacious secessionists. "Never was a people more united or more determined," a New Orleans resident wrote in the spring of 1861 to her brother-in-law, who was serving in Lincoln's cabinet. "There is but one mind, one heart, one action." Moreover, since the founding of the United States, the South had produced a disproportionate share of the nation's strong presidents: Washington, Jefferson, Madison, Monroe, Jackson, and Polk. Now President Jefferson Davis of the Confederacy, as a former war secretary and United States senator, possessed experience, honesty, courage, and what one officer described as "a jaw sawed in *steel*."

In contrast, the Union's list of political liabilities appeared lengthy. Loyal but contentious, northern Democrats wanted to prosecute the war without conscription, without the financial centralization represented by the National Bank Act, and without the abolition of slavery. Within the rival Republican party, Lincoln had trouble commanding respect. Unlike Davis, he had served in neither the cabinet nor the Senate, and his informal western manners inspired little confidence among eastern Republicans. Northern setbacks early in the war convinced most Republicans in Congress that Lincoln was an ineffectual leader. Vocal criticism of Lincoln sprang from a group of Republi-

President Abraham Lincoln

In this photo taken four days before Lincoln's assassination, the strains of the long wartime crisis show clearly on the president's face.

cans who became known as the Radicals and who included Secretary of the Treasury Salmon P. Chase, Senator Charles Sumner of Massachusetts, and Representative Thaddeus Stevens of Pennsylvania. The Radicals never formed a tightly knit cadre; on some issues they cooperated with Lincoln. But they did criticize him early in the war for failing to make the emancipation of the slaves a war goal and later for being too eager to readmit the conquered rebel states into the Union.

Lincoln's distinctive style of leadership encouraged and simultaneously disarmed opposition within the Republican party. Keeping his counsel to himself until ready to act, he met criticism with homespun anecdotes that caught his opponents off guard. The Radicals frequently concluded that Lincoln was a prisoner of the conservative wing of the party, while conservatives complained that Lincoln was too close to the Radicals. But Lincoln's cautious reserve had the dual benefit of leaving open his lines of communication with both wings of the party and fragmenting his opposition. Lincoln shrewdly brought several of his critics into

his cabinet, including Chase. Not only did Chase, once secure in the cabinet, moderate his criticism of the president, but he proved an excellent administrator.

In contrast, Jefferson Davis had a knack for making enemies. A West Pointer, he would rather have led the army than the government, and he used his sharp tongue to win arguments rather than to win over his foes. Davis's cabinet suffered from frequent resignations; the Confederacy had five secretaries of war in four years, for example. In particular, Davis's relations with his vice president, Alexander Stephens of Georgia, bordered on disastrous. A wisp of a man, Stephens weighed less than a hundred pounds and looked like a boy with a withered face. But he compensated for his slight physique with a tongue as acidic as Davis's. Leaving Richmond, the Confederate capital, in 1862, Stephens spent most of the war in Georgia, where he sniped at Davis as "weak and vacillating, timid, petulant, peevish, obstinate."

The conflict between Davis and Stephens involved not only a clash of personalities but also an ideological division, a rift, in fact, like that at the heart of the Confederacy. Although the Confederate Constitution, drafted in February 1861, resembled the United States Constitution in several ways, the southern charter explicitly guaranteed the sovereignty of the Confederate states and prohibited the Confederate Congress from enacting protective tariffs and from supporting internal improvements (measures long opposed by southern voters). For Stephens and other influential Confederate leaders—among them, governors Joseph Brown of Georgia and Zebulon Vance of North Carolina—the Confederacy existed not only to protect slavery but, equally important, to enshrine the doctrine of states' rights. (Brown condemned the Confederate Conscription Act as the most severe blow at constitutional liberty in American history.) In contrast, Davis's main objective was to secure the independence of the entire South from the North, a goal that frequently led him to override the wishes of state governors for the good of the Confederacy as a whole.

This difference between Davis and Stephens bore some resemblance to the discord between Lincoln and the northern Democrats. Like Davis, Lincoln believed that winning the war demanded an enhancement of the central government's power; like Stephens, northern Democrats resisted governmental centralization. But Lincoln could control his opponents more effectively than Davis, not only because, by temperament, he was more suited than Davis to conciliation but also because of the different nature of party politics in the two sections.

In the South the Democrats and the remaining Whigs agreed to suspend party rivalries for the duration of the war. However, this decision, made to promote southern unity, actually encouraged disunity. Without the institutionalization of conflict that party rivalry provided, southern politics tended to disintegrate along personal and factional lines. Lacking a party organization to back him, Davis could not mobilize votes to pass measures that he favored through the Confederate Congress, nor could he depend on the support of party loyalists throughout the slave states. In contrast, in the Union, northern Democrats' organized opposition to Lincoln tended to unify the Republicans. In the 1862 elections, which occurred at a low ebb of Union military fortunes, the Democrats won control of five large states, including Lincoln's own Illinois. Republican leaders drew the right conclusion from these Democratic gains: no matter how much they disdained Lincoln, they had to rally behind him or risk being driven from office by the Democrats. Ultimately, the Union would develop more political cohesion than the Confederacy, not because it had fewer divisions but because it managed its divisions more effectively.

Securing the Union's Borders

Even before large-scale fighting began, Lincoln moved swiftly to safeguard Washington, which was bordered by two slave states (Virginia and Maryland) and filled with Confederate sympathizers. A week after the firing on Fort Sumter, a Baltimore mob attacked a Massachusetts regiment bound for Washington, but enough troops slipped through to protect the capital. Lincoln then dispatched federal troops to Maryland, where he suspended the writ of habeas corpus*; in effect, federal troops could now arrest pro-secession Marylanders without formally charging them with specific offenses. Mind-

ful that strong Unionist sentiment flourished in the western part of the state, and cowed by Lincoln's bold moves, the Maryland legislature rejected secession. Delaware, another border slave state, quickly followed suit.

Next Lincoln authorized the arming of Union sympathizers in Kentucky, a slave state with a Unionist legislature, a secessionist governor, and a thin chance of staying neutral. Lincoln also stationed troops under General Ulysses S. Grant just across the Ohio River from Kentucky, in Illinois. When a Confederate army invaded Kentucky early in 1862, the state's legislature turned to Grant to drive it out. Officially, at least, Kentucky became the third slave state to declare for the Union. The fourth, Missouri, was ravaged by four years of fighting between Union and Confederate troops and between sundry bands of guerrillas and bushwackers, including William Quantrill, a Confederate desperado, and his murderous apprentices, Frank and Jesse James. Despite savage fighting and the divided loyalties of its people, Missouri never left the Union.[†]

By holding these four border slave states— Maryland, Delaware, Kentucky, and Missouri— in the Union, Lincoln kept open his lines to the free states and gained access to the river systems in Kentucky and Missouri that led into the heart of the Confederacy. (In 1862 invasions of the South by river would provide the North with most of its early military successes.) Lincoln's firmness, particularly in the case of Maryland, scotched charges that he was weak-willed, and it demonstrated how the crisis forced the president to exercise long-dormant powers. Although in the case *Ex parte* Merryman (1861), Chief Justice Roger B. Taney ruled that Lincoln had exceeded his authority in suspending the writ of habeas corpus in Maryland, the president, citing the Constitution's authorization of the writ's suspension in "Cases of Rebellion" (Article I, Section 9), insisted that he, rather than Congress, would determine whether a rebellion existed; and he ignored Taney's ruling.

---

*Habeas corpus: a court order requiring that the detainer of a prisoner bring the person in custody to court and show cause for his or her detention.

[†]Admitted to the Union in 1863, West Virginia became the fifth border state. This state originated in the refusal of thirty-five counties in the predominantly nonslaveholding region of Virginia west of the Shenandoah Valley to follow the state's leaders into secession in 1861.

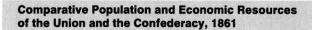

In Battle, 1861–1862

The Civil War was the first war to rely extensively on railroads, the telegraph, mass-produced weapons, joint army-navy tactics, iron-plated warships, rifled guns and artillery, and trench warfare. All of this lends some justification to its description as the first modern war. But to the participants, slogging through muddy swamps and weighed down with equipment, the war hardly seemed modern. In many ways, the soldiers had the more accurate perspective, for the new weapons did not always work, and both sides employed tactics that were more traditional than modern.

Armies, Weapons, and Strategies

Compared to the Confederacy's 9 million people, of whom over one-third were slaves, the Union had 22 million people in 1861. The North also had 3.5 times as many white men of military age, 90 percent of all U. S. industrial capacity, and two-thirds of its railroad track. Yet the Union faced a daunting challenge. Its goal was to force the South back into the Union, whereas the South was fighting merely for its independence. To subdue the Confederacy, the North would have to sustain offensive operations over an area comparable in size to the part of Russia that the French emperor Napoleon had invaded in 1812 with unforgettably disastrous results.

Measured against this challenge, the Union's advantages in population and technology shrank. The North had more men, but needing to defend long supply lines and occupy captured areas, it could commit a smaller proportion of them to frontline duty. The South, on the other hand, with black slaves as the basis of its labor force, could assign a higher proportion of its white male population to combat. As for technology, the North required, and possessed, superior railroads. Fighting defensively

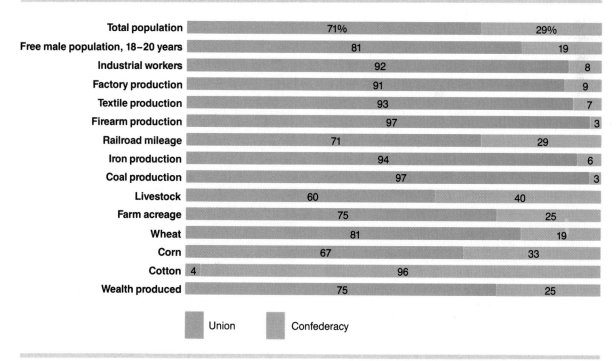

Comparative Population and Economic Resources of the Union and the Confederacy, 1861

	Union	Confederacy
Total population	71%	29%
Free male population, 18–20 years	81	19
Industrial workers	92	8
Factory production	91	9
Textile production	93	7
Firearm production	97	3
Railroad mileage	71	29
Iron production	94	6
Coal production	97	3
Livestock	60	40
Farm acreage	75	25
Wheat	81	19
Corn	67	33
Cotton	4	96
Wealth produced	75	25

At the start of the war, the Union enjoyed huge advantages in population, industry, railroad mileage, and wealth produced.

SOURCE: *The Times Atlas of World History* (New Jersey: Hammond, Inc., 1978).

Blacksmiths in Washington

These blacksmiths could shoe five hundred horses a day. Once finished with the horses, they would start on mules, of which the Union army had over one hundred thousand.

on so-called interior lines, the South could shift its troops relatively short distances within its defensive arc without relying on railroads, whereas the North had to move its troops and supplies huge distances around the exterior of the arc. To the North's disadvantage, not only could railroads easily be sabotaged by guerrillas, but once Union troops moved away from their railroad bases, their supply wagons often bogged down on wretched southern roads, which frequently became watery ditches in bad weather. Even on good roads, horses and mules, which themselves consumed supplies, were needed to pull wagons; an invading army of 100,000 men required 35,000 horses or mules. Finally, also to the Confederacy's benefit, southerners had an edge in soldiers' morale, for Confederate troops battled on home ground. "No people ever warred for independence," a Confederate general acknowledged, "with more relative advantages than the Confederates."

The Civil War witnessed experiments with a variety of newly developed weapons, including the submarine, the repeating rifle, and the multibarreled Gatling gun, the forerunner of the machine gun. Yet these futuristic innovations had less impact on the war than did the perfection in the 1850s of a bullet whose powder would not clog a rifle's spiraled internal grooves after a few shots. Like the smoothbore muskets that both armies had employed at the start of the war, most improved rifles had to be reloaded after each shot. But where the smoothbore musket had an effective range of only eighty yards, the Springfield or Enfield rifles widely employed by 1863 could hit targets accurately at four hundred yards.

The development of the rifle posed a challenge to long-accepted military tactics. The tactical manuals used at West Point in the 1840s and 1850s had identified the mass infantry charge against an opponent's weakest point as the key to victory. These manuals assumed that defenders armed with muskets would be able to fire only a round or two before being overwhelmed. The same assumption led tacticians to disdain trenches; against assaulting infantry, trenches would become mere traps for defenders. Armed with rifles, however, a defending force could fire several rounds before closing with the enemy. Attacking forces would now have far greater difficulty getting close enough to thrust bayonets; in fact, less than 1 percent of the casualties in the Civil War resulted from bayonet wounds.

Thus the rifle produced some changes in tactics during the war. Both sides gradually came to understand the value of trenches, which provided defenders with some protection against the withering fire of attacking forces. By 1865 trenches pockmarked the landscape in Virginia and Georgia. In addition, widening employment of the rifle forced generals to rely less on cavalry. Traditionally, the cavalry had ranked among the most prestigious components of an army, in part because cavalry charges were often devastatingly effective and in part because the cavalry helped to maintain

Life in the Field

The implements in this Union army–owned field surgical kit could remove bullets but not stop infection. The British-made five-shot revolver reached the South despite the Union blockade. A Confederate officer owned the brass-and-leather-adorned field glass.

The bullet-rent trousers belonged to a Union officer wounded at Peachtree Creek. Although he survived the war, he endured repeated operations in the remaining forty-five years of his life to remove tissue infected by the bullet.

class distinctions within the army. Indeed, at the start of the war, one of the clearest Confederate advantages lay in the quality of its cavalry. But rifles reduced the effectiveness of cavalry by increasing the firepower of foot soldiers. Bullets that might miss the rider would at least hit the horse. Thus as cavalry charges against infantry became more difficult, both sides adapted by relegating cavalry to reconnaissance missions and to raids on supply trains.

Although the rifle exposed traditional tactics to new hazards, by no means did it invalidate those tactics. The attacking army still stood an excellent chance of success if it achieved surprise. The South's lush forests provided abundant opportunities for an army to sneak up on its opponent. For example, at the Battle of Shiloh in 1862, Confederate attackers surprised and almost defeated a larger Union army despite the rumpus created by green rebel troops en route to the battle, many of whom fired their rifles into the air to see if they would work.

Achieving such complete surprise normally lay beyond the skill or luck of generals. In the absence of any element of surprise, disaster became a likely result for the attacking army. At the Battle of Fredericksburg in December 1862, Confederate troops inflicted appalling casualties on Union forces attacking uphill over open terrain, while at Gettysburg in July 1863, Union riflemen and artillery shredded charging southerners. But generals might still achieve partial surprise by hitting an enemy before it had concentrated its troops; in fact, this is what the North tried to do at Fredericksburg. Because surprise often proved effective, most generals continued to believe that their best chance of success lay in striking an unwary or weakened enemy with all the troops they could muster rather than in relying on guerrilla or trench warfare.

Much like previous wars, the Civil War was fought basically in a succession of battles during which exposed infantry traded volleys, charged, and countercharged. Whichever side withdrew from the field usually was thought to have lost the battle, but the losing side frequently sustained lighter casualties than the supposed victors. Both sides had trouble exploiting their victories, for neither had airplanes to hammer or tanks to envelop retreating columns. As a rule, the beaten army moved back a few miles from the field to lick its wounds; the winners stayed in place to lick theirs. Politicians on both sides denounced their generals as timorous fools for not pursuing a beaten foe, but these politicians rarely understood how difficult it was for a mangled victor to gather horses, mules, supply trains, and exhausted soldiers for a new attack. Until the end of the war, the only cases of entire armies actually surrendering arose from captured garrisons. Not surprisingly, for much of the war, generals on both sides concluded that the best defense was a good offense.

To the extent that the North had a long-range strategy in 1861, it lay in the so-called Anaconda plan. Devised by the Mexican War hero General Winfield Scott, the plan called for the Union to blockade the southern coastline and to thrust, like a huge snake, down the Mississippi River. Scott expected that this sealing off and severing of the Confederacy would make the South recognize the futility of secession and restore southern Unionists to power. The Anaconda plan promised a relatively bloodless end to the war, but Scott, himself a southern Unionist, exaggerated the strength of Unionist spirit in the South. Furthermore, although Lincoln ordered a blockade of the southern coast a week after the fall of Fort Sumter, the North hardly had the troops and naval flotillas to seize the Mississippi in 1861. Thus while the Mississippi remained an obvious objective, northern strategy did not unfold according to any blueprint like the Anaconda plan.

Early in the war, the pressing need to secure the border slave states, particularly Kentucky and Missouri, dictated Union strategy west of the Appalachian Mountains. Once in control of Kentucky, northern troops plunged southward into Tennessee. The Appalachians tended to seal this western theater off from the eastern theater, where the Confederacy's decision to move its capital from Montgomery, Alabama, to Richmond, Virginia, shaped the Union strategy. "Forward to Richmond" became the Union's first war cry.

Stalemate in the East

Before they could reach Richmond, one hundred miles southwest of Washington, Union troops would have to dislodge a Confederate army brazenly encamped at Manassas Junction, only twenty-five miles from the Union capital. Lincoln ordered General Irvin McDowell to attack his former West Point classmate, Confederate general P. G. T. Beauregard. "You are green, it is true," Lincoln told McDowell, "but they are green also; you are all green alike." In the resulting First Battle of Bull Run (or First Manassas),* amateur armies clashed in bloody chaos under a blistering July sun. The engagement was a spectacle that contrasted vividly with the picnicking of the well-dressed Washington dignitaries who had gathered to view the action. Aided by last-minute reinforcements and by the disorganization of the attacking federals, Beauregard routed the larger Union army.

After Bull Run, Lincoln replaced McDowell with General George B. McClellan as commander of the Union's Army of the Potomac. Another West Pointer, McClellan had served with distinction in the Mexican War and mastered the art of administration by managing various midwestern railroads in the 1850s. Few generals could match his ability to turn a ragtag mob into a disciplined fighting force. His soldiers adored him, but Lincoln quickly became disenchanted with his new commander. Lincoln believed that the key to a Union victory lay in simultaneous, coordinated attacks on several fronts. In this way, the North could exploit its advantage in manpower and resources and negate the South's advantage of interior lines. McClellan, a proslavery Democrat, hoped to maneuver the South into a relatively bloodless defeat and then negotiate a peace that would readmit the Confederate states with slavery intact.

McClellan soon got an opportunity to demonstrate the value of his strategy. After Bull Run,

---

*Because the North usually named battles after the nearest body of water and the South after the nearest town, many Civil War battles are known by two names.

the Confederates had pulled back behind the Rappahannock River and awaited the Union onslaught against Richmond. Rather than directly attack the Confederate army, McClellan formulated a plan in the spring of 1862 to move the Army of the Potomac by water to the tip of the peninsula formed by the York and James rivers and then move northwestward up the peninsula to Richmond. McClellan's plan had several advantages. Depending on water transport rather than on railroads (which Confederate cavalry could cut), the McClellan strategy reduced the vulnerability of northern supply lines. By dictating an approach to Richmond from the southeast, it threatened the South's supply lines. By aiming for the capital of the Confederacy rather than for the Confederate army stationed northeast of Richmond, finally,

McClellan hoped to maneuver the southern troops into a futile attack on his army in order to avert a destructive siege of Richmond.

By far the most massive military campaign in American history to that date, the Peninsula Campaign at first unfolded smoothly. Three hundred ships transported seventy thousand men and immense stores of supplies to the tip of the peninsula. Reinforcements soon swelled McClellan's army to one hundred thousand. Although Confederate reinforcements also poured into the peninsula, by late May McClellan was within five miles of Richmond.

If the war had been a chess game, McClellan would have become a grand master. But after luring the Confederacy to the brink of defeat, McClellan hesitated. Overestimating the Confed-

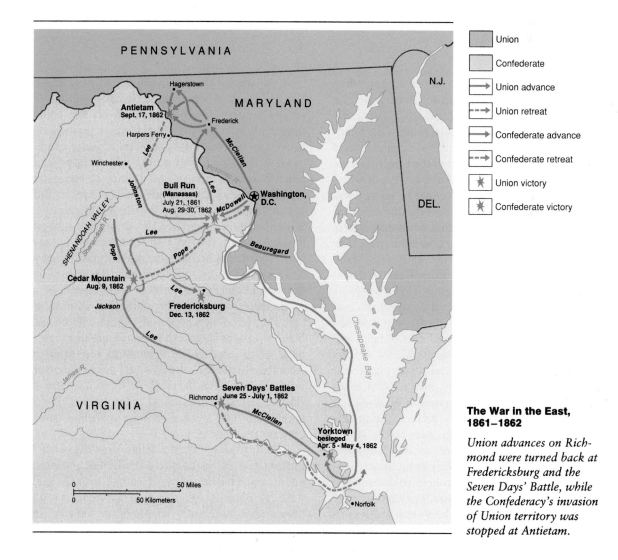

The War in the East, 1861–1862

Union advances on Richmond were turned back at Fredericksburg and the Seven Days' Battle, while the Confederacy's invasion of Union territory was stopped at Antietam.

Dead Soldiers at Antietam *These dead rebel gunners lie next to the wreckage of their battery at Antietam. The building, a Dunker church, was the site of furious fighting.*

erates' strength, he refused to launch a final attack on Richmond without the reinforcements that he expected, which were turned back by Confederate general Thomas "Stonewall" Jackson in the Shenandoah Valley. While McClellan delayed, General Robert E. Lee took command of the Confederacy's Army of Northern Virginia. An opponent of secession and so courteous that at times he seemed too gentle, Lee nevertheless possessed the qualities that McClellan most lacked, boldness and a willingness to accept casualties. Seizing the initiative, Lee attacked McClellan in late June. The ensuing Seven Days' Battles, fought in the forests east of Richmond, cost the South nearly twice as many men as the North and ended in a virtual slaughter of Confederates at Malvern Hill. But it was his own northern casualties that unnerved McClellan, and he began to send increasingly panicky reports to Washington. Lincoln, who cared little for McClellan's peninsula strategy, ordered McClellan to call off the campaign and return to Washington.

With McClellan out of the picture, Lee and his lieutenant, Stonewall Jackson, now boldly struck north and, at the Second Battle of Bull Run (Second Manassas), routed a Union army under General John Pope that had been held back from the peninsula to guard Washington. Lee's next stroke was even bolder. Crossing the Potomac River in early September 1862, he invaded western Mary-

land, where the forthcoming fall harvest could provide him with desperately needed supplies. By seizing western Maryland, moreover, Lee could threaten Washington, indirectly relieve pressure on Richmond, improve the prospects of peace candidates in the North's upcoming fall elections, and possibly induce Britain and France to recognize the Confederacy as an independent nation. But McClellan met Lee at the Battle of Antietam (or Sharpsburg) on September 17. Although a tactical draw, Antietam proved a strategic victory for the North, for Lee subsequently called off his invasion and retreated south of the Potomac. Heartened by the apparent success of northern arms, Lincoln then issued the Emancipation Proclamation, a war measure that freed all slaves under rebel control (see below). Talk of success, however, ignored the carnage of the twenty-four thousand casualties at Antietam that made it the bloodiest day of the entire war. A Union veteran recollected that one part of the battlefield contained so many bodies that a man could have walked through it without stepping on the ground.

Complaining that McClellan had "the slows," Lincoln faulted his commander for not pursuing Lee after the battle and replaced him with General Ambrose Burnside, who thought himself, and soon proved himself, unfit for high command. In December 1862 Burnside led 122,000 federal troops against 78,500 Confederates at the Battle of Fredericksburg. Burnside captured the town of Fredericksburg, northeast of Richmond, but then sacrificed his army in futile charges up the heights west of the town. Even Lee was shaken by the northern casualties. "It is well that war is so terrible—we should grow fond of it," he murmured to an aide during the battle. Richmond remained, in the words of a popular southern song, "a hard road to travel." The war in the East had become a stalemate.

The War in the West

The Union fared better in the West. Unlike the geographically limited eastern theater, the war in the West shifted over a vast and crucially important terrain that provided access to rivers leading directly into the South. The West also spawned new leadership. During the first year of war, an obscure Union general, Ulysses S. Grant, proved his competence. A West Point graduate, Grant had fought in the Mexican War and retired from the army in 1854 with a reputation for heavy drinking. He then had embarked on ventures in farming and in business, all of them dismal failures. When the Civil War began, he had gained an army commission through political pressure.

In 1861–1862 Grant retained control of two border states, Missouri and Kentucky. Moving into Tennessee, he captured two strategic forts, Fort Henry on the Tennessee River and Fort Donelson on the Cumberland. Grant then headed south to attack Corinth, Mississippi.

Corinth was a major railroad junction through which troops and supplies could be transported from the east to Memphis on the Mississippi River. In early April 1862, Confederate forces under generals Albert Sidney Johnston and P. G. T. Beauregard tried to relieve the Union pressure on Corinth by a surprise attack on Grant's army, encamped twenty miles north of the town, in southern Tennessee near a church named Shiloh. Hoping to whip Grant before the imminent arrival of twenty-five thousand Union reinforcements under General Don Carlos Buell, the Confederates exploded from the woods near Shiloh before breakfast and almost drove the federals into the Tennessee River. Beauregard cabled Richmond with news of a splendid Confederate victory. But Grant and his lieutenant, William T. Sherman, steadied the Union line. Buell's

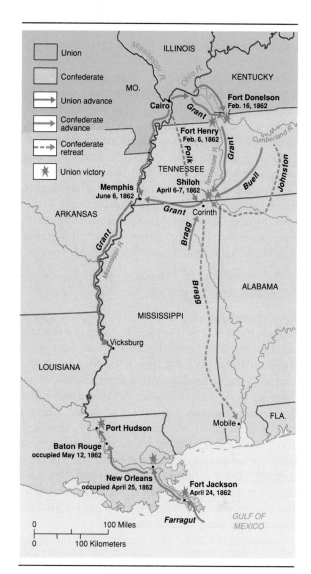

The War in the West, 1861–1862

By the end of 1862, the North held New Orleans and the entire Mississippi River except for the stretch between Vicksburg and Port Hudson.

reinforcements arrived in the night, and a Union counterattack drove the Confederates from the field the next day. Although Antietam would soon erase the distinction, the Battle of Shiloh was the bloodiest in American history to that date. Of the seventy-seven thousand men engaged, twenty-three thousand were killed or wounded, including Confederate general Albert Sidney Johnston, who bled to death from a leg wound. Defeated at Shiloh, the Confederates soon evacuated Corinth.

To attack Grant at Shiloh, the Confederacy had stripped the defenses of New Orleans, leaving only three thousand militia to guard its largest city. A combined Union land-sea force under General Benjamin Butler, a Massachusetts politician, and Admiral David G. Farragut, a Tennessean loyal to the Union, quickly capitalized on the opportunity. Blasting his way past two river forts south of New Orleans, Farragut took the city in late April and soon added Baton Rouge and Natchez to his list of conquests. Meanwhile, another Union flotilla moved down the Mississippi and captured Memphis in June. Now the North controlled the entire river, save for a two-hundred-mile stretch between Port Hudson, Louisiana, and Vicksburg, Mississippi.

Ironclads and Cruisers: The Naval War

By plunging its navy into the Confederacy like a dagger, the Union was exploiting one of its clearest advantages. The North began the war with over forty active warships against none for the South, and with the technology and industrial capacity to produce many more. Indeed, by 1865 the United States had the largest navy in the world. Steam-driven ships could penetrate the South's excellent river system from any direction and thereby turn a peacetime advantage into a wartime liability. For example, the Confederacy had stripped New Orleans's defenses in the belief that the real threat to the city would come from the north, only to find Farragut slipping in from the south.

Despite its size, the Union navy faced an extraordinary challenge in its efforts to blockade the South's thirty-five hundred miles of coast. Early in the war, small, sleek Confederate blockade-runners darted in and out of southern harbors and inlets with little chance of capture. The North gradually tightened the blockade by outfitting tugs, whalers, excursion steamers, and ferries as well as frigates to patrol southern coasts. The proportion of Confederate blockade-runners that made it through dropped from 90 percent early in the war to 50 percent by 1865. Even more than tightening the blockade, however, northern seizure of rebel ports and coastal areas shrank the South's foreign trade. In daring amphibious assaults during 1861 and 1862, the Union captured the excellent harbor of Port Royal, South Carolina, the coastal islands off South Carolina, and most of North Carolina's

river outlets. Naval patrols and amphibious operations contributed to a decline in the South's ocean trade to one-third its prewar level.

Although its resources were meager, the South made impressive efforts to offset the North's naval advantage. Early in the war, the Confederacy raised the scuttled Union frigate *Merrimac*, sheathed its sides with an armor of iron plate, rechristened it *Virginia,* and dispatched it to attack wooden Union ships in Hampton Roads, Virginia. The *Merrimac* quickly destroyed two northern warships but met its match in the hastily built Union ironclad the *Monitor.* In the first engagement of ironclads in history, the two ships fought an indecisive battle on March 9, 1862. The South constructed other ironclads and even the first submarine, which dragged a mine through the water to sink a Union ship off Charleston in 1864. Unfortunately, the "fish" failed to resurface and went down with its victim. But short of mechanics and iron-fabricating shops, the South could never build enough ironclads to overcome the North's supremacy in home waters. The Confederacy had more success

Deck of the *Monitor*

Although much smaller than its famous rival the Merrimac *(C.S.S. Virginia), the Union ironclad* Monitor *benefited from its shallow draft, speed, and maneuverability. Its flat, raftlike shape made it hard to hit.*

on the high seas, where wooden, steam-driven commerce raiders like the *Alabama* and the *Florida* (both built in England) wreaked havoc on the Union's merchant marine. Commerce raiding, however, would not tip the balance of the war in the South's favor, because the North, unlike its opponent, did not depend on imports for war materials. The South would ultimately lose the naval war.

The Diplomatic War

While armies and navies clashed in 1861–1862, conflict developed on a third front, diplomacy. At the outbreak of the war, the Confederacy began a campaign to gain European recognition of its status as an independent nation. Southern confidence in a swift diplomatic victory ran high. Planning to establish a colonial empire in Mexico, Napoleon III of France had grounds to welcome the permanent division of the United States. Moreover, the upper classes in France, and also in Britain, were widely viewed as sympathetic to the aristocratic South and eager for the downfall of the brash Yankee republic. Furthermore, for years such influential southerners as South Carolina's senator and governor James Henry Hammond had contended that an embargo of cotton exports would bring Britain to its knees. These southerners reasoned that Britain, dependent on the South for four-fifths of its cotton, would break the Union blockade and provoke a war with the North rather than watch its textile workers sink into revolutionary discontent under the weight of an embargo.

Leaving nothing to chance, the Confederacy in 1861 dispatched emissaries James Mason to Britain and John Slidell to France to lobby for recognition of the South as an independent nation. When a Union ship captain, acting without orders, boarded the British vessel the *Trent,* which was carrying Mason and Slidell, and brought the two men to Boston as prisoners, British tempers exploded. "You may stand for this," Britain's prime minister, Lord Palmerston, roared to his cabinet, "but damned if I will." But cooler heads soon prevailed. Recognizing that one war at a time was enough, President Lincoln released Mason and Slidell.

Settlement of the *Trent* affair did not eliminate friction between the United States and Britain. The construction in British shipyards of two Confederate commerce raiders, the *Florida* and the *Alabama,* evoked protests from Union diplomats. In 1863 the United States minister to London, Charles Francis Adams (the son of former president John Quincy Adams), threatened war if two British-built ironclads commissioned by the Confederacy, the so-called Laird rams, were turned over to the South. Armed with long spikes below the water, the powerful rams posed a genuine threat to the Union blockade of the South. Britain, however, capitulated to Adams's protests and purchased the rams for its own navy.

On balance, the South fell far short of its diplomatic objectives. While recognizing the Confederacy as a belligerent, neither Britain nor France ever recognized it as a nation. Basically, the Confederacy overestimated its hand. For several reasons, the South's vaunted "cotton diplomacy" failed dismally. The Confederate government talked of embargoing cotton exports in order to bring the British to their knees, but in reality, the government never controlled more than 15 percent of the South's cotton. Planters conducted business as usual by raising cotton and trying to slip it through the blockade. The South ultimately lost its share of the British market anyway; with 77 percent of that market in 1860, it held only 10 percent by 1865. But the South's declining share of the British cotton market resulted from forces beyond its control and yielded no political advantages. Bumper cotton crops in the late 1850s had glutted the British market by the start of the war and weakened British demand for cotton. In addition, Britain had responded to the threat of a cotton embargo by developing new suppliers in Egypt and India, thereby buffering itself from southern pressure. Gradually, too, the North's tightened blockade restricted southern exports.

The South also exaggerated Britain's stake in helping the Confederacy. As a naval power that had frequently blockaded its own enemies, Britain's diplomatic interest lay in supporting the Union blockade in principle; from Britain's standpoint, to help the South break the blockade would set a precedent that easily could boomerang. Finally, although France and Britain often talked of recognizing the Confederacy, the timing never seemed quite right. The Union's success at Antietam in 1862 and Lincoln's subsequent issuance of the Emancipation Proclamation dampened Europe's enthusiasm for recognition at a crucial juncture. By transforming the war into a struggle to end slavery, the Emancipation Proclamation produced an upsurge of pro-Union feeling in antislavery Britain, particularly among liberals and the working class. Workingmen in Manchester, England, wrote Lincoln to praise his resolve to free the slaves and to reassure him of "our warm and earnest sympathy." The proclamation, wrote Henry Adams (diplomat Charles Francis Adams's son) from London, "has done more for us here than all of our former victories and all our diplomacy."

Emancipation Transforms the War

"I hear old John Brown knocking on the lid of his coffin and shouting 'Let me out! Let me out!'" abolitionist Henry Stanton wrote to his wife after the fall of Fort Sumter. "The Doom of Slavery is at hand." In 1861 this prediction seemed wildly premature. In his inaugural address that year, Lincoln had stated bluntly, "I have no purpose, directly or indirectly, to interfere with the institution of slavery in the states where it exists." Yet in the space of two years, the North's priorities underwent a decisive transformation. A mixture of practical necessity and ideological conviction thrust the emancipation of the slaves to the forefront of northern war goals.

The rise of emancipation as a Union war goal reflected the changing character of the war itself. As late as July 1862, General George McClellan had written to Lincoln to restate his conviction that "neither confiscation of property . . . or forcible abolition of slavery should be contemplated for a moment." As the struggle dragged on, however, demands for the prosecution of "total war" intensified in the North. Even northerners who saw no moral value in abolishing slavery were starting to recognize the military value of emancipation as a technique to cripple the South's resources.

From Confiscation to Emancipation

Union policy on emancipation developed in stages. As soon as northern troops began to invade the South, questions arose about the disposition of captured rebel property, including slaves. Slaves who fled behind the Union lines were sometimes considered "contraband"—enemy property liable to seizure—and were put to work for the Union army. Whereas some northern commanders viewed this practice a useful tool of war, others did not, and the Lincoln administration was evasive. To establish an official policy, Congress in August 1861 passed the first Confiscation Act, which authorized the seizure of all property used in military aid of the rebellion, including slaves. By the terms of this act, slaves who had been employed directly by the Confederate armed services and who later fled to freedom became "captives of war." But nothing in the act actually freed these contrabands, nor did the law apply to contrabands who had not worked for the Confederate military.

Several factors underlay the Union's cautious approach to the confiscation of rebel property. Officially maintaining that the South's rebellion lacked any legal basis, Lincoln argued that southerners were thus still entitled to the Constitution's protection of property. The president also had practical reasons to walk softly. The Union not only contained four slave states but also held a sizable body of proslavery Democrats who flatly opposed turning the war into a crusade against the South's social institutions. If the North in any way tampered with slavery, these Democrats feared, "two or three million semi-savages" might come north and compete with white workers. Mindful of the considerable northern opposition to turning a limited policy of confiscation into a general program of emancipation, Lincoln assured Congress in December 1861 that the war would not become a "remorseless revolutionary struggle."

From the start of the war, however, Lincoln faced pressure from the loosely knit but determined Radical Republicans to adopt a policy of emancipation. Radicals hailed the war as a second American Revolution, one that would abolish slavery. Many subscribed to Pennsylvanian Thaddeus Stevens's urging that the Union "free every slave— slay every traitor—burn every Rebel mansion, if these things be necessary to preserve this temple of freedom." Radicals agreed with black abolitionist Frederick Douglass that "to fight against slaveholders without fighting against slavery, is but a half-hearted business."

With every new northern setback, support for the Radicals' point of view grew. Each Union military defeat reminded northerners that the confederacy, with a slave labor force in place to harvest southern crops and run southern factories, could commit a higher proportion of its white men to battle. As a measure conducive to total war, the idea of emancipation thus gained increasing favor in the North, and in July 1862 Congress passed the second Confiscation Act. This law authorized the seizure of the property of all persons in rebellion and stipulated that slaves who came within Union lines "shall be forever free." Finally, the law opened the door to blacks' military service by authorizing the president to employ blacks as soldiers.

Nevertheless, Lincoln continued to stall, even in the face of rising pressure for emancipation. "My paramount object in this struggle *is* to save the Union, and is *not* either to save or destroy slavery," Lincoln told antislavery journalist Horace Greeley. "If I could save the Union without freeing *any* slave, I would do it, and if I could save it by freeing *all* the slaves, I would do it; and if I could save it by freeing some and leaving others alone, I would also do that." Yet Lincoln had always loathed slavery, and by the spring of 1862, he had come around to the Radical position that the war must lead to the abolition of slavery. He hesitated principally because he did not want to be stampeded by Congress into a measure that might disrupt northern unity and because he feared that a public commitment to emancipation in the summer of 1862, on the heels of the northern defeat at Second Manassas and the collapse of the Peninsula Campaign, might be interpreted as an act of frantic desperation. After failing to persuade the Union slave states to emancipate slaves in return for federal compensation, he drafted a proclamation of emancipation, circulated it within his cabinet, and waited for a right moment to issue it. Finally, after the Union victory in September 1862 at Antietam, Lincoln issued the Preliminary Emancipation Proclamation, which declared all slaves under rebel control free as of January 1, 1863. Announcing the plan in advance softened the surprise, tested public opinion, and gave the states still in rebellion an opportunity to preserve slavery by returning to the Union—an opportunity that none, however, took. The final Emancipation Proclamation, issued on January 1, declared "forever free" all slaves in areas in rebellion.

The proclamation had limited practical impact. Applying only to rebellious areas, where the Union had no authority, it exempted the Union slave states and those parts of the Confederacy then in Union hands (Tennessee, West Virginia, southern Louisiana, and sections of Virginia). Moreover, it mainly restated what the second Confiscation Act had already stipulated: if rebels' slaves fell into Union hands, those slaves would be free. Yet the proclamation was a brilliant political stroke. By issuing it as a military measure, in his role as commander in chief, Lincoln pacified northern conservatives. Its aim, he stressed, was to injure the Confederacy, threaten its property, heighten its dread, sap its morale, and thus hasten its demise. By issuing the proclamation himself, Lincoln stole the initiative from the Radicals in Congress and mobilized support for the Union among European liberals far more dramatically than could any act of Congress. Further, the declaration pushed the border states toward emancipation: by the end of the war, Maryland and Missouri would abolish slavery. Finally, it increased slaves' incentives to escape as northern troops approached. Fulfilling the worst of Confederate fears, it enabled blacks to join the Union army.

Clearly, the Emancipation Proclamation did not end slavery everywhere or free "*all* the slaves." But it changed the nature of the war. From 1863 on, the war for the Union would also be a war against slavery.

Crossing Union Lines

The attacks and counterattacks of the opposing armies turned many slaves into pawns of war. Some slaves became free when Union troops overran their plantations. Others fled their plantations at the approach of federal troops to take refuge behind Union lines. A few were freed by northern assaults, only to be reenslaved by Confederate counterthrusts. One North Carolina slave celebrated liberation on twelve occasions, the number of times that Union soldiers marched through his area. By 1865 about half a million slaves were in Union hands.

In the first year of the war, when the Union had not yet established a policy toward contrabands (fugitive slaves), masters were able to retrieve them from the Union army. After 1862, however, the thousands of slaves who crossed Union lines were considered free. The continual influx of freedmen created a huge refugee problem for army

The Sea Island Experiments, 1861–1865

*I*n November 1861 a Union fleet sailed into Port Royal Sound, an inlet among the South Carolina Sea Islands, and bombarded the port's defenses. Before Union troops could occupy the islands, the white residents, many of them slaveowning planters, fled to the mainland. Left behind were elegant mansions, sprawling cotton plantations, and ten thousand slaves, who would remember the invasion as the "gun shoot at Bay Point."

The Sea Islands

The island chain, famous for the production of what had come to be called sea-island cotton, was the site of unique wartime experiments in new social policies.

Lying just off the southern coast between Charleston and Savannah, the conquered islands—including Port Royal, Hilton Head, and St. Helena—provided an operating base for the Union blockade fleet. They were of potential value to the Treasury Department, too. The Sea Islands were known for their high-grade cotton, which could be used to feed northern textile mills and to bolster the Union economy. But the takeover of the islands presented the Union with a challenge as well as a triumph.

Before the invasion, slaves had composed 83 percent of the Sea Island population. Long isolated from the mainland, they retained a distinctive culture and perpetuated many African customs. Their syntax and vocabulary were West Indian, and their Gullah dialect was almost incomprehensible to outsiders. Since the late eighteenth century, they had endured a harsh slave system similar to that of the West Indies. To the northerners who now arrived on the Sea Islands—army personnel, treasury agents, plantation managers, teachers, and missionaries—the very numbers of the black inhabitants seemed overwhelming. "Negroes, negroes, negroes," wrote Elizabeth Botume, a Boston teacher. "They hovered around like bees in a swarm. . . . Every doorstep, box, or barrel was covered with them." With the war barely under way and victory still a vision on the distant horizon, the Union suddenly had to forge a policy toward these thousands of "contrabands." While warfare occupied the rest of the nation, Sea

Island administrators embarked on a series of experiments in emancipation.

These experiments revealed deep divisions in northerners' thinking about the future of blacks. Some northerners on the scene focused on blacks' potential as soldiers. In May 1862 General David Hunter, who commanded the Union forces occupying the Sea Islands, formed a black army regiment; by August Sea Island men were being impressed into the First South Carolina "Volunteers," commanded by Massachusetts minister Thomas Wentworth Higginson. The drafting of blacks infuriated idealistic teachers and missionaries, who saw education as the blacks' primary need. "The negroes . . . will do anything for us, if we will only teach them," another teacher from Boston claimed. "The majority learn with wonderful rapidity," reported the free black Charlotte Forten of Philadelphia, "and they are said to be among the most degraded negroes of the South."

Equally sharp disagreements swirled around the question of economic opportunity for blacks. Edward Philbrick of Boston, an engineer who worked as a plantation superintendent on the islands, embodied one approach to the issue. Philbrick hoped to make the islands a showcase for free labor by turning the freedmen into wage earners on the large cotton plantations there. For blacks to produce more cotton as wage earners than they had as slaves, Philbrick reasoned, would squelch northern "gabble about the danger of immediate emancipa-

Sea Island School *Thousands of liberated slaves enrolled in the schools established by northern missionaries and teachers after the capture of the Sea Islands. This school was in Beaufort on Port Royal Island.*

tion" and buttress the position of those northerners who wanted emancipation to become the Union's main war goal. But the freedmen themselves had little enthusiasm for working in gangs on plantations, even if for wages. The practice smacked too much of their conditions under slavery. Instead, most Sea Island blacks would have preferred to plant food for themselves rather than cotton for northern factories, and many dreamed of owning their own land. "I should like to buy the very spot on which I live," an elderly freedman wrote to President Abraham Lincoln in a dictated letter. "I had rather work for myself . . . than work for a gentleman for wages."

Union administrators made some concessions to blacks' wishes. When, in the fall of 1863, Sea Island officials sold sixty thousand acres of confiscated rebel estates, only sixteen thousand acres were reserved for freedmen. The rest of the land was open to purchase by northern investors and speculators. Protesting the injustice of reserving a mere quarter of the acreage for those who composed the vast majority of the Sea Island residents, General Rufus Saxton, the islands' military governor and a "thoroughgoing Abolitionist, of the radical sort," secured approval in Washington to a plan to allow blacks to claim unsold land merely by squatting on it (a practice called preemption). Pressured by Saxton's rivals, however, the federal government reversed itself early in 1864 and forbade squatter claims.

The policy shifts continued. In December 1864 General William T. Sherman, fresh from his sweep across Georgia, arrived on the Sea Islands in the company of thousands of black camp followers who had gathered around his army during its march to the sea. To provide for these people, Sherman took steps to establish a class of black freeholders. General Sherman's Order No. 15 granted blacks the right to preempt unsold land not only on the Sea Islands but for thirty miles inland, on the mainland. By 1865 the islands had become a haven for black refugees from all over the South.

The new land policy would yet again be reversed: in August 1865 President Andrew Johnson would order all Sea Island lands returned to their original owners, thus dispossessing most of the blacks anew and leaving them no better or worse off than emancipated slaves elsewhere in the South. But during the Civil War, the islands had fulfilled a unique function. They had provided an arena wherein the Union first supervised emancipation and abolitionists first confronted large numbers of slaves. The scene of pioneer ventures in freedmen's education, black wage labor, and land redistribution, the Sea Islands had served as a testing ground for new social policies.

Sea Islands Enterprise

Garbed in castoff Union army uniforms, these newly liberated slaves cultivate a sweet-potato patch on a Hilton Head Island plantation.

commanders. "What shall I do about the negroes?" wrote a Union general in Louisiana to army headquarters in 1862:

> You can form no idea of . . . the appearance of my brigade as it marched down the Bayou. . . . Every soldier had a negro marching in the flanks, carrying his knapsack. Plantation carts, filled with negro women and children, with their effects; and of course compelled to pillage for their subsistence, as I have no rations to issue them. I have a great many more negroes in my camp now than I have whites.

As 1862 drew to a close, Union commanders in the South were appointing superintendents of freedmen to supervise large contraband camps. Many freedmen served in army camps as cooks, teamsters, and laborers. Some were paid to work on abandoned plantations or were leased out to planters who swore allegiance to the Union and who paid them wages stipulated by the army. Whether confined to contraband camps or working outside of them, many freedmen had reason to question the value of their liberation. Deductions for clothing, rations, and medicine ate up most, if not all, of their earnings. Labor contracts frequently tied them to individual employers for prolonged periods. Moreover, freedmen encountered fierce prejudice among Yankee soldiers, many of whom feared that emancipation would propel blacks north after the war. The best solution to the "question of what to do with the darkies," wrote one northern soldier, "would be to shoot them."

But this was not the whole story. Contrabands who aided the Union army as spies and scouts helped to break down ingrained bigotry. "The sooner we get rid of our foolish prejudice the better for us," a Massachusetts soldier wrote home. Before the end of the war, northern missionary groups and freedmen's aid societies sent agents into the South to work among the freedmen, distribute relief, and organize schools. In March 1865, just before the hostilities ceased, Congress created the Freedmen's Bureau, which had responsibility for the relief, education, and employment of former slaves. The Freedmen's Bureau law also provided that forty acres of abandoned or confiscated land could be leased to each freedman or southern Unionist, with an option to buy after three years. This was the first and only time that Congress provided for the redistribution of confiscated Confederate property.

Black Soldiers in the Union Army

During the first year of war, the Union had rejected black soldiers. Black applicants at northern recruiting offices were sent home, and black companies that had been formed in the occupied South were disbanded. After the second Confiscation Act, Union generals formed black regiments in occupied New Orleans and on the Sea Islands off the coasts of South Carolina and Georgia. Only after the Emancipation Proclamation, however, did large-scale enlistment begin. Leading blacks such as Frederick Douglass and Harvard-educated physician Martin Delany now worked as recruiting agents in northern cities. Douglass grasped the connection between recruiting blacks as soldiers and advancing their claims to citizenship. "Once let the black man get upon his person the brass letters, U.S.; let him get an eagle on his button, and a musket on his shoulder and bullets in his pocket, and there is no power on earth which can deny that he has earned the right to citizenship." Blacks were included in Union drafts, recruiting offices were set up in the loyal border states, and freedmen residing in refugee camps throughout the occupied South were enlisted. By the end of the war, 186,000 blacks had served in the Union army, one-tenth of all Union soldiers. Fully half came from the Confederate states.

White Union soldiers commonly objected to the new recruits on racial grounds. But some, including Colonel Thomas Wentworth Higginson, a liberal minister and former John Brown supporter who headed a black regiment, genuinely welcomed the black soldiers. "Nobody knows anything about these men who has not seen them in battle," Higginson exulted after a successful raid in Florida in 1863. "There is a fierce energy about them beyond anything of which I have ever read, except it be the French Zouaves [French troops in North Africa]." Even Union soldiers who held blacks in contempt pragmatically came to approve of "anything that will kill a rebel." Further, black recruitment offered new opportunities for whites to secure commissions, for blacks served in separate regiments under white officers.

Black soldiers suffered a far higher mortality rate than white troops. Typically assigned to labor detachments or garrison duty, blacks were less likely than whites to be killed in action but more likely to die of disease in the bacteria-ridden garrisons.

Flag of the Second Regiment of U.S. Colored Troops; Black Artillerymen

Black troops were organized late in the war and fought under flags such as these rare colors. The blacks in the photograph belonged to the Second U.S. Colored Light Artillery, which took part in the Battle of Nashville in 1864.

In addition, the Confederacy refused to treat captured black soldiers as prisoners of war, a policy that denied captured blacks the opportunity to be exchanged for Confederate prisoners. Instead, Jefferson Davis ordered all blacks taken in battle to be sent back to the states from which they came, where they were reenslaved or executed. In an especially gruesome incident, when Confederate troops captured Fort Pillow, Tennessee, in 1864, they massacred 262 blacks—an action that provoked outcries but no retaliation from the North.

Well into the war, black soldiers faced inequities in their pay. In contrast to white soldiers, who earned $13.00 a month plus a $3.50 clothing allowance, black privates received only $10.00 a month, with clothing deducted. "We have come out Like men and we Expected to be Treated as men but we have bin Treated more Like Dogs then men," a black soldier complained to Secretary of War Edwin Stanton. In June 1864 Congress belatedly equalized the pay of black and white soldiers.

Although fraught with hardships and inequities, military service was a symbol of citizenship for blacks. It proved that "black men can give blows as well as take them," Frederick Douglass declared. "Liberty won by white men would lose half its lustre." A black private explained: "If we hadn't become sojers, all might have gone back as it was

before. But now things can never go back because we have showed our energy and our courage . . . and our natural manhood." Above all, the use of black soldiers, especially former slaves, was seen by northern generals as a major strike at the Confederacy. "They will make good soldiers," General Grant wrote to Lincoln in 1863, "and taking them from the enemy weakens him in the same proportion they strengthen us."

Slavery in Wartime

Anxious white southerners on the home front felt as if they were perched on a volcano. "We should be practically helpless should the negroes rise," declared a Louisiana planter's daughter, "since there are so few men left at home." When Mary Boykin Chesnut of South Carolina learned that her cousin had been murdered in bed by two trusted house slaves, she became almost frantic. "The murder," Chesnut wrote, "has clearly driven us all wild." To maintain control over their 3 million black slaves, white southerners resorted to a variety of measures. They tightened slave patrols, at times moved entire plantations to relative safety in Texas or in the upland regions of the coastal South, and spread scare stories among the slaves. "The whites would tell the colored people not to go to the Yankees, for they would harness them to carts . . . in place of horses," reported Susie King Taylor, a black fugitive from Savannah.

Wartime developments had a mixed effect on the slaves. Some remained faithful to their masters and mistresses and helped hide treasured family belongings from marauding Union soldiers. Others were torn between loyalty and lust for freedom: one body servant, for example, accompanied his master to war, rescued him when he was wounded, and then escaped on his master's horse. Given a clear choice between freedom and bondage, slaves usually chose freedom. Few slaves helped the northern cause as dramatically as Robert Smalls, a hired-out slave boatman who turned over a Confederate steamer to the Union navy, but most slaves who had a chance to flee to Union lines did so. The idea of freedom had an irresistible attraction. Upon learning from a Union soldier that he was free, a Virginia coachman dressed in his master's clothes, "put on his best watch and chain, took his stick, and . . . told him that he might for the future drive his own coach."

The majority of slaves, however, had no escape and remained on their plantations under the nominal control of their masters. Despite the fears of southern whites, no general uprising of slaves occurred; and the Confederate war effort continued to depend heavily on slave labor. The Confederacy impressed thousands of slaves to work in war plants, to toil as teamsters and cooks in army camps, and to serve as nurses in field hospitals. But wartime conditions reduced the slaves' productivity. With most of the white men off at war, the master-slave relationship weakened on plantations. The women and boys who remained on plantations complained of their difficulty in controlling slaves, who commonly refused to work, performed their labors inefficiently, or spitefully destroyed property. A Texas wife contended that her slaves were "trying all they can, it seems to me, to aggravate me" by neglecting the stock, breaking plows, and tearing down fences. "You may give your Negroes away," she finally wrote despairingly to her husband in 1864.

Whether southern slaves fled to freedom or merely stopped working, they effectively undermined the plantation system. Thus southern slavery was disintegrating even as the Confederacy fought to preserve it. Hard pressed by Union armies, short of manpower, and deeply unsettled by the erosion of plantation slavery, the Confederate Congress in 1864 considered the drastic step of impressing slaves into its army as soldiers in exchange for their freedom at the war's end. Robert E. Lee favored the use of slaves as soldiers on the grounds that if the Confederacy did not arm its slaves, the Union would. Others, however, were adamantly opposed. "If slaves will make good soldiers," a Georgia general argued, "our whole theory of slavery is wrong." Originally hostile to the idea of arming slaves, Jefferson Davis changed his mind in 1865. In March 1865 the Confederate Congress narrowly passed a bill to arm three hundred thousand slave soldiers, although it omitted any mention of emancipation. With the end of the war a few weeks later, however, the plan was never put into effect.

Although the Confederacy's decision to arm the slaves came too late to affect the war, the debate over arming them damaged southern morale by revealing deep internal disagreements concerning war goals. Even before these conflicts had become obvious, the South's military position had started to deteriorate.

The Turning Point of 1863

In the summer and fall of 1863, Union fortunes dramatically improved in every theater of the war. Yet the year began badly for the North. The slide, which had started with Burnside's defeat at Fredericksburg, Virginia, in December 1862, continued into the spring of 1863. Burnside's successor, General Joseph "Fighting Joe" Hooker, a windbag fond of issuing grandiloquent proclamations to his troops, devised a plan to dislodge the Confederates from Fredericksburg by crossing the Rappahannock River north of the town and descending on the rebel rear. But Lee and Stonewall Jackson beat Hooker to the punch by attacking and routing him at Chancellorsville, Virginia, early in May 1863. The battle proved costly for the South, because Jackson was accidentally shot by Confederate pickets and died a few days later. Because Hooker had twice as many men as Lee, however, the Union defeat at Chancellorsville was especially humiliating for the North. "What will the country say?" Lincoln moaned. News from the West was no more

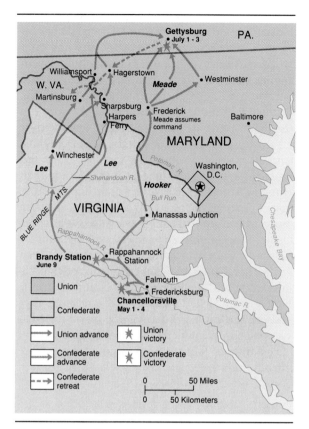

The War in the East, 1863

Victorious at Chancellorsville in May 1863, Lee again invaded Union territory but was decisively stopped at Gettysburg.

heartening for the Union. Although repulsed at Shiloh in western Tennessee, the Confederates still had a powerful army in central Tennessee under General Braxton Bragg. Further, despite repeated efforts, Grant was unable to take Vicksburg; the two-hundred-mile stretch of the Mississippi between Vicksburg and Port Hudson remained in rebel hands.

The upswing in Union fortunes began with Lee's decision after Chancellorsville to invade the North. The decision provoked dissent within the Confederate government, and Lincoln suspected that Lee was making a big mistake, but Lee had his reasons. He needed supplies that war-wracked Virginia could no longer provide, he hoped to panic Lincoln into moving troops from besieged Vicksburg to the eastern theater, and he thought that a major Confederate victory on northern soil would tip the balance in northern politics to the pro-peace Demo-

crats and gain European recognition of the Confederacy. Moving his seventy-five thousand men down the Shenandoah Valley, Lee crossed the Potomac into Maryland and pressed forward into southern Pennsylvania. At this point, with Lee's army now far to the west of Richmond, Hooker recommended a Union stab at the Confederate capital. But Lincoln brushed aside Hooker's advice. "Lee's *army,* and not *Richmond,* is your true objective," Lincoln shot back, and then the president replaced Hooker with the more reliable General George G. Meade.

Early in July 1863, Lee's offensive ground to a halt at a Pennsylvania road junction, Gettysburg. Confederates foraging for shoes in the town encountered some Union cavalry. Soon both sides called for reinforcements, and the war's greatest battle commenced. On July 1 Meade's troops installed themselves in hills south of town along a line that resembled a fishhook: the shank ran along Cemetery Ridge and a northern hook encircled Culp's Hill. By the end of the first day of fighting, most of the troops on both sides had arrived: Meade's army outnumbered the Confederates ninety thousand to seventy-five thousand. On July 2 Lee rejected advice to plant the Confederate army in a defensive position between Meade's forces and Washington and instead attacked the Union flanks, with some success. But because the Confederate assaults were uncoordinated, and some southern generals disregarded orders and struck where they chose, the Union was able to move in reinforcements and regain its earlier losses.

By the afternoon of July 3, believing that the Union flanks had been weakened, Lee attacked Cemetery Ridge in the center of the North's defensive line. After southern cannon shelled the line, a massive infantry force of fifteen thousand Confederates, Pickett's charge, moved in. But as the Confederate cannon sank into the ground and fired a shade too high, and as Union fire wiped out the rebel charge, rifled weapons proved their deadly effectiveness. At the end of the day, Confederate bodies littered the field. "The dead and the dying were lying by the thousands between the two lines," a dazed Louisiana soldier wrote. "The enemy seemed to be launching his cavalry to sweep the remaining handful of men from the face of the earth." A little more than half of Pickett's troops were dead, wounded, or captured in the horrible encounter.

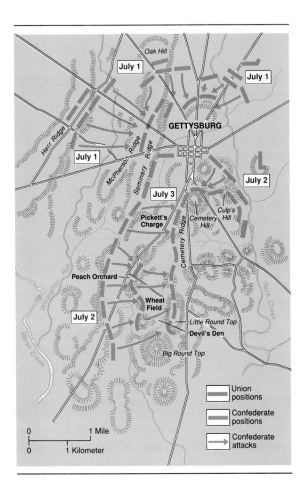

Gettysburg, 1863

The failure of Pickett's charge against the Union center on July 3 was the decisive action in the war's greatest battle.

When Lee withdrew to Virginia on July 4, he had lost seventeen generals and over one-third of his army. Total Union and Confederate casualties numbered almost fifty thousand. Despite the Confederate defeat, Gettysburg was not an exemplary Union victory, since Meade failed to pursue and destroy the retreating southern army. Still, because he had halted Lee's foray into the North, the Union was jubilant.

Almost simultaneously, the North won a less bloody but more strategic victory in the West, where Grant finally solved the puzzle posed by Vicksburg's defenses. Situated on a bluff on the east bank of the Mississippi, Vicksburg was protected on the west by the river and on the north by hills, forests, and swamps. Vicksburg could be attacked only over

a thin strip of dry land to its east and south. Positioned to the north of Vicksburg, Grant had to find a way to get his army south of the city and onto the Mississippi's east bank. His solution lay in moving his troops far to the west of the city and down to a point on the river south of Vicksburg. Meanwhile, Union gunboats and supply ships ran past the Confederate batteries overlooking the river at Vicksburg (not without sustaining considerable damage) to rendezvous with Grant's army and transport it across to the east bank. Grant then swung in a large semicircle, first northeastward to capture Jackson, the capital of Mississippi, and then westward back to Vicksburg. After a six-week siege, during which famished soldiers and civilians in Vicksburg were reduced to eating mules and even rats, General John C. Pemberton surrendered his thirty-thousand-man garrison to Grant on July 4, the day after Pickett's charge at Gettysburg. Port Hudson, the last Confederate holdout on the Mississippi, soon surrendered to another Union army. "The Father of Waters flows unvexed to the sea," Lincoln declared.

The War in the West, 1863: Vicksburg

Grant first moved his army west of Vicksburg to a point on the Mississippi south of the town. Then he marched northeast, taking Jackson, and finally west to Vicksburg.

Confederate Private James C. Gill

Gill fought at First Bull Run in 1861 and was wounded in 1862. With the help of his brother, who was killed pulling Gill from the field, Gill survived and was promoted to sergeant major. In the vanguard of Pickett's charge at Gettysburg, he was wounded again and died a few days after the battle.

Before the year was out, the Union won another crucial victory in the West. General William S. Rosecrans fought and maneuvered Braxton Bragg's Confederate army out of central Tennessee and into Chattanooga, in the southeastern tip of the state, and then forced Bragg to evacuate Chattanooga. Bragg defeated the pursuing Rosecrans at the Battle of Chickamauga (September 19–20, 1863), one of the bloodiest of the war, and drove him back into Chattanooga. But the arrival of Grant and of reinforcements from the Army of the Potomac enabled the North to break Bragg's siege of Chattanooga in November. With Chattanooga secure, the way lay open for a Union strike into Georgia.

Coming on the heels of reverses that had dri-

ven northern morale to its lowest point of the war, Union successes in the second half of 1863 stiffened the North's will to keep fighting and plunged some rebel leaders into despair. After hearing of the fall of Vicksburg, the Confederacy's ordnance chief, Josiah Gorgas, wrote in his diary: "Yesterday we rode the pinnacle of success—today absolute ruin seems our portion. The Confederacy totters to its destruction."

Totter it might, but the South was far from beaten. Although the outcome at Gettysburg quashed southerners' hopes for victory on northern soil, it did not significantly impair Lee's ability to defend Virginia. The loss of Vicksburg and the Mississippi cut the Confederate states west of the river—Arkansas, Louisiana, and Texas—off from those to the east; but these western states could still provide soldiers. Even with the loss of Chattanooga, the Confederacy continued to hold most of the Carolinas, Georgia, Florida, and Mississippi. Few contemporaries thought that the fate of the Confederacy had been sealed.

War and Society, North and South

Extending beyond the battlefields of Gettysburg and Vicksburg, the Civil War engulfed two economies and societies. By 1863 the progress of the war provided stark contrasts: with its superior resources, the Union could meet wartime demands as the imperiled Confederacy could not. But both regions experienced labor shortages and inflation. As the conflict dragged on, both societies confronted problems of disunity and dissent, for war issues opened fissures between social classes. In both regions war encroached on everyday life. Families were disrupted and dislocated, especially in the South. Women on both sides took on new roles at home, in the workplace, and in relief efforts.

The War's Economic Impact: The North

The war had an uneven effect on the Union's economy. Some industries fared poorly. For instance, the loss of southern markets damaged the shoe industry in Massachusetts, where output declined from 45 million pairs in 1855 to 32 million pairs in 1865. A shortage of raw cotton sent the cotton-textile industry into a tailspin that was only partly offset by a rise in the production of woolens. On the other hand, industries directly related to the war effort, such as the manufacture of arms and ready-made clothing, benefited from huge government contracts. By 1865, for example, the ready-made clothing industry was receiving orders for more than a million uniforms a year. Military demand also provided abundant business for the railroads. Some privately owned lines, which had suffered from excess capacity before the war, doubled the volume of their traffic during the war. In 1862 the federal government itself went into the railroad business by establishing the United States Military Railroads (USMRR) to carry troops and supplies to the front. "The quicker you build the railroad," Union general William T. Sherman told his troops, "the quicker you'll get something to eat." By 1865 the USMRR was the world's largest railroad.

The Republicans in Congress actively promoted business development during the war. Holding 102 of 146 House seats and 29 of 36 Senate seats in 1861, they overrode Democratic opposition and hiked the tariff in 1862 and again in 1864 to protect domestic industries. The Republican-sponsored Pacific Railroad Act of 1862 provided for the development of a transcontinental railroad, an idea that had foundered before the war on disagreements over which route such a railroad should follow. With the South out of the picture and no longer able to demand a southern route from New Orleans across the Southwest, Congress chose a northern route from Omaha to San Francisco. Chartering the Union Pacific and Central Railroad corporations, Congress then gave to each large land grants and generous loans. These two corporations combined received more than 60 million acres in land grants and $20 million in loans from the government. The issuance of greenbacks and the creation of a national banking system brought a measure of uniformity to the nation's financial system and facilitated the emergence of a truly national economy.

By raising the federal government's profile in the North's economy, the Republicans hoped to benefit a wide variety of social classes. To a degree, they succeeded. Republican measures like the Homestead Act, passed in 1862, embodied the party's ideal of "free soil, free labor, free men" by granting 160 acres of public land to settlers after five years of residence on the land. By 1865 twenty thousand homesteaders occupied new land in the West under the Homestead Act. To bring higher education within the reach of the common people, the Republicans secured passage in 1862 of the Morrill Land Grant Act. This law donated to the states proceeds from the sale of public lands—monies that would fund the establishment of universities emphasizing "such branches of learning as are related to agriculture and mechanic arts." The Morrill Act spurred the growth of large state universities, mainly in the Midwest and West. Michigan State, Iowa State, and Purdue universities, among many others, profited from its provisions.

Despite the idealistic goals behind some Republican laws, the war benefited the wealthy more than the average worker. Corrupt contractors grew fat by selling the government substandard merchandise such as the notorious "shoddy," clothing made from compressed rags, which quickly fell apart. Speculators who locked their patriotism in the closet made millions in the gold market. Because the price of gold in relation to greenbacks rose whenever public confidence in the government declined, those who bought gold in the hope that its price would rise actually benefited from Union defeats, and even more from Union disasters. Businessmen with access to scarce commodities also reaped astounding profits. For example, manpower shortages stimulated wartime demand for the mechanical reaper that Cyrus McCormick had patented in 1834. McCormick profited in addition from his distrust of the greenbacks. When paid in greenbacks for reapers, he immediately reinvested greenbacks in pig iron and then watched in glee as wartime demand drove the price of pig iron from twenty-three dollars to forty dollars a ton.

The war had a far less happy impact on ordinary workers. Protected from foreign competition by higher tariffs, northern manufacturers hoisted the prices of finished goods. Wartime excise taxes and inflation combined to push prices still higher. At the same time, wages lagged 20 percent or more behind cost increases for most of the war. This lag in wages, common in most periods of rapid inflation, became especially severe during the war because boys and women poured into government offices and factories as replacements for adult male workers who had joined the army. The proportion of women in the work force in manufacturing rose from one-quarter before the war to one-third during the war. Not only did boys and women draw lower pay than the men whom they had replaced, but employers' mere threats of hiring more youths and females undercut the bargaining power of the men who remained in the work force.

Some workers organized to decry their low wages. "We are unable to sustain life for the price offered by contractors who fatten on their contracts," Cincinnati seamstresses declared in a petition to President Lincoln. Cigar makers and locomotive engineers formed national unions, a process that would accelerate after the war. But organized protests had little impact on wages; employers often denounced worker protests as unpatriotic hindrances to the war effort. In 1864 army troops were diverted from combat to put down protests in war industries from New York to the Midwest.

The War's Economic Impact: The South

While stimulating some sectors of the North's economy, the war shattered the South's. Indeed, if the North and the South are considered together, the overall impact of the war was to retard *American* economic growth. For example, the commodity output of the American economy, which had registered huge increases of 51 percent and 62 percent in the 1840s and 1850s, respectively, rose only 22 percent during the 1860s. Even this modest gain depended wholly on the North, for in the 1860s commodity output in the South actually *declined* 39 percent.

Substantial wartime industrial growth by the South was more than offset by other factors. For example, the war wrecked the South's railroads; in 1864 Union troops, marching through Georgia under General William T. Sherman, tore up railroad tracks, heated them in giant ovens, and twisted them into "Sherman neckties." Cotton production, the foundation of the South's antebellum prosperity, sank from more than 4 million bales in 1861 to 300,000 bales four years later as Union invasions took their toll on production, particularly in Tennessee and Louisiana.

Invading Union troops also occupied the South's food-growing as well as cotton-producing regions.

Moreover, in agricultural areas under Confederate control, the drain of manpower into the army decreased the yields per acre of commodities like wheat and corn. Even the loss of a few carpenters and blacksmiths could disrupt the agricultural economy of rural districts. For example, the drafting of certain of their craftsmen, complained some Alabama petitioners to the federal government in 1863, had left their county "entirely Destitute of any man that is able to keep in order any kind of Farming Tules." Food shortages abounded late in the war. "The people are subsisting on the ungathered crops and nine families out of ten are left without meat," a Mississippi citizen lamented in 1864.

Agricultural shortages worsened the South's already severe inflation. By 1863 salt selling for $1.25 a sack in New York City cost $60.00 in the Confederacy. Food riots erupted in 1863 in Mobile, Atlanta, and Richmond; in Richmond the wives of ironworkers paraded to demand lower food prices.

Part of the blame for the South's food shortages rested with the planter class itself. While some planters heeded government pleas to shift from cotton to food production, many clung to the belief that cotton would never fail them. Although cotton production declined sharply overall, some individual planters still raised more cotton than they could market abroad. The consequences were far-reaching. Slave labor, which could have been diverted to army camps, where slaves might have relieved southern soldiers of menial tasks, remained essential on the labor-intensive cotton plantations, a circumstance that increased the Confederacy's reliance on its unpopular conscription laws. Moreover, cotton continued to sprout from land that could have been used for food production. To feed its hungry armies, the Confederacy had to resort to impressing food from civilians. This policy not only increased popular resentment of planters but also contributed to the South's mounting military desertions. Food-impressment agents usually concentrated on the easiest targets—farms run by the wives of active soldiers. Soldiers found it hard to resist the desperate pleas of their loved ones to return home. The wife of an Alabama soldier wrote to him: "We haven't got nothing in the house to eat but a little bit o meal. I don't want you to stop fighting them Yankees . . . but try and get off and come home and fix us all up some and then you can go back." By the end of 1864, half of the Confederacy's soldiers were absent from their units.

In one respect, the persistence of cotton growing did aid the South, because cotton became the basis for the Confederacy's flourishing trade with the enemy. The United States Congress virtually legalized this trade in July 1861 by allowing northern commerce with southerners loyal to the Union. In practice, of course, it proved impossible to tell whether receipts had fallen into the hands of loyalists or disloyalists, and for most traders it hardly mattered. As long as Union textile mills stood idle for lack of cotton, northern traders happily swapped bacon, salt, blankets, and other necessaries for southern cotton. The Union's penetration of the Confederate heartland both increased the need for trade and eased business dealings between the two sides; after its capture by the Union in 1862, Memphis became a major entrepôt for commerce that filled northern pockets and southern bellies. By 1864 traffic through the lines was providing the South with enough food daily to feed the entire Army of Northern Virginia. To a northern congressman, it seemed that the Union's policy was "to feed an army and fight it at the same time."

Trading with the enemy alleviated the South's food shortages but intensified its morale problems. The prospect of traffic with the Yankees gave planters an incentive to keep growing cotton, a decision that contributed to their unpopularity, and it fattened merchants and middlemen. "Oh! the extortioners," complained a Confederate war-office clerk in Richmond. "Our patriotism is mainly in the army and among the ladies of the South. The avarice and cupidity of men at home could only be exceeded by ravenous wolves."

Dealing with Dissent

Both wartime governments faced mounting dissent and disloyalty. Within the Confederacy, dissent took two basic forms. First, a vocal group of states' rights activists, notably Vice President Alexander Stephens and governors Zebulon Vance of North Carolina and Joseph Brown of Georgia, spent much of the war attacking Jefferson Davis's government as a despotism. Second, loyalty to the Union flourished among a segment of the Confederacy's common people, particularly those living in the Appalachian Mountain region that ran from western

North Carolina through eastern Tennessee and into northern Georgia and Alabama. The nonslaveholding small farmers who predominated here saw the Confederate rebellion as a slaveowners' conspiracy. Resentful of such measures as the "20-Negro" exemption from conscription, they were reluctant to fight for what a North Carolinian defined as "an adored trinity, cotton, niggers, and chivalry." "All they want," an Alabama farmer complained of the planters, "is to get you pupt up and to fight for their infurnal negroes and after you do there fighting you may kiss there hine parts for o they care." On the whole, the Confederate government responded mildly to popular disaffection from the war effort. In 1862 the Congress of the Confederacy gave Jefferson Davis the power to suspend the writ of habeas corpus, but Davis used his power only sparingly, by occasionally and briefly putting areas under martial law, mainly to aid tax collectors.

Lincoln faced similar challenges in the North, where the Democratic minority opposed both emancipation and the wartime growth of centralized power. Although "War Democrats" conceded that war was necessary to preserve the Union, "Peace Democrats" (called Copperheads by their opponents, to suggest a resemblance to a species of easily concealed poisonous snakes) disagreed. Demanding a truce and a peace conference, they charged that administration war policy was intended to "exterminate the South," make reconciliation impossible, and spark "terrible social change and revolution" nationwide.

Strongest in the border states, the Midwest, and the northeastern cities, the Democrats mobilized the support of farmers of southern background in the Ohio Valley and of members of the urban working class, especially recent immigrants, who feared losing their jobs to an influx of free blacks. In 1863 this volatile brew of political, ethnic, racial, and class antagonisms in northern society exploded into antidraft protests in several cities. By far the most violent eruption occurred in July in New York City. Catalyzed by the first drawing of names under the Enrollment Act, and by a longshoremen's strike in which blacks had been used as strikebreakers, mobs of Irish working-class men and women roamed the streets for four days until suppressed by federal troops. The city's laboring Irish loathed the idea of being drafted to fight a war on behalf of the slaves, who, once emancipated, might migrate north to compete with them for low-paying jobs. Too, they bitterly resented the provision of the draft law that allowed the rich to purchase substitutes. The Irish mobs' targets revealed the scope of their grievances. The rioters lynched at least a dozen blacks, injured hundreds more, and burned draft offices, the homes of wealthy Republicans, and the Colored Orphan Asylum.

President Lincoln's speedy dispatch of federal troops to quash these riots typified his forceful approach to dealing with dissent. Throughout the war, Lincoln imposed martial law with far less hesitancy than Davis. After suspending the writ of habeas corpus in Maryland in 1861, he barred it nationwide in 1863 and authorized the arrest of rebels, draft resisters, and those engaged in "any disloyal practice." The differing responses of Davis and Lincoln to dissent underscored the differences between the Confederacy's and the Union's wartime political systems. As we have seen, Davis lacked the institutionalization of dissent provided by party conflict and thus had to tread warily, lest his opponents brand him a despot. In contrast, Lincoln and other Republicans used dissent to rally patriotic fervor against the Democrats. After the New York City draft riots, for example, the Republicans blamed the violence on New York's antidraft Democratic governor, Horatio Seymour. When Seymour, rushing to the city to quell the disturbances, addressed a crowd of rioters as "my friends," the Republican press had a field day in branding the Democrats as disloyal.

Forceful as he was, Lincoln did not unleash a reign of terror against dissent. In general, the North preserved freedom of the press, speech, and assembly. In 1864 the Union became the first warring nation in history to hold a contested national election. Moreover, although some fifteen thousand civilians were arrested during the war, most were quickly released. A few cases, however, aroused widespread concern. In 1864 a military commission sentenced an Indiana man to be hanged for an alleged plot to free Confederate prisoners. The Supreme Court reversed his conviction two years later when it ruled that civilians could not be tried by military courts when the civil courts were open (*Ex parte* Milligan, 1866). Of more concern were the arrests of politicians, notably Clement L. Vallandigham, an Ohio Peace Democrat. Courting

arrest, Vallandigham challenged the administration, denounced the suspension of habeas corpus, proposed an armistice, and in 1863 was sentenced to jail for the rest of the war by a military commission. When Ohio Democrats then nominated him for governor, Lincoln changed the sentence to banishment. Escorted to enemy lines in Tennessee, Vallandigham was left in the hands of bewildered Confederates and eventually escaped to Canada. The Supreme Court refused to review his case.

The Medical War

Despite the discontent and disloyalty of some citizens, both the Union and the Confederacy witnessed a remarkable wartime patriotism that propelled civilians, especially women, to work tirelessly toward alleviating the suffering of soldiers. The United States Sanitary Commission, organized early in the war by civilians to assist the Union's medical bureau, consisted mainly of women volunteers. Described by one woman as a "great artery that bears the people's love to the army," the commission raised funds at "sanitary fairs," bought and distributed supplies, ran special kitchens to supplement army rations, tracked down the missing, and inspected army camps. The volunteers' exploits became legendary. One poor widow, Mary Ann "Mother" Bickerdyke, served sick and wounded Union soldiers as both nurse and surrogate mother. When asked by a doctor by what authority she demanded medical supplies for the wounded, she shot back: "From the Lord God Almighty. Do you have anything that ranks higher than that?"

The nursing corps also exemplifies how women on the home front reached out to aid the battlefront. Before the war ended, some thirty-two hundred women served the Union and the Confederacy as nurses. Already famed for her tireless campaigns on behalf of the insane, Dorothea Dix became the head of the Union's nursing corps. Clara Barton began the war as an obscure clerk in the United States Patent Office, but she, too, greatly aided the medical effort, in finding ingenious ways of channeling medicine to the sick and wounded. Catching wind of Union movements before Antietam, Barton showed up at the battlefield on the eve of the clash with a wagonload of supplies. When army surgeons ran out of bandages and started to dress wounds with corn husks, she raced forward with

Aiding the Sick and Wounded, North and South

Clean and gaily festooned, Carver Hospital in Washington, D.C., was a vast improvement over fetid field hospitals. Belle Boyd served the Confederacy as a nurse and a spy. Twice imprisoned by the Yankees, she later married a Union officer.

lint and bandages. "With what joy," she wrote, "I laid my precious burden down among them." After the war, in 1881, she would found the American Red Cross. The Confederacy, too, had its nurses extraordinary. One, Sally Tompkins, was commissioned a captain for her hospital work; another, Belle Boyd, served the Confederacy as both a nurse and a spy and once dashed through a field, waving her bonnet, to give Stonewall Jackson information. Few nurses got as close to the fighting as Clara Barton, who discovered a bullet hole in her sleeve after Antietam, and Belle Boyd, but danger stalked nurses even in hospitals far from the front. Author Louisa May Alcott, a nurse at the Union Hotel Hospital in Washington, D.C., contracted typhoid. Wherever they worked, nurses witnessed haunting, unforgettable sights. "About the amputating table," one reported, "lay large piles of human flesh— legs, arms, feet, and hands . . . the stiffened membrances seemed to be clutching oftentimes at our clothing."

Pioneered by British reformer Florence Nightingale in the 1850s, nursing was a new vocation for women and, in the eyes of many, a brazen departure from women's proper sphere. Male doctors were unsure about how to react to female nurses

and sanitary workers. Some saw the potential for mischief in attractive women's roaming around male hospital wards. But other doctors viewed nursing and sanitary work as potentially useful. The miasm theory of disease (see Chapter 11) commanded wide respect among physicians and stimulated some valuable sanitary measures, particularly in hospitals behind the lines. In partial consequence, the ratio of disease to battle deaths was much lower in the Civil War than in the Mexican War.

Despite improvements, for every soldier killed during the Civil War, two died of disease. "These Big Battles is not as Bad as the fever," a North Carolina soldier wrote. The scientific investigations that would lead to the germ theory of disease were only commencing in Europe during the 1860s. Arm and leg wounds frequently led to gangrene or tetanus, and typhoid, malaria, diarrhea, and dysentery raged through army camps.

Prison camps posed a special problem. Prisoner exchanges between the North and the South, common early in the war, collapsed by the middle of the war, partly because the South refused to exchange the black prisoners that it held and partly because the North gradually concluded that exchanges benefited the manpower-short Confederacy more than the Union. As a result, the two sides had far more prisoners than either could handle. Prisoners on both sides suffered gravely from camp conditions. "This cold weather is not just suited to Southern Constitutions," a Mississippian imprisoned in the Union camp at Rock Island, Illinois, wrote home. As much as southerners suffered in northern camps, the worst conditions plagued southern camps. Squalor and insufficient rations turned the Confederate prison camp at Andersonville, Georgia, into a virtual death camp; three thousand prisoners a month (out of a total of thirty-two thousand) were dying there by August 1864. After the war an outraged northern public demanded and secured the execution of Andersonville's commandant. Although the commandant was partly to blame for camp conditions, the deterioration of the southern economy contributed massively to the wretched state of southern prison camps. The Union camps were not much better, but the fatality rate among northerners held by the South exceeded that of southerners imprisoned by the North.

The War and Women's Rights

Female nurses and Sanitary Commission workers were not the only women to serve society in wartime. In both northern and southern government offices and mills, thousands of women took over jobs vacated by men. Moreover, home industry revived at all levels of society. "Old spinning wheels and handlooms were brought out from dusty corners," a Kentucky woman recalled. "Every scrap of leather was saved for the manufacture of rough shoes." In rural areas, where manpower shortages were most acute, women often did the plowing, planting, and harvesting.

Few women worked more effectively for their region's cause than Philadelphia-born Anna E. Dickinson. After losing her job in the federal mint (for denouncing General George McClellan as a traitor), Dickinson threw herself into hospital volunteer work and public lecturing. Her lecture "Hospital Life," recounting the soldiers' sufferings that she had witnessed, entranced audiences and brought her to the attention of Republican politicians. In 1863, hard pressed by the Democrats, these politicians invited Dickinson to campaign on

behalf of the Republican tickets in New Hampshire and Connecticut. This decision involved considerable risk, for Dickinson was a woman and scarcely twenty-one years old, but it paid handsome dividends for the party. Articulate and poised, Dickinson captured the hearts and votes of her listeners. Soon Republican candidates who had dismissed the offer of aid from a woman were begging her to campaign in their districts.

Mindful of the contributions of Dickinson and others to the Union cause, northern feminists hoped that the war would yield equality for women as well as for slaves. Not only should a grateful North reward women for their wartime services, these women reasoned, but it should recognize the intimate connection between equality for blacks and for women. In 1863 feminists Elizabeth Cady Stanton and Susan B. Anthony organized the National Woman's Loyal League. Although the league's main activity was to gather four hundred thousand signatures on a petition calling for a constitutional amendment to abolish slavery, Stanton and Anthony used the organization to promote woman suffrage as well as equality for blacks.

Despite high expectations, the war did not bring women significantly closer to economic or political equality. Women in government offices and factories continued to be paid less than men. Sanitary Commission workers and most wartime nurses, as volunteers, were paid nothing. Nor did the war produce a major change in the prevailing definition of woman's sphere. In 1860 that sphere already included charitable and benevolent activities; during the war the scope of benevolence was extended to embrace organized care for the wounded. But it was men who continued to dominate the medical profession, and for the remainder of the nineteenth century, nurses would be classified in the census as domestic help.

Feminists' keenest disappointment lay in their failure to capitalize on rising sentiment for the abolition of slavery to secure the vote for women. While the North had compelling reasons to abolish slavery in the rebellious areas of the South, northern politicians could see little practical value in woman suffrage. The *New York Herald,* which supported the Loyal League's attack on slavery, dismissed its call for woman suffrage as "nonsense and tomfoolery." Stanton wrote bitterly, "So long as woman

Southern Women Sewing, Cedar Mountain, Virginia

With their men off to war, southern women ran farms and sewed clothing for the soldiers at the front.

labors to second man's endeavors and exalt his sex above her own, her virtues pass unquestioned; but when she dares to demand rights and privileges for herself, her motives, manners, dress, personal appearance, and character are subjects for ridicule and detraction."

The Union Victorious, 1864–1865

Despite successes at Gettysburg and Vicksburg in 1863, the Union stood no closer to taking Richmond at the start of 1864 than in 1861, and most of the Lower South still remained under Confederate control. The constant press of Union invasion had taken its toll on the South's home front, but the North's persistent inability to destroy the main Confederate armies had eroded the Union's will to keep attacking. Northern war weariness strengthened the Democrats and jeopardized Lincoln's prospects for reelection in 1864.

The year 1864 proved to be crucial for the North. While Grant occupied Lee in the East, a Union army under General William T. Sherman attacked from Tennessee into northwestern Geor-

gia and took Atlanta in early September. The fall of Atlanta not only boosted northern morale but contributed to Lincoln's reelection. Now the curtain began to rise on the last act of the war. After taking Atlanta, Sherman marched unimpeded across Georgia to Savannah, devastated the state's resources, and cracked its morale. Pivoting north from Savannah, Sherman then moved into South Carolina. Meanwhile, having backed Lee into trenches around Petersburg and Richmond, Grant finally forced the evacuation of both cities and brought on the final collapse of the Confederacy.

The Eastern Theater in 1864

Early in 1864 Lincoln made Grant commander of all Union armies and promoted him to lieutenant general. At first glance, the stony-faced Grant seemed an unlikely candidate for so exalted a rank, held previously only by George Washington. Grant, a contemporary noted, "padlocks his mouth, while his countenance in battle or repose . . . indicates nothing." Grant's only distinguishing characteristics were his ever-present cigars and a penchant for whittling sticks into chips. "There is no glitter, no parade about him." But Grant's success in the West had made him the Union's most popular general, perhaps even the Union's most popular person. With his promotion, Grant moved his headquarters to the Army of the Potomac in the East and mapped a strategy for final northern victory.

Like Lincoln, Grant believed that the Union had to coordinate its attacks on all fronts in order to exploit its numerical advantage and prevent the South from shifting troops back and forth between the eastern and western theaters. (The South's victory at Chickamauga in September 1863, for example, had depended in part on reinforcements sent by Lee to Braxton Bragg in the West.) Accordingly, Grant planned a sustained offensive against Lee in the East while ordering William T. Sherman to move against the rebel army in Georgia commanded by Bragg's replacement, General Joseph Johnston. Sherman's mission was "to break it [the Confederate army] up, and to get into the interior of the enemy's country . . . inflicting all the damage you can."

In early May 1864, Grant led 118,000 men against Lee's 64,000 in a forested area near Fredericksburg, Virginia, called the Wilderness. After being checked by Lee in a series of bloody engagements (the Battle of the Wilderness, May 5–7), Grant tried to swing around Lee's right flank, only to suffer new reverses at Spotsylvania on May 12 and Cold Harbor on June 3. These engagements were among the fiercest of the entire war; at Cold Harbor, Grant lost 7,000 men in a single hour. Oliver Wendell Holmes, Jr., a young Union lieutenant and later a Supreme Court justice, wrote home how "immense the butcher's bill has been." But Grant refused to interpret repulses as defeats. Rather, he viewed the engagements at the Wilderness, Spotsylvania, and Cold Harbor merely as less than complete victories. Pressing on, he forced Lee to pull back to the trenches guarding Petersburg and Richmond.

Grant had accomplished a major objective, because once entrenched, Lee could no longer swing around to the Union rear, cut Yankee supply lines, or as at Chancellorsville, surprise the Union's main force. Lee did dispatch General Jubal A. Early on raids down the Shenandoah Valley, which the Confederacy had long used both as a granary and as an indirect way to menace Washington. But Grant countered by ordering General Philip Sheridan to march up the valley from the north and so devastate it that a crow flying over would have to carry its own provisions. The time had come, a Union chaplain wrote, "to peel this land." After defeating Early at Winchester, Virginia, in September 1864, Sheridan controlled the valley.

Sherman in Georgia

While Grant and Lee grappled in the Wilderness, Sherman advanced into Georgia at the head of 98,000 men. Opposing him with 53,000 Confederate troops (soon reinforced to 65,000), General Joseph Johnston retreated slowly toward Atlanta. Johnston's plan was to conserve his strength for a final defense of Atlanta while forcing Sherman to extend his supply lines. But Jefferson Davis, dismayed by Johnston's defensive strategy, replaced him with the more adventurous John B. Hood. Hood, having lost the use of an arm at Gettysburg and a leg at Chickamauga, had to be strapped to his saddle, but for all his physical impairments, he liked to take risks. During a prewar poker game,

he had bet $2,500 with "nary a pair in his hand." Hood promptly gave Davis what he wanted, a series of attacks on Sherman's army. These attacks, however, failed to dislodge Sherman and severely depleted Hood's own army. No longer able to defend Atlanta's supply lines, Hood evacuated his army from the city, which Sherman took on September 2, 1864.

The Election of 1864

Atlanta's fall came at a timely moment for Lincoln, who was in the thick of a tough campaign for reelection. Indeed, Lincoln had secured the Republican renomination with great difficulty. The Radicals, who had earlier flayed Lincoln for delay in adopting emancipation as a war goal, now dismissed his plans to restore the occupied parts of Tennessee, Louisiana, and Arkansas to the Union. The Radicals insisted that Congress, not the president, could alone set the requirements for the readmission of conquered states and criticized Lincoln's reconstruction standards as too lenient. While the Radicals rallied around Secretary of the Treasury Salmon P. Chase for the nomination, the Democrats attacked from a different direction. They had never forgiven Lincoln for making emancipation a war goal, and now the Copperheads, or Peace Democrats, demanded an immediate armistice, followed by negotiations between the North and the South to settle outstanding issues.

Although facing formidable challenges, Lincoln benefited from both his own resourcefulness and that of his political enemies. Playing his hand too quickly and openly, Chase turned the early boom for his nomination into a bust. By the time of the Republican convention in July, Lincoln's managers were firmly in control. Moreover, to isolate the Peace Democrats and attract prowar Democrats, the Republicans formed a temporary organization, the National Union party, and replaced Lincoln's vice president, Hannibal Hamlin, with a prowar southern Unionist, Democratic senator Andrew Johnson of Tennessee. This tactic helped exploit the widening division among the Democrats, who nominated George B. McClellan, the former commander of the Army of the Potomac and an advocate of continuing the war until the Confederacy's collapse, and then ran him on a platform written by the Peace Democrats. McClellan had to spend

The Election of 1864				
Candidates	Parties	Electoral Vote	Popular Vote	Percentage of Popular Vote
ABRAHAM LINCOLN	Republican	212	2,206,938	55.0
George B. McClellan	Democratic	21	1,803,787	45.0

much of his campaign trying to distance himself from his party's peace-without-victory platform.

Despite the Democrats' disarray, as late as August 1864, Lincoln seriously doubted that he would be reelected. Leaving little to chance, he arranged for furloughs so that Union soldiers, most of whom supported Lincoln, could vote in states lacking absentee ballots. But in the end it was chance, the timely fall of Atlanta, that immeasurably aided him. Although Hood's army had escaped from the city, a Richmond newspaper conceded that the "disaster at Atlanta" had punctured the antiwar movement in the North and saved Lincoln's presidency. With 55 percent of the popular vote and 212 out of 233 electoral votes, Lincoln swept to victory.

Sherman's March Through Georgia

Meanwhile, Sherman gave the South a new lesson in total war. After evacuating Atlanta, Hood led his Confederate army north toward Tennessee in the hope of luring Sherman out of Georgia. But Sherman did not rise to the bait. The war would never be won, he concluded, by chasing Hood around Tennessee and stretching his own supply lines to the breaking point. Rather, Sherman proposed to abandon his supply lines altogether, march his army across Georgia to Savannah, and live off the countryside as he moved along. He would break the South's will to fight, terrify its people, and "make war so terrible . . . that generations would pass before they could appeal again to it."

Sherman began by burning much of Atlanta and forcing the evacuation of most of its civilian population. This harsh measure relieved him of the need to feed and garrison the city. Then, sending enough troops north to ensure the futility of Hood's campaign in Tennessee, he led the bulk of his army, sixty-two thousand men, out of Atlanta to start the 285-mile trek to Savannah. Soon thousands of slaves were following the army. "Dar's de man dat rules the world," a slave cried on seeing Sherman. Sherman's four columns of infantry, augmented by

Sherman and His Generals

Sherman, shown here seated at center, was a moody and restless man, much like Grant. More than any other Union general, Sherman recognized that the best way to destroy the Confederacy was to undermine its ability to supply southern troops. Ruthless in his march through Georgia and the Carolinas, he nevertheless sought generous terms for the South after the war.

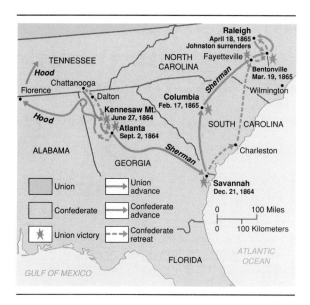

Sherman's March Through the South, 1864–1865

cavalry screens, moved on a front sixty miles wide and at a pace of ten miles a day. They destroyed everything that could aid southern resistance—arsenals, railroads, munitions plants, cotton gins, cotton stores, crops, and livestock. The ruin far exceeded Sherman's orders. Moreover, although Sherman's troops were told not to destroy civilian property, foragers carried out their own version of total war, ransacking and sometimes demolishing homes. Indeed, the havoc seemed a vital part of Sherman's own strategy. By the time that he occupied Savannah and made contact with the Union navy, he estimated that his army had destroyed about a hundred million dollars worth of property. After taking Savannah in December 1864, Sherman's army wheeled north toward South Carolina, the first state to secede and, in the general's view, one "that deserves all that seems in store for her." Sherman's columns advanced unimpeded to Columbia, South Carolina's capital. After fires set by looters, slaves, soldiers of both sides, and liberated Union prisoners gutted much of the city, Sherman headed for North Carolina. By the spring of 1865, his army had left over four hundred miles of ruin. Other Union armies moved into Alabama and Georgia and took thousands of prisoners. Northern forces had penetrated the entire Confederacy, except for Texas and Florida, and crushed much of its wealth. "War is cruelty and you cannot

refine it," Sherman wrote. "Those who brought war into our country deserve all the curses and maledictions a people can pour out."

Toward Appomattox

While Sherman headed north, Grant renewed his assault on the entrenched Army of Northern Virginia. Grant's main objective was Petersburg, a city south of Richmond through which most of the rail lines to the Confederate capital passed. Although Grant had failed on several occasions to overwhelm the Confederate defenses in front of Petersburg, the fall of Atlanta and Sherman's subsequent march through Georgia and into the Carolinas had taken their toll on Confederate morale. Rebel soldiers were accustomed to shortages of food, shoes, and clothing, but now they were burdened as well by a growing feeling of hopelessness. Rebel desertions, proportionately about the same as Union desertions until 1864, reached epidemic proportions in the winter of 1864–1865. Lee reported that hundreds of his men were deserting every night. Reinforced by Sheridan's army, triumphant from its campaign in the Shenandoah Valley, Grant late in March 1865 swung his forces around the western flank of Petersburg's defenders. Lee could not stop him. On April 2 Sheridan smashed the rebel flank at the Battle of Five Forks. A courier bore the grim news to Jefferson Davis, attending church in Richmond: "General Lee telegraphs that he can hold his position no longer."

Davis quickly left his pew, gathered his government, and fled the city. In the morning of April 3, Union troops entered Richmond, pulled down the Confederate flag, and ran up the Stars and Stripes over the capitol. As regiments of white and black troops entered in triumph, explosions set by retreating Confederates left the city "a sea of flames." "Over all," wrote a Union officer, "hung a canopy of dense smoke lighted up now and then by the bursting shells from the numerous arsenals throughout the city." Fires damaged the Tredegar Iron Works. Union troops liberated the town jail, which housed slaves awaiting sale, and its rejoicing inmates poured into the streets. On April 4 Lincoln toured the smoldering city and, for a few minutes, sat at Jefferson Davis's desk with a dreamy expression on his face.

Meanwhile, Lee was making a last-ditch effort to escape from Grant and from Sheridan's envel-

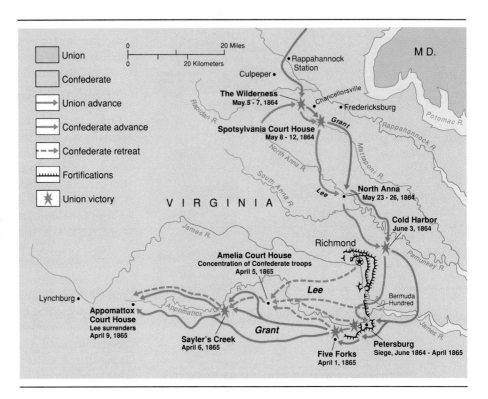

The Final Virginia Campaign, 1864–1865

Grant turned tactical reverses at the Wilderness, Spotsylvania, and Cold Harbor into strategic victories by refusing to abandon his campaign in the face of enormous casualties. He finally succeeded in pushing Lee into defensive fortifications around Petersburg, whose fall doomed Richmond. When Lee tried to escape to the west, Grant cut him off and forced his surrender at Appomattox Court House.

oping movements. Lee's destination was Lynchburg, sixty miles west of Petersburg. He planned to use the rail connections at Lynchburg to join General Joseph Johnston's army, which Sherman had pushed into North Carolina. But Grant and Sheridan swiftly choked off Lee's escape route, and on April 9 Lee bowed to the inevitable. He asked for terms of surrender and met Grant in a private home in the village of Appomattox Courthouse, Virginia, east of Lynchburg. While stunned troops gathered outside, Lee appeared in full dress uniform, with a sword. Grant entered in his customary disarray, smoking a cigar. When Union troops began to fire celebratory salutes, Grant put a stop to it. The final surrender of Lee's army occurred four days later. Lee's troops laid down their arms between federal ranks. "On our part," wrote a Union officer, "not a sound of trumpet . . . nor roll of drum; not a cheer . . . but an awed stillness rather." Grant paroled Lee's twenty-six thousand men and sent them home with their horses and mules "to work their little farms." The remnants of Confederate resistance collapsed within a month of Appomattox. Johnston surrendered to Sherman on April 18. While jubilation swept the North, Jefferson Davis was captured in Georgia on May 10.

Robert E. Lee

Posing in his uniform a few days after the war ended, Lee, as one historian has written, "looked like a perfect soldier, and was."

Grant headed back to Washington. On April 14 he turned down a theater date with the Lincolns, because Julia Grant found first lady Mary Lincoln overbearing. During an English comedy that night at Ford's Theater, an unemployed pro-Confederate actor, John Wilkes Booth, entered Lincoln's box and shot him in the head. Waving a knife, Booth leaped onto the stage shouting the Virginia state motto, *"Sic semper tyrannis"* ("Such is always the fate of tyrants") and then escaped, despite having broken his leg. That same night, one of Booth's accomplices stabbed Secretary of State Seward, who later recovered, while a third conspirator, who had been assigned to Vice President Johnson, failed to attack. Union troops hunted down Booth and shot him within two weeks, or else he shot himself. Of eight accused accomplices, including a woman boarding-house keeper, four were hanged and the rest imprisoned. On April 15, when Lincoln died, Andrew Johnson became president. Six days later Lincoln's funeral train departed on a mournful journey from Washington to Springfield, Illinois, with crowds of thousands gathering at stations to weep as it passed.

Conclusion

The Civil War took a larger human toll than any other war in American history. The death count stood at 360,000 Union soldiers and 260,000 Confederates. Most families in the nation suffered losses. Vivid reminders of the human toll remained to the end of the century and beyond. For many years armless and legless veterans gathered at regimental reunions. Citizens erected monuments to the dead in front of town halls and on village greens. Soldiers' widows collected pensions well into the twentieth century.

The economic costs were staggering, but the war did not ruin the national economy, only the southern part of it. The vast Confederate losses, about 60 percent of southern wealth, were offset by northern advances. At the war's end, the North had almost all of the nation's wealth and capacity for production. Spurring economic modernization, the war provided a hospitable climate for industrial development and capital investment. "The truth is," wrote Ohio senator John Sherman to his brother, General William T. Sherman, "the close of the war with our resources unimpaired gives an elevation, a scope to the ideas of leading capitalists, far higher than anything undertaken in this country before." No longer the largest slaveowning power in the world, the United States would now become a major industrial nation.

The war had political as well as economic ramifications. It created a "more perfect Union" in place of the prewar federation of states. The doctrine of states' rights did not disappear, but it was shorn of its extreme features. There would be no further talk of secession, nor would states ever again exercise their antebellum range of powers. The national banking system, created in 1863, gradually supplanted state banks. The greenbacks provided a national currency. The federal government had exercised powers that many in 1860 doubted that it possessed. By abolishing slavery and imposing an income tax, it asserted power over kinds of private property once thought untouchable. The war also promoted large-scale organization in both the business world and public life. The giant railroad corporation, with its thousands of employees, and the huge Sanitary Commission, with its thousands of auxiliaries and volunteers, pointed out the road that the nation increasingly would take.

Finally, the Civil War fulfilled abolitionist prophecies as well as Unionist goals. The war produced the very sort of radical upheaval within southern society that Lincoln originally said that it would not induce. Beaten Confederates had no idea of what to expect. Some wondered whether blacks and Yankees would permanently take over the South. The same thought occurred to the freedmen. "Hello, massa," a black Union soldier called out when he spotted his former owner among a group of Confederate prisoners whom he was guarding. "Bottom rail top dis time." The nation now turned its attention to the reconstruction of the conquered South and to the fate of 3.5 million newly freed slaves.

CHRONOLOGY

1861 President Abraham Lincoln calls for volunteers to suppress the rebellion (April).

Virginia, Arkansas, Tennessee, and North Carolina join the Confederacy (April–May).

Lincoln imposes a blockade on the South (April).

First Battle of Bull Run (July).

First Confiscation Act (August).

1862 Legal Tender Act (February).

George B. McClellan's Peninsula Campaign (March–July).

Battle of Shiloh (April).

Confederate Congress passes the Conscription Act (April).

David G. Farragut captures New Orleans (April).

Homestead Act (May).

Seven Days' Battles (June–July).

Pacific Railroad Act (July).

Morrill Land Grant Act (July).

Second Confiscation Act (July).

Second Battle of Bull Run (August).

Battle of Antietam (September).

Preliminary Emancipation Proclamation (September).

Battle of Fredericksburg (December).

1863 Emancipation Proclamation issued (January).

Lincoln suspends writ of habeas corpus nationwide (January).

National Bank Act (February).

Congress passes the Enrollment Act (March).

Battle of Chancellorsville (May).

Battle of Gettysburg (July).

Surrender of Vicksburg (July).

New York City draft riots (July).

Battle of Chickamauga (September).

1864 Ulysses S. Grant given command of all Union armies (March).

Battle of the Wilderness (May).

Battle of Spotsylvania (May).

Battle of Cold Harbor (June).

Surrender of Atlanta (September).

Lincoln reelected (November).

William T. Sherman's march to the sea (November–December).

1865 Sherman moves through South Carolina (January–March).

Grant takes Richmond (April).

Robert E. Lee surrenders at Appomattox (April).

Lincoln dies (April).

Joseph Johnston surrenders to Sherman (April).

For Further Reading

David Donald, *Lincoln Reconsidered: Essays on the Civil War Era,* 2d ed. (1956). Explorations of the gamut of Civil War topics, from Lincoln folklore to military history.

David Donald, ed., *Why the North Won the Civil War* (1960). Essays by major historians, analyzing the military, political, diplomatic, and economic reasons for Union victory.

Leon Litwack, *Been in the Storm So Long: The Aftermath of Slavery* (1979). A prizewinning examination of slaves' responses to the process of emancipation, continuing into the Reconstruction era.

James M. McPherson, *Battle Cry of Freedom: The Civil War Era* (1988). An award-winning study of the war years, skillfully integrating political, military, and social history.

Stephen B. Oates, *With Malice Toward None: The Life of Abraham Lincoln* (1977). The most recent one-volume study of Lincoln; an invaluable biography.

James G. Randall and David Donald, *The Civil War and Reconstruction,* 2d ed. (1961). The basic Civil War textbook for decades, notable for clarity and readability.

Emory M. Thomas, *The Confederate Nation, 1861–1865* (1979). An engaging narrative history, emphasizing the rise and fall of southern nationalism, with a complete bibliography.

Additional Bibliography

General

Daniel Aaron, *The Unwritten War* (1973); William L. Barney, *Flawed Victory: A New Perspective on the Civil War* (1975); William R. Brock, ed., *The Civil War* (1969); David P. Crook, *Diplomacy During the Civil War* (1975); Eric Foner, *Politics and Ideology in the Age of the Civil War* (1980); Paul G. Gates, *Agriculture and the Civil War* (1965); Harold Hyman, *A More Perfect Union: The Impact of the Civil War and Reconstruction on the Constitution* (1975); Eric L. McKitrick, "Party Politics in the Union and Confederate War Efforts," in William N. Chambers and Walter D. Burnham, eds., *The American Party System* (1975); James M. McPherson, *Ordeal by Fire: The Civil War and Reconstruction* (1982); Mary Elizabeth Massey, *Bonnet Brigades: American Women and the Civil War* (1966); Allan Nevins, *The War for the Union,* 4 vols. (1959–1971); Edmund Wilson, *Patriotic Gore* (1961).

The Military Experience

Michael Barton, *Good Men: The Character of Civil War Soldiers* (1981); Richard G. Beringer et al., *Why the South Lost the Civil War* (1986); Bruce Catton, *Mr. Lincoln's Army* (1951), *Glory Road* (1952), *A Stillness at Appomattox* (1953), and "Prison Camps of the Civil War," *American Heritage* 10 (August 1959): 4–13; Shelby Foote, *The Civil War: A Narrative,* 3 vols. (1958–1974); Herman Hattaway and Archer Jones, *How the North Won: A Military History of the Civil War* (1984); John T. Hubbell, *Battles Lost and Won: Essays from Civil War History* (1975); Gerald E. Linderman; *Embattled Courage: The Experience of Combat in the American Civil War* (1987).

The Black Experience

Dudley Cornish, *The Sable Arm: Negro Troops in the Union Army* (1956); John Hope Franklin, *The Emancipation Proclamation* (1963); Louis S. Gerteis, *From Contraband to Freedman: Federal Policy Toward Southern Blacks, 1861–1865* (1973); James M. McPherson, ed., *The Negro's Civil War* (1965) and *The Struggle for Equality: Abolitionists and the Negro in the Civil War and Reconstruction* (1964); Benjamin Quarles, *The Negro in the Civil War* (1953); Willie Lee Rose, *Rehearsal for Reconstruction: The Port Royal Experiment* (1964).

The Southern Experience

Thomas B. Alexander and Richard E. Beringer, *The Anatomy of the Confederate Congress* (1972); Paul D. Escott, *After Secession: Jefferson Davis and the Failure of Southern Nationalism* (1978); Douglas Southall Freeman, *R. E. Lee: A Biography,* 4 vols. (1934–1935); Clarence Mohr, *On the Threshold of Freedom: Masters and Slaves in Civil War Georgia* (1986); Robert M. Myers, ed., *The Children of Pride: A True Story of Georgia and the Civil War* (1972); James L. Roark, *Masters Without Slaves: Southern Planters in the Civil War and Reconstruction* (1978); Emory M. Thomas, *The Confederacy as a Revolutionary Experience* (1971); Bell I. Wiley, *The Plain People of the Confederacy* (1943) and *Road to Appomattox* (1956).

The Northern Experience

Adrian Cook, *The Army of the Streets: The New York City Draft Riots of 1863* (1974); Ann Douglas, "The War Within a War: Women Nurses in the Union Army," *Civil War History* 18 (1972), 197–212; George M. Fredrickson, *The Inner Civil War: Northern Intellectuals and the Crisis of the Union* (1965); David Gilchrist and W. David Lewis, eds., *Economic Change in the Civil War Era* (1965); Frank L. Klement, *The Copperheads of the Middle West* (1960) and *Dark Lanterns: Secret Political Societies, Conspiracies, and Treason Trials in the Civil War* (1984); William S. McFeely, *Grant: A Biography* (1981); James H. Moorhead, *American Apocalypse: Yankee Protestants and the Civil War* (1978); Joel Silbey, *A Respectable Minority: The Democratic Party in the Civil War Era, 1860–1868* (1977); George W. Smith and Charles Judah, eds., *Life in the North During the Civil War* (1968); Benjamin Thomas, *Abraham Lincoln* (1952); Hans L. Trefousse, *The Radical Republicans* (1968); T. Harry Williams, *Lincoln and the Radicals* (1942).

Personal Narratives

Eliza Frances Andrews, *Wartime Journal of a Georgia Girl* (1908); David Donald, ed., *Inside Lincoln's Cabinet: The Civil War Diaries of Salmon P. Chase* (1959); Rupert S. Hallard, ed., *The Letters and Diaries of Laura M. Towne* (1970); T. W. Higginson, *Army Life in a Black Regiment* (1867); John B. Jones, *A Rebel War Clerk's Diary* (1935); Mary Ashton Livermore, *My Story of the War* (1881); W. T. Sherman, *Memoirs,* 2 vols. (1886); C. Vann Woodward, ed., *Mary Chesnut's Civil War* (1982).

CHAPTER 15

The Crises of Reconstruction, 1865–1877

When the Civil War ended, parts of the South resembled a wasteland. The landscape "looked for many miles like a broad black streak of ruin and desolation," wrote a Union general, "the fences all gone; lonesome smoke stacks, surrounded by dark heaps of ashes and cinders." Homes, crops, and railroads had been destroyed; farming and business had come to a standstill; and uprooted southerners wandered about. As the Confederate armies dispersed, remnants of regiments made their way home. White refugees who had fled Union armies and burned-out plantations traveled the roads. So did black refugees. Some former slaves returned to areas where they had once lived, in search of relatives from whom they had been separated. Others moved off plantations to test their freedom, to look for work, or to seek relief. "Right off colored folks started on the move," a Texas freedman recalled. "They seemed to want to get closer to freedom—so they'd know what it was—like a place or a city."

The mood of the ex-Confederates was often as grim as the landscape. "The South lies prostrate—their foot is on us—there is no help," a Virginia woman lamented in her diary. Unable to face "southern Yankeedom," some planters considered emigrating to the American West or to Europe, Mexico, or Brazil, and a few hundred did. A large northern presence increased the rebels' dismay: two hundred thousand federal troops occupied the former Confederacy. Northern journalists and government officials also ventured south to investigate conditions and assess rebel attitudes. Their conclusions varied. Chief Justice Salmon P. Chase, on a self-appointed fact-finding mission, insisted that southerners were conciliatory and flexible. "The people are now in a mood to accept almost anything which promises of a definite settlement," he wrote from North Carolina in May 1865. A few days later, a *New York Tribune* reporter, also in North Carolina, sent his editor a harsher view of the ex-Confederates. "They are haughty, exacting, unsubdued, and if possible, *more* devilish than they ever were," he contended. "One would think that we were the subjugated and conquered people and not the rebels."

The mood of the vanquished had rarely, if ever, concerned victorious powers in previous wars. But the Civil War was a special case, for the Union had sought not merely victory but the return of national unity. The questions that the federal government faced in 1865 were therefore unprecedented. First, how could the Union be restored and the defeated South reintegrated into the nation? Would the Confederate states be treated as conquered territories, or would they quickly be readmitted to the Union with the same rights as other states? Who would set requirements for readmission—Congress or the president? Would Confederate leaders be punished for treason? Would their property be confiscated and their political rights curtailed? Most important, what would happen to the more than 3.5 million former slaves? The future of the freedmen constituted *the* crucial issue of the postwar era, for emancipation had set in motion the most profound upheaval in the nation's history. Before the war slavery had been the distinguishing feature of southern society. Both a labor system and a means of racial control, it had determined the South's social, economic, and political structure. What would replace slavery in the postwar South? The end of the Civil War, in short, posed two problems that had to be solved simultaneously: how to readmit the South to the Union and what status the free blacks would enjoy in American society.

Between 1865 and 1877, the drama of Reconstruction unfolded in several theaters. In Washington a conflict between President Andrew Johnson and Congress led to the enactment of a stringent Republican plan for restoring the South to the Union. In the defeated Confederate states, which were first readmitted to the Union under presidential directives, governments were reorganized according to the new congressional measures, and

Republicans took power. Throughout the localities of the South, the Reconstruction years spawned far-reaching social and economic changes. Emancipation reshaped black communities, where former slaves sought new identities as free people, and it transformed the southern economy as a new labor system replaced slavery. The North, meanwhile, hurtled headlong into an era of industrial expansion, labor unrest, and financial crises. By the mid-1870s northern politicians of both parties were ready to discard the Reconstruction policies that Congress had initiated in the 1860s. Simultaneously, the southern states were rapidly returning to "home rule," or Democratic control, as Republican regimes toppled one by one. In 1877 Reconstruction collapsed. But the nature and causes of its failure have engaged historians ever since.

Reconstruction Politics

At the end of the Civil War, President Johnson might have exiled, imprisoned, or executed Confederate leaders and imposed martial law indefinitely. Demobilized Confederate soldiers might have continued armed resistance to federal occupation forces. Freedmen might have taken revenge on former owners and the rest of the white community. But none of these drastic possibilities occurred. Instead, intense *political* conflict dominated the three years immediately after the war. In national politics unparalleled disputes produced two new constitutional amendments, a presidential impeachment crisis, and some of the most ambitious domestic legislation ever enacted by Congress, the Reconstruction Acts of 1867–1868. The major outcome of Reconstruction politics was the enfranchisement of black men, a development that few had expected when Lee surrendered.

That black suffrage became the pivot of federal Reconstruction policy proved a major surprise, for in 1865 only a small group of politicians supported such a controversial change. These advocates were all Radical Republicans, a minority faction that had emerged during the war. Led by Senator Charles Sumner of Massachusetts and Congressman Thaddeus Stevens of Pennsylvania, the Radicals had clamored for the abolition of slavery, just as they sup-

ported a demanding reconstruction policy, both in wartime and after. Any valid plan to restore the Union, Stevens contended, must "revolutionize Southern institutions, habits, and manners . . . or all our blood and treasure have been spent in vain." But the Radicals, outnumbered by moderate and conservative Republicans in the Thirty-ninth Congress, and opposed by the Democratic minority, seemingly had little chance of success. Nonetheless, in the complex political battles of 1865–1868, the Radicals managed to win the support of a majority of Republicans for parts of their Reconstruction program, including black male enfranchisement. Just as civil war had led to emancipation, a goal once supported by only a minority of Americans, so Reconstruction policy became bound to black suffrage, a momentous change that originally had only narrow political backing.

Lincoln's Plan

Conflict over Reconstruction began even before the war ended. In December 1863 President Lincoln issued the Proclamation of Amnesty and Reconstruction, which outlined a path by which each southern state could rejoin the Union. Under Lincoln's plan a minority of voters (equal to at least 10 percent of those who had cast ballots in the election of 1860) would have to take an oath of allegiance to the Union and accept emancipation. This minority could then create a loyal state government. But Lincoln's plan excluded some southerners from taking the oath: Confederate government officials, army and naval officers, as well as those military or civil officers who had resigned from Congress or from U.S. commissions in 1861. All such persons would have to apply for presidential pardons. Also excluded, of course, were blacks, who had not been voters in 1860. Lincoln hoped through his wartime "10 percent plan" to undermine the Confederacy by establishing pro-Union governments within it. Characteristically, the Republican Lincoln had partisan goals, too. He wanted to win the allegiance of southern Unionists (those who had opposed secession), especially former Whigs, and to build a southern Republican party.

Radical Republicans in Congress, however, envisioned a slower, more exacting readmission process that would exclude even more ex-Confederates from political life. Their plan won the backing of almost all Republicans, who agreed that Lincoln's program was too weak. Thus in July 1864 Congress enacted the Wade-Davis bill, which provided that each former Confederate state would be ruled by a military governor. Under the Wade-Davis plan, after at least half the eligible voters took an oath of allegiance to the Union, delegates could be elected to a state convention that would repeal secession and abolish slavery. But to qualify as a voter or delegate, a southerner would have to take a second, "ironclad" oath, swearing that he had never voluntarily supported the Confederacy. Like the 10 percent plan, the congressional plan did not provide for black suffrage, a measure then supported by only some of the Radicals. Unlike Lincoln's plan, however, the Wade-Davis scheme would have delayed the readmission process almost indefinitely.

Claiming that he did not want to bind himself to any single restoration policy, Lincoln pocket-vetoed* the Wade-Davis bill. The bill's sponsors, Senator Benjamin Wade of Ohio and Congressman Henry Winter Davis of Maryland, blasted Lin-

---

*Pocket veto: failure to sign a bill within ten days of the adjournment of Congress.

coln's act as an outrage. By the end of the war, the president and Congress had reached an impasse. Arkansas, Louisiana, Tennessee, and parts of Virginia under Union army control moved toward readmission under variants of Lincoln's plan. But Congress refused to seat their delegates, as it had a right to do. Lincoln, meanwhile, gave hints that a more rigorous Reconstruction policy might be in store. In his last speech (April 1865), he revealed that he favored some form of black suffrage, perhaps for blacks who had served in the Union army. He also entertained Secretary of War Stanton's proposal for temporary military occupation of the South. What Lincoln's ultimate policy would have been remains unknown. But at the time of his death, Radical Republicans turned with hope toward his successor, Andrew Johnson of Tennessee, in whom they felt that they had an ally.

Presidential Reconstruction Under Johnson

The only southern senator to remain in Congress when his state seceded, Andrew Johnson had worked amicably with Radical Republicans in wartime and had served as military governor of Tennessee from 1862 to 1864. He had taken a strong anti-Confederate stand, declaring, for example, that "treason is a crime and must be made odious," and had urged punishment of active Confederates. Above all, Johnson had long sought the destruction of the planter aristocracy, a goal that dominated his political career. A self-educated man of humble North Carolina origins, Johnson had moved to Greenville, Tennessee in 1826 and become a tailor. His wife, Eliza McCardle, had taught him how to write. An ardent Jacksonian, he had entered politics in the 1830s as a spokesman for nonslaveowning whites and risen rapidly from local official to congressman to governor to senator. Once the owner of eight slaves, Johnson reversed his position on slavery during the war. When emancipation became Union policy, he supported it, and as military governor, he assured Tennessee blacks that he would be their "Moses." But Johnson neither adopted abolitionist ideals nor challenged racist sentiments. He hoped mainly that the fall of slavery would injure southern aristocrats. Andrew Johnson, in short, had his own political agenda, which, as Republicans would soon learn, did not coincide

Andrew Johnson

When Vice President Johnson became president at Lincoln's death in April 1865, many Republicans expected him to impose "harsh terms" upon the defeated South.

with theirs. Moreover, he was a lifelong Democrat who had been added to the Republican, or National Union, ticket in 1864 to broaden its appeal and who had become president by accident.

Many Republicans voiced shock when Johnson announced a new plan for the restoration of the South in May 1865—with Congress out of session and not due to convene until December. The president presented his program as a continuation of Lincoln's plan, but in fact, it was very much his own. He explained in two proclamations how the seven southern states still without reconstruction governments could return to the Union. Almost all southerners who took an oath of allegiance would receive a pardon and amnesty, and all their property except slaves would be restored. Oath takers could elect delegates to state conventions, which would provide for regular elections. Each state convention, Johnson later added, would have to proclaim the illegality of secession, repudiate state debts incurred when the state belonged to the Confederacy, and ratify the Thirteenth Amendment,

which abolished slavery. (Proposed by an enthusiastic wartime Congress early in 1865, the amendment would be ratified in December of that year.) As under Lincoln's plan, all Confederate civil and military officers would be excluded from the oath needed for voting. But Johnson added a new disqualification. All well-off ex-Confederates, those with taxable property worth $20,000 or more, would also be barred from political life. Such an exclusion, said Johnson, would benefit "humble men, the peasantry and yeomen of the South, who have been decoyed . . . into rebellion." Johnson seemed to be planning a purge of aristocratic leadership. Poorer white southerners would now be in control.

Presidential Reconstruction took effect in the summer of 1865, supervised by provisional governors. But it had unforeseen consequences. Those southerners disqualified on the basis of wealth or high Confederate position applied for pardons in droves. Either gratified by their supplications or seeking support for reelection in 1868, Johnson handed out pardons liberally—some thirteen thousand of them. He also dropped plans for the punishment of treason. By the end of 1865, all seven states had created new civil governments to replace military rule, but in other ways the states had almost returned to the status quo ante bellum. Confederate army officers and large planters assumed state offices. Former Confederate congressmen, state officials, and generals were elected to serve in Congress. (Most of these new representatives were former Whigs who had not supported secession; southerners thought that they were electing "Union" men.) Georgia sent Alexander Stephens, the former Confederate vice president and a onetime Unionist, back to Congress as a senator. Some states refused to ratify the Thirteenth Amendment or to repudiate their Confederate debts.

Most important, all states took steps to ensure a landless, dependent black labor force—in one Alabamian's words, to "secure the services of the negroes, teach them their place." This goal was achieved through the "black codes," which replaced the slave codes, the state laws that had regulated slavery. Because the ratification of the Thirteenth Amendment was assured by the terms of Johnson's Reconstruction plan, all states guaranteed the freedmen some basic rights. They could marry, own property, make contracts, and testify in court against other blacks. But the important parts of the black codes were their restrictions, which varied from state to state. Some codes established racial segregation in public places; most prohibited racial intermarriage, jury service by blacks, and court testimony by blacks against whites. All codes included economic restrictions that would prevent former slaves from leaving the plantations. South Carolina required special licenses for blacks who wished to enter nonagricultural employment. Mississippi prohibited blacks from buying and selling farmland. Most states required annual contracts between landowners and black agricultural workers and provided that blacks without lawful employment would be arrested as vagrants and auctioned off to employers who would pay their fines.

The black codes established a halfway status for the southern freedmen, who, while no longer slaves, were not really liberated either. Although "free" to sign labor contracts, for instance, those who failed to sign them would be considered in violation of the law and swept back into involuntary servitude. The black codes thus solidified the alliance between planters and local law-enforcement agents—a white power structure with control over black labor. In practice, many clauses in the codes never took effect: the Union army and the Freedmen's Bureau swiftly suspended the enforcement of racially discriminatory provisions of the new laws. But the black codes were important indicators of white southern intentions. They showed what "home rule" would have been like without federal interference.

When former abolitionists and Radical Republicans decried the black codes, Johnson defended the codes and his restoration program. Ex-Confederates, he contended, should not be forced back into the Union as "a degraded and debased people." Many northerners, however, perceived signs of southern defiance: voters had elected ex-rebels to public office; southern conventions had been reluctant to repudiate secession or slow to pronounce slavery dead; and new laws had robbed freedmen of basic rights. "What can be hatched from such an egg but another rebellion?" asked a Boston newspaper. Republicans in Congress agreed. When the Thirty-ninth Congress convened in December 1865, it refused to seat the delegates of the ex-Confederate states. Establishing the Joint (House-Senate) Committee on Reconstruction,

Republicans prepared to dismantle the black codes and lock ex-Confederates out of power.

Congress Versus Johnson

The status of the southern blacks now became the major issue in Congress. "This is not a 'white man's government,'" exclaimed Republican congressman Thaddeus Stevens. "To say so is political blasphemy." But Radical Republicans like Stevens—who hoped to impose black suffrage on the former Confederacy, delay the readmission of the southern states into the Union, and transform the South into a biracial democracy—still constituted a congressional minority. Conservative Republicans, who tended to favor the Johnson plan, formed a minority too, as did the Democrats, who also supported the president. Moderate Republicans, the largest congressional bloc, agreed with the Radicals that Johnson's plan was too feeble. But they did not believe that northern voters would support black suffrage, and they wanted to avoid a dispute with the president. Since none of the four congressional blocs even approached the two-thirds majority required to overturn a presidential veto, Johnson's program would stay in place unless the moderates and the Radicals joined forces. The impetus for creating this alliance came from an unexpected source—Andrew Johnson himself, who soon alienated a majority of moderates and pushed them into the Radicals' arms.

The moderate Republicans supported two proposals drafted by one of their own, Senator Lyman Trumbull of Illinois, to invalidate the black codes. These measures won wide Republican support. In the first, Congress voted to continue the Freedmen's Bureau, established in 1865, whose term was coming to an end. This agency, headed by former Union general O. O. Howard and staffed mainly by army officers, was a major federal arm in the South. It provided relief, rations, and medical care; built schools for the freedmen; put them to work on abandoned or confiscated lands; and tried to protect their rights as laborers. Congress voted not only to extend the bureau's life for three years but to give it new power: it could run special military courts to settle labor disputes and could invalidate labor contracts forced on freedmen by the black codes. In February 1866 Johnson vetoed the Freedmen's Bureau bill. The Constitution, he declared, did not sanction military trials of civilians in peacetime, nor did it support a system to care for "indigent persons."

In March 1866 Congress passed a second measure proposed by Trumbull, a bill that made blacks U.S. citizens with the same civil rights as other citizens and gave the federal government the right to intervene in the states to ensure black rights in court. Johnson vetoed the civil-rights bill also. He argued that it would "operate in favor of the colored and against the white race." But in April Congress overrode his veto; the Civil Rights Act of 1866 was the first major law ever passed over a presidential veto. Then in July Congress enacted the Supplementary Freedmen's Bureau Act over Johnson's veto as well.

Johnson's vetoes bewildered many Republicans because the new laws did not undercut the basic structure of presidential Reconstruction. The president insisted, however, that both bills were illegitimate because southerners had been shut out of the Congress that passed them. His stance won support not only from the South but from northern Democrats, who were fast becoming the president's constituency. After the civil-rights veto, one New England Democrat praised Johnson for his opposition to "compounding our race with niggers, gypsies, and baboons." But the president had alienated the moderate Republicans, who rejected his arguments and began to work with the Radicals against him. Johnson had lost "every friend he has," one moderate legislator declared.

Some historians view Andrew Johnson as a political incompetent who, at this crucial turning point, bungled both his readmission scheme and his political future. Others contend that he was merely trying to forge a coalition of the center, made up of Democrats and non-Radical Republicans. In either case, Johnson underestimated the possibility of Republican unity. Once united, the Republicans moved on to a third step: the passage of a constitutional amendment that would prevent the Supreme Court from invalidating the new Civil Rights Act and would block Democrats in Congress from repealing it.

The Fourteenth Amendment

In April 1866 Congress adopted the Fourteenth Amendment, which had been proposed by the Joint Committee on Reconstruction. To protect blacks' rights, the amendment declared in its first clause that all persons born or naturalized in the United States were citizens of the nation and citizens of their states and that no state could abridge their rights without due process of law or deny them equal protection of the law. This section nullified the *Dred Scott* decision of 1857 (see Chapter 13), which had declared that blacks were not citizens. Second, the amendment guaranteed that if a state denied suffrage to any of its male citizens, its representation in Congress would be proportionally reduced. This provision did not guarantee black suffrage, but it threatened to deprive southern states of some of their legislators if black men were denied the vote. Third, the amendment disqualified from state and national office *all* prewar officeholders—civil and military, state and federal—who had supported the Confederacy, unless Congress removed their disqualifications by a two-thirds vote. In so providing, Congress intended to invalidate Johnson's wholesale distribution of amnesties and pardons. Finally, the amendment repudiated the Confederate debt and maintained the validity of the federal debt.

The Fourteenth Amendment was the most ambitious step that Congress had yet taken. It revealed the growing receptivity among Republican legislators to the Radicals' demands, including black enfranchisement. It reflected the Republican consensus that southern states would not deal fairly with blacks unless forced to do so. Most important, it was the first national effort to limit state control of civil and political rights. With its passage a huge controversy erupted. Abolitionists decried the second clause as a "swindle" because it did not explicitly ensure black suffrage. Southerners and northern Democrats condemned the third clause as vengeful. Southern legislatures, except for Tennessee's, refused to ratify the amendment, and President Johnson denounced it. His intransigence solidified the new alliance between the moderate and Radical Republicans. It also turned the congressional elections of 1866 into a referendum on the Fourteenth Amendment.

Over the summer Johnson set off on a whistle-stop train tour from Washington to St. Louis and Chicago and back, speaking to the public at railroad stations along the way. But this innovative campaign tactic—the "swing around the circle," as Johnson called it—was a debacle. Humorless and defensive, the president argued with his audiences and made fresh enemies. His hope of creating a new National Union party, composed of Democrats and conservative Republicans who opposed the Fourteenth Amendment, thus made little headway. Moderate and Radical Republicans, meanwhile, defended the amendment, condemned the president, and branded the Democratic party "a common sewer . . . into which is emptied every element of treason, North and South."

When the votes in the congressional elections were tallied, Republican candidates won in a landslide, often with even greater margins of victory than in 1864. In the Fortieth Congress, which would convene in March 1867, Republicans would outnumber Democrats almost two to one in the House and almost four to one in the Senate. In the interim the Republicans had secured a mandate to overcome southern resistance to the Fourteenth Amendment and to enact their own Reconstruction program, even if the president vetoed every part of it.

King Andrew

This Thomas Nast cartoon published in Harper's Weekly *just before the 1866 congressional elections conveyed Republican antipathy to Andrew Johnson. The president is depicted as an autocratic tyrant. Radical Republican Thaddeus Stevens, upper right, has his head on the block and is about to lose it. The Republic sits in chains.*

Congressional Reconstruction

The congressional debate over how to reconstruct the South began in December 1866 and lasted three months. To stifle a resurgence of Confederate power, Radical Republican leaders called for black suffrage, federal support for public schools, confiscation of Confederate estates, and an extended period of military occupation in the South. Reducing the ex-Confederate states to the status of territories, they believed, would enable Republicans to make the South over in the image of an idealized North, with "small farms, thrifty tillage, free schools . . . respect for honest labor and for equality of political rights." Moderate Republicans, who once would have rejected such a plan as too extreme, were now willing to accept parts of it. Legislators debated every ramification, including the constitutional question of whether the southern states had in fact seceded from the Union during the war; many issues grew so involved that one senator, who had lost the thread of a debate, complained that "the arguments seem to be drawn so fine that it [the subject at hand] has almost passed from my perception." In February 1867 after complex legislative maneuvers and many late-night sessions, Congress passed the Reconstruction Act of 1867, and, after Johnson vetoed it, repassed the law on March 2. Later that year and in 1868, Congress passed three further Reconstruction acts, all enacted over presidential vetoes, to refine and enforce the first.

The Reconstruction Act of 1867 invalidated the state governments formed under the Lincoln and Johnson plans and all the legal decisions made by those governments. Only Tennessee, which had ratified the Fourteenth Amendment and had been readmitted to the Union, escaped further reconstruction. The new law divided the other ten former Confederate states into five temporary military districts, each run by a Union general. Voters—all black men, plus those white men who had not been disqualified by the Fourteenth Amendment—

Major Reconstruction Legislation

Law	Provisions	Date of Congressional Passage	Purpose
Civil Rights Act of 1866	Declared blacks citizens and guaranteed them equal protection of the laws.	April 1866*	To invalidate the black codes.
Supplementary Freedmen's Bureau Act	Extended the life of the Freedmen's Aid Bureau and expanded its powers.	July 1866*	To invalidate the black codes.
Reconstruction Act of 1867	Invalidated state governments formed under Lincoln and Johnson. Divided the former Confederacy into five military districts. Set forth requirements for readmission of ex-Confederate states to the Union.	March 1867*	To replace presidential Reconstruction with a more stringent plan.
Supplementary Reconstruction Acts			To enforce the First Reconstruction Act.
Second Reconstruction Act	Required military commanders to initiate voter enrollment.	March 1867*	
Third Reconstruction Act	Expanded the powers of military commanders.	July 1867*	
Fourth Reconstruction Act	Provided that a majority of voters, however few, could put a new state constitution into force.	March 1868*	
Army Appropriations Act	Declared (in a rider to the main law) that military orders could be issued only by the general of the army.	March 1867*	To prevent President Johnson from obstructing Reconstruction.

(continued)

*Passed over Johnsons's veto.

Law	Provisions	Date of Congressional Passage	Purpose
Tenure of Office Act	Prohibited the president from removing any federal official without consent of the Senate.	March 1867*	To prevent President Johnson from obstructing Reconstruction.
Omnibus Act	Readmitted seven ex-Confederate states to the Union.	June 1868†	To restore the Union, under the terms of the First Reconstruction Act.
Enforcement Act of 1870	Provided for the protection of black voters.	May 1870‡	To enforce the Fifteenth Amendment.
Second Enforcement Act	Provided for federal supervision of southern elections.	February 1871	To enforce the Fifteenth Amendment.
Third Enforcement Act (Ku Klux Klan Act)	Strengthened sanctions against those who prevented blacks from voting.	April 1871	To combat the Ku Klux Klan and enforce the Fourteenth Amendment.
Amnesty Act	Restored the franchise to almost all ex-Confederates.	May 1872	Effort by Grant Republicans to deprive Liberal Republicans of a campaign issue.
Civil Rights Act of 1875	Outlawed racial segregation in transportation and public accommodations and prevented exclusion of blacks from jury service.	March 1875§	To honor the late senator Charles Sumner.

*Passed over Johnson's veto.
†Georgia was soon returned to military rule. The last four states were readmitted in 1870.
‡Sections of the law declared unconstitutional in 1876.
§Invalidated by the Supreme Court in 1883.

could elect delegates to a state convention that would write a new state constitution granting black suffrage. When eligible voters ratified the new constitution, elections could be held for state officers. Once Congress approved the state constitution, once the state legislature ratified the Fourteenth Amendment, and once the amendment became part of the federal Constitution, Congress would readmit the state into the Union—and Reconstruction, in a constitutional sense, would be complete.

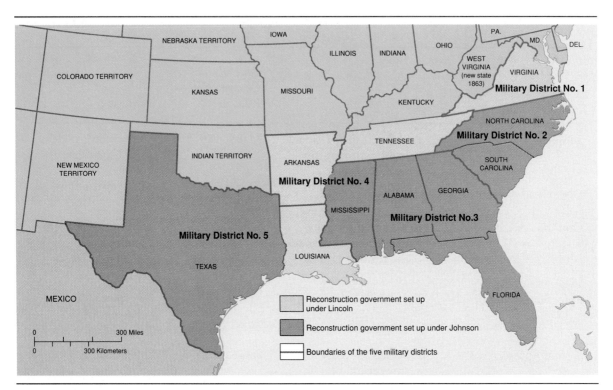

The Reconstruction of the South

The Reconstruction Act of 1867 divided the former Confederate states, except Tennessee, into five military districts and set forth the steps by which new state governments could be created.

The Reconstruction Act of 1867 was far more radical than the Johnson program because it enfranchised blacks and disfranchised many ex-Confederates. It fulfilled a central goal of the Radical Republicans: delaying the readmission of former Confederate states until Republican governments could be established and thereby preventing an immediate rebel resurgence. But the new law was not as severe toward former Confederates as it might have been. It provided for only temporary military rule. It did not prosecute Confederate leaders for treason or permanently exclude them from politics. Most important, it made no provision for the confiscation or redistribution of property.

During the congressional debates, Radical Republican congressman Thaddeus Stevens had argued for the confiscation of large Confederate estates to "humble the proud traitors" and to provide for the former slaves. In March 1867 he had proposed subdividing such confiscated property into forty-acre tracts to be distributed among the freedmen. The remainder of the confiscated land, some 90 percent of it, would be sold to pay off war debts.

Stevens wanted to crush the planter aristocracy and create a new class of self-sufficient black yeoman farmers. Political independence rested on economic independence, he contended; land grants would be more valuable to the freedmen than the right of suffrage, although both were deserved. Stevens's land-reform bill won the support of other Radicals, but it never made progress, for most Republicans held property rights sacred. Tampering with such rights in the South, they feared, would jeopardize them in the North. Moreover, Stevens's proposal would alienate southern ex-Whigs from the Republican cause, antagonize other white southerners, and thereby endanger the rest of Reconstruction. Thus land reform never came about. The "radical" Reconstruction acts were a compromise.

Congressional Reconstruction took effect in the spring of 1867. But it could not be enforced without military power, and Johnson, as commander in chief, controlled the army. When he impeded the congressional plan by replacing military officers sympathetic to the Radical cause with conservative ones, Republicans seethed. More suspicious than ever of the president and frustrated by his roadblocks, congressional moderates and Radicals once again joined forces to block Johnson from obstructing Reconstruction.

The Impeachment Crisis

In March 1867 Republicans in Congress passed two laws to limit presidential power. The Tenure of Office Act prohibited the president from removing civil officers without Senate consent. Cabinet members, the law stated, were to hold office "during the term of the president by whom they may have been appointed" and could be fired only with the Senate's approval. The goal was to bar Johnson from dismissing Secretary of War Stanton, the Radicals' ally, whose support Congress needed to enforce the Reconstruction acts. The second law, a rider to an army appropriations bill, prohibited the president from issuing military orders except through the commanding general, Ulysses S. Grant, who could not be removed without the Senate's consent.

The Radicals' enmity to Johnson, however, would not die until he was out of office. They began to look for grounds on which to impeach him and convict him and thereby remove all potential obstacles to congressional Reconstruction. The House Judiciary Committee, aided by private detectives, could at first uncover no valid charges against Johnson. On a second try, they produced some charges, but the House found them inadequate. Just as impeachment efforts seemed a lost cause, Johnson again came to his opponents' rescue by providing the charges that they needed.

In August 1867, with Congress out of session, Johnson suspended Secretary of War Stanton and replaced him with General Grant. In early 1868 the reconvened Senate refused to approve Stanton's suspension, and Grant, sensing the Republican mood, vacated the office. Johnson then removed Stanton and replaced him with another general, the aged Lorenzo Thomas. Johnson's defiance forced Republican moderates, who had at first resisted impeachment, into yet another alliance with the Radicals: the president had "thrown down the gauntlet," a moderate charged. The House approved eleven charges of impeachment, nine of them based on violation of the Tenure of Office Act. The other charges accused Johnson of being "unmindful of the high duties of office," of seeking to disgrace Congress, and of failing to enforce the Reconstruction acts.

Johnson's trial, which began in the Senate in March 1868, riveted public attention for eleven weeks. Seven congressmen, including leading Radical Republicans, served as prosecutors or "managers," while prominent attorneys represented the president. Johnson's lawyers maintained that he was merely seeking a court test by violating the Tenure of Office Act, which he thought was unconstitutional. They also contended, somewhat inconsistently, that the law did not protect Secretary Stanton, an appointee of Lincoln, not Johnson. Finally,

The Impeachment Managers

Seven Radical Republicans, chosen by the House of Representatives, served as impeachment "managers" at President Johnson's Senate trial in 1868. Benjamin F. Butler of Massachusetts, seated, far left, a criminal lawyer, assumed the role of chief prosecutor. Thaddeus Stevens, gaunt and haggard, seated next to Butler, spoke less but still dominated the proceedings. "If you don't kill the beast, it will kill you," he told Republican colleagues. Civil War photographer Mathew B. Brady captured the seven managers with his camera.

they asserted, Johnson was guilty of no crime indictable in a regular court.

The congressional "managers" countered that impeachment was a political process, not a criminal trial, and that Johnson's "abuse of discretionary power" constituted an impeachable offense. Although Senate opinion split along party lines and Republicans outnumbered Democrats, some Republicans wavered, fearing that the removal of a president would destroy the balance of power among the three branches of the federal government. They also distrusted Radical Republican Benjamin Wade, the president pro tempore of the Senate, who, because there was no vice president, would accede to the presidency if Johnson were thrown out.

Intense pressure from colleagues and constituents bombarded the wavering Republican senators, whose votes would prove crucial. Late in May 1868, the suspenseful trial reached its climax. The Senate voted against Johnson 35 to 19, one vote short of the two-thirds majority needed for conviction. Seven Republicans had risked political suicide and sided with the twelve Senate Democrats in voting against removal. In so doing, they set a precedent. Future presidents would not be impeached solely on political grounds or because two-thirds of Congress disagreed with them. But the anti-Johnson forces had also achieved their goal: Andrew Johnson had no future as president. After serving out his term, he returned to Tennessee, where he was reelected to the Senate five years later. Republicans in Congress, meanwhile, pursued their last major Reconstruction objective: to guarantee black suffrage.

The Fifteenth Amendment

Black suffrage was the linchpin of congressional Reconstruction. Only with the support of black voters could Republicans secure control of the ex-Confederate states, and only with the vote could southern blacks protect their own rights. The Fourteenth Amendment had promoted black suffrage indirectly, by threatening a penalty where it was denied. The Reconstruction Act of 1867, however, forced every southern state legislature to enfranchise black men as a prerequisite for readmission to the Union. But while black voting had begun in the South, much of the North had rejected it. At the end of the Civil War, only five New England states enfranchised black men; so did New York, on the condition that they owned property. Between 1867 and 1869, nine referenda in northern states defeated proposals for black suffrage. Iowa voters alone extended the franchise to blacks. Congressional Republicans therefore had two aims. They sought to protect black suffrage in the South against future repeal by Congress or the states and to enfranchise northern and border-state blacks, who would presumably vote Republican. To achieve these goals, Congress in 1869 proposed the Fifteenth Amendment, which prohibited the denial of suffrage by the states to any citizen on account of race, color, or previous condition of servitude.

Democrats argued that the proposed amendment violated states' rights by denying each state the power to determine who would vote. But Democrats did not control enough states to defeat the amendment and it was ratified in 1870. Four votes came from those ex-Confederate states—Mississippi, Virginia, Georgia, and Texas—that had delayed the Reconstruction process and were therefore forced to approve the Fifteenth Amendment, as well as the Fourteenth, in order to rejoin the Union. Some southerners contended that the new amendment's omissions made it acceptable, for it had, as a Richmond newspaper pointed out, "loopholes through which a coach and four horses can be driven." What were these loopholes? The Fifteenth Amendment did not guarantee black officeholding, nor did it prohibit voting restrictions such as property requirements and literacy tests. Such restrictions might be used to deny blacks the vote, and indeed, ultimately they were so used.

The controversy over black suffrage not only permeated national politics but drew new participants into the political debate. Since the end of the war, a small contingent of abolitionists, male and female, had sought to revive the cause of women's rights. In 1866, when Congress adopted the Fourteenth Amendment, women's rights advocates tried to join forces with their old abolitionist allies to campaign for both black suffrage and woman suffrage. Most Radical Republicans, however, did not want to be saddled with the woman-suffrage plank, for they feared that it would impede their primary goal, black enfranchisement.

This defection provoked disputes among women's rights advocates. Some, who continued

The Reconstruction Amendments

Amendment	Provisions	Date of Congressional Passage	Ratification
Thirteenth	Prohibited slavery in the United States.	January 1865	December 1865
Fourteenth	Defined citizenship to include all persons born or naturalized in the United States. Provided proportional loss of congressional representation for any state that denied suffrage to any of its male citizens. Disqualified prewar officeholders who supported the Confederacy from state or national office. Repudiated the Confederate debt.	June 1866	July 1868, after Congress made ratification a prerequisite for readmission of ex-Confederate states to the Union.
Fifteenth	Prohibited the denial of suffrage because of race, color, or previous condition of servitude.	February 1869	March 1870. Ratification required of Virginia, Texas, Mississippi, and Georgia for readmission to the Union.

to support black suffrage, contended that it would pave the way for the women's vote and that black men deserved priority. "If the elective franchise is not extended to the Negro, he is dead," explained Frederick Douglass, a longtime women's rights supporter. "Woman has a thousand ways by which she can attach herself to the ruling power of the land that we have not." But the women's rights leaders Elizabeth Cady Stanton and Susan B. Anthony, who repudiated black suffrage without attendant woman suffrage, decried the Fifteenth Amendment and denounced the Republicans for supporting it. The amendment, insisted Stanton, would establish an "aristocracy of sex." Moreover, she argued, if suffrage were extended without including women, their disabilities would merely increase. The battle over black suffrage and the Fifteenth Amendment divided women's rights

advocates into two rival suffrage associations, both formed in 1869. It also severed reformers such as Stanton and Anthony from the abolitionist tradition in which they had matured politically and inspired the development of an independent women's rights movement.

By the time that the Fifteenth Amendment was ratified in 1870, Congress could look back on five years of momentous achievement. Since the start of 1865, federal legislators had broadened the scope of American democracy by passing three constitutional amendments. The Thirteenth Amendment abolished slavery, the Fourteenth affirmed the rights of federal citizens, and the Fifteenth prohibited the denial of suffrage on the basis of race. Congress had also readmitted the former Confederate states into the Union. But after 1868 congressional momentum slowed. And in 1869, when Ulysses S.

Grant became president, the fierce battle between Congress and the executive ceased. The theater of action now shifted to the South, where an era of tumultuous change was under way.

Reconstruction Governments

During the unstable years of presidential Reconstruction, 1865–1867, the southern states had to create new governments, revive the war-torn economy, and face the impact of emancipation. Social and economic problems abounded. War costs had cut into southern wealth, cities and factories lay in rubble, plantation-labor systems disintegrated, and racial tensions flared. No sooner did legislatures enact the black codes than their impact was muted by the army, the Freedmen's Bureau, and a new civil-rights law. Beginning in 1865, freedmen organized black conventions, political meetings at which they protested ill treatment and demanded equal rights. These meetings took place in a climate of violence. Race riots erupted in major southern cities. In Memphis in May 1866, white crowds attacked black veterans, charged through black neighborhoods, and killed forty-six people; in New Orleans two months later, a white mob and police assaulted black delegates on their way to a political convention and left forty people dead. Even when Congress reimposed military rule in 1867, ex-Confederates did not feel defeated. "Having reached bottom, there is hope now that we may rise again to the surface in the course of time," a South Carolina planter wrote in his diary.

Congressional Reconstruction, supervised by federal troops, took effect in the spring of 1867. Despite efforts to stall it—many southern whites preferred military rule to the prospect of new civil governments based on black suffrage—the process moved forward. The Johnson regimes were dismantled, state constitutional conventions met, and voters elected new state governments, which Republicans dominated. In 1868 a majority of the former Confederate states rejoined the Union, and two years later, the last four states—Virginia, Mississippi, Georgia and Texas—followed.

Readmission to the Union did not end the *process* of Reconstruction, for Republicans still held power in the South. Republican rule was very brief, lasting less than a decade in all southern states, far less in most of them, and on average under five years. Opposition from southern Democrats, the landowning elite, thousands of vigilantes, and indeed, the majority of white voters proved insurmountable. But although short-lived, the governments formed under congressional Reconstruction marked a unique achievement, because black men, including former slaves, participated in them. In no other society where slaves had been liberated— neither Haiti, where slaves had revolted in the 1790s, nor the British Caribbean islands, where Parliament had ended slavery in 1833—had freedmen gained democratic political rights.

A New Electorate

The Reconstruction laws of 1867–1868 transformed the southern electorate by temporarily disfranchising 10 percent to 15 percent of potential white voters and by enfranchising more than seven hundred thousand freedmen. Outnumbering registered white voters by one hundred thousand, blacks gained voting majorities in five states.

The new electorate provided a base for the Republican party, which had never existed in the South. To their Democratic opponents, southern Republicans comprised three types of scoundrels: northern "carpetbaggers," who had allegedly come south seeking wealth and power (with so few possessions that they could be stuffed into traveling bags made of carpet material); southern "scalawags," predominantly poor and ignorant, who sought to profit from Republican rule; and hordes of uneducated freedmen, who where ready prey for Republican manipulators. Although the "carpetbag" and "scalawag" labels were derogatory and the stereotypes that they conveyed inaccurate, they remain in use as a form of shorthand. Crossing class and racial lines, the hastily established Republican party was in fact a loose coalition of factions with varied and often contradictory goals.

To northerners who moved south after the Civil War, the former Confederacy was an undeveloped region, ripe with possibility. The carpetbaggers' ranks included many former Union soldiers who hoped to buy land, open factories, build railroads, or simply enjoy the warmer southern climate. Albion Tourgee, a young lawyer who had served with the New York and Ohio volunteers, for example, relocated in North Carolina after the war to improve his health. There he worked as a journalist, poli-

The Carpetbaggers

Southern Democrats disparaged carpetbaggers as inter-lopers who hoped to "fatten on our misfortunes." In reality, most were Union army officers, businessmen, and professionals with capital and energy to invest in the South. This 1869 sheet-music cover caricatures the carpetbaggers by depicting a rather hungry-looking northern migrant casting a greedy eye upon the defeated Confederacy.

tician, and Republican judge, until Republican rule collapsed. Perhaps no more than twenty thousand northern migrants like Tourgee—including veterans, missionaries, teachers, and Freedmen's Bureau agents—headed south immediately after the war, and many returned north by 1867. But those who remained played a disproportionate part in Reconstruction politics, for they held almost one out of three state offices. Carpetbaggers recruited black support through a patriotic society called the Union League, which held meetings and rallies, urged blacks to vote, and escorted them to the polls.

Scalawags, white southerners who supported the Republicans, included some entrepreneurs who applauded party policies such as the national banking system and high protective tariffs as well as some prosperous planters, former Whigs who had opposed secession. They also comprised a few prominent politicians, among them James Orr of South Carolina and Mississippi's governor James Alcorn, who became Republicans for practical reasons: they wanted to retain influence and limit Republican radicalism. Republicans appreciated such important recruits and hoped to attract more of them. Most scalawags, however, were small farmers from the mountain regions of North Carolina, Georgia, Alabama, and Arkansas. Former Unionists who had owned no slaves and had no allegiance to the landowning elite, they sought to improve their economic position. Unlike carpetbaggers, they lacked commitment to black rights and black suffrage; most came from regions with small black populations and cared little whether blacks voted or not. Scalawags held the most political offices during Reconstruction, but they proved the least stable element of the southern Republican coalition: eventually, many drifted back to the Democratic fold.

Freedmen, the backbone of southern Republicanism, provided eight out of ten Republican votes. Republican rule lasted longest in states with the

American Citizens at the Polls,
by Thomas Waterman Wood, 1867

Black southerners voted for the first time in 1867, when the former Confederate states organized constitutional conventions. This painting conveys the enthusiasm that led up to 90 percent of eligible black voters to cast ballots. "The negroes voted their entire walking strength," an Alabama Republican reported, ". . . no one staying at home that was able to come to the polls."

The South Carolina Legislature

Although blacks served in all Reconstruction legislatures, only in South Carolina did they assume control. Forming a majority in the state House of Representatives, black legislators elected black speakers and ran major committees throughout Reconstruction. This scene depicts South Carolina lawmakers voting on an appropriations bill in 1873.

largest black populations, such as South Carolina, Mississippi, Alabama, and Louisiana. Introduced to politics in the black conventions of 1865–1867, the freedmen sought land, education, civil rights, and political equality. Even when land was not forthcoming, they continued to vote Republican. As an elderly freedman announced at a Georgia political convention in 1867, "We know our friends."

Although Reconstruction governments would have collapsed without black votes, freedmen held at most one in five political offices. Blacks served in all southern legislatures and filled many high posts in Louisiana, Mississippi, and South Carolina. They constituted a majority, however, only in the legislature of South Carolina, a state in which more than 60 percent of the population was black. No blacks won the office of governor, and only two served in the U.S. Senate, Hiram Revels and

Blanche K. Bruce, both of Mississippi. In the House of Representatives, a mere 6 percent of southern members were black, and almost half of these came from South Carolina.

Black officeholders on the state level, most of whom had risen to leadership roles in the black conventions, formed a political elite. They often differed from their black constituents in background, education, wealth, and complexion. A disproportionate number were literate blacks who had been free before the Civil War. (Many more former slaves held office on the local level than on the state level.) South Carolina's roster of elected officials illustrates some distinctions between high-level black officeholders and the freedmen who voted for them. Among those blacks sent to Congress, almost all claimed some secondary education, and some had attained advanced degrees. In South Carolina's state legislature, most black members, unlike the majority of their constituents, came from large towns and cities; many had spent time in the North; and some were well-off property owners or even former slaveowners. Color differences were evident, too: 43 percent of South Carolina's black state legislators, but only 7 percent of the state's black population, were mulattos.

The status gap between high-level black officials and black voters was significant. Most freedmen cared mainly about their economic future, especially about acquiring land, whereas black officeholders cared most about attaining equal rights. Still, both groups shared high expectations, and both prized enfranchisement. "We are not prepared for this suffrage," averred William Beverly Nash, an uneducated former slave, at the South Carolina constitutional convention. "But we can learn. Give a man tools and let him commence to use them and in time he will learn a trade. So it is with voting. We may not understand it at the start, but in time we shall learn to do our duty."

Republican Rule

Large numbers of blacks participated in American government for the first time in the state constitutional conventions of 1867–1868. The South Carolina convention had a black majority, and in Louisiana half the delegates were freedmen. The conventions forged democratic changes in their state constitutions. Delegates abolished property qualifications for officeholding, made many appointive offices elective, and redistricted state legislatures more equitably. All states established universal manhood suffrage, and some conventions offered further innovations: the new constitutions of Louisiana and South Carolina opened public schools to both races. These provisions integrated the New Orleans public schools as well as the University of South Carolina, from which whites withdrew. But most states did not provide for integrated education. Further, no state instituted land reform. When proposals for land confiscation and redistribution came up at the state conventions, they went down to defeat, as they had in Congress. Hoping to attract northern investment to the reconstructed South, southern Republicans hesitated to threaten property rights or to adopt land-reform measures that northern Republicans had rejected. South Carolina did set up a commission to buy land and make it available to freedmen, and several states changed their tax structures to force uncultivated land onto the market, but in no case was ex-Confederate land confiscated.

Once civil power shifted from the federal army to the newly formed state governments, the Republican administrations began ambitious programs of public works. They built roads, bridges, and public buildings; repaired broken-down facilities; promoted railroad development by endorsing railroad bonds; and funded institutions to care for orphans, the insane, and the disabled. The Republican regimes also expanded state bureaucracies, raised salaries for government employees, and formed state militia, in which blacks were often heavily represented. Finally, they created public-school systems, almost nonexistent in the South until then. In South Carolina prior to 1867, only one in eight white children, and hardly any blacks, had attended any school; but by 1875, with the advent of public schools, half the state's white children and 41 percent of its black children were enrolled.

Because rebuilding the devastated South and expanding the state governments cost millions, state debts and taxes skyrocketed. During the 1860s the southern tax burden rose 400 percent. State legislatures increased poll taxes or "head" taxes (levies on individuals); enacted luxury, sales, and occupation taxes; and imposed new property taxes. Before the war southern states had taxed property in slaves but had barely taxed landed property at all. Now for the first time, state governments assessed even small farmers' holdings, and big planters paid what they considered an excessive burden. Although northern tax rates still exceeded southern rates, southern landowners resented the new levies. In their view, Reconstruction strained the pocketbooks of the propertied, who were already beset by labor problems and falling land values, in order to finance the vast expenditures of Republican legislators, or what one Alabamian called the "no property herd."

Landowners complained about more than rising taxes. To Reconstruction's opponents, Republican rule was wasteful and corrupt, if not the "most stupendous system of organized robbery in history." A state like Mississippi, which had an honest government, provided little basis for such charges. But critics could justifiably point to Louisiana, where the governor pocketed thousands of dollars of state funds and corruption permeated all government transactions (as indeed it had before the war). Or they could cite South Carolina, where bribery ran rampant. The main postwar profiteers, besides the government officials who took bribes, were the railroad promoters who doled them out, and these were not necessarily Republicans. Nor did the Republican regimes in the South hold a monopoly on big spending or corruption. After the war bribery pervaded government transactions North and South, and far more money changed hands in the North. But Reconstruction's critics assailed Republican rule for additional reasons.

Counterattacks

Vexed as they were by northern interference, scalawag "treachery," and high taxes, ex-Confederates especially chafed at black enfranchisement and black officeholding and spoke with dread about the "horror of Negro domination." As soon as congressional Reconstruction took effect, a clamorous Democratic campaign began to undermine it. When the state constitutional conventions met, the Democratic press stood ready. Newspapers assailed North Carolina's delegates as an "Ethiopian minstrelsy ... baboons, monkeys, mules ... and other jackasses." They demeaned Louisiana's constitution as "the work of ignorant Negroes cooperating with a gang of white adventurers." A

Little Rock newspaper denigrated the Arkansas convention as "a foul gathering whose putridity stinks in the nostrils of all decency."

The Democrats delayed political mobilization until the southern states were readmitted to the Union. "The duty of the hour is to provide for our familys [sic] and avoid *politics*," declared Ella Thomas, the wife and daughter of Georgia planters, in 1868. Sharing such sentiments, perhaps one out of four eligible white voters abstained from voting. After readmission, however, the Democrats swung into action, calling themselves Conservatives so as not to repel those former Whigs who might join them. At first they sought to win the votes of blacks; but when that effort failed, they tried other tactics. In 1868–1869 Georgia Democrats challenged the eligibility of black legislators and expelled them from office. In response, the federal government reestablished military rule in Georgia, but determined Democrats still undercut Republican power. In every southern state, they contested elections, backed dissident Republican factions, and elected some Democratic legislators. They also made steady inroads among the scalawags, siphoning some of their votes from the Republicans.

Vigilante efforts to reduce black votes bolstered the Democrats' campaigns to win white ones. Antagonism toward free blacks, long a prominent motif in southern life, again flourished after the war. During presidential Reconstruction, when the white South sought to control freedmen's mobility, antiblack violence often erupted. Freedmen's Bureau agents in 1865 itemized a variety of outrages against blacks, including shooting, murder, rape, arson, roasting, and "severe and inhuman beating." Vigilante groups sprang up spontaneously in all parts of the former Confederacy under names like moderators, regulators, and in Louisiana, Knights of the White Camelia. A new group soon rose to dominance. In the spring of 1866, when the Johnson governments were still in power, six young Confederate war veterans in Tennessee formed a social club, the Ku Klux Klan, distinguished by elaborate rituals, hooded costumes, and secret passwords. New Klan dens spread through the state, and within a year Democratic politicians and former Confederate officers took control of them. By the election of 1868, when black suffrage had become a reality, Klan dens existed in all the southern states, and Klansmen embarked on night raids

to intimidate black voters. One of its founders now denounced the Klan as "perverted" and "pernicious," and indeed, it was no longer a social club but a widespread terrorist movement. Reminiscent of the antebellum slave patrols, the Ku Klux Klan became a violent arm of the Democratic party.

The Klan's goals were to suppress black voting, reestablish white supremacy, and topple the Reconstruction governments. Its members attacked Union League officers, Freedmen's Bureau officials, white Republicans, black militia units, economically successful blacks, and black voters. Concentrated in areas where the black and white populations were most evenly balanced and racial tensions greatest, Klan dens adapted their strategies and timing to local conditions. In Mississippi the Klan targeted black schools; in Alabama it concentrated on Republican officeholders. In Arkansas terror reigned in 1868; in Georgia and Florida Klan strength surged in 1870. Some Democrats denounced Klan members as "cut-throats and riff-raff." But prominent ex-Confederates were also known to be active Klansmen, among them General Nathan Bedford Forrest, the leader of the 1864 Fort Pillow massacre (see Chapter 14). Vigilantism united southern whites of different social classes and drew on the energy of many a Confederate veteran. In areas where the Klan was inactive, other vigilante groups took its place.

Republican legislatures outlawed vigilantism through laws providing for fines and imprisonment of offenders. But the state militia could not enforce the laws, and state officials turned to the federal government for help. In May 1870 Congress passed the Enforcement Act to protect black voters. Even this law was unenforceable, because witnesses to violations were afraid to testify against vigilantes, and local juries refused to convict them. The Second Enforcement Act, which provided for federal supervision of southern elections, followed in February 1871. Two months later Congress passed the Third Enforcement Act, or Ku Klux Klan Act, which strengthened the sanctions against those who prevented blacks from voting. It also empowered the president to use federal troops to enforce the law and to suspend the writ of habeas corpus in areas that he declared in insurrection. President Grant suspended the writ in nine South Carolina counties that had been devastated by Klan attacks.

After Congress enacted the three laws, a joint congressional committee launched a full-scale

The Ku Klux Klan

Disguised in long white gowns and hoods, Ku Klux Klansmen sometimes claimed to be the ghosts of Confederate soldiers. The Klan, which spread rapidly after 1867, hoped to end Republican rule, restore white supremacy, and obliterate, in one southern editor's words, "the preposterous and wicked dogma of Negro equality."

investigation of Klan activities. Victimized blacks and southern politicians of both parties testified. "I have heard of any quantity of horrible deeds," Henry M. Turner, a black minister, politician, and former Union army chaplain told government investigators. "Every man in Georgia who has got any brains must be satisfied, that there are organized bands of night assassins, murderous villains, who have banded themselves together and roam about and kill Republicans, kill any man who has got the name of radical attached to him." While Turner and others testified, the Ku Klux Klan Act generated thousands of arrests; most terrorists, however, escaped conviction.

By 1872 the federal government had effectively suppressed the Klan, but vigilantism had served its purpose. Only a large military presence in the South could have protected black rights, and the government in Washington never provided it. Instead, federal power in the former Confederacy diminished. President Grant steadily reduced troop levels in the South; Congress allowed the Freedmen's Bureau to die in 1869; and the Enforcement acts became dead letters. White southerners, a Georgia politician explained to congressional investigators in 1871, could not discard "a feeling

of bitterness, a feeling that the Negro is a sort of instinctual enemy of ours." The battle over Reconstruction was in essence a battle over the implications of emancipation, and it had begun as soon as the war ended.

The Impact of Emancipation

"The master he says we are all free," a South Carolina slave declared in 1865. "But it don't mean we is white. And it don't mean we is equal." Emancipated slaves faced extreme handicaps. They had no property, tools, or capital and usually possessed meager skills. Only a minority had been trained as artisans, and more than 95 percent were illiterate. Still, the exhilaration of freedom was overwhelming, as slaves realized, "Now I am for myself" and "All that I make is my own." At emancipation they gained the right to their own labor and a new sense of autonomy. Under Reconstruction the freedmen asserted their independence by seeking to cast off white control and shed the vestiges of slavery.

Confronting Freedom

For the former slaves, mobility was often the first perquisite of liberty. Some moved out of the slave quarters and set up dwellings elsewhere on their plantations; others left their plantations entirely. Landowners found that one freedman after another vanished, with house servants and artisans leading the way. "I have never in my life met with such ingratitude," a South Carolina mistress exclaimed when a former slave ran off. Field-workers, who had less contact with whites, were more likely to stay behind or more reluctant to leave. Still, flight remained tempting. "The moment they see an opportunity to improve themselves, they will move on," diarist Mary Chesnut observed.

Emancipation stirred waves of migration within the former Confederacy. Some freedmen left the Upper South for the Deep South and the Southwest—Florida, Mississippi, Arkansas, and Texas—where planters desperately needed labor and paid higher wages. Even more left the countryside for towns and cities, traditional havens of independence for blacks. Urban black populations sometimes doubled or tripled after emancipation; by 1866 Charleston had a black majority, and by 1870 almost equal numbers of blacks and whites lived in Atlanta, Richmond, Montgomery, and Raleigh. Overall during the 1860s, the urban black population increased by 75 percent, and the number of blacks in small rural towns grew as well. Many migrants eventually returned to their old locales, in search of their families or out of an attachment to the land. But they tended to settle on neighboring plantations rather than with their former owners. Freedom was the major goal. "I's wants to be a free man, cum when I please, and nobody say nuffin to me, nor order me roun'," an Alabama freedman declared to a northern journalist.

Freedmen's yearnings to find lost family members prompted considerable movement. "They had a passion, not so much for wandering as for getting together," a Freedmen's Bureau official commented. Parents sought children who had been sold; husbands and wives who had been separated by sale, or who lived on different plantations, reunited; and families reclaimed youngsters who were being raised in masters' homes. The Freedmen's Bureau helped former slaves get information about missing relatives and travel to find them. Bureau agents also tried to resolve entanglements over the multiple alliances of spouses who had been separated under slavery.

Reunification efforts often failed. Some fugitive slaves had died during the war or were untraceable. Other ex-slaves had formed new partnerships and could not revive old ones. "I am married," one husband wrote to a former wife (probably in a dictated letter), "and my wife [and I] have two children, and if you and I meet it would make a very dissatisfied family." But there were success stories, too. "I's hunted an' hunted till I track you up here," one freedman told his wife, whom he found in a refugee camp twenty years after their separation by sale.

Once reunited, freedmen quickly legalized unions formed under slavery, sometimes in mass ceremonies of up to seventy couples. Legal marriage had a tangible impact on family life. Men asserted themselves as household heads; wives and children of able-bodied men often withdrew from the labor force. "When I married my wife, I married her to wait on me and she has got all she can do right here for me and the children," a Tennessee freedman explained. Black women's desire to "play the lady," as southern whites described it, caused planters severe labor shortages. Before the war at least half of field-workers had been women; in 1866, a southern journal claimed, men performed almost all the field labor. Nevertheless, by the end of Reconstruction, many black women had returned to agricultural work as part of sharecropper families. Others took paid work in cities, as laundresses, cooks, and domestic servants. (Many white women sought employment as well, for the war had incapacitated white breadwinners, reduced the supply of future husbands, and left families destitute or in diminished circumstances.) Still, former slaves continued to view stable, independent domestic life, especially the right to bring up their own children, as a major blessing of freedom. In 1870 eight out of ten black families in the cotton-producing South were two-parent families, about the same proportion as among whites.

Black Institutions

The freedmen's desire for independence also led to the postwar growth of black churches. During the late 1860s, while some freedmen congregated at churches operated by northern missionaries in the

Freedmen's Schoolhouse

The establishment of freedmen's schools in the South represented the greatest triumph of the Freedmen's Bureau. Although underfunded and unable to reach many rural areas, the schools evoked tremendous support among blacks and laid a foundation for public-education systems in the southern states.

South, others withdrew from white-run churches and formed their own. The African Methodist Episcopal church, founded by Philadelphia blacks in the 1790s, gained thousands of new southern members. Negro Baptist churches sprouted everywhere, often growing out of plantation "praise meetings," religious gatherings organized by slaves.

The black churches, which offered a fervent, participatory experience, served many purposes. Beyond affording a closer communion among freedmen, they provided relief, raised funds for schools, and supported Republican policies. From the outset black ministers assumed leading political roles, first in the black conventions of 1865–1866 and later in the Reconstruction governments. After southern Democrats excluded most freedmen from political life at Reconstruction's end, ministers remained the main pillars of authority within black communities.

Black schools played a crucial role for freedmen as well. The ex-slaves eagerly sought literacy for themselves and above all for their children. At emancipation blacks organized their own schools, which the Freedmen's Bureau soon supervised. Northern philanthropic societies paid the wages of instructors, about half of whom were women. These teachers sometimes felt like pioneers in a foreign land. "Our work is just as much missionary work as if we were in India or China," a Sea Islands teacher commented. In 1869, just before it expired, the bureau reported more than four thousand black

schools in the former Confederacy. Within three years each southern state had a public-school system, at least in principle, generally with separate schools for blacks and whites. Advanced schools for blacks opened as well, to train tradespeople, teachers, and ministers. The Freedmen's Bureau and northern organizations like the American Missionary Association helped to found Howard, Atlanta, and Fisk universities (all started in 1866–1867) and Hampton Institute (1868).

Despite these advances, black education remained limited. Located in towns, most freedmen's schools could not reach the large black rural population. Black public schools, similarly inaccessible to most rural black children, held classes only for very short seasons. Underfunded and inferior, they were sometimes the targets of vigilante attacks. At the end of Reconstruction, illiteracy claimed more than 80 percent of the black population. Still, the proportion of youngsters who did not know how to read and write had declined and would continue to decline (see table on the following page). "Perhaps some *will* get an education in a little while. I *knows* de *next generation will*," a freedman told a missionary in 1865. "But . . . we has been kep down *a hundred years* and I think it will take *a hundred years to get us back again*."

School segregation and other forms of racial separation were taken for granted. Some black codes of 1865–1866 had segregated public-transit conveyances and public accommodations. Even after

Howard University

Founded by the Freedmen's Bureau in 1867, Howard University in Washington, D.C., was named after its first president, O. O. Howard, Union general and Freedmen's Bureau head. In 1870, the year this picture was taken, the pioneer black institution offered preparatory and collegiate programs, as well as training in law, pharmacy, and medicine.

the invalidation of the codes, the custom of segregation had continued on streetcars, steamboats, and trains as well as in churches, theaters, inns, and restaurants. On railroads, for example, whites could ride in the "ladies' car" or first-class car, while blacks had to stay in smoking cars or boxcars

Percentage of Persons Unable to Write, by Age Group, 1870–1890, in South Carolina, Georgia, Alabama, Mississippi, and Louisiana			
	1870	*1880*	*1890*
10–14			
black	78.9	74.1	49.2
white	33.2	34.5	18.7
15–20			
black	85.3	73.0	54.1
white	24.2	21.0	14.3
Over 20			
black	90.4	82.3	75.5
white	19.8	17.9	17.1

SOURCE: Roger Ransom and Richard Sutch, *One Kind of Freedom* (Cambridge: Cambridge University Press, 1978), 30.

with benches. In 1870 Senator Charles Sumner began campaigning in Congress for a bill that would desegregate schools, transportation facilities, juries, and public accommodations. After Sumner's death in 1874, Congress honored him by enacting a new law, the Civil Rights Act of 1875, which encompassed his program, except for the extremely controversial school-integration provision. But the law was largely unenforced, and in 1883 the Supreme Court invalidated it. The Fourteenth Amendment did not prohibit discrimination by individuals, the Court ruled, only that perpetrated by the state.

White southerners adamantly rejected the prospect of racial integration, which they insisted would lead to racial amalgamation. "If we have social equality, we shall have intermarriage," one white southerner contended, "and if we have intermarriage, we shall degenerate." Urban blacks, the most likely to be affected by segregation practices, sometimes challenged them, and black legislators promoted bills to desegregate public transit. Some black officeholders decried all forms of racial separatism. "The sooner we as a people forget our sable complexion," said a Mobile official, "the better it will be for us as a race." But most freedmen

548

were less interested in "social equality," in the sense of interracial mingling, than in black liberty and community. The newly formed postwar elite—teachers, ministers, and politicians—served black constituencies and therefore had a vested interest in separate black institutions. Rural blacks, too, widely preferred all-black institutions. They had little desire to mix with whites. On the contrary, they sought freedom from white control. Above all else, they wanted to secure personal independence by acquiring land.

Land, Labor, and Sharecropping

"The sole ambition of the freedman," a New Englander wrote from South Carolina in 1865, "appears to be to become the owner of a little piece of land, there to erect a humble home, and to dwell in peace and security, at his own free will and pleasure." Indeed, to freedmen everywhere, "forty acres and a mule" promised emancipation from plantation labor, from white domination, and from cotton, the "slave crop." Just as garden plots provided a measure of autonomy under slavery, so did landownership signify economic independence afterward. "We want to be placed on land until we are able to buy it and make it our own," a black minister had told General Sherman in Georgia during the war. Some freedmen defended their right to the land on which they lived, by pointing out that they and their forebears had worked on it for decades without pay.

But freedmen's visions of landownership failed to materialize, for, as we have seen, large-scale land reform never occurred. Proposals to confiscate or redistribute Confederate property failed in Congress as well as in the southern state legislatures. Some freedmen did obtain land with the help of the Union army or the Freedmen's Bureau, and black soldiers sometimes pooled resources to buy land, as on the Sea Islands (see Chapter 14). The federal government also attempted to provide ex-slaves with land. In 1866 Congress passed the Southern Homestead Act, which set aside 44 million acres of land in five southern states for freedmen and loyal whites. Not only did this acreage contain poor soil, but few former slaves had the resources to survive even until their first harvest. Thus although about four thousand blacks were resettled on homesteads under the law, most were unable to

establish farms. (White southern homesteaders fared little better.) By the end of Reconstruction, only a small minority of former slaves in each state owned working farms. In Georgia in 1876, for instance, blacks controlled a mere 1.3 percent of total acreage. Without large-scale land reform, the obstacles to black landownership remained overwhelming.

What were these obstacles? First, most freedmen lacked the capital to buy land and the equipment needed to work it. Further, white southerners on the whole opposed selling land to blacks. Most important, planters sought to preserve a black labor force. They insisted that freedmen would work only under coercion, and not at all if the possibility of landownership arose. As soon as the war ended, therefore, the white South took steps to make sure that black labor would remain available where it was needed, on the plantations.

During presidential Reconstruction, southern state legislatures tried to limit black mobility and to preserve a captive labor force through the black codes. Under labor contracts in effect in 1865–1866, freedmen received wages, housing, food, and clothing in exchange for fieldwork. With cash so short, wages usually took the form of a very small share of the crop, often one-eighth or less, divided among the entire plantation work force. Serving as mediators between former slaves and landowners, Freedmen's Bureau agents actively promoted the new labor system; they encouraged freedmen to sign labor contracts and tried to ensure adequate wages. Imbued with the northern free-labor ideology, which held that wage workers could rise to the status of self-supporting tradesmen and property owners, bureau officials and agents endorsed black wage labor as an interim arrangement that would lead to economic independence. "You must begin at the bottom of the ladder and climb up," Freedmen's Bureau head O. O. Howard exhorted a group of Louisiana freedmen in 1865.

But the freedmen disliked the new wage system, especially the use of gang labor, which resembled the work pattern under slavery. Planters had complaints, too. In some regions the black labor force had shrunk to half its prewar size or less, due to the migration of freedmen and to black women's withdrawal from fieldwork. Once united in defense of slavery, planters now competed for black workers. Moreover, their labor problems mounted, for the freedmen, whom planters often scorned as lazy

A Georgia Plantation, 1865–1881

The transformation of the Barrow plantation in Oglethorpe County, Georgia, illustrates in microcosm the striking changes that occurred in southern agriculture during Reconstruction. Before the Civil War, David Crenshaw Barrow had been the absentee owner of a two-thousand-acre plantation long known as the Pope Place. He had inherited the land through his first wife, Sarah Elizabeth Pope. The owner of several other plantations as well, Barrow had possessed some 400 slaves, about 135 of whom had lived on the "Pope Place." Assisted by slave foremen, an overseer had run the plantation. The overseer had lived in the main plantation house, from where he had kept a watchful eye on the slave quarters.

After the war the plantation changed in so many ways that by 1881, according to Barrow's son, David Crenshaw Barrow, Jr., "the place would now hardly be recognized." But the changes had occurred in stages.

The critical period immediately followed the war. At emancipation some of Barrow's former slaves had left the plantation, probably for nearby towns or other plantations. Those remaining had signed annual labor contracts with Barrow. Divided into two competing squads and supervised by a hired foreman, the freedmen grew cotton under the gang system. They received wages in the form of a share of the crop, with a reward going to the squad that worked more efficiently. Barrow liked the new system, but the freedmen did not. Within a few years, they rebelled against the hired foreman, "each man feeling the very natural desire to be his own 'boss' and farm to himself," Barrow's son wrote. The squads split into smaller groups and spread over the plantation. Still working for a small share of the crop, they continued to use the owner's mules and equipment. Now Barrow found the system unsatisfactory. He claimed that the freedmen mistreated the mules and failed to deliver his full share of the crop.

In the late 1860s, life on the Barrow plantation entered a third phase. One of the first planters in his area to subdivide his land, Barrow transformed the plantation into tenant farms of twenty-five to thirty acres. With this change, the freedmen moved their households from the old slave quarters to their own farms. They typically set up their log cabins at springs around the plantation and then added outhouses, stables, corncribs, and fodderhouses. Each head of family signed an annual contract, agreeing to pay a rent of 500 to 750 pounds of cotton plus varied amounts of other crops. As tenant farmers, the freedmen raised cotton (about half their crop), corn, and vegetables; the men did the plowing, and women and children the hoeing. Using uncultivated land for pasture, the tenants also raised hogs, chickens, and a few cattle. Barrow sold each farmer a mule on credit, and he set aside an acre on the edge of the plantation for a church and a school, which was open three months a year.

In 1881 David Crenshaw Barrow lived in the main house with two family members, probably his second wife (a former New Englander) and an unmarried daughter, Clara. The plantation's tenants

Tenants on the Barrow Plantation

Children pick cotton on the Barrow plantation in this late-nineteenth-century scene.

549a

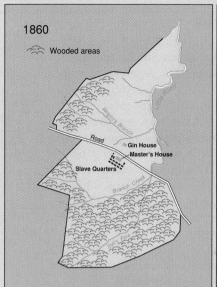

1860

🌿 Wooded areas

Road

Gin House

Master's House

Slave Quarters

Wight's Branch

Little River

Branch Creek

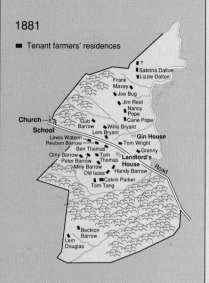

1881

■ Tenant farmers' residences

■ ?
■ Sabrina Dalton
■ Lizzie Dalton
Frank Maxey ◆
◆ Joe Bug
◆ Jim Reid
◆ Nancy Pope
◆ Cane Pope
Church— Gub Barrow ◆ ◆ Willis Bryant
School ◆ Lem Bryant
Lewis Watson ◆ Gin House
Reuben Barrow ◆ ◆ Tom Wright
Ben Thomas ◆ ◆ Granny
Orny Barrow ◆ ◆ Tom Thomas
Peter Barrow ◆ Landlord's House
Milly Barrow ◆ ◆ Handy Barrow
Old Isaac ◆ Road
◆ Calvin Parker
Tom Tang

◆ Beckton Barrow
Lem Douglas

The Barrow Plantation, 1860 and 1881

These maps show the changes that transformed the Barrow plantation after the Civil War.

numbered 162, at least half of them children. One out of four families was named Barrow. When David Crenshaw Barrow, Jr., summed up plantation life in 1881 for the readers of *Scribner's Monthly,* he emphasized "how completely the relations between the races at the South have changed." For instance, his father's tenants needed little supervision. "Very many negro farmers are capable of directing the working of their own crops," he explained, "and not a few object to directions." The younger Barrow expressed pride that no tenant on his father's land had joined the "exodus" movement that had drawn blacks out of the South in the late 1870s. He also took pleasure in the fact that the most troublesome slave, Lem Bryant, once beyond the overseer's control, had become the most industrious tenant—a transformation Barrow, Jr., attributed to the impact of freedom.

Claiming satisfaction with the changes that he and his father had seen, planter Barrow's son assured

David Crenshaw Barrow, Jr.

The young Barrow posed for this photograph around the time that his article in Scribner's Monthly *appeared.*

his readers that southern freedmen were content with their lives as tenant farmers. "In Georgia, the negro has adapted himself to his new circumstances, and freedom fits him

as if it had been cut out and made for him," he reported. "As a people, they are happy; they have become suited to their new estate and it to them." The younger Barrow's positive view of postwar farming arrangements might well have been challenged by the growing number of southerners, black and white, who had become mired in debt as sharecroppers. His article in *Scribner's,* however, written for a northern audience, was intended to convey a political message. Not only had the one-time slaves adjusted to emancipation, Barrow, Jr., suggested, but so had their former owners. This concession was part of the national celebration of reunion that followed the Compromise of 1877 (see below).

Few if any of David Crenshaw Barrow's nine offspring, all born on the "Pope Place," found a vocation in southern agriculture. Two sons had died as young men, and another in a Civil War battle. By 1881 the surviving Barrow children, save Clara, had moved away from their father's home and chosen a variety of occupations. Pope Barrow, the oldest, became a lawyer and a judge and would later serve as U.S. senator from Georgia. Thomas Barrow, who had fought with the Confederate army, first turned to business and then became a Baptist minister. Lucy Barrow married the son of a prominent Georgian, Howell Cobb, who had once been considered for the post of president of the Confederacy. Nellie Barrow also married and moved to Sapelo Island off the coast of Georgia. David Crenshaw Barrow, Jr., began his career as a lawyer but in 1879 became a mathematics teacher at the University of Georgia in Athens, not far from the Oglethorpe County plantation. Barrow, Jr., retained an avid interest in farming, which he later practiced in partnership with the son of his father's former overseer.

and incorrigible, did not intend to work as long or as hard as they had labored under slavery. One planter estimated that workers accomplished only "two-fifths of what they did under the old system"; and as productivity fell, so did land values. Some planters considered importing white immigrant labor, but they doubted that whites would perform black fieldwork for long. To top off the planters' problems, cotton prices plummeted, for during the war northern and foreign buyers had found new sources of cotton in Egypt and India, and the world supply had vastly increased. Finally, the harvests of 1866 and 1867 were extremely poor. By then an agricultural impasse had been reached: landowners lacked labor and freedmen lacked land. But free blacks, unlike slaves, had the right to enter into contracts—or to refuse to do so—and thereby gained some leverage.

Planters and freedmen began experimenting with new labor schemes, including the division of plantations into small tenancies (see "A Place in Time"). Sharecropping, the most widespread arrangement, evolved as a compromise. Under the sharecropping system, landowners subdivided large plantations into farms of thirty to fifty acres, which they rented to freedmen under annual leases for a share of the crop, usually half. Freedmen preferred this system to wage labor because it represented a step toward independence. The decentralized plan enabled heads of households to use the labor of family members. Moreover, a half-share of the crop far exceeded the fraction that freedmen had received as wages under the black codes. Planters often spoke of sharecropping as a capitulation, but they gained as well. Landowners retained power over tenants, because annual leases did not have to be renewed; they could expel undesirable tenants at the end of the year. Planters also shared the risk of planting with tenants: if a crop failed, both suffered the loss. Most important, planters retained control of their land and in some cases extended their holdings. The most productive land, therefore, remained in the hands of a small group of owners, as before the war. Sharecropping forced planters to relinquish day-to-day control over the labor of freedmen, but it helped to preserve the planter elite.

Sharecropping arrangements varied widely and were not universal. On sugar and rice plantations, the wage system continued. Some freedmen remained independent renters. Some landowners

leased areas to white tenants who then subcontracted with black labor. But by the end of the 1860s, the plantation tradition had given way to sharecropping in the cotton South, and the new system continued to expand. A severe depression in 1873 drove many black renters into sharecropping. By then thousands of independent white farmers had become sharecroppers as well. Stung by wartime losses and by the dismal postwar economy, they sank into debt and lost their land to creditors. Many backcountry residents, no longer able to get by on subsistence farming, shifted to cash crops like cotton and suffered the same fate. At the end of Reconstruction, one-third of the white farmers in Mississippi, for instance, worked as sharecroppers.

By 1880, 80 percent of the land in the cotton-producing states had been subdivided into tenancies, most of it farmed by sharecroppers, white and black. Indeed, white sharecroppers now outnumbered black ones, although a higher proportion of southern blacks, about 75 percent, were involved in the system. Changes in marketing and finance, meanwhile, made the sharecroppers' lot increasingly precarious.

Toward a Crop-Lien Economy

Before the Civil War, planters had depended on factors, or middlemen, who sold them supplies, extended credit, and marketed their crops through urban merchants. These long-distance credit arrangements were backed by the high value and liquidity of slave property. When slavery ended, the factorage system collapsed. The postwar South, with hundreds of thousands of tenants and sharecroppers, needed a far more localized network of credit.

Into the gap stepped the rural merchants (often themselves planters), who advanced supplies to tenants and sharecroppers on credit and sold their crops to wholesalers or textile manufacturers. Since renters had no property to use as collateral, the merchants secured their loans with a lien, or claim, on each farmer's next crop. They charged exorbitant interest of 50 percent or 60 percent or more and quickly drew many tenants and sharecroppers into a cycle of indebtedness. Owing part of the crop to a landowner for rent, a sharecropper also owed his rural merchant a large sum (perhaps

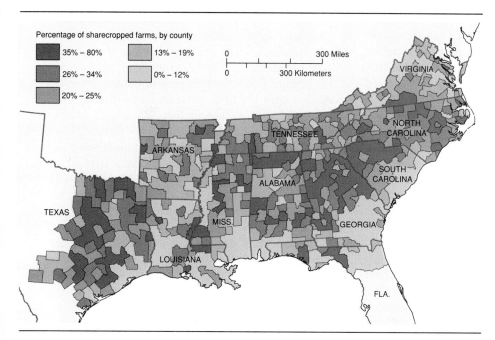

Percentage of sharecropped farms, by county

35% – 80%	13% – 19%
26% – 34%	0% – 12%
20% – 25%	

0   300 Miles

0   300 Kilometers

VIRGINIA

NORTH CAROLINA

TENNESSEE

ARKANSAS

SOUTH CAROLINA

ALABAMA

GEORGIA

TEXAS

MISS.

LOUISIANA

FLA.

Southern Sharecropping, 1880

The depressed economy of the late 1870s caused poverty and debt, increased tenancy among white farmers, and forced many renters, black and white, into sharecropping. By 1880 the sharecropping system pervaded most southern counties, with highest concentrations in the cotton belt from South Carolina to eastern Texas.

SOURCE: U.S. Census Office, Tenth Census, 1880, *Report of the Production of Agriculture* (Washington, D.C.: Government Printing Office, 1883) Table 5.

amounting to the rest of his crop, if not more) for supplies. Moreover, an illiterate tenant often could not keep track of his financial arrangements, and a merchant could easily take advantage of him. "A man that didn't know how to count would always lose," an Arkansas freedman later explained. Once a tenant's debts or alleged debts exceeded the value of his crop, he was tied to the land, to cotton, and to sharecropping.

By the end of Reconstruction, sharecropping and crop liens had transformed southern agriculture. They bound the entire region to staple production and prevented crop diversification, for despite plunging cotton prices, creditors—landowners and merchants—insisted that tenants raise only easily marketable cash crops. Short of capital, planters could no longer invest in new equipment or improve their land by such techniques as crop rotation and contour plowing. Soil depletion, land erosion, and agricultural backwardness soon locked much of the South into a cycle of poverty. Overall, postwar changes in southern agriculture left the region with extremely bleak economic prospects.

But the major victims of the new agricultural arrangements were the indebted tenant farmers, who had been trapped in a system of what has been called debt peonage. Raising cotton for distant markets, for prices over which they had no control, remained the only survival route open to poor farmers, regardless of race. But the low income thus derived often forced them into sharecropping and crop liens, from which escape was difficult. Black tenants, for whom neither landownership nor economic independence ever materialized, suffered further handicaps. Not only were their rights as workers limited, but when Reconstruction ended, their political rights dwindled too. As one southern regime after another returned to Democratic control, freedmen could no longer look to the state governments for protection. Nor could they turn to the federal government, for northern politicians were preoccupied with their own problems.

New Concerns in the North

The nomination of Ulysses S. Grant for president in 1868 launched a chaotic era in national politics. Grant's two terms in office featured political scandals, a party revolt, a massive depression, and a steady retreat from Reconstruction policies. By the mid-1870s, northern voters cared more about the economic climate, unemployment, labor unrest, and currency problems than about the "southern question." Responsive to the shift in popular mood, Republicans became eager to end sectional conflict and consequently turned their backs on the freedmen of the South.

Grantism

Republicans had good reason to pass over long-time party leaders and nominate the popular Grant. A war hero, Grant was endorsed by Union veterans and admired throughout the North. Although identified with Radical Republican views by 1867, he had nonetheless escaped the bitter feuds of Reconstruction politics. At first a Johnson adviser, Grant had broken with Johnson during the tenure-of-office crisis and had become his competitor. Even before Grant's nomination, important visitors to Washington were sure to call on him as well as on the president.

To oppose Grant in the 1868 election, the Democrats nominated New York governor Horatio Seymour, archcritic of the Lincoln administration during the war. Seymour opposed Reconstruction and advocated "sound money," or the withdrawal of greenbacks from circulation, a policy begun by Hugh McCulloch, Johnson's treasury secretary. Grant, who defended Reconstruction, ran on his personal popularity more than on issues. Although he carried all but eight states in the election, the popular vote was very close; in the South, the votes of newly enfranchised freedmen provided the margin of victory. When he was inaugurated, Grant vowed to execute all the laws whether he agreed with them or not, to support sound money, and to follow a humane policy toward the Indians.

A strong leader in war, Grant proved a passive president. Although he lacked Johnson's instinct for disaster, he had little skill at politics. Many of his cabinet appointees—business executives, army men, and family friends—were mediocre if not unscrupulous, and a string of scandals plagued his administration. In 1869 financier Jay Gould and his partner Jim Fisk attempted to corner the gold market with the help of Grant's new brother-in-law, a New York speculator. When gold prices tumbled, Gould salvaged his own fortune, but investors were ruined and Grant's reputation was tarnished. Then before the president's first term ended, his vice president, Schuyler Colfax, was found to be linked to the Crédit Mobilier, a fraudulent construction company created to skim off the profits of the Union Pacific Railroad. Using government funds granted to the railroad, the Union Pacific directors awarded padded construction contracts to the Crédit Mobilier, of which they were also the directors. Discredited, Colfax was dropped from the Grant ticket in the election of 1872. More trouble lay ahead. Grant's private secretary, Orville Babcock, was unmasked in 1875 after taking money from the "whiskey ring," a group of distillers who bribed federal agents to avoid paying millions in whiskey taxes. And in 1876 voters learned that Grant's secretary of war, William E. Belknap, had taken bribes to sell lucrative Indian trading posts in Oklahoma. Impeached and disgraced, Belknap resigned.

Although Grant was not personally involved in the scandals, he loyally defended his subordinates. To his critics, "Grantism" came to stand for fraud, bribery, and corruption in office. Such evils spread far beyond Washington. In Pennsylvania, for example, the Standard Oil Company and the Pennsylvania Railroad controlled the legislature. Urban politics also provided rich opportunities for graft and swindles. The New York City press revealed in 1872 that Democratic boss William M. Tweed, the "Grand Sachem" of Tammany Hall, led a ring that looted the city treasury and collected

The Election of 1868				
Candidates	Parties	Electoral Vote	Popular Vote	Percentage of Popular Vote
ULYSSES S. GRANT	Republican	214	3,013,421	52.7
Horatio Seymour	Democratic	80	2,706,829	47.3

Boss Tweed

Thomas Nast's cartoons in Harper's Weekly *helped topple New York Democratic boss William M. Tweed, who, with his associates, embodied corruption on a large scale. Known among reformers as the forty thieves, the Tweed Ring had granted lucrative franchises to companies they controlled, padded construction bills, practiced graft and extortion, and exploited every opportunity to plunder the city's funds.*

an estimated $200 million in kickbacks and pay-offs. When Mark Twain and coauthor Charles Dudley Warner published their satiric novel *The Gilded Age** (1873), readers recognized the book's speculators, self-promoters, and maniacal opportunists as familiar types in public life.

Grant had some success in foreign policy. In 1872 his competent secretary of state, Hamilton Fish, engineered the settlement of the *Alabama* claims with England. To compensate for damage done by British-built raiders sold to the Confederacy during the war, an international tribunal awarded the United States $15.5 million. But the

---

*The name Gilded Age was subsequently used to refer to the decades from the 1870s to the 1890s.

Grant administration undercut this success with a fiasco when it tried to add nonadjacent territory to the United States, as the Johnson administration had done. In 1867 Johnson's secretary of state, William H. Seward, had negotiated a treaty in which the United States bought Alaska from Russia at the bargain price of $7.2 million. Although the press mocked "Seward's Ice Box," the purchase kindled expansionists' hopes. In 1870 Grant decided to annex the Caribbean island nation of Santo Domingo. Formerly known as Hispaniola and today called the Dominican Republic, Santo Domingo had been passed back and forth since the late eighteenth century among France, Spain, and Haiti. Annexation, Grant believed, would promote Caribbean trade and provide a haven for persecuted southern blacks, who might settle among the Dominicans. American speculators, meanwhile, anticipated windfalls from land sales, commerce, and mining in Santo Domingo. But Congress disliked Grant's annexation plan. Senator Charles Sumner denounced the Santo Domingo scheme as an imperialist "dance of blood." The Senate killed the annexation treaty and further diminished Grant's reputation.

As the election of 1872 approached, dissident Republicans expressed fears that "Grantism" at home and abroad would ruin the party. Even Grant's new running mate, Henry Wilson, referred to the president privately as a millstone, or burden, on his fellow Republicans. The dissidents took action. Led by a combination of former Radicals—including Sumner (now Grant's enemy), Senator Carl Schurz of Missouri, and Congressman George Julian of Indiana—and Republicans left out of Grant's "Great Barbecue," the president's critics formed their own party, the Liberal Republicans.

The Liberals' Revolt

The Liberal Republican revolt marked a turning point in Reconstruction history. By splitting the Republican party, it undermined support for Republican southern policy. The Liberals attacked the "regular" Republicans on several key issues. Denouncing "Grantism" and "spoilsmen" (political hacks who gained party office), they demanded civil-service reform to bring the "best men" into government. Rejecting the usual Republican high-tariff policy, they espoused free trade. Most important, the Liberals condemned "bayonet rule" in the South. Even some Republicans once known for radicalism did a turnabout, claiming that Reconstruction had achieved its goal: blacks had been enfranchised and could henceforth manage for themselves. Corruption in government, North and South, they asserted, now posed a greater danger than Confederate resurgence. In the South, indeed, corrupt Republican regimes were *kept* in power, the Liberals said, because the "best men"—the most capable and experienced politicians—were ex-Confederates who had been barred from officeholding.

For president the new party bypassed Charles Sumner and nominated *New York Tribune* editor Horace Greeley, who had inconsistently supported both a stringent reconstruction policy and leniency toward former rebels. The Democrats endorsed Greeley as well, despite his longtime condemnation of them. Their campaign slogan explained their support: "Anything to Beat Grant." Republican reformers were suddenly allied with the Democratic party that they had recently castigated as a "sewer" of treasonous sentiments.

Horace Greeley proved so diligent a campaigner that he worked himself to death making speeches from the back of a campaign train. He died a few weeks after the election. Grant, who won 56 percent of the popular vote, carried all the northern states as well as a majority of the sixteen southern and border states. But the division among Republicans affected Reconstruction. To deprive the Liberals of a campaign issue, Grant Republicans in Congress, the "regulars," passed an amnesty act that effectively allowed all but a few hundred ex-Confederate officials to hold office. The flood of private amnesty acts that followed convinced white southerners that any ex-Confederate save Jefferson Davis could rise to power. During Grant's

second term, Republican desires to discard the "southern question" mounted as a depression of unprecedented scope gripped the nation.

The Panic of 1873

With the postwar years came accelerated industrialization, rapid economic expansion, and frantic speculation. Investors rushed to take advantage of rising prices, new markets, high tariffs, and seemingly boundless opportunities. Railroads provided the biggest lure. In May 1869 railroad executives drove a golden spike into the ground at Promontory Point, Utah, joining the Union Pacific and Central Pacific lines (see Chapter 16). The first transcontinental railroad heralded a new era. By 1873 almost four hundred railroad corporations crisscrossed the Northeast, consuming tons of coal and miles of steel rail from the mines and mills of Pennsylvania and neighboring states. Transforming the northern economy, the railroad boom led entrepreneurs to overspeculate, with drastic results.

Philadelphia banker Jay Cooke, who had helped finance the Union effort with his bond campaign during the Civil War, had taken over a new transcontinental line, the Northern Pacific, in 1869. Northern Pacific securities sold briskly for several years, but in 1873 the line's construction costs outran new investments. In September of that year, his vaults full of bonds that he could no longer sell, Cooke failed to meet his obligations, and his bank, the largest in the nation, shut down. Smaller firms collapsed as well, and so did the stock market. This Panic of 1873 triggered a shattering five-year depression that spread quickly, wreaking widespread devastation. Banks closed, farm prices plummeted, steel furnaces stood idle, and one out of four railroads failed. Within two years eighteen thousand businesses went bankrupt, and by 1878 3 million employees were out of jobs. Those still

The Election of 1872				
Candidates	Parties	Electoral Vote	Popular Vote	Percentage of Popular Vote
ULYSSES S. GRANT	Republican	286	3,596,745	55.6
Horace Greeley*	Democratic		2,843,446	43.9

*Upon Greeley's death shortly after the election, the electors supporting him divided their votes among minor candidates.

at work suffered repeated wage cuts, labor protests mounted, and industrial violence spread (see Chapter 17). The depression of the 1870s revealed the conflicts that would characterize a new, industrial America.

The depression also fed a dispute over currency that had begun in 1865. The Civil War had created fiscal chaos. During the war, Americans had used both national bank notes, yellow in color, which would eventually be converted into gold, and greenbacks, a paper currency not "backed" by a particular weight in gold. To stabilize the postwar currency, greenbacks would have to be withdrawn from circulation. This "sound-money" policy, favored by investors, was implemented by Treasury Secretary Hugh McCulloch with the backing of Congress. But those who depended on easy credit, both indebted farmers and manufacturers, wanted an expanding currency; that is, more greenbacks. Once the depression began, demands for such "easy money" rose. The issue divided both major parties and was compounded by another one: how to repay the federal debt.

During the war the Union government had borrowed what were then astronomical sums, on whatever terms it could get, mainly through the sale of war bonds—in effect, short-term federal IOUs—to private citizens. By 1869 the issue of war-debt repayment was straining the Republican party, whose support came from voters with diverse financial interests. To pacify bondholders, Senator John Sherman of Ohio and other Republican leaders obtained passage of the Public Credit Act of 1869, which promised to pay the war debt in "coin." Holders of war bonds expected no less; in fact, they expected payment in coin, although many had bought their bonds with greenbacks!

With investors reassured by the Public Credit Act, Sherman guided legislation through Congress that swapped the old short-term bonds for new ones payable over the next generation. In 1872 another bill in effect defined "coin" as "gold coin" by dropping the traditional silver dollar from the official coinage. Through a feat of ingenious compromise, which placated investors and debtors, Sherman preserved the public credit, the currency, and Republican unity. In 1875 he engineered the Specie Resumption Act, which promised to put the nation effectively on the gold standard in 1879, while tossing a few more immediate but less impor-

tant bones to Republican voters who wanted "easy money." Grant, no financial theorist, signed this act.

The Republican leadership acted not a moment too soon, because when the Democrats gained control of the House in 1875, with the depression in full force, a verbal storm broke out. Many Democrats and some Republicans passionately demanded that the silver dollar be restored in order to expand the currency and relieve the depression. These "free-silver" advocates secured passage of the Bland-Allison Act of 1878, which partially restored silver coinage. The law required the Treasury to buy $2 million to $4 million worth of silver each month and turn it into coin but did not revive the silver standard. In 1876 other expansionists formed the Greenback party, which adopted the debtors' cause and fought to keep greenbacks in circulation. But despite the election of fourteen Greenback congressmen, they did not get even as far as the free-silver people had. As the nation emerged from depression in 1879, the clamor for "easy money" subsided, only to resurge in the 1890s (see Chapter 20). The controversial "money question" of the 1870s, never permanently solved, gave politicians and voters another reason to focus on new northern issues and forget about the South.

Reconstruction and the Constitution

The Supreme Court of the 1870s also played a role in weakening northern support for Reconstruction. In the wartime crisis, few cases of note had come before the Court. After the war, however, constitutional questions surged into prominence.

First, would the Court support congressional laws to protect freedmen's rights? The decision in *Ex parte* Milligan (1866) suggested not. In this case, the Court declared that a military commission established by the president or Congress could not try civilians in areas remote from war where the civil courts were functioning. Thus special military courts to enforce the Supplementary Freedmen's Bureau Act were doomed. Second, would the Court sabotage the congressional Reconstruction plan, as Republicans feared? Their qualms were valid, for if the Union was indissoluble, as the North had claimed during the war, then the concept of *restoring* states to the Union would be meaningless. In *Texas* v. *White* (1869), the Court took a stand on this question, ruling that, although the

Union was indissoluble and secession was legally impossible, the process of Reconstruction was still constitutional. It was grounded in Congress's power to ensure each state a republican form of government and to recognize the legitimate government in any state.

The 1869 decision protected the Republicans' Reconstruction program. But during the 1870s, when faced with cases involving the Fourteenth and Fifteenth amendments, the Court backed away from Reconstruction policy. Significantly, most of the justices at this time were Republicans who had been appointed to the Supreme Court by Lincoln and Grant.

In the *Slaughterhouse* cases of 1873, the Supreme Court began to chip away at the Fourteenth Amendment. Although the cases involved a business monopoly rather than freedmen's rights, they provided the opportunity for a narrow interpretation of the amendment. In 1869 the Louisiana legislature had granted a monopoly over the New Orleans slaughterhouse business to one firm and had closed down all other slaughterhouses in the interest of public health. The excluded butchers brought suit. The state had deprived them of their lawful occupation without due process of law, they claimed, and such action violated the Fourteenth Amendment, which guaranteed that no state could "abridge the privileges or immunities" of U.S. citizens. The Supreme Court upheld the Louisiana legislature by putting forth a doctrine of "dual citizenship." The Fourteenth Amendment, declared the Court, protected only the rights of *national* citizenship, such as the right of interstate travel or the right to federal protection when on the high seas. It did not protect those basic civil rights that fell to citizens by virtue of their *state* citizenship. Therefore, the federal government was not obliged to protect such rights against violation by the states. The *Slaughterhouse* decision came close to nullifying the intent of the Fourteenth Amendment—to secure freedmen's rights against state encroachment.

The Supreme Court again backed away from Reconstruction in two cases involving the Enforcement Act of 1870. The case of *U.S. v. Reese* (1876) centered on Kentucky officials who, after barring blacks from voting, had been indicted in 1873 by a Kentucky federal court under the First Enforcement Act. In its decision in favor of the officials,

the Supreme Court stated that the Fifteenth Amendment did not "confer the right of suffrage upon anyone." It merely prohibited the hindrance of voting on the basis of race, color, or previous condition of servitude. Since the Enforcement Act prohibited the hindrance of *anyone* from voting for *any* reason (that is, since it did not repeat the exact wording of the amendment), the Court declared its crucial sections, and the Kentucky indictment, invalid. Another 1876 case, *U.S. v. Cruikshank,* concerned the indictment under the 1870 Enforcement Act of white Louisianians after the Colfax massacre, a battle between armed whites and black state militiamen in which seventy blacks had surrendered, half of whom were then murdered. The Fourteenth Amendment, contended the Court, prohibited only the encroachment on individual rights by a *state,* not by other individuals; "ordinary crime" was not the target of federal law. The decision threw out the indictments and, with them, the effectiveness of the Enforcement Act.

Continuing its retreat from Reconstruction, the Supreme Court in 1883 invalidated both the Civil Rights Act of 1875 and the Ku Klux Klan Act of 1871 and later upheld segregation laws (see Chapter 20). These decisions cumulatively dismantled the Reconstruction policies that Republicans had sponsored after the war. The 1870s rulings that initiated the judicial retreat had a more immediate impact as well. They confirmed rising northern sentiment that Reconstruction's egalitarian goals could not be enforced.

Republicans in Retreat

The Republicans did not reject Reconstruction suddenly but rather disengaged from it gradually. The withdrawal process began with Grant's election to the presidency in 1868. Although not an architect of Reconstruction policy, Grant defended that policy and tried to enforce the laws. But he shared with most Americans a belief in decentralized government and a reluctance to assert federal authority in local and state affairs.

During the 1870s, as the northern military presence shrank in the South, Republican idealism waned in the North. The Liberal Republican revolt of 1872 eroded what remained of radicalism. Although the "regular" Republicans, who backed Grant, continued to defend Reconstruction in the

1872 election, many held ambivalent views. Commercial and industrial interests now dominated both wings of the party, and Grant supporters had greater zeal for doing business in and with the South than for rekindling sectional strife. After the Democrats showed renewed strength by winning control of the House in the 1874 elections, in a nationwide sweep, Reconstruction became a political liability.

By 1875 the Radical Republicans, so prominent in the 1860s, had vanished from the political scene. Chase, Stevens, and Sumner were dead. Other Radicals had lost office or had abandoned their former convictions. "Waving the Bloody Shirt," or defaming Democratic opponents by reviving wartime animosity, now struck many Republicans, including former Radicals, as counterproductive. Party leaders reported that voters were "sick of carpet-bag government" and tiring of both the "southern question" and the "Negro question." Under such circumstances, it seemed pointless to continue the unpopular and expensive policy of military intervention in the South to prop up Republican regimes that even President Grant found corrupt. Finally, few Republicans shared the egalitarian spirit that had animated Stevens and Sumner. Politics aside, Republican leaders and voters generally agreed with southern Democrats that blacks, although deserving of freedom, were inferior to whites. To insist on black equality would be a thankless, divisive, and politically suicidal undertaking. Moreover, it would quash any hope of reunion between the regions. The Republicans' retreat from Reconstruction set the stage for its demise in 1877.

Reconstruction Abandoned

"We are in a very hot political contest just now," a Mississippi planter wrote to his daughter in 1875, "with a good prospect of turning out the carpet-bag thieves by whom we have been robbed for the past six to ten years." Similar contests raged through the South in the 1870s, as the resentment of white majorities grew and Democratic influence surged. By the end of 1872, the Democrats had regained power in Tennessee, Virginia, Georgia, and North Carolina. Within three years they won control in

Texas, Alabama, Arkansas, and Mississippi. As the 1876 elections approached, Republican rule survived in only three states—South Carolina, Florida, and Louisiana. Democratic victories in the state elections of 1876 and political bargaining in Washington in 1877 abruptly ended what little remained of Reconstruction.

Redeeming the South

After 1872 the Republicans' collapse in the South accelerated. Congressional amnesty enabled almost all ex-Confederate officials to regain office, divisions among the Republicans loosened their party's weak grip on the southern electorate, and attrition diminished Republican ranks. Some carpetbaggers gave up and returned North, while others, including supporters of Liberal Republicans in the divisive 1872 election, shifted to the Democratic party. Scalawags deserted in even larger numbers. Southerners who had joined the Republicans to moderate rampant radicalism tired of northern interference; once "home rule" by Democrats became a possibility, staying Republican meant going down with a sinking ship. As a Mississippian explained, *not* being a Democrat would condemn his family to "social isolation" and "political oblivion." Scalawag defections ruined Republican prospects for survival. In some states, as white southerners fled the Republican party, blacks became more powerful within it, thus polarizing voters into white and black camps. Unable to win new white votes or retain the old ones, the always precarious Republican coalition fell apart.

Meanwhile, the Democrats mobilized grassroots support and overcame the white voter apathy that had plagued the early days of Reconstruction. The resurrected southern Democratic party was not a pillar of unity. Within it, businessmen who envisioned an industrialized "New South" opposed an agrarian faction called the Bourbons, who represented the old planter elite. But all Democrats shared a major goal: to oust the Republicans from office. Their tactics varied from state to state. Alabama Democrats won by promising to cut taxes and by getting out the white vote. In Louisiana the "White League," a vigilante organization formed in 1874, undermined the Republicans' hold. Intimidation also proved effective in Mississippi, where violent incidents—like the 1874 slaughter in Vicksburg of

The White League

Alabama's White League, formed in 1874, strove to oust Republicans from office by intimidating black voters. To political cartoonist Thomas Nast, such vigilante tactics suggested an alliance between the White League and the outlawed Ku Klux Klan.

about three hundred blacks by rampaging whites—terrorized black voters. In 1875 the "Mississippi plan" took effect: local Democratic clubs armed their members, dispersed Republican meetings, patrolled voter-registration places, and marched through black areas. "Even in counties where there is no actual killing, the Republicans are paralyzed through fear and will not act," the anguished carpetbag governor of Mississippi wrote to his wife. "Why should I fight a hopeless battle . . . when no possible good to the Negro or anybody else would result?" In 1876, South Carolina's "Rifle Clubs" and "Red Shirts," armed groups that threatened Republicans, continued the scare tactics that had worked so well in Mississippi.

New outbursts of intimidation did not completely squelch black voting. Many blacks throughout the South continued to vote until the end of Reconstruction and after. But the Democrats deprived the Republicans of enough black votes to win state elections. In some counties they encouraged freedmen to vote Democratic at supervised polls where voters cast their ballots in public by placing a card with a party label in a box. In other instances white employers and landowners prevented blacks from voting. Labor contracts included clauses forbidding attendance at political meetings; planters used the threat of eviction to keep sharecroppers in line. Since the Enforcement acts could not be enforced, intimidation and economic pressure succeeded.

Redemption, the word that Democrats used to describe their return to power, meant more than a mere rotation in personnel. When the Democrats took office, they made changes as sweeping as those imposed by the Republicans in 1867–1868. Some

The Duration of Republican Rule in the Ex-Confederate States			
Former Confederate States	*Readmission to the Union Under Congressional Reconstruction*	*Democrats (Conservatives) Gain Control*	*Duration of Republican Rule*
Alabama	June 25, 1868	November 14, 1874	6½ years
Arkansas	June 22, 1868	November 10, 1874	6½ years
Florida	June 25, 1868	January 2, 1877	8½ years
Georgia	July 15, 1870	November 1, 1871	1 year
Louisiana	June 25, 1868	January 2, 1877	8½ years
Mississippi	February 23, 1870	November 3, 1875	5½ years
North Carolina	June 25, 1868	November 3, 1870	2 years
South Carolina	June 25, 1868	November 12, 1876	8 years
Tennessee	July 24, 1866*	October 4, 1869	3 years
Texas	March 30, 1870	January 14, 1873	3 years
Virginia	January 26, 1870	October 5, 1869†	0 years

*Admitted before start of Congressional Reconstruction.
†Democrats gained control before readmission.
SOURCE: John Hope Franklin, *Reconstruction After the Civil War* (Chicago: University of Chicago Press, 1962), 231.

Ho for Kansas!

Benjamin "Pap" Singleton, a one-time fugitive slave from Tennessee, returned there to promote the "exodus" movement of the late 1870s. Forming a real-estate company, Singleton traveled the South recruiting parties of freedmen who were disillusioned with the outcome of Reconstruction to settle the "fine rolling prairies" of Kansas. These emigrants, awaiting a Mississippi River boat, looked forward to midwestern homesteads, freedom from violence, and political equality.

states called constitutional conventions to reverse Republican policies. All cut back expenses, wiped out social programs, lowered taxes, and revised their tax systems to relieve landowners of large burdens. State courts limited the rights of tenants and sharecroppers. Most important, the Democrats used the law to ensure a stable black labor force. Legislatures restored vagrancy laws and revised crop-lien statutes to make landowners' claims superior to those of merchants. The redeemers extended their inventiveness to criminal law. Local ordinances in heavily black counties might restrict hunting, fishing, gun carrying, and ownership of dogs and thereby curtail the everyday activities of freedmen who lived off the land. States passed severe laws against trespassing and theft; stealing livestock or wrongly taking part of a crop became grand larceny with a penalty of up to five years at hard labor. By the end of Reconstruction, a large black convict work force had been leased out to private contractors, who profited from their labor.

For the freedmen, whose aspirations had been raised by Republican rule, the impact of redemption was dispiriting if not demoralizing. The new laws, Tennessee blacks contended at an 1875 convention, would "place the race in a condition of servitude scarcely less degrading than that endured before the late civil war." During the late 1870s, as the political climate grew more oppressive, an "exodus" movement spread through Mississippi, Tennessee, Texas, and Louisiana. "We looked around and we seed that there was no way on earth that we could better our condition," a Louisiana "colonization council" declared in 1877. Seeking a way out of the South, some freedmen decided to become homesteaders in Kansas. After a major outbreak of "Kansas fever" in 1879, four thousand "exodusters" from Mississippi and Louisiana joined about ten thousand who had reached Kansas in smaller groups earlier in the decade. But the vast majority of freedmen, devoid of resources, had no migration options or escape route. Mass movement of southern blacks to the North and Midwest would not gain momentum until the twentieth century.

The Election of 1876

By the autumn of 1876, with redemption almost complete, both parties moved to discard the heritage of animosity left by the war and Reconstruction. The Republicans nominated Rutherford B. Hayes, three times Ohio's governor, for president. Untainted by the scandals of the Grant administration and popular with all factions in his party, Hayes presented himself as a "moderate" on southern policy. He favored "home rule" in the South and a guarantee of civil and political rights for all—two planks that were by now clearly contradictory. The Democrats nominated Governor Samuel B. Tilden of New York, a millionaire corporate lawyer and political reformer. Known for his assaults on the rapacious Tweed Ring that had plundered New York City's treasury, Tilden campaigned against governmental fraud and waste. The candidates had much in common. As fiscal conservatives, both favored sound money. Both endorsed civil-service reform and decried corruption, an irony since the 1876 election would prove extremely corrupt.

Tilden won the popular vote by a small margin and seemed destined to capture the 185 electoral votes needed for victory. But the Republicans challenged the pro-Tilden returns from South Carolina, Florida, and Louisiana. If they could deprive the Democrats of these nineteen electoral votes, Hayes would become president. The Democrats, who needed only one of the disputed electoral votes for victory, challenged the validity of Oregon's single electoral vote, which the Republicans had won, on a technicality. Twenty electoral votes, therefore, were in contention. Republicans, however, still controlled the electoral machinery in the three unredeemed southern states, where they threw out enough Democratic ballots to declare Hayes the winner.

The nation now faced an unprecedented dilemma: each party claimed victory in the contested states, and each accused the other of fraud. In fact, both sets of southern results had been obtained by fraud: the Republicans had discarded legitimate Democratic ballots, while the Democrats had illegally prevented freedmen from voting. To resolve the conflict, Congress in January 1877 created a special electoral commission to determine which party would get the contested electoral votes. Made up of senators, representatives, and Supreme Court justices, the commission included seven Democrats, seven Republicans, and one independent, justice David Davis of Illinois. When

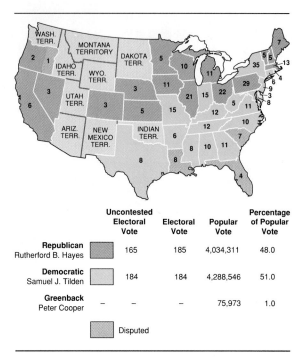

	Uncontested Electoral Vote	Electoral Vote	Popular Vote	Percentage of Popular Vote
Republican Rutherford B. Hayes	165	185	4,034,311	48.0
Democratic Samuel J. Tilden	184	184	4,288,546	51.0
Greenback Peter Cooper	–	–	75,973	1.0

Disputed

The Disputed Election of 1876

Davis resigned to run for the Senate, Congress replaced him with a Republican, and the commission handed the election to Hayes by an 8 to 7 vote.

Congress now had to certify the new electoral vote. But since the Democrats controlled the House, a new obstacle loomed. Some Democrats planned a filibuster to forestall approval of the electoral vote. Had they carried out their scheme, the nation would have been without a president on inauguration day. But there remained room for compromise, for many southern Democrats accepted Hayes's election. Among them were former scalawags with commercial interests, who still favored Republican financial policies, and railroad investors, who hoped that a Republican administration would help them build a southern transcontinental line. Other southerners cared mainly about Democratic state victories and did not mind conceding the presidency as long as the new Republican administration would leave the South alone. Republican leaders, although sure of eventual triumph, were willing to bargain as well, for candidate Hayes desired not merely victory but southern approval.

A series of informal negotiations ensued, at which politicians of both parties exchanged promises. Ohio Republicans and southern Democrats who met at the Wormley House, a Washington hotel, reached an agreement that if Hayes won the election, he would remove federal troops from South Carolina and Louisiana, and Democrats could gain control of those states. In other bargaining sessions, southern politicians asked for federal patronage, federal aid to railroads, and federal support for internal improvements. In return, they promised to drop the filibuster, to accept Hayes as president, and to treat freedmen fairly.

With the threatened filibuster broken, Congress ratified Hayes's election. Once in office, Hayes fulfilled some of the promises that his Republican colleagues had made. He appointed a former Confederate as postmaster general and ordered federal troops who guarded the South Carolina and Louisiana statehouses back to their barracks. Although federal soldiers remained in the South after 1877,

they no longer served a political function. The Democrats, meanwhile, took control of state governments in Louisiana, South Carolina, and Florida. When Republican rule toppled in these states, the era of Reconstruction finally ended, though more with a whimper than with a resounding crash.

But some of the bargains struck in the Compromise of 1877, such as the Democrats' promises to treat southern blacks fairly, were forgotten, as were Hayes's campaign pledges to ensure the freedmen's rights. "When you turned us loose, you turned us loose to the sky, to the storm, to the whirlwind, and worst of all . . . to the wrath of our infuriated masters," Frederick Douglass had charged at the Republican convention in 1876. "The question now is, do you mean to make good to us the promises in your Constitution?" The answer provided by the 1876 election and the 1877 compromises was "No."

Conclusion

The end of Reconstruction brought benefits to both political parties. Although unable to retain a southern constituency, the Republican party was no longer burdened by the unpopular "southern question." And it had firm support in New England, the Middle Atlantic states, and the Great Lakes states. The Democrats, who had regained power in the ex-Confederate states, would remain entrenched there for almost a century. To be sure, the South was now tied to sharecropping and economic backwardness as securely as it had once been tied to slavery. But "home rule," or Democratic control, was firmly in place.

Reconstruction's end also signaled a triumph for nationalism and the spirit of reunion. In the fall of 1877, President Hayes made a rousing goodwill tour of the South to champion reconciliation, and similar celebrations continued through the 1880s and 1890s. When former president Grant died in 1885, veterans of both Civil War armies served as pallbearers. Jefferson Davis, imprisoned for two years after the war but never brought to trial, urged young men to "lay aside all rancor, all bitter sectional feeling." The federal government turned battlefields into national parks where veterans of both armies could gather for reunions. As the nation applauded reconciliation, the reputation of Reconstruction sank. Looking back on the 1860s and 1870s, most late-nineteenth-century Americans dismissed the congressional effort to reconstruct the South as a fiasco—a tragic interlude of "radical rule" or "black reconstruction," fashioned by carpetbaggers, scalawags, and Radical Republicans.

With the hindsight of a century, recent historians continue to regard Reconstruction as a failure, though of a different kind. No longer viewed as a misguided scheme that collapsed because of radical excess, Reconstruction is now widely seen as a democratic experiment that did not go far enough. Historians cite two main causes. First, Congress did not promote freedmen's independence through land reform; without property of their own, southern blacks lacked the economic power to defend their interests as free citizens. Property ownership, however, does not necessarily ensure political rights, nor does it invariably provide economic security. Considering the depressed state of southern agriculture in the postwar decades, the freedmen's fate as independent farmers would likely have been perilous. Thus the land-reform question, like much else about Reconstruction, remains a subject of debate. A second cause of Reconstruction's collapse is less open to dispute: the federal government neglected to back congressional Reconstruction with military force. Given the choice between protecting blacks' rights at whatever cost and promoting reunion, the government opted for reunion. Reconstruction's failure, therefore, was the federal government's failure to fulfill its own goals and create a biracial democracy in the South. As a result, the nation's adjustment to the consequences of emancipation would continue into the twentieth century.

The Reconstruction era left some significant legacies, including the Fourteenth and Fifteenth amendments, both products of an extraordinary chain of postwar political crises. Although neither amendment would be used to protect minority rights for almost a century, they remain monuments to the democratic zeal that swept Congress in the 1860s. The Reconstruction years also hold a significant place in black history. During this brief respite between slavery and repression, southern blacks reconstituted their families, created new institutions, took part in the transformation of southern agriculture, and participated in government, for the first time in American history. The aspirations and achievements of the Reconstruction era left an indelible mark on black citizens, as is vividly conveyed in an excerpt from a federal document. In the 1880s a congressional committee investigating southern labor conditions solicited the testimony of James K. Green of Montgomery, Alabama, a black politician during Reconstruction and subsequently a carpenter and contractor. At the end of the war, Green reported,

> *I knew nothing more than to obey my master, and there were thousands of us in the same attitude, that didn't know the Lord's prayer, but the tocsin of freedom sounded and knocked at the door and we walked out like free men and we met the exigencies as they grew up, and shouldered the responsibilities.*

Green's proud memory of blacks' achievements reflected one kind of postwar experience. Consigning the Reconstruction era to history, other Americans of the 1880s turned their energies to their economic futures—to their railroads, factories, and mills, and to the exploitation of their bountiful natural resources.

CHRONOLOGY

1863 President Abraham Lincoln issues Proclamation of Amnesty and Reconstruction.

1864 Wade-Davis bill passed by Congress and pocket-vetoed by Lincoln.

1865 Freedmen's Bureau established.
Civil War ends.
Lincoln assassinated; Andrew Johnson becomes president.

1865 Johnson issues Proclamation of Amnesty and
(cont.) Reconstruction.

Ex-Confederate states hold constitutional conventions (May–December).

Black conventions begin in the ex-Confederate states.

Thirteenth Amendment added to the Constitution.

Presidential Reconstruction completed.

1866 Congress enacts the Civil Rights Act of 1866 and the Supplementary Freedmen's Bureau Act over Johnson's vetoes.

Ku Klux Klan founded in Tennessee.

Congress proposes the Fourteenth Amendment.

Tennessee readmitted to the Union.

Race riots in southern cities.

Republicans win congressional elections.

Thirty-ninth Congress begins debates over Reconstruction policy.

1867 Reconstruction Act of 1867.

William Seward negotiates the purchase of Alaska.

Constitutional conventions meet in the ex-Confederate states.

Howard University founded.

1868 President Johnson is impeached, tried, and acquitted.

Omnibus Act.

Fourteenth Amendment added to the Constitution.

Ulysses S. Grant elected president.

1869 Transcontinental railroad completed.

1870 Congress readmits the four remaining southern states to the Union.

Fifteenth Amendment added to the Constitution.

Enforcement Act of 1870.

1871 Second Enforcement Act.

Ku Klux Klan Act.

1872 Liberal Republican party formed.

Amnesty Act.

Alabama claims settled.

Grant reelected president.

1873 Panic of 1873 begins (September–October), setting off a five-year depression.

1874 Democrats gain control of the House of Representatives.

1875 Civil Rights Act of 1875.

Specie Resumption Act.

1876 Disputed presidential election: Rutherford B. Hayes versus Samuel B. Tilden.

1877 Electoral commission decides election in favor of Hayes.

The last Republican-controlled governments overthrown in Florida, Louisiana, and South Carolina.

1879 "Exodus" movement spreads through several southern states.

For Further Reading

Eric Foner, *Reconstruction: America's Unfinished Revolution, 1863–1877* (1988). A thorough exploration of Reconstruction that draws on recent scholarship and stresses the centrality of the black experience.

John Hope Franklin, *Reconstruction After the Civil War* (1961). An overview that dismantles the traditional view of Reconstruction as a disastrous experiment in radical rule.

William Gillette, *Retreat from Reconstruction, 1869–1879* (1979). A survey of the era's national politics, indicting Republican policy makers for vacillation and lack of commitment to racial equality.

Leon Litwack, *Been in the Storm So Long: The Aftermath of Slavery* (1979). A comprehensive study of the black response to emancipation in 1865–1866.

Michael Perman, *The Road to Redemption: Southern Politics, 1869–1879* (1984). Analysis of how the Democratic party gained power in the South and toppled the Reconstruction governments.

Roger L. Ransom and Richard Sutch, *One Kind of Freedom: The Economic Consequences of Emancipation* (1977). Two economists' assessment of the impact of free black labor on the South and explanation of the development of sharecropping and the crop-lien system.

Kenneth M. Stampp, *The Era of Reconstruction, 1865–1877* (1965). A classic recent interpretation of Reconstruction, focusing on the establishment and fall of Republican governments.

Allen W. Trelease, *White Terror: The Ku Klux Klan Conspiracy and Southern Reconstruction* (1971). An examination of postwar vigilantism in the southern states until the suppression of the Ku Klux Klan by the federal government in 1871–1872.

Joel Williamson, *The Negro in South Carolina During Reconstruction, 1861–1877* (1965). A pioneer study of black life and institutions after emancipation.

Additional Bibliography

Reconstruction Politics

Richard H. Abbott, *The Republican Party and the South, 1855–1877* (1986); Herman Belz, *Emancipation and Equal Rights: Politics and Constitutionalism in the Civil War Era* (1978); Michael Les Benedict, *A Compromise of Principle: Congressional Republicans and Reconstruction, 1863–1869* (1974) and *The Impeachment and Trial of Andrew Johnson* (1973); W. R. Brock, *An American Crisis: Congress and Reconstruction, 1865–1867* (1963); Fawn Brodie, *Thaddeus Stevens: Scourge of the South* (1959); LaWanda Cox and John H. Cox, *Politics, Principles, and Prejudice: Dilemma of Reconstruction in America* (1963); Richard O. Curry, ed., *Radicalism, Racism, and Party Realignment: The Border States During Reconstruction* (1969); David Donald, *Charles Sumner and the Rights of Man* (1970) and *The Politics of Reconstruction, 1863–1867* (1965); Ellen Carol DuBois, *Feminism and Suffrage: The Emergence of an Independent Women's Movement in America, 1848–1869* (1978), Chapters 2–6; William Gillette, *The Right to Vote: Politics and Passage of the Fifteenth Amendment* (1969); Harold Hyman, *A More Perfect Union: The Impact of the Civil War and Reconstruction on the Constitution* (1973); Stanley I. Kutler, *Judicial Power and Reconstruction* (1968); Eric McKitrick, *Andrew Johnson and Reconstruction* (1960); James M. McPherson, *Ordeal by Fire: The Civil War and Reconstruction* (1982); James C. Mohr, *Radical Republicans in the North: State Politics During Reconstruction* (1976).

The South

Dan C. Carter, *When the War Was Over: Self-Reconstruction in the South, 1865–1867* (1985); Richard Nelson Current, *Those Terrible Carpetbaggers* (1988); Stephen Hahn, *The Roots of Southern Populism: Yeoman Farmers and the Transformation of the Georgia Upcountry, 1850–1890* (1983); William C. Harris, *The Day of the Carpetbagger: Republican Reconstruction in Mississippi* (1979); Otto Olsen, ed., *Reconstruction and Redemption in the South* (1980); Michael Perman, *Reunion Without Compromise: The South and Reconstruction, 1865–1868* (1973); Mark W. Summers, *Railroads, Reconstruction, and the Gospel of Prosperity: Aid Under the Radical Republicans, 1865–1877* (1984); Ted Tunnell, *Crucible of Reconstruction: War, Radicalism, and Race in Louisiana, 1862–1877* (1984); Jonathan M. Wiener, *Social Origins of the New South: Alabama, 1860–1885* (1978).

Emancipation and the Freedmen

Ira Berlin et al., eds., *Freedom: A Documentary History of Emancipation,* No. 1 (1986) and No. 2 (1983); Carol Rothrock Bleser, *The Promised Land: The History of the South Carolina Land Commission, 1869–1890* (1969); LaWanda Cox, "The Promise of Land for the Freedmen," *Mississippi Valley Historical Review* 45 (1958): 413–440; W. E. B. Du Bois, *Black Reconstruction in America, 1860–1880* (1935); Barbara Jeanne Fields, *Slavery and Freedom on the Middle Ground: Maryland During the Nineteenth Century* (1985); Eric Foner, *Nothing but Freedom: Emancipation and Its Legacies* (1983) and *Politics and Ideology in the Age of the Civil War* (1980), Chapters 6–7; Herbert G. Gutman, *The Black Family in Slavery and Freedom, 1750–1925* (1976); Robert Higgs, *Competition and Coercion: Blacks in the American Economy, 1865–1914* (1977); Thomas Holt, *Black over White: Negro Political Leadership in South Carolina During Reconstruction* (1977); Jacqueline Jones, *Soldiers of Light and Love: Northern Teachers and Georgia Blacks, 1865–1873* (1980) and *Labor of Love, Labor of Sorrow: Black Women, Work, and the Family from Slavery to the Present* (1985), Chapter 2; Peter Kolchin, *First Freedom: The Responses of Alabama's Blacks to Emancipation and Reconstruction* (1972); Lawrence W. Levine, *Black Culture and Black Consciousness: Afro-American Folk*

Thought from Slavery to Freedom (1977); William S. McFeely, *Yankee Stepfather: General O. O. Howard and the Freedmen* (1966); Nell Irvin Painter, *Exodusters* (1977); James Roark, *Masters Without Slaves: Southern Planters in the Civil War and Reconstruction* (1978); William Preston Vaughan, *Schools for All: The Blacks and Public Education in the South, 1865–1877* (1974); Joel Williamson, *The Crucible of Race: Black-White Relations in the American South Since Emancipation* (1984).

National Trends

Paul H. Buck, *The Road to Reunion, 1865–1900* (1937); Adrian Cook, *The Alabama Claims* (1975); Ari M. Hoogenboom, *Outlawing the Spoils: A History of the Civil Service Reform Movement* (1961); William S. McFeely, *Grant: A Biography* (1981); David Montgomery, *Beyond Equality: Labor and the Radical Republicans, 1862–1872* (1967); Walter T. K. Nugent, *The Money Question During Reconstruction* (1967) and *Money and American Society, 1865–1880* (1968); Keith I. Polakoff, *The Politics of Inertia: The Election of 1876 and the End of Reconstruction* (1973); John C. Sproat, *"The Best Men": Liberal Reformers in the Gilded Age* (1968); Irwin Unger, *The Greenback Era: A Social and Political History of American Finance* (1964); Allen Weinstein, *Prelude to Populism: Origins of the Silver Issue, 1867–1878* (1970); C. Vann Woodward, *Reunion and Reaction: The Compromise of 1877 and the End of Reconstruction* (rev. ed., 1956).

CHAPTER 16

The Frontier West

Braving cold winter winds and deep snows in January 1855, forty-year-old John W. North (right), a New England abolitionist, lawyer, and land speculator, guided his horse along the Cannon River in the southern Minnesota Territory searching for a town site. At a river bend fourteen miles downstream from Faribault, he found the perfect place for a sawmill that might anchor his planned town's economy. North immediately began construction of the mill and a log house to serve as workmen's quarters. Six months later, the new community, bearing the name "Northfield" in honor of its founder, consisted of a small store, two mills, several houses, and a ramshackle hotel with a cloth roof.

The following year, town resident E. J. Doolittle, writing to a friend back east, glowingly described the community and the surrounding territory:

Northfield commenced new a year ago last April. we have one flowering mill that cost thirteen thousand dollars 1 water saw mill 1 steam saw mill with other machinery attached to it three hotels, one of them cost Eleven thousand dollars 4 stores well filled with goods & our other Building a school house that cost nine hundred a meeting house building about 40 good nice dwelling houses & twice as many poor houses & shanties there is quite a number of houses going up now the place is growing fast enough it is a very healthy place, & is going to be a great Farming country . . . we have no intoxicating drink sold in our town most all Yankees one colored family, two or three Dutch no Irish, Indians pass through town frequently

I wish you could take a trip out here. . . . I know you would like the country we do not have to dig stone nor cast manure to raise crops it does not cost any thing to pasture cattle here . . . I have just been up West of here about 75 miles I found it to be a fine country I set out to drive my team through a prairie to get to a piece of timbered land was obliged to stop the grass was so thick & high that I could not get through, it was on an average 9 feet high for some way, you may think it a great story If you don't believe it come out here & I will show to you wild geese, Ducks, Pigeons & fish in abundance.

Doolittle's enthusiastic letter expressed the wonderment and optimism that led many Americans in the second half of the nineteenth century to take part in one of the great migrations in modern history, exploring and developing nearly half the North American continent. Thirsting for a fresh start, they were lured west by the prospect of land and fortune.

Westward migration before the Civil War had helped create the image of the West as a land of adventure and opportunity. Trail-blazing pioneers had raced pell-mell across the huge expanses of the nation's midsection to reach the Pacific and join the gold rush of 1849, which brought quick prosperity to the West Coast. When California was admitted as a state in 1850, it boasted a population of more than three hundred thousand. Other mid-century pioneers—including farmers, land speculators, railroad developers, and various entrepreneurs—flooded into the fertile prairies of Iowa,

Minnesota, eastern Kansas, and Nebraska, carving the land into farms and communities.

By the end of the Civil War, the western frontier beckoned to a new generation. Over a million square miles lay within this region, which was bounded on the east by a line drawn roughly from St. Paul, Minnesota, to Fort Worth, Texas, and extended west across the Rocky Mountains to the Sierra Nevada and the Cascade Mountains. Elbowing aside the Indians, whose ancestors had inhabited the land for tens of thousands of years, the newcomers staked out mining claims or built the farms of their dreams in this last great West.

The part of the American heartland into which postwar settlers swarmed was called the Great Plains, a vast grassland of river valleys and plateaus extending to the eastern foothills of the Rockies. Travelers who ventured into this poorly charted region saw its terrain change sharply as they trekked westward. The eastern belt of the Plains comprised the rolling prairies of present-day Wisconsin, Illinois, Minnesota, Iowa, and eastern sections of the Dakotas, Nebraska, and Kansas—a land of fertile soil and life-giving rain. The easterners who settled there at first reveled in their role as pioneers. Novelist Hamlin Garland, recalling his boyhood in Wisconsin, Iowa, and South Dakota in the 1860s and 1870s, later wrote that the land's "lonely unplowed sweep" had given him "the satisfying sensation of being at last among the men who held the outposts, sentinels for the marching millions who were approaching from the east." But Garland's family, like many others, were soon shaken out of their optimism by hard times. Beyond the hundredth meridian, the landscape changed strikingly as the altitude gradually increased to produce the semiarid high Plains of the western Dakotas and western Nebraska and Kansas, on into eastern Montana, Wyoming, Colorado, and New

Mexico. Seared by hot winds in summer and lashed by blinding blizzards in winter, this stark, weather-beaten country quickly took the measure of all who ventured there. Scant rainfall (less than fifteen inches a year) and a timber shortage compounded the difficulties of establishing settlements and making a prosperous livelihood.

Beyond the Great Plains, in the Far West, rose the rugged Rocky Mountains, where farming was possible only in high-altitude windswept basins and a few river valleys; and still farther west lay the barren Great Basin of Nevada and the adjacent territories. In these forbidding regions, the inaccessibility of transportation further complicated the process of settlement.

In addition to minimizing the grimmer environmental realities of the Great Plains, would-be settlers and speculators brought with them cultural and racial blinders. They saw nothing unjust in appropriating native Americans' hunting and agricultural lands through flimsy, easily broken treaties. Moreover, most "Anglos" viewed the Mexicans who had lived in the Southwest for centuries, as well as the Chinese immigrants who helped work the West's mines and build its railroads, as alien and backward.

By 1900 it was obvious that the West's economic development required considerable support by the federal government in the form of military intervention, land subsidies, and aid to railroad builders. Investments by eastern banks and foreign capitalists were also crucial, as was access to international markets. Yet westerners clung to their ideal of the self-reliant, independent individual who could successfully contend with any obstacle, whether natural, human, or economic. That ideal, though often sorely tested, survived to form the bedrock of western Americans' outlook even a hundred years later.

Native Americans and the Frontier

The trans-Mississippi West was far from empty of human habitation when the newcomers arrived. An estimated 360,000 Indians lived in this region in the mid-nineteenth century. These native Amer-

ican cultures had been powerfully shaped by contact with non-Indians for centuries. Southwestern pueblo peoples such as the Hopis and Zuñis, who had been subjugated by Hispanic conquerors from the late sixteenth to early eighteenth centuries, had gradually achieved mutual accommodation with the relatively small Spanish-speaking population. Largely maintaining their traditional way of life based on intensive agriculture and sheepherding, the Hopis and Zuñis traded sheep and produce with the Mexican *rancheros* (ranchers) for metal hoes, glass beads, knives, and guns. Pueblo Indians and *rancheros* alike endured terrifying raids by the Jicarilla Apaches and the Navahos, although by the nineteenth century, even these fierce fighters were trading extensively with non-Indians for manufactured goods, and the Navahos were gradually giving up nomadism in favor of settled agriculture.

Among the Indians dwelling on the Great Plains, the introduction of horses by the Spanish at the end of the sixteenth century, and of firearms by British traders of the Hudson's Bay Company in the eighteenth century, had created the armed and mounted warrior tribes encountered by nineteenth-century westward migrants. Commercial and other contacts with the non-Indian world continued to be important to the Plains Indians as new settlers moved in.

But beyond these generally positive exchanges, contact with advancing non-Indians massively disrupted Indian life everywhere. Disease, which had devastated native Americans since the earliest European contact, continued its ravages among nineteenth-century western Indians. All tribes suffered severely from smallpox, measles, and diphtheria, as well as other diseases contracted from traders and settlers. By 1840 two major smallpox epidemics had reduced the Pawnees in Nebraska by nearly a third, to about six thousand people. The scattered tribes in California were similarly scourged by smallpox epidemics after the gold rush of 1849. Farther north, along the Oregon and Washington coasts, the peaceful Klamath, Chinook, Yurok, and Shasta tribes, who lived in permanent villages and fished extensively, were periodically decimated by disease. So were the native inhabitants of Nevada's starkly beautiful Great Basin.

However, by the mid-nineteenth century, it was the physical disruption of Indian life on the Great Plains, where nearly half the native Americans of the trans-Mississippi West dwelled, that was most in the public eye and on the public conscience. The non-Indians who descended on the Plains after 1850 had no understanding of traditional Indian culture and little inclination to respect or preserve the "savages'" ways. Military defeat and occasional massacres, forced removal to reservations, and devastation by disease, alcohol, and impoverishment—all this bewildered and wholly demoralized the Plains Indian peoples. Neither the occasional Indian victories over federal troops nor the well-meaning but misguided efforts of reformers to "uplift" the surviving Indians did much to reverse the downward spiral. By the 1890s relocation to distant, often inferior, and generally inadequate lands had become the fate of almost every Indian nation of the Great Plains. But there were also signs that the native Americans were evolving their own strong cultural response to conquest and forced modernization.

The Plains Indians

The Indians of the Great Plains inhabited two major subregions. The northern Plains, from the Dakotas and Montana southward to Nebraska, were dominated by several large tribes speaking Sioux languages, as well as by the Flatheads, Blackfeet, Assiniboins, northern Cheyennes, Arapahos, and Crows. Some of these were allies, but others were bitter enemies who fought one another endlessly.

The other major concentration of Plains Indians lived in the central and southern Plains. The so-called Five Civilized Tribes driven from the Southeast in the 1830s (see Chapter 8) pursued an agricultural life in their new home in the Indian Territory (present-day Oklahoma). In western Kansas the Pawnees maintained the older, more settled tradition characteristic of Plains river-valley culture before the introduction of horses, spending at least half the year in villages of earthen lodges along watercourses. Surrounding these were the truly nomadic tribes of western Kansas, Colorado, eastern New Mexico, and Texas—the Comanches, Kiowas, southern Arapahos, and Kiowa Apaches.

Considerable diversity flourished among the Plains tribes, and customs varied even within subdivisions of the same tribe. For example, the easternmost branch of the great Sioux Nation, the Dakota Sioux of Minnesota, who inhabited the wooded edge of the prairie, led a semisedentary

Plains Indians

In order to follow the buffalo herds on the Great Plains, the Blackfoot and Dakota tribes limited their possessions to easily transportable items. They made light, warm clothing from carefully tanned and softened deer and buffalo skins.

life based on small-scale agriculture, wild-rice harvesting, maple-sugar production, and deer and bison hunting. In contrast, the Lakota Sioux, who roamed the high Plains to the west, followed the buffalo migrations.

Despite the diversity, however, life for all the Plains Indians revolved around extended family ties and tribal cooperation. Within the various Sioux-speaking tribes, for example, children were raised without physical punishment and were taught to treat each adult clan member with the respect accorded to relatives. Families and clans joined forces to hunt and farm and reached decisions by consensus. Extended families, whose members followed the leadership of an older adult male in the tribe, gathered to form small winter villages or large summer encampments. Although non-Indians, steeped in their own notions of hierarchical social organization, called these men chiefs, the Indian leaders' power rested largely on persuasion. They reinforced their authority by example, giving their food and supplies to the needy and initiating projects in the hope that others would follow.

For the various Sioux bands, religious and harvest celebrations provided the cement for village and camp life. Sioux religion was complex and entirely different from the Judeo-Christian tradition. The Lakota Sioux thought of life as a series of circles. Living within the daily cycles of the sun and moon, Lakotas were born into a circle of relatives, which broadened to the band, the tribe, and the Sioux Nation. The Lakotas also believed in a hierarchy of plant and animal spirits that were often more powerful than human beings and whose help could be invoked in the Sun Dance. To gain access to spiritual power and to benefit the weaker members of the community, young men would "sacrifice" themselves by suffering self-torture—for example, by fastening skewers to their chest from which they dragged buffalo skulls; by hanging suspended from poles; or by cutting pieces of their own flesh and placing them at the foot of the Sun Dance pole. Painter George Catlin, who recorded Great Plains Indian life before the Civil War, described such a ceremony: "Several of them, seeing me making sketches, beckoned me to look at their faces, which I watched through all this horrid operation, without being able to detect anything but the pleasantest smiles as they looked me in the eye, while I could hear the knife rip through the flesh, and feel enough of it myself, to start involuntary and uncontrollable tears over my cheeks."

Many Plains tribes—not only the Lakota Sioux but also the Blackfeet, Crows, and Cheyennes—followed the buffalo migration. The huge herds, which at their peak contained an estimated 32 million bison, filled an amazing array of tribal needs. The Indians utilized every part of the animal. They ate its meat, either fresh or dried. They used its hide for tepee covers, shields, boats, shirts, and robes. Sinews became bowstrings; bones were fashioned into hoes, knives, awls, fishhooks, chisels, hide fleshers, spatulas, flint knapping tools, and wedges. They rendered buffalo fat into grease, ground up hooves to make glue, carved horn tips into toy tops for the children, and used buffalo dung ("chips") for fuel. They even used the skull for religious purposes, as in the Sun Dance.

By the 1870s the eastern vogue for wearing buffalo robes on carriages and sleighs, coupled with common use of the animals' hides for industrial belting, encouraged some Plains peoples to give up their nomadic existence and become professional hunters, with disastrous results. In contrast to the Pawnees, who carefully managed the buffalo herds to protect their food supply, the Blackfeet responded to the demand by hunting buffalo for profit. Polygyny spread as men took on additional wives to help with tanning the skins—a traditional task for Indian women. These increases in family size in turn obliged Blackfoot men to build bigger tepees and to spend more for horses and hunting supplies. At the height of the buffalo-hide trade between 1867 and 1873, a good Blackfoot hunter could make two thousand dollars a year, a small fortune for the time.

Swept up by their new prosperity, the Blackfeet thus modified their traditional way of life and became dependent on the buffalo trade, only to find the herds rapidly disappearing. Moreover, the Indians soon faced competition from white entrepreneurs who used the expanding railroad networks to hunt the animals and transport their prized pelts swiftly to market. William F. "Buffalo Bill" Cody, a famous scout, Indian fighter, and organizer of Wild West shows, in 1867–1868 killed nearly 4,300 bison in eight months to feed construction crews building the Union Pacific railroad. The herds dwindled further as eastern sport hunters and even sightseers chartered trains and headed west to shoot the animals for profit or adventure. Army commanders, seeing in the destruction of the buffalo a means of undermining the resistance of buffalo-dependent Indians, encouraged the slaughter. The carnage that resulted was almost inconceivable in its scale. Between 1872 and 1875, hunters killed 9 million buffalo, taking only the skin and leaving the carcass to rot. A railroad conductor of the period recalled that "one could have journeyed more than 100 miles along the railroad right-of-way, without stepping off the carcass of a slaughtered bison." By the 1880s the once thundering herds had been reduced to a few thousand animals, a native American way of life dependent on the buffalo had been ruined, and the path was cleared for American farmers to settle on former Indian hunting grounds.

The Transformation of Indian Life

Non-Indian hunters not only wiped out most of the buffalo but also increasingly encroached on the Plains Indians' lands in these years. In the Min-

Buffalo Head Trophies

To encourage buffalo hunting as a sport, railroads crossing the Great Plains had the animal heads mounted by their own taxidermists for display at ticket stations.

nesota Territory, for example, the Ojibwa Indians had controlled most of the land in the north as late as 1837, while various tribes of Dakota Sioux dominated the south. But over the next thirty years, under pressure as a result of mushrooming white settlement, these tribes ceded 24 million acres to the federal government in a series of treaties. These agreements established two large reservations (under the control of the Department of the Interior's Bureau of Indian Affairs) within the Minnesota Territory and promised the tribes annual government support. When the federal authorities failed to give the Dakota Sioux their yearly payments on time and neglected to provide promised agricultural aid, however, they returned to their former hunting grounds. Driven by hunger and angered by unfulfilled promises, they rose up in August 1862, killing nearly 500 white settlers. With reinforcements from the U.S. Army, the settlers retaliated, crushing the uprising in two weeks, hanging 38 Indians, and exiling the rest to poor-quality reservation land in the Dakotas and northeastern Nebraska. By 1866 the number of Sioux in Minnesota had been cut from 7,000 to 374.

By the 1860s the federal government had abandoned its previous policy of treating much of the West as a vast Indian reserve and had introduced a system of smaller, separate tribal reservations where the Indians were to be concentrated, by force if necessary, and where they were expected to exchange nomadism for a settled agricultural life. Some native Americans, like the Pueblos of the Southwest and the Crows of Montana, peacefully accepted their fate. Others, among them the Navahos of Arizona and New Mexico, as well as the Dakota Sioux, initially opposed the new policy, but to no avail.

The remaining tribes, however, with a population of nearly one hundred thousand, demonstrated the will and power to resist. From the 1860s through the 1880s, these tribes—the western Sioux, Cheyennes, Arapahos, Kiowas, and Comanches on the Great Plains; the Nez Percés and Bannocks in the northern Rockies; and the Apaches in the Southwest—faced the United States Army in a final battle for the West.

In this protracted and bitter conflict, precipitated by the expansion of western settlement and by Washington's new reservation policy, both sides committed atrocities. Two examples illustrate the tragic pattern. In 1859 the Cheyennes and Arapahos of southern Colorado began raiding the gold miners who had intruded upon their traditional lands in the Pike's Peak region. In 1864, weary of fighting, the tribes sued for peace and encamped by Sand Creek. There they were viciously attacked by the Colorado militia. In the ensuing slaughter, the militia clubbed and scalped the terrified Indian women and children even after the native Americans had raised a white surrender flag. "Kill and scalp all, big and little," shouted Colonel John M. Chivington, the militia leader; "Nits make lice." Two years later the Teton Sioux, defending land along Wyoming's Powder River that in their view had been fraudulently ceded to the United States by their Crow enemies, fought a ferocious war with the U.S. cavalry. Trying to stop construction of the Bozeman Trail (a new road angling northwestward from Fort Laramie, Wyoming, to the gold fields of Virginia City, Montana), the Teton Sioux lured Captain William J. Fetterman and the seventy-nine soldiers under his command out of their stockade, killed them, and horribly mutilated the bodies.

These two massacres—one, of Indians; the other, of whites—rekindled public debate over federal Indian policy. Western settlers had long pressed Congress to set up a tighter reservation policy controlled by the army rather than by the civilian "Indian agents" employed by the Bureau of Indian Affairs. Disturbed by the outright corruption and gross ineptitude of these federal agents who ran the reservations and of the local militia who policed them, some opponents of government policy argued that using trained West Point graduates to supervise the reservations would restore honest and efficient administration. Other critics, led by Wisconsin senator James R. Doolittle and supported by an Episcopal bishop from Minnesota, Henry Benjamin Whipple, opposed army control and simply urged a cessation of violence on both sides.

Responding to this debate in 1867, Congress halted construction of the Bozeman Trail, sent a peace commission to end the Sioux war in Montana, and set aside large districts on isolated western lands where, it was hoped, the Indians could be converted to Christianity and agriculture. As one peace commissioner told a delegation of Oglala Sioux:"The president desires to see you prosperous

Indian Chiefs

Early photographs of the Indian leaders Sitting Bull (left) and Joseph (right) captured both their pride and the frustration they felt after years of alternately negotiating and battling with the U.S. Army. "I don't want a white man over me," Sitting Bull insisted. "I want to have the white man with me, but not to be my chief. I ask this because I want to do right by my people. . . ."

and happy and has sent us here to devise means to secure this end. We have exercised our best judgment and adopted the best plan to improve your condition and save your people. Accept it and be happy." But behind the persuasion lay the threat of force. Any native Americans who refused to "locate in [the] permanent abodes provided for them," threatened Commissioner of Indian Affairs Ely S. Parker (himself a Seneca Indian), "would be subject wholly to the control and supervision of military authorities, [and] . . . treated as friendly or hostile as circumstances might justify."

At first it seemed that the plan would work. At their headquarters in Fort Laramie, Wyoming, the peace commissioners negotiated treaties with the Kiowas, Cheyennes, Arapahos, Sioux, Shoshones, Bannocks, Navahos, and Apaches providing for their removal to reservations in return for money and provisions. Representatives of fifty-four thousand northern Plains Indians agreed to settle on the so-called Great Sioux Reserve in the western part of present-day South Dakota. Representatives of sixty-eight thousand southern Plains Indians pledged to remain on reservations in present-day Oklahoma.

But Indian dissatisfaction with the treaties ran deep. As a Sioux chief, Spotted Tail, told the commissioners: "We do not want to live like the white man. . . . The Great Spirit gave us hunting grounds, gave us the buffalo, the elk, the deer, and the ante-

lope. Our fathers have taught us to hunt and live on the Plains, and we are contented." Rejecting the new system, many Indians refused to move to the reservations or to remain on them once there.

In August 1868 war parties of Cheyennes, Arapahos, and Sioux raided frontier settlements in Kansas and Colorado, burning homes and killing whites. As army troops, in retaliation, attacked any Indians who refused confinement, the soldiers made little distinction between those native Americans who had actually engaged in violence and those who simply wanted to be left in peace. That autumn, an army raiding party commanded by Lieutenant Colonel George Armstrong Custer attacked a sleeping Cheyenne village, killing more than a hundred warriors, shooting their nine hundred horses, and taking fifty-three women and children prisoner. Other hostile Cheyennes and Arapahos were pursued, captured, and returned to the reservations.

Spurred on by evangelical Christian reformers, Congress in 1869 established the Board of Indian Commissioners to mold reservation life along lines that the reformers thought desirable. The new board delegated to the major Protestant denominations the responsibility for appointing the agents who would run the reservations. The board's goal was to break, once and for all, the Indians' nomadic tradition and force them to remain on their reservations, where, under the supervision of benevolent agents, they would be Christianized, taught to farm, and given government assistance. Reformers hoped that, freed of dependency on the hunt, the Indians would cease to resist the settlers who wanted their lands. Completely failing to understand the nature of Indian culture, the board determined to achieve this transformation of the Indians into self-reliant, Christian farmers by establishing a policy of individual landownership. A comment by one federal official summed up the sense of cultural superiority that underlay U.S. Indian policy in these years: "A fundamental difference between Barbarians and a civilized people is the difference between a herd and an individual."

The new and inexperienced church-appointed Indian agents quickly encountered obstacles in trying to implement the board's policies. The pacifist Quaker agent Lawrie Tatum, a big-boned Iowa farmer, failed to persuade the Comanches and Kiowas to stay on their reservations in Oklahoma rather than raid Texas settlements; two Kiowa chiefs, Satanta and Big Tree, insisted that they could be at peace with the federal government while remaining at war with Texans. Other agents were unable to restrain scheming whites who, coveting reservation lands, fraudulently purchased them from the Indians. Moreover, the various Protestant denominations squabbled among themselves, all hoping to control the reservations that had the greatest number of potential converts. By the 1880s the federal government, frustrated with the churches, ignored their nominations for Indian agents and made its own appointments.

Caught in the sticky web of an ambiguous and faltering federal policy, and enraged by continuing non-Indian settlement of the Plains, defiant native Americans struck back in the 1870s. On the southern Plains, the Kiowas, Comanches, and Cheyennes raided a trading post called Adobe Walls in the Texas panhandle in 1874, thereby setting off the so-called Red River War. In this conflict regular army troops, in a fierce winter campaign, destroyed Indian supplies and slaughtered a hundred Cheyenne fugitives near the Sappa River in Kansas. With the exile of seventy-four "ringleaders" in this uprising to reservations in Florida, native American independence on the southern Plains came to an end. In the Southwest, in present-day Arizona and New Mexico, the Apaches fought an intermittent guerrilla war until their leader, Geronimo, surrendered in 1886.

Custer's Last Stand

Of all the acts of Indian resistance against the new reservation policy, none aroused more passion or caused more bloodshed than the conflict between the western Sioux tribes and the U.S. Army in the Dakotas, Montana, and Wyoming. The problems went back to the 1868 Treaty of Fort Laramie, which had ended the Powder River War and had set aside the Great Sioux Reserve "in perpetuity." But not all the Sioux bands had fought in the war or signed the treaty. For example, the highly respected chief Sitting Bull had carefully kept his band of Hunkpapa Sioux away from the fighting. Furthermore, certain western Sioux bands that did sign the treaty, among them the Oglala Sioux and the Brulé Sioux, had no intention of actually moving to the reservation.

Skillfully playing local officials against the federal government, Chief Red Cloud's Oglala band and Chief Spotted Tail's Brulé band in 1873 won

George Armstrong Custer and His Scouts, 1873

The U.S. Army cleverly exploited the traditional rivalries among the Plains Indian tribes by hiring scouts from one tribe to aid in the campaign against another. Colonel Custer's relaxed pose here foreshadowed the arrogance that led to his defeat at the Little Bighorn in 1876.

the concession of staying near the Indian agencies along the upper reaches of the White River in Nebraska, near their traditional hunting grounds. Shuttling back and forth between the agencies and the camps of Sitting Bull and the other nontreaty chiefs, they enjoyed the best of both worlds: they obtained government provisions but still hunted on their customary range. To protect these precious hunting grounds, they raided encroaching non-Indian settlements in Nebraska and Wyoming, intimidated federal agents, and harassed miners, railroad surveyors, and others who ventured onto their lands.

The Indian agents' inability to prevent the Sioux from entering and leaving the reservations at will, coupled with increasing pressures from would-be settlers and developers, prompted the army to take action. In 1874 General William Tecumseh Sherman sent a force under Colonel George Armstrong Custer into the Black Hills of South Dakota, near the western edge of the Great Sioux Reserve. Lean and mustachioed, with shoulder-length reddish-blond hair, the thirty-four-year-old Custer had been a celebrity since his days as an impetuous young officer in the Civil War, known for the black velvet uniform, embellished with gold braid, that he wore on the battlefield. Now for Indian combat, he had switched to a fringed buckskin uniform set off by a crimson scarf. Flamboyant and ambitious, he had just that year published an autobiography, *My Life on the Plains,* casting himself in the heroic mold of Davy Crockett and Kit Carson.

Custer's ostensible purpose was to find a location for a new fort and to keep an eye on renegade Indians. But his real objective was to confirm rumors about the existence of gold there. In this he was spurred on by the Northern Pacific Railroad, which was angling to attract settlers to the area. While Custer's troops mapped the lush meadows and chose a site for the fort, two "practical miners" whom Custer had brought along panned the streams for gold. In a report that he telegraphed to the *New York World,* Custer described the region as excellent farm country and casually mentioned finding "gold among the roots of the grass." The gold stampede that predictably followed gave the army a new justification for interceding against the Indians.

Custer had in fact become part of a deliberate army plan to force concessions from the Sioux. In November 1875, when negotiations to buy the Black

Hills broke down because the Indians' asking price was considered too high, President Ulysses S. Grant and his generals decided to physically remove all roadblocks to the entry of would-be miners. Every Indian outside the reservations by January 31, 1876, the government announced, would be hunted down by the army and taken in by force.

When the Indians refused to return to the reservations, the army mobilized for an assault, with Custer again in the thick of things. In June 1876, leading 600 troops of the Seventh Cavalry, Custer proceeded to the Little Bighorn River area of present-day Montana, a hub of Indian resistance. On the morning of June 25, seriously underestimating the Indian enemy and unwisely dividing his force into four separate units, Custer, with 211 men, recklessly advanced against a large company of Indians, later estimated at from 1,500 to 5,000 warriors, encamped along the Little Bighorn. Soon the outnumbered troops found themselves surrounded and under heavy fire. Desperately some of the men shot their own horses and tried to use the bodies as protection; but with bullets pelting them from all sides, their situation was hopeless. Custer and his entire force were wiped out. Two days later, another company of cavalry troops came upon the scene of carnage and buried the bodies where they lay. A single creature was found alive: a horse that had belonged to one of Custer's captains.

Americans reeled from this unexpected Indian victory. Metropolitan newspaper columnists groped to assess the meaning of "Custer's last stand." Some went beyond criticism of Custer's leadership to question the wisdom of current federal policy toward the Indians. Others worried that an outraged public would demand retaliation and the outright extermination of the Sioux. Most, however, endorsed the federal government's determination to quash the native American rebellion. "It is inconsistent with our civilization and with common sense," trumpeted a writer in the *New York Herald,* "to allow the Indian to roam over a country as fine as that around the Black Hills, preventing its development in order that he may shoot game and scalp his neighbors. That can never be. This region must be taken from the Indian."

The Indians' surprising coup at Little Bighorn made the army more cautious in its future campaigns. Taking over the Sioux reservations, the military sent further expeditions into Montana, where troops harassed various Sioux bands for more than five years, seeking to drive them onto the reservations. The army's most effective tactic was to attack Indian camps in the dead of winter and ruin the native Americans' supplies. Even Sitting Bull, a leader at Little Bighorn, who had led his tribe to Canada to escape the army, surrendered in 1881 for lack of provisions: the slaughter of the buffalo had wiped out his tribe's major food supply. For a time after his surrender, Sitting Bull suffered the ignominy of appearing as an attraction in Buffalo Bill's Wild West show.

Similar measures were used elsewhere in the West. In 1877 Chief Joseph and his Nez Percés of Oregon rebelled against the federal reservation policy. Attempting to escape to Canada with his band of about 250 warriors and 450 women, children, and aged people, Chief Joseph was closely pursued by the U.S. Army. He successfully stood off the troops for almost three months, when he ran out of ammunition and had to surrender forty miles short of the Canadian border. In his statement of surrender, Chief Joseph explained simply that "I am tired of fighting. . . . The old men are all killed. . . . The little children are freezing to death. . . . Hear me, my chiefs, I am tired; my heart is sick and sad. From where the sun now stands, I will fight no more forever." To punish him, the government relocated his tribe on the bleak Oklahoma plains, where many Nez Percés eventually died from disease.

Meanwhile, the Northern Cheyennes, too, had been forcibly transported to Oklahoma after the Battle of Little Bighorn, in which they had participated. Here, underprovisioned, unaccustomed to the searing heat, and grievously homesick, they died by the dozens. Some 150 survivors, including men, women, and children, led by Chief Dull Knife, escaped north in September 1878 to join the Sioux. But the army chased them down and took them, as prisoners, to Fort Robinson, Nebraska. When the army denied their request that they at least be allowed to stay on a reservation nearer their traditional northern lands, they refused to leave the fort. The post commander then withheld all food, water, and fuel. On a frigid night in January 1879, a desperate Dull Knife and his followers shot the guards and broke for freedom. Members of the startled garrison chased the Indians and gunned down half of them in the snow, including women and children as well as Dull Knife himself. The

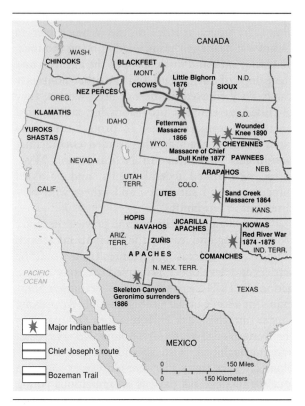

Major Indian-White Clashes in the West

Although they were never recognized as such in the popular press, the battles between native Americans and the U.S. Army on the Great Plains amounted to a major, undeclared war.

Atlanta Constitution condemned the incident as "a dastardly outrage upon humanity and a lasting disgrace to our boasted civilization." But although sporadic Indian resistance continued until the end of the century, these brutal tactics had sapped the Indians' will to resist.

"Saving" the Indians

Bloody massacres were not America's only answer to the "Indian problem." In 1879, the same year that Dull Knife led his followers on their doomed dash for freedom, army officer Richard H. Pratt founded the Carlisle Indian School in Pennsylvania. The school's objective seemed laudable: to equip individual Indians with the skills and cultural attitudes necessary to succeed in modern American society. As Pratt put it, he wanted to "kill the Indian and save the man." But the young Indians who came (voluntarily) to Pratt's boarding school were uprooted from their families and tribes, and teachers there made no pretense of respecting traditional Indian culture. Carlisle became the prototype for a number of other Indian schools that would be established, well into the twentieth century, with the avowed purpose of reeducating Indian youth in whites' skills and outlooks. Culturally, reeducation represented as determined an assault on the native American world as the slaughter of the buffalo, the seizure of hunting land, and military repression. Moreover, because it appealed to humanitarians' sincere concern for the Indians' well-being, it was more insidious.

These humanitarians, most of them well-educated easterners, were outraged not only by bloody atrocities like the Fort Robinson massacre but also by the federal government's flagrant abuse of its Indian treaties. A lecture tour by Chief Standing Bear, whose peaceful Ponca tribe had been driven from land north of the Missouri River guaranteed them by an 1865 treaty, further aroused the reformers' indignation. The Women's National Indian Rights Association, founded in 1883, and other groups took up the cause. Standing Bear's eloquence particularly affected Helen Hunt Jackson, a Massachusetts widow who had recently married a rich Quaker businessman and moved to Colorado. In *A Century of Dishonor* (1881), Jackson sought to rally public opinion against the government's record of broken treaty obligations. In the reform tradition of Harriet Beecher Stowe and her antislavery novel *Uncle Tom's Cabin*, Jackson angrily proclaimed: "It makes little difference . . . where one opens the record of the history of the Indians; every page and every year has its dark stain."

Genuinely concerned about the Indians' plight, well-intentioned humanitarians concluded that the Indians' interests would best be served by breaking up the reservations, ending all recognition of the tribes, and propelling the native Americans, as individuals, into mainstream society. In short, they proposed to eliminate the "Indian problem" by eliminating the Indians as a culturally distinct entity. Inspired by this vision, they threw their support behind a plan, devised by Massachusetts senator Henry L. Dawes, that resulted in the passage in 1887 of the Dawes Severalty Act.

The Dawes Act was designed to reform what well-meaning whites perceived to be the weaknesses of Indian life—the absence of private property, and the native peoples' nomadic tradition—by turning Indians into farmers and landowners. The law emphasized severalty, or the treatment of Indians as individuals rather than as members of tribes, and called for the breakup of the reservations. It provided for the distribution of 160 acres of reservation land for farming, or 320 acres for grazing, to each head of an Indian family who accepted the law's provisions. The remaining reservation lands (often the richest) were to be sold to speculators and settlers, and the income thus obtained would go toward purchase of farm tools for the Indians. To prevent unscrupulous persons from gaining control of the lands granted to individual Indians, the government would hold the property of each Indian in trust for twenty-five years. Under the Dawes Act, the Indians were also declared citizens of the United States with all the rights and responsibilities that attended such status, including the protection of federal laws and the requirement to pay taxes.

Western speculators who coveted reservation lands, as well as military authorities who wanted to break up the reservations for security reasons, had lobbied heavily for the Dawes Act. Nevertheless, the bill's strongest support had come from the "friends of the Indian"—advocates like Helen Hunt Jackson. Although they genuinely hoped that the law would alleviate the Indians' suffering, these reformers also believed in the innate superiority of American culture. Like those nineteenth-century social reformers who set up relief organizations to impose their own middle-class values on the urban poor (see Chapter 18), and like the would-be uplifters of the southern freedmen, the "friends of the Indian" believed that teaching Indians to speak English and to farm would open the doors of opportunity to them. Convinced that citizenship was the best protection for the Indians, and that full assimilation into the mainstream of society would enable them to get ahead, the reformers systematically tried to "civilize" the Indian peoples and wean them from their traditional culture. To publicize the success of his Carlisle Indian School, Richard H. Pratt published a series of "before" and "after" photographs in which Indian youths with long, braided hair and traditional tribal dress were transformed into proper young gentlemen who sported closely trimmed hair and wore suits and ties.

Like-a-Fishhook, 1845–1900

When Lewis and Clark visited the Hidatsa and Mandan Indians at the mouth of the Knife River in present-day North Dakota in 1804, they found a series of substantial villages, each protected by a palisade and consisting of forty to sixty large, round, earth-walled houses (earthlodges). The Mandans and the Hidatsas were closely knit, clan-oriented tribes that practiced subsistence agriculture supplemented with buffalo hunting. A century later, Goodbird, a Hidatsa, told a visiting anthropologist that "my family and I own four thousand acres of land, and we have money coming to us from the government. I own cattle and horses. I can read English, and my children are in school. . . . I am not afraid." In less than two generations, the Mandans and Hidatsas had abandoned ancient tribal ways closely adapted to the northern Plains and had become independent ranchers successfully making a living in a modern industrial society.

For Lewis and Clark, the communal nature of the traditional Mandan and Hidatsa cultures had been evident in every aspect of the native peoples' lives. Because members of the same clan, or extended kinship group, could not wed, marriage brought together a man and a woman from different clans. Chil-dren were thus tied to a large clan network, encompassing the members of both the mother's and the father's village. Clans were responsible for disciplining their members, providing for the sick and orphaned, and cooperating in sacred ceremonies. Children treated all elders with the respect accorded their own parents.

Tradition carefully defined social roles. Young Hidatsa girls learned to separate ordinary knowledge about growing crops, dressing skins, cutting wood, and cooking from ancient and sacred knowledge of basket weaving and pottery making, tepee and house construction, beading, and quill weaving. These sacred skills had to be purchased from tribal leaders, and those who mastered them became valued members of the community. For example, in return for paying an elder with a suit of finely tanned skins, a young woman might learn how to raise the four sacred foundation posts and the four great beams of an earthlodge. When another tribal member requested the young woman's help in construct-ing a new earthlodge, he in turn would pay her with softly tanned buffalo skins and food.

Young boys, too, learned the importance of reciprocal obligations. If a youth received his first bow and arrow from a maternal grandfather, he presented his elder with the first rabbits or prairie chickens killed with the weapons. At fifteen or sixteen, boys had to prove their toughness and willingness to go to war by fasting, enduring the torture of hanging from a tree by means of thongs laced through the skin, or cutting off a finger.

Religion pervaded the Hidatsa world. The people believed that they could acquire supernatural powers by practicing certain religious rites. Paralleling the seasons, their religious ceremonies celebrated the planting of corn in the spring and buffalo-hunting expeditions in the summer and winter. The buffalo-calling ceremony, staged during the winter, required the whole village to be silent so that the buffalo would be attracted into the rivers along which the tribe dwelled. If the tribe

Mandan Community, 1852

Although the Hidatsa and Mandan Indians of the Great Plains lived in tepees when following the buffalo herds, in the winter they dwelled in settled communities made up of large earthlodges, as painted here by George Catlin.

Hidatsa Earthlodge

The Hidatsas carefully divided the earthlodge interior into spaces for horses, for cooking and eating, and for the sacred bundle of relics that would bring good luck to the family.

failed to observe this ritual, a mild winter might set in. Unseasonably warm weather might in turn cause the buffalo to remain on the Plains, with the result that the Hidatsas might starve.

In 1837 a smallpox epidemic introduced by white settlers wiped out half the Hidatsa people and most of the neighboring Mandans. Then in 1845, the remaining members of both tribes formed the new village of Like-a-Fishhook. French fur traders moved in and exchanged cast-iron pots, knives, beads, guns, and other supplies for buffalo skins. In the 1850s, faced with the encroachment of non-Indian settlers on their hunting grounds and with the depletion of their wood supplies by the steamboats that plied the river and carried away timber for fuel, the Hidatsas signed a treaty with the U.S. government and were granted fifty thousand dollars a year for fifty years.

Contact with non-Indian peoples gradually reshaped Hidatsa culture. With each new influx of settlers, more wild game disappeared.

The Indians became dependent on the federal agents who distributed coffee, flour, sugar, and soap. To keep the Indians and non-Indians separated and to maintain the peace, the U.S. government set up Fort Berthold in 1864, established a permanent Indian agency there in 1868, sent in Congregational missionaries, and built schools. In 1887, under the Dawes Severalty Act, the government dispersed the communal villages and forced the Indians onto separate farms.

Those Indians who, like Goodbird, prospered, did so by adapting traditional culture to fit the government's regulations. Before establishing a separate farm, Goodbird first held a spiritual vigil to choose the site. Breaking with his Indian heritage, he lived in a wooden house but was careful to place the stove in the center and to leave the door open in good weather, following Hidatsa customs. Moreover, Goodbird also quickly learned how to work within the new federal system. He served in turn as a reservation policeman, an assistant farmer,

a distributor for government rations, a store owner, a cattle rancher, and a Congregational minister.

Some members of his family did not adapt as easily. His mother, Buffalo Bird Woman, a skilled house builder and gardener born before the move to Like-a-Fishhook, lost her valued status when the tribe became assimilated. Her brother, Wolf Chief, wrote yearly letters to the Bureau of Indian Affairs in which he chronicled the folly of a government policy that asked Indians to farm 160 acres of semiarid land. He also resisted regulations prohibiting Indians from leaving the reservation and buying cattle.

By 1900 many Hidatsa had become thriving ranchers, using modern equipment like horse-drawn wagons and threshers. But the tribe preserved elements of the communal society that its members had once so treasured—by accommodating traditions to the modern world. Hidatsa culture was not dead in 1900, but in less than fifty years, it had been transformed substantially.

(Left to right) Son of a Star, Goodbird, and Buffalo Bird Woman, 1906

Dressed in his best Sunday suit, Goodbird graphically demonstrates his movement away from the world of his parents. His father, Son of a Star, retains traditional garb, with the two feathers symbolizing his conquest of enemies in battle. Goodbird's mother, Buffalo Bird Woman, is wrapped in a traditional blanket.

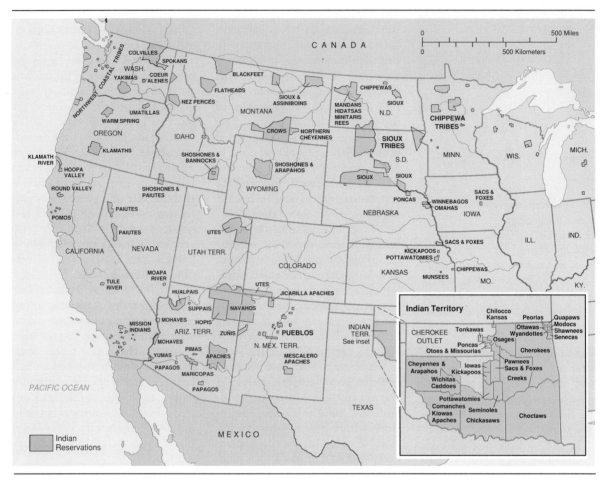

Western Indian Reservations, 1890

Native American reservations were almost invariably located on poor-quality lands. Consequently, when the Dawes Severalty Act broke up the reservations into 160-acre farming tracts, many of the semiarid divisions would not support cultivation.

The Dawes Act did not specify a timetable for the breakup of the reservations. Because land surveys took time, few allotments were made to the Indians until the 1890s. The act eventually proved to be a boon not to the Indians but to speculators, who commonly evaded the law and obtained the Indians' most arable land. By 1934 the act had slashed the total Indian acreage by 65 percent. Much of what remained in Indian hands was too dry and gravelly for farming.

Although some native Americans who received land under the Dawes Act prospered enough to expand their holdings and go into large-scale farm-ing or ranching, countless others languished. Hunting restrictions on the former reservation lands prevented many Indians from supplementing their limited farm yields. At the same time, various forms of government support extended to the Indians steadily increased their dependence on federal aid. Alcoholism, a continuing problem, and one exacerbated by the prevalence of whiskey as a trade item (and by the boredom that resulted from the disruption of hunting and other traditional pursuits), became more prevalent as native Americans strove to adapt to the constraints of reservation life.

The Ghost Dance and the End of Indian Resistance on the Great Plains

The plight of the Sioux became desperate in the late 1880s as the federal government reduced their meat rations and saddled them with more and more restrictions, and as disease killed a third of their cattle. The Sioux, who still numbered almost twenty-five thousand, turned to Wovoka, a new prophet popular among the Great Basin Indians in Nevada. Wovoka promised to restore the Sioux to their original dominance on the Plains if they performed the Ghost Dance.

Wearing sacred Ghost Shirts—leather vestments specially decorated to ward off evil—the dancers moved in a circle, accelerating until they became so dizzy that they passed out. In the resulting trancelike state, the Indians believed, they experienced visions of the future. Upon reviving, they explained their revelations to the rest of the tribe. In some cases, the dancers claimed special powers to kill non-Indian settlers. Many also believed that the Ghost Shirts would protect them

Ghost Dance Shirt

Constructed of white muslin adorned with red-dyed fringes and painted symbols, the Ghost Dance shirt, like the religious beliefs it represented, combined elements of white and Indian culture. The wearer believed that the shirt could ward off bullets.

from harm. Rituals such as the Ghost Dance enabled Indians to reaffirm their own culture.

In the fall of 1890, as the Ghost Dance movement spread among the Sioux in the Dakota Territory, Indian officials and military authorities grew alarmed. The local reservation agent, Major James McLaughlin, decided that Chief Sitting Bull, whose cabin on the reservation had become a rallying point for the Ghost Dance movement, must be arrested. On a freezing, drizzly December morning, McLaughlin dispatched a company of forty-two Indian policemen from the agency to take Sitting Bull into custody. As two policemen pulled the chief from his cabin, his bodyguard Catch-the-Bear shot one of them. As the policeman fell, he in turn shot Sitting Bull at point-blank range. Bloody hand-to-hand fighting immediately broke out between Sitting Bull's supporters and the police. As bullets whizzed by, Sitting Bull's horse sat down and began to perform the tricks remembered from its days in the Wild West show. Some observers were terrified, convinced that the spirit of the dead chief had entered his horse.

Sitting Bull's violent death preceded by only two weeks one of the bloodiest episodes of Indian-white relations on the Great Plains. On December 29, 1890, the Seventh Cavalry was in the process of rounding up 340 starving and freezing Sioux at Wounded Knee, South Dakota, when an excited Indian fired a gun that he had hidden under a blanket. The soldiers swiftly retaliated with Hotchkiss cannons. Within minutes 300 Indians, including 7 infants, were slaughtered. Three days later, a baby who had miraculously survived was found wrapped in a blanket under the snow. She was wearing a buckskin cap on which a beadwork American flag had been embroidered. Brigadier General L. W. Colby, who adopted the baby, named her Marguerite, but the Indians called her Lost Bird.

As the frozen corpses at Wounded Knee were dumped into mass graves, a generation of Indian-white conflict on the Great Plains shuddered to a close. Lost Bird, with her poignantly patriotic beadwork cap, highlights the irony of the Plains Indians' response to the tragic dilemma confronting them. Many did try, with varying success, to adapt to alien non-Indian ways. But few succeeded fully, and many others were understandably devastated at being forced to abandon age-old reli-

Wounded Knee

Piled up like cordwood, the frozen bodies of the Sioux Indians slaughtered at Wounded Knee were a grim reminder that the U.S. Army would brook no opposition to its control of Indian reservation life.

gious beliefs and a way of life rooted in hunting, cooperative living, and nomadism. Driven onto reservations, the Plains Indians were reduced to a status of almost complete dependency, as once strong cultural traditions, modes of survival, and forms of social organization were crushed. By 1900 the Plains Indian population had shrunk from nearly a quarter of a million to just over a hundred thousand. Nevertheless, after 1900 the population began slowly to rise. And against overwhelming odds, the pride, group memory, and cultural identity of the Plains Indians survived all efforts to trample them.

In contrast to the nomadic western Sioux tribes, for whom the encounter with the onrushing tide of white civilization was most traumatic, the more settled Navahos of the Southwest adjusted somewhat more successfully to the reservation system, preserving traditional ways while selectively incorporating elements of the new order in a complex process of cultural adaptation. By 1900 the Navahos had tripled their reservation land, dramatically increased their own numbers and the size of their herds, and carved out for themselves and their culture a distinct place in the deserts of Arizona and New Mexico.

These extraordinary changes were forced on the Indian population by the advance of non-Indian settlement. In the name of civilization and progress, non-Indians in the generation after the Civil War pursued a course that involved a strong mixture of sincere (if misguided) benevolence, coercion wrapped in an aura of legality, and outbursts of naked violence. Many white Americans felt toward the Indians nothing more complex than contempt, hatred, and greed for their land. Others, however, like General Colby in his gesture of adopting the infant survivor of a massacre in which he himself had participated, viewed themselves as divinely chosen instruments for uplifting, educating, and Christianizing the Indians. Both groups, however, were equally blind to any inherent value in Indian life and traditions. The humanitarians, no less than the most brutal advocates of extermination, played their part in shattering a proud people and an ancient culture. The fate of the Indians would weigh heavily on the American conscience for many generations.

Settling the West

The successive defeats of the native Americans opened up for settlement a vast territory that reached from the prairie Plains to the Sierra Nevada and the Cascade Mountains. In the 1840s, when nearly a quarter-million Americans had trudged overland to Oregon and California, they had typically endured a six- to eight-month trip in ox-drawn wagons with no springs, under whose canvas tops the temperature rose to 110 degrees by midday. Provisions were meager and the journey perilous. After 1870, as railroad expansion made the trip to the Great Plains and the Far West not only faster but considerably easier, migration accelerated. In the next three decades, new settlers started up 2.5 million farms in the Dakotas, Nebraska, and Kansas alone. More land was parceled out into farms than in the previous 250 years of American history combined, and agricultural production doubled.

The First Transcontinental Railroad

On May 10, 1869, church bells clanged and cannons boomed across the nation as Americans celebrated the completion of the first railroad spanning North America. As the two sets of tracks—the Union Pacific's, stretching westward from Omaha, Nebraska, and the Central Pacific's, reaching eastward from Sacramento, California—met at Promontory Point, Utah, beaming officials drove in a final ceremonial golden spike with a silver hammer. With the coming of the transcontinental, Americans could make in a week's time the same coast-to-coast journey that earlier took travelers to California several *months*.

Building the railroad took backbreaking labor. Finding American muscle in inadequate supply, the railroads turned to the immigrant masses. The Central Pacific employed Chinese in large numbers to swing their picks in the rugged Sierra Nevada, where the workers chipped and blasted railbed out of solid rock. The Union Pacific's construction gangs included countless brawny Irish immigrants who dug their way across Nebraska and Wyoming. Americans of many other national and racial backgrounds, including blacks and Mexican-Americans, also lent their might to the endeavor.

The Pacific Railroad Act of July 1, 1862, had authorized the construction of the transcontinental (see Chapter 14). The grants of land and other subsidies given to the railroads for each mile of track laid made them the single largest landholders in the West. Other railroads soon crisscrossed America, with nine major routes ultimately leading from the South or Midwest to the West.

Promoting the Railroads

This Pacific Railway panorama was designed to lure sightseers to visit the natural wonders of the Rocky Mountains. In the foreground are depicted the pigtailed Chinese immigrants who supplied much of the hard labor during the railroad's construction.

Settlers and the Railroad

By 1872, under the Pacific Railroad Act, Congress had awarded the railroads 170 million acres, worth at the time over half a billion dollars. By 1893 the states of Minnesota and Washington had also deeded to railroad companies a quarter of their state lands; Wisconsin, Iowa, Kansas, North Dakota, and Montana had turned over to them a fifth of their acreage. As mighty landowners, the railroads had a unique opportunity to shape settlement in the region—and to reap enormous profits.

The railroads used several different ploys to attract inhabitants. They created land bureaus and sent agents to the East Coast and Europe to recruit settlers. While the agents glorified the West as a new Garden of Eden, the land bureaus offered long-term loans and free transportation west to prospective buyers. The railroads commonly sold prime land at the rock-bottom price of two dollars to six dollars an acre and promised farmers low-cost transportation to market for their wheat, corn, and other crops. Meanwhile, a flood of promotional books egged on the hesitant. "How can any young man of spirit settle himself down to earning a bare existence," demanded one enthusiastic writer, "when all this vast region, . . . with its boundless, undeveloped resources before him, is inviting him

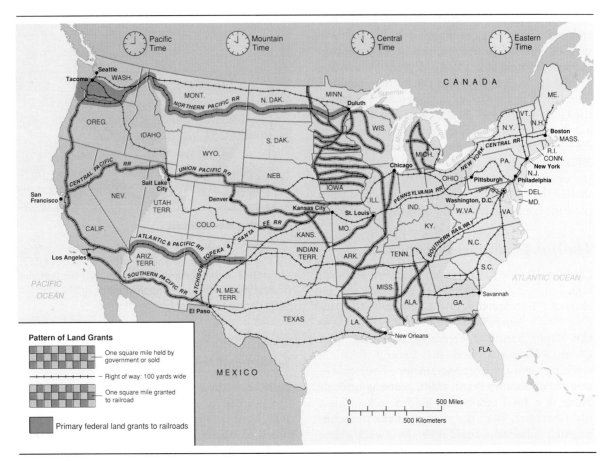

Transcontinental Railroads and Federal Land Grants, 1850–1900

Despite the laissez faire ideology that argued against government interference in business, Congress heavily subsidized American railroads and gave them millions of acres of land. As illustrated in the box, belts of land were reserved on either side of a railroad's right of way. Until the railroad claimed the exact one-mile-square sections it chose to possess, all such sections within the belt remained closed to settlement.

on? They will be nobodies where they are—they can be somebodies in building up a new society." Acknowledging that life on the Great Plains could be lonely, the promoters advised young men to bring their own wives (because "maidens are scarce") and to emigrate as entire families and with friends.

In addition to the millions of Americans who migrated from nearby states, the railroads between 1870 and 1900 helped bring nearly 2.2 million foreign-born settlers to the trans-Mississippi West. Some agents recruited whole villages of Germans and eastern Europeans to relocate to the North Dakota plains, where they found soils similar to those of their homelands. By 1905 the Santa Fe

Railroad alone had transported sixty thousand Russian Mennonites from the Ukraine (to which they had migrated long before from their original homeland in Germany) to the fertile Kansas plains.

With their extensive landholdings, the railroads enormously influenced the pattern of settlement. At regular intervals along their lines, they set up stations to replenish the coal and water needed for their trains; many of these became settlements, and later, major towns. New communities sprang up by the hundreds, their grid layouts and architectural styles virtually identical thanks to plans and supplies that the railroads furnished to arriving settlers. They were also, visually speaking,

Russian Peasants, Bozeman, Montana

Used to the cold winters of the steppes of their native Russia, these immigrants, still wearing traditional dress, sought out lands in the northern Dakota Territory where the landscape and climate were similar to those of their homeland.

unrelievedly dull, especially in comparison to the earliest western towns that had blossomed haphazardly along river courses.

The railroads influenced agriculture as well as architecture. To ensure quick repayment of the money owed to them, the railroads urged new immigrants to specialize in cash crops—wheat on the northern Plains, corn in Iowa and Kansas, cotton and tobacco in Texas. Although these crops initially brought in high revenues, many farmers grew dependent on income from a single crop and ultimately became vulnerable to fluctuating market forces.

Homesteaders on the Great Plains

Liberalized land laws were another powerful magnet pulling settlers westward. The Homestead Act, which Congress passed in 1862 to benefit small farmers and urban workers, had offered 160 acres of land to any individual who would pay a $10 registration fee, live on the land for five years, and cultivate and improve it. Because getting to the Great Plains was expensive, the typical settlers migrated from nearby states. In 1860 Kansas contained thirty-one thousand people from Illinois but only about forty-two hundred from New England. The majority had come from towns and small cities. On the Dakota frontier, only a third of the native-stock settlers had been farmers before they emigrated.

The Homestead Act also proved attractive to immigrants from the British Isles as well as from Scandinavia and other regions of Europe where good-quality land was prohibitively expensive. Urged on by land promoters, waves of English, Irish, Germans, Swedes, Danes, Norwegians, and Czechs immigrated to the United States in the 1870s and 1880s and formed their own communities. Soon the countryside in Minnesota and other states was dotted with towns bearing such names as New Ulm, New Prague, and New Sweden. Within a generation the Red River Valley in Minnesota could boast the largest Norwegian population outside Norway.

Although nearly four hundred thousand families claimed land under the provisions of the Homestead Act between 1860 and 1900, the law did not function as Congress had envisioned. Advance agents representing unscrupulous speculators filed false claims for the choicest locations, and railroads and state governments acquired huge expanses of land. Despite the good intentions of the Homestead Act's authors, only one acre in every nine went to the pioneers for whom it was intended.

A second problem resulted from the 160-acre limit specified by the Homestead Act. A 160-acre farm on the rich soils of Iowa or Minnesota was ample, but in the drier areas farther west, a prospective farmer needed more land. To rectify this problem, Congress in 1873 passed the Timber Culture Act, which gave homesteaders an additional 160 acres if they planted trees on 40 acres of it.

Homesteading in Nebraska, 1886

Not all Plains households were headed by males. The Chrisman sisters in Nebraska each staked a claim to 160 acres and took turns living with one another to fulfill the U.S. land office's residence requirements. Quilting was a relaxing diversion from the drudgery of farm work.

For the states with little rainfall, Congress also enacted the Desert Land Act in 1877, which made available 640 acres at $1.25 an acre on condition that the owner irrigate part of it within three years. However, this act, along with the Timber and Stone Act of 1878, which permitted the purchase of up to 160 acres of forest land for $2.50 an acre, was widely abused by grasping speculators, lumber-company representatives, and cattle ranchers seeking to expand their holdings. But even though individual families did not receive as much land as Congress had intended, federal legislation kept alive the dream of the West as a place for new beginnings.

New Farms, New Markets

Railroad expansion and the liberalization of the land laws coincided with advances in farm mechanization and the development of improved strains of wheat and corn. Progress on these fronts enabled farmers to boost production dramatically. Efficient steel plows; spring-tooth harrows that broke up the dense prairie soil more effectively than earlier models; specially designed wheat planters; and improved grain binders, threshers, and windmills all allowed the typical Great Plains farmer of the late nineteenth century to grow and harvest ten

times more wheat than would have been possible a few decades earlier. Another crucial invention was barbed wire, patented in 1874, which permitted farmers to keep roving livestock off their land—and which touched off violent conflicts between farmers and the cattle ranchers, who demanded the right to let their herds roam freely until the roundup. Generally the farmers won.

Fueling the leap in wheat production was a spiraling demand for the commodity, attributable to a 400 percent increase in the eastern urban population between 1870 and 1910. This demand was further stimulated by the development of milling techniques that improved the taste and texture of wheat flour. Before the 1870s, wheat was ground with large millstones that crushed the kernel to produce a coarse, strong-tasting, dark whole-wheat flour. Borrowing new milling techniques from Europe, the Archibald Mills in Dundas, Minnesota, in 1876 used steel rollers to crack the kernel, allowing the husk to be blown off and the bran to be separated. This technique produced a silky, all-white flour that won first prize at the Philadelphia World's Fair that year. The Washburn mills in Minneapolis (later called General Mills) soon adopted the new technology and produced tons of the better-tasting, though less nutritious, white flour.

584

Harnessing the water power of St. Anthony Falls on the Mississippi, and taking advantage of the shipping opportunities created by the fact that the Northern Pacific Railroad had its headquarters in Minneapolis, the Washburn mills quickly gained a national and even international market for their flour.

Farming seemed to be entering a period of unparalleled prosperity, and the claims of enthusiastic promoters nourished the idea that anyone could make an easy living in the West. Few fully understood the costs, difficulties, and perils of pursuing western farming as a livelihood. Land was expensive, even at the reduced prices offered by the federal government and the railroads. The cost of the horses, machinery, and seed needed to start up a farm could amount to at least twelve hundred dollars, far more than the annual earnings of the average industrial worker. Faced with substantial mortgage payments, many farmers had no choice but to specialize in a crop such as wheat or corn that would fetch high prices. This specialization, in turn, made them dependent on the railroads for shipping and put them at the mercy of the international grain market's shifting currents.

Far from being an independent producer, the western grain grower was a player in a complex world market economy. Railroad and steamship transport allowed the American farmer to compete in the international market. High demand could bring prosperity, but when world overproduction forced grain prices down, the heavily indebted western grower faced ruin. The emergence of a global grain trade also created economic pressures for peasant farmers in Europe—many of whom ultimately immigrated to the Plains, where their presence heightened the competition for land and for a slice of this tempting market. Faced with these complex realities, many a Plains farmer quickly abandoned the illusion of frontier independence and easy wealth.

Exacerbating homesteaders' difficulties on the western Great Plains, normal rainfall was less than twenty inches a year. Farmers compensated through "dry farming"—plowing deeply to stimulate the capillary action of the soils and harrowing lightly to raise a covering of dirt that would retain precious moisture after a rainfall. They also built windmills and diverted creeks for irrigation. But the onset of unusually dry years in the 1870s,

Cost of Establishing a Farm in Iowa, 1870	
Land (100 acres at $4 per acre)	$ 400
House (25% down payment on a $1,500 three-bedroom house)	375
Barn or stable (25% down payment on $500)	150
Team (horses or oxen)	150
Wagon and yoke or harness	150
Plow	30
Cultivator and harrow	20
Reaper-mower	200
Rakes, shovels, hammers, and other hand tools	40
Threshing machine (optional)	500
Total	**$2,015**

SOURCE: Allan G. Bogue, *From Prairie to Corn Belt* (Chicago: University of Chicago Press, 1963), 166–170.

together with grasshopper infestations and the major economic depression that struck the United States between 1873 and 1878 (see Chapter 15), made the plight of some midwesterners desperate.

Building a Society and Achieving Statehood

Whether they hailed from the East, the nearby Midwest, or foreign lands, homesteaders faced difficult psychological adjustments to frontier life. The arduous process of starting a farm discouraged many. Toiling to build a house, plow the fields, plant the first crop, and drill a well, the pioneers endured long hours of tedious, backbreaking work in isolated surroundings. Howard Ruede, a Pennsylvania printer who migrated to Kansas to farm, wrote home in 1877 complaining about the mosquitoes and bedbugs infesting his sod house. He nevertheless counseled his parents, "Don't publish my diary entire, . . . I don't care to let everybody know how I live, though it might deter some from coming who would otherwise throw away their money." The shining vision of an Edenic farm life quickly dimmed for Ruede and countless others rudely awakened by the severe Plains conditions. For black farmers who emigrated from the South to Kansas and other parts of the Plains after the Civil War, prejudice and racism compounded the psychological burdens of adjusting to a very different life.

Many middle-class women settlers, swept up in the romantic conventions of the day, found adaptation to Plains frontier life especially difficult. At least initially, some were enchanted by the haunting landscape, and in letters home they described the undulating open plains as arrestingly beautiful. But far more were struck by the "horrible tribes of Mosquitoes"; the violent weather—drenching summer thunderstorms with hailstones as "big as hen's eggs" and winter blizzards with blinding wind-driven snow; and the crude sod huts that served as their early homes because of the scarcity of timber. One woman burst into tears upon first seeing her new sod house. The young bride angrily informed her husband that her father had a better house for his hogs.

The high transiency rate on the frontier in these years reflected the frequent failures in adapting to the new environment. Nearly 66 percent of those who settled in Wapello County, Iowa, in 1850 had left within ten years. Seventy-nine percent of the families residing in a typical Wisconsin county in 1880 had moved on by 1895. Many were forced out by the rigors of frontier life, but others succumbed to speculative fever and sold out in the hope of finding better land farther west. However, in places, like Minnesota's Stearns County, that were populated largely by Germans and other immigrants with a tradition of family prosperity tied to continuous landownership, the persistence rate (or percentage of people staying for a decade or more) could be considerably higher.

Many of those who weathered the lean early years eventually came to identify closely with the land. Within a decade the typical Plains family that had "stuck it out" had moved into a new wood-frame house and had fixed up the front parlor. The women of these surviving households worked hard but learned to enjoy their lot. "Just done the chores," wrote one such woman to a friend. "I went fence mending and getting out cattle . . . and came in after sundown. I fed my White Leghorns, and then sat on the step to read over your letter. I forgot my wet feet and shoes full of gravel and giggled joyously." Despite their arduous existence, such settlers often spoke positively about life on the Great Plains. But they missed their old friends and the communities that they had left.

Some remote farm settlements blossomed into thriving communities. Churches and Sunday schools, among the first institutions to appear, became humming centers of social activity as well as of worship and religious teaching. Farmers gathered for barn raisings and group threshings, and families pooled their energies in quilting and husking bees. Neighbors readily lent a hand to the farmer whose barn had burned or whose wife or child was sick. Cooperation was a practical necessity and a form of insurance in a rugged environment where everyone was vulnerable to instant misfortune or even disaster.

As settlements grew into small towns, their inhabitants labored to reverse easterners' image of the Midwest as unrefined and backward. They eagerly set up lyceums and libraries to uplift and enlighten local residents. Masonic lodges and social clubs soon followed. Larger communities established fashionable hotels, the symbol of urban sophistication and culture, and brought in traveling entertainers to perform at their new "opera houses."

Like the farmers in the surrounding countryside, townspeople closed ranks when misfortune struck. At the first outbreak of fire or violence, the whole town mobilized. When the notorious ex-Confederate raider and outlaw Jesse James rode into Northfield, Minnesota, and held up the town bank in 1876, local merchants grabbed their shotguns and drove him off, killing two of his gang.

In their efforts to carry civilization to the frontier, the new settlers—on the Plains and farther west—tended to be conservative. They patterned their churches, schools, courts, and governmental structures after familiar institutions in the communities from which they had come. The process of achieving statehood required that the residents of a territory petition Congress to pass an enabling act establishing the territory's boundaries and

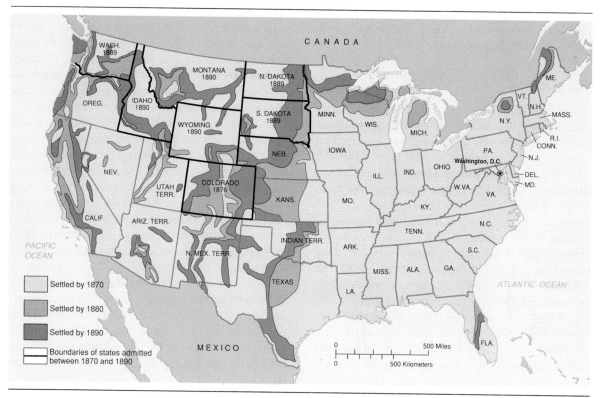

The Settlement of the Frontier, 1860–1890

The West was not settled by a movement of peoples gradually creeping westward from the East. Rather, settlers first occupied California and the Midwest and then filled up the nation's vast interior.

authorizing an election to select delegates for a state constitutional convention. Once the state constitution had been drawn up and ratified by popular vote, the territory applied to Congress for admission as a state.

Under these procedures Kansas entered the Union in 1861, followed by Nevada in 1864 and Nebraska in 1867. Colorado joined in 1876. Not until 1889 did the northernmost territories of North Dakota, South Dakota, Montana, and Washington gain statehood. Wyoming and Idaho came into the Union the following year. Utah, long prevented from joining because of the Mormon practice of polygamy, finally declared multiple marriages illegal and entered in 1896. With Congress's acceptance of Oklahoma's application for statehood in 1907 and those of Arizona and New Mexico in 1912, the process of creating permanent political institutions on the frontier was complete.

Although generally conservative, the new state governments were innovative in their support of woman suffrage. As territories became states, pioneer women, encouraged by women's rights activists like Susan B. Anthony and Elizabeth Cady Stanton, battled for the vote. Seven western states held referenda on this issue between 1870 and 1910. Success came first in the Wyoming Territory, where the tiny legislature enfranchised women in 1869 in hopes of improving the territory's reputation as a haven of rowdy mining camps by attracting females, who were outnumbered six to one. The Utah Territory followed in 1870 and reaffirmed its support for woman suffrage when it became a state. Nebraska in 1867, and Colorado in 1876, permitted women to vote in school elections. Although these successes were significant, by 1910 only four states—Idaho, Wyoming, Utah, and Colorado— had granted women full voting rights. The very newness of their place in the Union may have sensitized legislators in these states to women's important contributions to settlement and made them open to experimentation; but by and large, familiar institutions and traditions persisted.

The Grange

As we have seen, Plains farming proved far riskier than many had anticipated. Terrible grasshopper infestations between 1873 and 1877 consumed nearly half the midwestern wheat crop. Although overall production surged after 1870, the abundant harvests undercut prices. Wheat tumbled from a high of $2.95 a bushel in 1866 to $1.06 in 1880. Countless farmers who had borrowed heavily to finance their homesteads and expensive new machinery went bankrupt or barely survived. One struggling elderly Minnesota farmer wrote the governor in 1874: "[W]e can see nothing but starvation in the future if relief does not come."

When relief did not come, the farmers responded by setting up cooperative ventures. Under the leadership of Oliver H. Kelley, a Department of Agriculture clerk, midwestern farmers in 1867 formed the Grange, or "Patrons of Husbandry," as the organization was officially called. Membership climbed to more than 1.5 million in the trying years of the early 1870s. Patterned after the Masonic Order, the Grange offered a program of education, emotional support, and fellowship. For the inexperienced homesteader, it made available a library of the latest information on planting and livestock raising. For the exhausted farm family whose members put in an average of sixty-eight hours per week of backbreaking labor, the Grange organized biweekly social gatherings, including cooperative meals and lively songfests. Those who felt socially and culturally isolated on remote farms could find in the Grange "an opportunity for social, intellectual, and moral improvement."

But the heart of the Grange was concern over farmers' economic plight. An 1874 circular announced the organization's central purpose: to help farmers "buy less and produce more, in order to make our farms more self-sustaining." Grangers embraced the older Jacksonian belief that the products of the soil were the basis of all honorable wealth and that the producer classes—people who worked with their hands—formed the true backbone of society. Members sought to restore self-sufficiency to the family farm. Ignoring the con-

tradiction implicit in farmers' banding together to help individuals become independent tillers of the soil, they negotiated special discounts with farm-machinery dealers and set up "cash-only" cooperative stores and grain-storage elevators to cut out the "middlemen"—the bankers, grain brokers, and merchants who made money at their expense.

Grangers vehemently attacked the railroads, which not only routinely gave discounts to large shippers but also bribed state legislators for special land favors and charged higher rates for short runs than for long hauls. These practices sharply stung hard-pressed farmers. Although professing to be nonpolitical, Grangers in Illinois, Wisconsin, Minnesota, and Iowa lobbied state legislatures in 1874 to pass laws fixing maximum rates for freight shipments.

The railroads responded by appealing to the Supreme Court to declare these "Granger laws" unconstitutional. But in *Munn* v. *Illinois* (1877), the Court not only ruled against the railroads' objections but also upheld an Illinois law fixing a maximum rate for the storage of grain. The regulation of grain elevators, declared the Court's majority, was legitimate under the federal Constitution's clause granting police powers to states. When the Court in *Wabash* v. *Illinois* (1886) modified this position by prohibiting states from regulating *interstate* railroad rates, Congress passed the Interstate Commerce Act (1887), reaffirming the federal government's power to investigate and oversee railroad activities and establishing a new agency, the Interstate Commerce Commission (ICC), to do just that. Although the commission actually did little to curb the railroads' monopolistic practices, it did establish the principle of federal regulation of interstate transportation.

Despite promising beginnings, however, the Granger movement soon faltered. The railroads, having lost their battle on the national level, lobbied state legislatures and won repeal of most of the rate-regulation laws by 1878. Moreover, the Grange system of cash-only cooperative stores failed because few farmers had ample cash. Ultimately the Grange ideal of complete financial independence proved unrealistic. Under the conditions that prevailed on the Plains after the Civil War, it was impossible to farm without borrowing money.

How valid was the Grangers' analysis of the farmers' problems? The Grangers blamed greedy railroads and middlemen for their economic difficulties, but the situation was not that simple. The years 1873–1878 saw the entire economy caught in a grinding depression, in which railroad operators and merchant middlemen, no less than farmers, had to scramble to survive. And while farm commodity prices did fall between 1865 and 1900, the wholesale prices of manufactured goods, including items needed on the farm, fell in the same period as well—often faster than farm prices. Even the railroads' stiff freight charges could be justified in part by the thin pattern of western settlement and the seasonality of grain shipments.

Notwithstanding, the farmers and the Grange leaders who articulated their grievances had reasons aplenty to complain. Farmers who had no control over the price level of their crops were at the mercy of local merchants and farm-equipment dealers who exercised monopolistic control over the prices that *they* could charge. Similarly, railroads sometimes insisted on transporting wheat to only one mill. Occasionally they even refused to stop at small towns to pick up local wheat shipments. Policies like these struck the farmers as completely arbitrary and made them feel powerless. Hamlin Garland captured the hardship and despair of frustrated farmers in his *Main-Travelled Roads* (1891) and *Son of the Middle Border* (1917), describing barely surviving families who "rose early and toiled without intermission, till the darkness fell on the plain, then tumbled into bed, every bone and muscle aching with fatigue."

When the prices of corn, wheat, and cotton briefly revived after 1878, farmers deserted the Grange in large numbers. Although the Grange lived on as a social and educational institution, it lost its economic clout because it was ultimately unable to improve the financial position of the farmers whom it served. For all its weaknesses, however, the Grange movement did lay the groundwork for a second and even more powerful wave of agrarian protest in the 1880s and 1890s, to be discussed in Chapter 20.

The Southwestern Frontier

Until 1848, when the Treaty of Guadalupe Hidalgo ended the Mexican War and ceded to the United States an immense territory—part of which became California, Arizona, and New Mexico—Mexicans had controlled wide-open expanses of the Southwest. They had built their own churches, maintained large ranching operations, and as we have seen, traded with the Indians. Although the peace treaty pledged the United States to protect the liberty and property of those Mexicans who remained on American soil, in the next three decades, aggressive American ranchers and settlers took over the territorial governments and forced the Spanish-speaking population off much of the land. Those Mexicans who stayed behind adapted to the new Anglo society with varying degrees of success.

In Texas, where the struggle for independence from Mexico and the Mexican War had left a legacy of bitterness and misunderstanding, Anglos in the 1840s and 1850s frequently harassed local Mexican-Americans and confiscated their lands. Small numbers of Mexican bandits retaliated by raiding American communities, stealing from the rich and giving to the poor. Tensions peaked in 1859, when Juan Cortina, a local Mexican rancher, attacked the Anglo border community of Brownsville, Texas, and freed all the prisoners in jail. Pursued by the United States Army, Cortina battled the Americans for years, slipping back and forth across the border until the Mexican government, fearing a U.S. invasion, imprisoned him in 1875.

Similar violence erupted in California in the 1850s and 1860s after a cycle of flood and drought, together with a slumping cattle industry, ruined many of the large southern California ranches owned by the *californios*, the Spanish-speaking descendants of the original Spanish settlers. The collapse of the ranch economy forced many of these Hispanics to retreat into socially segregated urban neighborhoods, called barrios. In Santa Barbara, California, Spanish-surnamed citizens made up nearly half the town's 2,640 residents in 1870. Ten years later, however, overwhelmed by an influx of Anglos, they composed barely a quarter of the population. Maintaining a tenacious hold on their traditions, Spanish-speaking people in Santa Barbara and other towns survived by working as low-paid day laborers.

The cultural adaptation of Spanish-speaking Americans to Anglo society unfolded more smoothly in Arizona and New Mexico, where the initial Spanish settlement was sparse and a small class of wealthy Mexican landowners had long dominated

Adobe House, Santa Barbara, c. 1890

Although Spanish-speaking families in Santa Barbara were excluded from certain sections of town, they posed as proudly in front of their homes as did local Anglos.

a poor illiterate peasantry. Moreover, beginning in the 1820s, well-to-do Mexicans in Tucson, Arizona, had educated their children in the United States and had formed trading partnerships and business alliances with Americans. Perhaps the most successful was Estevan Ochoa, who began a long-distance freighting business in 1859 with a U.S. partner and then expanded it into a lucrative merchandising, mining, and sheep-raising operation.

The success of hard-working businessmen such as Ochoa, who became mayor of Tucson, helped moderate American settlers' antagonistic attitudes toward the indigenous Hispanic population. So, too, did the work of popular writers like Bret Harte and Helen Hunt Jackson. By sentimentalizing the old Spanish-Mexican ways in their writings, these authors increased public sympathy for Spanish-speaking Americans. Jackson's 1884 romance *Ramona,* a tale of doomed love set on a California Spanish-Mexican ranch overwhelmed by the on-rushing tide of Anglo civilization, proved enormously popular.

Not all was harmony, however. In Arizona and New Mexico, Mexican-American and Anglo ranchers became embroiled in fiery land disputes in the 1880s. Organizing themselves as *Las Gorras Blancas* (The White Caps) in 1888, Mexican-American ranchers intimidated and attacked Anglo newcomers who had fenced acreage in northern New Mexico previously considered public grazing land. But this vigilante action gained them little, as Anglo-dominated corporate ranching steadily

impinged on their operations. Relations changed in the urban centers as well, as Mexican-American businessmen increasingly restricted their business dealings to their own people, and the Hispanic population as a whole became more impoverished. Even in Tucson, where the Spanish-speaking elite enjoyed considerable economic and political success, 80 percent of the Mexican-Americans in the work force were laborers in 1880, taking jobs as butchers, barbers, cowboys, and railroad workers.

Violence and discrimination against Spanish-speaking citizens of the Southwest escalated in the 1890s, a time when racism in general was on the rise in the United States. Riots against Mexican-Americans broke out in the Texas communities of Beeville and Laredo in 1894 and 1899. Expressions of anti-Catholicism, as well as verbal attacks on the Mexican-Americans as violent and lazy, increased among hostile Anglos. For Spanish-speaking citizens, the battle for fair treatment and cultural respect would continue into the twentieth century.

Exploiting the West

For a generation of Americans that watched enviously as astounding fortunes were being made in railroading, steel, and other businesses (see Chapter 17), the spectacular gold-mining, cattle-raising, and farming enterprises that lit up the western landscape from the 1850s to the 1880s appeared to offer great opportunities for the individual to strike it rich. Publicized in banner headlines across the land, these "bonanzas" promised unheard-of wealth and seemed to confirm the myth of the frontier as a place of boundless opportunity. In reality, however, the bonanzas set in motion a boom-and-bust economy in which a few people became fabulously wealthy but most barely survived or lost their shirts. Of all the groups that surged onto the Great Plains and beyond in the late nineteenth century, none had to revise their expectations more radically than the speculators and adventurers thirsting for quick fortunes.

The Mining Frontier

Beginning with the California gold rush in 1849, a series of mining booms over the next three decades swept from the Southwest northward into Canada. The sensational discoveries in California's Sierra Nevada that produced more than $81 million worth of gold bullion in 1852 were followed by gold strikes on the Fraser River in British Columbia in 1857. The following year, Henry Comstock (who for obscure reasons bore the nickname "Old Pancake") stumbled upon the rich Comstock Lode along Nevada's Carson River. Months later, feverishly pursuing rumors of new strikes, prospectors swarmed into the Rocky Mountains near present-day Denver and uncovered deep veins of gold and silver along a little stream called Clear Creek. Over the next two decades, gold was discovered in Idaho, Montana, Wyoming, South Dakota, and, in 1896, in the Alaskan Klondike. Although the popular press clearly exaggerated reports of miners scooping up gold by the panful, by 1900 more than a billion dollars worth of gold had been mined just in California. The Comstock Lode alone produced more than $300 million worth of gold and silver.

The early discoveries of "placer" gold, panned from riverbeds and streams, reinforced the myth of the mining country as "a poor man's paradise." By 1860, when census takers asked Californians to report their occupations, more than 82,000 out of a population of 380,000 described themselves as miners. Of these, 35,000 were Chinese, many of whom were forced by prejudice to work poorer claims that others had abandoned.

Although a few prospectors became fabulously

wealthy, the experience of Henry Comstock, who sold out one claim for eleven thousand dollars and another for two mules, was more typical. The illusions of the frontier myth notwithstanding, most of the West's mining wealth fell into the hands of investment bankers and mining-company owners. Because the larger gold and silver deposits lay buried in veins of quartz deep within the earth, extracting them required huge investments in expensive equipment as well as substantial legal help for protection against competing claims. No sooner had the major discoveries been made, therefore, than large mining companies, backed by eastern or British capital, took them over.

But if the Comstock Lode, the Clear Creek strike, and the other ore discoveries failed to bring great riches to the average miner, they did stimulate flurries of secondary economic activity, and then wildly transformed normal patterns of social behavior. During the heyday of the Comstock Lode in the 1860s and 1870s, Virginia City, Nevada, erupted in an orgy of speculation and building.

Mining by Candlelight

These silver miners bore into rock by pounding in a steel drill; then they inserted a small dynamite charge to blow the rock up. Hand drilling, or "jacking," required fifty strikes per minute with an eight-pound hammer. Many miners bore the scars of missed hammer blows.

Like many boom towns near mining claims, it had sprung into being almost overnight. Started as a shantytown in 1859, it swelled by 1873 into a thriving metropolis of twenty thousand people, complete with elaborate mansions, a six-story hotel, an opera house, 131 saloons, 4 banks, and uncounted brothels. Males outnumbered females by three to one. Money quickly earned was even more rapidly lost.

In the chaotic rush to stake new claims, inhibitions about stealing and cheating fell by the wayside. Because Virginia City's police force was too small and too corrupt to maintain order, vigilantes took over the town during the economic downturn of 1871, hanged two notorious outlaws, and forced a number of others off the lode. Justice on the mining frontier was occasionally a rough affair, but most communities, unlike Virginia City, established stable police forces and a regular system of courts.

The boom-and-bust cycle evident in Virginia City was repeated in towns across the west between 1870 and 1900. Mark Twain captured the thrill of the mining "stampedes" in his book *Roughing It* (1872). "Every few days," wrote Twain, "news would come of the discovery of a brand-new mining region: immediately the papers would teem with accounts of its richness, and away the surplus population would scamper to take possession. By the time I was fairly inoculated with the disease, 'Esmeralda' had just had a run and 'Humboldt' was beginning to shriek for attention. 'Humboldt! Humboldt!' was the new cry, and straightway Humboldt, the newest of the new, the richest of the rich, the most marvelous of the marvelous discoveries in silver-land, was occupying two columns of the public prints to 'Esmeralda's' one."

Word of new ore deposits lured to the mining towns transient populations salivating to get rich. Miners typically earned about $2,000 a year at a time when teachers made $450 to $650 and domestic help $250 to $350. But meals and a tiny room cost between $480 and $720 annually. Further, mining was difficult and dangerous work. Serious accidents occurred daily. In less than two decades, more than three hundred workers died in the Virginia City mines. And when miners exhausted the major ore veins, they quickly packed up for new territories. By 1900 Virginia City's population had shrunk below four thousand. Although a few got rich, most miners at best earned only enough to go elsewhere, perhaps buy some land, and try again. But if the myth of the frontier exaggerated the opportunities of the mining West, it contained just enough reality to sustain people's hopes.

Cowboys and the Cattle Frontier

As Mark Twain had so colorfully related, the popular press's rousing accounts of big gold strikes had helped fuel the feverish expansion of the mining frontier during the 1860s and 1870s. Similar stories, romanticizing the life of the hardy cowboy, driving herds of longhorns northward from Texas through Oklahoma to markets in Dodge City and Abilene, Kansas, sparked the transformation of the cattle industry in these same decades. In this case, astute businessmen and railroad entrepreneurs, eager to fund their new investments in miles of track, promoted cattle herding as the new route to fame and fortune, and the eastern press took up the theme. The cowboy, once scorned as a ne'er-do-well and drifter, was now glorified as a man of rough-hewn integrity and self-reliant strength who lived a life of adventurous simplicity on the Shawnee, Chisholm, and other fabled cattle trails of the Southwest.

In 1868 Joseph G. McCoy, a young cattle dealer from Springfield, Illinois, shrewdly combined organizational and promotional skills to make the cattle industry a new bonanza. Having grown up in a moderately wealthy family, McCoy had avoided military service and reaped an enviable profit trading livestock during the Civil War. He was well aware that attempts in the 1850s to drive longhorn cattle from south Texas grasslands northward to markets in Arkansas, Illinois, and Missouri had been unprofitable and dangerous, owing to frequent Indian attacks and outbreaks of "Texas fever" that had killed thousands of cattle. But with the relocation of the Plains Indians onto reservations and the extension of the railroads into Kansas in the post–Civil War period, McCoy realized that the cattle-shipping business now had a renewed potential.

Forming a partnership in 1867 with his brothers' Illinois company that shipped cattle to New Orleans and New York, McCoy traveled to Kansas and oversaw the construction of a new stockyard in Abilene. First opposed by a hostile legislature that feared the northward spread of Texas fever, McCoy had to work hard to attract the trail-drover business to his yard. He gained the support of

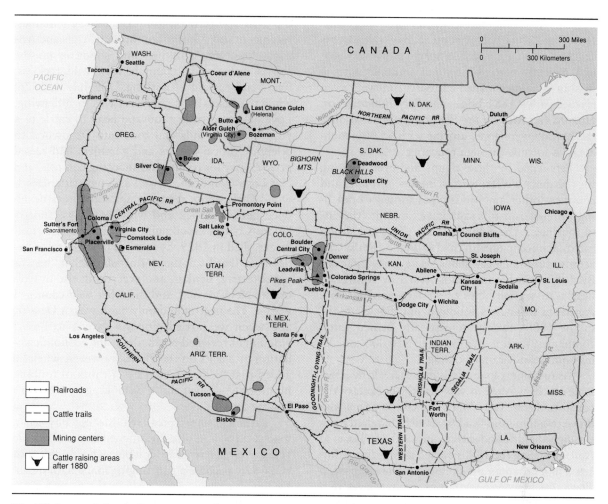

The Mining and Cattle Frontiers, 1860–1890

The western mining and ranching bonanzas lured thousands of Americans hoping to get rich quick.

neighboring ranchers by purchasing supplies from them at high prices and by reimbursing them for any of their own stock that died of Texas fever. By guaranteeing to transport his steers in railcars to hungry eastern markets, he obtained a five-dollar kickback from the railroads on each cattle car shipped. To make the overland cattle drives from Texas to Abilene easier, McCoy also helped survey and shorten the Chisholm Trail in Kansas. Finally, in a clever feat of showmanship, he organized the first Wild West show, sending four Texas cowboys to St. Louis and Chicago, where they staged roping and riding exhibitions that attracted exuberant crowds and eager buyers for the cattle he shipped. At the end of his first year in business, thirty-five thousand steers were sold in Abilene; the following

year the number more than doubled, to seventy-five thousand.

The great cattle drives of the 1860s and 1870s turned into a bonanza for herd owners. Steers purchased in Texas at $9 a head could be sold in Abilene, after deducting $4 in trail expenses, for $28. A herd of two thousand head could thus bring a tidy $30,000 profit. But the cattlemen, like the grain growers farther north on the Great Plains, lived at the mercy of high interest rates and an unstable market. During the financial panic of 1873, cattle drovers, unable to get extensions on their loans, teetered into bankruptcy by the hundreds. Glossing over the market's instability, railroad promoters kept investors interested by shamelessly exaggerating the potential for profit. In their *Hand-*

Book of Wyoming and Guide to the Black Hills (1877) and other publications, railroad sales agents suggested that a 25 percent yearly profit was normal, and a 50 percent profit not unusual. James S. Brisbin, a soldier-turned-entrepreneur, went even further in his 1881 book *The Beef Bonanza; or, How to Get Rich on the Plains,* arguing that once the buffalo were gone, anyone with $5,000 could amass a fortune through ranching.

Persuaded by these claims and ever questing for the quick dollar, former miners, farmers, and countless other ambitious types turned to ranching. Foreign investors sank huge sums into the cattle business. The English alone put $45 million into ranch companies in the 1870s and 1880s. One Scottish firm ran a half-million-acre ranch in Texas. By 1883 British companies owned or controlled nearly 20 million acres of western grazing land. American businesses followed suit. For example, in the 1880s twenty domestically owned cattle companies, each worth between $20,000 and $3 million, operated in Wyoming.

As in mining, little of the money made by large-scale ranchers found its way into the pockets of the cowboys themselves. The typical cowpunchers who drove two-thousand-head herds eight hundred miles through the dirt and dust from southern Texas to Abilene during the 1870s earned a mere thirty dollars a month, about the same as common laborers. They also braved the gangs of cattle thieves that operated along the trails. The most notorious of the cattle rustlers, William H. Bonney, better known as Billy the Kid, may have murdered as many as eleven men before he was killed by a sheriff in 1881 at the age of twenty-one. The long hours, low pay, and hazardous work discouraged older ranch hands from applying. Most cowboys were young men in their teens and twenties who worked for a year or two and then pursued different livelihoods. Lacking other skills, they had turned to cowpunching for quick money and for the strong friendships that developed along the trails.

Of the estimated thirty-five thousand to fifty-five thousand men who rode the trails in these years, nearly one-fifth were black or Mexican. Barred by discrimination from many other trades, black cowboys enjoyed the freedom of life on the trail. Although they were excluded from the position of trail boss, they distinguished themselves as resourceful and shrewd cowpunchers. Nat Love, the son of Tennessee slaves, left for Kansas after the Civil War to work for Texas cattle companies. As chief brander, he moved through Texas and Arizona "dancing, drinking, and shooting up the town." By his own account, he was "wild, reckless, free," and "afraid of nothing." On July 4, 1876, when the Black Hills gold rush was in full swing, Love delivered three thousand head of cattle to a point near the hills and rode into Deadwood to celebrate. Local miners and gamblers had raised prize money for roping and shooting contests, and Nat Love won both, as well as a new title, Deadwood Dick. Close relationships sometimes developed between black and white cowboys. Shortly before Charles Goodnight, a white pioneer trailblazer, died in 1929, he recalled of the black cowboy Bose Ikard, another former slave, that "he was my detective, banker, and everything else in Colorado, New Mexico, and the other wild country I was in. The nearest and only bank was at Denver, and when we carried money I gave it to Bose." Goodnight revealed much about the economic situation of blacks on the Plains, however, when he added that "a thief would never think of robbing him [Ikard]—never think of looking in a Negro's bed for money."

Although the typical real-life cowboy led a lonely, dirty, and often boring existence, a mythic version of the frontier cowboy who might with equal ease become a gunslinging marshal or a dastardly villain was glamorized in the eastern press as early as the 1870s. The image of the West as a wild and lawless land where vigilantes battled with brutish bandits fired easterners' imaginations. Edward L. Wheeler, a writer for the publishing house of Beadle and Adams, in 1877 penned his first dime novel, *Deadwood Dick, The Prince of the Road: or, the Black Rider of the Black Hills.* Over the next eight years, Wheeler turned out thirty-three Deadwood Dick novels relating the adventures of the muscular young hero who wore black clothes and rode a black horse. Cast alternately as outlaw, miner, gang leader, and cowboy, Deadwood Dick turned his blazing six-shooters on ruthless ruffians and dishonest desperadoes. He had much in common with the real-life Deadwood Dick except that Wheeler, to please his white readership, made him a white man. The vigilante justice and lynch law celebrated in these novels portrayed the western frontier as a throwback to a semi-legendary earlier age in which honor had triumphed when the righteous took matters into their own hands.

Cowpunchers on the Range *(detail)*

In his painting Breaking Camp *(1885), Charles M. Russell reinforced the myth of the carefree cowboy, cavorting with wild abandon and testing his strength against that of a bucking horse.*

The reality was a good deal less picturesque. Although Abilene, for example, went through an early period of violence and turmoil that saw cowboys pulling down the walls of the jail as it was being built, the town had quickly established a local police force to maintain law and order. City ordinances forbade the carrying of firearms and regulated saloons, gambling, and prostitution. James B. ("Wild Bill") Hickok served as town marshal in 1871, but his tenure was less eventful than legend had it. Dime novelists described him as "a veritable terror to bad men on the border," but during his term as Abilene's lawman, Hickok killed just two men, one of them by mistake.* Transient, unruly types certainly gave a distinctive flavor to cattle towns like Abilene, Wichita, and Dodge City, but the overall homicide rates there were not unusually high.

More typical of western conflicts were the "range wars" that pitted "cattle kings" (who thought that the open range existed for them alone to exploit) against farmers. Gaining the upper hand in state legislatures, farming interests sought to cripple the freewheeling cattlemen with quarantine laws and inspection regulations. Ranchers retaliated against the spread of barbed-wire farm fencing on the Plains, first by cutting the settlers' fences and then by buying up and enclosing thousands of acres of their own. Meanwhile, dozens of small-scale shooting incidents broke out between inhabitants of isolated farms and livestock drovers, as well as between rival cattlemen and sheep ranchers.

Peaking during 1880–1885, the bonanza produced more than 4.5 million head of cattle for eastern markets. Prices began to sag as early as 1882, however, and many ranchers, having expanded too rapidly, plunged heavily into debt. When President Grover Cleveland, trying to improve federal observance of Indian treaties, ordered cattlemen to remove their stock from the Cheyenne-Arapaho reservation in 1885, two hundred thousand more cattle were crowded onto already overgrazed ranges. That same year and the following, two of the coldest and snowiest winters on record combined with summer droughts and Texas fever to destroy nearly 90 percent of the cattle in some regions, pushing thousands of ranchers into bankruptcy. Those who survived were forced to irrigate, fence their lands, and raise cattle on smaller ranches. The cattle industry lived on, but railroad expansion and the increasing numbers of steers raised outside the Great Plains brought the days of the open range and the great cattle drives to an end. As had the mining frontier, the early years of the cattle frontier left behind memories of individual daring, towering fortunes for some, and hard times for many.

Bonanza Farms on the Plains

The heady enthusiasm that permeated mining and ranching in the 1870s and 1880s also percolated into agriculture. Like the gold rushes and cattle bonanzas, the wheat boom in the Dakota Territory started small but rapidly attracted large capital investments that produced the nation's first "agribusinesses."

The boom began during the Panic of 1873, when the failure of numerous banks caused the price of Northern Pacific Railroad bonds to plum-

---

*Hickok eventually moved on to Deadwood, where he was murdered in 1876 by Jack McCall as he played poker, ensuring his place in the pantheon of western heroes.

met. The railroad responded by exchanging land for its depreciated bonds. Speculators, including the railroad's own president, George W. Cass, jumped at this wonderful opportunity and purchased more than three hundred thousand acres in the fertile Red River valley of North Dakota for between fifty cents and a dollar an acre.

Operating singly or in groups, the speculators established enormous, factorylike ten-thousand-acre farms, each run by a hired manager, and invested heavily in labor and equipment. On the Cass-Cheney-Dalrymple farm near Fargo, North Dakota, which covered an area six miles long by four miles wide, fifty men did the initial plowing. An additional one hundred were hired for harvesting. Together they used 66 plows, 21 seeders, 60 harrows, 30 self-binding harvesters, and 5 steam-powered threshers. On a typical spring day, 50 or 60 plows rumbled across the flat landscape in unison. The *New York Tribune* reported that Cass, who had invested fifty thousand dollars for land and equipment, paid all his expenses plus the cost of the ten thousand acres with his first harvest alone.

The publicity generated by the tremendous success of a few large investors like Cass and Oliver Dalrymple, the "king" of the wheat growers, led to an unprecedented wheat boom in the Red River valley in 1880. Eastern banking syndicates and small farmers alike rushed to buy land. North Dakota's population tripled in the 1880s. Wheat production skyrocketed to almost 29 million bushels by the end of the decade. But the profits so loudly celebrated in the eastern press soon evaporated. By 1890 some Red River valley farmers were destitute.

The wheat boom collapsed for a variety of reasons. Overproduction, high investment costs, too little or too much rain, excessive reliance on one crop, and depressed grain prices on the international market all undercut farmers' earnings. Large-scale farmers who had invested in hopes of getting rich felt lucky just to survive. A discouraged Oliver Dalrymple lamented in 1889 that "it seems as if the time has come when there is no money in wheat raising."

The Oklahoma Land Rush

Even as farmers in the Dakotas and Minnesota were enduring poor harvests and falling prices, hard-pressed would-be homesteaders greedily eyed the enormous Indian Territory, as present-day Oklahoma was then known. The federal government, considering much of the land in this area virtually worthless, had reserved it for the Five Civilized Tribes, who had dwelled there since the 1830s. Because these tribes had sided with the Confederacy during the Civil War (except for some Cherokees), Washington had punished them by settling thousands of Indians from *other* tribes on lands in the western part of the territory. By the 1880s, recognizing the actual value of the Oklahoma lands, land-hungry non-Indians argued that the Civilized Tribes' betrayal of the Union justified further federal confiscation of their land.

Over the native Americans' protests, Congress in 1889 transferred to the federally owned public domain nearly 2 million acres in the central part of the Oklahoma Territory that had not been specifically assigned to any Indian tribe. At noon on April 22, 1889, thousands of men, women, and children in buggies and wagons stampeded into the new lands to stake out homesteads. (Other settlers, the so-called Sooners, had earlier infiltrated the lands illegally and were already plowing the fields.) Before nightfall tent communities had risen at Oklahoma City and Guthrie near stations on the Santa Fe Railroad. Nine weeks later, six thousand homestead claims had been filed. During the next ten years, as the Dawes Severalty Act freed up additional acres by breaking up the Indian reservations into individual allotments and opening the surplus to non-Indian settlement, homesteaders continued to pour into the territory.

The Oklahoma land rush demonstrated the continuing power of the frontier myth, which tied "free" land to the ideals of individual opportunity and self-determination. Despite early obstacles—the 1889 rush occurred too late in the season for most settlers to plant a full crop, and a drought parched the land the following year—Oklahoma farmers remained optimistic about their chances of "making it" on the last frontier. Most did survive, because they were fortunate enough to have obtained fertile land in an area where the normal rainfall was thirty inches, ten inches more than in the semiarid regions farther west. Still, a combination of exploitative farming, poor land management, and sporadic drought would within two generations place Oklahoma at the desolate center of what Americans of the 1930s would call the dust bowl.

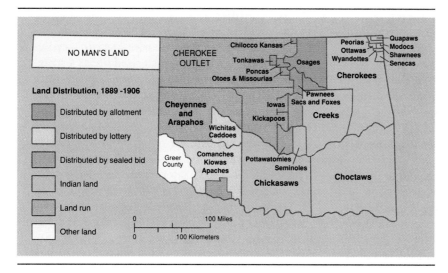

The Oklahoma Land Rush, 1889–1906

Lands in Oklahoma not settled by "sooners" were sold by lotteries, allotments, and sealed-bid auctions. By 1907 the major reservations had been broken up, and each native American had been given a small farm.

The Mythic West

In 1893, four years after the last major tract of Western Indian land, the Oklahoma Territory, was opened to non-Indian settlement, a young Wisconsin historian, Frederick Jackson Turner, delivered a lecture entitled "The Significance of the Frontier in American History." "[T]he frontier has gone," declared Turner, "and with its going has closed the first period of American history." Turner's lecture, which launched a new school of historical inquiry into the effects of the frontier on American history, was part of a broad popular awakening of interest in the frontier experience.

As farmers, miners, ranchers, Indian agents, and prostitutes had pursued their varied activities in the real West, a parallel mythic West had taken deep root in the American imagination. In the nineteenth century, this mythic West was a product of novels, songs, and paintings. In the twentieth century, it would be perpetuated by movies, radio programs, and television shows. The legend merits attention, for its evolution is fascinating, and its influence far-reaching.

The American Adam and the Dime-Novel Hero

In the early biographies of frontiersmen like Daniel Boone, and in the wilderness novels of James Fenimore Cooper, the western hero's personal development sometimes parallels, but more often runs counter to, the interests of society. Mid-nineteenth-century writers, extending the theme of the western wilderness as an alternative to society, presented the frontiersman as a kind of mythic American Adam—simple, virtuous, and innocent, untainted by a corrupt social order. For example, an early biographer of Kit Carson, the Kentucky-born guide who in 1830 made one of the first recorded crossings of California's Mojave Desert, depicted him as a perfect antidote to the evils of refined society, an individual of "genuine simplicity, . . . truthfulness . . . [and] bravery." At the end of Mark Twain's *Huckleberry Finn,* Huck rejects the constraints of settled society as represented by Aunt Sally and heads west with the declaration: "I reckon I got to light out for the territory ahead of the rest, because Aunt Sally she's going to adopt me and sivilize me, and I can't stand it. I been there before." In this version of the myth, the West is a place of adventure, romance, or contemplation where one can escape from society and its pressures.

But even as this conception of the myth was being popularized, another powerful theme had emerged as well. The authors of the dime novels that blanketed the nation in the 1860s and 1870s offered the image of the western frontiersman as a figure deeply immersed in society and its concerns. In *Buffalo Bill: King of the Border Men* (1869), a dime novel loosely based on real-life William F. ("Buffalo Bill") Cody, Edward Judson (who published under the name Ned Buntline) created an idealized hero who is a powerful force for morality and social order as he drives off treacherous Indians and rounds up horse thieves and no-good cattle rustlers.

So enthusiastically did the public welcome this new fictional frontiersman that Cody was inspired in 1883 to start his Wild West show. A former army scout and pony express rider, Cody was a natural showman, and his exhibitions proved immensely popular. In Chicago forty-two thousand people attended on the first day. Cody's elaborate productions offered demonstrations of steer roping and rodeo contests. For added authenticity, as we have seen, he even hired Sitting Bull, the Sioux chief who had helped wipe out Custer's force at the Little Bighorn, simply to sit and stare malevolently at the crowd. Cody also presented mock "battles" of army scouts and Indians—in effect, morality dramas of good versus evil. Along with entertainment, in short, the Wild West show reinforced the dime-novel image of the West as an arena of moral encounter where virtue always triumphed.

Revitalizing the Frontier Myth

Both versions of the myth—the West as a place of escape from society and the West as a stage on which the moral conflicts confronting society could be played out—figured prominently in the histories and essays of young Theodore Roosevelt, the paintings and sculptures of artist Frederic Remington, and the short stories and novels of writer Owen Wister. These three young members of the eastern establishment spent much time in the West in the 1880s, and each was intensely affected by the adventure. All three had felt thwarted by the constraints and enervating influence of the genteel urban world in which they had grown up, and each went West to experience the physical challenges and moral simplicities extolled in the dime novels. When Roosevelt arrived in 1884 at the ranch that he had purchased in the Dakota Badlands, he at once bought a leather scout's uniform, complete with fringed sleeves and leggings.

Each man also found in the West precisely what he was looking for. The frontier that Roosevelt glorified in such books as *The Winning of the West* (four volumes, 1889–1896), and that the prolific Remington portrayed in his work, was a stark physical and moral environment that stripped away all social artifice and tested an individual's true ability and character. Drawing on a popular version of English scientist Charles Darwin's evolutionary theory, which characterized life as a struggle in which only the fittest and the best survived, Roosevelt and Remington exalted the disappearing frontier as the last outpost of an honest and true social order.

This version of the frontier myth reached its apogee in Owen Wister's enormously popular novel *The Virginian* (1902), later reincarnated as a 1929 Gary Cooper movie and a 1960s television series. In Wister's tale the elemental physical and social environment of the Great Plains produces individuals like his unnamed cowboy hero, "the Virginian," an honest, strong, and compassionate man, quick to help the weak and fight the wicked. The Virginian is one of nature's aristocrats—ill-educated and unsophisticated but upright, steady, and deeply moral. The Virginian sums up his own moral code in describing his view of God's justice: "He plays a square game with us." For Wister, as for Roosevelt and Remington, the cowboy was the Christian knight on the Plains, indifferent to material gain as he upheld virtue, pursued justice, and attacked evil.

Needless to say, the western myth in all its forms was far removed from the actual reality of the West. Critics delighted in pointing out that not one scene in *The Virginian* actually showed the hard physical labor of the cattle range. The idealized version of the West also glossed over the darker underside of frontier expansion—the brutalities of Indian warfare, the forced removal of the Indians to reservations, the risks and perils of commercial agriculture and cattle growing, the boom-and-bust mentality rooted in the selfish exploitation of natural resources.

Further, the myth obscured the complex links between the settlement of the frontier and the emergence of the United States as a major industrialized nation increasingly enmeshed in a global economy. Eastern and foreign capitalists controlled large-scale mining, cattle, and agricultural operations in the West. The technical know-how of industrial America underlay the marvels of western agricultural productivity. And without the railroad, that quintessential symbol of the new industrial order, western expansion would have been unthinkable.

Conclusion

It is precisely the divergence between the mythic West and the real West that offers a clue to the power and importance of the myth. In an era when industrialization, urbanization, and immigration were altering the nation in ways unsettling to many, Americans embraced the legend of the West as an uncomplicated, untainted Eden of social simplicity and moral clarity. The mythic West represented what the entire society had once been like (or so Americans chose to believe), before the advent of cities, factories, and masses of immigrants.

The myth was the cumulative work of many hands, from dime-novel writers, newspaper correspondents, and railroad publicists to novelists, politicians, and artists. It sank deeply into the American consciousness and influenced the public response to social change. The more tenaciously Americans clung to the myth, the harder it became for them to understand and adjust to the transformations around them.

Of all the people who tried to come to terms with the meaning of the West, Frederick Jackson Turner remains one of the most fascinating. In his 1893 lecture, Turner went on to insist that the frontier experience was the key to understanding American history. "The expansion westward with its new opportunities, its continuous touch with the simplicity of primitive society," he argued, "furnish the forces dominating [the] American character." The frontier experience, he continued, had produced a practical, inventive, self-reliant people who valued individualism and freedom because they had experienced them firsthand in the wide-open spaces and face-to-face communities of the West.

As an actual description of social reality, Turner's analysis left much to be desired. Contemporary historians have moved away from his monolithic interpretation of the "American character" and his optimistic, broad-brush characterization of the frontier social order. But in his articulation and distillation of prevailing *ideas* about the West, Turner unconsciously demonstrated the powerful hold of the frontier myth on the national imagination. Caught up in the myth himself, Turner unwittingly became one of its most persuasive advocates.

The settlement of the West can thus be viewed from two perspectives: on the one hand, as a formidable episode in the social, economic, and political history of the United States, and, on the other, as a great mythic process that would live on in the American imagination long after the actual frontier had vanished, influencing our thinking about society, government, and ourselves.

CHRONOLOGY

1849 California gold rush.

1858 Henry Comstock strikes gold on the Carson River in Nevada.
Gold discovered at Clear Creek, Colorado.

1862 Homestead Act.
Sioux War breaks out in Minnesota.

1864 Nevada admitted to the Union.
Massacre of Cheyennes at Sand Creek, Colorado.

1866 Teton Sioux wipe out Captain William J. Fetterman's troops.
Railroad Enabling Act.

1867 Joseph McCoy organizes cattle drives to Abilene, Kansas.

1867   The Grange (Patrons of Husbandry) founded.
(cont.)   New Indian policy of smaller reservations adopted.

1869   Board of Indian Commissioners established to reform Indian reservation life.

1872   Mark Twain, *Roughing It.*

1873   Panic allows speculators to purchase thousands of acres in the Red River valley of North Dakota cheaply.

Timber Culture Act.

Biggest strike on Nevada's Comstock Lode.

1874   Invention of barbed wire.

Gold discovered in the Black Hills of South Dakota.

Red River War pits the Kiowas, Comanches, and Cheyennes against the U.S. Army.

Grasshopper infestations ruin crops in Iowa and Kansas.

1876   Colorado admitted to the Union, gives women the right to vote in school elections.

Massacre of Colonel George Armstrong Custer and his troops at Little Bighorn.

1877   *Munn* v. *Illinois.*

Desert Land Act.

1878   Timber and Stone Act.

1879   Massacre of northern Cheyennes at Fort Robinson, Nebraska.

1881   Helen Hunt Jackson, *A Century of Dishonor.*

1883   William ("Buffalo Bill") Cody organizes Wild West show.

1886   Severe drought on the Plains destroys cattle and grain.
Wabash v. *Illinois.*

1887   Dawes Severalty Act.

1888   *Las Gorras Blancas* (The White Caps) raid ranchers in northern New Mexico.

1889   Oklahoma Territory opened for settlement.

1889– Theodore Roosevelt, *The Winning of the West.*
1896

1890   Ghost Dance movement spreads to the Black Hills.

Massacre of Teton Sioux at Wounded Knee, South Dakota.

1891   Hamlin Garland, *Main-Travelled Roads.*

1893   Frederick Jackson Turner, "The Significance of the Frontier in American History."

1902   Owen Wister, *The Virginian.*

For Further Reading

Robert R. Dykstra, *The Cattle Towns* (1968). A lively analysis of the early stockyards and cattle towns in Kansas.

Gilbert G. Fite, *The Farmers' Frontier, 1865–1900* (1966). A spirited introduction to farming on the Great Plains.

Michael P. Malone, *Historians and the American West* (1983). A useful guide to the extensive literature about the West.

Sandra L. Myres, *Westering Women and the Frontier Experience, 1800–1915* (1982). An excellent brief survey of women's experiences on the frontier.

Russel Nye, *The Unembarrassed Muse: The Popular Arts in America* (1970). An entertaining study of popular literary and artistic culture in the nineteenth and twentieth centuries.

Rodman Wilson Paul, *Mining Frontiers of the Far West, 1848–1880* (1963). A fast-paced survey of the successive mining frontiers.

Mary Jane Schneider, *North Dakota Indians* (1986). A thorough guide to the culture and everyday life of the Plains Indians.

Richard Slotkin, *The Fatal Environment* (1985). A provocative exploration of the myth of the frontier and its relationship to Custer's last stand.

Robert M. Utley, *The Indian Frontier of the American West, 1846–1890* (1984). A history of the bitter Indian Wars of the post–Civil War West.

Additional Bibliography

The Western Mystique

William H. Goetzmann, *Exploration and Empire* (1966) and *The West of the Imagination* (1986); Robert V. Hine, *The American West* (2d ed., 1984); Howard R. Lamar, *The Far Southwest, 1846–1912* (1966); Howard R. Lamar and Leonard Thompson, eds., *The Frontier in History: North America and Southern Africa Compared* (1981); Leo Marx, *The Machine in the Garden: Technology and the Pastoral Ideal in America* (1964); Frederick Merk, *History of the Westward Movement* (1978); Roderick Nash, *Wilderness and the American Mind* (1973); Walter P. Webb, *The Great Plains* (1931).

Native Americans

Robert F. Berkhofer, Jr., *The White Man's Indian* (1978); Alfred W. Bowers, *Hidatsa Social and Ceremonial Organization* (1936); Roger Buffalohead and Priscilla Buffalohead, *Against the Tide of American History: The Story of the Mille Lacs Anishinabe* (1986); Leonard Dinnerstein, Roger L. Nichols, and David M. Reimers, *Natives and Strangers* (1979); Mario T. Garcia, *Desert Immigrants* (1981); Dwight L. Hoover, *The Red and the Black* (1976); Frederick E. Hoxie, *A Final Promise: The Campaign to Assimilate the Indians, 1880–1920* (1984); Robert H. Keller, *American Protestantism and United States Indian Policy, 1869–82* (1983); John G. Neihardt, *Black Elk Speaks* (1932); Francis Paul Prucha, *The Great Father: The United States Government and the American Indians* (2 vols., 1984); Glenda Riley, *Women and Indians on the Frontier, 1825–1915* (1984); James P. Ronda, *Lewis and Clark Among the Indians* (1984); Robert M. Utley, *Frontier Regulars: The United States Army and the Indian, 1866–1891* (1973) and *The Last Days of the Sioux Nation* (1963); Wilcomb E. Washburn, *The Indian in America* (1975); Richard White, *The Roots of Dependency: Subsistence, Environment, and Social Change Among the Choctaws, Pawnees, and Navajos* (1983); Gilbert H. Wilson, *The Hidatsa Earthlodge* (1934, reprint 1978) and *Waheenee: An Indian Girl's Story* (1920, reprint 1981).

The Process of Settlement

Ray Allen Billington, *Westward Expansion* (5th ed., 1982); Allen G. Bogue, *From Prairie to Corn Belt: Farming on the Illinois and Iowa Prairies in the Nineteenth Century* (1963); Solon J. Buck, *The Granger Movement* (1913); Albert Camarillo, *Chicanos in a Changing Society* (1979); Griswold del Castillo, *La Familia: Chicano Families in the Urban Southeast, 1848 to the Present* (1984); Arnoldo De Leon, *They Called Them Greasers: Anglo Attitudes Toward Mexicans in Texas, 1821–1900* (1983); John M. Faragher, *Women and Men on the Overland Trail* (1979) and "History from the Inside-Out: Writing the History of Women in Rural America," *American Quarterly* 33, no. 5 (Winter 1981): 537–557; Paul Wallace Gates, *Fifty Million Acres* (1954); Elizabeth Hampsten, *Read This Only to Yourself: The Private Writings of Midwestern Women, 1880–1910* (1982); Robert V. Hine, *Community on the American Frontier* (1980); June D. Holmquist, ed., *They Chose Minnesota: A Survey of the State's Ethnic Groups* (1981); Julie R. Jeffrey, *Frontier Women* (1979); Norton Juster, *So Sweet to Labor: Rural Women in America, 1865–1895* (1979); Leonard Pitt, *The Decline of the Californios* (1966); Robert J. Rosenbaum, *Mexicano Resistance in the Southwest* (1981); Lillian Schlissel, *Women's Diaries of the Westward Journey* (1982); Thomas Sheridan, *Los Tucsonenses: The Mexican Community in Tucson, 1854–1941* (1986); John F. Stover, *American Railroads* (1961); Joanna L. Stratton, *Pioneer Women: Voices from the Kansas Frontier* (1981); Louis B. Wright, *Culture on the Moving Frontier* (1955).

The Bonanza West

Anne M. Butler, *Daughters of Joy, Sisters of Misery* (1985); Hiram M. Drache, *The Day of the Bonanza* (1964); Harry Sinclair Drago, *The Great Range Wars* (1985); Philip Durham and Everett L. Jones, *The Negro Cowboys* (1965); Marion S. Goldman, *Gold Diggers & Silver Miners: Prostitution and Social Life on the Comstock* (1981); William S. Greever, *The Bonanza West: The Story of the Western Mining Rushes, 1848–1900* (1963); Marvin Lewis, *The Mining Frontier* (1967); Nat Love, *The Life and Adventures of Nat Love* (reprint, 1968); William R. Savage, *The Cowboy Hero* (1968); William R. Savage, ed., *Cowboy Life: Reconstructing an American Myth* (1980); Don Worcester, *The Chisholm Trail* (1980).

The Frontier Dream

Richard Slotkin, "Nostalgia and Progress: Theodore Roosevelt's Myth of the Frontier," *American Quarterly* 33, no. 5 (Winter 1981): 608–638; Henry Nash Smith, *Virgin Land: The American West as Symbol and Myth* (1950); Frederick Jackson Turner, *Frontier in American History* (1920); G. Edward White, *The Eastern Establishment and the Western Experience* (1968); Rupert Wilkinson, *American Tough: The Tough-Guy Tradition and American Character* (1984).

CHAPTER 17

The Rise of Industrial America

On October 21, 1892, before a crowd of more than two hundred thousand onlookers, presidential candidate Grover Cleveland stepped proudly into the Grand Court of Honor to open the World's Columbian Exposition in Chicago. After expressing satisfaction with the many remarkable achievements on display at the fair, Cleveland grasped a small electric key connected to a two-thousand-horse-power engine and proclaimed: "As by a touch the machinery that gives life to this vast Exposition is now set in motion, so in the same instant let our hopes and aspirations awaken forces which in all time to come shall influence the welfare, the dignity, and the freedom of mankind." A moment later, amid enthusiastic cheers and volleys from a military salute, electric fountains shot streams of water high into the air, officially marking the exposition's opening.

The Chicago world's fair represented the triumph of thirty years of industrial development. The country's largest corporations displayed their newest products. Machinery Hall housed two gigantic steam engines, each capable of pumping 12 million gallons of water daily. In the Electricity Building, the Westinghouse Company's dynamos mysteriously lit a model Egyptian temple and a tower of incandescent light bulbs; American Bell Telephone offered the first long-distance telephone calls to the East Coast; and Thomas A. Edison exhibited his latest phonograph.

The largest structure at the fair, the Manufactures and Liberal Arts Building, was a monument to American industrial development. Its immense size, the fair's guidebooks boasted, was emblematic of a generation of technological achievement. Containing more than forty-four acres of floor space, 3 million feet of lumber, and five railroad carloads of nails, and housing the exhibits of numerous corporations, the structure easily accommodated the thousands of people milling about expectantly at the opening ceremonies.

The fair's splendor dazzled the more than 25 million visitors who entered the gates between October 1892 and October 1893. General Lew Wallace, author of the popular novel *Ben-Hur*, described the exposition as "the fairest city that ever the sun shown [*sic*] on." Historian Henry Adams was especially impressed by the electrical dynamos, spinning silently at unbelievable speeds, which he saw as symbols for the infinite force and energy of the modern world. Possibly more typical was the reaction of Isabelle Garland, mother of writer Hamlin Garland, who visited the fair from a small midwestern farm community. "[M]y mother sat in her chair, visioning it all yet comprehending little of its meaning," Garland later observed. "Her life had been spent among homely small things, and these gorgeous scenes dazzled her, . . . letting in upon her in one mighty flood a thousand stupefying suggestions of art and history and poetry of the world. . . . At last utterly overcome, she leaned her head against my arm, closed her eyes and said, 'Take me home, I can't stand any more of it.' "

Isabelle Garland's emotional reaction captured the ambivalence of many late-nineteenth-century Americans, who found themselves at once exhilarated and unsettled as the nation was transformed by industrialization. In less than thirty years, through innovations in management, technology, production, and distribution, business leaders had built the United States into one of the world's great industrial powers. America's real gross national product grew between 1860 and 1900 by an average of nearly 4 percent annually, a rate one-third better than that of Germany and nearly double that of Great Britain. In these same years, U.S. textile and iron production doubled, the number of persons engaged in manufacturing quadrupled, rail production quintupled, and new companies, operating nationwide, brought a host of new products into urban, small-town, and rural homes across the country. Overall, manufacturing output soared from $1.8 billion in 1860 to $13 billion in 1900. All the more remarkably, this growth came amid the disruptions of a boom-and-bust business cycle that produced crippling depressions in 1873–1879 and 1893–1897.

For the next several chapters—indeed, in a very real sense, for the rest of this book—we shall examine the consequences of this remarkable period of industrial growth. But first, we will look more closely at how this transformation occurred and how it affected the men and women whose labor made it possible.

The Character of Industrial Change

Four dominating features marked the birth of modern industrial America after the Civil War: first, the rapid spread of technological innovation and the factory system; second, the constant pressure on firms to compete tooth and nail by cutting costs and prices—as well as the impulse to eliminate rivals and consolidate monopolistic power; third, the relentless drop in price levels (a stark contrast to the inflation of other eras); and finally, the failure of the money supply to keep pace with productivity, driving up interest rates and restricting the availability of credit.

All these factors were closely interrelated. Technological change enormously increased productivity and catalyzed the breathtaking industrial expansion. Technology also enabled manufacturers to cut costs and hire cheap unskilled or semiskilled labor. This cost cutting in turn drove firms to undersell each other, leaving weaker competitors by the wayside and prompting stronger, more efficient (and more ruthless) ones to consolidate. At least until the mid-1890s, cost reduction, new technology, and fierce competition forced down overall price levels. Farmers and industrial workers suffered from chronically low agricultural commodity prices and wages, but in their capacity as consumers, they (and all Americans) benefited as store-bought goods cheapened. Meanwhile, high interest rates and the difficulty of obtaining credit added to the burdens of farmers and small businessmen. And almost everyone suffered terribly during the depression years, when the government did nothing to relieve distress. Above all, business leaders' unflagging drive to maximize efficiency both created colossal fortunes at the top of the economic ladder and forced millions of wage earners to live near the subsistence level.

Out of the new industrial system poured dismal clouds of haze and soot—as well as the first tantalizing trickle of what would become an avalanche of alluring consumer goods. In turn, mounting demands for consumer goods stimulated heavy industry's production of "capital goods"—machines to boost farm and factory output. Together with the railroads, the corporations that manufactured capital goods, refined petroleum, and made the steel for railroads and industrial construction became the main driving force in the nation's economic growth.

A stunning expansion in the *scale* of industry offered tangible evidence of the magnitude of economic change. Until the 1870s most Americans would have considered a firm like the H. E. Bradford Company in Bennington, Vermont, which employed 110 operatives to make 18,000 shirts and other articles of clothing annually, to be a large business. But this was tiny compared to the mammoth corporations that by 1900 dominated industrial production and operated on an unprecedented scale. In 1905 the Singer Sewing Machine Company, for example, with capitalization (operating capital) of $20 million, boasted eight factories and more than 90,000 employees who made and sold 1.25 million sewing machines annually. Huge companies similarly achieved marvels of production in the railroad, meatpacking, steel, sugar, and oil industries.

Competition among the aggressive and innovative capitalists who headed American heavy industry was intense—and as the post–Civil War era opened, nowhere was it more intense than among the nation's railroads, which to many Americans most symbolized industrial progress.

Railroad Innovations

By 1900, 193,000 miles of railroad track crisscrossed the United States—more than in all of Europe, including Russia. These rail lines connected every state in the Union and opened up an immense new internal market. The omnipresent steam engine, rushing forward with what poet Walt Whitman called its "pant and roar," epitomized the new technological order. Most important, railroad companies pioneered crucial aspects of large-scale corporate enterprise, including the issuance of stock to meet their huge capital needs, the separation of ownership from management, the diversification of production facilities, the creation of national distribution and marketing systems, and the formation of new organizational and management structures.

Early railroad entrepreneurs such as Thomas A. Scott, who in the 1850s integrated seventy-three smaller companies and more than five thousand rail miles into the Pennsylvania Railroad, faced financial and organizational problems that would have ruined most smaller firms. The cost of buying land, laying track, building engines and cars, and setting up stations was horrendous. To meet these start-up costs and to carry on their extensive operations, railroads needed staggering sums. For large lines like the Pennsylvania, the necessary level of capitalization could approach $35 million.

Train Travel

Railroad companies established new standards for comfort, convenience, and speed. The Pullman Palace Car Company built special sleeping and dining cars that, according to one rider, made "traveling a pleasure and a recreation."

How were sums like this raised? The railroads, of course, received enormous land and loan subsidies from federal, state, and local governments. But even so, the larger lines had to borrow heavily by selling bonds to the public. By 1900 the combined debt of all U.S. railroads stood at an astounding $5.1 billion, nearly five times that of the federal government. Another way in which the railroads raised capital was by selling stock. Unlike bond holders, who earned a fixed rate of interest, stockholders received dividends only when the company earned a profit.

Although the stockholders owned the railroad, day-to-day operations remained in the hands of company officials. Because of the railroads' heavy indebtedness and the disastrous consequences of scheduling mistakes (at a time when a single track carried trains traveling in both directions), railroad managers had a high stake in systematizing their operations for maximum safety and efficiency. To coordinate the complex flow of cars across the country, railroads relied heavily on the magnetic telegraph. Invented in 1837, telegraph service had expanded quickly. By the end of the Civil War, Western Union's forty-four thousand miles of wire and more than a thousand offices formed the backbone of a communications network that linked the entire nation. To improve efficiency, the railroads set up clearly defined, hierarchical organizational structures and divided their lines into separate geographic units, each with its own superintendent. Elaborate accounting systems documented the cost of every operation for each division, from coal consumption to the repair of engines and cars. Using these reports, railroad officials could set rates and accurately predict profits as early as the 1860s, a time when most businesses had no idea of their total profit until they closed their books at year's end. Railroad management innovations thus became a model for many other businesses seeking a national market.

Creativity, Cooperation, and Competition

Collis P. Huntington, Jay Gould, James J. Hill, and the other larger-than-life figures who reorganized and expanded the railroad industry in the 1870s and 1880s were often depicted by their contemporaries as villains and robber barons who manipulated stock markets and company policies to line their own pockets. For example, one competitor scorned Jay Gould, the short, secretive president of the Union Pacific, as a "perfect eel," and newspaper publisher Joseph Pulitzer called him "one of the most sinister figures that have ever flitted bat-like across the vision of the American people." Recent historians, however, have pointed out that the great industrialists were a diverse group, and far from all bad. Although some were ironfisted pirates who engaged in deceptive and fraudulent practices, others were upstanding businessmen who managed their companies with sophistication and innovation. Indeed, some of their ideas were breathtaking in their originality and inventiveness.

The expansion and consolidation of railroading reflected both the ingenuity and the dishonesty flourishing on the corporate-management scene. Although by the 1870s railroads had replaced the patchwork of canal and stagecoach operations that dominated domestic transportation before the Civil War, the industry itself was in a state of chaos. Hundreds of small companies used widely different standards for car couplers, rails, track width, and engine size. Financed by large eastern and British banks, Huntington, Gould, and others devoured these smaller lines to create large, integrated track networks. In the Northeast four major trunk lines emerged. In the South four hundred small companies averaging less than forty miles of track apiece were consolidated into five major systems. West of the Mississippi five great lines—the Union Pacific (1869); the Northern Pacific (1883); the Atchison, Topeka, and Santa Fe (1883); the Southern Pacific (1883); and the Great Northern (1893)—controlled most of the track by 1893.

As they consolidated a hodgepodge of small railroads into a few interlocking systems, the masterminds of the giant trunk lines standardized all basic equipment and facilities, from engines and cars to outhouses (now provided in standard one-, two-, and three-hole sizes). The high costs of shifting cargo from the cars of one railroad to those of another led to the adoption of uniform specifications for automatic couplers, air brakes, and signal systems. In 1883, independently of the federal government, the railroads unilaterally divided the country into four time zones. This sweeping action outraged those, like Isabelle Garland, who believed in "God's time," based on the rising and setting of the sun. Then in May 1886 all railroads shifted

Jay Gould

In a commentary on Gould's vicious manipulation of the railway industry, a disapproving cartoonist depicted him as having amassed his fortune by destroying others' lives with as little concern as a bowler knocking down ninepins.

simultaneously to the new standard 4′ 8½″–gauge track. Finally, cooperative billing arrangements and accounting procedures enabled the railroads to ship cars from other roads, including dining and sleeping cars owned by the Pullman Palace Car Company, at uniform rates nationwide. Even steamship lines and urban commuter rail lines were incorporated into the railroads' tightly organized system.

This newly integrated transportation and communications network brought many advantages to factory owners and consumers. Companies gained access to a national market in which to buy their raw materials and sell their goods. Farmers and storekeepers across the country could buy food, hardware, and clothing once available only in the major East Coast cities.

But the expansion and consolidation of the railroads had its costs. Competition between lines became brutal and rancorous. Often it saddled the great trunk lines with massive debts. In 1879 Jay Gould, the guiding force behind the expansion of the Union Pacific, gained control of the Kansas Pacific Railroad. To squeeze out his southwestern competition, he ran tracks parallel to those of his rivals, engineered fluctuations in the price of their stock, and undercut their business by setting his rates below his own cost. One by one his compet-

itors toppled into bankruptcy while he consolidated his holdings. Meanwhile, to increase his own income, he "watered" the company's stock by issuing stock certificates far in excess of the actual value of the assets. By 1885 other unprincipled operators had watered a third of the nation's railroad stock, badly pinching small investors.

Entangled in heavy indebtedness, overextended systems, and crooked business practices, the railroads fought each other recklessly for traffic. Their ploys were many. They cut rates for large shippers, offered special arrangements for handling bulk goods, dispensed free passes to politicians who supported their operations, and granted substantial rebates and kickbacks to favored clients. Major customers soon learned to manipulate the rail carriers by negotiating their own lower prices. The competition became so ferocious that railroads tried to end it by establishing pools, or negotiated agreements to divide the traffic proportionally and to charge uniform rates.

None of these tactics, however, shored up the railroads' precarious financial position. A pooling agreement between two railroads would soon be undermined by pressure from a third. Rebates given by one system prompted retaliation from another. And the continuous push to expand drove some overbuilt lines into bankruptcy.

Caught in the middle of the railroads' tug-of-war, and stung by exorbitant rates and secret kickbacks, farmers and small business owners turned to state governments for help. Many midwestern state legislatures in the 1870s, responding to protests led by the Grangers, outlawed rate discrimination. Then in 1887, persuaded by Illinois senator Shelby M. Cullom's detailed study of devious railroad practices, Congress, as we have seen, passed the Interstate Commerce Act, which established the five-member Interstate Commerce Commission (ICC) to oversee the practices of railroads passing through more than one state. The law also banned monopolistic activity like pooling, rebates, and discriminatory short-distance rates. The railroads had the right to challenge the commission's rulings in the federal courts, however, and of sixteen cases brought to the Supreme Court before 1905, the justices found in favor of the railroads in all but one, essentially nullifying the ICC's regulatory clout. The Hepburn Act (see Chapter 21), passed in 1906, strengthened the ICC by finally empowering it to set rates.

The railroads' vicious competition did not abate until a national depression that began in 1893 forced a number of roads into the hands of the investment bankers on whom they had become increasingly dependent. Supported by the major investment houses in Boston, New York, and Philadelphia, J. Pierpont Morgan, a massively built man with piercing eyes and a commanding presence, took over the weakened systems, reorganized their administration, refinanced their debts, and built intersystem alliances by purchasing substantial blocks of stock in the competing roads. By 1906, thanks to the bankers' centralized management, seven giant networks controlled two-thirds of the nation's rail mileage.

In short, by the late nineteenth century, competition, corruption, mismanagement, and overextension had created a paradox in the railroad industry. The massive trunk systems had become the largest business enterprises in the world, towering over state and federal governments in the size and scale of their operations. They had pioneered the most advanced methods of accounting and large-scale organization. Their voracious appetite for rails and engines had stimulated the demand for iron, steel, and a host of secondary products. The integrated transportation network that they composed opened up exciting possibilities for the national distribution of new consumer products. Yet despite their enormous power and many innovations, the nation's railroads remained unstable. Cutthroat expansion had inflated operating costs, reduced revenues, and made them particularly vulnerable to economic downswings. During the depression of 1893, only intervention by investment bankers saved the industry from collapse.

Applying the Lessons of the Railroads to Steel

The close connections between railroad expansion and the growth of heavy industry are well illustrated in the career of steelmaker Andrew Carnegie. A diminutive dynamo of a man, only 5′ 3″ tall, Carnegie combined the business expertise of a Jay Gould with the showmanship of a P. T. Barnum. His achievements rested heavily on his salesmanship and his managerial skill, both of which played a major role in his success at transferring to steel

making the organizational and financial methods first developed in the railroad industry.

Carnegie's life was the embodiment of the rags-to-riches dream. Born in Dunfermline, Scotland, he had immigrated to America in 1848, at the age of twelve, and had taken a job at $1.20 a week as a bobbin boy in a Pittsburgh textile mill. Although he worked a sixty-hour week, the ambitious youngster also enrolled in a night course to learn double-entry bookkeeping.

The following year, Carnegie became a Western Union messenger boy. Taking over when the telegraph operators wanted a break, he soon became the city's fastest telegraph operator by "reading" the sound of the keys instead of deciphering individual letters. Because he had to decode the messages for every major business in Pittsburgh, Carnegie gained an insider's view of their operations.

Carnegie's big break came in 1852, when Tom Scott, superintendent of the Pennsylvania Railroad's western division, hired him as his secretary and personal telegrapher. Although only seventeen years old, Carnegie quickly mastered the complex details of what was the most innovative business at the time. When Scott became vice president of the Pennsylvania Railroad seven years later, Carnegie succeeded him as head of the line's western division.

A daring innovator, Carnegie, in his six years as division chief, used the complex cost-analysis techniques developed by Scott to more than double the road's mileage and quadruple its traffic. He set up the first night-train dispatchers and ran trains around the clock. When wrecks blocked the tracks, he burned the cars or laid new track around them to speed the resumption of service. He slashed commuter fares to keep ridership at capacity and developed various cost-cutting techniques. Shrewdly investing his earnings in telegraph, sleeping-car, and bridge companies, Carnegie by 1868 was earning more than fifty-six thousand dollars a year from his investments alone, a substantial fortune in that era.

In the early 1870s, Carnegie decided to build his own steel mill. His connections within the railroad industry, the country's largest purchaser of steel, made this a logical choice. Starting out during the depression years, when costs were low, he built the J. Edgar Thomson Mills, named for the president of the Pennsylvania Railroad. The mills incorporated the new Bessemer production technology, which shot a blast of air through an enormous crucible of molten iron to burn off carbon and impurities. Carnegie combined the new technology with the cost-analysis approach learned from his railroad experience. Introducing special scales to weigh the materials used in different parts of the mill, he became the first steel maker to establish the actual production cost per ton of steel. With the data generated, he not only cut expenses but also developed a solid basis for deciding when to invest in new furnaces and machine tools.

Carnegie's management philosophy was deceptively simple: "Watch the costs, and the profits will take care of themselves." From the start he priced his rails at sixty-five dollars per ton, five dollars below the competition. Then, through rigorous cost accounting, he lowered his production costs to fifty dollars per ton. Furthermore, he was not above asking for favors from his railroad-president friends or giving "commissions" to railroad purchasing agents. When other producers tried to get him to join a pool to fix prices, he initially agreed but then broke away; his efficient production methods enabled him to undersell his rivals.

Carnegie and his managers saved money in many ways. For example, they hired a chemist to ensure that they purchased only the highest-quality ore. They reprocessed the scrap that broke off as the steel went over the rollers—material that their competitors threw away. A true believer in technology, Carnegie installed the newest machines as swiftly as they were developed. In one instance this meant scrapping a three-month-old rolling mill when a better process came along.

As output climbed, Carnegie discovered the benefits of vertical integration—that is, controlling all aspects of manufacturing, from extracting raw materials to selling the finished product. In Carnegie's case this control embraced every stage from the mining and smelting of ore to the selling of steel rails. His movement toward vertical integration prompted him in 1881 to establish a partnership with Henry Clay Frick, the owner of a large coke* company, who in 1889 would become the chairman of Carnegie Steel while continuing as head of Frick Coke Company. In 1892 Carnegie also

---

*Coke: the solid residue obtained from coal after the removal of volatile material.

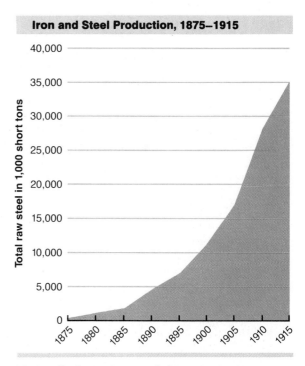

Iron and Steel Production, 1875–1915

New technologies, improved plant organization, economies of scale, and the vertical integration of production brought a dramatic spurt in iron and steel production.

SOURCE: *Historical Statistics of the United States.*

bought into an ore company in the newly opened Mesabi Range in Minnesota. Under Frick's aggressive leadership, Carnegie Steel's annual profits rose each year in the 1890s despite severe labor troubles and a crippling national depression, reaching $40 million in 1900. Carnegie Steel thus became the classic example of how sophisticated new technology might be combined with innovative management (and brutally low wages) to create a mass-production system that could slash consumer prices. By 1900 Carnegie was producing steel rails at a cost of $11.50 per ton.

Frick's management of daily operations left Carnegie free to pursue philanthropic activities. While still in his early thirties, Carnegie concluded that all great fortunes corrupted their possessors, and he resolved to donate his money to charitable projects. (He also knew full well that such actions would buttress his popularity.) Carnegie set up foundations and eventually donated more than $300 million for libraries, universities, and international-peace causes.

Andrew Carnegie Sums Up the Steel Business

The eighth wonder of the world is this:

two pounds of iron-stone purchased on
the shores of lake Superior and
    transported to Pittsburgh;

two pounds of coal mined in Connellsville
and manufactured into coke and
    brought to Pittsburgh;

one half pound of limestone mined
east of the Alleghenies and
    brought to Pittsburgh;

a little manganese ore,
mined in Virginia and
    brought to Pittsburgh.

And these four and one half pounds of
material manufactured into one pound of
solid steel and sold for one cent.

That's all that need be said
    about the steel business.

SOURCE: Harold C. Livesay, *Andrew Carnegie and the
Rise of Big Business* (Boston: Little, Brown, 1975), 189.

Andrew Carnegie

*Despite his well-polished image as a hard-working
industrial leader, Carnegie left the details of management to others and spent a considerable amount of
time playing golf near his castle in Scotland.*

By 1900 Carnegie Steel, employing twenty thousand people, had become the world's largest industrial corporation. Yet the company was torn by internal divisions and beset by newly aggressive rivals. Many of Carnegie's able lieutenants chafed under a management style that plowed most of the earnings back into new equipment and kept them in a subordinate position. In January 1900, when Frick, who had verbally agreed to sell coke to Carnegie Steel at a price considerably below the market rate, tried to raise his price, Carnegie forced him out in an angry confrontation. Said Carnegie of his former partner (who was fourteen years his junior): "He's too old, too infirm in health *and mind*. . . . I have nothing but pity for Frick." (Later, when Carnegie suggested that they renew their old friendship, Frick responded, "Tell Mr. Carnegie I'll meet him in Hell.") The competitive challenge came from Federal Steel, a large complex put together in

1898 by J. Pierpont Morgan, and from Illinois Steel. The success of these imposing rivals threatened to choke off Carnegie's sales to the wire, nail, and pipe industries.

Carnegie responded with typical cunning, by cornering the patents (exclusive rights to manufacturing and sales) on a new process for producing seamless pipes and by announcing plans to build a $12 million plant in which to manufacture them. The two competitors, Federal Steel and Illinois Steel, rushed to Carnegie's partners, seeking support for a compromise. At Morgan's request Charles Schwab, Carnegie Steel's president, met Carnegie on the golf course early in 1901 to ask what he wanted for his share of Carnegie Steel. The next day Carnegie gave Schwab a penciled note asking for nearly half a billion dollars. Morgan's response was simple: "Tell Carnegie I accept his price." Combining Carnegie's companies with Federal Steel, Morgan set up the

United States Steel Corporation, the first business capitalized at more than $1 billion. The corporation, with its two hundred member companies employing 168,000 people, marked a new scale in industrial enterprise.

Throughout his chain of corporate-world triumphs, Carnegie consistently portrayed himself as an entrepreneur who had risen through self-discipline and hard work. In a series of essays, he stressed that thrift, patience, and quick action in the face of opportunity were the keys to his success. The full story was more complex. He did not mention his uncanny ability to see the larger picture, his cleverness in hiring talented associates who would drive themselves (and the company's factory workers) mercilessly, his ingenuity in transferring organizational systems and cost-accounting methods from railroads to steel, and his callousness in keeping wages as low as possible. To a public little interested in corporate-management techniques, however, Carnegie's success simply reaffirmed the openness of the American economic system. For the new immigrants flooding the nation's shores, Carnegie's career gave credence to the idea that anyone might rise from rags to riches.

Consolidating the Industrial Order

Between 1870 and 1900, the same grasping competition that had stimulated railroad consolidation and reduced the number of iron and steel firms from 808 to 669 (see table) also swept the oil, salt, sugar, tobacco, and meatpacking industries. Like steel, these businesses required large capital investments and sold their products in a highly competitive market. Entrepreneurs in each industry therefore raced to reduce costs and enlarge their market share. Chicago meatpackers Philip Armour and Gustavus Swift, for example, raised to a high level of efficiency the process of turning hogs and cattle into bacon, pork chops, and steaks. Developing ingenious techniques of refrigerated shipping, Armour and Swift won a large share of the eastern urban market for meat.

The evolution of the oil industry typifies the consolidation process. After Edwin L. Drake drilled the first successful petroleum (or "crude-oil") well in 1859 near Titusville in northwestern Pennsylvania, entry into the oil business came relatively

Industrial Consolidation: Iron and Steel Firms, 1870 and 1900		
	1870	*1900*
No. of firms	808	669
No. of employees	78,000	272,000
Output (tons)	3,200,000	29,500,000
Capital invested	$121,000,000	$590,000,000

SOURCE: Robert L. Heilbroner and Aaron Singer, *The Economic Transformation of America: 1600 to Present*, 2d ed. (San Diego: Harcourt Brace Jovanovich, 1984), 92.

easily. Entrepreneurs sank wells, erected small refineries nearby, and distilled the petroleum into oil, which soon replaced animal tallow as the major lubricant, and into kerosene, which became the leading fuel for household and public lighting. By the 1870s the landscape near Pittsburgh and Cleveland, the sites of the first discoveries, was littered with rickety drilling rigs, assorted collection tanks, and ramshackle refineries. An almost festive atmosphere pervaded this early oil boom, as speculators flew homemade flags and banners over their rigs. One proclaimed the owner's intention to drill until he reached "Hell or China."

But few early hopefuls survived very long. In the contest for new markets and control of the oil industry, John D. Rockefeller, a young Cleveland merchant and devout Baptist, gradually achieved dominance. Although he did not share Andrew Carnegie's outgoing personality, the solemn Rockefeller resembled the opportunistic steel maker in other respects. Like Carnegie, Rockefeller had a passion for cost cutting and efficiency. Having founded the Standard Oil Company in 1870, he daily scrutinized every aspect of the firm's operation. Obsessed with the minutest details, he regularly harangued his refinery managers on improving production techniques. In one case he insisted that a manager find 750 missing barrel stoppers; in another he reduced from 40 to 39 the number of drops of solder used to seal a kerosene can. He realized that in a mass-production enterprise, small changes could save thousands of dollars.

Rockefeller constantly stressed the importance of providing a reliable product in winning consumer loyalty. He built a system of bulk depots and tank wagons for local kerosene distribution and insisted that all equipment be kept neat and clean.

Like Carnegie, he adopted the latest refining technologies to improve the quality of his fuels and lubricants. To boost sales volume, he advertised heavily. Packaged in a familiar red five-gallon can, Standard Oil kerosene was instantly recognizable by consumers.

Rockefeller resembled Carnegie, too, in his extraordinary ability to understand the inner workings of an entire industry. He particularly focused on transportation. The firm that controlled the shipment of oil between the well and the refinery, and between the refinery and the retailers, he realized, could dominate the industry. Accordingly in 1872 he purchased his own tanker cars and wangled not only a 10 percent rebate from the railroads for hauling his oil shipments but also a kickback on his competitors' shipments. When new pipeline technology made this a more efficient method of transporting oil, Rockefeller set up his own massive interregional pipeline network.

Like Carnegie, Rockefeller used aggressiveness and deception to force out his competitors. When local refineries rejected his offers to buy them out, he priced his product line below cost and strangled their business. If a storekeeper refused to sell Standard Oil's kerosene, the company supported the store's competitors and thus undercut the sales of uncooperative merchants. When rival firms teamed up against him, Rockefeller set up a pool—an agreement among several companies—that established production quotas and fixed prices. "The Standard Oil Company brooks no competition," a congressional investigating committee observed; ". . . its settled policy and firm determination is to crush out all who may be rash enough to enter the field against it; . . . it hesitates at nothing in the accomplishment of this purpose." Using such tactics, Rockefeller had seized control of 90 percent of the country's oil-refining capacity by 1879.

Convinced that competition wasted resources, Rockefeller tried to eliminate it in 1882 by establishing the Standard Oil Trust. Where the pool lacked legal status, the trust was a legal device that centralized control over a number of different companies by setting up a board of trustees to run all of them. To implement his trust, Rockefeller and his associates persuaded the stockholders of forty companies to exchange their stock for trust certificates. Within three years the Standard Oil Trust had consolidated crude-oil buying throughout its member firms and slashed the number of refineries

by half. In this way Rockefeller integrated the petroleum industry both *vertically,* by controlling every function from production to local retailing, and *horizontally,* by merging the competing oil companies into one giant system.

Having neutralized the competition, Rockefeller now reaped the profits. Standard Oil enlarged its refinery and pipeline capacity and expanded its distribution network not only in North America but also in Asia, Africa, and South America. Over the next decade, Rockefeller's personal fortune mushroomed to more than $800 million.

Taking a leaf from Rockefeller's book, companies in other industries such as copper, sugar, whiskey, and lead established their own trust arrangements. But their rapacious tactics, monopolistic control, and sky-high earnings soon provoked a public outcry. Beginning in New York State in 1879 and progressing to the federal level in 1888, legislative committees exposed the unscrupulous practices of these national trusts, and in the presidential election of 1888, both parties denounced them. When Rockefeller testified that the formation of the Standard Oil Trust had resulted in greatly reduced prices, his opponents pointed out that monopolies in the copper and sugar industries had pushed prices higher.

Fearful that the trusts would stamp out all competition, Congress, in 1890, under the leadership of Senator John Sherman of Ohio, passed the Sherman Anti-Trust Act, which outlawed trusts and any other contracts or combinations in restraint of trade and slapped violators with fines of up to five thousand dollars and a year in jail. But the loosely worded act failed to define clearly either *trust* or *restraint of trade.* As a result, between 1890 and 1904, the government prosecuted only eighteen antitrust suits. When Standard Oil's structure was challenged in 1892, its lawyers, invoking a New Jersey law that permitted corporations to own property in other states, simply reorganized the trust as an enormous holding company.* The same nine trustees became the new board of directors for Standard Oil (New Jersey), and the business made more money than ever.

The Supreme Court further hamstrung congressional antitrust efforts by interpreting the Sherman Act in ways sympathetic to big business.

---

*Holding company: a corporation that owns a controlling share of the stock of one or more other firms.

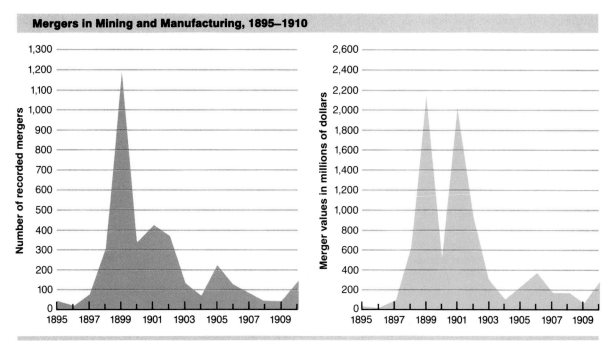

Mergers in Mining and Manufacturing, 1895–1910

A wave of business mergers occurred after the Supreme Court's 1897 and 1898 rulings that any firms concluding price-fixing or market-allocating agreements violated the Sherman Anti-Trust Act. But the merger mania died down when business leaders quickly discovered that companies could remain profitable only through vertical integration.

In 1895, for example, the federal government brought suit against the sugar trust in *United States v. E. C. Knight Company,* arguing that the Knight firm, together with four other corporations, controlled more than 90 percent of all U.S. sugar refining and therefore operated in illegal restraint of trade. The Court threw out the suit, however, drawing a distinction between commerce and manufacturing and defining the latter as a local concern, not a part of interstate commerce. The Court's decision ignored the fact that most trusts dominated the market through their extensive interstate distribution webs. Thus vindicated, corporate mergers and consolidations surged ahead at the turn of the century. By 1900 these mammoth firms accounted for nearly two-fifths of the capital invested in the nation's manufacturing sector.

The Triumph of Technology

Along with business mergers and consolidations, the invention and patenting of new machines offered another means of driving up profits, lowering costs, and improving efficiency. Further, mechanical inventions had the added advantage of piquing demand for new products. The development of a safe, practical system of generating electricity, for example, made possible an ever-growing range of electrical motors and household appliances. After 1870 business corporations stepped up their research efforts and introduced a remarkable variety of consumer goods.

The major inventions that stimulated industrial output and underlay mass production in these years were largely hidden from public view. Few Americans had heard of the Bessemer process for manufacturing steel or of the improved technologies that facilitated bottle and glassmaking, canning, flour milling, match production, and petroleum refining. Fewer still knew much about the refrigerated railcars that enabled Gustavus Swift's company to slaughter beef in Chicago and ship it east or about the Bonsack cigarette-making machine that could roll 120,000 cigarettes a day, replacing sixty skilled handworkers.

The innovations that people did see were the fruits of this technology—products like the sewing machine, mass-produced by the Singer Sewing Machine Company beginning in the 1860s; the telephone, developed by Alexander Graham Bell in 1876; and the light bulb, perfected by Thomas A. Edison in 1879. These inventions eased the drudgery of everyday life and in some cases reshaped social interactions. With the advent of the sewing machine, for example, clothing could be factory-stitched at high speed, and women were relieved of the tedium of sewing the family apparel by hand; inexpensive mass-produced clothing thus led to a considerable expansion in personal wardrobes. The spread of telephones—by 1900 the Bell Telephone Company had installed almost eight hundred thousand in the United States—not only transformed communication but undermined social conventions for polite behavior that had been premised on face-to-face or written exchanges. The light bulb, by further freeing people from dependence on daylight, made possible longer and more regular working hours. These wonders in turn inspired optimism that future technologies might lead to the betterment of society itself. The commissioner of patents proudly declared in 1892,

"America has become known the world around as the home of invention."

In the eyes of many, Thomas A. Edison epitomized the inventive impulse. Born in 1847 in Milan, Ohio, Edison, like Andrew Carnegie, was largely self-educated and got his start in the telegraphic industry. Also like the shrewd Scot, Edison was a born salesman and self-promoter. When he modestly averred that "genius is one percent inspiration and ninety-nine percent perspiration," he tacitly accepted the popular identification of himself as an inventing "wizard." Edison moreover shared Carnegie's vision of a large, interconnected industrial system resting on a foundation of technological innovation.

In his early work, Edison concentrated on the telegraph. His experimentation in the 1860s with machines that would send multiple messages on the same wire and automatically print the results led in 1868 to his first major invention, a stock-quotation printer. The money earned from the patents on this machine enabled Edison to set up his

Thomas A. Edison and His Inventions

At a time when Americans increasingly identified a corporation with a single individual, Edison made sure that he was directly associated with his inventions, either by being photographed with them or by using his name plainly on product labels.

first "invention factory" in Newark, New Jersey, which in 1876 he moved to nearby Menlo Park. Assembling a staff that included university-trained scientists, Edison boastfully predicted "a minor invention every ten days, and a big one every six months."

With the telegraph market undercut by Bell's invention of the telephone, Edison turned his attention to the electric light. He realized that practical electrical lighting had to be part of a complete system containing generators, voltage regulators, electric meters, and insulated wiring—a system that could be easily installed and repaired. It also had to be cheaper than lighting with natural gas, its main competitor.

Buoyed by the success and popularity of his invention in 1877 of a phonograph, or "sound writer" (*phono:* "sound," *graph:* "writer"), Edison set out to develop a new filament for incandescent light bulbs. Characteristically, he announced his plans for an electricity-generation process before he perfected his inventions and then scrambled feverishly, testing hundreds of materials before he found a carbon filament that would glow dependably in a vacuum. Backed financially by banker J. Pierpont Morgan, the Edison Illuminating Company in 1882 opened a power plant in the heart of New York City's financial district, furnishing lighting for eighty-five buildings.

On the heels of Edison's achievement, other inventors rushed into the electrical field. In 1887 engineer Frank J. Sprague used Edison's ideas to develop the first electric streetcar system, in Richmond, Virginia. But Edison competitors such as George Westinghouse, the inventor of the railroad air brake, were dissatisfied with the high cost of electrical transmission in Edison's system. Applying the ideas of the young electrical engineer and inventor William Stanley, Westinghouse designed a more efficient, high-voltage, alternating-current system, in the process stealing many of Edison's ideas. Edison angrily sued his competitors for patent violation. Although he successfully defended his electric light from patent infringement, the lawsuits cost him more than $2 million. Embittered by the legal battles, Edison relinquished control of his enterprises in the late 1880s. In 1892, with financier Morgan's help, Edison's company merged with a major competitor to form the General Electric Company. Four years later, GE and Westinghouse agreed to exchange patents under a joint Board of Patent Control. Such corporate patent-pooling agreements became yet another mechanism of market domination.

Although no longer a corporate leader, Edison continued to pump out invention after invention, including the mimeograph machine, the microphone, the motion-picture camera and film, and the storage battery. By the time of his death in 1931, he had patented 1,093 inventions and had amassed an estate worth more than $6 million. Yet Edison's greatest achievement remained his laboratory at Menlo Park. A model for the industrial research labs established at the turn of the century by Kodak, General Electric, and Du Pont, Edison's laboratory demonstrated that the systematic use of science in support of industrial technology paid large dividends. Invention itself, in short, had become big business.

Mass Production, Mass Marketing

The technological and managerial innovations of such figures as Edison, Carnegie, and Rockefeller proved readily adaptable throughout American industry, spurring marvels of productivity. Indeed, late-nineteenth-century industrialists often discovered that their factories were spewing out more goods than the market could absorb. This was particularly true in two kinds of businesses: those that manufactured devices for individual use such as sewing machines and farm implements, and those that mass-produced consumer goods such as matches, flour, soap, canned foods, and processed meats. Not surprisingly, these industries were pathbreakers in developing advertising and marketing techniques. Strategies for whetting consumer demand and for differentiating one product from another represented an important component of the post–Civil War industrial transformation. The sewing-machine and flour industries illustrate both the spread of mass production and the emergence of new marketing concepts.

Founded in New York City in 1851 by Isaac Merrit Singer, a part-time mechanic, the Singer Sewing Machine Company, like Carnegie Steel, plowed its profits back into operations. Also like Carnegie, it integrated vertically by establishing its own foundries and cabinetmaking operations. The introduction of interchangeable parts made possible the mass production of high-quality machines.

Product Merchandising

Eye-catching Quaker Oats and Ivory Soap advertisements helped turn the products they touted into household words.

Trademarks of Distinction

To develop easy product recognition and build consumer loyalty, companies such as Binney & Smith and Singer used bold packaging and memorable logos.

By 1880 annual production stood at a half-million units.

To market this Niagara of sewing machines, the company developed a vigorous advertising program, introduced installment buying, set up regional distribution centers, and opened a series of retail stores not only in the United States but also in Europe. (By 1885 Singer's plant in Scotland was turning out ten thousand machines a week for markets in England and continental Europe, including Russia.) Singer's sophisticated marketing operation included a corps of trained women who demonstrated the sewing machine's usefulness to potential buyers, and sales-support personnel who explained the machines' operations and repaired them. By such aggressive techniques, Singer's sales skyrocketed, and the company established overwhelming dominance in the sewing-machine industry.

The nation's flour mills proved equally adept at mass production. Adopting the most advanced European manufacturing technologies, they installed continuous-process machines that graded, cleaned, hulled, cut, and packaged their product in one rapid operation. As a result of these efficient methods, however, these companies, too, soon found that they were producing more flour than they could sell. How could they unload this excess and recoup production costs? One solution was product differentiation. The mills thought up a variety of new product lines, such as cake flours and breakfast cereals, and sold them through hard-hitting advertising. Flour miller Henry P. Crowell, for example, heavily advertised his new milled oat product under an easy-to-remember brand name, Quaker Oats. The advertisements of the Pillsbury Company of Minneapolis touted "Pillsbury's Best" flour as "strongly recommended by Eminent authorities—Physicians and Chemists—as a powerful Brain-Muscle and Bone forming food, particularly adapted for Brain workers, growing children and those suffering from digestive debility and disorders."

Through brand names, trademarks, guarantees, slogans, endorsements, and other gimmicks, manufacturers built demand for their products and won remarkable consumer loyalty. Americans bought Ivory Soap, first made in 1879 by Procter and Gamble of Cincinnati, because of the absurdly overprecise but impressive pledge that it was "99 and ⁴⁴/₁₀₀ths percent pure." James B. ("Buck") Duke's American Tobacco Company used trading cards, circulars, boxtop premiums, prizes, testimonials, and scientific endorsements to convert Americans to cigarette smoking.

In the photographic field, George Eastman in the 1880s developed a paper-based photographic film as an alternative to the bulky, fragile glass plates then in use. But professional photographers resisted the innovation, and Eastman realized that "in order to make a large business we would have to reach the general public and create a new class of patrons." Manufacturing a cheap camera for the masses, the Kodak, and devising a catchy slogan ("You press the button, we do the rest"), Eastman introduced a system whereby customers returned the one-hundred-exposure film *and the camera* to his Rochester factory, where the film was developed, the camera reloaded, and everything shipped back to them—for a charge of ten dollars. In marketing a new technology, Eastman had revolutionized an industry and democratized a visual medium previously confined to a few.

Many other companies with names well known today contributed to the production and marketing revolution—H. J. Heinz of Pittsburgh, Campbell Soup Company of Camden, Pabst Beer of Milwaukee, Borden Milk and Swift Meat Company of Chicago, to name a few. Benefiting from the savings made possible by new machinery, organizational efficiencies, high volume, and national distribution, such firms won a large share of the market with advertising that stressed their products' high quality and low cost.

Industrialization: Costs and Benefits

By 1900 the chaos of early industrial competition, when thousands of small companies had struggled to enter a national market, had given way to an economy dominated by a few enormous firms. An industrial transformation that had originated in railroading and expanded to steel and petroleum had spread to every nook and cranny of American business. For those who fell by the wayside in the era's unforgiving economic environment, the cost could be measured in ruined fortunes, bankrupted companies, and shattered dreams. John D. Rockefeller put things with characteristic bluntness. In the Standard Oil Trust, he said he wanted "only the big ones, only those who have already proved

they can do a big business. As for the others, unfortunately they will have to die."

The cost was high, too, for millions of American workers, immigrant and native-born alike. The new industrial order was built on the backs of a vast army of laborers who were paid subsistence wages and who could be fired on a moment's notice when hard times or new technologies made them expendable.

To be sure, what some called the second industrial revolution brought social benefits as well, in the form of labor-saving products, lower prices, and advances in transportation and communications. The benefits and liabilities sometimes seemed inextricably interconnected. The sewing machine, for example, created thousands of new factory jobs, made available a wider variety of clothing, and eased the lives of millions of housewives. At the same time, it encouraged avaricious entrepreneurs to operate sweatshops in crowded tenements and unsafe lofts where they heavily employed the immigrant poor—often vulnerable young women—to toil long hours for pitifully low wages.

Whatever the final balance sheet of social gains and costs, one thing was clear: the United States had muscled its way onto the world stage as an industrial titan. Between 1870 and 1900, the percentage of the world's manufactured goods produced by Americans jumped from under a quarter to nearly a third. The ambition and drive of countless inventors, financiers, managerial innovators, and marketing wizards had combined to lay the groundwork for a new social and economic order in the twentieth century.

The New South

The South entered the industrial era far more slowly than the North. As late as 1900, total southern cotton-mill output, for example, remained little more than half that of the mills within a thirty-mile radius of Providence, Rhode Island. Moreover, the South's $509 average per capita income was less than half the $1,165 income of northerners.

The reasons for the South's late economic blossoming are not hard to find. The Civil War's physical devastation, the scarcity of southern towns and cities, lack of capital, illiteracy, northern control of financial markets and patents, and a low rate of technological innovation crippled efforts by southern business leaders to promote industrialization and urban expansion.

Economic progress was also impeded by the myth of the Lost Cause, which, through its nostalgic portrayal of pre–Civil War society, perpetuated an image of the South as traditional and unchanging. So while sharing many features of northern industrial growth, including the use of new technology, southern industrialization inched forward haltingly and was shaped in distinctive ways.

Obstacles to Southern Economic Development

Much of the South's difficulty in industrializing stemmed from its lack of capital. Although the South had relatively few banks before the Civil War, the average loanable assets of southern banks had been quite high. Further, a long-standing self-sufficient barter economy had functioned well for whites living in hilly upcountry areas where, as small farmers, they had raised their own food and paid their bills through trade of farm produce. One blacksmith's ledger entries from the period before the Civil War recorded payment with a hundred pounds of seed cotton, fifteen pounds of flour, a hundred split rails, buttons, four bushels of corn, and small amounts of cash.

But the Civil War shattered the South's credit system. Four years of fierce fighting saw cities burned, fields trampled, livestock slaughtered, and farms and plantations ruined. Moreover, the war caused banks to fail in large numbers. By 1865 the South, with more than a quarter of the nation's population, possessed just 2 percent of its banks.

Additionally, federal government policies adopted during the war restricted the expansion of the southern banking system. The Republican-dominated wartime Congress, which had created a national currency and banking structure, required anyone wishing to start a bank to have fifty thousand dollars in capital in order to obtain a charter. Few southerners could meet this test after the war. Even those with the necessary capital faced obstacles, since federal laws passed by northerners prohibited the extension of mortgages on real estate. With limited assets and restricted loan options,

The Lost Cause

This engraving of 1868 mourns the South's tragic fate in the Civil War.

southern banks in effect were confined to urban centers and could lend only considerably smaller amounts than their northern counterparts.

With banks in short supply, country merchants and storekeepers became bankers by default, lending supplies rather than cash to local farmers in return for a lien, or mortgage, on their crops (see Chapter 15). Short of cash to pay their own debts, southern storekeepers, particularly in inland areas, insisted that farmers increase their cotton and tobacco acreage because those crops initially brought the highest returns. Yet even though they marked up the goods sold on credit to farmers by 40 to 70 percent, storekeepers rarely became rich. Few merchants in Georgia during the last quarter of the century had a net worth over five thousand dollars.

The shift from planting corn to raising cotton and tobacco made small southern farmers particularly vulnerable to the fluctuations of commercial agriculture. By the 1880s much of the South that had been largely self-sufficient now depended on outside producers for food, shoes, and agricultural implements. Selling cotton in a national and international market, postbellum farmers became prey to forces beyond their control. When the price of cotton fell from eleven cents per pound in 1875 to less than five cents in 1894, well under the cost of production, aggrieved southern farmers grew desperate.

The South not only suffered from an overspecialization in cash crops and a shortage of cash and banking facilities but also remained the victim of federal policies designed to aid northern industry. High protective tariffs raised the price of machine technology imported from abroad; the demonetization of silver (see Chapter 15) further limited capital availability; and discriminatory railroad freight rates hiked the expense of shipping finished goods and raw materials to outside markets.

The South's chronic shortage of funds affected the economy in indirect ways as well, by limiting the resources available for education. During Reconstruction northern philanthropists such as Georgia-born George Peabody, together with the Freedmen's Bureau, the American Missionary Association, and other relief agencies, had begun a modest expansion of public schooling for both blacks and whites. But Georgia and many other southern states operated segregated schools and refused to tax property for school support until 1889. As a result, school attendance remained low, severely limiting the number of educated persons able to staff technical positions in business and industry.

Southern states, like those in the North, often contributed what modest funds they had to war veterans' pensions. In this way, southern state governments built a white patronage system for Confederate veterans and helped reinforce southerners' lingering idealization of the old Confederacy—the South's Lost Cause. As late as 1911, veterans' pensions in Georgia ate up $1.2 million, or 22 percent of the state's entire budget, leaving little for economic or educational development.

The New South Creed and Southern Industrialization

Despite the limited availability of state and federal funds for industrialization, energetic southern newspaper editors such as Henry W. Grady of the

Atlanta Constitution and Henry Watterson of the *Louisville Courier Journal* beat the drums to encourage southern economic growth in the 1870s and proclaimed the boundless industrial potential of "this glorious sunny South." Fearful that the South would become an economic backwater, these writers and a cadre of planters, merchants, and industrialists championed what became known as the New South creed. The South's unprecedented natural resources and cheap labor, they argued, made it a natural site for industrial development. As one editor declared, "The El Dorado* of the next half century is the South. The wise recognize it; the dull and the timid will ere long regret their sloth or their hesitancy."

The movement to industrialize the South gained momentum in the 1880s. To attract northern capital, southern states offered tax exemptions for new businesses, set up industrial and agricultural expositions, and leased convicts from the state prisons to serve as cheap labor. Florida and Texas gave huge tracts of state lands to railroads, and southern rail mileage grew substantially. Other states sold forest and mineral rights on nearly 6 million acres of federal lands to speculators, mostly from the North, who significantly expanded output. The production of iron, sulfur, and coal catapulted. Denuding the forests of Alabama and Louisiana, northern lumber syndicates between 1869 and 1899 increased lumber production by 500 percent.

Following the lead of their northern counterparts, the southern iron and steel industries expanded as well. Birmingham, Alabama, founded in 1871 in the heart of a region blessed with rich deposits of coal, limestone, and iron ore, grew in less than three decades to a bustling iron-producing city with noisy railroad yards and roaring blast furnaces. By 1900 it was the nation's largest pig-iron shipper. In these same years, Chattanooga, Tennessee, housed nine furnaces, seventeen foundries, and numerous machine shops.

As large-scale recruiters of black workers, the southern iron and steel mills contributed to the migration of blacks cityward. By 1900, 20 percent of the southern black population was urban. While many of these urban blacks toiled as domestics or in similar menial capacities, others entered the

---

*El Dorado: a legendary place in Spanish America sought out for its precious metals and jewels.

industrial work force in places like Birmingham and Chattanooga. Southern industry reflected the patterns of racism permeating other aspects of southern life. The burgeoning textile mills of the piedmont were lily-white, while in the iron and steel industry, blacks, who composed 60 percent of the work force by 1900, had practically no chance of advancement. Nevertheless, in a rare reversal of the usual pattern, southern blacks in the iron and steel industry on average earned more than did southern white textile workers.

The Southern Mill Economy

Unlike the urban-based southern iron and steel industry, the textile mills that mushroomed in the South in the 1880s took southern industrialization down a path different from that which the North and Midwest were now following. Above the Mason-Dixon line, factories and mills were concentrated in cities. But the southern textile industry sprang up in the countryside and itself sometimes became a catalyst for the formation of new towns and villages. (This same pattern had occurred in rural New England in the 1820s.) In those southern districts that underwent the gradual transition from an agricultural to a mill economy, country ways and values suffused the new industrial workplace.

The cotton-mill economy grew largely in the piedmont, a beautiful country of rolling hills and rushing rivers stretching from central Virginia to northern Georgia and Alabama. Until the 1850s the piedmont had been the South's backcountry, a land of subsistence farming and limited roads, far from the thriving coastal plantations. The Civil War had disrupted even the modest gains in railroad expansion and factory construction that had come in the 1850s. Then, struggling to rebuild their farms and lives in the late 1860s, most of the piedmont's white yeoman farmers and freed blacks became ensnared in the crop-lien and sharecropping systems. In the two decades following the war, falling cotton and tobacco prices, laws that required the fencing of livestock, and higher taxes to support railway and road construction trapped farmers in the new commercial economy and undercut their semi-independent existence.

But postwar railroad construction also opened the region to outside markets and sparked a period of intense town building and textile-mill expansion. Between 1880 and 1900, track mileage in North Carolina grew more than 2½ times; the number of towns and villages jumped, quickening the pulse of commerce; and the construction of textile mills accelerated. During this same period, some 120 new mills were built in North Carolina alone; Augusta, Georgia, with twenty-eight hundred mill workers, became known as the Lowell of the South. The expansion of the southern textile industry nurtured promoters' visions of a new, more prosperous, industrialized South.

Merchants and newspaper editors hailed the prospect that proliferating cotton mills would lift the South out of its Civil War legacy of poverty and defeat. And sharecroppers and tenant farmers at first turned hopeful eyes toward mill work, realizing that a deepening agricultural depression was driving them into destitution and despair. Sharecropper Eula Durham, recalling a day spent picking cotton, vividly evoked the plight of the South's rural populace: "I got through picking that evening, . . . and [the owner of the cotton field] said 'Well, I don't know, I reckon you're worth a dime.' And he give me a dime for picking cotton all day. I went home and I cried, I was so mad. Papa said, 'If you don't sit down and hush I'm going to tear you all to pieces. That's all that old man had.' I said, 'Well, he ought to have told me that before I picked that cotton.'" For Eula Durham and countless others like her, the mills seemed to offer a way out of rural poverty.

But appearances were deceptive. The chief cotton-mill promoters were drawn from the same ranks of merchants, lawyers, doctors, and bankers who had profited from the commercialization of southern agriculture (and from the misfortunes of poor black and white tenant farmers and sharecroppers enmeshed in the new system). R. R. Haynes, a planter and merchant from North Carolina's Rutherford County, was typical of the new entrepreneurs. Starting out as a storekeeper, he expanded his operation to include a sawmill, cotton gins, and a wheat thresher. In 1884 he purchased land and water rights on Second Broad Creek and formed a company to finance construction of the Henrietta Mills. By 1913 Haynes owned not only one of the South's largest gingham-producing operations but also banks, railroads, lumber businesses, and a line of general stores.

Haynes and other prosperous southern textile industrialists had carefully mapped their path to success. They first constructed the mill itself—typically a narrow, three-story structure, fifty feet wide by two hundred feet long—along a fast-moving river that provided water power. Purchasing the most advanced cotton-spinning and cloth-weaving machinery from northern suppliers, and recruiting northern technicians and managers to set it up, they made low-skilled laborers the backbone of their operation.

Mill superintendents drew their workers from impoverished nearby farms and commonly hired whole families (almost exclusively poor whites). In their public pronouncements, they promised that textile work would free these families from poverty and instill in them the virtues of thrift, punctuality, and industrial discipline. While chanting the benefits of industrial progress, however, the cotton-mill entrepreneurs did not hesitate to shamelessly exploit the South's deep pool of cheap labor. By the 1880s, when the mills were earning their investors from 30 percent to 75 percent profit, the superintendents were paying young mill workers twelve to eighteen years of age from seven cents to eleven cents an hour, a rate 30 percent to 50 percent less than comparable mill wages in New England.

The mill dominated most piedmont textile communities. The mill operator not only built and owned the workers' housing and the company store but also supported the village church, financed the local elementary school, and pried into the morals and behavior of the mill hands. To keep the workers dependent and to curb their tendency to move from one mill to another seeking better opportunities, the mill owner usually paid workers just once a month, often in scrip—a certificate redeemable only in goods supplied by the company store. Since few families had enough money and supplies to get through a month without buying on credit, they usually overspent and fell behind in their payments. In these cases, the charges were deducted from the workers' wages the following month. In this way, the mill drew workers and their families into a cycle of indebtedness very much like that faced by sharecroppers and tenant farmers.

Southern mill superintendents accommodated themselves to local customs. Unlike northern mill workers, predominantly female and single, southern mill employees comprised men, married and single women, and children. Mothers commonly even brought babies into the mills and kept them

Textile Workers

Textile mills hired both adults and children. Here a man and two boys stand before the machines that they operated for sixty hours a week. Child laborers in the mills often went home so tired that they fell asleep before supper and could not be wakened until morning.

in baskets nearby while tending their machines. Little children visiting older siblings in the mills sometimes learned to operate the machines themselves. Laboring a twelve-hour day, the mill hands relieved their tedium by deliberately stationing themselves near friends so that they might converse as they worked. Ties among the workers were strong. One employee put it simply: "The mill community was a close bunch of people . . . like one big family. We just loved one another." The mill managers adjusted to other local practices as well. Since many southerners traditionally ate their major meal at midday, mills often let most of their hands go home between twelve and one. In addition, mill hands worked cooperatively, as they had during planting and harvesting on the farm, and watched over the looms of coworkers who were taking a break.

To help make ends meet, mill workers kept their own garden patches and raised chickens and an occasional cow and pig. Southern mill hands thus brought communal farm values, nurtured through cooperative planting and harvesting, into the mills and mill villages. Although they had to adapt to machine-paced work and received barely enough pay to live on, the working poor in the mill districts, like their counterparts in the North before the Civil War, eased the transition from rural to village-industrial life by clinging to a cooperative country ethic.

Like northern cotton mills before the Civil War, southern textile companies exploited the cheap rural labor around them, settling transplanted farm people in paternalistic company-run villages. Using these tactics, the industry underwent a period of steady growth. Between 1860 and 1900, cotton-mill capacity shot up 1,400 percent, and by 1920 the South was the nation's leading textile-mill center.

The Southern Industrial Lag

Still, industrialization in the South occurred on a smaller scale and at a slower rate than industrialization in the North and also depended far more on outside financing, technology, and expertise. Despite leaps in southern lumber, iron, and cotton production, the late-nineteenth-century southern economy remained essentially in a colonial status, subject to control by northern industries and financial syndicates. Except for the American Tobacco Company, southern industry was dominated by northern companies and northern bankers. U.S. Steel, for example, controlled the foundries in Birmingham, and in 1900 its executives began to price Birmingham steel according to the "Pittsburgh plus" formula based on the price of Pittsburgh steel, plus the freight costs of shipping from Pittsburgh. As a result, southerners paid higher prices for steel than did northerners, even though southern production was less costly.

Several factors thus combined to retard industrialization in the South. Unfavorable federal banking regulations, scarce capital, a staggering burden of wartime debt, and discriminatory business practices by profit-hungry northern-controlled enterprises all hampered the region's economic development. Dragged down by a poorly educated white population unskilled in modern technology and by an equally poorly trained, indigent black population excluded from skilled jobs, southern industry languished. Not until after the turn of the century did southern industry as a whole undergo the restructuring and consolidation that had occurred in northern business enterprise two decades earlier. Although Henry Grady's vision of a New South may have inspired many southerners to work toward industrialization, economic growth in the South, limited as it was by outside forces, progressed in its own distinctly regional way.

Industrial Work and the Work Force

As we have seen in the contrasting experiences of the North and South, industrialization proceeded unevenly nationwide. In fact, during the late nineteenth century, *most* Americans still worked in small factories and locally run businesses. In cities like Philadelphia and Cincinnati, a variety of small-scale work settings coexisted. Tiny sweatshops where women and children hand-stitched clothing operated in the same neighborhoods as small factories employing a mix of skilled and unskilled laborers. But in more and more locales as the century unfolded, there sprang onto the industrial scene large factories with armies of unskilled and semi-skilled workers who turned out leather soles for shoes, veneer-covered plywood for furniture, and castings for plows. Thus for all the variety, the pattern of change was evident. Between 1860 and 1900, the number of industrial workers jumped from 885,000 to 3.2 million, and the trend toward large-scale production became unmistakable.

From Workshop to Factory

The transition to a factory economy came not as an earthquake but rather as a series of jolts varying in strength and duration. But whether they occurred quickly or slowly, the changes in factory production had a profound impact on skilled craftsmen and unskilled laborers alike, for they involved a fundamental restructuring of work habits and a new emphasis on workplace discipline.

The impact of these changes can be seen by examining the boot and shoe industry. As late as

The Shoemakers
by E. B. and E. C. Kellogg, 1855

In antebellum America skilled shoemakers custom-made their products and sold them directly to the purchaser, cutting out the retailer. After the Civil War, the mass production of shoes spelled the end of many small shops, such as the one depicted in this lithograph.

the 1840s, almost every shoe was custom-made by a single skilled artisan, who worked in a small, independent shop where he and four or five other shoemakers set their own hours and agreed on the stint, or the number of pairs, to be produced each day. These shoemakers were aristocrats in the world of labor. Taught in an apprentice system, they took pride in their work and controlled the quality of their product. In some cases they hired their own helpers and paid them out of their own pockets.

Around these shoemakers there evolved a distinctive working-class culture, subdivided along ethnic lines. Foreign-born English, German, and Irish shoe workers each set up ethnic trade organizations and joined affiliated benevolent associations (see Chapter 8). They took time off for religious observances, funerals, and holidays; drank sociably on the job; and helped each other weather accidents or sicknesses. Bound together by their potent religious and ethnic ties, they also attended common churches, observed weddings and funerals according to old-country traditions, and relaxed together at the local saloon after work. Living in tenements and boarding houses within the same tight-knit ethnic neighborhood, they developed a strong ethnic and community pride.

As early as the 1850s, even before the widespread use of machinery, changes in the ready-made shoe trade began to affect the role and status of skilled labor. When Cincinnati's Filey and Chapin Company in 1851 moved its growing production

staff into a large warehouse, the owners broke down the manufacturing process into a sequence of repetitive, easily mastered tasks. Skilled shoe artisans now worked in a "team" of four men, each responsible for one function: putting the shoe on the last (a form shaped like a person's foot), attaching the heel, trimming the sole, "finishing" the leather with stain and polish, and so forth. Thus instead of crafting a pair of shoes from start to finish, each team member became a specialist in only one part of the process. The Ohio commissioner of labor statistics in 1878 voiced a common artisan lament about this narrowing of skills: "[F]ew machinists can build an engine, few shoemakers . . . can make a shoe. . . . The machinist may be a first class vise hand, the shoemaker may be a splendid trimmer . . . [but] their future is dependent upon their ability to secure employment at such a specialty."

Not only did the nature of the work change under the new factory system of shoe manufacture, but workers lost the freedom to drink on the job and to take time off for special occasions. A working-class culture that had reinforced group solidarity was now dismissed by owners and shop foremen as wasteful and inefficient.

In the 1880s, as shoe factories became larger and more mechanized, traditional skills largely vanished. Sophisticated sewing and buffing machines allowed shoe companies to replace skilled operatives with lower-paid, less skilled women and children. By 1890 women made up more than 35 percent of the work force in an industry once dominated by men.

In many other industries, skilled artisans found their responsibilities and relation to the production process changing. With the exception of some skilled construction crafts such as carpentry and bricklaying, artisans no longer participated in the production process *as a whole*. Like the laborer whose machine nailed heels on forty-eight hundred shoes a day, even "skilled" workers in the new factories specializing in consumer goods found themselves performing numbingly repetitive and monotonous tasks. Factory work, which writers and ministers had praised in the 1830s and 1840s as the foundation of happiness and the mark of social progress, had become specialized, machine-paced, and deadeningly routine.

The Hardships of Industrial Labor

The expansion of the factory system not only altered the nature of skilled work but also spawned an unprecedented demand for unskilled labor. By the 1880s nearly one-third of the 750,000 workers employed in the railroad and steel industries, for example, were common laborers.

In the construction trades, the machine and tool industries, and garment making, the services of unskilled laborers were procured under the so-called contract system. To avoid the problems of hiring, managing, and firing their own workers, large companies negotiated an agreement with a subcontractor to take responsibility for employee relations. A foreman or boss employed by the subcontractor supervised gangs of unskilled day laborers. These common workers were seasonal help, hired in times of need and laid off in slack periods. The steel industry employed them to shovel ore, coal, and lime around the yards and to move ingots inside the mills. The foremen drove the gangs hard; in the Pittsburgh area, the workers called the foremen "pushers."

Notoriously transient, unskilled laborers drifted from city to city and from industry to industry. As the first hired during good times and the first let go in bad, they sometimes worked for one-third the wages of a typical skilled artisan. In the late 1870s, unskilled laborers earned $1.30 a day, whereas bricklayers and blacksmiths earned more

than $3.00. Only unskilled southern mill workers, whose wages averaged a meager 84¢ a day in these years, earned less.

Unskilled and skilled workers alike not only put in up to twelve-hour shifts but also faced grave hazards to their health and safety. The alarming incidence of industrial accidents stemmed from a variety of circumstances, including dangerous factory conditions, workers' inexperience with the complicated machines, the rapid pace of the production process, and the employers' unconcern for plant safety. Hamlin Garland graphically described the perilous environment of a steel-rail mill at Carnegie's Homestead Steel Works in Pittsburgh (see "A Place in Time"). One steelworker recalled that on his first day at the mill, "I looked up and a big train carrying a big vessel with fire was making towards me. I stood numb, afraid to move, until a man came to me and led me out of the mill." Under such conditions the accident rate in the steel mills was extremely high.

In the coal mines and cotton mills, child laborers typically entered the work force at age eight or nine. These youngsters not only faced the same environmental hazards as adults but were especially prone to injury because of the pranks and play that they engaged in on the job. (When supervision was lax in the cotton mills, for example, child workers would grab the belts that powered the machines and see who could ride them farthest up toward the drive shaft in the ceiling before letting go and falling to the floor.) In the coal industry, children were commonly employed as slate pickers. Sitting at a chute beneath the breakers that crushed the coal, they removed pieces of slate and other impurities. The cloud of coal dust that swirled around them made them vulnerable to black lung disease—a disorder that could progress into emphysema and tuberculosis. Children and others who toiled in the cotton mills, constantly breathing in cotton dust, fell ill with brown lung, another crippling disease.

For adult workers, the railroad industry was one of the most perilous. In 1889, the first year that the Interstate Commerce Commission compiled reliable statistics, almost two thousand railwaymen were killed on the job and more than twenty thousand were injured.

Disabled workers and widows received only minimal financial aid from employers. Until the

Slate Pickers, 1911

Picking slate at a coal chute, their clothes and faces blackened with coal dust, these boys earned $2.50 for a sixty-hour work-week.

1890s the courts considered employer negligence to be one of the normal risks borne by the employee. Railroad and factory owners regularly fought against the adoption of state safety and health standards, on the grounds that the economic costs would be excessive. For sickness and accident benefits, workers joined fraternal organizations and ethnic clubs, part of whose monthly dues benefited those in need. But in most cases, the amounts set aside were too low to be of much help. When a worker was killed or maimed in an accident, the family became dependent on relatives or kindly neighbors for assistance and support.

Immigrant Labor

Outside the South factory owners turned to unskilled immigrant laborers for the muscle needed in the booming factories, mills, railroads, and heavy-construction industries. In Philadelphia, where native-born Americans and recent German immigrants dominated the highly skilled metal-working trades, Irish newcomers remained mired in unskilled horse-carting and construction occupations until

the 1890s, when the "new immigrants" from southern and eastern Europe replaced them (see Chapter 18). In the Northeast poverty-stricken French-Canadians filled the most menial positions in the textile mills. On the West Coast Chinese immigrants performed the dirtiest and most physically demanding jobs in mining, canning, and railroad construction.

Writing home in the 1890s, eastern European immigrants described the hazardous and draining work in the steel mills. "Wherever the heat is most insupportable, the flames most scorching, the smoke and soot most choking, there we are certain to find compatriots bent and wasted in toil," reported one Hungarian. Yet those immigrants disposed to live frugally in a boarding house and to work an eighty-four-hour week could save fifteen dollars a month, far more than they could have earned in the old country.

Intent on improving their families' economic standing, many immigrants readily accepted the steel mills' and factories' exhausting work schedules. One worker tersely summed up the typical routine: "A good job, save money, work all time, go home, sleep, no spend." Willing to make short-term sacrifices for long-term gains, immigrants commonly volunteered for overtime work on Sundays to maximize their income. If the immigrant workers stayed healthy and had no accidents, they often accumulated small savings and lived better than they ever had before.

While most immigrants worked hard, few adjusted easily to the rat race of the factory world. The rural peasants from southern and eastern Europe who immigrated after 1890 found it especially difficult to abandon their irregular work habits for the unrelenting factory schedules. Unlike farm routines, which allowed the changing daylight hours of the seasons, factory operations were dictated by the invariable speed of the machines. A brochure that the International Harvester Corporation used to teach English to its Polish workers attempted to instill the "proper" values. Lesson 1 read:

> *I hear the whistle. I must hurry.*
> *I hear the five minute whistle.*
> *It is time to go into the shop.*
> *I take my check from the gate board and hang*
>   *it on the department board.*
> *I change my clothes and get ready to work.*
> *The starting whistle blows.*
> *I eat my lunch.*
> *It is forbidden to eat until then.*
> *The whistle blows at five minutes of starting*
>   *time.*
> *I get ready to go to work.*
> *I work until the whistle blows to quit.*
> *I leave my place nice and clean.*
> *I put all my clothes in the locker.*
> *I must go home.*

As this "lesson" reveals, factory work tied the immigrants to a rigid timetable very different from the pace of farm life.

When immigrant workers resisted the tempo of factory work, drank on the job, or took unexcused absences, employers used a variety of tactics to enforce discipline. Some sponsored temperance societies and Sunday schools to teach habits of punctuality and sobriety. Others published rule books dictating specific codes of behavior. When efforts at persuasion proved ineffective, employers cut wages and put workers on the piecework system, paying them only for the items produced. Employers sometimes also provided low-cost hous-

ing to build employee allegiance to the company and gain leverage against work stoppages: if the workers went on strike, the boss could simply evict them. To keep skilled artisans from leaving, a few companies paid bonuses, set up pension plans, and promised steady employment.

In some cases workers fought attempts to tighten factory discipline by demanding a say in production quotas or asserting traditional rights, such as the custom in the cigar-making industry of allowing one employee to read to others as they worked. Seeking to re-create a village atmosphere in the workplace, immigrant factory help often persuaded employers to hire friends and relatives to work by their side. For factory workers who had come from farms where the entire family toiled together, a common goal became the employment of as many family members as possible.

In the face of immigrant labor's desires for a more sociable, humane working environment, the proliferation of machines in the factories frequently sparked employer-employee tensions. When the factory owner's interest in increasing output corresponded with the immigrant's desire to maximize income, the offer of long hours at the machines was accepted and even welcomed. But when the employer cut wages or unreasonably accelerated the work schedule, unrest boiled to the surface.

Young Women and Work in Industrializing America

In 1870 only 13 percent of all women worked outside the home. Sixty percent of these found jobs in domestic employment as cooks, maids, cleaning ladies, and laundresses. But most working women intensely disliked the long hours, dismally low pay, and social stigma attached to being a "servant." Therefore, when jobs in industry expanded in the last quarter of the century, growing numbers of women workers abandoned domestic employment for the better-paying, less demeaning work in the textile, food-processing, and garment industries. Between 1870 and 1900, the number of women working outside the home nearly tripled, and by the turn of the century, women made up 17 percent of the country's labor force.

A variety of factors propelled this rise in female employment. Changes in agriculture prompted many young farm women to seek employment in the industrial sector (see Chapter 18), while immigrant parents often sent their daughters to the factories to supplement their meager family incomes. The owners and managers of increasingly mechanized plants, in turn, welcomed young immigrant women as a ready source of inexpensive, unskilled labor. On the negative side, factory owners understood that many of these women would marry within a short time and leave the labor force, and thus treated them as temporary help and kept their wages low. Late in the century, young women in the clothing industry earned as little as five dollars for seventy hours of work.

Despite their paltry wages, long hours, and sometimes unpleasant working conditions, many young women relished the independence that they gained through factory employment. Even though in many cases most of their income went to their parents, they looked forward to having a little spending money for themselves. Mary Antin, a young Jewish immigrant, later captured in writing the excitement that she and her friends felt while shopping after a day of work in turn-of-the-century Boston, "noses and fingers on plate glass windows ablaze with electric lights and alluring with display."

When the typewriter and the telephone came into general use in the 1890s, office work became more specialized, and women with a high-school education moved into clerical and secretarial positions earlier filled primarily by men. They were attracted by the clean, safe working conditions and relatively good pay. First-rate typists could earn six dollars to seven dollars a week, which compared favorably with factory wages. Even though women were excluded from managerial positions, office work carried higher prestige and was generally steadier than work in the factory or shop.

Despite the growing number of women workers, when the late-nineteenth-century popular press touted the possibilities of moving up the ladder of success in industrial America, it left out young women completely. Women's work outside the home was seen as temporary. Their real achievement was defined in terms of marriage and the family. For women, success might be measured, for example, in the vicarious satisfaction that they experienced when a husband received a promotion or a son earned a raise. Few people even considered the possibility that a woman could attain national or even local prominence in the emerging corporate order.

Hard Work and the Gospel of Success

While women were generally excluded from the equation, influential opinion molders in these years preached that any man could achieve success in the new industrial era. In *Ragged Dick* (1867) and scores of later tales, Horatio Alger, a Unitarian minister turned dime novelist, recounted the adventures of poor but honest lads who rise through ambition, initiative, and self-discipline. Life is a struggle in Alger's fictional America, but the key to success lies in seizing the unexpected opportunities that fortune thrusts in one's path. In his stories shoeshine boys stop runaway horses or save children from drowning and are rewarded for their bravery by rich benefactors who give them a start in business. The career of Andrew Carnegie was often offered as proof that the United States remained the land of opportunity and "rags to riches."

Not everyone embraced this belief. In an 1871 essay, Mark Twain chided the public for its naïveté and cynically suggested that business success was more likely to come to those who lied and cheated. In testimony given in 1883 before a Senate committee investigating labor conditions, a New Yorker named Thomas B. McGuire dolefully recounted how he had been forced out of the horse-cart business by larger, better-financed concerns. Declared McGuire: "A man in the express business today owning one or two horses and a wagon cannot even eke out an existence. . . . The competition . . . from these monopolies . . . is too great. . . . I live in a tenement house, three stories up, where the water comes in through the roof, and I cannot better myself. My children will have to go to work before they are able to work. Why? Simply because this present system . . . is all for the privileged classes, nothing for the man who produces the wealth." Only with starting capital of ten thousand dollars —then a large sum—said McGuire, could the independent entrepreneur hope to compete with the large companies.

What are the facts? Certainly Carnegie's rise from abject poverty to colossal wealth was the rare exception, as recent studies of nearly two hundred of the largest corporations reveal. Ninety-five percent of the industrial leaders came from middle-

and upper-class backgrounds. However, even if skilled immigrants and native-born working-class Americans had little chance to move into management in the largest corporations, they did have considerable opportunity to rise to the top in *small* companies. In Paterson, New Jersey, the most successful owners of small- to medium-size iron, machinery, and locomotive companies between 1850 and 1880 invariably had started their careers as workers, broadened their skills through apprenticeship, and then opened their own factories. Although few of them reaped immense fortunes, many attained substantial incomes.

For unskilled immigrant laborers, the opportunities for advancement were considerably more limited. Many did, however, move to semiskilled or skilled positions. And with new jobs came higher earnings and sometimes the means to purchase a house. In nineteenth-century Boston, except for blacks, significant numbers of unskilled workers advanced into the next higher occupational stratum. Yet most immigrants, particularly the Irish and Italians, moved far more slowly than the sons of middle- and upper-class Americans who began with greater educational advantages and family financial backing. The upward mobility possible for such unskilled workers was generally mobility *within* the working class. Immigrants who got ahead in the late nineteenth century went from rags to respectability, not rags to riches.

One positive economic trend in these years was the rise in real wages, representing gains in actual buying power. Average real wages climbed 31 percent for unskilled workers and 74 percent for skilled workers between 1860 and 1900. Overall gains in purchasing power, however, were often offset by personal injuries and unemployment during slack times or economic slumps. The position of unskilled immigrant laborers was particularly shaky. Even during a prosperous year like 1890, one out of every five nonagricultural workers was unemployed at least one month. During the depressions of the 1870s and 1890s, wage cuts, extended layoffs, and irregular employment pushed those at the very base of the industrial work force to the brink of starvation.

Thus the overall picture of late-nineteenth-century economic mobility is complex. At the top of the scale, the rich grew even wealthier and amassed enormous fortunes. In 1890 a mere 10 percent of American families owned 73 percent of the nation's wealth. At the bottom of the scale, the most recent immigrants, particularly the unskilled, struggled to make ends meet. During the 1890s only about 45 percent of American industrial laborers earned more than the five-hundred-dollar poverty line annually. Nevertheless, in between the very rich and the very poor, skilled immigrants and small shopkeepers were swelling the ranks of the middle class. So while the standard of living for millions of Americans rose, the gap between the poor and the well-off remained a yawning abyss.

Labor Unions and Industrial Conflict

Toiling long hours for low wages, often under dangerous and degrading conditions, some late-nineteenth-century workers turned to labor unions for help. But the unions faced formidable obstacles to increasing their membership. With desperately poor immigrants pouring into the country, employers could always hire newcomers willing to work for lower wages and even to serve as strikebreakers.

Ethnic and racial divisions within the work force further hampered unionizing efforts. In mill towns like Troy, New York, for example, French-Canadian and Irish Catholic workers worshiped, socialized, and married largely within their own ethnic group. The same was true of Pennsylvania coal miners and steelworkers who had immigrated from various southern and eastern European countries.

Further, relatively prosperous skilled craftsworkers felt little kinship with low-paid common laborers. And even the skilled artisans were divided among themselves, depending on their particular craft. Iron molders, cigar makers, carpenters, and printers all worked in radically different environments and saw little reason for cooperative effort. Thus when craft-based unions did challenge management and go on strike, they represented only a tiny percentage of the work force.

Labor-organizing efforts reflected these realities. Two groups, the National Labor Union and the Knights of Labor, attempted to build a mass labor movement that would unite skilled and unskilled workers regardless of their specialty. After impressive initial growth, however, both efforts collapsed. The most successful labor movement of the period, the American Federation of Labor (AFL), represented an amalgamation of powerful independent craft unions. The AFL survived and grew, but it still represented only a small portion of the total labor force.

With unions so weak, labor unrest generally took the form of unplanned, wildcat walkouts when conditions became intolerable, and these actions born of desperation sometimes exploded into violence. This, in turn, whipped up middle-class fears of labor unrest, further impeding the development of a strong labor movement.

Organizing the Workers

The Civil War marked a watershed in the development of labor organizations. Labor unions in themselves were nothing new. From the eighteenth century on, carpenters, bricklayers, and other skilled workers had organized local trade unions to fight wage reductions and provide rudimentary benefits for their members in times of illness or accident. By the 1850s tradesmen in the printing, cigar-making, and ironworking businesses had even organized national associations along craft lines. But the effectiveness of these organizations was limited. The main challenge that labor leaders faced in the postwar period was how to boost the unions' clout. Some believed that this goal could be achieved by forming one big association that would transcend craft lines and pull in a mass membership.

One person inspired by this vision was Philadelphian William H. Sylvis, who in 1863 was elected president of the Iron Moulders' International Union, an organization of workers in stove factories and iron foundries. Strongly built and bearded, with a "face and eyes beaming with intelligence," Sylvis traveled the country exhorting iron molders to organize. When he had no money for train fare, he rode in the cab with the engineer. A compelling speaker, he lambasted "the monied aristocracy— proud, imperious and dishonest, . . . blasting and withering everything it [comes] in contact with." Within a few years, Sylvis had built his union from "a mere pygmy" to a membership of eighty-five hundred.

In 1866, acting on his dream of a nationwide association to represent all workers, Sylvis called a convention in Baltimore that formed the National Labor Union (NLU). The new organization not

Labor Unions

The idealism of the early labor movement is implicit in this 1899 membership certificate of the United Mine Workers.

only endorsed the eight-hour-day movement but also, reflecting the lingering aura of pre–Civil War utopianism, embraced a wide range of goals, including currency and banking reform, an end to convict labor, a federal department of labor, and restriction on immigration—especially Chinese immigration—since many regarded immigrants as responsible for driving wages down. The NLU under Sylvis's leadership also endorsed the cause of working women and elected the head of a Troy, New York, union of female laundry workers as one of its national officers. It urged black workers to organize as well, though in racially separate unions.

In the winter of 1866–1867 Sylvis's own iron founders' union became locked in a harrowing strike when the nation's foundry owners cut wages and laid off workers. After the strike failed miserably, Sylvis believed more deeply than ever before that the answer lay not in strikes but in national political reform. He invited a number of reformers to the 1868 NLU convention, including woman-suffrage advocates Susan B. Anthony and Elizabeth

Cady Stanton, who, according to a reporter, made "no mean impression on the bearded delegates." But the NLU suffered a shattering blow when Sylvis died suddenly in 1869. Despite a claim of three hundred thousand members, it faded quickly. After a brief incarnation in 1872 as the National Labor Reform party, it vanished from the scene.

But the dream of a national labor movement lived on in a new organization, the Noble and Holy Order of the Knights of Labor, founded in 1869 by nine Philadelphia tailors led by Uriah H. Stephens, head of the Garment Cutters of Philadelphia. A secret society modeled on the Masonic order (see Chapter 9), the Knights welcomed all wage earners or former wage earners; they excluded only bankers, doctors, lawyers, stockbrokers, professional gamblers, and liquor dealers. Calling for a great association of all workers, the Knights demanded equal pay for women, an end to child labor and convict labor, a graduated income tax, and the cooperative employer-employee ownership of factories, mines, and other businesses.

The Knights grew slowly at first, in part because the Catholic church forbade Catholics to join. But membership rocketed in the 1880s after the church lifted its prohibition and Terence V. Powderly replaced Stephens as the organization's head, or Grand Master Workman, in 1879. A young Scranton machinist of Irish-Catholic immigrant origins, Powderly was an unlikely labor leader. He was short and slight, with a blond drooping mustache, elegant attire, and a fastidious, somewhat aloof manner. One journalist expressed surprise at finding such a fashionable and sophisticated man as the leader of "the horny-fisted sons of toil." But Powderly's oratorical eloquence, coupled with a series of successes in labor clashes, brought in thousands of new members.

During its growth years in the early 1880s, the Knights of Labor reflected both its idealistic origins and Powderly's particular social vision. Powderly opposed strikes, which he considered "a relic of barbarism." His objective was a gradual end to the wage system and the reorganization of society on cooperative principles. Toward this end, he called on the Knights of Labor locals to form producer and consumer cooperatives. A strict teetotaler, he also urged temperance upon the membership. Powderly advocated the admission of blacks into local Knights of Labor assemblies, although he recognized the strength of racism and allowed local

"Between the Hammer and the Anvil"

Conservative, pro-business opponents sometimes used cartoons as the vehicle for scathing attacks on unions, condemning organized labor for depriving the worker of the ability to make independent decisions. Here a worker is caught between the hammer of the Knights of Labor and the anvil of capital.

assemblies to be segregated in the South. The Knights under Powderly also welcomed women workers; by 1886 women constituted an estimated 10 percent of the Knights' membership.

Powderly also supported restrictions on immigration—and a total ban on Chinese immigration. This policy reflected the widespread fear among union members of immigrants' working so cheaply that they would steal jobs from others. In the West such fears were directed particularly against the Chinese, and they were heightened when California railroad magnate Leland Stanford declared: "[O]pen the door and let everybody come who wants to come . . . until you get enough [immigrants] here to reduce the price of labor to such a point that its cheapness will stop their coming." In 1877 San Francisco workers demonstrating for an eight-hour workday destroyed twenty-five Chinese-run laun-

Ethnic and Racial Hatred

Although this Puck *cartoon lampoons the Irish, giving them an apelike appearance and showing them headed toward politics and prison (Sing Sing), it reserves even greater animosity for the Chinese, who are depicted as having little desire to remain in America once they have made some money.*

dries and terrorized the local Chinese population. In 1880 both major party platforms included anti-Chinese immigration plans. Two years later, Congress passed the Chinese Exclusion Act, placing a ten-year moratorium on Chinese immigration. Nevertheless, sporadic labor violence against the Chinese continued.

While inspired by Powderly's vision of a harmonious and cooperative future, most rank-and-file Knights of Labor were more interested in immediate issues such as wage cuts, production speedups, and deteriorating working conditions. Specifically, they strongly disagreed with Powderly's antistrike position. In 1883–1884 local branches of the Knights led a series of spontaneous strikes that elicited only reluctant support from the national leadership. In 1885, however, when Jay Gould tried to eradicate the Knights of Labor from

his Wabash railroad by firing workers active in the union, Powderly and his executive board recognized that the survival of their organization was at stake. They instructed all Knights employed by the Wabash line to walk off the job and those working for other lines to refuse to handle Wabash cars. This highly effective action crippled the Wabash's operations. To the nation's amazement, the arrogant Jay Gould met with Powderly and agreed to halt his campaign against the Knights of Labor. "The Wabash victory is with the Knights," declared a St. Louis newspaper; "no such victory has ever before been secured in this or any other country."

With this apparent triumph, membership in the Knights of Labor soared. By 1886 more than seven hundred thousand workers were organized in nearly six thousand locals. Turning to political action that fall, the Knights mounted campaigns in nearly two hundred towns and cities nationwide, electing several mayors and judges (Powderly himself had served as mayor of Scranton since 1878) and claimed a role in electing a dozen congressmen. In state legislatures they secured passage of laws banning convict labor, and at the national level they lobbied successfully for a law against the importation of foreign contract labor. Conservatives warned darkly that the Knights could cripple the economy and take over the country if they chose.

But in fact, the organization's strength soon waned. The leadership lost control of the membership during the period of explosive growth, and with the failure of a series of unauthorized strikes in 1886—including one targeted at Jay Gould, who had resumed his vendetta against the Knights — disillusionment spread. The national reaction to the Haymarket riot (see below) contributed to the decline. By the late 1880s, the Knights of Labor was but a shadow of its former self. Nevertheless, the organization had given a major impetus to the labor movement and had awakened in thousands of workers a sense of group solidarity and potential strength. Powderly, who survived to 1924, always remained proud of his role "in forcing to the forefront the cause of misunderstood and downtrodden humanity."

As the Knights of Labor weakened, another national labor organization, pursuing more immediate and practical goals, was gaining in strength. The skilled craft unions had long been uncomfortable with labor organizations like the Knights that welcomed skilled and unskilled alike. They were also concerned that the Knights' emphasis on broad reform goals would undercut their own commitment to better wages and to protecting the interests of their particular crafts. The break came in May 1886 when the craft unions left the Knights of Labor to form the American Federation of Labor.

From the first the AFL replaced the Knights' grand visions with practical tactics aimed at bread-and-butter issues. The AFL approach was aptly expressed in 1885 by Adolph Strasser, president of the International Cigar Makers' Union. Asked by a Senate labor committee about his union's "ultimate ends," Strasser responded: "We have no ultimate ends. We are going on from day to day. We fight only for immediate objectives. . . ."

This philosophy was vigorously pursued by Samuel Gompers, the English immigrant cigar maker who became head of the AFL in 1886 and led it for nearly forty years, until his death in 1924. Gompers believed in "trade unionism, pure and simple." The stocky, mustachioed labor leader had lost faith in utopian social reforms and catchall labor organizations in the 1870s, quickly recognizing that "the poor, the hungry, have not the strength to engage in a conflict even when life is at stake." To stand up to the corporations, Gompers asserted, labor would have to harness the bargaining power of the *skilled* workers, whom employers could not easily replace, and concentrate on the practical goals of raising wages and reducing hours.

A master tactician, Gompers believed that the trend toward large-scale industrial organization necessitated a comparable degree of organization by labor. He also recognized, however, that the skilled craft unions that had come together to form the AFL retained a strong commitment to controlling their own affairs. The challenge was to persuade the craftsworkers from the various trades to join forces without violating their sense of craft autonomy. Gompers's solution was to organize the AFL as a *federation* of trade unions, each retaining control of its own members but all linked by an executive council to coordinate strategy during boycotts and strike actions. "We want to make the trade union movement under the AFL as distinct as the billows, yet one as the sea," he told a national convention.

Focusing the federation's efforts on short-term improvements in wages and hours, Gompers carefully sidestepped divisive political issues. The new organization's platform did, however, demand an eight-hour workday, employers' liability, and mine-safety laws. By 1904, under Gompers's conservative tutelage, the AFL had grown to more than 1.6 million strong.

While the unions held up an ideal toward which many might strive, labor organizations as a whole in the late nineteenth century remained rather weak. Less than 5 percent of the work force joined union ranks. Split between skilled artisans and common laborers, separated along ethnic and religious lines, and divided over tactics, the unions battled with only occasional effectiveness against the growing power of corporate enterprise. Lacking financial resources, they typically watched from the sidelines during economic hard times as unorganized workers launched wildcat strikes that sometimes turned violent.

Strikes and Labor Violence

Americans had lived with a high level of violence from the nation's beginnings, and the nineteenth century, with its international and civil wars, urban riots, and Indian-white conflict, was no exception. Terrible labor clashes toward the end of the century were part of this continuing pattern, but they nevertheless shocked and dismayed contemporaries. From 1881 to 1905, there erupted close to thirty-seven thousand strikes, in which nearly 7 million workers participated. In some cases these strikes involved mobs, property damage, and looting. To a shaken middle class, America seemed on the verge of a class war.

In a period of chronic labor unrest, certain years stood out. One such year was 1877. The trouble actually began in 1873, when a Wall Street crash triggered a major depression. Six thousand businesses closed the following year, and many more cut wages and laid off workers in a desperate effort to survive. Striking Pennsylvania coal miners were fired and evicted from their homes. Tramps roamed the streets in New York and Chicago. The tension took a deadly turn in 1877 during a wildcat railroad strike. Ignited by a wage reduction on the Baltimore and Ohio Railroad in July, the strike exploded up and down the railroad lines, spreading quickly to New York, Pittsburgh, St. Louis,

Kansas City, Chicago, and San Francisco. Rioters in Pittsburgh torched Union Depot and the Pennsylvania Railroad roundhouse. By the time the newly installed president Rutherford B. Hayes had called out the troops and quelled the strike two weeks later, nearly one hundred people had died, and two-thirds of the nation's railroads stood idle.

The railroad strike stunned middle-class America. The religious press responded hysterically. "If the club of the policeman, knocking out the brains of the rioter, will answer, then well and good," declared one Congregational journal, "[but if not] then bullets and bayonets . . . constitute the one remedy. . . . Napoleon was right when he said that the way to deal with a mob was to exterminate it." The same middle-class Americans who worried about corporate abuse of power also grew terrified of mob violence from the bottom ranks of society.

Employers capitalized on the public hysteria to crack down on labor. Many required their workers to sign "yellow dog" contracts in which they promised not to strike or join a union. Some hired Pinkerton agents to serve as their own private police force and, when necessary, turned to the federal government and the U.S. Army to suppress labor unrest.

More strikes and violence followed in the 1880s. On May Day 1886, 340,000 workers walked off their jobs in support of the campaign for an eight-hour workday. Strikers in Cincinnati virtually shut down the city for nearly a month. Also in 1886, Chicago police shot and killed four strikers at the McCormick Harvester plant on May 3. At a protest rally the next evening in the city's Haymarket Square, someone threw a bomb from a nearby building, killing or fatally wounding seven policemen. The police in turn fired wildly into the crowd and killed four demonstrators.

Public reaction was immediate. Business leaders and middle-class citizens lashed out at labor activists and particularly at the sponsors of the Haymarket meeting, most of whom were associated with a German-language anarchist newspaper, the *Arbeiter Zeitung*. Eight were arrested and tried. Declared the Illinois attorney general: "Convict these men, make examples of them. Hang them, and you save our institutions." Although no evidence connected them directly to the bomb throwing, all were convicted, and four were executed. One committed suicide in prison. In Haymarket's

Labor Rally Poster, 1886

Business interests tried to smear labor unions as violence-prone and dominated by foreign radicals. Published in both German and English, this labor poster lent credence to such attacks.

aftermath still more Americans became convinced that the nation was in the grip of a deadly foreign conspiracy, and animosity toward labor unions intensified.

Stormy confrontations between business and labor continued into the 1890s. Federal troops were called out to crush a strike of silver miners in the Coeur d'Alene district of northern Idaho in 1892. Federal forces intervened again that same year when violence flared after managers cut wages and locked out the workers at the Carnegie Steel Company plant in Homestead, Pennsylvania (see "A Place in Time").

The most systematic use of troops to smash union power came in 1894, during a strike against the Pullman Palace Car Company. George Pullman, a self-taught entrepreneur who had pioneered in the manufacture of elegant dining, parlor, and sleeping cars for the nation's railroads, in 1880 had constructed a factory and town, called Pullman,

Homestead: The Town and the Mill, 1870–1907

On a rainy fall day in 1893, the writer Hamlin Garland crossed the Monongahela River on a ferry and debarked at a grimy industrial town near Pittsburgh. On assignment for *McClure's* magazine, Garland was investigating the "perilous trade" of steel making at Homestead, Pennsylvania, where the Carnegie Steel Company ran a major mill. One year before, state troops had suppressed a violent strike there. Garland had been sympathetic to the strikers, and he harbored grim expectations as he approached the plant.

From the banks of the polluted Monongahela, he could see the town and the mill sprawled over a hillside. Near the water's edge stood clusters of large sheds topped by tall smokestacks. Farther up the hill, Garland noted rows of dingy workers' houses, covered with soot and dust. All in all, the place seemed "as squalid and unlovely as could be imagined," he reported. "The streets of the town were horrible; the buildings were poor; the sidewalks were sunken and full of holes." Everywhere "groups of pale, lean men slouched in faded garments, grimy with the soot and grease of the mills."

Barely two decades earlier, the site of Homestead had been pastureland. In 1870 two large farms, the McClure and West homesteads, dominated the area, surrounded by smaller farms. The next year, a commercial venture, the Homestead Bank and Life Insurance Company, bought up the land and subdivided it into building lots. The

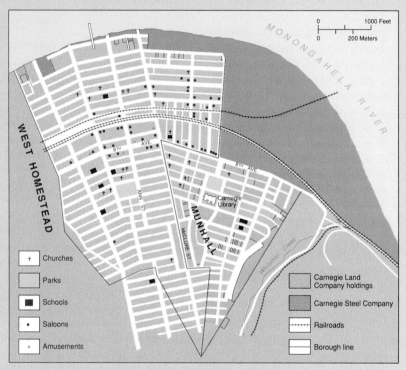

Homestead *The Carnegie Steel mills not only physically dominated the town but also occupied the most desirable land near the river. This location provided easy access to the barges that brought in supplies.*

SOURCE: Pittsburgh Survey. Maps under direction of Shelby M. Harrison, 1908.

company planned to create a residential suburb from which commuters could easily reach Pittsburgh—only seven miles away—on a new railroad line. But Homestead's suburban days were short-lived. In 1878, when the town's population reached six hundred, a glass factory was built. Three years later a steel mill was constructed on the riverbank, and in 1886 Carnegie's company purchased the mill. The Homestead facilities proved ideal for steel making. The Monongahela ensured an ample water

supply. Running through a region of bituminous coal mines, the river provided a conduit for fuel as well. New railroads brought in iron ore from Michigan mines and later from Minnesota. Within five years Carnegie had doubled the mill's capital and expanded its work force. By 1892 the sheds of the Carnegie works ranged over sixty acres. The town had eleven thousand residents, of whom thirty-eight hundred were mill employees.

As Garland learned, steel production had been broken down into

Homestead Life *An oppressive atmosphere hung over Homestead. The heat, particularly unbearable in summer, provided work for numerous water boys in the mills. As for the quality of the air, one observer noted that "the idiosyncrasy of this town is smoke. It rolls sullenly in slow folds from the great chimneys of the iron-foundries, and settles down in black, slimy pools on the muddy streets."*

many processes, spread out among the sheds. But all phases of steel making involved heat, noise, and hazard. At the blast furnaces, which processed raw iron, Garland found "pits gaping like the mouth of hell and ovens emitting a terrible degree of heat." Rising ninety feet into the air and surrounded by high stoves, the furnaces were worked by three men alternately. These puddlers stirred the molten iron with rods through holes in the furnace door. If cooled, the liquefied metal would become pig iron — so-called because the molds into which it was poured looked like suckling pigs around a "mother" furnace.

Homestead workers moved the molten iron on to other sheds and into Bessemer converters, two pear-shaped vessels that swung on pivots ten feet above the floor. When huge bursts of air were shot through the bottoms of the vessels, the twelve tons of liquid iron in each would become steel. "The thunder of the blast deafens you," wrote an awed observer. "The ever-brightening flame, flashing up finally as high as fifty feet, blinds you; sparks fall

everywhere." Encased in ingot molds, the hot steel was then placed on cars dawn by screeching engines, called donkeys, that lugged it off to the rolling mills. After the workers stripped off the molds, towering cranes lifted the red bars of steel and dropped them into a pit to be heated white-hot before being flattened. Emerging in rectangular slabs, or billets, the steel moved on to the finishing mills, where employees cut it into rails and beams. Although cooler than the furnace sheds, the rolling and finishing mills resounded with noise. Garland heard "the rumbling growl of rollers, the howls of horrible saws ... the crashing thunder of falling iron plate, the hoarse coughing of great engines, and the hissing of steam."

Accidents abounded throughout the sheds. Machinery sent off showers of sparks, liquid iron frequently spilled onto workers, and cranes hoisting tons of iron out of pits sometimes dropped their loads. During a single month in the 1890s, Homestead reported sixty-five accidents, of which seven were fatal. To survivors, the labor seemed endless,

for once the giant furnaces and converters were in operation, output had to be continuous. Most Homestead employees worked twelve-hour days, seven days a week. "How do they stand it?" asked another *McClure's* reporter, who had labored a few days in the sheds. "They all die young. Very few men well along in years are found anywhere in the mills."

After Garland left the "grim chimneys" and "belching smoke," he concluded that Homestead resembled a cancer. The mill and the town continued to grow. Fourteen years later Homestead claimed twenty-five thousand residents. The mills employed seven thousand of them, more than half recent Slavic immigrants. Although Andrew Carnegie and his top executives had built a library, a manual training school, and a hillside park, the smoke-enshrouded town remained a dismal place to work and live. "The trees are wasted and the foliage withered by the fumes," wrote a researcher for the *Pittsburgh Survey* in 1907. "The air is grey, and only from the top of a hill above the smoke is the sky blue."

ten miles south of Chicago. The carefully planned community provided solid brick houses for the workers; beautiful parks and playgrounds; a large central building housing a bank, a theater, and a public library; and even its own sewage-treatment plant. But despite the benefits that he gave the workers, Pullman closely policed their activities, outlawed saloons, and insisted that his properties turn a profit.

When the depression of 1893 hit, Pullman responded to a decline in orders by slashing workers' wages without reducing their rents. In reaction thousands of workers joined the newly formed American Railway Union and went on strike. They were led by a fiery young organizer, Eugene V. Debs, who vowed "to strip the mask of hypocrisy from the pretended philanthropist and show him to the world as an oppressor of labor." Union members working for the nation's largest railroads refused to switch Pullman cars, thus paralyzing rail traffic in and out of Chicago.

In response to the crisis, the General Managers' Association, an organization of top railroad executives, set out to break the union. The General Managers' first step was to import strikebreakers from among jobless easterners. Next they asked U.S. attorney general Richard Olney, who sat on the board of directors of three major railroad networks, for a federal injunction (court order) against the strikers for allegedly refusing to move railroad cars carrying U.S. mail.

In fact, union members had volunteered to switch mail cars onto any trains that did not carry Pullman cars, and it was the railroads' managers who were delaying the mail by refusing to send their trains without the full complement of cars. Nevertheless, Olney, supported by President Grover Cleveland and citing the Sherman Anti-Trust Act, secured an injunction against the leaders of the American Railway Union for restraint of commerce. When the union refused to obey the injunction and order its members back to work, Debs was arrested and federal troops poured in. During the ensuing rioting, seven hundred freight cars were burned, thirteen people died, and fifty-three were seriously wounded. By July 18 the strike had been crushed.

By playing upon a popular identification of strikers with anarchism and violence, crafty corporate leaders like Frick and Pullman persuaded state and federal officials to cripple organized labor's ability to bargain with business. When the Supreme Court (in the 1895 case *In re Debs*) upheld Debs's prison sentence and legalized the use of injunctions against labor unions, the judicial system gave business a potent new weapon with which to restrain labor organizers. Despite successive attempts by the National Labor Union, Knights of Labor, American Federation of Labor, and American Railway Union to build a strong working-class movement, the postwar labor turmoil sapped the vitality of organized labor and gave it a negative public image that it would not shed until the 1930s.

Social Thinkers Probe for Alternatives

The widespread industrial disorder was particularly unsettling when juxtaposed with the growing evidence of working-class destitution. In 1879, after observing three men rummaging through garbage to find food, Walt Whitman wrote: "If the United States, like the countries of the Old World, are also to grow vast crops of poor, desperate, dissatisfied, nomadic, miserably-waged populations, such as we see looming upon us of late years . . . , then our republican experiment, notwithstanding all its surface-successes, is at heart an unhealthy failure."

Whitman's bleak speculations were part of a general public debate over the social meaning of the new industrial order. At stake was a larger issue: should government become the mechanism for helping the poor and regulating big business?

Defenders of capitalism preached the laissez faire ("hands-off") argument, insisting that government should never attempt to control business. They buttressed their case by citing Scottish economist Adam Smith, who had argued in *The Wealth of Nations* (1776) that self-interest acted as an "invisible hand" in the marketplace, automatically regulating the supply of and demand for goods and services. In "The Gospel of Wealth," an influential essay published in 1889, Andrew Carnegie justified laissez faire by applying to human society the evolutionary theories of British scientist Charles Darwin. "The law of competition," Carnegie argued, "may be sometimes hard for the individual, [but] it is best for the race, because it insures the survival of the fittest in every department. We accept and welcome, therefore, . . . the concentration of business . . . in the hands of a few; and the law of competition between these, as being not only beneficial, but essential to the future progress of the race." Ignoring the scramble among businesses in the late nineteenth century to *eliminate* competition, Carnegie praised an unregulated competitive environment as a source of positive long-term social benefits.

Tough-minded Yale professor William Graham Sumner shared Carnegie's disapproval of governmental interference. In his combative book *What Social Classes Owe to Each Other* (1883) and a series of essays, Sumner asserted that inexorable natural laws controlled the social order: "A drunkard in the gutter is just where he ought to be. . . . The law of survival of the fittest was not made by man, and it cannot be abrogated by man. We can only, by interfering with it, produce the survival of the unfittest." The social theorists, sentimental humanitarians, and "labor fakers" intent on uplifting the poor and needy, he insisted, were actually harming the "forgotten man"—the hardworking individual whose taxes were expected to fund their do-good schemes. The state, declared Sumner, owed its citizens nothing but law, order, and basic political rights.

This conservative, laissez faire brand of Social Darwinism (as such ideas came to be called) did not go unchallenged. In *Dynamic Sociology* (1883), Lester Frank Ward, a geologist with the U.S. Geological Survey, argued that contrary to Sumner's claim, the supposed "laws" of nature *could* be circumvented by human will. Just as scientists had applied their knowledge to breeding superior livestock, government experts could use the power of the state to regulate big business, protect society's weaker members, and prevent the heedless exploitation of natural resources.

Henry George, a self-taught San Francisco newspaper editor and economic theorist, proposed to solve the nation's uneven distribution of wealth through what he called the single tax. In *Progress and Poverty* (1879), he noted that speculators reaped huge profits from the rising price of land that they neither developed nor improved. By taxing this "unearned increment," the government could obtain the funds necessary to ameliorate the misery and distress caused by industrialization. The result would bring the benefits of socialism—a state-controlled economic system that distributed resources according to need—without socialism's

great disadvantage, the stifling of individual initiative. George's program was so popular that he lectured widely around the country and only narrowly missed being elected mayor of New York in 1886.

The vision of a harmonious industrialized society evoked by labor leaders like William H. Sylvis and Terence V. Powderly was even more vividly expressed in the utopian novel *Looking Backward* (1888) by Massachusetts newspaper editor Edward Bellamy. Cast as a fantastic glimpse into the future, Bellamy's novel tells of Julian West, who falls asleep in the year 1888 and awakens in the year 2000 to find a nation without poverty or strife. In this future world, West learns, a completely centralized, state-run economy and a new religion of solidarity have combined to create a society in which everyone works for the common welfare. "Let but the famine-stricken nation . . . regulate for the common good the course of the life-giving stream," declares West, "and the earth would bloom like one garden, and none of its children lack any good thing." Bellamy's vision of a conflict-free society where all shared equally in industrialization's benefits so inspired middle-class Americans fearful of corporate power and working-class violence that nearly five hundred local Bellamyite organizations, called Nationalist clubs, sprang up to try to turn his dream into reality.

Ward, George, and Bellamy did not deny the benefits of the existing industrial order; they simply sought to humanize it. These utopian reformers envisioned a harmonious society whose members all worked together. Marxist socialists advanced a different view. Elaborated by German philosopher and radical agitator Karl Marx (1818–1883) in *Das Kapital* (1867) and other works, Marxism rested on the proposition (which Adam Smith had also accepted) that the labor required to produce a commodity was the only true measure of that commodity's value. Thus any profit made by the capitalist employer was "surplus value" appropriated from the exploited workers. As competition among capitalists increased, Marx predicted, wages would decline to starvation levels, and more and more capitalists would be driven out of business. At last society would be divided between a shrinking bourgeoisie (capitalists, merchants, and middle-class professionals) and an impoverished proletariat (the workers). At this point the proletariat would revolt and seize control of the state and of the means of production and distribution. While Marx's thought was dominated by an insistence on class struggle as the essence of modern history, his eyes were also fixed on the shining vision of the communist millennium that the revolution would eventually usher in—a classless utopia in which the state would "wither away" and all exploitation would cease. To lead the working class in its coming showdown with capitalism, Marx and his collaborator Friedrich Engels helped found a series of socialist parties in Europe, whose strength grew steadily beginning in the 1870s.

Despite Marx's keen interest in the United States, Marxism proved to have little appeal in late-nineteenth-century America outside a tiny group of primarily German-born immigrants. The Marxist-oriented Socialist Labor party (1877) had attracted only about fifteen hundred members by 1890. More alarming to the public at large was the handful of anarchists, again mostly immigrants, who rejected Marxist discipline and preached the destruction of capitalism, the violent overthrow of the state, and the immediate introduction of a stateless utopia. In 1894 Alexander Berkman, a Russian immigrant anarchist, attempted to assassinate Henry Clay Frick, the manager of Andrew Carnegie's Homestead Steel Works. Entering Frick's office with a pistol, Berkman shot him in the neck and then tried to stab him. But a carpenter by chance working in Frick's office overpowered him. Rather than igniting a workers' insurrection that would usher in a new social order, as he had hoped, Berkman's act simply earned him a long prison sentence and confirmed the middle-class stereotype of "labor agitators" as lawless and violent.

Conclusion

In the early years of the Republic, Thomas Jefferson had warned of the dangerous effects that industrialization could have on American virtue and democracy. At the same time, Jefferson's noted rival Alexander Hamilton had worked diligently to promote industrialization as essential to national prosperity and greatness. By 1900, with industrialization an omnipresent fact of life, Americans realized that both men had been right. As Hamilton had foreseen, industrialization had propelled the United States into the forefront of the world's major powers, lowered the cost of goods through mass production, generated many thousands of jobs, and made available a wide range of new consumer products. Few Americans would readily have given up their new material benefits.

Despite these advantages, all thinking persons recognized, as Jefferson had warned long before, that industrialization's cost was high. The rise of the giant corporations had been achieved through savage competition, exploited workers, shady business practices, and the collapse of an older economic order built on craft skills and a traditional apprenticeship system that had forged bonds between skilled and unskilled labor. Periodic outbursts of ugly labor violence, and the less dramatic but even more ominous phenomenon of urban slums and grinding poverty, offered stark evidence that all was not well in industrial America.

To improve their reputations, the great capitalists channeled at least a part of their fortunes into ostentatious public benefactions, including art museums, university endowments, and symphony orchestras. In contrast to Europe, where fortune remained within the family, some U.S. millionaires developed a lively tradition of private philanthropy.

Nevertheless, Americans remained profoundly ambivalent about the new industrial order. Caught between their desire for the higher standard of living that industrialization made possible and their fears of capitalist power and social chaos, Americans of the 1880s and 1890s sought strategies that would preserve those benefits while alleviating the undesirable social by-products. Efforts to regulate railroads at the state level, and such national measures as the Interstate Commerce Act and the Sherman Anti-Trust Act, as well as the fervor with which the ideas of a utopian theorist like Edward Bellamy were embraced, represented early manifestations of this impulse. In the Progressive Era of the early twentieth century (see Chapter 21), Americans would redouble their efforts to formulate political and social responses to the economic changes that had transformed the nation after the Civil War.

CHRONOLOGY

1837 Magnetic telegraph invented.

1859 First oil well drilled in Titusville, Pennsylvania.

1866 National Labor Union founded.

1869 First transcontinental railroad completed.
Knights of Labor organized.

1870 Standard Oil Company established.

1873 Panic of 1873 triggers a depression lasting until 1879.

1876 Alexander Graham Bell invents and patents the telephone.

Thomas A. Edison opens research laboratory at Menlo Park, New Jersey.

1877 Edison invents the phonograph.
Railway workers stage the first nationwide strike.

1879 Henry George, *Progress and Poverty*.
Edison perfects the incandescent lamp.

1881 Standard Oil Trust established.

1882 Edison opens the first electric power station on Pearl Street in New York City.
Chinese Exclusion Act.

1883 Railroads divide the country into time zones.
William Graham Sumner, *What Social Classes Owe to Each Other*.
Lester Frank Ward, *Dynamic Sociology*.

1886 American Federation of Labor (AFL) formed.
Police and demonstrators clash at Haymarket Square in Chicago.

1887 Interstate Commerce Act.

1888 Edward Bellamy, *Looking Backward*.

1889 Andrew Carnegie, "The Gospel of Wealth."

1890 Sherman Anti-Trust Act.

1892 Standard Oil of New Jersey and General Electric formed.
Steelworkers strike at Homestead, Pennsylvania.
World's Columbian Exposition opens in Chicago.
Miners strike at Coeur d'Alene, Idaho.

1893 Panic of 1893 triggers a depression lasting until 1897.

1894 Pullman Palace Car workers strike, supported by the National Railway Union.

1901 J. Pierpont Morgan organizes United States Steel.

For Further Reading

David Brody, *Steelworkers in America: The Nonunion Era* (1960). A perceptive analysis of the steelworkers' world.

Alfred D. Chandler, Jr., *The Visible Hand: The Managerial Revolution in American Business* (1977). A pathbreaking account of the innovative managerial changes in large-scale corporate enterprise.

Herbert G. Gutman, *Work, Culture, and Society in Industrializing America* (1976). Pioneering essays on the ways in which industrialization transformed the values and culture of working-class Americans.

David A. Hounshell, *From the American System to Mass Production, 1800–1932: The Development of Manufacturing Technology in the United States* (1984). A lively analysis of the evolution of mass-production techniques in the sewing-machine, agricultural-implement, and bicycle industries.

Alice Kessler-Harris, *Out to Work: A History of Wage-Earning Women in the United States* (1982). An important survey of women's entry into the paid labor force and its impact on family roles, cultural attitudes, and class distinctions.

Harold C. Livesay, *Andrew Carnegie and the Rise of Big Business* (1975). A sprightly brief biography of the country's most controversial industrialist.

David Montgomery, *The Fall of the House of Labor: The Workplace, the State, and American Labor Activism, 1865–1925* (1987). An insightful analysis of the transformation of industrial production and its impact on labor.

Daniel T. Rodgers, *The Work Ethic in Industrial America, 1850–1920* (1974). A thoughtful survey of meanings and values popularly associated with work.

Stephen J. Ross, *Workers on the Edge: Work, Leisure, and Politics in Industrializing Cincinnati, 1788–1890* (1985). An important community study of the changing world of work and its impact on politics.

Alan Trachtenberg, *The Incorporation of America: Culture and Society in the Gilded Age* (1982). A lively overview of post–Civil War social development.

Additional Bibliography

The Economy and Industrial Growth

Daniel Boorstin, *The Americans: The Democratic Experience* (1973); Robert W. Bruce, *Alexander Graham Bell and the Conquest of Solitude* (1973); David F. Burg, *Chicago's White City of 1893* (1976); Alfred D. Chandler, Jr., *Managerial Hierarchies: Comparative Perspectives on the Rise of the Modern Industrial Empire* (1980); George H. Daniels, *Science and Society in America* (1971); Carl Degler, *The Age of Economic Revolution* (1977); Samuel P. Hays, *The Response to Industrialism, 1885–1914* (1957); Robert L. Heilbroner, *The Economic Transformation of America* (1977); Ari Hoogenboom and Olive Hoogenboom, *A History of the ICC: From Panacea to Palliative* (1976); Thomas P. Hughes, *Networks of Power: Electrification in Western Society, 1880–1930* (1983); Maury Klein, *The Life and Legend of Jay Gould* (1986); Naomi R. Lamoreaux, *The Great Merger Movement in American Business, 1895–1904* (1985); David S. Landes, *The Unbound Prometheus: Technological Change and Industrial Development* (1969); Harold Livesay, *American Made: Men Who Shaped the American Economy* (1979); Allan Nevins, *Study in Power: John D. Rockefeller, Industrialist and Philanthropist* (2 vols., 1953); David F. Noble, *America by Design: Science, Technology, and the Rise of Corporate Capitalism* (1977); Jonathan Prude, *The Coming of Industrial Order: Town and Factory Life in Rural Massachusetts, 1810–1860* (1983); Leonard S. Reich, *The Making of American Industrial Research: Science and Business at GE and Bell, 1876–1926* (1985); Wyn Wachhorst, *Thomas Alva Edison: An American Myth* (1981); David O. Whitten, *The Emergence of Giant Enterprise, 1860–1914* (1983).

The New South

Wilbur J. Cash, *The Mind of the South* (1941); Paul M. Gaston, *The New South Creed: A Study in Southern Mythmaking* (1970); Steven Hahn and Jonathan Prude, eds., *The Countryside in the Age of Capitalist Transformation: Essays in the Social History of Rural America* (1985); Jacquelyn D. Hall et al., *Like a Family: The Making of a Southern Cotton Mill World* (1987); Robert Higgs, *Competition and Coercion: Blacks in the American Economy, 1865–1904* (1977); Melton A. McLaurin, *Paternalism and Protest: Southern Cotton Mill Workers and Organized Labor* (1971); Jay R. Mandle, *The Roots of Black Poverty: The Southern Plantation Economy After the Civil War* (1978); Howard N. Rabinowitz, *Race Relations in the Urban South* (1978); Roger L. Ransom and Richard Sutch, *One Kind of Freedom: The Economic Consequences of Emancipation* (1977); Peter Wallenstein, *From Slave South to New South: Public Policy in Nineteenth-Century Georgia* (1987); Jonathan M. Wiener, *Social Origins of the New South: Alabama, 1860–1885* (1978); C. Vann Woodward, *Origins of the New South, 1877–1913* (1951) and *The Strange Career of Jim Crow* (1966); Gavin Wright, *Old South, New South: Revolutions in the Southern Economy Since the Civil War* (1986).

Industrial Work and the Work Force

John Bodnar, *Immigration and Industrialization: Ethnicity in an American Mill Town* (1977); Milton Cantor and Bruce Laurie, eds., *Class, Sex, and the Woman Worker* (1977); John T. Cumbler, *Working-Class Community in Industrial America* (1979); Melvyn Dubofsky, *Industrialization and the American Worker* (1975); Melvin Dubofsky and Warren Van Tine, eds., *Labor Leaders in America* (1987); Leon Fink, *Workingmen's Democracy: The Knights of Labor and American Politics* (1983); David M. Gordon, Richard Edwards, and Michael Reich, *Segmented Work, Divided Workers: The Historical Transformation of Labor in the United States* (1982); Susan E. Kennedy, *If All We Did Was to Weep at Home: A History of White Working-Class Women in America* (1979); Daniel Nelson, *Managers and Workers: Origins of the New Factory System in the United States, 1850–1920* (1975); Peter R. Shergold, *Working Class Life* (1982); Stephan Thernstrom, *Poverty and Progress: Social Mobility in the Nineteenth Century City* (1964) and *The Other Bostonians: Poverty and Progress in the American Metropolis, 1880–1970* (1973).

Industrial Conflict

Paul Avrich, *The Haymarket Tragedy* (1984); Robert C. Bannister, *Social Darwinism: Science and Myth in Anglo-American Social Thought* (1979); Jeremy Brecher, *Strike!* (1977); Stanley Bruder, *Pullman* (1967); Mari Jo Buhle, *Women and American Socialism, 1870–1920* (1983); William M. Dick, *Labor and Socialism in America: The Gompers Era* (1972); Leon Fink, *Workingmen's Democracy: The Knights of Labor and American Politics* (1983); Gerald Grob, *Workers and Utopia: A Study of Ideological Conflict in the American Labor Movement, 1865–1900* (1961); Stuart B. Kaufman, *Samuel Gompers and the Origins of the American Federation of Labor* (1973); J. H. M. Laslett, *Labor and the Left: A Study of Socialist and Radical Influence in the American Labor Movement* (1970); Margaret M. Marsh, *Anarchist Women: 1870–1920* (1981); Henry F. May, *Protestant Churches and Industrial America* (1949); David Montgomery, *Workers' Control in America: Studies in the History of Work, Technology, and Labor Struggles* (1979); Nick Salvatore, *Eugene V. Debs, Citizen and Socialist* (1982); John L. Thomas, *Alternative America: Henry George, Edward Bellamy, Henry Demarest Lloyd, and the Adversary Tradition* (1983); Daniel J. Walkowitz, *Worker City, Company Town: Iron and Cotton Workers Protest in Troy and Cohoes, New York, 1855–1884* (1978); Norman J. Ware, *The Labor Movement in the United States, 1860–1895: A Study in Democracy* (1964); Leon Wolff, *Lockout: The Story of the Homestead Strike of 1892* (1965).

CHAPTER 18

The Transformation
of Urban America

Incensed by the appalling crowding in New York City tenement housing in 1890, newspaper reporter Jacob Riis exploded in anger. He had toured congested inner-city apartments, poking into attics and cellars where families were jammed together so tightly that their members had to sleep in shifts. Riis published his findings, documented with photographs and statistics, in a dramatic exposé entitled *How the Other Half Lives* (1890).

With a sure eye for the distressing detail, he guided the reader into a typical Cherry Street tenement. "Be a little careful, please!" he warned. "The hall is dark and you might stumble over the children pitching pennies back there. Not that it would hurt them; kicks and cuffs are their daily diet. They have little else. Here where the hall turns and dives into utter darkness is a step, and another, another. . . . Here is a door. Listen! That short hacking cough, that tiny, helpless wail—what do they mean? They mean that the soiled bow of white you saw on the door downstairs will have another story to tell— Oh! a sadly familiar story—before the day is at an end. The child is dying of measles. With half a chance it might have lived; but it had none. That dark bedroom killed it."

To Riis, such tenements were significant not only as the homes of the immigrant poor and destitute but also as the incubators of disease and vice. With three of its wards packing in more than 285,000 people per square mile on average, New York City in 1890 epitomized for Riis the depths to which conditions in urban America had sunk. "In the tenements all the influences make for evil," he warned, "because they are the hotbeds of the epidemics that carry death to rich and poor alike [and] the nurseries of pauperism and crime that fill our jails and police courts."

Riis's grim view of tenement life, which reflected his secure middle-class position, stood in marked contrast to many immigrants' remembrances of the tenement districts' vibrant street life, resonating with the melodies of organ grinders and the cries of peddlers, baked-potato and hot-corn vendors, and soda dispensers. Although the tenements were crowded, immigrants often congregated elbow-to-elbow in the hallways; left apartment doors open to invite visitors; and joked, sang, and played music to re-create the village intimacy remembered from their homelands. "How the people did enjoy that music," reminisced one East Sider from New York. "Everyone would be at their windows listening. . . . Then the people would clap their hands; it was inspiring in a neighborhood like that."

Their perspectives differed markedly, but Riis and the East Sider each recalled an era of bounding population growth that had transformed New York and other American cities in the late nineteenth century. Not only on the East Coast but south to New Orleans and west to San Francisco, cities had swelled at an astonishing pace. Between 1870 and 1900, New Orleans's population nearly doubled, Buffalo's tripled, and Chicago's increased more than fivefold. By the turn of the century, Philadelphia, New York, and Chicago had each passed the 1-million-person mark, and 40 percent of all Americans lived in cities. In 1900 New York's

3.4 million inhabitants alone almost exactly equaled the nation's entire urban population in 1850.

The spectacular urban growth, fueled by migration from the New England countryside and an influx of nearly 11 million foreign immigrants between 1870 and 1900, created a dynamic new environment for economic development. Lured by the expectation of bountiful jobs, these new arrivals on the urban scene provided an inexpensive work force for countless small businesses and industries. Mushrooming cities thus made possible an unparalleled concentration of resources and markets that in turn dramatically stimulated national economic expansion. Like the frontier, the city symbolized opportunity for all comers.

Yet the city's unprecedented scale and diversity threatened traditional American expectations about community life and social stability. Rural America had been a place of face-to-face personal relations, a clearly recognized social hierarchy, and a homogeneous population sharing the same likes and dislikes. In contrast, the city was a seething cauldron where a medley of immigrant groups contended with each other and with native-born Americans for jobs, power, and influence. Moreover, the same rapid growth that energized manufacturing and production strained city services, generating terrible housing and sanitation problems.

Native-born American city dwellers found the noise, stench, and congestion of this transformed landscape disturbing. Like Jacob Riis, they worried about the newcomers' squalid tenements, fondness for drink, and strange social customs. Thus when native-born reformers set about cleaning up the city and "Americanizing" the foreigners, they sought not only to improve the physical environment but also to destroy the distinctive habits and customs that made immigrant culture different from their own. Resenting the attack on their way of life, the recent arrivals fought back to protect their traditions and practices.

Still, despite deep conflict and controversy in these years, immigrant and native-born urbanites alike could boast about the city's rich economic, cultural, and social opportunities and claim, arguably, that the city had replaced the countryside as the center of American life. The late nineteenth century witnessed an intense struggle among these diverse urban constituencies to control the city politically and benefit from its economic and cultural potential. The stakes were high, for America was increasingly becoming an urban nation.

Urban Expansion

Between 1840 and 1900, the physical appearance of American cities was transformed. Responding to a critical need for housing and offices, land speculators, developers, and builders broke up urban space into residential neighborhoods, parks, downtown business districts, and commercial and manufacturing areas. Opportunistic business leaders built new transportation systems that moved thousands of urban commuters from home to work and back again by means of streetcars, trains, and eventually electric trolleys and subway cars. Working feverishly to keep pace with the demand for new housing, local carpenters and construction companies expanded the cities' boundaries by developing new suburban communities along railroad lines in the countryside, where land was less expensive and residents could enjoy a more pleasant environment than the bustling downtown afforded.

The New Urban World

The rapid growth of cities large and small after the Civil War created a national urban network—an interconnected web of regional metropolises, specialized manufacturing cities, and smaller subordinate communities of varying size and function. Linked by rail lines and waterways, major cities like Boston, New York, and Philadelphia on the East Coast and Chicago in the Midwest became regional centers that provided banking and financial services for surrounding towns and villages. Smaller cities often specialized in particular products or processes: for example, Holyoke, Massa-

Contrasting Views of Poverty

In the post–Civil War years, Americans tended to see urban poverty as a breeding ground for sin and crime while idealizing rural poverty. Jacob Riis's 1888 photograph Bandit's Roost *(left), suggests the wickedness lurking just below the surface of life in New York City's grim slum districts. Contrast this gritty scene with* Interior of an Adirondack Shanty *(c. 1880) by George B. Wood, Jr., which portrays the humble country life as the builder of strength and character.*

chusetts, in paper; Birmingham, Alabama, in steel; Minneapolis, Minnesota, in milling and lumber; Butte, Montana, in mining; Corning, New York, in glass; and Kansas City, Missouri, in the processing and shipment of beef.

Whatever the source of their growth, hundreds of cities expanded so briskly in the post–Civil War years that the nature of urban life was forever changed. In contrast to rural and small-town America, where the seasonality of agriculture dictated the rhythms of daily existence, cities pulsed with people rushing to meet schedules and beat deadlines. Moreover, whereas small-town residents knew their neighbors on a lifelong basis, shared their beliefs and traditions, and worshiped in the same local church, city dwellers lived in a world of strangers and at every turn confronted ethnic and class differences. Even the concept of time took on a new meaning in the city. Rural dwellers went to bed early, but urbanites walked about, played, and shopped late into the night. One social worker wrote, "Every night the brightly lighted main thoroughfares, with the gleaming store-windows and their lines of trucks in the gutters, provide a promenade for thousands who find in walk and

talk along the pavement a cheap form of social entertainment."

A Revolution in Transportation

Until the first quarter of the nineteenth century, most cities functioned as compact, densely settled communities covering perhaps a three-square-mile area. Within these "walking" cities, so called because a person could walk from one end to the other in an hour or two, rich and poor lived in close proximity, with the wealthy near the commercial center and the poor scattered in basements around town. The expansion of transportation systems, beginning in the 1830s with the stagecoach and continuing with the steam ferry and the horse-drawn streetcar, turned these older cities literally inside out. The rich and wellborn moved to the city's edge, while the poor migrated inward, settling in abandoned mansions and town houses that were subdivided and then subdivided again to accommodate their increasing numbers.

The first urban transportation networks, operating regularly scheduled omnibuses over fixed routes, appeared in New York, Boston, and Philadelphia in the 1830s. These uncomfortable horse-drawn coaches, which bounced along cobblestone-paved and deeply rutted city roads, were replaced in the next two decades with smoother-riding horse-drawn streetcars. Pulled by a single powerful horse along railway tracks in the streets, these "horse-cars" could carry thirty to forty passengers at a time. By the 1880s, 415 horsecar companies carried 188 million passengers a year over more than six thousand miles of track. The horsecars provided easy transportation between city dwellers' places of work and their residences, which increasingly were separated.

The horsecars were not without their drawbacks. Extra animals were sometimes needed to pull the cars up hills, and the hitching and unhitching process could take ten minutes. Observers recoiled as they watched panting horses, whipped by drivers eager to stay on schedule, strain to pull the crowded cars. Many looked away in disgust as creatures that had stumbled and fallen were destroyed where they lay. In New York alone, an estimated fifteen thousand overworked beasts died each year in the 1880s.

Horse droppings were another problem. Health officials in Rochester, New York, estimated in 1900 that the excrement produced yearly by the city's fifteen thousand horses would fill a hole one acre in circumference and 175 feet deep and would breed 16 billion flies. Added to the mud and garbage that befouled city streets, the stinking heaps of dung moved officials to explore alternate transportation options.

Steam railroads were an obvious first choice. As early as 1849, fifty-nine commuter trains were chugging into Boston daily from as far as fifteen miles away. But while steam engines could do the work of a hundred horses, they were designed for long hauls rather than short runs, and they functioned most efficiently when they pulled a large number of cars. To improve travel within the city, local officials explored more flexible alternatives that included cable cars and electric streetcars.

Chicago pioneered the most extensive cable-car system. Run by a circulating underground cable to which a conductor attached each vehicle, Chicago's cable cars by 1887 operated over more than eighty-six miles of track. More sanitary, better on hills, and quieter than the horsecars and the steam railways, cable cars marked a significant improve-

Los Angeles Cable Cars, 1889

Cable cars were quieter, cleaner, better ventilated, and less smelly than horsecars. As one customer commented, "On every warm summer evening the open cars are crowded with people riding solely to enjoy the cool and refreshing breeze."

ment in urban transportation. But high construction costs restricted cable operation to the most heavily traveled routes, and eventually cable cars proved profitable only in hilly cities. San Francisco's cable cars, now mainly a tourist attraction, provide a colorful reminder of a vanished era in urban transit.

By the 1890s electric streetcars, called trolleys because of the four-wheeled spring mechanism that trolled along the overhead wires, had replaced horsecars and cable cars in most cities. First installed in Richmond, Virginia, and Montgomery, Alabama, electric streetcar systems shaped the urban environment in important ways. Unlike European transportation companies, which charged according to the distance traveled, American streetcar firms adopted a flat-fee policy, usually five cents per ride with free transfers. By subsidizing commuting with a uniform-fare system, streetcar companies enabled families to move farther and farther from the city's center without increasing their transportation expenses, thereby encouraging urban sprawl. Recognizing that streetcar lines required a certain density of population to be profitable, and that the expansion of the lines would substantially raise land values, most streetcar companies ran their transportation operations at a loss, purchased land at the city's periphery, and earned towering profits from the sale of real estate. When the suburban lands became fully settled, however, many of these streetcar companies went broke.

Streetcar lines, which radiated outward from the heart of the city like spokes on a wheel, also helped revitalize the city center. With crosstown routes so limited, commuters who wished to visit a different part of the city had to pass through the downtown. The practical effect of this arrangement was to improve commercial opportunities in the central business district. In 1874 Philadelphia merchant John Wanamaker, recognizing the potential created by the growing streetcar network, turned an old downtown railroad freight depot into an elaborate department store. Wanamaker's success in Philadelphia was duplicated by Morris Rich in Atlanta, Adam Gimbel and Rowland H. Macy in New York, Marshall Field in Chicago, and Joseph L. Hudson in Detroit. The inexpensive convenience of traveling by trolley made shopping downtown a new form of recreation for millions of Americans after the Civil War.

A Mobile Population

The expansion of streetcar systems, coupled with the completion of regional railroad networks, dramatically affected urban residential stability. Historians have long recognized that the immigrants and transplanted farm people who flooded into American cities in the late nineteenth century tended to move frequently. Only recently has it been discovered that the old elites in most of these cities were highly transient as well. Indeed, a fever to move seized much of the population in these years.

The reasons for the frenzy of mobility were many. As city neighborhoods became crowded with people and congested with traffic, those with the means to do so headed for newer outlying residential areas, now conveniently accessible by streetcar, to gain open space and fresh air. Others pulled up

stakes in quest of the fashionable homes available on the city's periphery. Still others relocated because one could own a larger house for a lower cost in the new areas.

Omaha, Nebraska, typified many cities around the nation in the dizzying pace of its population's mobility. In the two decades before 1900, fewer than one-third of all Omaha residents lived in the same place for more than five years. In 1888 only 12.2 percent resided at the same address as they had in 1880. As the city's business district spread, rich and poor alike shifted residences rapidly.

A parallel movement *between* cities matched the frenetic residential shifts *within* cities. Both upper- and working-class urban families drifted from city to city in hopes of increasing their income or bettering their living conditions. Most cities, while growing in overall numbers because of the inpouring of newcomers, lost more than half their current inhabitants every decade. The actual population turnover was even greater, because many residents remained in town only a few months or a year or two and therefore never even showed up in decade-by-decade reports. Historical demographers calculate that most U.S. cities in this period experienced an astonishing turnover of about three or four times their total population every ten years.

Contemporaries like Jacob Riis deplored the unprecedented rapidity and scale of residential change. Riis viewed the migration of the middle and upper classes to the suburban fringe, away from downtown congestion, as a selfish attempt to escape responsibility for improving inner-city neighborhoods. An immigrant himself, Riis complained that the privileged classes were deserting the poor. In a sense, he was correct. Although many well-to-do city dwellers were concerned about the destitute, they placed the happiness, health, and safety of their own families first. They did not hesitate to move to neighborhoods with better housing and the promise of an improved quality of life.

Thus mobility and change were the norm in nineteenth-century urban society. New transportation systems facilitated considerable residential movement. Searching for new paths to comfort and success, both rich and poor freely changed residences and jobs. Just as the frontier West lured seekers of fresh beginnings and extravagant wealth, the city beckoned to the restless and ambitious with myriad exciting opportunities for advancement.

Migrants and Immigrants

The growing concentration of industries in urban settings produced demands for thousands of new workers in these years. The promise of good wages and a broad range of paid work drew many rural and small-town dwellers to the cities. So great was the migration from rural areas, especially New England, that some farm communities vanished from the map.

Young farm women led the exodus cityward. With the growing commercialization and specialization of farming in the late nineteenth century, farm work was increasingly male work. At the same time, rising sales of factory-produced goods through mail-order catalogs serving the countryside reduced rural needs for women's labor on subsistence tasks. So young farm women flocked to the cities, where they competed for jobs with immigrant, black, and native-born white women.

From 1860 to 1890, the prospect of a better life also attracted nearly 10 million northern European immigrants to East Coast and midwestern cities, where they joined the more than 4 million who had settled there in the 1840s and 1850s. Germans made up the largest group, numbering close to 3 million. Behind them nearly 2 million English, Scottish, and Welsh immigrants and almost 1.5 million Irish came in search of new jobs and new opportunities. Moreover, by 1900 more than 800,000 French-Canadians had migrated south to work in the New England mills, and close to a million Scandinavian newcomers were putting down roots in the rich farmlands of Wisconsin and Minnesota.

In the 1890s these recent arrivals from northern and western Europe, the "old immigrants," were joined by swelling numbers of "new immigrants." These comprised Italians, Slavs, Greeks, and Jews from southern and eastern Europe, as well as Armenians from the Middle East. In the next three decades, these new immigrants, often from peasant backgrounds, would boost America's foreign-born population by more than 18 million.

Whether old immigrants or new, the surge of foreigners owed much to improvements in steam-

Between 1865 and 1895, the majority of newcomers to America hailed from northern and western Europe. But the early twentieth century witnessed a surge of immigration from southern and eastern Europe.

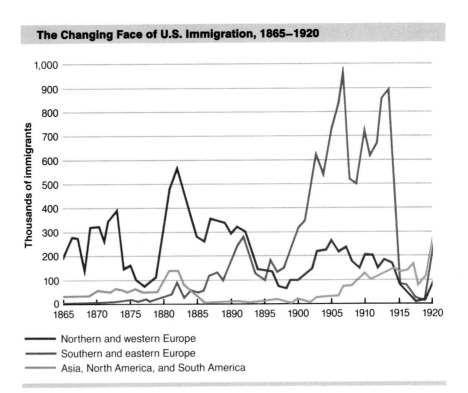

The Changing Face of U.S. Immigration, 1865–1920

Thousands of immigrants

——— Northern and western Europe
——— Southern and eastern Europe
——— Asia, North America, and South America

powered vessels. After the Civil War, the introduction of large, safe, swift, oceangoing steamships had not only reduced the time required for the Atlantic voyage from three months to two or three weeks but also spawned a free-for-all among competing lines that significantly drove down rates for ocean passage.

The overwhelming majority of both old and new immigrants settled in cities in the northeastern and north-central states. Fired up by the extravagant claims of the steamship lines, state immigrant bureaus, and railroad agencies, and by exuberant letters from countrymen who had emigrated earlier, the new Americans came in search of work and fresh beginnings. The impact of their numbers was staggering. In 1890 New York City (including Brooklyn, still a legally separate municipality) contained twice as many Irish as Dublin, as many Germans as Hamburg, half as many Italians as Naples, and 2½ times the Jewish population of Warsaw. That same year four out of five people living in greater New York had been born abroad or were children of foreign parents.

Many of these recent immigrants had come voluntarily, in pursuit of economic betterment. Others were forced out of their home countries by overpopulation, crop failure, famine, or industrial depression. Emigration from England, for example, spurted during downswings in the British economy in 1873 and 1883. On the Continent German peasants and artisans, squeezed by overpopulation and threatened by church reorganizations that they opposed, left in large numbers in the 1880s. In Norway severe job shortages coupled with a depression in agriculture and shipping drove out more than 260,000 people between 1879 and 1893.

Some ambitious individuals, including many single young men, immigrated in the belief that their opportunities for education would be better in the United States than in their homeland. Birger Osland, an eighteen-year-old Norwegian, explained his reasons for leaving to a friend: "My father is a schoolteacher and has, besides me, two younger sons, so that it often strains his resources to keep us in school here. . . . Besides . . . as I now probably have a foundation upon which I can build my own further education, I have come to feel that the most sensible thing I can do is to emigrate to America."

Women were less likely than men to come on their own. Wives and children often waited until the family breadwinner had secured a job and saved enough money to pay for their passage.

Would-be immigrants first had to travel to a European port city—Hamburg was a major port of embarkation—where they booked passage on a steamship. The cramped, often stormy Atlantic journey featured poor food, little privacy, and rudimentary sanitary facilities. Immigrants arrived tired, fearful, and in some cases very sick.

Further complications awaited the travelers upon reaching their destination, usually New York City. Before customs officials allowed them to enter the country, they inspected the newcomers for physical handicaps and contagious diseases. Those with "loathsome" infections such as leprosy, trachoma (a contagious viral disease of the eye), or venereal disease were refused admittance and deported. Immigrants who passed the physical examination then had their names recorded. If a customs inspector had difficulty pronouncing a foreign name, he often Anglicized it. One German Jew became flustered when asked for his name and mumbled "Schoyn vergessen [I forget]." The inspector, who did not understand Yiddish, wrote "Sean Ferguson" on the man's roster. In this manner, numerous immigrants ended up with "Americanized" names.

New York City established a special facility for admitting immigrants in 1855 at Castle Garden and in 1892 expanded it on Ellis Island. Here America's newest residents exchanged foreign currency for U.S. dollars, purchased railroad tickets, and arranged lodgings. In other cities immigrants were hounded by tavernkeepers, peddlers, and porters who tried to exploit their ignorance of the English language and American ways. "When you land in America," wrote one Swedish resident to friends back home, "you will find many who will offer their services, but beware of them because there are so many rascals who make it their business to cheat the immigrants."

Those who arrived with sufficient cash, including many German artisans and Scandinavian farmers, commonly traveled west to Chicago, Milwaukee, and the rolling prairies beyond. But most of the Irish, and later the Italians, who hailed largely from poor peasant backgrounds and were limited

Jakob Mithelstadt and Family, 1905

The Mithelstadts were Russian Germans who arrived in New York City on the S.S. Pretoria. The poorest immigrants traveled in steerage, below-deck cargo areas that lacked portholes and originally housed the cables to the ship's rudder.

by their meager resources, remained in eastern cities like Boston, New York, and Philadelphia, where they took the lowest-paying jobs. Those Irish and Italians who did go west typically made the trip in stages, moving from job to job on the railroad and canal systems.

Adjusting to an Urban Society

For many immigrants, the stresses of adjusting to the strangeness of urban life in a new society were eased by the fact that they could settle among compatriots who had preceded them. If a map of New York City's streets and neighborhoods were colored in by nationality, Jacob Riis observed in 1890, it "would show more stripes than on the skin of a zebra, and more colors than any rainbow." The streets of Manhattan between the West Side Irish neighborhoods and the East Side German neighborhoods teemed with tenements housing Poles, Hungarians, Russians, and Italians.

Late-nineteenth-century social commentators often assumed that each nationality group clumped together for reasons of national clannishness or the convenience of living among others who spoke the same language. But in fact, the process was far more subtle and complex. Most immigrants preferred to live near others not merely of their own nationality but from their own village or region in the old country. On New York's Lower East Side, for example, Italians did not form a single "Little Italy" but rather divided into many different subgroups: Neapolitans and Calabrians at Mulberry Bend, Genoese on Baxter Street, northern Italians west of Broadway, and Tyrolese Italians on Sixty-ninth Street near the Hudson River.

Within these ethnic neighborhoods, immigrants suffered incredibly crowded conditions. The congestion was worst in New York City, where, with real estate at a premium, landlords built four- and five-story buildings with few windows on lots only twenty-five feet wide. As early as 1853, the five-story Gotham Court tenement housed five hundred people. A decade later, when the owner added limited plumbing, the number of occupants jumped to eight hundred.

In 1879 upper-class New York reformers, concerned about the lack of light and fresh air in the tenements, secured passage of a law that forced landlords to construct buildings with central ten-foot by four-foot air shafts. Dubbed "dumbbell tenements" because of their shape, the new buildings squeezed stairs, halls, and common bathrooms into their narrowed central sections and represented only a slight improvement over their predecessors. By the 1890s a single New York City block typically contained ten dumbbell tenements with between two thousand and four thousand immigrant residents. Although overcrowding was worst in Manhattan, cramped, low-grade housing also characterized immigrant districts in Boston, Philadelphia, San Francisco, and other cities. In 1902 investigators in Buffalo, New York, found sixty Polish immigrants—men, women, and children—living in a single small row house. Mattresses were piled up in the daytime and at night spread out over every available inch.

For all the adversity, many immigrant families enjoyed satisfying and richly textured everyday lives. Ironically, crowded conditions fostered this richness. Within the tight ethnic neighborhoods of major U.S. cities, immigrants could speak their native language, purchase traditional foods, attend old-world church services, and celebrate the festivals that they had known in Europe. Despite the attempts of well-intentioned reformers to change their habits and behaviors, countless new Americans preserved their native language, dishes, and customs.

Other recent arrivals, however, eagerly learned English and shed the old ways, in hopes of blending quickly into the American mainstream. And indeed, for many immigrants and especially their children and grandchildren, the dream of upward mobility did become a reality. But cultural threats and sources of family conflict lurked in the larger urban world outside the familiar immigrant enclaves. Older immigrant women, confined to their tenement flats and immediate neighborhoods, often clung to traditional ways longer than did their husbands, sons, and daughters, whose work and social activities drew them into the broad currents of city life. As immigrant children learned English and "American" ways in the public schools, many rejected their parents' old-world accents, dress, and customs. For the second and third generation of immigrant families, the ethnic neighborhoods gradually lost their appeal. But still later, in the

Old New York: Shanties at 55th Street and 7th Avenue, *by Ralph Blakelock, c. 1870*

New York City immigrant housing was so crowded yet so expensive that some people resorted to living in temporary shacks on vacant land.

closing years of the twentieth century, many Americans would try to rediscover the lost world of their immigrant ancestors, finding in it long-neglected meaning and value.

Some immigrant groups adjusted far more easily than others. Those with a background in the skilled trades and a familiarity with Anglo-American customs had relatively few problems. English-speaking immigrants from the British Isles, particularly those from mill, mining, and manufacturing districts, found comparable work readily available in America's cities and established a comfortable life. Ethnic groups that formed a substantial percentage of a city's population also had a major advantage. The Irish, for example, who by the 1880s made up nearly 16 percent of New York's population, 8 percent of Chicago's, and 17 percent of Boston's, facilitated Irish immigrants' entry into the American mainstream by dominating Democratic politics and controlling the hierarchy of the Catholic church in all three cities. Similarly the Germans in Milwaukee, who composed nearly a third of the city's population in 1880, not only owned several major breweries, tanneries, and iron

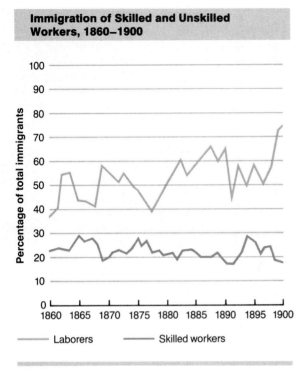

Immigration of Skilled and Unskilled Workers, 1860–1900

Laborers — Skilled workers

Far more laborers than skilled workers immigrated to American shores in the years from the Civil War to 1900.

NOTE: Laborers include unskilled workers, domestics, and farm hands.
SOURCE: Figure created by Thomas J. Archdeacon from data in U.S. Bureau of the Census, *Historical Statistics of the United States: Colonial Times to 1970* (Washington, D.C.: Government Printing Office, 1975), series C120–137.

foundries but held leadership positions in local government and civic organizations.

The larger the immigrant group, the more effectively organized were its churches, newspapers, schools, banks, and benevolent associations. Germans, Poles, Russian Jews, and other immigrants who arrived in large numbers in the 1880s and 1890s formed numerous self-help organizations. The New York Hebrew Free Loan Society, founded in 1892, gave interest-free loans of ten dollars to two hundred dollars to Jewish immigrants who wanted to set up their own businesses. By 1904 the society's treasury overflowed with more than a hundred thousand dollars donated by former loan recipients eager to support a benefactor that had helped them achieve their own prosperity.

Ironically, however, the larger immigrant groups' domination of urban institutions often made

the adjustment to American society *more* difficult for members of smaller immigrant groups. Germans and other well-organized and skilled foreigners tended to exclude less-skilled newcomers from lucrative jobs. English and German dominance of the building trades, for example, enabled those nationalities to limit the numbers of Italians hired. Not surprisingly, Italians accounted for only 18 percent of New York City's skilled brick masons in 1900 but made up 55 percent of the male barbers and 97 percent of the poorly paid bootblacks.

Another reason why smaller immigrant groups had difficulty adjusting to American society was that many of their members had no intention of staying permanently. Young Chinese and Italian males often journeyed to American shores simply to earn enough money to return home and buy land or set themselves up in business. Expecting only a brief stay, they made little effort to learn English or understand American customs. Of the Italians who immigrated to New York before 1914, nearly 50 percent went back to Italy. Although the rate of remigration was greatest among Chinese and Italians, significant numbers of immigrants of other nationalities eventually returned to their homelands as well.

A variety of factors thus influenced the ability of immigrants of different national origins to adapt to American urban society and improve their status. Nevertheless, as the number of foreigners in U.S. cities ballooned toward the turn of the century, all immigrant groups, irrespective of size, faced increasing hostility from native-born Americans, who not only disliked the newcomers' social customs but also feared their growing influence.

Slums and Ghettos

Every major city had its share of run-down, overcrowded slum neighborhoods. Generally clustered within walking distance of manufacturing districts near the city center, slums developed when landlords subdivided old buildings and packed in too many residents. The poorer the renters, the worse the slum. Slums became ghettos when laws, prejudice, and community pressure prevented the tenement inhabitants from moving out and renting elsewhere. During the 1890s Italians in New York, blacks in Philadelphia and Chicago, Hispanics in Los Angeles, and Chinese in San Francisco increasingly became locked in segregated ghettos.

For a number of reasons, foreigners of Italian origin in particular were pushed into substandard housing. As we have seen, most unskilled young Italian male immigrants in these years had little alternative to accepting the lowest-paying jobs. To maximize their meager savings, they took the cheapest housing available—generally badly deteriorated tenements. Because many viewed their stay in America as temporary, they endured terrible filth and congestion.

To urban reformers like Danish-born Jacob Riis, who brought their own cultural biases to the effort to improve urban sanitation and housing, the Italians themselves appeared to be at the heart of the slum problem. Riis despised the Italians' custom of congregating in the streets to purchase food, chat with friends, or simply pass the time. In *How the Other Half Lives,* he singled out a district called the Bend, at the intersection of Mulberry and Baxter streets, as the worst of New York's slums, and he emphasized its Italian character. "Half of the people in 'the Bend' are christened Pasquale . . . ," he wrote patronizingly. "When the police do not know the name of an escaped murderer, they guess at Pasquale and send the name out on an alarm; in nine cases out of ten it fits." While acknowledging the destructive effects of substandard housing, inadequate health care, unsanitary conditions, and the social disruption associated with immigration, Riis nonetheless blamed the Italian residents themselves for the district's crime, filth, disease, and appallingly high infant death rate. Other middle-class observers of urban poverty used the terms *slum* and *foreign colony* interchangeably. This tendency to fault the slum dwellers for their own plight, and to hold particular immigrant groups responsible for their living conditions, was characteristic of even well-intentioned reformers and helped shape—as well as distort—middle-class perceptions of the immigrant city.

Meanwhile, sobering evidence of the decay of urban America under the pressure of unremitting population growth mounted. Social workers in Chicago in the 1890s found conditions that matched those in New York City. Surveying a thirty-block section between Halsted Street and the Chicago River that was home to twenty-six different ethnic groups, they found that only about a quarter of the people had access to a bathroom with running water. The rest relied on repulsive outhouses, called privy vaults, located in yards or under porches. In

Homeless Children

Jacob Riis posed this picture of homeless barefoot boys, whom he called street arabs, to startle the public into aiding the poor. Note how the boys, with their eyes tightly closed, feign sleep.

an especially graphic report, the social workers deplored the district's "filthy and rotten tenements, the dingy courts and tumble-down sheds, the foul stables and dilapidated outhouses, the broken sewer-pipes, the piles of garbage fairly alive with diseased odors, and the numbers of children filling every nook, working and playing in every room, eating and sleeping in every window-sill, pouring in and out of every door, and seeming literally to pave every scrap of 'yard.' "

Health conditions in such districts almost defied description. Epidemics of typhoid fever, smallpox, and diphtheria periodically ravaged the slums, while slower killers like tuberculosis claimed many more victims (see "A Place in Time"). The immigrant city was particularly unsparing of its children. Juvenile diseases such as whooping cough, measles, and scarlet fever took a fearful toll, and infant mortality was very high. In one immigrant ward in Chicago in 1900, 20 percent of all infants died in their first year of life.

Further, because tenements often bordered the industrial districts, residents had to put up with the noise, pollution, and foul odors of tanneries,

Immigrant Milwaukee in the 1890s

On August 5, 1894, a mob of more than three thousand furious Polish citizens on Milwaukee's South Side fought a pitched battle with police and health-department officials. A smallpox epidemic had broken out in the city, and the health department had ordered infected persons to be taken by ambulance to a city isolation hospital. A distraught mother who had recently lost another child to smallpox refused to let the city "kill" her sick two-year-old daughter by hospitalizing her. "I can give better care and nourishment here than they can give in the hospital," she yelled at the authorities. Confronted by a violent crowd armed with clubs, knives, and stones, the health-department crew beat a hasty retreat. The local newspaper later reported that for more than a month after this incident, "mobs of Pomeranian and Polish women armed with baseball bats, potato mashers, clubs, bed slats, salt and pepper, and butcher knives, lay in wait all day for . . . the Isolation Hospital van."

The smallpox riots of 1894 reflected deep antagonisms between city officials and ethnic groups in Milwaukee. The confrontations pitted reform-minded middle-class political appointees and sanitary engineers seeking to establish city-wide health ordinances against immigrants seeking to preserve their traditions. The conflicts exposed the reformers' mixed motives, for beneath their drive to improve city sanitation lay a desire to destroy the foreign customs of Milwaukee's immigrants.

Tensions first surfaced in Milwaukee during a period of rapid growth. Settled in 1836 at a natural harbor formed on Lake Michigan, the city witnessed a tenfold population gain from 1850 to 1890, swelling from twenty thousand to more than two hundred thousand residents. Germans, who made up Milwaukee's largest immigrant group, predominated in the early years of settlement and concentrated heavily on the city's West Side. Then in the 1870s, large numbers of Poles and other eastern Europeans poured in, drawn by the unskilled jobs available in the rolling mills and blast furnaces of heavy industries such as the Milwaukee Iron Company and the E. P. Allis Company. Bartholomew Koperski, a Polish laborer, was typical of the many Poles who clustered in small, ill-ventilated houses in wards on the city's South Side. A railroad-car inspector, Koperski lived with his wife and six children in the upstairs of a twenty-two- by forty-foot cottage. He rented the basement to George Krzyżaniak, a twenty-nine-year-old Polish carpenter, his wife, and their two children. Although the city's health-department inspectors reported that most immigrants' homes were in "good sanitary condition," less than half had indoor plumbing.

The Koperskis and their compatriots belonged to a close ethnic

Immigrant Milwaukee

In most turn-of-the-century American cities, the boundaries of immigrant neighborhoods were tightly drawn. Neighbors often rallied together to drive outsiders away. Thus it was not unusual to have public authorities meet heated opposition when they attempted to enforce the law.

community whose ties were cemented by their common language and their powerful religious bonds. Milwaukee's Poles founded their own Catholic churches; published their own Polish-language newspaper, *Krytyka* (The Critic); and figured prominently in ward politics. During smallpox epidemics the Milwaukee health department tried to establish citywide health policies that quarantined infected houses, banned public funerals, and forced diseased persons into isolation hospitals, but the cohesive Polish wards fought back. Accustomed to nursing the sick at home, the Poles protested city efforts to cart invalids off to hospitals and then ban family members from visiting them. Further, with a strong tradition of elaborate church funerals for their deceased loved ones, they refused to accept the idea of burials without formal church rites.

At the height of the epidemic, a local alderman spoke out for his constituents. He raged that the Poles were being treated as "the scum of Milwaukee." "I don't blame the people down here for being worked up," he told a newspaper reporter. "The patients at the hospitals are not treated like human beings, and the way the dead are buried is brutal." He was particularly incensed by the position taken by Milwaukee's health commissioner, Walter Kempster, a native-born American who asserted, "I am here to enforce the laws, and I shall enforce them if I have to break heads to do it."

The debate over city quarantine policies between Kempster and Milwaukee's South Siders rekindled a conflict dating from nearly six months earlier, when Kempster was first appointed health commissioner. Hired because of his medical credentials, Kempster, a Republican, had ignored his party's suggested list of candidates to fill the twenty-six openings in his department. Incensed by Kempster's failure to reward any of their constituents with a job, Polish city-council members had agitated for his removal. Now the smallpox epidemic provided an additional avenue for those longing to unseat Kempster. In the crisis his adversaries denounced him as a symbol of arbitrary government authority and a subverter of immigrant culture and personal liberty.

As the deadly epidemic continued into the autumn months, the city council passed a new ordinance barring the health commissioner from hospitalizing victims without their consent. Still upset by his handling of the Polish South Siders, the council dismissed Kempster in February 1895. Milwaukee's battle over city health policies thus revealed a larger struggle between immigrant groups and public administrators: a tug-of-war for political control of the city.

Not until after 1900 did Milwaukee and other cities establish enforceable health regulations and vaccination policies that in time lowered the nationwide mortality rate from smallpox and other diseases. And only with massive educational campaigns in the Progressive Era were ethnic groups persuaded that local government had a legitimate need to interfere with their social customs in matters that concerned the welfare of all citizens.

Old Milwaukee

In this detailed scene of the city's commercial center, horsecars and horse-drawn wagons go about their business on busy East Water Street.

foundries, factories, and packing houses. After 1860 more and more factories used coal-fired steam engines as their energy source, and since coal was also the preferred heating fuel for most apartment houses and businesses, vast quantities of soot and coal dust drifted skyward daily. In tenements near factories and warehouses, the atmosphere was often hazy-gray with smoke, and the buildings themselves took on a dingy, grimy patina.

Although the immigrants' situation was grim, the position of blacks was worse. In contrast to most immigrants, who stayed in the shabbiest tenements only until they could afford better housing, blacks were trapped in segregated districts. Racist city dwellers used real-estate covenants and neighborhood pressure to exclude them from areas inhabited by whites. Because the numbers of northern urban blacks in 1890 remained relatively small— for example, they composed only 1.2 percent of Cleveland's population and 1.3 percent of Chicago's—they could not overcome whites' concerted campaigns to shut them out.

By the turn of the century, growing competition between immigrants and black migrants moving up from the South led to further efforts to segregate blacks in the poorest sections of northern cities—in Chicago, a long, narrow "Black Belt" on the South Side; in Cleveland, the Central Avenue District. Blacks in such cities faced intimidation as well as segregation. A Washington, D.C., black newspaper, the *Bee*, asserted in the 1880s that white police officers, particularly the Irishmen on the force, "delight in arresting every little colored boy they see on the street, who may be doing something not at all offensive, and allow the white boys to do what they please."

Rivalry over housing and jobs sometimes sparked racial violence. Most frequently the victim of an attack was a single individual, but sometimes interracial clashes escalated into a full-scale riot, as in New York City during the summer of 1900. The melee was touched off when Arthur J. Harris, a young black man, knifed and killed a plainclothes policeman in lower Manhattan who he believed was mishandling his wife. News of the murder spread quickly among whites, and the district seethed with anger. "Men and women poured by the hundreds from the neighboring tenements," reported a local newspaperman. "Negroes were set

upon wherever they could be found and brutally beaten."

Fashionable Avenues and Suburbs

As remains true today, the same cities that harbored slums, suffering, and violence also boasted neighborhoods of dazzling opulence. The very rich built monumental residences on what became exclusive thoroughfares just outside the downtown: Fifth Avenue in New York, Commonwealth Avenue in Boston, Euclid Avenue in Cleveland, and Summit Avenue in St. Paul. In Chicago after a devastating fire in 1871, the city's elite, including meatpacking magnate Philip Armour and department-store developer Marshall Field, moved south to Prairie Avenue around Eighteenth Street. Then in the 1880s, with the extension of Chicago's street-railway system, wholesale merchant and real-estate promoter Potter Palmer and other rich businessmen moved to Lake Shore Drive, the so-called Gold Coast on the near North Side, and the city's upper crust soon followed. The gradual northward migration of Chicago's well-to-do was paralleled by the expansion of the immigrant districts on the South Side, where once fashionable mansions were converted into cramped apartments and quickly filled with newcomers from Europe.

By the 1870s and 1880s, however, many wealthy and middle-income city dwellers were moving to the suburbs to distance themselves further from the crowded downtown and tenement districts with their motley ethnic populations, teeming streets, noisy saloons, and piles of garbage and excrement. Promoters of the suburban ideal, playing on the romantic rural nostalgia popular at the time, skillfully contrasted the rolling lawns and sheltered houses on the city's periphery with the right angles, sharp lines, and flat surfaces of the city proper. Cincinnati, wrote one suburban developer in 1870, is "surrounded with hills that are already blossoming like a rose. Beautiful cottages, stately residences, and princely mansions are springing up as if by magic. Villages are multiplying along the great thoroughfares." Similarly, in Lake Forest, north of Chicago, realtors praised the "pure air, peacefulness, quietude, and natural scenery." Soon many major cities could boast of their own stylish suburbs: Haverford, Ardmore, and Bryn

Dearborn Avenue, Chicago, c. 1890

Posh residential neighborhoods could be identified by the important civic institutions standing within them. Chicago's broad, tree-lined Dearborn Avenue was home to the magnificent Newberry Library and two imposing Protestant churches.

Mawr outside Philadelphia; Brookline near Boston; and Shaker Heights near Cleveland.

The suburbs, whether densely populated West Roxbury and Dorchester just outside Boston or the affluent Walnut Hills section of Cincinnati, provided an escape from the crime, congestion, and chaos of city life. In addition, cheaper suburban land values reduced housing costs. For between one thousand dollars and five thousand dollars, a skilled worker or a business clerk with a yearly income of a thousand dollars in the 1890s could purchase a small house away from the clogged heart of the city.

Middle-class city dwellers followed the precedents set by the wealthy. Skilled artisans, shopkeepers, clerks, accountants, and sales personnel moved either to new suburban developments at the city's edge or to outlying suburban communities (although those at the lower fringe of the middle class typically rented apartments or houses in neighborhoods closer to the city center). In the 1890s Chicago developer Samuel Eberly Gross created entire low-cost subdivisions north and west of the city and advertised homes for as little as ten dollars a month. Lawyers, doctors, small businessmen, and other professionals moved farther out along the main thoroughfares served by the street railway, where they purchased homes with large lots.

In time, a pattern of informal residential segregation by income took shape in the cities and suburbs. Built up for families of a particular income level, certain neighborhoods and suburbs developed remarkably similar internal standards for lot size and house design. Commuters who rode the new street railways out from the city center could identify the changing neighborhoods along the way as readily as a geologist might distinguish different strata on a washed-out riverbank.

So by 1900 whirring trolley cars and hissing steam-powered trains had burst the boundaries of the compact midcentury city. Within this expanded city, sharp dissimilarities in building height and neighborhood quality set off business sectors from fashionable residential avenues and strikingly differentiated squalid manufacturing districts from parklike suburban subdivisions. Musing about urban America in 1902, James F. Muirhead, a popular Scottish guidebook author, wrote that New York and other U.S. cities reminded him of "a lady in a ball costume, with diamonds in her ears, and her toes out at her boots." To Muirhead, urban America had become a "land of contrasts" in which the spatial separations of various social groups and the radically unequal living conditions for rich and poor had heightened the sense of ethnic and class consciousness. Along with the physical change in

American cities, in short, had come a new awareness of class and cultural disparities.

The Urban Challenge

Although middle- and upper-class Americans were abandoning their downtown residences in the 1880s and 1890s, the business and professional activities of countless merchants, journalists, manufacturers, lawyers, and others remained centered in the vibrant heart of the city. These old-stock citizens were deeply troubled by growing evidence there of social unrest. The occasional strikes and riots that swept through the cities were especially disturbing. Urban critics linked the disorder to the immigrant masses, who did not, they concluded, share their own cultural views on self-discipline and moral improvement. A chief target of the critics was the often corruption-riddled political machines that dominated city government in the Gilded Age.

Convinced that urgent steps must be taken to stem what seemed a rising tide of riot, robbery, and rotten government, concerned citizens waged a continuous battle in the late nineteenth century to eradicate urban crime, reform "boss" politics, and assimilate the immigrants into mainstream American society. Their efforts were catalyzed by a powerful blend of altruism and self-interest.

Policing the City

Would-be reformers worried not only about the organized mass protests of disgruntled workers but about the crime that inevitably increased as city populations grew denser. In his novel *Ragged Dick* (1868), Unitarian minister Horatio Alger detailed the variety of scams and tricks to which naive rural dwellers might fall prey when they visited the city. Shopkeepers swindled the unsuspecting by giving them incorrect change. Pickpockets and thieves stole handbags and purses. Con artists lured the unwary into giving them change for wallets stuffed with phony bills. Worst of all, Irish street gangs, led by toughs like Alger's fictional Mickey Maguire, threatened to beat up and rob the innocent.

Horatio Alger and other writers who associated crime with the growth of cities did not exaggerate. In Philadelphia, for example, which expanded in population from 409,000 to 1,294,000 between 1850 and 1900, the number of homicides nearly tripled in the second half of the century. As city dailies splashed reports of violence across their front pages, reformers worried publicly about urbanites' easy access to cheap handguns.

In their desire to maintain public order, city officials in the 1830s and 1840s had established police forces to supplement the traditional night watch that had patrolled the streets after dark to keep an eye out for fires. Unlike their European counterparts, these police forces were civilian enterprises, separate from the military and controlled by local officials. Following the example set by New York in 1853, other American cities had outfitted their municipal police forces with badges and uniforms and authorized officers to carry clubs and revolvers.

Initially, however, these new urban police forces had an odd, ill-defined assortment of responsibilities. Although officially hired to maintain order, prevent crime, and regulate morality by controlling drunks and other public nuisances, the police often performed additional functions. In New York City they cleaned streets and inspected boilers. In Baltimore, Philadelphia, and New York, they ran lodging houses for the homeless and distributed supplies to the poor. In St. Louis they supervised the sanitation of vegetable markets.

The police sometimes battled immigrant gangs like Baltimore's Blood Tubs and New York City's Bowery Boys, but they made little headway in suppressing the rowdy street life, drinking, gambling, and prostitution that flourished within the immigrant working class. Middle-class civic leaders grumbled about the "disorderly" crowds of laboring people noisily clustering on tenement stoops to talk politics or listen to street musicians. But they were most disapproving of the immigrants' neighborhood saloons, which offered a free lunch with a five-cent beer, provided meeting rooms, spread news of job openings, and sometimes, in back rooms, furnished gambling tables and offered prostitutes' services.

State legislatures, dominated in these years by rural, native-born citizens who deplored the immigrants' drinking and gambling, regularly passed laws banning these practices, curtailing Sunday business operations, and regulating saloons. Caught between moralistic state legislators and immigrant

Arresting a Hobo

In the late nineteenth century, "to be on the tramp" meant to be searching for work. Here a policeman arrests a disorderly tramp on New York City's Mulberry Street.

communities resentful of outside meddling, the police tried to steer a middle course, tacitly allowing the saloons to remain open on Sunday, for example, as long as their patrons behaved properly in public.

An investigation conducted in 1894 by New York State senator Clarence Lexow uncovered considerable evidence that the New York City police were not only failing to suppress illegal activities in the immigrant slums, they were licensing those activities. In return for regular payoffs, Lexow reported, the police permitted gamblers, prostitutes, and saloonkeepers to operate more or less at will in poor neighborhoods where little organized opposition existed, provided that they remained reasonably discreet. A portion of these payoffs, Lexow further revealed, ended up in the hands of local political bosses who hired and fired the police. Instead of fighting vice, a shocked Lexow concluded, the police were conniving in it.

The complex symbiosis between the police and those whom they were supposed to be policing manifested itself in other ways as well. By the 1870s,

in New York and most other major cities, police departments had squads of detectives who worked out of inner-city saloons. Often not easily distinguishable from the crooks and con men with whom they rubbed shoulders, these detectives sometimes even functioned as go-betweens for thieves and robbery victims, returning the stolen property in exchange for a reward. In some cities professional criminals reached an understanding with the detectives and gave back property stolen from individuals of high prestige and standing.

In city after city in the late nineteenth century, reformers strove to make law enforcement more professional by transferring the hiring and firing of police officers from political bosses to independent, nonpartisan boards of commissioners. Not until the 1890s, however, did most urban police forces begin to display a professional attitude toward their work. Pressured by reformers such as young Theodore Roosevelt, who headed New York City's Board of Police Commissioners from 1895 to 1897, civic leaders gradually removed the police department from the local political patronage system and adopted regular hiring procedures. But urban reformers had less success in legislating the stricter morality that the rural, native-born legislators so desired. Given the large immigrant populations within the cities, many police officers, especially those drawn from the immigrant ranks, remained sympathetic to the social customs of the ethnic groups among whom they circulated.

Governing the City

The competition for authority over the police revealed a deeper power struggle within urban politics. Amid the furiously haphazard growth of cities, political power had become fragmented and decentralized. The urgent demands placed on public utilities, rapid-transit systems, and fire and police departments forced cities to raise taxes, issue bonds, and create a host of new municipal departments and positions. Since large sums of money could be made by dominating any segment of this process, state and local politicians fought desperately for control of the city and the right to run these lucrative urban services.

Complicating the contest for control of city politics was the fact that both city governments and state legislatures claimed to have jurisdiction over the urban environment. Ostensibly to curb abuse in urban government, state legislatures altered city charters, bestowed special contracts and monopolies on certain railroad and utility magnates, and tried to minimize taxes by reducing the expenses of city government and limiting city services.

This kind of outside interference in local affairs had by midcentury encouraged the rise of a new kind of professional politician, the "boss." The boss presided over the city's "machine"—an unofficial political organization designed to keep a particular party or faction in office. Whether or not officially serving as mayor, the boss, assisted by local ward or precinct "captains," wielded enormous influence in city government. Often a former saloonkeeper or labor leader, the boss knew his constituents well. Cincinnati's George B. Cox was a typical boss, though more honest than many. The son of British immigrants, Cox worked his way up from being a newsboy and lookout for gamblers to tending bar and eventually acquired his own saloon. Elected to the Cincinnati city council in 1879, Cox in time became head of the city's Republican machine, which swung elections to the GOP, controlled key public offices, and acted as a broker among competing corporate and political interests.

For better or worse, the political machine was America's unique contribution to the challenge of municipal government in an era of pell-mell urban growth. Typified by Tammany Hall, the Democratic organization that dominated New York City politics from the 1830s to the 1930s, machines emerged in Baltimore, Philadelphia, Atlanta, San Francisco, and a host of other cities in the Gilded Age. Highly decentralized, the machine consisted of loosely affiliated and largely autonomous organizations in the local wards, the city's smallest political divisions. The ward captains, frequently saloonkeepers, turned out the vote at election time in return for jobs, contracts, and political appointments from city hall.

Within its orbit, the machine ruled supreme. The politicians who ran it controlled the jobs of thousands of policemen, firemen, sanitation workers, street crews, and other city employees; they exerted enormous influence over courts, schools, city hospitals, and other municipal agencies. Democratic in some cities and Republican in others, the machine hammered out compromises and resolved conflicts among competing urban interest groups.

Working through the local ward captains, the machine rode herd on the tangle of municipal bureaucracies, rewarding its friends and punishing its enemies through its control of taxes, licenses, and inspections. The machine gave tax breaks to favored contractors in return for large payoffs and slipped them insider information about upcoming street and sewer projects. At the neighborhood level, the ward captain doubled as a kind of welfare agent, helping the needy and protecting the troubled. He might intercede with a judge to secure clemency for a local boy caught running a gambling operation, dispense food to a family when the breadwinner was sick or injured, or provide a city job for an immigrant who could not find work. In this way, the machine helped compensate for failings in the Gilded Age's welfare system. In the process, however, essential municipal functions and urban social services became hopelessly entangled with corrupt politics.

A particularly effective precinct captain could work his way up from running the ward to running the city machine and eventually influence state and national politics as well. In Kansas City, Missouri, "Big Jim" Pendergast, an Irish hotelkeeper and saloonkeeper in one of the city's industrial wards, clawed his way to power in the 1890s by providing welfare services for his black, Italian, and Irish constituents. By controlling his ward's delegates to the city's Democratic convention, he rose to city alderman. When opposition interests threatened to use their pull in the state legislature to clamp down on the Kansas City police and root out gambling interests associated with Pendergast's saloon, he used his influence with the governor to engineer the appointment of a new city police chief sympathetic to his allies. By the turn of the century, Pendergast held near-absolute sway in Kansas City politics and wielded considerable clout at the state level as well.

Bosses like Cox and Pendergast—and even those in smaller cities such as Rochester, Omaha, and Memphis—transformed urban politics into a new form of entrepreneurship. They could be as ambitious and ruthless as any Gilded Age captain of industry. Like the Carnegies and the Rockefellers, the city bosses pioneered new forms of social organization and extemporized managerial innovations even as they consolidated their personal power, and in some cases they amassed vast fortunes. At times greedy and utterly unscrupulous, they nevertheless remained responsive to immigrant and working-class concerns in a society increasingly dominated by the middle and upper classes.

Under New York City's boss William Marcy Tweed, the Tammany Hall machine epitomized the slimy depths to which extortion and contract padding could sink. Although between 1869 and 1871, Tweed gave $50,000 to the poor and $2,250,000 to schools, orphanages, and hospitals, his machine also dispensed sixty thousand patronage positions and pumped up the city's debt by $70 million through graft and inflated contracts. The details of the Tweed ring's massive fraud and corruption were widely reported in newspapers and brilliantly satirized in *Harper's Weekly* by German immigrant cartoonist Thomas Nast, who in one cartoon portrayed Tweed and his cronies as vultures picking at the city's bones. The caption was "Let us prey." Tweed bellowed in fury. "I don't care a straw for your newspaper articles—my constituents don't

know how to read," he told *Harper's*, "but they can't help seeing them damned pictures." Convicted of fraud and extortion, Tweed was sentenced to jail in 1873, served two years, escaped to Spain, was reapprehended and reincarcerated, and died in jail in 1878.

Not all bosses were as crooked and covetous as Tweed. Boss Cox of Cincinnati, who steadfastly maintained that he had never received an illegal payoff, gained the backing of local good-government reformers—"goo-goos" to their opponents—by supporting voter-registration laws and by placing the police and fire departments under independent bipartisan boards. Cox helped remove police appointments from the patronage system and agreed to rules that required new recruits to undergo extensive training before they could join the force. He also supported the construction of a new city waterworks as well as the improvement of parks and other recreational facilities. Although Cox's opponents never believed that his administration was as free from corruption as he claimed, they did not overthrow his political machine until 1897.

Despite the stereotype of city bosses as coarse and crude—British observer James Bryce described them as "vulgar figures with good coats"—not all bosses fit that mold. San Francisco boss Abraham Ruef had graduated from the University of California at eighteen years of age with highest honors and spoke seven languages. Ed Flynn, the boss of the Bronx, New York, was a brilliant lawyer. Whatever their backgrounds, however, bosses represented a new political style that stressed grassroots ties to the neighborhood and ward. Standing amid the real-estate promoters, local businessmen, wealthy entrepreneurs, civic reformers, and other groups vying for power and pursuing their various agendas in the cockpit of urban politics, the boss made sure that the concerns of his constituents were heard. In this ceaseless struggle among competing groups with vastly different interests, the boss displayed a flexible, pragmatic, and opportunistic approach to meeting the day-to-day challenges of urban life.

Nevertheless, by the turn of the century, the bosses faced well-organized assaults on their power, led by an urban elite whose members sought to restore "good government." In this atmosphere the bosses increasingly forged alliances with civic organizations and reform leagues. The results,

"Let Us Prey," 1871

Cartoonist Thomas Nast hated William Marcy Tweed's ostentatious style. Pictured here as the chief vulture standing over the body of New York City, Boss Tweed wears an enormous diamond, a symbol of his insatiable greed.

although never entirely satisfactory to any of the parties involved, paved the way for new sewer and transportation systems, expanded parklands, and improved public services—a record of considerable accomplishment, given the magnitude of the problems created by urban growth.

Battling Poverty

Beginning at midcentury and continuing in this heyday of the political bosses, middle-class urban leaders, distressed by the rampant sickness and poverty around them, sought alternative solutions to the plight of the urban poor. These concerned citizens, comprising prominent reformers, church officials, and settlement-house workers, were convinced that cities were "putrefying" and that political bosses were only making matters worse.

The middle-class crusaders' attitudes toward poverty differed significantly from the political bosses' outlook. Rather than reacting, as the bosses did, to individual privation, the reformers developed independent organizations to help the poor systematically throughout the city. Moreover, far from viewing slum dwellers as friends and neighbors whose luck had gone bad, the charity workers eyed the destitute from a distance, frequently, like Jacob Riis, blaming them for their own troubles. Many of these do-gooders confused impoverished immigrants' social drinking with alcoholism and believed that their poverty was rooted in intemperance, gambling, and other vices caused by character flaws. Working from this premise, they focused their efforts on the moral improvement of the poor and ignored the fact that immigrants commonly held attitudes toward drinking, work, and leisure very different from their own. Thus, although genuinely concerned about the poor and disabled, the humanitarians ultimately turned their campaigns to help the destitute into missions to Americanize the immigrants and eliminate customs that they perceived as offensive and self-destructive.

Poverty-relief workers first targeted their efforts at the young, who were thought to be most malleable. Energized by the religious revivals of the 1830s and 1840s (see Chapter 9), early Protestant social reformers started charitable societies to help transient youths and street waifs. In 1843 Robert M. Hartley, a former employee of the New York Temperance Society, mobilized New York City's business and professional classes to support his newly founded New York Association for Improving the Condition of the Poor. Convinced that slum children learned bad habits from their parents, Hartley organized a system of "home visitation" that sent volunteers into inner-city tenements to urge poor families to change their ways. Expanding to Baltimore, Philadelphia, and Boston, Hartley's association also demanded pure-milk laws, public baths, and better housing.

Hartley's voluntaristic approach was supplemented at midcentury by the efforts of reformer Charles Loring Brace, who in 1853 founded the New York Children's Aid Society. Brace admired "these little traders of the city . . . battling for a hard living in the snow and mud of the street." But he also worried that the "bright, sharp [and] bold" gangs of boys who haunted New York's alleys, occasionally emerging to shine shoes or sell newspapers, would soon be corrupted by their tough environment and would join the swelling ranks of the city's "dangerous classes." To help them avoid this fate, and to spare the city from future upheavals, Brace established dormitories, reading rooms, and workshops where the boys could learn practical skills. A firm believer in individual self-help, Brace exhorted these youngsters to leave crowded New York and migrate west, where their talents and energy could be applied to good advantage. To further this goal, he set up a placement system that by the mid-1890s had transferred ninety thousand boys from the city to foster homes in such states as Illinois, Michigan, and Wisconsin, where local residents put them to work.

Where Brace's Children's Aid Society gave vulnerable adolescents an avenue of escape from city slums, the Young Men's Christian Association (YMCA), founded in England in 1841 and exported to America ten years later, provided decent housing and wholesome recreational facilities for country boys new to the city. More than any other institutions, the YMCA and later the YWCA (Young Women's Christian Association) worked to overcome the dislocation and strain experienced by the thousands of rural Americans who migrated to the city in the post–Civil War years. In the Protestant tradition of moral improvement, both organizations subjected their members to considerable supervision and expelled them for drinking and other forbidden behavior.

The departure of young people—especially farmers' daughters—from older rural areas was truly startling. Between 1840 and 1900, almost half the townships in Vermont lost more than a quarter of their population, and young adults led the exodus. In one Vermont town, 73 percent of those aged five to fourteen in the 1880 census had left by 1900. Like Carrie Meeber, the heroine in Theodore Dreiser's *Sister Carrie* (1900), youthful rural migrants drawn to the city's greater economic opportunities were awed by the glamour and glitter of urban life. Far from home, with few friends and no place to stay, they easily fell victim to the city's flashy con artists and fast talkers. The YMCA and the YWCA supplied such country innocents safe temporary lodgings and reassuring reminders of home.

By 1900 more than fifteen hundred YMCAs acted as a haven for nearly a quarter-million men. But YMCA (and YWCA) leaders reached only a small portion of the young adult population. Some whom they sought to help were put off by the organizations' close supervision and highly moralistic stance. Others, eager to assert their independence in the new urban environment, preferred not to ask for help. And although charity workers' attempts to direct their efforts toward children and young people made some progress, the strategy was too narrowly focused to stem the rising tide of urban problems.

New Approaches to Social Work

The inability of the Children's Aid Society, the YMCA, the YWCA, and other relief organizations to cope with the urban poor's explosive growth in the 1870s and 1880s convinced many middle-class Americans that urban poverty had reached epidemic proportions. The Reverend Josiah Strong, secretary of the American Home Missionary Society and minister of Cincinnati's Central Congregational Church, expressed this fear in his book *Our Country; Its Possible Future and Its Present Crisis* (1885). Asserting that the cities were "multiplying and focalizing the elements of anarchy and destruction," Strong attributed the urban menace to immigration and Catholicism. Critical of the immigrants' attachment to their saloons and beer halls, he pleaded for a cooperative effort among

the Protestant churches to battle the dual plagues of intemperance and destitution.

Even before Strong mounted the battlements, energetic social reformers were searching for solutions to urban poverty, especially among the immigrants. Perceiving that needy families usually ignored idealistic appeals to change their ways, reformers developed coercive strategies. The approaches of their various relief organizations differed, but all remained convinced that only bold measures could tear these unfortunates away from a lifestyle that bred dissipation and hardship.

One of the earliest and most effective agencies to combat poverty through tough-minded tactics was the Salvation Army. A church established along pseudomilitary lines in England in 1865 by Methodist minister "General" William Booth, the Salvation Army sent its uniformed volunteers to America in 1880 to provide food, shelter, and temporary employment for families. Known for its rousing music and attention-getting street meet-

Salvation Army Meeting

The Salvation Army combined fervent personal appeals with charitable services like soup kitchens, day nurseries, homes for prostitutes, and secondhand stores where the destitute could find employment.

ings, the group ran soup kitchens and day nurseries and dispatched its "slum brigades" to carry the message of morality to the immigrant poor.

Funded by donations, the Salvation Army functioned both to aid and to control an urban lower-class population whose fondness for saloons, dance halls, and streetside entertainment threatened the middle-class conception of a stable society. The organization's strategy was simple. Attract the poor with marching bands and lively preaching; follow up with offers of food, assistance, and employment; and then teach them the solid middle-class virtues of temperance, hard work, and self-discipline.

A similar approach to poor relief was implemented by the New York Charity Organization Society (COS), founded in 1882 by Josephine Shaw Lowell. Of a prominent Boston family, the strong-willed Lowell had been widowed when her husband of a few months was killed during the Civil War, and she wore black for the rest of her life.

Adopting what they considered a scientific approach to make aid to the poor more honest and efficient, the COS leaders divided New York City into districts, compiled files on all those who requested aid, and sent "friendly visitors" into the tenements to counsel families on how to improve their lives. Convinced that moral deficiencies lay at the root of poverty, and that the "promiscuous charity" of overlapping welfare agencies undermined poor people's desire to work, the Charity Organization Society tried to foster self-sufficiency in its charges.

Although the COS and similar groups in Boston, Philadelphia, and other cities did serve as useful coordinators for relief efforts, critics justly accused them of being more interested in controlling the poor than in alleviating their suffering. More often than not, the friendly visitors wore cultural blinders, failing to understand the real source of the difficulties faced by the poor and expecting to effect change by imposing middle-class standards. In the 1890s Chicago journalist George Ade cruelly ridiculed the typical friendly visitor as "235 pounds of Sunshine." The earnest Salvation Army workers and COS volunteers no doubt accomplished some good, but unable to see slum problems from the vantage point of the poor, they failed, for the most part, in their underlying objective: to convert the poor to their own standards of morality and decorum.

The Moral-Purity Campaign

The inability of Josephine Shaw Lowell and other like-minded social disciplinarians to eradicate urban poverty and crime prompted other reformers to push for even tougher measures against sin and immorality. In 1872 Anthony Comstock, a pious young dry-goods clerk, founded the New York Society for the Suppression of Vice. The organization demanded that municipal authorities close down gambling and lottery operations and censor obscene publications. Toward the end of his career in the early twentieth century, Comstock became a target of ridicule for his naive judgments about literature and art. (He dismissed George Bernard Shaw as "a foreign writer of filth" and raided the New York Art Students' League for displaying nude sculptures.) But in his heyday, Comstock's purity crusade gained widespread public support from middle- and upper-class civic leaders deeply frustrated by the lack of progress in flushing away urban vice.

Pursuing the same goal by different means, New York Presbyterian minister Charles Parkhurst, targeting the urban machines, organized the City Vigilance League in 1892 to attack the secret cooperation of city authorities with gambling dens, saloons, and brothels. Parkhurst blamed the "slimy, oozy soil of Tammany Hall" and the New York City police—"the dirtiest, crookedest, and ugliest lot of men ever combined in semi-military array outside of Japan and Turkey"—for the city's rampant criminal evil. When Senator Lexow's committee spearheaded the investigation of urban vice two years later, Parkhurst's league swamped the panel with evidence of officially tolerated corruption. In September 1894 a nonpartisan Committee of Seventy, among its members J. Pierpont Morgan, William Bayard Cutting, and the younger Cornelius Vanderbilt, elected a new mayor who pressured city officials to enforce the laws against prostitution, gambling, and Sunday liquor sales.

The purity campaign, however, lasted scarcely three years. Irish and German neighborhoods boisterously rallied in defense of their cherished saloons. Individuals who once championed Parkhurst's efforts scoffed at his self-righteous and bombastic rhetoric and deserted his movement; the city's reform coalition fell apart. Regaining power in 1897, Tammany Hall installed a new police chief who was once again content to regulate rather than root out vice. Even though Parkhurst politically controlled the mayor's office and had the backing of a reform coalition, his attempt to legislate morality had failed. New York City's population was too large, and its ethnic constituencies were too diverse, for the middle and upper classes to curb all the illegal activities flourishing within the sprawling metropolis.

The Social Gospel

Meanwhile, a handful of Protestant ministers in the 1870s and 1880s began to explore several radical alternatives for aiding impoverished city dwellers. Instead of focusing on their alleged moral flaws and character defects, these ministers argued that the rich and the wellborn deserved part of the blame for urban poverty and thus had a responsibility to do something about it.

William S. Rainsford, the Irish-born minister at New York City's Saint George's Episcopal Church, pioneered the development of the so-called institutional church movement, whereby large downtown churches in once elite districts that had been overrun by immigrants would provide their new neighbors with social services as well as a place to worship. With the financial help of his wealthy church warden J. Pierpont Morgan, Rainsford organized a boys' club, built church recreational facilities for the destitute on the Lower East Side, and established an industrial training program.

Some conservatives tongue-lashed the churchman and his unorthodox approach. Charles A. Dana of the *New York Sun* branded Rainsford a "conspicuous representative of a school of unwise and mischievous social agitators." Unfazed, Rainsford redoubled his criticism of middle-class churchgoers for their complacency and lack of concern about the immigrant poor. Dismissing the moralists' assumption that alcohol abuse resulted entirely from an individual's lack of will power, Rainsford argued that excessive drinking in immigrant wards was simply a by-product of the larger problem of the slums, where millions were trapped in often desperate circumstances. For Rainsford and those who shared his view, moral-purity campaigns to close saloons on Sunday were far less important than the prosecution of slum landlords and sweatshop owners who victimized the poor.

Although Rainsford and the members of his Institutional Church League could claim some successes in their own neighborhoods, their efforts in the end fell short, owing to the magnitude of slum conditions. But their sympathetic approach to urban destitution marked an important dimension of a crusade by a group of late-nineteenth-century ministers to awaken American Protestants to the realities of the immigrant city.

Supporting that drive were the leaders of the so-called Social Gospel movement, another effort within Protestantism to right contemporary social wrongs. The Social Gospel movement was launched in the 1870s by Washington Gladden, who for most of his career served as the minister of a large Congregational church in Columbus, Ohio. Dismayed by the way many middle-class churchgoers were turning a deaf ear to the plight of urban slum dwellers, Gladden insisted that true Christianity commits men and women to fight social injustice head on, wherever it exists. Thus, in response to the wave of violent strikes in 1877, he urged church leaders to become mediators in the conflict between business and labor.

If Gladden set the tone for the Social Gospel, Walter Rauschenbusch, a minister at a German Baptist church in New York's notorious "Hell's Kitchen" neighborhood, articulated the movement's central philosophy. Educated in Germany, Rauschenbusch returned to the United States in the 1880s and was strongly influenced by Henry George's and Edward Bellamy's criticism of laissez faire ideology. Enlarging the traditional Protestant focus on individual conversion, Rauschenbusch sought in such books as *Christianity and the Social Crisis* (1907) to apply Jesus's teachings to society itself. A truly Christian society, he said, would unite all churches, reorganize the industrial system, and work for international peace.

Although the Social Gospel's appeal for Christian unity led in 1908 to the formation of the Federal Council of Churches, the movement's biting attack on what its leaders blasted as the complacent Christian support of the status quo attracted only a handful of Protestants. But their earnest voices blended with a growing chorus of critics bemoaning the nation's urban woes.

The Settlement-House Movement

By the 1880s many concerned citizens had become convinced that reform pressures applied from the top down by the Charity Organization Society and the purity crusaders, however well intentioned, were not only ineffective but wrongheaded. Simple passage of laws did not ensure obedience. Rejecting Parkhurst's contemptuous attitude toward the poor, and the Charity Organization movement's tendency to blame poverty on individual moral failure, a younger generation of charity workers led by Jane Addams developed a new weapon against destitution: the settlement house. Like the Social Gospelers, they began by recognizing that the physical hardships of slum life were often beyond the control of individuals. Stressing the environmental causes of crime and poverty, settlement-house advocates insisted that relief workers take up residence in poor neighborhoods where, in Addams's words, they could see firsthand "the struggle for existence, which is so much harsher among people near the edge of pauperism."

The youngest daughter of a successful Illinois businessman, Addams had graduated from Rockford College in 1882 and toured Europe a year later with her friend Ellen Gates Starr. Impressed by Toynbee Hall, a charity workers' residence situated deep in a London slum, the two women returned to Chicago in 1889, purchased and repaired the dilapidated Charles J. Hull mansion on South Halsted Street, and opened Hull House as an experiment in the settlement-house approach. Living in the house themselves and working in daily contact with poor immigrants, they hoped to provide an exemplar of a creative outlet for college-trained women like themselves.

Jane Addams's hostility toward the methods and philosophy of the Charity Organization Society and other coercive agencies came from disillusioning personal experience. During her first years at Hull House, Addams had accepted Josephine Shaw Lowell's model for managing the poor. But in her autobiography, *Twenty Years at Hull House* (1910), Addams explained why she later rejected Lowell's self-assured methods. Once, attempting to get a jobless shipping clerk to help himself, she encouraged him to take a job as a canal digger. Following her advice, the clerk had contracted pneumonia and died a week later. "I learned," Addams wrote sadly, "that life cannot be administered by definite rules and regulations; that wisdom to deal with man's difficulties comes only through some knowledge of his life and habits as a whole; and that to treat an isolated episode is almost sure to invite blundering."

Drawing on the popular middle-class ideal of true womanhood as supportive and self-sacrific-

Hull House Nursery

Explaining why she set up a nursery for children born into poverty, Jane Addams wrote that "this slaughter of the innocents, this infliction of suffering on the newborn, is so gratuitous and so unfair, that it is only a question of time until an outraged sense of justice shall be aroused on behalf of these children."

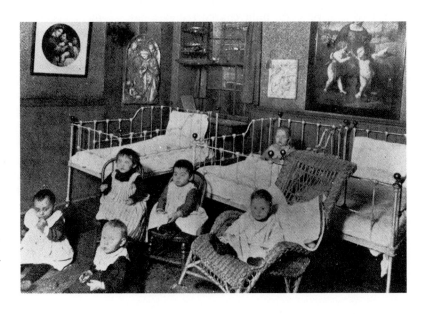

ing, the indefatigable Addams turned Hull House into a social center for recent immigrants and denied herself the luxuries that she might have purchased with her family wealth. Getting to know the Italian newcomers around her was a top priority. She invited them to plays; sponsored art projects; held classes in English, civics, cooking, and dressmaking; and encouraged them to preserve their traditional crafts. Disturbed by the depth of the neighborhood poverty that she witnessed, Addams set up a kindergarten, a laundry, an employment bureau, and a day nursery for working mothers. Hull House also sponsored recreational and athletic programs and dispensed legal aid and health care. In the hope of upgrading the shockingly filthy and overcrowded housing in the environs, Addams and her coworkers published systematic studies of city housing conditions and tirelessly pressured politicians to enforce sanitation regulations. For a time, demonstrating her principle of direct engagement with the lives of the poor, Addams even served as garbage inspector for her immigrant ward.

By 1895 at least fifty settlement houses had opened in cities around the nation. Settlement-house leaders trained a generation of young college students, many of whom would later serve as state and local government officials. Florence Kelley, for example, who had worked at Hull House, in 1893 became the chief factory inspector in Illinois. Many settlement-house veterans would later draw on their experience in these years and play an influential role in the regulatory movements of the Progressive Era (see Chapter 21). Through their sympathetic attitudes toward the immigrants and their systematic publication of data about slum conditions, settlement-house workers gave turn-of-the-century Americans new hope that the city's problems could be overcome.

But in their attempt to bridge the gap between rich and poor and to promote class cooperation and social harmony, settlement houses had far less success. Nor did the reformers succeed in increasing the neighborhood residents' political or economic power. Limited by their own commitment to social order and class harmony, settlement-house advisers tended to overlook immigrant organizations and their leaders, falling back instead on the ingrained tendency to impose their own middle-class taboos against drinking and gambling. While Hull House, one of the most successful of these efforts, attracted two thousand visitors per week

in 1894, this was only a fraction of the more than seventy thousand people who dwelled in a six-block radius of the building. "They're like the rest," complained one immigrant, "a bunch of people planning for us and deciding what is good for us without consulting us or taking us into their confidence."

Reshaping the Urban Environment

While reformers battled slum conditions and municipal corruption in the decades after the Civil War, landscape architects and city planners who shared the social workers' goal of a stable, orderly urban society took a different approach. In contrast to those who stressed people-oriented remedies, these architects and planners sought to reshape the urban masses by transforming their physical surroundings. In city after city, they redesigned the street system, installed new sewer and water mains, leveled hills, filled in swamps, and created broad boulevards and tree-lined parkways. Entire sections of America's metropolises were rebuilt in an attempt to restore beauty, dignity, and order to the urban environment.

Convinced that the level of urban education and cultural awareness must be raised, these self-proclaimed saviors of America's cities also established monumental public libraries with extensive book collections and endowed large art museums with treasured paintings and sculpture. To enhance appreciation of drama and music, they constructed theaters and symphony halls and founded professional orchestras. To encourage healthy outdoor exercise, they expanded urban park and recreational facilities. All the while, real-estate and business interests were remodeling the city in their own way, punctuating the urban skyline with great towers of commerce and finance that rose as high as thirty stories.

While the motivation behind the commercial construction was simple—profit and business growth—sponsors of the new urban landscape had more complex social objectives. Certainly they hoped that the improvement projects, cultural institutions, and recreational facilities that they were promoting would make the city a more appealing and attractive place. But they also wanted, through their physical reshaping of the city, to instill a sense of monumental order that would tame and restrain the urban masses. Although they never entirely achieved their aims, they did significantly restructure America's cities in the second half of the nineteenth century.

Parks and Public Spaces

Influenced by the work of English designers, and noting the popularity of parklike cemeteries such as Mount Auburn (1831) in Cambridge, Massachusetts, and Laurel Hill (1836) in Philadelphia, architects Andrew Jackson Downing and Frederick Law Olmsted envisioned a new urban landscape. With the backing of civic leaders, they proposed plans for the American city that contrasted sharply with the designs of the crowded, centralized cities of Europe. The ideal metropolis, they argued, should differentiate land use by clearly separating shopping and housing areas from the industrial district. The city should have a compact commercial nucleus, but even there spacious parks and roadways should open up the landscape. Most important, public buildings and boulevards should be built on a grand scale to inspire and awe ordinary citizens.

Olmsted was one of the earliest and most successful promoters of this vision. A self-taught scientific farmer, surveyor, and journalist, he had teamed up with English architect Calvert Vaux in 1858 to develop "Greensward," the original plan for Central Park in New York City (see Chapter 11). Olmsted and Vaux consciously designed the park as a spacious, tranquil country refuge within the city, a picturesque alternative to the monotonous straight-line regularity of the urban street grid. They intended Central Park to function as a rural antidote to the strains of urban life. Buoyed by their success with Central Park, they went on to design major parks for Brooklyn, Chicago, Philadelphia, and Boston.

But while Olmsted created his naturalistic oases within the urban desert, a quite different urban-design philosophy was advanced by Richard Morris Hunt, the first American graduate of the École des Beaux Arts, the famous school of architecture in Paris. Hunt embraced completely the École's neoclassical principles based on the models of ancient Greece and Rome. He was particularly influenced by Baron Georges Haussmann's monumental redesign of Paris in the mid-nineteenth

Boston Common at Twilight, *by Childe Hassam, 1885–1886*

Urban parks such as the Boston Common brought the country into the city, creating a peaceful refuge from the bustle of downtown life.

century. Applying his austere neoclassicism to Olmsted's Central Park, Hunt insisted that the park should shed its image as a "sylvan retreat fit for shepherds" and be converted instead into a "great open air gallery of Art," filled with impressive statuary mounted on large marble pedestals. As a step toward this goal, Hunt drew up plans for a series of elaborately formal gated entrances to the park. When this proposal was approved in 1863, a disgusted Olmsted resigned from the park's governing board.

Hunt and other devotees of French neoclassicism proposed to transform urban America by widening major thoroughfares, establishing uniform building heights, and sprinkling the cities with great public squares dominated by neoclassical monuments. In promoting the structured regularity of neoclassicism, Hunt and his upper-class backers hoped to make the city spacious and dignified, aesthetically uniform, and attractive to potential businesses. But they also viewed their proposals as a subtle form of urban social control. A formal, awe-inspiring urban environment, they believed, would encourage good citizenship and move the immigrant hordes to behave in a polite and restrained manner. As Chicago architect John Wellborn Root, a supporter of Hunt's ideas, put it, urban architecture should "convey in some large elemental sense an idea of the great, stable, conserving forces of modern civilization."

Boston's Back Bay

When Hunt, Root, and other architects called for revitalizing the urban environment through the application of planning and design principles, they

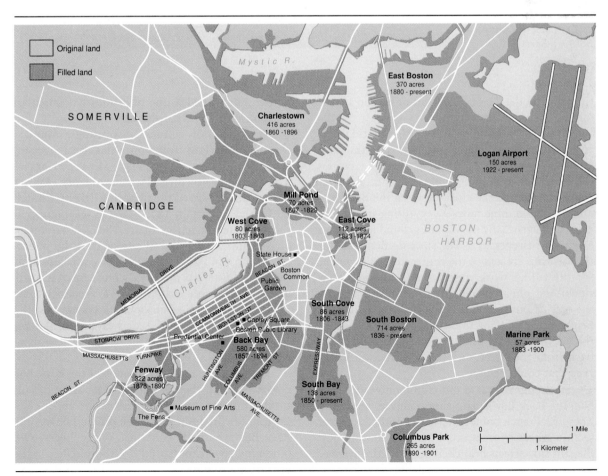

Urban Improvement: Expanding the City of Boston

Using round-the-clock gravel trains, Boston gained valuable new land by filling in swampy coastal flats.

Commonwealth Avenue, Back Bay, Boston, 1872

Built on wooden poles driven into the swampy earth, these elegant masonry townhouses lined the avenues of Boston's Back Bay.

took as a model the development of Boston's fashionable Back Bay district.

Until 1857 this area was a 450-acre tidal flat covered with water. Beginning that year, the state undertook a massive engineering project to reclaim the land. Between 1857 and 1900, special gravel trains ran around the clock between the Back Bay and Needham, nine miles away, filling in the low areas and eventually raising the ground level by an average of twenty feet. The state deeded some of the lots thus created to the contractors as payment for the filling work, reserved others for educational and philanthropic organizations, and sold the rest as building lots. Each deed specified the height of the building that could be constructed on the lot, the distance that the building should be set back from the street, and the construction materials that could be used.

State engineers laid out Commonwealth Avenue, the Back Bay's main thoroughfare, along the lines of a French boulevard, with a formal, central section graced by trees, stone benches, and statues. Elegant side streets branched off from the avenue, with back alleys for horse-cart deliveries. The uniform height of the district's five-story brownstone

houses established a line of vision that imparted both formality and consistency.

A variety of cultural institutions, founded through donations from upper-class businessmen, reinforced the Back Bay's image as a center of civilization and refinement. Architect Henry Hobson Richardson designed the imposing Trinity Church on Copley Square in 1875. Twelve years later, on the opposite side of the square, the New York firm of McKim, Mead, and White erected the monumental Boston Public Library. Space was also allocated for a fine-arts museum, a museum of science, and an orchestra hall. In 1881 Frederick Law Olmsted laid out the Fenway Park system near the Back Bay, building up the roadways to form dikes along the banks of the meandering, low-lying Muddy River.

Under the careful regulations of the Back Bay commissioners, the district, with its array of cultural attractions, became a mecca for upper-class Bostonians. In addition to the public library, the Back Bay eventually contained two colleges, two museums, five schools, and twelve churches. In the eyes of many businessmen, social reformers, and civic leaders, the Back Bay area thus represented the classic example of the charming, cosmopolitan urban environment that could be created through city planning.

Rebuilding Chicago

In contrast to Boston's achievements, the expansion of Chicago in the post–Civil War era was a planner's nightmare. Chicago was America's shock city, the extreme example of the kinds of problems that could be spawned by unregulated growth. Between 1850 and 1870, the city's population rose like a tidal wave, increasing from thirty thousand to nearly three hundred thousand. The influx not only strained city services but also inundated neighborhoods. So brisk was the rate of increase that architects, builders, and city officials, caught unprepared, could only react to crises as they arose. Nevertheless, the sheer magnitude of the changes forced Chicagoans to innovate in ways that were sometimes copied elsewhere.

For example, the expansion of the city in the 1840s left residents with swampy, unpaved streets that rested only slightly above the water table and remained quagmires for most of the year. To remedy this soggy situation, the city council in 1855 decided that the level of the streets must be raised. Over the next twenty years, owners jacked up their buildings to meet the new grade level. In 1857 one British traveler noted in amazement that "the Briggs House, a gigantic hotel, five stories high, solid masonry, weighing 22,000 tons, was raised four

and a half feet, and new foundations built below. The people were in it all the time, coming and going, eating and sleeping—the whole business of the hotel proceeding without interruption."

Chicago faced a new crisis in October 1871 when a raging fire destroyed more than sixty-one thousand buildings and leveled nearly four square miles in the central city. The entire commercial district was gutted, and nearly a hundred thousand people were left homeless. The urgent need for downtown reconstruction provided an unprecedented opportunity for Chicago architects, engineers, and businessmen. In the next two decades, these groups cooperatively pioneered exciting new methods for tall-office-building construction. Their experimentation made possible a new American building type, the skyscraper.

The skyscraper depended on three technological innovations: fireproofing, the internal metal frame, and the elevator. Although all three were available before the fire, not until the 1880s did Chicago architects, hectically rebuilding the city's business district, combine them in a distinctive commercial style. Given the city's recent experience, officials insisted that all new structures be built out of noncombustible materials. Stone was the obvious choice, but its great weight sharply limited the size of stone buildings that could be erected on the Chicago area's marshy soil. Louis Sullivan and other architects developed a far lighter alternative—a central metal skeleton, fireproofed with a fired-clay (or terra-cotta) tile, to support the

Raising Chicago's Briggs House

Raising the ground level where buildings already stood required clever engineering. In this case, hundreds of men, working in unison, slowly turned the large jack screws needed to lift the building from its foundation.

exterior walls. By placing the metal frame on an expanded foundation and installing motorized steam and electric elevators, Chicago architects increased the city's building heights from four to twenty-two stories. Once the commanding size and elevation of the Reliance Building (1890), Masonic Temple (1891), and other Chicago skyscrapers had demonstrated the technical feasibility and commercial advantages of constructing tall, metal-supported buildings on small, expensive urban lots, other American cities began to raise their skylines as well.

The dramatic rebuilding of the urban environment in Boston and Chicago, together with the inspiring example of Chicago's World's Columbian Exposition in 1892–1893 (see Chapter 17), encouraged businessmen and reformers in many smaller cities to swing into action. By the turn of the century, municipal-art societies, park and outdoor-art associations, and civic-improvement leagues had sprung up around the country. City after city launched planning programs to replace muddy streets and unsightly billboards in the downtown business districts with broad boulevards, sparkling fountains, and gleaming marble public buildings.

Known collectively as the city-beautiful movement, this crusade favored the interests of the well-born and the wealthy. Although advocates of the movement asserted that improving the urban landscape would benefit both rich and poor alike, they were less interested in upgrading the quality of immigrant housing and sanitary conditions in the slums than in making the city's public buildings impressive and even monumental. Like the followers of Richard Morris Hunt, they believed that attractive, more imposing civic architecture and landscape design would inevitably produce better citizens and reduce the dangers of urban immorality and social disorder. In the early twentieth century, the city-beautiful impulse would evolve into a comprehensive city-planning movement (see Chapter 21) inspired by even more soaring visions of a transformed urban environment.

Toward a Metropolitan America

While the city-beautiful advocates drafted their plans for the urban future, harried city-hall bureaucrats, municipal administrators, and civic engineers wrestled with such practical matters as inadequate water supplies, antiquated sewer systems, and basic municipal services that seemed continually to lag behind the pace of urban growth. As they worked to upgrade the quality of city services on many fronts, these administrators searched for more efficient and more centralized mechanisms of municipal organization and supervision. Little by little, new citywide agencies imperceptibly took over matters once handled at the neighborhood and ward level.

But while city administration became centralized, urban power remained widely dispersed. Urban elites, particularly business and real-estate interests, had difficulty cooperating. Immigrants often opposed the centralizing tendency, particularly when it disrupted familiar ties with the ward captain or involved plans to force them out of dilapidated though relatively inexpensive housing. Such conflicts among different segments of the urban population ultimately encouraged compromise arrangements necessary for the smooth functioning of the entire city.

Around midcentury, city dwellers began to recognize that the most dangerous aspect of urban life was the deplorable quality of the water and sewer systems. Most urbanites in the 1870s still relied on private wells, outhouses, and cesspools. Sewer systems, where they existed, were primitive and ineffective. One sanitary engineer described city sewer systems as "reservoirs of liquid filth, ever oozing through the defective joints, and polluting the very earth upon which the city stands."

Chicago poured its sewage directly into Lake Michigan, continually contaminating the source of its water supply and contributing directly to the frequent cholera, typhoid, and diphtheria epidemics that ravaged the city; Chicago's typhoid death rate alone reached 174 per 100,000 people in 1891. In New Jersey, Paterson and Passaic dumped their sewage directly into the Passaic River right above Newark's freshwater intakes.

Early attempts by city officials to construct interconnected sewer systems fell victim to local politics. In Washington, D.C., for example, the first contractors hired to build the system, who were chosen for their political contacts, proved grossly incompetent. They produced lateral sewers that could not run uphill into the main trunk lines. In New Orleans, a city subject to outbreaks of yellow fever and malaria, efforts to construct a citywide system in 1892 failed because of political ineptitude and contractor inexperience. Similarly, in St. Louis and Cincinnati, where politicians awarded contracts based on patronage, early, inadequate systems had to be replaced within a decade, at enormous expense.

Gradually and painfully, however, cities began to develop the centralized administrative structures that their size required, including the managerial tools to build and run effective sewer and water systems. To halt the further pollution of Lake Michigan, Chicago city officials in 1889 persuaded the state legislature to create a 185-square-mile sanitary district encompassing the city and its environs, supervised by elected officials with independent taxing authority. Between 1894 and 1899, the city built the enormous Ship and Sanitary Canal, which reversed the flow of the Chicago River to carry the city's processed sewage downstate. In Boston, too, engineers and civic officials in 1889 set up the centralized Metropolitan Sewage Commission, a permanent bureaucracy empowered to acquire land, oversee sewer construction, and formulate long-term expansion plans. By 1900 sewer and water systems established elsewhere had cut mortality rates from typhoid fever nationwide by 65 percent.

The movement to centralize control over water and sewer facilities was emblematic of a broader process of physical and political consolidation in urban America in the late nineteenth century. As cities exploded in size, they added unincorporated surrounding land (a process called annexation) and absorbed adjacent municipalities (consolidation). Through annexation and consolidation, city governments found that they could better coordinate transportation, water, and sewer networks and also increase tax revenues. In 1859 Philadelphia annexed five surrounding suburbs, quadrupling its population with the stroke of a pen. Chicago followed suit in 1889, adding 133 square miles in an area that is now the far South Side. The largest such consolidation occurred in 1898, when Brooklyn, Queens, Staten Island, and the Bronx joined Manhattan to form the New York City that we know today. In the process, New York added nearly 2 million people to its population and ballooned in size from forty-four to nearly three hundred square miles.

Practically every large American city broadened its boundaries in these years. The trend toward annexation was supported by merchants and business elites who saw it as another way to undercut the political power of the immigrant wards that in their view stood in the way of progress. The good-government reformers, waving the banner of civic efficiency, hailed annexation as a step toward making the police and fire departments and other municipal agencies more professional. Land speculators and real-estate promoters welcomed annexation as a way of securing the municipal water and sewer systems that would sharply increase the worth of their holdings. Most middle-class suburbanites, eager for access to efficient city services, went along with the process. Not until the mid-twentieth century would outlying suburban communities, valuing local autonomy and wary of big-city tax rates and social problems, successfully fight off annexation.

Conclusion   The movement toward a metropolitan America represented the culmination of a long struggle to control the changing urban world in the decades after the Civil War. The mind-boggling urban expansion of these years, drawing in millions of rural Americans and foreign immigrants alike, brought a concentration of economic power, an expansion of consumer markets, and a cornucopia of lucrative investment possibilities. For a nation in which seven out of ten people still lived on farms or in towns of fewer than twenty-five hundred inhabitants, as was true of America in 1880, the big cities' sheer size and diversity sometimes seemed overwhelming, while the battles for power and wealth that raged in urban America proved both exciting and deeply disturbing. It is hardly surprising that contemporary observers like Jacob Riis threw up their hands at conditions in the nation's metropolises.

While the social critics had their say, the urban population itself wrestled with the stresses and tensions of a social environment unfamiliar to many and undergoing tremendous flux. Middle- and upper-class urban residents were troubled not only by the new industrial city's massive physical problems—housing, schooling, transportation, sanitation, police and fire protection, and all the rest—but even more by the city's corrosive effect on traditional values and expectations. Migrants from America's farms and homogeneous small towns suddenly found themselves in an impersonal, ever-changing, fast-paced commercial world where antagonistic economic interests and ethnic and racial groups grappled for influence and power.

Predictably many of the native-born urban newcomers responded by attempting to re-create in the city the familiar features of rural life. They agitated for parks and playgrounds to bring nature into the metropolis, crusaded for temperance to dam the river of alcohol that washed over the immigrant wards, and campaigned for political reforms that would end boss rule and restore familiar forms of local government.

Immigrants, too, had to adjust to city life. Recently uprooted, in many cases, from centuries-old rhythms of peasant life or from the ghettos of eastern Europe, these newly arrived aliens had to adapt to the unremitting demands of industrial labor, to a babble of unfamiliar languages, to the mortal hazards and casual indignities of tenement-house life, and to the head-spinning diversity of the American urban scene. Faced with discrimination and hostility, the older immigrants clung as long as they could to their traditional ways, their ethnic foods, their street and saloon culture, and their cherished religious institutions. Remarkably impervious to the assaults of middle-class political opponents, the pieties of would-be uplifters, or the efforts of moral reformers to legislate behavior, the immigrants rallied round a familiar figure, the boss. Of all the urban actors in these years, the bosses demonstrated the most versatility in learning how to wield the levers of power in the strange new world of the Gilded Age city.

The city, then, was a place of constant contention among wildly different groups—poverty-stricken foreign immigrants, recent arrivals from the American hinterland, old urban elites, newly minted capitalist tycoons, an uneasy middle class, growing numbers of blacks—that eyed each other warily through layers of suspicion and mistrust. In view of these social realities, it is hardly surprising that the beautifiers and planners who sought through monumental architecture, classic statuary, and broad avenues to force the city into a single cultural mold only partially achieved their aims.

What finally emerged from the boisterous and bruising conflict was a gradual recognition that all city dwellers shared a basic interest in such mundane matters as clean water, adequate sewers, regular garbage collection, and reliable fire protection. Out of this realization blossomed a conception of what some called the service city—a city that could efficiently meet the collective needs of its diverse inhabitants while they pursued their personal or group interests. By 1900 cities across America had established administrative structures and developed trained bureaucracies with broad responsibility for sanitation, transportation, street lights, public health, parks, police, and so on. A metropolitan America had taken shape.

Despite dark warnings of chaos and social upheaval, a remarkable degree of order and stability prevailed in urban America as the nineteenth century closed. After a generation of unchecked growth, political struggle, and social unrest, the nation's cities had evolved governmental forms sufficient to assure at least an adequate quality of life for all and to intervene when necessary to protect the welfare of the urban populace. This enlarged conception of government only slowly penetrated the arena of national politics, but the lessons so painfully learned in the late-nineteenth-century cities would profoundly shape the progressive movement that lay ahead.

CHRONOLOGY

1843 Robert M. Hartley founds the New York Association for Improving the Condition of the Poor.

1851 The American branch of the Young Men's Christian Association (YMCA) opens.

1853 Charles Loring Brace founds the New York Children's Aid Society.

1855 New York opens its Castle Garden immigrant center.

1857 Filling in of Boston's Back Bay begins.

1858 Frederick Law Olmsted and Calvert Vaux design Central Park.

1859 Philadelphia annexes five surrounding suburbs.

1869 Boss William Marcy Tweed gains control of New York's Tammany Hall political machine.

1871 The Great Chicago Fire.

1872 Anthony Comstock founds the New York Society for the Suppression of Vice and leads a "purity" campaign.

1874 John Wanamaker opens his Philadelphia department store.

1875 Henry Hobson Richardson designs Trinity Church in Boston.

1879 The New York "dumbbell" tenement law is passed.

1880 William Booth's followers establish an American branch of the Salvation Army.

1882 Josephine Shaw Lowell founds the New York Charity Organization Society (COS).

1888 First electric-trolley line, in Richmond, VA.

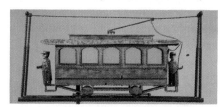

1889 Jane Addams and Ellen Gates Starr open Hull House.

1890 Jacob Riis, *How the Other Half Lives.*

1892 Immigrant-admitting station is opened on Ellis Island in the New York City harbor.

Reverend Charles Parkhurst organizes the City Vigilance League.

"Big Jim" Pendergast gains control of the Kansas City political machine.

1894 The Chicago Ship and Sanitary Canal is built.

Clarence Lexow's investigation of New York City reveals widespread police corruption.

1898 New York City consolidates five boroughs into Greater New York.

1900 Theodore Dreiser, *Sister Carrie.*

1907 Walter Rauschenbusch, *Christianity and the Social Crisis.*

1910 Jane Addams, *Twenty Years at Hull House.*

For Further Reading

Thomas J. Archdeacon, *Becoming American: An Ethnic History* (1983). An incisive overview of the immigrant experience.

Gunther Barth, *City People: The Rise of Modern City Culture in Nineteenth-Century America* (1980). A spritely account of popular city culture from newspapers to ballparks.

Paul Boyer, *Urban Masses and Moral Order in America, 1820–1920* (1978). A richly detailed analysis of reformers' attempts to control city life.

Allen F. Davis, *American Heroine: The Life and Legend of Jane Addams* (1973). A penetrating biography of a leader in the settlement-house movement.

Robert M. Fogelson, *Big-City Police* (1977). A provocative study, with useful comparative detail, of the evolution of urban police forces.

Kenneth T. Jackson, *Crabgrass Frontier: The Suburbanization of the United States* (1985). A stimulating comparative study of city expansion and suburban development in Europe and America.

Zane L. Miller, *Boss Cox's Cincinnati: Urban Politics in the Progressive Era* (1968). A detailed, balanced exploration of the functions served by an urban political boss.

Kathy Peiss, *Cheap Amusements: Working Women and Leisure in Turn-of-the-Century New York* (1986). A forceful and provocative analysis of immigrant women's lives.

Thomas L. Philpott, *The Slum and the Ghetto: Neighborhood Deterioration and Middle-Class Reform, Chicago, 1880–1930* (1978). An in-depth examination of the impact of ethnicity and race on one city.

Sam B. Warner, Jr., *Streetcar Suburbs: The Process of Growth in Boston, 1870–1900* (1962). A pioneering study of the factors that fueled suburban expansion.

Additional Bibliography

Urban Growth and Expansion

William L. Barney, *The Passage of the Republic* (1987); Gunther Barth, *Instant Cities: Urbanization and the Rise of San Francisco and Denver* (1975); Henry C. Binford, *The First Suburbs: Residential Communities on the Boston Periphery, 1815–1860* (1985); John E. Bodnar, *The Transplanted: A History of Immigrants in Urban America* (1985); Howard P. Chudacoff, *Mobile Americans: Residential and Social Mobility in Omaha, 1880–1920*

(1972) and *The Evolution of Urban Society* (2d ed., 1982); Donna R. Gabaccia, *From Sicily to Elizabeth Street: Housing and Social Change Among Italian Immigrants, 1880–1930* (1982); John S. Gilkeson, Jr., *Middle-Class Providence, 1820–1940* (1986); Charles N. Glaab and A. Theodore Brown, *A History of Urban America* (1967); Milton M. Gordon, *Assimilation in American Life* (1964); John Higham, *Send These to Me: Jews and Other Immigrants in Urban America* (1975); John Higham, ed., *Ethnic Leadership in America* (1978); Irving Howe, *World of Our Fathers: The Journey of the East European Jews to America and the Life They Found and Made* (1976); Joy J. Jackson, *New Orleans in the Gilded Age: Politics and Urban Progress, 1880–1896* (1969); Alan M. Kraut, *The Huddled Masses: The Immigrant in American Society, 1880–1921* (1982); Michael La Sorte, *La Merica: Images of Italian Greenhorn Experience* (1985); Judith W. Leavitt, *The Healthiest City: Milwaukee and the Politics of Health Reform* (1982); Odd S. Lovoll, *The Promise of America: A History of the Norwegian-American People* (1984); Roy Rosenzweig, *Eight Hours for What We Will: Workers and Leisure in an Industrial City, 1870–1920* (1983); Philip Taylor, *The Distant Magnet: European Emigration to USA* (1971); David Ward, *Cities and Immigrants: A Geography of Change in Nineteenth-Century America* (1971); Sam B. Warner, Jr., *The Private City: Philadelphia in Three Periods of Its Growth* (1968) and *The Urban Wilderness: A History of the American City* (1972).

The Problems of the City

Jane Addams, *Twenty Years at Hull House* (1910); Sydney E. Ahlstrom, *A Religious History of the American People* (2 vols., 1975); Robert Bremner, *From the Depths: The Discovery of Poverty in the United States* (1956); John W. Briggs, *An Italian Passage: Immigrants to Three American Cities, 1890–1930* (1978); Alexander B. Callow, Jr., *The Tweed Ring* (1966); Alexander B. Callow, Jr., ed., *The City Boss in America* (1976); Kathleen N. Conzen, *Immigrant Milwaukee, 1836–1860* (1976); Allen F. Davis, *Spearheads for Reform: The Social Settlements and the Progressive Movement, 1890–1914* (1967); Lyle W. Dorsett, *The Pendergast Machine* (1968); Robert Fisher, *Let the People Decide: Neighborhood Organizing in America* (1984); Melvin G. Holli, *Reform in Detroit: Hazen S. Pingree and Urban Politics* (1969); Morton Keller, *The Art and Politics of Thomas Nast* (1968); Kenneth L. Kusmer, *A Ghetto Takes Shape: Black Cleveland, 1870–1930* (1976); Roger Lane, *Policing the City: Boston, 1822–1885* (1967); Terrence J. McDonald, *The Parameters of Urban Fiscal Policy: Socioeconomic*

Change and Political Culture in San Francisco, 1860–1906 (1986); Henry F. May, *Protestant Churches and Industrial America* (1963); Gwendolyn Mink, *Old Labor and New Immigrants in American Political Development: Union, Party, and State, 1875–1920* (1986); Eric H. Monkkonen, ed., *Walking to Work: Tramps in America, 1790–1935* (1984); Humbert S. Nelli, *The Business of Crime: Italians and Syndicate Crime in the United States* (1976); Gilbert Osofsky, *Harlem: The Making of a Ghetto* (1963); James F. Richardson, *The New York Police: Colonial Times to 1901* (1970) and *Urban Police in the United States* (1974); Christine M. Rosen, *The Limits of Power: Great Fires and the Process of City Growth in America* (1986); Martin J. Schiesl, *The Politics of Efficiency: Municipal Administration and Reform in America, 1880–1920* (1977); Allan H. Spear, *Black Chicago: The Making of a Negro Ghetto, 1890–1920* (1967); Eugene J. Watts, *The Social Bases of City Politics: Atlanta, 1865–1903* (1978); Virginia Yans-McLaughlin, *Family and Community: Italian Immigrants in Buffalo, 1880–1930* (1977).

Transforming the City's Physical Environment

Bainbridge Bunting, *Houses of Boston's Back Bay* (1967); David F. Burg, *Chicago's White City of 1893* (1976); Carl W. Condit, *Chicago, 1910–29: Building, Planning, and Urban Technology* (1973); Albert Fein, *Frederick Law Olmsted and the American Environmental Tradition* (1972); David C. Hammack, *Power and Society: Greater New York at the Turn of the Century* (1982); Thomas S. Hines, *Burnham of Chicago: Architect and Planner* (1974); William H. Jordy, *American Buildings and Their Architects* (1972; vol. 3 of *Progressive and Academic Ideals at the Turn of the Century*); Harold M. Mayer and Richard C. Wade, *Chicago: Growth of a Metropolis* (1969); David Schuyler, *The New Urban Landscape: The Redefinition of City Form in Nineteenth-Century America* (1986); Jon C. Teaford, *City and Suburb: The Political Fragmentation of Metropolitan America, 1850–1970* (1979) and *The Unheralded Triumph: City Government in America, 1870–1900* (1984); Robert C. Twombly, *Louis Sullivan: His Life and Work* (1986).

CHAPTER 19

Daily Life, Popular Culture, and the Arts, 1860–1900

In 1894 Walter Teller Post, a recently married junior clerk for the Northern Pacific Railway in St. Paul, Minnesota, wrote in high spirits to his father on the family farm in Michigan. "I am hunting for a house," he noted. "Lillie and I have decided that it will be much nicer to go to housekeeping than to board. . . . We have to pay $35.00 per month for board. . . . We want to get a house [to rent] for about $15 or $20.00 per mo."

Several weeks later, Post proudly sent his father a sketch of their new rented house, showing the placement of all furniture and including stick figures of himself and his wife tucked cozily in their bed. The young couple had tried to furnish their home simply and inexpensively, turning down, for example, a "wonderful opportunity" to purchase a $300 piano for only $10 down and $10 a month. Nevertheless, they had run up a bill of more than $150 at a St. Paul department store. Post had put $100 down and promised to pay the balance in two months.

Post's father did not approve of the arrangement. Buying on credit was dangerous, he wrote back. And what about Walter's promise to send home ten dollars monthly to help out his parents? He was also troubled by Walter's enthusiasm for city life, with its myriad opportunities for amusement and shopping, and was particularly wary of his son's comment that someday "we [will] be rich enough to have more." Knowing only the long hours and hard work of farm life, the elder Post counseled restraint and warned his son not to spend beyond his means.

Post's father's concerns were well founded. Dazzled by the growing availability of consumer goods, and hoping that his material possessions would affirm his entry into the middle class, Walter had gotten in over his head. In less than two months, staggered by an unanticipated heating bill on his rented house, Post defaulted on his debt to the department store. Frustrated with his long hours and low pay, Post began to complain to his superiors. In September 1896 the railroad dismissed him. Soon he was searching for work among relatives in Indiana.

Walter Post's experience was hardly unique. Countless other Americans in the late nineteenth century faced similar difficulties in adjusting to changing patterns of consumption and work. In less than three decades, the American economy had undergone a fundamental reorganization and restructuring. For both the throngs of native-born Americans who, like Walter Post, moved from farm to city to work for national corporations, and the millions of foreigners who immigrated to the United States in these years, the process of readjusting expectations and learning to live in a rapidly industrializing society was not easy.

While the great era of consumer goods still lay ahead, a torrent of new products poured out of American factories, promising a transformation of everyday life and previously unimagined levels of comfort and convenience. Hot-air furnaces, electric lights, indoor plumbing, sewing machines, and cast-iron kitchen ranges eased the drudgery of running a home. Kellogg's Corn Flakes, Hires Root Beer, Jell-O, Borden's Evaporated Milk, and other prepared foods reduced meal-preparation time as well.

But these products were not equally accessible to everyone; their greater variety, in fact, widened the gulf between the haves and the have-nots and sharpened a latent sense of class consciousness among rich and poor. The middle and upper classes, which included lawyers, doctors, and other professionals, as well as accountants, store managers, engineers, and other white-collar workers, increasingly defined their status in terms of comfortable houses, material possessions, education, genteel cultural standards, and greater opportunities for leisure activities. In contrast, farmers and the urban working classes—the overwhelming majority of the population—although attracted (like Walter Post) to the new consumer products dangled before them, gained access to them slowly. Restricted in their purchasing power by low income and frequent lack of work, they struggled to acquire whatever small benefits they could.

Despite a roller-coaster economy and major depressions in 1873 and 1893, many men and women did succeed in improving their families' economic position and social standing. For all the upward mobility, however, the gulf between the classes remained wide. While the very rich lived in a world apart, and the middle class embraced its own particular behavior code and cultural pursuits, a vigorous working-class culture took form in the streets, churches, dance halls, saloons, vaudeville theaters, social clubs, and amusement parks of the bustling immigrant cities. Middle-class reformers strove to remake this working-class culture in its own image of propriety. In the long run, however, it was the culture of the masses that would prove the more influential in shaping modern America.

Everyday Life in Flux

In the closing decades of the nineteenth century, industrialization not only introduced an unprecedented range of innovative products but also opened up new jobs and destroyed older ones, in the process rearranging the occupational structure and altering the distribution of income within society. These changes, together with the expansion of white-collar occupations, created new expectations for family life and fostered a growing sense of class awareness. "The stratification of our society, and its crystallization into social groups," wrote New York lawyer John Jay Chapman in 1898, "is little short of miraculous."

Rising Standards of Living

In the second half of the nineteenth century, in virtually every industry, the increased output made possible by mechanization lowered prices and encouraged the development of new products that truly revolutionized daily life for many. The glass industry, for example, once dependent on skilled glassblowers, in the 1880s perfected new machines that could manufacture window glass in long sheets. These were then fashioned into the strikingly larger windows increasingly installed in department-store façades and private homes.

In the clothing trades, as we have seen, widespread use of sewing machines profoundly changed the industry. Before the Civil War, shirts had been made largely by hand. Each shirt required nearly thirty thousand stitches and took fourteen hours to complete. Most people wore hand-me-downs, and styles were simple. By the 1880s, however, complete shirts of standardized size and far more elaborate designs could be machine-sewn in less than two hours. For the elite and middle classes, personal wardrobes expanded dramatically. Clothes closets became commonplace household features, supplementing the small bureaus or armoires that had previously sufficed to hold the family apparel. Dress became an ever-more-important badge of social class. Immigrants and rural migrants rushed to purchase cheap factory-made clothes and lose the "greenhorn" or "hayseed" look.

Innovations in food technology, among them breakfast cereals, changed eating habits. In 1878, following on the heels of pre–Civil War dietary reformer Sylvester Graham (see Chapter 11), physician John Harvey Kellogg of Battle Creek,

The Lure of Advertising

These late-nineteenth-century advertisers promised to remake one's physique through padding and bustles and miraculously to improve health with chemical compounds.

Michigan, marketed Granola—a wheat, corn, and oat mixture that he advertised as healthier than the then standard breakfast of sausage, eggs, and potatoes. In the next three decades, Kellogg produced a variety of new cereals, including wheat flakes, shredded wheat, and Kellogg's Corn Flakes.

Soon competitors rushed into the field. Charles W. Post, for example, developed Grape Nuts Flakes and Postum, a breakfast drink made from bran, wheat, and molasses that he touted as an alternative to overstimulating, unhealthful coffee. By the turn of the century, those health-conscious middle- and upper-class Americans who could afford them had shifted to the new cereals and hot drinks as simpler, more easily prepared substitutes for the traditional heavy breakfast.

Not all inventions lived up to their promoters' claims. Lydia Pinkham's famous vegetable extract "for all those painful Complaints and Weaknesses so common to our best female population" contained nearly 23 percent alcohol. Other so-called health compounds featured significant amounts of opium. Countless patent medicines, including one that promised to "POSITIVELY CURE" backache in two hours and deafness in two days, were totally ineffective. But they were eagerly snatched up by

a society that had come to believe that material and physical improvements were now within everyone's reach.

Although some products failed to work as claimed, the overall impact of late-nineteenth-century industrialization was to significantly improve the level of comfort and convenience for many American families. In 1870 most urban women had shopped daily, because refrigeration did not exist to keep food from spoiling. Like farm wives, they had baked their own bread and canned their own fruits and vegetables. Hours and hours were spent in food preparation, doing laundry by hand, firing up smoky stoves and furnaces, and carrying "slop jars" containing human excrement to outdoor sewers or malodorous waste-collection tanks. By 1900, in contrast, the spread of indoor plumbing, better stoves and furnaces, commercially prepared foods, and mechanical washing machines had greatly eased this domestic burden. Urban middle- and upper-class families began to take for granted central heating, electric lights, telephone service, and a range of other household innovations unknown earlier. Also by the turn of the century, 90 percent of urban families ate store-bought bread, and two-thirds utilized commercial laundries.

New Improved Western Washer

Although the advertisements for mechanical washers implied that laundering clothes could be enjoyable, it still took considerable physical effort to crank the machine.

Refrigerated railroad cars brought fresh meat to local butchers, and housewives used iceboxes to store it for up to a week. In place of canning, homemakers purchased inexpensive commercially canned vegetables, Heinz pickles, and Campbell's soups. Campbell's jingle—"It only takes a ten-cent can to make enough for six"—targeted an economy-minded mass market.

Bringing New Commodities to Rural and Small-Town America

While the new products made possible by swift industrialization gradually changed the lives of city dwellers, mail-order houses and chain stores were expanding the horizons of rural and small-town Americans. The reorientation of rural consumer standards required nothing less than a massive educational campaign to introduce the nonurban population to the new products and conveniences, and the man who launched this campaign was Aaron Montgomery Ward, a traveling salesman from Chicago. In the 1860s Ward began to realize how dependent rural Americans were on local merchants selling a limited range of goods at high prices. Scraping together his savings and joining forces with the Grangers, who had pledged to reduce farmers' costs by cutting out the middleman (see Chapter 16), Ward in 1872 circulated a list of products for sale at a 40 percent discount. For farmers hesitant to deal with a distant, unknown merchant, he promised the unconditional right to return merchandise. By 1884 Ward's catalog offered nearly ten thousand items to rural customers.

Ward soon ran into competition from Richard Warren Sears, a flamboyant young Minnesota railroad agent whose first taste of marketing came when he obtained permission from a manufacturer to sell a case of watches left at his station. Moving to Chicago in 1887, he established a mail-order company (now Sears, Roebuck) that could ship farmers a wide range of products, including agricultural implements, clothing, medicine, furniture, stoves, guns, tools, and baby carriages. Sears built customer loyalty by guaranteeing low prices and publishing testimonials from satisfied patrons. The firm carried many products at different prices to suit all pocketbooks. Pump organs, for example, ranged from "Our AA Grade Home Favorite" at $64.95 to "Our Happy Home Organ, Grade B," at $22.00.

Distributed to millions of rural families, the encyclopedic Sears and Ward's catalogs, available in German and Swedish editions as well as English, opened the door to a new world of consumer goods and, coincidentally, educated their readers in the canons of middle-class taste. "The prevailing style in furniture," advised the 1897 Sears catalog, "is to have the various odd pieces upholstered in harmonizing colors of different shades." The same catalog provided a full-page lesson in the technique of making gold-filled watch cases and explained why they would outlast their cheaper gold-plated rivals. Similarly consumers had only to browse through the mail-order catalog to learn to distinguish a fish fork from a pickle fork or to appreciate the differences between cheap and expensive sewing machines, sleighs, and carriages.

Marketing like this inspired such trust in rural and small-town readers that they sometimes sought advice on personal problems. One lonely farmer wrote to Montgomery Ward's proposing marriage to the "girl wearing hat number ——— on p. 153 of your catalog."

The chain store offered another mechanism for bringing low-priced mass-produced goods to consumers outside large cities. F. W. Woolworth, a farm boy from upstate New York, in 1879 opened a "Five and Ten Cent Store" in Utica that sold goods like crochet needles, safety pins, soap, harmonicas, and thimbles from a "five-cent counter." Quickly increasing his volume and multiplying his stores, Woolworth appealed to those Americans who either lacked the money to buy more expensive goods or simply wished to economize. Woolworth's, together with the Great Atlantic and Pacific Tea Company (A&P), which consolidated several separate food stores into one operation in 1859, pioneered in the creation of nationwide "chains" that stressed low prices and consumer savings.

Under a barrage of advertising, consumers by the 1890s faced new choices daily about what they should buy. More conscious than ever before of the sparkling array of material options open to them, the American people were slowly drawn into a milieu in which the goods and services purchased increasingly dictated one's position and status in society. At the same time that material possessions made possible new realms of comfort and convenience, they also reinforced a pervasive sense of widening class differences.

A Shifting Class Structure

Patterns of consumption, culture, and everyday life reflect a society's class structure, and in late-nineteenth-century America, this structure underwent important modifications. From the colonial period on, social class had been loosely defined by occupation and income. Contemporaries readily identified the rich, the "middling ranks," and the poor in every community. But in the post–Civil War era, fundamental changes in the nature of work, together with shifts in residential location, massive immigration, and new patterns of consumption, redefined and sharpened the conception of social class.

In addition to income and occupation, lifestyle and self-identification now became important determinants of social rank.

The working class felt the impact of these changes first and most keenly. At midcentury skilled craftsmen, who exercised considerable authority over their work and viewed themselves as independent entrepreneurs, had dominated the working class. Common laborers, who exchanged simple muscle power for a daily wage, identified with the artisans above them and hoped eventually to acquire skilled positions themselves. Although skilled artisans earned between five hundred dollars and nine hundred dollars yearly, or from two to ten times the wages of common laborers, both segments of the working class shared a common outlook and sense of class identity. In Pittsburgh and other cities, craftsworkers and laborers lived on the same streets, attended the same churches, and patronized the same saloons. They believed in the value of hard physical labor, prided themselves on their physical strength, and helped each other in times of need.

Beginning in the 1870s, however, the bond between craftsworkers and unskilled laborers began to dissolve as new production methods restructured the work process. By the 1880s the widespread use of machinery had destroyed the jobs of many skilled artisans. The Bessemer steel-making process, for example, eliminated the need for the skilled puddlers who formerly had controlled production in the iron industry. With fewer skilled positions into which a worker might eventually move, the only people willing to undertake the dangerous, low-paying steel-mill jobs were unskilled foreign immigrants who desperately needed work. Thus by the turn of the century, a rift had developed within the working class. Craftsworkers now commonly looked down on the newcomers. Cut off from the common laborers who formed a substratum below them, skilled artisans identified more and more with the middle class.

As the working class fragmented, the expansion of the middle class, which would vastly accelerate in the early twentieth century, was already under way. After the Civil War, the demand for trained personnel increased in all economic sectors. Growing municipal bureaucracies, school systems, police forces, and fire departments required specially trained employees. Large businesses and

Training Secretaries, c. 1900

Thousands of young women, eager to obtain secretarial work, learned to type in courses such as this one run by the Remington Typewriter Company.

national corporations hired armies of clerks, accountants, and salespersons to manage their operations. Bustling department stores, insurance agencies, and food companies established accounting and sales divisions. These middle-class personnel worked in clean company headquarters and city offices physically separated from the sooty factories and dirty mills that employed manual laborers.

In contrast to members of the working class, who were paid by the hour or according to the level of production, middle-class clerical and professional workers received fixed weekly or monthly salaries. The salaries of the middle class, moreover, were considerably higher than even those of skilled craftsworkers. In Detroit, where very few skilled artisans took home more than $500 yearly, city clerks, bookkeepers, and inspectors earned between $500 and $1,000, while other middle-class jobs often paid more than $1,000 a year.

Middle-class employees' higher earnings and steady work significantly changed their outlook and expectations. Freed from worries about making ends meet, many adopted long-term strategies for improving their income and maximizing their purchasing power. They devoted more resources to educating their children, buying expensive items such as sewing machines and pianos on credit, and otherwise improving household comforts and conveniences. A shorter workweek, moreover, gave middle-class employees more time to spend with their families and greater opportunities for socializing and recreation.

The very wealthy, meanwhile, did not hesitate to flaunt their riches, thus honing public awareness of growing class divisions in industrial America. The Carnegies, Morgans, Rockefellers, Goulds, Huntingtons, and Fricks used their immense fortunes to build elaborate houses and country estates. Railroad financier Jay Gould, the owner of Lyndhurst—a Gothic castlelike home in Tarrytown, New York, with a 380-foot-long greenhouse filled with forty thousand dollars worth of exotic plants—was typical of a generation for whom a palatial house offered the ultimate proof of success on the capitalist battlefield. In Newport (Rhode Island), Bar Harbor (Maine), and other fashionable resort areas, the wealthy built great mansions (euphemistically called cottages), kept stables of racehorses, joined exclusive country clubs, and cruised on their magnificent personal yachts. Many also amassed lavish art collections, endowed museums, and traveled abroad.

As a result of workplace restructuring, the expansion of the middle class, and the rise in enormous fortunes, income distribution in America by the turn of the century had become severely skewed. Statistics are imprecise, but a knowledgeable observer estimated in 1896 that of the nation's 12.5 million families, approximately 5.5 million were working-class and earned less than $500 annually; 5.5 million were middle-class and had incomes from $500 to $5,000; and the remaining 1.5 million, or the 12 percent whose incomes were over $5,000, were rich. This privileged 12 percent, however, owned *86 percent* of the nation's wealth. In contrast, the middle class, whose families made up 44 percent of the population, possessed only 12.5 percent of the aggregate wealth, and the working class, who composed the bottom 44 percent of the nation's people, struggled to survive with a mere 1.5 percent of the wealth.

Everyday Life in Flux

The Changing Family

This skewed distribution of resources had an important impact on family life. The level of family income not only determined access to household technology and consumer goods but also affected family size, life expectancy, infant mortality, and relationships between parents and children. Historians are cautious in their use of aggregate federal census statistics from the era, which blur differences among social classes as well as between rural and urban Americans and between ethnic groups and the native-born. Nevertheless, such data *can* give us a broad overview of the changes in family structure in the post–Civil War years.

Between 1860 and 1900, these statistics revealed, most Americans lived in nuclear families; that is, families made up of only parents and children. Often boarders and servants resided with the nuclear family, but grandparents and other relatives typically did not. And families were becoming smaller, continuing a trend begun in the early nineteenth century. Family size shrank largely because mothers bore fewer children. For white women, the number of live births* fell from an average of 5.42 children in 1850 to 3.56 in 1900. But those children who were born had a better chance of surviving to adulthood, as indicated statistically by a rise in life expectancy from 38.4 years to 46.3 years for males and from 40.5 years to 48.3 years for females. Overall, the size of the average nuclear family stabilized at five or six members.

Like all averages, however, these figures obscure the significant differences created by social class, race, and ethnicity. For example, due to a very high rate of infant mortality among black males, their average life expectancy at birth in 1900, the first year for which we have statistics, was only 22.5 years, less than half that for whites. Similarly, the decline in family size was not uniformly distributed. Farmers and the urban working class, relying on the labor of their children to make ends meet, continued to have large families. Immigrant and farm families with six to eight children remained common. The urban middle and upper classes, by contrast, who had no need to send their children

off to work, chose to limit their family size. In Buffalo, New York, an industrial city with many immigrants, the difference in the average number of children in families of various occupational groups in 1900 was striking: 5.7 for laborers, 5.2 for skilled workers, and only 3.5 for business owners and company managers.

These statistics reveal how significantly middle- and upper-class families differed from their working-class counterparts. The correlation of high income with smaller family size indicates that the middle and upper classes were practicing birth control, either by periodically abstaining from sexual intercourse, by other forms of contraception, or by abortion. Whatever the method, smaller families meant more free time for women, more attention to the education and training of children, and greater opportunity for leisure and recreation.

Working-Class Family Life

The dramatic impact of income level on the nature of family life becomes most evident when we look at black and immigrant working-class households. Because many such households hovered at or fell below the poverty level, they had to rely on the labor of the children and on a network of relatives who could pitch in during times of need. The poorer the family, the more dependent it became on the cooperative work of all its members simply to survive.

Black families in the post–Civil War South, freed from slavery with few possessions and little money, relied heavily on their extended families for help and support. Although most blacks lived in nuclear, two-parent families, they counted on the close proximity of cousins, aunts, uncles, and other relatives to assist them with child care, housing, and expenses. For blacks, the extended kinship network replaced the nuclear family as the dominant institution in their daily lives. (In rural North Carolina and Mississippi, kinship networks containing between fifty and two hundred people practiced a remarkable degree of mutual cooperation, making decisions jointly, sharing economic resources, providing emotional support at funerals, and strengthening ties within the group through reciprocal visiting, family reunions, and membership in the same church.)

---

*As measured by the fertility rate: the average number of children born to each female between the ages of fourteen and forty-five.

The Walters, Lubert County, Georgia, 1896

Southern black families such as the Walterses depended on extended kin networks for assistance and emotional support.

The case of Joseph Sutton, who lived at Miles River Neck in Talbot County, Maryland, typified postwar blacks' reliance on relatives. In 1889, when Sutton was four, his father died. His mother, unable to run the farm by herself, moved to Baltimore to find work, leaving Sutton with his grandmother, who became, in effect, his surrogate parent. Three years later, at age seven, he moved in with his uncle, a nearby tenant farmer. There, for several years, Sutton took care of a baby cousin who was named after his great-grandmother, a common practice that symbolically reinforced the cohesiveness of the extended family. Thanks to these strong family bonds, Sutton overcame the loss of his own parents and eventually was able to buy a farm and form a stable family of his own.

Although often better off than their black counterparts, poor white farm families in the South and Midwest also depended heavily on the effort of all family members to survive. While the men and older boys worked in the fields, the farm wife with her younger children ran the house and dairy and kept up the kitchen garden. In addition to preparing meals, drawing water, tending the fire in the stove, cleaning the house, feeding chickens, taking care of the milk shed, and doing wash, farm women sewed and mended clothes, knitted hats and gloves, wove tablecloths, churned butter, made soap, and trimmed the oil lamps that illuminated the home in this age before electricity.

When necessary, white rural women and their daughters took over the duties normally performed by the men. "There were nine children in our family," reminisced Margaret Mitchell Womer about her childhood on the Great Plains, "six girls and three boys, and as the girls were older and my father not strong, the hard toil of the pioneer life fell to the lot of the girls. . . . Our house was made of logs and the girls helped in the construction of it." Some mothers and daughters occasionally plowed the fields, cared for the livestock, and pitched in at harvest time. Many farm families owed their survival to the hard work and resourcefulness of everyone involved.

The same was true for urban working-class families, for whom the contributions of women, young adults, and children often spelled the difference between survival and modest prosperity. The average urban family of five or six members in the 1890s needed an annual income of between six hundred and eight hundred dollars to live comfortably. Although prices for food, rent, and other necessities dropped between 1865 and 1890, and real wages increased by almost 50 percent, most working-class families still did not have a high enough income to live on the father's earnings alone. As in rural America, survival thus became a cooperative family effort.

To supplement their income, urban working-class families often rented rooms to boarders, and the women commonly took in laundry. Under the latter circumstance, washing became a heavy, all-day chore. Women had to draw water from a pump outside, carry it inside, heat it on the wood or coal stove, and boil the clothes. Working-class laundresses universally dreaded "blue Mondays," so named for the bluing or bleaching agents used in the laundry on Monday, the traditional washday. Beyond washing and cooking, urban working-class women who could not afford store-bought apparel continued to sew the family's clothes.

If a husband became sick or lost his job, a wife might even take a job in a garment factory alongside her elder daughters, who usually worked in manufacturing plants until they married. Immigrant children commonly went to work at the age of ten or twelve and were expected to turn over their earnings to their parents. Children grew up quickly under the weight of such responsibilities, but they also developed a strong family loyalty.

For many working-class families, the cooperative family ethic was the key to improving their financial position. In Detroit, for example, a fifty-year-old German carpenter and his three working children in the 1890s generated a combined income of $1,428, well within middle-class earning levels. The pooling of wages, by enabling working-class families to set aside part of their income for monthly mortgage payments, helps explain how many of them were able to purchase their own homes. (The greater availability of small, affordable houses was another factor.) Such working-class Americans turned homeownership into a kind of insurance. If the principal breadwinner fell sick or became unemployed, families could take in boarders or use the house as collateral on a loan.

Successful working-class families took pleasure not only in their material gains but also in their accomplishments in the face of difficult odds. "We had to live pretty close," proudly commented a Massachusetts carpenter in 1890 who was raising six children, "but we did it, and now we have the house all paid for, so there is no longer any rent." The cooperative family ethic, which stressed mutual support and reliance on a network of relatives, thus enabled working-class Americans to survive and in some cases even get ahead in the rapidly changing economic environment of the late nineteenth century. But the cooperative pattern also accentuated the differences between poor families and their middle- and upper-class counterparts who managed comfortably on the salary of the main breadwinner alone.

Middle-Class Society and Culture

Spared the struggle for survival confronted by the majority of Americans in the post–Civil War era, society's middle and upper ranks faced a different challenge. Those who had grown up during the first half of the century had been drilled by ministers and social reformers in the morality of a producer-oriented society. They were taught to work hard, practice self-discipline, save their money, and disdain people who flaunted their wealth. When postwar economic changes brought these standards into question, members of the middle and upper classes were forced to readjust their outlook and expectations. Uneasy about the gap in income and lifestyles between themselves and the poor, they searched for ways to rationalize their relative prosperity amid widespread destitution. To justify these conditions, ministers, advice-book writers, and other commentators appealed to Victorian morality, a set of social ideas widely influential among the privileged classes of England and America, as well as some sectors of the working class, during the long reign (1837–1901) of Britain's Queen Victoria.

Proponents of Victorian morality argued that the financial success of the middle and upper classes could be attributed to their superior talent, intelligence, morality, and self-control. They further insisted that the moral code and cultural standards of the richer classes, as well as their mastery of polite manners and genteel behavior, represented advanced outposts in society's general progress from barbarism to civilization and thus should be the standard for the poorer ranks. In defining the moral and spiritual role of the middle class, these opinion molders assigned a major role to women: while men engaged in the world's work, women would provide the gentle, elevating influence that would lead society in its upward march.

While authoritative voices preached the certitudes of Victorian morality, thereby justifying the status of America's upper classes, a network of institutions, from elegant department stores and hotels to elite colleges and universities, bore mute but eloquent witness to the privileged position of these groups in society.

Manners and Morals

The Victorian world view, which first took shape in the 1830s and 1840s, rested on several fundamental assumptions. Central to it were a belief in progress and a cautiously optimistic view of human nature. But progress would not come without strenuous moral effort. At its best the Victorian moral code energized reform movements against suffering and injustice, including slavery.

But this intense moralism could also take the form of an obsessive preoccupation with details of personal behavior. Since most members of the elite and middle classes had achieved their status (or so they believed) through sobriety, earnestness, industriousness, and self-restraint, they tended to place an extremely high value on these virtues. Thus "Victorian morality" became synonymous with an intense suspicion of spontaneity, self-indulgence, or spending time or money on short-lived pleasures. This moral outlook was often violated in practice, of course—especially among the very rich—but it was widely preached as the standard for all society. An elaborate moral vocabulary of middle-class virtues pervades the sermons, essays, and inspiring fiction of the period.

Another central Victorian tenet was the importance of "culture" (by which was meant a knowledge of the social graces, literature, the fine arts, and classical music) as an agency of social uplift. In the post–Civil War years, prominent clergymen like Henry Ward Beecher of Brooklyn and Phillips Brooks of Boston urged cultural refinement on both the middle class and those aspiring to middle-class status. Beecher proclaimed in 1876, "The laborer ought to be ashamed of himself" who after twenty years does not own his own house and

"who has not in that house provided carpets for the rooms, who has not his China plates, who has not his chromos [cheap copies of famous paintings], who has not some books nestling on the shelf." To further the cause, the elite founded, and the middle class supported, a network of cultural institutions in these years, including the Metropolitan Museum of Art in New York (1870), the Museum of Fine Arts in Boston (1870), and similar institutions in Philadelphia, Chicago, and other cities.

At its most petty, the middle-class focus on conduct and behavior often degenerated into a preoccupation with manners and social rituals. Middle- and upper-class families increasingly defined their own social standing in terms not only of income but also of behavior. Good manners, including a knowledge of proper etiquette in all social occasions, especially dining and entertaining, became an important badge of status.

In her popular advice book *The American Woman's Home* (1869), Catharine Beecher (the sister of Henry Ward Beecher) reflected a typical Victorian self-consciousness about proper manners. The following list of dinner-table behaviors, she said, should be avoided by those of "good breeding":

> *Reaching over another person's plate; standing up to reach distant articles, instead of asking to have them passed; using one's own knife and spoon for butter, salt, or sugar, when it is the custom of the family to provide separate utensils for the purpose; setting cups with the tea dripping from them, on the table-cloth, instead of on the mats or small plates furnished; using the table-cloth instead of napkins; eating fast, and in a noisy manner; putting large pieces in the mouth; . . . [and] picking the teeth at the table. . . .*

For Beecher and other molders of manners, meals became important rituals that differentiated the social classes. Not only were they occasions for displaying the elaborate china and silver that middle- and upper-class families exclusively possessed, but they also provided telltale clues to a family's level of refinement and sophistication.

The Victorian code—with its emphasis on morals, manners, and proper behavior—thus served to heighten the sense of class differences for the

Dining at Home, c. 1900

For middle- and upper-class families, dining rituals separated the cultured and the uncultured. Families that could afford them hired servants to help at mealtime.

post–Civil War generation and to create visible distinctions among social groups. Prominent middle- and upper-class Victorians made bold claims about their sincere interest in helping others improve themselves. More often than not, however, their self-righteous, intensely moralistic outlook simply widened the gap that income disparities had already opened.

The Cult of Domesticity

Victorian views on morality and culture, coupled with rising pressures on consumers to make decisions about a mountain of domestic products, had a subtle but important impact on middle-class expectations about women's role within the home. From the 1840s on, many architects, members of the clergy, and other promoters of the so-called cult of domesticity (see Chapter 8) had idealized the home as "the woman's sphere," a protected retreat where she could express her special maternal gifts, including a sensitivity toward children and an aptitude for religion. "The home is the wife's province," asserted one writer; "it is her natural field of labor . . . to govern and direct its interior management."

During the 1880s and 1890s, advocates of this cult of domesticity added a new obligation to the traditional woman's role as director of the household: to foster an artistic environment that would nurture her family's cultural improvement. For many Victorian Americans of the comfortable classes, houses became statements of cultural aspiration. Elaborately ornamented architectural styles were popular. Like intricate sculptures, these structures featured detailed, mass-produced spindle ornamentation on the front porches; windows of varying dimensions; and ornate projecting chimneys. Women took charge of arranging the furniture and the overflowing decoration of the front parlor, turning it into a treasure house whose furnishings and curios would reflect the family's social standing and refinement. Souvenir spoons and other knickknacks collected during family travels were displayed to demonstrate the household's cosmopolitanism. Excluded from the world of business and commerce, many middle- and upper-class women devoted considerable time and energy to decorating their home, seeking to make it, as one advice book suggested, "a place of repose, a refuge from the excitement and distractions of outside . . . , provided with every attainable means of rest and recreation."

Not all middle-class women pursued the domestic ideal. For some, the drudgery of housework and of running the family overwhelmed the

The Front Parlor, c. 1890

Called a thicket because of its profuse decoration, the Victorian front parlor was home to the piano. Victorian Americans widely viewed music as a source of inspiration and social improvement.

concern for artistic accomplishment. For others, the artistic ideal itself was simply not to their taste. Sixteen-year-old Mary Putnam complained privately to a friend that she played the piano because of "an abstract general idea . . . of a father coming home regularly tired at night (from the plow, I believe the usual legend runs), and being solaced by the brilliant yet touching performance of a sweet only daughter upon the piano." She then confessed that she detested the piano. Increasingly, women in the 1880s and 1890s sought other outlets for their creative energies.

Department Stores and Hotels

While the idealistic, moralistic emphasis of Victorian social thought helped justify the privileged status of the middle and upper classes, many who had been reared in the producer economy of the early nineteenth century, with its emphasis on thrift

and saving, at first found it difficult to accept the new preoccupation with the accumulation and display of material possessions. But changes in the psychology of merchandising in the 1880s and 1890s helped dull the pangs of guilt. By emphasizing the high quality and low cost of the goods that they sold, and by stressing that material acquisitions could promote artistic and cultural accomplishments, merchants, business leaders, and cultural promoters encouraged Americans to loosen their purse strings and enjoy prosperity without inner reservations.

A key agent in modifying attitudes toward consumption was the department store. In the final quarter of the nineteenth century, innovative entrepreneurs led by Rowland H. Macy in New York, John Wanamaker in Philadelphia, and Marshall Field in Chicago built the giant department store into an urban institution and transformed the shopping experience for the millions of middle- and upper-class consumers who were their greatest patrons.

The merchandising innovations of the large urban department store represented a radical departure from earlier techniques. Unlike the rural general store, which carried a limited supply of food and clothing, the department store prided itself on its diverse inventory and constant flow of new products. Borrowing the economy-of-scale principle from the new mass-production industries, the department-store magnates bought in large volume at low cost directly from manufacturers. In contrast to the small urban shops common at midcentury, each specializing in a narrow line of merchandise—whether fabric, lace, or umbrellas—the typical department store sold every conceivable household item and article of clothing. Where the small-shop owner haggled over prices and offered adjustments for unsatisfactory merchandise grudgingly if at all, the department store sold goods at a fixed price, allowed unconditional exchanges, and provided free delivery.

Merchants like Wanamaker and Macy helped overcome the middle and upper classes' reluctance to spend by advertising their products at "rock-bottom" prices and fighting price wars to convince customers of the validity of their claims. To avoid keeping their stock too long, they held giant end-of-the-season clearance sales at drastically marked-down prices.

The major downtown establishments sought to transform shopping from a humdrum activity into an adventure. Not only did the rapid turnover of merchandise create a sense of constant novelty, but the mammoth stores themselves became imitation palaces, complete with stained-glass skylights, marble staircases, brilliant chandeliers, and plush carpets. When it opened in 1876, John Wanamaker's Grand Depot in Philadelphia, which boasted a gaslit "tent" where women could examine silk evening gowns under ballroom conditions, welcomed more than seventy thousand people. Marshall Field's Chicago emporium contained a stained-glass dome made by Tiffany's, blue English carpets, and rare walnut paneling. Shopping here, patrons could escape the familiar routines of their daily lives and experience an aura of wealth and luxury that raised their expectations about interior decoration and served as a model for good taste and refinement. The stores' elevators, telephones, electric lights, ventilation systems, and modern bathrooms whetted the public's appetite for such up-to-the-minute conveniences in their own homes.

Department stores lavished care and attention on shoppers, especially women. Richly decorated lounges supplied with newspapers and stationery, elegant restaurants serving modestly priced lunches, salespersons who greeted shoppers at the door, and glittering holiday decorations enticed visitors to linger and buy on impulse. Brigades of female sales clerks answered questions and made women feel at home. Such personal attention suggested to middle- and upper-class customers that they were of the ranks that deserved to be served. The large urban department store thus functioned as a kind of social club and home away from home for comfortably fixed women.

The great department stores' merchandise, interior decor, and deferential staff reinforced middle-class standards of behavior and consumption. The lower-class heroine in O. Henry's short story "The Trimmed Lamp," Nan, who hopes to rise into the middle class by marrying the right suitor, explains to her friend Lou that her job as a department-store salesgirl has taught her proper manners and ideals. Although poor, she sews her jacket to match exactly that of a frequent customer, the well-to-do Mrs. Van Alstyne Fisher. Appealing to the status consciousness of their middle- and upper-class customers, department stores implicitly promised higher social standing and the psychological well-being of knowing the latest styles. For

Rike's Department Store, Dayton, Ohio, 1893

Department stores set new standards for customer comfort and service in this era.

the financially secure, shopping became an adventure, a form of entertainment, and a means of affirming one's place in society.

The stately metropolitan hotels that proliferated in the late nineteenth century provided further examples of high fashion and elite taste. After Boston's Tremont Hotel established a prototype for refined elegance and technological innovation in the 1830s by offering its guests indoor plumbing and speaking tubes (the predecessor of telephones), cities across America aspired to build top-notch hotels. By the 1880s innovative hotels were setting new standards for design excellence.

The Waldorf Astoria in New York, the Palmer House in Chicago, and San Francisco's Palace became public shrines, epitomizing efficient organization and upper-class taste. Built in 1892 in the German Renaissance style, the Waldorf Astoria was a self-contained community with offices, restaurants, ballrooms, courtyards, and five hundred guest rooms. Household reformers writing in the 1890s held up the highly organized restaurants and laundry systems of the big hotels as models for efficient cooperative-apartment complexes.

Whether one marveled at their efficiency or gazed in wonder at their splendid gilt mirrors and plush carpets, the grand hotels, like the giant department stores, set the pattern for luxury, convenience, and service. In his 1904 travel book *The American Scene,* writer Henry James described the first-class hotel as "a synonym for civilization." In a society that shunned aristocratic pretensions, hotels and department stores made luxury acceptable by clothing it in the guise of efficiency and simple good taste. They provided a setting where newly affluent members of society could indulge and pamper themselves, if only for a few minutes or a day.

The Transformation of Higher Education

At a time when relatively few Americans possessed even a high-school education, U.S. colleges and universities represented another institutional stronghold of the business and professional elite and of the moderately well-to-do middle class. In 1900, despite enrollment increases in the preceding decades, only 4 percent of the nation's eighteen- to twenty-one-year-olds were enrolled in institutions of higher learning.

Wealthy capitalists gained status and a measure of immortality by endowing colleges and universities. Leland Stanford and his wife Jane Lathrop Stanford launched Stanford University in 1885 with a bequest of $24 million in memory of a dead son; John D. Rockefeller donated $34 million to the University of Chicago in 1891. Industrialists and businessmen dominated the boards of trustees of many educational institutions and forced their conservative views on the faculty and administrators. Sardonic economist Thorstein Veblen called these business-oriented academic managers "Captains of Erudition."

Under these circumstances colleges were widely viewed as a training ground for future business and professional leaders. In the process of preparing affluent young people for later responsibilities, not only the classroom experience but also social contacts and athletic activities—especially football—played an important role. In these years football, which had been invented by American college students in 1869, was largely an elite sport, mainly the province of college teams. Adapted from English rugby, football quickly became popular on eastern college campuses. But the game, initially played without pads or helmets, was marred by violence in its early years. As late as 1905, eighteen students died of playing-field injuries. Concerned about the game's brutality, some college presidents dismissed football as a dangerous waste of time and money. When the University of Michigan in 1873 challenged Cornell to a game in Ann Arbor, Cornell's president Andrew D. White huffily telegraphed back: "I will not permit thirty men to travel four hundred miles merely to agitate a bag of wind."

But eager alumni and coaches strongly defended the new sport. Some—among them Henry Lee Higginson, the Civil War veteran and Boston banker who gave Harvard "Soldier's Field" stadium as a memorial to those who had died in battle—praised football as a character-building sport. A Social Darwinist who fervently believed that life was a struggle, Higginson insisted that football could improve the strength, courage, and self-discipline of American college youth. These defenders of the sport, including famed Yale coach Walter Camp, insisted that football could function as a surrogate frontier experience in an increasingly urbanized society. By 1900 football had become a popular fall ritual, and team captains were campus heroes. The sport served to stimulate alumni giving and built goodwill for these elite institutions that otherwise remained far outside the experience of the average American.

While postsecondary education remained confined to a small minority, more than 150 new colleges and universities were founded between 1880 and 1900, and enrollments more than doubled. The 4 percent of college-age youth actually enrolled in 1900 represented a jump from an even more minuscule 1.7 percent in 1870. A small but growing number of these newcomers to higher education were women. While wealthy capitalists endowed some institutions, others, such as the state universities of the Midwest, were financed largely through public funds. Many colleges, including some that would evolve into first-rate institutions, were founded and largely funded by various religious denominations.

These were years of fundamental debate in higher education over what should be taught and how it should be presented. Impetus for reform came from new discoveries in science, nowhere more conspicuously than in the field of medicine. Most physicians in the 1850s had attended medical school for only two sixteen-week terms. They typically received their degree without ever having visited a hospital ward or examined a patient. Then came the Civil War, which graphically demonstrated the abysmal state of American medical education. Twice as many soldiers died from infections picked up on the battlefield as from wounds. Doctors were so poorly trained and ignorant about sanitation that they often infected soldiers' injuries when they probed wounds with hands wiped on pus-stained aprons. "The ignorance and general incompetency of the average graduate of American medical schools, at the time when he receives the degree which turns him loose upon the community," wrote Harvard president Charles W. Eliot in 1870, "is something horrible to contemplate."

In the 1880s and 1890s, the public's well-justified skepticism about doctors encouraged leading medical professors, many of whom had studied in France and Germany, to begin radically restructuring American medical education. Using the experimental method developed by German scientists, they insisted that medical students be trained in biology, chemistry, and physics, including actual laboratory experience. By 1900 the practice of medicine in America had been placed on a firm professional foundation. Similar reforms took place in the teaching of architecture, engineering, and law.

These changes were part of a larger transformation in higher education after the Civil War that gave rise to a new institution, the research university. Unlike even the best of the mid-nineteenth-century colleges, whose narrow, unvarying curriculum focused on classical languages, theology, logic, and mathematics, the new research universities offered courses in a wide variety of subject areas, established various professional schools, and encouraged faculty members to pursue basic research. For Andrew D. White, the first president of Cornell University (1869), the objective was to create an environment "where any person can find instruction in any study." At Cornell, the University of Wisconsin at Madison, Johns Hopkins, Harvard, and other institutions, this new conception of higher education laid the groundwork for the central role that America's universities would play in the intellectual, cultural, and scientific life of the twentieth century. Despite these significant changes, with all their portents for the future, however, higher education still remained largely the privilege of a few as the nineteenth century ended. The era when college attendance would become the norm rather than the rare exception lay many years ahead.

Working-Class Leisure in the Immigrant City

In colonial America the subject of leisure time had arisen seldom—mainly when ministers condemned "idleness" as a dangerous first step leading to sin and wickedness. Disapproval of leisure also characterized the overwhelmingly rural culture of the early nineteenth century, in which the unremitting routines of farm labor left little time for relaxation. Family picnics, horse races, county fairs, revival meetings, and holiday observances such as the Fourth of July and Christmas had provided occasional permissible diversion, but most Americans continued to view leisure activities skeptically, and the line between relaxation and laziness was never clearly drawn. Henry Clay Work's popular song "Grand-father's Clock" (1876), which praised the ancient timepiece for "wasting no time" and working "ninety years, without slumbering," bore witness to the tenacity of this deep-seated reverence for work and suspicion of leisure.

After the Civil War, as immigration soared, urban populations shot up, and factories multiplied, striking new patterns of leisure and amusement emerged, most notably among the urban working class. Middle-class educators and moralists continued to ponder the distinction between "wholesome" and "unwholesome" recreation, but they were little heeded in the throbbing immigrant cities. After spending long hours in factories, mills, and behind department-store counters, or working as domestic servants in the homes of the wealthy, working-class Americans eagerly sought relaxation and diversion. They thronged the streets, patronized saloons and dance halls, went on Sunday excursions, cheered at boxing matches and baseball games, and organized boisterous group picnics and holiday celebrations. As amusement parks, vaudeville theaters, sporting clubs, and racetracks provided further outlets for workers' need for entertainment, leisure became a big business catering to a mass public.

With factory labor growing ever more routinized and impersonal, the casual social interactions that had thrived in earlier workplace environments became increasingly inhibited. Thus leisure time became especially important as an arena of freedom, spontaneity, and group solidarity where the time clock could be at least briefly forgotten. Ironically, the same ethnic divisions that fragmented the immigrant work force and retarded the emergence of a strong labor movement provided the foundation for a vigorous working-class culture beyond the factory gates, since ethnic bonds often underlay neighborhood-based pastimes.

Whereas many recreational activities involved both men and women, others particularly attracted one sex or the other. While the saloon offered an intensely male environment where patrons could share good stories, discuss and bet on sporting events, and momentarily put aside pressures of job and family, young working women shared confidences with friends in informal social clubs, tried out new fashions in street promenading, and found fun and excitement in neighborhood dance halls and amusement park excursions.

The Streets, the Saloon, and the Boxing Match

No segment of the population had a greater need for amusement and recreation than the urban working class. Hours of tedious, highly disciplined, and physically exhausting labor left workers tired at the end of the day but thirsting for excitement and escape from their cramped living quarters. A banner carried by the Worcester, Massachusetts, carpenters' union in an 1889 demonstration for the eight-hour workday summed up the importance of workers' leisure hours: "EIGHT HOURS FOR WORK, EIGHT HOURS FOR REST, AND EIGHT HOURS FOR WHAT WE WILL."

City streets provided recreation that anyone could afford. Relaxing and socializing after a day's work, shop girls and laborers clustered on busy corners, watching shouting pushcart peddlers and listening to organ grinders and buskers play familiar melodies. For a penny or a nickel, they could buy bagels, baked potatoes, soda, and a variety of other foods and drinks. Especially in the summer, when the heat and humidity within the tenements reached unbearable levels, the streets became a buzzing hive of neighborhood social life. One immigrant later fondly recalled his boyhood on the streets of New York's Lower East Side: "Something was always happening, and our attention was continually being shifted from one excitement to another."

The streets were open to all, but other leisure institutions drew mainly a male clientele. For example, in cities like Baltimore, Milwaukee, and Cincinnati with a strong German immigrant flavor, gymnastic clubs (called *Turnverein*) and singing societies (*Gesangverein*) provided both companionship and the opportunity to perpetuate old-world cultural traditions.

For workmen of all ethnic backgrounds, the saloon offered companionship, conviviality, and five-cent beer, often with a free lunch thrown in. New York City had an estimated ten thousand

McSorley's Bar, *by John Sloan, 1912*

Neighborhood saloons were places where friends could get together. In his novel Sister Carrie, *Theodore Dreiser admiringly described "the long bar . . . [with its] blaze of lights, polished woodwork, colored and cut glassware and many fancy bottles."*

saloons by 1900 and Denver nearly five hundred. (The Denver saloons, catering to the large German immigrant population, bore names like Edelweiss, Bavarian House, and Kaiserhof.) A recent study of working-class leisure in Worcester in these years estimates that on a typical Saturday night, one-quarter of the adult male population patronized the city's ninety-three saloons.

As gathering places in ethnic neighborhoods, the saloons reinforced group identity and became centers for immigrant politics. The saloonkeeper, who often doubled as the local ward boss, performed small services for his patrons, including in some cases writing letters for illiterate immigrants. Sports memorabilia and pictures of prominent prizefighters adorned saloon walls. With its rich mahogany bars, etched glass, shiny brass rails, and elegant mirrors, the saloon provided a taste of high-tone luxury to its factory patrons. Although working-class women rarely joined their husbands at the saloon, they frequently sent a son or daughter to the corner pub for a "growler"—a large tin pail of beer.

In earlier days workers had customarily taken occasional breaks from the job for a shared drink

and a few minutes of socializing. But in the highly disciplined factories of the late nineteenth century, drinking on the job was strictly forbidden, so a sharp distinction grew up between the world of work and the world of leisure. Thus the conventions of saloon culture stood in marked contrast to both the socially isolating routines of factory labor and the increasingly private and family-centered social life of the middle class. Nevertheless, it would be a mistake to view the old-time saloon through a haze of sentimental nostalgia. In the rougher saloons, prostitution and criminal activity flourished. Moreover, the problem of family violence related to drunkenness was a real one, and the widespread custom of "treating," or buying drinks for one's friends, while revealing an appealing spirit of comradeship, often meant that even less money from a workman's limited weekly pay was available to meet urgent family needs.

For working-class males, bare-knuckles prizefighting became one of the most popular amusements. Drawing its heroes from the poorer ranks of society, the ring became an arena where lower-class men could assert their individuality and physical prowess. In East Coast cities, blacks, Irish, and

Germans formed their own "sporting clubs" and used athletics to bolster their self-confidence and reaffirm their racial or ethnic identity. An enterprising publisher capitalized on boxing's popularity in 1873 with an illustrated history called *The American Fistiana,* full of stories of celebrated fighters.

Despite its origins and continued popularity within the working class, amateur boxing gained unexpected elite support in the 1880s and 1890s as an antidote to what some considered a dangerous tendency toward effeteness among males of the privileged classes. Theodore Roosevelt, a New York patrician and rising figure in Republican politics, did much to make the sport more respectable. The introduction of the Marquis of Queensbury code—a set of rules devised in England, requiring the use of gloves, outlawing wrestling holds, standardizing the three-minute round with a one-minute rest period, and changing the time required for a knockout from thirty seconds to ten—increased boxing's acceptability to the upper crust. Meanwhile, the sport, like other popular leisure-time diversions, was becoming increasingly professionalized.

The Rise of Professional Sports

Contrary to the prevailing myth, schoolboy Abner Doubleday did not invent baseball in Cooperstown, New York, in 1839. As an English game called rounders, the pastime had existed in one form or another since the seventeenth century. But if Americans did not create baseball, they unquestionably took this informal children's game and turned it into a major professional sport. The first organized baseball team, the New York Knickerbockers, was formed in 1845. Then in the 1860s the rules were codified, and the sport assumed its modern form. Overhand pitches replaced those formerly thrown underhand. Fielders, who now wore gloves, had to catch the ball on the fly to make an out instead of fielding it on one bounce. Games were standardized at nine innings, and bases were spaced ninety feet apart, as they are today.

In that same decade, promoters organized professional clubs and began to charge admission and compete for players. The Cincinnati Red Stockings, the first team to put its players under contract

Ball or Strike?

Early professional baseball had to fight to achieve respectability. The July 1898 issue of Outing *magazine critically observed that "the players are devoting their lives . . . to diversion instead of duty."*

for the whole season, gained fame in 1869 by touring the country and ending the season with fifty-seven wins and no losses. Clubs of professional players organized the National League in 1876, and soon crowds of from ten thousand to twelve thousand were turning out to watch professional games. By the 1890s baseball had become big business. As today, clubs scheduled doubleheaders, ran promotions such as children's day and ladies' day, and made money by selling beer, peanuts, and hot dogs.

Although baseball attracted a national following at all social levels, the working class particularly took the sport to heart. The most profitable teams were those from major industrial cities with a large working-class population. Workers attended the games when they could and avidly followed their team's progress when they could not. Some saloons reported scores on blackboards. In Cleveland just after the turn of the century, Mayor Tom

Johnson erected a bulletin board downtown that recorded game results. When the Spanish-American War broke out in 1898, a cartoon in a New York newspaper pictured a man about to enter a baseball stadium brushing aside a newsboy shouting "WAR EXTRA!" The caption read: "Your true 'fan' is not interested in such a trivial thing as war."

Newspapers thrived on baseball. Joseph Pulitzer introduced the first separate sports page when he bought the *New York World* in 1883, and much of the sporting news in the *World* and other papers was devoted to baseball. For the benefit of German immigrants, the New York *Staats Zeitung* published a glossary of German equivalents of baseball terms: for example, "umpire" was *Umparteiischer.* Baseball, declared novelist Mark Twain in a burst of hyperbole, had become "the very symbol . . . and visible expression of the drive and push and rush and struggle of the raging, tearing, booming nineteenth century."

Although no other organized sport attracted as large a following as baseball, horse racing and boxing contests were also widely covered in the popular press and drew big crowds of spectators and bettors. But while races like Louisville's Kentucky Derby became important social events for the rich, professional boxing aroused more passionate devotion among the working class. By far

the most popular sports hero of the nineteenth century was heavyweight fighter John L. Sullivan, "the Boston Strong Boy." Of Irish immigrant stock, Sullivan began boxing in 1877 at the age of nineteen. His first professional fight came in 1880 when he knocked out John Donaldson, "the Champion of the West," in a Cincinnati beer hall. With his massive physique, handlebar mustache, and arrogant swagger, Sullivan was enormously popular among immigrants. Barnstorming across the country, he vanquished a succession of local strong men, invariably wearing his trademark green tights with an American flag wrapped around his middle. His successes were minutely chronicled in *The National Police Gazette*, a sensational tabloid popular in working-class barbershops and saloons.

Sullivan loved drink and high living, and by the end of the eighties, he was sadly out of shape. But when the *Police Gazette* editor designed a new heavyweight championship belt—allegedly containing two hundred ounces of silver and encrusted with diamonds and pure gold—and awarded it to Sullivan's rival Jake Kilrain, the champion had to defend himself. The two met on a sweltering, hundred-degree day in New Orleans in July 1889, in the last bare-knuckles championship match. After seventy-five short but grueling rounds, Kilrain's managers threw in the towel. Newspapers around

st by Arthur T. Lumley, New York Illustrated News.

FOR THE HEAVY-WEIGHT CHAMPIONSHIP OF THE WORLD.

World's Heavyweight Boxing Championship, 1892

In dethroning ring champion John L. Sullivan, "Gentleman Jim" Corbett demonstrated that speed and finesse were more than a match for brute strength.

the nation banner-headlined the story. Contemptuously returning the championship belt to the *Police Gazette* after having had it appraised at $175, Sullivan went on the road in a melodrama written specifically for him. Playing the role of a blacksmith, he (in the words of a recent historian of bare-knuckles boxing) "pounded an anvil, beat a bully, and mutilated his lines." But his fans did not care: he was one of them, and they adored him. As one admirer wrote:

> *His colors are the Stars and Stripes,*
> *He also wears the green,*
> *And he's the grandest slugger that*
> *The ring has ever seen.*

Vaudeville, Amusement Parks, and Dance Halls

In contrast to the male preserve of saloons and prizefights, the world of vaudeville shows, amusement parks, and neighborhood dance pavilions not only welcomed all comers regardless of sex but in some cases proved particularly congenial to working-class women.

Vaudeville evolved out of the pre–Civil War minstrel shows, in which white comedians made up as blacks had performed songs and comic sketches (see Chapter 11). Vaudeville performances offered a succession of acts, all designed for mass appeal. The shows typically opened with a trained animal routine or a dance number, followed by a musical interlude featuring sentimental favorites such as "On the Banks of the Wabash Far Away" mixed in with new hits such as "Meet Me in St. Louis, Louis," a jaunty spoof of a young city wife's frustration with her stick-in-the-mud husband.

Comic skits followed, ridiculing the trials of urban life, satirizing the ineptitude of the police and municipal officials, poking fun at the babel of accents in the immigrant city, and mining a rich vein of broad ethnic humor and stereotypes. After further musical numbers and acts by ventriloquists, pantomimes, and magicians would come a "flash" finale such as flying-trapeze artists swinging against a black background. By the 1880s vaudeville was drawing larger crowds than any other form of theater, and understandably so: not only did it provide an inexpensive evening of light-

Amusement Park Rides, c. 1900

Spectacular boat slides provided weekend thrills for working-class people who spent most of their days at tedious factory jobs.

hearted entertainment, but in the comic sketches, immigrant audiences could laugh at their own experience as they saw it translated into slapstick and caricature.

Where vaudeville offered psychological escape from the stresses of working-class life by exploiting its comic potential, amusement parks provided physical escape, at least for a day. The prototype of the sprawling urban amusement parks was New York's Coney Island, a section of Brooklyn's oceanfront that in the 1870s evolved into a resort for the masses. At the turn of the century, the opening of several large amusement centers bearing names like Luna Park and Dreamland and featuring performers, fun houses, thrill rides, and games of skill boosted Coney Island's popularity. Taking the train from Manhattan, couples, families, and large excursion groups sponsored by fraternal societies poured into Coney Island by the thousands. By 1900 as many as half a million people would throng the beach, the boardwalk, and the amusement parks on a hot summer Saturday. Young couples who rode through the dark Tunnel of Love, sped down the dizzying roller coaster in Steeplechase Park, or watched belly dancers in the carnival atmosphere of the sideshows were encouraged to surrender to the spirit of exuberant play, forget the restrictions and demands of the industrial world, and lose themselves in fantasy.

By the end of the nineteenth century, New York City had well over three hundred thousand female wage earners, most of them young, unmarried women working as seamstresses, laundresses, typists, domestic servants, or department-store clerks. For this army of low-paid young working women and their counterparts in other cities, the amusement parks with their exhilarating rides and glittering dance pavilions, together with the dance halls that dotted the immigrant districts of most cities, exerted a powerful lure. Here they could meet friends, spend time with young men beyond the watchful eyes of parents, show off their new dresses, and try out the latest dance steps. As a twenty-year-old German immigrant woman who worked as a servant in a wealthy household observed: "I have heard some of the high people with whom I have been living say that Coney Island is not tony. The trouble is that these high people don't know how to dance. I have to laugh when I see them at their balls and parties. If only I could get out on the floor and show them how—they would be astonished." For such a woman, the brightly decorated dance pavilion, the exciting music, and the spell of a warm summer night could seem a magical release from the drudgery of daily life.

Ragtime

Since slavery days, black Americans had sustained a strong, creative musical culture, and thus it is not surprising that blacks made a major contribution to the popular music of the late nineteenth century, in the form of ragtime. Nothing could illustrate more sharply the differences between the cultural world of the middle class and that of the working class than the contrasting styles of popular music that each favored. The middle class preferred hymns or songs that taught a lesson or conveyed a moral. Ragtime, by contrast, which originated in the 1880s and 1890s with black musicians in the saloons and brothels of the South and Midwest, was played strictly for entertainment.

Ragtime developed out of the rich tradition of sacred and secular songs through which African-Americans had long eased the burdens of their lives. Like spirituals, ragtime used syncopated rhythms and complex harmonies, but it blended these with marching-band musical structures to create a distinctive style. Long a favorite of "honky-tonk" piano players, ragtime was introduced to the broader public in the 1890s by the music publishers of New York's Tin Pan Alley and quickly became a national sensation.

The reasons for the sudden ragtime craze were complex. Inventive, playful, with catchy syncopations and an infectious rhythm in the bass clef, the music displayed a fresh originality that had an appeal all its own. But part of ragtime's popularity also came from its origin in brothels and its association with blacks, who were widely stereotyped in the 1890s as sexual, sensual, and uninhibited by the rigid Victorian social conventions that restricted whites' behavior. The "wild" and complex rhythms of ragtime, therefore, were widely interpreted to be a freer and more "natural" expression of elemental feelings about love and affection. John Philip Sousa, the well-known composer of "Stars and Stripes Forever," reflected this common middle-class stereotype in his assertion that ragtime's "primitive rhythms . . . excite the basic human instincts." The rejection of ragtime by genteel critics like Sousa, however, made the new dance music all the more attractive to an urban working class that largely rejected the middle-class Victorian moral code.

Ragtime's best-known composer, Scott Joplin, a talented black piano player from St. Louis, introduced his music at Chicago's Columbian Exposition in 1893. "Maple Leaf Rag," published in 1899, earned him a national reputation. Hoping to win recognition as a serious composer, Joplin moved to New York in 1907 and wrote an opera, *Tremonisha*, which was never staged during his lifetime. He died a decade later, penniless and largely forgotten.

Ragtime's great popularity thus proved a mixed blessing for blacks. It testified to the achievements of brilliant composers like Joplin, helped break down the barriers faced by blacks in the music industry, and contributed to a spreading rebellion against the repressiveness of Victorian standards. But for some whites, ragtime simply confirmed their stereotype of blacks as primitive and sensual, a bias that underlay the racism of the period and helped justify segregation and discrimination.

In sum, from many perspectives the factories and immigrant slums of late-nineteenth-century America present a grim picture. The realities of overwork, poverty, disease, and inhumane living conditions hover darkly over the history of the period. Yet in the face of such realities, the laboring masses avidly pursued a colorful variety of leisure-time activities that affirmed their social solidarity and sustained their spirits. The vitality, gaiety, and sheer energy of this working-class culture remind us that however bleak their lives, the members of the urban working class remained strong and resilient in these years, conscious of their human worth and determined to assert it.

Cultures in Conflict

The late nineteenth century saw a United States embroiled in class conflict and cultural unrest. Part of this turmoil raged within the middle class itself. Victorian morality and genteel cultural standards were never totally accepted even within the elite and middle classes, and as the century ended, ethical questionings and new cultural stirrings intensified. Women stood at the very center of the era's cultural turbulence. Thwarted by a restrictive code of feminine propriety, middle-class women made their dissatisfactions heard. Developments as diverse as the rise of women's clubs, the growth of women's colleges, and an 1890s bicycle fad contributed to the emergence of what some began to call the new woman.

But while Victorian culture came under challenge from within the middle class itself, a widening chasm divided the well-to-do from the immigrant cities' teaming hordes of laborers. Perhaps in no period of American history have class conflicts—cultural as well as economic—been more open and raw. As native-born middle-class leaders nervously eyed the rambunctious and sometimes disorderly culture of city streets, saloons, boxing clubs, dance halls, and amusement parks, they correctly perceived a massive if unconscious challenge to their own cultural and social standing. While

some middle-class reformers promoted the public school as an institution for imposing middle-class values on the urban masses, others battled the hydra-headed manifestations of urban "vice" and "immorality." But ultimately it was the genteel mores of the middle class, not urban working-class culture, that proved the more vulnerable. By 1900 the Victorian social and moral ethos was crumbling on every front.

The Genteel Tradition and Its Critics

What was this genteel culture that aroused such opposition? In the 1870s and 1880s, a group of upper-class writers and magazine editors, led by Harvard art-history professor Charles Eliot Norton and New York editors Richard Watson Gilder of *The Century* magazine and E. L. Godkin of *The Nation,* codified Victorian standards for literature and the fine arts. With the support of artistic allies in Boston and New York, they joined forces in a campaign designed to improve American taste in interior furnishings, textiles, ceramics, wallpaper, and books. By fashioning rigorous criteria for excellence in writing and design, they hoped to create a coherent national artistic culture.

The drive to improve the arts was prompted in part by the flood of cheap reproductions and sensationalistic novels that poured off the nation's presses after the Civil War. Despondent about what Godkin called a "chromo civilization" enamored of trashy books and garish chromolithographic prints, Norton, Godkin, and Gilder, joined by the editors of other highbrow periodicals such as the *Atlantic Monthly* and *North American Review,* set up new guidelines for serious literature. They lectured the middle class about the value of high culture and the insights to be gained from the fine arts. They also censored their own publications to remove all sexual allusions, vulgar slang, disrespectful treatments of Christianity, and unhappy endings. In a characteristic gesture, Norton tried unsuccessfully to persuade dime-novel publisher Erastus Beadle to print Shakespeare's plays instead of western adventures and crime stories.

Expanding their combined circulation to nearly two hundred thousand copies and opening their magazines to a variety of new authors, Godkin and the other editors of these "quality" periodicals created an important forum for serious writing. Novelists Henry James, who published virtually all of

Sarah Orne Jewett and Mark Twain

Jewett and Twain not only broke from genteel literary standards but also created unique personal styles through their studied poses and distinctive attire.

his work in the *Atlantic,* and William Dean Howells, who served as editor of the same magazine, were both strongly influenced by this elite literary establishment. As James once wrote to a friend: "It is art that *makes* life, . . . and I know of no substitute whatever for [its] force and beauty. . . ." This so-called art for art's sake movement also made its influence felt through the work of architects, jewelers, and interior decorators.

But while the genteel magazines initially provided an important forum for new writers, their editors' strident elitism and imperialistic desire to control the nation's literary standards soon aroused opposition. Samuel Langhorne Clemens, better known as Mark Twain, spoke for many young writers when he declared as early as 1869 that he was through with "literature and all that bosh." Attacking aristocratic literary conventions, Twain and other authors who shared his concerns explored new forms of fiction and worked to broaden literature's appeal to the general public.

These efforts by a younger generation of writers to chart new directions for American literature rested on fundamental changes taking place in the publishing industry. To compete with elite periodicals costing twenty-five cents to thirty-five cents,

new magazines like *Ladies' Home Journal, Cosmopolitan,* and *McClure's* lowered their prices to a dime or fifteen cents and tripled or quadrupled their circulation. Supporting themselves through advertising rather than subscriptions, these magazines encouraged new trends in fiction while they mass-marketed new products and services. They provided an audience for young authors seeking to move beyond idealized romances and literary conventions to write about real people in everyday life.

Some of these authors have been labeled regionalists because they captured the distinctive dialect and details of local life in their environs. In *The Country of the Pointed Firs* (1896), for example, Sarah Orne Jewett wrote of the New England–village life that she knew from her own neighbors in South Berwick, Maine. Others, most notably William Dean Howells, have been called realists because of their focus on a truthful depiction of the commonplace and the everyday, especially in urban areas. Still others have been categorized as naturalists because their stories take on a fatalistic cast and stress the economic and psychological determinants of life. Stephen Crane's *Maggie: A Girl of the Streets* (1892), a bleak story of an innocent girl's exploitation and ultimate suicide in the harsh environment of an urban slum, is generally considered the first American naturalistic novel. Yet in practice, these categories are imprecise and often overlap. What many of these writers shared, irrespective of labels, was a skepticism toward established literary conventions and an intense desire to understand the society around them.

The careers of Mark Twain and Theodore Dreiser highlight the changes in the publishing industry and the evolution of new forms of writing. Both authors grew up in the Midwest, outside the East Coast literary establishment; Twain was born near Hannibal, Missouri, in 1835, and Dreiser in Terre Haute, Indiana, in 1871. As young men both worked as newspaper reporters and traveled widely in search of new financial opportunities. Both learned from direct and sometimes bitter personal experience about the greed, speculation, and fraud that figured centrally in Gilded Age life.

Of the two, Twain more incessantly sought a mass-market audience. With his drooping mustache, white hair, and white suits, Twain deliberately turned himself into a media personality, lecturing from coast to coast, founding his own publishing house, and selling his books through door-to-door salesmen. The name Mark Twain became his trademark, identifying him to readers as a literary celebrity much as the labels Coca-Cola and Ivory Soap won instant consumer recognition.* Although Dreiser possessed neither Twain's flamboyant personality nor his instinct for salesmanship, he, too, learned to crank out feature articles for mass magazines heavily dependent on advertising.

Drawing on their own experiences, Twain and Dreiser dealt in their writings with the human impact of the wrenching social changes taking place around them: the flow of people to the expanding cities and the relentless scramble for power, wealth, and fame. In the *Adventures of Huckleberry Finn* (1884), Twain presents a classic narrative of two runaways, the rebellious Huck and the slave Jim, drifting down the Mississippi in search of freedom. Their journey southward, which contrasts the idyllic life on the raft with the tawdry, fraudulent world

of the small riverfront towns, is at the same time a journey of identity that brings with it a deeper understanding of contemporary American society.

Dreiser's *Sister Carrie* (1900) also tells of a journey. But in this case, the main character, Carrie Meeber, an innocent and attractive girl on her way from her Wisconsin farm home to Chicago, is first seduced by a traveling salesman and then moves in with Hurstwood, the married proprietor of a fancy saloon. Driven by her desire for expensive department-store clothes and lavish entertainment, Carrie is an opportunist incapable of feeling guilt. She follows Hurstwood to New York, knowing that he has stolen the receipts from his saloon, abandons him when his money runs out, and pursues her own career in the theater.

Twain and Dreiser broke decisively with the genteel tradition's emphasis on manners and decorum. *Century* magazine readers complained that *Huckleberry Finn* was coarse and "destitute of a single redeeming quality." The publisher of *Sister Carrie* was so repelled by Dreiser's novel that he printed only a thousand copies (to fulfill the legal terms of his contract) and then stored them in a warehouse, refusing to promote them.

Growing numbers of scholars and critics similarly challenged the self-serving certitudes of aristocratic mores, including assumptions that moral worth and economic standing were closely linked and that the status quo of the 1870s and 1880s represented a social order decreed by God and nature alike (see "A Place in Time"). While Henry George, Lester Ward, and Edward Bellamy elaborated their visions of a cooperative and harmonious society (see Chapter 17), economist Thorstein Veblen in *The Theory of the Leisure Class* (1899) offered a caustic critique of the lifestyles of the new capitalist elite. The product of a poor Norwegian farm community in Minnesota, Veblen looked at the captains of industry and their families with a jaundiced eye, mercilessly documenting their ostentatious excess and "conspicuous consumption."

Within the new discipline of sociology, Annie MacLean exposed the exploitation of department-store clerks, Walter Wyckoff uncovered the hand-to-mouth existence of unskilled laborers, and W. E. B. Du Bois documented the suffering and hardships faced by blacks in Philadelphia. The publication of these social scientists' writings, coupled with the economic depression and seething labor agitation of the 1890s, made it increasing-

---

Mark Twain was originally a boatman's term indicating the two-fathom depth at which steamboats could safely navigate on the Mississippi River, which flows past Clemens's native Hannibal.

ly difficult for turn-of-the-century middle-class Americans to accept the smug, self-satisfied belief in progress and genteel culture that had been a hallmark of the Victorian outlook.

Modernism in Architecture and Painting

The challenge to the genteel tradition also found strong support among architects and painters. By the 1890s Chicago architects William Holabird, John Wellborn Root, and others had tired of copying European designs. Breaking with established architects such as Richard Morris Hunt, the designer of French chateaux for New York's Fifth Avenue, these Chicago architects followed the lead of Louis Sullivan, who argued that a building's form should follow its function. In their view, banks should look like the financial institutions that they were, not like Greek temples. Rejecting the pretentiousness of prevailing elite mores and striving to evolve

functional American design standards, the Chicago architects looked for inspiration to the future—to modernism—not to the past.

Frank Lloyd Wright's "prairie-school" houses, first built in the Chicago suburb of Oak Park in the 1890s, represented a typical modernist break with past styles. Wright scorned the bulky Victorian house with its wasted space and boxlike rooms. His designs, featuring broad, sheltering roofs and low silhouettes harmonious with the flat prairie landscape, used open, interconnecting rooms to create a sense of spaciousness.

The call of modernism, with its rejection of Victorian gentility, influenced late-nineteenth-century American painting as well. The watercolors of Winslow Homer, a magazine illustrator during the Civil War, revealed nature as brutally tough and unsentimental. In Homer's grim, elemental seascapes, lone men struggle against massive waves that constantly threaten to overwhelm

The Fog Warning, *by Winslow Homer, 1885*

By lowering the horizon line and placing the ship at a great distance from the rowboat, Homer creates the sense that this man is an insignificant speck in an immense and powerful natural world.

Lake Chautauqua, New York, in the 1880s and 1890s

*I*n the summer of 1874, Methodist minister John Heyl Vincent opened a special training institute for Sunday school teachers on Lake Chautauqua in southwestern New York State. In less than a decade, the Chautauqua assembly had expanded into a vast outdoor university, complete with lecture halls and recreational facilities, that offered to more than fifty thousand summer visitors courses on religion, science, art, ancient and foreign languages, and a variety of other subjects. Designed to provide spiritual and intellectual nourishment for all ages, the Chautauqua program functioned as a middle-class revival meeting, attracting Protestant families committed to the Victorian belief in self-improvement and moral uplift. Harvard philosopher William James described Lake Chautauqua as "a middle-class paradise," the perfect place to acquire knowledge of literature and the fine arts.

Visitors to Chautauqua in the 1880s found there an idyllic community in a peaceful wooded setting. Passing through a narrow gate, they entered a large encampment on 165 gently sloping acres near the lake. Scattered among the trees, they discovered a small city of cottages, tents, and wooden sheds with canvas extensions. A gracious, white four-story hotel, the Athenaeum,

William James

stood at the center of the campground. Rustic bridges spanned ravines overgrown with hemlock and underbrush. Tennis courts and a baseball field dotted the hillsides. On the lakefront a scale model of Palestine, complete with tiny towns

and cities, served as a basis for history and geography lessons. A nearby tent museum contained exhibits on biblical costumes and manners.

On the bluff overlooking the lake, a great barnlike structure housing the College of Liberal Arts served as the center for lectures and concerts. An audience of more than 7,000 would sit in its enormous sloping amphitheater and listen to speeches by leading scholars, reformers, and dignitaries on such topics as "Literature and Life" and "Jesus the Perfect Teacher." Beginning with Ulysses S. Grant, seven American presidents spoke there, as well as Frances Willard of the Woman's Christian Temperance Union, William James, inventor Thomas A. Edison, and Populist William Jennings Bryan. By the 1880s Lake Chautauqua was drawing nearly 75,000 campers each

Old Pier Building

Boats carrying visitors to Chautauqua arrived hourly at the Pier Building, built in 1886.

Lake Chautauqua *Chautauqua's programs reflected the middle-class belief that men and women should spend their leisure time productively. The combination of recreational and intellectual attractions made sojourners' stays memorable.*

summer and reaching an additional 250,000 people through its publications.

Besides a regular program of lectures, concerts, organ recitals, and public readings, Chautauqua offered an educational program in the College of Liberal Arts. "This is not, as it has been represented to be, a condensed university curriculum," one visitor commented, "but is designed for the assistance of students, young and old, who are ambitious for culture, but whose position debars them from the privilege of attending a regular university." Chautauqua prided itself on its commitment to educational self-help. By presenting sophisticated knowledge in a relaxed family recreational setting, it made learning a pleasurable activity and reinforced the middle-class belief that an education in literature and the arts could function as a powerful force for civilization and progress.

Not until the 1890s did visitors question the Chautauquan ideal. In that decade the devastating economic depression, the challenge to

the political system by the Populist party (see Chapter 20), and boiling labor unrest undermined the middle class's quiet confidence in the power of education to ensure society's progress. When William James visited there in 1896, the program appeared too good, too perfect, and too sheltered from the massive problems of the real world.

Riding back to Buffalo on the train, James tried to put his finger on just what the Chautauquan program lacked. From his railcar seat, he noticed a workman high on the iron scaffolding of a bridge. Suddenly the answer came to him. The Chautauquan leaders were too preoccupied with teaching about literature and the fine arts. Their educational system ignored not only the difficult social problems around them but also practical problems calling for courage and daring, much like that exhibited by the workman on the scaffolding. "As I awoke to all this unidealized heroic life around me," James confessed, "the scales seemed to fall from my eyes; a wave of sympathy greater than anything

I had ever before felt with the common life of common men began to fill my soul." The key to civilization, he concluded, lay not in abstract Victorian ideals like those preached at Chautauqua. Instead, it rested on developing a sharper, clearer understanding of the difficulties and challenges faced by all Americans.

James's rejection of Victorian idealism and his commitment to a more practical approach to solving everyday problems was typical of the major shift in outlook taking place at the turn of the century—a movement away from the detached values of high culture, with their implicit middle- and upper-class preoccupation with manners and behavior, to a tougher-minded concern for discovering the reality of lower-class poverty and suffering. Using this approach, James and other progressive thinkers would move beyond the complacent Chautauquan perspective to forge a new commitment to civic responsibility and social justice in the opening years of the new century.

them. Thomas Eakins's canvases of swimmers, boxers, and rowers (such as his well-known *Champion Single Sculls,* painted in 1871) similarly captured moments of vigorous physical exertion in everyday life. Obsessed with making his paintings strikingly realistic, Eakins studied anatomy at a medical school, did photographic studies and dissection on cadavers in preparation for painting, and insisted on using nude models in his drawing classes at the Pennsylvania Academy of Fine Arts. When he removed the loincloth of a male model, proper Philadelphians demanded his dismissal, even though his students overwhelmingly supported him. Albert Pinkham Ryder, a reclusive New York painter, turned to the inner world of dreams. The self-taught Ryder ignored popular artistic fashions and painted in a simple, almost primitive style. His landscapes blurred color and form, evoking a mood of reverie and mystery. Stubbornly independent, he escaped the pressures of the refined artistic establishment by retreating into a natural environment re-created from memory.

The revolt by architects and painters against Victorian standards was symptomatic of a larger shift in middle-class thought. This shift resulted from fundamental economic changes that had spawned a far more complex social environment than that of the past. As Protestant minister Josiah Strong perceptively observed in 1898, the transition from muscle to mechanical power had "separated, as by an impassable gulf, the simple, homespun, individualistic world of the . . . past, from the complex, closely associated life of the present." The increasingly evident gap between rural or small-town life—a world of quiet parlors and flickering kerosene lamps—and life in big, glittering cities of iron and glass made nineteenth-century Americans acutely aware of differences in wealth and upbringing. Given the disparities between rich and poor, between rural and urban, and between native-born Americans and recent immigrants, it is no wonder that pious Victorian platitudes about proper manners and the genteel arts seemed out of touch with the new social realities.

Distrusting the idealistic Victorian assumptions about social progress, middle-class journalists, novelists, artists, and politicians nevertheless remained divided over how to replace them. Not until the progressive period would social reformers draw on a new expertise in social research and an enlarged conception of the federal government's

regulatory power to break sharply with their Victorian predecessors' social outlook.

From Victorian Lady to New Woman

Although middle-class women figured importantly in the revolt against Victorian refinement, their role was complex and ambiguous. Dissatisfaction with the cult of domesticity did not necessarily lead to open rebellion. Many women, while chafing against the constraints of the genteel code and the assumption that they should limit their activities to the home, remained committed to playing a nurturing and supportive role within the family. In fact, early advocates of a "widened sphere" for women often fused the traditional Victorian ideal of womanhood with a firm commitment to political action.

The career of temperance leader Frances Willard illustrates how the cult of domesticity, with its celebration of special female virtues, could evolve into a broader view of women's social responsibilities. Like many of her contemporaries, Willard believed that women by nature were compassionate, nurturing, and sensitive to others. She was also convinced that drinking encouraged men to squander their earnings and profoundly threatened stable family life. Resigning her position as dean of women and professor of English at Northwestern University in 1874, Willard devoted her energies full-time to the temperance campaign. Five years later she was elected president of the newly formed Woman's Christian Temperance Union (WCTU).

Choosing as the union's badge a bow of white ribbon, symbolizing the purity of the home, Willard in 1880 launched a crusade to win the franchise for women so that they could vote to outlaw liquor. Women's participation in politics, she asserted, would help protect the family and improve public morality. Taking care not to challenge traditional Victorian views of women's proper role, Willard expanded the WCTU's activities to include welfare work, prison reform, labor arbitration, and public health. Under Willard's leadership the WCTU, with a membership of nearly 150,000 by 1890, became the nation's first mass organization of women. Through it, women gained experience as lobbyists, organizers, and lecturers, in the process undercutting the assumption of "separate spheres."

Pleading with a Saloonkeeper

Careful not to violate the popular image of the true woman as sweet and loving, Woman's Christian Temperance Union crusaders made it difficult for saloonkeepers to drive them away.

An expanding network of women's clubs offered another means by which middle- and upper-class women could hone their skills in civic affairs, public speaking, and intellectual analysis. In the 1870s many well-to-do women began to meet weekly to study topics of mutual interest. These club women soon became involved in social-welfare projects, public-library expansion, and tenement reform. By 1892 the General Federation of Women's Clubs, an umbrella organization established that year, boasted 495 affiliates and a hundred thousand members.

Another major impetus to an expanded role for women came from a younger generation of college women. Following the precedent set by Oberlin College in 1836, coeducational private colleges and public universities in the Midwest enrolled increasing numbers of women in these years, while Columbia, Brown, and Harvard universities in the East admitted women to the affiliated but separate institutions of Barnard (1889), Pembroke (1891), and Radcliffe (1894), respectively. Nationally, the percentage of colleges admitting women jumped from 30 percent to 71 percent between 1880 and 1900. By the turn of the century, women made up more than one-third of the total college-student population.

Initially, female collegiate education reinforced the prevailing concepts of femininity. The earliest women's colleges—Mount Holyoke (1837), Vassar (1865), Wellesley and Smith (1875), and Bryn Mawr (1884)—were founded to prepare women for marriage, motherhood, and Christian service. But participation in college organizations, athletics, and dramatics enabled female students to learn traditionally "masculine" strategies for gaining power. The generation of women educated at female institutions in the late nineteenth century developed the self-confidence to break with the Victorian ideal of passive womanhood and to compete on an equal basis with men by displaying strength, aggressiveness, and intelligence—popularly considered male attributes. By 1897 the U.S. commissioner of education noted: "[I]t has become an historical fact that women have made rapid strides, and captured a greater number of honors in proportion to their numbers than men."

Victorian constraints on women were further loosened at the end of the century when a bicycling vogue swept urban America. Fearful of waning vitality, middle- and upper-class Americans were exploring ways to improve their vigor, ranging from the use of health products such as cod liver oil and sarsaparilla for "weak blood" to enthusiastic participation in basketball, invented in 1891 by a physical-education instructor at Springfield College in Massachusetts to keep students in shape during the winter months, when bad weather limited outdoor activity. But bicycling, which could be done individually or in groups, quickly became the most popular sport for those who wished to combine exercise with recreation.

Bicycles of various designs had been manufactured since the 1870s, but bicycling did not become a national craze until the invention in the 1880s of the so-called safety bicycle, with its smaller wheels, ball-bearing axles, and air-filled tires. By the 1890s over a million Americans owned bicycles. In Boston alone more than twenty-five thousand cyclists jammed the streets on a typical Sunday afternoon, and thousands attended bike races in Franklin Park.

Bicycling especially appealed to young women who had chafed under the restrictive Victorian attitudes toward female exercise, which held that proper young ladies must never sweat, that the

Frances Willard's Cycling Lesson

An outspoken advocate of expanding women's opportunities, Frances Willard took up bicycling in her fifties and wrote about it in a best-selling book, A Wheel Within a Wheel: How I Learned to Ride the Bicycle.

female body must be fully covered at all times, and that physical exertion should take place, if at all, far from public view. The young women who rode bikes were immediately on display. Pedaling along without restrictive corsets or padded clothing, sporting instead a shirtwaist or "split" skirt, a woman bicyclist made an implicit feminist statement suggesting that she had broken with genteel conventions and wanted to explore new activities beyond the traditional sphere.

Changing attitudes toward femininity and women's proper role also found expression in gradually shifting ideas about marriage. Charlotte Perkins Gilman, a suffrage advocate and speaker for women's rights, asserted that women would make an effective contribution to society only when they won economic independence from men through work outside the home (see Chapter 21). One very tangible indicator of women's changing relationship to men was the substantial rise in the divorce rate between 1880 and 1900. In 1880 one in every twenty-one marriages ended in divorce. By 1900

the rate had climbed to one in twelve. Women who brought suit for divorce increasingly cited their husbands' failure to act responsibly and to respect their autonomy. Accepting such arguments, courts frequently awarded the wife alimony, a monetary settlement payable by the ex-husband to support her and their children.

Contemporary assessments of all these changes differed widely, often along gender lines. "Molly Donahue have up an' become a new woman!" complained Mr. Dooley, humorist Finley Peter Dunne's satirical newspaper character, in 1898. By riding a bicycle, demanding the vote, and "wearin' clothes that no lady shud wear," Molly had announced her independence. Another male critic, Chicago newspaperman George Ade, satirized the so-called new woman of the 1890s as a "fast girl": shallow, superficial, and heedless of social conventions. A more sympathetic male observer, magazine illustrator Charles Dana Gibson, captured the popular image of this new woman with his folio of "Gibson girls." In contrast to the stiff, corseted Victorian lady of formal engravings, the Gibson girl exuded a spirit of independence and freedom. Pictured playing tennis or riding her bicycle, Gibson's tanned, vigorous young woman enjoyed the healthy outdoor life and active participation in the community.

Women writers generally welcomed the new female commitment to independence and self-sufficiency. In the short stories of Mary Wilkins Freeman, for example, women's expanding role is implicitly compared to the frontier ideal of freedom. Freeman's characters fight for their beliefs without concern for society's reaction. Feminist Kate Chopin pushed the debate to the extreme by having Edna Pontellier, the married heroine of her 1899 novel *The Awakening*, violate social conventions by first falling in love with another man and then taking her own life when his ideas about women prove as narrow and traditional as those of her husband.

Despite the efforts of these and other champions of the new woman, attitudes changed slowly. The enlarged conception of women's role in society exerted its greatest influence on middle-class women who had enjoyed the privilege of higher education, possessed some leisure time, and could reasonably hope for success in the limited range of occupations open to them. Following this ideal, increasing numbers of young female college graduates postponed marriage to pursue careers in journalism, education, social work, and other fields. For female immigrant factory workers and for shop girls who worked sixty hours a week to try and make ends meet, however, the ideal remained little more than a distant fantasy. So while many women were seeking more independence and control over their lives, most still viewed the home as their primary responsibility.

Public Education as an Arena of Class Conflict

The agitation over women's role remained largely confined to the middle class, but a very different controversy, over the scope and function of public education, engaged Americans of all socioeconomic levels. This debate starkly highlighted the class and cultural divisions in late-nineteenth-century society. Viewing the public schools as an instrument for indoctrinating and controlling the lower ranks of society, middle-class educators and civic leaders from the 1870s on campaigned to expand public schooling and bring it under centralized control. Not surprisingly, the reformers' efforts aroused considerable opposition from ethnic and religious groups whose outlook and interests differed sharply from theirs.

Thanks to the crusade for universal public education started by Horace Mann and other antebellum educational reformers, most states by the Civil War had public-school systems, and more than half the nation's children were receiving some formal education. But most attended school for only three or four years, and few went on to high school. Concerned that many Americans lacked sufficient knowledge to participate wisely in public affairs or function effectively in the labor force, middle-class educational activists in the 1870s worked to raise the overall educational level and to increase the number of years that children spent in school.

One such reformer was William Torrey Harris, a Victorian moralist who viewed the public schools as a "great instrumentality to lift all classes of people into . . . civilized life." First as superintendent of the St. Louis public schools in the 1870s, and later as the federal commissioner of education, Harris urged teachers to instill in their students a sense of order, decorum, self-discipline, and civic loyalty. Believing that modern industrial society depended on citizens' conforming to the timetables of the factory and the train, he envisioned the

schools as models of punctuality and precise scheduling: "The pupil must have his lessons ready at the appointed time, must rise at the tap of the bell, move to the line, return; in short, go through all the evolutions with equal precision."

To achieve these goals and to wrest control of the schools from neighborhood leaders and ward politicians, reform-minded educators like Harris elaborated a philosophy of public education stressing punctuality and order, centralized administration, compulsory-attendance laws, and a tenure system to insulate teachers from political favoritism and parental pressure. By 1900 thirty-one states required school attendance of all children from eight to fourteen years of age.

But the steamroller methods used by Harris and like-minded administrators to systematize public education quickly prompted protests. New York pediatrician Joseph Mayer Rice, who in 1892 toured thirty-six cities and interviewed twelve hundred teachers, scornfully criticized an educational establishment that stressed singsong memorization and prisonlike discipline. Writing in *Forum* magazine, Rice told of a Chicago teacher who drilled her students mercilessly and yelled at them, "Don't stop to think, tell me what you know!" In city after city, he discovered teachers more concerned about students' posture than their learning.

Rice's biting attack on public education overlooked the real advances in reading and computation made in the previous two decades. Nationally, despite the influx of immigrants, the illiteracy rate for individuals ten years and older dropped from 17 percent in 1880 to 13 percent in 1890, largely because of the expansion of urban educational facilities. But Rice was on target in assailing many teachers' rigid emphasis on silence, docility, and unquestioning obedience to the rules. When a Chicago school inspector found a thirteen-year-old boy huddled in the basement of a stockyard building and ordered him back to school, the weeping boy blurted out: "[T]hey hits ye if yer don't learn, and they hits ye if ye whisper, and they hits ye if ye have string in yer pocket, and they hits ye if yer seat squeaks, and they hits ye if ye don't stan' up in time, and they hits ye if yer late, and they hits ye if yer ferget the page."

By the 1880s several different groups found themselves in opposition to centralized urban public-school bureaucracies. Although many working-class families valued education, those who depended

San Diego, California, Schoolhouse, c. 1890

The stained-glass windows, elaborate bell tower, and ornate entranceway of this San Diego school testified to the community's pride in and commitment to public education.

on their children's meager wages for survival resisted the attempt to force their sons and daughters to attend school past the elementary grades. While some immigrant families made great sacrifices to enable their children to get an education, many withdrew their offspring from school as soon as they had learned the rudiments of reading and writing, and sent them to work.

Further, Catholic immigrants objected to the overwhelmingly Protestant orientation of the public schools. Distressed by the use of the King James version of the Bible and by the schools' failure to observe saints' days, Catholics set up separate parochial-school systems. In response, Republican politicians, resentful of the Catholic immigrants' overwhelming preference for the Democratic party, tried unsuccessfully in 1875 to pass a constitutional amendment cutting off all public aid to church-related schools. Catholics in turn denounced federal aid to public schools as intended "to suppress Catholic education, gradually extinguish Catholicity in this country, and to form one homogeneous American people after the New England Evangelical type." In view of the Protestant outlook of many school administrators, the Catholics' commitment to educate their students in separate church-sponsored schools was understandable.

At the other end of the social scale were upper-class parents, particularly in the Northeast, who did not wish to send their children to immigrant-thronged public schools. They enrolled their daughters in female seminaries such as Emma Willard's in Troy, New York, and their sons in private academies and boarding schools like St. Paul's in Concord, New Hampshire. Shielding their privileged students from the temptations of urban life and preparing them to go on to college, these institutions reinforced the elite belief that higher education should be the preserve of the well-to-do.

The proliferation of private and parochial schools, together with the controversies over compulsory education, school funding, and classroom decorum, reveal the extent to which public education had become entangled in ethnic and class differences. Unlike Germany and Japan, which standardized and centralized their national education systems in the late nineteenth century, the United States, reflecting its social heterogeneity, instead created a diverse system of locally run public and private institutions that allowed each segment of society to retain some influence over the schools attended by its own children. Amid the disputes, school enrollments dramatically expanded. In 1870 fewer than seventy-two thousand students attended the nation's 1,026 high schools. By 1900 the number of high schools had jumped to more than 5,000, and the number of students, to more than half a million.

The Middle-Class Assault on Working-Class Culture

On many fronts well-to-do Americans tried to impose their values on the urban working class and to restrain what they deemed improper or immoral behavior in these years. (One reformer of the 1890s luridly described the immigrant city as a "cesspool" brimming with a "vile, debauched, . . . impure [and] besotted mass of humanity.") While charity workers preached middle-class virtues in the slums, and antivice societies battled against "indecent" books, magazines, and stage shows, other reformers waged war on gambling, prizefighting, Sunday baseball, and working-class Fourth of July celebrations featuring greased-pig races and other "brutish" diversions lubricated with ample kegs of beer.

Middle-class uplifters also denounced the immigrant dance hall and amusement park with its "Tunnel of Love" and bawdy sideshows. One reformer who visited a working-class dance hall later reported with alarm: "I saw one of the women smoking cigarettes, most of the younger couples were hugging and kissing, [and] there was a general mingling of men and women at the different tables."

Even public parks became arenas of class conflict. While the elite favored large, impeccably groomed urban parks that would serve as models of gentility and propriety, working people fought for neighborhood parks where they could picnic, play ball, drink beer, and escape the stifling heat of tenement apartments. In 1882 a worker in Worcester, Massachusetts, wrote the local newspaper to complain about the remoteness of the city's largest park and the "Keep Off" signs on the grass. While the rich could retreat to the mountains or seashore, this citizen asked, where could "the masses of people [find] . . . rest and recreation . . . and the refreshing breezes of summertime" if not in nearby, easily accessible parks?

No reform, however, attracted more middle-class support than the assault on that bastion of male working-class culture, the saloon. Organizations like the WCTU, the Anti-Saloon League (1893), and the powerful Methodist Board of Temperance and Morals led the charge. One popular strategy was to close saloons in specific cities through "local-option" referenda. In many industrial cities, bitter local-option battles pitted the immigrants against the well-to-do.

While alcohol abuse represented a serious social problem in late-nineteenth-century America, the antisaloon campaign, like other middle-class urban reforms, also involved a head-on clash between the customs and values of different social classes and ethnic groups. As the editor of an immigrant newspaper in Worcester cynically observed during a local-option campaign in 1881, many solid citizens who would vote to close the saloons themselves had cellars well stocked with liquor. One notable American who deplored the insensitivity to working-class culture betrayed by these strident middle-class reform efforts was the aged poet Walt Whitman. In his essay *Democratic Vistas* (1881), Whitman lamented how "certain portions of the people" were trying to force their cultural standards and moral values on the great mass of the population who were thereby made to feel "degraded, humiliated, [and] of no account."

Conclusion   Despite the assured sense of superiority that the elite classes brought to the cultural wars of the late nineteenth century, it was the culture of the immigrant masses that in the long run proved the more durable. Shabby vaudeville houses evolved into the nation's first movie theaters. Ragtime gave rise to jazz, America's greatest musical contribution. Primitive pleasure parks like Coney Island paved the way for such multimillion-dollar amusement complexes as Disneyland, Disney World, and similar enterprises scattered across the land. The early professional baseball teams and the much-maligned professional prizefights anticipated the ubiquitous, TV-based professional sports industry of our own day. In short, the raffish, disreputable, raucous, and frequently denounced working-class culture of the late-nineteenth-century immigrant city can be seen, in retrospect, as nothing less than the fertile seedbed of twentieth-century American mass culture.

CHRONOLOGY

1865 Vassar College founded.

1869 Cornell University founded.
First intercollegiate football game.
The Great Atlantic & Pacific Tea Company (A&P) organizes a chain of food stores.

1871 Thomas Eakins, *The Champion Single Sculls.*

1874 John H. Vincent creates the Chautauqua assembly.

1875 Smith College founded.
Frances Willard joins the Woman's Christian Temperance Union.
Henry Clay Work, "Grandfather's Clock."

1876 National League of baseball players organized.

1879 F. W. Woolworth opens his "Five and Ten Cent Store" in Utica, New York.

1884 Mark Twain, *Adventures of Huckleberry Finn.*
Bryn Mawr College founded.

1886 Richard Warren Sears starts Sears, Roebuck.

1891 Stanford University founded.
University of Chicago founded.
Columbia University adds Barnard College as a coordinate institution for women.
Basketball invented at Springfield College in Massachusetts.

1892 Joseph Mayer Rice writes his exposé of public education in *Forum* magazine.
General Federation of Women's Clubs organized.

1893 Stephen Crane, *Maggie: A Girl of the Streets.*

1895 Coney Island amusement parks open in Brooklyn.

1899 Scott Joplin, "Maple Leaf Rag."
Kate Chopin, *The Awakening.*
Thorstein Veblen, *The Theory of the Leisure Class.*

1900 Theodore Dreiser, *Sister Carrie.*

For Further Reading

Lois W. Banner, *American Beauty* (1983). A fascinating study of changing attitudes toward fashion and beauty.

Susan P. Benson, *Counter Cultures: Saleswomen, Managers, and Customers in American Department Stores, 1890–1940* (1986). An inside view of the grand department store and its male and female employees.

Clifford E. Clark, Jr., *The American Family Home, 1800–1960* (1986). An overview of the changing relationship between middle-class families and their homes.

Perry Duis, *The Saloon: Public Drinking in Chicago and Boston, 1880–1920* (1983). A comparative study of the economic and social functions of the saloon.

Harvey Green, *Fit for America: Health, Fitness, Sport, and American Society* (1986). A probing inquiry into America's preoccupation with health and physical fitness.

Charles Hamm, *Yesterdays: Popular Song in America* (1979). A colorful analysis of the changing vogues in popular music.

Stephen Hardy, *How Boston Played: Sport, Recreation, and Community, 1865–1915* (1982). A comprehensive survey, cutting across class lines, of sport and recreation in Boston.

Barbara Novak, *Nature and Culture: American Landscape and Painting, 1825–1875* (1980). A provocative analysis of the cultural assumptions behind nineteenth-century landscape painting.

Sheila M. Rothman, *Woman's Proper Place: A History of Changing Ideals and Practices, 1870 to the Present* (1978). A perceptive conceptualization of the shifting attitudes toward women's proper role in society.

David B. Tyack, *The One Best System: A History of American Urban Education* (1974). Analysis of the conflicting pressures behind the attempt to create a comprehensive urban public-education system.

Additional Bibliography

Daily Life

Daniel J. Boorstin, *The Americans: The Democratic Experience* (1973); Francis G. Couvares, *The Remaking of Pittsburgh: Class and Culture in an Industrializing*

City, 1877–1919 (1984); Daniel Horowitz, *The Morality of Spending: Attitudes Toward the Consumer Society in America, 1875–1940* (1985); Gerald D. Jaynes, *Branches Without Roots: Genesis of the Black Working Class in the American South, 1862–1882* (1986); Jacqueline Jones, *Labor of Love, Labor of Sorrow: Black Women, Work, and the Family from Slavery to the Present* (1985); Lawrence Levine, *Black Culture, Black Consciousness* (1977); David Montgomery, *The Fall of the House of Labor: The Workplace, the State, and American Labor Activism, 1865–1925* (1987); Nell I. Painter, *Standing at Armageddon: The United States, 1877–1919* (1987); Susan Strasser, *Never Done: A History of American Housework* (1982); Robert H. Walker, *Life in the Age of Enterprise* (1967); Olivier Zunz, *The Changing Face of Inequality: Urbanization, Industrial Development, and Immigrants in Detroit, 1880–1920* (1982).

The Culture of the Middle Class

Martha Banta, *Imaging American Women: Idea and Ideals in Cultural History* (1987); Ruth S. Cowan, *More Work for Mother: The Ironies of Household Technology from the Open Hearth to the Microwave* (1983); Carl N. Degler, *At Odds: Women and the Family in America from the Revolution to the Present* (1980); Deborah A. Federhen et al., *Accumulation and Display: Mass Marketing Household Goods in America, 1880–1920* (1986); Hugh Hawkins, *Between Harvard and America: The Educational Leadership of Charles W. Eliot* (1972); Dolores Hayden, *The Grand Domestic Revolution: A History of Feminist Designs for American Homes, Neighborhoods, and Cities* (1981); Robert Hendrickson, *The Grand Emporiums: The Illustrated History of America's Great Department Stores* (1979); Helen L. Horowitz, *Alma Mater: Design and Experience in Women's Colleges from Their Nineteenth-Century Beginnings to the 1930s* (1984); Daniel Walker Howe, ed., "Victorian Culture in America," *American Quarterly* 27 (December 1975), 507–32; Godfrey M. Lebhar, *Chain Stores in America, 1859–1962* (1952); Russell Lynes, *The Tastemakers* (1949); James McLachlan, *American Boarding Schools: A Historical Study* (1970); Steven Mintz, *A Prison of Expectations: The Family in Victorian Culture* (1983); Steven Mintz and Susan Kellogg, *Domestic Revolutions: A Social History of American Family Life* (1988); Ian M. G. Quimby, *Material Culture and the Study of American Life* (1978); Frederick Rudolph, *The American College and University: A History* (1962); Barbara M. Solomon, *In the Company of Educated Women: A History of Women and Higher Education in America* (1985); Laurence R. Veysey, *The Emergence of the American University* (1965); Susan Williams, *Savory Suppers and Fashionable Feasts: Dining in Victorian America* (1985); Gwendolyn Wright, *Moralism and the Model Home: Domestic Architecture and Cultural Conflict in Chicago, 1873–1913* (1980).

Working-Class Leisure and Recreation

John T. Cumbler, *Working-Class Community in Industrial America: Work, Leisure, and Struggle in Two Industrial Cities, 1880–1930* (1979); Elliot J. Gorn, *The Manly Art: Bare-Knuckle Prize Fighting in America* (1986); Allen Guttmann, *From Ritual to Record: The Nature of Modern Sports* (1978); John F. Kasson, *Amusing the Million: Coney Island at the Turn of the Century* (1978); Peter Levine, *A. G. Spalding and the Rise of Baseball: The Promise of American Sport* (1985); Russell Lynes, *The Lively Audience: A Social History of the Visual and Performing Arts in America, 1890–1950* (1985); Donald J. Mrozek, *Sport and American Mentality, 1880–1910* (1983); Kathy Peiss, *Cheap Amusements: Working Women and Leisure in Turn-of-the-Century New York* (1986); Roy Rosenzweig, *Eight Hours for What We Will: Workers and Leisure in an Industrial City, 1870–1920* (1983); David Q. Voigt, *American Baseball: From Gentleman's Sport to the Commissioner System* (1966); James C. Whorton, *Crusaders for Fitness: The History of Health Reformers* (1984).

The Clash of Cultures

Burton J. Bledstein, *The Culture of Professionalism: The Middle Class and the Development of Higher Education in America* (1976); Ruth Bordin, *Frances Willard: A Biography* (1986); Doreen B. Burke et al., *In Pursuit of Beauty: Americans and the Aesthetic Movement* (1986); Paul A. Carter, *The Spiritual Crisis of the Gilded Age* (1971); Lawrence A. Cremin, *The Transformation of the School: Progressivism in American Education, 1876–1957* (1961); Emory Elliott, ed., *Columbia Literary History of the United States* (1988); Neil Harris, ed., *The Land of Contrasts* (1970); Thomas Haskell, ed., *The Authority of Experts: Studies in History and Theory* (1984); Mary J. Herrick, *The Chicago Schools: A Social and Political History* (1971); Howard M. Jones, *The Age of Energy: Varieties of American Experience, 1865–1915* (1970); Wendy Kaplan, ed., *"The Art That Is Life": The Arts and Crafts Movement in America, 1865–1920* (1987); Alfred Kazin, *An American Procession: The Major American Writers from 1830–1930: The Crucial Century* (1984); T. J. Jackson Lears, *No Place of Grace: Antimodernism and the Transformation of American Culture, 1880–1920* (1981); Theodore Morrison, *Chautauqua: A Center for Education, Religion, and the Arts in America* (1974); David Nasaw, *Schooled to Order: A Social History of Public Schooling in the United States* (1979); Daniel J. Singal, *The War Within: From Victorian to Modernist Thought in the South, 1919–1945* (1982); John Tomsich, *A Genteel Endeavor: American Culture and Politics in the Gilded Age* (1971); Alan Trachtenberg, *The Incorporation of America: Culture and Society in the Gilded Age* (1982); Larzer Ziff, *The American 1890s: Life and Times of a Lost Generation* (1966).

CHAPTER 20

Politics and Expansion
in an Industrializing Age

Rain was falling in Chicago on June 6, 1884, as Republican delegates crowded into the city's cavernous convention hall. But the weather did not dampen excitement, for the party's presidential candidate was to be chosen. Visitors crowded the galleries; flickering gaslights illuminated the flags and the orators droning on stage. As the popular front-runner, Senator James G. Blaine, was nominated, the hall exploded in a tumultuous demonstration. The *New York Herald Tribune* reported:

> *Whole delegations mounted their chairs and led the cheering which instantly spread to the stage and deepened into a roar fully as deep and deafening as the voice of Niagara. The scene was indescribable. The air quivered, the gaslights trembled and the walls fairly shook. The flags were stripped from the gallery and stage and frantically raised, while hats, umbrellas, handkerchiefs and other personal belongings were tossed to and fro like bubbles over the great dancing sea of human heads.*

Late-nineteenth-century politics was an exuberant affair. Elections aroused enormous interest, and voters participated in record numbers. Songs, parades, banners, and buttons transformed presidential campaigns into national festivals. Politics, someone said, was to the United States what bullfights were to Spain.

The Republicans who gathered in Chicago in June 1884 could well cheer. Republican presidents had occupied the White House uninterruptedly since 1861. Despite the Republicans' stranglehold on the presidency, however, the two parties were very evenly matched. When they squared off in national elections, the outcome was never certain.

But beneath the hoopla, serious issues were at stake. Matters such as tariff rates, veterans' pensions, railroad development, and monetary policy vitally affected important interest groups as well as millions of ordinary Americans. Political feelings ran high over local issues as well. Religious, ethnic, and cultural differences between immigrant and native-born voters, and even between immigrant groups, shaped the politics of the big cities and of states like Wisconsin and Minnesota.

Yet while industrialization and urbanization were transforming the nation, politicians in Washington often seemed unable or unwilling to grapple with the social consequences. In part, this passivity reflected a deeply entrenched tradition of localism in American public life. To nineteenth-century Americans, "government" meant primarily the local authorities, not distant Washington.

But the federal government's lack of engagement with the social consequences of industrialization also arose from the fact that the nation's business elite played an important role in both major parties in this era, and these leaders firmly opposed governmental intervention in the economy. Wages, hours, working conditions, and even the appalling urban-slum conditions, they insisted, were determined by rigid "economic laws" that must not be tampered with. Of course, these same capitalists welcomed government economic policies that aided business, such as protective tariffs or railroad subsidies, but otherwise their theme was "hands off."

While government sidestepped social problems that in retrospect seem of central importance, politicians from the president down spent an amazing amount of time passing out government jobs. By the 1880s, the excesses of the spoils system, culminating in a shocking presidential assassination, had become so notorious that a demand for civil-service reform swept the nation.

Major social groups became either political outcasts or political victims. In the cotton South and on the wheat-growing western plains, natural catastrophes and economic grievances exploded in the 1880s in a grassroots farmers' alliance movement. Southern blacks, meanwhile, endured not only political disfranchisement but segregation, exploitation, and terrorism in an avowedly racist society.

Agrarian discontent turned even more political in the 1890s when the People's, or Populist, party emerged. The Populist platform of 1892 proposed far-reaching governmental programs to remedy economic and social problems. When a terrible depression struck a year later, unrest deepened. In 1896 voters for the first time in decades chose between two candidates, William McKinley and William Jennings Bryan, with radically different political and economic philosophies.

As the century ended, returning prosperity silenced domestic protest and fueled expansionist enthusiasm. Glowing with jingoistic fervor, millions cheered as the United States defeated Spain and acquired Caribbean and Pacific island territories, setting the stage for further expansion in Latin America and for confrontations in Asia. Only a minority of Americans protested as imperialist fever engulfed the nation.

Party Rivalries, Agrarian Stirrings, and Civil-Service Reform

Geography, ethnic loyalties, long-standing sectional conflict, and myriad state and local alignments shaped American politics in the 1870s and 1880s. Two major issues preoccupied lawmakers nationally. The first involved the nature and size of the money supply. As politicians clashed over "greenbacks" and silver coinage, economic grievances in the agricultural South and West—grievances that would dominate the politics of the 1890s—emerged.

The second issue was how to staff the government bureaucracy. In the 1870s critics began to attack the time-honored practice of awarding government jobs to the party faithful. These critics rallied around the banner of civil-service reform, and in 1883, in the Pendleton Act, they achieved their goal.

Patterns of Party Strength

Although American voters elected only one Democratic president, Grover Cleveland, between 1857 and 1912, presidential elections were often extremely close. In 1876 and again in 1888, the defeated Democrat actually received more popular votes than the Republican victor. In 1880 the triumphant Republican won by fewer than forty thousand votes. Control of the two houses of Congress was frequently divided between Republicans and Democrats.

Each party had its centers of regional strength. The Democrats' base was the South; southern sections of border states like Ohio, Indiana, and Illinois; and major northern cities with large immigrant populations. In the South the white elite that controlled the Democratic party dominated political life. The South's Democratic loyalties, dating to Andrew Jackson's day, had been massively strengthened by the Civil War. To white southerners, Republicans were villains who had devastated the South and then rubbed salt in the wound by setting up carpetbag governments in the defeated Confederacy and by electing General Grant as president. In election after election, the "solid South" rolled up overwhelming Democratic majorities. Similarly, in Boston, New York, and other northern cities, powerful Democratic bosses ensured the national party ticket strong support at election time. Not all big-city political machines were Democratic, but enough were to boost the Democratic cause mightily.

The bedrock of Republican strength was rural and small-town New England, Pennsylvania, and the upper Midwest. The Republicans could also

Immigrant Entrepreneurship

This wonderful 1888 photograph picturing the entire staff and stock of William C. Raue's house- and sign-painting business in Watertown, Wisconsin (a center of German immigrant culture), captures the expansive spirit of the 1880s—an exuberance also reflected in the era's politics.

count on a substantial vote in the northern cities from the native-born middle class and business and professional men, including the growing ranks of white-collar workers. Corporate tycoons like Carnegie, Rockefeller, and Morgan contributed liberally to the Republicans.

Northern Civil War veterans who after the war formed a social and political lobbying organization known as the Grand Army of the Republic (GAR) represented another potent Republican bloc. So faithfully did the GAR vote Republican that some suggested that its initials stood for "Generally All Republican." To solidify this vote, the Republicans ran a series of former Union Army generals for president and voted generous veterans' benefits.

These regional political divisions also reflected different economic interests. Politically powerful groups frequently clashed over the tariff, currency, public-land policy, and government support for railroads and internal improvements.

But these broad geographic concentrations of party strength masked a far more complex reality. The Republicans made frequent, if unsuccessful, efforts to dent the "solid South" and worked tirelessly to attract urban-immigrant voters. Democratic candidates often fared well in the Republican strongholds of New England and the Midwest. (In the election of 1880, for example, the Democrats nearly carried normally Republican New Hampshire.) Family tradition, ethnic ties, religious affiliation, and a host of local issues often determined how an individual voted. Nor did economic standing absolutely determine party affiliation. Most businessmen were Republican, but not all. During the campaign of 1888, a top Republican cautioned party workers not to assume that "the influence and money of the great corporation interest" would automatically flow to the Republicans.

State and local party leaders managed electoral campaigns. They chose the candidates, raised money, organized rallies, and—if their candidate won—distributed public jobs to party workers. Much depended on the state party organization. Pennsylvania's highly efficient Republican state committee kept detailed records on more than eight hundred thousand voters. In Indiana ten thousand Republican workers fanned out over the state in 1884, gathering information about party affiliation from every voter.

Powerful chieftains like the former saloon-keepers "Big Jim" Pendergast, the Democratic boss of Kansas City, and George B. Cox, the Republican boss of Cincinnati, controlled urban politics (see Chapter 18). These bosses turned out the vote at election time by taking care of constituents, keeping in close touch with ward leaders, rewarding followers with municipal jobs, and on occasion financing campaigns with "contributions" extracted from city employees or from companies doing business with the city.

With the two parties so evenly matched, "swing states" where elections could go either way—Connecticut, New York, New Jersey, Indiana, and Illinois—held the balance of power. By no coincidence, most presidential and vice-presidential candidates came from these critical states; party managers hoped that voters would support the native son.

Compared to the present, voter participation was remarkably high. Of course, most women did not yet have the vote, and blacks were losing it in the post-Reconstruction South. But among eligible northern voters, participation rates of more than 80 percent were not unusual, and in particularly hard-fought state and local elections, the rate could rise to 95 percent. Voter participation a century later would equal scarcely half that level.

Because only *men* could vote in most states, political parties functioned in part as male social organizations. Indeed, whatever their differences, males were linked simply by being involved in politics. Their enthusiastic participation in political rituals—conventions, debates in barbershops and taverns, rallies and parades—cemented that bond. This is one reason why woman suffrage aroused such resistance: it threatened the male political subculture that offered men so many material and emotional rewards.

The Stakes of Politics

Late-nineteenth-century electoral campaigns centered on issues that large numbers of voters considered important—among them the tariff, the nation's currency supply, and the benefits paid to army veterans. The import duties charged on hundreds of commodities, from steel to sugar, had a direct impact on powerful economic interests and even entire regions. Government policies affecting the money supply or veterans' pensions similarly concerned millions of Americans very directly.

To be sure, elections frequently involved emotional side issues. Orators often resorted to windy patriotic rhetoric or shamelessly flattered various immigrant groups. Southern office seekers made crude racist appeals to white voters, while Republican candidates in the North often "waved the bloody shirt," reminding voters that the Republicans had led the nation during the terrible Civil War and that the Confederacy's leaders had all been Democrats. As Rutherford B. Hayes advised a Republican campaigner in 1876: "Our strong ground is the dread of a solid south, rebel rule, etc., etc. I hope you will make these topics prom-

inent in your speeches. It leads people away from 'hard times,' which is our deadliest foe."

And while national party candidates of the 1870s and 1880s addressed some issues of contemporary concern, they rarely confronted the most glaring problems. Except for the Interstate Commerce Act of 1887 and the largely symbolic Sherman Anti-Trust Act of 1890, Washington generally ignored the social consequences of industrialization. Indeed, the nation's capital sometimes seemed caught in a time warp as the rest of society plunged headlong into the modern era.

There are understandable reasons for this neglect. Not only were the late-nineteenth-century presidents lackluster, but the presidency itself was much diminished. After Johnson's impeachment, Grant's passivity, and Hayes's disputed election, the political initiative in Washington not surprisingly passed from the White House to the legislative branch.

But in the legislative branch, virtual anarchy reigned. Party discipline hardly existed as senators jealously guarded their political turf and displayed little concern for large national issues. The parties were well organized to win elections, not to govern. One former senator, looking back on these years, recalled that each senator "kept his own orbit and shone in his sphere, within which he tolerated no intrusion from the President or from anybody else." As for the House of Representatives, political scientist (and future president) Woodrow Wilson described it in 1885 as a "mass of jarring elements" and wished that the United States could shift to a more disciplined parliamentary system, like Great Britain's.

Further, most Americans did not *expect* the federal government to intervene actively in economic or social affairs. The doctrine of laissez faire —the belief that unregulated competition represented the best path to progress—was widely preached. By this view, the federal government should promote economic development but not regulate the industries that it subsidized.

When people did want help from government, they tended to turn to local or state authorities. Some of the fiercest political contests of these years were fought far from Washington. On the Great Plains, angry farmers demanded that their state legislatures regulate exorbitant railroad rates. In the cities, immigrant groups contended for political power while native-born reformers periodically attempted to oust the political machines.

Moreover, city and state governments vied furiously with each other for control. In many states, cities could not change their system of government, alter their tax structure, or regulate municipal utilities without state approval. When Chicago wanted to issue permits to street popcorn vendors, a special act of the Illinois legislature was required. With the cities growing so rapidly, this archaic system of state control became intolerable, and city after city mounted campaigns for self-government.

To make matters worse, in most state legislatures the rural districts held disproportionate influence. In Connecticut, for example, where the legislature had last been reapportioned in 1818, villages of a few hundred people had the same voting strength in the legislature as cities like Hartford and Bridgeport. This issue, too, sparked countless political battles.

These grassroots political rivalries frequently pitted ethnic and social groups against one another. In New York City immigrant Catholics and native-born Protestants locked horns over tax support to parochial schools. In 1889 the native-born Republican legislators of Wisconsin passed a law requiring all children to attend English-language schools. This was a direct assault on the Catholic and Lutheran parochial schools where immigrant children were educated principally in German, Swedish, or Norwegian. Other states made similarly bald efforts to impose cultural and linguistic uniformity, leading many resentful immigrants to vote Democratic in 1890.

These electoral skirmishes between ethnic groups often centered on cultural differences, as native-born Protestants tried to force on the immigrants their own views on gambling, prostitution, temperance, and Sabbath observance. No issue aroused more conflict than prohibition. Irish whiskey drinkers, German beer drinkers, and Italian wine drinkers were equally outraged by anti-liquor legislation. In state after state, as well as in many cities and counties, prohibition proposals on the ballot roused passionate voter interest.

Thus Gilded Age politics formed an intricate mosaic of individuals, groups, and political parties pursuing varied interests in city halls, statehouses, and Washington, D.C. But despite all the activity, the political system still lagged behind in addressing the social problems of an increasingly urbanized and industrialized nation.

Hayes in the White House

In this era of locally based politics and a diminished presidency, the state leaders who controlled both major parties almost invariably chose appealing but pliable men as presidential candidates.

Rutherford B. Hayes (1877–1881) perfectly embodied this narrow view of the office. A lawyer and Civil War general wounded in action, Hayes had won admiration as an honest postwar governor of Ohio. His major presidential achievement was to restore respect for the office after the Grant scandals. With his flowing beard, the benevolent Hayes brought simplicity, dignity, and decorum to the White House. In part, this reflected the influence of his wife, Lucy, a highly intelligent, college-educated woman of great moral earnestness. The Hayeses and their five children often gathered in

The First Family

This carefully posed portrait of President Rutherford B. Hayes and his family was clearly intended to symbolize the virtues of domestic order and harmony highly prized in Gilded Age America, a time of turbulent social change.

the Red Room after dinner to sing hymns and then moved on to the Blue Room for prayers.

In contrast to Grant, whose periodic drinking bouts were legendary, Hayes was only a moderate drinker. He also recognized the political strength of the temperance movement. "Lemonade Lucy" Hayes actively supported the Woman's Christian Temperance Union (WCTU), and Hayes banished alcohol from the White House. Not everyone welcomed this reform; after one White House dinner, Hayes's secretary of state grumbled: "It was a brilliant affair. The water flowed like champagne."

Greenbacks and Silver

While Washingtonians groused about excessive White House sobriety, a political issue was brewing that would agitate American politics for decades: how to create a money supply adequate for a growing and diverse economy. Before the Civil War the nation's currency had consisted mainly of notes issued by state banks. With some sixteen hundred such banks in operation, the monetary situation was chaotic. A uniform national currency was needed, but what should the medium of exchange be? The only truly trustworthy money, many believed, was gold or silver, or certificates exchangeable for these scarce and precious metals. Reflecting this notion, all the *federally* issued currency in circulation in 1860, about $228 million, consisted of gold or silver coins or U.S. Treasury notes redeemable for gold or silver. Americans' deep-seated, almost superstitious, reverence for gold and silver added to the difficulty of establishing a coherent monetary policy.

To complicate matters, opposing groups clashed over the money question. Bankers and creditors, most business leaders, economists, and politicians believed that economic stability required a strictly limited currency supply. If too much money circulated, its value would drop, and inflation would jeopardize the wealth of the propertied classes and saddle working people with higher prices. But too tight a money supply drove interest rates up and prices down. Debtors—especially southern and western farmers—and some manufacturers favored expanding the money supply. Expansion would make it easier for them to pay off their obligations and also, by increasing consumer buying power, help maintain farm prices, which were falling alarmingly.

After the Civil War, these complex questions of federal monetary policy focused on a specific question: should the wartime greenbacks still in circulation be retained and even expanded, or cut back and ultimately eliminated, leaving only a currency backed by gold (see Chapter 15)? The hard times associated with the Panic of 1873 rendered this dispute even more bitter, and it continued despite the passage in 1875 of the Specie Resumption Act, a measure supported by the conservative, hard-money forces.

The money issue entered electoral politics in the mid-1870s with the formation of the Greenback party, whose platform included various measures, especially an expanded money supply, to benefit workers and debtor farmers of the West and South. The Greenback party's strength peaked in 1878, when it won the endorsement of labor organizations embittered by the government's hostility in the labor unrest of 1877. In the 1878 midterm elections, Greenback candidates garnered more than a million votes and won fourteen seats in Congress.

As prosperity returned after 1878, the Greenback party faded, but the money issue did not. An even longer-lasting controversy raged over the coinage of silver. Up to 1873 the U.S. Treasury regularly purchased and minted into coins all the gold and silver offered to it for sale. However, by the early 1870s little silver was being sold to the Treasury, and in the Coinage Act of 1873, Congress instructed the U.S. mint to cease making silver coins. Silver had been "demonetized." But just then, new discoveries in Nevada sharply increased the silver supply, and the same debtor groups agitating for more greenbacks now also demanded that the government resume the purchase and coinage of silver. Enthusiastically backed by the silver-mine owners, they denounced the demonetization of silver as "the Crime of '73."

Silver forces won a partial victory in 1878, when Congress passed the Bland-Allison Act over Hayes's veto. This measure required the Treasury to buy from $2 million to $4 million worth of silver each month and mint it into silver dollars. But the Treasury, dominated by monetary conservatives, sabotaged the law's intent by purchasing

A Cartoonist's Comment on the Silver Issue

The controversy over the coinage of silver, which surfaced in the 1870s, would convulse American politics for two decades. In this 1886 cartoon from the humor magazine Puck, *the artist uses the new national fad of bicycling to illustrate the ongoing disagreements over monetary policy.*

the minimum quantity of silver specified by the law and then refusing to circulate the silver dollars that it was obliged to mint.

Frustrated silver advocates tried a new approach in the Sherman Silver Purchase Act of 1890. This measure instructed the Treasury to buy, at current market prices, 4.5 million ounces of silver monthly—by no coincidence, almost precisely the amount then being produced by the nation's silver mines. It further required the government to issue Treasury notes, redeemable in gold or silver, equivalent to the cost of these purchases. The Sherman Silver Purchase Act did slightly increase the money supply; but as silver prices dropped, the government paid less each month for its purchases and

therefore issued fewer Treasury notes. The tangled controversy over silver went on.

The Spoils System

Since the Jacksonian era, successful candidates in national elections had rewarded supporters and contributors with government positions, ranging from cabinet posts and ambassadorships to post-office and customs-service jobs. The pattern of filling public jobs with political appointees also prevailed at the city and state level. This system was originally called rotation in office, and good arguments were offered in its defense: it seemed the most democratic means of filling government positions and provided upward mobility for lucky appointees.

But the system had its less desirable side. Unqualified and incompetent applicants sometimes received jobs simply because of their party loyalty. Once in office, these appointees often had to contribute to the reelection campaigns of their political patrons. Because of such abuses, this mode of filling public jobs came to be called the spoils system after the old expression "To the victor belongs the spoils."

Senators like Roscoe Conkling of New York and Benjamin Butler of Massachusetts were masters of the spoils system. They presided like monarchs over elaborate political organizations resting on thousands of patronage jobs. The battle over patronage among party chieftains led in the 1870s to a deep split in the Republican party between rival factions nicknamed the Stalwarts and the Half-Breeds. The two differed over little except who would control the party machinery and thus have the right to distribute patronage jobs. The Stalwarts' leader was the vain and strutting senator Roscoe Conkling, who had gained control of New York patronage in President Grant's day. Senator James G. Blaine of Maine led the Half-Breeds.

For years, a small but influential group of reformers of the native-born elite class had campaigned for a professional civil service based on merit. Well bred, well educated, and well heeled, these reformers had little understanding of the immigrants for whom the public payroll could be a ticket out of poverty. They favored a civil service staffed by "gentlemen . . . who need nothing and want nothing from government except the satisfaction of using their talents." But whatever their class biases, these conservative reformers had a point. As the functions of government grew more complex, a professional civil service became more essential.

Advocates of professionalization included Missouri senator Carl Schurz, editor E. L. Godkin, and social-welfare leader Josephine Shaw Lowell. Civil-service reformers displayed an almost religious fervor. "I have spent my life in fighting the spoils system," gasped one on his deathbed. They gave speeches, wrote editorials, and in 1881 founded the National Civil Service Reform League.

Cautiously aligning himself with the civil-service cause, President Hayes in 1877 launched an investigation of the corruption-riddled New York City customs office and demanded the resignation of two high officials who refused to cooperate. Both men had close ties to Conkling: one, Chester A. Arthur, was Conkling's top lieutenant in distributing patronage jobs. When the two ignored Hayes's resignation order, the president suspended them. Hayes's action won praise from civil-service reformers and Conkling's lasting hatred. The New York senator sneered about "snivel service" and Ruther*fraud* B. Hayes.

Civil-Service Reform

On taking office, Hayes had announced that he would not run for reelection, so at the Republican convention of 1880, the Stalwarts and the Half-Breeds competed to name his successor. Conkling nominated his old patron Ulysses S. Grant, and the former president led in the early balloting over the Half-Breeds' candidate, James G. Blaine. But both men lacked a majority, and on the thirty-sixth ballot, the convention turned to a dark horse, Congressman James A. Garfield of Ohio. Because Garfield had well-known links to the Half-Breeds, and to soften the blow to Conkling, the convention chose as Garfield's running mate Chester A. Arthur, the Conkling loyalist recently fired by Hayes! Since the forty-eight-year-old Garfield enjoyed excellent health, it seemed safe to put the totally unqualified Arthur on the ticket.

The Democrats nominated a 250-pound career army officer from Pennsylvania, Winfield Scott Hancock, while the Greenbackers gave the nod to Congressman James B. Weaver of Iowa. All three candidates had served as Civil War generals, Hancock with particular distinction at Chancellorsville and Gettysburg. Garfield's managers stressed not only his war record but also his humble log-cabin birth. Some Republican campaigners, appealing to Protestant prejudices, charged that Hancock's Catholic wife would fill the White House with priests, nuns, and monks. By a razor-thin margin of under 40,000 votes (of 9.2 million cast), Garfield edged out Hancock; Weaver trailed far behind with 308,578.

Garfield quickly grew to hate the spoils system. One observer described him as "fighting like a baited bull" against an invading horde of job seekers. When he chose James G. Blaine as secretary of state and named a Conkling opponent as the New York City customs collector, the Stalwarts concluded darkly that he was out to destroy their party influence.

Conkling tried a political maneuver that backfired. Together with New York's other senator, Thomas Platt, a Conkling loyalist nicknamed "Me Too," he resigned from the Senate. He hoped that the New York legislature would at once reelect him and thereby strengthen his political power. But Conkling miscalculated. The legislature chose

The Election of 1880				
Candidates	Parties	Electoral Vote	Popular Vote	Percentage of Popular Vote
JAMES A GARFIELD	Republican	214	4,453,295	48.5
Winfield S. Hancock	Democratic	155	4,414,082	48.1
James B. Weaver	Greenback-Labor		308,578	3.4

another senator and ended Conkling's career— and with it, the Stalwarts' influence.

But the civil-service reformers sought more than the defeat of individual spoilsmen; they wanted a civil-service law. A tragic event culminated in the realization of their wish. On July 2, 1881, President Garfield went to the Washington railway station to catch a train for Massachusetts. As he walked through the station, a man burst from the shadows, pulled a pistol, and shot him twice. It seemed at first that Garfield might survive, but the war veteran knew better. "I am a dead man," he told his doctors. He was right. After lingering in pain for some weeks, he died on September 19, 1881. Garfield's death brought to the White House Vice President Chester A. Arthur, the very symbol of the corrupt patronage system.

The assassin, a drifter named Charles J. Guiteau, was tried and hanged despite his obvious insanity, which took the form of a delusion that the Stalwarts would hail him as a hero and give him a prestigious job. At his arrest he had informed the police that he was a Stalwart, and he boasted that his deed had made Arthur president.

Civil-service reformers shrewdly capitalized on public shock at Garfield's assassination to build support for their cause, portraying the fallen president as a spoils-system martyr and exaggerating his saintly virtues. The reformers' campaign succeeded. In 1883 Congress enacted a civil-service law introduced by Senator George Pendleton of Ohio (Garfield's home state) and drafted by the Civil Service Reform League. The Pendleton Civil Service Act set up a civil-service commission to prepare competitive examinations and establish standards of merit for a variety of federal jobs; it also forbade political candidates from soliciting contributions from government workers.

The Pendleton Act initially covered only about 12 percent of federal employees but was gradually expanded. The establishment of a professional civil service independent of party politics marked an important step forward in the process by which the federal government gradually caught up with the modernizing trends transforming society.

As for Chester A. Arthur, the fact that he proved to be a mediocre president pleasantly surprised those who had expected him to be an utter disaster. Ex-president Hayes fumed that with Arthur in the White House, Conkling would be "the power behind the throne, superior to the throne," but in fact, Arthur supported civil-service reform and proved remarkably independent. Still, the easygoing and rather indolent Arthur was at best a caretaker president. Demonstrating their frustration with the feuding Republicans, the voters in 1882 gave the Democrats an overwhelming majority in the House of Representatives. In 1884, for the first time since the 1850s, they would put a Democrat in the White House, in the person of Grover Cleveland.

Politics of Privilege, Politics of Exclusion

Although hardly radical, Grover Cleveland challenged powerful interests by calling for cuts in the tariff and in veterans' pensions. Aroused interest groups rallied to defeat him in the 1888 election, one of the most corrupt in American history. During the Republican administration of Benjamin Harrison (1889–1893), big business and the veterans' lobby seemed firmly in the driver's seat. While Harrison and Cleveland fought their well-financed campaigns, debt-ridden, drought-stricken farmers from Georgia to the Dakotas mounted a spirited protest movement. And in the South so recently wracked by war, new forms of social and moral devastation emerged as the white majority used the machinery of politics to deny the region's black citizens their most basic rights.

The Election of 1884: Cleveland Victorious

At that tumultuous Chicago convention in 1884, the Republicans nominated their best-known party leader, James G. Blaine, a former United States representative and senator from Maine and Garfield's secretary of state. As an Augusta, Maine, newspaper editor in the 1850s, Blaine had helped found the Republican party. A gifted orator with a keen wit and a knack for remembering names and faces, Blaine represented the younger, more dynamic element of the Republican party eager to shed the taint of "Grantism" and build a truly national party that would promote economic development and take a greater interest in foreign policy.

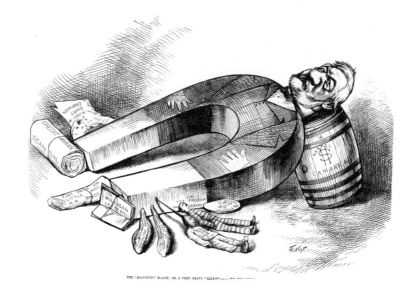

The "Magnetic" Blaine

James G. Blaine's admirers praised his "magnetic" personality, but political cartoonist Thomas Nast wittily turned the phrase against the Maine senator, calling attention to the allegations of financial impropriety that clung to him through much of his career.

But like many others, Blaine's name had been smirched in the tawdry political climate of the Gilded Age. Historian Henry Adams surely had Blaine in mind when he wrote that one could search the political history of this era "and find little but damaged reputations." In Blaine's 1876 senatorial campaign, his opponents had published incriminating letters in which Blaine, as Speaker of the House, appeared to offer political favors to a railroad company in exchange for stock. One of these communications ended with the directive "Burn this letter," which provided the Democrats a ready barb whenever Blaine ran for office thereafter. For civil-service reformers, Blaine epitomized the hated patronage system. To E. L. Godkin, he "wallowed in spoils like a rhinoceros in an African pool."

Sensing Blaine's vulnerability, the Democrats chose a sharply contrasting nominee, Grover Cleveland of New York. In a meteoric political rise as reform mayor of Buffalo and then as governor, Cleveland had fought the bosses and spoilsmen.

Short, rotund, and resembling a bulldog, Cleveland was his own man in an era of back-room political bargainers.

The shrewdness of the Democrats' choice became apparent when Godkin, Carl Schurz, and other Republican reformers bolted to Cleveland. These independent-minded Republicans were promptly nicknamed Mugwumps, an Algonquin Indian term for a renegade chief.

But Cleveland had liabilities. Early in the campaign, the Republicans charged that as a young man, he had fathered an illegitimate child. With characteristic honesty, Cleveland at once admitted the accusation, but the Republicans still used the incident against him. "Ma, Ma, where's my pa?" they chanted at rallies. "He's gone to the White House, ha, ha, ha!" responded defiant Democrats.

A more serious problem for Cleveland was opposition by Tammany Hall, the New York City Democratic machine that he had fought as governor. If Tammany's immigrant voters stayed home

The Election of 1884

Candidates	Parties	Electoral Vote	Popular Vote	Percentage of Popular Vote
GROVER CLEVELAND	Democratic	219	4,879,507	48.5
James G. Blaine	Republican	182	4,850,293	48.2
Benjamin F. Butler	Greenback-Labor		175,370	1.8
John P. St. John	Prohibition		150,369	1.5

on election day, Cleveland could lose his home state. But at a political rally on election eve, a prominent clergyman denounced the Democrats as the party of "Rum, Romanism, and Rebellion." Blaine failed to repudiate the remark immediately. The Cleveland campaign managers widely publicized this triple insult—to Roman Catholics, to patriotic Democrats tired of the "bloody shirt," and to drinkers. This blunder and the Mugwumps' defection allowed Cleveland to carry New York State by twelve hundred votes, and with it the election. Blaine, though seemingly destined for the presidency, would never make it to the White House. Cleveland, someone said, had, like Samson, slain his enemy "with the jawbone of an ass."

Cleveland's First Term

During his first term, the corpulent and rather lethargic Cleveland adapted comfortably to the dim role expected of Gilded Age presidents. He had early embraced the Jacksonian belief that progress and prosperity depended on the government's not meddling in the economy. In Andrew Jackson's day, laissez faire had been a radical idea, eagerly endorsed by a host of ambitious small entrepreneurs who wanted business conditions favorable to competition; by the 1880s it had become the rallying cry of an entrenched business elite staunchly opposed to any public regulation of corporate America.

Holding fast to the political views of his youth, Cleveland, though personally humane, displayed limited grasp of the impact of industrialization. Vetoing a bill that would have provided seeds to drought-stricken farmers in Texas, he warned that people should not expect the government to bail them out of their troubles. Given this orientation in top government, it is hardly surprising that ordinary working Americans often found national politics irrelevant. A trade-union leader, testifying in 1885 before a congressional committee investigating labor conditions, bewailed "the foolishness that the Republican party, and the Democratic party, too, have been indulging in for the past eight years." He challenged both parties to "take up some live issue instead of raking over the dead ashes of the past."

One public matter, however, did at least briefly arouse Cleveland's energies: the tariff. This hoary issue, dating from the 1790s, involved a tangle of conflicting economic and political interests. Tariff duties represented a major source of public revenue in this era before a federal income tax, but which imported goods should be subject to duties, and how high should rates be? Opinions diverged radically.

The producers of such commodities as coal, hides, timber, and wool unanimously demanded tariff protection against foreign competition. Manufacturers, on the other hand, were sharply divided. Industries that had prospered behind tariff walls—iron and steel, textiles, machine tools—wanted protection to continue. Many workers in these industries agreed, convinced that the tariff would bring higher wages. Other manufacturers, however, while seeking protection for their finished products, wanted low tariffs on raw materials utilized in manufacturing. Massachusetts shoe manufacturers, for example, urged high duties on imported shoes but low duties on imported hides.

Farmers of the West and South, by contrast, scathingly attacked the protective tariff, charging that it inflated the price of farm equipment and, by impeding international trade, made it hard to sell American farm products abroad. Critics of big business denounced the tariff as "the mother of trusts," and businessmen involved in foreign trade echoed the call for lower rates.

Above all, the tariff was a political football. The business-oriented Republicans generally advocated high tariffs, whereas the Democrats, with their agrarian base, generally favored lower rates. But much depended on which commodity was in question. A legislator's vote on a tariff bill depended almost entirely on the economic interests of his state or district. As a Democratic senator from Indiana put it in 1883, he supported his party's low-tariff position—except when it threatened Indiana's economic interests.

Cleveland's promotion of tariff reform arose initially from the fact that in the 1880s the high tariff, generating millions of dollars in annual federal revenue, was feeding a large and growing budget surplus. This surplus stood as a continual temptation to legislators to distribute it in the form of veterans' pensions or expensive public-works programs, commonly called pork-barrel projects, in their home districts. With his horror of paternalistic government, Cleveland became convinced that the budget surplus constituted a corrupting influence.

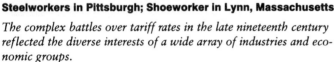

Steelworkers in Pittsburgh; Shoeworker in Lynn, Massachusetts

The complex battles over tariff rates in the late nineteenth century reflected the diverse interests of a wide array of industries and economic groups.

In 1887 Cleveland devoted his annual message to Congress entirely to the tariff issue. He argued that lower tariffs would not only cut the federal surplus but also reduce prices and slow the development of trusts. The high prices made possible by the protective tariff, he wrote, imposed a special burden on "those with moderate means, and the poor." Although the Democratic campaign of 1888 gave little attention to the issue, Cleveland's tariff message dismayed many corporate boardrooms, where talk of lowering the tariff seemed a dangerous assault on business prosperity.

Cleveland stirred up another hornet's nest when he took on the Grand Army of the Republic. Veterans' disability pensions cost the government millions of dollars annually, and in 1879, bowing to GAR pressure, Congress had eased the rules for securing them. No one opposed pensions for the deserving, but by the 1880s fraudulent claims had become a public scandal. The GAR actively encouraged veterans to file claims; and no matter how outrageous, these were routinely approved by Congress and the president. One veteran received a disability pension for poor eyesight that he attributed to wartime diarrhea. Not all Civil War vet-

erans abused the system, of course. When Samuel Whisler, an Ohio farmer and minister, received a pension check from Washington, he promptly returned it with a note: "I cannot prove that my disabilities were directly the result of the exposure and hardship of war; therefore, I cannot honestly accept this money from the government and must return the $400." But abuses were widespread enough to become a matter of partisan political controversy.

Unlike his predecessors, Cleveland investigated these claims—and rejected many of them. Early in 1887 he vetoed a bill that would have pensioned all disabled veterans (even if their disability had nothing to do with military service) and their dependents. The pension list should be an honor roll, declared Cleveland, not a refuge for frauds.

The Election of 1888

By 1888 some influential interest groups had concluded that Cleveland must go. He won renomination but faced a grimly determined Republican opposition. When Blaine decided not to run, the

Pre-television Presidential Campaigning

Pins, posters, banners, and bunting added a colorful note to nineteenth-century American political life.

Republican kingmakers turned to Benjamin Harrison of Indiana. The vice-presidential nomination went to Levi Morton of New York, the state that had cost the Republicans the 1884 election.

A corporation lawyer and former senator, Benjamin Harrison exhibited such personal coldness that some ridiculed him as the human iceberg. His campaign managers learned to whisk him away after speeches before anyone could talk with him or experience his flabby handshake. Capitalizing on the fact that he was the grandson of William Henry Harrison, they incongruously called their aloof candidate Young Tippecanoe.

Harrison's managers also developed a new style of electioneering. Instead of sending the candidate around the country, they brought delegations to Indianapolis, where Harrison read them flowery speeches appealing to their interests and vanity. Solemnly Harrison told an audience of awed little girls: "Some of the best friends I have are under ten years of age."

The Republicans focused tirelessly on the tariff issue. Falsely portraying Cleveland as an advocate of "free trade"—the elimination of all tariffs—they warned of the dire consequences of such a step. The high protective tariff, they argued, would ensure business prosperity, decent wages for industrial workers, and a healthy home market for the farmer.

The Republicans amassed $4 million in campaign contributions from worried business leaders. (Because the Pendleton Civil Service Act had outlawed the solicitation of campaign contributions from government workers, political parties depended more than ever on large business contributors.) This war chest purchased not only posters and buttons but also votes.

In one of the campaign's "dirty tricks," a California Republican leader, pretending to be a British-born naturalized citizen named Charles Murchison, wrote to the British ambassador to ask how he should vote. The ambassador fell into the trap and advised "Murchison" to vote for Cleveland. Capitalizing on the anti-British feeling then prevalent in the United States, especially among Irish immigrants, the Republicans gleefully publicized the "Murchison letter" as a shocking attempt by a foreign power to meddle in an American election.

Despite such Republican chicanery, Cleveland received almost one hundred thousand more votes than Harrison. But Harrison carried the key states of Indiana and New York and thus won in the electoral college. The Republicans held the Senate and regained the House. Harrison piously told his campaign chairman, Matthew Quay, that Providence had helped the Republican cause. "Providence hadn't a damn thing to do with it," Quay snorted; Harrison would never know "how close a number of men . . . approach[ed] the gates of the penitentiary to make him president."

Harrison swiftly rewarded his supporters. He appointed as commissioner of pensions a past GAR commander who on taking office declared "God help the surplus!" In 1890 Congress again passed, and Harrison signed, the pension bill that Cleveland had earlier vetoed. Within five years the pension rolls ballooned from 676,000 to nearly a million. So freely was money appropriated for pensions and pork-barrel legislation that the Republican Congress of 1890 became known as the Billion-Dollar Congress. In 1890 the triumphant Republicans also enacted the McKinley Tariff, which pushed rates to an all-time high. To pass the tariff, the Republican leadership did agree to one measure of interest to farmers and debtors: the Sherman Silver Purchase Act.

Rarely has the federal government been so subservient to entrenched economic interests, so sat-

The Election of 1888				
Candidates	Parties	Electoral Vote	Popular Vote	Percentage of Popular Vote
BENJAMIN HARRISON	Republican	233	5,477,129	47.9
Grover Cleveland	Democratic	168	5,537,857	48.6
Clinton B. Fisk	Prohibition		249,506	2.2
Anson J. Streeter	Union Labor		146,935	1.3

urated in the native-born Protestant cultural outlook, and so out of touch with the plight of the disadvantaged as during the 1880s. Grover Cleveland said it well: the masses had to learn "that while the people should . . . support their government, its functions do not include the support of the people."

But discontent was intensifying. Voters sharply rebuffed the Republicans in the midterm election of 1890, when the Democrats gained sixty-six congressional seats to win control of the House of Representatives. This voter response reflected not only a stinging rebuke of the Billion-Dollar Congress and the business-ruled Harrison administration but also immigrant resentment at the efforts of the WCTU and other organizations dominated by Protestant, native-born Americans to "uplift" newcomers by force of law. Above all, however, the 1890 election results awakened the nation to a tide of political activism engulfing the agrarian South and West.

Turmoil in Rural America

Millions of farmers felt abandoned by the political process in the late nineteenth century. Agricultural acreage and production grew impressively in these years (see Chapter 16), but many farmers confronted a demoralizing cycle of falling prices, scarce money, and debt. These problems hit the chronically impoverished South and the boom-and-bust Great Plains with stinging severity.

In the cotton South, small planters found themselves trapped by the crop-lien system, endlessly mortgaging future harvests to finance current expenses. Mired in debt, many had to give up their land and become tenants or sharecroppers. About a quarter of southern farmers were tenants

in 1880; by 1900, the figure had risen to one-third. One historian has aptly called the South in these years "a giant pawnshop."

Wheat farmers on the Great Plains also faced bewildering problems. Plunging into debt to buy land at high interest rates, many found themselves owing not only the bank but also the farm-implement dealer, the grain-elevator operator, and the railroad. In the 1870s farmers had looked to the Greenback and Granger movements for help, but by 1880 it was clear that these efforts had failed.

From these trying circumstances emerged the alliance movement, the most significant outburst of grassroots protest and reform in the late nineteenth century. It began in Texas in the late 1870s as poor farmers gathered to discuss their hardships. Soon an organization took shape, promoted by activists like farmer William Lamb, who organized more than a hundred local alliances. Though ill educated, Lamb ardently described the farmers' grievances. As he wrote in 1886: "We can't hold our pens still until we have . . . let it be known what it is we are working for."

The alliance idea advanced eastward across the lower South, especially after a farsighted Texan, Charles W. Macune, self-trained as both a lawyer and a physician, assumed leadership in 1887. By 1889 Macune had merged several regional farmers' organizations into a single body, the National Farmers' Alliance and Industrial Union, or Southern Alliance. A parallel organization of black farmers, the National Colored Farmers' Alliance, had meanwhile emerged in Arkansas and spread to other southern states.

Like the Grange, the alliance initially advocated farmers' cooperatives to purchase equipment and supplies for members and to market their cotton. These cooperatives mostly failed, however, because farmers lacked the capital to finance them.

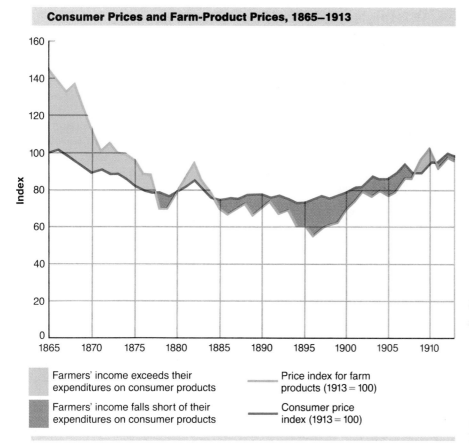

Consumer Prices and Farm-Product Prices, 1865–1913

Index

Farmers' income exceeds their expenditures on consumer products

Farmers' income falls short of their expenditures on consumer products

Price index for farm products (1913 = 100)

Consumer price index (1913 = 100)

Hard times battered rural America in the 1870s. Wrote a Kansas farmer: "At the age of 52, after a long life of toil, economy, and self-denial, I find myself and family virtually paupers."

Still, by 1890 the Southern Alliance boasted 3 million members, with an additional 1.2 million claimed by the National Colored Farmers' Alliance. Alliance members generally comprised not only the poorest farmers but also those most dependent on a single crop and most geographically isolated. As they attended alliance rallies and picnics, pored over the alliance newspaper, and listened to alliance speakers, hard-hit farm families felt less cut off—and increasingly recognized the political potential of their collective undertaking. As a member farmer in Hardy, Arkansas, wrote in 1889: "Reform never begins with the leaders, it comes from the people."

Meanwhile, alliance fever was burning across the Great Plains as well. In the drought-plagued years 1880 and 1881, alliances sprang up in Kansas, Nebraska, Iowa, and Minnesota. But the protest spirit faded as six years of abundant rainfall revived confidence and lured many thousands of

settlers to the northern plains. In parts of Kansas, the boom triggered frenzied land speculation; farms that had sold for $6.25 an acre in the 1860s went for $270.00 an acre in 1887. Railroads, eager to promote settlement along their routes, fed the boom mentality. "Follow the prairie dogs and Mormons and you will find good land," one promised.

In 1886–1887, however, came a painful awakening as killing winter blizzards and ice storms gave way to drought. From 1887 to 1897, only two Great Plains wheat crops were worth harvesting. Searing winds shriveled the half-ripe grain as locusts and chinch bugs gnawed away the rest. To make matters worse, wheat prices fell as world production increased.

Innumerable families packed up and returned East. "In God we trusted, in Kansas we busted," some scrawled on their wagons. Western Kansas lost 50 percent of its population between 1888 and 1892. But others hung on, prepared, in one his-

Nebraska Farm Family

For countless Great Plains farmers and their families, extreme weather conditions parched crops and froze livestock, and swarming grasshoppers seemingly devoured everything but the bills. The farm crisis that swept the South and West spawned a political protest movement that won the allegiance of both white and black farmers.

torian's words, "to fight nature, men, and the devil to keep their farms." The organization that is usually called the Northwestern Alliance, although never as large as its southern counterpart, grew rapidly. By 1890 the Kansas Alliance claimed a membership of 130,000, followed closely by alliances in Nebraska, the Dakotas, and Minnesota. Like the Southern Alliance, the Northwestern Alliance initially experimented with cooperatives and gradually turned to politics.

Both regional alliances attracted able speakers, writers, and economic thinkers. Macune, for example, devised an ingenious plan for coping with farmers' chronic debt and low prices. Under Macune's plan, called the subtreasury system, a farmer could store nonperishable crops in government warehouses and receive a government loan equivalent to 80 percent of their local market value. Later, when prices rose, he could sell these stored commodities on the open market and then repay the original loan plus storage fees and 1 percent interest.

Southern Alliance leaders Tom Watson of Georgia and Leonidas L. Polk of North Carolina urged southern farmers, black and white, to recognize their common plight and act together. For a time, this message of racial cooperation in the interest of reform offered promise.

In Kansas, meanwhile, Jerry Simpson, a witty, intelligent rancher who lost his stock in the hard winter of 1886–1887, became a major alliance leader. Mary E. Lease, a fiery Wichita lawyer, burst on the scene in 1890 as a spellbinding alliance orator.

As the movement swelled, the opposition turned nasty. When Jerry Simpson mentioned the expensive silk stockings of a conservative politician in his district and noted that *he* had no such finery, a hostile newspaper editor labeled him "Sockless Jerry" Simpson, the nickname he carried to his grave. When Mary Lease advised Kansas to "raise less corn and more hell," another conservative editor sneered: "[Kansas] has started to raise hell, as Mrs. Lease advised, and [the state] seems to have an overproduction. But that doesn't matter. Kansas never did believe in diversified crops."

From all this scalding rhetoric and feverish activity, a political agenda took form. In 1889 the Southern and Northwestern alliances arranged a loose merger and adopted a political litmus test for candidates in the 1890 midterm elections. Among their objectives were tariff reduction, a graduated income tax, public ownership of the railroads, federal funding for irrigation research, a prohibition on landownership by aliens, and "the free and unlimited coinage of silver."

The 1890 elections illuminated the depth of agrarian disaffection in the South and West. Southern Democrats who endorsed alliance goals won the governorships in Georgia, Tennessee, South Carolina, and Texas and gained control of eight state legislatures. On the Great Plains, alliance-endorsed candidates secured control of the Nebraska legislature and gained the balance of power in Minnesota and South Dakota. In Kansas the candidates of the alliance-sponsored People's party demolished all opposition. Three alliance-backed senators, together with some fifty congressmen (including Watson and Simpson), went to Washington in 1890 as angry winds from the hinterlands buffeted the political system.

Encouraged alliance representatives gathered at Ocala, Florida, in December 1890 and promulgated the Ocala Demands—in effect, a platform for the 1892 presidential election. But differences soon surfaced. While Northwestern Alliance leaders favored a third party, most Southern Alliance men, despite Watson and Polk's advice, rejected such a move, fearing that it would weaken the southern Democratic party, the bastion of white supremacy.

By 1892, however, some Southern Alliance leaders had reluctantly come around to the third-party idea, since many Democrats whom they had backed in 1890 had ignored the alliance agenda once in office. In February 1892 the top national alliance leaders organized the People's party of the United States—a title quickly shortened to the Populist party. At the party convention that August, thirteen hundred cheering delegates nominated for president the former Civil War general and Greenback nominee James B. Weaver of Iowa, now white-maned. Courting the South, they chose as Weaver's running mate the Virginian James Field, who had lost a leg fighting for the Confederacy.

The Populist platform reiterated the goals hammered out by the alliance leaders in 1889, with the addition of Macune's subtreasury plan and a call for the direct popular election of senators and other electoral reforms. Minnesota Populist Ignatius Donnelly's ringing preamble pronounced the nation on "the verge of moral, political, and material ruin" and declared: "[W]e seek to restore the government of the Republic to the hands of 'the plain people' with which class it originated."

Blacks After Reconstruction

The end of Reconstruction in 1877 and the restoration of power to the southern white elites, the so-called redeemers (see Chapter 15), spelled bad news for the nation's blacks, most of whom still lived in the South. The redeemer coalition of large landowners, merchants, and "New South" indus-

trialists had little interest in the ex-slaves except as a docile labor force or as political pawns. However, southern white opinion demanded an end to the hated "Negro rule," and local Democratic party officials methodically pursued this objective. Suppression of the black vote was a major goal. At first, black disfranchisement was accomplished by intimidation, terror, and blatant vote fraud, as blacks were either kept from the polls or forced to vote Democratic. Then in 1890 Mississippi amended its state constitution in ways that effectively excluded most black voters, and other southern states soon followed suit.

Because the Fifteenth Amendment (1870) guaranteed all male citizens' right to vote, disfranchisement had to be accomplished indirectly by such means as literacy tests, poll taxes, and property requirements. The racist intent of these devices became obvious when procedures were introduced to ensure that they affected only *black* voters. One stratagem, the so-called grandfather clause, exempted from these electoral requirements anyone whose ancestor had voted in 1860.

Black disfranchisement proceeded erratically over the South—North Carolina elected a black congressman as late as 1898—but by the early twentieth century, it was essentially complete. And it was effective. In 1896 some 130,000 blacks voted in Louisiana; in 1900, after passage of disfranchisement legislation, the number fell to 5,000.

Disfranchisement was only the keystone of the solid arch of white supremacy laboriously erected in the South. In a parallel development that culminated in the early twentieth century, state after state passed laws imposing strict racial segregation in many realms of life (see Chapter 21). Black caterers, barbers, contractors, bricklayers, carpenters, and other tradesmen lost their white clientele. An elaborate body of "scientific" thought allegedly proving blacks' innate inferiority gained a wide following.

Blacks who were sent to prison—sometimes for relatively minor offenses—faced the horrors of the convict-lease system, by which cotton planters, coal-mine operators, and other employers "leased" gangs of prisoners and forced them to labor under degraded conditions. One survivor of the system summed up his experience: "A Georgia [convict-lease] camp is hell itself!" But the ultimate enforcer of southern white supremacy was the lynch rope.

Black Prisoners Leased to a Road-building Contractor near Atlanta, Georgia, Around 1890

The convict-lease system in force throughout the South in the late nineteenth century gave rise to appalling abuses.

Through the 1880s and 1890s, an average of about a hundred blacks were lynched annually in the United States, overwhelmingly in the South. The stated reasons for this sadistic mob violence, often the rape of a white woman, frequently arose from rumor and unsubstantiated accusations. (The charge of "attempted rape" could refer to a wide range of loosely defined behavior unacceptable to whites.) The lynch mob actually functioned to exert social control, terrorizing blacks and demonstrating whites' absolute power. By no coincidence, lynching reached its high tide in 1892 as many poor blacks were embracing the farmers' alliance movement and rallying to the Populist party banner. Historian C. Vann Woodward has estimated that fifteen black Populists were killed in Georgia alone during the acrimonious campaign of that year.

The relationship between southern agrarian protest and white racism was complex. Some Populists, like Georgia's Tom Watson, sought to build a genuinely interracial movement. Watson denounced lynching and the convict-lease system.

When a black Populist leader pursued by a lynch mob took refuge in his house during the 1892 campaign, Watson summoned two thousand armed white Populists to defend him. But most white Populists, abetted by rabble-rousers like "Pitchfork Ben" Tillman of South Carolina, clung to racism; Watson complained that most poor whites "would joyously hug the chains of . . . wretchedness rather than do any experimenting on [the race] question." Farmers' alliance legislators in Mississippi and Georgia played a key role in disfranchising blacks and enacting segregation laws.

The white ruling elite, eager to drive a wedge in the protest movement, worked to inflame lower-class white racism. Addressing an alliance audience in 1889, conservative Atlanta editor Henry W. Grady warned against division among white southerners; the region's only hope, he said, was "the clear and unmistakable domination of the white race." But even as they raised the bugaboo of "Negro rule," the white elite manipulated the urban black vote as a weapon against agrarian radicalism, driving Tom Watson to despair. On balance, the rise of southern agrarian protest deepened racial hatred and ultimately worsened blacks' situation.

While southern blacks suffered racist oppression, the federal government largely stood aside. After a southern tour in 1877, President Hayes noted that black rights were being trampled by a variety of means, including lawless violence. But Hayes kept these observations to himself, and in this he was typical of a generation of northern politicians who paid lip service to egalitarian principles but failed to apply them to blacks.

The Supreme Court similarly abandoned blacks to their fate. The Fourteenth Amendment (1868) had granted blacks citizenship and the equal protection of the laws, and the Civil Rights Act of 1875 outlawed racial discrimination on juries and in public places such as hotels and theaters, as well as on railroads, streetcars, and other such conveyances; but the Supreme Court soon ripped gaping holes in these protective laws.

In the *Civil Rights Cases* (1883), the High Court declared the Civil Rights Act of 1875 unconstitutional. The Fourteenth Amendment protected citizens only from *governmental* infringement of their civil rights, the justices ruled, not from acts of discrimination by private citizens such as railroad conductors. In *Plessy* v. *Ferguson* (1896), the justices upheld a Louisiana law requiring segregated railroad cars. Racial segregation was constitutional, the Court held, provided that equal facilities were made available to each race. (In a prophetic dissent, Associate Justice John Marshall Harlan observed: "Our Constitution is color blind." Segregation, he added, was totally inconsistent with the constitutional principle of equality before the law.)

With the Supreme Court's blessing, the South proceeded to segregate its public-school system, totally ignoring the caveat that such separate facilities must be equal. (In reality, white children studied in nicer buildings, used newer equipment, and were taught by higher-paid teachers than black children.) Not until 1954 did the Court abandon this "separate but equal" doctrine. Rounding out their dismal record, the justices in 1898 upheld the poll tax and literacy tests by which Mississippi and other states had disfranchised blacks.

Few northerners protested the indignities that underlay the South's white-supremacist society. Until the North condemned lynching outright, declared the aged abolitionist Frederick Douglass in 1892, "it will remain equally involved with the South in this common crime." The restoration of sectional harmony, in short, came at a higher price: acquiescence by the North in the utter debasement of a people whose freedom had cost the lives of many thousands of northern young men.

Blacks responded in various ways to their plight. The best-known black southerner of the period, Booker T. Washington, counseled patience, accommodation, and the acquisition of useful skills (see Chapter 21). Many blacks did adapt to a racist society and even managed a precarious happiness. Black churches provided a haven of emotional support, as did black fraternal lodges like the Knights of Pythias.

Some blacks established businesses to serve their community. Two black-owned banks, in Richmond and Washington, D.C., were chartered in 1888. The North Carolina Mutual Insurance Company, organized in 1898 by John Merrick, a prosperous Durham barber, eventually evolved into a major enterprise. Carrying the logic of racial self-help to its extreme, Bishop Henry M. Turner of the African Methodist Episcopal church urged blacks to return to Africa and build a great Christian nation. Gloomily concluding that "there is no future in this country for the Negro," Turner made several trips to Africa in pursuit of his proposal.

"Five O'Clock Tea"

The pervasive racism of late-nineteenth-century America is graphically illustrated in this posed stereopticon photograph. Even among children pretending to be grown-ups, the only conceivable role for a small black girl clearly was as a servant.

The voices of black protest never wholly died out. Frederick Douglass urged that blacks press for full equality; "who would be free, themselves must strike the first blow," he proclaimed in 1883. If whites used violence to oppress blacks, insisted militant New York black leader T. Thomas Fortune, blacks could respond in kind.

Other blacks decided that the only answer to southern racism was to leave the South. In 1879 several thousand moved to Kansas (see Chapter 15), where they established farms and the town of Nicodemas. Some ten thousand migrated to Chicago between 1870 and 1890. Blacks who moved to the North soon found, however, that while white supremacy was not official policy there, public opinion sanctioned many forms of de facto discrimination. Northern black laborers, for example, like their southern counterparts, encountered widespread prejudice. Although the Knights of Labor welcomed blacks and by the mid-1880s had an estimated sixty thousand black members, its successor, the American Federation of Labor, played a far more ambiguous game. While officially forbidding racial discrimination, the AFL in practice looked the other way as many of its member unions informally excluded blacks.

The rise of the so-called solid South, firmly established on racist foundations, had important implications for American politics. For one thing, it made a mockery of the two-party system in a vast region of the nation. For years, the only meaningful election south of the Potomac was the Democratic primary. Further, the large bloc of southern Democratic senators and congressmen who trooped off to Washington each year, accumulating seniority and power, exerted a great and often reactionary influence on public policy. Above all, they mobilized instantly to quash any threat to southern white supremacy. Finally, the solid South wielded enormous clout in the national Democratic party. Since a two-thirds vote was required at the national nominating convention to choose the party's presidential nominee, no candidate unacceptable to the white South stood a chance. This "two-thirds rule" prevailed until 1936. Only in the 1970s, in the wake of sweeping social and economic changes, would a genuine two-party system emerge in the South.

But above all, the rigid caste system that evolved in the post-Reconstruction South profoundly shaped the consciousness of those immediately caught up in it, white and black alike. As white novelist Lillian Smith has written, describing her girlhood in turn-of-the-century Florida and Georgia: "From the day I was born, I began to learn my lessons. . . . I learned it is possible to be a Christian and a white southerner simultaneously; to be a gentlewoman and an arrogant callous creature at the same moment; to pray at night and ride a Jim Crow car the next morning; . . . to glow when the word *democracy* was used, and to practice slavery from morning to night."

The 1890s: Politics in a Depression Decade

The decade of the 1890s was one of the most difficult and unsettled in American history. Grover Cleveland, elected to a second term in 1892, at once had to cope with a business panic, a crisis of confidence in the government's fiscal stability, and a depression that took a terrible human toll. The early 1890s also brought bloody labor strikes as well as the emergence of the Populist party.

Amid these upheavals, Cleveland clung to his narrow view of government's proper role. He tried to rebuild confidence in the dollar by defending the gold standard, but otherwise neither he nor Congress provided leadership at a time of national crisis. The depression of the 1890s revealed with stark clarity that "politics as usual" was woefully inadequate to an industrializing society.

1892: Cleveland Revisited

The year 1892 brought evidence of gathering discontent. The Populist party platform, adopted in July, offered an angry catalog of agrarian demands. That same month, thirteen men died in a gun battle between strikers and strikebreakers at the Homestead steel plant near Pittsburgh, and President Harrison sent federal troops to Coeur d'Alene, Idaho, where a silver-mine strike had turned violent. Events seemed to justify the Populists' warnings of a nation verging on ruin.

Faced with a steady rise in domestic dissatisfaction and fearful that the powerful European socialist movement would spread to the United States, both major parties acted cautiously. The Republicans renominated Harrison and adopted a platform whose only answer to escalating unrest was praise for the high protective tariff. The Democrats turned again to Grover Cleveland, whose reputation for honesty remained untarnished but who in four years out of office had made clear his growing conservatism and his opposition to the Populists.

Apart from the Populist challenge, the 1892 election was a rerun of 1888, but with the tide this time flowing in the Democrats' direction. Harrison sparked no enthusiasm, and resentment still ran high toward his administration's identification with big business and the GAR. Cleveland won by more than 360,000 votes—a decisive margin in this era of close elections.

Superficially, the Populist party did not fare too badly. James B. Weaver got just over a million votes—8.5 percent of the total—and the Populists elected five senators, ten congressmen, and three governors. But Populist strength proved very spotty. The new party carried Kansas and showed some appeal in the West and in Georgia, Alabama, and

The Election of 1892				
Candidates	Parties	Electoral Vote	Popular Vote	Percentage of Popular Vote
GROVER CLEVELAND	Democratic	277	5,555,426	46.1
Benjamin Harrison	Republican	145	5,182,690	43.0
James B. Weaver	People's	22	1,029,846	8.5
John Bidwell	Prohibition		264,133	2.2

Texas, where the alliance movement had taken deep root. But it made no dent in New England or the urban East, did poorly in the traditionally Republican farm regions of the Midwest, and even failed to show broad strength in the upper Great Plains. "Beaten! Whipped! Smashed!" moaned the Minnesota Populist Ignatius Donnelly in his diary; ". . . Our followers scattered like dew before the rising sun."

Most disheartening of all was Populist showing in the South. Racism, ingrained Democratic loyalty, distaste for a ticket headed by a former Union general, and widespread intimidation and vote fraud kept the Populist vote under 25 percent through most of the South. This failure killed the prospects for interracial agrarian reform in the region. After 1892 southern politicians seeking to appeal to poor whites—including a disillusioned Tom Watson—stayed within the Democratic fold and laced their populism with virulent racism.

The Panic of 1893

No sooner did Cleveland take office than he confronted the worst crisis to face any president since the Civil War: an economic collapse in the railroad industry, which quickly spread. In the awesome industrial growth of the 1880s, railroads had led the way, unleashing a wave of speculation among hopeful investors. Some railroads had fed the speculative mania by issuing more stock (and enticing investors with higher dividends) than their business prospects warranted.

Weakened by agricultural stagnation, railroad growth slowed in the early 1890s. This, in turn, affected many related industries, including iron and steel. In 1893 the bubble burst. The first hint of trouble ahead came in February with the failure of the Philadelphia and Reading Railroad.

This bankruptcy would not alone have triggered a general business collapse if it had not come at a time of weakened confidence in the gold standard—the government's pledge to redeem paper money for gold on demand. This diminished confidence had several sources. First, when a leading London investment bank declared bankruptcy in 1890, hard-pressed British investors unloaded millions of dollars worth of stock in American railroads and other corporations and converted their dollars to gold. As a result, $68 million in U.S. gold reserves flowed across the Atlantic. Second, Congress's generous veterans' benefits and pork-barrel appropriations during the Harrison administration placed heavy demands upon the government's financial resources just as tariff revenues were dropping because of the prohibitively high McKinley Tariff. Third, the 1890 Sherman Silver Purchase Act further strained the gold reserve. This measure required the government to pay for its monthly silver purchases with Treasury certificates redeemable for either silver or gold and established the value of silver as one-sixteenth that of gold. In 1890 this sixteen-to-one ratio had approximated the actual market value of silver and gold. But new discoveries in the early 1890s pushed silver's market value down. This made it profitable for holders of Treasury certificates redeemable for gold or silver to convert them to gold, and many did so. Finally, the election of Grover Cleveland in 1892 eroded confidence in the dollar even more. Although Cleveland personally endorsed the gold standard, his party was known to harbor many advocates of inflationary policies.

With confidence in the gold standard waning, the well-to-do converted their paper currency to the precious metal. In January 1892 the gold reserve stood at $192 million. By the time Cleveland took office in March 1893, it had dwindled to $100 million, the minimum considered necessary to support the dollar. This decline alarmed those who believed—as most people did—that the gold standard offered the only sure evidence of the government's financial stability.

The collapse of a railroad early in 1893 thus simply acted as the catalyst for an economic crisis whose preconditions already existed. Fear now fed on itself as panicky investors converted their stock holdings to gold. Stock prices plunged in May and June; the gold reserve plummeted to $59 million; by the end of the year, seventy-four railroads and more than fifteen thousand commercial institutions, including six hundred banks, had failed. This was the Panic of 1893, the forerunner of four years of hard times.

The Depression of 1893–1897

The economic crisis worsened in 1894: by June nearly two hundred railroads had failed. By 1897 about a third of the nation's railroad mileage was in bankruptcy. Just as the railroad boom had been the key to the industrial prosperity of the 1880s, so the railroad crisis of the early 1890s sent shudders through the entire economy as hundreds more

banks and other businesses failed. A full-scale depression clamped down on the nation.

In human terms, the depression of 1893–1897 took a heavy toll. Estimates of industrial unemployment ranged from 20 percent to 25 percent. Upward of one-fifth of factory workers had no money with which to feed their families and heat their homes. Recent immigrants faced disaster. Jobless men tramped the streets and rode freight trains from city to city seeking work. For immigrant wives and mothers faced with the burden of caring for their families, the depression brought heartrending dilemmas. In *Maggie: A Girl of the Streets* (1896), novelist Stephen Crane told the fictional story of one such woman. She becomes an alcoholic, and her innocent daughter, seduced and abandoned by a street tough, turns to prostitution.

The unusually harsh winters of 1893 and 1894 aggravated the misery. In New York City, where the magnitude of the crisis quickly swamped local relief agencies, a minister reported numerous instances of starvation. Amid the suffering, a wealthy New Yorker named Bradley Martin threw a lavish costume ball costing several hundred thousand dollars. The partygoers spent as much as ten thousand dollars on their costumes. So grotesquely out of place did this highly publicized party seem

Coxey's Army

Jacob Coxey's "army" of the unemployed reaches the outskirts of Washington, D.C., in 1894. Note the new electrical or telephone poles.

in a prostrate city that public outrage forced Martin and his family to move abroad.

In rural America, already hard-hit by declining agricultural prices, the depression turned trouble into ruin. Farm prices dropped by more than 20 percent between 1890 and 1896. Corn plummeted from 50¢ to 21¢ a bushel; wheat, from 84¢ to 51¢. Cotton sold for a nickel a pound in 1894.

Some desperate Americans turned to protest. The populist movement, already strong, gained more adherents. In Boston six hundred jobless workers briefly occupied the statehouse in February 1894. In Chicago workers at the Pullman factory reacted to successive wage cuts by walking off the job in June 1894 (see Chapter 17). The strikers' statement summed up their plight: "We struck at Pullman because we were without hope." In Massillon, Ohio, self-taught monetary expert Jacob Coxey concluded that the answer to unemployment was a $500 million government public-works program funded with paper money not backed by gold but simply designated "legal tender" (just as it is today). A man of action as well as ideas, Coxey organized a march on Washington in March 1894 to lobby for his scheme. Thousands joined him en route, and several hundred actually reached Washington in late April.

Police arrested Coxey and other leaders when they attempted to enter the Capitol grounds, however; and his "army" broke up. Jacob Coxey may have been eccentric (he named a son Legal Tender Coxey), but his proposal closely resembled programs that the government would adopt during the depression of the 1930s. But in 1894 conservatives found the plan dangerously radical.

As unrest intensified, fear and anger clutched middle-class Americans. A California educator warned of "the great itinerant army of the unemployed" gathering across the nation. A church magazine demanded that troops put "a pitiless stop" to all outbreaks of unrest. To some observers, a bloody upheaval seemed imminent.

Defending the Gold Standard

In the face of mass suffering and turmoil, Cleveland retreated into a laissez faire fortress. He endlessly insisted that boom-and-bust economic cycles were inevitable and that the government could only hunker down and ride out the storm. These ideas represented the conventional wisdom of the day. Even Governor John Peter Altgeld of Illinois, known as a friend of working people, could see no role for government in alleviating hard times. Addressing Chicago workers in 1893, he warned of "suffering and distress" ahead and urged them to "bear it with the heroism and fortitude with which an American citizen should face and bear calamity."

Failing to grasp the complex causes of the depression, Cleveland focused on a single peripheral issue: defense of the gold standard. As the gold reserve dwindled, he became convinced that the Sherman Silver Purchase Act was entirely to blame, and in August 1893 he summoned a special session of Congress to repeal it. Although Senate silver advocates resisted fiercely, the act was repealed in October.

Nevertheless, the gold drain continued and the depression deepened. In early 1895, with the gold reserve down to $41 million, Cleveland turned to Wall Street. Bankers J. P. Morgan and August Belmont agreed to lend the government $62 million in exchange for U.S. bonds at a special discount. With this loan, the government purchased 3.5 million ounces of gold, half from foreign sources. Meanwhile, Morgan and Belmont resold the bonds to the public for a quarter-million-dollar commission and a substantial profit. Despite public indignation about Cleveland's hat-in-hand appeal to private bankers, this complicated deal did help restore confidence in the government's economic stability. The gold drain was stemmed, and when the Treasury offered $100 million in bonds in January 1896, they sold quickly.

Cleveland saved the gold standard, but at a high price. In clinging to his limited-government philosophy at a time of national crisis, he appeared unfeeling. His obsession with the gold standard seemed to show more concern for moneyed men than for the average American. His dealings with Morgan and Belmont, and the bankers' handsome profits on the gold-purchase deal, confirmed agrarian radicals' suspicions of an unholy alliance between Washington and Wall Street. Cleveland's readiness to use force against the Pullman strikers and Jacob Coxey's pathetic marchers suggested insensitivity to the downtrodden.

Cleveland was decent and able, but his conventional ideas had proved inadequate. He left the White House in 1897 discredited, even hated. Soon after, he visited a friend whose dog jumped up on his lap and began to lick his face. The friend tried to call off the dog, but Cleveland said: "No, let him stay. He, at least, likes me."

The failure of politics in the early 1890s was not limited to the presidency; Congress did no better. Even on tariff reform, to which Cleveland had committed his party, the Democratic Congress of 1893–1895 achieved little. The Wilson-Gorman Tariff of 1894 lowered duties somewhat but made so many concessions to protectionist interests that Cleveland disgustedly allowed it to become law without his signature.

One feature of the Wilson-Gorman Tariff that did suggest an enlarged vision of the government's role in an age of towering fortunes was a modest income tax of 2 percent on all income over $4,000 (about $40,000 in purchasing power today). But in 1895 the Supreme Court declared this measure unconstitutional. On a 5 to 4 vote, the Court held that the Constitution forbade direct federal taxation of individuals. Whether one looked at the executive, the legislature, or the judiciary, the paralysis of government in the face of economic tribulation seemed complete.

A further consequence of Cleveland's policies was to split the Democratic party. Having risen in three years from mayor to president with scant help from a regular party organization, Cleveland had little patience with the give-and-take of party politics. Convinced of the righteousness of his cause, he rebuffed those who urged compromise over repeal of the Sherman Silver Purchase Act. Predictably, agrarian leaders and silver Democrats condemned him. South Carolina's Ben Tillman, running for the Senate in 1894, proclaimed: "[T]his scoundrel Cleveland . . . is an old bag of beef and I am going to Washington with a pitchfork and prod him in his fat old ribs." This split in the Democratic ranks decisively affected the elections of 1894 and 1896 and led to a basic reshaping of political alignments as the century ended.

The depression shook the realm of ideas as well. Indeed, it contributed to a fundamental reorientation of social thought. Middle-class charitable workers who had been taught that individual defects of character caused poverty now realized —as socialists had long insisted and as the poor knew only too well—that even sober and hardworking people could be beaten down by eco-

nomic forces beyond their control. As the social-work profession took form in the early twentieth century, its members spent less time preaching to the poor and more time investigating the social sources of poverty and family disorganization.

Laissez faire ideology suffered a grievous setback in the 1890s as depression-worn Americans widely adopted a broadened conception of the proper role of government in dealing with large-scale economic and social problems. And after watching Grover Cleveland's feeble response to the economic calamity, many citizens concluded that a stronger, more active presidency was essential in the new industrial era. The depression was memorable, in short, not only for the suffering that it brought but also for the lessons that it taught.

The Watershed Election of 1896

Galloping Republican gains in the 1894 midterm election revealed the depths of popular revulsion against Cleveland and the Democrats, who were blamed for hard times. As politicians geared up for the 1896 presidential election, the monetary question became the overriding symbolic issue. While conservatives clung to the gold standard, agrarian radicals rallied to the banner of "free silver." The silverites' moment of triumph came at the 1896 Democratic convention, when the nomination went to a young champion of the silver cause, William Jennings Bryan. Despite Bryan's eloquence, Republican William McKinley emerged victorious. His triumph cemented the Republican gains of 1894 and laid the groundwork for a political realignment that would influence American politics for a generation.

1894: Repudiation of Cleveland

With the depression at its worst and President Grover Cleveland increasingly unpopular, the midterm election of 1894 spelled Democratic disaster. The blizzard of protest votes, commented one observer, left the Democrats "buried under the drift a thousand feet deep." Gaining 5 seats in the Senate and 117 in the House, the Republicans won both houses of Congress. At the state level, they secured control of several key states—including New York, Illinois, and Wisconsin—as immigrant workers, battered by the depression, abandoned their traditional Democratic allegiance in droves. Even such Democratic strongholds as Maryland, Missouri, and North Carolina fell into the Republican column. In New England the only Democratic congressman to survive was John Fitzgerald, grandfather of John F. Kennedy.

Populist candidates garnered nearly 1.5 million votes in 1894—an increase of more than 40 percent over their 1892 total. Populism's most impressive gains occurred in southern states such as North Carolina, Alabama, and Georgia. The Populists' advances in the South would probably have been even greater but for Democratic electoral fraud. "We had to do it," insisted one Democratic party operative; "those damned Populists would have ruined the country." Although several western states that had voted Populist in 1892 returned to their traditional Republican allegiance in 1894, the overall results that year heartened Populist leaders.

The Silver Issue

As serious economic divisions split Americans in the mid-1890s, Supreme Court justice Stephen J. Field described the situation as "a war of the poor against the rich: a war constantly growing in intensity and bitterness." But this "war" involved mostly words and was largely fought over a symbolic issue: free silver.

The silver issue dated from the 1870s, but it surged to prominence in 1893, thanks to Grover Cleveland. By clutching the gold standard so bull-doggishly, Cleveland forced his opponents into an equally exaggerated obsession with silver. Thus the genuine issues that divided rich and poor, creditor and debtor, and farmer and city dweller were obscured by murky debates over two semi-mythic precious metals. While conservatives warned of the nightmarish dangers of abandoning the gold standard, agrarian radicals in the South and West extolled silver as the remedy for poverty, debt, inequality, and the common cold. They were cheered and in some instances financed by western silver-mine owners who stood to profit handsomely if silver again became a monetary metal.

Beneath the rhetoric, each side had a point. Gold advocates recognized that a nation's paper money must be based on more than a government's ability to run printing presses and that uncontrolled inflation could be catastrophic. The silver advocates understood that basing the money supply on the number of gold bars in the Treasury's vaults could strangle a dynamic, growing economy. They knew from personal experience how tight-money policies depressed prices and devastated farmers. Unfortunately, these underlying realities were rarely expressed clearly.

The silverites' most influential piece of propaganda, William H. Harvey's *Coin's Financial School* (1894), explained the monetary issue in simplified partisan terms, denounced "the conspiracy of Goldbugs," and insisted that the free coinage of silver would banish debt and "revivify all the industries of the country." More than four hundred thousand copies of Harvey's booklet were sold or given away by silver-mine owners from 1894 to 1896. Gold-standard propagandists were equally misleading. One cartoon depicted the bleak conditions in various poverty-stricken nations that also had a silver coinage, implying that the United States would sink to the same deplorable level if it embraced free silver.

Silver Advocates Capture the Democratic Party

At the 1896 Democratic convention in Chicago, outnumbered Cleveland supporters protested in vain as western and southern delegates adopted a platform—including a demand for the free and unlimited coinage of silver at the ratio of sixteen to one—that in effect repudiated the Cleveland administration.

Who would be the nominee? The front-runner was Congressman Richard Bland of Missouri, long a pillar of the silver cause. But behind the scenes, the groundwork was being laid for the nomination of a dark horse: William Jennings Bryan of Nebraska. A thirty-six-year-old Illinois native, Bryan had entered Democratic politics in 1887 as a young lawyer in Lincoln, Nebraska. During two terms in Congress (1891–1895), he had fought for silver and against repeal of the Sherman Silver Purchase Act.

Bryan had discovered his oratorical talents in college debating contests and honed them in his early political campaigns. After his first political speech, he told his wife: "Mary, I have had a strange experience. Last night I found that I had power over the audience. I could move them as I chose." His moment at Chicago came when he delivered a major speech in the debate over the platform. In an era before television or electronic amplification, his booming voice and broad gestures easily reached the upper gallery of the spacious convention hall, where Mary Bryan, his most trusted adviser, was sitting. In this famous speech, Bryan praised western farmers as the bedrock of the nation and scorned advocates of the gold standard. By the time he reached his rousing conclusion—"You shall not press down upon the brow of labor this crown of thorns, you shall not crucify mankind upon a cross of gold"—the wildly cheering delegates had identified their candidate (see "A Place in Time").

The silverites' capture of the Democratic party presented a tough dilemma to the Populists, who held their convention two weeks later. They, too, advocated free silver, but only as one reform among many. To jump aboard the Bryan bandwagon would be to abandon the broad-ranging Populist program. Furthermore, fusion with the Democrats could destroy their influence as a third party. Yet the Populist leaders recognized that the most likely effect of a separate Populist ticket would be to siphon votes from Bryan and ensure the election of a conservative Republican. Reluctantly, the Populists endorsed Bryan, while preserving a shred of independence (and confusing voters) by naming their own vice-presidential candidate, Tom Watson, now a Georgia congressman.

The Republicans, meanwhile, had nominated former governor William McKinley, who as an Ohio congressman had given his name to the McKinley Tariff of 1890. The Republican platform extolled the high protective tariff and endorsed the gold standard, at least until other nations adopted bimetallism, a monetary system based on both silver and gold.

1896: McKinley Triumphant

Bryan did his best to sustain the momentum of the Chicago convention. Crisscrossing the nation by train, he delivered his free-silver campaign speech

"Dubious"

A Republican poster called voters' attention to poverty-stricken nations that had a silver coinage, implying that the United States would sink to the same level if it adopted Bryan's panacea.

to more than six hundred audiences in twenty-nine states. Not everyone found Bryan irresistible. One skeptical editor compared him to Nebraska's notoriously shallow Platte River: six inches deep and a mile wide at the mouth.

McKinley's campaign was shrewdly managed by his political mentor Mark Hanna, a Cleveland industrialist. A dignified, somewhat aloof figure, McKinley could not match Bryan's popular touch; to one critic, he always seemed to be "determinedly looking for his pedestal." Accordingly, Hanna built the campaign not around the candidate but around posters, pamphlets, and newspaper editorials that warned of the dangers of free silver, caricatured Bryan as a rabid radical, and portrayed McKinley and the gold standard as twin pillars of prosperity. One Republican poster pictured businessmen and factory workers carrying a giant gold coin on which stood a regal McKinley holding aloft the American flag as the sun of "PROGRESS" rose behind him.

Drawing on a war chest possibly as large as $7 million, Hanna spent lavishly on the campaign. J. P. Morgan and John D. Rockefeller together contributed half a million dollars, far more than Bryan's total campaign contributions. McKinley stayed home in Canton, Ohio, emerging from time to time to stand on his front porch and read pre-

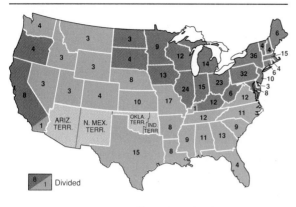

	Electoral Vote	Popular Vote	Percentage of Popular Vote
Republican William McKinley	271	7,102,246	51.1
Democratic William J. Bryan	176	6,492,559	47.7
Minor parties	–	–	315,398	1.2

The Election of 1896

pared speeches to a stream of visiting delegations. Carefully orchestrated by Hanna, McKinley's deceptively bucolic "front-porch campaign" was actually a marvel of organization. All told, some 750,000 people trekked to Canton that summer.

On election day, McKinley swamped Bryan by over six hundred thousand votes. He swept the Northeast and the Midwest and even carried three farm states beyond the Mississippi—Iowa, Minnesota, and North Dakota—as well as California and Oregon. Bryan's strength was limited to the solid South and the sparsely settled Great Plains and Rocky Mountain states. The Republicans retained control of Congress.

Seduced by free silver and Bryan's lung power, the Democrats had committed themselves to a platform and a candidate with little appeal for factory workers, the urban middle class, or the settled family farmers of the midwestern corn belt. The cities went heavily for McKinley. Urban voters realized that higher farm prices, a major free-silver goal, also meant higher food prices—hardly an attractive prospect. Bryan's weakness in urban America reflected cultural differences as well. To urban Catholics and Jews, this moralistic, teetotaling Nebraskan thundering like a Protestant revival preacher almost seemed a visitor from another planet.

The McKinley administration translated its conservative platform into law. The Dingley Tariff (1897) pushed rates to all-time high levels, while the Currency Act of 1900 officially committed the United States to the gold standard. With returning prosperity, rising farm prices after 1897, and the discovery of gold in Alaska and elsewhere, these measures aroused little protest. Bryan won renomination in 1900, but the fervor of 1896 was missing. The Republican campaign theme of prosperity, summed up in the slogan "A Full Dinner Pail," easily won McKinley a second term. Over 100,000 more Americans voted for McKinley in 1900 than in 1896, while nearly 140,000 fewer cast their ballots for Bryan.

The elections of 1894 and 1896 produced a Republican majority that, except for Woodrow Wilson's two presidential terms (1913–1921), would dominate national politics until the election of Franklin D. Roosevelt in 1932. Bryan's crushing defeat and the Republicans' emergence as the party of prosperity and the sound dollar left the Populist party a shambles and drove the Democrats back to their regional base in the South. But although populism collapsed after 1896, in its wake, a new reform movement called progressivism was picking up momentum. Populist veterans would find satisfaction in the fact that many of their reform proposals were enacted into law in the progressive years.

The Election of 1900

Candidates	Parties	Electoral Vote	Popular Vote	Percentage of Popular Vote
WILLIAM McKINLEY	Republican	292	7,218,491	51.7
William J. Bryan	Democratic; Populist	155	6,356,734	45.5
John C. Wooley	Prohibition		208,914	1.5

Chicago in the 1890s

Barely sixty years old in the 1890s, Chicago was already a booming, bustling city of more than 1.5 million people, second only in population to New York. The Midwest's commercial, industrial, railroad, and agricultural hub, its stockyards teemed with livestock destined for slaughter and the packing houses. Along fashionable North Side streets like Lake Shore Drive stood the proud mansions of the city's great tycoons—men like Leander McCormick, who made farm equipment; Potter Palmer, who built hotels; Marshall Field, who owned a big department store; and Philip Armour, who slaughtered hogs. In the sprawling South Side working-class wards, immigrants from scores of countries crowded in tenements but somehow preserved their distinctive ethnic identity.

Along the notorious Levee, saloons and brothels flourished, including the elegant Everleigh Club, run by two sisters from Kentucky, Ada and Minna Everleigh. A maze of elevated trains brought Chicagoans to the crowded downtown area, the Loop, where in the 1880s the world's first skyscrapers, thrusting eight and ten stories in the air, had transformed the skyline. Presiding over it all were colorful, easygoing politicians with nicknames like Bathhouse John and Hinky Dink.

Visiting Chicago in the nineties was a must for European tourists, who were invariably overwhelmed by its throbbing vitality and stark contradictions. A British journalist in 1897 called Chicago the "queen and guttersnipe of cities, cynosure and cesspool of the world," where public spiritedness and fla-grant civic corruption existed side by side.

Native-born writers, too, found the metropolis on Lake Michigan both alluring and repellent. The novelist Theodore Dreiser, who worked in Chicago as a journalist in the early 1890s, later tried to recapture his mixed impressions: "By its shimmering lake it lay, a king of shreds and patches, a maundering yokel with an epic in its mouth, a tramp, a hobo among cities, with the grip of Caesar in its mind, the dramatic force of Euripides in its soul. A very bard of a city this, singing of high deeds and high hopes, its heavy brogans buried deep in the mire of circumstance." A fictional Chicago reformer in Henry B. Fuller's *With the Procession* (1895) complains: "This town of ours labors under one peculiar disadvantage: it is the only great city in the world to which all its citizens have come for the one common, avowed object of making money."

In 1893 Chicago organized the magnificent Columbian Exposition, ostensibly to honor Christopher Columbus but mostly to celebrate itself. In a swampy area along Lake Michigan rose glistening exhibition halls, statuary, and a shimmering reflecting lagoon. A dizzying array of mechanical, artistic, and

South Water Street in the 1890s

Wrote Mark Twain in 1883: "It is hopeless for the occasional visitor to try to keep up with Chicago—she outgrows his prophecies faster than he can make them."

agricultural exhibits was on display from many states and nations. The Woman's Building, organized by Bertha Palmer, Potter Palmer's wife, housed exhibits from nearly fifty countries. Numerous conferences were held, including a "world's parliament of religions." On the Midway Plaisance—the fair's popular amusement section—farm folk gaped at belly dancers from the Middle East and rode the world's first Ferris wheel. At night the exhibition buildings were outlined by strands of electric lights—the first that many Americans had seen. For hundreds of thousands of visitors, the Chicago world's fair provided memories for a lifetime. For urban planners, the "White City" that sprang up as if by magic that summer was a tantalizing foretaste of beautiful cities of the future. The man chiefly responsible for the fair's design, Chicago architect Daniel H. Burnham, more than lived up to his motto: "Make no little plans, they have no magic to stir men's blood." The fair ended literally with a bang. On the last day, as Mayor Carter H. Harrison was attending the closing ceremonies, he was shot and killed by a disappointed office seeker.

The world's fair delayed the arrival of the depression of 1893–1897 to Chicago, but when the crisis hit, it hit hard. More than two hundred thousand Chicagoans were out of work during the winter of 1893–1894. Many crowded into city hall each night to sleep on the floor; there, at least, they could be warm. In the city's dumps, men, women, and even small children picked over the garbage, searching for food. Tension gripped the city. When Governor John Peter Altgeld, charging a miscarriage of justice, in 1893 pardoned three men sentenced to hang after the Haymarket bombing of 1886, he was denounced by the city's elite, and his political career was over. In 1894, when

The Columbian Exposition

The 1893 world's fair put Chicago on the map in a big way. Visitors gaped in awe at the lavish display of electric lighting (shown here in the painting by Childe Hassam) and rode the world's first Ferris wheel.

workers at George Pullman's factory went out on strike, federal troops put down the disturbances.

Then in the hot July of 1896, the Democrats poured into town for their convention. The Nebraska delegation arrived in a special fourteen-car train festooned with banners for William Jennings Bryan. Reflecting the desperate economic plight of the Great Plains, they took rooms at the Clifton House, a cheap, run-down hotel. The delegation of wealthy New York "Gold Democrats," led by millionaire financier and horse-racing enthusiast William C. Whitney, arrived in a special New York Central train and stayed at the city's finest hotel.

On the convention's second night, Bryan dined with his wife Mary and a friend at the Saratoga Restaurant. They watched as delegates surged along Dearborn Street, demonstrating for the Democratic front-runner, Missouri congressman Richard Bland. Said Bryan quietly: "These people don't know it, but they will be cheering for me just this way by this time tomorrow night. I will make the greatest speech of my life tomorrow." He was right.

The next day, he gave his rousing "Cross of Gold" speech, and the nomination was his.

Even for Chicago, the overgrown boom town of the West, it had been quite a week—and quite a decade.

William Jennings Bryan

All this lay in the future, however. The most stirring events of the McKinley years occurred abroad. As prosperity returned at home, the United States flexed its muscles beyond the seas.

Expansionist Stirrings and War with Spain

In the final decades of the nineteenth century, cries for American expansionism roared across the United States. Politicians, statesmen, editorial writers, and Fourth-of-July orators insisted that national greatness required America to match Europe's imperial powers in making its weight felt in the world. Farm leaders, religious writers, naval advocates, and business promoters joined the expansionist chorus. Fanned by sensationalistic newspaper coverage of a Cuban struggle for independence, the American public's enthusiasm for international assertiveness sparked a war between the United States and Spain in 1898.

Roots of Expansionist Sentiment

Since the early 1600s, when European settlers first established colonies along North America's Atlantic coast, the newcomers had been an expansionist people. By the 1840s the drive for territorial expansion had acquired a name: "Manifest Destiny." When Secretary of State William Seward purchased Alaska from Russia in 1867, many expected that Canada, too, would soon become part of the United States. The expansionist dream had faded somewhat after the Civil War as industrialization absorbed American energies, but it revived strongly after 1880 as innumerable politicians and other opinion molders hammered into the public mind the conviction that America had a global destiny.

The example set by European nations and Japan contributed to this welling-up of expansionist sentiment. In 1897, the sixtieth anniversary of Queen Victoria's reign, Great Britain held a splendorous celebration to remind the world of its far-flung colonial empire. Meanwhile, France, Belgium, Italy, Germany, and Japan were busily collecting colonies from North Africa to distant Pacific islands.

To achieve true greatness, many Americans concluded, the United States, too, must have an empire.

Others emphasized the economic argument and maintained that continued prosperity demanded overseas markets. Secretary of State James Blaine noted in 1890 that national productivity was outrunning "the demands of the home market" and insisted that American business must look abroad. Such arguments surfaced frequently during and after the depression of 1893–1897.

The proponents of a stronger navy contributed to the expansionist movement as well. In *The Influence of Sea Power upon History* (1890), Alfred T. Mahan, former head of the Navy War College at Newport, Rhode Island, equated sea power with national greatness and urged a U.S. naval buildup. Since a strong navy required bases abroad where vessels could dock for repairs, supplies, and fuel, Mahan and other naval advocates supported the movement to acquire foreign territories, especially Pacific islands with good harbors.

Some religious leaders chimed in, proclaiming America's divine mission to spread Christianity. American Protestant missionaries were already fanning out over the globe, and this call exerted a powerful appeal. The expansionist argument sometimes took on a racist tinge. As the Reverend Josiah Strong put it in his influential 1885 work *Our Country*: "God is training the Anglo-Saxon race for its mission"—a mission of bringing Christianity and civilization to the world's "weaker races."

All these themes were woven together by a group of Republican expansionists who tirelessly preached the gospel of imperial greatness and military might. Notable in this circle were Senator Henry Cabot Lodge of Massachusetts; diplomat John Hay; and Theodore Roosevelt, a rising New York Republican. "I should welcome almost any war," declared Roosevelt in 1897, "for I think this country needs one." A series of seemingly minor diplomatic skirmishes between 1885 and 1895 starkly revealed the newly assertive American mood and paved the way for the war that Roosevelt desired.

In the mid-1880s, quarrels flared up between the United States and Great Britain over fishing rights in the North Atlantic and in the Bering Sea off Alaska. These disputes reawakened Americans' latent anti-British feelings as well as the old dream of acquiring Canada. A poem published in the *Detroit News* supplied the nickname that critics would soon apply to the promoters of expansion —jingoists:

> *We do not want to fight,*
> *But, by jingo, if we do,*
> *We'll scoop in all the fishing grounds*
> *And the whole dominion too!*

The fishing-rights dispute was eventually settled by compromise in 1898, but by then attention had shifted to Latin America. In 1891 the United States seized a Chilean vessel that was attempting to buy guns in San Diego for one faction in a civil war then raging in Chile. A short time later, a mob

in Valparaiso, Chile, killed two unarmed American sailors and injured seventeen others on shore leave. Furious over this "insult . . . to the uniform of the United States," President Harrison practically called for a declaration of war against Chile. Only when the Chilean government apologized and paid an indemnity of seventy-five thousand dollars was the incident closed.

Another Latin American conflict, in 1895, arose from a dispute between Venezuela and Great Britain over the boundary line of British Guiana. The disagreement came to a head after gold was discovered in the contested territory. When the British rejected a U.S. arbitration offer, Secretary of State Richard Olney sent them a stern memoran-

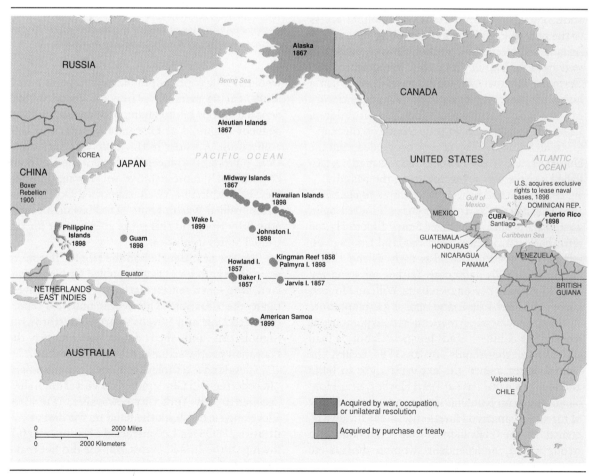

U.S. Territorial Expansion in the Late Nineteenth Century *The major period of U.S. territorial expansion abroad came in a short burst of activity in the late 1890s, when newspapers and some politicians beat the drums for empire.*

dum reminding them of the Monroe Doctrine. Delighted, President Cleveland described this lengthy note as "Olney's twenty-inch gun."

When the British eventually replied with a condescending message insisting that America's revered Monroe Doctrine had no standing in international law, a livid Grover Cleveland asked Congress to set up a commission to settle the disputed boundary even without Britain's approval. As patriotic fervor pulsed through the nation, the British decided to placate the United States and in 1897 accepted the findings of the American boundary commission.

Pacific Expansion

Meanwhile, the restless stirrings of the American giant were felt in the far-off Samoan Islands in the South Pacific, where the U.S. Navy sought access to the port of Pago Pago as a refueling station. But Britain and Germany had ambitions in Samoa as well, and in March 1889 the United States and Germany narrowly avoided a naval clash when a hurricane destroyed most of both fleets. Secretary of State Blaine's wife wrote to one of their children, "Your father is now looking up Samoa on the map." Once he found it, negotiations proceeded, and the United States, Great Britain, and Germany established a three-way protectorate on the islands.

Attention had by that time shifted to the beautiful Hawaiian Islands, twenty-five hundred miles west of California. The United States' link to Hawaii went back many years. New England trading vessels had stopped off there as early as the 1790s, and in the 1820s had come Yankee missionaries. In 1835 a young Boston merchant, William Hooper, had established a thousand-acre sugar plantation. Within a generation, American-owned plantations worked by Chinese and Japanese laborers had spread over the islands. By an 1887 treaty, the United States gained the exclusive right to build and fortify a naval base at Pearl Harbor, near Honolulu. American economic dominance and the influx of foreigners angered Hawaiians. In 1891 they welcomed to the Hawaiian throne Liliuokalani, a strong-willed, independent woman hostile to Americans.

Meanwhile, a crisis had come in 1890, when the framers of the McKinley Tariff, pressured by domestic sugar growers, had eliminated the duty-free status enjoyed by Hawaiian sugar. Hawaii's

Pineapple Industr

Hawaii

The lush Hawaiian Islands, with their industrious native peoples, considerable agricultural potential, and strategic importance, attracted the interest of American missionaries, entrepreneurs, and expansionists.

wholesale sugar prices plummeted 40 percent as a result. Facing ruin, the planters in January 1893 deposed Queen Liliuokalani, proclaimed the independent Republic of Hawaii, and requested U.S. annexation. A leader in this coup was Sanford B. Dole, a prominent pineapple planter. The U.S. State Department's representative in Hawaii, John L. Stevens, who had actively supported Dole's revolution, cabled Washington: "The Hawaiian pear is now fully ripe, and this is the golden hour for the United States to pluck it."

But the pear dangled on the tree for five more years. The grab for Hawaii troubled Grover Cleveland, who sent a representative to Hawaii to investigate the situation. This representative's report criticized Dole and Stevens's part in overthrowing Liliuokalani and shed doubt on whether the Hawaiian people actually desired annexation.

Cleveland's scruples infuriated expansionists. "In ordering Old Glory pulled down at Honolulu," declared a New York City newspaper, "President Cleveland turned back the hand on the dial of civilization." "Queen Lil" attracted a sentimental following in the United States, but she did not make matters easy for her American supporters by declaring that if restored to power, she would behead those who had conspired against her.

When McKinley succeeded Cleveland in 1897, the acquisition of Hawaii moved rapidly forward, and in 1898, by a joint congressional resolution, Hawaii was proclaimed an American territory. Sixty-one years later, it joined the Union as the fiftieth state. Liliuokalani lived to a ripe old age, revered as a link to Hawaii's past.

Crisis over Cuba

By 1898 American attention had shifted to an island much closer to home: the Spanish colony of Cuba, ninety miles off Florida, where, in 1895 an anti-Spanish rebellion had broken out. This revolt, organized by the brilliant Cuban writer José Martí and other Cuban exiles in New York City, won little support from U.S. business. Americans had $50 million invested in Cuba and annually imported $100 million worth of sugar and other products from the island, and turmoil could jeopardize these interests. Nor did the rebels initially secure the backing of either the Cleveland or the McKinley administration, both of which urged Spain to grant Cuba a degree of autonomy.

But the rebels' cause aroused much popular sympathy in the United States, and this support increased with revelations of the harsh tactics of the Spanish commander in Cuba, Valeriano Weyler. Particularly shocking was Weyler's herding of Cuba's civilian population into concentration camps to isolate the rebels. Brutality, malnutrition, and disease turned these camps into hellholes in which perhaps two hundred thousand Cubans died.

Fueling American anger was the sensationalized reporting of two New York City newspapers, William Randolph Hearst's *Journal* and Joseph Pulitzer's *World,* which were embroiled in a fierce circulation war. "Willie" Hearst, the son of a millionaire silver-mine owner, had been expelled from Harvard for sending chamber pots to his professors, with their names ornately painted in the bottom; he displayed the same outrageousness in the newspaper business. One of Hearst's gimmicks was a colored comic strip, "The Yellow Kid," which provided a name for his sensationalized editorial approach: yellow journalism. The Hungarian immigrant Pulitzer normally had higher standards, but in the cutthroat competition for readers, Pulitzer's *World* matched the *Journal*'s lurid sensationalism. The Cuban crisis was ready-made for Hearst and Pulitzer. Daily headlines screamed the latest developments, and feature stories detailed "Butcher" Weyler's horrifying atrocities. When a young Cuban woman was jailed for resisting a rape attempt by a Spanish officer, the papers trumpeted the story of the "Cuban Girl Martyr." In an excit-

Yellow Journalism

Joseph Pulitzer's World *(left) and William Randolph Hearst's* Journal—*whose comic-strip character "the Yellow Kid" (above) gave rise to the term* yellow journalism—*had a field day when an explosion ripped the U.S.S.* Main *in Havana harbor.*

ing climax, a daring Hearst reporter helped the woman escape and brought her triumphantly to a Madison Square Garden rally in her honor.

In 1897 a new, more liberal Spanish government made significant concessions in its Cuban policy, and for a time, a peaceful resolution of the crisis seemed possible. McKinley still pressed for a negotiated settlement, although he did order the battleship *Maine* to Havana. But Hearst and Pulitzer continued to inflame the public. On February 8, 1898, Hearst's *Journal* published a private letter written by Spain's minister to the United States, Dupuy de Lôme, which not only expressed reservations about Cuban independence but also described McKinley as "weak" and "a bidder for the admiration of the crowd." Many Americans would have agreed (Theodore Roosevelt once said that McKinley had "no more backbone than a chocolate eclair"), but they resented hearing it from a Spanish diplomat.

Irritation over the de Lôme letter turned to outrage when on February 15, 1898, a terrific explosion rocked the *Maine* in Havana harbor and killed 266 American crewmen. A painstaking review of all the evidence in 1976 concluded that a shipboard ammunition explosion, set off by a fire in a coal-storage bunker, had caused the blast. But in 1898 Americans were in no mood to view the tragedy as accidental. A navy inquiry blamed the blast on an underwater mine; newspaper headlines blazed with accusations of a "Spanish mine"; and war spirit flared high. On February 25 the young U.S. assistant secretary of the navy, Theodore Roosevelt, cabled Commodore George Dewey, chief of the U.S. Asiatic Squadron based at Hong Kong, to prepare for possible action against Spain's Asian colony, the Philippine Islands.

President McKinley still hung back from war. Genuinely anguished, he paced the White House at night and at least once broke down in tears. But in the last analysis, McKinley was not prepared to risk his popularity by resisting an aroused America. Of his sensitivity to public opinion, one Washington politician commented: "McKinley keeps his ear to the ground so close that he gets it full of grasshoppers much of the time."

Spain made further concessions to U.S. pressure, but too late. McKinley sent a war message to Congress on April 11, and legislators responded with a joint resolution recognizing Cuba's independence and authorizing force to expel the Span-

ish. An amendment introduced by Senator Henry M. Teller of Colorado declared that the United States had no desire for "sovereignty, jurisdiction, or control" in Cuba and pledged that America would leave the island alone once independence was assured.

The Spanish-American War

The conflict with Spain lasted just over three months, with only a few days of actual combat. The first action came on May 1, 1898, when Dewey's fleet steamed into Manila Bay in the Philippines and destroyed or captured all ten Spanish ships anchored there, at the cost of 1 American and 381 Spanish lives. In mid-August U.S. troops occupied the capital, Manila.

In Cuba the fighting centered on the Spanish military stronghold of Santiago de Cuba on the southeastern coast. On May 19 a Spanish battle fleet of seven aging vessels under Admiral Pascual Cervera sailed into the Santiago de Cuba harbor, where five U.S. battleships and two cruisers at once blockaded them. On July 1, in the war's only significant land action, American troops seized two strongly defended Spanish garrisons on El Caney Hill and San Juan Hill overlooking Santiago de Cuba. Leading the volunteer "Rough Riders" unit in the capture of San Juan Hill was none other than Theodore Roosevelt, who at last got his taste of war. "I am entitled to the medal of honor, and I want it," he wrote his friend Senator Lodge.

The final act came on July 3, when Cervera, under orders not to surrender, attempted to pierce through the American blockade to the open sea. American naval fire raked the archaic Spanish vessels and sank them. Spain lost 474 men in this gallant but doomed show of the flag. Americans might have found a cautionary lesson in this sorry end to four hundred years of Spanish rule in the Americas, but few had time for somber reflections on the Fourth of July, 1898. The *Washington Post* observed:

> *A new consciousness seems to have come upon us—the consciousness of strength—and with it a new appetite, the yearning to show our strength. . . . [t]he taste of empire . . .*

John Hay expressed the same thought more succinctly. It had been, he wrote Roosevelt, "a splendid little war."

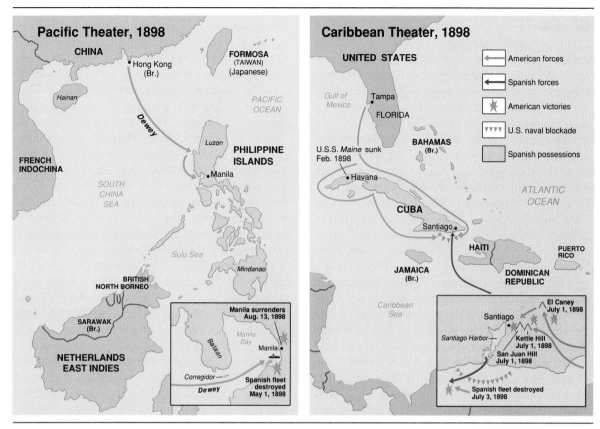

Pacific Theater, 1898

CHINA
Hong Kong (Br.)
FORMOSA (TAIWAN) (Japanese)
Hainan
PACIFIC OCEAN
Dewey
Luzon
PHILIPPINE ISLANDS
FRENCH INDOCHINA
SOUTH CHINA SEA
Manila
Sulu Sea
Mindanao
BRITISH NORTH BORNEO
SARAWAK (Br.)
NETHERLANDS EAST INDIES

Manila surrenders Aug. 13, 1898
Manila Bay
Bataan
Manila
Corregidor
Dewey
Spanish fleet destroyed May 1, 1898

Caribbean Theater, 1898

UNITED STATES
Gulf of Mexico
Tampa
FLORIDA
BAHAMAS (Br.)
U.S.S. *Maine* sunk Feb. 1898
Havana
CUBA
ATLANTIC OCEAN
Santiago
HAITI
PUERTO RICO
JAMAICA (Br.)
DOMINICAN REPUBLIC
Caribbean Sea

El Caney July 1, 1898
Santiago
Santiago Harbor
Kettle Hill July 1, 1898
San Juan Hill July 1, 1898
Spanish fleet destroyed July 3, 1898

American forces
Spanish forces
American victories
U.S. naval blockade
Spanish possessions

Major Battles in the Spanish-American War

The Spanish-American War was a short, sharp, one-sided encounter between the oldest European empire in the New World and the youngest power on the global stage. The conflict itself involved only a few limited U.S. engagements with out-matched Spanish forces in Cuba and the Philippines. The subsequent U.S. campaign to suppress an independence movement in the Philippines, however, proved long and costly.

The Scream of Shrapnel at San Juan Hill,

by Frederic Remington, 1898

Illustrator Frederic Remington, who went to Cuba as a war correspondent, helped to create a romantic image of the Spanish-American War and to promote the reputation of his friend Theodore Roosevelt.

For many who served in Cuba, Hay's blithe phrase was grotesquely inappropriate. Ill trained and poorly equipped, the troops went into summer combat in the tropics wearing heavy woolen uniforms. Medical care was abysmal. Food poisoning, yellow fever, malaria, and other diseases killed more than 5,000 American soldiers during and after the war; in contrast, 379 had died in battle.

Despite the racism they faced at base camps and on transport ships, blacks served with distinction. The black Tenth Cavalry, a part of the Rough Riders, played a crucial role in taking San Juan Hill. One enthusiastic New York newspaper exclaimed: "All honor to the black troopers of the gallant Tenth. . . . Firing as they marched, their aim was splendid, their coolness superb, and their courage aroused the admiration of their comrades."

With the defeat of Cervera's fleet, only the formalities remained. The Spanish sought an armistice on July 17, and in the peace treaty signed that December in Paris, Spain recognized Cuba's independence and, after much pressure and a payment of $20 million, ceded the Philippines, Puerto Rico, and the Pacific island of Guam to the United States. As 1899 dawned Americans possessed an island empire stretching from the Caribbean to the Pacific.

Deepening Imperialist Ventures: The Philippines, China, and Panama

The end of the Spanish-American War proved only an interlude in a period of intensifying world involvement for the United States. A few anti-imperialists protested expansionism, but they were no match for the jingoists. In the Philippines America fought a brutal and bloody four-year war against Filipinos struggling for independence. In China Washington took diplomatic and military steps to ensure an "open door" for U.S. commercial interests. Closer to home some highly dubious maneuvering by President Theodore Roosevelt cleared the way for the construction of an American canal across the Isthmus of Panama.

The Platt Amendment

For four years after the war (1898–1902), the U.S. Army governed Cuba under the command of the army surgeon General Leonard Wood. Wood's administration accomplished much in public health, education, and sanitation but nevertheless violated the spirit of the 1898 Teller Amendment, by which the United States had denied any intention of controlling Cuban affairs after Spain's expulsion.

The troops eventually withdrew, though under conditions that strictly limited Cuban sovereignty. An amendment to a 1901 army appropriations bill offered by Senator Orville Platt of Connecticut at the request of the War Department spelled out these conditions. The Platt Amendment authorized American withdrawal only after Cuba agreed not to make any treaty with a foreign power limiting its independence and not to borrow beyond its means. The United States also reserved the right to intervene in Cuba when it saw fit and to maintain a naval base there. With American troops still occupying the island, the Cuban constitutional convention of 1901 accepted the Platt Amendment, which remained in force until 1934. Under its terms the United States reoccupied Cuba in 1906–1909 and again in 1912 and established a large naval base at Guantanamo Bay, near Santiago de Cuba, which it still maintains. U.S. investments in Cuba, estimated at $50 million in 1898, soared to half a billion dollars by 1920.

Guerrilla War in the Philippines

An urgent problem confronted President McKinley as the Spanish-American War ended: what to do about the Philippines. This group of seven thousand remote Pacific islands, four hundred of them inhabited, had a population of more than 5 million in 1898. At the war's outset, few Americans knew that the Philippines belonged to Spain or even where they were. Without a map, McKinley later confessed, "I could not have told where those darn islands were within two thousand miles."

McKinley initially had little desire to keep the Philippines, but the victory over Spain whetted the public's appetite for expansion. To the American business community, the Philippines offered a steppingstone to the inviting China markets. Reflecting the prevailing mood as always, McKinley reasoned that it would be dishonorable to return the Philippines to Spain and dangerous to leave them on their own. The Filipinos were unready for self-government, he believed, and would be gobbled up if set adrift in the shark-infested waters of imperial rivalries. McKinley further persuaded

Manila in Flames

Despite the high-minded hopes of President McKinley, the U.S. repression of the Filipino independence movement after the Spanish-American War involved harsh and brutal actions, including the shelling and burning of large parts of Manila, the Philippines' capital.

himself that American rule would enormously benefit the Filipinos, whom he called "our little brown brothers." A devout Methodist who easily fell into the language of the pulpit, he explained that America's mission was "to educate the Filipinos, and to uplift and civilize and Christianize them, and by God's grace do the very best we could by them. . . ." (In fact, most Filipinos were already Christian— a legacy of centuries of Spanish rule.) Having prayerfully reached his decision, McKinley instructed the American peace negotiators in Paris to insist on U.S. acquisition of the Philippines.

But it soon became clear that uplifting the Filipinos would require a struggle. As early as 1896, twenty-seven-year-old Emilio Aguinaldo had organized a Filipino independence movement to drive out Spain. In the summer of 1898, with arms supplied by Commodore Dewey, Aguinaldo's forces had captured most of Luzon, the Philippines' main island. When the Spanish surrendered, Aguinaldo proclaimed Filipino independence and drafted a democratic constitution. Feeling betrayed when the Paris peace treaty ceded his country to the United States, Aguinaldo in February 1899 ordered his rebel force to attack Manila, the American base of operations. Seventy thousand more U.S. troops were ordered to the Philippines, and by the end of the year, this initial Filipino resistance had been crushed.

But these hostilities represented only the opening phase of a long guerrilla conflict. Before it ended, over 125,000 American young men had served in the Philippines, and 4,000 had been killed—more than ten times the American battle deaths in the Spanish-American War. As many as 20,000 Filipino independence fighters died. As in the later Vietnam War, casualties and suffering ravaged the civilian population as a result of U.S. military action. The American forces captured Aguinaldo in March 1901, but large-scale guerrilla fighting went on through the summer of 1902. Scattered resistance continued for several years more.

In 1902, under pressure from Senator George Frisbie Hoar of Massachusetts, a respected Republican anti-imperialist, a special Senate committee heard sobering testimony from soldiers back from the Philippines about the execution of prisoners, the torture of suspects, and the burning of Filipino villages. The humanitarian mood of 1898, when Americans had rushed to save Cuba from the Spaniards, seemed remote indeed.

Meanwhile, Washington had been wondering how to administer its new colony. By the Philippine Government Act (1902), Congress vested authority in a governor general to be appointed by the president. But the act also provided for an elected Filipino assembly and promised eventual self-government. Progress toward independence thereafter went forward, albeit at a snail's pace, with occasional intervals of semi-military rule. Among the strongest supporters of Philippine self-government were agricultural producers in the United States who realized that only with independence could tariff barriers be erected against Filipino agricultural products.

In 1933 Congress established a twelve-year timetable for the Philippines' independence. This goal was missed by one year because of World War II, but on July 4, 1946, independence finally came to the Filipinos. Emilio Aguinaldo not only lived to see this day but survived for nearly twenty years more, until 1964, when he died at age ninety-five.

Critics of Empire

Not all Americans applauded imperialism. Although few in number, the critics, like the Mugwumps who had challenged the spoils system, were influential. Indeed, some of them, like Carl Schurz and E. L. Godkin, *were* former Mugwumps. Other anti-imperialists included William Jennings Bryan, settlement-house founder Jane Addams, novelist Mark Twain, and Harvard philosopher William James. A somewhat unexpected recruit, steel king Andrew Carnegie, contributed thousands of dollars to the cause. As Carnegie wrote Carl Schurz: "You have the brains and I have the dollars. I can devote some of my dollars to spreading your brains." In November 1898, with the United States poised to take over not only Hawaii but perhaps the Philippines as well, these critics of empire formed the Anti-Imperialist League.

For the United States to gobble up foreign territories and subjugate other peoples, the anti-imperialists believed, was to violate the principles of human equality and self-government embodied in the Declaration of Independence and the Constitution. As one of them wrote: "Dewey took Manila with the loss of one man—and all our institutions." The argument that U.S. rule would force the Filipinos to accept "good government," Senator Hoar remarked, reminded him of slave traders' boasts about "new and easier . . . handcuffs or fetters to be worn by the slaves." The military fever that accompanied expansionism also dismayed the anti-imperialists. William James warned of "the power of the war demon"; Jane Addams reported that Chicago street children were

playing violent games and carrying out mock murders of "Spaniards" during the Spanish-American War.

In February 1899 the anti-imperialists failed by one vote to prevent Senate ratification of the expansionist peace treaty with Spain. McKinley's overwhelming reelection victory in 1900 and the defeat of the expansionist critic William Jennings Bryan eroded the anti-imperialists' causes. Nevertheless, at a time of jingoistic rhetoric and militaristic posturing, they had upheld an older and finer vision of America.

The Open Door Notes and the Boxer Uprising

As the Philippines war dragged on, American policy makers turned their attention still farther west —to China. Their objective was not territorial expansion but protection of U.S. commercial opportunities. Business interest in foreign markets had increased sharply with the depression of 1893–1897. With the nation's factories "outgrowing the home market," declared the newly founded National Association of Manufacturers in 1895, sales abroad offered "the only promise of relief." Proclaimed Indiana senator Albert J. Beveridge in 1898: "American factories are making more than the American people can use; American soil is producing more than they can consume. Fate has written our policy for us; the trade of the world must and shall be ours."

The China market seemed particularly inviting. Textile producers dreamed of massive sales to China's millions; investors saw opportunities for large-scale railroad construction. China was especially vulnerable to foreign intervention as the enfeebled Manchu Dynasty was tottering after a 250-year reign. When Japan defeated China in a war in 1894–1895, American business leaders sensed their opportunity. In 1896 a consortium of New York capitalists formed the American China Development Company to promote trade and railroad investment in China.

At the same time, however, other nations were hungrily eyeing the China market. Some went so far as to pressure the weak Chinese government to designate certain ports and even entire regions as spheres of influence where they would have exclusive trading and development rights. In 1896 Russia won both the right to build a railway across

Manchuria and a twenty-five-year lease on a large section of the region. In 1897 Germany forcibly secured a ninety-nine-year lease on the port of Chaozhou (Kiaochou) as well as mining and railroad rights in the adjacent Shandong (Shantung) province. The British won various concessions, too.

When it appeared that Americans might be squeezed out of China, the United States government stepped in. In September 1899 Secretary of State John Hay addressed notes to the major powers with economic interests in China—Russia, Germany, Great Britain, Japan, France, and Italy—asking them to take no actions interfering with American trading rights in China. Specifically, Hay requested that they open the ports within their spheres of influence to all nations and not grant special privileges to the traders of their own country. The six nations gave noncommittal answers, but Hay blithely announced that the principle of an "Open Door" to American business had been accepted.

These Open Door notes remain significant as evidence of the way in which commercial considerations influenced American foreign policy. They reflected what has been called a quest for "informal empire," in contrast to the acquisition of overseas colonies favored by the more openly imperialistic powers. In this kind of economic expansionism, Washington played a subordinate and supporting role to private enterprise—a kind of "imperialism" that fit neatly with the ideology of laissez faire. While U.S. trade with China remained minuscule in these years, visions of an enormous potential market there helped introduce a global perspective into American economic thinking.

At the very moment of Hay's Open Door notes, a more immediate and urgent threat to American interests—indeed, to all foreign interests—emerged in China. For years, antiforeign feeling had been building in China, fanned by an aged Manchu Dynasty empress disgusted by the growth of Western influence. In 1899 a fanatical antiforeign secret society known as the Harmonious Righteous Fists (called "Boxers" by Western journalists) went on a rampage throughout China and killed thousands of foreigners as well as Chinese converts to Christianity. In June 1900 the Boxers occupied Beijing (Peking), the Chinese capital, and laid siege to the district housing the foreign legations. The United States contributed twenty-five hundred soldiers to

Boxers in Tien Jin, China

The U.S. role in putting down the Boxer Rebellion was part of a pattern of deepening American involvement in Asia.

an international army that in August 1900 marched on Beijing, drove back the Boxers, and rescued the occupants of the besieged legations.

The defeat of the Boxer uprising further weakened China's government. Fearing total collapse of the regime, which would allow the imperial powers to carve up China, John Hay in 1900 issued a second, more important series of Open Door notes. He reaffirmed the principle of free and open trade in China for all nations and announced America's determination to preserve China's territorial and administrative integrity. In the 1930s, when Japanese expansionism menaced China's survival, John Hay's policy helped shape the American response.

Building the Panama Canal

The final episode in this cycle of foreign involvements left the most tangible legacy: the Panama Canal. People had long dreamed of a navigable canal across the ribbon of land joining North and South America. The commercial and strategic importance of a canal that would eliminate the long and hazardous voyage around South America was obvious. In 1879 a French company headed by Ferdinand de Lesseps, builder of the Suez Canal, had secured a twenty-five-year concession from Colombia to build a canal across the Isthmus of Panama, then part of Colombia. But corruption, mismanagement, and yellow fever plagued the project, and ten years and $400 million later, it went bankrupt, with the canal only half completed. Seeking to recoup some of its losses, the French company offered its assets, including the still-unexpired concession from Colombia, to the United States for $109 million.

In the expansionist climate of the 1890s, this offer aroused interest. An alternative route across Nicaragua also had its proponents, and lobbyists for both routes were active in Washington. But when the French lowered their asking price to $40 million in 1901, this turned the trick. In 1902 Congress authorized President Theodore Roosevelt* to accept the French company's offer and to negotiate with Colombia terms for the operation of a canal. The following year, Secretary of State Hay signed an agreement with the Colombian representative, Tomás Herrán, granting the United States a ninety-nine-year lease on a strip of land for the construction of a canal, in return for a down payment of $10 million and an annual fee of $250,000.

But the Colombian senate rejected the Hay-Herrán agreement. Colombian legislators had concluded that they should wait for the French concession to expire in 1904 and then negotiate a new concession with the United States. Although perfectly legal and quite shrewd, this action outraged Roosevelt, who privately denounced the Colombians as "greedy little anthropoids."

Determined to have his canal, Roosevelt found a willing collaborator in Philippe Bunau-Varilla,

---

*Elected vice president in 1900, Roosevelt had become president upon McKinley's assassination in September 1901.

an official of the bankrupt French canal company. Dismayed that his company might lose its $40 million, Bunau-Varilla, from his room in New York's Waldorf Astoria Hotel, organized a "revolution" in Panama. While his wife stitched a flag, he wrote a declaration of independence and a constitution for the new nation. Bunau-Varilla was in close touch with the Roosevelt administration, and when the "revolution" occurred as scheduled on November 3, 1903, an American warship hovered offshore as a warning to Colombia not to interfere. Proclaiming Panama's independence, Bunau-Varilla appointed himself its first ambassador to the United States. Three days later, Washington recognized the newly hatched nation. Twelve days after that, John Hay signed a treaty with Bunau-Varilla granting the United States a ten-mile-wide strip of land across Panama "in perpetuity" (that is, forever) in return for $10 million and an annual payment of $250,000—the same terms earlier rejected by Colombia. A few years later, Theodore Roosevelt concisely summarized the episode: "I took the Canal Zone, and let Congress debate, and while the debate goes on, the canal does also."

The first challenge confronting the U.S. canal builders was the persistence of the same yellow fever that had haunted the French. Under a rigorous drainage project directed by army colonel William Gorgas, the fever-bearing mosquito was eradicated—a remarkable public-health achievement. The Army Corps of Engineers began construction in 1906, and in August 1914 the first ship passed through the canal.

In 1921 implicitly acknowledging the dubious methods used to acquire the Canal Zone, the Senate voted a payment of $25 million to Colombia. But the price paid by the United States for the Panama Canal cannot be measured in dollars alone. For decades after, the ill feeling generated by Theodore Roosevelt's highhanded actions, combined with other instances of U.S. interventionism, shadowed U.S.–Latin American relations.

Conclusion   The opening of the Panama Canal concluded thirty years of expansionism that proclaimed the debut of the United States on the world stage. But foreign involvements never fully diverted attention from the fundamental question of late-nineteenth-century domestic American politics: could a government designed for the needs of a small agrarian society serve a nation of clanging factories and immigrant-crowded cities? Down to 1900, the answer was by no means clear. While issues such as the tariff, veterans' benefits, and monetary policy generated much oratory and some action, the dominant ideology of laissez faire severely limited governmental activism. For much of this period, interminable wrangling over patronage overshadowed far more important issues.

Rising agrarian discontent in the 1890s, sharpened by the depression of 1893–1897, underscored the urgency of certain social problems in these years. The Populist party, spawned by rural hardship, boldly challenged the assumptions of the laissez faire ideologists and corporate leaders who largely determined public issues. Although populism as an organized political force disintegrated after Bryan's ill-fated free-silver campaign of 1896, the movement's insistence that government play an assertive role in solving social and economic problems sank deep into the American consciousness. Indeed, this new and more activist outlook helped form the political environment of the progressive movement, to which we now turn.

CHRONOLOGY

1873 Panic of 1873.

Coinage Act demonetizes silver.

1877 Rutherford B. Hayes becomes president after disputed election.

1878 Bland-Allison Act requires Treasury to purchase silver.

1880 James Garfield elected president.

1881 Assassination of Garfield; Chester A. Arthur becomes president.

1883 Pendleton Civil Service Act.

1884 Grover Cleveland elected president.

1887 Cleveland urges tariff reform and vetoes veterans' pension bill.

1888 Benjamin Harrison elected president.

1889 United States, Great Britain, and Germany establish protectorate over Samoan Islands.

1890 Sherman Silver Purchase Act.

Sherman Anti-Trust Act.

McKinley Tariff pushes tariffs to all-time high.

1891 Crisis between United States and Chile over attack on U.S. sailors.

1892 Cleveland elected to second term as president.

1893 Panic of 1893; depression of 1893–1897 begins.

Drain of Treasury's gold reserve.

Repeal of Sherman Silver Purchase Act.

Overthrow of Queen Liliuokalani of Hawaii.

1894 "Coxey's Army" marches on Washington.

Pullman strike.

Wilson-Gorman Tariff.

1895 Supreme Court declares federal income tax unconstitutional.

Banker's loans end drain on gold reserve.

United States intervenes in Venezuela–Great Britain boundary dispute.

1896 Free-silver forces capture Democratic party and nominate William Jennings Bryan.

William McKinley elected president.

1897 Dingley Tariff.

1898 Spanish-American War.

1898– United States suppresses guerrilla uprising in
1902 Philippines.

1899 First United States Open Door notes on China.
United States helps put down Boxer uprising.

1900 Currency Act officially places United States on
gold standard.
Second Open Door notes on China.

1900 McKinley reelected; Theodore Roosevelt elected
(cont.) vice president.

1901 Platt Amendment retains U.S. role in Cuba.
Assassination of McKinley; Theodore
Roosevelt becomes president.

1902 Philippines Government Act.

1903 Hay-Herrán Treaty rejected by Colombia.
"Revolution" in Panama organized by Philippe
Bunau-Varilla.
Hay-Bunau-Varilla Treaty.

1914 Completion of Panama Canal.

For Further Reading

Robert L. Beisner, *From the Old Diplomacy to the New,
1865–1900*, 2d. (1986). A valuable recent study tracing the roots of expansionism.

Sean Dennis Cashman, *America in the Gilded Age: From
the Death of Lincoln to the Rise of Theodore Roosevelt* (1984). A good recent synthesis.

Carl N. Degler, *The Age of the Economic Revolution,
1876–1900,* 2d ed. (1977). A readable overview,
especially good on the economic context of Gilded
Age politics.

John Garraty, *The New Commonwealth, 1877–1890*
(1968). Well-written account focusing on the basic
transformations of the period.

Lawrence Goodwyn, *The Populist Moment: A Short History of the Agrarian Revolt in America* (1978). A carefully researched interpretive account focusing on the
political culture of the alliance movement.

Morton Keller, *Affairs of State: Public Life in Late Nineteenth-Century America* (1977). An excellent account
of politics and government.

Walter LaFeber, *New Empire: American Expansionism,
1860–1898* (1963). A basic and influential study.

H. Wayne Morgan, *Unity and Culture: The United States,
1877–1890* (1971). A good, brief study linking political and cultural trends.

George Brown Tindall, ed., *A Populist Reader* (1966).
A carefully chosen and well-edited selection of indispensable documents.

C. Vann Woodward, *The Origins of the New South,
1877–1913* (1971). A pioneering study, still unsur-
passed for the post-Reconstruction South.

Additional Bibliography

Gilded Age Politics and Voting Patterns: General

Peter H. Argersinger, "New Perspectives on Election Fraud
in the Gilded Age," *Political Science Quarterly* 100 (Winter
1985–1986): 669–687; Paula Baker, "The Domesti-
cation of Politics: Women and American Political Society, 1780–1920," *American Historical Review* 89 (June
1984): 620–647; Richard J. Jensen, *The Winning of the
Midwest: Social and Political Conflict, 1888–1896* (1971);
Paul Kleppner, *The Cross of Culture: A Social Analysis
of Midwestern Politics, 1850–1900* (1970); J. Morgan
Kousser, *The Shaping of Southern Politics: Suffrage
Restriction and the Establishment of the One-Party South,
1880–1910* (1974); Samuel McSeveney, *The Politics of
Depression: Political Behavior in the Northeast,
1893–1896* (1972); David J. Rothman, *Politics and
Power: The United States Senate, 1869–1901* (1966).

The Greenback Movement and the Silver Issue

Milton Friedman and A. J. Schwartz, *A Monetary His-
tory of the United States* (1963); Walter T. K. Nugent,
Money and American Society, 1865–1880 (1968); Allen
Weinstein, *Prelude to Populism: Origins of the Silver
Issue* (1970).

The Spoils System and Civil-Service Reform

Ari A. Hoogenboom, *Outlawing the Spoils: The Civil
Service Movement* (1961); Gerald W. McFarland, *Mug-
wumps, Morals, and Politics, 1884–1920* (1975); Allan
Peskin, *Garfield: A Biography* (1978); Thomas C. Reeves,
Gentleman Boss: The Life of Chester Alan Arthur (1975);
John Sproat, *"The Best Men": Liberal Reformers in the
Gilded Age* (1968).

Cleveland, the Tariff, and Agrarian Protest

Peter H. Argersinger, *Populism and Politics: William Alfred Peffer and the People's Party* (1974); Steven Hahn, *The Roots of Southern Populism: Yeoman Farmers and the Transformation of the Georgia Upcountry, 1850–1890* (1983); Horace S. Merrill, *Bourbon Leader: Grover Cleveland and the Democratic Party* (1957); Martin Ridge, *Ignatius Donnelly: Portrait of a Politician* (1962); Tom E. Terrill, *The Tariff, Politics, and American Foreign Policy, 1874–1901* (1973); C. Vann Woodward, *Tom Watson, Agrarian Rebel* (1938); C. Vann Woodward, "The Populist Heritage and the Intellectuals," in *The Burden of Southern History* (1960).

Black History in the Late Nineteenth Century

Louis R. Harlan, *Booker T. Washington: The Making of a Black Leader, 1865–1901* (1972); J. Morgan Kousser, *The Shaping of Southern Politics: Suffrage Restriction and the Establishment of the One-Party South* (1974); Rayford W. Logan, *The Negro in American Life and Thought: The Nadir, 1877–1901* (1954); August Meier and Elliott Rudwick, *From Plantation to Ghetto* (3d ed., 1976); Howard N. Rabinowitz, *Race Relations in the Urban South* (1978); C. Vann Woodward, *The Strange Career of Jim Crow* (3d ed., 1966).

The Election of 1896, McKinley, and Bryan

Peter H. Argersinger, " 'A Place on the Ballot': Fusion Politics and Antifusion Laws," *American Historical Review* 85 (April 1980): 287–306; Walter Dean Burnham, *Critical Elections and the Mainspring of American Politics* (1970); Paolo E. Coletta, *William Jennings Bryan* (3 vols., 1964–1969); Robert F. Durden, *The Climax of Populism: The Election of 1896* (1965); Paul W. Glad, *McKinley, Bryan, and the People* (1964); Lewis L. Gould, *The Presidency of William McKinley* (1980); Stanley L. Jones, *The Presidential Election of 1896* (1964).

Roots of American Expansion, U.S.–British Disputes, Anti-Imperialism

Robert L. Beisner, *Twelve Against Empire: The Anti-Imperialists, 1898–1900* (1968); Charles S. Campbell, *The Transformation of American Foreign Relations* (1976); Foster Rhea Dulles, *Prelude to World Power: Diplomatic History, 1860–1900* (1965); David Healy, *United States Expansionism: The Imperialist Urge in the 1890s* (1970); Ernest R. May, *American Imperialism* (1968); Thomas J. Osborne, *"Empire Can Wait": American Opposition to Hawaiian Annexation, 1893–1898* (1981); Bradford Perkins, *The Great Rapprochement: England and the United States, 1895–1914* (1968); Emily S. Rosenberg, *Spreading the American Dream: American Economic and Cultural Expansion, 1890–1945* (1982); Robert Seager II, *Alfred Thayer Mahan* (1977); Merze Tate, *The United States and the Hawaiian Kingdom* (1965); E. Berkeley Tompkins, *Anti-Imperialism in the United States: The Great Debate, 1890–1920* (1970); William A. Williams, *The Roots of the Modern American Empire* (1969).

The Spanish-American War and the Philippines

W. B. Gatewood, Jr., *Black Americans and the White Man's Burden* (1975); David Healy, *The United States in Cuba* (1963); Walter LaFeber, *Inevitable Revolutions: The United States in Central America* (1983); Gerald F. Linderman, *The Mirror of War: American Society and the Spanish-American War* (1974); Glenn A. May, *Social Engineering in the Philippines: The Aims, Execution, and Impact of American Colonial Policy, 1900–1913* (1980); Stuart Creighton Miller, *"Benevolent Assimilation": The American Conquest of the Philippines, 1899–1903* (1982); William J. Pomeroy, *American Neo-Colonialism: Its Emergence in the Philippines and Asia* (1970); Hyman Rickover, *How the Battleship Maine Was Destroyed* (1976); David R. Trask, *The War with Spain in 1898* (1981); Richard E. Welch, *Response to Imperialism: The United States and the Philippine-American War* (1979).

U.S.–Chinese Relations

Kenton Clymer, *John Hay: The Gentleman as Diplomat* (1975); Michael Hunt, *The Making of a Special Relationship: The United States and China to 1914* (1983); Akira Iriye, *Across the Pacific: An Inner History of American East-Asian Relations* (1967); Thomas J. McCormick, *China Market: America's Quest for Informal Empire, 1893–1901* (1967); Marilyn B. Young, *The Rhetoric of Empire: American China Policy, 1895–1901* (1968).

The Panama Canal

Walter LaFeber, *The Panama Canal* (1979); Sheldon B. Liss, *The Canal: Aspects of United States–Panamanian Relations* (1967); David McCullough, *The Path Between the Seas: The Creation of the Panama Canal, 1870–1914* (1977).

CHAPTER 21

The Progressive Era

It was late Saturday afternoon on March 25, 1911, but at the Triangle Shirtwaist factory on Washington Place in New York City, hundreds of young women and a few men were still at work. The clatter of fifteen hundred sewing machines jammed into the eighth- and ninth-floor workrooms filled the air. Suddenly fire broke out. Feeding on the bolts of cloth hanging over the sewing machines, the fire soon transformed the upper floors into an inferno. Panicked workers rushed for the doors, only to find some of them locked. Other doors opened inward (a violation of the fire laws) and were jammed shut by the crush of bodies.

There were a few miraculous escapes. Breaking through the outer doors of the elevator shaft, twenty-two-year-old Cecilia Walker and others slid down the elevator cable eight floors to ground level. Young Pauline Grossman crawled to safety across a narrow alleyway when three male employees formed a human bridge. As others tried to cross, however, the weight became too great, and the three men fell to their death. In desperation, dozens of workers leaped from the windows to certain death on the sidewalk below. One falling woman became entangled in a utility wire and hung there until the fire burned through her dress, when she plunged to the ground.

Distraught immigrant parents wandered amid the scenes of death all night, in search of their daughters; newspaper reporters could hear "a dozen pet names in Italian and Yiddish rising in shrill agony above the deeper moan of the throng." The next day, the *New York Times* summed up the horrible event in a banner headline:

141 MEN AND GIRLS DIE IN WAIST FACTORY FIRE; TRAPPED HIGH IN WASHINGTON PLACE BUILDING; STREET STREWN WITH BODIES; PILES OF DEAD INSIDE.

The Triangle fire offered terrible evidence that all was not well in urban-industrial America. Industrialization had brought many benefits, but it had also taken a heavy human toll and changed American life forever. The fabled "land of opportunity" seemed a thing of the past as large corporations grew increasingly powerful. For the immigrant millions in unsafe factories and unhealthy slums, life was often a desperate cycle of poverty, exhausting labor, and early death. At the same time, a new middle class of white-collar workers and urban professionals was consolidating its position, and a newly energized women's movement was demanding full participation in the political process.

From this volatile social stew surged a current of reform energy that came to be called the progressive movement. For decades, historians have argued about how to interpret this movement. Originally they portrayed progressivism in a kind of political-cartoon fashion as an inspiring triumph of "the people" over sinister corporations and crooked bosses. More recently, historians have added complexity to the picture, noting the role of special-interest groups (sometimes including big business) in promoting specific progressive reforms as well as the movement's darker side and its blind spots. Above all, historians now try to distinguish the diverse and sometimes contradictory impulses once lumped under the catchall label "progressivism."

But despite the interpretive shifts, historians have always recognized progressivism as a highly significant reform movement spawned by the vast changes that since the Civil War had obliterated many of the familiar contours of an older, simpler America. Whatever their specific reform agenda, all progressives grappled with the new social world of corporations, factories, cities, and immigrants.

Of course, reform was nothing new in the early 1900s; indeed, it is a constant in American history. From the time the Puritans dropped anchor in Massachusetts Bay in 1630 to the election of George Bush in 1988, Americans have struggled to correct what they perceived as dangerous social trends and to steer history back to its proper course as they saw it.

But if progressivism is part of a familiar American tradition, it was also quite different from earlier reform movements. For example, the reformers of the 1830s and 1840s had typically viewed government as irrelevant or even hostile to their purposes. Individuals and small, self-selected groups, they had insisted, must take the lead in achieving a better social order. The progressives, by contrast, viewed *government* as a major ally in the reform cause. And far from glorifying the individual or withdrawing from society, they saw organizations and social engagement as essential to reform.

Emerging around 1900, first at the city and state levels, myriad organizations, many composed exclusively of women, pursued their varied reform objectives. Under the influence of reform-minded journalists, novelists, religious leaders, social thinkers, and politicians, this diffuse progressive impulse quickly coalesced and took on national dimensions. At the federal level, a spirit of governmental activism radically different from the passivity of the late nineteenth century turned Washington into a hotbed of activity. By 1917, when reform gave way to war, American government and society had been altered in fundamental ways. In this chapter we shall look first at the social changes that spawned progressivism and then at the movement itself.

A Changing American Society and Economy

Explosive urban growth and corporate consolidation brought dramatic changes to the United States in the early years of this century. As native-born Americans poured cityward, they met a tide of immigrant newcomers, producing, in the words of one historian, "the same kind of swirling confusion that occurs in the mouth of a harbor when a river discharges its waters against the force of a rising ocean tide." The American city, with its business elite, its newly self-conscious middle class, and its recent immigrants, gave these early-twentieth-century decades their unique social character. Simultaneously, in these years of booming prosperity, new forms of business organization transformed the face of American capitalism. As we have seen in Chapter 17, however, not everyone benefited equally from economic growth. Millions of industrial workers endured long hours, low wages, dangerous working conditions, and demeaning pressures for ever greater productivity. Through labor unions and the ballot box, many workers organized to improve their lot.

Immigrant Masses and a New Urban Middle Class

Through all the political turbulence of the early twentieth century, humanity continued to flow inexorably toward the cities. By 1920, when the nation's urban population for the first time passed the 50 percent mark, sixty-eight American cities boasted more than 100,000 inhabitants. New York City grew by 2.2 million from 1900 to 1920, Chicago by 1 million, Detroit by 425,000.

Many of the new urbanites came from rural and small-town America. Like the heroine of Theodore Dreiser's novel *Sister Carrie* (1900), who left her rural home to find work in Chicago, millions of Americans seeking new opportunities took the train to the city. But the greatest source of

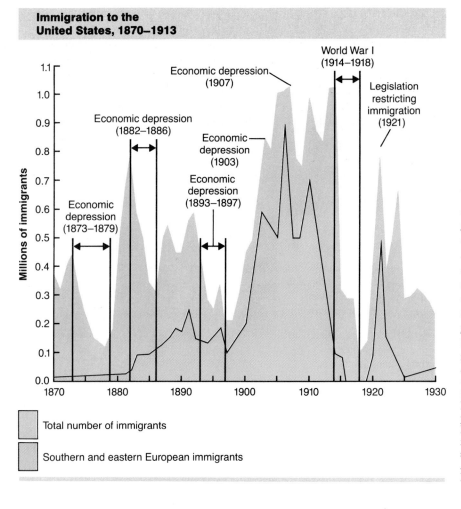

Immigration to the United States, 1870–1913

World War I (1914–1918)

Economic depression (1907)

Economic depression (1882–1886)

Economic depression (1903)

Legislation restricting immigration (1921)

Economic depression (1893–1897)

Economic depression (1873–1879)

Millions of immigrants

Total number of immigrants

Southern and eastern European immigrants

With the end of the depression of the 1890s, immigrants from southern and eastern Europe poured into America's cities, spurring an immigration-restriction movement, urban moral-control campaigns, and efforts to improve the physical and social conditions of immigrant life.

SOURCES: *Statistical History of the United States from Colonial Times to the Present* (Stamford, Conn.: Fairfield Publishers, 1965); and report presented by Senator William P. Dillingham, Senate document 742, 61st Congress, 3rd session, December 5, 1910: Abstracts of Reports to the Immigration Commission.

urban growth continued to be immigration. New York City's immigration center, Ellis Island, lying almost in the shadow of the Statue of Liberty, hummed busily at the start of the twentieth century, as immigration soared to all-time highs. More than 17 million newcomers arrived from 1900 to 1917, and most of them became city dwellers.

As in the 1890s, the influx was predominantly from southern and eastern Europe, but more than 200,000 Japanese and 40,000 Chinese also arrived between 1900 and 1920, as well as thousands of Mexicans who migrated northward to work on the railroad. As before, most immigrants came out of desperate economic necessity. But other factors influenced their decision as well. While many Mexicans fled revolutionary upheavals in their country, religious persecution figured importantly in the emigration of eastern European Jews. The Jews of the Russian Empire were forced to live in

a region of Poland and western Russia known as the Pale, and even in the best of times they suffered constant discrimination. Periodically, bloody anti-Semitic campaigns called pogroms swept over Russia, leading to the massacre of many Jews and forcing others literally to flee for their lives to America. Thousands of these eastern European Jewish immigrants settled on New York's Lower East Side, which by 1915 had a Jewish population of 1.4 million.

For the newly arrived immigrants of the early twentieth century, as for those of the preceding decades, city life often proved harsh and unforgiving as they crowded into crumbling slum tenements, row houses, and rickety three-story structures called triple deckers. Even in cities with reasonably honest governments, the authorities' ability to provide such basic necessities as safe water, sewage facilities, garbage collection, and fire pro-

Urban Immigrant Life

Houston Street on New York's Lower East Side was captured in a colorful 1917 painting by George Luks. A Chinese grocer stands at the window of his San Francisco market as a patron reads by the doorway.

tection—not to mention decent schools and parks —lagged behind the pace of urban growth. In many cities municipal corruption compounded the problem. Health conditions remained shockingly bad, with death rates in the most crowded immigrant wards twice the national average.

For years, Social Gospel ministers, settlement-house leaders, Salvation Army volunteers, and reform-minded journalists like Jacob Riis had been reminding middle-class America of the terrible conditions festering in the immigrant slums. In the early twentieth century, the message at last began to sink in and to affect the political process. A growing awareness of the seriousness of the urban problem helped lay the groundwork for the progressive reform movement.

While the immigrants attracted much attention, another, subtler change was transforming the cities as well: the vast expansion of a predominantly native-born middle class. From 1900 to 1920, the "white-collar" work force jumped from 5.1 million to 10.5 million—more than double the growth rate for the work force as a whole. As industry grew, the number of people in advertising doubled; the ranks of the civil engineers more than tripled; and the number of secretaries increased by nearly 600 percent, from 134,000 to 786,000.

Included in this new white-collar class were such disparate groups as the skilled engineers, technicians, and bureaucrats of big corporations; the owners and managers of medium-size local businesses; and professionals such as lawyers, physicians, and teachers. As these groups grew, so, too, did their sense of professional identity. Long-established professional societies such as the American Medical Association, the American Bar Association, and the National Education Association expanded rapidly in these years. Scores of new professional groups and business associations were formed, from the American Association of Advertising Agencies (1917) and the National Association of Accountants (1919) to the U.S. Chamber of Commerce (1912), the American Association of University Professors (1915), and the Farm Bureau Federation (1919). This truly was an age of organization.

As the professions gained in strength and self-confidence, they tightened their admission standards. For example, medical education became more rigorous following the publication in 1910 of a scathingly critical study conducted by Abraham Flexner for the Carnegie Foundation for the Advancement of Teaching. Thanks to the Flexner report, many weak medical schools folded, while others toughened admissions requirements and upgraded the quality of instruction.

The rise of this newly self-conscious middle class had wide-ranging effects. Ambitious, well educated, and valuing self-discipline and social stability, the members of this class were aware of their numbers and eager to make their influence felt. They had a keen and often uneasy sense of their rank in the urban social order: beneath the elite of aristocratic old families and new industrial tycoons, above the immigrant masses in the sprawling slums. For many middle-class Americans, membership in a national professional organization provided a sense of identity that might earlier have come from neighborhood, political-party affiliation, or local community standing.

For the women of this new urban middle class, the city offered both opportunities and frustrations. While immigrant girls took jobs as servants or factory operatives, middle-class young women became public-school teachers, secretaries, typists, librarians, clerks, and telephone operators. The number of women in such white-collar jobs surged from 5.3 million in 1900 to 8.6 million in 1920. Middle-class women's ideas about employment changed as well, as work outside the home began to be viewed not as a badge of shame or poverty but as rewarding and satisfying. Higher education offered another outlet for women. The number of women earning college degrees, although still a small proportion of the total female population, more than tripled in this twenty-year period. Of the 5 percent of college-age Americans attending college in 1910, 40 percent were women.

But for the married woman of the middle class, hedged in not only by the actual demands of home and children but by an ideology of female domesticity, city life could mean isolation and frustration. The divorce rate crept up, from one in twelve marriages in 1900 to one in nine by 1916. As we shall see, many middle-class women mired in boring, unchallenging domestic routines joined the new female white-collar workers and college graduates in leading the resurgent woman's movement of the early twentieth century.

Black Americans in a Racist Age

Of the nation's 10 million blacks at the turn of the century, more than two-thirds lived in the rural South as sharecroppers and tenant farmers. For them, infestations of the cotton boll weevil, which spread to the United States from Mexico in the

Women Enter the Work Force

A black nursemaid and her young charges watch cadets drill in Charleston, South Carolina; future telephone operators receiving switchboard training in 1915. Wrote one feminist in 1913: "The woman of the future—married or single—must be absolutely free to earn her livelihood, and must receive equal pay for equal service."

1890s, and devastating floods that periodically poured over eroded farmlands worsened an already difficult situation. Seeking economic betterment, many southern blacks left the land. By 1910 over 20 percent of the southern black population was urban-dwelling. While the black men in the cities who could find work took jobs in factories, mines, docks, and railroads or became carpenters, plasterers, or bricklayers, many black women became domestic servants, seamstresses, or workers in laundries and tobacco factories. By 1910, 54 percent of America's black women were employed.

For all blacks, legally enforced racism reached its peak during the first part of the twentieth century. A tangle of local "Jim Crow" laws imposed strict segregation on streetcars, trains, schools, parks, public buildings, and even cemeteries. The facilities provided for blacks, including the schools, were invariably far inferior. Legally imposed residential segregation also existed in a number of southern cities until the Supreme Court outlawed this practice in 1917. With a few exceptions, labor unions excluded black industrial workers, while skilled black craftsmen earned about one-third less than whites. In some courts, black and white witnesses took the oath on separate Bibles! Trapped in a cycle of poverty, poor education, and discrimination, and prevented from voting through a variety of stratagems, southern blacks faced very formidable obstacles, indeed.

For northern blacks, a group of just over a million, conditions were only slightly better. In northern cities, as in the South, open racism intensified after 1890, as economic depression and then massive immigration brought severe social tensions. (Ironically, the immigrants themselves, competing with blacks for jobs and low-cost housing, sometimes exhibited the most intense racial prejudice.) Segregation, while not imposed by law, was almost everywhere a fact of life, supported by informal social pressure and sometimes violence. Blacks lived in run-down "colored districts," attended dilapidated schools, and worked at the lowest-paying menial jobs. While blacks were permitted to vote, their votes—usually cast for the Republican party, the party of Lincoln—brought little political influence. The whites who ran the Republican party tolerated only those black politicians willing to confine themselves to distributing low-level patronage jobs and to remain silent on more fundamental issues. Even the newest of

Founding of the Ku Klux Klan as Portrayed in D. W. Griffith's *The Birth of a Nation* (1915)

Born in Kentucky ten years after the Civil War ended, Griffith based this film on a novel glorifying the KKK. Brilliant and innovative technically, the movie also reinforced racist attitudes.

the mass media, the movies, reinforced racism. David W. Griffith's 1915 classic *The Birth of a Nation* disparaged blacks and glorified the Ku Klux Klan.

Smoldering racism occasionally exploded in violence. In a terrible antiblack riot in Atlanta in 1906, four blacks were murdered, many black homes were burned, and a white police officer severely beat the president of a black theological seminary. Most horrible was the practice of lynching. The victims were usually black men accused or suspected of murder, rape, or some other crime. In certain cases, trumped-up charges justified the murder of blacks whose assertive behavior or economic aspirations whites found intolerable. Lynching peaked in the 1880s and 1890s, but from 1900 to 1920, an average of about seventy-five lynchings occurred yearly. Some involved incredible sadism, with large crowds in attendance, and the victim's body grotesquely mutilated, often before he was killed. Authorities did little to stop the practice. At a 1916 lynching in Texas, the mayor warned the mob not to damage the hanging tree, since it was on city property. Nor were all lynchings in the South. In Springfield, Ohio, in 1904, the body of a lynch victim was left hanging all day for the curious, including children, to see.

For all their adversity, or perhaps in part because of it, blacks developed self-reliance, group cohesion, and a vigorous cultural expression. Black religious life, centered in the African Methodist Episcopal (AME) church, was a bulwark of support for many. A handful of black colleges and universities such as Fisk in Nashville and Howard in Washington, D.C., carried on against heavy odds. In 1900 black educator and lawyer James Weldon Johnson collaborated with entertainer Bob Cole to compose the stirring "Lift Every Voice and Sing," sometimes called the black national anthem. The urban black community included several black-owned insurance companies and banks and boasted a small elite of entrepreneurs, teachers, ministers, and lawyers. A black achiever in a somewhat different field, Jack Johnson of Galveston, Texas, won the world's heavyweight boxing championship in 1908. Although major-league baseball excluded blacks, a thriving "Negro League" produced many stars and attracted a big following in black America.

Meanwhile, new black musical idioms were emerging. Scott Joplin transformed the music of black bars and "honky-tonks" into ragtime, a catchy rhythmic style that became highly popular. Another musical expression of black culture, the blues, rooted in the mournful chants of southern sharecroppers, gained recognition with the songs of W. C. Handy, including the classic "St. Louis Blues" (1914). Among urban blacks, another musical form, jazz, was taking shape in these years as well. Originating in New Orleans with the band of Buddy Bolden in the 1890s, jazz moved northward to Chicago and other cities around the First World War, eventually to win recognition as America's greatest musical achievement.

Corporate Boardrooms and Factory Floors

American business, like American society, was changing profoundly and rapidly. The late-nineteenth-century process of corporate consolidation that produced such behemoths as Carnegie Steel and the Standard Oil Trust accelerated in the early twentieth century. Indeed, this consolidation proceeded at such a mind-boggling rate that for a time around 1900, an average of more than 260 companies annually were swallowed up in mergers. This era also gave rise to holding companies—giant conglomerates that owned a number of corporations engaged in the same kind of business. The most famous holding company was created in 1901 when, as we have seen in Chapter 17, financiers led by J. P. Morgan of New York bought Andrew Carnegie's steel business and combined it with others that they owned to form the United States Steel Company. This corporate titan, initially capitalized at $1.4 billion, controlled 80 percent of all U.S. steel production. Following the same pattern, Morgan in 1902 consolidated six competing companies into the International Harvester Company to gain control of 85 percent of the farm-implement business. In the automotive field, William C. Durant in 1908 founded the General Motors Company, which, with financial backing from the Du Pont Corporation, bought up various independent automobile manufacturers, from the inexpensive Chevrolet to the luxury Cadillac.

A wide chasm separated the Morgans and the Durants from America's laboring masses. To be sure, many workers benefited from the prevailing good times. Industrial workers' average annual real wages (defined, that is, in terms of actual purchasing power, after allowing for inflation) rose from $532 in the late nineteenth century to $687 by 1915. In railroading and other unionized industries, wages climbed still higher. But even with the dollar's buying power many times greater than today (a loaf of bread cost seven cents in 1915), such wages could still barely support a wife and a family and left little cushion for emergencies.

To make ends meet, entire immigrant families went to work. Two-thirds of immigrant girls entered the labor force in the early 1900s, working at least for a time as factory help or domestics or in small establishments like laundries and bakeries. Families also supplemented their income with the earnings of children. Child-labor statistics are imprecise, but the available data (see table) suggest that in 1910 the nonfarm labor force included at least 1.6 million children aged ten to fifteen—15 percent of that age group—working in factories, mills, tenement sweatshops, and street trades such as shoe shining, flower selling, and newspaper vending (see "A Place in Time"). The total may have been higher, since many of the "women workers" listed in the census were in fact young girls. One investigator found a girl of five working at night in a South Carolina textile mill.

The Glass-Bottle Factories of Alton, Illinois, in the 1890s

*I*n 1803, when Meriwether Lewis and William Clark set out on the memorable expedition that would eventually bring them to the Pacific Northwest, they spent the first winter at a camp some twenty-five miles north of St. Louis, near the confluence of the Missouri and Mississippi rivers. The town of Alton, Illinois, which soon grew up near this site, saw a lot of history in the nineteenth century. In 1837 an abolitionist editor from Alton, Elijah Lovejoy, was murdered there by a proslavery mob and his printing press thrown into the river. Abraham Lincoln and Stephen A. Douglas debated there during their 1858 senatorial campaign. During the Civil War, Alton served as a major Union Army supply depot.

In the Progressive Era, however, Alton won a different kind of fame: it became notorious as an industrial center where child labor was exploited in a particularly blatant fashion. Alton was known for its glass-bottle manufacturing, and many boys as young as seven to ten years of age worked long, exhausting hours as "dogs" in the sweltering, smoky bottle factories. The dogs' job was to carry trays of red-hot glass bottles from the glassblowers' work stations to the cooling ovens. Since the glassblowers' income depended on their production rate, they continually pressured the dogs to trot faster, blowing loud whistles when a tray was ready.

The younger dogs earned forty cents a day for this labor, and the older ones received sixty cents a day. Dogs rarely advanced to the favored

Glassworker, 1909

Lewis Hine's camera captured the vulnerability and innocence of a very young glass-factory worker in 1909. Of such youthful workers Hine once noted: "I have heard their tragic stories, . . . and seen their fruitless struggles in the industrial game where the odds are all against them."

rank of apprentice, since the glassblowers usually reserved this position for their own sons, whom they kept in school. Illiterate and often in fragile health, the dogs faced grim prospects as they approached adulthood.

The bottle factories operated twenty-four hours a day, and when the Illinois factory inspector Florence Kelley (see below) visited Alton in the early 1890s, she found very young boys hard at work in the middle of the night. When she tried to interview them, they could not

stop for more than a few words, because they had to dart back and forth continually in response to urgent whistle blasts. At night the sleepy dogs often stumbled and ran into each other with their trays of red-hot glass. Kelley found many wearing bandages, and their mothers complained bitterly of burned clothing and shoes.

The work was not only dangerous but also unhealthy: as the boys came off the job and left the stifling factories, the chill air that they encountered caused severe res-

Alton Glass-Bottle Workers and Their "Dogs"

Posing for a group photograph provides a rare break in the routine for employees of the Illinois Glass Company of Alton, Illinois.

piratory ailments and other illnesses. When work was over, the young dogs often accompanied the glassblowers to the saloon, where they drank, swore, and chewed tobacco just like the men.

As Kelley investigated the Alton child-labor situation, she found that it had complex social ramifications. She learned that public officials in nearby towns often urged indigent families and widows with small children to move to Alton so the younger boys could work in the glass-bottle factories, thereby relieving the other municipalities of the expense of providing public aid to them. Kelley found one family with eleven children living in a tent near a bottle factory, with one shift of children working by day and the other by night, and the youngsters taking turns sleeping in the crowded tent.

When she interviewed the leading citizens of prosperous Alton, she found them convinced that the town's economic health depended on maintaining the status quo, and further that the dogs were so "tough" and "dissolute" that it was

pointless to try to educate them. The mayor defended the employment of underage workers, as did a school-board official who was also an executive in a glass-bottle factory.

In 1893, largely through Kelley's efforts, Illinois prohibited the employment of children under fourteen in factories. But unscrupulous men and women evaded this law by contracting to act as guardians for

Florence Kelley

children living in orphanages and poorhouses in the region around Alton. Swearing that their young charges were fourteen years of age, they sent the youths into the bottle factories. Some individuals gained control of several young boys in this fashion. These "guardians" would then live on the boys' meager earnings. In July and August, when the factories closed because the glass-blowers could not stand the heat of the ovens, the "guardians" and their wards took up residence in shantyboats along the Mississippi and survived by fishing and picking berries.

But Kelley and others continued to battle for reform, despite the stubborn opposition of the glass-bottle industry and the tightly organized glassblowers' union. (Because the individual trays of molten glass were not heavy, industry spokespersons insisted that the dogs' work was "light and easy.") In 1903 the Illinois legislature at last passed a tighter law that forbade night work for children under sixteen and allowed the employment of fourteen- and fifteen-year-olds only if a parent and a responsible school official signed a statement attesting that the would-be worker was at least fourteen, had attended school, and could read fluently and write legibly.

In her 1905 book *Some Ethical Gains Through Legislation,* Kelley told the story of the dogs of the Alton glass-bottle industry, which she denounced as "this child-destroying trade." Describing the other forms of child labor prevalent in America, including textile-mill work, sweatshop toil, and street trades such as newspaper vending, flower selling, and shoeshining, she challenged the nation to guarantee "the right of childhood" to its defenseless and exploited young. Accounts like hers, graphically describing the human cost of industrialization, helped awaken the conscience of the Progressive Era.

Children in the Labor Force, 1880–1930

Year	Children gainfully employed, nonagricultural work		
	Total number of children aged 10–15 (in millions)	Total number of children employed (in millions)	Percentage of children employed
1880	6.6	1.1	16.8
1890	8.3	1.5	18.1
1900	9.6	1.7	18.2
1910	10.8	1.6	15.0
1920	12.5	1.4	11.3
1930	14.3	0.7	4.7

SOURCE: *The Statistical History of the United States from Colonial Times to the Present* (Stamford, Conn.: Fairfield Publishers, 1965).

South Carolina Oyster Shuckers, 1911

For all laborers, the hours were long and the hazards great. Despite the 8-hour-workday movement of the 1880s, the average worker in 1900 still toiled 9 ½ hours a day, and considerably longer in certain industries. Some southern textile mills required workdays of 12 and even 13 hours. The Triangle fire was only a particularly gruesome reminder of the unsafe conditions in many industries. Few employers accepted any responsibility for the frequent work-related accidents and illnesses. Vacations and retirement benefits were practically unheard of. With rare exceptions, American capitalism extracted the maximum of labor from its work force and gave a bare minimum in return.

For immigrants and other new industrial workers accustomed to a casual, task-oriented pattern of rural labor, the inexorable demands of the time clock and the machine forced major and often bitterly resented adjustments. The routinization and speed up of factory work was promoted by a new specialist, the efficiency expert, who used time-and-motion studies to find the fastest way of performing each step in the production process.

The efficiency expert dreamed of making human workers as rational and predictable as machines. Inspiration came from Frederick W. Taylor, who in the 1870s had taken a managerial job in a Philadelphia steel mill, soon rising to chief engineer. Having long measured employees' performance with his ever-ready stopwatch, Taylor in his *Principles of Scientific Management* (1911) explained his ideas for increasing efficiency by standardizing job routines and rewarding the fastest workers. In both business circles and the larger culture, *efficiency* and *Taylorism* became popular catchwords.

Workers Organize; Socialism Advances

In view of such conditions, workers not surprisingly continued to organize to improve their lot and resist the dictates of the efficiency proponents. The American Federation of Labor (AFL) grew rapidly, from fewer than half a million members in 1897 to some 4 million by 1920. But this number still represented only about 20 percent of the nonfarm labor force. With thousands of immigrants hungry for jobs, unionizing activities could be risky. The boss could always fire an "agitator" and hire a docile newcomer instead. Judicial hostility also plagued the labor movement. In one of many anti-union court decisions, a unanimous Supreme Court in the 1908 *Danbury Hatters* case sharply limited unions' right to set up boycotts in support of strikes. A union boycott was a "conspiracy in restraint of trade," said the Court, and thus a violation of the Sherman Anti-Trust Act.

As in the past, the AFL's strength lay in the skilled trades and not in the factories and mills where most immigrants and women worked. A few unions did try to reach the laborers at the lower end of the scale. The International Ladies' Garment Workers' Union (ILGWU), organized in 1900 by immigrants working in New York City's needle trades, conducted a successful strike in 1909 and another after the 1911 Triangle fire.

For the young women who walked the picket lines, these strikes were emotional experiences, at once exhilarating and frightening. Some strikers were beaten by police; others lost their jobs. The 1909 strike began when a young garment worker, Clara Lemlich, herself a victim of police brutality, jumped to her feet as the speechmaking droned on at a protest rally and passionately called for a strike. Twenty thousand women garment workers stayed off the job the next day.

Another union that targeted the most exploited workers was the Industrial Workers of the World (IWW), nicknamed the Wobblies, founded in Chicago in 1905. The IWW's colorful leader was William D. "Big Bill" Haywood, a giant of a man and a compelling orator. After leading a knockabout life in Utah and Nevada, Haywood in 1893 joined the newly founded Western Federation of Miners. In 1895, after a heavily publicized trial, he and two other union leaders were acquitted on charges of complicity in the murder of the governor of Idaho. A black eyepatch that he sometimes wore to cover an old injury enhanced his formidable appearance.

Never large, and torn by dissent, the Wobblies' membership probably peaked at around thirty thousand, comprising mostly western miners, lumbermen, fruit pickers, and itinerant laborers. But it captured the imagination of middle-class sympathizers, including the cultural rebels of New York City's Greenwich Village, where Haywood often visited. Its greatest success came in 1912, when it won a bitter textile strike in Lawrence, Massachusetts. This victory owed much to two women: Elizabeth Gurley Flynn, a fiery Irish-American orator who had joined the IWW in 1906, and Margaret Sanger, a leader of the birth-control movement, who publicized the cause by sending strikers' children to sympathizers in New York City for temporary foster care.

In contrast to the conservative AFL, the IWW preached revolution. In 1908 it declared: "Between [the working class and the employing class] a struggle must go on until the workers of the world . . . take possession of the earth and the machinery of production, and abolish the wage system." Despite such fire-breathing rhetoric, however, the IWW's reputation for violence and sabotage was much exaggerated. Nevertheless, it faced unremitting harassment through arrests and prosecution by

Rumblings of Labor Militance

(Above) Emblem of a railroad union affiliated with the radical IWW; (left) striking garment workers, New York City, 1909. Declared young Clara Lemlich at a strike rally: "I am a working girl . . . on strike against intolerable conditions. I am tired of listening to speakers who talk in general terms."

government officials, and by 1920 its strength was broken.

Other workers, as well as some middle-class Americans dismayed by capitalism's human toll, turned to socialism. All socialists advocated an end to capitalism and backed public ownership of factories, utilities, railroads, and communications systems, but they differed sharply among themselves on how to achieve these goals. While the revolutionary ideology of German social theorist Karl Marx won a few converts, the vision of democratic socialism achieved at the ballot box attracted many adherents. In 1900 a group of democratic socialists formed the Socialist Party of America (SPA). These included Morris Hillquit, a handsome Russian-Jewish immigrant and New York City labor organizer; Victor Berger, the portly leader of the German socialists of Milwaukee; and Eugene V. Debs, the Indiana labor leader who had converted to socialism during his imprisonment following the 1894 Pullman strike. The SPA's most popular spokesperson, Debs was its presidential candidate five times between 1900 and 1920. The tall, kindly Debs won a following not only for his platform eloquence but also for his friendly manner and sympathy for the underdog.

The high tide of socialist strength came around 1912, when Socialist party membership stood at 118,000. Debs won over 900,000 votes for president that year (about 6 percent of the total), and the Socialists elected a congressman (Berger) and hundreds of municipal officials. The Intercollegiate Socialist Society, headed by eloquent lecturer Rose Pastor Stokes, a Russian-Jewish immigrant who had married a wealthy New Yorker with radical sympathies, carried the message to college and university campuses. The party also boasted thirteen daily newspapers and some three hundred weeklies, many published in foreign languages for immigrant members. Weakened by internal divisions (the IWW was expelled in 1912 for refusing to repudiate violence) and by defections to progressive reformism, the SPA faded after 1912. But as late as 1920, over 900,000 Americans again cast presidential ballots for Eugene V. Debs even as he sat in a federal penitentiary for his vocal opposition to America's entry into World War I.

The upsurge in Socialist votes represented only one sign of rising discontent with politics as usual. As the ill effects of rampant industrial growth became ever more palpable, the demand that government confront these consequences—a demand first voiced by the populists in the 1890s—grew insistent.

The Progressive Movement Takes Shape

At the start of the century, intellectuals increasingly challenged the ideological foundations of a business-dominated social order, and writers and journalists publicized the human toll of industrialization. Soon reform thundered over the nation as activists sought to make government more democratic, eradicate unhealthful and dangerous conditions in cities and factories, and curb corporate power. A bit overwhelmed by the diversity of these reform efforts, and awed at the political energies that they unleashed, Americans grouped them under a single label: the progressive movement.

Progressivism: An Overview

What was progressivism? On a few points, all students of the movement agree. First, it was a political response to industrialization and its social by-products: immigration, urban growth, the concentration of corporate power, the widening of class divisions. Second, despite important continuities, it was distinct from populism, the reform movement that preceded it. While populism attracted aggrieved farmers, progressivism's strength lay in the cities. Progressivism enlisted far more journalists, academics, and social theorists than did populism. Finally, the progressives were *reformers,* not radicals or revolutionaries. They wanted to remedy the social evils spawned by capitalism, not destroy the system itself.

But which aspects of the new urban-industrial capitalist order most needed attention, and what remedies were required? These basic questions stirred fundamental disagreements. Indeed, progressivism never constituted a cohesive movement with a unified program but rather a diverse array of reform activities that sometimes overlapped and sometimes diverged sharply. Many reformers insisted that the preservation of democracy required stricter regulation of business, from local transit companies to the almighty trusts. Others, emphasizing the humanitarian theme, pointed to the human toll of industrialization and called for legislation to protect workers and the urban poor. Other progressives concentrated on various schemes for reforming the structure of government, especially at the municipal level. Finally, some reformers, regarding immigration, urban immorality, and incipient social disorder as the central problems, fought for immigration restriction, the abolition of prostitution and the saloon, and other coercive social-control strategies. All this contributed to the mosaic of progressive reform.

And who were the progressives? Like the movement itself, they comprised a diverse lot, aligned in shifting coalitions that might unite on one issue, then divide on another. The native-born Protestant middle class, including the new white-collar professionals, was certainly central to progressivism, but on issues affecting the welfare of factory workers and city dwellers, the urban-immigrant political machines provided critical support. Even corporate leaders at times found it prudent to endorse and help shape business-regulation measures, especially when the pressure for such regulation became irresistible.

The initiative for these varied reform efforts came at first not from the political parties but from private groups with names like the Playground Association of America and the American League for Civic Improvement. In this era of organizations, it is not surprising to find the roots of progressivism in this organizational impulse. All the major progressive reforms, from woman suffrage and the abolition of child labor to antiprostitution and prohibition, drew strength from such private interest groups.

Closely related to this organizational dimension was the progressives' emphasis on a "scientific" approach to social problems. Scientific and technological expertise had transformed the nation's industrial system, and progressives tended to believe that such expertise would also solve the social problems that industrialism had left in its wake. Progressives marshaled scholarly evidence, expert opinion, and statistical data to support their various causes, and social research became a great vogue.

Some historians, stressing the technological and managerial aspects of progressivism, portray it as an example of a bureaucratic, organizational stage that all modernizing societies pass through. This is a useful way to think of the movement, provided that one realizes that progressivism was not some automatic process unfolding independently of human will. Eloquent leaders, gifted journalists, earnest ministers, and energetic organizers all made a difference. Human emotion—whether indignation over child labor, shock over a tragedy like the Triangle fire, optimistic visions of a happier future, or the ambition of an aspiring politician—propelled the movement forward. Progressivism, in short, is not an impersonal historical abstraction. It is a useful general term for the activities and concerns of many thousands of individual Americans in the early twentieth century.

Intellectuals Lay the Groundwork

Building on the writings of such figures as Lester Ward, Edward Bellamy, and the Social Gospel leaders, a brilliant group of turn-of-the-century thinkers helped reorient American social thought. In the process, they laid the ideological foundation for progressivism.

William Graham Sumner and other Gilded Age intellectuals had argued that Charles Darwin's theory of evolution through "survival of the fittest" supported an ideology of unrestrained economic competition. Lester Ward inaugurated the intellectual assault on this version of Social Darwinism, and the assault intensified in the opening years of the new century. As the old intellectual consensus collapsed, scholars in many different disciplines began to produce work skeptical of the established order and implicitly supporting far-reaching changes. As early as the 1880s, for example, the young Johns Hopkins University economist Richard T. Ely had attacked laissez faire ideas. A founder (1885) and later president of the American Economic Association, Ely steered it on a reformist course. Moving to the University of Wisconsin in 1892, Ely advocated reform legislation, supported organized labor, and worked closely with the state's innovative governor, Robert La Follette.

Another reshaper of economic thought was the eccentric, prickly, and brilliant Thorstein Veblen. A Norwegian-American from rural Minnesota,

Veblen earned a Ph.D. from Yale in 1884 but had trouble holding a job, partly because of sexual affairs that offended his colleagues' sense of propriety. Nevertheless, in *The Theory of the Leisure Class* (1899), Veblen produced a trenchantly satirical assault on the values and lifestyles of the Gilded Age business elite. In later writings he argued that engineers, shaped by the stern discipline of the machine, were better fitted to lead society than the business class. Veblen epitomized the admiration for efficiency, science, and technical expertise that lay at the heart of the progressive impulse.

Historians, too, contributed to the new currents of thought that fed into progressivism. In "The Significance of the Frontier in American History" (see Chapter 16), Frederick Jackson Turner argued that the central dynamic of American history was not the actions of Washington policymakers but the social and political experience of generations of western pioneers. Other historians generalized Turner's point. In *The New History* (1912), James Harvey Robinson eloquently argued that historians should probe beneath political and military events to explore the evolution of societies as a whole.

Highly influential in this process of historical revisionism were Mary Ritter Beard and her husband Charles A. Beard. In such books as *Woman's Work in Municipalities* (1915) and *A Short History of the American Labor Movement* (1920), Mary Beard spotlighted groups that traditional histories ignored. Meanwhile, in *An Economic Interpretation of the Constitution* (1913), Charles A. Beard gave ammunition to progressive reformers seeking to curb big business by arguing that the Constitution makers of 1787 had served the interests of the moneyed class of their day—the class to which they themselves for the most part belonged.

Harvard philosopher William James contributed to this process of intellectual reconstruction with his seminal 1907 work *Pragmatism,* which argued that truth emerges not from universal laws or abstract theorizing but from the stream of everyday experience, as we test our ideas in practice. Truth is what *works.* James's emphasis on the fluidity of knowledge and the importance of practical action contributed to the progressive mood of reformism and skepticism toward established ideologies.

James enormously admired Jane Addams, whose settlement-house career in Chicago's immigrant wards seemed a perfect illustration of his pragmatic philosophy. While others theorize about reality, he wrote her admiringly, "you *inhabit* reality." In *Democracy and Social Ethics* (1902), Addams rejected the old individualistic morality and called for a new social ideology rooted in awareness of modern society's complex interdependence.

No thinker better captured the progressive faith in the power of ideas to transform society than Herbert Croly. The son of Manhattan journalist David Croly and the woman's club founder Jane Cunningham, Croly grew up in a cosmopolitan world where social issues were hotly debated. In his masterpiece, *The Promise of American Life* (1909), Croly called for an activist federal government of the kind that Alexander Hamilton had advocated in the 1790s, but one that would serve *all* citizens, not merely the capitalist class. To build public support for such a transformed conception of government, Croly argued, intellectuals must redefine the popular understanding of such familiar terms in the American political vocabulary as *democracy, nationalism,* and *individualism.*

New Ideas About Education and the Law

With public-school enrollment leaping from about 7 million children in 1870 to more than 23 million in 1920, progressive intellectuals realized that here was a potential vehicle of social change. No one did more to transform educational ideas than John Dewey, a mild-mannered philosopher who taught at the University of Chicago and after 1904 at Columbia University. Dewey's boyhood in a small Vermont town shaped his social values. In numerous books, essays, and lectures over a long life, he insisted that a just and harmonious society could be built through the intelligent application of scientific method to social problems. Viewing intelligence as above all an instrument of social action, he called his philosophy Instrumentalism.

The public schools, Dewey maintained, could be significant instruments of reform, provided that they embraced the new ethic of social interdependence. Banishing bolted-down chairs and desks from the model school that he started at the University of Chicago in 1896, he encouraged children to move about the room, ask questions, and interact with each other as well as with the teacher. In such works

Progressive Era Social Thinkers

(Left to right) Oliver Wendell Holmes, Jr., Jane Addams, John Dewey, Thorstein Veblen. Wrote one reform-minded intellectual: "We shall demand perfection and never expect to get it."

as *Democracy and Education* (1916), Dewey argued that schools must not only *teach* the values of democracy and cooperation but *embody* those values through their methods and curriculum. The ideal school, he said, would be an "embryonic community" where children worked together in a harmonious process of intellectual inquiry and social growth.

The curricula of the nation's colleges and universities also reflected the new social thought. As courses in theology and the classics declined, new courses in the natural sciences, modern history, political science, social work, and sociology took their place. A mood of civic idealism spread across the campuses. No longer could the university be a "home of useless and harmless recluses," proclaimed the University of Michigan's president in 1899; it must dedicate itself to the public good. Princeton's president Woodrow Wilson summed up the new spirit in the title of his 1902 inaugural address: "Princeton for the Nation's Service."

Even the natural sciences felt the new rush of social activism. At the Massachusetts Institute of Technology, for example, Ellen Richards pioneered in applying chemistry to the issues of nutrition, food adulteration, and public hygiene. Statisticians used their skills to study labor conditions, epidemic diseases, and urban housing density.

New ideas influenced the legal profession as well. For decades, conservative judges, citing sacred legal principles and ancient precedents, had routinely upheld the interests of big business and struck down reform legislation. Here and there, however, a few jurists argued for a more flexible view. The most influential champion of the new legal philosophy was the patrician Boston law professor Oliver Wendell Holmes, Jr. In *The Common Law* (1881), Holmes insisted that law must evolve as society changes. In a famous aphorism much quoted by progressives, he declared: "The life of the law has not been logic; it has been experience."

Appointed to the Supreme Court in 1902, just as the progressive movement began, Holmes issued a series of eloquent dissents from the opinions of the conservative Court majority. In one case, challenging judges who worshiped precedent, Holmes declared in exasperation: "It is revolting to have no better reason for a rule of law than that it was laid down in the time of Henry IV. It is still more revolting if the grounds upon which it was laid down have vanished."

Novelists and Journalists Spread the Word

Thus intellectuals and academics chipped away at laissez faire ideology and laid the foundation for a new social ethic. Meanwhile, talented novelists and journalists helped transform progressivism into a national movement by conveying to middle-class readers the seamy details of corporate wrongdoing and the harsh reality of slum and factory life.

A path-breaking early work came in the turbulent depression year 1894, when Chicago journalist and reformer Henry Demarest Lloyd produced the highly influential *Wealth Against Commonwealth,* a biting exposé of the Standard Oil Company. In the wake of Lloyd's book, early-twentieth-century novelists offered fictionalized but compelling indictments of corporate greed and heedless urban growth. In *The Octopus* (1901), Frank Norris portrayed the struggle between ruthless railroad owners and the wheat growers of California's San Joaquin Valley. In *Susan Lenox: Her Fall and Rise* (1917), David Graham Phillips explored the links between slum life, political corruption, and prostitution. Theodore Dreiser's *The Financier* (1912) offered a memorable portrait of a business tycoon obsessed with money and power and utterly devoid of social consciousness.

Most influential of all in forging the progressive spirit were dozens of articles exposing urban political corruption and corporate wrongdoing published in mass-circulation magazines such as *McClure's, Cosmopolitan,* and *Everybody's.* President Theodore Roosevelt, who considered some of these articles too one-sided, disparagingly nicknamed the authors "muckrakers," after a character in John Bunyan's *Pilgrim's Progress* who spends all his time raking up filth; but the name stuck as a badge of honor. New York journalist Lincoln Steffens began the muckraking vogue in October 1902 with a *McClure's* article on political corruption in St. Louis, and soon such exposés were appearing everywhere.

The muckrakers' stark journalistic prose, emphasizing facts rather than abstractions, could be very powerful. In a 1903 series on working women, for example, Maria Van Vorst offered a gripping first-person account of posing as a laborer in a Massachusetts shoe factory where women's fingernails literally rotted off because they continually had to immerse their hands in caustic dyes.

The muckrakers touched a nerve. *McClure's* circulation soared to 750,000 and *Collier's* to more than 1 million during their heyday in 1901–1903. Many magazine exposés subsequently appeared in book form, including Lincoln Steffens's *The Shame of the Cities* (1904); the damning *History of the Standard Oil Company* (1904) by another star *McClure's* reporter, Ida Tarbell; and David Graham Phillips's *Treason of the Senate* (1906). A somewhat different journalistic contribution to

Progressive Era Journalism

Their investigative articles in magazines like McClure's *and* Collier's *made Ida Tarbell, Lincoln Steffens, and other "muckrakers" nationally famous. Ward boss George Washington Plunkitt of New York's Tammany hall dismissed the reformers as "morning glories" who would wilt in the noonday sun, but in fact their influence was profound.*

progressivism, the *New Republic* magazine, founded in 1914 by Herbert Croly with financial help from Wall Street banker Willard Straight, provided a forum for Croly, John Dewey, the young political writer Walter Lippmann, and other reform-minded intellectuals.

Reforming the Political Process

If one had to pinpoint a time and place for progressivism's beginning, it would probably be in the 1890s, in the well-to-do neighborhoods of America's cities. The urban bosses of the late nineteenth century, while often power-hungry and corruptly involved with corporate interests, did try, in their fashion, to help the immigrant masses at a time when few others showed much concern. But to the native-born urban elites and middle classes, "the boss system" represented the quintessence of evil, and in the 1890s a series of middle-class political reform crusades burst on the urban scene. New York City went through a succession of anti-Tammany reform spasms in which Protestant clergymen played an important role. Other cities, too, mobilized the forces of righteousness against the bosses. In Detroit, for example, the reform administration of Mayor Hazen Pingree (1890–1897) brought honesty to city hall, lowered transit fares, curbed powerful private utilities, and made the tax structure more equitable. Pingree also paved streets, provided public baths, and in other ways improved the quality of life. A shrewd politician as well as a reformer, he once slapped a health quarantine on a brothel where one of his political enemies, a local business leader, was paying a visit, and refused to let the embarrassed patron leave until he promised to drop his opposition to Pingree's reforms.

Stimulated by the writings of Lincoln Steffens and others, the municipal-reform impulse grew stronger after 1900. In 1907, for example, San Francisco newspaper editor Fremont Older led a crusade against the city's well-educated but notoriously corrupt political boss Abe Reuf. Attorney Hiram Johnson, who took over the prosecution of the Reuf machine when the original prosecutor was gunned down in court in a killing linked to San Francisco's underworld, obtained a conviction of the mayor and his cronies. Sternly self-righteous, Johnson perfectly embodied the reform fervor of the day—one observer called him "a volcano in perpetual eruption"—and he rode the fame of the Reuf case to the California governorship in 1910 and the U.S. Senate in 1916.

In Toledo, Ohio, a colorful eccentric named Samuel M. "Golden Rule" Jones led the reform crusade. A self-made businessman converted to the Social Gospel, Jones introduced profit sharing in his factory, and as mayor he established playgrounds, free kindergartens, lodging houses for tramps, and an open-air church for all faiths.

But as the urban political-reform movement matured, it came to mean more than simply "throwing the rascals out" or engaging in good works. It now also involved a systematic attack on the roots of urban misgovernment, including the uncontrolled private monopolies that provided such basic city services as water, gas, electricity, and public transportation. Municipal reformers passed laws regulating the rates that these utilities could charge, taxing them more equitably, and curbing their political influence. In some cases, reformers advocated complete public ownership of these companies. Public ownership of utilities, for example, was part of the reform program of Tom Johnson, Cleveland's popular mayor from 1901 to 1909, who was praised by Lincoln Steffens as "the best mayor of the best governed city in the United States."

Reflecting the Progressive Era enthusiasm for expertise and efficiency, some municipal reformers advocated *structural* changes in city government. Specifically, they wanted to substitute professional managers and administrators, chosen in citywide elections, for mayors and aldermen elected on a ward-by-ward basis. The chaos created by natural disasters sometimes gave a boost to this particular reform. Galveston, Texas, adopted a nonpartisan form of city administration after a terrible hurricane hit in 1901, and Dayton, Ohio, went to a city-manager system in the aftermath of a ruinous flood in 1913. Supposedly above politics, these experts were expected to run the city like an efficient business.

Who were these municipal reformers? Depending on the circumstances and the specific issue, virtually all elements of the urban population took part in reform efforts at one time or another. The native-born middle class, led by clergymen, newspaper editors, and other opinion molders, provided the initial impetus and continued to represent the core of support for urban beautification and political reform. Business interests frequently pushed for citywide elections and the city-manager system; the latter diminished the political influence of the immigrant wards and increased that of the corporate elite. On matters of immediate practical concern to the ordinary city dweller such as improved municipal services, the urban-reform movement won support from the immigrants and even from political bosses who realized that the old, informal system of providing for their constituents was being swamped by the influx of newcomers.

The municipal-reform movement soon expanded to a series of electoral reforms at the state level aimed at giving voters a greater voice in the governmental process. By 1910, for example, all states had replaced the old system of voting, by which the voter brought to the polls a preprinted ballot bearing the name of a specific candidate, with the new system of secret balloting, which made it hard to rig elections. Another widely adopted Progressive Era electoral reform was the direct primary, which originated in Wisconsin in 1903 and in which the members (rather than the leadership) of each party selected the party's nominees for public office.

Some western states inaugurated electoral reforms known as initiative, referendum, and recall, by which voters at election time could, respectively, enact laws directly, express their opinions on specific issues, and even kick out ("recall") public officials. The culmination of this flurry of electoral reform came in 1913 with the ratification of the Seventeenth Amendment to the Constitution, which shifted the election of U.S. senators from state legislatures to the voters at large.

These electoral changes produced mixed results. They were ostensibly intended to democratize voting, but in fact, party leaders and organized interest groups soon learned to manipulate the new electoral machinery very effectively. Ironically, the new procedures appear to have served mainly to weaken the ties of party loyalty and reduce voter interest. Overall voter-participation rates declined precipitously in the opening years of the twentieth century, while political activity by organized interest groups increased.

Reforming Society and City

If issues of municipal governance, utility regulation, and electoral reform represented the brain of progressivism, the impulse to improve the deplorable conditions in America's factories, mills, and sprawling slums represented its heart. By 1907, despite some employers' claims that abolishing child labor would produce "a nation of sissies," some thirty states had done just that. In 1903 Oregon enacted a law limiting women in industry to a ten-hour workday. Other industrial reformers concentrated on safety legislation, welfare programs, and disability benefits for workers injured on the job.

Legislation of this kind won strong support from political bosses in cities with heavy immigrant populations, such as New York, Boston, Cleveland, and Chicago. The New York State Factory Investigating Committee, set up after the 1911 Triangle fire, was headed by state senator Robert F. Wagner, a leader of Tammany Hall, New York

City's Democratic machine. As a result of this committee's investigations, New York enacted fifty-six worker-protection laws, including ones tightening factory-safety standards, permitting pregnancy leaves, and requiring chairs with backs for garment workers who toiled at sewing machines all day. New York also established a workers' compensation system that Wagner later praised as "the beginning of America's social security system." By 1914 twenty-five states had passed laws making employers liable for job-related injuries or deaths.

Other urban reformers worked for such practical goals as better garbage collection and street cleaning, milk inspection, public-health programs, and stricter housing codes. In an important reform measure that served as a model for many cities and states, the New York legislature in 1901 tightened the regulations governing tenement houses to make them somewhat safer and more livable. Building on the earlier efforts of Frederick Law Olmsted and others (see Chapter 18), urban-beautification advocates campaigned for more parks, boulevards, and street lights and called for legislation against billboards, smoky factories, and unsightly overhead electrical wires.

Among those who lobbied for urban beautification, Daniel Hudson Burnham, the chief architect of the 1893 Chicago world's fair, was the most influential. In 1902 Burnham and others organized a successful drive to revive Charles L'Enfant's beautiful original plan for Washington, D.C. Burnham also developed innovative city plans for Cleveland and San Francisco, though the latter effort was cut short by the 1906 earthquake and fire that left four square miles of San Francisco in ruins. But his most impressive achievement was his master plan of 1909 for Chicago.

Burnham recognized that such plans, if they were to capture the public imagination, had to be bold and comprehensive. Consequently, he proposed for Chicago a completely new layout that would make the city both efficient and aesthetically harmonious. Burnham recommended streamlining the city's rail traffic by running it through a central union terminus; transforming the lakefront by building a new park, museum, and recreational complex; speeding traffic flow by constructing diagonal avenues across the city's rigid street-grid system; eliminating slums by constructing wide streets and enforcing sanitation regulations; and revitalizing the city's congested major thoroughfare, Michigan Avenue, by raising the grade level to allow passage of cross traffic under it.

In Burnham's vision, Chicago's focal point would be a monumental new civic center containing a majestic neoclassical city hall and linked by a vast plaza to the cultural and recreational resources on Lake Michigan. Although the scale and grandeur of Burnham's plan made its implementation difficult, many of its features, including the museums and recreational facilities along the lake, eventually became a reality. Between 1910 and 1920, Chicago spent more than $300 million to extend Michigan Avenue and build Grant Park and Wacker Drive along the lakeshore. Burnham's soaring conviction that grand boulevards, imposing squares, monumental civic buildings, and extensive recreational facilities would restore the public's pride in metropolitan America, though unrealistically visionary, was shared by many urban beautifiers in the Progressive Era.

Corporate Regulation

Central to the progressive outlook was the conviction that big business was dangerously out of control. Inherited from the populists and reinforced by the muckrakers, this belief took deep root in society. Few Americans wanted to destroy the giant corporations, but many became convinced that these enterprises that had benefited so enormously from the government's economic policies should also be subject to government oversight. At the municipal and state level alike, reining in big business became the order of the day. In one state after another, legislation was enacted regulating railroads, mines and mills, telephone companies, and other businesses. Public-health officials, factory investigators, dairy inspectors, and other regulators monitored the nation's economy as never before.

In no state was this process more in evidence than in Wisconsin during the governorship of Robert La Follette (1901–1906). La Follette served in Congress in the 1880s as a loyal Republican, but he feuded with the senator who ran the state party and in 1900 was elected governor as an independent. Soon "Fighting Bob" began transforming state government just as Cleveland's Tom Johnson and other reform mayors were transforming municipal government. Challenging the business interests that had long dominated Wisconsin politics, the La Follette administration adopted the direct primary system, set up a commission to regulate railroads operating in the state, increased corporate taxes, and passed a law limiting campaign spending.

In formulating these regulatory measures, La Follette consulted regularly with Richard T. Ely, labor expert John R. Commons, and other professors at the nearby University of Wisconsin. He also set up a legislative reference library so that lawmakers could inform themselves about complicated issues rather than relying on political bosses or lobbyists. So novel was this approach to state government that it gained national attention as the "Wisconsin Idea."

Regulating national corporations at the municipal and even state level posed obvious problems. Once progressivism reached into national politics, however, the regulatory impulse, rooted in grassroots activism, moved to the center of the reform agenda.

Progressivism and Social Control: The Movement's Coercive Dimension

Although troubled by the social consequences of urban-industrial growth, most progressives believed that reformers like themselves could restore order through research, legislation, and enlightened social tinkering. But this outlook gave progressivism a repressive and strongly moralistic edge. While some progressives focused on such problems as child labor, industrial safety, and corporate regulation, others became obsessed as well with issues of personal behavior and morality.

Moral Control in the Cities

Fearful of urban social disorder, some reformers sought to impose morality by law. They campaigned against gambling, amusement parks, dance halls, and the newest moral menace, the movies. The first commercial films were brief comic sequences like *The Kiss* or *The Sneeze,* but with *The Great Train Robbery* (1903), which lasted for eight minutes, the movies began to tell stories. In

Theda Bara as Carmen

The blatant sexuality of many early movies gave rise to a strong movement for film censorship.

1914 came *A Fool There Was,* with its famous line "Kiss me, my fool!" (This movie starred Theda Bara, one of the first silent-movie stars; she was actually Theodosia Goodman, the daughter of a Cincinnati tailor.)

Quaint as they seem today, these early movies struck many middle-class Americans as dangerously immoral. The fact that they first won popularity in shabby, immigrant-district five-cent theaters called nickelodeons intensified such feelings. At the nickelodeon, immigrant children and youth could escape restrictive home environments. As a New York City garment worker who lived with her Italian-immigrant parents later recalled: "The one place I was allowed to go by myself was the movies. My parents wouldn't let me go anywhere else, even when I was twenty-four."

This freedom from moral oversight was precisely what worried progressives. Warning of "nickel madness," they demanded film censorship. Several states and cities did, in fact, set up censorship boards. Chicago's police chief was empowered to ban movies that he considered immoral.

Prostitution was another target of the moral-control impulse. In true progressive fashion, anti-prostitution reformers set out to investigate and quantify what they called "the social evil." The American Social Hygiene Association (1914), financed by John D. Rockefeller, Jr., sponsored medical research on venereal disease, underwrote "vice investigations" in various cities, and drafted model municipal statutes against prostitution.

At the popular level, a "white slave" hysteria engulfed the country. Sensationalized books, articles, and films warned darkly that innocent farm girls were being kidnapped and forced into a life of sin in the city. The Mann Act (1910) made it a federal crime to transport a woman across a state line "for immoral purposes," and amid much fanfare, the red-light districts of New Orleans, Chicago, and other cities were shut down or forced to operate more discreetly.

The Prohibition Movement

With the enormously important prohibition crusade, the progressive moral-control movement reached its zenith. Temperance had long loomed large on the American reform agenda, but in the Progressive Era the reformers' tactics and objectives shifted significantly. Earlier campaigns had focused on persuading individual drunkards to "take the pledge" and abandon their alcoholic ways. But with the founding of the Anti-Saloon League (ASL) in 1895, the emphasis shifted to the *legal* abolition of alcoholic beverages.

The ASL was in many ways a typical progressive organization. Full-time professionals staffed the national office, while Protestant ministers served on a network of state committees. From the ASL presses in Westerville, Ohio, poured tons of propaganda documenting the role of alcohol and the saloon in health problems, family disorder, child abuse, political corruption, and workplace inefficiency. Skillfully, the ASL promoted nationwide prohibition as the legislative cure-all for these problems.

Supported also by the Woman's Christian Temperance Union and influential church agencies, the ASL's crusade picked up steam. With the added impetus of the First World War, Congress in 1918 passed the Eighteenth Amendment, outlawing the manufacture, sale, or transport of alcoholic beverages anywhere in the United States (see Chapter 22). The last and most controversial of the great Progressive Era social reforms had achieved its goal.

Immigration Restriction

If the immigrant city posed threats, some reformers concluded, the obvious answer lay in excluding immigrants. As one reformer declared: "All the great problems . . . are tied up with the one great problem of foreign immigration." As early as 1894, a small group of prominent Bostonians formed the Immigration Restriction League to promote a literacy test for immigrants. Such a test (which revealed nothing except an individual's level of schooling) would have sharply reduced immigration from southern and eastern Europe. The American Federation of Labor, fearing immigrant job competition, also endorsed restriction.

This reform also won support from many, though not all, progressives. Characteristically, they documented their case with a flourish of scientific expertise. In 1911 a congressional commission produced a massive study bristling with statistical material allegedly proving the new immigrants' innate degeneracy. Sociologist Edward A. Ross, a distinguished progressive, in 1914 described the typical recent immigrants as "hirsute, low-browed, big-faced persons of obviously low mentality."

Led by Senator Henry Cabot Lodge of Massachusetts, Congress enacted literacy-test bills in 1896, 1913, and 1915, only to see them vetoed by a succession of presidents. In 1917, however, a clause excluding immigrants unable to read or write became law over President Woodrow Wilson's veto. This legislation, too, contributed to progressivism's ambiguous legacy.

The Eugenics Movement

The most sinister example of the perversion of "science" for illiberal and coercive purposes in the Progressive Era was the eugenics movement. Eugenics is the control of reproduction to alter the characteristics of a plant or animal species. Some American eugenicists believed that society itself could be improved through controlled breeding. In 1904, with funding from the Carnegie Foundation, leading eugenicists founded a research center on Long Island to study heredity and genetic manipulation. The director, Charles B. Davenport, was not only a well-known zoologist but also a racist, anti-Semite, and advocate of immigration restriction.

Inspired by Davenport and other eugenicists, certain states legalized the forced sterilization of criminals, sex offenders, and persons adjudged mentally deficient. In the 1927 case *Buck* v. *Bell*, the Supreme Court upheld the constitutionality of such laws.

This ugly underside of early-twentieth-century social thought emerged starkly in Madison Grant's *The Passing of the Great Race* (1916). In many respects, Grant appeared to represent the best in progressivism. The patrician son of an old-stock New York City family, he supported numerous civic causes. Yet in *The Passing* he stirred together a rancid brew of pseudoscientific data and spewed out a vicious diatribe against Jews, blacks, and southern and eastern Europeans. Jesus Christ, he insisted, was not really a Jew at all but an unrecognized "Nordic." Grant called for absolute racial segregation, immigration restriction, and the forced sterilization of "unfit" groups, including "worthless race types." Writing at the height of the Progressive Era, Grant chillingly previewed ideas that within a few years Adolf Hitler would bring to fruition.

Racism and Progressivism

As Grant's work suggests, racism rose to a high pitch during the Progressive Era. Although individual progressives like settlement-house leader Lillian Wald and muckraker Ray Stannard Baker spoke out against racial injustice, the progressive movement as a whole did little as blacks were lynched, disfranchised, and discriminated against. Like the immigrants, blacks represented for many progressives not potential reform allies but a source of social menace and danger to be studied, controlled, and kept out of public life.

In the South progressivism came with an explicit warning label: "For Whites Only." Southern progressive reformers often led the movement for black disfranchisement and segregation. Southern advocates of woman suffrage pointed out that with most blacks disfranchised in the region, granting women the franchise would strengthen white supremacy by doubling the white vote. Numerous southern politicians—including Governor James K. Vardaman of Mississippi and Senator Ben Tillman of South Carolina—supported a variety of progressive reforms while simultaneously pursuing viciously antiblack policies.

Progressive Era racism pervaded Washington during the presidential administration of Woodrow Wilson (1913–1921). Born in Virginia and reared in Georgia, Wilson displayed a patronizing attitude toward blacks throughout his life. He much admired the racist movie *The Birth of a Nation* and acquiesced as southerners in his cabinet and in the Congress (some of them powerful committee chairmen) imposed a rigid segregation on all levels of the government. Blacks who protested were fired or demoted.

Some progressives, however, eloquently spoke up for immigrants and blacks. For example, settlement-house worker Mary White Ovington helped found the National Association for the Advancement of Colored People (see below) and wrote *Half a Man* (1911), an important study of the effects of racial prejudice on New York City's blacks. Yet progressive social thought included a number of disturbing ingredients—an assurance of moral and intellectual superiority, an exaggerated confidence in the social applications of science, an uncritical acceptance of the use of state power to coerce individual behavior—that all too readily could turn repressive and destructive.

Blacks and Women Organize

For blacks and women, especially those of the urban middle class, the early twentieth century was a time of intense organizational activity and intellectual ferment. Both groups had ample reason for dissatisfaction about their situation, and in both groups movements flowered to address those grievances.

Controversy in Black America

The nation's foremost black leader from the 1890s until his death in 1915 was Booker T. Washington. Born in slavery in Virginia in 1856, the son of a black slave woman and a white plantation-owning father, Washington at the age of sixteen enrolled at a freedmen's school in Hampton, Virginia, founded by a Civil War general, Samuel Chapman Armstrong. In 1881 Washington organized in Tus-

kegee, Alabama, a state vocational school for blacks that eventually became Tuskegee University.

Washington attained national prominence in 1895 when he set forth his racial views in a famous address in Atlanta, Georgia. The first task of America's blacks, he insisted, must be to acquire useful vocational skills such as those taught at Tuskegee. Once blacks proved their economic value to society, he predicted, racism would fade away; meanwhile, they must patiently accept their lot in life. Although Washington in these years was secretly contributing to organizations fighting racial discrimination, the public message of his "Atlanta Compromise" speech was one of accommodation to segregation and disfranchisement.

White Americans much admired Washington, who traveled widely, lectured frequently, and once had dinner at the White House with Theodore Roosevelt. His acclaimed autobiography, *Up From Slavery* (1901), recounted his rise from poverty through honesty, hard work, and the help of kindly patrons like General Armstrong—themes familiar to a generation reared on the success stories of Horatio Alger.

Many blacks revered Washington as well, especially in the South, but among northern blacks his dominance came under increasing challenge after 1900. With racism escalating and blacks' status steadily worsening, Washington's philosophy of accommodation and his optimistic predictions seemed increasingly unrealistic. One outspoken critic, William Monroe Trotter, the editor of a black newspaper, the *Boston Guardian,* wrote in 1902 that Washington's acceptance of black disfranchisement was "a fatal blow . . . to the Negro's political rights and liberty." Another black who repudiated Washington's leadership was antilynching crusader and editor Ida Wells-Barnett. Driven from Memphis in 1892 when a mob destroyed her offices, she settled three years later in Chicago. A formidable woman with powerful flashing eyes, Wells-Barnett sharply criticized Washington's virtual silence on the subject of lynching.

Washington's most potent challenge came from W. E. B. Du Bois (1868–1963). The first black to be awarded a Ph.D. (from Harvard in 1895), Du Bois taught from 1896 to 1910 at Atlanta University, a black institution that competed with Tuskegee for contributions from northern philan-

A New Black Leadership

Ida Wells-Barnett, crusader against lynching, and W. E. B. Du Bois, outspoken critic of Booker T. Washington and author of the classic Souls of Black Folk. *The challenge, wrote Du Bois, was to find a way "to be both a Negro and an American."*

thropists. A cultivated scholar of refined manners and a distinguished appearance enhanced by a carefully trimmed goatee, Du Bois set forth his differences with Washington in *The Souls of Black Folk* (1903). Rejecting Washington's accommodationist call for patience and the exclusive cultivation of manual skills, Du Bois ringingly demanded for blacks full access to the same educational advantages and intellectual opportunities open to whites. Further, he declared, blacks must struggle ceaselessly against all forms of racial discrimination. Striking a new note of assertiveness and militance, Du Bois set the direction of black activism in the new century.

The Founding of the NAACP

For a time in the 1890s, an organization called the Afro-American Council served as a forum for blacks who favored vigorous resistance to racism. But when Booker T. Washington gained control of this organization around 1900, his opponents turned elsewhere. In 1905, under Du Bois's leadership, they held a strategy-making conference at Niagara Falls, and for the next few years, participants in the "Niagara Movement" met annually.

Meanwhile, a small group of white reformers was also growing dissatisfied with Washington's cautiousness and restraint. Prominent among them was newspaper publisher Oswald Garrison Villard, the grandson of abolitionist William Lloyd

Garrison. In 1909 Villard and his allies, together with Du Bois and other blacks from the Niagara Movement, formed the National Association for the Advancement of Colored People (NAACP). Rejecting Washington's accommodationist policy, the NAACP called for full political equality for blacks and an end to all racial discrimination. Attracting especially the urban black middle class, the NAACP by 1914 had six thousand members in fifty branches. The cause of racial equality had gained a robust new voice.

Revival of the Woman-Suffrage Movement

As late as 1910, women could vote in only four sparsely populated western states: Wyoming, Utah, Colorado, and Idaho. In six state referenda after 1896, woman suffrage went down to defeat each time. But rushing social and ideological currents infused the suffrage movement with new vitality after 1900. The growing ranks of middle-class women, increasingly well educated and in touch with current events, found it absurd that they could not vote, particularly when recently arrived immigrant men, often less well educated than themselves, enjoyed this right. A vigorous suffrage movement in Great Britain reverberated on this side of the Atlantic as well. Finally, the more general reform climate of the progressive movement,

GIVE YOUR CHILDREN EQUAL RIGHTS
VOTE YES Nov. 2
On the AMENDMENT ENABLING WOMAN TO VOTE
MASSACHUSETTS WOMAN SUFFRAGE ASSOCIATION

A Revived Women's Movement

A poster prepared by the Massachusetts Woman Suffrage Association; college women marching for suffrage in Philadelphia around 1915. "In slowly gathering numbers," wrote Charlotte Perkins Gilman in 1898, "women . . . are standing free."

in which women played a leading role, powerfully boosted the cause.

Like progressivism itself, the renewal of the women's movement started at the grassroots level. In New York, Chicago, Los Angeles, and other cities, local suffragists developed innovative forms of publicity, including street meetings and parades, and adopted an aggressive tone. Suffrage campaigns in California (1911) and New York (1915), though unsuccessful, gave evidence of a fresh drive and militancy.

A new generation of leaders, drawing on the rhetoric of progressive reform, translated this energy into a revitalized national movement. When the revered Susan B. Anthony retired in 1900 from the presidency of the National American Woman Suffrage Association (NAWSA), she passed the mantle to the talented and energetic Carrie Chapman Catt of Iowa. Although her husband's fatal illness forced her to resign in 1904, Catt remained active in NAWSA and in 1915 again became its president. Under her sagacious direction, NAWSA adopted the so-called Winning Plan: grassroots organization within a framework of tight centralized coordination.

Following an overall strategy devised in NAWSA's central office, women nationwide lobbied legislators, distributed literature, conducted referenda, and organized more parades and rallies. State after state, most in the Far West and Midwest, fell into the suffrage column. A key victory came in November 1917 when New York State voters approved a woman-suffrage referendum.

Not all women boarded the suffrage bandwagon. While some black women, immigrant women, and female factory workers participated at the grassroots level, NAWSA's membership remained predominantly white, native-born, and middle class. A few upper-class women even outspokenly opposed suffrage reform. Leader of the "Antis" was Josephine Dodge, widow of one of New York City's richest capitalists, who in 1911 formed the National Association Opposed to Woman Suffrage, based in her Fifth Avenue apartment. Women already had vast behind-the-scenes influence, Dodge and her friends argued; to invade the male realm of politics could only diminish their vital moral and spiritual role.

Nor did all suffragists accept Catt's strategy. One who did not was the young Alice Paul, who

Woman Suffrage Before the Nineteenth Amendment

Beginning with Wyoming in 1869, woman suffrage made steady gains in western states before 1920. In the East key breakthroughs came in New York (1917) and Michigan (1918). The South remained an anti-woman-suffrage bastion throughout the period.

as a student in Great Britain had come to admire the militant tactics of the British suffragists. Ambitious for leadership and impatient with NAWSA's state-by-state approach, Paul in 1913 founded the Congressional Union, later renamed the Woman's party, to bring direct pressure on the federal government to enact a woman-suffrage amendment. Insisting that "the party in power"—in this case, the Democrats under President Woodrow Wilson —must be held accountable for the continued denial of votes to women, Paul and her followers in the wartime year 1917 picketed the White House round the clock. They posted large signs that read:

PRESIDENT WILSON IS DECEIVING THE WORLD WHEN HE APPEARS AS THE PROPHET OF DEMOCRACY. . . . HE IS RESPONSIBLE FOR THE DISFRANCHISE-MENT OF MILLIONS OF AMERICANS. WE IN AMERICA KNOW THIS. THE WORLD WILL FIND HIM OUT.

Several of the demonstrators were arrested, jailed, and when they went on a hunger strike, force-fed.

Thanks in part to women's active participation in the American war effort of 1917–1918 (see Chapter 22), the tide turned at last. The Nine-teenth Amendment, granting women the vote, passed Congress by a narrow margin in 1919, and by August 1920 the ratification process was complete. That November, seventy-two years after the first American women's rights convention, in 1848, women across America could go to the polls.

Breaking Out of the "Woman's Sphere"

The suffrage movement did not exhaust the talents or organizational energies of American women. The 1890s had seen the founding of such groups as the General Federation of Women's Clubs, the National Council of Jewish Women, and the National Association of Colored Women; and these new organizations grew vigorously in the early twentieth century. Women's club members, settlement-house leaders, and individual female activists played a key role in a wide range of reform efforts. These included the campaigns to bring playgrounds and day nurseries to the slums, to abolish child labor, to improve conditions for women workers, and to eliminate health hazards posed by unsafe foods and quack remedies. Concern over such issues knew no gender boundaries. As Jane Addams observed, the same nurturing impulse that led women to care for their own children's needs drew them naturally into broader political activism in an industrial era when hazards often came from outside the home as well as inside.

Entrenched cultural assumptions about woman's proper "sphere" crumbled as women became active on many fronts. Penologist Katherine Bement Davis, with a Ph.D. from the University of Chicago, served as the innovative superintendent of a woman's reformatory in Bedford Hills, New York (1901–1914), and then as New York City's commissioner of corrections (1914–1917). Anarchist Emma Goldman crisscrossed the country delivering riveting lectures on politics, feminism, and modern drama while coediting a radical monthly, *Mother Earth*. And in 1914 Margaret Sanger began her crusade for birth control, a term that she coined. A nurse as well as a radical feminist, Sanger witnessed the tragedy of unwanted pregnancies among slum women. She fled to Europe in 1914 to escape arrest on obscenity charges directed against her militant journal *The Woman Rebel* but returned in 1916 to open the nation's first birth-control clinic, in Brooklyn, New York.

The leading feminist intellectual of these years was Charlotte Perkins Gilman. A Connecticut native related to novelist Harriet Beecher Stowe, Gilman was divorced and living in California when she wrote *Women and Economics* (1898). This influential work traced the history of sexual discrimination; explored the cultural process of gender stereotyping; and linked the legal, political, and social subordination of women to their economic dependence upon men. Giving a feminist twist to the ideas of Lester Ward and Edward Bellamy, Gilman argued that confining women to the domestic sphere, while necessary at an earlier stage of human evolution, had become outdated and inefficient. She advocated economic independence for women through equality in the workplace; the consolidation of cooking, cleaning, and other domestic tasks; and state-run nurseries and day-care centers.

Two women typify especially well the varied role of women in progressive reform: Alice Hamilton and Florence Kelley. Hamilton, a bacteriologist and professor at Northwestern University, was a close associate of Jane Addams at Hull House. In 1910, combining her scientific expertise with her social-welfare impulses, she conducted a pathbreaking investigation of lead poisoning in industry. Appointed an investigator for the U.S. Bureau

Birth-Control Pioneer Margaret Sanger

One of eleven children, Sanger saw her exhausted mother die at age forty-nine. Sanger's National Birth Control League was the forerunner of the Planned Parenthood Federation of America.

of Labor in 1911, she became a top expert on—and tireless campaigner against—work-related diseases and health hazards.

Florence Kelley, the daughter of an abolitionist congressman from Pennsylvania known as Pig Iron Kelley for his advocacy of high protective tariffs for iron, became a resident of Hull House in 1891. Investigating conditions in factories and tenement sweatshops, Kelley in 1893 helped secure passage of an Illinois law prohibiting child labor and limiting working hours for women. In 1899 Kelley became general secretary of the National Consumers' League, which sought to use organized consumer pressure to force improved factory conditions. Campaigning for a federal child-labor law, Kelley angrily asked: "Why are seals, bears, reindeer, fish, wild game in the national parks, buffalo, [and] migratory birds all found suitable for federal protection, but not children?" Thanks largely to her efforts, Americans awakened to the evils of child labor.

National Progressivism—Phase I: Roosevelt and Taft

By around 1905 many Americans were concluding that what had first seemed isolated and localized reform activities in fact constituted a national movement. Symbolically, in 1906 Robert La Follette left the Wisconsin state house to go to Washington as a U.S. senator. He arrived just as progressivism found its first national leader, Theodore Roosevelt.

Ambitious, bombastic, self-righteous, jingoistic, and opportunistic—but also brilliant, politically masterful, and endlessly interesting—Roosevelt, "TR," became president in 1901 and, for the next 7½ years, made the White House a storm center of political activism. The bustling political climate was far different from the rather somnolent days of Rutherford B. Hayes or Benjamin Harrison. Skillfully orchestrating public opinion as an instrument of political power, the popular young president pursued his goals: labor mediation, consumer protection, conservation, business virtue, and activism abroad. TR's hand-picked successor, William Howard Taft, lacked the master's political genius, however, and his administration was marked by nasty political sniping among former allies.

Roosevelt's Path to the White House

On September 6, 1901, in Buffalo, New York, an anarchist named Leon Czolgosz shot William McKinley. It seemed at first that the president would survive, and Vice President Theodore Roosevelt proceeded with a hiking trip in New York's rugged Adirondack Mountains. But several days later, a guide arrived with an urgent message: McKinley's condition was worsening. All night long, with only a local driver as a companion, Roosevelt traveled by horse and wagon the forty miles over rutted mountain roads to the nearest railroad station. Here, learning of McKinley's death, he boarded a special train for Buffalo. On September 14 the forty-two-year-old Roosevelt took the presidential oath of office.

Many politicians shuddered at the thought of the young and impetuous Roosevelt as president. Republican kingmaker Mark Hanna exclaimed: "My God, that damned cowboy in the White House!" Although not really a cowboy, Roosevelt did display many traits associated with the Wild West. The son of an aristocratic old New York family of Dutch origins, the sickly and nearsighted Roosevelt had seemed as a child almost a caricature of the pampered rich kid. But at the age of eleven, he began a body-building program that, combined with summers in Wyoming, transformed him into a paragon of physical fitness. When his young wife died in 1884, he stoically carried on. "I have never believed it did any good to flinch . . . from any blow," he wrote; "nor does it lighten the blow to cease from working." Two years on a Dakota ranch (1884–1886) further toughened him and assuaged his grief. For the rest of his days, he enthusiastically advocated what he termed "the strenuous life."

Plunging into politics at a time when most members of his social class considered it unfit for gentlemen, he served as a state assemblyman, New York City's police commissioner in an anti-Tammany reform administration, and a U.S. civil-service commissioner. In 1898, fresh from his Cuban exploits (see Chapter 20), he was elected New York's governor. Two years later, the state's Republican boss, unsettled by a governor whom he could not control, arranged for Roosevelt's nomination as vice president, little suspecting that Czolgosz's bullet would soon put Roosevelt in the White House. Far from pleased by this maneuver, Roosevelt wrote: "I would a great deal rather be anything, say a history professor, than Vice-President."

In contrast to some of his predecessors, who seemed worn down by the presidency, Roosevelt found it invigorating. "While President I have been President emphatically . . . ," he once boasted; "I believe in a strong executive." He enjoyed public life and loved the limelight. As a relative once observed: "When Theodore attends a wedding he wants to be the bride, and when he attends a funeral he wants to be the corpse." Most Americans were fascinated by their rambunctious young president with his toothy grin, machine-gun speech, and pas-

Theodore Roosevelt and the Teddy Bear

Roosevelt brought to the White House a vigor and energy it had not seen in decades. Wounded by a would-be assassin's bullet during a campaign speech, he declared: "I will make this speech or die. . . . [I]t takes more than that to kill a Bull Moose."

sion for the outdoors. When he refused to shoot a bear cub on a hunting expedition, a shrewd toy manufacturer introduced a cuddly new product, the Teddy bear.

After Theodore Roosevelt, the American presidency was never quite the same. He enlarged the office, both as a public forum and as a center of legislative initiative, in ways that permanently affected the balance of power within American government.

Roosevelt the Labor Mediator

The new president's political skills were quickly tested. In May 1902 the United Mine Workers Union (UMW) called a strike to gain not only higher wages and shorter hours but also recognition as a union. The mine owners refused even to talk to the UMW leaders. After five months, however, with winter looming and coal supplies dwindling, TR acted. Summoning the deadlocked parties to the White House and threatening to take over the mines, he won their reluctant acceptance of an arbitration commission to settle the dispute. The UMW called off the strike. The commission's findings, issued

in 1903, granted the miners a 10 percent wage increase and a reduction in the working day from ten to nine hours.

TR's approach to labor disputes, illustrated in the coal strike, differed sharply from that of his predecessors, who typically called out the troops to break strikes. He defended labor's right to organize, and when a prominent mine owner sanctimoniously proclaimed that the miners' welfare could safely be left to "the Christian men to whom God in his infinite wisdom has given control of the property interests of the country," Roosevelt bristled at such "arrogant stupidity."

Trustbusting and Corporate Regulation

With his privileged social background, TR neither feared nor much respected the upstart capitalists who had clawed their way to the top in Gilded Age America. The prospect of having to spend time with "big-money men," he once wrote a friend, "fills me with frank horror." Deeply conservative at heart, he had no desire to abolish America's big corporations, which he believed essential to national greatness. Nevertheless, as president, he came to

Roosevelt the Trustbuster

Roosevelt's goal was to break up the "bad" trusts—those that pursued only narrow, selfish objectives—without harming the "good" trusts that served the public interest. Sometimes the distinction was not entirely clear.

embrace the progressive conviction that corporate behavior must be carefully regulated. A strict moralist, he believed that corporations, like individuals, must be held to a high standard of virtue.

At the same time, Roosevelt the political realist understood well that many influential Washington figures did not share such views—among them, Senator Nelson W. Aldrich of Rhode Island, a seasoned defender of business interests. Roosevelt's presidency was thus a story of continuing tension between his aristocratic conservatism, his hesitant identification with progressive ideas, his moralistic side, and his recognition of the realities of power in capitalist America. The first test soon came.

The formation in 1901 of the United States Steel Company, the nation's first billion-dollar corporation, deepened public uneasiness over business consolidation. As always, TR dashed to the head of the parade. In his first State of the Union message, he gave a high priority to breaking up business monopolies, or "trustbusting." In February 1902 Roosevelt's attorney general filed suit against the Northern Securities Company, a mammoth holding company recently formed by giant railroad and banking interests. The Northern Securities Company controlled railroading in the Northwest and, in TR's view, clearly violated the Sherman Anti-Trust Act. Railroad tycoon E. H. Harriman struck back, ridiculing "political adventurers who have never done anything but pose and draw a salary." But Harriman was no match for Roosevelt. On a whirlwind speaking tour that summer, Roosevelt called for a "square deal" for all Americans and denounced special treatment for powerful capitalists. "We don't wish to destroy corporations," he insisted, "but we do wish to make them subserve the public good." In 1904, on a 5−4 vote, the Supreme Court ordered the dissolution of the Northern Securities Company.

During Roosevelt's presidency, forty-three other companies were sued for violating the antitrust law. In two key cases not finally decided until 1911, the Supreme Court ordered the breakup of the Standard Oil Company, the granddaddy of all the trusts, and the reorganization of the American Tobacco Company to make it less monopolistic.

As the 1904 election approached, Roosevelt made his peace with the Republicans' big-business wing, writing cordial letters to J. P. Morgan, E. H. Harriman, and other tycoons. The death of Mark Hanna early in 1904 removed a potential rival for the nomination. When the convention that unanimously nominated Roosevelt in Chicago adopted a conservative, probusiness platform, $2 million in corporate campaign contributions poured in.

Conservative Democrats, meanwhile, led by ex-president Grover Cleveland, maneuvered to rid their party of the free-silver heresies of William Jennings Bryan, the candidate in 1896 and 1900. To this end, they nominated a conservative New York judge and party loyalist, Alton B. Parker, and crafted a platform that firmly embraced the gold standard. The Democratic platform did attack the trusts and called for greater federal regulation of corporations, but on this issue Roosevelt ruled the field.

Easily defeating the lackluster Parker, Roosevelt turned to one of his major goals: railroad regulation. He had come to regard corporate regulation, rather than dramatic bursts of trustbusting, as a more promising long-term role for government, and this shift of outlook was reflected in the

The Election of 1904				
Candidates	Parties	Electoral Vote	Popular Vote	Percentage of Popular Vote
THEODORE ROOSEVELT	Republican	336	7,628,461	57.4
Alton B. Parker	Democratic	140	5,084,223	37.6
Eugene V. Debs	Socialist		402,283	3.0
Silas C. Swallow	Prohibition		258,536	1.9

central role that he played in the passage of the important Hepburn Act (1906). The Elkins Act (1903) had strengthened the Interstate Commerce Act of 1887 by stiffening the penalties against secret railroad rebates to favored shippers, and the Hepburn Act further tightened existing railroad regulation. This measure granted the Interstate Commerce Commission the power to set maximum railroad rates and to examine railroads' financial records. It also required standardized bookkeeping to make such inspection easier and strictly limited the railroads' distribution of free passes.

The Hepburn Act displayed TR's knack for political bargaining. When Senator Aldrich and other conservatives opposed the measure, Roosevelt fenced with them every step of the way. In one basic compromise, he agreed to put tariff reform aside in return for enactment of the Hepburn bill. Although the measure did not entirely satisfy reformers like La Follette, it did significantly increase the government's ability to regulate the railroads.

Consumer Protection, Racial Issues, and Conservation

No progressive reform aroused a more visceral popular response than the campaign against unsafe and falsely labeled food, drugs, and medicine. Upton Sinclair's *The Jungle* (1906) turned Americans' stomachs by describing the disgusting conditions under which their sausages and cold cuts were produced. Wrote Sinclair in one memorable passage: "It was too dark in these [packing-house] storage places to see well, but a man could run his hand over these piles of meat and sweep off handfuls of dried dung of rats. These rats were nuisances, and the packers would put poisoned bread out for them, they would die, and then rats, bread, and meat would go into the hoppers together." (The socialist Sinclair had intended his book to publicize the exploitation of immigrant workers as well as unsanitary packing-house conditions, but the latter message proved more potent. "I aimed at the nation's heart, but hit it in the stomach," he later lamented.)

Other muckrakers exposed useless and even dangerous patent medicines. Many popular nostrums, including children's medicines, contained cocaine, opium, or a large percentage of alcohol. "Colden's Liquid Beef Tonic," for example, "recommended for treatment of the alcohol habit," itself contained 26.5 percent alcohol! In the absence of regulation, the peddlers of these potions freely claimed that they could cure cancer, grow hair, and restore sexual potency.

Ever sensitive to the public mood, Roosevelt strongly supported the Pure Food and Drug Act and the Meat Inspection Act, both passed in 1906. The Pure Food and Drug Act outlawed the sale of adulterated foods or drugs and required accurate labeling of ingredients; the Meat Inspection Act established strict sanitary requirements for meatpackers, set up a meat-quality rating system (still in effect today), and created a program of federal meat inspection. A maverick Department of Agriculture chemist, Dr. Harvey W. Wiley, had for years waged war on adulterated foods, and by 1906 the larger food-processing, meatpacking, and medicinal companies, eager to regain public confidence, supported regulatory measures as well. Thanks to the muckrakers' revelations, TR's leadership, and pressure from the affected industries themselves, Wiley's lonely crusade at last succeeded.

On racial matters, Roosevelt's record was marginally better than that of many other politicians in this dismally racist age. On the positive side, he appointed a black as head of the Charleston customhouse despite white opposition, and he closed a Mississippi post office rather than yield to racist demands that he dismiss the black postmistress. In

The Fight Against Dangerous Food and Drugs

Consumer protection, typified by Collier's *1912 campaign for stricter enforcement of the laws against dangerous patent medicines, first became a major public issue in the Progressive Era.*

a gesture of symbolic importance, he invited Booker T. Washington to confer with him at the White House. The worst blot on his record came in 1906, when he summarily discharged an entire regiment of black army troops charged with rioting in Brownsville, Texas. The "Brownsville Incident" incensed black Americans. (In 1972, when most of the men involved were long dead, Congress reversed Roosevelt's unfair action and removed the dishonorable discharges from their service records.)

Roosevelt's most enduring domestic legacy may have been a heightened environmental awareness. By 1900 decades of rapid population growth and industrial expansion had taken a heavy toll on the land. Mining corporations, timber companies, ranchers, and settlers competed to exploit the West's limited natural resources. Deeply cherishing this region, Roosevelt wanted not only to preserve wilderness areas but also to see *all* natural resources managed by experts for the benefit of all, rather than "sacrificed to the short-sighted greed of a few."

In this spirit, TR helped secure passage of the National Reclamation Act (1902), which earmarked the proceeds from public-land sales to build irrigation projects in the arid Southwest. He also strongly supported his friend Gifford Pinchot, head

of the U.S. Forestry Service and an advocate of scientific resource management. With TR's backing, Pinchot's staff grew from 123 to 1,500. Following Pinchot's recommendations, Roosevelt set aside more than 200 million acres of public lands, including 85 million acres in Alaska, as national forests, mineral reserves, and potential water-power sites. A White House Conservation Conference in 1908, and the National Conservation Commission to which it gave rise, helped focus public attention on an issue that would grow in importance as the century wore on.

Taft in the White House

Roosevelt had pledged that he would not run in 1908, and to the disappointment of millions, he kept his promise. The Republican party's most conservative elements easily regained party control. They nominated Roosevelt's hand-picked successor, Secretary of War William Howard Taft, for president but chose a conservative vice-presidential nominee and, influenced by the National Association of Manufacturers, drafted an extremely conservative platform. (This document called for "revision" of the tariff but neglected to say in which direction.)

On the Democratic side, the defeat of conservative Alton B. Parker in 1904 opened the door for a last hurrah by William Jennings Bryan in 1908. Renominating the Nebraskan for a third White House run, the Democrats adopted a platform that called for a lower tariff, denounced the trusts, and embraced the cause of labor. In the campaign, Bryan espoused even more radical positions, including federal ownership of interstate railroads.

The Bryan of 1908 aroused neither the unreasoning horror nor the passionate support that he had generated in 1896. With Roosevelt's endorsement, Taft coasted to victory. But the Democrats made significant gains—Bryan bested Parker's 1904 vote total by 1.3 million—and progressive Republican candidates at the state level outran the conservative national ticket. Overall, the 1908 election outcome suggested a lull in the reform movement, not its end.

After the inaugural Roosevelt departed to hunt big game in Africa, to the delight of many conservatives. Quipped Senator Aldrich: "Let every lion do its duty." Even with TR on a distant continent, Taft at first seemed intimidated by his looming

The Election of 1908

Candidates	Parties	Electoral Vote	Popular Vote	Percentage of Popular Vote
WILLIAM H. TAFT	Republican	321	7,675,320	51.6
William J. Bryan	Democratic	162	6,412,294	43.1
Eugene V. Debs	Socialist		420,793	2.8
Eugene W. Chafin	Prohibition		253,840	1.7

shadow. "When I am addressed as 'Mr. President,'" he wrote Roosevelt, "I turn to see whether you are not at my elbow."

Taft, who hailed from an old political family in Cincinnati, differed markedly from Roosevelt. While TR rarely relaxed and kept in fighting trim, the sedentary Taft was grossly overweight. Roosevelt sparred in a boxing ring that he had set up in the White House; Taft preferred golf. The two politicians' leadership styles also differed. TR loved dramatic public donnybrooks with the forces of evil and greed; Taft had little taste for political conflict or rousing speeches. "I don't like the lime-light," he admitted. His happiest days would be spent after he left the presidency, as chief justice of the Supreme Court of the United States.

Pledged to carry on TR's reformist program, Taft supported the Mann-Elkins Act (1910), which strengthened the Interstate Commerce Commission's rate-setting powers and extended its regulatory authority to the nation's telephone and telegraph companies. On the antitrust front, the Taft administration actually outdid Roosevelt, prosecuting no fewer than ninety cases. But Taft characteristically pursued these cases without much publicity; and in the public mind, TR, not Taft, remained the quintessential "trustbuster."

President Taft Enjoying His Favorite Activity

One non-admirer described Taft in retrospect as "a large amiable island surrounded entirely by people who knew exactly what they wanted." In fact a man of considerable ability, he was buffeted by political crosscurrents that ended his presidential career after one term.

A Divided Republican Party

During the Roosevelt administration, a small but vocal group of reform-minded Republican legislators, nicknamed the Insurgents, challenged their party's congressional leadership. Influential Insurgents included senators La Follette and Albert Beveridge of Indiana and congressman George Norris of Nebraska. In 1909 the Insurgents turned against President Taft after a bruising battle over the tariff.

Taft at first shared the Insurgents' belief that the tariff should be lowered, and in 1909 a low-tariff bill passed the House. But high-tariff advocates in the Senate, led by Nelson W. Aldrich, pushed through a bill that raised the rates on hundreds of items. The compromise bill that emerged, the Payne-Aldrich Tariff, was close to the Senate version. At this point Taft abandoned the fight for tariff reduction. Signing the Payne-Aldrich Tariff into law, Taft, to the Insurgents' disgust, praised it as "the best tariff bill that the Republican party ever passed." The battle lines between conservative and progressive Republicans were drawn.

A major Insurgent target was the Speaker of the House, Joseph G. Cannon of Illinois, a poker-playing, tobacco-chewing Republican whose benevolent nickname, Uncle Joe, belied his reactionary ideas and ruthless politics. Wielding near-absolute power, Cannon prevented most reform measures from even reaching the House for a vote. The Insurgents' resentment against "Cannonism" burst out in March 1910, when they joined with the Democrats to pass an amendment to the rules, which George Norris introduced, removing the Speaker from the pivotal Rules Committee and stripping him of the power to appoint its members. This Insurgent victory was a direct slap at Taft, who supported Cannon.

Relations between Taft and Roosevelt degenerated rapidly in 1909–1910, as TR's Washington allies sent him stormy letters detailing Taft's ineptness and lack of reform zeal. The so-called Ballinger-Pinchot affair brought matters to a head. Taft's secretary of the interior, Richard A. Ballinger, was a conservative Seattle lawyer who disliked federal controls and believed in private development of natural resources. In one of a series of decisions galling to conservationists, Ballinger approved the sale, to a group of Seattle businessmen, of several million acres of public lands in Alaska containing rich coal deposits. This group in turn sold its holdings to a consortium of New York bankers that included J. P. Morgan, the very symbol of the money power. When a low-level Department of the Interior official, Louis R. Glavis, protested these actions, he was fired. In the best muckraking tradition, Glavis in November 1909 published an article in *Collier's* blasting Ballinger's actions. When Gifford Pinchot of the Forestry Service likewise criticized Ballinger in congressional testimony in January 1910, he, too, got the ax. TR's supporters were outraged.

When Roosevelt returned to the United States in June 1910, Pinchot rather than Taft met the boat in New York. In the 1910 midterm election, Roosevelt worked tirelessly for Insurgent candidates. In a speech particularly alarming to conservatives, the former president appealed for more federal regulation of business, censured judges who struck down progressive legislation, and even endorsed the radical idea of reversing judicial rulings by popular vote. Giving a name to his reviving political crusade, TR borrowed from Herbert Croly's *The Promise of American Life* and proposed a "New Nationalism" that would make the federal government a powerful reform instrument.

The Democrats captured the House of Representatives in 1910, while a coalition of Democrats and Insurgent Republicans controlled the Senate. The reform tide was rising, and Theodore Roosevelt was sounding more and more like a presidential candidate—though hardly a typical Republican one. Meanwhile, however, a new challenger for the national leadership of the progressive movement was coming forth, this time from the ranks of the Democrats.

National Progressivism—Phase II: Woodrow Wilson

In the election of 1912, ex-president Theodore Roosevelt and political newcomer Woodrow Wilson, together with Socialist Eugene Debs, offered competing visions of reform. Wilson won, and over the next four years, he played a pivotal leadership role as Congress enacted an imposing array of reform measures.

The Four-Way Election of 1912

In February 1912, now openly opposed to Taft, Theodore Roosevelt announced that he would seek the 1912 Republican nomination. But Taft had no intention of fading quietly into the sunset, and the stage was set for a Republican battle royal. Two other factors complicated the picture: the growing strength of the Socialist party and the presidential ambitions of Senator Robert La Follette. For a time, La Follette's candidacy found considerable support among reform-minded Republicans, but when Roosevelt entered the race, it quickly collapsed.

Challenging Taft in six state preferential primaries and four Republican state conventions, Roosevelt was almost uniformly victorious. But Taft controlled the party machinery, and the Republican convention that met in Chicago in June disqualified many of Roosevelt's hard-won delegates. Seething, TR's backers stalked out of the convention. In August they reassembled in Chicago to form a third party, the Progressive party. What had been the label of an amorphous reform movement now became the official name of a political organization.

Roosevelt exploited his posturing macho image to the hilt, declaring himself "stripped to the buff and ready for the fight." "I feel fit as a bull moose," he trumpeted, thereby giving his organization its nickname: the Bull Moose party. Carried along on a euphoric emotional high, the cheering, weeping delegates nominated their hero by acclamation, designated Hiram Johnson as his running mate, and adopted a platform that endorsed practically every reform cause that had stirred Americans for a decade, including tariff reduction, woman suffrage, business regulation, the abolition of child labor, the eight-hour workday, workers' compensation, the direct primary, and the popular election of senators. The convention's revivalistic mood was underscored as the delegates fervently joined in such songs as "Onward Christian Soldiers" and "The Battle Hymn of the Republic." The new party attracted a diverse array of followers, from a former partner of J. P. Morgan to settlement-house leader Jane Addams, drawn together by their admiration for the charismatic Roosevelt.

Meanwhile, the new political spirit had also infused the Democratic party and was producing reform administrations at the local and state level. One of these was in New Jersey, where in 1910 voters elected a political novice, Woodrow Wilson, as governor. In 1911–1912 a "Wilson for president" movement gained momentum, and when the Democrats assembled in Baltimore in late June, the Wilson boom proved irresistible.

In the electoral campaign, Taft more or less gave up, taking comfort that he had kept the Republican party safe for conservatism. While Debs championed an end to capitalism and a socialized economic order, Roosevelt and Wilson offered differing prescriptions for more moderate reform. TR continued to preach his New Nationalism: big business was here to stay, but government must regulate it and protect the public interest. Wilson, by contrast, speaking of the "New Freedom," evoked an earlier era of small entrepreneurs and uncontrolled competition. "The history of liberty is the history of the limitation of governmental power, not the increase of it," he declared.

Roosevelt did well for a third-party candidate, winning more than 4 million votes to Taft's 3.5 million, and eighty-eight electoral votes to Taft's

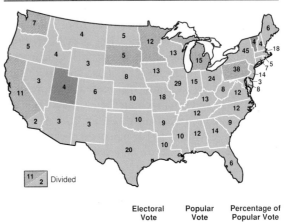

	Electoral Vote	Popular Vote	Percentage of Popular Vote
Democratic Woodrow Wilson	435	6,296,547	41.9
Progressive (Bull Moose) Theodore Roosevelt	88	4,118,571	27.4
Republican William H. Taft	8	3,486,720	23.2
Minor parties	–	–	1,135,697	7.5

The Election of 1912

eight. But the divided Republicans proved no match for the united Democrats. Wilson glided to victory with 6.3 million votes, and the Democrats also took both houses of Congress. More than 900,000 Americans cast their ballots for Debs and socialism.

The significance of the 1912 election ran deep. It revealed the drawing power of an attractive socialist candidate. It identified the triumphant Democrats firmly with reform (except on the issue of race), launching a tradition that Franklin D. Roosevelt would build upon in the 1930s. And finally, the breakaway Progressive party movement of 1912 demonstrated the strength of the reform impulse among grassroots Republicans while leaving the Republican party itself firmly in the grip of its most conservative elements.

Woodrow Wilson: The Scholar as President

The son, grandson, and nephew of Presbyterian ministers, Wilson grew up in various southern towns in a churchly atmosphere that shaped his oratorical style and his moral outlook. Although slow in school (probably because of the learning disorder dyslexia), Wilson graduated from Princeton in 1879 and went on to earn a Ph.D. in political science from Johns Hopkins University. In 1890 he became a professor at Princeton and in 1902 was chosen its president. Admired at first for his innovative educational ideas, Wilson gradually lost support because of a self-righteous unwillingness to compromise. In 1910, having lost several major battles at Princeton, he left the academic world. Two years later he was president of the United States.

As national leader Wilson exhibited the same strengths and weaknesses that he had earlier displayed at Princeton. With piercing gray eyes, impressive bearing, and an imposingly high forehead, he was an eloquent orator with a masterly command of language. But the same idealism that so inspired people could also alienate them. When he chose, Wilson could be a master of political statesmanship and compromise. "He can walk on dead leaves and make no more noise than a tiger," declared one awed politician. But he could also retreat into a fortress of absolute certitude that tolerated no opposition. During his eight years as president, the American people had ample opportunity to observe all these facets of his complex personality.

Tariff and Banking Reform

The first item on Wilson's agenda was tariff reform —a hot political issue and long a goal of southern and agrarian Democrats. Breaking a precedent dating from Thomas Jefferson's day, Wilson on April 8, 1913, read his tariff message to Congress in person. A low-tariff bill quickly passed the House, but as usual the Senate bill bogged down in a fierce partisan battle. Demonstrating his talent for dramatic leadership, Wilson publicly denounced the tariff lobbyists flooding into Washington. His censure led to a Senate investigation of lobbyists and of individual senators' financial interests in maintaining high tariffs. In the aftermath of all the publicity, the Senate passed a bill slashing tariff rates even more than the House version. The Underwood-Simmons Tariff, which Wilson signed in October 1913, reduced rates by an average of 15 percent and placed a number of items, including iron and steel, on the free list. It also imposed an income tax, as authorized by the newly ratified Sixteenth Amendment.

In June 1913, as the tariff battle raged, Wilson again went before Congress, this time to call for banking and currency reform. Everyone agreed that the nation's antiquated banking system was woefully inadequate for a modern industrial economy. Totally decentralized and independent, American banks needed a strong central bank—a "lender of last resort" to enable them to survive a fiscal crisis such as the Panic of 1907, in which many banks had failed. But beyond a general agreement on the need for reform, the consensus evaporated. The nation's bankers, whose Senate spokesman was Nelson W. Aldrich, favored a privately controlled central bank similar to the old Bank of the United States that Andrew Jackson had attacked in the 1830s. Others, including influential Virginia congressman Carter Glass, also supported a privately controlled banking system but thought that it should be decentralized. Progressive reformers believed that the central banking system should be completely under public control.

No monetary expert, Wilson listened to all sides. He did, however, insist that the central banking system must ultimately be under public control. Through the summer and fall of 1913, the complex bargaining went on, with Wilson playing a critical behind-the-scenes role. The result was the Federal Reserve Act of December 1913, Wilson's greatest legislative achievement.

A compromise among the various viewpoints considered by Congress, the Federal Reserve Act created a network of twelve regional Federal Reserve banks under mixed public and private control. Each regional bank was authorized to issue currency, called Federal Reserve notes, to the private banks in its district. These banks, in turn, could use this money to make loans to corporations and individual borrowers. (Look at a dollar bill: you will see the identification "Federal Reserve Note." In the circle to the left of Washington's portrait, you will find the name of the specific Federal Reserve Bank that issued your bill.) Overall control of the system was placed in the hands of the presidents of the twelve regional banks and a Washington-based Federal Reserve Board consisting of the secretary of the treasury, the comptroller of the currency, and seven other members appointed by the president for fourteen-year terms. As established in 1913, the Federal Reserve's decision-making authority was badly diffused. But eventually—and particularly

Woodrow Wilson

after the 1930s—"the Fed" would grow into a strong institution capable of directing the nation's monetary policy.

Corporate Regulation

Building on these achievements, Wilson and his congressional allies turned to that quintessential progressive cause, business regulation. Although as a candidate Wilson had shown little sympathy for the regulatory approach (with its implicit acknowledgment that giant corporations were here to stay), as president he shepherded through Congress two important regulatory measures. These embodied somewhat different strategies. The first, the Federal Trade Commission Act (1914), reflected an administrative approach. This law created a new five-member federal "watchdog" agency, the Federal Trade Commission (FTC), with power to investigate suspected violations of federal regulatory statutes, to require regular reports from corporations, and to issue "cease and desist" orders

(subject to court review) when it found unfair methods of business competition.*

The second of these measures, the Clayton Antitrust Act (1914), took the more traditional approach of listing specific illegal activities. The Sherman Anti-Trust Act of 1890, while outlawing all business practices "in restraint of trade," had remained vague about details. The Clayton Act spelled out such illegal practices, among them selling at a loss to monopolize a market and setting up interlocking directorates of supposedly competing companies.

Because some of the "watchdogs" whom Wilson appointed to the FTC were conservatives with big-business links, this agency did not play as active a role as reformers had hoped. But with the added clout of the Clayton Act, the Wilson administration filed antitrust suits against more than ninety corporations.

Labor Legislation and Farm Aid

Sympathetic to labor, and leading a party historically identified with working people, Wilson supported the American Federation of Labor, defended workers' right to organize, and endorsed a Clayton Act clause that explicitly exempted strikes, boycotts, and peaceful picketing from the antitrust laws' prohibition against actions "in restraint of trade." Somewhat exaggeratedly, AFL president Samuel Gompers hailed this clause as labor's Magna Carta. In September 1916, amid a presidential campaign, Wilson and the Democratic congressional leadership pushed through three important worker-protection laws: the Keating-Owen Act, barring from interstate commerce products manufactured by child labor;† the Adamson Act, establishing an eight-hour workday for interstate railway workers; and the Workmen's Compensation Act, providing accident and injury protection to federal workers.

Candidate Wilson also strongly supported the Federal Farm Loan Act and the Federal Warehouse

---

*The Federal Trade Commission replaced an earlier agency, the Bureau of Corporations, set up in 1903.

†This measure was declared unconstitutional in 1918. Later a 1919 law that placed a special tax on all goods manufactured by child labor was also ruled unconstitutional. But these laws paved the way for the final abolition of child labor by the Fair Labor Standards Act of 1938.

Act (1916), which made it possible for farmers, using land or crops as security, to secure long-term, low-interest credit from a network of regional Farm Loan Banks. The Federal Highway Act (1916), which matched federal funds with state appropriations for highway construction, benefited not only the new automobile industry but also farmers plagued by bad roads.

Progressivism and the Constitution

In the late nineteenth century, as we have seen, the courts usually sided with big business. This judicial conservatism came under increasing criticism in the Progressive Era. When the Supreme Court in *Lochner* v. *New York* (1905) declared unconstitutional a New York law establishing a ten-hour day and a sixty-hour week for bakery workers, Associate Justice Oliver Wendell Holmes, Jr., issued a sharp dissent.

Dramatic evidence of a moderating judicial climate came in *Muller* v. *Oregon* (1908), in which the Supreme Court upheld an Oregon ten-hour law for women laundry workers. Defending the constitutionality of the Oregon law was Boston attorney Louis Brandeis, who went beyond legal precedent to offer economic, medical, and sociological evidence of the harmful effects of long hours on women workers. This evidence came mainly from the research of Brandeis's sister-in-law Josephine Goldmark, a staff member of Florence Kelley's National Consumers' League. The Court's acceptance of this "Brandeis brief" marked a major breakthrough in making the nation's legal system more responsive to new social realities.

In 1916 Woodrow Wilson nominated Brandeis, who had helped fashion Wilson's New Freedom campaign theme in 1912, to the Supreme Court. The nomination set off a storm of protest.

Disapproving of Brandeis's innovative approach to the law, the conservative American Bar Association protested, as did the *New York Times,* the president of Harvard University, and the Republican leadership in Congress. Bigots opposed Brandeis because he was a Jew. But Wilson stood by his nominee, and after a fierce battle, the Senate approved.

The Progressive Era also produced four amendments to the Constitution, some of which we have already noted. The Sixteenth (ratified in 1913) granted Congress the authority to tax incomes. The Seventeenth (1913) mandated the direct election of U.S. senators. Nationwide prohibition was established by the Eighteenth (1919), while the Nineteenth (1920) granted women the vote. This remarkable wave of amendments, the first in a generation, vividly demonstrated how profoundly the progressive impulse had transformed the political landscape.

1916: Wilson Edges Out Hughes

Having compiled an enviable legislative record, Wilson easily won renomination in 1916. The Republicans turned to the bearded and handsome Charles Evans Hughes, a Supreme Court justice and former New York governor. The Progressive party leaders tried to nominate Theodore Roosevelt again, but TR's reformist interests had given way to an obsession with drawing the United States into the European war. At his urging, the Progressives endorsed Hughes and effectively ended their role as a third party. Because of the war, the issue of military preparedness figured importantly in the campaign.

With the Republicans now more or less reunited, the election outcome was extremely close.

The Election of 1916				
Candidates	Parties	Electoral Vote	Popular Vote	Percentage of Popular Vote
WOODROW WILSON	Democratic	277	9,127,695	49.4
Charles E. Hughes	Republican	254	8,533,507	46.2
A. L. Benson	Socialist		585,113	3.2
J. Frank Hanly	Prohibition		220,506	1.2

Wilson led comfortably in the popular vote (9.1 million votes to Hughes's 8.5 million), but the electoral-college outcome remained in doubt for several weeks as the California tally seesawed back and forth. Ultimately, Wilson carried the state by fewer than four thousand votes, and with it, the election. Many political observers believed that Hughes could have won California and gone to the White House if he had taken the time to make a gesture of friendship toward popular California senator Hiram Johnson during a western campaign swing. But he had failed to do so, and the thin-skinned Johnson, offended, had given Hughes only lukewarm support.

Conclusion

With the flurry of worker-protection legislation in the fall of 1916, the progressive movement lost momentum as the nation's attention turned from reform to war. A few reform measures enacted in the 1920s would offer reminders that progressivism had not died entirely, but the movement's zest and drive clearly waned with the coming of World War I.

Yet progressivism left a remarkable legacy, not only in specific laws but also in a changed view of government. To be sure, this altered perspective had ideological roots in the American past, including Jeffersonian optimism about human perfectibility, Jacksonian opposition to special privilege, conservative fears of "the masses," and the rising status of science and social research that had come with advances in higher education and the growing confidence of such academic disciplines as economics, sociology, and statistics.

But the progressives combined these diverse ingredients in creative new ways. By 1916 a consensus had taken hold that it was proper and necessary for government to play a central social and economic role. Thus a major progressive achievement was to expand the meaning of democracy and to challenge the cynical view that government was nothing but a tool of the economic elite. Theodore Roosevelt and Woodrow Wilson, together with governors like Robert La Follette and mayors like Tom Johnson, vastly enlarged the role of the executive in American government. But progressives did not seek "big government" for its own sake. Rather, they recognized that in an era of gargantuan industries, sprawling cities, and concentrated corporate power, government's role had to grow correspondingly if the public interest were to be served, a decent common life achieved, and the more vulnerable members of society protected.

Unquestionably, this high progressive ideal often faltered in practice. Moral indignation and a vision of social justice were sufficient to create reform laws and regulatory agencies, but those laws and agencies were often unable to fulfill their purpose, as emotional fervor gave way to bureaucratic routine. Indeed, reforms that the progressives originally envisioned as serving the larger society sometimes in practice mainly benefited special interests. Corporations that initially fought regulation proved remarkably adept at manipulating the new regulatory state to their own advantage. Unquestionably, too, progressivism had its repressive, illiberal, and coercive dimensions; and on the issue of racial justice, its record was generally dismal.

After all this has been acknowledged, however, the Progressive Era still shines forth as a time when American politics seriously began to confront the massive social upheavals wrought by industrialization. It was also a time when Americans learned to think of their government neither as remote and irrelevant nor as a plaything of the powerful but rather as an arena of possibility where public issues and social problems could be meaningfully addressed. Twenty years later, another great reform movement, the New Deal, would draw heavily on progressivism's legacy.

CHRONOLOGY

1895 Anti-Saloon League founded.

1898 Charlotte Perkins Gilman, *Women and Economics.*

1900 International Ladies' Garment Workers' Union (ILGWU) founded.

Socialist party of America organized.

Theodore Dreiser, *Sister Carrie.*

Carrie Chapman Catt becomes president of the National American Woman Suffrage Association (NAWSA).

1901 Assassination of McKinley; Theodore Roosevelt becomes president.

1902 Roosevelt mediates coal strike.

National Reclamation Act.

Jane Addams, *Democracy and Social Ethics.*

1903 W. E. B. Du Bois, *The Souls of Black Folk.*

1904 Roosevelt elected president.

Northern Securities case.

Lincoln Steffens, *The Shame of the Cities.*

Ida Tarbell, *History of the Standard Oil Company.*

1905 Industrial Workers of the World (IWW) organized.

Niagara Movement established by W. E. B. Du Bois and others.

1906 Hepburn Act.

Upton Sinclair, *The Jungle.*

Pure Food and Drug Act.

Meat Inspection Act.

Lochner v. *New York.*

1907 Walter Rauschenbusch, *Christianity and the Social Crisis.*

William James, *Pragmatism.*

1908 *Muller* v. *Oregon.*

William Howard Taft elected president.

1909 Payne-Aldrich Tariff.

Ballinger-Pinchot controversy.

National Association for the Advancement of Colored People (NAACP) founded.

Herbert Croly, *The Promise of American Life.*

1910 Mann Act.

Mann-Elkins Act.

1911 Triangle Shirtwaist Company fire.

Supreme Court orders dissolution of Standard Oil Company.

1912 Republican party split; Progressive (Bull Moose) party founded.

Woodrow Wilson elected president.

1913 Underwood-Simmons Tariff.

Federal Reserve Act.

Sixteenth Amendment added to the Constitution.

Seventeenth Amendment added to the Constitution.

Thirty thousand march for woman suffrage in New York.

1914 Federal Trade Commission Act.
Clayton Antitrust Act.

1915 D. W. Griffith, *The Birth of a Nation.*

1916 Federal Farm Loan Act.
Keating-Owen Act.
Adamson Act.
Workmen's Compensation Act.

1916 Wilson reelected.
(cont.) John Dewey, *Democracy and Education.*
Margaret Sanger opens nation's first birth-control clinic in Brooklyn, New York.

1919 Eighteenth Amendment added to the Constitution.

1920 Nineteenth Amendment added to the Constitution.

For Further Reading

John D. Buenker, John C. Burnham, and Robert M. Crunden, *Progressivism* (1977). A useful overview and survey of recent scholarship, stressing the movement's diversity.

John W. Chambers II, *The Tyranny of Change: America in the Progressive Era, 1900–1917* (1980). An interpretive work emphasizing the progressives' belief in intervention in the social and economic realms.

Gabriel Kolko, *The Triumph of Conservatism: A Reinterpretation of American History, 1900–1916* (1963). A seminal though controversial study that sees large corporate interests as underlying most progressive reforms.

Arthur S. Link and Richard L. McCormick, *Progressivism* (1983). Lucid, sensible unraveling of progressivism's diverse strands and comprehensive discussion of current interpretations.

Robert Wiebe, *The Search for Order, 1877–1920* (1967). A highly influential study treating progressivism as the response of a new middle class and professional groups to late-nineteenth-century urban-industrial changes.

Additional Bibliography

Society and the Economy

John Bodnar, *Immigration and Industrialization* (1977); David Brody, "The American Worker in the Progressive Age: A Comprehensive Analysis" in David Brody, *Workers in Industrial America: Essays on the Twentieth-Century Struggle* (2d ed., 1985); Irving Howe, *The World of Our Fathers* (1976); Alice Kessler-Harris, *Out to Work: A History of Wage-Earning Women in the United States* (1982); Alan M. Kraut, *The Huddled Masses: The Immigrant in American Society, 1860–1921* (1982); Elaine Tyler May, *Great Expectations: Marriage and Divorce in Post-Victorian America* (1980); William L. O'Neill, *Divorce in the Progressive Era* (1967); Glenn Porter, *The Rise of Big Business, 1860–1916* (1973); Bruno Ramirez, *When Workers Organize: The Politics of Industrial Relations in the Progressive Era, 1898–1916* (1978); Moses Rischin, *The Promised City: New York's Jews, 1870–1914* (1962); Elyce J. Rotella, *From Home to Office: U.S. Women and Work, 1870–1930* (1981); Nick Salvatore, *Eugene V. Debs* (1982); David Shannon, *The Socialist Party of America: A History* (1955).

The Progressive Impulse

John D. Buenker, *Urban Liberalism and Progressive Reform* (1973); David M. Chalmers, *The Social and Political Ideas of the Muckrakers* (1964); Lawrence A. Cremin, *The Transformation of the Schools: Progressivism in American Education, 1876–1957* (1971); Robert Crunden, *Ministers of Reform: The Progressives' Achievement in American Civilization* (1982); Allen F. Davis, *Spearheads for Reform: The Social Settlements and the Progressive Movement, 1890–1914* (1967); Charles Forcey, *The Crossroads of Liberalism: Croly, Weyl, Lippmann and the Progressive Era, 1900–1925* (1961); Dewey W. Grantham, *Southern Progressivism: The Reconciliation of Progress and Tradition* (1983); Samuel P. Hays, "The Politics of Reform in Municipal Government in the Progressive Era," *Pacific Northwest Quarterly* 55 (1964): 157–169; Melvin G. Holli, *Reform in Detroit: Hazen S. Pingree and Urban Politics* (1969); Justin Kaplan, *Lincoln Steffens: A Biography* (1974); Richard L. McCormick, *From Realignment to Reform: Political Change in New York State, 1893–1910* (1981) and "The Discovery That Business Corrupts Politics: A Reappraisal of the Origins of Progressivism," *American Historical Review* 86 (1981): 247–274; Thomas K. McCraw, "Regulation in America: A Review Article," *Business History Review* 49 (1975): 159–183; Jean B. Quandt, *From the Small Town to the Great Community: The Social Thought of Progressive Intellectuals* (1970);

Bradley R. Rice, *Progressive Cities: The Commission Government Movement in America, 1901–1920* (1977); Daniel Rodgers, "In Search of Progressivism," *Reviews in American History* 10 (1982): 113–132; Martin J. Schiesl, *The Politics of Efficiency: Municipal Administration and Reform in America, 1880–1920* (1977); David P. Thelen, *Robert La Follette and the Insurgent Spirit* (1976); Walter I. Trattner, *Crusade for Children* (1970); James Weinstein, *The Corporate Ideal in the Liberal State, 1900–1918* (1968); Robert Wiebe, *Businessmen and Reform: A Study of the Progressive Movement* (1962).

Progressivism's Darker Side

Paul Boyer, *Urban Masses and Moral Order in America, 1820–1920* (1978); Norman H. Clark, *Deliver Us from Evil: An Interpretation of American Prohibition* (1976); Mark T. Connelly, *The Response to Prostitution in the Progressive Era* (1980); Mark H. Haller, *Eugenics: Hereditarian Attitudes in American Thought* (1963); John Higham, *Strangers in the Land: Patterns of American Nativism, 1860–1925* (1955); Jack Temple Kirby, *Darkness at Dawning: Race and Reform in the Progressive South* (1972); J. Morgan Kousser, *The Shaping of Southern Politics: Suffrage Restriction and the Establishment of the One-Party South, 1880–1910* (1974); John F. McClymer, *War and Welfare: Social Engineering in America, 1890–1925* (1980); Charles E. Rosenberg, *No Other Gods: On Science and American Social Thought* (1976); James H. Timberlake, *Prohibition and the Progressive Movement, 1900–1920* (1963); C. Vann Woodward, *Origins of the New South, 1877–1913* (1951).

Blacks and Women

Eleanor Flexner, *Century of Struggle: The Women's Rights Movement in the United States* (1959); Linda Gordon, *Woman's Body, Woman's Right: A Social History of Birth Control in America* (1976); Louis R. Harlan, *Booker T. Washington: Wizard of Tuskegee, 1901–1915* (1983); Charles F. Kellogg, *NAACP: The History of the National Association for the Advancement of Colored People, 1909–1920* (1967); Aileen S. Kraditor, *The Ideas of the Women's Suffrage Movement, 1890–1915* (1963); Rosalind Rosenberg, *Beyond Separate Spheres: The Intellectual Roots of Modern Feminism* (1982); Elliott M. Rudwick, *W. E. B. Du Bois* (1969); Nancy Woloch, *Women and the American Experience* (1984).

Progressivism in National Politics

Paolo E. Coletta, *The Presidency of William Howard Taft* (1973); John Milton Cooper, Jr., *The Warrior and the Priest: Theodore Roosevelt and Woodrow Wilson* (1983); Samuel P. Hays, *Conservation and the Gospel of Efficiency: The Progressive Conservation Movement, 1890–1920* (1959); Arthur S. Link, *Woodrow Wilson and the Progressive Era* (1963); Albro Martin, *Enterprise Denied: Origins of the Decline of American Railroads, 1897–1917* (1971); Edmund Morris, *The Rise of Theodore Roosevelt* (1979); James Penick, Jr., *Progressive Politics and Conservation: The Ballinger-Pinchot Affair* (1968); Peter Temin, *Taking Your Medicine: Drug Regulation in the U.S.* (1980); Melvin I. Urofsky, *Louis D. Brandeis and the Progressive Tradition* (1981).

CHAPTER 22

World War I

Woodrow Wilson was somber on the evening of April 2, 1917, as he was driven from the White House to the Capitol to ask Congress for a declaration of war against Germany. The president spent the moments before his speech in a small room adjacent to the House of Representatives. Now flushed and trembling, he stared into a mirror until he had mastered his emotions and composed his features. At 8:32 P.M. he strode through the swinging doors into the House chamber and began his address.

Halfway through, Wilson uttered a memorable phrase: the world, he proclaimed, must be made "safe for democracy." Applause and shouts reverberated through the hall. Many senators and congressmen waved little silk American flags that someone had distributed beforehand. As the speech ended, a final burst of cheers echoed through the House chamber. Senator Henry Cabot Lodge of Massachusetts, one of Wilson's staunchest political opponents, rushed forward to shake his hand. "Mr. President," said Lodge, "you have expressed in the loftiest manner the sentiments of the American people."

But Wilson's own mood remained muted. "Think what it was they were applauding," he mused to an aide; "my message today was a message of death for our young men. How strange it seems to applaud that."

This message of death, which did indeed send many thousands of American young men to their graves, came reluctantly from Wilson, after months of trying to keep the United States out of war. Elected on a tide of reformist enthusiasm, Wilson found himself increasingly enmeshed in foreign affairs as his presidential term proceeded. Preoccupied at first with problems in Asia and Latin America, Wilson was soon caught up in—and ultimately consumed by—the struggle engulfing Europe. Wilson brought to these foreign crises the same self-assured moralism that he had long applied to issues closer to home.

While Woodrow Wilson's international involvements focused on Europe, his Republican predecessors in the White House, Theodore Roosevelt and William Howard Taft, had asserted a more active world role for the United States in Asia and Latin America. In contrast to William McKinley, a reluctant and clumsy imperialist, Theodore Roosevelt had no doubts about America's mission in Asia: to provide a balance of power, preventing any other nation from controlling the region. With his customary energy and highly personal approach, Roosevelt pursued this objective. President Taft, on the other hand, was guided less by a grand geopolitical design than by a practical desire to open the markets of the developing part of the world to American business. Taken together, the foreign policies pursued by each of these early-twentieth-century presidents—Roosevelt's balance-of-power chess game, Taft's concentration on business opportunities, and Wilson's moralism—illustrate the diverse and sometimes contradictory motives that would continue to shape the United States' world role as the twentieth century unfolded.

Defining America's World Role

U.S. involvement in Asia and Latin America, intensified by the Spanish-American War and the occupation of the Philippines, continued at a quickening pace in the first part of the new century. These foreign engagements clearly reflected the United States' growing determination to assert its might, to protect and vigorously extend American business investments abroad, and to impose its own standards of good government throughout the world.

The Roosevelt Corollary in Latin America and the Balance of Power in Asia

While the maneuverings that led to the building of the Panama Canal remain Theodore Roosevelt's most famous foreign-policy coup, his actions and pronouncements in response to other foreign crises further illuminated his belief that the United States must strengthen its world role, protect U.S. interests in Latin America, and preserve the balance of power in Asia.

In 1904, when several European nations threatened to invade the Dominican Republic, a small Caribbean island nation that had defaulted on its debts, Roosevelt concluded that such an assault would jeopardize American interests. If any big power were to intervene in Latin America, he believed, it should be the United States. Accordingly, in his annual message to Congress in December 1904, Roosevelt declared that while the United States had no territorial ambitions in Latin America, "chronic wrongdoing" by any Latin American nation would justify intervention by the United States, acting as an international policeman.

This pronouncement soon came to be known as the Roosevelt Corollary to the Monroe Doctrine. The original "doctrine," promulgated by President James Monroe in 1823, had warned European powers against meddling in Latin America; the Roosevelt Corollary announced that under certain circumstances, the United States had the right to precisely such meddling. Suiting actions to words, the United States operated the Dominican Republic's customs service for two years (1905–1907) and took over the management of its foreign debt.

Meanwhile, on the other side of the world, the imperial rivalries that swirled over China in the 1890s continued unabated in the new century, briefly casting President Theodore Roosevelt in the unfamiliar role of peacemaker. In 1900, taking advantage of the turmoil caused by the Boxer uprising (see Chapter 20), one hundred thousand Russian troops occupied the Chinese province of Manchuria, where Russia sought to promote its commercial interests by building railroads. This action alarmed the Japanese, who had their own plans for southern Manchuria and the nearby Korean peninsula. In February 1904 the Japanese launched a surprise attack that destroyed the Russian naval force at Port Arthur, Manchuria. In the Russo-Japanese War that followed, the Japanese completely dominated the Russians.

Roosevelt was quite happy to see Russian expansionism checked, but a total Japanese defeat of the Russians would disrupt the balance of power that TR considered essential to peace in the Far East and to the maintenance of America's role in the Philippines. Accordingly, in June 1905 TR invited Japan and Russia to send delegates to a peace conference at Portsmouth, New Hampshire, and in early September the two rivals signed a peace treaty. By its terms, Russia recognized Japan's rule in Korea, gave Japan control of the South Manchurian Railroad, and made other territorial concessions. After this outcome, restraining Japanese expansionism—peacefully, if possible— became America's major objective in Asia. For his role in ending the Russo-Japanese War, Theodore Roosevelt received the Nobel Peace Prize in 1906.

Meanwhile, American relations with Japan suffered when the San Francisco school board, in 1906, reflecting growing West Coast hostility to Asian immigrants, ordered all Asian children to attend segregated schools. Summoning the school-board members to Washington, Roosevelt persuaded them to reverse this discriminatory policy. In return, the Roosevelt administration in 1908 negotiated a "gentlemen's agreement" with Japan by which Tokyo pledged to stop the further emigration of Japanese laborers to the United States. Racist attitudes on the West Coast continued to poison U.S.-Japanese relations, however. In 1913 the California legislature prohibited Japanese aliens from owning land.

While Californians wrung their hands over the "yellow peril," Japanese journalists, looking at America's increasing military strength and involvements in Asia, began to speak of a "white peril." In 1907 Roosevelt ordered a flotilla of sixteen gleaming white U.S. battleships to set sail on a "training operation" to Japan and on around the world. Although officially treated as a courtesy call, the 1908 visit of this "Great White Fleet" to Japan pointedly underscored America's growing naval might.

Dollar Diplomacy in China and Nicaragua

The foreign policy of President William Howard Taft, who took office in 1909, focused mainly on advancing American commercial interests abroad —a policy that critics called dollar diplomacy. Since 1899, when Secretary of State John Hay wrote the first of his "Open Door" notes (see Chapter 20), Washington had tried with scant success to secure from the European powers and Japan a share in China's economic development. Pursuing this pol-

icy, the Taft administration persuaded a group of American bankers to explore investments in China. But when their agent in China, Willard Straight, proposed an American-financed railroad in northern Manchuria, he got nowhere. Not only did the American bankers reject the idea, but the Russians and Japanese at once signed a treaty dividing Manchuria between themselves for commercial purposes, effectively freezing out the Americans. When Woodrow Wilson took office in 1913, the Taft policy of aggressively promoting U.S. commercial expansion in China was, for the time being, shelved.

Closer to home, in Nicaragua, dollar diplomacy seemed to enjoy greater success. In 1911 a U.S.-supported revolution in Nicaragua brought to power Adolfo Díaz, an officer of an American-owned Nicaraguan mining property. "Under proper administration," suggested Díaz in a message to the United States, Nicaragua could be "a field for American commerce, instead of a pest under your nose." With encouragement from the U.S. Department of State, American bankers loaned the Díaz government $15 million in exchange for control of the Nicaraguan national bank, the customs service, and the national railroad.

When a revolt against Díaz broke out in 1912, Taft put the Roosevelt Corollary into action: he

U.S. Marines in Nicaragua, 1912

These troops were part of a 2500-man force sent by President William Howard Taft to support Nicaragua's pro-U.S. ruler, Adolfo Díaz. With one brief interval, the marines remained for twenty-one years.

ordered in twenty-five hundred marines to protect the American bankers' investment. Except for one brief interval, a contingent of marines remained in the Nicaraguan capital, Managua, until 1933 as a reminder of U.S. military might. Resistance against U.S. domination remained alive, however, led in the later 1920s and early 1930s by a general named Augusto Sandino. In 1979, when the U.S.-supported dictator of Nicaragua was overthrown, the rebel commanders took the name Sandinistas, to honor the resistance leader of a generation before.

Wilson and Latin America

Reprehending the expansionist policies of his Republican predecessors, Wilson pledged in 1913 that the United States would "never again seek one additional foot of territory by conquest." Nevertheless, Wilson, too, became deeply entangled in Latin American politics. In 1915, after bloody upheavals in Haiti and the Dominican Republic (two tiny nations sharing the same Caribbean island, Santo Domingo), Wilson ordered in the marines. The government's aim in Haiti, said Secretary of State William Jennings Bryan, was to encourage "American investment" by restoring "stability and order." A Haitian constitution favorable to U.S. commercial interests, for which the assistant secretary of the navy (and future president) Franklin D. Roosevelt later claimed credit, was ratified in 1918 by a margin of 69,377 in favor, 355 against—in a vote supervised by the marines. Under the command of Major General Smedley ("Old Gimlet Eye") Butler, marines brutally suppressed Haitian resistance to U.S. rule. The marines remained in the Dominican Republic until 1924, and in Haiti until 1934.

From 1911 to 1914, Wilson's major foreign preoccupation was with neighboring Mexico, a nation divided between a tiny elite of wealthy landowners and a mass of poor peasants. In a particularly turbulent era for Mexico, Wilson tried to promote good government in Mexico City, as he had at home; to protect the very large U.S. capital investments in the country; and ultimately, to safeguard the U.S. citizens traveling in Mexico or living along its border.

In 1911 rebels led by a democratic reformer and mystic named Francisco Madero unceremoniously ended the thirty-year rule of the autocratic president Porfirio Díaz. Forty thousand Americans had settled in Mexico under Díaz's regime, and U.S. investors had poured some \$2 billion into Mexican oil wells and other ventures. Madero briefly succeded Díaz, but early in 1913, just as Wilson took office, Mexican troops loyal to general Victoriano Huerta, a full-blooded Indian, overthrew and murdered Madero.

Reversing the long-standing American policy of recognizing all governments that clearly held power regardless of how they came to office, Wilson refused to recognize Huerta's regime: "I will not recognize a government of butchers," he declared. Authorizing arms sales to Huerta's rival, General Venustiano Carranza, Wilson also ordered the port of Vera Cruz blockaded to prevent a shipment of German arms from reaching Huerta. Announced Wilson, the former professor of political science: "I am going to teach the South American republics to elect good men."

In April 1914, seven thousand U.S. troops occupied Vera Cruz and began fighting Huerta's forces. Sixty-five Americans and some five hundred Mexicans were killed or wounded. Bowing to U.S. might, Huerta abdicated, Carranza took power, and the U.S. troops withdrew.

But the turmoil in Mexico continued, as local rebels and bandits challenged Carranza's authority. In January 1916 a bandit chieftain operating in northern Mexico, Pancho Villa, murdered sixteen young American mining engineers whom he had pulled from a train. Soon after, Pancho Villa's gang burned the town of Columbus, New Mexico, and killed nineteen of its inhabitants. Enraged, the American people demanded action. Wilson dispatched a punitive expedition that eventually totaled 12,000 U.S. troops into Mexico under the command of General John J. Pershing. Many of these troops were black, and Pershing, who expressed high regard for their abilities, thereafter carried the nickname Black Jack. When Pancho Villa not only eluded Pershing but brazenly staged another raid across the border into Texas, Wilson ordered 150,000 members of the National Guard into duty along the Mexican border. This massive military response to a comparatively minor problem would long prove a sore point in U.S.-Mexican relations.

Early in 1917, with the United States teetering on the brink of a far broader conflict in Europe, Wilson withdrew the U.S. forces from Mexico.

Pancho Villa with His Troops, 1914

A bandit chieftain and political opponent of Mexican leader Venustiano Carranza, Villa tried to provoke U.S. intervention in Mexico as a way of discrediting Carranza.

When Carranza was formally elected president later that year, Wilson extended U.S. recognition, thus opening the way to diplomatic exchange. That same year, in a move clearly aimed at curbing the free-wheeling operations of U.S. capitalists, Mexico adopted a new constitution that gave the central government rather than regional administrators control of the nation's oil and mineral resources and imposed strict regulations on foreign investors and developers.

Although soon overwhelmed by the larger drama of World War I, these seemingly minor early-twentieth-century involvements in Asia and Latin America illuminate the larger contours of American foreign-policy goals in these years. These goals reflected a search for world order on U.S. terms—an international system founded on the uniquely American ideological blend of liberalism, democracy, open trade, and capitalistic enterprise. Sometimes explicitly, often implicitly, Washington planners envisioned a harmonious, stable global order of democratic societies that would welcome both American political values and American corporate expansion.

These involvements in Asia and Latin America also foreshadowed future trends. The diplomatic maneuvering between the United States and Japan signaled a developing clash of interests, compounded by racism, that in 1924 would lead the United States to close the door to Japanese immigration and in 1941 culminate in war. The revolutionary and nationalistic energies stirring in Latin America portended developments that half a century later would explosively transform the politics of this region. And of more immediate concern, the vision of an American-based world order that underlay these episodes would soon find its fullest expression in Woodrow Wilson's response to the crisis now confronting him in Europe.

War in Europe

When war burst upon Europe in August 1914, most Americans initially wished only to remain aloof. For nearly three years, as the conflict raged in the trenches and on the high seas, the United States stayed officially neutral. But the tide of opinion gradually shifted. Deep-seated emotional ties to the British and French, powerful economic considerations, the vision of a world remade in America's image, and German violations of Woodrow Wilson's definition of neutral rights all combined by April 1917 to suck the United States into the maelstrom.

The Coming of War

With a few exceptions, Europe remained at peace through much of the nineteenth century and the early years of the twentieth. Some observers confidently prophesied that war was a thing of the past.

Beneath the surface, however, ominous developments gave such hopeful predictions a hollow ring. The European powers had aligned themselves in a complex network of alliances. As early as 1882, Germany, Austria, and Italy signed a mutual-defense treaty. In turn, France signed military treaties with Russia (1894) and with Great Britain (1904).

Beyond the formal treaties and alliances lay the sphere of imperial ambitions and nationalistic stirrings. The ancient Ottoman Empire, centered in Turkey, which had once controlled much of southeastern Europe, lost its grip in the 1870s, leaving in its wake such newly independent nations as Romania, Bulgaria, and Serbia (today part of Yugoslavia).

Nationalistic passions ran high in these new states, and particularly in Serbia, where patriots dreamed of achieving the cultural and political unification of the large ethnic group known as Slavs. This dream, called Pan-Slavism, powerfully molded turn-of-the-century politics in southeastern Europe. Many Pan-Slavic activists looked to Russia, the homeland of millions of Slavs, to lead the movement; the Russian government, for its part, vigorously supported the Pan-Slavic cause.

Meanwhile, however, the Austro-Hungarian Empire, with its capital in Vienna, also saw opportunities for expansion as the Ottoman Empire receded. In 1908 Austria-Hungary annexed Bosnia-Herzogovina, a Slavic region on its southern border, adjacent to Serbia. This move aroused alarm in Russia and fury in Serbia, which also had designs on Bosnia-Herzogovina.

Germany, under the leadership of Kaiser Wilhelm II, was also in an aggressive, expansionist mood. Many Germans believed that their nation, only recently forged from a collection of independent principalities, had fallen behind in the quest for national greatness and empire. Expansion, modernization, and military power became the order of the day in Berlin, the German Empire's capital.

At a level deeper than diplomacy and politics, many Europeans felt a vague restlessness in the opening years of the twentieth century. Life seemed soft, boring, and stale, devoid of challenge and danger. Like Theodore Roosevelt on the eve of the Spanish-American War, some openly speculated that a war might strengthen the national character and add excitement to a rather languid age.

These elements of European political culture combined to kindle an explosion that had horrendous consequences. In late June 1914 Archduke Franz Ferdinand of Austria made a state visit with his wife to Bosnia, which Austria had annexed six years earlier. As they rode in an open carriage through Sarajevo, the Bosnian capital, a young Serbian nationalist gunned them down. In response, Austria delivered a harsh ultimatum to Serbia on July 23. Five days later, pronouncing Serbia's answer unacceptable, Austria declared war on its eastern neighbor. Now Europe's intricate system of alliances came into play. Russia, which had a secret treaty with Serbia, mobilized for war. Germany declared war on Russia and on Russia's ally France. Great Britain, linked by treaty to France, declared war on Germany. A lone assassin's bullet had plunged Europe into a war that would transform history.

The American People's Initial Responses

President Wilson immediately proclaimed American neutrality and called on the nation to be neutral "in thought as well as in action." Most Americans supported Wilson's position. They felt gratitude that three thousand miles of salt water lay between them and the war. A popular song of the day summed up the national mood: "I Didn't Raise My Boy to Be a Soldier."

For Woodrow Wilson, the unfolding European crisis strangely paralleled a crisis in his own life. His wife, Ellen, had been in failing health for several months, and on August 6, 1914, she died. Thus while the president dealt with the international crisis, he also had to cope with his own grief and loss. Ellen Wilson had played an active role in her husband's career, providing wise advice and nurturing support.

While the majority of Americans fervently shared Wilson's desire to stay out of the war, his admonition to remain neutral in thought proved more difficult. The United States and Britain were linked by extensive economic ties. Many Americans of British ancestry, including Wilson himself and most members of his administration, felt an emotional connection with England. As early as August 1914, Wilson mused to his brother-in-law that a victory for militaristic Germany would spell a disaster for the world. Countless Americans had traveled in England. School textbooks stressed the English origins of American history and institutions. The English language itself—the language of Chaucer, Shakespeare, Dickens, and the King James version of the Bible—formed a strong common bond between Britons and Americans. The British government subtly reinforced this pro-British mood by a variety of informal contacts as well as by propaganda stressing the British-American link.

But not all Americans felt spontaneous ties with the British. Millions were of German origin, and many of them looked with sympathy on Germany's cause. Irish-Americans found little reason for dismay in the prospect of a German victory that might at last free Ireland from the British colonial yoke. Some Scandinavian immigrants initially identified more with Germany than with England.

However, while a variety of cultural and ethnic crosscurrents influenced American attitudes toward the war, they did not at first override the fundamental commitment to neutrality. For most Americans, as for the Wilson administration itself, keeping the United States out of the conflict became the chief goal.

The Perils of Neutrality

Despite its commitment to neutrality in 1914, the U.S. government went to war in 1917, with strong popular support. What factors underlay this turnabout?

First of all, Wilson's vision of a world order built on American political and economic values conflicted with his commitment to neutrality. The international system that he favored, based on liberalism, democracy, and freedom for American capitalistic enterprise, would have been impossible, he believed, in a world dominated by imperial Germany and its autocratic ruler Kaiser Wilhelm II. Further, Wilson gradually became convinced that even an Allied* victory would not ensure a liberal peace without U.S. participation in the postwar settlement. As the president put it in describing his ideas about the future international order: "America shall in truth lead the way." And if America were to help shape the peace, America would have to help fight the war.

This larger global vision influenced Wilson's handling of the issue that most obviously and

---

*During World War I, Great Britain, Russia, France, and later Italy were called the Allies. Germany and Austria-Hungary were called the Central Powers. The United States entered the war in 1917 as an "Associate Power" of the Allies, thereby distinguishing its war conduct and aims from those of the other nations with whom it sided.

immediately dragged the United States into the conflict: the question of neutral nations' rights on the high seas. Within days of the war's outbreak, the British had intercepted American merchant ships bound for Germany, declaring their cargo contraband that could aid Germany's war effort. Wilson had protested vehemently. These seizures evoked distant memories of the War of 1812 with England, fought partly over neutral rights. "Madison and I are the only two Princeton men that have become president," Wilson mused to an adviser; "the circumstances of the War of 1812 and now run parallel. I sincerely hope they will not go further."

Wilson's protests intensified in November 1914, when Britain declared the North Sea a war zone and planted it with deadly explosive mines. By choking off Germany's maritime imports, including food, Britain hoped to bring Germany to its knees. In March 1915 the British blockaded all German ports. Once more, the United States protested in vain. Britain was determined to exploit its naval advantage to the fullest, even if it meant alienating American public opinion.

But it was Germany, not England, that ultimately violated the American conception of neutral rights so grossly that the United States went to war. If Britannia ruled the waves, Germany controlled the ocean depths with an awesome new weapon: the torpedo-equipped submarine, or U-boat. In February 1915 Berlin proclaimed the waters around the British Isles a war zone and warned off all ships, including those of neutrals. Yet again Wilson protested; Germany would be held to "strict accountability," he declared, for any loss of American ships or lives. Nevertheless, several Americans died in the succeeding months as U-boats torpedoed British ships and a U.S. tanker.

Then on May 1, 1915, in a small announcement published in U.S. newspapers, the German embassy cautioned Americans against travel on British or French vessels. Six days later, a U-boat without warning sank the British liner *Lusitania* off the Irish coast, with the loss of 1,198 lives, including 128 Americans. As newspapers reported the news in bold headlines, U.S. public opinion turned sharply anti-German. (The *Lusitania*'s cargo holds, historians later discovered, had carried munitions destined for England.)

In increasingly strong messages to the German government, collectively called the *Lusitania* notes,

Woman's Peace Party Parade

With fans to symbolize their point, these marchers urged President Wilson to continue the search for peace despite German provocations on the high seas.

Wilson demanded specific pledges that Germany would cease unrestricted submarine warfare. In a speech a few days after the *Lusitania* sinking, Wilson insisted that America could persuade the belligerents to recognize the principle of neutral rights without resorting to force. Asserted the president: "There is such a thing as a man being too proud to fight."

The *Lusitania* disaster exposed deep divisions in U.S. public opinion. Many Americans, concluding that war with Germany had become inevitable, ridiculed Wilson's "too proud to fight" speech. Theodore Roosevelt, the Nobel Peace Prize winner, beat the drums for war and heaped scorn on the president's "abject cowardice and weakness." The organizers of a "preparedness" movement, led by a private lobby of bankers and industrialists called the National Security League, stirred up patriotism and promoted armament and universal military training. The National Security League organized great "preparedness" parades in New York, Washington, and other cities. By the fall of 1915, Wilson himself was calling for a military buildup.

Many others, however, including not only German-Americans and pacifists but millions who had taken Wilson's neutrality speeches seriously, deplored the drift toward war. Some leading feminists and social-justice reformers warned that the militant war spirit eroded the humanitarian values central to progressive reform. Jane Addams, for

example, pointed out that the international movement to reduce infant mortality and provide better care to the aged had been "scattered to the winds by the war."

As early as August 1914, fifteen hundred black-clad women had marched slowly down New York's Fifth Avenue, protesting the war. Early in 1915 Jane Addams, Carrie Chapman Catt, and other feminist leaders formed the Woman's Peace party to strengthen the peace cause. Late in 1915 automaker Henry Ford chartered the *Oscar II*—often called the Ford peace ship—which took a group of pacifists and other opponents of the war, including Addams, to Scandinavia in an abortive effort to persuade the belligerents to accept neutral mediation and fulfill Ford's dream of ending the war by Christmas.

Serious divisions even surfaced within the Wilson administration. Believing Wilson's *Lusitania* notes too hostile, and dismayed by what he saw as the abandonment of true neutrality, Secretary of State Bryan resigned in June 1915. His successor, the colorless and retiring Robert Lansing, was usually content to let Wilson act as his own secretary of state.

Some neutrality advocates concluded that incidents like the *Lusitania* crisis were inevitable if Americans continued to sail aboard belligerent ships. Early in 1916 a congressman and a senator introduced legislation to forbid such travel (the Gore-McLemore Resolutions), but it failed under strong opposition from President Wilson, who insisted that the principle of neutral rights must be upheld.

For a time, Wilson's firm but restrained approach seemed to work. While Germany did not specifically answer the *Lusitania* notes, it secretly ordered U-boat captains to spare passenger ships and eventually agreed to pay compensation for the loss of American lives in the *Lusitania* sinking. In August 1915, when a U-boat violated orders and sank a British passenger vessel, the *Arabic*, killing two Americans, Germany pledged that such incidents would not recur. In March 1916, however, a German sub sank a French passenger ship, the *Sussex*, in the English Channel, and several Americans were injured. This violation of the *Arabic* pledge provoked Wilson to threaten to break diplomatic relations—a first step toward war. In response, Berlin pledged not to attack merchant vessels without warning, although it added that the United States must compel Britain to observe "the rules of international law." Ignoring this qualification, Wilson announced Germany's acceptance of American demands; for the rest of 1916, the crisis over neutral rights eased.

The debate over the meaning of neutrality also involved questions of U.S. financial support to the warring nations. Soon after the war had begun, when banker J. P. Morgan sought permission to extend a loan to France, Secretary of State Bryan had rejected the request as "inconsistent with the true spirit of neutrality."

But towering economic considerations, combined with outrage over the *Lusitania* sinking, undermined this policy. In August 1915 Treasury Secretary William G. McAdoo warned Wilson of dire economic consequences if the Allied purchase of munitions and agricultural commodities in the United States was cut off by lack of funds. "To maintain our prosperity, we must finance it," McAdoo insisted. Secretary of State Lansing agreed, warning that only substantial loans to Great Britain could prevent "a serious financial situation" in the United States, including "general unrest and suffering among the laboring classes." Asked Lansing rhetorically: "Can we afford to let a declaration as to our conception of the 'true spirit of neutrality' made in the early days of the war, stand in the way of our national interests . . . ?"

Swayed by such arguments, and personally sympathetic to the Allied cause, Wilson permitted the Morgan bank to loan $500 million to the Brit-

ish and French governments. By April 1917 U.S. banks had loaned $2.3 billion to the Allies, in contrast to only $27 million to Germany. And while U.S. trade with the Central Powers dropped precipitously from 1914 to 1917, trade with the Allies increased nearly fourfold in these years. Despite American proclamations of neutrality, the Allies' economic dependence upon the United States grew progressively stronger. Although the United States still remained on the sidelines militarily, Wilson had taken full advantage of the Allies' credit needs to strengthen America's commercial and financial position in the world economy.

Stalemate in the Trenches

While Americans focused on neutral rights and the war at sea, the land war in Europe degenerated into a costly stalemate. The German high command initially planned to defeat the French and British in six weeks, but an autumn 1914 German drive across Belgium and into France bogged down along the Marne River in the face of dogged British and French resistance. The two sides then dug in, forming a line of trenches that snaked across France from the English Channel to the Swiss border. For more than three years, this line remained essentially unchanged. Occasional offensives gained little ground while taking a terrible human toll. A German offensive in February 1916 began with the capture of two forts near the town of Verdun and ended that June with the French recapture of the same two forts, now nothing but rubble, at a cost of hundreds of thousands of casualties. This war in the trenches was nightmarish for those caught up in it: a ghastly inferno of mud, lice, rats, artillery bursts, poison gas, and sudden, random death. British statesman David Lloyd George would later call this trench war "the most gigantic, tenacious, grim, futile, and bloody fight ever waged in the history of war."

In the struggle to capture the minds of Americans, the British stepped up their propaganda campaign. Posters and articles portrayed the atrocities allegedly committed by "the Huns" (a derogatory wartime term for the Germans), such as impaling babies on the tips of bayonets. After the war, much of this propaganda was exposed as false. German propaganda proved far less effective. Indeed, Americans who supported the German cause were increasingly stigmatized as potential traitors.

Documents seized in July 1915 revealing that German embassy officials were financing espionage in American war plants further discredited the German cause.

The Election of 1916

The war loomed large in the 1916 presidential election, in which Woodrow Wilson narrowly edged out Charles Evans Hughes to win a second term. The Democrats' campaign theme was set when their convention's keynote speaker, in describing Wilson's handling of a series of foreign crises, aroused wild applause as he ended each account with the refrain "We didn't go to war."

The Republican Hughes vacillated between criticizing Wilson for being insufficiently aggressive and rebuking him for pursuing policies that might lead to war. Some called him Charles Evasive Hughes. Hughes's major liability was an ever-more-bloodthirsty Theodore Roosevelt, who campaigned more for war than for the Republican ticket. The only difference between Wilson and the bearded Hughes, TR charged, was a shave. After the election some New York Democrats sent Roosevelt a taunting telegram of thanks: "Wilson ought to give you a Cabinet position, as you elected him, beyond doubt. . . . You made Wilson a million votes." Hughes did well among Irish-Americans and German-Americans, who considered Wilson excessively pro-British; Wilson's policies, on the other hand, won him solid support from women voters in those western states that had adopted woman suffrage.

Wilson's victory margin was fewer than 600,000 popular votes (out of more than 18 million votes cast) and a razor-thin 23 votes in the electoral college. Close as it was, the outcome revealed the strength of the American people's desire for peace as late as November 1916, five months before Wilson led the nation into war.

The United States Enters the War

Early in 1917 Germany's leaders took a fateful step: they resumed unrestricted submarine warfare. From 1914 on, a sharp debate had raged in Berlin between Chancellor Theobald von Bethmann-Hollweg, who favored limiting U-boat warfare to keep the United States neutral, and top military leaders who wanted to utilize Germany's U-boats to the maximum. As the war dragged on and a German victory seemed no nearer, Bethmann-Hollweg's position weakened. Even if the United States declared war, the generals argued, unrestricted U-boat use could bring victory before an American army reached the front. With billions in American loans already financing the Allied war effort, they further argued, a formal U.S. declaration of war meant little. The military significance of an American war declaration, said one German naval official, would be "zero, zero, zero."

Presidential Campaigning, 1916-Style

This Wilson banner, driven around New York City on a flag-bedecked truck, sums up the themes of the 1916 Democratic campaign: progressive reforms at home and avoidance of war abroad.

Representative Jeannette Rankin of Montana

A social worker, woman-suffrage advocate, and pacifist, Rankin was one of the fifty members of Congress who voted against Wilson's call for a declaration of war. Defeated in 1918, she won reelection in 1940, just in time to vote against war again.

The generals ultimately prevailed. The Germans resolved on January 9, 1917, to return to the earlier policy of unlimited U-boat attacks—a decision that would almost certainly pull the United States into the war.

Events now rushed forward with the rapidity of a torpedo speeding toward its target. Germany made its formal announcement on January 31. Three days later, Wilson broke diplomatic relations. During February and March, five American ships fell victim to U-boat assaults. On February 24 the United States learned through British intelligence of a telegram from the German foreign secretary, Alfred Zimmermann, to the German ambassador in Mexico. The cable proposed that, should the United States enter the war against Germany, a military alliance be formed among Germany, Mexico, and Japan, with Mexico promised the return of its "lost territories" of Texas, Arizona, and New Mexico.

On April 2 Wilson went before Congress with his solemn call for a declaration of war. A short but bitter debate followed. Senator Robert M. La Follette of Wisconsin gave an impassioned speech in opposition. The Senate voted 82–6 for war, and the House 373–50. Three key factors—German attacks on American shipping, U.S. economic investment in the Allied cause, and American cultural links to the Allies, especially England—had converged to draw the United States into the war.

Mobilizing at Home, Fighting in France

Compared to European nations, the United States was touched only lightly by World War I. The European states were at war for more than four years; the United States, for nineteen months. Their armies suffered casualties of 70 percent or more; the American army's casualty rate was 8 percent. The fighting left large parts of France brutally scarred; the American homeland was untouched. Nevertheless, the war marked a profound turning point in American history. Not only did it change the lives of the hundreds of thousands of young men who fought in it, but it deeply affected almost all Americans, men and women alike. As American youths struggled and died on the Western Front, the crisis of war mobilization transformed the nation's government and economy.

Raising an Army

The U.S. declaration of war in April 1917 found America's military woefully unprepared. The regular army consisted of 120,000 enlisted men, few with combat experience, plus some 80,000 recently federalized National Guardsmen. An aging officer corps dozed away the years until retirement. The last Civil War veteran in the army, Colonel John Clem (a drummer boy at the Battle of Shiloh), had retired only two years before. Enough ammunition was on hand for only two days of fighting. The War Department was a snake pit of jealous bureaucrats, one of whom hoarded twelve thousand typewriters as the war approached.

To raise an army and impose order on the War Department constituted the most immediate challenges. While the brilliant army chief of staff Peyton C. Marsh handled the latter task, Wilson's sec-

Draft Lottery, June 1917

World War I brought the first military draft to the United States since the Civil War. Nearly 10 million young men registered on the required date, June 5, 1917. They were drafted on the basis of numbers drawn from a fishbowl by blindfolded War Department officials.

retary of war, Newton D. Baker, took on the former. The fast-talking reform mayor of Cleveland, Baker was a poor administrator but a public-relations genius. The Selective Service Act of May 18, 1917, required all young men between twenty-one and thirty (later expanded to eighteen and forty-five) to register for military service. With memories of Civil War draft riots in many minds, Baker laid careful plans to make the first official draft-registration day, June 5, 1917, a "festival and patriotic occasion." To the government's relief, all went well.

Each registrant received a number, and draftees were chosen by lottery, with a blindfolded Newton D. Baker presiding. In contrast to the policy during the Civil War, local civilian draft boards rather than the military handled details of the draft. By November 1918 more than 24 million American men had registered, of whom nearly 3 million

were drafted. Volunteers and National Guardsmen swelled the total to 4.3 million.

Thanks to a precedent-breaking decision by Secretary of the Navy Josephus Daniels, eleven thousand women served in the navy in World War I, and several hundred in the marines. Although not assigned to combat duty, these women performed crucial support functions as nurses, clerical workers, and telephone operators.

The War Department's original plan called for several months of training, but some urgently needed draftees embarked for France after only a few weeks. The American Psychological Association saw this vast pool of draftees as ideal subjects for its new "IQ" (intelligence quotient) tests. Despite the army's suspicions (one general called the psychologists "mental meddlers"), thousands of draftees sweated through "intelligence" tests. From a present-day perspective, the results reveal not only the low educational level of many recruits but also the class and cultural biases of the test writers. One IQ question, for example, asked whether *mauve* was a drink, a color, a fabric, or a food. When the psychologists announced that 50 percent of the whites and 90 percent of the blacks taking the tests had scored at the "moron" level, editorial writers anxiously discussed the rising tide of imbecility supposedly sweeping the nation.

In the training camps, young men from all over America got their first taste of military discipline and, for many, their first experience of the world beyond their hometown or native farm. When not taking tests, doing calisthenics, peeling potatoes, or learning the uses of the bayonet, they watched movies, attended vaudeville shows, or read books supplied by the American Library Association. Entertainment and recreational facilities were provided by volunteer organizations coordinated by the Commission on Training Camp Activities, a War Department agency responsible for the recruits' moral welfare.

Organizing the Economy for War

The coming of war in 1917 brought not only military mobilization but also unprecedented government oversight of civilian life. For decades, reformers had called for greater governmental control of the economy, and now, under the stress of war emergency, an elaborate framework of control quickly took shape.

In 1916 Congress created an advisory body, the Council of National Defense, to oversee the government's preparedness program. In 1917 this council set up the War Industries Board (WIB) to coordinate military purchasing, fight waste, and ensure that the military's needs for weapons, equipment, and supplies were met. The WIB limped along until March 1918, when Wilson reorganized it and put Bernard Baruch in charge.

A tall South Carolinian of German-Jewish background, Baruch had made a fortune as a Wall Street stock speculator. Wilson, who much admired Baruch's practical knowledge, called him Dr. Facts. Under Dr. Facts, the WIB for a few months exercised enormous control over the industrial sector. In addition to allocating raw materials, the board established production priorities and introduced all kinds of efficiencies. As a war measure, the WIB induced companies that had been bitter competitors to standardize and coordinate their production processes to save steel, rubber, and other scarce

commodities. The standardization of bicycle manufacturing, for example, saved two thousand tons of steel. The elimination of the metal supports, called stays, from women's corsets allegedly saved enough steel for the building of two ships.

Another wartime conservation measure, daylight-saving time, was introduced by federal law in March 1918. Benjamin Franklin, in the 1770s, had originally proposed the idea of adjusting the clocks to take advantage of the longer summer daylight hours, but it took the war emergency to bring it about.

Baruch's counterpart on the agricultural front was Herbert Hoover, head of the Food Administration. Born in poverty in Iowa, Hoover had prospered as a mining engineer in Asia. He was organizing food relief in Belgium when Wilson brought him back to Washington. The Food Administration, created by Congress in August 1917, oversaw the production and allocation of food stuffs—especially wheat, meat, and sugar—to assure adequate supplies for the army as well as for the desperately food-short Allies. By Hoover's calcula-

The Home Front Gears Up for War

While Food Administration officials dreamed up clever slogans to encourage food conservation, women volunteers such as these Red Cross workers supported the war effort in a multitude of ways.

tions, in 1918 the Allies needed America to supply nearly 2 million tons of meat, 9 million tons of grain, and 1.5 million tons of sugar.

Hoover believed firmly in the voluntary approach. Like Newton D. Baker, he was a master of persuasion. A barrage of posters, magazine advertisements, and other propaganda urged Americans to conserve food. Volunteers distributed cards to millions of housewives pledging them to observe "meatless days" and "wheatless days." President Wilson pitched in by allowing a flock of sheep to be pastured on the White House lawn. Slogans such as "Serve Beans by All Means" and "Don't Let Your Horse Be More Patriotic Than You Are—Eat a Dish of Oatmeal" promoted substitutes for scarce commodities. In one Food Administration film, a young man wondering how he can help the war effort as he heaps sugar into his coffee is approached by a stern Uncle Sam, who challenges him: "Why don't you help save sugar?" The campaign was effective: sugar consumption dropped.

A key figure in the Food Administration was Harriot Stanton Blatch, a woman-suffrage leader and daughter of women's rights pioneer Elizabeth Cady Stanton. As head of the Speakers' Bureau of the Food Administration, Blatch spread the message of food conservation. She also organized the Woman's Land Army, which recruited female volunteers as replacements for male farm workers who had been drafted.

The War Industries Board and the Food Administration represented only the tip of the regulatory iceberg. Nearly five thousand government agencies supervised home-front activities during the war. The Overman Act of May 1918 gave President Wilson ultimate control of this vast tangle of federal agencies, including the Fuel Board, the Shipping Board, and the National War Labor Board, which resolved labor-management disputes that jeopardized production. When a massive railroad tie-up during the snowy winter of 1917–1918 threatened the flow of supplies to Europe, the government simply took over the system. Within a few months, the U.S. Railroad Administration, headed by Secretary of the Treasury William G. McAdoo, transformed the four hundred thousand miles of track owned by nearly three thousand competing companies into an efficient national transportation system.

American business, long a target of attack by progressive reformers, utilized the war emergency to improve its image. Corporate executives poured into Washington as consultants and advisers. Factory owners distributed prowar propaganda to their workers. Trade associations worked to mobilize the nation's productive strength behind the war.

In place of the trustbusting of a few years before, the government now waived the antitrust laws and actively encouraged industrial cooperation. The number of major corporate mergers in 1917 soared to nearly two hundred, more than twice the annual average for the immediate prewar years. Commenting in 1918 on the epidemic of "mergeritis," a magazine writer observed: "Never before has the civilized world been so committed as now to a policy of giant mergers in industry, to concentration, combination, and consolidation. . . . The war has accelerated . . . a tendency that was already irresistible. . . . Instead of punishing companies for acting in concert, the government is now in some cases forcing them to unite."

This colossal regulatory apparatus fell apart quickly when the war ended, but its influence lingered. The corporate mergers and coordination of the war years profoundly affected the future evolution of American business. And the old laissez faire suspicion of government, already much undermined, suffered further blows in 1917–1918. In the 1930s, when the nation faced a different kind of crisis, the governmental activism of World War I would be remembered.

With the AEF in France

About 2 million American soldiers went to France in 1917–1918 as members of the American Expeditionary Force (AEF) under General John J. Pershing. Ironically enough, Pershing was of German immigrant origins; his family name had originally been Pfoersching. A West Point graduate and commander of the 1916 Mexican expedition against Pancho Villa, Pershing was an iron-willed officer with a ramrod bearing, steely eyes, and trim mustache. The death of his wife and three of their four children in a San Francisco fire in 1915 had further hardened his personality.

For most young men of the AEF, the war at first seemed what Theodore Roosevelt called it: a great adventure. Most had never journeyed far from

JOIN THE
ARMY AIR SERVICE
BE AN AMERICAN EAGLE !
CONSULT YOUR LOCAL DRAFT BOARD. READ THE ILLUSTRATED
BOOKLET AT ANY RECRUITING OFFICE, OR WRITE TO THE CHIEF
SIGNAL OFFICER OF THE ARMY, WASHINGTON, D.C.

U.S. Army Air Service Recruiting Poster, 1918

Air skirmishes over the battle zone added a note of romance and derring-do to World War I, but most soldiers only watched from the mud and stench of the trenches.

home, and now they were en route to Europe! They made the voyage on crowded freighters or, for a lucky few, captured German passenger liners. Once in France, freight cars marked "HOMMES 40, CHEVAUX 8" (40 men, 8 horses) transported them to the front. Then began the routine of marching, training, becoming acquainted with the French—and waiting. The Young Men's Christian Association (YMCA), Red Cross, and Salvation Army provided recreation and a touch of home. Many young American women volunteered in these centers for servicemen.

The U.S. military conducted a massive propaganda campaign, including lectures, posters, and films, warning of the danger of venereal disease. One poster declared: "A German bullet is cleaner than a whore." When the French premier, Georges Clemenceau, wrote the Wilson administration with an offer to provide licensed houses of prostitution for the American troops (as was the custom for French soldiers), Secretary of War Baker exclaimed: "For God's sake, don't show this to the President, or he'll stop the war."

On the Western Front, aerial dogfights between German and Allied reconnaissance planes offered spectacular sideshows. The most famous of the World War I air aces, Germany's legendary "Red Baron," Manfred von Richthofen, shot down eighty British and French planes before his luck finally ran out in April 1918. In 1916 a group of American volunteers joined the French air corps as the *Lafayette Escadrille*. But although Secretary of War Baker was "thoroughly fascinated" by the recently invented airplane's military possibilities and persuaded Congress to appropriate large sums for plane construction, only thirty-seven were actually built. This was, in fact, one of the spectacular failures of the U.S. war production program.

The war would be won or lost on land and sea, however, and when the United States entered the conflict, Allied prospects looked bleak. Germany's resumption of unrestricted U-boat warfare took a horrendous toll in Allied shipping: six hundred thousand tons in March 1917, nine hundred thousand in April. A failed French offensive on the Marne that spring caused such high losses that French troops mutinied. A massive British offensive along the French-Belgian border ground to a halt near Paachendaele, Belgium, in November 1917, having gained four miles at a cost of more than 100,000 killed and wounded per mile. That same month, the Italian army suffered a disastrous defeat at Caporetto near the Austrian border, losing 275,000 prisoners.*

To make matters worse for the Allies in 1917, Russia left the war. Russia for years had been seething with discontent. Landless peasants, exploited industrial workers, university intellectuals inspired by Western liberal values, and revolutionaries inflamed by the communist ideology of Karl Marx were united in their hatred of the repressive and incompetent government of Czar Nicholas II. In March 1917 a revolutionary uprising including all these elements overthrew the czar and led to the establishment of a provisional government under the liberal Alexander Kerensky.

But the provisional government proved highly unstable as the Marxist revolutionaries maneuvered to seize power. The members of one faction of the divided revolutionary party, called bolsheviks (the Russian word for *majority*), gained the initiative in April when several top bolshevik lead-

---

*Initially neutral, Italy entered the war in 1915 on the side of the Allies.

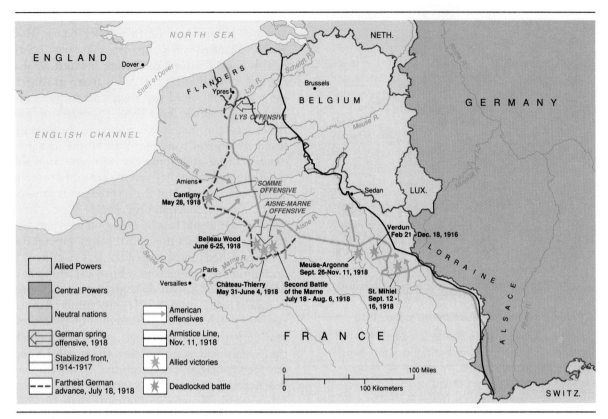

The United States on the Western Front, 1918

American troops first saw action in the campaign to throw back Germany's spring 1918 offensive in the Somme and Aisne-Marne sectors. The next heavy American engagement came that autumn as part of the Allies' Meuse-Argonne offensive that ended the war.

ers, including Vladimir Lenin, returned from exile in Switzerland. (The Germans, hoping that a victorious Lenin would take Russia out of the war, had permitted him and his party to pass through Germany in a sealed train.)

On November 6, 1917 (October 24 by the Russian calendar), a bolshevik armed coup led by Lenin and Leon Trotsky, another exiled bolshevik who had recently arrived from New York City, overthrew Kerensky and assumed control of the government. Capitalizing on the war weariness of the Russian people, the new leaders signed an armistice with Germany, which freed many thousands of German troops on the Russian front for fighting in France.

In these desperate circumstances, the French and British generals urgently wished to incorporate the Americans into already established units.

But for both military and political reasons, Pershing and his superiors in Washington insisted that the AEF be "distinct and separate." A believer in open, aggressive combat, Pershing abhorred the defensive mentality ingrained by three years of trench warfare. Further, he correctly surmised that America's voice at the peace table would be stronger if the AEF remained a distinct fighting force.

The first AEF units reached France in June 1917, but not until early 1918 did the Americans see much combat. In March Germany launched a major offensive along the Somme River, aimed at France's ports on the English Channel. When the Germans made alarming gains, the Allies created a unified command under French general Ferdinand Foch. Some American troops were thrown into the fighting around Amiens and Armentières that finally stemmed the German advance.

The second phase of Germany's powerful spring 1918 offensive came in May along the Aisne River. By the end of the month, the Germans had broken through to the Marne and faced a nearly open route to Paris, fifty miles away. The French government prepared for evacuation. At this critical moment, on June 4, American forces arrived in strength. Parts of three U.S. divisions* and a marine brigade helped stop the Germans at the town of Château-Thierry and nearby Belleau Wood, a huge German machine-gun nest.

Although both were halted, these two German offensives had punched deep holes (or *salients*, in military language) in the Allied line. A final German drive aimed at the ancient cathedral city of Rheims in the middle of the line between these two salients was stopped with the help of some eighty-five thousand American troops. This Allied rebuff represented the crucial turning point of the war. At enormous cost, the Germans' desperate effort to break the Allied line had been defeated.

Turning the Tide

The Allied counteroffensive that would end the war began on July 18, 1918. A million American soldiers were now on French soil, and 270,000 of them participated in a successful drive to push the Germans back from their advanced positions along the Marne. Rain pelted down as the Americans moved into position on the night of July 17. One wrote in his diary: "Trucks, artillery, infantry columns, cavalry, wagons, caissons, mud, MUD, utter confusion." Meanwhile, more than 100,000 AEF members joined in a renewed British offensive north of the Somme that at last expelled the Germans.

Pershing's first independent command came in September, when Foch authorized an American campaign to close a German salient around the town of St. Mihiel on the Meuse River, about 150 miles east of Paris. Welcoming this opportunity to vindicate his strategy of hard-hitting offense, Pershing assembled nearly 500,000 American and 100,000 French soldiers. Shelling of German positions began at 1:00 A.M. on September 11. Recorded

*In World War I an AEF division at full strength consisted of 27,000 men and 1,000 officers, plus 12,000 support troops. Each division was split into four infantry regiments.

an American in his diary: "It was zero hour and in one instant the entire front as far as the eye could reach in either direction was a sheet of flame, while the heavy artillery made the earth quake." Within four days the salient was closed, in part because some German units were already withdrawing when the attack began. Even so, St. Mihiel cost the United States 7,000 casualties.

The war's last great battle began on September 26, as some 1.2 million Americans joined in the struggle to drive the Germans from the Meuse River and the dense, ravine-filled Argonne Forest north of Verdun, a region scarred by four years of trench warfare. The stench of poison gas hung in the air, and bloated rats scurried in the mud, gorging on human remains.

The Allied high command assigned the AEF to advance to the city of Sedan and cut the four-track Sedan-Mezières Railroad, a major German supply route. In the way lay three long, heavily fortified German trenches, called *Stellung*. For weeks the battle raged. Teddy Roosevelt's joyous great adventure seemed far away in the Meuse-Argonne campaign. Wholesale death came in many forms, and without ceremony. Bodies, packs, rifles, photos of loved ones, and letters from home sank indiscriminately into the all-consuming mud. Adding to the horror was an influenza epidemic that took many lives on the battle front as well as in training camps and cities back home. The strain reached even the iron-willed Pershing. One day as he rode in his staff car, he buried his head in his hands and moaned his dead wife's name: "Frankie, Frankie, my God, sometimes I don't know how I can go on."

But the AEF at last overran the dreadful *Stellung*, and the survivors slogged northward. In early November the Sedan-Mezières railroad was cut. The AEF had fulfilled its assignment, at a cost of 26,277 dead.

Blacks in the AEF

More than 260,000 blacks volunteered or were drafted in World War I, and 50,000 of them went to France. Racism pervaded the military, as it did American society itself. The navy assigned blacks only to menial positions, and the marines excluded them altogether. When the war began, the army

Life at the Front

A battle-weary infantry corporal during the Argonne Forest campaign (left); a wounded Canadian being carried through the mud in the French countryside (right). Wrote Florence Bullard, working as a volunteer behind the lines: "I have had to write many sad letters to . . . mothers. I wonder if it will ever end."

hastily retired its senior black officer, Colonel Charles Young, on dubious medical grounds. Young rode on horseback from Ohio to Washington, D.C., to prove his fitness, but to no avail.

One racist senator from Mississippi, warning that the sight of "arrogant, strutting," black soldiers would trigger race riots, urged that blacks not be drafted at all. Indeed, blacks in many training camps experienced racial slurs and crude abuse. Tension reached the breaking point in Houston in August 1917, when some black members of the Twenty-fourth Infantry, endlessly goaded by local whites, seized weapons from the armory and killed seventeen whites. After a hasty trial with no opportunity for appeal, thirteen black soldiers were hanged and forty-one imprisoned for life. Not since the Brownsville Incident of 1906 (see Chapter 21) had black confidence in military justice been so shaken.

Once in France, blacks worked mainly as messboys (mealtime aides), laborers, or stevedores (ship-cargo handlers). Although reflecting a pattern of discrimination, these assignments in fact contributed significantly to the overall war effort. Working sometimes in twenty-four-hour shifts, black stevedores unloaded mountains of supplies from America with impressive efficiency.

One all-black division, the 92d, saw combat in the Meuse-Argonne. In addition, four black infantry regiments served with distinction under French command. One entire regiment (the 369th) received the French Croix de Guerre, while several hundred individual black soldiers were awarded French decorations for bravery.

The Germans showered the blacks of the 92d division with propaganda leaflets describing racism in America and urging them to cross over to the German lines, but none did. Some whites of the AEF, seeking to infect the French with their own racism, urged them to treat the blacks as inferiors. Most French people ignored this advice, however, and at least superficially treated whites and blacks the same. For black members of the AEF, this was an eye-opening experience that would remain with them when they returned home.

Promoting the War and Suppressing Dissent

After strong initial resistance to the war, patriotic fervor pervaded American society in 1917–1918. It reflected in part an elaborate government propaganda campaign to whip up enthusiasm for the war. As patriotism spread, it brought in its wake stifling intellectual conformity as well as intolerance for radical ideas and dissent of all kinds. Reflecting and even fostering this repressive spirit, governmental authorities and private vigilante groups hounded and arrested socialists, pacifists, and other dissidents and in the process trampled the basic constitutional rights of thousands.

Advertising the War

For President Wilson, the war at home was no less important than the war in France. "It is not an army we must shape and train for war, it is a nation," he declared. Underlying Wilson's rhetoric was his awareness that millions of Americans opposed the war. Indeed, immediately after Senator Lodge shook Wilson's hand so enthusiastically following the president's call for war, a thousand antiwar demonstrators besieged Lodge and his prowar congressional colleagues on the Capitol steps. One even punched the senator. The opponents of the war represented many diverse viewpoints, but collectively they posed a formidable barrier to Wilson's dream of rallying the nation behind his crusade for a new and finer world order.

Seeking initially to overcome domestic opposition by voluntary rather than coercive means, the Wilson administration drew upon the new professions of advertising and public relations to sell the war to Americans. Treasury Secretary William Gibbs McAdoo set the tone. McAdoo had married Woodrow Wilson's daughter Eleanor in 1914 and was presumed to have considerable White House influence. His penetrating eyes and sharp nose gave

him a hawklike look. One political humorist of this period wrote a whimsical poem that began: "William Gibbs, the McAdoo; He's always up and McAdooing."

McAdoo played a critical role in raising the enormous sums needed to defray the costs of the war. Including loans to the Allies, World War I cost the United States $35.5 billion—more than the government had spent in its entire first century of existence. About two-thirds of this amount was raised by a series of government bond drives, called Liberty Loans, orchestrated by McAdoo. The five Liberty Loan campaigns conducted between 1917 and 1919 succeeded phenomenally, raising more than $21 billion, or about 60 percent of the nation's war costs. As a consequence of this heavy wartime borrowing, the national debt rose from $1 billion in 1914 to nearly $27 billion in 1919.

A skilled promoter, McAdoo surrounded the Liberty Loan drives with enormous ballyhoo. Posters exhorted citizens, "FIGHT OR BUY BONDS." Monster Liberty Loan parades featured flags, banners, and marching bands. Movie stars like Douglas Fairbanks, Mary Pickford, and Charlie Chaplin worked for the cause. Schoolchildren contributed nickels and dimes for "thrift stamps" convertible into government bonds. They were inspired by a poem that began:

Hush little thrift stamp,
Don't you cry.
You'll be a war bond
By and by.

Beneath the good-natured hucksterism of McAdoo's war-bond campaigns ran an undercurrent of coercion. Only "a friend of Germany," declared the treasury secretary, would refuse to buy bonds.

The remaining one-third of the government's war costs came from the pockets of the American people in the form of higher taxes. Taking advantage of its new power to tax individual incomes granted by the Sixteenth Amendment (ratified in 1913), Congress imposed stiff wartime income taxes that rose as high as 63 percent at the top income levels. War-profits taxes, excise taxes on liquor and luxuries, and increased estate taxes also helped finance the war.

A progressive reformer and journalist named George Creel headed Washington's most effective wartime propaganda agency, the Committee on Public Information (CPI). Established in April 1917,

**Liberty Bond Rally,
New York City, 1917**

*The Wilson administration
was especially eager to persuade immigrant and ethnic
groups to support the war
effort. In this war-bond rally,
Chinese-Americans portray
(left to right) China, Miss Liberty, and Uncle Sam.*

ostensibly to combat wartime rumors by providing
authoritative information, the Creel committee in
reality functioned as a propaganda agency, tirelessly proclaiming the government's version of
reality and discrediting those who questioned that
version.

Brimming with energy and ideas, Creel set up
twenty-one separate divisions to handle different
aspects of the CPI's campaign. One division, for
example, distributed thousands of posters drawn
by leading illustrators. Still another wrote propaganda releases that appeared in the nation's newspapers as "news" with no indication of their source.
The *Saturday Evening Post* and other popular magazines published CPI ads that warned against spies,
saboteurs, and anyone who "spreads pessimistic
stories" or "cries for peace." Theaters screened CPI
propaganda films bearing such titles as *The Prus-
sian Cur* and *The Kaiser: The Beast of Berlin*.

To ensure the allegiance of recent immigrants,
who were presumed to be of dubious loyalty, the
CPI particularly targeted newcomers to America.
It poured foreign-language pamphlets into immigrant neighborhoods and supplied prowar editorials to the foreign-language press. At a CPI media
event held at Mount Vernon on July 4, 1918, an
Irish-born tenor sang "The Battle Hymn of the
Republic" while immigrants from thirty-three
nations filed reverently past George Washington's
tomb.

The CPI also targeted the working class. Factory posters refuted the socialists' charge that the
war was a capitalists' war. Creel's committee quietly financed an "American Alliance for Labor
and Democracy" headed by labor leader Samuel
Gompers.

Creel also hatched the idea of the "four minute
men": a network of seventy-five thousand speakers throughout the nation who gave short, pithy,
patriotic talks to audiences of all kinds on topics
assigned by the CPI. Creel later calculated that this
small army of propagandists delivered 7.5 million
speeches to audiences totaling 314 million.

Intellectuals, Cultural Leaders, and Reformers Present Arms

The nation's teachers, writers, religious leaders, and
magazine editors overwhelmingly supported the
war. These custodians of culture saw the conflict
as a struggle to defend threatened values and standards. Historians composed learned essays contrasting Germany's malignant power and glorification of brute force with the Allies' loftier, more
civilized ideals. Novelist Robert Herrick expressed
hope that the war would produce a "resurrection
of nobility" in modern life. In *The Marne* (1918),
expatriate American writer Edith Wharton expressed her love for her adopted nation, France.

The war poems of Alan Seeger enjoyed enormous popularity in wartime America. A young Harvard graduate who volunteered to fight for France in 1914 and died in action in 1916, Seeger held a romantic vision of war that many Americans longed to share. An artillery barrage was for him "the magnificent orchestra of war." The "sense of being the instrument of Destiny," wrote Seeger, represented the "supreme experience" of combat.

Many progressive reformers who had applauded Wilson's domestic program now cheered his war. The wartime climate of heightened government activism and sacrifice for the common good, they believed, would encourage further reform activity. Some of George Creel's most gifted coworkers in the Committee on Public Information were former muckraking writers. Herbert Croly, Walter Lippmann, and other progressive intellectuals associated with the *New Republic* magazine zealously supported the war. In gratitude, Wilson administration officials met regularly with the *New Republic*'s editors to brief them on the government's policies.

The most effective of these scholarly and journalistic champions of the war was John Dewey, whose ideas, as we have seen, had helped transform public education. Dewey exerted particular influence with the reform-minded younger generation. In a series of *New Republic* pieces in 1917–1918, he condemned the war's opponents. Socially engaged intellectuals, he said, must accept reality as they found it and shape it toward positive social goals, not stand aside in self-righteous isolation. The war, he went on, presented exciting "social possibilities" as an instrument for the advance of society at home and abroad. Domestically, the wartime growth of government power could be channeled to reform purposes once peace returned. Internationally, America's entry into the war could transform a crude imperialistic clash into a worldwide democratic crusade. Dewey's seductive arguments persuaded many former progressive reformers to support the war.

Wartime Intolerance and Hysteria

Responding to this drumfire of propaganda, some Americans became almost hysterical in their hatred of all things German, their hostility to aliens and dissenters, and their strident patriotism. Isolated actions by German saboteurs, including the blow-

ing up of a New Jersey munitions dump, fanned the flames. Americans of German ancestry, as well as citizens suspected of harboring pro-German sentiments, were forced to kiss the flag or recite the Pledge of Allegiance. A young woman in Canton, Ohio, was wrapped in a flag, marched to a bank, and ordered to buy a fifty-dollar war bond. In Collinsville, Illinois, a mob of five hundred lynched a German-born young man named Robert Prager in April 1918. When a jury exonerated the mob leaders, a jury member shouted: "Nobody can say we aren't loyal now." The *Washington Post*, while deploring the lynching, viewed it as evidence of "a healthful and wholesome awakening in the interior of the country."

An Iowa politician announced that "90 percent of all the men and women who teach the German language are traitors." German books vanished from libraries, towns with German names changed them, and on some restaurant menus, "liberty sandwich" and "liberty cabbage" replaced "hamburger" and "sauerkraut." A popular evangelist, Billy Sunday, proclaimed: "If you turn hell upside down you will find 'Made in Germany' stamped on the bottom."

Even the music world suffered. The Boston Symphony Orchestra dismissed its conductor, Karl Muck, for accepting a decoration from the kaiser. Leopold Stokowski of the Philadelphia Orchestra dropped German opera, songs, and contemporary orchestral music from the repertoire but asked President Wilson whether Bach, Beethoven, Mozart, and Brahms might not be retained.

The zealots of ideological conformity fell with special ferocity on war critics and radicals. A mob hauled a Cincinnati pacifist minister off to a woods and partially stripped and whipped him. Theodore Roosevelt branded antiwar senator Robert La Follette "an unhung traitor." Columbia University's president fired two antiwar professors. In Bisbee, Arizona, a vigilante mob forced twelve hundred miners who belonged to the Industrial Workers of the World onto a freight train and shipped them into the New Mexico desert without food, water, or shelter.

Opponents of the War

Despite the overheated conformist climate, a few Americans refused to support the war. Some were German-Americans with ties of memory and ancestry to the land of their forebears. Others were religious pacifists, including Quakers, Mennonites, and members of other historic peace churches. Of the more than sixty-five thousand young men who registered as conscientious objectors, twenty-one thousand were drafted. The army assigned most of these to "noncombatant" duty on military bases, such as cleaning latrines. In some camps these COs experienced great abuse. When two Hutterite brothers who had refused to wear military uniforms died in prison, their bodies were dressed in uniforms before they were shipped home.

Jane Addams, a founder of the Woman's Peace party in 1915, remained a pacifist throughout the war and thereby alienated many of her friends and reform colleagues. (She did, however, lecture for Harriot Stanton Blatch's Food Administration Speakers' Bureau, because she viewed increased food production as a means of aiding the war's innocent victims.) In *Peace and Bread in Time of War* (1922), Addams described the loneliness and ostracism that she experienced during the war as a result of her unpopular pacifist stance.

Woodrow Wilson heaped scorn on the pacifists. "What I am opposed to is not [their] feeling ..., but their stupidity," he told a labor audience in November 1917; "my heart is with them, but my mind has contempt for them. I want peace, but I know how to get it, and they do not."

Socialist party leaders, including Eugene V. Debs and Victor Berger, opposed the war on political grounds. They regarded it simply as a capitalist contest for world markets, with the soldiers on both sides as mere cannon fodder. The U.S. declaration of war, they insisted, reflected mainly Wall Street's desire to protect its loans to England and France.

The war produced deep fissures within the American women's movement. While some leaders like Jane Addams staunchly opposed the war, others patriotically endorsed it. Most offered at least qualified support while keeping their own goals firmly in view. Anna Howard Shaw, for example, president of the National American Woman Suffrage Association (NAWSA) from 1904 to 1915, agreed to chair the Woman's Committee of the Wartime Council of National Defense. Despite her seventy years, Shaw did her stubborn best in this largely symbolic post to bring a feminist perspective to bear on wartime policy.

Although Carrie Chapman Catt, Shaw's successor as president of NAWSA, joined Jane Addams in founding the Woman's Peace party in 1915, she supported U.S. entry into the war in 1917, sharing to some extent Wilson's vision of a more liberal postwar world order. But Catt continued throughout the war to direct her primary energies to the suffrage cause, insisting that this remained NAWSA's "number one war job." For this refusal to shelve the suffrage issue for the duration of the war, she was accused of disloyalty.

One of the fifty votes against Wilson's call for a declaration of war in the House of Representatives was cast by the committed pacifist Jeannette Rankin of Montana, the first woman elected to Congress. "I want to stand by my country," she declared in an emotional speech on the House floor, "but I cannot vote for war." The war's most incisive critic was Randolph Bourne, a young journalist. Although Bourne much admired John Dewey, he emphatically rejected his hero's prowar position and dissected his arguments in penetrating essays published in 1917–1918. Like moths near a flame, Bourne said, intellectuals were mesmerized by the lure of being near the center of action and power. He dismissed as a self-serving delusion the belief that liberal reformers could direct the war to their own purposes. War took on its own terrible momentum, he wrote, and could no more be controlled by intellectuals than a rogue elephant crashing through the bush. "If the war is too strong for you to prevent," he asked, "how is it going to be weak enough for you to control and mould to your liberal purposes?"

Ultimately, Dewey, Lippmann, and other prowar intellectuals came to agree with Bourne. By 1919 Dewey conceded that the war, far from promoting liberalism, had unleashed the most reactionary and intolerant forces in the nation. Randolph Bourne did not live to see his vindication, however. He died, at thirty-two, in the influenza epidemic that ravaged the nation in 1918–1919.

Suppressing Dissent by Law

Wartime intolerance also found expression in federal laws and in the actions of top government officials. The Espionage Act of June 1917 prescribed fines of up to ten thousand dollars and prison sentences of up to twenty years for a variety of loosely defined antiwar activities. The even more severe Sedition Amendment to the Espionage Act (May 1918) imposed heavy penalties on anyone convicted of using "disloyal, profane, scurrilous, or abusive language" about the government, the Constitution, the flag, or the military.

Wilson's reactionary attorney general, Thomas W. Gregory of Texas, employed these measures to stamp out dissent. Opponents of the war, proclaimed Gregory, should expect no mercy "from an outraged people and an avenging government." Under this sweeping legislation and similar state laws, the authorities arrested some fifteen hundred pacifists, socialists, and others whose only crime was to speak or write against the war. One socialist, Rose Pastor Stokes, found herself facing ten years behind bars (the sentence was later commuted) for telling an audience of women: "I am for the people, and the government is for the profiteers." Kate Richards O'Hare, a midwestern socialist organizer, served more than a year in prison for allegedly telling a small audience in Bowman, North Dakota: "The women of the United States are nothing more than brood sows, to raise children to get into the army and be made into fertilizer." (O'Hare denied having used these words, though she readily admitted to delivering antiwar lectures from coast to coast.) Eugene V. Debs was arrested in Cleveland and sentenced to ten years in a federal penitentiary for a non-inflammatory speech discussing the economic causes of war.

The Espionage Act also authorized the postmaster general to bar from the mail a wide variety of suspect material—a provision enthusiastically enforced by Wilson's postmaster general, Albert S. Burleson, a pompous, radical-hating superpatriot. Burleson suppressed a number of socialist periodicals. In January 1919 Congressman-elect Victor Berger received a twenty-year prison sentence (later set aside by the Supreme Court) and was denied his seat in the House of Representatives for publishing antiwar articles in his socialist newspaper, the *Milwaukee Leader*. According to socialist Norman Thomas, Burleson "didn't know socialism from rheumatism," but he blundered ahead with his one-man crusade.

A few citizens protested these actions. Muckraking journalist Upton Sinclair wrote to President Wilson to deplore that a man of Burleson's "pitiful and childish ignorance" should wield such power; but Wilson did little to restrain either his postmaster general or his attorney general. Nor did the U.S. Supreme Court. In three 1919 decisions, the Court upheld the Espionage Act convictions of per-

sons who had spoken out against the war. In one, *Schenck* v. *United States*, Justice Oliver Wendell Holmes, Jr., declared such repression justified when the exercise of the constitutional right of free speech posed a "clear and present danger" to the nation. In another decision, the Supreme Court upheld the conviction of Eugene V. Debs under the Espionage Act. Although the war was over, a vindictive Woodrow Wilson refused to commute Debs's sentence.*

The wartime mood, originally one of idealism and high resolve, had degenerated into fearful suspicion, narrow ideological conformity, and persecution of those who failed to meet the zealots' notions of "100 percent Americanism." The effects of this ugly wartime climate would linger long after the armistice was signed.

Economic and Social Trends in Wartime America

All wars bring unanticipated economic and social changes, and World War I proved no exception. The war affected the lives of millions of industrial workers, farmers, women, and blacks in important ways. The wartime mood also gave a significant boost to the moral-reform movement in American life.

Boom Times in Industry and Agriculture

For all its horrendous toll on the fighting front, World War I brought glowing prosperity to the American economy. Factory production in 1918 surged to a level more than one-third higher than in 1914. Despite the mobilization of several million young men into the military service, the civilian work force grew by 1.3 million from 1916 to 1918, including many women and blacks, and unemployment practically vanished. The "Help Wanted" signs appeared with the greatest frequency in war-related industries such as shipbuilding, munitions, steel, and textiles. Wages rose as

---

*President Warren Harding at last released the aging Debs in December 1921, but his rights as a U.S. citizen were not restored.

well, but for many workers not much faster than prices, which soared by 60 percent during the war. With manual labor in particular demand in factories and mills, however, the real wages of *unskilled* workers increased by nearly 20 percent from 1914 to 1918.

A no-strike rule prevailed in American industry during the war. Samuel Gompers, head of the American Federation of Labor and a strong supporter of the war, ordered AFL workers to stay on the job for the duration. The National War Labor Board also forbade strikes. (Some maverick AFL locals, as well as members of the more radical Industrial Workers of the World, ignored Gompers and went on strike anyway.) Even if the ban on strikes hampered unions, union membership rose significantly during these years, from 2.7 million in 1916 to more than 5 million by 1920. In part, this growth reflected the pro-union policies of the National War Labor Board, which guaranteed workers' right to organize and to bargain collectively with management. This federal agency also pressured war plants to introduce the eight-hour day, which by the war's end became the standard in American industry.

The booming wartime economy brought social disruption as well as prosperity. The stream of job seekers pouring into industrial centers strained housing, schools, and municipal services to the limit (see "A Place in Time"). The changes in social behavior during this period took many forms. For example, the consumption of cigarettes, which soldiers and workers could conveniently carry in their uniform pockets, increased nearly 350 percent, from 14 billion in 1914 to 48 billion in 1918. Automobile production quadrupled, from 460,000 in 1914 to 1.8 million in 1917. (The production of cars dipped briefly in 1918, when the government appropriated extra steel for military production.)

American agriculture profited, too. With European farm production disrupted by the war, U.S. agricultural prices more than doubled in 1913–1918, and farmers' real income rose significantly. Planters who sold cotton for 12¢ a pound in 1913 received 29¢ a pound by 1918. Corn prices soared from 70¢ a bushel to $1.52 a bushel in the same five-year period.

In the long run, this agricultural boom proved a mixed blessing. Many farmers borrowed heavily to expand wartime production, and when the artificially high prices of agricultural commodities col-lapsed after the return of peace, they found themselves in a credit squeeze. During the long years of agricultural depression in the 1920s and 1930s, many farmers would look back to the war years as the last time of real prosperity.

Blacks Migrate Northward

The war sharply accelerated the migration of southern blacks to northern cities. An estimated half-million blacks moved northward during the war, and most of them settled in cities. Each day, fresh arrivals from the South trudged through the cavernous railroad stations of Chicago, Cleveland, Philadelphia, New York, Detroit, and Pittsburgh. Chicago's black population grew from 44,000 in 1910 to 110,000 in 1920; Cleveland's, from 8,000 to 34,000.

What lured these thousands? Above all, they came for economic opportunity. The war sharply reduced the flow of new immigrant workers from Europe, and American industry turned to the black population, still heavily southern and rural, to help take up the slack. Black newspapers like the *Chicago Defender,* widely circulated in the South, spread the word of job opportunities. Some companies sent labor agents south to recruit black workers. Alarmed at the mass exodus of blacks, certain southern cities tried to hinder these agents. Jacksonville, Florida, for example, required them to pay a $1,000 fee. Letters and word-of-mouth reports helped swell the ranks of blacks heading north. One black, newly settled near Chicago, wrote his southern relatives: "Nothing here but money, and it is not hard to get." Another letter, this one from Pittsburgh, presented a more balanced picture: "They give you big money for what you do, but they charge you big things for what you get."

The economic inducements found a ready response. To the black sharecropper mired in chronic poverty and confronting blatant racism, the prospect of a salary of three dollars a day or more, in a region where racism seemed less intense, appeared a heaven-sent opportunity. The migration grew steadily larger; by 1920, 1.5 million American blacks were working in northern factories or other urban-based jobs.

These black newcomers brought with them their social institutions—above all, the church. In the black neighborhoods of the North, hundreds of storefront "holiness" churches sprang up to meet the spiritual needs of deeply religious migrants from the South. The growing concentration of blacks in New York City laid the groundwork for the Harlem Renaissance, a black cultural flowering of the 1920s. This migration also provided new recruits for black activist organizations. Membership in the recently founded National Association for the Advancement of Colored People (NAACP) doubled in 1918–1919. A Jamaican black nationalist named Marcus Garvey saw the opportunities of this wartime migration as well. In 1916 Garvey moved his recently founded Universal Negro Improvement Association (UNIA) from Jamaica to New York City. By 1919, with branches in most northern cities, the UNIA stood poised for explosive growth in the 1920s.

Once the initial elation faded, these blacks newly arrived in northern cities often found that they had exchanged one set of problems for another. White workers resented the labor competition, and white homeowners reacted in fear and hostility as crowded black neighborhoods spilled over into surrounding areas under the sheer weight of numbers.

A bloody outbreak of violence occurred on July 2, 1917, in East St. Louis, Illinois—home to ten thousand blacks who had recently come from the South. In a well-coordinated action, a white mob torched many black homes and then shot the residents as they fled for their lives. At least thirty-nine blacks perished, including a two-year-old infant who was shot and then thrown into the doorway of a burning house.

A few weeks later, a silent march down New York's Fifth Avenue organized by the NAACP protested racist violence. The marchers carried banners bearing such slogans as: "Mother, Do Lynchers Go to Heaven?" and "Mr. President, Why Not Make AMERICA Safe for Democracy?" Despite the protests, racial enmity in northern cities, like other wartime social trends, did not end with the signing of the armistice.

Women and the War

From one perspective, World War I seems a quintessentially male experience. Male politicians and statesmen made the decisions that led to war. Male generals issued the orders that sent untold thousands of other men to their death in battle. Yet any event as vast as the war touches all of society, not

just half of it. The war affected women differently than men, but it affected them profoundly.

Women's movement leaders like Carrie Chapman Catt and Anna Howard Shaw hoped that the war would lead to equality and greater opportunity for women. In *Mobilizing Woman-Power* (1918), Harriot Stanton Blatch offered a feminist variant of Woodrow Wilson's theme: women should actively support the war, she said, in order to have a role in shaping the peace.

For a bright, brief moment, the war did indeed seem to promise dramatic gains for women. Not only did thousands of women serve directly in the military and in volunteer agencies at home and in France, but an army of women workers invaded the war plants and munitions factories. About 1

Woman Lathe Operator

In 1917–1918 the patriotic slogan "A woman's place is in the war" temporarily replaced "A woman's place is in the home." Many women took jobs in war plants or served as Red Cross or Salvation Army volunteers.

Bridgeport, Connecticut, in 1916

*E*ven before the United States went to war in April 1917, the European conflict had transformed scores of American cities. Financed in part by loans from the Morgan bank and other U.S. financial houses, war orders rolled in from London and Paris—and, more rarely, Berlin—to factories in Pittsburgh, Schenectady, Dayton, Providence, Toledo, Birmingham, and the Du Pont Corporation's munitions plants in Delaware and New Jersey.

The city of Bridgeport, Connecticut, exemplifies both the prosperity and the disruption that the outbreak of hostilities brought to many U.S. industrial centers. Founded as a Puritan settlement on Long Island Sound in 1639, the community had grown slowly and sedately. In the nineteenth century, one of Bridgeport's major claims to fame was as the home of P. T. Barnum. When the irrepressible showman died in 1891, the city turned his lavish mansion, "Iranistan," into a museum.

Bridgeport had a good harbor at the mouth of the Poquonock River, and in the nineteenth century had come mills and factories that produced everything from corsets to Singer sewing machines. In 1914 Bridgeport was a stable, quiet city of about 100,000 inhabitants, its factory district balanced by solid middle-class neighborhoods and tree-lined suburbs.

But within a few months of the onset of war in Europe, Bridgeport found itself in a maelstrom of explosive growth as old factories expanded and new ones sprouted.

Main Street in Bridgeport

The Locomobile Company doubled its work force to manufacture thousands of open-bed military trucks (contemporaries called them motor wagons). After being tested on the city's streets with heavy loads of scrap iron, the vehicles were driven to the piers of New York City for the hazardous voyage to Europe. Most of the city's war production went to the Allies—but not all. One large firm, the Bridgeport Projectile Company, secured a major contract to make shells for the Central Powers. With the initiation of the U.S. preparedness program, military contracts from Washington supplemented those from abroad. Bridgeport's Torpedo Boat Company, for example, quadrupled its capacity in 1915 to manufacture submarines for the U.S. Navy.

Among Bridgeport's largest employers before the war was the Union Metallic Cartridge Company, owned by industrialist Marcellus Hartley Dodge. With close ties to the Rockefeller family as well as to the Morgan interests, Dodge secured millions of dollars in European war contracts, and employment at his cartridge company zoomed from 2,200 to 7,000. Early in 1915 Dodge decided to expand his Remington Arms Company in Bridgeport. By early autumn contractors had erected eighteen large interconnected buildings for the manufacture of bayonets and rifles. Hordes of would-be workers lined up at Remington's gates, and for several months the company hired a new person on the average of every ten minutes. By 1916 fifteen thousand men and women were working at Remington.

A Laborer at Bridgeport's Remington Arms Company Stamping out a Bayonet

Women War Workers in the Remington Arms Plant

This sudden prosperity, coming after a business slowdown in 1914, created a boom mentality in the nation's manufacturing belt. After the war the financiers and industrialists who prospered from these military contracts would be criticized as "merchants of death." But in 1915–1916 only a few socialists and pacifists pointed out that the munitions flowing from U.S. factories were contributing to an appalling slaughter on the Western Front. The talk was only of fat payrolls and humming factories. As the news magazine *World's Work* observed in January 1916: "Bridgeport bears witness . . . that war orders pay. . . . Each man, asking his neighbor, 'How's business?' gets the hearty response, 'Never better!' "

The war boom also ushered in unexpected social changes. As fifty thousand workers, most of them single young men and women, flooded Bridgeport, the population explosion strained the city's municipal services to the limit. Half the newcomers were recent immigrants from southern and eastern Europe who introduced strange languages and unfamiliar ways into this staid Yankee town. An obsession with loyalty and security gripped the city. Workers with German-sounding names were denied employment or fired unless they could prove their patriotism to the satisfaction of company management. The two hundred armed guards patrolling the Remington plant admitted workers by special pass only.

Housing posed an urgent problem. Rents and house prices shot sky-high, and soon no accommodations were available at any price. With the factories running twenty-four hours a day, landlords would rent a room to three different tenants, who would then occupy it in eight-hour shifts. When builders put up little new housing, fearing that the war boom would not last, Remington itself erected more than eighty brick residences, as well as temporary dormitories for four thousand young female employees.

Civic and religious leaders worried about the morals of the thousands of young people who thronged the city's streets after work. The few movie theaters and other recreational centers practically burst at the seams. Remington built a gymnasium and organized amateur baseball leagues for its workers. Moralists pointed out the necessity of banning alcohol and prostitutes from wartime Bridgeport.

The sudden boom spawned a series of labor disputes. Employees in the city's other factories demanded the same high wages as the war workers, and during the summer of 1916, no fewer than fifty-five strikes broke out in Bridgeport. Eager to keep their workers happy in an intensely competitive labor market, employers quickly granted their demands. Wages went up and working hours fell. By the end of 1916, the city's major employers had all adopted the eight-hour day.

Long before Woodrow Wilson's fateful war message to Congress, the conflict in distant France had transformed an American city. As a magazine writer observed in September 1916: "In the course of a few months, a typical New England town became one of the busiest hives of war industry in America." The ghost of P. T. Barnum, roaming the halls of "Iranistan," must have marveled at what was happening to Bridgeport.

million women worked in industry in 1917–1918, helping supply the nation's bounding labor needs. They held a variety of other jobs as well, from streetcar conductors to bricklayers. "Out of . . . repression into opportunity is the meaning of the war to thousands of women," wrote Florence Thorne of the American Federation of Labor in 1917; "[w]e ought to plan boldly for a splendid world after the war."

Such hopes grew stronger as the woman-suffrage movement sped toward victory in 1917–1918 on a tide of wartime idealism. "The services of women during the supreme crisis have been of the most signal usefulness and distinction," President Wilson wrote Catt; "it is high time that part of our debt should be acknowledged." New York in 1917 passed a state woman-suffrage referendum that had been rejected two years before. Twenty-six states in 1917–1919 petitioned Congress to pass a woman-suffrage amendment to the Constitution, and in 1919, by overwhelming margins, the House and Senate did just that. The Nineteenth Amendment was ratified in 1920.

Beyond this achievement, however, hopes that the war would bring permanent betterment in women's status proved unfounded. Relatively few women actually entered the work force for the first time in 1917–1918; most simply moved from poor-paying jobs to somewhat better-paying ones. And despite women's protests and War Labor Board rulings, even in these better-paying jobs most earned less than the men they replaced.

As soon as the war ended, women lost their jobs to make room for the returning men. As the New York labor federation put it: "The same patriotism which induced women to enter industry during the war should induce them to vacate their positions after the war." Male streetcar workers in Cleveland went on strike to force women conductors off the job. Twenty women judges in New York were compelled to resign; they had simply been hired as temporary wartime help, officials informed them.

Despite the short-lived rise in employment during the war, the percentage of working women actually declined slightly from 1910 to 1920. As industrial researcher Mary Van Kleeck wrote in 1921, when "the immediate dangers" ended, traditional male attitudes toward women "came to life once more." Randolph Bourne's bleak vision

again proved prophetic. The dark underside of the war spirit—the prejudice, the intolerance, the conformism—demonstrated remarkable tenacity after the return of peace; the war's more positive side effects, such as the beginnings of sexual equality in the workplace, were far more ephemeral.

Moral Reform in Wartime

War worked wonders for the prohibition movement. Nineteen states had already gone dry by 1917, owing to the efforts of such groups as the Woman's Christian Temperance Union and the Anti-Saloon League, but the war gave a decisive boost to the cause. Capitalizing on the anti-German hysteria, prohibitionists pointed out that most of the nation's biggest breweries bore such German names as Pabst, Schlitz, and Anheuser-Busch. Beer, they hinted, was part of a German plot to undermine America's moral fiber and fighting qualities. And with Herbert Hoover preaching the gospel of food conservation, they portrayed as dangerously unpatriotic the use of grain to manufacture whiskey and gin. Secretary of War Baker prohibited the sale of liquor near military camps and even forbade soldiers in uniform to buy a drink. Thus when the Eighteenth Amendment—banning the manufacture, transportation, or sale of alcoholic beverages—passed Congress in December 1917, it was widely seen as a war measure. Ratified in 1919, the prohibition amendment went into effect on January 1, 1920.

The war also strengthened the Progressive Era antiprostitution movement and encouraged strict standards of sexual morality. The War Department closed all brothels near military bases. The government's antiprostitution campaign also targeted war workers as Congress appropriated $4 million to combat prostitution and venereal disease on the home front. Sixty Young Women's Christian Association (YWCA) lecturers toured the nation for the Commission on Training Camp Activities, warning women not to let down their moral standards during the war. "Do Your Bit to Keep Him Fit," urged one wartime pamphlet addressed to women.

In San Antonio, Texas, a major military hub, the leader of a 1918 antiprostitution meeting reflected the war mood when he declared: "We propose to fight vice and its allies with the cold steel of the law, and to drive in the steel from the point to the hilt until the law's supremacy is acknowledged." Among the red-light districts closed on military orders was New Orleans's famed Storyville. Many jazz musicians who had been performing in Storyville's brothels and clubs moved up the Mississippi, carrying their music to Memphis, St. Louis, Kansas City, and Chicago. Thus the moral reformism of World War I contributed to the diffusion of jazz northward.

The wartime ground swell of moral-reform activity convinced some that traditional codes of behavior, under heavy challenge before the war, had now been restored to dominance. One anti-prostitution crusader wrote: "Young men of today . . . are nearer perfection in conduct, morals, and ideals than any similar generation of young men in the history of the world. Their minds have been raised to ideals that would never have been attained save by the heroism of . . . the World War."

Joyous Armistice, Bitter Aftermath

In November 1918 the war that had battered Europe for more than four years at last ground to a halt. Woodrow Wilson dominated the peace conference that followed, but the ill and exhausted president failed in his most cherished objective: American membership in the League of Nations. At home, wartime racism and intolerance grew worse in 1919–1920. In the election of 1920, the electorate repudiated Wilsonianism and sent Republican Warren G. Harding to the White House.

Wilson's Fourteen Points

From the moment the United States went to war, President Wilson planned to put a "Made in America" stamp on the peace that would follow. U.S. involvement, he and his liberal supporters believed, could transform a sordid power conflict into something higher and finer—nothing less than a struggle for a new, more democratic world order. Such a vision inspired many Americans as they applauded the departing troops, and they counted on the president to translate that vision into reality.

As the nation mobilized in 1917, Wilson strove to translate his vision into specific war aims. When the Allies failed to agree on a common statement

of purpose, Wilson recruited a group of scholarly advisers called the Inquiry and proceeded on his own. The need for a clear statement of America's war objectives grew urgent after the bolsheviks seized power in Russia late in 1917 and published many of the self-serving secret treaties signed by the European powers prior to 1914.

In a fourteen-point speech to Congress in January 1918, Wilson summed up U.S. war aims. That eight of these points dealt with territorial settlements in postwar Europe reflected Wilson's general belief in self-determination and autonomy for peoples formerly dominated by the Austro-Hungarian or the Ottoman Empire. A ninth point insisted that postwar colonial disputes must be resolved in the interests of the colonial peoples as well as of the European colonial powers. The remaining five points offered Wilson's larger postwar vision: a world of free navigation, lower trade barriers, reduced armaments, openly negotiated treaties rather than secret pacts of the kind that had helped bring on war in 1914, and "a general association of nations" to assure permanent peace and resolve conflicts by negotiation rather than war. The Fourteen Points helped solidify American support for the war, especially among liberals. The objectives seemed generous and high-minded proof that the nation had gone to war not for selfish reasons but out of noble objectives. Could Wilson achieve his goals? That remained to be seen.

Armistice

With the failure of Germany's spring 1918 offensive and Allied advances in the Meuse-Argonne and elsewhere along the line, the German high command saw the handwriting on the wall. In early October they proposed to Wilson an armistice based on the Fourteen Points. The British and French hesitated, but when Wilson threatened a separate peace, they agreed in early November to make peace on the basis of the Fourteen Points. Meanwhile, political turmoil in Berlin had brought the abdication of Kaiser Wilhelm II and the proclamation of a German republic.

As dawn broke over the Forest of Compiègne on November 11, 1918, Marshal Foch and his German counterparts, seated in Foch's private railway car, signed an armistice. Word spread quickly across the lines: hostilities would cease at 11:00 A.M. An

Peace, November 1918

The joy and relief with which Americans celebrated the Armistice are reflected in the expressions of members of the 369th black infantry regiment, shown returning to New York after the war. But for some, the war's conclusion meant a time to sort out the violence of the wartime experience, as The End of the War: Starting Home, *painted by black artist and ex-soldier Horace Pippin, reveals.*

American sky ace, Captain Edward Rickenbacker, flew over the lines at precisely 11:00 A.M. and watched as the booming guns fell silent and as French, British, American, and German youths cautiously emerged and approached each other. Rockets burst over the front that night, not in anger now but in relief and celebration. Back home, cheering throngs filled the streets, many carrying hand-lettered signs. "LONG LIVE PEACE," blazed one in Chicago. "Everything for which America has fought has been accomplished," Wilson's armistice message hopefully proclaimed.

The vast AEF, so laboriously assembled in France, now disbanded, and crowded troop transports carried proud and relieved soldiers home. One returnee, artillery captain Harry S Truman of Mis-

First Lieutenant Harry S Truman

Prevented by weak eyesight from enrolling at West Point, Truman served in the Missouri National Guard and commanded an artillery batallion in France during the First World War. The experience of leadership bolstered his confidence and helped lay the groundwork for his later political career.

souri, in a letter to his fiancée, Bess Wallace, described his feelings upon entering New York Harbor:

> *Dear Bess,*
>
> *I've never seen anything that looks so good as the Liberty Lady in New York Harbor and the mayor's welcoming boat, which came down the river to meet us. You know the men have seen so much and have been in so many hard places that it takes something real to give them a thrill, but when the band on that boat played "Home Sweet Home" there were not many dry eyes. The hardest of hard-boiled cookies even had to blow his nose a time or two.*

The Versailles Peace Conference

The fighting was over, but the challenge of forging a peace treaty still remained. Determined to play a central role, Wilson made a crucial decision: he would lead the American delegation to the peace conference. This was probably a mistake. Wilson's

oratorical skills far outstripped his talent for negotiation and compromise. The strain of protracted bargaining quickly took its toll on his frail nerves and slim reserve of energy.

Wilson compounded his mistake in the selection of his fellow peace commissioners: the sole Republican was an elderly diplomat who lacked influence in his party's circles. The appointment of one or two prominent Republicans to the peace commission might have spared Wilson much future grief. A further ill omen came in the November 1918 congressional elections. Despite Wilson's plea to the electorate to strengthen his hand at the peace conference by voting Democratic, the Republicans gained control of both houses of Congress.

Nevertheless, a festive mood prevailed on December 4, 1918, as the *George Washington,* a converted German liner, steamed out of New York bearing Woodrow Wilson to Europe—the first president to cross the Atlantic while in office. Ships' whistles blared; small planes buzzed overhead; and

Woodrow Wilson in Paris, December 1918

Citizens of the victorious Allied nations greeted Wilson deliriously, but back home the Republicans had gained control of both houses of Congress, and the political climate would soon turn sharply hostile.

a jaunty Wilson waved his hat to the crowd on the docks as the gleaming vessel eased out of the harbor. The giddy mood continued when the *George Washington* arrived at the French port of Brest. In Paris shouts of "Voodrow Veelson" rang out as Wilson and the French president rode in a parade up the Champs-Élysées, the city's elegant ceremonial boulevard. When Wilson visited England, children at the dock in Dover spread flowers in his path. In Italy an exuberant local official compared his visit to the Second Coming of Jesus Christ.

The exhilaration evaporated quickly, however, when the peace conference began on January 18, 1919, at the palace of Versailles near Paris. A so-called Council of Four, comprising the Allied heads of state, dominated the proceedings: Wilson; Italy's Vittorio Orlando; the aged and cynical Georges Clemenceau of France, determined to avenge Germany's humiliating defeat of France in 1871; and David Lloyd George of Great Britain, of whom Wilson said: "He is slippery as an eel, and I never know when to count on him."

These European statesmen represented bitter, vindictive nations that had suffered horrendously in the war. Their objectives bore little relationship to Wilson's vision of a liberal peace. As Clemenceau remarked: "God gave us the Ten Commandments and we broke them. Mr. Wilson has given us the Fourteen Points. We shall see."

Debates raged as the former Allies wrangled. Orlando demanded a port for Italy on the eastern Adriatic. Japan insisted on keeping the trading rights that it had seized from the Germans in the Chinese province of Shandong (Shantung). Clemenceau was obsessed with revenge. At one point, an appalled Wilson ordered the *George Washington* to stand by and threatened to leave the conference.

Reflecting this poisonous political climate, the peace treaty signed by a sullen German delegation in Versailles's Hall of Mirrors on June 28, 1919, was harshly punitive. Germany was disarmed, stripped of its colonies, forced to admit sole blame for the war, and saddled with whopping reparation payments to the Allies.* France regained the

---

*These reparations were initially set at $56 billion, including the pensions that the Allied governments would ultimately pay their veterans, but quickly negotiated downward. When Germany stopped reparations in 1932, only $9 billion had been paid.

provinces of Alsace and Lorraine lost to Germany in 1871 and took control for fifteen years of Germany's coal-rich Saar Basin. The treaty demilitarized a thirty-mile zone of Germany along the Rhine and transferred a large section of eastern Germany to Poland. All told, Germany lost one-tenth of its population and one-eighth of its territory under the Versailles treaty. The treaty granted Japan's Shandong claims and gave Italy a slice of Austrian territory around the Brenner Pass in which lived two hundred thousand German-speaking inhabitants.

Wilson's idealistic emphasis on self-determination and democracy influenced some of the treaty's provisions. Germany's former colonies (as well as those of Turkey in the Middle East) went to the various Allies under a "mandate" or trusteeship system by which they would eventually, at least in theory, become independent. The treaty also recognized the independence of Poland; the Baltic states of Estonia, Latvia, and Lithuania (territories that Germany had seized in a harsh peace treaty with bolshevik Russia in March 1918); and two new nations carved from the wreckage of the Austro-Hungarian and Ottoman empires: Czechoslovakia and Yugoslavia.

On balance, however, the Versailles treaty proved a disaster. Not only did its provisions arouse festering resentment in Germany, but its framers made little effort to come to terms with revolutionary Russia. Indeed, even as the Versailles conference was going on, Allied troops took part in a campaign to overthrow Russia's new bolshevik government. In August 1918 a fourteen-nation Allied force had landed at various Russian ports on the Baltic and at Vladivostok in Siberia, ostensibly to protect Allied war matériel and secure the ports from German attack. But these troops were soon assisting a counterrevolutionary Russian force (including both czarists and liberal democrats) seeking to overthrow Lenin.

U.S. troops, with Wilson's approval, participated in this intervention. By the end of 1918, seven thousand AEF members who had hoped to spend the holidays at home found themselves in Siberia, where they remained until April 1920. Like nearly every political leader of his day, Woodrow Wilson was strongly anti-bolshevik. Having welcomed the liberal Russian revolution of March 1917, he viewed Lenin's October coup, and Russia's subsequent

The Victors Assemble in Paris, December 1918

Seated (left to right), Orlando of Italy, Lloyd George of Great Britain, Clemenceau of France, and Wilson.

withdrawal from the war, as a betrayal of the Allied cause and of his hopes for a liberal Russian future.

The Versailles treaty reflected this hostility. Its territorial settlements in eastern Europe were designed to keep Russia as weak as possible. Before leaving Versailles, Wilson and the other Allied leaders agreed to support a Russian military leader, Admiral Aleksandr Kolchak, who was waging what would prove to be an unsuccessful campaign against the bolsheviks. Wilson, who had earlier refused to recognize Huerta and his government of "butchers" in Mexico, now refused to recognize Lenin's communist government. (The United States did not recognize the Soviet Union until 1933.)

The Fight over the League of Nations

Exhausted by months of bargaining and dismayed by the treaty's vindictive and unsatisfactory features, Wilson increasingly focused his attention in the summer of 1919 on his one shining achievement at Versailles: the creation of a new international organization, the League of Nations. The agreement or "covenant" to establish the League, written into the peace treaty itself, engaged Wilson's deepest emotions. The League represented the highest embodiment of his vision of a liberal, harmonious, and rational world order. As he wrote his adviser Edward House: "At least, House, we are saving the Covenant, and that instrument will

work wonders, bring the blessing of peace, and then when the war psychosis has abated, it will not be difficult to settle all the disputes that baffle us now."

But within a few months, Wilson's dream would lie in shattered ruins. Warning signs had come in February 1919, when several leading Republicans, including Senator Henry Cabot Lodge, expressed serious doubts about the League, and thirty-nine senators and senators-elect signed a "round-robin" letter rejecting the League in its present form. Wilson had retorted defiantly: "You cannot dissect the Covenant from the treaty without destroying the whole vital structure."

When Wilson returned to the United States in July 1919 and submitted the Versailles treaty to the Senate for ratification, Lodge bottled it up for weeks in the Foreign Relations Committee. Furious at Lodge's tactics, and convinced that he could rally popular opinion to his cause, Wilson abruptly left Washington on September 3 for a western speaking tour. Covering more than nine thousand miles by train, Wilson defended his beloved League in thirty-seven speeches in twenty-two days. Crowds were large and friendly. People wept as Wilson described his visits to American war cemeteries in France, and they warmly cheered his vision of a world free of war.

But the grueling trip took a terrible toll, and Wilson soon reached total exhaustion. On the night of September 25, as his train chugged eastward from Pueblo, Colorado, he collapsed. "I just feel as if I am going to pieces," the president, bursting into tears, told his personal physician, Cary Grayson. The train rushed back to Washington, where Wilson suffered a devastating stroke on October 2. For a time, he lay paralyzed and near death. Despite a partial recovery, Wilson spent most of the remainder of his term in bed or in a wheelchair, a reclusive invalid, his mind clouded, his fragile emotions betraying him into vindictive actions and petulant outbursts. He broke with his adviser Edward House; refused to see the British ambassador, Sir Edward Grey; and dismissed Secretary of State Lansing, whom he accused of disloyalty. In January 1920, Grayson advised resignation on medical grounds, but Wilson refused.

Wilson's strong-willed second wife, Edith Galt, whom the president had married in December 1915, played an important and not entirely constructive role during these difficult months. The second Mrs. Wilson fiercely guarded her incapacitated husband. She and Dr. Grayson concealed his condition from the public, controlled his access to information, and decided who could see him and who could not. Cabinet members, congressional leaders, and even the vice president, Thomas R. Marshall, were kept away from the White House. When the leader of one political delegation told Mrs. Wilson that "the welfare of the country" could be affected by the delegation's meeting with the president, she snapped: "I am not thinking of the country now, I am thinking of my husband."*

Under these trying circumstances, the tragic final act of the League drama played itself out. On September 10, 1919, the Foreign Relations Committee at last reported the Versailles treaty to the Senate, but with a series of amendments. The Senate split into three groups over the League issue: Democrats who supported the League covenant without changes; Republican "Irreconcilables," led by Hiram Johnson, Robert La Follette, and Idaho's William Borah, who opposed the League completely; and Republican "Reservationists" led by

Lodge, who demanded significant modifications in the League covenant before they would support U.S. membership. The Reservationists' key objection focused on Article 10 of the covenant, which pledged each member nation to preserve the political independence and territorial integrity of all other members. This blank-check provision, the Reservationists believed, infringed on America's freedom of action in foreign affairs and specifically on Congress's constitutional right to declare war. That right must be spelled out explicitly in the League covenant, they insisted.

Had Wilson been willing to compromise, the Senate would certainly have ratified the Versailles treaty, and the United States would surely have joined the League. But the invalid president dug in his heels as his physical and emotional condition now aggravated his tendency toward rigidity. From his isolation in the White House, Wilson instructed the Democratic senators to vote against the treaty with Lodge's reservations. Although international-law specialists believed that these reservations would not significantly weaken American participation in the League of Nations, Wilson rejected them as "a knife thrust at the heart of the treaty."

Despite the positive response of audiences on Wilson's aborted western tour, the American people did not rise up in support of the League. The reactionary political mood that Wilson's own administration had helped create during the war did not encourage a grand gesture of political idealism once the war was over. As the editor of *The Nation* magazine observed, "If [Wilson] loses his great fight for humanity, it will be because he was deliberately silent when freedom of speech and the right of conscience were struck down in America."

In a key Senate vote on November 19, 1919, a combination of pro-League Democrats loyally following Wilson's instructions and anti-League Irreconcilables joined forces to defeat the Versailles treaty with Lodge's reservations. The United States would not join the League. A second vote the following March produced the same result. A president elected amid soaring popular enthusiasm in 1912, applauded when he called for war in 1917, and adulated when he arrived in Europe in 1918, lay isolated and sick, his political leadership repudiated. What should have been Woodrow Wilson's

---

*The Twenty-fifth Amendment to the Constitution, ratified in 1967, set up procedures for the orderly transfer of power to the vice president from an incapacitated president unable to perform the duties of the office.

moment of supreme triumph had turned to ashes in his grasp.

Racism and Red Scare

The wartime spirit of "100 percent Americanism" left a bitter aftertaste in the United States. The years 1919–1920 saw new racial violence and fresh antiradical hysteria.

Lynch mobs murdered seventy-six blacks in 1919, the worst toll in fifteen years. The victims included ten veterans, several of them still in uniform. Some lynchings involved almost incredible brutality and sadism. In Omaha a mob shot a black prisoner more than a thousand times, mutilated him, and hanged his body in a busy intersection.

The bloodiest violence occurred in 1919 in Chicago, where a large influx of southern blacks had pushed racial tension to a high level. On a hot July afternoon, whites at a Lake Michigan beach threw stones at a black youth swimming offshore. When he subsequently sank and drowned, word quickly flashed through the black neighborhoods. A thirteen-day reign of terror followed as white and black marauders roamed the streets and randomly attacked innocent victims. Black gangs stabbed an Italian peddler; white gangs pulled blacks from streetcars and shot or whipped them. The violence and arson left fifteen whites and twenty-three blacks dead, over five hundred injured, and more than a thousand families, mostly black, homeless.

The wartime antiradical panic, reinforced by the fear and hatred of "bolshevism" so evident at Versailles, crested in the Red Scare of 1919–1920. Such emotions deepened when a rash of 3,630 strikes, representing an accumulation of grievances, broke out in 1919. When Seattle's labor unions organized an orderly general strike early in 1919, the mayor, accusing the strikers of seeking to "duplicate the anarchy of Russia," called for federal troops. Anxiety crackled again in April, when packages mailed to various public officials proved to contain bombs. One such bomb blew off the hands of a senator's maid; another damaged the home of the U.S. attorney general.

In September 350,000 steelworkers went on strike protesting low pay and a workweek that averaged nearly seventy hours. Mill owners broke the strike by using brutally repressive tactics and by taking out newspaper ads describing the walkout as a bolshevik plot engineered by "Red agitators."

The mounting frenzy over supposed radicals soon took political form. In November 1919 the House of Representatives refused to seat prominent Milwaukee socialist Victor Berger. Berger's district promptly reelected him, but the House stood firm. The New York legislature expelled several socialist members. The Justice Department, hastily setting up a new countersubversion division under young J. Edgar Hoover, future head of the Federal Bureau of Investigation, arrested hundreds of suspected communists and radicals. In December 1919, 249 Russian-born aliens were deported to their native land aboard the USS *Buford*, nicknamed the Red Ark. One deportee was the radical Emma Goldman, whose departure deprived the birth-control movement of an important leader. The government's antiradical crusade won enthusiastic support from the American Legion, a newly founded veterans' association, as well as the National Association of Manufacturers.

On January 2, 1920, in a national dragnet coordinated by the Justice Department, federal marshals and local police in thirty-two cities raided the homes of suspected radicals and the headquarters of radical organizations. Without bothering with search warrants or arrest warrants, these authorities arrested more than 4,000 persons (of whom some 550 were eventually deported), ransacked homes and offices, and seized reams of papers and records.

These lightning raids involved gross violations of civil rights and simple decency. Marshals barged into one woman's bedroom to arrest her. In Lynn, Massachusetts, police arrested thirty-nine men and women meeting to discuss the formation of a cooperative bakery. In Boston police paraded scores of arrested persons through the streets in handcuffs and chains. On Deer Island, a prison in Boston Harbor, the arrestees were confined in crowded, unheated, and unsanitary cells.

The rabidly antiradical and politically ambitious attorney general, A. Mitchell Palmer, coordinated these "Red raids." A Quaker who had compiled a strong reform record as a member of Congress, Palmer totally succumbed to the anticommunist hysteria of the early postwar period. Defending his actions, Palmer later described the menace that he believed the nation to face in 1919:

> *The blaze of revolution was sweeping over every American institution of law and order . . . eating its way into the homes of the American workman, its sharp tongues of revolutionary heat . . . licking at the altars of the churches, leaping into the belfry of the school bell, crawling into the sacred corners of American homes, seeking to replace marriage vows with libertine laws, burning up the foundations of society.*

The more outrageous manifestations of the Red Scare faded quickly as Palmer's irrational predictions failed to materialize and attention turned to other matters. When a bomb exploded in New York City's financial district in September 1920, killing thirty-eight people, most Americans concluded that it was the work of an isolated fanatic, not further evidence of approaching revolution.

The Election of 1920

In this disturbing climate, the nation prepared for the election of 1920. Wilson, now almost totally out of touch with political reality, toyed with seeking a third term but was dissuaded. At least two cabinet members, Treasury Secretary McAdoo and Attorney General Palmer, harbored presidential aspirations. But when the Democrats convened in San Francisco, the delegates sang "How Dry I Am" (prohibition had just taken effect), halfheartedly endorsed Wilson's League position, and nominated James M. Cox, who had compiled a mildly progressive record as governor of Ohio. They chose as Cox's running mate the young assistant secretary of the navy, Franklin D. Roosevelt, who possessed a potent political name.

The confident Republicans had trouble finding a candidate. After a few hopefuls failed to secure a majority at the Republican convention in Chicago, party leaders at last turned to Senator Warren G. Harding of Ohio, an amiable politician with few discernible qualifications except availability and a lack of enemies. As one Republican leader observed candidly, if ungrammatically: "There ain't any first raters this year. . . . We got a lot of second raters, and Harding is the best of the second raters." For vice president, they chose Governor Calvin Coolidge of Massachusetts, who had stirred the nation in 1919 with an outspoken denunciation of a Boston policemen's strike.

Wilson proclaimed the election a "solemn referendum" on the League, but his prediction of a landslide victory for Cox and Roosevelt proved wildly inaccurate. The nation was spiritually drained, both by the war and by the emotional roller-coaster ride—from lofty idealism to cynical disillusionment—on which Wilson had taken it. "The bitterness toward Wilson is everywhere and deeply rooted," wrote a Democratic campaign worker; "he hasn't a friend."

Sensing the popular longing for calm, Harding promised a return to "normalcy"—no more idealistic crusades, no more cavalcades of reform. His campaign addresses were empty of content but vaguely reassuring. William McAdoo would later describe Harding's speeches as "an army of pompous phrases moving over the landscape in search of an idea." Harding himself called them "bloviations."

Harding and Coolidge piled up one of the memorable landslide victories of American political history: 16 million popular votes against 9 million for Cox and Roosevelt. Nearly a million voters, at least in part to protest the wartime repression of radicals, defiantly cast their ballots for the socialist Eugene V. Debs, then serving time in an Atlanta penitentiary cell.

The Election of 1920				
Candidates	Parties	Electoral Vote	Popular Vote	Percentage of Popular Vote
WARREN G. HARDING	Republican	404	16,143,407	60.4
James M. Cox	Democratic	127	9,130,328	34.2
Eugene V. Debs	Socialist		919,799	3.4
P. P. Christensen	Farmer-Labor		265,411	1.0

The election dashed all hope for American entry into the League of Nations. During the campaign Harding hinted about some form of "international organization," but with victory assured, he bluntly announced that the question of American membership in the League was "dead." "Let it rest in the deep grave to which it has been consigned," he added for good measure in 1923. Senator Lodge exulted that the voters had ripped "Wilsonism" up by the roots. Two decades of reform at home and idealism abroad had come to a shockingly abrupt and embittered end.

Conclusion

By conservative estimate, the First World War cost 10 million dead and 20 million wounded worldwide. Included in this staggering toll were 112,000 American dead —49,000 in battle and the rest from influenza and other diseases. For those not in uniform, the war often produced a flush of prosperity but also hardships, ranging from sugar shortages to the loss of loved ones.

The war's social, political, economic, and technological impact extended far beyond the battlefield. The conflict brought marked advances in the technology of slaughter, for example, from U-boat torpedoes and primitive aerial bombs to devilishly toxic gases and chillingly more efficient machine guns.

In some ways, the war furthered the goals of progressivism. The wartime spirit helped bring to fruition such progressive reforms as prohibition and woman suffrage, for example, and for a time significantly enlarged the government's regulatory powers over the economy. But in a larger sense, the war and its aftermath severely undermined the best side of progressivism: its commitment to social justice and its humanitarian concern for the underdog. As conformism and fear of radicalism set in, the prewar reform impulse withered. This climate of reaction intensified in 1919–1920, as an emotionally spent American people sharply repudiated Woodrow Wilson and his idealism.

The war also introduced major changes in the lives of millions of ordinary workers, farmers, blacks, and women, while enhancing the standing of social workers, psychologists, engineers, public-relations specialists, advertisers, and other professionals who contributed expertise to the cause. Internationally, the conflict propelled the United States to the center of world politics and left the nation's businesses and financial institutions poised for global expansion.

Some of these changes endured, while others were fleeting. Cumulatively, however, their effect was profound. The United States that celebrated the armistice in November 1918 was a very different society from the one that Woodrow Wilson had so solemnly summoned to war only nineteen months earlier.

CHRONOLOGY

1905 President Theodore Roosevelt mediates the Russo-Japanese War.

1906 San Francisco segregates Asian schoolchildren.

1909 Roosevelt sends the "Great White Fleet" around the world.

1912 U.S. Marines occupy Nicaragua.

1914 U.S. troops occupy Vera Cruz, Mexico.

Archduke Franz Ferdinand assassinated.

World War I begins; President Woodrow Wilson proclaims American neutrality.

Wilson protests British interception of U.S. merchant ships.

1915 U.S. Marines occupy Haiti and the Dominican Republic.

Woman's Peace party organized.

Wilson's "strict accountability" note protests German U-boat attacks.

British liner *Lusitania* sunk by German U-boat.

"U.S. preparedness" movement begins.

Germany restricts U-boat campaign.

Wilson permits U.S. bank loans to Allies.

1916 U.S. punitive expedition invades Mexico, seeking Pancho Villa.

After *Sussex* sinking, Germany pledges not to attack merchant ships without warning.

Wilson reelected president.

1917 U.S. troops withdraw from Mexico.

Germany resumes unrestricted U-boat warfare; United States breaks diplomatic relations.

United States enters the war.

Selective Service Act sets up national draft.

War Industries Board, Committee on War Information, and Food Administration created.

Espionage Act passed.

NAACP march in New York City protests antiblack riot in East St. Louis and upsurge in lynchings.

1917 Bolsheviks seize power in Russia; Russia leaves **(cont.)** the war.

New York State passes woman-suffrage referendum.

U.S. government seizes the nation's railroads.

1918 Wilson outlines Fourteen Points for peace.

Sedition Amendment to Espionage Act.

American Expeditionary Force (AEF) helps stop Germans at Château-Thierry and Belleau Wood, closes St. Mihiel salient, and plays key role in the Meuse-Argonne campaign.

Armistice signed (November 11).

1919 Eighteenth Amendment added to the Constitution.

Peace treaty, including League of Nations covenant, signed at Versailles.

Racial violence in Chicago.

Wilson suffers paralyzing stroke.

Versailles treaty, with League covenant, rejected by Senate.

1920 "Red raids" organized by Justice Department.

Nineteenth Amendment added to the Constitution.

Warren G. Harding elected president.

For Further Reading

John M. Blum, *Woodrow Wilson and the Politics of Morality* (1956). Illuminating interpretive biography emphasizing Wilson's self-destructive personality traits.

Robert H. Ferrell, *Woodrow Wilson and World War I, 1917–1921* (1985). A vigorously written critical synthesis of the latest scholarship; especially good on the peace negotiations.

Frank Freidel, *Over There: The Story of America's First Great Overseas Crusade* (1964). Excellent, readable overview of the AEF experience based on soldiers' diaries and reminiscences.

David M. Kennedy, *Over Here: The First World War and American Society* (1980). Deeply researched interpretive study of the home front during the war.

Ernest R. May, *The World War and American Isolation, 1914–1917* (1966). Standard account of the steps from neutrality to intervention, stressing the role of Germany's shifting U-boat policies.

Arno Mayer, *Politics and Diplomacy of Peacemaking: Containment and Counterrevolution* (1967). Thoughtful analysis of the making of the Versailles treaty.

Additional Bibliography

The United States in Asia and Latin America

C. S. Campbell, Jr., *Special Business Interests and the Open Door Policy* (1951); C. C. Clenenden, *The United States and Pancho Villa* (1961); H. F. Cline, *The United States and Mexico* (1953); Raymond A. Esthus, *Theodore Roosevelt and the International Rivalries* (1970); Lester E. Langley, *The Banana Wars: An Inner History of American Empire, 1900–1934* (1983); Thomas

McCormick, *China Market, 1893–1901* (1967); D. G. Munro, *Intervention and Dollar Diplomacy in the Caribbean, 1900–1921* (1964); James Reed, *The Missionary Mind and America's East Asian Policy, 1911–1915* (1983).

The Road to War and Wartime Diplomacy

John L. Gaddis, *Russia, the Soviet Union, and the United States* (1978); Lloyd C. Gardner, *Safe for Democracy: The Anglo-American Response to Revolution, 1913–1923* (1984); N. Gordon Levin, Jr., *Woodrow Wilson and World Politics: America's Response to War and Revolution* (1968); Arthur S. Link, *Wilson the Diplomatist: A Look at His Major Policies* (1965); Arno J. Mayer, *Political Origins of the New Diplomacy, 1917–1918* (1963); Walter Millis, *The Road to War* (1935); Barbara Tuchman, *The Guns of August* (1962).

The Battlefield Experience

Arthur E. Barbeau and Henri Florette, *The Unknown Soldiers: Black American Troops in World War I* (1974); Edward M. Coffman, *The War to End All Wars: The American Military Experience in World War I* (1968); Robert Jackson, *At War with the Bolsheviks: The Allied Intervention into Russia, 1917–1920* (1972); Herbert M. Mason, Jr., *The Lafayette Escadrille* (1964); Laurence Stallings, *The Doughboys: The Story of the AEF, 1917–1918* (1963); Frank E. Vandiver, *Black Jack: The Life and Times of John J. Pershing* (1977).

The Government Mobilizes for War

Daniel R. Beaver, *Newton D. Baker and the American War Effort, 1917–1919* (1966); Kathleen Burk, *Britain, America and the Sinews of War* (1985); Edward M. Coffman, *The Hilt of the Sword: The Career of Peyton C. Marsh* (1966); Robert D. Cuff, *The War Industries Board* (1973); H. A. DeWeerd, *President Wilson Fights His War* (1968); Charles Gilbert, *American Financing of World War I* (1970); Daniel J. Kevles, "Testing the Army's Intelligence: Psychologists and the Military in World War I," *Journal of American History* 55 (1968): 565–581.

American Society and Culture in World War I

Allen F. Davis, "Welfare, Reform and World War I," *American Quarterly* 19 (1967): 516–533; Charles Forcey, *The Crossroads of Liberalism* (1961); Maurine W. Greenwald, *Women, War and Work* (1980); Ellis W. Hawley, *The Great War and the Search for a Modern Order: A History of the American People and Their Institutions, 1917–1933* (1979); Florette Henri, *Black Migration: Movement Northward, 1900–1920* (1975); Frederick C. Luebke, *Bonds of Loyalty: German-Americans and World War I* (1974); David Morgan, *Suffragists and Democrats: The Politics of Woman Suffrage in America* (1972); Elliott M. Rudwick, *Race Riot at East St. Louis, July 2, 1917* (1964); Barbara J. Steinson, *American Women's Activism in World War I* (1982).

Patriotism, Dissent, and Repression

Ray H. Abrams, *Preachers Present Arms: The Role of the American Churches and Clergy in World Wars I and II* (1969); George T. Blakey, *Historians on the Homefront: American Propagandists for the Great War* (1970); Charles Chatfield, *For Peace and Justice: Pacifism in America, 1914–1941* (1971); Alfred E. Cornebise, *War as Advertised: The Four Minute Men and America's Crusade, 1917–1918* (1984); Charles DeBenedetti, *Origins of the Modern Peace Movement* (1978); Carol S. Gruber, *Mars and Minerva: World War I and the Uses of Higher Learning in America* (1975); Michael T. Isenberg, *War on Film* (1981); Donald Johnson, *The Challenge to American Freedoms: World War I and the Rise of the American Civil Liberties Union* (1963); Michael Pearlman, *To Make Democracy Safe for America: Patricians and Preparedness in the Progressive Era* (1984); Harold C. Peterson, *Propaganda for War: The Campaign Against American Neutrality, 1914–1917* (1968); Harold C. Peterson and Gilbert Fite, *Opponents of War, 1917–1918* (1968); William Preston, Jr., *Aliens and Dissenters: Federal Suppression of Radicals, 1903–1933* (1966); Stephen Vaughn, *Holding Fast the Inner Lines: Democracy, Nationalism, and the Committee on Public Information* (1980).

Aftermath: Red Scare, Failed Peace, and Disillusionment

Wesley M. Bagley, *The Road to Normalcy: The Presidential Campaign and Election of 1920* (1962); David Brody, *Labor in Crisis: The Steel Strike of 1919* (1965); Zechariah Chafee, Jr., *Free Speech in the United States* (1941); Stanley A. Coben, *A. Mitchell Palmer: Politician* (1963); Stanley Cooperman, *World War I and the American Novel* (1970); Paul Fussell, *The Great War and Modern Memory* (1975); Arno Mayer, *Politics and Diplomacy of Peacemaking* (1967); Charles L. Mee, Jr., *The End of Order: Versailles 1919* (1980); Robert K. Murray, *Red Scare: A Study in National Hysteria, 1919–1920* (1955); Stewart I. Rochester, *American Liberal Disillusionment in the Wake of World War I* (1977); Klaus Schwabe, *Woodrow Wilson, Revolutionary Germany, and Peacemaking, 1918–1919* (1985); Ralph Stone, *The Irreconcilables: The Fight Against the League of Nations* (1970); William M. Tuttle, Jr., *Race Riot: Chicago in the Red Summer of 1919* (1970); William C. Widenor, *Henry Cabot Lodge and the Search for an American Foreign Policy* (1980); David Williams, "The Bureau of Investigation and Its Critics, 1919–1921," *Journal of American History* 68 (1981–1982): 560–579.

CHAPTER 23

The 1920s

Sam Groipen of Medford, Massachusetts, was washing the windows of his little grocery store, the Cooperative Cash Market, one day in June 1928 when he saw a meat truck pull up in front of the A&P supermarket next door. Sam knew the meaning of this seemingly ordinary event: his days as an independent grocer were numbered. A Jewish immigrant who had come from Russia with his family as a sixteen-year-old in 1914, Sam had opened his market in 1923, the year that he married. At first Sam and his wife did well. Sam served the customers; his wife did the bookkeeping. They knew their patrons by name, advertised in the local newspaper, and extended credit to those short on cash.

In 1925, however, the chain-store invasion began. A&P moved in next door, then First National and Stop & Shop across the street. In the beginning the chains did not hurt Sam's business too much. Small by today's standards, they carried only brand-name groceries, not meat or fish. But when the Medford A&P added meat and fish in 1928, Sam saw the handwriting on the wall. He wracked his brain to save his declining business, and at one point put a large "MAIN ENTRANCE" sign over the door of his small shop amid a forest of super-markets. But nothing helped. He watched his former customers—some of whom still owed him money—walk past his door on their way to a supermarket. "I felt like I was being strangled," he later recalled; "those bastard chains were destroying me."

In 1935 Sam Groipen sold out. Abandoning his dream of prospering as an independent busi-nessman, he took a sales job with the giant Prudential Life Insurance Company. Looking back years later, Sam still felt bitterness toward the chains, but his resentment had soft-ened. "When I bought the store I was young and ambitious," he recalled, "but I have been mellowed by the system."

Groipen's experience paralleled that of many thousands of Americans in the 1920s. Operators of "mom and pop" businesses and other independent entrepreneurs found themselves competing with, and in many cases swallowed up by, great consolidated corporations. This economic transformation was only one of many important developments in a decade that ushered in profound changes in American society.

It was in the 1920s that the nation's vast productive capacity, resting on the solid industrial base laid down in the late nineteenth century, burst forth with a tidal wave of automobiles, radios, electrical appliances, and other consumer goods. This torrent of new products brought a glow of prosperity to the economy and far-reaching changes to the lives of ordinary Americans. The prosperity proved fragile; the changes did not. Ingrained patterns of diet, dress, housekeeping, travel, entertainment, and even thought shifted markedly as a consequence of fundamental transformations in the economic order.

These technological changes, coming on the heels of several decades of immigration and rapid urban growth, also spawned severe social tensions. While Republican presidents espoused conservative political and cultural values, deep conflicts ripped at the fabric of society. But this same ferment also stimulated remarkable creativity in literature and the arts.

When the decade ended, Americans tried to sum up in a phrase their kaleidoscopic memories of these turbulent and change-filled years: they called them the Roaring Twenties.

A New Economic Order

Fueled by new consumer products, sophisticated advertising, and innovative forms of corporate organization, the economy surged ahead in the 1920s. But not everyone benefited. Key industries declined, workers lost jobs as factories were automated, and farmers suffered chronic economic troubles. Nevertheless, the overall picture seemed rosy, and the majority of Americans celebrated a thriving business culture.

A Decade of Prosperity

The war-induced boom continued until late 1920, when the rush of demobilization seriously disrupted the economy. As the government abruptly canceled contracts, and returning veterans swamped labor markets, a sharp recession struck. Consumers welcomed falling prices, but the recession's other effects hurt badly. Business activity slowed, bankruptcies increased, and unemployment jumped. Recovery came in 1922 with a boom in consumer-goods production, however, and for the next few years, the economy grew spectacularly. Unemployment declined to as low as 3 percent, prices held steady, and the gross national product climbed from about $70 billion in 1922 to nearly $100 billion in 1929. By mid-decade the 1920–1922 recession seemed only a minor setback.

An array of new consumer goods, including a wealth of home electrical products, contributed to

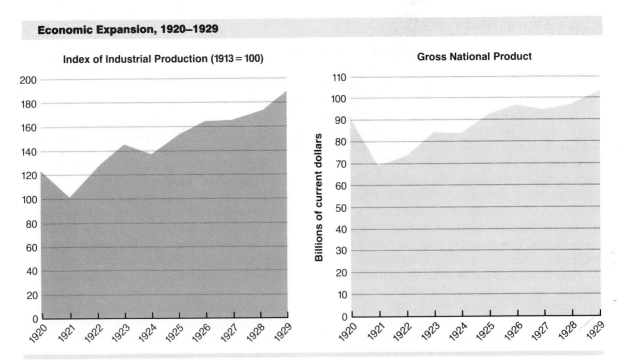

Economic Expansion, 1920–1929

After a brief postwar downturn, the American economy surged in the 1920s.

SOURCES: U.S. Department of Commerce, *Long-Term Economic Growth* (Washington, D.C.: U.S. Government Printing Office, October 1966), 169, and R. E. Lipsey, *Price and Quantity Trends in the Foreign Trade of the United States* (Princeton, N.J.: Princeton University Press, 1963), 424.

the general prosperity. Factories had started to electrify in the late nineteenth century; and with the construction of hydroelectric generating plants at Niagara Falls and elsewhere in the early twentieth century, the age of electricity dawned for urban American households as well. By the mid-1920s, with more than 60 percent of the nation's homes wired for electric power, a mind-boggling parade of electrical appliances, from refrigerators, ranges, washing machines, and vacuum cleaners to fans, razors, and mixers, stood gleaming in the stores. The annual production of refrigerators, which reached only about twenty-five hundred in 1920, surged to nearly half a million by 1928. The manufacture of such appliances, as well as of heavy-duty equipment for the electrical industry itself, provided a massive economic stimulus.

The 1920s business boom rested, too, on the automobile. At first a plaything of the rich, the automobile had started to reach a larger market even before the war. As early as 1904, Ransom E. Olds had sold five thousand of his sporty Oldsmobiles for $650 each. Henry Ford of Detroit, who had built his first prototype automobile in 1896, introduced the low-priced Model T in 1908; by 1916 seven hundred thousand had been sold.

But it was in the 1920s that the automobile came into its own. Total passenger-car registrations jumped from about 8 million in 1920 to more than 23 million in 1930. Ford led the market until middecade, when a reorganized General Motors Corporation spurted ahead by touting a range of colors (the Model T came only in black) and improved passenger comfort in its models. GM's lowest-priced car, named for French automotive designer Louis Chevrolet, proved especially popular. Responding to the challenge, Ford in 1927 introduced the stylish Model A in a variety of colors. By the end of the decade, the automobile industry accounted for about 9 percent of all wages in manufacturing and had stimulated such related industries as rubber, gasoline and petroleum, advertising, and highway construction.

In this growth-oriented business climate, American capitalism was vigorously expansionist. To supply their overseas markets more efficiently, Ford, General Motors, General Electric, and other big corporations not only expanded at home but also invested heavily in production facilities abroad. Other American firms acquired foreign processing facilities or sources of raw materials. Swift, Armour,

and other U.S. meatpackers built packing plants in Argentina; Anaconda Copper acquired Chile's biggest copper mine; and the mammoth United Fruit Company established processing factories throughout Latin America. By 1930 U.S. private investment abroad totaled over $15 billion.

New Modes of Producing, Managing, and Selling

Building on the industrial feats of the war years, the 1920s saw remarkable increases in productivity. Thanks to new assembly-line techniques of mass production, the per capita output of industrial workers grew by some 40 percent during this decade. At the sprawling Ford plants near Detroit, for example, workers stood in one place and performed simple, repetitive tasks as an endless chain conveyed the partly assembled vehicles past them. Engines and other components entered the final line from their own separate assembly lines.

Assembly-line production quickly spread. *Fordism* became a synonym worldwide for American industrial prowess. In the Soviet Union, which purchased twenty-five thousand Ford tractors in the 1920s, the people "ascribed a magical quality to the name of Ford," a 1927 visitor reported.

Prosperity and mass production stimulated a wave of corporate mergers rivaling that of the turn of the century. The war had spurred corporate consolidation, and this process continued in the 1920s. By the end of the decade, over a thousand companies a year disappeared through merger. A few corporate giants dominated the major industries: Ford, GM, and Chrysler in automobiles; GE and Westinghouse in electricity; U.S. Steel in the steel industry. In the public-utilities field, consolidation reached epidemic proportions. Samuel Insull of the Chicago Edison Company, for example, built an empire of local power companies that by 1929 had assets of $3.5 billion. By the end of the decade, one hundred corporations controlled nearly half the nation's business activity.

Merger mania was only one expression of the search for a more integrated corporate order adapted to the new economic era. Even when corporations did not actually merge, different companies that made the same product would often cooperate through trade associations on such matters as pricing, standardized specifications, and division of markets.

A Standard Oil Station in New Jersey, 1927

While the woman driver chats with friends on a rainy day, the attendant manually pumps the gasoline into the tank.

This effort by American capitalism to streamline its operations also led to the introduction of a more bureaucratic management structure within individual businesses. A few corporate leaders, to be sure, perpetuated the individualistic management style characteristic of the nineteenth century. Henry Ford, for example, ruled his company autocratically, mercilessly bullying his subordinates, including his own son Edsel, and making decisions largely by impulse. But this pattern was atypical. Like the federal government and many professional societies, corporations bureaucratized their management in the twenties. They set up specialized divisions, each with its own team of managers, with responsibility for such varied spheres as product development, market research, economic forecasting, and employee relations. The day-to-day oversight of this new corporate structure increasingly fell to professionals trained in the techniques of management.

The modernization of American business in the 1920s affected wage policies as well as production and organization. Rejecting the conventional economic wisdom, many "enlightened" business leaders began to argue that employers should not necessarily pay the lowest wages possible; higher wages, they suggested, would generate higher productivity. Henry Ford led the way in 1914 by paying his workers an unprecedented five dollars a day, and other companies followed his lead in the 1920s.

New systems for the mass distribution of goods emerged as well. Automobiles reached consumers through vast dealer networks. By 1926 the number of Ford dealerships approached ten thousand. Manufacturers pressured dealers to sell a specified quota of cars. As one ex–Ford dealer confessed in 1927: "There are always some people that you can sell anything to if you hammer them hard enough." Moreover, a rapidly expanding network of chain stores accounted for about a quarter of all retail sales by 1930. The spread of the automobile encouraged some family businesses such as roadside diners and tourist cabins, but in general, small, locally owned businesses like Sam Groipen's grocery store faded under relentless pressure from the chains. The A&P grocery chain expanded from 5,000 stores in 1922 to 17,500 in 1928. And installment buying represented another important mass-marketing innovation. By the end of the 1920s, credit purchases accounted for 75 percent of automobile sales.

Above all, the 1920s business boom bobbed along on a frothy sea of advertising. In 1929 corporations spent an estimated $1.8 billion promoting their wares, and the advertising business employed some six hundred thousand people. Radio, the newest of the mass media, relied entirely on advertising for its income.

The barons of the advertising business stood high among the corporate elite of the 1920s. Chicago advertising executive Albert Lasker owned

Merchandising, 1920s-Style

Evoking a world of elegance and sophistication, post–World War I advertisers offered a seductive vision of a new era of consumer abundance and material well-being.

the Chicago Cubs baseball team as well as his own eighteen-hole golf course. As early as 1918, Lasker's fame was such that Theodore Roosevelt invited him for a visit. ("Mr. Lasker, they tell me you are America's greatest advertising man," said the ex-president. "Colonel," replied Lasker, "no man can claim that distinction so long as you are alive.")

Like their counterparts today, the advertisers of the twenties used celebrity endorsements ("Nine out of ten screen stars care for their skin with Lux toilet soap"), promises of social success, and threats of social embarrassment. The fear strategy was employed with enormous effectiveness in the ads for Listerine mouthwash. Beneath a picture of a pretty but obviously unhappy young woman, for example, a 1923 Listerine ad proclaimed:

She was a beautiful girl and talented too. She had the advantages of education and better clothes than most girls of her set. She possessed that culture and poise that travel brings. Yet in the one pursuit that stands foremost in the mind of every girl and woman—marriage—she was a failure.

The young woman's problem, the ad made clear, was *halitosis,* a hitherto little-known term for bad breath. The remedy, of course, was Listerine, and lots of it.

A leading advertising copywriter of the 1920s was Helen Resor of New York's big J. Walter

Thompson Agency. Having worked her way up in a male-dominated business, Resor specialized in advertising copy directed to women. Her most famous slogan promoted Woodbury soap: "For the Skin You Love to Touch."

Beyond touting specific products, advertisers redefined popular aspiration by offering a seductive vision of a new era of consumption. Ads for automobiles, cigarettes, electrical conveniences, clothing, and home furnishings created a fantasy world of elegance, grace, and boundless pleasure. Enticing Americans to partake of the technological abundance, advertisers aroused desires that the new consumer-oriented capitalist system happily fulfilled. As one critic wrote in 1925:

[W]hen all is said and done, advertising . . . creates a dream world: smiling faces, shining teeth, school girl complexions, cornless feet, perfect fitting [underwear], distinguished collars, wrinkleless pants, odorless breath, regularized bowels, . . . charging motors, punctureless tires, perfect busts, shimmering shanks, self-washing dishes—backs behind which the moon was meant to rise.

Business influence in the 1920s extended far beyond the factory and the advertising pages; in fact, it saturated all areas of life. A 1921 article in *Independent* magazine summed up the prevailing mood: "Among the nations of the earth today

America stands for one idea: Business. . . . Thru business, properly conceived, managed, and conducted, the human race is finally to be redeemed."

Postwar America venerated the magnates of business and the new world of material comfort that they had created. Presidents Harding and Coolidge lauded business values and hobnobbed with businessmen. Magazines published admiring profiles of corporate leaders. A 1923 public-opinion poll placed Henry Ford far ahead of Warren Harding as a 1924 presidential prospect. In *The Man Nobody Knows* (1925), advertising executive Bruce Barton, son of a Protestant minister, described Jesus Christ as managerial genius who "picked up twelve men from the bottom ranks of business and forged them into an organization that conquered the world." Rarely have business standards and values so thoroughly pervaded American life. In *Middletown*, a study of Muncie, Indiana, published in 1929, sociologists Robert and Helen Lynd observed: "More and more of the activities of life are coming to be strained through the bars of the dollar sign."

Women in the New Economic Era

The lives of American women, as we shall see, were profoundly affected by the new electrical appliances, the automobile, and the other technological wonders of the 1920s. And clearly, too, women loomed large in the decade's ubiquitous advertising. In the ads glamorous women smiled behind the steering wheel, happily operated electric appliances, smoked cigarettes in romantic settings, and vacationed in exotic resorts. One resourceful ad man promoted cigarettes for women as "torches of freedom." In the advertisers' dream world, housework became an endlessly exciting technological challenge. As one ad put it: "Men are judged successful according to their power to delegate work. Similarly the wise woman delegates to electricity all that electricity can do."

But what of women in the workplace? The rise of the assembly line, offering work that was physically less demanding than many other forms of manual labor, theoretically should have increased job opportunities for women, but in fact, the work force in the automobile plants and other assembly-line factories remained overwhelmingly male. While the number of women holding jobs increased by more than 2 million in the 1920s, the *proportion* of women working outside the home continued essentially unchanged, hovering at about 24 percent.

When women did find work in industry, they sometimes faced wage discrimination. In 1929, for example, a male trimmer in the meatpacking

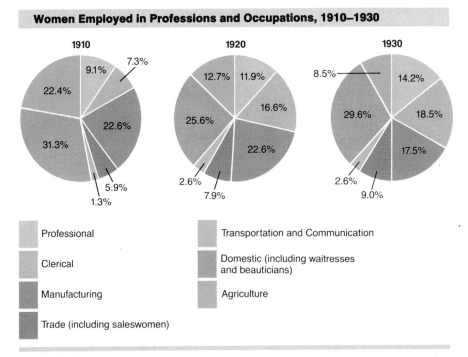

Women Employed in Professions and Occupations, 1910–1930

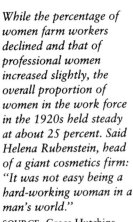

While the percentage of women farm workers declined and that of professional women increased slightly, the overall proportion of women in the work force in the 1920s held steady at about 25 percent. Said Helena Rubenstein, head of a giant cosmetics firm: "It was not easy being a hard-working woman in a man's world."

SOURCE: Grace Hutchins, *Women Who Work* (New York: International, 1934), 24.

industry received fifty-two cents an hour, a female trimmer, thirty-seven cents an hour. Even more pervasive was job segregation. Reflecting the widespread view that women were in the labor market for only a temporary period prior to marriage, employers relegated most women workers to low-paying piece-rate jobs.

The bureaucratization of business enlarged female employment opportunities somewhat. By 1930 some 2 million women had become secretaries, typists, or filing clerks. Very few women gained admission to capitalism's managerial ranks, however. Women like Helena Rubenstein, founder and head of a successful cosmetics empire, were exceptional. In the professions women rarely broke out of the strictly circumscribed spheres of nursing, librarianship, social work, and public-school teaching. With medical schools imposing a 5 percent quota on female admissions, the number of women physicians actually declined from 1910 to 1930.

Organized Labor in a Business Age

The labor movement faced tough sledding in the twenties. Very few women workers were unionized, and even among male workers, the statistics reflected organized labor's ebbing strength. Union membership declined from 5 million in 1920 to 3.4 million in 1929. Several factors underlay this decline. For one thing, overall wage rates moved steadily upward in the 1920s. In the steel industry, for example, real hourly wages rose about 17 percent from 1923 to 1929. The overall statistics on wage increases conceal many inequities and regional variations, but the prevailing pattern of fatter pay envelopes helped undermine the union movement.

Changes in the industrial process figured importantly as well. The trade unions' traditional strength lay in old, established industries like printing, railroading, coal mining, and the building trades. This older craft-based pattern of union organization was ill suited to the new mass-production industries.

The weakening of organized labor resulted also from management hostility. Sometimes this hostility took physical form. Henry Ford hired thugs and spies to intimidate would-be union organizers. In Marion, North Carolina, deputy sheriffs shot and killed six striking textile workers. The depu-

ties were acquitted, but a union organizer went to jail.

More typically, however, the anti-union campaign took subtler forms. Manufacturers' associations renamed the non-union shop the "open shop" and praised it as the "American Plan" of labor relations. Some firms set up company-sponsored employee associations and, in consultation with these groups, provided such benefits as cafeterias, better rest rooms, and recreational facilities. A few big corporations such as U.S. Steel and Standard Oil offered their workers company stock at special prices.

Some corporate leaders treated this new approach to labor relations as evidence of a heightened ethical awareness in American business. For example, the head of General Electric in the 1920s, Gerard Swope, insisted that workers' well-being stood next only to productivity in GE's hierarchy of values. "Welfare capitalism," a phrase sometimes used to describe this form of corporate paternalism, was clearly motivated in part by the desire to prevent the formation of independent unions with real clout.

Black membership in labor unions by the end of the 1920s stood at only about eighty-two thousand—mostly longshoremen, mine workers, and railroad porters. The American Federation of Labor officially prohibited racial discrimination, but in fact, the independent unions that made up the AFL discriminated against blacks in many ways. Some had clauses in their constitutions limiting membership to whites; others simply followed a de facto exclusionary policy. Corporations often hired blacks as strikebreakers, and this increased organized labor's hostility toward them. Black strikebreakers, denounced as "scabs," took such work out of dire need. As a jobless black character says in Claude McKay's 1929 novel *Home to Harlem*: "I got to live, and I'll scab through hell to live."

Had the climate been more favorable, a vast pool of workers would have been prime candidates for unionization. Amid the general prosperity, many industrial workers actually did not prosper at all. While overall wage rates increased, those of unskilled workers barely budged. Concluded one labor economist: "The failure of the unskilled to share in the general advance . . . is indeed startling."

Of the regional variations that skewed the wage picture, the most dramatic was that between North and South. In 1928, for example, the average

Railroad Employees of the 1920s

The Brotherhood of Sleeping Car Porters was one of the few unions with black members in a decade when the American workplace was strictly segregated along racial lines.

unskilled laborer in New England earned forty-seven cents an hour, while a person performing the same labor in the South received twenty-eight cents an hour. By the 1920s the growth of the southern textile industry finally forced the New England mills into active retreat. Many historic mill towns were devastated.

Not only women but also blacks, Mexican-Americans, and recent immigrants from southern and eastern Europe clustered at the bottom of the wage scale. Black workers, many of them recent migrants from the South entering the industrial labor force for the first time, faced special difficulties. The last hired and the first fired, they performed the most menial jobs and almost never held supervisory positions.

Agriculture: The Economy's Ailing Sector

Agriculture had prospered during the war, but in 1920 came the bitter aftermath. Prices of wheat, corn, and hay plummeted by 50 percent and more as the government's heavy wartime purchases for the army dwindled and as European agriculture revived. Between 1919 and 1921, farm income fell from $10 billion to just over $4 billion. When farmers tried to compensate for low prices by increasing production, large surpluses and still lower prices resulted. Farmers who had borrowed heavily to buy land and equipment during the war now felt the squeeze as loans and mortgage payments came due. Banking suffered, too, as farmers defaulted.

The major farm organizations, including the American Farm Bureau Federation (1920), turned to Washington for help. The farm groups backed a complicated price-support plan under which the government would annually purchase the surplus of six basic farm commodities—cotton, corn, rice, hogs, tobacco, and wheat—at the average price that these commodities had brought in 1909–1914 (when farm prices were high) and then sell these surpluses on the world market at prevailing prices. The government would make up the resulting losses through a tax, called an equalization fee, on domestic sales of these commodities—a tax that consumers would ultimately have paid in the form of higher food prices.

Backed by Secretary of Agriculture Wallace and a group of legislators known as the farm bloc, this plan was introduced in 1924 as the McNary-Haugen bill, so named for the chairmen of the House and Senate agricultural committees. After successive defeats in 1924 and 1926, the bill passed in 1927, but President Calvin Coolidge vetoed it. Repassed in 1928, the bill again died after another presidential veto.

Republicans in Power

Politics in the 1920s reflected the decade's business orientation. The Republican party controlled Congress and supplied two presidents who perfectly mirrored the prevailing cultural mood. In this climate former progressives and feminists faced difficult times.

Scandals and Silences: The Harding and Coolidge Years

The dominant Republican party continued in the 1920s to rely on its base of northern farmers, corporate leaders, small businesspersons, and some skilled workers. The Democrats, lacking a strong national organization, drew their votes mainly from the white South and the political machines of the immigrant cities.

With Republican progressives in the doghouse for having bolted to Theodore Roosevelt in 1912, party conservatives controlled the 1920 Republican convention. As presidential candidate, they settled upon Senator Warren Harding of Ohio. In 1891, struggling as editor of a failing newspaper, Harding had married the local banker's daughter, Florence Kling, and with her prodding launched the political career that brought him to the Senate in 1915. A genial backslapper largely unknown nationally, the floridly handsome Harding enjoyed good liquor, good stories, poker with his cronies, and occasional furtive encounters with his mistress, Nan Britton.

Yet this amiable second-rater won the presidency in a landslide, overwhelming his Democratic opponent and fellow Ohioan James M. Cox (see Chapter 22). Harding's very ordinariness appealed to voters longing for a return to familiar ways after the ordeal of war. Compared to Wilson's lofty sermons, even Harding's vacuous oratory had a certain soothing appeal.

Realizing his lack of qualifications, Harding in partial compensation made some notable cabinet appointments: Henry A. Wallace, the respected editor of an Iowa farm periodical, became secretary of agriculture; Charles Evans Hughes, former New York governor and 1916 presidential candidate, secretary of state; and Andrew W. Mellon, a prominent Pittsburgh banker and financier, treasury secretary. Herbert Hoover, the wartime food administrator, dominated the cabinet as secretary of commerce.

Unfortunately, Harding also made some disastrous appointments that returned to haunt him: his political manager, Harry M. Daugherty, as attorney general; a Senate pal, Albert B. Fall of

New Mexico, as secretary of the interior; and a wartime draft dodger whom Harding had met in Hawaii, Charles Forbes, as director of the Veterans' Bureau. These men, not the high-minded Hughes or Hoover, set the tone of the Harding years, creating an aura of back-room sleaze reminiscent of the Grant administration.

By 1922 Washington rumor hinted at criminal activity in high places. Increasingly distressed, Harding confessed to a journalist friend: "I have no trouble with my enemies. . . . But . . . my goddamn friends . . . , they're the ones that keep me walking the floor nights." Seeking escape, Harding in 1923 took a summer vacation to Alaska. Endlessly he played poker, trying to forget the clouds

President Warren G. Harding

Hamming it up in Baltimore, Harding pretends to be a movie cameraman for the amusement of onlookers. The president's unassuming friendliness won the affection of voters. Unfortunately, little substance lay beneath the surface charm.

gathering in Washington. In late July he suffered a heart attack, and on August 2, in the anonymity of a San Francisco hotel room, he died.

In 1924 a Senate investigation exposed the full dimensions of the scandals. Charles Forbes, convicted of stealing Veterans' Bureau funds, evaded prison by fleeing abroad. The bureau's general counsel committed suicide, as did an associate of Attorney General Daugherty who had been accused of influence peddling. Daugherty himself, forced from office in 1924 amid a welter of charges, escaped conviction in two criminal trials.

The seamiest scandal involved Interior Secretary Fall, who eventually went to jail for secretly leasing government oil reserves in Elk Hills, California, and Teapot Dome, Wyoming, to two oilmen while accepting "loans" from them totaling four hundred thousand dollars. Like "Watergate" in the 1970s, the phrase "Teapot Dome" became a shorthand label for an entire presidential legacy of scandals.

Vice President Calvin Coolidge learned of Harding's death while on a family visit in the village of Plymouth, Vermont. By flickering lantern light, he took the presidential oath from his father, a local magistrate. Coolidge brought a distinctly different style to the White House. Whereas Harding was talkative to the point of garrulity, Coolidge's silences became legendary. Once, as he was leaving for Washington, D.C., after a visit to California, a radio reporter asked for a parting message to the people of the state. "Goodbye," Coolidge responded. Coolidge is also said to have slept more than any other president. When he died in 1933, humorist Dorothy Parker asked: "How could they tell?"

Apart from matters of style, the advent of Coolidge brought little change. Governmental policies in the 1920s reflected the prevailing probusiness climate. The Fordney-McCumber Tariff (1922) and the Smoot-Hawley Tariff (1930) pushed rates on imported goods to all-time highs, benefiting domestic manufacturers. Thanks to the efforts of Treasury Secretary Andrew Mellon, Congress lowered the income-tax rates for the well-to-do. (To his credit, Mellon also balanced the federal budget every year from 1921 to 1928.) The Supreme Court under Chief Justice William Howard Taft, whom President Harding had appointed in 1921, overturned several progressive reform measures that

President Calvin Coolidge Throwing Out the First Ball

Even when he smiled, someone said, Coolidge looked as though he was sucking a lemon. Government's "greatest duty and opportunity," Coolidge once observed, "is not to embark on any new ventures."

had been opposed by influential business interests, including a 1919 federal law imposing punitive taxes on the products of child labor and a minimum-wage act for women workers in Washington, D.C. Coolidge rejected a request for aid from Mississippi River flood victims with the prim reminder that the government had no obligation to protect citizens "against the hazards of the elements."

Coolidge's veto of the McNary-Haugen farm bill further illuminated his philosophy of government. Warning of "the tyranny of bureaucratic regulation and control" that the plan would entail, he denounced the bill as an unconstitutional price-fixing scheme that would benefit a sector of American agriculture at the expense of "the general public welfare." Although his party had long championed the high protective tariff and other measures of benefit to business, Coolidge reacted in horror when farmers pursued the same kind of special-interest politics.

Despite their personal antipathy to progressivism, Harding and Coolidge could not dismantle the progressives' legacy of federal regulatory commissions. In some cases, however, they undercut these agencies by appointing individuals to run them who wholly opposed federal regulation.

Foreign Policy in an Isolationist Age

The arena of international relations produced one of the Harding presidency's few noteworthy achievements: the Washington Naval Arms Conference. After the war ended in 1918, the United States, Great Britain, and Japan found themselves edging toward a naval-arms race that none of them really wanted or could afford. In July 1921 President Harding called for a conference to deal with the problem. When the gathering convened in Washington that October, Secretary of State Hughes startled the delegates by proposing the destruction of specific vessels to achieve an agreed-upon ratio of ships among the world's naval powers. According to one observer, when the admiral heading the British delegation heard Hughes's proposal, he "came forward in his chair with the manner of a bulldog, sleeping on a sunny doorstep, who has been poked in the stomach."

Negotiations went forward, however, and in February 1922 the three nations, together with Italy and France, signed a treaty pledging to reduce their battleship tonnage by specified amounts and to observe a ten-year moratorium on battleship construction. The United States and Japan also agreed to respect each other's territorial holdings in the Pacific. Although this treaty ultimately failed to prevent war, it did represent a significant early arms-control effort.

Apart from the naval-arms conference, America followed a narrowly isolationist foreign policy in the 1920s. While U.S. corporate and financial interests extended their international involvements in the decade, politically the nation turned inward, joining neither Woodrow Wilson's cherished League of Nations nor the Court of International Justice (the World Court), a League-sponsored agency to resolve international disputes. The United States

did participate informally in some League agencies and sent observers to League-sponsored conferences; but in general, symbolic gestures replaced meaningful internationalist engagement. In 1928 the United States and France, eventually joined by sixty other nations, signed the Kellogg-Briand Pact renouncing aggression and calling for the outlawry of war. Lacking any enforcement mechanism, this high-sounding document did nothing to prevent the militarism that within a decade would again plunge the world into war.

U.S. insistence that its wartime allies repay their war debts in full produced much ill will. As President Coolidge laconically put it: "They hired [borrowed] the money, didn't they?" According to the calculations of a debt commission created by the Senate in 1922, the total bill came to $22 billion, including interest, with Great Britain and France the biggest debtors. With Europe's economy foundering, the United States sharply scaled down its debt demands in 1925–1926, but high U.S. tariff barriers made it difficult for foreign powers to earn the dollars necessary to pay even the reduced levies.

Progressive Stirrings, Democratic Divisions

The progressive spirit survived in the legislative branch. Congress staved off Andrew Mellon's proposals for even deeper tax cuts for the rich. Senator George W. Norris of Nebraska successfully prevented the Coolidge administration from selling a federal hydroelectric facility at Muscle Shoals, Alabama, to automaker Henry Ford for a fraction of its value. And with the creation of the Federal Radio Commission (1927), Congress extended to this new industry the progressive principle of governmental regulation of business activity.

In 1922, a midterm election year, labor and farm groups formed the Conference for Progressive Political Action (CPPA), which helped defeat a number of conservative Republican candidates. At a meeting in Cleveland in July 1924, CPPA delegates revived the Progressive party; adopted a strongly prolabor, profarmer platform that called for government ownership of railroads and water-power resources; and nominated Senator Robert La Follette for president. The Socialist party and the American Federation of Labor endorsed the nomination as well. Sidetracked by Teddy Roosevelt in 1912, "Fighting Bob" got his chance at last.

The Democratic party that assembled in New York City for its 1924 convention, meanwhile, was deeply split between its urban and rural wings. The closeness of this split became evident when a resolution condemning the Ku Klux Klan failed by one vote, 542 to 541. In the contest for the presidential nomination, Woodrow Wilson's treasury secretary, William G. McAdoo, emerged as the champion of the party's rural, Protestant, southern wing, while the big-city delegates rallied behind Governor Alfred E. Smith of New York, a Roman Catholic of Irish immigrant origins.

As the delegates cast ballot after ballot in the stifling convention hall that summer, neither McAdoo nor Smith could gain the necessary two-thirds majority. Joked humorist Will Rogers: "This thing has got to end. New York invited you folks here as guests, not to live." After 102 ballots the exhausted delegates nominated an obscure compromise candidate, John W. Davis, a conservative corporation lawyer. The Democratic platform called for tariff reduction, endorsed the League of Nations, and condemned the Harding scandals. In a gesture to the party's agrarian wing, Davis chose as his running mate Governor Charles Bryan of Nebraska, the younger brother of William Jennings Bryan.

Calvin Coolidge easily won the Republican nomination. The Republican platform praised the high Fordney-McCumber Tariff, urged reduced taxes and cuts in government spending, and applauded the Washington Naval Arms Conference as a contribution to peace. With the economy humming and the opposition divided, Coolidge swept to victory with nearly 16 million votes, about twice Davis's total. La Follette garnered 4.8 million votes—a significant achievement for a third-party candidate but far short of victory. The lopsided electoral-college vote—382 for Coolidge, 136 for Davis,

13 for La Follette—underscored the magnitude of the Republican landslide.

Women and Politics in the 1920s: A Dream Deferred

The belief of many suffragists that votes for women would transform politics survived the war only briefly. The major parties added women to their national committees and in 1920 endorsed several platform planks drafted by the newly organized League of Women Voters. Polling places shifted from saloons to schools and churches; states that had not earlier passed laws permitting women to serve on juries and hold public office now did so. The Women's Joint Congressional Committee, formed by a coalition of women's groups in 1919, lobbied for child-labor laws, protection of women workers, and federal support for education. The Sheppard-Towner Act (1921), passed in response to such lobbying, appropriated $1.2 million for rural prenatal and baby-care centers staffed by public-health nurses. Harriet Upton, national vice chairman of the Republican party, persuaded President Harding to support the measure.

Overall, however, the Nineteenth Amendment had less political impact than had been hoped. Women who had marched together in the suffrage campaign and worked together for other progressive reforms now scattered to all points on the political spectrum. Some voted Republican, others Socialist. Some joined the La Follette campaign in 1924, others worked to rebuild the Democratic party. Many withdrew from politics altogether. A midwestern women's club leader lamented that the hall where reformers once delivered passionate speeches "now rings with such terms as 'no trump' and 'grand slam.'"

As the women's movement splintered, it lost a unified focus. Drawing mainly middle-class and

The Election of 1924				
Candidates	Parties	Electoral Vote	Popular Vote	Percentage of Popular Vote
CALVIN COOLIDGE	Republican	382	15,718,211	54.0
John W. Davis	Democratic	136	8,385,283	28.8
Robert M. La Follette	Progressive	13	4,831,289	16.6

"The End of the Climb"

Having won women's right to vote, the American women's movement lapsed into a long quiescence. But a few women, among them Alice Paul, continued to fight for broader goals.

professional women, the League of Women Voters largely abandoned reform activism for the "nonpartisan" study of civic issues. Some feminists joined the peace movement. Carrie Chapman Catt founded the National Conference on the Cause and Cure of War, while Jane Addams channeled her energies into the Women's International League for Peace and Freedom.

Meanwhile, Alice Paul and her National Woman's party campaigned for an equal-rights amendment to the Constitution. Paul even opposed legislation protecting women workers because such laws supposedly implied women's inferiority. Most feminists, as well as radicals and labor activists, condemned her position. Florence Kelley of the National Consumers' League called the equal-rights amendment as defined by Paul "a slogan of the insane." The amendment might benefit professional women, these critics charged, but it could hurt female factory workers if it meant the abolition of protective legislation. The argument proved moot, however, because the proposed amendment got nowhere.

The conservative political atmosphere and materialistic mass culture of the 1920s underlay

this disarray. Jane Addams and other women's rights leaders faced accusations of communist sympathies by right-wing groups. Countless young women, bombarded by advertising that defined liberation in terms of a sophisticated lifestyle and the purchase of more consumer goods, found the prewar feminists' earnest civic idealism embarrassingly passé. One young woman in 1927 ridiculed "the old school of fighting feminists" for their lack of "feminine charm" and scorned the hard-core activists "who antagonize men with their constant clamor about maiden names, equal rights, [and] women's place in the world."

In such a climate, the few reforms achieved by organized women's groups often proved short-lived. The women's movement suffered serious setbacks when the Supreme Court struck down child-labor and women's protective laws. A 1924 child-labor constitutional amendment opposed by powerful business interests passed the Congress after heavy lobbying by women's organizations but won ratification in only a few states. And the Sheppard-Towner program of rural prenatal aid and baby care, denounced by the American Medical Association as an assault on physicians' monopoly of the health business, was terminated in 1929.

Mass Society, Mass Culture

The automobiles, electrical appliances, and myriad other products that flowed from the assembly lines in the 1920s reflected more than a change in the technological order. They heralded a new social and cultural era. Not only did these products themselves change Americans' everyday lives, but the standardized mass production that spawned them proved as adaptable to the realm of ideas as to the realm of roadsters and refrigerators.

A Nation of Cities, Consumer Goods, and Automobiles

The 1920 census confirmed that the United States had become a nation of cities. For the first time, the urban population outnumbered the rural. The census recorded a dozen cities of more than 600,000, with New York City, at nearly 6 million residents, heading the list.

Blacks figured importantly in the migration cityward. By 1930 more than 40 percent of the nation's 12 million blacks lived in cities, 2 million of them in Chicago, Detroit, New York, and other metropolitan centers of the North and West. Signaling political changes to come, the first black congressman since Reconstruction, Oscar DePriest, was elected in 1928 from Chicago's South Side.

This urban growth had wide cultural ramifications. While Americans remained strongly attached to rural and small-town values, the nation in the 1920s became increasingly urbanized, not only numerically but also, as one historian has written, "in the cast of its mind, in its ideals, and in its folkways." The powerful shaping agencies of the culture—radio, the movies, the corporations, the advertising agencies, the mass magazines—all operated from the urban centers. Even when these cultural voices nostalgically evoked rural values, they did so from big-city editorial offices and radio studios.

It was in the cities, too, that the new consumer goods, particularly electrical appliances such as refrigerators, ranges, and vacuum cleaners, had the most dramatic impact. While millions of farm families still lived without such conveniences, they were found in all but the poorest urban homes by 1930.

Technological and marketing innovations affected the daily life of city dwellers in innumerable ways. For women, these innovations significantly reduced the hours and sheer physical effort expended on housework. When Robert and Helen Lynd interviewed some working-class women in Muncie in 1925, nearly 75 percent said that they spent less time on housework than had their mothers. Vacuum cleaners supplanted brooms, dustpans, and carpet beaters. The time-consuming task of firing up a wood stove became a memory. Storebought clothes replaced laboriously sewn homemade apparel. Even the refrigerator saved labor. One young woman of the 1920s, Florence Hunt of Madison, Wisconsin, later recalled: "I remember when we got our first electric refrigerator. Before that, we had the old oak icebox with the big cake of ice in the metal-lined chest below. The ice would melt into a pan underneath, and unless you watched it carefully the pan would run over and make a big mess."

Electricity altered laundry routines as well. In the early twentieth century, many urban house-

"Give Her a Frigidaire for Christmas"

An array of labor-saving devices for the home became available to the urban middle class in the twenties.

wives had patronized commercial laundries to relieve themselves of the onerous chore of home laundering. But with the arrival of the electric washing machine and iron, this task moved back into the home. In this respect, the new technology reversed the trend toward the socialization of housework that reformers like Charlotte Perkins Gilman had welcomed.

Food preparation and even eating patterns also shifted under the impact of economic and technological change. The rise of the supermarket, for example, made sharp inroads on the annual ritual of canning. As one midwestern housewife commented in the mid-1920s: "You just spent your summer canning in 1890, but the canned goods you buy today are so good that it isn't worth your while." Similarly, before World War I, most housewives still baked their own bread. But in the 1920s, with commercial ovens turning out five thousand loaves an hour, all this changed. Nearly 75 percent of the Muncie housewives told the Lynds that they used commercially baked bread, much of it trucked in from other cities. In earlier times fresh fruits, vegetables, and salads had vanished from American tables in the long winter months. With the advent of refrigeration, supermarkets, and motor transport, fruits and vegetables became available year-round, significantly improving the national diet.

Rivaling urbanization and electrification in social and cultural impact was the automobile. Urban planners worriedly discussed traffic jams, parking problems, and the soaring accident rate. Over twenty-six thousand Americans died in traffic accidents in 1924, including about ten thousand children. A Muncie resident challenged the Lynds: "Why on earth do you need to study what's changing this country? I can tell you what's happening in just four letters: A-U-T-O."

Like the panoply of electrical appliances, the A-U-T-O reached into the lives of ordinary Americans. Family vacations, virtually unheard of a generation earlier, now enjoyed a great vogue. City dwellers rediscovered the natural beauty of the land—though they often found that thousands of their fellow Ford owners had precisely the same goal in mind! The automobile helped break down the isolation of rural life and gave farm dwellers far easier access to the city for shopping and entertainment.

While the automobile brought the family together for excursions and vacations, it could also erode family cohesion. Young people welcomed the freedom from parental oversight that it offered. As the Lynds observed, a young person could now jump into a car with friends and drive to a dance in a distant city on a whim, "with no one's permission asked." Complained one father, "It's getting so a fellow has to make a date with his family to see them."

The automobile's effects on individuality were similarly mixed. In contrast to train passengers, compelled to follow a predetermined route and schedule, car owners could travel where they wished, when they wished. But in other ways, the automobile dramatically accelerated the standardization of American life. Millions chugged around in identical black vehicles. The one-room schoolhouse was abandoned as buses carried children to consolidated schools. Neighborhood shops and markets declined as people drove to more distant chain stores. By no coincidence, the advent of the automobile age also brought the first suburban department stores, the first shopping center (in

The Automobile Age: Passenger Cars Registered in the United States, 1900–1986

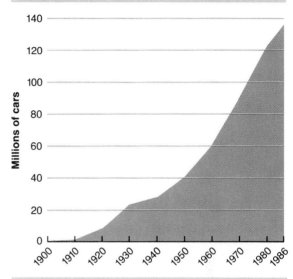

Henry Ford observed that the consumer could buy one "in any color so long as it is black." From a plaything for the rich, the automobile emerged after 1920 as the basic mode of transportation for the masses, in the process transforming American life in countless ways.

SOURCES: *Historical Statistics of the United States, Colonial Times to 1970* (Washington, D.C.: Government Printing Office, 1975), 716; *Statistical Abstract of the United States, 1988* (Washington, D.C.: Government Printing Office, 1987), 576.

Kansas City), and the first fast-food chain (A & W Root Beer).

Even at $300 or $400, the automobile remained too expensive for the poor. A thriving used-car market soon developed, but even so, car ownership only gradually penetrated the lowest economic ranks. Thus the "automobile suburbs" that sprang up beyond the streetcar lines attracted mainly the prosperous, while the urban poor, including the growing black population, remained behind. This pattern laid the groundwork for urban-suburban social divisions that would have important ramifications in the decades ahead.

At the same time, the automobile's farm cousin, the tractor, transformed agriculture. The number of tractors soared from 250,000 in 1929 to 920,000 in 1930, while the horse and mule population declined. But the tractor's advent was not an unmixed blessing. In this period of low farm

The Romance of the Automobile

Ads from the 1920s promised leisure and escape from urban congestion. When thousands flocked to rural "trails" such as those promoted by this 1925 brochure, however, traffic jams, exhaust fumes, and chugging engines could quickly undermine the sylvan charm.

prices, many farmers went into debt to buy mechanized equipment, thus contributing to the worsening agricultural crisis.

Routinized Work, Mass-Produced Pleasure

While mass production generated an abundance of consumer goods, the new assembly-line techniques also affected the way industrial employees viewed their work and themselves. The essence of the assembly line was repetitive labor, with a minimum of individual initiative or variation. Ironi-

cally, Henry Ford was comforted by his belief that most laborers preferred such work: "The vast majority of men want to stay put. They want to be led. They want to have everything done for them and have no responsibility. . . . [T]he average worker . . . above all . . . wants a job in which he does not have to think."

Ford managers actively discouraged expressions of individuality and even communication among employees. Because talking or laughter could divert workers from their task, Ford employees learned to whisper without moving their lips and adopted a fixed, impassive mask that some called "Fordization of the face."

As work became more routine, its psychic rewards diminished. Life on the assembly line did not foster pride in one's skills and the specialized knowledge that came from years of farming or mastering a craft. Nor did the assembly line offer much prospect of advancement. In Muncie, factories employing over four thousand workers announced only ten openings for foremen in 1924 and 1925—less than one chance in four hundred for upward job mobility. These changes in the nature of work may have contributed—along with higher wages and a shorter workweek—to the rising interest in leisure-time activities in these years, as workers sought in their free hours the fulfillment that jobs often failed to provide.

Thus the volume and variety of recreational diversions proliferated. Just as Henry Ford offered standardized transportation through new production techniques, so entrepreneurs in other fields offered standardized amusement. The mass production of culture was nothing new in the 1920s, of course. It had started at least as early as the 1830s, with the rise of the penny press, the dime novel, and the sentimental romance. But the process vastly accelerated in the twenties.

Mass-circulation magazines reached enormous audiences in this decade. By 1922 ten American magazines boasted a circulation of more than 2.5 million each. Some of these trumpeted sex, crime, and "true confessions"; others presented a blend of fiction, cartoons, and stories. The venerable *Saturday Evening Post,* with its bucolic Norman Rockwell covers and its fiction featuring small-town life, specialized in prepackaged nostalgia. Onetime muckraking magazines like *Collier's* now offered far more soothing fare.

A 1920s Magazine Stand

Mass weekly magazines like Collier's *opened new horizons for millions of readers while helping spread standardized social ideas and cultural values in post–World War I America.*

In 1921 the husband-and-wife team of Lila and DeWitt Wallace published the first issue of *Reader's Digest,* a compact magazine that condensed articles originally published elsewhere. Perfectly attuned to the times, the *Digest* offered traditionalist, probusiness views in a standardized format and highly simplified prose. Pitched to the mass market, it represented the journalistic counterpart of the Model T or the A&P.

Even the world of bookselling saw major changes. The old-style bookstores, with their musty, individualistic flavor, declined as book publishers increasingly marketed their products through department stores or mail-order distribution mechanisms such as the Book-of-the-Month Club (1924) and the Literary Guild (1926).

Radio and the movies, the newest of the media, contributed even more dramatically to the standardization of culture. As a mass-culture phenomenon, the radio era began on November 2, 1920, when station KDKA in Pittsburgh broadcast the news of Warren Harding's election. In 1921 New York's WEAF began a regular news program featuring H. V. Kaltenborn, and that autumn a Newark station broadcast the World Series (the Giants

beat the Yankees). In 1922 five hundred new stations began operations. "There is radio music in the air, every night, everywhere," proclaimed a San Francisco newspaper; "anybody can hear it at home on a receiving set." By 1927 radio sales approached 7 million.

Radio soon underwent the same consolidation process that was transforming the economy. In 1926 three big corporations—General Electric, Westinghouse, and the Radio Corporation of America—formed the first radio network, the National Broadcasting Company (NBC). The Columbia Broadcasting System (CBS) followed in 1927. The networks soon ruled radio broadcasting. Programming reflected audience preferences as revealed through elaborate market research. From Maine to California, Americans laughed at the same jokes, hummed the same tunes, and absorbed the same commercials at the same instant.

New York's WEAF broadcast the first commercially sponsored program in 1922, and soon the commercialization of the new medium was complete. The first network comedy show, the enormously popular (and mildly racist) "Amos 'n' Andy" (1928), brought millions in sales to its

George Burns and Gracie Allen

Comedy shows were enormously popular during the 1920s and 1930s, radio's "golden age." Like Burns and Allen, many of the most successful radio comedians got their start in vaudeville.

movie attendance stood at nearly 80 million. In Muncie nine theaters ran movies continuously from 1:00 P.M. to 11:00 P.M., seven days a week, fifty-two weeks a year.

Like radio programming, movie production became more and more standardized. By 1930 such Hollywood giants as Metro-Goldwyn-Mayer, Warner Brothers, and Columbia turned out the vast majority of American films. Predictable plots and typecast stars prevailed. An analogy drawn by one Hollywood mogul, while somewhat misleading, contained a kernel of truth as well: "The picture industry is no different from the underwear business, for example. It is completely governed by the law of supply and demand."

Moviegoers entered a celluloid world far removed from reality. One movie ad in the *Saturday Evening Post* promised "all the adventure, all the romance, all the excitement you lack in your daily life." These mass-produced fantasies helped shape popular behavior and values, especially those of the impressionable young. In the words of writer John Dos Passos, Hollywood offered a "great bargain sale of five-and-ten-cent lusts and dreams."

sponsor, Pepsodent toothpaste. NBC's 1929 income of $150 million came largely from the sale of advertising time.

The motion-picture business evolved along similar lines. The movies attracted a huge audience at all social levels in the 1920s as they expanded from the immigrant slums into elegant uptown theaters with names like "Majestic," "Ritz," and "Palace." First came the silent-film era, when such stars as the comedian Charlie Chaplin, the swashbuckling Douglas Fairbanks, the romantic Rudolph Valentino, and "America's sweetheart" Mary Pickford became national favorites. Director Cecil B. De Mille won fame and fortune for lavish biblical spectacles such as *The Ten Commandments* (1923) and *The King of Kings* (1927).

After Al Jolson's *The Jazz Singer* (1927) introduced sound to the movies (see "A Place in Time"), they became even more popular and spawned a new generation of screen idols, including the western hero Gary Cooper and the aloof Scandinavian beauty Greta Garbo. Another enduring Hollywood favorite, Mickey Mouse, made his debut in a 1928 animated cartoon, *Steamboat Willy*, produced by the young Walt Disney. By 1930 weekly

Rudolph Valentino and Agnes Ayres in The Sheik, 1921

A poor Italian immigrant, Valentino worked as a gardener and touring dancer before making his way to Hollywood, where he became a screen idol.

The film industry also stimulated consumption by presenting alluring images of the good life. As a black high-school freshman told a social researcher in the 1920s: "The movies have often made me dissatisfied with my neighborhood, because when I see a movie [with] the beautiful castle, palace, . . . and beautiful house, I wish my home was something like these."

Fads, Celebrities, and Heroes

In this era of mass communication, when news could reach every corner of the nation in a few seconds, a succession of fads and media-promoted events—or pseudoevents—preoccupied millions of Americans. In 1921 businessmen in Atlantic City promoted their resort with a bathing-beauty competition that they grandly called the Miss America Pageant. In 1922 came the vogue for a Chinese game called mah-jong. In 1924 a crossword-puzzle craze swept the country.

In professional sports massive publicity focused on a few larger-than-life celebrities: Babe Ruth of the New York Yankees, who hit sixty home runs in 1927; Ty Cobb, the Detroit Tigers' manager, whose earlier record of 4,191 major-league hits stood for many years; Red Grange, the Illinois halfback who helped make college (and later professional) football big business; Gertrude Ederle, the first woman to swim the English Channel; prizefighters Jack Dempsey and Gene Tunney, whose heavyweight title fights in 1926 and 1927 attracted crowds totaling more than two hundred thousand and radio audiences many times larger. When Tunney won the 1927 bout thanks to a famous "long count" by a referee, five radio listeners dropped dead of heart attacks.

The lives of some of these sports celebrities had a seamy side. Ruth was a coarse, heavy-drinking womanizer; Cobb (the first baseball player to become a millionaire), an ill-tempered racist. Yet the alchemy of publicity transformed them into exciting gladiators with lovable nicknames like the Sultan of Swat (Ruth) or the Georgia Peach (Cobb).

The ballyhoo extended to college sports as well. When Notre Dame played Army in 1924, sportswriter Grantland Rice memorably described Notre Dame's backfield:

Outlined against a blue-gray October sky, the Four Horsemen rode again. In dramatic lore, *they are known as Famine, Pestilence, Destruction, and Death. These are only aliases. Their real names are Stuhldreher, Miller, Crowley, and Layden.*

Another 1920s legend was born. The four young players, looking acutely uncomfortable, even posed on horseback in their football uniforms as a publicity stunt.

For all the media hype, this idolization of celebrities illuminates the anxieties and aspirations of ordinary Americans in these years. The girl uncertainly trying to define a role for herself in a period of confusing social change could find in the beauty pageants one kind of ideal to which she could aspire. For the man whose sense of mastery had been shaken by numerous developments from feminism to Fordism, the experience of cheering himself hoarse for a towering sports hero like Dempsey, Grange, or Ruth could momentarily restore a sense of personal importance and self-assurance.

The psychological meaning of this hero worship emerged with particular clarity in the public response to an event that stands by itself in this decade of manufactured celebrities: the solo Atlantic crossing on May 20–21, 1927, by an unknown young flyer named Charles A. Lindbergh. A Minnesotan of Swedish ancestry, Lindbergh spent the early twenties as a stunt flyer and airmail pilot and then decided to compete for a $25,000 prize offered by a New York hotel owner for the first nonstop New York–Paris flight. Lindbergh's daring flight eastward from Roosevelt Field, Long Island, in his silver-winged monoplane, *The Spirit of St. Louis*, captured the popular imagination. From the moment that he touched down in Paris, the glare of media attention enveloped him. In blasé New York, what one newspaper called "a surging ocean of people" turned out for a rousing ticker-tape parade. President Coolidge, foregoing his customary afternoon nap, held a White House reception; radio, newspapers, magazines, and movie newsreels provided saturation coverage. With his shy smile and self-effacing modesty, the "Lone Eagle" handled his celebrity with dignity. In an age of scandals and scams, he proved an authentic hero.

Coolidge praised Lindbergh's flight as a triumph of corporate technology, but many editorialists saw in his achievement reassuring evidence that the individual still counted in an era of

Hollywood in 1926

It was 1926, and the Warner brothers, Sam, Jack, and Harry, were worried. The motion-picture business had become intensely competitive in the 1920s, and the Warners' small upstart production company, Warner Brothers Pictures, Inc., was falling behind. But Sam Warner saw an opportunity to become more competitive: making movies that incorporated sound. The technology for sound movies had been available for years. In fact, an early experimental film made at Thomas Edison's laboratory in New Jersey, and designed to be shown in coordination with an Edison phonograph recording, featured two Edison technicians dancing in eerie slow motion while another played the violin.

But the larger Hollywood studios had resisted the transition to sound. The silent-movie business was flourishing, and the costs of switching to sound seemed a risky gamble. Expensive new equipment would have to be purchased, studios soundproofed, and new projectors installed in the nation's 20,000 movie theaters. No one knew how directors, actors, and actresses trained in the art of silent film would adapt to sound. And while silent movies could be distributed worldwide, sound films in American English would have a more limited market.

However, Warner Pictures, with little to lose, was willing to try anything, even sound. The technology that particularly interested the three brothers had been developed by the Western Electric Company, a sub-

Moviemaking at Warner Brothers Hollywood Studio

sidiary of the American Telephone and Telegraph Company. It involved amplified recordings on large discs mechanically synchronized to the film. Setting up a division called Vitaphone, Warner Brothers leased the rights to Western Electric's sound system. In August 1926 a Warner Brothers' feature called *Don Juan* and starring John Barrymore opened in New York with orchestral background music provided by the Vitaphone system rather than by the customary live theater orchestra, organ, or piano.

Don Juan was moderately well received, but the big breakthrough came in Warner Brothers' next film, *The Jazz Singer,* which featured not only music but also spoken dialogue. *The Jazz Singer* was based on a 1926 Broadway hit that told the story of a young Jewish immigrant who leaves his deeply religious parents to make a career in the world

of popular music. The prodigal son eventually returns, however, taking his dying father's place as synagogue cantor to chant the sacred "Kol Nidre" on the eve of Yom Kippur, the holiest day of the Jewish year. Appropriately, Sam Warner signed Al Jolson to star in the movie. Born Asa Joelson in St. Petersburg, Russia, Jolson was himself a Jewish immigrant and an ex-cantor who had become a musical-comedy star.

Warner planned *The Jazz Singer* as a silent movie except for six songs that Jolson would sing. On a July day in 1926, at a Warner studio on Sunset Boulevard in Hollywood, Jolson recorded one of the songs, "Blue Skies," on a special set designed so that the recording microphones would not pick up the loudly whirring movie cameras. As the song ended, Jolson, perhaps not even realizing that the recording equipment was still on, turned from

Al Jolson and Eugenie Besserer in The Jazz Singer

The Jazz Singer Screened in New York City, 1927

In one scene Jolson sang in blackface, a popular entertainment tradition dating back to nineteenth-century minstrel shows.

the piano to Eugenie Besserer, the elderly actress playing his mother. He ad-libbed: "Did you like that, Mama?" Startled, she replied, "Yes," and Jolson continued: "I'm glad. I'd rather please you than anybody I know of." He went on, still improvising, to describe the fine clothes and splendid house he would someday buy for her.

Sam Warner loved the effect of the accidentally recorded spoken passage and inserted some three hundred additional words of spoken dialogue throughout the movie, including Jolson's famous tag line, "You ain't heard nothin' yet." In the context, these words proved prophetic. Premièred in New York City in October 1927, *The Jazz Singer* became a tremendous hit. It opened in all the major cities that fall and remained for eight weeks rather than the customary three. One critic compared its star to the year's top celebrity: "Al Jolson's voice can now go ringing down the hallways of time. . . . Here is a show! To miss it would be like failing to catch a glimpse of Lindbergh."

Some critics considered the innovation a disastrous backward step. The advent of sound, an English critic wrote in 1928, "marks the most spectacular act of self-destruction that has yet come out of Hollywood. . . . The soul of the film—its eloquent and vital silence— is destroyed. The film now returns to the circus whence it came, among the freaks and the fat ladies."

But Warner Brothers forged ahead, in 1928 releasing its first "100 percent talkie," *The Lights of New York,* a tale of urban crime. The movie is stilted and awkward, as cast members speak slowly and self-consciously into microphones hidden in light fixtures and plants. In one scene the gangster boss, played by Hawk Miller, growls into a microphone concealed in a telephone and orders his henchmen to get rid of a rival with the ominous words: "Take him for a ride." The *New York Times* critic wrote, "While the picture could not be described as the best of entertainment, it may, in its halting manner, be pointing the way to the future."

When Warner Brothers' net profits jumped from $30,000 in the first eight months of 1927 to $17 million in the comparable period of

1929, the other studios got the message. By the end of 1929, three-quarters of Hollywood feature films had at least some sound sequences, and over half the movie theaters in the United States were equipped to show sound films. With New York banks financing the heavy costs, Wall Street's role in the newest entertainment medium expanded. American moviegoers enthusiastically embraced this latest innovation; they formed long lines to see the new sound movies, and they burst into spontaneous applause when they ended. Box-office receipts spurted by 50 percent from 1927 to 1930. By the mid-1930s the transition was complete, and the novelty of sound helped Hollywood weather the Great Depression of the 1930s.

Al Jolson's spur-of-the-moment ad lib had opened a new chapter in movie history. Director William C. De Mille, recalling years later the first talkie he saw, with its crackles and pops, described the dimensions of the revolution it portended: "It sounded like a grass fire, but it was to turn into a conflagration which swept away the Hollywood we had known and forced us to build a new city on the ruins of the old."

Charles A. Lindbergh Begins His Epic Flight, May 20, 1927

Lindbergh's achievement helped reassure Americans that the lone individual could still make a mark in an age of mass production and mass culture.

standardization and mechanization. To cultural conservatives Lindbergh's solid virtues proved that the old verities survived in a time of moral disarray. Native-born midwesterners embraced the Minnesota boy as one of their own and insisted that he, not urban immigrants, most truly represented America.

Clearly the social effects of the new mass media were neither all good nor all bad. The technologies of mass communication unquestionably promoted cultural standardization and uniformity of thought and to a degree stifled local and regional diversity. But radio, the movies, and the mass magazines also helped forge a national culture and introduced millions of Americans to fresh viewpoints and new ways of behaving. While they entertained, the mass media also hammered home a powerful message: an individual's horizons need no longer be limited by his or her immediate environment. The spread of mass culture in the 1920s opened a vastly larger world for ordinary Americans. If that world was often vacuous and tawdry, it was also sometimes exciting, stimulating, and provocative.

Cultural Ferment and Creativity

The American experience in the 1920s involved more than political scandals, triumphs of productivity, and short-lived fads. This was also a decade of bubbling cultural ferment and creativity. While some highly visible young people—and their parents—flouted the manners and morals of the prewar generation, writers, artists, musicians, and scientists compiled a record of remarkable achievement. American blacks, meanwhile, asserted their pride and collective energy through a remarkable cultural flowering known as the Harlem Renaissance. Pulsing through the decade were the rhythms of jazz, a black musical idiom that was winning wild popularity among whites as well as blacks.

The Jazz Age and the Postwar Crisis of Values

The war and its disillusioned aftermath brought to full boil the simmering cultural restlessness of the prewar years. As Randolph Bourne, one of the first to grasp the war's profound cultural implications, wrote in 1918: "One has a sense of having come to a sudden, short stop at the end of an intellectual era." The postwar period amply confirmed Bourne's premonition. In *The Wasteland* (1922), poet T. S. Eliot evoked images of a shattered culture. Another poet, Ezra Pound, made the same point more brutally in *Hugh Selwyn Mauberley* (1920). America had gone to war, he wrote, to save "a botched civilization; . . . an old bitch gone in the teeth."

The postwar crisis of values took many forms. Some members of the younger generation—especially affluent college students—boisterously assailed older conventions of decorous behavior. Taking advantage of the decade's prosperity and the freedom offered by the automobile, they threw noisy parties, consumed bootleg liquor, flocked to

Miss America Competitors, 1926

Their dimpled knees looking like so many baby faces, contestants pose for a publicity shot in front of the Golden State, a popular train of the day, as two male onlookers form their judgments.

jazz clubs, and danced the jitterbug and the Charleston. Asked her favorite activity, a California college student replied: "Of course, I adore dancing; who doesn't?"

The young also discussed sex more freely than their elders and in some cases indulged more openly in premarital sexual experimentation. Wrote novelist F. Scott Fitzgerald: "None of the Victorian mothers had any idea how casually their daughters were accustomed to be kissed." The ideas of Sigmund Freud, the Viennese physician whose studies of human sexuality first appeared in the 1890s, enjoyed a popular vogue in the 1920s—often in grossly oversimplified form.

Our knowledge of the 1920s "sexual revolution" derives largely from journalistic accounts and anecdotal reminiscences. Premarital sexual intercourse may have increased, but it was still exceptional, and widely disapproved by the young as well as the older generation. What can be documented is a change in courtship patterns. In earlier periods "courting" implied a serious intention of marriage. In the 1920s the more informal ritual of dating evolved. Casual dating allowed young people to test compatibility and gain confidence in relating to the opposite sex without necessarily contemplating marriage. The twenties also brought

greater erotic freedom, but within clear bounds. Despite moralists' charges of a total collapse of standards, most 1920s youth drew a quite distinct line between permissible and impermissible behavior.

The double standard, which held women to a stricter code of sexual conduct than men, remained very much alive. While young men could boast of their sexual adventures, young women who gained a reputation for being "fast" could face ostracism. The male's traditional role in initiating sexual activity also survived intact in the 1920s, as revealed by the decade's elaborate etiquette of kissing. One male student summed up this etiquette: "Although a girl will not always let you kiss her when you ask her, she usually appreciates your asking her, often so much that she has to tell her friends."

Despite the double standard, the postwar changes in behavior did have a liberating effect on women. Female sexuality was acknowledged more openly. Skirt lengths crept up, make-up (once the badge of a prostitute) appeared on many female faces, and the elaborate and confining armor of petticoats and corsets was drastically reduced. The awesome matronly bosom of the late nineteenth century—more intimidating than provocative in its suggestion of woman's maternal role—mysteriously deflated in the twenties as a trimmer, more boyish figure became the fashion ideal.

With the medical risks of smoking as yet undiscovered, many thousands of American young women took up this habit. In a survey at Ohio State University, one-third of the women students said that they had tried cigarettes. Many of these new female smokers consciously viewed the matter as a women's rights issue. As a woman student at the University of Illinois put it: "In this day one has a perfectly good right to ask why men should be permitted to smoke while girls are expelled for doing it."

Moral guardians protested these changes. A prominent Methodist bishop denounced the new dances that brought "the bodies of men and women in unusual relation to each other." When the president of the women's college Bryn Mawr permitted students to smoke on campus in 1925, denunciations rained down on her head. "Nothing has occurred in higher education that has so shocked our sense of social decency as the action of Bryn Mawr," fulminated the president of a Kansas teachers' college.

According to F. Scott Fitzgerald, around 1922 adults began to imitate the rebelliousness of the young. "[T]ired of watching the carnival with ill-concealed envy," wrote Fitzgerald, middle-aged Americans "discovered that young liquor will take the place of young blood, and with a whoop the orgy began." But cultural generalizations by novelists must be treated with care. They do not necessarily reflect the full historical reality. During the years of Fitzgerald's alleged national orgy, for example, the American divorce rate remained constant.

The most enduring twenties' stereotype is that of the flapper—the sophisticated, fashionable, pleasure-mad young woman. The term *flapper* apparently originated with a drawing by magazine illustrator John Held jr. depicting a young woman dressed in the latest fashion but with her rubber boots left open and flapping. (Held himself typified the 1920s. The product of a Mormon upbringing in Utah, he both lived and chronicled the fast life of this so-called Jazz Age. When that era suddenly ended in 1929, his career collapsed.)

Although enough young women conformed to the flapper stereotype to give it plausibility, it was largely a creation of journalists, fashion designers, and advertisers. But like all stereotypes, it played an important social role. In the nineteenth century, the idealized woman on her moral pedestal had symbolized an elaborate complex of cultural values. The flapper stereotype served a similar function. With her bobbed hair, defiant cigarette, dangling beads, heavy make-up, and shockingly short skirt, this semi-mythic figure epitomized the rebelliousness that composed at least a part of the youth culture of the twenties.

Indeed the entire Jazz Age was partially a mass-media and novelistic creation. F. Scott Fitzgerald's romanticized treatment of the affluent postwar young, *This Side of Paradise* (1920), spawned many imitators. A Catholic boy from St. Paul who left Princeton when he failed chemistry, Fitzgerald was only twenty-four when his best-selling novel appeared. With his sculpted good looks, wavy blond hair, and striking green eyes, he, like John Held jr., not only wrote about the Jazz Age but to a degree personified it. Flush with royalties, he and his wife Zelda partied away the early twenties in New York, Paris, and the French Mediterranean.

A moralist at heart, Fitzgerald both admired and deplored his Jazz Age contemporaries. His finest novel, *The Great Gatsby* (1925), brilliantly captures not only the gilded existence of the super-rich and the social climbers of the 1920s but also the cold-hearted selfishness and romantic illusions that ruled their lives.

As a description of the 1920s, the "Jazz Age" label must be applied with care. The upheaval in manners and morals was genuine but limited to a rather narrow social stratum. Old values did not vanish entirely in a hazy blur of alcoholic parties, suggestive dances, and backseat sex. Millions of Americans adhered to traditional ways and traditional standards. Most farmers, blacks, industrial workers, and recent immigrants found economic survival more pressing than the latest dance craze or the newest flapper fads and fashions.

American Writers of the Twenties

Like Fitzgerald, many young writers found the cultural turbulence of the 1920s a creative stimulus. The decade's most talented writers forged a remarkable body of work that was equally hostile to the moralistic pieties of the old order and the business pieties of the new.

The definitive literary skewering of postwar American society came in the novels of Sinclair Lewis, who had left his native Sauk Centre, Minnesota, in 1902 and rarely returned except in imagination. In *Main Street* (1920), Lewis caustically depicted the cultural barrenness and smug self-satisfaction of a fictional midwestern farm town, Gopher Prairie. In *Babbitt* (1922) he wielded his satirical scalpel upon a larger city, Zenith. In the character of George F. Babbitt, a middle-aged real-estate agent trapped in stifling middle-class conformity, Lewis created one of the memorable figures of American fiction.

The scorn for middle-class America that dripped from Lewis's novels found its journalistic counterpart in the work of H. L. Mencken, a Baltimore newspaperman of German immigrant stock who in 1924 founded and became coeditor of *The American Mercury* magazine, the bible of the decade's alienated intellectuals. A penetrating stylist and influential cultural arbiter, Mencken championed writers like Sinclair Lewis and Theodore Dreiser and heaped ridicule on small-town Americans, Protestant fundamentalists, the middle class (Mencken called it the Booboisie), and mainstream American culture generally. His devastating essays on Wilson, Harding, Coolidge, and Bryan are classics of American political satire. Asked why he remained in a nation so contemptible, Mencken replied: "Why do people visit zoos?"

A visual equivalent of Mencken's raucous iconoclasm was offered by photographer Alfred Stieglitz. In a 1923 show at his New York gallery, Stieglitz displayed a close-up photograph of a gelded horse's underside with the caption "Spiritual America."

Some young American writers spent the 1920s abroad, often in France. Even before the war, Eliot, Pound, and Gertrude Stein had become expatriates, and after the armistice other aspiring writers joined them. The most famous expatriate, Ernest Hemingway, had grown up in Oak Park, Illinois, become a reporter, and suffered serious wounds while serving as a Red Cross volunteer on the Italian front during the war. In 1921, at the age of twenty-two, Hemingway settled in Paris and began to write. In *The Sun Also Rises* (1926), he memorably evoked the experiences of a group of American and English young people, variously shattered by the war, as they drift around Spain. Even writers who stayed home often underwent a kind of spiritual expatriation, distancing themselves from the dominant business culture. Willa Cather, for example, produced a series of novels that implicitly repudiated modern mass society by evoking alternatives ranging from early New Mexico (*Death Comes for the Archbishop*, 1927) to seventeenth-century Quebec (*Shadows on the Rock*, 1931).

For this generation of writers, the war represented a seminal experience. The best of the war novels, Hemingway's *A Farewell to Arms* (1929), loosely based on the author's experiences in Italy, powerfully depicted the war's futility and the leaders' inflated rhetoric. Avoiding the elaborate descriptions and lofty abstractions characteristic of most prewar literature, Hemingway invented a terse, pared-down style. In a famous passage of *A Farewell to Arms*, the narrator says:

> *I was always embarrassed by the words sacred, glorious, and sacrifice and the expression in vain. We had heard them . . . and had read them, on proclamations that were slapped up by billposters over other proclamations, now for a long time, and I had seen nothing sacred, and the things that were glorious had no glory and the sacrifices were like the stockyards at Chicago if nothing was done with the meat except to bury it. There were many words that you could not stand to hear and finally only the names of places had dignity.*

But while writers gagged at Wilsonian rhetoric, village narrowness, and chamber-of-commerce cant, they remained at heart deeply American. A hopeful, often buoyantly confident desire to create a vital and authentic national culture inspired their literary efforts, just as it had earlier inspired Hawthorne, Melville, and Whitman.

Achievements in Architecture, Painting, and Music

The creative energies of the 1920s found other outlets as well. A burst of architectural activity, for example, transformed the urban skyline, especially in the larger cities. Chaotically eclectic in style, this architecture nevertheless displayed tremendous vitality. By the end of the decade, the United States boasted 377 buildings over 70 stories tall. The skyscraper, proclaimed one architectural writer, "epitomizes American life and American civilization."

Not everyone was enamored of the skyscraper and urbanization. Cultural critic Lewis Mumford, for example, lashed out at cities, with their "labyrinths of subways, . . . audacious towers, [and] . . . endless miles of asphalted pavements." As an alternative to ever more gargantuan and impersonal cities, Mumford advocated decentralization and a revitalization of the nation's regional roots.

American artists of the twenties turned to America itself for inspiration—either the real nation around them or the one that they held in memory. While muralist Thomas Hart Benton evoked a vanished, half-mythic America of cowboys, pioneers, and riverboat gamblers, Edward Hopper starkly portrayed a nation of faded small towns and lonely cities. In such paintings as *Sunday* (1926), in which an elderly man slumps on the curb of an empty sidewalk in front of a row of abandoned stores, Hopper conveyed both the dreariness and the potential beauty of urban America.

Other 1920s painters offered more upbeat images. John Sloan's *Main Street Gloucester* (1921), with its dazzling colors and vibrant energy, conveys a very different mood from that of Sinclair Lewis's novel *Main Street*, published the year before. Charles DeMuth painted boldly geometric grain elevators, factories, and urban scenes, while painter

and photographer Charles Sheeler recorded on film a dramatic series of images of Ford's River Rouge plant near Detroit. Wisconsin native Georgia O'Keeffe came to New York City in 1918 when Alfred Stieglitz (whom she married in 1924) mounted a show of her work. O'Keeffe's 1920s paintings evoked both the congestion and the excitement of Manhattan.

Musical performers and composers also contributed to the creativity of this extraordinary decade. And they, too, drew upon the cultural resources that they knew best. As composer Aaron Copland later recalled, describing his days as a music student in Paris in the early twenties: "The conviction grew inside me that the two things that seemed always to have been so separate in America—music and the life about me—must be made to touch."

While Copland and other composers drew upon folk-music traditions, still others evoked the new urban-industrial America. Composer Frederick Converse's 1927 tone poem about the automobile, "Flivver Ten Million," for example, featured such episodes as "Dawn in Detroit," "May Night by the Roadside," and "The Collision." Employing the new technology of radio, conductor Walter Damrosch brought classical music to millions with his "Music Appreciation Hour," introduced by NBC in 1928.

Above all, American music in the 1920s meant jazz. The Original Dixieland Jazz Band—five white

East River, *by Georgia O'Keeffe, 1928*

Best known for her abstract paintings of flowers and of animal skulls against a New Mexican desert background, O'Keeffe also painted some memorable urban scenes while living in New York City in the 1920s.

musicians imitating the black jazz bands of New Orleans—debuted at Reisenweber's Cabaret in New York City on January 26, 1917, and a jazz vogue soon was under way. "A college existence without jazz," insisted the University of Illinois student newspaper, "would be like a child's Christmas without Santa Claus."

The white bands that introduced jazz to a larger audience in the twenties also drained it of much of its energy. The most popular white band leader of the decade, Paul Whiteman, offered watered-down "jazz" versions of standard tunes and light classical works. Of the white composers who wrote in a jazz idiom, George Gershwin, with his *Rhapsody in Blue* (1924) and *An American in Paris* (1928), was the most original.

Meanwhile, black musicians were replenishing the creative springs of authentic jazz. Guitar picker Hudie Ledbetter (nicknamed Leadbelly) performed his field shouts and raw songs before appreciative black audiences in the South. Singers like Bessie Smith and Gertrude ("Ma") Rainey drew packed audiences on Chicago's South Side and sold thousands of records on black-oriented labels produced by the major record companies. Trumpeter Louis ("Satchmo") Armstrong and band leader Fletcher Henderson did some of their most creative work in the 1920s, while the enormously talented black pianist, composer, and band leader Duke Ellington performed to packed audiences at Harlem's Cotton Club.

Creativity in Black America

The growing concentration of blacks in the urban North, and especially in New York City, contributed to a black cultural flowering of the 1920s known as the Harlem Renaissance. This surge of artistic creativity took many forms. *Shuffle Along,* a 1921 Broadway musical review written and produced by blacks and featuring an all-black cast, enjoyed tremendous success. Tenor Roland Hayes, who excelled in both classical and folk songs; sculptor Aaron Douglas; and actor and singer Paul Robeson all contributed to the exciting ferment.

But above all, this was a literary movement in which gifted young writers produced an outpouring of novels, poems, and short stories exploring the black experience. Among the best of this work was Langston Hughes's *The Weary Blues* (1926); Claude McKay's *Home to Harlem* (1928); Nella Larsen's *Quicksand* (1928), dealing with the problems of young black women; and Jean Toomer's *Cane* (1923), an imaginative evocation of a black northerner's first encounter with the rural black South.

The Harlem Renaissance gained national visibility with the publication of *The New Negro* (1925), an anthology edited by Howard University professor Alain Locke. The NAACP provided a forum for black writers in its magazine *The Crisis.* Many Harlem Renaissance figures attended the memorable parties at Dark Towers, the elegant penthouse apartment of A'Lelia Walker, whose mother, known as Madame C. J. Walker, had made a fortune in the hair-preparation business.

For all its creative vitality, the Harlem Renaissance faced serious obstacles. The small black middle class and elite could give little support, and the Renaissance's artists and writers had scant contact with the black masses. The movement thus depended heavily on white patronage. Harlem was "in vogue" in the 1920s, yet often for distorted reasons. Alienated white intellectuals and rebellious Jazz Age youth idolized Harlem's black performers, artists, and writers for their supposed sensuality and "primitive" energy but ignored the ghetto's complex social problems. (Harlem's jazz clubs, ironically, excluded black customers.) Langston Hughes's white patron, a rich Park Avenue matron, supported him generously as long as his poems evoked the "African soul" but dropped him angrily when he began to write of black working people in Kansas City and New York.

Similar problems plagued the treatment of black themes by white artists and writers. *The Emperor Jones* (1920) by rising playwright Eugene O'Neill; Dorothy and DuBose Heyward's 1925 play *Porgy* (later transformed into an opera, *Porgy and Bess,* by George Gershwin); the first all-black movie, *Hallelujah* (1929); and Marc Connelly's popular folk drama *The Green Pastures* (1930) all drew upon the black experience in artistically creative ways, but all also perpetuated racial stereotypes. *Hallelujah,* for example, offered a dreamy, sentimentalized picture of the cotton plantations of the rural South, while viewing urban black life as a

The Diversity of Black Culture in the 1920s

(Above) Novelist and poet Langston Hughes (in a drawing by Winold Reiss); (center) Harlem's famed Cotton Club, where many legendary jazz artists performed; (right) blues singer Bessie Smith.

nonstop round of gambling, drinking, sex, and violence.

Although the Harlem Renaissance produced work of lasting significance, ultimately the movement proved a fragile cultural growth. With the stock-market crash of 1929, the Harlem "vogue" would end abruptly, and a new generation of black artists and writers would have to begin anew the task of expressing an authentic black voice.

Advances in Science and Medicine

The scientific developments of the 1920s would reverberate for decades to come. The first long-range television transmission, from New York City to Washington, occurred in 1927. In nuclear physics Arthur H. Compton of the University of Chicago won the Nobel Prize in 1927 for his studies on the nature of X-rays, while Ernest O. Lawrence of the University of California laid the theoretical groundwork that led to the construction of the first cyclotron in the early thirties.

The 1920s also witnessed important gains in medical research. Harvey Cushing of Harvard

Medical School made dramatic advances in neurosurgery, while at the University of Wisconsin, chemist Harry Steenbock discovered how to create vitamin D in milk by bombarding it with ultraviolet rays. Advances in the treatment of such killers as diphtheria, whooping cough, measles, and influenza helped produce a significant lengthening of life-expectancy rates.

Meanwhile, in 1919 an obscure physicist at Clark University in Massachusetts, Robert Goddard, published a little-noticed scientific article entitled "A Method of Reaching Extreme Altitudes." Throughout the 1920s Goddard studied the problem of rocketry and even performed rudimentary experiments including, in 1926, the first successful launch of a liquid-fuel rocket. Ridiculed at the time, Goddard's predictions of lunar landings and deep-space exploration proved prophetic.

A few observers sensed that a new era of scientific advance was dawning. In *Science and the Modern World* (1925), Harvard philosopher Alfred North Whitehead underscored science's growing role. Although "individually powerless," Whitehead concluded, scientists were "ultimately the rulers of the world." Although some found this prospect exhilarating, for many others it was simply one more of an array of disorienting social changes that made the 1920s an unusually stressful and conflict-ridden decade.

A Society in Conflict

Despite prosperity and superficial gaiety, American society faced deep stresses in the 1920s. The cultural homogeneity of an earlier day had collapsed under the combined assault of immigration, technology, urban growth, and Darwinian evolutionary theory. As a consequence, rural Americans uneasily surveyed the mushrooming cities; native-born Protestants apprehensively eyed the swelling ranks of Catholics and Jews; and upholders of traditional standards viewed the revolution in manners and morals with dismay. These complex crosscurrents manifested themselves in a series of highly charged episodes and movements that cast in harsh relief the social tensions of this decade.

Immigration Restriction

Fed by wartime superpatriotism, the long-standing impulse to turn America into a nation of like-minded, culturally identical people culminated in the 1920s. In 1921 Congress limited annual immigration to about 350,000. In 1924 it slashed the total to 164,000 and restricted immigration from any one nation to 2 percent of the total number of persons of that "national origin" already living in the United States in 1890. Since the great influx of southern and eastern Europeans had come after 1890, the intent of this provision was clear: to reduce the immigration of these people. As Calvin Coolidge observed upon signing the law: "America must be kept American." Further, by excluding Asians entirely, the 1924 law gratuitously insulted the Chinese and Japanese.

In 1929 Congress advanced the base year for determining "national origins" forward to 1920, but even under this slightly liberalized formula, the annual quota for Poland stood at a mere 6,500; for Italy, 5,800; and for Russia, 2,700. This quota system, which survived into the 1960s, represented the most enduring counterattack of rural, native-born America against the immigrant cities.

Because most restrictionists thought principally of Asia and southern and eastern Europe as the sources of "undesirables," the laws placed no restraints on immigration from the Western Hemisphere. In fact, immigration from French Canada and Latin America soared in the 1920s. Domestic political turmoil and economic necessity propelled many thousands of Mexicans northward. By 1930 at least 2 million Mexican-born persons lived in the United States, half of them in Texas, California, and Arizona. California's Mexican-American population soared from 90,000 to nearly 360,000 in the 1920s. Many of these newcomers to the Southwest became migratory farm workers who took up residence in rickety shacks and earned miserably low wages in the region's large-scale agribusinesses.

The Ku Klux Klan

The nativism of the immigration-restriction movement erupted even more viciously in the revived Ku Klux Klan. The original Klan had faded by the 1870s, but on Thanksgiving night in 1915, a group of hooded men gathered at Stone Mountain, Georgia, and revived it. William J. Simmons, a racist who loved secret societies, led the movement. D. W. Griffith's glorification of the Klan in *The Birth of a Nation* provided further inspiration.

The movement attracted little notice until 1920, when Simmons authorized two Atlanta public-relations specialists, Elizabeth Tyler and Edward Clarke, to organize a national membership drive. Sensing the appeal of the Klan's nativist, white-supremacist ideology and its fantastic secret ritualism, Tyler and Clarke devised a recruitment campaign involving a ten-dollar membership fee divided among the salesman (called the Kleagle) signing up new members, the local sales manager (King Kleagle), the district sales manager (Grand Goblin), and "Imperial Wizard" Simmons—with a rake-off to themselves. The enterprising pair also negotiated exclusive rights to sell Klan robes and masks ($6.50), the horse robe that every member had to buy whether or not he owned a horse ($8.00), and the genuine Chattahoochee River water used in initiation rites ($10.00 a bottle). This elaborate scam succeeded beyond anyone's wildest dreams, enrich-

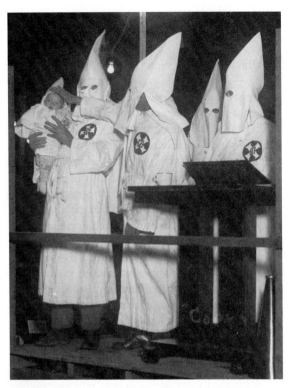

A Ku Klux Klan Ceremony on Long Island in the Early 1920s

The baby has been outfitted with its own white hood and robe. During its brief heyday after World War I, the revived Klan won many adherents all over the country to its message of white supremacy, moral purity, and 100 percent Americanism.

ing the promoters, Kleagles, and Goblins around the country.

Estimates of the new recruits to the Klan or its auxiliary, Women of the Klan, in the early twenties range from 2 million to 5 million. From its southern base, the Klan spread through the Midwest and Far West, especially in cities and towns where the native-born Protestant population remained dominant. Fifty thousand joined in Chicago; thirty-eight thousand in Indianapolis. Most newcomers were from the blue-collar ranks, although significant numbers of salesmen, clerks, and small businessmen joined as well.

During its brief heyday, the Klan exerted real political power in Texas, Oklahoma, Oregon, Indiana, and other states. In Oklahoma the Klan-controlled legislature impeached and removed an anti-Klan governor. The Klan elected a governor in

Oregon and pushed through legislation requiring public-school attendance of all children. Although the U.S. Supreme Court eventually judged this law unconstitutional, the state's Catholic school system suffered severely.

In 1922 a dentist from Texas, Hiram Wesley Evans, who described himself as "the most average man in America," dethroned William Simmons to become Imperial Wizard. Disarmingly admitting the Klan's image as a haven of "hicks" and "rubes" and "drivers of second-hand Fords," Evans urged the college-bred to support the great cause.

Under the umbrella term "100 percent Americanism," the particular thrust of Klan bigotry varied from region to region. In the South the anti-black theme loomed large. Klaverns in the North and West more often targeted Catholics and Jews. When an Illinois town changed its name to Mundelein to honor the newly chosen Roman Catholic cardinal of Chicago, a Klan newspaper thundered in outrage that Washington, D.C., might soon become "St. Patricksville," after Ireland's patron saint. In the Southwest much Klan violence was directed at violators of prohibition.

The Klan of the 1920s filled important needs for those who flocked to its banner. Although riddled with corruption at the top, it was not a movement of criminals or fanatics; observers invariably commented on the ordinariness of the members. The Klan's promise to restore the nation to an imagined earlier purity—ethnic, moral, and religious—exerted a powerful appeal to these ordinary Americans, the majority of whom were ill educated, deeply religious, of marginal economic standing, and disoriented by a rapidly changing social and moral order.

Klan membership also gave a sense of importance and group cohesion to rootless people who doubted their own worth. The ritual, the ceremonials, and the burning crosses lit up drab lives with drama and excitement. As one member wrote: "Who can look upon a multitude of white-robed Klansmen without thinking . . . of that throng of white-robed saints in the Glory Land?"

But if the individual Klansman seems more pitiable than sinister, the movement as a whole was far from benign. Investigators documented many cases of Klan intimidation, threats, beatings, and even murder in the grim quest for a purified America.

The Klan's collapse came with shocking suddenness. In March 1925 Indiana's politically influential Grand Dragon, David Stephenson, pressed bootleg liquor on a young secretary of his acquaintance, forced her on a Pullman train bound for Chicago, and raped her. When she swallowed poison the next day, Stephenson and his henchmen concealed her for days and refused to call a physician. The woman died several weeks later, and the Grand Dragon went to jail for first-degree manslaughter. From his prison cell, he revealed details of pervasive political corruption in Indiana. Its high moral pretensions ripped to shreds, the Klan faded rapidly. It did not die, however, and after World War II again surfaced as a malignant racist influence in American life.

The Garvey Movement

Among black Americans the decade's social strains produced a different kind of mass movement. For most blacks, escape from southern rural poverty made worse by racism led only to northern ghetto poverty made worse by racism. Many poor urban blacks turned to the spellbinding orator Marcus Garvey and his Universal Negro Improvement Association (UNIA). In a society where white represented the ideal, Garvey inverted the formula and glorified all things black. He urged black economic cooperation and founded a chain of UNIA grocery stores and other businesses. Finally, Garvey called on the world's blacks to return to "Motherland Africa" and establish a nation "strong enough to lend protection to the members of our race scattered all over the world."

An estimated eighty thousand blacks joined the UNIA, and many thousands more felt the lure of Garvey's hypnotic oratory; the uplift of the colorful UNIA parades, uniforms, and flags; and the seduction of Garvey's dream of a mass return to Africa.

In 1923 a federal court convicted Garvey of fraud in connection with the Black Star Steamship Company, one of his business ventures. In 1927, after two years' imprisonment, Garvey was deported to Jamaica. Without its charismatic leader, the UNIA collapsed. But as the first mass movement in black America, it revealed the discontent seething in the urban ghettos and the potential for large-scale activism. "In a world where black is despised,"

commented a black newspaper reporter upon Garvey's deportation, "he taught them that black is beautiful."

Fundamentalism and the Scopes Trial

American Protestantism had undergone severe trials in the half-century before 1920. The prestige of science had increased steadily, challenging religion's high cultural standing. Scholars had dissected the Bible's historical origins, while psychologists had explained the religious impulse in terms of human emotional needs. And all the while, Catholic and Jewish immigrants had poured in.

Liberal Protestantism had responded by accepting the findings of science and emphasizing social service to the immigrants. By around 1910 the Social Gospel seemingly had taken firm root. But a powerful reaction was building. This reaction came to be known as fundamentalism, after *The Fundamentals,* a series of pamphlets published in 1909–1914. Protestant fundamentalists insisted on the divine inspiration of every word in the Bible, on the Genesis version of Creation, and on the virgin birth and resurrection of Jesus. Social Gospelers and "modernists," they insisted, had abandoned these truths.

In the early 1920s, fundamentalists focused especially on a single symbolic issue: the theory of evolution. The evolutionary theory that Charles Darwin had advanced in *The Origin of Species* (1859) seemed to fundamentalists a blatant rejection of biblical truth. Fundamentalist legislators introduced bills to prohibit the teaching of evolution in the public schools in twenty states in 1921–1922, and several southern states enacted such legislation. In Texas, Governor Miriam ("Ma") Ferguson personally censored textbooks that discussed evolution. "I am a Christian mother," Ferguson declared, "and I am not going to let that kind of rot go into Texas textbooks." Fundamentalism's best-known champion in these years, aging politician William Jennings Bryan, vigorously endorsed the anti-evolution cause.

When the Tennessee legislature in 1925 outlawed the teaching of evolution in the public schools, the American Civil Liberties Union (ACLU) volunteered to defend any teacher willing to challenge this law. A young high-school biology teacher in the town of Dayton, Tennessee, John T. Scopes, accepted the offer. Scopes read to his class a text-book description of Darwin's theory, and his arrest duly followed.

Famed Chicago criminal lawyer Clarence Darrow headed the ACLU's team of lawyers, and William Jennings Bryan eagerly accepted an invitation to assist the prosecution. Journalists and photographers poured into Dayton, Chicago radio station WGN broadcast the proceedings live, and soon the Dayton "monkey trial" became another overnight sensation.

The trial's symbolic climax came when Darrow cross-examined Bryan on his religious beliefs and his scientific knowledge. As Bryan doggedly insisted on the literal accuracy of every story in the Bible, his ignorance of vast realms of human knowledge became painfully clear. Darrow amply succeeded in humiliating Bryan and ridiculing his "fool ideas." The local jury found Scopes guilty, but the larger verdict, the one that really counted, differed sharply. The Dayton trial, which Bryan had envisioned as a moment of triumph, in fact marked a decisive setback for fundamentalism. When Bryan died of a heart attack a few days after the trial's end, H. L. Mencken wrote a harshly satirical column in which he mercilessly derided Bryan and the "gaping primates" who idolized him.

Fundamentalism diminished as a force in mainstream Protestantism after the Scopes trial, but zealous new denominations and independent "full gospel" churches carried on the cause. Charismatic evangelist Aimee Semple McPherson, for example, regularly filled the fifty-two hundred seats of her Angelus Temple in Los Angeles and reached many thousands more by radio. Radiating drama and beauty, the white-gowned McPherson won an enormous following through her cheerful sermons and considerable theatrical talent. On one occasion she employed a gigantic electric scoreboard to illustrate the triumph of good over evil. Her followers, predominantly transplanted midwestern farmers, embraced her fundamentalist theology while reveling in her mastery of the techniques of mass entertainment. In many ways, McPherson anticipated the television evangelists of a later day. When she died in 1944, her International Church of the Foursquare Gospel had over six hundred branches in the United States and abroad. Fundamentalism suffered a severe blow at Dayton, but it was far from dead as the 1920s ended.

Aimee Semple McPherson

Offering a beguiling blend of religious fundamentalism, faith healing, and show-biz glitz, the Los Angeles–based McPherson won countless devoted followers.

The Sacco-Vanzetti Case

If the Scopes trial represented one battle in the cultural wars of the 1920s, the Sacco and Vanzetti case represented another. On April 15, 1920, robbers shot and killed the paymaster and guard of a shoe factory in South Braintree, Massachusetts, and stole two cash boxes containing $17,776.51. Three weeks later the police arrested two Italian immigrants, Nicola Sacco and Bartolomeo Vanzetti, and charged them with the murders. A jury found them guilty in 1921, and after repeated delays and appeals, they died in the electric chair on August 23, 1927.

These bare facts do not begin to convey the full texture of the case or the emotions that it aroused. Sacco and Vanzetti were not only immigrants but also avowed anarchists, and from the beginning the prosecution harped on their radicalism. The judge, a conservative Yankee Republican, made plain his hostility to the defendants, whom he privately referred to as "those anarchist bastards."

The Sacco-Vanzetti case encapsulated divisions in the larger society. Nativists dwelled on the defendants' immigrant origins. Conservatives, brushing aside issues raised by the defense, insisted that these alien anarchists must die. By contrast, prominent liberals such as Felix Frankfurter of the Harvard Law School (a future Supreme Court justice); socialist Eugene Debs; and writers and artists like John Dos Passos, Edna St. Vincent Millay, and Ben Shahn rallied around the convicted men.

In 1927 the governor of Massachusetts appointed a prestigious commission to review the case. The commission upheld the verdict, and twenty-seven days later, Sacco and Vanzetti went to the chair. Vanzetti had spent his final days on death row reading *The Rise of American Civilization* by Charles and Mary Beard.

On the day of the executions, John Dos Passos summed up his feelings in a bitter poem that concluded:

> All right you have won you will kill the brave
>   men our friends tonight
> . . . all right we are two nations.

Whether Sacco and Vanzetti actually committed the murders remains uncertain. The original case against them was circumstantial and far from airtight. However, recent findings, including ballistics tests on Sacco's gun, suggest that at least Sacco may have been guilty. But the poisonous political climate that tainted the trial remains indisputable, as does the case's symbolic importance in exposing the cleavages in American society in the 1920s.

Prohibition

A raging, decade-long controversy over the effort to rid the United States of alcoholic beverages further underscored those societal fissures. Temperance reform stretched far back into the nineteenth century, and, as we saw in Chapter 22, prohibition won wide support among progressives in the years before World War I as a legitimate way to deal with the serious social problems associated with alcohol abuse. But the prohibition cause also had a symbolic dimension, as a sign of the struggle of native-born Americans to maintain cultural and political dominance over the immigrant cities. Both components of the anti-alcohol crusade loomed large in the 1920s.

When the Eighteenth Amendment took effect in January 1920, prohibitionists rejoiced. Their cause had triumphed at last! Evangelist Billy Sunday proclaimed:

> *The reign of tears is over. The slums will soon be only a memory. We will turn our prisons into factories and our jails into storehouses and corncribs. Men will walk upright now. Women will smile and children will laugh.*

At first, Sunday's dream seemed attainable. Saloons closed; liquor advertising stopped; arrests for drunkenness dwindled. In 1921 alcohol consumption stood at about one-third the prewar level—an impressive decline. Yet prohibition was largely discredited by the end of the decade, and in 1933 it came to an end. What went wrong? Essentially, the prohibition debacle illustrates the virtual impossibility, in a democracy, of enforcing rules of behavior with which a significant portion of the population disagrees.

From the beginning, enforcement of the Volstead Act, the 1919 law that established a Prohibition Bureau within the Treasury Department, was underbudgeted and largely ineffective, especially in strongly antiprohibition states. New York, for example, repealed its prohibition-enforcement law as early as 1923.

Would-be drinkers grew bolder as enforcement faltered. For young people already rebelling against traditional standards, the illegality of alcohol simply added to its appeal. "Without doubt," declared a University of Wisconsin student, "prohibition has been an incentive for young folks to learn to drink. . . . It is the natural reaction of youth to rules and regulations." Every city boasted its well-known speakeasies where customers could buy drinks, and rumrunners routinely smuggled in liquor from Canada and the West Indies. Criminals sold flavored but highly toxic industrial-grade alcohol to an unsuspecting public. Many people concocted their own home brew, and the demand for sacramental wine increased at an amazingly fast pace. By 1929, thanks to such diverse stratagems, alcohol consumption had risen to about 70 percent of the prewar level.

Organized crime helped drinkers circumvent the law. In Chicago the police looked the other way as rival gangs engaged in bloody wars to control the city's liquor business. Chicago witnessed 550 gangland killings in the 1920s, with few arrests or

Skirting the Law

A garter safely hidden under a woman's skirt served as a convenient holder for a portable flask.

convictions. By 1929 Chicago mob king Al Capone controlled a vast network of speakeasies producing annual profits of $60 million. Although far from typical, Chicago's heavily publicized crime wave appeared to offer dramatic proof of prohibition's failure. A reform designed to produce a more orderly, law-abiding America seemed to be having precisely the opposite effect.

Thus prohibition, too, became a battleground in the decade's cultural wars. The "drys"—usually native-born Protestants—praised prohibition as a necessary and legitimate social reform. The "wets"— liberals, alienated intellectuals, Jazz Age rebels, big-city immigrants—condemned it as outrageous moralistic meddling.

On countless college and university campuses, prohibition was regarded as a joke. At Trinity College in Connecticut, the student newspaper suggested that as their class gift, the seniors erect a distillery on the campus "with the proceeds going to the college."

Prohibition figured prominently in the 1928 presidential campaign. While the Democratic platform halfheartedly endorsed prohibition, Democratic candidate Al Smith made no secret of his support for repeal of the Eighteenth Amendment. By contrast, Republican Herbert Hoover praised prohibition as "a great social and economic experiment, noble in motive and far-reaching in purpose." Once elected, Hoover appointed a commission to study the matter. In a confusing 1931 report, the commission acknowledged the breakdown of prohibition but nevertheless urged its retention. A New York journalist parodied the findings in a doggerel verse:

> *Prohibition is an awful flop.*
>   *We like it.*
> *It can't stop what it's meant to stop.*
>   *We like it.*
> *It's left a trail of graft and slime,*
> *It's filled our land with vice and crime,*
> *It don't prohibit worth a dime,*
>   *Nevertheless we're for it.*

Two years later, prohibition ended with the repeal of the Eighteenth Amendment. By 1933 the nation had other matters on its mind, and prohibition seemed little more than a relic from another age.

Hoover at the Helm

In 1928 the voters overwhelmingly chose Herbert Hoover as president. A gifted engineer, humanitarian, administrator, and cabinet member, Hoover seemed an excellent bet to perpetuate the nation's booming prosperity. Unlike his two predecessors, Hoover was no mere standpat conservative. He brought to the White House a distinctive social and political philosophy that reflected his background in technology and engineering.

The Election of 1928

A Hollywood casting agent could not have chosen two individuals who better personified the social and cultural schisms of the 1920s than the presidential candidates of 1928: Al Smith and Herbert Hoover. Although both were self-made men, in other ways they were "as far apart as Pilsner and Coca Cola," as H. L. Mencken put it.

In contrast to his experience in 1924, Al Smith, the four-term governor of New York, easily won the 1928 Democratic nomination. A Catholic and a wet, Smith, with his brown derby hat perpetually askew, exuded the flavor of immigrant New York City. Originally a machine politician, and fundamentally conservative in his social ideas, he represented progressivism's urban-immigrant component through his championing of social welfare and civil rights. His political intimates included several reform-minded women, notably Frances Perkins, the head of the state industrial board, and Belle Moskowitz, a key adviser.

Herbert Hoover won the Republican nomination with equal ease. In August 1927, when Calvin Coolidge cryptically announced, "I do not choose to run for president in 1928," Secretary of Commerce Hoover took him at his word and announced his own candidacy. Hoover faced no real competition, although some conservative party leaders remained suspicious of the highly intelligent but aloof progressive figure who had never run for public office and indeed who had spent much of his pre-1920 adult life abroad. Coolidge spitefully called Hoover "the Wunduh Boy."

Born in West Branch, Iowa, and orphaned at an early age, Hoover had put himself through Stanford University, made a fortune as a mining engineer in China and Australia, and was living in London when World War I began. His notable service as wartime food administrator helped win him a place in the Harding and Coolidge cabinets.

Stuffy, humorless, and invariably attired in a stiff high collar, Hoover disdained the handshaking and baby kissing of the campaign trail. Instead he issued "tons of reports on dull subjects" (in Mencken's jaundiced view) and delivered a series of laboriously composed radio speeches in a boring monotone. So maladroit was Hoover's campaign that the originality of some of his ideas went largely unnoticed. Smith, by contrast, campaigned spiritedly throughout the country, although in doing so he may actually have hurt his cause, because many Americans west of the Hudson did not warm to his big-city wisecracking or his unadulterated Lower East Side accent.

Smith's Catholicism figured importantly in the campaign. Whether, on balance, the religious issue helped or hurt his candidacy remains debatable, but he unquestionably faced a strong backlash of prejudice. While Hoover urged religious tolerance, and Smith denied any conflict between his faith and the duties of the presidency, to some staunch Protestants, especially rural southerners and urban fundamentalists, the issue seemed vital. Rumors circulated of the relocation of the Vatican to the United States if Smith won. (A post-election joke had the defeated Smith sending the pope a one-word telegram: "Unpack.") Long discredited anti-Catholic propaganda such as Maria Monk's *Awful Disclosures* of 1836 (see Chapter 12) circulated once again.

The decisive campaign issue, however, was probably neither alcohol nor religion, but prosperity. Republican orators freely took credit for the nation's flourishing economy and warned that a Smith victory would mean "soup kitchens instead of busy factories." In his nomination acceptance speech, Hoover predicted that "the final triumph over poverty" lay at hand. Seeking to defuse the prosperity issue, Smith chose as his campaign manager a General Motors vice president who moved the Democratic party headquarters to the GM building in New York and released lists of well-known capitalists who supported Smith.

Nevertheless, Hoover won in a landslide, grabbing 58 percent of the vote and even making deep inroads in the heavily Democratic "solid South." Smith won a meager 87 electoral votes, compared to a crushing 444 for Hoover. In a stark comment on the prevailing political climate, the Socialist party candidate, Norman Thomas, received only 267,000 votes—less than a third of Debs's 1920 total.

However, evidence of an emerging political realignment lay obscured by the torrent of Hoover votes. Smith did remarkably well in the midwestern farm belt, where financially strapped farmers abandoned their normal Republican allegiance. In northern cities, Catholic and Jewish immigrants (and their children, now coming of voting age) voted Democratic in record numbers (see table). In 1924 the nation's twelve largest cities had all gone Republican; in 1928 Smith carried all twelve.* Were

---

*The Republican sweep of the cities in 1924 was owing in part to La Follette's Progressive party candidacy, which divided the Democratic vote.

Presidential Voting by Selected Ethnic Groups in Chicago, 1924, 1928, and 1932

	Percent Democratic		
	1924	1928	1932
Blacks	10	23	21
Czechoslovaks	40	73	83
Germans	14	58	69
Italians	31	63	64
Jews	19	60	77
Lithuanians	48	77	84
Poles	35	71	80
Swedes	15	34	51
Yugoslavs	20	54	67

SOURCE: John M. Allswang, *A House for All Peoples: Ethnic Politics in Chicago, 1890–1936* (Lexington: University Press of Kentucky, 1971).

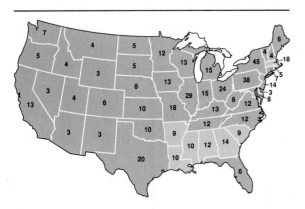

		Electoral Vote	Popular Vote	Percentage of Popular Vote
Republican Herbert C. Hoover		444	21,391,993	58.2
Democratic Alfred E. Smith		87	15,016,169	40.9
Minor Parties	–	–	330,725	0.9

The Election of 1928

prosperity to end, these portents suggested, the Republican party would be in trouble.

Herbert Hoover's Social Thought

As 1929 dawned, Americans looked hopefully to their new president, whom admirers proclaimed the Great Engineer. Not only had Hoover com-

piled a notable record of achievement, but he entered the White House with a well-developed social philosophy expounded most fully in his 1922 book *American Individualism.* Although his own life had followed the classic self-made-man pattern, Hoover did not mindlessly champion free competition. Nor in contrast to Harding and Coolidge, did he uncritically cheer for big business. His Quakerism, humanitarian activities, and engineering experience combined with his membership in a conservative political party to produce a unique social outlook.

Like Theodore Roosevelt, whom he had supported in 1912, the new president believed that cutthroat capitalist competition had become anachronistic. Rational economic development, he insisted, demanded corporate cooperation in marketing, wage policy, raw-material allocation, and product standardization. The economy, in short, should operate like a smoothly functioning machine.

Capitalism, he argued, had broad social obligations. He welcomed the growth of welfare capitalism and urged further movement in this direction. But above all, Hoover believed in voluntarism. The cooperative, socially responsible economic order that he envisioned must come about through the voluntary action of capitalist leaders, not through governmental coercion—in that way lay totalitarianism—or through power struggles pitting labor against management.

Hoover had put his philosophy into practice as secretary of commerce. Reorganizing the Commerce Department along more rational lines, he had made it a model for private industry. Seeking to accelerate the decade's trend toward corporate consolidation and cooperation, he had convened more than 250 conferences at which business leaders discussed such issues as unemployment, pricing policies, labor-management relations, and the virtues of trade associations. He urged higher wages to increase consumer purchasing power, and in 1923, arguing on grounds of efficiency, he persuaded the steel industry to shift to an eight-hour day. At the same time, he opposed the McNary-Haugen farm bill and other proposals for direct government intervention in the economy.

Hoover's ideology had its limitations. He displayed more interest in cooperation among capitalists than among consumers or workers. His conviction that American capitalism was embracing cooperation, social service, and enlightened labor policies overestimated the role of philanthropic considerations in business decision making. And his unqualified opposition to governmental economic intervention brought him to grief later in his administration when such intervention became urgently necessary.

Applying his ideology to specific issues, Hoover in his early months as president compiled an impressive record. He set up the President's Council on Recent Social Trends to gather data for policy makers' guidance. He created commissions to study public-policy issues. Responding to the farm problem, he secured passage of legislation that established a Federal Farm Board to promote cooperative commodity marketing. This, he hoped, would raise farm prices while preserving the voluntarist principle.

As the summer of 1929 turned to autumn, the Hoover administration seemed off to a promising start. But while Hoover methodically applied his engineering skills to the business of government, ominous long-term economic trends were converging toward a crisis that would overwhelm and ultimately destroy his presidency.

Conclusion

The 1920s stay vividly etched in America's historical consciousness partly because memorable events so decisively bracket the decade: World War I at the beginning, a catastrophic stock-market crash at the end. But another reason that the era remains restlessly alive is the stark picture that it presents of an entire people struggling to cope with massive technological and social change. Like world travelers made half-groggy by jet lag, Americans of the twenties sought to adapt to the rise of a mass-production, mass-culture metropolitan world that had emerged, seemingly almost overnight. Radio, the automobile, the movies, a parade of electrical appliances—so familiar to us that we hardly give them a second thought—were still exciting novelties in post–World War I America.

The most interesting responses to these sweeping changes unfolded outside the political arena. While the conservative political leadership of the twenties for the most part fell back on ideologies inherited from an earlier, less complex era, the rest of society seethed in ferment. Ironically, the same stresses and disorientation that produced bitter social conflicts in the decade also made it one of the most creative in American cultural and intellectual history. The champions of prohibition and fundamentalism, the troubled folk who donned the white robes of the Klan, the urban blacks who cheered Marcus Garvey, the artists and writers of the Harlem Renaissance, the early jazz musicians, and the young novelists and poets who revitalized American literature were all, in their different ways, trying to make sense of an unfamiliar and often threatening new social order. Historians have rightly deplored the political failures and reactionary social movements of the twenties, but that ought not obscure for us the positive and lasting aspects of this remarkable decade's achievements.

CHRONOLOGY

1915 Modern Ku Klux Klan founded.

1919 Volstead Act.

1920–
1921 Sharp postwar recession; agricultural prices plummet.

1920 Warren Harding elected president.

Radio station KDKA, Pittsburgh, broadcasts election returns.

Eighteenth Amendment added to the Constitution.

1920 F. Scott Fitzgerald, *This Side of Paradise*.
(cont.) Sinclair Lewis, *Main Street*.

1921 Recovery from recession; economic boom begins; agriculture remains depressed.
Sheppard-Towner Act.
National Woman's party founded by Alice Paul.
Shuffle Along, all-black musical review.

1921– Washington Naval Arms Conference.
1922

1922 Harding dies; Calvin Coolidge becomes president.
Supreme Court declares child-labor law unconstitutional.
Fordney-McCumber Tariff restores high rates.
Herbert Hoover, *American Individualism*.
Sinclair Lewis, *Babbitt*.
T. S. Eliot, *The Wasteland*.

1923 Supreme Court strikes down minimum-wage law for women.
Jean Toomer, *Cane*.

1924 Teapot Dome scandals investigated.
National Origins Act.
Coolidge elected president.
McNary-Haugen farm bill introduced.

1925 Scopes trial.
Ku Klux Klan scandal in Indiana.

1925 Alain Locke, *The New Negro*.
(cont.) Dorothy and DuBose Heyward, *Porgy*.
F. Scott Fitzgerald, *The Great Gatsby*.

1926 *The Jazz Singer*, first sound movie.
Ernest Hemingway, *The Sun Also Rises*.
Langston Hughes, *The Weary Blues*.

1927 Coolidge vetoes the McNary-Haugen bill.
Henry Ford introduces the Model A.
Willa Cather, *Death Comes for the Archbishop*.
Execution of Sacco and Vanzetti.

Charles A. Lindbergh's transatlantic flight.

1928 Kellogg-Briand Pact.
Herbert Hoover elected president.

1929 Federal Farm Board created.
Sheppard-Towner program ends.
Hallelujah, first all-black movie.
Ernest Hemingway, *A Farewell to Arms*.
Robert and Helen Lynd, *Middletown*.

1933 Repeal of the Eighteenth Amendment.

For Further Reading

Charles C. Alexander, *Here the Country Lies: Nationalism and the Arts in Twentieth Century America* (1980). A useful revisionist study whose chapters on the 1920s stress the decade's positive achievements.

Loren Baritz, ed., *The Culture of the Twenties* (1970). A rich collection of primary documents with an introductory essay stressing the conflict between "provincial" and "metropolitan" values.

John Braeman, Robert Bremner, and David Brody, eds., *Change and Continuity in Twentieth Century America: The 1920s* (1968). Interpretive essays by twelve historians offering fresh insights on the political, economic, and social history of the decade.

Paul Carter, *The Twenties in America* (1968) and *Another Part of the Twenties* (1977). Two essays surveying recent scholarship and offering refreshingly personal interpretive judgments.

Ellis W. Hawley, *The Great War and the Search for a Modern Order* (1979). An economic study, based on recent scholarship, that traces the emergence (and collapse in 1929) of the first mass-consumption society.

John D. Hicks, *Republican Ascendancy, 1921–1933* (1960). The best comprehensive survey of the decade's national politics.

William E. Leuchtenberg, *The Perils of Prosperity, 1914–1932* (1970). A cogent examination, rejecting popular stereotypes of the serious thinkers and mass culture of the twenties, by a distinguished intellectual historian.

George Soule, *Prosperity Decade: From War to Depression* (1947). A carefully documented, highly valuable economic history.

Additional Bibliography

Economic Trends

Guy Alchon, *The Invisible Hand of Planning: Capitalism, Social Science, and the State in the 1920s* (1985); Irving L. Bernstein, *The Lean Years: A History of the American Worker, 1920–1933* (1960); David Brody, "The Rise and Decline of Welfare Capitalism," in John Braeman et al., *Change and Continuity in Twentieth-Century America: The 1920s* (1968); Gilbert C. Fite, *American Farmers: The New Minority* (1981); Roland Marchand, *Advertising the American Dream: Making Way for Modernity, 1920–1940* (1985); Mira Wilkins, *The Maturing of Multinational Enterprise: American Business Abroad from 1914 to 1970* (1974).

Politics and International Relations

Susan D. Becker, *The Origins of the Equal Rights Amendment* (1981); Thomas Buckley, *The United States and the Washington Conference, 1921–1922* (1970); Nancy F. Cott, "Feminist Politics in the 1920s: The National Woman's Party," *Journal of American History* 71 (1984): 43–68; L. Ethan Ellis, *Republican Foreign Policy, 1921–1933* (1968); Betty Glad, *Charles Evans Hughes and the Illusion of Innocence* (1966); J. Stanley Lemons, *The Woman Citizen: Social Feminism in the 1920s* (1973); Donald R. McCoy, *Calvin Coolidge* (1967); Robert K. Murray, *The Politics of Normalcy: Governmental Theory and Practice in the Harding-Coolidge Era* (1973); Burl Noggle, *Teapot Dome* (1962); Francis Russell, *The Shadow of Blooming Grove: Warren G. Harding and His Times* (1968); Andrew Sinclair, *The Available Man* [Harding] (1965); Joan Hoff Wilson, *American Business and Foreign Policy* (1971).

Social Trends and the Mass Culture

Frederick Lewis Allen, *Only Yesterday* (1931); Lois W. Banner, *American Beauty* (1983); Eric Barnouw, *A Tour in Babel* [radio to 1933] (1966); William H. Chafe, *The American Woman: Her Changing Social, Economic and Political Roles, 1920–1970* (1972); Ruth Schwartz Cowan, *More Work for Mother* (1983); Robert Creamer, *Babe* (1974); Lawrence Cremin, *The Transformation of the School* (1961); James J. Flink, *The Car Culture* (1975); Estelle B. Freedman, "The New Woman: Changing Views of Women in the 1920s," *Journal of American History* 61 (1974): 372–393; Harry M. Geduld, *The Birth of the Talkies* (1975); Fred J. MacDonald, *Don't Touch That Dial* (1979); Lary May, *Screening Out the Past: The Birth of Mass Culture and the Motion Picture Industry* (1980); Frank Luther Mott, *American Journalism: A History* (3d ed., 1962); John B. Rae, *The American Automobile* (1965); Robert Sklar, *Movie-Made America* (1975); William H. Wilson *Coming of Age: Urban America, 1915–1945* (1974).

Jazz Age Youth, Dissident Writers and Intellectuals, Black Culture

Carlos Baker, *Ernest Hemingway* (1969); George H. Douglas, *H. L. Mencken* (1978); Paula Fass, *The Damned and the Beautiful: American Youth in the 1920s* (1977); Elton C. Fax, *Garvey* (1972); Frederick J. Hoffman, *The Twenties: American Writing in the Postwar Decade* (rev. ed., 1962); Nathan Huggins, *Harlem Renaissance* (1971); David L. Lewis, *When Harlem Was in Vogue* (1981); Arthur Mizener, *The Far Side of Paradise: A Biography of F. Scott Fitzgerald* (1951); Gilbert Osofsky, *Harlem: The Making of a Ghetto* (1968); Mark Schorer, *Sinclair Lewis* (1961); Daniel Scott Smith, "The Dating of the American Sexual Revolution: Evidence and Interpretation," in Michael Gordon, ed., *The American Family in Social and Historical Perspective* (2d ed., 1978); Theodore Vincent, *Black Power and the Garvey Movement* (1971).

Cultural Tensions and Symbolic Events

Charles C. Alexander, *The Ku Klux Klan in the Southwest* (1965); David M. Chalmers, *Hooded Americanism: The History of the Ku Klux Klan* (1965); Norman H. Clark, *Deliver Us from Evil: An Interpretation of American Prohibition* (1976); Ray Ginger, *Six Days or Forever?* [the Scopes trial] (1958); Robert A. Goldberg, *Hooded Empire: The Ku Klux Klan in Colorado* (1981); John Higham, *Strangers in the Land: Patterns of American Nativism, 1860–1925* (1955); Kenneth T. Jackson, *The Ku Klux Klan in the City, 1915–1930* (1967); K. Austin Kerr, *Organized for Prohibition: A New History of the Anti-Saloon League* (1985); Lawrence W. Levine, *Defender of the Faith; William Jennings Bryan: The Last Decade, 1915-1925* (1965); William G. McLoughlin, "Aimee Semple McPherson," *Journal of Popular Culture* 1 (1967): 193–217; George M. Marsden, *Fundamentalism and American Culture* (1980); Walter S. Ross, *The Last Hero: Charles A. Lindbergh* (1968); Francis Russell, *Tragedy in Dedham: The Story of the Sacco-Vanzetti Case* (1971); Andrew Sinclair, *Prohibition: The Era of Excess* (1962); John W. Ward, "The Meaning of Lindbergh's Flight," *American Quarterly* 10 (1958): 3–16.

Herbert Hoover and the 1928 Election

Peri Ethan Arnold, " 'The Great Engineer' as Administrator: Herbert Hoover and Modern Bureaucracy," *Review of Politics* 42 (July 1980): 329–348; David Bruner, *Herbert Hoover: The Public Life* (1979); E. Paula Elder, *Governor Alfred E. Smith: The Politician as Reformer* (1983); Ellis W. Hawley, ed., *Herbert Hoover as Secretary of Commerce* (1981); Joan Hoff-Wilson, *Herbert Hoover: Forgotten Progressive* (1975); Allan J. Lichtman, *Prejudice and the Old Politics: The Presidential Election of 1928* (1979).

CHAPTER 24

Crash, Depression, and New Deal

Rugged Campobello Island, lying in the Bay of Fundy off Eastport, Maine, was green and sunlit that August afternoon in 1921. In the sparkling waters off the island, a small sailboat bobbed and darted. At the helm, with several of his five children, was thirty-nine-year-old Franklin D. Roosevelt. A rising Democrat, Roosevelt had served as assistant secretary of the navy during World War I and as his party's vice-presidential candidate in 1920. But all that was far from his mind now. He loved sailing, and he loved Campobello Island. His parents had first vacationed there in 1883, and he had introduced his future wife Eleanor to the island in 1904.

Suddenly the idyllic afternoon took an ominous turn. First, Roosevelt, though an experienced sailor, unaccountably lost his footing and fell into the bay. "I never felt anything so cold as that water," he later recalled. Then he spotted the smoke of a fire on the heavily wooded island. Beaching the boat, he and the children frantically cut evergreen branches and beat back the spreading flames. As he remembered the scene: "Our eyes were bleary with smoke; we were begrimed, smarting with spark burns, exhausted." But with typical energy, Roosevelt insisted that he and the children jog the two miles to the family's rambling summer cottage on the beach.

That night, Roosevelt felt unusually fatigued —more tired than he had ever felt. Next morning his left leg dragged as he tried to walk. Soon all sensation in both legs disappeared. He had suffered an attack of poliomyelitis (infantile paralysis), a crippling viral infection that struck mostly children but sometimes adults as well. Except for a cumbersome shuffle with crutches and heavy metal braces, he would never walk again.

This illness changed the lives of both Franklin and Eleanor Roosevelt. For Franklin, confined to bed for months, it seemed the shattering end of his political career. But he exercised methodically, endured long hours of therapy, and gradually resumed political activity. In June 1928, laboriously mounting the podium at the Democratic National Convention, he nominated his friend Al Smith for president. Soon after, the New York Democratic party nominated Roosevelt for governor, and he went on to victory.

Somewhat superficial and even arrogant before 1921, this privileged only child became, through his ordeal, more thoughtful, more sensitive to others, more understanding of the disadvantaged, and far more determined. "If you had spent two years in bed trying to wiggle your big toe," he once said, "after that everything else would seem easy!"

Eleanor Roosevelt, too, was profoundly affected by her husband's illness. At first, she devoted herself entirely to his care—he could not even urinate without help with a catheter—and to the child-rearing responsibilities that now fell heavily upon her. But she also pushed him to resume a normal life and to return to politics. After years of subservience to her domineering mother-in-law, Anna Roosevelt, she firmly resisted Anna's efforts to take her son back to the family home at Hyde Park, New York, and turn him into a permanent invalid.

Eleanor became her handicapped husband's eyes and ears. Already actively involved with social issues, she now plunged into the affairs of the New York State Democratic party, serving on the executive board and editing the women's division newsletter. Though painfully shy, she forced herself to make public speeches, in the process overcoming an embarrassing tendency to giggle nervously at inappropriate moments.

The Roosevelts would soon need the strength and qualities of character that they had acquired during Franklin's fight back from incapacitating illness. Eight years after that August afternoon at Campobello, a devastating stock-market collapse signaled the onset of the worst depression in American history. Herbert Hoover grappled with the widening economic crisis through most of his term and then in 1933 made way for his successor: Franklin Roosevelt. Moving from the state house in Albany to the White House in Washington, Franklin and Eleanor, in their different ways, left their imprint on American history.

President Roosevelt dominated U.S. politics from 1933 until his death in 1945, first as leader of the government's effort to overcome the depression and then as wartime commander in chief. The depression-fighting phase of Roosevelt's presidency, commonly called the New Deal, was characterized by a dizzying array of laws, agencies, and programs that historians ever since have tried to whip into coherent form. And indeed, certain general patterns do emerge. In the years 1933–1935, sometimes called the First New Deal, the dual themes were relief and recovery. While Roosevelt urged national unity, his administration and a heavily Democratic Congress grappled with the immediate crises of massive unemployment, business stagnation, and agricultural distress. Around 1935, responding to political challenge on the Left and buoyed by a ringing endorsement in the 1934 midterm election, the New Deal shifted toward a more reformist course. In the so-called Second New Deal of 1935–1938, the administration placed less emphasis on unity and focused attention on business regulation and on social programs and tax policies benefiting working people, small farmers, sharecroppers, migrant laborers, and others at the lower end of the scale. Historians still argue over specific New Deal programs, and Americans of differing political persuasions even debate its overall merits. But few would disagree that the New Deal stands as a watershed in twentieth-century American history.

The many laws and agencies that made up the New Deal represented a complex amalgam of approaches drawn from diverse sources, shaped by many political crosscurrents, and reflecting the efforts of countless individuals. But in the public mind, the New Deal meant Roosevelt. Loved by some in his own day almost as a member of the family and reviled by others as a demagogue and an opportunist, Roosevelt is recognized today as a consummate politician whose administration set the national political agenda for at least a generation.

Crash and Depression

Like a joyride that ends in a blur of screeching tires and crunching metal, the prosperity of the 1920s came to a jolting climax in October 1929 with the disastrous collapse of the stock market. The Wall Street crash proved only the overture to a deep depression that reached into every household in the land. President Hoover, the "Great Engineer," struggled resolutely with the crisis, but his rigid ideological commitment to private initiative and his suspicion of governmental coercion sharply limited his effectiveness. In November 1932 a nation sorely disillusioned with Hoover gave an overwhelming electoral mandate to the Democratic party and its new leader, Franklin D. Roosevelt.

Black Thursday

Stock prices had risen steadily through much of the 1920s as investors responded optimistically to the many evidences of growing prosperity and advances in productivity. But beginning in 1928 and accelerating in 1929, this upward movement turned into a frenzied spiral as the lure of easy riches drew more and more speculators into the market. Prices of automotive, radio, aviation, and other glamour stocks floated into what one contemporary called "the blue and cloudless empyrean." Stock speculation in the early months of 1929 seemed the perfect form of gambling for an egalitarian society: everybody won.

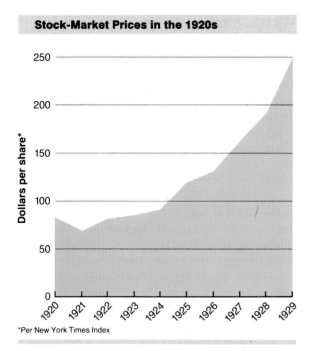

Stock-Market Prices in the 1920s

*Per New York Times Index

After rising moderately in the early 1920s, stock-market prices shot up later in the decade. Looking at such statistics, Herbert Hoover declared in 1929: "I have no fears for the future of our country. It is bright with hope."

In 1925 the market value of all stocks had stood at about $27 billion; by early 1929 the figure had surged to $67 billion. In early October it hit $87 billion. An estimated 9 million Americans played the market in these heady months, often on borrowed money. With stockbrokers willing to lend speculators up to 75 percent of a stock's purchase price, credit or "margin" buying became the rule. By the summer of 1929, such brokers' loans totaled $6 billion. The Federal Reserve Board's easy-credit policies and Treasury Secretary Andrew W. Mellon's continual pressure for income-tax cuts had increased the volume of money available for speculation.

A torrent of optimistic pronouncements drew more and more people into the market. "Everybody Ought to Be Rich," proclaimed General Motors executive John J. Raskob in the title of a *Ladies' Home Journal* article. President Calvin Coolidge, casting a final pearl of Yankee wisdom as he left office in March 1929, declared stocks "cheap at current prices."

With the nation's corporations eager for their share of the speculators' money, new securities, in the words of historian George Soule, "were manufactured almost like cakes of soap" simply because money could be made from their sale. Squadrons of salespersons earned fat commissions by selling securities at absurdly high prices to avid buyers. A few years before, Kleagles and Goblins had prospered by selling Ku Klux Klan memberships; now brokerage agents grew rich peddling American Can, Studebaker, Houston Oil, and Westinghouse. "Investment trusts," akin to the mutual funds of a later day, though totally unregulated, offered novices the benefit of the supposedly superior wisdom of more seasoned investors.

This speculative frenzy flew in the face of some hard economic realities. The prosperity on which it rested was in fact precarious. Agriculture remained depressed, as did mining, textiles, and other industries. Automobile production slowed as the 1920s wore on. The once booming construction industry declined by as much as 25 percent in 1928–1929 — an omen that few heeded.

In July 1928 the Federal Reserve Board tried to dampen speculation by increasing the interest rate on federal reserve notes, and early in 1929

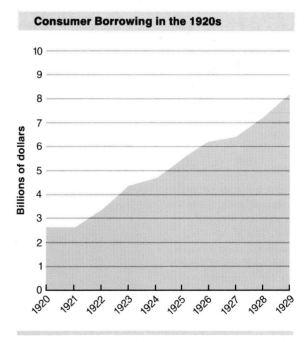

Consumer Borrowing in the 1920s

Americans plunged heavily into debt in the 1920s to play the stock market and to buy their new Fords, Chevrolets, and other consumer products. By 1929 their total debt stood at about $8 billion.

"the Fed" warned member banks not to lend money for stock-market speculation. But these measures did no good. With speculators willing to pay up to 20 percent interest for money to buy more stock, major banks and large corporations poured additional millions into the money market—an act akin to dumping gasoline on an already raging fire. The Fed tightened credit again in September. This time the action was effective, but with catastrophic consequences.

On October 24, 1929—"Black Thursday"—the collapse came. As prices suddenly dropped, trading grew more and more panicky. Some stocks found no buyers at all: they had literally become worthless pieces of paper. Mounted police broke up the uneasy crowds outside the New York Stock Exchange. Their faces frozen with anxiety, speculators huddled around the ticker-tape machines in brokers' offices—"like friends around the bedside of a stricken friend," according to the *New York Times*. At midday a group of powerful New York bankers temporarily stopped the hemorrhage on Wall Street by issuing a reassuring statement and ostentatiously buying some $30 million worth of shares of major stocks. But after a weak rally on Friday, prices plunged still lower early the next week. The climax came on Tuesday, October 29, when a record 16 million stocks changed hands in frantic trading, most at inconceivably low prices.

The big bankers who had tried to restore confidence the preceding Thursday remained grimly silent on Black Tuesday. In the weeks that followed, feeble upswings in stock prices alternated with further plunges.

On Black Thursday Herbert Hoover had issued the first of what would become a monotonous series of optimistic pronouncements. "The fundamental business of the country . . . ," declared the president, "is on a sound and prosperous basis." But Hoover was wrong. By mid-November, the low point for 1929, the loss in the market value of stocks stood at $30 billion. To one looking back from the ensuing depression of the 1930s, it appeared that the stock-market crash had triggered all the nation's economic woes. In fact, however, stock prices stabilized and even recovered somewhat in the 1930s. The worst appeared to be over. But the economy had deeper problems.

Onset of the Depression

Many economists shared Hoover's hope of quick recovery. After a shakeout of the stock market, analysts predicted, business activity would quickly revive. Instead, the economy went into a prolonged tailspin. The nation soon found itself locked in a full-scale depression that did not bottom out until 1933 and whose effects lingered through the decade.

1929

These two illustrations strikingly encapsulate the economic history of the year. The March 1929 magazine cover shows a young woman raptly reading the stock-market ticker tape, with its ever-rising prices; the cartoon "Sold Out," published on October 25, 1929, evokes the sickening panic triggered by the Wall Street collapse the day before.

Economists still debate the underlying causes of this depression. Some focus on the structural factors that made the prosperity of the 1920s fragile and unstable. They note, for example, that increased productivity did not generate corresponding wage increases for workers but rather took the form of higher corporate profits. Between 1920 and 1929, the proportional share of personal income going to the top 5 percent of America's income earners rose from 22 percent to 26 percent. By contrast, the 40 percent of Americans at the lower end of the economic scale received only about 12 percent of the total national income in 1929. The well-to-do spent a larger share of their income on nonessentials and luxuries, and this discretionary spending diminished sharply when the 1929 crash came. The decade's remarkable gains in productivity also encouraged overproduction. By the summer of 1929, the automobile, housing, textile, tire, and other durable-goods industries were overextended and cutting back.

Economists who trace the depression's causes to structural weaknesses in the economy also point to the protracted decline in farm prices in the 1920s as a major weak spot. Others argue that important sectors of industry—including railroads, steel, textiles, and mining—were lagging technologically as early as the 1930s and could not attract the kind of investment that would have helped stimulate recovery.

A second line of interpretation, the "monetarist" school launched by Milton Friedman and Anna Jacobson Schwartz in their 1963 work *Monetary History of the United States,* focuses on the collapse of the banking system in the early 1930s (see below), which they in turn blame on Federal Reserve System policies. The Fed, they charge, failed in its obligation to assure an adequate money supply that would have enabled the economy to bounce back from the shock of the crash. The money supply did indeed contract by 38 percent in the early 1930s, though how much the Federal Reserve System is to blame remains under debate.

Finally, all analysts emphasize that the U.S. depression occurred within the context of a global economic crisis. European economies—already enfeebled as a result of the First World War, massive debt payments, and a heavy trade imbalance with the United States—collapsed in 1931. Austria's biggest bank failed in May; Germany imposed currency controls in July; Great Britain abandoned the gold standard in September. This larger crisis had a variety of unpleasant effects upon the American economy and made an already bad situation worse.

While the depression's causes are complex and controversial, its chilling impact on the U.S. economy is all too clear. Statistics tell the bleak story. The gross national product (GNP) dropped from $104 billion in 1929 to $59 billion in 1932. Exports plummeted. Farm prices dropped still lower, falling by nearly 60 percent from 1929 to 1932. Wheat, which had sold for $1.04 a bushel in 1929, yielded only 51¢ a bushel in 1933. Railroad corporations controlling a third of the nation's track mileage fell into bankruptcy in the early thirties. The banking system tottered toward collapse. Between 1930 and early 1933, more than fifty-five hundred banks closed their doors. Industrial production rose slightly in the summer of 1932, but by the beginning of 1933, conditions had grown worse than ever. The unemployment rate rose from 3 percent in 1929 to 25 percent in 1933. This meant that the number of jobless Americans soared from 1.6 million to nearly 13 million in this four-year period. Many Americans who still had jobs faced severe cuts in pay and hours.

The Depression's Human Toll

The dark message embedded in these figures found confirmation as Americans looked around them —at idle factories, bankrupt farms, and closed banks; at the hopelessness etched in the expressions of the jobless, whether they were waiting in breadlines, sleeping on park benches, or trudging the streets looking for work.

Because most of those thrown out of work had families to support, the unemployment figures must be multiplied several times over to reflect the magnitude of the distress. Similarly, the epidemic of bank closings not only worsened the liquidity crisis but deprived millions of small depositors and their families of more than $3 billion in savings that they could ill afford to lose. Blacks, Mexican-Americans, southern sharecroppers, and other groups endured particular hardships in the depression (see Chapter 25).

Heart-rending scenes were played and replayed across rural America as thousands of farm families

Mason City Confronts the Depression

Mason City, a thriving community in north-central Iowa, had a proud record of growth and prosperity when the depression struck. Settled in the 1850s by Yankee farmers who belonged to the Masonic Order, Mason City had quickly become a hub for the fertile surrounding farmland. Immigrants from Scandinavia, Ireland, southern Europe, and later Mexico farmed the land and worked in the city's pork and beef packing-houses, beet-processing plants, and factories that utilized a high-grade local clay to produce tile, brick, and cement.

In the 1880s Mason City became the northern terminus of a shortline railroad, the Mason City & Fort Dodge Line, that was in turn part of a railroad link hauling coal from mines in southern Iowa to the yards of James J. Hill's Great Northern Railroad in Minneapolis. By 1890 four railroads converged on the city.

A confident, expansive mood prevailed among Mason City's residents in the early twentieth century. Farm homesteads originally purchased from the government for $2 or $3 an acre went for $100 an acre. As the urban center serving this booming agricultural region, Mason City prospered. In 1908 the town's business leaders hired the well-known architect Frank Lloyd Wright to design a downtown commercial complex including a bank, hotel, and office building.

The railroads declined as Iowa's coal deposits gave out, but in 1910 William Colby, the businessman son of Norwegian immigrant parents, announced plans to produce a new automobile, the Colby, in Mason City. The first car, called the Colby Model G, a five-passenger roadster selling for $1,650, emerged from Colby's plant that autumn. An improved version, dubbed the Model H and selling for $1,750, followed a year later. Visions of Mason City as the capital of an automotive empire fueled visions of prosperity. When a Colby driver completed a test run from Minneapolis to Mason City (130 miles) in under five hours, local boosters cheered. When the Colby racing team, driving the Colby Red Devil, placed second in a major race in the West, the town honored them with a lavish celebratory dinner. However, the bright dream was not to be. William Colby went bankrupt in 1914, and his humming plant fell silent. Only one Colby automobile, on display in a Mason City museum, is known to have survived.

But even this setback did not dampen Mason City's confidence for long. In 1918 the state's first fully paved cement interurban highway, an eleven-mile link between Mason City and nearby Clear Lake, brought out the entire town for dedication ceremonies, speeches, and a parade in which decorated bicycles, buggies, wagons, and automobiles made the triumphal drive to Clear Lake. Years later, Broadway composer

Mason City *The town's agricultural character is apparent in this undated photograph.*

Album Cover for The Music Man

Meredith Willson, born in Mason City in 1902, would capture the boomtime spirit of this era in his 1957 hit musical *The Music Man*, an affectionate tribute to his hometown, thinly disguised in the play as "River City."

The flush times of World War I intensified the feverish land speculation around Mason City. Prices shot up to $400 an acre, with little regard for the land's productive capacity. As one resident later wrote: "The town barber and the small-town merchant bought and sold options until every town square was a real estate exchange." In the glow of wartime prosperity, the town leaders founded a junior college in 1918. The speculative mania soon cooled, but confidence in the city's long-range prospects remained.

In October 1929, however, the nation's economy collapsed, dragging down with it Mason City and its twenty-three thousand residents. As the construction industry stagnated, the local factories laid off workers. Farm prices tumbled. Corn went for twelve cents a bushel; hogs, the basic cash crop, brought little more than two cents a pound; a load of oats would not buy a pair of shoes. In 1931–1932 a tidal wave of foreclosures and bankruptcies swept surrounding Cerro Gordo County. Industrious families that had sunk

every dollar into their farms faced disaster. The family outings, the easy conversations about crops, the pride in maintaining a handsome farm and well-repaired equipment all fell victim to the spreading miasma of fear. Milo Reno's Farm Holiday movement of 1931–1933, which urged farmers first to keep products off the market and then to prevent the foreclosures that were shattering lives and dreams across rural America, won a sympathetic following among the embattled farmers of Iowa, including Mason City's.

The county's leading landowning family, its roots dating to before the Civil War, lost almost all its holdings. A German immigrant who had married a local farmer's daughter and gradually built up holdings of nearly three hundred acres lost it all in bankruptcy court in 1932. "When the day was over," wrote the couple's lawyer, "this family went

out from the office the owner of an old team of horses, a wagon, a couple of cows and five hogs, together with their few sticks of furniture and no place to go." A retired farmer and his wife not only had to mortgage their Mason City home but saw the land that they had hoped to pass to their children sold at a tax sale.

Although Herbert Hoover was an Iowa native, the state turned resentfully against him as the depression deepened. Many solidly Republican voters in and around Mason City cast first-time Democratic ballots in 1932, helping to elect a Democratic governor and give the state's electoral vote solidly to Franklin Roosevelt.

By 1933, when the New Deal began, Mason City, like the rest of America, teetered on the brink of total collapse. The depression had struck the American heartland with devastating effect.

Mason City Turns Eighty-Five

Though badly stung by the depression, Mason City residents experienced some bright moments in the thirties. A mile-long parade capped the community's three-day celebration of its eighty-fifth anniversary in 1938. The festivities featured forty-seven visiting bands, thirty-six floats, and Shirley Morgan of Sheffield, Iowa, as queen.

Jobless Men Along the Chicago & Northwestern Tracks near De Kalb, Illinois

A local artist painted this haunting scene from a 1930s photograph.

lost their homes. In 1933 alone over 5 percent of the nation's farms underwent mortgage foreclosures or forced sales because of tax delinquency, with Iowa and the Dakotas especially hard hit (see "A Place in Time").

For the children of the depression, poor diet and inadequate medical and dental care often laid the groundwork for long-term health problems. City hospitals, health departments, and rural clinics reported alarming increases in malnutrition, rickets, pellagra, and other diet-related conditions among children. By early 1933, as local school boards stung by dwindling tax revenues shortened the school year and even closed schools, more than three hundred thousand children were out of school.

Newspapers of the early thirties conveyed the human meaning of the crisis by focusing on dramatic vignettes. The *New York Times* described "Hoover Valley"—a section of Central Park where jobless men had built makeshift shelters of boxes and packing crates. Journalists in Chicago wrote of several hundred homeless women who slept each night in the city's parks. Newspapers in Washington State told of an epidemic of forest fires deliberately set by men hoping to earn a few dollars as fire fighters. In a woods near Danbury, Connecticut, police discovered a woman and her daughter

near starvation. For five days they had eaten nothing but wild berries and apples.

Some gave up altogether. The suicide rate climbed nearly 30 percent between 1928 and 1932. In Youngstown, Ohio, a fifty-seven-year-old jobless father of ten jumped to his death from a bridge as the authorities prepared to evict his family from their home. On Christmas Eve, 1932, investigators found a young couple hiding without food in an empty summer cottage near a resort in upstate New York. Unable to secure work, they had decided to starve together rather than beg. Although extreme, such stories represented part of the terrible social cost of the nation's worst depression.

Hoover's Response

Historically, Americans had viewed economic depressions as acts of nature: little more could be done than to ride out the storm. Some members of Hoover's administration, including Treasury Secretary Mellon, continued to espouse such views. Hoover himself disagreed. Drawing upon the legacy of progressive reform and his experiences as U.S. food administrator during World War I, he initially responded to the economic crisis with energy and determination. But the steps that he

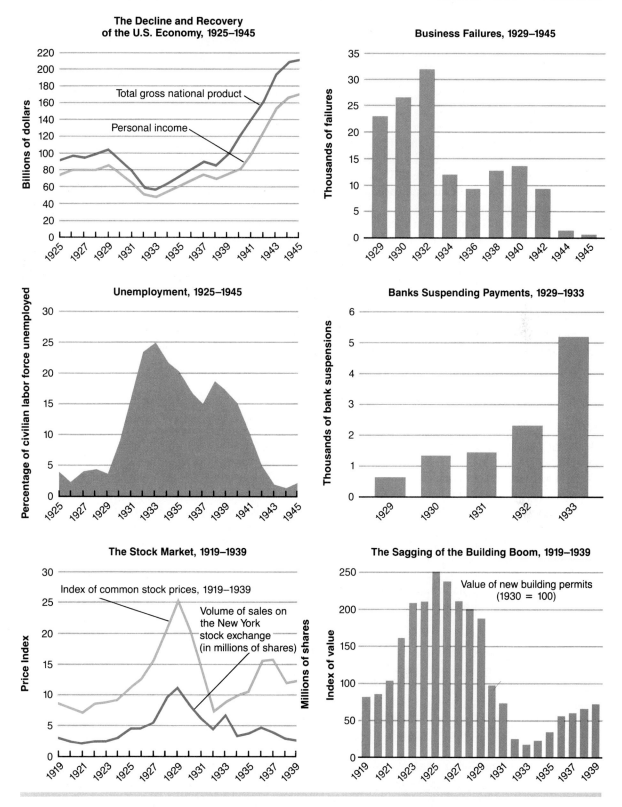

The Decline and Recovery of the U.S. Economy, 1925–1945

Total gross national product

Personal income

Business Failures, 1929–1945

Unemployment, 1925–1945

Banks Suspending Payments, 1929–1933

The Stock Market, 1919–1939

Index of common stock prices, 1919–1939

Volume of sales on the New York stock exchange (in millions of shares)

The Sagging of the Building Boom, 1919–1939

Value of new building permits (1930 = 100)

SOURCES: C. D. Bremmer, *American Bank Failures* (New York: Columbia University Press, 1935), 42; Thomas C. Cochran, *The Great Depression and World War II: 1929–1945* (Glen-view, Illinois: Scott, Foresman, 1968); *Historical Statistics of the United States, Colonial Times to 1970* (Washington, D.C.: Government Printing Office, 1975).

took also reflected his ideological commitment to localism and to private initiative. As he told an audience of Iowa farmers: "Every time we find solutions outside of government, we have not only strengthened character, but we have preserved our sense of real self-government."

Acting on these beliefs, Hoover summoned the nation's business leaders to the White House soon after the crash and won pledges from them to maintain wages and full employment. Viewing the unemployment crisis as a local issue, he called on municipal and state governments to create jobs through public-works projects. In October 1930 he set up an Emergency Committee for Employment to coordinate the efforts of voluntary relief agencies. Similarly encouraging a private rather than a governmental response to the liquidity crisis, Hoover in 1931 persuaded the nation's largest bankers to cooperate in setting up a private lending agency, the National Credit Corporation, from which hard-pressed smaller banks could borrow funds to make business loans.

But rather than improving, the crisis worsened. As early as November 1930, the voters rendered a harsh verdict on Hoover's policies. In the midterm election that year, the Republicans lost control of the House of Representatives and gave up eight Senate seats to the Democrats.

In fact, Hoover's well-intentioned antidepression strategy was a dismal failure. Unemployment mounted, and in 1931, pledges to the president notwithstanding, U.S. Steel, General Motors, and other big corporations announced major wage cuts. As for unemployment relief, private charities and local welfare agencies quickly proved inadequate to the crisis. In Philadelphia, where unemployment soared to more than three hundred thousand by early 1932, the city first cut relief payments to $4.23 per famly per week and then in June suspended them entirely. One charitable leader later described conditions in the city: "[People] kept alive from day to day, catch-as-catch-can, reduced for actual subsistence to something of the status of a stray cat prowling for food, for which a kind soul occasionally sets out a plate of table scraps or a saucer of milk."

By 1932, looking ahead to an election in the fall, with his voluntarist approach discredited, Hoover endorsed a series of measures that, taken together, constituted an unprecedented federal response to a national economic crisis. In January,

"You Stop Following Me!"

As the depression deepened, so did public resentment of Herbert Hoover. Admired in the 1920s as an administrative genius, the aloof president now struck millions of Americans as bumbling and uncaring.

at the president's recommendation, Congress set up and provided $2 billion in funding for a new agency, the Reconstruction Finance Corporation (RFC), to make loans to major economic institutions such as banks, insurance companies, and railroads. In its first six months of operation, the RFC pumped $1.2 billion into the economy. In February Hoover signed the Glass-Steagall Act, which made available $750 million of the government's gold reserves for loans to private businesses. And in July, although he had earlier vetoed similar measures backed by the Democrats, Hoover signed legislation authorizing the RFC to give $2 billion to state and local governments for job-creating public-works programs.

Ironically, however, Hoover reaped little political benefit from these measures. He supported the RFC idea only reluctantly, after the private National Credit Corporation's failure became obvious. He signed the $2 billion public-works bill very grudgingly, issuing a dire warning that it could open the door to "socialism and collectivism."

Hoover increasingly blamed the depression on great global forces and argued that only international measures would help. Some of the actions that he advocated, such as a one-year moratorium on war-debt and reparations payments by European nations, made sense, but they bore little immediate relevance to the urgent plight of ordinary Americans. Dreading an unbalanced budget, Hoover in 1931 called for a tax increase and thereby further alienated voters trying desperately to make ends meet.

Sensing the public's rising hostility, Hoover turned sullen and withdrawn. Avoiding personal contacts, he communicated with the American people through impersonal White House press releases that urged self-help and local initiative, denounced proposals for an expanded federal role, and endlessly saw prosperity "just around the corner." His relations with the news media soured. When his press secretary resigned and Hoover replaced him with a man heartily disliked by the Washington press corps, one reporter sardonically joked that the appointment was the first known instance of a rat joining a sinking ship.

The man once portrayed as a masterful manager and a humane philanthropist now emerged in the press as bumbling and hard-hearted. Hoover resented this characterization but seemed helpless to change it. Temperamentally unable to concede error, he told an aide: "No president must ever admit that he has been wrong." He even stubbornly continued to endorse prohibition long after its unpopularity had become obvious. A presidency launched so auspiciously in 1929 was ending in bitterness, recrimination, and failure.

Mounting Discontent and Protest

An ominous mood spread over the nation. In 1931 midwestern farmers devastated by plummeting agricultural prices organized the Farmers' Holiday Association to force prices up by withholding grain and livestock from the market. Declared the movement's leader, sixty-five-year-old Milo Reno of Iowa: "You can no more stop this movement than you could stop the revolution; I mean the Revolution of 1776." Dairy farmers who had watched wholesale milk prices sink to two cents a quart joined the protest, dumping thousands of gallons of milk in Iowa and Wisconsin. Farmers who did not participate in the boycott faced threats of violence.

The most alarming protest came from World War I veterans. In 1924 Congress had voted a veterans' bonus in the form of twenty-year endow-

ment policies against which the veterans might receive government loans. In 1931 a Texas Democratic congressman introduced a bill to change these endowments into immediate cash payments, and in June 1932 some ten thousand veterans, many jobless, descended on Washington to lobby for its passage. When Congress rejected the bill on June 17, most of the "bonus marchers" went home, but about two thousand stayed on, organizing protest parades and building a makeshift settlement in an outlying section of the city called Anacostia Flats. At one march, when a black veteran carrying an American flag was shoved and racially taunted, he shot back: "Don't try to push me, I fought for this flag in France and I'm going to fight for it here on Pennsylvania Avenue."

A nervous Herbert Hoover overreacted and ordered the army to confine the veterans to Anacostia Flats. The commander assigned this duty, General Douglas MacArthur, decided to break up the settlement entirely. On July 28, with a force of one thousand soldiers armed with tear gas, tanks, and even machine guns, MacArthur drove the veterans from their encampment and burned their shacks to the ground. For many Americans, the image of armed troops forcibly expelling peaceful demonstrators—and veterans at that—symbolized the Hoover administration's callous insensitivity to the depression's human dimension.

The Election of 1932

In the absence of other volunteers for the guillotine, Herbert Hoover easily won renomination at the 1932 Republican convention. Smelling defeat, the delegates gloomily adopted a platform offering perfunctory praise for Hoover's antidepression measures and endorsing a balanced budget, a protective tariff, and an end to national prohibition.

The Democrats, by contrast, scented victory as they spiritedly gathered in Chicago for their convention. The Democratic platform, cautiously crafted to erase the divisions that had weakened the party in the 1920s, appealed to the party's urban-immigrant wing with a call for an end to prohibition, to farmers with support for agricultural aid programs, and to fiscal conservatives with a demand for a balanced budget and a 25 percent reduction in federal spending.

The identity of the candidate remained unclear, however, as a number of Democratic hopefuls vied for the chance to challenge the vulnerable Hoover. These included Al Smith of New York, the party's 1928 standard-bearer; Texas's favorite son, John Nance ("Cactus Jack") Garner, Speaker of the House of Representatives; and Franklin D. Roosevelt, Smith's political protégé and the current governor of New York.

When Roosevelt, who led in the early ballots, failed to secure the necessary two-thirds majority, there arose the possibility of a dark-horse candidate. But then William Gibbs McAdoo of California, the former progressive who had served in Woodrow Wilson's cabinet and who in the 1920s had harbored presidential ambitions himself, announced his state's switch from Garner to Roosevelt. The Californians had not come to Chicago to see a deadlocked convention, he proclaimed, but to elect a president. The tide had turned; the nomination was Roosevelt's. Breaking precedent, FDR flew to Chicago to accept the nomination in person. Not realizing that he was naming an era, Roosevelt in his rousing acceptance speech pledged "a new deal for the American people."

Despite this ringing phrase, Roosevelt's campaign oratory gave no clear sense of his presidential agenda. He called for "bold persistent experimentation" and for more attention to "the forgotten man at the bottom of the economic pyramid," yet he also attacked Hoover's "reckless" spending and insisted that "only as a last resort" should the federal government play a larger economic role.

If his campaign lacked specifics, Roosevelt exuded confidence and good spirits. Above all, he was not Hoover! On November 8 FDR and his running mate John Nance Garner received nearly 23 million votes, as compared to fewer than 16 million for Hoover. (Roosevelt's margin in electoral votes was even more lopsided: 472–59.) Both the Senate and the House of Representatives went Democratic by heavy margins. After twelve years of Republican rule, the Democrats were back in the saddle. But what did this mean in terms of a program to fight the depression? During the lengthy interval between the election and Roosevelt's inauguration on March 4, 1933,* no one, probably

---

*The Twentieth Amendment, which shifted the date of the presidential inauguration from March to January 20, took effect after the 1933 inauguration.

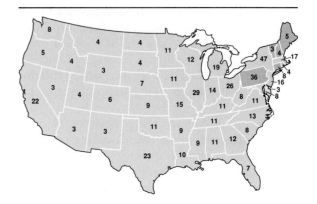

	Electoral Vote	Popular Vote	Percentage of Popular Vote
Democratic Franklin D. Roosevelt	472	22,809,638	57.4
Republican Herbert C. Hoover	59	15,758,901	39.7
Minor Parties	–	–	1,153,306	2.9

The Election of 1932

including Roosevelt himself, could confidently answer that question.

The New Deal Takes Shape

The Roosevelt years began on a note of feverish activity and high excitement. Enjoying overwhelming majorities in Congress, FDR proposed a staggering array of emergency measures in his early months in office, most of which passed by large margins. These measures reflected differing and sometimes contradictory policy perspectives. But through the confusion the contours of a depression-fighting strategy emerged. This strategy involved three components: industrial recovery through business-government cooperation and pump-priming federal spending; agricultural recovery through subsidized crop reduction; and short-term emergency relief for the jobless—funneled through state and local agencies when possible, but provided directly by the federal government if necessary. Hovering over this bustle loomed the larger-than-life figure of a smiling Franklin D. Roosevelt, cigarette holder jauntily tilted upward, for millions a symbol of endurance, confidence, and renewed hope.

New Beginnings

FDR's 1933 inaugural address vigorously set the tone of his administration. Although characteristically short on specifics, the new president dedicated his administration to helping the people in their time of crisis. "The only thing we have to fear," he intoned, "is fear itself." His own struggle to overcome a severe physical handicap lent added resonance to the phrase. Americans responded with an outpouring of support. Within days half a million approving letters deluged the White House.

Anticipating one Democratic campaign pledge, Congress a few days before the inaugural had passed an amendment to repeal the Eighteenth Amendment, which the states soon ratified. The nation's thirteen-year experiment with prohibition was over. Repeal would stimulate recovery, supporters argued, by producing a bonanza of local, state, and federal taxes on the sale of alcoholic beverages.

As the flurry of interest in repeal subsided, the nation's attention turned to the main event: fighting the depression. In some ways, Franklin Roosevelt seemed an unlikely figure to rally Americans in their moment of grave crisis. Like his distant cousin Theodore Roosevelt, FDR was of the social elite. His Dutch-immigrant ancestors had been merchants and landed aristocrats in New York for nearly three centuries, and he himself was the product of Groton Academy, Harvard College, and Columbia Law School. But during a term in the state senate (1911–1913) and especially as governor of New York, he had established close links with the urban-immigrant wing of the state Democratic party. When the depression struck, he had proposed to the New York legislature an innovative series of measures, including unemployment insurance, a public-works program, and emergency relief appropriations.

Roosevelt thus entered the Oval Office in March 1933 a seasoned, charmingly affable politician with a fine-tuned sensitivity to the public mood and a generalized desire to restore the nation to economic health within a framework of capitalism and liberal democracy. But he had no detailed agenda for achieving these goals. Little interested in abstract theorizing, Roosevelt approached his task by encouraging competing proposals, compromising (or papering over) differences, and then throwing his weight behind the measures that he sensed could be sold to Congress and the American people.

From his gubernatorial days, he had built up a circle of advisers nicknamed the brain trust. This group included Columbia University professors Raymond Moley and Rexford G. Tugwell and lawyer Adolph A. Berle. Of these, Moley was the most conservative; indeed, he eventually repudiated the New Deal. But Tugwell and Berle, heirs of the progressive reform tradition, rejected laissez faire ideology and advocated broad programs of federal economic planning and corporate regulation.

Roosevelt listened to his brain trusters, but they did not (as some critics fancifully charged) manipulate him like sinister puppet masters. In fact, the New Deal reflected many ideological and political crosscurrents. FDR by temperament sought a variety of opinions rather than relying on a single core of advisers.

Eleanor Roosevelt played a key White House role. A niece by birth of Theodore Roosevelt, the president's wife had politics in her blood, a keen social conscience, and a background in Progressive Era settlement-house work. She helped shape FDR's ideas not only directly but also by exposing him to the reformers, social workers, and advocates of minority rights whose causes she shared. Through Eleanor Roosevelt the ideas of a generation of women reformers found a voice in the White House. She traveled ceaselessly—40,000 miles in 1933 alone—and served as an astute observer for her wheelchair-bound husband. (With sly wit a Washington newspaper headlined midway through FDR's first term: "MRS. ROOSEVELT SPENDS NIGHT AT WHITE HOUSE.") In 1935 she began a regular syndicated newspaper column, "My Day."

Roosevelt's top political adviser, James Aloysius Farley, had managed FDR's two gubernatorial campaigns (1928 and 1930) and done the spadework that won his patron the presidential nomination in 1932. As postmaster general, he spent more time on politics than on the mails. He distributed patronage jobs, managed FDR's 1932 and 1936 campaigns, and oiled the friction points in White House relations with state and local Democratic machines. Bored by the substantive issues of the New Deal, the superficially jovial Jim Farley had a master's sense of the treacherous currents of presidential politics.

Roosevelt's cabinet reflected the New Deal's diversity. Secretary of Labor Frances Perkins, the first woman cabinet member, had served as state industrial commissioner during FDR's years as governor of New York. Interior Secretary Harold L. Ickes, a prickly but highly able Republican progressive from Chicago, had helped organize liberal midwestern Republicans for Roosevelt in 1932. Secretary of Agriculture Henry A. Wallace of Iowa held the same post that his father had occupied in the Harding and Coolidge administrations. Editor of an influential agricultural weekly, Wallace excelled as an agricultural economist, crop experimenter, and farm-policy theorist. Treasury Secretary Henry Morgenthau, Jr., FDR's neighbor and political ally from New York days, though a fiscal conservative, was prepared to tolerate unbalanced budgets if they were necessary to finance New Deal antidepression programs.

Below the cabinet rank, a host of newcomers poured into Washington in 1932, including former progressive social reformers, settlement-house workers, political scientists, economics professors, and bright young lawyers recommended by Felix Frankfurter of Harvard Law School. These newcomers energized the sometimes sleepy capital. They drafted bills, vied for the president's ear, and debated conflicting strategies of reform and recovery. From this hectic, pressure-cooker environment emerged a torrent of laws, programs, and agencies that historians somewhat awkwardly try to encompass within a single catchall label: the New Deal.

The Hundred Days

Between March 9 and June 16, 1933, as a parade of bills emanated from the Roosevelt White House, Congress enacted more than a dozen important measures, making the turbulent "Hundred Days" a period of legislative productivity unmatched in American history. Rooted in the political experience of the Progressive Era and World War I, and even in the Hoover presidency, these measures taken together led to an unprecedented level of federal involvement in the nation's economic life.

The frightening epidemic of bank failures presented FDR with his most immediate crisis. To gain time, the president on March 5 ordered all banks closed for four days. At the end of this so-called bank holiday, he proposed an Emergency Banking Act, which sailed through Congress in one day. This measure permitted healthy banks to reopen with a Treasury Department license, provided for the orderly handling of the affairs of failed banks, and enlarged the government's regulatory power over money and banking. The following Sunday evening, in the first of a series of informal radio talks dubbed "fireside chats," the president assured Americans that they could again entrust their money to banks. A second banking act, passed in June, further restored the nation's confidence in the banks by creating the Federal Deposit Insurance Corporation (FDIC) to insure all bank deposits up to five thousand dollars and to separate deposit banking from investment banking.

In keeping with the budget-balancing pledges of the Democratic platform, FDR on March 10 proposed, and Congress soon passed, an economy measure cutting federal workers' salaries, slashing veterans' pensions and benefits, and otherwise seeking to trim spending and reduce the budget deficit.

Other Hundred Days measures revealed the early New Deal's more experimental side. On March 31, for example, on FDR's recommendation Congress created the Civilian Conservation Corps (CCC) to employ jobless youths in such rural projects as reforestation, park maintenance, and erosion control. By 1935 half a million young men—no women were included—were at work in CCC camps from Maine to California, earning $35 a month plus room and board. Of all the New Deal agencies, the highly popular CCC, reflecting the traditional Jeffersonian belief in the virtues of country life, probably lay closest to FDR's heart.

Two important federal agencies established during the Hundred Days addressed the national tragedy of mortgage foreclosures. The Home Owners Loan Corporation (HOLC) helped needy Americans refinance their home mortgages. Eventually HOLC refinanced about one-fifth of all U.S. mortgages. The Farm Credit Administration did the same for rural Americans facing the loss of their farms.

The most comprehensive relief measure of the early New Deal, the Federal Emergency Relief Act (May 1933), revealed the continued strength of Herbert Hoover's conviction that relief must remain a local matter. This measure appropriated $500 million to replenish the empty relief coffers of states and cities. To administer this program, FDR appointed Harry Hopkins, a former social worker who would emerge as one of the New Deal's most powerful figures. A gaunt, acerbic, hyperactive chain smoker who enjoyed parties, sex, and the racetrack, Hopkins enlivened the Washington scene. In his first two hours on the job, operating from a makeshift desk in a hallway, he distributed $5 million to state and local relief agencies.

Another early New Deal measure incorporating ideas from the past was the Tennessee Valley Authority (TVA). During World War I, the government had built a hydroelectric facility on the Tennessee River at Muscle Shoals, Alabama, to power a nearby nitrate plant. Throughout the 1920s Senator George W. Norris of Nebraska had unsuccessfully urged the reactivation of this facility to supply electric power to the nearby farmers, most of whom still lived in a world of wood stoves and kerosene lamps.

With TVA the Roosevelt administration not only embraced Norris's idea but vastly expanded it through a commitment to the economic and social development of the entire Tennessee River valley —one of the nation's poorest areas. TVA built a hydroelectric network that supplied inexpensive power to the region while also developing a flood-control system, recreational facilities, and a soil-conservation program. Under director David E. Lilienthal, TVA proved one of the New Deal's most popular achievements.

The two most important measures of the Hundred Days, the Agricultural Adjustment Act and the National Recovery Act, addressed the fundamental challenge of economic recovery. Both measures evolved from debates among advocates of differing ideas that had been around for some time.

On the agricultural front, some favored the approach embodied in the McNary-Haugen bill of the 1920s by which the government would purchase agricultural surpluses and sell them abroad. Others, however, insisted that reduced production represented the key to agricultural recovery. They noted that farmers, seeking to maintain incomes, had responded to declining prices by *increasing* output, a process that drove prices still lower.

The advocates of production cuts won out. As a first step to this goal, the government in the summer of 1933 paid southern cotton planters to plow under much of their crop and midwestern farmers

to slaughter some 6 million piglets and pregnant sows. The wanton slaughter of pigs at a time when many people lacked adequate food proved a public-relations nightmare that the New Deal never fully lived down.

Pursuing the same goal in a more systematic and less emotion-laden fashion, the Agricultural Adjustment Act of May 1933 set up a program to go into effect in the 1934 growing season by which producers of the major agricultural commodities —including wheat, corn, cotton, hogs, and dairy products—received payments, called subsidies, in return for taking acreage out of production. A tax on processors of food, such as the mills that converted grain into flour or cereals, financed these subsidies. (Because the nation's consumers eventually paid this tax in the form of higher food prices, it was they who ultimately financed the New Deal's farm program.) A new federal agency, the Agricultural Adjustment Administration (AAA), supervised the complex program. The goal was *parity*: a restoration of farmers' purchasing power to what it had been in 1909–1914—a time of general prosperity in rural America.

The National Industrial Recovery Act (NIRA), passed in June 1933, drew upon the trade associations that President Hoover had promoted. It also embodied ideas of industrial self-regulation and business-government cooperation reminiscent of 1917–1918, when American business, prodded by Washington, had cooperated in the war-mobilization campaign. Now in 1933 the enemy was the depression rather than the German kaiser, but something of the same spirit of cooperation and shared purpose again united the nation—at least for a brief interval.

Under this law representatives of the major industries, granted immunity from antitrust prosecution, drafted codes of "fair competition" for their industries. These codes set production limits, prescribed wages and working conditions, and forbade price cutting and unfair competitive practices. To administer the codes, yet another federal agency, the National Recovery Administration (NRA), sprang into being.

As a promoter of recovery, the NRA aimed to break the cycle of wage cuts, falling prices, and layoffs. But reformers like Frances Perkins and union advocates like Senator Robert F. Wagner of New York saw further potential. Under pressure from Perkins, the NRA's textile-industry code banned

San Francisco Schoolchildren Form the NRA Blue Eagle, September 1933

Such stunts were part of NRA director Hugh Johnson's frenetic program to whip up public support for this controversial and cumbersome New Deal agency.

Major Measures Enacted During the "Hundred Days" (March 9–June 16, 1933)		
March	9	Emergency Banking Relief Act
	20	Economy Act
	31	Unemployment Relief Act (Civilian Conservation Corps)
May	12	Agricultural Adjustment Act
	12	Federal Emergency Relief Act
	18	Tennessee Valley Authority
	27	Federal Securities Act
June	13	Home Owners' Refinancing Act
	16	Farm Credit Act
	16	Banking Act of 1933 (Federal Deposit Insurance Corporation)
	16	National Industrial Recovery Act (National Recovery Administration; Public Works Administration)

child labor—a goal of reformers since the days of Florence Kelley. And through Wagner's efforts Section 7a of the law gave a boost to organized labor by prohibiting employers from discriminating against union members and affirming that workers had the right to organize and bargain collectively.

The head of NRA, Hugh Johnson, a retired general who had served with the War Industries Board in 1917–1918, brought to the job boundless energy, mercurial emotions, and a knack for publicity. Johnson quickly organized a whirlwind national campaign, complete with parades in major cities, to persuade consumers to buy only from companies that subscribed to an NRA code. The campaign's ubiquitous symbol, the blue eagle, and its slogan, "We Do Our Part," adorned billboards and magazine advertisements.

The National Industrial Recovery Act also appropriated some $3.3 billion for a federal public-works program that would employ the jobless and increase consumer purchasing power by pumping money into the economy. To oversee this vast program, the law created another new agency, the Public Works Administration (PWA). Under the leadership of Secretary of the Interior Harold

Ickes, the PWA eventually spent more than $4 billion on some thirty-four thousand public-works projects, many of them involving the construction of dams, bridges, and public buildings.

For the most part, the early New Deal was quite probusiness. In his speeches of 1933–1935, FDR always included the corporations as key players in the "all-American team" fighting the depression. The philosophy behind the NRA echoed Herbert Hoover's theme of business-government cooperation. Although the NRA codes, once signed by the president, had the force of law, Washington basically relied on voluntary business support for their implementation. Caught up in the spirit of national unity prevailing in 1933, most business leaders cooperated initially.

Moreover, the probusiness Reconstruction Finance Corporation, a carryover from the Hoover era, remained very active. FDR appointed as RFC chairman the millionaire Houston banker Jesse H. Jones. Under the forceful Jones, RFC loaned billions of dollars at favorable rates to banks, insurance companies, railroads, and even a large department-store chain. Jones not only helped endangered financial institutions but also extended government loans for new business ventures. According to historian Albert Romasco, Jones turned RFC into "the world's largest, most powerful bank" and made it a potent financial instrument serving corporate America.

A few early New Deal measures, however, anticipated a more adversarial approach to business—a theme that would soon loom larger. In fact, the 1929 crash had produced a bitter reaction against business executives. This reaction found expression, for example, in a Senate investigation of Wall Street conducted in 1932–1934 under the direction of a tough New York lawyer, Ferdinand Pecora. Pecora's probe revealed that not one of the twenty partners of the giant Morgan Bank had paid a penny of income tax in 1931 or 1932. The financier, a hero of the 1920s business culture, seemed less awe-inspiring in the political climate of 1933. People jeered when the president of the New York

Stock Exchange told a Senate committee considering regulatory legislation: "You gentlemen are making a big mistake. The Exchange is a perfect institution."

Reflecting this public mood, Congress in May 1933 passed the Federal Securities Act, stringently regulating the sale of stocks. This law required corporate executives to supply to the Federal Trade Commission full information on all stock offerings and made them personally liable for any misrepresentation of securities issued by their companies. This tough law, in turn, laid the groundwork for a measure the following year that sharply curbed the purchase of stock on credit (a practice that had contributed to the 1929 debacle) and created a powerful new federal agency, the Securities and Exchange Commission (SEC), to oversee the stock market.

Congress adjourned for the summer on June 16, 1933, and the Hundred Days ended. For many Americans this extraordinary initial burst of legislative activity came to symbolize the excitement and dynamism, as well as the confusion, of the Roosevelt years. The Hundred Days spawned an array of "alphabet-soup" agencies that few could keep straight. One cartoonist portrayed a harried Uncle Sam trying to juggle a dozen or more telephones labeled PWA, AAA, CCC, RFC, and so on. How would all these new programs and agencies work in practice? This remained to be seen.

The NRA Bogs Down

Responding to the stimulus of the Hundred Days, the economy improved briefly in the summer of 1933, but recovery proved illusory. Economic indicators remained bleak through 1934, and problems and controversy began to plague the New Deal.

The National Recovery Administration encountered particularly heavy seas. NRA's problems related in part to the erratic personality of its head, the hard-driving, hard-drinking Hugh Johnson. But NRA's difficulties went deeper. As the crisis-induced national unity of early 1933 faded, corporate America grew increasingly unhappy with NRA regulation. Charges of code violations increased. Small businesses objected that the codes served the interests of large businesses that wrote the codes and had less trouble meeting

Puzzling Out the New Deal

This 1934 cartoon makes clear that Americans of the 1930s, much like later history students, often had trouble keeping straight the new federal agencies that proliferated in Washington during the 1930s.

them. Republican leaders and some jurists attacked the NRA as unconstitutional. The agency itself, meanwhile, became bogged down in drafting trivial codes. The shoulder-pad industry had its own code; the nation's burlesque-house owners adopted an NRA code specifying the degree of nudity that strippers could display. Fundamentally, NRA provided no incentive to recovery. The trade associations that wrote and supervised the codes used them to restrict competition and maintain high prices, not to stimulate economic expansion.

Beset by myriad problems and failing in its essential task, NRA gradually sank of its own weight. Johnson departed in 1934, and in a May 1935 case, *Schechter* v. *United States,* involving a New York company convicted of violating the NRA's poultry code, the Supreme Court unanimously declared the NRA unconstitutional. The Court based its ruling on two grounds: first, the act delegated to the president regulatory powers that constitutionally belonged to the legislative branch; second, the NRA was regulating commerce within individual states, violating the constitutional provision limiting federal regulation to *inter*state commerce. Few New Dealers mourned. As an economic-recovery measure, the NRA had accomplished little.

Troubled Agriculture

The New Deal's early agricultural program proved more successful, but it, too, generated controversy. Aided by drought as well as by New Deal policies, agricultural production declined and commodity prices rose, as planners had hoped. From 1933 to 1937, total farm income increased by 50 percent.

But the AAA did little to help landless farm laborers, migrant workers, and the tenants and sharecroppers of the cotton South. Indeed, the AAA crop-reduction subsidies actually hurt tenants and sharecroppers, because the landowners in most cases simply banked the subsidy checks, removed the acreage from production, and left the sharecroppers to shift for themselves. One Georgia sharecropper, the father of seven, wrote Harry Hopkins: "I have Bin farming all my life But the man I live with Has Turned me loose taking my mule [and] all my feed. . . . I can't get a Job so Some one said Rite you."

Some victims of this process resisted. In 1934 the interracial Southern Tenant Farmers' Union, led by the Socialist party, emerged in Arkansas. Declared one elderly black sharecropper at the organizing meeting: "The same chain that holds my people holds your people too. . . . The landlord is always betwixt us, beatin' us and starvin' us and makin' us fight each other. There ain't but one way for us to get him where he can't help himself and that's for us to get together and stay together." The landowners struck back with a campaign of terror and nightriding, chasing down union organizers as their ancestors had hunted runaway slaves a century before.

Nature itself seemed to conspire against the farmers at the bottom of the economic ladder, as several years of parching drought in the mid-1930s turned the Great Plains into the so-called dust bowl. In Oklahoma the temperature rose above 100 degrees for thirty-five days in a row in the summer of 1934, and on the thirty-sixth day, it soared to 117 degrees. Rexford Tugwell, touring the Great Plains in the winter of 1933–1934, wrote of stunted winter wheat in arid fields looking "like stubble on an old man's beard." Under a searing sun and a rainless sky, dust storms rolled over the plains from the Dakotas to Texas. The choking, wind-driven clouds penetrated the tiniest cracks, covering furniture, clothing, and skin alike with a layer of fine dust. Drifting eastward, the clouds obscured the sky over Cleveland, dropped red snow in New England, and sifted yellow dust into the White House itself. Wrote one observer: "The country seems to brood as though death were touching it."

Battered by depression and drought alike, many poor farmers of the South and Great Plains abandoned the land. Some migrated to the cities, expanding the already huge relief rolls. Others packed their humble belongings into wheezing old cars and headed west to become migrant workers in the huge agricultural enterprises of California and Arizona. The hardships of these "Okies" (in fact, they came from many states, not just Oklahoma) became symbolic of the suffering and disruption of the 1930s.

In 1933–1935 debate raged between those New Dealers whose goal was to restore economic vitality to the agricultural sector as a whole and those, like Rexford Tugwell and Jerome Frank of the Department of Agriculture, who urged special

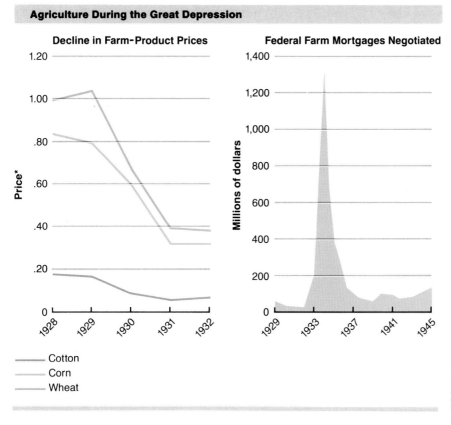

Agriculture During the Great Depression

Decline in Farm-Product Prices

Price*

Cotton
Corn
Wheat

Federal Farm Mortgages Negotiated

Millions of dollars

The depression hit rural America with brutal fierceness, as the farm-mortage statistics show. As agricultural income increased thanks to New Deal programs, however, farmers voted for Roosevelt in growing numbers.

*The graph shows the price per pound for cotton and the price per bushel for corn and wheat.

SOURCE: *Historical Statistics of the United States, Colonial Times to 1970* (Washington, D.C.: Government Printing Office, 1975), 511, 517.

attention to the plight of the nation's poorest farmers. At first FDR sided with those who took a less reformist view, and early in 1935 Jerome Frank and several of his allies in the Department of Agriculture were dismissed. The policy debate continued, however, and in the later New Deal, the advocates of a farm policy reflecting broader social objectives would score significant legislative victories (see below).

Controversy over Relief Strategy

Intense discussion focused, too, on the issue of aid for the unemployed. Relief administrator Harry Hopkins grew increasingly impatient with the slowness and inefficiency of many state and local relief agencies. By November 1933 Hopkins had convinced Roosevelt that only direct federal relief could prevent mass suffering and perhaps violent upheaval that winter. Accordingly, FDR put Hopkins in charge of a new but temporary public works

agency, the Civil Works Administration (CWA). Through the cold winter, CWA expended nearly a billion dollars on short-term work projects for the jobless. When the CWA check arrived, one Iowa woman recalled, "The first thing I did was to go out and buy a dozen oranges. I hadn't tasted any for so long that I had forgotten what they were like."

With the coming of spring, however, FDR abolished the CWA. No one would starve in warm weather, he believed. Although his conservative critics did not realize it, FDR shared with them a horror of creating a permanent underclass subsisting on welfare payments. But the persistence of mass unemployment, coupled with the inability of local agencies to cope with the challenge, rendered further federal relief programs nearly inevitable.

Hopkins's growing influence sharpened an intense behind-the-scenes struggle between him and Harold Ickes to control federal relief policy. Ickes, though a gifted administrator, was a cautious and suspicious man who scrutinized every PWA proposal for waste, corruption, and inefficiency. The PWA eventually did build many projects of enduring value, but in the short run the deliberate approach of "Honest Harold" left billions in relief funds stalled in the pipeline while he and his staff painstakingly reviewed every detail of their large-scale undertakings.

In contrast, the more impatient Hopkins sought above all to put people to work and get federal dollars circulating quickly. Even make-work projects like raking leaves, filling potholes, and collecting litter had merit, in his view, if they achieved these goals. Given the urgency of the unemployment crisis, Hopkins won the power struggle with Ickes. By mid-1934, although Ickes's PWA remained important, Hopkins dominated federal relief policy making.

The New Deal in Midstream: Popularity and Problems

As 1934 drew to a close, the first phase of the New Deal had ended. Despite the New Deal's brave beginnings, the depression continued. Major problems afflicted the NRA, conflict flared over the goals of the Roosevelt farm program, and the need for federal relief spending seemed to be expanding rather than tapering off as Roosevelt had hoped.

But the New Deal remained highly popular. This popularity reflected both the administration's achievements and FDR's enormous political skills. Assisted by gifted speechwriters and publicists, Roosevelt commanded the political stage, marshalling support for his programs with seemingly perpetual buoyancy, good humor, and self-assurance. Although many staunchly Republican newspaper publishers remained hostile, FDR enjoyed excellent relations with the working press. He loved bantering with reporters, and they reciprocated by presenting an overwhelmingly favorable picture of his administration.

In contrast to his tense and edgy predecessor, Roosevelt savored public appearances and took naturally to radio. He thought of the radio audience not as a vast, anonymous throng but as three or four family members in a living room, and in his conversational "fireside chats," he described his goals to the American people. To many, he seemed almost a family member himself. Frances Perkins later described his manner during these radio talks:

"His head would nod and his hands would move in simple, natural, comfortable gestures. His face would smile and light up as though he were actually sitting on the front porch or in the parlor with them." Roosevelt, in short, displayed an easy mastery of the new electronic medium—a mastery that his successors in the era of television would emulate.

The midterm election of November 1934 ratified the popular verdict on the New Deal. Reversing the usual midterm pattern, the incumbent Democrats *increased* their majorities in both the House and the Senate. As for FDR, Kansas journalist William Allen White observed: "He's been all but crowned by the people." Where would Roosevelt go now? Some observers viewed the New Deal as essentially complete and anticipated a period of cautious consolidation. But a different mood prevailed in the White House and in Congress. As the 1934 election returns rolled in, Harry Hopkins turned to a group of New Deal friends and declared: "Boys, this is our hour!" A new surge of activism, rivaling that of the Hundred Days, lay ahead.

The New Deal Changes Course

Depression still hobbled the country as 1934 ended, but the desperate conditions of early 1933 had eased. As the economy slowly revived, the mood of national unity faded, however, and the New Deal faced criticism from conservatives for going too far and from radicals for not going far enough. Shelving the unity theme, Roosevelt veered sharply leftward and took up the cause of the underdog. Buoyed by the results of the 1934 midterm election and with an eye on the forthcoming presidential contest, FDR in 1935 pushed through a bundle of reform measures so impressive that historians call this phase the Second New Deal. The landslide reelection victory that followed in 1936 cemented a new Democratic coalition that would long remain a potent political force.

Challenges from Right and Left

Although the early New Deal was hardly radical, some conservative business leaders soon concluded that it posed a mortal threat to the capitalist system. In 1934 several top corporate figures, joined by an increasingly conservative Al Smith and other disgruntled Democrats, formed an anti–New Deal organization called the American Liberty League, dedicated to the proposition that the Roosevelt program restricted individual freedom and pointed the way to socialism. Early in 1935 the U.S. Chamber of Commerce blasted the New Deal. Anti-Roosevelt jokes circulated among the rich. The *New Yorker* captured the mood with a cartoon picturing a group of elegantly dressed millionaires going off to the movie newsreels to hiss at Roosevelt. Members of the social elite denounced FDR as a traitor to his class; others could only sputter in rage at "that man in the White House."

More potent opposition came from spokespersons for those in the lower ranks of American life who demanded more radical social and economic changes. Detroit Catholic priest and radio spellbinder Charles E. Coughlin won an audience of some 40 million in the early thirties for his volatile brew of economics, politics, and piety. At first Coughlin supported the New Deal, but by 1935 he was condemning FDR as a "great betrayer and liar," making anti-Semitic allusions, and peddling his own panaceas, including nationalization of the banks and that old populist cure-all, free silver. As a priest and a native of Canada, Coughlin himself could not run for office, but his radio followers, organized as the National Union of Social Justice and drawn mainly from the ranks of the urban lower-middle class with a sprinkling of small businessmen, threatened FDR's 1936 electoral hopes.

Millions of older Americans, meanwhile, rallied to the banner of an elderly California physician, Francis E. Townsend. According to Townsend's deceptively simple plan, the government would pay two hundred dollars each month to all retired citizens over sixty, requiring only that the money be spent within thirty days. Such a plan would not only help elder Americans and stimulate the economy, Townsend insisted, but also open up jobs by encouraging early retirement. The fact that the scheme would have quickly bankrupted the nation did not prevent many older citizens, especially in southern California, from embracing it.

FDR's wiliest rival was Huey Long of Louisiana, a flamboyant political hell raiser. A country-boy lawyer who won the Louisiana governorship in 1928, Long ruled the state as his personal fiefdom while building highways, schools, and public

Huey Long Announces for President, August 1935

Administration strategists took Long's candidacy very seriously. A poll by the Democratic National Committee suggested that he might have won enough votes as a third-party candidate in 1936 to deny FDR reelection and hand the White House to the Republicans.

housing. He roared into Washington as a senator in 1932, preaching his "Share Our Wealth" program: a 100 percent tax on all annual incomes over $1 million and appropriation of all fortunes in excess of $5 million. With this money Long proposed to give every American family a comfortable income, a house, a car, old-age benefits, and free educational opportunities. While he sometimes played the buffoon, Long was highly intelligent. One senator, describing his debating style, compared him to a horsefly: "He would light on one part of you, sting you, and then, when you slapped at him, fly away to land elsewhere and sting again."

"Every man a king," proclaimed Long, and millions responded. Though he never translated his grand generalities into specifics, his baiting of the rich and powerful appealed to the many Americans sullenly resentful of the nation's gaping disparities of wealth. Like Father Coughlin, Long fleetingly endorsed the New Deal, but as his book *My First Days in the White House* (published posthumously in 1935) made clear, the presidential bug had bitten him badly. By 1935 "the Kingfish" (a nickname drawn from the radio comedy show

"Amos 'n' Andy") boasted 7.5 million supporters. An assassin's bullet cut Long down that September, but his close associate, the even more demagogic Gerald L. K. Smith, quickly took over his Share Our Wealth organization.

Adding to Roosevelt's worries, economic recovery was frustratingly elusive. National income in 1934 rose about 25 percent above the disastrous year 1933 but still hovered far below the 1929 level. Millions had now been jobless for three or four years and were deeply demoralized. As one observer described them: "They are ghosts that walk the street by day. They are ghosts sleeping with yesterday's newspapers thrown around them for covers at night." The rising frustration found expression, too, in nearly two thousand strikes, some of them communist-led, that disrupted labor in 1934, from New York taxi drivers to San Francisco dockworkers.

Rather than withdrawing in the face of adversity, as Hoover had done, Roosevelt outflanked his opponents and regained the political high ground in 1935 with an impressive series of legislative initiatives—the so-called Second New Deal.

The Second New Deal: Expanding Federal Relief

President Roosevelt set the stage for the Second New Deal in his January 1935 State of the Union address in calling for broad social reform. He soon fleshed out the rhetoric with a specific program involving six central elements: an enlarged and reorganized federal program of relief for the jobless, assistance to the rural poor, support for organized labor, social-welfare benefits for older Americans and other disadvantaged groups, stricter business regulation, and heavier taxes on the well-to-do.

With unemployment still alarmingly high, Congress in April 1935 passed the Emergency Relief Appropriation Act, granting Roosevelt a staggering $5 billion to spend more or less as he wished. He swiftly set up a new agency, the Works Progress Administration (WPA), headed by Harry Hopkins. Like the temporary Civil Works Administration that had helped the nation through the winter of 1933–1934, the WPA program involved the *direct* transfer of relief assistance from the federal government to individuals.

But Roosevelt's horror of what he called "the dole" led him to insist that the WPA provide *work* rather than handouts for the jobless. Over its eight-year life, the WPA extended essential support to more than 8 million unemployed American workers, pumped $11 billion into the economy, and completed a mind-boggling number of projects: 650,000 miles of roads constructed or improved; 124,000 bridges built or repaired; and 125,000 schools, hospitals, post offices, and other public buildings erected.

While most WPA workers performed manual labor, the agency also assisted writers, performers, and artists. The Federal Writers' Project employed out-of-work authors to produce a valuable series of state guides as well as the histories of various ethnic and immigrant groups. Black novelist Richard Wright's first book, a short-story collection called *Uncle Tom's Children* (1938), was written with support from the Federal Writers' Project. In Salem, Massachusetts, WPA workers transcribed hundreds of pages of handwritten legal documents from the witchcraft episode of 1692. In the South they collected the reminiscences of over two thousand aged ex-slaves.

The Federal Theatre Project, direct by Hallie Flanagan, a drama professor at Vassar College, put more than twelve thousand unemployed actors to work in theaters across the nation. One of the more controversial Federal Theatre Project undertakings, the Living Newspaper, which dramatized contemporary social issues, was dismissed by some critics as New Deal propaganda. But the FTP drama companies touring small-town America gave millions their first taste of live theater and offered a welcome respite from depression cares. Artists working for the Federal Art Project designed posters, taught painting in schools, and decorated post offices and courthouses with murals. These WPA arts agencies helped thousands of creative people survive the depression; they also enlivened a dismal decade and created an unprecedented federally supported popular-culture program.

Other New Deal agencies distributed relief funds as well. The National Youth Administration provided part-time work for more than 2 million high school and college youths. And Harold Ickes's Public Works Administration, after its agonizingly slow start, now picked up a full head of steam. Expending more than $4 billion over its entire life span, PWA employed many thousands of workers on some thirty-four thousand construction projects, including such diverse undertakings as the Triborough Bridge and the Lincoln Tunnel in New York City, the awesome Grand Coulee Dam on the Columbia River in Washington State, and a strikingly beautiful library for the University of New Mexico.

Monumental relief spending contributed to monumental budget deficits. The national debt soared from $21 billion in 1933 to $43 billion in 1940. According to John Maynard Keynes, an influential British economic theorist, this was just what the economy needed. Reversing the conventional budget-balancing wisdom, Keynes prescribed deficit spending as the key to economic recovery. In fact, however, although the deficits mounted each year, the New Deal, except perhaps toward the very end, never explicitly embraced Keynesianism. FDR reluctantly tolerated deficit spending as the price of other New Deal goals but never as an essential economic strategy valuable in itself.

The Second New Deal: Turning Leftward

Roosevelt's legislative proposals of 1935 also reflected his administration's sharp turn to the left. In 1933, buoyed by a short-lived but intense spirit

of national unity, the Roosevelt administration had played down class differences, stressed the common goal of recovery, and attempted an unprecedented degree of centralized economic planning and control. By 1935 the interlude of national harmony had ended, and the political struggles inevitable in a democracy made up of conflicting social classes and diverse interest groups had revived. Reflecting the new political reality, the Second New Deal abandoned the effort to devise programs with universal appeal. Stung by conservative criticism and confronting a broad spectrum of discontent, Roosevelt now offered a program frankly geared to the needs of the poor, the disadvantaged, and the laboring masses.

Social-justice advocates like Secretary of Labor Frances Perkins and federal Children's Bureau director Grace Abbott, as well as Eleanor Roosevelt, helped shape this program. But so, too, did hardheaded political calculations. Looking ahead to 1936, Roosevelt's political advisers feared that a coalition of the New Deal's radical critics could siphon off enough votes to deny Roosevelt a second term. The goal of winning over the followers of Coughlin, Townsend, and Long thus figured prominently in FDR's 1935 political agenda.

The New Deal's leftward turn was evident in its agricultural policy, as the plight of sharecrop-

Dust-Bowl Images: 1936 Ben Shahn Poster; Abandoned Farm in Hall County, Texas

Nature seemed to conspire with the economic cycle to batter Great Plains farmers in the 1930s. While many left the land to become migrants, a few stayed. "We made five crop failures in five years," one later recalled. "We scratched, literally scratched, to live."

Major Later New Deal Legislation (November 1933–1938)

1933 (Nov.)	Civil Works Administration	**1935**	Emergency Relief Appropriations Act (Works Progress Administration)
1934	Civil Works Emergency Relief Act		National Labor Relations Act (Wagner Act)
	Home Owners' Loan Act		Revenue Act of 1935
	Securities Exchange Act (Securities and Exchange Commission)		Social Security Act
	Communications Act (Federal Communications Commission)		Public Utilities Holding Company Act
	Federal Farm Bankruptcy Act		Banking Act of 1935
	National Housing Act (Federal Housing Administration)		Resettlement Administration
			Rural Electrification Act
		1937	National Housing Act of 1937
			Bankhead-Jones Farm Tenancy Act
		1938	Fair Labor Standards Act
			Agricultural Adjustment Act of 1938

pers, tenants, migrants, and other poor farmers aroused fresh attention. This plight, as we have seen, had been worsened by the New Deal's own AAA and its payments to large landowners to take acreage out of production. The Resettlement Administration, created by Congress in May 1935 and directed by Rexford Tugwell, made loans to help small farmers buy their own farms and to enable sharecroppers and tenants barely eking out a living from exhausted soil to resettle in more productive areas. Although Tugwell's agency accomplished less than he had hoped and lasted only two years, it did keep the difficulties of tenants and sharecroppers alive as an issue of governmental concern.

The Rural Electrification Administration (REA), another agency created in that busy spring of 1935, made low-interest loans to utility companies and farmers' cooperatives to extend electricity to the 90 percent of rural America that still lacked it. The REA compiled a record of significant achievements. By 1941, 40 percent of American farms enjoyed electric power.

Meanwhile, the New Deal's agricultural-recovery program suffered a setback in January 1936 when the Supreme Court declared the Agricultural Adjustment Act unconstitutional. The processing tax that funded the AAA's subsidies represented an illegal use of the government's tax power, the Court ruled. To replace the AAA, Congress soon passed the Soil Conservation and Domestic Allotment Act, under which farmers received payments for cutting production of soil-depleting crops such as wheat and cotton (which also happened to be the major surplus commodities) and planting soil-conserving grasses and legumes instead. When agricultural prices remained depressed, Congress passed another major farm law in 1938 (see below).

Organized labor won an important victory during the Second New Deal, again thanks to the efforts of New York senator Robert Wagner, himself a janitor's son who had risen to great power in Washington. At first FDR had opposed Wagner's campaign for a prolabor law, viewing such "special-interest" legislation as discordant with the early New Deal's national-unity theme. Wagner patiently built congressional support for his bill, however. In May 1935, when the Supreme Court ruled the NIRA unconstitutional, including Section 7a protecting union members' rights, FDR announced his support for a labor law that would survive constitutional scrutiny.

The National Labor Relations Act of July 1935 guaranteed collective-bargaining rights, permitted closed shops,* and outlawed such management

---

*In a closed shop, all employees must join the union as a condition of employment, so that the union bargaining agent can negotiate with management as the representative of the entire work force. In an open shop (advocated by so-called right-to-work groups today), union membership is not a requirement for employment.

practices as spying on unions and blacklisting labor "agitators." The law also created a new agency, the National Labor Relations Board (NLRB), to supervise shop elections and deal with labor-law violations. In the long struggle between labor and management, the Wagner Act, as it was called, gave powerful new weapons to labor and stimulated a wave of unionization (see Chapter 25).

Of all the path-breaking measures of the Second New Deal, one stands out for its long-range significance: the Social Security Act of 1935. Drafted by a committee chaired by Secretary of Labor Frances Perkins, this measure in fact had a complex parentage, including the ideas of Progressive Era reformers and the example of social-welfare programs in England and Germany. It established a mixed federal-state system of old-age pensions for workers; survivors' benefits for the victims of industrial accidents; unemployment insurance; and aid for dependent mothers and children, the blind, and the crippled.

Taxes paid in part by employers and in part by wages withheld from workers' paychecks funded the pension and survivors' benefit features of the program. In the short run, this payroll-withholding provision had a negative effect on the economy: it withdrew needed money from circulation and contributed to a sharp recession in 1937. But it made sense politically, because workers would fight any effort to repeal a social-security plan to which they themselves had contributed. As President Roosevelt put it: "With those taxes in there, no damned politician can ever scrap my social security program."

The Social Security Act was far from perfect. It set benefit payments at an extremely low level; contained no provision for health insurance; and excluded millions of farmers, domestic workers, and self-employed workers. However, the law did establish the principle of federal responsibility for social welfare and created the basic framework for a welfare system that would evolve and expand in the decades ahead.

The more radical thrust of the Second New Deal found expression, also, in two business regulatory measures of 1935. The Banking Act strengthened the Federal Reserve Board's control over the nation's banking system and money supply. The Public Utilities Holding Company Act regulated the interstate transmission of electricity and restricted gas and electric companies to one geographic region. The act dealt a mortal blow to the octopuslike public-utility empires that had proliferated in the 1920s for purely speculative purposes.

And finally, the Revenue Act of 1935 raised personal taxes at the higher income levels, increased corporate taxes, and boosted the levies on gifts and estates. Though this tax law had numerous loopholes and exceptions, and thus was not quite the "soak the rich" measure some believed, it did express the somewhat more class-conscious spirit of the Second New Deal.

By September 1935, when Congress finally adjourned, the Second New Deal was complete. A set of laws had been enacted promoting the interests of the jobless, the elderly, the rural poor, and the blue-collar workers; regulating major business enterprises more strictly; and somewhat increasing the taxes paid by the wealthy. Without fully embracing any of the radical panaceas espoused by Coughlin, Townsend, or Long, FDR had stolen their thunder by directing his program to the fears and inequities on which they had thrived. But despite the "antibusiness" label that his enemies pinned on him, FDR remained a firm supporter of the capitalist system. In his view the New Deal had saved capitalism by reforming its excesses and addressing some of its less desirable social consequences.

The Election of 1936: The New Deal at High Tide

With the Second New Deal in place and unemployment slowly declining, FDR faced the 1936 electoral campaign with confidence. "There's one issue in this campaign," he told an aide; "it's myself, and people must be either for me or against me."

The Republicans' presidential candidate, Governor Alfred Landon of Kansas, belonged to his party's progressive wing. A fiscal conservative who nevertheless believed that government must be responsive to social issues, Landon proved an earnest though inept campaigner. "Wherever I have gone in this country, I have found Americans," he revealed in one speech. In an unguarded moment, he conceded to a reporter that he had no hope of winning.

Recognizing the New Deal's popularity, the Republicans did not attack it frontally but simply asserted that they could administer it more efficiently than the Democrats. They lambasted Roosevelt's alleged dictatorial ambitions and charged that soon all workers would be forced to wear metal dog tags engraved with their social-security numbers.

Campaigning more against the fading memory of Herbert Hoover than against the inoffensive Alf Landon, FDR struck back with his usual zest. Only the forces of "selfishness and greed" opposed him, he declared at an election-eve rally in New York City, adding: "Never before in history have these forces been so united against one candidate as they stand today. They are united in their hatred for me—and I welcome their hatred."

The outcome was not even close. In the most crushing electoral victory since 1820, FDR carried every state but Maine and Vermont—precisely as campaign manager Jim Farley had predicted. Landon failed to carry even his home state of Kansas. Pennsylvania went Democratic for the first time since 1856. While Roosevelt was swamping Landon by a margin of 11 million popular votes, the Democrats increased their already top-heavy majorities in the Senate and the House of Representatives. The 1936 election underscored the message of 1932: decades of Republican dominance in national politics lay in ruin.

The Roosevelt landslide buried his minor-party opponents as well. Socialist Norman Thomas received under two hundred thousand votes. The Communist party's presidential candidate, Earl Browder, garnered only about eighty thousand votes despite the party's strenuous recruitment and organizing efforts. And Congressman William Lemke of North Dakota—the candidate of the coalition of Coughlinites, Townsendites, and Share Our Wealth enthusiasts that had appeared so formidable early in 1935—polled fewer than nine hundred thousand votes.

The New Democratic Coalition

As a minority party for most of the period from 1860 through the 1920s, the Democrats had historically counted on three bases of support: the white South, parts of the West, and some big-city Democratic organizations like Tammany Hall in New York City and the Kansas City machine of boss Tom Pendergast. FDR retained these centers of strength. Nearly three-quarters of the voters of the "solid South" went for Roosevelt in 1936, and the urban Democratic machines delivered equally lopsided victory margins.

FDR rarely challenged state or local Democratic leaders who could produce such large electoral pluralities, whether they supported the New Deal or not. In Virginia, for example, FDR withdrew support from a pro–New Deal governor who clashed with the state's conservative but powerful Democratic senators, Harry Byrd and Carter Glass. When the Democratic boss of Jersey City, New Jersey, Frank Hague, faced federal prosecution for mail tampering, FDR told Jim Farley: "Forget prosecution. . . . Tell Frank to knock it off . . . , but keep this thing quiet because we need Hague's support if we want New Jersey."

FDR pushed far beyond this traditional base in forging a new Democratic majority, however. Five partially overlapping voter groups made up the cornerstone of this new majority: farmers, urban immigrants, unionized industrial workers, northern blacks, and women.

The midwestern farm belt, long a Republican bastion, found the New Deal's agricultural program congenial and switched to Roosevelt. In Iowa, for example, where Democratic candidates had been lucky to garner a mere 20 percent of the vote in the 1920s, FDR won decisively in 1936.

Urban voters, many of them immigrants or the offspring of immigrants, followed the same pat-

The Election of 1936				
Candidates	Parties	Electoral Vote	Popular Vote	Percentage of Popular Vote
FRANKLIN D. ROOSEVELT	Democratic	523	27,752,869	60.8
Alfred M. Landon	Republican	8	16,674,665	36.5
William Lemke	Union		882,479	1.9

tern. Building on Al Smith's urban breakthrough in 1928, FDR carried the nation's twelve largest cities in 1936. Not only did the New Deal relief programs aid the urban masses, but Roosevelt wooed them persuasively at election time. When the presidential campaign entourage swept through cities like New York and Boston, cheering crowds lined the route for miles. Further solidifying his urban support, FDR appointed many representatives of the newer urban-immigrant groups, including unprecedented numbers of Catholics and Jews, to high New Deal positions.

Organized labor, led by prominent figures like Sidney Hillman of the Amalgamated Clothing Workers and John L. Lewis of the United Mine Workers, also lined up solidly in the New Deal coalition. The unions pumped many thousands of dollars into Roosevelt's reelection campaigns (although not nearly as much as big business gave to the Republicans), and the rank-and-file union members voted overwhelmingly for Roosevelt. Despite his early foot dragging on the Wagner bill, FDR's reputation as a "friend of labor" proved unassailable, particularly in contrast to Republicans.

The administration's increasing identification with organized labor had by 1936 helped give rise

to a strong anti–New Deal mood in business circles —especially in labor-intensive industries such as textiles, automobiles, and steel—where the prolabor thrust of the Second New Deal challenged management's entrenched power and raised production costs. But FDR did win significant support from some business leaders, particularly officials of corporations that benefited from his programs, such as the electrical companies that provided equipment for the TVA and PWA hydroelectric projects and exporters who profited from the later New Deal's aggressive free-trade policies.

While most southern blacks remained disfranchised by law and custom, the swelling black population of the northern cities was an increasingly important factor in electoral politics. As late as 1932, two-thirds of this northern black vote had gone to Hoover. One black editor, annoyed by the black voters' firm Republican allegiance, advised his readers: "My friends, go turn Lincoln's picture to the wall. That debt has been paid in full."

The advent of the New Deal produced a historic turnaround. Chicago's black voters signaled the new order in 1934 when they retired their popular Republican congressman, Oscar DePriest, and replaced him with a Democrat. The 1936 presi-

Harlem Voters, 1936

A rushing tide of northern black votes contributed mightily to Roosevelt's victory margin in his second presidential campaign.

dential election completed the transformation. Northern blacks voted in record numbers that year, and 76 percent of them cast their ballots for FDR, contributing to his overwhelming urban majorities. In Harlem Roosevelt won a crushing 81 percent of the vote.

Solid reasons underlay this turnaround. As the last hired and the first fired, blacks experienced unemployment rates in the depression even higher than those for the work force as a whole. Thus jobless blacks in the urban North benefited heavily from the New Deal's relief programs. (The AAA's crop-reduction program uprooted many southern black sharecroppers, but as a disfranchised group, they could not express their frustration at the polls.)

Many blacks also perceived the New Deal as a force for racial justice. In some respects, the record does not bear out this perception. The racially discriminatory clauses written into some NRA codes led black activists to dismiss the agency angrily as "Negroes Ruined Again." Some New Deal agencies tolerated racial discrimination. TVA, for example, barred blacks from Norris, the "model town" that it built in Tennessee.

Not only did Roosevelt propose no civil-rights legislation, but he kept himself aloof from a campaign to make lynching a federal crime. After declining in the 1920s, lynchings increased in the 1930s, as some Americans translated their economic woes into racial aggression. Fifty-seven blacks (as well as six whites) were lynched in 1933–1935.

In 1935 the NAACP declared a federal anti-lynching law its top legislative priority. Although an anti-lynching bill passed the House of Representatives that year, diehard southern racist senators—all Democrats—organized a filibuster against it. Concerned about his legislative program, and fearful of alienating southern white voters, FDR stood aside from the struggle. Concluded the NAACP bitterly: "[Blacks] ought to realize by now that the powers-that-be in the Roosevelt administration have nothing for them." Roosevelt remained similarly passive in 1938 when an anti-lynching bill again was narrowly defeated.

In other ways, however, FDR and the New Deal did work modestly to advance the black cause. Assuring an audience at Howard University, a black institution in Washington, D.C., that there would be "no . . . forgotten races" in his administration, Roosevelt supported those seeking to eradicate

Two Women of the New Deal

Eleanor Roosevelt, the president's active and influential wife, posed with Mary McLeod Bethune, an official of the National Youth Administration (a New Deal agency) and an important link between the White House and black America.

racism from New Deal agencies and appointed more than a hundred blacks to policy-level positions. The highest ranking of these, Mary McLeod Bethune, served as director of minority affairs in the National Youth Administration. The daughter of ex-slaves, Bethune graduated from Chicago's Moody Bible Institute; opened a girls' school in Daytona Beach, Florida, that evolved into Bethune-Cookman College; and from 1935 to 1949 headed the National Council of Negro Women. An influential figure in New Deal Washington and a close friend of Eleanor Roosevelt's, Bethune headed the so-called black cabinet that met regularly in her home and acted as a vital link between the Roosevelt administration and black organizations.

Roosevelt appointed William Hastie, a black NAACP lawyer, to a federal judgeship. In addition, the "Roosevelt Supreme Court" that took shape after 1936 made a series of important antidiscrimination rulings in cases involving voting rights, wage discrimination, jury selection, and real-estate transactions.

Thanks in large part to Eleanor Roosevelt, the New Deal supported racial justice in important symbolic ways. In 1938, for example, Mrs. Roosevelt attended a meeting in Birmingham, Alabama, of the interracial Southern Conference for Human Welfare. When police commissioner Eugene "Bull" Connor insisted that the meeting be segregated in compliance with the city's Jim Crow statutes, Mrs. Roosevelt pointedly placed her chair in the area separating the white and black delegates. In 1939, when the Daughters of the American Revolution denied black contralto Marian Anderson permission to perform in Washington's Constitution Hall, Mrs. Roosevelt resigned from the organization and New Deal officials arranged for an Easter Sunday concert by Anderson on the steps of the Lincoln Memorial. An audience of seventy-five thousand turned out.

Southern white racists, including many powerful Democrats, seethed at the New Deal's overtures to blacks. When a black minister rose to deliver the invocation at the 1936 Democratic convention in Philadelphia, Senator "Cotton Ed" Smith of South Carolina noisily stalked out. "This mongrel meeting ain't no place for a white man," he fumed. Describing his walkout to a sympathetic white audience back home, Smith declared: "It seemed to me that old John Calhoun leaned down from his mansion in the sky and whispered, 'You did right, Ed.'"

In short, black support for Roosevelt reflected more than purely economic calculations. While civil rights did not appear on the New Deal's legislative agenda, the causes of racial justice and black advancement did win significant support in the Roosevelt White House.

The Roosevelt administration worked more strenuously to attract women voters than any previous administration. The head of the Democratic party's women's division, Molly Dewson, a former National Consumers' League official and a close friend of the Roosevelts, spearheaded this effort. In the 1936 campaign, Dewson mobilized sixty thousand women precinct workers and fifteen thousand women who went door to door distributing more than 80 million colorful flyers describing New Deal programs. "[W]e did not make the old-fashioned plea that our nominee was charming," she later recalled; "instead we appealed to [women's] intelligence."

Dewson's campaign skills solidified her close links to the Roosevelts. Women's division memos received priority attention at the White House, and when Dewson wished to discuss matters personally with FDR, Mrs. Roosevelt seated her next to the president at dinner parties.

Dewson believed that women had a particular interest in issues relating to family and the home, and her campaign materials stressed how social security, the National Youth Administration, federally funded school-lunch programs, and other New Deal initiatives strengthened the family. Unlike earlier feminists, Dewson did not push a specifically feminist agenda or women's rights legislation. The New Deal programs of economic recovery and social welfare, she believed, offered the best promise of advancement for both men and women.

Dewson did, however, advocate the appointment of more women to federal policy-level positions, and she knew which strings to pull to place women in key New Deal posts. FDR appointed not only the first woman cabinet member (Frances Perkins) but also the first woman ambassador and more female federal judges than any of his predecessors. Through Dewson's efforts, the proportion of women postmasters increased significantly, and the 1936 Democratic platform committee reflected a fifty-fifty gender balance.

But despite the visibility of a few blacks and women in New Deal circles, and certain symbolic gestures of support, advancing the cause of these groups was not a major item on the New Deal agenda. Racism and sexism pervaded American society when FDR took office, and his administration, preoccupied with the economic crisis, did relatively little to change that state of affairs. Those conditions would await a later reform generation.

The New Deal Draws to a Close

No sooner had Roosevelt won reelection by a mountainous majority in 1936 than he launched an ill-conceived attack on the Supreme Court that weakened him politically. In the wake of this divisive fight, an embattled FDR confronted a newly energized conservative opposition that helped bring the New Deal to an end. But the New Deal's legacy remained; in the span of a few years, the nation's political agenda had been rewritten.

FDR and the Supreme Court

Fresh from electoral triumph, Roosevelt early in 1937 went after the one branch of government that seemed immune to his New Deal vision: the Supreme Court. The Court in 1937 consisted of nine elderly men; one had served as a justice since 1910, another since 1914. Four of the justices were archconservatives who abhorred the New Deal. Joined by others of more moderate views, these conservatives had invalidated not only the NRA and the AAA but progressive state laws as well. They seemed determined, in the words of Harlan Fiske Stone, a liberal member of the Court, to "tie Uncle Sam up in a hard knot."

Roosevelt feared that key measures of the Second New Deal, including the Social Security Act and the Wagner Act, would meet a similar fate. Indeed, some lawyers were so sure that the Social Security Act would be found unconstitutional that they advised their business clients to ignore it.

In February 1937 FDR put his political prestige on the line by proposing out of the blue a sweeping court-reform bill that would have allowed the president to appoint an additional Supreme Court member for each justice over the age of seventy, up to a total of six. Roosevelt blandly insisted that this proposal reflected his concern for the heavy workload of aging justices. However, his political motivation escaped no one.

FDR evidently believed that his enormous personal popularity would translate into a ground swell of support for his Court plan, but this did not happen. Congress and the public greeted it with skepticism that soon turned to sharp disapproval. The size of the Supreme Court (unspecified in the Constitution) had been modified several times in the early years of the Republic, but over the decades the membership of nine had taken on an almost sacrosanct quality. Conservatives were livid over the "court-packing" scheme. Some feared a Rooseveltian grab for power in the wake of the president's electoral triumph; others resented the disingenuous way that FDR had presented the plan. Even some staunch New Dealers abandoned the president on this issue.

For several months FDR stubbornly pushed his court-reform bill. Finally in July, he quietly gave up the fight. For one of the rare times in his long presidency, Roosevelt had suffered an embarrassing defeat.

But in fact, the Supreme Court had yielded to Roosevelt's pressure. One of the most conservative justices retired in May 1937; others announced retirement plans. In April and May, the Court upheld several key New Deal measures, including the Wagner Act (*National Labor Relations Board* v. *Jones and Laughlin Steel Corporation*) as well as a state minimum-wage law. This outcome may have been Roosevelt's objective all along. From 1937 to 1939, through retirement and death, FDR appointed four new members to the Supreme Court—Hugo Black, Stanley F. Reed, Felix Frankfurter, and William O. Douglas—laying the groundwork for a liberal majority that would endure long after Roosevelt and his New Deal had faded into history.

The Roosevelt Recession

Just as the Supreme Court fight ended, FDR confronted a far more serious crisis: after improving in 1936 and early 1937, the economy again plunged ominously in August 1937. Industrial production slumped to 1934 levels. Steel output sank from 80 percent to 19 percent of capacity. Menacing unemployment statistics again dominated the headlines: after dropping to around 7 million in early 1937, the jobless toll soared to 11 million in early 1938 —more than 20 percent of the work force.

What caused this short but severe relapse? Federal policies that steeply reduced consumer income played a role in the "Roosevelt recession." The new social-security program's payroll taxes withdrew some $2 billion from circulation. Further, FDR, concerned about mounting deficits, had seized upon the signs of recovery to terminate the PWA and to cut the WPA and other New Deal relief programs sharply. While these economies did reduce the federal deficit, they also contributed directly to the precipitous economic downturn of 1937–1938. So, too, did a drastic contraction of the money supply instigated by the Federal Reserve Board.

Echoing Hoover, FDR assured his cabinet: "Everything will work out all right if we just sit tight and keep quiet." Meanwhile, however, some key New Dealers had been persuaded by the Keynesian call for deficit spending as the key to recovery. Aware that FDR would have to be persuaded by political rather than economic arguments, they recruited Harry Hopkins to warn the president of a fierce political backlash if the breadlines and soup kitchens continued. Only a renewal of massive relief spending, Hopkins insisted, offered hope. Convinced, FDR in April 1938 authorized heavy new spending. Once more the WPA money machine clanked into action, and work-relief checks rained down on the parched economy. The PWA received a new lease on life. By the end of 1938, conditions were improving. Unemployment declined, and industrial output increased.

The End of the New Deal

Preoccupied by the Supreme Court fight, the 1937–1938 recession, and a menacing world situation (see Chapter 25), FDR offered few reform initiatives in his second term. Congress, however, enacted several significant measures. The Bankhead-Jones Farm Tenancy Act of 1937, for example, created a new agency, the Farm Security Administration (FSA), replacing Rexford Tugwell's short-lived Resettlement Administration. FSA made low-interest loans enabling tenant farmers and sharecroppers to buy their own family-size farms. Although the FSA did little to help the poorest tenants and sharecroppers, because they represented bad credit risks, it loaned more than $1 billion by the end of 1941, assisting many thousands of tenant families to become farm owners.

The FSA also established a network of well-run camps offering clean, sanitary shelter and medical services to migrant farm workers, many of whom lived in wretched, unhealthful conditions as they pursued their low-paying seasonal occupation. In its most innovative program, the FSA commissioned talented photographers, among them Dorothea Lange of San Francisco, to preserve on film the lives of tenants, migrants, and uprooted dust bowl families. In carrying out this assignment, Lange and other FSA photographers created a haunting album of stark depression-era images.

Other measures of the later New Deal set important precedents for the future. The National Housing Act of 1937, sponsored by Senator Wag-

ner, appropriated $500 million for urban slum clearance and public-housing projects. The Fair Labor Standards Act of 1938 banned child labor and established a national minimum wage of forty cents an hour and a maximum workweek of forty hours. Passed after intense political logrolling, this measure reflected not only humanitarianism but also some northern legislators' desire to undermine the competitive edge of the South, with its low wage scales. Although riddled with exceptions, this law did establish important regulatory precedents and improve conditions for some of the nation's hardest-working and lowest-paid workers.

The Agricultural Adjustment Act of 1938, adopted as surpluses and low prices continued to beset farmers, set up procedures for limiting production of basic agricultural commodities such as cotton, wheat, corn, and tobacco. It also created a mechanism by which the government, in years of big harvests and low prices, would make loans to farmers and store their surplus crops in government warehouses.* In years of poor harvests and higher prices, farmers could repay their loans and market their commodities at a profit. This measure helped stabilize farm prices and established the basic framework of federal agricultural policy for decades to come.

The later 1930s also brought a dramatic leap in union membership (see Chapter 25). This labor activism, stimulated in part by Section 7a of the NIRA and by the Wagner Act, demonstrated the New Deal's continuing role in transforming the social contours of American life.

Despite such achievements, the New Deal after 1935 clearly lost momentum. To a certain extent, the slackened pace reflected the growing strength of an anti–New Deal congressional coalition of Republicans and conservative southern Democrats. Sensing FDR's vulnerability after the Supreme Court fight, this opposition became more outspoken. Virginia Democrat Carter Glass, for example, in a denunciation of the New Dealers, proclaimed: "Thomas Jefferson would not speak to these people."

---

*These payments came directly from the federal treasury rather than from a processors' tax, a feature that had caused the Agricultural Adjustment Act of 1933 to be declared unconstitutional (see above).

Capturing the Migrant Experience

This family of Texas tenant farmers in a California migrant-labor camp was photographed in 1935 by Dorothea Lange (above), one of the gifted photographers who compiled a memorable visual record of the depression's human toll for the Farm Security Administration.

In 1937, at a moment when nerves were already rubbed raw by the Court fight, an aroused Congress rejected FDR's proposal to reorganize the executive branch by regrouping existing agencies, bureaus, and commissions into twelve superdepartments under the president's direct authority. The plan made administrative sense, but FDR's congressional critics claimed that it would create a virtual White House dictatorship.

The conservative coalition also slashed relief appropriations, launched an investigation of the NLRB, cut corporate taxes in 1938, and in July 1939 spitefully killed the WPA's Federal Theatre Project. Suspecting FDR of using WPA staff members for campaign purposes, the conservatives in 1939 passed the Hatch Act, forbidding federal workers from participating in electoral campaigns.

The Fair Labor Standards Act of 1938 made its way through Congress only after intense White House lobbying and much watering down by conservatives. As recovery proceeded, observed Harry Hopkins, Congress and the public at large seemed to become "bored with the poor, the unemployed, the insecure."

FDR struggled to reverse the anti–New Deal tide in the midterm election of 1938. Despite his active campaigning, however, the Republicans gained heavily in the House and Senate and won a net of thirteen governorships. Abandoning his earlier policy, Roosevelt also campaigned against several prominent anti–New Deal Democratic senators in 1938, but the major targets of his attempted purge, including senators Walter George of Georgia, "Cotton Ed" Smith of South Carolina, and Millard Tydings of Maryland, all won renomination and went on to victory in the general election.

Focusing mainly on ominous foreign developments in his January 1939 State of the Union message, FDR proposed no new domestic measures and spoke merely of the need to "preserve our reforms." The New Deal was over.

Conclusion

The New Deal in its six-year life compiled a stunning record of accomplishment. To be sure, not all New Deal programs succeeded. Nor did the New Deal demonstrate the capacity to achieve full economic recovery. As late as 1939, unemployment still hovered at around 9.5 million, or more than 17 percent of the labor force. Only in 1943, in the midst of a war-induced economic boom, did the vast pool of the jobless finally evaporate.

Yet when all this is acknowledged, the New Deal still constitutes a watershed in American history. The New Dealers may not have had all the right answers, but they asked many of the right questions. The Roosevelt administration began by assuming a fundamental governmental responsibility to promote economic prosperity and the well-being of all citizens. With such measures as social security, the Wagner Act, and the Fair Labor Standards Act, the basic contours of the modern activist welfare state were drawn.

In the 1920s, as indeed through much of post–Civil War U.S. history, the business class had exerted massive influence in Washington while other groups found themselves largely frozen out. Certainly the favored treatment of business did not suddenly end in 1933, as the Reconstruction Finance Corporation's massive loans to large corporations make clear. However, as the New Deal evolved, it increasingly acted as a broker for *all* organized interest groups—not just business, but also agriculture, labor, and other sectors. Although this still left the unorganized—the poorest sharecroppers and tenants of the rural South, for example—with little influence, government gradually became more responsive to varied interests.

The New Deal stood for reform, but reform of a new kind. The progressive reformers, convinced of the righteousness of their cause, had set out to eradicate evil from American life, whether the evil of exploitative corporate power or the evils of gambling, drink, and prostitution. The New Dealers, by contrast, in all their raucous diversity, felt few such impulses. Their aim was not to purify the nation by establishing the rule of the righteous but to bring their expertise to bear on the practical problems of business stagnation, unemployment, and the maldistribution of economic resources. The New Deal *style* differed markedly from that of earlier reform eras. As historian William E. Leuchtenberg has written: "If the archetypical progressive was Jane Addams singing 'Onward Christian Soldiers,' the representative New Dealer was Harry Hopkins betting on the horses at Laurel Race Track."

The New Deal vastly increased the power and prestige of the presidency. Roosevelt so dominated the politics of this era, and peppered Congress with so many messages and proposals, that Americans began to expect their president to formulate "programs" and to shape the terms of public debate. This development decisively altered the balance of power between the White House and Congress.

Any evaluation of the New Deal must come to grips with Franklin D. Roosevelt. Of course, not all reform in the 1930s originated with FDR. Nor was he a saint or a superman. He could be maddeningly devious, as in the Supreme Court fight, and his administrative skills left much to be desired. As agencies proliferated and overlapped, spectacular turf battles erupted. But Roosevelt's human strengths outweighed his liabilities. Unlike some of his challengers on the Left and ideologues of the Right like Hoover, he adopted an open, flexible, and experimental approach in grappling with the nation's problems. He once compared himself to a football quarterback, deciding which play to call next after seeing how the last one worked out. In the unprecedented and desperate conditions of the early depression years, the nation urgently needed such tolerance for innovation.

Above all, Roosevelt's infectious optimism brought renewed confidence to a demoralized people. This legacy of hope and activism is well summed up in an address that FDR delivered to an audience of young people in 1939: "We Americans of today . . . ," observed the president, "are characters in the living book of democracy. But we are also its author. It falls upon us now to say whether the chapters that are to come will tell a story of retreat or a story of continued advance."

CHRONOLOGY

1929 Stock market crash; onset of depression.

1930 President's Emergency Committee for Employment.

1931 Farmers' Holiday Association.

1932 Reconstruction Finance Corporation.
Veterans' bonus march.
Franklin D. Roosevelt elected president.

1933 Emergency Banking Act.
Civilian Conservation Corps (CCC).
Federal Emergency Relief Act (FERA).
Tennessee Valley Authority (TVA).
Agricultural Adjustment Administration (AAA).
National Recovery Administration (NRA).
Public Works Administration (PWA).
Civil Works Administration (CWA).

1934 Securities and Exchange Commission (SEC).
Civil Works Emergency Relief Act.
Democrats gain in midterm elections.

1935 Supreme Court declares NRA unconstitutional.
Emergency Relief Appropriation Act.
Works Progress Administration (WPA).
National Youth Administration.
Resettlement Administration.
Rural Electrification Administration (REA).
National Labor Relations Act (Wagner Act).
Social Security Act.

1935 Banking Act.
(cont.) Public Utility Holding Company Act.
NAACP campaign for federal anti-lynching law.
Huey Long assassinated.

1936 Supreme Court declares AAA unconstitutional.
Soil Conservation and Domestic Allotment Act.
Roosevelt wins landslide reelection victory.

1937 Roosevelt's "court-packing" plan defeated.
Hugo Black appointed to the Supreme Court.
Farm Security Administration (FSA).
National Housing Act.

1937– The "Roosevelt recession."
1938

1938 Fair Labor Standards Act.
Agricultural Adjustment Act of 1938.
Republicans gain heavily in midterm elections.
Stanley Reed appointed to the Supreme Court.

1939 Hatch Act.
Congress creates Executive Office of the Presidency.
Marian Anderson concert at the Lincoln Memorial.
Felix Frankfurter and William O. Douglas appointed to the Supreme Court.

For Further Reading

Paul Conkin, *The New Deal* (2d ed., 1975). A concise, balanced overview.

Frank Freidel, *Franklin Delano Roosevelt* (4 vols., 1952–1976). The definitive biography by a distinguished historian.

John Kenneth Galbraith, *The Great Crash, 1929* (1961). A lively account by a leading economist.

Otis L. Graham, Jr., ed., *The New Deal: The Critical Issues* (1971). Thoughtful interpretive essays on key themes.

William E. Leuchtenberg, *Franklin D. Roosevelt and the New Deal* (1983). A comprehensive, readable overview, rich in illuminating detail.

Albert U. Romasco, *The Politics of Recovery: Roosevelt's New Deal* (1983). A study particularly useful for the New Deal's policies toward business.

David A. Shannon, ed., *The Great Depression* (1960). Rich collection of newspaper stories and other primary documents.

Harvard Sitkoff, *A New Deal for Blacks* (1978). An exploration of the Roosevelt administration's policies toward black Americans.

Studs Terkel, *Hard Times* (1970). Oral-history interviews that poignantly convey the depression's human toll.

Susan Ware, *Beyond Suffrage: Women and the New Deal* (1981). A study of the network of women who held high office in the New Deal.

Additional Bibliography

Onset of the Great Depression

Robert Bendiner, *Just Around the Corner* (1968); David Burner, *Herbert Hoover: A Public Life* (1978); Roger Daniels, *The Bonus March* (1971); Milton Friedman and Anna J. Schwartz, *Monetary History of the United States, 1867–1960* (1963), Chapter 7, "The Great Contraction"; Susan Estabrook Kennedy, *The Banking Crisis of 1933* (1973); Albert U. Romasco, *The Poverty of Abundance: Hoover, the Nation, the Depression* (1965); John Shover, *Cornbelt Rebellion: The Farmers' Holiday Association* (1965); Peter Temin, *Did Monetary Forces Cause the Great Depression?* (1976); Joan Hoff Wilson, *Herbert Hoover: Forgotten Progressive* (1975).

The Early New Deal

Bernard Bellush, *The Failure of NRA* (1975); James MacGregor Burns, *Roosevelt: The Lion and the Fox* (1956); Searle F. Charles, *Minister of Relief: Harry Hopkins and the Depression* (1963); Otis L. Graham, Jr., *Toward a Planned Society: From Roosevelt to Nixon* (1976); Ellis Hawley, *The New Deal and the Problem of Monopoly* (1965); Mark Leff, *The Limits of Symbolic Reform: The New Deal and Taxation, 1933–1939* (1984); Robert Lekachman, *The Age of Keynes* (1966); Thomas K. McCraw, *TVA and the Power Fight* (1971); Raymond Moley, *After Seven Years* (1939); Van L. Perkins, *Crisis in Agriculture: The AAA and the New Deal* (1969); Eleanor Roosevelt, *This I Remember* (1949); John Salmond, *The Civilian Conservation Corps* (1959); Arthur M. Schlesinger, *The Coming of the New Deal* (1959); Donald Worster, *Dust Bowl* (1979) and *Rivers of Empire* (1986).

The Later New Deal

Sidney Baldwin, *Poverty and Politics: The Rise and Decline of the Farm Security Administration* (1968); Alan Brinkley, *Voices of Protest: Huey Long, Father Coughlin, and the Great Depression* (1982); David E. Conrad, *The Forgotten Farmers: The Story of the Sharecroppers and the New Deal* (1965); Jane DeHart-Mathews, *The Federal Theatre* (1967); Lyle Dorsett, *Franklin D. Roosevelt and the City Bosses* (1977); J. Joseph Huthmacher, *Robert F. Wagner and the Rise of Urban Liberalism* (1968); A. Cash Koeniger, "The New Deal and the States: Roosevelt vs. the Byrd Organization in Virginia," *Journal of American History* 68 (March 1982): 876–896; William E. Leuchtenberg, "Roosevelt's Supreme Court 'Packing' Plan," in Harold M. Hollingsworth and William F. Holmes, eds., *Essays on the New Deal* (1969); Richard Lowitt, *The New Deal and the West* (1984); Roy Lubove, *The Struggle for Social Security* (1968); Donald R. McCoy, *Landon of Kansas* (1966); William F. MacDonald, *Federal Relief Administration and the Arts* (1969); Charles McKinley and Robert W. Frase, *Launching Social Security* (1970); Michael Parrish, *Securities Regulation and the New Deal* (1970); Frank E. Smith, *The Politics of Conservation* (1966); Charles H. Trout, *Boston, the Great Depression, and the New Deal* (1977); Charles J. Tull, *Father Coughlin and the New Deal* (1965); Susan Ware, *Partner and I: Molly Dewson, Feminism, and New Deal Politics* (1987); Nancy J. Weiss, *Farewell to the Party of Lincoln: Black Politics in the Age of FDR* (1983); T. Harry Williams, *Huey Long* (1970); George Wolfskill, *The Revolt of the Conservatives: A History of the Liberty League* (1962); Robert L. Zangrando, *The NAACP Crusade Against Lynching, 1909–1950* (1980).

The End of the New Deal

Dewey W. Grantham, *The Democratic South* (1963); James T. Patterson, *Congressional Conservatives and the New Deal* (1967); Milton Plesur, "The Republican Congressional Comeback of 1938," *Review of Politics* 24 (1962): 525–562; Richard Polenberg, *Reorganizing Roosevelt's Government* (1966); Charles M. Price and Joseph Boskin, "The Roosevelt Purge . . . ," *Journal of Politics* 28 (1966): 660–670.

CHAPTER 25

American Life in a Decade of Crisis at Home and Abroad

It was January 11, 1937, and in Flint, Michigan, the temperature was sixteen above zero. For ten days some one hundred strikers had occupied Fisher Body plant No. 2, which made bodies for General Motors cars. A few miles away, other strikers were occupying the larger Fisher Body plant No. 1. Determined to force a showdown, GM executives cut off the heat to plant No. 2 and locked the main gate, preventing supporters from carrying food to the strikers inside. As evening fell, some 150 picketers and a crowd of onlookers milled about uneasily.

Around 8:00 P.M., after strikers had broken the lock on the main gate, thirty Flint policemen in riot gear rolled up in squad cars; some time later, they were joined by fifty more. When the police fired tear-gas canisters into the plant, the occupiers doused them with fire hoses.

Masterminding the strategy was Victor Reuther, a brother of Walter Reuther, president of the local United Auto Workers (UAW) union, who issued directions to the strikers through a loudspeaker powered by his car battery. One of the participants later recalled Victor Reuther's voice as "an inexhaustible, furious flood pouring courage into the men."

As the police moved closer, the occupying workers beat them back with a shower of empty bottles, nuts and bolts, and two-pound car-door hinges. When the picketers overturned a sheriff's car—with the overweight sheriff still inside—the outraged police fired into their ranks, injuring fourteen.

As Victor Reuther's battery grew weaker, Genora Johnson, the twenty-three-year-old wife of a striker, took the loudspeaker and emotionally urged women in the crowd to join the picketers. Many did so, running a gauntlet of police who tore at their coats. As the ranks of the picketers grew, the gunfire stopped. After a five-hour standoff, the police withdrew. Thanks in part to Victor Reuther's bullhorn and the quick thinking of Genora Johnson, the UAW's strike against GM went on to eventual victory.

In order to grasp the full meaning of the Great Depression, which touched so many millions of Americans, we must move from Wall Street, the halls of Congress, and the offices of New Deal agencies out into the world of auto plants, harvest fields, artists' studios, and ordinary people's homes. And we must turn our attention abroad as well, for in these economically cataclysmic years, powerful nations across the seas came under the control of brutal militaristic dictatorships that raised again the specter of war and added to the pervasive sense of crisis.

The American People in the Depression Decade

Like some uncontrollable natural catastrophe, the depression crashed over 1930s America. Unprecedented economic, social, and emotional havoc was left in its wake. A bird's-eye view of its awesome human toll conveys some of the reality, but a full understanding of the depression's impact also demands attention to particular groups of Americans—defined by occupation, gender, race, or ethnic origin—to whom the crisis brought special hardships and, in some cases, unique opportunities.

For millions of industrial workers, the New Deal's fresh political winds created a more favorable climate for unionization. But union growth still did not come easily. Workers in the nation's largest industries often had to fight a hostile management for the right to organize. Some female and minority members of the labor force shared in the solidarity and improved conditions that came with union membership, but others found that the depression worsened an already difficult situation. The 1930s witnessed a backlash against working women and against feminist goals in general, while the circumstances of hard-pressed blacks and Hispanic-Americans grew even more desperate.

Native Americans, meanwhile, became the objects of well-meaning but in some ways misguided attention from New Deal reformers. And the depression had a profound effect on the most basic social group of all, the family. Some families experienced conflict and disruption in these difficult years; others, however, grew closer and more supportive in the face of adversity.

The Plight of a People

In terms of human suffering, the depression took an enormous toll. For all the New Deal's efforts, unemployment in the 1930s never fell below about 14 percent, and during much of the decade, it was considerably higher. (A generation later, in the 1960s, the president's Council of Economic Advisers would define *5 percent* unemployment as the maximum tolerable level.) The percentages represent masses of jobless men and women; as late as 1939, the total stood at nearly 9 million. In rural America bankruptcies, foreclosures, and abandoned farms remained grim realities, and a quarter of all farm families had to accept public or private assistance during the 1930s.

In some cities the jobless rate soared far beyond the national average. In Toledo in 1932, for example, it stood at an incredible 80 percent. And many American workers remained employed only by taking jobs below their level of training: college alumni pumped gas; graduates of prestigious business schools sold furniture. A retired navy captain, employed as a ticket-taker in a movie theater, wore his usher's outfit with as much dignity as he had once worn his naval uniform.

Others eked out a few dollars by peddling products to neighbors as poor as themselves. "I'll never forget watching my mother trying to sell Two-in-One Shoe Polish door to door," one child of the depression later remarked.

While the death rate held steady through the 1930s (thanks to advances in combating infectious diseases), nutritional deficiencies and people's inability to pay for proper medical and dental care laid the groundwork for later problems—some of which showed up only after decades. "You have to have money to be sick—or [you] did then," novelist John Dos Passos recalled; "any dentistry also was out of the question, with the result that my teeth went badly to pieces. Without dough you couldn't have a tooth filled."

Psychologists counseled victims of "unemployment shock": jobless persons who compulsively walked the streets by day seeking work and then lay awake half the night worrying. Small humiliations provided a constant reminder of failure. When shoe soles wore out, cardboard or folded newspapers had to serve. Shoe tacks pierced worn rubber heels, cutting the skin. "You pass a thousand shoe-shops where a tack might be bent down," one young man recalled; "but you can't pull off a shoe and ask to have *that* done—for nothing."

The depression was no respecter of age: the savings of older Americans quickly evaporated when hard times hit. By the midthirties, 1 million Americans over sixty-five were on relief.

To the young, the depression brought a frustrating sense of lost opportunities. One observer has compared the younger generation of the 1930s

Unemployed Men Eating in a Chicago Baptist Church, 1930

The depression took an awful human toll. "What is to become of us?" wrote one discouraged man; "I've lost twelve and a half pounds this last month, just thinking. You can't sleep, you know. You wake up about 2 A.M., and you lie and think."

By no coincidence, advertisements of the 1930s, promoting products ranging from mouthwashes and deodorants to encyclopedias and correspondence courses, frequently exploited feelings of shame. The ads played on people's fears of being found out, of having their failings and pretenses exposed.

Decades later, survivors of the depression would recognize how deeply they had been marked by it. Habits of scrimping and saving acquired in the 1930s, for example, often survived into more affluent times. As Caroline Bird has written in *The Invisible Scar,* her aptly titled social history of the 1930s, the depression for many boiled down to "a dull misery in the bones."

Industrial Workers Unionize

The economic crisis energized and transformed American labor. Between 1900 and 1930, the number of unskilled or semiskilled factory workers had more than doubled, soaring from 3.7 million to 7.7 million. Yet at the outset of the depression, workers remained almost completely unorganized. For years the men who ruled such major industries as steel, automobiles, and textiles had successfully resisted all attempts to unionize their workers, seeing such efforts as a threat to their right to run their businesses as they saw fit. The prosperity and pro-business mood of the 1920s had further sapped the energies of the labor movement.

But in the 1930s hard times and a favorable government climate gave rise to a new labor militancy and a rushing tide of unionization. When the National Labor Relations Act of 1935 guaranteed labor's right to organize and to engage in collective bargaining, tremors of activism shook the rather stodgy American Federation of Labor. More militant AFL leaders like John L. Lewis of the United Mine Workers (UMW) and Sidney Hillman of the Amalgamated Clothing Workers, chafing at the AFL's slowness in organizing factory workers, decided to act. In November 1935 Lewis and Hillman established the Committee for Industrial Organization (CIO) within the AFL. Drawing upon a war chest supplied by the UMW, energetic young CIO activists preached the gospel of unionization to workers in Pittsburgh's steel mills, Detroit's auto plants, Akron's rubber factories, and southern textile mills. Unlike the restrictive, craft-based AFL unions, these CIO unions welcomed all

to a group of runners waiting impatiently for a starting gun that never sounded. High-school enrollment increased sharply, as many young people who would otherwise have entered the job market simply stayed on in school.

The depression counted among its victims many of the chronically disadvantaged, for whom it represented simply one more in a series of hardships. But the jobless rolls also included millions who had been earning good wages and had even achieved a measure of affluence before 1929. These newly impoverished individuals often experienced intense psychological stress as they tried to deal with their sudden decline in income and status. Some went to great lengths to maintain appearances, even when they had barely enough to eat. One carpet-cleaning firm made extra money by clandestinely renting out Oriental rugs, brought in for cleaning, to families that had been forced to sell their own carpets.

Striking Auto Workers Hold Impromptu Dance, March 1937

The campaign to organize auto workers, centered in Michigan, spread to other areas as well, reaching these workers at a Chevrolet body plant in St. Louis.

workers in a particular industry, regardless of race, gender, or degree of skill.

In 1936 a CIO-sponsored Steel Workers Organizing Committee (SWOC) headed by Lewis's lieutenant Philip Murray geared up for a major strike to win union recognition. SWOC's target was giant U.S. Steel, described by John L. Lewis as "the crouching lion in the pathway of labor." To the surprise of almost everyone, the crouching lion proved a pussycat. In March 1937 U.S. Steel recognized the steelworkers' union, granted a wage increase, and accepted a forty-hour week. Few knew at the time that earlier in 1937 Lewis had already worked out the settlement in secret meetings with the head of U.S. Steel, Myron C. Taylor, who had concluded that further opposition to unionization was futile in the face of labor militance and the strongly prolabor climate in Washington. Other big steel companies followed suit, and by the end of the year, four hundred thousand steelworkers had signed their union cards.

Meanwhile, a team of organizers led by the fiery, redheaded young autoworker and labor activist Walter Reuther had mapped an imaginative campaign to unionize General Motors, where

hostility to organized labor ran deep. In December 1936 thousands of workers at GM's two Fisher Body plants in Flint put aside their tools, sat down, and occupied the factories. This "sit-down strike" in two key plants paralyzed GM's production.

Determined to keep their action peaceful, the sit-down strikers carefully protected the equipment and the cars on the assembly lines. Recalled one striker: "If anybody got careless with company property—such as sitting on an automobile cushion without putting burlap over it—he was talked to."

Women played a key role in the Flint strike. While women workers did not participate in the actual occupation of the plants (to avoid gossip that might discredit the strike), they picketed on the outside. In addition, strikers' wives, sisters, and daughters organized the Women's Auxiliary to support the strike. This auxiliary not only opened a kitchen to feed the striking workers, but it undertook more direct activities as well. The women set up a speakers' bureau to present the union's version of the issues, paraded with their children through downtown Flint, and even produced a drama called *The Strike Goes On.*

The confrontation with the police at Fisher Body plant No. 2 on January 11, 1937, led to the formation of the Women's Emergency Brigade, whose members remained on twenty-four-hour alert for picket duty wherever needed. The four hundred brigade members ranged from the sixteen-year-old daughter of a striker to seventy-two-year-old Rebecca Goddard, a union sympathizer since her childhood in a southern coal-mining community. Complete with red berets and armbands, the Emergency Brigade played an important role during the rest of the strike. Though overall direction of the strike remained firmly in male hands, the women participants discovered the exhilaration of working with others on a common cause. As one woman wrote in the UAW newspaper, describing the anger that had propelled her into union activism: "I only wish I'd gotten mad long ago . . . , but I didn't have time for anything outside of my own small circle. I'm living for the first time with a definite goal."

At first, GM fought unionization. Not only did company officials use the police to harass the sit-down strikers, but they sent spies to union meetings and warned workers' families that strikers would be fired. GM also tried unsuccessfully to persuade the Roosevelt administration and the governor of Michigan, Frank Murphy, to call in troops and expel the strikers by force. While Roosevelt personally disapproved of the sit-down tactic, he refused to mobilize federal troops against the participants.

For six weeks the strikers held out. Then on February 11, powerful General Motors backed down. When GM signed a contract recognizing the United Automobile Workers (UAW), bearded workers who had vowed not to shave until victory was won streamed jubilantly out of the plants. Chrysler, another automotive leader, soon fell into line, and by the end of 1937, the UAW boasted more than four hundred thousand members. The unionization of the electrical and rubber industries moved forward rapidly as well.

In 1938 the deepening split in the labor movement came to a head as the Committee for Industrial Organization formally broke with the AFL to become the Congress of Industrial Organizations, a 2-million-member association of six major industrial unions including the autoworkers, steelworkers, and electrical workers. In response to the CIO challenge, the AFL itself showed new vigor

and flexibility in adapting to the changed nature of the American labor force. Overall, union membership in the United States shot from under 3 million in 1933 to well over 8 million in 1941, with much of the increase taking place after 1936.

These victories often came hard, as big corporations dug in their heels against unionization. Henry Ford, for example, hated unions, and his loyal lieutenant, a tough brawler named Harry Bennett, organized a squad of union-busting thugs— the "Service Department"—to keep the UAW out of the Ford Motor Company. In 1937, in a bloody encounter later memorialized as the "Battle of the Overpass," Bennett's hired enforcers viciously beat Walter Reuther and other UAW officials outside Ford's sprawling River Rouge plant near Detroit. Not until 1941 did Ford yield to the union's pressure.

Another holdout was the Republic Steel Company, headed by a union hater named Tom Girdler. Even after U.S. Steel and the other major steel makers signed with the CIO in March 1937, Republic and other smaller companies known collectively as "Little Steel" adamantly refused.

In May 1937 workers in twenty-seven Little Steel plants, including Republic's grimy factory along the Calumet River in South Chicago, walked off the job. Anticipating the strike, Girdler had assembled an arsenal of ninety-two riot guns, twenty-three hundred long-range tear-gas projectiles, and more than two thousand tear-gas hand grenades. The showdown came on May 30, Memorial Day, as a mass of strikers approached a force of 264 police guarding the factory. When someone in the crowd threw a large stick at the police, they responded with a hail of gunfire that left four strikers dead, six others dying, and more than eighty wounded. A local coroner's jury ruled the killings "justifiable homicide," but an investigative committee headed by Senator Robert M. La Follette, Jr., found that what the newspapers were branding the Memorial Day Massacre had been "clearly avoidable by the police." In 1941 Tom Girdler and the rest of Little Steel at last threw in the towel and signed union agreements with the CIO.

Another big holdout against unionization was the textile industry, with over six hundred thousand workers in 1930, mostly in the South and 40 percent female. The United Textile Workers (UTW), an AFL affiliate, had emerged from World War I with eighty thousand members, but it faltered badly

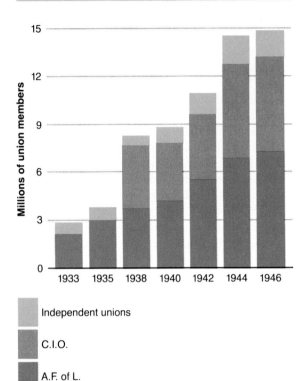

The Growth of Labor Union Membership, 1933–1946

Independent unions

C.I.O.

A.F. of L.

The 1930s witnessed bitter battles over unionization. Said steel executive Tom Girdler: "I won't have a contract . . . with an irresponsible, racketeering, violent, communistic body like the CIO. . . ." Despite such opposition, union membership increased dramatically.

in the 1920s owing to a series of failed strikes, a lack of strong AFL support, and a policy of admitting only skilled workers. After still another disastrous strike in 1934, John L. Lewis and Sidney Hillman of the CIO set up a Textile Workers Organizing Committee (TWOC) that in effect took over the feeble TWU. With high hopes TWOC organizers mapped a massive recruitment drive. Some plants were unionized, but the mill owners fought back viciously, and the 1930s ended with most textile workers still unorganized.

A large pool of workers remained virtually untouched by the unionizing wave of the 1930s, including most of those at the lower end of the wage scale—domestics; agricultural laborers;

department-store clerks; and restaurant, supermarket, and laundry workers, for example—who tended to be women, blacks, or recent immigrants. Yet when all the exceptions have been noted, the unionization of vast sectors of America's industrial work force in the 1930s must rank as one of the most memorable developments of a memorable decade.

Why did powerful corporations finally cave in to unionization after years of resistance? Certainly workers' militance and the tactical skill of a new generation of labor leaders played a major role. So, too, did management's fear of violence and sabotage. Although the unionizing campaigns remained overwhelmingly peaceful, the potential for violence was always present. In incidents such as the confrontation at Fisher Body plant No. 2, the "Battle of the Overpass," and the Memorial Day killings at Republic Steel, this potential seemed very close to the surface.

But above all, labor's dramatic successes after 1936 reflected a changed governmental climate. Where government officials had once lined up with the bosses to break strikes by force and legal intimidation, Roosevelt and key state officials like Governor Frank Murphy refused to intervene on the side of management. (The willingness of the South Chicago police to act as a kind of private army for Tom Girdler represents a rare exception to this pattern.) The Fair Labor Standards Act of 1938 and the role of the National Labor Relations Board in assuring fair union votes (see Chapter 24) made clear that Washington would no longer be an uncritical ally of management in labor disputes. Once the heads of the nation's major industries realized that the police power of the state would not be available to them, most quickly came to terms with the union leaders.

Mixed Blessings for Women

Senator Robert Wagner called the working woman in the depression years "the first orphan in the storm." Indeed, for many of the 25 percent of American women who were gainfully employed in 1930, the depression brought very difficult times. The female jobless rate eventually rose to more than 20 percent, and it hovered there through much of the decade. Women who were determined to continue working often could do so only by accepting lower-paying, lower-status jobs. A female factory worker who lost her job, for example, might take work as a sales clerk, waitress, or maid. Of the young women entering the job market for the first time, many had to settle for temporary, seasonal, or part-time work.

As a result of heavy competition from displaced male workers, the proportion of women in such white-collar professions as librarianship, social work, and public-school teaching declined in the 1930s. Like nearly all women workers, those professional women who did manage to cling to their jobs confronted blatant wage discrimination. In 1939, for example, the average woman school-teacher in the United States earned nearly 20 percent less than her male counterpart with comparable experience.

Married women who entered the job market encountered enormous resentment. They were accused of merely seeking to earn "pin money," whereas in fact the overwhelming majority worked out of economic necessity. Nevertheless, people complained that married women had no right to hold jobs with so many men out of work. A Kansas housewife whose husband could find no job wrote to President Roosevelt denouncing working wives as "thieving parasites." A 1936 Gallup poll found that 82 percent of Americans believed that a wife should not work if her husband had a job. Translating this thinking into public policy, many cities refused to employ married women as schoolteachers and even fired women teachers who got married.

The New Deal compiled a mixed record on women workers. Secretary of Labor Frances Perkins, though a woman and a long-time supporter of the Women's Trade Union League, lined up with the labor leaders and others critical of married women who worked. A number of the industrial codes adopted by the NRA gave the stamp of approval to lower pay for women workers. The minimum-wage clause of the Fair Labor Standards Act of 1938 helped thousands of women workers whose hourly wage fell below the new minimum but did not cover many categories of women workers, including the more than 2 million who worked for wages in private households.

The unionization drive of the later 1930s had a similarly mixed effect on women workers. Though not employed in great numbers in the mass-production industries where the organizing effort

was concentrated, significant numbers of women did work in some branches of these industries. For example, a big GM parts factory in Detroit employed more than six thousand women, and these female workers played a leading role in planning and carrying out the "slowdown" strategy that led to a union contract in 1937.

But those sectors of the labor force where women were most heavily concentrated—the textile industry and the clerical, service, and sales occupations—were, as we have seen, precisely the ones where the union movement made the least headway. The failure of the campaign to unionize the textile industry was paralleled by an equally unsuccessful drive to organize clerical workers. By the 1930s office work had been almost completely feminized, and most women office employees earned far less than male industrial workers. When the CIO chartered an office workers' union in 1937, many secretaries responded with enthusiasm, and several strikes were carried out. (The secretaries who struck a brassiere company in 1940 demonstrated a sense of humor as well as determination when they demanded, as their union newspaper reported, "an uplift in wages because their company keeps them flat-busted.") But the CIO campaign to improve the wages of clerical workers encountered the opposition not only of male bosses but also of many male union leaders, and it made little progress.

The depression also represented a low point for the women's movement. Battling the economic crisis, the nation had little patience for feminist issues or the struggle for gender equality. Despite the celebrity of a few women like Eleanor Roosevelt, Frances Perkins, and Amelia Earhart (the first woman to fly solo across the Atlantic), women achievers did not enjoy high visibility in this decade.

Notwithstanding the many roadblocks encountered by women, the proportion of women working for wages actually crept up slightly, from 25 percent in 1930 to 26 percent in 1940. Further, the percentage of gainfully employed *married* women increased markedly, from 11.7 percent in 1930 to 15.6 percent a decade later. In short, neither depression nor widespread criticism could reverse the long-term movement of women into the workplace; indeed, the economic crisis may have accelerated that movement, as married women took jobs to help their families weather the emergency.

As one working wife explained her particular motivation: "One day in '32 [my husband] just went fishing . . . and he fished for the rest of the bad times. . . . So at twenty-eight, with two little girls, I just had to go to work. I took a job as a salesclerk in the J. C. Penney, and worked through the Depression."

Blacks, Hispanic-Americans, and Indians Cope with Hard Times

While conditions for American blacks, Hispanics, and Indians in the thirties in many ways paralleled those of the white majority, the experiences of these minority groups also had unique features. For example, the depression markedly slowed the urbanization of black Americans. Some 400,000 southern blacks moved to northern cities in the 1930s—far fewer than in either the 1920s or the 1940s. In 1940 about 77 percent of the nation's 12 million blacks still lived in the South.

Rural and urban blacks alike endured extreme hardships. Not only did southern black tenant farmers and sharecroppers frequently face eviction, in part because of the New Deal's agricultural policies, but the jobless rate among black industrial workers far exceeded the rate for whites, largely because of deep-seated patterns of racism and discriminatory policies of unions intensified by fierce job competition in a depressed labor market. A 1936 study of unemployment patterns in Chicago reported "a prevailing sentiment that Negroes should not be hired as long as there are white men without work." While black workers benefited from the CIO's nondiscriminatory policy, the workplace racism remained an ugly fact of life.

Lynchings and miscarriages of justice continued as part of the reality of American life for blacks as well, especially in the South. Twenty-four blacks died by lynching in 1933, the year that President Roosevelt took office. In 1931 eight black youths were sentenced to death by an all-white jury in Scottsboro, Alabama, on highly suspect charges that they had raped two white women in a freight car. After heavy publicity and an aggressive defense, the Supreme Court in 1935 ordered a new trial for the "Scottsboro Boys" because of the unconstitutional exclusion of blacks from the jury and the denial of legal counsel to the defendants. Five of

the group were again convicted in 1936–1937, however, and served lengthy prison terms.

Blacks did not accept racism and discrimination passively. The National Association for the Advancement of Colored People battled strenuously, in courts and legislatures, against lynching, racial segregation, and the denial of black voting rights. For urban blacks the fact that whites owned most businesses in black neighborhoods and employed only whites represented a particular sore point. A campaign against this situation organized by the St. Louis Urban League in the early 1930s quickly spread to Chicago, Philadelphia, New York, and other cities. Under the banner "DON'T SHOP WHERE YOU CAN'T WORK," black protesters marched and boycotted businesses that hired only whites. In March 1935 hostility against white-owned businesses in Harlem, fueled by more generalized anger over racism and chronic unemployment, ignited a riot. This outburst, which resulted in an estimated $200 million in property damage, left three blacks dead and many Harlem businesses in ruin.

The American Communist party called attention to these racist conditions as part of an impassioned depression-era recruitment effort in the black community. The International Labor Defense Committee, a group linked to the Communist party, publicized the "Scottsboro Boys" case and supplied lawyers for the defense. But despite a few notable recruits (including, for a time, the young black writer Richard Wright), blacks did not join the Communist party at any higher rate than other Americans.

To some extent, the nation's preoccupation with the depression diverted attention from racial issues and the desperate economic straits of black Americans in the 1930s. But the Scottsboro case, the 1935 Harlem riot, and the rising tempo of NAACP activism gave warning that blatant racial discrimination and inequality could not be ignored forever.

The more than 2 million Hispanic-Americans, too, faced exceptionally trying times in the 1930s. Some of these were citizens who had long lived in the Southwest, but most were recent arrivals from Mexico, Puerto Rico, Cuba, and elsewhere in Latin America and South America. All but a handful of these 2 million were manual laborers. Some worked in the steel or meatpacking industries, while others, especially those from Mexico, were migratory

The "Scottsboro Boys" with Their Attorney

This celebrated Alabama case focused attention on blatant racial discrimination in the South's criminal-justice system.

agricultural laborers. As the depression deepened, the Mexican-born farm workers, welcomed for years as a source of cheap labor by the large produce growers of the Southwest, faced rising hostility. States that had formerly encouraged Mexican-American workers now slammed the door against them.

New Deal relief programs aided some Hispanic-Americans but excluded many others because they were not U.S. citizens. The influx into California and Arizona of thousands of "Okies" fleeing the dust bowl worsened the job crisis for the region's Mexican-American agricultural workers. By 1937 more than half the cotton workers of Arizona were out-of-staters who had supplanted the local Mexican-American laborers.

With their traditional patterns of migratory work disrupted, Mexican-Americans poured into the cities of the Southwest, swelling the population of the Hispanic urban neighborhoods, called barrios. In the cities, too, they met discrimination, sometimes in the form of such crudely expressed signs as "NO NIGGERS, MEXICANS, OR DOGS ALLOWED."

Finding themselves expendable pawns on the economic chessboard, some half a million Mexicans returned to their native land in the 1930s. Many did so voluntarily; others, through court-ordered repatriation. In 1932, for example, more

than two hundred thousand Mexican aliens were expelled by immigration officials and local authorities (see "A Place in Time").

Mexican-American agricultural workers who remained endured appalling labor conditions and near-starvation wages. A wave of protests and strikes (some led by Communist party organizers) swept California in these years. In 1933 strawberry pickers in El Monte struck for higher wages. Pea pickers in Hayward, cherry pickers in Mountain View and Sunnyvale, grape pickers in Lodi and Fresno, and eighteen thousand cotton workers in the San Joaquin Valley joined in as well. A labor organization called the Confederación de Uniones de Campesinos y Obreros Mexicanos (Confederation of Unions of Mexican Workers and Farm Laborers) emerged from the El Monte strike. Under the impetus of CUCOM, more strikes hit California's agricultural regions in 1935–1936, from the celery fields and citrus groves of the Los Angeles region to the lettuce fields of the Salinas Valley.

This labor activism was keenly resisted by the powerful owners of the region's big agribusinesses. Well-financed owners' organizations like the Associated Farmers of California and the California Fruit Growers Exchange (which marketed its citrus under the brand name Sunkist) fought the unions. With a war chest of $225,000, the Associated Farmers broke the Salinas Valley lettuce

The Los Angeles Barrio in the 1930s

*I*n the early 1930s, the depths of the depression, a party went on in the heart of Los Angeles's Mexican barrio. The members of the Nava family planned to return to their native Mexico the next day, and their friends bade them goodbye. Without work or money, the Navas had accepted an offer made to all barrio residents by the welfare authorities: free transportation back to Mexico . . . one-way only.

But as it happened, the Navas never boarded the train for Mexico. That night their eight-year-old son Julián suffered a ruptured appendix and was rushed to the hospital. He survived, but in the aftermath of the crisis, the family decided to remain in Los Angeles.

The Navas were only one of many thousands of Los Angeles families of Mexican origin whose lives were disrupted by the depression. Mexicans had first migrated to the city in large numbers in the early twentieth century, to take jobs laying track for the Pacific Electric Railroad. The 1910 census reported 8,917 Mexicans in Los Angeles, but knowledgeable local observers put the figure at closer to 20,000.

Mexicans continued to pour into the city even after the railroad-construction boom ended. They took the lowest-paying urban jobs and found seasonal employment as agricultural workers. By 1930 the Mexican population of Los Angeles County stood at 167,000—the largest concentration of Mexicans in the world outside Mexico City. Most lived in "Sonora Town," the sprawling barrio of East Los Angeles.

Mexican Men Outside Los Angeles Relief Office

When the depression hit, unemployment soared in the barrio, and the newcomers, once welcomed as a source of cheap labor, were now denounced as a drain on scarce relief funds. In January 1931 the Los Angeles County welfare director telegraphed Washington, asking that a team of immigration officials be sent to the city to supervise the deportation of Mexicans. The presence of federal representatives, he said, would "have a tendency to scare many thousands of alien deportables out of this district, which is the result intended."

Arriving as requested, immigration officers conducted dragnet raids in the barrio and made highly publicized arrests of Mexican aliens lacking proper documentation. In one raid in February 1931, police surrounded a downtown park popular with the Mexicans and held some four hundred adults and children captive for over an hour.

Meanwhile, Los Angeles welfare officials announced their plan of free one-way transportation to Mexico. The cost of sending a full trainload of returnees (called *repatriados*) to Mexico, they calculated, would be more than offset by annual savings in relief payments. Though the plan was "voluntary," those who refused to become *repatriados* found their relief payments cut off and, later in the 1930s, their applications for jobs in the WPA, PWA, or other New Deal work programs rejected. Under combined federal and local pressure, an estimated seventy thousand Mexicans left Los Angeles in 1931 alone.

Underlying this deportation drive was not only concern about welfare costs but prejudice. Some native-born Angelenos referred to the newcomers contemptuously as "greasers"; newspapers played up stories of barrio gang wars and crimes involving Mexicans. The Mexican community did not accept this injustice passively, however. The city's Spanish-language newspaper, *La Opinión,* and the barrio's business association denounced the intimidating tactics of immigration and welfare officials.

As the worst of the depression passed and the deportations and "voluntary" departures diminished, the rhythm of life in the barrio resumed, presenting a fascinating picture of a community suspended between two cultures. Radios covered with colorful *serapes* broadcast both the latest popular songs and the native folk melodies of Mexico, called *rancheros.* Supermarket food supplemented such traditional fare as enchiladas, tamales, and burritos. Though influenced by the cosmopolitan life around them, the Mexicans of Los Angeles spoke Spanish in the barrio, lit votive candles to the Virgin Mary in their churches, and perpetuated traditional remedies and folk beliefs dating back centuries.

The younger generation, gathering on the barrio's sidewalks in the warm southern California evenings, developed a distinctive street culture involving endless conversation, dramatic hairdos, a swaggering air of bravado, and flamboyant styles of dress: short skirts, black

Los Angeles Barrio, c. 1930

This photograph was taken in Chavez Ravine, now the site of Dodger Stadium.

stockings, and perilously high heels for the girls; widely draped, deeply pleated "zoot suits" for the boys.

While some of the barrio's young people turned to the vibrant street life, others concentrated on making their way in the larger society. Among the latter was Julián Nava. After high school and World War II naval service, Nava went on to Pomona College and Harvard University. In the 1960s, by then a history professor at San Fernando State College, he was elected to the Los Angeles School Board. In 1971 he became the board's president, with responsibility for a school system enrolling 650,000 students and operating on an annual budget of $750 million.

Julián Nava had come a long way since that depression-era night when an appendicitis attack had changed the course of his life. And Los Angeles had come a long way as well. The once despised Mexican minority had become an integral part of the city's fabric, affecting in countless ways its culture, its music, its religion, its cuisine, and the very texture of its life.

Designer's Sketch for a "Zoot Suit"

workers' strike of 1936. Sometimes the owners' anti-union resistance turned violent. In October 1933 bullets fired from a passing car ripped into a cotton pickers' union hall in Pixley, California, killing two men and wounding several others.

Fighting heavy odds, the labor movement among Mexican-American agricultural workers achieved a few notable successes. The El Monte strawberry pickers signed an agreement boosting their average wages from 9 cents to 20 cents an hour. Striking cotton pickers increased the rate for a hundred pounds of cotton to 75 cents—less than the $1 that they had demanded but 25 percent higher than the 60 cents that they had been receiving. These strikes also awakened at least some Americans to the inhumane working conditions and shamefully low wages of one of the nation's most exploited groups.

The 1930s also revived attention to the nation's 170,000 native Americans, most of whom existed in a world of dire poverty, scant education, inadequate health care, and bleak prospects. For nearly half a century, the government's Indian policy had been based on the Dawes Act of 1887 (see Chapter 16), which dissolved the tribes as legal entities and sought to promote the assimilation of Indians into the American mainstream by allocating tribal lands to individual Indians and offering the rest for sale to whites. Many native Americans, recognizing the threat to their cultural survival, had vocally protested this policy. Nevertheless, by the early 1930s, whites held about two-thirds of the land that native Americans had possessed in 1887, including much of the most valuable acreage.

Meanwhile, influential officials of the Bureau of Indian Affairs, among them several Quaker humanitarians appointed by Herbert Hoover, had become convinced that the Dawes Act approach should be reversed. One of the reformers outside government who supported change was John Collier, who had lived for a time among the Pueblo Indians of New Mexico. To preserve what he saw as the spiritual beauty and social harmony of traditional Indian life, Collier in 1923 had founded the American Indian Defense Association to promote and protect native American interests.

Appointed commissioner of Indian affairs in 1933, Collier translated into policy his vision of a renewed tribal life. Collier cadged funds from the CCC, the PWA, and the WPA to construct schools, hospitals, and irrigation systems on Indian reservations. These projects not only improved the quality of life on the reservations but also provided employment for many native American workers. In later years some older Indians would look back to the 1930s as a time of prosperity.

But Collier had larger goals. In 1934 he presented to Congress an omnibus bill halting the sale

A Navaho Family near Arizona's Grand Canyon

Under reformer John Collier, the Bureau of Indian Affairs in the 1930s sought a renewal of tribal life and an end to the gradual transfer of tribal lands to whites.

of tribal land to individuals, restoring the remaining unallocated lands to tribal control, creating new reservations, and expanding existing ones. Collier's bill would also have set up tribal councils with broad powers of home rule and required Indian schools to focus on native American history and to encourage traditional arts and handicrafts.

John Collier's visionary bill sparked angry opposition in western states, particularly among whites eyeing Indian lands. Some Indian leaders criticized it as a plan cooked up by well-meaning whites to transform the reservations into a kind of living museum and to treat native Americans as an exotic minority set apart from the mainstream of modern life. Collier's sweeping bill did, indeed, reflect primarily the sentimental idealism of a benevolent outsider who believed that he understood what was best for the Indians rather than the actual views and interests of the nation's highly diverse native American population.

The law that finally emerged from these complex crosscurrents, the Indian Reorganization Act of 1934, hailed by some as the Indians' New Deal, represented a compromise between Collier and his critics. The new law halted the sale of tribal lands to individuals and enabled tribes to regain title to their unallocated lands. But Congress sharply scaled back Collier's vision of tribal self-government and dropped the original bill's rhetorical calls for the renewal of traditional tribal culture.

As the New Deal ran out of gas in the later 1930s, so, too, did the cause of Indian reform. Collier faced increased opposition, congressional opponents slashed his agency's budget, and in 1945 he was forced to resign. By the late 1940s, John Collier's dream of a revitalized tribal life had mostly faded. The special standing of the Indian tribes with the federal government had been largely terminated, and native Americans were once more encouraged to abandon the reservation, give up traditional ways, and take their chances with everyone else in the treacherous currents of contemporary American life.

Family Life and Population Trends

For parents, including the women who remained at home as housewives and mothers as well as the many married women who worked, life in the 1930s often meant an endless struggle to make ends meet,

raise children on a shoestring, and hold the family together. They patched clothes, mended shoes, stretched food resources to the limit, and when all else failed, turned to public assistance. A young college-educated wife whose husband lost his job graphically described in a *Scribner's* magazine article the humiliation of welfare-office visits and the frustration of not being allowed to buy such "luxuries" as fresh fruit with her food coupons.

For the neediest, among them blacks, Hispanic-Americans, and the sharecropper families of the rural South (see Chapter 24), the depression imposed an added level of misery on lives already blighted by grinding poverty. In his powerful novel *Native Son* (1940), Richard Wright vividly conveyed, on the basis of grim personal experience, the desperate conditions of depression-era family life in the black slums of Chicago.

Ironically, however, life at the bottom had forced blacks, as well as others among the very poor, to develop psychological defenses and survival skills lacked by more affluent families. Social workers marveled at the emotional resilience and the patterns of mutual aid that helped black families get through the depression despite appallingly high unemployment rates. This cooperative spirit was institutionalized in New York's Harlem, where a charismatic black religious leader named Father Divine organized soup kitchens that distributed three thousand free meals a day.

Hard times disrupted courtship and marital patterns. The marriage rate tumbled in the early thirties, as couples confronted harsh economic realities. When young John Anderson graduated from the University of Wisconsin in 1931 with a degree in personnel management, for example, he fully anticipated finding a good job and marrying the classmate whom he had been dating. But months of eking out a living as a door-to-door salesman in Ohio shattered his hopes. "We corresponded for a couple of years," Anderson recalled, "but as time passed our letters were farther and farther apart. The . . . breaking up of young people who wanted to get married was the cause of much unhappiness and suffering during the Depression."

The birthrate also dropped sharply in the early depression years, as hard-pressed couples postponed a family or decided to have only one or two children. Such planning became easier with the increased availability and acceptance of birth-control devices such as condoms and diaphragms. The Federal Council of Churches, an association of Protestant denominations, declared contraception by artificial means morally acceptable in 1931, and in 1936 a federal court lifted the ban against importing or mailing birth-control information. Soon even the eminently respectable Sears, Roebuck catalog began to advertise contraceptives.

A declining birthrate combined with restrictions on immigration to retard population growth in the 1930s. In contrast to the growth rate from 1900 to 1930, when the population rose by more than 60 percent, the gain for the 1930s was a scant 7 percent. The economic crisis also temporarily slowed the growth of cities. The urban share of the population, after decades of dramatic increase, held steady in the 1930s at about 56 percent. In fact, many jobless young people returned to live with parents on farms.

By contrast, another long-term demographic trend, the westward movement, continued unabated in these years. Not only dust-bowl farmers but many thousands of American families responded to hard times by seeking brighter opportunities in the West, especially in California. The proportion of the population living in the Pacific region rose dramatically in this decade, and Los Angeles advanced from tenth to fifth among U.S. cities, leapfrogging such older urban centers as Boston, Baltimore, Cleveland, and St. Louis.

The depression's searing psychological effects struck families as well as individuals. In households with a strong tradition of male authority, the husband's loss of a job and consequent erosion of self-esteem often had a devastating impact. One man expressed the depression's threat to his masculinity in extreme form when he told a social investigator: "I would rather turn on the gas and put an end to the whole family than let my wife support me." Desertions increased, and the divorce rate, after a dip in the early and midthirties, edged upward, reaching a then all-time high by 1940.

Children found vacation plans canceled, hoped-for birthday presents not materializing, and the home atmosphere tense with anxious discussions of family finances. Maria Tighe of Long Island, who was seven years old when the stock-market crash threw her father, a construction worker, out of a job, could still recall, years later, sneaking to 6:00 A.M. mass so that her friends would not see her wearing ugly dresses and shoes provided by the welfare bureau. Elena Columbo, who grew up in Maynard, Massachusetts, in the thirties, remembered her dread at being sent to collect the food distributed to needy families by municipal authorities: "I used to cry. I didn't want to go, but I had to; I was the oldest. Everyone would see you there. I was ashamed."

But not all was bleak. Under the pressure of necessity, people rediscovered traditional skills. They painted their own houses and repaired their own cars. Home baking revived, and the sale of glass jars for canning fruits and vegetables shot upward. While hard times caused some people to turn inward, others would later look back on the depression as a time when adversity had strengthened social interdependence. Families in dire straits still found it possible to help others in the same plight. A man who grew up in a small town in Wisconsin said of those years: "The feeling among people was beautiful. Supposing some guy was a hunter. He'd go out and get a hold of some ducks or some game, [and] they'd have their friends over and share it."

Generosity, sharing, and making do could soften the depression's harsh impact on family life but not eliminate it entirely. The experience of a Cleveland railroad worker's family, recalled years afterward by one of the daughters, conveys that impact with particular vividness:

> I remember all of a sudden we had to move. My father lost his job and we moved into a double-garage. The landlord didn't charge us rent for seven years. We had a coal stove, and we had to each take turns, the three of us kids, to warm our legs. It was awfully cold when you opened those garage doors. We would sleep with rugs and blankets over the top of us [and] dress under the sheets. . . . In the morning we'd get out and get some snow and put it on the stove and melt it and wash around our faces. . . . [We] put on two pairs of socks on each hand and two pairs of socks on our feet, and long underwear and . . . Goodwill shoes. Off we'd walk, three, four miles to school.

Recollections such as this, endlessly repeated with subtle variations, make clear why the depression remained forever etched in the memory of those who lived through it.

Like all large-scale historical events, the depression had social effects undreamed of when the stock market crashed in 1929. Some reflected the conscious actions of individual leaders and organized groups: the unionization movement, the activism of California agricultural workers, the increased tempo of black protests against racism. Other social changes of the 1930s—the dip in the birthrate, the population movement westward, the entry of large numbers of married women into the work force—were the unplanned result of countless small decisions by ordinary Americans. Still other aspects of the social history of the thirties, such as the way some individuals and families broke under the strain while many discovered inner resources that carried them through, can never be precisely quantified. But whether planned or unplanned, measurable or immeasurable, these developments combined to influence the course of American history in important and unexpected ways.

The American Cultural Scene in the Thirties

Matching the depression's broad social effects was its profound cultural impact. While radio and the movies brought diversion to the masses, writers, artists, and social thinkers offered a more personal and probing view of American life and ideology. In the demoralized days of the early thirties, this view tended to be highly critical. But the tone shifted as the decade proceeded, and by the end of the thirties, the nation's cultural creators were discovering new value in America's history and traditions, and unexpected strength in its people. This more positive tone reflected the renewal of hope stimulated by the New Deal as well as the rallying of American intellectuals against the rise of militaristic dictatorships abroad—dictatorships that made American democracy seem both more fragile and more worth preserving than some intellectuals had once appeared to think.

The Golden Age of Radio

As an antidote to hard times, radio proved enormously popular. Each evening, millions of Americans gathered around their imposing Silvertone or Atwater Kent radio consoles to listen to their favorite network news commentators, musical programs,

and—above all—comedy shows. Radio humor reached its zenith in the 1930s, when the real world was hardly laughable. Comedians like Jack Benny, Fred Allen, and the husband-and-wife team George Burns and Gracie Allen won fiercely loyal audiences.

So, too, did the fifteen-minute afternoon domestic dramas known as soap operas (thus called because soap companies usually sponsored them). So deeply did many listeners become involved with these daily dollops of idealized romance and melodramatic crises that the line between fantasy and reality often blurred. Listeners wrote earnest letters to the soap-opera characters advising them how to handle their problems. When a New York City woman who was sentenced to be executed for murder lamented to a newspaper reporter that now she would miss the forthcoming episodes of her favorite soap opera, *Abie's Irish Rose,* the program's producers considerately gave her a synopsis of the next six months' fictional developments.

Housewives made up the overwhelming majority of soap-opera listeners. Identifying with the ordeals and traumas of the radio heroines, these women gained at least temporary escape from the difficulties of their own housebound lives. As one female listener put it: "I can get through the day better when I hear they have sorrows, too."

The standardization of mass culture, already under way in the 1920s, proceeded apace in the 1930s. As with television today, a successful radio show spawned a spate of imitations, producing a dead level of sameness across the radio band. Soap operas in particular took on a monotonous, assembly-line quality. Yet this formulaic and commercialized programming satisfied most listeners in the thirties, perhaps because they had experienced little else. One lonely lament over the lost possibilities of the new medium came from Lee De Forest, radio's inventor. "What have you done with my child?" he inquired plaintively.

The Silver Screen

The major movie studios tottered toward bankruptcy in 1931 and 1932, but in true Hollywood fashion, they staged a dramatic recovery in 1933 and for the rest of the decade enjoyed remarkable prosperity. Like radio, the movies proved extremely popular in depression America, when most people could still afford the quarter that it cost to see a show at the neighborhood Orpheum or Bijou. The introduction of the double features in 1931 and of drive-in theaters in 1933 also helped boost attendance. During some weeks in the 1930s, as many as 75 million Americans went to the movies. In 1939, 65 percent of the population attended at least once a week. The motion picture, declared one Hollywood executive, had become "as necessary as any other daily commodity."

What did these millions see? A few movies of the decade dealt realistically with such contemporary social issues as labor unrest in the coal industry (*Black Fury*) and the sharecroppers' plight (*Cabin in the Cotton*). Two brilliant documentaries made by Pare Lorentz for the Farm Security Administration, *The River* and *The Plow That Broke the Plains,* evoked the human and emotional toll of a century of westward expansion.

In contrast to the bleak pessimism of most movies of the early thirties that dealt with current social issues, Warner Brothers studio (which had close ties with the Roosevelt administration) made a series of movies in 1934–1936 that portrayed the New Deal in glowing terms. And in *Mr. Deeds Goes to Town* (1936) and *Mr. Smith Goes to Washington* (1939), director Frank Capra, the son of Italian immigrants, offered an unabashedly patriotic and idealistic message: that "the people" would always triumph over entrenched interests.

The gangster movies of the early thirties, drawing inspiration from real-life criminals like "Public Enemy Number One" John Dillinger and the legendary Bonnie Parker and Clyde Barrow, served up a different style of film realism. Photographed in stark black and white and taking advantage of the advent of sound, motion pictures like *Little Caesar* (1930) and *The Public Enemy* (1931) offered gritty, memorable images of urban America: looming skyscrapers; squealing tires in menacing, rain-swept streets; lonely bus depots and all-night diners; the rat-tat-tat of machine guns as rival gangs battled it out. When civic groups protested the glorification of crime in the gangster movies, Hollywood simply reversed the formula to make the police and "G-men" (FBI agents) the heroes, while retaining the same level of violence.

The lead characters in the gangster movies, especially those played by Edward G. Robinson and James Cagney, represented 1930s-style variants of the individualistic Horatio Alger heroes of an earlier day, fighting their way upward against incredible odds. Their portrayals struck a responsive chord with depression-era moviegoers, for whom the odds often seemed equally discouraging and the social environment equally menacing.

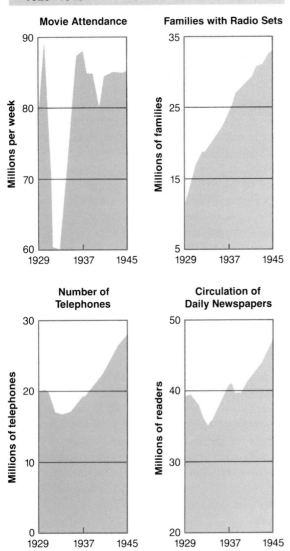

Mass Communication and Entertainment, 1929–1945

Movies, radio, and newspapers provided diversion amid hard times. Boasted one movie-industry leader in 1934: "No medium has contributed more greatly than film to . . . the national morale during a period featured by revolution . . . in other countries."

SOURCES: American Telephone and Telegraph Company, Federal Communications Commission, *The Film Daily,* and the National Broadcasting Company.

Movies in a Depression Decade

Hollywood prospered in the 1930s as Americans sought escape from economic worries. Shown are James Cagney and Jean Harlow in The Public Enemy *(1931); a poster for* Gone with the Wind *(1939); and the Marx Brothers in* Animal Crackers *(1930).*

But above all, the movies offered escape—the chance to forget the depression for a couple of hours. The Hollywood publicist who claimed that the movies "literally laughed the big bad wolf of the depression out of the public mind" obviously exaggerated, but cinema's narcotic function in the thirties is clear. Lush musicals such as *Gold Diggers of 1933* (with its theme song "We're in the Money") offered dancing, catchy tunes, and cheerful plots involving the triumph of luck and pluck over adversity. Walt Disney's *Snow White and the Seven Dwarfs* (1937) brought the technology of animation to a new level of sophistication, while *The Wizard of Oz* (1939) became an American classic, beloved by generations of children and adults alike.

The Marx Brothers, Groucho, Chico, and Harpo, provided some of the depression decade's finest movie moments. In such comedies as *Animal Crackers, Monkey Business, Duck Soup*, and *A Night at the Opera*, these zany vaudeville troupers of Jewish-immigrant origins created an anarchic world that satirized authority, fractured the English language, and hilariously demolished all known rules of logic. In *Animal Crackers*, for example, Groucho and Chico planned a search for a stolen painting:

> GROUCHO: *Suppose nobody in the house took the painting?*
>
> CHICO: *Go to the house next door.*
>
> GROUCHO: *Suppose there isn't any house next door?*
>
> CHICO: *Then we gotta build one.*

At a time when the established order and the traditional wisdom often seemed unreliable at best, the Marx Brothers' madcap mockery precisely matched the American mood.

Hollywood in the thirties dealt with blacks and women largely in stereotypes. Black actor and singer Paul Robeson pursued a brief movie career in the thirties, re-creating his stage role in *The Emperor Jones*, for example, but for the most part, talented black performers found themselves confined to such roles as the weepy, scatterbrained maid played by Butterfly McQueen in *Gone with the Wind* or the indulgent house servant patronized by child star Shirley Temple and played by tap dancer Bill Robinson in *The Little Colonel* (1935). Under the denigrating screen name Stepin Fetchit, black actor Lincoln Perry played a caricatured slapstick role as the slow-moving, slow-talking butt of humor in a long series of movies in the 1930s and later.

As for women, Hollywood continued to preach that they could find fulfillment only in marriage and domesticity. A few films, however, at least chipped away at the traditional stereotype. In the 1936 comedy *Wedding Present*, for example, Joan Bennett played a strong-willed professional. A top female star of the thirties, Mae West, invented a new, far more assertive stereotype. Tough, brassy, openly sexual, and fiercely independent, West in

I'm No Angel, She Done Him Wrong, and other hits mocked conventional morality, cut her suitors down to size with a razor-sharp wit, and made it clear that she would take orders from no one.

The Literature of the Early Thirties

Matching the nation's discouraged mood, the American fiction of the early depression years exuded disillusionment, cynicism, and despair. Sinclair Lewis and H. L. Mencken had satirized the middle class in the 1920s, but their successors in the early thirties challenged the fundamental premises of American ideology in far more radical ways.

In his bleak *Studs Lonigan* trilogy (1932–1935), Chicago-born James T. Farrell offered a depressing picture of the hero's empty existence. The product of a chaotic working-class Irish-immigrant neighborhood much like the one that Farrell himself had known as a boy, young Lonigan lacks any framework of meaning for making sense of his fragmented urban world. He simply stumbles through life, trying to piece together a coherent world view from the bits of mass culture that drift his way. At the end of the third volume, nearing thirty, jobless, and alone, Lonigan dies of tuberculosis in an impersonal hospital.

In *U.S.A.*, a highly innovative three-volume work published between 1930 and 1936, John Dos Passos drew a dark and intricate panorama of American history from 1900 through the early 1930s. Dos Passos's United States is a bloated, money-mad, exploitive society utterly lacking in social or spiritual coherence. As one character says, "Everything you've wanted crumbles in your fingers as you grasp it."

Of all these downbeat writers of the early thirties, the bleakest was surely Nathaniel West. Drawing on his experiences as a night clerk in a seedy Manhattan hotel, West in *Miss Lonelyhearts* (1933) created a nightmarish, surreal story of a newspaper advice columnist so oppressed by the stream of human misery endlessly flowing across his desk that he retreats into complete apathy and ultimately insanity. In West's *A Cool Million* (1934), a bitter parody of the Alger success novels, brave and virtuous young Lemuel Pitkin comes to New York to seek his fortune only to be cheated, betrayed, beaten, imprisoned, and eventually murdered.

Some radical novelists of the early thirties wrote even more explicitly of the decadence of capitalism, the exploitation of workers, and an approaching revolution. The American Communist party encouraged such writing through its John Reed* Clubs for writers and through contests to discover literary talent among the proletariat. Amid much dross, some interesting work emerged. Jack Conroy's *The Disinherited* (1933), a novel dealing with exploitation and labor violence in the Missouri coal fields, gained force from the fact that Conroy's own father and brother had died in a mine disaster. In a trilogy of novels beginning with *Pity Is Not Enough* (1933), Iowa-born proletarian writer Josephine Herbst offered a cold-eyed view of the shifting fortunes and muddled ideological gropings of a single American family from the Gilded Age through the 1930s.

Radical playwrights brought the class struggle to the stage. Clifford Odets's *Waiting for Lefty* (1935) offered cartoonlike stereotypes of noble workers and evil bosses and ended with the audience chanting "Strike! Strike! Strike!" Marc Blitzstein's radical musical *The Cradle Will Rock* (1937) was originally funded by the WPA's Federal Theatre Project. When nervous WPA officials ordered the performance postponed shortly before the opening-night curtain, the cast and audience defiantly walked down the street to another theater, and the show went on.

The Later Thirties: The Popular Front and Cultural Nationalism

In 1933 and 1934, the American Communist party vehemently attacked Franklin Roosevelt and the New Deal. But in 1935 Soviet dictator Joseph Stalin promulgated a new policy. Increasingly fearful of attack by Nazi Germany under its fascist[†] dictator Adolf Hitler, Stalin now called for a worldwide alliance, or "Popular Front," of all those who

opposed Hitler and his Italian fascist counterpart, Benito Mussolini. Responding to the new Soviet diplomatic line, American communist leaders began to praise Franklin Roosevelt, to describe communism as "twentieth century Americanism," and to recruit noncommunist writers and intellectuals to the antifascist cause.

For those who rallied to the Popular Front, and for many who did not, few events aroused more passionate emotions in these years than the Spanish Civil War of 1936–1939. In July 1936 Spanish army units led by fascist general Francisco Franco launched a revolt to overthrow Spain's legally elected left-wing government, a coalition of liberals, socialists, communists, and anarchists. Franco's cause won support from Spanish conservatives and monarchists, as well as from landowners, industrialists, and the Roman Catholic hierarchy. His fellow fascists Hitler and Mussolini provided extensive military aid.

The cause of the anti-Franco Spanish Loyalists (who continued to back the elected government in Madrid) won enthusiastic support from many writers, artists, and intellectuals who sympathized with the Popular Front. Archibald MacLeish, speaking at a writers' congress in New York City in 1937, pleaded eloquently for the Loyalist cause. No longer could writers stand aloof from their society, he insisted. The time for political commitment had come:

> These battles [in Spain] are not symbols of other battles to be fought elsewhere at some other time. They are the actual war itself. And in that war, that Spanish war on Spanish earth, we writers who contend for freedom are—whether we wish or not—engaged.

Writer Ernest Hemingway, who visited Spain as a war correspondent in 1936–1937, firmly supported the Loyalists. His novel *For Whom the Bell Tolls* (1940) told the story of a young American, Robert Jordan, who joins a Loyalist guerrilla band in the Spanish mountains and eventually dies for the cause. *For Whom the Bell Tolls* contrasted sharply with Hemingway's novels of the 1920s, with their disillusionment and skepticism about abstract ideals. Reflecting on his new-found capacity for political engagement, Hemingway later wrote: "The Spanish Civil War offered something which you could believe in wholly and completely, and

---

*John Reed (1887–1920) was a pre–World War I American radical who wrote *Ten Days That Shook the World* (1919), an account of the Bolshevik Revolution.

†Fascism (derived from the *Fascisti,* a political organization founded in Italy in 1919): a form of government involving one-party dictatorship, state control of production, extreme nationalism, hostility to minority groups, and the forcible suppression of all opposition, including labor unions.

in which you felt an absolute brotherhood with the others who were engaged in it."

The Popular Front suffered a shattering blow on August 24, 1939, when the Soviet Union and Nazi Germany signed a pact agreeing not to make war on each other and dividing Poland between them. Stalin's cynical exercise in power politics shocked idealistic Americans who had allied themselves with the Popular Front. Almost overnight, enthusiasm for cooperating with the communists under the banner of "antifascism" evaporated. Membership in the American Communist party dwindled as well. But although it was short-lived, the Popular Front significantly influenced U.S. politics and culture in the later 1930s and alerted Americans to the rise of fascism in Europe.

The emergence of fascism and the renewal of political faith summoned up by the Popular Front, coupled with the achievements of the Roosevelt administration, stimulated a broad shift in the American cultural climate in the mid-1930s. The New Deal's programs for writers, artists, and musicians contributed to this cultural resurgence as well. The bleakness and cynicism of the early depression years now gave way to a more positive and hopeful view of America—its people, its history, and its system of government. Abandoning the satirical tone characteristic of the 1920s, countless writers now voiced admiration for the fortitude, courage, and solid virtues of ordinary Americans. Even Sinclair Lewis, in a work far removed from the tone of *Main Street* and *Babbitt*, soberly warned of the dangers facing American democracy in his 1935 novel *It Can't Happen Here.*

This more affirmative cultural mood expressed itself in many ways. In John Steinbeck's *The Grapes of Wrath* (1939), for example, an uprooted dust-bowl family, the Joads, experience all kinds of misfortune as they make their way from Oklahoma to California along Route 66 in their battered old Hudson. But they never give up, and they never refuse help to others. As Ma Joad puts it: "They ain't gonna wipe us out. Why, we're the people— we go on."

Another eloquent expression of the new cultural spirit had its beginnings in 1936 when Tennessee-born journalist James Agee and photographer Walker Evans spent several weeks living with Alabama sharecropper families while researching an article on rural poverty for the business magazine *Fortune.* But *Fortune* rejected the intensely

Walker Evans Photograph

Together with contemporaries such as Dorothea Lange, Margaret Bourke-White, and Ben Shahn, Evans created a memorable portfolio of depression-era images for the Farm Security Administration. (At the time there was only one kind of Coca-Cola, it came in glass bottles, and it cost five cents.)

personal work that Agee produced, and not until 1941 did it appear under the title *Let Us Now Praise Famous Men.* Enhanced by Walker Evans's haunting photographs, Agee's beautifully written masterpiece evoked not only the precariousness of life at the bottom but also the strength and decency of Americans living at that level.

The more positive assessment of American life found expression on the stage as well. Thornton Wilder's play *Our Town* (1938) warmly portrayed a turn-of-the-century New England town where the deceptively ordinary routines of everyday life become, in memory, precious and full of meaning. In the same vein, William Saroyan's *The Time of Your Life* (1939) affectionately celebrated the foibles and virtues of a colorful collection of American "types" whom the playwright assembled in a San Francisco waterfront bar.

American music, too, reflected this swell of cultural nationalism. In such compositions as *Billy the Kid* (1938), Aaron Copland drew upon a rich store of American legends and folk melodies. George Gershwin turned to a popular 1920s play about black life in Charleston for the inspiration of his 1935 opera *Porgy and Bess*.

And jazz, that quintessentially American music, surged in popularity in the later thirties, thanks to the big bands of Benny Goodman, Count Basie, Glenn Miller, and others who developed a smoother, more flowing style of jazz known as swing. Goodman, the product of a Chicago immigrant upbringing, got his start on the clarinet at Jane Addams's Hull House. The beginning of the swing era dates from August 1935, when the Goodman band, at the end of a rather disappointing national tour, played to an enthusiastic sellout audience at the Palomar Ballroom in Los Angeles, featuring arrangements by the great Fletcher Henderson. Another unforgettable moment in jazz history came in 1938, when the Goodman band performed at New York's Carnegie Hall, citadel of the classical music establishment. Jazz had arrived. One of Goodman's important contributions to jazz was to include black musicians like pianist Teddy Wilson and vibraphonist Lionel Hampton in live performances as well as in recording sessions of his predominantly white orchestra.

The Count Basie band got its start at Kansas City's Reno Club, where, as Basie later recalled: "We played from nine o'clock in the evening to five or six the next morning, including the floor shows, and the boys in the band got eighteen dollars a week and I got twenty one." In 1936 Basie moved to a club on New York's Fifty-second Street called the Famous Door, and word soon spread that an exciting new band had hit town. For the next decade, swing dominated American popular music.

The cultural nationalism of the later 1930s also heightened interest in regional literature and art. Wallace Stegner wrote about Iowa in *Remembering Laughter* (1937), while Zora Neale Hurston's *Their Eyes Were Watching God* (1937) explored a black woman's search for fulfillment in her rural Florida community. In such works as *Absalom, Absalom!* (1936) and *The Hamlet* (1940), the best of the regional novelists, William Faulkner of Mississippi, continued the complex and often tragic saga of his mythic Yoknapatawpha County and its

fictional population of McCaslins, Compsons, Sartorises, and the upstart Snopses.

Artists Thomas Hart Benton of Missouri (a descendant of the nineteenth-century Missouri senator of the same name), John Steuart Curry of Kansas, and Grant Wood of Iowa contributed a strongly regional note to American painting. Wood's best ideas, he insisted, "came while milking a cow." But Curry, who taught art at the University of Wisconsin, always reminded his students that regionalism could not substitute for talent. As he put it: "Some of us . . . look forward to a great and alive art in the Middle West, but . . . [y]our greatness will not be found in Europe or in New York, or in the Middle West, or in Wisconsin, but within yourself."

Americans in these years also began to recognize the richness of their folk-art heritage. Galleries mounted shows of Amish quilts, New Hampshire weather vanes, itinerant portraiture from the colonial era, and lovingly crafted children's toys. Eighty-year-old Anna "Grandma" Moses of Hoosick Falls, New York, was only the best known of many folk artists "discovered" in this decade of cultural nationalism. In 1939 the Museum of Modern Art offered a major show, "Contemporary Unknown American Painters." Among the unknowns was Horace Pippin, a black Philadelphia laborer whose right arm had been shattered by a sniper's bullet in World War I. In such paintings as *John Brown Going to His Hanging,* Pippin revealed a genuine, if untutored, talent.

The patriotic absorption with all things American as the thirties ended generated a fascination as well with the nation's past. Americans flocked to historical re-creations such as Henry Ford's Greenfield Village near Detroit and Colonial Williamsburg in Virginia, the latter elaborately restored with money from the Rockefeller Foundation. Texans restored the Alamo in San Antonio, the "Cradle of Texas Liberty," between 1936 and 1939. Americans also made best sellers of historical novels like Margaret Mitchell's romantic epic of the Old South, *Gone with the Wind* (1936). Poet Carl Sandburg won a Pulitzer Prize in 1939 for a four-volume biography of Abraham Lincoln that elevated the martyred Civil War–era president to near-mythic status. And critic Van Wyck Brooks, who in the 1920s had dismissed the American literary tradition as pallid and second-rate, struck a new note with *The Flowering of New England* (1936),

Baptism in Kansas, by John Steuart Curry, 1928

In this early work portraying ordinary Americans' lives with affectionate respect, Curry anticipated the upbeat cultural nationalism of U.S. artists and writers in the later 1930s.

a warmly affectionate appreciation of the writers who had flourished in New England a century earlier.

As the 1930s drew to a close, Americans viewed their society, their history, and their political system with a newly appreciative eye. The nation had overcome the worst economic crisis in its history. The social fabric had not disintegrated; revolution had not come. As other societies collapsed into totalitarian dictatorships, American democracy seemed alive and well. Many intellectuals, writers, and creative artists who a decade earlier had appeared cut off and alienated from the rest of society now led the way in singing praises to America and its people.

The Age of Streamlining

This mood of restored confidence was neatly captured in an exciting style of industrial design called streamlining, which transformed the appearance of thousands of products. Streamlining originated in the 1920s with a visionary group of industrial designers including Norman Bel Geddes of Michigan, Walter Teague of Indiana, and Raymond Loewy, a native of Paris who emigrated to New York City in 1919. Inspired by the romance of flight,

Geddes, Teague, Loewy, and others fervently preached the gospel of streamlining: the elimination of all extraneous design features in favor of smoothly flowing surfaces. Graceful curves and parabolas replaced clunky, square shapes in their designs. The goal, said Geddes, was to reduce products to their "utmost simplification in terms of function and form."

Behind these aesthetic principles lay a social vision: that harmonious and functional consumer products would inspire a more harmonious and functional society. As cultural historian Jeffrey Meikle puts it: "The streamlined society would be as smooth and uncomplicated as an egg—a mechanical egg with no possibility of unruly life breaking out from within."

Streamlining appealed strongly to American business in the 1930s. It made products more attractive to consumers—a vital consideration at a time of economic stagnation. When Sears, Roebuck hired Raymond Loewy to streamline its line of Coldspot refrigerators in the 1930s, sales surged upward. Streamlining also helped business rebuild a reputation severely tarnished by the stock-market crash of 1929. At first, business had tried to bolster its image with advertisements and pronouncements in defense of the free-enterprise sys-

Streamlining

Innovative industrial designers of the 1930s whetted consumer demand and shaped the decade's aesthetics with their radically redesigned products. Shown is a New York Central locomotive of 1938, a gleaming triumph of streamlining.

The New York World's Fair, 1939

Like the 1893 Columbian Exposition in Chicago, the New York extravaganza attracted many thousands of visitors to glimpse "the world of tomorrow" and to admire the trylon and perisphere, its universally recognized symbols.

tem. But by mid-decade corporations began to stress the wonderful material benefits that business brought to society. The slogan of the Du Pont Corporation, "Better Things for Better Living Through Chemistry," summed up the new theme. The futuristic product designs of streamliners like Geddes, Teague, and Loewy fit in perfectly with this effort of corporate America to enhance its image as the benevolent shaper of the future.

Almost overnight, it seemed, products ranging from stoves and vacuum cleaners to toasters, alarm clocks, and cigarette lighters emerged in sleek new forms. The prosaic pencil sharpener metamorphosed into a gleaming, aerodynamically sound work of art poised for takeoff. By the mid-1930s streamlining had become a national vogue. Major art museums organized exhibits featuring streamlined product designs. Texaco hired Geddes to streamline its service stations. Geddes's sleekly modernistic stations, he boasted, would make lubrication "a stimulating experience" rather than merely "a casual necessity of motoring."

Under the theme "The World of Tomorrow,"

the New York World's Fair of 1939 represented the high point of both the streamlining vogue and corporate America's public-relations counteroffensive in the late 1930s. The heart of the fair, and its heavily publicized logo, was the Trylon and Perisphere: the former a seven-hundred-foot needle symbolizing the event's "lofty purpose" and the latter a smooth globe two hundred feet in diameter that seemed to float on a large circular pool of water. Inside the Perisphere, visitors found "Democracity," a large revolving diorama portraying an orderly, harmonious city of the future.

The hit of the fair, however, was Futurama, the exhibit that Norman Bel Geddes designed for the General Motors Corporation. Visitors to Futurama entered a cavernous, darkened circular auditorium where, to the accompaniment of piped-in music and a resonant recorded narration, a vision of America in the distant year 1960 slowly unfolded before their eyes—an America dominated by a complex interstate highway network complete with multiple lanes, cloverleafs, and stacked interchanges. For General Motors, Futurama represented a good public-relations investment, not only to promote GM vehicles but to build public support for the costly interstate highway system that the increasing number of cars and trucks would soon make essential—a system that would become a reality in the 1950s.

Along with a first glimpse of such wonders as television and automatic dishwashers, the 1939 World's Fair did, indeed, offer its millions of visitors a memorable vision of "The World of Tomorrow"—a benign, smoothly functioning technological utopia made possible by the nation's corporations. As one business magazine editorialized: "If there are any doubters left, a visit to the New York World's Fair should convince them that American business has been the vehicle which carried the discoveries of science and the benefits of machine production to the doorstep of American consumers." In one seductive, streamlined package, the fair epitomized corporate capitalism's version of the cultural nationalism and the reviving optimism that characterized the American mood as the thirties ended.

Undercurrents of Apprehension

But a muted note of uneasiness and fear belied the surface appearance of reviving confidence. For although the economic crisis had eased, dangers loomed on the international front. The anxiety triggered by the menacing world situation sometimes surfaced in unexpected ways. One such moment came on October 31, 1938—Halloween—when the Columbia Broadcasting System aired a dramatic adaptation of H. G. Wells's science-fiction story *War of the Worlds*. The program, an episode of a CBS dramatic series called the Mercury Theatre of the Air, was directed by twenty-three-year-old Orson Welles.

In highly realistic detail, the broadcast reported the landing of a mysterious space ship near Princeton, New Jersey, the emergence of strange creatures with deadly ray guns, and their advance toward New York City, destroying everything in their path. An actor playing the role of the secretary of commerce, but mimicking the voice of President Roosevelt with uncanny accuracy, urged citizens to flee for their lives.

This vivid dramatization sparked a national panic. For a few hours, horrified listeners from coast to coast firmly believed that aliens had landed, that New York had been obliterated, and that the end of the world was at hand. Newspapers the next day commented in awe on the "tidal wave of terror" that had overspread the country. Social scientists who later studied the event concluded that of an estimated listening audience of 6 million people, 20 percent had reacted in fear and even hysteria to what they believed to be an actual catastrophe. Some jumped in their cars and drove off into the night at breakneck speed. Others prayed. A few attempted suicide. As word of the alarm reached the CBS studio in New York, Welles inserted several announcements that the program was only a fictional dramatization. But by this time, many people had already fled their homes in fright, and not for several hours did the nation's heartbeat return to normal.

Beneath the panic about "Martians" that autumn night lay a far more rational fear: of approaching war. For a decade, while Americans had been preoccupied by the depression, the international situation had steadily worsened. By October 1938 global conflict seemed a distinct possibility. For weeks radio news bulletins had warned of impending war between Germany and England. In fact, some listeners to *War of the Worlds*, blurring the broadcast's details, concluded that a foreign nation had launched a surprise attack against the United States. Recalled one young woman: "People saw how excited I was and tried to quiet me, but I kept saying over and over again to everybody I met: 'Don't you know New Jersey is destroyed by the Germans—it's on the radio.' "

The panic triggered by Orson Welles's too-vivid dramatization quickly changed to sheepish embarrassment, but the fear aroused by more immediate and realistic dangers only escalated. By the time the New York World's Fair offered its shining vision of "The World of Tomorrow," the actual world of 1939 had become very scary indeed.

The United States in a Menacing World

Apart from efforts to improve relations with Latin America, the early Roosevelt administration remained largely aloof from the rest of the world. But while the United States grappled with the depression, Italy, Germany, and Japan pursued an increasingly aggressive and militaristic course. Americans reacted with ambivalence, torn between an impulse to resist fascism and an even stronger desire for peace. Vowing not to bumble into war once again as in 1917, millions in the United States supported neutrality and peace. Others, however, insisted that America should help embattled democracies abroad. All the while, Europe edged steadily closer to the precipice.

FDR's Nationalism and the Good Neighbor Policy

Concentrating on domestic recovery, President Roosevelt initially pursued a policy that put American economic interests above all other considerations. His secretary of state, Cordell Hull, believed passionately in free trade and international economic cooperation, but FDR at first showed little interest.

Indeed, in the summer of 1933, while Hull was representing the United States at a London economic conference called by the leading trading nations to stabilize the value of their currencies, Roosevelt dispatched his adviser Raymond Moley to England bearing a blunt message: the president had no interest in any currency-stabilization plans that might undercut his New Deal recovery program. Hull, a Tennessean famous for his salty language, was furious at being upstaged. He fumed to an associate: "That piss-ant Moley! Here he curled up at mah feet and let me stroke his head like a huntin' dog and then he goes and bites me in the ass." Without U.S. cooperation, the London conference broke up in angry frustration.

Roosevelt did, however, commit himself to an internationalist approach in Latin America, where bitterness over decades of "Yankee imperialism" ran high. In his 1932 inaugural address, FDR announced a "Good Neighbor" policy toward Latin America, rejecting the blustery "Big Stick" tactics of his cousin Theodore, who had moralistically insisted on Washington's right to use force to correct "wrongdoing" in Latin America. At a conference in Montevideo, Uruguay, in 1933, the United States endorsed a statement of principles that bluntly declared: "No state has the right to intervene in the internal or external affairs of another."

Under this policy Roosevelt withdrew the last

U.S. troops from the Dominican Republic and Haiti and persuaded the National City Bank of New York to transfer its control of Haiti's central bank to the Haitian government. He also worked out a treaty with the president of Panama reducing the U.S. role in Panamanian affairs and increasing Panama's commercial rights in the Canal Zone. At the same time, however, the United States remained closely identified with the repressive regimes of Raphael Trujillo in the Dominican Republic and Anastasio Somoza in Nicaragua.

The major tests of the Good Neighbor policy came in Cuba and Mexico. In Cuba falling sugar exports related to U.S. quotas imposed by the highly protectionist Smoot-Hawley Tariff of 1930 triggered an economic crisis. This in turn led to a revolutionary uprising in 1933 that brought to power a radical government headed by Grau San Martín. The United States opposed the San Martín government and refused to recognize it. But rather than sending in the marines as Theodore Roosevelt might have done, the Franklin Roosevelt administration pursued a less direct but no less effective course of action. Early in 1934, with the active connivance of the U.S. ambassador to Cuba, Sumner Welles, and after a "visit" by U.S. warships, San Martín was overthrown by a conservative coalition dominated by strongman Fulgencio Batista. Moving quickly to help the Batista regime, Washington lowered the tariff on Cuban sugarcane. As Cuban exports to the United States skyrocketed, Batista consolidated his power. He would rule Cuba on and off until 1959, when he was in turn overthrown by Fidel Castro.

In Mexico a reform government headed by Lázaro Cárdenas came to power in 1936 and promptly nationalized several big oil companies owned by U.S. and British corporations. Washington once again refrained from military intervention. Conceding Mexico's right to nationalize the oil companies but insisting on fair compensation, the United States pressured Cárdenas economically by suspending U.S. purchases of Mexican silver. After lengthy negotiations, Mexico and the oil companies hammered out a compensation figure agreeable to both parties.

In summary, while the Roosevelt administration continued to intervene in Latin America in various indirect ways, the Good Neighbor policy did bring an end to the more heavy-handed forms of interference, including direct military occupation.

The Rise of Fascism in Europe and Asia

Meanwhile, powerful political forces raged across much of the world—forces that would ultimately pull the United States once more into war. As early as 1922, taking advantage of Italy's postwar economic problems and social unrest, Benito Mussolini and his Fascist party came to power in Rome and within a few years suppressed all dissident voices and imposed one-party rule.

An even greater menace unfolded in Germany with the rise of the Austrian-born Adolf Hitler. An embittered war veteran with a gift for demagogic harangues, Hitler shrewdly capitalized on the German people's resentment against the harsh Versailles treaty and the inability of Germany's democratic government to control runaway inflation in the 1920s. Briefly jailed in 1923 after an unsuccessful grab for power, Hitler took the opportunity to dictate his political manifesto, *Mein Kampf* (My Struggle), replete with fanatic nationalism and anti-Semitism.

Depression struck Germany in 1929 as it did the United States, and in the aftermath of a deteriorating economic situation, Hitler's National Socialist (Nazi) party won broad support. On January 30, 1933, five weeks before Franklin Roosevelt took the oath as president of the United States, Hitler became the chancellor of Germany. Roosevelt and Hitler thus rose to power almost simultaneously, and their lives would fatefully intertwine for the next twelve years until they died within two weeks of each other in April 1945—Roosevelt as the powerful leader of a victorious nation; Hitler, a suicide in his Berlin bunker beneath the rubble of a destroyed capital.

Crushing potential rivals within his own movement, Hitler quickly clamped a brutal dictatorship on Germany. Young Nazis in the major cities staged towering bonfires to burn the works of authors—many of them Jewish—accused of expressing "un-German" ideas. A racist who believed that Germany must be purified of all "inferior" taint, Hitler instituted a program to drive out German Jews, whom he further blamed for Germany's defeat in World War I.

Pursuing a militaristic and expansionist foreign policy, Hitler in 1935 announced plans for a half-million-man army. A year later Nazi troops reoccupied the German-speaking Rhineland, a region that the Versailles treaty had ordered demil-

itarized. Early in 1938, to the cheers of Austria's Nazi sympathizers, Hitler proclaimed an *Anschluss* (union) between Austria and Germany, and German tanks rolled into Vienna, Austria's capital city. Mussolini, intent on building for Italy an African empire to match those of other European powers, invaded helpless Ethiopia in 1935. These moves by Germany and Italy caused much hand wringing, but little firm action, in London, Paris, Washington, and Geneva, the headquarters of the League of Nations.

Indeed, Hitler's only setbacks in these years came in the sports arena. At the 1936 Olympics in Berlin, black American track star Jesse Owens confounded Nazi racial theories by winning four gold medals and breaking or tying three world records. And then in 1938, black American boxer Joe Louis knocked out German fighter Max Schmeling in the first round of their heavyweight championship fight in New York City.

After Austria, Hitler turned his attention to the Sudetenland, a large region belonging to neighboring Czechoslovakia containing some 3 million ethnic Germans and 700,000 Czechs. Racially the Sudetenland was part of Germany, Hitler insisted, and he made clear his determination to take it, by force if necessary. At a conference in Munich on September 29–30, 1938—a conference that excluded the Czechs—British prime minister Neville Chamberlain and his French counterpart Edouard Daladier yielded to Hitler's demands and agreed to turn over the Sudetenland to Germany. A weakened Czechoslovakia, stripped of a third of its population and territory by this agreement, faced the massed tanks and troops of the German army. Interpreting this appeasement of the Germans as a diplomatic victory, a joyful Neville Chamberlain proclaimed "peace in our time." The world heaved a collective sigh of relief; war had been avoided.

Meanwhile, halfway around the world in Tokyo, fanatically nationalistic militarists had gained control of the Japanese government and inaugurated a fateful course of expansion. In 1931–1932 Japanese troops occupied the vast Chinese province of Manchuria, installed a puppet government, and gave the region a Japanese name: "Manchukuo." In July 1937 the Japanese launched a full-scale war against China itself.

Adolf Hitler

In this German magazine illustration from 1934, a belligerent Hitler was portrayed as his nation's savior.

European Aggression Before World War II

Less than twenty years after the end of World War I, war again loomed in Europe as Hitler launched Germany on a course of military and territorial expansion.

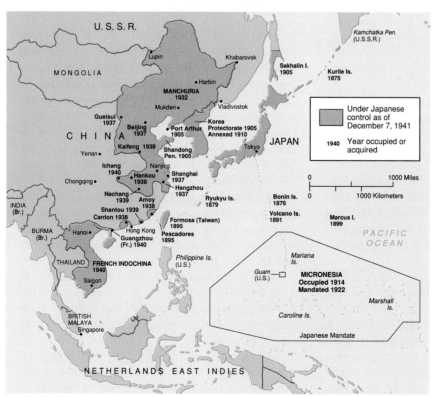

Japanese Expansion Before World War II

Dominated by militarists, Japan pursued an expansionist policy in Asia in the 1930s, extending its sphere of economic and political influence. In July 1937, having already occupied the Chinese province of Manchuria, Japan attacked China proper.

The individual pieces of this frightening puzzle had begun to come together in 1936, when Germany, Italy, and Japan signed treaties of political alliance and mutual defense. The alignment that would soon join forces in war had been forged.

The American Mood: No More War

The American people's response to these foreign developments reflected a deep revulsion against war. Novelists of the 1920s like Ernest Hemingway had repudiated the exalted wartime rhetoric of the World War I era, and by the mid-1930s, millions of Americans had concluded that the decision for war in April 1917 had been a ghastly mistake.

A series of books published around the middle of the decade reinforced this conclusion. The United States had been dragged into war, their authors argued, by banking and corporate interests desperate to protect their millions in loans and weapons sales to England and France. Walter Millis, a reporter for the *New York Herald Tribune,* carefully documented this charge in his sober work *Road to War: America, 1914–1917* (1935). More sensational exposés of the international arms traffic bore such titles as *Merchants of Death* and *One Hell of a Business.* Other works probed the propaganda techniques by which the American people had allegedly been brainwashed into supporting the war.

Public concern over the "merchants of death" issue led to the creation of a special congressional investigating committee headed by Senator Gerald Nye, a North Dakota Republican, to look into the charges. In a series of hearings between 1934 and 1936, the Nye committee compiled mountainous evidence of the heavy involvement of U.S. banks and corporations in financing World War I and supplying arms to the Allies. It also documented in detail these groups' lobbying and public-relations activities in support of U.S. intervention. In the Nye committee hearings, the old Progressive Era suspicions of "Wall Street" and "big business" resurfaced with particular intensity.

These books and investigations hit home. A Gallup poll in January 1937 revealed that an astonishing 70 percent of Americans believed that the United States should have stayed out of World War I. What had seemed at the time an act of high idealism now appeared to many a surrender to corporate interests.

All this produced a widespread determination to keep the United States out of future wars. Mistakenly equating Hitler with Kaiser Wilhelm, and the rise of fascism with the militaristic posturing of the pre-1914 European powers, many Americans concluded that the United States, protected by two oceans, could safely remain aloof from the upheavals convulsing other parts of the world. A *New York Times* book reviewer said that Walter Millis's *Road to War* should be made "required reading before anything more [is] said or written about American participation in another European war."

Reflecting this outlook, a peace movement spread across the nation's college and university campuses in 1935–1938. Led by the American Student Union and various peace groups, students organized antiwar rallies, held conferences, and marched with banners bearing such slogans as "SCHOLARSHIPS, NOT BATTLESHIPS." In a "peace strike" held in the spring semester of 1936, half a million students boycotted classes and attended antiwar events.

Novelists and playwrights expressed the national mood as well. As early as 1930, the German antiwar novel *All Quiet on the Western Front* became a best seller in the United States, and two popular antiwar dramas of 1936—Irwin Shaw's *Bury the Dead* and Robert E. Sherwood's *Idiot's Delight*—strengthened the mid-decade peace movement. In Shaw's play six American soldiers killed in battle refuse to be buried. The generals desperately try to get them underground, since "wars can be fought and won only when the dead are buried and forgotten."

A series of Neutrality Acts passed in 1935–1937 gave legislative expression to the popular longing for peace. Trying to prevent a repetition of the circumstances that had dragged the United States into war in 1917, these measures outlawed arms sales or loans to nations at war and forbade Americans from traveling on the ships of belligerent powers. In 1937, responding to the civil war in Spain, Congress extended the neutrality legislation to cover that conflict as well.

Critics of the Neutrality Acts (including President Roosevelt, who had signed them reluctantly) pointed out that these laws failed to distinguish between aggressors and victims, and might actually encourage a nation bent on conquest to attack its neighbors. When Japan invaded China in 1937, FDR refused to invoke the provisions of the Neutrality Act (on the technicality that neither side had formally declared war) in order to remain free to extend loans to the embattled Chinese.

The high point of the effort to promote peace legislatively came early in 1938, when Indiana congressman Louis Ludlow proposed a constitutional amendment requiring a national referendum on any U.S. declaration of war except in cases of actual attack. Only by a narrow margin, and after a direct appeal from President Roosevelt, did the House of Representatives reject the Ludlow Amendment.

Hesitant Response to the Fascist Challenge

The American people reacted only slowly to the fascist and militaristic regimes in Italy, Germany, and Japan. Indeed, many Americans at first regarded Mussolini with a kindly eye. He had imposed order and discipline, made the trains run on time, and in general energized Italy with a flurry of governmental activity.

Even Hitler found some American fans. As late as 1939, a pro-Nazi organization called the German-American Bund filled New York's Madison Square Garden with twenty thousand members and sympathizers. A Hollywood writer and anti-Semite named William Dudley Pelley organized a U.S. fascist movement called the Silver Shirts. (The initials deliberately echoed Hitler's S.S., an elite corps of Nazi fanatics.) Pelley's recruits, he boasted, represented "the cream, the head, the flower of our Christian manhood." Some Americans—including Joseph P. Kennedy, the U.S. ambassador to Great Britain (and father of future president John F. Kennedy)—found Hitler praiseworthy, or at least tolerable, because of his fanatic opposition to communism.

Even for Americans unsympathetic to fascism, Hitler and Mussolini seemed at first less figures of menace than of ridicule. Political cartoonists had a field day with Mussolini's jutting jaw. Children put black combs under their noses in imitation of Hitler's mustache and parodied the Nazi stiff-arm salute. The goose-stepping marches of fascist troops in Berlin and Rome appeared more like comic-opera

Benito Mussolini in a Characteristic Pose

The Italian facist leader initially won some American admirers for his dynamism and his stern insistence on order and discipline in Italian society.

routines than an omen of horrors. Through much of the thirties, the news magazine *Time* treated the Italian and German dictators as posturing demagogues more humorous than dangerous.

Not all Americans reacted this way. From the first, some viewed fascism with grave apprehension. The Popular Front was one expression of this antifascist impulse. As early as 1933, Harvard literature professor Howard Mumford Jones, addressing the American Library Association, warned that the Nazi book burnings and suppression of free speech menaced freedom everywhere. And influential newspaper columnist Dorothy Thompson, expelled from Nazi Germany in 1934, emerged as one of America's most powerful voices denouncing Hitlerism.

Whatever their feelings about fascism, most Americans strongly opposed a U.S. military response. Since neither the League of Nations nor Europe itself seemed capable of effective resistance to Hitler and Mussolini, why should the United States become involved?

What role did President Roosevelt play in all this? Fascinated by global politics and recognizing the role of power in world affairs, Roosevelt advocated adequate defenses and as early as 1933 promoted naval expansion. At the same time, personalizing international affairs just as he did domestic issues, he communicated constantly with world leaders, including Hitler and Mussolini, seeking avenues of accommodation.

Recognizing the strength of antiwar sentiment at home, FDR never pushed ahead of U.S. public opinion. Rather, in 1935 he assured a visiting Australian leader that America would never again enter a foreign war, regardless of the circumstances. In a 1937 speech, he suggested the possibility of a "quarantine" of aggressor nations to stop "the epidemic of world lawlessness," but when the public reacted coolly, he backed off.

Through much of the decade, FDR urged negotiations instead of confrontation as the best way to deal with Hitler. Accordingly, he sent a terse telegram of praise ("Good Man") to Prime Minister Chamberlain after the signing of the Munich Pact in September 1938 and wrote a State Department official that he was "not a bit upset" over the agreement to hand the Sudetenland over to Germany. The American public shared the president's support for the Munich Pact. A *New York Times* editorial summed up the prevailing consensus: "Let no man say that too high a price has been paid for peace in Europe until he has searched his soul and found himself willing to risk in war the lives of those who are nearest and dearest to him."

Significantly, Washington responded with more uneasiness to Japanese aggression against China than to the maneuverings of Hitler and Mussolini. Thanks to a long involvement in China by U.S. business interests and Christian missionaries, Americans regarded that nation with special sympathy and interest. While religious groups looked upon China as a vast mission field ripe for harvest, top government policy makers held firmly to the old dream of China's boundless economic potential as an outlet for American goods. As U.S. corporations increasingly felt "the need of foreign markets," Secretary of State Hull wrote FDR in

1935, they would inevitably turn to Asia, "for in that region lie the great potential markets of the world." On such grounds the United States had long advocated its famous Open Door policy, guaranteeing all nations equal commercial access in China.

Japan's expansionary moves of the 1930s, first in Manchuria and then against all China, threatened this Open Door principle. On a practical and immediate level, as Commerce Department officials pointed out, the closing of China to U.S. trade meant the loss of $100 million in annual cotton sales. Concern that Japanese goods, particularly textiles, might someday flood the world market sharpened Washington's uneasiness over Tokyo's aggressive policies. As early as 1934, General William "Billy" Mitchell, an advocate of air power, declared: "Japan is our most dangerous enemy, and our planes should be designed to attack her." At the same time, in the privacy of the cabinet, Roosevelt was speculating about the possibility of eventual war with Japan.

Publicly, however, Washington (which was in no position militarily to threaten war) reacted to Japan's moves in China with largely symbolic gestures. Both the Hoover and Roosevelt administrations refused to recognize Japan's puppet regime in Manchuria, and after the Japanese invasion of 1937, Washington extended modest loans to China and urged Americans to boycott Japanese silk. (At a student convention early in 1938, college women stripped off their silk hose and threw them in a bonfire, while the male students did the same with their silk neckties.) In October 1938 the U.S. ambassador to Japan, Joseph Grew, protested Japan's violation of the Open Door principle. The Japanese responded that the Open Door was "inapplicable" to the conditions of "today and tomorrow." Apart from these cautious steps, the United States did little as the Japanese tightened their grip on China.

1938–1939: The Gathering Storm

The interlude of reduced tension that followed the signing of the Munich Pact in September 1938 proved pathetically brief. Chamberlain's "peace in our time" lasted precisely 5½ months. At 6:00 A.M. on March 15, 1939, Nazi troops crashed across the border into Czechoslovakia. By evening they had lofted the Nazi swastika flag over the ancient hall of kings in Prague. Within another 5 months came the Nazi-Soviet Pact, giving Hitler a green light to invade Poland. Mused one American diplomat after the announcement of the pact: "These last two days have given me the feeling of sitting in a house where somebody is dying upstairs. There is relatively little to do and yet the suspense continues unabated."

In the United States, the worsening European situation intensified the debate over America's role. Some continued almost desperately to urge the United States to keep free of the approaching conflict. Recalling how U.S. involvement in the 1914–1918 war had shattered the progressive reform movement and spawned a climate of repressiveness and reaction, the opponents of intervention warned that the same thing could happen again. The nation should concentrate on its own social problems, they urged. As historian Carl Becker put it, "The place to save democracy is at home."

But opinion was shifting rapidly. As pacifist and neutralist sentiment weakened, the voices urging greater activism grew insistent. Warning of the "malignant character and cancerous spread" of fascism, cultural critic Lewis Mumford in 1938 issued "A Call to Arms" in the *New Republic* magazine. Archibald MacLeish, having earlier championed the cause of Spain, now exhorted his fellow citizens to mobilize against Hitlerism itself. After his appointment to the prestigious position of Librarian of Congress in 1939, MacLeish's pronouncements took on a quasi-official character. MacLeish coupled his calls for intervention with attacks on the alienated writers and intellectuals of the 1920s who, he claimed, had undermined American patriotism and made it harder for the nation to rouse itself against fascism.

After the fall of Czechoslovakia and Albania early in 1939, a now thoroughly aroused President Roosevelt publicly called on Hitler and Mussolini to pledge not to invade thirty-one specific nations, which he listed. A jeering Hitler, reading FDR's message before the German Reichstag (legislative assembly) as his Nazi followers roared with laughter, proclaimed sarcastically: "Mr. President, I fully understand that the vastness of your nation and the immense wealth of your country allow you to feel responsible for the history of the whole world and for the history of all nations. I, sir, am placed

in a much more modest and smaller sphere. . . ." In Rome Mussolini mocked Roosevelt's physical handicap, joking that the president's "creeping paralysis" had apparently reached his brain.

Roosevelt did more than send messages. In October 1938 he asked Congress for a $300 million military appropriation; in November he instructed the Army Air Corps to lay plans for an annual production of twenty thousand planes; in January 1939, calling for actions against "aggressor nations . . . more effective than mere words," he submitted to Congress a $1.3 billion defense budget. Hitler and Mussolini, he had now concluded, were "two madmen" who "respect force and force alone."

America and the Jewish Refugees

Once in power, Hitler and his followers had quickly translated their hatred of Jews into official policy. In 1935 a series of measures known as the Nuremberg Laws denied German Jews citizenship and many legal rights. In 1938 the anti-Semitic campaign became still more brutal, with the objective of forcing all Jews out of the country. The Nazis barred Jews from attending concerts or plays, expelled Jewish students from schools and universities, and required Jews to register all their property. Using as a pretext the assassination of a German official in Paris by a distraught Jewish youth, Hitler levied a "fine" of $400 million on the entire Jewish population of Germany.

This remorseless campaign reached a crescendo of violence on November 9–10, 1938: *Kristallnacht*, or "the Night of Broken Glass." In a systematic and well-coordinated rampage carried out all over Germany and Austria, Nazi loyalists vandalized Jewish homes, burned synagogues (while firemen stood by to make sure that adjacent structures did not ignite), and wrecked and looted thousands of Jewish-owned businesses. Not even Jewish hospitals, old persons' homes, or children's boarding schools escaped the terror.

No longer could anyone mistake Hitler's malignant intent. Indeed, this brutish repression foreshadowed the policy of outright extermination that would emerge during World War II as Hitler's "final solution" to the "Jewish problem." Jews, who had been leaving Germany in great numbers since 1933, now streamed out by the tens of thou-

Refugees from Nazism: Pianist Rudolph Serkin, Political Theorist Hannah Arendt

Thousands of Jewish writers, musicians, scientists, and scholars sought refuge in America from the tide of anti-Semitism unleashed by Adolf Hitler in the 1930s. Non-Jewish opponents of fascism like the novelist Thomas Mann immigrated to the United States as well.

sands, seeking whatever haven they could find. From 1933 through 1938, some sixty thousand came to the United States.

Among the victims of fascism who found refuge in America were several hundred distinguished scholars, musicians, writers, artists, and scientists. (While mostly Jewish, this group also included some non-Jews who had incurred Hitler's disfavor, such as novelist Thomas Mann and theologian Paul Tillich.) The remarkable company of illustrious immigrants included pianist Rudolph Serkin, composer Bela Bartok, architect Walter Gropius, political theorist Hannah Arendt, future secretary of state Henry Kissinger, and scores more of equal distinction. It also comprised a brilliant cadre of physicists—Leo Szilard, James Franck, Edward Teller, Enrico Fermi—who would soon play a central role in building the atomic bomb.

Although driven to America involuntarily, these men and women quickly rebuilt their smashed careers. As the director of one university art center commented wryly: "Hitler is my best friend. He shakes the tree and I collect the apples." American cultural and intellectual life in the second half of the twentieth century would have been immeasurably diminished had it not been for these talented refugees from the turmoil in Europe.

While welcoming famous and distinguished Jewish refugees, however, the United States proved far more reluctant to grant sanctuary to the mass of Nazism's Jewish victims. The sixty thousand Jews admitted to the United States by the end of 1938 composed but a small ripple of the refugee tide, and Congress consistently rejected all efforts to open the doors more widely by liberalizing the immigration law with its discriminatory quotas (see Chapter 23).

President Roosevelt bears some responsibility for this failure. To be sure, Roosevelt deplored Hitler's persecution of the Jews. Shocked by *Kristallnacht*, he told a news conference that he "could scarcely believe such things could occur in a twentieth-century civilization." And through Roosevelt's efforts, an international refugee conference held at Evian, France, in 1938 set up an Inter-Governmental Committee on Refugees. But apart from this essentially symbolic gesture, Roosevelt did little to translate his generalized sympathy for the Jews into political efforts to achieve a liberalization of the immigration statute.

What of the attitude of the American populace as a whole? While practically all Americans, according to the public-opinion polls, professed to deplore the persecution of the Jews, only a minority favored the admission of greater numbers of refugees. When the pollsters asked Americans early in 1938 if the immigration act should be amended to admit "a larger number of Jewish exiles from Germany," 75 percent responded no. The president of Sears, Roebuck wrote a senator: "I hope our natural sympathy with the plights of the Jews in Germany and Austria will not allow us to relax our immigration laws for one moment." When Senator Wagner and Congresswoman Edith Nourse Rogers of Massachusetts offered a joint bill in 1939 to admit twenty thousand German refugee children (most of whom would have been Jewish), 66 percent of Americans opposed even this humanitarian measure! Isolationist and anti-immigrant sentiments, perhaps intensified by latent anti-Semitism, severely circumscribed America's response to the tragedy of European Jewry.

The human meaning of such attitudes was graphically illustrated in June 1939 when the *St. Louis,* a vessel loaded with nine hundred Jewish refugees, after being denied a landing permit in Havana, asked permission to discharge its human cargo at Fort Lauderdale, Florida. Not only did immigration officials refuse this request, but according to the *New York Times,* a Coast Guard cutter stood by "to prevent possible attempts by refugees to jump off and swim ashore." With the lights of America within view, the *St. Louis* turned slowly eastward and sailed back across the Atlantic, carrying its stateless passengers to a fate that for many meant death at the hands of the Nazis.

Conclusion The terrible ordeal of the *St. Louis* provides an appropriately somber finale to a decade that began with Americans dazed by the stock-market crash and ended with the nation teetering on the brink of war. Between those bleak events, to be sure, the thirties brought bright moments of political creativity, social advance, and cultural achievement. The American family reeled under the impact of the depression but also displayed sturdy resilience. While hard times stimulated unionizing activity from the industrial plants of the East to the agricultural fields of the West, American business demonstrated its capacity for survival and renewal with bold design innovations in consumer goods and vigorous public-relations campaigns. The thirties was hardly a high point for black America, but the NAACP and other organizations continued the lonely struggle against lynching and discrimination, laying the groundwork for later advances. And while radio and the movies provided standardized amusement for the masses, writers, photographers, and painters not only conveyed the decade's sad realities but also rediscovered the vitality and richness of America's regional cultures. All the while, menacing events clouded the horizon. By 1939 the world looked dark; it would soon look darker still.

CHRONOLOGY

1930 *Little Caesar,* gangster movie starring Edward G. Robinson.

Animal Crackers, classic Marx Brothers comedy.

1930–1936 John Dos Passos, *U.S.A.* trilogy.

1931–1932 Japan invades Manchuria and creates puppet government

1932–1935 James J. Farrell, *Studs Lonigan* trilogy.

1933 Nathaniel West, *Miss Lonelyhearts.*

Jack Conroy, *The Disinherited.*

She Done Him Wrong and *I'm No Angel,* Mae West movie hits.

Roosevelt's economic nationalism sabotages London Economic Conference.

United States plays role in rise of Cuban strongman Fulgencio Batista.

Adolf Hitler becomes chancellor of Germany and assumes dictatorial powers.

1934 Indian Reorganization Act.

Nathaniel West, *A Cool Million.*

1934–
1936 Nye committee investigations.

Strikes by Mexican-American agricultural workers in the West.

1935 Supreme Court reverses conviction of the "Scottsboro Boys."

Harlem ghetto riot.

Clifford Odets, *Waiting for Lefty.*

Walter Millis, *The Road to War: America, 1914–1917.*

1935–1937 Neutrality Acts.

1935–1938 Peace movement sweeps U.S. campuses.

1935–1939 Era of the Popular Front.

1936 William Faulkner, *Absalom, Absalom!*

Sinclair Lewis, *It Can't Happen Here.*

Mr. Deeds Goes to Town, Frank Capra movie.

1936–
1937 Autoworkers' sit-down strike against General Motors (December 1936–February 1937).

1936–1939 Spanish Civil War.

1937 U.S. Steel, General Motors, and Chrysler sign union contracts.

Ten strikers shot dead in "Memorial Day Massacre" at Republic Steel Company in South Chicago.

Japan invades China.

1938 Formation of Congress of Industrial Organizations (CIO).

Thornton Wilder, *Our Town.*

1938 Carnegie Hall concert by Benny Goodman.
(cont.) *War of the Worlds* broadcast on CBS radio.

Nazis occupy Austria.

Munich Pact gives Sudetenland to Hitler.

Kristallnacht, night of Nazi terror against German and Austrian Jews.

United States protests Japanese violation of Open Door principle in China.

1939 John Steinbeck, *The Grapes of Wrath.*

New York World's Fair.

Nazis invade Czechoslovakia.

Nazi-Soviet Pact.

FDR submits $1.3 billion military budget.

1940 Richard Wright, *Native Son.*

William Faulkner, *The Hamlet.*

Ernest Hemingway, *For Whom the Bell Tolls.*

The Grapes of Wrath, movie directed by John Ford.

1941 James Agee and Walker Evans, *Let Us Now Praise Famous Men.*

For Further Reading

Charles C. Alexander, *Nationalism in American Thought, 1930–1945* (1969). Illuminating overview of trends in American thought and culture in the depression years and World War II.

Andrew Bergman, *We're in the Money: Depression America and Its Films* (1971). A lively interpretive study.

Irving Bernstein, *Turbulent Years: A History of the American Worker, 1933–1941* (1970). A thorough, well-researched account.

Caroline Bird, *The Invisible Scar* (1966). Moving look at the depression's human and psychological toll.

Robert Dallek, *Franklin D. Roosevelt and American Foreign Policy, 1932–1945* (1979). A fine study stressing FDR's responsiveness to domestic political currents.

Sidney Fine, *Sitdown: The General Motors Strike of 1936–1937* (1969). Classic account of a memorable and landmark strike.

Anthony Heilbut, *Exiled in Paradise: German Refugee Artists and Intellectuals in America from the 1930s to the Present* (1983). Good account of a refugee movement that profoundly influenced American culture.

Robert S. Lynd and Helen Lynd, *Middletown in Transition* (1937). A perceptive sociological study of Muncie, Indiana, in the depression.

Jeffrey Meikle, *Twentieth Century Limited: Industrial Design in America, 1925–1939* (1979). Fascinating study of the streamlining movement, with a good chapter on the New York World's Fair.

Russel Nye, *The Unembarrassed Muse: The Popular Arts in America* (1970). Useful treatment of radio and the movies in the 1930s.

Arnold A. Offner, *American Appeasement: United States Foreign Policy and Germany, 1933–1938* (1969). A comprehensive and well-written study.

Susan Ware, *Holding Their Own: American Women in the 1930s* (1982). A good overview incorporating recent scholarly research.

Additional Bibliography

American Society in the 1930s

Harold J. Alford, *The Proud Peoples: The Heritage and Culture of Spanish-Speaking Peoples in the United States* (1972); Robert F. Berkhofer, Jr., *The White Man's Indian: Images of the American Indian from Columbus to the Present* (1978); Dan T. Carter, *Scottsboro* (1964); William H. Chafe, *The American Woman: Her Changing Social, Economic and Political Roles, 1920–1970* (1972); Ruth Schwartz Cowan, "Two Washes in the Morning and a Bridge Party at Night: The American Housewife Between the Wars," *Women's Studies* 2 (1976):147–171; Melvyn Dubofsky and Warren Van Tine, *John L. Lewis: A Biography* (1977); Abraham Hoffman, *Unwanted Mexican-Americans in the Great Depression* (1974); Irving Howe and Louis Coser, *The American Communist Party: A Critical History* (1957); Robert S. McElvaine, ed., *Down and Out in the Great Depression* (1983); Matt S. Meier and Feliciano Rivera, *The Chicanos: A History of Mexican Americans* (1972); Ruth Milkman, ed., *Women, Work and Protest: A Century of U.S. Women's Labor History* (1985); Mark Reisler, *By the Sweat of Their Brows* (1976); Marjorie Rosen, *Popcorn Venus: Women, Movies, and the American Dream* (1971); Lois Scharf, *To Work and to Wed: Female Employment, Feminism, and the Great Depression* (1980); Lois Scharf and Joan M. Jensen, eds., *Decade of Discontent: The Woman's Movement, 1920–1940* (1983); Judith Sealander, *As Minority Becomes Majority: Federal Reaction to the Phenomenon of Women in the Work Place, 1920–1963* (1983); Bernard Sternsher, *Hitting Home: The Great Depression in Town and Country* (1970); Winifred D. Wandersee, *Women's Work and Family Values, 1920–1940* (1981); Patricia Yeghissian, "Emergence of the Red Berets," *Michigan Occasional Papers in Women's Studies* 10 (Winter 1980).

Cultural Trends in the Depression Decade

Daniel Aaron, *Writers on the Left: Episodes in American Literary Communism* (1961); Matthew Baigell, *The American Scene: Painting in the 1930s* (1974); Frederick Bensen, *The Literary Impact of the Spanish Civil War* (1967); Hadley Cantril, *Invasion from Mars: A Study in the Psychology of Panic* (1940); James M. Dennis, *Grant Wood: A Study in American Art and Culture* (1975); Malcolm Goldstein, *The Political Stage: American Drama and Theatre of the Great Depression* (1974); Nancy Helber and Julia Williams, *The Regionalists* (1976); Saul Maloff, "The Mythic Thirties," *Texas Quarterly* 11 (Winter 1968):109–118; Donald Meyer, *The Protestant Search for Political Realism, 1919–1941* (1961); Richard H. Pells, *Radical Visions and American Dreams: Culture and Social Thought in the Depression Years* (1973); Walter Rideout, *The Radical Novel in the United States, 1900–1954* (1956); Richard Schickel, *The Disney Version* (1968); Marshall W. Stearns, *The Story of Jazz* (1956); William Stott, *Documentary Expression and Thirties America* (1973); Warren Susman, "The Thirties," in *The Development of an American Culture*, edited by Stanley Coben and Lorman Ratner (1970); Allen Syles, *The Marx Brothers: Their World of Comedy* (1966); Frank A. Warren, *Liberals and Communism: The "Red Decade" Revisited* (1966).

U.S. Foreign Policy and the Fascist Challenge

Alan Bullock, *Hitler: A Study in Tyranny* (1952); Wayne S. Cole, *Roosevelt and the Isolationists, 1932–1945* (1983); Charles DeBenedetti, *The Peace Reform in American History* (1980); Robert A. Divine, *The Illusion of Neutrality* (1962) and *The Reluctant Belligerent* (1979); Robert H. Ferrell, *American Diplomacy in the Great Depression* (1957); Donald Fleming and Bernard Bailyn, eds., *The Intellectual Migration: Europe and America, 1930–1960* (1969); Lloyd C. Gardner, *Economic Aspects of New Deal Diplomacy* (1964); James B. Gilbert, *Writers and Partisans: A History of Literary Radicalism in America* (1968); Thomas N. Guinsburg, *The Pursuit of Isolation in the United States Senate from Versailles to Pearl Harbor* (1982); Allen Guttman, *The Wound in the Heart: America and the Spanish Civil War* (1962); Harvey Klehr, *The Heyday of American Communism: The Depression Decade* (1984); Arnold A. Offner, *The Origins of the Second World War: American Foreign Policy and World Politics, 1917–1941* (1975); Norman Holmes Pearson, "The Nazi-Soviet Pact and the End of a Dream," in *America in Crisis*, edited by Daniel Aaron (1952); Robert F. Smith, *The United States and Cuba* (1960); John E. Wiltz, *In Search of Peace: The Senate Munitions Inquiry, 1934–1936* (1963); David S. Wyman, *Paper Walls: America and the Refugee Crisis, 1938–1941* (1985).

CHAPTER 26

Waging Global War, 1939–1945

Americans who lived through World War II retained vivid images of the war's beginning and end long afterward. Even years later, most recalled their shock and indignation upon hearing the news on December 7, 1941, of the Japanese attack on the American naval base at Pearl Harbor, Hawaii, that brought the United States into the conflict. And they cherished their memories of the celebrations that greeted President Harry S Truman's announcement of the Japanese surrender on August 14, 1945.

Their forty-five months of global war finally over, Americans celebrated with exuberance. Virtually all Americans had considered the nation's participation in the war as just and necessary, and they now rejoiced in triumph. "Any girl . . . in downtown San Diego got kissed and thrown in Horton Plaza fountain," recalled Patricia Livermore. "I got thrown in ten times." Thousands of people snakedanced through a drenching thunderstorm in Salt Lake City, and nearly half a million cavorted in the streets in front of San Francisco's city hall. The society editor of the *Boston Herald,* Alison Arnold, remembered hearing the news on her car radio while driving home. "At almost every house the door opened and children poured out waving flags. The church bells were ringing. Everybody got in their cars and drove around town with the horns blowing." Some 2 million people frolicked in New York's Times Square. "The victory roar that greeted the announcement beat upon the eardrums until it numbed the senses," the *New York Times* reported the next day. "Restraint was thrown to the winds. Those in the crowds tossed hats, boxes and flags in the air. From those leaning perilously out of the windows of office buildings and hotels came a shower of paper, confetti, streamers. Men and women embraced—there were no strangers in New York yesterday."

For most Americans, it had been a "good war." Although the United States was no stranger to the war's tragedy—more than 300,000 Americans lost their lives in the conflict, perishing on faraway islands or in small European towns with quaint-sounding names—American losses paled beside the untold millions of casualties suffered by European and Asian nations. Moreover, the American home front was spared the devastation that swept Europe and Asia. In fact, the war made the United States once again a land of opportunity and hope. It lifted the nation out of the depression, redistributed income, and transformed the United States into a genuinely middle-class society. The war gave millions of Americans a second chance; and for millions more, a first chance. Women and blacks especially savored the novel joys of independence and freedom. At the same time, the experience of "total war" led to profound changes in the nation's behavior and institutions. It reshaped the nature of the economy and the role and power of the government. It disrupted family relationships and traditional social values. And it ended American isolationism, pushing the United States to the forefront of world affairs in a new era of Cold War and nuclear weapons.

Into the Storm, 1939–1941

Twenty years after the conclusion of World War I, Germany and Japan unleashed a campaign of international intimidation and aggression that ultimately sucked the United States into a second global conflict. The Roosevelt administration initially hoped that neutrality would keep America at peace and secure. When German victories in western Europe in the spring of 1940 pulverized that prospect, the president tried economic intervention as an alternative to military involvement, lending all possible aid to those nations resisting aggression by the so-called Rome-Berlin-Tokyo Axis. Moreover, as the fascist menace intensified, Roosevelt speeded up a rearmament campaign while simultaneously extending greater assistance to the Allies, stretching his executive authority to the legal limit and beyond. Although reluctant to ask a divided Congress for a declaration of war against the Axis, the president understood that his uncompromising conduct toward Germany and Japan could cause the United States to be "pushed," as he said, into a worldwide war. The push came with Japan's attack on the U.S. fleet at Pearl Harbor. As the New World girded to redress the balance of power in two older worlds in 1942, Americans suffered their grimmest year of the war. Victory seemed remote. American military officials gloomily contemplated a prolonged war of seven to fifteen years.

Storm in Europe

Adolf Hitler precipitated war by demanding that Poland restore to Germany the city of Danzig (Gdansk), lost after World War I. When Poland refused, the Führer's troops poured into Poland at dawn on September 1, 1939, while his *Luftwaffe* (air force) bombarded Polish cities. Two days later, Britain and France, honoring their commitments to Poland, declared war on Germany. Roosevelt dutifully invoked the Neutrality Acts, a series of laws passed in the mid-1930s to prohibit the specific actions, such as supplying arms to belligerents, that had drawn the United States into World War I. But the president did not repeat Woodrow

Wilson's appeal to Americans to be "impartial in thought as well as in action." Even a neutral, Roosevelt declared, "cannot be asked to close his mind or his conscience."

Determined to avoid an Allied defeat, which would force the United States to confront Nazi Germany alone, the president in mid-September 1939 asked a special session of Congress to revise the Neutrality Act's prohibition against the sale of weapons to belligerents. To allay fears that this measure might lead the country into war, the president also requested authorization to forbid American ships and travelers from sailing into designated combat zones and to prevent American merchant vessels from carrying cargoes to belligerents' ports. The amended neutrality law, which Congress adopted by large margins in November, further required that all supplies bought in America be paid for in cash and carried away by the Allies' own ships. Roosevelt had tailored the "cash-and-carry" provision to fit the public mood. Opinion polls that month revealed that while two-thirds of the American people favored aiding the Allies, the same percentage considered staying out of war even more important than saving England and France from defeat.

Suddenly in April 1940 Hitler unleashed his *Blitzkrieg* ("lightning war") on western Europe. The Germans first struck in the north, quickly occupying Denmark and crushing Norway. Then in May Hitler's panzer (armored) divisions seized the Netherlands, Belgium, and Luxembourg and drove the desperately retreating British Expeditionary Force back to the seacoast. Using every seaworthy vessel that they could commandeer, the British between May 28 and June 4 evacuated more than 338,000 troops across the English Channel from Dunkirk in northern France. The British saved their army, but now only France remained on the Continent to face the German onslaught. As Hitler's soldiers sliced through the undefended and presumably impassable Forest of Ardennes, outflanking the 3 million French soldiers along the Maginot Line,* Italy's fascist dictator Benito

---

*Maginot Line: an extensive system of fortifications built by France in the 1930s to guard against a German invasion.

Hitler's Blitzkrieg

(Left) A German soldier hurls a "potato-masher" grenade at resisting Poles; (right) a Belgian mother and her children walk through rubble left by a German air attack. In reaction to Germany's "lightning war" on Europe, Walter Lippmann wrote that Americans' "duty is to begin acting at once on the basic assumption that . . . before the snow flies again we may stand alone and isolated, the last great Democracy on earth."

Mussolini attacked France from the south. On June 22 France capitulated. A jubilant Hitler dictated the armistice to the French in the same railway car used by the Allies to compel Germany's surrender on November 11, 1918.

Hitler now took aim at Britain. Throughout the summer and fall of 1940, in the Battle of Britain, the Germans sought to terror-bomb the British into submission. Round-the-clock aerial bombing killed and wounded tens of thousands of British civilians, utterly destroyed the city of Coventry, and left parts of London in rubble. With Hitler's U-boats strangling Britain's lifelines, the new prime minister, Winston Churchill, unashamedly pleaded for all possible American aid short of troops. Most Americans favored additional support for Britain. But a large and articulate minority opposed such assistance, criticizing it either as a waste of mate-

rials needed by the United States for its own defense or as a subterfuge to involve Americans in a war not vital to their interests.

The Election of 1940

As the war escalated in Europe, Americans speculated about Roosevelt's political intentions. Would he run for an unprecedented third term? Not until the eve of the Democratic convention in July did the president reveal that given the world crisis, he could consent to a "draft" from his party. The Nazi menace forced most conservative anti–New Deal Democrats to accept FDR for another possible term and even to accept as his running mate Secretary of Agriculture Henry Wallace, an ultra-liberal disliked by many party professionals and moderates.

The dramatic German victories in Europe had an even greater impact on the Republicans' nominating process. While the anti-interventionist front-runners, Senator Robert A. Taft of Ohio and District Attorney Thomas E. Dewey of New York, criticized Roosevelt's handling of foreign affairs, a dark-horse candidate, Wendell L. Willkie of Indiana, outspokenly championed greater aid to the British. Backed by internationalists in the Republican party, especially those in corporate business and publishing, Willkie, a former Democrat and utility magnate, stampeded the GOP convention and won the nomination on the sixth ballot. Although he had never campaigned for elective office before, Willkie proved a formidable contender. Large crowds flocked to hear him denounce FDR's bid for a third term.

Roosevelt responded by adroitly playing the role of a national leader too busy with defense and diplomacy to engage in partisan politics. He undercut GOP criticisms by appointing Hoover's secretary of state, Henry L. Stimson, as his new secretary of war and Landon's running mate, Frank Knox, as his secretary of the navy. Encouraged by large bipartisan majorities in Congress, Roosevelt endorsed the nation's first peacetime draft and another dramatic increase in defense spending. Then in September, with Willkie's public support, the president concluded an executive agreement with Churchill to transfer fifty American destroyers used in World War I to Britain in exchange for leases on British air and naval bases in the Western Hemisphere. This arrangement bolstered American security and assisted England in its defense against a possible German invasion of the British Isles. In engineering it, Roosevelt evaded a congressional vote on the matter. Although he had taken the nation closer to war, Roosevelt explained his action as a way of averting American entry.

The president's anti-interventionist critics condemned Roosevelt's "dictatorial" methods and accused him of scheming to entangle the United States in the European conflict. To mobilize public opinion against the drift toward war, isolationists organized the Committee to Defend America First. Largely financed by Henry Ford and his associates, the America First Committee featured aviator Charles Lindbergh as its most popular speaker. Under the slogan "Fortress America," these isolationists claimed that the United States had the strength to stand alone regardless of Hitler's victories in Europe. Although America First attracted spokesmen from virtually every region, ideology, and ethnic group, most Americans supported Roosevelt's effort to assist Great Britain while avoiding active participation in the war.

With public-opinion polls showing Roosevelt securely ahead in late October, GOP leaders persuaded Willkie to drop bipartisanship and attack the president as an interventionist leading the country to war. He accused the president of secretly plotting war and unreservedly promised that if elected, "I will never send an American boy to fight in a European war." Stung, Roosevelt retorted, "Your president says this country is not going to war!" By a popular margin of almost 55 percent to Willkie's 45 percent, the voters returned Roosevelt to office with an electoral-college victory of 449 to 82.

From Isolation to Intervention

Assured of four more years in power, Roosevelt moved resolutely in support of Britain—the best way to defend the United States, the president declared in a fireside chat late in December 1940. Calling upon the United States to be the "great arsenal of democracy," he promised that there would be no slackening of America's determination to assist the Allies. In January 1941 Roosevelt proposed the lend-lease bill. Explaining that England did not have the money to purchase essential mate-

The Election of 1940				
Candidates	Parties	Electoral Vote	Popular Vote	Percentage of Popular Vote
FRANKLIN D. ROOSEVELT	Democratic	449	27,307,819	54.8
Wendell L. Willkie	Republican	82	22,321,018	44.8

rials, he asked Congress to rescind the "cash" provision of cash-and-carry and permit the president to lend or lease supplies to any country whose defense was deemed vital to American security. Although Roosevelt justified the measure as another step to avoid American participation in the fighting, the lend-lease bill actually amounted to the end of U.S. non-intervention and a declaration of economic war against Hitler. With polls showing nearly 80 percent of the public in favor of lend-lease, Congress approved the measure in March 1941 and initially appropriated $7 billion for supplies for Britain. Shipments to England began at once, and after Hitler invaded the Soviet Union in June, the Russians also started to receive American war matériel. Despite widespread American hostility to communism and to the Soviet Union, Roosevelt insisted that Germany remained the chief danger to the United States. To defeat Hitler, the president confided, "I would hold hands with the Devil."

The majority of Americans, while willing to take all steps short of war, remained determined to avoid a final commitment. The safe delivery of American supplies to Great Britain, however, brought the United States inexorably closer to an undeclared naval war with Germany. In April, with Nazi submarines that hunted their prey in "wolf packs" winning the Battle of the Atlantic and choking off the stream of aid to England, U.S. ships began to assist the British in tracking German U-boats. During the summer, as ten thousand tons of Allied merchant vessels sank to the bottom every day, the U.S. Navy started convoying British ships transporting lend-lease supplies, with orders to destroy enemy ships if necessary to protect the shipments. American forces also occupied Greenland and Iceland to keep these strategic Danish islands out of the hands of the Nazis, who had overrun Denmark itself.

In mid-August Roosevelt met with Churchill aboard a warship off Newfoundland to discuss joint military strategy. The two leaders' concluding public statement, soon known as the Atlantic Charter, expressed their mutual ideal of a postwar world. Recalling Woodrow Wilson's Fourteen Points (see Chapter 22), the charter condemned aggression, affirmed national self-determination, and endorsed the principles of collective security and disarmament. The following month, a German submarine opened fire on an American destroyer. Roosevelt denounced the Nazis as "the rattlesnakes of the Atlantic" and authorized naval patrols to shoot on sight at all Axis vessels operating between the United States and Iceland. In mid-October a second American destroyer was torpedoed, and on the final night of the month, a submarine sank the destroyer *Reuben James* and its 115 American sailors.

On a collision course with Germany, Roosevelt in November asked Congress to permit the arming of merchant ships and the transporting of lend-lease supplies to belligerent ports in previously prohibited war zones. By votes of 212 to 194 in the House and 50 to 37 in the Senate, Congress repealed the "carry" provision of cash-and-carry. Virtually nothing now remained of the neutrality legislation adopted by Congress in the 1930s to keep the United States out of war. Although not prepared for a major war, America was already fighting a limited one, and full-scale war seemed imminent. Yet because the bill to extend the draft for another year had passed the House by only a single vote in August 1941, the president still feared that any attempt to secure a declaration of war would be defeated, barring dramatic new developments. Hitler also hesitated to take the final step to declared belligerency, wanting no diversions from his life-and-death struggle with the Russians.

Toward Pearl Harbor

Hitler's triumphs in western Europe encouraged the Japanese to expand their aggression in Asia from China to the resource-rich British, Dutch, and French colonial possessions in Southeast Asia. It also left the United States virtually alone to oppose Japan's expansion. But always viewing Germany as the primary threat to American security, the Roosevelt administration sought to apply just enough pressure to deter the Japanese without provoking Tokyo to war before the United States had built the "two-ocean navy" authorized by Congress in 1940. "It is terribly important for the control of the Atlantic for us to keep peace in the Pacific," Roosevelt told Harold Ickes, his secretary of the interior, in mid-1941. "I simply have not got enough navy to go around—and every episode in the Pacific means fewer ships in the Atlantic." American military leaders agreed. As late as November 17, 1941, a report of the Joint Board of the Army and Navy counseled the president to prolong negotiations with Japan, emphasizing that "the most essential thing now, from the United States standpoint, is to gain time."

Both Japan and the United States hoped to avoid war, but neither would compromise its goals in return for peace. Japan's desire to create a Greater East Asia Co-Prosperity Sphere (an empire embracing much of China, Southeast Asia, and the western Pacific) matched America's insistence on the Open Door in China and the maintenance of the status quo in the rest of Asia. To the Japanese, Secretary of State Cordell Hull's demand that they give up their Asian conquests seemed just a smoke screen to thwart their legitimate national aspirations and deny them the raw materials and foodstuffs required by a rapidly growing and highly industrialized population. But to the Americans, Japan appeared a militaristic predator, brutalizing helpless Chinese peasants and bullying beleaguered Europeans to rob them of their imperial possessions in Asia.

Several decades of "yellow-peril" propaganda, as well as Tokyo's invasion of China, prompted Washington's bellicosity toward Japan. No American pressure groups organized to prevent a clash with Japan. There was no counterpart to the clamorous anti-interventionist critics who blasted U.S. involvement in Europe. Isolationists were as virulently anti-Japanese as internationalists. Repeatedly pictured in the media as skinny, bowlegged little people with buckteeth and thick spectacles, the Japanese appeared to be pushovers for the American navy. With virtual unanimity the American people applauded every step that the Roosevelt administration took to resist Japanese expansion.

To thwart Japan's entry into Southeast Asia after the fall of France in the spring of 1940, the United States allowed the Treaty of Trade and Navigation (1911) with the Japanese to expire. The president hoped that the threat of economic coercion would deflect Japan from its course of conquest. Japan, however, retaliated in July 1940 by initiating plans to implement its New Order in Asia. Roosevelt then imposed an embargo on the sale of aviation gasoline and scrap metal to Japan. Tokyo responded in September by occupying northern Indochina, a French colonial possession, and by concluding the Tripartite Pact with the Axis powers, Germany and Italy, in which each of the signatories pledged to help the others in the event of an attack by the United States. Washington answered by adding to the embargo list all metals as well as various chemicals, machine parts, and other products vital to Japan.

In July 1941 the Japanese overran the rest of Indochina. Roosevelt retaliated by freezing all Japanese assets in the United States and clamping a total embargo on trade with Japan. Tokyo now had to choose between submitting to the United States to gain a resumption of trade or conquering new lands to obtain the supplies vital to its war machine. In October the ardently expansionist war minister Hideki Tojo replaced the more conciliatory Fumimaro Konoye as prime minister of the imperial government. Tojo, who opposed compromise with the United States, set the first week in December as the deadline for Japanese forces to take the offensive if the United States did not capitulate and resume trade relations with Japan. The embargoed Japanese, watching their fuel meters drop toward empty, believed that they had no other option.

U.S. intelligence's deciphering of the top code used in messages sent to Japanese ambassadors alerted the Roosevelt administration by late November that war was imminent. It made no concessions, however, during the eleventh-hour negotiations still under way in Washington. Hull continued to insist that the resumption of American trade depended on the complete withdrawal of Japanese troops from China and Indochina. "I have washed my hands of it," Hull informed Stimson on November 27, "and it is now in the hands of you and Knox—the Army and the Navy." The Japanese, he added, "mean to fight and you will have to watch out." War warnings went out to all commanders in the Pacific that same day, advising that negotiations were deadlocked and that hostile Japanese action was possible at any moment. Most Americans expected Japan to continue its thrust to the south, attacking British Malaya or the Philippines. But the Japanese had decided to gamble on a knockout punch. They hoped that a surprise aerial raid on the U.S. naval base at Pearl Harbor would destroy the entire U.S. Pacific Fleet and compel a Roosevelt preoccupied with Germany to seek accommodation with Japan.

Destruction at Pearl Harbor

Several months prior to the air raid, army and navy officials in Hawaii had warned with uncanny accuracy that carrier-based Japanese bombers might attack at daybreak from about three hundred miles at sea.

Unopposed, waves of Japanese dive-bombers and torpedo planes soared across the Hawaiian island of Oahu on the morning of December 7 to bomb the ships anchored in Pearl Harbor and to strafe the planes parked wingtip to wingtip—as protection against sabotage—at the nearby air bases. American forces suffered their most devastating defeat in history. In less than three hours, 188 aircraft had been destroyed and nearly as many damaged, and eight battleships, three light cruisers, and three destroyers had been sunk or crippled. More than two thousand Americans had been killed. Japan's spectacular victory would open the way for an advance to the threshold of Australia by April 1942. It would also ensure Roosevelt an aroused

and united America to avenge what he termed this "day that would live in infamy."

When Roosevelt asked Congress to declare war on Japan on December 8, only one dissenting vote was cast—by Montana's Jeannette Rankin, who had also cast a nay vote against U.S. entry into World War I. The president still hesitated to request a declaration of war against Germany. Hitler quickly resolved his dilemma. Although the Tripartite Pact required Germany to assist Japan only if it was attacked first, and Hitler's advisers begged him not to add the United States to the already long list of anti-Nazi belligerents, he went before a cheering Reichstag on December 11 to declare war on the "half Judaized and the other half Negrified" American people. Mussolini immediately chimed in with his declaration of war against the United States, and Congress reciprocated that same afternoon. America now faced a global war that it was not yet ready to fight.

On the Defensive

In the days after Pearl Harbor, German U-boats wreaked havoc in the North Atlantic and freely prowled the Caribbean and the East Coast of the United States. Every twenty-four hours, five more Allied vessels went to the bottom. Scores of tankers and freighters flying the Stars and Stripes sank within sight of U.S. shores. U-boats even bottled up the Chesapeake Bay for nearly six weeks. By the end of 1942, Hitler's submarines had destroyed more than a thousand Allied ships, offsetting the tremendous pace of American ship production. The United States was losing the Battle of the Atlantic.

Similarly, the war news from Europe and Africa was, as Roosevelt admitted, "all bad." Hitler had planted the swastika across an enormous swath of territory, from the outskirts of Moscow and Leningrad—a thousand miles deep into Russia—to the Pyrenees on the Spanish-French border, and from the northern tip of Norway to the Libyan desert. In the spring of 1942, the onrushing Germans inflicted more than 250,000 casualties on the Soviet army in the Crimea, and Hitler launched a powerful offensive to seize the Caucasian oil fields. Just as relentlessly, German forces lunged eastward in North Africa, threatening to seize the Suez Canal, the British oil lifeline. It seemed only a matter of months before the Mediterranean would be an Axis sea and Hitler would be in India to greet Tojo marching across Asia from the east.

Apparently as invincible as the Nazis, the Japanese inflicted defeat after defeat on the Allied forces in the Pacific. Tojo immediately followed up his victory at Pearl Harbor with successful attacks on the Philippines, Malaya, and Thailand. By early 1942 the Japanese had also taken Hong Kong, Guam, Wake Island, the Gilbert Islands, Manila, and Singapore, the key to Southeast Asia. In February Tojo's naval squadrons utterly shattered Allied warships in the Battle of the Java Sea. March brought the fall of Java and the oil-rich Dutch East Indies, and the closing of the Burma Road, sealing off the only mainland link to China. By the middle

of May, when the last American soldiers in the Philippines surrendered, Japan's rising sun blazed over hundreds of islands in the central and western Pacific and over the entire eastern perimeter of the Asian mainland from the border of Siberia to the border of India.

America Mobilizes for War

The United States began to prepare actively for war after the fall of France in mid-1940. But many businesses, fearful that the demand for combat equipment might be short-lived, hesitated to convert to war production. Constant bickering among the military, industry, and labor also hindered preparedness, as each selfishly jockeyed for influence and power. And Roosevelt's own reluctance to speed mobilization, arising from his concern that his political opponents would depict him as a warmonger, further slowed the nation's preparations for global warfare. In December 1941 the American armed forces had a combined total of only 1.6 million men. With war production composing just 15 percent of industrial output, the military faced drastic shortages. Moreover, Washington had still not organized an efficient bureaucratic structure to direct mobilization.

Pearl Harbor changed everything. Within a week Congress passed the War Powers Act, granting the president unprecedented authority. Hundreds of special wartime agencies soon regulated almost every facet of American life. Increased draft calls and voluntary enlistments vastly enlarged the army and the navy. By the end of the war, more than 15 million men had been trained and equipped for the armed forces; and nearly 350,000 women had served in the women's branches of the military, especially the WAC (Women's Army Corps) and the WAVES (Women Accepted for Voluntary Emergency Service in the Navy). To direct this military complex, Roosevelt formed the Joint Chiefs of Staff, which, with Admiral William D. Leahy as chief, was made up of representatives of the army, the navy, and the army air force. Only a minor "corps" within the army as late as June 1941, the air force grew more dramatically than any other branch of the service and achieved virtual autonomy as it assumed a vital role in American combat strategy. The changing nature of modern warfare also led the Joint Chiefs of Staff to create the Office of Strategic Services (OSS) to conduct espionage, analyze the enemy's strengths and weaknesses, and gather the intelligence information required for strategic planning. In 1942 the managers of America's increasingly diversified and huge war machine moved into the world's largest building, the newly constructed Pentagon, in which some 35,000 military personnel worked. And like the Pentagon, the far-reaching domestic changes under way outlasted the war and significantly altered American attitudes, behavior, and institutions.

Organizing for Victory

Shortly after Pearl Harbor, Roosevelt called upon the American people to produce in 1942 an unprecedented 60,000 planes, 45,000 tanks, 20,000 anti-aircraft guns, 8 million tons of shipping, and immense quantities of other supplies for the American and the Allied fighting forces. To organize this herculean effort, Roosevelt established the War Production Board (WPB). Its tasks included allocating scarce materials, limiting or stopping the production of civilian goods, and distributing contracts among competing manufacturers. In addition, the War Manpower Commission (WMC) supervised the mobilization of men and women for the military, war industry, and agriculture; the National War Labor Board (NWLB) mediated disputes between management and labor, seeking to prevent strikes and runaway wage increases; and the Office of Price Administration (OPA) imposed strict price controls to check inflation as more and more personal income pursued fewer and fewer consumer goods.

In October 1942 Roosevelt persuaded James F. Byrnes to leave the Supreme Court to become the "assistant president" in charge of America's domestic war effort. His assignment was to increase the coordination of and cooperation between the many government agencies and representatives of industry and the military involved in carrying out the war effort. In May 1943 the president formally appointed Byrnes to head the new Office of War Mobilization (OWM), which exercised control over all aspects of the economy, as Bernard Baruch had done during World War I.

"The Americans can't build planes," a Nazi commander had jeered, "only electric iceboxes and razor blades." But soon after February 1942, when the last new civilian car came off a wartime assembly line, the United States achieved a miracle of war production. "It was not so much industrial conversion," observed a business leader, "as industrial revolution, with months and years condensed into days." Automobile manufacturers retooled to produce planes and tanks; a merry-go-round factory switched to fashioning gun mounts; a pinball-machine maker converted to armor-piercing shells. By the end of 1942, the proportion of the economy committed to war production had more than doubled, to 33 percent. When necessary, whole new industries were created from scratch. The government invested $700 million in some fifty new synthetic-rubber-making plants, to compensate for the loss of 97 percent of the nation's crude-rubber supply stemming from Japanese conquests in rubber-producing regions. By 1944 more than 80 percent of the rubber consumed in the United States came from the close to 1 million tons of synthetic rubber manufactured that year. At the war's close, Americans, once the world's largest importers of crude rubber, were the world's largest exporters of synthetic rubber.

The United States also became the world's greatest manufacturer of armaments. The nation produced more war matériel than its Axis enemies combined. By the end of the war, Americans had assembled some 300,000 military aircraft, as well as more than 86,000 tanks, 372,000 artillery pieces, 2.6 million machine guns, and 6 million tons of aircraft bombs. In addition, the United States turned out more than 5,000 cargo ships and 86,000 warships. When the government started its emergency crash shipbuilding program in 1941, it took about six months to produce a Liberty-class merchant ship. In 1943 Henry J. Kaiser, who had supervised the construction of Boulder Dam, used the revolutionary technique of prefabrication to reduce the time to less than two weeks; and in 1945 Kaiser, now dubbed "Sir Launchalot," and his fellow shipbuilders were completing a cargo ship a day.

Such breakneck production came at a significant cost. The size and powers of the government expanded far more than they had even during the New Deal, as the sum of defense spending zoomed from 9 percent of the GNP in 1940 to 46 percent in 1945, and the federal budget leaped from $9 business to convert to war production and to expand its industrial capacity, the government guaranteed profits through a system of cost-plus-fixed-fee contracts, generous tax write-offs, and suspension of antitrust prosecutions. Such measures chiefly benefited the giant corporations. Two-thirds of all federal war-production dollars went to the one hundred largest firms. The ten biggest businesses received 30 percent of the dollar total of all defense contracts (General Motors alone garnered 8 percent of all defense expenditures), greatly accelerating trends toward economic concentration in the United States.

A War Economy

The United States spent about $250 million a day to defeat the Axis. Federal expenditures totaled more than $320 billion between 1941 and 1945, ten times more than the cost of World War I and nearly twice the amount that had been spent by the government since its founding in 1788. Wartime spending and the military draft vanquished the unemployment of the Great Depression and stimulated an industrial boom that produced unprecedented prosperity for the majority of Americans. War spending doubled America's industrial output, created 17 million new jobs, and increased the GNP per capita from $573 in 1940 to $1,074 in 1945. By the end of the war, net farm income was more than twice what it had been in 1940; corporate profits after taxes had leaped 70 percent; and the real wages, or purchasing power, of industrial workers had risen 50 percent.

Full employment, longer workweeks, payment of time and a half for overtime, and the increased hiring of minorities, women, young people, and the elderly brought a middle-class standard of living to millions of families who had previously known privation. The war years produced the only significant shift in the distribution of American income in the twentieth century. Even without considering the effect on the most affluent of the graduated income tax, which went up sharply during the war, the fraction of total income going to the richest 5 percent sank from 26 percent to 20 percent, while the share of the least affluent 40 percent climbed from 13 percent to 16 percent of all income. The earnings of the bottom fifth of workers rose by 68 percent; and the size of the middle class doubled.

The Calship Yards, Los Angeles

Wartime shipbuilders told the story of a woman who was invited to christen a new ship. Escorted to an empty launching way, she was handed a bottle of champagne. "But where is the ship?" she asked. "You just start swinging the bottle, lady," a worker responded; "we'll have the ship there."

billion to $98 billion. The number of civilian employees of the federal government mushroomed from 1.1 million to 3.8 million. The executive branch, which managed the war effort, grew the most, and a close alliance formed between the defense industry and the military. (A generation later, Americans would call these concentrations of power the imperial presidency and the military-industrial complex.) And because the government was bent on achieving the greatest volume of war production in the shortest possible time, it encouraged corporate profits. "If you are going to try to go to war in a capitalist country," Secretary of War Stimson had pointed out, "you have to let business make money out of the process or business won't work."

"Dr. New Deal," Roosevelt aptly put it in 1943, had given way to "Dr. Win the War." To encourage

The war reversed the hard times of the 1920s and 1930s for American farmers. The parity rate paid by the government jumped from 72 percent in 1939 to 90 percent in 1942 and to 110 percent in 1943, and covered more commodities than ever before. At the same time, agricultural productivity soared. With over a million more new tractors in use in 1945 than in 1940, and with the utilization of improved fertilizers and cultivation techniques, by the end of the war, farmers produced 477 million more bushels of corn on the same acreage than they had at the start of the conflict, as well as 324 million more bushels of wheat and 500 million more pounds of rice. The combination of higher prices, increased productivity, and a 17 percent decline in the agricultural population enabled those who remained on the land to reduce their debts by $2 billion, to add $20 billion to the value of their farm property, and to accumulate $11 billion in savings. Radio comedians changed the words of an old nursery rhyme to sing "The farmer's in the dough." As mechanization and the consolidation of many small farms into fewer large ones proceeded, moreover, farming became "agribusiness," and organized agriculture took its seat in the council of power alongside organized labor, big government, and big business.

Meanwhile, organized labor expanded and grew wealthier. Union membership rose from 9 million workers in 1940 to 14.8 million in 1945 (to embrace 35 percent of nonagricultural employment). The jump resulted from the increase in the work force, combined with the National War Labor Board's "maintenance-of-membership" rule, which required all workers already enrolled in a union to continue their membership for the term of the existing contract. At the same time, the NWLB limited wage increases to restrain inflation. Many unions flexed their new muscles, however, to negotiate unprecedented fringe benefits for their members, including paid vacation time and health and pension plans. While most labor leaders obeyed the "no-strike" pledge that they had given the president immediately after Pearl Harbor, "wildcat" strikes not authorized by union officials periodically stopped work. Most were resolved with no marked effect on war production. The days lost during the war because of strikes amounted to less than one-tenth of 1 percent of total working time. The single major exception to the NWLB's success came in mid-1943 when the iron-willed head of

the United Mine Workers, John L. Lewis, led more than half a million coal-field workers out of the pits three times in two months. These coal strikes cost the union movement dearly. Over Roosevelt's veto Congress passed the Smith-Connally War Labor Disputes Act in June 1943, which limited workers' right to strike in any facility deemed essential to the war effort and empowered the president to seize and operate any such strike-bound plant. This legislation paved the way for the anti-labor laws enacted by state legislatures and Congress in the postwar years.

Far more than labor strikes, inflation threatened the health of the wartime economy. The Office of Price Administration fought a constant battle against the upward trend of wartime prices that was fueled by the combination of greater American spending power and fewer available goods and services. In the aftermath of Pearl Harbor, however, the OPA could do little but decry the steady 2-percent-a-month rise in prices. Gallup polls indicated that about 90 percent of Americans favored price controls, yet Congress hesitated to act. Each interest group resisted a maximum limit on its own wages or prices and demanded a ceiling on everyone else's. Not until the end of 1942 did Congress give the president the authority to freeze wages, prices, and rents. This freeze enabled the OPA to stop the upward spiral. Consumer prices rose only 8 percent in the last two years of the war; and the total 28 percent increase in the cost of living between 1940 and 1945 stood in marked contrast to the 62 percent rate of inflation between 1914 and 1918.

The OPA also instituted a rationing program to combat inflation and to conserve scarce materials. Under the government slogan "Use it up, wear it out, make it do or do without," the OPA rationed gasoline, coffee, sugar, butter, cheese, and meat. Accepting rationing as a contribution to the security of loved ones fighting the war, most Americans patriotically endured "meatless Tuesdays" and cuffless trousers. They formed car pools to decrease auto use, ate sherbet instead of ice cream, and put up with imitation chocolate that tasted like soap and imitation soap that did not lather. Only a minority patronized the illegal black market to purchase scarce items. Countless Americans also served as air-raid wardens, planted victory gardens, and organized collection drives to recycle paper, fats, rubber, and scrap metal.

BUY VICTORY BONDS

Display Bomb in New York City, 1943

(Above) Visiting British officers read from a "block-buster" bomb the signatures of those who have pledged donations to the government's war effort.

Victory Bonds

(Left) The government conducted a massive campaign to persuade Americans that by purchasing bonds they were buying the weapons to equip their loved ones on the front.

The sale of war bonds, by draining consumer purchasing power, helped decrease inflation; and the purchase of the bonds gave civilians a sense of personal involvement in the war effort. The Treasury Department sold about $40 billion in "E" bonds to small investors through payroll-deduction plans and organized bond drives, and nearly twice that amount in higher-denomination bonds to wealthy individuals and corporations. While the secretary of the treasury claimed that 60 percent of the reason for offering bonds was "to give the people an opportunity to do something" and to "make the country war-minded," the bonds actually raised half the money needed to pay for the war. Roosevelt sought to pay for the war as much as possible by increasing taxes. Congress, however, gave the president much less tax revenue than he wanted. Expenditures outstripped taxes by $22 billion in 1942 and by $57 billion in 1943. Congress also refused to legislate as progressive a tax system as Roosevelt called for. Still, the Revenue Act of 1942 raised the top income-tax rate from 60 percent to 90 percent and added most middle- and lower-income groups to the tax rolls for the first time, quadrupling the number of Americans who had to file returns and pay taxes. To make the collection of taxes more efficient, Congress in 1943 introduced the payroll-deduction system to withhold income taxes from wages and salaries. By 1945 the federal government was receiving nearly twenty times the tax revenue that it had in 1940.

Science and the War

To emphasize the decisiveness of scientific and technological developments in the Second World War, Winston Churchill dubbed it "a wizard war." The talents of scientists were extensively exploited, and even before the United States entered the war, Roosevelt had formed a National Defense Research

Committee to organize scientists for a weapons race against the Axis. Later in 1941 he created the Office of Scientific Research and Development (OSRD) as the contracting agency for the development of new ordnance and medicines. The OSRD spent more than $1 billion to produce improved radar and sonar devices, rocket weapons, flamethrowers, amphibious tanks, and proximity fuses for mines and artillery shells. Its funds advanced the development of jet aircraft, pressurized cabins for pilots, and high-altitude bombsights, and its employment of scientists to devise the best methods for utilizing new weapons resulted in a brand-new field called operational analysis. OSRD also hastened the widespread use of DDT and other insecticides, contributed to radical improvements in blood-transfusion techniques, and helped produce copious supplies of "miracle drugs" to combat infections, notably penicillin, and synthetic drugs like Atabrine to substitute for scarce quinine. The medical advances saved thousands of lives during the war and helped prolong life expectancy in peacetime.

The scientists' most notable undertaking was the development of the atomic bomb. In August 1939 physicist Albert Einstein, a Jewish refugee from Hitler's Germany, had warned Roosevelt that Nazi scientists were seeking to use the discoveries of atomic physics to construct a new weapon of extraordinary destructiveness. The president promptly established an advisory committee on uranium and in late 1941 launched a massive Anglo-American secret program—the Soviets were excluded—to produce an atomic bomb before the Germans did. With the aid of European colleagues, American physicists in 1942 successfully achieved a controlled atomic chain reaction and acquired the basic knowledge necessary to develop an atomic bomb. In 1943 and 1944 the Manhattan Engineering District—the code name given to the atomic research project—worked to stockpile U-235, a rare uranium isotope, and plutonium, a synthetic element, and in 1945 to assemble a bomb that could utilize the fissionable material for an atomic explosion. By July 1945 the Manhattan Project had secretly employed more than 120,000 people and spent nearly $2 billion unbeknownst to Congress.

Just before dawn on July 16, 1945, a blinding fireball, flashing with "the brightness of several suns at midday," arose over the desert at the Alamogordo, New Mexico, testing grounds. A huge,

billowing mushroom cloud followed. With a force of twenty thousand tons of TNT, the blast from the atomic test explosion could be felt more than a hundred miles from the detonation point. The awesome spectacle reminded J. Robert Oppenheimer, the Manhattan Project's scientific director, of a line from Hindu scripture: "Now I am become death, the destroyer of worlds." The atomic age had begun.

Propaganda and Politics

People as well as science and machinery had to be mobilized for the global conflict. To sustain a spirit of unity, the Roosevelt administration managed public opinion. Both to restrict the flow of secret military information and to intensify the American people's determination to destroy the Axis, the government regulated the media. In December 1941 Roosevelt established the Office of Censorship. This bureau examined all letters going overseas and worked with publishers and broadcasters to suppress information that might damage the war effort, such as details of troop movements. At its peak the Office of Censorship employed more than fourteen thousand people. Although Americans saw and heard more news coverage than in any previous war, much was concealed. A year passed before the casualty figures and the extent of damage to the naval fleet from the attack on Pearl Harbor were disclosed. Photographs of American dead on battlefields did not appear in newspapers until 1943, and only a few such pictures were approved for publication during the rest of the war years.

To shape public opinion, Roosevelt created the Office of War Information (OWI) in June 1942. Headed by respected pioneer radio news commentator Elmer Davis, the OWI employed more than four thousand artists, writers, and advertising specialists to explain the war and to counter enemy propaganda. But rather than stressing the U.S. commitment to the preservation of democratic values, the OWI played up the barbarism of the Axis nations and the need to crush them.

Hollywood producers answered the OWI directive—"Will this help win the war?"—by portraying American soldiers as freedom-loving heroes and vilifying Axis troops as sadistic murderers. Comics and cartoon strips illustrated similarly sinister and dehumanized enemies. Jukeboxes blared songs like "Let's Put the Axe to the Axis." Because

★ SILENCE MEANS SECURITY ★

Silence Means Security

Widespread wartime worries about domestic spies led propagandists to order up security posters like this one featuring a WAC.

the American home front was spared the terrible sufferings commonplace in Europe and East Asia, government propaganda emphasized the enemy's "bestiality" in order to motivate Americans to contribute to the war effort. Anti-Japanese propaganda contained a strong dose of racism.

While the Roosevelt administration concentrated on fostering unity and fighting the war, the president's Republican critics seized the initiative on domestic political matters. They were aided by the American people's tendency to blame wartime shortages and losses on the party in power and by the decreasing vitality of economic issues. Full employment and high wages undercut the Democrats' class appeal. The low voter turnout in the 1942 election, moreover, disproportionately hurt liberal Democrats. The Roosevelt coalition in urban areas relied heavily on draft-age and working-class men and women; but many of them in 1942 had recently migrated or gone into the armed services and failed to meet new residency requirements or to obtain absentee ballots.

The Republicans gained nine seats in the Senate and forty-six in the House in the 1942 elections, and congressional politics shifted to the right. The power to make or break legislation was now held by the conservative bloc of Republicans and southern Democrats. This coalition expressed resentment over the tremendous wartime expansion of executive authority as well as a desire to protect states' rights and to curb labor unions and welfare spending. The conservatives abolished such New Deal agencies as the CCC and the WPA and rebuffed all liberal proposals to extend the New Deal.

Despite the strength of the conservative coalition in Congress, the war expanded governmental and executive power to a degree that exceeded the hopes of the most ardent New Dealers. To an extent unimaginable in the 1930s, the federal government's budget, size, powers, and responsibilities ballooned during the war; to an unprecedented degree, Washington managed the economy, molded public opinion, funded scientific research, and intruded in the day-to-day lives of the American people.

But with more than $300 billion expended on the war effort, economic despondency gave way to buoyant prosperity. Unemployment ended. Millions moved above the poverty line, and millions more entered the middle class as organized labor and agriculture thrived. Big business also prospered and grew bigger, more highly concentrated, and increasingly intertwined with the military. The "miracle of production," as Americans termed their industrial success, strengthened confidence in business leaders and in the government's fiscal role in maintaining a robust economy. The achievements of mobilization made the United States second to none in economic and military power and fundamentally transformed the American people's expectations of what their federal government could and should be.

War and American Society

Some 15 million Americans went to war. Most had viewed themselves as civilians in uniform, and they called themselves GIs, after the "Government Issue" stamp on all their gear, to accentuate what they believed was the temporary nature of their military

Naval Recruits

The war brought together men and women from far-flung corners of the nation, in the process expanding personal horizons to an unprecedented degree.

status. Reluctant warriors, they had accepted their duty so that they could quickly return home to a familiar, secure America.

Despite these expectations, the war dragged on for almost four years, and servicemen and servicewomen were profoundly transformed by the military experience. In the course of the war, millions of GIs who had never been far from home traveled to unfamiliar cities, remote parts of the country, and foreign nations. Sharing tents, bunks, and foxholes with Americans of different religions, nationalities, and social backgrounds helped instill in them new perspectives that erased some pre-1941 regional and ethnic prejudices. Wartime service sowed the seeds of a more homogenized, national culture and broadened personal horizons. It modified how countless GIs saw themselves as well as their view of others. Many enlistees acquired skills in jobs

and professions that they had barely known existed. Under the Servicemen's Readjustment Act, or "GI Bill of Rights," enacted by Congress in June 1944, which provided living allowances, tuition fees, and supplies to veterans pursuing their new ambitions, several million ex-GIs who had been unable to afford education before the war would be studying for a high-school diploma or enrolled in college in 1946.

Returning GIs also found that America had changed as much as they had. "Home, the one really profound goal that obsesses every one of the Americans marching on foreign shores," wrote combat journalist Ernie Pyle, would never be the same again. Sweeping alterations in American society had challenged established values, redefined traditional relationships, and created unaccustomed problems and tensions. Readjustment to this strange new world would be difficult, often painful, and for some GIs even impossible.

The New Mobility

Nothing did more to transform the social topography than the vast internal migration of an already mobile people. Along with the 15 million men who moved about because of military service, as least as many Americans relocated to be near their husbands and fathers in the armed forces or to secure new economic opportunities. Throughout the country, women and men, young and old, black and white, pulled up stakes and swarmed to the centers of war production, especially to the Pacific Coast states, which did half the wartime shipbuilding and airplane manufacturing. California alone added nearly 2 million people to its growing population, many of them Chicanos from the Southwest or Mexico and farm families from the Midwest. Some 6 million people left agrarian America to work and live in the cities, particularly those near the manufacturing complexes of the Midwest and the West Coast. Several million poor whites and blacks from the South also migrated northward and westward, as well as to naval shipyards from Norfolk, Virginia, to Houston, and aircraft plants from Marietta, Georgia, to Fort Worth. This mass uprooting of people from familiar settings made Americans both more cosmopolitan and tolerant of different ethnic groups and ways of life, and more lonely, alienated, and frustrated. Further, lifestyles became increasingly freewheeling as

Americans moved far from their hometowns and their traditional values. Almost everywhere near war plants, housing shortages caused severe social problems. Millions of Americans took to living in converted garages, tent cities, dilapidated shacks, overpriced hotels and rooming houses, trailer camps, or even their own automobiles. Overcrowding as well as wartime separations placed enormous strains on family and community life. High rates of divorce, mental illness, family violence, and juvenile delinquency reflected the disruptions caused in part by the lack of privacy, the sense of impermanence, the absence of familiar settings, and the competition for scarce facilities. Few of the boom communities had the resources to supply their suddenly swollen populations with the needed transportation, recreation, and social services. Urban blight, as well as conflicts between newcomers and oldtimers, accelerated.

Education and Entertainment

The war-production boom that created both overcrowded communities and ghost towns played havoc with the nation's school systems. More than 350,000 experienced teachers quit their jobs to join the armed services or to take on better-paying war work. Many rural schools were left without any teachers, and countless schools in congested boom towns were understaffed. Students, too, abandoned the schools in record numbers. High-school enrollments sank as the full-time employment of teen-agers rose from 900,000 in 1940 to 3 million in 1944.

The loss of students to war production and the armed services forced colleges to admit an unprecedented number of women and to contract themselves out to the military. The navy's V-12 program and the army's specialized-training program sent nearly a million servicemen to college campuses during the war to acquire skills in engineering, foreign languages, economics, and the sciences. The military presence was all-pervasive. Harvard awarded four military-training certificates for every academic degree that it conferred, and the chancellor of the University of California announced that his school was "no longer an academic tent with military sideshows. It is a military tent with academic sideshows." Higher education became ever more dependent on the federal government, and most universities sought increased federal contracts and subsidies, despite their hav-

ing to submit to greater government interference and regulation.

The war also had a profound impact on American culture. All the media placed a stronger emphasis than ever before on mass production and mass audiences; and all emerged from the war more highly organized and with greater concentrations of power. Expenditures on books and theater entertainment doubled between 1941 and 1945. More than 60 million Americans attended movies weekly throughout the war, and the film industry reached its zenith in 1945–1946. Hollywood turned out a spate of war-oriented films in the aftermath of Pearl Harbor that reinforced the image of Nazis and Japanese as fiends and intensified Americans' appetite for unconditional victory. Such films as *Mission to Moscow* and *Song of Russia*, moreover, glorified Soviet heroism. As the war dragged on, however, and people tired of propaganda, Hollywood emphasized romance and adventure with such popular stars as Katharine Hepburn and Spencer Tracy, Gary Cooper and Ingrid Bergman. Numerous films, like *Meet Me in St. Louis* with Judy Garland, nostalgically portrayed a mythically serene and blissful America.

Similarly, popular music early in the war frequently featured militantly patriotic themes. Pub-

Wartime Cinema

In Keep Your Powder Dry, *a comedy promoting the Women's Army Corps, Lana Turner (left) becomes a WAC to prove that she deserves her large inheritance. She ultimately finds the military life fulfilling and receives an officer's commission.*

lished just ten days after the attack on Pearl Harbor, "Goodbye, Mama, I'm Off to Yokohama" became the first hit tune of 1942. As the war continued, themes of lost love and loneliness dominated song lyrics. Numbers like "They're Either Too Young or Too Old" expressed the laments and yearnings of millions of women separated from the men whom they loved. So, too, did the dozens of "dream songs," in which love denied by the real world could be achieved only in a dream. By 1945 bitterness rather than melancholy pervaded the lyrics of the best-selling records. Songs like "Saturday Night Is the Loneliest Night of the Week" revealed a frustrated impatience for the war's end.

In their reading habits, Americans turned increasingly to nonfiction during the war, although mysteries and historical romances remained popular. Few war novels were published, but Marion Hargrove's *See Here, Private Hargrove,* a semiautobiographical account of boot-camp experiences, and John Hersey's *A Bell for Adano,* the story of an Italian-American in the occupation of Sicily, became instant classics. Magazines, however, were the biggest sellers: every popular periodical increased its circulation. *Life, Look, The Saturday Evening Post,* and *Time* were the major fare to satisfy America's insatiable hunger for reports of battle actions and diplomatic analyses of the prospects for peace in the postwar world. Wendell Willkie's *One World* became the fastest-selling title in publishing history to that time, with 1 million copies snapped up in two months and 2 million in two years. A euphoric vision of a world without military alliances and spheres of influence, this brief volume by the 1940 Republican presidential candidate expressed the hope that an international organization would extend the blessings of peace and democracy throughout the postwar world. The military's needs for huge quantities of inexpensive reading materials led the Government Printing Office to publish the Armed Services Editions, reprints of classic novels and new works on every conceivable topic, in a double-column paperback format. The nearly 350 million copies distributed free to servicemen markedly speeded up the American acceptance of quality paperbacks, first introduced in 1939 by the Pocket Book Company.

An avid interest in wartime news also spurred a significant jump in radio listening during the war. The quest for up-to-the-minute information kept radio audiences at record levels. The voices of Edward R. Murrow and Eric Sevareid reporting from the battlefields became as familiar as those of Jack Benny and Eddie Cantor on their comedy shows; and programs analyzing current issues, like *Town Meeting of the Air,* reached the height of their popularity.

Women and the Family

While the soap operas and comedies continued to broadcast traditional images of family life, millions of American women donned pants, put their hair in bandannas, and went to work in defense plants. Reversing a decade of efforts to exclude women from the labor force, the federal government in 1942 began to urge women into war production and to pressure employers to hire them. Suddenly songs like "We're the Janes Who Make the Planes" were appealing to women to take up war work, and every avenue of mass propaganda was calling upon women to "do your share," to "help save lives," to "release able-bodied men for fighting." Millions of women who had never before held jobs outside the home now found employment in shops and factories, and millions more quit their menial positions as maids and clerks for the higher pay and union benefits of industry. More than 6 million women entered the labor force during the war, increasing the number of employed women to 19 million. The proportion of unionized female workers rose from 9 percent to 22 percent. Less than a quarter of the labor force in 1940, women constituted well over a third of all workers in 1945.

Even more startling to many, the characteristics of female wage earners changed. Predominantly young and single before the war, 75 percent of the new women workers were married, 60 percent were over thirty-five, and more than 33 percent had children under the age of fourteen. Women performed almost every kind of job, even those previously typed "man's work." They tended blast furnaces, ran lathes, operated cranes, greased locomotives, drove taxis, welded hulls, loaded shells, and worked in coke plants, rolling mills, and shipyards, once the exclusive preserves of men. "Rosie the Riveter," in overalls and cap, assembling airplanes and tanks, became the familiar symbol of the woman war worker; as a popular song put it, she was "making history working for victory."

Discrimination in employment, however, did not end. Despite government rules requiring equal

Woman Power

One female wartime worker related, "I never could handle the simplest can openers, or drive a nail without getting hurt, and now I put in half my nights armed with hammers and wrenches handling the insides of giant machines."

pay for equal work, women earned only about 65 percent of what men did for the same work. Few women during the war challenged the traditional view of gender roles; and gender equality was never a goal for the federal government or most employers. Government propaganda consistently portrayed women's war work as only a temporary response to an emergency. "A woman is a substitute," claimed a War Department brochure, "like plastic instead of metal." Training films stressed the similarity between operating industrial machinery and women's familiar work running sewing machines and vacuum cleaners. The work to be done, moreover, was pictured as an extension of women's traditional roles as wives and mothers. One American newspaperwoman wrote of the "deep satisfaction which a woman of today knows who has made a rubber boat which may save the life of her aviator husband, or helped fashion a bullet which may avenge her son!" Given the great concern about the availability of jobs for veterans after the war, moreover, the public attitude toward women's employment changed little in World War II. In 1945

only 18 percent of the respondents in a public-opinion poll approved of married women working.

Such traditional convictions about a woman's place were also reflected in the government's resistance to establishing child-care centers for women employed in defense work. "A mother's primary duty is to her home and children," the Labor Department's Children's Bureau stated. "This duty is one she cannot lay aside, no matter what the emergency." New York Mayor Fiorello LaGuardia proclaimed that the worst mother was better than the best nursery, and few officials publicly disagreed. Accordingly, funds for federal child-care centers covered fewer than 10 percent of defense workers' children, and the young suffered. Terms like *eight-hour orphans* and *latch-key children* entered the language to describe unsupervised children forced to fend for themselves. Movie theaters became dumping grounds for youngsters, and social workers' reports even cited instances of infants locked in cars in war-plant parking lots while their mothers completed their shifts. Further fueling the fears of those who believed that the employment of women outside the home would cause the family to disintegrate, juvenile delinquency increased fivefold during the war, and the divorce rate zoomed from 16 per 100 marriages in 1940 to 27 per 100 in 1944.

Yet the impact of war on women and the family proved multifaceted and even contradictory. As the number of divorces sailed to record heights, the marriage rate and birthrate increased to their highest levels in two decades. Although many women remained content to roll bandages for the Red Cross or tend victory gardens, more than three hundred thousand women joined the armed forces and for the first time in American history served in positions other than that of nurse. Despite the prevalence of traditional beliefs about gender roles and a woman's place, female workers gained unprecedented employment opportunities and public recognition. While millions of women eagerly gave up their jobs in defense plants in search of domestic stability at the end of the war, just as many did not relish losing the income and self-esteem that they had gained in contributing to the war effort. As Inez Sauer, who went to work for Boeing in Seattle, recalled:

My mother warned me when I took the job that I would never be the same. She said, "You will

*never want to go back to being a housewife."
She was right, it definitely did. At Boeing I found
a freedom and an independence I had never
known. After the war I could never go back to
playing bridge again, being a clubwoman and
listening to a lot of inanities when I knew there
were things you could use your mind for. The
war changed my life completely.*

Overall, women gained a new sense of their potential. They proved their capability and experienced the autonomy of participating in society outside the home. The war widened women's world as nothing ever had before.

Blacks and the War

Even more dramatically, the war opened doors of opportunity for many blacks. The wartime experience heightened blacks' aspirations and produced major cracks in the wall of white attitudes and policy.

Recognizing that the government needed the loyalty and labor of a united people, black leaders entered World War II determined to secure equal rights. Far from repeating W. E. B. Du Bois's call during World War I for blacks to put aside grievances and "close ranks" behind the president, in 1942 civil-rights spokesmen insisted that black support of the war hinged on America's commitment to racial justice. Black politicians demanded that the battle against the Axis be a "Civil War II" to destroy racism at home as well as Nazi racism abroad and that the fight be a "Double V" campaign waged for victory over racial discrimination as well as triumph on the battlefield. The NAACP urged blacks to use the war as an opportunity "to persuade, embarrass, compel and shame our government and our nation" to redress black grievances, and many responded to the slogan "democracy in our time" with a militancy rarely before seen in black communities.

Membership in the NAACP multiplied nearly ten times, reaching half a million in 1945, and the number of its chapters tripled. The association pressed for congressional enactment of anti–poll tax and anti-lynching legislation, combated racial discrimination in defense industries and in the armed services, and sought courtroom victories to end black disfranchisement. The campaign for black

voting rights gained momentum when the Supreme Court, in *Smith* v. *Allwright* (1944), ruled Texas's all-white primary unconstitutional. The decision eliminated a bar that had existed in eight southern states, although these states promptly resorted to other devices to minimize voting by blacks.

A new civil-rights organization, the Congress of Racial Equality (CORE), founded in 1942, advanced the strategy of nonviolent resistance to challenge Jim Crow. Employing the same forms of direct action that the Indian spiritual leader Mohandas Gandhi had been using in his campaign for India's independence, CORE staged a sit-in in 1942 in a Chicago restaurant that refused to serve blacks. CORE's sit-in tactic helped eliminate segregation in public accommodations in Detroit, Denver, and Chicago and inspired interracial groups in other cities to begin experimenting with nonviolent direct action to end racial discrimination. Also during 1942, A. Philip Randolph, president of the Brotherhood of Sleeping Car Porters, labored to build his March-on-Washington Committee into an all-black mass protest movement that would engage in civil disobedience to protest racial discrimination in every area of American life.

In 1941 Randolph had called for a "thundering march" of one hundred thousand blacks on Washington "to wake up and shock white America as it has never been shocked before." He warned Roosevelt that if the president did not abolish "discrimination in all government departments, army, navy, air corps, and national defense jobs," the nation would witness "the greatest demonstration of Negro mass power for our economic liberation ever conceived." Eager to have the proposed march canceled, the president agreed to compromise.

In June 1941 Roosevelt issued Executive Order 8802, the first presidential directive on race since Reconstruction. It prohibited discriminatory employment practices by federal agencies and all unions and companies engaged in war-related work, and it established the Fair Employment Practices Commission (FEPC) to enforce this new policy. Although the FEPC lacked effective enforcement powers, the combination of booming war production and a labor supply depleted by the draft resulted in the employment of some 2 million blacks in industry and another 200,000 in the federal civil service. Between 1942 and 1945, the proportion of blacks in war-production work rose from 3 percent to 9 percent. By the end of the war, black membership in labor unions had doubled to 1,250,000, and the number of skilled and semiskilled black workers had almost tripled. The average wage for blacks during the war increased from $457 to $1,976 a year, compared with a gain of $1,064 to $2,600 for white workers.

About 1 million black men and women served in the armed forces. Wartime needs slowly forced the military to end policies of excluding blacks from the marines and coast guard, restricting them to jobs as mess boys in the navy, and confining them to noncombatant units in the army. The all-black 761st Tank Battalion gained distinction fighting in Germany, and the 99th Pursuit Squadron won eighty Distinguished Flying Crosses for its combat against the *Luftwaffe* in Europe. In 1944 both the army and navy began experiments in integration in their training facilities, on ships, and on the battlefield. The great mass of blacks, however, served throughout the war in segregated service units commanded by white officers. Post exchanges, the USO, and the base chapels barred or discriminated against them. Most ironically, the Red Cross maintained separate black and white blood banks, even though a black physician, Dr. Charles Drew, had invented the process of storing blood plasma. The failure of military authorities to protect black servicemen off the post, and the use of white military police to keep blacks "in their place," sparked conflict and rioting on nearly every army base in the South and on many overseas. At least fifty black soldiers died in racial encounters in the United States during the war.

The violence within the military mirrored the growing racial tensions on the home front. As blacks militantly protested against discrimination and rejected all pleas to "go slow" in their campaign for first-class citizenship, many whites stiffened their resistance to any changes in blacks' inferior economic and social positions. Numerous clashes occurred, and in mid-1943 scores of cities reported pitched battles between whites and blacks. Race riots broke out in the Harlem section of New York City as well as in Mobile, Alabama, and Beaumont, Texas. In June Detroit exploded in an orgy of racial beatings, shootings, burning, and looting (see "A Place in Time"). The fear of continued violence stunted black leaders' militancy, and they began to concentrate on reducing blacks' aggressive behavior. They realized that few Americans would tolerate a war against racism at home that impeded the war effort overseas.

Yet the war brought revolutionary changes that would eventually result in a successful drive for black justice. Over seven hundred thousand blacks migrated from the South. This exodus turned a southern problem into a national concern. It created a new attitude of independence in blacks suddenly freed from the stifling constraints of a rigid caste structure. And greater educational and employment opportunities for the blacks who left the rural South engendered a spirit of hopefulness. As the growing numbers of blacks in the industrial cities of the North began to vote, moreover, they held the balance of power in close elections. This prompted politicians in both major parties to extend greater political recognition to blacks and to pay more attention than ever before to the civil-rights issue.

Blacks' optimism also flowed from the new prominence of the United States as a major power in a predominantly nonwhite world. Japanese propaganda appeals to the peoples of Asia and Latin America constantly emphasized lynchings and race riots in the United States, and most American newspapers deplored the Detroit race riots as a victory for Hitler. For the first time, Americans had to confront the peril that racism posed to their national security. In addition, the horrors of Nazi racism made Americans more sensitive to the harm caused by their own white-supremacist attitudes and practices. The frequent comparisons of Hitler's treatment of the Jews in Germany with the white South's behavior toward blacks further undermined American racism. As a former governor of Alabama privately complained: Nazism has "wrecked the theories of the master race with which we were so contented so long."

Summing up the developments catalyzed by the war, Swedish economist Gunnar Myrdal, in his massive study of race problems, *An American Dilemma* (1944), concluded that "not since Reconstruction had there been more reason to anticipate fundamental changes in American race relations." Black veterans especially, with a new sense of self-esteem that came from participating in the victorious war effort, returned to civilian life with high expectations. Like the athlete Jackie Robinson, who as a young lieutenant had refused to take a seat at the rear of a segregated bus and

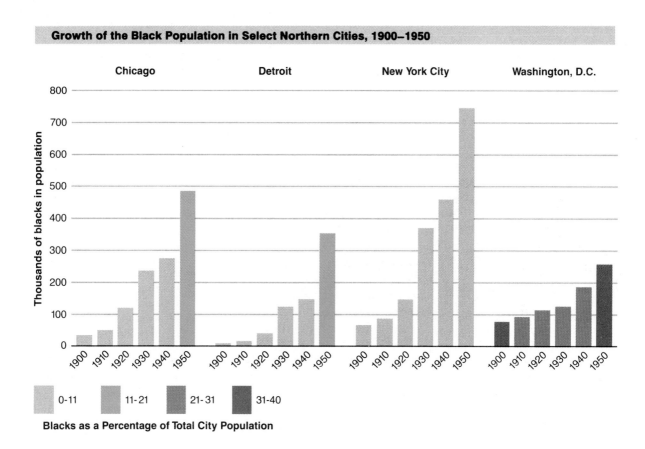

Growth of the Black Population in Select Northern Cities, 1900–1950

Chicago   Detroit   New York City   Washington, D.C.

Thousands of blacks in population

0-11   11-21   21-31   31-40

Blacks as a Percentage of Total City Population

The migration of blacks from the rural South to northern cities dramatically increased when the labor shortages of the Second World War created new opportunities in industry and the civil service for blacks.

had fought and won his subsequent court martial, and like the black enlistee who, after spending four years in the army, declared, "I'm damned if I'm going to let the Alabama version of the Germans kick me around," blacks faced the postwar era with a firm resolve to gain all the rights possessed by the white majority.

Native Americans, Mexican-Americans, and Jews in Wartime

The wartime winds of change also brought new opportunities as well as problems to other American minorities. Some twenty-five thousand native Americans served in the armed forces during the war. Many worked in combat-communication teams where they used Indian languages on telephones and radio equipment to confuse enemy

interceptors. Another seventy-five thousand Indians, mainly young men and women, left the reservations to work in defense plants and shipyards. It was the first time most of them had lived in a non-Indian world. After the war many preferred to remain in the cities and hoped gradually to become assimilated into mainstream life. The continuation of anti-Indian discrimination and of efforts to keep native Americans in a subordinate status, however, forced a majority of those who had left the reservations to return. They found that their reservations had suffered severely from congressional cuts in Indian budgets. Prodded by those who coveted Indian lands and resources, lawmakers demanded that Indians be taken off the backs of the taxpayers and that they be "freed from the reservations" to make their own way like other Americans. To mobilize against the campaign to

Wartime Detroit

*B*etween 1940 and 1943, about fifty thousand blacks and half a million whites, mainly from the South, flocked to Detroit. Attracted to the wartime capital of defense production by the prospect of jobs in the huge Chrysler Tank Arsenal and the new Ford factory in Willow Run—the world's largest bomber plant—most brought high expectations of a good life in the big city. But while many ultimately enjoyed prosperity for the first time, all had to face the reality of a critical housing shortage and inadequate facilities for transportation, education, and recreation. For blacks, discrimination made a difficult situation even worse. Confined to the congested ghetto of Paradise Valley, black newcomers to Detroit paid exorbitant rents for dirty, decrepit shacks served mainly by outdoor toilets.

The collision between aspirations and thwarted opportunities sparked militancy in migrants like Jesse Hall. Lured by the prospect of making more than $5 a day in a war-industry job, Hall moved his family to Detroit in February 1942. They left behind a lifetime of poverty and despondency in rural Desha County in southern Arkansas. Hall and his three children had picked and chopped cotton there from sunup to sundown to earn perhaps a dollar a day, while his wife, Josephine, cooked and cleaned in white people's homes for $2.50 a week.

Once in Detroit, Hall felt hope as his children attended school regularly for the first time in their lives, Josephine found employment as a

Panel from The Migration of the Negro #50, *by Jacob Lawrence, 1940–1941*

Lawrence, a black artist, painted a large series of canvases on blacks' movement to northern cities. Here he captures the brutality and hatred underlying the urban race riots such as those that rocked Detroit.

seamstress in a clothing store, and he himself proudly joined the UAW-CIO and worked in a Packard plant manufacturing engines for American bombers and PT boats. At the same time, however, he experienced virulent racism in his interactions with many Detroit whites. He grew bitter as the Detroit Real Estate Association stymied all his efforts to find decent housing, thus leaving his family no choice but to remain in their packed quarters in a segregated slum. He was enraged by the police's failure to take any

action to stop white gangs from attacking his children, and by a strike staged by some twenty-five thousand white Packard employees to protest the promotion of three blacks. In the course of the mass work stoppage, the strikers chanted, "We'd rather see Hitler and Hirohito win than work beside a nigger on the assembly line."

Resolved to make a better life for his family and himself, Jesse Hall soon registered to vote, joined the NAACP, and regularly attended rallies protesting racial discrimination. Joining forces with other activists, he pressed vigorously for equal access to new housing and better-paying jobs for blacks. Now whenever he was jostled by white passengers on crowded buses, Hall began to push back. Angered by the hypocrisy of blacks' fighting abroad for rights that they did not possess at home, Hall and many other Detroit blacks increasingly asserted themselves by matching the aggressiveness of whites. Throughout the spring of 1943, the two races clashed more and more frequently. The steadily mounting boldness that was displayed in interracial encounters in the city prompted a *Life* magazine reporter to describe wartime Detroit as "a keg of powder with a short fuse."

On Sunday, June 20, 1943, Detroit's racial turmoil ignited in violence. As more than one hundred thousand Detroiters thronged a park on Belle Isle to escape the steamy heat of the city's streets, one racial fight after another broke out. Stories of violent incidents and rumors of an impending race war blazed swiftly across every section of the city. Soon blacks were smashing and looting white-owned stores, and white mobs were assaulting blacks caught riding trolleys or sitting in movie theaters. When federal troops arrived late Monday to quell the riot, the toll included twenty-five blacks and nine whites killed, more than seven hundred injured, and over $2 million in property losses.

Dismissing Detroit's rampant racial discrimination and segregation, city and state politicians blamed the rioting on the black press and civil-rights groups who were agitating vocally against inequality. The Roosevelt administration maintained an official silence on the matter and ignored pleas for a presidential speech, a congressional investigation, or a government commission to study race relations. With a war to win, most of the nation resumed "business as usual." Nevertheless, the riot did bring greater, and more sympathetic, attention to the root causes of black militancy. In the summer of 1943 alone, more than a hundred local, state, and national interracial committees were established to study racial strife and a growing number of prominent whites supported blacks' drive for social justice. Although Detroit's blacks continued to encounter racial hatred and discrimination, many found doors of opportunity opening as the wartime labor shortage intensified. After 1943 blacks in Detroit enjoyed better jobs, higher wages, and improved living conditions. With these gains came a renewed determination to achieve the full benefits of citizenship. "We aren't going to go back to where we were before the war," vowed Jesse Hall. "We've shed our blood and proved our loyalty, and we're going to fight for all that is rightfully due us. We won't turn back."

Racial Violence *Police attempt to break up an incident in the June 1943 rioting in downtown Detroit.*

A Narrow Escape *A woman passenger climbs from a trolley to flee an angry mob that has stopped the conveyance in an effort to remove black riders.*

end all reservations, tribes, treaties, and trust protections, native Americans from various parts of the country organized the National Congress of American Indians.

To relieve critical wartime shortages in the labor supply, the United States negotiated an agreement with Mexico in 1942 for the importation of *braceros,* or temporary workers. In exchange for seasonal employment in Arizona, California, and Texas, the *braceros* were to be guaranteed adequate wages, medical care, and suitable living conditions. But large-scale growers frequently violated the terms of the contract and encouraged the massive influx of illegal immigrants desperate for employment. Unable to complain about their working conditions to government officials without risking their own arrest and deportation, hundreds of thousands of Mexicans became permanent, illegal, resident aliens, persistently exploited by southwestern agribusinesses. At the same time, an equally large number of Chicanos shifted from agricultural work to industrial and manufacturing jobs, especially in the defense plants, shipbuilding yards, and garment factories in and around Los Angeles. As their occupational status and material conditions improved, many became bilingual, and signs of acculturation grew. However, most Chicanos continued to run up against discrimination and remained in separate slum communities sealed off from the larger society.

Much of the prejudice against Chicanos became focused on the young men who wore "zoot suits"— a fashion that originated in Harlem and emphasized long, broad-shouldered jackets and pleated trousers tightly pegged at the ankles. Known as *pachucos,* the young zoot-suited Chicanos were repeatedly portrayed by newspapers as delinquents, dope addicts, and draft dodgers and were constantly blamed for attacks on servicemen. Throughout the first week of June 1943, bands of sailors from local naval bases and soldiers on leave rampaged through the streets of Los Angeles, stripping *pachucos,* cutting their long hair, and beating them. Military authorities looked the other way, and city police intervened only to arrest Chicanos. *Time* magazine described the violence as "the ugliest brand of mob action since the coolie race riots of the 1870s," yet Los Angeles officials praised the servicemen for having rioted, and the city council made the wearing of a zoot suit a misdemeanor.

Spanish-speaking Americans also suffered many of the same kinds of discrimination in the military as blacks did. Nevertheless, nearly 350,000 Chicanos served in the armed forces, volunteering in much higher numbers than that warranted by their percentage of the population and earning a disproportionate number of citations for distinguished service and Congressional Medals of Honor. And much like black and Indian veterans, returning Chicano veterans organized new groups, among them the American GI Forum, to press for equal rights after the war.

Despite the lip service paid to the ideals of tolerance, American Jews also discovered that even a war against Nazism did not end traditional prejudices. Anti-Semitism persisted in restrictive covenants to prevent the sale of homes to Jews, in employment ads that stated that only Protestants or Catholics need apply, in rigid quota systems to limit the number of Jews in universities, and in "gentlemen's agreements" to exclude Jews from certain professions. Public-opinion polls throughout the war revealed that a significant minority of Americans blamed either Wall Street Jews or Jewish communists for the war and thought Hitler justified in his treatment of Jews in Germany.

When reports of the Holocaust—the name later given to the Nazis' systematic effort to exterminate all European Jewry—became known in the United States early in 1942, most Americans viewed it as just a Jewish problem, a matter of small concern to them. Even well-intentioned people, remembering that accounts of German atrocities during World War I had often turned out to be propagandists' lies, tended at first to discount what they were now hearing of Nazi massacres. Not until late November, by which time some 2.5 million Jews had perished, did the State Department officially admit knowledge of Hitler's genocide. And then fourteen more months passed before Roosevelt established a special agency, the War Refugee Board (WRB), to assist in the rescue and relocation of those condemned to the death camps. The tardiness of the president's response reflected the wishes of the British to placate their Arab allies by keeping Jewish settlers out of Palestine, the congressional and public fears of an influx of destitute Jews into the United States, and the hesitancy of many American Jewish leaders to press the matter and risk incubating anti-Semitic hysteria at home. Despite the

The Holocaust

Entering Germany in 1945, American and Russian soldiers discovered the horrors that the Nazis had perpetrated on European Jews and others. One anonymous American GI wrote of the ghastly concentration-camp scenes: "I've seen what wasn't ever meant for human eyes to see."

State Department's obstruction of all rescue efforts, the WRB saved the lives of some 200,000 Jews and 20,000 non-Jews. But 6 million other Jews were gassed and incinerated.

The Abuse of Civil Liberties

Only a tiny minority of Americans refused to support the war effort, and the nation generally did not stoop to the mass assaults on aliens, repression of war dissenters, and strident advocacy of "100 percent Americanism" that had occurred during World War I. The glaring exception was the internment of 112,000 Japanese-Americans, two-thirds of them native-born U.S. citizens, in relocation centers guarded by military police. The policy reflected more than forty years of anti-Japanese sentiment on the West Coast, rooted in racial prejudice and economic rivalry, as well as fear of Japanese sabotage in the immediate aftermath of Pearl

Harbor. Self-seeking politicians and farmers who sought to take over the landholdings of Japanese-Americans had long decried the "yellow peril," and following the attack on Pearl Harbor, they whipped up the rage and fears of many white Californians. Numerous patriotic associations and newspapers clamored for action. The army general in charge of the Western Defense Command proclaimed: "A Jap is a Jap. It makes no difference whether he is an American citizen or not." In February 1942 Roosevelt gave in to the pressure and authorized the evacuation of all Japanese-Americans from the West Coast, despite the fact that not a single Japanese-American had been apprehended for espionage or sedition and neither the FBI nor military intelligence had uncovered any evidence of disloyal behavior by Japanese-Americans.

Forced to sell their lands and homes at whatever prices they could obtain, the Japanese-Americans were herded into barbed-wire-encircled detention camps in the most desolate areas of the West. Few Americans protested their incarcera-

Internment

These young Japanese-American brothers await the train that will carry them to a relocation center at Manzanar in California's Owens Valley.

tion. Stating that it would not question governmental claims of military necessity during time of war, the Supreme Court upheld the constitutionality of the evacuation in *Korematsu* v. *U.S.* (1944). By then, however, the hysteria had subsided, and the government had already begun a program of gradual release. In 1982 a special government commission formally blamed the Roosevelt administration's action on "race prejudice, war hysteria, and a failure of political leadership" and officially apologized to Japanese-Americans for "a grave injustice." In 1988 Congress voted to compensate all Japanese-Americans interned during World War II in the amount of twenty thousand dollars each.

The Second World War, 1942–1944

"No matter how long it may take us to overcome this premeditated invasion," President Roosevelt had promised in his war message to Congress on December 8, 1941, "the American people in their righteous might will win through to absolute victory." In the same spirit, as the new year began, Britain, the Soviet Union, the United States, and twenty-three other countries signed the Declaration of the United Nations. The "Grand Alliance" of 26 nations opposing the Axis promised to devote its full resources to battle to a triumphal conclusion. But in early 1942 the Allied outlook remained bleak. Nazi forces had conquered much of Europe and threatened the Suez Canal, and Japan controlled the western half of the Pacific and a large part of Asia.

The swift mobilization of America's military might turned the tides of war. Fighting on two oceans as well as in the hot desert sands of Africa, the snows of continental Europe, and the malarial jungles of Asian islands, Americans played a major role in stopping the Axis advance, driving back the enemy, and liberating conquered areas. Diplomacy followed the fortunes of war. The Allies' unity, strongest at the height of the Axis menace, gradually dimmed as Germany and Japan grew weaker and as the United States, Britain, and the Soviet Union each sought wartime strategies and postwar arrangements best suited to its own national interest.

The Allied Drive in Europe

Immediately after the raid on Pearl Harbor, British and American officials agreed to concentrate on defeating Germany first and then to smash Japan. But they differed on where to mount an attack against Hitler. To relieve the beleaguered Russians, who in 1942 were facing the full fury of the German armies, General George C. Marshall, army chief of staff, proposed an early invasion of France that would force Hitler to transfer troops to the west and thus lessen the pressure on the Red armies. But England's prime minister Churchill insisted on clearing the Mediterranean before invading France. Vividly recalling the frightful loss of a generation of young Britons in the bloody trench warfare of World War I, Churchill feared that a premature landing in France would only lead to another slaughterhouse. In addition, Churchill wanted to assist the British army fighting against the Germans in North Africa and protect England's control of the Suez Canal. Over Soviet protests the prime minister persuaded Roosevelt to attack the Germans in North Africa and to delay a "second front" in western Europe until the Allies had more

The Genial General

One American GI observed of Dwight Eisenhower: "He looks sort of like the guys you know at home."

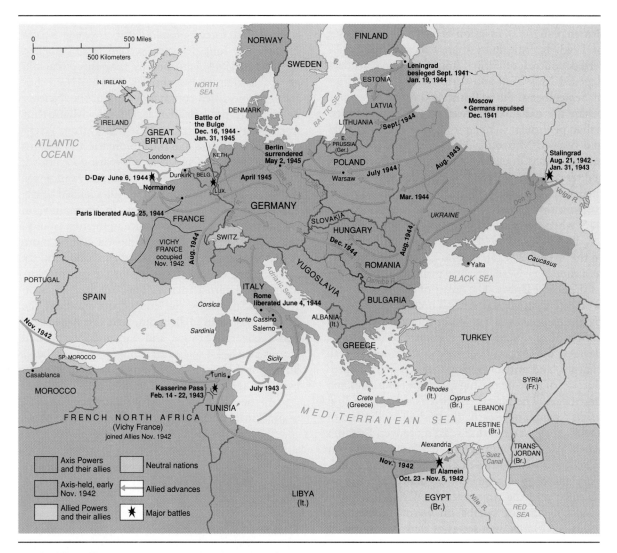

World War II in Europe and Africa   *The momentous German defeats at Stalingrad and in Tunisia early in 1943 marked the turning point in the war against the Axis. By 1945 the Allied conquest of Hitler's "thousand-year" Reich was imminent.*

ships and equipment. In November 1942, in Operation Torch, an Allied army of more than a hundred thousand American and British troops, commanded by General Dwight D. Eisenhower, landed in Morocco and Algeria. They pressed eastward to entrap the German army being pushed across Libya by British forces from Egypt. Eventually surrounded by Allied troops, over a quarter of a million Germans surrendered in Tunisia in May 1943, despite Hitler's orders to fight to the death.

Germany lost even more men on its eastern front. Thousands died every day as huge Russian and German armies fought the Battle of Stalingrad. By the end of 1942, the Russian snow had turned red with blood. In the house-to-house fighting at Stalingrad, the Soviet Union suffered more battle deaths in four months than the United States would lose in the entire war. Russia's Red Army, however, emerged victorious; it saved Stalingrad, hung on at besieged Leningrad, and went on the offensive across a front a thousand miles wide.

Stalin renewed his plea for a "second front" against Germany as the Soviet Union continued to bear the brunt of the fighting and dying. But when

Churchill again objected, Roosevelt agreed to the British plan for an invasion of Sicily in the summer of 1943. In little more than a month, the Allies seized control of Sicily. Italian military leaders deposed Mussolini and surrendered to the Allies on September 8. But as British and American troops began the exhausting crawl up the boot-shaped Italian peninsula, German soldiers poured into Italy and rescued Mussolini. Having to face elite German divisions in defensive positions in Italy's rugged terrain, the Allies spent eight months inching their way 150 miles to Rome. They would still be battling through the mud and snow of northern Italy when the war in Europe ended.

In 1943 and 1944, the Allies turned the tide in the Atlantic, began to send a thousand bombers at a time over Germany, and pushed the Nazis out of the Soviet Union. The Battle of the Atlantic was won by American science and industry as much as by the American navy. It depended on the utilization of advanced radar systems and new sonar devices; the invention of special torpedoes, depth charges, and antisubmarine rockets; and the production of ever-increasing quantities of planes and destroyers. The plague of Hitler's submarine "rat packs" would be greatly diminished by the end of 1943. At the start of that year, moreover, Britain's Royal Air Force and the United States Army Air Force began round-the-clock bombardment of military and civilian targets in Germany. The British by night and the Americans by day rained thousands of tons of bombs on German cities and industrial plants. In a series of raids on Hamburg in July 1943, Allied planes killed some sixty thousand people and leveled vast areas of the city, much as they had done earlier to Cologne.

Meanwhile, the Soviet offensive in 1943 reclaimed more and more Russian cities and towns held by the Nazis. In July German and Russian divisions fought the largest tank and infantry battle in history near the city of Kursk. The defeated Germans now faced perpetual retreat. By mid-1944 the Red Army had largely cleared the Germans out of the Soviet Union. The Russians advanced swiftly. They reached the outskirts of Warsaw, Poland, in July and established their own puppet government in Lublin, took control of Romania in late August and of Bulgaria two weeks later, and assisted the communist guerrilla forces led by Josip Broz Tito in liberating Yugoslavia in October.

As eastern Europe fell under Soviet domination, Allied forces prepared for a sweep across France. The long-delayed "second front" opened on June 6, 1944, launched by fifty-three-year-old general Dwight D. Eisenhower, who had been chosen supreme allied commander in Europe. Neither as inspirational a leader as Douglas MacArthur nor as heroic a warrior as George Patton, Eisenhower nevertheless had the diplomatic and administrative talents to supervise Operation Overlord, as the combined land-sea-air assault on France was called. At great cost in lives, the Allies landed nearly 150,000 men on five beach areas in Normandy, on the northwestern coast of France in the first twenty-four hours of the invasion. Almost a million more Allied soldiers waded ashore in the following six weeks. Late in July the Allies broke out of Normandy and thrust inland. They reached Paris on August 25; and by the end of the summer, the British had secured Belgium, and the Americans had recovered France and Luxembourg. Allied troops reached the German border a week later. Supply problems and stiff German resistance, however, brought the offensive to a halt.

As the Allies prepared for their attack on Germany, Hitler on December 16 threw the last of his

Camp Life in Normandy

Equipped with an American mess kit, a young French boy joins GIs in a Normandy "chow line."

reserves, a quarter of a million men, against the American position in the Forest of Ardennes in Belgium and Luxembourg. In ten days Hitler's troops drove a bulge eighty miles long and fifty miles deep into the Allied line. On Christmas Day the Allies stopped the last-gasp German counterattack and within a month had driven the Nazis back to the Rhine. Hitler had lost his final gamble in the Battle of the Bulge and had exhausted Germany's reserves. The way to Germany was now open. But the fierce fighting in the Ardennes took a toll of American casualties that eclipsed the Battle of Gettysburg as the bloodiest fight in American history: fifty-five thousand combatants killed or wounded and eighteen thousand taken prisoner.

The War in the Pacific

The day after the Philippines fell in mid-May 1942, an American naval force confronted a Japanese fleet in the Coral Sea off northeastern Australia. For the first time in history, a naval battle was fought entirely from aircraft carriers. Although both sides lost one large carrier and many planes, the Battle of the Coral Sea proved vital to the Allies in thwarting the Japanese advance on Australia. Less than a month later, the Japanese navy turned eastward toward Midway Island, the most important American outpost between Hawaii and Japan. A superior imperial armada of more than 160 ships aimed to knock out what remained of the decimated American fleet in the Pacific. But because the U.S. Signal Corps had deciphered the Japanese naval code, Admiral Chester Nimitz knew the plans and locations of the Japanese ships. In a decisive victory, American dive-bombers sank four major aircraft carriers and destroyed several hundred planes. The Japanese then reverted to the defensive, seeking to hold what they had previously won.

On August 7, 1942, marines waded ashore at Guadalcanal in the Solomon Islands to protect Australia from attack. They waged a savage fight for survival in the first of many steaming jungles they would encounter. Facing suicidal resistance—as well as rampant malaria, dysentery, fungus, and all the ravages of the disease-infested tropics—U.S. troops were stalemated for almost three months, until Admiral William Halsey's fleet destroyed the Japanese ships in the area, isolating those Japanese remaining on Guadalcanal. Yet it would take

The Island War

Marines and GIs gradually strangled Japan by a strategy of "leapfrogging" from one obscure Pacific island to another. Here an American takes shelter in a ditch on Okinawa to shield himself from enemy fire.

another three months before the Japanese were driven off the island, leaving behind more than twenty-five thousand of their dead—a gruesome preview of the island battles to come.

In the fall of 1943, the United States began a two-pronged advance toward Japan. Under General MacArthur, who had commanded the heroic but futile defense of the Philippines and had vowed that "I shall return" to the islands, the army advanced northward from Australia, "leapfrogging" from one strategic island to the next. A second force, led by Admiral Nimitz, "island-hopped" across the central Pacific, capturing key islands from which American aircraft could bomb Japan and isolating enemy troops left behind on the bypassed islands.

Although Pacific operations remained secondary to the defeat of Germany, the American forces under MacArthur and Nimitz steadily increased. By late 1944 the United States had deployed nearly 1.5 million marines and soldiers, as well as the navy's fastest and largest aircraft carriers, in the Pacific theater. Though suffering heavy casualties

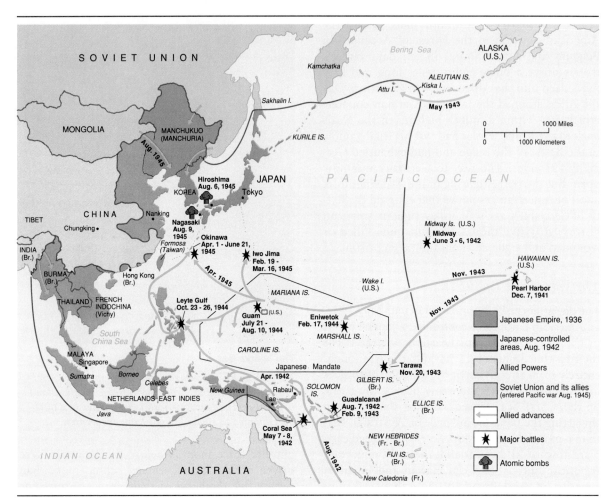

World War II in the Pacific *American ships and planes stemmed the Japanese offensive at the Battles of the Coral Sea and Midway Island. Thereafter, the Japanese were on the defensive against American amphibious assaults and air strikes.*

in capturing New Guinea before liberating Manila in early 1945, MacArthur lost less than 28,000 men in the Pacific war overall, fewer than the number killed in some individual battles in Europe. Nimitz, meanwhile, seized strategic bases on the Gilbert Islands in November 1943 and the Marshall Islands in February 1944, and captured the Marianas in the summer, putting Tokyo within range of the mighty B-29s, which could each carry seven tons of bombs. By late 1944 they were incinerating cities in Japan. Simultaneously, the American navy annihilated what remained of the imperial fleet at the battles of the Philippine Sea and Leyte Gulf. Japan's sea and air power was totally

shattered by the end of 1944. Despite their disastrous losses, however, Japanese military leaders stymied every attempt by civilians in the government to negotiate a peace.

The Grand Alliance

Roosevelt's overriding goals throughout the war had remained the total defeat of the Axis in Europe and Asia at the least possible cost in American lives, and the establishment of a new world order strong enough to preserve peace, open trade, and ensure national self-determination in the postwar era. Aware that only a common enemy fused the

Grand Alliance together, Roosevelt had tried to promote harmony by concentrating on military victory and postponing divisive postwar matters.

But Churchill and Stalin had other goals. Britain sought to retain its imperial possessions and a balance of power against Russia on the Continent. The Soviet Union aspired to weaken Germany permanently and to create a sphere of influence in Eastern Europe to protect Russia against possible future military attacks from the West. To hold this uneasy alliance together, Roosevelt put his faith in personal diplomacy and met frequently with foreign leaders to plan strategy and to mediate conflicts.

In January 1943, in the middle of the North African campaign, Roosevelt and Churchill had met at Casablanca, Morocco's main port. There they resolved to attack Italy before invading France and to proclaim that the war would be pursued until the Axis accepted "unconditional surrender." In this proclamation they had sought to reduce Soviet mistrust of the West, which had been worsened by the postponement of the promised "second front," and to deter Stalin from offering Hitler a separate peace. In Cairo, in November 1943, Roosevelt had met with Churchill and Jiang Jieshi (Chiang Kai-shek), the anticommunist head of the Chinese government. To induce Jiang to fight until Japan surrendered unconditionally, FDR had promised that Manchuria and Taiwan would be returned to China and that there would be a "free and independent Korea."

The president and prime minister had then continued on to Tehran, the capital of Iran, to confer with Stalin. The Allied triumvirate (known as the Big Three) set the invasion of France for May or June 1944, to coincide with the Russian offensive from the east, and tentatively agreed to divide Germany into zones of occupation and to impose reparations on the Reich. Most important to Roosevelt, Stalin had also promised to enter the

war against Japan after Hitler's defeat. On his return to the United States, the highly pleased president publicly predicted: "We are going to get along with him [Stalin] and the Russian people—very well indeed."

The Election of 1944

Roosevelt then turned his attention to domestic politics. The Republicans had made important gains in the 1942 congressional elections, and conservatives in both parties looked forward to consolidating their position in 1944. Although conservative Democrats could not deny Roosevelt renomination in 1944, they did force him to dump the liberal vice president, Henry Wallace, from the ticket and to accept instead Harry S Truman. A moderate senator from Missouri, Truman had gained national attention by chairing a subcommittee investigating waste in the defense effort. Not strongly opposed by any major faction in the party, Truman, "the new Missouri Compromise," restored a semblance of unity to the Democrats for the 1944 campaign.

Similarly hoping that party unity would carry them to victory, the GOP shunned the now outspokenly liberal and internationalist Wendell Willkie and nominated the moderate New York governor Thomas E. Dewey. To conciliate right-wing Republicans, Dewey selected John W. Bricker of Ohio as his running mate. More a contest of personalities than of issues, the campaign featured the Republicans harping in subtle ways on FDR's failing health and Roosevelt exploiting his role as commander in chief of the American military victories in Europe and the Pacific.

In November the electorate sent FDR back to the White House for an unprecedented fourth term. The president amassed 432 electoral votes to Dewey's 99. But with just 53 percent of the popular

The Election of 1944				
Candidates	Parties	Electoral Vote	Popular Vote	Percentage of Popular Vote
FRANKLIN D. ROOSEVELT	Democratic	432	25,606,585	53.5
Thomas E. Dewey	Republican	99	22,014,745	46.0

vote, Roosevelt won by his narrowest margin in four campaigns. As never before, he owed his triumph to the urban vote and to the extraordinary involvement of organized labor in Democratic politics. Most voters, eager to enjoy their new prosperity, showed little inclination for further New Deal programs. However reluctant Americans may have been to change leaders in the final phases of the war, they also left the power of the conservative coalition in Congress intact. A weary Roosevelt now directed his waning energies toward vanquishing the Axis and constructing a new international order that would prevent future wars.

Triumph and Tragedy, 1945

By the time of Roosevelt's last meeting with Churchill and Stalin, in February 1945 in the Soviet city of Yalta, the realities of the military situation and world power politics had changed in favor of the Soviet Union. Russia's victorious offensive was nearly complete, but American forces were still recovering from the Battle of the Bulge and were facing fanatical resistance on the route to Japan. The Red Army had overrun Eastern Europe; driven the Nazis out of Yugoslavia; begun to organize Poland, Romania, and Bulgaria as communist states; penetrated Austria, Hungary, and Czechoslovakia; and were poised only fifty miles from Berlin. Meanwhile, the Joint Chiefs of Staff insisted to Roosevelt that it was worth almost any price to obtain Russian military assistance in the Far East. They expected the invasion of Japan to cost a million American casualties. Stalin was in a position to make demands. He already dominated eastern Europe, and there was little that Churchill and Roosevelt could do to alter that; the United States still faced a long, bloody battle with the Japanese, and Stalin had the luxury of deciding whether or not to remain a nonparticipant in the Pacific war.

The Yalta agreements mirrored the new balance of power. Stalin again promised to declare war on Japan "two or three months" after the surrender of Germany, and in return Churchill and Roosevelt reneged on their arrangement with Jiang Jieshi, made at Cairo, and promised the Soviet Union concessions in Manchuria and the territories that

it had lost in the Russo-Japanese War forty years earlier. Stalin then recognized Jiang as the ruler of China and promised to persuade Mao Zedong's (Mao Tse-tung's) Chinese communists to end the nation's long civil war and cooperate with Jiang. The Soviet dictator also dropped his demands for $20 billion in reparations from Germany and the permanent dissolution of the Reich, accepting a temporary partitioning of Germany and future discussions by a reparations commission. On the matter dearest to Roosevelt's heart, Stalin approved plans for a United Nations Conference to be held in San Francisco in April 1945 to establish a permanent international organization for collective security.

The Soviet dictator, however, proved adamant on the issue of dominance in Eastern Europe, particularly Poland. Twice in the twentieth century, Poland had been the pathway for German troops invading Russia. Stalin would not expose Russia again, and after the Soviets had captured Warsaw in January 1945, he encouraged the Polish communists to brutally subdue a noncommunist majority. Roosevelt and Churchill refused to recognize the communist Lublin regime. But in consideration of the Soviet power in the area, they reluctantly accepted Stalin's pledge to reorganize the government to include "democratic leaders from Poland itself and from Poles abroad" and to allow free elections as soon as possible to determine the future government of Poland. Radio Berlin proclaimed Yalta "an unlimited triumph for Stalin," and many conservatives in the United States—then and afterward—agreed. But short of going to war against the Soviet Union while simultaneously battling Hitler and the Japanese, Roosevelt could only hope that Stalin would keep his promises.

The Defeat of Germany

As the diplomats at Yalta delayed resolving their differences, the Allied armies closed the vise on Germany. Early in March American troops captured Cologne and then poured across the Rhine River, quickly encircling the Ruhr Valley, Germany's industrial heartland. To counter the threat of Soviet power in a postwar Europe, Churchill now proposed a rapid, concentrated Anglo-American thrust to Berlin. General Eisenhower, with Roosevelt's backing, overruled the British. The Americans, wishing to minimize their casualties and to

Yalta

The palaces where Roosevelt, Churchill, Stalin, and their advisers gathered were still standing, but the rest of Yalta had been reduced to ruin during the German occupation.

reassure Stalin, who continued to fear that his allies might sign a separate peace with Germany, methodically advanced on a broad front extending from the North Sea to the border of Switzerland. In the last week of April, American and Russian troops joined hands at the Elbe River. By then, however, the Russians had taken Vienna and reached the suburbs of Berlin. On April 30 Hitler committed suicide in a secret bunker under the streets of Berlin, and the city fell to the Soviets on May 2. A hastily assembled new German government surrendered unconditionally on May 8.

Jubilant Americans celebrated Victory in Europe (V-E) Day on May 8 with ticker-tape parades and dancing in the streets. But the rejoicing quickly subsided. The United States now had to turn its attention to the war in the Pacific, where the fierce resistance from Japan continued to take a high toll in American lives. Moreover, in the last weeks of the German campaign, as Allied troops liberated those remaining in the concentration camps, Americans saw newsreels of the gas chambers in Auschwitz, the human ovens of Dachau, and the

corpses stacked high like cordwood in Belsen. They learned with horror that 6 million Jews and 1 million others had been systematically murdered in these Nazi death camps. And they mourned a tragedy closer to home, the death of Franklin Roosevelt. Throughout the early months of 1945, the once robust and vibrant leader of the New Deal had appeared increasingly frail and weary. On April 12 the exhausted president, sitting for a portrait at his second home in Warm Springs, Georgia, had abruptly clutched his head and moaned "I have a terrific headache." A cerebral hemorrhage had ended his life. His unprepared successor would inherit leadership of the most powerful nation in history as well as an escalating conflict with the Soviet Union that seemed more intractable every day.

A New President

"I don't know whether you fellows ever had a load of hay or a bull fall on you," Harry S Truman told reporters on his first full day in office, "but last night the moon, the stars, and all the planets fell on me." An unpretentious and uninspiring politician, awed by his new responsibilities, Truman struggled to continue FDR's policies. But Roosevelt had made no effort to familiarize his vice president with the course of world affairs. Truman distrusted the Russians and counted on American military power to maintain the postwar peace. In office less than two weeks, he lashed out at Soviet ambassador V. M. Molotov that the United States was tired of waiting for the Russians to carry out the Yalta agreement on free elections in Poland, and he threatened to cut off lend-lease aid if the Soviet Union did not cooperate. The Truman administration then reduced U.S. economic assistance to the Russians and stalled on the decision to grant them a $1 billion reconstruction loan. Yet Stalin continued to strengthen his domination of Eastern Europe, breaking the promises that the Soviet Union had made at Yalta. The boldness and bluster of both Stalin and Truman did nothing to arrest the steady dissolution of the Grand Alliance.

The United States would neither concede the Soviet sphere of influence in Eastern Europe nor take decisive steps to terminate it. While Truman insisted on a free Poland, he still eagerly sought Russian cooperation in establishing the United Nations and in defeating Japan. Diplomatic matters drifted and deteriorated. By June 1945, when the Allied countries succeeded in framing the United Nations Charter, official hopes for a new international order had dimmed, and the United Nations had already emerged as a diplomatic battleground for the Americans and Russians. Truman, Churchill, and Stalin met at Potsdam, Germany, from July 16 to August 2, to complete the postwar arrangements begun at Yalta. But the Allied leaders could barely agree even to demilitarize Germany and to punish Nazi war criminals. All the major divisive issues were postponed and left to the Council of Foreign Ministers to resolve later. Given the lack of effective negotiation, only military power remained to determine the contours of the postwar world.

The Atomic Bombs

Meanwhile, the war with Japan ground on. Early in 1945 an assault force of marines invaded Iwo Jima, a speck of an island 700 miles from Japan. There the marines battled thousands of Japanese soldiers hidden in tunnels and behind concrete bunkers and pillboxes. It took six weeks and twenty-six thousand marine casualties to secure the five-square-mile island. Then American troops waded ashore on Okinawa, only 350 miles from Japan and a key staging area for the planned American invasion of the Japanese home islands. They suffered nearly fifty thousand casualties before subduing the Japanese resistance.

If the capture of these small islands had been so bloody, what would the assault on Japan itself be like? Although a naval blockade and daily aerial pounding were exhausting Japan (on March 9–10 a fleet of B-29s had killed more than eighty thousand in Tokyo), the imperial government showed little disposition to surrender. Consequently, Truman scheduled an invasion of the Japanese island of Kyushu for late 1945 and one of Honshu, the main island, for early 1946.

The successful detonation of an atomic blast at Alamogordo in mid-July, however, gave Truman an alternative to the costly planned invasion. While meeting with Stalin at Potsdam, Truman issued an order on July 25 that an atomic bomb be dropped if Japan did not surrender before August 3. The next day he and Churchill warned Japan to surrender unconditionally or face "prompt and utter destruction." Japan rejected the Potsdam Declaration on July 28, and Truman gave the military the go-ahead. On August 6 a B-29 named the *Enola Gay* took off from the Marianas island of Tinian and dropped an atomic bomb on the city of Hiroshima. Nearly eighty thousand people died in the searing flash of heat and light, and many thousands more died later of radiation poisoning. On August 8, as promised, Russia declared war on Japan. The next day, at high noon, an atomic bomb was dropped on Nagasaki, incinerating some forty thousand and obliterating much of the city. On August 14 Japan accepted the terms of surrender, which left the emperor on the throne but subordinated him to the American commander of the occupation forces. On board the battleship *Missouri*, General MacArthur formally received the Japanese surrender on September 2, 1945. The long war was over.

Subsequently, many have questioned whether the fighting had to end with the United States resorting to the dreaded new atomic weapons. Some believe that racist American attitudes toward the Japanese motivated the decision to drop the bombs. Yet from the very beginnings of the Manhattan

Project, those involved regarded Germany as the target; and considering the indiscriminate ferocity of the Allied bombings of Hamburg and Dresden, there is little reason to assume that the Allies would have hesitated to drop atomic bombs on German cities if they had been available before the German surrender. Others contend that demonstrating the bomb's terrible destructiveness on an uninhabited island would have moved Japan to surrender. We will never know for sure. American policy makers had ruled against a demonstration bombing as impractical and too risky because the United States had an atomic arsenal of only two bombs, and they did not know whether the mechanism for detonating them in the air would work. Still others argue that Japan was ready to surrender and that an invasion of the home islands was unnecessary. Again, we cannot know for sure. All that is certain is that as late as July 28, 1945, Japan flatly rejected a demand for surrender, and not until after the bombing of Hiroshima did the Japanese government begin to discuss acceptance of the Potsdam Declaration.

The rapid worsening of relations between the United States and the Soviet Union, moreover, strengthened the conviction of some that Truman ordered the use of the atomic bombs primarily to intimidate Stalin. The failure of the Americans and Russians to resolve their differences had led Truman and his key advisers to seek an end to the war in the Pacific before Soviet entry into the conflict. They had also recognized the need to brandish an awesome weapon that might give the United States the leverage to oust the Russians from Eastern Europe. Referring to the Soviets, President Truman noted just before the atomic test at Alamogordo,

"If it explodes, as I think it will, I'll certainly have a hammer on those boys." Secretary of War Henry Stimson contended that the bomb was "a badly needed equalizer" in the struggle with the Soviet Union and that it emboldened the president to "get tough with the Russians." And Truman's new secretary of state, James Byrnes, thought that the bomb would "make Russia more manageable" and would "put us in a position to dictate our own terms at the end of the war."

The president and his advisers undoubtedly believed that the atomic bombs would strengthen their hand against the Soviets; but that was not the foremost reason why the bombs were dropped. As throughout the war, American leaders in August 1945 relied on production and technology to win the war with the minimum loss of American life. Every new weapon was put into use. No responsible official counseled that the United States should accept the deaths of thousands of Americans while not using a weapon developed with 2 billion taxpayer dollars. Indeed, to the vast majority of Americans, the atomic bomb was, in Churchill's words, "a miracle of deliverance" that shortened the war and saved lives. "I was a 21-year-old second lieutenant leading a rifle platoon," wrote one veteran later.

When the bombs dropped and news began to circulate that the invasion of Japan would not take place, that we would not be obliged to run up the beaches near Tokyo, assault-firing while being mortared and shelled, for all the fake manliness of our façades, we cried with relief and joy. We were going to live. We were going to grow up to adulthood after all.

Conclusion   The atomic bombs ended the deadliest war in history. More than 14 million men under arms, including more than 300,000 Americans, had died. Another 25 million civilians had perished. Much of Asia and Europe was reduced to rubble. Although the United States emerged physically unscathed, the war had had a profound impact on American life that would become starkly apparent in the postwar decades. Mobilization altered the structure of the economy; accelerated trends toward bigness in business, agriculture, and labor; and drastically enlarged the role of the military in many aspects of American life. World War II transformed the scope and authority of the federal government, especially the presidency. And it catalyzed vital changes in racial and social relations.

Isolationism all but disappeared as the United States became the strongest nation in the world and played a role in global affairs that would have seemed inconceivable to most Americans just five years before. Having stopped the Nazi onslaught in Europe and the Japanese conquest of Asia, many hoped that the newly established United Nations would ensure peace. But the mass destruction of the war and the total defeat of the Axis left in their wake a new international conflict—the Cold War. The mushroom clouds over Hiroshima and Nagasaki would lead to a spiraling atomic arms race that threatened nuclear nightmare. The revolutionary advances in wartime science and technology raised both hopes for a healthier and better world and fears of an end to all human life on earth. As the United States began a new era in 1945, facing unique problems and prospects, the nation was more powerful yet more insecure than ever before.

CHRONOLOGY

1939 Germany invades Poland; World War II begins.
Russia invades Poland.

1940 Germany conquers the Netherlands, Belgium, and France.
Germany, Italy, and Japan sign the Tripartite Pact.
Selective Service Act.
Franklin Roosevelt elected to an unprecedented third term.

1941 Lend-Lease Act.
Roosevelt establishes the Fair Employment Practices Commission (FEPC).
Germany invades the Soviet Union.
Japan attacks Pearl Harbor; the United States enters World War II.
War Powers Act.

1942 Battle of Midway halts Japanese offensive.
Internment of Japanese-Americans.
Revenue Act expands graduated income-tax system.
Allies invade North Africa (Operation Torch).

1942 (cont.) First successful atomic chain reaction.

1943 Soviet victory in Battle of Stalingrad.
Coal miners strike; Smith-Connally War Labor Disputes Act.
Detroit race riot.
Allied invasion of Italy.
Big Three meet in Tehran.

1944 Allied invasion of France (Operation Overlord).
GI Bill of Rights.
Roosevelt wins fourth term.
Battle of the Bulge.

1945 Big Three meet in Yalta.
Battles of Iwo Jima and Okinawa.
Roosevelt dies; Harry S Truman becomes president.
Germany surrenders.
Truman, Winston Churchill, and Joseph Stalin meet in Potsdam.
United States drops atomic bombs on Hiroshima and Nagasaki; Japan surrenders.

For Further Reading

John Morton Blum, *V Was for Victory: Politics and American Culture During World War II* (1976). A critical analysis of American society during the war.

James MacGregor Burns, *Roosevelt: The Soldier of Freedom* (1970). An incisive study of the president's wartime leadership.

Robert Dallek, *Franklin D. Roosevelt and American Foreign Policy, 1932–1945* (1979). A comprehensive view of U.S. foreign policy in the depression and war years.

Gabriel Kolko, *Politics of War: The World and U.S. Foreign Policy, 1943–1945* (1968). A revisionist view of the origins of the Cold War and American diplomacy.

Richard Polenberg, *War and Society: The United States, 1941–1945* (1972). A brief overview of major domestic developments.

Gordon W. Prange, *At Dawn We Slept: The Untold Story of Pearl Harbor* (1981). The most recent examination of the controversies surrounding the Japanese attack.

Martin Sherwin, *A World Destroyed: The Atomic Bomb and the Grand Alliance* (1975). A cogent explanation of atomic diplomacy's rise and consequences.

Additional Bibliography

General Works

A. Russell Buchanan, *The United States and World War II* (2 vols., 1964); Robert A. Divine, *Roosevelt and World War II* (1969); Martha Byrd Hoyle, *A World in Flames: The History of World War II* (1970); Gordon Wright, *The Ordeal of Total War, 1939–1945* (1968).

Military Operations

Stephen E. Ambrose, *The Supreme Commander: The War Years of General Dwight D. Eisenhower* (1970); John S. D. Eisenhower, *Allies: Pearl Harbor to D-Day* (1982); Kent R. Greenfield, *American Strategy in World War II* (1963); Akira Iriye, *Power and Culture: The Japanese-American War, 1941–1945* (1981); John Keegan, *Six Armies in Normandy: From D-Day to the Liberation of Paris, June 6–August 25, 1944* (1982); Charles B. MacDonald, *The Mighty Endeavor: American Armed Forces in the European Theatre in World War II* (1969); Gordon W. Prange, *Miracle at Midway* (1982); Bill D. Ross, *Iwo Jima: Legacy of Valor* (1985); Ronald H. Spector, *Eagle Against the Sun: The American War with Japan* (1984); Mark A. Stoler, *The Politics of the Second Front: American Military Planning and Diplomacy in Coalition Warfare, 1941–1945* (1977); John Toland, *The Rising Sun: The Decline and Fall of the Japanese Empire* (1970); Russell P. Weigley, *Eisenhower's Lieutenants: The Campaign of France and Germany, 1944–1945* (1981); William T. Y'Blood, *Red Sun Setting: The Battle of the Philippine Sea* (1981).

Mobilization

J. P. Baxter III, *Scientists Against Time* (1946); Alan Clive, *State of War: Michigan in World War II* (1979); George Q. Flynn, *The Mess in Washington: Manpower Mobilization in World War II* (1979); Paul A. C. Koistinen, *The Military-Industrial Complex: A Historical Perspective* (1980); Richard A. Landenbaugh, *American Steel Makers and the Coming of the Second World War* (1980); Nelson Lichtenstein, *Labor's War at Home: The CIO in World War II* (1983); Richard R. Lingeman, *Don't You Know There's a War On?* (1970); Steve Neal, *Dark Horse: A Biography of Wendell Willkie* (1983); Geoffrey Perrett, *Days of Sadness, Years of Triumph: The American People, 1939–1945* (1974); Joel Seidman, *American Labor from Defense to Reconversion* (1953); Brad-

ley F. Smith, *The Shadow Warriors: The OSS and the Origins of the CIA* (1983); Allan M. Winkler, *The Politics of Propaganda: The Office of War Information, 1942–1945* (1978).

American Society

Karen Anderson, *Wartime Women: Sex Roles, Family Relations, and the Status of Women During World War II* (1981); Richard M. Dalfiume, *Desegregation of the United States Armed Forces: Fighting on Two Fronts, 1939–1953* (1969); Roger Daniels, *Concentration Camps USA: Japanese Americans and World War II* (1981); Lee Finkle, *Forum for Protest: The Black Press During World War II* (1975); Susan M. Hartmann, *The Home Front and Beyond: American Women in the 1940s* (1982); Peter Irons, *Justice at War: The Inside Story of the Japanese-American Internment* (1983); Davis R. B. Ross, *Preparing for Ulysses: Politics and Veterans During World War II* (1969); Leila J. Rupp, *Mobilizing Women for War: German and American Propaganda, 1939–1945* (1978); Michi Weglyn, *Years of Infamy: The Untold Story of American's Concentration Camps* (1976); Neil A. Wynn, *The Afro-American and the Second World War* (1976).

Diplomacy

John H. Backer, *The Decision to Divide Germany: American Foreign Policy in Transition* (1978); Charles A. Beard, *President Roosevelt and the Coming of War* (1948); Diana S. Clemens, *Yalta* (1970); Wayne S. Cole, *Roosevelt and the Isolationists, 1932–1945* (1983); Robert A. Divine, *Second Chance: The Triumph of Internationalism in America During World War II* (1967); Herbert Feis, *Churchill, Roosevelt, Stalin* (2d ed., 1967); Charles E. Neu, *The Troubled Encounter: The United States and Japan* (1975); Raymond G. O'Connor, *Diplomacy During the Second World War, 1941–1945* (1965); Michael Schaller, *The United States Crusade in China, 1938–1945* (1979); Michael Sherry, *Preparing for the Next War: American Plans for Postwar Defense, 1941–1945* (1977); Christopher Thorne, *Allies of a Kind: The United States, Britain and the War Against Japan, 1941–1945* (1978); Paul Varg, *The Closing of the Door: Sino-American Relations, 1936–1946* (1973).

The Atomic Bomb

Gar Alperovitz, *Atomic Diplomacy* (1965); Barton J. Bernstein, ed., *The Atomic Bomb* (1976); Robert J. C. Butow, *Japan's Decision to Surrender* (1954); Herbert Feis, *The Atomic Bomb and the End of World War II* (1966); Gregg Herken, *The Winning Weapon: The Atomic Bomb in the Cold War, 1945–1950* (1980); John Hersey, *Hiroshima* (1946); Richard G. Hewlett and Oscar E. Anderson, *The New World* (1962); Chalmers M. Roberts, *The Nuclear Years* (1970); W. S. Schoenberger, *Decision of Destiny* (1969).

CHAPTER 27

Cold War America, 1945–1952

On the day that Franklin Roosevelt died, the new president, Harry S Truman, had hurried to console his predecessor's widow. "Is there anything *I* can do for you?" he inquired. "Is there anything *we* can do for you?" Eleanor Roosevelt had responded thoughtfully, "for *you* are the one in trouble now." The Truman administration, the first in a turbulent era that began with the atomic clouds over Hiroshima and Nagasaki, faced a long, almost uninterrupted succession of crises at home and abroad. Truman would often quip, "If you can't stand the heat, get out of the kitchen." And hot Truman's kitchen remained, as domestic discord deepened, his conflicts with Congress and the Republicans grew rancorous and vengeful, and U.S.–Soviet relations crackled with nuclear tensions.

Americans hoped that the postwar era would bring, in the words of the title of MGM's academy-award-winning 1946 film about servicemen's homecoming, "the best years of our lives." Optimistic that there would not soon be another war, confident that the nation could solve any problems that arose, Americans rushed to grab a share of the good life. They married, had babies, made Dr. Benjamin Spock's child-care manual the hottest-selling title since the sales lists began in 1895, took instant pictures of their families on the first Polaroid cameras, bought cars with automatic transmissions, and moved to split-level houses in suburbs that had shopping centers and families much like their own. But the peace of mind that they yearned for eluded them, for the Second World War had wrought decisive and disturbing changes in American society and in the global balance of power.

As never before, foreign developments profoundly affected American lives. Russian and American diplomats' failure to secure a reasonable solution to the problem of Eastern Europe's fate sparked a confrontation in which the Soviet Union and the United States each sought to reshape the postwar world in a way that would serve its own national interests. An uncompromising Truman squared off against an obsessive Stalin. Each action on the part of one seemed to intensify the insecurities of the other. A new form of international conflict—a Cold War—emerged, in which the two superpowers avoided a direct military clash yet used all their available resources around the globe to thwart the other's objectives.

The Cold War fundamentally changed America. Abandoning its historic aloofness from events outside the Western Hemisphere, the United States now plunged into a global struggle to contain the Soviet Union and stop communism. The nation that only a few years before had had no military alliances, a small defense budget, and no troops on foreign soil now built a massive military establishment, signed mutual-defense pacts with some forty countries, directly intervened in the affairs of allies and enemies alike, erected military bases on every continent, and embarked on a seemingly limitless nuclear-arms race with the Soviets. In the drive to halt the expansion of communism, the United States dispatched many thousands of Americans to fight in Korea, as their sons and younger brothers would later fight in Vietnam.

The Cold War's political and social effects proved equally drastic. The national preoccupation with the Soviet menace helped discredit socialists and others on the Left and sapped the vitality of New Deal liberalism. Focusing on the communist menace at home and abroad, the Truman administration had little time or inclination significantly to extend the New Deal reform agenda.

The Cold War affected the American Right as well. From the late nineteenth century through the 1930s, politically conservative Americans had deplored the growth of federal power and called for sharp limits on government. Conservatives of the Cold War era continued to hold these views on domestic social and economic issues, but when it came to military expansion, sniffing out domestic subversion and disloyalty, and leading the world fight against communism, they tolerated and even applauded a far-reaching expansion of governmental power. This ambivalence about the federal government's proper role would shape conservative ideology for decades to come.

The Cold War also stifled the free expression of ideas in America, as the anxieties of the early postwar period spawned a second "Red Scare" reminiscent of 1919. Provoked by popular fears of communist aggression abroad and of subversion from within the United States, a spate of public and private witch hunts undermined the liberties of the American people. The reckless hurling of unfounded charges of disloyalty added a new word to the American vocabulary—*McCarthyism*. Feeding the nation's paranoia about communism, McCarthyism destroyed careers and lives, stifled criticism of the status quo, and further fueled political intolerance. It also deeply discredited President Truman, who ironically had taken the lead in arousing American fears of communism. Renouncing Truman's leadership, the American people in 1952 turned hopefully to Dwight Eisenhower, a hero of the Second World War, to deliver the stability for which they so longed.

The Postwar Political Setting

Truman's sudden elevation to the presidency in 1945 caught both the new chief executive and the American people unprepared. Few outside his home state of Missouri or official Washington knew much about the new head of state, other than that in background and bearing he could not have been more unlike FDR. Born in 1884, the son of a Lamar, Missouri, horse and mule trader, Truman grew up in Independence, where he was remembered as a shy and bookish youth. After high school he worked mainly on his grandfather's farm until America's entry into the First World War gave him the opportunity to serve overseas as a captain in the field artillery. Returning to Kansas City after the war, Truman operated a men's clothing store and dabbled in local politics. When his haberdashery business failed in 1922, he became a full-time member of the party machine run by Tom Pendergast, the Democratic "boss" of Kansas City. First as county judge, and after 1934 as a U.S. senator, Truman gained a reputation as a diligent but colorless partisan, a supporter of Franklin Roosevelt yet not a

Truman's Haberdashery

Harry S Truman and friends posed in the future president's Kansas City shop around 1920.

committed New Dealer. Neither experienced in world affairs nor supported by any major interest group within the Democratic party, Truman won the vice-presidential nomination on the 1944 ticket because he was a safe alternative to the liberal Henry Wallace and the southern conservative James F. Byrnes. A mere five months after the election, Truman assumed the burden of leading the nation into the atomic age.

The very idea of this "usurper" in the White House initially dismayed liberals. "How I wish you were at the helm," the mayor of Minneapolis, Hubert H. Humphrey, wrote to Henry Wallace. "The country and the world don't deserve to be left this way," an equally disapproving David E. Lilienthal, chairman of the Tennessee Valley Authority, recorded in his journal. Their displeasure mounted as the feisty Truman let it be known that he intended to rule in his own way. He replaced New Deal liberals in the cabinet with moderates, and he gave key executive posts to old political cronies, whom the press, recalling Warren Harding's corrupt "Ohio Gang," dubbed the "Missouri Gang." At the same time, Truman unsettled conservatives by urging Congress to adopt a twenty-one-point economic-reform program and by emphasizing his role as the champion of the common people against the special interests.

Deeply concerned for the public welfare, Truman displayed on his desk a framed motto of Mark Twain: "Always do right. This will gratify some people, and astonish the rest." Indeed he wanted government to do more than in the past to help the average American—but without significantly altering the existing economic and social system. "I want to keep my feet on the ground," Truman confided to an aide. "I don't want any experiments; the American people have been through a lot of experiments and they want a rest." Neither rest nor an end to experiments would mark the Truman presidency, however. Despite his goal of moderate reform, Truman had to confront a resurgent Republican party more aggressive, and a fratricidal Democratic party more deeply divided into opposing northern-urban and southern-rural camps, than at any time since the 1920s. Because of congressional resentment of the enormous powers assumed by Roosevelt during the Second World War, moreover, Truman had to govern in an era of intense legislative suspicion of executive leadership.

Demobilization and Reconversion

As tangible proof of the war's end, most Americans wanted the 12 million men and women serving in the military "home alive in '45." The Truman administration announced plans for a gradual demobilization, but GIs and civilians alike clamored, "BRING OUR BOYS HOME—NOW!" Demonstrating for more transport ships to return them to the United States, American troops in Guam and Manila barraged members of Congress with threats of "no boats, no votes." In Paris and Frankfurt, thousands of other GIs surged through the streets chanting "Service yes, serfdom no!" Congress received hundreds of pairs of babies' booties with notes reading, "I Miss My Daddy." And on a single day in December, more than sixty thousand postcards arrived at the White House bearing the message "Bring the Boys Home by Christmas." Truman bowed to the pressure. By mid-1946 the navy had been reduced from 4 million to 1 million men, and the army from 8 million to fewer than 2 million. By 1948 the American military totaled just 1.5 million men. "The program we were following was no longer demobilization," Truman conceded in his memoirs; "it was disintegration of our armed forces."

The rapidity of demobilization pleased but also frightened Americans. Some members of Congress worried that returning veterans would bring back a blood lust for killing and proposed "demilitarization centers" to rehabilitate them before their release from the military. Hundreds of magazine articles focused on the readjustment problems that ex-GIs faced. *Sex Problems of the Returned Veteran* was an instant best seller. And the more than half a million divorces recorded in 1945 gave the United States the highest divorce rate in the world. The veterans came home, moreover, to a drastic housing shortage. Every city was plastered with "no vacancy" signs. In Chicago former servicemen were forced to live in coal sheds; in San Francisco they slept in automobiles parked on the city streets.

As the GIs became civilians and war plants closed their doors, Americans most feared the return of mass unemployment and economic depression.

Following the surrender of Japan, the government immediately canceled $35 billion in war contracts. Within ten days a million defense workers had lost their jobs. As defense spending plummeted from $76 billion in 1945 to less than $20 billion in 1946, worried economists forecast that postwar unemployment could top 11 million. Instead of a major depression, however, an economic boom began in late 1946. U.S. economic output, which had risen from $91 billion in 1939 to $200 billion in 1946, soared to $318 billion in 1950. The years of reconversion—the transition from wartime production to the manufacture of consumer goods—ushered in a quarter-century of expanding prosperity.

The Servicemen's Readjustment Act of 1944, popularly called the GI Bill of Rights, helped stimulate this economic growth. Under the GI Bill, 2.3 million veterans studied in colleges and universities between 1945 and 1950. The more than $15 billion they received in educational benefits, medical treatment, and loans to purchase homes or farms or to start new businesses aided the economic recovery. The rapid reconversion of industry further catalyzed economic activity. Benefiting from a 1945 tax cut of almost $6 billion and the accumulation of huge wartime profits, businesses invested massively in new factories and equipment.

The United States' emergence as economic leader of the noncommunist world had been signaled in 1944 when the Allied governments met at a New Hampshire resort to hammer out the Bretton Woods Agreement. Under this treaty, foreign currencies were to be valued ("pegged") in relation to the dollar, and several important institutions were created to oversee international trade and finance: the International Monetary Fund (IMF), the General Agreement of Tariffs and Trade (GATT), and the World Bank. Until the late 1960s, the Bretton Woods system functioned smoothly.

The United States' favorable position in international trade and finance bolstered the idea at home and abroad that the postwar years marked the beginning of "the American century" of worldwide peace and prosperity. Soon fears of an imminent postwar depression faded into vistas of limitless economic growth. With many nations in ruin, American firms could cheaply import raw materials; and with little competition from other industrial nations, they could increase their sales of export goods to record levels. In addition, wartime advances in science and technology, especially in electronics and synthetic materials, led to the development of whole new industries and radically boosted productivity in others.

Wartime savings and the pent-up demand for consumer goods further kindled postwar industrial growth and economic prosperity. The men and women who had endured the Great Depression and the Second World War yearned for the good life, and by the end of 1945, they possessed some $140 billion in bank accounts and government bonds. The rage to consume, and the widespread ability to do so, more than compensated for the decline in defense spending. Advertisements promising "a Ford in your future" and an "all-electric kitchen-of-the-future" quickly became reality as sales of homes, furniture, cars, appliances, and clothing skyrocketed. Scores of new products—televisions, filter cigarettes, electric clothes dryers, freezers, automatic transmissions, tubeless tires, air conditioners, hi-fis—suddenly became the hallmarks of the middle-class lifestyle.

Truman's Troubles

Americans' hunger to enjoy the fruits of affluence left them with little appetite for a resumption of New Deal economic and social reforms. The Employment Act of 1946 proved to be Truman's only major legislative accomplishment in the Seventy-ninth Congress. It committed the federal government to assuring economic growth and established the Council of Economic Advisers to assist the president in achieving "maximum employment, production, and purchasing power." Congress, however, equally fearful of federal deficit spending and increased presidential powers, gutted from the proposed bill both the goal of providing *full* employment and the broad executive authority necessary to attain that objective. Congress also blocked Truman's requests for public housing, a higher minimum wage, social-security expansion, a permanent Fair Employment Practices Commission, an anti–poll tax bill, federal aid to education, and government medical insurance.

Congressional eagerness to dismantle wartime controls, coupled with inconsistent leadership by the president, hobbled the administration's ability to deal with the major postwar economic problem: inflation. As consumer demand outran the supply of goods, the pressure on prices in the immediate postwar period grew intense. The wartime Office of Price Administration (OPA) continued to enforce price controls for a time after the end of the war, but food producers, manufacturers, and retailers opposed controls strenuously. While many consumers favored a continuation of OPA, others disliked it as a symbol of the hated system of wartime regulation. Reflecting these conflicting demands, Congress in June 1946 passed a bill that would have extended OPA's life while curtailing its powers. Truman vetoed the bill, effectively ending all price controls. Within a week food costs rose more than 16 percent. The price of beef doubled. "PRICES SOAR, BUYERS SORE, STEERS JUMP OVER THE MOON" headlined the *New York Daily News*. By the end of July, the cost-of-living index had shot up 6 percent.

At this point Congress passed a second bill extending price controls in weakened form, and Truman signed it. But the opponents of price controls toughened their tactics. Farmers and meat producers threatened to withhold food from the market. Observing that "meatless voters are opposition voters," Truman lifted controls on food prices just before the November 1946 midterm elections. This did his party little good, however, as Democratic candidates fared badly at the polls. On November 9, having pondered the election results, Truman announced the end of all price controls. By then the consumer price index had jumped nearly 25 percent since the end of the war, and food prices had risen at a far faster rate than that. Americans were paying 86 percent more for a round steak at the end of 1947 than they had in August 1945.

Meanwhile, the staggering rise in prices intensified organized labor's demands for higher wages. On top of inflation, workers faced a widespread decline in take-home pay because of the end of wartime bonuses and overtime, as well as employer resistance to large wage increases. As a result of these conditions, strikes tore across the postwar labor landscape: more hours were lost in work stoppages in the twelve months after V-J Day than in any previous year in all American history. In January 1946, 3 percent of the entire labor force was on strike, and more than 4.5 million men and women went on strike that year, including the powerful United Mine Workers, headed by John L. Lewis. Following forty days of economic paral-

John L. Lewis *(inset)* **and Illinois Coal Miners, 1946**

The 1946 strikes called by Lewis angered Truman and many other Americans, but the work stoppages led to a multimillion-dollar welfare fund for the United Mine Workers.

ysis, the president ordered government seizure of the mines. A week later, the miners returned to work, after Truman granted them most of the demands that he had earlier denounced as inflationary. Six months later, Lewis called for and got another strike, and again the government took over the mines.

In the spring of 1946, railway engineers and trainmen also struck and, for the first time in the nation's history, totally shut down the railroad system. Truman exploded. "If you think I'm going to sit here and let you tie up this whole country," the president shouted at the heads of the two unions, "you're crazy as hell." Emboldened by public hostility to unions ignited by the rampant work stoppages, Truman went before Congress on May 25, 1946, to demand authority to draft workers who struck in vital industries. Only when the rail employees gave in did the Senate reject Truman's proposal. His threat alienated labor leaders, and his encouragement of inflationary wage-price agreements between powerful unions and industries forced consumers to pay the bill in the form of higher prices.

By autumn of 1946, having antagonized virtually every major political interest group, Truman appeared nearly unable to govern. Only 32 percent of those surveyed in an October Gallup poll approved of the president's performance. "To err is Truman," some gibed. One commentator even suggested that the Democrats nominate Hollywood humorist W. C. Fields for president: "If we're going to have a comedian in the White House, let's have a good one." Summing up the public discontent with inflation, strikes, and shortages, the Republicans asked, "Had enough?" In the 1946 elections they captured twenty-five governorships and, for the first time since 1928, won control of Congress.

Anticommunism and Containment

Meanwhile, compounding Truman's problems, simmering antagonisms between Moscow and Washington had come to a boil by the end of 1946. With their common enemy, Hitler, dead in the rubble of his Berlin bunker, Russia and the United States abandoned their wartime alliance of expediency and vied for advantage in the power vacuum left by the defeat of Germany and Japan, the exhaustion and bankruptcy of Western Europe, and the crumbling of colonial empires in Asia and Africa. In a postwar setting ripe for misperception and misunderstanding, the two strongest nations to emerge from the war each sought security and safeguards for its national interest by means that fed the fears of the other. Fundamental ideological differences widened the chasm between the two powers. The stage was set for a protracted, complex, and dangerous conflict.

Confrontation and Polarization

As in the closing months of the war, the destiny of Eastern Europe, especially Poland, continued to be at the heart of U.S.–Soviet contention. Ravaged

twice in a quarter-century by German troops sweeping eastward across the plains of Poland, Russia wanted to ensure that it would never again be vulnerable to such invasions. Stalin insisted not only on a demilitarized and deindustrialized Germany but on a buffer of nations friendly to the Soviet Union along Russia's western flank. The communist dictator considered such a Soviet sphere of influence in Eastern Europe essential to Russian security, a just reward for Russia's bearing the brunt of the war against Germany, and no different from the American spheres of influence in Western Europe, Japan, and Latin America. Moreover, Stalin believed that the idea of a pro-Soviet zone in Eastern Europe had been implicitly accepted by Roosevelt and Churchill at Yalta.

With the 10-million-strong Red Army occupying roughly half of Europe at the end of the war, Stalin installed governments subservient to Moscow in Bulgaria, Hungary, and Romania. (Pro-Soviet revolutionary governments gained power independently of Moscow in Albania and Yugoslavia.) Disregarding the Yalta Declaration of Liberated Europe, moreover, the Russians in 1945 barred free elections in Poland and brutally suppressed the Polish democratic parties. The Soviet Union would tolerate no government in Poland that it could not totally control. In Stalin's view, Poland was "not only a question of honor for Russia, but one of life and death."

Stalin's refusal to abandon Russian dominance in Eastern Europe was matched by Truman's unwillingness to concede Soviet supremacy beyond Russia's own borders. What Stalin saw as critical to Russia's national security the Truman administration viewed as a violation of the right of nations to self-determination, a betrayal of democratic principles, and a cover for the spread of communism throughout Europe. Stalin's demands also seemed to violate a basic diplomatic tenet embraced by Truman and his foreign-policy advisers: that a policy of appeasement toward aggressive dictators leads not to peace but to greater violence and bloodshed. The infamous Munich conference of 1938, at which British prime minister Neville Chamberlain had capitulated to Hitler's territorial demands and thereby helped bring on World War II, was very much in their minds as they dealt with Stalin. America needed a tough policy on Poland, advised W. Averell Harriman, the American ambassador in Moscow, since any "generous and considerate attitude" by the United States would be regarded as weakness by Soviet leaders and would result in a "barbarian invasion of Europe." Moreover, many of Truman's advisers believed that traditional balance-of-power diplomacy and the division of the world into spheres of influence had caused the two world wars. Peace, they argued, could be ensured only through a new world order based on the self-determination of all nations working in good faith within the structure of the United Nations.

Truman believed that accepting the "enforced sovietization" of Poland and Eastern Europe would betray the U.S. war aims. Both the Atlantic Charter and the Yalta declaration had pledged self-government through free and open elections to the people of war-torn Europe. The president did not want the nations rescued from Hitler's tyranny to fall under the sway of another totalitarian dictatorship. Too, Truman worried that a Soviet stranglehold in Eastern Europe would imperil the American economy, whose health, he believed, depended on export outlets and on access to raw materials in the countries that Stalin appeared determined to control solely for Russia's economic betterment.

Domestic political considerations also shaped the Truman administration's response to Stalin. As had Roosevelt, Truman fully understood the political importance of the overwhelmingly Democratic 6 million Polish-Americans as well as of the millions of other Americans of Eastern European origin. Because these peoples retained a keen interest in the fates of their homelands, the Democratic party would face disaster, Truman realized, if the administration reneged on the Yalta conferees' declaration. The president also recognized the political strength of anticommunism in American politics and knew that any appearance of administration support for the Soviet control of Eastern Europe would give his conservative opponents an enormous advantage. Many Republicans had already grumbled about Roosevelt's concessions to the Russians at Yalta, and the new president was determined not to leave himself open to similar attacks by appearing "soft" on communism. Instead, he would align his administration with the nation's growing anti-Soviet sentiment and use it to fortify himself politically.

A combative posture fit the temperament of the feisty Truman. Eager to show his foes at home and abroad that he was in command, the president matched Stalin's intransigence on Polish elections with his own rigid demands for self-determination and the reorganization of Poland's government along democratic lines. Emboldened by America's monopoly of atomic bombs and its undisputed position as the world's economic superpower, the president assumed that the United States could control the terms of postwar settlements. His conviction that America's atomic power and Russia's need for economic assistance would force Stalin to retreat reinforced his insistence that there be no compromise on the Polish question.

The Cold War Begins

Truman's assertiveness, however, not only inflamed Stalin's compulsive mistrust of the West but also deepened the Russians' obsession with their own security. In reaction to the administration's hard line, Stalin both stepped up his confiscation of materials and factories from occupied territories and forced his Eastern European satellites to close their doors to Anglo-American trade and influence. In early February 1946, warning ominously that there could be no lasting peace with capitalism, the Russian dictator proclaimed new plans to make the Soviet Union secure against the challenge of the West and to overcome the American edge in weapons technology.

Two weeks later, a sixteen-page telegram from George Frost Kennan, the American chargé d'affaires in Moscow, arrived in Washington. A leading student of Soviet politics, Kennan, who had been stationed in Russia during the 1930s and throughout the war, had frequently called the State Department's attention to the historical factors underlying Soviet expansionism. After years of being at odds with the official policy of cooperation with the Soviet Union, Kennan's advocacy of toughness against the Russians now found a receptive audience. It particularly suited the mood of Truman, who a month earlier had insisted to his secretary of state James F. Byrnes that the time had come "to stop babying the Soviets" and "to get tough with Russia."

Kennan's telegram asserted the *inevitability* of American conflict with the Soviet Union. Stalin and his advisers, according to Kennan, would seek security for Russia by outmaneuvering the rival United States, but "never in compacts or compromises with it." It was foolish, Kennan concluded, to try to negotiate an accommodation with Moscow. Instead, he recommended a U.S. foreign policy based on the "long-term, patient, but firm and vigilant containment of Russian expansive tendencies." This policy of "containment," he predicted, would force the Soviets to act prudently by reinforcing their tendency to pull back "when strong resistance is encountered at any point."

In later years Kennan apologized for his telegram, admitting that it read "exactly like one of those primers put out by the Daughters of the American Revolution, designed to arouse the citizenry to the dangers of a communist conspiracy." But in early 1946 it nourished the appetite of many in Washington who insisted on "no compromise" with the Russians. Kennan's belief that only strong, sustained American resistance could contain Russian aggression quickly became unofficial Washington gospel. On February 27 Senator Arthur Vandenberg of Michigan, the top-ranking Republican on the Senate Foreign Relations Committee, condemned Soviet actions in Europe and Asia and demanded that the United States "draw the line"

with the Russians. The following day Secretary of State Byrnes, the target of Republican criticism for his attempts to accommodate the Soviets, so echoed the Michigan senator's call for a hard line that the press dubbed his speech "the Second Vandenberg Concerto."

A week later, Truman accompanied Winston Churchill to Westminster College in Missouri, where the former British prime minister, echoing the sentiments of the administration, delivered a memorable speech warning of a new threat to the democracies, this time from Moscow. Stalin, Churchill solemnly intoned, had drawn an iron curtain across the eastern half of Europe. "This is certainly not the liberated Europe we fought for," he exclaimed, and not one "which contains the essentials of permanent peace." Churchill called for an alliance of the English-speaking peoples against the Soviet Union and the maintenance of an Anglo-American monopoly of atomic weapons. "[T]here is nothing they admire so much as strength," he argued, "and nothing for which they have less respect than for military weakness."

Truman and Winston Churchill en route to Westminster College

Prior to delivering his "iron-curtain speech," Churchill had written Truman: "Under your auspices anything I say will command some attention, and there is an opportunity for doing some good to this bewildered, baffled, and breathless world."

Believing more than ever that American firmness could check Soviet expansionism, Truman in the spring of 1946 shifted his foreign policy in the direction prescribed by Kennan, Vandenberg, and Churchill. To force Stalin to keep an earlier promise to withdraw Soviet soldiers from the north of oil-rich Iran, Truman dispatched part of the Sixth Fleet to the Black Sea and threatened to send in American combat troops. Then in June, the president submitted an atomic-energy control plan to the United Nations, requiring the Soviet Union to cease all work on atomic weaponry and to submit to a comprehensive system of control and inspection by a U.N. agency. Only then, the administration's plan specified, would the United States destroy its own atomic arsenal. As expected, the Russians rejected the American proposal and offered an alternative plan equally unacceptable to the United States. With mutual hostility escalating, the Russians and Americans rushed ahead to develop their own doomsday weapons. In 1946 Congress passed the Atomic Energy Act, which established the Atomic Energy Commission (AEC) to control nuclear development and declared that the utilization of fissionable materials should be for civilian purposes "so far as practicable." From the outset, however, at least 90 percent of the AEC's effort focused on military weapons.

Thus, less than a year after American and Soviet soldiers had jubilantly joined hands at the Elbe River to celebrate the defeat of Nazism, the U.S.–Soviet peace had clearly been lost. The Cold War had begun. This conflict between the two superpowers and their allies throughout the world would be waged largely by economic pressure, nuclear intimidation, propaganda, and subversion rather than by direct U.S.–Soviet military confrontation. It would nevertheless affect American life as decisively as any military engagement that the nation had ever fought.

European Crisis, American Commitment

A formal proclamation of America's commitment to contain the Soviet sphere of influence came in early 1947. On February 21 the British informed the United States that they could no longer afford to keep up their assistance to the governments of Greece and Turkey in their respective struggles against a communist-supplied insurgent guerrilla movement and against Soviet pressure for access

to the Mediterranean. With more than half its industrial plants idled by a lack of fuel, a stricken Britain asked the United States to bear the costs of thwarting communism in the eastern Mediterranean. The harsh European winter, the most severe in memory, intensified the sense of urgency in Washington. The economies of Western Europe had come to a standstill. Famine and tuberculosis plagued the Continent. European nations' colonies in Africa and Asia were in revolt. Cigarettes and candy bars circulated as currency in Germany, and the communist parties in France and Italy appeared on the verge of toppling the precarious democratic coalition governments. Truman resolved to meet the challenge. "Inaction, withdrawal, 'Fortress America' notions could only result in handing to the Russians vast areas of the globe now denied them," he later recalled. "This was the time to align the United States of America clearly on the side, and at the head, of the free world."

The president's first task was to mobilize congressional and public support for a major departure from America's powerful tradition of no entangling alliances. In a tense meeting at the White House on February 27, Truman's new secretary of state, former army chief of staff George C. Marshall, presented the case for providing massive economic aid to Greece and Turkey. More concerned about inflation at home than about a civil war in Greece, however, most of the assembled members of Congress balked. Then Dean Acheson seized the moment. The newly installed undersecretary of state stunned his audience with dire predictions of the consequences of America's failure to intervene. "We are met at Armageddon," Acheson began dramatically. He defined the issue not as one of assisting the repressive Greek oligarchy and the Turkish military dictatorship but rather as a universal struggle of freedom against tyranny. "Like apples in a barrel infected by the corruption of one rotten one," he warned, the fall of Greece or Turkey would open Asia, Western Europe, and the oil fields of the Middle East to the Russian menace. "The Soviet Union [is] playing one of the greatest gambles in history," Acheson concluded. "We and we alone are in a position to break up that play." Shaken but still hesitant, the congressional leaders agreed to support the administration's request if the president could "scare hell out of the country."

Truman could and did. On March 12, 1947, in an address to a joint session of Congress, the president asked for $400 million in military assistance to Greece and Turkey. Truman starkly depicted a world endangered by the spreading tentacles of communism. The United States, he declared, must support free peoples everywhere who were "resisting attempted subjugation by armed minorities or by outside pressures." Called the Truman Doctrine—and meant to be as comprehensive as the Monroe Doctrine's "Keep Out" sign posted on the Western Hemisphere—the president's declaration committed the United States in theory to the role of global policeman facing an almost limitless confrontation with the Soviet Union and its allies. Endorsed by the Republican-controlled Congress in its mid-May vote in favor of military aid to Greece and Turkey, the Truman Doctrine laid the foundation for American Cold War policy for much of the next four decades.

A month later, the administration proposed massive American assistance for European recovery. The resulting program was called the Marshall Plan after the secretary of state, who had earlier advocated such aid in a Harvard commencement address. Truman envisioned the Marshall Plan as another weapon in the American arsenal against the spread of communism. With food in Western Europe scarce—millions were subsisting on less than fifteen hundred calories a day—the president

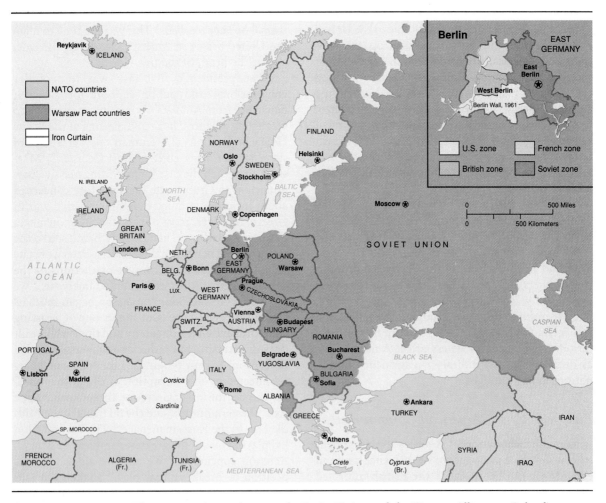

The Postwar Division of Europe

The wartime dispute between the Soviet Union and the Western Allies over Poland's future hardened after World War II into a Cold War that split Europe into competing American and Russian spheres of influence. Across an "iron curtain," NATO countries faced the Warsaw Pact nations.

wanted to end the economic devastation that could readily be exploited by communist revolutionaries. Although the Marshall Plan was ostensibly an effort to help the hungry and homeless of *all* the European countries, Truman correctly calculated that Russia and its communist allies would reject American economic assistance because of the conditions and controls linked to the aid. The administration also accurately predicted that economic recovery in Western Europe would expand sales of American goods abroad and thus promote prosperity in the United States. While denounced by the Left as a "Martial Plan" and by isolationist voices on the Right as a "Share-the-American-Wealth Plan," the Marshall Plan fulfilled its sponsors' hopes. Congress appropriated $17 billion for economic recovery in sixteen nations over a five-year period. By 1952 the economic and social chaos thought to provide a fertile seedbed for communism had been overcome in those nations, and the individual freedoms of their peoples preserved. Western Europe revived, prospered, and achieved an unprecedented unity, and U.S. business, not incidentally, boomed.

The Soviet Response

The Soviet Union reacted to the Truman Doctrine and Marshall Plan with swift, decisive moves that broadened its sphere of influence in Eastern Europe. In mid-1947 the Soviets rigged elections in Hungary to ensure a communist government. In February 1948 they added to their satellites by fomenting a general strike in Czechoslovakia, massing the Red Army on its border, and forcing the formation of a communist-dominated government that rapidly abolished other political parties and allowed the once democratic Czechoslovak nation to be absorbed into the Soviet orbit.

Following the seizure of Czechoslovakia, Stalin took bold action in the critical German area. The 1945 Potsdam Agreement had divided Germany into four separate zones (administered by France, Great Britain, the Soviet Union, and the United States) and had created a joint four-power administration for Germany's capital, Berlin, lying 110 miles within the Russian-occupied eastern zone. As the Cold War unfolded, however, the West refused to allow Stalin a role in administering the Ruhr Valley, the industrial heart of western Germany. Angered, Stalin felt that the West was reneging on wartime promises. In April 1948 the Soviets

began to impede the flow of supplies and people from the western zones of Germany into Berlin. Then on June 24, in reaction to the Allies' moves toward permanently uniting the three western zones into a pro-Western German state (which would also include West Berlin), the Russians blocked all rail and highway routes through the Soviet zone into Berlin. Stalin calculated that the Western powers, obstructed from provisioning the 2 million pro-Western Berliners under their control in the non-Russian sector of the city, would either have to abandon any plans to create an independent West Germany or withdraw and accept a communist Berlin.

Truman resolved neither to abandon Berlin to the Soviets nor to shoot his way into the city and possibly set off World War III. Instead he ordered a massive airlift to provide Berliners with the thousands of tons of food and fuel necessary for their survival. "We are going to stay, period," the president declared to end a cabinet discussion on the matter. American C-54 and C-47 cargo planes were soon landing at West Berlin's Templehof Airport almost every three minutes around the clock, bringing a mountain of supplies each day. To prevent the Russians from jamming American radar or shooting down the defenseless planes, Truman ordered a fleet of B29s, the only planes capable of delivering atomic bombs, to bases in England in July 1948. Although the planes were not actually armed with nuclear weapons, Truman bluffed that he would use "the bomb" if necessary. Tensions rose. The president confided in his diary his fear that "we are very close to war." Americans grew so uneasy in the summer of 1948 that a record number of people reported seeing flying saucers, and the air force launched an investigation of the alleged sightings. Meanwhile, for nearly a year, "Operation Vittles," as the Berlin airlift was called, provided the blockaded city with a precarious lifeline.

In May 1949 the Soviets suddenly ended the blockade. Stalin's gambit had failed. The airlift highlighted America's determination and technological prowess, revealed Stalin's stubborn willingness to use innocent citizens as pawns in pursuit of his goals, and drastically intensified anti-Soviet feelings in the West. Public-opinion polls in the United States in late 1948 revealed an almost unanimous belief that "Russia is an aggressive, expansion-minded nation" and an overwhelming demand

End of the Blockade

Jubilant American airmen celebrate the lifting of the Berlin blockade. American pilots had flown overworked and defenseless planes into Berlin day after day despite persistent Russian harassment.

for "firmness and increased 'toughness' in relations with Russia."

The continuing fear of a Soviet assault on Western Europe fostered support for a revitalized West German state and for an Atlantic collective security alliance. Thus in May 1949 the United States, Britain, and France ended their occupation of Germany and approved the creation of the Federal Republic of Germany (West Germany). A month earlier, ten nations of Western Europe had adopted the North Atlantic Treaty establishing a military alliance with the United States and Canada and declaring that an attack on any member of the alliance would be considered an attack against all. For the first time in its history, the United States had entered into a peacetime military alliance. Support for the treaty was not unanimous, however. Senator Robert Taft of Ohio, speaking for a small band of Republican senators, warned that such an agreement would provoke the Russians to respond in kind, stimulate a massive arms race,

and open the floodgates of American military aid to Europe. But the Senate overwhelmingly approved the treaty, and in July the United States officially joined the North Atlantic Treaty Organization (NATO), marking the formal end of U.S. isolationism.

Two days after the Senate ratification, Truman asked Congress to authorize $1.3 billion for military assistance to NATO nations. To underscore his determination to contain communism, especially after the outbreak of the Korean War in June 1950 (see below), the president persuaded General Dwight D. Eisenhower to become the supreme commander of the new mutual defense force and authorized the stationing of four American army divisions in Europe as the nucleus of the NATO armed force. The Soviet Union met the challenge by creating the German Democratic Republic (East Germany) in 1949, by exploding its own atomic bomb that same year, and by setting up a rival Eastern bloc military alliance, the Warsaw Pact, in 1955. A mere decade after the Second World War, the United States and the Soviet Union had divided Europe into two armed camps.

The Cold War in Asia

Moscow-Washington hostility similarly led to the division of Asia into contending military and economic camps. The Russians carved out a sphere of influence in Manchuria, the United States denied the Soviet Union any role in the postwar military occupation of Japan, and the two superpowers partitioned a helpless Korea.

Acting as Japan's unofficial dictator, General Douglas MacArthur transformed that nation into a prosperous constitutional democracy and set it firmly in the American orbit by the late 1940s. He barred communists from all government posts, sanctioned the American construction of major military bases and the stationing of American troops near the Soviet Union's Asian rim, and encouraged U.S. businesses to invest in Japan. Moreover, the United States took control of Japan's entire prewar island empire. Although the islands were technically administered under a U.N. mandate, the United States used them as air and naval bases and also as atomic-bomb testing sites. MacArthur could well boast in 1949 that the Pacific had become "an

Anglo-Saxon lake." As keen to contain the Soviets in Asia as in Europe, the Truman administration also aided the Philippine government in crushing a "procommunist" guerrilla movement and permitted the French to reestablish their colonial rule in Indochina (the region of Southeast Asia comprising Cambodia, Laos, and Vietnam), despite frequent American declarations in favor of national self-determination and in opposition to imperialism.

In China, however, U.S. efforts to stop the triumph of communism failed. The Truman administration initially tried to mediate the civil war raging in China between the Guomindang (Koumintang), or Nationalist, regime of Jiang Jieshi (Chiang Kai-shek) and the communist armies led by Mao Zedong (Mao Tse-tung). But American opposition to a communist victory in China led the administration to escalate its assistance to Jiang's eroding forces. The United States sent nearly $3 billion in aid to the Nationalists between 1945 and 1949. American dollars, however, could not force the inefficient Guomindang to reform itself and to win the support of the Chinese people. Jiang had alienated both peasants, by suppressing agrarian reform, and city dwellers, at whose expense he had profiteered. His armies, moreover, suffered from poor morale in response to these abuses. As Mao's well-disciplined and highly motivated forces marched south, Jiang's soldiers mutinied and surrendered without a fight. Jiang's armies "did not have to be defeated," said Dean Acheson; "they disintegrated." Unable to stem the growth of revolutionary sentiment or to hold the countryside—where the communists, in Mao's words, "swam like fishes in the peasant sea"—Jiang's regime collapsed. By the end of 1949, he had fled to an exile government on the island of Taiwan (Formosa).

Americans reacted with shock to Mao's establishment of the communist People's Republic of China. The most populous nation in the world, looked to as a counterforce to communism in Asia and a major market for American trade, had become "Red China." John Foster Dulles, a major Republican authority on foreign policy, called the communization of China "the worst defeat the United States has suffered in its history." Who was to blame? Who "lost" China? Denying that it could have done more to alter the outcome of the civil war, the Truman administration faulted Jiang's failure to achieve the reforms necessary to hold the Chinese

people's loyalty. But the government's explanation failed to persuade most Americans. The fall of China to communism particularly embittered midwestern and far western conservatives who had long believed that America's future lay in Asia rather than Europe. Many of them pointed the finger of blame at the State Department, among them former American ambassador to China Patrick Hurley, who railed at "pro-Communists in the State Department who . . . engineered the overthrow of our ally."

As the China debate raged, the president announced in September 1949 that the Soviet Union had successfully exploded an atomic bomb. In an instant the world had changed (see "A Place in Time"). The loss of the U.S. nuclear monopoly shattered all illusions of American invincibility. Taken together with the disturbing news of Mao's victory, the reports of Russia's atomic capability spawned sudden anticommunist hysteria in the United States and led to irrational searches for scapegoats and subversives (see below) to explain American setbacks in world affairs.

A reeling Truman administration began a major reassessment of its Cold War strategy. Stung by Republican charges that he was soft on communism, the president decisively ended the dispute among his scientific advisers in January 1950 by ordering the Atomic Energy Commission to mount an all-out effort to develop a fusion-based hydrogen bomb (H-bomb)—one with power measured in millions of tons of TNT rather than in thousands of tons like the existing A-bombs. Edward Teller, a Hungarian-born physicist who had worked on the Manhattan Project, had long argued for a fusion bomb, in which explosive power is created by forcing hydrogen atoms together. But leading scientists in America's nuclear establishment, led by J. Robert Oppenheimer and Harvard University president James B. Conant, had rejected Teller's proposed weapon as too complex to construct and too immorally destructive to use. In light of the fearful mood in Washington early in 1950, however, Truman took just seven minutes to accept the report of his secretaries of defense and state recommending a crash thermonuclear program. In November 1952 the United States exploded its first H-bomb in the Marshall Islands, projecting a radioactive cloud twenty-five miles into the stratosphere and blasting a canyon a mile long and 175 feet deep in the ocean floor. Nine months later the

Los Angeles Confronts the Atomic Age

*E*arly in January 1951, a Los Angeles construction company staged a major ground-breaking ceremony for the television cameras to promote its backyard family atomic-bomb shelters. As Hollywood stars applauded, Mrs. Ruth Calhoun, mother of three, smilingly dug the first spadeful of dirt. For $1,995 she had bought an underground cubicle at the edge of her patio that would include green plastic carpeting, beige-painted concrete walls, and even a light-weight Geiger counter to test for radioactivity. "I do a lot of canning and bottling in the summer," Mrs. Calhoun explained to reporters, "and it will make a good store-house." She added: "It will make a wonderful place for the children to play in, too."

Despite the reassuring tone of the ceremony, atmospheric nuclear testing and the possibility of nuclear war troubled Americans. Tales of the dire effects of radioactivity and images of mushroom-shaped clouds dominated the public consciousness. Country-music lyrics warned of "peace in the world, or the world in pieces." Radio programs offered chilling descriptions of the atomic destruction of American cities. An NBC broadcast on the hypothetical bombing of Chicago exclaimed:

Most of those in the center of the city were violently killed by the blast or by the following vacuum which explosively burst their stomachs and intestines, and violently ruptured their tissue. Those few who escaped the blast, but not the gamma rays, died slowly but inevitably after they

had left the ruined city. . . . No attempt at identification of bodies or burial ever took place. Chicago was simply closed, and the troops did not allow anyone to return.

Similarly graphic portrayals of people vaporized in a nuclear flash and the earth incinerated in a giant atomic fireball appeared in Ray Bradbury's 1950 science-fiction best seller *The Martian Chronicles*. Book titles by eminent scientists trumpeted *There Is No Defense, No Place to Hide,* and *One World or None.*

In September 1949 the White House had stunned the American people with a terse announcement that the Soviet Union had successfully detonated an atomic explosion: the United States had lost its

nuclear monopoly. When Soviet-supplied North Korean troops invaded South Korea in June 1950, apprehensive Americans, believing that the Soviet leaders were bent on world domination, sought security in renewed nuclear superiority, and safety in civil defense.

In 1950 the president created the Federal Civil Defense Administration (FCDA). The agency flooded the country with booklets, movies, and exhibits stressing that surviving an atomic war was possible through preparedness. It urged women to "never go out bare-legged" and cautioned men to wear wide-brimmed hats for protection against the "heat flash" of a nuclear attack. To reduce the nation's vulnerability, urban planners pro-

California Bomb Shelter Under Construction, 1951 *The manufacturer stocked this model with water, oxygen, and shovels.*

posed building "row cities" (50 miles long and a mile wide) and "donut cities" (hollow at the core). Public schools held routine air-raid drills and frequently showed the civil-defense film in which Bert the Turtle taught children to "duck and cover." New York City issued metal dog tags to all students so that their bodies might be identified in the event of a nuclear war. Four million Americans volunteered to be Sky Watchers, scanning the shorelines and rooftops for Russian planes; and millions more marked the numbers 640 and 1240 on their radio dials, where they could find communications in an atomic attack. Major corporations invested in underground facilities to safeguard their company records. Real-estate advertisements offered "good bomb immunity" in secluded parts of the country. Clever entrepreneurs found a market for aluminum pajamas and lead-foil brassieres.

Like Ruth Calhoun, many other Los Angeles residents purchased bomb shelters. For three thousand dollars, Sam Markell bought a "Kidde Kokoon." It came equipped with all that his family of five desired for a three-to-five-day underground stay, including a chemical toilet, nonelectric clock, canned food and water, protective apparel, and pick-and-shovel tool ("for digging out after the blast"). To reduce his

family's anxieties, Ronald Bates enlarged his backyard barbecue pit into a bomb shelter and stocked it with board games and puzzles as well as first-aid kits and other emergency supplies. Those who could not afford shelters learned the FCDA's "survival secrets" ("jump in any handy ditch or gutter . . . drop flat on the ground . . . bury your face in your arms . . . never lose your head").

The cease-fire in Korea in 1953 diminished the dread of imminent nuclear disaster that had gripped the nation. Resigned to living with the threat of nuclear destruction, Americans now laughed as Doris Day sang "Tic, Tic, Tic," poking fun at the dangers of radioactivity. Yet a sense of grim inevitability governed discussions of nuclear arms. Most Americans placed their hope in more and bigger bombs, and by the end of the 1950s, well over a million families had built or bought their own bomb shelters.

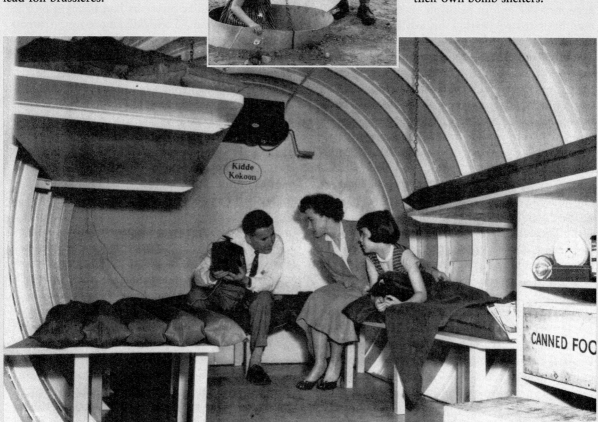

The Kidde Kokoon *The Kidde Kokoon's exterior hatch and interior living quarters are shown.*

Russians also detonated a hydrogen bomb. The balance of thermonuclear terror escalated.

Meanwhile, in early 1950 Truman also established a blue-ribbon committee of State and Defense Department officials to conduct a top-secret review of national defense policy. They devised NSC-68, a report emphasizing the Soviet Union's aggressive intentions and military strength. To counter what the report termed the Russian "design for world domination"—the mortal challenge posed by the Soviet Union "not only to this Republic but to civilization itself"—NSC-68 called for a massive American military buildup. The United States, the report advised, would have to maintain a large standing army and drastically increase its defense expenditures from the $13 billion allocated in 1950 to some $45 billion annually. The American people would have to be persuaded to support the higher taxes necessary to fund a 400 percent increase in military appropriations. The National Security Council, organized in 1947 to advise the president on all matters concerning America's preparedness, approved NSC-68 in principle in April. But Truman hesitated to swallow his advisers' expensive prescription. An aide to Secretary of State Acheson recalled: "We were sweating over it, and then, with regard to NSC-68, thank God Korea came along." By the end of 1950, Truman had ordered the implementation of NSC-68 and more than tripled the defense budget.

The Korean War

On June 24, 1950, as Truman pondered the implications of NSC-68, North Korean troops swept across the thirty-eighth parallel and began an invasion of the Republic of Korea (South Korea). Following Japan's defeat in 1945, the Korean peninsula, previously part of the Japanese Empire, had been temporarily divided at the thirty-eighth parallel for the purpose of military occupation by Soviet and American troops. This military dividing line had solidified into a political frontier between the Russian-backed People's Democratic Republic in North Korea and the American-supported Republic of Korea. Each sector of the Korean peninsula, nevertheless, had continued to hope that Korea would soon be a unified nation governed by its own regime.

But to Truman, North Korea's move seemed more a case of Soviet-directed aggression than an internal Korean matter. Although the Russians appeared to have been caught off guard by the North Korean attack and provided their ally with little aid after the outbreak of war, Truman never doubted that Stalin was using Korea to test the American containment policy.

"Korea is the Greece of the Far East," the president explained shortly after receiving the news of the invasion. "If we are tough enough now, if we stand up to them like we did in Greece three years ago, they won't take any next steps. But if we just stand by, they'll move into Iran and they'll take over the whole Middle East." Ever mindful of the failure of appeasement at Munich, Truman later stated that "communism was acting in Korea just as Hitler, Mussolini, and the Japanese had acted ten, fifteen, and twenty years earlier." Failure to oppose aggression would embolden the communists "to override nations closer to our own shores" and would lead to an even bloodier "third world war, just as similar incidents had brought on the second world war." Politically, moreover, Truman had to prove to Republican critics that the Democrats would stand up to "the Reds" and not allow another country to "fall" to the communists.

The president decided to intervene. Without consulting Congress, he sought the backing of the United Nations Security Council to repel the North Korean attack. U.N. approval was quickly gained, because Russia was then boycotting the Security Council to protest the United Nations' refusal to seat Mao Zedong's government in place of the exile Jiang Jieshi's regime in Taiwan. On June 27 Truman ordered American air and sea forces to the aid of the South Koreans and appointed seventy-year-old general Douglas MacArthur to command the U.N. effort in Korea. Three days later, American soldiers were fighting in Korea, despite the president's failure to ask Congress for a declaration of war. Although the intervention was officially a U.N. "police action," most of the naval and air support and nearly half the troops fighting under the U.N. flag came from the United States; South Korea supplied some 43 percent of the forces, and fourteen other nations contributed fewer than 10 percent of the U.N. troops.

The North Koreans rapidly pushed the U.N. forces back to the southeastern tip of the penin-

U.N. Troops in North Korea During the Offensive

From the start Truman believed that the Soviet Union had orchestrated the North Korean invasion of South Korea. He steadfastly maintained that "if the Russian totalitarian state was intending to follow in the path of the dictatorship of Hitler and Mussolini, they [had to] be met head on in Korea."

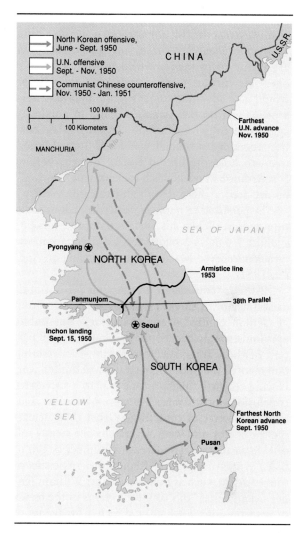

The Korean War, 1950–1953

The experience of fighting an undeclared and limited war for the limited objective of containing communism confused the generation of Americans who just fought an all-out war for the total defeat of the Axis. General MacArthur spoke for the many who were frustrated by the Korean conflict's mounting costs in blood and dollars: "There is no substitute for victory."

sula. Then in a brilliant amphibious maneuver on September 15, MacArthur's troops landed at Inchon, a port city near Seoul, and forced the North Koreans to retreat across the thirty-eighth parallel. Heartened by this military success, the Truman administration on September 27 permitted MacArthur to order the U.N. armies across the thirty-eighth parallel and toward the Yalu River, the boundary between North Korea and China. The police action to restore the original border between the two Koreas was now redefined as a war of liberation that would aim to create "a unified, independent, and democratic" single nation of Korea.

As MacArthur's troops neared the Yalu River, Mao Zedong angrily warned that China would not "stand idly by" if its border were threatened. Ignoring Mao's admonition, an overconfident MacArthur deployed the U.N. forces in a thin line below the river. On November 25 thirty-three Chinese divisions (about 300,000 men) counterattacked. Within two weeks they had driven MacArthur's stunned troops below the thirty-eighth parallel. By March 1951 the fighting had stabi-

lized at roughly the original border between North Korea and South Korea.

Truman again reversed course and in the spring of 1951 worked toward a negotiated peace based on the original objective of reestablishing the integrity of South Korea. But MacArthur rocked the boat. He urged that he be allowed to bomb and blockade China, to "unleash" Jiang Jieshi's troops against the communist regime, and to seek total victory even at the risk of an all-out war with China. Truman brusquely rejected such proposals: "We are trying to prevent a world war—not to start one." He further worried that the Soviet Union would take advantage of American involvement in a major war on the Asian mainland to pursue an aggressive course in Europe. Therefore, the conflict remained a limited war for a limited objective—to hold the line in Korea. But the defiant MacArthur had no stomach for stalemate. "In war," he declared, "there is no substitute for victory," and he persisted in publicly criticizing administration policy. When his inflammatory comments stymied Truman's progress toward negotiation, the president relieved MacArthur of command on April 10, 1951.

Truman considered MacArthur's insubordination a mortal threat to the American tradition of civilian control over the military. But public opinion strongly backed the general. Only 29 percent of those interviewed in a May 1951 Gallup poll favored the president's strategy of limited war. Having recently fought a total war to a successful conclusion, most Americans were baffled by Truman's objective of containing rather than defeating the enemy and were angered by the steady toll of U.S. casualties. An increasing number began to listen sympathetically to Republican criticisms of the president, such as Indiana senator William Jenner's charge that "this country today is in the hands of a secret coterie which is directed by agents of the Soviet Union."

The administration went on the offensive, forcefully stating its case before Congress. A showdown with the Chinese, testified General Omar Bradley, chairman of the Joint Chiefs of Staff, would lead only to "a larger deadlock at greater expense." The actions that MacArthur proposed, Bradley summarized, "would involve us in the wrong war at the wrong place at the wrong time and with the wrong enemy." Talk of total victory and of bombing China abated.

In July 1951 truce talks began in Korea, but they dragged on for two years as both sides fought a restricted yet deadly war. By the time the wrangling over prisoner repatriation and the location of the cease-fire line finally ended on July 26, 1953, this "limited" war had cost the United States 54,246 American lives, another 103,284 wounded and

missing, and some $54 billion. The conflict in Korea also speeded up the implementation of NSC-68 and the transformation of containment into a general global policy. Between 1950 and 1953, defense expenditures zoomed from $13 billion to just under $60 billion, from 5 percent to 13 percent of the gross national product, from one-third to two-thirds of the entire federal budget. In these years the United States also acquired new bases around the world, committed itself to rearm West Germany, and joined a mutual-defense pact with Australia and New Zealand. Significantly increased military aid flowed to Jiang Jieshi's beleaguered forces on Taiwan. Massive American military assistance was extended to the French army fighting the communist Ho Chi Minh in Indochina. With the United States now supporting any and all perceived enemies of communism, the State Department declared the French struggle against the guerrillas of the Vietminh (the league for Vietnamese independence) "an integral part of the worldwide resistance by the Free Nations to communist attempts at conquest." By 1954 the United States would be paying three-quarters of the French war costs in Vietnam.

Truman's intervention in Korea, ostensibly undertaken as an exercise in collective security under the United Nations Charter, in fact served mainly to preserve a precarious balance of power in one arena of Cold War conflict, by preventing the South Korean regime from falling to its rival in the north. The president's action also underscored the sweeping ramifications of the administration's commitment to the anticommunist struggle as well as the shift of that struggle's focus from Europe to Asia. George Kennan's containment doctrine, originally advanced to justify U.S. aid to Greece and Turkey, served in the early 1950s as the ideological foundation for a major war in Korea and, more ominously, for a deepening U.S. involvement with France's colonial war in Vietnam. Further, by committing American troops to battle with neither a declaration of war nor congressional approval, Truman set important precedents for future undeclared wars and enormously expanded presidential powers. Finally, the shock of China's fall and the frustrations of the inconclusive outcome in Korea heightened conservatives' unhappiness with Democratic rule and set off domestic shock waves that would have broad political and cultural ramifications in the 1950s and beyond.

The Truman Administration at Home

When Japan surrendered in 1945, most Americans wanted nothing more than to bring the boys home and enjoy the rewards of peace. Since the crash of 1929, the nation had known little but the privations of depression and the sufferings and shortages of war. Now it was time to forget the dark past and once again enjoy life! Widespread postwar affluence gave substance to these dreams. By 1953 the average American family enjoyed twice as much real income as in the go-go 1920s. Americans flocked to suburbia, launched a baby boom of howling proportions, and eagerly borrowed or saved to purchase the stoves, refrigerators, and new cars that had long been out of reach or unavailable. Sales of TV sets soared from fewer than 7,000 in 1946 to over 7 million by 1949; by 1953 half of all U.S. homes had at least one television set.

Fun, Forties-Style

After the war Americans grabbed for the good life, whether that meant enjoying a thrill-inducing ride at Coney Island, planning a family vacation, or jiving to a jukebox.

Not all Americans shared equally in the good times. Poverty remained a stark fact of life for millions in the cities and on the farms. Black Americans, who had loyally supported the war and in many cases fought on foreign battlefields, felt special bitterness as they experienced once again the grim reality of racism at home. Many refused to acquiesce, and this early postwar period saw the beginnings of a civil-rights movement that in a few years would sweep the nation.

But with the coming of peace, most Americans turned away from public issues and preoccupied themselves with career and family. The New Deal's achievements remained a proud memory, but the reform energies responsible for those achievements subsided into contentment and complacency.

The domestic politics of the Truman era reflected these social realities. Truman successfully preserved and consolidated the New Deal's liberal reforms; in 1948 and 1949, first as a part of his reelection strategy and then in the flush of his unexpected victory at the polls, Truman even proposed a series of bold measures, dubbed the Fair Deal, to push the reform tradition into new areas, including education, housing, health care, and civil rights.

But the spirit of the times was not reformist. Rather, a growing conservative trend in Congress supported a reduction of the power of both the federal government and groups such as organized labor that had surged to prominence in the 1930s. At the same time, rising anticommunist obsessions among the American people sharpened an ingrained tendency to associate radicalism with disloyalty and undercut liberal efforts to alter the status quo.

The administration's own priorities, especially after 1949, favored rearming for the struggle against the Russians rather than spending for social welfare. Anticommunism, not reform, more and more dominated the Truman administration's agenda. Fear of communism encircling the globe bred an atmosphere of fierce domestic repression that stifled dissent and placed a premium on unquestioning conformity. Perceptive observers recognized that when anticommunist rabble-rouser Senator Joseph McCarthy ran roughshod over the most basic principles of decency and fair play in the early 1950s, he was merely exploiting a climate of paranoia and mistrust that the White House itself had helped create.

The Eightieth Congress

The Republicans of the Eightieth Congress, which convened in January 1947, interpreted the 1946 elections as a mandate to reverse the New Deal. As "Mr. Republican," Senator Robert A. Taft of Ohio, declared: "We have got to break with the corrupting idea that we can legislate prosperity, legislate equality, legislate opportunity." The Republican-controlled Congress quickly passed tax measures favorable to the wealthy and defeated a proposal to raise the minimum wage. Vowing "to meat-axe government frills," Republicans and conservative southern Democrats also rebuffed Truman's requests for federal aid to education and a comprehensive housing program. The chief battleground between the president and conservatives, however, was the New Deal's pro-union Wagner Act of 1935 (see Chapter 24).

The rash of postwar strikes had created a national consensus—fostered by frequent media depictions of union leaders as labor barons, goons, and Reds—for curbing the unions' power. In 1947 more than twenty states passed laws to restrict union activities, and Congress responded that year with the Labor-Management Relations Act, better known as the Taft-Hartley Act. The new law significantly modified the Wagner Act by outlawing such union practices as the closed shop and by permitting the president to call an eighty-day cooling-off period to delay any strike that might endanger national safety or health. However, while the act eventually proved detrimental to certain unions and increased the difficulty of organizing non-unionized workers, it hardly became the "slave labor bill" that the union leadership had predicted. Still, the rank and file protested the act, and labor leaders demanded that Truman veto it.

Truman quickly returned the measure to Congress with a biting veto message. With his eye on the 1948 presidential election, he chided the lawmakers for "a shocking piece of legislation" biased against labor. Congress easily overrode the veto, but Truman had taken his first major step toward gaining organized labor's enthusiastic support for the election. He needed that support, and a lot more. Neither widely admired nor especially liked, Truman realized that his only hope in 1948 rested on his success in reforging FDR's New Deal coalition. He counted on the solid South to stay Democratic; shored up his support in the midwestern farm belt; and devoted most of his effort to winning the metropolitan areas, appealing particularly to laborers, liberals, ethnic Catholics, Jews, and blacks.

Playing the role of a staunch Rooseveltian New Dealer and casting his Republican congressional opponents as unfeeling villains, Truman proposed one liberal reform bill after another to the Eightieth Congress. He repeatedly urged legislators to extend the New Deal concept to such areas as housing, education, and health insurance. He promised labor a crusade to repeal the Taft-Hartley Act; and to woo agricultural America, he battled to maintain high farm-price supports. Courting various ethnic groups, he spoke out for laws that would admit thousands of displaced foreigners to the United States, and he repeatedly emphasized the Truman Doctrine's opposition to the spread of communism. In part to ensure the Jewish vote, moreover, immediately after the Jews proclaimed the independence of their homeland in Palestine on May 14, 1948, the president extended diplomatic recognition to Israel—overriding the vigorous objections of the State Department and America's European allies, who feared that recognition of the new nation would alienate the oil-rich Arab states.

The Politics of Civil Rights

Truman made the federal protection of civil rights a centerpiece of his reform agenda. Like his predecessor FDR, the president wished to retain the good graces of southern white Democrats and thus initially shied away from the race question. But the accelerating civil-rights movement, and the racial violence that it provoked, demanded a White House response.

After the war many blacks who had ably served in the armed forces or in the defense industry demanded the right to vote. In 1945 and 1946, the NAACP and local African-American groups conducted aggressive voter-registration drives. Particularly successful in Atlanta and the cities of North Carolina, these efforts raised the number of blacks registered to vote in the South to 12 percent in 1947, up from a mere 2 percent in 1940. The majority of southern blacks, however, still risked intimidation, repression, and even murder in pursuing their constitutional right to vote. Leading

white-supremacist politicians, among them Georgia governor Eugene Talmadge and Mississippi senator Theodore G. Bilbo, urged their followers to resort to any means to keep blacks from voting.

Fearful of blacks' assertiveness in seeking the vote, of their increasing refusal to move aside or doff their caps when white men approached, and of other signs of a bold new spirit among African-Americans, some southern whites struck out brutally to assert their dominance. In 1946 whites killed several black war veterans in rural Georgia who had voted that year, flogged to death an "uppity" black tenant farmer in Mississippi, blow-torched a young black in Louisiana for daring to enter a white woman's house, and blinded a black soldier for failing to sit in the rear of a bus in South Carolina. In Columbia, Tennessee, in 1946, whites rioted against blacks who insisted on their rights. In this incident police arrested seventy blacks and looked away as a white mob broke into the jail to murder two black prisoners. An aroused civil-rights movement called for federal action to end the violence.

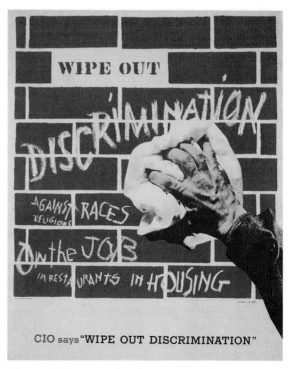

Wipe out Discrimination, *by Milton Ackoff, 1949*

The publication of To Secure These Rights *catapulted civil-rights issues to the forefront during the Truman years.*

Pickets outside the White House chanted, "SPEAK, SPEAK, MR. PRESIDENT!" Many liberals and leftists joined former first lady Eleanor Roosevelt in establishing the National Committee for Justice in Columbia, Tennessee, and nearly fifty religious and civil-liberties groups united with the NAACP in the National Emergency Committee Against Violence.

In September 1946 Truman met with a delegation from these organizations to discuss racial terrorism in the South. Horrified by their accounts, the president vowed to act. Not only did Truman personally believe that every American should enjoy the full rights of citizenship, but he also understood the importance of the growing black vote and took note of the continuing heavy migration of southern blacks to northern cities in states with large electoral votes. He realized, moreover, that white racism damaged American relations with much of the rest of the world. The Soviet Union repeatedly highlighted the ill treatment of blacks in the United States, both to undercut American appeals to the racially diverse peoples of Africa, Asia, and Latin America and to counter U.S. condemnations of repression behind the iron curtain. Shortly after the 1946 elections, therefore, Truman established the first President's Committee on Civil Rights to investigate race relations and to safeguard the rights of minorities.

The committee's report, *To Secure These Rights,* dramatized the inequities of life in Jim Crow America; underlined the compelling reasons— moral, economic, and international—why the government must act; and called for the eradication of racial discrimination and segregation from American life. The report also proposed anti-lynching laws, anti–poll tax legislation, and other specific measures. Hailing the report as "an American charter of human freedom," the president in February 1948 sent a special message to Congress urging the lawmakers to enact most of the committee's proposals.

In response, southern segregationists violently denounced Truman and damned his "stab in the back." A Texas congressman accused him of "kissing the feet of minorities." "Harlem is wielding more influence with the administration than the entire South," cried a representative from Georgia. Many key southern politicians warned of a boycott of the national Democratic ticket. The southern

revolt was on. Truman backtracked. Cowed by the prospect of a major southern defection from Democratic ranks, he dropped his plans to submit specific civil-rights bills to Congress and endorsed a weak civil-rights plank for the Democratic platform that made no mention of his own proposals.

But at the Democratic convention in July 1948, liberals and urban politicians who needed the backing of black voters rejected the president's watered-down civil-rights plank. They successfully amended the platform to include a clause forthrightly commending Truman "for his courageous stand on the issue of civil rights" and committing the party to press for action on Truman's initial proposals. Following a heated platform debate, thirty-five dissenting delegates from Mississippi and Alabama stalked out of the convention. They soon joined with other southern segregationists to form the States' Rights Democratic party and to nominate Governor J. Strom Thurmond of South Carolina for the presidency.

Running on a platform that emphasized opposition to civil rights, Thurmond's Dixiecrats, as they were nicknamed, hoped to win a hundred electoral votes in the South. If successful, they planned to use their political power as leverage to restore their dominance in the Democratic party and to protect "the southern way of life" against what they deemed an oppressive central government. Determined to preserve white supremacy, the Dixiecrats placed their electors on the ballot as the regular Democratic ticket in the several states in which they controlled the party machinery and thus erected a major roadblock to Truman's chances of victory.

The Election of 1948

Truman's hopes for election became even more remote when a band of Democratic left-wingers joined with the communists to launch a new Progressive party that nominated Henry A. Wallace for president. Truman had fired Wallace, his secretary of commerce and FDR's vice president (1941–1945), in September 1946 for publicly questioning the administration's "get tough" stance toward the Soviet Union. The Wallace candidacy especially threatened Truman's chances in the key populous northern states, where many urban Democrats viewed Wallace as the true heir of New Deal liberalism and supported his advocacy of increased federal funds for social-welfare programs and justice and equality for all minority groups.

Facing a divided Democratic party, the Republicans chose what seemed a sure path to victory. Although Senator Robert A. Taft of Ohio was the symbol and spokesman of the conservative heartland, the party leaders rejected this principled "Mr. Republican," who lacked the personal appeal to attract Democrats and independents, in favor of the opportunistic governor of New York, Thomas E. Dewey, as their standard-bearer. Playing it safe, the Republican platform also vaguely approved much of the New Deal and the administration's bipartisan foreign policy. Dewey and his vice-presidential running mate, the popular governor Earl Warren of California, confident of victory, ran a complacent campaign aimed at offending the fewest people. Dewey devoted most of his public appearances to bland appeals for national unity. Although sound in principle, the strategy backfired by making Dewey seem aloof, elusive, and smug.

In contrast, Harry Truman and his folksy running mate, Senator Alben Barkley of Kentucky, tirelessly kept up the offensive against the "nogood, do-nothing" Republican-controlled Eightieth Congress. To shouts of "Give 'em hell, Harry," the president spoke more than 350 times as his campaign train whistle-stopped across some thirty thousand miles. Ever on the attack, Truman hammered away at the GOP as the party of "privilege, pride, and plunder" just waiting "to do a hatchet job on the New Deal." While Truman earned applause for his spunk, pollsters and political pundits predicted a sure Dewey victory.

The experts, however, had failed to detect a swing to Truman late in the campaign. A surprised nation awoke the day after the election to learn that the president had squeaked to the biggest upset in U.S. political history. Truman received 24.1 million votes (49.5 percent) to Dewey's 22 million (45.1 percent). Ironically, the Progressives and the Dixiecrats had helped Truman. The prominence of the communists in the Wallace campaign forced most disgruntled liberals back into the Democratic column and also made the president and his program look moderate and mainstream by comparison. Wallace received only about a million popular votes and won no electoral votes. Likewise,

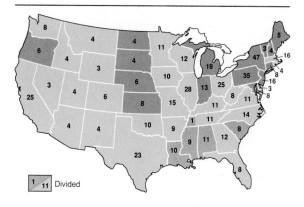

	Electoral Vote	Popular Vote	Percentage of Popular Vote
Democratic Harry S Truman	303	24,105,812	49.5
Republican Thomas E. Dewey	189	21,970,065	45.1
States' Rights Strom Thurmond	39	1,169,063	2.4
Minor parties	–	1,442,667	3.0

The Election of 1948

Thurmond collected fewer than 1.2 million votes and carried only the four southern states where the Dixiecrats ran under the regular Democratic party emblem. Although many white southerners despised Truman's advocacy of civil rights, they were not yet ready to revolt. As the attorney general of Virginia explained: "The only sane and constructive course to follow is to remain in the house of our fathers — even though the roof leaks, and there be bats in the belfry, rats in the pantry, a cockroach in the kitchen and skunks in the parlor." Moreover, Thurmond's failure to spark a major defection of southerners from the Democratic fold had freed Truman in the months before the election to campaign as a proponent of civil rights.

In July 1948 Truman had issued executive orders barring discrimination in federal employment and creating a committee to ensure "equality of treatment and opportunity for all persons in the armed services without regard to race, color, religion or national origin." This presidential edict proved good politics, though the navy, marine corps, and army moved haltingly to lower their racial barriers. Truman also benefited politically as a result of Supreme Court decisions in favor of civil rights. In 1946 the Court had declared segregation in interstate bus

Jackie Robinson

The talented slugger's joining the Brooklyn Dodgers in 1947 to become the first black major-league baseball player was the harbinger of countless other advances by blacks into areas from which they were previously barred.

transportation unconstitutional (*Morgan* v. *Virginia*); and in the election year of 1948, it outlawed restrictive housing covenants that forbade the sale or rental of property to minorities (*Shelley* v. *Kraemer*). Blacks similarly took heart in 1948 from the number of cities and states that had passed fair-employment-practices and public-accommodations laws and from the change in social attitudes symbolized by the Brooklyn Dodgers' signing of Jackie Robinson in 1947 to breach the color line in major-league baseball. They voted accordingly. Truman won a higher percentage of the black vote than had FDR in any of his four presidential victories.

Most of all, Truman won in 1948 because he re-created the New Deal coalition forged by Roosevelt. With the crisis in Berlin helping to rally the American people behind the president, Truman took every opportunity to remind farmers, ethnic groups, and laborers that the Republican "gluttons of privilege" planned to "turn the clock back" and deny them the benefits that they had gained under the New Deal. "In a sense," observed one political commentator in a post-mortem of Truman's success, "Roosevelt won his greatest victory after his death."

The Fair Deal

Although he had chalked up less than half the popular vote, winning by the narrowest margin since 1916, Truman regarded his election as a mandate for liberalism. In his 1949 State of the Union message, he proposed an ambitious social and economic program that he called the Fair Deal. The president asked Congress to enlarge the New Deal programs in the areas of economic security, conservation, and housing and to go far beyond Roosevelt's initiatives in civil rights, national health insurance, federal aid to education, and agricultural subsidies.

The Eighty-first Congress complied with most of Truman's appeals to extend existing programs. Lawmakers boosted the minimum wage to seventy-five cents an hour; increased social-security coverage and benefit payments; expanded appropriations for public power, reclamation, soil conservation, flood control, and slum clearance; and in the National Housing Act of 1949, authorized the construction of 810,000 subsidized low-income housing units. Congress also set up the National Science Foundation and approved a displaced-persons act admitting more than four hundred thousand refugees to the United States. But legislators rejected Truman's calls for repeal of the Taft-Hartley Act, federal aid to education, a comprehensive national health-insurance plan, and a crop-subsidy system that would both maintain farm income and hold down food prices. On the civil-rights front, southern Democratic lawmakers, with conservative Republican help, stymied all of Truman's efforts to enact anti-lynching and anti–poll tax laws and to establish a permanent Fair Employment Practices Commission.

Indeed, throughout Truman's presidency the conservative coalition in Congress stalemated liberal initiatives. Although Truman succeeded in preserving the New Deal, he failed to persuade the lawmakers to adopt his Fair Deal. In part, this reflected Truman's own lessening commitment to domestic reform as the Cold War and then the Korean War increasingly absorbed his time and energy. Further, the Cold War strengthened the conservative coalition's power by making the president ever more reliant on conservatives for their support of his military and foreign policies. In part, too, the postwar prosperity enjoyed by most Americans sapped the public enthusiasm that had sustained FDR's New Deal. In 1949, according to the Hickock Manufacturing Company, the belt size of the average American man had expanded to thirty-four inches, up from a depression-years average of thirty-one inches. The postwar Congresses mirrored the sense of well-being and complacency that most voting Americans felt. They also reflected the mounting popular apprehensions over communism that further doomed liberal hopes for a resurgence of reform.

The Politics of Anticommunism

As the Cold War evolved, a growing number of Americans came to believe that the country's foreign difficulties were rooted in treason and subversion at home. How else could the Chinese communists have gained power over all of China and the Russians have exploded their own atomic bomb? Unhinged by fear, millions of embittered Americans enlisted in a postwar crusade that blamed scapegoats for the nation's problems and equated dissent with disloyalty.

Similar intolerance had prevailed in the Know-Nothing campaign of the 1850s and the Red Scare of 1919–1920. The tendency to link radicalism with foreign conspiracies, moreover, was deeply rooted among American conservatives. Since its establishment in 1938, the House Committee on Un-American Activities (later called the House Un-American Activities Committee, or HUAC) had served as a platform for reactionaries' denunciation of the New Deal as a Russian plot to sovietize America. Only the extreme Right had taken such fulminations seriously at first. But after the Second World War, a growing number of Democrats as well as Republicans climbed on the anti-Red bandwagon to conduct a witch hunt in every corner of American life.

The second Red Scare deeply influenced both government actions and the behavior of ordinary Americans. Millions of men and women — in labor unions, schools and universities, and government jobs at every level — were subjected to oaths and security investigations. Anticommunist hysteria destroyed the Left, discredited liberalism, and undermined labor militancy. The trampling of civil liberties spawned a "silent generation" of college students and widespread political apathy, while the purge of controversial government officials ensured foreign-policy rigidity and the postponement of domestic reforms.

Loyalty and Security

As the Cold War began, reasons abounded for legitimate concern about American security. The Communist party had claimed some eighty thousand members at its height during the Second World War, and many more Americans, openly or secretly, had sympathized, and still sympathized, with its goals. No one knew how many of these individuals occupied sensitive government positions or directed their primary loyalty to the Soviet Union. In mid-1945 a government raid on the offices of a pro-communist magazine, *Amerasia,* uncovered a cache of classified documents that had been passed to the periodical by two State Department employees and a naval intelligence officer. Ten months later the Canadian government exposed a major spy network that had given American military information and atomic secrets to the Russians during the war. In response to the communist threat and to growing Republican criticism that the administration was lax in its internal security, Truman late in 1946 appointed a commission to study the loyalty problem.

Nine days after the president proclaimed a campaign against communism abroad in his "Truman Doctrine" speech of March 1947, he issued Executive Order 9835 establishing the Federal Employee Loyalty Program to root out subversives in government service. The order provided for an elaborate loyalty check on all government employees. Although the program initially had certain safeguards, the drive for absolute security quickly overrode concerns about the liberties of civil servants. Soon those suspected of disloyalty could neither face their accusers nor require the investigators to reveal the source of their information. Rather than focusing mainly on potential subversives in high-risk areas, the probe extended to the associations and beliefs of *every* government worker.

Local review boards sometimes accused employees of disloyalty solely because they criticized American foreign policy, advocated equal rights for women, or espoused the unionization of federal workers. "Of course the fact that a person believes in racial equality doesn't *prove* that he's a communist," mused an Interior Department loyalty board chairman, "but it certainly makes you look twice, doesn't it?" Government employees were asked whether they provided religious training for their children and what they thought of female chastity. Some were charged with disloyalty because they owned books on socialism or liked foreign films. Others lost their jobs because of guilt by association with radical friends and relatives, or because of previous membership in, or contributions to, organizations now listed by the attorney general as disloyal to the United States. Between 1947 and 1951, the loyalty boards forced nearly three thousand government employees to resign and fired some three hundred on charges of disloyalty. The probe uncovered no evidence of subversion or espionage. But it did spread fear and a mood of caution among government employees. "Why lead with your chin?" became a dominant reflex. "If communists like apple pie and I do," claimed one federal worker, "I see no reason why I should stop eating it. But I would."

The Anticommunist Crusade

The pall of conformity cast over the government by Truman's loyalty inquest fed the mounting anticommunist hysteria. The very existence of the federal investigation promoted widespread fears of communist infiltrators and legitimized other efforts to expose subversives. Universities banned controversial speakers. Popular magazines featured such articles as "Reds Are After Your Child" and "Communists Penetrate Wall Street." Even Marvel comics joined the fray: "Beware, commies, spies, traitors, and foreign agents! Captain America, with all loyal, free men behind him, is looking for you, ready

to fight until the last one of you is exposed for the yellow scum you are."

By the end of Truman's term, thirty-nine states had enacted antisubversion laws and loyalty programs with even fewer procedural safeguards than the federal government's. In legislation reminiscent of the Sedition Act of 1918, Connecticut made it a crime to print any "scurrilous or abusive matter" about the government, the armed forces, military uniforms, and the flag. Michigan invalidated all bequests to organizations judged subversive. Imprisonment awaited anyone in Massachusetts who knowingly allowed a meeting place to be used by communists. Schoolteachers, college professors, and state and city employees throughout the nation had to sign loyalty oaths or lose their jobs. In the name of "internal security," Americans were encouraged to snoop on their neighbors, colleagues, and relatives.

In 1947 a series of House Un-American Activities Committee hearings to expose communist influence in American life dominated the news. HUAC's probes blurred the distinctions between dissent and disloyalty, between radicalism and subversion. The committee perfected the tactic of threatening recalcitrant witnesses with the loss of their livelihoods. In Washington, D.C., a man lost his license to sell secondhand furniture because he had invoked the Fifth Amendment when questioned about his past; a woman who did the same was so effectively boycotted that she had to sell her thriving drugstore and leave town. HUAC also frightened labor unions into expelling communist members and steering clear of progressive causes. Fearing that to champion social justice would make them appear pro-communist, unions now concentrated solely on better pay and benefits for their members. Rather than the social-democratic movement that many unions aspired to become in the 1930s, postwar organized labor established itself as a highly bureaucratic special-interest pressure group.

HUAC also left its mark on the entertainment industry. When a group of prominent film directors and screenwriters refused to cooperate with the committee in 1947, HUAC had them cited for contempt and sent to federal prison. The threat of further investigations prompted the movie colony, financially dependent on favorable press and public opinion, to give in and exile its dissenters. Moreover, Hollywood established an unofficial

Hollywood Goes to Washington, 1947

Robert Taylor, Gary Cooper, and other stars testified that communists were at work in Hollywood's entertainment community.

blacklist barring the employment of anyone with even a slightly questionable past. Familiar faces disappeared from the movie screen; a similar blacklist in broadcasting silenced some of radio's most talented voices. Some Americans went to absurd lengths to avoid even the remotest hint of disloyalty. Considering an eight-year-old actress's father politically suspect, a producer fired the girl. A New York TV station refused to show Charlie Chaplin films produced in 1916 and 1917 because of the comedian's presumed radicalism. Between 1948 and 1954, Hollywood churned out more than forty anticommunist films, bearing such titles as *The Red Menace* and *I Married a Communist*. One studio even canceled a film on Longfellow, explaining that Hiawatha had tried to stop wars

between Indian tribes and that some might see the Indian's effort as communist propaganda for peace.

The presidential campaign of 1948 poured yet more fuel on the fires of national anxiety. Truman ran hard as the United States' number-one anticommunist. He described the international communist menace in the most demonic terms. He depicted rival candidate Henry Wallace as a Stalinist dupe, and Wallace's Progressive party as a tool of Moscow. Truman even accused the Republicans of being "unwittingly the ally of the communists in this country." The GOP responded in kind, dubbing the Democrats as "the party of treason." Republican Richard M. Nixon, running for reelection as a congressman from California, brazenly charged the Democrats with responsibility for "the unimpeded growth of the communist conspiracy in the United States."

To blunt the force of such accusations, Truman's Justice Department in 1948 prosecuted eleven top leaders of the American Communist party under the Smith Act of 1940, which outlawed any conspiracy to advocate the overthrow of the government. The result was the conviction and jailing of American citizens for their rhetoric, not for any actual acts of violence or espionage. In 1951 the Supreme Court added to the spiraling panic. Upholding the heavy fines and prison terms levied on the communist officials, the justices, in *Dennis v. U.S.*, described the Communist party as a "highly organized conspiracy" and narrowed the guarantees of the First Amendment by asserting that Congress had the power to curtail freedom of speech when its members concluded that the national security demanded such restriction.

Ironically, the Communist party was fading into obscurity at the very time when American leaders were most intent on magnifying the threat that it posed. By 1950 its membership had shrunk to fewer than thirty thousand. Yet Truman's attorney general that year warned that American Reds "are everywhere—in factories, offices, butcher stores, on street corners, in private businesses— and each carries in himself the germ of death for society."

Hiss and the Rosenbergs

No single episode did more to set off alarms of a diabolic Red conspiracy within the national government than the case of Alger Hiss. In the midst of the 1948 presidential campaign, HUAC conducted a hearing in which Whittaker Chambers, a senior editor at *Time* magazine and former Soviet agent who had broken with the communists in 1938, identified Hiss as an underground party member in the 1930s. The contrasts between the two men could not have been more dramatic. Chambers, the rumpled, repentant ex-communist, appeared a tortured soul crusading to save the West from the Red peril. The elegant Hiss seemed the very symbol of the liberal establishment. A distinguished graduate of Johns Hopkins University and Harvard Law School, Hiss had clerked for Supreme Court Justice Oliver Wendell Holmes before joining the Department of Agriculture in the New Deal. During World War II, he had worked for the State Department (even serving as a presidential adviser at Yalta and helping to organize the founding conference of the United Nations), and after the war he directed the Carnegie Endowment for International Peace, a private foundation promoting ways to avert war. Coolly and calmly, Hiss initially denied any communist affiliation and claimed not even to know Chambers.

Most liberals believed Hiss. They thought that he was being persecuted by a conservative congressional committee bent on tarnishing everything associated with New Deal liberalism. The administration rushed to his defense. Truman denounced Chambers's allegation as a "red herring" to deflect attention from the failures of the Republican Eightieth Congress in an election year.

But to many of those who harbored suspicions about the Rooseveltian liberal tradition, Chambers's persistence and Hiss's fumbling retreat intensified fears that the Democratic administration might be teeming with communists. Under rigorous questioning by Congressman Richard Nixon, a HUAC member, the former New Dealer relented and admitted that he had known Chambers and had even let Chambers have his car and live in his apartment. Still, Hiss denied ever having been a communist. When Chambers repeated his accusation on the national radio program "Meet the Press," Hiss sued him for slander. Chambers then broadened his accusation, claiming that Hiss had committed espionage in the 1930s by giving him secret State Department documents to be transmitted to the Soviet Union. To prove his charge, Chambers produced microfilm copies of confiden-

tial government papers that had been reproduced on a typewriter once owned by Hiss.

A now shaken Hiss protested his innocence, but a grand jury indicted him for perjury, or lying under oath. (The statute of limitations for espionage prevented a charge of treason.) A first trial ended in a hung jury, but a second resulted in a conviction in January 1950. Hiss was sentenced to five years in federal prison. Congressional conservatives were emboldened. Sympathetic to Nixon's characterization of the case as "the most treasonable conspiracy in American history," they relentlessly stalked other Hisses. Democrats were prime targets: Republican senator William E. Jenner charged that the rival party comprised a "crazy assortment of collectivist cutthroat crackpots and communist fellow-traveling appeasers." Who knew how many other bright young New Dealers had been spies? Who knew how many other privileged individuals in high places had betrayed the country?

Just as the Hiss affair ended, another shocking case of espionage alarmed Americans about their government's internal security. In early February 1950, the British arrested Klaus Fuchs, a German-born scientist involved in the Manhattan Project, for having passed atomic secrets to the Soviets during the Second World War. Fuchs's confession led to the arrest of his American accomplice, Harry Gold, who then implicated David Greenglass, a machinist who had worked at Los Alamos. After intensive questioning by the FBI, Greenglass named his sister and brother-in-law, Ethel and Julius Rosenberg, as co-conspirators in the wartime atomic spy network. The children of Jewish immigrants, the Rosenbergs lived on New York's Lower East Side, frequently spoke Yiddish, and strongly identified with the victims of Nazism. Refusing to confess, they insisted that they were victims of anti-Semitism and were being persecuted for their leftist political beliefs. Primarily on the testimony of their alleged accomplices, Gold and Greenglass, a jury in March 1951 found the Rosenbergs guilty of conspiring to commit espionage. The trial judge sentenced them to die by electrocution in New York's Sing Sing prison.

The severity of the punishment reflected the anticommunist fever that consumed the United States during the Korean War years. So did the opinion of the trial judge, who blamed the Rosenbergs for handing the Soviets the classified infor-

Ethel and Julius Rosenberg

The couple are shown in 1951 leaving the New York City federal court after their arraignment on spy charges.

mation that enabled them to build an A-bomb, thereby precipitating the communist aggression in Korea. Although offered clemency if they named other spies, neither Rosenberg would confess. "We are the first victims of American fascism," maintained Ethel Rosenberg in her last letter. On June 19, 1953, the Rosenbergs were executed.

At this point, few Americans could separate fact from fantasy. For many only a conspiracy theory could explain American weakness and Russian might. Republicans eagerly seized on such a theory. The "traitorous actions" of high government officials in the Roosevelt and Truman administrations had hobbled the United States and helped the Soviet Union, claimed GOP accusers, frustrated by their unexpected failure to unseat Truman in 1948. Doomed to four more years of what was already the longest exile from the White House that either party had endured since the Civil War, the GOP abandoned all restraint in 1949 in hurling accu-

sations that the "Commiecrats" had sold out America's security.

McCarthyism

No individual would scourge liberals and Democrats as audaciously and inflict as many mortal wounds as Republican senator Joseph R. McCarthy of Wisconsin. Desperate for a winning issue on which to run for reelection in 1952, McCarthy noted the attention accorded his fellow Republicans for their attacks on the Democrats as "soft on communism." Following suit, on February 9, 1950, McCarthy boldly trumpeted to a GOP women's meeting in Wheeling, West Virginia, that communists in the State Department were undermining American power in world affairs. "I have here in my hand a list of 205," McCarthy announced as he brazenly waved a laundry list, "a list of names known to the Secretary of State as being members of the Communist party and who nevertheless are still working and shaping policy." Although he could not produce evidence to back up his statement, the combination of his senatorial stature and sensational style gave him a national forum. McCarthy repeated his accusation in other speeches in the next few days, reducing his numbers to 81 and then 57 and toning down the rhetoric of his indictment from "card-carrying communists" to "subversives" to "bad risks." A Senate committee investigating the matter branded McCarthy's charges "a fraud and a hoax," but the junior senator from Wisconsin ranted on.

Buoyed by the partisan usefulness of Senator McCarthy's onslaught, Republicans encouraged even more accusations. "Joe, you're a dirty s.o.b.," declared Ohio senator John Bricker, "but there are times when you've got to have an s.o.b. around, and this is one of them." Even the normally fair-minded Robert Taft urged McCarthy "to keep talking, and if one case doesn't work, try another." He did just that, and *McCarthyism* quickly became a synonym for public charges of disloyalty without sufficient regard for evidence.

As the Korean War dragged on and Americans became irate and increasingly vulnerable to demogoguery, McCarthy's outlandish efforts to (in his words) "root out the skunks" escalated. He ridiculed Secretary of State Dean Acheson as the "Red Dean" and lashed out at Truman's dismissal of

General Douglas MacArthur as "the greatest victory the communists have ever won." In mid-1951 the senator charged that Secretary of Defense George C. Marshall, "a man steeped in falsehood," had "aided and abetted a communist conspiracy so immense as to dwarf any previous such venture in the history of man." A year later he referred to the Democratic governor of Illinois as "Alger—I mean Adlai—" Stevenson and accused him of being "Kremlin-directed."

McCarthy's underhanded attacks appealed most to midwestern Republicans indignant about the welfare state, restrictions on business, and the Europe-first emphasis of Truman's foreign policy. For them anticommunism was a weapon of revenge against the liberals and internationalists, and a bid to regain the controlling position that conservative forces had once held in American life. But McCarthy also won a devoted following among blue-collar workers who identified with the senator's charge that a person was either a true American or one of those "egg-sucking phony liberals." Laborers widely praised his insistence that the war against communism had to be fought with brass knuckles, not kid gloves. His flag-waving patriotic appeals held a special attraction for traditionally Democratic Catholic ethnics, who sought to gain acceptance as "100 percent Americans" through displays of anticommunist zeal. Countless Americans also shared McCarthy's hatred of privilege and gentility, of the "bright young men who are born with silver spoons in their mouths," of the "striped-pants boys in the State Department."

McCarthy's political power rested not only on the Republican establishment's support but also on Democrats' fears of antagonizing him. The widespread backing of McCarthy by his GOP colleagues made Democratic condemnations of the senator's ruthless tactics seem like mere partisan criticism. And when he helped several Republican candidates in the 1950 congressional elections to unseat prominent Democrats who had denounced him, McCarthy appeared politically invincible. He had campaigned primarily against Millard Tydings, the conservative Democratic senator from Maryland who had chaired the committee that dismissed McCarthy's initial accusations, and he contributed significantly to Tydings's defeat in 1950. "The ghost of Senator Tydings hangs over the Senate," a Washington reporter observed in 1951.

"Look out for McCarthy" became the Senate watchword. "Joe will go that extra mile to destroy you," warned the new majority leader, Lyndon B. Johnson of Texas. However much Democratic members of Congress detested him, few now dared incur his wrath.

The Korean War and the Rosenbergs' conviction further stoked the fires of hysterical anticommunism that sustained McCarthy. Such topics as civil rights and the admission of Communist China to the United Nations became taboo to discuss in public. Some who read liberal magazines chose to purchase them at a newsstand rather than appear on their subscription list. And Congress, which had cited only 113 witnesses for contempt from 1857 to 1949, named 117 from 1950 to 1952.

Over Truman's veto federal lawmakers in 1950 adopted the McCarran Internal Security Act, which required all organizations deemed to be communist by the attorney general to register with the Department of Justice and to furnish membership lists and financial statements. The measure also barred communists from employment in defense plants, empowered the government to deny passports to communists and to deport any alien suspected of subversion, and authorized the arrest and detention during a national emergency of "any person as to whom there is reason to believe might engage in acts of espionage or sabotage." The McCarran-Walter Immigration and Nationality Act, passed in 1952, again over the president's veto, reaffirmed the quota system based on national origins that severely restricted immigration from southern and eastern Europe. The measure also strengthened the attorney general's authority to exclude and deport aliens suspected of supporting communism.

The Election of 1952

By 1952 public apprehension about the loyalty of government employees combined with frustration over the Korean stalemate to sink Democratic presidential hopes to their lowest level since the 1920s. Moreover, both business and labor resented Truman's decision to freeze wages and prices during the Korean conflict. And evidence of corruption in government further plagued the Democratic party. Revelations of bribery and influence peddling by some of Truman's old political asso-

Dwight Eisenhower and Richard Nixon at the Republican Convention, 1952

The revelation that then-senator Nixon had benefited from a private fund raised by California businessmen posed a dilemma for Eisenhower, who had vowed that his administration would be as "clean as a hound's tooth." But Nixon's melodramatic appeal, which was nationally televised, saved the day, and the Republicans went on to win the election.

and wit made liberal intellectuals campaign "madly for Adlai." But Stevenson could not disassociate himself from the unpopular Truman, and his lofty speeches failed to stir the average voter. Most of all, he could not overcome the popular sentiment that twenty years of Democratic rule was enough and that, as the Republican propaganda proclaimed, "It's time for a change."

Compounding Democratic woes, the GOP nominated popular war hero Dwight D. Eisenhower. In 1948 the nonpartisan Eisenhower had rejected Democratic pleas that he head their ticket, insisting that "lifelong professional soldiers should abstain from seeking higher political office." But in 1952 he answered the call issued by the moderate eastern wing of the Republican party, which needed a strong candidate to challenge the isolationist and conservative forces arrayed with Ohio senator Robert A. Taft. Eisenhower's supporters outmaneuvered Taft's in a battle over contested delegates and succeeded in getting "Ike" nominated on the first ballot. As a concession to the hard-line anticommunist sentiment in the party, Eisenhower accepted as his running mate Senator Richard M. Nixon of California, the former HUAC Red hunter who had taken the lead in exposing Alger Hiss and had won a seat in the Senate in 1950 by redbaiting his opponent, Helen Gahagan Douglas, as "pink right down to her underwear."

Eisenhower and Nixon proved an unbeatable duo. With his captivating grin and unimpeachable record of public service, Eisenhower projected both personal warmth and the vigorous authority associated with military command. His smile, wrote one commentator, "was also a philosophical statement. It was a smile of infinite reassurance," promising benevolence and caring. In a time of uneasiness, Ike symbolized the stability for which Americans yearned. At the same time, Nixon kept public apprehensions at the boiling point. He accused the Democrats of treason, derided the

ciates, together with the president's stubborn insistence that "my house is always clean"—despite clear evidence to the contrary—gave the Republicans ammunition for charging the party in power with "plunder at home, and blunder abroad." In a late-1951 Gallup poll, Truman's standing dropped to an all-time low of 23 percent. Early in 1952 he announced that he would not seek reelection.

In his place the dispirited Democrats drafted the governor of Illinois, Adlai Stevenson. Although a reluctant candidate, Stevenson promised to "talk sense to the American people," and his eloquence

The Election of 1952

Candidates	Parties	Electoral Vote	Popular Vote	Percentage of Popular Vote
DWIGHT D. EISENHOWER	Republican	442	33,936,234	55.1
Adlai E. Stevenson	Democratic	89	27,314,992	44.4

Democratic candidate as "Adlai the appeaser . . . who got a Ph.D. from Dean Acheson's College of Cowardly Communist Containment," and charged that a Stevenson victory would bring "more Alger Hisses, more atomic spies."

The GOP ticket momentarily stumbled when newspapers revealed the existence of a secret "slush fund" collected by California business leaders to keep Richard Nixon in "financial comfort." However, Nixon saved his candidacy with a heart-tugging television defense of his actions. Identifying himself with the average American struggling to make it, a choked-up Nixon explained the gifts as intended to benefit his family. The bathos of his appeal won over the audience. Eisenhower then ensured a GOP landslide by his last-minute pledge to "go to Korea" to end the stalemated war. He won 55 percent of the popular vote and cracked the solid South to carry thirty-nine states, amassing 442 electoral votes to Stevenson's 89. Ike also managed to pull enough Republicans into office

on his coattails to give the GOP control of both houses of Congress, though by small margins.

Dan Collins was typical of the many Americans who voted for Eisenhower and Nixon in 1952. Collins had suffered through the Great Depression and fought overseas in World War II. In 1946 he returned to Boston and civilian status, "hoping to relax, get rich, and enjoy a bit of the good life." He earned more money in construction than he had previously dreamed possible and gained reassurance from his family values, religion, and patriotism. But recurrent international crises, Soviet expansionism abroad coupled with fears of communist infiltration at home, and the specter of atomic war intruded on his peace of mind. By 1951 Collins had concluded that "McCarthy must be on target in attacking those liberals in Washington." The following year, believing the Truman administration "riddled with Reds and corruption," Collins, a staunch Democrat, decided that "it was time to give the other guys a chance."

Conclusion

Thanks to voters like Dan Collins, the election of 1952 terminated two decades of uninterrupted Democratic rule in the White House. It also marked the close of the early postwar era. That era had seen some notable economic successes. Confounding the pessimists who had gloomily predicted that the depression would come roaring back once wartime production ended, the nation not only made the transition to a peacetime economy but achieved high levels of prosperity and employment.

But the postwar years were also a time of enormous ironies. The costly military triumph that Americans celebrated in 1945 opened the door to a different but seemingly equally dreadful conflict with the Soviet Union. Whether the Cold War would ignite a global nuclear war remained very much in doubt as the Truman administration ended. Domestically, the era that was to have ushered in tranquillity and harmony instead brought bitter partisanship and an ugly mood of suspicion and repression.

The early postwar period laid the groundwork for trends that would mold American history for half a century. The Cold War rhetoric of the Truman years influenced an entire generation's perceptions of the world. The imperatives of the anticommunist offensive provided the rationale for a vast strengthening of presidential power that would fundamentally reorient the nature of the federal government. And the first stirrings of civil-rights activism and of America's involvement in Vietnam represented overtures to the issues that would dominate American life in the 1960s.

But most Americans had little inkling of these long-term historical currents in 1952. They vaguely sensed that the bright promise of August 1945 had somehow slipped away, but they looked with hope to a new president and a new decade. Ike's infectious grin seemed an omen of better times ahead.

CHRONOLOGY

1945 Massive labor strikes.

Harry S Truman proposes twenty-one-point program of economic reforms.

1946 Full Employment Act.

Winston Churchill delivers his "iron curtain" speech.

Coal miners' strike.

More than a million GIs enroll in college.

Inflation soars to more than 18 percent.

Republicans win control of Congress.

1947 Truman Doctrine.

Truman orders Loyalty Review Program.

Taft-Hartley Act.

Marshall Plan proposed to aid Europe.

President's Committee on Civil Rights issues *To Secure These Rights*.

1948 Communist coup in Czechoslovakia.

State of Israel founded.

Soviet Union begins blockade of Berlin.

Congress approves Marshall Plan.

Truman orders an end to segregation in the armed forces.

Communist leaders put on trial under the Smith Act.

Truman elected president.

1949 North Atlantic Treaty Organization (NATO) established.

West Germany founded as a separate nation.

National Housing Act.

Communist victory in China.

Soviet Union detonates an atomic bomb.

1950 Truman authorizes building a hydrogen bomb.

Soviet spy ring uncovered at Los Alamos.

Alger Hiss convicted of perjury.

Joseph McCarthy launches anticommunist crusade.

Korean War begins.

Julius and Ethel Rosenberg arrested as atomic spies.

McCarran Internal Security Act.

Truman accepts NSC-68.

China enters the Korean War.

1951 Douglas MacArthur dismissed from his Korean command.

Supreme Court upholds Smith Act.

Rosenbergs convicted of espionage.

1952 First hydrogen bomb exploded.

Dwight D. Eisenhower elected president; Republicans win control of Congress.

For Further Reading

David Caute, *The Great Fear: The Anti-Communist Purge Under Truman and Eisenhower* (1978). A bitterly critical view of the impact of McCarthyism.

Robert J. Donovan, *Conflict and Crisis* (1977) and *Tumultuous Years* (1982). Highly readable narratives of the Truman presidency.

John L. Gaddis, *The United States and the Origins of the Cold War* (1972). The most comprehensive and dispassionate examination of the major issues.

Robert Griffith and Athan Theoharis, eds., *The Specter: Original Essays on the Cold War and the Origins of McCarthyism* (1974). A collection of revisionist interpretations.

Alonzo L. Hamby, *Beyond the New Deal: Harry S. Truman and American Liberalism* (1973). A positive assessment of Truman's efforts to preserve and extend the New Deal.

J. Joseph Huthmacher, ed., *The Truman Years* (1972). Balanced appraisals of key postwar problems.

Walter LaFeber, *America, Russia and the Cold War, 1945–1984* (rev. ed., 1984). The soundest and most succinct revisionist perspective on the course of American foreign policy.

Earl Latham, *The Communist Controversy in Washington* (1966). A thorough treatment of the second Red Scare that emphasizes Republican partisanship.

Theodore J. Lowi, *The End of Liberalism* (1969). A theoretical critique of the "interest-group liberalism" practiced after the New Deal.

Daniel Yergin, *Shattered Peace: The Origins of the Cold War and the National Security State* (1977). An explanation of the flaws in American policy that stem from misunderstandings.

Additional Bibliography

General Works

Robert H. Ferrell, *Harry S. Truman and the Modern American Presidency* (1983); Eric F. Goldman, *The Crucial Decade—and After* (1960); Joseph G. Goulden, *The Best Years, 1945–1950* (1976); Donald McCoy, *The Presidency of Harry S. Truman* (1984); Gary W. Reichard, *Politics as Usual: The Age of Truman and Eisenhower* (1988); Carl Solberg, *Riding High: America in the Cold War* (1973).

The Cold War

Terry H. Anderson, *The United States, Great Britain, and the Cold War, 1944–1947* (1981); Lynn Ethridge Davis, *The Cold War Begins: Soviet-American Conflict over Eastern Europe* (1974); Herbert Feis, *From Trust to Terror: The Onset of the Cold War* (1970); John L. Gaddis, *Strategies of Containment: A Critical Appraisal of Postwar American National Security Policy* (1982); Lloyd Gardner, *Architects of Illusion: Men and Ideas in American Foreign Policy, 1941–1949* (1970); Gregg Herken, *The Winning Weapon: The Atomic Bomb in the Cold War, 1945–1950* (1980); Timothy P. Ireland, *Creating the Entangling Alliance: The Origins of NATO* (1981); Joyce Kolko and Gabriel Kolko, *The Limits of Power: The World and United States Foreign Policy, 1945–1954* (1972); Bruce Kuklick, *American Policy and the Division of Germany* (1972); Bruce R. Kuniholm, *The Origins of the Cold War in the Near East* (1980); Robert L. Messer, *The End of an Alliance* (1982); Thomas G. Paterson, *On Every Front: The Making of the Cold War* (1979); Imanuel Wexler, *The Marshall Plan Revisited* (1983); Lawrence Wittner, *American Intervention in Greece, 1943–1949* (1982).

The Cold War in Asia

Robert M. Blum, *Drawing the Line: The Origins of the American Containment Policy in East Asia* (1982); Russell D. Buhite, *Soviet-American Relations in Asia, 1945–1954* (1982); Bruce Cumings, *The Origins of the Korean War* (1981); Charles M. Dobbs, *The Unwanted Symbol: American Foreign Policy, the Cold War, and Korea, 1945–1950* (1981); Joseph G. Goulden, *Korea: The Untold Story of the War* (1982); Akira Iriye, *The Cold War in Asia* (1974); Burton Kaufman, *The Korean War* (1986); Robert J. McMahon, *Colonialism and the Cold War* (1981); Lewis Purifey, *Harry Truman's China Policy: McCarthyism and the Diplomacy of Hysteria, 1947–1951* (1976); William W. Stueck, Jr., *The Road to Confrontation: American Foreign Policy Toward China and Korea, 1947–1950* (1981).

Domestic Issues and Problems

Jack S. Ballard, *The Shock of Peace: Military and Economic Demobilization After World War II* (1983); William C. Berman, *The Politics of Civil Rights in the Truman Administration* (1970); Bert Cochran, *Harry Truman and the Crisis Presidency* (1973); Richard Dalfiume, *Desegregation of the U.S. Armed Forces: Fighting on Two Fronts, 1939–1953* (1969); Susan M. Hartmann, *Truman and the 80th Congress* (1971); Francis H. Heller, ed., *Economics and the Truman Administration* (1981); Maeva Marcus, *Truman and the Steel Seizure Case: The Limits of Presidential Power* (1977); Norman D. Markowitz, *The Rise and Fall of the People's Century: Henry A. Wallace and American Liberalism, 1941–1948* (1973); Monte S. Poen, *Harry S Truman Versus the Medical Lobby* (1979); Athan Theoharis, ed., *The Truman*

Presidency: The Origins of the Imperial Presidency and the National Security State (1979); Allen Yarnell, *Democrats and Progressives: The 1948 Presidential Election as a Test of Postwar Liberalism* (1974).

The Cold War at Home

Michael Belknap, *Cold War Political Justice: The Smith Act, the Communist Party, and American Civil Liberties* (1977); Larry Ceplair and Steven Englund, *The Inquisition in Hollywood: Politics in the Film Community, 1930–1960* (1980); John P. Diggins, *Up from Communism* (1975); Robert Booth Fowler, *Believing Skeptics: American Political Intellectuals, 1945–1964* (1978); Richard Freeland, *The Truman Doctrine and the Origins of McCarthyism* (1972); Richard M. Fried, *Men Against McCarthy* (1976); Robert Griffith, *The Politics of Fear: Joseph R. McCarthy and the Senate* (1970); Stanley Kutler, *The American Inquisition* (1982); Mary Sperling McAuliffe, *Crisis on the Left: Cold War Politics and American Liberals, 1947–1954* (1978); William L. O'Neill, *A Better World: Stalinism and American Intellectuals* (1983); David M. Oshinsky, *A Conspiracy So Immense: The World of Joe McCarthy* (1983); Ronald Radosh and Joyce Milton, *The Rosenberg File* (1983); Thomas C. Reeves, *The Life and Times of Joe McCarthy* (1982); Michael P. Rogin, *The Intellectuals and McCarthy* (1967); Walter Schneir and Miriam Schneir, *Invitation to an Inquest* (rev. ed., 1983); Athan Theoharis, ed., *Beyond the Hiss Case: The FBI, Congress, and the Cold War* (1982); Allen Weinstein, *Perjury: The Hiss-Chambers Case* (1978).

CHAPTER 28

America at Midcentury

"It starts with these giant ants that crawl out of the ground from that place in New Mexico where they tested the atomic bomb—Alamogordo. They're desperate for sugar, and they rip apart anybody who gets in their way. It ends in the sewers of Los Angeles—and it's *really* scary!"

The year was 1954, and moviegoers all across America were shivering in terror at *Them!*, the giant-ant film that was part of a wave of mutant movies pouring out of Hollywood in the fifties. The atomic bomb and nuclear radiation played a big role in these productions. In *The Incredible Shrinking Man*, the unlucky hero is accidentally exposed to "atomic dust" and begins to shrink. In *The Attack of the Fifty-Foot Women*, the process is reversed; and nuclear testing spawns a giant octopus in *It Came from Beneath the Sea*.

These bizarre horror movies had their roots in a very real concern: the fear of radioactive fallout from atmospheric nuclear tests conducted in the Pacific by the United States and the Soviet Union. These tests pumped into the world's environment towering radioactive clouds containing strontium 90, a deadly cancer-causing chemical that accumulates in the teeth and bone marrow, especially of infants and children.

Deep public apprehension about nuclear tests was one component of this complex and fascinating period, sometimes called the Eisenhower Era after the president who served from 1953 to 1961. Oddly enough, however, the stark realities of the fifties quickly dimmed in the public consciousness in subsequent years. Indeed, the late sixties brought an outpouring of nostalgia for the "nifty fifties." In the distorting mirror of memory, the decade came to seem nothing more than a peaceful time of prosperity and easy living, of cheap gasoline and big cars, of comfortable suburban homes and family togetherness. The late-sixties mass media portrayed the preceding decade as a sunny time when almost everybody liked Ike and loved Lucy. Hollywood films and TV programs re-created the lives of the "typical" fifties teen-agers, who wore pedal pushers and circle skirts, did the bunny hop and hand jive, danced to "Sh-Boom" and "The Purple People-Eater," and idolized Elvis Presley.

Like most historical generalizations, this image of the fifties contains elements of truth. Many Americans did in fact enjoy the fruits of the decade's consumer culture. Having endured the hard times of the depression and war years, they reveled in a widespread prosperity presided over by a popular and trustworthy president. They had confidence in Dwight Eisenhower's vow to "wage peace" and welcomed the thaw in the Cold War that followed the end of the Korean War. And no doubt some high schoolers did lead the carefree, fun-filled existence captured in later media images.

Yet for a full picture of the fifties, we must look beyond the stereotypes. The decade had a darker side as well. Persistent worries not only about the dangers of radioactive fallout but also about the possibility of a nuclear holocaust tempered Americans' optimism. The nuclear-arms race loomed balefully over the decade and intensified popular longings for security.

In reality, this decade—sometimes portrayed as placid, uncomplicated, and worry-free—saw the birth of the space age, of hydrogen bombs and intercontinental ballistic missiles (ICBMs), of the African-American struggle for racial justice, and of an automated, computerized new industrial society. Television transformed life, as did the baby boom, mass suburbanization, and a remarkable internal migration. Midcentury America encompassed peace and a widening Cold War, prosperity and persistent poverty, civil-rights triumphs and rampant racism. So while the fifties were good years for many Americans, they were also a time when the seeds of future crises were sown.

The Eisenhower Presidency

Rarely in our history has a president better fit the national mood than did Dwight David Eisenhower. By 1953 Americans had endured a quarter-century of unrelenting upheaval—first a stock-market crash and crippling depression, and later a devastating world war and a menacing Cold War. Since the end of the war, they had craved peace and stability. This is what Eisenhower delivered. Ending "Truman's folly" in Korea, he kept the nation prosperous and out of war. Even the defeated Democratic candidate in the 1952 election conceded that the new president suited the temper of the times. "I agree that it is time for catching our breath," said Adlai Stevenson; "I agree that moderation is the spirit of the time." Although Eisenhower's moderate policies ultimately frustrated both conservatives and liberals, they proved to be just what most Americans desired. The people overwhelmingly approved Eisenhower's "middle way" between the "untrammeled freedom of the individual" and "government by bureaucracy." Seemingly an amateur outside the political fray, Eisenhower gave a people weary of partisanship a sense of unity. In place of continued turmoil, he encouraged tranquility; in place of insecurity, he inspired confidence.

Immensely popular throughout his two terms, Eisenhower epitomized the virtues as well as the hopes of many Americans. The most distinguished general of the Second World War, he nevertheless projected the image of a plain but good man. He expressed complicated issues in simple moral terms yet efficiently governed a highly complex urban, technological society. At once the hero who had vanquished Hitler and a grandfatherly figure with twinkling blue eyes and an ear-to-ear grin, Ike comforted an anxious people.

The General as Chief Executive

Born on October 14, 1890, in Denison, Texas, Dwight Eisenhower grew up in Abilene, Kansas, in a poor yet warmly loving, strongly religious family. More athletic than studious, he graduated from the U.S. Military Academy at West Point in 1915 and began his career as an army officer. Appointed primary aide to army chief of staff General George Marshall just five days after the bombing of Pearl Harbor, he quickly demonstrated his flair for war planning and organization. In 1942 he directed the American invasion of North Africa, and in 1944 he assumed the post of supreme commander of the Allied forces on the Western Front. Well liked during the war for his genial, democratic manner, and respected for his managerial ability and talent for conciliation, Ike emerged as an inspirational figure of heroic stature.

Eisenhower's approach to the presidency, reflecting his wartime leadership style, differed markedly from that of his Democratic predecessors. He devoted his time and energy to major matters only, and he worked hard to bring contending factions together. His restrained view of presidential authority stemmed in part from his respect for the constitutional balance of power, which he believed Franklin Roosevelt had abused by concentrating decision making in his own hands. It also reflected Eisenhower's sense of the dignity of the Oval Office, which he felt had been demeaned by Truman's propensity to feud with lawmakers.

Dwight David Eisenhower

"The public loves Ike," observed a columnist in 1959. "The less he does, the more they love him. That, probably, is the secret. Here is a man who doesn't rock the boat."

In stark contrast, the new president rarely intervened publicly in the legislative process, shunned using his office as a "bully pulpit," and assured his cabinet members that he would "stay out of [their] hair." He established an orderly chain of command in which everything moved through channels. "I am not one of those desk-pounding types that likes to stick out his jaw and look like he is bossing the show," Eisenhower explained. He delegated the affairs of government to subordinates, considered issues after they had been digested into single-page summaries, and conferred primarily with his top aides only.

Eisenhower's low-key style, taken in conjunction with his frequent fishing and golfing vacations, led Democrats to scoff at him as a leader who "reigned but did not rule." In truth, however,

Ike battled hard behind the scenes. His carefully cultivated image of passivity masked an active and occasionally ruthless politician. By sometimes deliberately talking in gobbledygook, he avoided unnecessary commitments and kept his options open. "Don't worry, Jim," he told his press secretary, who was nervously anticipating a query on a tough issue. "If that question comes, I'll just confuse them."

"Dynamic Conservatism"

Determined to govern the nation on sound business principles, Eisenhower staffed his administration predominately with corporate executives. "Eight millionaires and a plumber," jested one journalist describing the new cabinet. The president hoped to make good on one cabinet member's boast that "we're here in the saddle as an administration representing business and industry." To that end, Eisenhower in his first year worked with Congress to reduce farm-price subsidies, to cut the number of government employees, and to slash the federal budget. He also promoted private rather than public development of hydroelectric and nuclear power and won congressional approval of a bill that turned over to the coastal states some $40 billion worth of oil-rich "tidelands" that the Supreme Court had previously awarded to the federal government.

In the main, however, the Eisenhower administration stayed on a centrist, middle-of-the-road course. The corporate outlook espoused by Eisenhower rejected an extreme shift to the right or a return to pre–New Deal Republican policies. More pragmatic than ideological, he wished to reduce government spending and taxes, contain inflation, and govern efficiently. Having to deal with powerful pressure groups and, after 1954, with Democratic majorities in both houses of Congress, he accommodated himself to large-scale labor organizations and social welfarism. Summing up the president's views, his brother and adviser Milton Eisenhower declared: "We should keep what we have, catch our breath for a while, and improve administration; it does not mean moving backward."

Especially desirous of avoiding another depression, President Eisenhower vetoed conservative Republican senator Robert Taft's demand to abolish the Council of Economic Advisers. Indeed, under the leadership of Arthur Burns, who advocated a strong governmental effort to "fine-tune" the economy, the council emerged as Ike's key domestic agency. (Burns was the only government official other than the secretary of state who had a fixed weekly appointment with the president.) Although he had previously denounced deficit financing, the president now advocated using "any and all weapons in the federal arsenal, including changes in monetary and credit policy, modifications of the tax structure, and a speed-up in the construction of public works" to stimulate the economy and check business downturns. When recessions struck in 1953 and 1957, Eisenhower abandoned his goal of a balanced budget in favor of increased spending to restore prosperity.

The president labeled his credo "dynamic conservatism" and "modern Republicanism." He described his position as "conservative when it comes to money and liberal when it comes to human beings." Accordingly, he went along with Congress when it extended social-security benefits to more than 7 million Americans; raised the minimum wage from seventy-five cents to a dollar an hour; added 4 million workers to those eligible for unemployment benefits; and increased federally financed public housing for low-income families. He also approved construction of the St. Lawrence Seaway, linking the Great Lakes and the Atlantic Ocean, and the creation of the Department of Health, Education and Welfare. In 1956, moreover, Eisenhower backed the largest and most expensive public-works program in American history: the Interstate Highway Act, authorizing the building of a forty-one-thousand-mile system of expressways. The freeways that soon began to snake across the United States accelerated suburban growth, heightened Americans' dependency on cars and trucks, hastened the decline of the nation's rail lines, and contributed to the decay of its central cities.

The Republicans renominated Eisenhower by acclamation in 1956, and the electorate handed him a landslide victory. Running on a record of "peace, progress, and prosperity," Ike trounced Democrat Adlai Stevenson for a second time. With the GOP crowing "Everything's booming but the guns," the president even won two-thirds of the non-union labor vote and 45 percent of union members' ballots. Eisenhower garnered nearly 36 million popular votes to Stevenson's 26 million and carried all but seven states to win 457 of the 530 electoral votes.

The Downfall of Joseph McCarthy

Although the president despised Joseph McCarthy—whom he once derided as a "pimple on the path to progress"—Eisenhower feared confronting the senator. Instead, he tried to steal McCarthy's thunder by tightening security requirements for government employees; when that failed, he waited patiently, allowing McCarthy to grab plenty of rope in hopes that the demagogue would hang himself. Eventually McCarthy did just that, but meanwhile, utilizing the platform provided him by his new position as chairman of the Permanent Investigations Subcommittee of the Senate Committee on Government Operations, McCarthy rampaged through the Eisenhower administration. In 1953 he forced the discharge of hundreds of State Department employees whose views he opposed, although no proof existed that any had engaged in subversive activities. McCarthy denounced broadcasters for the Voice of America, a U.S. government radio station beamed at Eastern Europe, for quoting "controversial" authors. He demanded that the United States Information Agency's overseas libraries purge books by "communists, fellow travelers, et cetera." Suddenly banned, and even burned, were the works of such "et ceteras" as Ralph Waldo Emerson, Henry David Thoreau, Mark Twain, and

The Election of 1956				
Candidates	Parties	Electoral Vote	Popular Vote	Percentage of Popular Vote
DWIGHT D. EISENHOWER	Republican	457	35,590,472	57.6
Adlai E. Stevenson	Democratic	73	26,022,752	42.1

Joseph McCarthy

Despite the absurdity of McCarthy's accusations, reporters felt an obligation to report them. One recalled, "Joe couldn't find a communist in Red Square—he didn't know Karl Marx from Groucho— but he was a United States senator."

Whittaker Chambers. Riding high, McCarthy in 1954 even attacked the army for harboring communist spies. The army retaliated by accusing McCarthy of using his influence to gain preferential treatment for a member of his staff who had been drafted.

Congress voted to investigate the charges hurled by McCarthy and by the army, and on April 22, 1954, televised hearings commenced. A national audience that at times topped 20 million witnessed McCarthy's boorish behavior firsthand. His dark scowl, raspy voice, endless interruptions ("point of order, Mr. Chairman, point of order"), and disregard for the rights of others repelled many viewers. He behaved like the bad guy in a TV western, observed novelist John Steinbeck: "He had a stub-

ble of a beard, he leered, he sneered, he had a nasty laugh. He bullied and shouted. He looked evil." Near the end of the hearings, in June, McCarthy crudely slurred the reputation of a young lawyer assisting Joseph Welch, the army counsel. Suddenly the puckish, mild-mannered Welch turned his gentle wrath on McCarthy—"Until this moment, Senator, I think I really never gauged your cruelty or your recklessness. . . . Let us not assassinate this lad further, Senator. You have done enough. Have you no sense of decency, sir, at long last? Have you no sense of decency?" After a moment of silence, the gallery burst into applause.

The spell of the inquisitor thus broken, President Eisenhower now moved to destroy McCarthy. With the GOP no longer needing him to drive the "Commiecrats" from power, and the Democrats eager to be rid of their scourge, the Senate voted 67 to 22 in December 1954 to censure the Wisconsin senator for contemptuous behavior. This powerful rebuke—only the third in the Senate's history—demolished McCarthy as a political force. McCarthyism, Ike gloated, had become "McCarthywasism." Although McCarthy would sling disloyalty charges for several more years, most of his colleagues would leave the Senate chamber whenever he rose to speak, and the media would ignore him.

McCarthy died in 1957, but the fears that he had exploited lingered on. In the late 1950s, Congress annually funded the House Un-American Activities Committee's endless search for suspected radicals, while state and local governments still required teachers to take loyalty oaths. In the name of national security, Americans continued to ban books by left-wingers, to blacklist dissenters in the entertainment industry, and to demand the firing of radical professors.

McCarthyism also remained a rallying call of militant conservatives disenchanted with the postwar consensus on both foreign and domestic matters. The radio news commentaries of Fulton Lewis, Jr., and Clarence Manion; articles in the *National Review* (founded in 1955 by William F. Buckley, Jr., a recent Yale graduate); and the mailings of organizations like the Christian Anti-Communist Crusade and the John Birch Society all warned of a major subversive threat posed by domestic communism. Stressing victory over communism rather than its containment, the "new conservatives" (or radical right, as their opponents called them) also bemoaned the "creeping socialism" of Truman and Eisenhower and advocated a return to older moral standards. While few Americans took seriously the far right's contentions that gun control and fluoridation of drinking water were communist plots, or that Dwight Eisenhower was an agent of a leftist conspiracy, many sympathized with the general drift of conservative criticism. A particular target of that criticism was the nation's highest judicial body, the Supreme Court.

The Warren Court

Considerably liberalized in these years by the presence of a new chief justice, Earl Warren (1953), and three other Eisenhower appointees, the Supreme Court incurred conservatives' wrath for defending the constitutional rights of persons accused of subversive beliefs. In *Jencks* v. *United States* (1957), the Court held that the accused had the right to inspect government files used by the prosecution. In *Yates* v. *United States* (also 1957), the justices overturned the convictions of Communist party officials under the Smith Act (see Chapter 27) and underscored the distinction between the specific advocacy of unlawful acts and the teaching of general revolutionary ideology. Right-wing opponents denounced these and similar rulings, demanded limitations on the Court's powers, and plastered "Impeach Earl Warren" posters on highway billboards.

These condemnations, however, paled beside the bellowings of outraged segregationists following the Supreme Court's landmark decision in *Brown* v. *Board of Education of Topeka* (May 17, 1954). In a unanimous ruling reversing *Plessy* v. *Ferguson* (see Chapter 20), the Court held that separating schoolchildren "solely because of their race generates a feeling of inferiority as to their status in the community that may affect their hearts and minds in a way unlikely ever to be undone" and thus violated the equal-protection clause of the Fourteenth Amendment. "In the field of public education," the nine justices concluded, "the doctrine of 'separate but equal' has no place. Separate educational facilities are inherently unequal." A year later, the Court ordered the states to desegregate their schools "with all deliberate speed."

As the border states quietly complied, Eisenhower directed the school officials of Washington,

"Tsk Tsk — Somebody Should Do Something About That"

Eisenhower and School Integration

Cartoonist Herblock criticized Eisenhower's slowness to act in the crisis over school integration, depicting him as a fireman standing idly by as a building goes up in flames.

D.C., to end segregation in the public classrooms of the nation's capital. The president also mandated the desegregation of such federal facilities as navy yards and veterans' hospitals. But he refused to force white southerners to accept the Court's ruling. "I don't believe you can change the hearts of men with laws or decisions," he observed. Although not a racist, he never publicly endorsed the *Brown* decision, and he privately regretted his appointment of Earl Warren as "the biggest damn fool mistake I ever made."

Encouraged by the lack of presidential support for *Brown,* southern white opposition stiffened. White Citizens Councils committed to all-out defiance of the Court ruling sprang up; the Ku Klux Klan revived. Declaring *Brown* "null, void, and of no effect," southern legislatures claimed the right to "interpose" themselves against the federal government and adopted a strategy of "massive resistance" to thwart compliance with the law. They denied state aid to local school systems that chose to desegregate and even closed down desegregated public schools.

In 1956 more than a hundred members of Congress signed the Southern Manifesto, denouncing *Brown* as "a clear abuse of judicial power." The legislators pledged to "use all lawful means to bring about a reversal of this decision which is contrary to the Constitution and to prevent the use of force in its implementation." White southern politicians competed to "outnigger" each other in unyielding opposition to desegregation. When a gubernatorial candidate in Alabama promised to go to jail to defend segregation, his opponent swore that he would die for it. Many segregationists also resorted to violence and economic reprisals against blacks to maintain all-white schools. At the end of 1956, not a single black attended school with whites in the Deep South, and few did so in the Upper South.

The Laws of the Land

Southern resistance reached a climax in September 1957 when Arkansas governor Orval E. Faubus mobilized the state's National Guard to bar nine black students from entering Little Rock's Central High School under a federal court order. Despite this direct flouting of federal authority, Eisenhower initially did nothing. A new court order soon forced Faubus to withdraw the guardsmen, but their place was taken by a hysterical mob of nearly a thousand jeering whites who blocked the black students' entry.

That night, Eisenhower went on national television to reprehend this "disgraceful occurrence." He ordered the obstructors of federal law "to disperse forthwith." The next day, when the mob openly defied him, the president defended national supremacy and the prestige of his office by placing the Arkansas National Guard under federal command and, for the first time since Reconstruction, by dispatching federal troops to protect blacks' rights. To ensure the blacks' safety, troops patrolled the high school for the rest of the year. But rather than accept desegregation, Faubus shut down all of Little Rock's public high schools in 1958 and 1959. When a federal court ruling finally reopened them, only three blacks attended Central High School. As the fifties ended, fewer than 1 percent of the black students in the Deep South were enrolled in desegregated schools.

Even so, the *Brown* decision and Little Rock were crucial events in the emergence of the struggle for black civil rights. They galvanized the federal government's powers to use the law to mandate changes in the South. And Little Rock in particular foreshadowed television's vital role in the demise of Jim Crow. The contrast between the images of howling, often slovenly, white racists and those of the clean-cut and resolute black students, projected so vividly on the TV screen, immensely aided the civil-rights cause. According to a 1957 public-opinion poll, fully 90 percent of whites outside the South approved the use of federal troops in Little Rock.

Most nonsouthern whites also favored legislation to enfranchise southern blacks. Despite his personal reservations, Eisenhower proposed a voting-rights bill in the midst of the 1956 presidential campaign. Passed the following year, the Civil Rights Act of 1957, the first civil-rights law enacted since Reconstruction, established a permanent commission on civil rights with broad investigatory powers. Unfortunately, the law did little to guarantee the ballot to blacks. The Civil Rights Act of 1960, similarly pared down to appease strong white southern resistance, only slightly strengthened the first measure's enforcement provisions. Neither act empowered federal officials to register blacks to vote, and both proved largely ineffective. Like the *Brown* decision, however, they revealed a new attitude toward racial matters on the part of the federal government and further encouraged blacks to fight for their due.

The Cold War Continues

The Eisenhower administration maintained and consolidated the containment policy inherited from the Truman years. Joseph Stalin's death in 1953 and Dwight Eisenhower's resolve to reduce the risk of nuclear war gradually brought a thaw in the Cold War. But an icy ideological deadlock still powerfully gripped the United States and the Soviet Union. The Cold War did not end, nor did American determination to check communism. Changing times modified the East-West conflict, but containment remained the crux of American foreign policy throughout the 1950s.

Truce in Korea

As his first priority, Eisenhower honored his campaign pledge to go to Korea. Visiting American troops there in December 1952, he could not, however, bring home a settlement. The sticking point in negotiations remained the fate of the thousands of North Korean and Chinese prisoners of war, held by the U.N. forces, who did not want to return to communist rule. Eisenhower insisted on freedom of choice for these POWs, whereas the communist governments of Kim Il Sung and Mao Zedong (Mao Tse-tung) demanded the forcible repatriation of all captives. But in the summer of 1953, the Asian leaders agreed to a compromise, influenced primarily by the uncertainty reigning in the communist world following Stalin's death in March and by Eisenhower's veiled threat to use nuclear weapons to break the stalemate. The armistice signed on July 23, 1953, set the boundary between North and South Korea close to the thirty-eighth parallel, the prewar demarcation line, and established a panel of neutral nations to administer the POWs' return.

The end of the fighting brought relief to many Americans. But while reducing both domestic and international tensions, the peace left Korea divided and its political problems unresolved. Although Eisenhower believed that the United States had vindicated the principle of collective security, by checking aggression and preserving the sovereignty of South Korea, his right-wing critics condemned the truce as peace without honor.

Ike and Dulles

Eager to ease Cold War hostilities through diplomacy, Eisenhower first had to mollify the Republican Old Guard. A powerful phalanx of right-wingers in Congress rejected containment and clamored for more forceful efforts to roll back the Red tide. To placate them while he patiently sought to relax tensions with the Soviet Union, the president chose as his secretary of state John Foster Dulles, a stiff, self-righteous, and bellicose anticommunist.

A rigid Presbyterian whose humorlessness led some to dub him "Dull, Duller, Dulles," the secretary of state talked fervently of a holy war against "atheistic communism." Dulles's moralistic pronouncements led Eisenhower to liken him to "a patriarch out of the Old Testament." In the 1952

Republican platform, Dulles had depicted containment as a "negative, futile, and immoral" policy that sacrificed "countless human beings to a despotism and Godless terrorism." As secretary of state, he called for an offensive aimed at "liberating" the captive peoples of Eastern Europe and unleashing Nationalist leader Jiang Jieshi (Chiang Kai-shek) against Communist China. Condemning neutralism on the part of other nations as "immoral," he threatened "an agonizing reappraisal" of American commitments if its allies did not follow the U.S. lead in each twist and turn of the Cold War. Believing that the Soviet Union understood nothing but force, Dulles insisted on the necessity of "brinksmanship," the art of never backing down in a crisis, even if it meant risking war.

Such saber rattling pleased Republican extremists, but Eisenhower preferred conciliation over force to bring the Cold War under control. Partly because he feared a nuclear war with the Soviet Union, which had successfully tested its own H-bomb in 1953, Eisenhower refused to translate Dulles's rhetoric into action. The president insisted on making his administration's key foreign-policy decisions, often using Dulles as a lightning rod to deflect criticism. "There's only one man I know," he said, "who has seen more of the world and talked with more people and knows more than Dulles does—and that's me." Ike knew enough of war to hate it, and he understood the limits of American power. Thus when East German workers rioted in 1953 and the Hungarians revolted in 1956, the United States did nothing to prevent the Russians from crushing these insurrections. And despite talk of "unleashing" Jiang, the 1954 mutual-defense treaty concluded with Taiwan specifically prohibited the Nationalists from any aggressive ventures without prior consultation with the United States.

Waging Peace

As Hiroshima-size atomic bombs gave way to multimegaton thermonuclear weapons in the American and Soviet arsenals, Eisenhower labored to reduce the possibility of mutual extinction. As he eloquently put it in 1953: "[E]very warship launched, every rocket fired signifies, in the final sense, a theft from those who hunger and are not fed, those who are cold and are not clothed." He proposed before the United Nations an "atoms for

The Space-Age Toy Shop, 1950s

Through the eyes of two innocent children ogling a fantastic assortment of toy doomsday weapons, the cartoonist captured modern society's fascination with the space-age tools of global destruction.

peace" plan, whereby both superpowers would "serve the needs rather than the fears of mankind" by contributing fissionable materials to a new U.N. agency for use in industrial projects. Meanwhile, mounting fears over radioactive fallout from atmospheric atomic tests, especially the 1954 U.S. test series in the Pacific that spread radioactivity over a wide area, heightened world concern about the pell-mell nuclear-arms race.

In 1955 Eisenhower and the Soviet leaders met in Geneva for the first East-West summit conference since the Second World War. The discussions produced no concrete results, but mutual talk of "peaceful coexistence" led reporters to hail the "spirit of Geneva." Although the two nations could not agree on a specific plan for nuclear-arms control, Russia suspended further atmospheric tests of nuclear weapons in March 1958 and did not resume them for the remainder of Eisenhower's term. The United States, after a further test series that spring and summer, followed suit.

Still, the Cold War continued. To "contain" the Soviet Union, the United States encircled it with military bases and alliances. Dulles negotiated mutual-defense pacts with any nation that would join the United States in opposing communism. Thanks to Dulles's "pactomania," as some called it, Americans found themselves committed to the defense of forty-three nations. Primarily, however, the administration relied on the U.S. nuclear arsenal to deter the Soviets. Tailored to suit a cost-conscious president and a fiscally conservative Congress, Washington's "New Look" defense program emphasized nuclear bombs and the planes to deliver them while it cut back on the army and navy. The "New Look," in short, centered on threatening Moscow with "massive retaliation" rather than with the embroilment of U.S. troops in costly "brushfire" wars in remote places. "More bang for the buck," Republicans bragged. But the "New Look" simply spurred the Soviets to seek "more rubble for the ruble" by enlarging their own air force and nuclear stockpile.

Meanwhile, the focus of the Cold War shifted from Europe to the Third World, the largely non-white, developing nations in the southern half of the globe. There the two superpowers covertly waged war by proxy, using local guerrillas and military juntas to battle in isolated deserts and steamy jungles. To counter Soviet premier Nikita Khrushchev's threat of "wars of national liberation," the Eisenhower administration stepped up the role of the Central Intelligence Agency (CIA).

The Clandestine CIA

To command the CIA, Eisenhower chose Allen Dulles, a shrewd veteran of wartime OSS cloak-and-dagger operations and the brother of the secretary of state. Established by the National Security Act of 1947 mainly to conduct espionage and to analyze information on foreign nations, in the 1950s the CIA increasingly became involved in undercover operations to topple regimes believed hostile to the United States. In 1953 the agency successfully plotted with Iranian army officers to overthrow the popularly elected government that had taken possession of the rich oil resources long exploited by Britain. Fearing a precedent that might jeopardize Western oil interests in the Middle East, the CIA secretly returned the deposed shah of Iran to power and restored the oil wells to British firms. As a result, the United States gained a loyal ally on the Russian border, and American oil companies prospered from generous Iranian oil concessions. But the seeds of Iranian hatred of America had been sown—an enmity that would haunt the United States a quarter-century later.

In 1953, to ensure a pro-American government, the CIA also intervened in elections in the Philippines. In 1954 it equipped and trained a force of Guatemalans to stage a military coup against the incumbent regime, which had seized 225,000 acres from the American-owned United Fruit Company. After destroying the radical government, the CIA's Guatemalan agents instituted a military dictatorship subservient to the United States, restored United Fruit's properties, and trampled all political opposition.

The very few Washington officials who knew of these clandestine operations approved them. A congressional committee overseeing the CIA secretly reported in 1955: "It is now clear that we are facing an implacable enemy whose vowed objective is world domination by whatever means and at whatever cost. There are no rules in such a game. Hitherto acceptable norms of conduct do not apply." During his second term, Eisenhower allowed the CIA even greater leeway, and by 1957 more than half of the agency's personnel and 80 percent of its budget were devoted to "covert action." It subverted governments, bribed foreign politicians, and subsidized foreign newspapers and labor unions that hewed to a pro-American line. Unwilling to be pulled into long, costly military conflicts as Truman had been drawn into the Korean War, Eisenhower relied on clandestine CIA activities to bolster the United States' allies and weaken its opponents.

Conflict in Vietnam

Of all secret CIA operations in the second half of the 1950s, the most extensive were in Vietnam. Following Mao Zedong's victory in China in 1949, and especially after the outbreak of the Korean conflict, the United States had begun to view Indochina as an important arena of Cold War confrontation. The Truman administration had furnished the French (who were seeking to reconquer their former colony of Vietnam) with large-scale military assistance to wage war against the Vietminh, a broad-based Vietnamese nationalist coalition of guerrilla fighters led by the communist Ho Chi Minh (see Chapter 27). By 1954 American aid accounted for three-quarters of the French expenditures in the struggle. Still, the French tottered near defeat. In early 1954 the Vietminh trapped some twelve thousand French troops in the valley of Dienbienphu and besieged the garrison.

France appealed to the United States to intervene. Many high-ranking Eisenhower administration officials urged the use of American armed power, including atomic weapons, to assist the French. But the president demurred, prudently claiming that he could not act without the assent of the Democratic-controlled Congress and the cooperation of Britain. In truth, Eisenhower wanted to avoid committing American troops to the fight against a popular liberation movement in the jungles of Vietnam. "No one could be more bitterly opposed to ever getting the United States involved in a hot war in that region than I am," he told a press conference in 1954; "I cannot conceive of a greater tragedy for America." On May 7, 1954, the French surrendered at Dienbienphu, and in July an international conference in Geneva arranged a cease-fire and temporarily divided Vietnam at the seventeenth parallel pending elections in 1956 to determine the government of a unified nation.

Though opposed to committing the United States to another Asian land war, Eisenhower nevertheless feared the consequences of a communist victory in Vietnam. The president made his concern graphic in his "domino theory": "You have a row of dominoes set up, and you knock over the first one, and what will happen to the last one is the certainty that it will go over very quickly. So you have a beginning of a disintegration that would have the most profound influences." If Vietnam fell, Eisenhower warned, nearby Thailand, Burma, and Indonesia, and ultimately all of America's Asian allies, would follow.

Accordingly, Eisenhower had little compunction about ignoring the Geneva settlement. The CIA Mission in Vietnam, established in June 1954, helped install Ngo Dinh Diem, a fiercely anticommunist Catholic, first as premier of France's puppet state and then in 1955 as president of an independent South Vietnam. CIA agents worked closely with Diem to train his armed forces and secret police, to eliminate political opposition, and to block the election to reunify Vietnam that the Geneva agreements had specified. As Eisenhower candidly admitted later in his memoirs, the United States did not want the election held because "possibly 80 percent of the population would have voted for the communist Ho Chi Minh as their leader." Instead, Washington pinned its hopes on Diem to maintain a noncommunist South Vietnam.

But the aloof, autocratic Diem could never rally public support. His Catholicism alienated the predominantly Buddhist population; and his heavy-handed refusal to institute land reform for the peasants and to end massive government corruption created widespread opposition. Diem's repressive policies and his refusal to hold the promised elections led the former Vietminh guerrillas in 1957 to begin sporadic attacks against the Saigon government. In December 1960 the opposition to Diem coalesced in the National Liberation Front of South Vietnam (NLF); organized by the Vietminh and backed by North Vietnam, the insurgents attracted wide support. Diem's position, meanwhile, grew steadily weaker. In conflict with the peasantry, with much of the elite, and even with major units of his own army, he relied on the billions of dollars and the growing corps of U.S. advisers that the Eisenhower administration supplied. When Diem spurned U.S. requests to make the necessary reforms that would undercut the NLF's appeal and gain popular backing for his government, American officials unhappily dropped the matter. Diem was their only alternative to the NLF; so the United States would "sink or swim with Ngo Dinh Diem."

Crisis in the Middle East

Vietnam would become America's gravest world problem in the 1960s, but in the fifties Eisenhower faced his greatest crisis in the seething Middle East. In Egypt the fervent Arab nationalist Gamal Abdel Nasser came to power in 1954, determined to build a great dam at Aswan to harness the Nile River. The United States offered financing. But when Nasser declared neutrality in the Cold War and began to negotiate with the Soviet Union, an infuriated John Foster Dulles canceled the loan. Nasser retaliated by seizing the British-owned Suez Canal (a waterway in northeastern Egypt linking the Mediterranean and the Gulf of Suez) in July 1956,

announcing that he would finance the dam with tolls from the canal. England and France, dependent on the canal for the flow of more than half their oil supply, and Israel, fearful that a mighty Egypt would upset the delicate balance of power in the region, decided to force Nasser to give up the Suez Canal.

Israeli troops stormed into Egypt on October 29, 1956, and two days later, England and France invaded to seize the canal. Eisenhower was furious. He had not been consulted by America's allies, and with Russia vowing to stand by Egypt, he feared that the West's gunboat imperialism might trigger a nuclear war. The president quickly repudiated the Suez expedition and initiated a U.N. resolution condemning the aggression and calling for a British, French, and Israeli withdrawal from Egypt. At the same time, to deter Soviet interference, he ordered the Strategic Air Command on alert. "If those fellows start something, we may have to hit 'em—and, if necessary, with everything in the bucket," he commented. On November 6, with no hope of American support, the invaders announced that their troops would leave Egypt. Eisenhower had averted a larger, more ominous clash.

Nevertheless, the conflict had momentous consequences. First, it vastly swelled anti-West sentiment in the Third World. Second, in its wake the United States took over from England and France the role of protector of Western interests in the Middle East. Moreover, with the Soviet Union's building the Aswan Dam and supplying arms to Syria after the Suez crisis, the Cold War had spread to yet another global region.

"The existing vacuum in the Middle East," Eisenhower announced in January 1957, "must be filled by the United States before it is filled by Russia." Eager to secure oil for the industrial West, the president proclaimed what became known as the Eisenhower Doctrine. He declared that the United States would send military aid and, if necessary, dispatch troops to any Middle Eastern nation that asked for help to counter communist thrusts. Congress approved the doctrine in a joint resolution in March, and in April Eisenhower invoked it to shore up an anticommunist government in Jordan. In 1958 he sent fourteen thousand American marines into Lebanon to protect a pro–United States regime that was being challenged by Nasserite radicals.

Frustrations Abroad

Secretary of State Dulles boasted that such interventions reassured small nations "that they could call on us in a time of crisis." At the same time, however, the U.S. actions augmented the anti-Americanism of neutralists, nationalists, and reformers. When Vice President Nixon visited Peru and Venezuela in 1958, after the overthrow of dictators who had been personally decorated by Eisenhower, rabid crowds spat at him and stoned his car. The following year, Fidel Castro overturned a dictatorial regime in Cuba and denounced "yanqui imperialism," censuring the United States as a "vulture feeding on humanity." When anti-American rioting rocked Japan in 1960, Eisenhower canceled his announced trip to the United States' strongest Asian ally.

The beleaguered president suffered an even tougher blow on May 1, 1960, when, two weeks before a scheduled summit conference with Khrushchev in Paris, Russia shot down a high-altitude U.S. spy plane twelve hundred miles inside Soviet borders. Prior to this incident, Eisenhower had worked diligently to improve Soviet-American relations. His diplomacy in 1958 had defused a potential superpower crisis over the fate of Berlin. In 1959 Nixon had visited the Soviet Union, and Khrushchev had toured the United States. At the presidential retreat at Camp David, Maryland, the two heads of state had held a cordial meeting and agreed to confer in Paris during the coming year.

But they would never meet again. The plane's downing exposed the U-2 reconnaissance missions that the United States had been flying over the Soviet Union since 1956 to spy on Russian military installations. When Khrushchev announced the downing, the Eisenhower administration, denying the charge of espionage, initially maintained that a flight to collect weather data had simply strayed off course. An angry Khrushchev then displayed to the world the captured CIA pilot, the U-2's spy cameras, and photos taken of Soviet missile sites. Belatedly, Washington admitted the spying; but Eisenhower refused the Soviet premier's demands that he apologize for the flights, declaring that they were intended to prevent another Pearl Harbor. The summit collapsed, and Khrushchev canceled an invitation to the president to visit Moscow. A dispirited Eisenhower confided to an aide that "he saw nothing worthwhile left for him to do now until the end of his presidency."

The Eisenhower Legacy

Three days before leaving office, Eisenhower delivered a prophetic message to the American people. Like George Washington, he used the occasion of his farewell address to issue a somber warning. The demands of national security, observed the former soldier who had spent nearly two-thirds of his life in uniform, had produced the "conjunction of an immense military establishment and a large arms

Dulles and Eisenhower

Upon his selection as secretary of state, Dulles remarked to Eisenhower: "With my understanding of the intricate relationships between the peoples of the world and your sensitiveness to the political considerations involved, we will make the most successful team in history."

industry that is new in the American experience." Swollen Cold War defense budgets, he said, had made the health of the nation's economy dependent on military expenditures. Further, for scholars at hundreds of universities and research institutions, politicians from scores of congressional districts, and dozens of America's largest corporations, the U.S.–Soviet political tensions and military rivalry had made increased reliance on military contracts and grants a way of life. This intertwined combination of interests, Eisenhower believed, exerted enormous leverage in the councils of government and threatened the traditional subordination of the military in American life. He warned, "We must guard against the acquisition of unwarranted influence, whether sought or unsought, by the military-industrial complex. The potential for the disastrous rise of misplaced power exists and will persist."

The president concluded with an assessment of his foreign policy: he had avoided war but could not affirm that lasting peace was in sight. Most scholars agreed. He had ended the war in Korea, kept the peace for the next 7½ years, avoided direct military intervention in Vietnam, begun the process of relaxing tensions with the Soviet Union, and even cooperated in achieving a lull in the atmospheric testing of the doomsday weapons that he so abhorred. Yet he had also presided over an accelerating nuclear-arms race and expanded the Cold War; and he had given the CIA the green light to intervene in local conflicts around the globe and committed American power and prestige in Asia and the Middle East to a far greater extent than his predecessors. Eisenhower's failure to adjust American diplomacy to the needs and aspirations of Third World peoples would bequeath to his successors far more intractable problems abroad than even he had inherited.

Nevertheless, the moderate Eisenhower had prevented foreign-policy crises from escalating into conflicts that might have again drawn Americans into armed combat. Balance and restraint also characterized his mixed domestic record. But his middle-of-the-road policies pleased neither liberals nor conservatives. The president's acceptance of the social-welfare legislation of the New Deal and the Fair Deal so annoyed the Republican Right that conservatives grumbled that Ike's memoir of his first term should have been titled *More of the*

Same rather than *Mandate for Change*. Liberals, on the other hand, faulted Eisenhower for not doing enough to solve national problems. His reluctance to provide inspiring leadership in the efforts to quash McCarthyism and racism particularly troubled them. Clearly, however, Ike gave the majority of voters what they wanted, if not what reformers thought they should want. Most yearned for reassurance, and Eisenhower supplied it. He restored dignity to the presidency and a sense of harmony to the nation. As lucky as he was skillful, Eisenhower led the nation during the greatest economic boom in its history; and in an age of almost continuous upheaval and war, he furnished what Americans most desired: a breathing spell in which to relish stability and the comforts of life.

The Affluent Society

When Harvard economist John Kenneth Galbraith published a book about postwar America in 1958, he called it *The Affluent Society*. The title was well chosen: a booming, broad-based prosperity made the 1950s a period of economic abundance without historical parallel. The material aspects of the American dream had seemingly come true. By the end of the 1950s, about 60 percent of all American families owned homes; 75 percent, cars; and 87 percent, at least one TV. The total gross national product (measured in 1958 dollars) climbed from $318 billion in 1950 to $488 billion a decade later, mainly as a consequence of heavy government spending, a huge upsurge in productivity, and a steadily increasing demand for consumer goods and services.

Not all was rosy on the economic front. Three brief recessions marred the prosperity of the Eisenhower Era. In the 1957–1958 downturn, the unemployment rate inched up to 7.6 percent, the highest since the Great Depression. A rising national debt, which reached almost $290 billion by the end of 1960, evoked further worry.

But overall, the economic growth of the fifties brought the United States the highest standard of living the world had ever known. When corrected for inflation, the average American worker's real income in 1960 was 35 percent higher than it had

Gross National Product, 1950–1985

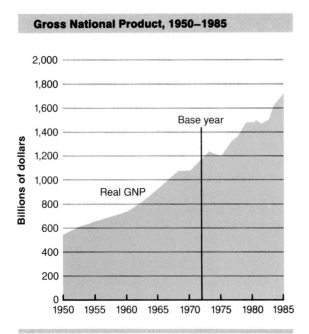

Following World War II, the United States achieved the highest living standard in world history. Between 1950 and 1970, the real GNP, *which factors out inflation and reveals the actual amount of goods and services produced, steadily increased. However, in 1972, 1974–1975, 1980, and 1982 the* real GNP *declined.*
SOURCE: *Economic Report of the President, 1985.*

been in 1945, and twice the level of the prosperous 1920s. With just 6 percent of the world's population, the United States produced and consumed nearly half of everything made and sold on earth.

The New Industrial Society

Government expenditures, a major source of the nation's economic growth and prosperity, nearly doubled in the 1950s. Federal spending leaped from less than $100 billion per year to more than $180 billion by the end of the decade, and the outlays of state and local governments more than kept pace. Although federal expenditures composed just 1 percent of the GNP in 1929, by the mid-1950s they had soared to 17 percent. Federal dollars constructed roads and airports, financed home mortgages, supported farm prices, paid pensions and unemployment benefits, and provided stipends for education. But more than *half* the federal budget

each year—about 10 percent of the GNP—went into the manufacture of bombs, planes, and weaponry. And with continued U.S.–Soviet rivalry in the production of atomic munitions, the development of missile-delivery systems, and the space race, the federal government was the nation's chief sponsor of scientific and technological research and development (R&D) in the 1950s.

Startling breakthroughs in physics, electronics, chemistry, and quantum mechanics revolutionized both the character and the productivity of American industry. As a result of ongoing R&D, chemicals surged from about the fiftieth-largest industry before the war to the nation's fourth largest in the 1960s. From such firms as Dow, Du Pont, and Monsanto came Dacron suits, Orlon shirts, Acrilan socks, Teflon pots and pans, and a host of other synthetic products that transformed the United States into a plastic society. Similarly, electronics grew swiftly to become the fifth-biggest industry

The TV Explosion

The Philco "Slender Seventeener" and other television models brought free entertainment into the home, providing Americans an escape from the anxieties of the fifties.

in the United States. Led by General Electric, Westinghouse, and RCA, the industry sold electrical equipment to other businesses and electrical appliances to consumers. Electric consumption tripled in the 1950s as industry turned to automation and as Americans purchased electric washers and dryers, freezers, blenders, television sets, phonographs, tape recorders, and stereos, as well as electric blankets, electric garage-door openers, and electric pencil sharpeners. Essential to the expansion in both the chemical and the electronics industry was the availability of inexpensive petroleum. With domestic crude-oil production increasing close to 50 percent and petroleum imports rising from 74 million to 371 million barrels between 1945 and 1960, gasoline prices stayed low in the fifties.

Bountiful cheap gasoline also underlay the expansion of the aircraft and automobile industries. The continued growth of aircraft manufacture, the nation's third-largest industry throughout the fifties, also rested on massive government defense spending, on the switch to jet propulsion by commercial aviation, and on the enormous sums poured into space research in the latter 1950s. The titan of the American economy, the automobile industry, profited from the engineering breakthroughs. Spending nearly one-fifth of their budget on R&D, carmakers utilized the latest technology to increase uniformity of product. Where the auto industry had once partially replaced human labor with machinery, it now used automation to control the machines themselves. Between 1945 and 1960, the industry halved the number of hours and workers required to produce a car. Other manufacturers followed suit, investing an average of $10 billion a year throughout the fifties on new labor-saving machinery and plants.

The Age of Computers

One key to the postwar technological revolution was the electronic computer. It brought, wrote an economist, "an advance in man's thinking as radical as the invention of writing." A new era dawned in 1944 when the International Business Machines Corporation (IBM), cooperating with scientists at Harvard University on devices to decipher the secret codes of the Axis powers, produced the Mark I calculator. Although slow, unable to perform many mathematical functions, and enormously cumber-

The ENIAC Computer

Despite its tangle of wires and tens of thousands of vacuum tubes, the original ENIAC had much less capacity than a tiny computer chip today.

some—a maze of five hundred miles of wiring and more than three thousand electromechanical relays—it proved a vital first step. Two years later, to improve artillery trajectory, the U.S. Army began operating ENIAC, the first electronic computer. Still vast and complex, with tens of thousands of vacuum tubes and resistors, ENIAC reduced the time required to multiply two tenth-place numbers from Mark I's three seconds to less than three-thousandths of a second. Then came the development of operating instructions, or programs, that could be stored inside the computer memory; the substitution of printed circuits for wired ones; and most vital, in 1948, the invention of tiny, solid-state components, called transistors, that ended reliance on radio tubes.

Steadily and surely, the computer fundamentally changed the American economy and society. Sales of electronic computers to industry rose from twenty in 1954 to more than a thousand in 1957, and to more than two thousand in 1960. By then, with the government as its major client, the electronic-computer industry had become a billion-dollar business. The government, which used three machines in computing the 1950 census returns, employed several hundred on the 1960 census. They became as indispensable to Pentagon strategists playing war games as to the Internal Revenue Service, as integral to the work of the Weather Bureau as to aerospace scientists "flying" rockets still on the drawing board. By the mid-1960s more than thirty thousand computers were being utilized by banks, insurance companies, airline- and hotel-reservation departments, stock-brokerage firms, hospitals, and universities. By making industrial automation possible, computers also transformed the nature of work. Greater quantities of products could be manufactured in less time and with fewer workers than ever before.

Concentration and Consolidation in Industry and Agriculture

Rapid technological advances accelerated a long-term economic trend: the growth and power of big business. Of the one hundred largest firms in 1950, twenty-two had assets of more than $1 billion; ten years later more than fifty did. By 1960 one-half of 1 percent of all companies earned more than half the total corporate income in the United States. The wealthiest, which could afford huge R&D outlays, became oligopolies as they swallowed up weak competitors. Just as three radio and television networks monopolized the nation's airwaves, so three automobile and three aluminum companies produced more than 90 percent of the cars and aluminum in the United States; and a handful of firms in steel, petroleum, aircraft, and office and electrical machinery controlled the lion's share of their industries' assets and sales. Major corporations also increased their power by forming conglomerates (mergers of companies in unrelated industries) and by acquiring facilities overseas, thus becoming "multinational" enterprises. Despite talk of "people's capitalism," the oil-rich Rockefeller family alone owned more corporate stock than all the nation's wage earners combined.

Along with growth and consolidation came further bureaucratization. In a process under way since the early twentieth century, "executives" continued to replace "capitalists," and by the mid-1950s American industry employed more than a quarter-million vice presidents. The new professional managerial class, largely divorced from ownership of the corporations they controlled, administered the many diverse departments involved in R&D, production, advertising, sales, accounting, investment, and labor relations. As standard-setters for the hosts of salaried, white-collar workers whom they supervised, this managerial elite placed a premium on conformist behavior—on giving in to social pressure rather than adhering to personal values. Sociologist David Riesman contrasted the "other-directed" behavior of the new middle class—its obsession to fit in and gain acceptance by bowing to the dictates of a group or organization—with the "inner-directed" orientation of small businesspersons and professionals of earlier years, who were guided by the values that they had learned in their youth. Deploring this development, radical sociologist C. Wright Mills depicted members of the white-collar class as selling "not only their time and energy but their personalities as well."

Changes in American agriculture paralleled those in industry. Farming grew increasingly scientific and mechanized. Between 1945 and 1960, technology cut the work-hours necessary to grow and harvest crops by more than half. With agricultural productivity outpacing demand, prices declined, and more and more farm families migrated to urban America. In 1956 alone one-eleventh of the farm population left the land. Between 1940 and 1960, the total number of farms dropped from above 6 million to just below 4 million, and the farm population fell from about 30 million (23.2 percent of the population) to about 15 million (8.7 percent). But the heavily capitalized big farm businesses prospered by employing sophisticated new agricultural machinery and improved chemical fertilizers, pesticides, and herbicides to raise productivity and the profitability of acreage. These large-scale agribusinesses also benefited handsomely from the $5 billion spent by the government on farm subsidies in the 1950s, since these payments were proportional to farm size and output. Moreover, a new soil-conservation program adopted in 1956, which paid farmers to take cropland out of production, primarily enriched the businesses that owned extensive property and could allow tens of thousands of their acres to lie fallow.

Blue-Collar Blues

Consolidation also transformed the labor movement. After twenty discordant years, the AFL and CIO merged in 1955. The new AFL-CIO brought

The American Farmer, 1940–1986

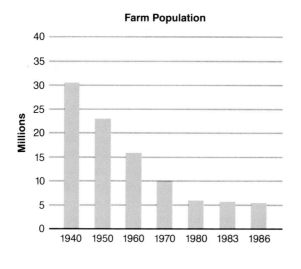

Farm Population

Millions

Number of Farms

Millions

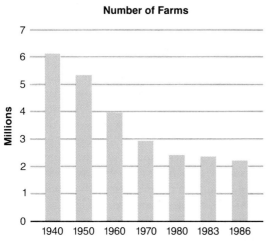

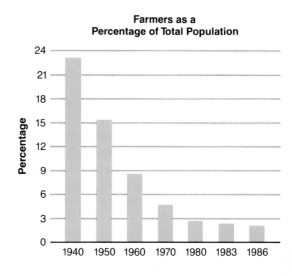

Farmers as a Percentage of Total Population

Percentage

Average Farm Size

Acres

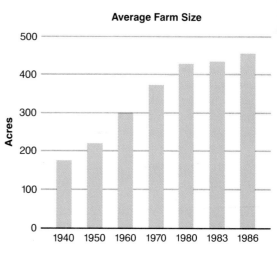

The postwar years saw a fundamental transformation of American agriculture. While the small family farmer joined the rural exodus to the cities, large farms prospered.
SOURCE: U.S. Bureau of the Census, *Statistical Abstract of the United States, 1985* (Washington, D.C., 1984), 628.

85 percent of all union members into a single administrative unit, with the AFL's George Meany as president and the CIO's Walter Reuther, a veteran of the labor wars of the 1930s, as senior vice president. The leadership promised aggressive unionism, but the movement could not recapture its old militancy.

In a sense, organized labor was a victim of its own past successes. Union victories at the bargaining table had secured so many benefits for workers

that their solidarity gave way to complacency. By the midfifties most unionized Americans earned decent wages and pensions, worked fewer than forty hours a week, and received paid vacations and sickness and hospitalization benefits. In the late 1940s, the United Automobile Workers and General Motors had signed a trend-setting contract providing for automatic wage hikes whenever productivity increased or the cost of living rose. Then in 1953, in negotiations with the Ford Motor

Company, the UAW led the way again, winning a guaranteed annual wage and the provision that laid-off workers would be paid two-thirds of their normal earnings in addition to government unemployment benefits. As unionized workers increasingly viewed themselves as comfortable members of an affluent society rather than as an aggrieved proletariat, the bitter strikes and labor turbulence of the depression era and the early postwar years gradually faded.

The labor movement's momentum was further sapped by a decrease in the number of blue-collar workers. As automation replaced more and more laborers in coal mines, auto plants, and steel mills, membership in those once mighty industrial unions dropped by more than half. Most of the new jobs in the 1950s were in the traditionally union-resistant white-collar service sector and in public employment, which banned collective bargaining by labor unions. Unwilling or unable to woo the unskilled and semiskilled black and Hispanic workers in the relatively low-paying service and agricultural jobs, organized labor saw its portion of the total labor force drop from a high of 28 percent in 1953 to 26 percent in 1960. In the nonagricultural sector, the proportion of unionized workers fell from 36 percent to 31 percent in this same seven-year period.

Prosperity, Suburbanization, and Mobility

As real purchasing power rose 22 percent between 1946 and 1960, Americans satisfied their desires for all the goods and services that they had longed for, but had been unable to attain, during the Great Depression and the Second World War, as well as for the many new gadgets and appliances now dangled before them. Spending less of their income on basic necessities, the American people enthusiastically purchased electric lawn mowers, air conditioners, and even striped toothpaste. They heaped their shopping carts with food that had been frozen, sprayed, dehydrated, and fortified and stocked up on aerosol air fresheners and hair sprays. When they lacked cash, they borrowed. Diners' Club issued the first credit card in 1950, and American Express soon followed. Installment buying, home mortgages, and auto loans raised Americans' total private indebtedness in the 1950s from $73 billion to $196 billion. A consumer culture now dominated American life. To further stimulate consumerism, advertising expenditures leaped nearly 250 percent in the fifties. Throughout the decade business annually allocated more for advertising than the nation spent on elementary and secondary education.

The car-selling slogan of the 1950s, "You auto buy now," encouraged Americans to purchase a record 58 million new cars that decade. The number of registered automobiles increased by 21 million, the total of motor-vehicle miles traveled rose by 75 percent, and critics complained of "auto-sclerosis"—the clogging of urban arteries. But the auto industry kept the public buying by promising glamour and status in newer, bigger, and flashier models. Henry Ford, who had insisted on no-frills black for all the cars he built, would have been aghast at the annual model changes of the 1950s and at car designers' emphasis on gleaming chrome, two-tone colors, and tail fins. Although seat belts remained an unadvertised extra-cost option, the 1955 Ford featured "Trigger-Torque 'Go' Power," and that year's Pontiac boasted the "Sensational Strato-Streak V–8!" Other models—sporting such names as "Fury," "Marauder," and "Barracuda"—came in colors ranging from "passion pink" to "horizon blue" to "lilac mist" and were powered by immense engines capable of propelling them more than twice as fast as any existing speed limit. Hand in hand with the increase in the number and power of automobiles came rises in highway deaths, air pollution, and oil consumption, as well as a creeping sprawl of motels, gas stations, and standardized fast-food outlets.

The greater availability of autos also spurred white Americans' exodus to suburbia. So did government policies. As federal spending on highways skyrocketed from $79 million in 1946 to $2.9 billion in 1960, and as state and local expenditures for roads kept pace, areas once considered too remote by urban workers suddenly became desirable places to live. The tax code further induced home buying by permitting deductions for home-mortgage interest payments and for property taxes. And the Federal Housing Administration (FHA) and the Veterans Administration (VA) stimulated home sales through policies requiring small down

EXCITING ESCAPE !

...this lion-hearted call to the open road

TOUCH a fingertip to Chrysler's pushbutton TorqueFlite transmission. Feel how smoothly, how instantly, power surges to your service.

...AND GO for the open road. Give this agile and adventurous car a chance to show you how exciting driving can be!

Chrysler's got the ride you want! From the pushbutton action of TorqueFlite transmission . . . the sure-footed control of Torsion-Aire Ride . . . the economy of Golden Lion engine . . . to the stop-on-a-dime safety of Total-Contact Brakes.

Chrysler's got the room you need! From the swing-aboard ease of optional Swivel Seats . . . the keep-your-hat-on head room, both front and back . . . the wider door openings and flatter floors . . . to leg-stretching lounging room all around.

Chrysler's got the style you can be proud of! Just look at Chrysler. Here's styling that set a trend in automotive design. And, underneath it all, Chrysler's superior engineering and quality construction standards give you the years-long reliability you deserve. You'll *always* be out front with this combination of stay-ahead style, quality, and lion-hearted way of going!

See your Chrysler dealer today . . . and answer that call to the open road.

CHRYSLER DIVISION OF CHRYSLER CORPORATION

lion-hearted **CHRYSLER**

. . . setting the pace in style and comfort

The Car Culture

This 1959 advertisement promised "exciting escape" to the buyer of a new Chrysler.

payments and offering low-interest loans. These government programs, creating a vast new market for private homes, in turn speeded up a construction-industry trend toward using modern industrial technology to mass-produce homes. Until 1945 the average contractor had built only 2 or 3 houses a year. But through standardized construction methods (see "A Place in Time"), the industry built a phenomenal 13 million new homes in the 1950s.

Eighty-five percent of this new-home construction took place in the suburbs. A variety of attractions lured Americans to suburbia. Some moved in search of affordable single-family dwellings. Others became suburbanites to escape the crime and grime of the central cities and to distance themselves from the millions of newly urbanized blacks and Hispanics, toward whom rampant prejudice continued. And many newly married Americans headed for suburbia in quest of communities oriented toward children and education.

Although social critics complained about endless acres of cookie-cutter houses inhabited by bored housewives and harried husbands desperate to keep up with their neighbors, most suburbanites enjoyed their comfortable new lifestyles, their clean, tranquil surroundings, and their like-minded neighbors. In the suburbia of the fifties, one could have a sense of belonging and of influence in the community. To a nation of immigrants, most from countries where property ownership was denied to all but an elite few, the desire to take title to a home of one's own formed the very core of the American dream.

While the population of central cities rose 10 percent during the 1950s, the number of suburban dwellers nearly *doubled*. About a million New Yorkers migrated to communities ringing the city. Bordering Los Angeles, Orange County doubled in population in the 1940s and then tripled that in the 1950s. Nationwide some 18 million moved to the suburbs. For the first time in the twentieth century, a majority of Americans lived in their own homes rather than in rented quarters. The suburban population of 60 million in 1960 equaled that of the central cities. And by 1970 the suburbs would contain two-thirds of the metropolitan-area population and the cities only one-third—exactly the reverse of 1950.

Americans migrated not only from city to suburb but from North to South and from East to West. Each year of the 1950s saw nearly one-fifth of the population change residences. Lured by burgeoning employment opportunities, droves of Americans descended on the Houston–Beaumont–Port Arthur complex, as well as on Phoenix and Mobile. Attracted by the plentiful jobs in the aircraft industry, others headed for the Northwest. Most, however, like the Brooklyn Dodgers and the New York Giants, migrated to California, which added some 5 million to its numbers and accounted for fully one-fifth of the nation's population growth in the 1950s. The fifth-largest state in 1940, California would supplant New York in 1963 as the most populous. The shift of millions from the frosty North and East to the balmy South and West altered the nation both economically and politically. Drawn to the Sunbelt by right-to-work laws, which outlawed the union shop, and by low taxes and energy costs, countless industrialists moved their plants

Levittown, U.S.A.

A braham Levitt and his sons Alfred and William symbolized for home construction what Henry Ford had meant to automobiles and Henry J. Kaiser to shipbuilding. The Levitts' pioneering mass-production techniques for constructing tract homes opened the gates to an exodus from the cities to the suburbs, and their immense success stimulated a host of imitators and a record 1.65 million housing starts in 1955.

Following the Second World War, Levitt & Sons purchased fifteen hundred acres of potato fields on Long Island's Hempstead Plain, some thirty miles from midtown Manhattan. In response to the postwar housing shortage, the Levitts quickly built 2,000 homes and rented them for just sixty-five dollars a month to married veterans eager to escape from their in-laws' residences or cramped apartments where landlords frowned on children. Using the standardized construction techniques that they had first employed in erecting low-cost housing units for wartime navy workers in Norfolk, Virginia, the Levitts then rapidly built and rented 2,000 more homes. In 1948 they began to offer the houses for sale. The company recognized that working Americans' ever-greater demand for suburban housing—a demand fueled by the easy availability of low-cost mortgages from the FHA and the VA, extensive car ownership, and the expanding U.S.

Levittown, Long Island, in 1949

The New York Times Magazine *described Levittown as having been "all previously planned in one of the most colossal acts ever of mortal creation."*

highway system—promised a bonanza of profits. By 1951 the Levitts had built and sold another 13,500 homes.

To erect their 720-square-foot Cape Cod or ranch-style houses as quickly and cheaply as possible, the Levitts established their own lumber mill, nail factory, and electrical-supply company. They employed mainly unskilled, non-union laborers, each of whom was trained to perform just one task. Everything moved on a fixed timetable as Levitt & Sons made "a factory of the whole building site." First came the bulldozers and trenching machines

to strip and ditch each 60- by 100-foot lot in twenty-seven minutes. Another crew poured the concrete foundation. Trucks then brought all the precut and preassembled materials to each site, where a succession of teams hammered the prefabricated siding, connected the plumbing, strung the electrical wires, fitted the windows, laid the flooring, shingled the roof, and spray-painted the walls.

Levittown radiated uniformity. Each house had two bedrooms; a bath; a kitchen equipped with an electric refrigerator, a range, and a washing machine; an expansion attic; and a living room with a fire-place, picture window, and built-in television set. Deeds to the property required door chimes, not buzzers, prohibited picket fences, mandated regular lawn mowing, and even specified when the wash could be hung to dry in the backyard. All the town streets curved at the same angle, and a tree was planted every twenty-eight feet.

Critics decried the tasteless, monotonous conformity of Levit-town; but young marrieds, as they were called, avidly purchased the Levitts' houses. Levittown's com-forts and conveniences sharply con-trasted with living conditions in the Quonset huts, trailer parks, and stuffy apartments to which many postwar Americans had become accustomed. One veteran, Wilbur Schaetzl, considered the crowded, violence-ridden Brooklyn neighbor-hood from which he had moved "so awful I'd rather not talk about it. Getting into this house was like being emancipated." Laura For-man, who had one child and was expecting a second, found Levit-town to be a "paradise for chil-dren—and mothers. Soon after we moved in, neighbors I hadn't even met yet came in to help. Because my husband was working, they packed my bags, drove me to the hospital, and took care of my other baby. And they wouldn't let me buy anything for the new baby either. That car-riage isn't mine and neither is the crib." Such small-town friendliness also appealed to Izzy Stark, who had previously lived in an apartment house without ever knowing his neighbors. Stark's Levittown friends "were closer than kin. When the girls go to a garden club meeting, we boys

The Suburban Explosion

Some suburban developments, including the Levittowns, rose up almost overnight. Invaders from the city did not lag far behind the bull-dozers and cement trucks.

get together and baby-sit and play poker. Or one night we'll all go bowling or to the movies. And now we're all taking some of these adult education courses down at the school one night a week. I'm taking 'How to Finish Your Attic' and Bob and Harry are learning photogra-phy." Despite the long commute to his office in Manhattan (he would travel half a million miles, or twenty times around the world, before he retired), Stark thought that he had achieved "his dream house."

To meet the galloping demand for its low-cost homes, in the early

1950s Levitt & Sons bought eight square miles of spinach farmland on the Delaware River in Bucks County, Pennsylvania, and constructed a second Levittown of sixteen thou-sand homes. Still another followed in Willingboro, New Jersey. Each endeavor mirrored the Levitts' con-cern for planned orderliness. In the Bucks County development, they situated schools, churches, baseball fields, shopping centers, parking lots, and offices for doctors and dentists at symmetrical points out-side the residential clusters. In Wil-lingboro they integrated the houses and the recreational and shopping facilities within the various neigh-borhoods. But that was all that the Levitts wished to integrate. Fearful that the admission of blacks would provoke "white flight" from the communities that they designed, Levitt & Sons excluded blacks. Not until the mid-1960s, when blacks brought suit to be allowed to pur-chase a home in Levittown, New Jersey, did the Levitts bow to a court order and sell their first home to a nonwhite.

The enormous success of the Levittown ventures reflected the shift in population in the 1950s. The United States in these years increas-ingly became a nation of white sub-urbs and nonwhite cities. As the suburbs attracted not only more and more private homeowners but also more and more commerce and industry, the cities fell victim to shrinking tax bases just as their need for social services zoomed. Levit-town and such similar suburban communities as Oak Meadows out-side Chicago and Parkmerced near San Francisco had changed the face of America.

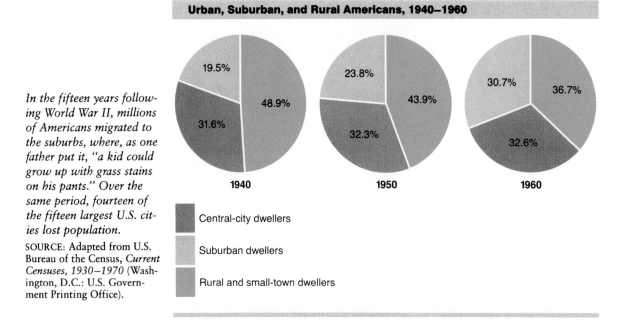

Urban, Suburban, and Rural Americans, 1940–1960

19.5%
48.9%
31.6%
1940

23.8%
43.9%
32.3%
1950

30.7%
36.7%
32.6%
1960

Central-city dwellers

Suburban dwellers

Rural and small-town dwellers

In the fifteen years follow-ing World War II, millions of Americans migrated to the suburbs, where, as one father put it, "a kid could grow up with grass stains on his pants." Over the same period, fourteen of the fifteen largest U.S. cit-ies lost population.

SOURCE: Adapted from U.S. Bureau of the Census, *Current Censuses, 1930–1970* (Wash-ington, D.C.: U.S. Govern-ment Printing Office).

and corporate headquarters there, in the process transplanting their conservative outlooks. By 1980 the population of the Sunbelt—an area stretching from the Old Confederacy across Texas and the Southwest to southern California—would exceed that of the North and East; and the political power of the Republican party would rise accordingly.

An American magically transported from the depression-wracked 1930s to the booming, pros-perous nation of twenty years later would have had trouble believing her eyes. For many (though far from all) Americans, penny-pinching financial worry had given way to a comfortable affluence. An industrial system rooted in the late-nineteenth-century era of cheap immigrant labor and the belching smokestack factories of the upper Mid-west was being transformed under the impact of automation, the computer, new management tech-niques, and the flow of people and businesses to the Sunbelt. A union movement that had long struggled for recognition and finally achieved it now found itself in decline, a victim of a changing economy and of the very working-class well-being that it had helped achieve. And a people that for a century had crowded in ever-greater numbers into city apartments, tenements, and town houses now turned its gaze to the green lawns and mass-pro-

duced houses of the suburbs. Gradually but inex-orably, all these changes were molding future social contours and political issues.

Consensus and Conservatism

Of course, not everyone embraced the fifties' mate-rialism or sank unquestioningly into a deep cush-ion of contentedness in these years. Throughout the decade disaffected intellectuals criticized American conformity and consumerism, especially in middle-class suburbia. They condemned Amer-ican religion for tepidness; denounced the young as a "silent generation"; bemoaned identical "ticky-tacky" suburban houses; and lampooned what they viewed as the shallow, insipid quality of life in "an America of mass housing, mass markets, massive corporations, massive government, mass media, and massive boredom." These critics complained that the consumer economy gave birth to "organization men" bent on getting ahead by going along, "status seekers" pursuing external rewards to compensate for inner insecurities, and "other-directed" per-sonalities highly vulnerable to peer-group pressure. The United States, the dissenters agreed, had become a "packaged society" and its people "all items in a national supermarket—categorized, processed, labeled, priced, and readied for merchandising."

But the attackers of homogeneity and materialism oversimplified the reality. They ignored the diversity of a society of distinct classes and ethnic groups, as well as the continued shaping influence of different races, religions, and regions. They overlooked the complacency and acquisitiveness of earlier generations and failed to notice the currents of dissent swirling just beneath the placid surface. Too eager to sneer at the middle class that shunned them, the disenchanted intellectuals of the 1950s made a caricature of American society.

Still, their criticism did spotlight the widespread elevation of comfort over challenge, safety over risk, and private pleasures over public affairs. Americans wanted a respite from the trials of the preceding decades. Moreover, terrified at the awful possibility of nuclear annihilation, they hungered for security, and they sought refuge in the good life.

Togetherness and the Baby Boom

In 1954 *McCall's* magazine coined the term *togetherness* to celebrate the "ideal" couple: the man and woman who married young, had a large family, and centered their lives on home and children. Confident of a bright future in a prosperous era, Americans in the 1950s wed at an earlier age than their parents, produced babies sooner, and had more of them. The number of births per thousand women rose from 80 in 1940 to 106 in 1950 and peaked at 123 in 1957, when an American baby was born every seven seconds. The baby boom was especially pronounced in suburbia: many referred to pregnancy as the "Levittown look."

At the same time, medical science made tremendous advances against childhood disease. Infection-fighting drugs—particularly streptomycin in 1945, aureomycin in 1948, and izoniazed in 1952—virtually eliminated diphtheria, influenza, and typhoid fever. Then in the mid-1950s the Salk and Sabin vaccines ended the dreaded poliomyelitis (polio), the major scourge of children. The dramatic drop in the mortality of the young helped raise life expectancy in the United States from 65.9

years in 1945 to 70.9 years in 1970. In tandem with the baby boom, this decline contributed to a 19 percent population increase. At a time of negligible immigration, the U.S. population jumped from 151 million to 180 million in the 1950s, the largest spurt in any previous decade. Most significantly, the percentage of children under fourteen in the total population leaped from less than a quarter in 1945 to nearly a third in 1960.

The sheer size of the baby-boom generation ensured its historical importance. In time it would become the Vietnam Generation and then the Me Generation. The baby boom helped fuel the economic boom and expand the nation's educational system. It also made child rearing a preeminent concern and reinforced the idea that women's proper place was in the home. With Americans increasingly convinced that early-childhood experiences influenced individuals psychologically for their entire lives, motherhood became a vital and demanding calling.

No one did more to emphasize the presumed close connection between full-time mothers and well-adjusted children than Dr. Benjamin Spock: only the Bible outsold his *Baby and Child Care* (1946) in the fifties. Popularizing the theories of Sigmund Freud and John Dewey, Spock urged mothers to create an atmosphere of warmth, intimacy, and trust for their children so that they could mature into happy, healthy adults. Crying babies were to be comforted so that they would not feel afraid or rejected. Breast feeding came back into vogue, and specially designed slings allowed babies to be carried close to the heart. Spock's advice often led to less scolding and spanking and more "democratic" family discussions. In some homes it produced a "filiarchy," where children's wants and needs dominated. Spock's teachings placed a premium on mothers' full-time devotion to child rearing; anything less, he argued, might result in insecurity. Spock even wanted the government to pay mothers so that they would not have to work outside the home. Seldom had the importance of motherhood been so exalted.

Domesticity

"No job is more exacting, more necessary, or more rewarding than that of housewife and mother," wrote a female journalist in *The Atlantic* in 1950,

Postwar Population Growth

As the baby boom took off, 1950s popular magazines placed a renewed emphasis on family life and commonly featured stories and portraits of five- and six-member families.

and countless others echoed that sentiment throughout the decade. The popular culture of the fifties glorified marriage and parenthood and depicted a woman's devotion to life in the home with her children as the most cherished goal. Television almost always pictured mother at home—usually in the kitchen. Hollywood films perpetuated the stereotype of career women as neurotics and of loving mothers and wife-companions as happy and healthy. As the "girl next door" star Debbie Reynolds explained in the film *The Tender Trap* (1955): "A woman isn't a woman until she's been married and had children." Or as the heroine of a 1957 *Redbook* story mused as she nursed her baby at 2 A.M., "I'm glad, glad, glad I'm just a housewife." Virtually without exception, American culture in the 1950s emphasized that women found their truest fulfillment, and made their greatest contribution to national life, as wives and mothers.

The nation's educational system promoted the same notion. While girls learned typing, stenography, etiquette, and cooking, boys were channeled into carpentry, auto mechanics, and courses leading to careers in law or medicine. Extracurricular activities reinforced the belief in males as leaders and females as assistants. Guidance counselors cautioned young women not to "miss the boat" of marriage by pursuing a higher education. "Men are not interested in college degrees, but in the warmth and humanness of the girls they marry," stressed one popular textbook on family living. "Men still want wives who will bolster their egos rather than detract from them." Overall, women constituted a smaller percentage of college students in the 1950s than in the twenties or thirties and received fewer advanced degrees than they had in those decades. Almost two-thirds of the college women in the fifties failed to complete a degree, and except in the most prestigious colleges, most of those who did graduate concentrated in such fields as home economics, child development, and primary-school education.

Likewise, popular psychology advocated the cult of domesticity, insisting that a contented woman was one who accepted her natural role as wife, mother, and homemaker. Such influential books as Helene Deutsch's *The Psychology of Women* (1944) and Ferdinand Lundberg's and Marynia Farnham's *Modern Women: The Lost Sex* (1947) argued that only "neurotic" women or "imitation men" avoided marriage and motherhood, and that feminists suffered from penis envy or some other psychological or sexual disorder. Joining the strident chorus, *Life* in 1956 attributed a rising divorce rate to "wives who are not feminine enough."

Yet even as the culture celebrated domesticity, profound changes were under way. Despite the mass layoffs of women immediately after World War II, women quickly returned to the labor force. By 1952, 2 million more women worked than had been employed during the war; and by 1960 nearly 40 percent of American women would hold full- or part-time jobs. The proportion of working wives, moreover, rose from 15 percent in 1940 to 30 percent in 1960. Strikingly reversing earlier patterns, some 40 percent of all working women in 1960 had school-age children.

Most worked to earn additional family income, however, not to challenge stereotypes of a woman's place. To help pay for the knotty-pine rumpus room or some other badge of success, most took low-paying, low-prestige sales and office jobs, where women remained "girls" whatever their age. In the main they accepted their status. Although the rise in female employment fostered conditions that would lead to a feminist resurgence in the late 1960s, organized feminism ebbed to its lowest point of the century during the fifties. The great majority of women responded to sudden prosperity and atomic jitters by concentrating on private satisfactions and trying to make the home a haven in an uncertain world.

Religion and Education

The quest for security and a sense of rootedness stimulated a renewed interest in religion. "Today in the U.S.," *Time* claimed in 1954, "the Christian faith is back in the center of things." Signs of the revival indeed abounded. Leading religious popularizers—such as the fiery evangelist Billy Graham, the riveting Roman Catholic bishop Fulton J. Sheen, and the soothing Protestant minister Norman Vincent Peale (with his message of "positive thinking")—had their own syndicated newspaper columns, best-selling books, and radio and television programs. Hollywood's biggest box-office attractions included *The Robe, The Ten Commandments, Ben Hur,* and other religious extravaganzas. *Modern Screen* magazine featured a series

entitled "How the Stars Found Faith." While popular singers crooned such hits as "I Believe" and "The Man Upstairs," billboards urged Americans to "bring the whole family to church" and TV commercials pronounced that "the family that prays together stays together."

The American Legion organized a "Back to God" campaign. Dial-a-Prayer offered formulaic telephone solutions for various spiritual problems. The Ideal Toy Company brought out a doll that genuflected. In the midfifties Congress added the phrase "under God" to the Pledge of Allegiance and made "IN GOD WE TRUST" mandatory on all U.S. currency. Church attendance swelled from 64.5 million (48 percent of the population) in 1940 to 110 million (63 percent) in 1958.

The resurgence of religion took many forms. Some prominent intellectuals, forsaking the Social Gospel's optimistic faith in progress and perfectibility, accepted modern forms of Calvinism ("neo-orthodoxy"). Augmenting a trend that would escalate in the future, millions of other Americans embraced evangelical fundamentalism and declared themselves "born-again" Christians. But most Americans turned to religion primarily for reassurance in an anxious age—for peace of mind and a sense of belonging. President Eisenhower himself opined, "Everybody should have a religious faith, and I don't care what it is." Thus, despite an aura of religiosity in the fifties, the *intensity* of religious belief diminished for many men and women as mainstream churches downplayed sin and evil and emphasized Americanism and fellowship.

Similarly, education flourished in the 1950s yet seemed more intellectually shallow than in previous decades. As a result of the baby boom, primary-school enrollment, which had risen by less than a million in the 1940s, jumped by nearly 10 million in the 1950s. By 1960 more than 30 million students attended primary school. California opened a new school an average of every seven days throughout the decade and still faced a classroom shortage. Likewise, the proportion of college-age Americans enrolled in institutions of higher learning soared from 15 percent in 1940 to 32 percent in 1957 and topped 40 percent in the early 1960s. At every level a watered-down version of the doctrine of "Education for Life Adjustment," attributed to education reformer John Dewey, held sway. Legions of Dewey disciples promoted sociability, health education, and self-expression over science, math, and history. For them, community needs took precedence over intellectual rigor, and the "well-rounded" student became more prized than the highly skilled and knowledgeable one.

Numerous surveys of college students in the 1950s described them as conservative, conformist, and careerist. The number of business majors swamped all other fields. Describing the student body as a "silent generation" more interested in security and comfort than in distinguishing themselves, *Time* reported in 1957: "No campus is without its atrocity story of intellectual deadness." Campus passivity was the norm as most students concentrated their nonacademic energies on listening to music, dating, and occasionally engaging in such pranks as panty raids and stuffing themselves into phone booths. Overall, their attitudes closely mirrored those of their elders in this decade of affluence and antiradicalism.

Affirmation and Anxiety: The Culture of the Fifties

American culture at midcentury reflected both the expansive, upbeat spirit of a prosperous era and an undercurrent of discontent with the quality of life. With increasing leisure and fatter paychecks, Americans spent one-seventh of the gross national product in 1950 on entertainment. Spectator sports boomed, new symphony halls opened, and book sales doubled during the decade.

But in the fiction of the 1950s, one finds a mood of doubt and alienation. Like the cool jazz of Miles Davis and the abstract expressionist paintings of Jackson Pollock (who dripped swirls of paint directly on the canvas), the novels of the fifties were characterized by introspection and highly personal yearnings. This set them decisively apart from the literature of the 1930s, with its social realism and political engagement. In such novels as Sloan Wilson's *The Man in the Gray Flannel Suit* (1955), John Cheever's *The Wapshot Chronicle* (1957), and John Updike's *Rabbit Run* (1960), the heroes feel vague dissatisfaction with their jobs and their domestic situation and long for a more vital and authentic existence. Updike's "Rabbit" Angstrom, for example, understandably finds his alcoholic wife and his job demonstrating the "MagiPeel"

kitchen implement frustrating in comparison with his glory days as a high-school basketball hero. But the stories end inconclusively; the protagonists seem emotionally drained and incapable of decisive action. J. D. Salinger's enormously popular *The Catcher in the Rye* (1951) offered an adolescent version of the alienated, ineffectual 1950s literary hero. Young Holden Caulfield, expelled from prep school, is repelled by the "phoniness" of the adult world and vaguely considers a break for freedom. But in the end he returns home, suffers a nervous collapse, and retreats to a narcissistic inner realm of imagined heroic exploits.

The most vital fiction of the fifties came from regional, black, and Jewish writers. William Faulkner continued his dense saga of the Snopses of Yoknapatawpha County, Mississippi, in *The Town* (1957) and *The Mansion* (1960), while Eudora Welty offered her evocation of small-town Mississippi life in *The Ponder Heart* (1954). Aspects of the black experience were memorably presented in James Baldwin's *Go Tell It on the Mountain* (1953), Lorraine Hansberry's *A Raisin in the Sun* (1959), and Ralph Ellison's brilliant and symbolically complex 1951 novel *Invisible Man*. Bernard Malamud's *The Assistant* (1957) explored the Jewish immigrant world of New York's Lower East Side, while Philip Roth's *Goodby Columbus* (1959) wittily dissected the very different world of wealthy, upwardly mobile Jews. The vividness and poignancy of works like these contrasted sharply with the colorlessness of much 1950s fiction.

Hollywood, too, reflected the diminished concern with social issues characteristic of postwar American culture. Movie moguls concentrated on westerns, musicals, and lavish biblical or historical costume spectacles. When film producers did turn from cavalry charges and chariot races to life in the 1950s, they generally portrayed Americans as one big, happy, white, middle-class family. The movies glorified material success and romantic love. And Hollywood now reserved the scarlet letter *A* for women intent on ambition rather than adultery. In place of the independent career-woman-in-tailored-suit types featured in films of the 1940s were the subordinated child-women roles played by Sandra Dee and June Allyson; the cute, cozy helpmates portrayed by Doris Day and Debbie Reynolds; and the "dumb blondes" whom "gentlemen preferred," especially as played by such cine-

Marilyn Monroe

Shown here in a poster promoting her 1956 film Bus Stop, *Monroe was the all-time movie sex symbol.*

matic bombshells as Marilyn Monroe and Jayne Mansfield.

But even as motion pictures entertained the American people, the industry declined. Between 1948 and 1960, as television viewing soared, weekly movie attendance dropped from nearly 90 million to about 45 million, the number of feature films produced fell from more than 400 to only 154, and a fifth of the nation's theaters stood empty or became bowling alleys and supermarkets. Hollywood desperately tried to recoup by developing such new visual techniques as Cinerama and CinemaScope. For the highly touted 3-D films, viewers donned special glasses that gave the illusion of depth. Suddenly the audience was hurtling down a roller coaster at 150 miles per hour or swerving to avoid a spear sailing right out of the screen. Nothing, however—including Smell-O-Vision and its rival Aroma-Rama, which emitted smells corresponding to what was depicted on the screen—could stem television's exploding popularity. By 1960 TV showed more than five times

as much film footage as Hollywood produced, and dozens of abandoned movie lots and theaters had been converted into TV locations and studios.

The Message of the Medium

No cultural medium ever grew so huge so quickly, and none so boldly reinforced the mood of the times as American television in the 1950s. The number of households with TV sets shot up from several thousand in 1946 to 5 million in 1950. Thereafter set ownership rose at a rate of some 5 million a year. By the midfifties more than two-thirds of all homes in the United States sported a rooftop television antenna; and early in the 1960s, 90 percent of all households had at least one TV, and 13 percent owned more than one. The number of transmitting stations jumped from six in 1946 to nearly five hundred in 1960.

American business capitalized on the phenomenon. Introduced in 1952, *TV Guide* soon outsold all other periodicals and by 1960 was published in fifty-three separate regional editions for its 7 million subscribers. The TV dinner, first marketed in 1954, altered the nation's eating habits. By the midfifties the three networks that controlled the television airwaves were each grossing larger advertising revenues than any other communications medium in the world.

In television's youth, sometimes also called its golden age, producers showcased talent and creativity. A spectrum of high-quality shows appeared during prime time, including opera performances, notable documentaries like the "See It Now" series hosted by famed news broadcaster Edward R. Murrow, sophisticated comedies like "Your Show of Shows," and critically acclaimed original dramas on "Playhouse 90" and "Studio One."

But all too soon, the networks' race for profits combined with McCarthy-era anxieties to transform the artistically innovative and sometimes politically challenging young medium into a cautious celebrator of conformity and consumerism. "The message of the media is the commercial," one critic noted, as corporations spent fortunes hawking their products. Expenditures for television advertising rose to $170 million in 1950, then doubled in 1951, passed $1 billion in 1955, and nearly doubled again in the next six years. To reap the greatest possible share of the revenue bonanza, the

The Television Revolution, 1950–1987

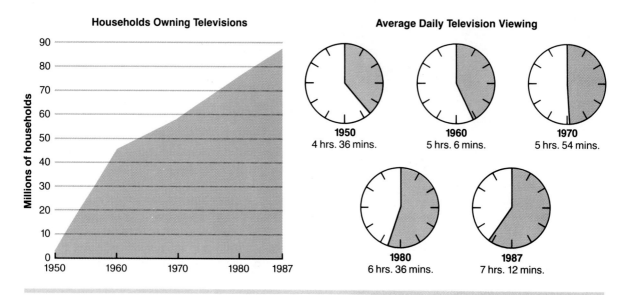

As televisions became commonplace in the 1950s, TV viewing altered the nature of American culture and politics.

SOURCE: *Statistical Abstracts of the United States.*

networks competed for the largest audiences by appealing to the lowest common denominator of taste. (As radio comedian Fred Allen observed: "They call television a medium because it's rare when it is well done.")

Upbraiding broadcasters for their mediocre programming in 1961, the head of the Federal Communications Commission dared them to try watching their shows for a whole day: "I can assure you that you will observe a vast wasteland." Others reviled the television set as the "one-eyed monster" and the "idiot box" rotting viewers' minds with a bland menu of inane quiz shows and situation comedies punctuated by outbursts of canned laughter. TV frequently portrayed women as either zany madcaps ("My Friend Irma," "I Love Lucy") or saccharine-sweet housewives ("The Donna Reed Show," "Ozzie and Harriet"). Such popular programs as "Father Knows Best" and "Make Room for Daddy" celebrated the family's paternal protector. Few of the complexities and tensions of modern family life were depicted. An ongoing pageant of police dramas and westerns, moreover, seemed to affirm the value of violence in overcom-

ing evil. And although millions of youngsters tuned in to "The Howdy Doody Show" and donned mousketeer ears as they watched "The Mickey Mouse Club," children's programs also regularly featured mayhem and gunplay.

The full extent of its impact on American life is difficult to gauge, but television certainly nurtured both consumerism and conformity in tastes, interests, and opinions. At best, it offered little to improve people; at worst, it reinforced racial and gender stereotypes and encouraged passivity. One domain hugely influenced by TV was politics; it became clear that in the political realm, video images were sometimes more powerful than reality. Viewers' perceptions based on events as depicted on the TV screen shaped their political responses mightily. The televised walkout of some southern delegates at the 1948 Democratic convention, for example, convinced many blacks that "Mr. Truman had, indeed, stuck out his neck for them," even though Truman was in fact backing away from a strong stand on civil rights at the time. Richard Nixon's televised appeal for support in 1952 saved his beleaguered vice-presidential candidacy even

TV Favorites from the Fifties

The Anderson family in "Father Knows Best" (left) and Lucy and Ricky in "I Love Lucy" (right) were popular visitors to America's living rooms in the 1950s.

though he never fully explained his alleged financial improprieties. In 1960 the "telegenic" image projected by candidate John F. Kennedy would help tip the presidential election in his favor. At yet another political level, TV's pervasive portrayal of the United States as a nation of supremely contented and comfortable citizens both reinforced that perception and obscured the existence of "the other America."

The Other America

"I am an invisible man," declared the black narrator of Ralph Ellison's *Invisible Man*; "I am invisible, understand, simply because people refuse to see me." Indeed, few white, middle-class Americans did perceive the extent of social injustice in the United States of the 1950s. Most never realized the pervasiveness of hunger and deprivation and

ignored the racism around them. "White flight" from cities to suburbs produced physical separation of the races and classes. Newly constructed expressways walled off decaying ghettos and pockets of rural poverty from middle-class motorists speeding by. The popular culture focused overwhelmingly on affluent Americans enjoying the "good life" and depicted blacks and Hispanics almost exclusively as servants, criminals, or figures of fun.

In the almost universal consensus of the Eisenhower Era, it had become practically an article of faith that the nation had eliminated inequality. "The jobless, distracted, and bewildered men of 1933," Richard Hofstadter, an eminent liberal historian, wrote in the midfifties, "have become homeowners, suburbanites, and solid citizens." Arthur Schlesinger, Jr., another leading exponent of liberalism, echoed the point in 1956: "[T]he central problems of our times are no longer problems of want and privation." Liberal and conservative thinkers alike believed that material abundance had made radicalism obsolete. Only a certain amount of fine-tuning, most agreed, was needed to perfect the existing democratic capitalist system. With the economy more prosperous than ever before in history, few doubted *Time* magazine's prediction that "nothing less than the elimination of poverty as a fact of life is in sight."

Poverty and Urban Blight

Some harsh economic realities, however, belied such optimism. True, the number of families living in poverty (defined by the federal government in the fifties as a family of four earning less than three thousand dollars a year) declined from 34 percent in 1947 to 22 percent in 1960, but some 35 million Americans, more than a fifth of the nation, still remained victims of malnutrition, disease, and squalor. Millions more survived on family incomes below four thousand dollars a year. While officially above the poverty line, they nevertheless constituted impoverished outsiders in "the affluent society." A Senate report in 1960 declared that at least one-half of all Americans aged sixty-five and over "cannot afford decent housing, proper nutrition, adequate medical care, or necessary recreation." Approximately 8 million of the aged had incomes below a thousand dollars a year, and a majority of senior citizens lacked both medical and hospital insurance.

At least a third of the poor worked on farms or lived in depressed rural areas like Appalachia. Tenant farmers and sharecroppers, and especially the 2 million migrant farm workers, experienced the most abject poverty. The secretary of labor in 1959 estimated their average hourly wage at fifty cents, but in fact, many worked for considerably less. Observing a Texas migratory-labor camp in 1955, a journalist reported that 96 percent of the children had consumed no milk in the previous six months; eight out of ten adults had eaten no meat; and most slept "on the ground, in a cave, under a tree, or in a chicken house." In California's Imperial Valley, the infant death rate among migrant workers was more than seven times the statewide average.

The bulk of the poor, however, huddled in spreading, decaying inner-city slums. Masses of Deep South blacks, Appalachian whites, Indians

forced off the reservations, Puerto Ricans, and Mexican migrants strained the cities' already inadequate schools and housing. Nearly two hundred thousand Hispanics herded into San Antonio's Westside barrio; a local newspaper described them as living like cattle in a stockyard, "with roofed-over corrals for homes and chutes for streets." A visitor to New York City's slums in 1950 found "25 human beings living in a dark and airless coal cellar ten feet below the street level. . . . No animal could live there long, yet here were 17 children, the youngest having been born here two weeks before." Trapped in a vicious cycle of want and a culture of poverty, the children of the poor started school at a disadvantage, quickly fell behind in their learning, and lacking encouragement or expectation of success, dropped out. Living, like their parents, with neither hope nor the necessary skills to enter the mainstream of American life, they bequeathed a similar legacy to their own children.

Incubators of poverty, many American cities also became social-service wastelands. The migration to the city by those most in need of greater municipal services paralleled the exodus of affluent residents and businesses to suburban areas. "We turned our cities into doughnuts," an urban planner commented, "with all the dough around the center and nothing in the middle." With their tax base shrinking, city governments watched helplessly as antiquated schools and mass-transit facilities deteriorated.

The pressing need for low-cost housing especially went unanswered. Slum-clearance and urban-renewal projects frequently shunted the poor from one ghetto to another to open up space for new parking garages and cultural centers. The Los Angeles barrio of Chavez Ravine was bulldozed to allow for construction of Dodger Stadium; the Hispanic community of South Phoenix was uprooted to make way for a highway. At the same time, landlords, realtors, and bankers deliberately excluded nonwhites from decent housing. Half of the housing in New York's heavily black Harlem predated 1900. There it was not uncommon for more than a dozen people to share a tiny apartment with broken windows, faulty plumbing, and gaping holes in the walls. Harlem's rates of illegitimate births, infant deaths, narcotics use, and crime towered above the averages for the city and the

The Other America

The quality of life for citizens like these poor white children and the black North Carolina grandmother substantiated Michael Harrington's claim that too much had been made of American affluence in the 1950s.

nation. "Where flies and maggots breed, where the plumbing is stopped up and not repaired, where rats bite helpless infants," black social psychologist Kenneth Clark observed, "the conditions of life are brutal and inhuman."

Blacks' Struggle for Justice

In the black South, meanwhile, the collision between the high hopes raised by the 1954 *Brown* decision and the daily indignities of persistent racial discrimination and segregation had sparked a dramatic new phase in the civil-rights movement. To sweep away the separate but rarely equal facilities that demeaned blacks in almost every aspect of life in the "Jim Crow" South, African-Americans developed new tactics, organizations, and leaders in the 1950s. Rejecting the NAACP's patient courtroom strategy and the Urban League's conciliatory negotiations, the southern movement devised direct-action confrontations with local power structures to engage large numbers of blacks

in their own freedom fight and to arouse the conscience of white Americans, on whom the enforcement of constitutional rights ultimately depended.

Symbolic of the racism that touched even the smallest details of everyday living in the 1950s, black passengers on the Montgomery, Alabama, public bus system had to surrender their seats so that no white rider would have to stand. Although they composed more than three-quarters of all passengers, blacks had to pay their fares at the front of the bus, leave and reenter through the back door, sit only in the rear, and then give up their seats to any standing white passengers. Early in December 1955, Rosa Parks, a strong-willed black who had worked for the local chapter of the NAACP, refused to get up so that a white man could sit. She was arrested. In protest, Montgomery's black leaders organized a massive boycott of the buses. "There comes a time when people get tired," intoned Martin Luther King, Jr., an eloquent twenty-seven-year-old black minister who articulated the anger and impatience of Montgomery blacks, "tired of being segregated and humiliated; tired of being kicked about by the brutal feet of oppression." The time had come, King continued, to cease being patient "with anything less than freedom and justice." Vowed King, who had recently earned a Ph.D. in philosophy at Boston University: "We will not retreat one inch in our fight to secure and hold onto our American citizenship." With this speech what would become a yearlong boycott by fifty thousand black Montgomerians began.

Both sides dug in for a protracted battle. Over difficult months a united black community walked to work or traveled in car pools. Whites tried to crush the boycott by intimidating and harassing blacks and by firebombing the homes of King and other black leaders, but the blacks stayed off the buses and gained greater self-respect. "My soul has been tired for a long time," an old woman told a minister who had stopped his car to offer her a ride; "now my feet are tired, and my soul is resting." Such fortitude impressed many whites. "One feels history is being made in Montgomery these days," commented a local librarian. "It is hard to imagine a soul so dead, a heart so hard, a vision so blinded and provincial as not to be awed with admiration at the quiet dignity, discipline, and dedication with which the Negroes have conducted the boycott."

But the city leaders would not budge, refusing the blacks' request for seating on a first-come, first-served basis, with blacks accommodated in the rear and whites in the front. This resistance forced the blacks to take their case to court and to file suit to challenge the constitutionality of bus segregation. In November 1956 the U.S. Supreme Court affirmed a lower-court decision outlawing segregation on the buses. Thirteen months after the boycott began, blacks boarded unsegregated buses in Montgomery. "The story of Montgomery," Martin Luther King would later write, "is the story of 50,000 Negroes who were willing to substitute tired feet for tired souls and walk the streets of Montgomery until the walls of segregation were finally battered by the forces of justice!"

The Montgomery bus boycott demonstrated black southerners' new strength and determination. It cracked the southern white myth that blacks liked segregation and that outside agitators alone sought to topple Jim Crow. It affirmed for blacks everywhere the real possibility of achieving social change. It gave the nation in Dr. King a persuasive African-American leader whose oratory could both inspire black militancy and touch the white conscience.

King's philosophy of civil disobedience fused the spirit and language of evangelical Christianity's sacrifice and redemption with the strategy of nonviolent resistance to authority. King's emphasis on direct action gave every black American an opportunity to become actively involved; and his insistence on nonviolence diminished the likelihood of bloodshed. Preaching that blacks must lay their bodies on the line to provoke crises that would force whites to confront their racism, he nevertheless urged his people to continue to love their enemies. "If we are arrested every day," declared King, "don't ever let anyone pull you so low as to hate them. We must use the weapon of love." By so doing, King prophesied, blacks would convert their oppressors and build a community of true brotherhood and love. To direct this new campaign against Jim Crow, King and a network of black ministers that had supported the Montgomery bus boycott formed the Southern Christian Leadership Conference (SCLC) in 1957.

The Hispanic-American and Native American Predicament

Meanwhile, although sensitized by the black struggle for civil rights, Hispanics and native Americans made little headway in ending discrimination against them. The newest minority group, Puerto Ricans (who are U.S. citizens), mushroomed from about seventy thousand in 1940 to three hundred thousand in 1950, and to nearly a million in 1960. Crowded mainly into the low-rent barrios of New York's East Harlem, Puerto Ricans suffered from inadequate schools, sanitation services, and police protection and were denied access to middle-class jobs and political influence. Still, like countless immigrants before them, they gained greater personal freedom in the United States while losing the security of a strong cultural tradition.

Family frictions flared in the transition from Puerto Rican to American ways. Parents commonly felt upstaged by children who learned English and obtained jobs that were closed to them. Moreover, the relationship between Puerto Rican husbands and wives changed as women found readier access to jobs than did men. One recent immigrant explained, "Whether I have a husband or not I work . . . and if my husband dare to complain, I throw him out. That is the difference; in Puerto Rico I should have to stand for anything a man asks me to do because he pays the rent. Here I belong to myself." However, although old values weakened and Puerto Ricans tried to embrace American ways, they encountered prejudice because of their skin color and Spanish language.

Mexican-Americans suffered the same indignities as did Puerto Ricans, with the additional disadvantage that "undocumented aliens" lacked all the civil liberties of citizenship. In the main, Chicanos attended inferior, segregated schools; and three out of four dropped out before finishing high school. Toiling primarily as agricultural stoop laborers and unskilled household or service workers, they were underpaid and overcharged, cheated and discriminated against, and excluded from the mainstream of American cultural and political life.

In 1953 the Eisenhower administration initiated Operation Wetback to locate and deport illegal Mexican aliens, who were often termed *wetbacks,* or *mojados,* because many thousands of them had swum across the Rio Grande to reach the United States. During the next three years, more than 3 million allegedly illegal entrants were apprehended and shipped across the border, many without recourse to due process. The Asociación Nacional México-Americana, established in 1950, sought to prevent the separation of family members and the sudden expulsion of individuals who had lived in the United States for more than a decade. But neither that organization nor the League of United Latin American Citizens (LULAC) could stop the abuses against aliens and the violations of the rights of Mexican-American citizens. The havoc and hardships caused by Operation Wetback reinforced Chicanos' mistrust of the government and intensified their alienation from Anglo society.

Overall, *La raza* (the community of the Spanish-speaking) proved powerless in the 1950s to improve the lot of Hispanics, one-third of whom lived below the poverty line. The millions of *mojados* who escaped detention contributed to the depression of wages for Chicanos in general, as did the continuation of the *bracero* program, which brought in nearly a half-million Mexicans a year to work for American growers on a temporary basis. With the continued influx of agricultural laborers, many Chicanos moved to the overcrowded urban American barrios during the 1950s. By 1960 more

than half a million Hispanics resided in the Los Angeles metropolitan area, and the barrios of Denver, El Paso, Phoenix and San Antonio were proportionately as large. The 1960 census estimated that Hispanics composed at least 12 percent of the combined population of Arizona, California, Colorado, New Mexico, and Texas.

Native Americans remained the poorest, most ignored minority. Between 1900 and 1930, Indian tribes had lost more than half the hundred million acres of land they possessed. In 1953, pressured by the agricultural, lumber, and mining interests that coveted the remaining Indian lands, Congress adopted House Concurrent Resolution 108. This measure ended the Indians' status as wards of the United States, granted them citizenship, and called for the liquidation of the reservation system and the termination of all special federal services to tribes. First applied to the Menominees of Wisconsin and the Klamaths of Oregon, tribes that owned valuable timberlands, the new policy proved disastrous. Further impoverishing the Indians whom it affected, the law transferred more than five hundred thousand acres of native American lands to non-Indians. To speed the sale of Indian lands to private developers, the government also established the Voluntary Relocation Program. Designed to lure Indians off the reservations and into urban areas, relocation offices provided native Americans with moving costs, assistance in finding housing and jobs, and living expenses until they obtained work. "We're like wheat," said one Hopi woman who went to the city. "The wind blows, we bend over. . . . You can't stand up when there's wind."

By the end of the decade, more than sixty thousand Indians had left the reservations for urban America. Some became middle-class; some ended up in the run-down shantytowns at the cities' edge; and nearly a third returned to their tribes. The National Congress of American Indians and many tribal councils officially protested termination and relocation. A Seminole petition to President Eisenhower voiced the native Americans' common concern: "We do not say that we are superior or inferior to the White Man and we do not say that the White Man is superior or inferior to us. We do say that we are not White Men but Indians, do not wish to become White Men but wish to remain Indians, and have an outlook on all things different from the outlook of the White Man." But the native Americans' pleas went unanswered. They remained the most invisible of America's "invisible" men and women. Another decade would pass before the nation began to recognize their plight.

Seeds of Disquiet

Still, for most white Americans, the Eisenhower years were a time of relative tranquility and prosperity. Nevertheless, by the late 1950s, feelings of apprehensiveness and a mood of self-scrutiny were rippling across the placid surface of life. Questioning the nation's very goals and purposes, critics spotlighted the shortcomings of American life and expressed impatience with Eisenhower's reluctance to tackle the problems of a radically transformed world. "We find ourselves as a nation on the defensive, and as a people seemingly paralyzed in self-indulgence," declared the president of Princeton University. Harvard's president seconded the notion that the United States was "adrift with little sense of purposeful direction, lacking deeply held conviction, wandering along with no more stirring thought in the minds of the people than the desire for diversion, personal comfort, and safety."

Some worrisome economic trends contributed to the uneasiness. Periodic business recessions, rising unemployment, and the growing national debt made Khrushchev's 1959 threat to bury the United States economically, and his boast that "your grandchildren will live under communism," ring in American ears. At the same time, successful anticolonial movements in the Third World, especially Fidel Castro's takeover of Cuba, diminished Americans' sense of national power, pride, and prestige. Adding to the disquiet were a rising discontent on the part of alienated American youth and a stunningly sophisticated display of technology by the United States' Cold War archrival.

Sputnik

On October 4, 1957, the Soviet Union successfully launched into orbit the first artificial earth satellite, called *Sputnik* ("Little Moon"). Weighing 184 pounds and measuring a mere twenty-two inches

in diameter, it circled the earth at a speed of eighteen thousand miles per hour. *Sputnik* dashed the comfortable American myth of unquestioned technological superiority; and when *Sputnik II,* carrying a live dog, went into a far more distant orbit on November 3, the event loosed a torrent of indignation that Eisenhower had allowed a "technological Pearl Harbor." Many warned that a "missile gap" between the United States and Russia now gravely imperiled the American republic.

The Eisenhower administration initially disparaged the Soviet achievement. One influential presidential adviser publicly quipped that the United States had no interest in the Soviets' "outer-space basketball game." But Eisenhower pushed behind the scenes to have the American Vanguard missile hastily readied to launch a satellite into orbit. On December 6, with many millions watching on TV, the Vanguard rose six feet in the air and then exploded. Newspapers around the globe mockingly rechristened the missile "Flopnik," "Sputter-

Sputnik

Russian citizens examine a replica of the first Sputnik *hanging in a Moscow exhibition hall in 1957.*

nik," and "Rearguard." When asked what Americans would find if they ever reached the moon, physicist Edward Teller joked, "Russians."

The humor masked a deep consternation that provoked Eisenhower to double the funds for missile development to $4.3 billion in 1958 and then raise the sum to $5.3 billion in 1959. To quiet the rampant national self-doubt, he also established the Science Advisory Committee, whose recommendations led to the creation of the National Aeronautics and Space Administration (NASA) in July 1958. By the end of the decade, the United States had launched several space probes and successfully tested the Atlas intercontinental ballistic missile (ICBM) system. But the national unease and humiliation that *Sputnik* left behind lingered on.

Part of the fallout from *Sputnik* was a feverish effort to reshape American education. Critics blamed the schools' emphasis on "life adjustment" for the fact that the Soviet Union was producing twice as many scientists and engineers as the United States. They compared the rigor and competitiveness of Soviet education with America's "soft" schools and complained that the United States reserved for its football stars the laurels that Russia awarded to outstanding students. Progressive education fell into disfavor. Vice Admiral Hyman Rickover, the father of the nuclear submarine, charged that the schools' failure to stress intellectual competence and a solid foundation in basic disciplines endangered national security. "There can be no second place in a contest with Russia," Rickover warned, "and there will be no second chance if we lose."

Sputnik provided the impetus for a crash program aimed at raising educational standards. It cultivated a consensus for change and swept aside the educational establishment's resistance to curriculum reform. Political barriers to federal aid to education tumbled as funds from Washington were swiftly diverted to construct new classrooms and laboratories, improve teacher salaries, and install instructional television systems in American schools. In 1958 Congress passed the National Defense Education Act, which provided nearly $300 million in loans to undergraduate and graduate students, as well as funds for teacher training and for the development of new instructional materials in the sciences, mathematics, and foreign languages.

Americans now banked on higher education to ensure national security. The number of college students, 1.5 million in 1940 and 2.5 million in 1955, skyrocketed to 3.6 million in 1960. That same year, the federal government funneled $1.5 billion to universities, a hundredfold increase over 1940.

This hike in education spending was directly linked to the nation's Cold War struggle with Russia. By 1960 nearly a third of the scientists and engineers on university faculties were engaged in full-time research for the federal government, mostly on defense projects. "This symbiosis between science and military," physicist I. I. Rabi claimed, was "the most important social and political development of this century." Although it channeled many millions of dollars to the nation's campuses, this new liaison between the Pentagon and America's colleges and universities raised unsettling questions. Some suggested that the military-industrial complex of which President Eisenhower warned was in reality a military-industrial-*educational* complex.

A Rebellion of Youth

Even as the education of America's children was undergoing harsh scrutiny, adolescents were experiencing a cultural restiveness that led them into a passionate search for self-definition. Few adults considered the social implications of their affluence on the young, or the consequences of having created a generation of teen-agers who could stay in school rather than have to go to work. Few gave much thought to the impact on children of growing up in an age when traditional values like thrift and self-denial had declining relevance, and of maturing at a time when young people had the leisure and money to shape their own subculture. Moreover, despite talk of family togetherness, fathers were often too busy to give much attention to their children, and mothers sometimes spent more time chauffeuring their young from place to place than communicating with them. Much of what adults knew about teen-age mores they learned from the mass media, which tended to focus on the sensational and the superficial.

The media thrived on accounts of juvenile delinquency, for example. News stories depicted high schools as war zones, city streets as jungles ruled by youth gangs, and teen-agers as zipgun-armed hoodlums. But while it is true that in the midfifties some four hundred thousand youths were annually being convicted of delinquency, this figure did not represent a dramatic spurt over the wartime delinquency rate. And although less than 10 percent of teen-agers had anything to do with gangs and switchblades, the many who sported tightly pegged pants, bandied street slang, and slicked back their hair in the "ducktail" look aroused adult disapproval and alarm.

Also dismaying to parents, young Americans passionately embraced rock-and-roll. While visiting a record store in 1951, Alan Freed, the host of a classical-music program on Cleveland radio, had observed white teen-agers enthusiastically dancing to and buying rhythm-and-blues records. Rhythm-and-blues had traditionally been recorded by and for blacks. Freed surmised that teens were being drawn to the music, with its heavy beat and sexually suggestive lyrics, because of its bold departure from the syrupy pop songs then flowing across the airwaves. In 1952 he started a new radio program called "Moondog's Rock and Roll Party." Its popularity soared, and in 1954 Freed took his program to New York City, where he propelled rock-and-roll—a newly emergent, livelier form heavily based on rhythm-and-blues—into a national craze.

Just as white musicians in the 1920s and 1930s had adapted black jazz for white audiences, so white performers in the 1950s transformed rhythm-and-blues into "Top Ten" rock-and-roll records that were devoured by white youth. Bill Haley and the Comets in 1954 dropped some of the sexual allusions from Joe Turner's version of "Shake, Rattle, and Roll," added country-and-western guitar riffs, and produced the first major rock-and-roll hit. The next year, the Comets had even greater success with "Rock Around the Clock." When Haley performed the song in *The Blackboard Jungle,* a 1955 film about juvenile delinquency, many parents linked rock-and-roll with violence and sex.

Nothing confirmed this connection more decisively in adults' minds than the phenomenal success of the king of rock-and-roll, Elvis Presley. Born in Tupelo, Mississippi, in 1935, Elvis Aron Presley was a nineteen-year-old truck driver in 1954 when, on impulse, he recorded two songs at a Memphis studio, "That's Allright Mama" and "Blue Moon of Kentucky." Melding the pentecostal music of his boyhood Assembly of God church with the hillbilly boogie that he heard on the "Grand Ole Opry"

The King

Elvis's on-stage gyrations won him the nickname "Elvis the Pelvis."

radio shows, and peppering in the frank sexuality of the black South's rhythm-and-blues, Presley added his voice to the exuberant cacophony transforming a popular music that had grown monotonous. His unique blend of musical traditions caught on at once with the restless youth of the fifties.

From January 1956, with the release of "Heartbreak Hotel," to March 1958, when he was drafted, Elvis produced an unprecedented fourteen consecutive million-selling records. Girls screamed at the sound of his voice and swooned at his poutysurly expression; boys adopted black-leather jackets and wore their hair long and greasy in imitation of the superstar.

Ironically, Presley himself craved traditional respectability. Even as his lyrics invited rebelliousness and freedom from parental constraints, Presley was collecting mainstream society's material symbols of success and status, including a fleet of pink Cadillacs and a Memphis mansion that would become a shrine for his fans after his death. In the sixties the raw energy and sexuality of his early songs gave way to saccharine romantic ballads.

But it was the Presley of the 1950s, with his raw delivery and swaggering sensuality, that shocked middle-class white adults, who saw in his smirking lips and bucking hips a fearsome threat to all they held dear. The more adults condemned Elvis and rock-and-roll in general, however, the more teenagers loved it. Record sales tripled between 1954 and 1960 as youths scooped up the 45-rpm recordings of their idols. They made Dick Clark's "American Bandstand," first broadcast nationwide in 1957, one of the decade's biggest TV hits.

Much as teens cherished rock-and-roll for its sexual frankness, immediacy, and exuberance, they elevated the characters played by Marlon Brando in *The Wild One* (1954) and by James Dean in *Rebel Without a Cause* (1955) to cult status for their overturning of respectable society's mores, and they delighted in *Mad* magazine's ridiculing of the phony, pretentious, and absurd in middle-class America. Rejecting Detroit's standards, teenagers customized their cars to make personal statements—which parents rarely understood.

Portents of Change

A group of nonconformist writers known as the Beats expressed an even more fundamental revolt against middle-class society. In such works as Allen Ginsberg's *Howl* (1956) and Jack Kerouac's *On the Road* (1957), the Beats scorned the competition and materialism of the fifties corporate world and scoffed at the "square" America described by Kerouac as "rows of well-to-do houses with lawns and television sets in each living room with everybody looking at the same thing and thinking the same thing at the same time." Romanticizing society's outcasts, they also glorified uninhibited sexuality, spontaneity, and spirituality.

The educated college-age youth who were among the Beats' greatest admirers worked to dissolve the increasingly fragile complacency and cautiousness of the era. Protesting capital punishment and the continuing investigations of the House Un-American Activities Committee, they also vocally decried the nuclear-arms race, and especially nuclear testing. In 1958 and 1959, thousands participated in Youth Marches for Integrated Schools in Washington. By 1960 the "silent generation" was sounding a note of vigorous dissent from stifling conformity. Together with the Beats and rock music, their activism heralded a youth movement and a counterculture that would explode in the 1960s.

Conclusion

The growing disquiet of the late fifties both accelerated the quest for national purpose and underlined the paradox of American society at midcentury. On the one hand, the United States was mightier than any nation in history and basked in a prosperity that enabled many citizens to enjoy "the good life." But on the other hand, Americans felt unease as the U.S.–Soviet arms race heated up and as their booming times brought unsettling social and technological changes.

Still, most Americans concentrated on the sunny facets of the 1950s. Applauding Dwight Eisenhower's moderation and genial leadership, they ignored his warnings about the military-industrial complex and largely closed their eyes to the persistent poverty within segments of society and to the dangerous concentration of power in the economy. Content and comfortable, America's white middle-class looked ahead confidently to continued affluence and peace. Tuning in to coverage of the 1960 campaign on their TV sets, they viewed two presidential candidates who themselves were glowing representatives of the consumer culture. The Democrat John Kennedy and the Republican Richard Nixon affirmed the premises on which America's consensus of anticommunism and economic abundance was based. Each promised to outdo his rival in expanding prosperity and containing communism. Few citizens who followed the campaign imagined that the United

States would soon be waging both a war against poverty and a land war in Asia, or anticipated that the rock-and-roll generation would help topple the South's institutions of white supremacy, challenge the older generation's most cherished values, and usher in an era of confrontation.

CHRONOLOGY

1944 Mark I computer begins operation.

1946 Dr. Benjamin Spock, *Baby and Child Care.*

1947 Levittown, New York, development started.

1948 Bell Lab develops the transistor.

1950 Asociación Nacional México-Americana established.

1952 Dwight D. Eisenhower elected president.

1953 Korean War truce signed.
CIA-supported coup in Iran.
Earl Warren appointed U.S. chief justice.
House Concurrent Resolution 108.

1954 Army-McCarthy hearings.
Brown v. *Board of Education of Topeka.*
Fall of Dienbienphu; Geneva Conference.
Southeast Asia Treaty Organization founded.
CIA intervention in Guatemala.

1955 Salk polio vaccine developed.
AFL-CIO merger.
First postwar U.S.–Soviet summit meeting.
James Dean stars in *Rebel Without a Cause.*
Montgomery bus boycott begins.

1956 Interstate Highway Act.
Suez crisis.
Soviet intervention in Poland and Hungary.
Allen Ginsberg, *Howl.*
Eisenhower reelected.

1957 Eisenhower Doctrine announced.
Civil Rights Act (first since Reconstruction).
Jack Kerouac, *On the Road.*
Little Rock school-desegregation crisis.
Soviet Union launches *Sputnik.*
Peak of "baby boom" (4.3 million births).

1958 U.S. troops sent to Lebanon.
National Defense Education Act.
United States and U.S.S.R. halt atomic tests.
National Aeronautics and Space Administration (NASA) founded.

1959 Fidel Castro comes to power in Cuba.
Khrushchev and Eisenhower meet at Camp David.

1960 National Liberation Front (NLF) established.
U-2 incident.
Second Civil Rights Act.

1961 Eisenhower notes military-industrial complex.

For Further Reading

Charles C. Alexander, *Holding the Line: The Eisenhower Era, 1952–1961* (1975). A balanced overview of Eisenhower's governmental programs and policies.

William H. Chafe, *The American Woman: Her Changing Social, Economic, and Political Roles, 1920–1970* (rev. ed., 1988). An incisive examination of discrimination against women and their efforts to overcome it.

Robert A. Divine, *Eisenhower and the Cold War* (1981). A sympathetic look at Eisenhower's foreign policy.

Dwight D. Eisenhower, *Mandate for Change, 1952–1956* (1963) and *Waging Peace* (1965). Eisenhower's memoirs of his presidency.

Emmet J. Hughes, *The Ordeal of Power* (1963). An enlightening inside account of Eisenhower's leadership.

Richard Kluger, *Simple Justice: The History of Brown v. Board of Education and Black America's Struggle for Equality* (1975). A magisterial history of the legal fight against school segregation.

Peter Lyon, *Eisenhower: Portrait of a Hero* (1974). An unflattering but highly detailed biography.

Walter A. McDougall, . . . *The Heavens and the Earth: A Political History of the Space Age* (1985). A probing investigation of the diplomatic and political factors affecting the space program.

Douglas Miller and Marian Novak. *The Fifties: The Way We Really Were* (1977). A critical, often caustic survey of social and cultural developments.

Geoffrey Perrett, *A Dream of Greatness: The American People, 1945–1963* (1979). A massive, richly evocative social history of the postwar era.

Additional Bibliography

The Eisenhower Administration

Stephen E. Ambrose, *Eisenhower* (2 vols., 1983–1984); Robert F. Burk, *The Eisenhower Administration and Black Civil Rights* (1984); Fred Greenstein, *The Hidden-Hand Presidency* (1982); Elizabeth Huckaby, *Crisis at Central High: Little Rock, 1957–1958* (1980); Stephen S. Lawson, *Black Ballots: Voting Rights in the South, 1944–1969* (1976); Herbert Parmet, *Eisenhower and the American Crusades* (1972); Gary W. Reichard, *The Reaffirmation of Republicanism: Eisenhower and the Eighty-third Congress* (1975); David W. Reinhard, *The Republican Right Since 1945* (1983); Elmo Richardson, *The Presidency of Dwight D. Eisenhower* (1979); Bernard Schwartz, *Super Chief: Earl Warren and His Supreme Court* (1983).

Foreign Affairs and Policies

Richard A. Aliano, *American Defense Policy from Eisenhower to Kennedy* (1975); Stephen E. Ambrose, *Ike's Spies: Eisenhower and the Espionage Establishment* (1981); Douglas S. Blaufarb, *The Counterinsurgency Era* (1977); Blanche Wiesen Cook, *The Declassified Eisenhower: A Divided Legacy* (1981); Robert A. Divine, *Blowing in the Wind: The Nuclear Test Ban Debate, 1954–1960* (1978); George C. Herring, *America's Longest War: The United States and Vietnam, 1950–1975* (1979); Richard Immerman, *The CIA in Guatemala* (1982); Burton Kaufman, *Trade and Aid: Eisenhower's Foreign Economic Policy* (1982); Donald Neff, *Warriors at Suez* (1981); John Stockwell, *In Search of Enemies* (1978).

The Economy and the Affluent Society

David P. Calleo, *The Imperious Economy* (1982); Gilbert C. Fite, *American Farmers* (1981); John Kenneth Galbraith, *The Affluent Society* (1958) and *The New Industrial State* (1971); Mark I. Gelfand, *A Nation of Cities* (1975); James R. Green, *The World of the Worker* (1980); Dolores Hayden, *Redesigning the American Dream* (1984); Kenneth T. Jackson, *The Crabgrass Frontier* (1986); Zane L. Miller, *Suburb: Neighborhood and Community in Forest Park, Ohio, 1935–1976* (1981); Ralph Parkman, *The Cybernetic Society* (1972); John B. Rae, *The Road and the Car in American Life* (1971); Gwendolyn Wright, *Building the Dream: A Social History of Housing in America* (1981).

Cultural Conservatism

Erik Barnouw, *The Image Empire* (1970); Peter Biskind, *Seeing Is Believing: How Hollywood Taught Us to Stop Worrying and Love the Fifties* (1983); Paul A. Carter, *Another Part of the Fifties* (1983); Barbara B. Clowse, *Brainpower for the Cold War: The Sputnik Crisis and the National Defense Education Act of 1958* (1981); Ruth Schwartz Cowan, *More Work for Mother* (1983); Richard A. Easterlin, *Birth and Fortune: The Impact of Numbers on Personal Welfare* (1980); Jeffrey Hart, *When the Going Was Good: American Life in the Fifties* (1982); Will Herberg, *Protestant, Catholic, Jew* (rev. ed., 1960); Landon Y. Jones, *Great Expectations: America and the Baby Boom Generation* (1980); Eugenia Kaledin, *Mothers and More: American Women in the 1950s* (1984); Susan Estabrook Kennedy, *If All We Did Was to Weep at Home: A History of White Working-Class Women in America* (1979); Alice Kessler-Harris, *Out to Work: A History of Wage-Earning Women in the United States* (1982); George Lipsitz, *Class and Culture in Cold War America* (1981); Richard Pells, *The Liberal Mind in a Conservative Age: American Intellectuals in the 1940s and 1950s* (1984); David Riesman, *The Lonely Crowd* (1950); Sheila M. Rothman, *Woman's Proper Place: A History of Changing Ideas and Practices, 1870 to the Present* (1978); Susan Strasser, *Never Done: A History of American Housework* (1982); William H. Whyte, *The Organization Man* (1956).

The Other America

Rodolfo Acuna, *Occupied America: A History of Chicanos* (1981); Larry W. Burt, *Tribalism in Crisis: Federal Indian Policy, 1953–1961* (1982); J. Wayne Flynt, *Dixie's Forgotten People: The South's Poor Whites* (1979); Simon Frith, *Sound Effects: Youth, Leisure and the Politics of Rock and Roll* (1981); Charlie Gillett, *The Sound of the City: The Rise of Rock 'n' Roll* (rev. ed., 1983); Michael Harrington, *The Other America* (1962); Alvin M. Josephy, Jr., *Now That the Buffalo's Gone* (1982); David Lewis, *King: A Critical Biography* (1970); Oscar Lewis, *La Vida* (1966); Manning Marable, *Race, Reform, and Rebellion: The Second Reconstruction in Black America, 1945–1982* (1984); Greil Marcus, *The Mystery Train* (1982); Stephen B. Oates, *Let the Trumpet Sound: The Life of Martin Luther King, Jr.* (1982); Elena Padilla, *Up from Puerto Rico* (1958); James T. Patterson, *America's Struggle Against Poverty, 1900–1980* (1981); Harvard Sitkoff, *The Struggle for Black Equality, 1954–1980* (1981).

CHAPTER 29

The Turbulent Sixties

In late January 1960, four black freshmen at North Carolina Agricultural and Technical (A & T) College in Greensboro discussed their humiliation over not being allowed to eat alongside white diners in restaurants and at lunch counters in the South. Middle class in aspirations, the children of urban civil servants and industrial workers, they believed that the Supreme Court's *Brown* decision of 1954 should have swiftly ended the indignities of racial discrimination and segregation. But the promise of change had outrun reality. Massive resistance to racial equality still proved the rule throughout Dixie. In 1960 most southern blacks could neither vote nor attend integrated schools. No matter how wealthy or educated, they could not enjoy a cup of coffee alongside whites in a public restaurant. Impatient yet hopeful, the A & T students could not accept the inequality that their parents had endured. They had been inspired by the Montgomery bus boycott led by Martin Luther King, Jr., in 1956, as well as by successful African independence movements in the late fifties in Ghana, the Belgian Congo, and other former European colonial possessions.

On the afternoon of February 1, the four young blacks entered the local Woolworth's and sat down at the lunch counter. "We don't serve colored here," the waitress replied when the freshmen asked for coffee and doughnuts. The students remained seated. They would not be moved. They vowed to sit in until the store closed and to repeat their request the next day and beyond, until they were served. On February 2 more than twenty A & T students joined them in their protest. The following day,

over sixty sat in. By the end of the week, the students overflowed Woolworth's and sat in at the lunch counter in the nearby S. H. Kress store. Six months later, after prolonged sit-ins, boycotts, and demonstrations, Greensboro's white civic leaders grudgingly allowed blacks to sit down at a restaurant and be served.

Meanwhile, the Greensboro "coffee party" had inspired similar sit-ins throughout North Carolina and in neighboring states. By April 1960 sit-ins had disrupted seventy-eight southern communities, and more than two thousand students had been arrested. Within a year both figures doubled; and by September 1961 some seventy thousand young blacks and whites had joined together to sit in to desegregate eating facilities as well as to "kneel in" in churches, "sleep in" in motel lobbies, "wade in" on restricted beaches, "read in" at public libraries, "play in" at city parks, and even "watch in" at segregated movie theaters.

The courage of the A & T students had transformed the struggle for racial equality. Their devotion to the cause emboldened black adults to voice their dissatisfaction, and it brought young blacks a new sense of self-respect and strength. "I myself desegregated a lunch counter, not somebody else, not some big man, some powerful man, but little me," claimed a black student. "I walked the picket line and I sat in and the walls of segregation toppled." Each new victory convinced thousands more that "nothing can stop us now."

The winds of change stirred by the sit-ins swept away the quiet complacency that characterized much of the 1950s. Watching the film footage of demonstrations and arrests each evening on his television set in Harlem in 1960, a young black teacher named Robert Moses felt their impact. "The students in that picture had a certain look on their faces, sort of sullen, angry, determined," recalled Moses, who would soon lead the drive to register black voters in Mississippi. "Before, the Negro in the South had always looked on the defensive, cringing. This time they were taking the initiative. They were kids my age, and I knew this had something to do with my life." Meanwhile, that same year, socialist Michael Harrington began to investigate the plight of the poor in an America that barely acknowledged their existence; Ralph Nader, a recent graduate of Harvard Law School, sounded the alarm that many automobiles were "unsafe at any speed"; marine biologist Rachel Carson was researching a book on the environmental hazards of pesticides, published in 1962 as *The Silent Spring*; and mother and writer Betty Friedan was beginning work on what would become a pathbreaking 1963 book on sexism, *The Feminine Mystique*.

These endeavors symbolized the sense of new beginnings that prevailed in the early sixties. Restless impatience and idealism, especially on the part of young Americans, led many to embrace John Kennedy's New Frontier and to rally behind Lyndon Johnson's Great Society. Both administrations' rhetorical emphasis on social justice generated fervent hopes and soaring expectations among the poorest Americans. But the assassinations of cherished national leaders, widespread racial strife, and U.S. involvement in Vietnam dampened optimism, and a reaction by the majority who opposed radical change ultimately curtailed social reform. The shimmering promise of a new decade would end in discord and disillusionment.

The New Frontier, 1960–1963

In 1960 John Fitzgerald Kennedy personified the energy, freshness, and self-confidence of American youth. On television, Kennedy projected an image of idealistic commitment and vigor (or "vigah," as he pronounced it). Capitalizing on his wealth, intelligence, and rugged good looks, he became the symbol of innovation, of imaginative new approaches to old problems.

His father, Joseph P. Kennedy, had earned a fortune from shipping, investment, liquor, and real-estate interests. A generous contributor to the Democratic party, he had secured several appointive posts from Franklin Roosevelt. But his prewar isolationism had prevented him from gaining elective office and admittance to the party's inner circles. Similarly, his Irish-Catholic roots and open pursuit of movie actresses had excluded the self-made multimillionaire from the nation's social elite. Seething with unfulfilled ambitions, the combative Joe Kennedy raised his four sons to attain the political power and social recognition that had eluded him. He drove them unrelentingly, instilling in each a passion to excel and to rule. Despite a severe back injury, John Kennedy played sports at Harvard and served in the navy during World War II. Behind the scenes the elder Kennedy promoted his son's career. He persuaded a journalist to rework John's senior thesis into the critically acclaimed book *Why England Slept* (for which John got full credit); and he prevailed upon a popular novelist to publish articles lauding John's heroism in rescuing sailors after their PT boat had been sunk in the South Pacific.

Esteemed as a war hero and scholar, John Kennedy employed his charm and his father's political connections to win election in 1946 to the House of Representatives from a Boston district where he had never lived. Yet Kennedy found committee work boring and did little to distinguish himself in the Congress. Despite his lackluster performance, the voters of Massachusetts were captivated by his personality and pleased with his moderately liberal voting record; they sent him to the Senate in 1952 and overwhelmingly reelected him six years later. By then Kennedy had a beautiful wife, Jacqueline, and a Pulitzer Prize for *Profiles in Courage,* a book written primarily by a staff member.

Only Kennedy's religion appeared to threaten his political future. No Catholic had ever been elected president; and the 1928 defeat of Alfred E.

Smith had convinced many politicians that none ever could be. Nevertheless, Kennedy's popularity and formidable political organization gained him a first-ballot victory at the 1960 Democratic convention in Los Angeles. Just forty-two years old when he accepted the nomination, Kennedy sounded the theme of a "New Frontier." Appealing to advocates of change, he issued an urgent summons for reform at home and victory abroad and called for "more sacrifice instead of more security" on the part of an America on "the frontier of unknown opportunities and perils."

The Election of 1960

The Kennedy challenge stirred the imagination of youth. "All at once you had something exciting," recalled Don Ferguson, a University of Nebraska student who joined the Kennedy campaign. "You had a guy who had little kids and who liked to play football on his front lawn. Kennedy was talking about pumping new life into the nation and steering it in new directions." But middle-aged, middle-class Americans, the bulk of the electorate, seemed to be looking for something else: stability, security, and the continuation of Eisenhower's "middle way" promised by the Republican candidate, Vice President Richard M. Nixon. Although scorned by liberals for his association with McCarthyism, Nixon had the advantage of being better known and more experienced than his Democratic rival. Further, he was a Protestant. Most important, he was closely identified with the still popular Ike.

Conducting an uninspiring campaign, however, Nixon fumbled his opportunity. He conceded that he and Kennedy shared the same policies and differed "only about the means to reaching those goals," and he devoted most of his time to defending the Eisenhower record. His greatest mistake, however, was agreeing to meet Kennedy in a series of four debates.

An audience of more than 70 million tuned in to the nation's first televised encounter between presidential candidates, an event that established the dominance of the mass media in American politics. The contrast between a haggard, pale Nixon, still recuperating from a knee infection that had hospitalized him for two weeks, and a dynamic, tanned Kennedy was striking. The telegenic Democrat radiated confidence and poise; his opponent appeared tense and insecure as he sweated visibly

under his pasty facial make-up. Although radio listeners considered the contest a draw, the far larger number that watched on TV believed that the Democratic challenger had bested the front-running vice president. Kennedy immediately shot up in the polls, and Nixon never regained the lead.

Kennedy benefited from the embarrassing U-2 incident and an economic recession that had marred Eisenhower's final year in office. He also boosted his chances by firmly endorsing the separation of church and state and supporting civil rights for blacks. His choice of Senate majority leader Lyndon B. Johnson, a Protestant and moderate from Texas, as his running mate, improved the likelihood of Democratic success in the South.

Still, the 1960 presidential election was the closest since 1888. Kennedy's hairbreadth margin of just 118,550 votes out of more than 68 million cast, 49.7 percent of the popular vote to Nixon's 49.5 percent, reflected a widespread desire to keep things as they were, as well as a hostility to the idea of a Catholic president. Post-election surveys revealed that Kennedy failed to secure the votes of more than 4 million usually Democratic Protestants, mainly in the South and trans-Mississippi West. This failure significantly lowered his popular tally, although most of the South remained in the

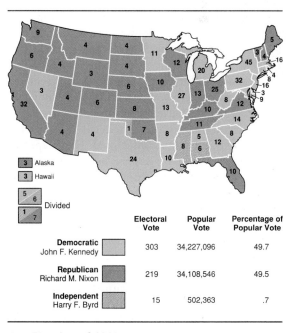

	Electoral Vote	Popular Vote	Percentage of Popular Vote
Democratic John F. Kennedy	303	34,227,096	49.7
Republican Richard M. Nixon	219	34,108,546	49.5
Independent Harry F. Byrd	15	502,363	.7

The Election of 1960

Democratic column. However, Kennedy's capture of 80 percent of the Catholic vote in the closely contested midwestern and northeastern states played a crucial role in his 303-to-219 margin in the electoral college. Although Nixon carried more states than Kennedy, the Democrat's popularity with Catholics, blacks, and other urban minorities gave Kennedy a slender victory.

"To Get America Moving Again"

Hatless and coatless in a snow-blanketed Washington, Kennedy set the tone of a new era at his inauguration: "Let the word go forth from this time and place, to friend and foe alike, that the torch has been passed to a new generation of Americans." The president surrounded himself with bright young academics and intellectuals who contrasted sharply with the staid businessmen of the Eisenhower administration. His advisers and cabinet members included McGeorge Bundy, a youthful dean of Harvard University, as special assistant for national-security affairs; Robert McNamara, a statistical wizard and president of the Ford Motor Company, as secretary of defense; and Walter Heller, a University of Minnesota professor, as chairman of the Council of Economic Advisers. For attorney general the president selected his closest confidant, his thirty-five-year-old brother Robert Kennedy. Replying to the criticism that his appointee lacked the background and maturity for the post, JFK quipped: "I see nothing wrong with giving Robert some legal experience before he goes out to practice law."

Kennedy adopted a dynamic style calculated to broaden his popular support and help him gain reelection. Exploiting television to the hilt, he exuded promise and purpose in his frequent TV speeches, interviews, and press conferences. Every appearance underscored the president's charisma and his urgent determination "to get America moving again." Kennedy, moreover, aided by his wife, adorned his presidency with the trappings of culture and intellectual excellence. He filled government posts with Rhodes scholars and invited distinguished artists to perform at the White House. Speechwriters like historian Arthur Schlesinger, Jr., embellished his addresses with quotations from Emerson and references to Aristotle. His taste and grace awed the media, and reporters endlessly extolled the first family's glamour and vitality.

John Fitzgerald Kennedy

Of the Kennedy years, historian Arthur Schlesinger observed: "Washington seemed engaged in a collective effort to make itself brighter, gayer, more intellectual, more resolute. It was a golden interlude."

Kennedy's Domestic Record

The media's image of a driving, innovative administration obscured the reality of Kennedy's unexceptional domestic record. There was hardly a New Frontier in legislation. Kennedy simply lacked the votes in Congress to knock down the barriers to reform erected by Republicans and southern Democrats, the same conservative coalition that had stifled Truman's Fair Deal.

Congress rejected the president's liberal proposals to fight poverty, provide federal aid to education, and finance medical care for the elderly through the social-security system. Conservative legislators even compromised his modest efforts to increase the minimum wage, authorize federal assistance for mass transit and middle-class housing, and establish manpower-training and redevelopment programs in chronically depressed areas. Constrained by the power of the conservative coalition and by his weak electoral mandate, Kennedy rarely pressed the legislators to enact his reform measures, maintaining that "there is no sense in raising hell and then not being successful."

Instead, JFK made economic growth his top domestic priority. To stimulate the flagging economy that he had inherited from Eisenhower, Kennedy combined increased defense and space expenditures with generous inducements to private enterprise to invest in capital growth. The president persuaded Congress in 1961 to boost the defense budget by nearly 20 percent, procuring not only five times more intercontinental ballistic missiles than Eisenhower had thought necessary but also a vastly augmented stockpile of medium-range missiles and nuclear submarines armed with Polaris missiles. Further, he pushed Congress to bolster America's ability to fight limited conventional wars and thereby, as Kennedy put it in July 1961, gave the nation "a wider choice than humiliation or all-out nuclear action." To checkmate insurgencies in the Third World—what the communists called wars of national liberation—the president strengthened the strategic reserves, added new combat-ready army divisions and tactical air wings, and established Special Forces units ("Green Berets") trained in guerrilla warfare. Both to stimulate the economy and to enhance American prestige, Kennedy persuaded Congress to finance a multibillion-dollar crash effort to place a man on the moon by 1970. (It would eventually cost the United States more than $25 billion to land astronaut Neil Armstrong on the lunar surface in 1969.)

Accepting unbalanced budgets as a price of stimulating long-term economic growth, Kennedy proposed lower business taxes through investment credits and generous depreciation allowances. Most business groups, however, remained suspicious of Kennedy and were quick to blame the White House whenever stock prices dipped. In April 1962 their uneasiness turned to wrath when Kennedy marshaled all the presidency's power to enforce informal wage-and-price restraints to curb inflation. Reacting angrily when U.S. Steel jacked up steel prices by six dollars a ton just after he had pressured the steelworkers' union to accept a non-inflationary contract with minimal wage increases, the president publicly denounced the steel company, threatened it with antitrust lawsuits and cancellation of government contracts, and mobilized the Federal Trade Commission and the FBI to investigate price agreements among steel produc-

ers. U.S. Steel backed down and rescinded its price hike. But the business community's resentment of the president's actions also forced Kennedy to relent. When the steel companies raised prices twice within a year, Kennedy said and did nothing. And in January 1963, when he announced his major effort to stimulate economic growth, the president explicitly rejected liberal proposals to increase expenditures on social programs; instead, he advocated holding federal spending constant while reducing both personal and corporate taxes as a way of encouraging private investment and consumption.

When the Kennedy presidency tragically ended in November 1963, his tax cut still remained bottled up in Congress. His management of the economy, however, had already more than doubled the rate of economic growth, decreased unemployment from 6 percent to 5 percent, and held inflation to just 1.3 percent a year. Fulfilling his promise to get the country moving again, he had introduced the longest uninterrupted era of economic expansion in American history. Still, liberal critics grumbled about "the third Eisenhower administration." They deplored Kennedy's failure to effect any redistribution of income or to plug the large tax loopholes that benefited the rich. They regretted that corporate profits had risen five times more than personal income and that Kennedy had promoted military spending at the expense of social welfare. They especially condemned Kennedy for neglecting the needs of the public sector. Mused John Kenneth Galbraith, one of the president's liberal economic advisers, who had sought a massive federal-spending program to create more jobs and improve public services: "I am not sure what the advantage is in having a few more dollars to spend if the air is too dirty to breathe, the water too polluted to drink, the commuters [unable] . . . to get in and out of the cities, the streets . . . filthy, and the schools so bad that the young, perhaps wisely, stay away, and hoodlums roll citizens for some of the dollars that they save in taxes."

Galbraith's allusion to dirty air and polluted water hinted at what by the early 1960s had become a matter of deepening public concern: environmental pollution. Awareness of the fragility of the earth's ecosystem, initially awakened during the fallout scare of the 1950s, intensified with the publication of Rachel Carson's *Silent Spring* in 1963. Carson's somber documentation of the hazards of DDT and other pesticides set off a national furor comparable to the impact of Upton Sinclair's 1906 exposé of the meat-packing industry, *The Jungle*. President Kennedy at once appointed an advisory committee on pesticides, and tough federal regulation eventually followed. Other environmental measures enacted by Congress in these years included the 1963 Clean Air Act, regulating automotive and industrial emissions, and a 1966 law forbidding the dumping of wastes and pollutants into the nation's lakes and rivers. An environmentally disastrous oil spill off Santa Barbara, California, led to the passage of an even stronger water-quality control act in 1970. After decades of heedless pollution, the nation was beginning to realize the heavy environmental risks that came with the advantages of a modern industrial order.

Kennedy and Civil Rights

When Kennedy enumerated the nation's "unfinished and neglected tasks" in his first State of the Union address, he did not even mention racial injustice. Clearly the president did not anticipate the intensity of the crusade for civil rights that would soon engulf the South, nor would he welcome it. Although Kennedy had claimed during the campaign that "if the president does not himself wage the struggle for equal rights—if he stands above the battle—then the battle will inevitably be lost," he straddled the issue for more than two years of his presidency. He worried that the fight for racial equality would divide Americans "at a time when the international scene required maximum unity." Most of all, Kennedy feared that the civil-rights issue would hopelessly split the Democratic party and entangle Congress in lengthy filibusters. Such a division would jeopardize the rest of his legislative program, not to mention his reelection hopes.

Accordingly, Kennedy treated racial problems as a thorny thicket to be tiptoed around rather than a preeminent moral issue requiring decisive leadership. He balanced his selection of an unprecedented number of blacks for high office with the appointment of white racists to federal judgeships. His Department of Justice greatly increased efforts to speed desegregation by litigation yet remained aloof from attempts by congressional liberals to enact civil-rights legislation. After stalling for two years on his campaign pledge to ban discrimination in federally financed housing with "a stroke

of the pen," the president issued a weak executive order that did little to lessen the residential segregation that both symbolically and in fact set blacks apart from white Americans. "If tokenism were our goal," wrote Martin Luther King, Jr., "this Administration has moved us adroitly toward its accomplishment."

But agitators for black rights kept pressure on the president. In the spring of 1961, the Congress of Racial Equality (CORE), an interracial protest group founded in 1942, organized a "freedom ride" through the Deep South to dramatize the widespread violation of a 1960 Supreme Court decision outlawing segregation in all bus and train stations used by interstate travelers. The freedom riders' efforts to desegregate terminals aroused the ire of southern whites. In Anniston, Alabama, Ku Klux Klansmen savagely beat the freedom riders and burned their bus; a white mob in Birmingham mercilessly mauled a CORE contingent. Not until rampaging whites in Montgomery even more viciously assaulted the freedom riders did Kennedy finally dispatch federal marshals to end the violence. And not until after scores more freedom rides and the arrest of hundreds of young protesters did the president press the Interstate Commerce Commission to enforce the Supreme Court's ruling.

Kennedy again used federal force to quell white racist violence in the fall of 1962. When a federal court ordered the University of Mississippi to enroll James Meredith, a black air-force veteran, angry whites, egged on by Mississippi's defiant governor Ross Barnett, rioted. Rallying behind Confederate battle flags, students and outside troublemakers attacked the federal marshals who had escorted Meredith to "Ole Miss." The Battle of Oxford left two dead, hundreds injured, and the campus shrouded in tear gas. Only the presence of thousands of federal troops finally restored order—and upheld the right of a black American to attend the university of his home state.

The Black Revolution

By 1963, with mounting numbers of blacks and whites determined to secure racial equality, Kennedy could hesitate no longer. The climax came in Birmingham, Alabama. Determined to provoke a confrontation that would fully expose the violent extremism of southern white racism and finally

Freedom Riders

In May 1961 stunned and shaken freedom riders watched their bus burn after it was set ablaze by a group of whites in Anniston, Alabama.

force the Kennedy administration's hand, Martin Luther King, Jr., initiated a series of marches, sit-ins, and pray-ins on Good Friday. With each protest bringing more and more arrests, Birmingham police commissioner Eugene "Bull" Connor scoffed that King would soon "run out of niggers." But as thousands of black schoolchildren joined King's crusade, Connor grew impatient and tried to crush the black movement with overwhelming force. He unleashed his men, armed with electric cattle prods, high-pressure water hoses, and snarling attack dogs, on the nonviolent demonstrators, many of them women and children. The ferocity of Connor's attacks, chronicled daily on the television news programs of many nations, filled the world with revulsion.

"The civil-rights movement should thank God for Bull Connor," JFK remarked. "He's helped it as much as Abraham Lincoln." Connor's vicious tactics seared the nation's conscience and at last impelled Kennedy to work to end segregation. Behind the scenes the president pressured Birmingham's economic and political leaders to accept a compromise settlement that ended the demonstrations in return for the desegregation of stores and the upgrading of black workers. By mid-1963 blacks and whites in hundreds of southern towns and cities had seized the initiative in the struggle for racial equality. The rallying cry "Freedom Now!" reverberated through the land as the number and mag-

nitude of the protests soared. Concerned about America's image abroad, and even more about the "fires of frustration and discord" raging at home, Kennedy believed that if the federal government did not lead the way toward "peaceful and constructive" changes in race relations, blacks would turn to far more militant leaders and methods. When Governor George Wallace refused to allow two black students to enter the University of Alabama in June 1963, Kennedy no longer temporized. He promptly forced Wallace—who had pledged "Segregation now! Segregation tomorrow! Segregation forever!"—to capitulate to a court desegregation order.

On June 11 the president went before television cameras to define civil rights as "a moral issue . . . as old as the Scriptures and . . . as clear as the American Constitution." Compassionately describing the plight of blacks in the Jim Crow America of 1963, he asked: "Who among us would be content to have the color of his skin changed and stand in his place? Who among us would then be content with the counsels of patience and delay?" The president concluded that the moral crisis "cannot be met by repressive police action" or "quieted by token moves or talk. It is time to act in the Congress, in your state and local legislative body, and, above all, in our daily lives." A week later Kennedy proposed a comprehensive civil-rights measure. Although House liberals quickly moved to broaden and toughen Kennedy's proposal, most members of Congress seemed immune to the president's plea.

To compel Congress to act, nearly 250,000 Americans converged on the Capitol on August 28 (see "A Place in Time"). But neither Kennedy's nor Martin Luther King's eloquence could quell the murderous rage of the bitterest opponents of civil rights. The same night of the president's civil-rights address, Medgar Evers, the head of the Mississippi branch of the NAACP, was shot by a sniper in Jackson, Mississippi. In September the bombing of a black church in Birmingham killed four girls attending a Sunday school class. And still, southern obstructionism kept the civil-rights bill stymied in Congress, with little hope of passage.

New Frontiers Abroad, 1960–1963

In his inaugural address, John Kennedy claimed to have been "granted the role of defending freedom in its hour of maximum danger." "[W]e shall pay any price, bear any burden, oppose any foe," he vowed, "to assure the survival and success of liberty." Soon after his inauguration, he launched a major buildup of the nation's military arsenal and adopted a new strategy of "flexible response." To "deter all wars, general or unlimited, nuclear or conventional, large or small," Kennedy tripled America's overall nuclear capabilities, augmented its conventional military strength, and formed the Green Berets to meet the challenge of procommunist guerrillas in the Third World.

At the same time, to reduce communism's appeal in Africa, Asia, and Latin America, Kennedy gained congressional backing for his expanded program of economic assistance to promote "peaceful revolution" in the Third World. A new Agency for International Development coordinated foreign aid. The Food for Peace program distributed surplus agricultural products. The Alliance for Progress envisioned a $100 billion joint public and private effort aimed at social reform and economic development in Latin America. Everyone in the Western Hemisphere had "a right to social justice," Kennedy affirmed, and this meant "land for the landless, and education for those who are denied education." In addition, the president in 1961 created the Peace Corps. By 1963 some five thousand volunteers were serving two-year stints as teachers, sanitation engineers, crop spe-

Peace Corps Volunteer in North Borneo

John Kennedy reinforced the soaring idealism of a new generation coming of age in the early 1960s. One student recalled that "we all . . . pictured dreams of a better world as simple and inevitably redemptive."

cialists, and health workers in more than forty Third World nations. Still, Kennedy clung to the containment policy of his predecessors. Determined to halt communism's spread, Kennedy emphasized power, toughness, and tests of will in his actions. "We must not tempt them with weakness," he declared in his inaugural.

Cold War Activism

Kennedy's first foreign-policy crisis came in the spring of 1961. To eliminate a communist outpost on America's doorstep, Kennedy approved plans, originally drawn up by the Eisenhower administration, for fifteen hundred anti-Castro exiles, "La Brigada," to storm Cuba's Bay of Pigs. The scheme, poorly conceived by the CIA but endorsed by the Joint Chiefs of Staff, assumed that the invasion would trigger a general uprising of the Cuban people to dethrone Fidel Castro. It was a fiasco.

The invaders never even established a defensible beachhead. Deprived of air support by a last-minute Kennedy decision aimed at concealing the United States' direct involvement in the invasion, the exiles were no match for Castro's superior forces. The Cuban people did not rise up, and the island's militia killed nearly five hundred invaders and captured the rest in less than three days. The president accepted blame for the failure. But he neither apologized for, nor desisted in, his effort to overthrow Castro. In violation of American treaty agreements, and to the outrage of many Latin Americans, Kennedy continued to interfere in Cuban affairs. He supported further raids by exiles, as well as CIA plots to assassinate Castro. The president did not want the Soviet leadership to interpret his abandonment of La Brigada as a sign of weakness.

An opportunity to prove his fighting ardor came in June 1961, when he met with Soviet leader Nikita Khrushchev to try to resolve the matters of a peace treaty with Germany and the presence of Western forces in Berlin (see Chapter 27). Comparing the American troops in that divided city to "a bone stuck in the throat," Khrushchev threatened war unless the West removed them. Perceiving the young American president as inexperienced and easily intimidated, Khrushchev, rather than negotiating, announced that he would sign a separate German peace agreement with East Germany that would imperil Western occupation rights in Berlin. A visibly shaken Kennedy returned to the United States and declared the defense of West Berlin essential to the Free World. Claiming that "Khrushchev wants to rub dirt in my nose," Kennedy ordered more than 150,000 reservists and National Guardsmen to active duty, sought an additional $3 billion in defense spending, and went on TV to announce a nationwide crash program of nuclear-fallout shelters. The sudden possibility of thermonuclear war steadily grew until mid-August, when the Soviets settled for a stalemate. Leaving unchanged the American role in West Germany and Berlin, the Russians signed a peace treaty with East Germany and constructed a wall of concrete and barbed wire to seal off their zone of Berlin. Designed to stop the flow of Germans from the communist sector (about a thousand refugees a day in July 1961), the Berlin Wall ended the exodus of brains and talent that had menaced the very economic survival of the East German state. Yet at the same time, it became an enduring symbol of communist failure and denial of personal freedom. Although neither the Soviets nor the Americans could claim total

victory, Kennedy believed that his toughness had paid off.

Missiles and Détente

In mid-October 1962 American aerial photographs revealed that the Soviet Union had begun to construct missile bases and to place both medium-range (one-thousand-mile) and intermediate-range (two-thousand-mile) missiles in Cuba. Smarting from the United States' loss of face at the Bay of Pigs, and fearing that unchecked Soviet interference in the Western Hemisphere would demolish American credibility around the globe, Kennedy resolved to respond strongly. After a week of intense secret discussions with his most trusted advisers, the president went on television on October 22 to inform the nation of "this clandestine, reckless, and provocative threat to world peace." Blasting the Soviets' actions as an "unjustified change in the status quo which cannot be accepted by this country, if our courage and our commitments are ever to be trusted again by friend or foe," Kennedy issued an ultimatum to the Kremlin that the missiles be removed. The United States would "quarantine" Cuba—that is, impose a naval blockade around the island—to prevent delivery of more missiles and would dismantle the missiles already in Cuba by force if the Russians did not do so themselves.

Kennedy's announcement alarmed the nation and the world. Never before had the two superpowers appeared to be moving on such a direct collision course toward a nuclear holocaust. Khrushchev denounced the quarantine as "outright banditry." For four days apprehension mounted as Soviet technicians worked feverishly to complete the missile launch pads and Russian missile-carrying ships steamed toward the U.S. blockade. Fearful of an impending nuclear attack, Americans remained close to their radio and television sets, hoping for a peaceful resolution of the crisis. As they waited, 180 U.S. naval ships in the Caribbean prepared to confront the Soviet freighters; B-52s armed with atomic bombs took to the air; and nearly a quarter-million troops assembled in Florida to invade Cuba. A solemn secretary of state Dean Rusk reported, "We're eyeball to eyeball."

Suddenly, on October 25, Rusk declared, "I think the other fellow just blinked." The Cuba-

Washington, D.C., in 1963

In 1963 the racially separate and unequal nation's capital more closely resembled a divided southern city than a showplace of democracy. Beyond the gleaming marble façades of Washington's public buildings lay a city of black slums as appalling as any in the nation. The flight of the white middle class to suburban Maryland and Virginia had abandoned large residential sections of Washington to blacks. Within the shadow of the Capitol, more than 40 percent of the city's families lived below the poverty level in a black ghetto of wretched, rat-infested rooming houses, poolrooms, and secondhand shops. No other American city exceeded the District of Columbia in rates of infant mortality, venereal disease,

and arrests for prostitution and drugs. And while, as the seat of the federal government, Washington could boast the highest per capita income of any American city, a large proportion of its citizens, including innumerable blacks, subsisted on welfare. Most blacks fortunate enough to have jobs held low-paying government posts or served as the waiters, maids, and cooks for the whites in power. But many had no work at all.

It was to the Washington of stately white monuments that civil-rights groups planned to march in 1963 to dramatize grassroots support for federal action against racial discrimination and segregation. To improve the chances of the civil-rights bill proposed by President

John Kennedy, they bypassed the drab streets of the black ghetto and rallied on the Mall, the very symbol of American nationhood and democracy.

As the sun rose over Washington on August 28, radio news bulletins predicted that the crowd would fall short of the 100,000 people expected. But throughout the morning a seemingly endless caravan of cars, buses, trains, and planes brought in an estimated quarter-million pilgrims from every part of the country and from abroad—powerful evidence of the new consensus in favor of a strong civil-rights act. More than 150,000 blacks mingled with some 75,000 whites on the grassy slopes surrounding the Washington Monument. In the spirit of church outing, they shared picnic lunches, sang songs of the movement, and then surged toward the Lincoln Memorial, holding aloft banners proclaiming such messages as "WE SEEK THE FREEDOM IN 1963 PROMISED IN 1863" and "A CENTURY-OLD DEBT TO PAY." Massed along the banks of the reflecting pool, the crowd gloried in its immense size and patiently endured several hours of speech-making by blacks deploring discrimination and whites confessing guilt over their belated commitment to racial justice.

Finally, in the late afternoon, after the wilting Washington heat and humidity had turned their clothes soggy, after many on the fringes of the crowd had withdrawn to the shade of old elms and oaks, the huge assemblage stilled as Mar-

A National Disgrace *Abject poverty flourished just minutes from the Capitol Building as the civil-rights crusaders gathered on the Mall.*

tin Luther King, Jr., stood at the lectern in the shadow of the Great Emancipator. In a confident, husky voice, King described the oppression of blacks, promised to continue the struggle until they gained all their civil rights, and in rising tones claimed that blacks would never be satisfied as long as they remained victimized by ghettoization and powerlessness. "[W]e will not be satisfied," King thundered, "until justice rolls down like the waters and righteousness like a mighty stream." As his followers shouted their approval, King put aside his text and, in the familiar cadences of the southern preacher that he was, spoke extemporaneously of a broader vision.

"I have a dream," King chanted again and again as the crowd roared amens in response, that someday, in the red hills of Georgia, the sons of former slaves and slaveowners could sit together at the table of brotherhood . . . that even Mississippi could become an oasis of freedom and justice . . . that boys and girls of both races in Alabama could join hands "and walk together as sisters and brothers" . . . that his four children could live in a nation where they would be judged on the basis of their character and not the color of their skin . . . that freedom could ring throughout America . . . that "all of God's children, black men and white men, Jews and Gentiles, Protestants and Catholics, will be able to join hands and sing in the words of that old Negro spiritual 'Free at last! Free at last! Thank God almighty, we are free at last!'"

King's oratory on that muggy August afternoon in 1963 did not speed the agonizingly slow progress of the civil-rights bill through Congress. It did not magically end racism in the United States or erase the poverty, joblessness, and despair pervading much of black America. It did not prevent the ghetto riots by angry young blacks that lay

The Marchers *The great demonstration, King remarked, "subpoenaed the conscience of a nation."*

Martin Luther King, Jr. *King warned of the "whirlwind of revolt" that would consume the nation if blacks' civil rights continued to be denied.*

ahead, or the white backlash that would ultimately slow the civil-rights movement and destroy King himself. But King had accomplished something perhaps even greater. He had turned a political rally into a historic event. In one of the great speeches of our history, he recalled America to the ideals of justice and equality and eloquently reminded us that the color of one's skin ought never be a burden or a liability in American life. In five years King would be dead, murdered by a white racist. But his dream lives. It is the promise of America, a shining reminder of what the United States could be.

bound Soviet ships stopped dead in the water, and Kennedy received a rambling yet conciliatory message from Khrushchev guaranteeing that the Russians would remove the missiles in exchange for an American promise never to invade Cuba. But just as Kennedy prepared to respond positively to the Soviet offer, he received a second letter from Khrushchev. Now the Kremlin insisted that the United States dismantle its missile sites in Turkey as part of the deal. Hours later an American U-2 reconnaissance plane was shot down over Cuba. It was "the blackest hour of the crisis," wrote a Kennedy aide. As the military pushed plans for the invasion of Cuba, Robert Kennedy persuaded his brother to accept Khrushchev's first letter and to ignore the second one. In the early morning hours of October 27, Khrushchev pledged to remove the missiles in return for Kennedy's non-invasion promise. The crisis had passed.

What might have happened if the Soviet government had *not* backed down? This question weighed on the minds of both Kennedy and Khrushchev. Staring over the brink of disaster had chastened both leaders. They agreed to install a "hot line" between the Kremlin and the White House so that Russian and American officials could instantly and directly communicate in time of future crisis. To promote a Cold War thaw, Kennedy authorized a major sale of U.S. surplus wheat to the Soviet Union. Then in an address at American University in June 1963, he advocated a step-by-step relaxation of superpower tensions:

> We are both caught up in a vicious and dangerous cycle in which suspicion on one side breeds suspicion on the other, and new weapons beget counterweapons. . . . If we cannot now end our differences, at least we can help make the world safe for diversity. For, in the final analysis, our most basic common link is that we all inhabit this small planet. We all breathe the same air. We all cherish our children's future. And we are all mortal.

Two months later, the United States and the Soviet Union agreed to a treaty outlawing the testing of nuclear weapons in the atmosphere and in the seas.

Building on Eisenhower's peaceful-coexistence theme, Kennedy's efforts ushered in a new phase of the Cold War, called détente. The two superpowers began to accept each other as adversaries

"No Caroline, Not Your Dollie—Your Daddy!"

Moscow-to-Washington Hot Line

The cartoonist whimsically imagined an anxious, perspiring Nikita Khrushchev reaching President Kennedy's daughter, Caroline, rather than the president himself in an urgent moment.

who would settle differences by negotiation rather than by armed confrontation. But while détente allayed nuclear terror in the world, it did not end the militarization of Soviet-American relations. U.S. leaders remained committed to a massive arms buildup to deter any possible Soviet threat to U.S. national security. Similarly, the Soviets' obsession with the American menace led in 1963 to a crash Soviet program to end the U.S. advantage in nuclear striking power. Despite détente, the arms race escalated and the contest for power in the Third World widened.

Kennedy and Indochina

On retiring from the presidency, Eisenhower had apologized to his successor for the "mess" that he was leaving in Laos, a tiny, landlocked section of former French Indochina that had been created by the Geneva agreement in 1954 (see Chapter 28). A civil war between an American-backed regime with little popular support and the procommunist Pathet Lao rebels appeared headed in early 1961 for a resounding communist triumph. Although convinced of the need to fight communists in "brushfire wars" in the Third World, Kennedy at this early stage in his presidency did not have the counterinsurgency forces to do so. Moreover, considering Laos strategically insignificant compared to Berlin and Cuba, Kennedy agreed to Soviet proposals for negotiation. After nearly a year and a half of diplomacy, the United States signed an accord in July 1962 that restored a neutralist premier to Laos but did little to weaken communist power in the countryside. Ironically, while stiffening Kennedy's resolve to allow no further communist gains in neighboring South Vietnam, the Laotian settlement served to confirm North Vietnam's impression of American weakness.

Determined not to give further ground in Southeast Asia, Kennedy in 1962–1963 expanded Eisenhower's assistance to South Vietnam into a major commitment. Like his predecessor, JFK thought that letting "aggression" go unchecked could lead to a wider war and believed that if communists forcibly took over one nation in a region, others would soon follow (the domino theory). Like Eisenhower, Kennedy assumed international communism to be a monolithic force, a single global enemy under the direct control of Moscow and Beijing. He viewed the conflicts fomented by the communist leadership as tests of America's, and his own, will. He would show the world that the United States was not the "paper tiger" that Mao Zedong (Mao Tse-tung) mocked.

As the unpopular South Vietnamese regime of Premier Ngo Dinh Diem, who had assumed power in 1954, came under attack from the National Liberation Front, or Vietcong, Kennedy endeavored to strengthen Diem by sending more American financial aid, supplies, and military advisers to Saigon. In 1962 the Americans initiated a "strategic hamlet" program to isolate the Vietcong by moving South Vietnamese peasants into fortified villages. As the corrupt and repressive Diem government steadily lost ground, Kennedy pressed Diem to make economic and political reforms that might win him the support of his people. Diem, however, failed to deliver on a promise of land reform and other crucial domestic changes. Instead, he brutally put down demonstrations by students, the urban middle class, and the Buddhist majority against his French-oriented Catholic ruling class. By mid-1963 Buddhist monks were immolating themselves in public to protest Diem's repression,

Vietnam: Deepening U.S. Commitment

The Kennedy years saw a significant expansion of the American commitment in Vietnam. Here a U.S. Army adviser inspects the inflation procedure for a three-man raft that will be used by troops for river crossings.

and Diem's own military leaders were plotting a coup to depose the premier and his associates.

In the fall of 1963, American policy makers concluded that their effort to stave off a Vietcong victory required a new government in Saigon. They gave assurances of support to South Vietnamese army officers planning Diem's overthrow. On November 1 the military leaders staged their coup, captured Diem and his brother, and shot them. The United States promptly recognized the new government (the first of nine South Vietnamese regimes in the next five years) but found it no better able than Diem's to win popular support or defeat the Vietcong. With some sixteen thousand military advisers now stationed in South Vietnam, and almost six hundred Americans already having lost their lives there, Kennedy would either have to use American combat forces to reverse the tide of war or withdraw and seek a face-saving negotiated settlement.

What he would have done next is unknown, for less than a month after Diem's murder, John F. Kennedy himself fell victim to an assassin's bullet. Many of his admirers contend that Kennedy's deepening disillusionment with South Vietnam's efforts to defend itself had led the president by late 1963 to advocate privately the complete withdrawal of American military advisers after the 1964 election. And the president in the fall of 1963 seemingly rejected publicly the sending of combat troops to Vietnam: "It is their war. We can help them, we can send them equipment, we can send our men out there as advisers, but in the final analysis it is their people and their government who have to win or lose the struggle."

Yet skeptics note that the president followed this utterance with a ringing restatement of his belief in the domino theory and a promise that America would not withdraw from the conflict. Virtually all his closest advisers, moreover, held that an American victory in Vietnam was essential to check the advance of communism in Asia. They would counsel Kennedy's successor accordingly.

The Thousand-Day Presidency

In November 1963, to improve his chances for victory in the upcoming presidential election, Kennedy traveled to Texas with Lyndon Johnson to unite warring conservative and liberal factions of

Mourning

"The death of a democratic prince, but a prince who . . . had become part of everyone's psychic and emotional life" was how one commentator described the fallen president. Jacqueline Kennedy and her children are shown on the morning of the funeral.

the state Democratic party. On November 22 a smiling, waving Jack Kennedy rode with his wife Jackie in an open car that swept past cheering crowds lining the streets of Dallas. As the motorcade slowed to make a turn, shots suddenly rang out. The president slumped forward. Bullets had shattered his skull and throat. While the driver sped the mortally wounded president to nearby Parkland Memorial Hospital—where the doctors soon pronounced Kennedy dead—Secret Service agents rushed a benumbed vice president Johnson to Air Force One to be sworn in as president.

In the aftermath of the assassination, sorrow and disbelief reverberated throughout the nation and around the globe. Most Americans ceased their regular activities for the next four days. They sat stunned in front of their televisions and stared at the countless replays of the shooting of the president; of the murder of his accused assassin, Lee Harvey Oswald, in the Dallas city jail by a minor underworld figure as Oswald was led to arraignment; of the somber state funeral, with the president's small son saluting his father's casket; of the grieving family lighting an eternal flame at Arlington National Cemetery. Few who watched would ever forget. TV's power to convey high national drama with incredible poignancy compounded the sense of both personal and national loss and raised the slain leader to heroic stature.

Kennedy loyalists still vigorously argue the president's potential for greatness, and what might have been had he lived. They stress his vitality and ability to change, emphasizing Kennedy's new directions in 1963 on Soviet relations and racial injustice. And they note that many of Lyndon Johnson's legislative successes, especially in the education and antipoverty areas, were initiated by Kennedy. His detractors, however, emphasize the gap between rhetoric and substance. The rocking chair that Kennedy used to ease his chronic back pain, they suggest, offers the most fitting symbol of his presidency—"you get the feeling of moving but you don't go anywhere."

Far from charting a "New Frontier" in foreign policy, Kennedy acted largely on his predecessors' assumptions. He championed a social revolution in Latin America but failed to fund it adequately. He spoke fervently of disarmament yet presided over a massive arms buildup. He opted for compromise in Laos but broadened U.S. involvement in Vietnam. Nevertheless, Kennedy had traveled a considerable distance in the thousand days of his presidency, far from the stance of an unabashed Cold Warrior who had sounded a bugle call to battle in his inaugural address. By word and deed in 1963, Kennedy had begun to question the necessity and value of conflict with the Soviets and appeared ready to take risks for peace.

Similarly, in domestic matters, until 1963, the "New Frontier" proved more rhetorical than real. Lacking a popular mandate and a liberal majority in Congress, Kennedy saw just one-third of his legislative proposals enacted into law. Although he helped launch the longest sustained economic recovery in the nation's history, this upturn resulted from spending far more on missiles than on human beings, more on the space race than on social wel-

fare. And even in 1963, when he planned a major attack on poverty, pressed for a tax cut to spur economic growth, and identified racial equality as the nation's top priority, Kennedy acted moderately enough to stay in tune with majority opinion.

Yet JFK also fired the energies and imaginations of millions of Americans. He gave reformers new hope, touched the poor and the powerless, and challenged the young to fight for what ought to be. His ideals helped stimulate a flowering of social criticism and activism in the 1960s that matched those of the Progressive Era and the New Deal. This was the legacy of rising expectations at home and complex entanglements in Southeast Asia that John Kennedy bequeathed to Lyndon Johnson, the man sworn in as the thirty-sixth president on the same plane that carried the murdered Kennedy's body back to Washington.

The Great Society

Lyndon Baines Johnson, who enjoyed being referred to by his initials in the manner of his idol FDR, immediately faced crises abroad and a stalled Kennedy program in Congress. Distrusted by liberals as "a Machiavelli in a Stetson," snidely regarded as a boor and a usurper by the Kennedy loyalists who surrounded him in the Oval Office, LBJ had achieved his highest ambition—yet he had achieved it through the assassination of a popular president in Johnson's home state. Only nine years older than Kennedy, he seemed nevertheless a relic of a past era, a back-room wheeler-dealer. Indeed, many Americans compared the crude and domineering Johnson unfavorably to Kennedy, who in death appeared even more elegant, urbane, and gifted than he had in life.

However, the new president did possess advantages that enabled him to provide healing balm and effective leadership for the mourning nation. Johnson had served in Washington almost continuously since 1932, as congressional aide, New Deal administrator, congressman, senator, majority leader, and vice president. No modern president came to office with more national political experience or had as deep and intimate an understanding of the workings of government. He displayed

LBJ with Hubert Humphrey

Visiting LBJ's Texas ranch in 1964, Johnson's Minnesotan vice president posed on horseback with the boss.

enormous energy and persuasive skill with politicians, wooing allies, neutralizing enemies, forging compromise among conflicting interests, and achieving legislative results. The fact that Johnson was a Protestant, a southerner, a reputed moderate, and a close associate of Capitol Hill power brokers, moreover, significantly improved the chances of the blocked Kennedy agenda. Above all, Johnson sought consensus. Having mastered the art of compromise, he tried to use his talents to unite the American people and win their devotion.

His first two years as president were extraordinarily successful. He deftly handled the awkward transition of power, won a landslide victory in 1964, and in 1965 guided through Congress the greatest array of social-reform legislation in American history.

But Johnson would not rest on his laurels. LBJ's swollen yet fragile ego could not abide the sniping of the Kennedy crowd, and he frequently complained that the media did not give him "a fair shake as president." Wondering aloud, "Why don't people like me?" Johnson pressed on—to do more, to do it bigger and better—to surpass his predecessors and vanquish all foes at home and abroad.

Ironically, in seeking consensus and the love of the American people, Johnson would hopelessly divide the nation and leave office repudiated.

Toward the Great Society

Five days after taking office, the new president called for early passage of the tax-cut and civil-rights bills as a memorial to John Kennedy. Johnson's masterful legislative strategy sidestepped the congressional obstacles that had stymied his predecessor. In February 1964 Congress passed a bill reducing income taxes by $10 billion. The measure spurred economic growth, as Johnson and his advisers anticipated, by driving up consumer spending and driving down unemployment. As a result, the budget deficit shrank from nearly $6 billion in 1964 to under $4 billion in 1966.

Eager to be viewed as a *national* leader rather than a parochial Texan, Johnson engaged in cloakroom bargaining to end a fifty-seven-day southern filibuster in June 1964 that resulted in the most far-reaching civil-rights legislation since Reconstruction. The 1964 Civil Rights Act outlawed segregation in public accommodations, granted the federal government new powers to fight black disfranchisement and school segregation, and created the Equal Employment Opportunity Commission (EEOC) to prevent job discrimination by race, religion, national origin, and sex.

In his boldest domestic initiative, Johnson then declared "unconditional war on poverty in America." The public approval that greeted this sweeping effort owed much to Michael Harrington's best-selling book *The Other America* (1962), an impassioned but well-documented work that argued persuasively that one-fifth to one-fourth of the nation lived in poverty. Largely invisible in an affluent America, said Harrington, some 40 million people—including destitute senior citizens, isolated farmers, blacks in urban ghettos, Hispanics in barrios and migrant-labor camps, Indians on reservations, miners in Appalachia, and families headed by a single mother —dwelled in substandard housing and subsisted on inadequate diets. Unaided or minimally assisted by a social-welfare bureaucracy, they lived with little hope in a culture of poverty, deprived of the education, medical care, and employment opportunities that most Americans took for granted.

To bring these "internal exiles" into the mainstream, President Johnson proposed a wide variety of training programs and support services, some of them earlier suggested by Kennedy, and championed a comprehensive $1 billion campaign to set them in motion. Enacted by Congress in August 1964, the Economic Opportunity Act far exceeded any previous government effort to aid the poor. The legislation established the Office of Economic Opportunity to fund and coordinate a Job Corps that would train young people in marketable skills; VISTA (Volunteers in Service to America), a domestic peace corps of young volunteers who would work in poverty areas; Project Head Start, which would provide compensatory education for preschoolers from disadvantaged families; the Community Action Program, to encourage the "maximum feasible participation" of the poor themselves in the decisions that affected them; and an assortment of public-works and training programs. With good reason the black novelist Ralph Ellison hailed Johnson as "the greatest American president for the poor and the Negroes."

Summing up his goals in 1964, Johnson offered a cheering crowd in Ann Arbor, Michigan, a vision of what he called the Great Society. First must come "an end to poverty and racial injustice," proclaimed LBJ, but that would be just the beginning:

> The Great Society is a place where every child can find knowledge to enrich his mind and to enlarge his talents. It is a place where leisure is a welcome chance to build and reflect, not a feared cause of boredom and restlessness. It is a place where the city of man serves not only the needs of the body and the demands of commerce but the desire for beauty and the hunger for community. It is a place where man can renew contact with nature. It is a place which honors creation for its own sake and for what it adds to the understanding of the race. It is a place where men are more concerned with the quality of their goals than the quantity of their goods.

A cornucopia of liberal programs targeting health, education, conservation, the environment, and racial equality appeared ready to flow from Washington if Johnson won election in November.

The Election of 1964

Lyndon Johnson's Great Society vision, with its plans for a sharp increase in federal programs and government spending, profoundly unsettled conservatives. Though lacking a leader of national stature since the death of Robert A. Taft in 1953, conservatism remained a potent force. Frederick Hayek's classic laissez faire manifesto *The Road to Serfdom* (1944), Whittaker Chambers's *Witness* (1952), and Russell Kirk's *The Conservative Mind* (1953) kept the conservative flame aglow. The movement's foremost journalist, William F. Buckley, impressed even opponents with his wit and intellectual rigor. The student organization Young Americans for Freedom was active on college campuses, and the *Reader's Digest* spread the message to millions of households. And from the Right's extremist fringe, the John Birch Society stridently denounced communist influence everywhere.

Leaders of the Right scorned not only the paternalism and welfarism that they saw as the central thread of the Roosevelt-Truman-Kennedy-Johnson brand of politics but also the moderate "me-too" Republicans (many put Eisenhower in this category) who often went along with the liberal Democrats. Still resisting the New Deal, conservatives railed against what they saw as an endless expansion of Washington's power. Most of them enthusiastically supported strong government and bountiful federal spending when the goal was defeating communism abroad, but they reacted in dismay at similar levels of governmental activism when the goal was to fight poverty, injustice, and lack of opportunity at home. To such conservatives, Johnson's Great Society was anathema—high-sounding rhetoric masking still more governmental infringement of basic American freedoms.

At the same time, the Great Society's racial liberalism frightened southern segregationists as well as a growing number of white blue-collar workers in northern cities. Fearful of the civil-rights movement's militancy, they resented the federal government's alliance with black protesters and dreaded the integration of their neighborhoods and schools. Their strong support of Alabama's segregationist governor George Wallace in democratic primaries in Maryland, Wisconsin, and Indiana in the spring of 1964 revealed the stirring of a significant "white backlash" against the civil-rights movement. At the Republican convention in July, these various dissatisfied groups coalesced to gain control of the GOP. They nominated the right-wing senator Barry Goldwater of Arizona as their presidential candidate and the equally staunch conservative congressman William Miller from upstate New York as his running mate and wrote a platform that repudiated moderate republicanism in every plank.

Determined to offer the nation "a choice, not an echo," Goldwater proudly defended his Senate votes against the civil-rights act and against the censure of Joseph McCarthy; suggested abolishing the graduated income tax and the Tennessee Valley Authority, one of the New Deal's showcase achievements; advocated the elimination of the union shop and of "compulsory" social security; and intimated that he favored the use of nuclear weapons against Cuba and North Vietnam if those nations did not accede to American demands.

Possessing a fortune from a family-owned Phoenix department store, Goldwater combined classical laissez faire ideology with a characteristically southwestern patriotism, individualism, and suspicion of Washington. He appealed to Americans disturbed by the Cold War stalemate and by the government's growing role in everyday life. His 1960 book *The Conscience of a Conservative* had urged a return to traditional values. With TV imagemaking increasingly shaping politics, Goldwater projected integrity, character, and refreshing forthrightness. His campaign slogan "In Your Heart You Know He's Right" summed up his supporters' feelings.

Goldwater's conservative crusade enabled Johnson to run as a liberal reformer yet still pose as the more moderate candidate. Together with his running mate, Senator Hubert Humphrey of Minnesota, Johnson depicted Goldwater as a trigger-happy extremist who would press the nuclear button in a crisis. When Goldwater charged that the Democrats had dillydallied in Vietnam rather than pursuing a total victory, Johnson appeared the apostle of restraint. "We are not going to send American boys nine or ten thousand miles from home," the president assured the American people in October, "to do what Asian boys ought to be doing for themselves."

To no one's surprise, LBJ surged to victory with 43 million votes to Goldwater's 27 million. The GOP carried only Arizona and five Deep South states. When the results revealed that the Republican party had lost more than five hundred of the state legislative seats that it previously held, many commentators proclaimed the death of both conservatism and the GOP. In fact, however, Goldwater's nomination and the support that he garnered from white southerners and blue-collar

The Election of 1964				
Candidates	Parties	Electoral Vote	Popular Vote	Percentage of Popular Vote
LYNDON B. JOHNSON	Democratic	486	43,126,506	61.1
Barry M. Goldwater	Republican	52	27,176,799	38.5

workers presaged the growing force of conservatism in American politics. Despite the Democrats' success in branding Goldwater an irresponsible reactionary whose election would lead to depression and nuclear war, nearly 40 percent of the electorate cast their ballots for an uncompromising conservative who demanded total victory over communism and an end to the welfare state. But in the short run, the Democrats secured huge majorities of 68 to 32 in the Senate and 295 to 140 in the House. The election of 70 first-term Democratic members of Congress, who owed their victory largely to LBJ's coattails, nullified the conservative coalition's power to block the president's proposals. For the first time in a quarter-century, the liberals had a working majority. Compromise was no longer necessary.

Triumphant Liberalism

"Hurry, boys, hurry," an exhilarated LBJ urged his aides. "Get that legislation up to the hill and out. Eighteen months from now ol' Landslide Lyndon will be Lame-Duck Lyndon." Wanting it all, and all at once, Johnson established a host of special task forces to flood Congress with Great Society proposals. In 1965 alone, the president bombarded Congress with sixty-three separate messages calling for social legislation. He got most of what he wanted (see box, next page).

The Eighty-ninth Congress—"the Congress of Fulfillment" to the president, and Johnson's "hip-pocket Congress" to his opponents—enormously enlarged the War on Poverty and passed another milestone civil-rights act. The Congress enacted a comprehensive plan of medical insurance for the elderly and allocated federal grants to the states to provide medical care to the needy. Reflecting the spirit of a nation confident of its boundless national resources and abilities, Congress established precedents for massive federal aid to education at every level from kindergarten to graduate school and funded a broad campaign for urban development, housing, and transit. The legislators also passed bills to liberalize immigration laws, to promote auto safety and highway beautification, to strengthen and extend restrictions on air and water pollution, and to establish new departments of transportation and of housing and urban development (the latter to be headed by Robert Weaver, the nation's first black cabinet member). Surveying the measures, Speaker of the House John McCormack intoned: "It is the Congress of accomplished hopes. It is the Congress of realized dreams."

Johnson's vision of an American society transformed by consensus seemed in sight. Instead of resorting to wealth-redistribution schemes that ran the risk of dividing the nation, the president expected continued economic growth to provide the United States with the funds necessary to achieve the Great Society. But the Great Society was not to be. Although some Johnson programs endured, significantly improving the quality of American life, as many proved ill conceived and rapidly faded from view. His major thrust, moreover, the desire to end poverty and provide economic opportunity for all, was, in the words of Martin Luther King, Jr., "shot down on the battlefields of Vietnam."

By 1966 Johnson would be spending twenty times more to wage war in Vietnam as to wage war on poverty. LBJ's shift of emphasis from welfare to warfare derailed his drive for consensus and enraged the millions still mired in poverty. A tide of black militancy and urban riots poured over America, and the turmoil alienated "middle America." At the same time, growing bitterness engendered by the war in Vietnam focused the wrath of liberals, particularly the young, on LBJ. The Democrats' loss of forty-seven seats in the House of Representatives in 1966 sealed the Great Society's fate.

The Warren Court in the Sixties

Although the Supreme Court remained a bulwark of the liberal tradition, by 1966 it, too, was under siege. Beginning with its epochal 1954 school-desegregation decision, and continuing with 1956–1957 rulings that affirmed the rights of alleged communists (see Chapter 28), the Court, headed by Chief Justice Earl Warren, had incensed the far right. By the time of Kennedy's election, "IMPEACH EARL WARREN" billboards, erected by the ultrareactionary John Birch Society (which had labeled Eisenhower a communist), already dotted American roadsides. Then, with Kennedy's substitution of two liberals for moderates on the High Court in 1962, and with Johnson's appointment

Major Great Society Programs

1964 **Tax Reduction Act** cuts by some $10 billion the taxes paid primarily by corporations and wealthy individuals.

Civil Rights Act bans discrimination in public accommodations, prohibits discrimination in any federally assisted program, outlaws discrimination in most employment, and enlarges federal powers to protect voting rights and to speed school desegregation.

Economic Opportunity Act authorizes $1 billion for a "war on poverty" and establishes the Office of Economic Opportunity to coordinate Head Start, Upward Bound, VISTA, the Job Corps, and similar programs.

1965 **Elementary and Secondary Education Act,** the first general federal-aid-to-education law in American history, provides more than $1 billion to public and parochial schools for textbooks, library materials, and special-education programs.

Voting Rights Act suspends literacy tests and empowers "federal examiners" to register qualified voters in the South.

Medical Care Act creates a federally funded program of hospital and medical insurance for the elderly (Medicare) and authorizes federal funds to the states to provide free health care for welfare recipients (Medicaid).

Omnibus Housing Act appropriates nearly $8 billion for low- and middle-income housing and for rent supplements for low-income families.

Immigration Act ends the discriminatory system of national-origins quotas established in 1924.

Appalachian Regional Development Act targets $1 billion for highway construction, health centers, and resource development in the depressed areas of Appalachia.

Higher Education Act appropriates $650 million for scholarships and low-interest loans to needy college students and for funds for college libraries and research facilities.

National Endowments for the Arts and the Humanities are created to promote artistic and cultural development.

1966 **Demonstration Cities and Metropolitan Development Act** provides extensive subsidies for housing, recreational facilities, welfare, and mass transit to selected "model cities" and covers up to 80 percent of the costs of slum clearance and rehabilitation.

Motor Vehicle Safety Act sets federal safety standards for the auto industry and a uniform grading system for tire manufacturers.

Truth in Packaging Act broadens federal controls over the labeling and packaging of foods, drugs, cosmetics, and household supplies.

---

of the even more liberal Abe Fortas and Thurgood Marshall—the latter, the Court's first black justice—the Warren Court handed down decisions in the 1960s that both changed the tenor of American life and further inflamed the heated political climate.

In a series of landmark constitutional rulings (see box), the Warren court elated liberals and offended conservatives. It prohibited Bible reading and prayer in public schools, limited the power of communities to censor objectionable books and films, and declared unconstitutional a state ban on the use of contraceptives. In *Baker* v. *Carr* (1962) and in subsequent related decisions, the Warren court ruled that the principle of "one man, one vote" must prevail in both state and national elections. The requirement that representation in all

Major Decisions of the Warren Court

1954 *Brown* v. *Board of Education of Topeka* rejects the separate-but-equal concept and outlaws segregation in public education.

1957 *Watkins* v. *U.S.* restricts Congress's investigatory power to matters directly pertinent to pending legislation.

Yates v. *U.S.* limits prosecutions under the Smith Act to the advocacy of concrete revolutionary action and disallows prosecutions for the preaching of revolutionary doctrine.

1962 *Baker* v. *Carr* holds that the federal courts possess jurisdiction over state apportionment systems to ensure that the votes of all citizens carry equal weight.

Engel v. *Vitale* prohibits prayer in the public schools.

1963 *Abington* v. *Schempp* bans Bible reading in the public schools.

Gideon v. *Wainwright* requires states to provide attorneys at public expense for indigent defendants in felony cases.

Jacobellis v. *Ohio* extends constitutional protection to all sexually explicit material that has any "literary or scientific or artistic value."

1964 *New York Times Co.* v. *Sullivan* expands the constitutional protection of the press against libel suits by public figures.

Wesberry v. *Sanders* and *Reynolds* v. *Sims* hold that the only standard of apportionment for state legislatures and congressional districts is "one man, one vote."

1966 *Miranda* v. *Arizona* requires police to advise a suspect of his or her constitutional right to remain silent and to have a counsel present during interrogation.

1967 *Loving* v. *Virginia* strikes down state antimiscegenation laws, which prohibit marriage between persons of different races.

1968 *Katzenbach* v. *Morgan* upholds federal legislation outlawing state requirements that a prospective voter must demonstrate literacy in English.

Green v. *County School Board of New Kent County* extends the *Brown* ruling to require the assignment of pupils on the basis of race, to end segregation.

legislative bodies be allocated on the basis of "people, not land or trees, or pastures," enhanced the political power of urban minorities at the expense of rural conservatives. Especially unsettling to many Americans was the Court's commitment to a rigorous standard of due process for everyone caught up in the criminal-justice system. Rulings decreeing that a poor defendant charged with a felony must be provided with an attorney, and that the accused had the right to counsel during interrogation, appeared to some to be handcuffing the law-enforcement process at a time of rising crime in the streets.

Criticism of the Warren court reached a climax in 1966 when it ruled in *Miranda* v. *Arizona* that police must warn all arrested suspects that anything they said could be used against them in court and that they could choose to remain silent. Public-opinion polls revealed that most Americans considered the Supreme Court to be an intrusive federal presence. The judicial activism of the Warren court, fundamentally altering the laws of the land in behalf of the underprivileged and the powerless, had stirred up a storm of opposition. Conservative candidates in 1966 frequently charged the liberal Court with overstepping its bounds, and two years later both Richard Nixon and George Wallace would appeal for votes by promising to appoint new justices who would emphasize "law and order" over individual rights and liberties.

The Changing Struggle for Equality, 1964–1968

Meanwhile, the drive for black equality unfolded. It crested and then rapidly receded in the two years following the 1963 March on Washington. Heartened by the belief that "we shall overcome some day," as the activists' anthem promised, the movement succeeded in ending legal discrimination and black disfranchisement and gaining improved opportunities for education and employment. But those victories did not vanquish the major problems that beset blacks because of caste and poverty: high rates of crime and drug addiction, family disorganization, and feelings of inadequacy rooted in three centuries of oppression. The persistence of white racism, moreover, discouraged blacks; they questioned whether they would ever be seen as equals in America. As a result, many who struggled for racial justice grew disenchanted with American society and increasingly hostile to whites. For some, the movement had generated aspirations that it could not fulfill and had kindled a spirit of racial pride that rejected integration as a desirable goal. "The paths of Negro-white unity that had been converging," wrote Martin Luther King, Jr., "crossed at Selma and like a giant X began to diverge."

The Civil Rights Act of 1965

Initially, Lyndon Johnson had proved as loyal an ally as the civil-rights movement could have hoped for. He had demonstrated his commitment to black justice by championing the sweeping Civil Rights Act of 1964. In outlawing racial discrimination in public accommodations and facilities, the act destroyed the legal basis of the South's caste system. By 1964, however, the young black activists in SNCC and CORE, believing that the ballot box held the key to power for southern blacks, had mounted a major campaign to register blacks to vote.

Focusing on the state most hostile to black rights, field workers for the two groups organized the Mississippi Summer Project of 1964 to dramatize the need for black enfranchisement. A thousand college-student volunteers assisted blacks in registering to vote and in organizing "Freedom Schools," which taught black history and emphasized black pride and self-worth. Harassed by Mississippi law-enforcement officials and Ku Klux Klansmen, the young volunteers endured the fire-bombing of scores of black churches and civil-rights headquarters, as well as arrests, beatings, kidnappings, and murders. Although they were able to add a mere twelve hundred blacks to the registration rolls, the volunteers enrolled nearly sixty thousand disfranchised blacks in the Mississippi Freedom Democratic party (MFDP) to take their case to the national Democratic convention that August. The protest party challenged the right of the lily-white Mississippi delegation to represent the state's Democrats and insisted that the Democratic nominating convention seat the MFDP delegates instead. Despite sympathy for their cause, President Johnson, concentrating on heading off a white southern walkout from the convention, proposed to grant two at-large seats to the MFDP and to bar delegations from states that disfranchised blacks at all future conventions. His compromise carried, but at the price of alienating militants in the movement.

Undeterred, Martin Luther King, Jr., and his Southern Christian Leadership Conference (SCLC) mapped strategy for a confrontation that would force the federal government to assure blacks of the franchise. Determined to gain a strong voting-rights law, they organized mass protests in Selma, Alabama. Blacks constituted approximately half the voting-age population of Dallas County, where Selma was located, but only 1 percent of them were registered to vote, in contrast to 65 percent of whites. Selma also had county sheriff Jim Clark, every bit as ill tempered and violence-prone as Birmingham's "Bull" Connor. As expected, Clark's men attacked black protesters and bystanders indiscriminately and brutally. Sheyann Webb, aged eight, recalled the troopers' charging of the blacks who attempted to march peacefully across a bridge: "I was terrified. I saw those horsemen coming toward me and they had those awful masks on; they rode right through the cloud of tear gas. Some of them had clubs, others had ropes, or whips, which they swung about them like they were driving cattle." Dramatically showcased on the television news, the vicious attack provoked yet another burst of

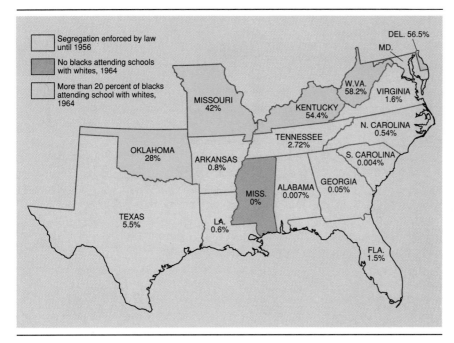

Segregation enforced by law until 1956

No blacks attending schools with whites, 1964

More than 20 percent of blacks attending school with whites, 1964

DEL. 56.5%
MD.
W.VA. 58.2%
VIRGINIA 1.6%
MISSOURI 42%
KENTUCKY 54.4%
N. CAROLINA 0.54%
TENNESSEE 2.72%
OKLAHOMA 28%
ARKANSAS 0.8%
S. CAROLINA 0.004%
MISS. 0%
ALABAMA 0.007%
GEORGIA 0.05%
TEXAS 5.5%
LA. 0.6%
FLA. 1.5%

School Segregation, 1964

White southern politicians launched a program of "massive resistance" to the 1954 Brown *decision. According to Mississippi senator James Eastland: "You are not required to obey any court which passes out such a ruling. In fact, you are obligated to defy it." By 1964 the southern states had made virtually no start toward school desegregation.*

national outrage and demands for a voting-rights bill.

On March 15, 1965, President Johnson addressed the Congress and a nationwide television audience. Comparing the encounter at Selma to the battle in 1775 at Lexington and Concord, he affirmed that the "real hero of this struggle is the American Negro," promised to exert all his power to wipe out prejudice, and called on the legislators to enact a strong voting-rights act. "[W]e *shall* overcome," concluded the president emphatically.

The resulting Voting Rights Act spectacularly expanded black suffrage in the South and transformed southern politics. Signed by the president in August 1965, the law authorized federal examiners to register qualified voters and to suspend devices like the literacy test in all areas where fewer than half the minority residents of voting age were registered. Together with the Twenty-third Amendment, ratified in 1964, which outlawed the poll tax in federal elections, and a 1966 Supreme Court decision striking down the poll tax in *all* elections, the 1965 Voting Rights Act boosted the number of registered Alabama blacks from 24 percent of those eligible in 1964 to 57 percent in 1968. In Mississippi in these four years, the proportion

Registering to Vote

Following passage of the Voting Rights Act of 1965, Time *observed that "there was a growing sentiment that perhaps it was time for the revolution to move off the streets."*

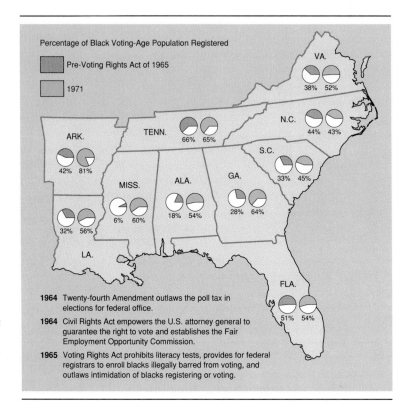

Percentage of Black Voting-Age Population Registered

▨ Pre-Voting Rights Act of 1965

☐ 1971

VA. 38% 52%

ARK. 42% 81%

TENN. 66% 65%

N.C. 44% 43%

S.C. 33% 45%

MISS. 6% 60%

ALA. 18% 54%

GA. 28% 64%

LA. 32% 56%

FLA. 51% 54%

1964 Twenty-fourth Amendment outlaws the poll tax in elections for federal office.

1964 Civil Rights Act empowers the U.S. attorney general to guarantee the right to vote and establishes the Fair Employment Opportunity Commission.

1965 Voting Rights Act prohibits literacy tests, provides for federal registrars to enroll blacks illegally barred from voting, and outlaws intimidation of blacks registering or voting.

Black Voter Registration in the South, 1964–1971

As blacks overwhelmingly registered to vote as Democrats, some former segregationist politicians, among them George Wallace, started to court the black vote, and many southern whites began to cast their ballots for Republicans, inaugurating an era of real two-party competition in the South.

of black registrants leaped from 7 percent to 59 percent; and the number of black voters throughout the South rose from 1 million to 3.1 million. For the first time since Reconstruction, blacks constituted a force to be reckoned with in southern politics.

The civil-rights movement had altered, though not perfected, race relations in America. Blacks' new voting power led to the defeat of Sheriff Jim Clark and numerous other white supremacists. Other once ardent segregationists found it politically prudent to change their stance and seek black support. Equal access to public accommodations gave blacks a new sense of dignity. "Now if we do want to go to McDonald's we can go to McDonald's," mused a black woman in Atlanta. "It's just knowing! It's a good feeling." But with discrimination lingering in many spheres and black unemployment still disproportionately high, the anger bubbling below the surface of the urban ghetto finally boiled over.

The Long, Hot Summers

On August 11, 1965, just five days after the voting-rights-bill signing ceremony at the White House, a confrontation between white police and young blacks in Watts, Los Angeles's largest black district, ignited the most destructive race riot in more than two decades. For six days and nights, nearly fifty thousand blacks, venting long-repressed anger, looted shops, firebombed white-owned businesses, and sniped at police officers, firefighters, and National Guard troops. When the melee ended, thirty-four people had been killed, some nine hundred injured, nearly four thousand arrested, and about $30 million worth of property devastated. In rapid succession blacks in Chicago and in Springfield, Massachusetts, took to the streets, looting, burning, and battling police.

Then in the summer of 1966, more than a score of ghetto outbreaks erupted in northern cities. Black youths rioted to force whites to pay heed to the squalor of the slums, the savage behavior of ghetto police, and other problems of urban poverty—issues that the civil-rights movement had ignored. Frustrated and furious, rampaging mobs of blacks stoned passing motorists, ransacked stores, put the torch to white-owned buildings, and hurled bricks at the troops sent to quell the disorder. The following summer brought nearly 150 racial outbreaks and 40 riots. It was the most intense and destructive outpouring of racial violence that the United States had ever witnessed. In Newark, New Jersey—the city with the nation's highest rates of black unemployment and maternal mortality—the arrest of a black taxi driver triggered five days of arson and looting that culminated in the killing of twenty-five blacks by the police. A week later Detroit, plagued by constant conflict between black citizens and white police, exploded in the bloodiest race riot in half a century: forty-three dead, more than a thousand wounded, nearly $50 million worth of property destroyed, and a large part of the country's fifth-largest city ravaged by some four thousand fires.

Within hours of the announcement of the assassination of Martin Luther King, Jr., in 1968 (see Chapter 30), black uprisings flared in the ghettos of over a hundred cities. The week's upheavals left another forty-six dead. Overall, the riot toll from 1964 to 1968 included nearly $200 million in destroyed property, forty thousand arrests, seven thousand injured, and some two hundred deaths.

A frightened, bewildered nation wondered why such widespread rioting was occurring just when blacks were beginning to achieve their goals. Militant blacks explained the riots as revolutionary violence to overthrow a racist, reactionary society. The extreme Right saw them as evidence of a communist plot. Conservatives described the riots as senseless outbursts—"engaged in by a few but bringing great distress to all"—by young troublemakers. An investigation conducted by the government's National Advisory Commission on Civil Disorders (the Kerner Commission) indicted "white racism" for fostering an "explosive mixture" of poverty, slum housing, poor education, and police brutality in America's cities. Warning that "our nation is moving toward two societies, one black, one white—separate and unequal," the commission recommended the creation of 2 million new jobs, the construction of 6 million units of public housing, an attack on de facto school segregation in the North, and massive funding for a "national system of income supplementation." However, President Johnson, aware of a swelling white backlash, ignored the advice of the commission that he had established, and most whites approved of Johnson's inaction. Alarmed by the demands for "Black Power" that had resounded during the recent riots, they preferred that their taxes be spent on strengthening local police forces rather than on new government programs to improve ghetto conditions.

"Black Power"

The so-called Black Power movement erupted within the civil-rights campaign in 1966. Paralleling the desperation expressed by urban blacks in the bloody street riots, the demand for Black Power flowed from years of disappointment and bitterness over the limited pace of racial change and the unyielding white opposition to the most minimal black advances.

The rhetoric of Black Power, less a formal ideology than a cry of fury and frustration, evolved from the teachings of Malcolm X. A former pimp, drug addict, and street hustler, Malcolm X had converted to the Nation of Islam, or Black Muslim, faith while in prison. Founded in Detroit in 1931 by Elijah Poole (who took the Islamic name Elijah Muhammad), the Nation of Islam insisted that blacks practice self-discipline and self-respect, and rejected integration as a goal. Exhorting blacks to separate themselves from the "white devil," Malcolm X urged them to be proud of their blackness and their African roots. Blacks, he proclaimed, must control their own destinies, rely on armed self-defense rather than nonviolence, and seize their freedom "by any means necessary." Malcolm X was assassinated by rival Black Muslims in February 1965, after he broke with Elijah Muhammad's Nation of Islam, but he was hardly silenced. His extraordinary account of his life and beliefs, *The Autobiography of Malcolm X* (1965), quickly became the preeminent text for the burgeoning Black Power movement.

In the summer of 1966, Stokely Carmichael led SNCC away from its original commitment to nonviolence when he told a rally of Mississippi blacks: "The only way we gonna stop them white men from whippin' us is to take over. We been saying freedom for six years and we ain't got nothin'. What we gonna start saying now is Black Power!" Carmichael's successor as head of SNCC, H. Rap Brown, went even further in encouraging black audiences "to get you some guns. . . . I mean, don't be trying to love that honky [white man] to death. Shoot him to death." Taking SNCC at its word, two college students in Oakland, California, Huey Newton and Bobby Seale, formed the Black Panther party in 1967. Brandishing firearms and wearing bandoliers, the Black Panthers patrolled black neighborhoods. They gained national publicity from a series of violent confrontations with the police, and from Newton's repeated claim that, "quoting from Chairman Mao . . . political power comes through the barrel of a gun."

Instantly dominating headlines and newscasts, the "Black Power" slogan was soon adopted by black leaders of virtually every persuasion. Revolutionaries used it to preach guerrilla warfare; liberals, to demand reform; and conservatives, to emphasize self-help. For many who adopted it, the phrase simply meant pride in oneself and a black person's control of his or her own identity and values. "Say it loud—I'm black and I'm proud," chanted soul singer James Brown, and a generation of blacks joyously affirmed that "black is beautiful." Rejecting skin bleaches and hair straighteners, young blacks donned dashikis, wore Afro hairstyles, enjoyed soul music and soul food, and established black-studies programs at colleges. Black Power reflected an insistence that blacks shape their own culture and define their own destiny. This was a new kind of radicalism that soon reverberated through all the major social movements of the sixties.

Indian and Chicano Power

The black movement inspired other minority groups to mobilize and aggressively press their claims. Activist native Americans, for example, whose peoples numbered nearly eight hundred thousand, half of them on reservations, organized demonstrations during the sixties to publicize their plight and to awaken self-respect and cultural pride in the Indian population. The Eisenhower termina-

tion policy, which had sought to assimilate Indians into the urban mainstream of American life, had enormously disrupted Indian ways. In 1961 representatives of sixty-seven tribes gathered in Chicago to draw up a Declaration of Purposes; three years later hundreds of Indians assembled in Washington to lobby for recognition in the War on Poverty. Native Americans, they pointed out, suffered the worst poverty, the highest disease and death rates, and the poorest education and housing of any group in the United States. President Johnson responded by establishing the National Council on Indian Opportunity in 1965, to channel antipoverty funds into Indian community improvement, job training, youth activities, and health services; in 1968 Johnson became the first president to send Congress a special message seeking greater federal aid for the Indians.

By then some Indian activists were demanding "Red Power" and insisting on the name "native American." They agitated for preferential hiring, native American studies in colleges, and government reimbursement for the lands that whites had illegally taken from them in violation of federal laws and treaties. Adopting the civil-rights movement's tactics of direct action and confrontation, Indians in 1968 clashed with officials of Washington State to assert old treaty rights to fish in the Columbia River and Puget Sound. Native Americans then also invaded Alcatraz Island, near San Francisco, mockingly claiming it "by right of discovery" and offering to buy it from the government for twenty-four dollars in beads and cloth (the sum allegedly paid by the Dutch to Indians for Manhattan Island in 1626). At the same time, Chippewa Indians in Minnesota inaugurated the American Indian Movement (AIM). Emphasizing Indians' right to control their own affairs, AIM, like the Black Panthers, established armed patrols to protect Indians from harassment by the police.

Mexican-Americans also challenged the dominance of whites. Their ethnic pride and solidarity were kindled by the efforts of César Chávez, founder of the United Farm Workers, to gain union recognition and improved working conditions for migrant farm laborers. A devout Roman Catholic, Chávez followed Martin Luther King, Jr., in utilizing religion and nonviolent resistance as weapons in the battle for social justice. Portraying the

Indian on Alcatraz Island, 1969

After taking over the island, native Americans proposed to develop it into a cultural center. In 1971 federal officials quietly removed the demonstrators.

César Chávez

Robert Kennedy called Chávez, union leader and the Chicanos' foremost spokesman, "one of the heroic figures of our time."

farm workers' struggle as part of the larger national movement for civil rights, Chávez organized a strike of grape pickers in California in 1965 and a nationwide consumer boycott of grapes picked by non-union workers. His efforts led to better wages for field hands and strengthened ethnic consciousness among Mexican-Americans. Like King, Chávez became the symbol of his people's cause.

Young Mexican-American activists criticized the moderation of their elders and shunned mainstream American values as the SNCC militants had done. They demanded that other Americans call them by their self-designation, *Chicanos*, as a mark of respect for their ethnic identity; they demanded bilingual and bicultural education in Chicano schools and Chicano studies in universities; and they insisted on Chicano-only organizations. In New Mexico, Chicanos founded the Alianza to recap-

ture territory usurped by whites. In Colorado the Crusade for Justice, and in Texas La Raza Unida, exemplified the new militancy. Young Chicanos in California organized the Brown Berets, modeled on the Black Panthers, and began to speak of "Chicano Power." The issue, they insisted, was control: "control over our environment; control over our schools so that our children can receive a better education; control over the agencies which are supposed to be administering to the needs of our people; control over the police whose salaries we pay but who continually brutalize our people."

The "Black Power," "Red Power," and "Brown Power" movements did not long sustain the intense activism and media attention that they attracted in the late sixties. But in elevating the consciousness and nurturing the confidence and self-assurance of the younger generation, each contributed significantly to the rise in political engagement, social cohesion, and cultural pride within their respective groups in the years ahead.

A Second Feminist Wave

Following the victory of the woman-suffrage campaign in 1920, the feminist movement in the United States had fallen on hard times. Individual feminists like Alice Paul, the advocate of a constitutional equal-rights amendment, had carried on the tradition of Susan B. Anthony and Elizabeth Cady Stanton, but the movement as a whole had lost momentum. In the 1950s, as we have seen, feminist consciousness hit a low point, as powerful cultural forces converged to elevate maternity and domesticity as the be-all and end-all of women's existence.

But with the rising tempo of social activism sparked by the civil-rights movement and other trends of the late fifties and early sixties, a new spirit of self-awareness and dissatisfaction began to stir among middle-class American women. The result was a revived feminist movement that profoundly altered women's view of themselves and their role in American life.

Several events served to coalesce the stirrings of discontent into a movement. President Kennedy, although he exploited numerous women in a series of fleeting sexual encounters both before and after his marriage, deserves part of the credit. In 1961, to offset criticism of his administration's poor record in appointing women to high office, Kennedy established the Presidential Commission on the Status of Women. The panel's 1963 report on sexual discrimination in employment documented occupational inequities suffered by women that were similar to those endured by minority groups. Women received less pay than men for comparable or even identical work and had far less chance of moving into professional or managerial careers. Although women composed 51 percent of the population, only 7 percent of the nation's doctors and less than 4 percent of its lawyers were female. Many of the women who served on the presidential commission and on the state commissions that it inspired strongly urged that the Civil Rights Act of 1964 prohibit sexual as well as racial discrimination in employment.

These women also monitored the Equal Employment Opportunity Commission's handling of discrimination complaints by women. Ultimately dismayed by EEOC's reluctance to enforce the ban on discrimination by sex, they formed the National Organization for Women (NOW) in 1966. Defining itself as a civil-rights group for women, NOW lobbied for equal opportunity, filed lawsuits against gender discrimination, and mobilized public opinion "to bring American women into full participation in the mainstream of American society NOW."

The popularity of NOW, and its rapid gains in membership, owed much to the publication in 1963 of Betty Friedan's *The Feminine Mystique*. Calling it "the problem that has no name," Friedan condemned the narrow postwar view that women should seek fulfillment solely as wives and mothers and "desire no greater destiny than to glory in their own femininity." The trap of suburban domesticity, Friedan argued, left many women with feelings of emptiness, with no sense of accomplishment, and afraid even to ask "the silent question— 'Is this all?'" To escape the mystique, Friedan asserted, women must pursue independent careers and establish "goals that will permit them to find their own identity." *The Feminine Mystique* revealed to disillusioned women that they were not alone in their unhappiness. Friedan's personal demand for "something more than my husband, my children, and my home" rang true to a growing number of educated middle-class American women who found the creativity of homemaking and the joys of motherhood exaggerated. *The Feminine Mystique* stimulated untold numbers of women to rethink their way of life.

Still another catalyst for feminism came from the involvement of younger, more militant women in civil-rights activism and in the antiwar crusade that had emerged to protest American involvement in Vietnam. Young women who joined these movements gained confidence in their own potential, an ideology to describe oppression and justify revolt, and experience in the strategy and tactics of organized protest. At the same time, their involvement made them conscious of their own second-class status, as men in these movements had monopolized the positions of power, relegated women to menial jobs like typing and making coffee, and sexually exploited them. In 1967 female veterans of the antiwar and civil-rights movements launched a new drive for women's liberation that borrowed the concept of class oppression from Marxist theory, the tactics and rhetoric of Black Power, and the loose organization of the student antiwar movement.

In 1968 radical feminists adopted the technique of "consciousness raising" as both a recruitment device and a means of transforming women's perceptions of themselves and society. Tens of thousands of women assembled in small discussion groups to share personal experiences and air grievances. As they talked among themselves, they gradually realized that others felt unhappiness and dissatisfaction similar to their own. "When I saw that what I always felt were my own personal hangups was as true for every other woman in that room as it was for me! Well, that's when *my* consciousness was raised," a New York City participant related. In this way, women increasingly learned to regard personal problems as shared problems with social causes and political solutions. "It makes you very sensitive—raw, even—this consciousness," wrote feminist Robin Morgan. "You begin

March for Equality

Throngs of women paraded down New York City's Fifth Avenue in August 1970 to demand equal employment opportunities and the right to legal abortions.

to see how all-pervasive a thing is sexism—the definition of and discrimination against half the human species by the other half." With this new consciousness came a sense of "sisterhood" and a determined commitment to eliminating sexism in American life.

Women's liberation interest groups sprang up in cities and college communities across the nation. They employed a variety of publicity-generating techniques and confrontation tactics to foster a supportive spirit of sisterhood and to fight sexism. In 1968 radical feminists crowned a live sheep Miss America to dramatize that such contests degraded women, and set up "freedom trash cans" in which women could discard high-heeled shoes, bras, curlers, and other items that they considered demeaning. They invaded all-male bars and social clubs and sat in at lawyers' associations and medical societies to call attention to discrimination against women in professional careers. "Women's libbers" also established health collectives and day-care centers, founded abortion-counseling services, demonstrated against advertisements that portrayed women as sex objects, and protested the use of sexist words like *chick* and *gal*.

Despite a growing ideological gulf between radicals and reformers in the women's movement, quarreling factions set aside their differences in August 1970 to join in the largest women's rights demonstration ever. Commemorating the fiftieth anniversary of women suffrage, the Women's Strike for Equality brought out tens of thousands of women nationwide to parade for the right to equal employment and safe, legal abortions. By then the women's movement had already pressured many financial institutions to issue credit to single women and to married women in their own name; filed suit against hundreds of colleges and universities to secure salary raises for women faculty members victimized by discrimination; ended newspapers' practice of listing employment opportunities under separate "Male" and "Female" headings; and gained government guidelines that required corporations receiving federal funds to adopt nondiscriminatory hiring practices and equal pay scales. By 1970, moreover, more than 40 percent of all women held full-time jobs.

In sharp contrast to the 1950s, when the ideologists of domesticity and "togetherness" had sought to force all women into a single mold, the changed consciousness born of the feminist movement of the sixties opened up for millions of young women—and many older women as well—a larger world of choices and opportunities. Of course, domesticity remained an option, but it was no longer the *only* option. Like the nation's minority groups, women were vigorously taking control of their own lives and defining their own goals.

The Lost Crusade in Vietnam, 1964–1968

The militancy of women, blacks, native Americans and Chicanos chipped away at the consensus that Lyndon Johnson so desired, but more than any other issue, America's deepening involvement in Vietnam unraveled his hopes for a united society. Although he had taken office with the intention of concentrating on domestic affairs, Johnson was sidetracked by the precarious situation in South Vietnam. Diem's successors proved unable to govern or to wage the war effectively. Taking advantage of the chaos, the Vietcong in 1964 stepped up attacks on noncommunist South Vietnam with sophisticated equipment supplied by North Vietnam.

Johnson had to choose either to intervene in a more decisive manner than his predecessors or to extricate the United States from Southeast Asia. The president was ambivalent. He privately described Vietnam as "a raggedy-ass fourth-rate country" undeserving of American blood and dollars. He feared that an all-out American military effort would provoke China's or Russia's entry and lead to World War III. And he foresaw that a full-scale American engagement in "that bitch of a war" would destroy "the woman I really loved—the Great Society." On the other hand, Johnson could not abide the thought that America might appear weak to its communist enemies. "We learned from Hitler at Munich that success only feeds the appetite of aggression," he told a press conference. If America abandoned Vietnam, he added, invoking the domino theory, "The battle would be renewed in one country and then in another country." Only American resolve and strength, Johnson believed, would deter a wider war. Having witnessed the harmful

impact on Truman and the Democratic party of the communist triumph in China, moreover, the president refused to consider a pullout or any move that would leave him vulnerable to conservative attack. "I am not going to lose Vietnam," he insisted. "I am not going to be the president who saw Southeast Asia go the way China went."

Trapped between unacceptable alternatives, Johnson gradually widened America's limited war, hoping that the measured application of American power would force Ho Chi Minh to the bargaining table. But the North Vietnamese were determined to win at any cost. They calculated that they would gain more by outlasting the United States than by negotiating. So the war ground on, devastating Southeast Asia and dividing the United States as no event in American history had since the Civil War.

The Gulf of Tonkin Resolution

In 1964 Johnson took bold steps to impress North Vietnam with America's commitment to defend South Vietnam and to block his vigorously anticommunist opponent, Barry Goldwater, from capitalizing on Vietnam in the presidential campaign. In February he ordered the Pentagon to prepare plans for air strikes against North Vietnam. In May his advisers drafted a congressional resolution authorizing an escalation of American military action, and in June the president appointed General Maxwell Taylor, a strong proponent of greater American involvement in the war, as ambassador to Saigon. Then, in early August, North Vietnamese patrol boats allegedly clashed with two American destroyers in the Gulf of Tonkin (see map). Evidence of an assault on the American ships was skimpy—LBJ privately admitted, "For all I know, our navy was shooting at whales out there." Nevertheless, Johnson announced on television that Americans had been victims of "open aggression on the high seas." Withholding the fact that the U.S. ships had been assisting South Vietnamese commando raids against two North Vietnamese islands in a clandestine operation planned by American advisers, the president condemned the attacks as unprovoked.

Ordering limited, retaliatory air strikes against North Vietnam for the first time, Johnson called on Congress to pass the previously drafted reso-

The Vietnam War, to 1968

Wishing to guarantee an independent, noncommunist government in South Vietnam, Lyndon Johnson remarked in 1965: "We fight because we must fight if we are to live in a world where every country can shape its own destiny. To withdraw from one battlefield means only to prepare for the next."

lution giving him the authority to "take all necessary measures to repel any armed attack against the forces of the United States and to prevent further aggression." Assured by the president that this meant no "extension of the present conflict," the Senate passed the so-called Gulf of Tonkin Resolution 88 to 2; the House vote was 416 to 0. Johnson had not only signaled America's determination to stand by its allies but also stymied Goldwater's effort to make Vietnam a campaign issue. He also now had a resolution that he likened to "grandma's nightshirt—it covered everything." His attorney general would soon describe the resolution as "the functional equivalent of a declaration of war," and the president would consider it a mandate to

commit American forces to Vietnam as he saw fit. But the Gulf of Tonkin Resolution also eventually created a major credibility problem for Johnson, as opponents of the war bitterly charged that he had deliberately misled Congress and misinformed the American public. Providing LBJ with a blank check to widen the conflict, moreover, the resolution made massive American military intervention more likely.

Americanization

Johnson moved hesitatingly toward cashing that blank check. He waited until 1965 to order the sustained bombing of North Vietnam, "Operation

Rolling Thunder." Rather than the immediate, massive assault that the military had recommended, Rolling Thunder left a broad range of targets in North Vietnam off limits, and expanded only gradually. Designed to inflict just enough damage to persuade Hanoi to negotiate, while simultaneously boosting the morale of the Saigon government and arresting the flow of soldiers and supplies southward from North Vietnam, it accomplished none of its purposes. Furthermore, for all of LBJ's concern about restraint, the United States dropped eight hundred tons of bombs daily on North Vietnam between 1965 and 1968, three times the tonnage that had rained on all of Europe, Africa, and Asia during World War II.

Unable to turn the tide by bombing, Johnson made a fateful decision: he committed American

United States Troops Under a Camouflage Net, 1967

Defense Secretary Robert McNamara and others had predicted a quick victory in Vietnam, but events proved otherwise. America's involvement in the faraway conflict grew dramatically in the Johnson years.

combat troops to Vietnam. In March 1965 he ordered two marine battalions to South Vietnam to defend American airfields. Then he expanded their mission to conduct offensive operations. When this action proved insufficient, the president dispatched an additional 125,000 troops in July. By the end of the year, 184,000 U.S. citizens found themselves in Vietnam. The war had been "Americanized," and the draft would soon summon a rising number of young Americans to arms.

LBJ did not stumble into the quagmire blindly. He knew the dangers. "Once on the tiger's back," Undersecretary of State George Ball had counseled him, "we cannot be sure of picking the place to dismount." The Democratic majority leader in the Senate, Mike Mansfield, had warned LBJ: "Remember, escalation begets escalation." But Johnson saw no other course. "I feel like a hitchhiker caught in a hailstorm on a Texas highway," he moaned; "I can't run, I can't hide, and I can't make it stop." As Mansfield predicted, each side continued to escalate its commitment. Prepared to battle on until the United States lost the will to fight, Hanoi stepped up its infiltration of troops into the South. Determined to prevent North Vietnam from winning, Johnson had stationed some 485,000 American troops in Vietnam by the end of 1967, a greater military force than the United States had in Korea at the peak of that war. Yet the end was still not in sight, and the Joint Chiefs of Staff kept asking for more fighting men.

Opposition to the War

First on college campuses and then in cities and small towns across the country, a steadily growing number of Americans doubted the wisdom of the nation's involvement in Vietnam and vocally opposed it. A week after the marines splashed ashore at Danang, South Vietnam, in March 1965, students and faculty at the University of Michigan conducted the first teach-in to raise questions about American intervention. All-night and two- or three-day discussions of the war soon followed at other universities; and some twenty-five thousand people, mainly students, attended a rally in Washington that spring to applaud the denunciation of an unjust and unnecessary war by senators Wayne Morse of Oregon and Ernest Gruening of Alaska,

LBJ's Vietnam Nightmare

The Vietnam War spelled Johnson's undoing. Young peace demonstrators made known their feelings about the president's role in the war during a massive antiwar protest at the Pentagon in October 1967 (top); a cartoonist caricatured Johnson as being haunted by the ghosts of Vietnam (inset).

the only members of Congress to vote against the Gulf of Tonkin Resolution.

The following year, paralleling new draft calls, large-scale campus protest against the war erupted. Students staged disruptive demonstrations against military recruitment and university research for the Pentagon and began a draft-resistance movement.

Likewise in 1966, a distinguished galaxy of intellectuals, members of the clergy, and liberal Democrats spoke out against the war. Some described it as a civil conflict in which the United

States had no business meddling. Others doubted that the United States could win at any reasonable cost and feared the prospect of spiraling escalation. And the negative impact of the war on U.S. relations with the rest of the world disturbed many Americans, as did the drastic cutbacks in Great Society programs necessitated by war costs that had quickly snowballed to more than $20 billion annually. The remonstrances of senators J. William Fulbright and Robert Kennedy, of foreign-policy experts like George Kennan and Walter

Lippmann, and of Dr. Benjamin Spock and Martin Luther King, Jr., spurred hundreds of thousands of Americans to participate in antiwar marches and demonstrations in 1967.

Critics also noted that the war's toll fell most heavily on the nation's poor. Thanks to college deferments, the subtle use of influence, and a military-assignment system that shunted the better educated to desk jobs, lower-class youths were twice as likely to be drafted and, if drafted, twice as likely to be assigned to combat duty as those from the middle class.

TV coverage of the war further eroded support for American involvement. Scenes of shocking cruelty, of fleeing refugees, of children maimed by U.S. bombs, and of dying Americans, replayed in the nation's living rooms night after night, laid bare the horror and futility of the war and undercut the official optimism of government press agents. Relentlessly pursuing action stories, TV crews uncovered the nastiest aspects of a dirty war. Americans shuddered as they watched napalm (a kind of burning glue that adheres to skin and clothing) and defoliants lay waste Vietnam's countryside and leave tens of thousands of civilians dead or mutilated. With abhorrence they viewed American troops, supposedly winning the hearts and minds of the Vietnamese, instead forcibly uprooting peasants, burning their villages, and desecrating their ancestral burial grounds. Telecasts showed enemy prisoners being treated barbarously and Vietnamese insurgents being slaughtered.

It would be a mistake, however, to conclude that all or even most Americans opposed the war. Even at the height of the antiwar movement—when campus and street demonstrations dominated the headlines and the TV screens—the majority of Americans, and especially blue-collar workers, initially either supported the war or remained undecided. But key sectors of the religious, academic, entertainment, and media communities were in opposition; and as casualty figures surpassed those of the Korean War, and total costs approached $100 billion, the war's unpopularity, even among the prowar or ambivalent majority, deepened. "I want to get out, but I don't want to give up" was a common response expressed to public-opinion pollsters. In mid-1967 Secretary of Defense Robert McNamara admitted that "the picture of the world's greatest superpower killing or seriously injuring a thousand noncombatants a week, while trying to pound a tiny backward country into submission on an issue whose merits are hotly disputed, is not a pretty one."

Equally disturbing was the manner in which the war had polarized the nation. Intelligent compromise, and even civil discourse, had become impossible. "Hawks" demanded a quick and total victory. "Doves" insisted on negotiating rather than fighting. All the while, the vast middle group of ordinary Americans, though not necessarily opposed to the war on principle, was being inexorably driven to the conclusion that it was unwinnable. As Johnson lashed out at his critics as "nervous Nellies" and refused to deescalate the conflict—"we are not going to shimmy"—the young paraded outside the White House taunting "Hey, hey, LBJ, how many kids did you kill today?" By 1968 Lyndon Johnson had become a virtual prisoner in the White House—unable to speak in public without drawing a crowd of hecklers—and his dream of a Great Society lay in ruins.

Conclusion

Despite President Johnson's mountain of woes in 1968, much had been accomplished during his administration. Under his predecessor, John Kennedy, high hopes prevailed that society could be reformed and communism contained. Idealistic Americans, especially the young, widely believed that the time had come to rid the nation of racism and poverty. The civil-rights movement that took form in the Kennedy years ultimately vanquished legally enforced segregation, disfranchisement, and racial discrimination, and it nurtured the self-respect of black Americans. Its triumphs also inspired other disadvantaged and minority Americans to fight for equality, develop self-pride, and determine their own destinies.

The reform impulse peaked during Lyndon Johnson's first two years in the White House. Millions benefited from Great Society legislation directed toward education, the arts, economic growth, environmental and consumer protection, and medical care and financial relief for the needy. The Great Society made the United States a more caring and just nation.

Yet the Great Society promised more than it could deliver. It depended too exclusively on continued economic growth. It sacrificed efficiency for haste. It spent too little money for too short a period to be effective. Despite LBJ's boast that the United States could afford both guns and butter (that is, fund a major war abroad while continuing a high level of spending on social programs at home), the skyrocketing costs of the war in Vietnam reduced the "War" on Poverty to a skirmish. By early 1966 the federal government was pouring $2 billion a month into the effort in Vietnam—more than the Johnson administration ever disbursed in a single year to combat poverty. As America's involvement in Vietnam escalated under the Democrats, angry blacks and college-age youth turned to violence to hasten social change, and a conservative reaction eroded support for further reform. Floundering in a futile, faraway war, Johnson and the Democratic party—like the American people as a whole—faced the election year of 1968 in confusion and disarray.

CHRONOLOGY

1960 Sit-ins begin.
John F. Kennedy elected president.

1961 Peace Corps and Alliance for Progress created.
Bay of Pigs invasion.
Freedom rides.
Berlin Wall erected.

1962 Michael Harrington, *The Other America*.
Cuban missile crisis.

1963 Civil-rights demonstrations in Birmingham.
March on Washington.
Test-Ban Treaty between the Soviet Union and the United States.
Kennedy assassinated; Lyndon B. Johnson becomes president.

1964 "Freedom Summer" in Mississippi.
Civil Rights Act.
Gulf of Tonkin incident and resolution.
Economic Opportunity Act initiates War on Poverty.
Johnson elected president.

1965 Bombing of North Vietnam and Americanization of the war begin.
Assassination of Malcolm X.
Civil-rights march from Selma to Montgomery.

Teach-ins begin.
Voting Rights Act.
Watts riot in Los Angeles.

1966 Stokely Carmichael calls for Black Power.
Black Panthers formed.
National Organization for Women (NOW) founded.

1967 Massive antiwar demonstrations.
Race riots in Newark, Detroit, and other cities.

For Further Reading

William Chafe, *The Unfinished Journey: America Since World War II* (1986). An interpretive history of social change emphasizing issues of class, gender, and race.

Sara Evans, *Personal Politics* (1979). An analysis of the roots of modern feminism in the civil-rights movement and in the New Left.

Michael Harrington, *The Other America* (1962). A classic examination of the persistence of indigence that helped launch the Johnson administration's War on Poverty.

Michael Herr, *Dispatches* (1977). Passionately felt essays by a journalist in Vietnam that elucidate the meaning of the war to those who fought it.

George Herring, *America's Longest War* (1979). A comprehensive account of the reasons for America's involvement and ultimate failure in Vietnam.

Peter Joseph, *Good Times* (1973). An oral history that conveys the emotional dimensions of the tragedies and traumas of the 1960s.

Allen Matusow, *The Unraveling of America: A History of Liberalism in the 1960s* (1984). A richly researched interpretation of liberal reform in the Kennedy-Johnson years.

Harvard Sitkoff, *The Struggle for Black Equality, 1954–1980* (1981). A dramatic account of the terror-laced struggle against white racism.

Milton Viorst, *Fire in the Streets: America in the 1960s* (1979). Biographical essays illuminating the social movements of the sixties.

Additional Bibliography

John F. Kennedy and the New Frontier

Henry Fairlie, *The Kennedy Promise* (1976); Jim F. Heath, *Decade of Disillusionment: The Kennedy-Johnson Years* (1975); David Knapp and Kenneth Polk, *Scouting the War on Poverty* (1971); Michael Kurtz, *Crime of the Century: The Kennedy Assassination from a Historian's Perspective* (1982); Donald Lord, *John F. Kennedy: The Politics of Confrontation and Conciliation* (1977); Bruce Miroff, *Pragmatic Illusions: The Presidential Politics of JFK* (1976); Lewis J. Paper, *John F. Kennedy: The Promise and the Performance* (1975); Herbert Parmet, *Jack* (1980) and *JFK* (1983); Bernard Schwartz, *Super Chief: Earl Warren and His Supreme Court* (1983); Anthony Summer, *Conspiracy* (1980); Gary Wills, *The Kennedy Imprisonment* (1983); Harris Wofford, *Of Kennedys and Kings: Making Sense of the Sixties* (1980).

Foreign Affairs in the Sixties

Desmond Ball, *Politics and Force Levels* (1981); Richard Barnet, *The Alliance* (1983); David Calleo, *Imperious America* (1982); Bernard Firestone, *The Quest for Nuclear Stability* (1982); John Girling, *America and the Third World* (1980); Walter LaFeber, *Inevitable Revolutions: The United States in Central America* (1985); Richard Mahoney, *JFK: Ordeal in Africa* (1983); Richard Walton, *Cold War and Counterrevolution* (1972); Peter Wyden, *Bay of Pigs* (1980).

Lyndon B. Johnson and the Great Society

Robert Caro, *The Path to Power* (1982); Richard Cloward and Frances Fox Piven, *Poor People's Movements* (1978); Ronnie Dugger, *The Politician: The Life and Times of Lyndon Johnson* (1982); Mark Gelfand, *A Nation of Cities* (1975); Doris Kearns, *Lyndon Johnson and the American Dream* (1977); Sar Levitan and Robert Taggert, *The Promise of Greatness* (1976); Harry McPherson, *A Political Education* (1975); Charles Morris, *A Time of Passion* (1984); Charles Murray, *Losing Ground: American Social Policy, 1950–1980* (1984); Stephen M. Rose, *The Betrayal of the Poor* (1972).

The Pursuit of Equality

Taylor Branch, *Parting the Waters: America in the King Years* (1988); Carl Brauer, *John F. Kennedy and the Second Reconstruction* (1977); James Button, *Black Violence: Political Impact of the 1960s Riots* (1978); Stokely Carmichael and Charles Hamilton, *Black Power: The Politics of Liberation in America* (1967); Clayborne Carson, *In Struggle: SNCC and the Black Awakening of the 1960s* (1981); William Chafe, *Civilities and Civil Rights: Greensboro, North Carolina, and the Black Struggle for Freedom* (1980); Joe F. Feagin and Harlan Hahn, *Ghetto Revolts: The Politics of Violence in American Cities* (1973); David J. Garrow, *Bearing the Cross: Martin Luther King, Jr., and the Southern Leadership Conference* (1986) and *Protest at Selma: Martin Luther King, Jr., and the Voting Rights Act of 1965* (1978); Steven F. Lawson, *Black Ballots* (1976); David L. Lewis, *King: A Critical Biography* (1970); Manning Marable, *Race, Reform, and Rebellion: The Second Reconstruction in Black America, 1945–1982* (1984); Anne Moody, *Com-*

ing of Age in Mississippi (1970); Victor Navasky, *Kennedy Justice* (1971); Stephen Oates, *The Trumpet Sounds* (1982); Howell Raines, *My Soul Is Rested* (1977); Mary Aickin Rothschild, *A Case of Black and White* (1982).

The Vietnam War at Home and at the Front

Lawrence Baskin and William Strauss, *The Draft, the War, and the Vietnam Generation* (1978); Larry Berman, *Planning a Tragedy* (1982); Gloria Emerson, *Winners and Losers* (1976); Bernard Fall, *The Two Vietnams* (1967); Frances FitzGerald, *Fire in the Lake* (1972); John Galloway, *The Gulf of Tonkin Resolution* (1970); Leslie Gelb and Archie Betts, *The Irony of Vietnam* (1979); David Halberstam, *The Making of a Quagmire* (1965) and *The Best and the Brightest* (1972); Alexander Kendrick, *The Wound Within* (1974); Gunter Lewy, *America in Vietnam* (1978); Jessica Mitford, *The Trial of Dr. Spock* (1969); Roger Morris, *Uncertain Greatness* (1978); Don Oberdoffer, *TET* (1977); Thomas Powers, *The War at Home* (1973); Herbert Schandler, *The Unmaking of a President: Lyndon Johnson and Vietnam* (1977); Neil Sheehan, *A Bright Shining Lie* (1988); Kathleen J. Turner, *Lyndon Johnson's Dual War: Vietnam and the Press* (1981).

CHAPTER 30

A Troubled Journey:
From Port Huron to Watergate

The Berkeley campus of the University of California was highly politicized in the fall of 1964. Locally, student activists were campaigning against the nearby *Oakland Tribune* and its conservative owner, whom they were accusing of racist hiring practices. And some Berkeley students had gone to the South over the summer to register blacks to vote, only to encounter white hostility and sometimes violence. Back in Berkeley that autumn, the civil-rights activists set up tables, organized rallies, collected money, and solicited new recruits on a strip of sidewalk near the campus gate traditionally open to such activities.

But on September 14, prodded by the *Tribune* editors and other local conservatives, nervous university officials banned these enterprises from the gate area. With the political climate already volatile, this move sparked a fierce reaction. Organizing under the general banner of the Berkeley Free Speech Movement (FSM), a coalition of student groups denounced the ban and insisted on the right to campus political activity. Matters came to a head on October 1, when the administrators ordered the arrest of Jack Weinberg, a graduate student and civil-rights activist who had set up a table in defiance of the ban. As the police dragged Weinberg off to a waiting cruiser, hundreds of students spontaneously surrounded the vehicle and sat down, blocking its exit.

The protesters found their voice in Mario Savio. A twenty-one-year-old junior philosophy major of Italian-American working-class background, Savio had participated that summer in the southern voter-registration drive. "I'm tired of reading about history," he had told a friend; "I want to make it." Savio got his wish. Clambering to the roof of the cruiser, he spoke to the pressing throng of students with humor, intelligence, and considerable tactical savvy. For thirty-two hours Weinberg and the officers remained in the police car while the sit-down demonstration continued. One student later recalled the scene: "I came out, and here's this huge rally going—just thousands of people—I've never seen so many people in my life—and in the middle there's this big bump. . . . I asked somebody, 'What the hell is going on?' and he said, 'There's a car there.' . . . Well, I sat there, and I got more excited about the thing. . . . I thought, 'If we hold out, maybe we can . . . get something changed.' "

After tense negotiations with FSM leaders, the Berkeley administrators dropped the charges against Weinberg and eight other students. But then in late November, they brought new charges against several students for illegal actions allegedly committed during the earlier demonstration. (Mario Savio was accused of biting a policeman.) This led to a mass occupation of the university administration building, Sproul Hall, and the arrest of more than five hundred students. As the ranks of the protesters grew to thousands, folk singer Joan Baez sang "We Shall Overcome," and Savio delivered an impassioned address placing the Free Speech Movement in a larger context. Students were being treated as interchangeable robots, he insisted, by an impersonal university bureaucracy that in turn served the larger interests of corporate America.

Calling for a humanistic educational environment that would encourage, not repress, political engagement, he proclaimed: "After a long period of apathy during the fifties, students have begun . . . to act. . . . There is a time when the operation of the machine becomes so odious, makes you so sick to heart, that . . . you've got to put your bodies upon the gears and upon the wheels, upon the levers, upon all the apparatus, and you've got to make it stop."

The ensuing weeks saw the Berkeley campus convulsed by picketing, rallies, sit-ins, and a strike by nearly 70 percent of the student body. Stabbing the air with signs bearing such messages as "Shut This Factory Down" and "My Mind Is Not the Property of the University," students protested what they viewed as a stifling educational environment nurtured by an institution all too willing to do the research and train the technicians required by American industry and government.

The Berkeley administration finally backed down early in 1965, rescinding its restrictions on campus political advocacy. By then, however, the spirit of protest had spread to other campuses. Mario Savio and his fellow activists had clearly touched a nerve. By the mid-1960s the post–World War II baby boomers were deluging the nation's colleges and universities, and many of these students did indeed encounter an impersonal, bureaucratized world. Endless registration lines, jammed classes, computer forms, and overcrowded dormitories did not mesh with their vision of college life.

These frustrations—as well as the turmoil of the 1960s—helped spawn a large-scale student movement that gave the decade its distinctive and memorable flavor. This movement had both political and cultural dimensions. Politically the key role fell to Students for a Democratic Society (SDS), an organization founded in 1962 at Port Huron, Michigan, by a small group of university students. Both influenced by and critical of the Kennedy-Johnson brand of political liberalism, and inspired by the civil-rights movement, SDS became the focal point for the activist wing of the student movement that consciously separated itself from the Democratic party's mainstream liberalism. Initially concentrating on domestic issues, SDS soon targeted its protests at the Vietnam War.

The cultural side of the movement was no less vital. Affluent young Americans expressed their alienation from the older generation in a variety of ways, from immersing themselves in a world of rock music and psychedelic posters to letting their hair grow long and wearing clothes purchased at Goodwill and army-surplus stores. Many experimented with marijuana and mind-altering drugs like LSD. The legendary 1969 rock-music festival at Woodstock, New York, embodied the spirit of the sixties no less than the escalating cycle of anti-war teach-ins and demonstrations.

But while the activism and cultural rebellion of some students won heavy media coverage, most Americans neither demonstrated nor experimented with drugs nor altered their lifestyles radically. Indeed, many citizens, especially of the working class, were dismayed by what they saw as a collapse of patriotism, morality, and "traditional values." It is thus not surprising that the chief political beneficiaries of the student movement were conservative Republicans. The widespread reaction against demonstrating students helped elect Ronald Reagan governor of California and Richard Nixon president of the United States. Appealing to the nation's "silent majority" with calls for law and order, Nixon revived his once tattered political fortunes and won a hotly contested presidential campaign in 1968.

Although a product of the nation's discord, Nixon as president won high marks for his management of world affairs. He inaugurated an era of détente with China and the Soviet Union, defused some of the tensions in the Middle East, and eventually ended U.S. involvement in Vietnam. Despite protests over the slow and circuitous process of disentangling the United States from the war, Nixon won a smashing reelection victory in 1972. In his second term, however, what had promised to be a memorable presidency shockingly disintegrated. A burglary of the Democratic National Committee headquarters at Washington's Watergate apartment/office complex during the 1972 campaign, and a subsequent White House cover-up, proved only the most visible part of an elaborate pattern of illegal and shady administration activities rooted in Nixon's personal and political obsessions. Pushing its executive powers beyond constitutional limits, the Nixon administration flouted the very law and order that it had so ostentatiously pledged to uphold. Facing impeachment, Nixon resigned in disgrace in 1974, bequeathing as his legacy a public disrespect for the political system seldom paralleled in American history.

The Rise and Fall
of the Youth Movement

Between 1950 and 1960, the number of American students pursuing higher education had risen from 1 million to 4 million. In the decade after 1960, this number doubled again, reaching 8 million in 1970. By then more than half the U.S. population was under the age of thirty. The baby boomers' sheer numbers and their unprecedented concentration in and around institutions of higher education gave these young people a sense of collective identity and ensured that their actions would have impact.

Most American youths of the 1960s embraced neither political nor cultural radicalism. Espousing hard work rather than what they considered student radicals' self-indulgence, apolitical or conservative-minded youths sought a secure place in the system, not its overthrow. They preferred beer to drugs (or disapproved of both) and drag racing

Fraternity Frolics

Despite the air of change, "Greek houses" remained a fixture on college campuses in the sixties.

or bowling to political demonstrations. They crowded into the campus fraternity and sorority houses and football stadiums, majored in subjects that would best equip them for the job market, and kept their ties to the religion in which they had been raised. A steadily growing number of college-age (and older) students enrolled in the nation's newly created system of community colleges, where, for a low tuition, working- and middle-class live-at-home students could study for a terminal vocational degree or prepare to transfer to a state university. Many other students found a congenial place in religious-oriented colleges. The majority of college-age young people, indeed, did not enroll in college at all. But whether they entered the work force or the military—or became young mothers—directly out of high school or whether they attended a vocational school, a community or religious college, or a state university, the vast majority of young Americans had their eyes steadily fixed on a good job, a new car, a family, and a pleasant suburban home. This left little incentive to turn radical. In fact, disdaining long-haired antiwar marchers with their beards, beads, and sandals, many of the young joined their elders in displaying bumper stickers proclaiming "My Country—Right or Wrong" or "America—Love It or Leave It."

Nevertheless, it was an insurgent minority of primarily liberal-arts majors and graduate students at the nation's more prestigious universities that attracted constant public notice. They were largely children of affluence who could afford to be idealistic; economically secure, they could reject the idea that the hard work, ambition, and self-denial that had helped to make their parents prosperous were necessary values for them. These well-off youths, moreover, raised with a conviction of their own importance in permissive, child-centered homes, resented restrictions on their behavior and expected quick gratification of their desires. Free of the need to earn a living after high school, they swelled college enrollments—and many stayed on the campuses for years, safe from the military draft.

Toward a New Left

The affluent, liberal-minded minority of American college students of the early sixties were highly receptive to the idealism of the civil-rights movement, the rousing calls of John F. Kennedy for service to the nation, and the campaign against nuclear testing that culminated in the test-ban treaty of 1963. Keenly aware that conformist students of the 1950s had been labeled the "silent generation," they were determined to change that stereotype. The figures whom they admired from the fifties were the mavericks, the mockers, and the outsiders: the witty and articulate liberal Adlai Stevenson; the iconoclastic comedian Mort Sahl; the Beat poet Allen Ginsberg; the radical sociologist C. Wright Mills; and pop-culture rebels like Elvis Presley and James Dean.

But if this generation of campus activists found some rays of hope in the nation's recent cultural and political history, they also saw ample reason for disillusionment and skepticism. John F. Kennedy's assassination in 1963 tragically cut down an idolized leader. While Lyndon Johnson tried to enact the liberal agenda with his domestic Great Society program, his coarse personal style, his political wheeling and dealing, and above all, his escalation of the war in Vietnam alienated most liberal students. This was particularly true of the so-called red-diaper babies, the offspring of politically active parents with roots in the radicalism of the 1930s. It was these students who provided the initial impetus for the campus political awakening of the 1960s, the so-called New Left. Indeed, Students for a Democratic Society evolved from the youth branch of an old-time socialist organization, the League for Industrial Democracy.

The Port Huron Statement—SDS's inaugural political manifesto—signaled the passing of the campus apathy of the Eisenhower years and proclaimed the launching of a new political movement. Written primarily by Tom Hayden, a twenty-two-year-old former editor of the University of Michigan student newspaper, and adopted in June 1962 by the sixty-odd founding members of SDS, the statement offered a broad critique of American society and expressed a yearning for more genuine human relationships: "We would replace power rooted in possession, privilege or circumstances, with power rooted in love, reflectiveness, reason and creativity." Citing the success of the students who had joined the southern sit-ins and freedom rides, SDS envisioned a nonviolent youth movement transforming the United States into a "participatory democracy": a society in which citizens would directly control the decisions on which their lives and well-being depended. Such a system, Hayden argued, would cure a Pandora's box of social ills, including empty careerism, materialism, militarism, and racism.

The red-diaper babies provided most of SDS's earliest recruits. These were altruistic youth, often raised in strongly Jewish or Christian homes that encouraged a sense of high ethics and political engagement. Many other idealistic students never joined SDS, preferring to be loosely associated with what they vaguely called the Movement. But whatever the label, a generation of activists found their agenda for change in the Port Huron Statement and other SDS manifestoes and publications. Suiting action to rhetoric, SDS volunteers, drawing on a modest grant from the United Auto Workers union, moved into working-class neighborhoods to lay the groundwork, they hoped, for a mass political awakening at the grassroots level.

Like the Berkeley free-speech activists, thousands of students in these years were similarly radicalized by what they perceived as the impersonality and rigidity of campus administrators, the insensitivity of the nation's bureaucratic processes, and mainstream liberalism's apparent inability to fulfill their expectations for swift, far-reaching change. Only by a radical rejection of the politics of compromise and consensus, many concluded, could the system be restructured along truly humane and democratic lines. By 1965 Mario Savio's call for students to throw their bodies upon the gears and levers of "the machine" until it ground to a halt was reverberating on campuses nationwide.

From Protest to Resistance

The movement took many forms. Students held sit-ins to halt racial discrimination in fraternities and sororities. They rallied to protest dress codes and other college rules. They marched to demand a relaxation of the grading system and a reduction in the number of required courses. And they threatened to close down universities that would not admit more minority students or cease research for the military-industrial complex. But more than any other issue, the escalation of the war in Vietnam in 1965 gave the New Left an opportunity to kindle a mass student revolt. When the Johnson administration abolished automatic student deferments from the draft in January 1966, more than two hundred new campus chapters of SDS appeared.

Popularizing the slogan "Make Love—Not War," SDS in 1966 disrupted ROTC (Reserve Officers' Training Corps) classes, organized draft-card burnings, and harassed campus recruiters for the military and for the Dow Chemical Company— the chief producer of napalm and Agent Orange, the chemicals used in Vietnam to burn villages and defoliate forests. The next year, as the organization adopted the rallying cries "From Protest to Resistance" and "The Streets Belong to the People," SDS leaders encouraged more provocative acts of defiance. They orchestrated civil disobedience at selective-service centers and openly counseled students to flee to Canada or Sweden rather than submit to the draft. At the Spring Mobilization to End the War in Vietnam, which attracted nearly a half-million antiwar protesters to New York's Central Park, SDS members led chants of "Burn cards, not people" and "Hell, no, we won't go!" as hundreds of supporters tossed their draft cards into a bonfire. By year's end SDS claimed about three hundred campus chapters.

In the spring of 1968, at least forty thousand students on some one hundred campuses took part in demonstrations or strikes against war and racism. Sometimes the confrontations turned violent, as in April at Columbia University. To denounce the university's proposed expansion into neigh-boring Harlem to construct a student gymnasium, militant blacks and SDS radicals, shouting "Gym Crow must go," occupied the administration building and held a dean against his will. The protest quickly expanded into a demonstration against the war and university military research. Almost a thousand students occupied other campus buildings, barricaded them, and converted them into "revolutionary communes." "We are fighting to recapture a school from business and war," wrote student James Kunen, "and rededicate it to learning and life." Outraged by the brutality of the police who retook the buildings by storm, the moderate majority of Columbia students then joined in a general boycott of classes that shut down the university. A pitched battle between police and some five thousand antiwar demonstrators at the Democratic National Convention in Chicago that summer (see below) offered further evidence that the antiwar movement in which student activists figured so prominently was pushing the nation toward increasingly emotional confrontation.

Even if passions ran high, the student movement was overwhelmingly peaceful. Although there was a tiny violence-prone fringe, the objective for the great mass of demonstrators was to build political pressure for an end to the war and racism by awakening the nation's conscience, not by provoking disorder and bloodshed. Opponents who warned darkly of revolutionary plots or trivialized the

The Columbia Strike, 1968

After police indiscriminately billy-clubbed a swath across the campus to evict demonstrators occupying college buildings, Columbia students launched a sympathy strike in protest, and the university shut down for the duration of the semester.

demonstrations as juvenile antics staged for television did an injustice to the earnestness of the effort and the planning that went into these actions.

A high point of the movement came in the autumn of 1969 with the New Mobilization, a series of mass antiwar demonstrations on campuses across the nation culminating in mid-November with the March Against Death in Washington, D.C. As three hundred thousand protesters descended on the wintry, drizzly city, thousands joined the nonstop march that began at Arlington National Cemetery, snaked past the White House, and ended at the Capitol, where twelve old-fashioned wooden coffins had been set up. For forty hours, from Thursday afternoon to Saturday morning, they marched in single file, each person carrying a candle and a cardboard plaque bearing the name of a soldier killed or a village destroyed in Vietnam. Writer Garry Wills, watching the slow line of young people move through Washington's darkened streets in the middle of the night, reflected: "They were ragged kids, comically self-important, a Halloween crew of trick-or-treaters; but the men they walked for could not be treated now, and they had no tricks to play—unless this were their last one, this haunting by proxy." After speeches, rallies, and several inconclusive skirmishes between police and a few demonstrators, the event came to a peaceful close. Richard Nixon, Lyndon Johnson's Republican successor in the White House, pointedly let it be known that he had spent the weekend watching football on TV.

The Waning of Student Radicalism

A crescendo of violence in the spring of 1970 marked the effective end of the student movement as a political force. On April 30, 1970, President Nixon jolted a war-weary nation with the announcement that he had ordered American troops to invade Cambodia. This neutral Southeast Asian nation, the president said, had become a staging area for North Vietnamese troops. Nixon's bold action was part of his plan for extricating the United States from Vietnam by "Vietnamizing" the ground conflict while stepping up the bombing to force the North Vietnamese to the negotiating table. His surprising expansion of the war stunned college students who had been lulled by his periodic

announcements of U.S. troop withdrawals from Vietnam. Infuriated, frightened, and feeling betrayed, they exploded in hatred for Nixon and the seemingly endless war.

At Kent State University in Ohio, as on scores of other campuses, these frustrations loosed a new wave of student turmoil, demonstrations, and speechmaking. A few hard-core radicals smashed windows, pelted police cars with rocks and bottles, and even attempted to firebomb the ROTC building. Reacting wrathfully to the tumult, Nixon lashed out at the college protesters as "bums," while his vice president Spiro Agnew compared them to Nazi storm troopers. In the same spirit, Ohio governor James Rhodes, who was waging an uphill campaign for the Republican senatorial nomination, slapped martial law on Kent State University and on May 3 ordered some three thousand National Guardsmen to the tense town of Kent. Donning full battle gear, the troops rolled onto the Kent State campus in armored personnel carriers, appropriated the gym for their headquarters, and pitched tents. Rhodes, presenting himself as the "law-and-order" candidate, hurried to Kent, where he denounced the protesters as "worse than the [Nazi] Brown Shirts and the communists" and vowed "to eradicate the problem."

The next day, May 4, about six hundred Kent State students held a peaceful demonstration against the escalation of the war. Catching the students by surprise, the voice of a campus police officer boomed through a bullhorn: "This assembly is unlawful! This is an order—disperse immediately!" Students shouted back: "Pigs off campus!" Some threw stones. "Prepare to move out," the guard commander ordered his men, "and disperse this mob." With bayonets outthrust, the inexperienced, nervous guardsmen moved toward the rally and laid down a blanket of tear gas. Hundreds of demonstrators and onlookers, choking and weeping, ran from the advancing guard. Near a pagoda on the top of a hill, the members of Troop G, apparently panicking, suddenly stopped, raised their rifles, and fired a volley.

"My God," a girl screamed, "they're killing us!" Thirteen seconds later, when the guardsmen stopped shooting at the students hundreds of yards away, fifteen bodies lay sprawled on the ground. Eleven students had been wounded, including one who was instantly paralyzed by a bullet entering

National Guardsmen at Kent State University, 1970

President Nixon's Commission on Campus Unrest concluded that "the [National Guard's] timing and manner of dispersal was disastrous. . . . The rally was peaceful and there was no impending violence."

his spine. Four were dead. None of those killed was a campus radical. Two had simply been passing by on their way to lunch.

The guardsmen later claimed that they had fired to protect themselves from a "charging mob." But an FBI investigation branded this defense a fabrication, and the commission appointed by Nixon to examine the incident denounced the action as "indiscriminate firing" and "unnecessary, unwarranted and inexcusable."

Nationwide, students and others reacted with stunned disbelief and then a torrent of angry protest demonstrations. On May 15 Mississippi highway patrolmen looking into a campus demonstration fired into a women's dormitory at Jackson State College, killing two students and wounding eleven. This senseless act heightened student resentment of the war and of the president who continued to wage it. About 80 percent of all American campuses thereafter experienced protests, although most of them were peaceful. More than four hundred colleges and universities suspended normal operations as students boycotted classes.

Popular reactions to the campus convulsions revealed the further polarization of an already divided nation. A majority of college students blamed Nixon for widening the war, and many applauded the demonstrators' goals. But far more Americans charged the *victims* with responsibility for the deaths at Kent State and criticized campus protesters for undercutting Nixon's foreign policy. Underlying the censure was a widespread, deep resentment of college students for their privileged status, political activism, and countercultural lifestyles, as well as impatience for an end to the social chaos of recent years. In reactions that were symptomatic of the nation's division, while Kent State students expressed profound alienation after the shootings, some Kent townspeople shared the sympathies of a local merchant who observed that the National Guard "made only one mistake—they should have fired sooner and longer." A local ditty promised, "The score is four, and next time more."

In fact, the campus protests after Kent State were the final spasm of an expiring, fragmenting movement. When a bomb planted by three antiwar radicals destroyed a science building at the University of Wisconsin in the summer of 1970, killing a graduate student (who himself opposed the war), the overwhelming majority of students, including those who were against the war, reacted with strong disapproval. When classes resumed that fall, the mood on the nation's campuses was dramatically different. A short-lived fad of "streaking"—racing across campus in the nude—more reminiscent of the twenties than the sixties, signaled the end of the student uprising. Frustrated by their failure to end the war, much less to revolutionize American society, former antiwar activists turned to other causes—especially the women's and ecology movements—to mystic cults and rural communes, or to careers and parenthood. The once influential SDS, having shunned doctrinaire ideology and authoritarian leadership, fell prey to disciplined, hard-line followers of Chinese communist leader Mao Zedong (Mao Tse-tung) or Cuban revolutionary Che Guevara. A handful of frustrated radicals went underground, planning and in a few cases carrying out acts of terrorism that provided a handy justification for governmental repression of the remnants of the antiwar movement. In 1970 FBI director J. Edgar Hoover added twelve hundred agents to the nearly two thousand FBI agents and many more paid informants already engaged in a crackdown on the New Left. The FBI, moreover, was just one of several government agencies then working, in Hoover's words, "to expose, disrupt, misdirect, discredit, or otherwise neutralize the activities" of young radicals. The New Left succumbed, a victim of government harassment, of its own internal contradictions, and of President Nixon's success in winding down the war in Vietnam (see below) and easing Cold War tensions. The movement's failure to win or hold the support of workers and students left it without adherents.

But the social and political aftereffects of the campus activism long outlived the New Left's demise. The student radicalism of the Vietnam years had stirred the fears and resentments of countless middle-class and working-class Americans, thus helping to stoke rising conservatism in the late sixties and early seventies. Indeed, common opposition to New Left activism would unite in a massive right-wing backlash such disparate groups as fundamentalist Protestants upset by changing moral standards, white southerners angered by court-order school desegregation, and ethnic Catholic blue-collar workers fed up with the Great Society's tax-and-spend policies.

Propelled to prominence was the conservative Ronald Reagan of California, who won his state's

governorship in 1966 in part because of his firm opposition to the Berkeley demonstrators. The actor-turned-politician then gained a resounding reelection victory by taking an even harder line than before against student militancy. Railing against the radicals who continued to disrupt the University of California, Reagan declared, "If it takes a bloodbath, let's get it over with. No more appeasement!" Sounding the same theme, conservatives gained elective office nationwide. Vivid memories of the student revolt would continue to weaken liberalism's appeal throughout much of the 1970s and 1980s.

Yet at the same time, the New Left spurred the growth of wider public opposition to the Vietnam War. The movement not only mobilized the campuses into a force that the government could not ignore but made continued American involvement in the Asian conflict more difficult. Too, the New Left's efforts aided in liberalizing many facets of student life and in rendering university governance less authoritarian. Following the campus protests, dress codes and curfews virtually disappeared; ROTC became an elective rather than a requirement; colleges vigorously recruited minorities; and students sat on the faculty committees that shaped the nature of their education, often pushing for "relevant" or contemporary courses as supplements to the traditional curriculum.

Some veterans of the New Left maintained their activism in the causes of the 1970s and 1980s: environmentalism, consumer advocacy, and the antinuclear movement. For example, Tom Hayden became a reforming California state legislator in the 1980s. Female students who learned organizing skills and also endured blatant male chauvinism in the sixties' antiwar movement formed the backbone of a resurgent women's movement in the seventies.

All this fell far short of the original New Left vision, however. The New Left never came near its goal of reconstructing the American social and political order. Students could be mobilized in the short run against the hated war in Vietnam, but only a few made a long-term commitment to radical politics. For the most part, the generation that the New Left had hoped to organize as the vanguard of radical change preferred pot to politics, and rock to revolution.

The Youth Culture

The same sense of alienation that drew some youth into radical politics led others to seek new meaning for their lives through lifestyles contrary to those of the dominant culture. For many young Americans, moreover, political and cultural rebellion became almost interchangeable. Scorning their elders' careerism and materialism, the young widely discounted the economic ambitions of "the Establishment." Some set up communes—group living arrangements in which the members strived to coexist in harmony and noncompetition. And many young people not only repudiated traditional notions of achievement and responsibility but also experimented with drugs and sex. Giving a name to this new pattern of behavior, historian Theodore Roszak wrote in the late 1960s, "It would hardly seem an

Communal Life

While many communes repudiated modern technology and the traditional nuclear family, they held in high esteem such quintessentially American values as personal independence, self-sufficiency, and a deep respect for nature.

exaggeration to call what we see arising among the young a 'counter culture': meaning, a culture so radically disaffiliated from the mainstream assumptions of our society that it scarcely looks to many as a culture at all, but takes on the alarming appearance of a barbarian intrusion."

The mores of these culturally radical youths owed a debt to the Beats of the fifties (see Chapter 28). Substituting the pleasure ethic for the work ethic, these "hippies" scandalized the middle class with their obscene language, sexual promiscuity, and indulgence in drugs. Some surveys estimated that at least half the college students in the late sixties tried marijuana and that a minority used hallucinogenic or mind-altering drugs, particularly LSD and mescaline. In the fifties the Beats had taken psychedelic drugs to heighten their creativity, but in the sixties LSD became a shortcut to a liberated consciousness. The high priest of LSD in the 1960s was Timothy Leary, a former Harvard psychologist fired in 1963 for encouraging students to experiment with drugs—to "tune in, turn on, drop out." On the West Coast, writer Ken Kesey and his followers, the Merry Pranksters, promoted hallucinogens by conducting "acid tests" (distributing free tablets of LSD in orange juice) and created the "psychedelic" craze of Day-Glo-painted bodies gyrating to electrified rock music under flashing strobe lights. Closely associated with Kesey, bands like the Grateful Dead and Jefferson Airplane launched the San Francisco sound of "acid rock." It blended a heavy beat with strident lyrics that extolled radical politics, drugs, and easy sexuality.

To further distance themselves from middle-class respectability, many young Americans flaunted outrageous new personal styles in these years. Young men and women alike showed their disdain for America's high-consumption society by dressing in surplus military garments, torn jeans, and tie-dyed T-shirts. Some embellished their secondhand outfits with love beads and Indian ornaments and went barefoot; others favored army boots or sandals. Especially galling to adults, young men sported long hair and beards. Indeed, long hair became the main badge of the countercultural lifestyle. To the young, it meant freedom to do as they pleased, but to parents it symbolized disrespect and contempt for social conventions.

New trends in popular music both echoed and shaped the changing moods of the youth culture. Early in the sixties, folk music had been the vogue on college campuses. Songs protesting racism and injustice—performed by Joan Baez, Pete Seeger, and others—mirrored the idealistic, nonviolent commitment of the civil-rights movement and the emerging New Left. Bob Dylan sang hopefully of changes "blowin' in the wind" that would transform American society. Then in 1964 Beatlemania swept the United States. Moving quickly beyond their early romantic songs like "I Want to Hold Your Hand" and "She Loves You," the English group frankly gloried in the youth culture's drugs ("I'd love to turn you on"), sex ("why don't we do it in the road?"), and radicalism ("you say you want a revolution").

The counterculture celebrated its vision of a life of freedom and harmony for all in August 1969, when nearly four hundred thousand young people gathered on farmland in New York's Catskill Mountains for the Woodstock festival. Despite soaking rains and food shortages, fans reveled for three days and nights in the music of Jimi Hendrix, Joe Cocker, and dozens of other rock stars. They swam nude in the lake and openly shared drugs, sexual partners, and their defiance of the Establishment. The counterculture heralded the festival as the dawning of an era of love and peace, the Age of Aquarius.

In fact, however, the counterculture's luster had already dimmed. The pilgrimage of the "flower children" to the Haight-Ashbury district of San Francisco (see "A Place in Time") and to New York's East Village in 1967 had brought in its wake a train of muggers, rapists, and dope peddlers pushing hard drugs. With the end of the decade came the shattering of the counterculture dream. In December 1969 the deranged Charles Manson and his "family" of runaways recruited in Haight-Ashbury ritually murdered a pregnant movie actress and four of her friends. One underground newspaper hailed Manson as its man of the year; others in the counterculture eulogized him as a diabolic hero. But to most of the young, the Manson tragedy revealed that something had gone profoundly wrong. Then a Rolling Stones concert at the Altamont Raceway near San Francisco deteriorated into a violent melee in which four young concertgoers died. In 1970 the Beatles disbanded. On his own, Beatle John Lennon sang, "The dream is over. What can I say?"

The Sexual Revolution

In the 1960s and early 1970s, the counterculture's "do your own thing" approach to sex blended with a relaxation of sexual taboos in the broader reaches of American culture. There was also evidence of a greater permissiveness in actual sexual behavior, although the media exaggerated such change. (To some extent Americans were simply becoming more open in pursuing previously hushed-up sexual activity.) Nevertheless, the result of these shifts in attitude and behavior was the widely trumpeted sexual revolution that flourished until the mid-1980s, when the AIDS epidemic—as well as the "graying" of the 1960s generation—chilled the ardor of open sexuality.

Most commentators linked the sixties' increase in sexual permissiveness to waning fears of unwanted pregnancy. In 1960 oral contraceptives came on the market. By 1970 "the Pill" was being taken by some 12 million women. Even more women used the intrauterine device (or IUD, subsequently banned as unsafe) or the diaphragm. Many states in the sixties repealed laws prohibiting the sale of contraceptives, and some legalized abortion. In 1970 in New York state, one fetus was being legally aborted for every two babies born. Then in 1973 the Supreme Court in *Roe* v. *Wade* struck down all remaining state laws that infringed on a woman's right to an abortion during the first trimester (three months) of pregnancy.

The mass culture eagerly embraced the new, more open sexuality. *Playboy* and similar male magazines in the late sixties featured ever-more-explicit erotica, and women's periodicals encouraged their readers to indulge in worry-free recreational sex. In several decisions of the later sixties, the Supreme Court extended First Amendment protection to books and films once banned as obscene. Hollywood's filmmakers were soon filling the movie screens with scenes of more or less explicit sex, provoking outrage from parental groups and religious organizations. These protests forced the Motion Picture Association to introduce a rating system in 1968 that indicated a film's suitability for viewers of different ages and sensibilities.

Sexually explicit films given "R" or "X" ratings were often box-office bonanzas. The enormous commercial success of such films led Broadway producers to present plays featuring frontal nudity, mimed sex acts, and mock orgies. Even television taboos tumbled as network censors allowed off-color jokes and frank discussions of previously forbidden subjects. By 1970, when the Federal Commission on Obscenity and Pornography recommended the end of all restrictions on pornographic materials available to adults, most barriers to public expressions of sexuality had already fallen.

The casual acceptance of sexuality undoubtedly influenced the general public's behavior. The divorce rate nearly doubled in the 1970s; more and more young couples chose to live together without benefit of a marriage license; and by the mid-1970s, according to surveys, three-quarters of all college students, male and female, had engaged in sexual intercourse before reaching their senior year. The use of contraceptives (and to some extent, even of abortion) spread to women of all cultural and religious backgrounds—including Roman Catholics, despite the Catholic church's impassioned stand against all forms of "artificial" birth control. And doubtless impelled downward by the Pill and by abortion, the national birthrate plunged steadily throughout the 1960s and 1970s. The diminished proportion of babies born during these two decades will significantly affect the American demographic profile well into the twenty-first century.

What some in the 1960s hailed as sexual liberation, most Americans bemoaned as moral decay. Offended by the proliferation of "topless" bars, X-rated pornographic theaters, and "adult" bookstores, millions of Americans who cherished monogamy and family applauded politicians who promised a war on smut. The sexual revolution—along with drugs, rock music, the Vietnam War, and political idealism—accentuated the "generation gap" that polarized the attitudes and behavior of many middle-class young people and those of their parents. Questions of morality and social behavior became volatile issues at the polls as images of pubescent promiscuity, frank sex education in the schools, rising abortion rates, and homosexuals "coming out of the closet" merged in many ordinary Americans' minds with pictures of student demonstrators and ghetto riots to form a collage of a civilization in collapse. In defense of embattled traditional values, a host of normally Democratic voters swelled the tide of conservatism as the decade ended.

1968: The Politics of Strife

The social and cultural turmoil of the sixties had unfolded against a backdrop of galling frustration with the course of events in Vietnam and an intensifying political crisis at home. The stormy year 1968 brought all of these developments together in a particularly explosive fashion. The year began with a thunderclap. In early January the North Koreans seized the American naval spy vessel USS *Pueblo* in international waters. They would hold the crew prisoners for almost a year. Even more jarring events followed. Political assassinations, escalating protests against the war, a presidential nominating convention marred by demonstrations and police violence, and rioting in the nation's ghettos dominated the news. Converging in the presidential campaign of that year, the swirling currents of strife precipitated the first major realignment in American politics since the New Deal.

The Tet Offensive in Vietnam

Early in January 1968, liberal senator Eugene McCarthy of Minnesota, an outspoken critic of the Vietnam War, surprised the Democratic party by announcing that he would enter the New Hampshire primary to challenge Lyndon Johnson for the presidential nomination. Early polls gave McCarthy less than 10 percent of the vote, and most experts thought that the candidate, a witty intellectual, had no chance of unseating Johnson, who had won the presidency in 1964 by the largest margin of votes in American history. The last time that such an insurgency had been attempted, in 1912, even the charismatic Teddy Roosevelt had failed. Yet McCarthy doggedly stuck to his course, determined that at least one Democrat would enter the primaries on an antiwar platform. "There comes a time when an honorable man simply has to raise the flag," he explained.

Haight-Ashbury in the Mid-1960s

*B*ordering Golden Gate Park by the bay, the Haight-Ashbury district of San Francisco in 1965 became a haven for college dropouts and young radicals seeking an alternative to the competitive, materialistic values of the "straight" world. They were attracted to the two-square-mile area of run-down Victorian homes by the seemingly carefree lifestyle of the artists and "beatniks" who had moved there after being forced out of nearby North Beach. Fittingly, in a city once notorious for its Chinatown opium dens, and whose original name,

"Yerba Buena," meant "good herb," Haight-Ashbury emerged as the capital of hippiedom, mainly because of the availability there of hallucinogenic drugs, which California did not outlaw until late 1966.

A distinctive counterculture developed in "Hashbury," as some called the district. The Psychedelic Shop on Haight Street supplied drug paraphernalia. Many restaurants served organic or macrobiotic meals. The Free Medical Clinic dispensed aid for bad drug trips and venereal diseases. Disciples of the Radha Krishna Temple roamed the streets

Janis Joplin with Big Brother and the Holding Company *Joplin once summed up her approach to her career and life for a reporter: "If I miss, I'll never have a second chance. . . . I gotta risk it. I never hold back, man. I'm always on the outer limits of probability."*

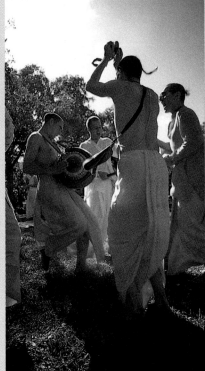

The Haight-Ashbury Scene

By 1967, as the popular song "Are You Going to San Francisco?" drifted over American airwaves, Haight-Ashbury was the scene of a mass immigration of youth. (Left) Two street people; (center) orange-gowned Hare Krishnas; (right) a Merry Prankster outside a bus adorned with psychedelic imagery.

in flowing orange robes, preaching universal peace and chanting the Hare Krishna. Underground newspapers like *The Oracle* provided commentaries on drugs, radical politics, mysticism, and rock music.

Such local groups as the Grateful Dead and Country Joe and the Fish gave free concerts in the park and popularized psychedelic ballrooms like the Fillmore West. The Diggers—who took their name from the seventeenth-century English radicals who defined property owning as theft—distributed free food and clothing. And many residents lived communally in "tribes" or "families," sharing work, meals, and sex.

Early in 1967, the first Human Be-In at Golden Gate Park made Haight-Ashbury a focus of media attention. Seeking to titillate their audiences, reporters and television crews dwelled on the twenty thousand "flower children" who rang bells, danced ecstatically, shared drugs, and handed sticks of smoking incense to the police.

Accounts of the festival played up Timothy Leary's preaching of the virtues of LSD, Beat poet Allen Ginsberg's chanting of Buddhist mantras, and the Jefferson Airplane's "acid rock." Soon everyone was talking about hippies. Thousands, then tens of thousands, of runaways, drug addicts, dope peddlers, and curious young people crowded into Haight-Ashbury for a "summer of love."

Close behind them came gawking tourists, "weekend hippies" looking for casual sex and cheap drugs, and a legion of robbers and rapists. The Haight-Ashbury deni-

zens' trust in strangers and faith in love and peace faded quickly as crime soared, drug users died, and narcotics agents cracked down on the abusers. "Love is the password in the Haight-Ashbury," observed one reporter, "but paranoia is the style. Nobody wants to go to jail."

"Hashbury" rapidly deteriorated into a slum overrun by drug addicts and criminals. Those who could, pursued their dream of living a life of love and sharing on communal farms in northern California and other less populous areas. But whether in the hills of Vermont or the deserts of New Mexico, they often found, as did one disillusioned hippie, that "we were together at the level of peace and freedom and love. We fell apart over who would cook and wash the dishes and pay the bills."

Suddenly America's hopes for victory in Vietnam sank, and with them LBJ's political fortunes. On January 31—the first day of Tet, the Vietnamese New Year—the National Liberation Front (NLF) and the North Vietnamese mounted a massive offensive. The communists attacked more than a hundred district towns and provincial capitals in South Vietnam, as well as a dozen American bases and even the U.S. embassy in Saigon. American troops eventually repulsed the offensive, regained the captured territory, and inflicted devastating casualties on the attackers. Vietcong guerrillas and North Vietnamese regulars apparently judged the offensive a failure because it had not toppled the Saigon government or ignited an uprising of disaffected southerners. General Westmoreland, announcing that thirty-seven thousand communists had been killed, boasted that "the enemy is on the ropes."

The media, however, emphasized the staggering number of American casualties and the audacious scope of the offensive. The realization that no area of South Vietnam was really secure from the enemy, and that a foe whom the president had repeatedly claimed was beaten could still initiate such daring attacks, jolted the American people. Many would no longer believe the reports of battlefield successes streaming from the White House and began to doubt that the United States could win the war at an acceptable cost.

After Tet increasing numbers of voters listened with newly sympathetic ears to McCarthy's criticism of the Johnson administration's handling of the war. *Time, Newsweek,* and the *Wall Street Journal* published editorials urging a negotiated settlement and an American withdrawal. A flood of photographs of the war's destruction revealed previously unimagined horrors. NBC anchorman Frank McGee concluded that "the grand objective—the building of a free nation—is not nearer, but further, from realization." The nation's most respected newscaster, Walter Cronkite of CBS, opined that "it seems now more certain than ever that the bloody experience of Vietnam is to end in a stalemate." "If I've lost Walter," President Johnson sighed, "then it's over. I've lost Mr. Average Citizen." Johnson's approval rating dropped to a shocking 35 percent after Tet, the lowest of any president since Truman's troubled times. The num-

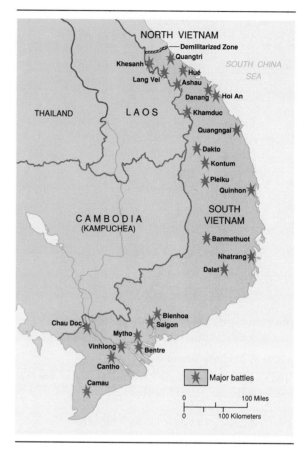

The Tet Offensive, January–February 1968

Although the Tet offensive proved a major tactical defeat for the communists, it effectively undermined American public support for the war.

ber of Americans who described themselves as pro-war "hawks" slipped from 62 percent in January to just 41 percent in March, while the proportion of antiwar "doves" climbed from 22 percent to 42 percent.

The Shaken President

A beleaguered Lyndon Johnson pondered a change in American policy. When the Joint Chiefs of Staff requested an additional 206,000 men for Vietnam, the president turned to old friends and advisers. Former secretary of state and venerable Cold Warrior Dean Acheson told the president that "the Joint Chiefs of Staff don't know what they're talking about." Clark Clifford, the new secretary of defense, also doubted the wisdom of further escalation. Questioning the top military commanders, Clifford became "convinced that the military course we were pursuing was not only endless but hopeless." Clifford later commented

> *"Will 200,000 more men do the job?" No one knew. "If the new troops were sent, could the North compensate with its own increases?" Probably. "Can bombing stop the war?" Never. "Should the bombing stop?" No. "Can bombing decrease American casualties?" Very little, if at all. "Did any of the military experts foresee any decline in the North's will to continue after four years of terrible casualties?" No.*

Clifford, Acheson, and other key foreign-policy experts urged the president to halt the bombing and to initiate negotiations.

Meanwhile, nearly five thousand college students had dropped their studies to stuff envelopes, telephone voters, and ring doorbells for Eugene McCarthy in the New Hampshire primary contest. To be "clean for Gene," they shaved their beards, cut their long hair, and dressed conservatively so as not to alienate potential supporters. McCarthy astonished the experts by winning nearly half the popular vote as well as twenty of the twenty-four nominating-convention delegates in a state regarded as conservative.

After this upset, twice as many students converged on Wisconsin to canvass its more liberal Democratic voters. They expected a resounding McCarthy triumph in the nation's second primary. Hurriedly, on March 16, Senator Robert Kennedy also entered the Democratic contest, and like McCarthy, he campaigned on a promise to end the war. Projecting the familiar Kennedy glamour and magnetism, Kennedy, who had resigned as attorney general and won election to the Senate from New York in 1964, was the one candidate who Johnson feared could deny him renomination. Indeed, millions of Americans viewed Kennedy as the rightful heir to the White House. Having secured the passionate support of minorities, the poor, and working-class ethnic whites, Kennedy was described by one columnist as "our first politician for the pariahs, our great national outsider." Yet he also attracted the backing of mainstream Democrats,

Robert Kennedy

Running an energy-charged campaign in 1968, the dynamic "Bobby" seemed to inspire either wild devotion or deep dislike.

many of whom responded as much to his charisma as to his commitments to end the war and to abolish poverty and racism.

On March 31, exactly three years after the marines had first splashed ashore at Danang, Johnson informed a surprised television audience: "I'm taking the first step to deescalate the conflict": a halt to the bombing in the North. Catching even his closest aides off guard, LBJ added that he wanted time to devote all his efforts to the search for peace. "Accordingly," he concluded, "I shall not seek, and I will not accept, the nomination of my party for another term as your president." Johnson, embittered by the personal abuse that he had suffered, and reluctant to risk further polarizing the Democrats and the nation, had called it quits. "The only difference between the [John F.] Kennedy assassination and mine," he lamented, "is that I am alive and it has been more tortuous." Two days later, pounding the final nail into Johnson's political coffin, McCarthy overwhelmingly trounced the president in the Wisconsin primary.

Assassinations and Turmoil

On April 4, just three days after the vote in Wisconsin, a stunned nation received chilling news from Memphis, Tennessee. Martin Luther King, Jr., who had gone to the city to support sanitation workers striking for union recognition and better working conditions, had been shot and killed as he stood on the balcony outside his motel room. The assassin was James Earl Ray, a white convict who had recently escaped from the Missouri state penitentiary. Ghetto blacks in nearly 125 cities surged through the streets in anger. As twenty blocks of Chicago's West Side went up in flames, Mayor Richard Daley ordered his police to shoot to kill arsonists. In Washington, D.C., more than 700 fires illuminated the night sky. Rampaging blacks in the nation's capital forced army units in full combat gear to set up machine-gun emplacements outside the Capitol and White House. The nationwide rioting left forty-six dead, more than three thousand injured, and nearly twenty-seven thousand in jail.

The violence stood in ironic contrast to King's message of peace and reconciliation. As the fallen civil-rights leader was buried in his native Atlanta, Americans recalled the prophetic and visionary biblical imagery of his words to a black audience in Memphis the night before his death: "I've been to the mountaintop. . . . I may not get there with you, but I want you to know that we as a people will get to the promised land."

Meanwhile, a three-cornered scramble developed for the Democratic presidential nomination. Johnson's vice president, Hubert Humphrey, entered the Democratic race as the standard-bearer of the Democratic coalition that had been forged in the New Deal. Humphrey's public support for the president's Vietnam policies, however, made his candidacy unacceptable to the antiwar liberal activists who had once lionized him for his courageous stands on civil rights and social justice. Avoiding the primaries, Humphrey utilized his popularity with labor chieftains, Johnson loyalists, and party bosses to line up convention delegates. Eugene McCarthy stood as the candidate of the "new politics"—a lofty moral crusade against war

and injustice directed mainly to affluent and educated liberals. And Robert Kennedy campaigned as the tribune of the less privileged, the sole candidate who appealed to various ethnic groups and the minority poor. But on June 5, 1968, as he celebrated his victory in the California presidential primary at a Los Angeles hotel, the brother of the murdered president was himself assassinated. A Palestinian refugee, Sirhan Sirhan, who loathed the senator for his pro-Israeli views, was apprehended at the scene and charged with the crime.

The assassination smashed the dream of the proponents of peace and racial justice to capture the Democratic party. As they tuned in to yet another state funeral on their television sets, many despaired of politics as an avenue of change. "I won't vote," one youth said, speaking for many of his generation. "Every good man we get they kill." A young black woman in Oregon experienced the same feeling as Kennedy was laid to rest in Arlington National Cemetery. "I knew it was all over, that there was no more reason for hope," she grieved. Several weeks later, she joined the Black Panthers. Kennedy's death also left the McCarthy forces dispirited and cleared the path for Humphrey, although some Democrats were furious that the party was about to nominate a prowar candidate who had not campaigned in a single primary.

Many more Americans, rejecting a Democratic party that seemed helpless in the face of mass disorder, turned to the third-party candidate George Wallace or to the Republican nominee Richard Nixon. The scrappy Nixon had battled ferociously to recover from two major defeats—his loss to John Kennedy in the 1960 presidential election and a failed bid for California's governorship in 1962. He had served the GOP faithfully and taken advantage of a pervasive sense of national disarray to emerge as the front-runner in 1968. To secure the Republican nomination, Nixon had fashioned a new image as a leader who would restore stability to a nation that seemed to be coming apart. "As we look at America," he proclaimed in his acceptance speech at the Republican convention,

we see cities enveloped in smoke and flame. We hear sirens in the night. We see Americans hating each other; killing each other at home. And as we see and hear these things millions of Americans cry out in anger: Did we come all this way for this?

Declaring that his leadership could end the civil discord, Nixon promised to listen to "the voice of the great majority of Americans, the forgotten Americans, the non-shouters, the non-demonstrators, those who do not break the law, people who pay their taxes and go to work, who send their children to school, who go to their churches, . . . who love this country."

Third-party candidate George Corley Wallace capitalized on the same wellspring of reaction as Nixon. The Alabama governor's acrimonious speeches intensified working-class whites' animosity toward militant blacks, antiwar protesters, and welfare recipients. Under the banner "STAND UP FOR AMERICA," Wallace promised to crack down hard on rioters, on "limousine liberals" who demanded that white laborers integrate their neighborhoods and schools, and on "long-hair, pot smoking, draft-card-burning youth."

Violence outside the Democratic National Convention in Chicago in August 1968 swelled the appeal of both Wallace and Nixon. Thousands had descended on the city to demonstrate their opposition to the Vietnam War. Most of the protesters were young idealists who hoped to pressure the delegates to repudiate the administration's Vietnam policy. Others, associated with the more radical faction within SDS, wanted to provoke a stormy confrontation that would force the Democrats into disrepute. A small number of alienated young Americans, seeking to discredit the system by ridicule, joined the largely mythical "Youth International party." These anarchistic "Yippies," led by Abbie Hoffman and Jerry Rubin, spoke airily of dumping LSD in the city's water system, releasing greased pigs in the crowded Loop area, and masquerading as hotel bellhops to seduce the wives and daughters of convention delegates.

Remembering the rioting that Chicago had suffered in the wake of King's assassination, Mayor Richard Daley turned the city into a war zone. "As long as I am mayor," he asserted, "there will be law and order." The savagery of the Chicago police, however, fulfilled the radicals' wish for mass disorder. On August 28, as a huge national television audience looked on and as participants chanted "The whole world is watching," Daley's bluecoats clubbed demonstrators and bystanders and broke into Senator McCarthy's campaign headquarters. The brutality on the streets overshadowed the con-

vention's nomination of Hubert Humphrey and ripped the Democrats further apart. The tumult fixed Americans' image of the Democrats as the party of dissent and disarray.

Conservative Resurgence

The Republican Nixon made the most of American hostility toward the Democrats. His television commercials flashed images of campus and ghetto uprisings. If elected, he promised to appoint a tough attorney general who would support "the peace forces" in their struggle against "the criminal forces" and to protect the "first civil right of every American . . . to be free from domestic violence." Indict-

George Wallace Supporters, Lansing, Michigan, 1968

As he chalked up primary victories in a string of southern states as well as in northern states such as Maryland and Michigan, Wallace proudly took credit for rattling "the eyeteeth of the Democratic party."

ing the Great Society, he insisted that it was "time to quit pouring billions of dollars into programs that have failed." Nixon made a special appeal to white southerners for their votes by muting the civil-rights issue and asserting that "our schools are for education—not integration." He cleverly straddled the Vietnam controversy, claiming that "new leadership will end the war and win the peace in the Pacific" but never revealing the substance of his secret Vietnam plan. Most of all, Nixon capitalized on a national desire for domestic calm.

George Wallace, likewise appealing to Americans' widespread revulsion against radicalism, raged across the political landscape in 1968. He fired up the fury of less-educated working-class men and women toward "those briefcase-totin' bureaucrats, ivory-tower guideline writers, bearded anarchists, smart-aleck editorial writers, and pointy-headed professors looking down their noses at us." Passionately, he denounced school integrationists, welfare mothers, and radical college professors alike. Promising to keep peace in the streets if it took "thirty thousand troops armed with three-foot bayonets," he vowed that "if any demonstrator ever lays [sic] down in front of my car, it'll be the last car he'll ever lie down in front of."

Wallace climbed steadily in voter-preference polls, inching up from 11 percent in February 1968 to 16 percent in July and to 21 percent in September. His selection of retired air-force general Curtis LeMay as his running mate in the American Independent party, however, completely doomed Wallace's small chance of election. Although many voters shared Wallace's views, most were terrified by LeMay's suggestion that the United States should "drop nukes on Vietnam." Even so, nearly 14 percent of the electorate—primarily young, lower-middle-class, small-town workers—rejected the two major parties and cast their vote for Wallace, despite reluctance to waste a vote on a candidate who had little likelihood of winning and despite an all-out effort by organized labor to discredit him.

With Nixon and Humphrey almost evenly splitting the remainder of the ballots, the Republican squeaked to victory with 43.4 percent of the popular vote. Nixon garnered only 301 electoral votes, the narrowest victory since Woodrow Wilson's slender triumph in 1916. Nevertheless, a new conservative majority had supplanted the long-dominant New Deal coalition, as Humphrey

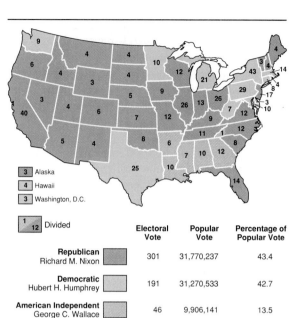

	Electoral Vote	Popular Vote	Percentage of Popular Vote
Republican Richard M. Nixon	301	31,770,237	43.4
Democratic Hubert H. Humphrey	191	31,270,533	42.7
American Independent George C. Wallace	46	9,906,141	13.5
Minor Parties	–	239,908	0.4

The Election of 1968

received just 38 percent of the white vote, not even half the skilled-labor vote, and only a third of the votes of unskilled and semiskilled workers.

The majority of voters, including such traditional Democratic loyalists as white southerners, union members, and ethnic Catholics, had cast their votes for law and order and respect for tradition. They had also decisively rejected any expansion of Great Society social-welfare programs. "I'm working my ass off," fumed a blue-collar worker in Boston, "and I'm supposed to bleed for a bunch of people on relief?" "People on relief got better jobs, got better homes than I've got," raged a white laborer in Milwaukee with wild exaggeration but deep-felt resentment; "The colored people are eating steak and this Polish bastard is eating chicken. Damn right I'm bitter."

The 57 percent of the electorate who voted for Nixon or Wallace would dominate American presidential politics into the 1990s. While the national Democratic party fractured into a welter of contending interest groups, the Republicans attracted a new majority of Americans who lived in the suburbs and the Sunbelt, regarded the federal government as too wasteful, disdained student radicalism and the forced busing of schoolchildren, and objected to further special efforts to assist minorities. As Kevin Phillips, a Republican political analyst and the architect of what would be called the southern strategy, foresaw in 1968:

> The great political upheaval of the nineteen-sixties is not that of Senator Eugene McCarthy's relatively small group of upper-middle-class and intellectual supporters, but a populist revolt of the American masses who have been elevated by prosperity to middle-class status and conservatism. Their revolt is against the caste, policies, and taxation of the mandarins of Establishment liberalism.

The 1968 election rang down the final act on one of the most dramatic and tragic years in American history. The Democrats' loss of some 12 million voters who in 1964 had cast ballots for LBJ heralded a major electoral shift. Although the traumatic events of the late sixties temporarily radicalized many Americans, far many more turned conservative. The controversial, stalemated war in Vietnam polarized American society and shattered the liberal consensus in support of domestic reform and U.S. global policing. A new majority now yearned for restraint abroad, a reduction of governmental activism at home, and—most of all— for Richard Nixon to restore domestic tranquillity and end the Vietnam War.

Nixon and World Politics

When Richard Milhous Nixon took the oath of office on January 20, 1969, after prayers by evangelist Billy Graham, he was already a familiar figure on the American political scene. A Californian of Quaker origins educated at Whittier College and Duke Law School, Nixon had worked briefly in wartime Washington with the Office of Price Administration before joining the navy and serving in the Pacific. Elected to Congress in 1946 on a strong anticommunist platform, he won national prominence as a member of the House Un-American Activities Committee for his role in the investigation of accused spy Alger Hiss. Nixon advanced to the Senate four years later in a campaign involving innuendos of disloyalty against his liberal Democratic opponent, Helen Gahagan Douglas,

whom he labeled "the Pink Lady." After two terms as Dwight Eisenhower's vice president, his loss to John Kennedy in 1960 and his unsuccessful bid for the California governorship two years later seemingly ended his political career. But Nixon slogged on, addressing local Republican gatherings and building up credits that he could draw on when the time came. In 1968 the crosscurrents of domestic unrest and an unpopular war created the conditions that at last propelled him to the pinnacle of American politics.

Although he came to the White House amid scenes of domestic chaos, Nixon sought primarily to make his mark in foreign affairs. An avid student of international relations, he considered himself a master of realpolitik—a pragmatic politics focusing on the advancement of the national interest. He shrewdly utilized his executive powers to promote a grand design that would both check Soviet expansionism and bring greater stability to the world, as well as limit the nuclear-arms race and enhance America's economic well-being. Nixon recognized that the continuing war in Vietnam had eroded American support for similar armed interventions and that the widening Sino-Soviet split had outdated his predecessors' monolithic anticommunist policies. He wished to accomplish what had eluded them: to get the United States out of Vietnam and begin a new era of détente—an easing of tensions—with the communist world.

To manage American diplomacy, Nixon chose Henry Kissinger. A Jewish refugee from Nazi Germany and a renowned professor of international relations at Harvard University, Kissinger served as the president's national security adviser until 1973, when he became secretary of state. He shared the president's distrustful view of human nature as well as the belief that power alone counted in world affairs. Both men, moreover, were disposed to act ruthlessly when obstacles blocked their goals. They expanded the authority of the National Security Council, thus accelerating the trend of concentrating foreign-policy decision-making authority in the White House rather than the State Department. Nixon and Kissinger particularly worried that others in the defense and intelligence bureaucracies might obstruct their initiatives or leak sensitive material to the press. Accordingly, they refashioned America's world primacy in a manner that kept their actions hidden from the American people and other key government officials. Two loners and outsiders, Nixon and Kissinger indulged their common penchant for intrigue and secrecy.

Vietnamization

The Nixon-Kissinger grand design, as a White House aide noted, required disgorging "the bone in the nation's throat" that Vietnam had become. Continued involvement in the war not only sapped America's military strength but also worsened mounting inflation in these years. In addition, it thwarted détente with the Soviet Union and the People's Republic of China and threatened to tarnish Nixon's reputation. "I'm not going to end up like LBJ," the new president vowed, "holed up in the White House afraid to show my face on the street. I'm going to stop that war." Speaking in Guam during an Asian tour in August 1969, the president unveiled what became known as the Nixon Doctrine, in which he redefined America's role in the Third World as that of a helpful partner rather than a military protector. Asian nations facing communist subversion, border clashes, or civil conflicts could count on American financial and moral support, but the United States would expect them to defend themselves, Nixon explained. In short, they would have to bear the main burden of their own security: "Asian hands must shape the Asian future."

The Nixon Doctrine reflected the president's understanding of the war weariness of both the electorate and the U.S. troops in Vietnam. Johnson's decision to stop escalating and start negotiating had dashed hopes for a communist defeat and left the American fighting men with a sense that nothing counted any longer but survival. Morale had plummeted, and discipline had collapsed. The number of army desertions had risen from twenty-seven thousand in 1967 to more than seventy-six thousand in 1970, and the desertion rate in the marines had increased even more precipitously. Racial conflict among American soldiers had become commonplace, and drug use had soared. Numerous instances of "fragging"—the killing of officers by enlisted men—were reported.

U.S. infantrymen's growing fears and frustrations also resulted in mounting American atrocities against the Vietnamese. A T-shirt popular among American soldiers read "KILL THEM ALL! LET GOD SORT THEM OUT!" Especially after 1967, instances of Americans' dismembering enemy bodies, torturing captives, wantonly torching villages, and murdering civilians came to light. In March 1968, in the hamlet of My Lai, an army unit under the command of an inexperienced lieutenant, William Calley, massacred 347 defenseless women, children, and old men. After stopping for a lunch break, the Americans then burned the village and killed the livestock. Public revelations of such incidents, and the increasing number of returning soldiers who joined the Vietnam Veterans Against the War and who dramatically renounced their medals and citations, undercut the already diminished public support for the war.

Despite the pressure on Nixon to end the long war quickly, he was determined to salvage America's pride and global prestige. "We would destroy ourselves if we pulled out in a manner that really wasn't honorable," the president told a journalist in May 1969. That spring, to achieve what he called "peace with honor," Nixon pursued three courses of action simultaneously. First, the president replaced American fighting forces with South Vietnamese troops, a process that became known as Vietnamization. By transferring responsibilities for the ground war to South Vietnam, Nixon reduced the number of American troops in Vietnam from more than half a million to fewer than thirty thousand by 1972. Second, taking the reins from the Saigon government, whose leaders rightly feared that any accord with the communists would doom them, Nixon sent Henry Kissinger to negotiate directly and secretly with North Vietnam's foreign minister, Le Duc Tho. Finally, to force the communists to compromise even as American forces withdrew, the president in March 1969 authorized a drastic escalation of American bombing. To maximize the harm done to the enemy—Kissinger called the tactic "jugular diplomacy"—Nixon secretly ordered the bombing of North Vietnamese supply routes in neighboring Cambodia and Laos, as well as the intensification of bombing raids on North Vietnam. By playing "the mad bomber," he hoped to force concessions from the enemy. As the president told an aide:

I want the North Vietnamese to believe I've reached the point where I might do anything to stop the war. We'll just slip the word to them

**"The Blind Leading the Blind,"
1971**

*Cartoonist David Levine
depicted four presidents as
being blind with regard to
American involvement in Vietnam: Eisenhower, who first
made an equivocal U.S. commitment in the faraway Asian
nation; Kennedy, who deepened
that commitment; Johnson,
under whose administration the
war escalated into a major conflict; and finally Nixon, who
expanded American bombing
targets to neutral Cambodia.*

*that "for God's sake, you know Nixon is obsessed
about communism. We can't restrain him when
he's angry—and he has his hand on the nuclear
button"—and Ho Chi Minh himself will be in
Paris in two days begging for peace.*

LBJ's War Becomes Nixon's War

The president's authorization of secret B-52 bombing raids against Cambodia (they would not become
public knowledge until reported by the *New York
Times* in 1972) neither convinced Hanoi of Nixon's dangerous unpredictability nor disrupted
communist supply bases in Cambodia. They did
help to undermine the precarious stability of that
tiny republic and to precipitate a civil war there
between pro-American and communist forces. To
aid the Cambodian communists (the Khmer Rouge)
and to facilitate North Vietnam's use of Cambodia
as a staging area for attacks on South Vietnam, the
North Vietnamese stepped up their infiltration of
troops into Cambodia in early 1970. In turn, to
demonstrate his toughness in what he viewed as a
contest of wills, Nixon ordered a joint American–South Vietnamese incursion into Cambodia
at the end of April. The invading soldiers captured
significant caches of enemy weapons, and their
success bought time for Vietnamization. But the

costs were high. The invasion ended Cambodia's
neutrality, widened the war throughout Indochina,
and provoked massive American protests against
the war, culminating in the student deaths at Kent
State and Jackson State universities.

The following year Nixon again combined the
continued withdrawal of American troops with
renewed blows against the enemy. In February 1971,
at the administration's initiative, the South Vietnamese army invaded Laos to destroy communist
bases there and to restrict the flow of supplies
southward from North Vietnam. The South Vietnamese, however, were routed. American television vividly conveyed their disorderly retreat and
their desperate attempts to escape the enemy by
clinging to the skids of departing American heli-
copters.

Emboldened by this success, communist forces
now moved quickly to occupy as much strategic
territory as possible. In April 1972 the North Vietnamese mounted a major offensive throughout
Cambodia and South Vietnam. With less than one
hundred thousand American troops remaining in
Vietnam, Nixon retaliated by mining North Vietnam's harbors and ports and by unleashing B-52s
on Cambodia as well as on North Vietnam's bases
and cities. "The bastards have never been bombed
like they are going to be bombed this time," he
vowed.

1945 Ho Chi Minh announces Declaration of Independence from France.

1950 French-controlled Vietnam receives U.S. financial aid and military advisers.

1954 Dienbienphu falls to Ho's Vietminh.

Geneva Accords end Indochina War and temporarily divide Vietnam at the seventeenth parallel.

Ngo Dinh Diem becomes South Vietnam's premier.

1955 Diem establishes the Republic of Vietnam.

U.S. advisers take over training of South Vietnamese army (ARVN).

1960 National Liberation Front (Vietcong) formed.

1961 President John Kennedy markedly increases military aid to South Vietnam.

1962 Strategic-hamlet program put in operation.

1963 Buddhist protests commence.

ARVN coup overthrows and assassinates Diem.

16,000 U.S. military personnel in Vietnam.

1964 General William Westmoreland takes charge of U.S. Military Assistance Command in South Vietnam.

Gulf of Tonkin incident and subsequent U.S. congressional resolution.

United States bombs North Vietnam.

23,300 U.S. military personnel in Vietnam.

1965 First American combat troops arrive in South Vietnam, at Danang.

184,000 U. S. military personnel in Vietnam.

1966 B-52s attack North Vietnam for first time.

Senate Foreign Relations Committee opens hearings on U.S. in Vietnam.

385,000 U.S. military personnel in Vietnam.

1967 Major antiwar demonstrations in New York and San Francisco; protest march on the Pentagon.

485,600 U.S. military personnel in Vietnam.

1968 North Vietnamese forces surround Khesanh.

Tet offensive.

My Lai massacre.

President Lyndon Johnson announces partial bombing halt and decision not to run for reelection.

Peace talks begin in Paris.

General Creighton Abrams replaces Westmoreland as commander of American troops in Vietnam.

536,000 U.S. military personnel in Vietnam.

1969	United States begins bombing of North Vietnamese bases in Cambodia.	**1972**	North Vietnam launches first ground offensive since 1968.

1969   United States begins bombing of North Vietnamese bases in Cambodia.

Provisional Revolutionary Government (PRG) formed by Vietcong.

First U.S. troop withdrawal announced after American military personnel in Vietnam reach peak strength of 543,400 in April.

Ho Chi Minh dies.

Nationwide antiwar protests in October.

475,200 U.S. military personnel in Vietnam.

1970   United States and South Vietnamese forces join in Cambodian incursion.

Student protests force some four hundred colleges and universities to close following Kent State killings.

Cooper-Church amendment limits U.S. role in Cambodia.

Senate repeals Gulf of Tonkin Resolution.

334,600 U.S. military personnel in Vietnam.

1971   United States provides air support for South Vietnamese invasion of Laos.

Antiwar rally of 400,000 in Washington.

Daniel Ellsberg releases Pentagon Papers to the *New York Times.*

1972   North Vietnam launches first ground offensive since 1968.

U.S. bombing and mining of North Vietnamese ports.

Last U.S. ground troops leave South Vietnam.

Preliminary peace agreement reached; National Security Adviser Henry Kissinger announces that "peace is at hand."

South Vietnam rejects peace treaty.

United States bombs Hanoi and Haiphong.

24,200 U.S. military personnel in Vietnam.

1973   Peace agreement signed in Paris by North and South Vietnam, the Vietcong, and the United States.

End of U.S. draft.

Congress passes War Powers Act.

First American POWs released in Hanoi.

U.S. bombing in Southeast Asia ends.

Fewer than 250 U.S. military personnel in Vietnam.

1974   South Vietnam announces new outbreak of war.

1975   North Vietnamese offensive captures Danang.

Senate rejects President Gerald Ford's request for emergency aid for South Vietnam.

South Vietnam surrenders following North Vietnam's capture of Saigon.

Khmer Rouge takes control in Cambodia.

Pro-Hanoi People's Democratic Republic established in Laos.

American Retreat from the War

The bombing raids in the spring of 1972 broke the impasse in the Paris peace talks, which had been stalemated since 1968. In October 1972 the North Vietnamese relented on their earlier demand that South Vietnam's President Thieu be replaced by a coalition government. A cease-fire agreement negotiated by Kissinger and Le Duc Tho required the withdrawal of all remaining American troops; provided for the return of American prisoners of war; and giving in to the communists' primary objective, allowed North Vietnamese troops to remain in South Vietnam. Shortly before the 1972 election, Kissinger announced to the nation that "peace is at hand."

Kissinger's negotiations enabled Nixon to campaign in 1972 as the architect of peace in Vietnam. Reassuringly the president announced that the draft would end in mid-1973. But the confident Kissinger had failed to gauge Thieu's obstinacy. The South Vietnamese president refused to sign a cease-fire agreement that permitted North Vietnamese troops to remain in the South. Meanwhile, Le Duc Tho, angered by Thieu's rebuff, pressed for even greater concessions at the negotiating table. Once again Nixon resorted to terror, authorizing the 1972 Christmas bombing of North Vietnam's major cities, Hanoi and Haiphong. The massive B-52 raids roused fierce opposition in Congress and in the United Nations but accomplished their purpose. The destructive aerial attacks dissolved the deadlock with North Vietnam while Nixon's secret assurances to Thieu that the United States would "respond with full force should the settlement be violated by North Vietnam" ended Saigon's recalcitrance.

On January 23, 1973, the day on which Lyndon Johnson died of a heart attack on his Texas ranch, President Nixon announced that a settlement agreement had been reached. The Paris Accords, signed four days later, essentially restated the terms of the October truce. The agreement ended hostilities between the United States and North Vietnam yet left unresolved the differences between North Vietnam and the Thieu regime, guaranteeing that Vietnam's future would yet be settled on the battlefield.

America's longest war had exacerbated national problems and deepened social divisions. It had cost at least $150 billion and taken a vast human toll. The fighting had resulted in some 58,000 American deaths and more than 300,000 wounded, including at least 10,000 paraplegics. Nearly half a million of the 2,700,000 Americans who served in the war, moreover, received less-than-honorable discharges—a measure of the high desertion rate, the rampant drug use at the front, the spread of antiwar sentiment even in the military, and the immaturity of the troops (the average U.S. soldier in Vietnam was just nineteen years old, seven years younger than the average American GI in World War II).

Further, virtually all who survived, wrote marine rifleman William Jayne, came back "as immigrants to a new world. For the culture we had known dissolved while we were in Vietnam, and the culture of combat we lived in so intensely . . . made us aliens when we returned." Reminders of a war that Americans wished to forget, these veterans were hardly greeted by parades and blizzards of confetti and ticker tape. Beyond occasional media attention to the psychological difficulties that they faced in readjusting to civilian life ("post-Vietnam syndrome"), which principally fostered an image of veterans as disturbed and dangerous, the nation paid little heed to those who had served and sacrificed.

Relieved that the long nightmare of war was past, most Americans quickly put the conflict aside. Few considered the extent to which American involvement in the war had physically devastated much of Vietnam, caused 2 million Vietnamese casualties, and brought severe human and material losses to Cambodia and Laos.*Even the bitterness of many Vietnam veterans faded. "We've adjusted too well," complained Tim O'Brien, a veteran and novelist of the war, in 1980. "Too many of us have lost touch with the horror of war. . . . It would seem that the memories of soldiers should serve, at least in a modest way, as a restraint on national bellicosity. But time and distance erode memory. We adjust, we lose the intensity. I fear that we are back where we started. I wish we were more troubled."

Détente

The disengagement of American troops from Vietnam helped Nixon and Kissinger to achieve a turnabout in Chinese-American relations and eventual détente with the communist superpowers. These dramatic developments marked the most significant shift in American foreign policy since the start

---

*The U.S. bombing and invasion of Cambodia, for example, had further disrupted an already divided nation and opened the door for the seizure of power by the communist Khmer Rouge rebels in 1975. The victorious communists renamed the country Kampuchea. The nation's new ruler, the fanatic Pol Pot, launched a program of mass executions, systematic terror, and forced relocation that, until his own overthrow following a Vietnamese invasion in 1979, left an estimated 3 million Cambodians dead—40 percent of the country's population. This genocidal horror, too, was part of the legacy of the Vietnam War.

Nixon in China, 1972

American TV networks covered Nixon's dramatic visits to legendary landmarks such as the Great Wall, as well as his impromptu conversations with the Chinese people. One reporter remarked that "the White House was playing [the visit] as a pageant, not as a news story."

of the Cold War and created a new relationship among the United States, the Soviet Union, and China.

Since the Korean War, presidents from Truman to Johnson had refused to recognize the People's Republic. Treating the mainland Chinese regime as an outlaw, the United States had vetoed the admission of "Red China" to the United Nations and pressured American allies to restrict trade with the communist giant. By 1969, however, a widening Sino-Soviet split made the prospect of improved relations attractive to both Nixon and Chinese leader Mao Zedong. That year armed clashes between Russian and Chinese troops along the border between the two countries prompted the Beijing government to seek better relations with Washington as security against Russian expansionism. Playing one communist power off against the other, the Nixon administration calculated that a new cordiality with China would constrain Soviet influence in Asia and push Moscow toward concessions in the continuing negotiations to limit nuclear arms.

As Nixon's first move in what Kissinger called "the three-dimensional game," the president in the fall of 1970 began to refer to China as the People's Republic rather than Red China. He also publicly intimated that he wished to visit "that vast, unknown land." Then in April 1971, the Chinese royally hosted an American table-tennis team that had been touring Japan. Behind this "ping-pong

diplomacy" lay serious maneuverings. Talks between the two nations' ambassadors in Poland led to a secret trip to Beijing by Kissinger in June and a startling mid-1971 announcement by Nixon that he would travel to the People's Republic "to seek the normalization of relations."

On February 22, 1972, the president's plane landed in China. Not since 1879, when Ulysses Grant had visited the faraway Eastern nation after leaving office, had an American president journeyed to China, now the most populous country in the world. Accompanied by a teeming entourage of news reporters and television camera crews, a beaming Nixon toured the Great Wall ("This truly is a great wall," he commented) and exchanged rice-liquor toasts with Mao Zedong and Chinese premier Zhou Enlai (Chou En-lai). Although significant remaining differences between the two powers delayed official diplomatic relations until 1979, the Nixon visit signaled the end of more than twenty years of Sino-American hostility. A historic milestone had been reached.

In an equally significant step, Nixon visited Moscow in May 1972. "There must be room in this world for two great nations with different systems to live together and work together," the president proclaimed. To that end, he concluded agreements with the Russians on trade[*] and technological

---

[*]Specifically the Soviets agreed to buy at least $750 million in American grain over a three-year period—a boon to U.S. farmers.

cooperation and, following the first Strategic Arms Limitation Talks (SALT I), signed two major arms-control pacts with Soviet leader Leonid Brezhnev. The SALT I agreement, overwhelmingly ratified by the Senate in October 1972, limited both nations to a maximum of two hundred antiballistic missiles (ABMs) and two ABM systems. The advent of the SALT I treaty indicated superpower acceptance of the idea that a mutual-deterrence policy afforded the surest guarantee against nuclear attack and that such mutuality could be preserved only by agreement on both sides not to build nation-wide missile defense systems. A separate agreement froze for five years the number of intercontinental ballistic missiles (ICBMs) and submarine-launched missiles that each power could have. Like the SALT I treaty, it allowed both nations to monitor each other by photo-reconnaissance satellites. The limitations slowed the costly and dangerous nuclear-arms race, reduced Cold War tensions, and in an election year, enhanced Richard Nixon's stature as a proponent of peace and stability.

American Self-Interest Abroad

A year after the SALT I agreement's ratification, the powder keg of Israeli-Arab relations again ignited in war. Israel's decisive triumph in the 1967 Six-Day War had left the Arabs humiliated and eager to reclaim the militarily strategic Golan Heights, taken from Syria; Egypt's Sinai Peninsula; and the West Bank and holy city of Jerusalem, seized from Jordan. The Israeli victory had also incited the homeless, embittered Palestinian Arabs to found the Palestine Liberation Organization (PLO), dedicated to destroying Israel and creating an Arab Palestinian nation in its place. Following a several-year-long Arab war of attrition against the Israelis, and concurrent bombing raids by Israel on its neighbors, Moscow-backed Syrian and Egyptian forces in 1973 launched an all-out attack against Israel on October 6—the most sacred Jewish holy day, Yom Kippur. Aided by massive U.S. shipments of highly sophisticated weaponry, the Israelis stopped the assault and then counterattacked. In retaliation, the oil-producing Arab states embargoed shipments of crude oil to the United States and its allies. This oil embargo, in effect from October 1973 to March 1974, spawned acute fuel shortages and startlingly increased the cost of

petroleum products in the United States. Petroleum imports remained high throughout the 1970s, driving inflation relentlessly upward.

The Nixon administration now shifted U.S. foreign policy from its traditional exclusive support for Israel to a more evenhanded relationship with the contending Middle Eastern nations. The dual shock of an energy crisis at home and renewed Soviet influence among the Arabs spurred Nixon and Kissinger to make a special effort to gain the backing of Arab countries previously hostile to the United States. Beginning in October 1973, Kissinger spent two years engaging in "shuttle diplomacy." Flying from one capital to another, he negotiated an Israeli-Egyptian cease-fire agreement in November 1973, engineered the withdrawal of Israel's troops from Egyptian and Syrian territories captured in 1973, and prevailed on the Organization of Petroleum Exporting Countries (OPEC) to end its embargo. Kissinger's diplomacy bore fruit in an expanding American influence in the Middle East, symbolized by Nixon's successful visit to Egypt, Saudi Arabia, and Syria in June 1974. Although the new direction in American diplomacy did not alter the root causes of Middle Eastern instability, especially the fate of the Palestinians, it did smooth relations between the Arabs and the United States and pave the way for Egypt, formerly a staunch Soviet ally, to expel its Russian advisers and side with Washington.

Recognizing the limits of U.S. power, Nixon and Kissinger also sought to strengthen America's allies. To counter Soviet influence and to protect American economic and strategic interests, the administration liberally supplied arms to the shah of Iran, Riza Pahlevi; to President Ferdinand Marcos in the Philippines; and to the white-supremacist regime of South Africa. The realpolitik of the Nixon-Kissinger diplomacy based American aid more on a nation's willingness to oppose the Soviet Union than on the nature of its government or the morality of its policies. Disregarding the U.N. human-rights covenants of 1966, the administration stepped up assistance to the repressive rulers of Argentina and South Korea, to the military dictatorships in Brazil and oil-rich Nigeria, and to the Portuguese colonial authorities in Angola.

After the election of the Marxist Salvador Allende to the presidency of Chile in 1970, Nixon secretly funneled $10 million to the CIA to fund

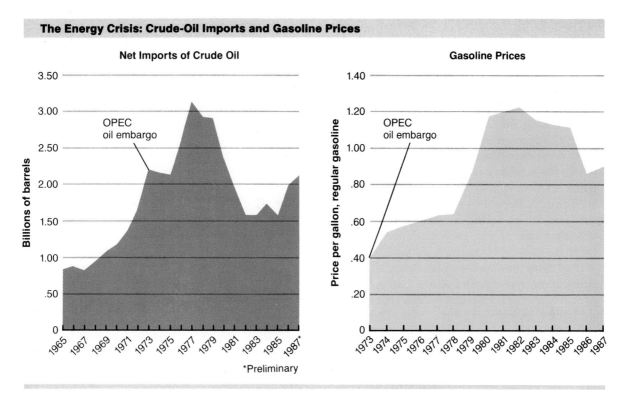

The Energy Crisis: Crude-Oil Imports and Gasoline Prices

Not until the 1980s, through the combination of a deep recession and fuel conservation, did U.S. petroleum imports finally begin dropping off (left). OPEC's ability to act as a supercartel in setting oil prices sent the cost of filling a car's gas tank skyrocketing in the 1970s (right).

SOURCE: Energy Information Administration, *Annual Energy Review*, 1987

opponents of the leftist Chilean government. "I don't see why we need to stand by and watch a country go communist due to the irresponsibility of its own people," Kissinger commented. The United States also cut off economic aid to Chile, blocked private banks from granting the nation loans, and successfully pressed the World Bank to drop Chile's credit rating. Believing that it had the tacit approval of Washington, a military junta in September 1973 overthrew the Chilean government and killed Allende. Nixon quickly recognized the new dictatorship, and substantial economic aid and private investment once again flowed to Chile.

The administration's active opposition to Allende reflected the extent to which American policy remained committed to containing communist influence. Whenever feasible, Nixon and Kissinger acted to enhance America's power abroad. At the same time, they understood the limits of American might and the changed realities of world

affairs. Discarding the model of a globe torn by a bipolar conflict between capitalism and communism—a perspective that had dominated State Department thought since 1945—they took advantage of the rift between China and the Soviet Union to improve U.S. relations with both communist nations. The Nixon administration also ended American involvement in the Vietnam War and improved the United States' position in the Middle East. Perhaps most significantly, the politician who had built his reputation as a hardline Cold Warrior initiated a new era of détente with the communist powers. The China opening and the arms limitation agreements with the Soviet Union dramatically abated Cold War tensions and reduced the risk of a nuclear holocaust. By adhering to a realistic diplomacy aimed at minimizing the likelihood of global war, Nixon and Kissinger negotiated with their adversaries to create a safer international environment.

Domestic Problems and Divisions

Richard Nixon hoped to be remembered primarily as an international statesman; yet his immersion in global politics could not prevent domestic affairs from pressing in. In some respects, Nixon displayed considerable resourcefulness and creativity in the domestic realm. He took significant initiatives in the areas of environmental protection and welfare reform and, rejecting the hands-off approach of traditional Republican conservatism, grappled with inflation and other complex economic problems that the nation confronted in the early seventies.

But there was another side to the Nixon administration that appealed to the darker recesses of the national character and exacerbated the fears and hatreds that divided Americans. This underside of the Nixon years was rooted in the complex character of Richard Nixon himself.

Richard Nixon: Man and Politician

Reporters who observed Richard Nixon invariably commented on the multiple levels of his personality: the calculated public persona of the politician, beneath which lurked a different and shadowy Nixon that rarely revealed itself. In both foreign and domestic policy, Nixon the politician exhibited many impressive traits. He was highly intelligent, with great analytic skills, phenomenal endurance, and a capacity for total concentration. A nickname from his navy days was "iron butt." He also had a zest for public life. "I like to be in the arena," he once said; "I have seen those who have nothing to do . . . , the people just lying around at Palm Beach. Nothing could be more pitiful." His political heroes were the scholarly Woodrow Wilson and the hyperactive Theodore Roosevelt.

Yet Nixon also displayed the watchfulness and rigid self-control of a man monitoring his own every move. Reporters noted the jerky, mechanical gestures; the darting, suspicious eyes; and what John Osborne of the *New Republic* called "the appalling on-order smile . . . , the upward twitch followed on the instant by a return to the usual sullen set of the mouth." Added Osborne, not unsympathetically: "The study of Richard Nixon . . . requires a steadfast clinging to the fact that he is

Richard Nixon

Dubbed "King Richard" by some commentators, Nixon pushed presidential authority to its furthest peacetime limit.

human." Occasionally the tight control slipped. One such moment came after his defeat in the 1962 California gubernatorial race, in a rambling, resentful, self-pitying "farewell" to reporters who had covered the campaign.

But the moments of self-revelation were rare. A basic rule of both Nixon and his staff, reported a journalist covering the Nixon White House, was to avoid any situation that would "expose to general view the man within the shell." Garry Wills, in his brilliant 1970 book *Nixon Agonistes,* carried the point even further: "With other politicians, informality exposes the man behind the office, a range of personality that extends beyond the political role. But Nixon does not exist outside his role, apart from politics: take off his clothes, he would be invisible."

When the private Nixon did emerge, he revealed himself to be suspicious, insecure, and full of anger. As a political associate observed: "Dick has great physical and moral courage, but there is an element of self-doubt very deep in him." Even in the White House, Nixon was almost paranoid in his conviction that enemies lurked on all sides, waiting to destroy him. He seethed with resentments, often acted as though he were locked in mortal combat, and viewed his life as a series of desperate crises met and surmounted. "I believe in the battle, whether it's the battle of a campaign or the battle of this office," he told an interviewer in 1972. "It's always there wherever you go. I, perhaps, carry it more than others because that's my way."

Driven as he was, Nixon sought to annihilate, not merely defeat, his partisan enemies, particularly those of the "eastern liberal establishment" who had long opposed him and whom he despised in return. "Nixonland," Adlai Stevenson had observed in the fifties, was a place of "slander and scare, of sly innuendo, of a poison pen, the anonymous phone call, and hustling, pushing, shoving—the land of smash and grab and anything to win." Nixonland lived on after Nixon's accession to the presidency, as he recruited staff members who shared his outlook. The art of politics, said his electoral adviser Kevin Phillips during the 1968 campaign, was the art of discovering who hates whom.

Probing for the source of the furies that gnawed at Nixon's innards, some perceptive observers viewed him as the classic outsider: reared in pinched surroundings, physically awkward, unable to relate easily to others. Even at tiny Whittier College, snubbed by the school's elite, he formed a club of underdogs called the Orthogonians (squares). But he was an outsider who propelled himself to the heights of national power by unremitting hard work and self-discipline. Teaching himself poker in the navy, he played it skillfully and methodically until he had built up a nest egg for the postwar years, and then dropped the game forever. Nixon was the quintessential self-made man, the consummate Horatio Alger hero, with all the strengths and weaknesses of the type.

At some level he always remained the outsider, sensing that he was not fully accepted, suspicious that others more graceful, more cultivated, more spontaneous than he, were laughing at his austere virtues, his stern self-discipline, his public gaucheries. When he sneered at those privileged persons who inhabited what he called "the so-called best circles in America," it was with the resentment of one who recognized that many in that charmed sphere held him in contempt.

Whatever the forces that shaped Nixon's personality, many Americans identified with his outlook, and this fact helped propel him to the White House. As Garry Wills put it, Nixon's strengths and deficiencies uncannily matched what was "best and weakest in America." Indeed, Wills concluded in 1970, "the last two decades seem almost to bear witness to a single trend: the inevitability of Nixon."

At the beginning of the Nixon years, it was the new president's strengths that were most apparent. He spoke of national reconciliation, appointed a well-qualified team, took bold initiatives in the international arena, and dealt with domestic problems responsibly and even creatively. But the darker side—the mean-spiritedness, the suspiciousness, the pitting of group against group for political advantage—soon came to the fore. This side of Nixon ultimately prevailed and in the end would drive him from office in disgrace.

The Nixon Presidency

Having urged Americans in his 1969 inaugural address to stop shouting at one another and to "speak quietly enough so that our words can be heard as well as our voices," Nixon began his presidency with a moderation and restraint reminiscent of Eisenhower. His calm rhetoric and appointment of a cabinet of flexibly conservative men of prominence promised the respite from unrest and rapid change that most Americans desired. Symbolic of this harmonious beginning, a united country joined the new president in celebrating the first successful manned space mission to the moon. Seven years after President John Kennedy had launched a massive effort to meet the Russian challenge in space (see Chapter 29), Apollo 11 landed its lunar module *Eagle* on the moon's Sea of Tranquillity. On July 21, 1969, astronaut Neil Armstrong walked on the moon's surface and announced to television audiences back on earth: "That's one small step for man, one giant leap for mankind." Americans took heartfelt pride in the fact that the United States had come from behind to win the space race and had accomplished a feat that rocket scientist Werner von Braun termed "probably as significant to the history of life on earth as aquatic life first crawling on land." Millions thrilled as astronauts Armstrong and Buzz Aldrin planted an American

Moonwalk, July 1969

In this photograph taken by fellow astronaut Neil Armstrong, Edwin Aldrin, Jr., descends the steps of the lunar-module ladder just before his historic walk on the moon.

flag and a plaque reading, "Here men from planet earth first set foot on the moon, July 1969 A.D. We came in peace for all mankind."

The only newly elected president since 1849 to face both houses of Congress controlled by the opposition party, Nixon had initially approved a moderate extension of Great Society programs. He signed bills to increase social-security benefits, to reform the tax system, to produce subsidized housing for low- and middle-income families, and to expand the Job Corps. The president also accepted Democrat-sponsored legislation to grant the vote to eighteen-year-olds and to clean up polluted waterways. Most disturbing to those conservatives who expected Nixon to honor his campaign pledge to reduce the regulatory powers of the federal government, he created the Environmental Protection Agency (EPA) and the Occupational Safety and Health Administration (OSHA) to enforce governmental standards for air and water quality and for work safety, respectively.

President Nixon truly jounced his party's right wing in August 1969 by unveiling the Family

Assistance Plan (FAP), tailored to reform the nation's antiquated welfare system. Crafted by Daniel P. Moynihan, a Great Society Democrat serving as Nixon's urban-affairs adviser, the FAP proposed to replace piecemeal handouts with a minimum annual income—sixteen hundred dollars for a family of four. Republicans swiftly criticized Nixon for promoting the liberal idea of a guaranteed annual wage for all and for sponsoring a measure that would increase total welfare costs. At the same time, liberal Democrats denounced the FAP for its low level of payments and its requirement that all heads of households on relief, mainly women, had to register for employment or job training. The Family Assistance Plan passed the House but, caught in ideological crossfire, expired in the Senate.[*]

Following the 1970 congressional elections, the administration's more conservative inclinations began to emerge. To cut federal expenditures, especially in the liberal social programs initiated by his Democratic predecessors, Nixon vetoed more than a score of measures enacted by the Ninety-second Congress. When his vetoes were overridden, he impounded (that is, refused to spend) the congressionally authorized funds. The president promised that his policy, which he called the New Federalism, would "reverse the flow of power and resources from the states and communities to Washington." To hasten that power shift from Washington to the states, Nixon proposed a revenue-sharing bill that would allocate some federal revenues to the states and to local municipalities. Despite the objections of some congressional Democrats who feared a dilution of their powers to control the federal purse, revenue sharing became law in October 1972. The president hailed the act for its invigoration of local government, but in the wake of the accompanying slashes in federal spending for social services, the nation's financially pressed cities complained that the new system left them worse off than before.

A Troubled Economy

During the 1968 campaign, Nixon had said, "I've always thought this country could run itself domestically without a president. All you need is a competent cabinet to run the country at home."

---

[*]In 1988 Moynihan, now a Democratic senator from New York, would finally see key elements of his Family Assistance Plan enacted into law.

Once in office, however, he found that he had to devote much of his attention to the nation's economic woes. Inheriting the bleak fiscal consequences of Lyndon Johnson's effort to wage the Vietnam War and carry on a program of heavy spending on social programs at home, all without hiking taxes, Nixon assumed the presidency facing what in those days was considered a whopping budget deficit ($25 billion) and an inflation rate of 5 percent. The cost of living rose more than 7 percent in 1969, and steadily mounting prices for energy, food, and raw materials threatened still worse inflation. Although anxious to check inflation, Nixon rejected proposals to manage wages and prices. "Controls, oh my God no!" he exclaimed, recalling his own World War II OPA experience with rationing and black markets. Instead, Nixon cut government expenditures and encouraged the Federal Reserve Board to force up interest rates.

The president intended to slow business and consumer spending as a means of reducing inflation. But despite falling industrial production, which raised unemployment to 6 percent in 1970 and brought the first major recession since the Eisenhower Era, inflation galloped forward. The head of the Democratic National Committee branded the alarming convergence of recessionary and inflationary trends "Nixonomics," complaining that "all the things that should go up—the stock market, corporate profits, real spendable income, productivity—go down, and all the things that should go down—unemployment, prices, interest rates—go up."

Early in 1971 Nixon startled the nation by declaring, "I am now a Keynesian." Fearing the political consequences of a worsening recession more than he feared the economic effects of inflationary prosperity, the president switched to the Keynesian tactic of reviving the economy through deficit spending. He deliberately proposed an unbalanced federal budget in the hope of stimulating recovery. He still held the line, however, against attempts to impose controls on wages and prices.

Then in August 1971 Nixon changed course again. Following a Commerce Department announcement of a major trade deficit—for the first time since 1890, the United States was importing more than it exported—the president announced a new set of measures to promote economic stabilization and deal with the trade imbalance. To

Inflation, 1920–1987

Inflation, which had been moderate during the two decades following the Second World War, began to soar with the escalation of the war in Vietnam in the mid-1960s. In 1979 and 1980 the nation experienced double-digit inflation in two consecutive years for the first time since World War I. Overall, between 1967 and 1987 the consumer price index more than tripled.

boost consumption of domestic goods, he levied a 10 percent surcharge on imports. To make the prices of U.S. goods more competitive abroad, Nixon declared that henceforth the value of the dollar would no longer be arbitrarily fixed in relation to other currencies (an arrangement devised by the major Western nations at an economic conference held at Bretton Woods, New Hampshire, in 1944); from now on, the dollar would be left to find its own level—it would "float"—in the international monetary exchanges.

Finally, in a startling reversal of his earlier absolute refusal to consider wage-and-price controls, Nixon decreed a ninety-day freeze on wages, prices, and rents, to be followed by federally imposed controls setting maximum annual increases of 5.5 percent for wages and 2.5 percent for prices and rents.

The new policies perked up the sluggish economy, sending the Dow-Jones stock index above one thousand for the first time in history, and then reduced inflation and the trade deficit enough to benefit Nixon in his reelection bid. In January 1973 the president reversed direction yet again, replacing wage-and-price ceilings with "recommended" guidelines and "voluntary" restraints. That year inflation soared to 9 percent. It would remain a major headache for the rest of the decade.

Law and Order

Nixon hoped that in combination with his flexible economic policies, the federal government's suppression of domestic disorder would forge an unbeatable voting coalition for the Republicans in 1972. Seeking support among nominally Democratic blue-collar laborers, white southerners, and members of white ethnic minorities, he proclaimed his opposition to court-ordered busing. Mindful of the ongoing appeal of Alabama populist and demagogue George Wallace, he took every opportunity to dramatize his tough stand on law and order and disapproval of radical activism. He cultivated the "silent majority" who feared the collapse of morality by affirming traditional values, ordering veterans' hospitals to cease performing abortions, and denouncing pornography and drugs. Courting the votes of those alarmed by judicial decisions that "coddled criminals," the administration sponsored numerous measures to strengthen the powers of the police.

To combat domestic radicalism, the president drew upon the full resources of the federal government. Under Nixon, the Internal Revenue Service audited the tax returns of prominent antiwar and civil-rights activists, and the Small Business Administration denied them loans. The Federal Bureau of Investigation illegally wiretapped individuals and organizations involved in leftist politics, and the National Security Agency intercepted their telecommunications. The FBI also infiltrated the ranks of the SDS and black radical groups with informers and agents who provoked violence within these movements to discredit them. The Justice Department and the FBI worked closely with local police forces in 1969–1970 to arrest Black Panthers on dubious charges and to disrupt their operations by disinformation programs. Gunfights between police and the Panthers killed some forty members of this radical black organization. Contrary to the specific prohibitions written into the National Security Act of 1947, moreover, the CIA investigated, and compiled dossiers on, thousands

of American dissidents. To focus the nation's fears on the radical threat, Nixon authorized the Department of Justice to prosecute antiwar activists and militant blacks in highly publicized trials.

Nixon also moved secretly to crush his opponents. Drawing from unspent 1968 campaign funds, he created a covert task force in 1969 to spy on liberal columnists and congressional critics of his administration. Viewing his political adversaries as personal assailants, the president compiled an "enemies list" of prominent Americans who would be harassed by the government. "Anyone who opposes us, we'll destroy," warned a top White House official. "As a matter of fact, anyone who doesn't support us, we'll destroy." To coordinate the government vendetta against his opponents, Nixon chose his aide Charles Colson, a self-described "anti-press, anti-liberal Nixon fanatic." Colson's task, explained the White House counsel, was to bring the full pressure of available federal machinery to bear against Nixon's foes.

Widening the offensive against the antiwar movement, Nixon in 1970 approved a scheme, known as the Huston Plan, which would employ the CIA and FBI in a wide variety of illegal missions. In the name of national security, the plan envisioned the recruitment of students to infiltrate radical organizations, extensive wiretapping and electronic surveillance, break-ins and burglaries to ferret out or plant evidence of illegal activity, and a new agency to centralize domestic covert operations under White House supervision. FBI chief J. Edgar Hoover, however, perceiving the Huston Plan as a threat to the FBI's independence, emphatically opposed it. Blocked, Nixon secretly created his own White House unit to discredit his opponents and ensure executive secrecy. Nicknamed "the plumbers" by White House insiders because of their assignment to stop government leaks, the team was headed by an ex-FBI agent, G. Gordon Liddy, and a former CIA operative, E. Howard Hunt.

The plumbers' first target was Daniel Ellsberg. Previously an analyst for the Department of Defense, Ellsberg in mid-1971 had turned over to the press the secret Pentagon Papers, a documentary account of American involvement in Vietnam prepared by the department during the Johnson administration. On June 13 the *New York Times* began to publish the papers. Although the documents contained nothing damaging about the Nixon administration, they revealed a long history of government lies—to foreign leaders, to Congress, and to the American people. Fearing that the Pentagon Papers would further undermine public trust in government statements about the war and establish a precedent for publishing other classified material, Nixon obtained a court injunction barring further publication of the papers. The *Times*, however, protesting the unprecedented use of prior restraint against the press, appealed to the Supreme Court. The High Court lifted the injunction, ruling that the First Amendment forbade such censorship. A livid Richard Nixon directed the Department of Justice to indict Ellsberg for theft and espionage and then ordered the plumbers to discredit him. In August 1971 Hunt and Liddy broke into the office of Ellsberg's psychiatrist to search for information that might denigrate the man who had become an instant hero to the antiwar movement.

The Southern Strategy

Concurrent with its attack on radicalism, the administration courted whites upset by the drive for racial equality, especially in the South. Nixon, who had won only 13 percent of the black vote in 1968, displayed little enthusiasm for trying to better that. The Republican legislator Edward Brooke of Massachusetts, the only black senator at the time, criticized the president for his "cold, calculated political decision to reject the needs of blacks." The administration testified before Congress against extending the Voting Rights Act of 1965 and in favor of modifications in the Fair Housing Act of 1968 that would have crippled its enforcement provisions. Moreover, it pleaded for a postponement in the desegregation of Mississippi's schools and argued against school busing as a means to reduce segregation. When the Supreme Court in 1971 upheld busing as a constitutional and necessary tactic to achieve racial balance in the schools (*Swann* v. *Charlotte-Mecklenburg Board of Education*), Nixon went on television to condemn the ruling and to ask Congress to enact a moratorium on busing.

In response to these roadblocks to racial equality, the heads of the U.S. Commission on Civil Rights and the Equal Employment Opportunity Commission, as well as top Justice Department lawyers, resigned in protest. "For the first time since Wood-

row Wilson," the NAACP's president charged, "we have a national administration that can rightly be characterized as anti-Negro."

The strategy of wooing the white South similarly dictated Nixon's approach to nominations for the Supreme Court. To reverse the liberalism of the Warren court, he tried to fill the Court with strict constructionists, judges who would not "meddle" in social issues or "be soft on criminals." In 1969 Nixon appointed Warren Burger, a conservative federal judge, to replace the retiring Earl Warren as chief justice. For the next vacancy that year, the president selected Clement Haynesworth of South Carolina. Disturbed by Haynesworth's anti-labor and anti-civil-rights rulings as a federal judge, seventeen Republican senators joined with most Democrats to reject his appointment. For the first time since the Hoover administration, the Senate voted down a Supreme Court nominee.

Nixon responded angrily, vowing to appoint someone with views similar to Haynesworth's. He chose G. Harrold Carswell of Florida, whose judicial record and vulnerability to charges that he had held racist views earlier in his career quickly elicited opposition from civil-rights groups, the American Bar Association, and most legal scholars. Thirteen Republicans again joined the opposition to reject the president's nominee; and Nixon again masterfully used the defeat to picture himself as sympathetic to the feelings of white southerners and to portray the Democrats as contemptuous of the white South. By 1972 Nixon finally succeeded in appointing three able and conservative justices to the Supreme Court: Harry Blackmun of Minnesota, Lewis Powell of Virginia, and William Rehnquist of Arizona. Joining forces with Chief Justice Burger, the Nixon appointees steered the Court in a moderate direction. While ruling liberally in cases involving abortion, desegregation, and the death penalty, the Burger court shifted to the right in rulings on civil liberties, community censorship, and the power of the police.

The Silent Majority Speaks

In his drive to build a Republican majority, Nixon aimed to capture the backlash vote that had gravitated to George Wallace in 1968. Playing the role of the moral defender of traditional values, he denounced the Democrats as the party of New Left "hooligans, hippies, and radical liberals" and blamed them for fostering drug use, supporting abortion, and cultivating social disorder. In an attempt to gain control of Congress in the off-year elections of 1970, Nixon encouraged his vice president, Spiro Agnew, to mount an attack on the liberal opposition. "It is time to rip away the rhetoric and to divide on authentic lines," pronounced Agnew in praise of political polarization. Crisscrossing the nation, the vice president assailed students as "parasites of passions," Democrats as "sniveling hand-wringers," and intellectuals as "an effete corps of impudent snobs." He relentlessly attacked the news media, which President Nixon viewed as bent on discrediting him and undermining his policies. Implying that the television networks were run by a "tiny and closed fraternity of privileged men," Agnew described newscasters as "curled-lip boys in eastern ivory towers" and, in a memorable epithet, "nattering nabobs of negativism."

Although liberals deplored Agnew's alarming alliterative allegations, many Democratic candidates joined their Republican opponents in appealing for law and order, patriotism, and a rejuvenation of traditional family values. As welcoming signs at working-class rallies across the nation proclaimed "SPIRO IS MY HERO," top Democrats reversed their previous positions on abortion, gun control, and the legalization of marijuana. The electoral result proved a draw. The Democrats gained eleven governorships and increased their majority in the House by nine, while the GOP picked up two Senate seats. Since the party of the president in power had suffered losses in every off-year congressional election except that of 1934, the White House took comfort in the standoff and confidently planned for the presidential race in 1972.

The Election of 1972

Nixon's reelection appeared assured. He counted on his diplomatic successes with China and Russia and his winding down of the war in Vietnam to attract moderate voters. He expected his southern strategy and law-and-order posture to appeal to the conservative Democrats who had voted for Wallace in 1968. Continued Democratic divisions and a succession of incidents embarrassing to Democratic presidential hopefuls boosted Nixon's

George McGovern and Supporters

McGovern was the candidate of choice for minorities, the poor, newly enfranchised college students, and for many of those who had championed Eugene McCarthy and Robert Kennedy in 1968. Kennedy once said of McGovern, "George is the most decent man in the Senate. As a matter of fact, he's the only one."

optimism. Hubert Humphrey could muster support only from old-line party bosses. Senator Edward Kennedy of Massachusetts had fallen from favor in 1969 after fleeing the scene of a nighttime accident on Martha's Vineyard in which a young woman passenger in his car drowned. The campaign of Senator Edmund Muskie of Maine collapsed when he wept publicly while responding to an accusation of prejudice against Canadian-Americans.

Nixon's only major worry, another third-party candidacy by George Wallace, dissolved on May 15, 1972. During a campaign stop at a Maryland shopping center, Wallace was shot by a deranged young man named Arthur Bremer. Paralyzed from the waist down, the Alabamian withdrew from the race, leaving Nixon a monopoly of the white-backlash, law-and-order vote.

The Senate's most outspoken dove, the "prairie populist" George McGovern of South Dakota, capitalized on the energetic support of antiwar activists to blitz the Democratic primaries. New party rules (adopted after the disastrous 1968 convention) that required every state delegation at the nominating convention to include minority, female, and youthful delegates in approximate proportion to their numbers among the populace also aided the liberal McGovern. One of his supporters, actress Shirley MacLaine, gleefully described California's convention delegation as "looking like a couple of high schools, a grape boycott, a Black Panther rally, and four or five politicians who walked in the wrong door." A disapproving labor leader grumbled about "too much hair and not enough cigars at this convention." McGovern easily won the nomination on the first ballot.

Perceptions of McGovern as inept and radical, however, drove away all but those most committed to him. After pledging to stand behind his vice-presidential running mate Thomas Eagleton "1,000 percent" when it became known that the Missouri senator had received electric-shock therapy for nervous depression, McGovern dumped him from the ticket and suffered the embarrassment of having several prominent Democrats publicly decline to run with him. McGovern's endorsement of income redistribution, the decriminalization of marijuana, an immediate withdrawal from Vietnam, and a whopping $30 billion defense-budget cut exposed him to GOP ridicule as the candidate of the radical fringe. Tagging McGovern the apostle of "abortion, acid, and amnesty" (he also advocated a pardon for the nearly 120,000 young Americans who had fled the United States to avoid the draft), the Republicans ensured that the Democrats never gained the offensive.

Questing for every possible vote, Nixon left no stone unturned. He created the Committee to Re-Elect the President (CREEP) and appointed his attorney general, John Mitchell, as its head. The many millions in contributions collected by CREEP financed a series of "dirty tricks" that spread dissension within Democratic ranks and paid for a special internal espionage unit to spy on the opposition. Led by Liddy and Hunt of the White House

plumbers, the Republican undercover team gained Mitchell's approval for a plan to wiretap the telephones at the Democratic National Committee headquarters in the Watergate apartment/office complex in Washington. Early in the morning of June 17, 1972, a security guard foiled the break-in to install the bugs. The police arrested James McCord, the security coordinator of CREEP, and several other burglars associated with Liddy and Hunt.

A White House cover-up began immediately. The president's press secretary dismissed the break-in as a "caper," a "third-rate burglary attempt." Nixon proclaimed "categorically" that "no one in the White House staff, no one in this administration, presently employed, was involved in this bizarre incident." Although the president had probably been unaware of the scheme, he well understood that Mitchell and other close aides could be implicated, jeopardizing his reelection hopes. Consequently (as the American people would learn after the election), Nixon ordered key staff members to expunge Hunt's name from the White House telephone directory, to buy the silence of those arrested with some four hundred thousand dollars in hush money (raised from private contributions) and hints of a presidential pardon, and to direct the CIA to halt the FBI's investigation of the Watergate break-in on the pretext that the inquiry would damage national security.

With the McGovern campaign a shambles and Watergate seemingly safely contained, Nixon won the election overwhelmingly. He polled nearly 61 percent of the popular vote and took the electoral college 520 to 17. He carried all of the once solidly Democratic South and won over a large majority of such traditionally Democratic voters as union members, ethnic minorities, and Catholics. McGovern edged Nixon out in just one state, Massachusetts, and the District of Columbia. Only blacks, Hispanics, Jews, and low-income voters

| **The Election of 1972** | | | | |
Candidates	Parties	Electoral Vote	Popular Vote	Percentage of Popular Vote
RICHARD M. NIXON	Republican	520	47,169,911	60.7
George S. McGovern	Democratic	17	29,170,383	37.5

strongly supported the Democratic contender. The 1968 realignment in presidential balloting had been solidified.

The GOP, however, gained only twelve seats in the House, and the Democrats added two more seats to bolster their majority in the Senate. This outcome demonstrated the growing difficulty of unseating incumbent legislators as well as the decline of party loyalty and the prevalence of ticket splitting among voters. In addition, in 1972, only 55.7 percent of the eligible electorate went to the polls (in 1960, 63.8 percent of those eligible had voted, and that figure had dropped in each intervening election). Whether indifferent to politics or disenchanted with the choices offered, a growing number of citizens no longer bothered to participate in the electoral process.

The Crisis of the Presidency

Nixon had campaigned in 1972 under the slogan "Four More Years." In his second inaugural address, he pledged "to make these four years the best four years in America's history." Ironically, they would rank among its sorriest, and the worst in Nixon's career. He would see his vice president resign in disgrace and his closest confidants go to jail. He himself would serve barely a year and a half of his second term before resigning office to escape impeachment and possibly a criminal trial.

The Watergate Cover-Up

The scheme to conceal the connection between the White House and the accused Watergate burglars had succeeded during the 1972 campaign. But after the election federal judge "Maximum John" Sirica, known for his tough treatment of criminals, refused to accept the claim of those on trial for the break-in that they had acted on their own. Threatening severe prison sentences, Sirica coerced James McCord of CREEP into confessing that highly placed White House aides had known in advance of the break-in and that the defendants had committed perjury during the trial. McCord also stated that the White House had pressured him and his codefendants "to plead guilty and remain silent."

Meanwhile, two *Washington Post* reporters, Carl Bernstein and Bob Woodward, following clues furnished by "Deep Throat,"* an unnamed informant in the Nixon administration, wrote a succession of front-page stories linking the break-in to illegal contributions and to "dirty tricks" against the Democrats paid for by CREEP.

In February 1973 the Senate established the Special Committee on Presidential Campaign Activities to investigate the alleged election misdeeds. As the trail of revelations led closer to the Oval Office, Nixon fired his special counsel, John Dean, after Dean refused to be a scapegoat. Then on April 30 the president announced the resignations of his two major assistants, H. R. Haldeman and John Ehrlichman, and pledged to get to the bottom of the scandal: "There can be no whitewash at the White House." To show that he meant business, he appointed Secretary of Defense Elliot Richardson, a Boston patrician of unassailable integrity, as his new attorney general. (Richardson replaced Richard Kleindienst, who had become attorney general in 1972 when John Mitchell resigned in order to chair Nixon's reelection campaign.) Bowing to Senate demands, moreover, the president instructed Richardson to appoint a special Watergate prosecutor with broad powers of investigation and subpoena. Richardson selected Archibald Cox, a Harvard law professor and a Democrat.

In May the special Senate committee began a televised investigation. Chaired by the wily Sam ("I'm just a plain country lawyer") Ervin of North Carolina, an expert on constitutional law, the hearings revealed a sordid tale of political corruption. Witnesses testified to the existence of a White House "enemies list," to the president's use of government agencies to harass his opponents, and to administration favoritism in return for illegal campaign donations. Most damaging to the president, the hearings exposed the White House's active involvement in the Watergate cover-up. But the Senate still lacked concrete evidence of the president's criminality, the so-called smoking gun that would prove Nixon's guilt. Because it was simply his word against that of his former counsel, John

---

Deep Throat was also the title of a notorious pornographic film of the time.

Sam Ervin

During the extraordinary national spectacle of the Watergate hearings, the North Carolina senator captured America's heart with his quick wit and country charm.

Dean, who had testified that Nixon personally directed the cover-up, the president expected to survive the crisis.

Then another presidential aide surprised the committee and the nation by revealing that Nixon had installed a secret taping system in the White House that recorded all conversations in the Oval Office. Both the Ervin committee and special prosecutor Cox insisted on access to the tapes, but Nixon refused, claiming executive privilege and national-security considerations. In October, when Cox sought a court order to obtain the tapes, Nixon ordered Attorney General Richardson to fire him. Instead, Richardson resigned in protest, as did the deputy attorney general. It was left to the third-ranking official in the Department of Justice, Solicitor General Robert Bork, to dump Cox. The furor stirred by what the press dubbed the Saturday Night Massacre sent Nixon's public-approval rating rapidly downward. Even as Nixon named a new special prosecutor, Leon Jaworski, under intense public pressure, the House Judiciary Committee began impeachment proceedings. In Massachusetts, the one state to vote for McGovern, bumper stickers proclaimed: "We Told You So."

A President Disgraced

Adding to Nixon's woes that October, Vice President Agnew, having been charged with income-tax evasion and accepting bribes, pleaded no contest—"the full equivalent to a plea of guilty," according to the trial judge. Dishonored, Agnew left government service with a three-year suspended sentence, a ten-thousand-dollar fine, and a letter from Nixon expressing "a great sense of personal loss." The president nominated the popular House minority leader, Gerald R. Ford of Michigan, to replace Agnew. Nevertheless, the unrelenting legal and political processes unfolding against Nixon made his continued residence at 1600 Pennsylvania Avenue highly uncertain.

In March 1974 special prosecutor Jaworski and the House Judiciary Committee subpoenaed the president for the tape recordings of Oval Office meetings following the Watergate break-in. Still trying to cover up the conspiracy, Nixon in April released edited transcripts of the tapes, filled with gaps and numerous repetitions of the phrase "expletive deleted." Despite the excisions, the president emerged as petty and vindictive. Senate Republican leader Hugh Scott of Pennsylvania referred to the tapes' revelations as "deplorable, disgusting, shabby, immoral." Even in the absence of a smoking gun implicating the president directly, what remained of Nixon's standing was destroyed. "We have seen the private man and we are appalled," declared the staunchly Republican *Chicago Tribune*.

Nixon's sanitized version of the tapes satisfied neither Jaworski nor the House Judiciary Committee. Both pressed for unedited recordings of key Oval Office conversations. In late July the Supreme Court rebuffed the president's claim to executive privilege. Citing the president's obligation to provide evidence necessary for the due process of law, Chief Justice Burger ordered Nixon to release the unexpurgated tapes.

On July 27 the House Judiciary Committee adopted the first article of impeachment. Six of the seventeen Republicans voted with the twenty-one Democrats to charge Nixon with obstruction of justice for impeding the Watergate investigation. An additional Republican voted with the majority on July 29 to condemn the president's abuse of power, particularly his partisan use of such agencies as the FBI and IRS. By a smaller margin, the committee on July 30 added as a third article of impeachment the president's contempt of Congress in refusing to obey a congressional subpoena to release the tapes.

Nixon stalled, pondering his next move. He was now checkmated at every position. On August 5, 1974, he conceded in a televised address that he had withheld relevant evidence from the special prosecutor and the Judiciary Committee. He then surrendered the subpoenaed tapes. They contained the smoking gun proving that the president had ordered the cover-up, obstructed justice, subverted one government agency to prevent another from

investigating a crime, and then lied about his role in the matter for more than two years. Shocked by the disclosures, even the diehard Nixon loyalists on the Judiciary Committee publicly rescinded their votes against presidential impeachment. Still, Nixon wavered, refusing to surrender. On August 7 Republican congressional leaders informed the president of the certainty of his impeachment and conviction. Two days later, Richard Milhous Nixon became the first American president to resign, and Gerald Ford took office as the nation's first non-elected president.

Conclusion

The sudden and shocking dénouement of the Watergate crisis marked the end of a period of extraordinary rancor in the nation's history. It capped a turbulent time in which a president elected by a majority that broke all records had feared to run for reelection, and his successor, who had garnered the next greatest percentage of the popular vote, resigned in disgrace. Coming on the heels of the U.S. withdrawal from Vietnam, festering national divisions, cultural conflicts, energy shortages, and rising inflation, Watergate deepened the insecurity of a nation no longer confident of its own government or sanguine about its destiny.

Coming to power when the voices of dissent had grown to a roar and the trickle of rebellion seemed to some a torrent, Nixon masterfully fashioned a new majority coalition to succeed the bloc forged by Franklin Roosevelt during the New Deal. With Henry Kissinger at his side, he significantly reduced international tensions in some key areas while planting the seeds of future problems in others.

The Nixon presidency brought both a revitalization and a redirection of American conservatism. On many fronts, especially those involving cultural values and matters of morality, he held firmly to classic conservative positions. He praised law and order and rejected radicalism in all its forms. In other ways, however, Nixon (aided by advisers like Daniel Moynihan) subtly reoriented conservative ideology. He administered the social-welfare programs of the New Deal and of later Democratic administrations with restraint, but he did not denounce them, as conservatives had been doing for forty years. And in his creation of a federal environmental agency, his Family Assistance Plan, and his Keynesian approach to the economy, he moved beyond the knee-jerk suspicion of "big government" to a recognition that the power of a strong federal government, if wisely used, could be employed to advance traditional conservative values; that the nation's air, water, and land could be protected for future generations; that able-bodied welfare recipients could be required to work; and that prudent governmental intervention could benefit the workings of a capitalist economic system. In these and other ways, Nixon sought to redefine the conservative agenda for the 1970s.

Yet a presidency committed to conservatism sucked the nation into one of its most radically disruptive crises. Promising to unite a divided people, Nixon and his alter ego Spiro Agnew polarized them still further. A man of great talents but even greater flaws, Nixon injected his personal obsessions into the stream of national politics. Under the guise of law and order, his administration chose dubious and illegal means to secure its goals and then tried to conceal the facts from lawful investigative bodies. Nearly fifty Nixon administration officials were indicted for fraud, extortion, perjury, obstruction of justice, and an assortment of other crimes, and more than a score of the president's associates, including several White House aides and Attorney General John Mitchell, went to prison.

The man left to pick up the pieces—Nixon's successor, Gerald Ford—proclaimed: "Our long national nightmare is over." Political commentators quickly emphasized that the outcome of Watergate proved that the constitutional system had worked. But as Americans contemplated the bicentennial of their Declaration of Independence in 1976, most believed that the recent flagrant abuse of presidential power offered little reason for confidence in Washington or its leaders. Watergate's legacy would be a disquieting malaise and distrust in government that would further erode the nation's self-confidence and limit the ability of Nixon's presidential successors to lead effectively.

CHRONOLOGY

1960 Birth-control pill marketed.

1964 Berkeley Free Speech Movement (FSM).

1965 Teach-ins against the Vietnam War.
Ken Kesey and Merry Pranksters stage first "acid test."

1966 Abolition of automatic student deferments from the draft.

1967 March on the Pentagon.

1968 Tet offensive.
President Lyndon Johnson announces that he will not seek reelection.
Martin Luther King, Jr., assassinated; race riots sweep nation.

1968 (cont.) Students take over buildings and strike at Columbia University.
Robert F. Kennedy assassinated.
Violence mars Democratic convention in Chicago.
Vietnam peace talks open in Paris.
Richard Nixon elected president.

1969 Apollo 11 lands first Americans on the moon.
Nixon begins withdrawal of American troops.
Woodstock festival.
March Against Death in Washington, D.C.
Lieutenant William Calley charged with murder of civilians at My Lai.

1970 United States invades Cambodia.
Students killed at Kent State and Jackson State universities.
Nixon proposes Huston Plan.

1971 United States invades Laos.
Swann v. *Charlotte-Mecklenburg Board of Education.*
New York Times publishes Pentagon Papers.
Nixon institutes wage-and-price freeze.

1972 Nixon visits China and Russia.
SALT I agreement approved.
Break-in at the Democratic National Committee headquarters in Watergate complex.
Nixon reelected in landslide victory.
"Christmas bombing" of North Vietnam.

1973 Vietnam cease-fire agreement signed.

Trial of Watergate burglars.

Senate establishes Special Committee on Presidential Campaign Activities to investigate Watergate.

President Salvador Allende ousted and murdered in Chile.

Vice President Spiro Agnew resigns; Gerald Ford appointed vice president.

Roe v. *Wade.*

Yom Kippur War; OPEC begins embargo of oil to the West.

Saturday Night Massacre.

1974 Supreme Court orders Nixon to release Watergate tapes.

1974 (cont.) House Judiciary Committee votes to impeach Nixon.

Nixon resigns; Ford becomes president.

For Further Reading

Morris Dickstein, *Gates of Eden: American Culture in the Sixties* (1977). An examination of the relationship between political and cultural radicalism.

David Harris, *Dreams Die Hard* (1983). The story of the antiwar and student movements as experienced by three participants.

Stanley Karnow, *Vietnam, A History* (1983). A balanced and comprehensive report on the war based extensively on interviews conducted by the author.

Jonathan Schell, *The Time of Illusion* (1975). A far-reaching and thought-provoking analysis of the ties between Nixon administration policies and the Watergate conspiracy.

Philip Slater, *The Pursuit of Loneliness* (1970). A contemporary account of the counterculture that incisively depicts the motives of its adherents.

I. F. Stone, *The Killings at Kent State* (1970). A gripping narration that fully captures the tragic dimensions of the incident.

Garry Wills, *Nixon Agonistes* (1970). A wide-ranging meditation on Richard Nixon's personality and pre-presidential career.

Bob Woodward and Carl Bernstein, *All the President's Men* (1974) and *The Final Days* (1976). Exciting journalistic accounts of the Watergate cover-up and of the events leading to Nixon's resignation.

Additional Bibliography

The New Left and Student Movements

Jerry Avorn et al., *Up Against the Ivy Wall* (1969); Edward Bacciocco, Jr., *The New Left in America* (1974); Ronald Berman, *America in the Sixties* (1968); Wini Breines, *Community and Organization in the New Left* (1983); Peter Clecak, *Radical Paradoxes* (1973); Joan Didion, *Slouching Towards Bethlehem* (1979); Todd Gitlin, *The Sixties: Years of Hope, Days of Rage* (1987) and *The Whole World Is Watching* (1980); Emmett Grogan, *Ringolevio: A Life Played for Keeps* (1972); Max Heirich, *The Beginning: Berkeley, 1964* (1968); Abbie Hoffman, *Soon to Be a Major Motion Picture* (1980); Ken Hurwitz, *Marching Nowhere,* (1971); Roger Kahn, *The Battle for Morningside Heights* (1970); Steven Kellman, *Push Comes to Shove* (1971); Joseph Kelner and James Munves, *The Kent State Coverup* (1980); Kenneth Kenniston, *Youth and Dissent* (1971); Richard King, *The Party of Eros* (1972); James Kunen, *The Strawberry Statement* (1968); Michael Lydon, *Rock, Folk* (1974); Klaus Mehnert, *Twilight of the Young* (1978); James Miller, *Democracy Is in the Streets* (1987); Ray Mungo, *Famous Long Ago* (1970); Philip Norman, *Shout! The Beatles in Their Generation* (1981); Thomas Powers, *The War at Home* (1973); Charles Reich, *The Greening of America* (1970); Michael Rossman, *The Wedding Within the War* (1971); Theodore Roszak, *The Making of a Counterculture* (1969); Jerry Rubin, *Do It!* (1971); Kirkpatrick Sale,

SDS (1973); Susan Stern, *With the Weathermen* (1975); Nicholas von Hoffman, *We Are the People Our Parents Warned Us Against* (1968); Jon Wiener, *Come Together* (1983); Tom Wolfe, *The Electric Kool-Aid Acid Test* (1968); Daniel Yankelovich, *The New Morality* (1974).

The Politics of 1968

Lewis Chester et al., *An American Melodrama* (1969); George Christian, *The President Steps Down* (1970); Marshall Frady, *Wallace* (1970); Richard Lemons, *The Troubled Americans* (1970); Samuel Lubell, *The Hidden Crisis in American Politics* (1970); Joe McGinniss, *The Selling of the President, 1968* (1969); Kevin Phillips, *The Emerging Republican Majority* (1969); Richard Scammon and Ben Wattenberg, *The Real Majority* (1970); Herbert Schandler, *The Unmaking of a President* (1977); Arthur M. Schlesinger, Jr., *Robert Kennedy and His Times* (1974); Irwin Unger and Debi Unger, *Turning Point: 1968* (1988); Richard Whalen, *Catch the Falling Flag* (1972); Jules Witcover, *The Resurrection of Richard Nixon* (1970).

Nixon-Kissinger Foreign Policies

Seyom Brown, *The Crises of Power* (1979); James Chace, *A World Elsewhere: The New American Foreign Policy* (1973); Lloyd Gardner, *A Covenant with Power* (1984) and *The Great Nixon Turnaround* (1973); Stephen Graubard, *Kissinger: Portrait of a Mind* (1973); Richard Hammer, *One Morning in the War* (1971); Arnold Isaacs, *Without Honor: Defeat in Vietnam and Cambodia* (1983); Henry Kissinger, *White House Years* (1979) and *Years of Upheaval* (1982); Robert Litwack, *Détente and the Nixon Doctrine* (1984); Timothy Lomperis, *The War Nobody Lost—and Won* (1984); Roger Morris, *Uncertain Greatness: Henry Kissinger and American Foreign Policy* (1977); Gareth Porter, *Vietnam* (1979); Stephen Rabe, *The Road to OPEC* (1982); William Shawcross, *Side-Show: Kissinger, Nixon, and the Destruction of Cambodia* (1979); Frank Snepp, *Decent Interval* (1977); John Stoessinger, *Henry Kissinger* (1976); Tad Szulc, *The Illusion of Peace* (1978).

The Nixon Administration

Fawn Brodie, *Richard Nixon: The Shaping of His Character* (1981); Vincent Burke, *Nixon's Good Deed: Welfare Reform* (1974); David Calleo, *The Imperious Economy* (1982); Jody Carlson, *George Wallace and the Politics of Powerlessness* (1981); Roland Evans, Jr., and Robert Novak, *Nixon in the White House* (1972); Leon Panetta and Peter Gall, *Bring Us Together* (1971); James Reichley, *Conservatives in an Age of Change: The Nixon and Ford Administrations* (1981); William Safire, *Before the Fall* (1975); Kirkpatrick Sale, *Power Shift* (1976); Leonard Silk, *Nixonomics* (1972); Michael Tanzer, *The Energy Crisis* (1974).

Watergate

Jimmy Breslin, *How the Good Guys Finally Won* (1975); John Dean, *Blind Ambition* (1976); James Doyle, *Not Above the Law* (1977); John Ehrlichman, *Witness to Power* (1982); Jim Houghan, *Secret Agenda: Watergate, Deep Throat and the CIA* (1984); J. Anthony Lukas, *Nightmare: The Underside of the Nixon Years* (1976); Richard Nixon, *RN: The Memoirs of Richard Nixon* (1978); John Sirica, *To Set the Record Straight* (1979); Maurice Stans, *The Terrors of Justice* (1984); Athan Theoharis, *Spying on Americans* (1978).

CHAPTER 31

New Problems, Old Verities: From Watergate to the Present

On December 14, 1986, a highly unconventional experimental airplane called *Voyager* took off from Edwards Air Force Base in California with twelve hundred gallons of gasoline and, jammed into the cramped cockpit, a two-person crew: Dick Rutan and Jeana Yeager. Rutan and Yeager, as well as the airplane's designer, Dick's brother Burt, had anticipated this moment for months. Their aim: to fly *Voyager* nonstop around the world without taking on additional fuel—a feat never before accomplished.

As the small, graceful white aircraft with the three cigar-shaped fuselages and the thin, elongated wings wended its way westward, Yeager and Rutan slept fitfully, fought exhaustion and stiff muscles, and kept an eye out for storms. Bad weather did batter *Voyager*; it bruised the crew badly and forced five course changes. In the flight's final hours, less than 1,000 miles from home, disaster nearly struck. The main engine stalled, and *Voyager* rapidly lost altitude. To avoid a watery crash, the pilots hastily started up the auxiliary engine. On December 23, after a bit more than nine days in the air, *Voyager* landed at Edwards before forty thousand cheering spectators. In a flight of 25,012 miles, at an average speed of only 115 miles per hour, Rutan and Yeager had fulfilled their mission.

Their achievement captured America's imagination. At a moment when heroes were in short supply and when people often seemed more intent on material success than on new challenges, the accomplishment of two obscure flyers united the nation in admiration. Editorial writers recalled Charles A. Lindbergh's solo flight across the Atlantic fifty-nine years earlier.

To thoughtful observers, the *Voyager* phenomenon offered revealing insights into America in the 1980s. Lindbergh, for example, had flown alone; this time, a man and a woman made the historic flight together. And *Voyager* was a small, simple craft, depending more on innovative design and human endurance than on massive power and complex technology. In a sense, this summed up a moment of transition in American history, when the nation was learning that bigger is not necessarily better and that technology can sometimes turn on its creators. Only months before, in January 1986, the great space shuttle *Challenger* had exploded on takeoff in Florida, killing all seven crew members.

While it stimulated reflections such as these, the *Voyager* achievement also helped reawaken Americans' capacity for awe at the resources of the human spirit and renew their ability to draw together to share a common experience. These were valuable lessons for a nation that had weathered some harsh and chastening ordeals since Watergate.

Inflation, Energy Worries, Hostages: The Frustrations of the Later 1970s

The post-Watergate era was not a happy time for the United States. In the wake of Richard Nixon's graceless departure from the White House, the nation appeared to lose spirit and direction. First Gerald Ford and then Jimmy Carter grappled with a tangle of seemingly insoluble domestic and foreign problems. As the Organization of Petroleum Exporting Countries (OPEC) forced up oil prices, the economy fell prey to inflation, unemployment, and recession. On the international scene, post-Vietnam America groped for a new role in a world where the old Cold War formulas appeared increasingly irrelevant. As Carter's term ended, Islamic religious fundamentalists seized and held hostage a group of Americans living in Iran—a sadly appropriate coda to a bleak decade.

The Caretaker Presidency of Gerald Ford

The nation breathed a collective sigh of relief when sixty-two-year-old Gerald R. Ford took the presidential oath on August 9, 1974. After months of unsavory revelations about the Nixon White House, Ford promised a refreshing change. A Michigan congressman who had served as minority leader before becoming vice president, Ford exuded human decency, if little evidence of brilliance. (Lyndon Johnson once remarked nastily that Ford had played too much football without a helmet in college.) TV comedians parodied Ford's verbal gaffes ("If Lincoln were alive today, he'd roll over in his grave") and his propensity for sending golf balls zooming in unexpected directions, but the visceral revulsion that many Americans felt toward Nixon never extended to his likable, if undistinguished, successor.

The nation's love affair with Ford underwent a severe strain a month into his term, however, when he fully pardoned Richard Nixon for "any and all crimes" committed while in office—thus shielding the ex-president from prosecution for his Watergate role. Ford insisted that this action would help the nation forget the scandal, but many Americans reacted with outrage.

On domestic issues Ford proved more conservative than Nixon. Having voted, as a congressman in the 1960s, against most Great Society pro-

grams, he now vetoed a variety of environmental, social-welfare, and public-interest measures, among them strip-mining regulation, aid to education, and a 1974 "freedom of information" bill granting citizens greater access to government records. The heavily Democratic Congress, however, overrode most of these vetoes.

Economic problems occupied much of Ford's attention. Beginning in 1973, oil prices shot up as a result of the Arab oil embargo (see Chapter 30) and stiff OPEC price hikes. The price of a barrel of crude oil more than tripled in 1973 and continued to rise through the decade. The impact of these increases on the United States, which imported more than one-third of its oil, was devastating. The soaring cost of gasoline, home heating oil, and other petroleum-based products drastically worsened already serious inflation. Consumer prices rose by 12 percent in 1974 and 11 percent in 1975.

Since the mandatory wage-and-price controls imposed by Richard Nixon in 1971 had failed to curb inflation, Ford tried a different approach. In October 1974 he unveiled a program of voluntary restraint dubbed "Whip Inflation Now" (WIN). Although Ford gamely wore his big "WIN" button at presidential functions, many Americans found this a trivial response to a grave crisis. Ford also cut federal spending and endorsed the Federal Reserve Board's effort to cool the overheated economy by raising the discount rate.

A severe recession resulted. The nation's economy stalled badly in 1974–1975, sinking to the worst levels since the 1930s. Unemployment hovered between 8 percent and 9 percent in 1974 and climbed to nearly 11 percent in 1975. Tax receipts dropped as business stagnated, and the federal deficit spurted to then record levels. Ford responded with proposals for a tax cut and other measures to stimulate consumer spending, but economic headaches plagued his administration to the end.

The oil crisis had a particularly devastating effect on the U.S. auto industry. As prices at the gas pump skyrocketed, Americans stopped buying the inefficient gas-guzzlers that Detroit had marketed for years. With domestic auto sales sagging, assembly lines fell silent. GM, Ford, and Chrysler laid off more than 225,000 workers in 1974.

President Gerald Ford Fights Inflation

In 1974 Ford proudly displayed his WIN button, the symbol of his administration's drive to "Whip Inflation Now" through voluntary effort.

Smaller, more fuel-efficient imports increased their share of the U.S. market from 17 percent in 1970 to 33 percent in 1980.

On the diplomatic front, Ford retained Henry Kissinger as secretary of state and supported the Nixon-Kissinger initiatives aimed at improving relations with China and the Soviet Union. Meeting at Vladivostok, Siberia, in 1974, Ford and Soviet leader Leonid Brezhnev made progress toward a new arms-control treaty, the SALT I agreement, limiting each side to twenty-four hundred nuclear missiles. When the departing Brezhnev admired Ford's Alaskan wolf coat, the American president impetuously gave it to him. The following year in Helsinki, Finland, Ford and Brezhnev joined thirty-one European nations in adopting a set of accords formalizing Europe's post-1945 political boundaries and avowing respect for human rights and freedom of travel.

The national morale, already battered by Watergate and economic problems, suffered a further blow in April 1975 when the South Vietnamese government fell, writing a bleak finis to two decades of U.S. effort to prevent just such an outcome. Once more the nation's TV networks chronicled depressing scenes from Vietnam: this time, desperate helicopter evacuations from the roof of the U.S. embassy in Saigon (soon to be renamed Ho Chi Minh City) as North Vietnamese troops closed in. A few weeks later, when the new communist government of Cambodia seized a U.S. merchant ship, the *Mayagüez,* a frustrated Ford ordered a military rescue. This hasty show of force freed the thirty-nine *Mayagüez* crew members but cost the lives of forty-one U.S. servicemen. As the nation entered the election year 1976—also the bicentennial of the Declaration of Independence—Americans found little cause for cheer and reasons aplenty to repudiate the party in power.

The Man from Georgia: Jimmy Carter in the White House

Gerald Ford won the Republican nomination in 1976 despite a strong challenge from the former governor of California, Ronald Reagan. With the Democratic party still in disarray from McGovern's controversial bid in 1972, a number of Democratic hopefuls emerged. The candidacy of Jimmy Carter, a wealthy Georgia peanut grower who had served as governor of his home state but remained unknown nationally, initially aroused scant attention. "Jimmy *who*?" many asked when they first heard his name. But Carter, who had planned his campaign carefully, swept the primaries in early 1976. A superficially affable man with a down-home manner, Carter stressed themes that appealed to post-Watergate America. He made a virtue of his status as an outsider to Washington, pledged never to lie to the American people, and freely avowed his religious faith as a "born-again" Christian. Beset by economic worries and still painfully aware of the Nixon scandals, voters responded warmly to this political newcomer.

Winning the nomination handily, Carter chose as his running mate Senator Walter Mondale, a liberal Democrat from Minnesota. Democratic campaigners invented the "misery index," a measure of current inflation and unemployment rates combined. But Carter's overwhelming initial lead in the polls gradually eroded as voters sensed a lack of clarity in his program and reacted against some of his mannerisms, including a toothy grin that seemed to flash on and off like a neon sign. Carter

The Election of 1976				
Candidates	Parties	Electoral Vote	Popular Vote	Percentage of Popular Vote
JIMMY CARTER	Democratic	297	40,827,394	49.9
Gerald R. Ford	Republican	240	39,145,977	47.9

hung on, however, aided by a puzzling Ford gaffe in a television debate ("There is no Soviet domination of Eastern Europe") that alienated voters of Eastern European origin.

Carter won by a narrow margin: 49.9 percent of the popular vote to Ford's 47.9. His electoral-college plurality was 297 to 240. (Less than 54 percent of those eligible had bothered to vote at all—an indicator of post-Watergate apathy.) The vote broke sharply along class lines: the well-to-do went for Ford; the disadvantaged, overwhelmingly for Carter. The Georgian swept the South and received 90 percent of the back vote.

As chief executive, Carter rejected the trappings of what some in Nixon's day had labeled the imperial presidency. On inauguration day, with his wife Rosalynn and daughter Amy, he walked from the Capitol to the White House. Carter occasionally taught Sunday school class at the Washington church that he attended and, in an echo of Franklin D. Roosevelt's radio chats, delivered some television speeches wearing a casual sweater and seated in an easy chair by a fireplace.

But populist symbolism alone could not ensure a successful presidency. Carter entered the White House without a clearly articulated political philosophy, and he never overcame this liability. Liberals and conservatives both claimed him; no one could be sure where he stood. Intensely private, Carter surrounded himself with a circle of young staff members from Georgia, few of whom had Washington experience. Disdaining conventional politics, he took little pleasure in socializing with politicians. "Carter couldn't get the Pledge of Allegiance through Congress," groused one senior legislator.

An intelligent, disciplined man who had worked as an engineer in the nuclear-submarine program after graduating from the U.S. Naval Academy, Carter was at his best when he focused on specific problems. But he lacked a larger political vision, or at least the capacity to convey such a vision. On one occasion he applied his formidable intellect to the pressing task of scheduling staff members' playing time on the White House tennis court.

As heir to a recession, Carter primed the economic pump during his first year with a tax cut and public-works programs. Thanks in part to these efforts, the unemployment rate dropped to around 5 percent by late 1978. But this activist strategy did not prove characteristic of Carter. He showed little sympathy for social-welfare measures involving federal spending. Liberals grumbled that he was the most conservative Democratic president since Grover Cleveland.

Like some early-twentieth-century progressives, Carter's logical, technocratic approach was best suited to issues of administrative efficiency, and he introduced notable reforms in the civil service and the executive branch of government. But his poor relations with Congress often frustrated even these efforts. His attempts to promote a national health-insurance program, overhaul the nation's welfare system, and reform the federal income-tax law—a loophole-ridden monstrosity that he had denounced in the campaign as "a disgrace to the human race"—met with little success.

Diplomacy in the Carter Years

Jimmy Carter's foreign-affairs achievements outshone his domestic record. As a candidate he had urged more attention to human-rights violations around the globe, implicitly rejecting Henry Kissinger's inclination to ignore repressive and even brutal conditions in other nations as long as they did not threaten U.S strategic interests. As president, Carter made human rights a high priority, and his secretary of state Cyrus Vance worked vigorously to combat abuses in Chile, Argentina, Ethiopia, South Africa, and other countries. (Human-rights problems in nations considered critical to U.S. security, such as South Korea and the Philippines, received more gingerly treatment.)

Carter also tried to adapt American foreign policy to the altered realities of a world no longer dominated by the superpowers. He sought better relations, for example, with the new black nations of Africa. As one State Department official summed up the administration's view: "It is not a sign of weakness to recognize that we alone cannot dictate events elsewhere. It is rather a sign of maturity in a complex world."

In a number of areas, Carter, like Ford, pursued initiatives launched by his predecessors. Since 1964, when anti-American riots had rocked Panama, successive administrations in Washington had been negotiating a more equitable treaty relationship between the United States and Panama. The Carter administration completed negotiations on two treaties transferring the Panama Canal and the Canal Zone to the Panamanians by 1999. Although these agreements amply protected U.S. security interests, conservatives attacked them as proof of America's post-Vietnam gutlessness. Why should the United States give up the Panama Canal, harrumphed a California senator; "We stole it fair and square." In a rare congressional success, Carter won Senate ratification of the Panama treaties by a vote of 68–32, 1 more than the two-thirds required.

The strengthening of ties with China accelerated after the death in 1976 of China's long-time communist leader Mao Zedong (Mao Tse-tung). Responding eagerly when Mao's successor, Deng Xiaoping, expressed interest in closer links with the United States, Carter restored full diplomatic relations with the People's Republic of China on January 1, 1979, thus opening the door to scientific, cultural, academic, and commercial exchanges.

Pullback from Détente

Carter showed both conciliation and toughness toward the Soviet Union, with toughness eventually winning out. In a June 1979 meeting in Vienna, Carter and Leonid Brezhnev signed the SALT II agreement, which Carter promptly submitted to the Senate for ratification. It immediately ran into trouble from advocates of a strong military, however, who charged that it gave the Soviets an edge in the nuclear balance of terror.

The fatal blow to the SALT II agreement came in January 1980 when the Soviet Union invaded Afghanistan, its neighbor to the south. The reasons were complex, including Moscow's desire to prop up a pro-Soviet Afghan regime and Russian uneasiness over the upsurge of Islamic religious fervor in both Afghanistan and the Islamic regions of the Soviet Union itself. But the invasion triggered a powerful reaction in the United States, where many viewed it as proof of Russia's expansionist designs on the Middle East. In this unfavorable political environment, Carter not only withdrew the SALT II agreement from the Senate but adopted a series of anti-Soviet measures, including a boycott of the 1980 Summer Olympics in Moscow.

Carter's hard-line Soviet policy reflected the influence of his national-security adviser, Zbigniew Brzezinski, a political scientist of Polish roots who harbored deep hostility toward the Soviet Union. Brzezinski viewed détente with suspicion and advocated a tough stance toward Moscow. Due in part to Brzezinski's influence, Carter in June 1979 endorsed an expensive and controversial new nuclear-missile system, the MX, and promulgated a new missile-targeting strategy, PD-59, that many considered dangerously provocative. Simultaneously, the administration's human-rights pronouncements focused increasingly on the Soviet Union.

Carter the Peacemaker

Jimmy Carter reaped his proudest achievement in the Middle East, where, despite Kissinger's efforts, a state of war prevailed between Israel and Egypt. Carter recognized the strategic threat posed by Middle Eastern instability, and his religious beliefs gave him a particular interest in these ancient biblical lands. When Egyptian leader Anwar el-Sadat surprised the world by flying to Israel in November 1977 to negotiate personally with Israeli prime minister Menachem Begin, Carter saw an opening. In September 1978, at Carter's invitation, Sadat and Begin met at Camp David, the presidential retreat in Maryland, where in thirteen days of intense negotiation, they hammered out the "framework" of a peace treaty. Months of further bargaining followed, but on March 26, 1979, as Carter flashed his widest smile, the two leaders signed a formal peace treaty at the White House.

A Step Toward Peace in the Middle East

In 1979 (left to right) President Anwar el-Sadat of Egypt, President Jimmy Carter, and Prime Minister Menachem Begin of Israel signed the Camp David Accords.

This achievement did not, as Carter hoped, produce a comprehensive Middle Eastern settlement. Indeed, in 1981 Islamic fanatics assassinated Sadat, in part because he had negotiated with the hated Israelis. But the Egyptian-Israeli peace treaty, limited though it was, represented the high point of the Carter presidency.

A Sea of Troubles as Carter's Term Ends

Inflation, already serious when Carter took office, assumed horrendous proportions as his term wore on. Prices increased by 10 percent in 1978 and by more than 13 percent in both 1979 and 1980. As before, the primary blame lay with staggering energy costs. The decade's second major oil crisis, which hit in 1979, made 1973–1974 pale by comparison. As OPEC boosted petroleum prices to more than $30 a barrel, Americans accustomed to paying 30¢ for a gallon of gasoline saw prices edging toward a dollar a gallon. Gripped by nightmares of gas pumps running dry, motorists kept their tanks full, fueling the very shortage that they dreaded. As long lines formed at gas stations, patience ran short and tempers flared. A wide array of energy-related costs jumped as well, feeding the runaway inflation. In 1979 alone, U.S. consumers paid $16.4 billion in added costs related to the oil-price

increases. Like Ford, Carter relied on voluntarism to curb the inflationary spiral. He established the Council on Wage and Price Stability, which exhorted workers and manufacturers to hold the line. But repeated oil-price hikes stymied his efforts.

The Federal Reserve Board pushed the discount rate higher and higher and bank interest rates followed, reaching an unheard-of 20 percent by 1980. With the cost of mortgages and business loans out of sight, economic activity remained in the doldrums, producing "stagflation"—a dismal combination of business stagnation and inflation. As the government borrowed money to make up for slumping federal tax revenues, the upward pressure on interest rates increased still more.

Pondering the oil crisis, Carter drew a larger lesson: for too long, Americans had been slurping up the world's dwindling fossil-fuel resources at a profligate rate; this wasteful approach must give way to a new national ethic of conservation. Carter recognized that two of the major factors underlying a generation of U.S. economic growth—cheap, unlimited energy and the lack of foreign competition—could no longer be counted on. Americans, he concluded, must learn to survive in a "zero-sum society" that had reached its economic limits and could no longer anticipate endless future expansion. Appointing himself the bearer of this bad news, he tried to formulate policies reflecting a philosophy of restraint.

Congress in 1975 had set fuel-efficiency standards for automobiles and established a national speed limit of fifty-five miles per hour, but Carter was convinced that more must be done. As early as 1977, he created the Department of Energy and proposed a comprehensive energy bill involving various forms of taxation on oil and gasoline consumption, tax credits for conservation measures, and research on alternative-energy resources. But Carter's poor relations with Congress undermined this initiative as well, and a considerably watered-down bill finally emerged in 1978.

As with Herbert Hoover in the early 1930s, Americans turned against the remote figure in the White House. When Carter's approval rating dropped to 26 percent in the summer of 1979 (lower than Nixon's at the depths of Watergate), the president retreated to Camp David for a period of reflection and consultation with some 130 public figures in all walks of life. He descended from the mountain to deliver a remarkable television address that seemed to shift the blame to the American people, in whom he discerned a collective "crisis of confidence." Carter followed up this appearance with a major cabinet reshuffle, but the whole exercise served mainly to deepen the spreading suspicion that Carter himself was a large part of the problem.

Carter's troubles worsened in the election year 1980. With double-digit inflation still raging and relations with the Soviets worsening, a fresh blow came from an unexpected source: Iran. For years, Iran had been ruled by a staunch U.S. ally, Shah Reza Pahlavi, who had come to power with CIA help in 1953 and built a repressive regime whose opponents were intimidated and tortured by the feared secret police, SAVAK. Resistance centered among the Islamic faithful of the militant Shiite sect, whose spiritual leader, Ayatollah Ruhollah

Khomeini, led the opposition from his exile in Paris. In January 1979, as the revolutionary movement reached a climax, the shah fled Iran. Khomeini, returning in triumph, imposed strict Islamic rule and preached fanatic hatred of the United States.

In early November Carter admitted the shah to the United States for cancer treatment. Shortly after, hundreds of militant Iranian students stormed the U.S. embassy in Tehran and seized more than fifty American hostages. Thus began the Iranian hostage crisis, a 444-day ordeal that traumatized Americans and nearly paralyzed the Carter administration. Endless TV images from Tehran of blindfolded hostages, rabidly anti-American mobs, and embassy occupiers using U.S. flags as garbage bags rubbed American nerves raw. A rescue attempt in April 1980 failed ignominiously as an American helicopter and transport plane collided in the Iranian desert, killing eight U.S. servicemen. Secretary of State Vance, who had opposed the high-risk rescue effort, resigned in its bitter aftermath. By mid-1980 Carter's approval rating had sunk to an appalling 23 percent. Just as the voters had vented their frustrations on Gerald Ford in 1976, they now turned on his successor.

Carter remains a fascinating yet somewhat tragic political figure. His story initially seemed one of amazing success. His sudden emergence in 1976 vividly illustrated how, in the TV era, a relative unknown could bypass the laborious process of amassing support among party power brokers and organized interest groups and instead gain formidable political strength almost overnight through direct TV appeals to local activists and ordinary voters. Pursuing the presidency at a moment when Americans longed to see integrity and competence restored to that tarnished, diminished office, he seemed at first to fill the bill precisely, pledging to bring compassion, competence, and human scale back to the White House.

But his limitations, while initially less evident than his strengths, ultimately undid him. Keenly analytical, he identified many fundamental issues that would dominate the national agenda in future years: energy policy; tax, welfare, and health-care reform; the need to redefine America's world role. But while he could pinpoint problems, he lacked the political skills that might have inspired the nation to confront those problems in a sustained way. By the end of his term, a victim both of his

Hanging Jimmy Carter in Effigy in Tehran

During the rule of Ayatollah Khomeini, frenzied anti-American demonstrations became a familiar feature of Iranian public life.

own flaws and of large-scale forces that might have overwhelmed even the ablest president, Carter was lonely and discredited. In time, Americans would arrive at a more balanced and more appreciative assessment, but when Carter left office in January 1981, few were sorry to see him go.

The Early Reagan Years: Conservatism in the Saddle

In 1980, as in 1976, voters turned to a presidential candidate who represented a sharp break with the recent past: the former actor and former California governor Ronald Reagan. Capitalizing on the economic and foreign-policy frustrations that had been building since the Vietnam War era, Reagan, like his one-time political hero Franklin Roosevelt, promised a new deal for the American people. But unlike the original New Deal of the 1930s, Reagan's version offered diminished governmental activism, reduced taxes and spending, and an unleashing of the free-enterprise system. Internationally, Reagan called for a restoration of U.S. leadership and pride. Fed up with a chain of setbacks culminating in the Iran hostage crisis, voters gave Reagan a chance to implement his vision of the American future.

Background of the Reagan Revolution

Several ideological and social trends underlay Reagan's victory in 1980. A belief in self-help and private enterprise had remained firmly entrenched in American thought despite the New Deal–Great Society ideology of governmental activism. Simultaneously, decades of Cold War rhetoric had imprinted deeply on the American consciousness a suspicion of the Soviet Union and a determination to remain ahead of the Russians militarily.

To these traditional conservative themes, the 1970s added the ideology of the so-called New Right: a cultural conservatism stressing social and moral issues. The social turmoil and sexual revolution of the 1960s, the women's movement, the rising rates of abortion and divorce, the more open expression of homosexuality, the pervasiveness of pornography on the newsstands, sex and violence in the mass media, and "secular humanism" in school textbooks—all gravely upset millions of Americans, who responded with a call for a restoration of morality and "traditional values." Jerry Falwell and other TV evangelists warned of the nation's imminent moral collapse. Falwell's Moral Majority was only one of many groups that had emerged to translate public concerns into political action.

A dramatic population shift in the seventies also played a role in Reagan's success. While New York City, Chicago, Detroit, and other cities of the Northeast and upper Midwest lost population during the decade, Texas, California, Florida, Arizona, and other "Sunbelt" states rapidly gained. These states represented regions that historically had been both intensely conservative politically and intensely suspicious of Washington. In 1978 Californians passed Proposition 13, a referendum calling for sharp cuts in state taxes. Elsewhere in the West, ranchers and developers organized the so-called Sagebrush Rebellion to demand a return of federal lands to state control.

The economic setbacks of the seventies, coupled with the uneasy feeling that the United States had lost prestige in the world, contributed as well to the shifting political climate. Waiting in the wings, ready to translate the nation's changing mood into a powerful force at the polls, was Ronald Wilson Reagan.

The Man Behind the Movement

Reagan grew up in Dixon, Illinois, the son of an alcoholic father and a pious mother active in the Disciples of Christ church. After graduating from Eureka College near Peoria, he worked as a sports announcer in Des Moines before striking out for Hollywood in 1937. His fifty-four films—including *Bedtime for Bonzo* (1951), in which he played opposite a chimpanzee—enjoyed only moderate success, but after 1954 he made a name for himself as a corporate spokesman for the General Electric Company, touting both GE's appliances and its conservative political ideas. An enthusiastic New Dealer in the 1930s, Reagan had moved to the right in the 1950s. He won national visibility in 1964 with a TV speech for presidential candidate

Bedtime for Bonzo (1951)

(Left to right) Ronald Reagan, Bonzo, Diana Lynn. Reagan's acting experience helped his political career, but sometimes reality and the movie world seemed to blur in his mind.

Barry Goldwater, in which Reagan eloquently praised American individualism and the free-enterprise system.

Recognizing Reagan's flair for politics, a group of California millionaires engineered his election as governor in 1966, a post that he held for eight years. In Sacramento he continued to popularize conservative ideas while proving himself flexible and capable of compromise. Reagan nearly won the Republican presidential nomination in 1976, and in 1980 he had little trouble disposing of his principal opponent, former CIA director George Bush. At the Republican convention, Reagan chose Bush as his running mate.

The Democrats glumly renominated Jimmy Carter, but with double-digit inflation, 20 percent interest rates, an 8 percent unemployment rate, and the Iranian hostage crisis on everyone's mind, the Georgian had no chance. Hammering away at the question "Are you better off now than you were four years ago?" Reagan garnered almost 51 percent of the popular vote to Carter's 41 percent. An independent candidate, liberal Republican congressman John Anderson, collected most of the balance.

Reagan's coattails helped in the Senate races, where Republicans gained eleven seats, and with them, for the first time since 1955, a majority. These Senate victories also revealed the power of conservative political-action groups (PACs), who

used computerized mass mailings focusing on emotional issues like abortion and gun control to defeat specifically targeted liberal Democrats, including Senator George McGovern, the 1972 Democratic presidential candidate. The Democrats retained control of the House of Represen-

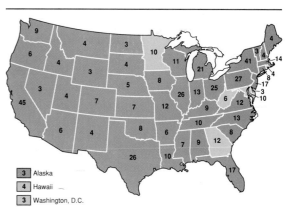

	Alaska
3	
4	Hawaii
3	Washington, D.C.

		Electoral Vote	Popular Vote	Percentage of Popular Vote
Republican Ronald Reagan		489	43,899,248	50.8
Democratic Jimmy Carter		49	35,481,435	41.0
Independent John B. Anderson		–	–	5,719,437	6.6
Minor Parties		–	–	1,395,558	1.6

The Election of 1980

tatives, but here, too, the Republicans made significant inroads. Reaping the benefits of a Republican southern strategy dating to Richard Nixon's day, Reagan carried not only every state west of the Mississippi but every southern state except Carter's own Georgia. Over half the nation's blue-collar workers voted Republican. Of the durable political alliance forged by Roosevelt in the 1930s, only black voters remained firmly Democratic.

Reagan's term began auspiciously: on inauguration day, January 20, 1981, the ordeal of the Iranian hostages ended, and they boarded planes for home. With this agonizing trauma past, the nation sized up its new leader. Although he would soon observe his seventieth birthday, Reagan seemed fit and vigorous. Few had a clear notion of his program beyond a rhetorical commitment to patriotism, military strength, the free market, and traditional values, but Reagan soon gave concrete substance to these generalities.

Reaganomics

Scoffed at as "voodoo economics" by George Bush during the 1980 primary campaign, and described by others simply as "Reaganomics," the new president's economic program boiled down to the belief that American capitalism, if freed from the burden of heavy taxes and government regulation, would surge to new heights of productivity. As Reagan's secretary of the treasury Donald Regan put it, America should unleash shackled free-enterprise energies that had "built everything from log cabins to high-rise apartments."

Budget director David Stockman, a former Michigan congressman and a true believer in Reaganomics, drafted Reagan's first budget message. The plan proposed a five-year, $750 billion tax cut built around a 30 percent reduction in federal income taxes over three years. Trimming down this proposal only slightly, Congress in May 1981 voted a 25 percent income-tax cut: 5 percent in 1981 and 10 percent in 1982 and 1983.

To compensate for the lost revenues, Reagan proposed massive spending reductions in such programs as school lunches, student loans, job training, and urban mass transit. Like Jimmy Carter, Reagan preached the message of settling for less, but with a different policy conclusion: that the nation could no longer afford the social programs to which it had been committed in the 1960s. Congress again went along, slashing more than $40 billion from domestic spending in 1981. Conservative Democrats, called boll weevils because so many of them were from the South, joined Republicans in voting these cuts. Journalists harked back to FDR's "Hundred Days" of 1933 to find a comparable time when government had shifted gears so dramatically. Although economists warned that a 25 percent tax cut, even with reduced spending, would produce catastrophic federal deficits, Reagan insisted that his program would so stimulate business growth that tax revenues would go up even with lower rates.

Reagan's appointees to head key agencies enthusiastically implemented another component of Reaganomics: drastic cutbacks in federal regulation of business. As Reagan put it: "Government is not the solution to our problems; government *is* the problem." Mark Fowler of the Federal Communications Commission (FCC) hacked away at federal rules governing the broadcast industry. Secretary of Transportation Drew Lewis cut back many of the regulations passed in the 1970s to reduce air pollution and improve efficiency and safety in cars and trucks. Secretary of the Interior James Watt, a leader in the Sagebrush Rebellion, opened federal wilderness areas, forest lands, and coastal waters to developers. (A biblical literalist who believed in the imminent Second Coming of Jesus Christ, Watt conceded that he saw little point in preserving the natural environment for future generations.) Ann Gorsuch Burford of the Environmental Protection Agency dedicated herself to undermining EPA's role as a watchdog monitoring the activities of corporate polluters. As director of the Occupational Safety and Health Administration (OSHA), Reagan chose a Florida supporter whose building firm had been cited by OSHA for nearly fifty violations in the 1970s.

Some of the more ardent of these officials did not last long. Watt left when his statements grew so outrageous that he became a liability. Burford resigned in 1983 amid a congressional inquiry into her handling of a $1.6 billion "superfund" intended to clean up toxic-waste sites. But although the faces changed, the deregulatory campaign went forward.

While implementing Reaganomics, the administration also had to cope with the immediate problem of inflation. The Federal Reserve Board led the charge, pushing the discount rate ever higher. This harsh medicine, coupled with a sharp drop in world oil prices, did its job. Inflation dropped to around 4 percent in 1983 and held steady thereafter.

But in a rerun of the 1970s, the high interest rates necessary to curb runaway inflation again spawned a severe recession. This downturn, which began late in 1981, exceeded even those of the Ford and Carter years. Factory utilization dropped to under 70 percent, and by late 1982 one of ten American workers was jobless. As funding for social programs dried up, the plight of the poor worsened. Blacks and Hispanics of the inner cities suffered severely.

The Reagan recession had another component as well: falling exports. As foreign investors bought dollars to secure the extremely high interest rates, the dollar rose in value vis-à-vis foreign currencies. This in turn made U.S. goods more expensive abroad. The decline in exports—coupled with big increases in imports of TVs, stereos, and automobiles from Japan and other countries—propelled the U.S. trade deficit (the gap between exports and imports) from $31 billion in 1981 to $111 billion in 1984. The trade gap with Japan alone widened to a staggering $33 billion in 1984.

The nation's industrial heartland, the so-called Rustbelt, reeled under the triple blow of slumping exports, aggressive foreign competition, and technological obsolescence. The aging, sluggish steel mills, machinery and automobile companies, and other smokestack industries of the Midwest and Great Lakes region laid off hordes of workers; some plants padlocked their doors forever. From 1979 through 1983, 11.5 million American workers lost jobs as a result of plant closings or slack work. While the recession hit the Sunbelt more lightly, plummeting oil prices brought hard times to cities like Houston (see "A Place in Time").

The drop in exports hurt farmers as well. Wheat exports fell 38 percent from 1980 to 1985, and corn exports by 49 percent. As grain prices plummeted, hardship and anguish seized rural America. In heartbreaking foreclosure sales, many Americans lost farms that their families had run for generations. By 1988 the farm population had fallen to under 5 million, the lowest since 1950.

Soaring federal deficits added to the economic muddle. Reagan's tax cuts reduced federal revenues

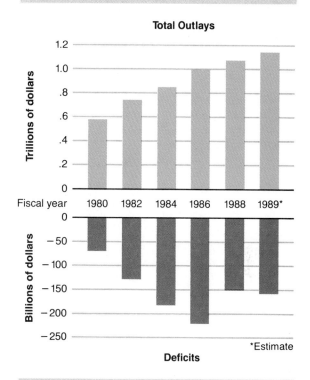

Federal Budget Expenditures and Deficits, Fiscal Years 1980–1989

After soaring to more than $200 billion in 1986, the runaway federal deficit declined somewhat thereafter. It is projected to continue at over $100 billion annually well into the 1990s, however, with unhappy implications for the U.S. economy.
SOURCES: U.S. Department of the Treasury; Office of Management and Budget.

without immediately bringing about the predicted business resurgence, while massive increases in military appropriations more than offset domestic spending cuts. With the economy in crisis, the government awash in red ink, and critics denouncing him as callous toward the poor, Reagan urged patience. His program would soon take effect, he insisted, and all would benefit. At the same time, in 1982 and early 1983, he accepted a reduced rate of military spending, a slowing of funding cuts in social programs, emergency job programs to relieve unemployment, and a smorgasbord of tax increases euphemistically called "revenue-enhancement measures."

Houston Weathers the Oil Crisis

The ups and downs of oil prices in the 1970s and 1980s took Houston, Texas, on a wild economic roller-coaster ride—a ride that reversed the experience of the rest of the country. While most of America reeled under skyrocketing energy costs, Houston's economy boomed. But when oil prices fell, stimulating recovery elsewhere, Houston suffered terribly.

Houston was no stranger to such boom-and-bust cycles. Founded in 1837 on Buffalo Bayou and named for Texas hero Sam Houston, the town flourished in the nineteenth century as a railroad center. But its history changed forever on January 10, 1901, when prospector Anthony Lucas brought in the world's mightiest oil well, Spindletop, in nearby Beaumont. For nine days the gusher roared on before it could even be capped. As more oil was discovered, new corporations emerged, including Gulf and Texaco, and Houston became the nerve center of the new industry. A channel to Galveston Bay in the Gulf of Mexico, completed in 1914, made the city a deep-water port. Hard times came in the early 1930s, however, when an oil glut combined with the Great Depression to drive oil prices down to ten cents a barrel.

World War II brought renewed growth, but the city's most spectacular boom came in the 1970s, when OPEC pushed world oil prices to unheard-of levels. Though Middle Eastern nations dominated OPEC, its pricing policies benefited U.S.

Houston's Dramatic Skyline at Dusk

petroleum companies as well, by increasing the value of *all* oil. The profits of the five biggest U.S. oil firms quadrupled in the seventies, reaching $14.5 billion by the end of the decade. Exxon's first-quarter profits in 1980 approached $2 billion, the largest ever recorded by any company in history.

Basking in the glow of unprecedented prosperity, Houston outdistanced its long-time rival Dallas. The city boasted more than 1.5 million inhabitants by 1980, a 26 percent increase in a decade, making it the fifth-largest in the United States. With 440,000 blacks and 280,000 Hispanics, the city reflected the Southwest's ethnic diversity. Unfet-

tered by zoning laws, sprawling Houston led the nation in new construction in the 1970s. Cloud-piercing skyscrapers formed a stunning downtown skyline. "If business takes you [to Houston]," advised *Forbes* magazine, "be prepared to work over lunch, dinner, and even breakfast."

Not all was work, however. In the exclusive suburb of River Oaks, where the oil barons' mansions stood in opulent array, the country club charged $35,000 for a membership—and had a long waiting list. Harold Farb built a $5.5 million white-marble supper club, the Carlyle, that one critic called "a cross between a red plush bordello, a neoclassical villa, and a hall of mirrors." Seeking to shed its rowdy boom-town image, Houston poured money into the symphony, the ballet, the opera, and a new cultural center. The nearby Johnson Space Center contributed to the city's prosperity as well, but above all, that prosperity rested on the sticky black substance that Houstonians persisted in calling "awl."

But petroleum prices plummeted in the 1980s, sinking to below fifteen dollars a barrel by 1988, less than half their peak in the late 1970s. The plunge unleashed havoc in the domestic oil industry. Three hundred thousand oil workers lost their jobs from 1982 to 1987. In Houston tens of thousands of jobs vanished. High-salaried young geologists took work as hotel bellhops, while unemployed drill hands had to poach game to feed their children. Houston's half-finished skyscrapers stood dark and silent; a multimillion-dollar suburban development, Heritage Plaza, looked like a ghost town. The exclusive Brae Burn Country Club slashed its membership fee from fifteen thousand dollars to eight thousand dollars.

By 1986 the Texas unemployment rate stood at 9 percent, two full percentage points above the national rate, and in Houston it was even higher. A national financial crisis in the savings and loan industry hit Houston hard, as several of the city's giant S&Ls, having extended millions of dollars in high-risk loans in the boom years, collapsed. In July 1988 one of Houston's biggest real-estate tycoons, J. R. McConnell, committed suicide in his jail cell as he awaited trial for fraud.

But even in hard times, Houstonians took a kind of perverse Texas pride in the magnitude of the disaster that had befallen them.

Oil Refineries, Houston's Life-Support System

Declared chamber of commerce president Gerald Griffin: "There is no other place on this planet hit as hard as Houston." The city on Buffalo Bayou had come through tough times before, and few doubted that it would weather this crisis as well.

Hard Times for Houstonians

Indeed, as the 1980s ended and oil prices turned up once again, signs of recovery began to appear. Houston's unemployment rate dropped, and fewer "For Sale" signs stood on front lawns. Houstonians were buoyed by the presidential victory of George Bush, who had once lived in the city and still maintained his legal residence there. The Bush administration, it was hoped, would channel federal contracts in Houston's direction. When the president appointed his former Houston neighbor, James A. Baker III, as secretary of state, the city's star seemed to be rising still higher in Washington.

But meanwhile, the great boom of the 1970s was only a fading memory, and for many, hard times remained a grim reality. Boom towns of the West commonly went through wild gyrations of prosperity and recession in the course of their history, though few in as spectacular a fashion as Houston.

A stock-market upturn in August 1982 hinted at a revival of economic confidence, but the recession's grip remained strong, and in the congressional elections that fall, the Democrats gained twenty-six House seats. Like so many other recent administrations, the Reagan presidency appeared headed for failure. But early in 1983 the economy rebounded. Encouraged by tax cuts, by a long-awaited decline in interest rates, and above all, by evidence that inflation had been licked at last, consumers went on a buying spree. The stock market surged, unemployment dropped, and the gross national product shot up by nearly 10 percent. Domestic auto sales picked up as the Japanese, under administration pressure, voluntarily limited auto exports to the United States.

To be sure, serious economic problems remained. The trade gap yawned ever wider; the deficit surpassed $200 billion in 1983; and millions of farmers, inner-city poor, and displaced industrial workers did not share in the renewed prosperity. But—just in time to brighten Reagan's reelection prospects—the general economic picture looked rosier by 1984 than it had in years.

Military Buildup

Convinced that the United States had grown dangerously weak militarily since Vietnam, Reagan launched the most massive military expansion in American peacetime history. Building on the increases in defense spending already introduced by Jimmy Carter in 1979–1980, the Pentagon's budget swelled from $171 billion in 1981 to more than $300 billion by 1985. Secretary of Defense Caspar Weinberger, warning darkly of the Soviet menace, appeared tirelessly before congressional committees in support of still greater increases. Congress showered more money on the military than could possibly be spent prudently. By 1985 the rate of Pentagon spending approached $500,000 *a minute,* round the clock, seven days a week.

This military buildup included a strong nuclear-weapons emphasis, as the administration shepherded the MX missile through key congressional votes in 1983 and 1985. To head the Arms Control and Disarmament Agency, Reagan appointed a sharp critic of the whole arms-control process. Sec-

Ronald Reagan, Outdoorsman

Though President Reagan was often photographed in natural settings, his administration gave little support to the cause of environmental protection.

retary of State Alexander Haig spoke of the utility of "nuclear warning shots" in a conventional war, and other administration officials speculated about the winnability of nuclear war. Over massive popular protests in England, Germany, and elsewhere, the administration in 1983 deployed 572 cruise and Pershing II missiles in Western Europe in fulfillment of a 1979 NATO decision, counterbalancing Soviet missiles in Eastern Europe.

The Federal Emergency Management Agency promulgated an elaborate civil-defense plan whereby city residents would flee to remote "host communities" when nuclear war threatened. A Defense Department official, T. K. Jones, argued that backyard shelters would save millions of people in a nuclear conflagration. "If there are enough shovels to go around," Jones asserted, "everybody's going to make it."

Confronting the "Evil Empire"

Unsettledness at the State Department, lurid anti-Soviet pronouncements, and setbacks in the Middle East characterized U.S. foreign policy in the early eighties. Secretary of State Haig alienated many administration leaders, including the outspoken U.N. ambassador, Jeane Kirkpatrick, with his flamboyant, self-promoting style. In 1982 Reagan replaced Haig with George Schultz, a seasoned administrator and team player who had served as secretary of labor and the treasury under Richard Nixon.

Détente had already started to fade in the late 1970s, but the level of anti-Soviet rhetoric intensified during Reagan's first term. The Russians would lie, cheat, and "commit any crime" to achieve their sinister purposes, Reagan insisted; without Soviet subversion, "there wouldn't be any hot spots in the world." Addressing a convention of Protestant evangelicals, he characterized the Soviet Union as an "evil empire" and "the focus of evil in the modern world." Anti-Soviet sentiment mounted when the Russians cracked down on the Polish labor movement Solidarity and crested in September 1983, when the Soviets shot down a Korean passenger plane that had entered Soviet airspace, killing all 269 aboard. The Soviets claimed that the plane had ignored several warnings and that spy planes sometimes followed a similar route, but to many Americans, the incident proved Moscow's brutality.

The Reagan administration's initial obsession with the Soviet menace shaped its policy toward El Salvador and Nicaragua, two poverty-stricken Central American nations caught up in revolutionary turmoil. In El Salvador the administration staunchly supported the ruling military junta in its ruthless suppression of a leftist insurgency backed by Cuba and Nicaragua. Right-wing "death squads" murdered thousands of suspected leftists. A moderate, José Napoleón Duarte, won the 1984 presidential election with U.S. support, but the killing went on. In early 1989 El Salvador voters rejected the ineffectual Duarte government and elected as president the candidate of the right-wing Arena

party, Alfredo Cristiani, a development that posed a headache for the incoming George Bush administration.

In Nicaragua the Carter administration at first extended financial assistance to the Sandinista revolutionaries who overthrew dictator Anastasio Somoza in 1979. But a strong dose of anti-Americanism in the Nicaraguan revolution, rooted in memories of past U.S. intervention, prevented American aid from having much political effect. In any event, Reagan quickly reversed this policy, claiming that the leftist Sandinistas were turning Nicaragua into a pro-communist state like Castro's Cuba and a staging area for Soviet expansion. Under director William Casey, the Central Intelligence Agency in 1982 organized and financed a ten-thousand-man anti-Sandinista guerrilla army, called the contras, based in neighboring Honduras and Costa Rica. The contras, many with links to the deposed Somoza regime, conducted raids, planted mines, and carried out sabotage inside Nicaragua, in the process killing many innocent people. The CIA mined Nicaraguan harbors and

Contra Training Camp on the Honduras-Nicaragua Border, 1986

The CIA-funded contras, targeted to overthrow Nicaragua's Sandinista government, enjoyed the enthusiastic support of President Reagan, but Congress and many Americans had serious reservations.

prepared a handbook describing techniques for assassinating Sandinista officials.

Fearing another Vietnam, Americans grew alarmed as details of this U.S.-run "covert" war leaked out. Congress voted a yearlong halt in U.S. military aid to the contras in December 1982 and imposed another ban from October 1984 to October 1986. But Reagan's enthusiasm for the contras, whom he lauded as "the moral equivalent of our Founding Fathers," held steady. Secret contra aid, funded from private right-wing sources and foreign governments, and organized within the White House itself, continued despite congressional prohibitions. When Nicaragua brought the United States before the World Court for mining its harbors, Washington simply refused to participate in the case.

Reagan's militarization of American foreign policy fell heavily on the tiny West Indian island of Grenada, where a 1983 coup had replaced the leftist government with an even more radical—and unpopular—administration. On October 23, 1983, two thousand U.S. Marines invaded Grenada, overthrew the offending government, and installed a regime friendly to the United States. Democrats voiced sharp criticism, but the administration claimed that U.S. strategic interests in the region justified the action. Most Grenadians, as well as other West Indian governments, expressed their approval.

Frustration and Tragedy in the Middle East

Tensions between Israel, the Palestinians, and the surrounding Arab nations remained high as Reagan took office. Using its clout as a major supplier of aid to Israel, the administration promoted a comprehensive Middle Eastern peace settlement involving creation of a Palestinian homeland on the West Bank, the region seized by Israel in the 1967 war (see map). This initiative got nowhere, however; Israel not only rejected the idea but actively promoted Jewish settlement in the disputed territory.

The cycle of Mideast violence escalated in June 1982, when Israel invaded Lebanon to expel the Palestine Liberation Organization (PLO) from its headquarters in southern Lebanon. This devastating raid did force the PLO to withdraw, but it worsened the turmoil in Lebanon, a nation already

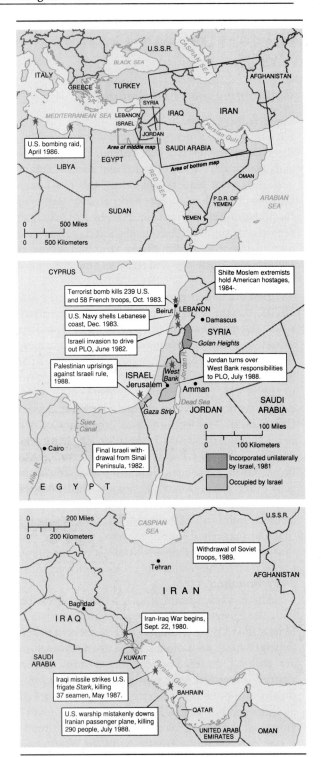

The Mideast Crisis in the 1980s

A maelstrom of ethnic and religious hatreds as well as a region of vital strategic importance because of its oil resources, the Middle East remained a major world hotspot in the Reagan years and beyond.

wracked by fighting between rival Christian and Moslem militia groups.

President Reagan ordered 2,000 U.S. Marines to Lebanon in 1982 as part of an international force to oversee the PLO's departure to Tunisia and help restore order to the war-torn country. But the Moslem militia leaders viewed the United States as favoring Israel and the Christian-dominated Lebanese government, and they began to fire on the marines. While leaving this small and vulnerable U.S. force in its exposed position, Reagan failed to explain how its deployment served America's larger interests in the region. The tragic climax came in October 1983, when a Moslem terrorist drove a truck loaded with explosives into the marines' poorly guarded barracks at the Beirut airport. In the blast that followed, 239 marines died. This disaster underscored the bankruptcy of Reagan's Middle Eastern policy; by early 1984 the remaining marines had been withdrawn.

The Nuclear-Freeze Movement

The military buildup of the early 1980s, the collapse of the arms-control process, and Reagan's anti-Soviet rhetoric sparked a grassroots reaction as millions of Americans perceived a growing threat of nuclear war. This response took the form of a campaign for a verifiable superpower freeze on the manufacture and deployment of nuclear weapons. The brainchild of Randall Forsberg, a young Massachusetts arms-control expert, the freeze movement represented the first sustained popular challenge to Reaganism. Early in 1982 several New England town meetings adopted freeze resolutions; that summer, eight hundred thousand antinuclear protesters—the largest political demonstration in American history—rallied in New York's Central Park; in the fall elections, freeze resolutions passed in nine states, including California and Wisconsin. Rising concern about nuclear war found other outlets as well. "We need a 'moral about-face,'" declared the American Roman Catholic bishops in 1983; "the whole world must summon the moral courage and the technical means to say no to nuclear conflict."

Responding to the antinuclear clamor, the administration in June 1982 proposed the total removal of medium-range nuclear missiles from Europe and belatedly began talks with the Soviets in Geneva on strategic-arms reductions. In a different approach to neutralizing the growing peace movement, Reagan in March 1983 proposed the Strategic Defense Initiative (SDI), a vast system of space-based lasers and other high-tech defenses against nuclear missiles. Quickly nicknamed "Star Wars" after a popular 1977 movie, SDI drew upon Americans' deep faith in technology as well as upon Reagan's own past. A 1940 Reagan film called *Murder in the Air* featured the "Inertial Projector," an SDI-like secret weapon that destroyed incoming enemy aircraft by invisible rays. The Pentagon launched an SDI research program, but critics pointed out not only the project's prohibitive cost and technical implausibility but also the likelihood that it would simply provoke another escalation in the nuclear-arms race. To the end of the Reagan years, Star Wars generated fierce debate.

Reagan's First Term: A Summing Up

As the 1984 election approached, liberal Democrats and many independents found much to criticize in the Reagan presidency, including runaway military spending, worsening Cold War tensions, massive budget deficits, a cavernous foreign-trade gap, sharp cuts in social programs, and the assault on the government's well-established regulatory function. As the United States floundered in the Middle East, Nicaraguans suffered under a U.S.-funded war. To critics, jingoism abroad and selfishness at home summed up the meaning of Reaganism.

But the administration had some solid achievements to its credit, notably an end to inflation. Despite serious underlying problems, the economy was booming. And Reagan's personal popularity proved remarkably impervious to the ups and downs of his policies. Some called him the Teflon president—nothing seemed to stick to him. Even his bitterest opponents found occasional reasons to applaud. For example, feminists who generally deplored Reagan's program welcomed his 1981 nomination of Sandra Day O'Connor as the first woman justice on the U.S. Supreme Court. Most Americans found Reagan personally likable, and they admired his courageous and even jaunty response to a brush with death on March 30, 1981, when a ricocheting bullet fired by a mentally disturbed young man struck him in the chest as he left a Washington hotel. Rushed to the hospital, Reagan walked in under his own steam, quipping to the physicians: "Please tell me you're all Republicans."

By 1984 many Americans believed that Reagan had indeed delivered on his promise to revitalize the free-enterprise system, rebuild U.S. military might, and make the nation once again "stand tall" in the world. If he had done relatively little to enact the social agenda of the New Right, he often rhetorically praised its moral vision. Buoyed by evidence of broad public support, Reagan confidently prepared to campaign for a second term.

The Changing Contours of Society and Culture in Contemporary America

The United States that celebrated the bicentennial of the Constitution in 1987 was a very different nation from that of 1945 or even 1960. In contrast to the political activists of the sixties, the generation that came of age in the seventies seemed cautiously intent on personal goals and financial success. These years also saw unprecedented numbers of women enter the work force, enroll in professional schools, and launch careers. Black Americans joined the middle class in record numbers, while ethnic pride and a sense of new possibilities stirred the American Indian population.

But social problems persisted. While some Americans prospered, millions in the inner cities, often nonwhite minorities, remained stuck in poverty. For many citizens, the emotional issue of abortion and the stark reality of AIDS forced revisions in sexual ideology and behavior. Throughout the contemporary era, the unsettling pace of change led to a search for moral certitude and spiritual solace that produced a remarkable resurgence of religion in American life.

America Turns Inward: The Era of the Yuppie

In the aftermath of the 1960s—when young activists had fought racism, sexism, war, and injustice—the mood of the seventies and eighties changed dramatically. Social engagement did not disap-

pear, but it diminished in intensity and shifted in focus. The heightened environmental consciousness of the early 1970s remained central as Americans expressed rising concern about air and water pollution and the peril to endangered species. The campaign to save the whales from extinction at the hands of the highly sophisticated whaling fleets of various nations won many recruits. The hazards of nuclear power aroused particular attention in the later 1970s, culminating in 1979 when a near-catastrophic accident crippled the Three Mile Island nuclear-power plant near Harrisburg, Pennsylvania.

But millions of young people turned from public to private concerns in these years. The political climate of the seventies did not inspire the kind of civic idealism that John F. Kennedy and Martin Luther King, Jr., had once aroused, and Ronald Reagan's message of individualism and his suspicion of "the government" easily translated into a self-centered materialism. Apart from calls for more military spending, Reagan offered little in the way of a common national agenda or vision. In these circumstances, the "campus radical" of the 1960s gave way to a new social stereotype, the "yuppie" (young urban professional), preoccupied with physical fitness, psychic harmony, a tasteful "lifestyle," and money. Reversing the middle-class flight from the city that had slowed and then practically halted the long national process of urbanization, many yuppies purchased run-down inner-city apartments or town houses and expensively restored them. This process, known as gentrification, often had the effect of pushing out poorer residents, including countless elderly citizens.

Jogging became a middle-class fad. James Fixx's *Complete Book of Running* sold well until Fixx dropped dead of a heart attack while pursuing his favorite activity. Actress Jane Fonda, an antiwar activist in the sixties, won a new following for her videocassettes demonstrating exercise techniques. A vogue for "natural" foods free of pesticide residues and chemical additives spread, and the rate of cigarette smoking declined as medical evidence linked the habit to lung cancer, heart disease, and other maladies. Thomas Harris's 1969 best seller *I'm OK, You're OK* heralded the shift to personal preoccupations; transcendental meditation (TM) and other "consciousness-raising" techniques won devoted followers in the seventies. Historian Christopher Lasch summed up his view of the era in the title of his 1979 book *The Culture of Nar-*

cissism; writer Tom Wolfe called it simply the Me Generation.

A revolution in consumer electronics shaped the era as well. The TV set, of course, remained the living-room icon. In 1986 the average American spent thirty hours a week watching the tube. Prime-time soap operas like "Dallas," chronicling the steamy affairs of a Texas oil family, captivated millions each week. The Super Bowl, the annual confrontation of professional-football gladiators, invariably won vast audiences. All-time viewing records fell on February 28, 1983, when 50 million households tuned in for the final episode of "M*A*S*H," a long-running CBS comedy featuring a Korean War medical unit.

Transmitting via satellite, "super stations" like Ted Turner's WTBS in Atlanta went national, while the rise of cable television gave birth to a variety of new channels offering everything from business reports to rock music. For an added fee, viewers had a still broader choice, including first-run films on HBO (Home Box Office) and sexually explicit movies on the Playboy Channel. Faced with such competition, the networks' share of the market declined to under 75 percent by the late 1980s.

The introduction of the videocassette recorder (VCR) enabled Americans to tape TV shows for later viewing and to rent movies on cassette. By 1988 nearly half of U.S. households had VCRs; entertainment had become highly privatized. Instead of going out to the movies, many families now spent Saturday night at home with the VCR. In the music field, the compact disc, in which tiny laser beams "read" millions of dots molded into three miles of concentric circles on each disc, offered remarkably high-quality sound. Americans bought some 7 million CD players in 1986–1987 alone.

And this was the era of the personal computer. A product of World War II, the computer moved into the home in the late 1970s when two young Californians, Steven Jobs and Stephen Wozniak, working in Jobs's garage, developed a small-scale model. In 1977 the Apple II computer hit the market. Sales soared, reaching $118 million by 1980, and computer businesses mushroomed in a region south of San Francisco nicknamed "Silicon Valley" (after the silicon computer chip). Jobs and Wozniak became overnight heroes: the American dream still lived. (Pushed aside when Apple sales lagged in 1985, Jobs resigned from his own company.) IBM, which launched its PC (personal computer) in 1981, quickly grabbed 40 percent of the market. By the late 1980s, small computers adorned thousands of business offices, and millions of individual Americans used them on a regular basis, particularly students, teachers, scholars, and writers.

The Great Bull Market

Keeping body and mind in shape and acquiring the latest electronic playthings did not come cheaply. The post-Vietnam generation sought out careers that would support them in the lifestyle to which they aspired. In the nation's colleges, humanities courses lost enrollments as students targeted their academic programs toward specific vocational objectives. Law-school and business-school applications skyrocketed.

Reviving prosperity unleashed a wave of stock-market speculation reminiscent of the 1920s. The great bull market began on August 12, 1982, when the Dow Jones average stood at 777, and it lasted for five years. In the "get-rich-quick" climate of the day, entrepreneurs like Donald Trump, the Manhattan real-estate tycoon, and Ivan Boesky, who seemed to have a magic touch when it came to stock transactions, became celebrities. Brokerage firms like E. F. Hutton advertised heavily to lure more people into the market. The Horatio Alger–like 1984 autobiography of Lee Iacocca, who had rescued Chrysler Corporation from near bankruptcy (thanks to a federal bailout program in 1980), enjoyed many weeks on the best-seller list. Reports of corporate mergers filled newspaper business columns. Chevron bought Gulf for $13 billion in 1984; GE acquired RCA (and its NBC subsidiary) for $6.3 billion in 1986. Through it all, the stock market roared on; the Dow surged to an unheard-of 2,669 on August 12, 1987, more than three times its level when the boom began.

Meanwhile, however, the downside of the Wall Street feeding frenzy had surfaced. In 1985 E. F. Hutton officials pled guilty to manipulating funds in ways that defrauded hundreds of banks. Ivan Boesky went to prison after his 1986 conviction for insider trading (profiting through advance knowledge of planned corporate actions). Then on October 19, 1987, "Black Monday," came a devastating stock-market crash. In the largest single-day drop in stock-market history, the Dow plunged 508 points as one-fifth of the paper value of the nation's stocks evaporated. Newspapers recalled

Black Monday on the Stock Market, October 19, 1987

The 1987 collapse of stock prices—the shattering end of a five-year bull market—reminded older Americans of the crash of 1929. The long-term effects, however, proved minimal.

the 1929 crash that had ushered in the Great Depression. The 1987 collapse had no such long-term effects (indeed, by August 1989 the Dow had again soared to over 2,700, a level not seen since October 1987), but it did provide a useful reminder to a new generation of eager investors that stocks can go down as well as up.

By the late 1980s, the self-absorption and materialism of the preceding two decades seemed on the wane, but they remained influential. In a 1987 survey of some three hundred thousand college freshmen, 76 percent identified "being very well off financially" as a top goal—nearly double the percentage that had embraced this objective in 1970. Only 39 percent (in contrast to 83 percent in 1967) ranked "developing a meaningful philosophy of life" as particularly important.

The Women's Movement: Gains and Uncertainties

The most permanent legacy of the 1960s was a revitalized women's movement and a fundamental change in the status of women in American life. As early as 1963, Betty Friedan's *The Feminine Mystique* had heralded a new cycle of feminist activism, and as the civil-rights and antiwar move-

ments politicized thousands of middle-class young women, many began to examine their own subordinate status in society. The resulting feminist ferment represented a rare source of social involvement in the generally quiescent 1970s. The National Organization for Women (NOW), founded by Friedan and others in 1966, boasted nearly fifty thousand members by the mid-1970s. Feminist support groups met in city apartments and college dorm rooms; Gloria Steinem's *Ms.* magazine (founded in 1972) spread the message.

With the movement's growth came new-found political clout. The National Women's Political Caucus (1971) endorsed candidates and promoted a feminist agenda in Washington and state capitals. By 1972 many states had liberalized their abortion laws and outlawed sex discrimination in hiring. That same year, Congress passed an Equal Rights Amendment (ERA) to the Constitution ("Equality of rights under the law shall not be denied or abridged by the United States or any State on the basis of sex"). When twenty-eight states quickly ratified it, ultimate adoption seemed assured. In *Roe* v. *Wade* (1973), the Supreme Court proclaimed women's constitutional right to abortion.

The women's movement remained strong in the later 1970s and the 1980s, but the early unity diminished. Never very cohesive, the movement increasingly splintered into radical and moderate camps. While both camps espoused gender equality, moderates deplored the radicals' sometimes strident antimale rhetoric. Movement activists also remained overwhelmingly educated, middle-class, and white. Black women, generally more centrally concerned with racism than sexism, kept their distance; and many homemakers were put off by some feminists' tendency to downgrade domesticity and family values while praising female autonomy and careerist goals. In *The Second Stage* (1981), Betty Friedan urged feminists to add family issues to their agenda and not leave this potent theme to their opponents.

As the movement gained visibility, its opposition hardened. In 1972 President Nixon vetoed a bill that would have set up a national network of day-care centers; its "communal approach to child-rearing," he charged, was "family weakening." After the initial spurt of support for the ERA, the ratification process bogged down. In 1979 Congress gave advocates an additional three years to achieve ratification, but the amendment died in 1982, three states short of the required three-fourths.

No issue relating to women aroused more anguished controversy, both among feminists and in society at large, than abortion. In the wake of *Roe* v. *Wade*, a well-organized "Right to Life" movement pressed for a constitutional amendment outlawing abortions. This effort, led by Roman Catholic and conservative Protestant groups, generated virulent controversy. Abortion, opponents charged, undermined respect for human life; it was "the murder of the unborn." "Pro-life" advocates picketed pregnancy-counseling centers; a fanatic fringe even bombed a few abortion clinics. The amendment campaign failed, but in 1976 Congress cut off Medicaid funding for most abortions, in effect putting this procedure out of reach of the poor.

Most feminists adopted a "pro-choice" stance, arguing that while abortion ought never to be undertaken lightly, the decision should rest with the individual woman and her physician and not be made a matter of legal prohibition. Public-opinion polls reflected the nation's polarization over

Anti-Abortion Demonstration in Washington, D.C., January 1989

In the years following the Roe *v.* Wade *decision (1973), a well-organized anti-abortion movement emerged in the United States.*

the issue, but a majority favored the "pro-choice" position. The actual number of women seeking abortions rose from about 750,000 in 1973 to over 1.5 million in 1980 and then leveled off.

As debate raged over the ERA and abortion, women streamed into the workplace. The proportion of women working outside the home leaped from 35 percent in 1960 to about 60 percent in 1988. Fifty-one percent of women with infants under the age of one were in the work force. Although many remained at the lower end of the pay scale, in traditional "women's jobs," this pattern, too, was changing. From 1977 to 1987, the proportion of corporate-management positions held by women rose from 24 percent to 37 percent (though *top* management still remained an overwhelmingly male preserve). The ratio of female lawyers and physicians edged upward after 1960, reaching about 18 percent by 1986 (see table). In that year, too, 36 percent of college and university professors were women. Steeply rising female enrollments in medical schools, law schools, and Ph.D. programs guaranteed a continuation of this trend.

Changing patterns of fertility, marriage, and divorce also shaped women's lives. After the postwar baby boom's peak in 1960, the birthrate dropped steadily for sixteen years, reaching a low in 1976. Couples not only were marrying later but postponed starting a family and had fewer children. By 1980 the statistically average American family had 1.6 children. The number of unmarried couples living together—most of them childless—jumped from 523,000 in 1970 to nearly 2 million in 1985. And 1987 saw 487 divorces for every thousand marriages, up from 258 per thousand in 1960.

While these demographic trends had many underlying causes, conservatives often blamed them on the women's movement. Like Richard Nixon, they worried that women's changing role would lead to a weakening of the family. Working women themselves acknowledged the stresses of their situation. Torn between career and family pressures, some yielded to the "superwoman" syndrome, pushing themselves to be successful professionals, attentive mothers, superb cooks, efficient housekeepers, and seductive wives all at the same time.

Some feminists worried that younger women, benefiting from opportunities won in earlier strug-

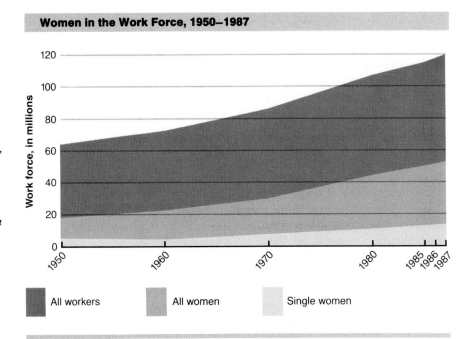

Women in the Work Force, 1950–1987

Since 1960 the proportion of American women who are gainfully employed has surged upward. As a result, young women coming of age in the 1990s have far different expectations about their lives than did their grandmothers or even their mothers.

SOURCES: *Statistical Abstract of the United States, 1988* (Washington, D.C.: Government Printing Office, 1987), 373; *World Almanac and Book of Facts, 1989* (New York: Pharos Books, 1988), 152.

All workers   All women   Single women

Women Enter the Professions:
Percentage of Women Employed in Selected Professions, 1970 and 1986

Profession	Percentage of Women Workers	
	1970	1986
Social scientists and urban planners	22.5	46.0
Mathematical and computer scientists	16.7	36.2
Natural scientists	13.6	22.5
Lawyers and judges	4.9	18.1
Physicians	9.7	17.6
Architects	4.0	9.7
Engineers	1.7	6.0

SOURCE: U.S. Bureau of the Census, *Statistical Abstract of the United States, 1988* (Washington, D.C.: U.S. Government Printing Office, 1987), 376–377.

gles without having participated in those struggles, were losing sight of the movement's original goals. Could women function as equals in the male world, they asked, without absorbing the competitiveness, the status preoccupations, the single-minded careerism, and other characteristics of that world once deplored by feminists? Feminists recognized, too, that a long road lay ahead in overcoming ingrained patterns of gender discrimination. The lack of adequate day-care facilities made life hard for working mothers. Working women's average earnings still lagged well behind those of men. And though the pattern was shifting, the workplace remained largely gender-segregated. Such fields as nursing and secretarial work overwhelmingly employed women, while the higher-prestige professions like law and medicine, particularly at the upper ranks, were dominated by men.

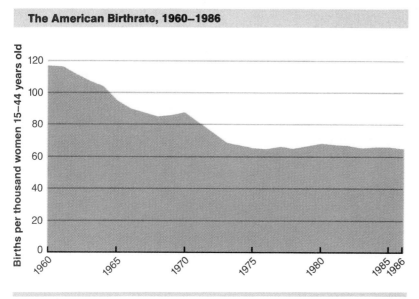

The American Birthrate, 1960–1986

Families of four or five children or even more were once common in the United States. But from 1960 to the mid-1970s, the U.S. birthrate fell by nearly half.
SOURCE: U.S. Department of Commerce, Bureau of the Census.

The Dilemmas of the Modern Woman

As this New Yorker *cartoon suggested, juggling a career and family commitments could be stressful.*

The eighties was not a favorable decade for confronting these inequities. The Reagan administration, deeply suspicious of governmental activism on social issues, opposed many feminist (and black) goals. Reagan's appointees to the United States Civil Rights Commission, the agency charged with enforcing the nation's civil-rights laws, shared his doubts about government's role in such matters. The Reagan budget cuts fell especially harshly on social-welfare programs serving women and children. As women heading single-parent families increasingly swelled the welfare rolls, observers spoke of the "feminization of poverty."

Reflecting the changed political and cultural atmosphere, *Good Housekeeping* magazine in 1988 hailed a "new traditionalism" reportedly gaining ground among American women. Focused on husband, children, and home, it seemed very much like the old traditionalism. Feminists, while recognizing that many goals remained unfulfilled and that American women differed sharply among themselves about the kinds of lives that they wished to lead, could nevertheless take satisfaction in real gains achieved.

The Two Worlds of Black America

The story of contemporary black America is really two very different stories. On one hand, millions of blacks have experienced significant upward

Florence Griffith-Joyner

A superb athlete, Griffith-Joyner won three gold medals in track at the 1988 Summer Olympic Games.

mobility. Thanks to the civil-rights movement, blacks can now pass through doors long bolted shut. In 1965 black students accounted for under 5 percent of college enrollments; by 1985 the figure had risen to nearly 10 percent, as the proportion of black high-school graduates going on to college nearly matched that of their white classmates. By the mid-1980s more than 40 percent of black workers held white-collar jobs, and about 45 percent of blacks owned their own homes. TV's *Cosby Show,* a popular family comedy of the later 1980s in which Bill Cosby played an obstetrician married to a lawyer, portrayed this successful, upwardly mobile black world.

But outside this charmed circle lay another, much grimmer black world—one of inner-city slums where blacks who had missed the "Up" escalator found themselves trapped. In this world, comprising about a third of the black population, up to half the young people never finished high school and the jobless rate in the late 1980s hovered as high as 60 percent.

While racism contributed to this situation, economic trends played a role as well. Structural

changes in the economy since World War II had eliminated many unskilled jobs once held by the urban poor. The recessions of the 1970s and early 1980s hit the already struggling black underclass with special ferocity, and even amid the prosperity and rising employment of Reagan's second term, the poverty rate among blacks edged higher.

Cocaine, including the particularly potent "crack," pervaded the urban ghettos (as well as other levels of American life) in the 1980s. Black children as young as eight or nine earned up to a hundred dollars a day working as lookouts for drug dealers. By their early teens, some became dealers themselves, earning in two days what they would make in a year working at McDonald's.

This was also a violent world. In the 1980s a young black male was six times as likely to be murdered as a young white male. Sixty black children under the age of seventeen were murdered in Detroit in 1987, most in gang-related violence. In Los Angeles two major gangs, the Bloods and the Crips, accounted for more than four hundred killings that year. Each gang had its distinctive colors, and some innocent young people died simply because they wore clothes of the wrong shade. Jewelle Taylor Gibbs of the School of Social Welfare at Berkeley summed up the situation in 1988: "Young black males in America's inner cities are an endangered species. . . . They are [the] rejects of our affluent society."

Among unmarried young black women of the slums, the pregnancy rate reached astronomical proportions. Single women—most of them young, poor, and uneducated—accounted for more than half of all black births in 1986. Millions of these single mothers, many scarcely beyond childhood themselves, depended on welfare payments for survival. Total AFDC (Aid to Families with Dependent Children) payments in 1986 stood at just under $16 billion. The AFDC caseload of 3.7 million families (a nearly 500 percent increase since 1960) represented more than 7 million children. Caught in a vicious cycle of dependence, these millions threatened to become a permanent undercaste in American society that would transmit the culture of poverty from one generation to the next.

While unemployment, drug use, illegitimacy, and welfare dependency affect Americans of all races and ethnic groups, these problems present themselves most starkly among inner-city black and

Hispanic populations. In 1980 some 43 percent of all mothers receiving AFDC payments were black, and another 13 percent Hispanic. In 1987–1988, when the illegitimacy rate among white women stood at just over 15 percent, the comparable figure for black women was around 56 percent. Buffeted by complex social and economic forces, America's predominantly nonwhite inner cities pose a major social challenge now and in the future.

New Patterns of Immigration

America's recent population growth—from 204 million in 1970 to 246 million in 1988—reflects a steady influx of immigrants, both legal and illegal. In contrast to former eras, when most immigrants came from Europe, some 45 percent of the new arrivals since 1960 have come from the Western Hemisphere and 30 percent from Asia.

Thanks to both immigration and a high birthrate, Hispanics compose the nation's fastest-growing ethnic group. Precise figures are uncertain, because many illegal Hispanic residents evade the census takers, but the Census Bureau estimated the 1985 Hispanic population at 17.5 million (up from 9 million in 1970), consisting mainly of Mexican-Americans concentrated in the Southwest and Cubans, Puerto Ricans, Haitians, and other West Indians living mainly in New York, Florida, Illinois, and New Jersey.

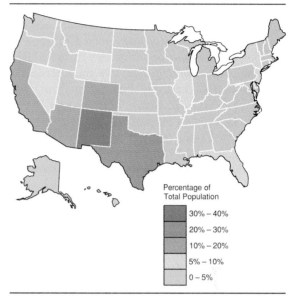

Percentage of
Total Population

- 30% – 40%
- 20% – 30%
- 10% – 20%
- 5% – 10%
- 0 – 5%

The Hispanic Population of the United States, 1980

The Hispanic population continues to expand rapidly. From 1980 to 1985, according to Census Bureau estimates, it grew by some 30 percent in California and Florida and by 23 percent in Texas, with high rates of increase in other states as well.

As with immigrants of the past, desperate economic conditions at home propel these newcomers to America. In oil-rich Mexico, for example, with its appalling unemployment and per capita annual

New Americans

(Left) A young Asian woman at a naturalization ceremony in California; (right) Cubans at a similar event in Florida.

income of just over two thousand dollars, the collapse in world oil prices in the 1980s worsened the nation's chronic poverty and spurred the down-and-out to seek new opportunities in the north. But these recent immigrants, like their predecessors, often face hardship and poverty in their adopted land as well. Nearly 20 percent of Mexican-Americans and 30 percent of Puerto Ricans live below the poverty line.

Clinging proudly to their language and traditions, these Hispanic newcomers are strongly influencing American culture. In Los Angeles, with nearly a million Mexican-Americans, one could drive for miles in the 1980s and see only Spanish business signs and movie marquees; large parts of Miami, such as the open-air market of the Calle Oche district, seemed wholly Hispanic.

Estimates of the number of illegal aliens in the United States ranged as high as 12 million by the end of the 1980s. Working long hours under harsh conditions with few legal protections, these impoverished migrants, mostly Mexicans and Haitians (as well as Puerto Ricans, who are U.S. citizens), performed hard manual labor, sweated in the gar-

ment trades, cleaned houses and cared for children, and bent their backs in agricultural fields under the blazing southwestern sun. Addressing this growing problem, the Immigration Reform and Control Act of 1986 outlawed the hiring of illegal aliens and strengthened immigration controls at the border. At the same time, the new law offered legal status to aliens who could prove that they had lived in the United States since January 1, 1982.

Immigration from Asia has also climbed steadily as newcomers from Korea, Vietnam, and the Philippines joined already well-established Japanese and Chinese communities in California and spread eastward. These newest Americans worked hard, sought higher education, and moved up rapidly. The younger generation, torn between the new and the old, faced stresses and tensions but generally has retained a strong group identity while taking advantage of the larger society's opportunities. All these ethnic trends made the United States of the 1980s a far more diverse, vibrant, and interesting place than it had been a generation earlier.

Brightening Prospects for Native Americans

The status of American Indians reached a low point in the 1950s, when the federal government sought to terminate all Indian-aid programs and promote Indians' relocation in cities—where, it was tacitly hoped, they would gradually disappear as a distinct ethnic group. Aroused by this destructive and ill-conceived policy, and influenced by the social-protest climate of the sixties, members of the militant American Indian Movement (AIM) dramatized their cause by occupying Alcatraz Island in San Francisco Bay in 1969, the Bureau of Indian Affairs in Washington in 1972, and a trading post at Wounded Knee, South Dakota (site of the terrible 1890 Indian massacre by the U.S. Army), in 1973.

This militance helped bring about an important shift in federal policy. Rejecting both the disastrous "termination" approach and Washington's traditional paternalism toward Indians, President Nixon in 1970 called for greater autonomy for the native Americans in managing their own affairs. Nixon's commissioner of Indian affairs, himself a Sioux-Mohawk, helped draft the Indian Self-Determination Act of 1974, granting tribes the right

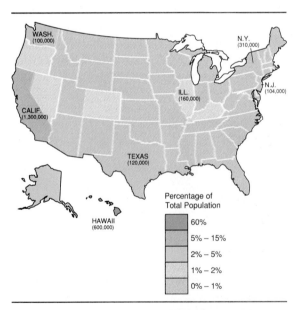

The Asian Population of the United States, 1980

Asian newcomers face the age-old immigrant challenge of adapting to a different culture. One Korean preparing to immigrate to the United States in 1979 told a journalist: "I am familiar with Western food. I have eaten hamburgers."

to manage federal-aid programs on the reservations and to oversee their own schools.

The seventies also brought a heightened sense of Indian pride and tribal loyalty. Nearly 1.4 million persons identified themselves as American Indians in the 1980 census, in contrast to fewer than 800,000 in 1970. Since natural increase could not account for this rate of growth, census analysts concluded that thousands of people simply chose to identify themselves as Indians who had not done so a decade before.

This flowering of ethnic pride inspired efforts to promote economic development on the chronically poverty-stricken reservations. Federal legislation in 1961 had given tribes the right to buy or develop land for commercial or industrial projects, and a number of tribes undertook commercial ventures ranging from resorts to mining and logging operations. Other tribes permitted food-processing companies, electronics firms, and other businesses to build factories on tribal lands, providing much-needed jobs.

Indian tribes have also enjoyed remarkable success in asserting long-ignored treaty rights. The creation of the Indian Claims Commission by the federal government in 1946 laid the groundwork for this process, but the major claims settlements have come since 1970. In 1971 the Eskimos, Aleuts, and other native peoples of Alaska won 40 million acres of land and nearly $1 billion in settlement of their long-standing claims. In 1980 the Sioux were awarded $107 million for lands in South Dakota illegally taken from them more than a century earlier, and the Penobscot Indians in Maine received $81 million for claims based on a federal law of 1790. In 1988 the tiny Puyallup tribe of Washington State received $162 million in settlement of their claim that much of the city of Tacoma occupied land that they had been granted by treaty in the 1850s. The Puyallups at once announced plans to restore the salmon runs on the Puyallup River and construct a deep-water port on Puget Sound. "With this settlement . . . ," declared a tribal leader, "our people . . . will always have a future."

Yet not all was rosy for the Indians. High rates of unemployment, alcoholism, and disease persisted both on the reservations and in the cities. But the renewal of tribal life, the new direction of federal policy, and the willingness of the white majority to recognize the validity of ancient trea-

ties clearly represented an advance over past neglect and blatant injustice. By the end of the eighties, those who had feared or hoped that native Americans would gradually vanish had clearly been proved wrong.

Changing Sexual Patterns in the Era of AIDS

The greater openness about sex that was one of the sixties' legacies had a particular impact on the homosexual community. Beginning in the 1970s, many gay men and lesbians "came out of the closet" and openly acknowledged their sexual preference. They rallied, paraded, and formed choruses in New York, San Francisco, and elsewhere. They also organized to demand legal protection against job discrimination and other forms of harassment. As one leader told a throng of fifty thousand demonstrators in Washington, D.C., in 1979: "We are twenty million strong in this nation. We are moving from gay pride to gay politics."

Religious conservatives, meanwhile, deplored the growing tolerance of homosexuality as evidence of the disintegration of society's moral fabric. Declared evangelist Jerry Falwell: "Homosexuality is so grievous, so abominable in the sight of God that he destroyed the cities of Sodom and Gomorrah because of this terrible sin."

The loosening of traditional sexual mores received a jolting setback in the 1980s, however, with the proliferation of various sexually transmitted diseases (STDs), including AIDS (acquired immune deficiency syndrome), first diagnosed in the United States in 1981. By mid-1989 some 97,000 U.S. cases had been reported, and at least 46,000 Americans had died. An exhaustive government study in 1989 projected from 300,000 to 480,000 cases by 1991. Public-health officials warned that a vaccine against the deadly virus lay far in the future. Despite widespread fears of a "breakout" into the general population, AIDS through the late eighties remained confined mainly to sexually active homosexuals and bisexuals, intravenous drug users sharing needles, a few individuals who acquired the virus through blood transfusions, and those having sexual intercourse with members of these high-risk groups. Nevertheless, medical authorities, including Surgeon General C. Everett Koop, soberly warned everyone of the need for caution and urged the wider use of condoms.

The AIDS scare provided some Americans with an excuse to express their hatred of homosexuals. But others responded admirably. The disease's mysterious nature stimulated a massive medical-research effort. By 1983 Dr. Robert Gallo of the National Cancer Institute (simultaneously with a French scientist) had isolated the AIDS virus. Hospices in many communities provided care and support to sufferers; a large AIDS quilt bearing the names of victims toured the nation; candlelight marches memorialized those who had died.

The impact of AIDS on sexual behavior remained unclear. Certainly many gays grew more cautious. In San Francisco and other cities, bath houses catering to the gay community closed their doors. The awareness of risk penetrated the general population more slowly—indeed some data suggest rising rates of sexual activity among unmarried heterosexuals in the 1980s—but even this group presented evidence of shifting patterns. Surveys of sexually active unmarried women, for example, found that the number relying on the condom as their chief contraceptive method nearly doubled between 1982 and 1987. The exuberant slogan of the 1960s, "Make Love, Not War," had given way to a more somber exhortation, "Safe Sex," that seemed likely to live on in the 1990s.

The Evangelical Renaissance

A most striking aspect of post-1970 American society has been the high visibility of religion. In a time of unsettling, sometimes tumultuous social change, many Americans have sought the assurance of a clear-cut belief system that would give meaning to life and resolve ethical dilemmas. Religious faith has always loomed large in American history, but since 1970 it has played a more decisive cultural and political role than it had for years.

This intensification of religious interest has assumed various forms. Some have joined cults such as L. Ron Hubbard's Scientology, the Reverend Sun Myung Moon's Unification church (whose adherents some called "moonies"), and the International Society for Krishna Consciousness, whose chanting, saffron-robed followers added an exotic note on city streets and college campuses. The more significant expression of this religious resurgence was the rapid growth of evangelical Protestant denominations such as the 2-million-member Assemblies of God church and the 14-million-strong Southern Baptist Convention. While these groups differed among themselves—the so-called charismatic or Pentecostal churches, for example, favoring a highly emotional form of worship that included "speaking in tongues"—they all believed in the Bible's verbatim truth, in "born-again" religious experience, and in an earthly life governed by personal piety and strict morality.

Evangelical Christians had actively pursued social reform before the Civil War. Many twentieth-century evangelicals also turned to political activity, but of a conservative variety. As a California evangelical minister observed in 1985: "I always thought that churches should stay out of politics. Now it seems almost a sin *not* to get involved." Jerry Falwell's pro-Reagan Moral Majority registered an estimated 2 million new voters in 1980 and 1984. While targeting specific issues such as abortion, homosexuality, pornography, and public-school prayer, evangelicals also embraced a strongly conservative, anticommunist world view.

Evangelicalism's rejuvenation was fueled by a network of religious bookstores, by more than a thousand radio stations featuring religious pro-

The AIDS Quilt, Washington, D.C., 1987

Each panel commemorates a person who died of AIDS. Wrote one woman who quilted a panel in honor of her grandson: "We were so close. I was there when he was born, and I was there when he passed away."

gramming, and above all, by television evangelists. Along with Falwell's "Old Time Gospel Hour," popular broadcasts included Pat Robertson's "700 Club," Jim and Tammy Bakker's "PTL" (Praise the Lord) program, Oral Roberts's telecasts from Oklahoma, and Jimmy Swaggart's from Louisiana. Many of these shows aired on Robertson's CBN (Christian Broadcast Network), the nation's fourth-largest cable network. These television "ministries" often spawned collateral enterprises, such as Oral Roberts University in Tulsa, Oklahoma; Falwell's Liberty University in Lynchburg, Virginia; and the Bakkers' religious theme park and hotel in South Carolina. With their endless pleas for money, the televangelists repelled many Americans but millions of others found their spiritual message reassuring.

The "electronic church" suffered severe jolts in 1987–1988. Jim Bakker resigned after acknowledging a sexual encounter with a church secretary and subsequent payoffs to buy her silence. The fiercely moralistic Jimmy Swaggart fell from grace when his trysts with a New Orleans prostitute became public knowledge. But the TV preachers' tribulations could not obscure the growing influence of evangelical religion. Politicians ignored it at their peril, as did anyone seeking to understand the post-1970 cultural scene. Confronting change on all sides, evangelicals found certitude in their faith. In the process, they profoundly influenced American life in the late twentieth century.

The Later Reagan Years and Beyond

Sweeping to victory in 1984, Ronald Reagan at seventy-three (the oldest person ever elected president) hoped that his second term would solidify the "Reagan revolution." In fact, however, problems abroad and embarrassments at home plagued his final White House years. Still, much of the controversy faded when Reagan signed a historic arms-control treaty with the Soviet Union and established a warm personal relationship with Soviet leader Mikhail Gorbachev. Winning the presidency in his own right in 1988, Vice President George Bush confronted complex challenges as he strove to emerge from Reagan's looming shadow.

The Election of 1984

The 1984 Republican convention, carefully staged for television, highlighted the themes of the forthcoming campaign: patriotism, prosperity, and the personality of Ronald Reagan. The Democrats' candidate-selection process, by contrast, more accurately reflected the diversity of American society. The early favorite, former vice president Walter Mondale, approached the race in traditional fashion, soliciting endorsements from labor unions, party bigwigs, and various interest groups. But he faced strong challenges from two unconventional candidates, Gary Hart and Jesse Jackson. Hart, a former Colorado senator, assiduously imitated John Kennedy's speech and mannerisms and, like Kennedy, appealed to the young. Jackson, a black Chicago minister and onetime associate of Martin Luther King, Jr., in the civil-rights movement, tried to build a "rainbow coalition" of blacks, Hispanics, displaced workers, and other outsiders in Reagan's America.

While beating back these challenges, Mondale failed to ignite much enthusiasm. His campaign's high point came when he announced his vice-presidential choice, New York congresswoman Geraldine Ferraro, who clearly savored her role as the first woman ever to run on a major-party presidential ticket. Mondale and Ferraro campaigned gamely, but the Reagan slogan "Morning in America" hit a responsive chord among the people. Carried along on a tide of prosperity, the Reagan-Bush

The Election of 1984				
Candidates	Parties	Electoral Vote	Popular Vote	Percentage of Popular Vote
RONALD REAGAN	Republican	525	54,451,521	58.8
Walter Mondale	Democratic	13	37,565,334	40.5

ticket won 59 percent of the popular vote and carried every state but Mondale's Minnesota and the District of Columbia. Once again, many traditionally Democratic voters, especially blue-collar workers, defected to Reagan and gained prominence as the Reagan Democrats. The "gender gap" that had emerged in earlier polls measuring Reagan's support largely dissolved in 1984. Despite Ferraro's presence on the Democratic ticket, a higher percentage of women voted Republican in 1984 than in 1980.

Rising Foreign Problems

An array of troubles reflecting a world no longer neatly divided between East and West confronted Reagan in his second term. In the Philippines, an important U.S. ally, resistance to the corrupt government of President Ferdinand Marcos intensified following the 1983 assassination of the popular opposition leader Benigno Aquino. After a fraud-ridden election in 1986, Aquino's widow Corazon rejected Marcos's victory assertions and proclaimed herself president. While Marcos went into exile in Hawaii, the United States recognized Aquino's government and supported her program of land reform. Plagued by poverty, a communist insurgency, and a military skeptical of democracy, the Philippines faced a clouded future. But for the moment, U.S. support for Aquino seemed the wisest choice.

With Congress obviously unenthusiastic about funding Reagan's undeclared war against the Sandinista government of Nicaragua, President Oscar Arias Sánchez of Costa Rica, joined by other Central American political leaders, arranged a cease-fire between the Sandinistas and the contras beginning in March 1988. This fragile truce won only

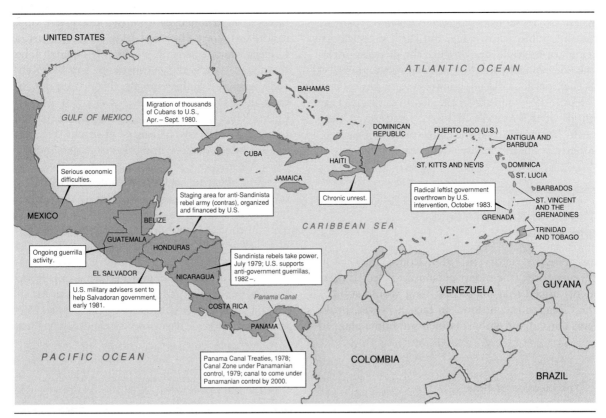

The United States in Central American and the Caribbean

Plagued by grinding poverty, massive social problems, and repressive regimes, Latin America saw turmoil and bloody conflict in the 1980s.

grudging support from Reagan, who still dreamed of a contra victory. In Panama, meanwhile, revelations emerged in 1987 that a U.S.-backed military strongman, General Manuel Noriega, had been profiting from the illicit flow of drugs through his country. Noriega's regime, charged New York's Senator Alphonse D'Amato, was "a total criminal empire." After Noriega rejected a State Department plan for a quiet exile, a U.S. grand jury indicted him on various drug charges. Nevertheless, he clung to power, an embarrassment to an administration that had made the war on drugs a high priority.

Growing opposition to South Africa's racist government posed further dilemmas for Washington as Anglican bishop Desmond Tutu, a leader of South Africa's blacks, rallied American support for his people's cause. While critical of apartheid (South Africa's policy of racial separation), the administration opposed efforts to impose sanctions against it. In October 1986, however, overriding a Reagan veto, Congress passed a series of sanctions, including a ban on South African products and a prohibition on business investments in South Africa.

The Middle East remained a chronic trouble spot. Secretary of State Schultz made a final effort at a settlement in 1988 based on the formula "land for peace," by which Israel would give up the West Bank in return for security guarantees by the Arab states. But the Israelis showed no interest, and the Arabs, citing America's role as Israel's chief ally, refused to accept Schultz as a disinterested mediator.

Meanwhile, a bloody religious war between Iran and Iraq further complicated America's Middle Eastern role when Reagan ordered the navy to assist in the risky task of escorting oil tankers through the Persian Gulf. In May 1987 an Iraqi missile struck the U.S. frigate *Stark,* killing thirty-seven sailors. And in July 1988, in an incident uncomfortably reminiscent of the Soviets' earlier destruction of a Korean airliner, the U.S. warship *Vincennes,* under fire from Iranian gunboats in the gulf, shot down an Iranian passenger plane that it mistook for an F-14 fighter, killing all 290 aboard. A Pentagon investigation found the *Vincennes* crew to blame but took no disciplinary action, concluding that the stress of first-time combat helped explain the tragic error.

Reagan's second term also saw a rash of airplane hijackings and other terrorist acts by Palestinians demanding the release of prisoners. In June

1985 hijackers seized a TWA flight en route from Athens to Rome and murdered one passenger, a U.S. sailor. That October, terrorists commandeered an Italian cruise ship, the *Achille Lauro,* near Port Said, Egypt, and brutally shot an elderly wheelchair-bound Jewish American and threw his body overboard. Twenty persons, including several Americans, died in terrorist attacks on the Rome and Vienna airports that December. In September 1986 Palestinians seized a Pan Am jetliner in Karachi, Pakistan; twenty-one passengers died in a bungled rescue attempt. In December 1988, in the waning months of Reagan's term, a Pan Am jet flying from London to New York crashed in Scotland, killing all 259 aboard, including a great many Americans. Authorities quickly established that a concealed bomb had caused a midflight explosion. Strong circumstantial evidence pointed to Palestinian extremists operating in Germany.

Like the Iranian hostage crisis, these incidents both infuriated and frustrated Americans. But public opinion did not turn against Reagan as it had against Jimmy Carter, in part because the administration struck against a major fomenter of world terrorism, Libyan leader Muammar Qaddafi. In April 1986, after a Libya-directed bombing of a Berlin nightclub popular with American GIs, U.S. bombers attacked five Libyan sites, damaging military targets and causing civilian casualties as well. Airports tightened security, but terrorism remained a hard-to-combat tactic by which shadowy underground groups in the Mideast and elsewhere expressed their hatred of U.S. policy by striking at innocent American citizens.

Deficits and Supreme Court Battles at Home

On the domestic front, 1986 brought some significant legislative achievements, including a new immigration law (see above) and an administration-sponsored tax-reform law that made the system fairer by eliminating many deductions and establishing uniform rates for persons at comparable income levels. The law also removed some 6 million low-income Americans from the income-tax rolls and shifted the tax burden somewhat from individuals to corporations. Meanwhile, sky-high federal deficits—the legacy of Reaganomics—remained a serious problem. The deficit gushed to over $200 billion in 1985 and 1986 and hovered at about $150 billion in 1987 and 1988. The Gramm-Rudman Act of 1985, a draconian measure aimed at producing a balanced budget by 1990, reflected congressional frustration with massive deficits. It mandated automatic, across-the-board spending cuts if the normal budget process did not achieve the budget-balancing goal. But when the Supreme Court in 1986 declared key provisions of the law unconstitutional, its effectiveness fell into doubt. Gargantuan federal deficits, coupled with an enormous trade gap, represented long-term economic problems bequeathed by Reagan to his successor.*

Like most presidents, Reagan sought to perpetuate his philosophy through his Supreme Court appointments, but he achieved mixed results. In addition to the O'Connor nomination, he elevated William Rehnquist to chief justice, replacing the retiring Warren Burger, and chose another judicial conservative, Antonin Scalia, to fill the Burger vacancy. When a third vacancy opened in 1987, Reagan nominated Robert Bork, a brilliant but controversial judge and legal scholar whose intellectual rigidity and doctrinaire opposition to judicial activism led many to conclude that he lacked both a judicial temperament and a sufficient awareness of the Supreme Court's role in protecting individual liberties. After exhaustive Judiciary Committee hearings, the Senate rejected the Bork nomination, 58–42. Reagan's next nominee, Douglas Ginsburg, withdrew after admitting that he had smoked marijuana as a law student and a professor. (The Ginsburg nomination, some observed, gave new meaning to the phrase "High Court.") Reagan's third choice, Anthony Kennedy, won quick confirmation.

The impact of the Reagan appointments became evident in 1989. In four 5–4 rulings, the Supreme Court imposed confining new definitions on widely used civil-rights laws aimed at protecting the employment rights of women and minorities and remedying past abuses. But even with three Reagan appointees, the Supreme Court displayed a mind of its own. In a key 1988 ruling, the Court overwhelmingly rejected the administration's efforts to overturn a law authorizing the appointment of independent special prosecutors to investigate wrongdoing in the executive branch. Writing the majority opinion, Chief Justice Rehnquist stingingly rejected the administration's audacious claim that the president should have the power to dismiss such prosecutors.

The Iran-Contra Scandal

On November 3, 1986, a Beirut newspaper reported that in 1985 the United States had shipped, via Israel, 508 antitank missiles to the violently anti-American government of Iran. Thus began the worst scandal of the Reagan administration. Acknowledging the sale, Reagan said that the aim had been to encourage "moderate elements" in Tehran and to secure the release of American hostages (including the CIA's Beirut bureau chief) held in Lebanon by pro-Iranian radical groups. In a February 1987 report, a presidentially appointed investigative panel, headed by former Texas senator John Tower, placed heavy blame on the administration—particularly on Donald Regan, then chief of staff, who promptly resigned.

But more details soon spilled out, including the bizarre sidelight that national-security adviser Robert McFarlane had accompanied a second arms shipment to Tehran in May 1986, bringing with him, for presentation to the Ayatollah Khomeini, a Bible autographed by President Reagan and, for obscure reasons, a key-shaped cake. The most explosive revelation, however, was that Lieutenant Colonel Oliver North, a National Security Council aide, had diverted millions in profits from the Iran arms sales to pay for military assistance to the Nicaraguan contras at a time when Congress had forbidden such aid. In November 1986, just before FBI investigators arrived, North and his secretary Fawn Hall, as they later acknowledged, held a "shredding party" to destroy incriminating documents. Hall smuggled other papers out of the White House under her clothing.

In the summer of 1987, a joint House-Senate investigative committee chaired by Senator Daniel Inouye of Hawaii took 250 hours of testimony from twenty-eight witnesses. The nation watched in fascination as Fawn Hall asserted that sometimes one must "go above the written law"; as the gung-ho "Ollie" North, resplendent in his bemedaled marine uniform, portrayed himself as a true patriot; and

---

*The trade deficit bottomed out in 1987, when it reached $154 billion. The gap began to shrink thereafter, thanks to stronger U.S. exports. In early 1989, however, it was still running at an annual rate of over $100 billion.

as portly, pipe-smoking former national-security adviser John Poindexter testified that he had deliberately concealed the fund-diversion scheme from Reagan to provide the president "future deniability . . . if it ever leaked out." North's emotional, self-serving testimony elicited a short-lived wave of popular support.

The Inouye committee's report found no evidence that Reagan had personal knowledge of illegalities but roundly criticized the casual managerial style and general disregard for the law that had fed the scandal. (Eight Republicans dissented from the report, arguing for a stronger affirmation of Reagan's personal innocence.) Meanwhile, early in 1988, a court-appointed special prosecutor, Lawrence Walsh, issued criminal indictments against Poindexter, North, and others. In May 1989 a federal jury convicted North of obstructing a congressional inquiry, destroying and falsifying Security Council documents, and accepting an illegal gratuity. Federal judge Gerhard Gesell fined North $150,000 and ordered him to perform twelve hundred hours of community service but did not send him to prison. North's Iran-contra role declared Gesell, was that of "a low-ranking subordinate working to carry out initiatives of a few cynical superiors."

While less damaging than Watergate, the Iran-contra scandal dogged the administration's final years. Ironically, however, Reagan's passive presidential style, and his notorious vagueness about details, helped him through the crisis: people had no trouble believing that he had been oblivious to crimes committed a few feet from the Oval Office. As a Kansas City physician commented to a public-opinion pollster: "He doesn't have his finger on what's going on. He tells somebody else to do it and goes back to bed."

More Scandals and Embarrassments

Other disturbing revelations plagued Reagan's second term. In June 1988, after a two-year investigation, Justice Department officials revealed evidence of bribery and conspiracy in scores of military-procurement contracts involving billions of dollars and some of the Pentagon's largest suppliers. Although some downplayed the matter as a case of a few rotten apples, others saw systematic corruption in Pentagon procurement, worsened by the free-spending tendencies of the early eighties. Evidence of more subtle forms of influence buying also surfaced. In 1986, for example, the top ten defense contractors paid nearly $250,000 in "honoraria" to lawmakers with direct oversight of military spending.

Ironically, Reagan's closest associates caused some of his worst problems. Two key advisers were convicted of influence peddling after leaving the White House. Reagan's old friend Attorney General Edwin Meese became a target of investigation for allegedly using his influence to promote various ventures in which he and a close associate had an interest, including a billion-dollar oil-pipeline project in Iraq. Meese finally resigned in July 1988, declaring himself "vindicated" when a special prosecutor decided not to press criminal charges.

Memoirs published by several former White House aides proved highly embarrassing as well. In *For the Record* (1988), former chief of staff Donald Regan, still smarting over his abrupt departure and his feuds with the president's wife, Nancy, pictured Reagan as little more than an automaton: "Every moment of every public appearance was scheduled, every word was scripted, every place where Reagan was expected to stand was chalked with toe marks." Then in 1989, revelations surfaced that during the Reagan years prominent Republicans had been paid hundreds of thousands of dollars for interceding with the Department of Housing and Urban Development on behalf of developers seeking federal subsidies. Former Interior Secretary James Watt, for example, received over $400,000 for making several phone calls to HUD officials.

Reagan's popularity seemed unaffected by all this dirty linen. His admirers did not really look to him for administrative brilliance or conventional political skills; the sources of his popularity lay far deeper. Drawing on his own conservative convictions as well as on his years of training as an actor, Reagan possessed an uncanny ability to articulate the beliefs, aspirations, and fears of millions of Americans. For that, they were ready to forgive him almost any lapse.

Mission to Moscow

A dramatic warming of Soviet-American relations counterbalanced the presidential setbacks. Meeting at Geneva in 1985 and Reykjavík, Iceland, in 1986, Reagan and Soviet leader Mikhail Gorbachev explored the arms-control issues that the two nations had been negotiating off and on since 1983. The prospects of agreement at first appeared bleak, for Gorbachev insisted on Reagan's abandonment of Star Wars as the price of arms-control progress. But the Soviet, beset by a sluggish economy and an entrenched bureaucracy at home, eagerly pursued an easing of big-power tensions to provide a breathing space for domestic reform.

In 1987 negotiators reached agreement on a treaty providing for the removal of twenty-five hundred American and Soviet missiles from Europe. This Intermediate Nuclear Forces (INF) Treaty, signed by Gorbachev and Reagan in Washington that December, did not end the nuclear threat; indeed, it left about 95 percent of the world's nuclear arsenal in place. But it did revive the long-dormant arms-control process and for the first time actually eliminated an entire class of *existing* nuclear weapons rather than merely putting a limit on the deployment of *future* weapons as SALT I had done. In another first, the INF Treaty provided for on-site inspection to verify compliance.

This agreement, in turn, led to Reagan's historic visit to Moscow in May 1988. Not only did the two leaders sign the final version of the INF Treaty (which had meanwhile won Senate ratification), but they established a cordial personal relationship. Asked about his 1983 "evil empire" remark, Reagan responded amiably that he had been talking about an earlier era, not Gorbachev's Russia. A smiling Gorbachev, embodying his policy of *glasnost* (openness), escorted his visitor around Red Square, stopping to chat with reporters. Resolving one sticky point in U.S.–Soviet rela-

---

Milestones in Nuclear-Arms Control

	Event	*Provisions*
1963	Limited Test Ban Treaty	Prohibits atmospheric, underwater, and outer-space nuclear testing.
1967	Outer Space Treaty	Prohibits weapons of mass destruction and arms testing in outer space.
1968	Non-Proliferation Treaty	Promotes peaceful international uses of nuclear energy; aims to stop the global proliferation of nuclear weaponry.
1972	Strategic Arms Limitation Treaty (SALT I)	Limits for five years U.S. and Soviet deployment of strategic weapons systems.
	Anti-Ballistic Missile (ABM) Treaty	Restricts U.S. and Soviet testing and deployment of defensive systems.
1974	Threshold Test Ban Treaty	Establishes limits on size of underground tests.
1979	Strategic Arms Limitation Treaty (SALT II) (Unratified)	Establishes limits on strategic launch vehicles and delivery craft and restricts the development of new missiles. (Treaty was never ratified, but its terms are observed by the United States and the Soviet Union.)
1982	Strategic Arms Reduction (START) Talks	Seeks 50 percent reduction in U.S. and Soviet strategic nuclear weapons.
1988	Intermediate-Range Nuclear Forces (INF) Treaty	Commits the United States and the Soviet Union to withdraw their intermediate-range nuclear missiles from Eastern and Western Europe and to destroy them.

tions, Gorbachev announced Soviet withdrawal from Afghanistan.

In explaining the remarkable easing of Cold War tensions symbolized by Reagan's Moscow visit, observers noted not only the domestic considerations that underlay Gorbachev's quest for better relations with the United States but also Reagan's personal friendliness and the rapport between the two heads of state. While conservatives pointed to the Reagan military buildup as the key to the improved big-power climate, peace activists suggested that the nuclear-freeze movement had played an important role in persuading the administration to renew arms-control talks. Still others emphasized the influence of Nancy Reagan, whose concern for her husband's place in history led her to promote his image as a man of peace.

Whatever its sources, few denied the monumental importance of this shift. Détente, derailed in the late 1970s, was not only back on track but barreling ahead at a rate hardly imaginable a few years earlier. Americans reacted to Reagan's role in this process with applause that must have warmed the old actor's heart. Many who remained sharply critical of Reagan's domestic policies praised the INF Treaty and the Moscow summit. The vigorous Cold Warrior, denouncer of earlier arms-control treaties, and champion of massive military spending seemed destined to be remembered for his part in bettering relations with the Soviets, signing an important arms agreement, and reducing the risk of global war. Such are the paradoxes of politics and the endless fascination of history.

The Election of 1988

As the Reagan era wound down, his would-be successors emerged. On the GOP side, Vice President George Bush's strongest rival, Kansas senator Robert Dole, won the Iowa primary but lost in New Hampshire and elsewhere. Soon Bush had the nomination sewn up.

A large group of contenders nicknamed "the seven dwarves" battled for the Democratic nomination. Gary Hart, an early favorite, dropped out after the *Miami Herald* revealed his affair with a Florida model, including a Caribbean cruise on a yacht aptly named *Monkey Business*. The field eventually narrowed to two: Jesse Jackson and Massachusetts governor Michael Dukakis. Jack-

Jesse Jackson

A spellbinding orator and Democratic presidential contender in 1984 and 1988, Jackson won heavy black support and also the backing of many whites with his call for more attention to the needs of the nation's poor and disadvantaged.

son, preaching concern for the poor and urging a full-scale war on drugs, ran well in the primaries, winning not only the black vote but a larger margin of white votes than in 1984. But Dukakis victories in major primary states like New York and California proved decisive. As his running mate, Dukakis chose Texas senator Lloyd Bentsen, a courtly sixty-seven-year-old conservative who brought regional and ideological balance to the ticket.

The Democrats exuded confidence as they assembled for their convention in Atlanta. "Poor George, he can't help it. He was born with a silver foot in his mouth," jeered the keynote speaker, state treasurer Ann Richards of Texas, needling the vice president for both his privileged background and his penchant for silly remarks. To the relief of delegates who found Dukakis unexciting, "the Duke" delivered a rousing acceptance speech that fired them with enthusiasm.

At the Republican convention in New Orleans, the only suspense involved the vice-presidential choice. Bush surprised everyone by selecting a little-known young senator from Indiana, J. Danforth Quayle III, the golf-playing son of a wealthy newspaper publisher. Bush apparently hoped that Quayle's boyish good looks would appeal to the younger generation and to women voters. Feminists bristled at the patronizing assumption that a handsome candidate could win them over. Moreover, controversy descended on Quayle with the revelation that in 1969, when his family's newspapers had strongly supported the Vietnam War, he had pulled strings to evade service in Vietnam. But the issue soon faded; indeed, it may have helped Quayle by casting him as a victim of media persecution.

Accepting the nomination, Bush called for a "kinder, gentler America" and pledged no new taxes. Campaigning with a vigor that belied his bumbling reputation, Bush stressed Reagan's achievements while distancing himself from the Iran-contra scandal and other embarrassments. Emphasizing peace and prosperity, he pointed with pride at the INF Treaty, better Soviet relations, low inflation, and the 14 million new jobs created during the eighties—an achievement unmatched by any other industrial nation.

Setting out to discredit Dukakis, Bush denounced the New Englander as a liberal soft on crime and itching to raise taxes. Bush TV commercials, playing on latent racist stereotypes, featured a black man who committed rape and murder after his release under a Massachusetts prisoner-furlough program. In his most demagogic attack, Bush assailed Dukakis's veto of a bill requiring Massachusetts schoolchildren to recite the Pledge of Allegiance, even though the Supreme Court had long ago declared such laws unconstitutional. "What is it about the Pledge of Allegiance that so upsets him?" Bush asked darkly.

Thrown on the defensive, Dukakis emphasized his accomplishments as governor. "This election is not about ideology, it's about competence," he insisted. He hammered at the failures of the "Swiss-cheese" Reagan economy and, with appeals to organized labor and emphasis on patriotism and the family, wooed the "Reagan Democrats" who had deserted the party in 1980 and 1984.

But Dukakis had trouble getting his campaign in gear. He seemed edgy and defensive, and his dismissal of ideology made it difficult for him to define his vision of America. He denounced Bush's "soft-on-crime" charges as "garbage," but the garbage stuck. Even Dukakis's own backers wearied of his vague generalities, stock phrases ("good jobs at good wages"), and repeated reminders of his managerial skills. In two TV debates, Bush taunted

Rating the Candidates

A cartoonist's comment on the 1988 campaign.

his rival as a passionless technocrat: "Wouldn't it be nice to be perfect? Wouldn't it be nice to be the iceman so you never make a mistake?"

Both candidates avoided serious issues in favor of TV-oriented "photo opportunities" and "sound bites." Bush visited flag factories and military plants while Dukakis turned up at labor rallies, in classrooms, and—to prove that he opposed crime—at a Florida ceremony honoring state-police trainees. To demonstrate his toughness on defense, he posed in a tank. Editorial writers grumbled about the "junk-food" campaign, but in an era when fleeting impressions counted for everything, the memorable visual image, the catchy phrase, and the twenty-second spot on the evening news had become the essence of presidential politics.

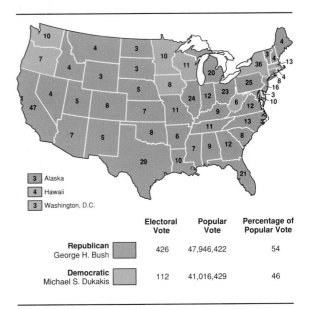

		Electoral Vote	Popular Vote	Percentage of Popular Vote
Republican George H. Bush		426	47,946,422	54
Democratic Michael S. Dukakis		112	41,016,429	46

The Election of 1988

Bush Victorious

When the polls closed on November 8, Bush emerged as the victor, with 54 percent of the vote. Dukakis's 46 percent was better than that of the Democratic candidates in 1968, 1972, 1980, and 1984 but still well short of victory. Bush carried forty states, whereas Dukakis prevailed in ten plus the District of Columbia; the electoral-college vote was a lopsided 426–112. Bush took the South and the Rocky Mountain states and squeaked through in the key states of California, Illinois, and Pennsylvania. His negative campaign, coupled with Americans' generally upbeat mood and Dukakis's weakness as a campaigner, turned the tide.

But the Democrats fared well otherwise, widening their control of both houses of Congress, gaining a net of one governorship, and retaining majorities in most state legislatures. As in other recent elections, the turnout was low. Only about 50 percent of the total eligible voters actually went to the polls—the lowest percentage since 1924, and far lower than in the other Western democracies.

The politics of race figured in the outcome. While Dukakis, like Mondale in 1984, won 90 percent of the black vote, under 40 percent of white voters cast their ballots for him. Dukakis proved especially weak among white southerners and the white working class. A major challenge for the Democrats clearly lay in rebuilding the old New Deal coalition of blacks and of working-class and ethnic whites. When a 1989 mayoral race in Dem-

ocratic Chicago split strictly along racial lines, with Jesse Jackson supporting the losing black candidate, that goal seemed more elusive than ever.

George Bush represented a long tradition of patricians in politics, embodied in earlier days by Theodore Roosevelt and Franklin D. Roosevelt. The son of a Republican senator from Connecticut, he attended an exclusive private school, graduated from Yale, and fought in World War II before breaking into the Texas oil business. Bush's Texas years added a distinctive tang to his style and opened the door to politics. He served in the House of Representatives, lost a Senate race (to Lloyd Bentsen), held various appointive offices (including the directorship of the CIA), and ran unsuccessfully for the Republican presidential nomination in 1980 before being tapped as Ronald Reagan's running mate that year.

In his cabinet selections, Bush turned to trusted associates and Washington insiders. The key post of secretary of state went to James Baker III, a Texas friend who had been Reagan's White House chief of staff and secretary of treasury, as well as Bush's campaign manager. Elizabeth Dole, the wife of Bush's defeated rival Robert Dole, became secretary of labor. Dr. Louis W. Sullivan, dean of the Morehouse University Medical School, a predominantly black institution in Atlanta, was named secretary of health and human services. And Bush chose retired air-force general Brent Scowcroft as national security adviser. Scowcroft had held the same position under Gerald Ford. But the Senate rejected Bush's first choice for secretary of defense, former senator John Tower of Texas, because of concerns about Tower's drinking habits, his sexual peccadilloes, and his close links to large military contractors. Bush next nominated Congressman Richard Cheney of Wyoming, a respected conservative who won quick confirmation.

Abandoning his harsh campaign tones, Bush in his inaugural emphasized harmony, criticized materialism, and returned to the "kinder, gentler nation" theme of his New Orleans acceptance speech. Again television's power to shape political reality was underscored. In six months' time, Bush's image had evolved from that of a spineless wimp (columnist George Will ridiculed him as "Reagan's lap dog"), to the ruthless campaigner willing to say anything to win, to the kindly leader championing goodwill and reconciliation.

Americans eager to believe that the latter was the "real Bush" soon found support for their hopes. Making clear that his would be a "hands-on" presidency, Bush expressed a readiness to cooperate with the Democratic Congress: "The American people want action," he declared; "they did

President George Herbert Walker Bush

With his wife Barbara at his side, Bush is sworn in as the United States' forty-first president.

not send us here to bicker." In the same let's-get-serious vein, the new first lady, the matronly, white-haired Barbara Bush, showed no interest in matching the high-fashion glitter of the Reagans.

Edging away at least slightly from Reagan's shadow, Bush proposed to cut 1990 military appropriations $2.7 billion below the Reagan figure and to slash Reagan's proposed funding for SDI research by 22 percent. As for the Nicaraguan contras, the cause so dear to Reagan's heart, Bush and congressional Democratic leaders agreed on ten months of nonmilitary funding aimed at reintegrating the contras into Nicaraguan life and politics. This plan paralleled the peace proposals advanced in 1987 by a group of five Latin American presidents. Of Reagan's program of military support for the contras, Secretary of State Baker observed: "I think we all have to admit that the policy basically failed."

Responding to national concern about drugs, Bush named William Bennett, Reagan's secretary of education, as "drug czar" to coordinate federal programs in this area. Bennett's first target was the warring druglords and drug gangs of Washington, D.C., notorious as America's "murder capital."

For the most part, Bush avoided the hard budget and tax choices that might have given substance to his "kinder, gentler" rhetoric. Despite campaign pledges to be the "education president," for example, his first budget requested $3 billion less for education than Reagan proposed in his last budget. With the Congressional Budget Office projecting several years of federal deficits in the $100 billion range, either higher taxes or far deeper cuts in military spending seemed the only source of funds for pressing social needs, yet neither course had strong political support in the early Bush years.

On the volatile abortion issue, Bush echoed Reagan in criticizing *Roe* v. *Wade*. In April 1989 over 300,000 "pro-choice" marchers rallied in Washington in support of the landmark 1973 decision. Abortion opponents, meanwhile, erected 4,400 crosses on Capitol Hill in a "Cemetery of the Innocents," symbolizing the number of fetuses aborted each day in America. The Supreme Court's new conservative majority made itself felt again in July 1989 in a 5–4 decision upholding a Missouri law restricting women's access to abortion. The Court also agreed to hear three more cases that could result in a reversal of *Roe* v. *Wade* itself. While anti-abortionists cheered, pro-choice activists geared up for further protests and political action. Clearly, this emotional issue would remain a divisive one for years to come.

Another continuing problem, environmental pollution, was spotlighted in March 1989 when a 987-foot oil tanker, the *Exxon Valdez,* ran aground in Alaska's beautiful Prince William Sound and spilled over 10 million gallons of crude oil. The accident fouled six hundred square miles of coastline and marine habitats, killed thousands of sea otters and shore birds, and jeopardized Alaska's vital herring and salmon industries. Bush called the spill a "major tragedy" but insisted that oil exploration and drilling must go on at an unabated rate.

Bush seized the initiative on environmental issues in June 1989 by proposing a strengthened Clean Air Act to combat acid rain and tighten regulations on toxic-air pollution. This recommendation contrasted sharply with the Reagan administration's open hostility to environmental concerns. With industrial polluters pouring out some 2.7 billion pounds of toxic and even carcinogenic substances each year, such action was urgently needed.

Internationally, the new administration confronted chronic problems in the Middle East and momentous changes in the Soviet Union and China. On the Middle Eastern front, the Bush administration persuaded PLO leader Yasir Arafat to acknowledge Israel's right to exist, while meanwhile pressuring Israel to make concessions to the Palestinians to further the stalled peace process.

The death in June 1989 of Iran's America-hating leader, the Ayatollah Khomeini, raised hopes of improved U.S.–Iranian relations, but the Middle East situation worsened in July when a pro-Iranian Shiite Moslem group in Lebanon hanged an American hostage, marine colonel William Higgins, and threatened other hostage hangings in retaliation for Israel's kidnapping of a prominent Shiite cleric and anti-Israeli terrorist leader. Pronouncing Americans "shocked right to the core," President Bush, like other presidents before him, groped for an effective U.S. policy in a region seething with ancient hatreds, bitter grievances, and fanatic religious ferment.

Elsewhere, the thawing of the Cold War presented both opportunities and problems. Americans watched closely as ethnic and nationalistic unrest swept parts of the Soviet Union and as Poland's Solidarity organization and other movements for democracy and independence gained ground in Eastern Europe. In 1989, as U.S. and Soviet negotiators resumed the much delayed START talks on reducing long-range nuclear missiles, West German chancellor Helmut Kohl not only rejected plans to modernize NATO's short-range nuclear missiles based in Germany but urged talks with the Soviets on the elimination of all nuclear weapons from Europe. When the Soviets announced plans to remove five hundred short-range nuclear weapons from Eastern Europe, the controversy with NATO intensified. President Bush, in Europe for NATO's fortieth anniversary in June 1989, delivered an important speech in Mainz, West Germany, proposing big reductions in conventional military forces by NATO and the Soviets, with negotiations on short-range nuclear weapons to follow. East and West should move beyond military confrontation to address their common environmental problems, Bush asserted.

America's improved relations with China suffered a grievous setback in 1989, when the Chinese army brutally crushed a pro-democracy demonstration by masses of unarmed Chinese students in Beijing's central square. A wave of repression, arrests, and public executions followed the initial attack, which killed an estimated 400 to 800 students. The Bush administration protested sharply, halted arms sales to Beijing, curtailed high-level diplomatic contacts, and urged international financial institutions to postpone loans to China. Washington refrained, however, from breaking diplomatic relations. Clearly, the upheavals shaking the communist world would long preoccupy U.S. diplomacy as the major powers tentatively groped toward a new and less dangerous structure of international relationships.

Conclusion   The fifteen years from the resignation of Richard Nixon in 1974 to the début of the Bush administration in 1989 brought profound economic, social, and political changes to America. The energy shocks of the 1970s eventually faded, but more chronic problems of budget deficits, trade imbalances, and industrial decline shadowed the economic boom of the later 1980s. While many Americans prospered, enjoying the new electronic technology of computers, VCRs, and CD players, the minorities of the inner cities lagged further behind, a fact that deepened fears of a sharply divided population. Amidst all these changes, women poured into the work force in record numbers, with far-reaching consequences for the future. Politically, Ronald Reagan dominated the era, demonstrating extraordinary political gifts but also a tendency to retreat from hard issues into a world of fantasy and anecdote. But confronted by fundamental transformations in the Soviet Union, Reagan showed a capacity for change and flexibility in helping to thaw Cold War hostilities, and for that he would be remembered.

As Reagan's political heir, George Bush faced daunting challenges. Lacking his predecessor's charisma, Bush entered the White House without an overwhelming mandate, a strong personal following, or the kind of global strategic vision that Richard Nixon, for example, had brought to the office. Americans watched cautiously as the Bush years began. The *New York Times* asked: "Is Bush prepared to imagine the future?"

Globally, the United States confronted serious problems in Latin America, the Middle East, Africa, and even Europe, where the relaxation of Cold War tensions had triggered a reassessment of NATO and of America's military role. Domestically, problems as diverse as the federal deficit, the foreign-trade gap, diminished economic competitiveness, environmental hazards, inner-city social breakdown, and disturbingly low levels of educational achievement all posed major challenges. How Americans and their elected representatives would deal with these issues and others only beginning to emerge remained for the future to tell.

CHRONOLOGY

1963 Betty Friedan, *The Feminine Mystique.*

1966 Founding of National Organization for Women (NOW).

1972 Equal Rights Amendment passed by Congress.

1973 Major rise in OPEC prices; Arab oil boycott.
Roe v. *Wade.*

1974 Richard Nixon resigns presidency; Gerald Ford sworn in.
Whip Inflation Now (WIN) program.

1975 South Vietnamese government falls.

1976 Jimmy Carter elected president.

1977 Panama Canal treaties ratified.
Introduction of Apple II computer.

**1978– **
1980 Double-digit inflation and soaring interest rates.

1979 Menachem Begin and Anwar el-Sadat sign peace treaty at White House.
Second round of OPEC price increases.
Accident at Three Mile Island nuclear plant.
Carter and Leonid Brezhnev sign SALT II agreement in Vienna.

1980 Carter withdraws SALT II agreement from Senate after Soviet invasion of Afghanistan.
Iran hostage crisis preoccupies nation.
Ronald Reagan elected president.

1981 Major cuts in taxes and domestic spending, coupled with large increases in military budget, launch Reagan era.

1981–
1983 Severe recession (late 1981–early 1983).

spoke of the "booming, buzzing confusion" of the universe; and American history, too, when viewed from too close up, can seem merely a mass of facts and dates, signifying nothing. When considered more broadly, however, our national experience furnishes reason for encouragement. Despite wrong turns and missed opportunities, the story of the United States is the story of challenges confronted and problems solved.

Underlying this record of achievement is the strength and adaptive capacity of American government. The Constitution drafted in Philadelphia in the hot summer of 1787 for a struggling new nation of 4 million people, most of them British in origin and most of them farmers, today provides a strong and responsive government for a modern industrial society of 240 million people drawn from the four corners of the earth. The intricate political machinery invented by the founders—with checks and balances among the three branches of the federal government and a further parceling-out of power among federal, state, and local authorities—still works remarkably well. It provides a continuity and stability almost unheard of in the world's troubled political history.

American democracy has also become more and more inclusive. In 1787 the franchise was confined to white male property owners. By 1920— after workingmen's movements in the Jacksonian era, the bloody Civil War, and a long battle for woman suffrage—all adult Americans had the constitutional right to vote regardless of race, gender, or economic standing. For blacks, that right was often denied in practice, and not until the civil-rights struggles of the 1950s and 1960s did it become a full reality. The process of translating the franchise into meaningful political power is a matter of organization, and this process, too, has been a continuing one. Many different groups have played a part, from the Civil War veterans and farmers of the late nineteenth century to the industrial workers of the 1930s to the Hispanics, feminists, evangelicals, elderly Americans, and gay-rights organizations of the 1980s.

While the much discussed "lessons of history" are rarely simple or obvious, it is important to realize that Americans of earlier generations confronted circumstances that in interesting ways parallel those that bedevil us today. Their success in coping with the challenges of their day offers reason for confidence as we nervously anticipate future problems.

Large-scale economic change, for example, is nothing new to Americans. The transformations of the nineteenth century, when industrialization altered the very nature of society, were as sweeping as any that we face in the foreseeable future. The vast technological processes that turned an agrarian society into an urban-industrial one surely seemed as unsettling to those who experienced them as the problems with which we wrestle today. Yet our forebears not only survived this era of radical change; they emerged from it with their government and their fundamental social institutions robustly intact.

Similarly, present-day environmental and public-health menaces had their counterparts in earlier times, when vile factory smoke blackened urban skies, open sewers spewed their noisome content into rivers, freewheeling entrepreneurs pillaged the wilderness, dangerous machines killed and maimed thousands of workers, horses deposited tons of excrement and gallons of urine on city streets each day, and unscrupulous firms foisted tainted food and dangerous medicines on an unsuspecting public. But the nation took action. Stimulated by journalistic exposés, laws were enacted and agencies created in the Progressive Era to protect society against the treacherous side effects of the new industrial order. The hazards today differ, of course, but the tradition of rising to the challenge remains strong and vital.

The distressing betrayals of the public trust that we have witnessed in recent years can be more than matched in the historical record, from the treasonous machinations of Vice President Aaron Burr to the corruption of the Tweed Ring in New York City to the Harding scandals. The remedy in each case has been the democratic process itself, reinforced by the vigilance of a free press. The "excesses of the media" are often attacked today, sometimes with justice, yet the independence and investigative zeal of our newspaper reporters and television correspondents stand as essential safeguards against the political misdeeds and corruption that will persist as long as human nature remains what it is.

Even the debate over the federal government's regulatory power that so preoccupies us today has deep roots in the American past. Through much

The Democratic Impulse

Chinese students and workers pressed for greater liberty in the late spring of 1989 (left); East German youths helped one another to climb the Berlin Wall as they celebrated the opening of the East German borders in November 1989 (right).

of our history, particularly during the nineteenth century, that regulatory function atrophied as energetic capitalists enjoyed free reign. But our history has also seen periods when the nation awakened to the need for more rigorous public oversight and control to protect the general welfare against private abuses. This cyclical process can prove instructive as we continue to seek a balance between individual freedom and the larger social interest.

Another invaluable asset from our past is the tradition of respect for human rights—a hard-won legacy rooted in Judeo-Christian religious teachings, the English common law tradition, the Bill of Rights, and a host of landmark judicial decisions. To be sure, this legacy has often been betrayed, as victims of racist bigotry or political oppression knew all too well. Still, the legacy lives on, and it sets us apart from millions the world over who live under far more repressive regimes.

The year 1989—two hundred years after the launching of the American Republic and the beginning of the French Revolution—may be another major landmark in history. Up to a million Chinese demonstrated for democracy in Beijing before being repulsed in a bloody military assault. Winds of change blew ever more fiercely in the Soviet Union. And as Moscow's grip loosened, Eastern Europe made a breathtaking dash for freedom—and except in Romania, almost without violence. A noncommunist government took office in Poland, and Hungary prepared for free elections. In November East Germany began virtually to collapse after opening the hated Berlin Wall, and German reunification loomed on the horizon. After massive popular demonstrations, dissident playwright Václav Havel moved from prison to the presidency of Czechoslovakia; in a moving speech to a cheering U.S. Congress in February 1990, Havel invoked Thomas Jefferson and Abraham Lincoln as his inspiration. In South Africa, meanwhile, apartheid seemed finally to be crumbling.

For Americans, appreciation of their nation's place in the nurturing of democracy is no cause for complacency or smugness. Rather, this realization invites a quiet determination to live up more fully to our national ideals, and to pass on to future generations the enduring vision of freedom that others have transmitted to us from the past.

APPENDIX

Declaration of Independence

IN CONGRESS, JULY 4, 1776

THE UNANIMOUS DECLARATION OF THE THIRTEEN UNITED STATES OF AMERICA

When, in the course of human events, it becomes necessary for one people to dissolve the political bands which have connected them with another, and to assume, among the powers of the earth, the separate and equal station to which the laws of nature and of nature's God entitle them, a decent respect to the opinions of mankind requires that they should declare the causes which impel them to the separation.

We hold these truths to be self-evident: That all men are created equal; that they are endowed by their Creator with certain unalienable rights; that among these are life, liberty, and the pursuit of happiness; that, to secure these rights, governments are instituted among men, deriving their just powers from the consent of the governed; that whenever any form of government becomes destructive of these ends, it is the right of the people to alter or to abolish it, and to institute new government, laying its foundation on such principles, and organizing its powers in such form, as to them shall seem most likely to effect their safety and happiness. Prudence, indeed, will dictate that governments long established should not be changed for light and transient causes; and accordingly all experience hath shown that mankind are more disposed to suffer, while evils are sufferable, than to right themselves by abolishing the forms to which they are accustomed. But when a long train of abuses and usurpations, pursuing invariably the same object, evinces a design to reduce them under absolute despotism, it is their right, it is their duty, to throw off such government, and to provide new guards for their future security. Such has been the patient sufferance of these colonies; and such is now the necessity which constrains them to alter their former systems of government. The history of the present King of Great Britain is a history of repeated injuries and usurpations, all having in direct object the establishment of an absolute tyranny over these states. To prove this, let facts be submitted to a candid world.

He has refused his assent to laws, the most wholesome and necessary for the public good.

He has forbidden his governors to pass laws of immediate and pressing importance, unless suspended in their operation till his assent should be obtained; and, when so suspended, he has utterly neglected to attend to them.

He has refused to pass other laws for the accommodation of large districts of people, unless those people would relinquish the right of representation in the legislature, a right inestimable to them, and formidable to tyrants only.

He has called together legislative bodies at places unusual, uncomfortable, and distant from the depository of their public records, for the sole purpose of fatiguing them into compliance with his measures.

He has dissolved representative houses repeatedly, for opposing, with manly firmness, his invasions on the rights of the people.

He has refused for a long time, after such dissolutions, to cause others to be elected; whereby the legislative powers, incapable of annihilation, have returned to the people at large for their exercise; the state remaining, in the mean time, exposed to all the dangers of invasions from without and convulsions within.

He has endeavored to prevent the population of these states; for that purpose obstructing the laws of naturalization of foreigners; refusing to pass others to encourage their migration hither, and raising the conditions of new appropriation of lands.

He has obstructed the administration of justice, by refusing his assent to laws for establishing judiciary powers.

He has made judges dependent on his will alone, for the tenure of their offices, and the amount and payment of their salaries.

He has erected a multitude of new offices, and sent hither swarms of officers to harass our people and eat out their substance.

He has kept among us, in times of peace, standing armies, without the consent of our legislatures.

He has affected to render the military independent of, and superior to, the civil power.

He has combined with others to subject us to a jurisdiction foreign to our constitution, and unacknowledged by our laws, giving his assent to their acts of pretended legislation:

For quartering large bodies of armed troops among us;

For protecting them, by a mock trial, from punishment for any murders which they should commit on the inhabitants of these states;

For cutting off our trade with all parts of the world;

For imposing taxes on us without our consent;

For depriving us, in many cases, of the benefits of trial by jury;

For transporting us beyond seas, to be tried for pretended offenses;

For abolishing the free system of English laws in a neighboring province, establishing therein an arbitrary government, and enlarging its boundaries, so as to render it at once an example and fit instrument for introducing the same absolute rule into these colonies;

For taking away our charters, abolishing our most valuable laws, and altering fundamentally the forms of our governments;

For suspending our own legislatures, and declaring themselves invested with power to legislate for us in all cases whatsoever.

He has abdicated government here, by declaring us out of his protection and waging war against us.

He has plundered our seas, ravaged our coasts, burned our towns, and destroyed the lives of our people.

He is at this time transporting large armies of foreign mercenaries to complete the works of death, desolation, and tyranny already begun with circumstances of cruelty and perfidy scarcely paralleled in the most barbarous ages, and totally unworthy of the head of a civilized nation.

He has constrained our fellow-citizens, taken captive on the high seas, to bear arms against their country, to become the executioners of their friends and brethren, or to fall themselves by their hands.

He has excited domestic insurrection among us, and has endeavored to bring on the inhabitants of our frontiers the merciless Indian savages, whose known rule of warfare is an undistinguished destruction of all ages, sexes, and conditions.

In every stage of these oppressions we have petitioned for redress in the most humble terms; our repeated petitions have been answered only by repeated injury. A prince, whose character is thus marked by every act which may define a tyrant, is unfit to be the ruler of a free people.

Nor have we been wanting in our attentions to our British brethren. We have warned them, from time to time, of attempts by their legislature to extend an unwarrantable jurisdiction over us. We have reminded them of the circumstances of our emigration and settlement here. We have appealed to their native justice and magnanimity; and we have conjured them by the ties of our common kindred, to disavow these usurpations, which would inevitably interrupt our connections and correspondence. They, too, have been deaf to the voice of justice and of consanguinity. We must, therefore, acquiesce in the necessity which denounces our separation, and hold them, as we hold the rest of mankind, enemies in war, in peace friends.

We, therefore, the representatives of the United States of America, in General Congress assembled, appealing to the Supreme Judge of the world for the rectitude of our intentions, do, in the name and by the authority of the good people of these colonies, solemnly publish and declare, that these United Colonies are, and of right ought to be, FREE AND INDEPENDENT STATES; that they are absolved from all allegiance to the British crown, and that all political connection between them and the state of Great Britain is, and ought to be, totally dissolved; and that, as free and independent states, they have full power to levy war, conclude peace, contract alliances, establish commerce, and do all other acts and things which independent states may of right do. And for the support of this declaration, with a firm reliance on the protection of Divine Providence, we mutually pledge to each other our lives, our fortunes, and our sacred honor.

JOHN HANCOCK [*President*]
[*and fifty-five others*]

The Articles of Confederation and Perpetual Union

BETWEEN THE STATES OF NEW HAMPSHIRE, MASSACHUSETTS BAY, RHODE ISLAND AND PROVIDENCE PLANTATIONS, CONNECTICUT, NEW YORK, NEW JERSEY, PENNSYLVANIA, DELAWARE, MARYLAND, VIRGINIA, NORTH CAROLINA, SOUTH CAROLINA, GEORGIA.*

Article 1.

The stile of this confederacy shall be "The United States of America."

Article 2.

Each State retains its sovereignty, freedom and independence, and every power, jurisdiction, and right, which is not by this confederation expressly delegated to the United States, in Congress assembled.

Article 3.

The said states hereby severally enter into a firm league of friendship with each other for their common defence, the security of their liberties and their mutual and general welfare; binding themselves to assist each other against all force offered to, or attacks made upon them, or any of them, on account of religion, sovereignty, trade, or any other pretence whatever.

Article 4.

The better to secure and perpetuate mutual friendship and intercourse among the people of the different states in this union, the free inhabitants of each of these states, paupers, vagabonds, and fugitives from justice excepted, shall be entitled to all privileges and immunities of free citizens in the several states; and the people of each State shall have free ingress and regress to and from any other State, and shall enjoy therein all the privileges of trade and commerce, subject to the same duties, impositions, and restrictions, as the inhabitants thereof respectively; provided, that such restrictions shall not extend so far as to prevent the removal of property, imported into any State, to any other State of which the owner is an inhabitant; provided also, that no imposition, duties, or restriction, shall be laid by any State on the property of the United States, or either of them.

If any person guilty of, or charged with treason, felony, or other high misdemeanor in any State, shall flee from justice and be found in any of the United States, he shall, upon demand of the governor or executive power of the State from which he fled, be delivered up and removed to the State having jurisdiction of his offence.

Full faith and credit shall be given in each of these states to the records, acts, and judicial proceedings of the courts and magistrates of every other State.

Article 5.

For the more convenient management of the general interests of the United States, delegates shall be annually appointed, in such manner as the legislature of each State shall direct, to meet in Congress, on the 1st Monday in November in every year, with a power reserved to each State to recall its delegates, or any of them, at any time within the year, and to send others in their stead for the remainder of the year.

No State shall be represented in Congress by less than two, nor by more than seven members; and no person shall be capable of being a delegate for more than three years in any term of six years; nor shall any person, being a delegate, be capable of holding any office under the United States, for which he, or any other for his benefit, receives any salary, fees, or emolument of any kind.

Each State shall maintain its own delegates in a meeting of the states, and while they act as members of the committee of the states.

In determining questions in the United States, in Congress assembled, each State shall have one vote.

---

*This copy of the final draft of the Articles of Confederation is taken from the *Journals,* 9:907–925, November 15, 1777.

Freedom of speech and debate in Congress shall not be impeached or questioned in any court or place out of Congress: and the members of Congress shall be protected in their persons from arrests and imprisonments, during the time of their going to and from, and attendance on Congress, *except for treason*, felony, or breach of the peace.

Article 6.

No State, without the consent of the United States, in Congress assembled, shall send any embassy to, or receive any embassy from, or enter into any conference, agreement, alliance, or treaty with any king, prince, or state; nor shall any person, holding any office of profit or trust under the United States, or any of them, accept of any present, emolument, office or title, of any kind whatever, from any king, prince, or foreign state; nor shall the United States, in Congress assembled, or any of them, grant any title of nobility.

No two or more states shall enter into any treaty, confederation, or alliance, whatever, between them, without the consent of the United States, in Congress assembled, specifying accurately the purposes for which the same is to be entered into, and how long it shall continue.

No State shall lay any imposts or duties which may interfere with any stipulations in treaties entered into by the United States, in Congress assembled, with any king, prince, or state, in pursuance of any treaties already proposed by Congress to the courts of France and Spain.

No vessels of war shall be kept up in time of peace by any State, except such number only as shall be deemed necessary by the United States, in Congress assembled, for the defence of such State or its trade; nor shall any body of forces be kept up by any State, in time of peace, except such number only as, in the judgment of the United States, in Congress assembled, shall be deemed requisite to garrison the forts necessary for the defence of such State; but every State shall always keep up a well regulated and disciplined militia, sufficiently armed and accoutred, and shall provide, and constantly have ready for use, in public stores, a due number of field pieces and tents, and a proper quantity of arms, ammunition and camp equipage.

No State shall engage in any war without the consent of the United States, in Congress assembled, unless such State be actually invaded by enemies, or shall have received certain advice of a resolution being formed by some nation of Indians to invade such State, and the danger is so imminent as not to admit of a delay till the United States, in Congress assembled, can be consulted; nor shall any State grant commissions to any ships or vessels of war, nor letters of marque or reprisal, except it be after a declaration of war by the United States, in Congress assembled, and then only against the kingdom or state, and the subjects thereof, against which war has been so declared, and under such regulations as shall be established by the United States, in Congress assembled, unless such States be infested by pirates, in which case vessels of war may be fitted out for that occasion, and kept so long as the danger shall continue, or until the United States, in Congress assembled, shall determine otherwise.

Article 7.

When land forces are raised by any State for the common defence, all officers of or under the rank of colonel, shall be appointed by the legislature of each State respectively, by whom such forces shall be raised, or in such manner as such State shall direct; and all vacancies shall be filled up by the State which first made the appointment.

Article 8.

All charges of war and all other expences, that shall be incurred for the common defence or general welfare, and allowed by the United States, in Congress assembled, shall be defrayed out of a common treasury, which shall be supplied by the several states, in proportion to the value of all land within each State, granted to or surveyed for any person, as such land and the buildings and improvements thereon shall be estimated according to such mode as the United States, in Congress assembled, shall, from time to time, direct and appoint.

The taxes for paying that proportion shall be laid and levied by the authority and direction of the legislatures of the several states, within the time agreed upon by the United States, in Congress assembled.

Article 9.

The United States, in Congress assembled, shall have the sole and exclusive right and power of determining on peace and war, except in the cases mentioned in the 6th article; of sending and receiving ambassadors; entering into treaties and alliances, provided that no treaty of commerce shall be made, whereby the legislative power of the respective states shall be restrained from imposing such imposts and duties on foreigners as their own people are subjected to, or from prohibiting the exportation or importation of any species of goods or commodities whatsoever; of establishing rules for deciding, in all cases, what captures on land or water shall be legal, and in what manner prizes, taken by land or naval forces in the service of the United States, shall be divided or appropriated; of granting letters of marque and reprisal in times of peace; appointing courts for the trial of piracies and felonies committed on the high seas, and establishing courts for receiving and determining, finally, appeals in all cases of captures; provided, that no member of Congress shall be appointed a judge of any of the said courts.

The United States, in Congress assembled, shall also be the last resort on appeal in all disputes and differences now subsisting, or that hereafter may arise between two or more states concerning boundary, jurisdiction or any other cause whatever; which authority shall always be exercised in the manner following: whenever the legislative or executive authority, or lawful agent of any State, in controversy with another, shall present a petition to Congress, stating the matter in question, and praying for a hearing, notice thereof shall be given, by order of Congress, to the legislative or executive authority of the other State in controversy, and a day assigned for the appearance of the parties by their lawful agents, who shall then be directed to appoint, by joint consent, commissioners or judges to constitute a court for hearing and determining the matter in question; but, if they cannot agree, Congress shall name three persons out of each of the United States, and from the list of such persons each party shall alternately strike out one, in the petitioners beginning, until the number shall be reduced to thirteen; and from that number not less than seven, nor more than nine names, as Congress shall direct, shall, in the presence of Congress, be drawn out by lot; and the persons whose names shall be drawn, or any five of them, shall be commissioners or judges to hear and finally determine the controversy, so always

as a major part of the judges who shall hear the cause shall agree in the determination; and if either party shall neglect to attend at the day appointed, without shewing reasons which Congress shall judge sufficient, or, being present, shall refuse to strike, the Congress shall proceed to nominate three persons out of each State, and the secretary of Congress shall strike in behalf of such party absent or refusing; and the judgment and sentence of the court to be appointed, in the manner before prescribed, shall be final and conclusive; and if any of the parties shall refuse to submit to the authority of such court, or to appear or defend their claim or cause, the court shall nevertheless proceed to pronounce sentence or judgment, which shall, in like manner, be final and decisive, the judgment or sentence and other proceedings being, in either case, transmitted to Congress, and lodged among the acts of Congress for the security of the parties concerned: provided, that every commissioner, before he sits in judgment, shall take an oath, to be administered by one of the judges of the supreme or superior court of the State where the cause shall be tried, "well and truly to hear and determine the matter in question, according to the best of his judgment, without favour, affection, or hope of reward": provided, also, that no State shall be deprived of territory for the benefit of the United States.

All controversies concerning the private right of soil, claimed under different grants of two or more states, whose jurisdictions, as they may respect such lands and the states which passed such grants, are adjusted, the said grants, or either of them, being at the same time claimed to have originated antecedent to such settlement of jurisdiction, shall, on the petition of either party to the Congress of the United States, be finally determined, as near as may be, in the same manner as is before prescribed for deciding disputes respecting territorial jurisdiction between different states.

The United States, in Congress assembled, shall also have the sole and exclusive right and power of regulating the alloy and value of coin struck by their own authority, or by that of the respective states; fixing the standard of weights and measures throughout the United States; regulating the trade and managing all affairs with the Indians not members of any of the states; provided that the legislative right of any State within its own limits be not infringed or violated; establishing and regulating post offices from one State to another throughout all the United States, and exacting such postage on the papers passing through the same as may be requisite to defray the expences of the said office; appointing all officers of the land forces in the service of the United States, excepting regimental officers; appointing all the officers of the naval forces, and commissioning all officers whatever in the service of the United States; making rules for the government and regulation of the said land and naval forces, and directing their operations.

The United States, in Congress assembled, shall have authority to appoint a committee to sit in the recess of Congress, to be denominated "a Committee of the States," and to consist of one delegate from each State, and to appoint such other committees and civil officers as may be necessary for managing the general affairs of the United States, under their direction; to appoint one of their number to preside; provided that no person be allowed to serve in the office of president more than one year in any term of three years; to ascertain the necessary sums of money to be raised for the service of the United States, and to appropriate and apply the same for defraying the public expences; to borrow money or emit bills on the credit of the United States, transmitting, every half year, to the respective states, an account of the sums of money so borrowed or emitted; to build and equip a navy; to agree upon the number of land forces, and to make requisitions from each State for its quota, in proportion to the number of white inhabitants in such State; which requisitions shall be binding; and, thereupon, the legislature of each State shall appoint the regimental officers, raise the men, and cloathe, arm, and equip them in a soldier-like manner, at the expence of the United States; and the officers and men so cloathed, armed, and equipped, shall march to the place appointed and within the time agreed on by the United States, in Congress assembled; but if the United States, in Congress assembled, shall, on consideration of circumstances, judge proper that any State should not raise men, or should raise a smaller number than its quota, and that any other State should raise a greater number of men than the quota thereof, such extra number shall be raised, officered, cloathed, armed, and equipped in the same manner as the quota of such State, unless the legislature of such State shall judge that such

extra number cannot be safely spared out of the same, in which case they shall raise, officer, cloathe, arm, and equip as many of such extra number as they judge can be safely spared. And the officers and men so cloathed, armed, and equipped, shall march to the place appointed and within the time agreed on by the United States, in Congress assembled.

The United States, in Congress assembled, shall never engage in a war, nor grant letters of marque and reprisal in time of peace, nor enter into any treaties or alliances, nor coin money, nor regulate the value thereof, nor ascertain the sums and expences necessary for the defence and welfare of the United States, or any of them: nor emit bills, nor borrow money on the credit of the United States, nor appropriate money, nor agree upon the number of vessels of war to be built or purchased, or the number of land or sea forces to be raised, nor appoint a commander in chief of the army or navy, unless nine states assent to the same; nor shall a question on any other point, except for adjourning from day to day, be determined, unless by the votes of a majority of the United States, in Congress assembled.

The Congress of the United States shall have power to adjourn to any time within the year, and to any place within the United States, so that no period of adjournment be for a longer duration than the space of six months, and shall publish the journal of their proceedings monthly, except such parts thereof, relating to treaties, alliances or military operations, as, in their judgment, require secrecy; and the yeas and nays of the delegates of each State on any question shall be entered on the journal, when it is desired by any delegate; and the delegates of a State, or any of them, at his, or their request, shall be furnished with a transcript of the said journal, except such parts as are above excepted, to lay before the legislatures of the several states.

Article 10.

The committee of the states, or any nine of them, shall be authorized to execute, in the recess of Congress, such of the powers of Congress as the United States, in Congress assembled, by the consent of nine states, shall, from time to time, think expedient to vest them with; provided, that no power be delegated to the said committee for the exercise of which, by the articles of confederation, the voice of nine states, in the Congress of the United States assembled, is requisite.

Article 11.

Canada acceding to this confederation, and joining in the measures of the United States, shall be admitted into and entitled to all the advantages of this union; but no other colony shall be admitted into the same, unless such admission be agreed to by nine states.

Article 12.

All bills of credit emitted, monies borrowed and debts contracted by, or under the authority of Congress before the assembling of the United States, in pursuance of the present confederation, shall be deemed and considered as a charge against the United States, for payment and satisfaction whereof the said United States and the public faith are hereby solemnly pledged.

Article 13.

Every State shall abide by the determinations of the United States, in Congress assembled, on all questions which, by this confederation, are submitted to them. And the articles of this confederation shall be inviolably observed by every State, and the union shall be perpetual; nor shall any alteration at any time hereafter be made in any of them, unless such alteration be agreed to in a Congress of the United States, and be afterwards confirmed by the legislatures of every State.

These articles shall be proposed to the legislatures of all the United States, to be considered, and if approved of by them, they are advised to authorize their delegates to ratify the same in the Congress of the United States; which being done, the same shall become conclusive.

Constitution of the United States of America

PREAMBLE

We the people of the United States, in order to form a more perfect union, establish justice, insure domestic tranquillity, provide for the common defense, promote the general welfare, and secure the blessings of liberty to ourselves and our posterity, do ordain and establish this CONSTITUTION for the United States of America.

Article I

Section 1. All legislative powers herein granted shall be vested in a Congress of the United States, which shall consist of a Senate and a House of Representatives.

Section 2. The House of Representatives shall be composed of members chosen every second year by the people of the several States, and the electors in each State shall have the qualifications requisite for electors of the most numerous branch of the State Legislature.

No person shall be a Representative who shall not have attained to the age of twenty-five years, and been seven years a citizen of the United States, and who shall not, when elected, be an inhabitant of that State in which he shall be chosen.

Representatives and direct taxes shall be apportioned among the several States which may be included within this Union, according to their respective numbers, *which shall be determined by adding to the whole number of free persons, including those bound to service for a term of years and excluding Indians not taxed, three-fifths of all other persons.* The actual enumeration shall be made within three years after the first meeting of the Congress of the United States, and within every subsequent term of ten years, in such manner as they shall by law direct. The number of Representatives shall not exceed one for every thirty thousand, but each State shall have at least one Representative; *and until such enumeration shall be made, the State of New Hampshire shall be entitled to choose three, Massachusetts eight, Rhode Island*

and Providence Plantations one, Connecticut five, New York six, New Jersey four, Pennsylvania eight, Delaware one, Maryland six, Virginia ten, North Carolina five, South Carolina five, and Georgia three.

When vacancies happen in the representation from any State, the Executive authority thereof shall issue writs of election to fill such vacancies.

The House of Representatives shall choose their Speaker and other officers; and shall have the sole power of impeachment.

Section 3. The Senate of the United States shall be composed of two Senators from each State, *chosen by the legislature thereof,* for six years; and each Senator shall have one vote.

Immediately after they shall be assembled in consequence of the first election, they shall be divided as equally as may be into three classes. The seats of the Senators of the first class shall be vacated at the expiration of the second year, of the second class at the expiration of the fourth year, and of the third class at the expiration of the sixth year, so that one-third may be chosen every second year; *and if vacancies happen by resignation or otherwise, during the recess of the legislature of any State, the Executive thereof may make temporary appointments until the next meeting of the legislature, which shall then fill such vacancies.*

No person shall be a Senator who shall not have attained to the age of thirty years, and been nine years a citizen of the United States, and who shall not, when elected, be an inhabitant of that State for which he shall be chosen.

The Vice President of the United States shall be President of the Senate, but shall have no vote, unless they be equally divided.

Note: Passages that are no longer in effect are printed in italic type.

The Senate shall choose their other officers, and also a President *pro tempore,* in the absence of the Vice President, or when he shall exercise the office of the President of the United States.

The Senate shall have the sole power to try all impeachments. When sitting for that purpose, they shall be on oath or affirmation. When the President of the United States is tried, the Chief Justice shall preside: and no person shall be convicted without the concurrence of two-thirds of the members present.

Judgment in cases of impeachment shall not extend further than to removal from the office, and disqualification to hold and enjoy any office of honor, trust or profit under the United States; but the party convicted shall nevertheless be liable and subject to indictment, trial, judgment and punishment, according to law.

Section 4.   The times, places and manner of holding elections for Senators and Representatives shall be prescribed in each State by the legislature thereof; but the Congress may at any time by law make or alter such regulations, except as to the places of choosing Senators.

The Congress shall assemble at least once in every year, and such meeting *shall be on the first Monday in December, unless they shall by law appoint a different day.*

Section 5.   Each house shall be the judge of the elections, returns and qualifications of its own members, and a majority of each shall constitute a quorum to do business; but a smaller number may adjourn from day to day, and may be authorized to compel the attendance of absent members, in such manner, and under such penalties, as each house may provide.

Each house may determine the rules of its proceedings, punish its members for disorderly behavior, and with the concurrence of two-thirds, expel a member.

Each house shall keep a journal of its proceedings, and from time to time publish the same, excepting such parts as may in their judgment require secrecy; and the yeas and nays of the members of either house on any question shall, at the desire of one-fifth of those present, be entered on the journal.

Neither house, during the session of Congress, shall, without the consent of the other, adjourn for more than three days, nor to any other place than that in which the two houses shall be sitting.

Section 6.   The Senators and Representatives shall receive a compensation for their services, to be ascertained by law and paid out of the treasury of the United States. They shall in all cases except treason, felony and breach of the peace, be privileged from arrest during their attendance at the session of their respective houses, and in going to and returning from the same; and for any speech or debate in either house, they shall not be questioned in any other place.

No Senator or Representative shall, during the time for which he was elected, be appointed to any civil office under the authority of the United States, which shall have been created, or the emoluments whereof shall have been increased, during such time; and no person holding any office under the United States shall be a member of either house during his continuance in office.

Section 7.   All bills for raising revenue shall originate in the House of Representatives; but the Senate may propose or concur with amendments as on other bills.

Every bill which shall have passed the House of Representatives and the Senate, shall, before it become a law, be presented to the President of the United States; if he approve he shall sign it, but if not he shall return it with objections to that house in which it originated, who shall enter the objections at large on their journal, and proceed to reconsider it. If after such reconsideration two-thirds of that house shall agree to pass the bill, it shall be sent, together with the objections, to the other house, by which it shall likewise be reconsidered, and, if approved by two-thirds of that house, it shall become a law. But in all such cases the votes of both houses shall be determined by yeas and nays, and the names of the persons voting for and against the bill shall be entered on the journal of each house respectively. If any bill shall not be returned by the President within ten days (Sundays excepted) after it shall have been presented to him, the same shall be a law, in like manner as if he had signed it, unless the Congress by their adjournment prevent its return, in which case it shall not be a law.

Every order, resolution, or vote to which the concurrence of the Senate and House of Representatives may be necessary (except on a question of adjournment) shall be presented to the President of the United States; and before the same shall take effect, shall be approved by him, or being disapproved by him, shall be repassed by two-thirds of the Senate and House of Representatives, according to the rules and limitations prescribed in the case of a bill.

Section 8.   The Congress shall have power

To lay and collect taxes, duties, imposts, and excises, to pay the debts and provide for the common defense and general welfare of the United States; but all duties, imposts and excises shall be uniform throughout the United States;

To borrow money on the credit of the United States;

To regulate commerce with foreign nations, and among the several States, and with the Indian tribes;

To establish an uniform rule of naturalization, and uniform laws on the subject of bankruptcies throughout the United States;

To coin money, regulate the value thereof, and of foreign coin, and fix the standard of weights and measures;

To provide for the punishment of counterfeiting the securities and current coin of the United States;

To establish post offices and post roads;

To promote the progress of science and useful arts by securing for limited times to authors and inventors the exclusive right to their respective writings and discoveries;

To constitute tribunals inferior to the Supreme Court;

To define and punish piracies and felonies committed on the high seas and offenses against the law of nations;

To declare war, grant letters of marque and reprisal, and make rules concerning captures on land and water;

To raise and support armies, but no appropriation of money to that use shall be for a longer term than two years;

To provide and maintain a navy;

To make rules for the government and regulation of the land and naval forces;

To provide for calling forth the militia to execute the laws of the Union, suppress insurrections, and repel invasions;

To provide for organizing, arming, and disciplining the militia, and for governing such part of them as may be employed in the service of the United States, reserving to the States respectively the appointment of the officers, and the authority of training the militia according to the discipline prescribed by Congress;

To exercise exclusive legislation in all cases whatsoever, over such district (not exceeding ten miles square) as may, by cession of particular States, and the acceptance of Congress, become the seat of government of the United States, and to exercise like authority over all places purchased by the consent of the legislature of the State, in which the same shall be, for erection of forts, magazines, arsenals, dock-yards, and other needful buildings;—and

To make all laws which shall be necessary and proper for carrying into execution the foregoing powers, and all other powers vested by this Constitution in the government of the United States, or in any department or officer thereof.

Section 9.   *The migration or importation of such persons as any of the States now existing shall think proper to admit shall not be prohibited by the Congress prior to the year 1808; but a tax or duty may be imposed on such importation, not exceeding $10 for each person.*

The privilege of the writ of habeas corpus shall not be suspended, unless when in cases of rebellion or invasion the public safety may require it.

No bill of attainder or ex post facto law shall be passed.

No capitation, or other direct, tax shall be laid, unless in proportion to the census or enumeration herein before directed to be taken.

No tax or duty shall be laid on articles exported from any State.

No preference shall be given by any regulation of commerce or revenue to the ports of one State over those of another; nor shall vessels bound to, or from, one State, be obliged to enter, clear, or pay duties in another.

No money shall be drawn from the treasury, but in consequence of appropriations made by law; and a regular statement and account of the receipts and expenditures of all public money shall be published from time to time.

No title of nobility shall be granted by the United States: and no person holding any office of profit or trust under them, shall, without the consent of the Congress, accept of any present, emolument, office, or title, of any kind whatever, from any king, prince, or foreign state.

Section 10.   No State shall enter into any treaty, alliance, or confederation; grant letters of marque and reprisal; coin money; emit bills of credit; make anything but gold and silver coin a tender in payment of debts; pass any bill of attainder, ex post facto law, or law impairing the obligation of contracts, or grant any title of nobility.

No State shall, without the consent of Congress, lay any imposts or duties on imports or exports, except what may be absolutely necessary for executing its inspection laws: and the net produce of all duties and imposts, laid by any State on imports or exports, shall be for the use of the treasury of the United States; and all such laws shall be subject to the revision and control of the Congress.

No State shall, without the consent of Congress, lay any duty of tonnage, keep troops or ships of war in time of peace, enter into any agreement or compact with another State, or with a foreign power, or engage in war, unless actually invaded, or in such imminent danger as will not admit of delay.

Article II

Section 1.   The executive power shall be vested in a President of the United States of America. He shall hold his office during the term of four years, and, together with the Vice President, chosen for the same term, be elected as follows:

Each state shall appoint, in such manner as the legislature thereof may direct, a number of electors, equal to the whole number of Senators and Representatives to which the State may be entitled in the Congress; but no Senator or Representative, or person holding an office of trust or profit under the United States, shall be appointed an elector.

The electors shall meet in their respective States, and vote by ballot for two persons, of whom one at least shall not be an inhabitant of the same State with themselves. And they shall make a list of all the persons voted for, and of the number of votes for each; which list they shall sign and certify, and transmit sealed to the seat of government of the United States, directed to the President of the Senate. The President of the Senate shall, in the presence of the Senate and the House of Representatives, open all the certificates, and the votes shall then be counted. The person having the greatest number of votes shall be the President, if such number be a majority of the whole number of electors appointed; and if there be more than one who have such majority, and have an equal number of votes, then the House of Representatives shall immediately choose by ballot one of them for President; and if no person have a majority, then from the five highest on the list said house shall in like manner choose the President. But in choosing the President the votes shall be taken by States, the representation from each State having one vote; a quorum for this purpose shall consist of a member or members from two-thirds of the States, and a majority of all the States shall be necessary to a choice. In every case, after the choice of the President, the person having the greatest number of votes of the electors shall be the Vice President. But if there should remain two or more who have equal votes, the Senate shall choose from them by ballot the Vice President.

The Congress may determine the time of choosing the electors and the day on which they shall give their votes; which day shall be the same throughout the United States.

No person except a natural-born citizen, *or a citizen of the United States at the time of the adoption of this Constitution,* shall be eligible to the office of President; neither shall any person be eligible to that office who shall not have attained to the age of thirty-five years, and been fourteen years a resident within the United States.

In case of the removal of the President from office or of his death, resignation, or inability to discharge the powers and duties of the said office, the same shall devolve on the Vice President, and the Congress may by law provide for the case of removal, death, resignation, or inability, both of the President and Vice President, declaring what officer shall then act as President, and such officer shall act accordingly, until the disability be removed, or a President shall be elected.

The President shall, at stated times, receive for his services a compensation, which shall neither be increased nor diminished during the period for which he shall have been elected, and he shall not receive within that period any other emolument from the United States, or any of them.

Before he enter on the execution of his office, he shall take the following oath or affirmation:— "I do solemnly swear (or affirm) that I will faithfully execute the office of the President of the United States, and will to the best of my ability preserve, protect and defend the Constitution of the United States."

Section 2. The President shall be commander in chief of the army and navy of the United States, and of the militia of the several States, when called into the actual service of the United States; he may require the opinion, in writing, of the principal officer in each of the executive departments, upon any subject relating to the duties of their respective offices, and he shall have power to grant reprieves and pardons for offenses against the United States, except in cases of impeachment.

He shall have power, by and with the advice and consent of the Senate, to make treaties, provided two-thirds of the Senators present concur; and he shall nominate, and by and with the advice and consent of the Senate, shall appoint ambassadors, other public ministers and consuls, judges of the Supreme Court, and all other officers of the United States, whose appointments are not herein otherwise provided for, and which shall be established by law: but Congress may by law vest the appointment of such inferior officers, as they think proper, in the President alone, in the courts of law, or in the heads of departments.

The President shall have power to fill up all vacancies that may happen during the recess of the Senate, by granting commissions which shall expire at the end of their next session.

Section 3. He shall from time to time give to the Congress information of the state of the Union, and recommend to their consideration such mea-

sures as he shall judge necessary and expedient; he may, on extraordinary occasions, convene both houses, or either of them, and in case of disagreement between them, with respect to the time of adjournment, he may adjourn them to such time as he shall think proper; he shall receive ambassadors and other public ministers; he shall take care that the laws be faithfully executed, and shall commission all the officers of the United States.

Section 4. The President, Vice President and all civil officers of the United States shall be removed from office on impeachment for, and on conviction of, treason, bribery, or other high crimes and misdemeanors.

Article III

Section 1. The judicial power of the United States shall be vested in one Supreme Court, and in such inferior courts as the Congress may from time to time ordain and establish. The judges, both of the Supreme and inferior courts, shall hold their offices during good behavior, and shall, at stated times, receive for their services a compensation which shall not be diminished during their continuance in office.

Section 2. The judicial power shall extend to all cases, in law and equity, arising under this Constitution, the laws of the United States, and treaties made, or which shall be made, under their authority;—to all cases affecting ambassadors, other public ministers and consuls;—to all cases of admiralty and maritime jurisdiction;—to controversies to which the United States shall be a party;—to controversies between two or more States; —*between a State and citizens of another State;*—between citizens of different States;—between citizens of the same State claiming lands under grants of different States, and between a State, or the citizens thereof, and foreign states, citizens or subjects.

In all cases affecting ambassadors, other public ministers and consuls, and those in which a State shall be party, the Supreme Court shall have original jurisdiction. In all the other cases before mentioned, the Supreme Court shall have appellate jurisdiction, both as to law and fact, with such exceptions, and under such regulations, as the Congress shall make.

The trial of all crimes, except in cases of impeachment, shall be by jury; and such trial shall be held in the State where said crimes shall have been committed; but when not committed within any State, the trial shall be at such place or places as the Congress may by law have directed.

Section 3.   Treason against the United States shall consist only in levying war against them, or in adhering to their enemies, giving them aid and comfort. No person shall be convicted of treason unless on the testimony of two witnesses to the same overt act, or on confession in open court.

The Congress shall have power to declare the punishment of treason, but no attainder of treason shall work corruption of blood, or forfeiture except during the life of the person attainted.

Article IV

Section 1.   Full faith and credit shall be given in each State to the public acts, records, and judicial proceedings of every other State. And the Congress may by general laws prescribe the manner in which such acts, records, and proceedings shall be proved, and the effect thereof.

Section 2.   The citizens of each State shall be entitled to all privileges and immunities of citizens in the several States.

A person charged in any State with treason, felony, or other crime, who shall flee from justice, and be found in another State, shall on demand of the executive authority of the State from which he fled, be delivered up, to be removed to the State having jurisdiction of the crime.

No person held to service or labor in one State, under the laws thereof, escaping into another, shall, in consequence of any law or regulation therein, be discharged from such service or labor, but shall be delivered up on claim of the party to whom such service or labor may be due.

Section 3.   New States may be admitted by the Congress into this Union; but no new State shall be formed or erected within the jurisdiction of any other State; nor any State be formed by the junction of two or more States, or parts of States, without the consent of the legislatures of the States concerned as well as of the Congress.

The Congress shall have power to dispose of and make all needful rules and regulations respecting the territory or other property belonging to the United States; and nothing in this Constitution shall be so construed as to prejudice any claims of the United States, or of any particular State.

Section 4.   The United States shall guarantee to every State in this Union a republican form of government, and shall protect each of them against invasion; and on application of the legislature, or of the executive (when the legislature cannot be convened), against domestic violence.

Article V

The Congress, whenever two-thirds of both houses shall deem it necessary, shall propose amendments to this Constitution, or, on the application of the legislatures of two-thirds of the several States, shall call a convention for proposing amendments, which, in either case, shall be valid to all intents and purposes, as part of this Constitution, when ratified by the legislatures of three-fourths of the several States, or by conventions in three-fourths thereof, as the one or the other mode of ratification may be proposed by the Congress; provided *that no amendments which may be made prior to the year one thousand eight hundred and eight shall in any manner affect the first and fourth clauses in the ninth section of the first article;* and that no State, without its consent, shall be deprived of its equal suffrage in the Senate.

Article VI

All debts contracted and engagements entered into, before the adoption of this Constitution, shall be as valid against the United States under this Constitution, as under the Confederation.

This Constitution, and the laws of the United States which shall be made in pursuance thereof; and all treaties made, or which shall be made, under the authority of the United States, shall be the supreme law of the land; and the judges in every State shall be bound thereby, anything in the Constitution or laws of any State to the contrary notwithstanding.

The Senators and Representatives before mentioned, and the members of the several State legislatures, and all executive and judicial officers, both of the United States and of the several States, shall be bound by oath or affirmation to support this Constitution; but no religious test shall ever be required as a qualification to any office or public trust under the United States.

Article VII

The ratification of the conventions of nine States shall be sufficient for the establishment of this Constitution between the States so ratifying the same.

Done in Convention by the unanimous consent of the States present, the seventeenth day of Sep-

tember in the year of our Lord one thousand seven hundred and eighty-seven and of the Independence of the United States of America the twelfth. In witness whereof we have hereunto subscribed our names.

[Signed by]
G° WASHINGTON
Presidt and Deputy from Virginia
[*and thirty-eight others*]

Amendments to the Constitution

Article I*

Congress shall make no law respecting an establishment of religion, or prohibiting the free exercise thereof; or abridging the freedom of speech, or of the press; or the right of the people peaceably to assemble, and to petition the government for a redress of grievances.

Article II

A well-regulated militia being necessary to the security of a free State, the right of the people to keep and bear arms shall not be infringed.

Article III

No soldier shall, in time of peace, be quartered in any house without the consent of the owner, nor in time of war, but in a manner to be prescribed by law.

Article IV

The right of the people to be secure in their persons, houses, papers, and effects, against unreasonable searches and seizures, shall not be violated, and no warrants shall issue but upon probable cause, supported by oath or affirmation, and particularly describing the place to be searched, and the persons or things to be seized.

*The first ten Amendments (Bill of Rights) were adopted in 1791.

Article V

No person shall be held to answer for a capital, or otherwise infamous crime, unless on a presentment or indictment of a grand jury, except in cases arising in the land or naval forces, or in the militia, when in actual service in time of war or public danger; nor shall any person be subject for the same offense to be twice put in jeopardy of life or limb; nor shall be compelled in any criminal case to be a witness against himself, nor be deprived of life, liberty, or property, without due process of law; nor shall private property be taken for public use without just compensation.

Article VI

In all criminal prosecutions, the accused shall enjoy the right to a speedy and public trial, by an impartial jury of the State and district wherein the crime shall have been committed, which district shall have been previously ascertained by law, and to be informed of the nature and cause of the accusation; to be confronted with the witnesses against him; to have compulsory process for obtaining witnesses in his favor, and to have the assistance of counsel for his defense.

Article VII

In suits at common law, where the value in controversy shall exceed twenty dollars, the right of trial by jury shall be preserved, and no fact tried by a jury shall be otherwise reexamined in any court of the United States, than according to the rules of the common law.

Article VIII

Excessive bail shall not be required, nor excessive fines imposed, nor cruel and unusual punishments inflicted.

Article IX

The enumeration in the Constitution, of certain rights, shall not be construed to deny or disparage others retained by the people.

Article X

The powers not delegated to the United States by the Constitution, nor prohibited by it to the States, are reserved to the States respectively, or to the people.

Article XI

[*Adopted 1798*]

The judicial power of the United States shall not be construed to extend to any suit in law or equity, commenced or prosecuted against one of the United States by citizens of another State, or by citizens or subjects of any foreign state.

Article XII

[*Adopted 1804*]

The electors shall meet in their respective States, and vote by ballot for President and Vice President, one of whom, at least, shall not be an inhabitant of the same State with themselves; they shall name in their ballots the person voted for as President, and in distinct ballots the person voted for as Vice President, and they shall make distinct lists of all persons voted for as President, and of all persons voted for as Vice President, and of the number of votes for each, which lists they shall sign and certify, and transmit sealed to the seat of government of the United States, directed to the President of the Senate;—the President of the Senate shall, in the presence of the Senate and House of Representatives, open all the certificates and the votes shall then be counted;—the person having the greatest number of votes for President shall be the President, if such number be a majority of the whole number of electors appointed; and if no person have such majority, then from the persons having

the highest numbers not exceeding three on the list of those voted for as President, the House of Representatives shall choose immediately, by ballot, the President. But in choosing the President, the votes shall be taken by States, the representation from each State having one vote; a quorum for this purpose shall consist of a member or members from two-thirds of the States, and a majority of all the States shall be necessary to a choice. And if the House of Representatives shall not choose a President whenever the right of choice shall devolve upon them, before *the fourth day of March* next following, then the Vice President shall act as President, as in the case of the death or other constitutional disability of the President.

The person having the greatest number of votes as Vice President shall be the Vice President, if such a number be a majority of the whole number of electors appointed; and if no person have a majority, then from the two highest numbers on the list the Senate shall choose the Vice President; a quorum for the purpose shall consist of two-thirds of the whole number of Senators, and a majority of the whole number shall be necessary to a choice. But no person constitutionally ineligible to the office of President shall be eligible to that of Vice President of the United States.

Article XIII

[*Adopted 1865*]

Section 1.   Neither slavery nor involuntary servitude, except as a punishment for crime whereof the party shall have been duly convicted, shall exist within the United States, or any place subject to their jurisdiction.

Section 2.   Congress shall have power to enforce this article by appropriate legislation.

Article XIV

[*Adopted 1868*]

Section 1.   All persons born or naturalized in the United States, and subject to the jurisdiction thereof, are citizens of the United States and of the State wherein they reside. No State shall make or enforce any law which shall abridge the privileges or immunities of citizens of the United States; nor shall any State deprive any person of life, liberty, or property, without due process of law; nor deny to any person within its jurisdiction the equal protection of the laws.

Section 2. Representatives shall be apportioned among the several States according to their respective numbers, counting the whole number of persons in each State, excluding Indians not taxed. But when the right to vote at any election for the choice of Electors for President and Vice President of the United States, Representatives in Congress, the executive and judicial officers of a State, or the members of the legislature thereof, is denied to any of the male inhabitants of such State, being twenty-one years of age and citizens of the United States, or in any way abridged, except for participation in rebellion, or other crime, the basis of representation therein shall be reduced in the proportion which the number of such male citizens shall bear to the whole number of male citizens twenty-one years of age in such State.

Section 3. No person shall be a Senator or Representative in Congress or Elector of President and Vice President, or hold any office, civil or military, under the United States, or under any State, who, having previously taken an oath, as a member of Congress, or as an officer of the United States, or as a member of any State legislature, or as an executive or judicial officer of any State, to support the Constitution of the United States, shall have engaged in insurrection or rebellion against the same, or given aid and comfort to the enemies thereof. Congress may, by a vote of two-thirds of each house, remove such disability.

Section 4. The validity of the public debt of the United States, authorized by law, including debts incurred for payment of pensions and bounties for services in suppressing insurrection or rebellion, shall not be questioned. But neither the United States nor any State shall assume or pay any debt or obligation incurred in aid of insurrection or rebellion against the United States, or any claim for the loss or emancipation of any slave; but all such debts, obligations, and claims shall be held illegal and void.

Section 5. The Congress shall have the power to enforce, by appropriate legislation, the provisions of this article.

Article XV
[*Adopted 1870*]

Section 1. The right of citizens of the United States to vote shall not be denied or abridged by the United States or by any State on account of race, color, or previous condition of servitude.

Section 2. The Congress shall have power to enforce this article by appropriate legislation.

Article XVI
[*Adopted 1913*]

The Congress shall have power to lay and collect taxes on incomes, from whatever source derived, without apportionment among the several States, and without regard to any census or enumeration.

Article XVII
[*Adopted 1913*]

Section 1. The Senate of the United States shall be composed of two Senators from each State, elected by the people thereof, for six years; and each Senator shall have one vote. The electors in each State shall have the qualifications requisite for electors of [voters for] the most numerous branch of the State legislatures.

Section 2. When vacancies happen in the representation of any State in the Senate, the executive authority of such State shall issue writs of election to fill such vacancies: Provided, that the Legislature of any State may empower the executive thereof to make temporary appointments until the people fill the vacancies by election as the Legislature may direct.

Section 3. This amendment shall not be so construed as to affect the election or term of any Senator chosen before it becomes valid as part of the Constitution.

Article XVIII
[*Adopted 1919; repealed 1933*]

Section 1. *After one year from the ratification of this article the manufacture, sale, or transportation of intoxicating liquors within, the importation* *thereof into, or the exportation thereof from the United States and all territory subject to the jurisdiction thereof, for beverage purposes, is hereby prohibited.*

Section 2.   *The Congress and the several States shall have concurrent power to enforce this article by appropriate legislation.*

Section 3.   *This article shall be inoperative unless it shall have been ratified as an amendment to the Constitution by the legislatures of the several States, as provided by the Constitution, within seven years from the date of the submission thereof to the States by the Congress.*

Article XIX
[*Adopted 1920*]

Section 1.   The right of citizens of the United States to vote shall not be denied or abridged by the United States or by any State on account of sex.

Section 2.   The Congress shall have the power to enforce this article by appropriate legislation.

Article XX
[*Adopted 1933*]

Section 1.   The terms of the President and Vice President shall end at noon on the 20th day of January, and the terms of Senators and Representatives at noon on the 3d day of January, of the years in which such terms would have ended if this article had not been ratified; and the terms of their successors shall then begin.

Section 2.   The Congress shall assemble at least once in every year, and such meeting shall begin at noon on the 3d of January, unless they shall by law appoint a different day.

Section 3.   If, at the time fixed for the beginning of the term of the President, the President-elect shall have died, the Vice President-elect shall become President. If a President shall not have been chosen before the time fixed for the beginning of his term, or if the President-elect shall have failed to qualify, then the Vice President-elect shall act as President until a President shall have qualified; and the Congress may by law provide for the case wherein neither a President-elect nor a Vice President-elect shall

have qualified, declaring who shall then act as President, or the manner in which one who is to act shall be selected, and such persons shall act accordingly until a President or Vice President shall have qualified.

Section 4.   The Congress may by law provide for the case of the death of any of the persons from whom the House of Representatives may choose a President whenever the right of choice shall have devolved upon them, and for the case of the death of any of the persons from whom the Senate may choose a Vice President whenever the right of choice shall have devolved upon them.

Section 5.   Sections 1 and 2 shall take effect on the 15th day of October following the ratification of this article.

Section 6.   This article shall be inoperative unless it shall have been ratified as an amendment to the Constitution by the Legislatures of three-fourths of the several States within seven years from the date of its submission.

Article XXI
[*Adopted 1933*]

Section 1.   The eighteenth article of amendment to the Constitution of the United States is hereby repealed.

Section 2.   The transportation or importation into any State, Territory, or Possession of the United States for delivery or use therein of intoxicating liquors, in violation of the laws thereof, is hereby prohibited.

Section 3.   This article shall be inoperative unless it shall have been ratified as an amendment to the Constitution by conventions in the several States, as provided in the Constitution, within seven years from the date of submission thereof to the States by the Congress.

Article XXII
[*Adopted 1951*]

Section 1.   No person shall be elected to the office of President more than twice, and no person who has held the office of President, or acted as President, for more than two years of a term to which some other person was elected President shall be elected to the office of President more than once. But this article shall not apply to any person holding the office of President when this article was proposed by the Congress, and shall not prevent any person who may be holding the office of President, or acting as President, during the term within which this article becomes operative from holding the office of President or acting as President during the remainder of such term.

Section 2. This article shall be inoperative unless it shall have been ratified as an amendment to the Constitution by the legislatures of three-fourths of the several States within seven years from the date of its submission to the States by the Congress.

Article XXIII
[*Adopted 1961*]

Section 1. The District constituting the seat of Government of the United States shall appoint in such manner as the Congress may direct:

A number of electors of President and Vice President equal to the whole number of Senators and Representatives in Congress to which the District would be entitled if it were a State, but in no event more than the least populous State; they shall be in addition to those appointed by the States, but they shall be considered for the purposes of the election of President and Vice President, to be electors appointed by a State; and they shall meet in the District and perform such duties as provided by the twelfth article of amendment.

Section 2. The Congress shall have the power to enforce this article by appropriate legislation.

Article XXIV
[*Adopted 1964*]

Section 1. The right of citizens of the United States to vote in any primary or other election for President or Vice President, for electors for President or Vice President, or for Senator or Representative in Congress, shall not be denied or abridged by the United States or any State by reason of failure to pay any poll tax or other tax.

Section 2. The Congress shall have the power to enforce this article by appropriate legislation.

Article XXV
[*Adopted 1967*]

Section 1. In case of the removal of the President from office or of his death or resignation, the Vice President shall become President.

Section 2. Whenever there is a vacancy in the office of the Vice President, the President shall nominate a Vice President who shall take office upon confirmation by a majority vote of both Houses of Congress.

Section 3. Whenever the President transmits to the President pro tempore of the Senate and the Speaker of the House of Representatives his written declaration that he is unable to discharge the powers and duties of his office, and until he transmits to them a written declaration to the contrary, such powers and duties shall be discharged by the Vice President as Acting President.

Section 4. Whenever the Vice President and a majority of either the principal officers of the executive departments or of such other body as Congress may by law provide, transmit to the President pro tempore of the Senate and the Speaker of the House of Representatives their written declaration that the President is unable to discharge the powers and duties of his office, the Vice President shall immediately assume the powers and duties of the office as Acting President.

Thereafter, when the President transmits to the President pro tempore of the Senate and the Speaker of the House of Representatives his written declaration that no inability exists, he shall resume the powers and duties of his office unless the Vice President and a majority of either the principal officers of the executive department[s] or of such other body as Congress may by law provide, transmit within four days to the President pro tempore of the Senate and the Speaker of the House of Representatives their written declaration that the President is unable to discharge the powers and duties of his office. Thereupon Congress shall decide the issue, assembling within forty-eight hours for that purpose if not in session. If the Congress, within twenty-one days after receipt of the latter written declaration, or, if Congress is not in session, within twenty-one days after Congress is required to assemble, determines by two-thirds vote of both

Houses that the President is unable to discharge the powers and duties of his office, the Vice President shall continue to discharge the same as Acting President; otherwise, the President shall resume the powers and duties of his office.

Article XXVI

[*Adopted 1971*]

Section 1.   The right of citizens of the United States, who are eighteen years of age or older, to vote shall not be denied or abridged by the United States or by any State on account of age.

Section 2.   The Congress shall have power to enforce this article by appropriate legislation.

Growth of U.S. Population and Area

Census	Population	Percentage of Increase over Preceding Census	Land Area, Square Miles	Population per Square Mile
1790	3,929,214		867,980	4.5
1800	5,308,483	35.1	867,980	6.1
1810	7,239,881	36.4	1,685,865	4.3
1820	9,638,453	33.1	1,753,588	5.5
1830	12,866,020	33.5	1,753,588	7.3
1840	17,069,453	32.7	1,753,588	9.7
1850	23,191,876	35.9	2,944,337	7.9
1860	31,443,321	35.6	2,973,965	10.6
1870	39,818,449	26.6	2,973,965	13.4
1880	50,155,783	26.0	2,973,965	16.9
1890	62,947,714	25.5	2,973,965	21.2
1900	75,994,575	20.7	2,974,159	25.6
1910	91,972,266	21.0	2,973,890	30.9
1920	105,710,620	14.9	2,973,776	35.5
1930	122,775,046	16.1	2,977,128	41.2
1940	131,669,275	7.2	2,977,128	44.2
1950	150,697,361	14.5	2,974,726*	50.7
†1960	178,464,236	18.4	2,974,726	59.9
1970	204,765,770	14.7	2,974,726	68.8
1980	226,504,825	10.6	2,974,726	76.1
‡1987	243,396,000	7.5	2,974,726	81.8

* As remeasured in 1940.
† Not including Alaska (pop. 226,167) and Hawaii (632,772).
‡ As of July 1, 1987.

Admission of States into the Union

State	Date of Admission	State	Date of Admission
1. Delaware	December 7, 1787	26. Michigan	January 26, 1837
2. Pennsylvania	December 12, 1787	27. Florida	March 3, 1845
3. New Jersey	December 18, 1787	28. Texas	December 29, 1845
4. Georgia	January 2, 1788	29. Iowa	December 28, 1846
5. Connecticut	January 9, 1788	30. Wisconsin	May 29, 1848
6. Massachusetts	February 6, 1788	31. California	September 9, 1850
7. Maryland	April 28, 1788	32. Minnesota	May 11, 1858
8. South Carolina	May 23, 1788	33. Oregon	February 14, 1859
9. New Hampshire	June 21, 1788	34. Kansas	January 29, 1861
10. Virginia	June 25, 1788	35. West Virginia	June 20, 1863
11. New York	July 26, 1788	36. Nevada	October 31, 1864
12. North Carolina	November 21, 1789	37. Nebraska	March 1, 1867
13. Rhode Island	May 29, 1790	38. Colorado	August 1, 1876
14. Vermont	March 4, 1791	39. North Dakota	November 2, 1889
15. Kentucky	June 1, 1792	40. South Dakota	November 2, 1889
16. Tennessee	June 1, 1796	41. Montana	November 8, 1889
17. Ohio	March 1, 1803	42. Washington	November 11, 1889
18. Louisiana	April 30, 1812	43. Idaho	July 3, 1890
19. Indiana	December 11, 1816	44. Wyoming	July 10, 1890
20. Mississippi	December 10, 1817	45. Utah	January 4, 1896
21. Illinois	December 3, 1818	46. Oklahoma	November 16, 1907
22. Alabama	December 14, 1819	47. New Mexico	January 6, 1912
23. Maine	March 15, 1820	48. Arizona	February 14, 1912
24. Missouri	August 10, 1821	49. Alaska	January 3, 1959
25. Arkansas	June 15, 1836	50. Hawaii	August 21, 1959

Presidential Elections, 1789–1988

Year	States in the Union	Candidates	Parties	Electoral Vote	Popular Vote	Percentage of Popular Vote
1789	11	GEORGE WASHINGTON	No party designations	69		
		John Adams		34		
		Minor candidates		35		
1792	15	GEORGE WASHINGTON	No party designations	132		
		John Adams		77		
		George Clinton		50		
		Minor candidates		5		
1796	16	JOHN ADAMS	Federalist	71		
		Thomas Jefferson	Democratic-Republican	68		
		Thomas Pinckney	Federalist	59		
		Aaron Burr	Democratic-Republican	30		
		Minor candidates		48		
1800	16	THOMAS JEFFERSON	Democratic-Republican	73		
		Aaron Burr	Democratic-Republican	73		
		John Adams	Federalist	65		
		Charles C. Pinckney	Federalist	64		
		John Jay	Federalist	1		
1804	17	THOMAS JEFFERSON	Democratic-Republican	162		
		Charles C. Pinckney	Federalist	14		
1808	17	JAMES MADISON	Democratic-Republican	122		
		Charles C. Pinckney	Federalist	47		
		George Clinton	Democratic-Republican	6		
1812	18	JAMES MADISON	Democratic-Republican	128		
		DeWitt Clinton	Federalist	89		
1816	19	JAMES MONROE	Democratic-Republican	183		
		Rufus King	Federalist	34		
1820	24	JAMES MONROE	Democratic-Republican	231		
		John Quincy Adams	Independent Republican	1		
1824	24	JOHN QUINCY ADAMS	Democratic-Republican	84	108,740	30.5
		Andrew Jackson	Democratic-Republican	99	153,544	43.1
		William H. Crawford	Democratic-Republican	41	46,618	13.1
		Henry Clay	Democratic-Republican	37	47,136	13.2
1828	24	ANDREW JACKSON	Democratic	178	642,553	56.0
		John Quincy Adams	National Republican	83	500,897	44.0
1832	24	ANDREW JACKSON	Democratic	219	687,502	55.0
		Henry Clay	National Republican	49	530,189	42.4
		William Wirt	Anti-Masonic	7 ⎱	33,108	2.6
		John Floyd	National Republican	11 ⎰		
1836	26	MARTIN VAN BUREN	Democratic	170	765,483	50.9
		William H. Harrison	Whig	73 ⎱		
		Hugh L. White	Whig	26	739,795	49.1
		Daniel Webster	Whig	14		
		W. P. Mangum	Whig	11 ⎰		
1840	26	WILLIAM H. HARRISON	Whig	234	1,274,624	53.1
		Martin Van Buren	Democratic	60	1,127,781	46.9
1844	26	JAMES K. POLK	Democratic	170	1,338,464	49.6
		Henry Clay	Whig	105	1,300,097	48.1
		James G. Birney	Liberty		62,300	2.3
1848	30	ZACHARY TAYLOR	Whig	163	1,360,967	47.4
		Lewis Cass	Democratic	127	1,222,342	42.5
		Martin Van Buren	Free Soil		291,263	10.1

Because candidates receiving less than 1 percent of the popular vote are omitted, the percentage of popular vote may not total 100 percent. Before the Twelfth Amendment was passed in 1804, the electoral college voted for two presidential candidates; the runner-up became vice president.

Year	States in the Union	Candidates	Parties	Electoral Vote	Popular Vote	Percentage of Popular Vote
1852	31	FRANKLIN PIERCE	Democratic	254	1,601,117	50.9
		Winfield Scott	Whig	42	1,385,453	44.1
		John P. Hale	Free Soil		155,825	5.0
1856	31	JAMES BUCHANAN	Democratic	174	1,832,955	45.3
		John C. Frémont	Republican	114	1,339,932	33.1
		Millard Fillmore	American	8	871,731	21.6
1860	33	ABRAHAM LINCOLN	Republican	180	1,865,593	39.8
		Stephen A. Douglas	Democratic	12	1,382,713	29.5
		John C. Breckinridge	Democratic	72	848,356	18.1
		John Bell	Constitutional Union	39	592,906	12.6
1864	36	ABRAHAM LINCOLN	Republican	212	2,206,938	55.0
		George B. McClellan	Democratic	21	1,803,787	45.0
1868	37	ULYSSES S. GRANT	Republican	214	3,013,421	52.7
		Horatio Seymour	Democratic	80	2,706,829	47.3
1872	37	ULYSSES S. GRANT	Republican	286	3,596,745	55.6
		Horace Greeley	Democratic	*	2,843,446	43.9
1876	38	RUTHERFORD B. HAYES	Republican	185	4,034,311	48.0
		Samuel J. Tilden	Democratic	184	4,288,546	51.0
		Peter Cooper	Greenback		75,973	1.0
1880	38	JAMES A. GARFIELD	Republican	214	4,453,295	48.5
		Winfield S. Hancock	Democratic	155	4,414,082	48.1
		James B. Weaver	Greenback-Labor		308,578	3.4
1884	38	GROVER CLEVELAND	Democratic	219	4,879,507	48.5
		James G. Blaine	Republican	182	4,850,293	48.2
		Benjamin F. Butler	Greenback-Labor		175,370	1.8
		John P. St. John	Prohibition		150,369	1.5
1888	38	BENJAMIN HARRISON	Republican	233	5,477,129	47.9
		Grover Cleveland	Democratic	168	5,537,857	48.6
		Clinton B. Fisk	Prohibition		249,506	2.2
		Anson J. Streeter	Union Labor		146,935	1.3
1892	44	GROVER CLEVELAND	Democratic	277	5,555,426	46.1
		Benjamin Harrison	Republican	145	5,182,690	43.0
		James B. Weaver	People's	22	1,029,846	8.5
		John Bidwell	Prohibition		264,133	2.2
1896	45	WILLIAM McKINLEY	Republican	271	7,102,246	51.1
		William J. Bryan	Democratic	176	6,492,559	47.7
1900	45	WILLIAM McKINLEY	Republican	292	7,218,491	51.7
		William J. Bryan	Democratic; Populist	155	6,356,734	45.5
		John C. Wooley	Prohibition		208,914	1.5
1904	45	THEODORE ROOSEVELT	Republican	336	7,628,461	57.4
		Alton B. Parker	Democratic	140	5,084,223	37.6
		Eugene V. Debs	Socialist		402,283	3.0
		Silas C. Swallow	Prohibition		258,536	1.9
1908	46	WILLIAM H. TAFT	Republican	321	7,675,320	51.6
		William J. Bryan	Democratic	162	6,412,294	43.1
		Eugene V. Debs	Socialist		420,793	2.8
		Eugene W. Chafin	Prohibition		253,840	1.7
1912	48	WOODROW WILSON	Democratic	435	6,296,547	41.9
		Theodore Roosevelt	Progressive	88	4,118,571	27.4
		William H. Taft	Republican	8	3,486,720	23.2
		Eugene V. Debs	Socialist		900,672	6.0
		Eugene W. Chafin	Prohibition		206,275	1.4

*When Greeley died shortly after the election, his supporters divided their votes among the minor candidates.

Because candidates receiving less than 1 percent of the popular vote are omitted, the percentage of popular vote may not total 100 percent.

Year	States in the Union	Candidates	Parties	Electoral Vote	Popular Vote	Percentage of Popular Vote
1916	48	WOODROW WILSON	Democratic	277	9,127,695	49.4
		Charles E. Hughes	Republican	254	8,533,507	46.2
		A. L. Benson	Socialist		585,113	3.2
		J. Frank Hanly	Prohibition		220,506	1.2
1920	48	WARREN G. HARDING	Republican	404	16,143,407	60.4
		James N. Cox	Democratic	127	9,130,328	34.2
		Eugene V. Debs	Socialist		919,799	3.4
		P. P. Christensen	Farmer-Labor		265,411	1.0
1924	48	CALVIN COOLIDGE	Republican	382	15,718,211	54.0
		John W. Davis	Democratic	136	8,385,283	28.8
		Robert M. La Follette	Progressive	13	4,831,289	16.6
1928	48	HERBERT C. HOOVER	Republican	444	21,391,993	58.2
		Alfred E. Smith	Democratic	87	15,016,169	40.9
1932	48	FRANKLIN D. ROOSEVELT	Democratic	472	22,809,638	57.4
		Herbert C. Hoover	Republican	59	15,758,901	39.7
		Norman Thomas	Socialist		881,951	2.2
1936	48	FRANKLIN D. ROOSEVELT	Democratic	523	27,752,869	60.8
		Alfred M. Landon	Republican	8	16,674,665	36.5
		William Lemke	Union		882,479	1.9
1940	48	FRANKLIN D. ROOSEVELT	Democratic	449	27,307,819	54.8
		Wendell L. Willkie	Republican	82	22,321,018	44.8
1944	48	FRANKLIN D. ROOSEVELT	Democratic	432	25,606,585	53.5
		Thomas E. Dewey	Republican	99	22,014,745	46.0
1948	48	HARRY S TRUMAN	Democratic	303	24,105,812	49.5
		Thomas E. Dewey	Republican	189	21,970,065	45.1
		Strom Thurmond	States' Rights	39	1,169,063	2.4
		Henry A. Wallace	Progressive		1,157,172	2.4
1952	48	DWIGHT D. EISENHOWER	Republican	442	33,936,234	55.1
		Adlai E. Stevenson	Democratic	89	27,314,992	44.4
1956	48	DWIGHT D. EISENHOWER	Republican	457	35,590,472	57.6
		Adlai E. Stevenson	Democratic	73	26,022,752	42.1
1960	50	JOHN F. KENNEDY	Democratic	303	34,227,096	49.7
		Richard M. Nixon	Republican	219	34,108,546	49.5
		Harry F. Byrd	Independent	15	502,363	.7
1964	50	LYNDON B. JOHNSON	Democratic	486	43,126,506	61.1
		Barry M. Goldwater	Republican	52	27,176,799	38.5
1968	50	RICHARD M. NIXON	Republican	301	31,770,237	43.4
		Hubert H. Humphrey	Democratic	191	31,270,533	42.7
		George C. Wallace	American Independent	46	9,906,141	13.5
1972	50	RICHARD M. NIXON	Republican	520	47,169,911	60.7
		George S. McGovern	Democratic	17	29,170,383	37.5
1976	50	JIMMY CARTER	Democratic	297	40,827,394	49.9
		Gerald R. Ford	Republican	240	39,145,977	47.9
1980	50	RONALD W. REAGAN	Republican	489	43,899,248	50.8
		Jimmy Carter	Democratic	49	35,481,435	41.0
		John B. Anderson	Independent		5,719,437	6.6
		Ed Clark	Libertarian		920,859	1.0
1984	50	RONALD W. REAGAN	Republican	525	54,451,521	58.8
		Walter F. Mondale	Democratic	13	37,565,334	40.5
1988	50	GEORGE H. W. BUSH	Republican	426	47,946,422	54.0
		Michael S. Dukakis	Democratic	112	41,016,429	46.0

Because candidates receiving less than 1 percent of the popular vote are omitted, the percentage of popular vote may not total 100 percent.

Vice Presidents and Cabinet Members, 1789–1989

The Washington Administration (1789–1797)

Vice President	John Adams	1789–1797
Secretary of State	Thomas Jefferson	1789–1793
	Edmund Randolph	1794–1795
	Timothy Pickering	1795–1797
Secretary of Treasury	Alexander Hamilton	1789–1795
	Oliver Wolcott	1795–1797
Secretary of War	Henry Knox	1789–1794
	Timothy Pickering	1795–1796
	James McHenry	1796–1797
Attorney General	Edmund Randolph	1789–1793
	William Bradford	1794–1795
	Charles Lee	1795–1797
Postmaster General	Samuel Osgood	1789–1791
	Timothy Pickering	1791–1794
	Joseph Habersham	1795–1797

The John Adams Administration (1797–1801)

Vice President	Thomas Jefferson	1797–1801
Secretary of State	Timothy Pickering	1797–1800
	John Marshall	1800–1801
Secretary of Treasury	Oliver Wolcott	1797–1800
	Samuel Dexter	1800–1801
Secretary of War	James McHenry	1797–1800
	Samuel Dexter	1800–1801
Attorney General	Charles Lee	1797–1801
Postmaster General	Joseph Habersham	1797–1801
Secretary of Navy	Benjamin Stoddert	1798–1801

The Jefferson Administration (1801–1809)

Vice President	Aaron Burr	1801–1805
	George Clinton	1805–1809
Secretary of State	James Madison	1801–1809
Secretary of Treasury	Samuel Dexter	1801
	Albert Gallatin	1801–1809
Secretary of War	Henry Dearborn	1801–1809
Attorney General	Levi Lincoln	1801–1805
	Robert Smith	1805
	John Breckinridge	1805–1806
	Caesar Rodney	1807–1809
Postmaster General	Joseph Habersham	1801
	Gideon Granger	1801–1809
Secretary of Navy	Robert Smith	1801–1809

The Madison Administration (1809–1817)

Vice President	George Clinton	1809–1813
	Elbridge Gerry	1813–1817
Secretary of State	Robert Smith	1809–1811
	James Monroe	1811–1817
Secretary of Treasury	Albert Gallatin	1809–1813
	George Campbell	1814
	Alexander Dallas	1814–1816
	William Crawford	1816–1817

Secretary of War	William Eustis	1809–1812
	John Armstrong	1813–1814
	James Monroe	1814–1815
	William Crawford	1815–1817
Attorney General	Caesar Rodney	1809–1811
	William Pinkney	1811–1814
	Richard Rush	1814–1817
Postmaster General	Gideon Granger	1809–1814
	Return Meigs	1814–1817
Secretary of Navy	Paul Hamilton	1809–1813
	William Jones	1813–1814
	Benjamin Crowninshield	1814–1817

The Monroe Administration (1817–1825)

Vice President	Daniel Tompkins	1817–1825
Secretary of State	John Quincy Adams	1817–1825
Secretary of Treasury	William Crawford	1817–1825
Secretary of War	George Graham	1817
	John C. Calhoun	1817–1825
Attorney General	Richard Rush	1817
	William Wirt	1817–1825
Postmaster General	Return Meigs	1817–1823
	John McLean	1823–1825
Secretary of Navy	Benjamin Crowninshield	1817–1818
	Smith Thompson	1818–1823
	Samuel Southard	1823–1825

The John Quincy Adams Administration (1825–1829)

Vice President	John C. Calhoun	1825–1829
Secretary of State	Henry Clay	1825–1829
Secretary of Treasury	Richard Rush	1825–1829
Secretary of War	James Barbour	1825–1828
	Peter Porter	1828–1829
Attorney General	William Wirt	1825–1829
Postmaster General	John McLean	1825–1829
Secretary of Navy	Samuel Southard	1825–1829

The Jackson Administration (1829–1837)

Vice President	John C. Calhoun	1829–1833
	Martin Van Buren	1833–1837
Secretary of State	Martin Van Buren	1829–1831
	Edward Livingston	1831–1833
	Louis McLane	1833–1834
	John Forsyth	1834–1837
Secretary of Treasury	Samuel Ingham	1829–1831
	Louis McLane	1831–1833
	William Duane	1833
	Roger B. Taney	1833–1834
	Levi Woodbury	1834–1837
Secretary of War	John H. Eaton	1829–1831
	Lewis Cass	1831–1837
	Benjamin Butler	1837
Attorney General	John M. Berrien	1829–1831
	Roger B. Taney	1831–1833
	Benjamin Butler	1833–1837
Postmaster General	William Barry	1829–1835
	Amos Kendall	1835–1837

Secretary of Navy	John Branch	1829–1831
	Levi Woodbury	1831–1834
	Mahlon Dickerson	1834–1837

The Van Buren Administration (1837–1841)

Vice President	Richard M. Johnson	1837–1841
Secretary of State	John Forsyth	1837–1841
Secretary of Treasury	Levi Woodbury	1837–1841
Secretary of War	Joel Poinsett	1837–1841
Attorney General	Benjamin Butler	1837–1838
	Felix Grundy	1838–1840
	Henry D. Gilpin	1840–1841
Postmaster General	Amos Kendall	1837–1840
	John M. Niles	1840–1841
Secretary of Navy	Mahlon Dickerson	1837–1838
	James Paulding	1838–1841

The William Harrison Administration (1841)

Vice President	John Tyler	1841
Secretary of State	Daniel Webster	1841
Secretary of Treasury	Thomas Ewing	1841
Secretary of War	John Bell	1841
Attorney General	John J. Crittenden	1841
Postmaster General	Francis Granger	1841
Secretary of Navy	George Badger	1841

The Tyler Administration (1841–1845)

Vice President	None	
Secretary of State	Daniel Webster	1841–1843
	Hugh S. Legaré	1843
	Abel P. Upshur	1843–1844
	John C. Calhoun	1844–1845
Secretary of Treasury	Thomas Ewing	1841
	Walter Forward	1841–1843
	John C. Spencer	1843–1844
	George Bibb	1844–1845
Secretary of War	John Bell	1841
	John C. Spencer	1841–1843
	James M. Porter	1843–1844
	William Wilkins	1844–1845
Attorney General	John J. Crittenden	1841
	Hugh S. Legaré	1841–1843
	John Nelson	1843–1845
Postmaster General	Francis Granger	1841
	Charles Wickliffe	1841
Secretary of Navy	George Badger	1841
	Abel P. Upshur	1841
	David Henshaw	1843–1844
	Thomas Gilmer	1844
	John Y. Mason	1844–1845

The Polk Administration (1845–1849)

Vice President	George M. Dallas	1845–1849
Secretary of State	James Buchanan	1845–1849
Secretary of Treasury	Robert J. Walker	1845–1849
Secretary of War	William L. Marcy	1845–1849

Attorney General	John Y. Mason	1845–1846
	Nathan Clifford	1846–1848
	Isaac Toucey	1848–1849
Postmaster General	Cave Johnson	1845–1849
Secretary of Navy	George Bancroft	1845–1846
	John Y. Mason	1846–1849

The Taylor Administration (1849–1850)

Vice President	Millard Fillmore	1849–1850
Secretary of State	John M. Clayton	1849–1850
Secretary of Treasury	William Meredith	1849–1850
Secretary of War	George Crawford	1849–1850
Attorney General	Reverdy Johnson	1849–1850
Postmaster General	Jacob Collamer	1849–1850
Secretary of Navy	William Preston	1849–1850
Secretary of Interior	Thomas Ewing	1849–1850

The Fillmore Administration (1850–1853)

Vice President	None	
Secretary of State	Daniel Webster	1850–1852
	Edward Everett	1852–1853
Secretary of Treasury	Thomas Corwin	1850–1853
Secretary of War	Charles Conrad	1850–1853
Attorney General	John J. Crittenden	1850–1853
Postmaster General	Nathan Hall	1850–1852
	Sam D. Hubbard	1852–1853
Secretary of Navy	William A. Graham	1850–1852
	John P. Kennedy	1852–1853
Secretary of Interior	Thomas McKennan	1850
	Alexander Stuart	1850–1853

The Pierce Administration (1853–1857)

Vice President	William R. King	1853–1857
Secretary of State	William L. Marcy	1853–1857
Secretary of Treasury	James Guthrie	1853–1857
Secretary of War	Jefferson Davis	1853–1857
Attorney General	Caleb Cushing	1853–1857
Postmaster General	James Campbell	1853–1857
Secretary of Navy	James C. Dobbin	1853–1857
Secretary of Interior	Robert McClelland	1853–1857

The Buchanan Administration (1857–1861)

Vice President	John C. Breckinridge	1857–1861
Secretary of State	Lewis Cass	1857–1860
	Jeremiah S. Black	1860–1861
Secretary of Treasury	Howell Cobb	1857–1860
	Philip Thomas	1860–1861
	John A. Dix	1861
Secretary of War	John B. Floyd	1857–1861
	Joseph Holt	1861
Attorney General	Jeremiah S. Black	1857–1860
	Edwin M. Stanton	1860–1861
Postmaster General	Aaron V. Brown	1857–1859
	Joseph Holt	1859–1861
	Horatio King	1861
Secretary of Navy	Isaac Toucey	1857–1861
Secretary of Interior	Jacob Thompson	1857–1861

The Lincoln Administration (1861–1865)

Vice President	Hannibal Hamlin	1861–1865
	Andrew Johnson	1865
Secretary of State	William H. Seward	1861–1865
Secretary of Treasury	Samuel P. Chase	1861–1864
	William P. Fessenden	1864–1865
	Hugh McCulloch	1865
Secretary of War	Simon Cameron	1861–1862
	Edwin M. Stanton	1862–1865
Attorney General	Edward Bates	1861–1864
	James Speed	1864–1865
Postmaster General	Horatio King	1861
	Montgomery Blair	1861–1864
	William Dennison	1864–1865
Secretary of Navy	Gideon Welles	1861–1865
Secretary of Interior	Caleb B. Smith	1861–1863
	John P. Usher	1863–1865

The Andrew Johnson Administration (1865–1869)

Vice President	None	
Secretary of State	William H. Seward	1865–1869
Secretary of Treasury	Hugh McCulloch	1865–1869
Secretary of War	Edwin M. Stanton	1865–1867
	Ulysses S. Grant	1867–1868
	Lorenzo Thomas	1868
	John M. Schofield	1868–1869
Attorney General	James Speed	1865–1866
	Henry Stanbery	1866–1868
	William M. Evarts	1868–1869
Postmaster General	William Dennison	1865–1866
	Alexander Randall	1866–1869
Secretary of Navy	Gideon Welles	1865–1869
Secretary of Interior	John P. Usher	1865
	James Harlan	1865–1866
	Orville H. Browning	1866–1869

The Grant Administration (1869–1877)

Vice President	Schuyler Colfax	1869–1873
	Henry Wilson	1873–1877
Secretary of State	Elihu B. Washburne	1869
	Hamilton Fish	1869–1877
Secretary of Treasury	George S. Boutwell	1869–1873
	William Richardson	1873–1874
	Benjamin Bristow	1874–1876
	Lot M. Morrill	1876–1877
Secretary of War	John A. Rawlins	1869
	William T. Sherman	1869
	William W. Belknap	1869–1876
	Alphonso Taft	1876
	James D. Cameron	1876–1877
Attorney General	Ebenezer Hoar	1869–1870
	Amos T. Ackerman	1870–1871
	G. H. Williams	1871–1875
	Edwards Pierrepont	1875–1876
	Alphonso Taft	1876–1877

Postmaster General	John A. J. Creswell	1869–1874
	James W. Marshall	1874
	Marshall Jewell	1874–1876
	James N. Tyner	1876–1877
Secretary of Navy	Adolph E. Borie	1869
	George M. Robeson	1869–1877
Secretary of Interior	Jacob D. Cox	1869–1870
	Columbus Delano	1870–1875
	Zachariah Chandler	1875–1877

The Hayes Administration (1877–1881)

Vice President	William A. Wheeler	1877–1881
Secretary of State	William M. Evarts	1877–1881
Secretary of Treasury	John Sherman	1877–1881
Secretary of War	George W. McCrary	1877–1879
	Alex Ramsey	1879–1881
Attorney General	Charles Devens	1877–1881
Postmaster General	David M. Key	1877–1880
	Horace Maynard	1880–1881
Secretary of Navy	Richard W. Thompson	1877–1880
	Nathan Goff, Jr.	1881
Secretary of Interior	Carl Schurz	1877–1881

The Garfield Administration (1881)

Vice President	Chester A. Arthur	1881
Secretary of State	James G. Blaine	1881
Secretary of Treasury	William Windom	1881
Secretary of War	Robert T. Lincoln	1881
Attorney General	Wayne MacVeagh	1881
Postmaster General	Thomas L. James	1881
Secretary of Navy	William H. Hunt	1881
Secretary of Interior	Samuel J. Kirkwood	1881

The Arthur Administration (1881–1885)

Vice President	None	
Secretary of State	F. T. Frelinghuysen	1881–1885
Secretary of Treasury	Charles J. Folger	1881–1884
	Walter Q. Gresham	1884
	Hugh McCulloch	1884–1885
Secretary of War	Robert T. Lincoln	1881–1885
Attorney General	Benjamin H. Brewster	1881–1885
Postmaster General	Timothy O. Howe	1881–1883
	Walter Q. Gresham	1883–1884
	Frank Hatton	1884–1885
Secretary of Navy	William H. Hunt	1881–1882
	William E. Chandler	1882–1885
Secretary of Interior	Samuel J. Kirkwood	1881–1882
	Henry M. Teller	1882–1885

The Cleveland Administration (1885–1889)

Vice President	Thomas A. Hendricks	1885–1889
Secretary of State	Thomas F. Bayard	1885–1889
Secretary of Treasury	Daniel Manning	1885–1887
	Charles S. Fairchild	1887–1889

Secretary of War	William C. Endicott	1885–1889
Attorney General	Augustus H. Garland	1885–1889
Postmaster General	William F. Vilas	1885–1888
	Don M. Dickinson	1888–1889
Secretary of Navy	William C. Whitney	1885–1889
Secretary of Interior	Lucius Q. C. Lamar	1885–1888
	William F. Vilas	1888–1889
Secretary of Agriculture	Norman J. Colman	1889

The Benjamin Harrison Administration (1889–1893)

Vice President	Levi P. Morton	1889–1893
Secretary of State	James G. Blaine	1889–1892
	John W. Foster	1892–1893
Secretary of Treasury	William Windom	1889–1891
	Charles Foster	1891–1893
Secretary of War	Redfield Proctor	1889–1891
	Stephen B. Elkins	1891–1893
Attorney General	William H. H. Miller	1889–1891
Postmaster General	John Wanamaker	1889–1893
Secretary of Navy	Benjamin F. Tracy	1889–1893
Secretary of Interior	John W. Noble	1889–1893
Secretary of Agriculture	Jeremiah M. Rusk	1889–1893

The Cleveland Administration (1893–1897)

Vice President	Adlai E. Stevenson	1893–1897
Secretary of State	Walter Q. Gresham	1893–1895
	Richard Olney	1895–1897
Secretary of Treasury	John G. Carlisle	1893–1897
Secretary of War	Daniel S. Lamont	1893–1897
Attorney General	Richard Olney	1893–1895
	James Harmon	1895–1897
Postmaster General	Wilson S. Bissell	1893–1895
	William L. Wilson	1895–1897
Secretary of Navy	Hilary A. Herbert	1893–1897
Secretary of Interior	Hoke Smith	1893–1896
	David R. Francis	1896–1897
Secretary of Agriculture	Julius S. Morton	1893–1897

The McKinley Administration (1897–1901)

Vice President	Garret A. Hobart	1897–1901
	Theodore Roosevelt	1901
Secretary of State	John Sherman	1897–1898
	William R. Day	1898
	John Hay	1898–1901
Secretary of Treasury	Lyman J. Gage	1897–1901
Secretary of War	Russell A. Alger	1897–1899
	Elihu Root	1899–1901
Attorney General	Joseph McKenna	1897–1898
	John W. Griggs	1898–1901
	Philander C. Knox	1901
Postmaster General	James A. Gary	1897–1898
	Charles E. Smith	1898–1901
Secretary of Navy	John D. Long	1897–1901
Secretary of Interior	Cornelius N. Bliss	1897–1899
	Ethan A. Hitchcock	1899–1901
Secretary of Agriculture	James Wilson	1897–1901

The Theodore Roosevelt Administration (1901–1909)

Vice President	Charles Fairbanks	1905–1909
Secretary of State	John Hay	1901–1905
	Elihu Root	1905–1909
	Robert Bacon	1909
Secretary of Treasury	Lyman J. Gage	1901–1902
	Leslie M. Shaw	1902–1907
	George B. Cortelyou	1907–1909
Secretary of War	Elihu Root	1901–1904
	William H. Taft	1904–1908
	Luke E. Wright	1908–1909
Attorney General	Philander C. Knox	1901–1904
	William H. Moody	1904–1906
	Charles J. Bonaparte	1906–1909
Postmaster General	Charles E. Smith	1901–1902
	Henry C. Payne	1902–1904
	Robert J. Wynne	1904–1905
	George B. Cortelyou	1905–1907
	George von L. Meyer	1907–1909
Secretary of Navy	John D. Long	1901–1902
	William H. Moody	1902–1904
	Paul Morton	1904–1905
	Charles J. Bonaparte	1905–1906
	Victor H. Metcalf	1906–1908
	Truman H. Newberry	1908–1909
Secretary of Interior	Ethan A. Hitchcock	1901–1907
	James R. Garfield	1907–1909
Secretary of Agriculture	James Wilson	1901–1909
Secretary of Labor and Commerce	George B. Cortelyou	1903–1904
	Victor H. Metcalf	1904–1906
	Oscar S. Straus	1906–1909
	Charles Nagel	1909

The Taft Administration (1909–1913)

Vice President	James S. Sherman	1909–1913
Secretary of State	Philander C. Knox	1909–1913
Secretary of Treasury	Franklin MacVeagh	1909–1913
Secretary of War	Jacob M. Dickinson	1909–1911
	Henry L. Stimson	1911–1913
Attorney General	George W. Wickersham	1909–1913
Postmaster General	Frank H. Hitchcock	1909–1913
Secretary of Navy	George von L. Meyer	1909–1913
Secretary of Interior	Richard A. Ballinger	1909–1911
	Walter L. Fisher	1911–1913
Secretary of Agriculture	James Wilson	1909–1913
Secretary of Labor and Commerce	Charles Nagel	1909–1913

The Wilson Administration (1913–1921)

Vice President	Thomas R. Marshall	1913–1921
Secretary of State	William J. Bryan	1913–1915
	Robert Lansing	1915–1920
	Bainbridge Colby	1920–1921
Secretary of Treasury	William G. McAdoo	1913–1918
	Carter Glass	1918–1920
	David F. Houston	1920–1921
Secretary of War	Lindley M. Garrison	1913–1916
	Newton D. Baker	1916–1921

Attorney General	James C. McReynolds	1913–1914
	Thomas W. Gregory	1914–1919
	A. Mitchell Palmer	1919–1921
Postmaster General	Albert S. Burleson	1913–1921
Secretary of Navy	Josephus Daniels	1913–1921
Secretary of Interior	Franklin K. Lane	1913–1920
	John B. Payne	1920–1921
Secretary of Agriculture	David F. Houston	1913–1920
	Edwin T. Meredith	1920–1921
Secretary of Commerce	William C. Redfield	1913–1919
	Joshua W. Alexander	1919–1921
Secretary of Labor	William B. Wilson	1913–1921

The Harding Administration (1921–1923)

Vice President	Calvin Coolidge	1921–1923
Secretary of State	Charles E. Hughes	1921–1923
Secretary of Treasury	Andrew Mellon	1921–1923
Secretary of War	John W. Weeks	1921–1923
Attorney General	Harry M. Daugherty	1921–1923
Postmaster General	Will H. Hays	1921–1922
	Hubert Work	1922–1923
	Harry S. New	1923
Secretary of Navy	Edwin Denby	1921–1923
Secretary of Interior	Albert B. Fall	1921–1923
	Hubert Work	1923
Secretary of Agriculture	Henry C. Wallace	1921–1923
Secretary of Commerce	Herbert C. Hoover	1921–1923
Secretary of Labor	James J. Davis	1921–1923

The Coolidge Administration (1923–1929)

Vice President	Charles G. Dawes	1925–1929
Secretary of State	Charles E. Hughes	1923–1925
	Frank B. Kellogg	1925–1929
Secretary of Treasury	Andrew Mellon	1923–1929
Secretary of War	John W. Weeks	1923–1925
	Dwight F. Davis	1925–1929
Attorney General	Henry M. Daugherty	1923–1924
	Harlan F. Stone	1924–1925
	John G. Sargent	1925–1929
Postmaster General	Harry S. New	1923–1929
Secretary of Navy	Edwin Denby	1923–1924
	Curtis D. Wilbur	1924–1929
Secretary of Interior	Hubert Work	1923–1928
	Roy O. West	1928–1929
Secretary of Agriculture	Henry C. Wallace	1923–1924
	Howard M. Gore	1924–1925
	William M. Jardine	1925–1929
Secretary of Commerce	Herbert C. Hoover	1923–1928
	William F. Whiting	1928–1929
Secretary of Labor	James J. Davis	1923–1929

The Hoover Administration (1929–1933)

Vice President	Charles Curtis	1929–1933
Secretary of State	Henry L. Stimson	1929–1933
Secretary of Treasury	Andrew Mellon	1929–1932
	Ogden L. Mills	1932–1933

Secretary of War	James W. Good	1929
	Patrick J. Hurley	1929–1933
Attorney General	William D. Mitchell	1929–1933
Postmaster General	Walter F. Brown	1929–1933
Secretary of Navy	Charles F. Adams	1929–1933
Secretary of Interior	Ray L. Wilbur	1929–1933
Secretary of Agriculture	Arthur M. Hyde	1929–1933
Secretary of Commerce	Robert P. Lamont	1929–1932
	Roy D. Chapin	1932–1933
Secretary of Labor	James J. Davis	1929–1930
	William N. Doak	1930–1933

The Franklin D. Roosevelt Administration (1933–1945)

Vice President	John Nance Garner	1933–1941
	Henry A. Wallace	1941–1945
	Harry S Truman	1945
Secretary of State	Cordell Hull	1933–1944
	Edward R. Stettinius, Jr.	1944–1945
Secretary of Treasury	William H. Woodin	1933–1934
	Henry Morgenthau, Jr.	1934–1945
Secretary of War	George H. Dern	1933–1936
	Henry A. Woodring	1936–1940
	Henry L. Stimson	1940–1945
Attorney General	Homer S. Cummings	1933–1939
	Frank Murphy	1939–1940
	Robert H. Jackson	1940–1941
	Francis Biddle	1941–1945
Postmaster General	James A. Farley	1933–1940
	Frank C. Walker	1940–1945
Secretary of Navy	Claude A. Swanson	1933–1940
	Charles Edison	1940
	Frank Knox	1940–1944
	James V. Forrestal	1944–1945
Secretary of Interior	Harold L. Ickes	1933–1945
Secretary of Agriculture	Henry A. Wallace	1933–1940
	Claude R. Wickard	1940–1945
Secretary of Commerce	Daniel C. Roper	1933–1939
	Harry L. Hopkins	1939–1940
	Jesse Jones	1940–1945
	Henry A. Wallace	1945
Secretary of Labor	Frances Perkins	1933–1945

The Truman Administration (1945–1953)

Vice President	Alben W. Barkley	1949–1953
Secretary of State	Edward R. Stettinius, Jr.	1945
	James F. Byrnes	1945–1947
	George C. Marshall	1947–1949
	Dean G. Acheson	1949–1953
Secretary of Treasury	Fred M. Vinson	1945–1946
	John W. Snyder	1946–1953
Secretary of War	Robert P. Patterson	1945–1947
	Kenneth C. Royall	1947
Attorney General	Tom C. Clark	1945–1949
	J. Howard McGrath	1949–1952
	James P. McGranery	1952–1953
Postmaster General	Frank C. Walker	1945
	Robert E. Hannegan	1945–1947
	Jesse M. Donaldson	1947–1953

Secretary of Navy	James V. Forrestal	1945–1947
Secretary of Interior	Harold L. Ickes	1945–1946
	Julius A. Krug	1946–1949
	Oscar L. Chapman	1949–1953
Secretary of Agriculture	Clinton P. Anderson	1945–1948
	Charles F. Brannan	1948–1953
Secretary of Commerce	Henry A. Wallace	1945–1946
	W. Averell Harriman	1946–1948
	Charles W. Sawyer	1948–1953
Secretary of Labor	Lewis B. Schwellenbach	1945–1948
	Maurice J. Tobin	1948–1953
Secretary of Defense	James V. Forrestal	1947–1949
	Louis A. Johnson	1949–1950
	George C. Marshall	1950–1951
	Robert A. Lovett	1951–1953

The Eisenhower Administration (1953–1961)

Vice President	Richard M. Nixon	1953–1961
Secretary of State	John Foster Dulles	1953–1959
	Christian A. Herter	1959–1961
Secretary of Treasury	George M. Humphrey	1953–1957
	Robert B. Anderson	1957–1961
Attorney General	Herbert Brownell, Jr.	1953–1958
	William P. Rogers	1958–1961
Postmaster General	Arthur E. Summerfield	1953–1961
Secretary of Interior	Douglas McKay	1953–1956
	Fred A. Seaton	1956–1961
Secretary of Agriculture	Ezra T. Benson	1953–1961
Secretary of Commerce	Sinclair Weeks	1953–1958
	Lewis L. Strauss	1958–1959
	Frederick H. Mueller	1959–1961
Secretary of Labor	Martin P. Durkin	1953
	James P. Mitchell	1953–1961
Secretary of Defense	Charles E. Wilson	1953–1957
	Neil H. McElroy	1957–1959
	Thomas S. Gates, Jr.	1959–1961
Secretary of Health, Education, and Welfare	Oveta Culp Hobby	1953–1955
	Marion B. Folsom	1955–1958
	Arthur S. Flemming	1958–1961

The Kennedy Administration (1961–1963)

Vice President	Lyndon B. Johnson	1961–1963
Secretary of State	Dean Rusk	1961–1963
Secretary of Treasury	C. Douglas Dillon	1961–1963
Attorney General	Robert F. Kennedy	1961–1963
Postmaster General	J. Edward Day	1961–1963
	John A. Gronouski	1963
Secretary of Interior	Stewart L. Udall	1961–1963
Secretary of Agriculture	Orville L. Freeman	1961–1963
Secretary of Commerce	Luther H. Hodges	1961–1963
Secretary of Labor	Arthur J. Goldberg	1961–1962
	W. Willard Wirtz	1962–1963
Secretary of Defense	Robert S. McNamara	1961–1963
Secretary of Health, Education, and Welfare	Abraham A. Ribicoff	1961–1962
	Anthony J. Celebrezze	1962–1963

The Lyndon Johnson Administration (1963–1969)

Vice President	Hubert H. Humphrey	1965–1969

Secretary of State	Dean Rusk	1963–1969
Secretary of Treasury	C. Douglas Dillon	1963–1965
	Henry H. Fowler	1965–1969
Attorney General	Robert F. Kennedy	1963–1964
	Nicholas Katzenbach	1965–1966
	Ramsey Clark	1967–1969
Postmaster General	John A. Gronouski	1963–1965
	Lawrence F. O'Brien	1965–1968
	Marvin Watson	1968–1969
Secretary of Interior	Stewart L. Udall	1963–1969
Secretary of Agriculture	Orville L. Freeman	1963–1969
Secretary of Commerce	Luther H. Hodges	1963–1964
	John T. Connor	1964–1967
	Alexander B. Trowbridge	1967–1968
	Cyrus R. Smith	1968–1969
Secretary of Labor	W. Willard Wirtz	1963–1969
Secretary of Defense	Robert F. McNamara	1963–1968
	Clark Clifford	1968–1969
Secretary of Health, Education, and Welfare	Anthony J. Celebrezze	1963–1965
	John W. Gardner	1965–1968
	Wilbur J. Cohen	1968–1969
Secretary of Housing and Urban Development	Robert C. Weaver	1966–1969
	Robert C. Wood	1969
Secretary of Transportation	Alan S. Boyd	1967–1969

The Nixon Administration (1969–1974)

Vice President	Spiro T. Agnew	1969–1973
	Gerald R. Ford	1973–1974
Secretary of State	William P. Rogers	1969–1973
	Henry A. Kissinger	1973–1974
Secretary of Treasury	David M. Kennedy	1969–1970
	John B. Connally	1971–1972
	George P. Shultz	1972–1974
	William E. Simon	1974
Attorney General	John N. Mitchell	1969–1972
	Richard G. Kleindienst	1972–1973
	Elliot L. Richardson	1973
	William B. Saxbe	1973–1974
Postmaster General	Winton M. Blount	1969–1971
Secretary of Interior	Walter J. Hickel	1969–1970
	Rogers Morton	1971–1974
Secretary of Agriculture	Clifford M. Hardin	1969–1971
	Earl L. Butz	1971–1974
Secretary of Commerce	Maurice H. Stans	1969–1972
	Peter G. Peterson	1972–1973
	Frederick B. Dent	1973–1974
Secretary of Labor	George P. Shultz	1969–1970
	James D. Hodgson	1970–1973
	Peter J. Brennan	1973–1974
Secretary of Defense	Melvin R. Laird	1969–1973
	Elliot L. Richardson	1973
	James R. Schlesinger	1973–1974
Secretary of Health, Education, and Welfare	Robert H. Finch	1969–1970
	Elliot L. Richardson	1970–1973
	Caspar W. Weinberger	1973–1974
Secretary of Housing and Urban Development	George Romney	1969–1973
	James T. Lynn	1973–1974
Secretary of Transportation	John A. Volpe	1969–1973
	Claude S. Brinegar	1973–1974

The Ford Administration (1974–1977)

Vice President	Nelson A. Rockefeller	1974–1977
Secretary of State	Henry A. Kissinger	1974–1977
Secretary of Treasury	William E. Simon	1974–1977
Attorney General	William Saxbe	1974–1975
	Edward Levi	1975–1977
Secretary of Interior	Rogers Morton	1974–1975
	Stanley K. Hathaway	1975
	Thomas Kleppe	1975–1977
Secretary of Agriculture	Earl L. Butz	1974–1976
	John A. Knebel	1976–1977
Secretary of Commerce	Frederick B. Dent	1974–1975
	Rogers Morton	1975–1976
	Elliott L. Richardson	1976–1977
Secretary of Labor	Peter J. Brennan	1974–1975
	John T. Dunlop	1975–1976
	W. J. Usery	1976–1977
Secretary of Defense	James R. Schlesinger	1974–1975
	Donald Rumsfeld	1975–1977
Secretary of Health, Education, and Welfare	Caspar Weinberger	1974–1975
	Forrest D. Mathews	1975–1977
Secretary of Housing and Urban Development	James T. Lynn	1974–1975
	Carla A. Hills	1975–1977
Secretary of Transportation	Claude Brinegar	1974–1975
	William T. Coleman	1975–1977

The Carter Administration (1977–1981)

Vice President	Walter F. Mondale	1977–1981
Secretary of State	Cyrus R. Vance	1977–1980
	Edmund Muskie	1980–1981
Secretary of Treasury	W. Michael Blumenthal	1977–1979
	G. William Miller	1979–1981
Attorney General	Griffin Bell	1977–1979
	Benjamin R. Civiletti	1979–1981
Secretary of Interior	Cecil D. Andrus	1977–1981
Secretary of Agriculture	Robert Bergland	1977–1981
Secretary of Commerce	Juanita M. Kreps	1977–1979
	Philip M. Klutznick	1979–1981
Secretary of Labor	Ray F. Marshall	1977–1981
Secretary of Defense	Harold Brown	1977–1981
Secretary of Health, Education, and Welfare	Joseph A. Califano	1977–1979
	Patricia R. Harris	1979
Secretary of Health and Human Services	Patricia R. Harris	1979–1981
Secretary of Education	Shirley M. Hufstedler	1979–1981
Secretary of Housing and Urban Development	Patricia R. Harris	1977–1979
	Moon Landrieu	1979–1981
Secretary of Transportation	Brock Adams	1977–1979
	Neil E. Goldschmidt	1979–1981
Secretary of Energy	James R. Schlesinger	1977–1979
	Charles W. Duncan	1979–1981

The Reagan Administration (1981–1989)

Vice President	George Bush	1981–1989
Secretary of State	Alexander M. Haig	1981–1982
	George P. Shultz	1982–1989
Secretary of Treasury	Donald Regan	1981–1985
	James A. Baker III	1985–1988
	Nicholas Brady	1988–1989

Attorney General	William F. Smith	1981–1985
	Edwin A. Meese III	1985–1988
	Richard Thornburgh	1988–1989
Secretary of Interior	James Watt	1981–1983
	William P. Clark, Jr.	1983–1985
	Donald P. Hodel	1985–1989
Secretary of Agriculture	John Block	1981–1986
	Richard E. Lyng	1986–1989
Secretary of Commerce	Malcolm Baldridge	1981–1987
	C. William Verity, Jr.	1987–1989
Secretary of Labor	Raymond Donovan	1981–1985
	William E. Brock	1985–1988
	Ann Dore McLaughlin	1988–1989
Secretary of Defense	Caspar Weinberger	1981–1988
	Frank Carlucci	1988–1989
Secretary of Health and Human Services	Richard Schweiker	1981–1983
	Margaret Heckler	1983–1985
	Otis R. Bowen	1985–1989
Secretary of Education	Terrel H. Bell	1981–1985
	William J. Bennett	1985–1988
	Lauro F. Cavazos	1988–1989
Secretary of Housing and Urban Development	Samuel Pierce	1981–1989
Secretary of Transportation	Drew Lewis	1981–1983
	Elizabeth Dole	1983–1987
	James L. Burnley IV	1987–1989
Secretary of Energy	James Edwards	1981–1982
	Donald P. Hodel	1982–1985
	John S. Herrington	1985–1989

The Bush Administration (1989–   )

Vice President	J. Danforth Quayle III	1989–
Secretary of State	James Baker III	1989–
Secretary of Treasury	Nicholas Brady	1989–
Attorney General	Richard Thornburgh	1989–
Secretary of Interior	Manuel Lujan	1989–
Secretary of Agriculture	Clayton Yeutter	1989–
Secretary of Commerce	Robert Mosbacher	1989–
Secretary of Labor	Elizabeth Dole	1989–
Secretary of Defense	Richard Cheney	1989–
Secretary of Health and Human Services	Louis W. Sullivan	1989–
Secretary of Education	Lauro Cavazos	1989–
Secretary of Housing and Urban Development	Jack Kemp	1989–
Secretary of Transportation	Samuel Skinner	1989–
Secretary of Energy	James Watkins	1989–
Secretary of Veterans' Affairs	Edward Derwinski	1989–

Supreme Court Justices

Name	Terms of Service	Appointed By
JOHN JAY	1789–1795	Washington
James Wilson	1789–1798	Washington
John Rutledge	1790–1791	Washington
William Cushing	1790–1810	Washington
John Blair	1790–1796	Washington
James Iredell	1790–1799	Washington
Thomas Johnson	1792–1793	Washington
William Paterson	1793–1806	Washington
JOHN RUTLEDGE*	1795	Washington
Samuel Chase	1796–1811	Washington
OLIVER ELLSWORTH	1796–1800	Washington
Bushrod Washington	1799–1829	J. Adams
Alfred Moore	1800–1804	J. Adams
JOHN MARSHALL	1801–1835	J. Adams
William Johnson	1804–1834	Jefferson
Brockholst Livingston	1807–1823	Jefferson
Thomas Todd	1807–1826	Jefferson
Gabriel Duvall	1811–1835	Madison
Joseph Story	1812–1845	Madison
Smith Thompson	1823–1843	Monroe
Robert Trimble	1826–1828	J. Q. Adams
John McLean	1830–1861	Jackson
Henry Baldwin	1830–1844	Jackson
James M. Wayne	1835–1867	Jackson
ROGER B. TANEY	1836–1864	Jackson
Philip P. Barbour	1836–1841	Jackson
John Cartron	1837–1865	Van Buren
John McKinley	1838–1852	Van Buren
Peter V. Daniel	1842–1860	Van Buren
Samuel Nelson	1845–1872	Tyler
Levi Woodbury	1845–1851	Polk
Robert C. Grier	1846–1870	Polk
Benjamin R. Curtis	1851–1857	Fillmore
John A. Campbell	1853–1861	Pierce
Nathan Clifford	1858–1881	Buchanan
Noah H. Swayne	1862–1881	Lincoln
Samuel F. Miller	1862–1890	Lincoln
David Davis	1862–1877	Lincoln
Stephen J. Field	1863–1897	Lincoln
SALMON P. CHASE	1864–1873	Lincoln
William Strong	1870–1880	Grant
Joseph P. Bradley	1870–1892	Grant
Ward Hunt	1873–1882	Grant
MORRISON R. WAITE	1874–1888	Grant
John M. Harlan	1877–1911	Hayes
William B. Woods	1881–1887	Hayes
Stanley Matthews	1881–1889	Garfield
Horace Gray	1882–1902	Arthur
Samuel Blatchford	1882–1893	Arthur
Lucious Q. C. Lamar	1888–1893	Cleveland
MELVILLE W. FULLER	1888–1910	Cleveland

NOTE: The names of Chief Justices are printed in capital letters.
*Although Rutledge acted as Chief Justice, the Senate refused to confirm his appointment.

Name	Terms of Service	Appointed By
David J. Brewer	1890–1910	B. Harrison
Henry B. Brown	1891–1906	B. Harrison
George Shiras, Jr.	1892–1903	B. Harrison
Howell E. Jackson	1893–1895	B. Harrison
Edward D. White	1894–1910	Cleveland
Rufus W. Peckham	1896–1909	Cleveland
Joseph McKenna	1898–1925	McKinley
Oliver W. Holmes	1902–1932	T. Roosevelt
William R. Day	1903–1922	T. Roosevelt
William H. Moody	1906–1910	T. Roosevelt
Horace H. Lurton	1910–1914	Taft
Charles E. Hughes	1910–1916	Taft
EDWARD D. WHITE	1910–1921	Taft
Willis Van Devanter	1911–1937	Taft
Joseph R. Lamar	1911–1916	Taft
Mahlon Pitney	1912–1922	Taft
James C. McReynolds	1914–1941	Wilson
Louis D. Brandeis	1916–1939	Wilson
John H. Clarke	1916–1922	Wilson
WILLIAM H. TAFT	1921–1930	Harding
George Sutherland	1922–1938	Harding
Pierce Butler	1923–1939	Harding
Edward T. Sanford	1923–1930	Harding
Harlan F. Stone	1925–1941	Coolidge
CHARLES E. HUGHES	1930–1941	Hoover
Owen J. Roberts	1930–1945	Hoover
Benjamin N. Cardozo	1932–1938	Hoover
Hugo L. Black	1937–1971	F. Roosevelt
Stanley F. Reed	1938–1957	F. Roosevelt
Felix Frankfurter	1939–1962	F. Roosevelt
William O. Douglas	1939–1975	F. Roosevelt
Frank Murphy	1940–1949	F. Roosevelt
HARLAN F. STONE	1941–1946	F. Roosevelt
James F. Byrnes	1941–1942	F. Roosevelt
Robert H. Jackson	1941–1954	F. Roosevelt
Wiley B. Rutledge	1943–1949	F. Roosevelt
Harold H. Burton	1945–1958	Truman
FREDERICK M. VINSON	1946–1953	Truman
Tom C. Clark	1949–1967	Truman
Sherman Minton	1949–1956	Truman
EARL WARREN	1953–1969	Eisenhower
John Marshall Harlan	1955–1971	Eisenhower
William J. Brennan, Jr.	1956–	Eisenhower
Charles E. Whittaker	1957–1962	Eisenhower
Potter Stewart	1958–1981	Eisenhower
Byron R. White	1962–	Kennedy
Arthur J. Goldberg	1962–1965	Kennedy
Abe Fortas	1965–1970	L. Johnson
Thurgood Marshall	1967–	L. Johnson
WARREN E. BURGER	1969–1986	Nixon
Harry A. Blackmun	1970–	Nixon
Lewis F. Powell, Jr.	1971–	Nixon
William H. Rehnquist	1971–1986	Nixon
John Paul Stevens	1975–	Ford
Sandra Day O'Connor	1981–	Reagan
WILLIAM H. REHNQUIST	1986–	Reagan
Antonin Scalia	1986–	Reagan
Anthony Kennedy	1988–	Reagan

PHOTOGRAPH CREDITS

The following abbreviations are used for some sources from which several illustrations were obtained:
BA—Bettmann Archive. CHS—Chicago Historical Society. CP—Culver Pictures. GC—Granger Collection. HSP—Historical Society of Pennsylvania. LC—Library of Congress. MMA—Metropolitan Museum of Art. NA—National Archive. NPG—National Portrait Gallery. NYHS—New-York Historical Society. NYPL—New York Public Library. SI—Smithsonian Institution. UPI/Bettmann—UPI Bettmann Newsphotos. WW—Wide World. YU—Yale University.

Prologue p. xxxiii, Frank Whitney/The Image Bank; p. xxxv, Eric Meola/The Image Bank; p. xxxix(top), Cara Moore/The Image Bank; p. xxxix(bottom), Steve Proehl/The Image Bank; p. xl, Mike Malyszko/Stock, Boston; p. xli, Alan Becker/The Image Bank; p. xliii(top), Nathan Benn/Stock, Boston, p. xliii(bottom), Gary S. Chapman/The Image Bank; p. xliiia(top), Allen Russell/Profiles West; p. xliiia(bottom), Tim Haske/Profiles West; p. xliiib(top), Tim Haske/Profiles West; p. xliiib(bottom), Jerry Jacka Photography; p. xliv(top), Denver Museum of Natural History; pp. xliv–xlv, Eric Meola/The Image Bank; p. xlv(top), Georg Gerster/Comstock; p. xlv(bottom), Mound City Group National Monument, National Park Service, Michael Bitsko; p. xlvii(top), Don Landwehrle/The Image Bank; p. xlvii(center), Al Satterwhite/The Image Bank; xlvii(bottom), H. Wendler/The Image Bank; p. xlviii(top), John Aldridge/The Picture Cube; p. xlviii(bottom), Peter Cole/New England Stock Photo; p. il, Steve Dunwell/The Image Bank; p. l, Ken Dequaine/Third Coast Stock Source.

Chapter 1 p. liv, St. Louis Science Center, Photo: Dirk Bakker, Detroit Institute of Arts; p. 1, MMA, Gift of J. P. Morgan; p. 5(top), National Gallery of Art; p. 5(bottom left, center, and right), Jerry Jacka Photography; p. 8(left), Werner Foreman Archive; p. 8(right), Werner Foreman Archive/Museum of Anthropology with British Columbia; p. 11, Lee Boltin; p. 13, The Marquess of Salisbury at Hatfield House/The Fotomas Index; p. 14, GC; p. 15, GC; p. 18, GC; p. 19, GC; p. 21, Lee Boltin; p. 22, Lee Boltin; p. 25, Bodleian Library; p. 26, GC; p. 29, National Maritime Museum, Greenwich, England; p. 31a, GC; p. 31b(all), GC; p. 33(all) Flowerdew Hundred Foundation; p. 35, CP; p. 37, Massachusetts Historical Society; p. 39, GC.

Chapter 2 p. 42, Massachusetts Historical Society; p. 43, GC; p. 46, American Antiquarian Society; p. 48(left), Pilgrim Society, Boston; p. 48(right), Eliot Elisofon/Life Picture Service; p. 49, Massachusetts Historical Society; p. 53(both), Mick Heles; p. 55, Frank Siteman/Stock, Boston; p. 56(left), Massachusetts Historical Society; p. 56(bottom right), Museum of Fine Arts, Boston, Gift of Leverett Saltonstall; p. 56(top right), Pilgrim Society, Plymouth, MA; p. 59, Huntington Library; p. 62, Essex Institute, Salem, MA; pp. 66–67, John Carter Brown Library; p. 71, GC; p. 74, Trustees of British Museum; p. 75, GC; pp. 75a–75b(all), Photos courtesy of Louise E. Gray, The Middlesex County Historical Society, Sarah Streetman, photographer; p. 77(both), GC.

Chapter 3 p. 80, Brookline Historical Society; p. 81, GC; p. 87, Collection Albany Institute of History and Art, Gift of Governor and Mrs. Averell Harriman and Three Anonymous Owners; p. 89(left), Library Company of Philadelphia; p. 89(right), HSP; p. 91, Peabody Museum, Harvard University; p. 93, Bob Daenmrich/Stock, Boston; p. 94(both), NYPL Manuscript Division; p. 97(both), GC; p. 99, Colonial Williamsburg; p. 103a, Museum of the American Indian; p. 103b(top), Public Archives of Canada; p. 103b(bottom), Rochester Museum and Science Center; p. 104, GC; p. 105, Henry du Pont Winterthur Collection of Earl of Shaftsbury; p. 107, NYHS MacDonald/Aldus Archive; p. 110, GC; p. 111, MMA, Edward W. C. Arnold Collection of New York Prints, Maps, and Pictures. Bequest of Edward W. C. Arnold, 1954; p. 113, Newport Historical Society; p. 115(both), David R. White/Stockfile; p. 119(left), YU Bequest of Eugene Phelps Edwards, 1938; p. 119(right), NYPL Rare Book Division; p. 121, The Princeton University Library; p. 123, GC.

Chapter 4 p. 126, HSP(detail); p. 127, GC; p. 128, HSP; p. 130, Collection Brown University, MacDonald/Aldus Archive; p. 134, GC; p. 137(left), NYPL Emmett Collection; p. 137(right), Massachusetts Historical Society; p. 141, North Wind Picture Archives; p. 145, Museum of Fine Arts, Boston, Deposited by City of Boston, 1876; p. 147, GC; p. 149 Corcoran Gallery, Washington, D.C.; p. 150, GC; p. 151, GC; p. 155, GC; p. 156, GC; p. 159(left), HSP; p. 159(right), Robert Llewellyn; p. 159a, American Antiquarian Society; p. 159b(top), GC;

p. 159b(bottom), John Carter Brown Library; p. 160, LC; p. 161(left), HSP; p. 161(right), GC.

Chapter 5   p. 164, MMA Bequest of Charles Allen Munn, 1924; p. 165, Museum of Fine Arts, Boston, Deposited by City of Boston, 1876; p. 168, NYHS; p. 169, NYPL Print Collection, Astor, Lenox and Tilden Foundations; p. 171, HSP; p. 174, Independence National Historical Park, Philadelphia; p. 175a, The Filson Club, Louisville, KY; p. 175b, Kentucky Military History Museum; p. 177, Detroit Public Library, Burton Historical Collection, Photo: Thomas Featherstone; p. 182, Virginia Museum of Fine Arts, Boston, Gift of Miss Dorothy Payne; p. 184(right), The Friends Historical Library of Swarthmore College; p. 184(center), Frick Art Reserve Library; p. 184(left), YU, Bequest of Mrs. Katherine Rankin Wolcott Verplanck; p. 186, HSP; p. 192, National Gallery of Canada, Ottawa; p. 193, New Orleans Museum of Art, Museum Purchase, Art Acquisition Fund Drive; p. 195, Anne van der Vaeren/Image Bank; p. 196, Colonial Williamsburg; p. 198, Virginia Museum of Fine Arts, Boston; p. 201(left), Museum of Fine Arts, Boston, Boston, Bequest of Winslow Warren, 1931; p. 201(right), GC.

Chapter 6   p. 204, National Gallery of Art, Washington, Gift of Edgar William and Bernice Chester Garbisch; p. 205, BA; p. 208, Maryland Historical Society; p. 209a, Mr. and Mrs. Karolik Collection, Museum of Fine Arts, Boston; p. 209b, Maryland Historical Society; p. 209(left), Worcester Art Museum, Worcester, MA; p. 209(right), Maryland Historical Society; p. 210, HSP; p. 215, NYHS; p. 216, Donaldson, Lufkin & Jenrette Collection of Americana; p. 221, Boston Public Library; p. 223, NYPL, Print Collection; p. 224, CHS; p. 226, Brooklyn Museum, Gift of the Crescent Hamilton Athletic Club; p. 227, Winterthur Museum; p. 229, Robert Llewellyn; p. 231(left), Adams National Historical Site, Jeffrey Dunn Photographer; p. 231(right), SI, National Museum of American Art, Adams-Clement Collection, gift of Mary Louisa Adams in memory of her mother, Louisa Catherine Adams Clement; p. 235, Henry Francis du Winterthur Museum; p. 239(left), HSP; p. 239(right), Museum of Fine Arts, Boston, George Nixon Black Fund.

Chapter 7   p. 242, Minneapolis Institute of Arts, William Hood Dunwoody Fund; p. 243, GC; p. 245, Maryland Historical Society; p. 245(both), Robert Llewellyn; p. 246, Franklin D. Roosevelt Library; p. 248, Boston Atheneum; p. 252(both), Independence National Historical Park Collection; p. 253, Peabody Museum, Harvard University. Photo by Hillel Berger; p. 258, Peabody Museum; p. 260, GC; p. 264, The New Haven

Historical Society, Gift of Mrs. Philip Galpin, 1886; p. 266, The Pennsylvania Academy of Fine Arts, Harrison Earl Fund; p. 267a, Charles Bulfinch by Mather Brown, 1786, Harvard University Art Museums, Gift of Francis V. Bulfinch, 1933; p. 267b(top), plan of State House by Bulfinch, 1787, Phelps Stokes Collection, NYPL; p. 267b(bottom), Gift of Mrs. Horatio A. Lamb in memory of Mr. and Mrs. Winthrop Lamb, Museum of Fine Arts, Boston, Boston; p. 268, BA; p. 274(left), Harvard University Portrait Collection, Bequest Ward Nicholas; p. 274(right), Anne S. K. Brown Military Collection, Brown University Library.

Chapter 8   p. 276, The St. Louis Art Museum Purchase, Ezra H. Lilly Fund (detail); p. 277, GC; p. 279(left) Walters Art Gallery; p. 279(top), Buffalo Bill Historical Center; p. 279(bottom), Missouri Historical Center; p. 280, MMA, Rogers Fund 1942; p. 281a, NYHS; p. 281b(top), State Historical Society of Wisconsin; p. 281b(bottom), National Museum of American Art, SI, Gift of the Misses Henry; p. 286, National Museum of American Art, SI, Harriet Cane Johnston Collection; p. 288, Museum of Natural History, Le Havre, France; p. 290, NYHS; p. 296, Rhode Island Historical Society; p. 297, University of Lowell; p. 300, St. Louis Art Museum, Loan from Collection of Arthur Ziern, Jr.; p. 302, New York State Historical Association, Cooperstown; p. 307, Cheekwood Botanical Gardens and Fine Arts Center, Nashville, TN; p. 310, YU, Gift of George Hoadley.

Chapter 9   p. 312, Walters Art Gallery; p. 313, Cornell University Library, Department of Rare Books; p. 316, MMA; p. 320(both), GC; p. 325, NYHS; p. 328, NYHS; p. 329, SI, Division of Political History; p. 331, SI; p. 334, Church Museum, Brigham Young University; p. 335, Lightfoot Collection; p. 337, New York State Historical Association; p. 337a, Museum of Art, Rhode Island School of Design, Jesse Metcalf Fund; p. 337b(top), NYPL, Stokes Collection; p. 337b(bottom), Memorial Art Gallery of the University of Rochester, Gift of Thomas J. Watson, photo, James Via; p. 340, Collection of the Museum of American Folk Art, New York City, Promised Bequest of Dorothy and Leo Rabkin; p. 343(both), GC; p. 344, Free Library of Philadelphia; p. 347, GC; p. 348, LC.

Chapter 10   p. 350, The Historic New Orleans Collection(detail); p. 351, GC; p. 357, The Historic New Orleans Collection; p. 360, Helga Photo Studio; p. 361, Louisiana State Museum; p. 364, Everson Museum of Art of Syracuse and Onondaga County, Gift of Hon. Andrew D. White; p. 367, NYHS; p. 369a(both), South Caroliniana Library; p. 369b, South Caroliniana Library; p. 371(top), Historical Society of

New York City; p. 371(bottom), Peabody Museum, Harvard University; p. 372, from The Whitney Museum of American Arts, exhibit "The Painter's America," Collection of Hon. and Mrs. John Heinz, III, Washington, DC/Laurie Platt Winfrey, Inc.; p. 373, LC; p. 377, NYPL; p. 380, Virginia State Library; p. 382, Hampton University Museum; p. 383, BA; p. 384(right), Collection of Glenbow Museum, Calgary, Alberta, Canada; p. 384(left), Virginia State Library.

Chapter 11 p. 386, Edison Institute, Henry Ford Museum & Greenfield Village; p. 387, State Historical Society of Wisconsin; p. 388, WW; p. 390, BA; p. 392, GC; p. 396, International Museum of Photography at George Eastman House; p. 398, Clarence Davies Collection, Museum of the City of New York; p. 399, BA; p. 402, National Museum of American Art, SI, Gift of Frederick Weingeroff; p. 405, BA; p. 406, CP; p. 409(left), YU; p. 409(right), National Gallery of Art, Andrew W. Mellon Collection; p. 411, National Portrait Gallery; p. 413, Cleveland Museum of Art; p. 413a, GC; p. 413b(top), Olmstead Office Portfolio; p. 413b(bottom), J. Clarence Davies Collection, Museum of the City of New York; p. 416, NPG, SI, transfer from National Gallery of Art, Gift of Andrew W. Mellon, 1942.

Chapter 12 p. 418, Museum of Fine Arts, Boston, Boston(detail); p. 419, LC; p. 422, Levi Stauss; p. 424, GC; p. 427, GC; p. 431, GC; p. 432, NPG, SI; p. 433, National Park Service, Scotts Bluff National Monument; p. 434, CHS; p. 437, SI, Division of Political History; p. 443, Amon Carter Museum, Fort Worth; p. 444(left), National Academy of Design; p. 444, GC; p. 447a, International Museum of Photography at George Eastman House; p. 447b, Bancroft Library, University of California, Berkeley, CA; p. 450, Oakland Museum, Gift of Concours d'Antiques Art Guild, Oakland, CA/Laurie Platt Winfrey, Inc.

Chapter 13 p. 452, MMA, Arthur Hoppock Hearn Fund, 1950, Courtesy of Kathleen Curry; p. 453, LC; p. 455, LC; p. 458, SI, Division of Political History; p. 459, Detroit Institute of the Arts, Gift of Mrs. Jefferson Butler and Miss Grace R. Conover; p. 466, SI, Division of Political History; p. 471, NPG, SI, transfer from the National Gallery of Art; p. 474(left), GC; p. 474(right), NPG, SI; p. 476, MMA Gift of Mr. and Mrs. Carl Stoeckel, 1897; p. 479a, Charlestown Museum; p. 479b(top), GC; p. 479b(bottom), Gibbes Museum of Art; p. 480, Museum of the Confederacy; p. 482, GC; p. 484(top), Missouri Historical Society; p. 484(bottom), SI, Division of Political History.

Chapter 14 p. 486, Meed Art Gallery, Amherst College, Museum Purchase; p. 487, Index of American Design, National Gallery of Art; p. 488, NYHS; p. 490, Cook Collection, Valentine Museum; p. 493, Lincoln Collection, John Hay Library, Brown University; p. 496, Meserve Collection; p. 497(right), Bill Dekker, photo by Henry Groskinsky; p. 497(center left), Russ Pritchard, photo by Larry Sherer; p. 497(bottom left), Confederate Memorial Hall; p. 497(top left), Historical Collections, National Museum of Health and Medicine, Armed Forces Institute of Pathology; p. 500, LC; p. 502, BA; p. 505b(top), Historical Pictures Service, Inc.; p. 505b(bottom), Western Reserve Historical Society; p. 507(left), National Infantry Museum; p. 507(right), CHS; p. 511, Dale C. Wheary; p. 516(left), NA; p. 516(right), GC; p. 518, LC; p. 520, Brady Collection, NA; p. 522, GC.

Chapter 15 p. 526, YU, Gift of William W. Garretson; p. 527, The Museum of the Confederacy; p. 530, NPG, SI; p. 533, GC; p. 537, GC; p. 541(top), GC; p. 541(bottom), Wood Art Gallery, Montpelier, VT; p. 542, North Wind Picture Archives; p. 545, Tennessee State Library and Archives; p. 547, LC; p. 548, Moorland Spingarn Research Center, Howard University; p. 549a, Georgia Department of Archives and History; p. 549b, Hargrett Rare Book and Manuscript Library, University of Georgia Libraries; p. 558, GC; 559(left), Kansas State Historical Society; p. 559(right), LC; p. 563, GC.

Chapter 16 p. 566, National Museum of American Art, lent by SI, NMNH, Department of Anthropology; p. 567, Minnesota Historical Society; p. 570(left), SI; p. 570(right), Western History Collections, University of Oklahoma Library; p. 571, Kansas Pacific Railway Album, DeGolyer Library, Southern Methodist University; p. 573(left), BA; p. 573(right), SI, National Anthropological Archives; p. 574, BA; p. 577a, American Museum of Natural History; p. 577b(top), Joslyn Art Museum, Omaha, Nebraska; p. 577b(bottom), Minnesota Historical Society; p. 579, Museum of the American Indian, Heye Foundation, W. E. Richards Collection; p. 580, SI, Bureau of American Ethnology; p. 581, GC; p. 583, Haynes Foundation, Montana Historical Society, Helena; p. 584(right), Art Collections, The State Museum of History, Nebraska; p. 584(left), Nebraska State Historical Society No. 8801–128/Quilt made by Isabella Barnes of Abion, Nebraska, 1880; p. 590, Santa Barbara Historical Society; p. 591, University of Idaho Library, Special Collections; p. 595, Amon Carter Museum, Fort Worth; p. 600, GC.

Chapter 17 p. 602, LC; p. 603, GC; p. 605(left), CHS; p. 605(right), LC; p. 607, BA; p. 610, LC; p. 614(right), Edison

National Historic Site, photo: Joseph S. Cavotta, III; p. 614(left), GC; 616(top right), LC; p. 616(bottom left), Singer Sewing Machines Co. Inc.; p. 616(bottom right), LC; p. 618, Louisiana Historical Association Collection, Manuscripts Section, Howard-Tilton Memorial Library, Tulane University; p. 621, LC; p. 623, The Connecticut Historical Society; p. 625, International Museum of Photography at the George Eastman House; p. 629, LC; p. 630, GC; p. 631, LC; p. 633, GC; p. 633b(both), LC; p. 637(left), Bell Telephone Company; p. 637(right), NPG.

Chapter 18 p. 640, The Toledo Museum of Art, Ohio, Gift of Florence Scott Libbey(detail); p. 641, BA; p. 643(right), Museum of the City of New York; p. 643(left), The Adirondack Museum; p. 644, Huntington Library, San Marino, CA; p. 648, National Park Service: Statue of Liberty National Monument; p. 649, Milwaukee Art Museum; p. 651, Museum of the City of New York, Jacob A. Riis Collection; p. 651a, LC; p. 651b, Milwaukee County Historical Society; p. 653, North Wind Picture Archives; p. 655, BA; p. 657, GC; p. 659, North Wind Picture Archives; p. 662, Jane Addams Memorial Collection, University of Illinois, Chicago, The University Library; p. 664, Museum of Fine Arts, Boston, Boston, Gift of Miss Maude E. Appleton; p. 666, Print Department, Boston Public Library; p. 667, CHS; p. 671(top), Henry Ford Museum and Greenfield; p. 671(bottom), NPG.

Chapter 19 p. 674, Museum of Fine Arts, Boston, Boston, Charles Henry Hayden Fund(detail); p. 675, Minnesota Historical Society; p. 677(left), GC; p. 677(right) GC; p. 678, BA; p. 680, GC; p. 682, Bancroft Library, University of California, Berkeley; p. 685, GC; p. 686, Museum of the City of New York, Byron Collection; p. 687, BA; p. 691, Detroit Institute of Arts; p. 692, North Wind Picture Archives; p. 693, Henry Ford Museum and Greenfield Village; p. 694, LC; p. 697(left), GC; p. 697(right), North Wind Picture Archives; p. 699, Museum of Fine Arts, Boston, Otis Norcross Fund; p. 699a(top), GC; p. 699a(bottom), Chautauqua Historical Collection, Smith Memorial Library, Chautauqua, NY; p. 699b, Chautauqua Historical Collection, Smith Memorial Library, Chautauqua, NY; p. 701, North Wind Picture Archives; p. 702, Used by permission of National Woman's Christian Temperance Union, Evanston, Illinois; p. 704, San Diego Historical Society, Ticor Collection.

Chapter 20 p. 708, Brigham Young University Photo Archives; p. 709, BA; p. 713, Rutherford Hayes Presidential Center; p. 715, BA; p. 718, North Wind Picture Archives; p. 720(left), NYPL; p. 720(right), LC; p. 721, University of Hartford Collection; p. 724, Division of Domestic Life, SI;

p. 726, LC; p. 730, GC; p. 734, Division of Political History, SI; p. 735a, Curt Teich Postcard Collection, Lake County Museum; p. 735b(top), CHS; p. 735b(bottom), BA; p. 738, Curt Teich Postcard Collection, Lake County Museum; p. 739(left), LC; p. 739(right), GC; p. 741, YU(given by the artist, 1900); p. 743, LC; p. 745, Lightfoot Collection; p. 747, BA; p. 747(top), GC.

Chapter 21 p. 750, Skip Liepke, American Heritage(detail); p. 751, GC; p. 754(left), St. Louis Art Museum; p. 754(right), LC; p. 755(left), LC; p. 755(right), GC; p. 756, BA Springer Film Archive; p. 757a, International Museum of Photography at George Eastman House; p. 757b(top), Robert K. Graul; p. 757b(bottom), Illinois State Historical Library; p. 759(right), Wayne State University, Archives of Labor and Urban Affairs; p. 758, LC; p. 759(left), Brown Brothers; p. 763(left to right), BA, NPG, BA, GC; p. 764, LC; p. 768, BA; p. 771(left), University of Chicago Library; p. 771(right), GC; p. 772(left), SI, Division of Political History; p. 772(right), CP; p. 774, GC; p. 776(left), Historical Pictures Service; p. 776(right), GC; p. 777, GC; p. 779, GC; p. 780, BA; p. 784, GC; p. 787(left), Sophia Smith Collection, Smith College; p. 787(right), BA.

Chapter 22 p. 790, Sophia Smith Collection; p. 791, GC; p. 793, BA; p. 795, GC; p. 800, BA; p. 801, UPI Bett; p. 802, NA; p. 803(left), CP; p. 803(right), SI, Division of Political History; p. 805, GC; p. 808(left), NA; p. 808(right), GC; p. 810, Encyclopedia Britannica Inc; p. 815, BA; p. 815a, Bridgeport Public Library; p. 815b(left), UPI/Bett; p. 815b(right), Bridgeport Public Library; p. 818(top), BA; p. 818(bottom), Philadelphia Museum of Art, Gift of Robert Carten; p. 819(top), Truman Library; p. 819(bottom), GC; p. 821, GC; p. 825, Sagamore Hill National Historic Site.

Chapter 23 p. 828, GC; p. 829, BA; p. 832, BA; p. 833(left), BA; p. 833(right), CP; p. 836, BA; p. 837, LC; p. 838, LC; p. 841, GC; p. 842, GC; p. 844, Henry Ford Museum and Greenfield Village; p. 845, CP; p. 846(top), CP; p. 846(bottom), GC; p. 847a, BA; p. 847b(top), GC; p. 847b(bottom), BA; p. 848, GC; p. 849, CHS; p. 852, New Britain Museum of Art, Connecticut, Stephen Lawrence Fund, photo, E. Irving Blomstrann; p. 854(left), GC; p. 854(center), BA; p. 854(right), CP; p. 856, BA; p. 858, BA; p. 860, UPI/Bett; p. 864, BA.

Chapter 24 p. 866, FDR Library; p. 867, LC; p. 870(left), Boston Athenaeum; p. 870(right), GC; p. 871a, State Historical Society of Iowa, p. 871b(top), GC; p. 871b(bottom), State Historical Society of Iowa; p. 872, Painting from photo taken by Ivan E. Prall; p. 874, Historical Pictures Service; p. 880, UPI/

Bett; p. 881, GC; p. 885, UPI/Bett; p. 887(left), GC; p. 887(right), LC; p. 891, UPI/Bett; p. 892, FDR Library; p. 896(left), GC; p. 896(right), LC; p. 898(left), Social Security Administration; p. 898(right), UPI/Bett.

Chapter 25 p. 900, Phoenix Art Museum, Gift of the IBM Corporation; p. 901, UPI/Bett; p. 903, CHS; p. 904, WW; p. 909, WW; p. 909a, LC; p. 909b, Dick Whittington; p. 910, BA; p. 915(top left), BA Springer Film Archive; p. 915(top right), Henry Ford Museum and Greenfield Village; p. 915(bottom), BA Springer Film Archive; p. 918, LC; p. 920, Whitney Museum of American Art, Gift of Gertrude Vanderbilt Whitney; p. 921(left), Henry Dreyfuss Symbols Archive, Cooper-Hewitt Museum of Design, SI; p. 921(right), Henry Ford Museum and Greenfield Village; p. 925, GC; p. 930(left), GC; p. 930(right), UPI/Bett; p. 932, BA Springer Film Archive.

Chapter 26 p. 934, © CPC 1989, Courtesy Judy Groffman, Fine Art, New York, NY; p. 935, A. Eisenstadt/Time, Inc.; p. 937(left), U.S. Army/Captured German records; p. 937(right), UPI/Bett; p. 941, NA; p. 944, CP; 946(left), LC; p. 946(right), LC; p. 948, NA; p. 949, University of Louisville Photographic Archives; p. 950, Photofest; p. 952, LC; p. 955a, Lawrence, Jacob. *The Migration of the Negro #50.* "Race riots were numerous all over the North because of the antagonism that was caused between the Negro and the white workers. Many of these riots occurred because the Negro was used as a strike breaker in many of the Northern industries." (1940−41) Tempera on gesso on composition board, 18 × 12″. Collection, the Museum of Modern Art, Gift of Mrs. David M. Levy; p. 955b(top), WW; p. 955b(bottom), WW; p. 957(top), U.S. Army; p. 957(bottom), UPI/Bett; p. 958, UPI/Bett; p. 960, BA; p. 961, NA; p. 965, U.S. Army/FDR Library.

Chapter 27 p. 970, MMA, Arthur Hoppock Hearn Fund, 1950; p. 971, Harry S Truman Library; p. 972, Harry S Truman Library; p. 975(inset), UPI/Bett; p. 975, WW; p. 978, WW; p. 982, WW; p. 983a, Loomis Dean/*Life Magazine* © 1951 Time, Inc.; p. 983b(top), UPI/Bett; p. 983b(bottom), UPI/Bett; p. 985, WW; p. 987(top), WW; p. 987(left), Henry Ford Museum and Greenfield Village; p. 987(right), LC; p. 989, Ackoff, Milton. *Wipe out Discrimination,* 1949. Offset lithograph, 43 7/8 × 32 3/4″. Collection, The Museum of Modern Art, Gift of the Congress of Industrial Organizations; p. 992, UPI/Bett; p. 997, UPI/Bett; p. 995, UPI/Bett; p. 999, WW; p. 1001(left), SI, Division of Political History; p. 1001(right), WW.

Chapter 28 p. 1004, Courtesy of Robert Wale/The Illustration House, Inc.(detail); p. 1005, Photofest; p. 1007, UPI/Bett; p. 1009, Robert Phillips/Black Star; p. 1010, Herblock/The Washington Post; p. 1013, cover drawing Sykovarsky, © 1961, 1989 The New Yorker Magazine, Inc.; p. 1016, Eisenhower Library; p. 1018, GC; p. 1019, SI; p. 1023, GC; p. 1023a, UPI/Bett; p. 1023b, Elliott Erwitt/Magnum Photos, Inc.; p. 1026, UPI/Bett; p. 1029, GC; p. 1031(left), Photofest; p. 1031(right), Photofest; p. 1033(right), Leonard Freed/Magnum Photos, Inc.; p. 1033(left), Elliott Erwitt/Magnum Photos, Inc.; p. 1036, WW; p. 1038, UPI/Bett.

Chapter 29 p. 1042, Dan Budnik/Woodfin Camp and Associates, Inc; p. 1043, UPI/Bett; p. 1046, JFK Library; p. 1049, UPI/Bett; p. 1050, Tor Eigeland/Black Star; p. 1051a, UPI/Bett; p. 1051b(top), Steve Shapiro/Black Star, 1051b(bottom), Bob Adelman/Magnum Photos Inc.; p. 1052, JFK Library; p. 1053, U.S. Army; p. 1054, Fred Ward/Black Star; p. 1056, LBJ Library; p. 1063, Eve Arnold/Magnum Photos, Inc., p. 1067(left), WW; p. 1067(right), Bob Fitch/Black Star; p. 1069, WW; p. 1072, James Pickerell/Black Star; p. 1073(top), UPI/Bett; p. 1073(inset), LC, The Swann Collection of Caricature and Cartoon; p. 1075(left), SI, Division of Political History; p. 1075(right), Ivan Messar/Black Star.

Chapter 30 p. 1078, Larry Burrows/Life Picture Service; p. 1079, Burt Glinn/Magnum Photos, Inc.; p. 1081, Elliott Erwitt/Magnum Photos, Inc.; p. 1083, Steve Shapiro/Black Star; p. 1085, WW; p. 1087, Photo Trends (Time/Life); p. 1089a(top), Gene Anthony/Black Star; p. 1089a(bottom); Elliott Landy/Magnum Photos, Inc.; p. 1089b(left), Matsumoto/Black Star; p. 1089b(center), M. L. Carlebach/Black Star; p. 1089b(right), Gene Anthony/Black Star; p. 1091, Cornell Capa/Magnum Photos, Inc.; p. 1093, H. Kubota/Magnum Photos; p. 1097, drawing by David Levine. Reprinted with permission from *The New York Review of Books.* Copyright © 1971 NYREV, Inc.; p. 1098(top), James Pickerell/Black Star; p. 1098(bottom), Bill Strode/Black Star; p. 1099, Leonard Freed/Magnum Photos, Inc.; p. 1101, Sygma; p. 1104, J. P. Leffont/Sygma; p. 1106, NASA; p. 1110, S. Trerza/Magnum Photos, Inc.; p. 1113, Fred Hard/Black Star; p. 1115, Burt Glinn/Magnum Photos, Inc.; p. 1116, Dennis Brack/Black Star.

Chapter 31 p. 1118, Shepard Sherbello/Picture Group; p. 1119, John Barr/Gamma Liaison; p. 1121, UPI/Bett; p. 1124, Sygma; p. 1125, Henri Bureau/Sygma; p. 1127; Sygma; p. 1129a, Paul S. Howell/Gamma Liaison; p. 1129b(top), Kaluzny/Gamma Liaison; p. 1129b(bottom), Kaluzny/Gamma Liaison; p. 1130, The White House; p. 1131, Jason Bleibtreu/Sygma; p. 1136, WW; p. 1137, A. Tannenbaum/Sygma; p. 1139, © 1987 R. Chast, The New Yorker; p. 1140, Charlie Nye/Sygma; p. 1141(left), Bill Nation/Sygma; p. 1141(right), Johnson/Gamma Liaison; p. 1144, J. L. Atlan/Sygma; p. 1151, UPI/Bett; p. 1152,

© 1988 Miami News; p. 1154, Pamela Price/Picture Group; p. 1157(left), Bill Pierce/Sygma; p. 1157(right), Abe Frajndlich/Sygma.

Epilogue p. ii, © 1989 Bill Day/Detroit Free Press; p. iv(left), J. Langevin/Sygma; p. iv(right), J. Langevin/Sygma.

Table of Contents p. xi(top), Steve Dunwell/The Image Bank; p. xi(bottom), Jerry Jacka Photography; p. xii, Huntington Library; p. xiii, GC; p. xiv, HSP; p. xv, GC; p. xvi, Collection of Glenbow Museum Calgary, Alberta, Canada; p. xvii, International Museum of Photography at George Eastman House; p. xviii, Dale C. Wheary; p. xix, LC; p. xx, LC; p. xxiii, GC; p. xxiv, GC; p. xxv, GC; p. xxvi, UPI/Bett; p. xxvii, JFK Library; p. xxviii, Bill Strode/Black Star; p. xxix, Johnson/Gamma Liaison.

INDEX